Preventing Irreparable Harm. Provisional Measures in International Human Rights Adjudication

Eva Rieter

 intersentia

Antwerp – Oxford – Portland

Eva Rieter
Preventing Irreparable Harm. Provisional Measures in International Human Rights Adjudication

ISBN 978-90-5095-931-5
D/2010/7849/9
NUR 828

© 2010 Intersentia
www.intersentia.com

To my mother
Ella Verhamme
(1943-1990)

To Mark

ACKNOWLEDGMENTS

It has been a great privilege that Prof. Theo van Boven, whose life's work is to show that 'people matter', was willing to act as my doctoral advisor. The issue of provisional measures in human rights adjudication evidently is close to his heart and, as I argue in this book, conceptually related to the issue of reparations, an area of his particular expertise. Our discussions were interesting and inspiring. Moreover I would like to thank him for his unfailing support throughout the many years of the project that finally resulted in this book.

I have been incredibly fortunate in my family and friends. I cannot name them all here, but I will just mention Marion Golany-Wilbers, Nannet Heilhof, Marloes van den Akker and Denise Prévost who each in their own way, and from different places in the world, continue to show that 'people matter'. The regular thesis discussions, exchanging parts of chapters, with Denise have been great. Equally, several other friends have read and commented on various drafts. I would like to mention in particular Ilse Van Den Driessche, Alette Smeulers and Harald Quadvlieg.

Special mention deserve my research assistants, in particular Folkert de Vries, Sebastiaan van der Zwaan, Hansje Plagman, Nora Paulke, Amra Avdic and Pam Nicolai who worked for me over extended periods in a manner that was both intelligent and enjoyable. Several friends and family were willing to lend me a hand in a similar manner, among them Titia Rieter, Olivier Rieter, Hanneke Jacobs and Katrijn Hamakers.

Former colleagues at Maastricht University and my colleagues at the Department of International and European law of Radboud University Nijmegen have made me feel very welcome. What has been particularly important to the eventual completion of this book was the encouragement of Prof. Karel Wellens, Chair of the department of International and European Law and of Prof. Piet Hein van Kempen, professor of criminal law and procedure and of human rights law, at the Radboud University Nijmegen. Professor Wellens has been involved closely in the last stages of completion of the book. I am very grateful for the manner in which he read the complete manuscript and gave pertinent suggestions. Of the many others who have been supportive at crucial stages, I will just mention Prof. Fred Grünfeld, Prof. Fons Coomans and Prof. Ellen Vos of the Maastricht University department of International and European law and Henri de Waele of Radboud University department of International and European law. Fiorina Argante, Marion Grevinga, Nannet Heilhof and Ilse Van Den Driessche have painstakingly helped me out with some of the most tedious finalisations of the book. Finally I would like to thank Marina Jodogne who swiftly and competently prepared the voluminous manuscript for publication.

The support of the Netherlands Organisation for Scientific Research (NWO) is gratefully acknowledged for enabling me to visit the Inter-American Commission and Court in Washington, D.C. and San José, Costa Rica, respectively. I am indebted to the various practitioners I spoke with, such as (former) members of adjudicatory bodies and staff members at the relevant secretariats (Geneva, San José, Washington DC, Strasbourg). They are mentioned in Chapter II in the respective sections discussing the availability of information on provisional measures. In this respect I would like to single out for sharing their insights with me Prof. Scheinin, who has also been very helpful in the process of gaining access to information on the practice of the HRC with regard to provisional measures, Judge Thomas Buergenthal and Judge Cançado Trindade, both former Presidents of the Inter-American Court, Commissioners Goldman, Mendez and Grossman, and finally Brian Tittemore, scholar and staff member at the Inter-American Commission, whose particularly intelligent and kind assistance was very much appreciated. He died in 2007, but he has made an important contribution to the Inter-American jurisprudence.

This book is dedicated to my mother, who died a long time ago but whose memory continues to be present, gentle, with a love for people and words, quiet humour and insistence on respect. Crucial to me are always my family (Toon, Titia and Olivier Rieter, aunts and uncles, etc.) and friends. This book is dedicated to them as well. It is meant in particular for my partner Mark Kirkels, our daughter Julia, who was born in April 2009, and her brother and sister Luuk and Hester. Thank you Mark for supporting me in many ways in completing this book. Our love reminds me of what is important.

This manuscript was completed in December 2008, with incidental references to subsequent events.

TABLE OF CONTENTS

CHAPTER VIII
ENSURING PROCEDURAL RIGHTS TO PROTECT THE RIGHT TO LIFE AND PERSONAL INTEGRITY

CHAPTER IX
PROTECTING AGAINST DEATH THREATS AND HARASSMENT

CHAPTER XIII
PROTECTION

PART IV: RESPONSES

LIST OF ABBREVIATIONS

ACHR	American Convention on Human Rights
ACHPR	African Commission on Human and Peoples' Rights
AI	Amnesty International
CAT	UN Committee against Torture
CEDAW	UN Committee on the Elimination of All Forms of Discrimination against Women
CEJIL	Center for Justice and International Law
CERD	UN Committee on the Elimination of all Forms of Racial Discrimination
CIDH	Inter-American Commission on Human Rights (Comisión Internacional de Derechos Humanos)
CoE	Council of Europe
ECHR	European Convention on Human Rights
EComHR	European Commission on Human Rights
ECtHR	European Court of Human Rights
Fed. BiH	Federation of Bosnia and Herzegovina
HRC	UN Human Rights Committee
IACHR	Inter-American Court of Human Rights
ICAT	UN Convention against Torture and other Cruel, Inhuman or Degrading Treatment of Punishment
ICCPR	International Covenant on Civil and Political Rights
ICJ	International Court of Justice
ICTY	International Criminal Tribunal for the Former Yugoslavia
ILC	International Law Commission
ITLOS	International Tribunal on the Law of the Sea
JCPC	Judicial Committee of the Privy Council
PCIJ	Permanent Court of International Justice
State of BiH	State of Bosnia and Herzegovina
UNHCR	United Nations High Commissioner for Refugees
VCCR	Vienna Convention on Consular Relations
VCLT	Vienna Convention on the Law of Treaties
WTO	World Trade Organisation

GENERAL INTRODUCTION

1   TAKING URGENT ACTION IN INTERNATIONAL HUMAN RIGHTS ADJUDICATION

This book aims to clarify and further develop a legal concept of provisional measures as used by international adjudicators dealing with individual complaints about human rights violations. Various international adjudicators take action on behalf of individuals facing imminent or ongoing human rights violations. Often the need arises to take action as fast as possible. Such urgent action is particularly necessary when the imminent or ongoing violation would cause irreparable harm to persons. Examples of irreparable harm are disappearances, torture or executions.

An urgent action to prevent such irreparable harm generally takes place in the form of a message, sent as quickly as possible, to the State concerned, calling upon it to prevent the alleged imminent violation. If a United Nations (UN) Special Rapporteur, such as the Special Rapporteur on Extra-Judicial, Summary or Arbitrary Executions (hereinafter: Special Rapporteur on Executions),[1] sends such a message, it is usually called an 'urgent appeal'. On the other hand, if it is sent during the course of judicial or quasi-judicial proceedings, it is called an interim or provisional measure. Such measure may traditionally be defined as a measure taken (or 'indicated')[2] by an adjudicator and sent to the State concerned in order to safeguard the rights of the petitioner pending the final determination of the case. In international law the terms 'interim measures' and 'provisional measures' are used interchangeably,[3] but the Statute of the International Court of Justice (ICJ) speaks of provisional measures (Article 41) and this is the term generally used in this book. An exception is made only when discussing the practice of the Inter-American Commission on Human Rights because this Commission uses the term 'precautionary measures' to distinguish its own provisional measures from those of the Inter-American Court of Human Rights.[4]

---

[1]   Such Rapporteurs are independent experts appointed by the Chairperson of the UN Commission on Human Rights, a body of State representatives. They are appointed as part of the thematic proceedings based on the UN Charter. In relation to complaints sent to these Rapporteurs by individuals or NGOs reference is often made to more 'humanitarian', 'Charter-based proceedings' in order to distinguish them from the 'treaty based' individual complaint proceedings, based on specific treaties such as the International Covenant on Civil and Political Rights.

[2]   This term is found in Article 41(1) of the Statute of the International Court of Justice. Several other adjudicators have copied its use. Generally the term 'indicate' is used to refer to the process of communicating a provisional measure to the State concerned. The meaning of this term in the context of provisional measures has been controversial. In its *LaGrand* decision (*Germany* v. *United States*) of 27 June 2001, the International Court of Justice has now clarified its own use of the term. See Chapter I on the ICJ's provisional measures to protect persons.

[3]   The 1978 Rules of the International Court of Justice use the term provisional measures (articles 73-78), but the title of the subsection relating to Article 41 Statute is 'Interim Protection': Part III, Section D (Incidental Proceedings), Subsection 1.

[4]   See Chapter II, section 4 on provisional measures in the Inter-American system. The 'precautionary measures' taken by the Inter-American Commission on Human Rights during the course of adjudication are simply provisional measures by another name. They do not refer to the

The idea of provisional measures is based on a procedure used in national jurisdictions where an individual may, pending litigation, request a court to provide for preventive measures, injunctions, or other relief. A decision to take such measures does not prejudice the eventual legal determination of the conflict. It is relief *pendente lite*.

Various international adjudicators have the power to 'indicate', 'take', 'issue' or 'use' provisional measures during their proceedings. It can be necessary to use them pending international proceedings in order to preserve the respective rights of the parties or to prevent aggravation of the dispute. The most prominent international adjudicator making use of provisional measures is the ICJ.[5] Although individuals cannot appeal to that Court, its procedures are nevertheless relevant for conceptual reasons. Furthermore, some of the ICJ's case law on provisional measures, such as the *Hostages* case,[6] the *Genocide Convention* case[7] and *Armed activities on the territory of the Congo (Congo* v. *Uganda)*,[8] has dealt with the issue of irreparable harm to persons,[9] an issue directly relevant to human rights law. The Court has even indicated provisional measures in order to postpone the execution by one State of a national of another State.[10] Other adjudicators with no specific human rights competence taking provisional measures are the International Tribunal on the Law of the Sea (ITLOS),[11] the European Union's European Court of Justice (ECJ)[12] and international (arbitral) tribunals in commercial law.[13]

The Inter-American Court of Human Rights (IACHR) and European Court of Human Rights (ECtHR) and supervisory bodies to human rights treaties,[14] such as the Human Rights Committee (HRC) to the International Covenant on Civil and Political Rights (ICCPR), can indicate provisional measures in order to avert a deterioration of the alleged victim's position.[15] Human rights courts as well as other supervisory bodies to human rights treaties with an individual complaint mechanism are adjudicators determining a legal conflict between an individual and a State on the basis of law and rules of procedure.[16] They have used provisional measures as part of their judicial function.[17]

'precautionary' principle'. See Chapter I, section 5.3.3 and Chapter XV (Immediacy and risk), discussing the relationship between provisional measures and the precautionary principle.

[5] See Article 41 of the Statute of the International Court of Justice.

[6] ICJ *Case concerning United States Diplomatic and Consular Staff in Tehran (US* v. *Iran)*, Order of 15 December 1979.

[7] ICJ *Case concerning application of the Convention on the Prevention and Punishment of the Crime of Genocide (Bosnia and Herzegovina* v. *Yugoslavia (Serbia and Montenegro)*, Orders of 8 April 1993 and 13 September 1993; see further Higgins (1997).

[8] ICJ *Armed activities on the territory of the Congo (Congo* v. *Uganda)*, Order of 1 July 2000.

[9] The various reasons for provisional measures given by the ICJ are discussed more closely in Chapter I.

[10] ICJ *Case concerning the Vienna Convention on Consular Relations (Paraguay* v. *United States of America)*, Order of 9 April 1998; *LaGrand (Germany* v. *United States)*, Order of 5 March 1999 and Judgment of 27 June 2001 and *Avena and other Mexican Nationals (Mexico* v. *US)*, Order of 5 February 2003 and Judgment of 31 March 2004.

[11] See Article 290 UN Convention on the Law of the Sea and Article 25 of Annex VI.

[12] See Articles 242 and 243 EC Treaty.

[13] The case law of the ECJ and of international tribunals in commercial law falls outside the scope of this book.

[14] These are often called quasi-judicial bodies.

[15] This research will show that provisional measures can be used also to protect others than the petitioner.

[16] By analogy, according to the European Court of Human Rights (ECtHR) a 'tribunal' is a body exercising judicial functions, established by law to determine matters within its competence on the basis of rules of law and in accordance with proceedings conducted in a prescribed manner, see e.g. ECtHR *Sramek* v. *Austria*, Judgment of 22 October 1984, §36 and *Le Compte, Van*

The first urgent decisions of human rights adjudicators provide the historical background of the practice by human rights adjudicators. The HRC used so called 'informal provisional measures' in the 1970s and 1980s, requesting information on medical treatment in detention or on the whereabouts of alleged victims without explicitly invoking its rule on provisional measures, as well as a formal provisional measure to halt an expulsion, dating from 1977.[18] In the 1970s and 1980s the Inter-American Commission on Human Rights intervened informally on behalf of disappeared persons.[19] Since 1988, virtually as of its first case, the Inter-American Court has ordered provisional measures to protect against death threats.[20] The European Court of Human Rights (ECtHR) initially did not often use provisional measures because the Commission (when it was still active) normally did so. The earliest known occasion on which the European Commission on Human Rights used (informal) provisional measures was to prevent the execution of Nicolas Sampson in 1958. The European Court did use them to halt the extradition of *Soering* in January 1989.[21]

For one of the systems discussed in this book, the Inter-American human rights system, Professor Buergenthal, President of the Inter-American Court between 1985 and 1987[22] has expressed the importance of provisional measures as follows:

> "It is quite clear that the power of the Court to grant provisional measures has proved to be a very useful enforcement tool in the inter-American system. In a region of the world where serious violations of human rights are by no means a thing of the past, provisional measures can save lives, and they have done so on a number of occasions".[23]

Professor Cançado Trindade, President of the Inter-American Court between 1999 and 2003,[24] has referred to provisional measures as a 'procedural remedy of crucial importance to the protection of the fundamental rights of the human person'.[25]

Leuven and De Meyere v. *Belgium*, 23 June 1981, §55. This reasoning may apply to international adjudicators such as the Human Rights Committee as well. See further Chapter XVI (Legal status).

[17] While the theoretical issue of what should be the role of the judiciary and what powers it should have in a democracy is relevant, its discussion would require a separate study, especially in relation to the specific nature of the international system with its additional legitimacy problems. This study is based on the premise that the international system of supervision of human rights treaties – with all its flaws – is a given for those States that have accepted it.

[18] See Chapters V (Expulsion), VI (Disappearances) and VII (Health in detention).

[19] Interview by the author with Juan Méndez, Washington D.C., 17 October 2001. See further Chapters II (Systems) and VI (Disappearances).

[20] IACHR *Velásquez Rodríguez, Fairén Garbi and Solís Corrales, and Godínez Cruz Cases*, Orders for provisional measures of 15 and 19 January 1988.

[21] ECtHR *Soering* v. *UK* Judgment of 7 July 1989. See further Chapter IV (Part 2), discussing the early case of *Bönisch* v. *Austria*, Judgment of 6 May 1985.

[22] Member of the Court from 1979 to 1991.

[23] Buergenthal (1994), p. 93.

[24] Member of the Court from 1995 to 2006.

[25] Cançado Trindade, preface by the President of the Inter-American Court of Human Rights to Provisional Measures Compendium II (2000), p. XVII, §29. See further, e.g., Cançado Trindade (2003), pp. 162-168 and Pasqualucci (1993), pp. 803-864, in particular pp. 844-846.

2 PROVISIONAL MEASURES IN HUMAN RIGHTS ADJUDICATION: CHANGING THE TRADITIONAL CONCEPT?

This book examines the legal concept of provisional measures in human rights adjudication. Apart from the conceptual questions raised by these provisional measures, there is their evident practical significance. Yet, a systematic analysis of the situations in which they may be relied on is currently lacking.[26] Such analysis of the nature of the various types of provisional measures is of importance to alleged victims,[27] to organisations representing them, as well as to the adjudicators themselves.

The question arises whether the concept of provisional measures has been adapted to fit the context of international human rights law or is generally the same as under traditional international law. The purposes of provisional measures as used under the UN and the regional human rights systems may differ from the traditional purposes of provisional measures as used by the ICJ. It is assumed, for instance, that one traditional purpose, preventing irreparable harm, is more relevant in human rights cases than are other purposes such as preventing aggravation of the dispute or preserving the respective rights of the parties.

Thus Chapter I examines the concept as applied by two international tribunals with no specific human rights mandate: the ICJ (and its predecessor) and ITLOS. The subsequent chapters analyse the practice with regard to specific aspects of provisional measures (set out in section 4 of this introduction) of certain international and regional human rights adjudicators (mentioned in section 5). This is done in order to determine whether it is possible to identify a core to the concept of provisional measures that the human rights systems have in common and, if so, what this common core entails. Clearly the book does not only deal with the similarities and differences between the various systems that are immediately apparent from the treaty texts and Rules of Procedure but also discusses common developments, a certain convergence of approaches towards the concept of provisional measures in human rights cases. At the same time the scope of application, or outer limits, of provisional measures could vary from system to system. The exigencies of the situation in a specific region or the particular task of an adjudicator in a given system may require the use of provisional measures that go beyond the core common to all systems.

This book discusses the extent of the convergence or divergences in the approaches of the adjudicators. It examines not only the core common to provisional measures in the human rights systems, but also the outer limits of such measures. In this respect it may contribute to the ongoing discussion about the proliferation of international adjudicators and the risk of fragmentation of international law.

The outer limits are assumed to be wider in a regional rather than in an international system, due to the greater interest in mutual compliance displayed by other States parties and because in a regional system the adjudicator is geographically and culturally somewhat closer to the situations pending before it. Often a regional adjudicator may be able to apply mechanisms for fact-finding, monitoring and conciliation in a more focused way as well.

To the extent that there is a difference between the concept of provisional measures in human rights adjudication and in other situations the book discusses whether the concept as used by human rights adjudicators could also be relevant to adjudicators with a general competence, not limited to human rights issues, when they are dealing with issues involving irreparable harm to

---

[26]   The secondary literature on provisional measures in international adjudication that does exist, deals mostly with the ICJ. See Chapter I. There are some articles dealing with the practice of using provisional measures in some of the human rights systems. See Chapter II.

[27]   In practice the term 'alleged victim' is used also in the context of potential victims. Obviously, in the context of an impending violation, if the provisional measure works as intended, the violation does not take place at all or at least is not continued.

persons. In this sense this book is part of the discussion about the humanization of international law.[28]

3   PUBLICATION AND MOTIVATION

Most human rights adjudicators do not publish or motivate their provisional measures.[29] In this light the phenomenon that scholars sometimes read more into decisions than may have been intended by adjudicators[30] applies even more to decisions on provisional measures than to decisions on jurisdiction or merits.[31] Even if the adjudicator would publish and motivate them, there is obviously little time for contemplation. The urgency of the situation does not allow for exhaustive study and discussion. Still, in order to interpret the concept, potential petitioners, States, the adjudicator itself in later cases, other adjudicators as well as commentators depend on the information made available on the use of provisional measures. Consequently, their interpretations, actions and submissions could improve if adjudicators would include reasoning in their decisions on provisional measures, as sent to the State and the petitioner. It would also be useful if they would make available to the public more information on their use of provisional measures.

It may be argued that provisional measures in human rights cases do not have to be reasoned and the practice of using them does not need to be coherent because they are by definition adopted to address a situation of urgency. In that sense they would have a character that would be more humanitarian than judicial. Such an argument could explain why provisional measures are used in a certain situation vis-à-vis a certain State but not in similar situations vis-à-vis another State. The adjudicator may have envisaged something could be achieved exactly in that State but not in other States. Apart from the lack of time for elaboration, the wish to maintain maximum flexibility may also account for the lack of transparency in the decision-making on provisional measures by human rights adjudicators.

Evidently the above argument is not the approach taken in this book. While the aim of using provisional measures is not as such to proclaim the law or have general application, but rather to help one or more specific individuals,[32] explaining their use and increasing their accessibility is likely to make them more persuasive and to enhance their credibility. States and petitioners are now often unclear about the types of cases in which they are used. Some flexibility for the adjudicator would indeed remain necessary, but this does not rule out clarification of the use of provisional measures. The aim of flexibility does not justify secrecy and lack of explanation.[33]

Sometimes States (including domestic courts) are uncertain about the concept of provisional measures. States may invoke arguments applicable not just in the context of provisional measures. They may argue that domestic courts are better placed to assess risk of irreparable harm, for

---

[28]   See e.g. Van Boven (1982); Simma (1993); Buergenthal (1997); Higgins (1998); Flinterman (2000); Kamminga (2001); Seiderman (2001); Meron (2003/2006); Cançado Trindade (2004) and Kamminga (2008).

[29]   See Chapter II on the human rights systems.

[30]   Secretariat staff of the European Commission on Human Rights in Strasbourg (October 1997), the HRC in Geneva (October 1998) and the Inter-American Commission on Human Rights in Washington D.C. (September/October 2001) have also stressed this.

[31]   Thirlway (1994), p. 6 points out with regard to the provisional measures by the ICJ: "Provisional measures Orders are prepared under pressure of time and in order to deal with the immediate situation". As a result, he considers that the 'texts of such Orders should not be put under the magnifying glass on the assumption that every word has been weighed'. See also Sztucki (1983), p. 278.

[32]   See Conclusion Part II (Purpose).

[33]   See further Chapter II.

instance in expulsion or extradition cases or cases involving indigenous peoples and the environment. They may also argue that international adjudicators should not interfere in democratic decisions, for instance in death penalty cases, or that domestic resources do not allow for certain expenditures to be made, for instance in cases involving protection against death threats or access to health care.

Substantiation of the use of provisional measures and making the decisions ordering them accessible to the public would help increase their coherence and credibility for everyone involved.[34] In the face of a particular threat, information about the use of provisional measures in similar cases would provide States and petitioners with some idea about the concept of irreparable harm employed by the adjudicator and about the way risks are assessed. It could also be useful to know, for instance, the number of times provisional measures are requested by petitioners and the number of times they are granted. Knowing in what type of situations adjudicators will intervene urgently could be equally useful to NGOs and to State authorities so that they could already anticipate this domestically, making recourse to an international adjudicator unnecessary because the situation would already be addressed. This would allow the State to be pro-active in the protection of human rights. After all, that is what is explicitly required under the respective provisions involving the undertakings of State parties to respect and ensure the rights and provide effective remedies and reparations[35] and implicitly in the requirement to exhaust domestic remedies.[36] Thus, the State would avoid the situation that many similarly situated persons would have to resort to international complaint proceedings in urgent cases.

The relevant information on the practice of the respective systems used for this book is presented in the subsequent Chapters. The practice of the various human rights adjudicators shows that they often do not indicate the criteria for the use of provisional measures, let alone the order in which they deal with these criteria, and that their approach is not always coherent. Still, at a more abstract level some underlying principles and ideas can be found in the human rights systems. These have been used to clarify and develop a legal concept of provisional measures in human rights cases. These principles and ideas are linked to the existing doctrine on provisional measures in general international law.[37] Thus, based on more abstract principles that seem to be common in the approach of the adjudicators, this book aims to fill gaps in the doctrine.[38]

---

[34] See further Chapter II on transparency and Chapter XVII on the official responses of States.

[35] See e.g. Article 2 ICCPR, Articles 2 and 6 ICERD, Article 24 CEDAW, Article 2 ICAT, Articles 1, 13 and 50 ECHR, Articles 1, 2 and 63(1) ACHR and Article 1 ACHRPR.

[36] See e.g. Article 2 OP to the ICCPR, Article 11(3) ICERD, Article 4 OP to the CEDAW, Article 22(4)(b) ICAT, Article 35(1) ECHR, Article 46(1)(a) ACHR, Articles 50 and 56 ACHRPR and Article 6 Protocol African Court.

[37] Several scholars have contributed to the interpretation and development of this doctrine in non human rights law. See e.g. Guggenheim (1931 and 1933); Dumbauld (1932); Mendelson (1972-1973); Oellers-Frahm (1975); Elkind (1981); Sztucki (1983); Collins (1992); Thirlway (1994), Merrills (1995); Rosenne (2005) and Brown (2007), pp. 119-151. As noted, within the constraints of this book it was not feasible to deal with the extensive case law of arbitral tribunals and the European Court of Justice. For an account of the latter see, e.g. De Schutter (2005), pp. 93-130; Tridimas (1999); Jacobs (1994), pp. 37-68 and Collins (1992). For an account of the case law of arbitral tribunals see e.g. Collins (1992). See Chapter I for a discussion of approach by the PCIJ, ICJ and ITLOS.

[38] Given the lack of information available on the practice of the human rights adjudicators with regard to provisional measures, in particular their reasoning, the subsequent chapters sometimes refer to the arguments of the parties, on the assumption that these played a role in the adjudicator's decision-making. As ICJ Judge Shahabuddeen has observed, it is indeed 'not proper mechanically to impute to the Court the position taken or assumed by counsel, particularly where

4   ASPECTS OF PROVISIONAL MEASURES IN HUMAN RIGHTS ADJUDICATION

As this book aims to clarify and further develop a legal concept of provisional measures, used by international human rights adjudicators, it analyses the choices made by these adjudicators with regard to the use of provisional measures. Since the existing records of their decisions to take provisional measures, as well as the responses by Addressee States are mostly found in case law, it is case law that is used as the main source. This is complemented by some information derived from secondary literature, visits of the secretariats/Registries in Washington D.C., San Jose, Geneva and Strasbourg[39] and, for the HRC, information from the case files in Geneva.[40] The approach of the various adjudicators is compared, among others as to type of cases in which provisional measures are used. Exhaustive discussion is neither possible – most provisional measures are not published – nor necessary as this book takes a qualitative rather than a quantitative approach.

The cases discussed have been selected because they are informative about a particular aspect of provisional measures.[41] The book discusses typical cases providing insight into the features of provisional measures that the various systems have in common. In addition, it mentions similar cases in which other adjudicators indeed confirm the approach taken in these typical cases or choose to take a different approach. The book also examines atypical cases (Chapter XI) to explore the outer limits of the concept.

Certain aspects of provisional measures have been selected that seem pertinent both with regard to the concept of provisional measures in general and in the context of human rights adjudication. These are: the protection required and the relationship with reparation and the (group of) beneficiaries; the relevance of admissibility and jurisdiction on the merits, assessment of temporal urgency and risk, legal status, the official responses of addressee States and the follow-up by adjudicators. The discussion focuses on irreparable harm, an aspect of the concept that may help explain the other aspects as well. Thus, the emphasis is on the situations in which human rights adjudicators have used provisional measures. Implicitly or explicitly an adjudicator facing a request for provisional measures not only determines the applicable purpose of provisional measures, but also the protection required, the relationship between provisional measures and forms of reparation and the group of beneficiaries involved.

At the same time the adjudicator assesses temporal urgency and risk. Obviously, without the competence to use provisional measures it would be a fruitless exercise to consider whether they are warranted. In that sense the competence or jurisdiction to use provisional measures is a prerequisite rather than a criterion for the use of provisional measures. With regard to the ICJ the relevance of admissibility and jurisdiction on the *merits* has sometimes been considered to be not just an aspect, but a prerequisite as well. Some human rights adjudicators have discussed non-exhaustion of domestic remedies, (non-)admissibility of the claim and the duration of provisional measures as well as the role of reservations in cases in which provisional measures were used.

---

the Court has not spoken'. 'On the other hand', he noted 'it is equally not right to seek to appreciate the positions taken by the Court abstracted from their forensic context'. "As is well known, it is frequently the case that recourse to the arguments of counsel is necessary for an understanding of what in fact a court was doing". Separate Opinion of Judge Shahabuddeen in *Passage through the Great Belt* (*Finland* v. *Denmark*), Order of 29 July 1991.

[39] Washington D.C., September-October 2001; San José Costa Rica, October-December 2001; Geneva, October 1998, April and October 2002; and Strasbourg, October 1997. See also Chapter II (Systems).

[40] A reason to pay particular attention to the practice of the HRC lies in the special difficulty of obtaining information on the use of and rationale for its provisional measures. Much information was derived from the case files rather than from publicly available documents. See Chapter II.

[41] See about purposive sampling Patton (2002), pp. 230-243.

While these discussions have some bearing on the concept of provisional measures, it is obvious from the practice that admissibility and jurisdiction on the merits are not a prerequisite for the use of provisional measures in human rights cases.[42]

In addition, the adjudicator considers the legal status of provisional measures, the responses of the Addressee State in the past and the best ways to monitor compliance. A separate discussion of each of these aspects is important in order to understand the concept of provisional measures in human rights adjudication. Yet in practice they obviously must be taken into account simultaneously. After all, in the concept of provisional measures procedural and substantive law are intertwined.[43]

A question that sometimes arises is whether the adjudicator is the appropriate body to deal with the situation on an urgent basis.[44] If a request for provisional measures is made the adjudicator itself probably cannot avoid taking this policy question into account, at least to some extent. Individual petitioners could take it into account in order to find out what would be the most appropriate course of action to avoid irreparable harm and whether this includes resorting to international adjudicators. Petitioners could take into account as well the anticipated impact of the adjudicator's use of provisional measures on future cases and the responses of States.[45]

In addition to examining the choices by the adjudicators with regard to the use of provisional measures, classical legal research is applied: finding and analysing relevant law with regard to provisional measures (case law as well as the applicable standards and rules of procedure), comparing the jurisprudence in order to find the underlying rationale for the use of provisional measures. This is then put in a conceptual framework interpreting the convergence and divergence of the practice of the various adjudicators with regard to provisional measures. This framework is based, on the one hand, on the factual question whether two or more adjudicators have used provisional measures in a given context (e.g. halting executions) and on the other hand on the underlying rationale that the provisional measures of the various adjudicators appear to have in common.

5   HUMAN RIGHTS SYSTEMS

The Human Rights Committee (HRC) is the only adjudicator in a system that is applicable to States in various regions of the world.[46] Its practice serves as a basis for the discussion of the common core of provisional measures. Apart from the HRC the most important UN adjudicator whose cases are discussed is the Committee against Torture (CAT). A discussion of the practice of CAT as well as that of the European Court of Human Rights (ECtHR) helps clarify the assess-

---

[42]   See Chapter I (in Part I 'Setting') on this aspect of the general concept and Chapter XIV (in Part III 'Consequences') with regard to human rights adjudication.

[43]   The Inter-American Court considers its provisional measures jurisdictional rather than procedural. Maybe the point where substantive and procedural law meet in order to prevent irreparable harm could be called a 'jurisdictional guarantee'.

[44]   See also Part II on the purpose of provisional measures and the discussion in Chapter I on non-aggravation of the dispute including the relevance of simultaneous diplomatic activities.

[45]   Sometimes NGOs are themselves the petitioner, but not the victims, as in the Inter-American and African systems, see Chapter II.

[46]   Of the international treaties the ICCPR is the only one comparable to the regional conventions in the range of rights involved. The only other international human rights adjudicator with an established practice of using provisional measures is the Committee against Torture, but this involves a single-issue treaty. As of yet there is no (extensive) practice of using provisional measures by the Committee on the Elimination of Racial Discrimination and the Committee on the Elimination of Discrimination against Women.

ment of risk before using provisional measures in non-refoulement cases.[47] The ECtHR, more-over, has recently elaborated on the legal status of provisional measures, making reference to the practice of some other adjudicators as well.[48] The most important regional system, however, is the Inter-American system. This is the only system with a clearly developed practice of dealing with urgent cases. The practice of the Inter-American Commission and Court helps clarify the group of beneficiaries of provisional measures, the specificity of these measures – ordering to refrain from action or instead to take positive action – their purpose as well as their relationship to obligations on the merits and reparation.[49]

To the extent information is available, a few references are made to the African human rights system and its provisional measures.[50] As noted, the case law of the ECtHR and the former European Commission is mainly relevant with regard to the legal status of provisional measures and assessment of risk in non-refoulement cases, although some atypical cases are discussed as well (Chapter XI). Finally, a brief reference is made to the approach of the Bosnia Human Rights Chamber, established under the Dayton Peace Agreement, particularly in relation to forced evic-tion and cultural rights. In its application of provisional measures this Chamber interprets the European Convention on Human Rights (ECHR) in a different way than the European Court of Human Rights (ECtHR).[51]

Apart from an occasional reference to the urgent actions by UN thematic mechanisms, such as the Special Rapporteur against Executions and the Special Rapporteur on Human Rights De-fenders, an examination of other types of urgent actions not constituting provisional measures is beyond the scope of this book.[52] Thus, the urgent actions by the UN High Commissioner on Hu-man Rights, by country mechanisms, by the ILO, preventive action (or preventive diplomacy) by the UN Secretary-General, urgent actions by the Security Council in individual cases,[53] and EU, Commonwealth and OSCE actions, most of them more 'humanitarian' than adjudicatory, will not be discussed. Urgent procedures before national courts, such as summary proceedings and injunc-tions, have likewise been excluded from this research.[54]

For several of the human rights systems, the lack of direct information necessitates an ap-proach drawing information from the rights claimed, the decisions on the merits and reparations in the cases in which the adjudicators took provisional measures. In other words, information on

---

[47]   See Chapter XV (Immediacy and risk).

[48]   See Chapter XVI (Legal status).

[49]   See Chapters XII and XIII.

[50]   This necessarily is brief given the lack of information on the individual petitions dealt with by the Commission supervising the African Convention on Human and People's Rights (ACHPR).

[51]   Within the scope of this book the specific human rights procedures of international governance applicable to Kosovo are not discussed.

[52]   The independent experts based their activities on international rules, but they often use more diplomatic methods than the treaty monitoring bodies to convince States to respect these rules. Regularly they request governments to act in a certain way, or abstain from action, 'for humanitarian reasons'. It can be inferred from their yearly reports to the United Nations Human Rights Commission that (thematic) Special Rapporteurs and Working Groups often receive more, and more positive replies from governments to their urgent appeals than to their normal communications. See Van Boven (1994), pp. 72-73 referring to the 1990 and 1992 reports by several Charter-based mechanisms. See also, e.g., Decaux (2005), pp. 241-275 and debate, pp. 277-281; Rodley (2001), pp. 279-283 and Van Boven (1995), pp. 98-105.

[53]   For instance in relation to imminent executions of anti-apartheid activists in South Africa.

[54]   Obviously provisional measures ordered by international adjudicators find their way back to domestic courts, which may implement them through injunctions, etc. See also Chapter XVII (Official responses).

the rationale of their provisional measures often is construed from the case law, rather than taken directly from it.

6 THE COMMON CORE AND OUTER LIMITS OF PROVISIONAL MEASURES: AN OUTLINE OF THE BOOK

While some theoretical works are available on provisional measures in general, writings on the theory of provisional measures in human rights cases are scarce. Part I of this book consists of two chapters. The first Chapter discusses the concept of provisional measures in traditional international law, as used in adjudication of conflicts between States. In this respect the current practice of the ICJ and the International Tribunal on the Law of the Sea (ITLOS) may already show how the traditional concept has evolved. This Chapter distinguishes those situations in which provisional measures aim to protect individuals, with a focus on their use to halt executions. Subsequently, Chapter II briefly sets out the use of provisional measures by human rights adjudicators in the context of the different human rights treaties. While this book is based on the premise that the possibility to resort to provisional measures is part of the judicial function,[55] this Chapter discusses the competence of each adjudicator to use provisional measures, based on the relevant treaty text and Rules of Procedure. For each system it also refers to promptness and transparency of decision-making. It briefly notes the types of situations in which provisional measures are used in each system (Chapter II). Parts II and III are organised by aspect (situations in which provisional measures have been used and the concept of irreparable harm; protective measures and relationship obligations on the merits and with reparation; beneficiaries; admissibility and jurisdiction; assessment of temporal urgency and risk; legal status; official responses of addressee States and follow-up) in order to find the common core and outer limits of provisional measures in human rights adjudication.

Part II focuses on the situations in which provisional measures are used, culminating in a conclusion on the purpose of provisional measures in human rights adjudication. There are situations that have triggered provisional measures in most of the systems. In other situations only one or two adjudicators have, thus far, used provisional measures. An attempt is made to assess the relevance of these cases for the practice of the other human rights adjudicators. Chapters III-XI discuss the following situations: halting executions, halting corporal punishment, halting expulsion or extradition, timely intervention in disappearance cases, timely intervention in detention situations involving risks to health, timely intervention to deal with death threats and harassment, ensuring procedural rights to protect the right to life and personal integrity, protecting cultural rights of indigenous peoples, halting mass expulsion, halting internal displacement or forced eviction and other, more incidental, cases that may help establish the outer limits of the concept of provisional measures. Chapter XII on protection deals with the substantive obligations of States. It is based on the situations discussed in the previous chapters. On the one hand it focuses on the specificity of the provisional measures and the question whether action (positive obligations) or abstention is required. On the other hand it discusses the relationship between provisional measures and obligations on the merits as well as forms of reparation. It also deals with the beneficiaries of provisional measures, representation and consultation and the addressees of provisional measures. Part II concludes with a substantive discussion of the purpose of provisional measures.

Part III deals with what could be seen as the consequences of the findings regarding the purpose of provisional measures in human rights adjudication. Chapter XIV discusses jurisdiction on the merits and admissibility. Chapter XV deals with assessment of temporal urgency and risk

---

[55]   See also Chapter XVI (Legal Status).

and Chapter XVI with the legal status of provisional measures. Recent case law has drawn international attention to the latter aspect of the concept.[56]

Another question with regard to provisional measures in human rights adjudication is whether (and how) they actually work. This is a question of causality that falls outside the scope of this research. Nevertheless, the available case law provides some information on the official responses of addressee States (discussed in Chapter XVII) and the follow-up by adjudicators (Chapter XVIII). Rather than analysing causality as such this book simply discusses this information, as this may help clarify the legal concept of provisional measures in human rights cases.

Exactly because provisional measures in human rights adjudication concern the fate of human beings at risk, their individual situations and narratives have been the points of departure in this book. Still, for the sake of presenting the concept of provisional measures, the stories of the people involved have sometimes been split up over different Chapters. Nevertheless, the course of some of these stories may be followed throughout the Chapters, discussing various aspects of the concept.

By way of conclusion this book presents the common core of provisional measures in human rights adjudication and their outer limits and discusses what steps could be taken to improve the functioning of provisional measures in human rights adjudication. The latter is based, among others, on the best practices found in the various systems. It does this by taking into account, where relevant, the following criteria to determine how provisional measures could best assist a beneficiary: accessibility, motivation and consistency, responsiveness to the specific situation, consultation and follow-up. The criteria of accessibility, motivation and consistency have been selected for use in this study as they are thought to make provisional measures more convincing vis-à-vis addressee States. Responsiveness to the specific situation and consultation are considered necessary for the effectiveness of these measures in protecting the individual and follow-up by the adjudicators is used as a criterion because it has generally been regarded essential in treaty monitoring.[57]

---

[56]   See e.g. ICJ *LaGrand* (*Germany* v. *US*), Judgment of 27 June 2001 and ECtHR (Grand Chamber) *Mamatkulov and Askarov* v. *Turkey*, Judgment of 4 February 2005. This confirmed the first section's Judgment of 6 February 2003 in *Mamatkulov* v. *Turkey*, reversing *Cruz Varas and Others* v. *Sweden*, Judgment of 20 March 1991.

[57]   On the general importance of follow-up in human rights cases see e.g. Boerefijn (1999), pp. 101-112.

PART I

SETTING

INTRODUCTION

This Part examines the setting of the concept of provisional measures as developed by human rights adjudicators. This setting provides the basis for an examination of the purpose of provisional measures (Part II), as well as the impact of the irreparable nature of the harm on the aspects of jurisdiction and admissibility, immediacy and risk and legal status (Part III) and the responses by States and the follow-up by the adjudicators (Part IV).

Implicitly or explicitly the use of provisional measures by the human rights adjudicators appears to have been inspired by the practice of the ICJ. While obviously the humanization of international law is expressed in the practice of the human rights adjudicators, the practice of the ICJ reflects this humanization as well. In order to see to what extent the human rights adjudicators have adapted the traditional concept of provisional measures this study takes as a point of departure the ICJ practice with regard to provisional measures. At the same time it discusses the fact that to some extent the ICJ itself has taken into account the special position of the individual as well (Chapter I). Among others Chapter I discusses the authority to order provisional measures in adjudication of conflicts between States, issues of promptness and transparency of decision-making and the purpose of provisional measures in general international law. It deals with the relation to the merits, the problem of prejudgment, the protective measures required and their relation to reparations. Furthermore it addresses the question who are the beneficiaries, the relevance of jurisdiction on the merits, the assessment of urgency, the legal status, the official responses of addressee States and the follow-up by the ICJ and ITLOS.

Before examining what the use of provisional measures may have in common in all the systems, it is necessary to examine how these measures function in each specific system. The particularities of the systems may help explain differences in the practice developed with regard to provisional measures. Chapter II introduces the various human rights adjudicators, putting their use of provisional measures in the context of the specific human rights system in which they operate. The chapter concludes by more specifically discussing the authority to use provisional measures, publication and motivation of these measures and convergence and divergence of case law. The latter is an issue relevant to the question of the 'common core' and 'outer limits' of the concept of provisional measures, discussed in Part II and to the legal status of these measures, discussed in Part III.

CHAPTER I
DEVELOPMENT OF THE CONCEPT OF PROVISIONAL MEASURES BY THE ICJ AND ITLOS

1   INTRODUCTION

This Chapter discusses the development of the traditional concept of provisional measures, as used in adjudication of conflicts between States. It focuses on the practice of the International Court of Justice (ICJ) and its predecessor the Permanent Court of International Justice (PCIJ), with an occasional reference to the International Tribunal on the Law of the Sea (ITLOS). Both are international adjudicators not specifically focussing on human rights, one a court of general jurisdiction, the other dealing with the law of the sea. As noted in the Introduction to this book, the question arises whether the concept of provisional measures has been adapted to fit the context of international human rights law or is generally the same as under traditional international law. The assumption is that the traditional concept of provisional measures differs from that developed by the UN and regional human rights adjudicators because the purpose is different. Thus this chapter focuses on the (development of) the traditional purpose of provisional measures by the ICJ and ITLOS.

The chapter first discusses the authority to order provisional measures in adjudication of conflicts between States. It also briefly refers to the issues of promptness and transparency of decision-making. Subsequently it deals with the purpose of provisional measures in general international law. It discusses separately those situations in which provisional measures by the ICJ aim to protect individuals. In fact the protection of the individual already played some role in the case law of the PCIJ. Nevertheless this chapter focuses on their more recent use to halt executions. It then refers to the relation to the merits, prejudgment, the protective measures required and their relation to reparations. Furthermore it addresses the beneficiaries, the relevance of jurisdiction on the merits, assessment of urgency, legal status, the official responses of addressee States and the (relative lack of) follow-up by the ICJ.

2   THE AUTHORITY TO USE PROVISIONAL MEASURES

2.1   Introduction

Article 41 of the Statute of the International Court of Justice (ICJ) provides in its first paragraph:

> "The Court shall have the power to indicate, if it considers that circumstances so require, any provisional measures which ought to be taken to preserve the respective rights of either party".[1]

As Merrills has noted, partly because of its brevity Article 41 is one of the most difficult articles of the ICJ Statute. It leaves unanswered 'questions concerning both the basis of interim measures

---

[1]   The relevant Rules of Court are Articles 73-78 in section D. (Incidental Proceedings, Subsection 1. Interim protection), *reproduced in* 17 *ILM* 1286 (1978).

and the scope and exercise of the power'.[2] This chapter first deals with the authority to use provisional measures *proprio motu*, then with the issues of transparency and promptness and the authority to delegate the use of provisional measures.

2.2   *Proprio motu* use

Adjudicators normally take provisional measures following a request by a party. Nevertheless, several adjudicators can do so *proprio motu* as well. The term *proprio motu* seems to be used to refer to the situation in which there was no (specific) request by one of the parties to use provisional measures, but the adjudicator used them on its own motion. The term *ex officio* is always used together with terms such as 'authority' or 'power'. In other words here the emphasis is on the authority of the adjudicator to use provisional measures. This relates to the function of the adjudicator. In fact such an adjudicator has the authority *ex officio* to use provisional measures *proprio motu*.[3] Sometimes a reference to provisional measures taken *proprio motu* seems to denote a discretionary power to do so while the reference to provisional measures taken *ex officio* denotes an obligation on the part of the adjudicator.

In 1932 Dumbauld wrote that in cases already brought before it, in accordance with Article 40 PCIJ Statute, the PCIJ had the power to indicate provisional measures *ex officio*. However, if the main action had not yet been brought, it could not do so on its own initiative. In passing he pointed out that (one of) the parties could request provisional measures already before the main action was brought, but without such request the Court could not indicate them in such case.[4]

Different from the PCIJ the present Court can only order provisional measures once the complaint itself has already been instituted.[5] Like the PCIJ, the ICJ may equally indicate provisional measures *proprio motu* 'at any time' (Article 75(1) of the Rules of Court). Moreover, the substance of the measures may be different from that asked by the parties. Thus far the ICJ itself has only once indicated provisional measures *proprio motu*.[6] It has only done so in the

---

[2]   Merrills (1995), p. 90. The ICJ has never used provisional measures in the course of advisory proceedings. See about this power Sztucki (1983), pp. 136-143. See also Merrills (1995), p. 145 referring to the *Applicability of the obligation to arbitrate under section 21 of the UN Headquarters Agreement of 26 June 1947*, Order of 9 March 1988 (holding that in the circumstances of the case it was not appropriate for the Court 'to consider whether or not provisional measures may be indicated in proceedings on a request for an advisory opinion').

[3]   Sometimes the term *sua sponte* is used instead of *proprio motu*.

[4]   Dumbauld (1932), p. 155.

[5]   Thirlway (1994), p. 17 notes that different from some other international tribunals, there must be an established case before the ICJ. Sztucki (1983), p. 13 refers to Mixed Arbitral Tribunals allowing requests for provisional measures before an application is filed.

[6]   See ICJ *LaGrand (Germany* v. *US)*, Order of 3 March 1999. See Merrills (1995), p. 143, referring to the Orders until 1995. The Orders decided by the ICJ subsequent to 1995 were equally on request of a party, Rosenne (2005), p. 177. In 1975 Oellers-Frahm, pp. 14-16 argued that the possibility of *ex officio* use would remain a dead letter because, according to the author, at the stage of provisional measures the Court does not undertake a summary analysis of the conflict in light of the need for protection of certain rights. Yet once the Court is (made) aware that it is at the stage of provisional measures, it does undertake such a summary analysis. It is true, however, that thus far it only dealt with the issue of *proprio motu* use when the imminence of the harm risked would seem to require provisional measures without first organising a hearing. In the *Bosnia* case such use of Article 75(1) of the Court's Rules was requested unsuccessfully. The Court in fact considered that the parties had made specific requests for provisional measures and therefore Article 75(1) did not apply. ICJ *Application of the Convention on the prevention and punishment of the crime of genocide (Bosnia and Herzegovina* v. *Yugoslavia (Serbia and*

LaGrand case because Germany had brought the case so close to the actual execution date that a hearing could not be held.[7] It has used its power to modify or 'tone down' the provisional measures requested by (one of) the Parties.[8] After all Article 75(2) of the Rules of the Court stipulates that 'the Court may indicate measures that are in whole or in part other than those requested, or that ought to be taken or complied with by the party which has itself made the request'. It invoked this Rule in its Order for provisional measures in the *Genocide Convention* case[9] and in *Cameroon* v. *Nigeria*.[10] It has also included new aspects in its Orders for provisional measures, which had not been requested by either of the parties. Judge Ajibola confirmed that the 'purpose and content of Article 41 of the Statute is not and cannot be restricted only to the preservation of the prospective rights of the parties in a matter like the one before the Court'. Thus he voted with the majority of the ICJ on the first operative part of the Order for provisional measures in *Cameroon* v. *Nigeria*, noting that the situation called for an Order *proprio motu* under Article 75 of the Rules of Court. In this context he emphasized the Court's power to order provisional measures in order to prevent the aggravation or extension of the dispute.[11]

According to Judge Laing, in his separate opinion to the Order for provisional measures by ITLOS in the *M/V 'Saiga'* case (1998), the ICJ has now affirmed that it has the power to order provisional measures to prevent aggravation or extension of the dispute even when the parties did not request this. He pointed out that there was no doubt that ITLOS had this authority as well.[12] On the other hand, the next year ad hoc Judge Shearer questioned whether ITLOS could prescribe provisional measures not requested by the parties. According to him the situation of ITLOS differed significantly from that of the ICJ.[13] He noted that Article 290(3) of the UN Convention on the Law of the Sea stipulates that the ITLOS could only prescribe, modify or revoke provisional measures taken under this article 'at the request of a party to the dispute and after the parties have been given an opportunity to be heard'. He considered, therefore, that 'if article 89,

---

      Montenegro)), Order of 13 September 1993 (second request). See Wellens (1998), p. 428 commenting on this approach.

[7]   See ICJ *LaGrand (Germany* v. *US)*, Order of 3 March 1999. Note that it took a different approach here from that taken in the *Bosnia* case. See also Separate Opinion of President Schwebel attached to this Order, still questioning the appropriateness of the use of Article 75(1) of the Rules in this context.

[8]   See e.g. Merrills (1995), p. 144 and Oellers-Frahm (1975), p. 15 (the latter noting that for those adjudicators that, unlike the ICJ, are not allowed to order provisional measures different from those requested (*ultra petita*), *ex officio* authority may be used to change the protective measures required). See section 3.7 (Protection).

[9]   ICJ *Application of the Convention on the prevention and punishment of the crime of genocide (Bosnia and Herzegovina* v. *Yugoslavia (Serbia and Montenegro))*, Order of 13 September 1993 (second request). See section 3.3.6 (gross human rights violations).

[10]   ICJ *Land and maritime boundary between Cameroon and Nigeria (Cameroon* v. *Nigeria)*, Order of 15 March 1996, §§41 and 48. See section 3.3.4 (border conflict cases).

[11]   ICJ *Land and maritime boundary between Cameroon and Nigeria (Cameroon* v. *Nigeria)*, Order of 15 March 1996, Separate Opinion of Judge Ajibola. He referred to *Nicaragua* v. *US*, Order of 10 May 1984, *Frontier Dispute case (Burkina Faso* v. *Mali)*, Order of 10 January 1986 and the *Application of the Convention on the prevention and punishment of the crime of genocide (Bosnia and Herzegovina* v. *Yugoslavia (Serbia and Montenegro))*, Order of 8 April 1993. See section 3 on the purpose of provisional measures.

[12]   ITLOS Separate Opinion Judge Laing, *M/V 'Saiga'* (No. 2), Order of 11 March 1998.

[13]   He noted that in its Order for provisional measures in the *M/V 'Saiga' (No. 2)* case ITLOS invoked Article 89(5) of the Rules. This stipulates that it may prescribe measures 'different in whole or in part from those requested' and that it may indicate 'the parties which are to take or to comply with each measure'. This Rule was modelled on Article 75 of the 1978 ICJ Rules of Court.

paragraph 5, of the Rules of the Tribunal truly purports to give a power to the Tribunal to act beyond the bounds of what has been requested (*ultra petita*)', the Rule would not be authorised by the Convention and would thus be invalid.

> "If, on the other hand, it is properly to be interpreted as meaning only that the Tribunal may, in addition to the alternatives of acceding completely to, or rejecting completely, the requested measures, prescribe measures that represent a partial grant or modified version of the requested measures, then the rule would be within power. I would include among such permitted measures, even if not formally requested by the parties, such "traditional" provisional measures as non-aggravation of the dispute, and – in the special circumstances of the present case – the measure directing the parties to seek agreement with other States and fishing entities engaged in fishing for southern bluefin tuna, since this measure is closely related to other measures sought by the parties".[14]

Nevertheless in the *MOX Plant* case (2001) both ITLOS and the Arbitral Tribunal constituted pursuant to the UN Convention on the Law of the Sea to deal with this case did consider that they may prescribe measures different from those requested by the parties. ITLOS simply referred to Article 89(5) of its Rules.[15] The Arbitral Tribunal equally referred to this article. It also noted that any question of procedure not expressly governed by the Convention or the Rules were to be decided by the Tribunal after consulting the parties. Since the parties did not comment on this issue the Tribunal considered that it was competent to prescribe provisional measures other than those sought by a party.[16]

---

[14] ITLOS *Southern Bluefin Tuna Cases,* (*New Zealand* v. *Japan; Australia* v. *Japan*), 27 August 1999, Separate Opinion of Judge ad hoc Shearer.

[15] ITLOS the *MOX Plant* case (*Ireland* v. *UK*), Order for provisional measures of 3 December 2001, §83.

[16] Arbitral Tribunal constituted pursuant to Article 287, and Article 1 of Annex VII, of the United Nations Convention on the Law of the Sea for the dispute concerning the MOX Plant, international movement of radioactive materials, and the protection of the marine environment of the Irish Sea, The *MOX Plant* case (*Ireland* v. *UK*), Order No. 3, suspension of proceedings on jurisdiction and merits and request for further provisional measures, 24 June 2003, §43. The Arbitral Tribunal stated 'its willingness', during the hearings in June 2003, 'to consider the possibility of prescribing provisional measures if either Party considers that such measures are necessary to preserve the respective rights of the Parties or to prevent serious harm to the environment'. It did so after it announced its decision to suspend further proceedings in the case on the basis of considerations of mutual respect and comity, given possible proceedings before the European Court of Justice. Subsequently Ireland indeed submitted a request for further provisional measures. See Arbitral Tribunal constituted pursuant to Article 287, and Article 1 of Annex VII, of the United Nations Convention on the Law of the Sea for the dispute concerning the MOX Plant, international movement of radioactive materials, and the protection of the marine environment of the Irish Sea, The *MOX Plant* case (*Ireland* v. *UK*), Order No.3, suspension of proceedings on jurisdiction and merits and request for further provisional measures, 24 June 2003, §§31 and 32. See also ITLOS *Land Reclamation by Singapore in and around the Straits of Johor (Malaysia* v. *Singapore)*, Order of 8 October 2003.

2.3 Transparency, promptness and delegation

The Orders of the ICJ are published and include reasoning.[17] Obviously provisional measures should be taken in a timely fashion.[18] Sometimes this necessitates delegation of the authority to take provisional measures. Moreover, the discussion on transparency and due process is also influenced by considerations of promptness. Article 74 of the ICJ's Rules stipulates that requests for provisional measures shall have priority over all other cases and that the Court shall be convened 'forthwith' and 'as a matter of urgency'. Pending the meeting of the Court, its President may call upon the parties to take into account the request. Merrills points out that until 1995 the period between the request and the Order granting provisional measures varied from eight to 31 days. For the cases in which the ICJ refused the request the period ranged from 42 to 68 days.[19] More recently it took 27 days in *Avena*, one day in *LaGrand* and six days in *Breard*.[20] Notice for Orders for provisional measures shall go 'forthwith' to the Parties and the Security Council.[21] In the *Lockerbie* and *Genocide Convention* cases the ICJ only dealt with the request for provisional measures after it had notified all Parties to the Montreal Convention and the Convention against Genocide, respectively, of the filing of the applications.[22] Given the urgency involved, sending these notifications after the proceedings on provisional measures would seem more appropriate, especially in cases involving the fate of human beings.[23]

It is the ICJ President who fixes a date for the hearing about the request for provisional measures. In some cases (s)he arranges a hearing within a very short period of time. Thirlway mentions the *Hostages* case (ten days) and contrasts this to the *Great Belt* case (40 days). He notes that the President presumably takes into account the degree of urgency as well as other material considerations, such as *audi alteram partem*. The Parties must have the opportunity to attend the hearing.[24]

As noted, the possibility of delegation was introduced in order to address the need for promptness.

Initially the Presidents of the PCIJ and ICJ had the power to make provisional interim orders. In 1927 President Max Huber granted the request for provisional measures in the *Sino-Belgian Treaty* case.[25] Since the Rules of Court of 1978, Rule 74(4) stipulates that the President can only send a telegram requesting the States involved 'to act in such a way as will enable any

---

[17] Since 1999 the Orders for provisional measures (and the written and oral pleadings) are easily accessible on the website of the ICJ (<www.icj-cij.org>). The Court's judgments and provisional measures, as well as the texts of the hearings are made available on the internet in full. The PCIJ case law is also made available on this website. ITLOS case law is available at <www.itlos.org>.

[18] About promptness see e.g. Merrills (1995), p. 142. About assessment of temporal and material urgency see section 5.

[19] Merrills (1995), p. 142.

[20] See further section 3.3 on the ICJ's provisional measures to protect persons.

[21] Article 73(2) ICJ Rules of Procedure; Article 94 ITLOS Rule of Procedure; see further Rosenne (2005), pp. 153-154. In exceptional cases the Geneva human rights adjudicators might at some point decide to do the same, but it remains to be seen whether the Security Council will formally deal with the information received. On follow up by the human rights adjudicators see Chapter XVIII.

[22] See further Rosenne (2005), p. 166.

[23] See e.g. ICJ *LaGrand (Germany* v. *US)* and *Avena (Mexico* v. *US)*. See further Rosenne (2005), p. 166.

[24] Thirlway (1994), p. 26.

[25] PCIJ Denunciation of the Treaty of 2 November 1865 between China and Belgium, Order of 8 January 1927. See further section 3.3.2.

order the court may make (…) to have its appropriate effects'.[26] As Rosenne observes, in all cases in which the President sent such a telegram, provisional measures were later used and in those cases in which the President did not send telegrams, the ICJ subsequently denied the request for provisional measures. The *Avena* case is an exception: the ICJ used provisional measures to halt the execution of several Mexican nationals in the US. The President previously had not sent a telegram simply because the execution dates were not imminent.[27] Chambers of the ICJ do have the power to order provisional measures. In the *Frontier Dispute* case (1986) between Burkina Faso and Mali the Chamber constituted to deal with the dispute indeed did so.[28]

Article 29 ICJ Statute stipulates that, (w)ith a view to the speedy dispatch of business', the Court 'shall form annually a chamber composed of five judges which, at the request of the parties, may hear and determine cases by summary procedure'. While this Chamber is formed annually it does not appear to be used in the context of requests for provisional measures, possibly also because provisional measures are generally requested by one of the parties rather than by both parties together.

In the context of requests for provisional measures it may be necessary to streamline the standard proceedings in the interest of promptness, as long as both parties have an opportunity to address procedural and substantive concerns upon the Court's first indication of provisional measures. In any case both parties must have equal access to information, also at the provisional measures stage. Both parties must have the opportunity to be heard.[29] Yet, if the respondent does not respond or fails to appear this is not an obstacle to the use of provisional measures.[30] In general the ICJ has tried to allow the parties full opportunity to present their observations on the request for provisional measures.[31] 'The most usual practice', as Dumbauld put it in 1932 (with regard to the PCIJ), 'is to provide for a hearing if the matter is not too urgent'.[32] He referred to the statement by Judge Guerrero that 'time might not always permit a hearing'.[33] Nevertheless he noted that urgency as a result of the applicant party's 'lack of diligence' in making a timely

---

[26] See also Rules 13 and 32. Initially the power was delegated to the President when Court was not sitting (1922 Rules of Court, Article 57); later the power could not be delegated (1931 revision of the Rules); subsequently the President could 'take such measures as may appear to him to be necessary in order to enable the Court to give an effective decision' (1936 Rules of Court, Article 61(3) and 1946 ICJ Rules of Court); the present Rule provides: "Pending the meeting of the Court, the President may call upon the parties to act in such a way as will enable any order the Court may make on the request for provisional measures to have its appropriate effects" (1978 ICJ Rules of Court: Article 74(4)). See Wellens (1998), pp. 428-429 on the President's proactive use of this power in the *Genocide Convention* case.

[27] Rosenne (2005), pp. 169-170. For a recent example see also ICJ Press release of 15 August 2008, Proceedings instituted by Georgia against Russia, Urgent Communication to the Parties from the President under Article 74, paragraph 4, of the Rules of Court.

[28] ICJ *Frontier Dispute* case (*Burkina Faso* v. *Mali*), Order for provisional measures of 10 January 1986.

[29] See e.g. Merrills (1995), p. 143.

[30] See e.g. ICJ *Fisheries Jurisdiction* cases (*UK* v. *Iceland*; *Germany* v. *Iceland*, Order of 17 August 1972; *US Diplomatic and Consular Staff in Tehran* (*US* v. *Iran*) (*Hostages* case), Order of 15 December 1979.

[31] See, however, the discussion by Judge Schwebel on the short notice in the *LaGrand* case (*Germany* v. *US*), Order of 3 March 1999. See also Judge Buergenthal in *LaGrand* case (*Germany* v. *US*), Judgment of 27 June 2001.

[32] Dumbauld (1932), p. 159.

[33] Ibidem.

complaint would be 'duly discounted' by the Court.[34] The *LaGrand* case shows that the ICJ has taken a different approach when the life of an individual is at stake.[35]

In 1995 Merrills noted that States without a national as a member of the Court had generally insisted on an *ad hoc* Judge already at the stage of provisional measures, with the exception of Nicaragua in the *Nicaragua* case.[36] This trend has continued since 1995, albeit again with some exceptions in particularly urgent cases.[37] This is consistent with the ICJ statement in the *South-Eastern Greenland* case that the presence of *ad hoc* Judges would depend on the urgency of the case.[38]

ITLOS normally sends the information about the requests for provisional measures on the same day that a party requests them, generally to the relevant Ministry or Secretary of State and to the Embassy (or Consulate) of that State in Germany (where the ITLOS is seated).[39] It generally takes three weeks for it to Order provisional measures.

ITLOS has elaborated more than the ICJ on the possibilities of delegation. The Tribunal is composed of 21 members with a quorum of eleven members. Like the ICJ, annually it forms a chamber of five of its members that may hear and determine disputes by summary procedure.[40] Article 25 of the ITLOS Statute provides that ITLOS and its Seabed Disputes Chamber shall both have the power to prescribe provisional measures and that this power is delegated to the Chamber of Summary Procedure when the Tribunal is not in session or when there are insufficient members to constitute a quorum.[41] Like the Chamber of the ICJ, this Chamber is composed of the President and the Vice-President, 'acting *ex officio*' and three other members.[42] ITLOS may adopt provisional measures at the request of any party to the dispute and they shall be subject to its review and revision.

Pursuant to Article 16 of the Statute, ITLOS adopted Rules specifying, among others, its approach to urgent cases. The Rules stipulate that in case of urgency the President may convene the Tribunal at any time.[43] If the Tribunal is not sitting it is the President who shall fix the earliest

---

[34]   Ibidem.
[35]   ICJ *LaGrand* (*Germany* v. *US*), Order of 3 March 1999. See further section 3.3 (protection of the individual).
[36]   Merrills (1995), p. 145.
[37]   Since 1995 in most cases States that did not have a Judge of their nationality in the Court proposed an *ad hoc* Judge already at the provisional measures stage (*Land and Maritime Boundary between Cameroon and Nigeria* (*Cameroon* v. *Nigeria*), Order of 15 March 1996; *Legality of the use of force* (*Serbia and Montenegro* v. *Belgium/Canada/France/Germany/Italy /Netherlands/Portugal*), Order of 2 July 1999; *Arrest warrant of 11 April 2000* (*Congo* v. *Belgium*), Order of 8 December 2000; *Armed activities on the territory of the Congo* (*Congo* v. *Rwanda*), Order of 10 July 2002; *Certain criminal proceedings in France* (*Congo* v. *France*), Order of 18 July 2003; *Case concerning pulp mills on the river Uruguay* (*Argentina* v. *Uruguay*) Orders of 13 July 2006 and 23 January 2007. Yet in *Breard* (*Paraguay* v. *US*), Order of 9 April 1998, *Avena et al.* (*Mexico* v. *US*), Order of 5 February 2003 and *Armed activities on the territory of the Congo* (*Congo* v. *Uganda*), Order of 1 July 2000 no *ad hoc* Judges were appointed at the provisional measures stage.
[38]   PCIJ *Legal status of the South-Eastern Territory of Greenland*, Order for provisional measures of 3 August 1932, p. 280. See also Dumbauld (1932), p. 157 and Rosenne (2005), p. 137.
[39]   See e.g. ITLOS *MOX plant* case, §3. See also Rosenne (2005), p. 154.
[40]   See Article 15 Statute of the International Tribunal for the Law of the Sea, also stipulating that two alternative members shall be selected for the purpose of replacing members who are unable to participate in a particular proceeding.
[41]   See e.g. ITLOS Press Release 100, 6 October 2005.
[42]   See Article 28 Rules of the Tribunal. For the ICJ see Article 29 ICJ Statute.
[43]   Article 41(6) Rules of the Tribunal, adopted 28 October 1997 (amended 15 March and 21 September 2001).

possible date for a hearing. Pending the meeting of the Tribunal he may 'call upon the parties to act in such a way as will enable any order the Tribunal may make on the request for the provisional measures to have its appropriate effects'.[44] Within 15 days of the prescription of the measures, at the written request of a party, the Tribunal shall review or revise them. It may also review or revise them *proprio motu*.[45]

3   THE PURPOSE OF PROVISIONAL MEASURES IN GENERAL INTERNATIONAL LAW

3.1   Introduction

Article 41 ICJ Statute gives the ICJ the power to order provisional measures 'if it considers that circumstances so require'. The power to order such measures is discretionary.[46] Nevertheless, certain criteria have been applied to assess the appropriateness of their use. In that sense, the decision to use them is 'not purely discretionary'.[47] Reference is often made to their use to prevent irreparable harm and to the criterion of 'urgency'.[48] Obviously the concepts of irreparable harm and urgency are interrelated. They can only be understood in light of the rights claimed and the possible form of reparation. This raises issues involving the purpose of provisional measures, the risk of prejudgment and the question how urgency must be assessed. These issues are discussed in different sections. In order to clarify the criteria of irreparable harm and urgency this book distinguishes between the purpose of provisional measures and the assessment of temporal and material urgency. Temporal urgency relates to immediacy and material urgency to assessment of risk. The other criterion is that of irreparable harm, which adjudicators have found difficult to define.[49] Moreover, this concept is not always explicitly referred to in each international legal conflict.[50]

This Chapter not only discusses the purpose of preventing irreparable harm, but also other traditional purposes. It then discusses the relationship between provisional measures, the rights

---

[44]   Article 90(2) and (4) Rules of the Tribunal.

[45]   Article 91 Rules of the Tribunal.

[46]   See e.g. Sztucki (1983), p. 111; Merrills (1995), p. 109 and with regard to ITLOS, in *M/V 'Saiga'* Judge Laing who has pointed out that 'the view is well known that the power to order provisional measures is in principle discretionary', §6. He notes that such measures are 'discretionary and equitable' and that the 'open-ended' language of the Convention on the Law of the Sea facilitates this by stating: 'if it considers that the circumstances so require', §27. *M/V 'Saiga'* (N o. 2), Order for provisional measures of 11 March 1998, Separate Opinion Judge Laing.

[47]   Elkind (1981), p. 209.

[48]   See e.g. Rosenne (2005), pp. 135-148; Elkind (1981), pp. 209-219; Sztucki (1983), pp. 104-122; Beirlaen (1979-1980), pp. 97-101 and pp. 256-261; Merrills (1995), pp. 106-113 and Thirlway (1994), pp. 8-10 and pp. 25-27.

[49]   Also called irreparable damage, injury or prejudice. See further Elkind (1981), p. 216.

[50]   See e.g. ITLOS Judge Laing arguing 'there seems to be no *a priori* universal requirement of substantive urgency'. He believes that the notion of irreparability should not replace the textual requirement of the preservation of rights. With regard to a requirement of substantive urgency he notes that this 'has received some tepid encouragement under the twin influences of the requirements of procedural urgency and the notion that irreparability, with its connotations of gravity, has largely replaced the textual requirement of preservation of rights'. He believes that this idea is inaccurate and points out that the Order 'gives no credence to it'. *M/V 'Saiga'* (No. 2), Order for provisional measures of 11 March 1998, Separate Opinion Judge Laing, §26.

claimed and the eventual form of reparation, an issue closely related to that of prejudgment and the interests of the respondent State.

3.2 Adjudication of conflicts between States: the traditional purpose of provisional measures

3.2.1 Introduction

The ICJ's provisional measures aim to provide States with an expeditious remedy. At a minimum they serve to protect the *status quo ante* pending international adjudication. Elkind gives a broader expression of the function of provisional measures: "No party to a pending action may take advantage of a delay in settlement procedures by taking actions which will frustrate those procedures. This general norm is the real 'general principle'".[51] He also notes that this principle could be seen as 'a corollary to the principle *nemo judex in sua causa* (no one may be judge in his own cause) since a defendant who takes an action anticipating the judgment of the court or prejudicing the outcome of the dispute is, in effect, deciding in his own favour'.[52] This statement serves as an example of a broader approach to provisional measures that takes into account the fairness of the proceedings.

The way in which the ICJ uses provisional measures 'has an important bearing on its ability to assist States in managing and resolving their disputes by peaceful means'.[53] Upon receipt of a request for provisional measures it must examine, to some extent, the substance of the case.[54] In some of these cases it subsequently finds that it lacks jurisdiction or that the case must be discontinued. In these situations the provisional measures phase provides the only opportunity for the Court to perform its judicial function. Rosenne has referred to the *Southern Bluefin Tuna* case in which the Annex VII arbitral tribunal had pointed out that revocation of the ITLOS Order for provisional measures did 'not mean that the Parties may disregard the effects of that Order or their own decisions made in conformity with it'.[55]

---

[51] Elkind (1981), p. 30. See in general his discussion of irreparable injury, the maintenance of the status quo, protection of the environment and aggravation or extension of the dispute, pp. 209-233.

[52] Elkind (1981), p. 33 (footnote 53). See also section 3.6 of this Chapter on provisional measures and prejudgment.

[53] See Merrills (1995), p. 142.

[54] See further section 4 on the relationship with the rights claimed and section 5 on provisional measures and prejudgment.

[55] Annex VII Arbitral Tribunal *Southern Bluefin Tuna* case, Award on Jurisdiction and Admissibility of 4 August 2000, §67, referring to ITLOS *Southern Bluefin Tuna* cases (*New Zealand* v. *Japan, Australia* v. *Japan*), Order of 27 August 1999. Rosenne (2005), pp. 157-158, noted that 'carefully drafted provisional measures prescribed by ITLOS may have an implication for the future actions of the parties and lay the basis for the final solution of the dispute, even when the arbitral tribunal does not have jurisdiction over the dispute. There is no reason why this notion should not be given a wider application'. Thus 'carefully crafted provisional measures' may 'lay the basis for the final solution of the dispute', even when the adjudicator subsequently determines that it has no jurisdiction. In other words, proceedings on provisional measures constitute 'an important element in the general procedures available to States for the pacific settlement of their international dispute'. This does not mean that States could start proceedings simply in order to obtain provisional measures as some sort of interim judgment. Thus far this was a practice mainly before the Inter-American Commission on Human Rights, before the introduction of new Rules of Procedure, see Chapter II of this book. If proceedings started before the ICJ are disingenuous, the ICJ is likely to dismiss them or in any case to deny requests for

Section 3.1 mentioned the notion of preventing irreparable harm and noted that adjudicators have found it difficult to define the concept. The PCIJ initially referred to it. Subsequently, however, in 1939 it failed to mention it as a purpose of its provisional measures. In 1951 the ICJ did not mention it either, but since 1972 it has generally been accepted to constitute one of the main purposes of its provisional measures. This section briefly refers to some of the important early cases, starting with the two cases in which the purpose of preventing irreparable harm was not mentioned.

3.2.2   Preservation of rights and prevention of prejudice

In *Electricity Company of Sofia and Bulgaria* (1939) the PCIJ decided to use provisional measures to prevent prejudice to Belgium. The Court referred to Article 41 of the Statute and noted that this provision applied the principle 'universally accepted by international tribunals and likewise laid down in many conventions to which Bulgaria has been a party – to the effect that the parties to a case must abstain from any measure capable of exercising a prejudicial effect in regard to the execution of the decision to be given and, in general, not allow any step of any kind to be taken which might aggravate or extend the dispute'.[56] What it seems to have had in mind is the preservation of rights. The Parties shall not cause prejudice to the execution of the decision to be given by the Court. The decision also seems to regard non-aggravation of the dispute as a universally accepted principle. Thirlway speculates that this is 'either a restatement of something which in the Permanent Court's view was inherent in judicial procedures, or as something which was implied in Article 41 of the Statute'.[57] The Court referred to prejudice to the Applicant (Belgium) but there was no indication that this prejudice would have been irreparable.[58] In the *Anglo-Iranian Oil Co.* case (1951) the ICJ equally referred to the rights that may be 'subsequently adjudged by the Court to belong either to the Applicant or to the Respondent'.[59]

In a previous case brought by Belgium (1927) the PCIJ did order provisional measures exactly because the violation of certain rights 'would not be made good simply by the payment of an indemnity or by compensation or restitution in some material form'.[60] Equally, in the *South-Eastern Greenland* case (1932), in which the Court denied a request for provisional measures, it pointed out that the object of provisional measures 'contemplated by the Statute of the Court' was to preserve the respective rights of the Parties insofar as 'the damage threatening these rights would be irreparable in fact or in law'.[61] In 1972 the ICJ confirmed this approach in its Order for provisional measures in the *Fisheries Jurisdiction* cases. It referred to the purpose of preservation of the respective rights of the Parties pending the decision of the Court and pointed out that this presupposed that irreparable prejudice should not be caused to rights that are the subject of dispute in judicial proceedings. If Iceland would undertake the action planned it would anticipate

provisional measures. If a request for provisional measures is aimed at preventing irreparable harm to persons and there is no *prima facie* inadmissibility it is suggested in this book that the proceedings started are not to be regarded as disingenuous and if such serious cases can be solved as a consequence of provisional measures ordered by the Court this should only be welcomed.

[56]   PCIJ Electricity Company of Sofia and Bulgaria (*Belgium* v. *Bulgaria*), Order of 5 December 1939, p. 199.
[57]   Thirlway (1994), p. 13.
[58]   See Elkind (1981), pp. 209-210. See also section 3.6.
[59]   ICJ *Anglo-Iranian Oil Co.* case, Order of 5 July 1951.
[60]   See e.g. PCIJ *Sino-Belgian Treaty* case, Order of 8 January 1927, p. 7.
[61]   PCIJ *South-Eastern Greenland* case, Order of 3 August 1932, p. 284.

the Court's judgment and prejudice the rights claimed by the UK and Germany. This would 'affect the possibility of their full restoration in the event of a judgment in its favour'.[62]

3.2.3 Preservation of or return to the status quo/non-anticipation of the judgment

Thirlway refers to the idea of preservation as probably the most essential element of the concept of provisional measures, preserving rights that are threatened with irreparable harm.[63] This, in turn, raises the question of the *status quo*. In the *Hostages* case, for instance, the US had argued that it obviously was not requesting the Court to maintain the *status quo* 'as created by the Government of Iran of the past days and weeks', but rather a return to the *status quo ante*.[64] The US referred to Dumbauld's reference to 'the last uncontested status prior to the controversy'.[65] In the *Frontier Dispute* case the request for provisional measures related to the restoration of the *status quo ante*. The Parties only requested these measures a few years after they referred the boundary dispute to the Court.[66] They did so in light of subsequent incidents. Thirlway points out that non-anticipation is 'another way of putting the idea of preserving the *status quo*'. He then raises the question what is the *status quo* and whether it is necessarily the *status quo* that has to be preserved in order to protect the relevant rights.[67] He notes that 'preservation of rights' means that 'it must be shown that there is a right', that there is a threat to this right that must be prevented because it will not be sufficient 'to wait and recompense the holder of the right afterwards'. This obviously implies an 'anticipation' to some extent. In this respect he makes a distinction between a request to 'restrain one party from taking some step to change the status quo' and a request to 'require a form of restraint which itself involves a departure from the status quo'.[68] Merrills considers that 'there is no reason in principle why actual or impending economic damage should not be a sufficient reason for obtaining interim protection'. Clearly the requesting State should

---

[62]   ICJ *Fisheries Jurisdiction* cases, Orders of 17 August 1972. About those cases see Thirlway (1994), pp. 11-12 who regrets the brevity of the Court's finding. He refers to the UK's request in which it 'explained very clearly the economic consequences of exclusion of British vessels from the Icelandic fishing grounds, and why those consequences would be irreversible'. He suggests that it was this that justified the Court's Order for provisional measures. "Even if the economic consequences had been purely transitory, and therefore capable of redress by monetary reparation, the Icelandic action would be just as much an anticipation of the Court's judgment". In other words, he argues that even if there is no risk of irreparable harm (because redress by monetary reparation would be possible) the ICJ could still use provisional measures simply to prevent a State from anticipating the Court's judgment.

[63]   Thirlway (1994), p. 3, referring to the French term *mesures conservatoires,* and pp. 8-10.

[64]   ICJ *Hostages* case (*US* v. *Iran*), Oral pleadings of 10 December 1979, p. 33.

[65]   Dumbauld (1932), p. 187. Elkind (1981) discusses these statements at pp. 219-220.

[66]   ICJ *Frontier Dispute* case (*Burkina Faso* v. *Mali*), Order of 10 January 1986.

[67]   In the context of the *Passing through the Great Belt* (1991) case he notes that it 'could be said that the *status quo* was the fact of the Great Belt remaining open; but Finland argued in fact that the mere continuation of the works was creating a situation in which it would be, as it were, too late for Denmark to turn back, and that therefore the *status quo* was a *status quo* in which Denmark was not planning a bridge, or was at least not proceeding with construction work of a bridge'. In reference to the fact that the ICJ found that the interference would not take place 'until after the Court would foreseeably have given judgment on the merits', he concludes that the Court considered that the *status quo* was that of the Great Belt and not of Denmark's plans, Thirlway (1994), p. 12.

[68]   Thirlway (1994), p. 11.

show that the harm is irreparable 'in the sense that it could not be adequately dealt with by a subsequent award of compensation'.[69]

Recently the ICJ denied requests for provisional measures in two cases instigated by Congo in relation to arrest warrants and criminal proceedings in Belgium and France, respectively.[70] The second case is still pending, but in the first the ICJ eventually found in favour of Congo[71] Nevertheless, pending the proceedings provisional measures were not warranted because the situation was not irreversible,.

3.2.4 Non-aggravation or extension of the dispute

Non-aggravation or extension of the dispute was already mentioned as a purpose of provisional measures in the PCIJ *Electricity Company of Sofia and Bulgaria* case (1939).[72] Yet the *Fisheries Jurisdiction* cases (1972), summing up the purposes of provisional measures, did not mention this aspect.[73] In the *Aegean Sea* case (1976) Greece argued that the purpose of preventing aggravation or extension of the dispute is a general consideration underlying the right to order provisional measures. All actions of the parties that might aggravate or extend the dispute fall under the jurisdiction of the Court. This power is not 'merely another way of phrasing the idea that interim measures are intended to avoid prejudice in regard to the execution of the decision later to be given'. In other words, 'these are clearly independent grounds for the Court's intervention'.[74]

According to Elkind the most important function of interim protection is indeed the prevention of violence,[75] yet in all cases provisional measures must aim at preserving the rights of the parties.[76] A decade later Merrills wrote that the idea appeared to be firmly established 'that, in addition to the unique features of each situation', the ICJ 'should take into account the general value of containing disputes.[77] On the other hand, Thirlway suggests that the obligation not to aggravate or extend an existing dispute 'might be seen as a parallel' to the obligation laid down in Article 18 Vienna Convention on the Law of Treaties or to the obligation not to defeat the object and purpose of an existing treaty between signature and ratification.[78] He notes that 'you have, as it were, a legal kernel of obligation or asserted obligation contained in the original dispute, or in the treaty, and you have in parallel to that an obligation or asserted obligation not to enlarge, spoil, or defeat the kernel of law'.[79] The question remains whether non-aggravation of the dispute

---

[69]   Merrills (1995), p. 112. In ICJ *Arbitral Award of 31 July 1989* (*Guinea-Bissau* v. *Senegal*), Order of 2 March 1990, the ICJ rejected the argument that Article 41 should be used to protect interests as well as rights, see Merrills (1995), p. 143. See further section 3.5 on the relationship with the rights claimed.

[70]   ICJ *Arrest warrant of 11 April 2000* (*Congo* v. *Belgium*), Order of 8 December 2000 and Certain criminal proceedings in France (*Congo* v. *France*), Order of 17 June 2003.

[71]   ICJ *Arrest warrant of 11 April 2000* (*Congo* v. *Belgium*), Judgment of 14 February 2002. See on this case e.g. Van Alebeek (2006), esp. pp. 333-337 and p. 477.

[72]   PCIJ *Electricity Company of Sofia and Bulgaria* (*Belgium* v. *Bulgaria*), Order of 5 December 1939; see also Dumbauld (1932), pp. 167-168 and Thirlway (1994), p. 7 pointing out that the 1907 Washington Convention that introduced the Central American Court and the Bryan Treaties (US) did not refer to preservation of rights but instead to the purpose of non-aggravation of the dispute and of preservation of *status quo*.

[73]   ICJ *Fisheries Jurisdiction* cases, Orders of 17 August 1972.

[74]   O'Connell's arguments on behalf of Greece in the ICJ *Aegean Sea* case (*Greece* v. *Turkey*), Order of 11 September 1976, referred to in Elkind (1981), p. 225.

[75]   See Elkind (1981), p. 229.

[76]   Elkind (1981), p. 228.

[77]   Merrills (1995), p. 122.

[78]   Thirlway (1994), p. 13.

[79]   Thirlway (1994), p. 14.

can be a purpose in itself sufficient for the Court to use provisional measures or whether it is part of or related to the power to use provisional measures to preserve the rights of the parties.

In the *Nicaragua* case the US argued that the use of provisional measures was 'particularly inappropriate at this time' because it could 'irreparably prejudice the interests of a number of states and seriously interfere with the negotiations'.[80] The US considered that the fact that the UN Security Council and the OAS were addressing the conflict was another reason to refuse the provisional measures requested. Merrills notes that the ICJ did not discuss the relevance of the above-mentioned diplomatic activity for the 'circumstances' to be taken into account for the use of provisional measures. The fact, however, that it did order provisional measures shows that it did not consider that this was inappropriate. Merrills suggests that the Court may have agreed with Nicaragua's argument that the fact that the question before it is linked with political questions should not force it to decline the 'essentially judicial task' before it.[81] Subsequently the ICJ pointed out, in its judgment on jurisdiction and admissibility, that the UN Charter does not confer *exclusive* responsibility on the Security Council for the maintenance of international peace and security. There was no provision in the Charter demarcating between the functions of the Security Council and the ICJ. "The Council has functions of a political nature assigned to it, whereas the Court exercise purely judicial functions. Both organs can therefore perform their separate but complementary functions with respect to the same events".[82] Merrills concludes that legal and political processes complement each other and 'there need be no contradiction between the pursuit of diplomatic means of settlement and the ordering of interim protection under Article 41'. At the same time there may be circumstances in which diplomatic efforts satisfy the Court that there is no longer a threat of irreparable harm, that here is no urgency anymore or that provisional measures would indeed prejudice ongoing negotiations.[83] In the *Genocide Convention* case the ICJ again did not consider the use of provisional measures inappropriate, despite Serbia's argument that the Security Council was already dealing with the case under Chapter VII.[84]

On the other hand, in the *Lockerbie* case, after the Security Council issued Resolution 748 under Chapter VII of the UN Charter, it did not consider the use of provisional measures appropriate, although several judges had argued that it could still have used them *proprio motu* with the purpose of preventing the aggravation of the dispute and in order to reduce tension.[85] According to Thirlway's interpretation of the case law until and including the decision not to use provisional measures in the *Lockerbie* case (1992), either the Court has no independent power to use provisional measures only to prevent the aggravation or extension of the dispute or, if it exists

---

[80]   ICJ *Military and paramilitary activities in and against Nicaragua* (*Nicaragua* v. *US*), Judgment on jurisdiction and admissibility, 26 November 1984, §33 and Merrills (1995), p. 127.

[81]   Merrills (1995), p. 128. See further Rosenne (2005), pp. 196-201 and Gray (2003).

[82]   ICJ *Military and paramilitary activities in and against Nicaragua* (*Nicaragua* v. *US*), Judgment on jurisdiction and admissibility, 26 November 1984, §95.

[83]   Merrills (1995), p. 128.

[84]   ICJ *Application of the Convention on the prevention and punishment of the crime of genocide* (*Bosnia and Herzegovina* v. *Yugoslavia (Serbia and Montenegro)*), Order of 8 April 1993, §33.

[85]   ICJ *Questions of Interpretation and Application of the 1971 Montreal Convention arising from the Aerial Incident at Lockerbie* (*Libya* v. *US and UK*), Order of 14 April 1992. See the Dissenting Opinions of Judges Bedjaoui, Ranjeva, Ajibola, Weeramantry and *ad hoc* Judge El-Kosheri. As Merrills (1995), p. 131 points out, the ICJ could only have used provisional measures based on a finding that the Resolution was unconstitutional. 'Whatever the Court's powers to deal with such questions, it is difficult to see how they could be properly addressed in incidental proceedings'. He notes that the ICJ left open the question whether the ICJ could use provisional measures if the Security Council is acting in the same manner, but under Chapter VI. He refers in agreement to the statement by four individual members that this would indeed be possible (pp. 131-132).

it 'should be exercised very sparingly'.[86] Subsequently, however, the ICJ has pointed out that, by virtue of Article 41, it does have the power to indicate provisional measures 'with a view to preventing the aggravation or extension of the dispute whenever it considers that circumstances so require'. It has this power 'independently of the requests for the indication of provisional measures submitted by the parties to preserve specific rights'.[87]

In other words, in cases involving armed struggle the ICJ has used provisional measures to prevent aggravation of the conflict, but in the *Lockerbie* case it has not. According to Merrills, the fact that the Court refused to use them for that purpose in the latter case 'must be explained by its different assessment of the facts'.[88] Moreover, it might also be explained by the idea that the ICJ 'should be extremely cautious' in its decision to use provisional measures *proprio motu* if a dispute was already dealt with under Chapter VII of the UN Charter.[89]

In *Congo* v. *Uganda* (2000) the ICJ ordered provisional measures and noted that Security Council resolutions do not, as such, preclude the ICJ 'from acting in accordance with its Statute and with the Rules of Court'.[90] After all the ICJ exercises 'purely judicial functions'. "Both organs can therefore perform their separate but complementary functions with respect to the same events".[91] Already in the *Frontier Dispute* case (1986) the Chamber noted that 'independently of the requests submitted by the Parties for the indication of provisional measures, the Court or, accordingly, the Chamber possesses by virtue of Article 41 of the Statute the power to indicate the provisional measures with a view of preventing the aggravation or extension of the dispute whenever it considers that circumstances so require'.[92] The ICJ repeated this statement in 2000 in its Order for provisional measures in *Armed Activities on the Territory of the Congo (Congo* v. *Uganda)*.[93] It now seems to be generally accepted that the need to prevent the aggravation or extension of a dispute could be taken into account in deciding whether provisional measures are necessary.[94]

One situation in which this need is triggered is in cases where there is a risk of armed conflict. Yet Judge Buergenthal has pointed out that the ICJ must 'be deemed to have the requisite powers vested in courts generally, powers that in my view find expression in Article 41 of its

---

[86]   Thirlway (1994), pp. 14-16.

[87]   See e.g. ICJ *Certain criminal proceedings in France (Congo* v. *France)*, Order of 17 June 2003 (finding no need to use provisional measures) and *Land and maritime boundary between Cameroon and Nigeria (Cameroon* v. *Nigeria)*, Order of 15 March 1996, §41. See also the Court's statement in *Frontier Dispute (Burkina Faso* v. *Mali)*, Order of 10 January 1986, §18.

[88]   Merrills (1995), pp. 124-125. He also referred to the Separate Opinion of Judge Shahabuddeen, in *Lockerbie (Libya* v. *US/UK)*, Order of 14 April 1992.

[89]   Merrills (1995), p. 125. See also Wellens (1998), p. 422. In general on provisional measures and 'international crisis management': Rosenne (2005), pp. 218-222 and Gray (2003).

[90]   ICJ *Armed Activities on the Territory of the Congo (Congo* v. *Uganda)*, Order of 1 July 2000, §44.

[91]   ICJ *Armed Activities on the Territory of the Congo (Congo* v. *Uganda)*, Order of 1 July 2000, §44. See also *Cameroon* v. *Nigeria*, Order of 15 March 1996, §36.

[92]   ICJ *Frontier Dispute* case *(Burkina Faso* v. *Mali)*, Order of 10 January 1986, §18. Merrills (1995), p. 123 notes that this remark 'served to underline the importance of the issue of aggravation and extension on the particular facts, as well as to confirm the existence of residual powers which might be significant in other cases'. See also the discussion of the *proprio motu* use of provisional measures in section 2 of this Chapter.

[93]   ICJ *Armed Activities on the Territory of the Congo (Congo* v. *Uganda)*, Order of 1 July 2000, §44. See also *Cameroon* v. *Nigeria*, Order of 15 March 1996, §41.

[94]   Judge Laing even argues that ITLOS should not prescribe provisional measures without a reference to this purpose because they 'might otherwise themselves become the source of tension between the parties', ITLOS *M/V 'Saiga'* case (No. 2), Order of 11 March 1998, Separate Opinion of Judge Laing, §§31-32.

Statute, to ensure that the orderly adjudication of cases pending before it is not aggravated or undermined by extrajudicial coercive measures resorted to by one party to the dispute against the other'.[95] This applies to a broader range of cases than just those involving possible armed conflict. It would also mean that a provisional measure could be ordered 'just' to prevent aggravation of the dispute without also ordering measures to prevent irreparable harm to the rights that are the subject of the dispute.

He notes that in such cases 'the test would not be whether there is an imminent threat of irreparable harm to the subject matter of the dispute, but whether the challenged actions are having a serious adverse effect on the ability of the party seeking the provisional measures to fully protect its rights in the judicial proceedings'.[96]

In any case, even if the ICJ decides not to use provisional measures, for a State the act of requesting provisional measures could have a value in itself. Merrills gives the following examples: the fact that they allow for the opportunity to generate publicity, that they may allow an increase in the pressure on the other States, that they may provoke a debate and even remove the requesting State's fear that it is about to be attacked.[97]

3.2.5 Preserving the integrity of the proceedings/preserving the evidence

Reference has also been made to preserving the integrity of the proceedings and the preservation of evidence.[98] According to Dumbauld (1932) provisional measures 'protect *rights* of the parties, not the *evidence* by which a party expects to establish its rights, unless such evidence is indispensable and its loss would mean the loss of a right'.[99] The PCIJ President's Order in the *Sino-Belgian* case did refer to the obligation to provide judicial safeguards for Belgian nationals.[100] Yet this is a substantive obligation for China that could help protect the individual rights of the Belgian nationals rather than just obligations necessary to preserve the procedural rights of Belgium in the case before the PCIJ.

While in the *Frontier Dispute* case (1986) the ICJ did refer to the risk of destruction of evidence that might be material to the dispute, Thirlway considers this a purely procedural justification for provisional measures, 'not of great importance'.[101] In this case both Parties (Burkina Faso and Mali) had agreed to bring the case before the ICJ and had also agreed on a cease-fire. In the *Land and Maritime Boundary between Cameroon and Nigeria* case (1996), however, this was not the case. Still the ICJ ordered, among others, that 'both parties should take

---

[95] ICJ *Pulp Mills* (*Argentina* v. *Uruguay*), Order of 27 January 2007, Declaration of Judge Buergenthal, §7. See also Declaration by Judge Koroma to the same order, §4.

[96] Id., Declaration of Judge Buergenthal, §11. See also the discussion in Chapter XIII (Protection) with regard to the problem with equality of arms when one of the parties in a legal conflict (the petitioner) is executed by the other (the State) pending a case before a human rights adjudicator.

[97] See Merrills (1995), pp. 140-141, referring to the *Aegean Sea* case and the *Lockerbie* case in relation to the fear of being attacked. For a contrary view, aiming at discouraging States to resort to the Court, see the two Concurring Opinions of Judges Dugard and Buergenthal in *Congo* v. *Rwanda*, Order of 10 July 2002.

[98] See e.g. Sztucki (1983), pp. 73-74.

[99] Dumbauld (1932), p. 164.

[100] PCIJ *Sino-Belgian Treaty* case, Order of 8 January 1927.

[101] ICJ *Frontier Dispute* case (*Burkina Faso* v. *Mali*), Order of 10 January 1986. Thirlway (1994), p. 16. Yet as Merrills (1995), p. 108 points out, given the armed clashes that have taken place following reference of the boundary dispute to the Court, 'it was plainly important to restore the situation on the ground and to facilitate the gathering of evidence if the final judgment was to be effective'. See also Chapter XII, section 2.10 for an instance in which the European Commission on Human Rights used provisional measures to preserve evidence.

all necessary steps to conserve evidence relevant to the present case within the disputed area' and that they 'should lend any assistance to the fact-finding mission which the Secretary-General of the United Nations has proposed to send to the Bakassi Peninsula'.[102]

3.2.6 Preventing serious harm to the (marine) environment

In its provisional measures in the *Nuclear Test* cases (1973) the ICJ ordered France to halt its nuclear tests and referred to claims that 'the uncertain physical and genetic effects to which contamination exposes the people of New Zealand causes them acute apprehension, anxiety and concern; and that there could be no possibility that the rights eroded by the holding of further tests could be fully restored in the event of a judgment in New Zealand's favour in these proceedings'.[103]

The early work of Elkind (1981) already suggested protection of the environment as one of the circumstances that might warrant the use of provisional measures.[104] He referred to the pleadings of New Zealand in the *Nuclear test* cases about the 'irreversible contribution which such tests make to the pollution of the human environment'. To some extent it seemed, thereby, to be 'asserting some world community interest'.[105] He has also pointed out that '[e]nvironmental damage in most cases involves the unendurable rather than the irreparable'.[106] While the environmental and world community interests may certainly have played a role in the ICJ's Order to France to halt its nuclear tests, at the time environmental protection, as an interest in itself, was not yet generally considered to constitute a reason for the use of provisional measures. Later, in *Pulp Mills*, the ICJ did stress the 'great significance' it attached to respect for the environment.[107] It noted the 'general obligation of States to ensure that activities within their jurisdiction and control respect the environment of other States or of areas beyond national control is now part of the corpus of international law relating to the environment'.[108] It pointed out that the case

---

[102] ICJ *Land and Maritime Boundary between Cameroon and Nigeria* case (1996), Order of 15 March 1996, §49 (Judge Ajibola voted against this part of the Order, considering that while the order was formally directed to both Parties, in fact it 'can only refer to Cameroon', resulting in unequal treatment of the Parties).

[103] ICJ *Nuclear Tests* case (*New Zealand* v. *France*), Order of 22 June 1973, §28. See also section 3.6 (prejudgment) and 3.7.4 (relation to reparation). In 1994 Wellens referred to the 'potential irreversibility of many forms of environmental damage' and considered that 'one would expect a more widespread acceptance and provision for mechanisms indicating interim measures of protection upon emergence of a dispute, although the need for such a mechanism could in the first place be reduced by the application of the precautionary principle to the maximum extent possible', Wellens (1994), p. 25. See also section 5.3 on assessment of material urgency and the precautionary principle.

[104] Elkind (1981), pp. 220-224.

[105] Elkind (1981), p. 222. See the *Nuclear Test* cases, Orders of 22 July 1973 (the six Dissenting Opinions related to the issue of jurisdiction rather than to the purpose of provisional measures). For Elkind's evaluation of the concept of irreparable harm see the discussion in section 3.3 of this Chapter.

[106] Elkind (1981), p. 224.

[107] ICJ *Pulp Mills*, Order of 13 July 2006, §72. Yet it denied the request for provisional measures because Argentina had not persuaded it that the construction of the mills posed 'an imminent threat of irreparable damage', §73. See also on lack of imminence, ICJ *Pulp Mills*, Order of 23 January 2007, §§42 and 50.

[108] It referred to ICJ *Advisory Opinion on the Legality of the Threat or Use of Nuclear Weapons*, 8 July 1996. See further, e.g. Kwiatkowska (1996). See also section 5.3 on assessment of material urgency and the precautionary principle.

highlighted the importance of the need to ensure environmental protection of shared natural resources while allowing for sustainable economic development'.[109]

The introduction of Article 290(1) UNCLOS specifically recognized environmental protection as one of the aims of provisional measures. The article provides the criterion that the provisional measures prescribed by ITLOS must be 'appropriate under the circumstances to preserve the respective rights of the parties to the dispute or to prevent serious harm to the marine environment'. This means that there could be two different reasons for provisional measures by ITLOS. If it takes measures to prevent such harm to the marine environment and these measures have been requested by one of the Parties the two reasons coincide. It explicitly provides the tribunal with the authority to take into account a general interest going *beyond* the rights of the Parties to the conflict. This is the interest of the protection of the marine environment. ITLOS does not use the criterion of preventing irreparable harm. As is clear from the text, instead it uses the more lenient criterion of preventing *serious* harm. This is also the criterion generally used in international environmental law.[110] This means that, just like in human rights treaties, States have now explicitly assigned to an international adjudicator the task to determine conflicts about the interpretation and application of rights and interests that surpass those of the State alone.

In the *MOX Plant* case Ireland argued that the commissioning of the plant would itself be 'a near-irreversible step'.[111] It would not be possible 'to return to the position that existed before the commissioning of the MOX Plant simply by ceasing to feed plutonium into the system'.[112] The UK, on the other hand, contended that 'neither the commissioning of the MOX Plant nor the introduction of plutonium into the system' would be irreversible, 'although decommissioning would present the operator of the plant with technical and financial difficulties, if Ireland were to be successful in its claim before the Annex VII arbitral tribunal'.[113] ITLOS placed on record the assurances given by the UK that there would be no additional marine transports to or from Sellafield as a result of the commissioning of the MOX Plant and that there would be no export of MOX fuel until October 2002 nor import 'to the THORP plant of spent nuclear fuel pursuant to contracts for conversion to the MOX plant'. In the circumstances, and in the short period before the constitution of the Annex VII arbitral tribunal, it did not find that the urgency of the situation required the prescription of the provisional measures requested by Ireland. As discussed in section 3.7 on the substance of provisional measures it instead ordered the parties to cooperate.[114]

3.2.7 Preventing irreparable harm

Dumbauld pointed out in 1932 that it is not necessary for provisional measures to be 'absolutely indispensable'. It is 'sufficient if they serve as a safeguard against substantial and not easily reparable injury'.[115] "The degree of necessity required varies with the nature of the measure. The more serious the hardship to defendant, the stricter the scrutiny of plaintiff's wants".[116]

---

[109]   ICJ *Pulp Mills*, Order of 13 July 2006, §80.

[110]   See also the discussion on the relationship between provisional measures and the precautionary principle in section 5.3.3.

[111]   ITLOS *MOX Plant* case (*Ireland* v. *UK*), Order of 3 December 2001, §70.

[112]   Ibid.

[113]   ITLOS *MOX Plant* case (*Ireland* v. *UK*), Order of 3 December 2001. The discussion on the provisional measures in the *Southern Bluefin Tuna* cases (*New Zealand* v. *Japan*; *Australia* v. *Japan*) Order of 27 August 1999 is also relevant in this respect.

[114]   ITLOS *MOX Plant* case (*Ireland* v. *UK*), Order of 3 December 2001, §§77-89.

[115]   Dumbauld (1932), p. 163.

[116]   Ibid.

Half a century later Elkind noted that the likelihood of irreparable injury to be caused to (one of) the Parties was indeed 'the most commonly accepted circumstance' justifying the use of provisional measures.[117]

Even when the ICJ does not use the phrase 'irreparable harm', this seems to underlie its use of provisional measures, or in the words of Rosenne, the ICJ will regard a case as urgent only if the 'potential damage would be irreparable'.[118] The next section will refer to the Court's case law regarding rights that surpass those of the State alone, in particular to protect the individual. In those cases reference is often made exactly to the purpose of preventing irreparable harm.

3.3 Conflicts between States with regard to the protection of the individual

3.3.1 Introduction

The ICJ is not a human rights court and not even an international court of general jurisdiction, receiving individual complaints. Yet a State may request it to indicate provisional measures for the protection of individuals. This means that the Court can address individual rights in so far as they are asserted by a State, through diplomatic protection, but always in function of the relationship between the rights of an individual and those of a State.[119]

Both under customary international law and in conventions such as the Vienna Convention on Consular Relations (1963), States have the fundamental right to protect their subjects abroad, if these are injured, or are about to be injured, by acts of another State, in violation of international obligations. The State may accord diplomatic protection against an act or omission by a foreign State causing injury to its subjects.[120] In 1924 the PCIJ already called this 'an elementary principle of international law'.[121] The State is entitled to communicate with its national who is arrested or charged with a crime in another State, to give him or her assistance and to have a representative present at the trial. Moreover, international law has recognised the right of States to demand reparation for damage suffered by their nationals abroad. In this respect, citizens are still seen as a constituent element of the State itself – and, ideally, the primary reason for the State's existence. On the other hand, the changing nature of international law may even change the doctrine of diplomatic protection, exactly where human rights are concerned.[122] The individual is increasingly gaining prominence in international law, which is particularly relevant in connection with dignity rights and the right to life. To some extent this is also reflected in the decisions of the ICJ.[123]

This section discusses the PCIJ Order in *China* v. *Belgium*, and ICJ Orders involving consular issues, border conflicts and mass human rights violations.

---

[117]   Elkind (1981), p. 210. For Elkind's evaluation of the concept of irreparable harm see the discussion in section 3.3 of this Chapter. For another discussion of the early case law see also Beirlaen (1979-1980), pp. 262-270.

[118]   Rosenne (2005), p. 135.

[119]   On diplomatic protection and attempts of the ILC Special Rapporteur Dugard to emphasize human rights aspects, see e.g. his reports A/CN.4/514 (2001), A/CN.4/538 (2004); A/CN.4/546 (2005) and A/CN.4/567 (2006). See also Vermeer-Künzli (2007) and Pronto (2007).

[120]   ALI Restatement (Third) of the Foreign Relations Law of the United States, (1987) par 713, Comment c. See more closely on the issue of diplomatic protection and its relation to human rights the reports by ILC Rapporteur Dugard and Vermeer-Künzli (2007).

[121]   PCIJ *Mavrommatis Concessions* cases, Judgment of 30 August 1924, p. 12.

[122]   See Kamminga (1992).

[123]   See also, e.g., Milano (2004), Pinto (2002), Bedjaoui (2000), Higgins (1998), Schwebel (1996b) and Goy (1995).

3.3.2 Protecting nationals

In 1927 Belgium claimed that the Treaty of Friendship, Commerce and Navigation with Belgium, which had been denounced by China, was still in force. President Huber of the PCIJ ordered provisional measures, noting that, should this claim later be found to be correct, a violation of the rights of the Belgian nationals in China 'could not be made good simply by the payment of an indemnity or by compensation or restitution in some other material form'.[124] Thus he ordered provisional measures, upholding, at least during the proceedings, certain basic rights contained in this treaty. These rights included the right of any Belgian who lost his passport or had committed an offence 'to be conducted in safety to the nearest Belgian consulate' and protection of Belgians against insult or violence. They also included their right not to be arrested except through a consul, 'nor to be subjected, as regards the execution of any penalty involving personal violence or duress, to any except the regular action of Belgian law'. Finally the provisional measures ordered China to ensure the right to a fair trial (legal proceedings) heard by 'the modern courts', with the right of appeal, 'in accordance with the regular legal procedure and with the assistance of advocates and interpreters chosen by them and duly approved by the said courts'.[125] As Higgins puts it:

> "[v]arious rights that today we would term human rights were protected by the interim measures, exactly because they were the claimed rights by one party under the dispute (...) The protection of human rights was the concomitant of the perceived need to protect the rights claimed in the dispute under litigation; it was not ancillary to them or separate from them".[126]

3.3.3 Protecting diplomats and other nationals

In *US Diplomatic and Consular Staff in Tehran* (1979) the US had claimed violations of its diplomatic and consular rights, as well as the rights of its nationals to 'life, liberty, protection and security'.[127]

Early November 1979 a strong-armed group of several hundred people had attacked the US embassy and took hostage all the diplomatic and consular personnel, as well as other persons present in the premises. Later, they seized US personnel and one US private citizen in other places in Tehran and brought them to the embassy as well. Reportedly, the Iranian security personnel had simply disappeared from the scene and the government made no attempt to clear the embassy premises or to rescue the hostages. They did not even attempt to persuade the militants to terminate their actions. Two weeks after the attack thirteen hostages were released, but at the time of the request for provisional measures several people were still being held hostage: at least 28 persons with the status of 'member of the diplomatic staff', at least twenty persons recognized as 'member of the administrative and technical staff' and two US citizens with no diplomatic or consular status.

The US alleged inhumane treatment of the hostages. In its Order the Court noted the assertions by both the militants and the Iranian authorities that the hostages were well treated and that special visits had been allowed by religious personalities and representatives of the ICRC.

---

[124] PCIJ *Denunciation of the Treaty of 2 November 1865 Between China and Belgium*, Order of 8 January 1927, p. 7.

[125] Id., p. 8. Subsequently President Huber revoked the Order 'in its entirety', upon request of Belgium, now that Belgium and China had agreed to a provisional regime of protection, Order of 15 February 1927.

[126] Higgins (1997), p. 95.

[127] ICJ *United States Diplomatic and Consular Staff in Tehran (US v. Iran)*, 15 December 1979, p. 19.

The Court also pointed out that Iran had not refuted the concrete allegations of ill treatment. It referred to examples, mentioned in some of the sworn declarations, of hostages who had been released in November 1979. Some hostages 'were paraded, bound and blindfolded before hostile and chanting crowds; at least during the initial period of their captivity, hostages were kept bound and frequently blindfolded, denied mail or any communication with their government or with each other, subjected to interrogation, threatened with weapons'.[128] Seventeen days later the Court unanimously issued an Order for provisional measures. While the ICJ ordered provisional measures on the basis of the diplomatic and consular conventions alone, it did add, that 'the continuance of the situation [which is] the subject of the present request exposes the human beings concerned to deprivation, hardship, anguish and even danger to life and health and thus to a serious possibility of irreparable harm'.[129]

The *Hostages* case is known mainly for its discussion of state responsibility, including responsibility for inaction[130] and for the Court's determination that 'diplomatic law itself provides the necessary means of defence against, in sanction form, illicit activities by members of diplomatic or consular missions'.[131] At the time the US filed the Application, however, US nationals were still being held hostage in Iran, requiring immediate protective action. For this reason the US also requested provisional measures under Article 41 of the ICJ Statute and Article 73 Rules of Court.[132] The US had requested, in particular, the immediate release of its nationals detained in the embassy and at the Iranian Ministry of Foreign Affairs. It had also requested the restoration of the embassy premises to the US authorities. Before the Court was able to convene to discuss this request the President sent the governments of Iran and the US a telegram requesting them 'to act in such a way as will enable any order the court may make (…) to have its appropriate effects'.[133]

Subsequently, in its judgment on the merits, the ICJ pointed out:

> "Wrongfully to deprive human beings of their freedom and to subject them to physical restraint in conditions of hardship is in itself manifestly incompatible with the principles of the Charter of the United Nations, as well as with the fundamental principles enunciated in the Universal Declaration of Human Rights".[134]

In its order for provisional measures the Court considered that, contrary to Iran's argument, the hostage taking and detention of internationally protected persons was far from 'secondary and marginal'. The Court referred to the UN Secretary General's statement that it was a 'grave situation' posing 'a serious threat to international peace and security' as well as Security Council resolution 457 in which the Council expressed its deep concern about the dangerous level of tension between the two States, a tension which 'could have grave consequences for international peace and security'.[135] Iran had also put forward that the matter was one of domestic jurisdiction. The Court responded that 'a dispute which concerns diplomatic and consular premises and the

---

[128] ICJ *US Diplomatic and Consular Staff in Tehran (US v. Iran) (Hostages* case), Order of 15 December 1979, §§17, 18, 22 and 23.

[129] Id. p. 20.

[130] ICJ *US Diplomatic and Consular Staff in Tehran (US v. Iran) (Hostages* case), Order of 15 December 1979, §§61-67 (due diligence) and 69-79 (acts of state).

[131] ICJ *US Diplomatic and Consular Staff in Tehran (US v. Iran) (Hostages* case), Order of 15 December 1979, §§83 and 86.

[132] It requested provisional measures on 29 November 1979, the day it filed its Application.

[133] On the basis of Rule 74(4) of the Rules of Court (1978).

[134] ICJ *US Diplomatic and Consular Staff in Tehran (US v. Iran) (Hostages* case), Judgment of 24 May 1980, §91.

[135] ICJ *US Diplomatic and Consular Staff in Tehran (US v. Iran)*, Order of 15 December 1979, §23.

detention of internationally protected persons, and involves the interpretation or application of multilateral conventions codifying the international law governing diplomatic and consular relations, is one which by its very nature falls within international jurisdiction'.[136]

The Court also disposed of Iran's argument that provisional measures were intended to protect the interests of both Parties and could not be granted to one side only. It pointed out that the terms of Article 41 of the Statute explicitly refer to 'the respective rights of *either* party' (italics by the Court), that 'the whole concept of an indication for provisional measures, as Article 73 of the Rules recognizes, implies a request from one of the parties for measures to preserve its own rights against action by the other party calculated to prejudice those rights *pendente lite*'. It concluded that a request for provisional measures is 'by its nature unilateral'.[137]

The State did not argue these points during the hearing, as it chose not to appear before the Court. Instead, the Court derived these arguments from a letter Iran had sent one day before the hearing.[138]

After emphasising the fundamental importance of respect for the inviolability of envoys and embassies for the conduct of relation between States, in particular the reciprocal obligation to assure the personal safety of the diplomats, the US pointed out the danger of irreparable harm.

> "Whereas continuance of the situation the subject of the present request exposes the human beings concerned to privation, hardship, anguish and even danger to life and health and thus to a serious possibility of irreparable harm".[139]

The Court unanimously found that the situation required the indication of provisional measures in order to preserve the rights claimed.[140] Firstly, Iran should immediately return to the exclusive control of US authorities the premises of the US Embassy, Chancery and Consulates and ensure their inviolability and effective protection as required by the treaties in force between the two States as well as by customary international law. Secondly, Iran 'should ensure the immediate release, without any exception, of all persons of United States nationality who are or have been held in the Embassy of the United States of America or in the Ministry of Foreign Affairs in Tehran, or have been held as hostages elsewhere, and afford full protection to all such persons, in accordance with the treaties in force between the two States, and with general international law'. Thirdly, Iran 'should, as from that moment, afford to all the diplomatic and consular personnel of the United States the full protection, privileges immunities to which they are entitled under the treaties in force between the two States, and under general international law, including immunity from any form of criminal jurisdiction and freedom and facilities to leave the territory of Iran'. Finally, it also ordered both parties not to take any action and to 'ensure that no action is taken which may aggravate the tension between the two countries or render the existing dispute more difficult of solution'.[141]

Thirlway asks in what way the rights asserted by the US would be 'preserved' by the measures requested:

---

[136] Id., §25.

[137] Id., §29.

[138] According to Oellers-Frahm, in light of the fact that the defendant State often does not appear before the Court, it became customary in proceedings for provisional measures for the Court to take into consideration any available materials, even without any specific provision to that effect in the Rules of Court. Oellers-Frahm (1981), p. 283. See also Chapter XV (Immediacy and risk).

[139] ICJ *US Diplomatic and Consular Staff in Tehran* (*US* v. *Iran*), Order of 15 December 1979, §42.

[140] It referred to the provisions of the Convention on the Prevention and Punishment of Crimes against Internationally Protected Persons, including Diplomatic Agents (1973).

[141] ICJ *US Diplomatic and Consular Staff in Tehran* (*US* v. *Iran*), Order of 15 December 1979, §47.

"Setting aside for the moment the rights of individuals concerned, the other rights had already been grossly and flagrantly infringed; it was certainly right that the infringement should cease, but whether this took place following an order of interim measures or following judgment on the merits would not be a question of preservation of the rights, but rather a damage-limitation exercise. In neither event would the injury suffered be an irreparable one".[142]

It seems evident, however, that the Court's main interest was in fact the protection of the individuals concerned against further harm. While noting that 'nothing could be more irreparable than the taking of life', Thirlway questions whether the rights of the US were at stake now that some of the persons at risk of being executed were not US citizens.[143] He notes that the Court 'moved imperceptibly from the international legal rights of the United States to the injury to the persons, health and life of the individuals concerned; the Order provides no link between these two considerations'.[144]

Indeed, in Higgins' words: '[e]schewing formalism, the Court thus made the connection between harm to the individuals concerned and obligations owed by Iran to the United States under the Vienna Conventions'.[145]

3.3.4 Protecting people in border conflict cases: collateral human beings

In the *Frontier Dispute* case (1986) the ICJ Chamber pointed out that, in the face of 'force which is irreconcilable with the principle of the peaceful settlement of international disputes' it had the 'power and duty to indicate, if need be, such provisional measures as may conduce to the due administration of justice'.[146] Moreover, in this case 'the armed actions in the territory in dispute could result in the destruction of evidence material to the Chamber's eventual decision'.[147] Finally the facts that had ' given rise to the requests of both Parties for the indication of provisional measures exposes the persons and property in the disputed area, as well as the interests of both States within that area, to serious risk of irreparable damage'.[148] Thus the risk of irreparable harm to persons and property was sufficient for the use of provisional measures, 'even though, it must be said, that harm could not of itself affect where the frontier line might run or the implementation of a judgment on the frontier line'.[149]

In *Cameroon* v. *Nigeria* (1996) the ICJ noted that it was clear from submissions of both Parties 'that there were military incidents and that they caused suffering, occasioned fatalities – of both military and civilian personnel – while causing others to be wounded or unaccounted for, as well as causing major material damage'.[150] It pointed out that the rights at issue were 'sovereign rights which the Parties claim over territory' and that these rights also concerned persons.[151] It noted that especially the killing of persons had already 'caused irreparable damage to the rights that the Parties may have over the Peninsula' and persons in the disputed area were 'exposed to

---

[142]   Thirlway (1994), p. 8. He pointed out that 'if the Iranian intruders had not already gained access to the secret files in the Embassy vaults, to prevent them doing so would be to forestall an injury which would be irreparable'.

[143]   Thirlway (1994), p. 8.

[144]   Id., p. 9.

[145]   Higgins (1997), p. 100. For ICJ *DRC* v. *Uganda*, Order of 1 July 2000. See section 3.3.6 of this Chapter.

[146]   ICJ *Frontier Dispute* case (*Burkina Faso* v. *Mali*), Order of 10 January 1986, §19.

[147]   Id., §20. See also section 3.2.

[148]   Id., §21.

[149]   Higgins (2007), p. 102.

[150]   ICJ *Land and maritime boundary between Cameroon and Nigeria* (*Cameroon* v. *Nigeria*), Order of 15 March 1996, §38.

[151]   Id., §39.

serious risk of further irreparable damage'. As a consequence the rights of the Parties within that area were exposed to such risk. Armed actions 'could jeopardize the existence of evidence relevant to the present case'.[152] Judge Oda attached a declaration to the Order, expressing some concern about this statement. He noted that the purpose of provisional measures was to preserve the rights that were to be considered at the merits stage and which constituted, or were 'directly engaged by, the subject of the application'. "The anticipated or actual breach of the rights to be preserved ought to be one which could not be erased by the payment of reparation of compensation to be ordered in a later judgment on the merits". He believed 'that loss of life in the disputed area, distressing as it undoubtedly is, does not constitute the real subject matter of the present case'.[153]

Judge Koroma, on the other hand, considered that the Court had indeed sufficient reason to grant this provisional order 'on its own accord', because of 'the possibility of a further military engagement resulting in irreparable damage to the rights of either Party, including further loss of human life'.[154] Ad hoc Judge Ajibola did not agree with the contents of the provisional measures in several respects, but he did confirm that protection and preservation of human life has often been an important aspect of provisional measures and he agreed that the Court should indeed order provisional measures to the effect that Parties would cease acts of aggression in order to alleviate the sufferings and loss of life and property caused by the dispute between two States.[155]

As noted, analysing this case Higgins pointed out that '[t]he risk of irreparable harm to persons', was 'enough for provisional measures – even though, it must be said, that harm could not of itself affect where the frontier line might run'.[156] She argues that this case and *Frontier Dispute* case (*Burkina Faso* v. *Mali*) (1986),[157] taken together, 'go beyond the series of cases in which provisional measures that protect human life were indicated because the dispute in question was exactly about such rights'.[158] In other words, even if the dispute before the Court is not exactly about the protection of human life or dignity, provisional measures for the protection of these rights may still be indicated.[159]

---

[152] Id., §42.

[153] ICJ *Land and maritime boundary between Cameroon and Nigeria* (*Cameroon* v. *Nigeria*), Order of 15 March 1996, declaration of Judge Oda.

[154] ICJ *Land and maritime boundary between Cameroon and Nigeria* (*Cameroon* v. *Nigeria*), Order of 15 March 1996, declaration of Judge Koroma. In a joint declaration Judges Weeramantry, Shi and Vereshchetin express concern about one aspect of the courts border, because of the dispute about the location of the respected armed forces, while Judge Mbaye was 'delighted' by the approach taken by the Court.

[155] ICJ *Land and maritime boundary between Cameroon and Nigeria* (*Cameroon* v. *Nigeria*), Order of 15 March 1996, Separate Opinion of Judge Ajibola (He referred to the *Fisheries Jurisdiction* case and the *Hostages* case. "Evidently those indications of provisional measures whether simply for the preservation of rights, the avoidance of an aggravation or extension of the dispute or an act such as might cause irreparable harm or prejudice to the parties have always had an element of protection and preservation of human life and/or property").

[156] Higgins (1998), p. 699.

[157] ICJ *Frontier Dispute* case (*Burkina Faso* v. *Mali*), Order of 10 January 1986 and *Land and Maritime Boundary between Cameroon and Nigeria* (*Cameroon* v. *Nigeria*), Order of 15 March 1996.

[158] Higgins (1997), pp. 107-108. See also Rosenne (2005), pp. 194-196 and Ghandhi (2004).

[159] For a different approach see Yoshiyuki Iwamoto (2002), p. 364.

3.3.5 Releasing crew and the protection of the (marine) environment

As discussed in section 3.2 the ICJ and ITLOS have dealt with requests for provisional measures to prevent serious harm to the (marine) environment. This section refers to the authority of ITLOS to order the release of crew and its wearing on the authority to order provisional measures.

In his separate opinion in the *M/V 'Saiga'* case (1998) ITLOS Judge Laing 'catalogued' the types of cases in which provisional measures have been used in public international law. He referred to a wide variety of rights that have been recognized in provisional measures in relation to: 'armed conflicts, threats to peace, injuries to property and persons; human rights violations; commercial and consular/diplomatic rights of aliens; environmental protection and maritime freedoms'. He considered that 'perhaps the existing jurisprudence reflects that rights or claims of a generally high order have received cognition'. In addition, he argued that Article 290 UNCLOS would have to protect 'non-traditional asserted rights'. However, in the *'Saiga'* case 'the rights in issue fall within the catalogue set forth above or clearly involve specific entitlements and claims under UNCLOS, plus, in one situation, general notions of human rights'.[160] The 'one situation' referred to involved the rights and freedoms of crew members on board vessels that were entered by other States.[161]

The urgent action to be undertaken by ITLOS may take two different forms. One is the 'prescription' of provisional measures and the other is the delivery of an urgent judgment ordering the release of vessels or crews. Article 90 of the ITLOS Rules stipulates: 'subject to article 112, paragraph 1, a request for the prescription of provisional measures has priority over all other proceedings before the Tribunal. Article 112(1) of the Rules provides that applications for releases of vessels or crews have priority over all other proceedings before the Tribunal. Yet it also provides that 'if the Tribunal is seized of an application for release of a vessel or crew and of a request for the prescription of provisional measure, it shall take the necessary measures to ensure that both the application and the request are dealt with without delay'.

The fact that there is an urgent procedure for the release of vessels or crews, together with the fact that decisions for such release take the form of a judgment, shows the importance attached by ITLOS to the plight of persons in detention. Had it not introduced a specific provision on this issue, ITLOS could have used Article 290 UNCLOS, on the prescription of provisional measures, to intervene in such cases. The Rules imply that the requests for provisional measures have priority over all other proceedings *except* those involving the release of vessels or crews. At the same time they leave some possibility to examine a request for provisional measures prior to a request for release of vessels or crews.

Circumstances triggering a request for provisional measures may be more serious than those triggering a request for the release of crew and certainly more serious than those triggering a request for the release of vessels only. After all, a request for provisional measures could involve threats of irreparable harm to the environment as well as to the inhabitants of an Applicant State, for instance if one State claims that a nuclear facility of another State lacks any form of basic protection against leakage of waste into adjacent waters. In my view examination of such a request for provisional measures to intervene against irreparable harm should have priority over examination of a request for the release of crew, unless crew members are in danger of life and limb.

---

[160] ITLOS *M/V 'Saiga'* case (No. 2), Order of 11 March 1998, Separate Opinion of Judge Laing, §21.

[161] See more closely on the prompt release procedure Tanaka (2004) and Escher (2004).

3.3.6 Halting gross human rights violations

Bosnia brought a case before the ICJ requesting it to order provisional measures to the effect, among others, that Yugoslavia and its agents in Bosnia 'must immediately cease and desist from all acts of genocide' and that Bosnia had the right to seek and receive support in order to defend itself, including through obtaining military supplies. The ICJ found that it had *prima facie* jurisdiction to deal with the submission in so far as it was based on the Genocide Convention. It avoided the issue of the effect of the UN arms embargo on Bosnia's right to self-defence by considering that it had established the existence of 'a basis on which its jurisdiction might be founded' and 'ought not to indicate measures for the protection of any disputed rights other than those which might ultimately form the basis of the judgment in the exercise of that jurisdiction'.[162] It ordered Yugoslavia (Serbia and Montenegro) to immediately take all measures within its power to prevent commission of the crime of genocide, in particular to 'ensure any military, paramilitary or irregular armed units which may be directed or supported by it, as well any organizations and persons which may be subject to its control, direction or influence, do not commit any acts of genocide, of conspiracy to commit genocide, of direct and public incitement to commit genocide, or of complicity in genocide, whether directed against the Muslim population of Bosnia and Herzegovina or against any other national, ethnical, racial or religious group'. In addition neither Party should take action that could aggravate or extend the existing dispute.[163] A few months later Bosnia submitted a further request for provisional measures. Instead, the Court reaffirmed its previous provisional measures, 'which should be immediately and effectively implemented'.[164] Many years later the Court found Serbia responsible not for complicity but for failure to prevent the genocide in Srebrenica. It also noted the State's failure to observe its provisional measures.[165]

In *Armed Activities on the Territory of the Congo* (2000) the ICJ unanimously ordered provisional measures, among others, to the effect that both Parties (Congo and Uganda) 'must, forthwith, take all measures necessary to ensure full respect within the zone of conflict for fundamental human rights and for the applicable provisions of humanitarian law'.[166] The Court noted that it must focus its attention on the rights claimed in the Congo's application, which included the right to respect for the rules of international humanitarian law and for the instruments relating to the protection of human rights.[167] Five years later, in its judgment in this case, it found 'that the DRC put forward no specific evidence demonstrating that after July 2000 Uganda committed acts in violation of each of the three provisional measures indicated by the Court'. Nevertheless, the Court observed 'that in the present Judgment it has found that Uganda is responsible for acts in violation of international human rights law and international humanitarian law carried out by its military forces in the territory of the DRC (…). The evidence shows that

---

[162] ICJ *Application of the Convention on the Prevention and Punishment of the Crime of Genocide (Bosnia and Herzegovina* v. *Yugoslavia),* Order of 8 April 1993, §35.

[163] Id., §52.

[164] ICJ *Application of the Convention on the Prevention and Punishment of the Crime of Genocide (Bosnia and Herzegovina* v. *Yugoslavia),* Order of 13 September 1993. See further on this issue section 7 (follow-up), and the Separate Opinions of Judges Lauterpacht, Weeramantry, Ajibola and Shahabuddeen. For comment on these Orders see e.g. Toufayan (2005), Gaffikin (1995), Wiebalck (1995), Gray (1994), Maison (1994) and Warbrick (1993).

[165] ICJ *Application of the Convention on the Prevention and Punishment of the Crime of Genocide (Bosnia and Herzegovina* v. *Yugoslavia),* Judgment of 26 February 2007. See also later in this Chapter, e.g. sections 3.7.4 and 7.

[166] ICJ *Armed Activities on the Territory of the Congo (Congo* v. *Uganda),* Order of 1 July 2000.

[167] Id., §40. Congo had requested the Court to order much more detailed provisional measures directed only at Uganda.

such violations were committed throughout the period when Ugandan troops were present in the DRC (..).The Court thus concludes that Uganda did not comply with the Court's Order on provisional measures of 1 July 2000".[168] It further noted that 'that the provisional measures indicated in the Order of 1 July 2000 were addressed to both Parties. The Court's finding in paragraph 264 is without prejudice to the question as to whether the DRC did not also fail to comply with the provisional measures indicated by the Court'.[169]

The ICJ also expressed its awareness of the 'complex and tragic situation which had long prevailed in the Great Lakes Region'. "There has been much suffering by the local population and destabilisation of much of the region".[170] The Court noted that it had to pronounce on the violations committed by Ugandan military forces on the territory of the Congo, but it nevertheless observed 'that the actions of the various parties in the complex conflict' had 'contributed to the immense suffering faced by the Congolese population'. It made the following general remark in this respect: "The Court is painfully aware that many atrocities have been committed in the course of the conflict. It is incumbent on all those involved in the conflict to support the peace process in the DRC and other peace processes in the Great Lakes area, in order to ensure respect for human rights in the region".[171]

In August 2008 Georgia submitted a case against Russia to the ICJ under the International Convention on the Elimination of Racial Discrimination (CERD). Subsequently it requested the ICJ to order provisional measures against Russia 'to protect its citizens against violent discriminatory acts by Russian armed forces, acting in concert with separatist militia and foreign mercenaries the context of violations of CERD'.[172] The next day the President of the Court invoked Article 74(4) of the Rules of Court and 'having considered the gravity of the situation' called upon the parties 'to act in such a way as will enable any order the Court may take on the request for provisional measures to have its appropriate effects'.[173] In October 2008 the Court ordered provisional measures to the effect that both Parties shall refrain from any act of racial discrimination and from sponsoring, defending or supporting such acts; that they shall facilitate humanitarian assistance; and that they shall refrain from any action which might prejudice the respective rights of the Parties or might aggravate or extend the dispute.[174]

---

[168] ICJ *Armed Activities on the Territory of the Congo* (*Congo* v. *Uganda*), Judgment of 19 December 2005, §264.

[169] Id., §265.

[170] Referring to the security implications for Uganda and some other neighbouring States the Court was aware that 'the factional conflict' within the Congo required a 'comprehensive settlement of the conflict of the region'. Yet the Court was to respond to the particular legal dispute brought before it. 'As it interprets and implies the law, it will be mindful of context, but its task cannot go beyond that'. ICJ *Armed Activities on the Territory of the Congo* (*Congo* v. *Uganda*), Judgment of 19 December 2005, §26. On the judgment in general see e.g. Gathii (2007) and Savadogo (2002).

[171] ICJ *Armed Activities on the Territory of the Congo* (*Congo* v. *Uganda*), Judgment of 19 December 2005, §221.

[172] ICJ Press release of 14 August 2008, 'Georgia submits a Request for the indication of provisional measures'.

[173] ICJ Press release of 15 August 2008, 'Proceedings instituted by Georgia against Russia Urgent Communication to the Parties from the President under Article 74, paragraph 4, of the Rules of Court'.

[174] ICJ *Application of the International Convention on the Elimination of Racial Discrimination* (*Georgia* v. *Russian Federation*), 15 October 2008 (by a 8-7 vote).

3.3.7 Protecting nationals: halting executions

The safety of its nationals abroad is a vital interest of a State. In the three death penalty cases before the ICJ the interests of States coincided with those of the individuals involved. In these cases about violations of the Vienna Convention on Consular Relations (VCCR) the very lives of their citizens were at stake. In the *Breard, LaGrand* and *Avena* cases against the US, initiated by Paraguay, Germany and Mexico respectively, the ICJ ordered provisional measures to halt the execution of an individual.[175] Here the interests of the State, namely being able to assist its citizen entangled in the laws of a foreign country, overlapped with the interest of the individual concerned.

This section focuses on the Order for provisional measures in the *Breard* case, as it marks the first time the ICJ ordered provisional measures to suspend the execution of an individual.[176] The case, brought before the Court by Paraguay, concerned the US failure to observe the Vienna Convention on Consular Relations (VCCR) and its failure to remedy past violations of it. Under US domestic law, there is no legal recourse available to remedy this violation if a foreign national is only informed of his consular rights at the stage of federal proceedings for post-conviction relief.

The application stated that the authorities of Virginia had arrested Paraguayan national Breard in 1992 and that he was charged, tried and convicted of culpable homicide and sentenced to death in 1993. It stated that all this happened while he was not informed of his right to consular access under Article 36 VCCR.[177] When Paraguay found out about his case, by its own means, his state *habeas* appeals (before the Courts of the Commonwealth of Virginia) had already been concluded and he could no longer raise a VCCR claim, for reasons of procedural default. Yet he could not raise his claim any earlier, since he was not informed of his rights, which was also his claim.[178] For this reason, Paraguay demanded 'restitution in kind' in the form of a retrial of its national in conformity with the VCCR.

On 9 April 1998 the ICJ unanimously indicated provisional measures in *Breard*. It used the following sentence:

> "The United States should take all measures at its disposal to ensure that Angel Francisco Breard is not executed pending the final decision in these proceedings, and should inform the Court of all the measures which it has taken in implementation of this Order".

The ICJ ordered provisional measures to ensure that Breard was not executed pending the proceedings. It stated that its power to indicate provisional measures under Article 41 of its Statute presupposed that 'irreparable prejudice shall not be caused to rights which are the subject

---

175   ICJ *Case concerning the Vienna Convention on Consular Relations* (*Paraguay* v. *US*), Order of 9 April 1998; *LaGrand* (*Germany* v. *US*), Order of 3 March 1999; *Avena and other Mexican nationals* (*Mexico* v. *US*), Order of 5 February 2003. On the ICJ and the VCCR see e.g. Künzli (2005); Orakhelashvili (2005); Aceves (2004); Ghandhi (2004); Cassel (2002); Jennings (2002); Orakhelashvili (2002); Rieter (2002a); Schabas (2002b); Stephens (2002); Yoshiyuki Iwamoto (2002); Feria Tinta (2001); Van Boven/Rieter (2000); Addo (1999); Cassel (1999b); Mani (1999) and Uribe (1996-97). See also *Request for interpretation of the judgment of 31 March 2004 in the case concerning Avena and other Mexican nationals* (*Mexico* v. *US*), Order of 16 July 2008, discussed *infra*.

176   On this Order and the US response see more closely 'Agora' (AJIL 1998), pp. 666-712 and Rieter (1998), pp. 475-494.

177   ICJ *Case concerning the Vienna Convention on Consular Relations* (*Paraguay* v. *US*), Order of 9 April 1998, and Verbatim Record of public sitting, CR 98/7, 7 April 1998.

178   On the federal proceedings for post-conviction relief in the US see e.g. Bal/Rieter (2001).

of a dispute in judicial proceedings'.[179] It must, therefore, be concerned 'to preserve by such measures the rights which may subsequently be adjudged by the Court to belong either to the Applicant, or to the Respondent'.[180] Such measures, it stated, are only justified if there is urgency. Breard's execution was ordered for 14 April 1998 and 'such an execution would render it impossible for the Court to order the relief that Paraguay seeks and thus cause irreparable harm to the rights it claims'.[181]

The Court pointed out that 'the function of this Court is to resolve international legal disputes between States, inter alia when they arise out of the interpretation or application of international conventions, and not to act as a court of criminal appeal'.[182] It ruled, furthermore, that the measures indicated by the Court for a stay of execution 'would necessarily be provisional in nature and would not in any way prejudge findings the Court might make on the merits'. They would preserve the respective rights of both Paraguay and the US. Finally, it indicated that it was 'appropriate that the Court, with the co-operation of the Parties, ensure that any decision on the merits be reached with all possible expedition'.[183]

Judge Oda's declaration was rather confusing. He believed that the US was released from its responsibility for violating the Convention by apologising to Paraguay and giving an assurance of non-repetition. He also believed the Court had no *prima facie* jurisdiction in this case and he emphasized that 'the request for provisional measures should not be used to ensure that the main Application continue'. This is puzzling, as exactly this is generally seen as a very good reason for using provisional measures. Yet in his view, 'given the fundamental nature of provisional measures, those measures should not have been indicated upon Paraguay's request'. He voted, nevertheless, in favour of the Order, 'for humanitarian reasons, and in view of the fact that, if the execution were to be carried out on 14 April 1998, whatever findings the Court might have reached might be without object'.[184]

The US, however, disregarded the provisional measures. This included a decision by the US Supreme Court not to postpone the execution. By way of its constituent State, the commonwealth of Virginia, the US executed Angel Francisco Breard on 14 April 1998.[185] While the Paraguayan case was not pursued after the execution of Breard, it set the standard for the ICJ. In fact the Court's reasoning in this case was not based on human rights law, but rather more generally on international law concepts such as *restitutio in integrum*. Human rights concerns, however, are not alien to these concepts and the provisional measures, if respected, advanced the protection of human rights.[186] In its subsequent Orders for provisional measures in the *LaGrand* and *Avena* cases the ICJ confirmed the approach taken in *Breard*.

The executions of Breard and, subsequently, of LaGrand raised the question again as to whether the Court's provisional measures were legally binding. This issue was finally affirmatively determined in the Court's judgment in *LaGrand* (2001)[187] Germany had brought this case before the ICJ on behalf of the brothers *LaGrand*, who had been sentenced to death in violation of the VCCR. Karl LaGrand had already been executed. Germany requested and the ICJ ordered provisional measures on behalf of Walter LaGrand.[188] Texas nevertheless executed him. In its judgment in *LaGrand* the Court found that 'when the sending State is unaware of the

---

179   ICJ *Vienna Convention on Consular Relations* (*Paraguay* v. *US*), Order of 9 April 1998, §35.
180   Ibid.
181   ICJ *Vienna Convention on Consular Relations* (*Paraguay* v. *US*), Order of 9 April 1998, §37.
182   Id., §38.
183   Id., §40.
184   ICJ *LaGrand* case (*Germany* v. *US*), Judgment of 27 June 2001, Declaration Judge Oda.
185   See also section 7 of this Chapter (follow-up).
186   See also, e.g., Schabas (2002), Orakhelashvili (2002) and Van Boven/Rieter (2000).
187   ICJ *LaGrand* case (*Germany* v. *US*), Judgment of 27 June 2001.
188   ICJ *LaGrand* case (*Germany* v. *US*), Order of 3 March 1999.

detention of its nationals due to the failure of the receiving State to provide the requisite consular notification without delay, (...) the sending State has been prevented for all practical purposes from exercising its rights under Article 36'.[189] Article 36(1) VCCR 'creates individual rights, which, by virtue of Article I of the Optional Protocol, may be invoked in this Court by the national State of the detained person. These rights were violated in the present case'.[190] It was not necessary to show 'whether the LaGrands would have sought consular assistance from Germany, whether Germany would have rendered such assistance, or whether a different verdict would have been rendered'. It was 'sufficient that the Convention conferred these rights, and that Germany *and the LaGrands* [italics ER] were in effect prevented by the breach of the United States from exercising them, had they so chosen'.[191] The ICJ decided it need not discuss the issue whether the individual right to consular notification also was a human right.[192]

The US had not given 'full effect' to the rights in paragraph 1 and had, thus, violated paragraph 2: "Under these circumstances, the procedural default rule had the effect of preventing 'full effect [from being] given to the purposes for which the rights accorded under this article are intended', and thus violated paragraph 2 of Article 36".[193] The Court found that 'although United States courts could and did examine the professional competence of counsel assigned to the indigent LaGrands by reference to United States constitutional standards, the procedural default rule prevented them from attaching any legal significance to the fact, *inter alia*, that the violation of the rights set forth in Article 36, paragraph 1, prevented Germany, in a timely fashion, from retaining private counsel for them and otherwise assisting in their defence as provided for by the Convention'.[194] Thus the Court found that while the rule of procedural default 'as such' did not violate Article 36 VCCR, its specific application in the present case did.

> "The problem arises when the procedural default rule does not allow the detained individual to challenge a conviction and sentence by claiming, in reliance on Article 36, paragraph 1, of the Convention, that the competent national authorities failed to comply with their obligation to provide the requisite consular information 'without delay', thus preventing the person from seeking and obtaining consular assistance from the sending State".[195]

In the Order for provisional measures in *Avena* the ICJ had ordered provisional measures to halt the execution of three persons.[196] The US respected this order. In its Judgment the ICJ again found violations of Article 36 VCCR and specified that 'the appropriate reparation in this case

---

[189]   Paragraph 1 (a) VCCR refers to the right of communication and access and paragraph 1 (c) 'sets out the measures consular officers may take in rendering consular assistance to the nationals in custody of the receiving State', ICJ *LaGrand* case (*Germany* v. *US*), judgment of 27 June 2001, §74. The ICJ noted that the breach of paragraph 1 (b) 'had the consequence of depriving Germany of the exercise of the rights accorded it under Article 36, paragraph 1 (a) and paragraph 1 (c) and thus violated the provisions of the Convention', §73. It did not say that a violation of paragraph 1 (b) would always result in the breach of provisions of that Article, but in this case it did. The Court referred to paragraph 1 as establishing an 'interrelated régime' designed to facilitate implementation of the system of consular protection, §74.

[190]   ICJ *LaGrand* case (*Germany* v. *US*), Judgment of 27 June 2001, §77.

[191]   Id., §74.

[192]   Id., §78. This was the Court's reply to the further contention of Germany, at the hearings, then the right of the individual to be informed without delay and article 36, paragraph 1, of the Vienna Convention was not only in individual rights, but has today assumed 'the character of a human right'.

[193]   ICJ *LaGrand* case (*Germany* v. *US*), Judgment of 27 June 2001, §91.

[194]   Ibid.

[195]   ICJ *LaGrand* case (*Germany* v. *US*), Judgment of 27 June 2001, §90.

[196]   ICJ *Avena and other Mexican Nationals* (*Mexico* v. *US*), Order of 5 February 2003.

consists in the obligation of the United States of America to provide, by means of its own choosing, review and reconsideration of the convictions and sentences of the Mexican nationals' mentioned in the judgment.[197]

In response the US President issued a Memorandum to the Attorney General determining that the US 'will discharge its international obligations' under this judgment 'by having State courts give effect to the decision in accordance with general principles of comity in cases filed by the 51 Mexican nationals addressed in that decision'.[198] Then again, the next day the US withdrew from the Optional Protocol to the VCCR, in order to prevent any new claims against it by other States in case they would consider that the international obligations of the US based on the VCCR were not properly discharged. A State Department spokesman pointed out: 'we have a system of justice that provides people with due process and review of their cases, and it's not appropriate that there should be some international court that comes in and reverses decisions of our national courts'.[199]

In June 2008 Mexico requested the ICJ to interpret the appropriate reparation referred to in its 2004 *Avena* Judgment because the US apparently understood it only as an obligation of means, while Mexico understood it as an obligation of result.[200] Mexico noted that since *Avena* (2004) '[o]nly one state court had provided the required review and consideration'.[201] In addition, in March 2008 the US Supreme Court, 'while acknowledging that the *Avena* judgment constitutes an obligation under international law on the part of the United States, ruled that "the means chosen by the president of the United States to comply were unavailable under the US constitution" and that "neither the *Avena* Judgment on its own, nor the Judgment in conjunction with the President's memorandum, constituted directly enforceable federal law" precluding Texas from "applying state procedural rules that barred all review and consideration of Mr. Medellín's Vienna Convention claim"'.[202] Mexico added that the Supreme Court referred to alternative means by which the US could still comply with its obligations, 'in particular, by the passage of legislation by Congress making a "non-self-executing treaty domestically enforceable" or by "voluntary compliance by the State of Texas".[203]

---

[197] ICJ *Avena and other Mexican Nationals* (*Mexico* v. *US*), Judgment of 31 March 2004, §153(9).

[198] US President's Memorandum for the Attorney General on compliance with the decision of the ICJ in *Avena*, 28 February 2005. See also Kirgis (2005). Texas prosecutors, however, questioned the President's authority to 'force courts' to reopen cases. A spokesman for the Attorney General of Texas was quoted in the New York Times: "The State of Texas believes no international court supercedes the laws of Texas or the laws of the United States". See further Anaya Valencia/Jackson/Van de Putte/Ellis (2005); Young (2005); Brook (2004); Murphy (2004); Shelton (2004a); Carter (2003); Ray (2003); Babcock (2002).

[199] See 'U.S. quits foreign inmate accord', CNN.com, 11 March 2005 (quoting State Department spokesman Ereli). See further e.g. Liptak, 'U.S. says it has withdrawn from world judicial body', New York Times 10 March 2005 (with Professor Koh commenting that this move was counterproductive and Professor Spiro that it was a 'sore-loser kind of move' and 'If we can't win, we're not going to play').

[200] ICJ *Request for interpretation of the judgment of 31 March 2004 in the case concerning Avena and other Mexican nationals* (*Mexico* v. *US*), Order of 16 July 2008 (Judges Simma and Parra-Aranguren, acting under Article 24(1) ICJ Statute, had informed the Court that they would not sit in this case).

[201] This was the case of Osvaldo Torres Aguilera. It added that in another case, that of Rafael Camargo Ojeda, Arkansas had 'agreed to reduce' his death sentence to life imprisonment 'in exchange for his agreement to waive his right to review and reconsideration under the *Avena* judgment'. ICJ *Request for interpretation of the judgment of 31 March 2004 in the case concerning Avena and other Mexican nationals* (*Mexico* v. *US*), Order of 16 July 2008, §2.

[202] Id., §4.

[203] Ibid.

Mexico also requested provisional measures because 'a Texas court had declined the stay of execution requested by counsel for Mr. Medellín in order to allow Congress' to pass such legislation.[204] It indicated that 'the paramount interest in human life is at stake' and that 'that interest would be irreparably harmed if any of the Mexican nationals whose right to review and reconsideration was determined in the *Avena* judgment were executed without having received that review and reconsideration'.[205] The ICJ indeed ordered the US to 'take all measures necessary to ensure' that Medellín and four others 'are not executed pending judgment on the Request for interpretation submitted by the United Mexican States, unless and until these five Mexican nationals receive review and reconsideration' consistent with the Court's *Avena* judgment of 2004.[206]

This is the first time the Court has ordered provisional measures in the context of a request for interpretation of an earlier ICJ judgment under Article 60 ICJ Statute. There was no other basis for jurisdiction as the US is no longer a party to the Optional Protocol to the VCCR. The decision to order these measures was made despite the US argument that there was in fact no dispute as to the meaning and scope of the Court's *Avena* Judgment, as required by Article 60 ICJ Statute. The US argued that the dispute was not about interpretation, as it agreed with Mexico that it was facing an obligation of result, but about implementation. The majority of the Court (five judges dissented) considered that 'while it seems both Parties regard paragraph 153(9) of the *Avena* Judgment as an international obligation of result, the Parties nonetheless apparently hold different views as to the meaning and scope of that obligation of result, namely whether that understanding is shared by all United States federal and state authorities and whether that obligation falls upon those authorities'.[207] As it considered it could deal with the request for interpretation, it was able to order provisional measures.[208]

Indeed, the fact that something is a dispute about implementation does not rule out per se that it is also a dispute on interpretation. The question is whether or not it matters for the existence of a legal dispute that what the State says formally, differs from what it does or fails to do in practice or whether that is solely a matter of supervision of implementation. Some human rights adjudicators have created follow-up mechanisms such as maintaining a case on the docket pending implementation.[209] The Inter-American Court, for instance, has pointed out that it is a power inherent in its jurisdictional function to supervise compliance with its decisions.[210] It

---

[204] ICJ *Request for interpretation of the judgment of 31 March 2004 in the case concerning Avena and other Mexican nationals* (*Mexico* v. *US*), Order of 16 July 2008, §5.

[205] Id, §19.

[206] Id., §80 (referring specifically to the obligation of review and reconsideration 'consistent with paragraphs 138 to 141' of the 2004 Judgment).

[207] Id., §55.

[208] Yet five judges dissented, all of them stressing that no executions should take place before review and reconsideration, based on the US obligations as expressed in the *Avena* judgment. They argued, however, that Article 60 ICJ Statute could not be a basis upon which to found jurisdiction in this case, considering there was no dispute on the interpretation of the *Avena* judgment. See the dissenting opinion of judge Buergenthal (arguing, among others, that the Order 'adds no additional protection' and that '(h)umanitarian considerations which clearly underlie the decision cannot override the legal requirements of the Statute of the Court'); the joint dissenting opinion of judges Owada, Tomka and Keith and the dissenting opinion of Judge Skotnikov. See further section 7 of this Chapter on Follow up. Subsequently, in its judgment of 19 January 2009, the Court found it could not accede to Mexico's request for interpretation.

[209] See Chapter XVIII on Follow up by the human rights adjudicators.

[210] See e.g. IACHR Order on supervision of compliance in the cases *Fermín Ramírez* v. *Guatemala* and *Raxcacó Reyes* v. *Guatemala* and on the request to expand the provisional measures in *Raxcacó Reyes y otros*, 9 May 2008, 1st 'Considering' clause.

appears that in cases of a continuing or sudden risk of irreparable harm relating to violations that have already been established by the ICJ in a judgment,[211] Article 60 ICJ Statute could be construed as a device for follow-up by the ICJ in order to enhance compliance with its Judgments in those cases where there is no longer jurisdiction for the Court to take up a new case regarding non-implementation. Yet this could only be so as long as there is some link to a 'dispute' between the parties regarding the interpretation of their obligations under the judgment. In this context it might be argued, at least at the stage of provisional measures, that a State's arguments involving contradictions in the behaviour of the executive of another State (or in the behaviour of the various branches) – with regard to its public expressions of legal commitment meant for a domestic as opposed to a 'foreign' or international audience – do indeed show the existence of a 'legal dispute' on interpretation.[212]

3.4   Preventing irreparable harm and the humanization of international law

3.4.1 Introduction

The PCIJ and the ICJ have shown to be open to interests beyond those of individual States. They may concern peace and security, the rights of other States or organisations, the (marine) environment, the 'collateral damage' to individuals or minority groups and the rights of individuals vis-à-vis the main claim of the Applicant State.

As Elkind already put it in 1981, 'desperation defines the boundaries of interim protection'. Even though the ICJ deals only with complaints between States, the 'government of a State must cope with the desperation of its people'. He noted that 'irreparable injury and unendurable situations are only the two most acute situations likely to lead to violence', meaning that the ICJ is 'under a duty to grant interim measures in any dispute where the threat of violence is imminent'. He referred to the *Hostages* case as the one 'most fraught with desperation', also underlining 'the nexus between desperation and urgency'.[213] Elkind published his work on provisional measures in 1981, when the *Hostages* case was indeed one of the few specifically dealing with the plight of individual human beings. Subsequent to the *Hostages* case the ICJ has

---

[211]   In this context the Inter-American Court, which has on occasion also used provisional measures following a Judgment on the merits, and even on reparation, has recently decided, instead of ordering provisional measures, simply to order compliance with the obligation not to execute 25 persons based on its previous Judgments. In other words it now clearly distinguishes between supervision of its judgments on the merits and reparation and the use (and supervision, expansion or termination) of its provisional measures. See e.g. IACHR Order on supervision of compliance of the cases *Fermín Ramírez* v. *Guatemala* and *Raxcacó Reyes* v. *Guatemala* and on the request to expand the provisional measures in *Raxcacó Reyes y otros*, 9 May 2008.

[212]   Subsequently the ICJ considered it appropriate to review again whether there exists a dispute and whether there was a difference of opinion between the parties, see the discussion in §§21-47. From this it concluded that it could not accede to Mexico's request after all. Yet it did observe that 'considerations of domestic law which have so far hindered the implementation of the obligation incumbent upon the United States, cannot relieve it of its obligation'. It noted that a 'choice of means was allowed to the United States in the implementation of its obligation and, failing success within a reasonable period of time through the means chosen, it must rapidly turn to alternative and effective means of attaining that result'. With regard to the execution of Medellín in contravention of its provisional measures, it found that the US 'did not discharge of its obligation' under its Order. It also reiterated that 'its Avena Judgment remains binding and that the United States continues to be under an obligation fully to implement it'.

[213]   Elkind (1981), p. 258.

dealt with cases involving border conflicts and gross human rights violations.[214] Apart from provisional measures aimed to help relieve the situations in these cases, the ICJ has now also used provisional measures to halt executions of death sentences of the nationals of one State by another State. Elkind put it as follows "Not all cases involving interim measures are as desperate, as urgent or as critical as the *Hostages Case*. But interim protection is best understood in conditions of desperation, crisis and urgency because these are the conditions with which it must be able to cope if it is to fulfil its function".[215]

3.4.2 Humanization

In *DRC* v. *Rwanda* (2006) the ICJ recognized the prohibition of genocide as a peremptory norm (*ius cogens*). As Judge Dugard has noted, norms of *ius cogens* 'affirm the high principles of international law, which recognize the most important rights of the international order – such as the right to be free from aggression, genocide, torture and slavery and the right to self determination'.[216] He also observed that in its choice of precedent, in *Congo* v. *Uganda* (2005), the ICJ was influenced by 'the gravity of the issues raised', even though it did not make explicit that its choice 'was influenced by the fact that norms of *jus cogens* were involved in this case'.[217]

Judge Simma agreed with the Court's judgment in *Congo* v. *Uganda*, but he considered that it should have found that the 'victims of the attacks at the Ndjili International Airport remained legally protected against such maltreatment irrespective of their nationality'. International human rights law and humanitarian law applied in this case as well.[218] His discussion of this issue affirms that the Court has a task in the protection of persons caught up in conflicts between States, independent of the intentions of the States bringing a claim on their behalf, acknowledging that Uganda's claim regarding the seventeen victims at the airport may not have been based on a 'genuine concern for the fate of the persons concerned'.[219] He specifically pointed out 'that legal arguments clarifying that in situations like the one before us no gaps exist in the law that would deprive the affected persons of any legal protection, have, unfortunately never been as important as at present, in the face of recent deplorable developments'.[220] He noted that the events at the airport 'were factually connected to the armed conflict' and that 'the application of international humanitarian law would be consistent with the understanding of the scope' of this law as

---

[214]   ICJ *Nicaragua* case, Order of 10 May 1984, *Frontier Dispute* case (*Burkina Faso* v. *Mali*), Order of 10 January 1986, *Application of the Convention on the Prevention and Punishment of the Crime of Genocide* (*Bosnia and Herzegovina* v. *Yugoslavia (Serbia and Montenegro)*), Order of 8 April 1993, *Land and maritime boundary between Cameroon and Nigeria* (*Cameroon* v. *Nigeria*), Order of 15 March 1996, *Armed Activities on the Territory of the Congo* (*DRC* v. *Uganda*), Order of 1 July 2000.

[215]   Elkind (1981), p. 258.

[216]   ICJ *Armed Activities on the Territory of the Congo* (new application: 2002) (*DRC* v. *Rwanda*), Judgment on jurisdiction of the Court and admissibility of the application of 3 February 2006, Separate Opinion of Judge Dugard, §10.

[217]   ICJ *Armed Activities on the Territory of the Congo* (new application: 2002) (*DRC* v. *Rwanda*), Judgment on jurisdiction of the Court and admissibility of the application of 3 February 2006, Separate Opinion of Judge Dugard, §11. He pointed out that the ICJ, in *Congo* v. *Uganda*, relied on the *Certain Phosphate Lands* case rather than referred to the controversial *Monetary Gold* case. *Monetary Gold removed from Rome in 1943* (*Italy* v. *France, UK and US*), Judgment of 15 June 1954 and *Certain Phosphate Lands in Nauru* (*Nauru* v. *Australia*), Judgment of 26 June 1992 (preliminary objections).

[218]   ICJ *Armed Activities on the Territory of the Congo* (*Congo* v. *Uganda*), Judgment of 19 December 2005, Separate Opinion of Judge Simma, §17.

[219]   Id., §18.

[220]   Id., §19.

developed by the ICTY Appeals Chamber.[221] He invoked provisions on the prohibition of cruel, inhuman or degrading treatment or punishment, the right to liberty and security of persons and the freedom of movement in the ICCPR, the Convention against Torture and the African Charter on Human and Peoples' Rights. Uganda could have raised these violations before the ICJ.[222] Moreover, the contemporary law of state responsibility confirmed that a State has standing to bring a claim regarding human rights violations committed against persons that might not possess the nationality of that State.[223] Finally, he argued that while Uganda 'chose the avenue of diplomatic protection and failed', the ICJ should have pointed out the applicability of international humanitarian and human rights law and Uganda's standing in this respect.[224]

3.4.3 The concept of irreparable harm

Elkind believes it is not always helpful to speak of irreparable harm because this criterion may be too difficult for the Applicant State to meet when arguing for the use of provisional measures. He refers to the *Hostages* case (1979) and to 'most cases of environmental injury', pointing out:

> "Irreparable injury is a reference to a final result and is quite beside the point. In this respect, the basis of the complaint is not so much that the injury is irreparable, but that it is unendurable. The complainant cannot be expected to put up with it pending the outcome of the dispute. The *status quo* is intolerable".[225]

Agreeing with the ICJ's refusal to take provisional measures in the *Arbitral Award* case (1990) Judge Evensen wrote separately, pointing out that the risk of irreparable damage should not be a condition for the stipulation of interim measures. He noted that neither Article 41 ICJ Statute nor Article 73 Rules of Court contained any reference to 'irreparable damage' and considered that the Court's discretionary powers should not be limited in such manner.[226]

In *M/V 'Saiga'* (1997), the first Order for provisional measures by ITLOS, Judge Laing referred to Elkind's suggestion that the applicable phrase should be 'unendurable' rather than 'irreparable'. He agreed that 'irreparability arguably does not adequately cover such situations as that of the U.S. hostages' in the *Hostages* case (1979) and that of the case at hand. In this case the applicant State had requested provisional measures to the effect, among others, that the M/V 'Saiga' and her crew would be released. Previously, ITLOS had already ordered their prompt release under the 'prompt release' proceedings of the Convention on the Law of the Sea.[227] During the public hearing held the next month the applicant specified this request. Subsequently

---

[221] Id., §§21-23. He referred to Article 75 of Protocol I Additional to the 1949 Geneva Conventions and Article 3, common to the four Geneva Conventions. Regarding the application of human rights law he quoted the ICJ in its Advisory Opinion on the *Wall in the occupied Palestinian Territory* stating that 'the protection offered by human rights conventions does not cease in case of armed conflict', §30, referring to ICJ *Legal Consequences of the Construction of a Wall in the Occupied Palestinian Territory*, Advisory Opinion of 9 July 2004, §106.

[222] ICJ *Armed Activities on the Territory of the Congo (Congo v. Uganda)*, Judgment of 19 December 2005, Separate Opinion of Judge Simma, §§31-32.

[223] Id., §35, referring to Article 48 of the ILC's 2001 draft on State Responsibility.

[224] Id., §37.

[225] Elkind (1981), p. 223. See further section 3.3 (protection of the individual).

[226] ICJ *Arbitral Award of 31 July 1989 (Guinea-Bissau v. Senegal)*, Order of 2 March 1990 (dismissed by fourteen votes to one).

[227] The *M/V 'Saiga'* case *(St. Vincent and the Grenadines v. Guinea)*, Judgment of 4 December 1997, §§79 and 86. See Article 292 of the Convention. See about 'prompt release' Tanaka (2004) and Escher (2004).

Guinea released the vessel and its crew. Hence ITLOS noted in its Order that the prescription of a provisional measure for their release would no longer serve a purpose. Nevertheless, 'the rights of the Applicant would not fully be preserved if, pending the final decision, the vessel, its Master and the other members of the crew, its owners or operators were to be subjected to any judicial or administrative measure in connection to the incidents leading to the arrest and detention of the vessel and to the subsequent prosecution and conviction of the Master'. It unanimously prescribed provisional measures to the effect that Guinea would refrain from such actions.[228] In his Separate Opinion Judge Laing noted that this case showed that the standard of irreparability was not applicable. He referred to the treaty language of 'the preservation of the respective rights' and the addition, in Article 290(1) UNCLOS of 'the institution of prevention of "serious" harm to the marine environment'. This language 'strongly reinforces the view that the rather grave standard of irreparability is inapt for universal use, at least in many situations under UNCLOS'. He considered that ITLOS should indicate very clearly the subsidiary or supplementary nature of the standard of irreparable harm if it would decide to use it in the future.[229]

Elkind has pointed out 'that the motivating force behind interim protection is urgency. Its purpose is to prevent irreparable injury, terminate unendurable situations, and generally to prevent violence by providing an effective alternative to self-help'.[230] He specified that provisional measures must order the prevention of irreparable injury by maintaining the *status quo*. On the other hand, they could also order to put a halt to an unendurable or intolerable situation, because the complaining Party 'cannot reasonably be expected to endure the *status quo* pending judicial settlement of a dispute'.[231] This approach seems useful, also in the context of the ensuing discussion of the purpose of the provisional measures in human rights adjudication.[232] It comes down to maintaining the *status quo* in the face of threats of irreparable harm as well as returning to the *status quo ante* to deal with an ongoing unendurable situation. Such provisional measures aim to prevent (further) human suffering.

Nevertheless, thus far the ICJ and the human rights adjudicators have only referred to the concept of irreparable harm, which appears to cover both of the abovementioned situations. For this reason this book refers to the latter concept also in the context of ongoing unendurable situations that must be halted.[233]

3.5 The relation to the rights claimed and the possible judgment on the merits

In 1932 Dumbauld already pointed out that provisional measures 'always constitute an exceptional remedy'.[234] The proceedings for provisional measures are subsidiary to the main claim. They simply aim to preserve the rights that are in dispute. As the ICJ has pointed out the purpose of the use of provisional measures is 'to safeguard the rights of each party'. It 'presupposes the possibility of irreparable damage being caused to the rights at issue in judicial

---

228   ITLOS *M/V 'Saiga'* (No. 2) case (*St. Vincent and the Grenadines* v. *Guinea*), Order of 11 March 1998, §§41 and 52.

229   ITLOS *M/V 'Saiga'* (No. 2) case (*St. Vincent and the Grenadines* v. *Guinea*), Order of 11 March 1998, Separate Opinion of Judge Laing, §28.

230   Elkind (1981), p. 229. This qualification, dating from 1981, has not lost its significance.

231   Elkind (1981), pp. 229-230.

232   See Part II of this book.

233   On the distinction between irreparability in law and irreparability in fact, see e.g. Sztucki (1983), pp. 108-110.

234   Dumbauld (1932), p. 184. See also Judge Shahabuddeen in the *Passage through the Great Belt* case (*Finland* v. *Denmark*), Order of 19 July 1991, p. 29.

proceedings'.[235] There is no formal requirement that the Parties before the ICJ or ITLOS specify the rights claimed in their request for provisional measures. There should, however, be sufficient information for the adjudicators to conclude that there is 'a *prima facie* basis' for the 'probable jurisdiction of the Tribunal on the underlying merits'.[236]

Some respondent States have argued that the applicant State should show the likelihood of success on the merits.[237] In the *Hostages* case (1979) the ICJ considered that it was the purpose of provisional measures to preserve 'rights which are the subject of dispute in judicial proceedings'.[238] Thus generally speaking the rights to be protected by provisional measures must be linked closely to (or be identical to) the rights claimed in the main case.[239] The main dispute in the *Arbitral Award* case (1990) related to the validity of an arbitral decision about maritime delimitations. However, Guinea-Bissau's application for provisional measures included a request to direct the Parties to abstain from all actions in the disputed area. The Court rejected this request because 'the alleged rights sought to be made the subject of provisional measures are not the subject of the proceedings before the Court on the merits of the case'.[240] According to Merrills this decision 'reflects the traditional conception of interim measures as concerned with rights rather than interests'.[241] After all, Guinea-Bissau would not be able to bring the dispute on maritime delimitation before the ICJ because Senegal had made reservations in this respect.

Thirlway notes that the *Genocide Convention* case (1993) 'made clear that even the rights claimed in the Application cannot be protected by provisional measures unless they are rights in respect of which the Court would have jurisdiction under the title which the Court regards as prima facie established'.[242] The ICJ pointed out that 'the Court, having established the existence of a basis on which its jurisdiction might be founded, ought not to indicate measures for the protection of any disputed rights other than those which might ultimately form the basis of a judgment in the exercise of that jurisdiction'.[243] At the same time, as discussed in section 3.3.4, the ICJ has been prepared to order provisional measures to protect the lives of persons on the

---

[235] ICJ *Frontier Dispute* case (*Burkina Faso* v. *Mali*), Order of 10 January 1986 (Chamber), §13. See further e.g. *the Passage through the Great Belt* case, (*Finland* v. *Denmark*), Order of 19 July 1991, §21 and *US Diplomatic and Consular Staff in Tehran* (*US* v. *Iran*) (*Hostages* case), Order of 15 December 1979, §36.

[236] Separate Opinion of Judge Laing in the *M/V 'Saiga'* (No. 2), Order of 11 March 1998, §20, also noting that 'parties will sometimes request measures to protect rights not directly located in the Convention but arising under customary international law' and considering that the 'difficulty of identifying the precise content and even existence of customary rules might further influence a tolerant approach of decision-makers to this requirement'.

[237] See further section 3.6 on the issue of prejudgment and section 5.3 on assessment of material urgency.

[238] ICJ *US Diplomatic and Consular Staff in Tehran* (*US* v. *Iran*) (*Hostages* case), Order of 15 December 1979, §36. See also, e.g., *Fisheries Jurisdiction* cases (*UK* v. *Iceland*; *Germany* v. *Iceland*), Order of 17 August 1972, §21; *Frontier Dispute* case (*Burkina Faso* v. *Mali*), Order of 10 January 1986, §13 and *the Passage through the Great Belt* case, Order of 29 July 1991, §16.

[239] See also Wellens (1998), pp. 420-421, p. 424. Generally on this issue Beirlaen (1979-1980), pp. 270-283.

[240] ICJ *Arbitral Award of 31 July 1989* (*Guinea-Bissau* v. *Senegal*), Order of 2 March 1990, §26 (Judge *ad hoc* Thierry dissenting).

[241] Merrills (1995), p. 102. See also Thirlway (1994), p. 17.

[242] Thirlway (1994), p. 35. See also the criticism expressed by Toufayan (2005), Gaffikin (1995); Maison (1994) and Wiebalck (1995).

[243] ICJ *Application of the Convention on the prevention and punishment of the crime of genocide* (*Bosnia and Herzegovina* v. *Yugoslavia (Serbia and Montenegro)*), Order of 8 April 1993, §35. See section 3.3.

basis of existing obligations of the Respondent State, even though these obligations were not the *direct* subject matter of the Application.

The rights claimed may have already earned clear recognition. In that case the party requesting provisional measures should just give some indication of the violation of these rights. In the alternative, the Applicant State should make an effort to show that the rights claimed indeed exist.[244] After all the use of provisional measures would be 'a pointless exercise in empty authority' if there were 'no possibility of the claimed rights being substantiated as having an existence in law'.[245]

By contrast, in other cases States have complained that a request for provisional measures was too much a request for an instant decision.[246] Moreover, as noted, there have been Orders for provisional measures regarding the plight of human beings, not directly linked to the rights in dispute. This all indicates that the ICJ takes a sufficiently flexible approach to its competence to order provisional measures, taking into account the rights of (groups of) persons, as long as it has *prima facie* jurisdiction vis-à-vis the obligations of the State in this regard.[247]

3.6 Provisional measures and prejudgment

States have sometimes argued that provisional measures were intended to protect the interests of both Parties and could not be granted to one Party only.[248] On the other hand, in the *Hostages* case (1979) the ICJ pointed out that the terms of Article 41 ICJ Statute explicitly refer to 'the respective rights of *either* party' (italics by the Court). '[T]he whole concept of an indication for provisional measures, as Article 73 of the Rules recognizes, implies a request from one of the parties for measures to preserve its own rights against action by the other party calculated to prejudice those rights *pendente lite*'. It concluded that a request for provisional measures is 'by its nature unilateral'.[249] This is different for ITLOS because it is authorised, under Article 290 UNCLOS, to order provisional measures that are appropriate 'to preserve the respective rights of the parties'.[250]

Still according to Mendelson 'the risk of prejudice to one or other of the parties is a real one, which cannot be glossed over by the simple incantation of the formula that the grant or

---

[244] See also Goldie (1973-74), p. 501 who notes that in the latter case the State 'would have a very heavy burden of proof to discharge'.

[245] Goldie (1973-74), p. 502.

[246] See also the next section on prejudgment (section 3.6).

[247] See e.g. *Questions relating to the obligation to prosecute or extradite* (*Belgium* v. *Senegal*), Order of 28 May 2009, §57 "Whereas the power of the Court to indicate provisional measures should be exercised only if the Court is satisfied that the rights asserted by a party are at least plausible". The Court added there was no need to establish definitively the existence of the rights claimed by Belgium or to consider Belgium's capacity to assert such rights before the Court' and that this State's rights 'begin grounded in a possible interpretation of the Convention against torture, therefore appear to be plausible', §60. Not all members of the Court have been comfortable with the Court's approach to the relation with the merits, see Judge Oda in ICJ *Land and maritime boundary between Cameroon and Nigeria* (*Cameroon* v. *Nigeria*), Order of 15 March 1996, §2. See also Yoshiyuki Iwamoto (2002).

[248] See also Fitzmaurice (1986), p. 544, arguing that the ICJ should preserve the interests of 'both parties equally' and Judge Ajibola in his Separate Opinion in *Land and maritime boundary between Cameroon and Nigeria* (*Cameroon* v. *Nigeria*), Order of 15 March 1996, under IV (III).

[249] ICJ *Hostages* case: *United States Diplomatic and Consular Staff in Tehran* (*US* v. *Iran*), Order of 15 December 1979, §29.

[250] Judge Laing considers that a general requirement to balance the right of the parties would be consistent with the language of Article 290(1), Separate Opinion Judge Laing, ITLOS *M/V 'Saiga'* (No. 2), Order of 11 March 1998, §23. See also section 3.7 on protection and reparation.

refusal of interim measures does not prejudge subsequent decisions in other phases of the proceedings'. The ICJ should 'weigh up the risks to both parties and try to achieve the fairest solution'. In this context he noted: "If there is a strong chance of jurisdiction on the merits, the risk of prejudice to the rights of the plaintiff will be relatively greater if interim measures are not indicated, than the risk of prejudice to the rights of the defendant, if they are. Conversely, if there is little prospect of a positive finding on jurisdiction, there will be little prejudice to the plaintiff in refusing interim measures, because the Court will probably not be in a position to grant it a remedy on the merits at the end of the day, whereas the granting of interim measures may cause substantial prejudice to the interests of an unwilling defendant".[251]

In 1932 Dumbauld wrote that the PCIJ's provisional measures do not constitute a provisional judgment. The Applicant 'can not demand that his legal position be bettered'. He did note 'a seeming exception' when the relief sought in the principal case is simply aimed at forbidding 'a flagrant wrong or violation of right, rather than an exercise of "judicial jurisdiction" to decide a truly doubtful question of law'. In such case, he acknowledges, 'the only object of the final judgment is to forbid the illegal act, definitively and with force of *res judicata*'. Thus, 'it may well come to pass that the interim order temporarily prohibiting unlawful conduct threatening irreparable damage will in fact, though not in law, be equivalent to giving applicant the very same thing he hopes to secure by final judgment'.[252]

The requirement of non-anticipation by one of the Parties of a decision on the merits means that neither of the Parties shall pre-empt the final determination of the case. This is one of the traditional reasons for courts to use provisional measures.[253] Provisional measures to prevent anticipation by one of the parties, in the sense of pre-empting the final determination that could otherwise have been made by the adjudicator, may at the same time trigger the different rule that the adjudicator itself shall not anticipate the final determination and must 'avoid any appearance of pre-judgment'.[254] However, this does not mean that the provisional measures may not give an indication of substantive law to the extent this is already clear.

Thirlway notes that 'the rights sought to be protected must be, to put it at its lowest, closely linked with the rights which are the subject of dispute in the main proceedings'. Hence, 'to some extent an "anticipation" is only to be expected in every case'. The Court has to find the necessary *degree* of anticipation to justify provisional measures. What is important here, according to Thirlway, is who took the initiative: 'it is one thing to restrain one party from taking some step to change the status quo, and quite another to require a form of restraint which itself involves a departure from the status quo'.[255]

If a request for provisional measures is in fact a request for an interim judgment they should not be ordered because they could be seen to prejudice the decision on the merits and would be incompatible with Article 41.[256] In *Chorzów Factory* (1927) the PCIJ rejected a request by Germany as 'designed to obtain an interim judgment in favour of part of the claim' rather than a request for interim protection proper.[257] Thirlway suggests that the ICJ could refer to this decision in order to prevent applications for provisional measures that would simply cause 'short-term tactical advantage' to one of the Parties. Otherwise 'the fact that neither jurisdiction nor the claim itself have to be proved up to anywhere near the hilt for measures to be granted must offer a

---

[251] Mendelson (1972-73), pp. 313-314.

[252] Dumbauld (1932), pp. 163-164.

[253] See e.g. Elkind (1981), p. 210. See also section 3.2 of this chapter on the traditional purposes of provisional measures.

[254] See Judge Shahabuddeen in *the Passage through the Great Belt* case, Order of 29 July 1991.

[255] Thirlway (1994), p. 11.

[256] See e.g. Merrills (1995), p. 104 and Sztucki (1983), pp. 95-96.

[257] PCIJ *Factory at Chorzów* (*German interests in Polish Upper Silesia* cases), Order of 21 November 1927, p. 10.

temptation where a case can be made for urgency even if the merits of the claim are shaky or the jurisdictional title dubious'.[258]

Judge Gros referred to attempts to obtain an 'interim judgment' in his dissenting opinion on the Order for provisional measures in the *Nuclear Test* cases (1973). He considered that 'it would indeed, by definition, be contrary to the nature of interlocutory proceedings if they enabled the dispute of which they were only an accessory element to be disposed of'.[259] Thirlway points out that the result of this argument is curious. After all, the measures must relate to the rights claimed.

> "Could the Court refuse to indicate measures requiring the temporary cessation of nuclear tests merely because the claim was for a permanent cessation of such tests? Assuming that there was sufficient evidence of urgency and the prospect of irreparable damage, the mere coincidence of the request for measures with the terms of the claim would be a strange and artificial reason for refusal".[260]

He also notes that the ICJ could prevent complacency of the beneficiary once provisional measures have been taken, by including in the Order for provisional measures a provision to review the measures in light of, among others, the progress of the proceedings on the merits.[261] With regard to the *Chorzów Factory* case and its reference to 'an interim judgment in favour of a part of the claim' he explains that this turned on the basis of the German request. Germany 'was not so much asking for protection pendente lite of the rights asserted in the Application, as asking for immediate satisfaction of what it regarded as an indisputable part of the claim'.[262]

In the *Hostages* case (1979) Iran had objected that the US was, in fact, requesting a judgment on the merits of the case during the interim measures phase. The Court distinguished this case from the *Chorzów Factory* case (1927), where the PCIJ had declined a request for provisional measures as being 'designed to obtain an interim judgment in favour of a part of the claim'.[263] The ICJ noted that the circumstances in that case were 'entirely different from those of the present one, and the request there sought to obtain from the Court a final judgment on part of a claim for a sum of money'. It pointed out as well that a request for provisional measures must in fact 'by its very nature relate to the substance of the case since, as Article 41 expressly states, their object is to preserve the respective rights of either party'. In other words, the relationship between the rights to be protected at the provisional measures phase and the rights claimed on the merits in fact is one of the requirements of Article 41.[264] It concluded that 'in the present case the purpose of the United States request appears to be not to obtain a judgment, interim or final, on the merits of its claims but to preserve the substance of the rights which it claims *pendente lite*'.[265] Oellers-Frahm put it as follows:

---

[258]   Thirlway (1994), p. 27.

[259]   Dissenting Opinion Judge Gros, ICJ *Nuclear tests* cases (*New Zealand* v. *France/Australia* v. *France*), Order of 22 June 1973, p. 123 (Australia) and p. 158 (New Zealand). The ICJ *denied* the request, but Judge Gros proposed additional/different reasons for this denial.

[260]   Thirlway (1994), p. 27.

[261]   Thirlway (1994), pp. 27-28. He pointed out that the ICJ had in fact done so in the ICJ *Fisheries Jurisdiction* cases (*UK* v. *Iceland*; *Germany* v. *Iceland*), Order of 17 August 1972.

[262]   Thirlway (1994), p. 28.

[263]   PCIJ *Factory at Chorzów* (*German interests in Polish Upper Silesia* cases), Order of 21 November 1927, p. 10.

[264]   See also section 3.5.

[265]   ICJ *US Diplomatic and Consular Staff in Tehran* (*US* v. *Iran*), Order of 15 December 1979, §28.

"That there may even be identity between the objects of those two procedures is self-evident, since often the claim on the merits concerns the re-establishment of the *status quo ante*".[266]

In 1981 Elkind considered that in the *Hostages* case (1979) 'it was precisely the status quo existing at the time the application and request were filed which was intolerable from the standpoint of international law'. This triggered the question of the restoration of the *status quo ante*. The attempt in this case 'might have constituted an interim judgment'. "If the Court, after granting interim measures, later found for Iran on the question of jurisdiction, it could not revoke that particular measure. What could it do? Order the hostages returned to Iran? That would have been absurd. Yet it was one of the most urgent situations that the Court has ever faced".[267] In fact this case already showed that the ICJ takes a more flexible approach regarding the use of provisional measures when the urgent situation involves fundamental rights of individuals.

In the *Genocide Convention* case (1993) Serbia and Montenegro argued that Bosnia Herzegovina was really seeking an interim judgment, but the ICJ pointed out that the rights of both Parties 'to dispute the facts alleged against it, and to submit arguments in respect of the merits, must remain unaffected by the Court's decision'. At the stage of provisional measures it could not make definitive findings of fact or imputability, but it merely determined whether the circumstances required the use of provisional measures to protect rights under the Genocide Convention.[268]

In 1991 the ICJ denied a request for provisional measures in the *Passage through the Great Belt* case. It did so for lack of temporal urgency.[269] The Respondent State had also argued that the Applicant State should be able to 'substantiate the right it claims to a point where a reasonable prospect of success in the main case exists'. The Applicant, on the other hand, argued that the ICJ 'may not enter into the merits of a particular case at the stage of deciding whether or not to indicate provisional measures'. It denied that its case could be considered as *prima facie* unfounded.[270] Clearly the Applicant is not in a position to argue that the Court should not take into account the rights claimed, implying that this would prejudge the decision on the merits.[271] Indeed the ICJ noted that it is the purpose of the provisional measures to preserve rights that are subject to dispute.[272] With regard to the Respondent's argument that the type of reparation in this case could only be satisfied by damages, because 'restitution in kind would be excessively onerous', it pointed out that it was 'not at present called upon to determine the character of any decision which it might make on the merits'. It did point out, however, that the possibility of a judicial finding that the construction of works involving an infringement of a legal right 'must not be continued or must be modified or dismantled' could and should 'not be excluded a priori'.[273] It noted that it was for Denmark to consider the impact a judgment upholding Finland's claim could have on the implementation of the Great Belt project. It was therefore also for Denmark 'to decide

---

[266] Oellers-Frahm (1981), p. 284.
[267] Elkind (1981), pp. 219-220.
[268] ICJ *Application of the Convention on the prevention and punishment of the crime of genocide* (*Bosnia and Herzegovina* v. *Yugoslavia (Serbia and Montenegro)*), Order of 13 September 1993 (second request), §44. Only according to Judge Tarassov the Order that Serbia was to ensure that forces under its control or influence would refrain from acts of genocide was 'very close to a pre-judgment of the merits'. See also Merrills (1995), p. 105, remarking that this does not seem very convincing. See on the other hand, Gray (2003), p. 893.
[269] See further section 5.2.
[270] ICJ *Passage through the Great Belt* case (*Finland* v. *Denmark*), Order of 29 July 1991, §21.
[271] See also ICJ *Passage through the Great Belt* case (*Finland* v. *Denmark*), Order of 29 July 1991, Separate Opinion of Judge Shahabuddeen, pp. 29-30.
[272] ICJ *Passage through the Great Belt* case (*Finland* v. *Denmark*), Order of 29 July 1991, §22.
[273] Id., §31.

whether or to what extent it should accordingly delay or modify that project'.[274] Merrills pointed out:

> "Although the question of possible remedies was a subsidiary point, it provides a striking illustration of how questions of interim protection can become bound up with those relating to the merits, and of how the Court, while not anticipating its future judgment, may nevertheless have to give an issue such as remedies its early attention".[275]

Judge Shahabuddeen has noted that the ICJ is only considering whether the State requesting provisional measures has shown any possibility of the existence of the right sought to be preserved, not whether it definitively exists. "A finding that such a possibility exists clearly falls short of constituting an interim judgment".[276]

When taking provisional measures the ICJ has to consider the circumstances drawn to its attention as requiring such measures, but it cannot make definitive findings of fact.[277] It emphasises that 'the right of the respondent State to dispute the facts alleged and to submit arguments in respect of the merits must remain unaffected by the Court's decision'.[278] In its decisions to order provisional measures for a stay of execution of death sentences, for instance, it has pointed out that the measures 'would necessarily be provisional in nature and would not in any way prejudge findings the Court might make on the merits'. Such measures would preserve the respective rights of the Parties and the Court would ensure, with the cooperation of the parties, that any decision on the merits would be reached 'with all possible expedition'.[279]

In its decisions to *refuse* provisional measures it also points out that 'the decision given in the present proceedings in no way prejudges any question relating to the merits of the case' and leaves unaffected the rights of both States to submit arguments. In *Congo* v. *France* (2003), for instance, it denied a request for provisional measures to the effect that the proceedings by a French investigating judge against a Congolese politician would be suspended immediately. It pointed out that this decision 'in no way prejudges the question of the jurisdiction of the Court to deal with the merits of the case or any questions relating to the admissibility of the Application, or relating to the merits themselves'. It added the customary remark that the decision 'leaves unaffected the right of the Governments of the Congo and France to submit the arguments in respect of those questions'.[280]

---

[274] Id., §32-33. See further section 3.2 on the traditional purposes of provisional measures.

[275] Merrills (1995), p. 113.

[276] ICJ *Passage through the Great Belt* case (*Finland* v. *Denmark*), Order of 29 July 1991, Separate Opinion of Judge Shahabuddeen, p. 30.

[277] See further section 5.3 on assessment of material urgency.

[278] See e.g. ICJ *Military and Paramilitary Activities in and against Nicaragua* (*Nicaragua* v. *US*), Order of 10 May 1984, §§29-31.

[279] ICJ *Breard* (*Paraguay* v. *US*), Order of 9 April 1998, *LaGrand* (*Germany* v. *US*), Order of 3 March 1999, §27, *Avena et al.* (*Mexico* v. *US*), Order of 5 February 2003. See also *Armed activities on the territory of the Congo* (*Congo* v. *Uganda*), Order of 1 July 2000, §90.

[280] ICJ *Certain criminal proceedings in France* (*Congo* v. *France*), Order of 17 June 2003, §40. See also *Arrest warrant of 11 April 2000* (*Congo* v. *Belgium*), Order of 8 December 2000, §77.

3.7 Protection and reparation

3.7.1 Introduction

Clearly the discussion of the protection required by provisional measures is related to the purpose of these measures. Often it is a matter of perspective whether provisional measures are seen as requiring maintenance of, change of or return to the status quo. They may constitute requests or orders to provide information in order to preserve the evidence. The question whether and to what extent provisional measures require positive measures is equally a matter of perspective. The substance of provisional measures must be regarded as based on a continuum between negative and positive measures. Moreover, provisional measures may vary with regard to the level of specificity.

3.7.2 Action and abstention: positive obligations in Orders for provisional measures

International adjudicators have ordered States to abstain from acting as well as to take positive action, with varying degrees of detail.[281] In order to prevent prejudice to the rights of Belgian nationals in China, in 1927 the President of the PCIJ ordered China, among others, to accompany any Belgian who may have lost his passport or committed some offence against the law, 'in safety to the nearest Belgian consulate', to provide 'effective protection' of Belgian missionaries and 'in general, protection of Belgians against any insult or violence'. Any legal proceedings against Belgians were to be heard by 'modern courts', with a right of appeal and with the assistance of counsel and interpreters of choice.[282] This provisional measure is reasonably detailed and includes both obligations to act and to refrain from acting.

Equally, in the *Fisheries* cases (1972) the ICJ not only ordered Iceland to refrain from certain acts, but it also ordered the Applicant States (the UK and Germany) to 'ensure' that vessels registered in their State did not take an annual catch of a certain amount and to 'furnish' both Iceland and the Registry of the ICJ with all the relevant information.[283]

In the *MOX Plant* case (2001) ITLOS used provisional measures aimed precisely at preserving the rights arising from the duty to cooperate, referred to as a fundamental principle in relation to the prevention of environmental harm.[284] Ireland had contended that its rights under certain specified conditions would be 'irrevocably violated' if the UK would start the operation of the MOX power plant at that time. Ireland considered that these operations would have irreversible consequences. Eventually, rather than ordering the provisional measures requested by Ireland, ITLOS ordered both Parties to exchange further information with regard to the possible consequences for the Irish Sea, to monitor risks and devise measures to prevent the radioactive pollution that 'might result from the operation of the Mox plant'.[285] It ordered the Parties to cooperate and 'enter into consultations forthwith' to '(a) exchange further information with regard to possible consequences for the Irish Sea arising out of the commissioning of the MOX plant; (b) monitor risks or the effects of the operation of the MOX plant for the Irish Sea; (c) devise, as appropriate, measures to prevent pollution of the marine environment which might result from the

---

[281]   See already Dumbauld (1932), p. 167: "Interim measures afford protection not only against acts but also against omissions to act which threaten a right". See also p. 195.

[282]   PCIJ *Sino-Belgian* case, Order of the President of 8 January 1927.

[283]   ICJ *Fisheries Jurisdiction* cases (*UK* v. *Iceland*; *Germany* v. *Iceland*), Order of 17 August 1972.

[284]   ITLOS *MOX plant case* (*Ireland* v. *UK*), Order of 3 December 2001, §83.

[285]   ITLOS *MOX plant* case (*Ireland* v. *UK*), Order of 3 December 2001, §89.

operation of the MOX plant'.[286] The duty to cooperate also plays a role in the specific context of risk assessment.[287]

3.7.3 Specificity of decisions about provisional measures

As noted, the PCIJ was rather specific in its Order for provisional measures in the *Sino-Belgian* case (1927).[288] Yet traditionally the ICJ has not specified the contents of its provisional measures.[289] In later cases this changed. As discussed, the ICJ (Chamber) decided in the *Frontier Dispute* case (1986) not to order exactly those measures as requested by Burkina Faso. Rather than the withdrawal of the Parties' forces to a specific line it ordered a withdrawal of the forces, the terms of which should be determined by agreement between the Parties. Only if such agreement would fail the ICJ itself would set the terms of the specific line for withdrawal.[290] The effect of this approach was 'conciliatory in the sense that the onus is placed on the parties to negotiate a *modus vivendi*, pending judicial resolution of the dispute'.[291] The substance of the Order was particularly attuned to the context, in which a regional organisation was actively involved in addressing the situation. The Order recognised this involvement and 'the Chamber's task was essentially one of co-ordinating its application of Article 41 with the parties' outside activities'. By choosing this approach to the substance of provisional measures the ICJ also avoided accusations of prejudgment.[292] As Merrills points out, the approach of the Chamber in this case was 'clearly a legitimate exercise' of its powers under Article 41.[293]

---

[286] Ibid.

[287] See section 5.3 of this Chapter (urgency).

[288] PCIJ *Sino-Belgian* case, Order of the President of 8 January 1927.

[289] See e.g. PCIJ *Electricity Company of Sofia and Bulgaria* (*Belgium* v. *Bulgaria*), Order of 5 December 1939, see further Elkind (1981), pp. 97-98. See also ICJ *Nuclear tests* cases (*New Zealand* v. *France* and *Australia* v. *France*), Order of 22 June 1973, on the *Nuclear Tests* cases see further Elkind, pp. 117-122.

[290] In the *Frontier Dispute* case (1986) Burkina Faso requested the Chamber to order the withdrawal of the Parties to a specific line also proposed on the merits. Mali pointed out that this request could not be seen as 'provisional' as it would amount to granting the claim on the merits. The ICJ responded by distinguishing 'between withdrawal as a matter of principle and the determination of its extent'. In other words it ordered the withdrawal of the forces and determined that the terms of this withdrawal should be determined by agreement between the Parties.

[291] Merrills (1995), p. 133.

[292] ICJ *Frontier Dispute* case (*Burkina Faso* v. *Mali*), Order of 10 January 1986. See also Merrills (1995), pp. 105-106 and p. 126. See also section 3.6 on provisional measures and prejudgment. As Merrills notes, at the time the issue was under consideration 'within the framework of a regional organisation'. Thus 'this was a constructive way of discharging the Chamber's function while avoiding any accusation of prejudgment', Merrills (1995), p. 105. This was the organisation ANAD, which stands for Accord de non-agression et d'assistance en matière de défense. Burkina Faso had also requested the Chamber to order that each Party should refrain from any act of territorial administration beyond that same specific line. The Chamber noted that it did not consider itself empowered, at the stage of provisional measures, to modify the situation that prevailed before the armed actions. Rather it was necessary to avoid prejudging the existence of any specific line, ICJ *Frontier Dispute* case (*Burkina Faso* v. *Mali*), Order of 10 January 1986, 11, §29. Instead it ordered that administrative acts in the disputed areas should not modify the situation that prevailed before the armed actions. If it would have ordered the provisional measures requested by Burkina Faso it would have gone 'beyond a restoration of the status quo', Merrills (1995), p. 105.

[293] Id., p. 133.

Obviously the discussion on the specificity of provisional measures is closely related to that on the authority of adjudicators to order provisional measures *proprio motu*. Article 75(1) of the ICJ Rules of Procedure refers to an action *proprio motu* if provisional measures are ordered in the absence of any request.[294] Modification of the contents of the provisional measures requested by one of the Parties, including by ordering the preservation of the rights involved 'by other means than those proposed', or by concluding that 'rights other than those invoked in the request', required provisional measures, 'in addition to or instead of those rights' (footnotes omitted).[295] Such modification of provisional measures was 'a matter of routine in the Court's practice'. This mainly comes down to condensing and consolidating requests that were originally very detailed, granting the measures requested only in particle The Court also routinely adds specific protective measures in order to preserve the rights of the Respondent State, as well as measures of general restraint directed to both Parties, also in cases in which the requesting Party had only requested such measures to be taken vis-à-vis the Respondent. Finally, it may indicate general measures of restraint that were not included in the request for provisional measures at all.[296]

Regarding the substance of provisional measures, Judge Shahabuddeen has noted that they 'should be framed in self-executing terms, in the sense that [they] should contain all the legal elements required for [their] interpretation and application'.[297] In *Cameroon* v. *Nigeria* (1996) Judge Ajibola argued that the Court was correct in ordering both Parties to take no action that might prejudice rights of the other or that might aggravate or extend the dispute. After all, it was the 'cardinal duty of the Court to preserve peace'. However, he disagreed with the other four operative parts of the Order. He considered that the Court should 'refrain from orders with diplomatic or political content or matters concerning mediation or negotiation, since strictly speaking there issues are apparently outside the legal assignment of the Court'. Leaving aside the relation between 'strictly speaking' and 'apparently', it is clear that he was concerned that some of the operative parts may actually 'do more harm or damage than good' and that 'the Court should not issue an order in vain, that is, an order that is difficult or impossible to implement'.[298] The latter criterion is not very convincing. While it is obvious that an Order should be capable of being implemented, the Court should not be led by the expectation that the State concerned might not be willing to implement such Order. Authoritative Orders of the Court already are important simply in order to back up arguments made in domestic courts and other fora. In addition, even though that is not their main purpose, they are significant building blocks for the development of international law in general.

Dumbauld has pointed out that provisional measures 'should go no further than necessary to fulfil their purpose'. The adjudicator should choose, from equally effective measures, those that 'least harm' the Addressee State.[299] He referred to a range of protective measures relating to the preservation of peace, including the establishment of neutralised zones, and concluded that the 'Court may use its discretion in indicating any sort of measure which will attain the end desired and prove acceptable in practice'.[300]

As to substance the Order for provisional measures often is less far reaching than the original request by (one of) the Parties and the ICJ often takes into account the rights of the respondent

---

[294] See also section 2 (authority).

[295] Sztucki (1983), p. 158.

[296] Id., p. 159. See also section 3.3.4 (border conflict cases).

[297] ICJ *Land and maritime boundary between Cameroon and Nigeria* (*Cameroon* v. *Nigeria*), Order of 15 March 1996, declaration of Judge Shahabuddeen.

[298] ICJ *Land and maritime boundary between Cameroon and Nigeria* (*Cameroon* v. *Nigeria*), Order of 15 March 1996, Separate Opinion of Judge Ajibola. On the official responses of States, see section 7 of this chapter.

[299] Dumbauld (1932), p. 167. See also section 3.8 on the rights of the addressee Parties.

[300] Dumbauld (1932), p. 168.

as well.[301] At the same time it has pointed out the obligations of the addressee by specifying that the Respondent State should transmit the Court's order to its constituent parts, such as the Governor of Arizona in *LaGrand* and report on implementation.[302]

The Court's recommendations in Orders denying provisional measures, for instance by stressing the importance of preventing aggravation of the dispute (which is also one of the purposes of provisional measures) is, as Merrills put it, a type of 'conciliatory function' related to 'the kind of implied power referred to in the *Free Zones* case'.[303] The ICJ has made such recommendations, for instance, in the case of *Armed Activities in the territory of the Congo* (*Congo v. Rwanda*) (2002).[304] Judge Buergenthal disagreed with the expression of the Court's deep concern regarding 'deplorable human tragedy, loss of life, and enormous suffering' resulting from the continued fighting in East Congo. He also disputed the Court's emphasis on the obligations of all Parties to proceedings before it to act in conformity with their obligations under the UN Charter and other rules of international law. The Court had pointed out in particular, the obligations by Congo and Rwanda under the Geneva Conventions and the First Additional Protocol.[305] It had also noted, referring to a range of UN Security Council resolutions, that whether or not States accept its jurisdiction, 'they remain in any event responsible for acts attributable to them that violate international law'.[306] Buergenthal considered that the ICJ had no jurisdiction to address these matters once it had ruled that it lacked *prima facie* jurisdiction to order provisional measures: "The Court's function is to pronounce itself on matters within its jurisdiction and not to voice personal sentiments or to make comments, general or specific, which, despite their admittedly 'feel-good' qualities, have no legitimate place in this order".[307] He pointed out that the Court's own responsibilities under the UN Charter for the maintenance of peace and security are not general, but 'strictly limited to the exercise of its judicial functions in cases of which it has jurisdiction'.[308]

Judge Koroma responded to Buergenthal by stating that the Court had 'rightly and judiciously' expressed its deep concern and rightly emphasized the responsibilities of all Parties.[309] Judge Dugard pointed out that the Order made no judgment on the conduct of either Party, but rightly expressed concern about the human suffering in the region of the Eastern Congo as well as called upon States in the region 'to abide by the rule of law'. The Court's call applied to

---

[301] See section 3.6 on prejudgment and section 6.1 on the beneficiaries. See also Merrills (1995), p. 143.

[302] ICJ *LaGrand* case (*Germany v. US*), Order of 3 March 1999, §28. See also Wellens (1998), pp. 428-429 on the possibility for the President of the Court to specify the required action or abstention, for instance by way of follow up, based on the President's discretionary powers in Article 74(4) of the Rules.

[303] Merrills (1995), p. 133, noting that in the *Free Zones* case the PCIJ considered that 'it is for the Court to facilitate, so far as is compatible with its Statute, such direct and frankly settlement'.

[304] ICJ *Armed Activities in the territory of the Congo* (new application: 2002) (*Democratic Republic of the Congo v. Rwanda*), Order of 10 July 2002. See generally about this case Kritsiotis (2001); Savadogo (2002); Tatulli (2003); Gray (2003) and Mampuya (2004).

[305] ICJ *Armed Activities in the territory of the Congo* (new application: 2002) (*Democratic Republic of the Congo v. Rwanda*), Order of 10 July 2002, §§54-56.

[306] Id., §93.

[307] ICJ *Congo v. Rwanda*, Order of 10 July 2002, Declaration of Judge Buergenthal, §§3-4. According to Buergenthal the Court's expression of concern 'in a formal Order of the Court' presupposed that the Court had the 'requisite jurisdiction to deal with that subject-matter', §5.

[308] ICJ *Congo v. Rwanda*, Order of 10 July 2002, Declaration of Judge Buergenthal, §6.

[309] ICJ Congo v. Rwanda, Order of 10 July 2002 (denying provisional measures), Declaration of Judge Koroma, §12.

all States in the region and did 'not in any way prejudge the issue raised in the present proceedings'.[310]

Judge Buergenthal warned that the Court's statement 'might also encourage States to file provisional measure requests, knowing that, despite the fact that they would be unable to sustain the burden of demonstrating the requisite prima facie jurisdiction, they would obtain from the Court some pronouncements that could be interpreted as supporting their claim against the other Party'.[311] This indeed seems a real possibility, indicating that the Court must stay alert in its formulations. Yet it appears that the ICJ considers it may insert recommendations in its Orders denying provisional measures.

A more recent example (2006 and 2007) in which it did so was in its Orders denying requests by Argentina for provisional measures *Pulp Mills*, where the Court reminded the parties of their responsibilities under international law and stressed the need for Argentina and Uruguay 'to implement in good faith the consultation and co-operation procedures' provided for in a treaty concluded between them in the 1970s. It encouraged both parties 'to refrain from any actions which might render more difficult the resolution of the present dispute'.[312]

An earlier case in which the question was brought up whether the Court could insert general recommendations to the Parties in its Orders denying the use of provisional measures, was the *Aegean Sea* case (1976).[313] In this case Judge Lachs considered that the ICJ should, even when it did not indicate provisional measures, have acted *proprio motu*. It should have stressed the need for restraint and have made its own contribution to help 'pave the way to the friendly resolution of a dangerous dispute'.[314] In the *Arbitral Award* case (1990) Judge Evenson drew attention to the Parties to 'make every effort to enter into provisional arrangements'.[315] In the *Passage through the Great Belt* case (1991), the ICJ itself, in reference to the PCIJ decision in the *Free-Zones* case, noted that 'pending a decision of the Court on the merits, any negotiation between the Parties with a view to achieving a direct and friendly settlement is to be welcomed'.[316] Subsequently this case was indeed settled by negotiation and Merrills points out that the Court's suggestion 'was well justified and may have served a useful purpose'.[317]

---

[310]   ICJ *Congo* v. *Rwanda*, Order of 10 July 2002, Separate Opinion of Judge Dugard, §13.

[311]   ICJ *Congo* v. *Rwanda*, Order of 10 July 2002, Declaration of Judge Buergenthal, §9.

[312]   ICJ *Case concerning Pulp Mills on the River Uruguay* (*Argentina* v. *Uruguay*), Order of 13 July 2006 (denying provisional measures), §82. In its subsequent Order it reiterated 'its call to the Parties' in respect to both aspects. Order of 23 January 2007 (denying provisional measures), §53.

[313]   ICJ *Aegean Sea* case (*Greece* v. *Turkey*), Order of 11 September 1976. On the protection required in the Court's provisional measures see also section 3.7.

[314]   Judge Lachs suggested that the ICJ 'could have made its own constructive, albeit indirect, contribution, helping to pave the way to the friendly resolution of a dangerous dispute'. It could have done so by acting *proprio motu*, laying 'greater stress on, in particular the need for restraint on the part of both States and the possible consequences of any deterioration or extension of the conflict', even without indicating provisional measures proper. ICJ *Aegean Sea* case (*Greece* v. *Turkey*), Order of 11 September 1976, Separate Opinion Judge Lachs, p. 20. Yet Sztucki noted in 1983 that the Court had been 'consistently reluctant (*South-Eastern Greenland, Right of Passage, Aegean Sea*) to accept general prevention as the sole object of its interlocutory decisions', Sztucki (1983), p. 78.

[315]   ICJ *Arbitral Award of 31 July 1989* (*Guinea-Bissau* v. *Senegal*), Order of 2 March 1990, Separate Opinion of Judge Evenson.

[316]   ICJ *Passage through the Great Belt* case (*Finland* v. *Denmark*), 29 July 1991, §95. Judges Tarassov and Broms would have preferred an even more concrete proposal. Judge Broms also pointed out that the Parties could take up the suggestion for negotiations without loss of face exactly because such negotiations were recommended in the Court's Order.

[317]   Merrills (1995), p. 136.

With regard to cases in which it denied provisional measures because it considered them inappropriate in the circumstances, the above arguments indeed seem to justify the insertion of general recommendations. The same applies in cases where it denies a request for provisional measures because of *prima facie* inadmissibility, without removing the case form its docket (General List) altogether. On the other hand, in cases in which the ICJ *manifestly* has no jurisdiction under Article 41 to order provisional measures it could be argued to be inappropriate to insert such recommendations. An obvious example would be when an individual person requests the ICJ to order provisional measures. To be sure, exactly because of the lack of jurisdiction *ratione personae* the ICJ does not even list such a request in its List of cases. In that sense a better example would be an Order by the Court to deny provisional measures for manifest lack of jurisdiction combined with a decision to remove the case from the List.[318] In such Order it would be inappropriate to insert recommendations to the Parties, despite the fact that the Court has a role to play under the UN Charter for the maintenance of international peace and security. After all, it could only perform this as part of the case pending before it to settle a contentious proceeding. If jurisdiction is so manifestly lacking that the Court removes the case from the List, it could be argued it has no jurisdiction either to insert recommendations in its Order denying a request for provisional measures. On the other hand, if the case is still on the List this means there is still a possibility of jurisdiction on the merits.

Thus generally speaking the issue goes to the appropriateness of inserting a recommendation, not to the power to do so. D' Aspremont has rightly pointed out that, contrary to the operative part of an Order for provisional measures, recommendations 'have no legal consequences'.[319] No 'apparent basis for jurisdiction over the merits' is needed for the Court to make such recommendations 'as they do not make a final finding of facts or imputability'.[320] Moreover, a reference to the general human rights obligations of States or to their obligations under the UN Charter does not interfere with the purpose of preventing damages to the States involved.

According to Rosenne '[r]estraint and careful crafting of the judicial pronouncement are certainly necessary' in cases in which the Court decided not to grand judicial measures for lack of *prima facie* jurisdiction. "But the real test for the Court in considering whether to include such general statements in any order of provisional measures, in any other judicial pronouncement is whether the statement is likely to contribute to the peaceful settlement of the dispute".[321]

3.7.4 Relation to reparation

As Collins has pointed out, in *Chorzów Factory* (1927) the PCIJ did *not* decide that it was precluded from ordering provisional measures by 'the mere fact that the Applicant State seeks the same remedy in the interim measures phase as it seeks on the merits'. Instead the Court simply decided that Article 41 PCIJ Statute could not serve as a basis for an award of interim damages, because this would require 'some form of determination on the merits' and not because the remedy somehow paralleled the final judgment.[322]

Apart from a relationship to the rights claimed, it is also important to examine the possible obligations and forms of reparation in the event of a finding of a violation on the merits.[323] After

---

[318] That is, if the Court would enter into a discussion on the request at all. It might also simply start with removing the case from the List.

[319] D' Aspremont (2007), p. 190.

[320] Id., p. 192.

[321] Rosenne (2005), p. 221.

[322] Collins (1993), p. 229. See PCIJ *Factory at Chorzów* (*German interests in Polish Upper Silesia* cases), Order of 21 November 1927. See also Rosenne (2005), p. 190.

[323] In general on judicial remedies, including reparation, see e.g. Gray (1987).

all the use of provisional measures could be warranted if the respondent would otherwise pre-empt any meaningful reparation.[324] At the same time the adjudicator must also be able to provide the relief requested.[325] In that sense the substance of the eventual obligation (cessation, assurances of non-repetition) or form of reparation and that of the temporary relief pending the case (*pendente lite*) are closely related.[326] In the *Sino-Belgian Treaty* case (1927) the PCIJ considered that the violation of certain rights 'would not be made good simply by the payment of an indemnity or by compensation or restitution in some other material form'.[327] In its Order for provisional measures in the *Nuclear Tests* cases (1973) the ICJ referred to claims that 'the uncertain physical and genetic effects to which contamination exposes the people of New Zealand causes them acute apprehension, anxiety and concern; and that there could be no possibility that the rights eroded by the holding of further tests could be fully restored in the event of a judgment in New Zealand's favour in these proceedings'.[328]

Merrills noted that 'on a narrow view' prejudice to a State 'is irreparable only if it cannot be adequately compensated for in the final judgment'. The ICJ took such a narrow view in the *Aegean Sea* case (1976). The Court considered that the exclusive right to information on the natural resources of the continental shelf 'might be capable of reparation by appropriate means'.[329] Merrills emphasised that 'such an interpretation of the concept of irreparable prejudice, if applied generally, would have the effect of restricting the scope for interim protection very severely'.[330] He noted that the Court took a different approach when it ordered provisional measures in the *Nicaragua* case (1984). This, however, was not surprising given the seriousness of the allegations. Nevertheless, the 'alleged violations of Nicaragua's sovereignty could have been compensated by an award of reparation (which was in fact being sought) and thus in the strict sense this did not constitute "irreparable prejudice"'. Merrills presumed that the ICJ used provisional measures 'on the ground that in a case involving allegations of flagrant violations of international law the applicant's rights should be protected whether or not it might eventually succeed in its claim for damages'.[331]

There is no need for a provision on restitution in kind in each particular Convention. The right to restitution in kind is a general rule of international law. As early as 1928, the Permanent Court of International Justice established that this form of reparation was to be preferred:

---

[324] Dumbault (1932), p. 165 has referred to 'irreparable in money' and situations in which 'pecuniary redress' would be 'inadequate', also referring to Guggenheim (1931), p. 12.

[325] See e.g. Goldie (1973-74), p. 504.

[326] See also Wellens (1998), p. 421 ('the kind of measures requested must be such that they can be subsumed by the Court's judgment').

[327] PCIJ *Sino-Belgian* case, Order of the President of 8 January 1927, p. 7. Common law may be instructive in order to clarify the relation between irreparable harm and the prospect of reparation: harm is considered irreparable when 'there is no certain pecuniary standard for the measure of damages', for instance when the interest of the Party requesting provisional measures is primarily subjective, Elkind (1981), p. 216.

[328] ICJ *Nuclear tests* case (*New Zealand* v. *France*), Order of 22 June 1973, §28.

[329] Merrills (1995), p. 108. See also ICJ *Pulp mills on the river Uruguay (Argentina* v. *Uruguay)*, Order of 13 July 2006, in which the Court found that the circumstances did not require the use of provisional measures. Among others, it was 'not at present convinced' any violation at issue 'would not be capable of being remedied at the merits stage of the proceedings', §70. See also §§72 and 76.

[330] Merrills (1995), p. 108. See also Elkind's criticism (1981), pp. 211-215 discussed in section 3.4. See further section 5.3 on assessment of material urgency.

[331] Merrills (1995), pp. 108-109. See also Sztucki (1983) p. 112, referring to the *Hostages* case.

> "The essential principle contained in the actual notion of an illegal act -a principle which seems to be established by international practice and in particular by the decisions of arbitral tribunals- is that reparation must, as far as possible, wipe out all the consequences of the illegal act and re-establish the situation which would, in all probability, have existed if that act had not been committed. Restitution in kind, or, if this is not possible, payment of a sum corresponding to the value which a restitution in kind would bear".[332]

Article 35 of the International Law Commission's Articles on State Responsibility confirms that the injured State is entitled to the 're-establish the situation which existed before the wrongful act was committed'.[333]

In cases of mass human rights violations the ICJ has sought cessation and guarantees of non-repetition, rather than the compensation traditionally requested in diplomatic protection cases. In such cases of mass violations compensation would be a particularly inappropriate as the sole form of reparation and this would in fact be reflected in the use of provisional measures pending the proceedings.[334] On the other hand, the Court has shown an awareness of the appropriateness of forms of reparation other than compensation also in cases involving fewer individuals, brought in the evolving exercise of 'diplomatic protection'. The US hostages were to be released immediately. The Paraguayan, German and Mexican nationals were not to be executed before their cases had been submitted to a review taking into account the lack of consular assistance. In view of the object of the aforementioned VCCR, namely the protection of nationals abroad, it is not surprising that the wronged State expected some form of 'restitution in kind'. By indicating provisional measures, the ICJ acknowledges that if it were to decide *restitutio in integrum* was indeed warranted, this decision would be rendered useless if irreparable harm had already been inflicted. Thus the ICJ ordered provisional measures in the cases *Breard, LaGrand* and *Avena*.[335] The execution of Breard and LaGrand, in contravention of these Orders, made impossible this restitution in kind. As noted, Paraguay subsequently withdrew its case against the US, but Germany persisted. The purpose of Germany's claim in *LaGrand* had been to 'ensure that German nationals will be provided with adequate consular assistance in the future, and thus be protected against the fatal consequences following from breaches of Article 36 in circumstances allowing those leading to the death of the brothers LaGrand'.[336] After the execution of Walter LaGrand Germany focused on its right to satisfaction. It considered that an apology alone did not suffice and would be no help in future cases. Instead, it asked the Court to pronounce the obligation to provide Germany with assurances of non-repetition. As the first reason for its insistence on satisfaction, it referred to the International Law Commission's

---

[332] PCIJ *Factory at Chorzów* (*German interests in Polish Upper Silesia* cases), Order of 21 November 1927, p. 41.

[333] ILC Articles on Responsibility of States for Internationally Wrongful Acts, adopted at the 53rd session, November 2001, A/56/10, Chapter IV E.2. Article 34 stipulates that restitution is the first of the forms of reparation available to an injured State.

[334] Apart from its appropriate emphasis on the continued obligation to punish genocide and cooperate fully with the ICTY, the ICJ's approach in the *Genocide Convention* case, 27 February 2007, was surprising in this respect. See e.g. Milanović (2007), pp. 689-691, also referring to the case law of the Inter-American and European Court of Human Rights and the Bosnia Human Rights Chamber. These adjudicators are introduced in the Chapter II of this book. Gattini (2007), p. 712 also noted that a look at the case law of the Inter-American Court 'could have provided a useful source of obligation'. See further Chapter XIII on the approaches of the various adjudicators to the relation with reparation.

[335] ICJ *Breard* (*Paraguay v. US*), Order of 9 April 1998; *LaGrand* case (*Germany v. US*), Order of 3 March 1999 and *Avena et al.* (*Mexico v. US*), Order of 5 February 2003.

[336] See ICJ *LaGrand* case (*Germany v. US*), verbatim record CR 2000/27 of 13 November 2000, p. 15.

statement that satisfaction is a remedy designed especially for those cases in which injury cannot be made good by restitution or compensation. As its second reason to request the ICJ to oblige the US to render satisfaction, Germany referred to 'the particularly grave character of the moral damage inflicted upon Germany'.[337] In short Germany claimed that adequate assurances were warranted against repetition. This would mean a guarantee of non-repetition requiring preventive action, rather than 'simple' verbal assurances.

Indeed, the ICJ considered that an apology by the US was not sufficient in this case. It also considered that an apology would not be sufficient *in other cases* where 'foreign nationals have not been advised without delay of their rights under Article 36, paragraph 1, of the Vienna Convention and have been subjected to prolonged detention or sentenced to severe penalties'.[338]

The Court stressed the importance of the information the US had provided on its programme to ensure compliance. "If a State, in proceedings before this Court, repeatedly refers to substantial activities which it is carrying out in order to achieve compliance with certain obligations under a treaty, then this expresses a commitment to follow through with the efforts in this regard".[339]

In relation to the other two types of assurances sought by Germany, the Court considered that:

> "if the United States, notwithstanding its commitment referred to in paragraph 124 above, should fail in its obligation of consular notification to the detriment of German nationals, an apology would not suffice in cases where the individuals concerned have been subjected to prolonged detention or convicted and sentenced to severe penalties. In the case of such a conviction and sentence, it would be incumbent upon the United States to allow the review and reconsideration of the conviction and sentence by taking account of the violation of the rights set forth in the Convention. This obligation can be carried out in various ways. The choice of means must be left to the United States".[340]

Although this was less than Germany requested, in cases involving German nationals who are sentenced to severe penalties, the Court did confirm the obligation of the US to review and reconsider convictions and sentences in cases where Article 36(1)(b) has been denied despite the US assurances.[341] Two years later the ICJ specified this by pointing out that the 'freedom in the choice of means for such review and reconsideration is not without qualification'.[342] It should be effective, take account of the rights in the VCCR and 'guarantee that the violation and the possible prejudice caused by that violation will be fully examined and taken into account'. The

---

[337] See ICJ *LaGrand* case (*Germany* v. *US*), verbatim record CR 2000/27 of 13 November 2000, pp. 15 and 16.

[338] ICJ *LaGrand* case (*Germany* v. *US*), Judgment of 27 June 2001, §123.

[339] On the other hand, the Court noted that such question could not provide an assurance that the US will never again fail to observe the obligation of notification under Article 36. It also noted that no State could give such a guarantee and that Germany did not seek it, but the US had met 'Germany's request for a general assurance of non-repetition'. The Court confirmed that it was indeed within its authority and jurisdiction to determine the existence of a violation of international obligation and, if necessary, to hold that a domestic law has been the cause of this violation. It stated that 'it has not found that a United States law, whether substantive or procedural in character, is inherently inconsistent with the obligations undertaken by the United States in the Vienna Convention', ICJ *LaGrand* case (*Germany* v. *US*), Judgment of 27 June 2001, §125.

[340] Ibid.

[341] See e.g. Aceves (2003), Jennings (2002), Orakhelashvili (2002), Palmisano (2002), Tams (2002) and Cassel (1999b).

[342] ICJ *Avena* (*Mexico* v. *US*), Judgment of 31 March 2004, §131.

'review and reconsideration should be both of the sentence and of the conviction' and 'should occur within the overall judicial proceedings relating to the individual defendant concerned'.[343] It pointed out that 'the clemency process as currently practiced within the United States criminal justice system, does not appear to meet the requirements (…) and is therefore not sufficient in itself to serve as an appropriate means of "review and reconsideration" as envisaged by the Court in the *LaGrand* case'.[344] As discussed, Mexico requested the ICJ to interpret the *Avena* judgment and in this context it also requested provisional measures to halt the execution of Medellín and four others. The Court, by a narrow majority, found that the Parties 'apparently hold different views as to the meaning and scope of th[e] obligation of result [in *Avena*], namely whether that understanding is shared by all United States federal and state authorities and whether that obligation falls upon those authorities'.[345] Subsequently Texas executed Medellín. Clearly, the executions of Breard, LaGrand and Medellín caused irreparable harm not only to the claim, but in fact to the persons involved.

3.8 The beneficiaries of provisional measures and the rights of the addressees

3.8.1 Introduction

The Court's recent use of provisional measures aimed to prevent human suffering may be roughly divided into cases involving individuals sentenced to death who had been deprived of consular protection by their State of nationality on the one hand and cases involving armed 'territorial' conflicts on the other hand. In the latter type of cases the group of beneficiaries generally is considerably larger. Moreover, the Court's involvement may partially be explained by the ICJ's role, under the UN Charter, in the maintenance of peace.

Even if the applicant State fails to convince the Court to use provisional measures it may still benefit from the Court's examination of the case, as this may draw public attention to the conflict, enable it to publicly make arguments and bring the conflict 'into sharper legal focus'.[346] In some cases it may strengthen the State's bargaining position, especially if the adjudicator, while denying the request, nevertheless gives some general recommendations.

3.8.2 Rights by proxy (diplomatic protection)

Evidently States normally institute proceedings and request provisional measures to protect their own rights, although in the majority of cases, in one way or other the interests of the Applicant State's citizens are involved (and subsumed in those of the State).[347] In *Avena* the Court had also stressed that it had 'been addressing the issues of principle (…) from the viewpoint of the general application of the Vienna Convention, and there can be no question of an *a contrario* argument'. "In other words, the fact that in this case the court's ruling has concerned only Mexican nationals

---

[343] Id., §§138 and 141.

[344] Id., §143. See also e.g. Shelton (2004) and Aceves (2003).

[345] ICJ Request for interpretation of the judgment of 31 March 2004 in the case concerning *Avena and other Mexican nationals* (*Mexico* v. *US*), Order of 16 July 2008, §55. See further section 3.3.7.

[346] See e.g. Merrills (1995), p. 113.

[347] As Cançado Trindade put it in a dissent to the ICJ's decision not to order provisional measurs in *Questions relating to the obligation to prosecute or extradite* (*Belgium* v. *Senegal*), Order of 28 May 2009, the rights invoked by the contending parties 'have a direct relationship with the legitimate expectations of thousands of human beings', §14.

cannot be taken to imply that the conclusions reached by it in the present Judgment do not apply to other foreign nationals finding themselves in similar situations in the United States".[348] This 'indicates that the Court is more concerned about the international rule of law than about strictly contractual relations between two states parties'.[349]

In cases involving the lives of persons the approach of the ICJ to the group of beneficiaries to be protected by its provisional measures should not be overly strict. The infusion of human rights norms in the law on diplomatic protection in fact warrants a flexible approach to the group of beneficiaries, rather than a strict interpretation of the 'nationals' to be protected.[350] The point of departure should be the protection required rather than a narrow concept of nationality or an otherwise limited approach. In the *Hostages* case, for instance, the ICJ had ordered Iran to immediately release all US nationals, not just those held in the US Embassy or in the Ministry of Foreign Affairs in Tehran, but also those who 'have been held as hostages elsewhere'.[351] In other words it took the scope of the group of beneficiaries to be rather wide to include all US nationals being held as hostage anywhere in Iran.

In the context of the law of the sea ITLOS Judge Laing has also noted 'potential beneficiaries include non-States, often in a commercial context' and argued that provisional measures must protect 'non-traditional asserted rights'.[352]

3.8.3 General interest

Often the measures requested could also serve the general interest, such as in cases involving gross and widespread human rights violations or in cases involving environmental degradation. Already in the early cases of the PCIJ there were discussions on the question whether provisional measures could be used in 'proceedings instituted by the requesting State not in defence of its own rights but in the 'public interest', as a member of the Council of the League'.[353] If the State has standing to do so, without reference to its 'own rights', and the ICJ has jurisdiction to hear its particular human rights claim,[354] this Court should also be able to Order provisional measures. After all this would still preserve the respective rights of either party to ensure protection of the human rights standards invoked. The prevention of aggravation of the dispute is but one example.[355]

3.8.4 Third parties' rights and obligations

Applicant States may also refer to the rights and obligations of third parties. In some cases third parties have even submitted information separately.[356] With regard to the relief sought in the *M/V*

---

[348] ICJ *Avena et al.* (*Mexico* v. *US*), Judgment of 31 March 2004, §151. See on the confusion created in *Avena* on State rights, diplomatic protection and individual rights Künzli (2005), pp. 55-56 and Milano (2004), pp. 124-132. See also Shelton (2004a), p. 561.

[349] Shelton (2004a), p. 565.

[350] See also Judge Simma in ICJ *Armed activities on the territory of the Congo* (*Congo* v. *Rwanda*), Order of 10 July 2002. Generally on diplomatic protection, see the various reports by ILC Rapporteur Dugard; see also Vermeer-Künzli (2007).

[351] ICJ *US Diplomatic and Consular Staff in Tehran* (*US* v. *Iran*), Order of 15 December 1979, §47.

[352] ITLOS *M/V 'Saiga'* (No.2) case, Order of 11 March 1998, Separate Opinion Judge Laing, §21.

[353] Sztucki (1983), pp. 228-229.

[354] See e.g. Milano (2004), p. 114, pp. 118-119.

[355] See section 3.2.

[356] See e.g. the applications for permission to intervene by Australia, Samoa, Solomon Islands, the Marshall Islands and the Federal States of Micronesia in the *Request for an examination of the*

'Saiga' case ITLOS Judge Laing wrote about third parties that situations involving them had no direct bearing on the case but 'incidents involving non-parties may provide evidence of (…) similar facts and conduct, raising the inference that the actions in issue may have occurred'.[357]

An applicant State's interest in the clarification of a legal issue may also be at stake, as was the case in the two requests for provisional measures by Bosnia, dealing with the legality of the UN arms embargo. As the ICJ considered that the clarification of this issue was meant for members of the Security Council rather than for Serbia and Montenegro, it decided not to order provisional measures to this effect,[358] Bosnia declared its intention to institute legal proceedings against one 'third State' with permanent membership in the Security Council.[359] In November 1993 it argued that the UK had 'failed and refused to prevent genocide, had imposed and maintained an arms embargo in violation of Article 51 of the UN Charter and had abetted ongoing genocide by opposing the efforts of others to have the embargo lifted'. It considered that these actions amounted to 'complicity in genocide'. The next month, however, Bosnia and UK issued a joint statement in which Bosnia announced that it would not institute such legal proceedings.[360]

3.8.5 Rights of the addressee States

The Court's Order for provisional measures in the *Anglo-Iranian Oil Co.* case (1951) has been criticised as arguably 'contrary to the usual practice' of the ICJ and the PCIJ, 'especially because the decree created an opportunity for the company to deplete Iran's oil reserves further'. In that sense it 'patently failed to protect the status quo in an even-handed way'.[361] Respondents need to be protected as well, but the question is to what length.

It has been suggested to include in the Order the condition that the requesting State will compensate the respondent for (some of the) losses sustained in compliance, should the Court subsequently reject the submission on the merits.[362] In domestic systems injunctions often include such condition. Different from domestic rules and regulations the ICJ Statute and Rules of Court do not expressly confer such a power on the ICJ. It has been pointed out that even if such a power could be implied it had never been exercised.[363] Elkind has considered that one way to protect the

---

situation in accordance with paragraph 63 of the Court's judgment of 20 December 1974 in the Nuclear Tests (New Zealand v. France) case, Order of 22 September 1995.

[357] M/V 'Saiga' (No.2) case, Order of 11 March 1998, Separate Opinion Judge Laing, §24. He remarked, however, that the issue played no part in the Order in this case.

[358] ICJ Application of the Convention on the prevention and punishment of the crime of genocide (Bosnia and Herzegovina v. Yugoslavia (Serbia and Montenegro)), Orders of 8 April 1993 and 13 September 1993.

[359] It referred to the Separate Opinion of Judge Lauterpacht, to the Order of 13 September 1993, §§98-115.

[360] See 'editor's note', p. 43 International and Comparative Law Quarterly p. 714 (1994). See also Toufayan (2005).

[361] ICJ Anglo-Iranian Oil Co. (UK v. Iran), Order of 5 July 1951. See Goldie (1974), p. 496. As Rosenne (2005), p. 155 put it 'the fact that important provisional measures were indicated in the case and that later the Court held itself to be without jurisdiction over the application has troubled both the Court and publicists'. See also Fisheries jurisdiction cases, Orders of 17 August 1972.

[362] Merrills (1995), p. 117 refers to the argument of Denmark in the Passage through the Great Belt case. The Court did not order provisional measures and therefore did not deal with this request.

[363] Mendelson (1972-73), pp. 312-313. Collins (1992), pp. 229-231, points out that 'there can be little doubt that a principle of compensation for the unjustified grant of an injunction in private litigation is a general principle of law'. Dumbauld (1932), p. 162 considers that the PCIJ had an implied power to condition its use of provisional measures this way. Merrills (1995), p. 117 has noted that such a 'provision of security can be thought of as a general principle of law'. In his Separate Opinion to ITLOS Land reclamation by Singapore in and around the straits of Johor

respondent State is 'to balance the convenience of the parties in a case involving interim protection'. "If compliance with the measures involves a greater hardship than denial of the measures, then they should be denied".[364] About the aforementioned conditional relief he mentioned that in many domestic jurisdictions courts can order plaintiffs to 'post security' against any damage the respondent might suffer 'by virtue of compliance with the Order if the Court later decides for respondent at the jurisdiction or the merits phases'. He suggested that the ICJ could consider this because the power to do so is 'functionally inherent' in the power to order provisional measures. At the same time he emphasized that Parties that fail to appear before the Court cannot raise matters such as balance of convenience nor can they ask the Court to order the Applicant State to post security.[365]

The ICJ has not yet decided the issue whether a Party may receive compensation for injuries resulting from compliance with provisional measures if the Court later determines it had no jurisdiction on the merits or if it finds in favour of the addressee of the provisional measures.[366] In the *Great Belt* case (1991) Judge Shahabuddeen recalled that it was not settled whether the jurisprudence of the ICJ allowed for 'compensating a party for any injuries suffered in complying with an interim measure should the latter be eventually found to have been unjustified'. He pointed out that this made even more significant the exceptional character of provisional measures.[367] The discussion in the next section on the existence of *prima facie* jurisdiction on the merits is particularly relevant from the perspective of the rights of the addressee State.

In the *Lockerbie* and *Genocide Convention* cases the (Acting) President denied the Applicant States' request to accelerate the proceedings, and did not invoke Article 75(1) of the Rules in order to ensure the effectiveness of any provisional measures that might be taken.[368] In *LaGrand*, on the other hand, the Court did decide to order provisional measures immediately, as the execution of the death sentence against Walter LaGrand was so imminent that a formal hearing could not have been planned until after the execution. Judges Schwebel and Buergenthal were correct in criticising Germany for not bringing the case and the request for provisional measures before the Court sooner.[369] This would have allowed the US to adequately prepare its response and present it during a hearing. Nevertheless, as the life of a person was involved the Court could not have taken a different approach. Moreover, the ICJ was fully aware of the US arguments in this respect because this was the second request for provisional measures to halt an execution the ICJ had dealt with within a limited period of time. In the previous case the US had extensively argued against the use of provisional measures in its written and oral submissions and subsequently disrespected the proceedings before the ICJ by executing the Paraguayan national in square violation of the Court's provisional measures.[370]

(*Malaysia* v. *Singapore*), Order of 8 October 2003, §20 Judge Lucky wrote: "Although there is no international precedent that I can find, I think the time has come to consider whether applicants for provisional measures, as in some municipal systems, should provide a guarantee in their applications that if the measures sought are granted, but discontinued if the substantive matter is determined in the respondent's favour, they will pay damages incurred and costs to the respondents".

[364] Elkind (1981), p. 259.
[365] Elkind (1981), pp. 259-260. See also pp. 238-241 and p. 57.
[366] See section 3.6 on prejudgment. See further section 3.7 on protection and reparation. See also the purpose of protecting collateral rights, section 3.3.4.
[367] ICJ *Passage through the Great Belt* case (*Finland* v. *Denmark*), Order of 29 July 1991, Separate Opinion Judge Shahabuddeen, p. 29.
[368] See also Rosenne (2005), pp. 163-164 and Sztucki (1983), pp. 156-157.
[369] ICJ *LaGrand* case (*Germany* v. *US*), Order of 3 March 1999, Separate Opinion Judge Schwebel and Judgment of 27 June 2001, Dissenting Opinion Judge Buergenthal.
[370] See also Addo (1999), p. 720.

When the rights involved are the same for both States it is not difficult to order provisional measures that have an equal impact on both Parties. If, on the other hand, the case does not relate to a territorial question but to the international responsibility of a Respondent State, it is more difficult to fully achieve equal treatment in the text of the provisional measure.[371]

It could be argued that in balancing the rights of the Parties in a conflict, a State's interest in the protection of life and limbs of its citizens must outweigh the procedural problems arising under the national law of the other State when, for instance, that other State has to retry a foreign national in compliance with international law. At the time of its Order to halt the execution of Breard and LaGrand, however, the ICJ had not yet reached a decision on this issue. It merely indicated provisional measures so that the effectiveness of a possible decision on the merits would not be precluded.[372] Its judgment in *LaGrand* (2001) indeed confirmed the importance of protection of life and limbs.[373]

4 JURISDICTION ON THE MERITS AND THE USE OF PROVISIONAL MEASURES

Section 2 noted that while the authority of the adjudicator to use provisional measures is a prerequisite, the possibility of jurisdiction on the merits relates to the appropriateness of their use.[374]

The discussion of the relationship between jurisdiction and provisional measures can be divided in two categories: the authority to use such measures in the particular system in the first place and their use in relation to the jurisdiction on the merits. The first relates to the implicit or explicit legal basis for provisional measures, the authority to use them in inter-state proceedings, the authority to use them *proprio motu* and the delegation of the authority to an individual judge. The second already relates to the question whether provisional measures are warranted. It involves the concept of *prima facie* jurisdiction and the use of provisional measures. This section

---

[371]   Merrills (1995), p. 117.

[372]   This is also observed by Wilson (1998), p. 8: "[The ICJ ruling] didn't say that Breard should go free. It didn't pass any judgment on the validity of the death sentence imposed in his case. It didn't even say that he should get a new trial. Moreover, it didn't reach any decision as to the ultimate question before the ICJ-that is, what should be done when the Vienna Convention is violated. It simply said that Angel Breard should not be executed until the court had a chance to hear the full arguments on the application of the Vienna Convention in the context of Breard's case, a legal dispute over which the U.S. government had explicitly agreed that the ICJ had jurisdiction".

[373]   ICJ *LaGrand* (*Germany v. US*), Judgment of 27 June 2001. See also *Avena* (*Mexico v. US*), Judgment of 31 March 2004 and Mexico's argument in ICJ *Request for interpretation of the judgment of 31 March 2004 in the case concerning Avena and other Mexican nationals* (*Mexico v. US*), Order of 16 July 2008, §20 ('any delay in an execution would not be prejudicial to the rights of the United States as all of the above-mentioned Mexican nationals would remain incarcerated and subject to execution once their right to review and reconsideration has been vindicated'.)

[374]   Obviously there are also levels of appropriateness. In the context of the practice of ITLOS Devine has suggested the following methodology: 1. Is there prima facie jurisdiction? 2. Has jurisdiction been excluded by (one of) the parties? 3. Is the exercise of jurisdiction admissible in this case? 4. Is it appropriate in this case (criteria of urgency, respective rights and serious harm to the marine environment)? 5. What measures should be taken? See Devine (2003), pp. 274-275.

deals with the second category: the relevance of the jurisdiction on the merits as established by the ICJ.[375]

If an individual, a company, or an organisation would request provisional measures, however much warranted to prevent irreparable harm, the ICJ obviously would have no authority to indicate them because 'only States may be parties in cases before the Court' (Article 34(1)). In other words the ICJ clearly would have no jurisdiction *ratione personae.*[376]

Yet in the context of provisional measures the ICJ normally does not have to concern itself with jurisdiction *ratione personae*, because almost all States are Party to the ICJ Statute.[377]

Generally speaking, however, the ICJ mainly deals with the question whether there is *prima facie* jurisdiction *ratione materiae.*

The power of the ICJ to indicate provisional measures is 'separate and independent from jurisdiction over the action in chief'.[378] It must be seen independently from the jurisdiction on the

---

[375] Chapter II of this book deals with the competence, procedure, promptness and transparency of the human rights adjudication, while Chapter XV deals with the relation between provisional measures and jurisdiction on the merits as well as admissibility.

[376] Elkind points out that Article 35 of the ICJ Statute stipulates that 'the Court shall be open to States Parties to the present Statute'. It therefore deals with jurisdiction *ratione personae*. Read together with Article 94 of the UN Charter (providing that all members of the UN are *ipso facto* parties to the ICJ Statute) it identifies 'over whom the Court has inherent jurisdiction with regard to interim measures', Elkind (1981), p. 259 and p. 177. He further supports this approach by reference to domestic systems with some form of interim remedy, in which this remedy has been based on jurisdiction *ratione personae*, Elkind (1981), p. 177. He notes that the consent of a State to be brought before the ICJ is usually expressed through Article 36 of the Statute, which is primarily concerned with jurisdiction *ratione materiae*. He notes that interim protection is an urgent remedy and the Court 'cannot be bogged down by complicated questions of Article 36 jurisdiction at the interim protection stage', Elkind (1981), p. 259.

[377] This was different in the *Genocide Convention* case: ICJ *Application of the Convention on the prevention and punishment of the crime of genocide* (*Bosnia and Herzegovina* v. *Yugoslavia (Serbia and Montenegro)*), Order of 8 April 1993. In this case the ICJ itself raised the question of jurisdiction. Thirlway (1994), p. 34 points out that the Court found it necessary to raise the issue ex officio, at the stage of provisional measures. The Respondent (the Republic of Yugoslavia) had chosen not to raise it, obviously because it in fact claimed to be a member of the UN, as successor of the 'old' Yugoslavia, and therefore claimed to be a party to the Statute. The ICJ repeated that there should be prima facie jurisdiction and added that this includes jurisdiction ratione personae as well as ratione materiae. Resolutions of the Security Council and the General Assembly had denied the continuity of Yugoslavia (the Respondent State) and pointed out that it should reapply for UN membership. The ICJ noted that it was not necessary, at the phase of provisional measures, to determine definitely whether the Respondent was still a party to the ICJ statute. It noted that the compromissory clause to a multilateral treaty, such as Article XI of the Genocide Convention could be regarded prima facie within its jurisdiction ratione personae. With regard to the Applicant State, Bosnia-Herzegovina, it equally concluded that Article XI appeared to afford a basis on which its jurisdiction might be founded, see Order of 8 April 1993, §19. It rejected another basis for jurisdiction relied on by Bosnia-Herzegovina, namely a treaty dating from 1919, because it appeared to be limited to the present territory of Yugoslavia. In other words, there was no jurisdiction ratione loci based on this treaty. Neither was there prima facie jurisdiction based on the doctrine of forum prorogatum. See further Merrills (1995), pp. 95-100. See also Elkind (1981) arguing that the only prerequisite for the use of provisional measures is jurisdiction ratione personae, while with regard to jurisdiction ratione materiae the Court should only satisfy itself that there is no manifest absence of jurisdiction, p. 177 and p. 192. Doubts on jurisdiction on the merits ratione temporis does not necessarily hinder the use of provisional measures as orders for such measures are 'oriented towards the present and the future', Wellens (1998), p. 435.

merits exactly because of the aim to 'provide an expeditious remedy' and, in the words of Merrills, it 'is therefore well established that the Court can consider whether to order interim measures without first resolving contested issues of jurisdiction and, as a corollary, that such consideration in no way prejudices its later decision on jurisdictional questions'.[379]

In the 1930s Dumbauld pointed out that jurisdiction to grant protection *pendente lite* did not depend on jurisdiction in the main action. A Court could provide such a remedy in advance of determination about its jurisdiction.[380] He noted that it was 'sufficient that want of jurisdiction is not obvious *prima facie*'.[381] In other words, he argued that it is sufficient that there is no *a priori* lack of jurisdiction.[382]

It is important to examine the issue of jurisdiction on the merits at least to a certain extent. Eli Lauterpacht has observed that the ICJ could not 'disregard altogether the question of its competence on the merits' although it did not need to satisfy itself at that stage that it had such

---

[378] Dumbauld (1932), p. 165. See e.g. ICJ *Anglo-Iranian Oil Co.* case Judgment on preliminary objections of 22 July 1952, pp. 102-103. The Court held that it was competent to indicate provisional measures if the dispute did not *a priori* fall 'completely outside the scope of international jurisdiction'. Judges Badawi Pasha and Winiarski dissented. They considered that if 'there is no jurisdiction on the merits, there can be no jurisdiction to indicate interim measures of protection' (p. 97). They agreed, however, that the ICJ did not have to finally pronounce on the question of jurisdiction before indicating provisional measures, because requests for provisional measures 'might well become pointless' in such cases. Cheng (1953), p. 271 refers to the Czechoslovak-Hungarian Mixed Arbitral Tribunal's statement that refusing provisional measures 'for the sole reason that the jurisdiction of the Tribunal is challenged' would 'open a very simple way for any party wishing to avoid interim measures of protection being taken against him. The power of the Tribunal (...) would thus be rendered absolutely futile'. Sztucki (1983), p. 230 also quotes from (the French version) of this case: 'Il suffit que son incompétence ne soit pas manifeste, évidente'. About the phrasing in the *Anglo-Iranian* case Cheng points out, at p. 272, that it would have been preferable if the Court would have said that the dispute could not *a priori* be excluded from *its* (rather than 'international') jurisdiction.

[379] Merrills (1995), p. 91. See section 3.6 about the issue of prejudgment.

[380] Dumbauld (1932), p. 165 and p. 186. In the 1920s the President of the PCIJ, who at the time had the power to indicate provisional measures, noted that the Court, in its final decision, would 'either declare itself to have no jurisdiction or give judgment on the merits': PCIJ *Denunciation of the Treaty of 2 November 1865 between China and Belgium*, Order of 8 January 1927. According to Cheng this means that 'he was evidently of the opinion that he was competent to indicate such measures, even before the question of jurisdiction had been decided, but when prima facie the dispute came within, or at least did not fall outside the Court's jurisdiction'. Cheng (1953), p. 272, also referring to PCIJ *Administration of the Prince von Pless* case, Order of 11 May 1933, A/B 54, p. 153 and *Polish Agrarian Reform and the German minority* case, 29 July 1933, A/B 58, p. 179.

[381] Dumbauld (1932), p. 165.

[382] According to Sztucki the *Sino-Belgian* case, the *Polish Agrarians* and the *Pless* cases do not mean that the Court has the power to order provisional measures unless there is a manifest lack of substantive jurisdiction. He argues that these cases have limited value as a precedent in the context of jurisdictional issues, Sztucki (1983), pp. 226-227. He points out that at the time (until 1936) preliminary objections were not filed immediately upon the notification of an application and the request for provisional measures, Sztucki (1983), pp. 222-223 and pp. 225-229. Moreover, he argues, the President in the *Sino-Belgian* case used provisional measures 'on personal conviction that the application and request met very high jurisdictional requirements; but at the same time felt it necessary to reflect the fact that competence in the matters of interim protections and substantive jurisdiction was divided in that case, and that the latter question, if necessary, would be decided by the full Court unbound by the decision or conviction of its President' (footnotes omitted), Sztucki (1983), pp. 226-227.

jurisdiction. As a reason for this he noted that 'Governments ought not to be discouraged from undertaking, or continuing to undertake, the obligations of judicial settlement as the result of any justifiable apprehension that by accepting them they may become exposed to the embarrassment, vexation and loss, possibly following upon interim measures, in cases in which there is no reasonable possibility, *prima facie* ascertained by the Court, of jurisdiction on the merits'.[383]

Sztucki points out that there is always a risk that the ICJ, for jurisdictional reasons, will deny provisional measures that may otherwise be warranted, while it may eventually uphold jurisdiction. On the other hand, the ICJ may also renounce jurisdiction after having indicated provisional measures. In that case the Respondent would have been 'called upon to submit to a restraint on his freedom of action in a matter on which the Court really has had nothing to say from the very beginning'.[384] Yet Sztucki notes that indicating provisional measures before the final decision on jurisdiction is nevertheless appropriate because 'requests for interim protection are regarded as a matter of urgency while jurisdictional questions are not'. Exactly because 'the question of jurisdiction is so important in inter-State litigation and therefore requires a scrupulous

---

[383] The claim, he considered, must be based on an instrument that *prima facie* confers jurisdiction upon the Court and that incorporates 'no reservations obviously excluding its jurisdiction'. ICJ *Interhandel* case (*Switzerland* v. *US*), Order of 24 October 1957, Separate Opinion Lauterpacht, pp. 118-119. The ICJ had determined that the question of jurisdiction on the merits was to be dealt with in the phase of Preliminary Objections. While the majority did not consider the issue of jurisdiction to be an obstacle, the Court determined that there was no need for provisional measures. Four members (Judges Lauterpacht, Klaestad, Hackworth and Read) disagreed and considered that the ICJ had no jurisdiction to take provisional measures in this case. See also the *Nuclear Test* cases, Orders of 22 June 1973, Declaration of Judge Singh pointing out that there must be a '*possible* valid base for the Court's competence' and that the application must be 'prima facie entertainable'. Even at the stage of *prima facie* examination the ICJ 'has to examine the reservations and declarations' referred to as the basis for the Court's jurisdiction. As a result the ICJ could either find that 'there is no possible base' for the Court's jurisdiction or 'a possible base exists, but needs further investigation'. In the latter case 'the Court is inevitably left no option but to proceed to the substance of the jurisdiction of the case to complete its process of adjudication which, in turn, is time-consuming and therefore comes into conflict with the urgency of the matter coupled with the prospect of irreparable damage to the rights of the parties. It is this situation which furnishes the "raison d'être" of interim relief', *Australia* v. *France*, pp. 109-110 and *New Zealand* v. *France*, p. 146. In other words he argued that if there is no such *prima facie* jurisdiction provisional measures should not be taken. See also Merrills (1995), pp. 91-92 pointing out that 'despite the incidental character of the proceedings, the consent of the respondent, and hence the question of substantive jurisdiction, cannot be entirely ignored', exactly because of the 'exacting consequences' of provisional measures. After all, their aim is 'to make States act, or more usually refrain from acting, in certain ways for a period of months, or possibly years, until the case is finally disposed of'. See further section 3.7 of this Chapter on the protective measures required.

[384] Sztucki (1983), pp. 255-256. He points out that this was the case in the *Anglo-Iranian Oil Co.* case, Judgment of 22 July 1952, p. 114. He acknowledges that the ICJ 'convalidated the indication of interim measures by stating in his judgment on jurisdiction that the order was lapsing *ex nunc* and not *ex tunc*'. He also refers to the Separate Opinion of Judge Fitzmaurice in the *Northern Cameroons* case regarding this situation, as Sztucki puts it, 'as perfectly regular'. He confirms that this 'may be so from the point of view of formal logic based on the general concept of incidental jurisdiction' but from the point of view of common sense the situation is 'highly undesirable'.

and time-consuming examination, the Court is compelled to be less scrupulous with respect to the determination of that very question when it considers requests for interim protection'.[385]

In the *Anglo-Iranian Oil Co.* (1951) case the ICJ granted provisional measures, but later decided it had no jurisdiction.[386] According to Elkind, since then 'many judges and scholars have been timid about the Court's power to indicate interim measures without sufficient assurance that the Court actually has jurisdiction to hear the merits of the case'. He notes that 'no clear theory has emerged from either the Court or from scholars' as to the basis of the Court's jurisdiction to grant provisional measures under Article 41.[387] Yet he considers that in conditions of urgency even the test of a *prima facie* chance of success on the merits is too strict. The better rule would be 'that the action must not be manifestly without merit'.[388] In other words, he argues for 'a very light standard of proof as to jurisdiction under Article 36 at the interim protection phase'.[389] With regard to this jurisdiction the Court should go no further than 'satisfy itself that the absence of jurisdiction under Article 36 is not manifest'.[390]

In the *Nuclear Test* cases (1973) the ICJ established the criterion that provisional measures may be used if there is no *a priori* lack of jurisdiction.[391] In the *Fisheries Jurisdiction* cases (1972) it pointed out that it need not finally satisfy itself that it had jurisdiction on the merits, but ought not to act 'if the absence on the jurisdiction of the merits is manifest'. It concluded by stating that it could take provisional measures as long as it 'could identify an instrument which appeared *prima facie*, to afford a possible basis on which the jurisdiction of the Court might be founded'.[392] This means that the possibility of such jurisdiction is sufficient.[393] In the *Hostages* case (1979) the ICJ 'regarded the so-called 'positive' *prima facie* test as sufficient for the interim

---

[385] Sztucki (1983), pp. 253-254. For a general discussion on the likelihood of jurisdiction on the merits and the use of provisional measures, see also Beirlaen (1978-1979), pp. 425-459.

[386] ICJ *Anglo-Iranian Oil Co.* case, Order of 5 July 1951. See also Cheng (1953), p. 273 who notes that there are differences of opinion 'as to whether there must be a probability that the Court has jurisdiction or whether a mere possibility is sufficient'. "The reason why an international tribunal may exercise this power even when its jurisdiction as to the merits is yet uncertain must be sought in the fact that the duty of the parties to maintain the status quo already exists independently of any judicial intervention". At the other end of the spectrum it has sometimes been asserted that the Court must fully satisfy itself that it has jurisdiction. Elkind (1981), p. 179 mentions the approach of Judge Forster in the *Nuclear Test* cases (*Australia* v. *France*; *New Zealand* v. *France*), Orders of 22 June 1973. He also refers to the suggestion of Judge Gros that Article 53 ICJ Statute requires the Court to fully satisfy itself that it had jurisdiction when one of the parties failed to appear. Vice-President Singh and Judge Morosov accepted this approach in the *Aegean Sea* case, Order of 11 September 1976, p. 17 and p. 22. Elkind points out, however, that the Court unanimously applied the *prima facie* test in the *Hostages* case, despite the non-appearance of Iran before the Court. Judges Forster, Gros and Singh all took part in this decision.

[387] Elkind (1981), p. 167.

[388] Elkind (1981), p. 192. See also p. 259: "The best rule is that interlocutory injunctive relief will be granted unless the claim is frivolous or vexatious". At p. 182 he points out that *prima facie* is a slippery concept.

[389] Elkind (1981), p. 207.

[390] Elkind (1981), p. 259.

[391] ICJ *Nuclear Test* cases (*Australia* v. *France*; *New Zealand* v. *France*), 22 June 1973, §23. See further Cheng (1953), pp. 270-271.

[392] ICJ *Fisheries Jurisdiction* cases, Order of 22 June 1973, §17.

[393] See Merrills (1995), p. 92, referring to the *Nuclear Test* cases and pointing out that more recent cases confirmed this. See pp. 92-100 for his discussion of the *Nicaragua, Arbitral Award, Passage through the Great Belt* and *Genocide Convention* cases. See also Collins (1992), pp. 220-222.

protection stage, namely that there must be an instrument in force between the parties conferring jurisdiction upon the Court without reservations concerning the question at issue'.[394]

In the *Nicaragua* case (1984) the ICJ pointed out that it had given the issue of jurisdiction over the merits of the case the 'fullest consideration compatible with the requirements of urgency'.[395] In the *Legality of the use of force* cases (1999) the ICJ applied the stricter test of existing *prima facie* evidence rather than the more lenient test of absence of manifest lack of jurisdiction or of *prima facie* not to be excluded.[396] Thirlway has noted that it is 'impossible to arrive at a water-tight definition' of the jurisdiction required and that the general trend seems to be towards a very low standard of proof.[397] After all, extensive deliberations about the question

---

[394] Oellers-Frahm (1981), p. 283. The ICJ found that the Vienna Convention on Diplomatic Relations (1961) and the Vienna Convention on Consular Relations (1963), as well as Article I of the Optional Protocols to both treaties (on the compulsory settlement of disputes), furnished a basis on which the jurisdiction of the Court 'might be founded'. It pointed out that it was sufficient at this stage of the proceedings 'if the provisions invoked by the Applicant appear, *prima facie*, to afford a basis on which the jurisdiction of the Court might be founded'. ICJ *United States Diplomatic and Consular Staff in Tehran (US* v. *Iran)*, Order of 15 December 1979, §§14 and 15.

[395] ICJ *Military and Paramilitary Activities in and against Nicaragua (Nicaragua* v. *US)*, Order of 10 May 1984, §§24 and 25 (while the ICJ unanimously decided it was competent to use provisional measures, while several members later questioned one of the grounds for jurisdiction. Judge Schwebel dissented regarding both grounds for jurisdiction). Again, in its decision whether or not to take provisional measures the ICJ merely examined whether it had *prima facie* jurisdiction on the merits. It need not finally satisfy itself that it has such jurisdiction, 'yet it ought not to indicate such measures unless the provisions invoked by the applicant appear, *prima facie* to afford a basis on which the jurisdiction of the Court might be founded'. See also *Arbitral Award of 31 July 1989 (Guinea-Bissau* v. *Senegal)*, Order of 2 March 1990; *Passage through the Great Belt (Finland* v. *Denmark)*, Order of 29 July 1991, §14; *Application of the Convention on the Prevention and Punishment of the Crime of Genocide (Bosnia and Herzegovina* v. *Yugoslavia (Serbia and Montenegro))*, Order of 8 April 1993; *Land and Maritime Boundary between Cameroon and Nigeria (Cameroon* v. *Nigeria)*, Order of 15 March 1996, §31 (In fact the declaration made by both Parties under Article 36(2) ICJ Statute, constituted 'a prima facie basis upon which its jurisdiction in the present case might be founded'; Nigeria had also argued that provisional measures should not be ordered because the case was inadmissible. The Court pointed out that while it did not rule on the question whether it should decide on *prima facie* admissibility before ordering provisional measures, it considered that the case did 'not appear prima facie to be inadmissible', §33); *Certain criminal proceedings in France (Congo* v. *France)*, Order of 17 June 2003, §20; for older cases see *Nuclear Test* cases, Orders of 22 June 1973, §§13 and 17 and *US Diplomatic and Consular Staff in Tehran (US* v. *Iran) (Hostages* case), Order of 15 December 1979, §§15, 18 and 20. In some of these cases the judgment on the merits also illustrates the approach of the members of the Court towards provisional measures. In the ICJ *Anglo-Iranian Oil Co.* case, Order of 5 July 1951 the ICJ ordered provisional measures while later it found it had no jurisdiction on the merits.

[396] ICJ *Legality of the use of force (Serbia and Montenegro* v. *Belgium and seven other States)*, Order of 2 July 1999. In this case Serbia had requested it to take provisional measures against the member States of NATO to halt military action in the Kosovo conflict. The ICJ considered that it manifestly lacked jurisdiction to take such measures because, among others, there was no *prima facie* evidence that Article IX of the Genocide Convention constituted a basis of jurisdiction. With regard to the cases against Spain and the US (the ninth and tenth cases submitted) it found a manifest *absence* of jurisdiction and these cases were removed from the General List (see §42 *Yugoslavia* v. *Spain* and §34 *Yugoslavia* v. *US*). The other eight cases remained on the Court's List of cases.

[397] Thirlway (1994), p. 22.

whether an adjudicator has jurisdiction or competence to deal with a given case on the merits would conflict with the need for urgent action.[398]

In 1991 Judge Shahabuddeen pointed out, in reference to the 'circumstances' mentioned in Article 41 ICJ Statute, that the question of *prima facie* jurisdiction in fact does not relate to the power to order provisional measures, but rather 'whether the case is a fit and proper one for exercising that power'.[399] Commentators have equally noted that 'one cannot treat the possible jurisdiction over the merits as a precondition to the indication of provisional measures without confusing the two sorts of jurisdiction'.[400] Indeed, the question rather is whether it is *appropriate* for the ICJ to order provisional measures in light of the evidence of likelihood of substantive jurisdiction.

4.1   Decision-making on jurisdictional issues

Sztucki notes that the ICJ does not decide on provisional measures as a *collective* body. Rather, the judges decide individually. He refers to the 1978 Hague Academy course by Judge Jiménez de Aréchaga equally pointing out that each judge decides individually: 'theories, attempting to determine the collective criteria followed on this matter, do not reflect accurately the reality nor the way the Court operates at this stage'. He notes that while the judges may discuss the question together, a 'formal and collective decision on the jurisdictional issue is not possible'. Judges will vote for or against provisional measures taking into account the views they have formed individually on the issue of jurisdiction. They may later change their minds in the light of further pleadings. The Court will grant provisional measures only if 'a majority of judges believes at the time that there will be jurisdiction over the merits'.[401]

4.2   Removing cases from the Court's List (docket) to discourage requests for provisional measures

The question has arisen whether cases in which provisional measures were denied should be removed from the List only for manifest or also for *prima facie* lack of jurisdiction. In *Congo* v. *Rwanda* (2002) the ICJ did not grant Congo's request for provisional measures finding it lacked

---

[398] See also section 2.

[399] Separate opinion of Judge Shahabuddeen in *Passage through the Great Belt* case (*Finland* v. *Denmark*), Order of 29 July 1991.

[400] Thirlway, among others, has referred to the Court's 'distinct statutory jurisdiction' under Article 41 to use provisional measures, Thirlway (1994), p. 22. Only incidentally it has been argued that jurisdiction on the merits is a prerequisite for the use of provisional measures and that the Court cannot take provisional measures before jurisdiction is established. See e.g. Judge Morozov in the *Aegean Sea* case (*Greece* v. *Turkey*), Order of 11 September 1976, disagreeing with the argument 'that the Court allegedly has a right to consider the request for the indication of interim measures of protection before it has considered and settled the question of its jurisdiction', p. 21 and considering that 'neither the Statute nor the Rules of Court contain any provisions which provide that the request for interim measures for protection has any priority over the question of jurisdiction', p. 22. Sztucki (1983), p. 152 points out that four years previously, in the *Fisheries Jurisdiction* cases (*UK* v. *Iceland*; *Germany* v. *Iceland*), Order of 17 August 1972, Morozov had voted in favour of the indication of provisional measures before the Court had 'settled' the question of its jurisdiction.

[401] Sztucki (1983), p. 257 quoting Jiménez de Aréchaga, 'International Law in the Past Third of a Century', 159 RCADI 161(1978).

prima facie jurisdiction.[402] Judge Dugard, who had voted with the majority, considered that the Court should have removed the case from the List, as requested by Rwanda.[403] He referred to the Court's judgment in *LaGrand*, finding that its Orders for provisional measures are binding upon States. He pointed out: "As a consequence of this decision, provisional measures will assume a greater importance than before and there will be a greater incentive on the part of States to request such measures". 'In these circumstances,' he argued, the case should have been removed from the List for manifest lack of jurisdiction. Dugard referred to the Separate Opinion of Judge Higgins in *Yugoslavia* v. *Belgium* (1999) explaining cases manifestly lacking jurisdiction as cases in which 'it is clear beyond doubt that no jurisdiction exists in a particular case'. In such situation 'a good administration of justice requires that the case be immediately struck off the List'.[404] Considering that the Court, by failing to find manifest lack of jurisdiction, set a dangerous precedent that could result in the Court being 'inundated with requests for provisional measures',[405] he noted that the applicant State was 'clutching at straws to found jurisdiction'. "It has clutched at eight straws in the hope that their cumulative effect might compensate for the failure of each one individually to offer a basis for jurisdiction. The Court should show its displeasure for this strategy by striking the Application from the list".[406] Yet this approach to jurisdiction appears overly strict. Rather the ICJ should seriously consider all possible grounds for jurisdiction, especially in cases of grave human suffering. In any case, even when it denies a request for provisional measures it should not declare a case manifestly lacking jurisdiction and remove it from the List if there are serious jurisdictional issues remaining to be discussed. The aim of discouraging States from submitting requests for provisional measures should not interfere with the Court's task in this respect. In *Congo* v. *Rwanda* there seem to have been at least two such jurisdictional issues, one based on the Genocide Convention and the other based on the Convention on the Elimination of

---

[402] ICJ *Congo* v. *Rwanda*, Order of 10 July 2002. Judge Elaraby dissented, considering that the progressive shift that the Court had made in its approach to jurisdiction had not been reflected in the Order. Judge Mavungu also dissented.

[403] ICJ *Congo* v. *Rwanda*, Order of 10 July 2002 (Dugard dissenting).

[404] ICJ *Congo* v. *Rwanda*, Order of 10 July 2002, Separate Opinion of Judge Dugard, §5, referring to *Legality of Use of Force (Yugoslavia* v. *Belgium)*, Order of 2 June 1999, Separate Opinion of Judge Higgins, §29. Dugard suggested that the case 'should be removed from the List where there is no reasonable possibility, based on the facts and circumstances of the unsuccessful Application, that the Applicant will at some future date be able to establish the jurisdiction of the Court on the instruments invoked for jurisdiction in the Application for provisional measures'.

[405] In his view, six of the instruments relied on by the Congo manifestly did 'not provide the remotest basis for jurisdiction'. Regarding the first remaining 'possible ground', the Montreal Convention for the Suppression of Unlawful Acts against the Safety of Civil Aviation, he pointed out that the 'accumulation of objections to the establishment of jurisdiction' indicated that it '*manifestly*' did not constitute a basis for jurisdiction. He also referred to other factors demonstrating that there was 'no real possibility' that a reasonable connection between the dispute submitted to the Court and Article 14 of the Montreal Convention could be established at subsequent stages of the proceedings', ICJ *Congo* v. *Rwanda*, Order of 10 July 2002, Separate Opinion of Judge Dugard, §10. Regarding the second 'possible ground' he questioned whether the Convention on the Elimination of All Forms of Discrimination against Women was an appropriate instrument for the protection of women in armed conflict and noted that it imposed no effective procedures for its enforcement, §11. He referred to the never used Article 11 CERD as an example of such an effective procedure. He considered that 'none of the eight instruments advanced by the Applicant to found jurisdiction in the present proceedings, viewed separately, offers, prima facie, a basis for jurisdiction in the present dispute, either now or in future'. He concluded that '(t)he absence of jurisdiction is therefore manifest' and that '(t)his conclusion is even stronger if one views the eight instruments cumulatively'.

[406] ICJ *Congo* v. *Rwanda*, Order of 10 July 2002, Separate Opinion of Judge Dugard, §12.

Discrimination against Women (CEDAW).[407] The next heading discusses the validity of the reservations to Article IX Genocide Convention (the jurisdictional clause) made by Rwanda.[408] The subsequent heading refers to the possible jurisdictional basis of CEDAW.

4.3 The development of international law and Article IX Genocide Convention as a jurisdictional basis for provisional measures

Subsequent to the denial of the request for provisional measures in *Congo* v. *Rwanda* (2002) the Court rendered a judgment on jurisdiction and admissibility in this case. The Dissenting Opinion of Judge Koroma and the joint Separate Opinion of Judges Higgins, Kooijmans, Elaraby, Owada and Simma confirmed that absence of jurisdiction under the Genocide Convention was not manifest. The Separate Opinion argued against a 'laissez faire' interpretation of the ICJ's 1951 Advisory Opinion on reservations to the Genocide Convention. Instead this 1951 Opinion should be read in its particular context, without being allowed to freeze the development of international law.[409] At the time, the Court 'had no occasion to address the application of the law of treaties to issues of severability in the context of reservations to human rights treaties'.[410] Moreover, the Court's present judgment, in *Congo* v. *Rwanda* (2006), should not be understood to suggest that a reservation to a jurisdictional clause will always be compatible with the object and purpose of a Convention.[411]

> "It is thus not self-evident that a reservation to Article IX could not be regarded as incompatible with the object and purpose of the Convention and we believe that this is a matter that the Court should revisit for further consideration".[412]

---

[407]   ICJ *Congo* v. *Rwanda*, Order of 10 July 2002 and Judgment of 3 February 2006. See also Kritsiotis (2001); Savadogo (2002); Tatulli (2003) and Mampuya (2004).

[408]   See also Chapter XIV (Jurisdiction and admissibility).

[409]   They pointed out that the 1951 Opinion must be understood against the background of the specific questions put to it by the General Assembly and that the problems that it 'could already envisage in 1951 have turned out to be vastly greater than it could have foreseen'. They also noted that the vast majority of States have failed to engage in the task of scrutinizing and objecting to reservations, often giving rise to 'serious concern as to compatibility with the object and purpose of the treaty concerned'. ICJ *Armed Activities on the Territory of the Congo* (new application: 2002) (*Congo* v. *Rwanda*), Judgment on jurisdiction of the Court and admissibility of the application of 3 February 2006, Separate Opinion Judges Higgins, Kooijmans, Elaraby, Owada and Simma, §§10-11. "The Court itself was not in 1951 asked to pronounce on the compatibility of particular reservations to the Genocide Convention with its object and purpose (...) Since 1951 many other issues relating to reservations have emerged, that equally were not and could not have been before the Court at that time". They mentioned two related questions, one regarding the role of UN bodies monitoring human rights treaties in the assessment of the compatibility with object and purpose and the other concerning the scope and powers of regional human rights courts, §12. See also Chapter XIV (Jurisdiction, admissibility and provisional measures in human rights adjudication).

[410]   Separate Opinion Judges Higgins, Kooijmans, Elaraby, Owada and Simma, §12.

[411]   Neither should the Court's previous Order denying Congo's request for provisional measures. They also explained that the ICJ did not pronounce on the issue in *Yugoslavia* v. *US*, since Yugoslavia had not introduced any arguments to this effect, Separate Opinion Judges Higgins, Kooijmans, Elaraby, Owada and Simma, §18.

[412]   Judges Higgins, Kooijmans, Elaraby, Owada and Simma suggested some of the considerations the Court had in mind 'in its findings thus far, that a reservation to Article IX is not incompatible with the objects and purposes of the Convention'. Yet they pointed out that the ICJ has an

The joint Separate Opinion referred to the ensuing evolution of international law, emphasizing that to observe the reality that the Court did not settle all matters relating to reservations in its 1951 Advisory Opinion 'is not to attempt to fragment a mythical overarching law on all questions of reservations'. After all the 1951 opinion just 'set out the law as to what it was asked, and no more, and did not foreclose legal developments in respect of hitherto uncharted waters in the future'.[413]

Human rights courts and tribunals had 'not regarded themselves as precluded by this Court's 1951 Advisory Opinion from doing other than nothing'. This development did not constitute a 'deviation' from general international law by 'these various courts and tribunals'.[414] 'Rather, it is to be regarded as developing the law to meet contemporary realities'. The specific findings of the Court in 1951 did not prohibit this. "Indeed, it is clear that the practice of the International Court itself reflects this trend for tribunals and courts themselves to pronounce on compatibility with object and purpose, when the need arises".[415]

In his Dissent Judge Koroma argued that the reservation to Article IX of the Genocide Convention was indeed invalid. He considered that it is contrary to the object and purpose of the treaty to make reservations to a provision on dispute settlement, if that provision is the raison d'être of the treaty.[416] He pointed out that 'States are often remiss in fulfilling their duties of objecting to reservations which they consider invalid'. "Moreover, the failure of a State to object should not be regarded as determinative in the context of human rights treaties like the Genocide Convention that are not based on reciprocity between States but instead serve to protect individuals and the international community at large".[417] He referred to the General Comment on reservations by the Human Rights Committee interpreting the ICCPR, which was equally relevant for the interpretation of the Genocide Convention. Congo's failure to object to Rwanda's reservation at the time it was made had 'no bearing on the Court's ability to consider it'.[418] Judge Koroma also emphasized that Rwanda, from a moral perspective, should have consented to the Court's jurisdiction.[419]

Despite the unimpressive practice of objecting to reservations contrary to the object and purpose of human rights treaties, various States have indeed objected against the reservations made by certain States to Article IX Genocide Convention.[420] The UK, for instance, has 'consistently stated' that it is 'unable to accept reservations in respect of article IX of the said Convention'; it 'is not the kind of reservation which intending parties to the Convention have the right to make'. It also specifically pointed this out vis-à-vis Rwanda, emphasizing that it does not

---

important role to play under the Genocide Convention and that Article IX of the Convention not only speaks of disputes regarding its interpretation and application, but also regarding the 'fulfilment of the Convention', Joint Separate Opinion, §§26-29.

[413] ICJ *Armed Activities on the Territory of the Congo* (new application: 2002) (*Congo v. Rwanda*), Judgment on jurisdiction of the Court and admissibility of the application of 3 February 2006, Separate Opinion Judges Higgins, Kooijmans, Elaraby, Owada and Simma, §13.

[414] Id., Separate Opinion Judges Higgins, Kooijmans, Elaraby, Owada and Simma, §22.

[415] Id., Separate Opinion Judges Higgins, Kooijmans, Elaraby, Owada and Simma, §23.

[416] Id., Dissenting Opinion Judge Koroma, §11, referring to ILC Report A/CN.4/558/Add.2, §3.1.13, 14 June 2005.

[417] Id., Dissenting Opinion Judge Koroma, §14.

[418] Id., §15.

[419] Id., §§24-25.

[420] Article IX stipulates: "Disputes between the Contracting Parties relating to the interpretation, application or fulfillment of the present Convention, including those relating to the responsibility of a State for genocide or for any of the other acts enumerated in article III, shall be submitted to the International Court of Justice at the request of any of the parties to the dispute".

accept the reservation.[421] The Netherlands went a step further. When it declared the reservations made by a range of States to Article IX incompatible with the object and purpose of the Convention, it explicitly stated, also referring to Rwanda, that it did 'not deem any State which has made or which will make such reservation a party to the Convention'.[422]

4.4 Armed conflict and CEDAW as a jurisdictional basis for provisional measures

The jurisdictional ground of Article 29 Convention on the Elimination of Discrimination against Women (CEDAW), invoked in *Congo* v. *Rwanda* (2002), did have some merit.[423] Indeed, the ICJ did not completely dismiss it in its Order for provisional measures. After all it did not remove the case from the List. It simply stated that 'at this stage in the proceedings the Congo has not shown that its attempts to enter into negotiations or undertake arbitration proceedings with Rwanda' concerned the application of Article 29 CEDAW and the Congo had not specified either 'which rights protected by that Convention have allegedly been violated by Rwanda and should be the object of provisional measures'.[424] The latter argument, on the specification of the relevant treaty provisions, has rightly been criticized by Judge Higgins. Especially in situations involving human beings in conditions of hardship, it is for the Court to specify these rights.[425] She noted that it is well-established in the case law of international human rights adjudicators that it is not necessary for a petitioner 'to identify which specific provisions of the treaty said to found jurisdiction are alleged to be breached'. She considered that '*a fortiori*' there was 'no reason' for the ICJ 'to suggest a more stringent test' for establishing whether it had *prima facie* jurisdiction for the use of provisional measures. It is not clear why there was no reason '*a fortiori*'. Nevertheless, Higgins correctly invokes the practice of the human rights adjudicators and indeed there appears to be no reason for the ICJ to take a different approach. As Higgins pointed out:

> "It should rather be for the Court itself, in accordance with the usual practice, to see whether the claims made by the Congo and the facts alleged could prima facie constitute violations of any particular clause in the Conventions on the Elimination of All Forms of Discrimination against Women, the instrument relied on by the Congo as providing the Court with jurisdiction over the merits".[426]

---

[421] Objections of 26 August 1983. See also Mexico's objection of 4 June 1990 pointing out that 'the reservation made by the United States Government to article IX of the aforesaid Convention should be considered invalid because it is not in keeping with the object and purpose of the Convention, nor with the principle governing the interpretation of treaties whereby no State can invoke provisions of its domestic law as a reason for not complying with a treaty'. Moreover, application of the reservation 'would give rise to a situation of uncertainty as to the scope of the obligations which the United States Government would assume with respect to the Convention'.

[422] Declaration made upon accession to the Convention, 20 June 1966; Objections of 27 December 1989 to the reservations of the US.

[423] Article 29 CEDAW stipulates: "Any dispute between two or more States concerning the interpretation or application of the present Convention which is not settled by negotiation shall, at the request of one of them, be submitted to arbitration. If within six months from the date of request for arbitration the parties are unable to agree on the organization of the arbitration, any one of those parties may refer the dispute to the International Court of Justice by request in conformity with the Statute of the Court".

[424] ICJ *Congo* v. *Rwanda*, Order of 10 July 2002, §79.

[425] ICJ *Congo* v. *Rwanda*, Order of 10 July 2002, Declaration of Judge Higgins.

[426] Ibid.

While CEDAW may not be the most appropriate instrument for the protection of women in armed conflict, this does not mean it cannot create a jurisdictional basis. It is true that the most effective procedures for the enforcement of this Convention are found in its recent Optional Protocol, which has not yet been ratified by Congo and Rwanda. Yet the supervisory committee to this treaty has also dealt with the issue of violence against women in its Concluding Observations and in a General Recommendation, interpreting the State obligations under the Convention to prevent violence against women.[427] The newly developed practice under its Optional Protocol has only confirmed this.[428]

What made Congo's argument based on CEDAW less convincing was the apparent lack of attempts by it to submit for arbitration a dispute with Rwanda regarding the application of CEDAW before bringing it before the ICJ. Yet at the provisional measures stage doubts regarding the existence of these attempts should not as such mean that Article 29 CEDAW manifestly does not constitute a basis for the Court's jurisdiction.[429] Moreover, as Judge Kooijmans pointed out, the position of the Court that Congo should have explicitly referred to CEDAW in its attempts to settle the dispute by negotiation is unrealistic, 'in particular in the case of a multifaceted conflict like the present one'.[430] He referred to a complaint brought by Congo before the African Commission on Human and Peoples' Rights (ACHPR), as well as to many complaints brought before the UN Security Council.[431]

> "In view of the character and mandate of the international institutions to which these grievances were addressed, the complaints could not be expected to itemize on a treaty-by-treaty basis the provisions allegedly breached".[432]

The ICJ had no choice, he noted, 'but to ascertain whether a precondition, explicitly laid down by the Contracting States, is met and to decline jurisdiction if it is not'. Nevertheless, the Women's Convention did not 'set out any specific criteria for the element of "not settled by negotiation"'.[433] This meant that the Court would have had 'sufficient room' to interpret this element less rigidly.[434]

In other words, *prima facie* CEDAW could serve as a jurisdictional basis, which could even have justified the use of provisional measures. In any case, the ICJ only removes a case from the List in exceptional cases.[435]

---

[427]   It has also published statements regarding the rights of women in, for instance, Iraq and Afghanistan.

[428]   CEDAW has made a public inquiry and published a report involving violence against women in Mexico, among others discussing murders and disappearances (CEDAW/C/2005/OP.8/MEXICO). It also published a decision on an individual complaint regarding domestic violence: *A.T.* v. *Hungary*, 26 January 2005. See further Chapter II (Systems) and IX (Threats).

[429]   ICJ *Armed Activities on the Territory of the Congo* (new application: 2002) (*Congo* v. *Rwanda*), Judgment on jurisdiction of the Court and admissibility of the application of 3 February 2006, §91 points out that the evidence had not satisfied the Court that the Congo had 'in fact sought to commence negotiations in respect of the interpretation or application of the Convention'.

[430]   ICJ *Certain criminal proceedings in France* (*Congo* v. *France*), 17 June 2003, Declaration of Judge Kooijmans, §7.

[431]   Id., §5.

[432]   Id., §7.

[433]   Id., §15.

[434]   Id., §15. For a different approach see the Separate Opinion of Judge Dugard, §18.

[435]   See also Rosenne (2005), pp. 132-134.

4.5   Provisional measures and forum prorogatum

In the case concerning *Certain criminal proceedings in France* (2003) Congo 'proposed to found the jurisdiction of the Court upon on a consent thereto yet to be given by France', under Article 38(5) Rules of Court. Subsequently France indeed explicitly consented to the jurisdiction of the Court in this case.[436] With regard to the request for provisional measures the ICJ in this case initially followed a different procedure exactly because there was no evidence yet of consent to the Court's jurisdiction. The application was simply sent to France and both States were informed that the case would not be entered in the General List and no action would be taken in the proceedings until the ICJ was informed of the consent of France. Upon receipt of this consent, four months later, the case was entered in the General List and hearings were fixed for that same month. Subsequently the ICJ decided not to indicate provisional measures.[437]

4.6   ITLOS and prima facie jurisdiction

Under Article 290 UNCLOS the adjudicator deciding on provisional measures should first determine that the adjudicator deciding on the merits 'has or would have *prima facie* jurisdiction'.[438] According to Judge Laing 'the juridical understanding of "*prima facie*" is that at first sight or impression (on its face), the evidence adduced by the Applicant sufficiently establishes the Tribunal's jurisdiction'. He adds that 'a *prima facie* finding has no bearing whatsoever on the Tribunal's final determinations at the merits stage'.[439]

A dispute on the admissibility of the claim in the *MOX Plant* case illustrates some difficulties that could arise if different adjudicators may deal with a case.[440] The UK had argued that the matters of which Ireland complained 'were governed by regional agreements providing for alternative and binding means of resolving disputes'.[441] ITLOS, however, considered that the dispute settlement procedures under those treaties dealt with 'disputes concerning the

---

[436]   ICJ *Certain criminal proceedings in France* (*Congo* v. *France*), Order of 17 June 2003, §21. See also Rosenne (2005), p. 151.

[437]   ICJ *Certain criminal proceedings in France* (*Congo* v. *France*), Order of 17 June 2003, §§5-7. See Rule 38(5) stipulating "When the applicant State proposes to found the jurisdiction of the Court upon a consent thereto yet to be given or manifested by the State against which such application is made, the application shall be transmitted to that State. It shall not however be entered in the General List, nor any action be taken in the proceedings, unless and until the State against which such application is made consents to the Court's jurisdiction for the purposes of the case". See also Sztucki (1983), p. 221 and Rosenne (2005), p. 120. France also consented to the Court's jurisdiction in *Djibouti* v. *France*, ICJ press release 10 August 2006, but there was no request for provisional measures, probably because the ICJ had previously denied such requests (*Congo* v. *France*, Order of 17 June 2003; *Congo* v. *Belgium*, Order of 8 December 2000).

[438]   In its first Order for provisional measures, in *M/V 'Saiga'* (No. 2) of 11 March 1998 ITLOS adopted the formulation of the ICJ that it need not finally satisfy itself that it has jurisdiction on the merits 'and yet it may not prescribe such measures unless the provisions invoked by the Applicant appear *prima facie* to afford the basis on which the jurisdiction of the Tribunal might be founded' (§29). Judge Laing points out that ITLOS could simply have quoted Article 290(1) UNCLOS, Separate Opinion Judge Laing, §10.

[439]   ITLOS *M/V 'Saiga'* (No. 2), Order of 11 March 1998, Separate Opinion Judge Laing, §10.

[440]   In 1983 Sztucki, p. 222 still noted that 'the concept of parallel jurisdictions in the same case' appeared to be 'rather remote from international realities'.

[441]   It argued that Ireland could not bring the case before the 'Annex VII arbitral tribunal', constituted pursuant to Article 287 and Article 1 Annex VII UNCLOS. It referred to the Convention for the Protection of the Marine Environment of the North-East Atlantic (the OSPAR Convention) and the EC and Euratom Treaty.

interpretation or application of those agreements, and not with disputes arising under the Convention'.[442] ITLOS first satisfied itself that *prima facie* the Annex VII arbitral tribunal would have jurisdiction.[443] It then considered whether provisional measures were required *pending* the constitution of this tribunal.[444] Subsequently the Arbitral Tribunal agreed with the finding by ITLOS that it had jurisdiction *prima facie*. It noted that both States were Parties to UNCLOS, that the Tribunal had been duly constituted, that Ireland had presented its case on the basis of various provisions of the Convention, that the dispute concerned the interpretation and application of this Convention and that there was 'nothing which manifestly and in terms excludes the Tribunal's jurisdiction'. Nevertheless it decided to suspend further proceedings on jurisdiction and merits in light of certain areas of European Community law 'as they appear to affect the dispute between the Parties before this Tribunal'. It noted that these had become more acute because the European Commission was examining the question whether to institute proceedings under Article 226 of the EC Treaty.[445] The Tribunal suspended the proceedings 'bearing in mind considerations of mutual

---

[442]   It considered that 'even if the OSPAR Convention, the EC Treaty and the Euratom Treaty contain rights or obligations similar to or identical with the rights or obligations set out in the Convention, the rights and obligations under those agreements have a separate existence from those under the Convention'. ITLOS *MOX plant case (Ireland* v. *UK)*, Order of 3 December 2001, §§49 and 50.

[443]   ITLOS *MOX plant case (Ireland* v. *UK)*, Order of 3 December 2001, §§61-62. ITLOS does this on the basis of Article 290(5) of UNCLOS, stipulating that it may prescribe, modify or revoke provisional measures 'if it considers that *prima facie* the tribunal which is to be constituted would have jurisdiction'. Given the fact that this function is specifically laid down by treaty and as long as ITLOS does not presume to determine anything more than the *prima facie* jurisdiction of such an arbitral tribunal, it does not violate the principle of *compétence de la compétence*. See Dumbauld (1932), p. 186 about a related situation, pointing out that because the power of the PCIJ to order provisional measures did not depend upon jurisdiction 'in the principal action', 'one court may provide a remedy *pendente lite* in aid of an action of which another court has cognizance'. This would be so in order to prevent a denial of justice in a case in which the other tribunal (with the jurisdiction on the merits) had no jurisdiction to grant provisional measures, provided that the parties were also bound by the obligatory jurisdiction of the PCIJ. An exception would apply if 'an inconsistent intention on the part of the parties was manifested', pp. 155-156. In the MOX Plant case the other Tribunal did not lack jurisdiction to use provisional measures, but had not yet been constituted, which made ITLOS the only tribunal to prevent the denial of justice referred to by Dumbauld.

[444]   It did not prescribe the provisional measures requested by Ireland, because it considered that in the short period before the constitution of the arbitral tribunal the urgency of the situation did not require these measures. Yet it did prescribe provisional measures of different nature. It referred to the duty to cooperate as a fundamental principle in the prevention of pollution of the marine environment under both the Convention and general international law. Under Article 290 UNCLOS it was appropriate to preserve the rights arising from this duty. Thus ITLOS ordered the cooperation of the Parties, which were to enter into consultation at once and to exchange information, monitor risks and devise preventive measures. ITLOS *MOX Plant* case (*Ireland* v. *UK)*, Order of 3 December 2001. See in particular §§81, 82 and 89. See also section 3.7 on protection.

[445]   "In these circumstances there is a real possibility that the European Court of Justice may be seized of the question whether the provisions of the Convention on which Ireland relies are matters in relation to which competence has been transferred to the European Community and, indeed, whether the exclusive jurisdiction of the European Court of Justice, with regard to Ireland and the United Kingdom as Member States of the European Community, extends to the interpretation and application of the Convention as such and in its entirety". Arbitral Tribunal constituted pursuant to Article 287, and Article 1 of Annex VII, of the United Nations Convention on the Law of the Sea for the dispute concerning the MOX Plant, international

respect and comity which should prevail between judicial institutions both of which may be called upon to determine rights and obligations as between two States'.[446]

4.7   The duration of provisional measures

Provisional measures end with the final decision of the Court. The ICJ has determined that an Order for provisional measures may not continue following the adjudicator's decision that it has no jurisdiction.[447] Moreover, proceedings for interpretation and revision of judgments by the ICJ are technically regarded as a new case.[448]

In his Separate Opinion in the *Tuna* cases ITLOS Judge Treves pointed out that Article 290(1) UNCLOS stipulates that provisional measures are meant to apply 'pending the final decision'. He considered that 'this expression should be read as meaning up to the moment in which a judgment on the merits has been rendered'. He noted that in case of measures requested under Article 290(5) UNCLOS, providing for the possibility that ITLOS prescribes provisional measures pending the institution of an arbitral tribunal for the resolution of a conflict between States, the provisional measures could apply until 'the judgment on the merits by the arbitral tribunal'. Of course the competent adjudicator[449] may decide to revoke or modify the measures before the final decision on the merits.[450]

---

[446]   movement of radioactive materials, and the protection of the marine environment of the Irish Sea, The *MOX Plant* case (*Ireland* v. *UK*), Order No. 3, suspension of proceedings on jurisdiction and merits and request for further provisional measures, 24 June 2003, §21.
It observed that both the decisions of the ECJ and its own decision under the Convention would be final and binding. Arbitral Tribunal constituted pursuant to Article 287, and Article 1 of Annex VII, of the United Nations Convention on the Law of the Sea for the dispute concerning the MOX Plant, international movement of radioactive materials, and the protection of the marine environment of the Irish Sea, The *MOX Plant* case (*Ireland* v. *UK*), Order No. 3, suspension of proceedings on jurisdiction and merits and request for further provisional measures, 24 June 2003, §§27 and 28. ITLOS Judge Treves had already referred to considerations of comity and 'economy of legal activity' in his Separate Opinion in the *MOX Plant* case, Order of 3 December 2001, Separate Opinion Judge Treves, §5. See further on the *MOX Plant* case Forster (2003) and Lavranos (2006). More generally see Treves (1999).

[447]   The ICJ has decided that its provisional measures lapse once it determines it has no jurisdiction, *Anglo-Iranian Oil Co.* case, Judgment of 22 July 1952. See generally on the duration of provisional measures Rosenne (2005), pp. 149-158.

[448]   Rosenne (2005), pp. 149-150. For an example see ICJ Request for interpretation of the judgment of 31 March 2004 in the case concerning *Avena and other Mexican nationals* (*Mexico* v. *US*), Order of 16 July 2008.

[449]   Under 290(1) or 290(5) UNCLOS.

[450]   Separate Opinion of Judge Treves, ITLOS *Southern Bluefin Tuna* cases, Order of 27 August 1999. The issue of duration is also relevant in the context of the related precautionary principle. The SPS Agreement provides in Article 5(7) that review of measures taken on the basis of precautionary principle shall take place 'within a reasonable period of time'. The European Commission, in its communication on the precautionary principle, has stressed that the temporary measures taken when scientific data are inadequate are provisional but that 'the provisional nature is not bound up with a time limit but with the development of scientific knowledge'. Commission of the European Communities, Communication from the Commission on the precautionary principle, 2 February 2000, COM (2000) 1, pp. 12 and 21. It notes on p. 28 that the WTO Appellate Body pointed out in the *Hormones* case that what constitutes 'a reasonable period of time' to review a precautionary measure was 'to be established on a case-by-case basis and depends on the specific circumstances of each case, including the difficulty of obtaining the

The Annex VII Arbitral Tribunal instituted under UNCLOS has pointed out that the Parties to the conflict before it must still respect the effects of the Orders of ITLOS prescribing provisional measures and 'their own decisions made in conformity with it' even after such Orders have been revoked. It noted that its Orders and the subsequent developments have had an impact on the perspectives and actions of the Parties.[451] Rosenne suggests, correctly, that '[t]here is no reason why this notion should not be given a wider application, in that way making the provisional measures proceedings an important element in the general procedures available to States for the pacific settlement of their international disputes.[452]

5   ASSESSMENT OF URGENCY

5.1   Introduction

Provisional measures show that adjudicators believe the matter to be so urgent that measures should be taken, although they have not yet been able to evaluate all the evidence and arguments. For provisional measures an exhaustive and definitive examination of the evidence is not necessary. Waiting too long before taking them defeats their purpose. Still, how are the interests of urgency, on one hand, and reliability of information, on the other, balanced off against each other? In deciding whether or not to indicate provisional measures, a balance must be struck between the two.

This section sets out discussing the practice of the ICJ involving Parties that are more or less equal, at least in comparison to the situation of an individual requesting provisional measures against a State. Before the ICJ States may make requests for the use of provisional measures 'at any time during the course of the proceedings' (Article 73(1) Rules of Court). Obviously, if they request provisional measures later in the proceedings rather than at the initial stages, the States in question must equally show that the case is urgent. If a request has previously been denied, they must also show that the renewed request is based on 'new facts' (Article 75(3) Rules of Court).

In 1991 the ICJ noted that provisional measures are only justified if there is urgency 'in the sense that action prejudicial to the rights of either party is likely to be taken before such final decision is given'.[453] This brief description could refer to two types of urgency: material and temporal. The term 'likely' obviously refers to material urgency, but could also refer to the immediacy of the risk. The phrase 'before such final decision is given' relates to the initially indeterminate duration of provisional measures, in the sense that it is not clear when the final decision will be given.

This book distinguishes between criteria for assessment of temporal and material urgency.[454] The first relates to the immediacy of risk and is discussed in section 5.2. The

---

additional information necessary for the review *and* the characteristics of the provisional SPS measure'.

[451]   Annex VII Arbitral Tribunal *Southern Bluefin Tuna* case, Award on Jurisdiction and Admissibility of 4 August 2000, §67, referring to ITLOS *Southern Bluefin Tuna* cases (*New Zealand* v. *Japan; Australia* v. *Japan*), Order of 27 August 1999.

[452]   Rosenne (2005), pp. 157-158.

[453]   ICJ *Passage through the Great Belt* (*Finland* v. *Denmark*), 22 July 1991, §23.

[454]   The term temporal urgency or urgency in the temporal sense is taken from Judge Treves (ITLOS) who distinguishes between the 'temporal dimension of the requirement of urgency' and the 'qualitative dimension'. See his Separate Opinion in the *Southern Bluefin Tuna* cases, Order of 27 August 1999. See further Rosenne (2005), pp. 135-148, esp. p. 136.

discussion of assessment of material urgency also includes the relationship with the preventive and precautionary principles.

5.2   Assessment of temporal urgency

In the *Interhandel* case (1957) the ICJ found there was no need to use provisional measures, relying upon a statement by the respondent State, made during the hearings on provisional measures, that it was not taking action at that time.[455] Equally, in another case, upon the Applicant State's request to postpone further consideration of its earlier request for provisional measures, the ICJ considered that there was no urgency anymore.[456]

In the *Passage through the Great Belt* case (1991) the ICJ noted provisional measures are 'only justified if there is urgency in the sense that action prejudicial to the rights of either party is likely to be taken before such final decision is given'.[457] Finland had objected to the construction of a bridge that could obstruct passage through the Great Belt, but the ICJ did not take the provisional measures requested. Instead it 'placed on record' Denmark's assurance that before the end of 1994 it would not cause physical obstruction of the East Channel. This meant that although Finland could not convince the ICJ to take provisional measures it did obtain 'a significant benefit from its request'.[458] Moreover, the ICJ itself decided to accelerate the proceedings.[459] It simply decided not to use provisional measures because of the abovementioned assurances by Denmark and because it expected the conclusion of the case before the end of 1994. Denmark had argued as well that, even upon completion of the bridge, there was no risk of irreparable prejudice and therefore no urgency. The Court, however, agreed with Finland that it might have a case for provisional measures if the passage would be obstructed before the decision on the merits. This meant that 'if the bridge was completed early (contrary to the respondent's assurances), or the decision on the merits were delayed beyond the end of 1994, Finland would be entitled to renew its request for interim protection with every prospect of success'.[460]

In *Gabcikovo-Nagymaros* (1997), when discussing whether there was a 'peril' referred to the requirement that a state of necessity (for the non-fulfilment of an international agreement) had to be 'grave' and 'imminent'. It noted that 'imminence' was synonymous with 'immediacy' or 'proximity' and went 'far beyond' the concept of 'possibility'. This did not exclude 'that a "peril" in the long term might be held to be "imminent" as soon as it is established, at the relevant point

---

[455]   ICJ *Interhandel* case (*Switzerland* v. *US*), 24 October 1957 (about this case see also section 2.3 of this chapter on provisional measures and jurisdiction on the merits). See also, e.g. ICJ *Pulp mills on the river Uruguay* (*Argentina* v. *Uruguay*), Order of 13 July 2006 denying the provisional measures requested by Argentina, among others, for lack of imminence, §75. The approach of the human rights adjudicators generally is equally strict, but exceptions have been developed in certain death penalty and expulsion cases where it is unclear how soon after a domestic decision execution of the death sentence or expulsion order will take place. In addition, in some death penalty cases provisional measures have been used when there was no imminent execution date, apparently in order to express moral condemnation. See further Chapter XV (Immediacy and risk).

[456]   ICJ *Trial of Pakistani Prisoners of War* (*Pakistan* v. *India*) 1973, §14. Petrén dissented because Pakistan did not withdraw its request.

[457]   ICJ *Passage through the Great Belt* (*Finland* v. *Denmark*), 22 July 1991, §23.

[458]   Merrills (1995), p. 112. On 10 September 1992 the case was removed from the Court's List of cases after the parties had settled the dispute.

[459]   See ICJ *Passage through the Great Belt* (*Finland* v. *Denmark*), 22 July 1991 and Merrills (1995), p. 112.

[460]   Merrills (1995), pp. 111-112.

in time, that the realisation of that peril, however far off it might be, is not thereby any less certain and inevitable'.[461]

In 2003 Mexico requested the ICJ to take provisional measures on behalf of 52 Mexican nationals on death row in the US. The ICJ ordered provisional measures on behalf of three of them for whom an execution date was imminent because domestic remedies had been exhausted. They 'were at risk of execution in the following months, or even weeks'. The other Mexican detainees had not yet exhausted domestic remedies meaning that their executions were not impending and that there was no need yet for provisional measures.[462]

Most requests for provisional measures discussed by ITLOS relate to Article 290(5) UNCLOS.[463] This is a provision dealing with the time period before the arbitral tribunal is installed. Eventually it is this tribunal that should determine the case. Once installed, this tribunal itself could also use provisional measures. While statements made by ITLOS or individual judges relate to this situation specifically, they still provide some information on the assessment of temporal urgency in general.

In the *MOX plant case* (2001) ITLOS decided not to order the provisional measures exactly the way Ireland had requested them. It did not consider that the urgency of the situation required this in the short period before the arbitral tribunal would be instituted. It referred specifically to the assurances given by the UK during the public hearings to the effect that there would be no import or export of fuel to and from the plant until a given date. It also noted that the UK had stated its hope to reach agreement on the institution of the arbitral tribunal 'within a short space of time'.[464] Instead of ordering the provisional measures requested by Ireland it ordered different provisional measures relating to the duty to cooperate.[465] In *Malaysia v. Singapore* (2003) it incorporated the assurances of Singapore in the prescription for provisional measures.[466]

---

[461]   ICJ *Gabčíkovo-Nagymaros (Hungary v. Slovakia)*, Judgment of 25 September 1997, general list 1992, §54 (no provisional measures because of an agreement between the parties). Yet see ICJ *Pulp mills on the river Uruguay (Argentina v. Uruguay)*, Order of 13 July 2006 denying the provisional measures requested by Argentina, among others, for lack of imminence, §75. See also *Pulp mills on the river Uruguay (Argentina v. Uruguay)*, Order of 23 January 2007 (denying the provisional measures requested by Uruguay against the blockades by Argentinean citizens), §42.

[462]   ICJ *Avena and other Mexican nationals (Mexico v. US)*, Order of 5 February 2003, *Avena and other Mexican nationals (Mexico v. US)*, Judgment of 31 March 2004, §21. See also e.g. ICJ *Pulp mills on the river Uruguay (Argentina v. Uruguay)*, Order of 13 July 2006 (denying provisional measures, among others because 'the threat of any pollution is not imminent as the mills are not expected to be operational before August 2007 (Orion mill) and June 2008 (CMB mill), §75.

[463]   See ITLOS *Southern Bluefin Tuna Cases (New Zealand v. Japan; Australia v. Japan)*, Order of 27 August 1999; *MOX Plant case (Ireland v. UK)*, Order of 3 December 2001; *Land reclamation by Singapore in and around the straits of Johor (Malaysia v. Singapore)*, Order of 8 October 2003, *M/V 'Saiga'* (No. 2) case *(St. Vincent and the Grenadines v. Guinea)*, Order of 11 March 1998 did not relate to Article 290(5).

[464]   ITLOS *MOX plant case (Ireland v. UK)*, Order of 3 December 2001, §§77-81.

[465]   This in itself indicates that it considered that there was some form of temporal urgency. See the individual and dissenting opinions for some background on this decision. See also Rosenne (2005), pp. 147-148. See further section 3.7 (protection and reparation).

[466]   ITLOS *Land reclamation by Singapore in and around the straits of Johor (Malaysia v. Singapore)*, Order of 8 October 2003. In an earlier case judge Treves pointed out that the requirement of urgency is 'inherent in the very nature of provisional measures'. He noted that Article 290(5) UNCLOS nevertheless explicitly mentions the requirement of urgency, which is therefore different from the normal requirement. It is stricter than when provisional measures are requested under Article 290(1) UNCLOS, which is the general provision on the competence of ITLOS to use provisional measures. This is so because 'there is no "urgency" under paragraph 5

5.3   Assessment of material urgency

5.3.1   Introduction

Apart from temporal urgency it is important to determine material urgency or risk of irreparable harm. The question arises to what extent evidence of risk and *prima facie* evidence of such risk differ or, more generally speaking, whether and how the evidentiary requirements on the merits could shed some light on the assessment of risk of irreparable harm *pending* the proceedings. The term 'evidentiary requirements' is used here to refer to the criteria to be met in order to prove a case as well as to the standard and burden of proof. These issues are interrelated and normally adjudicators do not clearly distinguish between them. Apart from the issue of evidentiary requirements there is also the issue of how the adjudicators evaluate this evidence, in other words the standard of review.[467] Adjudicators have the inherent authority to determine which party carries the burden of proof.[468] They also determine the related issue of the sources of legal presumption[469] and point out the duty of cooperation.[470] They are free to determine the

---

[467] if the measures requested could, without prejudice to the rights to be protected, be granted by the arbitral tribunal once constituted'. If there is such urgency pending the constitution of the arbitral tribunal, provisional measures may be used. Once constituted this tribunal may modify, revoke or affirm the measures taken under Article 290(5) UNCLOS and it may also order new provisional measures, ITLOS *Southern Bluefin Tuna* cases, Order of 27 August 1999, Separate Opinion of Judge Treves.

[467] International adjudicators normally have a fact-finding authority. They may examine the facts *proprio motu*. Depending on the facts found by the adjudicator the claimant and respondent party may have to provide more, or less, evidence. Adjudicators may order the parties to provide information and documents and submit pleadings. Sometimes they have the power to examine witnesses and conduct *in situ* investigations. They may appoint independent experts and determine whether expert witnesses proposed by one of the parties can be heard. Moreover, they can take 'judicial notice', which means that certain facts do not need further proof.

[468] The traditional approach to the burden of proof is that the party alleging certain facts must prove them. See e.g. Kazazi (1996), pp. 232-235 and pp. 369-370. The principle concerned is that of *actori incumbit probatio/onus probandi actori incumbit*. The 'burdens of proof and of persuasion lie on the party that advances a point for adjudication'. They must do so by a preponderance of the evidence, Highet (1992), p. 46 and p. 70. Bringing indirect evidence is also allowed as long as it leads to reliable and reasonable conclusions. The parties usually have to prove issues of fact only, not the law itself. International tribunals are expected to take 'judicial notice' of international law. The principle concerned is that of *iura novit curia*.

[469] Kazazi mentions general principles of law as the main source of legal presumptions in international procedure. When evaluating the evidence the adjudicator takes into account applicable presumptions 'in favour of the party that carries the burden of proof and not refuted by the other party'. The burden may then shift from one party to the other because 'presumptions affect the burden of proof insofar as they create *prima facie* evidence or proof in favour of the party that benefits from them'. He points out that presumptions may shift the burden but do not reverse it. Instead they create *prima facie* evidence in favour of the party claiming certain facts. It is possible that the other party cannot bring evidence against the presumption in question and the adjudicator rules in favour of the claimant party. This applies in particular when the presumption concerns a rule of *ius cogens*. "In such a case, an irrebuttable legal presumption has conclusive probative value and, depending on whether it supports the claim or not, it either relieves the proponent from the burden of proof or makes its burden impossible to meet". Kazazi (1996), pp. 370-371.

[470] Kazazi argues that the 'duty of parties to cooperate in good faith in matters of evidence does not shift the burden of proof, as it is not the purpose of the rule to relieve the claimant of its obligation to prove its claims'. "It is only after the claimant has apparently done its best and all in

admissibility of evidence and are not limited by certain technical rules of evidence that can be found in domestic law. Finally, they 'determine the probative value to be given to each piece of evidence available to them'.[471]

The issue of material urgency again triggers the question of the relationship between provisional measures, the rights claimed and the forms of reparation.[472] It is equally related to the issue of prejudgment.[473] This section also discusses the relevance of the precautionary and preventive principles to understanding the concept of provisional measures.

5.3.2 Material urgency

Traditionally courts and other adjudicators have had to deal with urgent situations involving risk assessment. Assessment of material urgency for the use of provisional measures often implies an initial assessment of the main claim.[474] If it does not, it is still important to clarify the substantive

---

its power to secure evidence, and has actually produced some *prima facie* evidence in support of its case, that the duty of the respondent to produce the evidence exclusively in its possession commences". He also notes that international tribunals do not have specific sanctions at their disposal to force a party to produce information and documents, Kazazi (1996), pp. 372-373. The duty of cooperation in providing information and documentation or the 'collaboration of parties' aims to 'enable the tribunal to base its decision on as much evidence as possible' and to preserve peace 'through establishing justice and truth'. As a last resort measures such as taking note of a State's failure to provide information or 'drawing reasonable adverse inferences therefrom' could be used 'as a deterrent in order to encourage the parties to provide more information and documents'. He explains that adjudicators have sometimes drawn such an adverse inference against a party withholding evidence, but that mixed claims commissions have resorted to this more often than 'international tribunals dealing solely with the claims of States in their own rights', Kazazi (1996), pp. 373-374 and p. 380. This is not surprising given the fact that international tribunals dealing exclusively with the interests of States may assume equality between the parties with regard to the magnitude of the consequences of a finding as well as equality of arms in the production of evidence. On the other hand, as discussed in section 3.3 on the ICJ and the protection of the individual and in Part III of this book, proceedings involving individuals as well as States have to take into account the principle of effective protection of the individual. See in this respect the comments on the standard of proof used by the ICJ in the *Genocide Convention* case, 26 February 2007, e.g. the dissenting opinion of Vice-President Al-Khasawneh, §42; Gaeta (2007a), pp. 278-280 and Gaeta (2007b), p. 643; for a different approach see Milanović (2006), p. 595 and Gattini (2007), pp. 894-895. See also Chapter XV (Immediacy and risk), section 3.2.2 as well as Chapter VI (Disappearances). In its Judgment in *Congo* v. *Uganda* the ICJ also considered evidence contained in certain UN documents 'to the extent that they are of probative value and corroborated, if necessary by other credible sources'. ICJ *Armed Activities on the Territory of the Congo (DRC v. Uganda)*, judgment of 19 December 2005, §207. It referred to a 'coincidence of reports from credible sources', 'persuasive evidence' in the form of UN reports, consistent in the presentation of facts, supporting each other and 'corroborated by other credible sources'. In this respect it referred to the Human Rights Watch Report 'Ituri: covered in blood, ethnically targeted violence in northeastern DR Congo', July 2003. See ICJ *Armed Activities on the Territory of the Congo (DRC v. Uganda)*, Judgment of 19 December 2005, §209, See section 3 of this Chapter, focusing on this purpose of provisional measures in general international law and Part II of this book on the purpose of provisional measures in human rights cases.

[471] Kazazi (1996), pp. 374-376. See further on the issues of fact-finding and fact and law e.g. Lillich (1992) and Highet (1987), p. 75.

[472] Discussed in section 4.

[473] Discussed in section 5 of this chapter.

[474] See also section 3 of this chapter on the purpose of provisional measures.

law invoked, implicitly or explicitly, with the provisional measures.[475] Sometimes respondent States have referred to the obligation of the party requesting provisional measures to show a reasonable prospect of success on the merits.[476] Urgency and the gravity of the harm risked are interlinked. If the ICJ finds that the potential harm 'would be irreparable', this triggers a discussion of the 'urgency' criterion.[477] In 1932 Dumbauld already considered that delay for the purpose of a hearing 'is not unlimited, and must not be incompatible with the essentially urgent character of interim protection'. "In view of the summary nature of the procedure, the rules of evidence should be relaxed rather than made more rigid than usual". In any case, apparently all that was required was a 'prima facie showing of probable right and probable injury'.[478]

In the Nuclear Test cases (1973) the ICJ noted that the information did not exclude the possibility that the deposit on Australia's territory of radioactive fall-out resulting from the tests performed by France could cause irreparable damage.[479] Elkind pointed out that in these cases the ICJ 'was willing to accept very slight proof as to the likelihood of irreparable injury' while in the Aegean Sea case (1976) it required a 'much stricter standard of proof' of irreparable harm.[480]

In his Separate Opinion Judge Elias criticized the Court's approach in that case because, as he put it, it meant that 'the State which has the ability to pay can under this principle commit wrongs against another State with impunity, since it discounts the fact that the injury by itself might be sufficient to cause irreparable harm to the national susceptibilities of the offended State'. He considered that 'might' should no longer be 'right' in 'today's inter-State relations'.[481] While the ICJ considered that rights claimed by States might be protected through provisional measures, even though they concern the nature and extent of rights rather than their existence, in this case it found that circumstances did not require such measures.[482]

Elkind criticised the Court's decision in the Aegean Sea case (1976) and considered that Greece had the burden to allege and prove irreparable injury and that 'demonstrating that the interests sought to be protected were subjective or incapable of pecuniary ascertainment should have satisfied that onus'. Following this, 'the burden of coming forward with the evidence to negate the claim of irreparable injury shifted to Turkey'. Because Turkey did not appear and did not present evidence to the contrary 'the Court should have held that the case for irreparable

---

[475] See also section 3.5 and 3.7 on the relationship with the rights claimed and the forms of reparation.

[476] See also section 3.6 on prejudgment.

[477] See Rosenne (2005), p. 135.

[478] Dumbauld (1932), pp. 160-161.

[479] ICJ Nuclear Tests cases (Australia v. France), Order of 22 June 1973, §29. Shahabuddeen acknowledges that the ICJ did not say that the possible damage might violate some possible right of the applicant. However, given the fact that the Court recognised the possibility that the Applicant might be able to show irreparable damage it was improbable that it did not assume that its rights might be at stake as well. Passage through the Great Belt (Finland v. Denmark), Order of 29 July 1991, Separate Opinion Judge Shahabuddeen, pp. 25-33. See further Goldie (1972-73), p. 497, also referring to the PCIJ Sino-Belgian Treaty case, Order of 8 January 1927.

[480] Elkind (1981), p. 223. See, however, ICJ Nuclear Tests follow-up case, Order of 22 September 1995.

[481] ICJ Aegean Sea case, Order of 11 September 1976, Separate Opinion Judge Elias, p. 31.

[482] According to Thirlway (1994), p. 24 this decision seems to imply that the question whether there is a prima facie case on the merits does not arise if the other party has admitted the existence of the right to be protected. In reference to the Nuclear test cases, 'where the very existence of a right to redress for damage caused by fall-out from nuclear tests was disputed', he considered the criterion chosen by the ICJ, 'while appropriate for the facts before it, does not lend itself for generalization'. As a ground rule he proposes that 'if there is any requirement that a prima facie case be made out as a condition of provisional measures, this must be so in principle even where it is asserted as an extension of a recognized right'.

injury was established'. He pointed out that Article 53 did not require the ICJ either 'to coddle the non-appearing respondent to the extent of raising defences *proprio motu*'.[483]

Thus, Elkind considered that the ICJ erred in the *Aegean Sea* case with regard to the burden of proof for the likelihood of irreparable harm. He referred to two findings of law that were implicit in the Court's holding: '(a) that the question of what constitutes irreparable injury is solely a question of fact and (b) that the burden of proving irreparable injury rests with the plaintiff'. However, he noted, the Court only stated that the Turkish explorations 'might be' capable of reparation, which meant that it also might *not* be capable of such reparation.[484]

According to Sztucki, writing in the early 1980s, the ICJ was not strict about *prima facie* cases. He noted that it could order provisional measures without requiring the Applicant to show a *prima facie* case, while this was normally required under national laws and in the practice of the European Court of Justice.[485]

In 1991 Denmark argued that Finland's request for provisional measures in the *Passage through the Great Belt* case was inappropriate because there was 'not even a prima facie case' in favour of the Finnish claim. It argued that Finland should substantiate the right it claims 'to a point where a reasonable prospect of success in the main case exists'.[486] Merrills notes that the ICJ 'was prepared to regard Finland as having satisfied any *prima facie* test that might be necessary, but stopped short of endorsing Denmark's argument that the merits of the principal claim are in fact relevant in proceedings relating to interim protection'.[487] In his separate opinion Judge Shahabuddeen considered that the Applicant State indeed had to show a *prima facie* case 'in the sense of demonstrating a possibility of existence of the specific right'. Given the exceptional character of the procedure he argued that it was necessary for the requesting State to show some arguable basis for the existence of the right sought to be protected.[488]

At the same time it is often the Respondent that raises the question whether the right claimed indeed exists. In such situations there is no question of prejudgment. Moreover, a finding by the ICJ that there is a possibility of the existence of a right does not, in itself, constitute an interim judgment.[489] Judge Shahabuddeen pointed out that it 'is improbable that the Court is bound by a mere assertion of rights even where these are manifestly incapable of existing in law'. In that sense 'the Court must be concerned with satisfying itself affirmatively of the possible existence of the rights claimed, the required degree of proof being dependent on the character and circumstances of the particular case'.[490] He did not suggest that the requesting State 'should

---

483   Elkind (1981), p. 206.
484   Elkind (1981), p. 214.
485   Sztucki (1983), p. 259 (also for early examples of case law by the European Court of Justice).
486   ICJ *Passage through the Great Belt* (*Finland* v. *Denmark*), Order of 22 July 1991, §21.
487   ICJ *Passage through the Great Belt* case, Order of 22 July 1991. Merrills (1995), p. 114 points out that in the approach suggested by Denmark the strength of the case on the merits should be treated as a relevant circumstance. 'Although superficially attractive, such an approach would present many problems and has never been endorsed by the Court'. The ICJ noted that Denmark had not challenged the existence of a right of Finland of passage through the Great Belt. Instead the dispute was about the nature and extent of the passage. It found that 'such a disputed right may be protected by the indication of provisional measures' if it 'considers that circumstances so require', *Passage through the Great Belt* (*Finland* v. *Denmark*), Order of 22 July 1991, §22.
488   ICJ *Passage through the Great Belt* (*Finland* v. *Denmark*), Order of 22 July 1991, Separate Opinion Judge Shahabuddeen, p. 29. He also referred to Dumbauld's remark that provisional measures always constitute 'an exceptional remedy', (1932), p. 184.
489   ICJ *Passage through the Great Belt* (*Finland* v. *Denmark*), Order of 22 July 1991, Separate Opinion Judge Shahabuddeen, p. 30. See about prejudgment section 3.6.
490   ICJ *Passage through the Great Belt* (*Finland* v. *Denmark*), Order of 22 July 1991, Separate Opinion Judge Shahabuddeen, p. 30.

anticipate and meet each and every issue which could arise at the merits'. This would depend on the nature and circumstances of the case. He suggested the following standard: "What is important is that enough material should be presented to demonstrate the possibility of existence of the right sought to be protected".[491] Judge Shahabuddeen argued that it is reasonable to order provisional measures only if the Applicant State can show some possibility of success on the merits. After all, such measures often have an unequal impact on the parties.[492] The 'need to avoid any appearance of prejudgment' is 'of special importance in the sensitive field of litigation between States'.[493] He reiterated that it is only necessary to show 'the possibility of the existence of the right claimed'. According to Merrills this means that 'the *prima facie* test could be satisfied (at least in theory) without going into the merits of the case in any detail'. He welcomes, however, the Court's reluctance to take this approach because 'if a *prima facie* test were to be formally required it would probably be impossible to prevent the parties from devoting a significant amount of their argument to the merits'. At the same time he acknowledges that, informally, it 'would be surprising if a preliminary view of the merits did not in practice influence the Court's approach to requests for interim protection to some degree'.[494]

In the *Great Belt* case (1991) Shahabuddeen referred to the Court's remark in its Order for provisional measures in the *Hostages* case (1979) that 'a request for provisional measures must by its very nature relate to the substance of the case since, as article 41 expressly states, their object is to preserve the respective rights of either party'.[495] He discussed the fact that the Court goes into the merits of cases at the stage of provisional measures. This means that the Court considers that the State requesting provisional measures 'must satisfy the Court that it has an arguable case in favour of the existence of the rights sought to be preserved pending a final decision'.[496] In this case, however, he agreed with the ICJ that there was no urgency. After all, Denmark showed full cooperation and undertook not to complete the disputed bridge before the Court's decision on the merits.

If the Respondent State provides assurances that it will avoid causing irreparable harm this can play a role in the determination that there is no urgency.[497] In this context Merrills has pointed out that 'in an appropriate case the fact that the parties, and especially the respondent, are demonstrating a co-operative, responsible and law-abiding attitude is a factor which can be and has been given weight'. At the same time he stressed that 'if rights are genuinely threatened, something more than vague assurances of goodwill will be necessary before a request is refused'.[498]

---

[491] Id., p. 31.

[492] Merrills (1995), p. 115, notes that this approach would be consistent with the use of the *prima facie* test for jurisdiction to use provisional measures.

[493] ICJ *Passage through the Great Belt* (*Finland* v. *Denmark*), Order of 22 July 1991, Separate Opinion Judge Shahabuddeen, p. 29. See about prejudgment section 3.6.

[494] Merrills (1995), pp. 115-116.

[495] ICJ *US Diplomatic and Consular Staff in Tehran* (*US* v. *Iran*) (*Hostages* case), Order of 15 December 1979, §28. See also section 3.5 on the relationship between provisional measures and the claim.

[496] ICJ *Passage through the Great Belt* (*Finland* v. *Denmark*), Order of 22 July 1991, Separate Opinion Judge Shahabuddeen, p. 33.

[497] See e.g. ICJ *Great Belt* case, Order of 22 July 1991 and ITLOS *MOX Plant* case, Order of 3 December 2001.

[498] Merrills (1995), p. 121. In *Questions relating to the Obligation to Prosecute or Extradite* (*Belgium* v. *Senegal*), Order of 28 May 2009, the ICJ took note of the assurances given by Senegal that it would not allow Mr. Habré to leave its territory before the Court has given its final decision, and found that the risk of irreparable prejudice to the rights claimed by Belgium was 'not apparent on the date of this Order', §§71-72 (Judge Cançado Trindade dissenting).

Thirlway referred to Judge Shahabuddeen's Separate Opinion, concluding that the State requesting provisional measures 'is required to establish the possible existence of the rights sought to be protected'.[499] Judge Shahabuddeen himself referred to a statement by Judge Anzilotti who wrote that the Court, for its decision on provisional measures, takes 'into account the *possibility* of the right claimed (...) and the *possibility* of the danger to which that right was exposed'.[500] While this statement was a dissent by a PCIJ Judge, Judge Shahabuddeen considered in 1991 that 'the general pattern of advocacy employed by counsel, and also the reaction of the Court on some occasions, as in the United States Diplomatic and Consular Staff in Teheran case, would appear to be objectively consistent with Judge Anzilotti's understanding of the law' as expressed above.[501] He noted that the interests of the respondent State required the Court to examine whether there was a possibility of the right claimed and a possibility of the danger to which that right was exposed. He considered that the requirement of *prima facie* evidence of the possible existence of the right would not be the same as a full examination on the merits. He pointed out that the 'possibility formula' proposed by Judge Anzilotti was to be preferred over the requirement of *prima facie* evidence because it implied even less risk of prejudgment.

Nevertheless, in international litigation the distinction between a *prima facie* test, a test whether there is a serious issue to be tried and a test whether there is a possible danger to a possible right is not that great.[502] In any case the risk of irreparable harm must be shown to some extent. Merrills has pointed out that the ICJ may have to consider 'both the probability of a certain event occurring and the consequences which may be expected if it does'.

> "It is worth noting that any future event does not have to be certain, a probability is sufficient".[503]

In relation to the *Southern Bluefin Tuna* cases (1999) by ITLOS, Judge Treves noted that it seemed reasonable to hold 'that the prevention of serious harm to the southern bluefin tuna stock is the appropriate standard for prescribing measures'. He pointed out that this standard could apply to measures for the preservation of the rights of the parties exactly 'because these rights concern the conservation of that very stock'. In that sense he would have preferred that ITLOS had mentioned the prevention of serious harm to the stock as the *standard* for ordering provisional measures rather than (only) as the *purpose* of action to be taken by the parties.[504] In the context of the provisional measures in the *M/V 'Saiga'* case ITLOS Judge Laing pointed out that comparable ICJ jurisprudence did not suggest that there is a '*prima facie* standard by which this Tribunal must adjudge the existence and sufficiency of the circumstances and other elements which relate to the discretion to prescribe measures'. He considered that there was no persuasive doctrine to suggest this either. If jurisprudence about a *prima facie* standard at the provisional measures stage would exist, it 'would be unreliable, since such circumstances, elements and contextual situations are too varied to be submitted to a sole, and probably simplistic, standard'.

---

[499]   Thirlway (1994), p. 24.
[500]   PCIJ *Polish Agrarian Reform and German Minority* case, Order of 29 July 1933, Dissenting Opinion by Judge Anzilotti, series A/B, No. 58, p. 181.
[501]   ICJ *Passage through the Great Belt* case (*Finland* v. *Denmark*), Order of 19 July 1991, Separate Opinion of Judge Shahabuddeen, p. 34.
[502]   ICJ *Passage through the Great Belt* case (*Finland* v. *Denmark*), Order of 19 July 1991, Separate Opinion of Judge Shahabuddeen, pp. 28-36. See also section 3.6 on provisional measures and prejudgment.
[503]   Merrills (1995), p. 107.
[504]   Separate Opinion of Judge Treves, referring to §§70 and 77 of ITLOS *Southern Bluefin Tuna* cases, Order of 27 August 1999.

He noted that this conclusion was confirmed by 'the discretionary nature of the functions of the Tribunal in proceedings on provisional measures'.[505]

Indeed, international adjudicators sometimes use the standard of *'prima facie* evidence', but they do not indicate exactly what this means. According to Kazazi the stage of evidence referred to as *prima facie* is 'an inevitable stage for the distribution of the burden of proof, without which there will be no case to require the respondent's answer'.[506] Judge Laing is correct in pointing out that to use a single inflexible standard at the stage of provisional measures would do no justice to the different contexts. Nevertheless, it does seem that international adjudicators apply some standard, and the concept of *prima facie* evidence for purposes of provisional measures seems sufficiently flexible.[507]

5.3.3 The preventive and precautionary principles

Provisional measures by the ICJ (and ITLOS) are often based on the principle of prevention of irreparable harm.[508] The preventive and precautionary principles are principles that could trigger a policy (or judicial) decision to take temporary measures or that relax the evidentiary requirements for taking measures to prevent harm.[509] If adjudicators apply these principles in their decisions on the merits, this approach may equally be reflected in their decisions on provisional measures. After all, the standard of risk to be met for provisional measures is anyhow more relaxed than the evidentiary standard in the main case. Since provisional measures and the preventive and precautionary principles have the common aim of *preventing* harm, information on the latter principles could potentially be useful to clarify the criteria for the use of provisional measures as well.

References to the precautionary principle in international documents on environmental law are of more recent date (second half of the 1980s) than references to the preventive principle. The latter principle can be traced back to international environmental documents of the 1930s.[510] The preventive principle is broader than the precautionary.[511] References are normally made to the preventive principle when a causal relationship can already be established between the act or omission and serious or irreparable harm and when the probability of the risk can be established either quantitatively or qualitatively. In the latter case it should be possible to indicate, for

---

[505]   ITLOS *M/V 'Saiga'* (No. 2), Order of 11 March 1998, Separate Opinion of Judge Laing, §§2-13.

[506]   Kazazi (1996), pp. 326-327.

[507]   Black's Law Dictionary, providing definitions on the basis of US law, defines *prima facie* as follows: at first sight; on the first appearance; on the face of it; so far as can be judged from the first disclosure; presumably; a fact presumed to be true unless disproved by some evidence to the contrary. It defines prima facie evidence, among others, as evidence good and sufficient on its face. "Such evidence as, in the judgment of the law, is sufficient to establish a given fact, or the group or chain of effects constituting the party's claim or defence and which if not rebutted or contradicted, will remain sufficient". Black's Law Dictionary, West Publishing Co., St. Paul, Minn., 1990 (6th ed.).

[508]   See section 3 of this Chapter, focusing on this purpose of provisional measures in general international law.

[509]   See for in-depth discussions of various aspects of the precautionary principle e.g. Wibisana (2008); Vos/Van Calster (eds.) (2004); Douma (2003); Faure/Vos (eds) (2003); Marr (2003); Trouwborst (2002); O'Riordan/Cameron/Jordan (2001) and Freestone/Hey (1996). In literature on risk assessment 'risk' relates to cause and effect and refers to the probability or likelihood that this damage will indeed be caused as well as to the magnitude of this damage. This cannot be measured exactly. The term 'uncertainty' is used for a situation in which the probability and magnitude of the harm cannot be pinpointed.

[510]   Sands (2003), p. 267.

[511]   Trouwborst (2002), p. 35.

instance, whether the risk is negligible, small or high. Depending on the value attached to a certain right or interest even scientific evidence of a slight risk could be sufficient to trigger the preventive principle and halt the act or remedy the omission. The preventive principle 'seeks to minimise environmental damage as an objective in itself'.[512] This means that States may be obliged to prevent harm to the environment not only if it involves cross-border harm but also if it involves harm to the environment within their own jurisdictions.[513] In that respect there is a clear correlation between human rights law and the preventive principle in environmental law.[514] Sands notes that the preventive principle 'prohibits activity which causes or may cause damage to the environment in violation of the standards established under the rules of international law'.[515] The preventive principle is reflected in State practice, supported by domestic legislation and international standards as well as by the emphasis in international legal documents on the need to carry out environmental impact assessments and provide access to environmental information.[516]

There is no generally accepted definition of the precautionary principle. In fact various States, adjudicators and commentators use 'approach', 'principle', 'preventive' and 'precautionary' in different ways. The precautionary principle becomes relevant if there is insufficient or conflicting evidence (e.g. conflicting risk assessments) on the causal relationship. It could also play a role if the probability of the risk cannot be determined although there is indeed scientific evidence about a causal relationship.[517] Traditionally the party alleging the risk was forced to provide sufficient scientific evidence of such risk, necessitating urgent action. This often meant that by the time such evidence was available the harm had already been done. This harm could be long lasting or even irreversible. The precautionary principle, first found in the legal systems of certain States,[518] was introduced exactly to deal with situations of scientific uncertainty about risks to the environment or to health. Given the gravity of the harm that could otherwise result, certain acts should be halted or certain omissions addressed without the obligation to wait for full scientific certainty about the risk.

One interpretation of the principle has been laid down in the Rio Declaration.[519] Principle 15 stipulates:

> "In order to protect the environment, the precautionary approach shall be widely applied by States according to their capabilities. Where there are threats of serious or irreversible damage, lack of full scientific certainty shall not be used as a reason for postponing cost-effective measures to prevent environmental degradation".

Many international and regional instruments, binding and non-binding, have referred to the principle.[520] It is not yet firmly established as a rule of customary international law although it has widely been resorted to by policy makers. Many international legal documents (mainly involving environmental law) have referred to it, some of them in binding provisions.[521]

---

[512]   Sands (2003), p. 246.
[513]   See Sands (2003), p. 246 (setting it off against Principle 21 of the Rio Declaration, a principle flowing from State sovereignty).
[514]   See further Chapter XV on Immediacy and risk in human rights adjudication, with specific references to the preventive and precautionary approach.
[515]   Sands (2003), p. 247.
[516]   For references see Sands (2003), p. 247. See also Chapter XIII on beneficiaries and consultation.
[517]   See e.g. Trouwborst (2002), pp. 35-44.
[518]   E.g. the *Vorsorgeprinzip* in Germany.
[519]   Rio Declaration on environment and Development, June 1992, A/CONF.151/26 (Vol. I).
[520]   For an overview of such references see Trouwborst (2002).
[521]   See the references in Sands (2003). Trouwborst (2002) and Douma (2003) argue that, in environmental law, the principle has acquired customary international law status.

As Sands puts it in relation to the Rio Declaration on Environment and Development (1992) and its statement that lack of full scientific certainty 'shall not be used' to prevent action:

> "What remains open is the level at which scientific evidence is sufficient to override arguments for postponing measures, or at which measures might even be required as a matter of international law".[522]

If precautionary or preventive measures would be *required* under international law the adjudicator could order them. If they are only allowed, the adjudicator could accept them as a justification by States for certain acts or omissions. The precautionary principle could be argued to support 'shifting the burden' of proof (even if not formally) so that companies or States planning to carry out a certain activity must show that there is no (impermissible) risk to the environment. While in some interpretations the damage risked does not need to be 'serious' or 'irreversible', in other interpretations the burden only shifts from the party alleging to the party allegedly causing the threat once it has been established that the damage risked would indeed be 'serious' or 'irreversible'.[523]

Thus far the ICJ has not referred to the precautionary principle, even though in the 1995 French *Nuclear Tests* cases New Zealand and the intervening States had invoked it.[524] In his dissent Judge Weeramantry did consider the precautionary principle and the fact that it could shift the burden of proof.[525] Two years later, in *Gabcikovo-Nagymaros* (1997), the ICJ again failed to take into account the precautionary principle. This case dealt with Hungary's argument that the suspension of works on a hydroelectric dam (under a bilateral treaty) could be justified because of a 'state of necessity'. It invoked the argument of ecological necessity. According to the ICJ a state of necessity could not exist without a 'peril'. It acknowledged that this word evoked the idea of 'risk' and that this was what distinguished 'peril' from material damage. However, 'the mere apprehension of a possible "peril" could not suffice in that respect'.[526] On the other hand, as Sands points out, the ICJ was examining the legal situation in 1989 when Hungary had suspended

---

[522] Sands (2003), p. 273.

[523] See e.g. the examples given by Sands (2003), pp. 270-272. Sands notes about shifting the burden in the latter context that there is 'growing evidence to suggest that this interpretation is beginning to be supported by state practice, even if it still falls short of having sufficient support to allow it to be considered a rule of general application', p. 273 and references therein.

[524] See ICJ Request for an examination of the situation in accordance with paragraph 63 of the Court's judgment of 20 December 1974 in the *Nuclear Tests* case (*New Zealand* v. *France*), request by New Zealand, §105.

[525] Request for an examination of the situation in accordance with paragraph 63 of the Court's Judgment of 20 December 1974 in the *Nuclear Tests* cases, Order of 22 September 1995, Dissenting Opinion of Judge Weeramantry, pp. 317-362, in particular pp. 342-344. "New Zealand has placed materials before the Court to the best of its ability, but France is in possession of the actual information. The principle then springs into operation to give the Court the basic rationale for considering New Zealand's request and not postponing the application of such means as are available to the Court to prevent, on a provisional basis, the threatened environmental degradation, until such time as the full scientific evidence becomes available in refutation of the New Zealand contention". He considered that New Zealand would have been entitled to a consideration of its request for provisional measures. See also the Dissenting Opinion of Judge Ad Hoc Palmer, pp. 381-421, in particular p. 412.

[526] ICJ *Gabcikovo-Nagymaros* (*Hungary* v. *Slovakia*), Judgment of 25 September 1997, §54. This case had been brought before the ICJ by common Agreement between the parties. It was included in this Agreement that the parties would not request provisional measures.

its work on the dam project and at that time 'the precautionary principle had not yet emerged and could not realistically be applied as general international law'.[527]

The International Tribunal for the Law of the Sea (ITLOS) has been more willing to relax the evidentiary standard for the party claiming risk to the environment and, implicitly, to apply the precautionary principle. It seems to have taken provisional measures on the basis of the precautionary principle, or at least the precautionary approach, in the *Southern Bluefin Tuna* cases (1999). In this case it noted that the parties should act with 'prudence and caution' to prevent 'serious harm'.[528] It also noted that there was 'scientific uncertainty' about the measures to be taken.[529] While it could not conclusively assess the scientific evidence presented by the parties, 'measures should be taken as a matter of urgency to preserve the rights of the parties and to avert further deterioration of the southern bluefin tuna stock'.[530] It ordered the parties, among others, not to conduct experimental fishing programs.[531] In their separate opinions Judge Treves and ad hoc Judge Shearer explicitly referred to the precautionary approach.[532]

While the precautionary principle involves situations of scientific uncertainty it is still necessary to provide some evidence of risk before it can be used as a justification for halting certain developments.

A question that has arisen, apart from the status of the principle and its applicability to health and other issues outside of environmental law,[533] is whether it is mainly a principle to be used by policy makers or whether it also serves a function before the courts and other adjudicators. Clearly international adjudicators have to deal with it if States use it as a justification for an infringement upon the rights claimed by the other party. Yet in my view adjudicators may take into account the precautionary approach not just as a justification by States for their policy making (including certain acts or omissions) but also as an indication of how to approach the evidentiary requirements when dealing with a request for provisional measures.[534]

---

[527] Sands (2003), p. 275.

[528] See ITLOS *Southern Bluefin Tuna* cases (*New Zealand v. Japan; Australia v. Japan*), Order of 27 August 1999, §77.

[529] Id., §79.

[530] Id., §80.

[531] For the protective measures required in provisional measures see section 3.7 of this Chapter.

[532] Judge Treves noted in his Separate Opinion that he would have preferred it if the tribunal had explicitly stated that in the case at hand 'the requirement of urgency' was 'satisfied only in the light of such precautionary approach', §8; Ad Hoc Judge Shearer noted that the provisional measures were 'rightly based upon considerations deriving from a precautionary approach', p. 6. See about the precautionary principle or approach and the law of the sea Marr (2003).

[533] In the *Beef Hormones* case the WTO Appellate Body noted that it was not clear whether the precautionary principle could already be considered a rule of customary international law. It pointed out, however, that it was 'unnecessary, and probably imprudent' for it to take a position on this question and that 'the precautionary principle, at least outside the field of international environmental law, still awaits authoritative formulation'. WTO Appellate Body, report of 16 January 1998, WT/DS48/AB/R, §123. The industry has criticised the use of the precautionary principle in relation to policy on food safety as creating an impossible burden of proof for food products and ingredients, see e.g. Hathcock (2000).

[534] As Treves notes, 'the precautionary approach can be seen as a logical consequence of the need to ensure that, when the arbitral tribunal decides on the merits, the factual situation has not changed'. Separate Opinion of Judge Treves, ITLOS *Southern Bluefin Tuna* cases (*New Zealand v. Japan; Australia v. Japan*), Order of 27 August 1999, §9. He noted that the Order of the Tribunal had hinted at a precautionary approach, in particular in §77 in relation to the future conduct of the parties. He regretted that the order did not explicitly state that a precautionary approach was also necessary in the Tribunal's assessment of urgency.

6   THE LEGAL STATUS OF PROVISIONAL MEASURES

It has not always been clear whether the provisional measures by the ICJ were legally binding. This was due mainly to the wording of Article 41 ICJ Statute, referring to the power to 'indicate' provisional measures, which 'ought' to be taken. Different from the ICJ Statute the more recent UN Convention on the Law of the Sea (UNCLOS) stipulates the power to 'prescribe' rather than 'indicate' provisional measures.[535] In other words, its provisional measures are clearly legally binding.

The legal controversy on the legal status of provisional measures by the World Court had already started with the PCIJ Statute.[536] Scholarly views differed as to the question whether the provisional measures of the PCIJ and ICJ were legally binding. Dumbauld, for instance, considered the provisional measures of the PCIJ not to be legally binding.[537] Other authors adhered to a functional interpretation and argued that even if the wording of Article 41 was ambiguous (e.g. 'indicate'), the power itself to indicate provisional measures was a necessary attribute of the judicial function. Fitzmaurice wrote that '(t)he whole logic of the jurisdiction to indicate interim measures entails that, when indicated, they are binding – for this jurisdiction is based on the absolute necessity, when the circumstances call for it, of being able to preserve, and to avoid prejudice to, the rights of the parties, as determined by the final judgement of the Court'.[538] Various authors regard the obligation to respect provisional measures a general principle of law.[539]

---

[535] See Article 290 UNCLOS and Article 25 of Annex VI of UNCLOS (Agreement relating to the implementation of Part XI of the United Nations Convention on the Law of the Sea of 10 December 1982, New York, 28 July 1994).

[536] In ICJ *Military and Paramilitary Activities in and against Nicaragua (Nicaragua v. US)*, Judgment of 27 June 1986 it re-emphasized its Order of 10 May 1984. It noted that it was 'incumbent upon each party to take the Court's indications seriously into account'. "Particularly is this so in a situation of armed conflict where no reparation can efface the results of conduct which the Court may rule to have been contrary to international law", §§288-289. In *Application of the Convention on the prevention and punishment of the crime of genocide (Bosnia and Herzegovina v. Yugoslavia (Serbia and Montenegro))*, Order of 13 September 1993 (second request) the ICJ noted in passing that, unlike its final judgments, its Orders had no 'binding force' or 'final effect' 'in the decision of any dispute'. It referred to the PCIJ decision in *Free Zones of Upper Savoy and the District of Gex*, Order of 19 August 1929. Nevertheless, it reiterated that Yugoslavia must immediately and effectively implement its 'first order to prevent and cease any act of genocide'. But see the Separate Opinions by Judges Weeramantry and Ajibola, discussed infra. In a 1996 article Judge Oda wrote that the Court 'has never taken an overt position in this respect but, as a matter of principle, the Court's "Order" ought to be properly observed' and '(i)f the later judgement on the merits is rendered in favour of the applicant State, the respondent State may be made responsible for any action taken in defiance of the provisional measures', Oda (1996), p. 555. See also Beirlaen (1984-1985), pp. 739-775 and Rosenne (2005), p. 157 (on the *Nicaragua* case) and p. 179 (on the consequences of disrespect for the Court's provisional measures before *LaGrand*).

[537] Dumbauld (1932), p. 169. See also p. 173 (in the absence of express wording).

[538] Fitzmaurice (1986), p. 584. See in general on the functional approach Elkind (1981).

[539] See e.g. Collins (1992-III), p. 216. See also the remarks of Pescatore and Oellers-Frahm at the colloquium in Bernhardt (ed.) (1994b), pp. 121-122 and pp. 146-147 respectively. For the opposite view, see, eg. Herdegen, id., p. 126. Cançado Trindade recently observed a 'doctrinal trend' to consider provisional measures as 'equivalent to a true general principle of law, common to virtually all national legal systems, and endorsed by the practice of national, arbitral, and international tribunals', ICJ *Questions relating to the obligation to prosecute or extradite*

A provisional measure has no force of *res iudicata* as the decision on the merits still needs to be taken. It is, however, a general principle of law that, pending the proceedings before a Court, the status quo must be maintained.[540] In 1953 Cheng put it as follows:

> "The reason why an international tribunal may exercise this power even when its jurisdiction as to the merits is yet uncertain must be sought in the fact that the duty of the parties to maintain the status quo already exists independently of any judicial intervention".[541]

In the words of Crockett '(a)lthough [provisional measures] are not res iudicata, they do enrich or diminish a party's legal position so that (...) monetary or restitutionary liability for a violation of an order indicating interim measures would be entailed. To hold that interim measures have no legal effect would be tantamount to rendering them nullities'.[542]

In his Separate Opinion in the *Genocide Convention* case (1993) Judge Weeramanty argued that provisional orders are part of the inherent authority of a judicial tribunal, as a general principle and for reasons of practical necessity. One of the principles he mentioned in support of this view is 'the wide and universal recognition of the enjoining powers of courts as an inherent part of their jurisdiction'.[543] Equally, Judge Ajibola pointed out that provisional measures influence the outcome of the adjudication and should therefore be considered part of the judgment.[544] After all 'an order, like a judgement (and being incidental to it) ought not to be ineffective, artificial or illusory. It should be binding and enforceable, otherwise, *ab initio*, there may be a good and reasonable ground to question it being issued at all. The Court, it is submitted, should not be seen to act in vain'.[545]

In its judgment in *LaGrand* (2001) the ICJ finally determined that its provisional measures were legally binding. It applied a purposive interpretation to deal with the ambiguities of Article 41 ICJ Statute.[546] It followed from the object and purpose of the Statute and from 'the terms of Article 41 when read in their context', that the power to indicate provisional measures entailed 'that such measures should be binding, inasmuch as the power in question is based on the

---

(*Belgium* v. *Senegal*), Order of 28 May 2009, dissenting opinion of Judge Cançado Trindade, §13.

[540] See PCIJ *Electricity Company of Sofia and Bulgaria* (*Belgium* v. *Bulgaria*), Order of 5 December 1939, p. 194.

[541] Cheng (1953), p. 273.

[542] Crocket (1977), p. 384.

[543] ICJ *Application of the Convention on the Prevention and Punishment of the Crime of Genocide* (*Bosnia and Herzegovina* v. *Yugoslavia (Serbia and Montenegro)*), Order of 13 September 1993, Separate Opinion Judge Weeramantry.

[544] ICJ *Application of the Convention on the Prevention and Punishment of the Crime of Genocide, Provisional Measures* (*Bosnia and Herzegovina* v. *Yugoslavia (Serbia and Montenegro)*), Order of 13 September 1993, Separate Opinion Judge Ajibola, §5.

[545] Ibid. See also Ajibola (1996).

[546] It noted that it was faced with two texts (the French and the English), which were not 'in total harmony'. It pointed out that both texts were equally authentic. It then referred to Article 33(4) Vienna Convention on the Law of Treaties, 'which in the view of the Court again reflects customary international law'. This provision reads: "When a comparison of the authentic texts discloses a difference of meaning which the application of Articles 31 and 32 does not remove the meaning which best reconciles the texts, having regard to the object and purpose of the treaty, shall be adopted". It then considered the object and purpose of the ICJ Statute together with the context of Article 41 Statute: "The context in which Article 41 has to be seen within the Statute is to prevent and Court from being hampered in the exercise of its functions because the respective rights of the parties to a dispute before the Court are not preserved". ICJ *LaGrand* (*Germany* v. *US*), Judgment of 27 June 2001, §102.

necessity, when the circumstances call for it, to safeguard, and to avoid prejudice to, the rights of the parties as determined by the final judgment of the Court'.[547] "The contention that provisional measures indicated under Article 41 might not be binding would be contrary to the object and purpose of the Article".[548]

The ICJ also referred to the principle 'universally accepted by the international tribunals and likewise laid down in many conventions (...) to the effect that the parties to a case must abstain from any measure capable of exercising a prejudicial effect in regard to the execution of the decision to be given, and, in general, not allow any step of any kind to be taken which might aggravate or extend the dispute'.[549] It noted that it has frequently indicated Orders designed to avoid aggravating or extending disputes, which it had 'indicated with the purpose of being implemented'.[550]

The Court considered that there are no other sources or interpretations contradicting the Court's conclusions as drawn from the terms of Article 41, read in their context and in the light of the object and purpose of the Statute. Article 94 UN Charter did not prevent Orders made under Article 41 from having a binding character and neither did the preparatory work.[551]

Since the Court's judgment in *LaGrand* its provisional measures cannot be considered other than legally binding.[552] Its decision did not seem to depend on the nature of the rights to be protected. In other words, the ICJ 'did not equivocate' in holding that its provisional measures were legally binding, 'nor did it narrow the application of its holding to death penalty cases, nor even danger to life cases'. It attributed 'legal effect to all its orders for provisional measures, irrespective of content and context'.[553] In sum, the text of the ICJ Statute includes a reference to

---

[547]   ICJ *LaGrand* (*Germany* v. *US*), Judgment of 27 June 2001, §102.

[548]   Ibid.

[549]   It referred to PCIJ *Electricity Company of Sofia and Bulgaria*, Order of 5 December 1939.

[550]   The ICJ refers to several of its Orders, see §103 of *LaGrand* (*Germany* v. *US*), Judgment of 27 June 2001.

[551]   See ICJ *LaGrand* (*Germany* v. *US*), Judgment of 27 June 2001, §109. Given the conclusions reached in interpreting the text of Article 41 in the light of its object and purpose, the Court did not consider it necessary to resort to the preparatory work in order to determine meaning of the Article. It did, however, point out that the preparatory work of the Statute did not preclude the conclusion that orders under Article 41 are binding. See §§104 and 105-107, discussing the *travaux*. With regard to the US claim that this particular Order was not legally binding because of the way it was phrased the ICJ pointed out that in fact this Order 'was not a mere exhortation'. "It had been adopted pursuant to Article 41 of the Statute". Thus it was legally binding and 'created a legal obligation for the United States', §110. Jennings (2002), p. 35 considers the Court should have paid more attention to the question of Article 94 UN Charter, as manifestly 'of crucial and practical importance'. See further Crocket (1977), p. 376. See in general on the Court's approach to the binding nature of provisional measures in *LaGrand*; Orakhelashvili (2002), pp. 116-121, pointing out, correctly, that the Court's approach can be explained by the principle of effectiveness, p. 119.

[552]   For varying views on the reasoning of the Court, see e.g Weckel (2005); Oellers-Frahm (2001a); Jennings (2002), Mennecke and Tams (2002) and Kammerhofer (2003). For a different approach see Yoshiyuki Iwamoto (2002), p. 365, somehow arguing that provisional measures should nevertheless 'have *no* binding force in cases where the criteria for indicating measures have not been satisfied, including the situation in which the rights to be protected may not fall within the scope of *prima facie* jurisdiction'. In such case, he considers, 'an order on provisional measures should not be conceived as a proper one'. "If it were, it would pose the risk of creating an' interim judgment' or a binding decision over a matter which might be irrelevant to the actual dispute before the Court". Naming *Breard* and *LaGrand* as possible examples of such cases he seems to imply that it is for States to consider whether the criteria have been satisfied.

[553]   Harrington (2003), p. 76.

provisional measures and the Court's purposive interpretation of this text has resulted in the finding that provisional measures are binding in all cases.

7   FOLLOWING UP ON OFFICIAL STATE RESPONSES

The general rate of compliance with the ICJ's provisional measures is not impressive.[554] It is not clear to what extent this relates to the fact that it was only in 2001 that the ICJ established the obligatory character of its provisional measures, but in the context of the *Genocide Convention* case (1993-2007) this has certainly been suggested.[555]

Apart from the responses of other States and other actors as well as the media, the follow-up of the ICJ itself is important because it indicates how seriously it takes its own Orders. What may also play a role in increasing effectiveness is the transparency of the Court's decision-making, particularly its reasoning. Judge Kooijmans has noted that 'a court should make clear in its reasoning that it is fully aware of the wider context and the complexity of the issues involved'. This would help 'make its legal assessments and conclusions comprehensible and thereby acceptable to litigant States whose leaders are no trained lawyers (even though they may be assisted by legal professionals), but are the main actors in the process of implementing the judgement'.[556] This section, however, deals with the Court's monitoring of the implementation of its own provisional measures.

7.1   ICJ Rules on follow-up

In 1978 the ICJ formally included a Rule on follow-up in its Rules of Court. Article 78 stipulates that the ICJ 'may request information from the parties on any matter connected with the implementation of any provisional measures it has indicated'. The ICJ has generally requested such information in its initial Order, but Article 78 does not rule out the use of subsequent Orders, indicated *proprio motu*, to remind States of their obligations under Orders for provisional measures. The inclusion of Article 78 does not seem to have been inspired by humanitarian considerations, but rather more generally by considerations of effectiveness.[557] In the *Hostages* case (1979) the ICJ for the first time noted in an Order for provisional measures that it would keep the case continuously under review.[558] Later, in the context of Orders to halt the execution of a death sentence, it also specifically noted that the addressee States should inform it of the measures taken to comply with its Order.[559] On the other hand, despite the serious nature of the

---

[554]   See e.g. Savadogo (2002), pp. 378-380. On compliance with its judgments see e.g. Paulson (2004) and Ajibola (1996) and Schwebel (1996a). For a thorough discussion of compliance with the ICJ's judgments and provisional measures, see in particular Schulte (2004).

[555]   ICJ *Application of the Convention on the Prevention and Punishment of the Crime of Genocide (Bosnia and Herzegovina v. Yugoslavia (Serbia and Montenegro))*, Order of 13 September 1993, Separate Opinion Judges Weeramantry and Ajibola. See also, e.g., Gaffikin (1995), p. 460 and p. 468.

[556]   ICJ *Armed Activities on the Territory of the Congo (Congo v. Uganda)*, Judgment of 19 December 2005, Separate Opinion of Judge Kooijmans, §4. See also Cassel (1999b), p. 887.

[557]   See Rosenne (2005), p. 178, referring to the two Orders in the *Fisheries Jurisdiction* cases, requesting the Applicant States to provide both the Court and the Respondent with all relevant information.

[558]   ICJ *US Diplomatic and Consular Staff in Tehran (US v. Iran)* (*Hostages* case), Order of 15 December 1979.

[559]   ICJ *Breard (Paraguay v. US)*, Order of 9 April 1998, *LaGrand (Germany v. US)*, Judgment of 27 June 2001; Avena et al. (*Mexico v. US*), Order of 5 February 2003 and ICJ *Request for*

cases in question, in its Orders in the *Genocide Convention* case (1993) and *Congo* v. *Uganda* (2000), it did not include a specific requirement for the addressee States to inform it of the measures taken in compliance.[560]

7.2 ITLOS Rules on follow-up

ITLOS does include in its Orders for provisional measures a formal obligation to report on measures taken in compliance. In Rule 95 of the ITLOS Rules of Procedure each Party 'shall inform the Tribunal as soon as possible as to its compliance (...). In particular, each party shall submit an initial report upon the steps it has taken or proposes to take'. In its Orders prescribing provisional measures ITLOS includes the date by which the Parties are to submit their initial reports. It may also request further information.[561]

7.3 Follow-up in death penalty cases

The US death penalty cases are particularly relevant in the context of a discussion on compliance. In the first case the ICJ ordered the US to halt the execution of Paraguayan national Angel Breard. The only step undertaken by the US in response was a letter sent by the Secretary of State Madeleine Albright to Jim Gilmore, the Governor of Virginia, asking him to halt the execution temporarily, because carrying it out at that time 'could lead some countries to contend incorrectly that the US does not take seriously its obligations'.[562] At the same time, however, the Clinton administration urged the US Supreme Court *not* to halt the scheduled execution.[563] Administration lawyers said the sole measure available to the US government for complying with the provisional measures was 'persuasion', not 'legal compulsion through the (US) judicial system'.[564] Angel

---

     interpretation of the judgment of 31 March 2004 in the case concerning Avena and other Mexican nationals (Mexico v. US), Order of 16 July 2008. See also *Frontier Dispute case (Burkina Faso v. Mali)*, Order of 10 July 1986.

[560] ICJ *Application of the Convention on the prevention and punishment of the crime of genocide (Bosnia and Herzegovina v. Yugoslavia (Serbia and Montenegro))*, Order of 8 April 1993 (Bosnia had invoked Article78 Rules of Court in both requests for provisional measures, but without response by the Court, see Rosenne (2005), p. 178) and *Armed activities on the territory of the Congo (Congo v. Uganda)*, Order of 1 July 2000. See also *Land and maritime boundary between Cameroon and Nigeria (Cameroon v. Nigeria)*, Order of 15 March 1996.

[561] See Rosenne (2005), p. 180.

[562] Reuters, 14 April 1998. A reference was also made to the rather unfair justice systems in many parts of the world, see Amnesty International (1998), p. 4.

[563] See e.g. Amnesty International (1998), p. 4, describing that the US government told the Supreme Court that the assistance of consular officials would not have changed the outcome of the proceedings and that for this reason no stay of execution should be granted despite the ICJ's provisional measure. Thus, it seems, the same arguments were used by the US before the US Supreme Court (*after* the provisional measures were indicated), that were rejected by the ICJ. The Solicitor General argued, among others, that 'the ICJ's Order indicating provisional measures should not be accorded comity, not should it be considered binding by the Supreme Court', Aceves (1998), p. 520. See also footnote 17: "David Andrews, the Legal Adviser of the Department of State, co-signed the amicus brief on behalf of the United States. Mr Andrews had appeared as the U.S. Agent before the ICJ barely a week earlier". See also Wilson (1998), p. 9: "These government lawyers, who had purported to honor the international court's jurisdiction the week before, now argued to the highest domestic court in the United States that the ICJ's ruling was "not binding" and that its order was merely "precatory" in nature-in other words, that the ICJ's ruling was not entitled to any legal deference in the U.S. courts".

[564] Reuters, 14 April 1998.

Francisco Breard was executed, as planned, on 14 April 1998 by the commonwealth of Virginia. After his execution Albright apparently said the US 'did the right thing'.[565]

In cases in which provisional measures are requested and ordered, often the arguments of the Parties on the merits and those on the provisional measures are linked together. The US invoked arguments of federalism, separation of powers and domestic rules of procedure. Its Supreme Court had indicated that it must decide questions presented to it 'on the basis of law'. 'The Executive Branch, on the other hand,' it stated, 'in exercising its authority over foreign relations may, and in this case did, utilize diplomatic discussion with Paraguay. Last night the Secretary of State sent a letter to the Governor of Virginia requesting that he stay Breard's execution. If the Governor wishes to wait for the decision of the ICJ, that is his prerogative. But nothing in our existing case law allows us to make that choice for him'.[566] In effect this means it considered that a decision by the ICJ is not 'law', the US Supreme Court never makes new law, and the issue was solely a matter for 'diplomatic discussion'. The US Supreme Court's decision marked the end of Breard's life, since the US government felt it could not do anything apart from requesting the Governor of Virginia to postpone the execution and urging the Supreme Court not to do that.[567] The ICJ's provisional measures were meant to ensure that the execution would not take place during the course of the proceedings before it. By ignoring these and executing Breard, the US not only showed disrespect for the ICJ, but also rendered it impossible to award the specific remedy claimed by Paraguay, namely *restitutio in integrum*.[568]

The ICJ did not have an opportunity to comment on the US disrespect for its Order to halt the execution of Paraguayan citizen Breard, as Paraguay requested a discontinuance of the case several months after Breard's execution.[569] In a way the Court's Order to halt the execution of German citizen Walter LaGrand could be seen as a follow-up on the US non-compliance in Breard in that the Court pointed out that the responsibility of the Respondent State is engaged by the actions of all its composite parts and that the federal authorities must transmit the Order to, in this case, the Governor of Arizona, who was in turn obliged to act in compliance with the ICJ's Order.[570]

Nevertheless, Walter Lagrand was executed. Different from Paraguay Germany maintained the case. Thus, in its judgment in *LaGrand* the ICJ did have the opportunity to follow-up on its Order for provisional measures. It determined that the US had not complied. It did note that this measure did not create an obligation of result and agreed that 'due to the extremely late presentation of the request for provisional measures, there was certainly very little time for the

---

[565] Reuters, 16 April 1998.

[566] US Supreme Court, *Breard v. Greene*, 523 U.S. 371 (1998) (14 April 1998).

[567] See also Aceves (1998) p. 523 calling it 'disquieting' that the final decision on compliance with treaty obligations and provisional measures are entrusted to state rather than federal authorities and Wilson (1998), p. 1 wondering why it fell to a state governor 'to effectively decide the legal force of a decision of an international tribunal'.

[568] See further Rieter (1998) as well as the contributions in Agora, *American Journal of International Law* (1998); Aceves (1998); Klabbers (1998) and Wilson (1998). For a different approach see Bradley (1998-1999) arguing that the 'internationalist conception' of the relation between international and US law is inconsistent with the traditionally 'dualist' approach and unlikely to be to be accepted by US authorities.

[569] ICJ *Breard (Paraguay v. US)*, Order of 9 April 1998; Request by Paraguay for a discontinuance (2 November 1998); Order of 10 November 1998 to remove the case from the List. As Paraguay initially expressed its intention to continue the case after the execution of its national, there has been speculation on possible pressure subsequently exerted on this State that could explain its request to remove the case from the List.

[570] ICJ *LaGrand (Germany v. US)*, Order of 3 March 1999, §28.

United States authorities to act'.[571] Nevertheless it observed that 'the mere transmission of its Order to the Governor of Arizona without any comment, particularly without even so much as a plea for a temporary stay and an explanation that there is no general agreement on the position of the United States that orders of the International Court of Justice on provisional measures are non-binding, was certainly less than could have been done even in the short time available'.[572] It also commented on the Solicitor General's letter to the US Supreme Court:

> "The same is true of the United States Solicitor General's categorical statement in his brief letter to the United States Supreme Court that 'an order of the International Court of Justice indicating provisional measures is non-binding and does not furnish a basis for judicial relief'".[573]

The ICJ reflected on the decision of the Governor of Arizona as well:

> "It is also noteworthy that the Governor of Arizona, to whom he Court's Order had been transmitted, decided not to give effect to it, even though the Arizona Clemency Board has recommended a stay of execution for Walter LaGrand".[574]

Finally, it commented on the decision of the Supreme Court which had rejected a separate application by Germany for a stay of execution, although 'it would have been open to the Supreme Court, as one of its members urged, to grant a preliminary stay'.[575] The ICJ summarised the situation as follows: 'the various competent United States authorities failed to take all the steps they could have taken to give effect to the Court's Order'. The Order did not require the US to 'exercise powers it did not have', but it did impose the obligation to 'take all measures at its disposal to ensure that Walter LaGrand is not executed pending the final decision in these proceedings'. It found that the US did not discharge this obligation.[576]

In other words, in its judgment in *LaGrand* the ICJ clearly followed up the non-compliance with its Order, by singling out the roles of various US authorities and explain that it had not ordered anything out of the ordinary. Yet for several reasons it did not attach additional consequences to its finding of non-compliance. It observed that Germany, in its third submission, only requested the Court to 'adjudge and declare' that the US violated its international legal obligation to comply with the Order. It contained no other request regarding that violation. "Moreover, the Court points out that the United States was under great time pressure in this case, due to the circumstances in which Germany had instituted the proceedings". It further noted that 'at the time when the United States authorities took their decision the question of the binding character of orders indicating provisional measures had been extensively discussed in the literature, but had not been settled by its jurisprudence. The Court would have taken these factors into consideration had Germany's submission included a claim for indemnification'.[577]

The US attitude towards the provisional measures by the ICJ displayed in *Breard* and subsequently in *LaGrand* may be explained by a (latent) hostility towards international law and a high level of ignorance by some members of Congress and of some domestic courts as to its

---

[571] ICJ *LaGrand* (*Germany* v. *US*), Judgment of 27 June 2001, §111.

[572] Id., §112.

[573] Id., §112.

[574] Id., §113.

[575] Id., §114.

[576] Id., §115.

[577] Id., §116. See also on the *LaGrand* Judgment: Orakhelashvili (2005); Cassel (2002); Fitzpatrick (2002); *LaGrand* Symposium (2002); Mckie (2002); Mennecke/Tams (2002); Orakhelashvili (2002); Rieter (2002); Schiffman (2002); Hirsch Ballin (2001); Oellers-Frahm (2001a).

contents and meaning.[578] To some extent this situation appeared to be changing. Combined with the fact that some actors may gradually have become used to the idea of the ICJ's provisional measures and judgments in *LaGrand* and *Avena*, more and more critical voices in the US itself resort to arguments based on international and comparative law.[579] The US respected the Order for provisional measures in *Avena* (2003).[580] In response to the Judgment (2004) in this case the President this time gave a clear message to the Attorney General about the need to comply.[581]

Yet, as noted, at the same time the US withdrew from the Optional Protocol to the VCCR, blocking any future efforts by other States to bring a conflict regarding this treaty to the ICJ for resolution.[582] In addition, the US Supreme Court has now found that 'neither the *Avena* Judgment on its own, nor the Judgment in conjunction with the President's memorandum, constituted directly enforceable federal law' precluding Texas from "applying state procedural rules that barred all review and consideration of Mr. Medellín's Vienna Convention claim"'.[583]

As discussed, the subsequent Order for provisional measures by the ICJ was based on a request for interpretation of the *Avena* judgment. In this context the discussion arose as to whether one could speak of a legal dispute on interpretation as required by Article 60 ICJ Statute.[584] In its provisional measure itself the Court again included the obligation of the State to inform it of the implementation measures undertaken.[585] In any case, subsequently both the US Supreme Court and the State of Texas ignored the ICJ's Order for provisional measures and Medellin was

---

[578]   See e.g. the reaction at the ICJ's provisional measures by a spokesperson for Jesse Helms (chairman of the Senate Foreign Relations Committee) who, as Amnesty International puts it, 'appeared to have forgotten that the USA entered into the terms of the Vienna Convention voluntarily'. He condemned the Court's decision in the following words: "It is an appalling intrusion by the United Nations into the affairs of the State of Virginia. (…) There is only one court that matters here. That's the Supreme Court. There's only one law that applies. That's the United States Constitution". Cited in *Amnesty International* (1998), p. 4.

[579]   The US Supreme Court itself, for instance, has referred to international and comparative law in its decision on the death penalty for minors. Yet with regard to the VCCR it confirmed its earlier decision in *Breard* v. *Greene*, 523 U.S. 371, see *Sanchez-Llamas* v. *Oregon*, 548 U.S. 331 (2006). See also *Medellin* v. *Dretke*, 544 U.S. 660 and Kirgis (2006). See further Chapter XVII (Official responses) and opinion poll conducted by Knowledge Networks, 'Americans on International Courts and their Jurisdiction over the US', 11 May 2005, <www.worldpublicopinion.org/pipa/pdf/may06/Tribunals_May06_rpt.pdf>.

[580]   ICJ *Avena* (*Mexico* v. *US*), Order of 5 February 2003. The death sentence against Torres was commuted to life imprisonment and the other two beneficiaries were not executed either. See e.g. Murphy (2004), pp. 581-584 and Shelton (2004a).

[581]   See section 3.3.7 of this Chapter.

[582]   Most significant in this respect was the aforementioned quote of State Department spokesman Ereli: 'we have a system of justice that provides people with due process and review of their cases, and it's not appropriate that there should be some international court that comes in and reverses decisions of our national courts' in: 'U.S. quits foreign inmate accord', CNN.com, 11 March 2005. This indicates at least a double message on the meaning of US obligations, this one meant for an internal rather than international audience.

[583]   US Supreme Court *Medellín v. Texas*, [US] 552 U.S. _ (2008), 128 S. Ct. 1346 (25 March 2008). See also section 3.3.7 of this Chapter.

[584]   ICJ *Request for interpretation of the judgment of 31 March 2004 in the case concerning Avena and other Mexican nationals* (*Mexico* v. *US*), Order of 16 July 2008. See further section 3.3.7 of this Chapter.

[585]   ICJ *Request for interpretation of the judgment of 31 March 2004 in the case concerning Avena and other Mexican nationals* (*Mexico* v. *US*), Order of 16 July 2008, §80.

executed.[586] The Court has observed that the US failed to discharge of its obligation under its Order. This is not a very strong response, but at least it is combined with the observation that it is for the Court and not the parties to determine the Court's jurisdiction.

When States have agreed, under international law, to have the ICJ resolve any conflicts they may have regarding the interpretation of a treaty, these conflicts are certainly not resolved if individual states in a federation choose to ignore its Orders or Judgments and if they do so, the State concerned bears full responsibility.

7.4   Follow-up in the context of armed conflict

In its judgment in the *Nicaragua* case (1986) the ICJ specifically discussed the failure of the Parties to fully comply with its Order of provisional measures.[587] In its judgment in *Burkina Faso* v. *Mali* (1986) the ICJ Chamber referred to its Order of January 1986 and noted 'with satisfaction that the Heads of State of Burkina Faso and the Republic of Mali have agreed "to withdraw all their armed forces from either side of the disputed area and to effect their return to their respective territories"'.[588]

In the *Genocide Convention* case (1993) Bosnia requested additional provisional measures within four months of the Court's first Order. Instead, the ICJ reaffirmed that its previous Order

---

[586]   US Supreme Court 552 U.S. _ (2008), 128 S. Ct. 1346 (25 March 2008) (5-4 *per curiam* decision). One of the dissenters, Justice Breyer, pointed out that the execution should have been stayed, among others because of the ICJ Order; because 'legislation has been introduced in Congress seeking to provide the legislative approval necessary to transform our international legal obligations into binding domestic law. See *Avena* Case Implementation Act of 2008, H. R. 6481, 110th Cong., 2d Sess. (2008) (referred to committee, July 14, 2008)'; because 'prior to *Medellín*, Congress may not have understood the legal need for further legislation of this kind. That fact, along with the approaching election, means that more than a few days or weeks are likely necessary for Congress to determine whether to enact the proposed Legislation' and because 'to permit this execution to proceed forthwith places the United States irremediably in violation of international law and breaks our treaty promises'. He also pointed out that 'different Members of this Court seem to have very different views of what this case is about. In my view, the issue in this suit – what the majority describe as the "beginning premise" – is not whether a confession was unlawfully obtained from petitioner'(..). 'Rather, the question before us is whether the United States will carry out its international legal obligation to enforce the decision of the ICJ. That decision requires a further hearing to determine whether a conceded violation of the Vienna Convention (Texas' failure to inform petitioner of his rights under the Vienna Convention) was or was not harmless'. Obviously, the fact that non-compliance with the Court's judgment may be brought before the UN Security Council is simply one method of enforcement that cannot be used as an excuse for domestic courts not to implement international law obligations, especially those obligations that should indeed be regarded as self-executing for the reasons provided in the dissent by Breyer, in a domestic system in which treaties are in any case considered the supreme law of the land. See further on this case the contributions of the *Medellín* symposium (*Suffolk Transnational Law Review* 2008) such as the pertinent remarks by Paust, pp. 303-333 on the supremacy clause, self-execution and, in particular the role of the UN Security Council.

[587]   ICJ *Military and Paramilitary Activities in and against Nicaragua* (*Nicaragua* v. *US*), Judgment on the merits of 27 June 1986, §§286-291. See also Reichler (2001). See on Nicaragua's attempt to renew its request for provisional measures Rosenne (2005), pp. 170-172.

[588]   ICJ *Burkina Faso* v. *Mali*, Judgment of 22 December 1986, §§177-178.

'should be immediately and effectively implemented'.[589] In this light its response in its judgment on the merits to Serbia's non-compliance with its provisional measures was rather weak (2007).[590]

In its judgment in *Congo* v. *Uganda* (2005) it dealt with the issue of non-compliance, but only on request by the applicant State. It concluded that Uganda had not complied with its Order of July 2000. Congo had requested the Court to declare so, but it had not submitted specific evidence in this regard. Yet the Court pointed out that it had just found Uganda responsible for acts of killing, torture and other forms of inhuman treatment in violation of international human rights and humanitarian law carried out by its military forces against Congolese civilians.[591] Specifically it found violations of the right to life and the prohibition of torture and cruel treatment in international and African human rights treaties.[592] These violations had been continued after the Court's Order for provisional measures.[593] The ICJ added that it had in fact addressed its provisional measures to both Parties and that its finding on the non-compliance by Uganda did not mean that the Congo 'did not also fail to comply' with its measures.[594]

In a separate opinion Judge Kooijmans considered that the Court should have dismissed Congo's submission on Uganda's non-compliance, as it had not met the burden of proof. He noted that the formulation chosen by the Court seemed 'to indicate an awareness' that neither Uganda nor the Congo had respected the provisional measures. He considered that it would have been 'judicially sound' not to have found that Uganda had not complied with its Order on provisional measures, although he had 'no doubt whatsoever that Uganda breached its obligations under the Order'. Yet the evidentiary requirements and the purpose of provisional measures to protect the 'legal interests of either party' caused him to regret the ICJ's finding that one of the Parties had violated the Order for provisional measures.[595]

The claims brought by the Congo related to acts that took place after the provisional measures were ordered while the counter-claims by Uganda, to the extent they were accepted by the Court, did not, making it more difficult for the Court to comment on violations of the provisional measures by Congo. The ICJ may have considered that its freedom to deal with information not based on the applications of the Parties is more limited at the stage of the merits

---

[589] ICJ Application of the Convention on the prevention and punishment of the crime of genocide (*Bosnia and Herzegovina* v. *Yugoslavia (Serbia and Montenegro)*), Order of 13 September 1993 (second request), §53. See further Toufayan (2005), Gaffikin (1995) and Wiebalck (1995). See also Wellens (1998), p. 424 ("This conclusion not only reinforces the view of the Court as to the effects to be given to any order indicating provisional measures, but it also exemplifies sound judicial reasoning, keeping the balance between the awareness of the limits of the Court's power over effective implementation and the need to closely reassess all the circumstances since the making of the previous order").

[590] Of course this also related to the fact that it did not find Serbia responsible for complicity, but only for failure to prevent. In this context it referred to the failure to observe its provisional measures as an element in establishing the State's responsibility for failure to prevent. Yet it appeared to attach no other consequences to the State's failure to observe its provisional measures.

[591] ICJ *Armed Activities on the Territory of the Congo* (*Congo* v. *Uganda*), Judgment of 19 December 2005, §345.

[592] Articles 6 (1) and 7 ICCPR; Articles 4 and 5 ACHPR; Article 38 (2) and (3) Convention on the Rights of the Child and Articles 1, 2, 3 (3), (4), (5) and (6) of its Optional Protocol on child soldiers. See ICJ *Armed Activities on the Territory of the Congo* (*Congo* v. *Uganda*), Judgment of 19 December 2005, §219.

[593] ICJ *Armed Activities on the Territory of the Congo* (*Congo* v. *Uganda*), Judgment of 19 December 2005, §264.

[594] Id., §265.

[595] ICJ *Armed Activities on the Territory of the Congo* (*Congo* v. *Uganda*), Judgment of 19 December 2005, Separate Opinion of Judge Kooijmans §§74-78.

than at the stage of provisional measures. Nevertheless, this may not be the case in the context of following up on its own Orders for provisional measures. The Court itself appears to be the most appropriate body to monitor compliance with its provisional measures. *Proprio motu* examination of publicly available materials is in fact warranted in this context even if the Parties fail in bringing such materials to the Court's attention. In addition, international organisations could take a more active approach, assisting the Court in its function of monitoring compliance with its provisional measures by invoking the possibility of Article 69(2) Rules of Court. This Article stipulates:

> "When a public international organization sees fit to furnish, on its own initiative, information relevant to a case before the Court, it shall do so in the form of a Memorial to be filed in the Registry before the closure of the written proceedings. The Court shall retain the right to require such information to be supplemented, either orally or in writing, in the form of answers to any questions which it may see fit to formulate, and also to authorize the parties to comment, either orally or in writing, on the information thus furnished".

Moreover, in certain cases the Court could implicitly invite such organisations to provide pertinent information by notifying them of relevant pending cases.[596]

Ad hoc judge Kateka attached a dissenting opinion to the Court's judgment. He invoked the 'clean hands' theory and considered that the Court's finding of Uganda's non-compliance showed a 'lack of concern' for the actions taken by the Congo to raise this issue against Uganda when it itself had committed grave violations of human rights and international humanitarian law.[597]

Yet when discussing the protection of human beings even-handedness should not play the role suggested by Kateka. Otherwise the actor suffering the consequences of this approach would be the individual, who in the present constellation can only be represented by his State. Rightly, the Court was not swayed by the 'clean hands' argument, which would have left the individual without any form of legal protection just because his State did not have clean hands.

Indeed, if a 'clean hands' theory would have a role to play, the Court could easily address it in its phrasing of provisional measures, as it did in this case by ordering *both* Parties to take the necessary measures to ensure full respect for fundamental human rights and the applicable provisions of humanitarian law. Moreover, the subsequent expression by the Court in its Judgment of an awareness that both Parties may have failed to comply with its Order seems sufficient to deal with any disingenuousness on the part of the Congo.

While the ICJ did point out that its Orders on provisional measures under Article 41 had binding effect[598] and that they 'created legal obligations which both Parties were required to comply with', it simply found,[599] that Uganda did not comply with its Order of 2000. It did not attach any specific consequences to this finding.[600] As noted, in its judgment in the *Genocide Convention* case (2007) took a similar approach.[601] In any future cases of non-compliance it is to be hoped that the Court will take an approach that is gradually more robust.

---

[596] See Article 43(2) of the Rules of Court, as amended 29 September 2005. The international organisations referred to in Article 69 are organisations of States.

[597] ICJ *Armed Activities on the Territory of the Congo* (*Congo* v. *Uganda*), Judgment of 19 December 2005, Dissenting Opinion of Judge Kateka, §61.

[598] Referring to *LaGrand* (*Germany* v. *US*), Judgment of 27 June 2001, §109.

[599] It did so by 15 votes to 2 (Judge Kooijmans and Judge ad hoc Kateka dissenting).

[600] Its finding on the obligation to make reparation for the injury caused was made before its finding on non-compliance with its provisional measures.

[601] CJ ICJ *Application of the Convention on the prevention and punishment of the crime of genocide* (*Bosnia and Herzegovina* v. *Yugoslavia (Serbia and Montenegro)*), 26 February 2007. More

8   CONCLUSION

As Judge Higgins wrote in 1997, 'the evolving jurisprudence on provisional measures shows a growing tendency to recognize the human realities behind disputes of states'.[602] Generally speaking the rationale behind the use of provisional measures is to ensure a meaningful outcome of a case brought before a court or other adjudicator. More specifically, the traditional purposes of provisional measures as used by the ICJ are twofold. The first is the preservation of rights, the breach of which is both imminent (or already taking place) and likely to cause irreparable harm to the rights claimed. The second, applied only incidentally, is the preservation of proper legal proceedings. In other words, in the first case there should be a link between the right and remedy claimed and the provisional measure and in the second case there should be a link between the provisional measure and the purpose of having a fair and accurate procedure.[603]

On the other hand the ICJ has occasionally used provisional measures for reasons not necessarily closely related to the rights claimed or to the proceedings. It has taken provisional measures in border conflict cases, not only to maintain the status quo in relation to the claim, but also to prevent irreparable harm to civilians living in the border area. Their rights were not the (main) subject of a State's request for provisional measures against another State but 'collateral' to the dispute.[604] This would indicate that the ICJ, as an adjudicator not primarily dealing with human rights, has developed a certain sensitivity towards the plight of human beings caught up in conflicts between States. In any case it shows that in the practice of the ICJ the traditional twofold distinction may have been extended to a threefold distinction: to prevent irreparable harm to the claim, to the procedure or to individuals not central to the dispute.

Cançado Trindade has noted that human rights treaties have set limits to State voluntarism, creating a 'new vision of the relations between public power and the human being, which is summed up, ultimately, in the recognition that the State exists for the human being, and not vice-versa'.[605]

As Crocket already pointed out in 1977, referring to the Court's general power to order provisional measures, jurisdiction to do so 'would appear to be more closely related to the inherent power of an international tribunal to determine its own jurisdiction than to the doctrine that jurisdiction is conferred through the consent of the parties'.[606]

The ICJ is not a human rights court. It does not even deal with individual complaints. Yet in spite of the limitations it is faced with as an adjudicator dealing only with inter-State complaints, it does seem to realise the importance of the protection of groups and individuals. Moreover, for conceptual reasons its use of provisional measures is relevant to the practice of the human rights adjudicators. It may be, for instance, that the unequivocal confirmation of the binding nature of its provisional measures in *LaGrand* will contribute to better compliance by States, not just of its own provisional measures,[607] but also in the context of provisional measures by other international adjudicators. After all the ICJ referred to the inherent function of adjudicators to order preservation of the status quo pending the proceedings, invoking the general principle that States must not allow any step to be taken that might aggravate the dispute.

---

generally on this case, see e.g. Amerasinghe (2008); Ben-Naftali/Sharon (2008); Goldstone/Hamilton (2008); Dupuy (2007); Sivakumaran (2007); Sorel (2007) and Weckel (2007).

[602]   Higgins (1997), p. 108.

[603]   This includes hearing both parties on the basis of equality of arms and preserving the evidence.

[604]   Higgins (1997), pp. 101-102 and pp. 107-108.

[605]   IACHR *Blake* v. *Guatemala*, Judgment on reparations of 22 January 1999, Separate Opinion Judge Cançado Trindade, §33.

[606]   Crocket (1977), p. 379.

[607]   Indeed, the US respected the subsequent provisional measures in *Avena*.

The ICJ's finding in *LaGrand* that its provisional measures are legally binding is not made dependent on the fact that basic rights of the human person were involved, but is simply part of its traditional function. The power to indicate binding provisional measures is required by the object and purpose of Article 41 ICJ Statute and 'based on the necessity, when the circumstances call for it, to safeguard, and to avoid prejudice to, the rights of the parties as determined by the final judgment of the Court'.[608]

At the same time some of the conflicts between States in which the ICJ orders provisional measures may indeed concern the rights of individuals and the (human rights) obligations of States towards them.[609] This only underscores the importance of the inherent powers of adjudicators in this respect. In such cases its provisional measures may either aim to halt measures that could result in irreparable harm to a large group of people (armed activities, nuclear tests, etc), or aim at the (diplomatic) protection of specific individuals (halt execution of a death sentence; release persons held hostage).

Various aspects of the Court's orders for provisional measures specifically show its receptiveness to the fate of human beings. In the *Chorzów factory* (1927) case, concerning a request to grant a pecuniary claim at the provisional measures stage, rather than to secure rights basic to the human being, the PCIJ was strict and refused to order provisional measures. It considered that the request coincided with the claim on the merits and was in fact a request for an interim judgment. On the other hand, without breaking with *Chorzów factory*, the ICJ did take provisional measures in the *Nuclear Test* cases (1973).[610] While it did not explain the difference, it is likely, especially in light of subsequent cases, that it took into account the enormity of the possible consequences to the environment and population of the Applicant States. In the *Hostages* case (1979) it again ordered provisional measures overlapping to a great extent with the main claim. What distinguishes these cases from the *Chorzów factory* case is that they involved the fate of human beings.

The ICJ equally has relaxed the strict requirement that the Applicant State should not only specify the rights invoked in the context of the request for provisional measures, but that these should also be related to the main claim. This involves cases, for instance, of armed conflict in which the States may not necessarily be as interested in the fate of the people living in the disputed areas as the Court itself. It is particularly relevant in border conflict cases in which the Court has added references to so-called 'collateral' claims, involving 'collateral damage' to people. It may even be argued that the Court could introduce *proprio motu* a reference to the obligations of States vis-à-vis these people, based on the merest opening in this respect in one of the submissions of one of the Parties.[611]

In some cases, at the stage of provisional measures, the Court was yet to determine on the merits whether a certain act or omission by a State would indeed constitute a violation of the rights invoked by the other State (e.g. the *Nuclear Test* cases). In other cases it was clear that certain acts or omissions constituted a violation of the rights invoked, but the dispute related to evidence and/or imputability (e.g. *Hostages* case and *DRC* v. *Uganda*).

The ICJ has also taken into account the basic rights of the individual in its attitude towards procedural requirements. In a particularly urgent case it has used provisional measures in advance of a hearing on the use of provisional measures: in an Order to halt the imminent execution of an individual it was prepared to 'reward' the State involved for submitting the claim and request for provisional measures strategically late, as the individual facing execution could hardly be punished for his State being procedurally remiss. Had the claim only involved pecuniary interests, rather than the life of an individual, such decision would have been unlikely.

---

[608] ICJ *LaGrand* (*Germany* v. *US*), Judgment of 27 June 2001, §102.

[609] See generally e.g. Sohn (1982).

[610] Only two of the judges considered this approach incorrect, as rewarding an attempt to obtain an 'interim judgement'.

[611] For a different approach see Yoshiyuki Iwamoto (2002).

In some cases States may invoke human rights treaties. Even if they act on the basis of diplomatic protection rather than *erga omnes* obligations they in fact ask the ICJ to interpret State obligations under human rights treaties and, therefore, to take into account the rights of the individuals concerned. In such cases the assessment of the risk involved and the role of the beneficiaries may differ from the approach normally taken by the ICJ in its use of provisional measures and approximate more closely the provisional measures taken by human rights adjudicators.[612] At the same time, as noted, States may sometimes be involved in legal disputes that have developed into military conflict, with their citizens caught in the middle. If the States involved bring the case before the Court and request provisional measures, not particularly invoking the rights of the individuals, the ICJ nevertheless takes into account the basic rights of the individual. As a result the provisional measures ordered may differ from those requested. In general the Court seems to be more resourceful in drafting Orders for provisional measures different from those requested when the case involves the fate of human beings: it refers to the obligations of both Parties and it adds the obligation not to aggravate the dispute, referring to its task in the maintenance of peace and security.

The more recent decisions to take provisional measures in the consular protection/death penalty cases, on the one hand, and on mass human rights violations, on the other, are a confirmation of the progressive developments described by Higgins.[613] In this sense they constitute examples of the humanization of international law observed by various authors.[614]

Already in 1960, in *Honduras* v. *Nicaragua*, the ICJ noted that the reference to 'judicial decisions' in Art 38(1)(d) of the ICJ Statute is not limited to ICJ case law alone. At the time the ECtHR was barely in existence and the other international adjudicators were not even established yet.[615] The subsequent Chapters deal with the judicial decisions by the human rights adjudicators in urgent cases since 1960. International human rights law may considerably enhance public international law in general and the ICJ extensively referred to it in its Advisory Opinion on the *Wall in the occupied Palestinian territory* (2004). It considered the text and object and purpose of human rights treaties, referred to the 'constant practice' of the supervisory bodies to these treaties, invoking their authoritative case law, General Comments and Concluding Observations.[616]

---

[612] The most interesting source for comparison would be the practice of the human rights adjudicators of using provisional measures in inter-State proceedings, but there is not much practice in this regard. Only the ECtHR has had to deal with requests for provisional measures in inter-State proceedings.

[613] Higgins (1997). For discussion of subsequent developments see e.g. Rieter (1998); Addo (1999); Feria Tinta (2001); Rieter (2002); Schabas (2002b); Orakhelashvili (2002); Shelton (2004a); Ghandhi (2004); Milano (2005); Dugard (2007); Higgins (2007); Pronto (2007); Bedi (2007). For an approach considering the Court's new reasoning 'artificial' see Jennings (2002) and Yoshiyuko Iwamoto (2002).

[614] See e.g. Buergenthal/Sohn (1973); Van Boven (1982); Simma (1993); Buergenthal (1997); Higgins (1998); Meron (2000); Flinterman (2000); Kamminga (2001); Seiderman (2001); Cançado Trindade (2004); Meron (2006).

[615] ICJ *Arbitration Judgment of the King of Spain of 1906* (*Honduras* v. *Nicaragua*), Judgment of 18 November 1960, pp. 204-217. See also the Separate Opinion of Judge Cançado Trindade in the judgment on preliminary objections in IACHR *Constantine et al.* v. Trinidad and Tobago, 1 September 2001, §34.

[616] ICJ Advisory Opinion on the Legal Consequences of the Construction of a Wall in the Occupied Palestinian Territory, 9 July 2004, §§107-114 and 136.

Cançado Trindade has pointed out that human rights law enables the law of treaties to evolve and to regulate legal relations between and within States and that by affirming contemporary legal principles human rights law in fact enriches and legitimises general international law.[617]

Indeed, the practice of the ICJ indicates, albeit tentatively, that adjudicators not exclusively dealing with human rights may develop sensitivity for the plight of human beings caught up in conflicts between States, with its consequential effects on the concept of provisional measures.[618]

---

[617] IACHR *Blake* v. *Guatemala*, Judgment on reparations of 22 January 1999, Separate Opinion Judge Cançado Trindade §§27-28. He also considered that the emphasis on positivism and on States as the main subjects of international law is simply a product of the time, rather than 'eternal and immutable truths'. In fact, given the growing importance of human rights, the 'almost mechanical application' of so-called truths, such as the autonomous will of the State, has become inappropriate. IACHR *Blake* v. *Guatemala*, Judgment on reparations of 22 January 1999, Separate Opinion Judge Cançado Trindade, §§28-29.

[618] As a Judge at the ICJ Cançado Trindade subsequently observed that 'we are living the infancy' of the ICJ's jurisprudential development relating to provisional measures. He noted that the Court had not yet pronounced on the autonomy of its Orders for provisional measures, nor on the legal consequences of non-compliance, nor on issues of state responsibility in this respect. *Questions relating to the Obligation to Prosecute or Extradite (Belgium v. Senegal)*, Order of 28 May 2009, dissenting opinion Judge Cançado Trindade, §97.

CHAPTER II
THE USE OF PROVISIONAL MEASURES IN THE CONTEXT OF THE VARIOUS HUMAN RIGHTS SYSTEMS

1   INTRODUCTION

This Chapter introduces the human rights adjudicators referred to in this book: the Human Rights Committee (HRC), the Committee against Torture (CAT), the Inter-American Commission (CIDH)[1] and Court of Human Rights (IACHR), the African Commission on Human and Peoples' Rights (ACHPR), the European Commission and Court of Human Rights (ECtHR) and the Bosnia Human Rights Chamber. The other two UN Committees, the Committee on the Elimination of Racial Discrimination (CERD) and the Committee on the Elimination of Discrimination against Women (CEDAW) are only mentioned briefly, lacking extensive practice with regard to the use of provisional measures. The same applies for the recently established African Court of Human and Peoples' Rights.

The Chapter sets out the rules on provisional measures in the context of the respective individual complaint systems. For each system it briefly sums up the situations in which provisional measures have been used, their context (institutional setting and the right of individual complaint), the power of the adjudicator to use provisional measures and the promptness with which it uses them and, finally, the sources about provisional measures used for this book (under the heading 'transparency or the lack thereof').[2]

The Chapter concludes with a brief discussion of the authority to use provisional measures, the importance of motivating them and the general issue of convergence and divergence.[3] As to the latter, the overview presented in this Chapter serves to highlight commonalities as well as differences between the systems. This contextual information may help explain why the respective practices of the adjudicators, discussed in the subsequent chapters, converge or diverge.

2   HUMAN RIGHTS COMMITTEE

2.1   Introduction

The HRC, supervising compliance with the ICCPR, has mostly used provisional measures to halt execution of the death penalty. In addition it has used provisional measures to inquire about the health situation of detainees, to halt expulsions and corporal punishment, to find a missing person and to ensure access to counsel. Moreover, it has used them in cases involving indigenous culture (e.g. when a company is allowed to log trees in a traditional grazing area), in a family life case, in

---

[1]   The Spanish acronym CIDH is used: Comisión Interamericana de Derechos Humanos, so as to distinguish it from IACHR. In this book IACHR stands for Inter-American Court of Human Rights.

[2]   Because of variations in the availability of information the discussion on procedure and promptness is more extensive with regard to some systems than with regard to others.

[3]   The subsequent Chapters more extensively discuss the practice of the adjudicators. While this Chapter, for instance, deals with the competence of the various adjudicators to use provisional measures, Chapter XIV deals with the relevance of jurisdiction on the merits for the use of provisional measures and Chapter XVI deals with the legal status of these measures.

a case involving death threats and in a freedom of expression case (to halt the destruction of a painting).

This section discusses the institutional setting of the provisional measures as used by the HRC and the right of individual petition, the power to order provisional measures, the promptness of the adjudicator in deciding on the use of provisional measures and the availability of information on the use of these measures.

2.2 The right of individual complaint: the HRC and the OP to the ICCPR

The ICCPR entered into force in 1976 and has 160 States parties.[4] The HRC, consisting of 18 independent experts, supervises to what extent the States parties respect the ICCPR. The first Optional Protocol (OP) to the ICCPR lays down the right of individual complaint. It does not explicitly refer to the power to take provisional measures, but in 1977 the HRC included this possibility in its Rules of Procedure.[5]

In order to clarify the Committee's use of provisional measures it is sometimes helpful to consult not just its case law on the merits and inadmissibility, but also other sources of information on its interpretation of rights. The Committee's activities under the reporting procedure are one of three sources of information on its interpretation of rights. As part of the reporting procedure (under Article 40 ICCPR) States parties must periodically send in reports explaining how their legislation and practice answer to the obligations they assumed under the treaty. In a discussion that takes place in public a delegation of the State answers questions posed by Committee members. The HRC then publishes its official comments on the State report as Concluding Observations.[6] The second source of information is the publication by the HRC of General Comments on specific rights or issues.[7] In order to clarify the concept of provisional measures the third source of information is obviously the most important: the decisions of the HRC on individual complaints.

Bringing a case (an individual complaint) before the Committee is only possible if the State against which the complaint is directed has pre-committed itself to the individual complaint procedure under the first Optional Protocol (OP) to the ICCPR. Under this Protocol, 110 States have recognised the right of persons under their jurisdiction to submit individual complaints to the Committee.[8]

---

[4]   Treaty concluded in 1966, entered into force 1976, 160 States Parties according to the data provided by the UN High Commissioner on Human Rights (last updated 20 July 2007): <http://untreaty.un.org> (accessed 29 November 2007).

[5]   It did so as Rule 86. In August 2004 its Rules of Procedure were renumbered. Now Rule 92 is the Rule on provisional measures. Still, most of the quotes are from cases published prior to that date and they refer to Rule 86. This list provides an overview of the most relevant Rules:

Provisional measures	Rule 86 (old) →Rule 92 (new)
Transmission to State/request for information	Rule 91 (old) →Rule 97 (new)
Designation of Special Rapporteurs	Rule 89 (old) →Rule 95 (new)
Confidentiality	Rule 96 (old) →Rule 102 (new)

[6]   Where relevant this book also refers to these Concluding Observations. See generally Boerefijn (1999a).

[7]   Where relevant reference is made to these General Comments throughout this book.

[8]   Treaty concluded in 1966, entered into force 1976, 110 States Parties according to the data provided by the UN High Commissioner on Human Rights (last updated 11 October 2007): <http://untreaty.un.org> (accessed 29 November 2007). On exhaustion see Article 5 OP. As Harrington puts it, States have granted the right of individual petition to over a billion people in the world, Harrington (2003), p. 64.

The petitioners must claim to be a victim of a provision of the ICCPR. Individuals claiming such a violation before the HRC can do this only after they have exhausted domestic remedies. In other words, they must first try and get redress before the courts of the State against which they are bringing a claim. This way, this State has the opportunity to resolve and remedy the situation before it ends up at the international level. Only when they have exhausted domestic remedies or when no effective remedies are available, victims of human rights violations may resort to the Committee to find redress.[9] Victims initiate such a complaint by writing a letter to the Committee's Secretariat in Geneva. When the letter contains insufficient information, the Secretariat specifies to the petitioner (usually called 'author' and sometimes 'applicant') the additional information necessary for the registration of the complaint.[10] Petitioners do not need to travel to Geneva as the procedure is conducted entirely in writing. Both the petitioner and the respondent State have the opportunity to respond to each other's submissions. It is an adversary procedure based on equality of arms. The parties must comply with certain procedural requirements. The Committee has denied many claims as *prima facie* unsubstantiated. It has denied other claims because the alleged facts occurred before the ICCPR entered into force for the State in question. It also declares a complaint inadmissible if it is not based on any provision of the Covenant or is even contrary to the Covenant or if it includes insulting language to the State concerned.

For many individuals the Committee is the first (quasi-) judicial body dealing with their complaint about violations of Covenant provisions, because these were never properly addressed before domestic courts. In other cases domestic courts may have been uncertain about the proper interpretation of certain provisions. In such situations the Committee can provide the necessary clarifications.

The State parties against which complaints have been lodged vary considerably. Examples are Canada, Argentina, the Netherlands, Zambia, and Georgia. The subject matter varies as well. The Committee has ruled about issues ranging from disappearances to the right to equality. Many cases have dealt with the right to a fair trial or detention issues. The first cases under the OP, in the late 1970s and early 1980s, were almost all directed against Uruguay.[11]

2.3 The power and promptness of the HRC to take provisional measures

2.3.1 Introduction

This section discusses the power to use provisional measures, the need to delegate this power, the promptness of the intervention with regard to certain issue areas, possible explanations for tardiness, the manner in which the Addressee State is contacted, other relevant Rules of Procedure and the possibility to take provisional measures *proprio motu*.

---

[9] More generally on ICCPR law and the proceedings under the OP see e.g. Barkhuysen/Van Emmerik/Rieter (2008); Nowak (2005); Joseph/Schultz/Castan (2004); Vandenhole (2004); Conte/Davidson/Burchill (2004); Carlson/Gisvold (2003); Bayefsky (2002); Young (2002); Bayefsky (2001); De Zayas (2001); pp. 67-121; Scheinin (2001), pp. 129-145; Bayefsky (2000); Evatt (1998), pp. 86-115; Ghandhi (1998); Schmidt (1998), pp. 13-18; O'-Flaherty (1996); McGoldrick (1994); Zwart (1994); and Schmidt (1992), pp. 645-659.

[10] This book uses the term petitioner.

[11] Other Latin American countries such as Argentina, Chile or Paraguay ratified the OP much later, namely in 1986, 1992 and 1995 respectively.

2.3.2 The power of the HRC to use provisional measures

While the text of the OP itself does not include a reference to the use of provisional measures, the HRC has developed a practice of using them. Under Article 39(2) ICCPR the HRC shall establish its own rules of procedure. In March 1977 the HRC discussed these, including the introduction of a rule on provisional measures.[12] The issue that came up most often was the question whether the HRC had indeed the power to take provisional measures and, if so, whether it could delegate this power to subsidiary organs.[13] It drafted the following Rule, then Rule 86, now Rule 92:

> "The Committee may, prior to forwarding its Views on the communication to the State party concerned, inform that State of its Views as to whether interim measures may be desirable to avoid irreparable damage to the victim of the alleged violation. In doing so, the Committee shall inform the State party concerned that such expression of its Views on interim measures does not imply a determination on the merits of the communication".

2.3.3 Promptness and delegation

The Committee is only in session three times a year. In 1977, during the drafting process of the Rule on provisional measures, Committee member Espersen (Denmark) already referred to the delays involved in the Committee's procedures and mentioned the issue of the death penalty as an example. He emphasised the need to avoid irreparable harm to the petitioner. These delays 'made it quite possible that the execution of a sentence by a State, especially the execution of the death penalty, would make the whole case obsolete'. The Rule should be such that 'the Committee or a subsidiary group should be able to reach a quick decision on interim measures'.[14] Several members of the HRC indeed considered that there should be an arrangement to deal with provisional measures in between sessions.[15] Cold War politics, however, initially prevented the inclusion of a rule allowing delegation of the competence to take provisional measures to a Rapporteur or Working Group.[16] Nevertheless, the text of the Rule did not exclude the possibility of a subsidiary

---

[12] In February and March 1977 the Secretary General had submitted 'preliminary draft provisional rules of procedure'. These included the following rule on provisional measures: "The Committee, or the Group referred to under rule 88 below after consultation with the Chairman of the Committee, may at any time request the State party concerned to take interim measures in order to avoid irreparable damage to the victim of the alleged violation. In doing so, the Committee or the Group shall inform the State concerned that such a request does not imply a determination as to the admissibility or the substantive validity of the communication". Preliminary draft provisional rules of procedure submitted by the Secretary-General, CCPR/C/L.2 and Add. 1 and 2, 28 February, 2 and 4 March 1977; draft Rule 86 was initially issued in CCPR/C/L.2/Add. 2 on 4 March 1977. See Yearbook of the Human Rights Committee 1977-1978, Vol. II, 1986. It was partly inspired by the Rules of Procedure of the Committee on the Elimination of Racial Discrimination. During its thirteenth and seventeenth meeting, chaired by Mavrommatis (Cyprus), the members of the Committee discussed this proposal.

[13] Summary records of the meetings of the first session, thirteenth meeting, 29 March 1977 and seventeenth meeting, 31 March 1977, Yearbook of the HRC 1977-1978, Vol. I, CCPR/1 pp. 44-46 and 54.

[14] Ibidem.

[15] See Sir Vincent Evans (UK); Uribe Vargas (Colombia); Prado Vallejo (Ecuador); Espersen (Denmark); Opsahl (Norway) and Tomuschat (Federal Republic of Germany).

[16] Several members, predominantly of Eastern European States, did not want to delegate the power to use provisional measures: Graefrath (former German Democratic Republic); Koulishev (Bulgaria); Movchan (USSR). See summary records of the meetings of the first session, 13th meeting, 29 March 1977 and 17th meeting, 31 March 1977, Yearbook of the HRC 1977-1978,

body contacting the State on urgent matters. The summary records indicate that the Committee preferred to leave open this question for the time being.[17]

In response to the increasing number of petitions by persons on death row the HRC finally introduced a Special Rapporteur in 1987. This Rapporteur could then take provisional measures (at least those involving death penalty cases) in between sessions.[18] After all, execution dates are not centred on HRC sessions.

Thus, after about ten years the HRC finally determined the unfinished discussion about the delegation of the power to issue provisional measures. As Tomuschat puts it:

"The death row cases made it abundantly clear that the original line of construing the Protocol, which led to the deletion, in Rule 86, of any reference to subsidiary bodies of the Committee,

---

Vol. I, CCPR/1, pp. 44-46 and 54. Ganji (Iran) considered that any group the HRC would establish would keep it informed of any views communicated to States. If the full Committee disagreed with those views, it could always adopt its own position. "Such instances were likely to be rare, however, since rule 86 provided that views on interim measures should be formulated after consultation with the Chairman of the Committee. It might be useful, nevertheless, to add a sentence in rule 86 stipulating that the views communicated to States concerning interim measures should be brought to the attention of the Committee at its first meeting after the transmission of the views in question". Note that the eventual formulation does not refer to consultation with the Chairman.

[17] The Annual Report 1977 to the General Assembly, describing the adoption of the Rules of Procedure at the Committee's first session, presents the rule on provisional measures as providing that only the Committee but not a subsidiary body may inform a State party of its views whether such measures may be desirable. A/32/44, §56. The next Annual Report to the General Assembly refers to a decision the HRC did take to improve promptness in deciding on urgent cases. It notes that it 'was suggested' that the Committee's application of Rule 86 'should not be subject to the prior inclusion of the communications in the lists of communications'. These lists were prepared by the Secretariat for the Committee's convenience. The persons who suggested this were considering the urgency factor and wished to avoid the hurdle of this formal procedure: '(t)hus the Committee would be in a position to apply rule 86 at an early stage in urgent cases' A/32/44, §175. While the Report does not explain whether all members agreed with this suggestion, it did not refer to any disagreement either. This could be interpreted as an acknowledgment of the possibility to use provisional measures at least prior to the admissibility declaration. See Chapter III on the relevance of admissibility and jurisdiction on the merits.

[18] A/43/40, 28 September 1988, §656, in: Official Records of the Human Rights Committee 1987-1988, Vol. II, CCPR/7/Add. 1. The first 31 sessions the HRC used provisional measures only during sessions. It did so more than 20 times. Its speed ranged from twelve days to almost six months. The first time the HRC used provisional measures was on 21 July 1986, on behalf of Earl Pratt, 210/1986. This was the only time it did so that year. For budgetary reasons there was no proper meeting in the fall of 1986. This may account for the fact that the second time the HRC took provisional measures to halt an execution was seven months later. On the other hand, the Working Group of the HRC did convene between 8 and 10 December 1986 in order to deal with 'urgent cases'. Apparently this did not result in the use of provisional measures. It was in 1987 that it was suddenly faced with many death penalty complaints. Seven months after its first provisional measure on this issue it used a provisional measure again, this time on behalf of Ivan Morgan, 225/1987, 24 March 1987. That same year it used twenty other such provisional measures. *Lloyd Reece* v. *Jamaica* (247/1987), (disc. 1993); *Reid* v. *Jamaica*, 20 July 1990; *A.A.* v. *Jamaica*, 30 October 1989; *Kelly* v. *Jamaica*, 8 April 1991; *W.W.* v. *Jamaica*, 26 October 1990; *Carlton Linton* v. *Jamaica* 22 October 1992; *Michael and Desmond McLean* v. *Jamaica*, 11 April 1991 and *Campbell* v. *Jamaica*, 30 March 1992. On 12 November alone it used provisional measures in eight different cases, all in order to halt an execution. On this day it decided to appoint one of its members as a Special Rapporteur on Death Penalty Cases.

was incompatible with the object and purpose of Rule 86 to enable the Committee swiftly and effectively to address any situation where irreparable harm is looming".[19]

Possibly to satisfy those members of the Committee who were wary of delegating this power to a Rapporteur, the HRC decided to appoint Mr. Mavrommatis (Cyprus), known for his diplomatic approach, to this post. He was not very active in his use of provisional measures.[20] In fact, the pre-session Working Group took most of the provisional measures.[21] It is not clear why he did not take provisional measures more often, since it was in fact his task to deal with the urgent cases when the HRC was not in session.

As of spring 1989 the Committee replaced the Special Rapporteur on Death Penalty cases with a Special Rapporteur on New Communications in order to deal with its increasing caseload. Her task was not only to deal with urgent cases in between sessions but also to authorize registration of all new cases and transmit them to States.[22]

2.3.4 Explaining promptness and tardiness

2.3.4.1 INTRODUCTION

To examine the Committee's promptness in taking provisional measures the first provisional measure decision in a given case, in relation to the date of initial submission, was taken as a point

---

[19] Tomuschat (1995), p. 628.

[20] Presumably Mavrommatis started in his new function at the end of the Committee's session, in December 1987. Only five cases are known in which he used provisional measures. In two of these, almost three months passed before he used them but in one case he took provisional measures within a day. Possibly the Secretariat sent telegrams on his behalf in other cases as well, but if this is the case the HRC failed to mention it in the final decision.

[21] This involved more than 20 cases.

[22] In its Annual Report 1989 the Committee does not yet mention the Special Rapporteur's role with regard to provisional measures. A/44/40, §620 and Annex IX. While in another section the Report refers to the HRC's requests not to carry out death sentences, it does not specify whether the full Committee, a Working Group, the old Special Rapporteur on Death Penalty Cases or the Special Rapporteur on New Communications decided on the provisional measures. In July 1991 the Committee adopted revised terms of reference for the mandate of the Special Rapporteur on New Communications. This included (b) 'to issue rule 86 requests, whether coupled with a request under rule 91 or not' and (c) 'to inform the Committee at each session on action taken under rules 86 and 91'. The Special Rapporteur now takes the decision to transmit a complaint to the State party and to request provisional measures. Annex X, Mandate of the Special Rapporteur on New Communications, revised terms of reference adopted at the 1087th meeting, 24 July 1991, A/46/40, 10 October 1991, in: Official Records of the Human Rights Committee 1990/1991, Vol. II, CCPR/10/Add. 1. In 1987 the HRC requested the State not to carry out the death sentence before it had had an opportunity to consider further the question of admissibility. As of spring 1988 it used a different formulation, by requesting the State not to carry out the death sentence while it was considering the communication. This allowed for a longer duration of the provisional measure. This way the Committee would not need to renew the use of provisional measures after the case was declared admissible. Instead, it could just reiterate them in situations where a State seemed to move towards non-compliance. Even during sessions it is the Special Rapporteur on New Communications rather than the full Committee who decides on the use of provisional measures. Information obtained at the HRC Secretariat in Geneva, September 2003.

of reference.[23] After 1993 the HRC saw an increase in the use of provisional measures.[24] The actions of the subsequent Special Rapporteurs on New Communications have shown that, on occasion, it was possible to intervene within days. Yet it was only over time and with the introduction of modern communication methods that a practice developed of prompt intervention.[25] Since the Rapporteurs became accustomed to the use of e-mail, the HRC often used provisional measures within a day[26] or even on the same day,[27] depending also on resources and alertness at the Secretariat.[28]

---

[23]   While it is possible that the petitioner initially did not request provisional measures, but did so at a later date, not mentioned in the View, in the large majority of cases he requests this as part of his initial communication. Of course in some of these cases the HRC repeats its provisional measures. It must be noted that the promptness of the provisional measure may often depend more on the situation at the Secretariat in Geneva than on the attitude of the Rapporteur.

[24]   In 1998 the number of provisional measures decreased. This may be related to the withdrawal of Jamaica from the Optional Protocol. Jamaica withdrew on 23 October 1997. This became effective on 23 January 1998. On 22 January 1998 the Rapporteur still took provisional measures in HRC *Howell* v. *Jamaica* (2003). The last example of such a decision sent to Trinidad and Tobago dates from 15 January 1999. See *Rawle Kennedy* v. *Trinidad and Tobago*, 28 March 1992. Trinidad and Tobago initially withdrew and re-entered with reservations on 26 May 1998. This would have become effective on 26 August 1998, but the HRC decided to declare admissible a complaint following that date. This decision, of 5 November 1999, related to a case submitted on 7 December 1998 and transmitted to the State with a provisional measure on 15 January 1999 (see 845/1998). Trinidad and Tobago denounced the Optional Protocol once more on 27 June 2000 (now without re-entering). This became effective on 27 September 2000. Some cases submitted before that date may still be pending and, upon final determination, may disclose information about the use of provisional measures.

[25]   Promptness only improved substantially as of 1995. The majority of provisional measures were then issued within days.

[26]   See e.g. HRC *Michael Robinson* v. *Jamaica*, 29 March 2000, initial submission of 9 December 1996, Rule 86/91 of 10 December 1996. In *Brown* v. *Jamaica*, 23 March 1999, the Secretary to the Governor General of Jamaica even commented to counsel on the 'commendable dispatch' of the Committee's request for a stay (letter by counsel of 20 November 1997). Counsel had submitted the request for provisional measures on 12 November 1997 and the Rapporteur transmitted the case under Rule 86/91 on 13 November 1997 (on file with the author).

[27]   See e.g. HRC *Mansaraj et al.; Gborie et al. and Sesay et al.* v. *Sierra Leone*, 16 July 2001. Initial submission of 12 and 13 October 1998; Rule 86 equally on 12 and 13 October 1998; the 18 petitioners had all been sentenced to death on 12 October 1998. There was no right of appeal. See section 5 on the State party's attitude.

[28]   Apart from the lack of resources at the Secretariat and the difficulty to obtain a response from the Rapporteur (initially because of more primitive means of communication) the lack of promptness in the use of provisional measures in the first years might also be explained by the decision of the Rapporteur only to intervene in the face of an actual execution date rather than upon receipt of the complaint. In the autumn of 1995 the HRC 'declared that the competence of the Special Rapporteur to issue, and if necessary to withdraw, provisional measures would continue up until the moment the Working Group on Communications took up the question of admissibility. When the Committee was not in session that competence would be exercised by the Chairman until the Working Group on Communications considered the substance of the case, in consultation, where necessary, with the Special Rapporteur', A/51/40, Vol. I, 1996, §381. It seems that in such cases the Chairman takes over the Rapporteur's task, while the Rapporteur deals with similar new cases. Subsequently the HRC did not provide any information that would indicate changes in the practice of taking provisional measures as a result of this decision. Rapporteur Scheinin reports that there would be at most two days a year in which he could not check his e-mail. Moreover,

In a presentation before CAT, Special Rapporteur Scheinin gave some information about the practical procedure before the HRC:

> "Language problems, which could be very real, were resolved by the Secretariat; the Special Rapporteur needed to know only the essential elements of each case, which was set out for him by the Secretariat in a language at his command. A member of the Human Rights Committee could theoretically continue to serve as a special rapporteur for the duration of his term of office. In practice, the matter was reviewed every two years when the bureau of the Committee was convened, where upon, the Special Rapporteurs for New Communications and for Follow Up on Views were appointed".[29]

Scheinin noted that the Special Rapporteur of the HRC responsible for provisional measures intervenes at a much earlier stage than the pre-sessional working group reviewing draft decisions on admissibility. He intervened 'at the moment when it became necessary to decide to register a communication, and it was generally then that a request addressed to the State party under rule 86 might be appropriate'.[30]

2.3.4.2 DEATH PENALTY CASES

In some cases the HRC seems to have skipped several sessions before it used provisional measures. Any time it takes more than four months to use them it means not only that the Rapporteur did not deal with the case but also that the HRC itself skipped an earlier opportunity to deal with it.[31] This may indicate the role of the Secretariat in suggesting cases for discussion. In any case, apart from exceptional circumstances, the Secretariat only approaches the Special Rapporteur and not the full Committee, even during sessions.[32]

Tardiness of the full Committee or the Special Rapporteur in adopting provisional measures may relate to late receipt of information by the petitioner, to the question whether the Rapporteur can be reached quickly (e.g. through e-mail or by mobile phone) and to the question whether the Rapporteur reacts quickly.[33] It may also relate to shifts within the Secretariat in Geneva or to holiday periods at the Secretariat.[34] If the State only received the Note Verbale with the request for the provisional measures the day before the planned execution or on the day itself, this may also play some role in cases of non-compliance, at least to the extent that the State may use the late receipt as an excuse for having executed the petitioner in defiance of the Committee's provisional measures.[35] Nevertheless, the HRC has determined that the State breaches its obligations

---

the Secretariat could also get hold of him through mobile phone. Interview with Martin Scheinin, Geneva, April 2003.

[29] CAT Summary Records, 27th session, 13 November 2001, CAT/C/SR.487, 10 March 2003, §19.

[30] Id., §17.

[31] See e.g. HRC *A. H.* v. *Trinidad and Tobago*, 31 October 1990 (more than eight months between submission and the use of provisional measures).

[32] Information obtained at the Secretariat in Geneva, September 2003.

[33] At least one Special Rapporteur preferred to receive the complete file rather than the case summaries before he would make decisions. This may have resulted in delay.

[34] An example of the latter is 732/1997. Measures were taken within 18 days, while most provisional measures used during the period Pocar was Rapporteur were taken within days. In this case, however, the Christmas holiday took place subsequent to the submission and previous to the provisional measure.

[35] See HRC *Glenn Ashby* v. *Trinidad and Tobago*, 21 March 2002. Yet the main reason for disregarding the provisional measure in that case seems to be the fact that the deadline set by the JCPC was approaching, beyond which domestic law would forbid execution. In this case the

under the OP when it executes an alleged victim knowing that a case has been brought before the Committee, even if the Committee has not yet itself contacted the State with provisional measures.[36]

In two Belarus cases the HRC was particularly tardy in requesting provisional measures. In fact it requested them only after the executions. In the one case it took provisional measures nine and a half months after the initial submission, while the execution had taken place at least three months earlier.[37] In the other case the interval between initial submission and the provisional measure was eleven months. Seven months previously Belarus had executed the petitioner. The Committee referred to the lack of promptness in its use of provisional measures in the following, rather oblique, terms:

> "The Committee notes with regret that, by the time it was in a position to submit its Rule 86 request, the death sentence had already been carried out. The Committee understands and will ensure that cases susceptible of being subject of Rule 86 requests will be processed with the expedition necessary to enable its requests to be complied with".[38]

It is not clear what caused the extreme tardiness, but unavailability of resources at the Secretariat, in particular in relation to complaints in languages other than English, French or Spanish, may have played a role.[39]

2.3.4.3 DETENTION AND DISAPPEARANCE CASES

The above discussion of prompt intervention involved death penalty cases. Obviously this promptness is also relevant in expulsion,[40] detention and disappearance cases as well as in those

---

[36] Secretariat handed the Rapporteur's combined Rule 86/91 request to the Permanent Mission of Trinidad and Tobago in Geneva at 4.05 p.m. Geneva time on 13 July 1994. This was 10.05 a.m. Trinidad and Tobago time. According to the Permanent Mission this request was transmitted by facsimile to the Port-of-Spain authorities between 4.30 and 4.45 p.m. that day, Geneva time. In Trinidad and Tobago it was between 10.30 and 10.45 a.m. Mr. Ashby's counsel continued the efforts to obtain a stay of execution throughout the night of 13 to 14 July 1994, both before the Court of Appeal in Trinidad and Tobago and before the JCPC in London. The JCPC issued an order to stay the execution shortly after 11.30 a.m. (London time) on 14 July. It appeared, however, that by that time Mr. Ashby had already been executed. It was 6.30 a.m. in Trinidad and Tobago when the JCPC issued its order. The Court of Appeal was also in session at the time of the execution, deliberating on whether it would order a stay of execution.

[36] See e.g. HRC *Piandiong et al.* v. *the Philippines*, 19 October 2000; *Mansaraj et al.* v. *Sierra Leone*, 16 July 2001 and *Glenn Ashby* v. *Trinidad and Tobago*, 21 March 2002. See further Chapters XVI (Legal status) and XVII (Official responses).

[37] HRC *Anton Bondarenko and Natalia Schedko (submitted by the latter on behalf of her deceased son and herself)* v. *Belarus*, 3 April 2003.

[38] HRC *Igor Lyashkovich and Mariya Staselovich (submitted by the latter on behalf of her deceased son and herself)* v. *Belarus*, 3 April 2003 §1.3. See also *Anton Bondarenko and Natalia Schedko (submitted by the latter on behalf of her deceased son and herself)* v. *Belarus*, 3 April 2003, §1.3.

[39] About this case see also Chapter XVII (Official responses) and Chapter XVIII (Follow-up by the adjudicators).

[40] In one early case (1978), in which there was no Special Rapporteur yet, the HRC seized the earliest opportunity to take provisional measures to halt an expulsion. This was around a month after initial submission. HRC *O.E.* v. *S.*, 25 January 1978. In this case the petitioner had submitted a complaint on behalf of his son on 30 December 1977. The HRC used provisional measures on 25 January 1978, meaning that it took action within a month. In some cases

involving indigenous culture. The discussion of prompt intervention and the use of provisional measures in detention cases relates to lack of medical treatment, whereabouts and access to counsel. In this type of cases the HRC has also used so-called 'informal' provisional measures, requesting information on the treatment and whereabouts under the rule on the transmission of cases and requests for clarification, rather than formally under the Rule on provisional measures.[41]

---

involving alleged threats to life and security in the receiving State the HRC did not use provisional measures. One such case was HRC P. L.-B. v. Canada, 556/1993, discontinued 17 April 1996 (request for urgent measures of 4 October 1993, initial submission of 5 October 1993, information about his deportation on 7 October 1993 and Rule 91 of 18 January 1994, letter State of 19 July 1994: the petitioner was not deported but he disappeared; on file with the author). In this case it did not use them partly because the timeframe between submission and the date of deportation appeared too short and the Secretariat was unable to contact the Rapporteur in time. Counsel for the petitioner had informed the HRC that he had 'just learned a few minutes ago' that his client's removal from Canada would most likely take place in the evening of 7 October 1993. The HRC received this fax on this date. It was sent two days previously and refers to a submission of 4 October 1993. By the time it registered the case it had already received reports that the petitioner had been deported. Hence it only referred to Rule 91. Transmission under Rule 91 of 18 January 1994. In 2003 a petitioner was extradited subsequent to the initial submission of his case. In this case the HRC had not used provisional measures. Both the initial submission and the extradition took place on the same day, meaning that only a 'same day Rule 86' could have been effective. Technically this case involved a deportation, but with the same risk as extradition because a death sentence had already been pronounced against the petitioner in the receiving State. While the petitioner had requested provisional measures, the time-period for contacting the Rapporteur or another member of the HRC apparently was too short. HRC *Judge* v. *Canada*, 5 August 2003. See Chapter V (Expulsion) for a discussion of the Committee's View in this case. It appears from the case file that the Secretariat attempted to contact two different members of the Committee on the day the case was submitted. As noted, the petitioner was deported on the same day. The reason Rule 86 was not used may lie in the difficulty of reaching the Special Rapporteur in the timeframe of hours rather than days. The Special Rapporteur transmitted the case to the State party more than a year later, on 20 August 1999.

[41] The issues of lack of medical treatment in detention and unclear whereabouts of detained persons were among the early cases dealt with by the Committee, when the examination of individual complaints by international adjudicators was still new and more sensitive than it is now. This may account for the fact that it initially did not formally invoke its Rule on provisional measures in these cases. See the discussion in Chapter VI (Locating and protecting disappeared persons) and Chapter VII (detention). The case *Juan E. Zelaya Blanco and Myriam Zelaya Dunaway (on behalf of Roberto Zelaya who later joined)* v. *Nicaragua,* 20 July 1994, indicates that the practice of using informal rather than formal provisional measures, once developed in a given context (e.g. detention) continued to be used into the 1990s. Initially the petitioners (the brother and sister of Mr. Zelaya) wrote to the Secretary General of the UN in July 1988, among others referring to death threats made against their detained brother by a lieutenant. Five days later they received information that this lieutenant had been transferred following an investigation. While they observed that he was still in active military service and could continue to put other people at risk, the Committee could indeed conclude that the immediate threat against the alleged victim no longer existed. Letters of 22 and 26 July and 2 September 1988 (on file with the author). The *official* initial submission was sent two months later, in September 1988. The focus of the complaint was on the health of the alleged victim and in particular on the risk of prolonged experimentation with cortisones. The Working Group dealt with the case at the earliest opportunity, since there was not yet a Special Rapporteur on New Communications who could deal with cases in between sessions. Special Rapporteur Mavrommatis had only been appointed to deal with death penalty cases. At this time there was no longer a need to intervene in relation to the death threat, although it is not clear whether the HRC would have enquired about this

The urgency of some of the situations was not met with the requisite promptness. In *Setelich* it took the HRC four months to decide on the petitioner's first request to use provisional measures. Although it did not use provisional measures but inquired about the alleged victim's health instead, it would have been useful had it been able to move in a more timely fashion. Yet it must be borne in mind that this is an early case, brought before the HRC during the period before it had assigned one of its members with the task of dealing with communications in between sessions.[42] Since the installation by the HRC of a Special Rapporteur dealing first with death penalty cases only and later with all new communications, the promptness has gradually increased.[43]

Prompt intervention is also particularly important in disappearance cases. Different from the UN Working Group on Enforced Disappearances (WGED), the HRC has no specific guidelines on prompt intervention in disappearance cases. The WGED directly transmits cases that occurred within the three months preceding receipt of the information by the Group to the Minister of Foreign Affairs 'by the most direct and rapid means'.[44]

---

otherwise. On the issue of death threats and the use of provisional measures see Chapter IX. While decision-making by the Working Group was prompt, in the circumstances, its implementation by the Secretariat was not. Between the Committee's decision to enquire about the alleged victim's health situation and access to medication and the transmittal of this decision to the State party there was an interval of more than three weeks. Rule 91 decision of 24 October 1988, CCPR/C/WG/34/D/328/1988, 8 November 1988 and Note Verbale of 17 November 1988 (on file with the author). The HRC requested, among others, information on the current state of health of Mr. Zelaya. In particular it requested the State to forward copies of his medical reports and to indicate the medication he was receiving. Zelaya was detained until March 1990. After his release he went to the US. The HRC declared the case admissible after he had already been released. See also *Dave Marais* v. *Madagascar*, 24 March 1984 in which the HRC used informal provisional measures to ensure access to counsel, two years after initial submission. In *Muteba* v. *Zaire*, 24 July 1984 a request for information about such access, together with requests about the state of health of the alleged victim, was sent within eight days. Informal provisional measures were sent on the same date as those in the case of HRC *Manera Lluberas* v. *Uruguay*, 6 April 1984. The decision to use provisional measures in *A. et al.* v. *Angola*, 810/1998, discontinued 1 August 2000 (initial submission of 13 February 1998; provisional measures of 10 March 1998) to provide access to counsel and court, was taken within a month of receipt of initial submission.

[42] In *Altesor* v. *Uruguay*, 29 March 1982 the HRC was able to act within three weeks because it was in session at the time. Still, in some cases harm to a detainee's health could clearly become irreparable in three weeks time. In HRC *Lafuente Penarrieta et al.* v. *Bolivia*, 2 November 1987, it is not clear why the HRC did not request informal provisional measures in 1984, upon receipt of initial submission, or during or following the time the alleged victims were on a hunger strike, but rather in 1985.

[43] At least seven times before the introduction of a Special Rapporteur the HRC did not intervene during the upcoming session but instead skipped one or more sessions. Nine times it did indeed intervene at the upcoming session. Once this was even within eight days of the initial submission. See *Muteba* v. *Zaire* (124/1982).

[44] Working Group on Enforced or Involuntary Disappearances, Revised methods of work of the Working Group, adopted 14 November 2001. The UN Working Group, not a treaty body, but one of the thematic mechanisms, has specifically delegated its power to the Chairperson, who can authorise the urgent appeals. If a person disappeared more than three months but less than a year previous to receipt of the information by the Secretariat the Chairperson may authorise transmission of the case in between sessions. In such cases there should be some connection with a case that did occur within the three-month period and the method of transmission is by letter. See <www.ohchr.org>. In this respect there does not appear to be extensive cross-fertilization between the adjudicator and the Working Group. See also Chapter VI on the practice of adjudicators with regard to using provisional measures in disappearance cases.

The case of *Ana Rosario Celis Laureano* v. *Peru* (1996) involved the urgent intervention of the UN Working Group on Disappearances as well as that of the HRC.[45]

In *Almeida de Quinteros* v. *Uruguay* (1983)[46] the petitioner had submitted the case on be-half of her daughter and herself five years after her daughter was last seen. The HRC requested the State to confirm that Elena Quinteros, whose whereabouts had been unknown since 1976, was in detention. It requested the State to make known the place of detention.[47] Because five years had passed since her disappearance it is not surprising that the HRC did not use provisional measures. The likelihood that a disappeared person has died increases with every month the disappearance persists. The Committee's request to be informed of her whereabouts seems to be more a matter of principle and a necessary stage in acquiring information for a final determination than it is an attempt to informally intervene pending the proceedings in order to prevent irreparable harm.[48]

---

[45] HRC *Laureano Atachahua (on behalf of his granddaughter Ana Rosario Celis Laureano)* v. *Peru*, 25 March 1996. The victim, who was a minor, had disappeared in August 1992. Her grandfather submitted his complaint to the HRC more than two months later, in October 1992. By then the UN Working Group had already registered her case. The HRC determined that it was not prevented from dealing with this case because, in light of the difference in the mandates of the Working Group and itself, the case could not be seen as dealing with the 'same matter'. In November 1992 the Peruvian Government informed the UN Working Group that the Prosecutor's Office in Huacho was investigating the case and that the Government had requested information from two Ministries: those of Defence and the Interior. The Prosecutor's Office had not yet found Ms. Laureano nor identified those responsible for her disappearance. More than half a year leter, the HRC Special Rapporteur transmitted the case to the State party. By that time the UN Working Group had already appealed to the State twice. It is not clear whether the Rapporteur enquired about her health and whereabouts since the Committee's View does not provide information about the substance of the transmission. In its admissibility decision, in July 1994, the HRC only requested detailed information on the investigations carried out by the authorities. Given the lack of response by the State the likelihood of finding her alive after November 1992 seemed limited. The State party responded on 10 June 1993 drawing on information provided by its Ministry of Defence. "On 8 September 1992, the commander of the military base in Ambar inquired with the judge about the status of the case; on 11 September 1992, the judge confirmed that the girl had been abducted one month earlier, and that the judicial authorities seized of the matter attributed responsibility for the event to members of the military. On 21 September 1992, the Attorney-General of the Second Prosecutor's Office (Fiscal de la Segunda Fiscalía de la Nación) reported on the action taken by the Office until then; he issued a list of eight police and military offices and concluded that Ms. Laureano was not detained in any of these offices". HRC *Laureano Atachahua (on behalf of his granddaughter Ana Rosario Celis Laureano)* v. *Peru*, 25 March 1996, §4.1. Although the submission was two months after the disappearance and the Working Group on Disappearances had already been involved for a month, the HRC could have reacted immediately upon receipt of the submission instead of several months later. Beyond this report of 21 September 1992, the State does not seem to have investigated the matter. This also appears from the information provided by the UN Working Group, which had not been updated beyond November 1992. See also Chapter XI on the attitudes of addressee States and the follow-up by the adjudicators. See also *Mojica* v. *Dominican Republic*, 15 July 1994.

[46] HRC *Almeida de Quinteros* v. *Uruguay*, 21 July 1983.

[47] HRC *Almeida de Quinteros* v. *Uruguay,* 21 July 1983, com. no. 107/1981, CCPR/C/OP/2, at 138 (Rule 91 of 14 October 1983).

[48] See also HRC *Thevaraja Sarma (submitted by his father S. Jegatheeswara Sarma)* v. *Sri Lanka*, 16 July 2003. In this case the victim had been abducted in June 1990. The State party ratified the OP in October 1997 and the initial submission was of October 1999. See also *Alfredo and Samuel Sanjuán Arévalo (submitted by their mother Elcida Arévalo Perez)* v. *Colombia*, 3 November 1989, CCPR/C/37/D/181/1984, 22 November 1989 (no informal provisional measures, probably because the disappearance took place more than two years before initial submission).

Before the HRC introduced the Special Rapporteur on New Communications it intervened informally several times, requesting information on the whereabouts of an alleged victim.[49] In In *Tshishimbi* v. *Zaire* (1996) the Special Rapporteur took *formal* provisional measures to discover the whereabouts of the alleged victim and prevent irreparable harm.[50] Subsequently the Committee expressed particular concern about the absence of cooperation in relation to the provisional measure by the Rapporteur.[51] Nevertheless, the full Committee did not itself use formal provisional measures to follow-up on those of the Special Rapporteur. Instead, it reiterated the Rule 91 (current Rule 97) request 'to provide detailed information on the whereabouts of Mr. Tshishimbi and to indicate whether he was covered by the terms of the amnesty announced by the State party's new Government in the summer of 1994'. After all, nothing had been heard from him for two years, making it less likely that he was still alive. The use of provisional measures is particularly warranted in the context of recent disappearances or in the face of other indications that the alleged victim may still be alive.[52] A relevant example is *El Megreisi* v. *Libya* (1994).[53] The petitioner had submitted a case on behalf of his brother almost two years after his disappearance. The HRC only requested information on his whereabouts and health seven months after initial submission.[54] Subsequently the El-Megreisi family learned that the petitioner's brother was still alive in April 1992, when he was suddenly allowed a visit by his wife. During this visit he could not comment on his conditions of detention. It was then that the HRC requested information on his health and whereabouts.[55]

2.3.4.4 CASES INVOLVING THREATS TO INDIGENOUS CULTURE

The HRC has not been particularly prompt in its intervention on behalf of indigenous culture. The time between initial submission and the use of provisional measures varied from two and a half months (*Länsman II*)[56] to almost three and a half years (*Lubicon Lake Band*).[57] Waiting such a period before taking them considerably diminishes their practical use. When it did use provisional measures in the latter case it did so in light of the seriousness of the claim that the Lubicon Lake Band was on the verge of extinction.[58] In that light it would have been helpful if it had made the assessment earlier in the proceedings. It must be remembered, however, that this was the first

---

[49] Promptness varied from a few days to four months.

[50] In this case there was an interval of one month between the initial submission and the provisional measure.

[51] HRC *Tshishimbi* v. *Zaire*, 25 March 1996.

[52] See also Chapter VI (Locating and protecting disappeared persons).

[53] HRC *Mohammed Bashir El-Megreisi (submitted by his brother Youssef El-Megreisi)* v. *Libya*, 23 March 1994.

[54] It is not clear from the decision on the merits why it did not make this request immediately upon receipt of the complaint. Possibly it assumed that the disappearance was not sufficiently recent and therefore did not warrant provisional measures. It is also possible that the Rapporteur simply did not deal with the case sooner or that the Rapporteur preferred the use of informal provisional measures under Rule 91 (old) in this case. The View only refers to Rule 91, not to Rule 86, but it is also possible that Rule 86 was used nevertheless.

[55] Five months later the petitioner stated that at that time his brother was detained in a military camp in Tripoli of which the name and location were unknown. The next month, in its admissibility decision, the HRC repeated its request to the State about the current whereabouts, state of health and conditions of detention.

[56] HRC *Länsman* v. *Finland (Länsman II)*, 30 October 1996.

[57] HRC *Lubicon Lake Band* v. *Canada*, 26 March 1990.

[58] See also Chapter X (Culture).

time the HRC formally used provisional measures in a case not involving the death penalty, expulsion or extradition. Moreover, there was no Rapporteur yet dealing with new communications in between sessions, which meant that the case was a recurring topic only during official sessions.

2.3.4.5 URGENCY AFTER REGISTRATION OF THE PETITION

In 2003 Special Rapporteur Scheinin acknowledged that the Secretariat does not inform him about new developments after he has authorised registration of a case. To his knowledge, no Rapporteur assigned to prepare a specific case for determination on the merits has intervened to alert the HRC about such developments that might warrant the use of provisional measures. Provisional measures taken after registration follow up on earlier provisional measures, rather than deal with new situations. He agreed that it would be useful to arrange for a procedure to deal with those urgent issues coming up following registration. As an example he referred to risks to a detainee on the verge of turning blind.[59]

2.3.5 Contacting the addressee State with provisional measures

Especially if the treaty body only informs the agent of the State in Geneva (Permanent Mission) of the provisional measure, it is important to allow for time to transmit this information from there, by way of the Ministry of Foreign Affairs, to the relevant (prison) authorities, often through the Ministry of Justice as well.[60]

Within the United Nations it is diplomatic practice to address the diplomatic missions representing States, based in Geneva, rather than the governments directly. In urgent cases, however, this is not very practicable. By the time the provisional measure reaches the relevant authorities, irreparable harm may already have occurred. Hence, even in some of the early cases the HRC

---

[59] Interview by author with Special Rapporteur Scheinin, Geneva, April 2003. Thus far it does not appear that a formal decision has been made to arrange for such a procedure. Indeed HRC *Polay Campos (submitted by his wife Espinoza de Polay)* v. *Peru,* 6 November 1997 appears to be a rare exception in which the case rapporteur eventually suggests the use of provisional measures. On 5 March 1993 Ms. Espinoza de Polay submitted the case on behalf of her husband who was detained in Peru. She sent her submission from France. Only when the Committee declared this case admissible, three years after the initial submission, it requested the State to ensure medical treatment. While three Rapporteurs theoretically could have intervened (the initial submission in *Polay Campos* v. *Peru* was in March 1993, just before the session ending the Rapporteurship of Lallah and starting that of Chanet. Pocar started his Rapporteurship as of spring 1995), the practice at the Secretariat seems to have been such that the Rapporteur authorizing registration and transmission of the new case to the State *may* be informed about urgent matters at the same time. More importantly, the Special Rapporteur on New Communications does not receive information about subsequent developments that could put at risk the health of the petitioner, while the member of the Committee who is responsible for drafting the decision on the merits does not have the task of intervening urgently. Eventually, in *Polay Campos* the HRC did urge the State to provide medical treatment, but it only did so when it declared the case admissible. It is evident that it did not act with the same sense of urgency as it tends to do when it uses formal provisional measures. It eventually intervened upon a suggestion by Committee member Prado Vallejo who became the case Rapporteur. Letter of Prado Vallejo to the Geneva Secretariat, 2 July 1996 (on file with the author).

[60] The issuance of a provisional measure may also be useful information to submit in domestic court.

already sent a telegram directly to the Minister of Foreign Affairs as well as to the Deputy Prime Minister.[61]

In other cases the HRC also sent the provisional measure to the Advocate General of the State. It may address him as follows: 'please find enclosed the text of the urgent note verbale which we delivered to the Permanent Mission today'.[62] In cases against Jamaica it developed the practice to address the Minister of Foreign Affairs and External Trade directly and send a copy to the Permanent Mission of Jamaica in Geneva. According to Special Rapporteur Scheinin, however, there is no consistent practice on whether the Secretariat contacts only the Permanent Mission or whether it contacts the Ministry of Foreign Affairs, other government ministries, prison wardens etc. as well.[63]

Jamaica's attitude towards the manner in which it was informed of provisional measures in the early years becomes apparent in *Reece* v. *Jamaica* (disc. 1993).[64] Jamaica pointed out it wished to receive all the information together with the request for provisional measures. Its response serves as a reminder of the importance of providing full information with any decision to use provisional measures and, preferably, some motivation.[65] It also serves as a historical background showing that initially the means of communication were rather inefficient.[66]

---

[61] HRC *O.W.* v. *Jamaica*, 26 July 1988, and *Earl Pratt and Ivan Morgan* v. *Jamaica*, 6 April 1989.

[62] HRC *Ramcharan Bickaroo* v. *Trinidad and Tobago*, 29 October 1997, Rule 86/91 decision of 5 October 1993 (on file with the author).

[63] Interview by the author with Special Rapporteur Scheinin, Geneva, April 2003.

[64] HRC *Lloyd Reece* v. *Jamaica*, 247/1987, discontinued upon receipt of the petitioner's instructions to withdraw, 28 April 1993; initial submission of 18 June 1987; Rule 86/91 of 25 November 1987 of 12 November 1987 (separate unpublished HRC decision, on file with the author). His death sentence was commuted on 6 June 1995. See also the follow-up case *Lloyd Reece* v. *Jamaica*, 14 July 2003.

[65] See further section 8.3 of this Chapter on publication and motivation. The HRC decided to take provisional measures on 12 November, but this decision was only transmitted to the State on 25 November 1987. It pointed out that a person under sentence of death had submitted the complaint. At the same time it noted that further factual information from the petitioner was necessary before the HRC could consider the question of admissibility. It relied on the State's willingness to cooperate with the HRC 'at this early stage in the consideration of the subject-matter'. Apparently, however, the State only received this decision thirteen days after the HRC had decided on it. On 8 December 1987 an official Note Verbale confirmed the message in the telegram. It was only with this Note Verbale that the Secretariat also transmitted the text of the complaint itself. Decision under Rule 86/91, 12 November 1987, CCPR/C/31/D/247/1987, transmitted on 25 November 1987 (by telegram) and Note Verbale by UN Secretariat to Jamaican Ministry of Foreign Affairs with a copy to the Permanent Mission, 8 December 1987 (on file with the author). In other words, there was an interval between the Committee's decision to take provisional measures and the Secretariat's action to inform the State, first by telegram and later by transmittal of the Note Verbale. A month later the Jamaican Ministry of Foreign Affairs, Trade and Industry responded to the telegram. While the Note Verbale referred to a telegram, the response referred to a telex. It may be assumed that the UN Centre for Human Rights sent its telegrams through its own telex system before it changed to using the fax. It noted that the telegram included the text of the Committee's decision to take provisional measures, which mentioned that a copy of the petitioner's communication would be transmitted separately. The State acknowledged that, under the Rules of Procedure, the HRC was only required to ensure that the text of a complaint is sent to the State party before it made a declaration on admissibility. It nevertheless felt that the HRC should make such communications available to the Government 'at the earliest possible opportunity, or at any rate, contemporaneously with the first request by the Committee for action by the State Party under the Protocol and its Rules'. It gave as an example the Committee's request under Rule 86. The Ministry of Foreign Affairs felt 'that from

The case of the late *Rockliff Ross* v. *Guyana* (disc. 1997)[67] shows the lengths to which the Secretariat of the HRC sometimes has to go in trying to get the message to the relevant authorities. Even though the pains taken were to no avail, the case serves as an interesting example showing the sequence of events in contacting the State party. Aguilar Urbina, the Chairperson of the HRC, had authorised both the registration of the case and the use of provisional measures. These were to be sent directly to the State party, more precisely to the Presidency and the Office of the Attorney General, because there was no Permanent Mission of Guyana in Geneva and the Permanent Mission in New York would only start its daily business after the execution. A member of the Geneva Secretariat dictated the contents of the Note Verbale with the provisional measure to an assistant of the Superintendent of the State Prison. The Superintendent himself could not be reached anymore, being 'out in the yard'. Earlier the Superintendent of the prison had said he could not interfere with the process and emphasised he was carrying out an executive order. Rockliff Ross was executed as planned.[68]

---

that stage the relevant State Party should at least be seized of the nature of the complaint that has been made against it'. "Indeed, although Rule 86 has no express provisions on this question, it appears to proceed on the assumption that the State Party would already have been seized of the communication and hence of the complaint by the time a request for its action under that Rule has been made". Letter of the Ministry of Foreign Affairs, Trade and Industry of Jamaica to the Director of the United Nations Centre for Human Rights, 24 December 1987, reference number 50/151/1 regarding Lloyd Reece (247/1987) (on file with the author). From the Secretariat's reply to the Jamaican Ministry of Foreign Affairs it becomes apparent that Jamaica had made the same observation with regard to twelve other cases. These were 237/1987, 246/1987, 248/1987, 249/1987, 250/1987, 251/1987, 252/1987, 253/1987, 254/1987, 255/1987, 256/1987 and 257/1987.The Secretariat agreed with the State's argument that the text of a communication should be transmitted simultaneously with the relevant decision.

[66] "Nevertheless, given the special nature of the cases in question, the Committee requested the Secretariat, as an exception to the normal practice, to transmit the text of the decisions first by telegram, to be followed by a retransmittal of the decisions as soon as possible, under cover of Notes Verbales, enclosing at that time copies of the communications themselves. This, the Secretariat has tried to do as expeditiously as possible". It also suggested a solution for this problem: "Should the Ministry of Foreign Affairs consider it helpful, the Secretariat would be quite willing to consider the possibility of effecting transmittal of the Committee's decisions together with copies of the communications by telefax (if further cases of this nature do arise). For this purpose, the Secretariat would be grateful for learning the telefax number of the Ministry of Foreign Affairs". Note Verbale by the UN Secretariat (Centre for Human Rights) to the Ministry of Foreign Affairs of Jamaica of 15 January 1988 concerning 237/1987, 240/1987 and 246/1987 to 257/1987 (on file with the author).

[67] HRC *(The late) Rockliff Ross* v. *Guyana*, discontinued 10 December 1997, 703/1996 (on file with the author).

[68] At approximately 11:30 a.m. Chairperson Aguilar Urbina had authorised the provisional measures. Mr. Schmidt of the UN Secretariat would contact the Superintendent of the Prison. At 12:15 p.m. the Secretariat transmitted the Note Verbale of Aguilar to the Presidency by fax. Seven successive attempts to send this to the Attorney General failed. At 12:30 p.m. Schmidt was on the phone with the Superintendent of the prison, who said he could not interfere with the process and emphasised he was carrying out an executive order. Schmidt suggested him at least to check with the President's or the Attorney General's Office, which the Superintendent promised to do. Subsequent attempts (between 12:30 – 14:15 p.m.) to contact the Office of the Attorney General by phone and to reach the Presidency and the Chief Justice failed as well. Between 12:35 and 12:45 p.m. Schmidt dictated the contents of the Note Verbale with the provisional measure to an assistant of the Superintendent of the State Prison. The Superintendent himself could not be reached anymore, being 'out in the yard'. The request to have him paged or call back remained without result. The assistant promised to deliver the handwritten transcript to

Sometimes a long time-span does not mean that the HRC did nothing. It may have taken action informally. *A.A.T.* v. *Hungary* (disc. 1994) serves as an example.[69] In this deportation case it took the HRC ten months to decide affirmatively on the use of provisional measures.[70] Yet this case hints at the importance of informal interventions. The Geneva Secretariat emphasised to the petitioner that if the authorities would decide to expel or extradite him to Iraq he should not hesitate to contact the Committee. Upon inquiry in Hungary the Committee found that there was indeed a valid court order for the expulsion of the petitioner and that a date had been set. Apparently, informal interventions on behalf of the HRC resulted in a stay of this domestic court order. Nevertheless, once it appeared that the expulsion was still imminent, the Special Rapporteur did transmit the case to the State party and requested it to halt deportation. Obviously, for this type of informal intervention there should be knowledge about the domestic situation and personal access to State decision-makers by a member of the HRC or its Secretariat.

2.3.6 Related Rules of Procedure

Next to the Rule on provisional measures itself (now Rule 92, previously Rule 86) there are some other Rules of Procedure with particular relevance to provisional measures: the Rule on the transmittal of a complaint to the State party and the possible enquiry of the Committee on specific points needing clarification by the State or the petitioner (now Rule 97, previously Rule 91), the Rule on the designation of special rapporteurs (now Rule 95, previously Rule 89), and the Rule on confidentiality (now Rule 102, previously Rule 96). Generally the Committee's provisional measures[71] are simply included at the end of a Note Verbale directed to the respondent government. This Note Verbale normally transmits the complaint to the State concerned and provides it with the communication number of the case.[72] The HRC sometimes uses provisional measures as part

---

[69] the Superintendent in the yard. At 14:15 p.m. the HRC received a reply from the Attorney General's Office, but none from the Superintendent's Office. The London-based NGO Interights sent Mr. Schmidt a fax on 6 June 1996 informing him that the execution took place at 8:00 a.m. Guyana time. Initial submission 2 June 1996 (received 3 June); telephone call by counsel at 11:00 a.m. Geneva time on 4 June; submission under Rule 86 on 4 June at 11:30 a.m. Geneva time: client scheduled for execution same day 8:00 a.m. (2:00 p.m. Geneva time), from file notes of 4 June 1996 and telephone chart (on file with the author) in: *Rockliff Ross* v. *Guyana*, discontinued 10 December 1997, 703/1996.

[69] HRC *A.A.T.* v. *Hungary*, 543/1993 (disc. 1994); initial submission of 10 August 1992; Rule 86/91 of 2 June 1993.

[70] The petitioner had requested provisional measures in August 1992 but the Rapporteur only used provisional measures in June 1993.

[71] In its Views and Annual Reports the HRC itself tends to use the term 'interim measures'. As noted in the Introduction for the sake of consistency this book normally uses the term provisional measures.

[72] Note Verbale is the term generally used to refer to official letters sent to the State involved, usually to the State's diplomatic representative at the UN in Geneva. This representative is expected to channel such letters to his government (usually the Ministry of Foreign Affairs). Often it also requests certain information from the State. The HRC usually includes its provisional measures in this 'transmission' to the State. In July 1991 the Committee adopted revised terms of reference for the mandate of the Special Rapporteur on New Communications. This included 'to issue rule 86 requests, whether coupled with a request under rule 91 or not' and 'to inform the Committee at each session on action taken under rules 86 and 91'. Annex X, Mandate of the Special Rapporteur on New Communications, revised terms of reference adopted at the 1087th meeting, 24 July 1991, A/46/40, 10 October 1991, in: Official Records of the Human Rights Committee 1990/1991, Vol. II, CCPR/10/Add. 1.

of its decision on admissibility rather than together with its earlier decision to transmit the case to the State. Sometimes it does both.

The Rule on confidentiality clarifies the level of access to information. Since 1997 the Committee has formally excluded provisional measures from its confidentiality rules. It declared decisions relating to provisional measures to be public information, not hampered by confidentiality limitations. Its paragraph 5 provides:

> "Subject to paragraph 4, the Committee's decisions on inadmissibility, merits and discontinuance shall be made public. The decisions of the Committee or the Special Rapporteur designated pursuant to rule 95 paragraph 3, under rule 92 of this rule shall be made public. No advance copies of any Committee decision shall be issued".

Paragraph 6 stipulates:

> "The Secretariat is responsible for the distribution of the Committee's final decisions. It shall not be responsible for the reproduction and the distribution of submissions concerning communications".

A limited interpretation of paragraph 6, making the Secretariat only responsible for the distribution of the HRC's final decisions, would make it difficult to envisage the implementation of the obligation to make public decisions on provisional measures.

2.3.7 Proprio motu use of provisional measures

Often petitioners submit hand-written complaints, without assistance of a lawyer, sometimes from death row. They may invoke any particular article of the Covenant. However, the HRC can derive the applicable rights from the facts of the case even if the petitioner did not specifically claim them. It is customary for the HRC, or rather initially its Secretariat, to indicate *proprio motu* under which articles issues seem to arise. For instance, based on the initial petition the HRC has inquired about the health of the petitioner's detained relatives while the petitioner apparently did not specifically request this.[73] On the basis of the facts mentioned in the complaint it also seems to have requested information on the whereabouts of a petitioner's relative.[74] In other words it took an informal provisional measure *proprio motu*.[75]

Equally, if the complaint refers to the imposition of corporal punishment on the alleged victim, but the specific claims do not relate to it, the HRC can include an Article 7 claim *proprio motu* and use provisional measures to prevent the execution of the punishment. In the first two corporal punishment cases it is likely that members of the Committee noticed only at a rather late stage of the proceedings that the petitioner had been sentenced to corporal punishment. Then they raised the issue *proprio motu*. They could also have used provisional measures, but at this late

---

[73] See e.g. HRC *Valentini de Bazzano* v. *Uruguay*, 15 August 1979. In *Martinez Machado* v. *Uruguay*, 4 November 1993, however, it did not inquire about the alleged victim's state of health, despite the great concern expressed by the petitioner. In *Almirati Nieto (submitted by Almirati Garcia)* v. *Uruguay*, 25 July 1983 it did not intervene *proprio motu* either, probably because of the lack of specificity about the urgency of the concern. See further Chapter VII (Detention).

[74] HRC *Martinez Machado* v. *Uruguay*, 4 November 1993.

[75] On this flexible approach, not applying *non ultra petita* in a strict manner, or not regarding as *non ultra petita* this type of assistance to the lay petitioner in formulating his claim, as long as it is based on the facts in the petition, is based on the protective function of the adjudicator and on the particular context. See further Chapter XIV (Jurisdiction). About informal provisional measures see Chapters VI (Disappearances) and VII (Detention).

stage the Committee may no longer have taken into account the possibility of taking provisional measures because the decision to take such measures is normally made during the initial stages of the proceedings. Now that the HRC has clearly found violations in the context of specific claims about corporal punishment it is likely that any mention of this punishment in a petition will trigger action by the Secretariat contacting the Special Rapporteur about the use of provisional measures in cases in which the punishment has not yet been executed.[76]

The Committee has also used provisional measures upon request, but on the basis of a different right than that claimed by the petitioner. It introduced this *proprio motu*. This was the case in the *Lubicon Lake Band* v. *Canada* (1990) involving cultural survival. In this case the petitioner claimed a violation of Article 1 ICCPR and requested provisional measures. Before deciding on the request for provisional measures the HRC first introduced Article 27 ICCPR *proprio motu* as an alternative to the Article 1 ICCPR claim, which it held inadmissible. Then it took the provisional measures, requested, but on the basis of the claim it had introduced *proprio motu*.[77]

---

[76] See further Chapter IV (Corporal punishment). In a case published the year before *Sooklal* (2001), the case *Osbourne* v. *Jamaica* (2000), it appears from the files in Geneva, but not from the View itself, that the Committee did use provisional measures. It did so on 23 June 1997. The petitioner had submitted his complaint that same month, on 12 June 1997. It was in this case that the HRC pointed out, for the first time, that imposition of corporal punishment in itself already constituted a violation of Article 7, even without the execution of this punishment. While the Committee published *Matthews* v. *Trinidad and Tobago*, the first case dealing with corporal punishment, in March 1998, more than two months after it used its provisional measure to prevent flogging in *Osbourne* v. *Jamaica*, it is unlikely that it already used provisional measures in *Matthews*. The complaint was of 11 October 1993 and the Committee declared it admissible, also with regard to the corporal punishment issue, two years later. Indeed the file does not refer to the use of provisional measures.

[77] HRC *Bernard Ominayak, Chief of the Lubicon Lake Band* v. *Canada*, 26 March 1990 (destruction of the natural habitat and Article 27). See also Chapters X (Culture) and XIV (Jurisdiction and admissibility). In situations claiming *ongoing* violations the HRC has sometimes taken into account new developments. In *Bakhtiyari family* v. *Australia* (2003) the Rapporteur adjusted his provisional measures in light of procedural developments. See HRC *Bakhtiyari family* v. *Australia*, 29 October 2003, §2.1: "On 27 March 2002, the Committee, acting through its Special Rapporteur for New Communications, pursuant to Rule 86 of the Committee's Rules of Procedure, requested the State party to refrain from deporting Mrs Bakhtiyari and her children, until the Committee had had the opportunity to consider their claims under the Covenant, in the event of a negative decision by the Minister for Immigration on their request in October 2001 to exercise his discretion to allow them to remain in Australia. Following the Minister's adverse decision and advice that Mrs Bakhtiyari and her children had applied to the High Court of Australia, this request to refrain from deportation was adjusted by the Special Rapporteur on New Communications, on 13 May 2002, to be conditional on an adverse decision on the application by the High Court". Later the Committee observed that certain claims under Articles 17 and 23 'deriving from a separation of the family unit' had been withdrawn after the father had been placed with his family. However, 'the most recent information suggests that the State party is moving to remove Ms. Bakhtiyari and her children while proceedings in relation to Mr Bakhtiyari are in process'. HRC *Bakhtiyari family* v. *Australia*, 29 October 2003, §8.5. Thus, *proprio motu* it regarded these claims as still relevant and considered them sufficiently substantiated for purposes of admissibility.

2.3.8 Withdrawing provisional measures

Generally human rights adjudicators take provisional measures for a limited period and, based on the facts, they may decide to extend them or not to renew them at all after this period has lapsed. In some cases a specific decision was made to withdraw provisional measures.

In the *Jouni Länsman* v. *Finland II*, involving Sami culture, the Rapporteur had used provisional measures in August 1995, but had immediately invited the State to inform him in case it did not agree with such measures, which the State promptly did. In November 1996 the Rapporteur set aside his provisional measures, apparently accepting the State's arguments. Later the case was declared admissible.[78] When a case is declared inadmissible the provisional measures are generally assumed to be set aside, unless a statement to the contrary is made.[79] Yet in another case involving the Sami *Sara et al.* v. *Finland*, the provisional measures were first maintained upon admissibility, but when the case was subsequently declared inadmissible, the Committee specifically noted that the provisional measures were set aside as well.

With regard to a discontinued extradition case, *E.G.* v. *Canada* (unpublished, but discontinued in 1997),[80] it appears from the file that the State party was keen on withdrawal of the provisional measures and the Rapporteur indeed decided that there was no need to maintain them. He had made this decision 'after careful consideration and upon reflection' and 'on the basis of the assurances obtained by the Canadian Government from United States authorities, to the effect that the death penalty will not be sought against and imposed on' the petitioner. As the Rapporteur normally points out in his decision to take provisional measures, he noted here as well that the withdrawal did not imply that the HRC had reached a decision on admissibility.[81] In the letter sent by the Secretariat to counsel it was noted that the Rapporteur was 'satisfied that the Government of Canada has obtained the appropriate assurances from the United States authorities, both at the Federal and at the State level'.[82] In May 1997 the petitioner withdrew his communication before the HRC. 'The answers provided by Canada in response to the communication have helped to clarify his legal situation and he feels that the assurances are now sufficient that the death penalty will not be imposed'.[83]

---

[78] See the discussion in Chapter X (Protecting (indigenous) cultural and religious rights).

[79] The latter is further discussed in Chapter XIV (Jurisdiction and admissibility).

[80] *E.G.* v. *Canada*, 738/1997, disc. 17 November 1997, initial submission 5 January 1997, received 7 January 1997 with newspaper clipping of the Orlando sentinel of 18 September 1996, Rule 86/91 of 17 January 1997; withdrawal of Rule 86 (on file with the author).

[81] Note verbale by the Special Rapporteur to the Permanent Mission of Canada in *E.G.* v. *Canada* (738/1997), 28 April 1997 (on file with the author).

[82] Letter by the Secretariat to the petitioner's counsel, 28 April 1997 (on file with the author). The fact that in federal systems it is also important to take into account implementation at the level of the constituent State is something not only the human rights adjudicators, but also the ICJ has had to face. See e.g. its provisional measures to halt executions in *LaGrand* and *Avena*. See Chapter I.

[83] Letter by counsel to the HRC, 26 May 1997; In November 1997 the HRC decided to discontinue examination of the case, letter by the Secretariat to counsel informing about the decision, taken at the 61st session, to discontinue the case, 17 November 1997 (on file with the author).

2.4 Decisions of the HRC to take provisional measures: transparency or the lack thereof?

2.4.1 Introduction

The fact that the proceedings are conducted entirely in writing obviously means that the HRC does not conduct public hearings on the use of provisional measures. The request for provisional measures is usually included in the last paragraph of a Note Verbale sent to the State party. This request is not motivated[84] and Notes Verbales are not published.[85] In its Annual Report to the General Assembly it provides some general information on the use of provisional measures.[86] However, the main information about its use of provisional measures must be derived from its case law. This section refers to the different sources and shows that the Committee has not been very transparent in its use of provisional measures.

2.4.2 Secondary literature and visit of the Geneva Secretariat

There is no literature systematically analysing the HRC's use of provisional measures. Some general literature on the HRC has referred to provisional measures.[87] Only a handful of authors have more extensively dealt with the issue.[88] In addition some information was obtained at the Committee's secretariat in Geneva.[89]

---

[84] There may be a recent change in this respect, judging from HRC *Dissanayake, Mudiyanselage Sumanaweera Banda* v. *Sri Lanka*, 22 July 2008, where the Committee notes in its decision on the merits that the petitioner had requested provisional measures to the effect that he be granted respite from the execution of the sentence of hard labour, but that in March 2005 the Special Rapporteur denied this request 'on the ground that working in a print shop did not appear to come within the terms of article 8, paragraph 3(b)', §1.2.

[85] This section deals with the available information on the Committee's provisional measures. Only in the early years it sometimes separately published a provisional measure.

[86] See the paragraph in the Report on the Committee's consideration of communications under the Optional Protocol. Incidentally the HRC also mentions provisional measures in its Concluding Observations on certain States Parties' reports.

[87] Literature discussing the HRC's procedure in general only briefly refers to provisional measures. See, e.g. Bayefsky (2002), pp. 64 and p. 165; De Zayas (2001), pp. 79-81; O'Flaherty (1996) p. 28; Zwart (1994), pp. 14-16; McGoldrick (1994), pp. 131-132, p. 202; Zwaak (1991), p. 82. Discussion is more extensive in Joseph/Schultz/Castan (2004), pp. 25-28; Barkhuysen/Van Emmerik/Rieter (2002), pp. 84-89 and (2008), pp. 106-112; Ghandhi (1998), pp. 57-65 and p. 425; the following articles have also referred to the HRC's use of provisional measures: Pasqualucci (2005); Schmidt (1998); Kamminga (1996) and Van Boven (1994). As apparent from the title, Interim Measures Indicated by International Courts, Bernhardt (ed.) (1994) does not deal with the HRC's provisional measures but only with measures indicated by courts.

[88] Harrington (2003), pp. 55-87 and Tomuschat (1995), pp. 624-634. See also Malinverni (2005), pp. 63-75; Schabas (2005), pp. 77-90; Naldi (2004), pp. 445-454 (on legal status); Van Boven/Flinterman/Rieter (1999), pp. 908-909 and Rieter (1999), pp. 1136-1145 (both on Dutch compliance with provisional measures by CAT).

[89] The author visited the Geneva Secretariat on 12-22 October 1998; 29 March-5 April 2003 and 24-30 August 2003. She wishes to thank HRC members Martin Scheinin, Sir Nigel Rodley (April 2003), Fausto Pocar and Cecilia Medina Quiroga (October 1998) as well as various (former) staff members dealing predominantly with the HRC, but also with CAT, including Marcus Schmidt, Paul Oertly, Antonie Cardon, Carla Edelenbosch and Jacob Möller. In October 1998 only the files recently closed (and some pending files) were available, not those already archived. Some

2.4.3 Drafting history Rule 86 (current Rule 92)

The drafting history of Rule 86 provides some information on the Committee's approach towards the concept of provisional measures in the first years of its existence. In this respect the HRC discussed three issues: its authority to use provisional measures; urgency and delegation of the authority to use provisional measures to subsidiary organs;[90] and the relationship of provisional measures with the admissibility and merits of a case pending before it.[91]

2.4.4 Separate publication of decisions on provisional measures

While the HRC normally does not publish its Notes Verbale, including the references to Rule 86, in the early stages it took separate decisions to issue provisional measures and published some of them.[92] This provides additional information on how the HRC has approached the issue, at least in the early years. In 1978 it made public a provisional measure to halt a deportation.[93] In 1986, moreover, on two separate occasions it made public a specific provisional measure to halt an execution.[94] These provisional measures are separate decisions instead of a sentence in an unpublished Note Verbale to the government concerned. It is clear from these decisions that the request for information (then under Rule 91) and the use of provisional measures are closely interrelated. In the first death penalty case, *X* v. *S* (1986), the HRC considered that it had insufficient information to deal with the admissibility of the case. It requested the State party to clarify certain matters involving the right of appeal to the Judicial Committee of the Privy Council (JCPC) in London and the issue of statutory time limits. Apart from this it requested the State party not to carry out the death sentence against the petitioner before the HRC had had the opportunity to consider further the question of admissibility. The Committee indicated that this further consideration would take place during its next session.[95] It later joined the case with another.[96] The final deci-

---

files, moreover, were missing. In one week in March/April and one in August 2003 it was made possible to consult several archived files (some of them relating to files that had been pending in October 1998). The author is grateful for the decision of March 2003 by a meeting of members of the HRC and HRC staff granting her access to these archived files with regard to decisions about the use of provisional measures. This decision was based on what was then Rule 96(5) of the Rules of Procedure (currently Rule 102(6)). Within the limited time period available a selection was made on the basis of death penalty cases from the time period in which the HRC did not mention its use of provisional measures in its decisions on the merits and inadmissibility, other cases in which questions arose about the use of provisional measures, recently discontinued cases (of which the communication numbers were available) and cases the author was alerted to in October 1998 that could not be properly consulted then. It must be noted that case files do not always provide information about the use of provisional measures either: until about 1995 there was no formal exchange between Secretariat and Special Rapporteur about these measures. There would just be a phone call and, normally, a note in the file about the decision taken.

90 See later in this Chapter.

91 See Chapter XIV (Jurisdiction and admissibility).

92 The reason that it did so in the early stages may have been that, different from subsequently, these were decisions by the full Committee.

93 HRC *O.E.* v. *S.*, 25 January 1978 and 26 July 1978, com. no. 22/1977, CCPR/C/OP/1 at 5 and 6. See further Chapter V on halting refoulement.

94 HRC *X* v. *S* (210/1986 of 21 July 1986) and *X* v. *S* (252/1987 of 13 November 1987), both published in *Selected Decisions* vol. II, under the heading 'interlocutory decisions', CCPR/C/OP/2.

95 HRC *X* v. *S*, 210/1986. Since 210/1986 was one of the cases in *Pratt and Morgan* v. *Jamaica* it is now clear that the State in *X* v. *S* was Jamaica. It is not clear why the HRC initially chose to keep the State anonymous. Possibly, it did so because it was publishing the decision on provisional

sion in both cases is *Pratt and Morgan* v. *Jamaica* (1989).[97] The second time it separately published a provisional measure in a death penalty case was in a case that was also called *X* v. *S* (1987).[98] This case is different in the sense that here the HRC requested the information from the petitioner and not from the State. This request for information and the provisional measures request to the government are nevertheless interrelated.[99] Similarly, there have been separate publications in relation to early detention cases in which the HRC requested information about the health and/or whereabouts of the alleged victims.[100]

Unlike the Committee did initially, when it decided for provisional measures in full session, the Rapporteurs, first the one on Death Penalty Cases and later the one on New Communications, do not draft formal transmission and provisional measures decisions. Clearly they do not provide a motivation why provisional measures would be necessary. In the weeks preceding a session the Working Group on Communications could also decide on provisional measures. It does not motivate its provisional measures either.

2.4.5 Information in the Annual Reports

The HRC gives some cursory information on its use of provisional measures in its Annual Reports. It mentioned that during its 29th and 30th sessions (22 March-27 July 1987) it had used them to halt executions vis-à-vis two States parties.[101] It also mentioned a mysterious situation in which it invoked provisional measures 'in a case concerning a group of persons, in respect of whom the State party was requested to take steps to avoid irreparable damage'.[102]

In its Annual Report of 1988 the HRC clarified an issue brought up when the Rule was drafted. The Committee finally determined what to do with urgent situations arising in between sessions.[103]

In its 1989 Annual Report it also pointed out that some petitioners sentenced to death and awaiting execution 'claimed to be innocent of the crimes of which they were convicted and further allege that they were denied a fair hearing'. The Committee used provisional measures 'in view of the urgency of the communications'. Again, the report indicated that during that period there were only two addressee States.[104]

---

measures when it had not yet decided on the merits and it believed the State would be more willing to cooperate if the Committee did not yet identify it.

[96] See 225/1987.

[97] HRC *Earl Pratt and Ivan Morgan* v. *Jamaica*, 6 April 1989.

[98] See 252/1987.

[99] As yet there is no inadmissibility decision or final View available on this interlocutory decision *X* v. *S*. It is most likely that the case was discontinued.

[100] See Chapter VII (Detention). In the third volume of the Selected Decisions of the HRC the table of contents refers to 'interlocutory decisions', with the subheading 'decisions transmitting a communication to the State party (rule 91) and requesting interim measures of protection (rule 86)'. In fact under this heading two inadmissibility decisions simply refer to provisional measures in death penalty cases. *O.W.* v. *Jamaica*, 26 July 1988 (inadm.), 227/1987 and *N.A.J.* v. *Jamaica*, 26 July 1990 (inadm.), 246/1987, CCPR/C/OP/3, pp. 11-16.

[101] A/42/40, §404, in: Yearbook of the Human Rights Committee 1987, Vol. II, CCPR/6/Add. 1.

[102] A/42/40, §405, in: Yearbook of the Human Rights Committee 1987, Vol. II, CCPR/6/Add. 1, referring to the 30th session. This may be the case of *Bernard Ominayak, Chief of the Lubicon Lake Band* v. *Canada*, 26 March 1990, CCPR/C/38/D/167/1984, 28 March 1990 because in 1986 the HRC used provisional measures in that case, see Chapter X on protecting cultural survival.

[103] See under 'timing and procedure', section 2.3 of this Chapter.

[104] A/44/40, 29 September 1989, §634, in: Official Records of the Human Rights Committee 1988/1989, Vol. II, CCPR/8/Add. 1.

Apart from some information on the HRC's practice of issuing provisional measures, including information about the delegation of the authority to issue them to a Special Rapporteur,[105] the Annual Reports also provide the names of the Special Rapporteurs during the period in question.[106]

2.4.6 Information in the Committee's Views and inadmissibility decisions

The fact that there is no complete record of its provisional measures, let alone of the substance of these measures, does not mean that the HRC did not use them. Closer investigation of its case law uncovers many of these measures. Whether or not provisional measures were used in individual cases must normally be ascertained from references made in the Committee's decisions on the merits (Views) and its inadmissibility decisions.[107] Apart from such references, the HRC rarely discusses provisional measures. At times it does not even mention in its Views that it has used them.[108]

---

[105] A/52/40, Vol. I, 1997, §467 (Pocar transmitted 46 new communications under Rule 91 and an unspecified number of Rule 86 decisions); A/53/40, 1998, §433 (Pocar transmitted 57 new communications under Rule 91, while 'in other cases' he used Rule 86); A/54/40, 1999, §398 (Kretzmer transmitted 44 new communications under Rule 91 and used Rule 86 in 10 cases). A/55/40, Vol. II, 2000, §§14 and 546 (Kretzmer transmitted 66 communications and used provisional measures 11 times); A/56/40, Vol. I, 2001, §15 (Kretzmer transmitted 32 communications and used provisional measures twice. Scheinin transmitted 31 communications, four times he also used Rule 86; in §99 the Committee mentions that during the period covered by this Annual Report, the Special Rapporteurs transmitted 60 new communications (not 63) and issued provisional measures in 7 cases (not 6)).

[106] As noted, the Annual Reports only provide general information. See e.g. A/46/40, 1991, §§669 and 692 (this report does not mention how many communications were transmitted to the State, let alone how many provisional measures); A/47/40, 1992, §617 (Lallah transmitted 30 new communications under Rule 91); A/48/40, 1993, §772 (Chanet transmitted 35 new communications under Rule 91); A/49/40, Vol. I, 1994, §386 (Chanet transmitted 26 communications under Rule 91); A/50/40, Vol. I, 1995, §492 (Chanet and Pocar transmitted 38 new communications); A/51/40, Vol. I, 1996, §378 (Pocar transmitted 62 new communications under Rule 91).

[107] The Committee's Views and inadmissibility decisions are found in the Annexes to the HRC's Annual Report to the General Assembly. Admissibility decisions, on the other hand, are not made public, not even after publication of the Committee's decision on the merits. One exception is *Rawle Kennedy* v. *Trinidad and Tobago*, public admissibility decision of 2 November 1999. It is therefore not possible to refer systematically to useful information included in these decisions. In this book incidentally references are made based on information from the files in Geneva.

[108] Sometimes the HRC appears to have used provisional measures only as part of the admissibility decision. This seemed to be the case in HRC *Bernhard Lubuto* v. *Zambia* (1995), meaning it took the HRC three and a half years before it used its provisional measures. *Bernhard Lubuto* v. *Jamaica*, 31 October 1995. In §4.4 of the View, the Committee notes that it declared the communication admissible on 30 June 1994 and it also notes that it had requested the State party, under Rule 86, not to carry out the death sentence against the petitioner pending the case. The initial submission was of 1 January 1990. From the references to Rule 86 in this paragraph one would almost conclude that it only used the provisional measure as part of the admissibility decision. Nevertheless, the file shows provisional measures were used already on 23 February 1990. The case file, however, shows provisional measures were used within two months. In other words, the assumption based on the View is incorrect and can be explained by the Committee's failure to provide the exact information in this decision. Equally, in *George Graham and Arthur*

2.4.7 Dividing decisions in time-periods depending on the availability of information

Depending on the information they provide, the decisions of the Committee may be divided in several categories. The first category covers the period *between August 1977 and April 1991*. These older Views and inadmissibility decisions mention all decisions of the Committee in relation to the case, including decisions to take provisional measures.[109] In other words, the format of the cases is such that information on their use can be identified in the View or decision itself.

Apart from the interlocutory decisions mentioned above, on provisional measures separately published, for this period this research examined the Committee's use of provisional measures in twenty inadmissibility decisions and three Views dealing with the death penalty,[110] all in the early period from 1988 to April 1991. There was also one case dealing with deportation,[111] one dealing with the protection of indigenous culture[112] and several informal provisional measures (under Rule 91) dealing with the health of detainees.[113]

During the period *from April 1991 to March 1996* the format of the decisions changed. The HRC did no longer provide the information on the use of provisional measures in the text of the Views itself. In his 1995 article Tomuschat qualifies this change in format as 'deplorable'. He points out that 'the measure in which requests under Article 86 are made and heeded or disregarded by States is an important feature of any proceeding'.[114] Fortunately, in this period it is often still possible to find out whether provisional measures were taken in a certain case because the HRC mentions this on the cover page of the View in question.[115] Research with regard to this period uncovered provisional measures in a large number of inadmissibility decisions and Views.[116]

In the period from *July 1996 to August 1998* the Committee again changed the format of its Views, but this did not improve matters. As a general rule, the Committee did not mention prior

---

Morrison v. *Jamaica*, 25 March 1996 the HRC did not immediately use provisional measures, but seemingly only several years after the initial submission, after one of the petitioners had died during a prison incident. In fact the file shows that it did not use them at the admissibility stage in October 1994, but earlier, in October 1992. The initial submission was of 18 March 1991; Rule 86/91 was of 25 October 1992.

[109] They can be found under 'Documentation References' on the cover page, with a reference to the document number.

[110] In this period the HRC published 206 Views and inadmissibility decisions. Between 1988 (when it started to use provisional measures in death penalty cases) and April 1991 it published 89 of these 206 cases.

[111] HRC *O.E.* v. *S* (22/1977).

[112] HRC *Ominayak* v. *Canada*, 26 March 1990.

[113] See Chapter VII.

[114] Tomuschat (1995), p. 629.

[115] As of July 1994 the Committee's Views inform the reader (on the cover page) that the provisional measure 'is not issued in document form'. This means that they no longer include the (internal) document number of the decision of provisional measures on the cover page of the View. The date of the transmittal of the provisional measure to the State Party is still mentioned.

[116] In total, in the approximately 200 Views and inadmissibility decisions published during this period, the HRC referred to provisional measures more than 60 times. It did so mainly, but not exclusively, in death penalty cases. Sometimes the HRC describes the transmittal of the communication under (former) Rule 91, but fails to mention its use of provisional measures in this respect. The use of these measures may still be mentioned on the cover page or in the text of the decision. In relation to the admissibility decision, the HRC may mention its renewed request for interim protection under Rule 86, although the cover page does not mention the Rule 86 of that date. See e.g., *Michael Sawyers and Michael and Desmond McClean* v. *Jamaica*, 11 April 1991.

decisions on the cover page anymore and did not refer to them in the decision itself either.[117] This means that it is not clear from the case law whether it used provisional measures during this period and, if so, in which cases. Although from the situations involved one could assume the HRC had used them, this could only be confirmed through information collected at the Secretariat of the Committee in October 1998, April and August 2003.[118] This period covers more than 100 inadmissibility decisions and Views, none of them referring to provisional measures while, in fact, the HRC had indeed used provisional measures in at least 50 cases. Since 1997 the Rule on publicity and confidentiality stipulates that decisions to use provisional measures 'shall be made public'. In this light one might have expected the Committee, in addition to mentioning the use of provisional measures in its Views, to publish these measures separately as well or otherwise to summarise them in its Annual Reports. Surprisingly, however, this new rule initially did not even trigger a restoration of the old format of the Committee's Views, at least mentioning in which cases provisional measures had been used.

It took two years, until the October 1998 session, before the HRC mentioned its use of provisional measures on the cover page again. These cover pages, however, were published neither on the treaty body database of the High Commissioner on Human Rights nor in the Committee's Annual Report.[119] *Between October 1998 and March 2002* the HRC published 147 inadmissibility decisions and Views. In more than 20 of these cases the HRC used provisional measures.[120] The foregoing means that the information about the use of provisional measures during the six-year period from July 1996 until March 2002 has been particularly inaccessible. The HRC remedied this lack of transparency in March 2002 when it started to refer again to its provisional measures in a way that is accessible to the public, in other words, on publicly available cover pages and/or in the text of the Views themselves.[121]

---

[117] It concerned the period from 16 July 1996 to 19 August 1998.

[118] The author visited the secretariat in Geneva in October 1998. At the time only the files recently closed (and some pending files) were available, not those already archived. Some files, moreover, were missing. In one week in March/April and one in August 2003 it was made possible to consult several archived files (some of them relating to files that had been pending in October 1998). The author is grateful for the decision of March 2003 by a meeting of members of the HRC and HRC staff granting her access to these archived files with regard to decisions about the use of provisional measures. This decision was based on what was then Rule 96(5) of the Rules of Procedure (currently Rule 102(6)). Within the limited time period available a selection was made on the basis of death penalty cases from the time period in which the HRC did not mention its use of provisional measures in its decisions on the merits and inadmissibility, other cases in which questions arose about the use of provisional measures, recently discontinued cases (of which the communication numbers were available) and cases the author was alerted to in October 1998 that could not be properly consulted then. It must be noted that case files do not always provide information about the use of provisional measures either: until about 1995 there was no formal exchange between Secretariat and Special Rapporteur about these measures. There would just be a phone call and, normally, a note in the file about the decision taken.

[119] Category IV in the table of cases (from 19 August 1998 to March 2002). It seems that, mistakenly, these cover pages had not been included in the decisions as made public. Consultation of the internal search system in Geneva ('ODS search') in April 2003, by entering communication numbers of cases in which Rule 86 was expected to have been used, uncovered only twelve cases mentioning Rule 86 on the (internal) cover page. There are, however, several other cases in which provisional measures were used during this period. Only a search of the case files uncovered this. There was even one case (614/1995) in which the internal cover pages did in fact mention previous decisions, including under Rule 91, but failed to mention that the Rapporteur had used Rule 86 as well.

[120] Again, this number it not necessarily exhaustive.

[121] Category V in the table of cases (as of March 2002).

It must be kept in mind that this division is based on the type of information available. It only indicates the format in which the HRC has presented its decisions, but is not meant to indicate possible trends in its use of provisional measures.[122]

2.4.8 The relevance of discontinued cases

Provisional measures have not just been used in cases that were subsequently published (in Views and inadmissibility decisions), but also in cases that were later discontinued. If death penalty cases are discontinued this is usually because counsel had no other intention than to halt the execution. Following the stay a new avenue for appeal may have been opened or, as is often the case, the Secretariat was unable to contact the petitioners or their counsel. In death penalty cases this may equally indicate that the death sentence has been commuted so that counsel lost interest in the case. In expulsion cases, however, the fact that the alleged victim cannot be reached, clearly does not mean that the case has been solved. He may have been forcibly returned. In cases in which counsel is unable to contact his clients (usually after deportation, sometimes after prison transfers) the HRC has sometimes tried to find them through the Office of the UN High Commissioner for Refugees. Usually, however, the search remains ineffective. This means that once a petitioner has been removed from the territory of the addressee State, this often marks the end of the individual complaint proceeding against that State. In relation to the death penalty and expulsion there are many discontinued cases, such as the above.

By September 1997 the HRC reported a total number of 115 discontinued or withdrawn cases.[123] As the communication numbers of these cases are not known it is not possible to check in which of them the HRC used provisional measures. It is only since the fall of 1998 that the HRC mentions the communication numbers of those cases it decided to discontinue.[124] This was the result of the new rule concerning confidentiality and it meant, among others, that all final decisions would be made public, including decisions to discontinue a case. Still, the HRC does not indicate whether provisional measures were used in these cases. Thus, it is only possible to refer to these cases incidentally.[125] This chapter refers to known cases in which the HRC used provisional measures, as well as those in which counsel requested the use of provisional measures to no avail.[126]

---

[122] The drop in provisional measures under Category IV as compared to Category III, for instance, seems to relate more to the denunciation of the OP by Jamaica and Trinidad and Tobago, dramatically diminishing the number of provisional measures than to the difference in source.

[123] A/52/40, §456.

[124] A/53/40.

[125] See e.g. HRC *A.A.T.* v. *Hungary* (543/1993) for an example of a case in which provisional measures were used but that was later discontinued because it had been solved (on file with the author). In some cases counsel asked for discontinuance after, for instance, the promise that permanent residence visas would be granted, or after the victim's release and changes in the law.

[126] See e.g. HRC *A.B.* v. *Canada* (622/1995); *J.P.A.F.* v. *Canada* (620/1995); *P.L.-B.* v. *Canada* (556/1993) and *J.C.A.* v. *Costa Rica* (725/1996) and *X.* v. *Australia* (776/1997), for examples of discontinued cases in which counsel's request for provisional measures had been denied. In some cases it is not clear whether provisional measures were used. *O.* v. *France* (715/1996), for instance, concerned an impending deportation to Spain but it is not clear whether they were used. In one case, *R.* v. *Canada* (652/1995), the petitioner did not request provisional measures and the HRC did not grant them, but there was a discussion about serious hardship. It was possible to examine the case files of eight discontinued cases mentioned in the Committee's reports to the General Assembly relating to sessions 53-56. In fact provisional measures were not applied in these cases. See e.g. *HRC Coloma* v. *Russia* (607/1995); *Schier* v. *New Zealand* (892/1999); *Lee-*

2.4.9 No information on pending cases

On the basis of the available material it is possible to draw tentative conclusions about the situations the HRC has dealt with and the protective measures required by its (informal) decisions on provisional measures. No comprehensive information is available on the direction the *present* Committee is taking, by way of its Rapporteur. This is so, exactly because it is necessary to await the publication of the cases on the merits. It is only occasionally that information becomes available in advance of publication of the decision on the merits.

In some cases involving executions in violation of its provisional measures the HRC has made public *official* statements.[127] In other cases counsel or others may have informed the press.[128]

Alexander v. *Australia* (723/1996); *Huat* v. *Australia* (681/1996); *Nielson* v. *Australia* (545/1993); *Espinosa* v. *Ecuador* (551/1993). One of the cases mentioned as discontinued was in fact concluded with a View. In *Gutierrez Vivanco* v. *Peru* (678/1996) the HRC found a violation of Article 14. Provisional measures played no role. There were two cases that related to deportation. In one of them the petitioner did not request provisional measures and the HRC did not grant them, but there was a discussion about serious hardship, see *Richardson* v. *Canada* (652/1995). In the other the petitioner did request Rule 86 but the HRC did not grant it. The case was discontinued following the petitioner's expulsion, see *A.B.* v. *Canada* (622/1995). Four other case files relating to these sessions were not available. According to Secretariat staff at least two of these four cases were not applicable: HRC *Agatanova* v. *Latvia* (764/1997) and *Kravchenko* v. *Latvia* (713/1996). While the latter case related to deportation, the petitioner's wife had already been deported before he submitted the case. In *Williams* v. *New Zealand* (773/1997) the petitioner had requested the HRC to use provisional measures to request the State to make available kidney dialysis so as to prevent irreparable harm. The HRC did not do so and eventually the case was discontinued. See Chapter XII (Other situations). The fourth case, *O.* v. *France* (715/1996) concerned an impending deportation to Spain. It is not clear whether provisional measures were used. It was also possible to examine some other files of discontinued cases, some of earlier periods, on the assumption that they might relate to deportation or death penalty cases. Two of these cases appeared to be inapplicable. HRC *Nunes* v. *Jamaica*, (745/1997) and *Sahli* v. *France* (629/1995). Five of them did involve the use of provisional measures to halt an execution. See e.g. HRC *Frank McKnight* v. *Jamaica* (729/1996), Rule 86 of 4 December 1996; case discontinued on 29 July 2003. In *H.M.* v. *Jamaica*, (595/1994) the HRC used provisional measures on 8 November 1994. In April 1995 the petitioner withdrew the case following reclassification of his sentence from capital to non-capital on 20 March 1995. His counsel pointed out that their client's sentence had been commuted to life imprisonment. They withdrew the case because their objective for requesting the Committee's recommendations had been fulfilled. Letter of 18 April 1995. Hence, at its 54th session the HRC decided to discontinue the case, letter of 3 August 1995. See also *E.P.* v. *Trinidad and Tobago* (636/1995), Rule 86 of 27 June 1995, discontinued 29 July 2003 (on file with the author). In *Rockliff Ross* v. *Guyana*, 703/1996, the State executed the petitioner despite provisional measures. See also *Reece* v. *Jamaica*, 247/1987, both discussed Chapter III (Executions). In several cases the HRC failed or refused to use provisional measures to halt a deportation. See e.g. HRC *P.L.-B* v. *Canada* (556/1993); *J.P.A.F.* v. *Canada* (620/1995); *A.B.* v. *Canada* (622/1995); *J.* v. *Canada* (685/1996) and *J.C.A.* v. *Costa Rica* (725/1996). In total, this book refers to nine discontinued cases in which the HRC used provisional measures. As noted, five of them dealt with halting executions. One dealt with halting the execution of a detention order. HRC *V.* v. *Spain*, 495/1992. Three cases dealt with halting expulsion or extradition. HRC *O.E.* v. *S.*, 22 /1977; *A.A.T.* v. *Hungary*, 543/1993 and *E.G.* v. *Canada*, 738/1997. One case, finally, dealt with providing access to counsel and court. HRC *A. et al.* v. *Angola*, 810/1998.

[127]   See public statements following the execution of Ashby, HRC Summary Record of the 1352nd meeting: Trinidad and Tobago, 26 July 1994; *Dante Piandiong et al.* v. *the Philippines,* 19

Until the HRC decides to publish its provisional measures separately for those who wish to consult them, to issue press releases in some of these cases or at least an overview of its provisional measures in its Annual Report, the information on the use of provisional measures will become available only upon publication of its final Views and inadmissibility decisions.[129]

In my view, after publication of the final Views, the previous admissibility decision should be made available as well. If it is advisable to 'anonymise' the (alleged) victim, initials could be used instead of the full names. Moreover, the Committee should always discuss the procedure under a separate heading and include references to the provisional measures taken. It would be preferable if it also provided a short explanation of the purpose of the provisional measure. In any case a specification should be included in the note verbale sent to the State. In my opinion this would enhance the authoritativeness of the provisional measure.

2.4.10 Construing the purpose of provisional measures from the Committee's case law

The lack of consistent references to and explanations for the use of provisional measures necessitates an approach drawing conclusions from the factual situations, the rights claimed and the eventual decisions on the merits and reparation. In this light, it is necessary not only to present the conclusions, together with references to the sources, but to present as well the construction of this source material. This is so precisely because the findings are construed and cannot be found as such in the text of the decisions.

If sufficient case law is available on certain issues, for instance on the death penalty, it is not necessary to present the issue on a case-by-case basis. If there are only a limited number of (diverse) cases available on an issue, however, such approach is indeed warranted. In some cases the context provided in the relevant Views themselves is insufficient and additional information is

---

October 2000. See also *Mansaraj et al.; Gborie et al. and Sesay et al.* v. *Sierra Leone*, 16 July 2001 and *Glenn Ashby* v. *Trinidad and Tobago*, 21 March 2002. See further press release, 'Human Rights Committee deplores the execution of six individuals in Uzbekistan', 24 July 2003. The petitioners who were executed were Muzaffar Mirzaev (case 1170/2003), Shukrat Andasbaev (case 1166/2003), Ulugbek Ashov (case 1165/2003), Ilkhon Babadzhanov and Maksud Ismailov (case 1162/2003), and Azamat Uteev (case 1150/2003). In addition see *Barno Saidova* v. *Tajikistan*, 8 July 2004. In other cases NGOs sometimes make available information. While the case of *Ahani* was still pending, sources other than the HRC had already made available information about the provisional measures and the fact that Canada nevertheless deported him. Amnesty International urgent action of 17 May 2002 and Amnesty International Annual Report 2003, p. 67. *Mansour Ahani* v. *Canada*, 29 March 2004, CCPR/C/80/D/1051/2002, 15 June 2004. See the discussion of this case in Chapter V (Expulsion). The Asian Human Rights Commission made public information about the use of provisional measures to the effect that Sri Lanka would protect Michael Anthony Fernando and his family against threats. See e.g. the urgent appeals on its website, <www.ahrchk.net> (consulted on 5 August 2004). See further about this case Chapter IX (Threats).

128 An example is a newspaper article referring to a 'Geneva based United Nations human rights panel', which agreed to examine the Bakhtiyari family's case on 28 March 2002 and had recommended Australia not to deport the children until it had been able to determine the case. Richard C. Paddock, 'A family apart in Australia', Los Angeles Times, 10 April 2002, reproduced at <www.carad-wa.org> (consulted 9 April 2003). The HRC published its decision on the merits in 2003: *Bakhtiyari* v. *Australia*, 29 October 2003. See further in Chapter V on halting expulsion and Chapter VII on detention situations involving risks to health and safety.

129 In September 2002 the Special Rapporteur reported he had used more than 20 provisional measures, many of them involving conditions of detention (health care) and expulsion. Interview of author with Special Rapporteur Martin Scheinin, Maastricht 20 September 2002.

derived from other sources such as NGO reports and Concluding Observations by the HRC in relation to State reports under Article 40 ICCPR.

3 CAT, CEDAW AND CERD

3.1   Introduction

In light of their adjudicatory function, in light of the object and purpose of the treaties and the individual petition system, the Committee on the Elimination of Racial Discrimination (CERD), supervising the International Convention on the Elimination of All Forms of Racial Discrimination (ICERD),[130] and the Committee against Torture (CAT) supervising the Convention against Torture and other Cruel, Inhuman or Degrading Treatment or Punishment (ICAT),[131] have included in their Rules of Procedure the possibility of taking provisional measures.

For the Convention on the Elimination of All Forms of Discrimination against Women (CEDAW),[132] the possibility of individual complaint was only recently introduced, by way of an Optional Protocol. This Protocol includes an explicit article on provisional measures. The same applies to the even more recent UN Convention against Disappearances, which has not yet entered into force. It explicitly provides for the possibility (and obligation) to take urgent action.

CAT has an established practice with regard to provisional measures while CERD has never used them and the Committee on the Elimination of Discrimination against Women (CEDAW) has only just started its practice. Dealing with complaints under the most recent individual complaint mechanism, CEDAW has used provisional measures in 2003, requesting the State to take protective measures to prevent irreparable harm to the petitioner because of domestic violence.[133]

CAT takes almost all its provisional measures under Article 3 (non-refoulement).[134] Yet there is one case in which it took them in order to protect family members and witnesses against threats and another case in which it did so in the context of the State's obligation to act against impunity.[135] As the majority of its case law deals with the question whether or not there would be a real risk of torture in the receiving or requesting State, most of its case law will be dealt with in Chapter XV about provisional measures and assessment of risk.

While CERD has never used provisional measures as of yet there are situations in which it could feasibly use them in the future.[136] Article 2(1)(a) CERD stipulates that States refrain from

---

[130]   ICERD was concluded in 1965 and entered into force in 1969. It has 173 States parties (as of 18 July 2007).

[131]   ICAT was concluded in 1984 and entered into force in 1987. It has 145 States parties (as of 2 October 2007).

[132]   CEDAW was concluded in 1979 and entered into force in 1981. There are 185 States parties (as of 20 July 2007).

[133]   CEDAW *A.T.* v. *Hungary*, 26 January 2005. See further Chapter IX (Threats).

[134]   Between 1993 and 2003 CAT took provisional measures in more than 80 cases involving non-refoulement. See Chapter V (Non-refoulement) and Chapter XV (Immediacy and risk).

[135]   CAT *B.M'.B* v. *Tunisia* (inadm.), 5 May 1994 and *Suleymane Guengueng et al.* v. *Senegal* (involving former Chadian dictator Habré), Press release Human Rights Watch, 23 April 2001, 'United Nations asks Senegal to hold Ex-Chad Dictator', <www.hrw.org/justice/habre> (accessed 22 June 2005); confirmed formally in Note Verbale CAT to HRW of 27 April 2001, <http://www.hrw.org/french/themes/habre-legal.htm> (accessed 22 June 2005).

[136]   Until 2000 the number of cases decided by CERD was extremely small. See Van Boven (2000a) and Van Boven (2001a), also referring to the 'modest number of communications received and considered'. Before 2000 the Committee published decisions (views and inadmissibility

racial discrimination and ensure that public authorities and institutions refrain from such discrimination. Article 3 obliges States to prevent racial segregation and apartheid and Article 4 to take immediate and positive measures against incitement of racial hatred. Article 5 lays down the security of the person including the protection from violence or bodily harm (Article 5(b)),[137] the right to vote (Article 5(c)) and social, economic and cultural rights such as the right to housing, health care and education (Article 5(e)). This right is of particular importance when children are involved.[138] Article 6 refers to the undertaking to ensure effective protection and remedies including reparation and satisfaction.

If CERD would decide to take provisional measures this would likely be in the context of widespread and systematic discrimination or in an extreme individual case.[139] In this respect there may be similarities with its practice to take preventive measures including early warning and urgent procedures with regard to situations requiring its immediate attention outside of the regular process of commenting on State reports.[140] When it initiated this practice in 1993 it referred to the conclusion by the fourth meeting of the chairpersons that the human rights treaty bodies had an important role to play not only in responding to human rights violations but also in seeking to prevent them. Each treaty body should consider whether procedural innovations would be required to enable it to take all possible measures within its competence in order to prevent human rights violations and monitor more closely emergency situations.[141]

It is perhaps not surprising that the treaty body dealing with the smallest number of individual petitions was the first and, thus far, only body to institute a formal process for urgent situations. The HRC did decide, in April 1991 that it could request periodic emergency reports, but has

---

decisions) in nine cases. Between 2000 and August 2007 another 29 cases were concluded with an inadmissibility decision or decision on the merits (based on UN statistical survey of 15 August 2007).

[137] See Chapter IX (Threats) on the use of provisional measures by other adjudicators to protect against such threats.

[138] See also Chapter XIII (Protection).

[139] See Chapter XI discussing provisional measures in the Inter-American system to prevent mass expulsion and by the Bosnia Chamber to halt forced eviction. As noted in Chapter I (ICJ), in October 2008 the ICJ ordered provisional measures to the effect that both Parties shall refrain from any act of racial discrimination and from sponsoring, defending or supporting such acts; that they shall facilitate humanitarian assistance; and that they shall refrain from any action which might prejudice the respective rights of the Parties or might aggravate or extend the dispute. ICJ *Application of the International Convention on the Elimination of Racial Discrimination*, (*Georgia v. Russian Federation*), 15 October 2008 (by a 8-7 vote).

[140] This became part of its regular agenda in 1994. See its working paper on this issue, A/48/18, Annex III. The General Assembly has supported this approach, see e.g. General Assembly resolution 48/90, 20 December 1993, A/RES/48/90, 16 February 1994: "Encourages the Committee to continue to exert its efforts to enhance its contributions in the area of prevention of racial discrimination, including early warning and urgent procedures". The distinction between early warning measures and urgent procedures is not always clear in practice, but the former would be aimed at addressing existing problems in order to prevent escalation while the latter would respond to 'problems requiring immediate attention to prevent or limit the scale or number of serious violations of the Convention'. See e.g. the Annual Report of CERD to the General Assembly, 22 September 1995, A/50/18, §§20-24. See e.g. Van Boven (1998), pp. 165-182.

[141] Fourth meeting of Chairpersons of the human rights treaty bodies, 42nd session, A/47/628, §44.

not often used this method.[142] The other treaty bodies have, on occasion, asked for special reports.[143]

This section discusses the right of individual petition and the power of CERD, CAT and CEDAW to order provisional measures, the promptness of CAT in deciding on the use of provisional measures and the availability of information on the use of these measures.[144]

3.2   The right of individual complaint and CERD, CAT and CEDAW

CERD consists of eighteen, CAT of ten and CEDAW of twenty-three independent experts. Like the decisions of the HRC, the decisions of the other UN supervisory bodies dealing with individual complaints must be seen in their wider context, including the tasks of these bodies under the reporting procedure.[145] Similar to the HRC they publish Concluding Observations on State reports as well as General Comments on specific issues.[146]

CAT's Rapporteur for follow-up to State party reports and gender issues has pointed out that the follow-up procedure has been established to ensure compliance with Article 2 ICAT. Matters for which CAT requested measures in the context of its follow-up procedure should meet three criteria: 'they must be urgent, protective and achievable within one year'.[147] These references, especially to urgency and to the criterion of protective measures, are relevant as well in the context of provisional measures. Also relevant is the response by the Chairperson of CAT to a remark by the representative of China. The Chairperson noted:

---

[142] See A/50/40, §§36 and 39. For examples see Boerefijn (1999a), pp. 255-283 (on reporting under exceptional circumstances).

[143] The International Federation for Human Rights (FIDH) notes that the UN Committee on Economic, Social and Cultural Rights (a committee not currently dealing with individual petitions) 'is the quickest at examining situations, which are not dealt with by state party reports'. These 'consist in sending letters to the relevant governments, expressing the concern of the Committee in relation to the information gathered and asking for factual information in response'. The FIDH adds that these examinations are 'carried out outside any well-defined procedure'. In this respect the Committee seems to prefer 'to justify its reaction within the framework of its follow-up to earlier recommendations' although urgency is indeed 'one of the factors in sending letters of concern'. International Federation for Human Rights, Progress report on implementation of FIDH program (2000-2001), treaty monitoring bodies: mechanisms to be supported, report 322/2, December 2002, p. 20.

[144] On 4 April 2008 the UN Working Group on the Optional Protocol adopted by consensus a draft for an Optional Protocol to the International Covenant on Economic, Social and Cultural Rights and sent it for consideration to the Human Rights Council. This draft also includes an Article 5 on interim measures, which refers to the discretion of the supervisory committee to 'transmit to the State Party concerned for its urgent consideration a request that the State Party take such interim measures as may be necessary in exceptional circumstances to avoid possible irreparable damage to the victim or victims of the alleged violations'.

[145] See e.g. Flinterman (2003), pp. 621-624; Bayefsky (2002); Bayefsky (2001); Ingelse (2001); Alston/Crawford (2000); Bayefsky (2002); O' Flaherty (1996).

[146] CERD and CEDAW have regularly issued General Comments. CAT, thus far, has only published a General Comment on Article 3 ICAT (non-refoulement) and one on Article 2 on Implementation of Article 2 by States Parties, see further Chapter XV (Immediacy and risk).

[147] See CAT Summary Record of the 662nd Meeting, 19 May 2005, CAT/C/SR.662, 2 June 2005, §5 (Ms. Gaer, US, Rapporteur for follow-up to State party reports and gender issues).

"It was standard practice to raise questions about individual cases during the dialogue with States parties, most of which had not been reluctant to reply. However, as a rule, such cases were not mentioned in the conclusions and recommendations".[148]

Article 22 ICAT lays down the right of individual complaint against States that have specifically recognised CAT's competence in this regard.[149] The same applies to Article 14 ICERD.[150] The individual complaint procedure under the Optional Protocol to the Women's Convention entered into force on in December 2000.[151] CEDAW's first decision on the merits concerned protection against domestic violence.[152] In this case it also used provisional measures. The proceedings of CERD, CAT and CEDAW do not significantly differ from those of the HRC.[153]

3.3 Power and promptness of CAT and CEDAW to take provisional measures and the possibilities of the new Committee against Disappearances

3.3.1 Introduction

As noted, CERD was the first UN treaty body introducing provisional measures in its Rules of Procedure. Rule 94(3) is phrased as follows:

"In the course of its consideration, the Committee may inform the State party of its views on the desirability, because of urgency, of taking interim measures to avoid possible irreparable damage to the person or persons who claim to be victim(s) of the alleged violation. In doing so, the Committee shall inform the State party concerned that such expression of its views on interim measures does not prejudice either its final opinion on the merits of the communication or its eventual suggestions and recommendation".

---

[148] See CAT Summary Record of the 662nd Meeting, 19 May 2005, CAT/C/SR.662, 2 June 2005, §32.

[149] Of the States parties to the ICAT 61 have also recognised the right of individual petition, 17 of them since 2000. Japan, the UK and the US have only recognised the inter-State procedure that has never been used as of yet. See UN statistical survey, updated 23 November 2007 untreaty.un.org (accessed 11 July 2005). About the treaty itself and the process leading up to its conclusion and ratification see Burgers/Danelius (1988) and Boulesbaa (1999). About the individual complaint procedure and case law see Doerfel (2005); Gorlick (1999); pp. 479-495, esp. pp. 484-492; Ingelse (2001); Gorlick (2000), pp. 117-177, esp. pp. 150-164.

[150] Since 2000, the number of States parties to the ICERD that recognised the competence of CERD to receive and consider communications under Article 14 ICERD increased from 31 to 51. See UN statistical survey, 15 August 2007.

[151] The right of individual complaint under the OP to the CEDAW has been recognised by 89 States. See UN statistical survey, 8 November 2007.

[152] CEDAW *A.T.* v. *Hungary*, 26 January 2005. See also Boerefijn (2005a), pp. 470-480.

[153] See section 2 of this Chapter on the HRC. See also Chapter XIV on admissibility and jurisdiction. CAT often refers to the 'complainant', CEDAW to the 'author' and CERD to the 'petitioner'. Generally about the proceedings see Complaint Procedures, Fact Sheet No. 7/Rev.1 and The United Nations Human Rights Treaty System: An introduction to the core human rights treaties and the treaty bodies, Fact sheet no. 30, June 2005; Hannum (2004); Bayefsky (2002); Barkhuysen/Van Emmerik/Rieter (2008); Amnesty International Handbook to combat racial discrimination (2001); Tanaka/Nagamine (2001); O'Flaherty (1996); Zwaak (1991).

While CERD has never invoked it as of yet, the Rule did serve as a source of inspiration when the HRC was drafting its Rules of Procedure.[154]

Rule 108 of CAT's Rules of Procedure stipulates:

"1. At any time after the receipt of a complaint, the Committee, a working group, or the Rapporteur(s) for new complaints and interim measures may transmit to the State party concerned, for its urgent consideration, a request that it take such interim measures as the Committee considers necessary to avoid irreparable damage to the victim or victims of alleged violations.

2. Where the Committee, the Working Group, or Rapporteur(s) request(s) interim measures under this rule, the request shall not imply a determination of the admissibility or the merits of the complaint. The State party shall be so informed upon transmittal.

3. Where a request for interim measures is made by the Working Group or Rapporteur(s) under the present rule, the Working Group or Rapporteur(s) should inform the Committee members of the nature of the request and the complaint to which the request relates at the next regular session of the Committee.

4. The Secretary-General shall maintain a list of such requests for interim measures.

5. The Rapporteur for new complaints and interim measures shall also monitor compliance with the Committee's requests for interim measures".

As noted, the OP to the Women's Convention explicitly refers to the power to take provisional measures. Its Article 5 stipulates:

"1. At any time after the receipt of a communication and before a determination on the merits has been reached, the Committee may transmit to the State Party concerned for its urgent consideration a request that the State Party take such interim measures as may be necessary to avoid possible irreparable damage to the victim or victims of the alleged violation.

2. Where the Committee exercises its discretion under paragraph 1 of the present article, this does not imply a determination on admissibility or on the merits of the communication".[155]

Article 31 International Convention for the Protection of All Persons from Enforced Disappearance[156] provides for an optional individual complaint procedure. Its section 4 stipulates:

---

[154] See section 2.4 of this Chapter.

[155] Rule 63 Rules of Procedure CEDAW-Committee (A/56/38, Annex 1): "1. At any time after the receipt of a communication and before a determination on the merits has been reached, the Committee may transmit to the State party concerned, for its urgent consideration, a request that it take such interim measures as the Committee considers necessary to avoid irreparable damage to the victim or victims of the alleged violation. 2. A working group or rapporteur may also request the State party concerned to take such interim measures as the working group or rapporteur considers necessary to avoid irreparable damage to the victim or victims of the alleged violation. 3. When a request for interim measures is made by a working group or rapporteur under the present rule, the working group or rapporteur shall forthwith thereafter inform the Committee members of the nature of the request and the communication to which the request relates. 4. Where the Committee, a working group or a rapporteur requests interim measures under this rule, the request shall state that it does not imply a determination of the merits of the communication". CEDAW's Working Group on Communications under the OP to the CEDAW has recommended deletion of the words 'or rapporteur' in this rule, leaving it for the working group to deal with requests for provisional measures, see its Report of its ninth session, 26 February 2007, in: Sessional/Annual Report of Committee CEDAW/C/2007/111/WGCOP/L.1, §8(g).

[156] Adopted 20 December 2006, not yet entered into force (by December 2008: 71 signatories and one ratification (Albania)).

"4. At any time after the receipt of a communication and before a determination on the merits has been reached, the Committee may transmit to the State Party concerned for its urgent consideration a request that the State Party will take such interim measures as may be necessary to avoid possible irreparable damage to the victims of the alleged violation. Where the Committee exercises its discretion, this does not imply a determination on admissibility or on the merits of the communication".

Yet in urgent cases the Committee may address even States parties that have not recognized the individual complaint procedure under Article 31. The innovative Article 30 introduces the possibility for the Committee to intervene upon a request 'by relatives of the disappeared person or their legal representatives, their counsel or any person authorized by them, as well as by any other person having a legitimate interest' that 'a disappeared person should be sought and found'. In fact when it considers that a range of procedural requirements is met, it 'shall request the State Party concerned to provide it with information on the situation of the persons sought, within a time limit set by the Committee'.[157]

3.3.2 Promptness and delegation

In 2002 CAT introduced its new Rules of Procedure, creating the Special Rapporteur on New Complaints and Interim Measures to enhance consistency and speed. Following a proposal by Committee member Mavrommatis Rule 108 refers to 'Rapporteur(s)' rather than to 'Rapporteur'. Mavrommatis had pointed out that 'in view of the urgency of requests for interim measures the Committee should envisage having an alternate to such a rapporteur, who would be able to deal immediately with a case in the absence of the Rapporteur for New Complaints'.[158]

Previously the Secretariat transmitted each new communication to the Chairman, 'who consulted the other members of the Committee about it'.[159]

"In appointing the rapporteur for a given communication, language considerations were taken into account, since the rapporteur often had to examine the dossier in depth. The procedure was therefore pragmatic rather than systematic, but was perhaps less effective than that of the Human Rights Committee".[160]

Most information about the promptness of CAT's provisional measures is available over the period 1993-2003 and is unlikely to reflect the increased promptness suggested by the 2002 decision to assign one member of CAT with the task to deal with provisional measures. In the period under review it generally took the Committee a few weeks to decide on provisional measures. There are some instances in which it was able to take them on the day on which it received the petition.[161] There are also cases in which it took them half a year after the petitioner requested

---

[157] On the procedural requirements see Chapter XIV (Jurisdiction and admissibility).
[158] CAT Summary Records 28th session, 6 May 2002, CAT/C/SR.513, 15 May 2002, §92.
[159] Summary Records 27th session, 13 November 2001, CAT/C/SR.487, 10 March 2003, §20 (Burns, Canada).
[160] Ibidem.
[161] See CAT *Mutombo* v. *Switzerland*, 27 April 1994 (petition and provisional measure 18 November 1993) and *P.S.S.* v. *Canada*, 13 November 1998 (petition and provisional measure 5 May 1997).

them.[162] In one case it took provisional measures within a day, but the petitioner was deported on that same day. The State argued that it had received the Note Verbale too late.[163]

Initially CAT used provisional measures almost automatically in any Article 3 case. Later a Special Rapporteur was introduced. As provisional measures are considered to be 'fairly intrusive' the Rapporteur would ask the secretariat to make a quick assessment on the substance of the complaint and whether there was prima facie evidence of risk. This resulted in the use of provisional measures in a lower percentage of cases.[164]

In 2005 the representative of Sweden pointed out that when CAT requested provisional measures 'it would be helpful if the request was forwarded at a reasonable time, in other words before 6 p.m. on a Friday evening'.[165] The Rapporteur on interim measures pointed out that 'while he always tried to observe the 24 hour rule, it was sometimes necessary to ask the State party for further information'.[166] This seems to indicate that, since the institution of a Rapporteur, an attempt is made to take provisional measures within a day of receipt of a request to that end.

The Rules of Procedure by the CEDAW foresee delegation of the authority to take provisional measures to a working group or rapporteur, but the Working Group on Communications has suggested the deletion of the reference to 'or rapporteur'.[167] On 20 October 2003 the used provisional measures for the first time.[168]

---

[162] See e.g. *X, Y and Z* v. *Sweden*, 6 May 1998 (provisional measures on behalf of Z on 22 November 1996; initial submission 27 June 1996).

[163] CAT *J.A.G.V.* v. *Sweden*, 11 November 2003 (provisional measure and expulsion of 23 July 2002); see also *Z.T.* v. *Australia*, 19 November 2003 in which the petition dated from 4 January 2000 and the provisional measure was sent on 26 January 2000, on which day the State expelled the petitioner.

[164] About 60 to 70 % according to an estimate made at the secretariat in Geneva in October 2003. Yet see Chapter XV (Immediacy and risk), section 3.2.4 under the heading 'assessment of risk by CAT.

[165] See Summary Record of the 662nd Meeting, 19 May 2005, CAT/C/SR.662, 2 June 2005, §24 (Ms. Sundberg, representative Sweden).

[166] See Summary Record of the 662nd Meeting, 19 May 2005, CAT/C/SR.662, 2 June 2005, §36 (Mr. Mavrommatis, Rapporteur on interim measures). See also Chapter XV on immediacy and risk.

[167] See Rule 63. Yet its Working Group on Communications under the Optional Protocol has suggested the deletion of the words 'or rapporteur', see its Report of its ninth session, 26 February 2007, in: Sessional/Annual Report of Committee CEDAW/C/2007/111/WGCOP/L.1, §8(g).

[168] See CEDAW *A.T.* v. *Hungary*, 26 January 2005 (the petitioner sent a request on 10 October; 2003; 10 days later provisional measures were used; a corrigendum was sent on 17 November 2003 and a follow-up on 13 July 2004). Based on information provided by Prof. Flinterman, member of the Working Group, Maastricht 10 June 2005, Beate Schöpp-Schilling, Chairperson of the Working Group on individual petitions, used these provisional measures upon consultation with other members of the Working Group. At the time CEDAW was the only UN treaty body based in New York rather than Geneva. When the Optional Protocol introducing the right of individual complaint entered into force, members of its staff visited Geneva for two weeks to inform themselves about the practices of the other treaty bodies. Obviously this included the practices with regard to provisional measures. There were weekly contacts (e-mail and phone) for purposes of coordination. The person with overall responsibility for the individual petition procedures in Geneva was previously active for CEDAW in New York, which may also be helpful for the integration of working methods. In 2008 the Committee transferred to Geneva.

3.3.3 Proprio motu

The text of the CAT's Rule on provisional measures does not exclude their *proprio motu* use and as most complaints involve Article 3 (non-refoulement) it would be very rigid, and disagree with the purpose of the Rule, to insist on an explicit invocation by the petitioner in such cases where the petitioner already mentions a date of expulsion and argues before CAT that such expulsion would violate the principle of non-refoulement.[169] The text of the OP to the Women's Convention does not preclude *proprio motu* use of provisional measures either and neither does the text of CEDAW's Rules of Procedure.

3.3.4 Withdrawing provisional measures

As noted, generally human rights adjudicators take provisional measures for a limited period and, based on the facts, they may decide to extend them or not to renew them at all after this period has lapsed. Moreover, in practice the HRC, the Inter-American Commission and Court and the ECtHR have been known to lift provisional measures upon receipt of pertinent information on changed circumstances or lack of urgency or risk.[170] Nevertheless, since 2002 the CAT's Rule on provisional measures (Rule 108) explicitly invites the State to protest against the use of provisional measures:

> "6.The State party may inform the Committee that the reasons for the interim measures have lapsed or present arguments why the request for interim measures should be lifted.
> 7.The Rapporteur, the Committee or the Working Group may withdraw the request for interim measures".[171]

A reason for the inclusion of this rule may be the letters received by a few states threatening withdrawal from the individual complaint system. These States had done so at a strategic moment in time, just after the withdrawals by Jamaica and Trinidad and Tobago from the OP to the ICCPR. This may have been why CAT formally introduced this 'mini procedure' in which the State is informed of the possibility to request a withdrawal of the provisional measures.

In 2003 some members of the secretariat expressed the fear that this new rule would be used by States as a tool for taking provisional measures less seriously.[172] Indeed, discomfort about the

---

[169]   CAT has also declared petitions admissible in which the petitioner, not assisted by counsel, does not specifically invoke Article 3 ICAT but indicates a fear of torture upon expulsion. In such cases it has also used provisional measures. See e.g. CAT *V.L.* v. *Switzerland*, 20 November 2006 (provisional measures 14 January 2005).

[170]   See e.g. Chapter XV on immediacy and risk.

[171]   Former Rules 108(9) and 110(3) of CAT's Rules of Procedure did not contain such invitation. Rule 108(9) was as follows: "In the course of the consideration of the question of the admissibility of a communication, the Committee, or a working group or a special rapporteur designated under rule 106, paragraph 3, may request the States parties to take steps to avoid possible irreparable damage to the person or persons who claim to be victim(s) of the alleged violation. Such a request addressed to the State party does not imply that any decision has been reached on the question of the admissibility of the communication". Former Rule 110(3) stipulated: "In the course of its considerations, the Committee may inform the State party of its views on the desirability, because of urgency, of taking interim measures to avoid possible irreparable damage to the person or persons who claim to be victim(s) of the alleged violation. In doing so, the Committee shall inform the State party concerned that such expression of its views on interim measures does not prejudice its final views on the merits of the communication". See Rules of Procedure 1984 as amended during the 13th session, A/50/44 Annex 4.

new rule also appears from the statements by members of the Committee itself. During the drafting process of the mandate of the Rapporteur on New Complaints and Interim Measures Committee member Mariño (Spain) had argued that it would 'be more prudent to authorise the Rapporteur to act in conjunction with the plenary or the Bureau or, at the very least, in consultation with the Chairman' when deciding to withdraw provisional measures. 'Given that a person's life could be at stake' the Rapporteur should not be empowered to act alone on this matter. While he did not wish to 'cast doubts on the sound judgment of the Rapporteur', he did wish to 'make sure that appropriate safeguards were in place'.[173] González Poblete (Chile) responded that 'the most important task was to establish uniform criteria and uniform jurisprudence'. To achieve this 'the Rapporteur would report to the Committee on his or her decisions and Committee would indicate what corrective action needed to be taken in the future, if required'.[174] The full Committee did not adopt the suggestion by Mariño about the need for consultation before provisional measures would be withdrawn.

The reference in each 'request' for provisional measures by the Special Rapporteur to the fact that this 'request could be reviewed in the light of observations provided by the State party on the admissibility or on the merits' would indeed appear to trigger more requests for withdrawal. Yet the new Special Rapporteur certainly did not automatically heed to States' requests for such withdrawals. In April 2002 the Special Rapporteur denied a request by Germany to withdraw the Committee's provisional measures.[175] Germany had taken this course of action while it was the first time provisional measures had ever been requested against it.

Another example of CAT not immediately heeding to a State's request for a withdrawal of provisional measures is one taken in December 2003 in which a reference to the possibility of withdrawal had been added: "The Rapporteur indicated that this request could be reviewed in the light of new arguments presented by the State party". CAT also noted that the State party acceded to this request.[176] In February 2004 'the State party challenged the admissibility of the communication and requested the Committee to withdraw its request for interim measures, pursuant to Rule 108, paragraph 7, of the Committee's rules of procedure'. The View notes that the petitioner objected to the State party's motion for withdrawal of the provisional measures, but it does not specify what was the Committee's response. It only notes that the Secretariat informed the State party that admissibility and merits would be examined separately.[177] Subsequently it found the

---

[172]   Yet it was also suggested that the Committee would not mention any withdrawals in its Views because then it would look like CAT made a mistake if it had to withdraw and it could discourage petitioners. In fact it appears that the Committee has referred to withdrawals and State's requests for withdrawals and to the extent that it has not, such lack of transparency would not enhance the Committee's credibility.

[173]   CAT Summary Records, 28th session, 16 May 2002, CAT/C/SR.527, 29 May 2002, §25.

[174]   CAT Summary Records, 28th session, 16 May 2002, CAT/C/SR.527, 29 May 2002, §26.

[175]   In November 2002 the State party had submitted its observations on the admissibility of the complaint 'together with a motion asking the Committee to withdraw its request for interim measures, pursuant to Rule 108, paragraph 7, of the Committees rules of procedure'. Counsel asked the Committee to *maintain* its provisional measures 'until a final decision on the complaint has been taken'. 'On 4 April 2002, the Committee, through its Rapporteur on new communications and interim measures, decided not to withdraw its request for interim measures'. See §1.3. Eventually in this case it did not find a violation of Article 3 ICAT. The petitioner had 'failed to establish a foreseeable, real and personal risk of being tortured if he were to be returned to Turkey'. CAT did welcome the 'State party's readiness to monitor the complainant's situation following his return to Turkey' and requested it to 'keep the Committee informed about said situation'. CAT *M.A.K.* v. *Germany*, 12 May 2004, §13.9.

[176]   CAT *R.T.* v. *Switzerland*, 24 November 2005 (inadm.), §1.2.

[177]   Id., §1.3.

claim manifestly unfounded and declared the case inadmissible. In light of cases such as these it would seem that informing States of the possibility to request withdrawal of provisional measures is simply a gesture to placate them.

3.4   Decisions of CAT and CEDAW to take provisional measures: transparency or the lack thereof?

Like the HRC, CEDAW and CAT do not publish their provisional measures separately.[178] The request is usually included in the last paragraph of a Note Verbale to the State party.

Unless one of the parties decides to make public the information on the use of provisional measures pending the case information will only be available upon publication of the decision on the merits.[179] References to the use of provisional measures in their decisions usually are not very

---

[178]   Rule 74 Rules of Procedure CEDAW (Confidentiality of communications) provides: "1. Communications submitted under the Optional Protocol shall be examined by the Committee, working group or rapporteur in closed meetings. 2. All working documents prepared by the Secretariat for the Committee, working group or rapporteur, including summaries of communications prepared prior to registration and the list of summaries of communications, shall be confidential unless the Committee decides otherwise. 3. The Committee, working group or rapporteur shall not make public any communication, submissions or information relating to a communication prior to the date on which its views are issued. 4. The author or authors of a communication or the individuals who are alleged to be the victim or victims of a violation of the rights set forth in the Convention may request that the names and identifying details of the alleged victim or victims (or any of them) not be published. 5. If the Committee, working group or rapporteur so decides, the name or names and identifying details of the author or authors of a communication or the individuals who are alleged to be the victim or victims of a violation of rights set forth in the Convention shall not be made public by the Committee, the author or the State party concerned. 6. The Committee, working group or rapporteur may request the author of a communication or the State party concerned to keep confidential the whole or part of any submission or information relating to the proceedings. 7. Subject to paragraphs 5 and 6 of the present rule, nothing in this rule shall affect the right of the author or authors or the State party concerned to make public any submission or information bearing on the proceedings. 8. Subject to paragraphs 5 and 6 of the present rule, the Committee's decisions on admissibility, merits and discontinuance shall be made public. 9. The Secretariat shall be responsible for the distribution of the Committee's final decisions to the author or authors and the State party concerned. 10. The Committee shall include in its annual report under article 21 of the Convention a summary of the communications examined and, where appropriate, a summary of the explanations and statements of the States parties concerned, and of its own suggestions and recommendations. 11. Unless the Committee decides otherwise, information furnished by the parties in follow-up to the Committee's views and recommendations under paragraphs 4 and 5 of article 7 of the Optional Protocol shall not be confidential. Unless the Committee decides otherwise, decisions of the Committee with regard to follow-up activities shall not be confidential". The Rules of Procedure of CAT do not specifically refer to confidentiality pending the individual complaint proceedings.

[179]   For an example of information about provisional measures by CAT made available pending the proceedings, see CAT *Suleymane Guengueng et al.* v. *Senegal* (involving former Chadian dictator Habré), Press release Human Rights Watch, 23 April 2001, 'United Nations asks Senegal to hold Ex-Chad Dictator', <www.hrw.org/justice/habre> (accessed 22 June 2005); confirmed formally in Note Verbale CAT to HRW of 27 April 2001, <http://www.hrw.org/french/themes/habre-legal.htm> (accessed 22 June 2005) About this case see Chapter XII (Other cases).

extensive. In the secondary literature reference is made to provisional measures only in passing.[180] CEDAW published its decision on the merits in *A.T.* v. *Hungary* in January 2005. It did devote a separate section to the provisional measures it had taken in accordance with Article 5(1) of the Optional Protocol.[181] In addition, different from the HRC, CAT does seem to refer more consistently to situations in which it refused to take provisional measures.

In May 2001 the CAT had a discussion about its use of provisional measures. This discussion may have been triggered by critical comments of certain States. Committee member Camara (Senegal), who presented a background paper, pointed out that the Rules of Procedure 'did not specify the kind of interim measures to be taken in order to prevent irreparable damage resulting from a violation of the Convention'.

> "He had therefore reviewed the Committee's practice, which was often based on individual decisions by the rapporteurs for the communications concerned, in an attempt to identify a general rule".[182]

The background paper itself is not available, but apparently it listed the circumstances in which Rapporteurs in individual cases had recommended the use of provisional measures, as well as the conditions in which they did not.[183] Camara noted that when a State had accepted the right of individual petition, 'it accepted that an external body might take decisions it would not like'.[184]

> "There was no point in having a Convention if the Committee was always supposed to condone the action of States. An effort should be made to improve communications with States, since they appeared willing to accept interim measures whenever an explanation of the reasons for them was provided".[185]

Initially CAT planned to draft a General Comment 'on interim measures requested by the Committee under article 22 of the Convention'.[186] Apparently it later decided against drafting such a Comment.[187] In November 2001 the Committee had a meeting with the Special Rapporteur

---

[180]   O'Flaherty (1996), pp. 162-163 briefly mentions the possibility of provisional measures. See more specifically Barkhuysen/Van Emmerik/Rieter (2008), pp. 106-112 and Ingelse (2001), p. 179, p. 180, p. 188. See also the references in Chapter XV on assessment of risk. The author visited the Geneva Secretariat on 12-22 October 1998; 29 March-5 April 2003 and 24-30 August 2003. She would like to thank various staff members dealing predominantly with the HRC, but also with CAT, including Marcus Schmidt, Paul Oertly, Antonie Cardon, Carla Edelenbos and Carmen Rueda Castañon.

[181]   CEDAW *A.T.* v. *Hungary*, 26 January 2005, §§4.1-4.8. As to other requests by petitioners for provisional measures, see the information that the five member Working Group on Communications under the Optional Protocol turned down a request for provisional measures (unspecified), see its Report of its ninth session, 26 February 2007, in: Sessional/Annual Report of Committee CEDAW/C/2007/111/WGCOP/L.1, §4.

[182]   CAT Summary Record, 26th session, 15 May 2001, CAT/C/SR.479/Add.1, 25 May 2001, §5.

[183]   See further Chapter XV on assessment of risk.

[184]   CAT Summary Record, 26th session, 15 May 2001, CAT/C/SR.479/Add.1, 25 May 2001, §5.

[185]   Summary Record, 26th session, 15 May 2001, CAT/C/SR.479/Add.1, 25 May 2001, §27. See further Chapter XVII (Official responses).

[186]   The Summary Records refer to document CAT/C/XXVI/Misc.11, which is not publicly available.

[187]   Committee member Gaer (US) criticised the background paper. She 'suggested that it was unnecessary to identify countries or cases by name when citing the Committee's jurisprudence'. She also questioned the references to the General Comments of another supervisory body and pointed out that the text 'should be carefully revised to ensure that it was gender-neutral'.

for New Communications of the HRC to hear about that Committee's practice with regard to provisional measures. HRC Special Rapporteur Scheinin discussed the authority of the HRC, the range of cases in which it used provisional measures and other related issues. CAT member El Masry (Egypt) asked Scheinin whether the same Rapporteur was responsible for registering a petition and for the procedure with regard to provisional measures and whether 'he received guidelines' from the HRC. Scheinin confirmed that the same Rapporteur dealt with both issues, about which there were no written guidelines.

> "[T]he rapporteurs applied the criteria set out in the Optional Protocol and the Committee's jurisprudence, which was often very extensive, although in certain cases the rapporteur had to innovate".[188]

Scheinin pointed out that having a Special Rapporteur to take such measures 'had the dual advantage of ensuring consistency' and 'of proceeding rapidly in urgent cases'.

> "Another practical advantage of the institution of Special Rapporteur for New Communications was that there was no need to justify the requests for interim measures of protection. The Special Rapporteur had full latitude in making such requests and, where necessary, withdrawing them".[189]

It is not clear why the institution of a Special Rapporteur diminishes the need to justify provisional measures. Given the reference to 'full latitude' the reason for wishing not to justify provisional measures may lie in the need for ultimate flexibility. It is also possible that in this context the term 'justify' specifically relates to 'justify oneself' or 'answer to' the State, rather than to 'motivate', 'provide reasoning' or 'substantiate'. After all, motivation or substantiation are requirements inherent to authoritative adjudication, while international adjudicators, being independent, do not have to 'answer to' a State. Some form of substantiation of their provisional measures should be possible without losing too much flexibility. Nevertheless, Burns, the Chairman of CAT, and Mavrommatis, who subsequently became its Special Rapporteur on New Complaints and Interim Measures, seemed to agree with Scheinin. Burns pointed out that the CAT 'could only endorse the reasons given – consistency and speed – to explain the usefulness of having a special rapporteur' and that 'he himself never gave explanations when addressing requests for interim measures to States parties'.[190] According to Mavrommatis:

> "[I]t would be desirable to avoid making such requests too systematically to States parties because some of them would be likely, especially for the sake of shortening the proceedings, to denounce the Optional Protocol, as had happened in the past. Ways had to be found to reconcile that imperative with the need to avoid having to justify the request for interim measures".[191]

Rather than substantiating its provisional measures in order to enhance their authority and persuasiveness, Mavrommatis' advice would be to limit the number of provisional measures. When he refers to 'the need to avoid having to justify the requests for interim measures' he must mean

---

[188] Summary Records, 26th session, 15 May 2001, CAT/C/SR.479/Add.1, 25 May 2000, §8 (see also §26).
[189] Summary Record, 27th session, 30 November 2001, CAT/C/SR.487, 10 March 2003, §§21-22.
[190] Id., §4.
[191] Id., §7.
Id., §8.

something else than the conviction that the adjudicator does not have to 'answer to' the State. It may be that he simply fears additional resources would be necessary if they were to do so.[192]

A few years later Mavrommatis noted, as the Special Rapporteur for New Communications and Interim Measures, that '(a)lthough some States had requested the Committee to establish guidelines on criteria for requesting interim measures, the Committee considered that guidelines could be restrictive'. Instead he emphasized that CAT did not take provisional measures automatically in non-refoulement cases.[193]

4   THE INTER-AMERICAN HUMAN RIGHTS SYSTEM

4.1   Introduction

The situation in which precautionary and provisional measures have been used in the Americas most often is for the protection of witnesses, human rights defenders and others against threats. Other measures related to halting the execution of a death sentence, locating and protecting disappeared persons, halting a deportation and protecting the health and dignity of detainees. The precautionary and provisional measures of the Inter-American Commission and Court show the seriousness of the situation in which these adjudicators must operate, in particular in countries such as Colombia and Guatemala.

In the Inter-American system precautionary and provisional measures have been used as well to protect indigenous culture, judicial independence or even freedom of speech. There have also been cases involving arbitrary detention, mass expulsion and the psychological well-being of minors whose biological parents had disappeared. Often the provisional and precautionary measures, particularly those involving protection against threats, aim at protecting a large number of beneficiaries and they are sometimes maintained over a long period of time. In most cases the President of the Court first used urgent measures, which were later ratified by the full Court.

This section explains the obligations of members of the OAS under the American Convention on Human Rights and the American Declaration on the Rights and Duties of Man. It also describes the right of individual complaint and the different roles of the Commission and Court in the Inter-American system, the power of the Commission and Court to order provisional measures and their promptness in doing so and, finally, the transparency of the information they make available on the use of provisional measures.

---

[192]   See further section 8.3 of this Chapter. Scheinin pointed out that the withdrawal by some Caribbean States from the OP to the ICCPR was not due to the Committee's practice with regard to provisional measures, but had arisen 'from a complex situation in which the States involved had also been subject to the jurisdiction of the Privy Council in London', Summary Record, 27th session, 30 November 2001, CAT/C/SR.487, 10 March 2003, §13. It seems that certain critical States have simply exploited CAT's fear for similar withdrawals from the individual petition system under the ICAT, a system not facing this complex situation. See further Chapter XVII on the official responses of Addressee States.

[193]   "If there was no prima facie case for the threat of torture, the complaint was refused. Interim measures would be refused if the Committee considered that persons were attempting to use the procedure to prolong their stay in a certain country. Each case was considered very carefully, and as much information as possible was requested from all parties. A new procedure had been introduced whereby, if there was no prima facie case, the State party concerned was informed that the case might be reviewed at a later date pending receipt of further information". Summary Records, 34th session, 19 May 2005, CAT/C/SR.662, 2 June 2005, §4 (Mavrommatis). See further Chapter XIII on reparations and XV on immediacy and risk.

4.2 Right of individual complaint and the Inter-American Commission and Court

4.2.1 Introduction

Of the 35 countries of the Americas, 34 countries are active members of the Organisation of American States (OAS).[194] The Inter-American Human Rights system has two supervisory organs, the Commission and the Court. The OAS created the Commission in 1959, long before the Court came into existence. The Court was introduced in 1969 by the American Convention on Human Rights (ACHR). In 1969 the General Assembly agreed on the text of the ACHR.[195] At present 21 of the 24 State Parties have recognised the contentious jurisdiction of the Court.[196] This includes important countries such as Brazil and Mexico (both federal States), Colombia, Peru, Argentina and Chile and non-Latin American countries such as Suriname and Haiti.

Different from the complaint system under the ICCPR and the ECHR the petitioner does not need to be the actual victim. Article 44 of the American Convention provides:

> "Any person or group of persons, or any nongovernmental entity legally recognised in one or more member states of the Organization, may lodge petitions with the Commission containing denunciations or complaints of violation of this Convention by a State Party".

Before the entry into force of the ACHR, in 1978, the member States of the OAS already had human rights obligations under the OAS Charter and the American Declaration on the Rights and Duties of Man. Equally, those OAS members that have not ratified the Convention, or have ratified it without recognising the jurisdiction of the Court to deal with individual complaints, still have obligations under the American Declaration.

At present, ten OAS members have not ratified the American Convention: six Caribbean Islands, Guyana, Belize, The United States and Canada. This list of non-members now includes Trinidad and Tobago as well. Trinidad used to be a State party to the ACHR but it denounced the Convention.[197]

4.2.2 Inter-American Commission

As noted, the establishment of the Commission pre-dates the entry into force of the ACHR. It is an organ of the OAS under the OAS Charter (Article 53). The Commission is composed of seven members elected in their individual capacity by the General Assembly of the OAS. The General Assembly is the supreme organ of the OAS that, among others, has the power to decide the gen-

---

[194] The participation of the government of the 35th country, Cuba, has been suspended since 1962: Resolution VI in: "Eighth Meeting of Consultation of Ministers of Foreign Affairs, serving as Organ of Consultation in application of the Inter-American Treaty for Reciprocal Assistance, Punta del Este, Uruguay, January 22-31, 1962, Meeting Documents," Organization of American States, OEA/Ser.F/II.8, doc. 68, pp. 17-19. According to the Commission the State itself is still a party to OAS Charter and, thus, has obligations under the American Declaration. See, e.g., its Report on Cuba, Chapter IV, Annual Report 2001. See in general about the OAS and human rights: Gómez (1998), pp. 173-197. See also Taillant/Picolotti (1998), pp. 117-134.

[195] It entered into force on 18 July 1978.

[196] As of 24 December 2007. On 26 May 1998 (effective a year later), Trinidad and Tobago denounced the ACHR. Before that time there were 22 States that had recognized the competence of the Court and 26 State parties. Dominica, Grenada and Jamaica have ratified the ACHR, but not the competence of the Court.

[197] Denunciation of 26 May 1998, which became effective on 26 May 1999. The Court may still deal with cases initiated before this.

eral action and policy of the OAS and determine the structure and function of its organs (Article 54a OAS Charter). Article 106 of the OAS Charter provides that the principal function of the Inter-American Commission 'shall be to promote the observance and protection of human rights and to serve as a consultative organ of the Organization in these matters'. This article also announces the creation of an Inter-American Convention on human rights that shall determine 'the structure, competence, and procedure of this Commission, as well as those of other organs responsible for these matters'.[198]

Roughly, the monitoring function of the Commission can be divided in a reporting task, an adjudicatory task and the task to represent the petitioners in the cases it decides to send to the Court. As part of its reporting task, its delegations visit countries. Afterwards, the Commission prepares country reports. This is especially important in dealing with gross and systematic violations.[199] Furthermore, the Commission adjudicates individual complaints. It may do so based either on the Declaration or on the ACHR. According to Article 20 of the Statute of the Inter-American Commission of Human Rights, approved by the General Assembly of the OAS in October 1979, the Commission monitors compliance with the American Declaration of the Rights and Duties of Man for those States that have not yet ratified the ACHR.[200] The Declaration already dates from 1948. The Ninth International Conference of American States, the same Conference that created the OAS, approved it several months before the Universal Declaration of Human Rights.

The Inter-American Commission's competence to take action and examine individual complaints with respect to member States of the OAS that are not party to the ACHR is based on the OAS Charter and on the practice the Commission has established. The General Assembly's adoption of the Statute of the Commission has confirmed this practice.[201]

In addition the ACHR has assigned the Commission with a clear function monitoring the rights contained in it. Under this Convention the Commission may examine cases brought under Article 44 ACHR and may subsequently decide to bring a case before the Court, if the State involved has recognised the competence of the Court. States parties to the Convention that have not

---

[198] Charter of the Organisation of the American States, as amended by the "Protocol of Buenos Aires", signed on February 27, 1967, at the Third Special Inter-American Conference; by the "Protocol of Cartagena the Indias", approved on December 5, 1985, at the Fourteenth Special Session of the General Assembly; by the "Protocol of Washington", approved on December 14, 1992, at the Sixteenth Special Session of the General Assembly; and by the "Protocol of Managua", adopted on June 10, 1993, at the Nineteenth Special Session of the General Assembly.

[199] See generally Medina Quiroga (1988).

[200] This Article stipulates that the Commission has the following specific powers in relation to those member States of the OAS not parties to the ACHR: "a. to pay particular attention to the observance of the human rights referred to in Articles I, II, III, IV, XVIII, XXV and XXVI of the American Declaration of the Rights and Duties of Man; b. to examine communications submitted to it and any other available communication, to address the government of any member state not a Party to the Convention for information deemed pertinent by this Commission, and to make recommendations to it, when it finds this appropriate, in order to bring about more effective observance of fundamental human rights; and, c. to verify, as a prior condition to the exercise of the powers granted under subparagraph b. above, whether the domestic legal procedures and remedies of each member state not a Party to the Convention have been duly applied and exhausted".

[201] See the Inter-American Commission's Annual Reports. See generally Buergenthal (1982), pp. 231-245 and Buergenthal (1975), pp. 828-836. About a similar argument with regard to the UN Charter and the Universal Declaration see e.g. Sohn (1982), pp. 1-64. See further Chapter XVI (Legal Status).

recognised the competence of the Court still have obligations under the Convention, as monitored by the Commission.

The Commission takes admissibility decisions and decisions on the merits. In urgent cases, it may take a decision to request a State to take precautionary measures or (in cases where the State involved has recognised the competence of the Court) request the Court to order provisional measures.

Article 51 ACHR stipulates that if the matter discussed in the Commission's report, setting forth the facts and stating its conclusions (under Article 50 ACHR), has not been settled or submitted to the Court, the Commission makes pertinent recommendations and prescribes a period within which the State is to take remedial measures.[202] Upon expiry of such period the Commission shall decide (by an absolute majority of its members) whether the State has taken adequate measures and whether to publish its report.

Initially the Commission deals with all individual complaints.[203] The Commission or a State Party may bring a case before the Court, but the petitioner may not. In the past the Commission brought cases before the Court only sparingly, but during the last decade the number has increased. With its new Rules (2001/2003) a significant change is introduced in how the Commission will deal with cases against States that have recognised the contentious jurisdiction of the Inter-American Court. While for a long period most cases were *not* sent to the Court, by now most of them are.[204] Article 43 of the Rules, dealing with the report on the merits and Article 44, dealing with referral of the case to the Court, establish that the petitioner has one month to present a position as to whether the case should be submitted to the Court. Article 44 specifically lays down that the Commission 'shall' refer the case to the Court when it considers that the State has not complied with the recommendations of its report on the merits.[205] This leads exception only

---

[202] Following the examination of the evidence, the Commission prepares a report stating the facts and conclusions regarding the case (Article 46 (2)). It then transmits the report with its recommendations (Article 47 (1)). When the matter has not been settled within three months from the date of the transmittal of the report to the state, the Commission may submit it to the Court or, in the alternative, the Commission may set forth its opinion and conclusions, including its pertinent recommendations. It then prescribes a period within which the government in question must take the measures that are incumbent upon it to remedy the situation examined (Article 47). Upon expiry of the prescribed period the Commission decides by the vote of an absolute majority of its members whether the State has taken suitable measures and whether to publish its report (Article 48).

[203] Article 61 ACHR, See §2.2.

[204] About the case law of the Commission see the Commission's website (<www.cidh.org>), with the Annual Reports, the cases published by the Commission (since 1974), press releases (since 1993), information on Rapporteurships, etc. and see the Inter-American Human Rights Digest, Repertorio de Jurisprudencia by Grossman/Goldman/Martin/Rodríguez-Pinzón (only in Spanish): <http://www.wcl.american.edu/humright/hracademy/iadigest.cfm> and database for Inter-American Commission reports (session reports 1960-1969), Annual Reports (1970-1998) and Special Reports (1962-2001) at: <http://www.wcl.american.edu/pub/humright/digest/Inter-American/index.html>. See further Wilson (2001), Index of individual case reports of the Inter-American Commission (1994-1999), pp. 353-647.

[205] The Court and several commentators had criticised the fact that the Commission used to send only some cases to the Court. Some members of the Commission's staff, however, considered that sending all cases to the Court would delude from the standing of the Commission. Interview with Christina Cerna, Washington D.C., 18 October 2001. See in general about the procedure before the Commission and/or the Court: Medina Quiroga/Nash Rojas (2007); Pasqualucci (2003); Gomez (2001), pp. 111-126; Faúndez Ledesma (1999); Buergenthal/Cassel (1998), pp. 539-571; Krsticevic (1998), pp. 413-448; Farer (1998), pp. 515-536; Gomez (1998a), pp. 213-240; Harris/Livingstone (1998); Cançado Trindade (1998a), pp. 133-149 and (1998b), pp. 1-27

when an absolute majority of the members of the Commission decides not to refer the case. As only the State and the Commission can act before the Court, the Commission's role changes from that of an 'adjudicator' to that of a 'litigator'. It turns into the representative of the petitioner. In an attempt to remedy the (appearance of) conflict in this regard it has established the practice, during the Court hearings, to include the petitioner in its team and to take on the more generally formulated role to act to defend the Inter-American system. The Commission and the petitioner may in fact have different positions and bring different arguments.

To sum up, the Commission can take on different roles to promote the observance and protection of human rights (Article 111 OAS Charter): a conciliatory, an informal advisory and an adjudicatory role.[206] In addition it has the completely different task of representing the petitioners before the Court in cases it had previously adjudicated itself.

4.2.3 The Inter-American Court

The Inter-American Court has distinguished itself in its proactive use of provisional measures to prevent irreparable harm to persons.[207] It consists of seven judges 'elected in an individual capacity from among jurists of the highest moral authority and of recognised competence in the field of human rights, who posses the qualifications required for the exercise of the highest judicial functions in conformity with the law of the state of which they are nationals or of the State that proposes them as candidates'.[208] The OAS General Assembly elects them from a panel of candidates proposed by the States Parties to the Convention.[209]

The Court applies and interprets the ACHR. To do this, it has both an adjudicatory jurisdiction and the competence to issue Advisory Opinions, for instance on the interpretation of certain articles.[210] As part of its adjudicatory role it takes decisions on provisional measures, preliminary objections, merits and reparations.[211] Since the political organs of the OAS do not play a role in follow-up it also tries, together with the Commission, to supervise and monitor the compliance of States with its Judgments and provisional measures. The flexibility of the Commission and Court in this respect may help achieve effective protection of persons against human rights violations.[212]

The Court can only examine those individual complaints that the Commission has previously examined.[213] In other words, the Commission deals with all individual complaints first.

---

and (1998c), pp. 573-604; Dulitzky (1998), pp. 363-390; Nikken (1996), pp. 25-44; Pinto (1998), pp. 169-184; Vivanco (1998), pp. 51-72; Davidson (1997); Fix-Zamudio (1996), pp. 19-32; Nieto Ravia (1996), pp. 397-418; Nieto Navia (1994), pp. 369-418 and Fix-Zamudio (1989), pp. 8-64.

[206] The informal advisory role is not related to the Inter-American Court's function, later introduced in the ACHR, to issue Advisory Opinions upon request.

[207] It has equally distinguished itself on two interrelated levels, firstly through its analysis of human rights obligations both in its Advisory Opinions and in contentious cases. Worth mentioning are the 1988 landmark cases of *Velásquez Rodríguez*, Judgment of 29 July 1988 and *Godínez Cruz*, Judgment of 20 January 1989, both against Honduras. The Court established State responsibility for disappearances, which were violations of the right to personal freedom, personal integrity as well as the right to life. Ever since it has emphasised the obligation to prevent, to investigate and punish human rights violations. Secondly it has distinguished itself in its Judgments on remedies and reparations, see also Chapter XIII (Protection).

[208] Article 52 ACHR. See also, e.g. Faúndez Ledesma (1998), pp. 185-210; Picado (1996), pp. 19-32; Pasqualucci (1996a), pp. 877-899; Pasqualucci (1995), pp. 794-806; Gros Espiell (1988), pp. 456-466.

[209] Article 53 ACHR.

[210] See e.g. Buergenthal (1985), pp. 1-27.

[211] If necessary, it also issues Interpretations of Judgments on the Merits or on Reparations.

[212] See also Chapter XVIII (Follow-up).

[213] Article 61 ACHR.

Only the Commission or a State Party may bring a case before the Court. In the past the Commission did so only sparingly,[214] yet during the last decade the number of cases brought before the Court has increased. The Commission's new Rules of Procedure have laid down that it shall refer a case to the Court when it considers that the State has not complied with its decision on the merits. In the last decade, within the confines of the Convention text, the Court is increasingly giving the petitioners (and victims) the possibility to directly contact the Court in cases pending before it.[215] As of June 2001, when the Court's new Rules of Procedure became applicable, the petitioner is able to present arguments and claims independently, once the Commission (or the State) has brought a case before the Court.[216]

4.3 Power and promptness of the Inter-American Commission and Court

4.3.1 Introduction

Article 63(2) deals with provisional measures to prevent irreparable harm to persons:

> "In cases of extreme gravity and urgency, and when necessary to avoid irreparable damage to persons, the Court shall adopt such provisional measures as it deems pertinent in the matters it has under consideration. With respect to a case not yet submitted to the Court, it may act at the request of the Commission".

It appears from the last sentence that the Commission may request the Court to act with respect to a case not yet submitted to the Court.[217] Obviously the Commission cannot do this in relation to

---

[214] See e.g. Buergenthal (2005), p. 15.

[215] See in general about the case law and proceedings before the Commission and Court: Shelton (2004b), pp. 127-141; Pasqualucci (2003); Faúndez Ledesma (1999); Buergenthal/Cassel (1998), pp. 539-571; Cançado Trindade (1998a), pp. 133-149; Pinto (1998), pp. 169-184; Davidson (1997) and Volio Jiménez (1996), pp. 287-298.

[216] Rules of Procedure December 2000, with amendments that entered into force January 2003. About procedural changes see Pasqualucci (2003), pp. 18-25; Gomez (2001), pp. 111-126; Cançado Trindade (1998), pp. 1-27; Gomez (1998a), pp. 213-240; Krsticevic (1998), pp. 413-448; Méndez/Cox (1998); Nikken (1996), pp. 25-44; Vivanco (1998), pp. 51-72 and Padilla (1995). See e.g. the Court's refusal to order an extension of its provisional measures in the *Raxcacó Reyes et al.* case (Gatemala), on behalf of Mr Valenzuela Ávila, 20 April 2006, because his case was unrelated to the *Raxcacó Reyes et al.* case and the pending provisional measures, and involved a case still pending before the Commission, meaning that it was the Commission that could request the Court to order provisional measures involving that matter, but not the petitioner. See further Chapter XIII (Protection), the section on beneficiaries. For the case law of the Court see the Court's website <http://www.corteidh.or.cr/> as well as <http://www1.umn.edu/humanrts/iachr/iachr.html> (basic documents, case law, Annual Reports, Press Releases). See also the Inter-American Human Rights Digest, Repertorio de Jurisprudencia by Grossman/Goldman/Martin/Rodríguez-Pinzón (only in Spanish): <http://www.wcl.american.edu/humright/hracademy/iadigest.cfm>; the contributions on the Inter-American system by Medina Quiroga, Martín and Rodríguez Pinzón in the Netherlands Quarterly of Human Rights; Buergenthal/Shelton (1995).

[217] The Statute of the Commission provides in Article 19 (c) that the Commission shall have the power 'to request the Inter-American Court of Human Rights to take such provisional measures as it considers appropriate in serious and urgent cases which have not yet been submitted to it for consideration, whenever this becomes necessary to prevent irreparable injury to persons', Statute of the Inter-American Commission on Human Rights, approved by Resolution N1 447 taken by

States that have not ratified the ACHR or States that have ratified the Convention but have not accepted the compulsory jurisdiction of the Court.[218]

The Commission usually takes its own precautionary measures before it applies to the Court to take provisional measures. Its authority to do so is based on its function of adjudicating petitions under the OAS Charter as well as under the ACHR.[219] It formally laid down this possibility in its Regulations of 1980 and it can be found in Article 25 of the Commission's new Rules, which entered into force on 1 May 2001. This Article provides:

> "1. In serious and urgent cases, and whenever necessary according to the information available, the Commission may, on its own initiative or at the request of a party, request that the State concerned adopt precautionary measures to prevent irreparable harm to persons.
> 2. If the Commission is not in session, the President, or, in his or her absence one of the Vice-Presidents, shall consult with the other members, through the Executive Secretariat, on the application of the provision in the previous paragraph. If it is not possible to consult within a reasonable period of time under the circumstances, the President, or, where appropriate, one of the Vice-Presidents shall take the decision on behalf of the Commission and shall so inform its members.
> 3. The Commission may request information from the interested parties on any matter related to the adoption and observance of the precautionary measures.
> 4. The granting of such measures and their adoption by the State shall not constitute a prejudgment on the merits of a case".[220]

---

the General Assembly of the OAS at its ninth regular session, held in La Paz, Bolivia, October 1997.

[218] The last sentence ('a case not yet submitted') could also be interpreted to imply that the Commission may only request provisional measures if it will later bring the case before the Court on the merits as well. On the other hand, the inclusion of the word 'yet' may also simply distinguish between cases already pending before the Court and those still pending before the Commission, without implying anything more than an assumption that, at a later stage, the latter will be submitted to the Court as well. In any case, the word does not justify lifting a provisional measure when the Commission has not yet submitted a case to the Court within a certain time frame.

[219] About their legal status see Chapter XVI.

[220] Rules of Procedure of the Inter-American Commission on Human Rights, approved by the Commission at its 109th special session held from December 4 to 8, 2000. Entry into force on 1 May 2001 according to Article 78. The Spanish and English texts are equally authentic. Its previous Rules, then called Regulations, dealt with precautionary measures in Article 29: "The Commission may, at its own initiative, or at the request of a party, take any action it considers necessary for the discharge of its functions. In urgent cases, when it becomes necessary to avoid irreparable damage to persons, the Commission may request that provisional measures be taken to avoid irreparable damage in cases where the denounced facts are true. If the Commission is not in session, the Chairman, or in his absence, one of the Vice-Chairmen, shall consult with the other members, through the Secretariat, on implementation of the provisions of Paragraphs 1 and 2 above. If it is not possible to consult within a reasonable time, the Chairman shall take the decision on behalf of the Commission and shall so inform its members immediately. The request for such measures and their adoption shall not prejudice the final decision". Regulations of the Inter-American Commission of Human Rights, Approved by the Commission at its 660th Meeting, 49th Session, held on 8 April, 1980, and modified at its 64th Session, 840th Meeting, held on 7 March, 1985, at its 70th Session, 938th Meeting, held on 29 June, 1987, and at its 90th Session, 1282nd Meeting, held on 21 September, 1995. The text of this regulation about its precautionary measures used the term 'provisional measures'. Article 25 of the new Rules does not reproduce the first paragraph of Article 29 of the old Regulations because that paragraph was

The reason for the increase in precautionary and provisional measures in the last decade is not that they were not necessary in the past. In the 1970s and 1980s few States in the hemisphere even had elected governments and evidence of gross human rights violations in that period is abundant. The changes seem to lie in the institutional development of the tool.

Commissioner Juan Mendez refers to two advantages of taking precautionary measures first and going to the Court for provisional measures only later. Firstly, if the Commission does not go to the Court directly, it has more ammunition. The other advantage is that the Commission, through the Executive Secretariat, can do it directly from Washington D.C. It can be done in one hour, while when the Commission applies to the Court it has to prepare a statement and so does the Court. When the Court is not in session the Secretariat of the Court contacts the President. Even though the Court's Secretariat will usually act on it swiftly, it still takes another couple of steps. Mendez notes that if the matter is very urgent the Commission probably requests the Court to take provisional measures and takes its own precautionary measures at the same time, without waiting for the Court's reaction. According to him the benefit of the system is that it is so flexible that you can adapt it to the degree of emergency.[221]

In the last decade the Commission's practice in using the tool of precautionary measures has become more elaborate. There are a few different layers of decision-making providing some extra flexibility. NGOs are aware that under its Rules of Procedure and practice, the Commission has to make a 'case' of any petition received, including of an originally free-standing petition for precautionary measures. Often, however, they file a petition and at the same time they file separately for precautionary measures. This is to emphasise the urgency of the case, possibly for fear that the Executive Secretariat will take less seriously such request when it is filed as part of a petition.[222] For instance, when a case deals with the displacement of communities, petitioners may say that this is going to happen any time soon, it may even happen tomorrow. In such cases the President of the Commission may take precautionary measures without first consulting the rest of the Commission.

Another approach is not to act on the urgent petition for precautionary measures but to act immediately on the formal petition by giving it a number and passing it on to the government. Even though in that case the Commission itself does not say it is taking a precautionary measure, because of the fact that it is passing the petition on to the government so quickly and because the petitioners' request for urgent measures is included, the State knows that it is a matter to which they have to pay attention.

The third possibility is to inform the State that it has received a request for precautionary measures and to request it to give its version of the situation so that the Commission can decide whether or not to act on the request. Several times States have solved the problem at that stage. For instance, they have released persons in detention. This way, this third possibility is an intermediate step that is not a formal decision but it may work nevertheless.

The fourth possibility is indeed taking a precautionary measure asking a State to act in a certain way or to refrain from acting and giving it several weeks or months to comply.

The fifth possibility the Commission has when it is faced with urgent situations, is to go directly to the Court and request it to take provisional measures. Governments tend to fear the Court's provisional measures more that the Commission's precautionary measures.[223]

---

not specific to the issue of precautionary measures. The addition 'under the circumstances' following 'within a reasonable period of time' in Article 25(2) is already implicit in 'reasonable' and seems redundant

[221] Interview by author with Commissioner Juan Mendez, Washington D.C., 17 October 2001.

[222] Id.

[223] Commissioner Juan Mendez mentioned these five layers of decision-making during an interview by the author in Washington D.C., on 17 October 2001.

The first case in which the Commission went straight to the Court to request a provisional measure was the case *Bustíos Rojas*. Upon request of the petitioners (Americas Watch), the Commission went to the Court without first using its own precautionary measures.[224]

States may want to avoid placing the Commission in a position where it has to go to the Court. Generally they fear having to attend the Court's hearings, where they have to account for their acts or omissions in public. If they comply with the Commission's precautionary measures, or even anticipate them, they may be able to avoid the attention of the press as well.

As part of its considerations the Court often specifically refers to the fact that the State failed to respond to the Commission's precautionary measures as one of the indications of urgency warranting an Order by the Court.[225] Yet strong views have also been expressed arguing against the Commission's use of precautionary measures before going to the Court to request provisional measures: '(t)he Commission's insistence in its practice with regard to prior precautionary measures may, in some case, have negative consequences for the potential victims and create one more obstacle for them. In certain cases, it can constitute a denial of justice at the international level'.[226]

In the *Matter of Children Deprived of Liberty in the "Complexo do Tatuapé" of FEBEM* regarding Brazil the Commission had continued using its own precautionary measures for a long time while repeatedly receiving reports of beneficiaries killed.[227]

4.3.2 The Commission's Rules of Procedure (2000/2003)

In 2000 the Commission substantially amended its Rules of Procedure.[228] The new Rules on the Commission's admissibility decisions and the criteria for sending a case to the Court are important in the context of its precautionary measures.

The possibility to take precautionary measures is useful not only in relation to States that have not recognised the compulsory jurisdiction of the Court, but also to those that have. It gives the Commission more flexibility. Of course this is the case only inasmuch as the Commission does not fail to resort to the Court when the case is ready or when the exigencies of the situation so require. With the present Rules of Procedure this risk is considerably diminished.

4.3.3 The Court's competence

First and foremost Article 63(2) ACHR establishes the Court's competence. The Statute of the Court does not further elaborate on its competence to take provisional measures.[229]

---

[224] See the urgent measures ordered by the Court's President in *Bustíos Rojas*, 5 June 1990, as confirmed by the full Court in its Order for provisional measures of 8 August 1990.

[225] See, e.g., IACHR *James, Briggs, Noel, Garcia and Bethel* cases, Order for provisional measures, 14 June 1998, *James et al.* cases, Order of the President for urgent measures, 25 October 2001 and Order for provisional measures, 26 November 2001.

[226] See Cançado Trindade's individual opinion in IACHR *Matter of the persons imprisoned in the "Dr. Sebastião Martins Silveira" Penitentiary in Araraquara, São Paulo* regarding Brazil, Order of 30 September 2006, §30, referring to his Separate Opinion in the *Matter of Mery Naranjo et al.*, §§5-11 and in the *Matter of Gloria Giralt de García-Prieto et al.*, §§7-13.

[227] See IACHR *Matter of Children Deprived of Liberty in the "Complexo do Tatuapé" of FEBEM*, Order of 17 November 2005, Separate Concurring Opinion of judge Cançado Trindade criticizing this.

[228] The Statute, as approved by the General Assembly provides that the 'Commission shall prepare and adopt its own Regulations, in accordance with the present Statute'. Indeed, the Commission previously called its Rules of Procedure 'Regulations'. It amended the Rules slightly in 2003. These Rules, as amended, entered into force in January 2004.

As is clear from Article 25 of the Rules, the President of the Court may use so-called 'urgent measures' when the Court is not in session. The President basically grants 'provisional measures' provisionally so that any provisional measures later decided by the full Court may still have their intended function. Later, usually following a public hearing in the matter, the full Court ratifies these in an Order for provisional measures. Thus far, there are no known instances where the full Court decided not to ratify the President's urgent measures other than for reasons that the situation meanwhile had been solved already. The Court lifts its provisional measures when they are no longer necessary.

4.3.4 Delegation and consultation

Different from the Rules of Procedure of the HRC and CAT, the Rules of the Inter-American Commission specifically refer to consultation within the Commission about the use of provisional measures.[230] Article 6 of the Rules provides that the Commission shall have as its board of officers a President, a first Vice-President and a second Vice-President. If consultation on the use of precautionary measures has not been possible within a reasonable period of time, the President or one of the Vice-Presidents shall take the decision on behalf of the Commission. Since 2001 the

---

[229] Statute of the Inter-American Court of Human Rights, adopted by the General Assembly of the OAS at its Ninth Regular Session, held in La Paz, Bolivia, October 1979 (Resolution 4.4.8). Article 25 of its Rules of Procedure, dating from 2000 (with paragraphs 3 and 6 added in 2003), provides: "1. At any stage of the proceedings involving cases of extreme gravity and urgency, and when necessary to avoid irreparable damage to persons, the Court may, at the request of a party or on its own motion, order such provisional measures as it deems pertinent, pursuant to Article 63(2) of the Convention. 2. With respect to matters not yet submitted to it, the Court may act at the request of the Commission. 3. In contentious cases already submitted to the Court, the victims or alleged victims, their next of kin, or their duly accredited representatives, may present a request for provisional measures directly to the Court. 4. The request may be made to the President, to any judge of the Court, or to the Secretariat, by any means of communication. In every case, the recipient of the request shall immediately bring it to the President's attention. 5.If the Court is not sitting, the President, in consultation with the Permanent Commission and, if possible, with the other judges, shall call upon the government concerned to adopt such urgent measures as may be necessary to ensure the effectiveness of any provisional measures that may be ordered by the Court at its next session. 6. The beneficiaries of urgent measures or provisional measures ordered by the President may address their comments on the report made by the State directly to the Court. The Inter-American Commission of Human Rights shall present observations to the State's report and to the observations of the beneficiaries or their representatives. 7. The Court, or its President if the Court is not sitting, may convoke the parties to a public hearing on provisional measures. 8. In its Annual Report to the General Assembly, the Court shall include a statement concerning the provisional measures ordered during the period covered by the report. If those measures have not been duly implemented, the Court shall make such recommendations as it deems appropriate". Rules of Procedure of the Inter-American Court of Human Rights, approved by the Court at its 49th Regular Session held from 16 to 25 November 2000, entered into force on 1 June 2001, amended November/December 2003 (including the addition of §§3 and 6), entered into force 1 January 2004. The Permanent Commission referred to in Rule 25 (5) is composed of 'the President, the Vice-President and any other judges the President deems it appropriate to appoint, according to the needs of the Court'. See Article 6 (1) Rules.

[230] As noted, Rule 63(3) of CEDAW's Rules of Procedure stipulates that when a Working Group or Rapporteur has decided to take provisional measures they 'shall forthwith thereafter inform the Committee members of the nature of the request and the communication to which request relates'.

Vice-Presidents can now take this decision as well. As becomes clear from Article 25(2) the other members of the Commission must be informed when the President or either Vice-President has requested a State to adopt precautionary measures. Apart from a special provision on precautionary measures (Article 25), the Rules of Procedure also include specific references to serious or urgent cases in Articles 29 and 30. Article 29, on the initial processing of individual petitions, lays down in paragraph 2 that the Executive Secretary shall immediately notify the Commission in serious or urgent cases. Article 50 of the Rules stipulates that this provision, just like the Rule on precautionary measures, also applies to the procedure of petitions with regard to OAS member States not a party to the ACHR.[231]

Article 30, on the admissibility procedure, provides in paragraph 4: 'In serious or urgent cases, or when it is believed that the life or personal integrity of a person is in real or imminent danger, the Commission shall request the promptest reply from the State, using for this purpose the means it considers most expeditious'. The Commission may refer here to the means of communication (telephone, fax, etc.) of precautionary measures, as well as to other measures such as an informal request during a country visit or simply giving priority to examining that case.

While responsiveness sometimes depends slightly on the efficiency of the individual staff members, the CIDH generally is capable of responding quickly and in a manner that is focused on the situation.[232]

The CIDH was the first international body to speak out on the situation of the 'unlawful combatants' at Guantanamo Bay. Subsequently various UN special mechanisms and treaty bodies have dealt with their situation, yet the CIDH remains the only international adjudicator with competence to deal with complaints against the US. Indeed it has shown its 'capacity to respond quickly and effectively to urgent concerns raised by counter-terrorism measures, when domestic mechanisms of protection may be absent or ineffective'.[233]

Whereas in its adjudicatory role the Court deals only with States that have recognised its contentious jurisdiction, the Commission deals with all members of the OAS. This is relevant in relation to the Commission's competence to take precautionary measures. It can take them both with regard to States that have ratified the ACHR and with regard to those that have not. As discussed in the previous section member States of the OAS who have not ratified the ACHR must still answer to the Inter-American Commission on Human Rights.

With respect to State parties to the Convention, the Commission's competence is based on the ACHR. The Statute provides in Article 19 that the Commission has several special powers with respect to the States parties to the American Convention on Human Rights. One of these is

---

[231]   With regard to the initial processing of petitions Article 34(2) of the old Regulations had provided that 'in serious or urgent cases or when it is believed that the life, personal integrity or health of a person is in imminent danger, the Commission shall request the promptest reply from the government, using for this purpose the means it considers most expeditious'.

[232]   In the context of disappearances it was the Inter-American Commission that was the first to use provisional measures, in the 1970s and 1980s. In any case it had authorised the Executive Secretary to intervene in some urgent cases in its name. Generally this happened when someone had claimed that a person had disappeared after an arrest. Such intervention normally consisted of writing a letter, sometimes sending a telegram. At other times it was a telephone-call to the relevant State's Ambassador to the OAS, based in Washington D.C. and sometimes even a long distance call to the Foreign Ministry or to some other contact in the State. The Commission used these methods to express an interest in the fate and whereabouts of the recently disappeared person. It seems that the Executive Secretary did this quite often but the practice was also very discretionary. It may well be that many urgent complaints just received the regular case treatment. Interview of author with Juan Méndez, Washington D.C., 17 October 2001. In the 1980s he was working as a practitioner at the NGO Human Rights Watch.

[233]   Tittemore (2006), p. 401.

'to request the Inter-American Court of Human Rights to take such provisional measures as it considers appropriate in serious and urgent cases which have not yet been submitted to it for consideration, whenever this becomes necessary to prevent irreparable injury to persons'.

The Commission can only ask the Court to take provisional measures when the State concerned has recognised the Court's jurisdiction, but it may use precautionary measures with regard to all member States of the OAS.[234]

The terminology used by the Commission in relation to its precautionary measures differs. The Commission sometimes says it 'issued' precautionary measures and sometimes it says it decided to 'take' them. Often it simply states it requested a government to take the necessary steps to prevent irreparable harm to persons. Generally, petitioners request the Commission to 'take' or 'issue' precautionary measures, while the Commission, in turn, asks the State to 'take' or 'adopt' precautionary measures. In other words both the Commission's decision itself to take precautionary measures and the protective measures required are called 'precautionary measures'. The Commission holds periodic meetings determining whether precautionary measures must be maintained or not. When it does not maintain them, it often also notes that it 'filed' the case, meaning lifted or archived it.

4.3.5 Promptness

Since the Inter-American Court is not permanently in session it is usually the President who takes action in urgent cases in the periods between the sessions. The first time the Court became involved in the issue of provisional measures to prevent the execution of a death sentence was when the President of the Court ordered urgent measures in the cases of *James, Briggs, Noel, Garcia and Bethel* in May 1998. Judge Salgado-Pesantes, who was President of the Court at the time, ordered Trinidad and Tobago to take all necessary measures to preserve the lives of these six persons 'so that the Court may examine the pertinence of the provisional measures requested by the Inter-American Commission on Human Rights'. The President sometimes refers to his consultation with the other members of the Court.[235] In any case, the Rules of Procedure provide that the President consults with the Permanent Council before he orders urgent measures. The full Court has confirmed such Orders and has sometimes noted that the President had used them 'in conformity with the provisions of the Convention and the Rules of Procedure and the information presented in the matter'.[236] It has also noted that it was 'convenient to hear the arguments of the State and the Commission with regard to this matter in a public hearing'.[237]

Trinidad' first six reports, responding to the Court's Orders and to those of the President, argued that Trinidad could not stay an execution until the Warrant of Execution had been issued and read.[238] The Commission pointed out that the fact that there were only five to seven days between the reading of a Warrant of Execution and the execution itself 'would impede the Court's

---

[234] See further Chapter XVI (Legal status).

[235] IACHR *James et al.* cases, Order of the President for urgent measures, 29 June 1998; *James et al.* case, Order of the President for urgent measures, 13 July 1998; *James, Briggs, Noel, Garcia and Bethel* cases, Order of the President for urgent measures, 22 July 1998 and Order of the President for urgent measures, 25 October 2001 all refer to consultation; the President's Orders of 11 May and 19 June 1999, on the other hand, do not refer to consultation.

[236] IACHR *James et al.* cases, Orders for provisional measures, 14 June and 29 August 1998, 25 May and 25 September 1999 and 26 November 2001.

[237] IACHR *James, Briggs, Noel, Garcia and Bethel* cases, Order for provisional measures, 14 June 1998 ('convenient' is the literal translation used in the official English text of the original 'conveniente', but it is likely that the Court meant something like 'suitable').

[238] See IACHR *James et al.* cases, Order for provisional measures, 29 August 1998.

ability to issue effective provisional measures'.[239] Trinidad's professed impossibility to stay an execution in advance of the reading of the Execution Warrant, combined with the fact that there is only a limited period of time (e.g. five to seven days) between this reading and the intended execution, indeed makes it very difficult for the Court to order provisional measures in a timely manner. The death row prisoner must first contact the NGO or lawyer dealing with his case who, in turn, must contact the Commission, which in turn approaches the secretariat of the Court. The Court's staff then communicates with the President who orders urgent measures. These must arrive in time to halt the execution.[240] As noted, in cases that are themselves already pending before the Court the petitioners may now directly approach the Court without having to go through the Commission.

The Inter-American Court does not normally provide information on the time span between the Commission's receipt of urgent information on an execution and its resort to the Court. Yet some cases have shown that the Commission is able to respond very swiftly.[241] The State is generally late in informing a prisoner of his execution date. Sometimes the Commission leaves the Court little time to deal with an urgent case.[242] In other instances, it is the Court that waits until the day before the execution with its order for provisional measures.[243]

4.3.6 Proprio motu

The Inter-American Commission can take precautionary measures *proprio motu*.[244] An example is the *La Tablada* case, which did not arise from any individual submission. The petitioner just

---

[239] IACHR *James et al.* cases, Order for provisional measures, 29 August 1998.

[240] See also under the heading 'timing' in this paragraph.

[241] On 25 June 1998 Mr. Thomas had been informed that he would be hanged in five days. The next day the petitioners informed the Commission about this. On the same day the Commission unsuccessfully appealed to the Court to include him as a beneficiary in the *James et al.* provisional measures. *James et al.* cases, Order of the President for urgent measures, 29 June 1998. Another example is when on 17 June 1999 the Commission informed the Court that on that same date the State had read a warrant of execution to one of the beneficiaries of the Court's provisional measures, Mr. Briggs, and that this execution would be carried out in five days. *James et al.* cases, Order for provisional measures, 16 August 2000.

[242] There have also been times when the Commission was not that swift and did not leave the Court much reaction time. One of them also concerns the case of Mr. Briggs. In February and May 1999 Trinidad requested the Court to 'confirm' that he was not a beneficiary any more. On that same day the Secretariat requested the Commission to submit an urgent report on the situation of Mr. Briggs within 24 hours. The Commission requested an extension of four days, which included the weekend. The President granted this extension. *James et al.* case, Order for provisional measures, 25 May 1999. On the day the Commission presented its report the Court ordered the provisional measures to be maintained. In his Concurring Opinion Judge Cançado Trindade referred to the little time that was available to the Court to decide on this Order: 'the few hours that the Court disposed of' (in fact, the Spanish text says 'de que dispuso la Corte', referring to the little time the Court had, rather than the time it 'disposed of') 'the merciless pressure of time' and the Commission's document 'submitted to the Court a couple of hours ago'.

[243] On 29 June 1998 the President of the Court ordered urgent measures on behalf of Mr. Thomas. His execution was scheduled early the next morning, which meant that these measures were barely in time. *James et al.* cases, Order of the President for urgent measures, 29 June 1998. The Commission requested the Court to include Mr. Hilaire as a beneficiary, four days before his scheduled execution. The President ordered urgent measures on his behalf three days later, again only on the day before his scheduled execution. *James et al.* cases, Order of the President for urgent measures, 13 July 1998.

[244] See Article 25(1) of the Commission's Rules of Procedure ('on its own initiative').

asked for a provisional measure.[245] Yet the Commission seldom uses such precautionary measures *proprio motu*. It already deals with a great number of cases and it also considers it is in a better position when it can say that there was a specific request to take action, even if it is only a telephone call. In theory, however, the Commission could act upon its own initiative if something comes to its attention, for instance based on public knowledge.[246]

Since the introduction of the Office of the OAS Special Rapporteur on Freedom of Expression the Commission has been more pro-active in the use of precautionary measures to protect journalists and it has even informed specific journalists of the possibility of requesting the Commission's precautionary measures.[247] While this is not the same as *proprio motu* use of provisional measures, it clearly is approaching the potential beneficiary *proprio motu*.

The Commission can also go to the Court and ask for provisional measures on its own initiative. An example of where the Commission acted without a request is the *Chipoco* case. Yet the Court observed that this was a matter still pending before the Commission, which had 'not submitted information to the Court sufficient to support the adoption of such measures, which requires the Commission to have gathered preliminary evidence to support a presumption of the truth of the allegations and of a situation whose grave seriousness and urgency could cause irreparable harm to persons'.[248]

As to the Court, if a case is still pending before the Commission it cannot order provisional measures *proprio motu*. It can only order them upon request by the Commission. Once a case is pending before the Court the Rules of Procedure have given the petitioner a more independent role. Not only the Commission, but also the petitioner can request provisional measures. At this stage the Court can also order them *proprio motu*.[249] Thus, the monopoly of the Commission with regard to triggering the Court's decision whether or not to order provisional measures only applies to those cases that are not yet pending before the Court. In such cases the petitioner depends

---

[245] See also Chapter VII (Detention situations) and Chapter XIII (Protection).

[246] Interview of author with Juan Mendez, Washington D.C., 17 October 2001.

[247] See e.g. CIDH Annual Report 2006, 3 March 2007, Volume II, Report of the Office of the Special Rapporteur for Freedom of Expression, p. 1, §§7-8 and p. 9, §18.

[248] IACHR *Chipoco* (Peru), Order of 27 January 1993 (refusing request for provisional measures). Previously the President had already decided not to order urgent measures, Order of President of 14 December 1992. On evidentiary requirements see Chapter XV (Immediacy and risk).

[249] See Article 63(2) ACHR and 25(3) of the Court's Rules of Procedure. In its Annual Report 2005, p. 76, the Court included charts indicating that provisional measures were requested 96 times (including requests for extensions) and rejected three times; in six cases the Court used them *proprio motu* (see also section 4.3 of Chapter XIII (Protection) on the importance of ascertaining the wishes of the beneficiaries in this respect), nine were on request of the victim, 80 on request of the Commission and one based on an agreement by the petitioners, the State and the Commission. 75 % of the provisional measures relates to cases pending before the Commission and 25 % to cases pending before the Court. The Court's Annual Report 2007 referred to a total of 118 requests for provisional measures. It noted that in 10 cases the measures requested were rejected and that 32 belonged to requests to *expand* provisional measures already adopted. It also pointed out that 26 % of the provisional measures requested were related to contentious cases processed before the Court, while 74 % related to proceedings still pending before the Commission. The great majority (93) of the provisional measures were requested by the Inter-American Commission. Again the Court mentioned that it ordered six provisional measures on its own motion (meaning that it did not use them *proprio motu* since the publi8cation of its Annual Report 2005); again it mentioned that one was requested by common agreement by the Commission, the alleged victims and the State and 18 were requested by the alleged victims or their representatives, indicating that the number of such requests doubled since 2005. See Annual Report 2007, p. 76.

on the Commission's decision that its own precautionary measures are insufficient and that, pursuant to the last sentence of Article 63(2), the Court's provisional measures are warranted.

At the end of 2001 the Secretary of the Inter-American Court decided to assign the task to prepare provisional measures to one staff member. The question arises whether this is a desirable approach. After all, provisional measures constitute an integral part of the case. For a decision whether or not to take them it is necessary to examine all information available. Such a division of labour would mean a duplication of work. Nevertheless, this approach has been suggested with regard to the ECtHR as well and it could have benefits.[250] According to Garry instituting a separate body with expertise in analysing requests for provisional measures 'might also be beneficial to the individual applicants for whom a thoroughly knowledgeable and expeditious review of the request is often a matter of life or death'.[251] Expertise on provisional measures is necessary, but these measures should not be dealt with in a manner divorced from the main case.

During an on-site visit in Peru the Inter-American Commission had received information about harassment to which Mr. Mezarina was subjected, allegedly by members of the Peruvian army. There had been an attack on his life in November 1998. Unknown persons had fired at him twice when he was leaving his home. In February 1999 the Commission granted precautionary measures on his behalf and on behalf of his family. In light of the Commission's reference to its country visit, it may be that it more or less decided this precautionary measure on a *proprio motu* basis. In March 1999 Peru informed the Commission that it had adopted specific measures. Subsequently, 'the parties' continued presenting information on the issue.[252] The reference to 'the parties' may either mean that there indeed had been a petitioner from the start (which probably means that the Commission did not use its power to take precautionary measures *proprio motu*) or that later an NGO came forward to represent the beneficiary.[253]

4.4 Decisions by the Inter-American Commission and Court to take provisional measures: transparency or the lack thereof?

4.4.1 Introduction

Different from the UN adjudicators the Inter-American Commission and the Inter-American Court (especially the latter), have been more forthcoming in providing information about their use of provisional measures.[254] Secondary literature has addressed the issue as well.[255]

---

[250] See e.g. Buquicchio-de Boer (1998), p. 236.

[251] Garry (2001), p. 402.

[252] CIDH Annual Report 1999, Chapter III C.1, §49.

[253] In the alternative the beneficiary himself remained in touch with the Commission and was referred to as a party.

[254] As set out in this section they have published more information on their use of provisional measures than the UN committees. The author visited the Secretariat of the Inter-American Commission, Washington, D.C. (18 September-22 October 2001). She would like to thank members of the Commission Robert Goldman, Juan Mendez and Claudio Grossman; staff members Brian Tittemore, Veronica Gomez, Elisabeth Abi-Mershed, Ignacio Alvarez, Ariel Dulitzky and Christina Cerna; as well as Rick Wilson (Washington College of Law), Viviana Krsticevic (CEJIL), the Guatemala Human Rights Commission, Diego Rodríguez (Washington College of Law) and Claudia Martín (Washington College of Law). She also would like to thank Judge Thomas Buergenthal (The Hague, 19 July 2001) and Douglas Cassel (then Northwestern University School of Law, Chicago, 7 September 2001). She visited the Secretariat of the Inter-American Court, San José, Costa Rica (23 October-10 December 2001). She would like to thank President Cançado

4.4.2 The Commission

Official information on the Commission's early use of precautionary measures is lacking.[256] Apparently, during the 1970s the Commission's President would sometimes – very informally – contact a State if the Commission felt a person was at risk. He did so simply for humanitarian reasons and did not specifically refer to the State's obligations under the OAS Charter or the ACHR.[257] In 2001 one of the members of the Commission recalled that in the 1970s and 1980s, when he himself brought cases before the Commission as a petitioner, the Commission developed a practice of urgent intervention in the context of the disappearances.[258]

Between 1979 and 1989 the Commission focused primarily on other activities, such as preparing Country Reports, rather than on individual petitions. Yet as part of its other activities the Commission has intervened in urgent situations as well.

Since 1989, when the Court issued its first Judgments, not only the Court, but also the Commission has dealt more intensively with individual complaints. This may mean that it has used precautionary measures more often since then, although references to precautionary measures prior to 1996 are only found incidentally.[259]

It is only since its Annual Report 1996, published in March 1997, that the Commission includes a specific section on its use of precautionary measures. In this Annual Report the Commis-

---

Trindade and staff members Pablo Saavedra-Alessandri, Emilia Segares-Rodríguez, Paula Lizano, Olger González-Espinoza, María Auxiliadora Solano, Lilly Ching; former under-Secretary of the Court Victor Rodriguez, Charles Moyer (Inter-American Institute of Human Rights, formerly Secretary of the Court and Commission); and Alejandra Nuño (CEJIL Costa Rica). She also attended the public hearings on provisional measures in the *Centro Pro* case against Mexico, where the murder of human rights lawyer Digna Ochoa was discussed (after the withdrawal of provisional measures), and the hearings on reparations in the *Bamaca* case against Guatemala (a case in which witnesses were in need of protection against threats also after the judgment on the merits was published).

[255] See e.g. Medina Quiroga/Nash Rojas (2007), pp. 70-71 (precautionary measures) and pp. 93-94 (provisional measures); Bonifaz Tweddle (2006), pp. 55-97; Pasqualucci (2005), pp. 1-49; Cançado Trindade (2005), pp. 145-163; Shelton (2005b), pp. 165-176; Pasqualucci (2003), pp. 219-325; Cançado Trindade (2003), pp. 162-168; González-Espinoza (2002), pp. 1189-1196; Buergenthal (1994), pp. 69-94; Aguiar-Aranguren (1994), pp. 19-37.

[256] In general the Commission's early decisions on admissibility and merits are difficult to access. See Wilson (American University), in his introduction to the 1994 version of an index to the Inter-American Commission's case law, at the University of Minnesota search database <http://www1.umn.edu/humanrts/cases/commission.htm>. See also Gilman (1998), pp. 261-290.

[257] Interviews by author with Christina Cerna, Washington D.C., 18 October 2001 and Charles Moyer, San José, Costa Rica, 20 November 2001.

[258] Interview by author with Commissioner Juan Méndez, Washington D.C., 17 October 2001. In the 1980s he was working as a practitioner at Human Rights Watch.

[259] The 1997 case docket of CEJIL, the main NGO bringing cases before the Inter-American Commission and Court, gives some information on the cases it has dealt with prior to 1998. This case docket is simply a reference document used within CEJIL. It was not intended for publication and it does not claim to be complete. It mentions 153 cases. In 36 of these it requested the Commission to take precautionary measures. It is not clear whether the Commission always followed this request. In seven of these cases CEJIL also requested the Commission to seek provisional measures from the Court. It requested the Commission to take precautionary measures in eight cases involving Colombia and in ten cases involving Guatemala. The other countries were Mexico (five), El Salvador and Dominican Republic (three times each), Honduras and Bolivia (twice each) and Peru, Brazil and Guyana (once each). CEJIL case docket 1997, on file with the author.

sion presented its precautionary measures in the order in which it received requests for such measures by petitioners.[260] In later Annual Reports the Commission presents the precautionary measures per State in chronological order.[261] Its presentation generally includes the name of the person(s) on whose behalf the Commission used precautionary measures and usually a very brief summary of facts. Furthermore, the Commission mentions the rights of the persons exposed to grave and imminent danger, the number it has assigned to the case (if any) as well as the name of the State involved and the date on which the Commission decided on the precautionary measures.[262]

The quality of the information given in the Annual Reports on the Commission's use of precautionary measures seems to depend on the desk officer at the Executive Secretariat, working on a specific country. This is particularly relevant in light of the question to what extent the Annual Report provides an explanation for the use of precautionary measures in the cases it describes. It is possible that for budgetary reasons the Commission has chosen not to coordinate the information it presents.[263]

As the Commission does not formally reject petitioners' requests for precautionary measures, there is no documentation available on its decision *not* to take them.[264] This means that its conditions for taking precautionary measures must be derived from the information it provides on those situations where it did take them.

Before 2000 the Commission already published both its Admissibility and its Inadmissibility Reports, with 'the essential purpose of establishing clear and objective criteria for the process-

---

[260] See CIDH Annual Report 1996, Chapter II, §4.

[261] See e.g. CIDH Annual Report 1997, Chapter III, §2(a).

[262] As of Spring 2008 the Commission also provides a functioning link on its website through which the sections of its Annual Reports discussing precautionary measures may be accessed directly.

[263] In 2002, for instance, the Commission received 4.1 % of the total OAS budget. Speech by Dr. Juan Méndez, President of the Inter-American Commission of Human Rights at the inauguration of the 114th regular session of the Inter-American Commission of Human Rights, 25 February 2002, <www.cidh.org/discursos>. Méndez noted that the Commission's overall budget for that financial year was $ 3.1 million USD and that it spent approximately two-thirds on staff salaries and benefits. He pointed out that '[t]he remainder barely covers the costs of preparing and holding two regular sessions and one special session publishing an annual report, covering performance contract fees, and paying for supplies and similar items'. "As a result on-site visits, dealings with the Inter-American Court, and the Commission's other activities in promoting and protecting human rights have to be financed with voluntary contributions from member states and assistance from observer nations". The Court's Annual Report 2005, published in 2006, referred to the Commission's budget at constituting 4.29 % of the OAS budget. The Commission has since included a link to 'Financial resources' on its website, which presents a graph for the OAS 2006 adjusted budget indicating 4.6 % of the budget distributed to the Commission ($ 3,728.3). See <http://www.cidh.org/financiro.eng.htm> (consulted 10 August 2008).

[264] Cançado Trindade has pointed out that 'the decisions of the Commission and the Court concerning both precautionary and provisional measures, respectively, should always be motivated, as a guarantee of respect for the adversary principle – which is a general principle of law – so that the petitioners have certainty that the matter they submitted has been duly and carefully considered by the international instance, and so that the meaning of the decision taken by the latter is clear'. This applied also to the Commission's decision to deny a request for precautionary measures: 'this decision should be duly justified'. IACHR *Matter of the persons imprisoned in the "Dr. Sebastião Martins Silveira" Penitentiary in Araraquara, São Paulo* (Brazil), Order of 30 September 2006, Separate Opinion Judge Cançado Trindade, §30, referring to his Separate Opinions attached to *Mery Naranjo et al.* (Colombia), Order of 22 September 2006, §§5–11 and *Gloria Giralt de García Prieto et al.* (El Salvador), Order of 26 September 2006, §§7-13.

ing of individual petitions both for the states and for the representatives of the victims of human rights violations'.[265] Nevertheless, there sometimes is a lack of transparency, both with regard to the decision-making on which cases to speed up and send to the Court and with regard to the use of precautionary measures.[266]

In order to address the problem of the lack of transparency of the procedure in 2000 the Commission introduced a provision in its Rules of Procedure. Article 44(2) reads as follows:

> "The Commission shall give fundamental consideration to obtaining justice in a particular case, based, among others, on the following factors: (a) the position of the petitioner; (b) the nature and seriousness of the violation; (c) the need to develop or clarify the case law of the system; (d) the future effect of the decision within the legal systems of the Member States; and, (e) the quality of the evidence available".

The petitioner and the representative of the State attend the hearings before the Inter-American Commission. The Commission does publicize that it has had a hearing as well as some of its contents. Both parties are free to publicize their visions on the matter but the meetings themselves are not open for the public and the press.

In some of its admissibility decisions the Inter-American Commission refers to its use of precautionary measures and sometimes it provides information on State replies, etc. Since 1996 it includes a short section on its use of precautionary measures in its Annual Report. This has already improved the transparency of the Commission's use of this tool. The information provided, however, is not very consistent and does not generally analyze the replies of States. It is possible that the Commission fears that more detail on State replies would diminish the effectiveness of its precautionary measures because State parties could use non-compliance by other States as an excuse for their own non-compliance. It may also be possible to explain the inconsistency in reporting by the chronic lack of resources under which the Commission's Secretariat is forced to operate.

Obviously, the Secretariats of the various adjudicators have an important role to play in the day to day proceedings and drafting of documents, including the preparation of decisions on provisional measures. After all the petitions and State responses arrive at these Secretariats and the adjudicators can only function effectively when their members are assisted by the staff working at these Secretariats.[267] The Inter-American Commission has expressed itself publicly about this and related issues, partly to address speculations in domestic press. In 2005 it published a Resolution in which it distanced itself from public statements made by one of its members both involving the status of its precautionary measures and with regard to its decision-making on these measures. Commissioner Gutiérrez had publicly indicated to a Mexican newspaper that the relevant province in Mexico 'had no obligation to comply with precautionary measures', because

---

[265] CIDH Annual Report 1997, Chapter III, §§5-6.

[266] In the past, when there was no policy to send cases to the Court, the lack of transparency with regard to decision-making on when to send a case to the Court was even greater. On the one hand the need for transparency and motivation required the Commission to give reasons in its Annual Report for not having sent a case to the Inter-American Court. On the other hand, some members of the Commission and its staff perceived a risk that doing this might undermine the integrity and effectiveness of the Commission's final decisions, for instance when the Commission did not deem a case strong enough to present to the Court. Nevertheless, in my view providing no information and explanation why a case was not sent to the Court might actually enhance the risk of speculation, which could also undermine effectiveness.

[267] This observation could equally be made with regard to *permanent* international courts as well as domestic courts.

they were 'only observations issued from the Secretariat, not from the Commission'.[268] The remark had caused alarm among the petitioners and others in Mexico. The beneficiary of the precautionary measures reportedly decided to leave the province in question because of the statements. Gutiérrez had also attacked the Executive Secretary as having 'usurped' the Commission's functions, being the person who 'decides to admit and process all the files in relation to questions on the merits and precautionary measures'.[269] Moreover, while he was in Colombia, in November 2004, he had stated that precautionary measures were not binding. The remarks by the Commissioner were particularly problematic in light of the serious situations in Colombia, involving death threats, and the fact that this State had never protested that the Commission's precautionary measures would not be legally binding. Finally, he had publicly commented on statements of the Inter-American Commission with regard to his State of nationality (Venezuela).

In the Resolution the Commission noted that the various opportunities it had given Gutiérrez to comply with his juridical and ethical obligations had been to no avail. It pointed out that it had 'the legal and moral obligation to report on this situation to the member States, the organs of the OAS and civil society, and to respond publicly to the notions put forth by Commissioner Freddy Gutiérrez Trejo'.[270] The Commission reaffirmed the international obligation of member States to comply with its precautionary measures.[271] The Resolution also reiterated the ethical and legal commitment of members of the Commission to refrain from participating in the discussion of a matter if they are nationals of the State concerned.[272] With regard to its decision-making it noted that the precautionary measures had in fact been adopted with the majority vote of its members and that when the Commission was not in session such vote would take place through conference calls or by electronic means, in accordance with Article 17(5) of its Rules of Procedure.[273]

In July 2007 the Commission referred the same Commissioner once more. It stated that he had repeatedly abused his position as a Rapporteur in order to attack the institutional integrity of the Commission. It also stated that he had made false statements regarding matters and cases pending and had made numerous public statements even with regard to cases pending involving his own country. The other members of the Commission decided to replace him in the functions and responsibilities that were assigned to him as a Rapporteur.[274]

In July 2008 the Commission adapted and expanded Article 15 of its Rules of Procedure regarding Rapporteurships and Working Groups, which originally consisted of two paragraphs only. Among others the article now includes parameters for the designation of Rapporteirships and membership in Working Groups and it includes the explicit option to replace a special rapporteur 'for reasonable cause' by an absolute majority.

For its discussion of precautionary measures this chapter predominantly draws on the information provided in the Commission's Annual Reports since 1996. In 1996 the Commission

---

[268] CIDH Resolution 1/05, 8 March 2005.
[269] Ibidem.
[270] CIDH Resolution 1/05, 8 March 2005.
[271] See further Chapter XVI on legal status.
[272] See more generally about the independence and impartiality of members of the Commission and the Court e.g. Faúndez Ledesma (1998), pp. 185-210.
[273] CIDH Resolution 1/05, 8 March 2005, by all members of the Commission other than Gutiérrez. The latter's comment was attached to the Resolution.
[274] CIDH Resolution 3/07, 17 July 2007.

took less than thirty precautionary measures.[275] In the next five years it took fifty or more precautionary measures each year.[276]

Two approaches of the Commission (and its staff) are particularly helpful with regard to transparency: the fact that it now publishes statistics about its precautionary measures in its Annual Reports and the fact that it sometimes publishes press releases specifically about compliance with its own precautionary measures and with the Court's provisional measures.[277] Recently it has even made available video and audio of hearings involving a State's compliance with its precautionary measures.[278] It has also made a separate link to 'precautionary measures' on the main page of its website, providing information even on recent precautionary measures that have not yet been included in an Annual Report.[279]

4.4.3 The Court

Despite the lack of any meaningful budget the Court has been able to make its decision-making on the use of provisional measures more transparent than any other human rights adjudicator.[280]

---

[275] Annual Report 1996. These were Brazil (4), Colombia (4), Dominican Republic (3), Ecuador (1), El Salvador (1), Guatemala (8), Honduras (2), Mexico (5) and US (1).

[276] In its Annual Report 2006, published in March 2007, the CIDH included a table referring to 57 precautionary measures in 1997; 54 in 1998; 52 both in 1999 and in 2000; 50 in 2001; 91 in 2002; 56 in 2003, 37 in 2004; 33 in 2005 and 37 in 2006.

[277] See e.g. CIDH, Press Release, 'IACHR Expresses concern over the situation of Yvon Neptune', 19/05, 6 May 2005; 'Inter-American Commission on human Rights expresses its concern over the situation in the Urso Branco prison in Brazil', 13/04, 19 March 2004; 'Executive Secretary of the IACHR concerned over the death threats against Human Rights Defenders in Haiti', 28/01, 9 November 2001; 'Inter-American Commission on Human Rights requests precautionary measures to protect Claudy Gassant, the judge investigating the murder of reporter Jean Dominique', 13/01, 6 July 2001 and Press release (urging the OAS to call off the execution of federal death row inmate Garza), 11/01, 15 June 2001; all at: <www.cidh.org>. Furthermore it is interesting to note that, in the press releases on precautionary measures, the Commission has introduced a practice of attaching background information (less than half a page) on its mandate and composition, evidently intended to inform the media. See e.g. press release 'IACHR calls upon the United States to postpone execution of juvenile offender Alexander Williams', 7/02, 19 February 2002. See also Chapters XVII (Official State responses) and XVIII (Follow up).

[278] See e.g. CIDH Video and Audio of the hearing on Precautionary Measures for the Detainees at the Guantánamo Bay Naval Base, held on October 28, 2008, during the Commission's 133rd period of sessions, link provided in CIDH press release 02/09, 'IACHR welcomes order to close Guantanamo detention center', 27 January 2009, at <http://www.cidh.org/Comunicados/English/2009/02-09eng.htm> (consulted 27 January 2009).

[279] See e.g. <http://www.cidh.org/medidas/2009.eng.htm> (consulted 27 Jnauary 2009).

[280] In 2005 the Court received less than two percent of the OAS budget. Following the presentation by the President of the Court of the 1999 Annual Report on the work of the Court to the Committee on Juridical and Political Affairs of the Permanent Council of the OAS, Annual Report of the Inter-American Court 2000, III.6, sixteen delegations congratulated the Court for the excellent work performed during 1999 and hoped that the OAS would continue to support the Court. "In this respect, they expressed themselves in favor of reintegrating at least US$ 100,000.00 of the US$ 150,500.00 cut form the Court's budget for 2000 by the OAS Program-Budget Committee, so that the Court could conduct at least three sessions in 2000 and translate and publish its annual report for that year. Likewise, they expressed the hope that the Court's budget would be increased as of 2001, as it has been frozen since 1998". On 12 October 2000 the OAS General Assembly approved the Court's budget for the year 2001in a total of US$ 1,284,700. In other words the Court must work with a little over a million US dollars, Annual Report Inter-American Court 2000, Chapter VII. See also the General Secretariat's Report on the

From the start the Inter-American Court has published its provisional measures separately, first in its Annual Reports, later also in its 'Series E' on provisional measures.[281] The same applies to the President's decision to take urgent measures in advance of any Court decision.

The Court hearings on provisional measures are public and contribute significantly to the persuasiveness of its Orders for provisional measures. Moreover, since September 2001 its provisional measures are also accessible directly on the website of the Court.[282] They are motivated, references are made to public hearings held on requests for provisional measures and they regularly include concurring opinions.[283] The Court also issues press releases specifically referring to its provisional measures and both the Commission and the Court provide overviews of their provisional measures in their Annual Reports.[284]

Yet given the relevance of the Court's provisional measures for other systems as well as for the English speaking petitioners and States of the American system it would be substantially increase the accessibility of the information if good translations were regularly provided.[285]

---

budget execution of the regular fund 2001 as presented to the Committee on Administrative and Budgetary Affairs, 18 September 2001(MAN/AS/150/01), p. 6, <www.oas.org/consejo/CAAP/documentos.htm>. The latter Report speaks of a total OAS budget of 76 million US dollars, which means that the Court received 1.7 % in 2001. In a table published in its 2005 Annual Report, published in 2006, the IACHR refers to 1,82 % of the OAS Annual Budget that is reserved for the Court. Both in 2005 and 2006 the budget was US$ 1,391,300. The budget set by the OAS clearly did not take account of the increased case load of the Court. The budget for 2007 was somewhat larger: 1,656,300 and for 2008 it was 1,756,300 (IACHR Annual Report 2007, p. 6). In a speech of 27 November 2006 President Sergio García Ramírez referred to the 26.3 percent increase in the Court's regular budget and the increase in the funds from external donations, Annual Report 2007, p. 55.

[281] This includes introductions by the President of the Inter-American Court: Fix-Zamudio (1996), pp. V-IX; Cançado Trindade (2000), pp. VII-XVIII; Cançado Trindade (2001), pp. V-XX. See also the separate publication on the Court's website (often only in Spanish; in cases involving Brazil often only in Portuguese).

[282] See <http://www.corteidh.or.cr>. The website of the University of Minnesota Human Rights Library is an accessible alternative, though not up-to-date: <http://www1.umn.edu/humanrts/iachr/iachr.html>.

[283] On dissenting and separate opinions before the Inter-American Court generally see Gros Espiell (1988), pp. 456-466.

[284] They both provide statistics as well. See e.g. IACHR Annual Report 2005, with 25 tables, pp. 65-81, including tables relating to provisional measures, such as the number of public hearings held on provisional measures, p. 79. In addition, in 2007 the Court introduced the practice of making available on its website the official pleadings of several cases. Again the Court is the first human rights adjudicator doing so in a manner comparable to that of the ICJ.

[285] The translation into English of provisional measures that were originally written in Spanish has sometimes been unclear or inaccurate. Moreover, quotations in these provisional measures from earlier decisions on the merits or reparations (and even from provisions of the treaty) often appeared to have been translated anew, rather than copied from the original translation or official text. In spite of a chronic lack of resources some oversight on the accuracy and consistency of translations would be useful. A fully functioning search system of the case law, including the provisional measures, would be the next step.

5   THE AFRICAN HUMAN RIGHTS SYSTEM

5.1   Introduction

An African Court on Human and Peoples' Rights was installed in 2006 with an explicit mandate to order provisional measures. In July 2008 the African Union (AU) adopted a Protocol aimed at the merger of this Court with the Court of Justice. The new African Court of Justice and Human Rights also has the power to order provisional measures. Lacking Court practice this book only refers to the practice of the Commission, whose mandate to use provisional measures is based on its Rules of Procedure.

The African Commission, monitoring compliance with the African Charter on Human and Peoples' Rights (ACHPR), has used provisional measures to halt executions; to protect against threats and ensure security; to intervene in a detention situation and ensure medical treatment; to halt deportation; to protect indigenous culture; to allow the return of a person to his home country and to allow the return of a body for burial; to intervene on behalf of journalists detained without charge and to release detainees or bring them before a court.

This section discusses the institutional setting of the provisional measures as used in the African system and the right of individual petition, the power to order provisional measures, the promptness in deciding on the use of provisional measures and the availability of information on the use of these measures.

5.2   The right of individual complaint before the African Commission and Court

In 1981 the Organisation African Unity, the predecessor of the AU,[286] adopted the African Charter on Human and Peoples' Rights (ACHPR). This Charter entered into force in 1986. It has 53 States parties (all AU member States). The African Commission, monitoring compliance with its provisions, consists of 11 members. Its Secretariat was inaugurated in June 1989 and is based in Banjul (The Gambia), yet its sessions are often held in other States in Africa.[287] Its function is both promotional (Article 45(1)) and protective (Article 45(2)). Under its protective mandate it must 'ensure' the protection of human and peoples' rights. In this context it examines State Reports and individual communications.[288] The African Commission has also instituted Special Rapporteurs on prisons and prison conditions; on women's rights; on freedom of expression; on human rights defenders; on extra-judicial, summary or arbitrary executions; on refugees, asylum seekers and internally displaced persons in Africa. Some of these Rapporteurs also apply an urgent action procedure. These urgent actions may relate to persons that have not submitted any

---

[286]   Constitutive Act of the African Union, Lomé, Togo, 11 July 2000 (based on the Sirte Declaration of the Organisation of African Unity's Assembly of Heads of State and Government, Fourth Extraordinary Summit, Libya, 9 September 1999). The Constitutive Act entered into force 26 May 2001. The headquarters of the AU are in Addis Ababa (Ethiopia). See generally about Africa and human rights Heyns (2004); Zeleza/McConnaughay (2004); Lloyd/Murray (2004), pp. 165-187; Bekker (2004), pp. 293-299; Naldi (1999); Welch (1995); specifically on the African Union and human rights: Murray (2004) and Udombana (2002), pp. 1177-1261. About the role of the African Union's predecessor, the OAU, see e.g. Naldi (2002), pp. 1-35.

[287]   See Ouguergouz (2003), pp. 505-507.

[288]   Formally its mandate is to examine State communications and 'other communications'.

complaint before the Commission.[289] The interrelation between the Commission's provisional measures and the urgent actions by its Special Rapporteurs has not yet been formally clarified.

The ACHPR also includes a provision on early warning in emergency situations. Under Article 58(3) the Commission should refer cases of emergency to the Chairman of the Assembly of Heads of State and Government. As Ankumah observes, this Assembly had 'a reputation of failing to condemn human rights abuses by African governments'. She speculates about what Idi Amin would have done with a complaint about violations in Uganda in the late 1970s, when he was the Chairman of the Assembly.[290]

As noted, part of the Commission's mandate is 'protective' (Article 45(2)). Under this mandate it must 'ensure' the protection of human and peoples' rights. The main procedure discussed in the Charter is the inter-State complaint procedure, which has rarely been used (Articles 47-54).[291] On the basis of the phrase 'communications other than those of States parties' in Article 55 ACHPR the Commission has accepted individual complaints. It accepts complaints by individuals and by NGOs and it does not apply a victim requirement. In this respect the practice developed by the Commission is similar to that of the Inter-American Commission, although for the latter the absence of victim requirement is apparent from Article 44 ACHR.

The procedure is otherwise similar to that of the other adjudicators.[292] In the *Ogoni* case (2002) the African Commission made clear that the 'uniqueness of the African situation and the special qualities of the African Charter on Human and Peoples' Rights imposes upon the African Commission an important task. International law and human rights must be responsive to African circumstances'.[293]

In 1998 the Heads of State and Government of the OAU (now AU) adopted the Protocol to the African Charter establishing an African Court on Human and Peoples' Rights. It has been installed in Arusha, Tanzania and the new judges were sworn in on 2 July 2006. The African Commission or States that have ratified the Protocol can bring cases before the Court (Article 5). In addition the Court can provide Advisory Opinions.[294] Direct access to the Court is possible for individuals and NGOs when the State against which they complain has made a declaration to this effect accepting the competence of the Court to receive cases under Article 5(3) Protocol.[295] As

---

[289]   About the Rapporteurs see e.g. Evans/Murray (2002), pp. 280-304; Harrington (2001), pp. 247-267 and Murray (2000), pp. 22-24.

[290]   Ankumah (1996), p. 40. See also Murray (2000), pp. 24-25.

[291]   See ACHPR *Congo* v. *Rwanda, Burundi and Uganda*, com. nr. 227/99, 15th Annual Activity report 1001-2.

[292]   See e.g. ACHPR, Information Sheet No. 2 Guidelines of the submission of communications (10 pp.) and No. 3 Communication Procedure (10 pp.). See in general about the case law and proceedings before the Commission Heyns & Killander (2006), pp. 509-543; Murray (2004), pp. 193-204; Flinterman/Ankumah (2004), pp. 171-188; Heyns/Viljoen (2004), pp. 129-143; Mugwanya (2003); Ouguergouz (2003); Udombana (2003a), pp. 1-37; Evans/Murray (2002); Pityana (2002), pp. 219-245; Naldi (2001), pp. 109-118; Nmehielle (2001); Odinkalu (2001), pp. 225-246; Umozurike (2001), pp. 707-712; De Wet (2001), pp. 713-729; Murray (2000); Heyns/Viljoen (1999), pp. 421-445; Umozurike (1997) and Ankumah (1996).

[293]   "Clearly, collective rights, environmental rights, and economic and social rights are essential elements of human rights in Africa. The African Commission will apply any of the diverse rights contained in the African Charter. It welcomes this opportunity to make clear that there is no right in the African Charter that cannot be made effective". ACHPR *The Social and Economic Rights Action Center and the Center for Economic and Social Rights* v. *Nigeria* (Ogoni case), October 2001, §68.

[294]   See e.g. Van der Mei (2005b), pp. 27-46.

[295]   "The Court may entitle relevant Non Governmental organizations (NGOs) with observer status before the Commission, and individuals to institute cases directly before it, in accordance with article 34 (6) of this Protocol". As of 15 October 2007, 24 States had ratified the Protocol on the

noted, in July 2008 the AU adopted a Protocol aimed at the merger of this Court with the Court of Justice.[296] The Protocol on the African Court of Human and Peoples' Rights will remain in force for a transitional period. The new Protocol does not make provision for direct access to the Court by individuals or NGOs either. Once more they can only bring petitions to the Human Rights Section of the new Court against States that have made a specific declaration to this effect. In addition to State parties and the African Commission the African Committee of Experts on the Rights and Welfare of the Child, African Intergovernmental Organizations accredited to the Union or its organs and African National Human Rights Institutions can also bring petitions (Article 30 of the 2008 Protocol).

As there is not practice so far, the interrelationship between the African Commission and either African Court is not yet clear.[297]

5.3 Power and promptness in the African system

The African Charter does not contain a specific article on provisional measures, but Rule 111 of the Commission's Rules of Procedure stipulates:

> "1. Before making its final views know to the Assembly on the communication [sic], the Commission may inform the State party concerned of its views on the appropriateness of taking provisional measures to avoid irreparable damage being caused to the victim of the alleged violation. In so doing, the Commission shall inform the State party that the expression on its views on the adoption of those provisional measures does not imply a decision on the substance of the communication.
> 2. The Commission, or when it is not in session, the Chairman, in consultation with other members of the Commission, may indicate to the parties any interim measure, the adoption of which seems desirable in the interest of the parties or the proper conduct of the proceedings before it.
> 3. In case urgency when the Commission is not in session, the Chairman in consultation with other members of the Commission, may take any necessary action on behalf of the Commission. As soon as the Commission is again in session, the Chairman shall report to it on any action taken".[298]

African Court on Human and Peoples' Rights. See the official website of the African Union: <www.africa-union.org>. This source does not indicate which of those States specifically recognised the competence of the Court to receive cases under Article 5(3) Protocol. Some States that have ratified the Protocol had not previously explicitly recognized an individual complaint mechanism, such as the individual complaints procedure under the ICCPR (e.g. Rwanda, Burundi and the Comoros).

[296] The Protocol on the Statute of the African Court of Justice and Human Rights was adopted at the 11th African Union (AU) Summit of July 2008. It merges the 1998 Protocol on the African Court of Human and Peoples' Rights and the 2003 Protocol of the African Court of Justice (ratified by 15 AU States).

[297] On the creation of the 1998 Protocol and the potential of the African Court on Human and Peoples' Rights (given the text of the Protocol), see e.g. Padilla (2005), pp. 185-194; Van der Mei (2005), pp. 113-129; Ouguergouz (2003), pp. 681-683; Pityana (2003), pp. 110-129; Harrington (2002), pp. 305-334; Udombana (2000), pp. 1-5 and Krisch (1998), pp. 713-726. On the announced institution of a Court of the African Union see e.g. Viljoen/Baimu (2004), pp. 241-267.

[298] ACHPR Rules of Procedure of 6 October 1995 (<www.achpr.org>). Previously this was Rule 109, Rules of Procedure, 1 February 1988, see Murray/Evans (2001), p. 161.

Article 27(2) of the Protocol to the African Charter establishing the African Court on Human and Peoples' Rights (1998) stipulates:

> "In cases of extreme gravity and urgency, and when necessary to avoid irreparable harm to persons, the Court shall adopt such provisional measures as it deems necessary".

The words 'shall adopt' indicate the importance attached to provisional measures while 'such provisional measures as it deems necessary' refers to the discretion of the Court. It is not yet clear how the complementarity between the Commission and the Court would work out with regard to provisional measures. In the text of the 1998 Protocol there is no arrangement similar to that in Article 63(2) ACHR whereby the Commission requests the Court's provisional measures in cases that *can* be brought before the Court but at that time are still pending before the Commission.[299]

Article 35 of the Protocol on the Statute of the African Court of Justice and Human Rights (2008) stipulates:

> "1. The Court shall have the power, on its own motion or on application by the parties, to indicate, if it considers that circumstances so require any provisional measures which ought to be taken to preserve the respective rights of the parties.
> 2. Pending the final decision, notice of the provisional measures shall forthwith be given to the parties and the Chairperson of the Commission, who shall inform the Assembly".

It is assumed that the change in phrasing from 'cases of extreme gravity and urgency, and when necessary to avoid irreparable harm to persons', in the 1998 Protocol, to 'if it considers that circumstances so require any provisional measures which ought to be taken to preserve the respective rights of the parties', in the 2008 Protocol, aims at a broader range of situations than just those to prevent irreparable harm to persons, because the provision applies to both the Human Rights Section and to the General Affairs Section.

The text of Article 27(2) of the 1998 Protocol does not rule out the *proprio motu* use of provisional measures by the African Court and neither does the text of Article 111 of the Commission's Rules of Procedure for provisional measures by the Commission. The text of Article 35 of the 2008 Protocol explicitly refers to *proprio motu* use.

The available primary sources provide insufficient information on the promptness of the Commission's interventions.[300] In light of the lack of resources and other problems at the Commission's secretariat, it may be assumed that promptness in a given case depends also on the resourcefulness of individual Commissioners.[301]

---

[299] See Articles 2 and 8 Protocol to the African Charter on Human and Peoples' Rights.

[300] See section 5.4. Some decisions do provide information relevant as to promptness, see e.g. ACHPR *B.* v. *Kenya*, November/December 2004 (inadm.), 2004 AHRLR 67. In this case the request was received on 21 October 2003. The Secretariat prepared a draft appeal to the State (in a case involving judicial independence) and sent it to the chairperson of the Commission on 24 October. The latter replied by e-mail on 28 October, determining that an appeal letter should not be sent until the Commission had examined the matter during the next session in November. In March 2004 the petitioner withdrew the complaint, considering that the State was now addressing the situation.

[301] While discussing the practice of Special Rapporteurs in the context of the African Commission, Harrington (2001), pp. 247-267 lists several criteria, such as expertise, resources, willingness to devote time and the independence of the Commissioner. These criteria may also play a role in the Commission's use of provisional measures. The 2005 Guidelines excluding senior civil servants and diplomatic representatives from Commission membership, BC/OLC/66/Vol. XVIII will be

5.4 Decisions to use provisional measures: transparency or the lack thereof?

As part of human rights adjudication in the African system provisional measures could help prevent irreparable harm, but thus far they have received little attention.[302] Initially it was difficult even to access the decisions on the merits by the African Commission in individual cases, also because the drafters of the Charter had not intended to create easy access.[303] Yet the Commission has now made available on its website its Annual Activity Reports including its decisions in individual cases.[304] Moreover, in July 2004 the Centre for Human Rights of the University of Pretoria published the first volume of African Human Rights Law Reports and it has continued these publications since.[305]

The Commission does not publish information on its use of provisional measures, let alone the texts themselves of the communications sent to the States under Rule 111.[306] It has published few press releases, especially in comparison to the Inter-American Commission, and the press releases it did publish, did not relate to provisional measures. Recently the Special Rapporteur on human rights defenders in Africa has published a range of press releases that sometimes refer to ongoing threats and therefore aim at prevention. These may also be indicative of how communications under Rule 111 are formulated.[307] Yet this is only the case to the extent that these press releases were prepared by the Secretariat and not by the Rapporteur herself. The Annual Activity Reports or the publication of the University of Pretoria, with the relevant case law, sometimes do

---

helpful to ensure independence, see Heyns/Killander (2006), pp. 524-525. See also Udombana (2003b), pp. 485-488, discussing the lengthy proceedings before the African Commission and the 'absolute necessity' of the power of a human rights tribunal to order provisional measures, p. 488.

[302] For a discussion see e.g. Flauss (2005a), pp. 231-239; Ouguergouz (2003), pp. 741-742; Udombana (2003b), pp. 479-532 (discussing various systems, but paying due attention to the African system); Naldi (2002), pp. 1-9, Nmehielle (2001), pp. 232-236 (and pp. 299-301 about the Court); for references see e.g. Murray (2000a), p. 20 (footnote 99) and Ankumah (1996), p. 41 (the rule on provisional measures is an 'effort to give meaning to the provisions guaranteed by the Charter').

[303] Article 59(3) ACHPR stipulates that the Assembly formally adopts the Commission's annual Activity Reports, which include its decisions in individual cases: Article 59(1) "All measures taken within the provisions of the present Chapter shall remain confidential until such a time as the Assembly of Heads of State and Government shall otherwise decide. (2) The report on the activities of the Commission shall be published by its Chairman after it has been considered by the Assembly of Heads of State and Government".

[304] See <www.achpr.org>. About openness/ confidentiality and resource limitations see e.g. Murray (2000b), pp. 169-173 and pp. 160-161. See also Ouguergouz (2003), pp. 680-681.

[305] The 2004 publication included 97 findings of the African Commission before 31 December 2000. See African Human Rights Law Reports, <www.chr.up.ac.za> (African Human Rights Centre, University of Pretoria). The African Human Rights Centre has since published subsequent African Human Rights Law Reports. Previously the Institute for Human Rights and Development, a pan-African NGO, also published a compilation of the Commission's decisions between 1994 and 1999. Very useful is also the website of the University of Minnesota's African Human Rights Resource Center, which lists the case law of the African Commission alphabetically: <http://www1.umn.edu/humanrts/africa/comcases/allcases.html>. Another useful internet source is <http://www.chr.up.ac.za/hr_docs/themes/theme02.html>. See further the documents in Heyns (2005) and Murray/Evans (2001).

[306] On the lack of transparency see also Julia Harrington (2001), pp. 247-267.

[307] See ACHPR Special Rapporteur on human rights defenders in Africa, Adv. Reine Alapini-Gansou, on specific cases of harassment, detention, assassination. E.g. Press release on the harassment of Mr. Jean-Paul Noël Abdi, Djibouti, 16 March 2007.

not refer to (informal) provisional measures while they may have been taken, because the official publication of the decision on the merits or inadmissibility does not always refer to procedural decisions.[308] Yet some additional information about the use of provisional measures by the African Commission can be found in press releases by NGOs.[309]

6   THE EUROPEAN HUMAN RIGHTS SYSTEM

6.1   Introduction

Most provisional measures by the (former) European Commission and by the European Court involve halting expulsion and extradition (Articles 2 and 3 ECHR). There are also a few provisional measures involving direct violation of Articles 3 and 4 by the addressee State (halting executions or intervening in detention situations and intervening in the conditions of 51 asylum seekers in tents in the burning sun, without sanitation in no-man's land between Spain and Morocco). Incidentally the Commission or Court have also used provisional measures in situations varying from ensuring access to court, halting the destruction of an embryo in an IVF case and preserving evidence.

This section discusses the institutional setting of the provisional measures as used in the European system and the right of individual petition, the power to order provisional measures, the promptness of the adjudicator in deciding on the use of provisional measures and the availability of information on the use of these measures.

6.2   The right of individual complaint

The European human rights system is the oldest regional system. It has been instituted under auspices of the Council of Europe. This organisation was inaugurated in 1949. Presently it has 47

---

[308]   In earlier, unofficial, versions of the decisions references were sometimes made to provisional measures. This appears to have been the case e.g. in *Vera and Orton Chirwa* v. *Malawi*, 1995, §3: "After international protest, the sentences were commuted to life imprisonment. The Chirwas were held in almost complete solitary confinement, given extremely poor food, inadequate medical care, shackled for long periods of time within their cells and prevented from seeing each other for years". See also *Degli (on behalf of Corporal N. Bikagni) et al.* v. *Togo*, published in abbreviated undated version, 7th Annual Activity Report and (2000) AHRLR 315 (ACHPR 1994). See e.g. <http://dcregistry.com/users/ACHPR/index3.html> (consulted 20 October 2007) for the initial decision of March 1995, §14 ("On 19 September 1994, the Commission, under Rule 109, called on the government of Togo to take the necessary measures to prevent irreparable prejudice to Corporal Bikagni".). Thus, in some cases, given the subject matter, (informal) provisional measures may have been used.

[309]   See e.g. Minority Rights Group, Statement on the human rights situation of Endorois of Kenya 36th session of the African Commission on Human and Peoples' Rights (23 November-7 December 2004) and press release, 24 January 2005, <www.minorityrights.org> (accessed on 25 July 2005). In this submission it drew attention to the provisional measures that the Commission had granted during its 35th session on 1 June 2004, urging the government of Kenya 'to take immediate steps to ensure that no further issuance of mining concessions or transfers of parts to the land occurred prior to the case being concluded' in order to prevent irreparable damage to the traditional lands of the Endorois community around the Lake Bogoria region, through government sanctioned mining operations. See further Chapter X (cultural rights).

members.[310] The Council of Europe has introduced almost 200 treaties, the most important of which is the European Convention on Human Rights (ECHR). The Convention was concluded in 1950 and entered into force in 1953. The permanent European Court of Human Rights (ECtHR) consists of 47 judges, a number equal to the number of Contracting States (Article 20 ECHR). The Court is divided in Chambers of seven judges. The Grand Chamber (seventeen judges) handles important cases referred to it by the Chamber to which a case was initially brought or through a system of internal appeal.[311]

The Court only deals with civil and political rights, which have been interpreted to include positive obligations as well.[312] The range of rights covered is more limited than that of the Inter-American and, especially, the African human rights system, but its individual complaint system is being used to the full. The ECHR 'represents a very distinct form of international instrument and – in many respects – its substance and process of application are more akin to those of national constitutions than to those of 'typical' international treaties'.[313]

Protocol 11 to the ECHR entered into force in 1998 and introduced a complete overhaul of the European human rights system, predominantly in order to address the ever increasing case-load of the Court. In the original system a European Commission on Human Rights, set up in 1954 and comparable to the Inter-American and African Commissions, initially dealt with cases. It declared them (in)admissible and published reports on the merits (so-called Article 31 reports). The Commission and the State concerned could decide to take the case to the European Court of Human Rights, in existence since 1959. If not, the Committee of Ministers of the Council of Europe would finally decide on the question whether there had been a violation or not. Sometimes it would take a decision different from that of the Commission. This old system is still relevant because the European Commission often used provisional measures. In this respect it set the stage for the practice of the current permanent Court.

With the entry into force of the 11th Protocol the Commission was abolished.[314] The Court became permanent and its jurisdiction became compulsory for all States parties to the Convention. The Committee of Ministers now only monitors compliance with the Court's judgments, a

---

[310] To understand the broader context of provisional measures taken in the human rights system of the Council of Europe two other regional organisations in Europe must be mentioned that sometimes deal with human rights issues: the Organization for Security and Co-operation in Europe (OSCE), a 55 member security organisation (including non-European States), including its High Commissioner on National Minorities, the Office for Democratic Institutions and Human Rights, the High Commissioner on Freedom of the Media and the Conflict Prevention Centre of the Secretariat of the OSCE, on the one hand, and the European Union on the other hand.

[311] Given the excessive workload of the Court, in 2004 Protocol 14 was accepted to streamline proceedings. It will enter into force upon ratification by Russia.

[312] See e.g. Mowbray (2004); Van der Velde (2002); Vlemminx (2002); Lawson (1995) and Forder (1992). See further Chapter XIII on the protective measures required. In addition to the rights in the Covenant the following Protocols are in force: Protocol 1 (property, education and elections), Protocol 4 (no imprisonment for debt, freedom of movement; no expulsion of citizens, no collective expulsion of aliens), Protocol 6 (abolition of the death penalty, war time exception possible), Protocol 7 (appeal in criminal cases; procedural safeguards expulsion aliens; compensation for wrongful conviction; no double jeopardy; equality between spouses), Protocol 12 (general prohibition of discrimination) and Protocol 13 (abolition of the death penalty without exceptions). The Council of Europe also introduced the European Social Charter and its Protocols (including a collective complaint system).

[313] ECtHR Concurring Opinion Judge Garlicki, §4, ECtHR (Grand Chamber), *Öcalan* v. *Turkey*, Judgment of 12 May 2005.

[314] While the new Court started functioning in November 1998, the Commission continued to exist until the end of October 1999 in order to deal with those cases it had previously declared admissible.

role more suitable for a political body.[315] While the new Court took over the functions of the Commission, it seems that it does not always have the opportunity to fulfil all of the fact-finding and conciliatory functions previously fulfilled by the Commission.[316]

Article 34 ECHR (right of petition) stipulates protection for the alleged victims in unhindered submission of complaints and participation in the proceedings. Moreover, anyone participating in the proceedings (as petitioners, counsel, witnesses, experts, advisers, etc.) enjoys immunity from legal process in respect of acts before the Court, as well as freedom to correspond with the Court and freedom to travel in order to attend hearings in Strasbourg.[317]

Different from the Inter-American and African system there is a so-called 'victim requirement', meaning that for the complaint to be declared admissible the petitioner must in fact allege to be the victim of the violations complained of. This means that the role of NGOs is less prominent than in the other two regional systems.[318]

As noted, one of the main purposes of Protocol 11 was to be able to deal with the steadily increasing caseload, which by 1997 amounted to 4,750. At present, however, the Court is struggling to keep up with an even more staggering stream of applications.[319] To address the problem of overburdening various proposals have been made, including the introduction of a *certiorari* system similar to that used by the U.S. Supreme Court. Yet a pick-and-choose approach would not do justice to the petitioner's right to redress about violations of the ECHR.

If a certiorari system would be introduced, the Court should still address all claims involving risks of irreparable harm to persons. Introduction of a certiorari system that does not take into account urgent cases would constitute an irreparable blow to the protective function of the Court. At the same time when such a system *would* still address all urgent claims, clarity about the types of cases suitable for the use of provisional measures would then be even more warranted, lest some petitioners would try and infuse an urgent element in a claim that might otherwise be denied.

---

[315] On follow-up see Chapter XVIII. In general about the supervisory mechanism applied at the time and the proposed changes see Klerk (1995).

[316] In 1999 the Office of the Commissioner for Human Rights was established. This Commissioner does not only have a role in the sphere of promoting and facilitating, but is also mandated to identify problems, visit member States and publish reports.

[317] European Agreement relating to Persons Participating in Proceedings of the European Court of Human Rights (ETS no. 161), adopted 1996, entered into force 1999, 35 State parties as of 3 September 2007.

[318] Different from the system under the OP to the ICCPR, companies and other non-governmental entities may petition the ECtHR as long as they claim to be victims of a violation against themselves.Obviously NGOs may represent or assist the alleged victims and submit *amicus curiae* briefs. See further on the role of NGOs Chapter XIII (Protection), section 4 on the beneficiaries of provisional measures. More generally on the law and procedure before the ECtHR (and the old Commission) see e.g. Practice Direction on Institution of Proceedings, 1 November 2003, supplementing Rules 45 and 47 of the Rules of Court, see <www.echr.coe.int>, under 'Basic texts', 'Practice Directions'; Mowbray (2007); Leach (2007); Ovey/White (2006); Van Dijk/Van Hoof/Van Rijn/Zwaak (2006); Van de Lanotte/Haeck (2005); Barkhuysen/Van Emmerik/Rieter (2002/2008); Clements/Mole/Simmons (1999); Van der Velde (1997); Harris/Boyle/Warbrick (1995); Gomien/Harris/Zwaak (1997); Schokkenbroek (1996); Klerk (1995); Cohen-Jonathan (1994), pp. 97-111; Zwart (1994); Lawson/deBlois (1994); Zwaak (1991) and Ergec/Velu (1990), pp. 818-991.

[319] In 2006 the Court had delivered 1560 judgments and struck out or declared inadmissible 28,160; 89,887 cases were pending, see ECtHR Annual Report 2006, May 2007, p. 115.

6.3   Power and promptness in the European system

6.3.1   Introduction

When the ECHR was drafted in the late 1940s and early 1950s no provision was made for the possibility to take provisional measures.[320] The International Juridical Section of the European Movement had included a provision on such measures in its draft convention of 12 July 1949, but if discussion took place on the issue this is not reflected in the *travaux préparatoires*. The proposed Article 35 was similar to Article 41 ICJ Statute.[321]

It was not long after the Convention entered into force, in 1953, that it became clear that if the rights in the Convention were to have practical meaning and if the Convention-bodies were to truly perform their task, these bodies should have the possibility to indicate to the Parties that provisional measures are warranted in a given case.

As early as 1957, the Commission sent an urgent request to the Government of the United Kingdom not to execute Nicolaos Sampson until the Commission had been fully informed of the circumstances of the case. The Commission stated it had decided to make this request in order to prevent "any irreparable act".[322] This could be called an informal provisional measure, not based on a specific Rule on provisional measures. Yet in two less serious cases, decided in 1958 and 1963, the Commission refused to take provisional measures, considering that the Convention did not give it the competence to order them.[323]

In 1964 it again took informal provisional measures, this time to halt an extradition.[324] In fact since then an informal practice developed in which the Commission requested – and obtained – the cooperation of Governments in urgent cases involving extradition or expulsion.

In 1970 the Acting President of the Commission once more requested a State not to execute persons, in this case any of the 34 suspects in a criminal case in Greece, during the proceedings before the Commission.[325] The executions did not take place.[326] In 1974 the Commission decided

---

[320]   The Convention was signed in Rome, 4 November 1950.

[321]   See Nørgaard (1994), pp. 278-297 and references therein.

[322]   See EComHR *Application of the ECHR to the Island of Cyprus (Greece* v. *United Kingdom),* Article 31 report of the Commission, No. 176/56, 26 September 1958, p. 34. This request was respected, see further Chapter III (Executions).

[323]   EComHR *X.* v. *Federal Republic of Germany,* 22 March 1958 ("Whereas the Convention does not contain any such obligations binding upon the High Contracting Parties as invoked by the Applicant; whereas, moreover, the Convention does not contain any provision giving the Commission competence to order provisional measures; whereas it therefore appears that the application is in this respect incompatible with the provisions of the Convention; whereas it should, in pursuance of Article 27, paragraph 2, of the Convention, accordingly be rejected".) and *X. and Y.* v. *Belgium,* 18 December 1963 ('whereas the fact that the Commission is dealing with a case does not have suspensive effect and the Commission is not empowered to order protective measures (see the decision on the admissibility of Application No. 297/57, Volume II, p. 213); whereas, far from obliging national courts to wait for the Commission to complete its work before they complete theirs, the Convention, in principle, provides for the opposite solution (Article 26) and assigns a mainly subsidiary role to the collective guarantee machinery set up by it').

[324]   EComHR *X* v. *Austria and Yugoslavia,* 30 June 1964 (inadm.); provisional measure on 14 February 1964. See also *S.B.* v. *FRG,* 19 December 1969 (struck off), provisional measure on 7 January 1965 and 24 April 1965.

[325]   See Partial Decision of the Commission as to the admissibility of the application, *The Second Greek case,* application No. 4448/70, *Denmark, Norway and Sweden* v. *Greece,* report of the Commission on the present state of the proceedings, adopted on 5 October 1970, p. 11. Both cases and both requests for provisional measures were brought before the Commission by States,

to make official its theretofore informal practice of using provisional measures by including a provision on provisional measures in its Rule 36 of its Rules of Procedure.[327] The Court did so in 1982. Almost all provisional measures taken before the entry into force of Protocol 11 were the Commission's. The old Court did not often deal with provisional measures. Yet its Rules of Procedure did include a rule on provisional measures: Rule 36, which entered into force in January 1983. The President could take provisional measures at the request of one of the parties, the Commission, the petitioner or 'any other person concerned', or *proprio motu*. Nevertheless, most cases in which provisional measures were used were either solved at the admissibility stage and struck out, or declared inadmissible so that the provisional measure did not apply any longer. Moreover, of those cases in which the Commission did make a decision on the merits, not all were later determined by the Court.[328]

Presently the Court's procedure on provisional measures is called 'Rule 39 procedure'. Rule 39 stipulates:

> "The Chamber or, where appropriate, its President may, at the request of a party or of any other person concerned, or of its own motion, indicate to the parties any interim measure which it considers should be adopted in the interests of the parties or of the proper conduct of the proceedings before it".[329]

On the basis of the wording of the Rule on provisional measures, one may conclude that many circumstances could give rise to a request for provisional measures. As will be seen in the subsequent chapters, however, the Commission and Court have interpreted this provision rather strictly. They have been taken mostly in cases of imminent expulsion or extradition involving *prima facie* evidence of a real risk of torture, inhuman treatment or life threatening situation in the receiving State.[330] The President of the Section may consult the other members of the seven judge panel constituted for the case in order to decide on the use of provisional measures.[331] It has been

---

under the state complaint procedure (Article 24 ECHR (pre-Protocol 11), rather than by individuals under the individual complaint procedure (Article 25 ECHR pre-Protocol 11).

[326] See also Chapter XVIII (Official responses). EComHR *Amerktane* v. *UK* (1973) was only submitted to the Commission after the UK authorities had already sent the alleged victim from Gibraltar to Morocco. The petitioners claimed he had subsequently been tortured and sentenced to death. The Commission decided to give priority to the case, possibly because he was still facing execution at the time of submission. No information is available about whether it informally inquired with the UK government about the situation of Amerktane in Morocco, including possible diplomatic interventions on his behalf by the government to prevent his execution. In fact he was executed in January 1973. The case was subsequently settled with his widow. *Amekrane* v. *UK*, 11 October 1973 (adm.).

[327] Article 36 ECHR (pre-Protocol 11) stating that the Commission shall draw up its own rules of procedure. It did so on 13 December 1974. In its 1993 Rules of Procedure, Rule 36 was phrased as follows: "The Commission, or when it is not in session, the President may indicate to the parties any interim measure the adoption of which seems desirable in the interest of the parties or the proper conduct of the proceedings before it". Revised version as adopted by the Commission on 12 February and 6 May 1993 and entered into force on 28 June 1993.

[328] The old Court did take provisional measures in *Soering* v. *UK, Vijayanathan & Pusparajah* v. *France, Chahal* v. *UK* and *Ahmed* v. *Austria*. See Chapter V (Non-refoulement).

[329] "2. Notice of these measures shall be given to the Committee of Ministers. 3. The Chamber may request information from the parties on any matter connected with the implementation of any interim measure it has indicated".

[330] Articles 2 and 3 ECHR.

[331] See Garry (2001), p. 401, referring to an interview with Judge Pellonpää, Section IV, 16 June 2000.

pointed out by one of the judges of the permanent Court, in reference to the *Öcalan* case, that the efficiency of decision-making on the use of provisional measures would have been influenced negatively if the judges had not been available on a permanent basis.[332]

When provisional measures were used, the former Commission often decided to give the case precedence as well, according to Rule 33:

> "The Commission shall deal with applications in the order in which they really become ready for examination. It may, however, decide to give precedence to a particular application".

Precedence or priority, however, was not only given simultaneously with provisional measures to prevent irreparable harm, but also in other cases, such as where priority treatment of a case could ensure that petitioners with terminal illnesses could still be informed of the decision on the merits.[333] Under Rule 41 the current permanent Court can give priority to urgent cases too.[334] It has the policy to do so in cases in which it also decided to order provisional measures, but it does give priority in other cases as well.[335]

6.3.2 Inter-State cases

As noted, the UN adjudicators have never dealt with complaints brought by States against other States. Regionally, thus far, only the European system has dealt with a few significant inter-State cases.[336] In two of the very early inter-State cases the European Commission used provisional measures to halt the execution of death sentences.[337]

---

[332] See Thomassen (2008), p. 931. Wilhelmina Thomassen was a member of the Court between 1998 and 2004.

[333] See e.g. EComHR *B.* v. *France*, 12 July 1991 (adm.) (priority decision 19 April 1991). This case subsequently came before the ECtHR on 18 October 1991 as *X* v. *France*, undated priority decision; petitioner died 2 February 1992; judgment of 31 March 1992. See also, e.g., EComHR *R.M.* v. *UK,* 14 April 1994 (inadm.), priority decision of 21 October 1993.

[334] See e.g. ECtHR *Pretty* v. *UK*, 29 April 2002.

[335] Judge Myjer provides a non-exhaustive list that is applied by the Court with some measure of flexibility. The Court considers that 'cases should be considered as urgent and granted priority under Rule 41', if: "a. the existing situation which the applicant complains about poses a risk to his life or health; b. there exist other circumstances connected with the applicant's person, warranting special urgency in dealing with the application; c. the case concerns particularly serious violations of human rights that might require a fact-finding mission; d. Rule 39 was applied in the case". Other situations referred to include those concerning systemic or endemic problems or cases considered as appropriate for being dealt with as a pilot case, cases where the applicant 'is in a precarious situation by reason of his or her age or state of health' or 'is in detention and there is a prima facie indication attending to the right to liberty and security of a person'. See Myjer (2007), p. 1074.

[336] Recently see the ECtHR's provisional measures in *Georgia* v. *Russia*. ECtHR Press release issued by the Registrar, 'European Court of Human Rights grants request for interim measures', 12 August 2008. Both the African and Inter-American Commission have now dealt with an inter-State case as well, but in these cases no provisional measures were used. See ACHPR *Congo* v. *Rwanda, Burundi and Uganda*, com. nr. 227/99, 15th Annual Activity report 1001-2 and CIDH *Nicaragua* v. *Costa Rica*, 8 March 2007 (inadm.).

[337] See the aforementioned *Application of the ECHR to the Island of Cyprus* (*Greece* v. *United Kingdom*), Article 31 report of the Commission, No. 176/56, 26 September 1958, p. 34 (to halt the execution of Sampson in Cyprus) and Partial Decision of the Commission as to the

6.3.3 Delegation and promptness

In the old system of a non-permanent Commission and Court, the decision-making procedure for when the request for provisional measures arrived at the Commission's Secretariat, the slightly differed depending on whether the Commission was or was not in session at the time. If the Commission was in session, one of its members was instantly appointed as a rapporteur. He would examine the case – a further enquiry might be made by telephone or fax – and present a proposal to the Commission. If the case was 'particularly urgent', he could do this at any time during the session.[338] When the Commission was not in session, the Commission's President or Acting President (the President of either Chamber) dealt with the request.[339] At the Secretariat, the 'lawyer best qualified to deal with it' – given his or her language or legal system – obtained relevant information from the petitioner or his or her lawyer (on the basis of a questionnaire to be filled in by the petitioner or otherwise by completing a check-list on the basis of the available information)[340] and, among others, made a brief summary of the case and gave a provisional opinion as to the merits of the request.[341] This was then discussed with the Secretariat's senior lawyer responsible for all provisional measures. Following this, the senior lawyer, or someone standing in for her, would immediately contact the President or Acting President by telephone. Relevant documents might be sent by fax. As soon as the Commission was again in session, any action undertaken was brought to its attention.[342]

Once the decision to apply Rule 36 was made, the Government concerned was contacted immediately, usually by fax, but sometimes also by telephone. When provisional measures were used the respondent Government was usually notified of the petition at the same time and invited to comment on its admissibility and merits. Rule 46 laid down that:

> 'In any case of urgency, the Secretary of the Commission, may, without prejudice to the taking of any other procedural steps, inform a High Contracting party concerned in an application, by any available means, of the introduction of the application and of a summary of its objects'.

The Secretary did not send this 'communication' to the respondent government, however, when a Commission session was imminent, so that the matter could be discussed by the Commission as a whole.[343] In that case the President or Acting President did not 'communicate' the case, but he did already take the provisional measure.

The promptness of the Commission's earliest – informal – provisional measures varied from more than four months to the same day. Its promptness subsequently varied as well from around eight months to the same day.

---

admissibility of the application, *The Second Greek case* (*Denmark, Norway and Sweden* v. *Greece*), 5 October 1970, §11 (to halt the execution of Karageorgas).

[338] EComHR Directive concerning the implementation of interim measures pursuant to rule 36 of the Commission's Rules of procedure, January 1997, p. 3, point III, §2.

[339] The President or Acting President could not take a decision on provisional measures where this concerned their own state of citizenship: Directive concerning the implementation of interim measures pursuant to rule 36 of the Commission's Rules of procedure, January 1997, p. 1, point I, §1.

[340] EComHR Directive concerning the implementation of interim measures pursuant to rule 36 of the Commission's Rules of procedure, January 1997, p. 2, point II§2.

[341] Id., p. 1, point I §1.

[342] See Rule 34(3) of the Commission's Rules of Procedure.

[343] EComHR Directive concerning the implementation of interim measures pursuant to rule 36 of the Commission's Rules of procedure, January 1997, p. 3, point II §3 sub (b).

Soering v. *UK* (1989) was the first case in which the Court faced a situation in which it it-self was called upon to take provisional measures.[344] In this case the Commission had used provisional measures. Subsequently, after the case had been brought before the Court, the President decided to use provisional measures as well. Yet, there was a period of time in which the petitioner was without the protection of provisional measures. This was not problematic in this particular case because the UK, in a good faith application of the Convention, decided not to extradite Soering. Nevertheless, the Court decided to amend its Rules of Procedure so that, unless the President of the Court would decide differently, the Commission's provisional measures would remain applicable when the case was sent to the Court.

Different from the Inter-American system, the former European system did not specifically take into account situations considered urgent by the *Commission* that were not yet pending before the *Court*.

Buquicchio-de Boer has noted that the Commission often received requests for provisional measures by fax on Friday afternoons 'just hours before an expulsion'. Some Member States carried out deportations on weekends.[345] The permanent Court has a greater chance to deal promptly with requests. Nevertheless, petitioners are informed that requests for provisional measures should be sent during working hours (8am-6pm Monday through Friday), this should not be done outside of working hours 'unless this is absolutely unavoidable'. In addition, petitioners are recommended to already submit their urgent request in advance of the final domestic decision, so as to enable the Court to act as quickly as possible in case a person will be removed soon after the final domestic decision has been given.[346]

The European Commission would put on hold its normal planning and examine the request as soon as possible. When not in session the President would decide 'in collaboration with a senior member of the Commission's legal Secretariat'.[347]

Since the entry into force of Protocol 11 petitioners address their requests to the Registry of the Court and the underlying cases are immediately assigned to a Section. The President of the Section in question will decide on the request for provisional measures. Some Presidents consult with other members of their Section. Judge Pellonpää, for instance, would bring the case before the Section for a vote, if he had any doubts and if time permitted him to do so. Often Presidents will at least consult 'a judge familiar with the country at issue (who will give a recommendation on acceptance or refusal of the application with supporting reasons) and its law in addition to analysing documentation provided in the application'.[348]

In this respect the approach of the HRC is rather different. If the Special Rapporteur has the nationality of the State against which the complaint is made the Secretariat contacts the Chairperson or another member of the Committee to decide on the use of provisional measures.[349] It seems that the emphasis of the ECtHR is on acquiring as much information as possible, on the assumption that the national judge would indeed be able to provide inside information. The emphasis of the HRC, on the other hand, is on independence and impartiality.

At times the European Court and its staff have to take a range of actions in order to ensure that the relevant government is informed of the use provisional measures. In the *Shamayev* case (2005), the petitioners were removed from their cells and the request for provisional measures on behalf of eleven of them in order to prevent their extradition to Russia was received by the Court

---

[344]   ECtHR *Soering* v. *UK*, Judgment of 7 July 1989.

[345]   Buquicchio-de Boer (1998), pp. 229-236.

[346]   ECtHR Practice Direction, Requests for interim measures, 5 March 2003. See further Chapter XV (Immediacy and risk). See also Chapter XVI (Legal status), and XVII (Official responses) on the tendency by some States to make sure petitioners are unable to send a request to the Court.

[347]   Buquicchio-de Boer (1998), pp. 233-234.

[348]   Garry (2001), p. 414, referring to an interview of 16 June 2000.

[349]   See e.g. HRC *Länsman III* v. *Finland*, 17 March 2005.

around 4 PM. At 6 PM the government of Georgia was informed, through its permanent representative in Strasbourg, that the Court had ordered provisional measures. The names of the persons concerned were dictated to the representative of the permanent representation by phone. Given technical problems and failed attempts by the staff to have them resolved, the decision of the Court was formally repeated to the vice-president of justice of Georgia only at 7:45 PM, which could only be confirmed by telecopy at 7:57 PM. Meanwhile, at 7:10 PM the petitioners were extradited.[350]

6.3.4 Proprio motu

Sometimes petitioners who are not represented by a lawyer are less likely to request provisional measures, but they might, nevertheless, ask for the adjudicator's intervention. This was already the case with the former European Commission, which regarded this as a request for such measures as well.[351]

On occasion the Court has even addressed itself to the petitioner under Rule 39, requesting a halt to a hunger strike. It does so *proprio motu*, often in response to a request by the petitioner about improvements in detention conditions, a prison transfer etc.[352]

Rule 39 stipulates that the relevant Chamber of the ECtHR, or its President, may take provisional measures on its own initiative or on the request of the petitioner. They may also do so on the request of 'any other person concerned'. In this respect the possibilities for NGOs are wider than is generally the case in the European system. Moreover, apart from NGOs, individuals such as witnesses to the human rights violation complained of may approach the ECtHR when they receive threats, requesting provisional measures on their behalf, also if they are not themselves parties to the case.[353]

6.4   Decisions to use provisional measures: transparency or the lack thereof?

Most handbooks on the ECHR only refer to provisional measures in passing.[354] A few articles have paid specific attention to the practice of the former European Commission on Human Rights and/or the current Court with regard to provisional measures.[355] A few articles also refer to statis-

---

[350]   ECtHR *Chamaïev et autres c. Géorgie et Russie*, 12 April 2005, §§474-475.

[351]   See: EComHR Directive concerning the implementation of interim measures pursuant to rule 36 of the Commission's Rules of procedure, January 1997 ("(w)here the applicant requests the Commission, expressly or in substance") and Nørgaard (1994), pp. 280-281. See also EComHR *Ennslin, Baader and Raspe* v. *FRG*, 8 July 1978 (inadm.), discussed in Chapter XII (Other situations), section 2.10 (preserving evidence).

[352]   Following the example of the Commission, in 1983 the old Court introduced a reference to addressing the petitioner in its Rule 36. The present Court may do so as well. See also Chapter XIII (Protection), section 4 (beneficiaries).

[353]   See also Pasqualucci (2005), p. 36. See Chapter IX on the use of provisional measures to protect against death threats and harassment.

[354]   Recent handbooks devote more attention to the issue, see e.g. Barkhuysen/Van Emmerik/Rieter (2008), pp. 48-53; Van Dijk/Van Hoof/Van Rijn/Zwaak (2006), pp. 110-119; Leach (2005), pp. 38-42; VandeLanotte/Haeck (2005), pp. 435-486 and Barkhuysen/Van Emmerik/Rieter (2002), pp. 39-44.

[355]   Haeck/Burbano Herrera/Zwaak (2008), pp. 41-63; Rieter (2007); Rieter (2006), pp. 736-739; De Salvia (2005), pp. 177-194; Rieter (2005a), pp. 25-44; Rieter (2005b), pp. 320-324; Rieter (2004), pp. 73-87; Rieter (2003a), pp. 1074-1076; Rieter (2003b), pp. 23-27; Spielmann/Spielmann (2000), pp. 1346-1358; Buquicchio-de Boer (1998); pp. 229-236,

tics provided by the ECtHR following the entry into force of Protocol 11.[356] The Registry of the Court itself has indicated that in 2007 the Court had received 'approximately 1,060 requests for interim measures and granted 252 of them'.[357]

The available information on the use of provisional measures by the European Commission is haphazard at most.[358] Specific information about decision-making with regard to provisional measures often is only made available when a State did not respect them.[359]

Following the entry into force of Protocol 11 and Rule 39 the Court's Registry adapted its practice by automatically registering requests for provisional measures rather than only after the decision is made to accept or reject a request. According to Garry '[a]utomatic registration has the

---

[356] Nørgaard (1994), pp. 278-297; Bernhardt (1994a), pp. 95-114; Giardina (1993), pp. 791-802; MacDonald (1992), pp. 703-740; Nørgaard/Krüger (1988), pp. 109-117; Zwart (1985a), pp. 562-571; Rogge (1977), pp. 1569-1570; Eissen (1969), pp. 252-256.

[356] See Haeck/Burbano Herrera (2003), pp. 625-676 and Garry (2001), pp. 399-432. There are various articles and case notes specifically discussing *Cruz Varas v. Sweden* (1991) and *Mamatkulov and Askarov v. Turkey,* 4 February 2005 (Grand Chamber), see also Chapter XVI on the legal status of provisional measures.

[357] ECtHR Press release issued by the Registrar, 'Inappropriate use of interim measures procedure', 21 December 2007.

[358] See e.g. Nørgaard/Krüger (1988), pp. 109-117; EComHR *Cruz Varas v. Sweden,* Report of 7 June 1990 and Buquicchio-de Boer (1998), pp. 229-236.

[359] A case in point is EComHR *Lynas v. Switzerland,* 6 October 1976 (inadm.). In this case the petitioner claimed that the Swiss authorities, in deciding on his extradition to the United States, exposed his life to danger since CIA agents were after him. On the morning of 22 December 1975 the Secretary of the Commission learnt of the application (sent 18 December) and immediately submitted the petitioner's request 'for an immediate approach to the Swiss Government' to the President of the Commission. At 10.45 the Secretary informed the Swiss Government that the application had been lodged. At 12.10 the President of the Commission was contacted. He immediately made an order for provisional measures and decided that the petition should be given precedence. The Federal Justice Division of the Swiss Government was notified by telephone at 12.15. The representative of the Justice Division informed the Secretary that the petitioner had just been taken to a plane, which had not yet taken off; he stated that the Federal Councillor in charge of the Justice and Police Department would be immediately informed of the order made by the President of the Commission. The notification of the order was confirmed the same day (22 December 1975) by a letter from the Secretary. The Commission was subsequently informed that the petitioner had been extradited to the US on 22 December 1975. Another example is EComHR *Cruz Varas v. Sweden,* 7 June 1991, §§65-70. The President of the European Commission decided to apply Rule 36 on 6 October 1989, 9 AM. Ten minutes later the agent of the Swedish Government was informed by telephone. At noon the Commission confirmed this by telefax. In the meantime the Secretariat of the competent Ministry had been informed (at 9.20 AM). At 12.45 PM the matter was presented to the competent Minister. "However, according to information given by the Government, the Minister could not take any action since the matter had already been decided by the Government and was pending before another authority". In the meantime the petitioner had requested the National Immigration Board to stay the enforcement of the expulsion. "At that time the Board was aware of the present application to the Commission and of the Commission's indication under Rule 36". At 4.40 PM Mr. Cruz Varas was deported to Chile. His wife and son went into hiding in Sweden. That same year Sweden also ignored a provisional measure on behalf of a petitioner who was subsequently deported to Jordan. The agent of the Government had been informed by phone at 4.10 pm. The decision was confirmed by fax on 5.38. Two days later Sweden nevertheless expelled the petitioner. Provisional measure of 19 October 1989 in: *Mansi v. Sweden,* 9 March 1990 (struck out) and 7 December 1989 (adm.)

effect of making applications available to the public from the very beginning'.[360] Indeed such registration would be a prerequisite for making such information available. Nevertheless, this effect seems overstated given the fact that members of the public would have to travel to Strasbourg and indicate which specific case file they would like to consult.

In general, since the entry into force of Protocol 11, memorials and other documents filed with the Court's Registry in principle are accessible to the public (Article 40(2) ECHR).[361] As noted, potential petitioners and other interested persons have to travel to Strasbourg and should indicate beforehand exactly which documents they need. General requests to look, for instance, at files on cases against one particular State are not granted. This applies equally to requests to consult all files in a given period involving requests for provisional measures by petitioners, or to all decisions to grant such request by the Court.[362] In most cases no hearings are held, but if they are held, they are public. Thus far, however, there is no public information on cases in which the Court held such a hearing at the stage of provisional measures.

A brief reference to the use of provisional measures may be found in decisions on the merits and inadmissibility decisions. Decisions *not* to grant provisional measures generally are not mentioned at all. Case law is available on the internet through the HUDOC search database.[363] Older cases are available to a certain extent, but if necessary, one may make a copy of a particular case from the bound volumes of unpublished cases at the Court's library in Strasbourg. The information on many cases of the former Commission that were struck from the roll can only be consulted in bound volumes at the Registry in Strasbourg.[364]

Decisions to take provisional measures are not published separately and do not include an explanation. Some cases are pending for a long time. This means that a new practice may develop with regard to provisional measures with which most practitioners, governments and scholars are unfamiliar because most information on the use of provisional measures is only published in judgments on the merits and inadmissibility decisions. The Information Notes prepared by the Court do have an entry on the use of Rule 39 from which some information can be derived on the use of provisional measures in ongoing cases.

For attorneys that take asylum cases only occasionally and for others interested in the developments, information with regard to provisional measures simply is not very accessible. Even for seasoned asylum attorneys who keep each other informed about the Court's use of provisional measures, it would be useful if the Court itself made available this information as most attorneys are not yet in touch with all asylum attorneys in all member States of the Council of Europe.

A helpful development was the publication, in 2003, of a Practice Direction on provisional measures by the President of the Court.[365] Moreover, there have been a few cases in which the

---

[360]   Garry (2001), p. 414.

[361]   For exceptions see Rules 33(3) en 99(4).

[362]   "You must give the details of each case you wish to consult. It is not possible to deal with general requests, for example to consult the files of all cases against a particular State or all the files relating to a particular subject". See: Consultation of files, 7 November 2002, <www.echr.coe.int/eng/General.htm> (consulted 22 July 2004).

[363]   See <www.echr.coe.int>.

[364]   The author visited the Secretariat of the European Commission on Human Rights, Strasbourg (13-17 October 1997). She would like to thank Maud Bucchiccio-de Boer, Nico Mol, Agnes van Steijn, Marie-Therèse Schoepfer, Wolfgang Peukert, Michèle De Salvia, Caroline Ravaux, Wolfgang Larcher, Wolfgang Strasser and Leo Zwaak. She also would like to thank Ties Prakken (counsel in the *Öcalan* case, Maastricht, interview of 18 March 1999) and the late Henry Schermers (Leyden, interview of 3 March 1998) as well as Yvonne Klerk, Stijn Franken, Jouke Osinga, René Bruin and Mark Jansen who have been helpful in providing information.

[365]   ECtHR Practice Direction on Interim Measures, 5 March 2003. See <www.echr.coe.int> 'Basic texts', 'Practice Directions'.

Court issued a press release about the (non)-use of provisional measures, but these are exceptional.[366]

In addition, the cause of transparency was served in two provisional measures directed against the Netherlands involving expulsion to Somalia in 2004, in which the Court gave some explanation of its use of provisional measures.[367] It added an explanatory remark to the State in order to stem an increasing number of individual complaints by persons similarly situated.

> "The President had regard to the current situation in northern Somalia and in particular to the absence of an effective public authority capable of providing protection to the applicant, who submits that he belongs to a minority and that he has no family or clan ties in northern Somalia. The President further noted that there was no guarantee that the applicant would be admitted to northern Somalia".[368]

In the second case it added the following explanation for its use of provisional measures: it had used them 'in the light of the information currently available concerning the situation of internally displaced persons in Puntland'. The measures would apply until the Court had studied the new Dutch country report on Somalia, on the basis of which the Dutch executive decides on asylum petitions. Depending on the information in this Report the Court would then decide to hold a fact-finding hearing in Strasbourg, hearing experts with personal knowledge about Somalia.[369] Subsequently the Court was faced with a flood of cases against the UK involving the situation in Sri Lanka. Here the Court issued a press release providing some reasoning referring to the general situation of risk.[370]

---

[366] See the first provisional measure in the case *Öcalan*, press release 4 March 1999 (access to his Turkish counsel) and ECtHR (Section 2) *Shamayev and 12 others* v. *Georgia and Russia*, 36378/02, Rieter (2003b). See also ECtHR press release 337 of 30 June 2004 in which the Court referred to a decision of the previous day not to grant the request by lawyers of Saddam Hussein to order the UK not to transfer him to the Iraqi interim government without prior receipt of a declaration that the death penalty would not be imposed. See <www.echr.coe.int/eng/General.htm>.

[367] See Rieter (2005a), pp. 25-44. This concerned cases against the Netherlands to prevent expulsion of persons to Somalia. See also Rieter (2006), pp. 736-739.

[368] See President ECtHR, Note Verbale with provisional measure, 3 May 2004, in case 15243/04, published in the Dutch journal JV 226 (Jurisprudentie Vreemdelingenrecht). Asylum counsel in the Netherlands make a scan of the Notes Verbales they receive with information about provisional measures directed to the State and make these available at 'Vluchtweb' <www.vluchtweb.nl>, a subscription-based website maintained by the Dutch NGO Vluchtelingenwerk (Dutch Council for Refugees). Some information is also freely available at the website of the Vereniging Asieladvocaten en -juristen Nederland, <www.vajn.org> (organization of Dutch asylum lawyers). Moreover, one attorney has made available examples of procedures before the ECtHR, listing several procedures initiated by various attorneys and posting the text of some Notes Verbales with provisional measures, see <http://www.collet.nu/ehrm.htm>.

[369] Ibid. In the context of these cases members of the Strasbourg staff wrote a brief advisory for Dutch attorneys. See Kempees/Mol/Van Steijn (2004), pp. 299-300. On provisional measures in non-refoulement cases see Chapter V. On the group of beneficiaries see section 4 of Chapter XIII (Protection).

[370] ECtHR *NA.* v. *UK*, 17 July 2008, §§21-22. In this case the Court's request fell on deaf ears. The UK refused to halt the deportation of Tamils to Sri Lanka as a general measure and the Court was forced to order provisional measures 342 times. See also Chapter XIII (Protection), section 4.4.2.

In order to strengthen the provisional measures decisions it sends to States, it appears that the ECtHR has, at least since 2006, added references to the fact that ignoring provisional measures could constitute a violation of Article 34 ECHR.[371]

At the end of 2007 the Registrar of the ECtHR also published a Press Release warning petitioners not to submit inappropriate requests for provisional measures.[372]

7 THE BOSNIA HUMAN RIGHTS CHAMBER

7.1 Introduction

The Bosnia Human Rights Chamber was introduced in the General Framework Agreement for Peace in Bosnia and Herzegovina (Dayton Peace Agreement) in 1995, as part of a transitional justice approach.[373] It has ordered provisional measures to halt executions, find a disappeared person, ensure medical examination in detention and improve health conditions in a refugee camp, but most of its provisional measures relate to halting forced evictions. It has also used them to halt exhumation of the body of the petitioner's deceased wife from a Muslim cemetery, to protect religious sites, to secure ballots, to suspend constructions, to safeguard documentary evidence and in the context of legislation.

This section discusses the institutional setting of the provisional measures as they were used by the Bosnia Chamber and the right of individual petition, the power to order provisional measures, its promptness in deciding on the use of provisional measures and the availability of information on the use of these measures.

7.2 The right of individual complaint

In 1995 the State of Bosnia and Herzegovina (State of BiH) had not yet ratified the ECHR. Annex 6 to the Dayton Peace Agreement instituted the Human Rights Commission encompassing the Office of the Ombudsperson and the Human Rights Chamber. The Chamber was a temporary hybrid tribunal for the settlement of disputes about human rights during the first post-war period in the former Yugoslavia. Other relevant initiatives, part of the Dayton Agreement, are the Constitutional Court of BiH, the Commission for Real Property Claims (under Annex 7) and the ombudspersons of the Federation of BiH and Republika Srpska.

---

[371] See e.g. ECtHR *Ben Khemais* v. *Italy*, 24 February 2009, §18; *C.B.Z.* v. *Italy*, 24 March 2009, §13; *O.* v. *Italy*, 24 March 2009, §16 as well as several other judgments against Italy published on 24 March 2009. On the violation of Article 34 see the discussion of the case *Mamatkulov* in Chapter XVI (Legal status).

[372] ECtHR Press release issued by the Registrar, 'Inappropriate use of interim measures procedure', 21 December 2007.

[373] General Framework Agreement for Peace in Bosnia and Herzegovina, signed and entered into force Paris 14 December 1995, agreed between the Republic of Bosnia and Herzegovina, the Republic of Croatia and the Federal Republic of Yugoslavia (the "Parties"). See in general, for instance: Küttler (2003), pp. 47-68; Gomien (2001), pp. 763-770; Nowak (2001), pp. 778-780; O'Flaherty (2001), pp. 749-762; Nowak (2000a), pp. 141-208; Nowak (1999a), pp. 285-289; Nowak (1999b), pp. 95-106; Benedek (1999); Gomien (1999), pp. 107-120; Haller (1999), pp. 25-29; Hicks (1999), pp. 127-148; Kälin (1999), pp. 59-66; Leuprecht (1999), pp. 15-18; Neussl (1999), pp. 290-302; O'Flaherty (1999), pp. 6-13; Pajic (1998), pp. 1-12 and Nowak (1997), pp. 174-178.

Several international organisations and institutions played a role in the post-conflict period, including the operation of the Chamber. The Office of the High Representative was created under the Dayton Peace Agreement. The High Representative is at the same time the EU's Special Representative.[374] Other existing organisations, such as the OSCE, the Council of Europe, the NATO and the United Nations Mission in BiH (including the International Police Task Force) also play (or have played) a role in the transition process (and economy) in Bosnia.[375]

The facts complained of should fall within the jurisdiction of the parties to the Annex: the State of Bosnia and Herzegovina (BiH) with its constituent parts: the Federation of BiH and the Republica Srpska.

The Chamber could consider allegations of violations of the ECHR and its Protocols,[376] as well as allegations about discrimination under several other international treaties, including the ICCPR (and its two Protocols), ICESCR, ICAT, ICERD and CEDAW, the Geneva Conventions I-IV and Protocols I and II, the Convention on the Reduction of Statelessness and the Framework Convention for the Protection of National Minorities.

The Bosnia Chamber was a hybrid tribunal because it consisted of both international and domestic members applying international norms directly in the national system. Eight of the fourteen members of the Chamber were international members, appointed by the Committee of Ministers of the Council of Europe. Four members were appointed by the Federation of BiH and two by the Republica Srpska. Michèle Picard (France) was the President. The staff of the Secretariat numbered around 45 in 2002.[377] Approximately ten of them were international staff.

The Chamber could also be called an adjudicator *sui generis*. It was instituted on the basis of an international treaty, at the same time it is considered an institution of the State of BiH, but is not its Constitutional Court: "One must, therefore, assume that it is an institution sui generis with a predominantly international element".[378]

The Rules of Procedure have largely been inspired by those of the ECtHR and the former Commission, but 'the procedure is less formalistic and contains important differences'.[379] There are also separate Rules dealing with particular institutions, for instance, about the relations with the Ombudsperson. The Ombudsperson could submit cases to the Chamber, but petitioners could also directly resort to it without going through the Ombudsperson first.[380]

In April 2002 the State of BiH became a member of the Council of Europe and ratified the ECHR. In a Press Release of June 2003 Amnesty International emphasized the importance of the Bosnia Chamber. It noted that the 'unique mandate of the Chamber has enabled it to consider issues relating to human rights violations specific to the context of Bosnia-Herzegovina, where discrimination in the enjoyment of many human rights has been widespread and access to justice minimal'. It added: "The continuing and rising number of applications being submitted to the Chamber indicates that for people in Bosnia-Herzegovina, the Chamber is acting as a last and possibly only avenue of justice".[381]

---

374 See the website of the High Representative: <http://www.ohr.int/>.

375 See e.g. Alefsen (1999), pp. 149-154 and Hicks (1999), pp. 127-148.

376 See e.g. Pajic (1999), pp. 33-44 and Mol (1998), pp. 27-69.

377 Bosnia Chamber Annual Report 2002, p. 8.

378 Nowak (1997), p. 176.

379 Ibid.

380 See Title IV. On the relation with the ombudsperson, see e.g. Gelmamez, (1999), pp. 277-329. See also Haller (1999), pp. 25-32. For the website of the current Office of the Ombudsperson see <www.ohro.ba>. In general about the procedure and case law of the Chamber see Küttler (2003); Dakin (2002); Nowak (2001), pp. 771-793; Nowak (2000a), pp. 182-190; Berg (1999); Neussl (1999), pp. 290-302; Aybay (1997), pp. 529-558 and Nowak (1997), pp. 174-178.

381 Amnesty International, Press Release, Bosnia-Herzegovina: Abolition of Human Rights Chamber leaves citizens unprotected, 11 June 2003.

Despite these and similar arguments put forward in favour of extending the Chamber's mandate, it was decided not to do so. The mandate of the Chamber expired on 31 December 2003. Those cases received by the Bosnia Chamber on or before that date were dealt with by a Human Rights Commission within the Constitutional Court of BiH in 2004. The Constitutional Court is meant to deal with all human rights cases received after that date.

7.3   The power and promptness of the Bosnia Human Chamber

7.3.1 Introduction

Article X (1) of Annex 6 to the Dayton Peace Agreement provides (in relevant part):

> "The Chamber shall have the power to order provisional measures, to appoint experts, and to compel the production of witnesses and evidence".

Article VIII, 2(f) on the jurisdiction of the Chamber stipulates:

> "Applications which entail requests for provisional measures shall be reviewed as a matter of priority in order to determine (1) whether they should be accepted and, if so (2) whether high priority for the scheduling of proceedings on the provisional measures request is warranted".[382]

This means that the authority to take provisional measures was granted in the treaty itself. Rule 36 of the Chamber's own Rules of Procedure then specifies:

> "1. Applications entailing requests for provisional measures shall be reviewed as a matter of priority. The Chamber, or when it is not in session, the President, shall determine in particular whether such applications should be accepted and, if so, whether high priority for the scheduling of proceedings on the provisional measures requested is warranted.
> 2. The Chamber or, when it is not in session, the President, shall decide whether, in the interest of the parties or the proper conduct of proceedings, any provisional measures should be ordered under Article X para. 1 of the Agreement.
> 3. The Chamber or, when it is not in session, the President, shall bring any such order to the notice of the party concerned by any available means with a view to ensuring its effective implementation in accordance with the Agreement.
> 4. Where the President has ordered any provisional measures she or he shall report her or his action to the Chamber under para. 3 of Rule 33".[383]

Article XI, 1(b) of Annex 6 also refers to provisional measures. At first sight this is a strange provision, because it grants the Chamber the power 'to include an order for provisional measures

---

[382]   See also Article XI (Decisions): "1. Following the conclusion of the proceedings, the Chamber shall promptly issue a decision, which shall address: (a) Whether the facts found indicate a breach by the Party concerned of its obligations under this Agreement; and if so (b) what steps shall be taken by the Party to remedy such breach, including orders to cease and desist, monetary relief (including pecuniary and non-pecuniary injuries), and provisional measures". And Article XII (Rules and Regulations) "The Chamber shall promulgate such rules and regulations, consistent with this Agreement, as may be necessary to carry out its functions, including provisions for preliminary hearings, expedited decisions on provisional measures, decisions by panels of the Chamber, and review of decisions made by any such panels".

[383]   Rule 36 Rules of Procedure of the Human Rights Chamber, Sarajevo, adopted on 13 December 1996.

in its final decision on the merits of a case'. Chapter XIII discusses the relationship between the protective measures required pending the proceedings and as a form of reparation, but in order to indicate a relationship between concepts it is generally useful to distinguish them first. The Chamber seems to have found a way to interpret this provision: "This power might be used to regulate the position of the parties before the decision becomes final and binding, or pending the full implementation of the decision".[384] Indeed, pending implementation it may often be useful to follow up on the situation of the victims in order to make sure that nothing happens that could prevent further implementation.[385]

7.3.2 Delegation

Pursuant to the reference in the Dayton Peace Agreement about priority treatment of requests for provisional measures the Chamber gives precedence to such requests.[386] With the reference to the situation when the Chamber is not in session this system also made included a reference to delegation of the authority to take provisional measures from the Chamber to its President, in order to ensure prompt and effective protection. Rule 33, on action by the Chamber in specific cases, specifies in section 3 that the Vice-President may also 'take any necessary action on behalf of the Chamber', if the President is 'prevented from carrying out his duties'. The Vice-Presidents of the two Panels were the next in line to take such action and, in case they were not available, a judge with seniority.[387] Whoever took the decision to take provisional measures in between sessions shall inform the full Chamber during the next session.

In urgent cases the Chamber could order provisional measures within one or two days.[388] A Handbook drafted by the former Registrar of the Chamber notes:

> "In order to enable the secretariat to act quickly on such a request, the applicant's submissions must be as complete as possible. They may initially be sent by facsimile. It is highly advisable not to leave the intervention request to the last minute, as the secretariat has no duty officers processing a request during a weekend or a public holiday".[389]

Another provision that takes into account promptness is Rule 48, providing that 'in any case of urgency, the Registrar may, without prejudice to the taking of any other procedural steps, inform the respondent Party in an application, by any available means, of the introduction of the application and of a summary of its subject-matter'.

If the Chamber orders provisional measures, it normally immediately transmits the application itself to the respondent Party for 'factual or legal observations to be submitted by that party as a matter of urgency'.[390]

---

[384] See Bosnia Chamber Annual Report 2000 (under the heading 'provisional measures').
[385] The Inter-American Court only considers a case closed once the State has fully implemented it. Before such time it may maintain provisional measures, for instance to protect witnesses. See further Chapter XIV discussing jurisdiction and Chapter XVIII on follow-up.
[386] See also Rule 35.
[387] See e.g. Rules 9, 10 and 4, Bosnia Chamber Annual Report 1999 and Berg Handbook (1999), p. 9.
[388] Response by Peter Kempees, Registrar of the Chamber, 8 March 2001, by e-mail (on file with the author).
[389] Berg Handbook (1999), p. 9.
[390] See Berg Handbook (1999), p. 10, referring to 'President's Standing Order no. 1'.

7.3.3 Proprio motu use and withdrawal of provisional measures

Rule 36 itself does not refer to the authority to take provisional measures *proprio motu*, but Rule 33(1) states that the Chamber may, *proprio motu* or at the request of a party, take any action which it considers expedient or necessary for the proper performance of its duties under the Agreement.[391]

Rule 36(5) stipulates that the Chamber shall withdraw an order for provisional measures whenever it is 'no longer justified'. It is the Chamber as a whole that decides so, 'by formal decision'. In deciding whether or not to maintain provisional measures information provided by other international organisations plays a role, for instance from OSCE officers, officers of the UN International Police Taskforce or the Human Rights Field Operation of the Office of the UN High Commissioner for Human Rights.[392]

7.3.4 Continuity

To put the Chamber's provisional measures in context it is useful to know that, under Rule 16 of the Rules of Procedure, the Ombudsperson may also take such measures.[393]

As noted, upon expiry of the Chamber's mandate, on 31 December 2003, a Human Rights Commission within the Constitutional Court of BiH dealt with those cases received by the Bosnia Chamber on or before that date.[394] It could not accept new applications, but in ongoing cases that require provisional measures this Commission, or its President may take provisional measures.[395]

---

[391] The Berg Handbook (1999), p. 10 simply notes that Rule 36 may also be applied on the Chamber's own motion. It then adds that an 'injunction could also be issued against an applicant'. It does not give examples in which the Chamber had done so. It is not clear whether the Chamber formally decided that it could do so, or whether the author of the handbook, legal secretary of the ECtHR and legal officer of the former European Commission, has assumed this based on the fact that the Chamber has taken over many rules and practices of the Strasbourg bodies. In a footnote the Handbook refers to the practice of the former European Commission to recommend petitioners to stop their hunger strike. See further on this issue Chapter XIII, section 4 on the beneficiaries of provisional measures.

[392] Berg Handbook (1999), p. 10. OSCE officers also play a role in monitoring compliance with Chamber decisions, including Orders for provisional measures, see e.g. Annual Reports 1999 and 2000 of the Bosnia Chamber, in its overview of cooperation with international institutions in BiH and Periodic Report of the Human Rights Field Operation in the former Yugoslavia of the Office of the High Commissioner for Human Rights, April 1998, §§27-29.

[393] See e.g. the Ombudsperson's Annual Reports, under 'Interim measures'. Between May 1997 and the end of January 1998, for instance, she took provisional measures 59 times. On the ombudsperson see also Raguz (1999), pp. 121-124.

[394] As of July 2005 the website of this Commission <http://www.hrc.ba/commission> only refers to three members. It refers to two other persons from BiH that must be appointed, while 2(1) of its Rules of Procedure refers to 'the two international members'.

[395] See Rule 34 Rules of Procedure Human Rights Commission within the Constitutional Court of BiH, adopted January 2004: "(1) Applications entailing requests for provisional measures shall be reviewed as a matter of priority. The Commission, or when it is not in session, the President, shall determine in particular whether such applications should be accepted and, if so, whether high priority for the scheduling of proceedings on the provisional measures requested is warranted. (2)The Commission or, when it is not in session, the President, shall decide whether, in the interest of the parties or the proper conduct of proceedings, any provisional measures should be ordered under Article X paragraph 1 of the Agreement. (3)The Commission or, when it is not in session, the President, shall bring any such order to the notice of the Party concerned by any available means with a view to ensuring its effective implementation in accordance with the

The Constitutional Court of BiH consists of six citizens of the State of BiH (four selected by the Federation of BiH and two by Republica Srpska) and three international judges appointed by the President of the ECtHR. It started its work in 1997.[396]

7.4   Decisions to use provisional measures: transparency or the lack thereof?

Like all other human rights adjudicators, apart from the Inter-American Court, the Bosnia Chamber did not publish its provisional measures separately. References to these measures are instead found in the decisions on inadmissibility and merits.[397] These decisions refer to all requests for provisional measures, also those it did not grant, making it possible to examine the type of cases in which it does not consider them warranted. Another useful approach by the Chamber was its specific, though brief, discussion of its use of these measures in its Annual

---

Agreement. (4) Where When [sic] the President has ordered any provisional measures he or she shall report her his or heris [sic] action to the Commission under paragraph 3 of Rule 31. (5) Whenever an order for provisional measures is no longer justified, the Commission shall, by a formal decision, withdraw it". See also Rule 33 (on priority) and 31(1) (on action in specific cases).

[396]   See Rule 78 Rules of Procedure Constitutional Court BiH: (1) The Chamber may, until the adoption of a final decision, upon a request of a party, issue any interim measure it deems necessary in the interest of the parties or the correct conductance of the proceedings before the Court. (2) Exceptionally, the President of the Court may, if it is not possible to convene a session of the Chamber, issue an interim measure such as is referred to in paragraph 1 of this Article. (3) The plenary Court may, on its own motion, issue an interim measure such as is referred to in paragraph 1 of this Article. (4) A decision on an interim measure such as is referred to in paragraph 1 of this Article shall be submitted immediately to the adopter of the challenged act and to the parties to the proceedings. (5) The Chamber or President of the Court, if they find it appropriate, may also decide to forward a decision on a measure such as is referred to in paragraph 1 of this Article to other authorities. (6) The Chamber or the President of the Court shall submit a decision on an interim measure referred to in paragraph 1 of this Article to the plenary Court for information. (7) A decision on an interim measure such as is referred to in paragraph 1 of this Article shall have legal effect, until the plenary Court decides otherwise. (8) The Chamber or the President of the Court may request information from the parties on every issue relating to an interim measure. (9) In the event that an interim measure is no longer justified, the Chamber or the President of the Court shall annul it. (10) Proceedings for the adoption of an interim measure shall be urgent. See also Rule 10 (1) The Chamber shall consist of the President of the Court and two Vice-Presidents from among the judges elected by the competent legislative authorities of the Entities. The President of the Court shall preside over the Chamber. (2) The Chamber shall decide by a majority of votes of the members of the Chamber on the joining or separation of cases and on requests for the adoption of interim measures. The Chamber shall adopt a proposal for a decision on admissibility which shall be submitted to the Grand Chamber or the plenary Court for verification. (3) The Chamber shall submit a decision on an interim measure to the plenary Court for information.

[397]   Different from the HRC, it is the practice of the Chamber to mention any Orders (and requests for such Orders) in the final decision (Peter Kempees, 12 March 2001, by e-mail (on file with the author). The bound volumes of these decisions are not widely available outside of BiH, but the cases can be accessed on the internet. The Chamber shares its site with that of the human rights commission within the constitutional court of BiH. The site includes a search database with all the decisions of the former Human Rights Chamber see: <http://www.hrc.ba/> (last accessed 10 January 2008).This database includes all decisions until July 2003, as well as decisions on admissibility and merits until May 2005.

Reports.[398] In the secondary literature only Berg, the legal secretary of the ECtHR and former Registrar of the Human Rights Chamber, devotes some more specific comments to 'intervention in urgent matters'.[399]

8 CONCLUSION

8.1 The authority to use provisional measures

8.1.1 Introduction

The Inter-American Court is able to order provisional measures based on the explicit text of the treaty. The same applies to CEDAW and the new African Court, as well as to the former Bosnia Chamber. The Inter-American Commission, African Commission, European Commission and Court, HRC, CAT and CERD have included in their Rules of Procedure the possibility to use provisional measures. Indeed, even if the text of the treaty is not explicit about the authority to use provisional measures in the context of individual complaints, in practice this authority is deemed part of the function of the adjudicator assigned to deal with individual complaints under a given human rights treaty. Apart from CERD, all human rights adjudicators regularly use provisional measures. Just with regard to the inter-State complaint proceedings in the human rights treaties, which have not often been used in any case, the practice of using provisional measures is very limited.[400]

It is submitted that human rights adjudicators have the implied power to use provisional measures.[401] After all human rights adjudication has the function of determining, on the basis of a legal procedure, the obligations of States in a legal conflict with an individual or individuals involving human rights. This function is particularly pressing in the face of threats of irreparable harm to persons.[402] Provisional measures are necessary in order to prevent such harm pending the proceedings.

If the human rights treaty also includes inter-State proceedings it should be possible to use provisional measures in these proceedings as well. After all, even the ICJ – the obvious inter-State adjudicator – has used provisional measures in the face of irreparable harm to persons.[403]

---

[398]   See especially its Annual Reports 2000, 1999 and 1998 (on average devoting half a page on the issue). These Reports are accessible at the website of the human rights commission within the constitutional court of BiH: <http://www.hrc.ba/> (last accessed 10 January 2008).

[399]   Berg (1999), pp. 8-11. See further Küttler (2003), pp. 70-72; Nowak (2001), p. 777; Gelmamez (1999), pp. 309-310 and Aybay (1997), p. 545. The author would like to thank Jacob Möller (judge in the Bosnia Chamber, Geneva 1998), Therese Nelson and Peter Kempees (staff of the Chamber) for the information they provided.

[400]   See Chapter III (Executions) with two early examples from the European system.

[401]   In this respect Pasqualucci (2005), distinguishes between the inherent authority of courts and the implied power of quasi-judicial bodies. In this book, however, the argument is made that all human rights adjudicators (courts and so-called 'quasi-judicial bodies') have the implied power to take provisional measures to properly perform their function of addressing individual complaints. Chapter XVI on the legal status of provisional measures further elaborates on this.

[402]   For a discussion of the purpose of provisional measures in human rights cases (in relation to irreparable harm) see conclusion Part II.

[403]   See Chapter I on the ICJ and provisional measures to protect individuals.

8.1.2 Proprio motu use

The HRC often receives information on the basis of which it concludes that the petitioner is asking for provisional measures. An example is a hand-written note with the text: 'I am going to be executed on 5 March', without a specific request for provisional measures. On the other hand it is not clear whether the HRC could use provisional measures based on information from sources other than the petitioner. Different from the HRC the rules on provisional measures by the Inter-American Commission and Court and the European Court of Human Rights specifically provide for the possibility of *proprio motu* use of provisional measures.

In a human rights approach the authority to use provisional measures should indeed include the authority to use them *proprio motu*. Especially in cases in which potential beneficiaries are unable to contact the adjudicator directly, the adjudicator should be able, in light of the purpose of provisional measures, to intervene on its own motion on the basis of other credible information.

8.1.3 Delegation

If a court or other adjudicator only convenes periodically it becomes necessary to delegate the authority to use provisional measures to one member of the court or adjudicatory body. Without this option the usefulness of provisional measures is seriously reduced because they are tardy or even used only after the irreparable harm has already been done.[404] In other words, without the possibility to delegate the power to use provisional measures these measures will be deprived of their protective function.

Once the HRC started to receive a substantial number of urgent petitions (relating to impending executions) it decided to delegate its authority to use provisional measures to one of its members, who as the Special Rapporteur on New Communications could then deal with these in between sessions. The Committee against Torture waited somewhat longer with taking a similar decision, but has now assigned a Special Rapporteur to deal with these cases as well. In some systems the provisional measures taken in between sessions have a different status and name, for instance 'urgent measures'. The President of the Inter-American Court, upon consultation with other members of the Court, only takes 'urgent measures' and calls for a meeting of the full Court. It is the Court that uses the provisional measures proper. While such approach is interesting, it is not necessary as long as the member to whom the authority has been delegated indeed reports about the use of all provisional measures. Following this, the adjudicator should ratify, expand upon or lift the provisional measure. An obligation to consult other members of the Court or Committee in advance could be useful as well, but this should not be required at the cost of expedience.

8.2   Publication and motivation of provisional measures

In the context of the ICJ's provisional measures it has been argued that, generally speaking, international adjudicators should hold public hearings on the use of provisional measures.[405] Such hearings may indeed help enhance the persuasive force of provisional measures and play a role in follow-up, because they would offer a formalized forum for dialogue between the parties on this issue. Nevertheless, they are not always practicable and their absence does not significantly diminish the authority of provisional measures that are substantiated and publicly accessible. In

---

[404]   See also Pasqualucci (2005), p. 36.

[405]   See the individual opinion of judge Buergenthal in *LaGrand* (*Germany* v. *US*), Judgment of 27 June 2001. See also Addo (1999), pp. 713-732 and Cassel (2002), p. 886.

practice, however, only the Orders of the Inter-American Court are published and motivated.[406] In the other systems the use of provisional measures is simply mentioned in the decision on the merits or inadmissibility. The unpublished letters to the parties informing them of decisions about provisional measures normally do not clarify the criteria for their use either.

Most adjudicators do not formally reject requests by petitioners to take provisional or precautionary measures. Thus, it is not possible to systematically trace failed attempts to convince them to take such measures. Systematic references to refusals to use provisional measures are only found in the decisions by the Inter-American Court, the Bosnia Chamber and, to some extent, the Committee against Torture.[407] This lack of references by the other adjudicators is unfortunate because cases in which the petitioners failed to convince the adjudicators to take provisional measures could give particular insight into their approach to the concept.

Many provisional measures in the European system have been taken in cases that were not published. These cases can only be examined in Strasbourg. This book makes reference mainly to those cases that are easily verifiable. An exception is made for the practice of the HRC because for several years it failed to mention its use of provisional measures in its final decision altogether. Without reference to information derived from the case files the practice discussed would not be representative. Because eventually an opportunity was offered to examine case-files in Geneva on the Committee's practice with regard to provisional measures it was decided to make them more widely available in this book.[408]

It is remarkable that information about the use of urgent appeals by Special Rapporteurs under the non-legal proceedings is more systematically made available, at the latest in their Annual Reports. Often Special Rapporteurs also make use of press releases. The international and regional adjudicators, on the other hand, do not regularly issue press releases and they do not consistently make available information on the particular protective measures required. It could be argued that adjudicators should have even more reason than theme Rapporteurs to motivate and publish their decisions on provisional measures.

This book emphasises the importance of motivation and accessibility of an adjudicator's provisional measures, increasing the authority of the measures used and providing insight in the approach of the adjudicators to the concept.[409] This transparency and accessibility is all the more important because, as is argued in Chapter XVI, provisional measures are legally binding.[410] This provides more concrete tools to domestic courts as well.[411]

It might be said that providing a motivation for the use of provisional measures would already anticipate the final determination of the case. Yet in that case it would be the use itself of the measures rather than the motivation that would anticipate the decision on the merits. Motivation only serves to clarify the basis for using provisional measures and to make visible the most important criteria applied by the adjudicator. If this already indicates a certain direction the adju-

---

[406] See Rieter (2005a), p. 42. The Inter-American Court is also the only human rights adjudicator that convenes hearings specifically to deal with requests for provisional measures.

[407] The HRC did not keep record of these requests, meaning that statistical data are not available either. In its Information Notes the ECtHR occasionally also refers to cases in which it refused to take provisional measures.

[408] This book indicates which information is on file with the author.

[409] Rieter (2005a), p. 40. See also Rieter (2003), p. 24.

[410] On the importance of motivation in response to the increased status of these measures in the European system in particular, Rieter (2005a), pp. 41-42.

[411] For an example see Rieter (2005a), pp. 29-32. The need for motivation of provisional measures in the European system was confirmed in Haeck/VanDeLanotte (2005), pp. 468-469, in which it was noted that the binding nature of provisional measures as well as the need to enable domestic courts to act in the face of failure by the executive both argue in favour of motivating provisional measures. See also Rieter (2006), pp. 736-739.

dicator may take, this is very likely to happen as well if he omits making explicit such a motivation. Adjudicators like the ICJ, with a more general mandate, not only involving human rights, have also motivated their orders for provisional measures. The motivation and publication of the Orders of the Inter-American Court of Human Rights is commendable and States have never complained that this anticipated the eventual decision. In human rights cases involving the risk of irreparable harm to persons the rule of non-anticipation by the adjudicator of the decision on the merits simply means that provisional measures should not *dictate* the direction of the ultimate determination of the main conflict. This approach is based on the threat of irreparable harm to persons on the one hand and the difference in availability of evidence and time for evaluation of this evidence at different stages of the proceedings. The assessment of the evidence for the purpose of provisional measures should not prejudice the eventual decision. It should be clear, for instance, that the final decision is based on an evaluation of all the available evidence and arguments on the basis of the principle *audi alteram partem*.[412] After all adjudicators should make available the information to both parties and allow them the opportunity to respond. In fact this principle should apply already *pending* the proceedings to any follow-up decision with regard to the provisional measures initially taken.

On the other hand, because provisional measures cannot go further in the required protection than an eventual decision on reparations would, they already give an indication on substantive law. This is all the more reason for the adjudicator to motivate its decisions to use provisional measures. If the rationale of provisional measures is explained these measures become more persuasive. Moreover, both the State and the petitioner may be able to provide a more focused response. The provisional measure would be substantiated by referring to the *authority* to use it, the purpose of preventing irreparable harm to persons[413] and the applicable articles as well as by noting that the decision is made in light of the urgency of the situation and based on *prima facie* evidence of an imminent risk of irreparable harm. The adjudicator could also refer to previous decisions on the legal status of provisional measures, indicate the follow-up information required as well as the relevant time limits.[414] For adjudicators that do not yet motivate their use of provisional measures substantiation in this form would not imply an inordinate increase of the workload of the adjudicator and its staff. It would only require one extra page in a Note Verbale or order to the government (sent for information to the petitioners) that could partially be standardised.[415]

Accessibility, transparency, coherence and consistency in the use of provisional measures should be increased, among others by making public the decisions and by including reasoning. One of the aims of the research is in fact to assist in this process by collecting, systematizing and analysing the relevant information.

8.3   Convergence or divergence?

The introduction to this chapter noted that the overview was aimed to serve to highlight commonalities as well as differences between the systems. As to the commonalities, the systems are facing

---

[412]   The principle *audi alteram partem/audiatur et altera pars* (both parties are to be heard in the course of a judicial procedure), may be considered a general principle of law. Cheng (1953) has pointed out that the principle translates into practice 'the fundamental requirement of equality between the parties in judicial proceedings', p. 291.

[413]   This is further discussed in the Conclusion to Part II.

[414]   For a discussion of the official responses by addressee States, the legal status of provisional measures and follow-up see the subsequent Chapters.

[415]   The Inter-American Court uses such a standardised model, adding the relevant information for the case at issue.

common problems and issues, which may sometimes result in converging interpretations, occasionally consciously (often referred to as 'dialogue' or 'cross-fertilization'), at other times more indirectly.[416] As to the possible divergences in the approaches of the adjudicators with regard to provisional measures these are mainly due to the differences between the systems.[417] These divergences are explored to clarify the use of provisional measures that are situated, as discussed in Chapter XII, on a continuum beyond the common core, but still within the outer limits of the concept.[418]

In other words, the differences and commonalities in the systems may help to explain why the respective practices of the adjudicators converge or diverge with regard to the use of provisional measures. Awareness of convergence and divergence may in turn enhance the understanding of the common core and outer limits of the current concept of provisional measures in human rights adjudication.[419] The question also arises whether (regional) context could fully determine the outer limits of the concept of provisional measures in human rights cases or whether there are outer limits beyond which adjudicators cannot go in any system without depriving the concept of independent meaning.[420]

To the extent information is available, the subsequent chapters examine the divergences and convergences in the approaches of the human rights adjudicators towards provisional measures with regard to the aspects mentioned in the Introduction to this book (the protection required, the relationship with reparation and the (group of) beneficiaries; the relevance of admissibility and jurisdiction on the merits, the assessment of temporal urgency and risk, the legal status, the official responses of addressee States and the follow-up).

Are the international and regional adjudicators moving towards a more uniform approach to the concept of provisional measures? This study aims to identify what, if any, is the underlying

---

[416] See e.g. Weiser (2004), pp. 116-117 (and references therein): "[T]he human rights domain is especially conducive to international and transnational influences because of the numerous 'genealogical' links between national, regional and international human rights standards". See further Slaughter (2003), pp. 191-219; Slaughter (2000), pp. 1103-1124; Slaughter (1994), pp. 99-135. In general on comparing various human rights systems, see e.g. Buergenthal (2005); Cançado Trindade (2004); Udombana (2003b), pp. 479-532; Jayawickrama (2002); Fix-Zamudio (2000), pp. 507-533; Ramcharan (2000), pp. 324-326; Helfer (1999), pp. 285-379; Pool/Mayhew (1999), also referring to the domestic case law made accessible through the NGO Interights; Carozza (1998), pp. 1217-1237 (discussing uses and misuse of comparative law in international human rights, taking the ECtHR as an example); Dulitzky (1997), pp. 33-74; Helfer/Slaughter (1997), pp. 273-391; Sohn (1996), pp. 33-56; Ni Aolain (1995), pp. 101-142; Merrills (1993); Partsch (1989), pp. 1-9 and Cançado Trindade (1987).

[417] As ITLOS pointed out in its Order for provisional measures in the *Mox Plant* case, 'the application of international law rules on interpretation of treaties to identical or similar provisions of different treaties may not yield the same results, having regard to, *inter alia*, differences in the respective contexts, objects and purposes, subsequent practice of parties and *travaux préparatoires*'. ITLOS the *MOX Plant* case (*Ireland* v. *UK*), Order for provisional measures of 3 December 2001, §51.

[418] In this respect regional systems may set the stage and move forward at a greater pace, possibly to be followed by international adjudicators. See e.g. Van Boven (1995), p. 23: 'in devising regional (or sub-regional) systems for the promotion and protection of human rights, the following three criteria should duly be taken into account so as to give the regional approach a value additional to the universal approach: (1) its pioneering or innovative character, (ii) the introduction of a higher level of protection, (iii) the fulfilment of clearly established needs of a particular region (or sub-region)'.

[419] It is assumed that the concept is dynamic rather than frozen in time.

[420] The latter refers to the ability of the phrase to be used in communication resulting in some form of common understanding.

interpretative approach as to the nature of provisional measures that the human rights adjudicators have in common. As the adjudicators generally do not make explicit the rationale for using provisional measures, an attempt is made to derive it from their judgments on the merits and admissibility. The conclusions drawn with regard to a possible underlying interpretative approach are supported by the fact that this book also examines whether more than one system has used provisional measures in a given circumstance.

As noted in the Introduction, when the underlying approaches of all adjudicators, as well as the specific practice of at least two of them converge, this study speaks of a common core.

It is assumed that if the adjudicators indeed move towards a more uniform approach this will make the provisional measures more persuasive to domestic courts, the executive and the legislator. In addition it presumably is more 'costly' for a State's international image to ignore such provisional measures because of their enhanced legitimacy.

States dealing with supervisory mechanisms under various human rights treaties have sometimes emphasized the importance of coordination. This does not just apply to coordination between the UN treaty bodies,[421] but also between regional and international human rights adjudicators, as well as human rights and general international adjudicators, such as the ICJ.[422] For instance, States have sometimes referred to the case law of the ECtHR implying that CAT or the HRC should follow its example. Even States that are not themselves subject to the jurisdiction of the ECtHR have sometimes argued that the UN bodies should take the same approach as that Court.[423] The Dutch government has tried to justify ignoring a provisional measure by CAT, among others, by pointing to the different case law of the ECtHR.[424] The case law of the two petition mechanisms 'differed in terms of the extent to which the burden of proof lay with the State party'. There was a 'clear need' for the international and the European body 'to reach some measure of agreement on their interpretation of the rules, since it was essential for asylum-seekers and European Governments to know the exact limits of the protection provided by international law'.[425]

As an example of an international law concept on which the approaches of the various adjudicators may differ, this research on provisional measures aims to contribute to the ongoing discussion on the proliferation of international adjudicators and the 'fragmentation' of international

---

[421] On this see e.g. Rasmussen, member of CAT, who has argued for additional meeting time. He pointed out that the lack of contact with the UN Special Rapporteur against torture and other UN bodies 'was attributable to time constraints, not to the fact that the Committee did not find such cooperation beneficial'. Summary Records, 34th session, 19 May 2005, CAT/C/SR.662, 2 June 2005, §63.

[422] Specifically on the relation between human rights case law and general international law, see e.g. Borgen (2005); Toufayan (2005); Caflisch/Cançado Trindade (2004), pp. 5-62; Oellers-Frahm (2001b), pp. 67-104; Cohen-Jonathan (1999), pp. 767-789; Simma (1995), pp. 153-235; Cançado Trindade (1987) and Sohn (1982), pp. 1-64. See also Kamminga's Final Report on the Impact of International Human Rights Law on General International Law, presented on behalf of the Committee of Human Rights Law and Practice of the International Law Association (ILA), July 2008, made available on SSRN: <http://ssrn.com/abstract=1150664> (consulted 5 August 2008); on the role of international and regional adjudicators, including issues such as subsidiarity, judicial activism and restraint, see e.g. Carozza (2003), pp. 38-79; Benvenisti (1999), pp. 843-854; Mahoney (1990), pp. 57-88 and Schachter (1983), pp. 813-821.

[423] See e.g. the remarks by Canada in the context of proceedings before the HRC, CAT and Inter-American Commission (see Chapter XVII (Official responses)).

[424] See further Chapter XVI (Legal status).

[425] Statement by Mr. Dumoré (Netherlands), Summary Record of the Committee against Torture, 24th meeting, 11 May 2000, CAT/C/SR.426, 13 February 2001, §4, see also Chapter XV on assessment of risk and XVII (Official responses).

law, or in any case the importance of coherence in the application of international law.[426] Already in 1971 the ICJ stated: 'an international instrument has to be interpreted and applied within the framework of the entire legal system prevailing at the time of its interpretation'.[427]

Article 31(3)(c) Vienna Convention on the Law of Treaties (VCLT) is particularly relevant as an expression of the aim of increasing coherence in the law applied to different subject matters. It reflects the principle of systemic integration, referring to 'any relevant rules of international law applicable in the relations between the parties' as an element that must be taken into account with the context when interpreting a treaty provision. A presumption exists of consistency of the text to be interpreted with general international law, unless this would undermine the object and purpose of the particular system.[428]

International human rights law may to some extent be seen as a 'regime'. Krasner has explained 'regime' as 'a set of implicit or explicit principles, norms, rules, and decision-making procedures around which actors' expectations converge in a given area of international relations'.[429] Indeed, human rights adjudicators, alleged victims, NGOs and States appear to have assumed, even if implicitly, the principle of effective protection to prevent irreparable harm to persons as a fundamental norm around which the human rights system is built. At the same time, in light of the principle of systemic integration, this special 'regime' does not, and should not weaken general international law.

As the purpose of this regime is the protection of human rights, any resort to 'external' general rules, also applicable outside of the regime, is legitimate in any case as long as this is conducive to their protection. Insofar as general international law is truly in the process of humanization,[430] resort to international law rules that harm the effective protection of human rights is becoming increasingly less likely. From a systematic perspective it is important for the human rights adjudicators as well to pursue consistency and coherence in the application of general concepts and principles of international law. The Conclusion to this book will return to the issue of consistency and coherence for those instances in which this situation does occur and the object and purpose of the human rights system would in fact be undermined by applying the interpretation advanced by general international adjudicators such as the ICJ.[431]

---

[426]   See e.g. ILC, Report of the Study Group, Finalized by Martti Koskenniemi, Fragmentation of international law: difficulties arising from the diversification and expansion of international law, A/CN.4/L.682, 13 April 2006; Conclusions of the ILC Study Group, Fragmentation of international law: difficulties arising from the diversification and expansion of international law, A/CN/.4/L.702, 18 July 2006; Wellens/Huesa-Vinaixa (2006); Simma (2004), pp. 845-847; Pauwelyn (2003); Slaughter (2003), pp. 191-219; Higgins (2003), pp. 21-51; Charney (2002), pp. 369-380; Dupuy (2002); Koskenniemi/Leino (2002), pp. 553-579; Reed (2002), pp. 219-237; Buergenthal (2001), pp. 267-275; Sands (2001), pp. 527-558; Hafner (2000); speech of ICJ President Guillaume to the UN General Assembly, 27 October 2000; the various contributions in NYU Symposium Issue 'The Proliferation of International Tribunals: Piecing Together the Puzzle', (1999), pp. 679-933; Helfer/Slaughter (1997), pp. 273-391; Charney (1999a); Heyns/Killander (2006), pp. 540-543; Wellens (1994), pp. 3-37; Partsch (1989), pp. 1-9.

[427]   ICJ Advisory Opinion Legal Consequences for States of the Continued Presence of South Africa in Namibia (South West Africa) notwithstanding Security Council Resolution 276 (1970), 21 June 1971, §53.

[428]   See Sands (1999), p. 104. The rule invoked must both be relevant and applicable between the parties. The latter means that it must be legally binding (based on customary law, treaty or general principle). For an explicit reference to Article 31(3)(c) see e.g. ICJ Oil Platforms (Iran v. US), 6 November 2003, §41. See further e.g. McLachlan (2005), pp. 279-320; Higgins (2003), pp. 1-20; Pauwelyn (2003); Conforti (2007), pp. 6-18.

[429]   Krasner (1983), p. 2.

[430]   See also Chapter I, section 3.4.

[431]   See the suggestion by Sands (1999), p. 104.

The African Commission is explicitly authorized to 'draw inspiration from' rules of international law other than those found as such in the ACHPR or to take those 'into consideration' (see Articles 60 and 61 ACHPR). The African Court even 'shall apply' the provisions of the ACHPR as well as 'other instruments ratified by the States concerned' (Article 7 Protocol).[432] The older instruments, in particular the ECHR, are not explicit in this respect, but nevertheless cross-fertilization does appear to take place. In some cases even the ECtHR has explicitly referred to the case law of other adjudicators.[433]

Obviously it is more difficult to find a common understanding of legal concepts and achieve convergence in interpretation with regard to a large number of States from different regions of the world. Yet if all adjudicators have a similar interpretative approach to certain phenomena and legal texts, this would validate that interpretation for the time being.[434] Cross-fertilization can make an interpretation more convincing and more coherent from the perspective of the development of a body of international case law.

The practice that has been developed by human rights adjudicators in the application of the human rights treaties subsequent to their entry into force is relevant when a given treaty is applied domestically, as well as when other international adjudicators invoke the provisions of that treaty. International adjudicators may do so either directly, as the ICJ has done,[435] or in order to inform the meaning of the particular treaty they supervise. In both cases they consider the subsequent practice of the relevant treaty bodies as well.[436]

The drafters of the Vienna Convention on the Law of Treaties (VCLT) did not take into account the fact that many modern treaties, such as those aimed at the protection of human rights, have introduced expert bodies interpreting the meaning of the treaty provisions, often even through adjudication of complaints by individuals against States parties.[437] Nevertheless, even the text of Article 31(3)(b) VCLT, 'any subsequent practice in the application of the treaty which establishes the agreement of the parties regarding its interpretation', does not preclude a dynamic interpretation involving subsequent developments. After all, it may be assumed that States parties ratified human rights treaties, including the supervisory mechanisms, in good faith, meaning that the human rights adjudicators established by these treaties have genuinely been assigned the task of monitoring compliance with and therefore interpret the provisions of the treaty.[438] Thus the practice developed by the human rights adjudicators could be said to establish the agreement of the parties regarding their interpretation, exactly because these adjudicators were created under

---

[432] See also Ouguergouz (2003), p. 735.

[433] See e.g. ECtHR *Kurt* v. *Turkey*, 25 May 1988 (on disappearances); *Issa* v. *Turkey*, 16 November 2004 (on extraterritorial application); and, specifically on provisional measures: *Mamatkulov and Askarov* v. *Turkey*, 4 February 2005 (Grand Chamber). On the latter judgment see also Chapter XVI (Legal status). For overviews of references by domestic (and international) adjudicators to international case law, see e.g. Final and Interim Reports of the Committee on International Human Rights Law and Practice of the International Law Association (ILA) on the impact of findings of the United Nations human rights treaty bodies, 2004 and 2002.

[434] As noted, it is assumed that the concept of provisional measures is dynamic rather than frozen in time.

[435] See e.g. ICJ *Legal consequences of the construction of a wall in the occupied Palestinian territory*, Advisory Opinion of 9 July 2004, §§107-113.

[436] See e.g. Report of the Committee on International Human Rights Law and Practice of the International Law Association, at the Berlin Conference (2004), pp. 629-630; McCorquodale (2004), pp. 477-504; Herdegen (2004), p. 125; Simma (1995), p. 234.

[437] See also Report of the Committee on International Human Rights Law and Practice of the International Law Association, at the Berlin Conference (2004), p. 629.

[438] See also Helfer/Slaughter (2005), pp. 3-58.

the treaty in order to interpret it.[439] In light of the object and purpose of the human rights treaty, which is not traditionally inter-State, as well as of the individual complaint mechanism included in the treaty, one may conclude that there is no need for the consent of each State party with each and every finding by these adjudicators.[440] They have agreed to, and signed up for, a 'process' of treaty interpretation by an expert body functioning as an adjudicator in the context of the individual complaint procedure.[441]

In 1948 ICJ Judge Alvarez already noted 'that an institution, once established, acquires a life of its own, independent of the elements which have given birth to it, and it must develop, not in accordance with the views of those who created it, but in accordance with the requirements of international life'.[442] Two years later he pointed out that, because of the 'exigencies of modern life', there is a rapid elaboration of new rules of law, 'effected by means which are different from those of former times'. "The common view that international law must be created solely by States is, therefore, not valid to-day – nor indeed has it ever been".[443]

---

[439] See also Report of the Committee on International Human Rights Law and Practice of the International Law Association (ILA), at the Berlin Conference (2004), p. 629 and the HRC agreeing with this approach in its draft General Comment 33 (2nd revised version, 18 August 2008), §18 (arguing this in relation to the 'general body of jurisprudence' generated by the HRC and referring to the Berlin Conference report). This position is no longer reflected, though, in the advance unedited version of its General Comment 33, CCPR/C/GC/33, 5 November 2008. See further ILA Committee on International Human Rights Law and Practice Final Report on the Impact of International Human Rights Law on General International Law, July 2008, §3.2, also noting that '(a)lthough the International Court of Justice has not formally endorsed such an approach implicitly it has adopted this course of action, e.g. in its advisory opinion on *The Wall* in which it closely follows the findings of the UN human rights treaty bodies'. Of course States will sometimes argue that adjudicators overstepped their mark and tried to create rather than interpret the law, which is still an argument that strikes a chord with many. This is a discussion that cannot be avoided. It means in any case that adjudicators must motivate their findings, with a thorough and coherent legal analysis. See also Mahoney (1990), pp. 57-88, arguing, in the context of the practice of the ECtHR, that judicial activism and judicial self-restraint are two sides of the same coin.

[440] In his discussion of Article 31 VCLT Sorel (2006), pp. 1289-1334, extensively deals with the teleological and dynamic/evolutive interpretation by various adjudicators (e.g. ICJ, ICTY, ECJ, ECtHR) and notes that Article 31 has left behind traditional voluntarism. An argument has also been made that States may be understood to have acquiesced in the role of the supervisory bodies as interpreting the law to such effect that it comes to constitute subsequent practice. See Report of the Committee on International Human Rights Law and Practice of the International Law Association, at the Berlin Conference (2004), p. 629. This may be different only when there is considerable protest by a range of States parties. After all, different from the traditional system of issuing objections to treaty reservations by other States, in this context States would indeed have a self-interest in voicing their disagreement with the interpretation by an international *adjudicator*, as this may have an impact on their own obligations under the treaty in question. This study does not address the question what is the level and range of such protest and what are its consequences.

[441] On the law as a process approach in general see Higgins (1994), pp. 1-16, esp. p. 8. See further Hey (2003).

[442] ICJ *Conditions of admission of a State to membership in the United Nations* (Article 4 of the Charter), Advisory Opinion of 28 May 1958, Individual Opinion Judge Alvarez, p. 68.

[443] ICJ *Competence of the General Assembly for the admission of a State to the United Nations*, Advisory Opinion of 3 March 1950, Dissenting Opinion Judge M. Alvarez, p. 13. He also pointed out that '(i)t would be meaningless to speak of solidarity, interdependence, co-operation, the general interest, human happiness, etc., if States could continue to exercise all their rights freely and without restriction' , p. 14. Next to the institutions he referred to in 1948, he now noted that a

Apart from the relevance of the subsequent practice developed by the adjudicators to the interpretation of treaty provisions, 'judicial decisions' also constitute 'subsidiary means for the determination of international law' (Art 38(1)(d) ICJ Statute). These may be domestic or international judicial decisions. The phrase 'judicial decisions' is used, rather than 'court decisions'. This potentially includes the decisions made in individual cases by treaty monitoring bodies or WTO Panels and Appellate Body. The argument is often made that such decisions are 'quasi-judicial', but even if that is the case, what could be argued to be most relevant is the range of States whose obligations are covered by the interpretation, rather than the exact legal status of the findings.[444] In other words, a decision of a domestic court, which may be binding on one particular State, certainly has less legal authority vis-à-vis other States, than the interpretation by a treaty monitoring body. Nevertheless, the findings by domestic courts and other domestic adjudicators may be used as subsidiary means for the determination of international law. In this vein the decisions of treaty bodies on individual complaints against States could equally, and more suitably, serve as subsidiary means for the determination of this law.

A joint Separate Opinion attached to the ICJ Judgment in *Congo* v. *Rwanda* (2006) made some important remarks about the case law of the human rights adjudicators.[445] It pointed out, among others, that 'the treaty bodies set up under certain United Nations conventions may well be central to the whole efficacy of those instruments'.[446] It also drew attention to new trends discernable from the practice of human rights adjudicators, which 'have not followed 'the laissez faire' approach to reservations attributed to the International Court's Advisory Opinion of 1951'.[447] Significantly, it pointed out:

> "The practice of such bodies is not to be viewed as 'making an exception' to the law as determined in 1951 by the International Court; we take the view that it is rather a development to cover what the Court was never asked at that time, and to address new issues that have arisen subsequently".[448]

---

treaty itself acquires a life of its own. "Consequently, in interpreting it we must have regard to the exigencies of contemporary life, rather than to the intentions of those who framed it". ICJ *Competence of the General Assembly for the admission of a State to the United Nations,* Advisory Opinion of 3 March 1950, Dissenting Opinion Judge M. Alvarez, p. 18. In other words, the 'interpretation of treaties must not remain immutable'. Ibid.

[444] On the legal status of provisional measures see Chapter XVI.

[445] On the case law by the various human rights systems regarding Jurisdiction, admissibility and provisional measures in human rights adjudication see Chapter XIV.

[446] ICJ *Armed Activities on the Territory of the Congo* (new application: 2002) (*DRC* v. *Rwanda*), Judgment on jurisdiction of the Court and admissibility of the application of 3 February 2006, Separate Opinion Judges Higgins, Kooijmans, Elaraby, Owada and Simma, §21.

[447] They referred to the practice of the European Court of Human Rights, the Inter-American Court of Human Rights and the Human Rights Committee supervising the ICCPR, with its General Comment 24.

[448] Separate Opinion Judges Higgins, Kooijmans, Elaraby, Owada and Simma, §16.

CONCLUSION

Part I provides the basis on which the development of the concept of provisional measures in human rights adjudication is examined.

For conceptual reasons the ICJ's use of provisional measures is relevant to the practice of the human rights adjudicators. The practice of the ICJ is discussed in Chapter I. The chapter found that the practice of the ICJ with regard to provisional measures shows that adjudicators not exclusively dealing with human rights may develop sensitivity for the plight of human beings caught up in conflicts between States. This has also helped develop the concept of provisional measures. In cases involving the fate of human beings the ICJ has ordered provisional measures overlapping to a great extent with the main claim. In other cases, but for the same reason, it has also relaxed the strict requirement that the Applicant State should not only specify the rights invoked in the context of the request for provisional measures, but that these should be related to the main claim as well. The ICJ has further taken into account the basic rights of the individual in its attitude towards procedural requirements for the use of provisional measures. Finally, when the case involves the fate of human beings the Court seems to be more resourceful in drafting Orders for provisional measures different from those requested: it refers to the obligations of both Parties and it adds the obligation not to aggravate the dispute, referring to its task in the maintenance of peace and security.

From the practice of the ICJ three purposes of provisional measures may be perceived to prevent irreparable harm, namely to the claim, to the procedure or to individuals not central to the dispute. The question arises whether this is the case as well in the practice of the human rights adjudicators. This question is addressed in Part II.

The ICJ's finding in *LaGrand* that its provisional measures were legally binding is not made dependent on the fact that basic rights of the human person were involved, but is simply part of its traditional function. The power to indicate provisional measures was required by the object and purpose of Article 41 ICJ Statute and 'based on the necessity, when the circumstances call for it, to safeguard, and to avoid prejudice to, the rights of the parties as determined by the final judgment of the Court'.[1] The question arises whether the binding nature of provisional measures in human rights adjudication is dependent on the purpose of the specific provisional measures or equally applies across the board, even though the particularly serious nature of the harm to be prevented in some cases may have played a role in the finding provisional measures legally binding. This question is dealt with in Part III.

Finally the practices developed by the human rights adjudicators with regard to provisional measures and discussed in the subsequent Parts in turn are relevant to the ICJ. After all the reference to 'judicial decisions' in Article 38(1)(d) of the ICJ Statute is not limited to ICJ case law alone.

Chapter II of Part I discussed the use of provisional measures by the human rights adjudicators in the context of the right to individual complaint. Human rights adjudicators have the inherent authority to use provisional measures. If the human rights treaty also includes inter-State proceedings it should be possible to use provisional measures in these proceedings as well. As appears already from the practice before the ICJ, States may also institute proceedings (partly) involving human rights violations. Pending these proceedings the ICJ has also granted provisional

---

[1]   ICJ *LaGrand* (*Germany* v. *US*), Judgment of 27 June 2001, §102.

measures. The authority to use provisional measures includes the authority to use them *proprio motu*. Especially in cases in which potential beneficiaries are unable to contact the adjudicator directly, the adjudicator should be able to intervene on its own motion on the basis of other credible information. The inherent authority to order provisional measures, based on the principle of effective protection, also implies the possibility of delegation. Without the possibility to delegate the power to use provisional measures to one member of the court or adjudicatory body these measures will be deprived of their protective function. After all, various adjudicators only convene periodically. Generally speaking over time the human rights adjudicators have improved the promptness with which they decide on provisional measures. They have done so indeed partly by introducing a mechanism of delegation and partly because of an improvement in rapid communication methods.

This book emphasises the importance of motivation and accessibility of an adjudicator's provisional measures. In most systems the transparency of decision-making on provisional measures is insufficient. The availability of information is not very balanced over the different bodies. The Inter-American Court of Human Rights publishes its decisions on provisional measures separately and these decisions are motivated. The other systems, however, offer virtually no explanations on the use of provisional measures. Their use is simply mentioned in the decision on the merits or inadmissibility. The unpublished letters to the parties informing them of decisions about provisional measures normally do not clarify the criteria for their use either. In addition, most adjudicators do not formally reject requests by petitioners to take provisional measures. Thus it is not possible to systematically trace failed attempts to convince them to take such measures. Systematic references to refusals to use provisional measures are only found in the decisions by the Inter-American Court, the Bosnia Chamber and, to some extent, the Committee against Torture. The lack of references by the other adjudicators is unfortunate because cases in which the petitioners failed to convince the adjudicators to take provisional measures could give particular insight into their approach to the concept. Accessibility, transparency, coherence and consistency in the use of provisional measures should be increased, among others by making public the decisions and by including reasoning. One of the aims of this research is to assist in this process by collecting, systematizing and analysing the relevant information.

The current lack of transparency in the practice of most adjudicators made an impact on the methodology used in this book. Given the breadth of systems and subject matters discussed, and as most provisional measures are not published, exhaustive discussion of the practice with regard to all subject matters dealt with by all the adjudicators when using provisional measures is not possible. It is not necessary either since this book takes an illustrative rather than an exhaustive approach. The cases discussed are selected because they are informative about a particular aspect of provisional measures. Typical cases are discussed providing insight into the features of provisional measures that the various systems have in common. Similar cases are also mentioned in which other adjudicators confirmed the approach taken in these typical cases or in which they chose to take a different approach. The book also examines atypical cases (Chapter XI) in order to explore the outer limits of the concept. It makes reference mainly to those cases that are easily verifiable. An exception is made for the practice of the HRC because for several years it failed to mention its use of provisional measures in its final decision altogether. Without reference to information derived from the case files the practice discussed would not be representative. Because eventually an opportunity was offered to examine case files in Geneva on the Committee's practice with regard to provisional measures it was decided to make the information retrieved more widely available in this book.

In the context of requests by petitioners for provisional measures the systems are facing common problems and issues, which may sometimes result in converging interpretations, occasionally consciously (often referred to as 'dialogue' or 'cross-fertilization'), at other times more indirectly. Are the international and regional adjudicators moving towards a more uniform approach to the concept of provisional measures? This study aims to identify what, if any, is the underlying interpretative approach as to the nature of provisional measures that the human rights adjudicators have in common. This is particularly relevant for the assessment of the provisional measures used by an adjudicator while its constituent treaty does not explicitly mention this possibility. As the adjudicators generally do not make explicit the rationale for using provisional measures, an attempt is made to derive it from their judgments on the merits and admissibility. The conclusions drawn with regard to a possible underlying interpretative approach are supported by the fact that this book also examines whether more than one system has used provisional measures in a given circumstance. As noted in the Introduction, when the underlying approaches of all adjudicators, as well as the specific practice of at least two of them converge, this study speaks of a common core.

Awareness of convergence and divergence may enhance the understanding of the common core and outer limits of the current concept of provisional measures in human rights adjudication. As to the possible divergences in the approaches of the adjudicators with regard to provisional measures these are mainly due to the differences between the systems. These divergences are explored to clarify the use of provisional measures that are situated, as discussed in Chapter XII, on a continuum beyond the common core, but still within the outer limits of the concept. The question also arises whether (regional) context could fully determine the outer limits of the concept of provisional measures in human rights cases or whether there are outer limits beyond which adjudicators cannot go in any system without depriving the concept of independent meaning.

It may be more difficult to find a common understanding of legal concepts and achieve convergence in interpretation with regard to a large number of States from different regions of the world. Yet if all adjudicators have a similar interpretative approach to certain phenomena and legal texts, this would validate that interpretation for the time being.[2] Cross-fertilization can make an interpretation more convincing and more coherent from the perspective of the development of a body of international case law. It is assumed that if the adjudicators indeed move towards a more uniform approach this will make the provisional measures more persuasive to domestic courts, the executive and the legislator. In addition it presumably is more 'costly' for a State's image to ignore such provisional measures because of their enhanced legitimacy.

Article 31(3)(c) Vienna Convention on the Law of Treaties (VCLT) is particularly relevant as an expression of the aim of increasing coherence in the law applied to different subject matters. It reflects the principle of systemic integration, referring to 'any relevant rules of international law applicable in the relations between the parties' as an element that must be taken into account with the context when interpreting a treaty provision. A presumption exists of consistency of the text to be interpreted with general international law, unless this would undermine the object and purpose of the system.

The practice that has been developed by human rights adjudicators in the application of the human rights treaties subsequent to their entry into force is relevant when a given treaty is applied domestically, as well as when other international adjudicators refer to the provisions of that treaty. International adjudicators may do so either directly, as the ICJ has done in its *Wall* opinion, or in order to inform the meaning of the particular treaty they supervise. In both cases they consider the subsequent practice of the relevant treaty bodies as well. This is so either as law applicable in the relations between the parties or as the authoritative interpretation of a treaty provision that is conceptually similar, which interpretation could therefore serve as a source of inspiration or even indicate underlying general principles of law or interpretation.

In addition, apart from the relevance of the subsequent practice developed by the adjudicators to the interpretation of treaty provisions, 'judicial decisions' also constitute 'subsidiary means for the determination of international law' (Article 38(1)(d) ICJ Statute). These may be domestic

---

[2]   As noted, it is assumed that the concept of provisional measures is dynamic rather than frozen in time.

or international judicial decisions. The term 'judicial decisions' is used, rather than 'court decisions'. Judicial decisions potentially include the decisions made in individual cases by treaty monitoring bodies or WTO Panels. The argument is often made that such decisions are 'quasi-judicial', but even if that is the case, what could be argued to be most relevant is the range of States whose obligations are covered by the interpretation, rather than the exact legal status of the findings. In other words, a decision of a domestic court, which may be binding on one particular State, certainly has less legal authority vis-à-vis other States, than the interpretation by a treaty monitoring body. Nevertheless, the findings by domestic courts and other domestic adjudicators may be used as subsidiary means for the determination of international law. In this vein the decisions of treaty bodies on individual complaints against States could equally, and more suitably, serve as subsidiary means for the determination of this law.

The subsequent Parts discuss the practice of the human rights adjudicators with regard to their use of provisional measures. Further dialogue about the concept within, as well as between the various systems, will undoubtedly enhance the quality and persuasiveness of provisional measures by human rights adjudicators. Meanwhile, for this research 'information-rich' cases have been selected in order to gain insight into the concept of provisional measures in human rights adjudication. Some of them relate to situations in which (almost) all human rights adjudicators have used provisional measures, others concern unusual situations.

By abstracting from individual cases and systems the subsequent chapters examine patterns with regard to the various aspects mentioned in the introduction and, if possible, point out best practices. As noted in the Introduction to this book, the latter are based on the following criteria: accessibility, motivation and consistency, responsiveness to the specific situation, consultation and follow-up. These criteria are selected as they are considered either to make provisional measures more convincing to the addressee State or to be necessary for the effectiveness of these measures in protecting the individual.

PART II

PURPOSE

INTRODUCTION

Provisional measures in international human rights adjudication have been referred to as 'a practical and necessary device for preventing irreversible harm to either party's case such as the destruction of crucial evidence pertaining to the facts or danger to an individual applicant's health and well-being (…). They are also important for ensuring that the proceedings of the case are properly handled'.[1] As Cançado Trindade, judge at the Inter-American Court, has pointed out, in human rights law excessive formalism is unwarranted. In the past such formalism has sometimes given the impression that procedure was an end in itself, rather than a means to achieve justice, while in fact provisional measures are judicial guarantees of a preventive character. The concept is evolutive. The transposition of preventive measures from national to international law did not appear to have changed the object of provisional measures, at least not in interstate relations. Yet the most recent transposition from inter-State relations to international human rights law has indeed changed the purpose of provisional measures.[2]

Part I, discussing the practice of the ICJ and ITLOS (Chapter I) and introducing the human rights systems dealt with in this book (Chapter II), provided the setting for a discussion of the purpose of provisional measures as used by the human rights adjudicators.

The question arises whether the purpose of provisional measures used in the human rights systems differs from the purpose of such measures as applied by the ICJ and ITLOS.

The ICJ has ordered provisional measures also when there would be no irreparable harm to the claim but instead to rights 'collateral' to the claim. It may be assumed that adjudicators specifically dealing with human rights may equally take provisional measures in such circumstances. Like the ICJ, the human rights adjudicators have generally invoked the traditional concept of 'irreparable' rather than 'intolerable' or 'unendurable' harm.[3] As this Part will show, preventing irreparable harm is in fact the *main* purpose of the provisional measures by human rights adjudicators, while it is just *one* of the purposes of provisional measures in general international law.[4]

There is less clarity, however, about the types of situations that would result in such harm. Adjudicators have used provisional measures in a wide variety of situations, generally without specifying their approach to the concept of irreparable harm. One question that arises, for instance, is whether they use provisional measures to prevent irreparable harm to a wide range of human rights (referred to in this book as irreparable harm to the claim), or to prevent irreparable

---

[1]   Garry (2001), p. 404.

[2]   The Inter-American Court now uses this argument, which was introduced by Cançado Trindade, in its Orders for provisional measures, see e.g. *Peace Community of San José de Apartadó*, Order of 24 November 2000, 12th Considering Clause, following the previous Order of the President in the same case, 9 October 2000, ninth Considering Clause and referring to the Order of the President in the *Constitutional Court* case (Peru), 7 April 2000, §§10-11.

[3]   Elkind has pointed out with regard to the provisional measures by the ICJ, that these measures are necessary when the injury is 'unendurable' or 'intolerable,' rather than 'irreparable'. The petitioner 'cannot be expected to put up with it pending the outcome of the dispute'. Elkind (1981), p. 223. See further Chapter I (ICJ). Elkind's terminology has not been adopted, but in fact it seems incorporated in the concept of irreparable harm as used by the adjudicators.

[4]   See further Chapter I of this book.

harm to a smaller range of human rights intimately related to basic conditions of life in dignity (referred to in this book as irreparable harm to persons).

Most constituent documents or Rules of Procedure for different adjudicators have specified irreparable harm simply as harm to the victim of the alleged violation.[5] The criterion for the Inter-American Court specifically is to prevent irreparable harm to *persons*.[6] This is also the relevant criterion for the Inter-American Commission.[7] The Protocol to the African Charter, instituting an African Court, applies a similar reference.[8]

The Rules of Procedure of the ECtHR (and the former Commission), on the other hand, do not refer to irreparable harm at all. Instead the Rule on provisional measures is formulated broadly: 'any interim measure, the adoption of which seems desirable in the interest of the parties or the proper conduct of the proceedings before it'. Rule 111 of the Rules of Procedure of the African Commission has it both ways. In the first paragraph it refers to avoiding 'irreparable damage being caused to the victim' and in the second to 'any interim measures, the adoption of which seems desirable in the interest of the parties or the proper conduct of the proceedings before it'.

While Annex 6 of the Dayton Peace Agreement specifically includes an entry on provisional measures, it gives no indication of their purpose and the text of the Rule on provisional measures in the Chamber's Rules of Procedure is taken from the Rules of Procedure of the ECtHR. This means that the text does not specify the type of situations in which the Bosnia Chamber is expected to take provisional measures.

On the basis of the wording of the Rules on provisional measures of the ECtHR and the European Commission one may conclude that many circumstances could give rise to their use of provisional measures. In practice, however, both adjudicators have interpreted this provision rather strictly. They have taken provisional measures mostly in cases of imminent expulsion or extradition involving *prima facie* evidence of a real risk of torture, inhuman treatment or life

---

[5]   For the HRC the Rule on provisional measures speaks of avoiding 'irreparable damage to the victim of the alleged violation' (Rule 92/Rule 86 old). Both Rule 108(1) of CAT's Rules of Procedure and Article 5 of the Optional Protocol to the Women's Convention speak of avoiding irreparable damage to the victim or victims of the alleged violations. CERD does so as well, only more circumspectly. Rule 94(3) of CERD's Rules of Procedure refers to avoiding 'possible irreparable damage to the person or persons who claim to be victim(s) of the alleged violation'. The African Commission also speaks of avoiding irreparable damage 'to the victim of the alleged violation' (Rule 111 Rules of Procedure).

[6]   Article 63(2) ACHR.

[7]   "In serious and urgent cases, and whenever necessary according to the information available, the Commission may, on its own initiative or at the request of a Party, request that the state concerned adopt precautionary measures to prevent irreparable harm to persons". The significance of the comma, followed by the word 'and' is unclear. It may be that the Commission can order precautionary measures both in 'serious and urgent cases' and 'whenever necessary according to the information available'. In any case, the precautionary measures still aim at the prevention of irreparable harm to persons. It is not clear how 'urgent cases' are clarified by the addition of 'and whenever necessary according to the information available' and by the addition of 'serious' nor is it clear whether the Commission intends to extend or restrict the possibility to take precautionary measures. See Rule 25.

[8]   Article 27(2) OP to the ACHPR: "In cases of extreme gravity and urgency, and when necessary to avoid irreparable harm to persons, the Court shall adopt such provisional measures as it deems necessary". Article 35 of the Protocol on the Statute of the African Court of Justice and Human Rights (2008) does not include this reference, probably because the power to order provisional measures is broader because the provision applies to both the Human Rights Section and to the General Affairs Section.

threatening situation in the receiving State.[9] Yet it turns out that, based on the same text, the Bosnia Chamber has in addition used provisional measures to halt forced eviction.[10]

Chapter II, introducing the human rights systems, pointed out that the Inter-American Court is the only adjudicator that publishes its provisional measures as well as motivates them. In addition, even though the Inter-American Commission does not publish its precautionary measures themselves, it does publish in its Annual Report a yearly overview of its practice in using these measures. Moreover, in its decisions on the merits it adds a brief explanation of its use of precautionary measures. It appears, furthermore, that like the Inter-American Court in its Orders, the Commission does motivate, to some extent, the measures themselves in its Notes Verbales to the Addressee States. Generally the Commission points out in its letter to the petitioner informing it about the precautionary measures taken vis-à-vis the State that it considers necessary the adoption of concrete measures, with an urgent character, in order to protect the life and personal integrity of certain people, often mentioned by name. Sometimes it refers to a particular group of people. Such letter also notes that the precautionary measure is without prejudice to other actions deemed pertinent by the government.[11] The Commission considers that all concrete measures 'need be' or 'must be'[12] adopted urgently[13] in order to protect the personal integrity and the life of the persons mentioned.[14]

The other human rights adjudicators neither publish nor motivate their provisional measures. In a few situations the HRC has provided information about its approach towards provisional measures, but generally this must be derived from the context as apparent from its decisions on the merits. The object and purpose of a treaty, the essence of a right and the prevention of irreparable harm are issues that are closely related. Hence when discussing the HRC's practice with regard to the use of provisional measures it is helpful to refer to its General Comments dealing with the issue of reservations, states of emergency and the meaning of Article 2 ICCPR (general legal obligations). These may help determine which actions or omissions it would consider to cause irreparable harm. The HRC emphasises, for instance, that limitations of rights may in no case 'be applied or invoked in a manner that would impair the essence of a Covenant right'.[15] In its General Comment on Article 4 ICCPR (states of emergency) it affirmed that Articles 6 (right to life) and 7 (prohibition of torture and cruel treatment) are non-derogable. It pointed out that the inclusion in the Covenant of these rights as rights that could not be derogated from even during emergency situations was recognition of the peremptory nature of these rights.[16] In other words, the Committee qualifies these rights as rules of *ius cogens*. This statement may also reflect its awareness of the irreparable nature of violations of these rights.

---

[9]   Articles 2 and 3 ECHR.

[10]   See Chapter XI on halting mass expulsion and forced eviction.

[11]   Information derived from viewing several such letters at the Offices of the NGO CEJIL in Washington, DC (October 2001) and San Jose, Costa Rica (December 2001). Most cases involve a request to the government to protect certain people against threats to their life or physical integrity.

[12]   The Commission uses phrases like: *'que deben adoptarse'* or *'considera necesaria'*.

[13]   The phrase used is *'con carácter urgente'*.

[14]   In such cases the Commission also seeks that the government takes timely measures for the immediate investigation of the denounced acts so as to identify and punish those responsible. See further Chapter XIII (Protection and reparation).

[15]   See HRC General Comment No. 24 on reservations, 4 November 1994; General Comment No. 29 on states of emergency, 24 July 2001 and General Comment No. 31, 'The nature of the general legal obligation imposed on States parties to the Covenant' (on Article 2), 29 March 2004.

[16]   HRC General Comment 29 on Article 4 (states of emergency), 31 August 2001, §11.

The following statement gives some indication as to the Committee's approach to the purpose of provisional measures.

> "Flouting of the Rule, especially by irreversible measures such as the execution of the alleged victim or his/her deportation from the country undermines the protection of Covenant rights through the Optional Protocol".[17]

The statement emphasises the importance of provisional measures for the prevention of actions of an irreversible nature. It is not clear whether the use of the word 'especially' means that the Committee could also use provisional measures in contexts not constituting irreversibility. It is clear, however, that flouting its provisional measures would always undermine the protection, through the Optional Protocol, of Covenant rights and *especially* in cases in which the provisional measures were intended to halt irreversible measures.

Beyond such specific statements, information about the purpose of the provisional measures by the relevant adjudicators and the precise protection required must be derived from the claims, the findings on the merits[18] and the recommendations for reparation.[19]

The HRC has pointed out that provisional measures are essential to the Committee's role under the OP.[20] Its general reference to the obligation of States not to frustrate its consideration of a case[21] may be seen as an obligation not to harm the procedure, but it does not indicate whether this obligation eventually relates to harm to the person or the claim. The reference, on the other hand, to the obligation not to prevent the HRC from expressing its Views[22] may be seen as an obligation not to cause irreparable harm to the claim.

In *Mamatkulov* (2005) the ECtHR pointed out: "Even before the provisions regulating the question of interim measures came into force, the Commission had not hesitated to ask respondent Governments for a stay of execution of measures liable to make the application pending before it devoid of purpose".[23] This statement from the European system equally seems to refer to preventing irreparable harm to the claim.

Part II examines whether in *practice* the irreparable harm to be prevented is harm to the claim or to persons. Even if irreparable harm to the victim of the alleged violation (the criterion for the international adjudicators and the African Commission) is understood as irreparable harm to persons (the criterion for the Inter-American Commission and Court and the African Court), this in itself does not clarify the types of situations in which the adjudicators would use provisional measures to prevent such harm. Part II discusses those situations in which most human rights adjudicators have used provisional measures on the one hand and those that are specific mainly to one system on the other. It analyses known instances of provisional measures in a variety of situations, examining what type of urgent action the adjudicator has undertaken and, if there is no explicit reference to provisional measures, whether this action may nevertheless amount to such measures. Occasionally, it also refers to situations in which provisional measures would have been feasible or in which petitioners unsuccessfully requested them.[24]

---

[17] HRC *Dante Piandiong, Jesus Morallos and Archie Bulan* v. *the Philippines*, 19 October 2000, §5.4.

[18] See further section 3 in the Chapters III-XI.

[19] See Chapter XIII (Protection).

[20] See e.g. HRC *Dante Piandiong et al.,* 19 October 2000, §5.4.

[21] Id., §5.2.

[22] Id., §5.1.

[23] ECtHR (Grand Chamber) *Mamatkulov and Askarov* v. *Turkey*, 4 February 2005, §106.

[24] Clearly, decisions by the adjudicators *not* to use provisional measures could help clarify their approach towards the concept of these measures, in particular their outer limits. Public information about such decisions, however, is rare.

All chapters pay attention to the relationship between provisional measures and the merits of the relevant cases. After all, the question arises whether provisional measures should be taken in cases in which a finding of a violation is unlikely. This does not relate to evidentiary requirements alone, an issue discussed in Chapter XV on assessment of risk, but also to substantive issues. If the adjudicators would never find on the merits that States have obligations under these articles, the purpose of provisional measures could not be preventing irreparable harm to the claim. Their purpose would only be the protection of the right of individual petition as such.

The argument in this book rests on the assumption that provisional measures are taken to prevent a violation from taking place or to stop a continuing violation. Thus, for cases in which provisional measures have been requested, it is important to establish what type of obligations the adjudicators have found on the merits, in order to see whether an order to take provisional measures pending the proceedings may be justified by the case law on the merits. The question must be addressed whether there is an apparent right and whether its violation would result in irreparable harm.

Another assumption in this book is that provisional measures are aimed at ensuring that if the adjudicator would subsequently find that a given act or omission would constitute a violation, the most adequate form of reparation could still be implemented.

The term 'irreparable' appears to be the generic term applied in the context of provisional measures. Yet it is argued that a distinction must be made between *irreversible* harm to the claim (or procedure), on the one hand and *irreparable* harm to the person(s) involved on the other. The subsequent chapters will clarify this distinction. The destruction of a painting, for instance, is discussed as irreversible harm to the claim of the artist not to have it destroyed.[25] The destruction of evidence is discussed as an example of irreversible harm to the procedure.[26] Part II argues that in certain cases irreversible harm to the claim in fact would constitute irreparable harm to persons as well.[27] Moreover, in some cases irreversible harm to the procedure would equally constitute irreparable harm to persons, albeit to persons other than the petitioner.[28] This book will argue that the use of provisional measures to prevent acts that are reversible is beyond the outer limits of the concept of provisional measure, while their use to prevent acts that are not only irreversible, but also irreparable is more likely to fall within the core common to the practice of all human rights adjudicators. Violations of rights causing irreparable harm must be prevented since a return to the *status quo ante* is impossible after the irreversible has taken place (irreversibility), while the nature of the harm implies that such violations can never be repaired by financial compensation (irreparability).

In order to establish the common core and outer limits of the concept of provisional measures currently applied by human rights adjudicators Part II discusses a selection of cases in which the human rights adjudicators have referred to the use of provisional measures.

Separate chapters are devoted to those situations in which the use of provisional measures by human rights adjudicators seems widespread, or in which their use is at least more than incidental, as long as more than one adjudicator has used them in that situation. Examples of situations in which only one system has used them are all discussed together in one chapter. Yet apart from the practice of the adjudicators with regard to the actual use of provisional measures, their practice with regard to the case law on the merits is deemed relevant as well, in order to establish the underlying rationale that the use of provisional measures may have in common.

In order to clarify the development of the concept, the selection of cases discussed covers the range of human rights claims in the context of which provisional measures are known to have been used or refused. Examples that could have particular relevance to an international context of

---

[25] See Chapter XII, section 2.11.
[26] See Chapter XII, section 2.10.
[27] See Chapters III-XI.
[28] See Chapter IX on protecting against death threats and harassment.

counterterrorism measures are referred to as well. Moreover, cases were selected involving individual as well as collective beneficiaries of provisional measures and State obligations to act as well as to abstain from acting.

Part II starts with Chapter III on provisional measures to halt executions, Chapter IV on provisional measures to halt corporal punishment and Chapter V on provisional measures to halt expulsion or extradition in non-refoulement cases. They show that such measures have been used by all relevant adjudicators, not just in the post 2001 counter-terrorism era but already from the inception of the individual complaint proceedings. Chapters VI (Locating and protecting disappeared persons) and VII (Intervening timely in detention situations involving risks to health and dignity) discuss provisional measures to protect the life and personal integrity of persons in (secret) detention. Again, from the start human rights adjudicators have used provisional measures is such circumstances, but their current relevance is evident as well. A less obvious type of provisional measures, incidentally used by some adjudicators, involves respect for procedural rights such as due process in detention. Chapter VIII discusses this practice and shows that in fact these measures have only been used in cases ultimately aimed at the protection of life and personal integrity.

While Chapters III to VIII all involve the protection of persons that already are under the physical control of government authorities (in some form of detention), Chapter IX deals with the protection of persons that generally are not (yet) detained but whose lives and personal integrity are at risk because of their views, activities or belonging to a particular group. It discusses the practice, firmly established in the Inter-American system, of ordering provisional measures to protect against death threats and harassment. It notes that more recently most other adjudicators have begun to use such provisional measures as well, the ECtHR being the last. This Chapter argues that in the European system this type of provisional measure is indeed warranted as well. Death threats do not just take place outside of the Council of Europe. Certain of the member States of this organisation also fail to protect persons against death threats and harassment. Some governments refer to the 'war on terror' in order to justify labelling human rights defenders, journalists and others as 'enemies of the State'. This makes these people vulnerable to threats and attacks against their lives and physical integrity.

Chapters X and XI discuss provisional measures of a different type. They are different because they partly involve collective rights and because strictly speaking they do not relate to the right to life and personal integrity. Chapter X deals with the practice, established in some systems, of ordering provisional measures for the protection of (indigenous) cultural and religious rights. Chapter XI discusses the (limited) practice, developed in the Americas and by the Bosnia Chamber, to halt mass or arbitrary expulsion and forced eviction.

Chapter XII deals with the continuum between common core and outer limits of the concept of provisional measures by discussing examples of situations in which only one human rights adjudicator has used provisional measures as well as some examples of cases in which adjudicators have explicitly refused to use them.

The last chapter of Part II discusses the relation between the substance of the provisional measures on the one hand (e.g. act or abstention) and the measures or forms of reparation that could possibly be ordered upon an eventual finding of a violation (Chapter XIII) on the other hand. This chapter also discusses some issues with regard to the beneficiaries of provisional measures.[29]

Based on common elements relevant to the concept of provisional measures in human rights cases, the Conclusion to be found at the end of this Part presents a theoretical framework for the purpose of provisional measures in human rights adjudication. It clarifies the meaning of

---

[29]   It also briefly refers to the addressees of provisional measures. The *official responses* of addressee States are discussed in Chapter XVII.

irreparable harm to the claim, persons or the procedure and indicates which of them is crucial to the use of provisional measures in human rights adjudication.

While the conclusions to the individual chapters already take the first step in this respect, the Conclusion to Part II argues more closely what types of provisional measures belong to the common core, what types may be situated somewhere beyond the common core but still within the outer limits and what currently constitute the outer limits of the concept.

It combines theoretical with practical criteria. While the argument is based on what seems to be a common underlying rationale for the use of provisional measures in human rights adjudication, this book qualifies as belonging to the common core those types of provisional measures that not only share the underlying common rationale but are also actually used by more than one adjudicator.

Thus, with regard to the purpose of provisional measures the Conclusion to Part II indeed presents the current common core of the concept as well as its outer limits, applying the criteria of irreversible and irreparable harm.

Chapter III
Halting Executions

1   Introduction

The international and regional human rights adjudicators dealing with a range of human rights have all used provisional measures to halt executions.[1] Even the ICJ, which does not have a specific human rights function, has made use of provisional measures to halt executions.[2] This chapter discusses the practice of the human rights adjudicators in this regard. The issue of prejudgment discussed in Chapter I (ICJ) is also relevant in the practice of the human rights adjudicators. Provisional measures to halt an execution serve as an example. Thus this chapter deals with the issue of prejudgment as well. The subsequent chapters on provisional measures used in specific situations will not return to this issue as no new aspects are highlighted in the case law regarding those situations.

The question arises whether provisional measures should be taken in cases in which a finding of a violation is unlikely. This does not relate to evidentiary requirements alone,[3] but also to substantive issues. As noted in the introduction to Part II, the argument in this book rests on the assumption that there is a link between provisional measures and the possible decision on the merits. In this approach the first question to be dealt with is whether certain conduct would constitute a violation of any of the treaty provisions invoked or at least whether the rights invoked are *capable* of being interpreted such that a violation could be concluded. If not, this book argues that the use of provisional measures would be inappropriate.

The next question, which is addressed in Chapter XIII, is whether a violation of the rights invoked would result in the impossibility of an appropriate form of reparation. In other words, could such violations constitute irreparable harm? If answered in the affirmative this would warrant the use of provisional measures in order to prevent or halt these violations.[4]

Most of the practice discussed in section 2 is based on provisional measures only mentioned in the decisions on the merits, but not published separately. One reason for discussing decisions on the merits to help explain the use of provisional measures (section 3) thus is the fact that these decisions constitute the only information publicly available. This chapter concludes by discussing available information on the relationship between provisional measures and the decision on the merits.

---

[1]   Even for the specialized treaty bodies (CAT, CEDAW, CERD) an intervention would be feasible in the context of a death sentence based on statements extracted under torture or based on a discriminatory trial.

[2]   ICJ *Case concerning the Vienna Convention on Consular Relations* (*Paraguay* v. *US*), Order of 9 April 1998 (*Breard* case); *LaGrand* (*Germany* v. *US*), Order of 27 June 2001; *Avena and other Mexican Nationals* (*Mexico* v. *US*), Order of 5 February 2003 and *Interpretation Avena*, Order of 16 July 2008, as discussed in Chapter I.

[3]   See Chapter XV (Immediacy and risk).

[4]   See Chapter XIII (Protection).

2   PRACTICE

2.1   Introduction

Provisional measures to halt executions have been used in all three regional human rights systems, as well as by the HRC.[5] The European Commission was the first to use them, as discussed under the next heading. The African Commission[6] and the Bosnia Chamber have used provisional measures to halt executions as well.[7] The HRC and the Inter-American Commission and Court, finally, have used provisional measures to halt the execution of a great number of persons. While briefly referring to the European system first, this section takes as a point of reference the practices of the HRC and the Inter-American Commission and Court.

2.2   ECHR

The first known example of a provisional measure to halt an execution dates from 1957. The European Commission on Human Rights sent an urgent request to the Government of the United Kingdom not to execute Nicholaos Sampson, a twenty-two year old journalist from Cyprus, until it had been fully informed of the circumstances of the case.[8] Under the provisions of the Emergency Regulations the Nicosia Special Court had sentenced him to death for carrying firearms.[9]

---

[5]   The other specialized UN conventions (ICAT, CEDAW and ICERD) do not deal specifically with the death penalty.

[6]   See e.g. ACHPR (African Commission) *Constitutional Rights Project* (*in respect of Akamu and Others*) v. *Nigeria*, provisional measure of 22 October 1991; *Constitutional Rights Project* (*in respect of Lekwot and 6 others*) v. *Nigeria*, provisional measure of 16 February 1993; *International Pen, Constitutional Rights Project, Interights on behalf of Ken Saro-Wiwa Jr. and Civil Liberties Organisation* v. *Nigeria*, provisional measure somewhere between 2 and 9 November 1995 (secret execution 10 November 1995); *Avocats sans Frontières* (*on behalf of Bwampamye*) v. *Burundi*, provisional measure of 13 December 1999; *Interights et al.* (*on behalf of Mariette Bosch*) v. *Botswana*, provisional measures of 27 March 2001 (execution on 31 March 2001) and *Interights* (*on behalf of Husaini et al.*) v. *Nigeria*, provisional measures of 6 and 8 February 2002 (also sent to the African Union).

[7]   See Bosnia Chamber *Sretko Damjanović* v. *Fed. BiH*, provisional measure of 16 December 1996; *Nail Rizvanović* v. *Fed.BiH*, provisional measure of 2 September 1997 and *Borislav Herak* v. *Fed. BiH*, provisional measure of 10 November 1997.

[8]   See also Chapter II (Systems).

[9]   Earlier he had been found not guilty of the murder of a police sergeant. The previous year the Government of Greece had lodged a complaint against the UK in connection with Cyprus. In the beginning of July the Commission received an urgent letter by Greece pointing out that Sampson's execution appeared imminent. Letter by the Agent of the Greek Government, 1st July 1957, also mentioning that this case has 'deeply stirred the population of the island, which is apparently very anxious and disturbed about the fate of the young journalist'. EComHR *Application of the ECHR to the Island of Cyprus* (*Greece* v. *UK*), 26 September 1958 (Article 31 report), p. 33. It was on that day that the Sub-Commission intervened. During the hearings, in July 1957, President of the Commission drew the attention to this decision. "In addition, the Sub-commission received on 1st July 1957 an urgent letter from the Agent of the Greek Government regarding the case of Nicolas Sampson. This letter gave rise to the Sub-commission's decision of the same day, a Decision which has already been communicated to you. The Sub-Commission desired to be thoroughly informed of the facts of the case". EComHR *Application of the ECHR to the Island of Cyprus* (*Greece* v. *UK*), 26 September 1958 (Article 31 report), p. 37.

The Commission stated it decided to make this request in order to prevent 'any irreparable act'.[10] The UK did not carry out the execution.

The next time the European Commission intervened to halt an execution was equally in an inter-State case but this time it was to halt an execution by Greece itself. In 1970, during the Greek Colonels' regime, the Acting President of the Commission requested the State not to execute any of the 34 suspects in a criminal case during the proceedings before the Commission.[11] The executions did not take place.

The Convention organs did not have to intervene in death penalty cases anymore until the Court was faced with the case of *Öcalan* v. *Turkey*. In 1999 it ordered Turkey not to execute Öcalan during the proceedings before it.[12] At the time this State was the only original member of the Council of Europe that still retained the death penalty. It abolished it in 2002.

2.3   Inter-American Commission and Court

At least since the early 1990s the Inter-American Commission makes use of precautionary measures to halt executions.[13] An example is its first precautionary measure on behalf of Shaka Sankofa, at the time still called Gary Graham.[14] This is one of the many cases before the Commis-

---

[10]   See EComHR *Application of the ECHR to the Island of Cyprus* (*Greece* v. *UK*), 26 September 1958 (Article 31 report), p. 34 (the death sentence should not be carried out until the Sub-commission had been fully informed as to the facts of the case and had had the opportunity to present its observations). The European Commission did not have a Rule on provisional measures at the time. See generally Chapter XVII on official responses. See also Eissen (1969), p. 254 and p. 258. The death sentence of Nikolaos (or Nikos) Sampson was commuted to a life sentence, to be served in the UK. Later he received amnesty and when Cyprus gained formal independence from the UK in 1960, he returned. In 1974 he was installed as President of Cyprus by a coup d'état staged by Greek-Cypriot nationalists and remained so for eight days, until the Turkish invasion of Northern Cyprus. He was sentenced to a prison term, which for medical reasons he was allowed to serve in France (Encyclopedia Brittannica 2001). He did not serve this sentence and upon return to Cyprus in 1990 he was briefly detained. In March 1992 he brought a case before the European Commission for a violation of Article 5 ECHR: *Sampson* v. *Cyprus*, 9 May 1994 (inadm.).

[11]   On 8 April 1970 the public Prosecutor requested the death penalty for Karageorgas. The European Commission used informal provisional measures on 11 April, requesting Greece to suspend the execution of the death sentences against the thirty-four accused persons. On 12 April the domestic court sentenced Karageorgas to life imprisonment. See Partial Decision of the Commission as to the admissibility of the application, *The Second Greek case* (*Denmark, Norway and Sweden* v. *Greece*), 5 October 1970, §11. Both cases and both requests for provisional measures were brought before the Commission by States, under the State complaint procedure (former Article 24 ECHR), rather than by individuals under the individual complaint procedure (former Article 25 ECHR).

[12]   ECtHR *Öcalan* v. *Turkey*, Judgment of 12 May 2005 (second provisional measure of 30 November 1999 in order to stay the execution (first provisional measure: access to his Turkish counsel, see press release 4 March 1999).

[13]   As discussed in Chapter II the Inter-American Commission's provisional measures are called 'precautionary measures'.

[14]   CIDH *Gary T. Graham, now known as Shaka Sankofa* v. *US*, 15 June 2000 (adm.). The initial petition was of 26 April 1993 by the International Human Rights Law Clinic at the Washington College of Law, American University. The state of Texas had first scheduled him to be executed on 29 April 1993. On 27 April 1993 the Commission sent a note to the Governor of Texas requesting a stay. His execution was subsequently stayed 'as a consequence of various domestic

sion involving the US death penalty. It was a case involving juvenile death penalty and a credible claim of innocence. In October 1993 the Commission took precautionary measures noting that the beneficiary was 17 years old at the time of the offence for which he was sentenced to death, that his case 'dealt with the most important right, the right to life, and a mistake on the part of the authorities could result in irreparable harm'.[15]

In October 2004 the US Supreme Court decided that the Constitution did not allow the execution of offenders who were below the age of 18 when their crimes were committed.[16] Until that time the Inter-American Commission had continued to take precautionary measures to halt the execution of juvenile offenders. In February 2002, for instance, it did so on behalf of Alexander Williams whose execution by the State of Georgia was scheduled for the next day. It alleged that the execution of a person who was below the age of eighteen when he committed the offence would violate his right to life under Article I of the American Declaration. Moreover, it would also violate fundamental norms of customary law.[17]

Another case involving the US relates to the federal death penalty. In *Garza* the Inter-American Commission took precautionary measures and in its admissibility decision (2001) it held that the failure of an OAS Member State 'to take steps to preserve a condemned man's life while his case was being reviewed by the Commission was inconsistent with the state's basic human rights obligations'.[18] It also took precautionary measures on behalf of Victor Saldaño, an Argentine citizen sentenced to death in Texas. His Hispanic background had been taken into account in determining 'future dangerousness'.[19] Despite the fact that the US generally does not respect the Commission's precautionary measures, many individuals and NGOs in the US con-

---

legal proceedings'. His first new execution date had been set for 3 June 1993. On 1 June the Commission again requested the Governor to stay his execution. The Commission formally opened his case on 3 August 1993 and transmitted the pertinent parts of the petition to the State. On the same day it requested the Governor of Texas once more to suspend the execution. During a hearing on 4 October the petitioners requested the Commission to take precautionary measures pursuant to Article 29(2) of its Regulations. This may lead to the conclusion that the petitioners (and the Commission itself) considered the notes the Commission sent before only as informal precautionary measures.

[15] CIDH *Gary T. Graham, now known as Shaka Sankofa* v. *US*, 15 June 2000 (adm.), §15. He was executed on 22 June 2000.

[16] US Supreme Court, *Roper* v. *Simmons*, 543 U.S. 551 (2005). This ruling affected 72 juvenile offenders in 12 US states. Between 1985 and 2003 Texas executed 13 juvenile offenders, Virginia 3 and Oklahoma 2. South Carolina, Florida, Georgia and Missouri each executed one person who was below 18 at the time of the offence.

[17] Several days after it received the initial petition, on 6 December 2000, the Commission issued precautionary measures for the first time in order to investigate his claim. It reiterated these on 15 February 2002 and again on 19 February, the day before the scheduled execution.

[18] CIDH *Juan Raúl Garza* v. *US*, 4 April 2001 (adm.).

[19] On 5 June 2000 the US Supreme Court revoked his death sentence and returned his case to the Texas Court of Criminal Appeals. By letter of 10 November 2000 the US informed the Commission that it had received information from the Texas Court of Criminal Appeals about a public hearing that would be held on 30 December 2000, later postponed until 8 February 2001, Annual Report 2000, §50. This Court has since affirmed his death sentence finding that, among others, the confession of error by the prosecutor in his case, in admitting expert testimony at the sentencing face that race or ethnicity was a factor in determining future dangerousness, did not permit it on remand to consider the admissibility of that testimony as the defendant should have objected against the use of this expert testimony at trial, *Saldaño* v. *State*, 70 S.W. 3d 873 (Tex. Crim. App. 2002) (13 March 2002).

tinue to resort to it.[20] It is the only international adjudicator that examines complaints against the US.[21]

The Commission has dealt with many death penalty cases, mainly from the United States and Trinidad and Tobago, but also with regard to Guatemala, Jamaica, Grenada and the Bahamas. Of the Caribbean States, Jamaica and Trinidad and Tobago are the most notable. The Commission has requested a stay of execution in many cases 'so that it could investigate thoroughly the charges made in connection with the case and the presumed violation' of their fundamental rights.[22] It has also formulated the rationale for the use of the precautionary measures by stating that executing petitioners before the Commission has been able to examine their claims would cause irreparable harm.[23]

Apart from Guatemala and Barbados, and initially Trinidad and Tobago, none of the death penalty States in the Americas have recognised the jurisdiction of the Inter-American Court. In 1998 the Court ordered provisional measures for the first time in order to halt executions on behalf of several persons from Trinidad and Tobago, whose cases were pending before the Commission.[24] Trinidad had recognised the Court's jurisdiction in 1991 and withdrew its recognition in May 1998.[25] The Court has since dealt with one situation involving Barbados[26] and two involving Guatemala, currently the only State in Latin America imposing the death penalty.[27]

---

[20]   See Chapter II on the obligations of OAS States under the American Declaration. See also Chapter XVII on the official responses of addressee States.

[21]   The US has not ratified the OP recognising the right of individual complaint under the ICCPR. It has not ratified the ACHR either. The Inter-American Commission deals with complaints against the US on the bases of the US obligations under the OAS Charter, including the American Declaration. See further Chapter II (Systems) and XVI (Legal status).

[22]   For CIDH Annual Report 1997 see e.g. Neville Lewis, Case 11.825, 20 November 1997; Leroy Lamey, Case 11.826, 20 November 1997; Peter Blaine, Case 11.827, 19 November 1997.

[23]   See e.g. CIDH *Denton Aitkin* v. *Jamaica* (2 May 2000) and Dave Sewell (4 December 2000), Annual Report 2000, §§38-39.

[24]   It had previously taken precautionary measures on their behalf but these proved unsuccessful. The provisional measures can be found as the *James et al.* v. *Trinidad and Tobago* cases. In 2002 the Court issued its Judgment in *Hilaire, Constantine et al. and Benjamin et al.* Not all beneficiaries protected under the *James et al.* Order for provisional measures are included in this Judgment of 21 June 2002. This book discusses this Judgment to the extent it may clarify the purpose of provisional measures. See section 4 of this Chapter. See further Chapter XIV (Jurisdiction and admissibility).

[25]   See Chapter XIV (Jurisdiction and admissibility).

[26]   IACHR *Case of Boyce et al.* v. *Barbados*, Judgment of 20 November 2007 (ordering, among others, a commutation of the death sentence of the victim that was still facing the death penalty, in order to guarantee the non-repetition of the violations of the rights addressed in the judgment, §127). See the previous Orders for provisional measures of 25 November 2004 and 14 June 2005. In the judgment the Court referred to these measures as follows: "The Court had ordered the State to adopt provisional measures on behalf of all four victims for the purpose of preserving their "lives and physical integrity [...] so as not to hinder the processing of their cases before the Inter-American system" (*supra*, paras. 31-33). Since their cases have now reached this Tribunal, which has already analyzed violations of the American Convention by Barbados to their detriment in accordance with its contentious jurisdiction, the Court considers that the purpose of the provisional measures has been met. In light of the above, and further considering that Mr. Atkins passed away in 2005, that Messrs. Boyce and Joseph's death sentences have been commuted to life in prison, and that the Court has ordered the State to formally commute the death sentence of Mr. Huggins, this Court hereby lifts the provisional measures ordered on behalf of all of the victims. Accordingly, the Tribunal considers that the State's obligations within the framework of these procedural measures are superseded by those that are ordered in the present Judgment as of

In its Orders for provisional measures the Court generally refers to Article 1(1) ACHR, stating that this article 'imposes on States Parties the obligation to respect the rights and freedoms set out in that treaty and to ensure to all persons subject to their jurisdiction the free and full exercise of the said rights and freedoms'.[28] Moreover, 'as the Court has repeatedly held, it is the responsibility of the State to adopt measures to protect all persons subject to its jurisdiction'[29] and 'this duty is particularly compelling in the case of persons currently the subject of a proceeding before the supervisory organs of the American Convention'.[30]

In Orders involving death penalty cases it also considers that 'if the State were to execute the alleged victims, this would lead to an irreparable situation, as well as constitute conduct incompatible with the object and purpose of the Convention'.[31]

In his Concurring Opinion to the Court's Order to halt executions in *James et al.* Cançado Trindade elaborated on the 'eminently preventive dimension' of the Court's provisional measures. He pointed out that the constitutive elements of provisional measures (extreme gravity and urgency on the one hand and the prevention of irreparable harm to persons on the other) to date were 'present and persistent' in this case. These elements 'transform the provisional measures of protection into a true jurisdictional guarantee of preventive character'.[32]

In light of the constitutive elements of provisional measures and their legal nature Cançado disagreed with 'the doctrinal trend which beholds in the provisional measures ordered by the Inter-American Court at the request of the Commission measures of an exceptional order, to be restrictively interpreted by virtue of their innovating character'.[33] He considers this doctrinal trend to be static and conservative.[34] It is difficult to see how provisional measures could still have an innovative character, as he claims, in such an approach. He may mean that scholars normally tend to take a cautious approach to the use of provisional measures, cherishing their exceptional character exactly because the protection required in those measures is indeed innovative. In that light, his statement indicates his belief that such measures should, contrary to this trend, nevertheless be ordered more often and in new types of situations as well.

2.4 HRC

The great majority of provisional measures by the HRC deals with the death penalty. More than 160 cases were examined in which the HRC used provisional measures in the context of this

---

the date of its notification". IACHR *Case of Boyce et al.* v. *Barbados*, Judgment of 20 November 2007, §129.

[27] Guatemala accepted the Court's contentious jurisdiction on 9 March 1987.

[28] See e.g. IACHR *Boyce and Joseph* v. *Barbados*, Order of 25 November 2004.

[29] See e.g. IACHR *Raxcacó et al.* v. *Guatemala*, Order of 30 August 2004, 5th 'Considering' clause and *Sarayaku Indigenous Community* v. *Ecuador*, Order of 6 July 2004, 4th 'Considering' clause.

[30] IACHR *Raxcacó et al.* v. *Guatemala*, Order of 30 August 2004, 5th 'Considering' clause; *Gómez Paquiyauri* v. *Ecuador*, Order of 7 May 2004, 6th 'Considering' clause; and *Urso Branco Prison* v. *Brasil*, Order of 22 April 2004, 5th 'Considering' clause.

[31] See IACHR *James et al.*, Order of 26 November 2001, 12th 'Considering' clause; *Raxcacó et al.*, 30 August 2004, 9th 'Considering' clause; *Boyce and Joseph* v. *Barbados*, 25 November 2004, 9th 'Considering' clause.

[32] See e.g. IACHR *James et al.* cases, Order of 25 May 1999.

[33] See IACHR *James et al.* cases, Order of 25 May 1999, Concurring Opinion Cançado Trindade, §10.

[34] IACHR *James et al.* cases, Order of 25 May 1999, Concurring Opinion Cançado Trindade, §11.

penalty.[35] Most of them were taken since spring 1993.[36] While in death penalty cases this international adjudicator has virtually always used them, this research is based on the premise that the decision to do so is, or should be, related to its case law on the merits.[37] The petitions in death penalty cases in which provisional measures were taken generally invoked the right to a fair trial. The HRC has been extensive in its case law on fair trial and the right to life. Section 4 on the relationship between provisional measures and the merits, first refers to more general remarks on this link and then focuses on the most important claims made in death penalty cases before the HRC, in order to clarify the function of provisional measures to halt executions.

3   RELATION BETWEEN PROVISIONAL MEASURES TO HALT EXPULSION OR EXTAN EXECUTION AND THE EXPECTED DECISION ON THE MERITS

3.1   Introduction

What is the relation between a *prima facie* claim and the use of provisional measures? Do human rights adjudicators use provisional measures in all cases involving petitioners facing the death penalty or is the decision to use them based on the existence of an apparent right?

The first step in addressing this question is to make explicit the rights invoked for the use of provisional measures to halt an execution.

Article 6(1) ICCPR recognises the inherent right to life of every human being. No one shall be arbitrarily deprived of his life. Article 6(2) stipulates that in 'those countries which have not abolished the death penalty' this sentence may only be imposed under strict conditions in conformity with the provisions of the ICCPR and only for the most serious crimes. Article 6(4) lays down the right of all persons sentenced to death to seek pardon or commutation. It establishes that amnesty, pardon, or commutation may be granted in all cases. In conjunction with 14(5) it provides that no execution should take place pending appeal or other recourse procedure, nor pending pardon or commutation proceedings. Article 6(5) forbids the death penalty for persons who were

---

[35]   This section discusses the Committee's decisions in death penalty cases over the period July 1986 to July 2003. Occasionally, references are made to case law decided after this period. In almost all cases referred to the HRC used provisional measures pending the proceedings. There are some death penalty cases, however, in which it did not use provisional measures because the State had already commuted the sentence. See Chapter II on the accessibility of information on provisional measures. The HRC may equally have used provisional measures in cases that have not yet been concluded. In all but one case it seems to have used provisional measures in order to halt an execution. The exception was a request to halt the imposition itself of the sentence rather than just its execution: *Victor Domukovsky, Zaza Tsiklauri, Petre Gelbakhiani and Irakli Dokvadze* v. *Georgia*, 6 April 1998 (provisional measures of 10 March 1995 and 5 July 1996).

[36]   There is no great difference in the frequency with which the HRC used provisional measures previous to and following the institution of the Special Rapporteur on Death Penalty Cases. Subsequently, with the institution of the Special Rapporteur on New Communications, frequency initially diminished, but later increased. Apart from factors such as an increase in the number of petitions, this may also depend on the personal attitude of the Rapporteur in question. While the introduction of a Special Rapporteur on Death Penalty cases opened a possibility to deal with urgent cases in between sessions, the Rapporteur did not make use of this possibility as often as he could have. On the other hand, pending sessions the HRC took provisional measures quite often during the period this Rapporteur was in function. See also Chapter II.

[37]   Equally, there should be such a link with the reparation eventually recommended, see Chapter XIII (Protection).

below the age of 18 when the crime occurred for which they stand trial or are convicted. Article 6(6) emphasises that nothing in the article shall be invoked to delay or prevent the abolition of capital punishment. A contemporary interpretation of the prohibition of cruel treatment and the right to life is evidenced in both the Second Optional Protocol (Second OP) abolishing the death penalty and decisions by national and international courts.[38] The last 15 years an increasing number of States have abolished the death penalty, 67 of which have ratified the Second OP.[39] Jamaica has been the State that the HRC has dealt with most often to halt an execution. It has also dealt with Trinidad and Tobago, Barbados, Guyana, St. Vincent and the Grenadines (the Americas), Zambia and Sierra Leone (Africa), South Korea and The Philippines (Asia), Belarus, Russia, Ukraine, Uzbekistan, Tajikistan (Europe and Central Asia).[40]

In the regional systems provisional measures have also been used to halt executions. The African system is not very elaborate on the right to life. Article 4 ACHPR simply stipulates that human beings are inviolable and that every human being 'shall be entitled to respect for his life and the integrity of his person'. "No one may be arbitrarily deprived of his right". Fourteen African States have abolished the death penalty for all crimes, nineteen States are not actively applying the death penalty and 21 others retain and apply this penalty.[41]

Article 2(1) ECHR lays down that every one's life shall be protected by law. "No one shall be deprived of his life intentionally save in the execution of a sentence of a court following his conviction of a crime for which this penalty is provided by law". Subsequently the Member States of the Council of Europe adopted Protocol No. 6 on the abolition of the death penalty in peace time (1983).[42] This development was completed with its adoption of Protocol No. 13 on the abolition of the death penalty in all circumstances (2002).[43] The Commission and Court have only dealt with three States: UK, Greece and Turkey. Presently, all Member States of the Council of Europe, except Russia, have abolished the death penalty.[44] Abolition has become a condition of membership of the Council of Europe.[45]

Of the Members of the Organisation of American States (OAS) that still apply the death penalty only Guatemala and Barbados have also recognised the competence of the Inter-American Court. Until May 1999 this applied to Trinidad and Tobago as well.[46] Article 4 ACHR provides

---

[38]   See e.g. the abolition of the death penalty by the South African Constitutional Court: *S v Makwanyane and Mchunu*, 1995 (2) SACR 1 (CC). Generally on the death penalty in international law see e.g. Schabas (2002a); Schabas (1996) and Hood (2002).

[39]   Ratification status as of 3 September 2008. According to Amnesty International by 2007 137 countries in the world had abolished the death penalty in law or practice, Amnesty International report 2008.

[40]   In general about international developments see the reports of the UN Special Rapporteur on Summary and arbitrary executions, also referring to the Rapporteur's urgent appeals to halt executions. Trinidad & Tobago and Jamaica have now withdrawn from the individual complaint proceedings under the First OP. See e.g. Chapters XIV (Jurisdiction and admissibility) and XVII (Official responses).

[41]   See Chenwi's book (2007) on the abolition of the death penalty in Africa, referring to 13 abolitions in law and practice, p. 25 (and referring to 7 African countries having ratified the 2nd OP to the ICCPR), pp. 51-52. In addition Rwanda abolished the death penalty in July 2007.

[42]   Council of Europe Treaty Series 114; concluded 28 April 1983; entry into force 1 March 1985 (ratified by all member States of the Council of Europe except Russia, which has signed but not yet ratified).

[43]   Council of Europe Treaty Series 187; concluded 3 May 2002; entry into force 1 July 2003 (40 ratifications as of 7 September 2008).

[44]   Ukraine ratified Protocol No. 6 in 2000 and since also ratified Protocol 13. The membership of retentionist Belarus is pending since 1993.

[45]   Council of Europe Resolution 1044 (1994).

[46]   This State denounced the ACHR on 26 May 1998. This became effective on 26 May 1999.

that no one shall be arbitrarily deprived of his life. This Convention, which was signed in 1969, stipulates that States that have abolished the death penalty shall not re-establish it (Article 4(3) ACHR). Countries that have not abolished the death penalty may only impose this penalty for the most serious crimes, in accordance with a law establishing such punishment, enacted prior to the commission of the crime. They may only impose this penalty, moreover, pursuant to a final judgment. States shall not extend their death penalty law to 'crimes to which it does not presently apply'. They shall in no case inflict capital punishment for political offences or related common crimes (Article 4(4)). They shall not impose this punishment upon persons who were below the age of eighteen or more than seventy years of age at the time the crime was committed, nor to pregnant women (Article 4 (5)). Finally, this article provides that every person condemned to death shall have the right to apply for amnesty, pardon or commutation of sentence. States shall not impose capital punishment 'while such a petition is pending a decision by the competent authority' (Article 4 (6)). In 1990 a separate Protocol on the abolition of the death penalty was adopted.[47]

The American Declaration is less elaborate on the right to life than the ACHR. Article I provides: "Every human being has the right to life, liberty and the security of his person". The Commission and the Court have considered that the Declaration must be interpreted in light of the Convention.[48] They have specified the obligations of States with regard to Article 1 of the Declaration and Article 4 ACHR. While States in the Americas generally have an abolitionist tradition, this applies mainly to the Latin-American States.[49] Many common law countries in the Americas, with the notable exception of Canada, have not abolished the death penalty. The United States (US) and several Caribbean States still actively apply it.

Apart from the right to life the international and regional treaties also include a prohibition of torture and cruel or degrading treatment or punishment. This has also been relevant in the context of death penalty cases.[50] Article 7 ICCPR stipulates that no one shall be subjected to torture or to cruel, inhuman or degrading treatment or punishment. The text of Article 3 ECHR is similar, but without reference to 'cruel'. Article 5 ACHPR provides that 'every individual shall have the right to the respect of the dignity inherent in a human being' and that 'all forms of exploitation and degradation of man particularly slavery, slave trade, torture, cruel, inhuman or degrading punishment and treatment shall be prohibited'. Article 5 ACHR, finally, stipulates in paragraph 1: "Every person has the right to have his physical, mental and moral integrity respected". Paragraph 2 specifically prohibits torture and cruel, inhuman or degrading punishment or treatment.

As noted, none of the human rights adjudicators, apart from the Inter-American Court (and to some extent the Inter-American Commission), have published or motivated their provisional measures. After mentioning a few cases by the Inter-American Court this section attempts to derive information from the decisions on the merits in death penalty cases about the types of death penalty situations in which the adjudicators use provisional measures. The focus is on the practice of the HRC, but in the context of the right to life references are also made to the approach of the ECtHR and the Bosnia Chamber. It specifically examines whether the practice of the HRC makes sense in light of its general approach towards the purpose of its provisional measures.

---

[47]   OAS Treaties Series No. 73, adopted 8 June 1990. As of September 2008 there were 9 ratifications, <www.cidh.org>.

[48]   See also Chapter II (Systems).

[49]   The only Latin-American country still applying it is Guatemala.

[50]   Specifically about the death penalty as cruel punishment, see e.g. Nowak (2000b) and Schabas (1996).

After all it has made some explicit statements about this purpose in some cases involving non-compliance with its provisional measures.[51]

3.2   Prejudgment

If in a request by petitioners for provisional measures the facts complained of relate to other aspects of the main case, not directly constituting a situation of urgency, the adjudicator will declare (this part of) the request for provisional measures inadmissible. The Inter-American Court has emphasized that it may not examine 'any arguments other than those which are directly and strictly related to situations of extreme gravity and urgency which require the adoption of protection measures to avoid irreparable damage to persons. Any other arguments or facts may only be examined and determined by the Court when considering the merits of contentious cases brought before the Court'.[52]

This means that if it is 'not possible to assess the facts at issue without giving an opinion on the merits of the case' using provisional measures 'implies revising the conformity of the facts denounced by the alleged victims to the American Convention'. "The opinion on the merits of a case submitted to the Court must be issued in the judgment rendered in that case rather than in a decision regarding the adoption of provisional measures. In fact, the latter may imply a prior judgment via an interlocutory proceeding, determining some of the facts submitted to the consideration of the Court and their consequences".[53]

Yet the situation is different when the irreparable harm is related to the main claim. The Inter-American Commission and Court have made some statements regarding provisional measures to halt executions that may clarify the issue of prejudgment and provisional measures.

In death penalty cases the Inter-American Commission requested stays of execution 'to give it time to fully examine the allegations made in the petition, on the grounds that, executing (…) before the Commission could investigate the case would cause irreparable harm'.[54] It bases its request 'on the fact that, should the State execute the victim before the Commission had an opportunity to examine the case, any eventual decision would be rendered moot in terms of the efficacy of potential remedies'.[55] It referred to remedies such as a recommendation of commutation of sentence and pointed out that such mootness would cause the victim irreparable harm.[56]

---

[51]   About the legal status of provisional measures see Chapter XVI and about the follow-up by the adjudicators see Chapter XVIII.

[52]   IACHR Matter of *Adrián Meléndez-Quijano et al.* (El Salvador), Order of 26 November 2007, 9th 'Considering' clause, referring to various cases including *Matter of Luisiana Ríos et al.* (Venezuela), Order of 3 July 2007, 9th 'Considering' clause.

[53]   IACHR Matter of *Adrián Meléndez-Quijano et al.* (El Salvador), Order of 26 November 2007, 10th 'Considering' clause, referring to *Matter of Castañeda-Gutman (*Mexico), Order of 25 November 2005, 6th 'Considering' clause and *Matter of Luisiana Ríos et al.* (Venezuela), Order of 3 July 2007, 11th 'Considering' clause. In *Meléndez-Quijano* the previous provisional measures to protect the beneficiaries were reiterated, but the Court found inadmissible the petitioners' request 'for the provisional suspension of "all the administrative and judicial proceedings started against Adrián Meléndez-Quijano"'.

[54]   E.g. CIDH Annual Report 2000, §47.

[55]   Ibid.

[56]   See e.g. CIDH 6 January 1999, Wayne Matthews, Case 12.076; 21 January 1999, Alfred Frederick and Natasha De Leon, Cases 12.082 and 12.093; 4 March 1999, Vijay Mungroo and Phillip Cholatal, Cases 12.11 and 12.112; 12 April 1999, Naresh Boodram and Joey Ramiah, Case 12.129; 28 April 1999, Nigel Mark, Case 12.137; 1 May 1999, Wilberforce Bernard and Steve Mungroo, Cases 12.140 and 12.141; 8 May 1999, Peter Benjamin and Krishendath

In the operational part of its Order the Court often orders the State to take all necessary measures to preserve the life (and physical integrity) of the beneficiaries 'so as not to hinder the processing of their cases before the Inter-American system'.[57] In his first Order for urgent measures the President of the Inter-American Court pointed out:

> "It is imperative to note that this does not imply a declaration on the merits of the request, but simply acknowledges the possibility of such a decision, which leads to the conclusion that the stay of the executions of the petitioners is necessary to guarantee the integrity of the Inter-American system for the protection of human rights".[58]

This also refers to the procedural considerations aimed at safeguarding the Inter-American human rights system as a whole. Both the Inter-American Court and its President have noted the relationship between the merits and the provisional measures, often in connection with the remark that the cases included in the Commission's request have not yet been submitted to the Court. The Court noted, for instance, that for that reason its consideration of 'the issues at hand' is:

> "based not upon the merits of said Cases but upon the State's procedural obligations as a Party to the American Convention. Therefore, the Court cannot, in a provisional measure, consider the merits of any arguments pertaining to issues other than those which relate strictly to the extreme gravity and urgency and the necessity to avoid irreparable damage to persons. Such other issues are properly brought before the Court only through contentious cases or requests for advisory opinions".[59]

At other times the President simply stated that since the case had not been submitted to the Court, 'the adoption of urgent measures does not imply a decision on the merits of the existing controversy by the petitioners and the State'.[60] In the first example the Court noted that its consideration of the issues was not *based* on the merits of the cases but on the State's procedural obligations under the ACHR. In the second example a decision on the merits is not *implied* by the adoption of urgent measures. In other words, their adoption does not result, implicitly, in a determination on the merits. In both cases the result is that 'the Court will study the request of the Commission in light of the existence of a situation of extreme gravity and urgency and the necessity to avoid irreparable damage to persons, elements to be taken into account in conformity with Article 63(2) of the Convention'.[61]

Seepersad, Cases 12.148 and 12.149; 11 May 1999, Calvin Dial and Andrew Dottin, Case 12.145; 20 May 1999, Anthony Johnson and Allan Phillip, Cases 11.718 and 12.115; 21 May 1999, Narine Sooklal, Case 12.152; 25 May 1999, Amir Mowlah, Case 12.153; 3 June 1999, Mervyn Parris and Francis Mansingh, Cases 12.156 and 12.157.

[57] See e.g. IACHR *James et al.* cases, Order for provisional measures, 14 June 1998, 29 August 1998, 25 May 1999 and 26 November 2001.

[58] IACHR *James, Briggs, Noel, Garcia and Bethel* cases, Order of the President for urgent measures, 27 May 1998.

[59] IACHR *James et al.* cases, Order for provisional measures, 29 August 1998. See also, Order for provisional measures, 26 November 2001.

[60] IACHR *James et al.* cases, Order of the President for urgent measures, 29 June 1998. See also those of 27 May 1998, 13 July 1998 and 25 October 2001.

[61] IACHR *James et al.* cases, Order for provisional measures, 26 November 2001.

The President of the Inter-American Court has pointed out that by adopting urgent measures, this Presidency is ensuring that the Court may carry out effectively its conventional mandate'.[62] The full Court simply considered:

> "That the cases included in the request for amplification have not been submitted to the Court and the consideration of the issues at hand is, consequently, based upon the State's procedural obligations under the Convention in relation to the processing of the Provisional Measures of protection and therefore does not imply a prejudgment on the merits. As a result, the Court will study the request of the Commission in light of the existence of a situation of extreme gravity and urgency and the necessity to avoid irreparable damage to persons, elements to be taken into account in conformity with Article 63(2) of the Convention".[63]

Indeed, the Inter-American Court has considered that the cases in which it took provisional measures were 'not before the Court'. It noted that the purpose of provisional measures in international human rights law was 'to protect fundamental human rights by seeking to avoid irreparable damage to persons'. Their adoption 'does not imply a decision on the merits of the controversy between the petitioners and the State'. "Upon ordering such measures, this Tribunal is ensuring only that it may faithfully exercise its mandate pursuant to the Convention in cases of extreme gravity and urgency".[64]

While the Inter-American Court explains that its consideration is 'based upon the State's procedural obligations under the Convention in relation to the processing of the Provisional Measures of protection and therefore does not imply a prejudgment on the merits', it does refer to the Commission's statement that the claims pending before it 'if proven, tend to establish violations of the American Convention'.[65]

Since the President's first Order for urgent measures to halt executions, the Court and its President have pointed out that the execution of the death penalty in the cases of the alleged victims 'would necessarily affect the Court's consideration of the Commission's request by rendering moot the object of any eventual decision in their favor'.[66] Thus, there is a relationship between the merits of the case (and possible reparation)[67] and the prevention of irreparable harm intended with the Court's provisional measures.

The relationship between the merits of the case and the prevention of irreparable harm is also relevant because provisional measures may be used to prevent a State from anticipating the Court's Judgment and pre-empting it. Some consideration of substantive law is relevant in this

---

[62] IACHR *James et al.* cases, Order of the President for urgent measures, 25 October 2001.

[63] IACHR *James et al.* cases, Order for provisional measures, 26 November 2001.

[64] See e.g. IACHR *Raxcacó et al.*, Order of 30 August 2004 (11th 'Considering' clause); *Carlos Nieto et al.*, Order of 9 July 2004 (10th 'Considering' clause); and *Sarayaku Indigenous Community*, Order of 6 July 2004 (2nd 'Considering' clause) and *Boyce and Joseph*, Order of 25 November 2004 (10th 'Considering' clause).

[65] IACHR *James et al.* cases, Order of the President for urgent measures, 26 November 2001. See also *James et al.* case, Order of the President for urgent measures, 11 May 1999. That same month, on the other hand, the Court had also pointed out that when it considers requests for provisional measures in cases still pending before the Commission its 'consideration of the issues at hand' is 'based upon the State's procedural obligations as a Party to the American Convention, rather than on the merits of each Case'. Thus, the elements the Court takes into account when it studies the Commission's request are 'the existence of a situation of extreme gravity and urgency and the necessity to avoid irreparable damage to persons'. See e.g. *James et al.* case, Order of 25 May 1999.

[66] See IACHR *James, Briggs, Noel, Garcia and Bethel* cases, Order of the President for urgent measures, 27 May 1998 and further Orders.

[67] See also Chapter XIII (Protection).

respect. At the same time the Inter-American Court itself is expected not to predetermine its decision on the merits by ordering provisional measures. Traditionally, courts have tried to balance those two conflicting rules (non-anticipation and no predetermination), in light of the importance of balancing the interests of the parties in a conflict pending before them. Yet the situation is different for adjudicators dealing with human rights issues, exactly because the parties are not two States but the State on the one hand and an individual or group of individuals on the other. This makes the situation inherently unequal, increasing the task of the adjudicator. In this respect the statements of the Inter-American Court are sufficiently general in nature to be relevant as well to the situation of the other human rights adjudicators.

3.3   The published Orders of the Inter-American Court to halt executions

In its Orders for provisional measures the Inter-American Court specifically refers to the rights claimed. An examination of the various Orders in the *James et al.* case shows that the omission, in some cases, of a reference to the protection of physical integrity in addition to the protection of life is not necessarily based on a specific decision on the part of the Court and its President.[68]

With regard to five new beneficiaries in the *James et al.* case the Court noted that they all complained about the mandatory nature of the death penalty.[69] Other complaints included failure to supply full disclosure to the defence, delay in bringing the person involved to trial (3x), improper treatment in detention (5x), conditions of detention (2x), statements taken by coercion (3x), failure to advise right to an attorney, inadequacy of counsel and no trial by a competent, independent and impartial tribunal. The Court pointed out that if the State would execute the petitioners 'it would create an irremediable situation'. It 'would be incompatible with the object and purpose of the Convention'.[70] In the reports Trinidad initially supplied to comply with the Court's Order it pointed out that it had followed due process in all the cases in which the Court had now ordered provisional measures.[71]

With regard to those beneficiaries involved in the Court's Judgment in *Hilaire* etc. (2002) it is possible to illustrate a relationship with the merits. First of all, all cases included in the Judgment dealt with the *mandatory* death penalty. The Commission also claimed other violations.[72] In two cases it claimed a violation of Article 5(6) for failure to take efforts for the reform and 'social re-adaptation' of the petitioner as an essential aim of his punishment. This request is interesting

---

[68]   See for instance IACHR *James et al.* case, Order for provisional measures, 27 May 1999 and Order of President for urgent measures, 19 June 1999 and Order of 25 October 2001 in which the Court ordered the State to take all necessary measures to preserve the lives of the beneficiaries without mentioning their physical integrity. See the Orders of 25 September 1999, 16 August 2000 and 24 November 2000 for examples where physical integrity is explicitly mentioned. In this light not too much meaning must be attached either to the change from the phrase 'physical integrity' to that of 'personal integrity' used in the Court's Order of November 2001 and in most Orders involving other situations. It seems reasonable to assume that the Inter-American Court intended to include the protection of physical integrity in all its Orders to halt executions.

[69]   IACHR *James et al.* cases, Order of the President for urgent measures, 25 October 2001; Order for provisional measures, 26 November 2001. In one case the Commission had already declared admissible the claims of the petitioner: Case of Balkissoon Roodal, 10 October 2001 (adm.).

[70]   IACHR *James et al.* cases, Order for provisional measures, 26 November 2001. The majority of beneficiaries was later included in the cases *Hilaire, Constantine et al.* and *Benjamin et al.*

[71]   IACHR *James et al.* cases, Order for provisional measures, 29 August 1998.

[72]   E.g. a violation of the right to respect for the physical, mental and moral integrity, as laid down in Article 5(1), the right not to be subjected to cruel, inhumane or degrading punishment or treatment in violation of Article 5(2).

because it means that the Commission, at least in certain circumstances, takes the approach that the death penalty as such or, alternatively, the death row phenomenon, or certain aggravated forms of this phenomenon would run counter to the essential aims of punishment laid down in human rights treaties. Earlier, British lawyers had suggested this approach in cases before the HRC.

In June 2002 the Court issued its Judgment. It found that the State had violated the right to life of all 32 petitioners (Articles 4(1) and 4(2)) in conjunction with Article 1(1). It also found a violation of Article 2 ACHR (obligation to adopt the necessary legislative or other measures). Trinidad had violated, moreover, their right to humane treatment (Articles 5(1) and 5(2)). Finally, it found 32 violations of the right of every person condemned to death to apply for amnesty, pardon or commutation of sentence, laid down in Article 4(6). With regard to 30 of them, the Court found a violation of the right to trial within a reasonable time (Articles 7(5) and 8(1)) and with regard to eleven of them a violation of the right to judicial protection (Articles 8 and 25). On top of all these violations the Court found that Trinidad arbitrarily deprived Joey Ramiah of his right to life in violation of Article 4 ACHR by executing him pending the proceedings.[73] Subsequently the provisional measures were maintained on behalf of those petitioners still under sentence of death.[74]

In *Boyce and Joseph* v. *Barbados* (2004) the Inter-American Court pointed out that 'in this case the measures mandated are designed to allow the organs of the Inter-American system of human rights protection to evaluate the possible existence of a violation of Articles 2, 4, 5 and 8 of the American Convention'.[75] In 2007 the Court found the State in violation of various provisions of the ACHR.[76] It ordered, among others, that the State must commute the death sentence of Michael McDonald Huggins and adopt the necessary measures to ensure that the death penalty is not imposed in a way that violates the rights and freedoms guaranteed in the ACHR and, in particular, that it not be imposed by means of a compulsory judgment; it must also take legislative or other measures to eliminate the effect of a provision in its Constitution that makes it impossible to contest 'existing laws'; and, the State's obligations arising from the Court's provisional measures in this case should be replaced by the obligations specified in the judgment.[77]

Already in 1983 the Inter-American Court had pointed out that States that still applied the death penalty were not to extend it to situations to which it did not previously apply. Its unanimous advice was 'that the Convention imposes an absolute prohibition on the extension of death penalty and that, consequently, the State Party cannot apply the death penalty to crimes for which such a penalty was not previously provided for under its domestic law'. The Court also found, unanimously, 'that a reservation restricted by its own wording to Article 4(4) of the Convention does not allow the Government of a State Party to extend by subsequent legislation the applica-

---

[73]   See IACHR *Hilaire, Constantine and Benjamin et al.* v. *Trinidad & Tobago*, 21 June 2002.

[74]   See e.g. IACHR *James et al.*, Order of 28 February 2005. See further on maintaining provisional measures e.g. Chapter XIV (Jurisdiction and admissibility).

[75]   IACHR *Boyce and Joseph* v. *Barbados*, Order of 25 November 2004, 7th 'Considering' clause. See also 1st 'Having seen' clause: the provisional measures are taken so as not to hinder the processing of their cases before the Inter-American system.

[76]   IACHR *Boyce et al.* (*Barbados*), Judgment on Preliminary Objection, Merits, Reparations and Costs, 20 November 2007 (finding that Barbados had violated the Articles 4(1) and 4(2) ACHR (Right to Life), in relation to Article 1(1) (obligation to respect rights); it had also violated Article 2 (Domestic Legal Effect), in relation to Articles 1(1), 4(1), 4(2) and 25(1) (Judicial Protection); and Articles 5(1) and 5(2) ACHR (Right to Humane Treatment) in relation to Article 1(1), all to the detriment of Lennox Ricardo Boyce, Jeffrey Joseph, Frederick Benjamin Atkins and Michael McDonald Huggins).

[77]   IACHR *Boyce et al.* (*Barbados*), Judgment on Preliminary Objection, Merits, Reparations and Costs, 20 November 2007.

tion of the death penalty to crimes for which this penalty was not previously provided'.[78] In *Rax-cacó Reyes* v. *Guatemala* (2005) the Court found a violation of the prohibition to extend the death penalty to situations to which it did not previously apply (Article 4(2)).[79] It also found that this State's domestic legislation, punishing by death any type of kidnapping, violated the principle in Article 4(2) that the death penalty should be limited to the worst crimes only.[80]

3.4 Unpublished provisional measures to halt executions

3.4.1 Introduction

In order to clarify the relationship with the merits in the unpublished provisional measures by the HRC (and most other human rights adjudicators), it is all the more important to know what the claims were in cases in which provisional measures were taken. An examination of known cases in which the HRC took provisional measures in death penalty cases shows that apart from the right to life itself (Article 6), the rights most regularly claimed by detainees on death row are the right to a fair trial (Article 14), the security of person and pre-trial rights (Article 9), the prohibition of torture or cruel treatment (Article 7) and the right to humane treatment in detention (Article 10).

The subsequent sections deal with various components of the case law on the death penalty. The focus is on the approach of the HRC, but where relevant references are made to other adjudicators. Section 3.4.2 deals with the right to life as such and refers to the case law of the ECtHR and Bosnia Chamber. Section 3.4.3 discusses rights relating to the person sentenced to death: juvenile death penalty and mandatory death penalty. Section 3.4.4 involves rights relating to the death penalty proceedings and, finally, section 3.4.5 deals with the significance of the death row phenomenon, including its impact on individual petitioners.

---

[78] See IACHR *Restrictions to the death penalty*, Advisory Opinion OC-3/83, 8 September 1983. Before its provisional measures in *James et al.* and its Judgment in *Hilaire, Constantine and Benjamin et al.*, the Inter-American Court only dealt with the issue of the death penalty as part of its advisory function. In this Advisory Opinion the Commission had requested the Court's Advisory Opinion in light of three cases pending before it in which Guatemala has executed persons on the basis of trials before Courts of Special Jurisdiction. On the basis of its reservation to Article 4(4) ACHR Guatemala had justified its extension of the death penalty to crimes for which this penalty was not previously provided under its domestic law. Article 4(4) stipulates: "In no case shall capital punishment be inflicted for political offences or related common crimes". In reference to the Court's Advisory Opinion the Commission subsequently found Guatemala in violation of Article 4 ACHR. Resolution 15/84 of the Commission against Guatemala (cases 8094, 9083 and 9080), 3 October 1984, Informe Anual 1984-1985. Only the Commission could deal with these cases as a contentious matter, because Guatemala just accepted the Court's contentious jurisdiction in March 1987.

[79] IACHR *Raxcacó Reyes* v. *Guatemala*, 15 September 2005, §§57-66.

[80] IACHR *Raxcacó Reyes* v. *Guatemala*, 15 September 2005, §§67-72. See also *Hilaire, Constantine et al., Benjamin et al.* v. *Trinidad & Tobago*, 21 June 2002, §§106-108. See further on the case of *Case of Raxcacó Reyes et al.* (Guatemala), the Court's Order of 21 November 2007 deciding, among others, to lift the provisional measures adopted by the Court in favor of Pablo Arturo Ruiz Almengor, but to reiterate to the State that it must maintain the necessary measures to project the life of Bernardino Rodríguez Lara so as not to obstruct the processing of his case before the inter-American system for the protection of human rights; and to remind the State that, in its judgment *Raxcacó Reyes* v. *Guatemala*, 15 September 2005, as a measure of non-repetition it had ordered the State abstain from applying the death penalty and executing those convicted of the crime of kidnapping or abduction.

3.4.2 The right to life as such

The adjudicators have to deal with treaty texts on the right to life that were drafted when the death penalty was still common in many States. Thus, these texts often refer to States in which the death penalty is still applied, simply posing limitations to their use. The question arises whether provisional measures have been taken also in cases in which a violation was later found on the basis of a more dynamic interpretation of the provisions on the right to life or only in such cases in which there would likely be a violation even on the basis of a restrictive interpretation.

3.4.2.1 ECtHR

In the *Soering* case (1989) the ECtHR established that capital punishment under certain conditions was still permitted by Article 2(1) ECHR.[81] It acknowledged that subsequent practice could remove a textual limit on the scope for dynamic or evolutive interpretation of Article 3 ECHR. In the circumstances of the case it found that the extradition of Soering to the US would violate Article 3 because of the death row phenomenon in the state of Virginia.[82] In this case both the Commission and the ECtHR used provisional measures. The decisions on the merits do not further clarify whether they would equally use such measures in other cases involving the death penalty.

Only very recently the ECtHR slightly adapted its approach to the right to life as such. In *Öcalan* v. *Turkey* (2005) the Grand Chamber agreed with the First Section of the ECtHR, which decided in 2003 that both the concepts of inhuman and degrading treatment and the legal position with regard to the death penalty had 'undergone a considerable evolution' since the entry into force of the Convention and indeed since its *Soering* judgment.

> "The *de facto* abolition noted in that case in respect of twenty-two contracting States in 1989 has developed into a *de jure* abolition in forty-three of the forty-four Contracting States and a moratorium in the remaining State which has not yet abolished the penalty, namely Russia".

All States have signed and all but three have ratified Protocol No. 6. The practice is 'further reflected' in the policy of the Council of Europe creating a death penalty free zone by requiring abolition as a condition of membership.

> "Such a marked development could now be taken as signalling the agreement of the Contracting States to abrogate, or at the very least to modify, the second sentence of Article 2 §1, particularly when regard is had to the fact that all Contracting States have now signed Protocol No. 6 and that it has been ratified by forty-one States. It may be questioned whether it is necessary to await ratification of Protocol No. 6 by the three remaining States before concluding that the death penalty exception in Article 2 has been significantly modified. Against such a consistent background, it can be said that capital punishment in peacetime has come to be regarded as an unacceptable ... form of punishment which is no longer permissible under Article 2".[83]

Yet it subsequently retracted somewhat from this statement by replaying its argument that by opening for signature Protocol No. 13 (on the abolition of the death penalty in all circumstances)

---

[81] ECtHR *Soering* v. *United Kingdom*, Judgement of 7 July 1989.

[82] See later in this Chapter under the heading 'death row phenomenon'. On provisional measures to halt extradition see Chapter V.

[83] ECtHR Grand Chamber *Öcalan* v. *Turkey*, Judgment of 12 May 2005, §163, quoting *Öcalan* v. *Turkey* (First Section), 12 March 2003, §§189-196.

the Contracting States had 'chosen the additional method of amendment of the text of the Convention in pursuit of their policy of abolition'. It did acknowledge that 'this final step toward complete abolition of the death penalty' could also 'be seen as confirmation of the abolitionist trend in the practice of the Contracting States'. Thus, Protocol 13 'does not necessarily run counter to the view that Article 2 has been amended in so far as it permits the death penalty in times of peace'.[84] Taken together this statement seems to lean towards construing Article 2 as no longer permitting the death penalty. Nevertheless, the Grand Chamber subsequently agreed with the Chamber that there was no need to reach 'any firm conclusion' on this issue because 'even if Article 2 were to be construed as still permitting the death penalty' it would in any case be contrary to the Convention 'to implement a death sentence following an unfair trial'.[85] It agreed with the Chamber's reasoning that the implementation of the death penalty following an unfair trial would not be permissible.[86] The Chamber had pointed out that Article 2 'ranks as one of the most fundamental provisions of the Convention'.

> "Even if the death penalty were still permissible under Article 2, the Court considers that an arbitrary deprivation of life pursuant to capital punishment is prohibited".

The Chamber determined that Öcalan had not had a fair trial so that his execution would have resulted in a violation of Article 2. This conclusion 'must inform' the Court's opinion when it considers whether the imposition of the death penalty had resulted in a violation of Article 3 ECHR. The Court found such a violation because Öcalan had spent several years facing execution on the basis of an unfair trial.

> "In the Court's view, to impose a death sentence on a person after an unfair trial is to subject that person wrongfully to the fear the he will be executed. The fear and uncertainty as to the future generated by a sentence of death, in circumstances where there exists a real possibility that the sentence will be enforced, must give rise to a significant degree of human anguish. Such anguish cannot be dissociated from the unfairness of the proceedings underlying the sentence which, given that human life is at stake, becomes unlawful under the Convention".[87]

In *Öcalan* the ECtHR indicated that the execution of the petitioner would constitute a violation of Article 2 because his trial had been unfair. The Inter-American Court has equally considered that, as long as the execution itself is not carried out, the imposition of the death penalty without due process does not result in a violation of the right to life.[88] Like the ECtHR this Court has held that

---

84 ECtHR (Grand Chamber), *Öcalan* v. *Turkey*, Judgment of 12 May 2005, §164.

85 ECtHR (Grand Chamber), *Öcalan* v. *Turkey*, Judgment of 12 May 2005, §165. The Grand Chamber continues its approach in *Soering* with regard to the traditional method of amendment and the interpretation of Article 3 ECHR. It considers that 'the fact that there are still a large number of States who have yet to sign or ratify Protocol No. 13' may presently prevent it 'from finding that it is the established practice of the Contracting States to regard the implementation of the death penalty as inhuman and degrading treatment' contrary to Article 3. It believes that this may be so because the rights in Article 3 are non-derogable, 'even in times of war'.

86 The Court imposing the penalty must be independent and impartial and 'the most rigorous standards of fairness' must be observed 'in the criminal proceedings both at first instance and on appeal'. Grand Chamber, *Öcalan* v. *Turkey*, Judgment of 12 May 2005, §166, quoting *Öcalan* v. *Turkey* (First Section), 12 March 2003, §§201-204. The Court referred to the irreversible nature of an execution, ECOSOC Resolution 1984/50, the decisions of the HRC, the Inter-American Court judgment *Hilaire, Constantine and Benjamin et al.* v. *Trinidad and Tobago* and that Court's Advisory Opinion on consular assistance.

87 ECtHR (Grand Chamber), *Öcalan* v. *Turkey*, Judgment of 12 May 2005, §164.

88 See IACHR *Fermín Ramírez* v. *Guatemala*, 20 June 2005, §103.

having suffered adverse conditions of detention and having been sentenced to death after a trial in violation of the principle of due process constituted a violation of the right to respect for each person's physical, mental and moral integrity and the prohibition of cruel, inhuman or degrading treatment (Article 5 (1)(2)).[89]

Thus, the Court did not find a violation of Article 2 for the imposition of the death penalty following an unfair trial, but only indicated that the execution of the petitioner would constitute such violation. Its alternative argument based on Article 3 is somewhat strained because there would be anguish in any case, independent of the fairness of the proceedings. Moreover, the first sentence seems to imply that a person can also *rightfully* be subjected to the fear of execution, while the Chamber previously emphasized that capital punishment in peace time has come to be regarded as unacceptable. While the Court was unwilling to explicitly construe Article 2 as excluding the death penalty, replicating the conundrum created in *Soering* with the 'traditional method of amendment' approach,[90] it would have been more convincing for it to have found a violation of Article 2 for imposition of the death penalty after an unfair trial rather than a violation of Article 3. The Court's approach perpetuates an unclear situation with regard to provisional measures that could arise particularly in non-refoulement cases. The question arises whether it would use provisional measures in cases in which imposition of the death penalty would be likely, but execution may not necessarily follow because the death penalty is not applied actively at the time of the decision on provisional measures. The ECtHR, for instance, refused to take provisional measures to halt the transfer of Saddam Hussein to the Iraqi Interim Government, which did not actively apply the death penalty at the time. After he was handed over the Interim Government re-instated the penalty. While this may be predominantly an issue of assessment of risk, the Court's complicated reasoning, regarding Articles 2 and 3 may in itself have repercussions for the use of provisional measures.

The interpretation by the ECtHR of Articles 2 and 3 ECHR in the *Soering* and *Öcalan* judgments is not entirely convincing. The Court's acknowledgment, in *Soering*, that subsequent practice could remove a textual limit on the scope for dynamic or evolutive interpretation of Article 3 is indeed consonant with the longstanding view that the ECHR is a living instrument. Nevertheless, the Court used Protocol No. 6 (on the abolition of the death penalty in peace time) not to show a practice and conviction on the part of the member States of the Council of Europe, but to establish that the Contracting Parties intended the normal method of amendment of the text in order to introduce a new obligation to abolish the death penalty. Protocol 6, however, was adopted to lay down and secure, and certainly not to limit, the interpretation of Article 2 ECHR. Reflecting the contemporary standards of justice in Europe, the Protocol takes into account the subsequent practice and codification. In his Concurring Opinion Judge De Meyer considered that the death penalty is not consistent with the present state of European civilisation. 'Extraditing somebody in such circumstances', he said, 'would be repugnant to European standards of justice, and contrary to the public order of Europe'.[91] It is unfortunate that in *Öcalan* the Court stuck with its traditional inter-state 'treaty amendment' approach. Its members seem to have in mind images of politicians conspiring together to indicate to the Court that it should not meddle. While there may be some truth to such images in other contexts, including with regard to human rights issues, given the general attitude within the Council of Europe vis-à-vis the death penalty, the approach of judge Garlicki in his Concurring Opinion appears more realistic. He points out that 'it can no longer be disputed that – on the European level – there is a consensus as to the inhuman nature of the death penalty'.

---

[89] IACHR *Fermín Ramírez* v. *Guatemala*, 20 June 2005, §§114-120.

[90] Or as Garlicki calls it, 'a doctrine of pre-emption', ECtHR (Grand Chamber), *Öcalan* v. *Turkey*, Judgment of 12 May 2005, Concurring Opinion Judge Garlicki, §5.

[91] ECtHR *Soering* v. *United Kingdom*, Judgement of 7 July 1989, Concurring Opinion Judge De Meyer.

"Therefore, the fact that governments and politicians are preparing a formal amendment to the Convention may be understood more as a signal that capital punishment should no longer exist than as a decision pre-empting the Court from acting on its own initiative".[92]

In fact the Court is not acting on its own initiative, but simply interpreting the provisions invoked. Yet in its interpretation it should not box itself into a corner, away from its normal 'living instrument' approach. This living instrument approach is particularly warranted in the context of the right to life and the prohibition of cruel treatment. After all the Court considers Articles 2 and 3 to be the most fundamental rights in the Convention. Garlicki correctly points out that the Court 'seems to be convinced that there is no room for the death penalty even within the original text of the Convention [b]ut at the same time, it has chosen not to express that position in a universally binding manner'. He considers the Court 'could and should have gone further in this case'.[93] The ECHR 'represents a very distinct form of international instrument and – in many respects – its substance and process of application are more akin to those of national constitutions than to those of 'typical' international treaties'.[94]

"[A]s long as the member States have not clearly rejected a particular judicial interpretation of the Convention', it is 'legitimate to assume' that 'the Court has the power to determine the actual meaning of words and phrases which were inserted into the text of the Convention more than fifty years ago'. "In any event, and this seems to be the situation with regard to the death penalty, the Court may so proceed when its interpretation remains in harmony with the values and standards that have been endorsed by the member States".[95]

While the Court could have gone further on the merits, it did use provisional measures, which indicates that they have been taken also in cases in which a violation later could have been found on the basis of a more dynamic interpretation of the provisions on the right to life.

3.4.2.2 BOSNIA AND PROTOCOL NO. 6 TO THE ECHR (ABOLITION IN PEACE TIME)

The Bosnia Chamber has specifically interpreted Protocol No. 6 to the ECHR on the abolition of the death penalty in peace time. The petitioner had submitted that his execution would violate his human rights as guaranteed by Annex 6 of the Peace Agreement. The respondent Party had argued that the execution would be covered by Article 2 of Protocol No. 6 and would not involve any violation of the petitioner's rights. The Chamber used provisional measures in 1996 and 1997. On the merits it pointed out that Article 1 of the Protocol prohibited both the imposition and the execution of the death penalty. This prohibition is absolute and subject only to the exception in Article 2. The obligations under the Protocol became effective in December 1995 when the General Framework Agreement entered into force. The Chamber then proceeded with its interpretation of Article 2 of the Protocol. It noted that, as an exception to the rule, it should be 'narrowly interpreted'. After all the right to life was one of the most fundamental provisions in the ECHR.[96] It considered that before the exception could apply 'there must be specific provision in

---

92   ECtHR (Grand Chamber), *Öcalan* v. *Turkey*, Judgment of 12 May 2005, Concurring Opinion Judge Garlicki, §5.

93   Id., §2.

94   Id., §4.

95   Ibid.

96   Bosnia Chamber *Sretko Damjanović* v. *Fed. BiH*, 5 September 1997 (merits), §29. See also *Herak* v. *Fed. BiHH*, 12 June 1998, §§ 50-51.

domestic law authorising the use of the death penalty in respect of defined acts committed in time of war or of imminent threat of war'.

> "The law must define with adequate precision the acts in respect of which the death penalty may be applied, the circumstances in which it may be applied, and the concepts of 'time of war or imminent threat of war'. Article 2 requires that before it can apply the legislature should have considered and defined the circumstances in which, exceptionally in the context of a legal system where the death penalty has been abolished, such penalty may nevertheless be applied in respect of acts committed in time of war or imminent threat thereof".[97]

The provisions on the basis of which the petitioner was sentenced to death were not restricted to 'time of war or imminent threat of war'. Neither did they have the necessary precision.[98] Moreover, the obligation in the Constitution to secure the rights and obligations in the international agreements listed in Annex I made the death penalty provisions inapplicable as a matter of national law, because of the Second OP to the ICCPR.[99] The Second OP imposed 'an absolute prohibition, without the possibility of any reservation or exception, on the imposition or carrying out of the death penalty in time of peace'. Since Bosnia was not in a state of war anymore, executing the petitioner would be contrary to the Second OP.[100] The domestic law authorising execution of the death penalty in peace time was inconsistent with the Constitution because of the Constitution's general obligation to 'secure the highest level of internationally recognised human rights'. According to the Bosnia Chamber the obligation to secure the other human rights agreements (including the Second OP to ICCPR) without discrimination included 'both an obligation to secure the rights in question to all persons and an obligation to do so without discrimination'.[101]

> "Where one of the human rights agreements referred to imposes a clear, precise and absolute prohibition on a particular course of action, the only way in which the obligation to secure the right in question to all persons without discrimination can be carried out is by giving effect to the prohibition".[102]

---

[97]   Bosnia Chamber *Sretko Damjanović* v. *Fed. BiH*, 5 September 1997 (merits), §32. See also *Herak* v. *Fed. BiH*, 12 June 1998, §49.

[98]   Bosnia Chamber *Herak* v. *Fed. BiHH*, 12 June 1998, §§ 50-51.

[99]   Id., 12 June 1998, §§52-56, referring to Articles I, II(4) and II(1) of the Constitution (as set out in Annex 4 to the General Framework Agreement). In the earlier case *Damjanović* the Chamber's formulation was less precise, triggering a concurring opinion by Nowak and Möller. They pointed out that under the Constitution the right not to be executed 'is an absolute right and all organs of the State of BH and its entities have the constitutional obligation to secure this right'. Referring to Article II(4) of the Constitution they explained that the Constitutional obligation to secure the right not to be executed had to be distinguished from the international obligations under Annex 6 and the jurisdiction of the Chamber to consider complaints about violations of the Second OP to the ICCPR only in case of alleged or apparent discrimination.

[100]   Bosnia Chamber *Sretko Damjanović* v. *Fed. BiH*, 5 September 1997 (merits), §36 and *Herak* v. *Fed. BiHH*, 12 June 1998, §54.

[101]   Bosnia Chamber *Sretko Damjanović* v. *Fed. BiH*, 5 September 1997 (merits), §37 and *Herak* v. *Fed. BiH*, 12 June 1998, §56.

[102]   Bosnia Chamber *Sretko Damjanović* v. *Fed. BiH*, 5 September 1997 (merits), §37 and *Herak* v. *Fed. BiH*, 12 June 1998, §56.

3.4.2.3 HRC AND THE RIGHT TO LIFE AS SUCH

The HRC has struggled with issues similar to those of the ECtHR. In the extradition cases *Kindler* v. *Canada* and *Ng* v. *Canada* (1993) it had to decide on the right to life and the relationship between Articles 6(1) and (2) as well as on the relevance of the death row phenomenon in the context of Article 7. It has, thus far, interpreted Article 6 ICCPR rather than the Second Optional Protocol (1987), abolishing the death penalty (Second OP).[103]

In fact the HRC took the same approach of reading Article 7 in light of Article 6(2). It concluded that 'capital punishment as such, within the parameters of Article 6, paragraph 2, does not *per se* violate Article 7'.[104] Moreover, it referred to its previous jurisprudence on the death row phenomenon and interpreted the ECtHR decision on the death row phenomenon, *Soering* v. *UK*, restrictively, by emphasizing this Court's analysis of the specific situation of Soering over its discussion of the death row phenomenon in general. It then distinguished Kindler's situation from Soering's by stating that the facts of the case differed as to age, mental state and conditions on death row, which in Kindler's case was in Pennsylvania, and in Soering's case in Virginia. It also noted that in *Soering* there was a simultaneous request for extradition by a State where the death penalty would not be imposed.[105] In *Ng* v. *Canada* the Committee reasoned along the same lines as in *Kindler* (1993). The dissenters, similarly, followed their reasoning in that case. The Committee stated that it was aware that 'by definition, every execution of a sentence of death may be considered to constitute cruel and inhuman treatment within the meaning of Article 7 of the Covenant'. At the same time it noted that Article 6(2) permitted the imposition of capital punishment. It also pointed out, however, that any method of execution must be designed in such a way as to avoid conflict with Article 7. The petitioner had provided 'detailed information that execution by gas asphyxiation may cause prolonged suffering and agony and does not result in death as swiftly as possible, as asphyxiation by cyanide gas may take over 10 minutes'. The HRC pointed out that the State had had the opportunity to refute these allegations, but had failed to do so.[106] It considered that Canada could reasonably have foreseen that the petitioner, if sentenced to death, would be executed in a way that amounts to a violation of Article 7, because execution by gas asphyxiation did not meet the test of 'least possible physical and mental suffering'.[107] Consequently Canada had failed to comply with its obligations under the Covenant by extraditing Ng without having sought assurances that he would not be executed.[108]

---

[103] Adopted 15 December 1987, entered into force 11 July 1991, G.A. Res. 44/128, 44 UN GAOR Supp. (No. 49) at 206, A/44/49 (1989). The reason for this is the fact that the extradition cases dealing with this issue were all against Canada. While this State has abolished the death penalty it is not yet a party to the OP2. Australia is a party, but in *A.R.J.* v. *Australia* the HRC concluded that there was no real risk of the death penalty. This meant it did not need to discuss the Second OP. From the View it is not clear whether it may have used provisional measures, with this Protocol in mind but the files show that the HRC indeed did so in light of the Second OP (on file with the author).

[104] HRC *Kindler* v. *Canada*, 30 July 1993.

[105] Id. Note that the Supreme Court of Zimbabwe, for instance, has interpreted *Soering* much less restrictively. Section 3.4.5 of this Chapter discusses the issue of the death row phenomenon.

[106] HRC *Ng* v. *Canada*, 5 November 1993, §16.3. "Rather, the State party has confined itself to arguing that in the absence of a norm of international law which expressly prohibits asphyxiation by cyanide gas, 'it would be interfering to an unwarranted degree with the internal laws and practices of the United States to refuse to extradite a fugitive to face the possible imposition of the death penalty by cyanide gas asphyxiation'".

[107] HRC *Ng* v. *Canada*, 5 November 1993, §16.4.

[108] Five members of the HRC would have found a violation of Article 7 on different grounds. Pocar and Lallah considered that because they would find a violation of Article 6, they would necessarily find a violation of Article 7 as well. Aguilar Urbina pointed out that the death penalty

In *Judge* v. *Canada* (2003) the HRC reversed *Kindler*. It recognised that it should ensure consistency and coherence of its jurisprudence but noted that 'there may be exceptional situations in which a review of the scope of application of the rights protected in the Covenant is required'. As examples it mentioned situations 'where an alleged violation involves that most fundamental of rights – the right to life – and in particular if there have been notable factual and legal developments and changes in international opinion in respect of the issue raised'. The *Kindler* decision dated from ten years prior. It noted that 'since that time there has been a broadening international consensus in favour of abolition of the death penalty, and in states which have retained the death penalty, a broadening consensus not to carry it out'.

Paragraphs 2 to 6 'have the dual function of creating an exception to the right to life in respect of the death penalty and laying down limits on the scope of that exception'. The HRC acknowledged that by interpreting paragraphs 1 and 2 of Article 6 in this way abolitionist and retentionist States parties were treated differently. This was 'an inevitable consequence of the wording of the provision itself'. It also pointed out that many delegates participating in the drafting process already saw the death penalty as an 'anomaly' or a 'necessary evil'. The Committee noted that it would appear logical to interpret the rule in Article 6(1) 'in a wide sense' and to interpret Article 6(2) narrowly.[109]

Given the fact that the HRC overturned its previous case law it is not surprising that some members attached an individual opinion.[110] Lallah underscored the importance of the decision and

---

as such constituted cruel, inhuman and degrading treatment in violation of that article and not only in case of gas asphyxiation. In any case he considered that the application of the death penalty was subsumed by the violation of Article 6. See §11 of *Ng* v. *Canada*. Chanet considered that the HRC had engaged in 'questionable discussion' when it assessed the suffering caused by cyanide gas and took 'into consideration the duration of the agony'. She wondered whether it would find no violation if the agony lasted nine minutes, now it has deemed unacceptable an agony lasting more than ten minutes. She noted that a strict interpretation of Article 6 could have prevented this debate. Wennergren, finally, quoted one of the dissenting justices of the US Supreme Court in a 1992 case denying an individual a stay of execution by gas asphyxiation in California. Justice John Paul Stevens wrote: "The barbaric use of cyanide gas in the Holocaust, the development of cyanide agents as chemical weapons, our contemporary understanding of execution by lethal gas, and the development of less cruel methods of execution all demonstrate that execution by cyanide gas is unnecessarily cruel". Wennergren considered that this summarised 'in a very convincing way' why the use of this method amounts to a violation of Article 7. He also explained that he did not consider execution by lethal injection acceptable either 'from a point of view of humanity' but at least this did 'not stand out as an unnecessarily cruel and inhumane method of execution, as does gas asphyxiation'. On the other hand, two other members of the HRC would not have found a violation of Article 7 at all. Herndl emphatically disagreed with the HRC's finding of a violation of Article 7 because of the execution method. He criticised the fact that the HRC gave only one reason to substantiate its finding of a violation, namely that the execution method did not meet the test of the 'least possible physical and mental suffering'. He considered it futile to attempt to establish categories of execution methods, because it was 'futile to attempt to quantify the pain and suffering of any human being subjected to capital punishment'. This was so, as long as 'such methods were not manifestly arbitrary and grossly contrary to the moral values of a democratic society, and as long as such methods are based on a uniformly applicable legislation adopted by democratic processes'. Ando equally disagreed with the finding of a violation of Article 7. The only thing he was certain of was that the article 'prohibits any method of execution which is intended for prolonging suffering of the executed or causing unnecessary pain to him or her'.

[109] HRC *Judge* v. *Canada*, 5 August 2003, §10.5.

[110] Committee member Solari Yrigoyen, for instance, provided an alternative text. He would have preferred an approach in which the Committee had found a violation of Article 14(5) because of

added three observations. He recalled that while it was 'encouraging' to note a 'broadening international consensus in favour of the abolition of the death penalty', it was 'appropriate to recall that, even at the time when the Committee was considering its views in Kindler some 10 years ago, the Committee was quite divided' in relation to Article 6. He pointed out that no less than five members of the Committee dissented in that case 'precisely on the nature, operation and interpretation of Article 6(1) of the Covenant'. To illustrate this he appended their individual opinions in *Kindler* (1993) to his separate opinion in *Judge* (2003).[111] While Judge was deported to the US before the HRC could take provisional measures, this case clarifies that such measures vis-à-vis non-death penalty States should always be used in refoulement cases involving a real risk of imposition of the death penalty.

3.4.3 The right to life and the person of the petitioner

This section focus on two issues pertaining to the person of the petitioner: the death penalty for minors and the mandatory death penalty. The first issue is that of the death penalty for minors. The Inter-American Commission has found that not only had a norm of customary international law emerged prohibiting juvenile death penalty, but that this norm was of 'a sufficiently indelible

---

the automatic review of the petitioner's death sentence in absentia. This would result in a violation of Article 6. His approach may originate from a wish not to overrule previous case law. Chanet clearly subscribed to the Committee's new approach, which she had advocated more than ten years previously in Kindler, but considered that the Committee should not have given an opinion in this case about Article 14(5). She considered that while the HRC could 'declare itself competent to assess the degree of risk to life (death sentence) or to physical integrity (torture), it is less obvious that it can base an opinion that a violation has occurred in a State party to the Covenant on a third State's failure to observe a provision of the Covenant'. The HRC had examined this claim and declared it inadmissible for failure to substantiate. In other words, Chanet considered that the HRC should not have examined this claim for admissibility *ratione materiae* in the first place. She argued that now that the HRC directly addressed the fundamental question of the compatibility with Article 6 of extradition without assurances, the issue of the irregularity of the procedure followed in the third State became irrelevant because an abolitionist State cannot expel or extradite a petitioner to a State where he could be executed. About deportation and extradition in the face of risks of an unfair procedure in the receiving or requesting State (the third State) Chanet noted that while the HRC 'can ascertain that a State party has not taken any undue risks, and may perhaps give an opinion on the precautions taken by the State party to that end, it can never really be sure whether a third State has violated the rights guaranteed by the Covenant if that State is not a party to the procedure'. She mentioned some of the other problems involved: what if the third State is not a party to the ICCPR or the OP? 'Does the obligation of a State party to the Covenant in its relations with third States cover all the rights in the Covenant or only some of them? Could a State party to the Covenant enter a reservation to exclude implementation of the Covenant from its bilateral relations with another State?'.

[111] HRC *Judge* v. *Austria* (2003). He also observed that other provisions of the ICCPR may be relevant in interpreting Article 6(1). He noted in particular Articles 5(2) and 26. Finally, he observed that the Supreme Court of Canada's decision in *Burns* was encouraging, although he wondered about its remark that assurances against the death penalty must be obtained 'subject to exceptions'. He was not sure whether it was possible conceptually to envisage such exceptions, 'given the autonomy of Article 6(1) and the possible impact of Article 5(2) and also Article 26 which governs the legislative, executive and judicial behaviour of States parties'. "That, however, is a bridge to be crossed by the Committee in an appropriate case". The dissents by Ando and Solari Yrigoyen did not relate to the interpretation of Article 6(1). All members participating in the decision agreed with this interpretation. Pursuant to Rule 85 Wedgwood (US) did not participate in the adoption of the View.

nature' to constitute a norm of *ius cogens*.[112] Imposition of the death penalty for crimes committed below the age of 18 constitutes a violation of the right to life under Article I of the American Declaration. Execution of a person in such circumstances would be 'a further grave and irreparable violation' of the right to life.[113]

The HRC has also found a violation of Article 7 in a case of a minor on death row. In *Johnson* v. *Jamaica* (1998) the petitioner's age was not a factor in finding a death row phenomenon in violation of Article 7, but the imposition of the death sentence itself was void *ab initio* – and as such in violation of Article 7 – because of the violation of Article 6(5) forbidding the death penalty for persons under 18 at the time of the crime.[114]

The other issue that has arisen is whether the mandatory death penalty is prohibited or not. The Inter-American Commission[115] and Court have considered it is indeed prohibited.[116] The Court, for instance, found a violation of Article 4(1) ACHR because domestic legislation prevented courts from establishing the degree of culpability of a convicted person and compelled the

---

[112] Apart from the fact that the rejection by States of the juvenile death penalty was virtually uniform, it referred to the non-derogable nature of the relevant treaty provisions and pointed out that 'the acceptance of this norm crosses political and ideological boundaries and efforts to detract from this standard have been vigorously condemned'. CIDH *Domingues* v. *US*, 22 October 2002, §85. When discussing on the merits whether the American Declaration prohibits the execution of persons convicted of a crime committed when they were below the age of 18 the Inter-American Commission has interpreted its provisions 'in the context of pertinent developments in customary international law and the norms of jus cogens'. It has taken into account 'evidence of relevant state practice as disclosed by various sources, including recitals in treaties and other international instruments, a pattern of treaties in the same form, the practice of the United Nations and other international governmental organisations, and the domestic legislation and judicial decisions of states'. CIDH *Domingues* v. *US*, 22 October 2002, §54. See further e.g. *Shaka Sankofa* (*Gary Graham*) v. *US*, 29 December 2003 and *Patterson* v. *US*, 7 March 2005. For an earlier approach by the Commission see *Roach and Pinkerton* v. *US*, 22 September 1987.

[113] See e.g. CIDH *Domingues* v. *US*, 22 October 2002, §§87 and 112.

[114] HRC *Clive Johnson* v. *Jamaica*, 20 October 1998. See also *Alfredo Baroy* v. *the Philippines*, 31 October 2003 (inadm.). In this case the HRC used provisional measures both to halt the petitioner's execution and to speedily determine his age and treat him as a minor in the meantime. Subsequent to this provisional measure a domestic court reduced his sentence, 'for reasons other than alleged minority', to *reclusion perpetua*. Thus, the HRC considered that the issues with regard to alleged violations of Article 6 had become moot. Nevertheless it observed that 'sentencing a person to death and placing him or her on death row in circumstances where his or her minority has not been finally determined raises serious issues under articles 10 and 14, as well as potentially under article 7, of the Covenant'. It noted, however, that at the time of its consideration of the case domestic remedies had not been exhausted.

[115] See e.g. CIDH *Lamey, Mykoo, Montique & Daley* v. *Jamaica*, 4 April 2001 (the mandatory death penalty, excluding consideration of the individual circumstances of each offender and offence results in arbitrary deprivation of life in violation of Article 4 (1) ACHR; this also precludes 'any effective review by a higher court as to the propriety of a sentence of death in the circumstances of a particular case', which cannot be reconciled with the fundamental principles of due process under Articles 4 and 8; moreover, it 'deprives an individual of the most fundamental rights without considering whether this exceptional form of punishment is appropriate in the circumstances of the individual's case', which is contrary to the essential respect for the dignity of the individual, underlying Article 5) and CIDH *Thomas* v. *Jamaica*, 3 December 2001.

[116] IACHR *Hilaire, Constantine et al., Benjamin et al.* v. *Trinidad & Tobago*, 21 June 2002, §105 and IACHR *Raxcacó Reyes* v. *Guatemala*, 15 September 2005.

indiscriminate imposition of the death penalty.[117] The international adjudicator has taken a similar approach. In fact both the Inter-American Commission and Court have referred to the HRC's case law in this respect, while it, in turn, seems to have been inspired by the Inter-American case law. In all cases involving the mandatory death penalty the HRC also used provisional measures, even when it had not yet interpreted Article 6 as prohibiting such penalty. In *Thompson v. St. Vincent & the Grenadines* (2000)[118] it found the mandatory death penalty, as applied in this State, in violation of Article 6(1), since it was 'based solely upon the category of crime for which the offender is found guilty, without regard to the defendant's personal circumstances or the circumstances of the particular offence'.[119] In *Kennedy v. Trinidad and Tobago* (2002)[120] the Committee confirmed the decision in *Thompson* by establishing that mandatory capital punishment for certain categories of crime may indeed constitute a violation of Article 6(1).[121] Counsel had argued, following the decision of the Inter-American Commission in *Hilaire v. Trinidad and Tobago* (1999),[122] that the mandatory death sentence constituted a violation of Articles 6(1), 7 and 26 ICCPR. This decision seems to have followed US Supreme Court decisions declaring the mandatory death sentence to be unconstitutional.[123] The HRC has considered that 'such a system of mandatory capital punishment would deprive the author of the most fundamental of rights, the right to life, without considering whether this exceptional form of punishment is appropriate in the circumstances of his or her case'. Discretionary measures by the executive, such as the right to

---

[117] IACHR *Hilaire, Constantine et al., Benjamin et al.* v. *Trinidad & Tobago*, 21 June 2002, §103.

[118] HRC *Mr. Eversley Thompson* v. *St. Vincent & the Grenadines*, 18 October 2000.

[119] Lord Colville dissented. He considered that the HRC was diverting from its earlier Views. He believed that the majority had founded its opinion on civil law rather than common law and disagreed with the view that there could be full compliance with Article 6(4) and still a violation of Article 6(1). Kretzmer wrote the second dissent, co-signed by Amor, Yalden and Zakhia. Note that, apart from Lord Colville himself, one of the other dissenters, Yalden, indeed came from a common law country (Canada), while some of the others may have been influenced by common law thinking. At the same time Bhagwati (India), Evatt (Australia) and Henkin (US) who were in the majority, all are from common law countries as well. Moreover, it is the US Supreme Court that initiated the jurisprudence on the mandatory death penalty. For an earlier case in which the HRC found a violation of Article 6(2) rather than 6(1) see: *Lubuto* v. *Zambia*, 31 October 1995.

[120] HRC *Kennedy* v. *Trinidad and Tobago*, 26 March 2002.

[121] In HRC *Xavier Evans* v. *Trinidad and Tobago*, 21 March 2003, the death sentence was commuted several years before the petitioner submitted his case to the HRC. This means that Rule 86 was not used. Because of this commutation the HRC determined that the application of mandatory capital punishment in this case did not give rise to a claim under the OP.

[122] See CIDH *Hilaire v. Trinidad & Tobago*, 21 April 1999 (Report 66/99) as referred to in IACHR *Hilaire, Constantine et al., Benjamin et al.* v. *Trinidad & Tobago*, 21 June 2002, §23. The Commission brought the case before the Court on 23 May 1999, arguing that the mandatory death penalty violated Articles 1(1), 4(1), 5(1), 5(2), 5(6) and 8(1) ACHR. In its subsequent submissions of *Constantine et al.* and *Benjamin et al.* it omitted the reference to Article 5(6) on social re-adaptation etc.).

[123] See e.g. US Supreme Court, *Woodson v. North Carolina* 428 U.S. 280 (1976), arguing that respect for human dignity, underlying the relevant provision in the constitution, required 'consideration of aspects of the character of the individual offender and the circumstances of the particular offense as a constitutionally indispensable part of imposing the ultimate punishment of death'. The statute in question 'impermissibly treats all persons convicted of a designated offense not as uniquely individual human beings, but as members of a faceless, undifferentiated mass to be subjected to the blind infliction of the death penalty', pp. 303-305).

seek pardon or commutation, while obligatory under the ICCPR, were insufficient to secure adequate protection of the right to life.[124]

In *Carpo et al.* v. *the Philippines* (2003) the HRC raised the issue of the mandatory death
penalty *proprio motu*. The Rapporteur may intuitively take provisional measures in a case in
which, based on the facts, the HRC later invokes a claim *proprio motu*.[125] Wedgwood and Ando
did not agree with the Committee's choice to deal with the claim *proprio motu* nor with the
Committee's approach towards the mandatory death penalty.[126] On the other hand, they did agree
with the use of provisional measures in this case. In subsequent cases the HRC raised the issue of
the mandatory death penalty again.[127] In *Pagdayawon Rolando* v. *the Philippines* (2004), for
instance, the Committee first used provisional measures and later found a violation of Article
6(1).[128] The UN Special Rapporteur on arbitrary executions has confirmed this approach by the
HRC, Inter-American Commission and Court and several domestic courts. "Making such a penalty mandatory – thereby eliminating the discretion of the court – makes it impossible to take into
account mitigating or extenuating circumstances and eliminates any individual determination of
an appropriate sentence in a particular case". "The adoption of such a black and white approach is
entirely inappropriate where the life of an accused is at stake. Once the sentence has been carried
out it is irreversible".[129]

---

[124] HRC *Thompson* v. *St. Vincent and the Grenadines*, 18 October 2000 and *Kennedy* v. *Trinidad
and Tobago*, 26 March 2002. See also *Jaime Carpo et al.* v. *Philippines*, 28 March 2003 (Ando
and Wedgwood dissenting). In this case Amor and Yalden were in fact with the majority and did
neither join Ando's dissent nor that of Wedgwood. The other three dissenters in the earlier two
cases are no longer members of the HRC.

[125] HRC *Jaime Carpo et al.* v. *Philippines*, 28 March 2003 (Ando and Wedgwood dissenting).

[126] Wedgwood pointed out that the initial communication by the petitioners was 'well after
publication of the Committee's earlier opinions on the question of mandatory death penalties'.
They had had the advice of professional legal counsel who had decided not to raise such a claim.
However, it is in fact normal practice of the HRC to take up issues *proprio motu* and the
argument that counsel should have known about the HRC's earlier decisions on the mandatory
death penalty also works the other way around, because it should have come as no surprise to the
State either that the HRC would bring up this issue based on its earlier Views. Nevertheless,
Wedgwood correctly points out that the HRC could have referred the issue of mandatory
sentencing to the State party for comment. In other words, the case law is clear on the principle of
mandatory death penalty and the HRC could easily bring it up as part of its practice to raise
issues *proprio motu*, deriving from the facts of the case, without violating procedural equality. It
could, however, have requested the State party to provide it with a copy of the opinion of the trial
court in order to determine whether the facts of the case indeed amounted to mandatory
sentencing.

[127] It noted from the domestic judgments that the death penalty was imposed automatically and
found a violation of Article 6(1) ICCPR. Only Committee member Ando objected, referring to
his individual opinion in *Carpo*. The Committee's Special Rapporteur had used provisional
measures in *Rayos* as well. HRC *Ramil Rayos* v. *the Philippines*, 27 July 2004. While Scheinin,
Chanet and Lallah fully agreed with the Committee's finding that the petitioner's mandatory
death penalty was an arbitrary deprivation of life, they considered that the HRC should have
followed its interpretation in *Judge* v. *Canada*. It should have found that the State equally
violated Article 6 by re-introducing capital punishment in 1993 after abolishing it in 1987. They
pointed out that the distinction between abolition and a moratorium was decisive in this respect.

[128] HRC *Pagdayawon Rolando* v. *the Philippines*, 3 November 2004 (Wedgwood and Ando
dissenting).

[129] See e.g. Press release of the Special Rapporteur on extrajudicial, summary or arbitrary
executions, 'Expert on arbitrary executions calls on Singapore government not to carry out

3.4.4 The right to life and the fairness of the proceedings

The provision that a death sentence may be imposed only in accordance with the law and not contrary to the provisions of the ICCPR implies that 'the procedural guarantees therein prescribed must be preserved, including the right to a fair hearing by an independent tribunal, the presumption of innocence, the minimum guarantees for the defence, and the right to review by a higher tribunal'.[130] Consequently, if no further appeal is available, the imposition of a death sentence 'upon the conclusion of a trial in which the provisions of the Covenant have not been respected' constitutes not only a violation of Article 14 (fair trial) but a violation of the right to life (Article 6) as well. Thus, the HRC has pointed out that if the final death sentence was passed without due respect for the requirements of Article 14 it must hold that there has also been a violation of Article 6.[131] These requirements include 'the right to a fair hearing by an independent tribunal, the presumption of innocence, the minimum guarantees for the defence, and the right to review of conviction and sentence by a higher tribunal'.[132]

In its General Comment on the right to a fair trial, the Committee pointed out that the rights specifically enumerated in Article 14 ICCPR are 'minimum' guarantees. Their observance does not always ensure the fairness of a hearing. The right to a fair trial is broader than the sum of the individual guarantees, and depends on the entire conduct of the trial.[133]

Thus, the HRC considers that any violation of the right to a fair trial in a death penalty case automatically results in a violation of the right to life as well. Chapter XIII (Protection) shows that this relationship with the right to life is reflected also in the remedy the HRC considers warranted if it finds a violation. This is relevant as well for the use of provisional measures.

Death penalty cases in which the adjudicators have taken provisional measures relate to a range of claims. This section first discusses specific issues regarding the fairness of the proceedings dealt with by the regional adjudicators: trial in public and the prohibition of forced confessions, the right to consular notification, freedom from *ex post facto* laws, the independence and impartiality of the judiciary, rights of amnesty, pardon or commutation and the prohibition to execute persons pending judicial or administrative proceedings. It then specifically refers to the most important claims in death penalty case in which the HRC has taken provisional measures: right to counsel, adequate time and facilities to prepare a defence, right to appeal and effective

---

mandatory death sentence', 15 November 2005. The appeal by Rapporteur Alston was made on behalf of Nguyen Tuong Van, awaiting execution for attempting to traffic almost 400 grams of pure heroin. He pointed out that while the Singapore Court of Appeal had considered several cases decided by the JCPC 'it failed to examine the most important case of all', which was *Boyce and Joseph* v. *the Queen* (2004), pointing out that "No international human rights tribunal anywhere in the world has ever found a mandatory death penalty regime compatible with international human rights norms".

[130] HRC General Comment 6, 30 April 1982, §7.

[131] See, e.g., HRC *Daniel Pinto* v. *Trinidad and Tobago*, 20 July 1990 (Wennergren dissenting); *Carlton Reid* v. *Jamaica*, 20 July 1990 (Wennergren dissenting); *Paul Kelly* v. *Jamaica*, 8 April 1991; *Trevor Collins* v. *Jamaica*, 25 March 1993; *Garfield Peart and Andrew Peart* v. *Jamaica*, 19 July 1995; *George Graham and Arthur Morrison* v. *Jamaica*, 25 March 1996; *Clifford McLawrence* v. *Jamaica*, 18 July 1997; *Abdool Saleem Yasseen and Noel Thomas* v. *Republic of Guyana*, 30 March 1998; *Silbert Daley* v. *Jamaica*, 31 July 1998; *Clarence Marshall* v. *Jamaica*, 3 November 1998; *Conroy Levy* v. *Jamaica*, 3 November 1998; *Christopher Brown* v. *Jamaica*, 23 March 1999 and *Azer Garyverdy Ogly Aliev* v. *Ukraine*, 7 August 2003.

[132] HRC General Comment 6, 30 April 1982, §7.

[133] HRC General Comment 13, 13 April 1982, §5. The HRC has since replaced this General Comment with its General Comment 32, 23 August 2007, see §31. For specific references to necessary aspects for the right to fair trial in cases involving the death penalty see §§10, 17, 38, 51.

representation on appeal, fair trial aspects of detention and delay and undue delay and the lack of a written judgment by domestic courts.

3.4.4.1 TRIAL IN PUBLIC AND THE PROHIBITION OF FORCED CONFESSIONS

While the African Charter does not specifically mention the right to public trials, the African Commission, drawing guidance from international human rights law and practice, has found that Article 7 does not allow *in camera* trials.[134]

The rule that no one shall be compelled to testify against himself or to confess guilt (Article 14(3)(g) ICCPR) is closely related to Article 7 on the prohibition of torture and cruel treatment. The HRC has noted that Article 14(3)(g) 'must be understood in terms of the absence of any direct or indirect physical or psychological pressure from the investigating authorities on the accused, with a view to obtaining a confession of guilt. *A fortiori*, it is unacceptable to treat an accused person in a manner contrary to Article 7 of the Covenant in order to extract a confession'.[135] Hence the HRC has found that for the purpose of guaranteeing a fair trial Article 14(3)(g) also implies the prohibition of torture and cruel treatment.[136]

3.4.4.2 THE RIGHT TO CONSULAR NOTIFICATION

An example of a claim dealt with in the Inter-American system involves the right of consular notification. In 1999 the Inter-American Court issued an Advisory Opinion dealing with the human rights obligations of the members of the OAS who were also States Parties to the Vienna Convention of Consular Relations. The Court considered that executing a foreign national who had not been notified of his or her right to contact his consulate, and had not been able to remedy this violation once informed of this right was an arbitrary deprivation of life.[137] The Inter-American Commission has used precautionary measures several times to halt executions of persons who had not been informed of their right of consular notification.[138]

---

[134] ACHPR *Civil Liberties Organisation et al.* v. *Nigeria*, April/May 2001, §§35-39.

[135] See e.g. HRC *Paul Kelly* v. *Jamaica,* 8 April 1991; *Glenford Campbell* v. *Jamaica*, 30 March 1992, and *Albert Berry* v. *Jamaica*, 7 April 1994.

[136] See e.g. HRC *Paul Kelly* v. *Jamaica*, 8 April 1991 and General Comment 32, on Article 14, 23 August 2007, §§6, 41 and 60. See also ACHPR *Malawi African Association et al.* v. *Mauritania*, May 2000, §95 and *Civil Liberties Organisation et al.* v. *Nigeria*, April/May 2001, §40.

[137] IACHR The right to information on Consular assistance in the framework of guarantees of the due process of law, Advisory Opinion OC-16/99, 1 October 1999. See also the ICJ *LaGrand* judgment of 27 June 2001, discussed in Chapter I.

[138] See e.g. CIDH *Humberto Leal García* v. *US*, 30 January 2007, §47; *Rubén Ramírez Cárdenas* v. *US*, 30 January 2007, §48; *Heriberto Chi Aceituno* v. *US*, 28 September 2007, §50 (see also CIDH press release 35/08, 8 August 2008 condemning his execution) and *José Ernesto Medellín* v. *US*, 6 December 2006 and 3 January 2007. See also decision on the merits, 24 July 2008 (determining 'that the State violated Articles I, XVIII and XXVI of the American Declaration of the Rights and Duties of Man against Mr. Medellín, with respect to the criminal conviction that led to his death sentence. Among other aspects, the IACHR determined that as a result of the State's failure to fulfill its obligation, under Article 36.1 of the Vienna Convention on Consular Relations, to inform Mr. Medellín of his right to consular notification and assistance, the criminal process against him did not meet the minimum standards of due process and a fair trial required under Articles XVIII and XXVI of the American Declaration. The Commission concluded that if

3.4.4.3 FREEDOM FROM EX POST FACTO LAWS

The Inter-American Court has also dealt with freedom from *ex post facto* laws. In *Fermín Ramírez* v. *Guatemala* (2005) it pointed out that the procedural guarantees delimiting the State's power to prosecute and punish individuals in a democratic society are particularly important in the context of the death penalty.[139] In order to establish his dangerousness, the sentencing tribunal had changed the legal qualification of the crime and introduced (and held as established) new facts and circumstances that the petitioner had not been charged with.[140] The Inter-American Court added that the introduction of the criterion of future dangerousness in the domestic legislation was incompatible with the freedom from *ex post facto* laws in Article 9 ACHR.[141]

3.4.4.4 INDEPENDENCE AND IMPARTIALITY OF THE JUDICIARY

One very important claim relates to the independence and impartiality of the judiciary. In *Öcalan* the ECtHR found that the petitioner had not been tried by an independent and impartial tribunal within the meaning of Article 6(1) ECHR, which was not in conformity 'with the strict standards of fairness required in cases involving capital sentence'.[142] He had to 'suffer the consequences of the imposition of that sentence for nearly three years'. The imposition of the death penalty 'following an unfair trial by a Court who's independence and impartiality were open to doubt amounted to inhuman treatment in violation of Article 3'.[143]

Although it had already found that the execution of the petitioner would violate Protocol No. 6 the Bosnia Chamber considered whether the execution would be in conformity with Article 2 ECHR.[144] It pointed out that the procedural guarantees in death penalty cases must be 'of the

---

the State executed Mr. Medellín based on those proceedings, it would commit an irreparable violation of his fundamental right to life, protected by Article I of the American Declaration. The IACHR thus recommended, among other things, that the State vacate the death penalty imposed on Mr. Medellín and hold a new trial in accordance with the protections prescribed under the American Declaration-equality, due process, and a fair trial, including the right to competent legal representation', see press release 33/08 of 6 August 2008, condemning his execution). See also the ICJ's provisional measures in the *Avena interpretation* case, Chapter I.

[139] IACHR *Fermín Ramírez* v. *Guatemala,* 20 June 2005, §78.

[140] Id., §§65-80. It referred to the principle of coherence or correlation between the charge and the sentence, meaning that the sentence should be based only on the facts and circumstances in the original charges. It referred to ECtHR *Pelissier and Sassi* v. *France,* 25 March 1999, §§51-54 (observing that Article 6 (3)(a) ECHR gives the defendant the right 'to be informed no only of the cause of the accusation, that is to say the acts he is alleged to have committed and on which the accusation is based, but also the legal characterization given to those acts').

[141] IACHR *Fermín Ramírez* v. *Guatemala,* 20 June 2005, §§87-98. The Court also found a violation of a minimum guarantee of prior notification of the charges (Article 8 (2)(b)) and of adequate time and means for the preparation of the defence (Article 8 (2)(c)).

[142] ECtHR Grand Chamber *Öcalan* v. *Turkey,* Judgment of 12 May 2005, §174.

[143] ECtHR Grand Chamber *Öcalan* v. *Turkey,* Judgment of 12 May 2005, §§174 (but see partly Dissenting Opinion Wildhaber, Costa, Caflisch, Türmen, Garlicki and Borrego Borrego arguing that the domestic court had been independent and impartial; see also the partly Dissenting Opinion by Costa, Caflisch, Türmen and Borrego Borrego arguing that even if the domestic court had not been independent and impartial this would not have constituted a breach of Article 3).

[144] Bosnia Chamber *Sretko Damjanović* v. *Fed. BiH,* 5 September 1997 (merits). See, however, the concurring opinion of Nowak and Möller pointing out that it was irrelevant whether the imposition of the death penalty before December 1995 was in accordance with the law at that time and whether the sentence was imposed by an independent and impartial court after a fair

highest order'.[145] A strict approach must be taken to the requirements of independence and impartiality of judges. It pointed out that members of the District Military Court that convicted the petitioner were not legally protected against removal. Such protection 'must normally be considered an essential requirement of independence'. In this case the relevant court 'lack a sufficient appearance of independence' and could therefore not be regarded as a 'court' for the purposes of Article 2(1) ECHR.[146] The African Commission has also emphasized the importance of an independent and impartial judiciary.[147] In the *Saro-Wiwa* case it found that the special tribunals in Nigeria violated Article 7(1)(d) African Charter 'because their composition is at the discretion of the executive branch'.[148] In violation of this article, tribunals composed of persons belonging largely to the executive branch of government create the 'appearance, if not actual, lack of impartiality', simply by their composition and '(r)egardless of the character of the individual members of such tribunals'.[149] It has also found that the composition alone of the Special Courts in Sudan violated Article 7 (1)(d) by creating 'the impression, if not the reality, of lack of impartiality'. The government had the duty to provide the structures necessary for the exercise of this right. "By providing for courts whose impartiality is not guaranteed, it has violated article 26". The Commission added that the State had violated both articles as well by dismissing more than 100 'judges who were opposed to the formation of special courts and military tribunals' "To deprive courts of the personnel qualified to ensure that they operate impartially thus denies the right to individuals to have their case heard by such bodies".[150]

---

trial or not because after the entry into force of the Dayton Peace Agreement execution of a death penalty would constitute 'a violation of the constitutional obligation to secure the absolute right not to be executed', as contained in Article 1 Second OP, listed in Annex I of the Constitution.

[145] Bosnia Chamber *Sretko Damjanović* v. *Fed. BiH*, 5 September 1997 (merits), §38.

[146] Id., §§40-42. See also *Herak* v. *Fed. BiH*, 12 June 1998.

[147] See also Chapter XII, section 2.9, discussing provisional measures to protect independence of the judiciary.

[148] ACHPR *International PEN et al.* (*on behalf of Ken Saro-Wiwa*) v. *Nigeria*, 31 October 1998, §86.

[149] ACHPR *Constitutional Rights Project* (*in respect of Zamani Lakwot and 6 others*) v. *Nigeria*, October 1994, §§13-14. See also *Constitutional Rights Project* (*in respect of Akamu et al.*) v. *Nigeria*, undated/8th Annual Activity Report/1995, §12. It also found a violation in a case against Mauritania. "Withdrawing criminal procedure from the competence of the Court established within the judicial order and conferring it to an extension of the executive necessarily compromises the impartiality of the Court, to which the African Charter refers. Independent of the quality of the persons sitting in such jurisdictions, their very existence constitutes a violation of the principles of impartiality and independence of the judiciary and, thereby, of article 7(1)(d)". Moreover, by establishing a section within the special domestic tribunal, responsible for matters relating to state security, Mauritania was 'reneging on its duty to guarantee the independence of the Court' in violation of Article 26 ACHPR. ACHPR *Malawi African Association et al.* v. *Mauritania*, 11 May 2000, §§98-100.

[150] ACHPR *Amnesty International et al.* v. *Sudan*, November 1999, §§68-69. In an unedited version of a decision against Malawi (that cannot be found as such in the official version) the Commission considered that under Article 7(1)(a) and (c) ACHPR individuals have a right to be tried by a court that is not only impartial, but also competent. This 'follows from the other articles and the spirit of the Charter' "To fail to ensure that judges have legal training and that rules of evidence are applied illustrates that the government has neglected its duty to provide courts that are of sufficient competence to satisfy Article 26 of the Charter". *Achutan* (*on behalf of Aleke Banda*) and *Amnesty International* (*on behalf of Orton and Vera Chirwa*) v. *Malawi*, October/November 1994, at <dcregistry.com/users/ACHPR/index2.html>.

3.4.4.5 RIGHTS OF AMNESTY, PARDON OR COMMUTATION AND THE PROHIBITI-ON TO EXECUTE PERSONS PENDING JUDICIAL OR ADMINISTRATIVE PRO-CEEDINGS

There have also been claims about the procedural rights involving requests for amnesty, pardon or commutation. The HRC seems to take a more restrictive approach than the Inter-American Court. In *Fermín Ramírez* v. *Guatemala* (2005) the Inter-American Court found a violation of Article 4(6) because an appropriate possibility for requesting clemency was lacking. It pointed out that clemency formed part of the international *corpus iuris*.[151] In *Kennedy* v. *Trinidad and Tobago* (2002) the HRC decided that the right to seek commutation was not governed by the procedural guarantees of Article 14 and that it was within the discretion of States to spell out the modalities of the exercise of this right.[152]

Yet, no execution should take place pending appeal or other recourse procedure, nor pending pardon or commutation proceedings (Article 6(4) jo. 14(5) ICCPR). A similar provision can be found in Article 4(6) ACHR. This is directly related to the purpose of the provisional measures: halting executions pending the proceedings before the HRC. As one member of the Committee put it, its Rule on provisional measures 'had in fact been designed to guarantee' that those sentenced to death should be able to exhaust all remedies.[153]

3.4.4.6 RIGHT TO COUNSEL

The extensive case law of the HRC, in cases in which it previously used provisional measures, indicates the types of situations in which provisional measures are likely to be invoked in the future as well. One situation obviously is that involving complaints regarding the right to counsel.

The HRC has determined it is 'imperative' or 'axiomatic' that 'legal assistance be available at all stages of the proceedings in capital cases'.[154] This includes any preliminary hearings and the relevant appeals as well.[155] Equally, the absence of an assigned counsel during summing up constitutes ineffective assistance of counsel in violation of this article.[156] The HRC has equally noted

---

[151] IACHR *Fermín Ramírez* v. *Guatemala*, 20 June 2005, §§104-110.

[152] HRC *Kennedy* v. *Trinidad and Tobago*, 26 March 2002.

[153] HRC Summary Record of the 1352nd meeting: Trinidad and Tobago, 26 July 1994, CCPR/C/SR/1352, 31 July 1996, §21 (Bruni Celli; Venezuela).

[154] See e.g. HRC *Frank Robinson* v. *Jamaica*, 30 March 1989 (provisional measures were not applied in this case since his death sentence was already commuted before he petitioned the HRC). See further *E.B.* v. *Jamaica*, 26 October 1990, §5.4. See also *W.W.* v. *Jamaica*, 26 October 1990; *Daniel Pinto* v. *Trinidad and Tobago*, 20 July 1990; *Carlton Reid* v. *Jamaica*, 20 July 1990; *Paul Kelly* v. *Jamaica*, 8 April 1991; *Raphael Henry* v. *Jamaica*, 1 November 1991; *Glenford Campbell* v. *Jamaica*, 30 March 1992; *Trevor Collins* v. *Jamaica*, 25 March 1993; *Robinson LaVende* v. *Trinidad and Tobago*, 29 October 1997; *Abdool Saleem Yasseen and Noel Thomas* v. *Republic of Guyana*, 30 March 1998; *Clarence Marshall* v. *Jamaica*, 30 November 1998 and *Christopher Brown* v. *Jamaica*, 23 March 1999.

[155] See e.g. HRC *Osbourne Wright and Eric Harvey* v. *Jamaica*, 27 October 1995 and *Clarence Marshall* v. *Jamaica*, 3 November 1998 (a violation of Article 14(3)(d) because the court commenced and proceeded through a whole day of the preliminary hearing without informing the petitioner of his right to legal representation).

[156] HRC *Christopher Brown* v. *Jamaica*, 23 March 1999. The Committee recalled that the State party should ensure that counsel, once assigned, provide effective representation of the accused. It considered that 'it should have been apparent to the trial judge that counsel was not providing

that the denial of legal aid constitutes a violation of Article 14(1) jo. 2(3).[157] Still, 'the mere absence of the defence counsel at some limited time during the proceedings does not in itself constitute a violation of the Covenant'. It 'must be assessed on a case-by-case basis whether counsel's absence was incompatible with the interests of justice'.[158] It is axiomatic in capital cases that the accused be represented not only for the trial but also for the preliminary inquiry.[159] In a case against Ukraine the HRC considered a violation of Article 14(1) that the petitioner had no counsel during the first five months of detention. During this period he had been interrogated by police officers and the capital crime of which he was accused was being reconstructed without his participation. In the same case it also found a violation of Article 14(3)(d) because the Supreme Court heard his case in his absence and in the absence of his counsel.[160] Indeed, Article 14(3)(d) also stipulates the right to be tried in one's presence. In one case against Georgia the HRC noted that it was uncontested that the petitioners were forced to be absent during long periods of the trial, that one of the petitioners was not represented for part of the trial and that two others were represented by lawyers whose services they had refused. They were not allowed to conduct their own defence or to be represented by lawyers of their choice.[161] The HRC has also pronounced itself on the availability of information to the defendant. In a 1997 case against Jamaica the petitioner did not have the documents of a statement in which someone else confessed to the murder for which the petitioner had been sentenced to death. The Committee noted that the State party had not explained why this alleged statement was never made available to him or to his counsel. It found that the failure to provide him with legal aid had denied him the opportunity to have inquiries made about the matter and to pursue such domestic legal remedies as may have been available to him.[162]

Regional adjudicators have also dealt with this issue. In *Öcalan*, for instance, the ECtHR found a violation of the rights of the defence because the petitioner had no access to a lawyer while in police custody, he 'was unable to communicate with his lawyers out of the hearing of officials, restrictions had been imposed on the number and length of his lawyers' visits to him, he

---

effective representation of the accused'. This should have been apparent 'at the latest when he noticed that counsel was absent when he started his summing-up'.

[157] HRC *Rawle Kennedy* v. *Trinidad and Tobago*, 26 March 2002.

[158] HRC *Clarence Marshall* v. *Jamaica*, 3 November 1998.

[159] HRC *Steve Shaw* v. *Jamaica*, 2 April 1998. See also *Clive Johnson* v. *Jamaica*, 20 October 1998. In this case the State party had not contested that the petitioner was not represented during the preliminary hearing but had merely stated that there was no indication that he had requested a lawyer. The Committee considered that "when the author appeared at the preliminary hearing without a legal representative, it would have been incumbent upon the investigating magistrate to inform the author of his right to have legal representation and to ensure legal representation for the author, if he so wished". See further *Christopher Brown* v. *Jamaica*, 23 March 1999. In this case the HRC noted from the trial transcript that the petitioner's representative was absent during the deposition of two prosecution witnesses at the preliminary hearing and that the magistrate continued the hearing of the witnesses and only adjourned when the petitioner indicated that he did not wish to cross-examine the witnesses himself. After two adjournments where the lawyer again did not turn up, the judge appointed new counsel for the petitioner, but this counsel declined to cross-examine the witnesses. The Committee found a violation of Article 14(3)(d). "In the present case, the Committee is of the opinion that the magistrate, when aware of the absence of the author's defence counsel, should not have proceeded with the deposition of the witnesses without allowing the author an opportunity to ensure the presence of his counsel".

[160] HRC *Azer Garyverdy ogly Aliev* v. *Ukraine*, 7 August 2003.

[161] It found a violation of Article 14(3)(d) in respect of all four petitioners. HRC *Victor P. Domukovsky, Zaza Tsiklauri, Petre Gelbakhiani and Irakli Dokvadze* v. *Georgia*, 6 April 1998.

[162] This amounted to a violation of Article 14(3)(d) in conjunction with Article 2(3) ICCPR. HRC *Maurice Thomas* v. *Jamaica*, 3 November 1997.

was unable to consult the case-file until an advanced stage of the proceedings and his lawyers did not have sufficient time to consult the file properly'.[163]

The African Commission has noted that 'especially in serious cases, which carry the death penalty, the accused should be represented by a lawyer of his choice'. "The purpose of this provision is to ensure that the accused has confidence in his legal counsel. Failure to provide for this may expose the accused to a situation where he will not be able to give full instructions to his counsel for lack of confidence".[164] Assigning of military counsel to accused persons, against their objections, 'and especially in a criminal proceeding which carries the ultimate punishment' violates Article 7(1)(c) ACHPR.[165] Giving sentencing tribunals the power to veto the choice of counsel of defendants is 'an unacceptable infringement' of the right to freely choose one's counsel. "There should be an objective system of licensing advocates, so that qualified advocates cannot be barred from appearing in particular cases. It is essential that the national bar be an independent body which regulates legal practitioners, and that the tribunals themselves not adopt this role, which will infringe on the right to defence".[166] The African Commission added that it was desirable for indigent defendants that they were represented 'at state expense', but 'even in such cases, the accused should be able to choose from a list the preferred independent counsel "not acting under the instructions of government but responsible only to the accused"'.[167]

3.4.4.7 ADEQUATE TIME AND FACILITIES TO PREPARE A DEFENCE

The HRC explains the right to have adequate time and facilities for the preparation of the defence as an important element of the guarantee of a fair trial and a corollary or 'emanation' of the principle of equality of arms. Particularly in capital cases it is axiomatic that sufficient time must be granted to the accused and counsel and this requirement applies to all stages of the judicial proceedings.[168] At the same time 'the State party cannot be held accountable for lack of preparation or alleged errors made by defence lawyers unless it has denied the author and his counsel time to prepare the defence or it should have been manifest to the court that the lawyers' conduct was incompatible with the interests of justice'.[169] In the absence of information or objection from the State party the HRC found a violation of Article 14(2) in *Saidov* v. *Tajikistan*

---

[163] This constituted violations of Article 6(1), together with Article 6 (3)(b)(c). See ECHR (Grand Chamber), *Öcalan* v. *Turkey*, Judgment of 12 May 2005, §173.

[164] ACHPR *Civil Liberties Organisation et al.* v. *Nigeria*, April/May 2001, §28.

[165] Id., §31.

[166] ACHPR *Amnesty International et al.* v. *Sudan*, November 1999, §64. See also *Constitutional Rights Project* v. *Nigeria*, 26th ordinary session, 13th Annual Activity Report, §12.

[167] ACHPR *Civil Liberties Organisation et al.* v. *Nigeria*, April/May 2001, §29. The Commission referred to early case law of the HRC involving Uruguay and to its own Resolution on the Right to Recourse and Fair Trial (1992). See also ACHPR *Malawi African Association et al.* v. *Mauritania*, May 2000, §96 (no access or restricted access to counsel and insufficient time to prepare for the defence in violation of Article 7(1)(c)) and idem, §97 (Article 7(c)(1) requires charges in language defendants understand).

[168] HRC *Clifton Wright* v. *Jamaica*, 27 July 1992; *Paul Kelly* v. *Jamaica*, 8 April 1991; *Aston Little* v. *Jamaica*, 1 November 1991; *Leaford Smith* v. *Jamaica*, 31 March 1993 and *Alrick Thomas* v. *Jamaica*, 31 March 1992.

[169] See e.g. HRC *Errol Smith and Oval Stewart* v. *Jamaica*, 8 April 1999. It has discussed Article 14 (3)(b) and (e) in other situations as well. See e.g. *Yasseen and Thomas* v. *Guyana*, 30 March 1998.

(2004). 'Due to the extensive and adverse pre-trial coverage by state-directed media' the petitioner's right to be presumed innocent had been violated.[170]

3.4.4.8 RIGHT TO APPEAL AND EFFECTIVE REPRESENTATION ON APPEAL

In some States the issue of the availability of legal aid for constitutional motions is of crucial importance.[171] The ICCPR does not require States to provide for several instances of appeal, but *if* domestic law provides for further instances Article 14(5) requires that the convicted person indeed has access to each of them.[172] In death penalty cases the availability of legal representation is a prerequisite for a fair hearing. This also applies to hearings on constitutional issues, especially as these are often quite complicated. When the HRC refers to the requirements of a fair hearing in such cases, it does not argue that Article 14(3)(d) is directly applicable, but it states that in death penalty cases the requirements found in Article 14(3)(d) must be read into Article 14(1).[173]

The right to a fair trial extends to the right to review by a higher tribunal according to law (Article 14(5) ICCPR). The Committee takes 'according to law' in Article 14(5) to mean that when domestic law provides for more than one instance of appeal in criminal cases, the convicted person must indeed have effective access to each of these instances of appeal.[174] Of course it is a prerequisite for Article 14(1) that the petitioner is informed about the date of the appeal hearing before it takes place.[175] The most important factor the HRC has examined in relation to the right to effective representation during appeal is whether counsel had abandoned (grounds for) the appeal. It has found violations of Article 14(3)(d) and (5) when counsel had abandoned all grounds of appeal and when the court had not ascertained whether this was in accordance with the wishes of the client.[176]

---

[170]   HRC *Gaibullodzhon Ilyasovich Saidov* (*submitted by his wife Barno Saidova*) v. *Tajikistan*, 8 July 2004.

[171]   See the discussion of exhaustion of domestic remedies and the use of provisional measures, Chapter XIV, section 2.2.2.

[172]   See, e.g., HRC *Anthony Currie* v. *Jamaica*, 29 March 1994; *Lloyd Grant* v. *Jamaica*, 31 March 1994; *Patrick Taylor* v. *Jamaica*, 18 July 1997; *Desmond Taylor* v. *Jamaica*, 2 April 1998 (Ando, Bhagwati, Buergenthal and Kretzmer dissenting) and *Steve Shaw* v. *Jamaica*, 2 April 1998 (Ando, Bhagwati, Buergenthal and Kretzmer dissenting). See also *Clive Johnson* v. *Jamaica*, 20 October 1998 (in this case the Committee considered that, in light of its other findings it was not necessary to address counsel's claim that the absence of legal aid for the purpose of filing a constitutional motion *in itself* constituted a violation of the Covenant).

[173]   The HRC has also found a violation of Article 14(3)(d) because of the denial of legal aid 'which contributed to the further delay in the author's application for leave to appeal to the Privy Council'. *Maurice Thomas* v. *Jamaica*, 3 November 1997. See further *Raphael Henry* v. *Jamaica*, 1 November 1991 and *Robinson LaVende* v. *Trinidad and Tobago*, 29 October 1997. The Inter-American Commission has made a similar argument, invoking Articles 8(1) and 25 ACHR, see e.g. CIDH *Lamey, Mykoo, Montique and Dalton* v. *Jamaica*, 4 April 2001, (fifth recommendation); *Joseph Thomas* v. *Jamaica*, 3 December 2001 (fourth recommendation); *Denton Aitken* v. *Jamaica*, 21 October 2002 (fifth recommendation) and *Sewell* v. *Jamaica*, 27 December 2003 (fourth recommendation).

[174]   HRC *Raphael Henry* v. *Jamaica*, 1 November 1991.

[175]   HRC *Alrick Thomas* v. *Jamaica*, 31 March 1992.

[176]   HRC *Carlton Reid* v. *Jamaica*, 20 July 1990; *Paul Kelly* v. *Jamaica*, 8 April 1991; *Trevor Collins* v. *Jamaica*, 25 March 1993; *Tony Jones* v. *Jamaica*, 6 April 1998. See also e.g. *George Graham and Arthur Morrison* v. *Jamaica*, 25 March 1996; *Rickly Burrell* v. *Jamaica*, 18 July 1996; *McCordie Morrison* v. *Jamaica*, 3 November 1998, and *Errol Smith and Oval Stewart* v. *Jamaica*, 8 April 1999. On this issue see also Spronken (2001), pp. 447-449.

The African Commission has pointed out about the right of appeal that Article 7(1)(a) ACHPR is clearly violated by the 'foreclosure of any avenue of appeal to competent national organs in a criminal case attracting punishment as severe as the death penalty'.[177] "For an appeal to be effective, the appellate jurisdiction must, objectively and impartially, consider both the elements of fact and of law that are brought before it".[178] All provisions of Article 7(1) are 'mutually dependent, and where the right to be heard is infringed, other violations may occur, such as detentions being rendered arbitrary'. "Especially sensitive is the definition of 'competent', which encompasses facets such as the expertise of the judges and the inherent justice of the laws under which they operate".[179] In 2000 the African Commission found Sierra Leone in violation of due process (Article 7(1) (a) ACHPR) for executing 24 soldiers without having granted them the right of appeal.[180] Moreover, it found a violation of the right to life (Article 4), stressing this right 'is the fulcrum of all other rights. It is the fountain through which other rights flow, and any violation of this right without due process amounts to arbitrary deprivation of life'.[181]

3.4.4.9 UNDUE DELAY

There is a clear link between the right to be brought promptly before a judicial officer (Article 9(3) ICCPR) and the right to habeas corpus (Article 9(4)). This link often shows itself in the issue of access to legal representation.[182] Moreover, the right of persons charged with a criminal offence to be informed promptly and in detail of the charges against them (Article 14 (3)(a)) is closely related to, but more precise than, Article 9(2). Article 9(2) stipulates that anyone who is arrested shall be informed, at the time of arrest, of the reasons for his arrest and shall be promptly informed of any charges against him. However, as long as Article 9(3) is indeed complied with, a violation of Article 9(2) does not necessarily imply a violation of Article 14(3)(a).[183] In other words, as long as the authorities have complied with Article 9(3), Article 14(3)(a) does not require them to provide the details of the nature and cause of the charge immediately upon arrest.[184]

---

[177] ACHPR *Civil Liberties Organisation et al.* v. *Nigeria*, April/May 2001, §35. See also *Constitutional Rights Project* (*in respect of Lakwot and 6 others*) v. *Nigeria*, 1995, §11 and *Constitutional Rights Project* (*in respect of Akamu et al.*) v. *Nigeria*, undated/8th annual activity report 1995, §11.

[178] ACHPR *Malawi African Association et al.* v. *Mauritania*, 11 May 2000, §94.

[179] ACHPR *Amnesty International et al.* v. *Sudan*, November 1999, §61.

[180] They were executed on 19 October 1998, some of them in violation of provisional measures by the HRC, see e.g. Chapter XVII (Official responses). The Sierra Leonean NGO Forum of Conscience brought the case before the African Commission five days after the executions took place.

[181] ACHPR *Forum of Conscience* v. *Sierra Leone*, October/November 2000, §19. As noted, the initial submission in this case was five days after the execution, which explains why no provisional measures were used.

[182] HRC *Stephens* v. *Jamaica*, 18 October 1995. The HRC found a violation of Article 9(3) because of a delay of eight days, but it did not find a violation of Article 9(4) because there was no evidence that the petitioner or his legal representative had requested a prompt decision on the lawfulness of his detention. The availability of counsel seems crucial, since in other cases in which it found violations of Article 9(3) the HRC mentioned the denial of access to legal representation as an aggravating factor. In such cases it did find a violation of the right to habeas corpus (Article 9(4)). See also *Glenford Campbell* v. *Jamaica*, 30 March 1992; *Albert Berry* v. *Jamaica*, 7 April 1994 and *Clifford McLawrence* v. *Jamaica*, 18 July 1997.

[183] HRC *Clifford McLawrence* v. *Jamaica*, 18 July 1997, see especially §5.9.

[184] Id. In this case, however, the Committee *had* found a violation of Article 9(3) when it stated that a delay of one week in a capital case could not be deemed compatible with that paragraph and

The General Comment on the right to liberty and security of persons (Article 9) stipulates that 'pre-trial detention should be an exception and as short as possible'.[185] The Committee has found that, in the absence of a satisfactory explanation by the State party, a delay ranging from 23 months to more than three years in bringing the petitioner to trial, during which he is kept in pre-trial detention, constituted not only a violation of Article 14(3)(c) but also of the entitlement to trial within reasonable time or release (Article 9(3)).[186] The HRC may also find a violation of Article 9(3) but not of 14(3)(c). If the HRC only recommends commutation in the context of a violation of Article 14, this choice is significant as provisional measures used in cases involving a claim of a violation of Article 9 alone do not seem to be related to the right to reparation.[187] It has concluded that a delay of almost four years between the judgment of the Court of Appeal and the beginning of the retrial, a period during which the petitioner was kept in detention, cannot be deemed compatible with the provisions of Articles 9(3) and 14(3)(c), 'in the absence of any explanations from the State party justifying the delay'.[188] In other cases it declared the claim inad-

---

neither could the pre-trial detention of more than 16 months. The Committee had indeed found a violation of Article 9(2) when it stated that it must rely on the petitioner's statement that he was only apprised of the charges for his arrest when he was first taken to the preliminary hearing almost three weeks after the arrest. It noted that the duty to inform the accused under Article 14(3)(a) is 'more precise' than that for arrested persons under Article 9(2). Given the fact that in this case the Committee had concluded that the State had not complied with Article 9(3) its reasoning in declaring no violation of Article 14(3)(a) is puzzling.

[185] HRC General Comment No. 8 on the right to liberty and security of persons (Article 9), 30 June 1982.

[186] See e.g. HRC *Christopher Brown* v. *Jamaica*, 23 March 1999; *Steve Shaw* v. *Jamaica*, 2 April 1998; *Beresford Whyte* v. *Jamaica*, 27 July; *Anthony Finn* v. *Jamaica*, 31 July 1998; *Clive Smart* v. *Trinidad and Tobago*, 29 July 1998; *Zephiniah Hamilton* v. *Jamaica*, 23 July 1999; *Desmond Taylor* v. *Jamaica*, 2 April 1998; *E. Henry and E. Douglas* v. *Jamaica*, 25 July 1996 and *Oral Hendricks* v. *Guyana*, 22 October 2002.

[187] See further Chapter XIII (Protection). In the following two cases provisional measures were used, but the claim was not based on Article 9 ICCPR alone. *Andrew Perkins* v. *Jamaica*, 30 July 1998, the petitioner was only brought to trial after one year and nine months, and remanded in custody for that period. The HRC found a violation of Article 9(3) but deemed that, in the circumstances, there was no need to address the question of whether the delay also constitutes a violation of Article 14(3)(c). See also *Everton Morrison* v. *Jamaica*, 27 July 1998. The delay of 1,5 year between arrest and trial was only a 'matter of concern' but did not amount to a violation of Article 9(3) 'since he was detained on a murder charge' nor of Article 14(3)(c) 'because the preliminary enquiry took place during that period'. Medina Quiroga dissented on this issue arguing that 'if a delay is a matter of concern the Committee cannot conclude that there is no violation unless the State has given an explanation about the reasons for the delay'. She pointed out that the Committee itself had taken this position when it decided on the admissibility of the claim and invited the State 'to provide more precise information as to the investigations carried out during the period between the arrest and the preliminary enquiry and to inform the Committee of the exact dates of the preliminary hearings'. As the State simply responded to this request by repeating its earlier statement, she concluded that the Committee should have found a violation of Article 9(3).

[188] HRC *Leroy Shalto* v. *Trinidad and Tobago*, 4 April 1995. See also *Sahadeo* v. *Guyana*, 1 November 2001. In another case it found that the delay of one year and nine months between the Court of Appeal judgment that a re-trial should take place and the beginning of the re-trial could not be attributed solely to the State party and thus did not disclose a violation of the Covenant. *Christopher Brown* v. *Jamaica*, 23 March 1999. In the absence of any circumstances justifying it, the HRC did consider that a delay of one year and eleven months between trial and appeal constituted a violation of Article 14(3)(c) and (5). *Samuel Thomas* v. *Jamaica*, 31 March 1999; see also *Clifford McLawrence* v. *Jamaica*, 18 July 1997 (delay of two years and seven months; in

missible noting that it was clear that such delays in the appeal proceedings were essentially attributable to the petitioner.[189]

About the relevance of the economic situation as a justification for undue delay the HRC has pointed out that 'the rights set forth in the Covenant constitute minimum standards which all States parties have agreed to observe'.[190]

3.4.4.10 THE LACK OF A WRITTEN JUDGMENT BY DOMESTIC COURTS

Some claims based on Article 14(3)(c) and 14(5) ICCPR have related specifically to the lack of written judgment by domestic courts.[191] This has been relevant in many cases involving Jamaica. In *Clement Francis* v. *Jamaica* (1995)[192] the HRC found that the 'inordinate delay in issuing a note of oral judgment' entailed a violation of Article 14 paragraphs 3(c) and 5, 'although it appears that the delay did not ultimately prejudice the author's appeal to the Judicial Committee of the Privy Council'.

The lack of written judgment on appeal results in a denial of the possibility to effectively appeal to the Judicial Committee of the Privy Council (JCPC) in London. The JCPC allegedly routinely dismisses petitions that are not accompanied by the written judgment of the lower court. The Jamaican Constitution provides for appeals from a decision of the Jamaican Court of Appeal to the JCPC. Thus, the failure of the Court of Appeal to issue a written judgment resulted in a violation of Article 14(5).[193] Equally, the HRC has determined that the dismissal of an application for leave to appeal, 'without reasons given and in the absence of a written judgment' constitutes a violation of Article 14(5).[194] When the Court of Appeal does not produce a written judgment the petitioner is prevented from effectively petitioning the JCPC for special leave to appeal.[195]

---

this case it even observed that in the absence of any State party justification it would make such a finding in similar circumstances in other cases. This was a clear warning to the State party for future cases); *Silbert Daley* v. *Jamaica*, 31 July 1998 (delay of two years and seven months); *Errol Smith and Oval Stewart* v. *Jamaica,* 8 April 1999 (delay of two years and one month) and *Errol Johnson* v. *Jamaica*, 22 March 1996 (delay of four years and three months).

[189] HRC *Clive Smart* v. *Trinidad and Tobago*, 29 July 1998. The Committee referred to the contents of an addendum in the Court of Appeal judgement that stated: "It was clear to us all that the appellant was attempting by this manoeuvre to beat the *Pratt and Morgan* deadline as best he could". Sometimes it has noted that delays were not entirely attributable to the State party, as the petitioners themselves had requested adjournments. See e.g. *Abdool Saleem Yasseen and Noel Thomas* v. *Republic of Guyana*, 30 March 1998 and *Lennon Stephens* v. *Jamaica*, 18 October 1995.

[190] HRC *Bernhard Lubuto* v. *Zambia*, 31 October 1995. It acknowledged the difficult economic situation of the State party, but considered that the period of eight years between the arrest and the final decision of the Supreme Court, dismissing his appeal, was incompatible with the requirements of Article 14(3)(c).

[191] See also Chapter XIV on the relationship with admissibility and jurisdiction.

[192] HRC *Clement Francis* v. *Jamaica*, 25 July 1995. See also *Aston Little* v. *Jamaica*, 1 November 1991, finding a violation of Article 14(5).

[193] HRC *Raphael Henry* v. *Jamaica*, 1 November 1991.

[194] HRC *George Winston Reid* v. *Jamaica*, 8 July 1994.

[195] HRC *Raphael Henry* v. *Jamaica*, 1 November 1991. See also *Victor Francis* v. *Jamaica*, 24 March 1993. In *Anthony Currie* v. *Jamaica*, 29 March 1994 the petitioner pointed out fifteen years had passed since he was originally charged with murder and almost thirteen years since the Court of Appeal orally dismissed his appeal. No written judgment had been issued as yet. Challenging Jamaica's statement that the JCPC had examined his case, he stated that the Privy

3.4.5 The death row phenomenon

There are at least four levels at which the death row phenomenon may come into play. The first level consists of being sentenced to death and waiting to be executed at a predetermined point in time in a predetermined, often routinised and 'medicalised' manner. The second level consists of the length of the wait (days/5 years/18 years/32 years?).[196] The third level relates to the circumstances of the wait, such as a separate death row and a rigid regime.[197] The final level consists of individual circumstances such as age, mental history. If step one triggers the death row phenomenon, the other steps (the length of the wait, the circumstances on a specific death row and personal factors) simply show types of aggravation. The question arises whether the HRC would use provisional measures in any or all of these situations.

While in the more recent *Öcalan* case the ECtHR took provisional measures to halt an execution, in *Soering* v. *UK* it did so to halt extradition to a death penalty State.[198] On the merits it found that the UK would violate Article 3 ECHR rather than Article 2 on the right to life (since, as noted, the majority had a strictly textual interpretation of the latter article). Its argument for finding a violation of Article 3 was based on the risk of exposure to a so called 'death row phenomenon'.[199] This issue may become relevant as well in the context of a person not awaiting extradition, but already on death row, awaiting execution. As established in the Court's case law, ill treatment must attain a minimum level of severity if it is to fall within the scope of Article 3.[200] The ECHR concluded that the circumstances relating to a death sentence could give rise to an issue under Article 3. It gave as examples the manner in which the sentence is imposed or executed, the personal circumstances of the condemned person and disproportionality to the gravity of the crime committed, as well as the conditions of detention while awaiting execution.

> "Present day attitudes in the Contracting States to capital punishment are relevant for the assessment whether the acceptable threshold of suffering or degradation has been exceeded".

The Court concluded that extradition of Soering would result in a violation of Article 3.

> "Having regard to the very long period of time spent on death row in such extreme conditions, with the ever present and mounting anguish of awaiting execution of the death penalty, and to the personal circumstances of the applicant, especially his age and mental state at the time of the offence, the applicant's extradition to the US would expose him to real risk of treatment going beyond the threshold set by art. 3. A further consideration of relevance is that in the particular

---

Council merely denied him leave to appeal, because he was unable to meet the requirements of its rules of procedure.; see also *Paul Kelly* v. *Jamaica,* 8 April 1991; *Lenford Hamilton* v. *Jamaica,* 21 March 1994 and *Trevor Collins* v. *Jamaica,* 25 March 1993.

[196] In the case *S* v. *Makwanyane and Mchunu* of the Constitutional Court of South Africa, 1995 (2) SACR 1 (CC), Justice Kentridge, for instance, has said: 'the mental agony of the criminal, in its alternation of fear, hope and despair must be present even when the time between sentence and execution is measured in months or weeks rather than years'.

[197] In Missouri persons sentenced to death are incarcerated together with other long-term prisoners, rather than on a separate death row, see: Lombardi, Sluder & Wallace (1997), pp. 2-11. If it would be the physical circumstance of a separate death row alone that would trigger the death row phenomenon, Missouri would not produce it.

[198] On provisional measures to halt refoulement see Chapter V.

[199] The following discussion is partly based on Rieter (2002b). See on the death row phenomenon, e.g. Schmidt (2000); Schabas (1996) and Schabas (1994).

[200] ECtHR *Ireland* v. *United Kingdom,* Judgment of 13 Dec. 1977; *Tyrer* v. *United Kingdom,* Judgment of 25 April 1978 (the Court, referring to the convention as a 'living instrument' declared birching minors to be contrary to article 3 of the Convention).

instance the legitimate purpose of extradition could be achieved by another means which would not involve suffering of such exceptional intensity or duration".

It noted, moreover:

"However well-intentioned and even potentially beneficial is the provision of the complex of post-sentence procedures in Virginia, the consequence is that the condemned prisoner has to endure for many years the conditions on death row and the anguish and mounting tension of living in the ever-present shadow of death".

The strength of the wording used by the Court indicates the importance that must be accorded to this anguish and mounting tension. It seems Soering's youth and his mental state at the time are only taken into account as *contributory* factors.[201] They are not necessary to establish that the death row phenomenon violates Article 3.[202] Thus, in this interpretation any situation that could expose a person to the death row phenomenon would constitute a violation of Article 3.

In *Reyes* v. *Guatemala* (2005) the Inter-American Court found the conditions of detention of a person sentenced to death to violate his right to physical, psychological and moral integrity. In reference to testimony by a psychologist that the detainee was suffering from post traumatic stress and psychosomatic illnesses caused by his situation, awaiting his execution, the Court found a violation of the prohibition of cruel, inhuman and degrading treatment contrary to Article 5(2) ACHR.[203]

Unlike the ECtHR and the Inter-American Court the HRC, as the only international adjudicator, has not accepted that the so called death row phenomenon violates the prohibition of cruel treatment under the ICCPR. The HRC usually declares inadmissible claims relating to the death row phenomenon, without even discussing them on the merits.[204] The remoteness of a favourable decision on the merits would make doubtful the use of provisional measures involving only a claim about this phenomenon.

Thus, different from domestic and regional courts,[205] the HRC has thus far maintained that detention for a specific period of time does not amount to a violation of Article 7 and 10(1) 'in the

---

[201]   See also Shea (1992) (convincingly arguing that the death row phenomenon, rather than the specific facts in the case, was the main criterion in the *Soering* judgment); for a different approach see: Lillich (1991); see also Quigley/Shank (1989).

[202]   As subsequent cases on removal to a death penalty State often were struck out or declared inadmissible, they do not clarify the position of the Strasbourg organs, see e.g. *Venezia* v. *Italy*, 21 October 1996 (struck out as domestic court had forbidden the extradition); *Aylor-Davis* v. *France*, 20 January 1994 (inadm.), (inadmissible for lack of real risk of exposure to death penalty, thanks to recipient State party's credible assurances against the death penalty) In such cases involving possible removal to a death penalty State, the Commission always used provisional measures to prevent the removal while the case was pending. However, this does not need to be linked to the prevention of irreparable harm in the context of the death row phenomenon: all States involved have now ratified Protocol 6, meaning that the provisional measure could have been to prevent irreparable harm to the right to life of the petitioner. The fact that the Court used provisional measures to prevent Turkey from executing Öcalan may be more significant, as Turkey had not ratified Protocol 6 at the time. See Grand Chamber *Öcalan* v. *Turkey,* 12 May 2005.

[203]   IACHR *Raxcacó Reyes* v. *Guatemala*, 15 September 2005, §§94-102.

[204]   Part of this discussion is derived from Rieter (2002b). See further Nowak (2000b) and Schmidt (2000).

[205]   Such as the Judicial Committee of the Privy Council and the Zimbabwe Supreme Court.

absence of some further compelling circumstances'.[206] The Committee has been unwilling to consider detention conditions in relation to the death row phenomenon. These complaints, it considered, must be addressed separately.[207]

The HRC has often found violations of Articles 7 and/or 10 for beatings, threats and general conditions on death row.[208] The Committee has not yet found a circumstance that is so compelling

---

[206]   See e.g. HRC *Errol Johnson* v. *Jamaica*, 22 March 1996. See further *Ramcharan Bickaroo* v. *Trinidad and Tobago*, 29 October 1997 (almost 16 years); *Ramcharan Bickaroo* v. *Trinidad and Tobago*, 29 October 1997 and *Robinson LaVende* v. *Trinidad and Tobago*, 29 October 1997 (in an individual opinion Bhagwati, Chanet, Prado Vallejo and Yalden criticised the majority's lack of flexibility; this joint individual opinion covered the cases of *Bickaroo* and *LaVende*; Gaitan de Pombo also approved the individual opinion but did not sign it; see also Henkin in *Simpson* v. *Jamaica*, 31 October 2000, attaching an individual opinion noting that, like several of his colleagues, he continued to be troubled by the Committee's formulation of the relevant principles with regard to the death row phenomenon; nevertheless, he concurred in the Committee's conclusion that the circumstances of the petitioner's case did not constitute a violation of Article 7, 'according to the jurisprudence of the Committee as formulated in previous cases' because he did not consider the present case 'an appropriate vehicle for re-examining and reformulating' the principles involved). In the extradition case *Cox* v. *Canada*, 31 October 1994 Committee member Ban (Hungary) emphasised that the decisive factor for the death row phenomenon should be psychological rather than physical. "Although I accept the notion that physical conditions play an important role when assessing the overall situation of prison inmates on death row, my conviction is that the decisive factor is rather psychological than physical; a long period spent awaiting execution or the granting of pardon or clemency necessarily entails a permanent stress, an ever increasing fear which gradually fills the mind of the sentenced individual, and which, by the very nature of this situation, amounts -depending on the length of time spent on death row- to cruel, inhuman and degrading treatment, in spite of every measure taken to improve the physical conditions of the confinement". He disagreed with the Committee's holding that the petitioner had adduced no evidence showing, for instance, that there would be unreasonable delays imputable to Pennsylvania. He referred to counsel's submission that 'nobody had been executed in Pennsylvania for more than twenty years, and there are individuals awaiting execution on death row for as much as fifteen years'. Wennergren pointed out that Pennsylvania had not executed anyone in more than twenty years. Prisoners sentenced to death are segregated from other prisoners. The fact that they are awaiting execution for so many years can be explained by the fact that Pennsylvania does not consider it appropriate to proceed with executions, rather than because those on death row avail themselves of all types of judicial appellate remedies. If this State 'considers it necessary, for policy reasons, to have resort to the death penalty as such but not necessary and not even opportune to carry out capital sentences, a condemned person's confinement to death row should, in my opinion, last for as short a period as possible, with commutation of the death sentence to life imprisonment taking place as early as possible'. "A stay for a prolonged and indefinite period of time on death row, in conditions of particular isolation and under threat of execution which might by unforeseeable changes in policy become real, is not, in my opinion, compatible with the requirements of article 7, because of the unreasonable mental stress that this implies".

[207]   See e.g. HRC *Christopher Brown* v. *Jamaica*, 23 March 1999.

[208]   See e.g. HRC *McTaggart* v. *Jamaica*, 31 March 1998 (severe beatings, belongings burnt including letters from his lawyers, a trial transcript and a copy of his petition to the Privy Council); *Michael Freemantle* v. *Jamaica*, 24 March 2000; *Carlton Linton* v. *Jamaica*, 22 October 1992 (physical abuse, a mock execution set up by prison wardens and denial of adequate medical care); *Irvine Reynolds* v. *Jamaica*, 3 April 1997; *Everton Morrison* v. *Jamaica*, 27 July 1998; *Willard Collins* v. *Jamaica*, 1 November 1991; *Tony Jones* v. *Jamaica*, 6 April 1998; *Randolph Barrett and Clyde Sutcliffe* v. *Jamaica*, 30 March 1992; *Michael Robinson* v. *Jamaica*, 29 March 2000 (excessive force) and *Victor Domukovsky, Zaza Tsiklauri, Petre Gelbakhiani and*

that, in combination with the length of time spent on death row, it would result in inhuman or degrading treatment. In most cases if it pronounces on inhuman treatment, the Committee generally finds a separate violation of the Covenant. The fact that this inhuman treatment took place on death row seems to have no specific significance for the Committee.

Short of finding a death row phenomenon, the HRC sometimes did find violations in cases of ill treatment that are specific to persons on death row. It found, for instance, that waiting almost 20 hours before informing prisoners of a stay of execution and removing them from the death cell was a violation of Article 7.[209] It also found violations of Articles 7 and 10(1) in a case where the petitioner was repeatedly taunted and threatened about his impending execution, in graphic detail.[210]

Possibly the HRC did find a death row phenomenon in some very specific cases. In *Francis* v. *Jamaica* (1995)[211] it found a violation of Articles 7 and 10(1).

> "Whereas the psychological tension created by prolonged detention on death row may affect persons in different degrees, the evidence before the Committee in this case, including the author's confused and incoherent correspondence with the Committee, indicates that his mental health seriously deteriorated during incarceration on death row. Taking into consideration the author's description of the prison conditions, including his allegations about regular beatings inflicted upon him by warders, as well as the ridicule and strain to which he was subjected during the five days he spent in the death cell awaiting execution in February 1988, which the State party has not effectively contested, the Committee concludes that these circumstances reveal a violation of Jamaica's obligations under Articles 7 and 10, paragraph 1, of the Covenant".[212]

The petitioner was entitled to an 'effective remedy, including appropriate medical treatment, compensation and consideration for an early release'.

Another case in which the Committee mentioned the psychological impact of death row is *Williams* v. *Jamaica* (1997).[213] It found violations of Articles 7 and 10(1) because the material before it indicated that the petitioner's mental condition seriously deteriorated during his incarceration on death row. He did not receive any, or at least inadequate, medical treatment for his mental condition.[214] At the time of the decision the petitioner had been removed from death row,

---

Irakli Dokvadze v. *Georgia*, 6 April 1998 (a finding of torture for severe beatings, physical and moral pressure including concussion and broken bones, wounding and burning, scarring, torture and threats to family). See also Chapter VI on ongoing detention situations and Chapter IX on death threats and harassment.

[209] HRC *Earl Pratt and Ivan Morgan* v. *Jamaica*, 6 April 1989.

[210] HRC *Dwayne Hylton* v. *Jamaica*, 15 July 1994.

[211] HRC *Clement Francis* v. *Jamaica*, 25 July 1995 (no provisional measures because the death sentence had already been commuted; provisional measures were used on behalf of other petitioners in earlier case, *C.F.* v. *Jamaica*, 28 July 1992 (inadm.).

[212] HRC *Clement Francis* v. *Jamaica*, 25 July 1995.

[213] HRC *Nathaniel Williams* v. *Jamaica*, 4 November 1997 (classified as non-capital in 1992; the petitioner was re-sentenced to serve a further ten years at the General Penitentiary before becoming eligible for parole).

[214] Counsel had indicated that the petitioner had already displayed signs of mental disturbance at the time of the trial in December 1988. He also referred to correspondence from inmates on death row stating that the petitioner had severe mental problems and was unable to write himself. He referred to a report of a psychiatric examination in March 1992 observing that the petitioner 'had four sticks of wooden matches occluding his left external auditory conduct (ear) which he explained was to shut out the 'voices' which he constantly heard discussing him'. This doctor diagnosed Williams as 'suffering from schizophrenia of a paranoid type, unspecified personality

but he was still suffering this mental condition. The Committee noted that in this case the requisite remedy for the violation of Articles 7 and 10(1) included, in particular, an entitlement to appropriate medical treatment.

In both cases the Committee took into account the psychological impact of detention on death row on the convicted prisoner. Still, it did not literally call this impact a 'death row phenomenon'. It simply condemned the lack of adequate medical treatment and called for appropriate medical treatment. The difference in remedy between the two cases can be explained by the fact that in *Francis* the Committee had also found a violation of Article 14(3)(c) and (5) in relation to the 'inordinate delay in issuing a note of oral judgment in his case'.

Thus, at present the HRC does not consider that a State is in violation of the Covenant if it executes a petitioner after a long period on death row. Its comments imply that it should strive to prevent executions. At the same time it recommends commutation or release only if it finds a specific violation of Article 14. It has not found that a violation of other articles, such as Articles 7 and 10, also resulted in a violation of Article 6, and that, therefore, a death sentence must be commuted.[215] Nor did it find, between 1991 and 1998, that violation of articles other than Article 14, should result in a commutation even if not a violation of Article 6. Paradoxically, this reasoning leads to the conclusion that declaring that the death row phenomenon does *not* violate Article 7 is the only method used by the Committee itself to reduce recourse to the death penalty in cases where it did not find a violation of Article 14. Of course, the Committee does act to reduce recourse to the death penalty in cases of unfair trial. Clearly, if a State executes a prisoner in an expedited manner, without remedying an unfair trial, this will violate the Covenant. The real dilemma for the HRC is not the legal implication of a decision that the death row phenomenon would violate Article 7, but the actual implication that the State would decide to execute a prisoner before he has had a chance to communicate to the HRC about such a violation. Such situation would only leave the HRC the option of deciding in its Concluding Observations to the State party's report under Article 40 ICCPR, that a prisoner had been executed in violation of the right of petition. If the HRC found a violation of Article 14, it would be particularly unsatisfactory if the HRC only had the possibility to refer to this as part of its Concluding Observations to the State party's report. It might very well be the case, moreover, that this way the Committee will never know of these cases.

In cases in which a prisoner would be able, after all, to petition the HRC if it would have set a clear deadline for the stay on death row, this fact could 'provide' the State party with the argument that it was respecting this deadline in executing the prisoner in disregard of provisional measures indicated by the Committee. In my view, these factual implications are the real dilemma. It did not matter what the HRC did, as the JCPC decision in *Pratt and Morgan* v. *Attorney General* (1993) had already triggered the aforementioned negative effect. More recently, this domestic court has tried to remedy this effect by clearly establishing that States could not execute prisoners in violation of the right to fair trial arguing this is necessary in order to limit the length of time on death row so as not to violate the prohibition of cruel treatment. The HRC could take a similar approach. Nevertheless, as long as there is no indication that it may be ready to change its case law in this respect, the Rapporteur should not use provisional measures in cases only claiming a death row phenomenon, because on the merits the Committee would not find a violation.

---

disorder and anxiety and depression, in keeping with the circumstances of his incarceration. He recommended that the author should benefit from regular psychotropic medication'. Counsel visited the petitioner on death row on 18 December 1992. He noted that Williams did not understand the questions he put to him and a senior prison officer as well as other inmates on death row told counsel that the petitioner was ill. His repeated requests for authorisation of a further medical examination had been unsuccessful.

[215] See further Chapter XIII (Protection), discussing the relationship between provisional measures and reparation.

This way the provisional measures would serve no function, within the individual complaint system, other than to postpone the inevitable.

The ECtHR has taken an approach that is different from that of the majority of the HRC. The European Court stated about the long period of time on death row: 'just as some lapse of time between sentence and execution is inevitable if appeal safeguards are to be provided to the condemned person, so it is equally part of human nature that the person will cling to life by exploiting those safeguards to the full'.[216]

An element of delay between the lawful imposition of a death sentence and the exhaustion of available remedies is inherent in the review of a death sentence. Therefore even prolonged periods of detention under a severe custodial regime on death row cannot generally be considered to constitute cruel, inhuman or degrading treatment if the convicted person is merely availing himself of appellate remedies.[217]

Committee member Chanet noted in dissent: 'I consider that the author can not be expected to hurry up in making appeals so he can be executed more rapidly'.

The HRC does attach importance to the question of what caused the delay. It considers that 'prolonged periods of detention under a severe custodial regime on death row cannot generally be considered to constitute cruel, inhuman or degrading treatment if the convicted person is merely availing himself of appellate remedies'.[218]

That a convicted person makes use of a constitutional right for review of his case does not make his stay on death row less cruel. The fact that the prisoner clings to his life is only natural and cannot be used to argue that the time-period spent in expectation of his execution does not subject him to cruel, inhuman and degrading treatment. The prisoner's only choice is between death and death row.

4   CONCLUSION

The three regional systems, the HRC and the Bosnia Chamber have all used provisional measures to halt executions. Especially the HRC and the Inter-American Commission and Court have used such measures very often.

All adjudicators have stressed that their use of provisional measures does not imply a decision on the merits. The Inter-American Court has acknowledged the relationship between the merits of the case and the provisional measures used pending the case. It must be ensured that the State does not anticipate the case by taking action pre-empting that which is requested on the merits. At the same time the adjudicator may not prejudge the case at the stage of provisional measures. What this means in practice is that, as the Inter-American Court has put it, it 'cannot, in a provisional measure, consider the merits of any arguments pertaining to issues other than those which relate strictly to the extreme gravity and urgency and the necessity to avoid irreparable damage to persons'.[219]

---

[216]   The Supreme Court of Zimbabwe, like the European Court, considered the likely effect of the delay to be the proper test, and not the cause of the delay. When the sentence was death, the cause of the delay was immaterial, because the dehumanising character of the delay was unaltered. Per curiam it was decided '(i)t was highly artificial and unrealistic to discount the mental agony and torment experienced on death row on the basis that the condemned prisoner could have shortened his suffering by not making maximum use of the judicial process available. The cause is irrelevant for it fails to lessen the degree of suffering of the condemned person'. In approval, the Supreme Court an Indian case and the ECtHR *Soering* case.

[217]   HRC *Randolph Barrett and Clyde Sutcliffe* v. *Jamaica*, 6 April 1992.

[218]   See HRC *Earl Pratt and Ivan Morgan* v. *Jamaica*, 30 March 1992.

[219]   IACHR *James et al.* cases, Order for provisional measures, 29 August 1998.

This chapter focussed on the unpublished provisional measures by the HRC, dealing with various components of the case law on the death penalty. Among others it dealt with the right to life as such, also referring to the case law of the ECtHR and Bosnia Chamber. The chapter observed that the ECtHR did use provisional measures in cases in which it subsequently could have gone further on the merits. In other words they have been taken also in cases in which a violation later was not, but could have been found on the basis of a more dynamic interpretation of the provisions on the right to life. The Bosnia Chamber's use of provisional measures to halt an execution fits clearly in its case law on the merits. The case law by the HRC on the right to life as such has only recently been clarified. *Judge* v. *Canada* (2003) shows that vis-à-vis non-death penalty States such measures should always be used in refoulement cases involving a real risk of imposition of the death penalty, also when there are no specific concerns regarding the fairness of the proceedings or the person to be sentenced to death in the requesting State. Yet before this clarification the HRC had already used provisional measures in such cases.

Next to the right to life as such this chapter also discussed rights relating specifically to the person sentenced to death. Both the Inter-American Commission and Court and the HRC have found that the death penalty for minors and the mandatory death penalty are forbidden. This makes it obvious that provisional measures should be used pending proceedings involving such claims. It then examined case law referring to several aspects affecting the fairness of death penalty proceedings. The most important claims in death penalty cases in which the HRC has taken provisional measures involve the right to counsel, adequate time and facilities to prepare a defence, right to appeal and effective representation on appeal, fair trial aspects of detention, undue delay and the lack of a written judgment by domestic courts. The chapter indicated the varying prospect of success with such claims. Finally, this chapter dealt with the significance of the death row phenomenon, including its impact on individual petitioners and discussed the limited prospect of success on the merits. In this respect the question arises why the HRC decided to take provisional measures virtually automatically in all death penalty cases to halt executions. In view of the fact that in many cases it may then have to declare, on the basis of its previous case law, that there was no violation, one may wonder whether the object of the provisional measure was simply to postpone the suffering until after the expected finding. This would be an unsatisfactory approach to the concept of provisional measures. If the HRC (in majority) does not consider a certain situation to be in violation of the Covenant and the claim only relates to this issue while there is no indication that it will change its case law, the Rapporteur should not use provisional measures. The main example is the death row phenomenon claim. While there would be good reasons for the Committee to change its case law and find a violation of Article 7 ICCPR in at least some circumstances, as long as there are no indications that it might do so, the Rapporteur should not use provisional measures in relation to such claims.

CHAPTER IV
HALTING CORPORAL PUNISHMENT

1   INTRODUCTION

Thus far only the HRC and the Inter-American Commission have used provisional measures to halt corporal punishment. It is argued that the other human rights adjudicators would also order such provisional measures if faced with a complaint regarding the impending execution of a sentence (or disciplinary measure) of corporal punishment. After all, the prohibition of corporal punishment is widespread and based on the existing case law on the merits.[1]

On the one hand, provisional measures to halt the execution of corporal punishment are similar to those to halt the execution of a death sentence. In both cases these measures appeal to the State to refrain, pending the proceedings, from carrying out a practice that, as Rodley has put it, applies rather than violates *national* law.[2] On the other hand, in the relation of these measures to the merits provisional measures to halt the execution of corporal punishment differ from those halting the execution of a death sentence. As becomes clear in section 3 of this chapter, with regard to corporal punishment the case law on the merits is rather more straightforward and un-controversial, while the previous chapter showed that the case law on the merits regarding the situations in which the death penalty is prohibited is more complicated and therefore the choice to use provisional measures is too.

2   THE PRACTICE OF THE ADJUDICATORS TO TAKE PROVISIONAL MEASURES TO HALT CORPORAL PUNISHMENT

In June 1997, in *Osbourne* v. *Jamaica* (2000), the HRC ordered Jamaica to halt the execution of a sentence of 10 strokes of the tamarind switch.[3] Counsel had argued that the use of this switch was an inherently cruel, inhuman and degrading punishment and that the actual procedure employed for flogging and whipping 'appears to be largely at the discretion of the implementing prison authorities'.[4] This also emphasized the risk of abuse of power.[5] In response, Jamaica invoked the

---

[1]   See section 3.

[2]   Rodley (1999), p. 309.

[3]   HRC *Osbourne* v. *Jamaica*, 15 March 2000. This is also the first case published by the HRC that deals specifically with the issue of corporal punishment. The legislation described the tamarind switch as 'three lengths of twigs of the tamarind tree, each forty-four to forty-eight inches long and not more than one-quarter of one inch in diameter, trimmed smoothly so that there shall be no protrusion of knots or joints and bound together with cotton twine', Article 244(A)(3)(a) The Prison (Amendment) Rules, 7 April 1965, No 115, reproduced at <http://www.corpun.com/japrr1.htm> (consulted 26 April 2007).

[4]   In both Trinidad and Tobago and Jamaica flogging has taken place with the so-called cat-o-nine tails. In Jamaica the Prison (Amendment) Rules, no. 105 of 1965 explain this instrument as follows: 'a rope whip consisting of a round wooden handle twenty inches long, and one to one and on-half inches in diameter with nine thongs of cotton cord and not more than three sixteenths of an inch in diameter and knotted at the end or whipped at the end with cotton twine'. In Jamaica the prison director could choose whether the disciplinary punishment would consist of flogging

permissibility of the sentence under domestic law as a justification for a violation of the ICCPR. The HRC, however, pointed out on the merits that 'the constitutionality of the sentence is not sufficient to secure compliance also with the Covenant'.[6] The second time the HRC used provisional measures to stop a State from carrying out a sentence of corporal punishment (six strokes of the tamarind switch) was in 1998 in the case of *Higginson* v. *Jamaica* (2002).[7]

The Inter-American Commission has also used precautionary measures at least once in order to halt the execution of a flogging sentence, in a case against the Bahamas. It did so in February 2003 immediately upon confirmation from the petitioner that his sentence had not yet been

---

or whipping. Flogging would be inflicted with the cat-o-nine tails on the back of the prisoner between the shoulders and the waist. Whipping would be inflicted with a tamarind switch on the prisoner's buttocks.

[5] He invoked the affidavit of a former detainee who had already suffered the execution of a sentence of corporal punishment. E.P. had been sentenced to four years hard labour and six strokes of the tamarind switch. He was scheduled for release on 1 March 1997 after he had been granted a remission of his sentence for good behaviour. In his affidavit he stated that on the day before his release more than twelve correctional officers took him from his cell to another section of the prison. He protested when he realised that they were going to carry out the sentence of flogging. As a result, one of the officers hit him in the stomach. He stated that 'an unnecessary number of prison warders (25) were present at the time of the whipping and that this added to his humiliation', *Osbourne* v. *Jamaica*, 15 March 2000, §3.3. "He was then seized, blindfolded and ordered to remove clothing from the lower part of his body. When this was done, he was forced to lean forward across a barrel and one of the warders placed his penis in a slot in the barrel. He was then strapped in that position and struck across the buttocks with an instrument that he was unable to see". Affidavit as discussed in *Osbourne* v. *Jamaica*, 15 March 2000, §3.3. He also noted that the doctor was the only outsider present and that this doctor did not examine him after the whipping. Affidavit as discussed in *Osbourne* v. *Jamaica*, 15 March 2000, §3.3. The Amnesty International report 'Jamaica; a summary of concerns: a briefing for the Human Rights Committee', October 1997, AI Index: AMR 38/07/97 referred on p. 15 to petitions filed with the HRC by Errol Pryce and George Osbourne, which were still pending at the time. The petition of Errol Pryce included an affidavit describing the circumstances of his whipping. He was the first person whipped by court order in over 20 years. Amnesty International describes the same circumstances as mentioned in the affidavit by E.P. to which the HRC refers in its View in *Osbourne* v. *Jamaica*. The only additional information it provides is that the person whipping Errol Pryce was wearing a hood covering his face and a long gown concealing his body. Newspaper articles have also referred to this case, e.g. 'Court of appeal to decide on flogging', B. Gayle, staff reporter, The Gleaner, 28 April 1998 and 'Jamaican court abolishes flogging', Reuters, CNN, 18 December 1998. In 2004 the HRC published its Views in this case, finding a violation of Article 7: *Errol Pryce* v. *Jamaica*, 15 March 2004.

[6] HRC *Osbourne* v. *Jamaica*, 15 March 2000, §9.1. It was its firm opinion that the imposition of corporal punishment constituted cruel, inhuman and degrading punishment in violation of Article 7 ICCPR, even if it had not been carried out. Under Article 2(3)(a) ICCPR Jamaica was 'under an obligation to provide Mr. Osbourne with an effective remedy, and should compensate him for the violation. The State party is also under an obligation to refrain from carrying out the sentence of whipping upon Mr. Osbourne. The State party should ensure that similar violations do not occur in the future by repealing the legislative provisions that allow for corporal punishment'.

[7] HRC *Higginson* v. *Jamaica*, 28 March 2002. Higginson submitted his complaint in January 1997. He had been sentenced to several years of imprisonment with hard labour as well as six strokes of the tamarind switch. In this case the petitioner was not represented by counsel in the proceedings before the HRC. The Rapporteur used provisional measures a year later. Jamaica's denunciation of the OP did not play a role yet as it became effective only on 23 January 1998.

carried out. The State acknowledged receipt of this request, noting that it had been 'referred to the relevant authorities for their attention'.[8]

3   RELATION BETWEEN PROVISIONAL MEASURES TO HALT CORPORAL PUNISHMENT AND THE EXPECTED DECISION ON THE MERITS

As to punishments for disciplinary offences, Article 31 UN Standard Minimum Rules for the Treatment of Prisoners points out that corporal punishment 'shall be completely prohibited'.[9] The aversion against corporal punishment is apparent as well in UN Rules dealing with juveniles in detention.[10] Moreover, the punishment is prohibited in international humanitarian law.[11] Doctrinally it is not surprising that the HRC used provisional measures to halt corporal punishment. Already in its General Comment on Article7 ICCPR (1992) it had pointed out that the prohibition of cruel, inhuman or degrading punishment must extend to corporal punishment.[12]

---

[8]   CIDH *Prince Pinder* v. *Bahamas,* 12 October 2005 (adm.), §11. The petition was based on the American Declaration. The Commission repeated its request almost two months later, but received no response other than an acknowledgment of receipt, §13 (precautionary measures of 4 February, acknowledgment of receipt of 8 April 2003; reiteration of precautionary measure on 30 May 2003; acknowledgment of receipt 30 June 2003). No information is provided in the 2003 Annual Report's overview of precautionary measures. See also decision on the merits of 15 October 2007.

[9]   Standard Minimum Rules for the Treatment of Prisoners, Adopted by the First United Nations Congress on the Prevention of Crime and the Treatment of Offenders, held at Geneva in 1955, and approved by the Economic and Social Council by its resolution 663 C (XXIV) of 31 July 1957 and 2076 (LXII) of 13 May 1977. On the language used see Rodley (1999), p. 316.

[10]   See e.g. United Nations Rules for the Protection of Juveniles Deprived of their Liberty, G.A. res. 45/113, annex, 45 U.N. GAOR Supp. (No. 49A), p. 205, A/45/49 (1990); United Nations Guidelines for the Prevention of Juvenile Delinquency (The Riyadh Guidelines), G.A. res. 45/112, annex, 45 U.N. GAOR Supp. (No. 49A), p. 201, A/45/49 (1990) and Standard Minimum Rules for the Administration of Juvenile Justice ("The Beijing Rules"), G.A. res. 40/33, annex 40 U.N. GAOR Supp. (No. 53), p. 207, A/40/53 (1985). The Commentary to the latter notes: "The provision against corporal punishment is in line with article 7 of the International Covenant on Civil and Political Rights and the Declaration on the Protection of All Persons from Being Subjected to Torture and Other Cruel, Inhuman or Degrading Treatment or Punishment, as well as the Convention against Torture and Other Cruel, Inhuman or Degrading Treatment or Punishment and the draft convention on the rights of the child".

[11]   See e.g. Rodley (1999), pp. 314-316.

[12]   See e.g. HRC General Comment 20, 4 March 1992, §5. Like the HRC, CAT has equally shown a special interest in the abolition of corporal punishment. Such punishment 'could constitute in itself a violation in terms of the Convention'. CAT Concluding Observations on Jordan, A/50/44, 1 May 1995, §169. See also, e.g., its Concluding Observations on Namibia, A/52/44, 6 May 1997, §150. In addition, the Committee on the Rights of the Child, supervising the Convention on the Rights of the Child, has confirmed 'the obligation of all States parties to move quickly to prohibit and eliminate all corporal punishment and all other cruel or degrading forms of punishment of children'. Committee on the Rights of the Child General Comment No. 8 (2006) on "The right to protection from corporal punishment and other cruel or degrading forms of punishment (Articles 19; 28(2); and 37)", CRC/C/GC/8, 2 March 2007, §2. UN Charter-based bodies have confirmed this approach: Commission on Human Rights, Res. 1997/38, E/CN.4/1997/150, April 1997 and Res. 2000/43, E/CN.4/Res. 2000/43, 20 April 2000: "Corporal punishment, including of children, can amount to cruel, inhuman or degrading punishment or even to torture". The consecutive Special Rapporteurs on Torture (Kooijmans, Rodley, Van

The individual cases in which the HRC dealt with corporal punishment all relate to Jamaica and Trinidad and Tobago.[13] In the latter State the punishment is still possible.[14] No one but the court and the President can repeal a prisoner's flogging sentence. Flogging is also used as a means of prison discipline.[15] The case of *Errol Pryce* v. *Jamaica* (2004) had been submitted in May 1997, subsequent to the carrying out of corporal punishment on the petitioner in February of that year.[16] While the HRC only published its Views in 2004, this case had triggered considerable interest in 1997 and may have drawn the attention of the HRC to the possibility of using provisional measures to halt corporal punishment.[17]

Boven, Nowak) have taken the view that corporal punishment is inconsistent with the prohibition of torture and other cruel, inhuman or degrading treatment or punishment enshrined in the Universal Declaration of Human Rights. See e.g. Rapporteur Van Boven's interim report to the General Assembly A/57/173, 2 July 2002, §48, confirming the approach of the other Rapporteurs. The urgent action sent by Rapporteur Nowak to the Bahamas on behalf of a person sentenced to eight lashes with a 'cat-of-nine-tails', on 10 October 2006, confirms this view, A/HRC/4/33/Add.1., 20 March 2007, p. 16.

[13] In most Caribbean States corporal punishment is a remainder of slavery times and was used mainly until the Second World War. For information on other sentences of flogging, next to that of Osbourne, see Amnesty International's Annual Reports 1995, 1996 and 1998. See also Amnesty's report 'Jamaica: A summary of concerns, A briefing for the Human Rights Committee, October 1997, AI Index: AMR 38/07/97. In later Annual Reports, following 1998, Amnesty International does not further discuss corporal punishment in Jamaica (the Jamaica Court of Appeal declared corporal punishment unconstitutional in December 1998).

[14] Amnesty International's Annual Report 1994 refers to the case of an eleven-year-old boy who was sentenced to twenty strokes with a leather belt for possession of cocaine. He had no opportunity to appeal the sentence as it was carried out immediately. Its Annual Report 1995 mentions that subsequently there was a court hearing in this case in which the boy sought redress and compensation. See further Annual Reports 1996, 1997 and 1998. See also Amnesty International, Trinidad and Tobago: woman sentenced to corporal punishment, March 1996, AI Index: AMR 49/07/96. In its Annual Report 1999 it pointed out that at least three people may have been whipped in 1998. They had been sentenced that same year. It noted that the Court of Appeal reportedly described as 'monstrous' the fact that in August one person received fifteen lashes while the appeal of his conviction and sentence was still pending.

[15] Flogging is mainly carried out at the maximum-security prison of Carrera Island, which has a special 'whipping room'. "The naked prisoner is placed face down on an adjustable bench and handcuffed. He never knows who delivers the blows – the officer is masked or the prisoner's face is turned. Many people are present during a flogging, including the prison doctor, the infirmary officer, the prison superintendent, and several other senior officials. The doctor is responsible for examining the prisoner's heart rate, blood pressure, respiratory rate and other signs both before and after the flogging. S/he can suspend the flogging or whipping if s/he considers that the prisoner is physically unfit to withstand the punishment". Amnesty International, Trinidad and Tobago: woman sentenced to corporal punishment, March 1996, AI Index: AMR 49/07/96, p. 2.

[16] HRC *Errol Pryce* v. *Jamaica*, 15 March 2004 (finding a violation of Article 7). Amnesty International had earlier reported on this case: Amnesty International report 'Jamaica; a summary of concerns: a briefing for the Human Rights Committee', October 1997, AI Index: AMR 38/07/97. The Special Rapporteur on Torture had equally referred to it: E/CN.4/1999/61, §§399-403.

[17] See further HRC *Higginson* v. *Jamaica*, 28 March 2002. Again it pointed out that it was its 'consistent opinion' that corporal punishment violates Article 7, 'irrespective of the nature of the crime that is to be punished or the permissibility of corporal punishment under domestic law'. In its Concluding Observations, under the reporting procedure (Article 40), it has also addressed the issue: see e.g. its Concluding Observations in relation to Sudan CCPR/C/79/Add. 85, 5 November 1997: "Flogging, amputation and stoning, which are recognised as penalties for

In *Matthews* v. *Trinidad and Tobago* (1998)[18] the petitioner had claimed violations of Art. 10(1) ICCPR because of the conditions of detention, in particular the sanitary conditions. In passing, he mentioned that he had been sentenced to 20 years imprisonment and 20 strokes with a birch. While he did not claim a violation with respect to corporal punishment, the Committee raised the issue *proprio motu*, recalling its General Comment on Article 7 ICCPR. In its admissibility decision it requested Trinidad and Tobago to inform it whether the punishment had already been carried out.[19] The HRC may have used provisional measures in this case, but given the fact that it only raised the issue *proprio motu* when discussing admissibility it is unlikely that it did so.[20]

The Committee could also have concluded already in this case that the imposition of the punishment *in itself* was a violation of Article 7. It could have pointed out in the decision on the merits that the State party was under an obligation not to carry out the sentence of 20 strokes with a birch, as it indeed did in the later case of *Sooklal* v. *Trinidad and Tobago* (2001).[21] In that case the petitioner was serving a prison sentence and was sentenced to twelve strokes with the birch. His complaint related to Articles 9(3) and 14(3)(c) but the Committee pointed out, again *proprio motu*, that the facts of the case also raised an issue under Article 7 ICCPR. It referred to its decision in the abovementioned *Osbourne* v. *Jamaica* (2000), a case in which it had used provisional measures. In that case it had decided on the merits that, irrespective of the brutality of the crime that was to be punished, it was 'the firm opinion of the Committee' that corporal punishment constituted cruel, inhuman or degrading punishment.[22] In the *Sooklal* case it found that by imposing the sentence of whipping with the birch Trinidad had violated Article 7 ICCPR. In other words, the imposition of the sentence was already a violation, even if it had not been carried out. This time it did point out, in the paragraph discussing the entitlement to an effective remedy, that if the State had not yet executed the sentence of corporal punishment it was under an obligation not to do so.[23] It appears, however, that pending the proceedings before it, it did not order provisional measures *proprio motu* in this case, while it could have done so.

The ECtHR already determined in *Tyrer* v. *UK* (1978) that Article 3 ECHR did not allow for corporal punishment:

---

criminal offences, are not compatible with the Covenant. (...) By ratifying the Covenant, the State party has undertaken to comply with all its articles; penalties which are inconsistent with articles 7 and 10 must be abolished". See also Concluding Observations about Iraq's fourth periodic report CCPR/C/79/Add.84, 5 November 1997 (expressing deep concern about the use of punishment such as amputation and branding, pointing out that such punishments should cease immediately).

[18] HRC *Matthews* v. *Trinidad and Tobago*, 31 March 1998.

[19] When it discussed the merits, however, it noted that the State had not provided any information on the issue and that the petitioner himself had not raised it. It considered that this implied 'that the punishment, if imposed on him, may not have been carried out'. The Committee noted that it 'maintains that corporal punishment is incompatible with the provisions of article 7 of the Covenant, but makes no finding in this respect in the present case'. HRC *Matthews* v. *Trinidad and Tobago*, 31 March 1998, §7.2.

[20] This is a case from the time period during which the HRC did not provide information on the use provisional measures in its Views. A consultation of the file in Geneva confirms that the note verbale to the State party of 5 January 1994 was transmitted under Rule 91 (transfer of petition to State and requests for information) alone. A further Rule 91 decision of 4 April 1995 did not refer to the issue either (on file with the author).

[21] HRC *Boodlal Sooklal* v. *Trinidad and Tobago*, 25 October 2001.

[22] HRC *Osbourne* v. *Jamaica*, 15 March 2000.

[23] HRC *Boodlal Sooklal* v. *Trinidad and Tobago*, 25 October 2001.

"The very nature of judicial corporal punishment is that it involves one human being inflicting physical violence on another human being. Furthermore, it is institutionalised violence that is in the present case violence permitted by the law, ordered by the judicial authorities of the State and carried out by the police authorities of the State (...). Thus, although the applicant did not suffer any severe or long-lasting physical effects, his punishment – whereby he was treated as an object in the power of the authorities – constituted an assault on precisely that which it is one of the main purposes of Article 3 (art. 3) to protect, namely a person's dignity and physical integrity. Neither can it be excluded that the punishment may have had adverse psychological effects".[24]

As judicial corporal punishment and disciplinary corporal punishment in detention (administrative punishment) no longer exist in Europe, the ECtHR has dealt with no further cases in this respect.

In *Doebbler* v. *Sudan* (2003) the African Commission found that the punishment of flagellation was a violation of the right to respect for physical integrity and human dignity (Article 5 ACHPR).[25] In this light, should it deal with a complaint involving a sentence of corporal punishment that has not yet been executed, its use of provisional measures may be expected.

As discussed in section 2 of this Chapter in 2003 the Inter-American Commission has already used provisional measures to halt corporal punishment in a complaint involving the American Declaration. In this case it found on the merits (2007) that:

"While there is no evidence before the Commission that Mr. Pinder has actually been subjected to corporal punishment, the Commission considers that the jurisprudence makes it palpably clear that the mere anticipation of flogging is within the parameters of the cruel, inhuman and degrading elements of judicial corporal punishment. Corporal punishment is not simply about the actual pain or humiliation of a flogging, but also about the mental suffering that is generated by anticipating the flogging".[26]

---

[24] ECtHR *Tyrer* v. *UK*, 25 April 1978, §33. It added, also at §33: "The institutionalised character of this violence is further compounded by the whole aura of official procedure attending the punishment and by the fact that those inflicting it were total strangers to the offender. Admittedly, the relevant legislation provides that in any event birching shall not take place later than six months after the passing of sentence. However, this does not alter the fact that there had been an interval of several weeks since the applicant's conviction by the juvenile court and a considerable delay in the police station where the punishment was carried out. Accordingly, in addition to the physical pain he experienced, Mr. Tyrer was subjected to the mental anguish of anticipating the violence he was to have inflicted on him". Moreover, at §35: "The indignity of having the punishment administered over the bare posterior aggravated to some extent the degrading character of the applicant's punishment but it was not the only or determining factor".

[25] ACHPR *Curtis Francis Doebbler* v. *Sudan*, May 2003.

[26] CIDH *Prince Pinder* v. *Bahamas*, 15 October 2007 (merits), §35. Both the Court of Appeal of the Bahamas and the Judicial Committee of the Privy Council had identified flogging as inhuman and degrading, but because of a so-called 'savings clause' they decided to nevertheless dismiss the complaint. They had held that corporal punishment is permitted under the Constitution of the Bahamas by virtue of Article 17 (2), which provides that 'nothing contained in or done under authority of law shall be held inconsistent with or in contravention of this Article to the extent that the law in question authorizes the infliction of any description of punishment that was lawful in the Bahama Islands immediately before 10 July 1973'. See CIDH *Prince Pinder* v. *Bahamas*, 12 October 2005 (adm.), §§14 and 17, referring to the Court of Appeal judgment of 29 January 1999 and the Privy Council judgment of 15 July 2002. See also the criticisms of a similar 'savings clause', which 'has the past prevail into the future', by Judge García Ramírez in his Separate Opinion to IACHR *Caesar* v. *Trinidad and Tobago*, 11 March 2005, §§24-28 and by Judge Jackman.

By this time the Inter-American Court itself, in *Caesar v. Trinidad and Tobago* (2005) had confirmed unequivocally that such punishment is prohibited under the ACHR. In this case, involving a punishment of 15 strokes with the 'cat-o-nine-tails', the Commission had not used precautionary measures as the punishment had already been carried out. The Commission had found a violation of the right to humane treatment (Article 5 ACHR) and subsequently brought the case before the Court. The Court pointed out that the practices of torture as well as other cruel, inhuman or degrading treatment or punishment all 'constitute a violation of peremptory norms of international law', independent of any codification.[27] The Court noted 'the growing trend towards recognition, at international and domestic levels, of the impermissible character of corporal punishment, with regard to its inherently cruel, inhuman and degrading nature'.[28] Consequently, State Parties to the ACHR, under Articles 1(1) and 5, are 'under an obligation *erga omnes* to abstain from imposing corporal punishment, as well as to prevent its administration, for constituting, in any circumstance, a cruel, inhuman or degrading treatment or punishment'.[29] It considered that judicial corporal punishment by flogging, as applied in the law and practice of Trinidad and Tobago, by its very nature reflected 'an institutionalization of violence, which although permitted by the law, ordered by the State's judges and carried out by its prison authorities, is a sanction incompatible with the Convention'.[30] In fact, corporal punishment by flogging constituted as such a from of torture and therefore was 'a violation *per se* of the right of any person subjected to such punishment to have his physical, mental and moral integrity respected, as provided in Article 5(1) and 5(2), in connection with Article 1(1) of the Convention'.[31] The Court determined that 'the corporal punishment by flogging, as it was examined in the instant case, must be considered as a form of torture and is, therefore, contrary *per se* to Article 5(1) and 5(2) of the Convention and to peremptory norms of international law'.[32] The Court's finding that corporal punishment constitutes a violation of the prohibition cruel treatment (and in some cases, such as that of *Caesar* involving flogging, even torture)[33] brings any provisional measures ordered to halt the execution of such punishment firmly within the common core of the concept. This is confirmed by the Court's express reference to peremptory norms of international law. Thus, should the Inter-American Court deal with a complaint involving a sentence of corporal punishment, imposed at a time when the State party had recognized the jurisdiction of the Court,[34] but which has not yet been executed, the Court would most certainly order provisional measures.

4   CONCLUSION

Only two adjudicators, the HRC and the Inter-American Commission, have used provisional measures to order a halt to the execution of a sentence of corporal punishment and their practice in this regard is limited. Yet the existing case law on the prohibition of corporal punishment is straightforward. This punishment is contrary to the prohibition of torture and/or cruel treatment, as has been widely accepted among the various human rights adjudicators. The fact that they have

---

[27]   IACHR *Caesar* v. *Trinidad and Tobago*, 11 March 2005, §70.
[28]   Id., §70.
[29]   Id., §70.
[30]   Id., §73.
[31]   Id., §73.
[32]   Id., §88. See also §73.
[33]   The Court spoke of flogging as 'in absolute contravention to the Convention' and it spoke of the 'aberrant character of such punishment', IACHR *Caesar* v. *Trinidad and Tobago*, 11 March 2005, §130.
[34]   See further Chapter XIV (Jurisdiction).

not developed an extensive practice of using provisional measures in this regard seems to be based more on the fact that they have not received requests to this effect. Those States that still use corporal punishment (several States applying a version of *shari'a* law and a decreasing number of Caribbean States) mostly have not recognized individual complaint mechanisms and in most of the States that have recognized such mechanisms, this punishment has been abolished. Moreover, in those States in which corporal punishment is still applied that *have* recognized international mechanisms for individual complaint a tradition to resort to such mechanisms is yet to be developed. What is clear from the case law on the merits, as well as from other international statements and legal documents, is that would they be faced with requests for provisional measures to halt corporal punishment, the human rights adjudicators would grant these requests. In fact this type of provisional measures belongs to the common core of the concept as it aims to prevent irreparable harm to persons.[35]

---

[35]   See further Conclusion Part II.

Chapter V
Halting Expulsion or Extradition in Non-Refoulement Cases

1   Introduction

Human rights adjudicators take provisional measures to halt a deportation, expulsion or extradition pending the proceedings, based on the requirement of non-refoulement. The non-refoulement principle is laid down, among others, in the UN Refugees Convention. Article 33(1) defines this principle as follows:

> "No Contracting State shall expel or return ("refouler") a refugee in any manner whatsoever to the frontiers of territories where his life or freedom would be threatened on account of his race, religion, nationality, membership of a particular social group or particular political opinion".[1]

The human rights adjudicators have also read this principle into the prohibition of torture and cruel treatment included in the respective human rights treaties and virtually all human rights adjudicators have used provisional measures in the context of claims involving non-refoulement.

The previous chapter on halting executions already discussed the treaty provisions and case law involving the right to life and the prohibition of cruel treatment, which are also relevant in the context of non-refoulement. This chapter specifically addresses the question which situations involving claims of non-refoulement have warranted provisional measures. In expulsion or extradition, are the rights invoked at least *capable* of being interpreted such that a violation could be concluded? As noted, this book argues that the use of provisional measures would otherwise be inappropriate.

2   Practice

2.1   Introduction

CAT and the ECtHR have used provisional measures almost exclusively to ensure respect for the principle of non-refoulement. Yet most of the case law of these adjudicators is devoted to the evidentiary requirements for finding a violation, an issue which is further discussed in Chapter XV (Immediacy and risk), rather than to the interpretation and scope of the rights. The Inter-American Commission and the HRC have used provisional measures less often to halt expulsion or extradition, but their practice in this regard nevertheless provides useful information on preventing irreparable harm.

---

[1]   See 1951 Convention relating to the status of refugees, entered into force 22 April 1954 (143 State Parties as of 1 September 2005); 1967 Protocol relating to the status of refugees, entered into force 4 October 1967 (143 State Parties as of 1 September 2005); some States have ratified the Protocol but not the Convention itself, see e.g. the US and Venezuela. About the UN High Commissioner on Refugees see e.g. <www.unhcr.ch>. Generally about the rights of refugees see e.g. Macklin (1995), pp. 251-277; Cançado Trindade (1997); Gorlick (1999); Clark (1999); Nicholson/Twomey (1999); Smeulers (2002), pp. 45-52 and references and Goodwin-Gill (2007).

2.2 CAT

The UN Committee against Torture has used its provisional measures almost exclusively to halt expulsion and extradition. Article 3 UN Convention against Torture stipulates:

> "No State Party shall expel, return ('*refouler*') or extradite a person to another State where there are substantial grounds for believing that he would be in danger of being subjected to torture".

This is the article most often invoked in petitions to the CAT. The Committee has devoted a specific General Recommendation to Article 3.[2] Many cases have been submitted especially from Canada, Switzerland and Sweden. Other addressee States have included Australia, Venezuela, France and the Netherlands. The reason why the Committee has not yet dealt with complaints against some of the other States Parties that have nevertheless recognised its competence to do so may simply be that lawyers from those States have not yet found their way to Geneva.[3]

The UN Convention against Torture is the only human rights treaty with a specific provision on non-refoulement. As noted, on the merits the cases dealt with by CAT are particularly relevant for the discussion of evidentiary requirements and most often the reason for the use of provisional measures or for denying petitioners' requests in this respect simply lies in CAT's preliminary assessment of the evidence of risk.[4]

In 1993 it started to examine the first petitions. It became clear immediately that most complaints would involve the principle of non-refoulement and would include a request for provisional measures. During the first years the Committee took provisional measures in almost all of these cases and very often it found a violation on the merits. Some of the States involved showed their unhappiness about this, which appears to have resulted, at least for a period of time, in decisions by the Committee to decrease the number of cases in which it would find a violation. It also took provisional measures less often.[5] Nevertheless it has used them regularly and has also made some strong statements on the merits both with regard to the need to protect petitioners with and without refugee status against refoulement.

In *Agiza* v. *Sweden* (2005) CAT recalled 'that the Convention's protections are absolute, even in the context of national security concerns, and that such considerations emphasise the importance of appropriate review mechanisms. While national security concerns might justify some adjustments to be made to the particular process of review, the mechanism chosen must continue to satisfy article 3's requirements of effective, independent and impartial review'.[6]

It has also confirmed the authority of the UNHCR when it comes to petitioners who have been recognized as a refugee. In *Elif Pelit* v. *Azerbaijan* (2007) it noted that the petitioner 'was

---

[2] CAT General Comment No. 1: Implementation of Article 3 of the Convention in the context of Article 22, 21 November 1997. See further Chapter XV (Immediacy and risk).

[3] Of the States parties to the ICAT 61 have also recognised the right of individual petition. See <http://www2.ohchr.org/english/bodies/ratification/9.htm> (last updated 18 April 2008). The Committee has dealt with individual complaints against 21 of these States, mostly involving the issue of non-refoulement. About the individual complaint procedure and case law see Doerfel (2005); Ingelse (2001); Gorlick (2000); Gorlick (1999).

[4] See Chapter XV (Immediacy and risk). In some cases States ignored the provisional measures decided upon by CAT, see e.g. *Tebourski* v. *France*, 1 May 2007; *Dar* v. *Norway*, 11 May 2007 (in which the State subsequently facilitated the petitioner's return to Norway) and *Singh Sogi* v. *Canada*, 16 November 2007. State party responses are further discussed in Chapter XVII and the legal status of provisional measures in Chapter XVI.

[5] This is further discussed in Chapter XV on immediacy and risk.

[6] CAT *Ahmed Hussein Mustafa Kamil Agiza* v. *Sweden*, 20 May 2005, §13.8. See also Van Boven (2006), pp. 746-758 and Joseph (2005), pp. 339-346.

recognised as a refugee in Germany, as it had been concluded that she would be at risk of persecution if she was returned to Turkey. Her refugee status remained valid at the time of her deportation to Turkey by the State party authorities'. The Committee recalled Conclusion No. 12 of the UNHCR's Executive Committee 'On the extraterritorial effect of the determination of refugee status", pursuant to whose letter (f) "the very purpose of the 1951 Convention and the 1967 Protocol implies that refugee status determined by one Contracting State will be recognized also by the other Contracting States".[7]

2.3   HRC

Apart from CAT, with its explicit reference to non-refoulement, the other human rights adjudicators read the principle of non-refoulement into the prohibition of torture and cruel treatment. The HRC has recognised the principle on the basis of the obligations of States under Article 7 ICCPR (prohibition of torture and cruel treatment) and Article 6 (right to life), in light of the undertaking in Article 2 to ensure the rights in the Covenant to all individuals within its territory and subject to its jurisdiction.

It has also dealt with requests for provisional measures to halt an impending extradition, expulsion, deportation or other form of forced return until it had been able to determine whether this would result in a violation of the principle of non-refoulement underlying Articles 6 and 7 ICCPR.

The earliest known expulsion case in which it used provisional measures dates from 1978, a year after it had published its first decision on the merits. It involves an unspecified State. The Committee intervened almost nine months after it adopted its Rules of Procedure. In this case, *O.E.* v. *S.* (1978), it decided to inform the State of the Committee's view 'that pending further consideration of the case, the alleged victim, having sought refuge in S, should not be handed over or expelled to country X'.[8] The case represents the earliest *explicit* use of provisional measures by the HRC, not only in expulsion cases but in general. Insufficient information is available about the existing threat in country X. It is not clear whether there was a real risk of the death penalty in that country or a real risk of torture or ill treatment.

Since this case the HRC has taken provisional measures on behalf of a number of persons in extradition cases. Most of them were facing the death penalty in the requesting State.[9] Canada extradited both Kindler and Ng to the United States in September 1991 after the Supreme Court of Canada had rendered judgment in their cases. It did so in spite of the Committee's provisional measures taken earlier that month.[10] The HRC used provisional measures not only in the cases *Kindler* v. *Canada* and *Ng* v. *Canada* but also in a few other extradition cases. In *K.C.* v. *Canada*

---

[7]   CAT *Elif Pelit* v. *Azerbaijan*, 1 May 2007, §11.

[8]   In the same letter, but before mentioning Rule 86, it already asked the State party to inform the HRC whether it was contemplating the deportation or extradition of the alleged victim to country X. It also requested the petitioner to provide information in substantiation of his claim of violation of the Articles 7, 9, 13, 14 and 15 ICCPR. *O.E.* v. *S.*, 25 January 1978.

[9]   See HRC *Kindler, Ng, Cox* and *E.G.* v. *Canada* and *Weiss* v. *Austria*. Weiss was not facing the death penalty. All other cases relate to Canada and to extradition requests from the US. Canada abolished the death penalty in 1976. Article 6 of the 1976 Extradition Treaty between Canada and the US provides: "When the offence for which extradition is requested is punishable by death under the laws of the requesting State and the laws of the requested State do not permit such punishment for that offence, extradition may be refused unless the requesting State provides such assurances as the requested State considers efficient that the death penalty shall not be imposed or, if imposed, shall not be executed".

[10]   See also Chapter XVII on the official State responses.

(inadm. 1992) and in the follow-up case *Cox* v. *Canada* (1994), for instance, the petitioner equally requested the HRC 'to adopt interim measures of protection because extradition of the author to the United States would deprive the Committee of its jurisdiction to consider the communication, and the author to properly pursue his communication'. This means that counsel clearly provided a specific rationale for the use of provisional measures, relating to the right to individual complaint and the consequent possibility for the HRC to properly consider such complaints. The HRC Special Rapporteur took provisional measures 'to defer the author's extradition until the Committee had had an opportunity to consider the admissibility of the issues placed before it'.[11] *E.G.* v. *Canada* (disc. 1997), another extradition case in which provisional measures were used, equally involved the death penalty.[12] The petitioner had submitted he had 'an arguable case' of a breach of the ICCPR. One of the arguments related to execution by electric chair. Another argument was that of the risk of a death sentence for a federal drugs charge involving large quantities of marijuana, which would not meet the 'most serious crimes' standard in the ICCPR.[13]

There are also *expulsion* cases in which the HRC used provisional measures to halt refoulement (regarding Articles 6 and 7 claims) and one case in which it requested the State to halt the return of the petitioner in light of the right to family life (Articles 17 and 23 claim).[14]

As noted, the HRC first took provisional measures to halt an expulsion in 1978. Surprisingly, according to the available information the next time it used provisional measures in an expulsion case was in 1993.[15] In *A.A.T.* v. *Hungary* (disc. 1994)[16] the petitioner submitted that a deportation to Iraq would jeopardise his life and security. Apparently the authorities had already issued a deportation order. He had been a soldier in the Iraqi army for two years. He claimed that he deserted at the outbreak of the Gulf war in 1991, because he refused to fight for Saddam Hussein in what he felt was a senseless war. He added that he lost five members of his family during the war. Several months after his arrival in Hungary he was arrested by the police and charged with robbery. He claimed to be innocent and the victim of confusion. Following informal inter-

---

[11] HRC *K.C.* v. *Canada*, 29 July 1992 (inadm.); *Cox* v. *Canada*, 31 October 1994. In the View the HRC mentions 12 January 1993 (§4.1). On the cover page, on the other hand, it mentions 20 April 1993.

[12] HRC *E.G.* v. *Canada* (738/1997), initial submission of 5 January 1997 (received 7 January 1997), Rule 86/91 of 17 January 1997; withdrawal of Rule 86 on 28 April 1997; petitioner's request to withdraw the case of 26 May 1997. On 17 November 1997 the HRC informed the petitioner that it had discontinued the case (on file with the author).

[13] The Canadian Minister of Justice had authorised his extradition without asking assurances against the death penalty, in reference to a sworn affidavit by a State prosecutor stating that the prosecution declined to seek the death penalty for the murder he had been charged with under Florida law. The petitioner noted, however, that he might be sentenced to death under federal law. From the court file establishing probable cause, rather than from the extradition request itself, it appeared that the US government had evidence that the petitioner was involved in a conspiracy to posses marijuana involving a quantity in excess of 1.000 kilos. The petitioner had been advised that if the US could prove that the killing for which he was charged in State court was part of the overall drug activity, the federal prosecutor could seek the death penalty pursuant to federal law. The federal prosecutor had refused to indicate whether he would seek the death penalty and Canada had not obtained assurances from him that it would not be imposed. The petitioner requested the HRC to use provisional measures under Rule 86 and ten days after the receipt of this request the HRC indeed used Rule 86. Initial submission of 5 January 1997; note verbale to the Permanent Representative of Canada of 17 January 1997 (on file with the author). In general on *Kindler, Ng* and *Cox*, see e.g. Harrington (2006), pp. 82-134.

[14] The latter case is discussed in Chapter XII (Other situations).

[15] As noted, in 1991 and 1992 it used provisional measures to halt extraditions.

[16] HRC *A.A.T.* v. *Hungary*, 543/1993 (disc. 1994); initial submission of 10 August 1992; Rule 86/91 of 2 June 1993 (on file with the author).

ventions the Special Rapporteur used provisional measures in June 1993. Apparently the case was subsequently solved.[17]

The petitioner's husband in *G.T.* v. *Australia* (1997),[18] a case similar to *A.R.J.* v. *Australia* (1997),[19] had been convicted for importing around 240 grams of heroin from Malaysia into Australia. While he was in prison he applied for refugee status. The Refugee Tribunal refused his application because, although it considered that there was indeed a 'real chance' that he would face imposition of the death penalty in Malaysia, this did not constitute persecution in terms of the Refugee Convention.[20] The Note Verbale to the State referred explicitly to the fact that Australia had abolished the death penalty and had acceded to the Second OP on the abolition of the death penalty.[21]

In the later case of *Ahani* v. *Canada* (2004)[22] the HRC used provisional measures for the State to refrain from deporting the petitioner to Iran 'until the Committee has had an opportunity to consider the allegations, in particular those that relate to torture, other inhuman treatment or even death as a consequence of the deportation'. Mansour Ahani feared torture and ill treatment if he were to be returned. The State nevertheless deported him.[23] Reportedly he was briefly detained upon his return to Iran and has not been heard from since. There have been several other cases as well in which the HRC used provisional measures to halt refoulement. These include cases against Australia,[24] Canada,[25] France,[26] Denmark[27] and Kyrgyzstan.[28]

---

[17] In August 1994 the HRC sent the petitioner the message that it had discontinued examination of his case. This was sent to him at an address in Hungary, which may mean that he had not been deported. Correspondence from 10 August 1992 to 17 August 1994 in *A.A.T.* v. *Hungary* (543/1993), (on file with the author).

[18] HRC *Mrs. G.T.* v. *Australia*, 4 November 1997.

[19] HRC *A.R.J.* v. *Australia*, 28 July 1997. The alleged victim was an Iranian citizen detained in Western Australia. The Australian Refugee Review Tribunal did express sympathy for the applicant 'in that should he return to Iran it is likely that he would face treatment of an extremely harsh nature', yet he could not be considered a refugee because he did not have a well-founded fear of being persecuted for one of the reasons stated in the Refugee Convention. Instead, his fear arose out of his conviction for a criminal act. The Federal Court of Australia, in turn, determined that the Refugee Review Tribunal had not erred 'in finding that he did not attract Refugee Convention protection'. It pointed out that it was not dealing with the question whether or not the petitioner could be returned to another country or be permitted to remain in Australia on another basis. Like the Refugee Review Tribunal it noted that the risk of unfair trial, imprisonment and torture was 'a matter of serious concern'. Finally, on 11 January 1996, the petitioner was informed that the Minister for Immigration and Ethnic Affairs was not prepared to exercise his discretion to allow him to remain in Australia. The HRC used provisional measures on 3 April 1996.

[20] The petitioner expected the federal court to confirm her husband's deportation and referred to a letter from the Australian office of Amnesty International opposing his forcible return since it believed that he would face the death penalty in Malaysia as a result of his conviction in Australia. Pending the case the HRC requested the State not to deport the petitioner's husband to Malaysia 'or to any country where he would likely face the death sentence'. See §4.1.

[21] HRC Note Verbale of 17 June 1996 in *G.T.* v. *Australia*, 706/1996 (on file with the author).

[22] HRC *Mansour Ahani* v. *Canada*, 29 March 2004.

[23] See Chapter XVII (Official responses).

[24] See HRC *Omar Sharif Baban* (*also on behalf of his son Bawan Heman Baban*) v. *Australia*, 6 August 2003 (initial submission of December 2000, provisional measures of September 2001 after receiving information that the case was listed for a domestic court hearing in October 2001). Apparently, however, the petitioner and his son had escaped from Villawood Detention Centre already in June. 'Their current precise whereabouts are unknown' (see §§1.2, 2.1 and 2.6). Subsequently the HRC concluded that domestic remedies were still available in respect of the

claim under Article 7 and therefore declared it inadmissible (§6.4). It did find violations of Article 9(1) and (4) ICCPR. See further about this case Chapter VII (detention situations involving risks to health and safety). In *Ali Aqsar Bakhtiyari and Roqaiha Bakhtiyari* (*also on behalf of their five children*) v. *Australia*, 29 October 2003 the HRC used provisional measures to halt the deportation of Mrs. Bakhtiyari and her children in March 2002. Subsequently, the Special Rapporteur adjusted his provisional measures 'to be conditional on an adverse decision on the application by the High Court'. This case too is particularly relevant in the context of another type of provisional measures, discussed in Chapter VII (Detention). Nevertheless, the petitioners had also argued that the State had been in error in finding that they were not Afghan nationals and that if returned to Pakistan they would be sent on to Afghanistan where they feared exposure to violations of Article 7 (see §§1.2 and 3.1). In that light the Rapporteur had used provisional measures to halt their expulsion. In May 2003 the petitioners again requested provisional measures because the removal would amount to a breach of Articles 7, 17, 23(1) and 24. The Rapporteur renewed his request not to expel them (see §7.2). In October 2003 the HRC declared inadmissible the claim under Article 7 for failure to substantiate. It found violations of Article 9(1) and (4). Given 'the number and age of the children, including a newborn, the traumatic experiences of Mrs Bakhtiyari and the children in long-term immigration detention in breach of article 9 of the Covenant, the difficulties that Mrs Bakhtiyari and her children would face if returned to Pakistan without Mr Bakhtiyari and the absence of arguments by the State party to justify removal in these circumstances', the HRC considered that removing them without the final determination in Mr Bakhtiyari's proceedings would constitute arbitrary interference in the family of the petitioners in violation of Articles 17(1) and 23(1) (§9.6). See also Chapter XIII on the relationship with forms of reparation. In *D. and E. and their two children* v. *Australia*, 11 July 2006, pending the proceedings, on 12 February 2002, the Special Rapporteur requested the State to provide information, 'on an urgent basis', on whether the petitioners were under a real risk of deportation while their case was being considered by the HRC; the Committee trusted that the State would not deport them before it had received such information and had an opportunity to consider whether the request for provisional measures should be granted. Two months later the State replied that 'it was in the process of considering the request for information by the Special Rapporteur on the possibility of whether there is a real risk or removal' of the petitioners from Australia while the HRC was examining the case. It announced that it would not remove the petitioners until the request had been considered, §1.2. On 11 April 2006 counsel informed the HRC that the petitioners had obtained a temporary protection visa and therefore there was no need to proceed with the case under Article 7, §3.3. They did wish to maintain the case under Articles 9 and 24. On the merits the Committee found a violation of Article 9(1) ICCPR for their continued immigration detention for three years and two months 'without any appropriate justification', §7.2.

[25] In HRC *Daljit Singh* v. *Canada*, 30 March 2006 (inadm.), on 5 November 2004, the Committee had used another qualified provisional measure, namely for the State not to deport the petitioner before providing the HRC with information on whether it intended to remove him to India and before providing it with its observations pursuant Rule 97 (old Rule 91). On 9 November 2004, following a request for clarification, the HRC requested the State not to deport the petitioner to India before the State had made its observations on admissibility and merits and before the HRC had acknowledged receipt of these observations, §1.2. Subsequently the HRC declared the case inadmissible as insufficiently substantiated.

[26] In HRC *Samira Karker on behalf of her husband Salah Karker* v. *France*, 26 October 2000, it is not evident from the text of the View why the HRC used provisional measures. The case involved an islamist sentenced to death in Tunisia in 1997. He had refugee status since 1998, but the Minister of the Interior decided to expel him in order to protect French territory. This expulsion did not appear to be imminent. The HRC used Rule 86 half a year after the initial submission of 18 September 1998. It appears from the case file that the provisional measure was to halt his expulsion to Tunisia pending the examination of the case. In other words, the Rapporteur decided

In a case against Sweden the HRC has also used provisional measures of a different nature, but in the context of the refoulement of a petitioner (who was handed over by the Swedish authorities to 'some ten foreign agents in civilian clothes and hoods' where later 'investigations by the Swedish Parliamentary Ombudsman, disclosed that the hooded individuals were United States' and Egyptian security agents') and the subsequent ill treatment and torture he had suffered, as well as the risks his Swedish counsel considered he was facing because of Swedish authorities contacting him in Egypt. Counsel had noted this in response to arguments by Sweden against the admissibility of the case (with regard to, e.g. counsel's authorization and the delay in the submission before the HRC). In response the HRC, on 16 January 2006, 'in light of counsel's comments on the State's submissions (…) and of the material before the Committee related to the author's situation, requested, pursuant to Rule 92 of its Rules of Procedure, that the State party take necessary measures to ensure that the author was not exposed to a foreseeable risk of substantial personal harm as a result of any act of the State party in respect of the author'.[29] Thus this is not a provisional measure to halt refoulement, as the deportation had already taken place before the case was submitted to the HRC. It could be seen as a provisional measure to protect against death threats and harassment, but the difference is that Sweden must abstain from action in respect of the petition so that he would not be exposed to a risk of 'substantial personal harm'.

To return to the issue of halting refoulement, Section 3.3 discusses cases in which the HRC took provisional measures to halt expulsion in the context of 'lack of proper care' in the receiving State.

2.4 European Commission and Court

Most of the provisional measures taken by the European Commission on Human Rights have involved the principle of non-refoulement. At least since 1964 it has used provisional measures in this context.[30] An example of an early case is *Becker* v. *Denmark* (1976), involving the impending expulsion of 199 children to Vietnam. The Commission decided to request the State 'not to take any steps in the meanwhile' that 'might prejudice the conduct of the present proceedings' and, more specifically, to delay 'any final movement of the children' pending the proceedings before

---

to use this provisional measure just in case his expulsion would become imminent after all. Hence, the provisional measure did not relate to the question, also raised by the Working Group, about 'which measures the State party has taken to review regularly the situation of Mr. Karker and the necessity of the continuation of the order against him'. See §6.2. Eventually, the HRC found no violation of Articles 12 and 13 and considered that the claim under Article 9 was inadmissible *ratione materiae*. See also Chapter XV (Immediacy and risk).

[27] HRC *Jonny Rubin Byahuranga* v. *Denmark*, 1 November 2004. On 9 July 2004 the HRC used provisional measures not to deport him before it had had an opportunity to address the continued need for these measures and on 30 July 2004 it prolonged these until the closing date of the session in November of that year. On the merits it found that expulsion would indeed result in a violation of Article 7 ICCPR (Wedgwood and Yalden dissenting).

[28] HRC *Maksudov & Rakhidov; Tashbaev & Pirmatov* v. *Kyrgyzstan*, 16 July 2008 (provisional measures of 6 March 2006, 8 June 2006 and 13 June 2006; on 9 August 2006 they were nevertheless handed over to Uzbek law enforcement authorities). See §§1.2, 8.1-8.9 and 10.1-10.3.

[29] HRC *Mohammed Alzery* v. *Sweden*, 25 October 2006, §2.3.

[30] See EComHR *X* v. *Austria and Yugoslavia*, 30 June 1964 (inadm.), provisional measure of 11 March 1964 (previously, on 14 February 1964, already communicated by phone).

it. At the same time it decided to give precedence to the petition.[31] Initially, some provisional measures were taken informally, rather than based explicitly on the Rules of Procedure.[32]

Often cases in which the European Commission had used provisional measures were subsequently closed or by the time they were brought before the Court there was no longer any risk of expulsion or extradition. Thus, the previous ECtHR did not often have occasion to use provisional measures. It did so for the first time in 1989 in the extradition case *Soering* v. *UK*.[33] The new permanent Court was suddenly faced with many more requests for provisional measures because there was no longer a Commission to deal with the bulk of these requests. The European Commission and Court have taken provisional measures on behalf of persons alleging a real risk of cruel treatment or torture or to their life itself upon deportation to a specific State for reasons as varied as membership of a persecuted minority, being charged with adultery[34] or with membership of a terrorist organisation[35] or because they were risking female genital mutilation.[36] Exceptionally, they have also done so in the context of a risk of 'lack of proper care' in the receiving State.[37]

The Court has pointed out that the protection afforded by Article 3 ECHR is wider than that provided by Article 33 Refugees Convention.[38] This means that it has also used provisional measures on behalf of persons not considered refugees.[39]

The Court denies most of the requests for provisional measures, mostly in light of an assumed lack of 'evidence' of future risk,[40] but also because while it may be convinced that the situation complained of will indeed occur, it does not consider that this would constitute a type of harm that would be irreparable.[41]

---

[31] EComHR *Becker* v. *Denmark*, 3 October 1975 (inadm.), provisional measure of 18 July 1975.

[32] See e.g. EComHR *X.* v. *Austria and Yugoslavia*, 30 June 1964 (inadm.); *X* v. *Federal Republic of Germany*, 22 December 1967 (adm.) and 19 December 1969 (Article 31 report); *Mohamed Kerkoub* v. *Belgium,* 15 December 1971 (inadm.); *Tossum Dolani* v. *Belgium*, 31 May 1972 (inadm.) (invoking provisional measures 'conformément à la pratique généralement suivie dans des affaires analogues') and *X.* v. *the Netherlands*, 27 May 1974 (struck out; invoking provisional measures 'conformément à la pratique de la Commission dans des cas de ce genre').

[33] ECtHR *Soering* v. *UK*, 7 July 1989.

[34] See e.g. EComHR *Jabari* v. *Turkey*, 11 July 2000 (provisional measure of 26 February 1998).

[35] See e.g. ECtHR *Shamayev et al.* v. *Georgia and Russia*, 16 September 2003 (inadm.) (provisional measures to Georgia on 4 October 2002).

[36] See e.g. ECtHR *Lunguli* v. *Sweden*, 1 July 2003 (struck out) (provisional measures of 13 September 2002).

[37] See further section 3 of this Chapter on the relationship with the merits.

[38] See e.g. ECtHR *Ryabikin* v. *Russia*, 19 June 2008, §118 and *Ahmed* v. *Austria*, 17 December 1996, §41.

[39] See e.g. the provisional measures ordered in *Ryabikin* in March 2004 (they were lifted in September 2005, probably for lack of immediacy of the risk, as subsequently the Court did find that extradition to Turkmenistan would result in a violation of Article 3) and the measures used by the Commission on behalf of Ahmed on 15 December 1994 and by the Court on 2 October 1996, *Ahmed* v. *Austria*, 17 December 1996.

[40] See further Chapter XV (Immediacy and risk).

[41] See e.g. *Gary McKinnon* v. *UK*, initial decision of 12 August 2008 by the Acting President to apply Rule 39 to the effect that the petitioner should not be extradited to the US before a given time so as to allow the Court to examine the request at the earliest opportunity (28 August). On 28 August 2008 the Court decided to refuse his request. ECtHR press release, 'European Court of Human Rights refuses request for interim measures by Gary McKinnon', 28 August 2008. McKinnon was alleged to have gained unauthorised access to military computers in the US from his home in the UK. His complaint was mainly under Article 3 ECHR about the conditions of detention he would face if he were convicted in the US.

While the Court normally does not provide reasoning for its use of provisional measures, on occasion it has included some explanatory sentences in certain Notes Verbales to States in order to prod these States to take action and prevent a flood of cases from petitioners in a similar position.[42] Indeed, on the merits it has pointed out that in case of group persecution there is no need to show that the petitioner has been especially 'singled out' for persecution, the test used in *Vilvara-jah* (1991).[43] If the Court deals with a situation of large scale violations concerning a whole minority there is no need for establishing 'further special distinguishing features'.[44]

In 2008 the ECtHR confirmed the absolute nature of the prohibition of refoulement, also in the context of persons suspected of terrorism.

> "The concepts of 'risk' and 'dangerousness' in this context do not lend themselves to a balancing test because they are notions that can only be assessed independently of each other. Either the evidence adduced before the Court reveals that there is a substantial risk if the person is sent back or it does not. The prospect that he may pose a serious threat to the community if not returned does not reduce in any way the degree of risk of ill treatment that the person may be subjected to on return".[45]

2.5   African Commission

In 1969 the Organisation of African Unity (OAU), the predecessor of the African Union, adopted a specific convention on refugees, with an expanded refugee definition encompassing those who

---

[42]   See e.g. President ECtHR, Note Verbale with provisional measure, 3 May 2004, in case 15243/04, published in the Dutch journal JV 226 (Jurisprudentie Vreemdelingenrecht). See further Rieter (2005a), pp. 25-44 and Rieter (2006), pp. 736-739. This concerned cases against the Netherlands to prevent expulsion of persons to Somalia. Upon the motivated provisional measures, a return moratorium was decided for members of minority groups and persons who had no family or clan relations in northern Somalia and subsequently, following a provisional measure on behalf of a Somali petitioner belonging to a majority clan, and relating to all Somali who would be internally displaced upon being sent to Northern Somalia, a deportation moratorium for all Somali asylum-seekers who do not originate from one of the so-called safe areas. See also *NA.* v. *UK*, 17 July 2008, which concerned even a greater number of cases involving imminent expulsion to Sri Lanka. After 20 provisional measures, on 23 October 2007 the Court pointed out that, 'having regard to the security situation in Sri Lanka 'Rule 39 had been applied on each occasion an interim measure had been requested by an ethnic Tamil'. It referred to 'the strain which the processing of numerous Rule 39 applications places on judicial time and resources' and 'concluded that, pending the adoption of a lead judgment in one or more of the applications already communicated, Rule 39 should continue to be applied in any case brought by a Tamil seeking to prevent his removal'. The hope was expressed that the Government would 'assist the Court by refraining for the time being from issuing removal directions in respect of Tamils'. The State responded that it was 'not in a position to assist the Court by refraining from issuing removal directions in all such cases on a voluntary basis'. See §21. The Court had since used provisional measures in 'respect of three hundred and forty-two Tamils', §22. See also Chapter XIII (Protection) and XVII (Official State responses).

[43]   ECtHR *Vilvarajah* v. *UK*, 30 October 1991.

[44]   ECtHR *Salah Sheekh* v. *the Netherlands*, 11 January 2007. See also Chapter XV (Immediacy and risk).

[45]   ECtHR (Grand Chamber), *Saadi* v. *Italy*, 28 February 2008, §139 (confirming ECtHR *Chahal* v. *UK*, 15 November 1996). The Inter-American Court had previously confirmed the absolute nature also in the context of detention, see e.g. Medina Quiroga (2005), pp. 142-143.

fled armed conflict and civil war.[46] This indicates that the Commission may take a more elaborate approach to non-refoulement than the 1951 United Nations Convention on the Status of Refugees and its 1967 Protocol.

Moreover, similar to the ICCPR and the other two regional human rights treaties the African Convention on Human and Peoples' Rights itself includes provisions on the right to life and integrity (Article 4 ACHPR), the prohibition of cruel treatment and torture (Article 5) and safeguards against expulsion (Article 12(4)), which seem to imply a prohibition of refoulement. Indeed, the practice of the African Commission appears to confirm the approach of the HRC and the ECtHR in this respect. An example of a case in which the African Commission used provisional measures to halt a deportation involves the allegation that a deportation from Namibia (where the alleged victim had lived for the last 25 years) to Angola would put him at a 'real risk of torture and extra judicial death'. Angola had accused him of being a UNITA rebel. The petitioner alleged a violation of Articles 4 (life and integrity), 5 (prohibition of cruel treatment and torture) and 12(4) ACHPR (safeguards against expulsion). In February 2001 the African Commission wrote to the minister of foreign affairs of Namibia expressing concern over the impending deportation. While the next year it declared the case inadmissible for non-exhaustion of domestic remedies, the fact that it used provisional measures to halt deportation suggests that its approach to the prohibition of cruel treatment and the right to life is similar to that of the other human rights adjudicators.[47] In this case the Commission did not expressly invoke Rule 111 but in substance its action pending the case constitutes a provisional measure.[48] At the end of the decision it specifically added a note about its intervention. Its arguments emphasize the importance of preventing irreparable harm to the victim.[49]

2.6 Inter-American Commission

In the Americas the Cartagena Declaration expanded upon the 1951 United Nations Convention on the Status of Refugees and its 1967 Protocol.[50] It was inspired, among others, by the work of

---

[46] OAU Convention Governing the Specific Aspects of Refugee Problems in Africa, 1001 UNTS 45, signed 10 September 1969, entered into force 20 June 1974. Article 1(2): "The term 'refugee' shall also apply to every person who, owing to external aggression, occupation, foreign domination or events seriously disturbing public order in either part or the whole of his country of origin or nationality, is compelled to leave his place of habitual residence in order to seek refuge in another place outside his country of origin or nationality". Article 2(3) provides: "No person shall be subjected by a Member State to measures such as rejection at the frontier, return or expulsion, which would compel him to return to or remain in a territory where his life, physical integrity or liberty would be threatened for the reasons set out in Article 1, paragraphs 1 and 2".

[47] ACHPR *Interights (on behalf of Jose Domingo Sikunda)* v. *Namibia*, May 2002 (inadm.). It has also used provisional measures on behalf of persons who had already been deported; for one person to the effect that he would be allowed to return, for the other, who had since died, that his body could be returned to Zambia for burial, *Amnesty International* v. *Zambia*, 5 May 1999 (on behalf of William Banda and John Chinula). See also Chapter XIII (Protection) and Chapter XI (Mass expulsion).

[48] About the informal provisional measures of the HRC see Chapter VII (Detention).

[49] See further Chapter XIV (Jurisdiction and admissibility).

[50] Several Latin American countries have collaborated to face the situation of refugees and displaced persons in the Americas. In 1984 ten governments and experts from twelve countries held a colloquium in Cartagena de Indias (Colombia) on the international protection of refugees in Central America, Mexico and Panama. This resulted in the Cartagena Declaration on Refugees, adopted at 'Coloquio Sobre la Proteccion Internacional de los Refugiados en America

the Inter-American Commission on Human Rights[51] and by the OAU Convention. The Declaration extended its definition of a refugee in Central America to people threatened by, among others, internal conflicts, massive violations of human rights and generalised violence.[52]

Unlike the ECtHR, the Inter-American Court has not yet used provisional measures to halt refoulement, but this appears to be due to the types of cases that have been brought before it by the Commission and not to any lack of underlying rationale for their use in this context. Were the Commission to deal with a non-refoulement case against a State that has recognized the Court, and request the Court's provisional measures, it is likely that the Court would order these, given its general approach to the prevention of irreparable harm to persons. Thus far the Court has used

---

Central, México y Panamá: Problemas Jurídicos y Humanitarios', Cartagena, Colombia, 22 November 1984.

[51] In conclusion 3 of the Cartagena Declaration it was noted that 'in view of the experience gained from the massive flows of refugees in the Central American area, it is necessary to consider enlarging the concept of a refugee, bearing in mind, as far as appropriate and in the light of the situation prevailing in the region, the precedent of the OAU Convention (Article 1, paragraph 2) and the doctrine employed in the reports of the Inter-American Commission of Human Rights'. See also the Commission's Annual Report 1981-1982: Informe Anual 1981-1982, Capítulo 6, §4 referring to the 1965 Annual Report.

[52] "Hence the definition or concept of a refugee to be recommended for use in the region is one which, in addition to containing the elements of the 1951 Convention and the 1967 Protocol, includes among refugees persons who have fled their country because their lives, safety or freedom have been threatened by generalised violence, foreign aggression, internal conflicts, massive violation of human rights or other circumstances which have seriously disturbed public order". Conclusion 3 of the Cartagena Declaration on Refugees. Conclusion 5 reiterated 'the importance and meaning of the principle of non-refoulement (including the prohibition of rejection at the frontier) as a corner-stone of the international protection of refugees. This principle is imperative in regard to refugees and in the present state of international law should be acknowledged and observed as a rule of jus cogens'. In 1987 the Presidents of five Central-American States signed the Esquipulas II Accord to collaborate in their attempts to find solutions to displacement and to device plans for social and economic development alleviating 'the poverty, landlessness, and social exclusion that were at the roots of the conflicts'. Statement by UN Deputy High Commissioner for Refugees Gerald Walzer, San José, 5 December 1994, to mark the 10th anniversary of the Cartagena Declaration on Refugees, 'the Cartagena Declaration: a decade of progress', Refugees Magazine, 1 March 1995 (<www.unhcr.ch/cgi-bin/texis/vtx/>, consulted on 11 June 2002). In this Accord the participating States committed to give refugees and displaced persons immediate protection and assistance, especially with regard to health, education, work and security and to facilitate their repatriation or resettlement, always on a voluntary and individual basis. Acuerdo de Esquipulas II, point 8, Guatemala, 7 August 1987 (see the website of the Central-American Parliament: <www.parlacen.org.gt>, consulted 15 June 2002). Based on these political commitments, the UN was able to organise the first International Conference on Central American Refugees (CIREFCA) in 1989. The governments involved signed a Plan of Action in which they committed themselves to enact specific measures with respect to refugees, displaced persons and repatriates. They also promised to treat refugees in a non-discriminatory way. See: Declaration and Concerted Plan of Action in Favour of Central American Refugees, Returnees and Displaced Persons, Report of the Secretary-General, Office of the UNHCR, 31 October 1989; and Resolution of the OAS General Assembly, Los Refugiados Centroamericanos y la Conferencia Internacional sobre Refugiados Centroamericanos, 18 November 1989, ANG/RES. 1021 (XIX-0/89). Yet as we will see one of the main refugee problems in the 1990s, involving Haitians fleeing to the US and the Bahamas, concerned States not involved in CIREFCA.

provisional measures to halt deportation in the context of complaints about arbitrary and mass expulsion.[53]

The Inter-American Commission, on the other hand, has taken various precautionary measures in the context of the principle of non-refoulement inherent in Article 5(2) ACHR and explicit in the more limited Article 22(8) ACHR (on the right to asylum).[54] Information about the precautionary measures used by the Inter-American Commission in non-refoulement cases is available as of the early 1990s. The addressee States have included the US, Canada, the Bahamas, Peru and the Dominican Republic. Some of these States have not yet ratified the ACHR, necessitating resort to the American Declaration. Evidently, in such cases there is no recognition of the Court either, making the Commission the only adjudicator capable of intervening in urgent situations.[55]

This section devotes particular attention to the information-rich *Haitian refugees* case in which the Inter-American Commission specifically discussed its use of precautionary measures in its decision on the merits.[56] This case against the US clearly illustrates the fact that Article I of the

---

[53] See Chapter XI on mass expulsion and forced eviction. In his concurring opinion to the Court's Advisory Opinion on the Juridical conditions and rights of undocumented workers, 17 September 2003, Judge Cançado Trindade did refer to the principle of non-refoulement.

[54] As noted in Chapter II (Systems), the Inter-American Commission has been involved with the problem of refugees on the basis of provisions in the Declaration and the Convention. Both documents include articles dealing with asylum and non-refoulement. Article XXVII of the Declaration provides: "Every person has the right, in case of pursuit not resulting from ordinary crimes, to seek and receive asylum in foreign territory, in accordance with the laws of each country and with international agreements". According to the Commission this article contains two criteria, which are cumulative. The first is that the right to seek and receive asylum must be in accordance with the laws of the country of which asylum is sought. The second is that this right must be in accordance with international agreements. It found that the effect of the dual cumulative criteria in the article was that 'if the right is established in international but not in domestic law, it is not a right which is recognised by Article XXVII of the Declaration'. Article 22(7) ACHR lays down a similar provision. In other words, the Commission observes that, were it only to consult these articles, the Inter-American system would not provide, directly or indirectly, the rule of non-refoulement. These provisions, however, are not the only ones that are relevant. For State Parties to the Convention the principle of non-refoulement is expressly laid down in Article 22(8) ACHR: "In no case may an alien be deported or returned to a country, regardless of whether or not it is his country of origin, if in that country his right to life or personal freedom is in danger of being violated because of his race, nationality, religion, social status, or political opinions". Moreover, it is implied in Article 5(2) ACHR: "No one shall be subjected to torture or to cruel, inhuman, or degrading punishment or treatment".

[55] See also Chapter II (Systems).

[56] CIDH *The Haitian Centre for Human Rights et al.* v. *United States* (Haitian refugees case), 13 March 1997, §1 (referring to 1 October 1990 as the day the Commission received the petition) and §12 (referring to 3 October 1990). For a background on this case, focussing on the proceedings in the US, see e.g. Ratner (1998), pp. 187-220; Koh (1994b), pp. 139-173 and Koh (1994), pp. 999-1025. The Inter-American Commission has not only dealt with the problems of refugees as part of its adjudicatory function but also in its Annual Reports. In its Annual Report 1993 the Commission made special mention of the military coup in Haiti in 1991 and the massive exodus of Haitians to which the ensuing severe repression and difficult economic conditions had led. It noted that more than 50.000 of them went to countries such as the US and the Bahamas and many of them died at sea. "Thousands others were 'turned back' on the high seas in keeping with the United States' controversial policy for screening the Haitian boat people". CIDH Annual Report 1993, Chapter II. Already in 1985, the Commission noted that the principle of non-refoulement in Article 22(8) ACHR could not protect directly those refugees dealing with a State not a party to the ACHR. Of course, according to the Cartagena Declaration, the general principle of non-refoulement 'should be' observed as a rule of ius cogens. Yet there was no political

American Declaration complements the UN Refugee Convention. Several organisations representing Haitian refugees had filed a petition against the US in 1990. This petition concerned the US practice of stopping ('interdicting') boats with Haitians on the high seas and returning them to Haiti. It alleged that many of these boat people had a reasonable fear that they would be persecuted if returned to Haiti. The authorities nevertheless denied them a proper forum to process their refugee claims. While the petition was pending before the Commission the representatives made certain requests, including:

> "To seek immediate, interim relief from the United States Government in the form of temporary suspension of the Haitian Migrant Interdiction program, and the deportation of interdicted Haitians to Haiti until the restoration of lawful order in Haiti, and the subsiding of the grave personal danger that now faces Haitians from random and state-sponsored violence".[57]

In response, the Commission sent several notes to the US, including a telex of 4 October 1991 sent to the US Secretary of State, James Baker. In this telex it issued an emergency request that could be qualified as a precautionary measure. It did not, however, identify specific victims but rather challenged the policy as such. The interesting aspect is that the Commission based itself on a Resolution of the OAS Ad Hoc Meeting of Ministers of Foreign Affairs:

> "It has decided pursuant to paragraph 4 of Resolution 1/91 of the Ad Hoc Meeting of Ministers of Foreign Affairs, entitled 'Support to the Democratic Government of Haiti,' to request that the United States Government suspend its policy of interdiction of Haitian Nationals who are attempting to seek asylum in the United States and are being sent back to Haiti, because of the danger to their life, until the situation in Haiti has been normalized".[58]

The telex presumably was the Commission's reply to the petitioners' Emergency Application for Provisional OAS Action to Halt the United States' Policy of Interdicting and Deporting Haitian Refugees, filed on 3 October 1991. Among others, this petition stated that the US policy deprived Haitians 'of a fair opportunity to articulate and substantiate claims for political asylum'. The petitioners pointed out that a Haitian who avoided interdiction at high sea and arrived in the US had at least a five percent chance of 'being considered to possess a legitimate asylum claim', while an interdicted Haitian would only have a .005 percent likelihood to be so considered. They argued that '(t)he strength of the asylum claim did not suddenly change once Haitian boat people

---

mechanism monitoring those States that had not ratified the Convention. CIDH Informe Anual 1984-1985, Capítulo IV, Desplazamientos en la Región y Protección de Refugiados.Vis-à-vis OAS member States that have not yet ratified the ACHR it is not only the abovementioned right to seek and receive asylum in the American Declaration (Article XXVII) that is relevant with regard to the principle of non-refoulement, but especially Article I of the Declaration, providing that every human being has the right to life, liberty and the security of his person. In fact, in the Inter-American system this article complements the provisions of the UN Refugee Convention and its Protocol. Not only the Commission's Annual Reports and its case law but also its Special Country Reports may clarify the obligations of States under the Convention or the Declaration. A case in point is the Commission's Special Report on Canada (2000). In this Report it pointed out that the right to asylum in Article XXVII of the Declaration was itself a means to safeguard the fundamental right to liberty, integrity and life in Article I. It pointed out as well that 'the effective protection of substantive rights requires an adequate procedural framework for their implementation'. Such framework must provide mechanisms effectively establishing whether a person meets the applicable standard of risk. CIDH Canada Report 2000, §104.

[57] CIDH *The Haitian Centre for Human Rights et al.* v. *United States* (Haitian refugees case), 13 March 1997, §11(a).

[58] Id., §13.

got around the interdiction programme, instead, what changed was the opportunity to be heard'.[59] The Commission sent its telex the day after receipt of the petitioners' request.

In February 1992 the petitioners filed another Emergency Application. They argued that the US, by maintaining its interdiction programme despite the coup, had 'deprived Haitians fleeing the military junta of a fair opportunity to articulate and substantiate claims of political asylum'. Five days later they submitted a Supplemental Filing in Support of this Emergency Application pointing out that Haitian soldiers were present on the docks when the interdictees were repatriated and asked for their names and addresses. Later many of them were arrested at home or at pre-established roadblocks. Several of them were killed and some were tortured.[60] On that same day the Commission sent a note to James Baker to the effect that:

> "The Inter-American Commission on Human Rights notes that the return of the Haitians from the United States recommenced on February 3, 1992 and that the implementation of the present policy will result in the transfer of some 12,000 Haitians. Given the uncertain situation in Haiti, the Members of the Commission unanimously and respectfully request the United States Government to suspend, for humanitarian reasons, the return of Haitians".[61]

During a hearing, a year later, the petitioners argued the admissibility of the petition, requested precautionary measures and presented documentary evidence about the health condition of the Haitians held at Guantanamo Bay. They also presented three witnesses who testified, among others, on why the 'in country processing' by the US of the asylum requests in Haiti itself was not working. Two weeks later the Commission approved a report in which it took the following precautionary measures:

> "a. It called upon the United States Government to review, as a matter of urgency, its practice of stopping on the high seas vessels destined for the USA with Haitians and returning them to Haiti without affording them an opportunity to establish whether they qualify as refugees under the Protocol relating to the Status of Refugees, or as asylum-seekers under the American Declaration of the Rights and Duties of Man.
> b. It called upon the United States Government to ensure that Haitians who were already in the United States are not returned to Haiti without a determination being made as to whether they qualify for refugee status, under the Protocol Relating to the Status of Refugees, or as asylees [sic] under the American Declaration of the Rights and Duties of Man.
> c. It placed itself at the disposal of the parties concerned with a view to reach a friendly settlement of this matter on the basis of respect for the human rights recognized in the American Declaration of the Rights and Duties of Man.
> d. It stated that this request is without prejudice to the final decision in this case".[62]

---

[59]   Id., §6.

[60]   Id., §§7-10.

[61]   Id., §14. See also Press Communiqué 2/92, following the 81st session of the Commission, which closed on 14 February 1992: 'the Commission studied with concern the situation of the boat people, i.e., those Haitian citizens who are being returned to Haiti, particularly from the base at Guantanamo. It asked its Chairman to address a letter to the Secretary of State of the United States, asking that the return of Haitian citizens to their country be suspended on humanitarian grounds, so long as the danger and systematic human rights violations by now known to exist in that country persist', Annual Report 1991 (Annex).

[62]   CIDH precautionary measures of 12 March 1993, *The Haitian Centre for Human Rights et al.* v. *United States* (Haitian refugees case), 13 March 1997, §17. The Commission also dealt with the situation of the Haitian refugees more generally, rather than only as part of this case. In its Annual Report 1993, for instance, it refers to a Declaration it issued on their situation. It called on

Seven months later the Commission declared the petition admissible and pointed out that its precautionary measures of March 1993 remained in force.[63] Six months afterwards the petitioners urged the Commission to issue a decision on the merits as soon as possible because of the 'continuing deterioration of the human rights situation in Haiti and ongoing reports of abuse of Haitians forcibly repatriated by the Government of the United States without political asylum interviews'.[64] The petitioners did not ask the Commission to repeat its precautionary measure, but instead they urged it to give the case priority.[65] Nevertheless, the Commission did not specifically respond to the petitioners' request and it decided on the merits only three years later.

2.7   Bosnia Chamber

The Bosnia Chamber has also taken provisional measures ordering the respondent Parties 'to take all necessary steps to prevent the applicants from being taken out of the territory of Bosnia and Herzegovina by the use force'. It did so in the context of a petition invoking a range of rights: the prohibition of torture or inhumane or degrading treatment, the right to liberty and security of person, the right to a fair trial, the right to respect for family life, the prohibition of expulsion of nationals, procedural safeguards in relation to the expulsion of aliens and Protocol 6 on the abolition of the death penalty. The petitioners were nevertheless handed over to the US forces based in Bosnia as part of the Stabilization Force led by the NATO. They were then transferred to the US military detention centre at Guantanamo Bay.[66] In two other cases the petition was lodged after the alleged victims had already been transferred to Guantanamo. In one the petitioner's wife requested the Chamber to order a provisional measure to the effect that he would be 'treated humanely whilst in any form of detention'. The Chamber decided to reject this request.[67] In the

---

member States 'to take emergency measures to prevent the dangers suffered by Haitians fleeing repression and persecution who are nonetheless being repatriated', Annual Report 1993 (1a).

[63]   CIDH *The Haitian Centre for Human Rights et al.* v. *United States* (Haitian refugees case), 13 October 1993 (adm.); see also merits report of 13 March 1997, §19(d).

[64]   Letter of 26 April 1994, CIDH *The Haitian Centre for Human Rights et al.* v. *United States* (Haitian refugees case), 13 March 1997 (merits), §42. In September 1994 the Commission still informed the petitioner that it would decide on the merits later that year. See Koh (1994), p. 1018 (footnote 84).

[65]   See also Chapter XVII (Official responses).

[66]   Bosnia Chamber *Boudellaa, Lakhdar, Nechle and Lahmar* v. *BiH and Fed.BiH*, 11 October 2002 (adm. & merits).

[67]   Bosnia Chamber *Mustafa Ait Idir* v. *BiH and Fed. BiH*, 4 April 2003 (adm. & merits). Such provisional measures would, however, have been appropriate given the responsibility of the respondent parties for having allowed him to become exposed to the situation at Guantanamo Bay. Apparently the Chamber is reluctant to recognize that extraterritorial obligations may continue beyond the transfer of authority over a detainee to a third State. After all, it did use provisional measures to halt the deportation of the other petitioners, confirming the approach of the ECtHR and the other human rights adjudicators about the responsibility of the sending State. In this case it could not order such measures because the petitioner had already been transferred. Because the respondent parties ignored the provisional measures in the first case, by February 2002 the petitioners were still in the same situation, detained at Guantanamo Bay. The request of Mustafa Ait Idir's wife was appropriate. Some form of intervention by the State responsible for exposing a petitioner to serious violations by another State is certainly warranted. Such an approach is in fact to be preferred over simply waiting until the decision on the merits and granting (financial) compensation upon the finding of a violation. In other words it would have been appropriate for the Chamber to order some form of intervention. Even before the specific reports about torture and ill-treatment in Iraq (e.g. the Abu Graib prison operating under US

other case the petitioner's lawyer also requested provisional measures, but this request seemed less appropriate. His counsel requested the Chamber, 'as a provisional measure, to issue a decision declaring that the criminal investigation against the applicant was not in accordance with the law'. The Chamber rejected this request.[68]

The next section specifically discusses some situations that indicate a relationship between the provisional measures taken pending the case and the (expected) decision on the merits.

3 RELATION BETWEEN PROVISIONAL MEASURES TO HALT EXPULSION OR EXTRADITION AND THE EXPECTED DECISION ON THE MERITS

3.1 Introduction

How do the decisions on the merits by the various adjudicators clarify the types of non-refoulement claims for which adjudicators are likely to use provisional measures? This section discusses the responsibility for future violations in another State and the specific issue of whether non-death penalty States are allowed to extradite persons without asking assurances against the death penalty. It then deals with the scope of the principle of non-refoulement. The focus is on the question whether the principle of non-refoulement extends to the prohibition of ill treatment and whether provisional measures have been used in such cases. The discussion mainly involves the issue of life imprisonment and so-called 'lack of proper care' issues. This is discussed under the heading *ratione materiae*, as it deals with more substantive issues. The other issues involving the scope of the principle are taken together and briefly discussed under the heading *ratione personae*. They relate more to issues involving the addressee and victim. The focus here is on issues of extra-territorial obligation (intermediary States, non-State actors and extraordinary renditions). In all these cases the question arises whether provisional measures may be used.

3.2 Future violations in another State

3.2.1 Introduction

A discussion on the use of provisional measures to ensure respect for the extraterritorial obligations of States starts with the issue of future violations in another State. After a general discussion of the State's obligation 'to ensure', a question will be singled out that arose in the earlier practice of the HRC: the ICCPR and the reintroduction of the death penalty through extradition.

---

authority) and Cuba (the US facility at Guantanamo Bay) it was clear that the detainees at Guantanamo had no access to court and counsel and were not even informed of the charges against them, nor were they aware of what would happen to them. It is well known that such situations exponentially increase the risk of ill-treatment and torture. Moreover, information about attempts by the US to limit the internationally recognised interpretation of the prohibition of torture was already publicly available. See also Chapters XIII (Protection) and XV (Immediacy and risk).

[68] Bosnia Chamber *Belkasem Bensayah* v. *BiH and Fed. BiH*, 4 April 2003.

3.2.2 Obligation 'to ensure'

Article 3 UN Convention against Torture is more explicit than the other human rights treaties in laying down a prohibition of non-refoulement. This also makes obvious the Committee's use of provisional measures to halt such refoulement. As noted, the CAT devoted a General Recommendation to this principle. For treaties other than the UN Convention against Torture, with its explicit inclusion of the principle of non-refoulement, it is important to address the issue of the responsibility of States not only to deal with past violations, but also with violations that are likely to take place in the future and in another State. When an adjudicator were to determine on the merits that the sending State has no responsibility for exposing a petitioner to violations in another State, the use of provisional measures to halt such expulsion pending the proceedings would be inappropriate.

The Inter-American Commission, the European Commission, the ECtHR and the Bosnia Chamber have equally recognized the principle of non-refoulement in the context of the prohibition of torture and inhuman treatment, the right to life and the obligation of State Parties to secure these rights to everyone within their jurisdiction.

Already in 1959 the European Commission pointed out that ratification of the ECHR must be understood as agreeing to restrict the right to control the entry and exit of foreigners.[69] A few years later it confirmed this, specifically mentioning the prohibition of inhuman treatment in Article 3.[70] It had used provisional measures in this case in 1964.[71] Although the Commission declared the case inadmissible, it confirmed that it had 'frequently held that expulsion and, considering this case holds that, repatriation of a person may in certain exceptional circumstances raise an issue under the Convention and in particular under Art. 3'.[72] Later it specified that a decision to deport, extradite or expel a person to face conditions falling within the scope of Article 3 incurred the responsibility of the contracting State under Article 1 ECHR.[73] This interpretation 'is based upon the unqualified terms of Article 3 of the Convention, and the requirement which read in conjunction with Article 1 imposes upon the Contracting Parties to the Convention to protect 'everyone within their jurisdiction' from the real risk of such treatment, in the light of its irremediable nature'.[74]

The European Court addressed the responsibility issue when it decided in *Soering* v. *UK* (1989) that State Parties have an 'inherent obligation' under Art. 3 ECHR not to extradite a person facing a real risk of exposure to torture, inhuman or degrading treatment or punishment.[75] As Judge De Meyer stated in his concurring opinion in this case:

---

[69]   EComHR *X* v. *Sweden*, 30 June 1959.

[70]   EComHR *Kuzbari* v. *Germany*, 26 March 1963 (it is not clear whether provisional measures were used) and *X* v. *Austria and Yugoslavia*, 30 June 1964 (inadm.), provisional measures 14 February and 11 March 1964.

[71]   EComHR *X.* v. *Austria and Yugoslavia*, 30 June 1964 (inadm.), provisional measures 14 February and 11 March 1964. See also *X.* v. *Germany*, 22 December 1967 (adm.); 19 December 1969 (struck out), informal provisional measures in April 1965. See also *Amekrane* v. *UK*, 11 October 1973 (adm.). In this case there were no provisional measures as the removal had already taken place. See further *X* v. *Belgium*, 29 May 1961 (inadm.). In this case no information is available about the use of provisional measures.

[72]   EComHR *Becker* v. *Denmark*, 3 October 1975, p. 233. See further Chapter XV (Immediacy and risk).

[73]   EComHR *Altun* v. *Germany*, 3 May 1983 (adm.), p. 219. See also 7 March 1984 (struck out).

[74]   See EComHR *Kirkwood* v. *UK*, 12 March 1984 (inadm.), under 'the law', §3 (last paragraph).

[75]   ECtHR *Soering* v. *UK*, 7 July 1989. While Article 3 of the UN Convention against Torture spells out a specific obligation, based on the 'abhorrence of torture', this 'does not mean that an

"When a person's right to life is involved, no requested State can be entitled to allow a requesting State to do what the requested State itself is not allowed to do".[76]

Moreover, a departure from the principle that the Convention institutions would not discuss 'potential violations' was necessary 'in view of the serious and irreparable nature of the alleged suffering risked, in order to ensure the effectiveness of the safeguard provided' by Article 3.[77]

Soering was the first case in which the ECtHR used provisional measures to halt an extradition. Moreover, *Soering* illustrates the special character of Article 3. The ECtHR pointed out that the sending State has no power over the practices of the receiving State and that Art. 1 ECHR 'cannot be read as justifying a general principle to the effect that, notwithstanding its extradition obligations, a Contracting State may not surrender an individual unless satisfied that the conditions awaiting him in the country of destination are in full accord with each of the safeguards of the Convention'.[78] Thus, it is the fundamental nature of Article 3 that triggers the responsibility of the sending State, rather than its human rights obligations in general.[79] The HRC has taken a similar approach. Article 2 ICCPR stipulates that each State party 'undertakes to respect and ensure to all individuals within its territory and subject to its jurisdiction' the rights recognised in the ICCPR. According to the General Comment on this article (2004) this obligation 'entails an obligation not to extradite, deport, expel or otherwise remove a person from their territory, where there are substantial grounds for believing that there is a real risk of irreparable harm, such as that contemplated by Articles 6 and 7 of the Covenant, either in the country to which removal is to be effected or in any other country to which the person may subsequently be removed'.[80] This also means that the State should make the relevant judicial and administrative authorities aware of the need to ensure such compliance with the ICCPR.

More than ten years previously, in its General Comment on Article 7 ICCPR (1992), the HRC already noted that States must not, by extraditing or expelling persons, expose them to the danger of torture or cruel, inhuman or degrading treatment or punishment. Moreover, before it published this General Comment the HRC had used provisional measures three times in an extradition case and once, in 1978, in an expulsion case.[81] This shows that already in 1978 the HRC implicitly accepted the principle of non-refoulement.[82] Like the European Commission before it, the HRC made this decision at the provisional measures stage. It considered there was no need to

---

essentially similar obligation is not already inherent in the general terms of Article 3'. The Court pointed out that another interpretation 'would plainly be contrary to the spirit and intendment of the Article' and 'hardly be compatible with the underlying values of the Convention', §88.

[76] Compare also Article 16 ILC Articles on State Responsibility (aid or assistance in the commission of an internationally wrongful act).

[77] ECtHR *Soering* v. *UK*, 7 July 1989, §90. See also *Cruz Varas et al.* v. *Sweden*, 20 March 1991 and *Vilvarajah et al.* v. *UK*, 30 October 1991, confirming this approach with regard to expulsion.

[78] ECtHR *Soering* v. *UK*, 7 July 1989, §86.

[79] Strictly speaking Lawson (1999), p. 245 is correct in considering that the responsibility of the UK is based on its failure, in violation of Article 1, to ensure Soering's rights under Article 3. Thus, a failure to ensure other rights in the Convention could also trigger State responsibility. In light of similar approaches by the ECtHR in other contexts – including its approach to provisional measures, see the Conclusion to Part II and see Chapter XVI (Legal status) – the fact that it refers to Article 3 specifically may indicate that its underlying rationale for its interpretation of Article 1 may be the exceptional importance of certain rights in the Convention.

[80] HRC General Comment on Article 2 ICCPR, the nature of the general legal obligation imposed on States parties to the Covenant, 21 April 2004, §12.

[81] For the expulsion case see HRC *O.E.* v. *S.*, 25 January 1978, for the extradition cases see *Kindler* v. *Canada* and *Ng* v. *Canada*, provisional measures of 26 September 1991 and *K.C.* v. *Canada*, provisional measure of 12 March 1992.

[82] It did not publish any information, however, on whether it discussed this issue at the time.

await determination of this legal issue on the merits before using provisional measures for the first time in such a case.

The HRC has determined that State parties must ensure that they carry out all other legal commitments, including bilateral treaty obligations, 'in a manner consistent with the Covenant'.[83]

> "The starting point for consideration of this issue must be the State party's obligation, under article 2, paragraph 1, of the Covenant, namely, to ensure to all individuals within its territory and subject to its jurisdiction the rights recognized in the Covenant. The right to life is the most essential of these rights".[84]

It noted that extradition as such was outside the scope of the Covenant but that 'a State party's obligation in relation to a matter itself outside the scope of the Covenant may still be engaged by reference to other provisions of the Covenant'.[85]

Kindler v. *Canada* (1993) is the first case the HRC decided *on the merits* on the existence of future violations in another State.[86] The issue in such cases is not whether the alleged victim's rights have been or are likely to be violated by the receiving State, which often is not even a party to the OP, but whether the sending State would expose him to a real risk of a violation of his rights under the Covenant by extraditing him. The HRC found that the State returning the potential victim could be held responsible under the Covenant for exposing him to danger to his life or physical integrity in the receiving State, perpetrated by persons unrelated to the sending State.[87] While a State party is 'not required to guarantee the rights of persons within another jurisdiction', it may be in violation of the ICCPR if it 'takes a decision relating to a person within its jurisdic-

---

[83] HRC *Ng* v. *Canada,* 5 November 1993, §14.1.

[84] Ibid.

[85] See HRC *Kindler* v. *Canada*, 25 October 1993, §6.1; *Ng* v. *Canada*, 5 November 1993, §6.1 and *Cox* v. *Canada*, 31 October 1994, §10.3, all referring to *M.A.* v. *Italy*, 10 April 1984 (inadm.), §13.4: "There is no provision of the Covenant making it unlawful for a State party to seek extradition of a person from another country". See also, e.g., *Aumeeruddy-Czieffra et al.* v. *Mauritius*, 9 April 1981, §9.2. Yet Aguilar Urbina has pointed out that the Committee's statement that extradition as such was outside the scope of application of the Covenant was 'remiss-and even dangerous'. He considered that, in a narrow sense, extradition would be included within the procedures regulated by Article 14 ICCPR (fair trial). See *Ng* v. *Canada*, 5 November 1993, dissenting opinion Aguilar Urbina, §1-3.

[86] Referring to human rights treaties as living instruments, HRC *Kindler* v. *Canada*, 25 October 1993, §9.2; *Ng* v. *Canada*, 5 November 1993, §9.2; *Cox* v. *Canada,* 31 October 1994, §7.1. In *Cox* v. *Canada* Herndl and Sadi dissented, seemingly considering that the reference to 'in good faith' in Article 31 Vienna Convention on the Law of Treaties did not refer to the way States should interpret and carry out a treaty but rather to the way international bodies such as the HRC should ascertain and carry out the intention of the parties to the treaty.

[87] See e.g. HRC *Kindler* v. *Canada*, 25 October 1993. In *Cox* v. *Canada*, 31 October 1994 Committee member Ban (Hungary) pointed out that his position (on a violation of Article 7) was 'strongly motivated by the fact that through Mr. Cox's surrender to the United States, the Committee would lose control over an individual at present within the jurisdiction of a State party to the Optional Protocol'. See also decisions by domestic courts, not only confirming the 'non-refoulement' principle, but also determining that removal without assurances against the death penalty could not be allowed: South African Constitutional Court *Mohamed and another* v. *President of Republic of South Africa and others*, 28 May 2001, CCT 17/01 (2001); Canadian Supreme Court, *United States v. Burns*, [2001] 1 S.C.R. 283 (15 February 2001); Hoge Raad (Dutch Supreme Court) 30 maart 1990 RvdW 1990, 76, Nederlandse Jurisprudentie 1991, No. 249, March 30 1990 (the *Short* case, also reported in English, in ILM 29 (1990), pp. 1375 ff.).

tion, and the necessary and foreseeable consequence is that that person's rights under the Covenant will be violated in another jurisdiction'.[88]

> "That follows from the fact that a State party's duty under article 2 of the Covenant would be
> negated by the handing over of a person to another State (whether a State party to the Covenant
> or not) where treatment contrary to the Covenant is certain or is the very purpose of the handing
> over. For example, a State party would itself be in violation of the Covenant if it handed over a
> person to another State in circumstances in which it was foreseeable that torture would take
> place. The foreseeability of the consequence would mean that there was a present violation by
> the State party even though the consequence would not occur until later on".[89]

The Inter-American Commission has equally read the principle of non-refoulement in the right to
life and security of Article I of the Declaration. In the *Haitian Refugees* case (1997) it found that,
pursuant to this Article, the US had violated the right to life 'of those unnamed Haitian refugees
identified by the petitioners' who 'were interdicted by the United States, repatriated to Haiti, and
later lost their lives after being identified as "repatriates"'. In this respect it also noted the international case law on a specific type of extra-territorial obligations, providing that if a State party's
extradition or expulsion of a person within its jurisdiction would result in a real risk of violation
of this person's human rights in another jurisdiction, the State party may itself be in violation of
this treaty.[90] The Commission also concluded that the act of interdicting the Haitians on the high
seas and 'placing them in vessels under their jurisdiction, returning them to Haiti, and leaving
them exposed to acts of brutality by the Haitian military and its supporters constitutes a breach of
the right to security of the Haitian refugees' under Article I.[91]

---

[88]   HRC *Kindler* v. *Canada*, 25 October 1993, §6.2.

[89]   Ibid.

[90]   It also referred to ECtHR and HRC case law.

[91]   Still, in this case the Commission started out examining the aforementioned Article XXVII of the
Declaration laying down the right to seek and receive asylum. It dealt first with the criterion of
conformity with international instruments and referred to the 1951 Convention relating to the
Status of Refugees and its 1967 Protocol. It noted its belief 'that international law had developed
to a level at which there is recognition of a right of a person seeking refuge to a hearing in order
to determine whether that person meets the criteria in the Convention'. *The Haitian Centre for
Human Rights et al.* v. *United States* (Haitian refugees case), 13 March 1997, §155. The
Commission referred to Article 33 (1) of the Refugees Convention, laying down the principle of
non-refoulement. It noted that the US Supreme Court had 'construed this provision as not being
applicable in a situation where a person is returned from the high seas to the territory from which
he or she fled'. This domestic court had held specifically, that the principle of non-refoulement in
Article 33 'did not apply to the Haitians interdicted on the high seas and not in the United States'
territory'. US Supreme Court, *Sale, Acting Commissioner, Immigration and Naturalization
Service, et al.* v. *Haitian Center Council, INC, et al.*, 509 U.S. 155, (21 June 1993). The
Commission did not agree with the US Supreme Court's finding and pointed out that it shared the
view of the United Nations High Commissioner for Refugees in her *amicus curiae* brief to the
Supreme Court, that 'Art. 33 had no geographical limitations', §157. The finding, however, that
the US had breached its treaty obligations under Article 33 Refugee Convention did not suffice
for finding a breach of Article XXVII Declaration. Under that article the right to seek and receive
asylum must be in accordance with the domestic laws of the country in which refuge is sought.
The Commission noted that in fact the US had recognised and acknowledged the right of Haitian
refugees to seek and receive asylum in the US both prior to and subsequent to the Supreme Court
decision. It also noted that the article provides for a right to seek and receive asylum in 'foreign
territory' and that the US had, by interdicting Haitians on the high seas, violated their right to
seek and receive asylum in some foreign territory other than the US, such as the Dominican

The Commission has specified that an 'essential aspect' of the right to personal security in Article I of the Declaration is the 'absolute prohibition of torture, a peremptory norm of international law creating obligations *erga omnes*'.[92] It pointed out that while a person could be deprived of his refugee status under the Refugee Convention, the prohibition of torture as a norm of *ius cogens* applied 'beyond the terms of the 1951 Convention'. Returning to their home country 'persons who have been subject to certain forms of prosecution such as torture', it noted, 'would place them at a risk which is impermissible under international law'. It referred to the American Declaration and Article 3 UN Convention against Torture and emphasised:

> "The fact that a person is suspected of or deemed to have some relation to terrorism does not modify the obligation of the State to refrain from return where substantial grounds of a real risk of inhuman treatment are at issue".[93]

The Bosnia Chamber has confirmed the abovementioned approach by the ECtHR in *Soering* and pointed out that the respondent Parties are liable for extradition or expulsion giving rise to an issue under Articles 2 and 3 ('or, exceptionally, under Articles 5 and/or 6'). This liability 'arises from the positive obligation enshrined in Article I of the Agreement and Article 1 of the Conven-

---

Republic, Jamaica, the Bahamas, Cuba, Venezuela, Suriname, Honduras, etc. The Commission found that the US 'summarily interdicted and repatriated Haitian refugees to Haiti without an adequate determination of their status, and without granting them a hearing to ascertain whether they qualified as "refugees"'. It found that the dual criteria test of the right to seek and receive asylum in 'foreign territory' had been satisfied and, hence, the US had violated the article, §162. It is clear, however, from its case law, that even when the asylum seeker is not intercepted on the high seas but in a State that always denied the right to seek and receive asylum in its domestic law (so that it would not be possible to claim a violation of Article XXVII), the Commission could still find a violation of Article I, because this article implies the principle of non-refoulement.

92   CIDH Canada Report 2000, §118.

93   CIDH Canada Report 2000, §154. The Inter-American Commission also referred to a judgment of the ECtHR: *Chahal* v. *United Kingdom*, 15 November 1996, §§79-80. In its Concluding Observations to the fourth periodic report of Canada the HRC equally expressed concern 'that Canada takes the position that compelling security interests may be invoked to justify the removal of aliens to countries where they may face a substantial risk of torture or cruel, inhuman or degrading treatment'. It referred to its General Comment on Article 7 and recommended a revision of this policy 'in order to comply with the requirements of article 7 and to meet its obligation never to expel, extradite, deport or otherwise remove a person to a place where treatment or punishment that is contrary to article 7 is a substantial risk'. See CCPR/C/79/Add. 105, adopted on 6 April 1999, §13. In HRC *Ahani* v. *Canada*, 29 March 2004, counsel had pointed out that the Canadian Supreme Court had envisaged extraordinary situations in which Canada could return a person even when there was a substantial risk of torture. She emphasised that this was contrary to the absolute ban on torture in international law, §6.4. In the context of the Supreme Court of Canada's decision in *Suresh* Weiser (2004), p. 141 (accompanying footnote) considers that 'it is particularly astounding for the court to suggest that the prohibition against torture can ever be derogated from'. The Inter-American Commission also dealt with the case of Suresh albeit only initially in the context of non-refoulement, see its precautionary measures of 16 January 1998, CIDH *Suresh* v. *Canada*, 27 February 2002 (adm.), §8. In *Ahani* v. *Canada*, 29 March 2004, neither the domestic courts nor the HRC itself had determined whether a substantial risk of torture existed in the case of the petitioner. Thus, the latter would express 'no further view on this issue other than to note that the prohibition of torture, including as expressed in article 7 of the Covenant, is an absolute one that is not subject to countervailing considerations'. *Ahani* §10.10.

tion to secure the rights and freedoms in regard to all persons within their jurisdiction'. To extra-dite a person to another State where there was a substantial risk of a violation of the above articles 'would be against the general spirit of the Convention and of the Agreement'.[94]

The obligation to cooperate in the international fight against terrorism did not relieve the re-spondent Parties from their obligation to ensure respect for the rights protected in the Agreement. The Chamber referred to the 'Guidelines of the Committee of Ministers of the Council of Europe on human rights and the fight against terrorism' (2002), as 'an authoritative clarification of the principles deriving from the Convention'. The Committee of Ministers recalled that 'it is not only possible, but also absolutely necessary, to fight terrorism while respecting human rights'. The Guidelines restated Convention principles: an extradition may only be granted if there are ade-quate guarantees that the requested person will not be sentenced to death. Moreover, extradition 'may not be granted when there is serious reason to believe that the person whose extradition has been requested will be subjected to torture or to inhumane or degrading treatment or punish-ment'.[95]

In the three cases involving petitioners detained in Guantanamo Bay the Chamber, among others, found violations of their right not to be subjected to the death penalty (Protocol 6). Con-siderable uncertainty existed regarding the charges that would be brought against the petitioners, the applicable law and what sentence would be sought. This uncertainty did not exclude the impo-sition of the death penalty. "This risk is compounded by the fact that the applicants face a real risk of being tried by a military commission that is not independent from the executive power and that operates with significantly reduced procedural safeguards". The Chamber also referred to the potentially unlimited duration of the petitioners' detention. The uncertainties involved gave rise to an obligation by the respondent Parties to seek assurances from the US against imposition of the death penalty. Yet, BiH and Fed. BiH had failed to do so.[96]

Similar reasoning applies to the African Commission's use of provisional measures to halt a deportation.[97] All human rights adjudicators have used provisional measures in these circum-stances before deciding on the merits on the principle of non-refoulement. While the case in which the African Commission took provisional measures was later declared inadmissible, this decision was unrelated to the merits of the case.[98] The principle of non-refoulement has equally

---

[94]   Bosnia Chamber *Boudellaa, Lakhdar, Nechle and Lahmar v. BiH and Fed. BiH*, 11 October 2002, §259. The Chamber pointed out that the cases involving handing over the petitioners to US forces did not call for 'extra-territorial application' of the Agreement. The Agreement did not cover the actions of the US nor require the Parties to impose observance of the rights protected in the Agreement on the US, §258. See also *Bensayah v. BiH and Fed. BiH*, 7 March 2003, §182.

[95]   Bosnia Chamber *Boudellaa, Lakhdar, Nechle and Lahmar* v. *BiH and Fed. BiH*, 11 October 2002, §259. The Chamber pointed out that the cases involving handing over the petitioners to US forces did not call for 'extra-territorial application' of the Agreement. The Agreement did not cover the actions of the US nor require the Parties to impose observance of the rights protected in the Agreement on the US, §§265-267. See also *Bensayah v. BiH and Fed. BiH*, 7 March 2003, §183.

[96]   Bosnia Chamber *Boudellaa, Lakhdar, Nechle and Lahmar* v. *BiH and Fed. BiH*, 11 October 2002, §§270-300; *Bensayah* v. *BiH and Fed. BiH*, 4 April 2003, §§185-199; *Ait Idir* v. *BiH and Fed. BiH*, 4 April 2003, §§139-153. It recalled the relationship in international human rights law between the fairness of the trial and the imposition of the death penalty. It found that 'as a matter of experience intimately related' to the 'principle of human rights law' as laid down in Safeguard No. 5 of the 1984 'Safeguards guaranteeing protection of the rights of those facing the death penalty', courts that are 'not fully independent from the executive power and that offer reduced procedural safeguards and limitations on the right to legal assistance' are more likely to impose the death penalty.

[97]   ACHPR *Interights (on behalf of Jose Domingo Sikunda)* v. *Namibia*, May 2002 (inadm.).

[98]   The case was declared inadmissible for non-exhaustion of domestic remedies.

been recognized by the UN Special Rapporteur on Torture[99] and the ICTY.[100] In fact, the prohibition of torture, from which the principle of non-refoulement is derived, is a peremptory norm of international law or *ius cogens*.[101]

3.2.3 The ICCPR and re-introduction of the death penalty through extradition

With regard to the HRC another issue to be addressed when discussing the appropriateness of provisional measures is its approach to the right to life and the relationship between Article 6(1) and (2) ICCPR.[102] Article 6 ICCPR prohibits the expansion of the scope of the death penalty. The article is often interpreted as not allowing reinstatement of the death penalty after it has been abolished.[103] Yet in *Kindler* v. *Canada* (1993), in *Ng* and in *Cox*, the HRC argued that Article 6(1) must be read together with 6(2).[104] This meant that Article 6(2), rather than Article 6(1), was applicable in case of extradition of a non-death penalty State to a death penalty State. Canada would only violate Article 6(1) '(i)f Mr. Kindler had been exposed, through extradition from Canada, to a real risk of a violation of Article 6(2) in the United States'.[105] In light of its analysis

---

[99]   See e.g. UN Special Rapporteur on Torture, Theo van Boven, (the 'principle of non-refoulement is an inherent part of the overall absolute and imperative nature of the prohibition of torture and other forms of ill-treatment'), 1 August 2004, A/59/324, §28 and UN Special Rapporteur on Torture Manfred Nowak, 30 August 2005, A/60/316, §29 (referring to the 'absolute principle'of non-refoulement).

[100]   See ICTY *Prosecutor* v. *Furundzija*, case IT-95-17/I-T, 10 December 1998, 38 ILM 317 (1999) where the Yugoslavia Tribunal pointed out that the prohibition of torture as laid down in human rights treaties was an absolute right, which could not even be derogated from in times of emergency. It noted that this was linked to the fact that it is a peremptory norm. It then stated: "This prohibition is so extensive that States are even barred by international law from expelling, returning or extraditing a person to another State where there are substantial grounds for believing that the person would be in danger of being subjected to torture", §144. See also Manfred Nowak, referring to the principle of non-refoulement as 'an important general principle of international law': *Ait Idir* v. *BiH and Fed. BiH*, 4 April 2003, §1 of his partly dissenting opinion.

[101]   See e.g. ICTY *Prosecutor* v. *Furundzija*, case IT-95-17/I-T, 10 December 1998, 38 ILM 317 (1999), §§144-154; *Prosecutor* v. *Delacic and Others*, case IT-96-21-T, 16 November 1998, §454; *Prosecutor* v. *Kunarac*, cases IT-96-23-T and IT-96-23/1, 22 February 2001, §466; ECtHR *Case of Al-Adsani* v. *the United Kingdom*, 21 November 2001, §61; HRC General Comment 29 (under 11); IACHR *Cantoral Benavides* v. *Peru*, Judgment of 18 August 2000 and *Maritza Urrutia* v. *Guatemala*, Judgment of 27 November 2003 ('The absolute prohibition of torture, in all its forms, is now part of international jus cogens', §92); Cartagena Declaration, Conclusion 5, which calls the non-refoulement principle itself a rule of *ius cogens*; CIDH Special Report on Canada (2000), §154; see also Allain (2002), pp. 533-558 (concluding that the principle of non-refoulement itself has become a rule of *ius cogens*); see also the various references to decisions of domestic courts in Smeulers (2002), p. 83 and see e.g. Seiderman (2001), p. 275; Bassiouni (1996), p. 68; Alleweldt (1996), p. 1 ; Burgers/Danelius (1988), p. 12; Verdross/Simma (1984), p. 819; O'Boyle (1977), p. 687.

[102]   See also Chapter III on halting executions.

[103]   See e.g. HRC General Comment no. 6, CCPR/C/21/Rev. 1, pp. 4-5; UN Special Rapporteur on Extra-judicial, Summary or Arbitrary Executions Report on his mission to the USA, UN Doc. E/CN.4/1998/68/Add.3, 22 January 1998, p. 3.

[104]   See HRC *Kindler* v. *Canada*, 30 July 1993; *Chitat Ng* v. *Canada*, 5 November 1993; *Cox* v. *Canada*, 31 October 1994.

[105]   HRC *Kindler* v. *Canada*, 30 July 1993.

of the requirements of Article 6(2) the Committee pointed out that the petitioner had not claimed a violation of Article 14 (fair trial), that he was over eighteen years of age when the crime was committed and that the penalty was imposed for a very serious crime.

The majority opinion in *Kindler* is surprising since it would seem that the exception of Article 6(2) is not applicable to Canada, which does not have the death penalty.[106] Indeed, *Kindler* gave rise to several strong dissents.[107] The same happened in other cases involving the death penalty.[108] The decision led to a construction of Art. 6 that made its constituent parts meaningless,

---

[106] See HRC *Roger Judge* v. *Canada*, 5 August 2003, in which the HRC indeed reversed its case law on this point.

[107] HRC *Kindler* v. *Canada*, 30 July 1993. Wennergren emphasised that Article 6(1) guaranteed to every human being the *inherent* right to life. "The other provisions of article 6 concern a secondary and subordinate object, namely to allow States parties that have not abolished capital punishment to resort to it until such time they feel ready to abolish it (...). It would appear to be logical to interpret the fundamental rule in article 6(1) in a wide sense, whereas paragraph 2, which addresses the death penalty, should be interpreted narrowly". Article 6(2), he argued, is merely an exception or 'dispensation' for those States that have not abolished the death penalty but 'what article 6, paragraph 2 does not', he noted, 'is to permit States parties that have abolished the death penalty to reintroduce it at a later stage'. The fact that Article 6(2) is applicable to the US, he considered, should not be construed so as to absolve Canada from its own obligations under Article 6(1). Lallah, in his dissent, also stated that Article 6(2) is not applicable to Canada, since Canada had abolished the death penalty. Pocar equally stated that Article 6(2) merely tolerates the death penalty, within certain limits and in view of future abolition, and that States that have abolished it should not reintroduce it, neither directly nor indirectly. Chanet observed that the HRC, in order to conclude that Canada had violated Article 6, was forced to undertake a joint analysis of paragraphs 1 and 2 of Article 6. The fact that the Committee found it necessary to use both paragraphs in support of its argument, 'clearly shows that each paragraph, taken separately, led to the opposite conclusion, namely, that a violation had occurred'. Since Article 6(2) only refers to countries in which the death penalty has not been abolished, this 'rules out the application of the text to countries which have abolished the death penalty' (italics omitted). The Committee erred, she said, by subjecting Canada, 'as if it were a non-abolitionist country, to a scrutiny of the obligations imposed on non-abolitionist States'. 'This analysis shows', she noted, 'that, according to the Committee, Canada, which had abolished the death penalty on its territory, has by extraditing Mr. Kindler to the United States re-established it by proxy in respect of a certain category of persons under its jurisdiction'. She did not think this type of 'reintroduction by proxy' was authorised by the Covenant. Being merely an implicit recognition of the existence of the death penalty, Article 6(2) could not be regarded as an authorisation to re-establish this penalty. Aguilar Urbina noted that the majority had interpreted the exception extensively by reading Article 6(1) in light of Article 6(2). He pointed out that it should be the reverse as Article 6(2) is the exception to the rule in Article 6(1) and should therefore be interpreted restrictively. Article 6(2) constituted a limitation on the application of the death penalty for those States that had not abolished it, while for those that had abolished it, Article 6 'represents an insurmountable barrier' against reintroduction. He noted that the spirit of the article was to eliminate the death penalty as a punishment and he emphasised the absolute nature of the article as a non-derogable right. He pointed out that Canada's abolition of the death penalty prevented it from applying it directly or indirectly ('through the handing-over to another State').

[108] Apart from being an unwarranted extensive interpretation of the provision itself, it ran counter to the proviso in Article 6(6) that 'nothing in this article shall be invoked (...) to prevent the abolition of capital punishment'. Dissenting opinion Chanet, HRC *Kindler* v. *Canada*. In *Cox* v. *Canada*, 31 October 1994, she noted that by undertaking a joint analysis of Article 6(1) and Article 6(2) ICCPR the HRC made three legal errors. The first was that it applied to an abolitionist State a text that has been, 'expressly and without ambiguity, reserved exclusively' to

while human rights provisions should be interpreted in such a way as to provide individuals with the most meaningful protection.[109] The majority interpretation over-emphasised one paragraph in the Covenant, thereby ignoring the overall purpose of the article and the Convention as a whole, including the prohibition of cruel treatment in Art. 7. The HRC acknowledged this when it over-turned *Kindler* (1993) in *Judge* v. *Canada* (2003).[110]

As noted, the HRC used provisional measures in all extradition cases involving risk of the death penalty. It did so in *K.C.* and *Cox* while the complaint did not seem to be based on arguments other than those that had already been dismissed in *Kindler* and *Ng*. This means that the HRC would be unlikely to find a violation on the merits if the petitioner would be extradited. Nevertheless, pending the proceedings it used provisional measures. In *Judge* v. *Canada* (2003) this friction between the provisional measures and the end result was solved.[111]

---

non-abolitionist States. The second was that it considered the simple implicit recognition of its existence as an authorisation to re-establish the death penalty in a State that has abolished it. This is an extensive interpretation that clashes with the meaning of Articles 6(6) and 5(2) ICCPR. Those texts, taken together, forbid a State to selectively apply the death penalty. The third mistake was a consequence of the previous two. When the HRC considers that Canada is implicitly authorised by Article 6(2) to re-establish the death penalty and apply it in certain cases, the Committee submits Canada to the obligations imposed on non-abolitionist States as if it had not abolished the death penalty. She also pointed out that the State could have requested assurances under the bilateral treaty and the fact that it did not do so meant that it deliberately exposed persons in the situation of Mr. Cox to the application of the death penalty in the requesting State. This constituted discrimination as well, in violation of Articles 2(1) and 26 ICCPR. She considered the approach of Canada, leaving the choice of requesting assurances or not in the hands of a government deciding on the basis of its criminal law policies, an arbitrary deprivation of the right to life in violation of Article 6(1).

[109] It is clear that, even when the Convention was formulated, the underlying goal was the abolition of the death penalty. This would make a major contribution to respect for the right to life. Subsequent developments, including the adoption of the Second OP, only enhanced this view.

[110] HRC *Judge* v. *Canada*, 5 August 2003. As a significant factor the HRC referred to the fact that, since *Kindler*, Canada itself, in the Supreme Court case of *US* v. *Burns* (2001), had recognised 'the need to amend its own domestic law to secure the protection of those extradited from Canada'. It noted that the ICCPR should be interpreted as a 'living instrument' and the rights protected under it 'should be applied in context and in the light of present-day conditions', §10.3. In reference to the provision on interpretation in the Vienna Convention on the Law of Treaties, it pointed out that Article 6(1) ICCPR constitutes the general rule. Its purpose is to protect life. States that have abolished the death penalty are obliged under this paragraph to protect life in all circumstances. As noted, paragraphs 2 to 6 'have the dual function of creating an exception to the right to life in respect of the death penalty and laying down limits on the scope of that exception'. "Among these limitations are that found in the opening words of paragraph 2, namely, that only States parties that 'have not abolished the death penalty' can avail themselves of the exceptions created in paragraphs 2 to 6. For countries that have abolished the death penalty, there is an obligation not to expose a person to the real risk of its application. Thus, they may not remove, either by deportation or extradition, individuals from their jurisdiction if it may be reasonably anticipated that they will be sentenced to death, without ensuring that the death sentence would not be carried out". See §10.4.

[111] Two cases against Australia, a State party that had abolished capital punishment and had ratified the Second OP, had already indicated its evolving position on this particular issue. Rather than the question whether the application of capital punishment would violate the Covenant it addressed the question 'whether there was a real risk of capital punishment as such'. See HRC *G.T.* v. *Australia*, 4 November 1997 and *A.R.J.* v. *Australia*, 28 July 1997. The reasoning of the HRC was similar in both cases. It did not find violations of Articles 6 and 7. In one case it noted Article 1 of the Second OP, but it established that Australia would not violate this article because

Judge was a fugitive who had been sentenced to death in Pennsylvania, but he escaped and fled to Canada. Following conviction for two robberies Canada ordered him to be deported. He requested a stay until Canada would seek and receive an extradition request from the US, but he was removed on the day of his submission to the HRC. The Special Rapporteur was not in a position to use provisional measures.[112] If he had been removed under the bilateral extradition treaty between the US and Canada the latter could have asked for assurances against execution. The HRC noted that the speed of the removal appeared to have been an 'attempt to prevent him from exercising his right of appeal to the Court of Appeal'.[113] It found that the State party 'failed to demonstrate that the author's contention that his deportation to a country where he faces execution would violate his right to life, was sufficiently considered'. The decision to deport the petitioner was taken arbitrarily and in violation of Article 6 together with Article 2(3) ICCPR.[114] He was entitled to an appropriate remedy 'which would include making such representations as are possible to the receiving state to prevent the carrying out of the death penalty on the author'.[115]

3.3 Findings ratione materiae

3.3.1 Introduction

While the prohibition of refoulement is explicitly included in the UN Convention against Torture (ICAT) it is considered only to relate to the limited definition of torture in Article 1 of the Convention. As noted, according to CAT the principle of non-refoulement does not apply to the prohibition of cruel, inhuman or degrading treatment or punishment in Article 16 ICAT.[116]

---

the death penalty was not a foreseeable and necessary consequence of his deportation. There were some other claims in this case, relating to the right to family life (Articles 17 and 23), but the Committee found that they were inadmissible for insufficient substantiation. Although it declared the Article 9 claim admissible, it found that the deportation would not amount to a violation by Australia of that article. The State party had argued that preventive detention was not automatic in Malaysia and was 'not likely to occur in the instant case, taking into account T.'s limited knowledge of the trafficking in which he was involved'. Since the petitioner had not challenged this information and only relied on the existence of certain legislation, the State's information was the decisive factor in the Committee's assessment of the risk involved. See more generally Chapter XV on assessment of risk.

[112]   See Chapter II (Systems), section 2.4 on the power and promptness of the HRC.

[113]   HRC *Judge* v. *Canada*, 5 August 2003, §10.8.

[114]   Id., §10.9. Irrespective of the fact that it had not yet ratified the second OP (aiming at the abolition of the death penalty) Canada, as a State party that has abolished the death penalty, had violated Article 6(1) by deporting the petitioner to the US 'without ensuring that the death penalty would not be carried out'. Thus, it established 'the crucial link in the causal chain that would make possible the execution of the author', §10.6. The State had submitted that its conduct should be assessed in light of the law applicable at the time when the alleged violation took place. However, the HRC considered that the protection of human rights was evolving and that 'the meaning of Covenant rights should in principle be interpreted by reference to the time of examination', §10.8.

[115]   See HRC *Judge* v. *Canada*, 5 August 2003, §12. Solari Yrigoyen suggested a different, more precise, remedy. The State party was 'to do everything possible, as a matter of urgency to avoid the imposition of the death penalty or to provide the author with a full review of his conviction and sentence'. He also added the customary obligation to ensure that similar violations do not occur in the future. See further Chapter XIII (Protection).

[116]   See CAT *B.S.* v. *Canada*, 14 November 2001 and *T.M.* v. *Sweden*, 18 November 2003 (but see partly dissenting opinion by Fernando Mariño Menéndez).

It does not apply either to situations that do not fit the limited definition of torture in this Convention (only if 'inflicted by or at the instigation of or with the consent or acquiescence of a public official or other person acting in an official capacity'; only pain or suffering not arising from, inherent in or incidental to 'lawful sanctions'). Thus, Article 3 ICAT only deals with non-refoulement in case of risk of torture and it refers to the limited definition of torture in Article 1.[117] Obviously, this approach has implications for the use of provisional measures. CAT has only used them in the context of claims about a real risk of torture in the receiving or requesting State. Article 7 ICCPR, on the other hand, is not restricted by a limited definition of torture. Moreover, it also prohibits expulsion in the face of cruel, inhuman or degrading treatment or punishment.[118] The same applies for the provisions in the regional human rights treaties.[119]

In its General Comment on Article 7 ICCPR (1992) the HRC pointed out that the distinctions between the different kinds of punishment or treatment would depend on the nature, purpose and severity of the treatment applied. It was not necessary 'to draw up a list of prohibited acts or to establish sharp distinctions'. In any case, the prohibition of Article 7 extends to corporal punishment as well as to acts that cause mental suffering to the victim. Moreover, prolonged solitary confinement may amount to a violation of Article 7 as well.[120]

In light of the Committee's interpretation of Article 6 ICCPR in the decades before *Judge* v. *Canada* (2003) the question arises how it interpreted Article 7. After all, in these cases it had used provisional measures to halt deportations in death penalty cases while it did not accept on the merits that this would constitute a violation of Article 6 (right to life). As discussed in the chapter on halting executions, in *Ng* v. *Canada* the HRC considered that Canada could reasonably have foreseen that the petitioner, if sentenced to death, would be executed in a way that amounts to a violation of Article 7, because execution by gas asphyxiation did not meet the test of 'least possible physical and mental suffering'.[121] Consequently Canada had failed to comply with its obliga-

---

[117]   Yet 'lawful' has been argued to refer to international law as well. After all, international human rights norms may not be violated either. See e.g. Smeulers (2002), p. 53 and Alleweldt (1996), p. 94. CAT has pointed out that corporal punishment does not fall under the exception of 'lawful sanctions'. See further Ingelse (2001), p. 278.

[118]   See also Ingelse (2001), p. 397 (pointing out that most provisions in the Convention against Torture and their interpretation by CAT 'did not extend beyond and sometimes do not even extend as far as the case law of the Human Rights Committee').

[119]   See e.g. ECtHR *Soering* v. *UK*, 7 July 1989, §88 and *Vilvarajah et al.* v. *UK*, 30 October 1991, §103.

[120]   HRC General Comment 20 [44], 3 April 1992, A/47/40 (1992), annex VI, p. 193, §§6 and 11. See *El-Megreisi* v. *Libya*, 23 March 1994, §5.4 ('by being subjected to prolonged incommunicado detention in an unknown location', the petitioner was the victim of torture and cruel and inhuman treatment). See also *Mukong* v. *Cameroon*, 21 July 1994, §9.4. The ECtHR (third section) has found a violation of Art. 3 when a petitioner was 'kept in solitary confinement for an excessive and unnecessarily protracted period, that he was kept for at least seven months in a cell that failed to offer adequate protection against the weather and the climate, and that he was kept in a location from which he could only gain access to outdoor exercise and fresh air at the expense of unnecessary and avoidable physical suffering'. See *Mathew* v. *the Netherlands*, 29 September 2005, §217. If there is a general practice in a requesting State of exposing certain (extradited) persons to such treatment provisional measures to halt their extradition would be appropriate. See also an earlier case like *Dhoest* v. *Belgium*, 14 May 1987 (no violation Article 3), in which the European Commission on Human Rights had refused to take provisional measures and later found no violation of Article 3 (for evidentiary reasons) and just noted that prolonged solitary confinement was 'undesirable', §116. See also Ingelse (2001), p. 256.

[121]   HRC *Ng* v. *Canada*, 5 November 1993, §16.4.

tions under the Covenant by extraditing Ng without having sought assurances that he would not be executed.[122]

Specific issues of contention regarding the prohibition of ill treatment are the death row phenomenon, life imprisonment and expulsion of a person facing 'lack of proper care' in the receiving State. These issues have played a role in decision making on provisional measures.[123]

3.3.2 Death row phenomenon

Chapter III (halting executions) discussed the approach of the European Court and the HRC to the death row phenomenon. The HRC does not consider this phenomenon, as such, to constitute a violation of the prohibition of cruel treatment. Since its judgment in *Soering* v. *UK* (1989) the ECtHR does. The European Commission had previously found that exposing a petitioner to the death row phenomenon did not constitute a violation of the prohibition of cruel treatment. Nevertheless, it had used provisional measures in *Soering*, as it did in the previous case of *Kirkwood* v.

---

[122]   Five members of the HRC would have found a violation of Article 7 on different grounds. Pocar and Lallah considered that because they would find a violation of Article 6, they would necessarily find a violation of Article 7 as well. Aguilar Urbina pointed out that the death penalty as such constituted cruel, inhuman and degrading treatment in violation of that article and not only in case of gas asphyxiation. In any case he considered that the application of the death penalty was subsumed by the violation of Article 6. See §11 of *Ng* v. *Canada*. Chanet considered that the HRC had engaged in 'questionable discussion' when it assessed the suffering caused by cyanide gas and took 'into consideration the duration of the agony'. She wondered whether it would find no violation if the agony lasted nine minutes, now it has deemed unacceptable an agony lasting more than ten minutes. She noted that a strict interpretation of Article 6 could have prevented this debate. Wennergren, finally, quoted one of the dissenting justices of the US Supreme Court in a 1992 case denying an individual a stay of execution by gas asphyxiation in California. Justice John Paul Stevens wrote: "The barbaric use of cyanide gas in the Holocaust, the development of cyanide agents as chemical weapons, our contemporary understanding of execution by lethal gas, and the development of less cruel methods of execution all demonstrate that execution by cyanide gas is unnecessarily cruel". Wennergren considered that this summarised 'in a very convincing way' why the use of this method amounts to a violation of Article 7. He also explained that he did not consider execution by lethal injection acceptable either 'from a point of view of humanity' but at least this did 'not stand out as an unnecessarily cruel and inhumane method of execution, as does gas asphyxiation'. On the other hand, two other members of the HRC would not have found a violation of Article 7 at all. Herndl emphatically disagreed with the HRC's finding of a violation of Article 7 because of the execution method. He criticised the fact that the HRC gave only one reason to substantiate its finding of a violation, namely that the execution method did not meet the test of the 'least possible physical and mental suffering'. He considered it futile to attempt to establish categories of execution methods, because it was 'futile to attempt to quantify the pain and suffering of any human being subjected to capital punishment'. This was so, as long as 'such methods were not manifestly arbitrary and grossly contrary to the moral values of a democratic society, and as long as such methods are based on a uniformly applicable legislation adopted by democratic processes'. Ando equally disagreed with the finding of a violation of Article 7. The only thing he was certain of was that the article 'prohibits any method of execution which is intended for prolonging suffering of the executed or causing unnecessary pain to him or her'.

[123]   Obviously there have been other issues as well, such as that of female genital mutilation. The ECtHR has pointed out in this context that 'it is not in dispute that subjecting a woman to female genital mutilation amounts to ill-treatment' contrary to Article 3 ECHR. What is the issue in such cases is whether the petitioner is facing a real risk of such treatment. ECtHR *Collins and Akaziebie* v. *Sweden*, 8 March 2007 (inadm. by a majority). In this case on 8 July 2005 provisional measures were used but withdrawn in the finding on inadmissibility.

UK (inadm. 1984). In the latter case it had first taken and renewed provisional measures, but five months after it had initially taken them it decided not to renew them and only to resume its examination of the case more than two months later. The next month the petitioner informed it that the State had signed the relevant extradition warrant. Counsel requested the President to take provisional measures 'in view of the proximity of the Commission's resumption of its examination of the admissibility of the matter'. The President declined to do so. On the day the proceedings before the Commission were to resume the petitioner once more requested the use of provisional measures. Counsel invoked Art. 13 ECHR and noted the unsuccessful outcome of the proceedings for habeas corpus. Again the Commission declined to use provisional measures.

The fact that it used provisional measures initially indicates its willingness to do so also when the case law on the merits is not yet clear. The fact that it later decided not to renew the measures may indicate that by then the Commission had already deliberated about it and the likelihood of a majority for finding a violation on the merits seemed too limited to continue asking the UK to postpone the extradition.

Given that a few years later, in the *Soering* case, the Commission again used provisional measures, several members may have believed that *Soering* could be distinguished from *Kirkwood*. It may also be that it was clear, already at the stage of provisional measures, that there had been a shift in approaches within the Commission or that a different approach by the Court would be likely. Eventually, the Commission concluded by 6 votes to 5 that Soering's extradition would not constitute a violation of Article 3, while the ECtHR concluded unanimously that it would.[124] Should the Commission have decided not to take provisional measures in this case, the petitioner would already have been extradited. This would have made redundant the *Court's* provisional measures.

As noted, thus far the HRC has not found the death row phenomenon as such to be in violation of Article 7 ICCPR. Nevertheless, it has found violations of this article in the context of detention situations on death row. An argument may be made that States should not be allowed to extradite someone to a situation such as those in which the HRC found violations of Article 7 ICCPR in Jamaican cases involving death row inmates. In such a case provisional measures could be used in order to prevent irreparable harm and the decision on the merits would forbid the State to extradite. In result for the petitioner this would be strikingly different from the Committee's case law relating to persons who are already on death row. In the latter cases its eventual decision on the merits does not indicate that the State should abstain from executing persons who have experienced violations of Article 7 on death row.[125]

The fact that CAT has not used provisional measures to halt refoulement in cases involving a real risk of inhuman treatment rather than torture does not mean that its interpretation is not significant to help understand the concept of provisional measures in human rights adjudication generally. Under Article 16 Convention against Torture, the obligation to take general measures against cruel, inhuman or degrading treatment or punishment, CAT has expressed its concern about solitary confinement and, even more so, incommunicado detention. In the latter situation the detainee is not only deprived of all contact with the outside world, but equally of all contact with other detainees. CAT has found that such detention violated Article 2(1), because such situations were conducive to torture. Torture and other cruel, inhuman or degrading treatment is more likely to occur in situations in which there is no access to court and counsel, family members or independent medical assistance. The longer the period before a detainee is brought before a court, the greater the risk of ill treatment. Detainees are normally tortured most severely in the first days

---

124   EComHR *Soering* v. *UK*, 19 January 1989; ECtHR *Soering* v. *UK*, 26 June 1989. For a discussion of the case see e.g. Van der Wilt (1995), pp. 53-80; Shea (1992), pp. 85-138; Lillich (1991), pp. 128-149; Van den Wyngaard (1990), pp. 757-779 and Quigley/Shank (1989), pp. 241-272.

125   See Chapter XIII (Protection).

of their detention. Moreover, a lengthy period of detention may make it difficult to find visible traces of ill treatment.[126]

3.3.3 Life imprisonment

Petitioners have also requested the use of provisional measures to prevent extradition facing long prison sentences rather than the death penalty. While the *evidentiary* issues are similar to those in other extradition cases, the *type* of harm threatened is different. In *S.I.G.* v. *the Netherlands* (1985) the European Commission had taken provisional measures to halt an extradition to the US for someone awaiting a prison sentence of 50 years.[127] In another case, a few years later, it refused to take provisional measures and pointed out, when it subsequently declared the case inadmissible, that Article 3 'cannot be interpreted in the sense that it would require a procedure for the reconsideration of a life sentence with a view to its remission or termination in any country to which extradition from a Convention State is envisaged'.[128] In *Einhorn* v. *France* (2001) the Court had taken provisional measures, but lifted them only a few days later. On the merits it pointed out that it did 'not rule out the possibility that the imposition of an irreducible life sentence may raise an issue under Article 3'. "Consequently, it is likewise not to be excluded that the extradition of an individual to a State in which he runs the risk of being sentenced to death without any possibility of early release may raise an issue under Article 3".[129] This case did not relate to such a situation. In other words, the fact that the Court lifted its provisional measures may relate to evidentiary requirements rather than to expectations on a decision on the merits. In *Weiss* v. *Austria* (2002) the petitioner had been tried *in absentia* for fraud, racketeering and money laundering. He was sentenced to a period of 845 years without opportunity for release until having served at least 711 years. ECtHR first used provisional measures to halt his extradition, but then, on request of Austria, it decided not to prolong them. The petitioner subsequently withdrew the case in order to submit it to the HRC.[130] In May 2002 the Special Rapporteur of the HRC used provisional measures to halt his extradition until the Committee 'had received and addressed the State party's submission on whether there was a risk of irreparable harm to the author, as alleged by counsel'.[131] The ECtHR had not indicated how it had phrased the provisional measure nor why it subsequently did not prolong them. The HRC, on the other hand, did specify its provisional measure, the phrasing of which was more cautious than usual. Instead of requesting the State to halt the extradition until the HRC had examined the merits (or admissibility) it requested it to halt the extradition until the Committee had dealt with the State's comments about the existence of a risk of irreparable harm. In fact adjudicators may always withdraw, or decide not to prolong, their provisional measures upon receipt of information showing that there was no risk or the circumstances had since changed and there was no longer any imminence or risk.[132] In this case, how-

---

[126]   See also Chapter VIII (Procedural rights).

[127]   EComHR *S.I.G.* v. *the Netherlands*, 10 October 1985 (inadm.).

[128]   ECtHR *P. and R.H. and L.L.* v. *Austria*, 5 December 1989 (inadm.). See also *Nivette* v. *France*, 3 July 2001 (inadm.). While it is unclear whether provisional measures were requested in *Nivette*, the Court indicated that the relevant criterion is whether there is a risk of a sentence of life imprisonment 'without any possibility of early release'.

[129]   ECtHR *Einhorn* v. *France*, 16 October 2001 (inadm.). Among others it referred to Council of Europe documents that were 'not without relevance', §27.

[130]   ECtHR *Weiss* v. *Austria*, 13 June 2002 (struck out).

[131]   HRC *Sholam Weiss* v. *Austria*, 3 April 2003. (initial submission 24 May 2002, Rule 86 of 24 May 2002; extradition 9 June 2002). See also Chapter XIII on the protection required.

[132]   See Chapter XV on Immediacy and Risk.

ever, the cautious phrasing appears to be related to doubts not about the risks involved, but about whether these would warrant the use of provisional measures.[133]

An example in which the HRC Special Rapporteur refused to use provisional measures to prevent a long prison sentence is that of *J. v. Canada* (disc. 2003).[134] The case was submitted in March 1996 on behalf of an American citizen who had fled to Canada after he was charged with drug trafficking. His counsel requested the HRC to use provisional measures in order to prevent his extradition if the Supreme Court of Canada would decide so. Counsel argued that the petitioner could be condemned to at least 20 years imprisonment in the US while the sentence for the same crime would be substantially lower in Canada. The argument appeared to be that the sentence would be disproportionate, in violation of Articles 7 and 10. A week later the Special Rapporteur registered the case under Rule 91 (current Rule 97), but refused to use provisional measures. Subsequently, the HRC did not hear anything from the State until July 1998, when it informed the Committee that in March 1996 the Supreme Court of Canada had decided to allow the extradition which would take place the same day. The refusal to use provisional measures shows the Committee's reluctance to use them other than in the most extreme circumstances.[135]

The HRC has not yet determined on the merits whether life imprisonment without the possibility of parole would constitute a violation of Article 7 ICCPR, either generally or in the specific circumstances of the case.[136] In *Weiss v. Austria* (2003),[137] it considered that the petitioner's conviction and sentence were not yet final, 'pending the outcome of the re-sentencing process which would open the possibility to appeal against the initial conviction itself'. In this light it considered it was premature for it to decide, on the basis of hypothetical facts, whether his extradition to serve life imprisonment without the possibility of early release gave rise to the State's responsibility under the ICCPR.[138] The petitioner had submitted that a sentence of 845 years for offences of fraud was 'grossly disproportionate' and amounted to inhuman punishment and that a life sentence without parole for a non-violent offence was inhuman *per se*.[139]

---

[133] For a recent example see ECtHR Press release 4 August 2008 regarding *Mustafa Kamal Mustafa* (*Abu Hamza*) v. *UK*. His complaint was that if extradited he would be exposed to treatment in breach Article 3 ECHR 'because he risks a life sentence without parole and, particularly in view of his health problems, as a result of the fact that he might be detained in a so-called "supermax" detention facility'. In other words the life imprisonment claim was combined with a claim involving health issues.

[134] HRC *J. v. Canada* (685/1996) discontinued in April 2003 (on file with the author).

[135] Equally, it shows that some States indeed extradite a person immediately upon exhaustion of domestic remedies, warranting the use of provisional measures in advance of such exhaustion. See Chapter XV on immediacy (assessment of temporal urgency). In April 2003, after several reminders sent to counsel, the HRC decided to discontinue the case. The case also illustrates the main reason for discontinuance other than that the case has been solved. When a person has been extradited or expelled it is very difficult to contact the petitioner, even if expelled or extradited to an accessible State like the US.

[136] See Ingelse (2001), p. 279 on the CAT and life imprisonment as cruel treatment.

[137] HRC *Sholam Weiss* v. *Austria*, 3 April 2003 (initial submission 24 May 2002, Rule 86 of 24 May 2002; extradition 9 June 2002).

[138] HRC *Sholam Weiss* v. *Austria*, 3 April 2003, §9.4.

[139] Id., §6.7. The HRC did find a violation of Article 14(1) on equality before the courts, taken together with the right to an effective and enforceable remedy under Article 2(3), because the petitioner was extradited in breach of a stay issued by the Administrative Court and because he had not been able to appeal the decision of the Upper Regional Court, while the prosecutor could and did appeal an earlier judgment of this Court, §9.6. It also reiterated that the State had violated its obligations under the OP by extraditing the petitioner before the HRC had been able to address his allegation that this would cause irreparable harm, §10.1. See Chapter XVI (Legal status) and XVII (Official responses).

Given its reluctance to interpret the death penalty and the death row phenomenon as a violation of Article 7 presently it is not likely that the HRC would find a violation of this article in the context of imprisonment for life. In this context the use of provisional measures seems less appropriate.[140]

Austria did not respect the provisional measure and extradited Weiss.[141] Irrespective of doubts about the appropriateness of these measures in a given case, respect for the HRC and good faith application of the obligations arising under the individual complaint procedure demands compliance with the Committee's provisional measures.[142] The HRC pointed out once more, but this time in the context of extradition and expulsion, that these measures are essential to the its role under the OP. Flouting the rule on provisional measures undermines the protection of Covenant rights under the OP, especially if States did this 'by irreversible measures such as the execution of the alleged victim or his/her deportation from the country'.[143] On the one hand the reference to 'especially' indicates that the HRC considers that States could ignore their obligations also through reversible measures. One might think of ignoring deadlines for response or stating disagreement but, on the basis of factors other than the Committee's provisional measures, refraining from taking irreversible action. On the other hand, the word 'especially' indicates the particularly reprehensible nature of irreversible acts in cases in which it had used provisional measures. At the same time it is noteworthy that the HRC does not use the term 'irreparable'. By using the term irreversible instead it potentially extends the range of cases in which it could use provisional measures. This could indicate that it is not ready to reverse its approach taken in *Stewart* v. *Canada* (1996) in which it used provisional measures in family life cases.[144]

3.3.4 Lack of proper care

Both the European Commission and the ECtHR have used provisional measures to prevent deportation in some cases of 'lack of proper care' in the receiving State, but only very exceptionally. An early case in which the European Commission took such provisional measures was *Taspinar* v. *the Netherlands* (1985).[145] In July 1984 the Commission had taken provisional measures and requested information 'concerning the grounds on which the Government considered it justified to conclude that the applicant's child would be taken care of if returned to Turkey'. This question, relating to a seven year old child, helps explain the rationale for the use of provisional measures to halt the expulsion pending further examination of the case.[146] The European Commission subsequently used provisional measures in other cases involving lack of proper care as well. It pointed out that it did 'not exclude that a lack of proper care in a case where someone is suffering from a serious illness could in certain circumstances amount to treatment contrary to Article 3'.[147]

The Commission was unlikely to take provisional measures because of the psychological condition of a petitioner, including the risk of suicide.[148] Yet it did use provisional measures

---

[140] This may explain the cautious phrasing of its provisional measures in this case. Yet, it does not justify Austria's non compliance. See Chapter XVII (Official responses).

[141] See Chapter XVII (Official responses).

[142] See further Chapter XVI (Legal status).

[143] HRC *Sholam Weiss* v. *Austria*, 3 April 2003, §7.2.

[144] HRC *Stewart* v. *Canada*, 1 November 1996. See Chapter XII on provisional measures in other situations, under the heading 'halting deportation in family life cases'.

[145] EComHR *Taspinar* v. *the Netherlands*, 9 October 1985 (struck out after a statement by the authorities that they would grant the 7 year old son a residence permit).

[146] The provisional measure was taken under Rule 36 and the question was asked under Rule 42.

[147] See e.g. EComHR *Tanko* v. *Finland*, 19 May 1994 (inadm.).

[148] See e.g. EComHR *Choudry* v. *UK*, 13 May 1996 (inadm.). This case involved a risk of serious deterioration of the psychiatric illness of one petitioner upon deportation of her husband, as well

because of the age (unaccompanied child)[149] or physical condition of the petitioner and in light of the availability of (medical) care in the receiving State (e.g. claims of lack of proper care for deaf petitioner with little communication skills;[150] of lack of medication to prevent a petitioner from losing his eyesight;[151] or of adverse circumstances for terminally ill persons).[152]

The ECtHR has been less forthcoming in this context. It did use provisional measures to halt the expulsion of D. who was in the final stages of a terminal illness (AIDS) and had no prospect of family support nor medical care upon expulsion. On the merits in *D.* v. *UK* (1997) it first pointed out that 'aliens who are subject to expulsion cannot in principle claim any entitlement to remain in the territory of a Contracting State in order to continue to benefit from medical, social or other forms of assistance provided by the expelling State'. However, it then found that compelling humanitarian considerations may exceptionally result in a violation of Article 3. In this case expulsion of the petitioner to St. Kitts would violate this article. The lack of family support and medical care upon expulsion would hasten his death and subject him to acute mental and physical suffering.[153] Subsequently, in another case still dealt with by the Commission, deportation of a

---

as a claim of lack of proper care for the husband regarding his leg and arm prostheses. The President refused to take provisional measures in July 1995. Two months later the Commission did give the case priority, but the petitioners subsequently moved to Ireland and were no longer at risk of deportation to Pakistan. The case was declared inadmissible. Yet see *D. et al.* v. *Sweden*, 8 September 1993 (struck out) and *Harron and Alayo* v. *Sweden*, 7 March 1996 (adm.) and 3 December 1996 (struck out) in which the Commission did use provisional measures on behalf of petitioners claiming a real risk of permanent physical and mental injuries upon their expulsion to Uganda. In this case there was a suicide risk as well.

[149] See the above EComHR *Taspinar* v. *the Netherlands*, 9 October 1985. On the other hand, on 31 January 1994, in *Nsona* v. *the Netherlands*, the President of the Commission decided *not* to use provisional measures to halt the expulsion of nine year old Francine Nsona to Zaire (Congo) (he 'found no basis' for a Rule 36 decision). That same day she was sent to Switzerland where Swiss Air decided to provide shelter in its nursery. Subsequently she was sent to Kinshasa, apparently travelling alone. A business relation of Swiss Air collected her at the airport and brought her to the immigration authorities in Zaire. On the merits the Commission accepted that her removal to Zaire 'might have exposed her to some hardship' but not to the risk of treatment prohibited by Article 3, see Rule 31 Report, 2 March 1995 (20 votes to 4). The ECtHR found no violation of Article 3 either, Judgment of 26 October 1996 (dissenting opinion by judge De Meyer arguing that her removal did give rise to an issue under Article 3 because of the haste to remove such a young child without appropriate investigation and because the State handed over to others all responsibility for her welfare as soon as she had left its territory; this was not merely an 'attitude' that was 'open to criticism', but treatment 'difficult to consider human').

[150] See EComHR *Nasri* v. *France*, 13 July 1995 (provisional measure more than three years previously).

[151] See EComHR *Tanko* v. *Finland*, 19 May 1994 (inadm.). In this case the petitioner invoked risk of losing his eyesight in view of the inadequate facilities for treating him and possibly operating on him in Ghana. The Commission took provisional measures in March 1994 and prolonged these in April. Subsequently it did not find it established that the petitioner could not obtain his medication in Ghana or bring it with him from Finland. Thus, it declared the case inadmissible. More generally about the assessment of risk see Chapter XV (Immediacy and risk).

[152] See e.g. EComHR *D.* v. *UK*, 15 October 1996 (Rule 31 report); *Harron and Alayo* v. *Sweden*, 7 March 1996 (adm.) and 3 December 1996 (struck out); ECtHR *D.* v. *UK*, 2 May 1997; ECtHR *Tatete* v. *Switzerland*, 18 November 1999 (adm.) and 6 July 2000 (Judgment) (the first provisional measure was still taken by the Commission); ECtHR *S.C.C.* v. *Sweden*, 15 February 2000 (inadm.); ECtHR *Taskin* v. *Germany*, 22 May 2001 (adm.) and 23 July 2002 (struck out); ECtHR *Cardoso and Johansen* v. *UK*, 5 December 2000 (struck out).

[153] ECtHR *D.* v. *UK*, 2 May 1997, §§51-54.

person to Congo would also violate Article 3. His HIV infection had 'already reached an advanced stage necessitating repeated hospital stays' and the care facilities in Congo were precarious.[154] On the other hand, in *S.C.C. v. Sweden* (2000) the ECtHR declared inadmissible a claim under Article 3. In this case there were no exceptional circumstances in which removing the petitioner may result in a violation 'owing to compelling humanitarian considerations'. She was not in the advanced stages of AIDS, her children and other family members were living in Zambia and, according to a report from the Swedish Embassy, AIDS treatment was available.[155] In this case the Court did use provisional measures.

Bensaid v. *UK* (2001) is another example of the strict approach of the ECtHR on the merits.[156] This case involved a petitioner suffering from a serious and long-term mental illness. On the merits the Court expressed awareness of the difficulties of obtaining medication in Algeria and 'the stress inherent in returning to that part of Algeria, where there is violence and active terrorism'. Nevertheless, it considered that medical treatment was available in Algeria and the fact that his circumstances would be 'less favourable than those enjoyed by him in the United Kingdom is not decisive' from the point of view of Article 3. The Court emphasised the 'high threshold' set by Article 3, 'particularly where the case does not concern the direct responsibility of the Contracting State for the infliction of harm'. Thus, it did not find 'a sufficiently real risk' because the case did not disclose the exceptional circumstances of *D.* v. *UK*. Yet, pending the proceedings it had taken provisional measures.[157]

More recently the ECtHR has confirmed its strict approach.[158]

Even if it initially did use provisional measures pending the proceedings in these cases, it sometimes let itself be easily swayed by the State's submissions and decided not to prolong these measures.[159] In *N.* v. *UK* (2008), the Court apparently did use and continue to use provisional

---

[154] EComHR *B.B.* v. *France*, 8 September 1997 (adm.), 9 March 1998 (Article 31 report finding by 29 to 2 votes that there would be a breach of Article 3) and 7 September 1998 (struck out after French undertaking not to deport him). The provisional measures were of 2 April 1996.

[155] ECtHR (first section) *S.C.C.* v. *Sweden*, 15 February 2000 (inadm.).

[156] ECtHR *Bensaid* v. *UK*, 6 February 2001.

[157] The Court does not specify the date on which it took provisional measures in this case. It simply indicates that it used them.

[158] See e.g. ECtHR *Arcila Henao* v. *the Netherlands*, 24 June 2003 (inadm.); *Ndangoya* v. *Sweden*, 22 June 2004 (inadm.); *Amemignan* v. *the Netherlands*, 25 November 2004 (inadm.); *Hida* v. *Denmark*, 19 February 2004 (inadm.); *Haliti et al.* v. *Denmark*, 19 February 2004 (inadm.); *Muratovic* v. *Denmark*, 19 February 2004 (inadm) (involving PTSD); *Kaldik* v. *Germany*, 22 September 2005 (inadm. by a majority) (involving PTSD) and *N.* v. *UK*, 27 May 2008 (Grand Chamber). While in these cases no mention is made of petitioners' requests for provisional measures nor of the Court's decision to use or not to use Rule 39, the dissenting opinion by Judges Tulkens, Bonello and Spielmann in ECtHR (Grand Chamber), *N.* v. *UK*, 27 May 2008 points out that provisional measures were used in that case. More generally they point out that '(a) glance at the Court's Rule 39 statistics concerning the United Kingdom shows that, when one compares the total number of requests received (and those refused and accepted) as against the number of HIV cases, the so-called "floodgate" argument is totally misconceived', §8. They discuss the statistics in a footnote, noting that of the more than 300 provisional measures used between June 2005 and April 2008 less than 30 involved HIV cases; while this shows that this is a minority, it nevertheless indicates that the Court *has* used provisional measures in these 'lack of proper care' cases.

[159] See e.g. ECtHR *Salkic et al.* v. *Sweden*, 29 June 2004 (inadm.), §2. In this case the President initially used provisional measures and considered it necessary to obtain information on the question whether there was anyone that would assist the family upon their arrival in Sarajevo and the State responded that 'no arrangements had been made for assistance to the applicants upon their arrival in Sarajevo. However, the Migration Authority had scheduled a meeting with them

measures, but subsequently found that the case was not sufficiently 'exceptional' for a finding of a violation of Article 3 ECHR for lack of proper care in the receiving State. In its discussion of general issues in this case the Court noted that the decision 'to remove an alien who is suffering from a serious mental or physical illness to a country where the facilities for the treatment of that illness are inferior to those available in the Contracting State may raise an issue under Article 3, but only in a very exceptional case, where the humanitarian grounds against the removal are compelling'.[160] The Court has decided to maintain the 'high threshold' it set in D. v. UK, only finding a violation of Article 3 in 'very exceptional circumstances' (D., for instance, was critically ill and appeared to be close to death, no nursing or medical care was available, nor family 'willing or able to care for him or provide him with even a basic level of food, shelter or social support').[161] As a reason for using this high threshold it noted that 'the alleged future harm would emanate not from the intentional acts or omissions of public authorities or non-State bodies, but instead from a naturally occurring illness and the lack of resources to deal with it in the receiving country'.[162] It considered that while many of the rights in the ECHR 'have implications of a social or economic nature', the Convention' is essentially directed at the protection of civil and political rights'.[163] It concluded its general discussion of the issue by pointing out that it is 'necessary, given the fundamental importance of Article 3 in the Convention system, for the Court to retain a degree of flexibility to prevent expulsion in very exceptional cases'. Nevertheless, Article 3 'does not place an obligation on the Contracting State to alleviate such disparities through the provision of free and unlimited health care to aliens without a right to stay within its jurisdiction. A finding to the contrary would place too great a burden on the Contracting States'.[164] The Court even referred to the 'search for a fair balance between the demands of the general interest of the community and the requirements of the protection of the individual's fundamental rights'.[165] This is a controversial statement as Article 3 ECHR is absolute and does not allow for such a balance.[166] It has been suggested, therefore, that it might be more appropriate to discuss lack of proper care cases under Article 8 ECHR, where such a balance would be possible.[167] It is argued in this book that in those exceptional cases where the Court would be likely to find a violation on the merits, the use of provisional measures would be appropriate also in the context of an Article 8 claim as it does concern risk of irreparable harm to persons.

The use of provisional measures to halt expulsion in cases involving lack of proper care in the receiving State has not remained a practice, albeit modest, of the Strasbourg organs alone. The HRC has equally used provisional measures to halt deportation in the face of an expected lack of

---

on 12 March 2004 where the issues would be discussed and similar meetings had taken place on earlier occasions'. On 9 March 2004 the Chamber reconsidered the petition 'in the light of the information provided by the Swedish Government' and decided not to prolong the provisional measure. A few days later the petitioners informed the Court that the meeting with the Migration Authority had been cancelled. In addition they 'disputed that any such meetings had been held on earlier occasions'. Subsequently they were deported.

160   ECtHR (Grand Chamber) N. v. UK, 27 May 2008, §42.
161   Ibid.
162   Id., §43.
163   Id., §44.
164   Ibid.
165   Ibid.
166   See e.g. ECtHR Saadi v. Italy, 28 February 2008, §127. See also the dissent by Judges Tulkens, Bonello and Spielmann in N. v. UK, §7 and, e.g. Terlouw (2008) and Bruin (2008).
167   See the annotation of N. v. UK, 27 May 2008, by Battjes (HBA) in Jurisprudentie Vreemdelingenrecht JV 2008/266, §5.

proper medical treatment in the receiving State. In *C. v. Australia* (2002)[168] the petitioner was an Assyrian Christian with a psychiatric condition, which he incurred in immigration detention. During this detention as a 'non-citizen' without an entry permit he had developed a serious psychiatric illness.[169] Only in August 1994, after more than two years, he was released from detention into his family's custody, on the basis of his special (mental) health needs. At this point he was behaving delusional and in May 1996 he was convicted for aggravated burglary and threats to kill. Subsequently he was sentenced to a prison term. Following this the State planned to deport him to Iran.[170] In December 1999 the HRC used provisional measures to stay his deportation and the State respected them. Almost three years later, in its decision on the merits, the HRC indeed considered that the petitioner's continued detention, when the State was aware of his mental condition and failed to take the necessary steps to ameliorate his mental deterioration, constituted a violation of Article 7 ICCPR.[171] Moreover, it found that his deportation would amount to a separate violation of this article. It attached weight to the fact that he 'was originally granted a refugee status on the basis of well-founded fear of persecution as an Assyrian Christian, coupled with the likely consequence of return of his illness'. The State had 'not established that the current circumstances in the receiving State are such that a grant of refugee status no longer holds validity'. It further observed that the domestic courts had accepted 'that it was unlikely that the only effective medication (Clorazil) and back-up treatment would be available in Iran' and found the petitioner 'blameless for his mental illness' that was 'first triggered while in Australia'. Thus, the

---

[168] HRC *C. v. Australia*, 28 October 2002 (initial submission 23 November 1999, Rule 86, 2 December 1999).

[169] He was detained in July 1992 and psychologically assessed for his deteriorating psychiatric condition since August 1993.

[170] In October 1996 he underwent psychiatric assessment. The assessment report noted that 'no previous illness was apparent and that his morbid-origin persecutory beliefs developed in detention'. It found 'little doubt that there was a direct causal relationship between the offence for which he is currently incarcerated and the persecutory beliefs that he held on account of his [paranoid schizophrenic] illness'. 'As a result of treatment' it found 'a decreasing risk of future acts based on his illness, but an ongoing need for careful psychiatric supervision'. A subsequent assessment came to similar conclusions. On this basis the minister ordered his deportation. See §2.8. The Administrative Appeals Tribunal found that his case fell outside the provisions of the Refugee Convention because 'while he could suffer a recurrence of his delusional behaviour in Iran which given his ethnicity and religion could lead to a loss of freedom, this would not be 'on account of' his race or religion'. Moreover, it made no findings on the standard of health care facilities in Iran, although it found a 'lack of certainty' that the petitioner 'would be able to obtain Clorazil in Iran'. See §2.10. The Federal Court equally noted that 'while [his] illness can be controlled by medication available in Australia [Clorazil], the medication is probably not available in Iran'. See §2.11.

[171] The HRC noted that the psychiatric 'evidence was essentially unanimous' about the fact that the psychiatric illness 'developed as a result of the protracted period of immigration detention'. It pointed out that the State was aware of this at least since August 1992 and that by August 1993 'it was evident that there was a conflict between the author's continued detention and his sanity'. "Despite increasingly serious assessments of the author's conditions in February and June 1994 (and a suicide attempt), it was only in August 1994 that the Minister exercised his exceptional power to release him from immigration detention on medical grounds". By that time his 'illness had reached such level of severity that irreversible consequences were to follow'. HRC *C. v. Australia*, 28 October 2002, §8.4. Among others, the HRC also considered that given the circumstances, 'whatever the reasons for the original detention, continuance of immigration detention for over two years without individual justification and without any chance of substantive judicial review was in the Committee's view, arbitrary and constituted a violation of article 9, paragraph 1', §8.1.

HRC considered that his deportation 'to a country where it is unlikely that he would receive the treatment necessary for the illness caused, in whole or in part, because of the State party's violation' of his rights would amount to a violation of Article 7.[172]

The second time the HRC used provisional measures in the context of lack of proper care in the receiving State was in December 2001. In *Romans* v. *Canada* (2004) it requested the State not to deport a petitioner to Jamaica. His family had expressed fear for his life and physical integrity because of his mental illness and the situation in Jamaican prisons.[173] This provisional measure was taken before the decision on the merits in the aforementioned *C.* v. *Australia* (2002), indicating an expectation that the full Committee would indeed find a violation in the circumstances.[174]

Some failed requests for provisional measures could also provide insight in the approach of an adjudicator. A subcategory of a 'lack of proper care' case relates to claims of risk to the family members of the person to be deported. In *Choudry* v. *UK* the main claim related to the risk of a serious deterioration of the psychiatric illness of the wife of the person to be deported. The ECtHR refused to take provisional measures in this case.[175] In *P.L.-B.* v. *Canada* (disc. 1996)[176]

---

[172] HRC *C.* v. *Australia*, 28 October 2002, §8.5. Ando, Klein and Yalden dissented with regard to the finding of a violation of Article 7. They considered that arguing that the conflict between the petitioner's continued detention and his sanity could only be solved by his release would expand the scope of Article 7 too far. They did not think that the fact that the State did not immediately order the release of the petitioner amounted to a violation of Article 7. They did not agree either with the other ground the HRC had found for a violation of Article 7. They considered that the State had provided 'detailed arguments' to the effect that the petitioner, as an Assyrian Christian, would not suffer a persecution in Iran and would be able to receive an effective medical treatment.

[173] HRC *Steven Romans* v. *Canada*, 9 July 2004. By 1995 this petitioner had been diagnosed to suffer from chronic paranoid schizophrenia and from substance abuse and personality disorders. At the end of 1996 he was convicted of assault. A deportation order was issued in July 1999. The Appeal Division of the Immigration Board accepted that there would be 'great emotional hardship' inflicted on his family if he were deported, but 'on balance of probabilities' he himself would not suffer 'undue hardship'. His counsel argued that he was mentally incompetent to act on his own and to care for himself, which was recognised by the Appeal Division. Deportation would leave him with 'virtually no treatment facilities'. "Bellevue Hospital in Jamaica had advised that it could not treat violent patients, and such persons are placed in regular prison facilities". Counsel before the HRC also argued that Jamaica had a long history of mistreating the mentally ill in correctional facilities. Counsel had referred to the ECtHR case *D.* v. *UK*. In May 2002 the State contended that the case was inadmissible for failure to exhaust domestic remedies. Apart from this it considered that 'an alleged deterioration of his condition after return was largely speculative' and that he had presented 'no evidence that death would be a necessary and foreseeable consequence of a return to Jamaica'. Eventually the HRC declared the case inadmissible for non-exhaustion of domestic remedies. See also Chapter XIV on the relationship with admissibility and the issue of suspensive effect.

[174] Even CAT, which does not recognize the application of the principle of non-refoulement in the context of cruel treatment, as it makes a formal link between non-refoulement in Article 3 ICAT and the definition of torture in Art. 1 ICAT, has nevertheless taken into account medical evidence of the psychological state of the petitioner who 'does not appear capable of coping with a forcible return' which 'would entail a definite risk to his health' when determining on the merits that the petitioner could not be returned to Libya. Yet the Committee equally pointed out the petitioner's political activities subsequent from his departure from Libya 'and the persistent reports concerning the treatment generally meted out to such activists when they are forcibly returned'. CAT *Gamal El Rgeig* v. *Switzerland*, 15 November 2006, §7.4.

[175] ECtHR *Choudry* v. *UK*, 13 May 1996 (inadm.).

one of the arguments of counsel related to the risk of irreparable harm to the petitioner's children if he would be separated from them, also given the fact that their mother was terminally ill.[177] The HRC was unable to use provisional measures in time.[178] The case provides useful information on counsel's argument about irreparable harm to both the alleged victim and the children under his care. The fact that in this case the petitioner did not report for removal and could not be found at his home address taking care of his children does not diminish the value of an argument about threats of irreparable harm to family members of the petitioner. Such argument may apply when they are in a vulnerable position, for instance because of their age, illness or disability.

3.4 Findings ratione personae

3.4.1 Introduction

Several aspects of findings *ratione personae* are also relevant in a discussion on the issue of provisional measures to halt expulsion. One is the issue whether provisional measures are used to halt removal to a safe State that may subsequently remove the petitioner to a State where she runs the risk of irreparable harm. Another is whether they are used when the risk of harm emanates from non-State actors, and yet another whether they have been used to deal with the phenomenon of extraordinary rendition.

3.4.2 Indirect danger through removal

The HRC, CAT and ECtHR have specifically noted that sending States are responsible for exposing a person to a real risk of ill-treatment 'either in the country to which removal is to be effected

---

[176]   HRC *P. L.-B.* v. *Canada*, 556/1993, discontinued 17 April 1996, request for urgent measures of 4 October 1993, initial submission of 5 October 1993, information about his deportation on 7 October 1993 and Rule 91 of 18 January 1994 (on file with the author).

[177]   Counsel had further requested the HRC to take provisional measures because the petitioner would face irreparable harm should he be returned to Angola. She pointed out that, 'given the medical support for his account of detention and torture in 1991', it was reasonable to infer that his collaboration with the UNITA rebels was known to the Angolan authorities and that he ran the risk of being detained upon his return. She pointed out that, once he had been expelled, even if the HRC would eventually decide favourably on the merits, it would be unlikely that he could be found and returned to Canada. She also referred to the rise in hostilities in Angola and the risk that he would not survive a forced return. She concluded that the removal of the petitioner at this stage 'would effectively frustrate any possible good that could come out of the submission of a communication to the Committee'. She emphasised that granting provisional measures in this case 'would not have any adverse impact on the public interest in Canada' as it was 'a unique factual situation'. They 'would have no generalised effect on the operation of Canada's immigration system'. Submission of 5 October 1993, in *P. L.-B.* v. *Canada* (556/1993), discontinued 17 April 1996 (on file with the author).

[178]   See Chapters II (Systems) and XV (Immediacy and risk). Subsequently, the Rapporteur requested the State to clarify the circumstances of the petitioner's deportation in October 1993. The State responded six months later. Apart from providing information and arguments about admissibility and the domestic law and proceedings, it also noted that 'contrary to the impression which the Committee may have' immigration officials had not removed the petitioner from Canada. The State did acknowledge that he was scheduled for removal in October 1993, but pointed out that he did not appear and that his current whereabouts were unknown. Note verbale transmitting the case under Rule 91 of 18 January 1994; Submission of the State of 19 July 1994, in *P. L.-B.* v. *Canada* (556/1993), discontinued 17 April 1996 (on file with the author).

or in any country to which the person may subsequently be removed'.[179] This is often referred to as indirect removal to third States or removal to intermediary States. In *T.I.* v. *UK*, for instance, the ECtHR took provisional measures to halt expulsion to Germany in order to prevent an expulsion from Germany to Sri Lanka.[180]

As a precondition for a State's reliance on an 'internal flight alternative' the Court has also listed certain guarantees that have to be in place: 'the person to be expelled must be able to travel to the area concerned, to gain admittance and be able to settle there, failing which an issue under Article 3 may arise, the more so if in the absence of such guarantees there is a possibility of the expellee ending up in a part of the country of origin where he or she may be subject to ill-treatment'.[181]

3.4.3 Threats by non-State actors

CAT deals with a limited definition of the prohibition of torture, which it has found to exclude torture by non-State actors. This has repercussions for its use of provisional measures. In fact it has not used them in such cases.[182] The HRC and the ECtHR, on the other hand, have used provisional measures in situations involving threats by non-state actors.[183]

---

[179] See HRC General Comment No. 31 [80], Nature of the General Legal Obligation Imposed on States Parties to the Covenant, CCPR/C/21/Rev.1/Add.13, 26 May 2004, §12; See also CAT *Korban* v. *Sweden*, 16 November 1998 and CAT General Comment 1 on Article 3 ICAT.

[180] ECtHR *T.I.* v. *UK*, 7 March 2000. The Commission did not always take into account the possibility that the State would return a petitioner to another State where he would also be at risk. In e.g. EComHR *Barir et al.* v. *France*, 18 October 1993, the Commission had used provisional measures (on 27 March 1992) for France not to expel the petitioners to Somalia, upon which France proceeded to expel four of them to Syria (on 29 March 1992). The petitioners had stressed from the start that their expulsion to Syria or Egypt would also expose them to ill treatment.

[181] ECtHR *Salah Sheekh* v. *the Netherlands*, 11 January 2007, §141 (provisional measures were used pending the proceedings).The Court added that there was no guarantee that once there the petitioner would be able to stay in the territory and 'with no monitoring of deported rejected asylum seekers taking place, the Government have no way of verifying whether or not the applicant will have succeeded in gaining admittance'. "In view of the position taken by the Puntland and particularly the Somaliland authorities, it seems to the Court rather unlikely that the applicant would be allowed to settle there. Consequently there is a real chance of his being removed, or of his having no alternative but to go to areas of the country which both the Government and UNHCR consider unsafe", §141. See more closely on this case, e.g. Terlouw (2007), pp. 185-194.

[182] See e.g. CAT *Rocha Chorlango* v. *Sweden*, 22 November 2004, §5.2 and *S.S* v. *the Netherlands*, 5 May 2003, §6.4 (in this case provisional measures were used, but the claim not only related to risks originating from a non-governmental entity but also related to risks originating from the State). See further on non-governmental entities Ingelse (2001), p. 400, pp. 403-404.

[183] See e.g. ECtHR *Ahmed* v. *Austria*, 17 December 1996. See also e.g. *Sheekh* v. *the Netherlands*, 11 January 2007, in which provisional measures were used pending the proceedings and where the Court stated on the merits, at §137: "Owing to the absolute character of the right guaranted, Article 3 of the Convention may also apply where the danger emanates from persons or groups of persons who are not public officials. However, it must be shown that the risk is real and that the authorities of the receiving State are not able to obviate the risk by providing appropriate protection". In *Ahani* v. *Canada*, 29 March 2004, §10.7 the HRC emphasized that both the right to life and the right to be free from torture also required the State to take 'steps of due diligence to avoid a threat to an individual of torture from third parties'(finding a violation of Article 13 in conjunction with Article 7 ICCPR for the failure to provide the petitioner with 'the procedural

3.4.4 Extraordinary renditions and other forms of transfer

It may be assumed that the human rights adjudicators will take provisional measures in situations involving involuntary return, independent of the term used for this return (expulsion, extradition, rendition, removal, etc.), or involuntary transfer (from the authority of one State to those of another, on the same territory). The risk facing the person involved should be the determining factor. So-called extraordinary renditions, for instance, could violate the principle of non-refoulement even more than an extradition or expulsion following the appropriate procedures.[184] In the face of a growing practice of making use of these extraordinary renditions alertness by the relevant human rights adjudicators would be warranted, including with regard to (*proprio motu*) use of provisional measures in pending cases.

With regard to Article 3 of Protocol 4 to the ECHR (prohibition of expulsion of nationals) and Article 1 of Protocol 7 to the ECHR (procedural safeguards in relation to expulsion of aliens) the Bosnia Chamber has clarified the terms 'expelled' and 'expulsion'. It has pointed out that the protection afforded by these two articles 'applies also in cases in which a person is deported, removed from the territory in pursuance of a refusal of entry order or handed over to officials of a foreign power'. In one case it found that the respondent Parties had not followed the requirements of a legal expulsion procedure arising from the domestic law. The violations fell within the responsibility of both respondent Parties. The factual actions taken by them, with regard to the revocation of citizenship, the decision on refusal of entry and 'the handing-over the applicant for expulsion to the US forces, after making sure in diplomatic contact that those forces would take him into custody and bring him out of the country, involved action of both Parties which constitutes a violation of the applicant's rights'.[185]

The request for provisional measures by lawyers acting on behalf of Saddam Hussein and refused by the ECtHR in June 2004 did not relate to transporting people from one State to another to be 'interrogated', but involved the transmission of a former dictator to a transitional government (Iraq's interim government) in a State that has not abolished the death penalty. Lawyers acting on behalf of Saddam Hussein asked the ECtHR 'to permanently prohibit the United Kingdom from facilitating, allowing for, acquiescing in, or in any other form whatsoever effectively participating, through an act or omission, in the transfer of the applicant to the custody of the Iraqi Interim Government unless and until the Iraqi Interim Government has provided adequate assurances that the applicant will not be subject to the death penalty'. They relied on Articles 2 and 3 ECHR and on Protocols 6 (abolition in times of peace) and 13 (abolition in all circumstances) to the Convention, arguing that the UK 'has an obligation to ensure individuals are not subject to the death penalty and therefore not to surrender legal or physical custody of individuals to a country

---

protections' required to prevent irreparable harm, §10.8; given this finding there was no need to determine the extent of the risk of torture prior to Ahani's deportation nor was there a need to determine whether he suffered torture or ill treatment subsequent to his return, §10.10). See also the Concluding Observations of the HRC to the report by France, CCPR/C/60/FRA/4, 31 July 1997, §20: "The Committee is particularly concerned by the restrictive definition given to the concept of 'persecution' for refugees by the French authorities as it does not take into account possible prosecution proceedings from non-state actors".

[184] See e.g. 'Torture by proxy', the report by the Association of the Bar of the City of New York and the Center for Human Rights at New York University (2004); American Civil Liberties Union (2005), pp. 10-12 and pp. 25-36; Human Rights Watch (2005); Amnesty International (2005); Mayer (2005). See further e.g. Special Rapporteur on the promotion and protection of human rights and fundamental freedoms while countering terrorism, Martin Scheinin, e.g. Mission to the US, A/HRC/6/17/Add.3, 22 November 2007, p. 18.

[185] Bosnia Chamber *Bensayah* v. *BiH and Fed.BiH*, 7 March 2003, §§111-127. See also *Ait Idir* v. *BiH and Fed.BiH*, 4 April 2003, §101 and *Boudellaa, Lakhdar, Nechle and Lahmar* v. *BiH and Fed.BiH*, 11 October 2002 (adm. & merits), §§177-205.

or jurisdiction where they would face such consequences and other breaches of the Convention'. The ECtHR decided not to grant this request.[186] Press agency Reuters, observing that the decision was not motivated,[187] noted that a spokesperson for the Court had indicated to it that it only takes provisional measures if it is convinced that there is a risk of physical harm that is very important, irreversible and imminent.[188]

The question arises whether the Court refused to take provisional measures mainly for political reasons, because of the person involved, or for policy reasons, fearing a flood of new submissions regarding extraordinary renditions. In light of its *Bankovic* judgment it is also possible that it considered itself incompetent to deal with human rights violations committed by Member States outside their own territory. In that case it would consider itself *prima facie* incompetent to take provisional measures.[189] Yet since that time it has used provisional measures, e.g. to halt transfer of detainees by UK authorities in Iraq to the Iraqi authorities.[190] The most plausible reason may be the fact that the Provisional Coalition Authority did not actively implement the death penalty at the time of the intended transmission. Just a few weeks after the ECtHR refused to take provisional measures the new Iraqi Interim Government re-instated the death penalty. It was one of its first decisions following the transfer of sovereignty. The ECtHR may not have foreseen this risk.

---

[186] ECtHR Press release 337, 'European Court of Human Rights rejects requests for interim measures by Saddam Hussein', 30 June 2004.

[187] On the lack of publication and motivation in most systems see also Chapter II.

[188] See Reuters, 'Conseil de l'Europe: pas de "mesures provisoires" pour Saddam Hussein', 30 June 2004 ('*n'impose à un État des «mesures provisoires », en vertu de l'article 39 de son règlement, que lorsqu'elle est «convaincu qu'il y a un risque de préjudice physique très important, irrémédiable et imminent»*'), posted on <www.peinedemort.org> (accessed on 13 August 2004).

[189] See ECtHR *Bankovic et al.* v. *Belgium and 16 other States*, 12 December 2001 (inadm.). The Court's approach to extraterritorial obligations as it appears from *Bankovic* seems to be contrary to its normal interpretation methods. Moreover, the Court put itself outside present day reality. See e.g. Lawson (2004), pp. 83-123. Subsequent to *Bankovic* it seems to have adapted its approach somewhat, gravitating more towards the approach of the Inter-American Commission, HRC and ICJ. See e.g. ICJ *Legal consequences of the construction of a wall in the occupied Palestinian territory* (Advisory Opinion), 9 July 2004, holding that the ICCPR is applicable in respect of 'acts done' by a State in the exercise of its jurisdiction outside its own territory, §§107-113; *Armed Activities on the Territory of the Congo (Congo* v. *Uganda)*, judgment of 19 December 2005, §§179-180 and *Case concerning the application of the International Convention on the Elimination of All Forms of Racial Discrimination (Georgia* v. *Russia)*, Order for provisional measures of 15 October 2008, §109. The Working Group on Enforced or Involuntary Disappearances has equally expressed concern about the 'extraordinary renditions' that had been used to 'transport terrorist suspects to other States for aggressive interrogation'. Report of the Working Group on Enforced or Involuntary Disappearances, E/CN.4/2006/56, 27 December 2005, §22. See also e.g. Gondek (2005) and Coomans/Kamminga (2004). For a different approach see O'Boyle (2004), pp. 125-139. Further on jurisdiction and provisional measures see Chapter XIV.

[190] Provisional measures in case of *Faisal al-Saadoon and Khalef Mufdhi* v. *UK*, 30 December 2008 (by the Acting President of the Fourth Section). A scan of the ECtHR letter to counsel confirming its use of provisional measures was posted at <http://humanrightsdoctorate.blogspot.com/2009/01/uk-breaches-provisional-measures.html>. The provisional measure was ignored by the UK in reference to a decision of a domestic court. See also Chapters XIV (Jurisdiction) and XVII (Official responses).

4   CONCLUSION

The HRC and CAT, the adjudicators in the three regional systems as well as the Bosnia Chamber have all used provisional measures to halt refoulement. This means that they consider that they can use such measures to prevent a State from exposing an alleged victim to future violations in another State. Moreover, it may be expected that all adjudicators would be able to take provisional measures also to halt removal to a third State that is likely to subsequently remove the alleged victim to a State where he is at risk of torture. It may equally be expected that all adjudicators could use provisional measures in the context of extraordinary renditions and other forms of transfer. CAT has not used provisional measures in the face of risk of torture by non-State actors and in light of its case law on the merits is unlikely to do so. The other adjudicators may indeed use them in such circumstances. When the petitioner claims a real risk not of torture but of cruel treatment CAT does not use provisional measures either. The HRC and ECtHR have used provisional measures in the face of a real risk of cruel treatment in the receiving or requesting State and in light of the relevant provisions and case law the other adjudicators may do so as well.

In the European system provisional measures have been used on occasion to halt expulsion of a person facing lack of proper care in the receiving State. The HRC has recently confirmed this approach on the international plane and it is not unlikely that the other adjudicators, with the exception of CAT, will interpret the obligations under the respective treaties in a similar manner. Nevertheless the use of provisional measures by these adjudicators in cases involving lack of proper care is by no means certain, for instance because the ECtHR, the only adjudicator with some established practice on the issue, has a very strict approach on the merits. Nevertheless, the use of provisional measures would tie in with what they could do on the merits.

Both the HRC and the ECtHR have been ambivalent with regard to the issue of life imprisonment. This is also reflected in their provisional measures to halt extradition of people facing this punishment. They are reluctant to take such measures and, if they do, are likely to be convinced by the State's arguments not prolong them.

The ECtHR has used provisional measures to halt extradition of a person facing the death penalty in light of the death row phenomenon. In *Soering* it eventually determined that this phenomenon could constitute cruel treatment. As virtually all Member States of the Council of Europe have ratified at least one of the two Protocols on the death penalty by now, extradition to face such a penalty would in any case constitute a violation of the right to life. Moreover, the Court has now acknowledged that the developments regarding the attitudes towards the death penalty may have removed textual limitations in the interpretation of the right to life in the ECHR itself. This means that there is no longer a need to take provisional measures just in order to halt exposure to the death row phenomenon. This is not yet the case in the interpretation of the ICCPR by the HRC. While it has not yet recognised the death row phenomenon as such to constitute a violation of Article 7, some of its members would be willing to do so and counsel for petitioners is likely to continue invoking the argument. Thus, the issue is bound to recur in the context of provisional measures.

In the range of situations involving claims of non-refoulement provisional measures have been used by various adjudicators. Given their case law on the merits some of these claims are almost certain to trigger the use of provisional measures because the adjudicators consider that expulsion or extradition would result in irreparable harm to the claim. Of course the actual use of the provisional measures then still depends on whether the adjudicator considers there is a real and immediate risk of such harm.[191] For other claims, such as those involving lack of proper care

---

[191]   See Chapter XV (Immediacy and risk).

or life imprisonment, the case law on the merits is not so clear and neither is the likelihood of adjudicators using provisional measures pending the proceedings to prevent irreparable harm.

CHAPTER VI
LOCATING AND PROTECTING
DISAPPEARED PERSONS

1   INTRODUCTION

Several of the adjudicators have used provisional measures to intervene in disappearance cases. The term 'disappearance' refers to a technique of unacknowledged detention, often followed by extrajudicial execution, generally 'as the result of a deliberate plan, carefully executed, either directly by government authorities or with their tacit approval, in a manner designed to avoid accountability'.[1] Disappearances are not restricted to military regimes although they often take place 'in countries where the military establishment is either in power or has a high degree of autonomy from civilian authority'.[2] The preamble to the UN Declaration on the Protection of all Persons from Enforced Disappearance describes the phenomenon as follows: 'persons are arrested, detained or abducted against their will or otherwise deprived of their liberty by officials of different branches or levels of Government, or by organized groups or private individuals acting on behalf of, or with the support, direct or indirect, consent or acquiescence of the Government, followed by a refusal to disclose the fate or whereabouts of the persons concerned or a refusal to acknowledge the deprivation of their liberty, which places such persons outside the protection of the law'.[3]

The Inter-American Commission has used precautionary measures several times in disappearance cases. The HRC has intervened occasionally in such cases, albeit generally without formally invoking its rule on provisional measures. The Bosnia Chamber has used provisional measures in this context as well. The ECtHR, on the other hand, while having dealt with petitions relating to disappearances, has not yet done so through the use of provisional measures.

The phenomenon of disappearances is very relevant still. While it first became known in the 1970s in the Americas, it has since become a serious human rights issue in various other parts of

---

[1]   Berman/Clark (1982), p. 532.

[2]   Méndez/Vivanco (1990), pp. 510-511; see also Grossman (1992) and Brody/González (1997).

[3]   Preamble to the UN Declaration on the Protection of all Persons from Enforced Disappearance, General Assembly resolution 47/133, 18 December 1992. Thus far this has been the international instrument generally referred to internationally, e.g. by the UN Working Group on Enforced and Involuntary Disappearances. See e.g. Brody/González (1997). The UN Working Group on Enforced and Involuntary Disappearances 'deems that it should construe the definition provided by the Declaration, in a way that is most conducive to the protection of all persons from enforced disappearance'. Definition of enforced disappearance, General Comment by WG, during 81st session, 20 March 2007. The International Convention for the Protection of All Persons against Enforced Disappearances, adopted 20 December 2006, but not yet entered into force, provides a working definition in Article 2: 'the arrest, detention, abduction or any other form of deprivation of liberty by agents of the State or by persons or groups of persons acting with the authorization, support or acquiescence of the State, followed by a refusal to acknowledge the deprivation of liberty or by concealment of the fate or whereabouts of the disappeared person, which place such a person outside the protection of the law'. By 1 November 2008, 79 States had signed and five States had ratified this treaty. It will enter into force upon 20 ratifications or accessions. Often a reference is also made to the definition in Article 7(2)(i) of the Rome Statute of the International Criminal Court, which is similar to the definition found in the new Convention.

the world as well, including in the context of the 'war on terror' launched after the 9/11 terrorist attacks in the US (2001).[4] This chapter first discusses the practice of the human rights adjudicators in urgently dealing with disappearance cases. Then it explores how this practice relates to their decisions on the merits.

2 PRACTICE

Several delegations in the working group drafting the International Convention for the Protection of All Persons from Enforced Disappearance[5] had argued in favour of the inclusion of a reference to provisional measures in the treaty itself, for the purpose of emphasising the importance of such measures in the context of disappearances, 'especially in order to avoid irreparable harm and preserve evidence'.[6] Indeed, Article 31, which provides for an optional individual complaint procedure, specifically includes the possibility of using provisional measures. Article 31(4) stipulates:

> "At any time after the receipt of a communication and before a determination on the merits has been reached, the Committee may transmit to the State Party concerned for its urgent consideration a request that the State Party will take such interim measures as may be necessary to avoid possible irreparable damage to the victims of the alleged violation. Where the Committee exercises its discretion, this does not imply a determination on admissibility or on the merits of the communication".

Yet in urgent cases the Committee introduced by this treaty may address even States parties that have not recognized the individual complaint procedure under Article 31. The innovative Article 30 introduces the possibility for the Committee to intervene upon a request 'by relatives of the disappeared person or their legal representatives, their counsel or any person authorized by them, as well as by any other person having a legitimate interest' that 'a disappeared person should be sought and found'. In fact when it considers that a range of procedural requirements is met, it 'shall request the State Party concerned to provide it with information on the situation of the

---

[4]   See e.g. Paust (2004), pp. 79-96. See further Berman/Clark (1982). See also the discussion on secret detention centres, e.g. the Marty report presented on behalf of the Parliamentary Assembly of the Council of Europe, Committee on Legal Affairs and Human Rights, Document 10957 and Add.; AS (2006) CR 17, 27 June 2006; Res. 1507 (2006), 27 June 2006 and Rec. 1754 (2006), 27 June 2006; Amnesty International, Below the radar: secret flights to torture and disappearance, 5 April 2006, AI Index: AMR 51/051/2006; Amnesty International, Partners in crime: Europe's role in US renditions, 14 June 2006, AI Index: EUR 01/008/2006; Amnesty International, Secret detention in CIA 'Black Sites', 8 November 2005, AI Index: AMR 51/177/2005; Amnesty International, USA: Torture and secret detention, testimony of the 'disappeared' in the 'war on terror', 4 August 2005, AI Index: AMR 51/108/2005; Amnesty International urgent action regarding the possible 'disappearance' of Canadian national Maher Arar, 21 October 2002, AI Index: AMR 51/159/2002 and subsequent actions; Human Rights Watch, The United States' Disappeared; the CIA's long-term ghost detainees', a Human Rights Watch briefing paper, October 2004. The issue discussed here is obviously related to those discussed in the chapters on non-refoulement (Chapter V, in particular its discussion of 'extraordinary renditions'), treatment in detention (Chapter VII), ensuring procedural rights to protect the right to life and personal integrity (VIII) and jurisdiction (Chapter XIV).

[5]   Adopted 20 December 2006, not yet entered into force (by 1 November 2008: 79 signatories and 5 ratifications).

[6]   E/CN.4/2005/WG.22/CRP.9/Rev.1, 22 September 2005, §24. On this new treaty see also Chapters II (Systems) and XVI (Legal status).

persons sought, within a time limit set by the Committee'.[7] A related provision is Article 34 on widespread disappearances:

> "If the Committee receives information which appears to it to contain well-founded indications that enforced disappearance is being practised on a widespread or systematic basis in the territory under the jurisdiction of a State Party, it may, after seeking from the State Party concerned all relevant information on the situation, urgently bring the matter to the attention of the General Assembly of the United Nations, through the Secretary-General of the United Nations".[8]

2.1   HRC

In the early detention cases, mostly involving Uruguay, the HRC often not only requested information regarding the state of health of detainees but also regarding their whereabouts. In those cases it did not formally invoke its rule on provisional measures, but instead it used its rule on the transmission of cases. Yet it did so at least partially to intervene in ongoing situations. Under this rule the HRC informs the State concerned of the case brought against it, in order to allow it to respond.[9] In other words, it used 'informal provisional measures' rather than formal provisional measures under Rule 86 (current Rule 92). The very first enquiry of this kind dates from 1978 and concerned an unspecified State.[10] The next of such inquiries were made between 1979 and 1981 in cases involving Uruguay. An example of an enquiry in one of the early cases is *Martinez Machado* v. *Uruguay* (1983). The petitioner was a Uruguayan national living in France acting on behalf of his brother. Eight years after his brother, a history teacher, was arrested, he was sentenced by a military court to nine and a half years imprisonment. Subsequently, in November 1980, he disappeared from Libertad prison.[11] His family had no contact with him and 'felt great concern for his state of health'. Within a month the HRC transmitted the case and also requested information on his whereabouts. This decision seems to have been taken *proprio motu* on the basis of the facts mentioned in the complaint.[12] Mr. Martinez only resurfaced more than five months later. In 1983 the HRC found that Uruguay had violated the Covenant, including Article 10(1) ICCPR, because it had held him incommunicado for more than five months.[13]

A decade later, with no information on the intervening period, it was Libya that was requested to provide the Committee with information on the whereabouts of an alleged victim. As

---

[7]   On the procedural requirements see Chapter XIV (Jurisdiction and admissibility).

[8]   See also Chapter XIII (Protection), section 4 on the group of beneficiaries. The treaty also contains a compromissory clause for submission to the ICJ, see Article 42.

[9]   Rule 91, current Rule 97.

[10] HRC *M.A.* v. *S.*, 24 April 1979.

[11] As he noted, previously the same had happened to Teti Izquierdo, see Chapter VI on intervention in detention situations involving risks to health and safety.

[12] The HRC did not enquire, however, about the alleged victim's state of health, although the petitioner had noted the family's great concern: *Martinez Machado* v. *Uruguay*, 4 November 1983.

[13] In the decision on the merits the HRC determined the State was under an obligation to take immediate steps to ensure strict observance of the Covenant. It must also treat him with humanity as required by Article 10(1). It was expected, moreover, to transmit a copy of the Committee's decision to the victim. See further HRC *Drescher Caldas (represented by his wife Ibarburu de Drescher)* v. *Uruguay*, 21 July 1983; *Sendic Antonaccio (submitted by Setelich)* v. *Uruguay*, 28 October 1981; *Teti Izquierdo* v. *Uruguay*, 1 April 1982; *Martinez Machado* v. *Uruguay*, 4 November 1983, but also *Dave Marais* v. *Madagascar*, 24 March 1984.

the full Committee had done in the previous cases, when there was not yet a Special Rapporteur on New Communications, the request was made under its rule on the transmission of cases.[14]

Thus far there is only one case involving the health and/or whereabouts of the alleged victim in which the HRC *explicitly* used provisional measures, requesting the State to 'avoid any action which might cause irreparable harm to the alleged victim'. This was the case *Tshishimbi* v. *Zaire* (1996).[15] In April 1993 the petitioner, residing in Belgium, had submitted a complaint to the HRC on behalf of her husband. He had been abducted in Zaire (Democratic Republic of the Congo) the previous month. He was a career military officer who had been imprisoned in 1973 for his refusal to obey orders. Since the late 1970s he had sympathized with the opposition parties. In 1992 Etienne Tshisekedi, the leader of the main opposition movement, became Prime Minister and appointed Tshishimbi as his military advisor. President Mobutu did not recognise the new Government and the petitioner noted that the military and especially the members of the special presidential division, loyal to President Mobutu, subjected the new Prime Minister, his Cabinet and his special advisors to 'constant surveillance, and at times harassment and bullying'. In this context, she claimed, her husband was abducted.[16] The disappearance took place after he had left the residence of the Prime Minister to go home. A month later Belgian press reported that he was believed to be detained at the headquarters of the National Intelligence Service. Ill treatment apparently was common in this place. It was on that day that his wife petitioned the HRC and requested provisional measures.[17] The Special Rapporteur transmitted the case to the State Party requesting information on the whereabouts and state of health of the alleged victim, as the full Committee had done in the previous six cases. The difference was that the Rapporteur used formal provisional measures under Rule 86 (current Rule 92) as well. She did so a month after receipt of the initial submission, urging the State 'to avoid any action which might cause irreparable harm to the alleged victim'.[18] It is remarkable that, next to the provisional measure proper, the Rapporteur posed a question under the general rule on transmission and inquiry. She asked the State 'to clarify the circumstances' of his abduction, to investigate the allegations and 'to provide

---

[14]   HRC *Mohammed Bashir El-Megreisi* (*submitted by his brother Youssef El-Megreisi*) v. *Libya*, 23 March 1994. The petitioner's brother had disappeared in January 1989. Almost two years later, he submitted a complaint to the HRC. The Optional Protocol entered into force for Libya on 16 August 1989. Seven months later the Special Rapporteur requested information under Rule 91 on the whereabouts of the brother and his state of health.

[15]   HRC *Tshishimbi* v. *Zaire*, 25 March 1996.

[16]   Early April 1993 Belgian press reports mentioned that he had been arrested. The exact circumstances of his abduction, however, remained unknown.

[17]   The submission pointed out that his family and the Government of Prime Minister Tshisekedi had been without news about Colonel Tshishimbi since 28 March 1983 when he was taken to an unknown destination where they expected him to be tortured. The petitioner expressed great anxiety about his fate. She referred to the activities by President Mobutu against those close to Prime Minister Tshisekedi. She also requested the Committee to use an urgent admissibility procedure in light of the risks to the life of Tshishimbi (submission of 21 April 1993, on file with the author). In its View the Committee pointed out that counsel for the petitioner did not indicate whether any steps had been taken in Kinshasa to pursue domestic remedies, but it concluded that it was apparent that the petitioner and her counsel considered any resort to such remedies to be futile, 'given in particular the absence of reliable information about the whereabouts of Mr. Tshishimbi'.

[18]   "*Par ailleurs, conformément à l'article 86 du règlement intérieur du Comité, le Gouvernement de son excellence est prié de prendre toutes les mesures appropriées pour éviter qu'un préjudice irréparable ne soit causé à la victime de la violation alléguée*". Note verbale of 21 May 1993 (on file with the author).

information about Mr. Tshishimbi's whereabouts and state of health'.[19] It may be that she intended to maintain the practice of requesting information on the whereabouts and state of health under that Rule and reserve the use of Rule 86 (current Rule 92) to very exceptional cases. It is also possible that she wished to maintain some continuity with the previous cases or that she considered that provisional measures could draw the attention of the State only to the obligation to *refrain* from acting and not to any positive obligations. The latter would then be within the purview of the rule on the transmission of cases.

2.2   Inter-American Commission

As discussed in Chapter II the first precautionary measures taken by the Inter-American Commission dealt with disappearances, but its use of (informal) precautionary measures was often rather discretionary.[20] The Commission is the adjudicator that has used precautionary measures most often in order to locate disappeared persons. It is very sensitive to the experiences of the American continent with disappearances that took place mainly in the 1970s and 1980s. Since then the number of disappearances decreased but once in a while the Commission did request a State to ascertain the whereabouts of a person recently disappeared. The use of precautionary measures in these cases is not always clearly documented. More information is available as of the late 1990s. There have been several cases in Colombia in which the Commission took precautionary measures in order to find disappeared persons.[21] Other addressee States have included Guatemala, Mexico and Guyana.[22]

---

[19] It was phrased as follows: '*et d'informer le Comité sur l'adresse ainsi que l'état de santé actuel de l'auteur de la communication*'. Note verbale of 21 May 1993 (on file with the author).

[20] Author's interview with Commissioner Juan Méndez, Washington D.C., 17 October 2001. In the 1980s he was working as a practitioner at Human Rights Watch.

[21] See e.g. CIDH lawyers collective '*José Alvear Restrepo*' v. *Colombia*, precautionary measures of 14 March 1997 (probably informally), on 15 March 1997 the beneficiary was released (see Case of Mr. Vilalba Vargas, CEJIL case docket 1997); *4 Investigators Popular Training Institute* v. *Colombia*, precautionary measure of 28 January 1999, they were released on 11 and 19 February 1999, Annual Report 1999, §17; *Robinson Ríos Uribe and José Gregorio Villada* v. *Colombia* ("they were last seen at a Medellín metropolitan police checkpoint on November 27, 2001, as they were travelling toward Cali. Some days later, the two young men contacted their families and told them they had been abducted by a paramilitary group. The Commission undertook a series of steps toward clearing up this situation during its on-site visit (December 7-13, 2001); finally, on December 18, 2001, it asked the Colombian government, as a matter of urgency, to take the steps necessary to reveal the whereabouts and guarantee the lives and persons of the aforesaid individuals and to launch a prompt and effective investigation using the urgent search mechanism established by Law 589/2000"), Annual Report 2001, §26; *Luis Alberto Sabando Véliz* v. *Colombia*, precautionary measure of 19 October 2004, Annual Report 2004, §27; More than 9 members of the *Embera Katio indigenous community of Alto Sinú* v. *Colombia*, precautionary measure of 4 June 2001, Annual Report 2001, §17.

[22] See e.g. CIDH *Jorge Alberto Rosal Paz* v. *Guatemala*, 11 March 2004 (friendly settlement), precautionary measures of 10 August 1983, 30 May 1984, 19 February 1985 and 1 August 1985; *Franz Britton* (*Collie Wills*) v. *Guyana*, precautionary measures of 4 & 5 April 2000, 24 August 2000, 4 February 2001, 10 October 2001 (adm.), Annual Report 2000, §34 and *Franz Britton AKA Collie Wills* v. *Guyana*, 10 October 2001 (adm.), §§11 and 18; *Faustino Jiménez Alvarez* v. *Mexico*, precautionary measures of 13 July 2001 and extension of 28 November 2001 to protect his wife and a witness against threats, Annual Report 2001, §39 and *Oscar Umberto Duarte Paiz* v. *Guatemala*, precautionary measures of 5 July 2006, 18 (12) Guatemala Human Rights Update, 13 July 2006, pp. 4-5.

Chapter VI

In March 1997 lawyers collective 'José Alvear Restrepo' in Colombia[23] requested the Commission to take precautionary measures on behalf of one of its lawyers. Members of the National Police in Bogotá had arbitrarily detained him after a demonstration involving professors and students. The Commission immediately requested information from the Colombian government with regard to his detention. The government responded and he was freed the next day.[24] It is not clear whether the Commission simply requested information or indeed took actual precautionary measures. This example does not necessarily fall within the category of protecting disappeared persons but the detention took place in unclear circumstances conducive to disappearance.[25]

In January 1999 the Commission was informed that a group of armed civilians had forcefully entered the headquarters of the Popular Training Institute (IPC) in Medellin, Antioquia and had abducted four of its investigators.[26] The Commission took precautionary measures that same afternoon. It urgently contacted Colombia to take the necessary measures to ascertain the whereabouts of the victims and protect their lives, physical integrity and liberty. Two of them were freed within two weeks and the two others a week later.[27]

In November 1999 the Commission requested Colombia to ascertain the whereabouts of two spokesmen for the peasant migration[28] and ensure their life and physical integrity. Military units had apparently arrested them the previous day. According to eyewitness accounts they had been tied to a tree and tortured. Following this, the self-defence units ('Autodefensas') had kept them in detention, publicly acknowledging their participation in the incident.[29] In its Third Report on the human rights situation in Colombia, published in March 1999, the Commission noted that it had taken precautionary measures on behalf of these two persons, but had received no further news on their whereabouts.[30] This case is an example of the close links these self-defence units can have with the police, military or other government authorities in certain areas of Colombia. It indicates also how clearly interrelated the different types of violations are, as well as the reasons for the perpetrators to commit them. The case related to issues of migration and possibly land rights and involved human rights defenders and witnesses to human rights violations. In such situations the Commission may order a State to ascertain the whereabouts of certain disappeared persons, but also to protect persons against attacks, often by members of paramilitary groups.[31]

In March 2000 the Commission requested Colombia to protect the life, physical integrity and liberty of a human rights defender who had disappeared six days earlier. He had held various

---

[23]   The submission was made together with CEJIL.

[24]   CIDH Case of Mr. Vilalba Vargas, CEJIL case docket 1997 (on file with the author).

[25]   On provisional measures in detention cases, see Chapter VI.

[26]   The 'Autodefensas' (paramilitaries) of Córdoba and Urabá had claimed responsibility for the kidnappings.

[27]   CIDH Annual Report 1999, Chapter III.C.1, §17.

[28]   They were from the Middle Magdalena region.

[29]   CIDH Annual Report 1999, Chapter III.C.1, §23. The Autodefensas described one of these human rights defenders as a 'terrorist of the ELN'.

[30]   CIDH Annual Report 1999, Chapter V – Colombia, §120.

[31]   The Commission had also requested the State to guarantee the lives and physical integrity of the residents of La Vereda La Placita who had witnessed and denounced the acts of torture. Several days later, on 6 December 1999, it requested Colombia to amplify the precautionary measures to include eight other persons who had also served as spokespersons for the peasant migration. Their personal security was in danger as well. During the period covered by the 1999 Annual Report the petitioner and the State continued to present information on the precautionary measures. Annual Report 1999, Chapter III.C.1, §§23-24.

elected positions and was working in marginalised, black and indigenous communities. Prior to his disappearance, several actors in the armed conflict had threatened him.[32]

In June 2001 the Commission took precautionary measures to clarify the whereabouts and protect the lives and personal integrity of nine named persons as well as 'other members of the Embera Katio indigenous community of Alto Sinú' who had been abducted from the community's main town and the neighbouring areas.[33]

Since 1996 the Annual Reports mention only a few States other than Colombia with regard to which the Inter-American Commission had used a precautionary measure requesting to locate a disappeared person. In April 2000 it took such a measure on behalf of Franz Britton, also known as Collie Wills. The petitioner reported that Mr. Britton had not been seen since his re-arrest in Guyana on 25 January 1999.[34] Earlier he had been arrested, and released four days later. Upon request, he reported to the police station the next day and was re-arrested by Leon Fraser, the Commissioner of Police. Eyewitnesses subsequently claimed they had seen him in the company of Mr. Fraser, who was head of the dreaded 'Black Clothes' police. They claimed he was being bundled into a silver grey car. According to the petitioner the 'Black Clothes' police unit was responsible for most of the extra-judicial killings in Guyana. A week later a domestic court ordered the Commissioner of Police to bring Mr. Britton before a court, by a writ of habeas corpus. In an affidavit the Commissioner stated that he had released him two days after his re-arrest and that he was no longer in police custody. The Commission took precautionary measures, requesting the State to take the appropriate measures to protect the life of Mr. Britton. The Commission also requested information on his health status, the reason for his arrest and detention and the location of the detention facilities where he was being held.[35] It is noteworthy that when the petitioner requested it to take provisional measures he had already been disappeared for more than a year.[36] The question arises whether this disappearance was still so recent that a precautionary measure could prevent irreparable harm. Still, in October 2001, when the Commission declared the case admissible, it also decided to maintain in effect its precautionary measures.[37]

In July 2001 the Commission took precautionary measures on behalf of someone who had been violently detained in Mexico the month before, without a warrant. His family had witnessed how agents of the judicial police had abducted him in an operation involving several vehicles also marked as belonging to this police force. They filed complaints with the Attorney General of the state of Guerrero, who apparently took no effective steps to locate him. Upon the petitioners' request the Commission's precautionary measures asked for intervention by the *federal* Attorney General because the petitioners suspected complicity between the kidnappers and the public prosecution service of Guerrero. In August Mexico responded that an investigation had begun, with the involvement of the wife of the disappeared man. The next month the petitioners informed the Commission that there were still irregularities in the investigation. In November Mexico

---

[32] CIDH Annual Report 1999, Chapter III.C.1, §25.

[33] On behalf of the other members of that indigenous community who had not yet been abducted but who were working together with the petitioners, the Commission took precautionary measures as well, to the effect that the State should protect them against further attacks. The Commission also requested Colombia to investigate, prosecute and punish those responsible for the attacks against the indigenous community. CIDH Annual Report 2001, §17.

[34] The petitioner was the Chairman for Economic Empowerment in Guyana.

[35] CIDH *Franz Britton AKA Collie Wills* v. *Guyana*, 10 October 2001. By letters of 4 and 5 April 2000, 24 August 2000 and 4 February 2001 the Commission requested information about the adoption of the precautionary measures, the admissibility of the petition and the merits. It did not receive a reply, §§11 and 18.

[36] Commission took precautionary measures one year and two months after the alleged disappearance, which was ten days after they were requested by the petitioner.

[37] CIDH *Franz Britton AKA Collie Wills* v. *Guyana*, 10 October 2001, §§11 and 18.

reported that it was continuing its search to locate him and it had arrested two suspected perpetrators. Subsequently the Commission extended its precautionary measures to cover the wife of the disappeared man, who was in grave danger because of her search. The precautionary measure also came to include a former officer of the judicial police in Guerrero who was under arrest and whose life was being threatened if he continued to make allegations about the involvement of judicial police officers and their superiors in kidnappings.[38]

2.3   European system

While the European Commission and Court have dealt with disappearance cases as well they do not seem to have used formal provisional measures in this context.[39] The next section examines their case law in disappearance cases to assess whether it would give occasion to the use of provisional measures.

2.4   Bosnia Chamber

Many disappearances took place in former Yugoslavia between 1991 and 1995. According to conservative estimates 'some 17,000 persons in Bosnia-Herzegovina are still recorded as missing'.[40] Nevertheless, the only known occasion in which the Bosnia Chamber used provisional measures was in 1996, requesting Republika Srpska to find a priest and his parents who had disappeared.[41] Families of disappeared persons may have focussed their efforts on other types of recourse, in particular the International Commission on Missing Persons (ICMP). In 1996 this Commission was specifically instituted to assist these families in order to 'secure the co-operation

---

[38]   CIDH Annual Report 2001, §39. Another example is the Commissions precautionary measure on behalf of Oscar Umberto Duarte Paiz who was kidnapped on 24 May 2006, requesting 'an expedited transfer of any information' regarding his whereabouts. Mr. Duarte Paiz was the leader of the San Juan Integral Association for the Development of Quetzal City and Bordering Communities (ASIDECQ). It also asked for protection of his family members and seven members of his organization, Guatemala Human Rights Commission (US), 18 (12) Guatemala Human Rights Update, 13 July 2006, pp. 4-5. On provisional measures to protect against death threats and harassment generally, see Chapter IX.

[39]   There is one case, ECtHR *Istrate* v. *Moldova*, 13 June 2006 (4th section), in which the ECtHR, dealing with a case involving Article 6 ECHR, approximately 2 years after the initial submission, received a letter signed by the petitioner, 'dated 1 September 2003', posted 7 April 2005, in which he stated 'that he had previously been the victim of an attempted murder, that he was afraid for his life and that he sought the Court's protection'. 'He had also stated that the letter had been given to a third person who had been instructed to post it in case of his disappearance'. Subsequently the ECtHR inquired with the State, asking it to comment on the letter. In June 2005 the petitioner contacted the Court again and the case was pursued under Article 6 ECHR without further reference to the right to life. See also the Court's request for information on 8 March 2004, asking Georgia and Russia to 'provide information on the disappearance of Mr Khashiev and Mr Baymurzayev and, if applicable, on their health and place of detention in Russia'. ECtHR *Shamayev et al.* v. *Georgia and Russia*, 12 April 2005, §45.

[40]   Amnesty International, 'Bosnia-Herzegovina: Human Rights Chamber decision on Srebrenica – a first step to justice', AI Index: EUR 63/007/2003, 7 March 2003.

[41]   Bosnia Chamber *Matanović* v. *Srpska*, 6 August 1997; in other disappearance cases (*Balić* v. *Srpska*, 10 September 1998 (adm.) and *Grgić* v. *Srpska*, 3 September 1997) no mention is made of the use of provisional measures.

of Governments and other authorities in locating and identifying persons missing as a result of armed conflicts, other hostilities or violations of human rights and to assist them in doing so'.[42]

3 RELATION BETWEEN PROVISIONAL MEASURES LOCATE AND PROTECT DISAPPEARED PERSONS AND THE EXPECTED DECISION ON THE MERITS

3.1 Introduction

In some of the cases in which adjudicators used provisional measures to locate disappeared persons a decision on the merits is available as well that could shed light on the relation between the case law on the merits and the use of provisional measures. Moreover, disappearance cases in which no provisional measures were used could still help clarify the practice of the adjudicators vis-à-vis such measures. After all provisional measures may not have been used simply because the disappearance was not recent, but the decision on the merits could still justify future use of such measures in imminent cases, indicating likelihood of success on the merits.

3.2 HRC

From the start of its activities the HRC has dealt with claims in which the whereabouts of the alleged victims were unclear. It has emphasised the positive obligations of States under the right to life in Article 6 ICCPR.[43] The obligation under this article to take preventive measures against disappearances, combined with the obligation to protect the right to security of person under

---

[42] See the website of the ICMP: <http://www.ic-mp.org/home>. Subsequently its mandate was expanded. It is headquartered in Sarajevo, BiH, but also has offices in the Republic of Croatia, Serbia and Montenegro, and Kosovo.

[43] See e.g. HRC *Dermit Barbato* (*submitted by Mr. Gilmet Dermit on behalf of his cousins*) v. *Uruguay*, 21 October 1982. The HRC concluded that the Uruguayan authorities were responsible for not taking adequate measures to protect the life of one of the alleged victims, either by act or by omission. He had served his sentence in July 1980 but he was still in detention in December of that year. He was last seen alive on 24 December. On 28 December the authorities showed his mother his dead body for identification. His brother, a medical doctor, had disappeared earlier that month, on 2 December 1980. Only on 19 December 1980 his detention was officially announced. The authorities described him as belonging to a group of relatives of prisoners who had carried out 'agitation and propaganda activities'. He continued to be held incommunicado. The petitioner claimed a violation of Article 10 ICCPR 'because the treatment of detainees in Uruguay did not conform to this provision'. He pointed out that he was unable to provide more detailed information about his treatment in detention because he was being held incommunicado. The HRC found a violation of Article 6 with regard to the brother who died in detention, and of Articles 9(3) (not being brought promptly before a judge), 9(4) (incommunicado detention and violation of right habeas corpus) and 14(3)(c) (undue delay). It did not further address the Articles 10 and 7 claims. Only in the paragraph on reparations it pointed out that the State was obliged to take effective steps, among others, to ensure strict observance of the rights of detained persons set forth in Articles 7, 9 and 10 ICCPR. In light of the circumstances of his brother's continued detention and death and in light of the circumstances of his own arrest and incommunicado detention the HRC could have requested information about his health status under Rule 91 (currently Rule 97).

Article 9 ICCPR, underlines the importance of the State's duty to take positive measures to protect persons against threats to their life and dignity.[44]

In *Almeida de Quinteros* v. *Uruguay* (1983) the HRC not only found violations of the rights of the disappeared person, but also of the rights of this person's family.[45] It confirmed this approach in subsequent cases.[46] In *El-Megreisi* v. *Libya* (1994), in which the HRC had taken 'informal' provisional measures in 1989, it found on the merits that the prolonged incommunicado detention in an unknown location constituted a violation of Article 7 ICCPR (prohibition of torture and cruel and inhuman treatment).[47] In the case of *Tshishimbi* v. *Zaire* (1996), the only known case in which the HRC formally used provisional measures, the State had not responded at all. Three years later, in its decision on the merits the HRC found that the State had failed to ensure his liberty and security of person, in violation of Article 9(1). It referred to its previous jurisprudence that an interpretation of Article 9(1) limited to the context of arrest and detention would render ineffective the guarantees of the Covenant by allowing States parties to 'tolerate, condone or ignore threats made by persons in authority to the personal liberty and security of non-detained individuals within the State party's jurisdiction'. The HRC also found that the removal of the victim and the prevention of contact with his family and with the outside world constituted cruel and inhuman treatment in violation of Article 7. It urged the State party to thoroughly investigate the circumstances of the abduction and unlawful detention and to bring to justice those responsible. The State party was under an obligation to ensure that similar violations did not occur in the future.[48] In *Thevaraja Sarma* v. *Sri Lanka* (2003) it found violations of Articles 7 and 9 ICCPR with regard to the disappeared son and of Article 7 with regard to the petitioner and his

---

44 HRC General Comment 6 (16) about Article 6 ICCPR points out that States should take 'specific and effective' measures to prevent disappearance. They should also establish 'facilities and procedures to investigate thoroughly, by an appropriate and impartial body, cases of missing and disappeared persons'. In the case of *Ana Rosario* the HRC found violations of Articles 6(1), 7 and 9(1), all *juncto* Article 2(1) and of Article 24(1). Her abduction and disappearance and the prevention of contact with her family and the outside world constituted cruel and inhuman treatment. Eight days before her disappearance a court had provisionally released her into the custody of her grandfather and the armed State agents who abducted her from her home had not acted on the basis of an arrest warrant or the orders of a judicial officer. The State, moreover, had ignored the HRC's request for information about the results of her grandfather's petition for habeas corpus, all in violation of Article 9. Finally, in violation of Article 24(1), the State did not adopt any particular measures of protection to investigate her disappearance and ensure her security and welfare. Such special measures were required because of her status as a minor. *Ana Rosario Celis Laureano* (*submitted by her grandfather Laureano Atachahua*) v. *Peru*, 25 March 1996. See also *Alfredo and Samuel Sanjuán Arévalo* (*submitted by their mother Elcida Arévalo Perez*) v. *Colombia*, 3 November 1989.
45 HRC *Almeida de Quinteros* v. *Uruguay,* 21 July 1983. "The Committee understands the anguish and stress caused to the mother by the disappearance of her daughter and by the continuing uncertainty concerning her fate and whereabouts. The author has the right to know what has happened to her daughter. In these respects, she too is a victim of the violations of the Covenant suffered by her daughter, in particular of article 7". By letter of 15 June 1987 the victim's mother informed the Committee that the State had failed to implement its Views and requested the Committee to urge the State to comply with its Views. By note of 31 October 1991 the State party only referred to the relevant paragraphs of Law 15.848 of 22 December 1996, without providing any further information on her daughter's case.
46 See e.g. HRC *J. Thevaraja Sarma* (*submitted by his father S. Jegatheeswara Sarma*) v. *Sri Lanka,* 16 July 2003.
47 HRC *Mohammed Bashir El-Megreisi* (*submitted by his brother Youssef El-Megreisi*) v. *Libya*, 23 March 1994.
48 HRC *Tshishimbi* v. *Zaire,* 25 March 1996. See also Chapter XVII (Official responses).

wife. It noted, however, that the petitioner had not asked the HRC to conclude that his son was dead and that, while invoking Article 6, he also asked for 'the release of his son, indicating that he has not abandoned hope for his son's reappearance'. The HRC considered that in such circumstances it would be inappropriate to presume his death and make a finding with respect to Article 6. It pointed out that the State was under an obligation to provide the petitioner and his family with an effective remedy, 'including a thorough and effective investigation into the disappearance and fate of the author's son' and 'his immediate release if he is still alive'.[49] The HRC also referred to the UN Declaration on the Protection of all Persons from Enforced Disappearances (1992). Moreover, it referred to the definition of enforced disappearance contained in Article 7(2)(i) of the Rome Statute of the International Criminal Court and noted that disappearance constitutes a violation of many of the rights in the ICCPR, including the right to liberty and security of person (Article 9), the right not to be subjected to torture or ill treatment (Article 7) and the right of persons deprived of their liberty to be treated with humanity and respect for their inherent dignity (Article 10). Finally it pointed out that disappearance constitutes a grave threat to the right to life (Article 6).[50]

The standard phrase used by the HRC in reference to the burden of proof is that it 'cannot rest on the author of the communication alone, especially considering that the author and the State party do not always have equal access to the evidence and that frequently the State party alone has access to relevant information'. It then continues with: "It is implicit in article 4(2) of the Optional Protocol that the State party has the duty to investigate in good faith all allegations of the violation of the Covenant made against it and its authorities, and to furnish to the Committee the information available to it".[51] Moreover, according to McGoldrick the HRC does not apply a standard of 'beyond a reasonable doubt', but rather a standard 'approximating to' a 'balance of probabilities'.[52]

Not only does the case law of the HRC comport with the State's obligation to ensure that similar events do not occur in the future, as traditionally mentioned in the paragraph on reparations in the Committee's Views,[53] it also underlines the State's duty to act swiftly in the face of threats against persons rather than await the HRC's final determination. While the case is pending this certainly justifies a reminder of the State's positive obligations by the HRC, through the use of provisional measures.

3.3 Inter-American system

Already in the early 1970s the Inter-American Commission has denounced the act of disappearing people.[54] Since then it has consistently denounced the phenomenon in strong terms. In 1983 the political organs of the OAS became involved as well. The OAS General Assembly declared that forced disappearance was 'an affront to the conscience of the Hemisphere and constitutes a crime

---

[49]   HRC *J. Thevaraja Sarma* (*submitted by his father S. Jegatheeswara Sarma*) v. *Sri Lanka*, 16 July 2003.

[50]   Ibid. See also Blaauw (2002) and Froidevaux (2002). In *Louisa Bousroual* (*on behalf of her husband Salah Saker*) v. *Algeria*, 30 March 2006 the petitioner assumed that her husband, who had been disappeared in 1994, had died. In this case the HRC found a violation of the right to life as well.

[51]   See e.g. HRC *Marais* v. *Madagascar*, 24 March 1983; *Bleier* v. *Uruguay*, 29 March 1982 and *Mukong* v. *Cameroon*, 21 July 1994.

[52]   McGoldrick (1994), para. 4.36. Generally see Chapter XV (Immediacy and risk).

[53]   See also Chapter XIII on the relationship between provisional measures and forms of reparation.

[54]   CIDH Annual Report 1974.

against humanity'.[55] In 1994 the OAS General Assembly adopted the Inter-American Convention on Forced Disappearance of Persons.[56]

In *Velásquez Rodríguez* (1988) the IACHR set out its influential doctrine of state responsibility with regard to disappearances. Taking into account the systematic practice of disappearances and the general human rights situation in Honduras, it found that the disappearance of Mr. Velásquez Rodríguez constituted a violation of the right to life, humane treatment, personal liberty and security.[57] It found that the act of disappearing people and the subsequent failure to investigate these disappearances constituted a violation of a range of rights.

Subsequently it dealt with various other disappearance cases.[58] In *Bámaca Velásquez* (2000), for instance, the Court also found that Guatemala had violated a range of rights: the right to personal liberty (Article 7 ACHR) of the disappeared person, Efraín Bámaca Velásquez, as well as his right to humane treatment (Article 5(1) and 5(2) ACHR), the right of his wife and immediate family to humane treatment, his right to life (Article 4 ACHR), his right to judicial guarantees and judicial protection (Articles 8 and 25 ACHR) as well as that of his wife and immediate family. Moreover, the State neither complied with the general obligations of Article 1(1) ACHR – in connection with the violations of the aforementioned substantive rights –, nor with the obligation to prevent and punish torture (Articles 1, 2, 6 and 8 of the Inter-American Convention to Prevent and Punish Torture).[59]

The Inter-American Commission has dealt with a considerable range of cases involving disappearances. As noted, it has regularly used precautionary measures in such cases as well.[60] The Commission and Court have both referred to the UN Declaration against disappearances and to other international and regional instruments as well.

They have also referred to the concept of the burden of proof, which could be relevant not only as an indication of the evidence of risk to life required for the use of provisional measures,[61] but also to indicate the general attitude of the adjudicator towards the phenomenon of disappearances. This, in turn, could help clarify the use of provisional measures. The IACHR noted that 'because the Commission is accusing the Government of the disappearance of Manfredo Velásquez, it, in principle, should bear the burden of proving the facts underlying its petition'.[62] It seems, however, that the Court simply wished to point out that the Commission should make a *prima facie* case. As Kokott points out, human rights treaties have a 'non-reciprocal, law-making character'. This makes individual complaint proceedings under human rights treaties less adver-

---

55   OAS Resolution AG/RES. 666 (XVIII-0/83), 18 November 1983, §5.

56   Adopted at Belém do Pará, 9 June 1994; entered into force on 28 March 1996; 12 State parties as of 30 July 2006.

57   IACHR *Velásquez Rodríguez* (Honduras), 29 July 1988.

58   See e.g. IACHR *Godínez Gruz* (Honduras), 20 January 1989; *Caballero Delgado and Santana* (Colombia), 8 December 1995; *Garrido and Baigorria* (Argentina), 2 February 1996; *Castillo Páez* (Peru), 3 November 1997. In *Blake* (Guatemala), 24 January 1998, it emphasized the rights of the next of kin.

59   IACHR *Bámaca Velásquez* case (Guatemala), Judgment of 25 November 2000 (merits). See also e.g. *Juan Humberto Sanchez* (Honduras), 7 July 2003 (violations of Articles 4, 5, 7, 8 and 25); *Molina Thiessen* (Guatemala), 4 May 2004 (right to life, humane treatment, right to personal liberty, fair trial, rights of the family, rights of the child and judicial protection); *Case of 19 Merchants* disappeared in 1987 (Colombia), 5 July 2004 (violations personal liberty, personal integrity and life); *Serrano Cruz sisters* (El Salvador), 1 March 2005 (violations of Articles 5, 8, 17, 18, 19, 25).

60   See e.g. CIDH *Juan de la Cruz Núñez Santana et al.* v. *Peru*, 13 April 1999; *Ignacio Ellacuría et al.* v. *El Salvador*, 22 December 1999.

61   See generally Chapter XV (Immediacy and risk).

62   IACHR *Velásquez Rodríguez* case, 29 July 1988, §123.

sarial than most domestic proceedings. The non-reciprocal or universal character of human rights treaties warrants an approach in which the individual petitioner does not bear the burden of proof, but rather only the burden of presenting a *prima facie* case.[63] Referring to the burden of proof of an individual 'evokes a perception of a technical burden of producing evidence which is not found in human rights law'. Rather than the burden of proof the petitioner has, as Kokott calls it 'the "burden" of presenting a *prima facie* case in supporting one's claim (*commencement de preuve*) or the risk of non-persuasion'.[64]

The IACHR has 'set the standard' on the standard of proof in serious human rights cases:

> "The international protection of human rights should not be confused with criminal justice. States do not appear before the Court as defendants in a criminal action. The objective of international human rights law is not to punish those individuals who are guilty of violations, but rather to protect the victims and to provide for the reparation of damages resulting from the acts of the States responsible".[65]

In light of the purpose expressed in the relevant treaties of effective protection of human rights it indeed appears 'illogical' to apply the high standard of 'beyond a reasonable doubt' to international adjudication.[66] Kokott referred to decisions by international adjudicators showing that these in fact are willing to accept a lower standard of proof than that of 'beyond a reasonable doubt', at least in cases concerning the most serious human rights violations.[67]

The Commission's as well as the Court's case law on the merits, finding disappearances to constitute a violation of a combination of rights, referring to regional and international instruments and taking into account the position of the individual in the assessment of the evidence, clearly confirms the appropriateness of the use of provisional measures.

3.4 European system

Both the Inter-American Court and the HRC – as discussed under the previous subheading – have found that enforced disappearances could constitute a violation of the rights to life, humane treatment and personal liberty and security.[68] Similar to the approach of the HRC and the Inter-American Commission and Court, the European Commission and Court have found that disappearances violate the rights of the next of kin as well.[69] In *Kurt* v. *Turkey* (1996/98), for instance, the European Commission and Court found that the State had violated the prohibition of cruel

---

63   Kokott (1998), p. 211.

64   Ibid.

65   IACHR *Velásquez Rodríguez*, Judgment of 29 July 1988, §§134-135.

66   See Kokott (1998), pp. 205-206.

67   Id., pp. 196-205.

68   The African Commission does not seem to have had occasion to deal with disappearances on the merits, but see ACHPR *Africa Legal Aid* (*on behalf of Mr. Lamin Waa Juwara*) v. *the Gambia*, 209/97, found inadmissible in May 2000 (no reference to the use of provisional measures in this case, which was submitted 1,5 years after the disappearance).

69   See e.g. ECtHR *Timurtas* v. *Turkey*, 13 June 2000, §95; and *Çakici* v. *Turkey*, 8 July 1999, §98. In subsequent cases it has sometimes found a violation to the disappeared person himself, but it has not considered the disappearance itself to be a form of torture or ill treatment.

treatment with regard to the mother of the disappeared person. On the other hand they did not examine separately whether the disappeared person *himself* was a victim of such treatment.[70]

This context it may be significant that the European Commission and Court do not seem to have used provisional measures in order to help find the disappeared person alive. In fact they have generally taken a more restrictive approach towards disappearances than the HRC and the Inter-American Commission and Court, possibly because they were less attuned to dealing with particularly serious and systematic human rights violations. The subsequent paragraphs will further refer to differences between the approach in the European system and that of the other systems.

In the inter-State case *Cyprus* v. *Turkey* (1999) the European Commission did emphasize the positive obligations of States to protect human rights and recalled that the HRC stressed that States should take 'specific and effective measures to prevent disappearances and establish effective facilities and procedures to investigate early, by an appropriate and impartial body, cases of disappearances that may involve a violation to the right to life'.[71] Subsequently, when the ECtHR dealt with this case in 2001, it invoked its distinction between substantive and procedural violations of the right to life. It found that there had been no breach of Art. 2 ECHR 'by reason of an alleged violation of a substantive obligation under that Article in respect of any of the missing persons'.[72] At the same time it found that 'there has been a continuing violation of Article 2 of the Convention on account of the failure of the authorities of the respondent State to conduct an effective investigation into the whereabouts and fate of Greek-Cypriot missing persons who disappeared in life-threatening circumstances'.[73] It equally found that 'there has been a continuing violation of Article 5 of the Convention by virtue of the failure of the authorities of the respondent State to conduct an effective investigation into the whereabouts and fate of the Greek-Cypriot missing persons in respect of whom there is an arguable claim that they were in Turkish custody at the time of their disappearance'.[74] Yet it held that 'no breach of Article 5 of the Convention has been established by virtue of the alleged actual detention of Greek-Cypriot missing persons'.[75] In fact the 'combination-approach' taken in the Inter-American system and by the HRC is to be preferred.[76]

Apart from creating an evidentiary hurdle, as discussed in the subsequent paragraph, the European Commission and Court initially did not consider disappearances as the complex mix of multiple and continuous human rights violations recognized by the Inter-American Court and HRC. They simply found a particularly serious violation of Article 5 ECHR (personal liberty and security) *in the context of the* right to life and the prohibition of cruel treatment, rather than a violation of these rights taken together.[77]

Yet this has since changed. The ECtHR has begun finding violations of the right to life as well, not only procedurally, but also substantively. It has held that lengthy periods of unacknowledged detentions went 'beyond a mere irregular detention' in violation of Article 5 ECHR[78] and

---

[70]   EComHR *Kurt* v. *Turkey*, 5 December 1996, §§197 and 221. See also ECtHR *Kurt* v. *Turkey*, 25 May 1998. In his concurring opinion in *Matanović et al.* v. *Republika Srpska*, 6 August 1997 Nowak notes that this approach was 'somewhat surprising', Concurring Opinion, §6.

[71]   EComHR *Cyprus* v. *Turkey*, 4 June 1999, §202.

[72]   ECtHR *Cyprus* v. *Turkey*, 10 May 2001, §130. See also EComHR *Cyprus* v. *Turkey*, 4 June 1999.

[73]   ECtHR *Cyprus* v. *Turkey*, 10 May 2001, §136.

[74]   Id., §150.

[75]   Id., §151.

[76]   See also Taqi (2001), pp. 940-984 and the discussion under the next heading ('Bosnia Chamber').

[77]   ECtHR *Kurt* v. *Turkey*, 25 May 1998, §201 (a forced disappearance 'raises fundamental and grave issues under Article 5'). See also EComHR *Cyprus* v. *Turkey*, 4 June 1999, §119.

[78]   See e.g. ECtHR *Timurtaş* v. *Turkey*, 13 June 2000, §83.

also examined such allegations from the perspective of Article 2 ECHR (right to life), albeit without taking into account the prohibition of torture and ill treatment (Article 3 ECHR).[79]

On the other hand, the ECtHR has not yet done away with the evidentiary hurdle it created in its earlier case law. By 2006 it still used the evidentiary standard of 'beyond reasonable doubt'.[80] Such a standard is in fact more appropriate as imposed on a State in the context of a criminal law case than on a petitioner for proving the responsibility of a State in a disappearance case.[81] The standard does not seem to be required by the text of the ECHR itself. Its context, object and purpose certainly do not require it.

Moreover, the ECtHR has indeed shown an awareness of the special responsibility of the State by pointing out that 'Convention proceedings do not in all cases lend themselves to a rigorous application of the principle *affirmanti incumbit probatio* (he who alleges something must prove that allegation)'.[82] It has also noted that this standard 'should not be interpreted as requiring such a high degree of probability as in criminal trials'.[83] In this context dropping the reference to the criterion of 'beyond reasonable doubt' would be the next logical step. After all, when 'the events in issue lie wholly, or in large part, within the exclusive knowledge of the authorities', 'the burden of proof may be regarded as resting on the authorities to provide a satisfactory and convincing explanation'.[84] If it can be established that someone was 'officially summoned by the military or the police, entered a place under their control and has not been seen since' the onus is indeed 'on the Government to provide a plausible explanation as to what happened on the premises and to show that the person concerned was not detained by the authorities, but left the premises without subsequently being deprived of his or her liberty'.

---

[79]   See e.g. ECtHR *Orhan* v. *Turkey*, 18 June 2002, §§328-332.

[80]   See e.g. ECtHR *Akdeniz* v. *Turkey*, 31 May 2005 (4th section), §96 ("the Court has generally adopted up to now the standard of proof "beyond reasonable doubt". Such proof may follow from the coexistence of sufficiently strong, clear and concordant inferences or of similar unrebutted presumptions of fact; in addition, the conduct of the parties when evidence is being obtained may be taken into account"); *Bazorkina* v. *Russia*, 27 July 2006 (1st section), §106; *Uçar* v. *Turkey*, 11 April 2006 (2nd section), §74; *Şeker* v. *Turkey*, 21 February 2006 (2nd section), §§64-65; *Nesibe Haran* v. *Turkey*, 6 October 2005 (3rd section), §65; *Özgen et al. v. Turkey*, 20 September 2005 (2nd section), §36; *Taniş et al. v. Turkey*, 2 August 2005 (4th section), §160; *Türkoğlu* v. *Turkey*, 17 March 2005 (3rd section), §116 and *Orhan* v. *Turkey*, 18 June 2002 (1st section), §264.

[81]   For a critical discussion of the case law until 2000 see Taqi (2001), pp. 940-984 (discussing EComHR *Kurt* v. *Turkey*, 5 December 1996; ECtHR *Kurt* v. *Turkey*, 25 May 1998; *Cakici* v. *Turkey*, 8 July 1999 and *Timurtas* v. *Turkey*, 13 June 2000). In *Labita* v. *Italy*, Grand Chamber Judgment of 6 April 2000, a Dissenting Opinion of eight judges pointed out that the 'test, method and standard of proof in respect of responsibility under the Convention are different from those applicable in the various national systems as regards responsibility of individuals for criminal offences', Joint Partly Dissenting Opinion of Judges Pastor Ridruejo, Bonello, Makarczyk, Tulkens, Strážnická, Butkevych, Casadevall and Zupančič, §1. See also *Veznedaroglu* v. *Turkey*, Judgment of 11 April 2000, Partly Dissenting Opinion of Judge Bonello, §12: 'in other fields of judicial enquiry, the standard of proof should be proportionate to the aim which the search for the truth pursues: the highest degree of certainty, in criminal matters; a workable degree of probability in others' and *Tahsin Acar* v. *Turkey*, 8 April 2004 with concurring opinion by Judge Bonello, pointing out: "Unacceptable that the applicant is told by a court of justice that he cannot win against the State, as he failed to produce evidence which the state had wrongly failed to produce".

[82]   ECtHR *Taniş et al.* v. *Turkey*, 2 August 2005 (4th section), §163.

[83]   ECtHR *Nachova and Others* v. *Bulgaria*, 26 February 2004, §166.

[84]   See ECtHR *Salman* v. *Turkey*, 27 June 2000 (Grand Chamber), §100; see also *Taniş et al.* v. *Turkey*, 2 August 2005 (4th section), §160; as well as *Çakıcı* v. *Turkey*, 8 July 1999 (Grand Chamber), §85; *Timurtaş* v. *Turkey*, 13 June 2000, §82.

"In the absence of such an explanation, the Court's examination of the case may extend beyond Article 5 to encompass, in certain circumstances, Article 2 of the Convention".[85]

In a recent case, of July 2006, the ECtHR found Russia in violation of the right to life (both substantively and procedurally), personal liberty and an effective remedy for a disappearance that took place in Chechnya.[86] Nevertheless, while it found the authorities responsible for his death, it found 'the exact way in which he died and whether he was subjected to ill-treatment while in detention' were 'not entirely clear'.[87] It found insufficient evidence for a violation of Art. 3 ECHR 'since the information before it' did 'not enable the Court to find beyond all reasonable doubt that the applicant's son was subjected to treatment contrary to Article 3'.[88]

This is the first of many disappearance cases regarding Chechnya pending before the Court.[89]

3.5 Bosnia Chamber

With regard to the disappearance of the Roman Catholic priest and his parents, mentioned in the previous section for its use of provisional measures in 1996, in 1997 the Bosnia Chamber found that Republika Srpska had failed to secure the petitioners' right to liberty and security of person.[90] It decided not to consider whether a forced disappearance also constituted a violation of Articles 2 and 3 ECHR. In his concurring opinion Nowak rightly pointed out that the Chamber was not bound by the restrictive approach taken by the Ombudsperson, only alleging violations of Article 5. After all the case did not only deal with arbitrary deprivation of personal liberty and security, but in fact dealt with enforced disappearance as a larger phenomenon encompassing a wider range of rights. This criticism in fact also applies to the approach of the ECtHR at the time. As discussed, it only started to change this approach around 2000. Nowak noted that while the UN Declaration on the Protection of all Persons from Enforced Disappearance was not legally binding, it did constitute 'the most elaborate and authoritative international instrument in this field'.[91] Enforced disappearances were human rights violations not explicitly referred to in the ECHR (1950) and the Declaration should be taken into account when applying the Convention. He pointed out that the 'very act of enforced disappearance is a particularly serious violation of human rights which clearly goes beyond mere arbitrary deprivation of personal liberty and security'.[92] Such disappearances constitute 'a violation of the rules of international law guaranteeing, inter alia, the right to recognition as a person before the law, the right to liberty and security of the person and the right not to be subjected to torture and other cruel, inhuman or degrading treatment or punishment. It also violates or constitutes a grave threat to the right to life'.[93] There

---

85   ECtHR *Taniş et al.* v. *Turkey*, 2 August 2005 (4th section), §160.

86   ECtHR *Bazorkina* (*regarding the disappearance of her son Yandiev*) v. *Russia*, 27 July 2006. See also ECtHR *Gongadze* v. *Ukraine*, 8 November 2005, finding violations of Article 2, 'both in its substantive and procedural aspects', as well as of Articles 3 and 13. Generally about the evidentiary requirements for provisional measures see Chapter XV (Immediacy and risk).

87   ECtHR *Bazorkina* v. *Russia*, 27 July 2006, §131.

88   Id., §133.

89   See e.g. Human Rights Watch, 'Russia condemned for 'disappearance' of Chechen,' 27 July 2006; International Herald Tribune, 'European Court blames Russia for missing Chechen', 27 July 2006; <bbc.co.uk>, 'Russia censured over Chechen man', 27 July 2006.

90   Bosnia Chamber *Matanović et al.* v. *Srpska*, 6 August 1997.

91   Bosnia Chamber *Matanović et al.* v. *Srpska*, 6 August 1997, Concurring Opinion Nowak, §3.

92   Bosnia Chamber *Matanović et al.* v. *Srpska*, 6 August 1997, Concurring Opinion Nowak §4.

93   Ibid.

was 'ample evidence' that the disappearance of the petitioners was 'not an isolated case'.[94] Nowak provided some relevant contextual information about the 'special process on missing persons in the territory of the former Yugoslavia'.[95] He pointed out that the Chamber should have taken into account the provisions of the UN Declarations and the relevant international case law as a tool for interpreting the ECHR. Just like the Inter-American Court and the HRC the Bosnia Chamber should have found violations of the right to life and the prohibition of cruel treatment as well.[96] Again, this comment may well apply to the ECtHR too.

In this same case the Chamber *did* refer to the presumption of responsibility of the State that is created when someone has disappeared from official custody. It recalled the statement by the European Commission that Article 5 ECHR could be understood as a guarantee against disappearances and any 'unaccounted disappearance of a detained person' must be considered as a particularly serious violation of this Article.[97] Finally the Bosnia Chamber expressed its agreement with the approach to evidence taken by the Inter-American Court of Human Rights in *Velasquez Rodriguez*.[98]

In the *Srebrenica* cases (2003) the Bosnia Chamber found that Republika Srpska had violated the human rights of their family members by the continued refusal to inform them of the fate of their loved ones.[99] It had done 'almost nothing to clarify the fate and whereabouts of the presumed victims of the Srebrenica events, or to take other action to relieve the suffering of their surviving family members, or to contribute to the process of reconciliation in Bosnia and Herzegovina'.[100] This time the Chamber extensively referred to the ICTY decision *Prosecutor* v. *Radoslav Krstć*, international instruments, including the UN Declaration, and international and domestic activities and decisions. Moreover, it ordered Republika Srpska, in accordance with the 'guiding principles' on reparation developed by the IACHR,[101] 'as a matter of urgency', to release immediately 'any such missing persons who are still alive and held in detention unlawfully'.[102]

Although the Bosnia Chamber initially took an overly limited approach on the merits in *Matanović et al.* v. *Srpska* (1997), only finding a violation of Article 5 ECHR, it *did* take provisional measures while this case was still pending.

Moreover, whatever improvements could still be made, the subsequent case law of the ECtHR, also finding violations of Articles 2 and 3 ECHR in certain disappearance cases, in fact confirms the relationship with the right to life and the prohibition of cruel treatment that seems to underlie the Chamber's use of provisional measures in *Matanović*. Finally, the relationship between the protection required in orders for reparation and for provisional measures was clearly

---

[94] Bosnia Chamber *Matanović et al.* v. *Srpska*, 6 August 1997, Concurring Opinion Nowak §5.

[95] Ibid.

[96] In this case Nowak would also have found a violation of Article 3 because 'the prolonged period of incommunicado detention' to which the petitioners had been exposed constituted as such inhuman treatment. Moreover, he would have found a violation of Article 2(1) jo. 1 'because the enforced disappearance of the applicants for a period of one and a half years as from the entry into force of the Dayton Peace Agreement constitutes a grave threat to the right to life, because there are certain indications that one or more of the applicants might have died in detention, and because the respondent Party has failed to secure and protect the applicants' right to life', Bosnia Chamber *Matanović et al.* v. *Srpska*, 6 August 1997, Concurring Opinion Nowak, §9.

[97] EComHR *Cyprus* v. *Turkey*, Application No. 8007/77, 72 DR, p. 38.

[98] Bosnia Chamber *Matanović et al.* v. *Republika Srpska*, 6 August 1997, §35.

[99] Bosnia Chamber *Srebrenica* cases (49 petitions), 7 March 2003. It did find that it had no jurisdiction *ratione temporis* vis-à-vis the disappeared persons themselves since the violations took place before the Dayton Peace Agreement was signed (14 December 1995).

[100] Bosnia Chamber *Srebrenica* cases (49 petitions), 7 March 2003, §188.

[101] See Bosnia Chamber *Srebrenica* cases (49 petitions), 7 March 2003, §211.

[102] Ibid.

confirmed in the Chamber's judgment in the *Srebrenica* cases (2003). Sadly, the order to release those missing persons that are still alive, while very appropriate, must have been made for rhetorical purposes rather than the expectation that persons would still return alive.

4   CONCLUSION

The HRC has mainly used informal provisional measures in its early political detention cases, when the whereabouts of the detainee were unclear. It once used provisional measures formally. The Inter-American Commission has regularly used precautionary measures on behalf of disappeared persons. The Bosnia Chamber has also used provisional measures at least once in a disappearance case. The ECtHR, on the other hand, does not appear to have used them yet in the context of the disappearance cases that it has dealt with.

The discussion in section 3, on the relation to the case law on the merits under the various international and regional human rights treaties, confirms that the right to life and the prohibition of cruel treatment underlie the use of provisional measures by the HRC, the Inter-American Commission and Court and the Bosnia Chamber.

The human rights adjudicators have all confirmed that given the inequality between the individual and the State the burden of proof cannot rest solely with the individual, particularly in relation to claims about the right to life. Unfortunately they have not always been that clear on the standard of proof. After all, in order to achieve an early shift in the burden of proof from the petitioner to the State, the petitioner should not have to meet the standard of evidence 'beyond a reasonable doubt'. The State always has the monopoly of power vis-à-vis the individual. It normally also has a monopoly on information, especially in relation to disappearances and torture. Exactly given this unequal situation between the two, both as to the consequences of any finding and in light of the possibility to obtain evidence, the standard of proof in cases between unequal parties should vary according to the allocation of the burden of proof. It should be higher if the initial burden is on the State (e.g. in a criminal trial, where the State has to prove an individual's guilt in order to deprive him of his freedom). It should be lower if the initial burden is on the individual (e.g. in disappearance or torture cases claiming state responsibility). In the latter case the burden shifts from the individual to the State once the individual has made a *prima facie* case. After all the individual claims human rights violations of a very serious nature often involving the right to life and the prohibition of cruel treatment while the consequences for the State simply involve refraining from acting, providing access, releasing a person, providing compensation, etc. Moreover, the State is able to retrieve and make disappear information and evidence and therefore is at a much stronger position than the individual claiming a human rights violation.[103]

The best way to urgently deal with disappearances is to prevent them from taking place by adequately responding to threats against persons. As discussed in Chapter VII, this includes taking measures to physically protect persons as well as investigating and prosecuting previous threats. Once a disappearance has occurred, the chance of finding the person involved diminishes with each day. Intervention in the first days of a disappearance thus has the greatest chance of finding the person alive.

The UN Working Group on Enforced and Involuntary Disappearances[104] has introduced the rule that it would issue an urgent appeal in each case on which it received information within three months of the last time the person was seen. Different from the Working Group, however, the Inter-American Commission did not regulate its urgent procedure in this respect. As dis-

---

[103]   See also Chapter XV (Immediacy and risk).

[104]   For a brief reference to this Working Group see Chapter II (Systems), section 2.4 'Power and promptness of the HRC to take provisional measures', under the subheading 'prompt intervention in disappearance and detention cases'.

cussed, at least on one occasion it took precautionary measures to locate the person concerned more than a year after he had last been seen. Later it even decided to maintain these measures when it declared the case admissible. One may speculate on the Commission's reasons. It may be that it considered this disappearance an unusual occurrence in the State involved and either believed that there was still a chance to find the disappeared person alive, or at least wished to preserve evidence of the disappearance, or more generally wished to emphasise the seriousness of the situation by using precautionary measures in a symbolic gesture aimed at the prevention of *new* disappearances.

The fact that the ECtHR has not yet used provisional measures to locate disappeared persons may relate to its functioning in general, especially its fear for a flood of urgent disappearance cases. Yet it is unlikely that such fear would prod the overworked Court simply to dismiss a well-reasoned request for provisional measures in a recent disappearance case, in the context of a pattern of disappearances with the ensuing impunity. It is more likely that the Court simply has not yet received such requests. The reason may be that not just the Court and its staff, but also domestic counsel and NGOs are in a 'non-refoulement mode' vis-à-vis the Court. The Court is accustomed to use provisional measures mainly in expulsion and extradition cases. A related explanation may be found in the case law on the merits on this particular subject matter, which has been more restrictive than that of the other human rights adjudicators. It has generally assigned a heavy burden to the petitioner for proving the State's direct responsibility for a disappearance. Moreover, those NGOs dealing specifically with disappearances may simply assume that they may only submit a case upon exhaustion of domestic remedies, even when domestic habeas corpus proceedings are ineffective in locating the disappeared person in time to prevent his or her extrajudicial execution.

Given the importance of the rights involved, the ECtHR should indeed follow the example of the other adjudicators and use provisional measures as well when faced with a petition regarding a recent disappearance. This could be relevant not just for disappearances in traditional conflict areas within Council of Europe States,[105] but also in light of recent reports on the disappearance of persons in the context of the 'war on terror'.[106]

Petitioners may bring complaints against Council of Europe States in which disappeared persons were last seen or on the basis of reports about secret detention centres on their territory.[107]

---

[105] See e.g. Human Rights Watch, Russia/Chechnya, Swept under: torture, forced disappearances, and extrajudicial killings during sweep operations in Chechnya, February 2002; Human Rights Watch, Russia, Last seen…: continued 'disappearances' in Chechnya, April 2002; Amnesty International Urgent Action on behalf of at least 34 men from an unofficial settlement for internally displaced persons in Altievo, Nazran region, Ingushetia, 24 June 2004, AI Index EUR 46/039/2004.

[106] The Working Group on Enforced or Involuntary Disappearances has also referred to 'the existence of secret detention centres where terrorist suspects are held in complete isolation from the outside world'. In this context it pointed out that it was 'well documented' that disappearance was 'often a precursor to torture and even to extrajudicial execution'. Report of the Working Group on Enforced or Involuntary Disappearances, E/CN.4/2006/56, 27 December 2005, §22.

[107] See also the references in the Introduction to this Chapter. The Working Group on Enforced and Involuntary Disappearances has interpreted Article 10 of the Declaration (stipulating that persons 'deprived of liberty be held in an officially recognized place of detention') to mean that such place must always be 'clearly identifiable'. "Under no circumstances, including states of war or public emergency, can any State interests be invoked to justify or legitimize secret centres or places of detention which, by definition would violate the Declaration, without exception" E/CN.4/1997/34, 13 December 1996, §24. See further Chapter V (Non-refoulement) on extraordinary renditions. At the same time complaints may be brought before the Inter-American Commission against the US. See further Chapter VIII on procedural rights and Chapter XIV on jurisdiction and admissibility.

In fact, as ICJ Judge Simma pointed out in his Separate Opinion in *Congo* v. *Uganda* (2005), this concerns obligations *erga omnes* in which not just individual petitioners, but also other States have a legal interest:

> "If the international community allowed such interest to erode in the face not only of violations of obligations *erga omnes* but of outright attempts to do away with these fundamental duties, and in their place to open black holes in the law in which human beings may be disappeared and deprived of any legal protection whatsoever for indefinite periods of time, then international law, for me, would become much less worthwhile".[108]

---

[108]   ICJ *Armed activities on the territory of the Congo* (*Congo* v. *Uganda*), Judgment of 19 December 2005, Separate Opinion Judge Simma, §41.

CHAPTER VII
INTERVENING IN DETENTION SITUATIONS INVOLVING RISKS TO HEALTH AND DIGNITY

1   INTRODUCTION

Most adjudicators, even the ICJ and ITLOS, have dealt with situations regarding persons deprived of their liberty.[1] The human rights adjudicators have used provisional measures not only on behalf of disappeared persons,[2] but also on behalf of persons whose place of detention was known. In both cases provisional measures are taken in order to prevent the (further) torture, ill-treatment and death of the persons involved.

The HRC has intervened in detention cases very frequently, especially in the 1970s and 1980s, but also more recently. In the Inter-American system provisional measures have been used repeatedly as well. Examples from these systems, as well as from the European and African systems will be given in section 2.

These provisional measures do not generally entail a direct intervention to prevent a specific interrogation-method[3] or punishment.[4] Instead they entail the prevention of and putting a stop to ongoing ill-treatment.[5] Most often they require positive measures to prevent the further deterioration of the health of a detainee, for instance by providing access to medical care and by paying special attention to particularly vulnerable detainees, such as minors, detainees in mental distress and detainees on a hunger strike.

As pointed out in the Introduction to Part II, the argument in this book rests on the assumption that there is a link between provisional measures and the decision on the merits. Hence in order to explain the use of provisional measures there must be a likelihood of finding a violation on the merits with regard to the right to life and personal integrity, in this case of detainees. Section 3 deals with that issue.

---

[1]   See Chapter I, referring to ICJ *Hostages* case and ITLOS case law regarding release of a vessel or crew.

[2]   See Chapter VI. For death threats and harassment in detention see Chapter IX. The use of provisional measures in cases of lack of access to court and counsel are discussed in Chapter VIII.

[3]   For a case in which such intervention was requested see section 2.2 of this Chapter. See also the Cleveland Principles on the Detention & Treatment of Persons in Connection with 'The Global War on Terror' adopted at a Conference at Case Western Reserve University School of Law, Ohio, 7 October 2005 and subsequently endorsed by many other experts. See further Chapter VIII (Procedural rights) on extraterritorial detention (e.g. Guantanamo) and Chapter VII (Expulsion) on so-called extraordinary renditions, both in the context of counter-terrorism measures.

[4]   On provisional measures to prevent corporal punishment see Chapter IV.

[5]   See section 2.2 of this Chapter.

2 PRACTICE

2.1 Introduction

Most human rights adjudicators have used provisional measures in one way or other in the context of detention. Section 2 briefly refers to specific measures to protect against ill-treatment,[6] including certain interrogation methods. It then focuses on the use of (informal) provisional measures relating to the health situation of detainees, sometimes in the form of requests for information, sometimes explicitly in order to ensure access to medical care. This section also pays attention to the protection of particularly vulnerable detainees, with a focus on minors, as well as to requests for provisional measures by or on behalf of detainees on a hunger strike. Some cases involve a request by petitioners to halt the execution of a detention order rather than to ensure access to medical treatment.[7] The discussion of the use of provisional measures in detention situations concludes with a discussion of situations, dealt with by the HRC in the context of death row, in which provisional measures could have been used.

2.2 Protecting against certain interrogation methods and other ill treatment

2.2.1 European system

There is one famous case involving the legality of interrogation methods in which the adjudicator had been requested to intervene pending the proceedings. In *Ireland* v. *United Kingdom* (1972) the European Commission was requested to order the UK to halt a specific interrogation method. This was at a time when the Commission had indeed used provisional measures previously, generally in the context of halting an expulsion, extradition or the execution of a death sentence, but the possibility to do so had not yet officially been included in its Rules of Procedure.[8]

The request to take provisional measures in this case was made as part of the inter-State complaint procedure. Ireland had invoked this procedure against the UK in December 1971, arguing that the latter's use of five interrogation techniques ((a) wall-standing;[9] (b) hooding;[10] (c) subjection to noise;[11] (d) deprivation of sleep; (e) deprivation of food and drink) against suspected IRA terrorists was incompatible with Article 3 ECHR.[12]

That same month the Commission decided to give priority to the application.[13] Three months later Ireland referred to reports by detained persons and by Amnesty International that the ill treatment was continuing despite the fact that Ireland's Article 3 claim was pending before the

---

[6]   See also Chapter IX (protecting against death threats and harassment).

[7]   In general about the specific protection required by provisional measures see Chapter XIII (Protection).

[8]   The European Commission did so in 1974.

[9]   '(F)orcing the detainees to remain for periods of some hours in a "stress position", described by those who underwent it as being "spread eagled against the wall, with their fingers put high above the head against the wall, the legs spread apart and the feet back, causing them to stand on their toes with the weight of the body mainly on the fingers"'.

[10] '(P)utting a black or navy coloured bag over the detainees' heads and, at least initially, keeping it there all the time except during interrogation'.

[11] '(P)ending their interrogations, holding the detainees in a room where there was a continuous loud and hissing noise'.

[12] The techniques were sometimes referred to as 'disorientation' or 'sensory deprivation' techniques. ECtHR *Ireland* v. *UK*, Judgment of 18 January 1978, §96.

[13] See Rule 38(1) of the Commission's Rules of Procedure.

Commission. It requested provisional measures to ensure that such ill treatment was discontinued pending a decision in the case, in order to prevent irreparable harm.[14] While Ireland recognized that the ECHR did not expressly empower the Commission to order or direct a Government to adopt such measures, it submitted that the Commission did possess the power to take provisional measures as this was 'the necessary attribute of its judicial functions and therefore covered by the doctrine of implied powers'. It also referred to previous cases in which the Commission had requested Governments to take provisional measures. In particular it requested the Commission to seek an undertaking by the UK that all treatment of detainees complained of under Article 3 should be discontinued; to seek permission for attendance by observers nominated by the Commission at centres of custody 'to ascertain whether these persons were subjected to such treatment'; and to seek 'an undertaking that all such persons in custody should be taken to the centres where these observers would be located and that the observers should at all times be given access to such persons'.

Ireland considered that 'the object of interim measures is generally the preservation of the rights of the parties, pending adjudication, insofar as the damage threatened to these rights would be irreparable'. It submitted that 'the measures suggested would not in any way prejudice the rights of the respondent Government, but that they would on the other hand protect from irreparable damage the right to physical integrity of those persons in custody who had been and were still being subjected to ill-treatment'.[15]

In response the UK observed that the Commission should first decide on the admissibility of the case.[16] It also noted that the proposal was made in respect of 'new and unspecified allegations' and not on the material already supplied to the Commission. Finally, it submitted that the Convention did not include a provision 'conferring on the Commission competence to order interim measures of the kind that were being sought'.[17] With this formulation, adding 'of the kind that were being sought', the UK seemed to have left leave the door slightly ajar. It could be argued that this State mainly disagreed with the specific measures of protection requested by Ireland, rather than disputed the overall competence of the Commission. It is also possible that it considered the Commission should only use provisional measures to halt activities that, if they indeed are taking place, undisputedly violate Article 3. After all, in the latter situation a provisional measure would indicate a likelihood that the Commission would determine that these activities constitute ill-treatment as forbidden under Article 3. In the former situation it would indicate a likelihood that this treatment (which is forbidden under Article 3) is in fact taking place or will occur.

That same month, in March 1972, the Commission decided that it 'did not have the power, consistent with its functions under the Convention, to meet the request made in the applicant Government's letter'.[18] Apart from noting that it made the decision after considering Ireland's letter and the response by the UK it did not explain its decision. It did not say that it did not have the power to order provisional measures at all, only that it could not meet the specific request made by Ireland.[19]

The ECtHR eventually found that '(t)he five techniques were applied in combination, with premeditation and for hours at a stretch; they caused, if not actual bodily injury, at least intense physical and mental suffering to the persons subjected thereto and also led to acute psychiatric disturbances during interrogation. They accordingly fell into the category of inhuman treatment within the meaning of Article 3 (art. 3). The techniques were also degrading since they were such

---

14   See ECHR Yearbook 23, p. 82.
15   Id., p. 84.
16   Ibid. See further Chapter XIV (Jurisdiction and admissibility).
17   It referred to the Commission's decision in *X* v. *FRG*, 20 March 1958, 297/57.
18   ECHR Yearbook 23, p. 88.
19   See further Chapter XIII (Protection).

as to arouse in their victims feelings of fear, anguish and inferiority capable of humiliating and debasing them and possibly breaking their physical or moral resistance'.[20] This recourse to the five techniques amounted to a practice of inhuman and degrading treatment in violation of Article 3.[21]

Thus far the judgments and decisions of the ECtHR do not seem to indicate similar cases involving requests to order a halt to certain interrogation methods while the case is pending before it, but provisional measures are certainly feasible in this respect.

There could also be other forms of ill treatment unrelated to interrogation methods. To take but one example, on the merits the ECtHR has had to deal with the issue of force-feeding. It found that a measure that 'was considered to be medically necessary – such as force-feeding a detainee to save her/his life – could not in principle be regarded as inhuman and degrading'. Yet, 'such a measure had to have been proved to be medically necessary and the procedural guarantees for the decision to force-feed had to be complied with'. "Moreover, the manner in which the applicant is subjected to force-feeding during the hunger strike shall not trespass the threshold of a minimum level of severity envisaged by the Court's case law under Article 3 of the Convention".[22] While it is feasible that a petitioner on hunger strike would request the Court to order a State to halt force-feeding, the Court would not easily do so unless faced with information of persistent use of force-feeding that is not medically warranted or done in a manner in itself contrary to Article 3.[23] An example of a case where the Court found a State in violation of Article 3 for such force-feeding is *Ciorap* v. *Moldova* (2007). In this case it concluded that the petitioner's 'repeated force-feeding, not prompted by valid medical reasons but rather with the aim of forcing the applicant to stop his protest, and performed in a manner which unnecessarily exposed him to great physical pain and humiliation, can only be considered as torture'.[24] Were it to receive a claim in an ongoing situation of such type of force-feeding the use of provisional measures would be warranted.

2.2.2 Inter-American system

Adjudicators have regularly dealt with allegations of ill treatment that, once proven, would immediately constitute violations of international law. Often this concerns ill treatment in detention and sometimes it is ongoing. In response the Inter-American Commission has used various precau-

---

[20]   ECtHR *Ireland* v. *UK*, Judgment of 18 January 1978, §167.

[21]   Id., §168. CAT has also pointed out that suspects must not be blindfolded during interrogation and that using 'moderate physical pressure' is completely unacceptable as a method of interrogation because allowing this, together with the secrecy of the standards of interrogation, would create conditions leading to a risk of ill treatment and torture. See e.g. Ingelse (2002), pp. 254-255 and the references therein.

[22]   See ECtHR *Nevmerzhitsky* v. *Ukraine*, 5 April 2005, §94. At §93 it noted: "When, however, as in the present case, a detained person maintains a hunger strike this may inevitably lead to a conflict between an individual's right to physical integrity and the High Contracting Party's positive obligation under Article 2 of the Convention – a conflict which is not solved by the Convention itself" (see *X* v. *Germany* (1984) 7 EHRR 152). "In the instant case, the Court finds that the force-feeding of the applicant, without any medical justification having been shown by the Government, using the equipment foreseen in the decree, but resisted by the applicant, constituted treatment of such a severe character warranting the characterisation of torture", §98. See also ECtHR *Herczegfalvy* v. *Austria*, Judgment of 24 September 1992, §83.

[23]   About the role of physicians in this respect see e.g. World Medical Association, Declaration on hunger strikers, November 1991, <www.wma.net/e/policy/h31.htm> and Oguz and Miles (2004). For a commentary by the Dutch branch of the International Commission of Jurists on force-feeding, see Wijnakker (2006), pp. 434-449.

[24]   ECtHR *Ciorap* v. *Moldova*, 19 June 2007, §89.

tionary measures to protect detainees against ill treatment by prison officials and others. The Inter-American Court has equally dealt with such issues.[25]

In August 1992 the Inter-American Commission took precautionary measures in a case against Peru, aimed at the protection of the prisoners who had been at the 'Miguel Castro Castro Prison' in Lima during an attack by the Army that took place in May 1992. In particular, it requested information on the whereabouts and medical condition of the inmates who had been wounded. Formally, the Commission had received the first communication twelve days after the attack.[26]

In fact, it appears from the Commission's 1993 Report on Peru that its Executive Secretariat received reports about the events already in early April 1992. Unsuccessfully, the Commission made several attempts to convince the government to allow it to use its good offices. Apparently, the ICRC had not been allowed to play a role at all in the earlier stages of the military operation of early May. Only in the night of 8 May was it allowed a brief visit. Reportedly, the prosecutor was the only non-military presence in the prison. No institution or individual had been allowed to enter the prison as independent observer.[27] The Commission noted that, as reported by independent sources, on 7 May and especially on 8 May the inmates had asked for the presence of institutions such as the ICRC and the Commission, whose good offices could help implement the prison transfer. The authorities, however, did not accept these suggestions and on 9 May the 'combined army and police forces' used force against the inmates, including explosives and weapons of war. Four days later the Chairman of the Commission sent the following letter to Peru's Minister of Foreign Affairs:

> "I have the honor to address your Excellency in connection with the events that occurred at the 'Miguel Castro Castro' prison starting on May 6, 1992 to request that you kindly adopt the following measures at soon as possible:
> Provide the Inter-American Commission on Human Rights with a complete list of the male and female inmates who were in cellblocks 1A and 4B of that institution on May 5 last.
> Provide the Inter-American Commission on Human Rights with a complete list of the individuals who were killed, wounded, or who have been missing since May 6.
> Provide the Inter-American Commission on Human Rights with a complete list of the survivors, and where they are at the present time.
> Re-establish, as soon as possible, visits from relatives of the inmates, so that they provide them with any clothing, medications and toiletries that they may need.
> Take the necessary measures to provide the wounded with the medical care they require".[28]

As indicated before, the Commission formally opened the case relating to the incident in June 1992. In its Special Report on Peru it noted that the next month the 'disturbing information' it received concerning the situation of the inmates prompted it to request Peru, in August 1992, to take measures to protect the rights of the detainees.[29] Indeed its admissibility report in the *Castro*

---

[25] Obviously this is closely related to the discussion in Chapter IX (threats).

[26] The Commission alleged that 500 troops of the Peruvian army had entered the prison to transfer the inmates to the 'Santa Mónica' prison. During the attack by the Army 34 inmates died and 18 others were wounded. The Commission also received information from 'a variety' of other sources including letters sent by inmates. The Commission opened the case the next month. See CIDH *Hugo Juarez Cruzat et al.* (*Miguel Castro Castro Prison*) v. *Peru*, 5 March 2001 (adm.).

[27] CIDH Special Report on Peru 1993, §95.

[28] Id., §97.

[29] Before providing the complete text of the precautionary measures taken, the Commission listed the situation as denounced by the petitioners and NGOs: "a.That a group of around 80 inmates in cellblock 4-B and 2 members of Tupac Amaru Revolutionary Movement had been transferred to Yanamayo prison Puno. b. That prison does not have the facilities to provide inmates with the

Castro Prison case notes that it took precautionary measures on 18 August 1992. It decided to do so '(i)n view of the information supplied and the fact that there had been no reply from the Government of Peru'.[30] It requested Peru to send an official list of the persons who died or disappeared during the incidents in May. It also requested information on the whereabouts and medical condition of the surviving inmates.[31]

The Commission pointed out that it had received additional information with regard to the case 'to the effect that inmates in the Miguel Castro Castro penal institution were in very bad condition, very poorly fed – far below the minimum requirements – and that the sick and those in need of medical attention were living alongside healthy inmates. No inmate was allowed to receive visits from relatives or their attorneys. In general, conditions were such that they posed a serious threat to the inmates' personal security and even their lives'.[32]

According to the petitioners, during (and after) the Army attack of May 1992, Peru rejected the proposal by the inmates to form a committee with representatives of the ICRC and the Inter-American Commission. The petitioners pointed out that 'the prisoners made every effort to resolve the situation differently and even went so far as to sign a document with Attorney General Mirtha Campos, where the main point was the Red Cross' presence as a minimum requirement to guarantee the lives of the prisoners at the time of surrender'. The petitioners added that they only revolted when they realised 'that the real objective of the Army and police troops was to kill everyone'. They stated that the confrontation continued from 6 May to 9 May 1992, 'when the Army troops began to selectively execute prisoners, despite the fact that they had surrendered and

---

minimum protection needed to cope with the very low temperature at that altitude and the inhospitable climate. c. The individuals being held have been taken to Yanamayo with only the clothes on their backs, after having spent several weeks exposed to the elements, poorly fed, and subjected to various types of serious mistreatment; a number of them were also wounded. d. No authorisation has been given to allow relatives to visit those being held in Yanamayo and they are not allowed to send them the food, clothing, coats or medicine the prisoners need to cover their basic needs. e. Two inmates have already died as result of the inadequate facilities, their very weakened physical condition at the time they were transferred and because of the authorities' refusal to permit the vital necessities of those being held at Yanamayo prison to be supplied by those outside. f. Members of rival armed groups are said to be held inside the same facilities, which poses a serious threat to their personal safety and life should serious violence occur". CIDH Special Report on Peru 1993, §99.

[30] They consisted of the following: "1. That the Government of Peru authorize the Inter-American Commission on Human Rights to conduct an on site inspection of the Yanamayo prison facilities in the Department of Puno. 2. That the Government of Peru authorize the Inter-American Commission on Human Rights to speak with persons deprived of their liberty in that penal institution. 3. That the Government of Peru authorize relatives and attorneys to visit prisoners in that and other detention centers and that it allow clothing, medicine, coats and toiletries that the inmates require to meet their vital needs to enter. 4. That the Government of Peru provide persons suffering from health problems with needed medical care and that such persons be transferred to establishments where they can receive proper medical attention. 5. That the Government of Peru adopt measures to keep separate persons who are considered members of rival armed groups, so as to avoid the kind of violence that could threaten the safety or life of the inmates. 6. That the Government of Peru forward to the Inter-American Commission on Human Rights the official list of persons who died and disappeared as a result of the events that occurred at the Miguel Castro Castro penal institution, as well as a list of the wounded and the whereabouts of those transferred". CIDH Special Report on Peru 1993, §100.

[31] While it remains unclear whether the exact date was 14 or 18 August, it seems likely that the precautionary measures mentioned here are the same as the aforementioned of 14 August reproduced in the Commission's Special Report on Peru.

[32] CIDH Special Report on Peru 1993, §§101-102.

were leaving the facility to be transferred to another facility'. The petitioners maintained that the Prison Warden, the Assistant Warden and another commander they identified were immediately to blame for the events leaving dead 34 prisoners and wounding 13 others. According to them 'these three had a plan to isolate and annihilate the inmates'. The petitioners also mentioned another incident, later in May 1992, where 500 Army troopers entered the prison again, heavily armed and wearing hoods in order to move 300 prisoners. Allegedly, prisoners were ill-treated and beaten. This exacerbated the conditions of those who had already been wounded during the attack of 6 May. The petitioners claimed that the detainees were held incommunicado and some of them without clothing or shoes. 'There were few mattresses and blankets, little food and no proper medical attention'.[33] They argued that they had submitted their petition before domestic remedies had been exhausted 'because of the urgency of the situation and to avoid further and possibly irreparable harm to the inmates at Miguel Castro Castro prison'.

Among others, the State contended that the operation was conducted by National Police troops and the Army troops were simply guarding the outside perimeter of the prison and never directly intervened. It alleged that the police only intervened because the male inmates, who were members of Sendero Luminoso (Shining Path), had rejected earlier attempts to persuade the inmates to cooperate in the transfer. It also maintained that a document shows that ICRC representatives were present. It reiterated that its Army 'did not selectively and summarily execute the prisoners as they were leaving the prison, since the Army troops did not have a direct hand in the operation (…) instead, they confined their activities to security outside the prison'.

In December 1992 the President of the Inter-American Court decided not to take urgent measures in the *Peruvian Prisons* cases.[34] The Court confirmed this in plenary session by a decision not to order provisional measures for lack of evidence of risk.[35]

In its 1993 Special Report on Peru the Commission pointed out that it had received additional information with regard to the case 'to the effect that inmates in the Miguel Castro Castro penal institution were in very bad condition, very poorly fed – far below the minimum requirements – and that the sick and those in need of medical attention were living alongside healthy inmates. No inmate was allowed to receive visits from relatives or their attorneys. In general, conditions were such that they posed a serious threat to the inmates' personal security and even their lives'.[36] It was only in 2001 that the Commission declared the case admissible.[37] It determined that Peru had waived the requirement to exhaust national remedies because it had not asserted this requirement in a timely manner.[38]

---

[33] In this context they claimed that the treatment of inmates in this prison was 'inhumane, given the scarcity of food, the lack of heating in the cells, the lack of medical care for sick prisoners, the absolute ban on visits – both by family members and prisoners' attorneys –, the harassment, abuse and brutality of the guards charged with the custody of the prisoners and the safety of prisons'.

[34] IACHR *Peruvian Prisons* cases, Resolution of the President of 14 December 1992.

[35] IACHR *Peruvian Prisons* cases, Order of the Court of 27 January 1993. According to the Commission the Inter-American Court did order provisional measures in December 1992, in connection with the situation at the Peruvian prisons in general (including the 'Miguel Castro Castro Prison'): *Hugo Juarez Cruzat et al. (Miguel Castro Castro Prison)* v. *Peru*, 5 March 2001 (adm.), §5. See further Chapter XV (Immediacy and risk).

[36] CIDH Special Report on Peru 1993, §§101-102.

[37] CIDH *Hugo Juarez Cruzat et al. (Miguel Castro Castro Prison)* v. *Peru*, 5 March 2001 (adm.).

[38] It pointed out, moreover, that in July 1992 the habeas corpus petition relating to the events had been declared inadmissible by the Peruvian court.

Another case in which the Inter-American Commission took precautionary measures, at least according to its Annual Report 1998, was that of Damion Thomas.[39] The case alleged on-going ill-treatment by prison officials in the St. Catherine Prison in Jamaica.[40] Yet in its Final Report the Commission did not refer to the precautionary measure previously mentioned in its Annual Report. In fact it related to its *refusal* to heed to the petitioners' repeated requests for such measures. It noted that in their original petition and subsequent communications the petitioners requested such measures 'based upon an immediate threat posed to Mr. Thomas' mental and physical health'. In April 2000 the Commission responded to the various requests by stating that 'based upon the information provided by both parties in the matter, it considered that it could effectively address the concerns raised by the petitioners through the Commission's complaint procedure and without the need to adopt precautionary measures at that time'.[41]

The petitioners apparently had requested the Commission to ensure their client's transfer to a prison in Jamaica other than St. Catherine's District Prison.[42] A month after the Commission's refusal to adopt precautionary measures, Jamaica sent a communication arguing that 'the Petition-ers should be disallowed from applying for precautionary measures until such time as they in-tended to open a full case before the Commission'. In the alternative, it argued, that 'the informa-tion provided by the Petitioners did not substantiate the occurrence or threat of irreparable dam-age necessary to support the adoption of precautionary measures by the Commission'.[43]

Here the State argued that there should be a connection between a request for precautionary measures and opening a full case before the Commission. In fact, petitioners have often requested precautionary measures before sending in a formal petition in a full case. The Commission, more-over, has often resorted to precautionary measures before opening a case and in many of these situations a case was never formally opened.[44] Only in death penalty cases the Commission now opens a case immediately and assigns a case number. What is interesting here is that the State believed the petitioners should not even be allowed to apply for precautionary measures if they did not intend to open a full case.[45]

In any case, the Commission seemed to agree with regard to the State's position that the in-formation provided by the petitioners did not substantiate the occurrence or threat of irreparable harm necessary to support the adoption of precautionary measures.[46] Yet in its Final Report the

---

[39]   CIDH Annual Report 1998, §43 (to take the necessary measures to prevent him from suffering irreparable harm), case 12.069.

[40]   Normally, precautionary measures addressed at Jamaica aim at halting the execution of a death sentence.

[41]   CIDH *Damion Thomas* v. *Jamaica*, 4 April 2001 (merits), §14.

[42]   CIDH *Damion Thomas* v. *Jamaica*, 15 June 2000 (adm.), §3. The petitioner in this case was Allen & Overy, a law firm in London.

[43]   Id., §13.

[44]   See in general about the proceedings Chapter II (Systems).

[45]   The petitioners themselves had 'expressed the view that he communication filed on Mr. Thomas' behalf was not a request to open a full case on their complaint, but rather a request for precautionary measures to protect Mr. Thomas' life and physical integrity'. CIDH *Damion Thomas* v. *Jamaica*, 15 June 2000 (adm.), §5. The Commission, however, had already opened the case in December 1998 and the petitioners had consistently taken part in the procedure set by the Commission. In this light the State's reference to the original intention of the petitioners is particularly intriguing.

[46]   According to both the Admissibility and the Final Report it never took precautionary measures. It is not clear whether the reference in its discussion of precautionary measures in its Annual Report 1998 to such measures, as taken on 9 December 1998 is mistaken or whether the reports on admissibility and merits simply fail to mention that the Commission initially did take them. If the Commission indeed took precautionary measures on 9 December, it did so two days before it formally opened the case, which was on 11 December 1998.

Commission concluded that Jamaica was responsible for failing to respect the physical, mental and moral integrity of Mr. Thomas, thereby subjecting him to cruel or inhuman punishment or treatment in violation of Articles 5(1) and 5(2) jo. 1(1) ACHR.[47] If it never took such measures earlier during the proceedings it must either have believed that no irreparable harm had occurred or that, at the time, there was no sufficient substantiation of a threat of such occurrence.

Another example of Commission involvement to protect detainees against ill treatment is reported by CEJIL. On an unspecified date this NGO requested the Commission to take precautionary measures to protect the physical integrity of almost 150 labour union members who had been arbitrarily detained upon their attendance of an assembly. Allegedly, the Bolivian authorities had taken them to various military camps. At these camps they were subjected to torture and mistreatment and deprived of access to medical attention. At the same time, the government declared a state of emergency, so that they could not file writs of habeas corpus and were denied the assistance of counsel. The Commission took precautionary measures in May 1995 and eventually the detainees were freed.[48] Clearly, this precautionary measure did not only relate to prison conditions and access to health care but also to the prevention of torture and disappearances.

In April 1996 the President of the Inter-American Court requested Ecuador to adopt forthwith the measures necessary 'to effectively ensure the physical and moral integrity of Mr. Rafael Iván *Suárez-Rosero*, so that any provisional measures that the Inter-American Court may take can have the requisite effect'.[49] The beneficiary was detained at that time. In June 1996 the Court lifted the urgent measures, having received note from the Commission that 'it was desisting from its requests for provisional measures on the grounds that the circumstances of extreme gravity and urgency that had inspired the adoption of urgent measures no longer existed, a fact demonstrated by the release of Mr. Rafael Iván Suárez-Rosero by the Government of Ecuador, and that there was currently no risk to the safety of Mr. Suárez-Rosero and his family'.[50]

More recently the Inter-American Court has also ordered provisional measures in serious detention situations of a general nature, affecting larger groups of people.[51] In the *Urso Branco*

---

[47] CIDH *Damion Thomas* v. *Jamaica*, case 12.069, Final Report 50/01, 4 April 2001, §VII. It recommended Jamaica to grant the petitioner an effective remedy, including compensation, to investigate the facts, determine responsibility and undertake 'appropriate remedial measures'. It also recommended it to ensure that detention officials are appropriately trained with regard to standards of humane treatment and that complaints about ill treatment and other conditions of detention are properly investigated and resolved.

[48] CEJIL case docket 1997 (on file with the author).

[49] IACHR *Suárez-Rosero* (Ecuador), Order of 12 April 1996 (President). Later that same month the President expanded the urgent measures to include the family members of the detainee.

[50] IACHR *Suárez-Rosero* (Ecuador), Order of 28 June 1996.

[51] For a range of Orders dealing with requests for provisional measures in the context of detention see e.g. IACHR *Matter of the Penitentiary Center of the Central Occidental Region* (*Uribana Prison*) (Venezuela), Order of 2 February 2007; *Matter of Urso Branco prison* (Brazil), Orders of 2 May 2008, 21 September 2005, 7 July 2004, 22 April 2004, 29 August 2002 and 18 June 2002; *Matter of the Mendoza prisons* (Argentina), Orders of 27 November 2007, 30 March 2006, 18 June 2005, 22 November 2004; *Matter of the persons imprisoned in the "Dr. Sebastião Martins Silveira" Penitentiary in Araraquara São Paulo* (Brazil), Order of the President of 10 June 2008; Order of 30 September 2006; *Matter of Children Deprived of Liberty in the "Complexo do Tatuapé" of FEBEM* (Brazil), Order of President 10 June 2008, Orders of 3 July 2007, 4 July 2006, 30 November 2005 and 17 November 2005; *Matter of Yare I and Yare II Capital Region Penitentiary Center* (Venezuela), Orders of 8 February 2008, 30 November 2007 and 30 March 2006; *Matter of Capital El Rodeo I & El Rodeo II Judicial Confinement Center*, Order of 8 February 2008; *Matter of Monagas Judicial Confinement Center* (*'La Pica'*) (Venezuela), Order of 3 July 2007 and 9 February 2006; *Case of the Miguel Castro-Castro Prison* v. *Peru*, Orders of 29 January 2008 and 30 January 2007.

Prison case, for instance, it ordered Brazil to immediately take all necessary measures to protect the lives and personal integrity of all persons detained in certain detention centers, as well as those working there and visitors.[52] Moreover, in its Order for provisional measures in *Las penitentiarías de Mendoza* v. *Argentina* the Court required the State to take the necessary measures to protect the life and personal integrity of all detainees from the detention centers involved, as well as employees and visitors.[53] The Court has noted that the State must 'make the appropriate adjustments to deal with the structural problems', but meanwhile, sometimes the situation makes it necessary that detainees 'who are being affected by such flaws, be protected by provisional measures if their condition is of extreme seriousness and urgency'.[54] In any case extreme seriousness 'should be assessed taking into account the specific context', as 'it is clear that if the fundamental rights such as the right to life and physical integrity are subjected to such type of threat, an order for provisional measures should be considered'.[55] The urgency criterion 'refers to special and exceptional situations that deserve an immediate measure and response aimed at averting the threat'. This involves 'circumstances that because of their own nature imply an imminent risk'. A 'lack of response would mean a danger *per se*'.[56]

In January 2006 the Court took provisional measures on behalf of those persons deprived of their liberty by Venezuela, detained in the Detention Centre of Monagas, known as 'La Pica'. The State should efficiently and immediately take measures to prevent violence in La Pica to the effect that no-one would die and the personal integrity of the detainees and others present in La Pica would be respected. As usual, the measures required should be planned and implemented with the participation of the representatives of the beneficiaries. The State was also requested to provide an up-to-date list of all persons detained and indicate the circumstances of their detention.[57] Finally, the State should investigate and prosecute the acts that led to the adoption of the provisional measures.[58]

2.3 Requests for information on the health situation of detainees

It has mainly been the HRC that has requested information on the health situation of detainees without explicitly requesting States to ensure medical attention. There are at least twenty cases involving political prisoners in which the HRC used such informal provisional measures to intervene in ongoing detention situations. The first time it did so was in 1977. Most interventions took place in the 1970s and early 1980s and involved Uruguay. There have also been cases against Zaire (now the Democratic Republic of Congo), Madagascar, Bolivia, Nicaragua and Peru.

The Rule 91 (current Rule 97) requests for information about the health of an alleged victim clearly aim at ensuring proper proceedings and safeguarding the evidence. At the same time,

---

[52]   IACHR *Cárcel de Urso Branco* (Brazil), Order of 21 September 2005. See also the Orders of 18 June and 22 August 2002, 22 April and 7 July 2004. See further Chapter XIII (Protection). On 21 October 2006 the Commission declared this case admissible. Its report includes a list of the 96 inmates who had died in the Urso Branco prison between 3 November 2000 and 8 February 2006.

[53]   IACHR *Las penitentiarías de Mendoza* (Argentina), Order of 22 November 2004.

[54]   IACHR *Matter of Capital El Rodeo I and El Rodeo II Judicial Confinement Center*, 8 February 2008, 14th 'Considering' clause.

[55]   Id., 17th 'Considering' clause.

[56]   Id., 18th 'Considering' clause.

[57]   More generally on the group of beneficiaries see Chapter XIII.

[58]   CIDH *Caso del internado judicial de Monagas ('La Pica')* (Venezuela), Order of 13 January 2006. Yet analysing compliance with this requirements is a matter to be dealt with on the merits. See infra referring to IACHR *Matter of the Children Deprived of liberty in the "Complexo do Tataupé" of FEBEM*, Order of 3 July 2007, 12th 'Considering' clause and 7th 'Decisional' clause.

however, these requests seem to have the additional purpose of preventing irreparable harm to the persons involved. Hence, the requests for information on the health and 'whereabouts' of alleged victims, as found in these communications, seem to function as informal requests for provisional measures. If this implies preventing irreparable harm, the next question is whether this means *refraining* from acting or taking *positive* measures to prevent irreparable harm. In fact the substance of the HRC's informal provisional measures in the above cases illustrates a continuum between negative and positive action in respect of the obligations under the ICCPR and the OP.[59]

The case of *M.A.* v. *S* (1978) is one of the first cases in which the HRC requested information on the alleged victim's whereabouts and state of health. It is also one of the few cases in which it published such a decision separately,[60] although it did not specify the addressee State.[61]

The first occasion in which the petitioners explicitly requested the HRC to use provisional measures on behalf of a detainee was in 1977 in the case of *Altesor* v. *Uruguay* (1982).[62] Four months after the initial submission they requested the HRC to take provisional measures to avoid irreparable harm to their father's health and life in light of his 'very poor state of health'.[63] The

---

[59] See also Chapter XIII (Protection).

[60] HRC *M.A.* v. *S.*, 24 April 1979, com. no. 20/1977, CCPR/C/OP/1 at 5 and 20. Its decision was of 25 January 1978. On that same day it also requested a State to halt the expulsion of another petitioner. This case was published as well: *O.E.v. S*, 25 January 1978, 22/1977, CCPR/C/OP/1 at 5 (1984); 26 July 1978, CCPR/C/OP/1 at 6; 27 October 1978, CCPR/C/OP/1 at 35. In December 1977 Ms. M.A. had submitted a complaint on behalf of her husband. Only very little information is available in this case. She stated that her husband was arrested in the unspecified State 'S' two months previously. He allegedly was detained incommunicado and attempts to resort to domestic resources, including habeas corpus, had been unsuccessful. The HRC requested the petitioner to inform it whether a case concerning her husband had been submitted to the Inter-American Commission on Human Rights. It requested the State to provide information on the state of health of the petitioner's husband. The State party responded, among others, with the observation that the alleged victim was a 'wanted person' and that the same matter had also been submitted to the Inter-American Commission. The petitioner acknowledged this but did not respond to the Committee's request whether it was her intention to withdraw the case from the Inter-American Commission. On 24 April 1979 the HRC decided to declare the case inadmissible.

[61] Around 25 January 1978, when it had requested information about his whereabouts and state of health, it also dealt with the abovementioned cases *Valentini de Bazzano* and *Altesor*. It is not clear why the HRC kept anonymous the State involved even after it had declared the case inadmissible. Given the state of ratifications of OAS members in 1979 this case may relate to Uruguay as well. See also *Drescher Caldas (represented by his wife Ibarburu de Drescher)* v. *Uruguay*, 21 July 1983. In January 1979 Ms. Ibarburu de Drescher had submitted a complaint against Uruguay on behalf of her husband Mr. Drescher Caldas. Among others, she requested that a medical examination should be permitted by doctors suggested by her husband's family. In April 1979 the HRC transmitted the case under Rule 91 and also 'drew the State party's attention to the concern expressed by the petitioner with regard to the state of health and whereabouts of her husband'. It requested the State 'to furnish information to the Committee thereon'. For another case in which it enquired about the health of the petitioner see *Pietraroia* v. *Uruguay*, 27 March 1981. The HRC did so two months after initial submission, when it declared the case admissible.

[62] HRC *Altesor* v. *Uruguay*, 29 March 1982.

[63] The petitioners were Uruguayan nationals residing in Mexico acting on behalf of their father, a former trade union leader and member of the Chamber of Deputies. In their initial letter of 10 March 1977 they stated that he was arrested in 1975 without any formal charges. Shortly before his arrest, they noted, 'he had undergone a heart operation which saved his life but at the same time made it necessary for him to observe very strict rules regarding work, diet and medication'.

HRC did not formally take provisional measures, but that same month it transmitted the complaint to the State party and included a request for information about the alleged victim's state of health.[64]

Another case, besides that of *Altesor*, in which a petitioner specifically requested the use of provisional measures in order to avoid irreparable harm to the health of the alleged victim, was *Sendic* v. *Uruguay* (1981).[65] The petitioner was Violeta Setelich, a Uruguayan national living in France. She submitted the complaint on behalf of her husband, detained in Uruguay. He had been the main founder of the Movimiento de Liberación Nacional Tupamaros. She stated that in all places of detention where he had been kept between 1973 and 1976 he was subjected to ill treatment. She mentioned solitary confinement, lack of food and harassment. In one of these places he developed a hernia as a result of a severe beating by the guards. She also declared that, as of February 1978, he was again subjected to inhuman treatment and torture. He was forced to do the 'plantón' (to stand upright with his eyes blindfolded) throughout the day. He was only allowed to rest for a few hours at a time. He was beaten and received insufficient food.[66] She noted that because of his hernia he could only take liquids and was unable to walk without help. Apart from this he also suffered from heart disease. His state of health continued to deteriorate and she feared for his life.[67] In this light she requested the Committee to apply provisional measures 'to avoid irreparable damage to his health'.[68] Four months later, in March 1980, the HRC transmitted the communication to the State party and also requested it to inform it about the state of health of Mr. Sendic, the medical treatment given to him and his exact place of detention.[69]

On the merits the Committee found violations of, among others, Articles 7 and 10(1) because Sendic was 'held in solitary confinement in an underground cell, was subjected to torture for three months in 1978 and is being denied the medical treatment his condition requires'. In this respect the State was under an obligation to extend to him the treatment required under Articles 7 and 10. 'The State party must also ensure that Raúl Sendic receives promptly all necessary medical care'.[70] It was not until its decision on the merits that it requested the State to *provide* the necessary medical care. In other words, pending the proceedings it only requested information

---

[64] Allegedly he was subjected to beatings and electric shocks and later remained handcuffed, hooded and in absolute solitary confinement.
Four months later it did request the State to ensure adequate medical treatment. Subsequently, at the admissibility stage, it requested information again regarding the state of health of the alleged victims.

[65] HRC *Sendic Antonaccio* (*submitted by his wife Violeta Setelich*) v. *Uruguay*, 28 October 1981.

[66] After three months, when he received his first visit, his state of health was alarming. She stressed that his situation had not changed since the entry into force of the ICCPR and the Optional Protocol on 23 March 1976. With regard to his medical health she alleged that he had needed an operation for his hernia since 1976. There had been, she pointed out, a medical order to perform such an operation, but the military authorities had refused to take him to a hospital.

[67] The HRC noted that she 'even thought that it had been decided to kill him slowly, notwithstanding the official abolition of the death penalty in Uruguay in 1976'.

[68] At the time of writing (28 November 1979) she was also unsure about her husband's whereabouts and requested the HRC to obtain information from the State party about his place of detention and the conditions of his imprisonment.

[69] In three further letters Ms. Setelich emphasised her deep concern about her husband's state of health. "She reiterated that after soldiers had struck him in the lower abdomen with gun butts at Colonials barracks in mid-1974 her husband had developed an inguinal hernia and that there was a risk that the hernia might become strangulated".

[70] HRC *Sendic Antonaccio* (*submitted by his wife Violeta Setelich*) v. *Uruguay*, 28 October 1981. By note of 31 October 1991 the State party informed the Committee that it had released the author on 14 March 1985.

about medical health, but it did not formally request the provision of medical care. Nevertheless, it seems likely that this was, at least partially, underlying the request for information.[71]

In another Uruguayan case concerning political prisoner a Brazilian national living in the Netherlands submitted a complaint on behalf of her son detained in Uruguay. She expressed deep concern about her son's state of health, mentioning that he suffered from a heart disease, had received two operations and urgently needed a third one and that the authorities were denying him proper medical attention. The Working Group of the HRC transmitted the case two months after initial submission and requested information on the alleged victim's health at the same time.[72] In most cases the Committee requested information on the health of the alleged victim when it transmitted the case as well as when it declared the case admissible.[73] On several subsequent occasions the HRC did specifically ask Uruguay to ensure access to medical care,[74] but in the last two cases against Uruguay the HRC again simply inquired about the health of alleged victim. It neither repeated nor intensified this request later.[75]

---

[71]   See also Chapter XIII on the relationship with the forms of reparation.

[72]   HRC *Estradet Cabreira* v. *Uruguay*, 21 July 1983. She stated that her son had been detained in Libertad prison since January 1973. Just like in previous communications by family members of political prisoners detained in Libertad, she complained about conditions of imprisonment including the small size of the cell, the fact that he was kept there 23 hours a day and about the punishments inflicted on detainees, such as being sent for solitary confinement at 'La Isla'. She claimed that 'the worst part of her son's imprisonment is the continuous harassment by the guards and the severe punishment for such actions as reporting to relatives on prison conditions or speaking with other inmates without authorization'. She alleged, furthermore, that 'detainees are continuously kept in a state of anxiety and tension because they live in constant fear of being again interrogated in connection with the prior conviction or with purported political activities in prison'. This situation seriously endangered the physical and mental health of the detainees at Libertad. She mentioned the names of several detainees in poor health who died.

[73]   HRC *Vasilskis* v. *Uruguay*, 31 March 1983. Despite the fact that the HRC initially did not enquire about the health of the alleged victim, the State did respond to the allegations in this respect. Her living conditions were the same as those of the other female prisoners and she was 'not subject to the slightest discriminatory treatment and it is completely untrue to state that she received insufficient food or is subject to ill-treatment'. The State acknowledged that she suffered from Raynaud's disease and pointed out that she was receiving the necessary treatment: 'her present condition can be described as compensated'. See also *Dave Marais* v. *Madagascar*, 24 March 1984. In one case it initially did not enquire about the health of the victim, but when it declared the case admissible it did request 'further information about her health'. See e.g. *Larrosa Bequio* v. *Uruguay*, 29 March 1993.

[74]   See section 3.4.

[75]   HRC *Lucia Arzuaga Gilboa* (*submitted by her aunt Felicia Gilboa de Reverdito*) v. *Uruguay*, 1 November 1985. Ms. Gilboa de Reverdito submitted a case on behalf of her niece Ms. Arzuaga Gilboa, a university student who was detained in Uruguay from June 1983 until early September 1984. The petitioner stated that her niece suffered from the consequences of meningitis contracted in 1982 and required special medical treatment. The case was initially submitted in July 1983. That same month the Working Group transmitted the case to the State under Rule 91 and requested to inform it of the alleged victim's state of health. In a submission of September of that year she gave specific information about torture and various forms of cruel and degrading treatment to which she claimed her niece had being submitted. She pointed out that she was unable to specify its effect 'because it has not yet been possible to attain any clinical information or to have her examined by a reliable doctor'. She did refer to some symptoms, which gave her cause for alarm. For instance, after they had strung her up by the chain of her handcuffs, naked, in an open yard, in mid winter, she suffered attacks of vomiting. She was then taken for examinations the nature of which has remained unclear. "It is known, however, that some of the examinations involved electro-encephalograms. In this regard, it should be borne in mind that, as

A relevant health inquiry case not involving Uruguay is *Jaona* v. *Madagascar* (1985).[76] In this case counsel claimed that the petitioner, a 77-year-old politician, was arrested 'on the pretext that demonstrations organised in his support were endangering public order and security' and taken to a military camp. He was not brought before a judge. Counsel claimed violations of Articles 9, 18 and 19. The Working Group decided to transmit the case and requested the State to inform it of the petitioner's state of health. Two months later counsel submitted additional information about the petitioner's state of health and alleged that the authorities were refusing him the necessary medical care and had not authorized specialist professors, including the Dean of the Faculty of Medicine of Tananarive, to examine him. He also referred to the petitioner's hunger strikes of January 1983. The claim itself related to arbitrary detention and freedom of expression, but the informal provisional measures related to the health of the detainee.[77] In *Marais* v. *Madagascar* (1983) the HRC also requested the State to provide information about the whereabouts and health of the alleged victim. In this case, it found violations of Articles 7 and 10 as well.[78]

Another case was *Lafuente Penarrieta et al.* v. *Bolivia* (1987).[79] In April 1984 eight Bolivian citizens, one of them living in the US, submitted a complaint on behalf of four of their relatives and three others who were being held at the San Jorge Barracks in Bolivia. Their submission stated that members of the armed forces arrested the alleged victims in October 1983 on suspicion of being *guerrilleros*. Allegedly, they were severely tortured during the first two weeks, kept incommunicado for 44 days under inhuman conditions and held in solitary confinement. The

---

I stated in my initial communication, my niece contracted meningitis last year. The blows to the head which she received were there particularly dangerous in her case". In the last health case against Uruguay, *Raul Cariboni* (*submitted by his wife Ruth Magri de Cariboni*) v. *Uruguay*, 27 October 1987, the alleged victim's wife submitted a case in October 1983. Her husband, a former professor of history and geography, was detained from 1973 until 13 December 1984. She mentioned that he had suffered two heart attacks during torture and that in December 1976 the medical board at the Central Hospital of the Armed Forces had concluded that only heart surgery could save him. Examinations in 1978 and 1982 resulted in an advice to have special examinations, in the form of phonocardiograms, every six months. Such examinations, however, were not made possible in the prison. She also stated that, after visits made in 1980 and 1983, the ICRC had listed him 'among the prisoners in most precarious state of health'. She pointed out that 'he was in danger of dying suddenly unless he received adequate medical attention and could enjoy conditions of life different from those he was subjected to in prison'. Four months after the initial submission the Working Group transmitted the case to the State under Rule 91 and requested information on alleged victim's state of health.

[76] HRC *Monja Jaona* v. *Madagascar*, 1 April 1985. The petitioner was represented by Maître Eric Hammel, who was a lawyer in Madagascar until his expulsion in February 1982. He was now assisting the petitioner from France. Hammel was also counsel in the cases *Marais* v. *Madagascar*, 24 March 1983 and *Wight* v. *Madagascar*, 1 April 1985 (in those cases referred to as Hamel). He claimed that his own expulsion by order of the Ministry of Justice had related, among others, to his involvement in representing the petitioner in relation to a previous arrest. This time Jaona was arrested on 15 December 1982 and taken to the military camp of Kellivondrake. Counsel pointed out that the arrest followed Jaona's public denunciation of election fraud and his call for new elections. The HRC was informed of his release on 26 March 1984. Hammel himself submitted a case against Madagascar in August 1983. See *Eric Hammel* v. *Madagascar*, 3 April 1987.

[77] On the merits the HRC found violations of Articles 9 and 19 and considered that the petitioner should be granted compensation under Article 9(5). After being elected deputy of Madagascar Joana was released.

[78] HRC *Dave Marais* v. *Madagascar*, 24 March 1984.

[79] HRC *Lafuente Penarrieta, Rodriguez Candia, Ruiz Caceres and Toro Dorado* v. *Bolivia*, 2 November 1987.

authorities had denied them proper medical attention and their state of health was very poor. One of them was suffering from a skull fracture, which was only attended to four months later. In October 1984 they started a hunger strike, which lasted a month. The Working Group on New Communications requested the State to inform the HRC about the state of health of the alleged victims when it transmitted the case to the State, more than a year after the first submission.[80]

In 2003 the Special Rapporteur on New Communications noted that he had used what he called a 'Pocar type' request for information about the medical situation and medical attention of a petitioner who had requested provisional measures to release him so that he could receive medical attention.[81] This remark shows that Pocar also intervened in medical situations when he was a Special Rapporteur between 1995 and 1999. Information about such cases is not yet readily available.

2.4   Ensuring access to health care in detention

2.4.1   Introduction

The HRC, the Inter-American Commission and Court, the African Commission, the (former) European Commission and the European Court have all used provisional measures in order to ensure access to health care in detention.

2.4.2   HRC

At the end of January 1978 the HRC requested the State to *ensure* adequate medical treatment in the aforementioned case of *Altesor* (1982).[82] As noted, the previous year it had already requested information on the state of health of the alleged victim in February 1978. Around the same time as its request for positive measures in *Altesor* it requested such measures in *Valentini de Bazzano* v. *Uruguay* (1979) as well.[83] When it declared the complaint admissible it requested the State

---

[80]   At this stage the Working Group determined that the petitioners could act on behalf of the four alleged victims who were their relatives. With regard to the other three persons, including the man who was suffering from a skull fracture, it requested the petitioners to provide written evidence of their authority to act. In April 1986 the HRC declared the case admissible in so far as it related to the relatives of the petitioners. The petitioners had not submitted evidence on their authority to act on behalf of the other three persons. At this stage the group of beneficiaries of this request for information had been reduced from seven to four persons. Initially the group of beneficiaries for the informal provisional measures was larger. Obviously, in the face of insufficient information the HRC initially took the better safe than sorry approach. Only after it had given the petitioners the opportunity to show their authority to act on behalf of these three persons it decided to declare that part of the case inadmissible for insufficient evidence. For another example of an informal provisional measure to enquire about the state of health of a detainee see *Juan E. Zelaya Blanco and Myriam Zelaya Dunaway* (*on behalf of Roberto Zelaya who later joined*) v. *Nicaragua*, 20 July 1994.

[81]   Interview by author with Special Rapporteur Scheinin, Geneva, April 2003.

[82]   HRC *Altesor* v. *Uruguay*, 29 March 1982.

[83]   HRC *Valentini de Bazzano* v. *Uruguay*, 15 August 1979. The petitioner did not specifically request the HRC to use Rule 86 on provisional measures or request information about their health under Rule 91 and, initially, the Committee did not do so *proprio motu* either when it transmitted the case to the State under Rule 91. The petitioner claimed that her husband, Mr. Bazzano Ambrosini, had been tortured upon his arrest in 1975. A judge granted him conditional release after a one-year detention, but without the judge's knowledge he had been removed from the place of detention and taken to an unknown place. Later he was once more taken to an

party *proprio motu* to arrange for the medical examination of the petitioner's husband and stepfather and to give them 'all necessary medication and treatment if this had not already been done'.[84] One and a half years later it adopted its View, which included a reference only to the health of the petitioner's husband, not to that of the other two alleged victims. It noted that the husband 're-mained imprisoned in conditions seriously detrimental to his health' and found violations of Articles 7 and 10(1) in this respect.[85] Even more remarkable than the fact that, pending the proceedings, the HRC had inquired *proprio motu* about the health of the petitioner's relatives, was that at the admissibility stage it also requested the State to *provide* all necessary treatment and medication. In other words, this encompasses more than requesting the necessary information for the conclusion of proceedings under the OP.

Teti Izquierdo v. *Uruguay* (1982)[86] related to a disappearance[87] and to access to medical care, entailing informal provisional measures to act rather than abstain from acting.[88] The petitioner specifically discussed the treatment of her detained brother, and enclosed, among others, the testimony of a former detainee who was released and expelled to France in April 1980:

---

unidentified place and confined incommunicado. In February 1977 he was charged with 'subversive association' and remained 'together with four other political prisoners in a cell measuring 4.50 by 2.50 meters in conditions seriously detrimental to his health'. With regard to her stepfather, Mr. Massera, a professor of mathematics and former Deputy to the National Assembly, she noted, among others, that he had been forced to remain standing with his head hooded for long hours. When he lost his balance he fell down and broke his leg. Since he did not immediately receive medical treatment the leg that was broken is now several centimetres shorter than the other leg. The health related complaint on behalf of her mother, Ms Valentini de Massera, was that she had been subjected to ill treatment and had suffered from inadequate diet and unhealthy working conditions.

[84] The HRC did not mention the health of the petitioner's mother.

[85] It gave its own summary of the facts on which it would base its views and noted that the State party had not contradicted these. It found several other violations with regard to all three of them, including of Article 10(1) for the denial to receive visits by any family member. Some of these violations might also bear a relationship with the Committee's request, pending the proceedings, about the health of the author's husband and stepfather. One was that the State had held her husband incommunicado for months in violation of Article 10(1) and another was that it was responsible for the torture of her stepfather who suffered permanent physical damage as a result, in violation of Articles 7 and 10(1). Using the general expression it would often use in subsequent findings of violations of various types the HRC considered that the State party was 'under an obligation to take immediate steps to ensure strict observance of the provisions of the Covenant and to provide effective remedies to the victims'.

[86] HRC *Teti Izquierdo* v. *Uruguay*, 24 October 1980 (Rule 91 decision), 73/1981, CCPR/C/OP/1 at 7 (1984). *Teti Izquierdo* v. *Uruguay*, 1 April 1982.

[87] See Chapter VI on intervention in disappearance cases.

[88] See also Chapter VI on (informal) provisional measures in disappearance cases. Ms. Teti Izquierdo had submitted a case on behalf of her brother Mario on 7 July 1980. She was an Uruguayan national residing in France. Her brother was detained in Uruguay. He held dual nationality, Urugayan and Italian. She stated that he was a medical student arrested on 24 May 1972. After his arrest he was held incommunicado and tortured several times, as a result of which he suffered serious physical and psychological injury. In 1974 he attempted suicide. In 1978 he was sentenced to ten years imprisonment, a sentence that he would have served in May 1982. Because of good conduct and his advanced studies in medicine, the prison authorities had allowed him to provide medical treatment to the other prisoners. He did this for several years, earning him the esteem of his fellow prisoners.

"It was towards the end of 1979 that Major Maurino took over the post of Prison Director. He questioned Mario several times. The Major knew him already because he was the officer who had tortured him during the interrogations".

The petitioner alleged that this Major held her brother responsible 'for having instigated statements made by prisoners to the Red Cross Mission which visited the prisoners in the Libertad Prison in February/March 1980'. Consequently, a group of prisoners including her brother was subjected to reprisals, consisting of death threats and physical attacks. Ms. Teti alleged that in June 1980 her brother was forced to sign a statement in connection with new charges against him. In August 1980 they moved him to a punishment cell, in total isolation. The above-mentioned former detainee also testified that her brother was questioned again by the Major after the Red Cross delegation left. He 'accused Mario of being responsible for the complaints allegedly made by the prisoners to the Red Cross that he was a torturer. Until the day I left, Mario was constantly harassed and threatened'. While this indicated ongoing threats the HRC only used informal provisional measures after it was informed of the petitioner's disappearance.[89] Subsequently the petitioner submitted some more information about her brother's removal from the Libertad Prison. Afterwards, 'neither his relatives nor the international agencies nor the Italian Embassy in Uruguay had managed to see him or to obtain any definite information regarding his situation and place of detention'. It was only towards the end of May 1981, however, that he was brought back to the Libertad Prison. He had been kept incommunicado for eight months.[90] The State did not provide any of the information requested.[91]

---

[89] See also Chapter IX on death threats and harassment. Three months after her initial submission the petitioner sent a telegram informing the HRC that her brother had disappeared from Libertad prison. She expressed fear for his physical safety. Two weeks afterwards the HRC decided to use 'informal' provisional measures by transmitting the case while requesting information on the whereabouts and state of health of the alleged victim. There was no Special Rapporteur on New Communications yet and only the full Committee decided on such issues. About prompt decision-making see also Chapter II.

[90] A week later the petitioner expressed extreme alarm about her brother's health. When he was moved from Libertad Prison he weighed 80 kilograms and upon his return he weighed only 60 kilograms. She was afraid that 'if he continued to be subjected to unsatisfactory conditions of imprisonment, his health might suffer even more, to the point where his life might be in danger'. More than four months after the HRC's request about the health and whereabouts of Teti Izquierdo, the State Party submitted that the military examining magistrate had ordered another inquiry because further evidence had appeared that would warrant new proceedings. The authorities had identified 'new ringleaders of the "Tupamaros Extremist Movement"'. Accordingly the State pointed out he 'was moved from Military Detention Establishment No. 1 to another Detention Establishment, with the agreement and knowledge of the competent court, for the purpose of the requisite investigation, interrogation and inquiries, and also for reasons of security, with a view to dismantling the said plan. His state of health is good'. On 6 May 1981 it stated the same.

[91] See generally Chapter XVII (official responses). Ms. Teti alleged that General Rafela had revealed the new charges against her brother in a press communiqué denouncing an alleged invasion plan organised from Libertad Prison. The authorities brought several charges against her brother that they said would justify a retrial. During the time he was removed from Libertad Prison the authorities did not mention his whereabouts and he was not allowed any contact with his defence lawyer or relatives. She pointed out that the military authorities had also charged several other political prisoners who were, like her brother, close to the end of their full sentences. She mentioned as examples professor Raul Martinez and psychologist Orlando Pereira. She also noted that any 'invasion plan' against Libertad Prison was very unlikely given the conditions at this prison. It was one of the prisons with the most efficient security systems.

When the HRC declared the case admissible in July 1981 it not only requested the State Party to inform it (for the second time) 'of Mario Teti's state of health' but also 'to ensure that he was given suitable medical treatment'. In September 1981 the petitioner informed the HRC that her brother received an electrocardiogram upon his return to Libertad. This 'revealed that the heart attack he had suffered in 1980 had resulted in a blockage of the left artery'. Because of his chronic asthmatic condition, she pointed out, it was very difficult to treat his cardiac disease. Apart from this, her brother was suffering from thrombophlebitis in both legs. The HRC did not intervene with regard to his health any further until its decision on the merits almost a year later when it noted that the State party should also ensure that he 'receives promptly all necessary medical care'.

Thus the HRC intensified its request for information in its admissibility decision by asking the State to 'ensure he was given suitable medical treatment'.[92]

In *Marais* v. *Madagascar* (1983) the HRC also used informal provisional measures of a positive nature. It did so first in October 1981.[93] In its admissibility declaration the Committee reiterated its request to provide it with detailed information about the alleged victim's state of health. '[W]ithout prejudging the merits of the case', it pointed out that the State party 'should ensure that Mr. Marais was held under humane conditions of imprisonment' in accordance with Article 10 ICCPR.[94] On the merits the HRC found violations of Articles 7 and 10(1) and pointed out that it 'would welcome a decision by the State party to release Mr. Marais, prior to completion of his sentence, in response to his petition for clemency'.

In *Muteba* v. *Zaire* (1990)[95] the HRC's Working Group sought information about the alleged victim's state of health and it specifically requested the State to 'ensure that Tshitenge Muteba received adequate medical care'.[96] In March 1983 the full Committee confirmed this, when it declared the case admissible, it once more sought information about his state of health and requested the State to ensure he received adequate medical care.[97]

---

[92]   See also HRC *Raul Sendic Antonaccio (submitted by his wife Violeta Setelich)* v. *Uruguay*, 28 October 1981.

[93]   HRC *Dave Marais* v. *Madagascar*, 24 March 1984.

[94]   See also Chapter VIII on ensuring procedural rights to protect the right to life and personal integrity, discussing the Committee's informal provisional measure to ensure access to counsel.

[95]   HRC *Muteba* v. *Zaire*, 24 July 1984. Nina Muteba submitted the case on 13 June 1982 on behalf of her husband who was being detained in Zaire at the time of submission. Later, her husband was able to leave for France and joined her in the submission before the HRC. In February 1982 she received a copy of a note from her husband sent to the ICRC. He explained that he had been arrested on 31 October 1981, that he had no contact with the outside world and that food was insufficient. In addition, Ms. Muteba informed the HRC that she received information from one of her brothers and from a former detainee 'that her husband had been subjected to such severe torture that he became unrecognizable and that he continued to be held under inhuman prison conditions'. She explained that her husband could not take legal steps to address the situation locally because he 'had never been allowed to establish contact with a lawyer or a judge', and 'no member of his family dared to do anything on his behalf because they were afraid of retaliation'.

[96]   See also the inquiry into access to court and the ability to contact a lawyer.

[97]   In March 1984 Mr. Muteba informed the Committee that he was released following an amnesty and had joined his family in France in August 1983. He submitted 'a detailed report on his detention substantiating the allegations made by his wife and legal representative'. He was able to mention names of persons responsible for torturing him. He also referred to mock executions and the expectation by the regime that certain 'special treatment' would result in madness or death by torture, starvation or sickness. He alleged he was able to survive with the help of some discontented soldiers of Mobutu's presidential guard. The HRC found violations of Articles 7 and 10(1) because he was subjected to torture and not treated 'with humanity and the inherent dignity of the human person, in particular because he was held incommunicado for several months'.

A more recent case in which the HRC urged a State, pending the proceedings before it, to provide the alleged victim with adequate medical treatment is *Polay Campos* v. *Peru* (1997).[98] In July 1992 the authorities had transferred petitioner's husband to the Miguel Castro Castro Prison in Yanamayo, situated at an altitude of 4000 meters. In April 1993, a month after initial submission, a tribunal of faceless judges, established under special anti-terrorist legislation, sentenced him to life imprisonment. The HRC noted that it appeared from the file that he was convicted of 'aggravated terrorism'.[99] At the end of that month he was transferred to the Maximum Security Prison in the Callao Naval base in Lima. The petitioner provided the HRC with a newspaper clipping showing her husband handcuffed and locked up in a cage. She claimed that he was beaten and had received electric shocks during this transfer. He was now held 'in a subterranean cell where sunlight only penetrates for 10 minutes a day, through a small opening in the ceiling'. She also pointed out that his lawyer was himself imprisoned in June 1993, allegedly for defending her husband. The case was transmitted to the State in May 1994. At this point the Rapporteur did not yet make a request about the health situation of Polay Campos.[100] In June 1994 the petitioner noted that her mother-in-law had finally been able to visit her son the previous month. She described his situation as very serious. He lost about twenty kilos, was detained incommunicado and, because of the lack of sunlight (except for fifteen minutes), his vision had been seriously affected. The petitioner also noted that her mother-in-law had initiated a habeas corpus action, which she enclosed. In this appeal extreme worry was expressed about his life, health and physical and psychological integrity. This domestic appeal also noted that Vladimir Montesinos had visited him at the naval base, told him he would only leave his cell in a coffin, for which he should already arrange payment. Allegedly Montesinos also noted that once the death penalty would have been approved in the new Constitution Polay Campos would be the first to be executed.[101]

When it declared the case admissible in March 1996 (three years after the first submission), the HRC requested information not only about the operation of special tribunals under the anti-terrorist legislation but also about 'the victim's current conditions of detention'. It was at this point that it also enquired about his medical condition and urged the State to provide him with adequate medical treatment.[102] Similar to the cases previously discussed, such inquiry could serve the examination of the merits. At the same time, however, it could also be seen as an act to keep the State on guard concerning any failure to ensure the right to life and humane treatment of the alleged victim pending the proceedings. The fact, finally, that the Committee not only requested

---

[98] HRC *Polay Campos* (*submitted by his wife Espinoza de Polay*) v. *Peru*, 6 November 1997. On 5 March 1993 Ms. Espinoza de Polay submitted the case on behalf of her husband who was detained in Peru. She sent her submission from France.

[99] The petitioner's husband was the leader of the Movimiento Revolucionario Túpac Amaru (MRTA).

[100] The Committee's View does not provide information about its transmission of the case to the State, but the file shows the Rapporteur transmitted it in May 1994, fourteen months after initial submission. Note verbale of 5 May 1994 (on file with the author).

[101] 'Accion de habeas corpus' brought before the Superior Court of Callao, 3 June 1993, sent to the Committee on 20 June 1994 (on file with the author). General Montesinos was infamous during the Fujimori reign, for orchestrating (and participating in) torture and for fraud. See e.g. National Security Archive, a non-governmental foreign policy documentation centre at George Washington University, <http://www.gwu.edu/~nsarchiv/NSAEBB/NSAEBB37/> (consulted 25 August 2008).

[102] The inquiry about his health consisted of a request to forward copies of the relevant reports of the ICRC delegates and of the District Attorney and doctor who had visited and examined him in December 1994. It also consisted of a request to forward reports of subsequent visits. See §6.5 of the View.

information but urged Peru to *provide* the alleged victim with adequate treatment, clearly establishes this case as one in which the HRC, used positive provisional measures informally, without mentioning the Rule on provisional measures.[103]

In November 1997 the HRC adopted its View in this case. With regard to the victim's detention in the Miguel Castro Castro prison it found that the State had not refuted the allegation that he had been detained incommunicado, also implying he had been unable to talk to a legal representative. Another allegation the State had not refuted was that he was kept in an unlit cell for 23 and a half hours a day in freezing temperatures. The Committee concluded this amounted to a violation of Article 10(1). During the last month of the victim's stay in this prison his case was already under examination by the HRC, but it did not intervene at the time to prevent irreparable harm.

Regarding his transfer to the prison at Callao the HRC also found that the fact that the authorities displayed him to the press in a cage was a degrading treatment contrary to Articles 7 and 10(1). About his detention at Callao the HRC concluded that his total isolation for a period of a year and the restrictions on correspondence with his family violated Articles 7 and 10(1). It discussed the general conditions of detention at this prison and noted Peru's detailed information about the medical treatment 'as well as his entitlements to recreation and sanitation, personal hygiene, access to reading material and ability to correspond with relatives'. It concluded, on the other hand, that the State party had not provided any information about the claim that he continued 'to be kept in solitary confinement in a cell measuring two metres by two, and that apart from his daily recreation, he cannot see the light of day for more than 10 minutes a day'. In this respect it found violations of Articles 7 and 10(1) as well. It did not make the usual comment about the obligation to treat the detainee with the respect required under Article 10, to ensure adequate medical care and take the necessary steps to prevent any further violations. This could be explained by the fact that it had found a violation of Article 14 as well, because of his trial by a special tribunal of 'faceless judges'. In this light it considered that the victim should be released 'unless Peruvian law provides for the possibility of a fresh trial that does offer all the guarantees required by article 14 of the Covenant'.[104]

In one case the HRC used provisional measures on behalf of a person who tried to prevent the execution of a detention order. Within a month of receipt of the initial communication Special Rapporteur Lallah contacted the Ministry of Justice of Spain on behalf of a sixty-four-year-old petitioner claiming violation of Article 14. He mentioned that the petitioner had presented a medical affidavit indicating he was suffering from cancer and other grave illnesses.[105] The State responded ten days later arguing, among others, that a domestic court had considered that he could receive adequate medical treatment while in detention. It summarised the situation by concluding that there appeared to be no case of irreparable harm. It also noted that once it would have received relevant medical information it would adopt the appropriate measures and that it had sent the Committee's provisional measures to the relevant judicial body.[106]

---

[103] It was Prado Vallejo, member of the HRC (Ecuador) and Rapporteur in this specific case who suggested the inclusion of a formal request in the admissibility decision to the effect that the victim would receive the requisite medical attention, letter Julio Prado Vallejo to Secretariat, 2 January 1996 (on file with the author).

[104] See also Chapter XIII (Protection).

[105] HRC *V.* v. *Spain*, 495/1992 (disc. 1995), provisional measures of 22 May 1992. The telegram to the Ministry of Justice contained more information than the official Note Verbale to the Permanent Representative, but probably the other information could be found in the annexes to the Note Verbale (on file with the author).

[106] Letter Ministry of Justice to the Special Rappporteur, 1 June 1992 (on file with the author).

2.4.3 Inter-American system

The Inter-American Commission and Court have also taken provisional measures in detention cases involving access to health care. Moreover, during a country visit the Inter-American Commission sometimes requests certain authorities to take action in urgent cases. This approach is not unlike what the European 'prison visiting' Committee against torture (CPT Committee) does in urgent cases, as well the activities of UN Special Rapporteurs and other UN officials taking part in a country mission.

Occasionally the Inter-American Commission has taken precautionary measures for access to health care in detention.[107] In April 2001 the Commission took precautionary measures on behalf of a prisoner in Cuba. In its Annual Report the Commission quoted from the petitioners' request for precautionary measures that 'his health is delicate because of a tumor on his right lung' and that the prisoner began a hunger strike in February 2001 in demand of medical care.[108] The Commission requested Cuba:

> "(1) To transfer inmate [...] to a hospital specializing in the kind of physical ailments from which he is suffering. (2) To grant him specialized medical attention, to be administered in collaboration with a physician selected by his family".[109]

In February 1997 Mr. Cesti-Hurtado was detained in the Simón Bolívar barracks in Peru without contact with the outside world. He was 'prevented from receiving food or medicines', despite the fact that his wife had arranged with the Public Defender to bring him these herself three times a day as he was suffering from heart problems (cardiac ischemia) since 1994. The Commission's petition before the Inter-American Court argued that this could 'pose a threat to his life, given the tense situation to which he has been subjected'.[110] The Commission requested the Court to order Peru to comply with a domestic habeas corpus ruling, but the President decided not to issue such urgent measures.[111] Invoking Article 5 ACHR (respect for physical, mental and moral integrity and the prohibition of cruel treatment) he nevertheless ordered urgent measures *proprio motu*. He concluded 'from the content of the Commission's request', 'that in reference to the state of health of Mr. Cesti Hurtado, it is necessary to request the Government of Peru to take urgent measures to ensure his physical, psychological and moral integrity by providing adequate medical treatment

---

[107] The case of Mr. Esquina Mendoza and others, in preventive detention in Sololá in Guatemala, serves as an example. In April 1998 the Commission took precautionary measures requesting Guatemala to take the necessary measures to protect their physical integrity. They were seriously ill and the poor conditions of their detention resulted in a dangerous health situation. Annual Report 1998, §24. Other examples date from October 1998 and January 1999 when the Commission requested Peru to take the necessary measures for the medical care of two gravely ill detainees. Case 11.167 of Mr. Morales Zapata. Annual Report 1998, §49 and case 12.171 of Mr. Tulich Morales, Annual Report 1999, Chapter III C.1, §48. In 2002 they were pardoned for humanitarian reasons. CIDH, Press Release 16/00, 20 October 2002, §13 (the Commission noted that it had previously adopted precautionary measures 'pertaining to their medical care'). See also e.g. on behalf of a detainee at the Miguel Castro Castro prison (Peru), apparently suffering from diabetes and kidney disease, CIDH Annual Report 2005, Chapter III, §35 and on behalf of a detainee in Suriname apparently suffering from 'complete occlusion of the aorta and gangrene in the lower limbs', CIDH Annual Report 2004, chapter III, §44.

[108] Generally on hunger strikes see section 2.5.4 of this chapter.

[109] CIDH Annual Report 2001, §28. On Cuba's response see Chapter XVII (official responses).

[110] IACHR *Cesti Hurtado* (Peru), Order of the President of 29 July 1997, (having seen clause 2(f)).

[111] See further Chapter XI on provisional measures in other situations.

for his heart problems'.[112] In September 1997 the Inter-American Court confirmed this by ordering provisional measures to ensure the physical, psychological and moral integrity of Mr Cesti-Hurtado, in detention in Peru. It subsequently ordered Peru to maintain the provisional measures it had adopted to ensure his personal integrity and 'permit him to receive the medical treatment of his choice'. In addition, in June 1999 it ordered the State to expand the provisional measures to ensure the physical and psychological integrity of three of his family members.

The Court's discussion of Article 5 in the judgment on the merits (1999) is significant in the context of the provisional measures taken while the case was still pending. The State had declared that it has always respected the right to physical safety and that Cesti Hurtado enjoyed 'special treatment in compliance with the orders of the Court itself, is subject to medical evaluations, and has a series of amenities enjoyed by no other prisoner in Peru'.[113] The Court observed 'that the substance of this alleged violation was closely connected to the objective of the provisional measures adopted in favor of Gustavo Cesti Hurtado'. Therefore, it would 'study the allegations of the parties in the light of the information contained in the State's latest reports' and the observations presented by the Inter-American Commission.[114] Among others, it found that Peru should indeed comply with the domestic decision on habeas corpus, but also that 'based on the evidence in the proceedings', it had not been shown that the treatment received by Gustavo Cesti Hurtado during his detention has been inadequate in violation of Article 5(2) ACHR.[115]

Two months later Peru released him, but the Court decided to maintain the provisional measures for his protection and that of his family. The next year the Commission acquiesced in the State's request to lift them, noting that the victim had already been released and that it had included in its application for reparations 'a chapter on the deterioration of Mr. Cesti's health because of his imprisonment and the medical care that had been offered him'. In August 2000 the Court indeed lifted its provisional measures.[116]

2.4.4 African system

There have been several cases involving detainees, but it is not always clear whether the African Commission had taken provisional measures. The death sentences of political prisoners *Orton and Vera Chirwa* had been commuted due to international pressure, but they remained in prison in Malawi in extremely adverse conditions.

They had been in detention since 1981, the year when the African Charter was adopted. It is not clear when the case was first brought before the Commission, but the Commission decided to bring it to the attention of Malawi early March 1992. Orton Chirwa died in prison in October of that year. His wife was released in January 1993, 'for strictly humanitarian reasons', after a period of 12 years in prison. She later became a member of the African Commission and its Special Rapporteur on Detention. In December 1993 the Commission 'decided that the communications

---

[112] IACHR *Cesti Hurtado* (Peru), Order of the President of 29 July 1997, (7-9th considering clauses). See further XIII (beneficiaries) which also addresses the rights of addressees.

[113] IACHR *Cesti Hurtado* (Peru), Judgment of 29 September 1999, §155. The State pointed out that Captain Cesti Hurtado had received 'due and adequate medical attention in the Military Hospital', where he went to the dentist and the doctor every week. All the specialized examinations that he requested for his heart condition had been carried out in the Military Hospital. It had not been possible to agree to his request to be treated in a private clinic 'because it was necessary to avoid making distinctions between prisoners', §157.

[114] Id., §158.

[115] Id., §160.

[116] IACHR *Cesti Hurtado* (Peru), Orders of 11 September 1997, 21 January 1998, 3 June 1999, 19 November 1999 and 14 August 2000; Judgment of 29 September 1999. See also Chapter XII (other situations), referring to a follow-up request by the Commission.

gave evidence of a series of serious or massive violations of human rights in Malawi'. It resorted to the Assembly of Heads of State of the Organization of African Unity (now African Union), under Article 58 ACHPR.[117] The official version of its decision on the merits does not mention its use of provisional measures, but in an older version mention is made of Rule 109, which used to be the rule on provisional measures.

On the other hand, in December 1993 official action regarding Malawi may indeed have been useful, but intervention to alleviate the detention situation of Orton and Vera Chirwa would have been futile, as Orton had already died in October 1992 and Vera was released in January 1993. It is possible that the Commission tried to intervene previously, but there is no public record in this regard.

In its decision on the merits, taken in 1994, the Commission found that they had been tortured and ill treated, including by a 'reduction in diet, chaining for two days of the arms and legs with no access to sanitary facilities, detention in a dark cell without access to natural light, water or food, forced nudity, and beating with sticks and iron bars'. The Commission found that these acts, jointly and separately, clearly constituted violations of Article 5 ACHPR. It also found a range of general prison conditions in violation of this article, including 'shackling of hands in the cell so that the prisoner is unable to move (sometimes during the night and day), serving of rotten food, solitary confinement, or overcrowding such that cells for 70 people are occupied by up to 200'.[118]

A known case in which the African Commission has taken provisional measures is that of *Constitutional Rights Project and Others* v. *Nigeria*.[119] The health of the detainees involved was deteriorating and early 2005 the Commission invoked Rule 109 on provisional measures to call upon Nigeria to ensure that their health was not in danger.[120] In other detention cases, sometimes explicitly including claims of lack of access to medication and medical attention, it is again unclear whether provisional measures were used. On the merits it has found a violation of Article 5 for 'deprivation of light, insufficient food and lack of access to medicine or medical care'.[121]

---

[117] ACHPR *Amnesty International on behalf of Orton and Vera Chirwa* v. *Malawi*, 16th session, October/November 1994, §16, referring to Rule 109 of the Rules of Procedure (on the use of provisional measures).

[118] Id., §§33-34. The UN Working Group on Arbitrary Detention notes in Decision 13/1993 that the 'very harsh conditions of detention might have been the cause of death of Orton Chirwa'. This 'justified the Working Group's urgent appeal to the Government of Malawi concerning Chihana Chakfwa, an appeal that has unfortunately gone unanswered', E/CN.4/1994/27.

[119] ACHPR *Constitutional Rights Project and Others* v. *Nigeria,* decided at the 26th ordinary session, 13th Annual Activity Report 2000. This was part of a range of cases involving detention: *Constitutional Rights Project and Others* v. *Nigeria,* 140/94, Decided at the 26th ordinary session, 13th Annual Activity Report and (2000) AHRLR 227; *Constitutional Rights Project* v. *Nigeria* (*I*), 148/96, decided at the 26th ordinary session, 13th Annual Activity Report and (2000) AHRLR; *Constitutional Rights Project and Another* v. *Nigeria,* 150/96, decided at the 26th ordinary session, 13th Annual Activity Report and (2000) AHRLR 235; *Civil Liberties Organisation* v. *Nigeria,* 151/96, decided at the 26th ordinary session, 13th Annual Activity Report and (2000) AHRLR 243.

[120] ACHPR *Constitutional Rights Project and Others* v. *Nigeria,* decided at the 26th ordinary session, 13th Annual Activity Report 2000, §17. In March 1997 it sent a Mission to Nigeria, which also took up the complaints. On the merits it found violations of Article 5 ACHPR.

[121] ACHPR *Civil Liberties Organisation* v. *Nigeria,* 151/96, decided at the 26th ordinary session, November 1999, 13th Annual Activity Report and (2000) AHRLR 243, §27.

2.4.5 European system

Worth mentioning here is that already in 1957 the Commission has dealt with a request for provisional measures on account of the poor state of health of a detainee. In this case, however, the Commission simply considered itself incompetent to order provisional measures (these were not included in the Rules of Procedure at the time) and rejected the petition in this respect as incompatible with the provisions of the Convention.[122]

Obviously, since that time provisional measures have been taken, also in the context of detention. The case of *Demir et al.* v. *Turkey* is an example in which the European Commission intervened on the basis of a request for information on the petitioners' health situation and access to medical examination, as has been the practice with the HRC.[123]

This attention to the health situation of detainees was confirmed in subsequent cases. In *Paladi* v. *Moldova*, for instance, the European Court used provisional measures to the effect that the petitioner should not be transferred from a medical centre back to a prison hospital. The next day he was nevertheless so transferred and only a few days later was he allowed to return to the medical centre. On the merits both the fourth section and the Grand Chamber determined that a delay in the implementation of a provisional measure constituted a violation of the right of individual petition as well.[124]

With regard to general conditions of detention the Court has not been keen to intervene.[125] In *Ghvaladze* v. *Georgia*, for instance, initially it refused a request for provisional measures. Nevertheless, several months later it did decide to use provisional measures. In addition it noted 'the existence of other applications before it, which it had already communicated to the respondent Government' It 'put a question to the parties asking whether there existed within the Georgian prison system an administrative practice consisting of keeping detainees in unsatisfactory conditions, and/or a structural problem underlying the lack of medical treatment in provision'. It pointed out that in that case the petitioner would be exempted from the requirement to exhaust

---

[122]   EComHR *X.* v. *FRG*, p. 212, Yearbook 2, pp. 204-214, 22 March 1958 (inadm.).

[123]   It did so on 15 February 1993, on the basis of Rule 48(2a) of its Rules of Procedure. EComHR *Hüseyin Demir, Faik Kaplan, Sükrü Süsin* v. *Turkey*, Report of 29 May 1997.

[124]   ECtHR *Paladi* v. *Moldova*, 10 July 2007 (referring to provisional measures of 10 November 2005) (unanimous finding of a violation of Article 3, 6-1 on a violation of Article 34, Judge Bratza dissenting). ECtHR *Paladi* v. *Moldova* (Grand Chamber) 10 March 2009 (15-2 on the violation of Article 3; 9-8 on the violation of Article 34). See also *Kotsaftsis* v. *Greece*, in which provisional measures were used on 9 March 2007 requesting Greece 'to order the transfer of the applicant to a specialized medical centre so that he could undergo all the necessary tests and remain in hospital until his doctors considered that he could return to prison without his life being endangered'. On 15 March 2007 the petitioner was indeed so transferred. ECtHR Press Release 431 of 12 June 2006 on Chamber judgment in *Kotsafstis* v. *Greece*, 12 June 2008, §§4 and 32-37. On the merits the Court found that for a certain period Greece had not fulfilled its obligation to safeguard the petitioner's physical integrity, in violation of Article 3 ECHR.

[125]   In the alternative it intervenes but only uses Rule 41 on priority. See e.g. *Sarban* v. *Moldova*, Fourth Section Annual Report 2005, p. 9. The judgment on the merits indicates that in January 2005 the petitioner had asked for provisional measures 'requesting his immediate release from detention on remand in order to undergo medical treatment', *Sarban* v. *Moldova*, 4 October 2005, §5. Early February the Chamber communicated the case to the State (apparently without provisional measures). Later that month the petitioner withdrew his request for provisional measures after he was given access to his doctor and wife, §5. On the merits the Court found that 'the failure to provide basic medical assistance to the applicant when he clearly needed and had requested it, as well as the refusal to allow independent specialised medical assistance, together with other forms of humiliation' amounted to degrading treatment contrary to Article 3 ECHR, §90.

domestic remedies for purposes of his complaints under Article 3 ECHR.[126] This may also mean that in this context provisional measures are taken sooner and with increased specificity, possibly also covering a larger group of detainees, as in the Inter-American system.[127] Other relevant instances of the use of provisional measures in the context of detention are discussed under section 2.5 on protecting particularly vulnerable detainees.

2.5 Protecting particularly vulnerable detainees

2.5.1 Introduction

This section provides examples of provisional measures on behalf of particularly vulnerable detainees. It discusses situations of minors and of detainees in psychological distress (e.g. mental illness). It also discusses how the Inter-American and European systems deal with the situation of detainees on a hunger strike pending the proceedings and how the HRC deals with the question of access to health care by death row inmates pending the proceedings before it.

2.5.2 Protecting the health and safety of minors in detention

Because of the vulnerability of children circumstances of detention more rapidly result in irreparable harm to children than to adults. This may explain why the HRC and the Inter-American Commission and Court have often used provisional measures on their behalf.

In most health cases examined the HRC has invoked Rule 91 (current Rule 97) rather than used provisional measures proper. It did invoke formal provisional measures in a case involving detained children.[128]

In 2001-2002 the Special Rapporteur on New Communications received various requests to use provisional measures on behalf of refugees detained in Australia. In some of these cases he did indeed use them. In other cases he simply made enquiries into their health status, similar to the Committee's early practice.[129]

Several news accounts have provided information about specific cases involving risk of irreparable harm.[130] A ten-year-old boy had reportedly tried to hang himself and was cut down by detention centre staff.[131] A six-year-old boy reportedly stopped eating and drinking and was admitted to hospital. He was diagnosed with chronic posttraumatic stress disorder. A leaked report by the Human Rights and Equal Opportunity Commission noted that there was insufficient evidence that the Commonwealth had taken all appropriate measures to prevent the boy from witnessing self-harm and riots. It considered his human rights had been violated by the failure of the Department and the Minister to remove him from detention 'despite strong medical advice'.[132] If

---

[126] See ECtHR Case law information note No. 100, 30 September 2007, p. 10.

[127] In general on the specificity of provisional measures and the group of beneficiaries, see Chapter XIII (Protection).

[128] See *infra*.

[129] Interview by author with Martin Scheinin, Maastricht 20 September 2002.

[130] An example is the denial of medication to asylum seekers taking part in a hunger strike at Woomera detention centre. They were denied medication unless they drank two glasses of milk first. This applied to a sixty-year-old schizophrenic woman as well. AAP, 'Hunger strikers denied medicine', 27 March 2003, <www.news.com.al> (consulted 9 April 2003).

[131] AAP, 'Suicide bid by detention boy, 10', the Age, 20 July 2002, <www.theage.com.au> (consulted 9 April 2003).

[132] AAP, 'Boy detainees rights breached', the Age, 9 May 2002, <www.theage.com.au> (consulted 9 April 2003).

the HRC would be involved in such cases it would be feasible that it would use provisional measures.

The case of the *Bakhtiari family* (2003) was brought before the HRC in March 2002. The plight of the two eldest boys received particular attention in the media.[133] The fourteen-year-old Almadar and twelve-year-old Mentazer Bakhtiari escaped the detention centre twice.[134] They attempted to claim political asylum at the British Consulate, but they were returned after the British Government had rejected their claim.[135]

An employee of Australasian Correctional Management said that when Almadar arrived at Woomera he turned up regularly for activities and was a lively, inquisitive, 'proud and happy' child who was 'excited to be in Australia'.

> "But as the months in detention passed and the family's claim for asylum turned down he seemed to lose his grip on things (...). He fell under the influence of older men who were organising the riots and hunger strikes and who themselves were committing acts of self-harm. He witnessed grown men slashing themselves and others attempting to harm themselves".[136]

Initially the Special Rapporteur only used provisional measures to halt their deportation.[137] Subsequently, the petitioners provided the Committee with several reports,[138] finding that 'ongoing detention was causing deep depressive effects upon the children'. In particular these reports referred to several instances of self-harm, including where Almadar and Mentazer stitched their lips together, slashed their arms, 'voluntarily starved themselves and behaved in numerous erratic ways, including drawing disturbed pictures'. The Department of Human Services 'strongly recommended' that the children and their mother should have 'ongoing assessment *outside* the Woomera facility'.

Five days after receipt of these reports the Special Rapporteur used provisional measures requesting the State to 'inform the Committee within 30 days of the measures it had taken on the basis of evaluation by the State party's own expert authorities that, as a result of incidents of self harm inflicted by at least two of the children upon themselves, Mrs. Bakhtiyari and her children should have ongoing assessment outside of Woomera detention centre, in order to ensure that further such acts of harm were not suffered'.[139]

In September 2002 the petitioners provided the HRC with an Assessment Report of the Department of Human Services, recommending that the children and their mother 'be released into the community in order to prevent further social and emotional harm being done to the children, especially the boys'. It was the Department of Immigration and Multicultural and Indigenous Affairs that had requested this assessment. However, the Rapporteur did not repeat the provisional measures.[140]

---

[133] HRC *Bakhtiari family* v. *Australia*, 29 October 2003.

[134] The HRC itself did not mention that the detention centre was privately run.

[135] Alamdar had told ABC radio: "In camp, we didn't learn English; we learned too many bad things (...) we learn how to cut ourselves, how to drink shampoo, how to suicide. Two times I killed myself by razor, two times I suicide me". Larissa Dubecki, Andra Jackson, 'Boys despair over return to Woomera', 20 July 2002, <www.theage.com.au> (consulted 9 April 2003).

[136] Russell Skelton, 'No happy ending in sight for two young boys', 20 July 2002, <www.theage.com.au> (consulted on 9 April 2003).

[137] See Chapter V on halting expulsion or extradition.

[138] A psychologist's report, a report of the South Australian State government's Department of Human Services and a report of an Australian Correctional Management Youth Worker.

[139] Provisional measures of 3 May 2002.

[140] In its submission of October 2002 the State party pointed out that the family did not cooperate with the assessment that took place in August 2002. 'Mrs Bakhtiyari did not allow the authorities

It is possible that the petitioners in the Bakhtiari case asked the HRC to request the State to release the children.[141] In the European and the Inter-American human rights system the Commission and/or Court have indeed requested release in a few instances. Even the HRC itself has once requested a State, as a formal provisional measure, to take into account the health of one petitioner and not to execute the detention order against him while it was examining the admissibility of the case.[142] It is unlikely, however, that Australian counsel would have been aware of this case because it was discontinued and the HRC does not publish information about such cases.[143]

In August 2003 the Full Bench of the Family Court ordered the immediate release of all the children, pending resolution of the final application to the High Court. They were released on that day.[144] More than two months later the HRC published its decision on the merits. Apart from violations of Article 9 (1) and (4), it also found violations of Article 24(1) and, potentially, of Articles 17(1) and 23(1) ICCPR.

It pointed out that, under Article 24(1) ICCPR, 'the principle that in all decisions affecting a child, its best interests shall be a primary consideration, forms an integral part of every child's right to such measures of protection as required by his or her status as a minor'. It observed that in this case the children 'have suffered demonstrable, documented and on-going adverse effects of detention'. It noted that this had been so until their release, that their detention had been arbitrary and in violation of Article 9(1) and that the two eldest sons had suffered in particular. Among others, the state was obliged to pay appropriate compensation to the children. The State should also refrain from deporting the children and their mother while their father was pursuing domestic proceedings, because any such action would result in violations of Articles 17(1) and 23(1) ICCPR.

Awareness of the vulnerability of children caused the Inter-American Commission on Human Rights to intervene in situations where minors (unaccompanied by their families) were detained, not segregated from adults.[145] The HRC has also dealt with such cases but, thus far, the only information available on the use of provisional measures in this context is in the case of *Baroy* v. *the Philippines* (inadm. 2003). The petitioner had been sentenced to death and allegedly was seventeen years old at the time of the submission of the case in January 2002. The Rapporteur used provisional measures to halt his execution and 'further requested the State party speedily to determine the age of the author and meanwhile to treat him as a minor, in accordance with

---

to speak to the two eldest sons, which compromised the assessment. An independent psychologist made an assessment on 2 and 3 September 2002, and made recommendations the Department is considering'.

[141]   The State reported in the press its view that the lawyers were aggravating the situation of the children. A situation such as this is not easy to assess by a non-permanent international body based in another continent.

[142]   HRC *V.* v. *Spain*, disc. 1995. The official Note Verbale to the State was less specific than the telegram sent to the Ministry of Justice. The latter referred to an affidavit indicating that the petitioner suffered from cancer and other grave illnesses. It also specified that this request was made for humanitarian reasons. On 1 June 1992 the Ministry of Justice responded that, according to the information it had received, there appeared to be no case of irreparable harm if the petitioner would be detained and that the State would adopt the appropriate measures once it had received the medical information. It noted that the Committee's provisional measure was sent to the relevant judicial body for determination (on file with the author).

[143]   The letter to the petitioner, moreover, referred only to Rule 91 and did not mention that the Rapporteur had used provisional measures under Rule 86 in the Note Verbale sent to the State on the same date.

[144]   See further Chapter XVII (Official responses).

[145]   See *infra*.

the provisions of the Covenant'.[146] The case *Damian Thomas* v. *Jamaica* (1999) was not a death penalty case. At the time of submission of the communication the petitioner was a minor.[147] Pending the proceedings the HRC did not use provisional measures to stop or prevent an Article 24 violation. Later it did find violations of Articles 24 and 10(2) and (3) requiring an effective remedy 'entailing his placement in a juvenile institution, separated from adult prisoners if Jamaica legislation authorises it'.[148] The Committee had mentioned that it had received a letter from several inmates at the General Penitentiary, requesting that it act on behalf of the petitioner. The petitioner himself had written to the Commissioner for Prisons requesting that he be removed from the General Penitentiary, an adult prison. Yet when he was moved it was to St. Catherine District Prison, again an adult prison. In a later submission the petitioner added that he had been systematically beaten by warders both at the General Penitentiary and at St. Catherine District Prison.[149] The petitioner had not invoked any particular articles of the Covenant, but the communication appeared to raise issues under Articles 7, 10 and 14. It is customary for the Committee, or rather its Secretariat, to indicate under which articles issues seem to arise in such complaints. In this case, however, at the merits stage, the HRC added that another article of the Covenant was at stake as well. It concluded *proprio motu* that the facts of the present case also constituted a violation of Article 24 of the Covenant, since the State party has failed to provide to Damian Thomas 'such measures of protection as are required by his status as a minor'. It regretted the State party's lack of cooperation with respect to the non-segregation of the petitioner from adult prisoners.[150]

---

146 HRC *Alfredo Baroy* v. *the Philippines*, 31 October 2003 (inadm.).

147 In §1 the HRC mentions he was sixteen years old at the time, while in §6.5 it concludes he was seventeen years old.

148 HRC *Damian Thomas* v. *Jamaica*, 8 April 1999 (no Rule 86).

149 The HRC declared part of the claim inadmissible because of Jamaica's denunciation of the OP. This was the claim relating to ill treatment by warders on specific dates. On the merits the Committee noted that the petitioner had made precise allegations of ill treatment by warders on specific dates, about which he had complained to the prison authorities. It noted that these claims had not been refuted by the State party, which had promised to investigate these but had failed to forward its findings to the Committee, eleven months after promising to do so and in spite of a reminder by the HRC. It recalled that a State party is under the obligation to investigate seriously allegations of violations of the Covenant made under the OP. In this case, however, the Committee considered the claims inadmissible under Article 1 of the OP since the allegations were transmitted to the State party after Jamaica's denunciation of the OP came into force on 23 January 1998. Committee member Solari Yrigoyen dissented. He would have concluded a violation of Articles 10(1) and 7 in relation to the treatment suffered by the petitioner. He stated that although the State party denounced the OP, the events described in the complaint occurred before that date and were handled in the same manner as the original complaint. For this reason, he argued, the terms of the OP continued to apply to the communication. At the same time the HRC did declare admissible the remainder of the claim, which had been transmitted to the State party before Jamaica's denunciation of the OP came into force. See §6.4. The HRC referred to the State party's contention that the circumstances under which the author was being held were not clear and observed that 'given the name, date of birth, date of arrest and of conviction and the location in 1998 in St. Catherine District Prison, all in relation to the author, the State party should have no difficulty in identifying the details relevant to this matter'.

150 The petitioner was entitled to an effective remedy for the violation of Articles 10(2) and (3) and 24 'entailing his placement in a juvenile institution, separated from adult prisoners if Jamaican legislation authorises it'. This remedy, moreover, was to include compensation for his non-segregation from adult prisoners while he was a minor. One may wonder what the remedy may entail when Jamaican legislation does not authorise separation from adult prisoners.

It would be interesting to know whether, if the possibility of a violation of Article 24 had been mentioned at an earlier stage, the Special Rapporteur on New Communications would have taken provisional measures in order to prevent a 'further violation of Art. 24', especially when there are allegations of abuse or threats by adults. The HRC could have intervened for the petitioner's protection and requested his segregation from adult prisoners and treatment appropriate to his age and legal status. If the rationale of Article 24 is to protect minors from abuse by adult prisoners, in that way it is also a means to prevent torture and cruel treatment.

In the Inter-American human rights system, the Commission and Court have indeed intervened in an increasing number of cases in order to ensure segregation of minors from adults or, more generally, to prevent irreparable harm.[151]

In one early case against Paraguay the beneficiaries were 255 minors who had been held at the Panchito López re-education centre for minors. After a fire had broken out in which nine minors died, the Commission used precautionary measures and the minors were transferred.[152]

One case involving Honduras has generated information that may be useful to clarify the meaning of the Commission's precautionary measures on behalf of minors in detention. In 1995 the Commission dealt with a case against Honduras alleging the unlawful arrest of street children and their incarceration in the Central Penitentiary of Tegucigalpa. These children were detained together with in each cell approximately 80 adult prisoners. One of the NGOs that brought the case noted that it was 'of great interest because of the international and national media coverage it has received'. "This case is representative of an urgent situation wherein minors suffer serious mistreatment in detention centres, including sexual abuse and torture. Children have also been killed in detention centres meant for adults".[153]Nine days after the initial submission the petitioners urgently requested the Commission to adopt precautionary measures to guarantee the life and physical safety of the juveniles held in that prison and 'to ensure that they were housed in facilities that were appropriate to their status'. The petitioners requested that the juveniles be separated from the adult prisoners. The State should provide medical and psychological treatment to juveniles who had been the victims of physical, sexual and psychological abuse and that it should take the necessary security measures to guarantee the lives and safety of the juveniles detained in the Central Penitentiary.[154] In response, the State noted that it was under enormous economic con-

---

[151] For precautionary measures by the Inter-American Commission see e.g. Annual Report 1996, Chapter II, §4a (*Minors in detention* v. *Brazil); Annual Report 2001, §48 (255 minors in detention* v. *Paraguay*); Annual Report 2004, §36 (*62 children held in the Juvenile Center of Provisional Confinement* v. *Guatemala*); Annual Report 2004, §14 (*Children confined in the State Foundation for the Well-being of Children* v. *Brazil*).

[152] During the fire a guard shot one youngster, who later died. On 8 August 2001 the Commission took precautionary measures. See Instituto "Coronel Panchito López", case 11.666. Subsequently the Court became involved as well. IACHR "*Instituto de Reeducación del Menor*" (Paraguay), Judgment of 2 September 2004.

[153] CEJIL case docket 1997 referring to street children detained with adults at the Central Penitentiary of Tegucigalpa (Honduras). See also Chapter XVII (Official responses).

[154] According to CEJIL's own case docket this case began with a petition for precautionary measures in February 1995, while the Commission's final report mentions 13 April 1995 as the day the petition itself was submitted and 22 May 1995 as the day on which the petitioners requested precautionary measures. The Commission notes that this request was amplified on 6 June 1996 to include three children in the Choluteca jail and 34 children in the San Pedro Sula Prison. CIDH *Minors in detention* v. *Honduras*, 10 March 1999 (merits), §49. While the phrasing is unclear, the context leads one to conclude that the Commission indeed used the precautionary measures requested and later amplified them. Literally, the Commission reports that the petitioners' request was amplified.

straints but was making 'supreme efforts' to comply with international obligations.[155] It pointed out the alarming rate of juvenile felonies.[156]

On the basis of Article 29 ACHR (on interpretation) and the consistent practice of the Commission and Court, the Commission combined the regional and the universal human rights systems to interpret the Convention. It pointed out that other international instruments contained even more specific rules with regard to the protection of children. The Commission concluded that the practice of incarcerating minors in adult penal institutions, thereby endangering their physical, mental and moral health, was indeed a violation of Article 19 ACHR. It pointed out that the obligation to provide special protection for children was a non-derogable obligation under Article 27(2) ACHR. It also referred more generally to the non-derogable rights of the child.[157]

The Commission pointed out that the State's duty to house minors and adults in separate detention facilities was based on Article 5(5) jo. Article 19 ACHR. It also noted that the 'essential aim of reform and social rehabilitation of prisoners' under Article 5(6) was 'absolutely impossible to achieve in penal institutions in which children are forced to live alongside adult criminals'. It then continued discussing the obligations under Article 5(1) (right to respect for physical, mental and moral integrity) and 5(2) (prohibition of torture, cruel, inhuman or degrading punishment or treatment and the right of all person deprived of their liberty to be treated with respect for their inherent dignity). It considered that 'the cohabitation of juvenile and adult inmates is a violation of the human dignity of these minors and has led to abuses of the juveniles' personal integrity. The physical superiority of the adult inmates enables them to force themselves upon the juveniles and abuse them'.[158] In conclusion Honduras had violated the 'special right of minors' to have their physical, moral and mental integrity respected. It had subjected the juveniles in question to inhuman and degrading treatment and had failed to take the necessary steps to prevent adult inmates from physically and sexually assaulting or abusing the juvenile inmates.[159]

---

[155] In this case they had alleged that the situation of the children violated the international law relating to the detention of minors including Articles 5, 7, 19 and 29(b) ACHR, Articles 7 and 10(b) ICCPR, Articles 3(1), 19(1) and 37 Convention on the Rights of the Child and Article 13(4) of the UN Standard Minimum Rules for the Administration of Juvenile Justice (Beijing Rules).

[156] More generally on official State responses see Chapter XVII.

[157] CIDH *Minors in detention* v. *Honduras*, 10 March 1999, §98.

[158] The Commission mentioned as evidence the reports represented by the petitioners, several newspaper articles with statements by judges and prosecutors (included in the Commission's merits report) and the statements of the juveniles themselves. It pointed out that the acts or omissions by prison, police and judicial officials in relation to the allegations were directly imputable to the State. CIDH *Minors in detention* v. *Honduras*, 10 March 1999, §125-130. It also referred to statements made to the press by a Supreme Court justice. These confirmed that the authorities were aware of the fact that juveniles were being raped in the Central Penitentiary but nevertheless transferred them (upon the discovery of one particular case of rape) to another cell occupied by adults, 'where they would continue to face similar risks'. *Minors in detention* v. *Honduras*, 10 March 1999, §133.

[159] In its decision declaring admissible a complaint against Peru on the detention of juveniles, the Commission made no mention of precautionary measures. The complaint concerned insufficient separation from adult detainees, inadequate conditions of detention and lack of regular access to health care. In this case, however, the complaint was only brought after the youths had already left the detention facility complained of). CIDH *Leoncio Florian López et al.* v. *Peru*, 3 October 2000 (adm.). With regard to Paraguay the Tekojoja Foundation and CEJIL petitioned the Commission, on 14 August 1996, alleging adverse prison conditions and 'extreme physical and psychological violence' to which children and young people were subjected in the Panchito López Penitentiary for minors. Previously, the Tekojoja Foundation had brought a habeas corpus proceeding before the courts in Paraguay with the aim to stop the detention of minors in that penitentiary. They had provided evidence of the uninhabitable conditions of this penitentiary and

The Inter-American Court ordered Brazil, among others, to protect the lives and personal integrity of those minors detained in a detention centre in Brazil as well as others present, in particular to prevent further violent outbursts, to guarantee safety, maintain order and prevent cruel treatment. Moreover, the State should take the necessary measures to reduce overcrowding, confiscate any arms, separate the detainees in accordance with the relevant international standards and keeping in mind the best interests of the child, provide the necessary medical care, periodically monitor the detention conditions and the physical and moral conditions of the children detained.[160] It has pointed out that 'problems relating to detention centers require medium and long-term actions to adapt their conditions to the corresponding international standards'. Yet States also have the obligation to take immediate action in order to 'guarantee the physical, mental and moral integrity of the inmates, as well as their right to life and their right to enjoy the minimum conditions for a decent life, especially in the case of children, who require special attention from the State'.[161] It specified that the measures to be adopted based on its Order for provisional measures must be adopted 'immediately and effectively'.[162] On the other hand, 'the analysis of the effectiveness of the investigations and proceedings relating to the facts that gave rise to these provisional measures' corresponded to the examination of the merits of the case, which was pending before the Commission.[163] In other words, while the State was expected to investigate the facts as part of the provisional measures, in order to prevent (further) irreparable harm, it would not analyse the effectiveness of the measures undertaken by the State in this respect, as this was reserved for the merits.[164]

In its Orders for provisional measures the Inter-American Court has also included general statements on existing law, such as that 'as a consequence of its positive obligation to protect the right to life and physical integrity, the State has the duty to prevent that individuals under its custody be subject to conditions such as overcrowding'.[165] It has observed that, together with the

---

the degrading treatment to which the minors were subjected. This included overcrowded conditions, continuous violence and malnourishment, a lack of beds or mattresses and insufficient basic medical attention. The Supreme Court of Paraguay, however, 'paralyzed' the case, which prompted the Foundation and CEJIL to bring a complaint before the Commission. CEJIL case docket 1997 (on file with the author). Apparently, the petitioners did not request and the Commission did not take precautionary measures.

[160] IACHR *Case of the children and adolescents deprived of their liberty in the 'Complexo do Tatuapé' of FEBEM* (Brazil), Orders of 17 and 30 November 2005. Attached to the 17 November Order is a Concurring Opinion by Judge Cançado Trindade criticizing the long period of adverse detention circumstances before the Commission finally resorted to the Court for provisional measures. See also IACHR *Jorge Castañeda Gutman* (Mexico), Order of 25 November 2005, Concurring Opinion by Judges Cançado Trindade and Ventura Robles, §§4 and 8.

[161] See e.g. IACHR *Matter of Yare I and Yare II Capital Region Penitentiary Center*, Order of 30 March 2006, 17th 'Considering' clause; *Matter of the Monagas Judicial Detention Center ('La Pica')*, 9 February 2006, 19th 'Considering' clause; *Matter of the Children Deprived of liberty in the "Complexo do Tataupé" of FEBEM*, Order of 4 July 2006, 12th 'Considering' clause and Order of 3 July 2007, 10th 'Considering' clause.

[162] IACHR *Matter of the Children Deprived of liberty in the "Complexo do Tataupé" of FEBEM*, Order of 3 July 2007, 11th 'Considering' clause.

[163] Id., 12th 'Considering' clause and 7th 'Decisional' clause.

[164] See also Chapter XIII (Protection).

[165] IACHR *Matter of the persons imprisoned in the "Dr. Sebastião Martins Silveira" Penitentiary in Araraquara, São Paulo* (Brazil), Order of 30 September 2006, 15th 'Considering' clause. See also IACHR *Las penitenciarías de Mendoza* (Argentina), Order of 22 November 2004. Here the Court noted that in light of the relation between the conditions of detention and the right to life and personal integrity it was possible to protect detainees thorough its provisional measures, 11th 'Considering' clause.

precarious detention situation in a case and the State's failed 'duty to divide inmates into different categories', these circumstances 'may give rise to violent events (…) and might cause an immediate loss of lives and generalized attacks affecting the inmates' personal integrity'.[166] After all the State's obligation to protect in the detention context extends to the protection against threats and harassment originating from third parties, like other detainees.[167] "Given the characteristics of the detention centers, the State must protect prisoners from violent acts which, if there is no State control, might take place among the detainees".[168] In this light the Court has stressed that 'the acts of the state security officers, specially those aimed at keeping order', or at the referral from one detention centre to the other, 'must be carried out strictly respecting the human rights of the prisoners and preventing unduly violent acts'.[169]

2.5.3 (Method of) confinement and protecting detainees in psychological distress

Precautionary and provisional measures may also be warranted because of the specific vulnerability of people for reasons other than their age.[170] In December 1994 a petitioner requested the Inter-American Commission to intervene on behalf of an Argentine citizen detained in Bolivia. She had been arrested for possession and transportation of cocaine. Despite her long and documented medical history of mental illness the Bolivian authorities detained her at a women's prison facility lacking the capability to provide the special treatment required by her condition. During this detention she was raped several times. The Bolivian judiciary refused to transfer her to a specialised psychiatric facility. While it is not clear whether the Commission took the precautionary measures requested to safeguard her physical integrity, it did start an investigation *in loco*.[171] In February 1995 a domestic court acquitted her because of mental incompetence. Yet she remained in detention awaiting fulfilment of procedural requirements. According to CEJIL she was transferred from the women's prison to a psychiatric facility as a result of pressure from international groups and eventually could return home to the care of her family.[172]

In *Cesti Hurtado* the Commission requested the Inter-American Court twice to order Peru to release Mr. Cesti. The Court did not do this as this would constitute an anticipation of the merits of the case.[173] Instead it noted that 'the President of this Court, in his Order, instructed the State of Peru to adopt urgent measures by providing Mr. Cesti-Hurtado with proper medical treatment for

---

[166]   IACHR *Matter of the persons imprisoned in the "Dr. Sebastião Martins Silveira" Penitentiary in Araraquara, São Paulo* (Brazil), Order of 30 September 2006, 15th 'Considering' clause.

[167]   IACHR *Las penitentiarías de Mendoza* (Argentina), Order of 22 November 2004, 12th considering clause.

[168]   IACHR *Matter of the persons imprisoned in the "Dr. Sebastião Martins Silveira" Penitentiary in Araraquara, São Paulo* (Brazil), Order of 30 September 2006, 16th 'Considering' clause.

[169]   Id., referring to *Matter of Yare I y Yare II Capital Region Penitentiary Center*, Order of 30 March 2006, 14th 'Considering' clause; *Matter of Monagas Judicial Confinement Center ('La Pica')*, Order of 9 February 2006, 16th 'Considering' clause and *Matter of Children Deprived of Liberty in the "Complexo do Tatuapé" of FEBEM*, Order of 17 November 2005, 14th 'Considering' clause.

[170]   See e.g. CIDH *Jorge Bernal, Julio César Rotela and 458 patients of the Neuro-psychiatric Hospital* v. *Paraguay*, Annual Report 2003, §60.

[171]   SERPAJ, a human rights organization from her home country (Argentina), initially submitted the request and was subsequently supported by CEJIL.

[172]   CEJIL case docket 1997.

[173]   See IACHR *Cesti Hurtado* (Peru), Order of the President, 29 July 1997, 5th and 6th 'Considering' clauses and Order of the Court of 11 September 1997, 5th 'Considering' clause.

his heart disease, with a view to protecting his physical, psychological and moral integrity. The Court ratifies that order and decides to maintain those measures'.[174]

A famous early detention case dealt with by the Inter-American Court is that of María Elena *Loayza Tamayo*, who was serving a 20-year prison sentence. Pending the case the Court had ordered Peru to take 'all provisional measures necessary for the effective safeguard of her physical, psychological and moral integrity'.[175] In light of the danger to her physical, psychological and moral health, it ordered Peru to modify her prison conditions, in particular with regard to her solitary confinement. It also expected Peru to provide her with medical treatment, both physical and psychiatric, without delay. On the merits the Court found, among others, that Peru had violated her right to humane treatment, as recognized in Article 5 jo. 1(1) ACHR.[176]

In *Patanè* v. *Italy* (1986) the European Commission took provisional measures on behalf of a petitioner serving a five year prison sentence 'who was suffering from a severe state of depression and whose health was, according to medical certificates submitted, continuously deteriorating to the point where there existed an acute threat to her life'.[177]

In *Keenan* v. *UK* (2001) a mentally ill detainee had committed suicide in detention. His mother complained of failure by the detention authorities to protect his life. While the ECtHR considered that there had indeed been a particular risk of suicide in this case, of which the authorities could have been aware, it did not find a violation of the right to life in this case. It did, however, find that the treatment of the detainee had violated the prohibition of cruel treatment.[178]

---

[174]   IACHR *Cesti Hurtado* (Peru), Order of the Court of 11 September 1997, 6th 'Considering' clause. Subsequently the Commission brought the casse before the Court on the merits and again requested provisional measures for the provisional release of Mr Cesti. Once more the Court denied this, Order of 29 January 1998, calling upon Peru 'to permit Mr. Cesti Hurtado to receive the medical treatment of his choice', 2nd 'Decisional' clause. On 3 June 1999 the Court expanded its provisional measures to protect his family against threats and harassment. Shortly upon Cesti's release, on 11 November 1999, the Court decided to maintain its provisional measures for the protection of Cesti and his family. By Order of 14 August 2000 it lifted its provisional measures. See further the Court's decisions on the merits and reparations: Judgment on the merits, 29 September 1999, Interpretation of judgment of 29 January 2000; Judgment on Reparations of 21 May 2001 and Interpretation of that judgment of 27 November 2001; Resolution on Compliance of 17 November 2004 (continuing supervision of compliance) and Order by the President of 21 December 2005 (denying renewed request for provisional measures aimed at ensuring compliance with the Court's judgments).

[175]   IACHR *Loayza Tamayo* (Peru), Orders for provisional measures of 2 July and 13 September 1996. Clearly provisional measures taken in the context of incommunicado detention could also help prevent disappearances and torture. Ms Loayza was released on 16 October 1997. On 11 November 1997 the Court ordered the provisional measures closed. In 2000 the Court ordered provisional measures on her behalf again, but this time relating to her socioeconomic circumstances: 13 December 2000 (President) and 3 February 2001. In 2001 (28 August 2001) these were lifted on request of the State (see also Chapter XII on provisional measures in other situations).

[176]   IACHR *Loayza Tamayo* (Peru), Judgment of 17 September 1997.

[177]   While the Commission had not specified its provisional measures of 15 October 1985 and the State decided to release the petitioner, who subsequently disappeared. EComHR *Patanè* v. *Italy*, 3 December 1986 (struck out). See more generally Chapter XIII (Protection) and XVII (Official responses). See also, in a different factual situation involving a risk of suicide) and a possible transfer to communist East-Germany, 27 May 1974, *Brückmann* v. *FRG*, EuRGZ 1974, p. 113 and 1976, p. 451.

[178]   ECtHR *Keenan* v. *UK*, 3 April 2001.

In a situation similar to that occurring in *Keenan* it is feasible that a petitioner, having exhausted domestic remedies, would request the intervention of the ECtHR.[179]

Indeed in more recent cases the Court had used provisional measures to protect detainees in psychological distress. In *Prezec* v. *Croatia* (2008), the ECtHR had used provisional measures in September 2007, ordering the State to provide a prisoner with the requisite psychiatric treatment. In response, in January 2008 the State carried out a psychiatric examination. "The report drawn up on 15 January 2008 concluded that the applicant suffered from a personality disorder and was in need of an active, permanent and differential psychiatric treatment". In March 2008 he was placed in a psychiatric hospital with a treatment programme specifically designed for him. It includes 'compulsory psychiatric treatment of the applicant in the Zagreb Prison Hospital, con-sisting of intensive psychiatric treatment in small groups and therapeutic communities, organised art and computer workshops as part of the applicant's therapy and his preparation for the return to the normal life'. The treatment was to last until his release.[180]

In some other contexts requests for provisional measures have remained unsuccessful. In *Lorsé et al.* v. *The Netherlands* (2003)[181] counsel had requested the ECtHR to take provisional measures to the effect that Lorsé would be immediately transferred from the maximum security prison (EBI) in Vught to an ordinary prison. Alternatively the Court was requested to take provi-sional measures of a more general nature, namely those 'necessary to put an end to the continuing violation of Article 3 of the Convention'.[182] The President of the first section decided not to take any provisional measures.[183]

Counsel for the petitioner had noted that the request for provisional measures was made in light of the physical and mental situation of the petitioners.[184] A letter by the Secretariat respond-ing to the request for provisional measures informed counsel for the petitioner 'that such a request can normally be acceded to only if there is imminent danger of harm that cannot subsequently be remedied or made good, as can be the case, in particular, if the applicant is in danger of being expelled or deported'.[185] Subsequently the Court examined the request and informed counsel officially that it had decided 'not to indicate to the Government the measure you suggest'.[186]

In earlier cases the ECtHR had held that 'complete sensory isolation, coupled with total so-cial isolation, can destroy the personality and constitutes a form of inhuman treatment which cannot be justified by the requirements of security or any other reason'.[187]

---

[179] See also e.g. ECtHR *Dybeku* v. *Albania*, 18 December 2007.

[180] ECtHR *Prezec* v. *Croatia*, 28 August 2008 (struck out after friendly settlement).

[181] ECtHR *Lorsé et al.* v. *The Netherlands*, judgment of 4 February 2003 (former first section). See also *Van der Ven* v. *The Netherlands*, judgment of 4 February 2003 (former first section).

[182] ECtHR *Lorsé et al.* v. *The Netherlands*, letter of 19 November 1999 (on file with the author).

[183] ECtHR *Lorsé et al.* v. *The Netherlands*, 18 January 2000 (adm.).

[184] A recent domestic decision had had a profound psychological impact on him and he was on hunger strike since 15 November 1999. ECtHR *Lorsé et al.* v. *The Netherlands*, initial petition of 19 November 1999 (on file with the author). The Court did not further discuss the petitioner's hunger strike. Its description of the facts in admissibility decision of 18 January 2000 briefly notes that he began a hunger strike on 17 November 1999.

[185] ECtHR *Lorsé et al.* v. *The Netherlands*, letter by the Secretariat of 19 November 1999 (on file with the author).

[186] ECtHR *Lorsé et al.* v. *The Netherlands*, letter by Registrar section 1, 30 November 1999 (on file with the author).

[187] See e.g. ECtHR *Messina* v. *Italy*, 8 June 1999 (inadm. as to the conditions of detention claim), 1st 'As to the law' clause (10th paragraph).

"On the other hand, the removal from association with other prisoners for security, disciplinary or protective reasons does not in itself amount to inhuman treatment or degrading punishment".[188]

In January 2000 the first section began its examination of the admissibility of the *Lorsé* case. It did decide to give it priority under Rule 41.[189] The admissibility decision indicates that the President of the first section decided not to take provisional measures.

On the merits the Court did not find that the petitioner was subjected to sensory isolation or total isolation. In fact, it noted, that the Italian special regime in an earlier case 'was significantly more restrictive'.

It found that the combination of the routine strip-searching and the other security measures amounted to inhuman or degrading treatment in violation of Article 3. It considered 'that in the situation where Mr Lorsé was already subjected to a great number of control measures, and in the absence of convincing security needs, the practice of weekly strip-searches that was applied to Mr Lorsé for a period for more than six years diminished his human dignity and must have given rise to feelings of anguish and inferiority capable of humiliating and debasing him'.

The judgment on the merits does not refer to the request for provisional measures and the admissibility decision only notes that the President decided not to take them. It might be feasible, in future, to use provisional measures to halt such strip-searches that are performed routinely even on those occasions in which the petitioner has not been in contact with the outside world.

2.5.4 Protecting detainees on a hunger strike

In the Inter-American and European systems provisional measures have also been requested by or on behalf of detainees on a hunger strike.[190] The protection requested may still have been improvement of prison conditions or investigation of specific mistreatment.

There are some examples in which the Inter-American Commission took precautionary measures in hunger strike cases.[191] It has, for instance, intervened on behalf of a prisoner in Cuba who had a tumor on his lung. Two months previously he had begun a hunger strike demanding medical care.[192]

It is not always clear what role is played by the hunger strike, but it seems unlikely that the Inter-American Commission admonishes the beneficiaries of the precautionary measures to end their hunger strike, as the European Commission and Court have done in the past.[193]

In December 2000 the Commission took precautionary measures on behalf of the petitioners in the case of *Juan Carlos Abella* v. *Argentina*,[194] or the *La Tablada* case, on which it had made public its final Report three years before. The precautionary measures involved twenty of the eleven persons whose right to humane treatment the Commission had found violated in 1997.

---

[188] Ibid.

[189] ECtHR *Lorsé et al.* v. *The Netherlands*, letter by Registrar section 1, received 25 January 2000 (on file with the author).

[190] See also Chapter XIII (Protection), section 4.2, on beneficiaries and addressees (under the heading 'the petitioner as addressee') and Chapter XV (Immediacy and risk), section 3.2.5 on health in detention and assessment of risk.

[191] See e.g. CIDH precautionary measures of 16 December 1998 on behalf of María Emilia de Marchi (Brazil), case 12.002, Annual Report 1998, §14 and on 27 December 2000 on behalf of eleven detainees in case 11.137 (Argentina), Annual Report 2000, §9; See also Chapter XIII (Protection, discussing beneficiaries and addressees in section 4).

[192] CIDH Annual Report 2001, §28.

[193] See also Chapter XIII (Protection), section 4.

[194] CIDH *Juan Carlos Abella et al.* v. *Argentina* (*La Tablada* case), 18 November 1997.

With regard to these eleven persons the Commission had also found violations of the right to appeal their conviction to a higher court and the right to a simple and effective remedy. It had recommended Argentina to 'take the most appropriate measures to repair the harm suffered' by them.[195] Yet apparently, they were still imprisoned in December 2000. They were in an advanced stage of a hunger strike and the issue became very important in Argentina. The Commission initiated a follow-up in this case.[196] Given the urgency of the situation (some of them might die) the Commission took precautionary measures asking the government to act and resolve the situation so that the detainees would abandon their hunger strike. In its Annual Report 2000 the Commission notes that both Argentina and the petitioners later informed it that the State had taken measures leading them to stop the hunger strike.[197] In a press release of 11 December 2000 the Commission had already noted it issued the following precautionary measure to Argentina: "The immediate adoption of the necessary measures to implement fully the recommendation of Report 55/97". It reproduced these recommendations and noted that, in the past three years, it had repeatedly taken steps to ensure their implementation, including visiting Argentina and holding three follow-up hearings. It pointed out that the persons involved had been on a hunger strike than 90 days, reportedly because of the non-implementation of the Commission's recommendation. "Although the Commission is not in favor of a hunger strike that compromises the health and threatens the lives of the persons involved, it believes that the way to resolve this grave situation is to implement the recommendations fully and without further delay".[198] This was the first case where the Commission used precautionary measures as part of a follow-up of a case that ended three years previously. It shows an approach to the use of these measures that is integrated in the Commission's other activities and takes into account the other obligations of the State as previously established.

Thus, with regard to the addressees of the its precautionary measures in cases involving hunger strikes it is relevant to note that the Inter-American Commission is not in the habit of telling detainees to give up a hunger strike. In the *Tablada* case such 'order' clearly would have been awkward as the prisoners started their hunger strike because Argentina was not following the Commission's recommendations that had been based on its findings of violations.

The approach is quite different in the European system. In April 1981 one of the sisters of Robert (Bobby) Sands, MP, urgently contacted the European Commission on his behalf. He was in the 54th day of a hunger-strike 'which he had no choice but to undertake as a more conventional domestic remedy was not open to him to protest against prison conditions which he regarded as intolerable'. She stated that her brother's life was in danger. His state of health was 'such that he is unable himself to make an application directly'. In addition she requested an immediate fact-finding investigation. The Acting President of the Commission took provisional measures, 'in view of the urgency of the situation'. He requested the State 'to take the necessary steps to enable a Delegation from the Commission' to meet with her brother in prison in order to find out whether he indeed intended to make the petition and, if so, to further discuss the substance and proceed-

---

[195] Id. In §115 the Commission notes that on 14 May 1993 the petitioners had requested it to visit the prisons to verify the status of the prisoners involved as they considered that the lives of these prisoners were in danger. The Commission does not provide information on its reaction to this request.

[196] In Rule 46 of its Rules of Procedure (2000) the Commission has ratified its practice on follow-up and compliance with its recommendations in cases not referred to the Court.

[197] CIDH Annual Report 2000, §9.

[198] CIDH 'Inter-American Commission on Human Rights Requests Precautionary Measures in the "*La Tablada*" Case', Press Release 20/00, 11 December 2000, <www.cidh.oas.org/comunicados/english/2000/Press20-00.htm>. The Commission's Annual Report 2000 notes that the Commission took precautionary measures on 27 December 2000, while the press release announcing these measures is from 11 December.

ings.[199] This was an a-typical provisional measure. It could be considered to aim at the safeguarding of the evidence.[200] Yet, the urgency of the situation related to the fact that the life of a possible petitioner was at risk. The Commission meant to ascertain whether Bobby Sands himself agreed with the petition filed by his sister. Meanwhile his life was at risk and the claims involved Articles 2 and 3.

The next day a Delegation of the Commission consisting of the Acting President, Mr Nørgaard and Mr Opsahl indeed travelled to London for discussions with officials from the Northern-Ireland Office. On 25 April the delegation travelled to Belfast to visit the Maze Prison. The prison doctor informed them that Bobby Sands was 'lucid and capable of following events' but 'physically very weak'. They also spoke with Marcella Sands and her solicitor and with another prisoner. In the end, however, they did not speak with Sands himself. Through the intermediary of his sister's counsel it was established 'that he did not wish to associate himself' with the petition.[201] Bobby Sands died from the effects of his hunger-strike on 5 May 1981. On the basis of the information provided by the Delegates the Commission considered that his state of health did not prevent him from validly indicating his wish not to be associated with the petition and understanding the implications. It struck out the case.[202]

The European Commission and Court have responded to requests for provisional measures by detainees on a hunger strike by invoking its Rule on such measures vis-à-vis the petitioner instead in order for them to stop their hunger strike.[203]

More recently, the ECtHR has used provisional measures to halt re-imprisonment of petitioners who had been hospitalized because of the after-effects of long-term hunger-strikes.[204]

---

[199] EComHR *Marcella Sands and Robert Sands* v. *the UK*, 14 October 1981 (struck out).

[200] See also Chapter XII (Other situations).

[201] See further Chapter XIII (Protection), section 4 on beneficiaries.

[202] EComHR *Marcella Sands and Robert Sands* v. *the UK*, 14 October 1981 (struck out).

[203] See EComHR *S., R., A. and C.* v. *Portugal*, 15 March 1984 (inadm.); *Vakalis* v. *Greece* (petitioner was in deteriorating health resulting from hunger strike; the provisional measure of 3 April 1992 did not aim for his release, but it did address both the State and the petitioner), 15 January 1993 (struck from the role upon release) and *Ilijkov* v. *Bulgaria* (complaint about continue pre-trial detention and the conditions in which he was force-fed; provisional measure of 20 October 1997 only to the petitioner to stop his hunger strike; Article 31 Report of 29 October 1998; Judgment of 26 July 2001). The Court has confirmed the Commission's approach, see e.g. ECtHR *Ilaşcu and others* v. *Moldova and Russia*, 8 July 2004, §11 and ECtHR *Taner Tanyeri et al.* v. *Turkey*, 6 December 2005 (struck out). In May and June 2001 the three petitioners in this case started a hunger strike protesting their solitary confinement in so-called F-type prison cells in Turkey. In August they applied to the Court for provisional measures under Rule 39 requesting the Court to order that their detention in these F-type prison cells cease. A month later the President of the Chamber notified the Government of the respondent Party of the introduction of the application under Rule 40 of the Rules of Court and 'invited the applicants, under Rule 39 of the Rules of Court, to discontinue their hunger strike'. In May 2002 the Court was informed by the representative of the petitioners that they had suspended their hunger strike and that they had been released from detention. See also *Rodić et al.* v. *Bosnia and Herzegovina*, 27 May 2008. On 24 June one of the petitioners and on 29 June 2005 the other three were 'invited' under Rule 39 to end their hunger strike; they did so on 1 July 2005; on 13 September 2005 the case was granted priority under Rule 41, see §4. See further Chapter XIII (Protection), section 4.

[204] See Press release ECtHR 412, 'Fact-finding mission to Turkey in hunger-strike cases', 6 September 2004, referring to this case and '52 other cases'. A report by the Human Rights Foundation of Turkey, September 2004, notes that the ECtHR delegation examined 54 prisoners at the hospital of Istanbul University. The report specifically named petitioners Yanick, Gençay, Balyemez, Kör, Kuruçay, Gürbüz, Uyan, Yildiz and Hun. With regard to Balyemez it noted that

2.6 Access to health care for death row inmates?

In light of its practice of using informal provisional measures enquiring about the health situation of political detainees, sometimes specifically requesting the State to take positive measures, it is interesting to note that the HRC never used such measures on behalf of death row inmates. After all, in some of the death penalty cases there is an apparent lack of medical assistance. On the merits the HRC often specifically recommended, as part of the remedy, the humane treatment of the petitioner in detention. While provisional measures were used in the following cases they were only meant to halt the petitioner's execution and not to intervene to ensure medical assistance. While certain requests by the HRC to the State for information may have triggered changes in treatment or access to medication, there are no known cases of informal provisional measures comparable to those used on behalf of political (and immigration) detainees. One death row prisoner, for instance, asked the HRC whether it could assist him in convincing the Commissioner of Prisons to transfer him to a cell where there was adequate natural light. The Secretariat noted: "I regret to inform you that the Centre for Human Rights is not in a position to request the prison authorities to place you in another cell. You are kindly advised to bring your complaints to the Commissioner of Prisons".[205]

As noted, it has found violations of Articles 7 and 10(1) in relation to ill treatment on death row that included lack of medical attention. A case in point is *Henry and Douglas* v. *Jamaica* (1996).[206] Henry was kept in a cold cell after being diagnosed with cancer and Douglas after he incurred medical problems caused by a gunshot wound. The HRC found that the conditions of incarceration under which Henry continued to be held until his death, 'even after the prison authorities were aware of his terminal illness' and the lack of medical attention to Douglas' gunshot wound, constituted a violation of Articles 7 and 10(1).[207] It would have been possible, at an earlier stage, to take provisional measures to request medical treatment on their behalf, had the HRC been inclined to do so in death penalty cases.

In other cases the Committee only found a violation of Article 10(1). An example is *Hamilton* v. *Jamaica* (1999).[208] In this case the petitioner had been shot in the lower area of his spine by a police officer after a hearing by a Magistrate as part of the preliminary enquiry. He became paralysed in both legs and was unable to move from his cell, unless he was carried by other inmates. He was also unable to remove his slop bucket (serving as a toilet) from the cell himself and had therefore been obliged to pay other inmates to remove it. Sometimes he was forced to remain in his cell until he had obtained the necessary funds. Counsel submitted that the petitioner's rights under Artsicles 7 and 10 of the Covenant were being violated, because the failure of the prison authorities to take into account his paralysed condition and to make proper arrangements for him.

---

the Court had already taken provisional measures on 5 February 2004 to halt his re-imprisonment. See also provisional measures not to re-imprison in the cases of Hun Kuruçay, Gürbüz, Uyan and Yildiz, all following the fact-finding mission of September 2004, Report Human Rights Foundation of Turkey, <www.tihv.org.tr/report/2004_09/septprison.html>, §4.1. On the merits see e.g. ECtHR *Yildiz* v. *Turkey*, 20 October 2005. See also Chapter XV (Immediacy and risk) on the fact-finding mission dealing with the compatibility with Articles 2 and 3 of their continued detention, section 3.2.5. Generally on hunger strikes in Turkey, see Sevinç (2008).

[205] HRC Letter by the HRC Secretariat of 12 March 1993 (on file with the author).

[206] HRC *Henry and Douglas* v. *Jamaica*, 25 July 1996.

[207] It observed that 'the issues raised in the initial communication concerning lack of medical treatment and unsatisfactory conditions of detention relate directly to the circumstances of Henry's death'. The Committee considered that, in the circumstances, counsel had standing to continue his representation on the communication despite the fact that Henry had died.

[208] HRC *Zephiniah Hamilton* v. *Jamaica*, 23 July 1999.

This 'lack of proper care'[209] was also said to be a violation of the UN Standard Minimum Rules for the Treatment of Prisoners. The Committee found a violation of Article 10(1).[210]

Not only in case of disability or terminal illness would medical treatment be required but also, for instance, in case of allergies with serious consequences.[211] In *Brown* v. *Jamaica* (1999)[212] the petitioner had claimed that the warders had destroyed his belongings, including an asthma pump and other medication and that he had been denied assistance in case of an asthma attack.[213] When the petitioner brings specific allegations that the prison conditions cause serious detriment to his health and that he did not receive medical treatment, despite repeated requests, or that the authorities made it impossible to keep the appointment for an operation, the HRC indeed finds a violation of Article 10(1).[214] It often notes in such cases that the State party had not refuted these specific allegations, nor forwarded any results of the announced investigation into the allegations. Sometimes the HRC not only finds a violation of Article 10 in this respect but also of Article 7. In one case the petitioner had stated that the sanitary conditions of the prison 'are dreadful, that the quality and quantity of the food is grossly inadequate and that he has been denied access to non-legal mail'. Moreover, he had stated that he had been subjected to inadequate medi-

---

[209] Note that the HRC uses the same terminology here as the ECtHR (in non-refoulement cases), or repeats terminology used by counsel, see Chapter V.

[210] In yet other cases the HRC found that the evidentiary requirements for a claim of denial of medical treatment had not been fulfilled. It noted, for instance, that 'the State party observes that its investigations showed that the author *did* receive treatment for his arthritic condition, while the author denies that *any* treatment was provided. In the circumstances, the Committee considers that a violation of Article 10 in this respect has not been established'. HRC *Tony Jones* v. *Jamaica*, 6 April 1998. The State party had asserted that its investigations had shown that 'within the resources available the author was treated for his arthritis'. Counsel had observed that the authorities were informed of the petitioner's arthritic condition in September 1994 and 1995 and in August 1996. "In spite of visits by the Inspector (of Prisons) in April and September 1996, Mr. Jones has still not received any medications for his arthritic condition".

[211] In one case counsel had claimed that the petitioner was allergic to dust and to the paint used in St. Catherine Prison and that his allergy provoked attacks of asthma and burning eyes. He claimed that he did not receive any treatment for this. The petitioner had also described the conditions of detention on death row as inhumane and degrading and claimed that he was beaten on two specific occasions and did not receive medical attention for his injuries. Since the State party had not answered to any of these allegations, the Committee considered that due weight must be given to the petitioner's claims. It found that the treatment to which he had been subjected and the conditions of detention as described by him constituted a violation of Articles 7 and 10(1) ICCPR. HRC *Beresford Whyte* v. *Jamaica*, 27 July 1998.

[212] HRC *Christopher Brown* v. *Jamaica*, 23 March 1999.

[213] If the petitioner had not provided any further information regarding a claim, the HRC will dismiss it for lack of substantiation. See e.g. HRC *Everton Morrison* v. *Jamaica*, 27 July 1998; (lack of substantiation that the difficulties in obtaining proper treatment for deteriorating eyesight amounted to violation of Article 10(1)).

[214] See e.g. HRC *Clarence Marshall* v. *Jamaica*, 3 November 1998. In this case it is not clear why the unsanitary prison conditions, the lack of medical treatment and especially treatment such as being hit in the side by a warden 'to such an extent that he was taken to the prison surgeon', only amounted to a violation of Article 10(1) and not of Article 7 as well. *Nicholas Henry* v. *Jamaica*, 20 October 1998; *Conroy Levy* v. *Jamaica*, 3 November 1998 and *Leroy Morgan and Samuel Williams* v. *Jamaica*, 3 November 1998.

cal attention, which had caused the loss of his sight in one eye.[215] The HRC found that these circumstances disclosed a violation of Articles 7 and 10(1) ICCPR.[216]

In *Leslie* v. *Jamaica* (1998)[217] the HRC noted that the petitioner had made very precise allegations about various beatings and deplorable conditions of detention. Among others, he claimed to have been the victim of several assaults. He reported these assaults to the prison authorities and repeatedly requested medical attention to no avail. He wrote to the prison Ombudsman and was finally taken to hospital early 1992. He claimed that warders had told him on several occasions 'that there was no point in providing him with medical treatment, because he was about to be executed'. He submitted that this cost him 'great embarrassment and depression'. He also submitted (providing dates and times) that a warder harassed him, reportedly because he had complained about his treatment to the Ombudsman and the 'Human Rights Office'. He further alleged that a warder had stuck a finger in his eye and kicked him several times.[218] The HRC found violations of Articles 7 and 10(1).[219]

These cases indicate the *range* of detention situations in which the HRC could have used (informal) provisional measures. The Committee's attitude towards reparation for violations relating to conditions of detention and access to medical assistance is important as well.[220]

In *Neptune* v. *Trinidad and Tobago* (1996)[221] the HRC found that the victim should be released for the violation of Article 14. It also found violations of Articles 9(3) and 10(1). Pending this release it expected the immediate improvement of the circumstances of his detention. In order to avoid similar violations in the future, it also recommended the State party to improve the general conditions of detention. This fits into the specific form of reparation called 'assurances of non-repetition'. The HRC normally refers to this type of reparation simply by noting the obliga-

---

[215] The State party had not refuted 'the specific allegations' and had not, 'in spite of its explicit promise' and the principle in Article 4(2) OP, forwarded results of the investigation. *Errol Smith and Oval Stewart* v. *Jamaica*, 8 April 1999.

[216] A related issue is that of access to medical records. In HRC *Zheludkova* v. *Ukraine* 29 October 2002 (no Rule 86) the HRC considered that Article 10(1) had been violated because of the 'consistent and unexplained denial of access to medical records'. Rivas Posada, Ando and Bhagwati disagreed with this, considering that the interpretation of Article 10(1) should not be stretched that far. Medina Quiroga, however, considered that the Committee's reasoning 'excessively restricts' the interpretation of Article 10(1) 'by linking the violation of that provision to the possible relevance which the victim's access to the medical records might have had for the medical treatment that he received in prison'. She pointed out that the right to have access to medical records 'forms part of the right of all individuals to have access to personal information concerning them'. She considered that the denial of the victim's request for access to the medical records in itself constituted a violation of the right in Article 10 to be 'treated with humanity and with respect for the inherent dignity of the human person', independent from the question 'whether or not this refusal may have had consequences for the medical treatment of the victim'.

[217] HRC *Junior Leslie* v. *Jamaica*, 31 July 1998.

[218] Allegedly the same warder subjected him to further physical and verbal abuse on subsequent dates. The HRC pointed out that the State party had not contested this 'except to say some 14 months later that it would investigate'.

[219] In later cases with regard to prison conditions the HRC would only find violations of Article 10(1). It would point out that it was not necessary to consider separately the claims arising under Article 7, because Article 10 specifically 'deals with the situation of persons deprived of their liberty and encompasses the elements set out generally in article 7'. This may still be different in situations where petitioners have been beaten. *Devon Simpson* v. *Jamaica*, 31 October 2001. See also *R. S.* v. *Trinidad and Tobago*, 2 April 2002.

[220] For examples of cases in which provisional measures were indeed used see Chapter XIII on the relationship between provisional measures and possible forms of reparation.

[221] HRC *Clyde Neptune* v. *Trinidad and Tobago*, 16 July 1996.

tion to ensure that similar violations do not occur in the future. In this case it also gave a recommendation on how to do this, namely by improving the general conditions of detention. In subsequent cases this form of reparation (assurances of non-repetition) could lay a foundation for taking provisional measures to intervene in certain prison situations with a specific impact on a petitioner.[222] The immediate improvement of the circumstances of detention pending release, as a form of specific reparation upon the finding of a violation, may serve as additional argument for the use of provisional measures, to intervene in certain detention circumstances threatening irreparable harm, also on death row. In *Henry and Douglas* v. *Jamaica* (1996)[223] the HRC considered that, in the circumstances, counsel was allowed to continue his representation despite the fact that Henry had died. It observed that 'the issues raised in the initial communication concerning lack of medical treatment and unsatisfactory conditions of detention relate directly to the circumstances of Mr. Henry's death'. Subsequently Jamaica indicated that it had ordered an investigation into the complaints that medical attention had been denied to the petitioners. In relation to this issue, counsel had argued that the abuse of convicted prisoners had been a common occurrence for at least 20 years and that the fear of reprisals prevented prisoners from submitting official complaints. The HRC noted that the State party had not contested the allegation that Henry was being kept in a cold cell after being diagnosed for cancer nor that Douglas had received insufficient medical attention for a gunshot wound. It found violations of Articles 7 and 10(1). Pursuant to Article 2(3)(a) ICCPR it pointed out that Douglas was entitled to an effective remedy entailing compensation for the conditions of his detention, in particular for the inadequate medical attention he received for his gunshot wound. It reaffirmed that the obligation in Article 10 to treat individuals deprived of their liberty with respect for their inherent dignity 'encompasses the provision of adequate medical care during detention; this obligation, obviously, extends to persons under sentence of death'. In this particular case the HRC could have used provisional measures to intervene pending the case to allow Eustace Henry, who was in the final stages of cancer, to die in more humane circumstances and it could have requested the State as well to provide medical attention to Everald Douglas. Such measures would be similar to those it used on behalf of political prisoners.[224]

In *R. S.* v. *Trinidad and Tobago* (2002)[225] the HRC noted the information provided by counsel, showing 'that the author's mental state at the time of the reading of the death warrants was obvious to those around him and should have been apparent to the prison authorities'. The State had not contested this information. In the circumstances, issuing a warrant for the author's execution constituted a violation of Article 7.[226]

---

[222] See the provisional measures by the IACHR and ECtHR in the context of detention.
[223] HRC *Henry and Douglas* v. *Jamaica*, 25 July 1996.
[224] Another case in point is *Williams* v. *Jamaica* (1997), 4 November 1997. In this case the HRC found violations of Articles 7 and 10(1) for failure to provide medical treatment for the victim's mental condition while on death row. An effective remedy included, in particular, an entitlement to appropriate medical treatment. In relation to the finding of violations of Articles 7 and 10(1) in *Nicholas Henry* v. *Jamaica*, 20 October 1998, the State party was equally obliged to provide the petitioner with an effective remedy 'including immediate medical examination and treatment if necessary, compensation, and consideration for early release'.
[225] HRC *R. S.* v. *Trinidad and Tobago*, 2 April 2002. Since it had no further information about his state of mental health at the earlier stages of the proceedings it was not in a position to decide whether the State had also violated Article 6 ICCPR. It also found a violation of Article 10 because of prison conditions. At the time of the View the victim's death sentence had already been commuted. As a form of reparation the HRC mentioned appropriate medical and psychiatric care and improvement of conditions of detention in accordance with Article 10 or release.
[226] HRC *R. S.* v. *Trinidad and Tobago*, 2 April 2002. *McCordie Morrison* v. *Jamaica,* 3 November 1998, related to ongoing illness in prison. The petitioner developed synovitis, which caused

Questions have also been raised on the circumstances of the death of one of the petitioners involved in *Champagnie, Palmer and Chisholm* v. *Jamaica* (1994).[227] In letters to the HRC inmates pointed out they were frightened and concerned over his death, mainly because the cause was unknown. They noted that inmates serving longer sentences apparently were not entitled to go the hospital 'on the outside'. They mentioned certain guards who, they considered, should not have a medical function at the prison clinic. Some of them also noted that whenever an ex-death row inmate complained about something the guards would tell them that they should have hanged them.[228] In *Khomidov* v. *Tajikistan* (2004) the HRC had used provisional measures in September 2002. In March 2004 the petitioner informed the Committee that she had met her son and found him in bad health and adverse psychological condition. 'He was very nervous, shouted throughout the meeting, and stated that he could no longer live in such uncertainty and prefer to be executed'. She also referred to several health problems for which he received no medical assistance or examination. The HRC did not comment on this in its decision on he merits and did not refer to medical assistance as part of the remedy.[229]

---

swelling of the joints. In its final View the HRC found that the State party had failed to provide additional information, despite its promise to do so. Again it recalled that States are under an obligation to conduct a serious investigation of alleged violations of the ICCPR made under the OP procedure. It referred to *Herrera Rubio* v. *Colombia*, 2 November 1987. It specified that this entails 'forwarding the outcome of the investigations to the Committee, in detail and without undue delay'. "Consequently, due weight must be given to the author's allegation that he was denied medical treatment, and the Committee finds that the lack of medical treatment to the author constitutes a violation of article 10 of the Covenant". It did not mention provision of medical treatment as part of the remedy, probably because it recommended release. *Devon Simpson* v. *Jamaica*, 31 October 2001, related to prison conditions. As a remedy for the violation of Article 10 the HRC referred to 'adequate compensation, an improvement in the present conditions of detention and due consideration of early release'. By this time the HRC had changed its approach, pointing out that in detention situations it was sufficient to refer to Article 10. It was not necessary anymore to mention Article 7 as well. It would have been feasible to use Rule 86 in relation to disability and prison conditions. In *Hamilton* v. *Jamaica* (1999), the case by the petitioner who was paralysed, the HRC found violations of Articles 9(3), 14(3)(c) and 10(1) and considered that the State party was under an obligation to provide the victim with 'an effective remedy, entailing compensation and placement in conditions that take full account of his disability'. *Zephiniah Hamilton* v. *Jamaica*, 23 July 1999. Between the issuance of provisional measures and the final View, the death sentence had been commuted.

227   HRC *Champagnie, Palmer and Chisholm* v. *Jamaica*, 18 July 1994.
228   In this case the HRC found violations of the right of appeal. Palmer had been transferred from death row to the general penitentiary. He died in May 1994. The HRC did not mention this in its View of July 1994, but in September of that year his counsel provided it with information and suggested it to make representations to the Government in relation to his death. The information consisted of several letters of inmates received by the Jamaica Council for Human Rights. His fellow inmates pointed out that Palmer had been feeling sick already for a month. His condition worsened on 6 May after lunch. He was only brought to the hospital section of the prison where he was given some 'yellow colour pills'. On the morning of 7 May the inmates were told he had died. Allegedly guards had tried to force a prisoner to give him an injection, which this prisoner refused to do. He said to the guards: "You nuh see that the man sick bad and a hospital the man fe go". The officer's response was: "A dead him fi dead". It was also noted that Palmer was bawling the whole night. Counsel received this information on 16 September and sent it to the HRC by letter of 26 September 1994 (on file with the author).
229   HRC *Bakhrom Khomidov* (*submitted by his mother Saodat Khomidova*) v. *Tajikistan*, 29 July 2004.

Thus far the HRC has never used provisional measures in order to remedy detention situations for prisoners on death row (such as relating to a deteriorating health situation), although it has sometimes suggested such measures in decisions on the merits. One reason for this may be that the Secretariat only consults the Special Rapporteur on New Communications to initiate the case for registration and for any provisional measures taken. It may also consult this Rapporteur to follow-up on provisional measures already taken, e.g. upon information of a new execution date. However, it generally does not consult the Rapporteur on New Communications when it receives information relating to threats or lack of medical treatment. It simply prepares this information for the Committee member assigned to the case when it will be discussed on admissibility and merits.[230]

Obviously, not only in response to claims of lack of medical attention for political prisoners or death row inmates, but also in detention situations of other persons an argument for the use of provisional measures could be made.[231]

3 RELATION BETWEEN PROVISIONAL MEASURES TO INTERVENE IN DETENTION SITUATIONS AND THE EXPECTED DECISION ON THE MERITS

3.1 Introduction

As the chapters on executions, expulsion and disappearances have already dealt extensively with the relationship between provisional measures and the eventual decision on the merits involving

---

[230] In April 2003 the Special Rapporteur indicated his intention to request the Secretariat to start contacting him with information relating to new threats of irreparable harm in pending cases. Interview by author with HRC Special Rapporteur Scheinin, Geneva, April 2003.

[231] The case of Patterson Matthews serves as an example. He had submitted a complaint not about the fact that he had been sentenced to corporal punishment but about, among others, the deterioration of his eyesight and the lack of access to medical care. The HRC transmitted the case under Rule 91 more than two months after submission. The Rapporteur did not request specific information in relation to the condition of his eye and the medical assistance he received in this regard. The petitioner attributed the lack of medical attention to the fact that he had written about an incident in the prison in November 1988 in which prison warders had killed an inmate. In April 1995 the HRC decided, under Rule 91, to request the State party to provide copies of the petitioner's medical file at the prison as well as his medical file at the eye clinic. It also requested the petitioner to provide more detailed information about the treatment he received for his eye disease and, 'in particular, whether he was ever operated on, or whether an operation was recommended, after May 1991. *Patterson Matthews* v. *Trinidad and Tobago*, 4 April 1995. In its admissibility decision of October 1995 the HRC noted that it had not received a reply from the State party, despite a reminder sent to it of that year. It recalled that it was implicit in the OP that States make available to the HRC all information at their disposal and it regretted the lack of cooperation. Nevertheless, it noted that it appeared from the file that the petitioner had visited the eye clinic regularly and that he underwent an eye operation between March and May 1992. Despite the fact that it had this information already when it requested the State to provide it with the medical file, it considered that the petitioner had failed to advance a claim under Article 2 OP. *Patterson Matthews* v. *Trinidad and Tobago*, 13 October 1995 (adm.), CCPR/C/55/D/569/1993, 25 October 1995 (initial submission 12 October 1993; Rule 91 of 5 January 1994; unpublished document on file with the author). See also *Boodoo* v. *Trinidad and Tobago*, 2 April 2002 (claim about prison conditions, including that a physician recommended his placement in a brightly-lit room in order to prevent the blindness that had begun to set in, and assaults/death threat as a result of his correspondence with the UN Centre for Human Rights, only Rule 91, no Rule 86).

the right to life and personal integrity, this section addresses this issue only briefly. In cases involving provisional measures on behalf of detainees the relevant rights are those involving the right to life (Article 6 ICCPR; Article 4 ACHR; Article 4 ACHPR; Article 2(1) ECHR), the prohibition of torture and ill-treatment (Article 7 ICCPR; Articles 4, 11 and 16 ICAT; Article 5(2) ACHR; Article 5 ACHPR; Article 3 ECHR) and humane treatment in detention (Article 10 ICCPR).[232] Rather than discussing detention rights in general, this section simply refers to some case law that could shed light on the use of provisional measures on behalf of detainees.

3.2   HRC

From the start of its activities the HRC has faced many ongoing detention situations involving risks to health and safety. It has pointed out that Article 10 'applies to any one deprived of liberty under the laws and authority of the State who is held in prisons, hospitals-particularly psychiatric hospitals-detention camps or correctional institutions or elsewhere'.[233] It has often found a violation of both Articles 7 and 10(1) without making a clear distinction between the two. Article 10(1) complements Article 7 ICCPR and both articles impose positive obligations. However, there have been some cases that dealt with Article 10 (1) on its own without also finding a violation of Article 7.[234]

The HRC has reaffirmed that Article 10(1) 'encompasses the provision of, *inter alia*, adequate medical care during detention'. It also considered that the provision of basic sanitary facilities equally fell within the ambit of Article 10. "The Committee further considers that the provi-

---

[232]   Article 10 ICCPR stipulates: "1. All persons deprived of their liberty shall be treated with humanity and with respect for the inherent dignity of the human person. 2. (a) Accused persons shall, save in exceptional circumstances, be segregated from convicted persons and shall be subject to separate treatment appropriate to their status as unconvicted persons; (b) Accused juvenile persons shall be separated from adults and brought as speedy as possible for adjudication. 3. The penitentiary system shall comprise treatment of prisoners the essential aim of which shall be their reformation and social rehabilitation. Juvenile offenders shall be segregated from adults and be accorded treatment appropriate to their age and legal status". See also, e.g., Articles 37 and 25 Children's Convention, Standard Minimum Rules for the Treatment of Prisoners (First UN Congress on the Prevention of Crime and the Treatment of Offenders, Geneva 1955; approved by the Economic and Social Council, resolutions 663 C (XXIV), 31 July 1957 and 2076 (LXII), 13 May 1977); Body of Principles for the Protection of All Persons under Any Form of Detention or Imprisonment (General Assembly res. 43/173, 9 December 1988); United Nations Standard Minimum Rules for the Administration of Juvenile Justice ("The Beijing Rules"; GA res. 40/33, 29 November 1985); in general see e.g. Penal Reform International (2001) and Medina Quiroga (2005).

[233]   HRC General Comment 21 on the right to humane treatment in detention (Article 10), 10 April 1992.

[234]   In HRC *Valentini de Bazzano (also on behalf of her husband Bazzano Ambrosini, her stepfather Massera and her mother Valentini de Massera)* v. *Uruguay*, 15 August 1979, the Committee found that prolonged incommunicado detention violated Article 10(1), §37. A few years later, in a case against Panama, it determined that the detention of the petitioner in a special cell with a mentally disturbed prisoner violated Article 10(1). *Wolf* v. *Panama*, 26 March 1992. Moreover, in a case against Hungary the Committee found that limiting exercise and hygiene periods to five minutes a day violated Article 10(1). See HRC *Parkanyi* v. *Hungary*, 27 July 1992. As a last example, in *Abdool Saleem Yasseen and Noel Thomas* v. *Republic of Guyana*, 30 March 1998, detainees were required to share mattresses and were deprived of natural lighting except for their one hour of daily recreation. This constituted a violation of Article 10(1) as well.

sion of inadequate food to detained individuals and the total absence of recreational facilities does not, save under exceptional circumstances, meet the requirements of Article 10".[235]

Just like the UN Standard Minimum Rules for the Treatment of Prisoners,[236] Article 10 ICCPR sets some very basic minimum standards that fall below, for instance, those of the Committee to the European Convention against Torture. These minimum standards must be safeguarded 'regardless of a State party's level of development'. This means that 'lack of resources' is no excuse.[237] The Inter-American Commission, the African Commission and the ECtHR have expressed themselves similarly.[238] The Inter-American Commission, for instance, has pointed out that the minimum standards laid down in Article 5 ACHR 'apply irrespective of the nature of the conduct for which a particular individual had been imprisoned'.[239] They must be satisfied, moreover, 'even if the economic or budgetary circumstances of a State Party may render compliance difficult'.[240] This case law on the positive obligations of States to guarantee minimum standards of detention, including access to health care, also underlies the use of provisional measures pending detention cases.

Sometimes a complaint submitted to the HRC refers to Article 10(3) ICCPR.[241] The main message of Article 10(3) is that 'no penitentiary system should be merely retributory'. Each peni-

---

[235] HRC *Paul Kelly* v. *Jamaica*, 8 April 1991. See also *Daniel Pinto* v. *Trinidad and Tobago*, 20 July 1990.

[236] Standard Minimum Rules for the Treatment of Prisoners (resolution 1955/1977 adopted by the First United Nations Congress on the Prevention of Crime and the Treatment of Offenders, 30 August 1955; approved by United Nations Economic and Social Council resolution 663 C (XXIV) of 31 July 1957; and amended by ECOSOC resolution 2076 (LXII) of 13 May 1977) (a new rule 95 was added). See also: Body of Principles for the Protection of All Persons under any form of Detention or Imprisonment, adopted by the General Assembly, 9 December 1988, Resolution 43/173; Principles of Medical Ethics relevant to the role of Health Personnel, particularly Physicians, in the protection of prisoners and detainees against torture and other cruel, inhuman or degrading treatment or punishment, Adopted by the General Assembly of the United Nations on 18 December 1982, resolution 37/194; Code of Conduct for Law Enforcement Officials, adopted by United Nations General Assembly resolution 34/169 of 17 December 1979.

[237] The HRC determined this in a case against Cameroon, in which it also referred to the aforementioned Standard Minimum Rules for the Treatment of Prisoners: "It should be noted that these are minimum requirements which the Committee considers should always be observed, even if economic or budgetary conditions may make compliance with these obligations difficult". HRC *Albert Womah Mukong* v. *Cameroon*, 8 July 1992, §9.3.

[238] On other case law of these adjudicators see later in this section.

[239] CIDH *Damion Thomas* v. *Jamaica*, 4 April 2001 (merits), §37. The Commission points out that the ECtHR takes a similar approach: *Ahmed* v. *Austria*, Judgment of 17 December 1996, §38.

[240] CIDH *Damion Thomas* v. *Jamaica*, 4 April 2001 (merits), §37. The Commission referred here to its previous case law including *Baptiste* v. *Grenada*, Final Report 38/00, 13 April 2000, §136.

[241] Regarding political detainees see HRC *Vasilskis* v. *Uruguay*, 31 March 1983 and *Oxandabarat Scarrone* v. *Uruguay*, 4 November 1983. In *Vasilskis* the petitioner alleged on behalf of his sister 'that the penitentiary system is not aimed at reformation and social rehabilitation of prisoners but at the destruction of their will to resist. They are given a number and are never called by their name. Elena Beatriz Vasilskis is No. 433 of Sector B. Psychological pressures on the inmates are allegedly designed to lead them to denounce other inmates'. Two years later, on 20 March 1985, the victim's brother informed the Committee about her release. By note of 25 March 1985 the State party itself informed the Committee about her release on 12 March 1985 on the basis of the amnesty act of 8 March 1985, which it confirmed by note of 31 October 1991. In *Oxandabarat Scarrone* a Uruguayan national living in Spain submitted, on 30 June 1981, a complaint on behalf of her father, detained in Uruguay. The complaint included specific allegations relating to her father's health, including the statement of a medical doctor who had himself been detained at

tentiary system should 'essentially seek the reformation and social rehabilitation of the prisoner'.[242]

In this respect, when examining State reports, the Committee expects to receive information on work and education programmes and post release programmes, but it has never really addressed this issue as part of an individual complaint, nor has it used provisional measures specifically in this context.

The HRC considers that there are elements in certain provisions of the ICCPR that could not be made subject to lawful derogation under Article 4, even though those provisions themselves are not listed in Article 4(2). It has mentioned some 'illustrative examples'. These indicate the importance the HRC attaches to certain rights in the Covenant. It referred to the obligation, in Article 10, to treat all persons deprived of their liberty with humanity and with respect for the inherent dignity of the human person. This article expressed 'a norm of general international law not subject to derogation'. This is 'supported by the reference to the inherent dignity of the human person in the preamble to the Covenant and by the close connection between articles 7 and 10'.[243] The Committee's provisional measures based on Article 10, relating to the health of detainees, reflect this awareness of the irreparable nature of violations of this article, as discussed in the previous section.

The HRC has often dealt with complaints by death row prisoners about their conditions of detention. These complaints are often based upon Articles 7 and 10 ICCPR and involve beatings, threats and ill treatment upon arrest or in pre-trial detention. Thus far it has not used provisional measures to halt torture and ill treatment pending such cases. Some complaints have dealt not so much with inhumane conditions of detention as such, but rather with the death row phenomenon as a form of cruel treatment. The HRC has often declared them inadmissible because they were not properly raised in the domestic proceedings.[244] It declared other claims inadmissible for insufficient substantiation.[245] In such cases it has never used provisional measures either.

Libertad prison. He had examined several prisoners there, including the alleged victim. The report stated that the petitioner's father had suffered a cranioencephalic traumatism in 1976-1977. Since then his 'faculty of perceiving time and space is impaired'. She also alleged that 'the prison regime to which her father is subjected is not designed to produce any kind of reform of rehabilitation but aims at psychological and physical annihilation'.

[242] HRC General Comment 21 on the right to humane treatment (Article 10), 10 April 1992.

[243] HRC General Comment 29 on states of emergency (Article 4), 24 July 2001.

[244] HRC *Beresford Whyte* v. *Jamaica*, 27 July 1998 (Medina Quiroga and Scheinin dissenting, considering respectively that the claim of beatings should have been dealt with on the merits and that a violation of Article 7 should have been established).

[245] See e.g. HRC *Samuel Thomas* v. *Jamaica*, 31 March 1999. The petitioner had claimed that he was badly beaten by police officers or threatened with further physical violence. Jamaica informed the Committee that it had been unable to investigate the petitioner's allegation 'in the absence of additional information, such as the place where the author was held, the time at which the incident allegedly occurred and if possible the name(s) of the officers involved'. The Committee noted that the allegations in relation to the treatment while he was in police detention were very vague and it considered that it was incumbent upon an alleged victim to provide sufficient information so that a State party may investigate an allegation. The HRC also noted that the State party did in fact request additional information in order to investigate the claims. It found that the information provided by the author and his counsel was insufficient for the State party to be able to adequately investigate the matter. Although this position seems clear, it could have asked the State party why it did not know the place where the petitioner was held. While in the absence of additional information the State party cannot be expected to know how to investigate allegations, a State party should be able to find out in which place it has held a person in police detention. About the consequences of failure of counsel during the hearing before the

In a case against Georgia the Committee found the State responsible for severe beatings and physical and moral pressure. This included concussion and broken bones, wounding and burning, scarring, torture and threats to family members.[246] It is acknowledged internationally that not only physical treatment can amount to torture and ill treatment, but also psychological pressure. As Rodley explains in his standard work on the treatment of prisoners in international law, psychological torture is more sophisticated than physical torture in that it leaves little physical trace. Examples of psychological torture are: deprivation of light, deprivation of darkness, deprivation of sound or sleep, general disorientation, threats of mutilation or death, mock execution and, of course, the threat that physical abuses will be extended to persons close to the prisoner.[247] On the basis of its traditional jurisprudence, if the HRC would find a violation of Articles 7 and 10 this would not warrant 'an appropriate remedy including commutation'.[248] Apart from a few cases involving corporal punishment,[249] as of yet there are no known cases in which the HRC intervened to put an end to (psychological) torture and ill treatment pending the proceedings.

3.3   Inter-American system

The law of the Inter-American system is comparable to Article 7 jo. 10 ICCPR as Article 5 ACHR not only prohibits torture and ill treatment but also provides that every person has the right to respect for his physical, mental and moral integrity. Among others, the Inter-American Court has pointed out that '(i)n the context of health care institutions, whether they are public or private centers, the staff in charge of the care of patients exercise a strong control or dominance over persons who are under their custody. The intrinsic imbalance in power between hospitalized patients and the persons having authority over them is usually greater in psychiatric institutions'.[250] It also noted that 'the personal features of an alleged victim of torture or cruel, inhuman, or degrading treatment should be taken into consideration when determining whether his or her personal integrity has been violated, for such features may change the insight of his or her individual reality and, therefore, increase the suffering and the sense of humiliation when the person is subjected to certain types of treatment'.[251]

With regard to persons deprived of their liberty Article 5 ACHR provides in particular that they shall be treated with respect to their inherent dignity.[252] Among others, it stipulates that

---

[246] domestic court to substantiate the assault, as well as the lack of medical documents corroborating the assault see also *Clarence Marshall* v. *Jamaica*, 3 November 1998.
HRC *Victor Domukovsky, Zaza Tsiklauri, Petre Gelbakhiani and Irakli Dokvadze* v. *Georgia*, 6 April 1998.

[247] See Rodley (1999), p. 10. It is troubling to note that prisoners in the US cannot appeal to even a domestic court when they are subjected to psychological torture (Prison Litigation Reform Act (1996)). See e.g. Tushnet/Yackle (1997) and Robertson (2000). About the importance of access to Court and counsel, also to prevent ill-treatment, see e.g. the precautionary measures by the Inter-American Commission with regard to the extraterritorial detention by the U.S. at Guantanamo, see Chapter VIII (Procedural rights).

[248] See the discussion about the relationship between provisional measures and the decision on reparation in Chapter XIII.

[249] See Chapter XII (Other situations), section 2.

[250] IACHR *Ximenes-Lopes* v. *Brazil*, Judgment of 4 July 2006, §107. See also §129 and §140.

[251] Id., §127.

[252] As the IACHR noted in *Neira Alegría et al.* (Peru), Judgment of 19 January 1995: "In essence, Article 5 refers to the rule that nobody should be subjected to torture or to cruel, inhuman, or degrading punishment or treatment, and that all persons deprived of their liberty must be treated with respect for the inherent dignity of the human person".

'(m)inors while subject to criminal proceedings shall be separated from adults and brought before specialised tribunals, as speedily as possible, so that they may be treated in accordance with their status as minors'. This special attention to minors has been important in the practice of the Inter-American system with regard to provisional measures. Article 5 ACHR also provides that '(p)unishments consisting of deprivation of liberty shall have as an essential aim the reform and social readaptation of the prisoners'. In the American Declaration of the Rights and Duties of Man provides in Article I: "Every human being has the right to life, liberty and security of his person". Article XXV lays down the right to humane treatment of everyone in custody and Article XXVI prohibits 'cruel, infamous or unusual punishment'.[253] In addition, in 2008 the Inter-American Commission adopted Principles and Best Practices on the Protection of Persons Deprived of Liberty in the Americas.[254]

The Inter-American Commission has often dealt with complaints about prison situations and the obligations of OAS member states. Section 2 has already discussed many Inter-American cases. What underlies these cases is the general approach of the Commission and Court towards the right to life and respect for personal integrity, which is in turn comparable to that of the other human rights adjudicators. The Court has pointed out that the right to life is fundamental to the ACHR, as all other rights depend upon it.[255] States have the obligation to guarantee the creation of the necessary conditions for the full exercise of this right. Moreover, the right to respect for personal integrity is of such importance that its protection is particularly emphasized in the ACHR, among others by the prohibition of torture, cruel, inhuman or degrading treatment and the impossibility to suspend this prohibition during times of emergency.[256] The right to life and respect for personal integrity do not just imply negative obligations, but positive obligations as well, in order for States to comply with the general obligation laid down in Article 1(1) ACHR.[257]

Apart from this general attention, the Court has pointed out the particular obligations vis-à-vis detainees.[258] Persons deprived of their liberty are in a special situation of powerlessness vis-à-vis the authorities so that States have a special obligation towards them.[259] The duty to adopt security measures 'is more evident since these persons are detained in the state detention centers, and under such circumstances the State plays a special role as guarantor of the rights of the persons that remain under its custody'.[260] Detainees have the right to live in conditions of detention

---

[253] In a resolution of 5 June 2001 the OAS General Assembly expressed its concern over the state of penitentiary systems and detention centres in various countries of the Americas. It noted that 'this situation hinders and can even prevent the social rehabilitation of convicts, which is the essential aim of prison sentences, according to the Pact of San José'. It pointed out that 'the topic of all aspects of health in prisons is part of the hemispheric agenda'. It only resolved, however, to instruct the Permanent Council to consider the advisability of a study on this issue. General Assembly Resolution 'Study of the rights and care of persons under any form of detention or imprisonment', 5 June 2001, AG/RES.1816 (XXXI-O/01).

[254] CIDH Resolution 1/08, 13 March 2008, OEA/Ser/L/V/II.131 doc. 26.

[255] See e.g. IACHR *"Instituto de Reeducación del Menor"* (Paraguay), Judgment of 2 September 2004, §156.

[256] Id., §157, referring to Articles 5 and 27 ACHR.

[257] Id., §158.

[258] See e.g. IACHR *Asunto de la Cárcel de Urso Branco* (Brasil), Resolución de 2 de mayo de 2008, 19th 'Considering' clause.

[259] IACHR *"Instituto de Reeducación del Menor"* (Paraguay), Judgment of 2 September 2004, §152. Significantly, the Court also refers to its Order for provisional measures in the *Gómez Paquiyauri brothers* case, Order of 7 May 2004, 13th 'Considering' clause.

[260] See IACHR *Matter of the persons imprisoned in the "Dr. Sebastião Martins Silveira" Penitentiary in Araraquara, São Paulo* (Brazil), Order of 30 September 2006, 11th 'Considering' clause, referring to *Matter of Children Deprived of Liberty in the "Complexo do Tatuapé" of FEBEM*, Order of 17 November 2005, 7th 'Considering' clause; *Matter of Urso Branco Prison,*

that are compatible with their personal dignity. The State has the obligation to respect and ensure their right to life and personal integrity.[261] It must do so, among others, by guaranteeing minimum conditions of detention compatible with their dignity.[262] As Judge García Ramírez has pointed out, the State cannot avoid the peremptory duty to 'protect the life and integrity of individuals who are subjected to its immediate, complete and constant control and lack, by themselves, the effective ability of self-determination and defence'.[263] In detention situations the role of the State as guarantor is particularly intense and it is thus reasonable to 'require that the State must avoid, immediately and absolutely, losing human lives as a consequence of violent conditions ruling in prisons, as the result of a direct action by State's agents, or as actions of other people, that the State should avoid and prevent'.[264]

The Court has also stressed that upon a finding of a violation the Court must, as a guarantee of non-repetition, 'take all necessary actions to allow prison conditions to conform to international standards'.[265]

The Court has also pointed out that the protection of the life of the child 'requires the State to pay special attention to the conditions of a child's life while it is deprived of liberty, because this right has not extinguished or been restricted owing to detention or imprisonment'.[266]

Previously, in a case against Honduras dealing with the detention of minors, the Commission referred to the Judgment of the Inter-American Court in *Neira Alegría*,[267] emphasising that the State is the institution responsible for detention establishments and the guarantor of the right to life and humane treatment of prisoners.[268] In this light the Commission elaborated on the position of detainees in general and the ensuing responsibility of the State.

> "[T]he State, by depriving a person of his liberty, places itself in the unique position of guarantor of his right to life and to humane treatment. When it detains an individual, the State introduces that individual into a "total institution" – such as a prison – where the various aspects of his life are subject to an established regimen; where the prisoner is removed from his natural and social milieu; where the established regimen is one of absolute control, a loss of privacy, limitation of living space and, above all, a radical decline in the individual's means of defending himself. All this means that the act of imprisonment carries with it a specific and material commitment to protect the prisoner's human dignity so long as that individual is in the custody of the State, which includes protecting him from possible circumstances that could imperil his life, health and personal integrity, among other rights".[269]

---

[261] Order of 21 September 2005, 6th 'Considering' clause; and *Matter of the Mendoza Prisons*, Order of 18 June 2005, 6th 'Considering' clause. See also e.g. *Matter of Capital El rodeo I and El Rodeo II Judicial Confinement Center*, Order of 8 February 2008, 11th 'Considering' clause.

[262] See e.g. IACHR *"Instituto de Reeducación del Menor"* (Paraguay), Judgment of 2 September 2004, §151 and *Hilaire, Constantine, Benjamin et al.*, Judgment of 21 June 2002, §165.

[263] IACHR *"Instituto de Reeducación del Menor"* (Paraguay), Judgment of 2 September 2004, §159.

[264] IACHR *Matter of Capital El Rodeo I and el Rodeo II Judicial Confinement Center*, Order of 8 February 2008, separate opinion Judge García Ramírez (joined by Judge Medina Quiroga), §15.

[265] Id., §16.

[266] See IACHR *Montero Arangunen et al.* (*Detention Center of Catia*) v. *Venezuela*, Judgment of 5 July 2006.

[267] IACHR *Bulacio* case, Judgment of 18 September 2003, §126 and *Matter of children deprived of liberty in the 'Complexo do Tataupé' of FEBEM*, Order of 4 July 2006, 9th 'Considering' clause and of 3 July 2007, 8th 'Considering' clause.

[268] IACHR *Neira Alegría et al.*, Judgment of 19 January 1995, §60.

[269] Given the reasoning this would also apply in case of privatization.

CIDH *Minors in detention* v. *Honduras*, 10 March 1999, §135.

According to Article XI American Declaration "Every person has the right to the preservation of his health through sanitary and social measures relating to food, clothing, housing and medical care, to the extent permitted by public and community resources". The Commission has emphasised that 'as the state exercises exclusive control over all aspects of a prisoner's life and well-being, it is subject to an enhanced obligation to supervise and secure for prisoners the minimum standards of humane treatment prescribed under Art. 5 of the Convention'.

In light of the specific commitment derived from the act of imprisonment, the Commission pointed out that the State had a specific obligation to protect prisoners from attacks by third parties including other inmates. If it failed to do so, it violated Article 5 ACHR and incurred international responsibility. This was all the more so with regard to prisoners who are defenceless or at a disadvantage, 'as in the case of juveniles'.[270] The Commission was very clear in this respect:

> "In the Commission's view, the State's duty to protect the personal integrity of any person deprived of liberty includes the obligation to take all measures necessary to prevent attacks and assaults against a prisoner by agents of the State or private individuals. These obligations become all the more compelling when juveniles are involved. In such cases, the State must not only endeavour to protect their personal integrity, but also to promote the full development of their personality and their reintegration into society".[271]

The Inter-American system has dealt extensively with the rights of minors in detention. It added to the general responsibility of the State to protect persons, and the specific responsibility to protect the personal integrity of persons in detention, the even greater responsibility to protect minors in detention. Thus the Inter-American Court has pointed out that when children are detained, the State has yet additional obligations under Art. 19 ACHR, taking into account the special position of children and the concept of 'best interest of the child'.[272] Articles 6 and 27 UN Children's Convention include in the right to life the obligation to 'ensure to the maximum extent possible the survival and development of the child'. The UN Committee supervising this Convention has interpreted the term 'development' broadly, encompassing the physical, mental, spiritual, moral, psychological and social.[273] In that light States have the obligation to ensure detained children are not deprived of their 'project of life'.[274] In that sense, the Inter-American Court has noted that Rule 13 of the UN Rules for the Protection of Juveniles Deprived of their Liberty[275] establishes that 'Juveniles deprived of their liberty shall not for any reason related to their status be denied the civil, economic, political, social or cultural rights to which they are entitled under national or international law, and which are compatible with the deprivation of

---

[270] Id., §§136-137.

[271] Id., §140. The Commission also referred here to article 40 of the Children's Convention.

[272] IACHR *"Instituto de Reeducación del Menor"* (Paraguay), Judgment of 2 September 2004, §160; see also e.g. its Advisory Opinion on the Legal Position and Rights of Children, 28 August 2002, §§56 and 60.

[273] UN Committee on the Rights of the Child, General Observation of 27 November 2003, §12.

[274] IACHR *"Instituto de Reeducación del Menor"* (Paraguay), Judgment of 2 September 2004, §161, among others referring to its Advisory Opinion on the Legal Position and Rights of Children, 28 August 2002, §§80-81, 84 and 86-88 and Rule 13.5 of the UN Standard Minimum Rules for the Administration of Juvenile Justice, ('The Beijing Rules'), GA 40/33, 29 November 1985. On the notion of 'project of life' see e.g. IACHR *Loayza Tamayo* (Peru), 27 November 1998 (Reparations), §§147-148, referring to the project of life as 'akin to the concept of personal fulfilment, which in turn is based on the options that an individual may have for leading his life and achieving the goal that he sets for himself', §148. See further Chapter XI (Mass expulsion), section 2 and Chapter XII (Other situations), section 2.1.

[275] G.A. res. 45/113, annex, 45 U.N. GAOR Supp. (No. 49A) at 205, U.N. Doc. A/45/49 (1990).

liberty'.[276] Closely related to the argument that the right to life to some extent entails a certain quality of life are the obligations of the State regarding the personal integrity of detained children. In determining whether treatment or punishment is cruel, inhuman or degrading the fact that those subjected to it are children must by necessity be taken into account.[277] These findings on the merits clearly support the use of provisional measures to protect the life and personal integrity of minors in detention.

3.4   African system

The African Charter on Human and Peoples' Rights contains a provision that is similar to Article 5 ACHR and Article 7 jo.10 ICCPR and, as the African Commission has noted, Article 5 ACHPR 'prohibits not only torture, but also cruel, inhuman or psychological suffering'. "This includes not only actions which cause serious physical or psychological suffering, but which humiliate the individual or force him or her to act against his will or conscience".[278] The African Commission has a Special Rapporteur on prisons and prison conditions who visits States and prepares reports.[279] The Rapporteur may also intervene in urgent cases. In 2002 the African Commission, the Association for the Prevention of Torture (APT) and several other NGOs, institutions and experts adopted the 'Robben Island Guidelines' for the Prohibition and Prevention of Torture, Cruel, Inhuman or Degrading Treatment or Punishment in Africa. Regarding conditions of detention these Guidelines reiterate the importance of separating pre-trial detainees from convicted persons and of ensuring that 'juveniles, women, and other vulnerable groups are held in appropriate and separate detention facilities'. Moreover States should encourage the use of non-custodial sentences for minor crimes and take other measures to reduce over-crowding in places of detention.[280]

Like the aforementioned Article XI of the American Declaration Article 16 ACHPR stipulates that every individual shall have the right to enjoy the 'best attainable state of physical and mental health' and States parties shall take the necessary measures to 'ensure that they receive medical attention when they are sick'. Analogous to the Inter-American Commission the African Commission has pointed out that the State's responsibility under Article 16 ACHPR is even more evident in detention situations 'to the extent that detention centres are its exclusive preserve, hence the physical integrity and welfare of detainees is the responsibility of the competent public authorities'.[281] Denying a detainee access to doctors while his health is deteriorating is a violation of Article 16. After all 'the authority of the government is heightened in cases where the individual is in its custody and therefore someone whose integrity and well-being is completely dependent on the activities of the authorities'.[282]

---

[276]   IACHR *"Instituto de Reeducación del Menor"* (Paraguay), Judgment of 2 September 2004, §161.

[277]   Id., §162. The Court also referred to the *Gómez Paquiyauri Brothers* case (Peru), 8 July 2004, §170 as well as Rule 26(2) of the UN Standard Minimum Rules for the Administration of Juvenile Justice, ('The Beijing Rules'), GA 40/33, 29 November 1985.

[278]   ACHPR *International Pen and Others* (*on behalf of Ken Saro-Wiwa*) v. *Nigeria*, 31 October 1998, §79.

[279]   Until recently this was Commissioner Vera Chirwa who had previously been the subject of a petition before the Commission.

[280]   Guidelines and Measures for the Prohibition and Prevention of Torture, Cruel, Inhuman or Degrading Treatment or Punishment in Africa (The Robben Island Guidelines, §§ 35-37).

[281]   ACHPR *Malawi African Association and Others* v. *Mauritania*, 11 May 2000, §120.

[282]   ACHPR *Media Rights Agenda and others* v. *Nigeria*, 31 October 1998, §91.

The African Commission has confirmed that the prohibition of torture, cruel, inhuman or degrading treatment or punishment is absolute.[283] It has emphasized, in reference to the UN Body of Principles, that the obligations under Article 5 are to be interpreted 'so as to extend the widest possible protection against abuses, whether physical or mental'.[284] Denying medical attention 'under health-threatening conditions' and denying 'access to the outside world' showed lack of respect for the 'dignity inherent in a human being' and for the 'recognition of his legal status'. Such denial did not respect principles 1 and 6 of the UN Body of Principles for the Protection of all Persons under any form of detention or imprisonment. Thus it also constituted a breach of Article 5 ACHR.[285] All of this serves as a foundation for the Commission's use of provisional measures in detention cases.

3.5 European system

Apart from many cases on the lawfulness of detention[286] the case law on detention of the European Commission and Court has involved the prohibition of torture and cruel treatment in (police) detention. Sometimes this specifically related to positive obligations of the State, once more indicating that their provisional measures in detention cases can be based on substantive case law. In the *Greek Case*, for instance, the European Commission found that overcrowding, inadequate heating, inadequate sleeping and toilet facilities, insufficient food, recreation and contacts with the outside world constituted a violation of Article 3 ECHR.[287] In *Cyprus* v. *Turkey* the European Commission found the failure to provide sufficient food, water and medical assistance in detention centres constituted inhuman treatment contrary to Article 3 ECHR.[288] In *Hurtado* v. *Switzerland* it found a violation because the State had failed to provide appropriate medical assistance during the first six days after his arrest to a prisoner whose rib was fractured.[289]

As noted, in *Lorsé et al.* v. *the Netherlands* (2003) the ECtHR had refused to take provisional measures for a prison transfer or, more generally, to take measures to halt further violations of Article 3. While the Court did not find that the petitioner had been subjected to sensory isolation, it pointed out that it did 'not diverge from the view' expressed by the European Committee for the Prevention of Torture and Inhuman or Degrading Treatment or Punishment (CPT) that the situation in the prison in Vught 'is problematic and gives cause for concern'. Moreover, the Court noted it was 'struck by the fact that Mr Lorsé was submitted to the weekly strip-search in addition to all the other strict security measures within the EBI'. It considered that this systematic strip-searching required more justification than the Dutch government had provided, exactly because of the awareness by the authorities of the petitioner's 'serious difficulties coping with the regime' and the fact that nothing untoward was ever found during the strip searches. Thus, it found that the combination of routine strip-searching with the other stringent security measures amounted to inhuman or degrading treatment in violation of Article 3.[290]

Even if, in the circumstances, it decides not to indicate the specific measures suggested by counsel (such as in this case prison transfer), it could decide to take more generally worded meas-

---

[283] See e.g. ACHPR *Huri-Laws* v. *Nigeria*, October/November 2000, §41.

[284] ACHPR *Huri-Laws* v. *Nigeria*, October/November 2000, §40.

[285] Id., §41.

[286] See e.g. ECtHR *Conka* v. *Belgium*, Judgment of 5 February 2002 and *Amuur et al.* v. *France*, Judgment of 25 June 1996.

[287] EComHR *Greek Case* (first), 5 November 1969.

[288] EComHR *Cyprus* v. *Turkey*, 10 July 1976.

[289] EComHR *Hurtado* v. *Switzerland*, 26 January 1994.

[290] ECtHR *Lorsé et al.* v. *The Netherlands*, Judgment of 4 February 2003 (former first section). See also *Van der Ven* v. *The Netherlands*, Judgment of 4 February 2003 (former first section).

ures, as counsel had suggested in this case as well. Provisional measures that are more specific might be possible as well, especially in systems with a well-developed jurisprudence on reparations.[291] Pending the proceedings the adjudicator could order a State to re-examine its strip-search practice with regard to a petitioner and inform it urgently on the security concerns requiring this practice. It could subsequently order a halt to such searches taking place routinely even when the petitioner has had no contact with the outside world.

While the European Commission has sometimes intervened in the past in cases involving psychological distress, the case law on the merits is not that liberal. In *Kudla* v. *Poland* (2000) the petitioner had complained, among others, that he had not received adequate psychiatric treatment during his detention on remand. The Commission considered Article 3 had been violated, but the Court found otherwise. It pointed out that Article 3 cannot be interpreted 'as laying down a general obligation to release a detainee on health grounds or to place him in a civil hospital to enable him to obtain a particular kind of medical treatment'.[292] "Nevertheless, under this provision the State must ensure that a person is detained in conditions which are compatible with respect for his human dignity, that the manner and method of the execution of the measure do not subject him to distress or hardship of an intensity exceeding the unavoidable level of suffering inherent in detention and that, given the practical demands of imprisonment, his health and well-being are adequately secured by, among other things, providing him with the requisite medical assistance".[293] In this case it accepted that 'the very nature' of 'his psychological condition made him more vulnerable than the average detainee and that his detention may have exacerbated to a certain extent his feelings of distress, anguish and fear'. It also took note of the fact that he was kept in custody for six weeks 'despite a psychiatric opinion that continuing detention could jeopardize his life because of a likelihood of attempted suicide'. Yet 'on the basis of the evidence before it and assessing the relevant facts as a whole,' it did not find it established that the petitioner was subjected to 'ill-treatment that attained a sufficient level of severity to come within the scope of Article 3 of the Convention'.[294]

On the other hand, the Court does take into account the work of the prison visiting Committee introduced under the European Convention for the Prevention of Torture and Inhuman or Degrading Treatment or Punishment. This treaty introduced non-judicial preventive machinery to protect detainees. It is based on a system of visits of prisons and other facilities in which people are deprived of their liberty by the European Committee for the Prevention of Torture and Inhuman or Degrading Treatment or Punishment (CPT).[295] This Committee sometimes intervenes informally in pressing health situations of individual (groups of) detainees, especially in the context of prison visits. Moreover, Rule 32 of its Rules of Procedure, on ad hoc visits stipulates that in addition to its regular visits, 'the Committee may carry out such ad hoc visits as appear to it to be required in the circumstances'. When the Committee is not in session, the Bureau (consisting of a smaller group of CPT members and several staff members servicing the Committee) may, 'in case of urgency, decide on the Committee's behalf on the carrying out of an ad hoc visit'. "The President of the Committee shall report to the Committee at its next meeting on any action which has been taken under this paragraph".[296] The activities of CAT under the new Optional Protocol Optional Protocol to the Convention against Torture and other Cruel, Inhuman or Degrading

---

[291]   See further Chapter XIII (Protection).

[292]   ECtHR *Kudla* v. *Poland*, Judgment of 26 October 2000, §93.

[293]   Id., §94.

[294]   Id., §99.

[295]   See also Recommendation (2006)2 of the Council of Europe Committee of Ministers to member States on the European Prison Rules, adopted 11 January 2006 (952nd meeting).

[296]   CPT Rules of Procedure CPT/Inf/C (2008) 1.

Treatment or Punishment[297] (comparable to the European Convention against Torture) will likely confirm this. Its entry into force may also trigger cases being brought before CAT under the individual complaint proceedings, with the ensuing possibility of CAT using provisional measures in detention cases in a manner similar to that of the other adjudicators.

4   CONCLUSION

In several cases the human rights adjudicators have shown sensitivity towards the health and safety of detainees pending the proceedings.

The HRC has used (informal) provisional measures mainly, but not exclusively, on behalf of political detainees. It seems to have used requests to ensure access to medical care and requests for information interchangeably. The HRC has not clarified why it used informal provisional measures dealing with medical treatment (either requests for information or requests to ensure) under Rule 91 (current Rule 97) rather than formal provisional measures under Rule 86 (current Rule 92), but this may be explained by the fact that it initiated the tradition in its early years. It has not clearly distinguished those situations in which it only enquires about the health situation of a detainee from those in which it requests the State to take positive measures to ensure adequate medical care. In general its approach has been cumulative, first only inquiring, later also requesting positive measures. There are several cases in which the HRC requested the State to *ensure* adequate medical treatment pending the proceedings. Sometimes it has also mentioned the need to ensure this in its decision on the merits. Hence, in such cases there is a clear correlation between the 'procedural' request and the final determination of the case.

A request by the HRC for information about the health situation of a detainee is partly based on the Committee's hope that it will influence the State to pay more attention to the health of the detainees involved, partly simply meant to help make a decision on the merits. A request to provide treatment, on the contrary, amounts to specifically asking the State for *positive* action. Such action clearly is required not just on behalf of the proceedings but on behalf of the alleged victim. In other words, it relates to the possible final outcome of the case.

Thus far the HRC has never used (informal) provisional measures in order to remedy detention situations for prisoners on death row (such as relating to a deteriorating health situation), although it has sometimes suggested such measures in decisions on the merits. One reason for this may be that the Secretariat only consults the Special Rapporteur on New Communications to initiate the case for registration and for any provisional measures. It generally does not consult the Rapporteur on New Communications when it subsequently receives information relating to threats or lack of medical treatment. It simply prepares this information for the Committee member assigned to the case when it will be discussed on admissibility and merits. It is recommended that the HRC should change this approach.

The Inter-American Commission and Court, the European Commission and Court and the Bosnia Chamber have also used provisional measures on behalf of 'non-political' detainees. Apart from demanding information adjudicators have also specifically requested States to ensure access to health care in detention. Because of the vulnerability of children circumstances of detention more rapidly result in irreparable harm to children than to adults. In their provisional measures, the HRC, the Inter-American Commission and the Inter-American Court have dealt with the specific situation of children in detention.

---

[297]   Adopted on 18 December 2002 at the fifty-seventh session of the General Assembly of the United Nations by resolution A/RES/57/199.

Provisional measures have been used to order a halt to violent situations in detention. This chapter also argued that the use of provisional measures to order a halt to disputed interrogation methods or treatment in detention is certainly feasible as well.

On occasion the European Commission and Court have used provisional measures vis-à-vis the petitioners instead of the State in order for them to stop their hunger strike. The Inter-American Commission and Court do not use provisional measures to this end.[298] The European Court has incidentally used provisional measures to halt re-imprisonment of petitioners who had been hospitalized because of the after-effects of long-term hunger-strikes, which indicates its focus on preventing irreparable harm.

Both the texts of the respective provisions and the interpretation of the adjudicators in decisions on the merits confirm the fundamental nature of the prohibition of torture and cruel treatment, the special position of detainees and the positive obligations of States to ensure their access to health care and respect their dignity. The use of provisional measures requiring States to take protective measures on behalf of detainees in various contexts, while the case is pending, is firmly based on this case law.

---

[298] See also Chapter XIII, section 4, criticizing the European approach.

CHAPTER VIII
ENSURING PROCEDURAL RIGHTS TO PROTECT
THE RIGHT TO LIFE AND PERSONAL INTEGRITY

1 INTRODUCTION

The HRC, the Inter-American Commission and the ECtHR have used provisional measures requesting States to provide information on and ensure access to court and counsel for persons detained incommunicado.[1] At first sight these measures relate to due process and arbitrary detention and are not aimed at preventing irreparable harm to persons, but rather to the claim and, indirectly, to the individual complaint procedure. Yet this chapter argues that these provisional measures also aim at preventing irreparable harm to persons. They appear to have been based on fears for the life and physical integrity of the persons detained.

The issues of incommunicado detention and access to court and counsel have received increasing attention in the context of the counter-terrorism measures introduced by the US after the terrorist attacks of 11 September 2001, mainly in the context of extra-territorial detention of so-called 'unlawful combatants', for instance at Guantanamo Bay.[2]

The provisional measures used in order to ensure procedural rights[3] could be considered a very rudimentary form of international habeas corpus, aimed at helping ensure domestic habeas corpus in the most serious cases. Indeed, one could also consider, as Cançado Trindade does, that all provisional measures are a 'kind of an embryo of an international habeas corpus',[4] not just those aimed at ensuring procedural rights, but this chapter just deals with the latter.

---

[1]   Similar to its requests to provide information about and medical attention for an alleged victim or to protect against threats, mentioned in the previous chapters.

[2]   See e.g. Joint Report on the Situation of detainees at Guantánamo Bay prepared by the Chairperson of the UN Working Group on Arbitrary Detention, the Special Rapporteur on torture, the Special Rapporteur on the independence of judges and lawyers, the Special Rapporteur on freedom of religion or believe and the Special Rapporteur on the right of everyone the enjoy the highest attainable standard of physical and mental health, E/CN.4/2006/120, 27 February 2006. See in general about the respect for human rights in this context e.g. Report of the UN Special Rapporteur on the promotion and protection of human rights and fundamental freedoms while countering terrorism, Martin Scheinin, E/CN.4/2006/98, 28 December 2005 and Communications with Governments, E/CN.4/2006/98/Add. 1, 23 December 2005; Report, UN Independent Expert Robert Goldman on the promotion and protection of human rights and fundamental freedoms while countering terrorism, E/CN.4/2005/103, 7 February 2005; UN High Commissioner's Digest of Jurisprudence on Terrorism, 28 July 2003, <http://www.unhchr.ch/html/menu6/2/digest.doc> (last consulted 2 October 2006); CIDH report on terrorism and human rights, OEA/Ser.L/V/II.116, Doc. 5 rev.1 corr., 22 October 2002; Guidelines of the Committee of Ministers of the Council of Europe on human rights and the fight against terrorism, 11 July 2002. See also The Berlin Declaration of the International Commission of Jurists on Upholding Human Rights and the Rule of Law in Combating Terrorism, 28 August 2004 and The Cleveland Principles on the Detention & Treatment of Persons in Connection with 'The Global War on Terror', adopted at a Conference at Case Western Reserve University School of Law, Ohio, 7 October 2005 and subsequently endorsed by many other experts.

[3]   This book deals with procedural rights.

[4]   Interview of author with IACHR President Cançado Trindade, San José, Costa Rica, December 2001.

As in the previous chapters, section 3 deals with the relation of these provisional measures to the decisions on the merits. They all involve procedural rights cases linked to the right to life and the prohibition of torture and cruel treatment.

2 THE PRACTICE OF THE ADJUDICATORS

2.1 Introduction

The HRC, the Inter-American and African Commissions and the ECtHR have all used provisional measures ensuring procedural rights.

2.2 HRC

There have been a few cases in which the HRC has used formal or 'informal' provisional measures concerning the right of habeas corpus, access to counsel, family and consul.[5]

In *Marais* v. *Madagascar* (1983) the alleged victim, a South African national, had been a passenger on a chartered aircraft that had been forced to make an emergency landing in Madagascar in January 1977, because of lack of fuel. Together with the pilot he was arrested and tried for flying over Malagasy territory and sentenced to five-year imprisonment.[6] In March 1981, two years after initial submission, the HRC noted with concern that it had received no further information or clarifications in response to two earlier requests. It 'strongly urged' the State to provide this information without delay, including on the alleged victim's state of health and whereabouts. In addition it requested information on his access to his legal representative, Maître Eric Hammel. It requested the State to remove any obstacles barring Hammel's access to his client, 'should there hitherto have been any obstacles'. The State should 'ensure that the lawyer and his client had the proper facilities for effective access to each other'.[7] When the HRC declared the case admissible it reiterated that the State party should ensure proper access to legal counsel and on the merits it found a violation of Article 14(3)(b) and (d) ICCPR because the authorities had denied the petitioner adequate opportunities to communicate with his counsel, Maître Hammel.[8]

In *Muteba* v. *Zaire* (1990)[9] the HRC requested the State, almost a month after initial submission in 1982, to inform it whether Mr. Muteba had been able to contact a lawyer and whether he had been brought before a court.[10] This was a request additional to the usual request for copies of court decisions. Possibly the HRC decided to ask this additional question not just because it needed it in order to make a determination on the merits, but also as an informal intervention, pending the proceedings before it, to remind the State to ensure access to counsel as well as the right to habeas corpus. In March 1983 the HRC declared Muteba's case admissible. Again it requested the State to inform it whether the alleged victim 'had effective contacts with a lawyer and whether he had been brought before a court'.[11] Subsequently it found violations of Articles 7

---

[5]   See about 'informal' provisional measures Chapter VI (Disappearances).

[6]   See also HRC *John Wight* v. *Madagascar*, 1 April 1985.

[7]   See also Chapter VII on intervention in detention situations involving risks to health and safety.

[8]   On 11 February 1982 Maître Hammel was expelled from Madagascar. From France he continued to represent Dave Marais before the HRC.

[9]   HRC *Muteba* v. *Congo (Zaire)*, 24 July 1984.

[10]   See also the health inquiry and request to ensure adequate medical care.

[11]   HRC admissibility decision of 25 March 1983 as referred to in *Muteba* v. *Congo (Zaire)*, 24 July 1984, §7.

386

and 10, in particular in light of his incommunicado detention. He was entitled to 'effective remedies, including compensation' and the State was required to halt an inquiry, punish those responsible and to 'take steps to ensure that similar violations do not occur in the future'.[12]

A. et al. v. *Angola* (disc. 2000) was another case relating to a private airplane from South Africa, 21 years after the case against Madagascar.[13] The plane had been forced to land by the Angolan authorities. Counsel for five passengers and three crew members on board the aircraft approached the South-African Department of Foreign Affairs as well as the HRC. She pointed out that her clients had been detained for almost four weeks without formal charge, during which time the South-African consulate had not been allowed access to them. Neither the South-African authorities nor the families had received any information about their detention or about legal assistance. She noted that family members of three of them had flown to Angola but had been denied access to the detainees. She emphasized that due to the lack of information, family members feared for the safety of the detainees.[14] She requested urgent attention to her clients' plight, as they had already been detained for almost a month. She pointed out that, according to the information available, there had been no military equipment or cargo of a dubious nature on board the aircraft, but rather foodstuffs and building materials. She pointed out that the Angolan authorities had not afforded consular access to the South-African authorities. There was no information whatsoever on the reasons for their detention or what was going to happen to them. Because of this they were also unable to appoint a legal representative in Angola: there were neither instructions nor factual information on the basis of which such a representative could represent the detainees effectively and properly. In light of the unwillingness to provide information and allow access to them she argued her clients should be released immediately.[15] A few weeks later counsel pointed out that the captain, the co-pilot and the flight engineer had been released and sent back to South-Africa. Counsel spoke with two of them, from which conversation it appeared that they were not aware of the reasons for their release and did not know the whereabouts of the passengers. According to counsel it appeared from this conversation that the persons still detained were passengers 'who could quite possibly not have been aware as to where the flight was going to go and what the purpose of the flight was'. She requested advice on what could be done to secure their prompt release.[16]

Upon receipt of this submission by counsel the Special Rapporteur transmitted the case to the State in as far as it concerned the five persons still detained. He also formally used provisional measures requesting the State to bring the detainees 'before a court without delay, and to allow them access to their legal representative, family and the South-African consul'.[17]

These three cases dealt with by the HRC may be linked to lack of information and fears for the lives and physical integrity of detainees, often detained incommunicado.

---

[12]   HRC *Muteba* v. *Congo* (*Zaire*), 24 July 1984, §13.

[13]   HRC *A. et al.* v. *Angola*, disc. 1 August 2000.

[14]   HRC Letter by counsel of 13 February 1998 in *A. et al.* v. *Angola* (on file with the author).

[15]   HRC Submission of 18 February 1998 in *A. et al.* v. *Angola* (on file with the author).

[16]   HRC Submission of 10 March 1998 in *A. et al.* v. *Angola* (on file with the author).

[17]   HRC Note Verbale to the State of 10 March 1998, *A. et al.* v. *Angola* (on file with the author). In May and August of that year the HRC requested information from counsel and in January 2001 it informed her that it had decided to discontinue the case in the absence of replies to its letters. Letter to counsel of 3 January 2001 informing her of the decision at the Committee's 69th session to discontinue the case (on file with the author).

2.3 Inter-American system

In February 2002 US NGOs filed a petition with the Inter-American Commission calling illegal the detention at Guantanamo Bay (the US naval base in Cuba) of al-Qaeda and Taliban suspects without charge and without the protection of prisoner of war status.[18] They stated:

> "Although the United States has an obligation and right to arrest and try the perpetrators of the horrendous crimes of Sept.11, it must do so in compliance with fundamental principles of national, human rights and humanitarian law".

The Bush administration had refused to consider any of the 300 (at the time) detainees from 26 countries as prisoners of war.[19] It said that they were fighting for an illegal terrorist group and for a government that was not recognised. The detainees apparently might be tried in closed military tribunals (i.e. by 'faceless' judges) that could sentence them to death with a simple two-thirds vote from a military commission.[20] They had no access to counsel and had not been informed of the charges against them. The petitioners requested the Commission to demand that the US give the detainees official prisoner of war status. The Vice-President of the Centre for Constitutional Rights, one of the petitioners in this case, stated 'either they were picked up on the battle field, in which case they're POWs, or they did something criminal, in which case they should be charged. There is no legal limbo status'.[21]

In March 2002 the Inter-American Commission (CIDH) took precautionary measures and requested the US 'to take the urgent measures necessary to have the legal status of the detainees at Guantanamo Bay determined by a competent tribunal'.[22] It wrote that the available information suggested that the detainees were at the 'unfettered discretion' of the US government. It concluded that without clarification of their legal status, their rights under international and domestic law '[could not] be said to be the subject of effective legal protection'. No person under the authority and control of a State could be deprived of his fundamental and non-derogable rights and in this case humanitarian law might be relevant next to human rights law. It concluded that the precautionary measures were 'both appropriate and necessary in the present circumstances, in order to ensure that the legal status of each of the detainees is clarified and that they are afforded

---

[18] See on the legal status of the detainees or the various proposals for military commissions to try them e.g.: Gill/Van Sliedrecht (2005); Amann (2004); Paust (2004a); Steyn (2004); Dahlstrom (2003); Paust (2003); see also Amnesty International, 'Bosnia-Herzegovina. Unlawful detention of six men from Bosnia-Herzegovina in Guantánamo Bay', AI Index Eur 63/013/2003, 30 May 2003; for a defense of the US policies see Yoo/Ho (2003).

[19] By October 2005 the number of persons detained at Guantanamo was reported to be 595, see CIDH Precautionary measure of 28 October 2005 (all precautionary measures in this case have been made available at the website of the Center for Constitutional Rights, one of the petitioners in this case: <http://www.ccr-ny.org/v2/legal/september_11th/sept11Article.asp?ObjID= 7lt0qaX9CP&Content=134>; consulted 5 october 2006).

[20] The term 'faceless judges' became colloquial in the context of Fujimori's reign in Peru, where suspects accused of terrorism were tried by a panel of anonymous judges, whose faces had also been made unrecognisable.

[21] Associated Press (Ian James), 25 February 2002.

[22] CIDH *Guantanamo Bay* case, Precautionary measures of 12 March 2002, 41 *ILM* (2002), p. 532, also published in 23(1-4) *Human Rights Law Journal* 15 (2002), pp. 14-15 and 96 *American Journal of International Law* (2002), pp. 730-731. See on the Commission's precautionary measures in this case e.g. Tittemore (2006); Cerone (2005); Cerna (2004) and Shelton (2002).

the legal protections commensurate with the status that they are found to possess, which may in no case fall below the minimum standards of non-derogable rights'.[23]

In its precautionary measure the CIDH pointed out that by depriving the detainees at Guantanamo Bay of their right to an independent determination of their status, the US had also 'effectively deprived them of any other due process rights to which they might be entitled'.[24]

Indeed the ICRC has noted that international humanitarian law currently does not recognise the status of 'unlawful combatant'. Thus, the detainees should have either prisoner of war or civilian status. As the ICRC put it *"There is no* intermediate status; nobody in enemy hands can be outside the law".[25]

Among others the US had claimed that the Commission's precautionary measures were inappropriate because they did not involve cases in which the life or physical integrity were under 'imminent threat of immediate harm'.[26] It requested the Commission to reverse its precautionary measures. The petitioners, on the other hand, observed that the CIDH was not obliged to 'confine itself to situations in which there is a threat to life and personal integrity'.[27] Moreover, they pointed out that their lives and personal integrity were indeed at risk and that judicial review was essential to the protection of these rights. It noted that the government did not cite independent sources to substantiate its claims that the detainees were treated humanely. They also referred to the reported increase in mental disorders among the detainees.[28] The petitioners noted that the

---

[23] Ibid. See also the follow-up precautionary measure of 23 July 2002. According to the Vice-President of the Centre for Constitutional Rights the Commission's decision was 'a victory for advocates of the rule of law and due process. Failure to abide by the Commission's recommendation would be a lawless act and a violation of the US' treaty obligations'. Press Release Center for Constitutional Rights, 13 March 2002 (on file with the author; archived press releases at <www.ccr-ny.org> only go back to November 2002; consulted 5 October 2006). See also Chapters XVII (Official responses) and XVIII (Follow-up).

[24] See CIDH *Guantanamo Bay* case, Observations by the Center for Constitutional Rights, the Human Rights Clinic at Columbia Law School and the Center for Justice and International Law on the US response to the Commission's precautionary measures of 12 March 2002, 13 May 2002, p. 19, available at <http://www.ccr-ny.org/v2/legal/september_11th/docs/5-13-02ObservationsonGovtResponse.pdf> (consulted 5 October 2006). See also e.g. Special Raporteur on the promotion and protection of human rights and fundamental freedoms while countering terrorism, Martin Scheinin, Mission to the US, A/HRC/6/17/Add.3, 22 November 2007, pp. 9-11.

[25] ICRC Commentary on Geneva Convention IV relative to the protection of civilian persons in time of war, Geneva 1958, p. 51 and further references in CIDH Detainees at *Guantanamo Bay*, Observations by the Center for Constitutional Rights, the Human Rights Clinic at Columbia Law School and the Center for Justice and International Law on the US response to the Commission's precautionary measures of 13 March 2002, 13 May 2002, p. 20.

[26] CIDH Detainees at *Guantanamo Bay*, US response to the Commission's precautionary measures of 12 March 2002, §32.

[27] CIDH Detainees at *Guantanamo Bay*, Observations by the Center for Constitutional Rights, the Human Rights Clinic at Columbia Law School and the Center for Justice and International Law on the US response to the Commission's precautionary measures of 12 March 2002, 13 May 2002, p. 23.

[28] CIDH Detainees at *Guantanamo Bay*, Observations by the Center for Constitutional Rights, the Human Rights Clinic at Columbia Law School and the Center for Justice and International Law on the US response to the Commission's precautionary measures of 12 March 2002, 13 May 2002, pp. 24-25.

majority of Guantanamo detainees were still detained incommunicado.[29] Moreover, the US had not disputed the fact that none of the detainees had had access to counsel.[30] The CIDH subsequently confirmed and expanded its measures.[31]

As the CIDH already stressed in its first precautionary measure regarding the 'unlawful combatants' at Guantanamo Bay, 'no person under the authority and control of a state, regardless of his or her circumstances, is devoid of legal protection for his or her fundamental and non-derogable human rights'.[32] It explained its precautionary measures as appropriate and necessary 'in order to ensure that the legal status of each of the detainees is clarified and that they are afforded the legal protections commensurate with the status that they are found to possess, which may in no case fall below the minimum standards of non-derogable rights'.[33]

This indicates that, from the start, the importance of protecting the non-derogable rights of detainees was the rationale for the use of precautionary measures. Without legal recourse (regarding their status and detention) and access to counsel the detainees were at risk of irreparable harm.

To some extent, as a scholar and staff member of the Commission put it, the precautionary measures by the CIDH may be seen as injunctive measures taken in order to prevent prejudice to the positions of the parties. Yet there are many situations in which they should be regarded more as a 'protective mechanism to preclude the imminent perpetration of human rights violations against the life or personal integrity of a person or group of persons'.[34] In other words, they aim to 'prevent imminent violations of substantive human rights' or preserve the Commission's 'ability to adjudicate upon consummated violations'.[35]

In July 2002 CIDH reiterated its precautionary measures for the first time. Moreover, it noted that additional information had augmented its concerns. "In particular, as indicated by the Petitioners and as reported in the media, the manner in which certain detainees at Guantanamo Bay were captured raises reasonable doubts concerning whether they belong to the enemy's armed forces or related groups". Among others it referred to information about the presence of six Algerian citizens arrested by US authorities in Bosnia.[36]

Two years later, in July 2004, the CIDH pointed out that information had surfaced 'suggesting that U.S. government officials and agencies have developed legal policies and guidelines concerning the methods of treatment and interrogation that are inconsistent with well-established international standards governing humane treatment'.[37] In a very important statement it observed

---

[29] In January 2002 the ICRC only spoke with an 'unspecified handful of detainees' and the 'almost complete lack of contact' of the detainees 'with the outside world may violate the non-derogable right to be free from cruel, inhuman or degrading treatment'.

[30] CIDH Detainees at *Guantanamo Bay*, Observations by the Center for Constitutional Rights, the Human Rights Clinic at Columbia Law School and the Center for Justice and International Law on the US response to the Commission's precautionary measures of 12 March 2002, 13 May 2002, pp. 25-26.

[31] CIDH Detainees at *Guantanamo Bay*, Precautionary measures of 23 July 2002, 18 March 2003, 29 July 2004 and 28 October 2005.

[32] CIDH Detainees at *Guantanamo Bay*, Precautionary measures of 12 March 2002, p. 4.

[33] CIDH Detainees at *Guantanamo Bay*, Precautionary measures of 12 March 2002, pp. 4-5.

[34] Tittemore (2006), p. 381.

[35] Tittemore (2006), p. 382.

[36] CIDH Detainees at *Guantanamo Bay*, Precautionary measures of 23 July 2002. See also Chapter IV (Non-refoulement), referring to the transfer by the Bosnian to the US authorities contrary to a provisional measure by the Bosnia Chamber.

[37] CIDH Detainees at *Guantanamo Bay*, Precautionary measures of 29 July 2004, p. 2, referring among others to the defense department memo on 'Counter-resistance techniques' prepared by Pentagon general counsel William J. Hayes II and approved by the US secretary of defense on 2 December 2002, available at <http://www.cdi.org/news/law/memos-release.cfm> and <http://www.defenselink.mil/news/Jun2004/d20040622doc6.pdf> (consulted 5 October 2006).

that this information 'appears to contradict previous assurances provided to the Commission by Your Excellency's government that it is the United States' policy to treat all detainees and conduct all interrogations, wherever they may occur, in a manner consistent with the commitment to prevent torture and other cruel, inhuman or degrading treatment or punishment, and, if correct, may also have contributed to an environment in which a lack of clarity in standards of treatment facilitated the possible perpetration of abuses'.[38] The Commission also requested information regarding the allegation that persons under the age of eighteen were detained in Guantanamo and that they had not been segregated from the adult population.[39]

In addition, in October 2005 the Commission expanded its precautionary measures specifically emphasizing the importance of investigating allegations of torture. The Commission also pointed out that the US should not use 'diplomatic assurances' to circumvent its non-refoulement obligations.[40]

The measures referred not only to the importance of clarifying the legal status of the detainees and of granting them legal recourse and access to counsel, but also expressed concern regarding reports about the possible ill-treatment of detainees, requesting specific information on the whereabouts, status and treatment of detainees in places other than Guantanamo Bay.[41] Moreover, the Commission emphasized the principle of non-refoulement from Guantanamo to other States where detainees would be at risk of irreparable harm to their life or personal integrity. It specified the procedural rights that should help prevent this refoulement. Moreover diplomatic assurances should not be used to circumvent the obligation of non-refoulement. Regarding the treatment of detainees in Guantanamo Bay itself, it emphasized the need for thorough and impartial investigations and prosecutions. The authorities were not to use statements obtained through torture (unless in proceedings to prosecute acts of torture).[42] The consecutive expansions of the precautionary measures by the CIDH in the Guantanamo case illustrate further the underlying rationale of provisional measures in that they relate to non-refoulement (Chapter V), disappearances (Chapter VI) and detention (Chapter VII) as well.

In a Resolution of July 2006 the CIDH concluded that the US failure to give effect to its precautionary measures had 'resulted in irreparable prejudice to the fundamental rights of the detainees at Guantanamo Bay including the rights to liberty and to humane treatment'. It urged the US, among others, to close Guantanamo without delay.[43]

---

[38] CIDH Detainees at *Guantanamo Bay*, Precautionary measures of 29 July 2004, p. 2 (with footnote referring to the US submission of 24 December 2003, pp. 13-17).

[39] CIDH Detainees at *Guantanamo Bay*, Precautionary measures of 29 July 2004, p. 3.

[40] CIDH Detainees at *Guantanamo Bay*, Precautionary measures of 28 October 2005.

[41] CIDH Detainees at *Guantanamo Bay*, Precautionary measures of 18 March 2003 and 29 July 2004. See also CIDH Precautionary measures of 22 September 2002 on behalf of an unknown number of foreign nationals detained in the US itself following 11 September 2001.

[42] CIDH Detainees at *Guantanamo Bay*, Precautionary measures of 28 October 2005.

[43] CIDH Resolution 1/06 in Press Release 27/06, 'Inter-American Commission urges to close Guantanamo without delay', 28 July 2006, available at <http://www.cidh.org/Comunicados/English/2006/27.06eng.htm> (consulted 6 October 2006. Several developments took place domestically, which cannot be discussed extensively here. In *Hamdan* v. *Rumsfeld* (2006), for instance, the US Supreme Court finally determined that the military commissions constituted under the Military Order were unlawful. It found that they had not been expressly authorised by the US Congress and were in violation of both international law and US military law. US Supreme Court *Hamdan* v. *Rumsfeld*, 548 U.S. 557 (2006) (29 June 2006). Available at <www.supremecourtus.gov/opinions/05pdf/05-184.pdf> (consulted 6 October 2006). In September 2006 the US President successfully proposed new legislation and confirmed that the CIA had been using secret detention and 'alternative' interrogation techniques. He remarked that 'unfortunately, the recent Supreme Court decision put the future of this program in question, and we need this legislation to save it'. US President's Radio Address of 12 September 2006,

In August 2008 a case was brought before the Inter-American Commission on behalf of Djamel Ameziane who had been detained at Guantanamo for more than six years. As part of this complaint a request was made for precautionary measures. On 20 August 2008 the Commission indeed used precautionary measures. Rather than involving the auxiliary rights of access to court and counsel, these measures dealt directly with the prevention of ill-treatment in detention and with the prohibition of refoulement.[44] The Commission requested the State to immediately take all measures necessary to ensure that he is not subjected to ill-treatment or torture, that he has access to medical care, that he is not transferred to Algeria contrary to the principle of non-refoulement. The Commission also noted that diplomatic assurances could not serve to circumvent the prohibition of refoulement.[45]

Even once Guantanamo is closed (as it had been for a brief period before 11 September 2001),[46] any official (or unofficial) continuation of the secret detention policy and the use of certain interrogation methods would warrant continued monitoring by the CIDH and others and may trigger further precautionary measures also involving access to court and counsel.

2.4 African system

In April 2002 a petition had been filed against Eritrea on behalf of eleven former government employees who had been detained in September 2001 and were since being held incommunicado. It was alleged that they could be prisoners of conscience, that their whereabouts were 'currently unknown' and that they had 'not been given access to their families or lawyers'. The petitioners feared for their safety.[47] The African Commission took several increasingly specific provisional measures in this case. In May 2002 it took a provisional measure requesting the President of Eritrea 'to intervene in the matter being complained of pending the outcome of the consideration of the complaint before the Commission'.[48] Later that month the Ministry of Foreign Affairs responded that the alleged victims 'had their quarters in appropriate government facilities, had not been ill-treated, have had continued access to medical services and that the government was making every effort to bring them before an appropriate court of law as early as possible'.[49] In October of that year the Commission followed up on its 'urgent appeal' by reminding the State

---

<http://www.whitehouse.gov/news/releases/2006/09/20060916.html>. For a critical discussion of the compromise reached between three Republican senators and President Bush see Paust (2006). See also Amnesty International, 18 September 2006. The Military Commissions Act was accepted in October 2006 and it notes that the 'habeas stripping' provisions apply to all cases without exception. The military Commissions Act also allows the use of evidence extracted from certain 'interrogation techniques' as long as these were used before the end of 2005 when the Detainee Treatment Act became law. On 12 June 2008, in *Boumediene v. Bush*, 553 U.S._ (2008), 128 S. Ct. 2229 (12 June 2008), with a 5-4 majority the US Supreme Court found that detainees at Guantanamo did have habeas corpus rights and that the Detainee Treatment Act (2005) did not provide an adequate and effective substitute for such habeas.

[44] See Chapters VII (Detention) and V (Non-refoulement).

[45] See Center for Constitutional Rights, press release, 21 August 2008, <http://ccrjustice.org/newsroom/press-releases/inter-american-commission-human-rights-moves-halt-torture-guantanamo%3A-orders>.

[46] See CIDH press release 02/09 on the decision by the new US President, Barack Obama, 'IACHR welcomes order to close Guantanamo detention center', 27 January 2009, at <http://www.cidh.org/Comunicados/English/2009/02-09eng.htm> (consulted 27 January 2009).

[47] African Commission *Liesbeth Zegveld and Mussie Ephrem v. Eritrea*, November 2003.

[48] Id., §10.

[49] Id., §12.

that it was its General Prosecutor's responsibility to bring the accused 'before a competent court of law in accordance with the rules guaranteeing fair trial under relevant national and international instruments'.[50] In June 2003 the Chairperson of the Commission once more appealed to the President of Eritrea 'to intervene in this matter and urge the authorities holding the 11 individuals to release them or bring them before the courts in Eritrea'.[51] This example indicates that the African Commission has also used provisional measures to ensure access to court and counsel. Equally, in this case the prevention of ill treatment and disappearances seems to have been an underlying rationale for the use of this type of provisional measure.

2.5 European system

With regard to the European system two cases are discussed, one against Turkey, involving access to counsel and the right to life, and the other against Russia, about access to counsel and the protection of personal integrity. The first case relates to the situation of PKK leader Öcalan subsequent to his arrest. A case was brought before the ECtHR on his behalf in which his (Dutch) counsel requested the Court to take provisional measures to ensure access to counsel.[52] Despite counsel's emphasis on the serious threat of torture or disappearance, and the importance of immediate access of Turkish and foreign lawyers to the petitioner, as well as immediate medical examination, initially the ECtHR did not take provisional measures.[53]

Yet a remarkable aspect of this case is the fact that the Registry of the Court immediately issued a press release on the submission of the case and the request for provisional measures.[54] Subsequently it issued another press release pointing out that a Chamber of seven judges deliberated on the request and decided that 'at this stage' the use of provisional measures was 'not appropriate'. At the same time, given 'the gravity of the allegations', the Court decided 'to seek clarification from the Turkish authorities on a number of points concerning the circumstances of Mr Öcalan's arrest and detention'. In particular it asked the Turkish Government for a speedy response to a request for information on the question of Mr Öcalan's access to lawyers.[55] In the

---

[50]   Id., §15.

[51]   Id., §19. During the 33rd Ordinary Session of the Commission petitioner Zegveld submitted that local counsel were unable to pursue the case domestically for fear of jeopardising their legal practice and even personal persecution. The State responded that the petitioners' assertion in this respect was 'speculative' and that Zegveld herself 'should accredit herself to the courts in Eritrea to enable her to bring this matter before the local courts', §32. In October 2002 the Commission also took a provisional measure on behalf of journalists detained without charge in Liberia. The nature of this provisional measure was not specified. African Commission *Samuel Kofi Woods, II and Kabineh M. Ja'neh* v. *Liberia,* October 2002 (this may have been an informal rather than a formal provisional measure).

[52]   See generally Prakken (2005), Chapter 5 and Böhler (2000).

[53]   ECtHR Application by Dutch counsel Britta Böhler and Ties Prakken of 16 February 1999 and follow-up fax of 17 February 1999 by counsel Stijn Franken pointing out not only that Böhler and Prakken were staying in the transit area of Istanbul airport, not being allowed to enter, but also that domestic counsel were besieged by Turkish police or security forces, that several attorneys had already been arrested and that Mr Öcalan had not been granted access to counsel (on file with the author).

[54]   ECtHR Press Release 96, 18 February 1999, available at <http://cmiskp.echr.coe.int/tkp197/view.asp?item=8&portal=hbkm&action=html&highlight=&sessionid=8696144&skin=hudoc-pr-en> (consulted 6 October 2006).

[55]   It invoked Rule 54 §3 (a) of its Rules. See ECtHR Press Release 106, 23 February 1999, available   at   <http://cmiskp.echr.coe.int/tkp197/view.asp?item=1&portal=hbkm&action=

Court's letter to the petitioner's counsel providing information on the clarification sought from the Government, the gravity of the allegations was specified by reference to Articles 2 and 3 ECHR. In addition, the Court pointed out that it attached particular importance to the possibility of the petitioner to be assisted by lawyers both in the criminal proceedings against him and in the proceedings before the ECtHR. It requested the State to provide such information within three days.[56]

While initially it had refused the provisional measures requested, the next month the ECtHR did decide to take such measures with regard to compliance with the requirements of Article 6 ECHR. In its letter informing counsel of these measures it explained that it took its decision '[b]earing in mind that the applicant risks being tried by a tribunal which the Court has found in two cases not to be in conformity with Article 6 of the Convention and that procedural guarantees assume even greater importance in a case, such as the present, involving the death penalty'. As part of the provisional measure it requested the State to take all necessary steps to secure Öcalan's rights under Article 6 ECHR, to fully respect the rights of the defence, particularly Öcalan's right 'to have effective consultations in private with the lawyers representing him' in the proceedings brought against him in Turkey. Moreover, the State should also enable him effectively to exercise his right of individual petition to the ECtHR, 'through the lawyers of his choice'.[57]

Turkey, however, did not wish to comply with this provisional measure because it considered that it 'went far beyond the scope of interim measures within the meaning of Rule 39'.[58] In its submission to the Court it stressed that the provisional measures were unprecedented. The practice of the former Commission had always related to issues of non-refoulement, whereby one could speak of an irreversible situation. The criterion of irreparable harm, inherent in the notion of provisional measures, had never been verified in the present case and the Court had not put forward any other justification. The State added that domestic recourse had not even been initiated at this stage and that the provisional measures constituted a 'grave anticipation' of the case, hindering the domestic proceedings. It regretted that the Court had decided to take provisional measures 'based on unfounded allegations by foreign counsel' and considered that the Court's 'unjustified and unmotivated' decisions risked harming the credibility of the system, the most important attribute of which ought to be the legal certainty of the proceedings, avoiding that the Court would succumb to external pressure.[59] In other words, the State seemed to imply that the provisional measures were unrelated to Articles 2 and 3 ECHR, that Öcalan should first exhaust domestic remedies and that the provisional measures relating to a fair trial and access to counsel would somehow hinder domestic proceedings. The State also suggested that the Court's provisional measures harmed legal certainty by taking seriously the petitioner's allegations.

Different from what was suggested by the State the Court does appear to have had in mind the protection of the right to life and the prohibition of torture and cruel treatment in its use of

---

html&highlight=%F6calan&sessionid=8696144&skin=hudoc-pr-en> (consulted 6 October 2006).

[56] Letter by Secretariat ECtHR to counsel Ties Prakken, 23 February 1999 (on file with the author). According to this Letter the State had also been requested to provide information, among others, on the conditions of his (incommunicado) detention, the frequency of the interrogations and the medical supervision of his treatment and state of health.

[57] Letter Registry to counsel Ties Prakken, 4 March 1999 referring to its use of Rule 39 (on file with the author). The Court's Press Release of 4 March 1999, announcing these provisional measures, is not currently available at the website of the ECtHR, but see Information Note No. 5 on the case-law of the Court, April 1999, available at <http://www.echr.coe.int/Eng/InformationNotes/INFONOTEN005.html> (consulted 6 October 2006). See also Garry (2001), p. 402 and Spronken (2001), p. 442.

[58] ECtHR Information Note 5, April 1999, p. 6.

[59] Submission by Turkey of 8 March 1999 (on file with the author).

provisional measures in this case, even specifically referring to the fact that the case involved the death penalty. Indeed the Court was not the only non-national body making the link between the importance of access to counsel and the right to life and prohibition of torture and cruel treatment. On the day the case was brought before the Court the UN Special Rapporteur on Torture already appealed to Turkey to ensure Öcalan's right to physical integrity, requesting information on his circumstances and calling for 'immediate access to legal counsel'.[60] Moreover, the European Committee for the Prevention of Torture and Inhuman or Degrading Treatment or Punishment (CPT) visited him on 2 March 1999, concluding that his 'somatic health' was good, but expressing concern about the potentially negative effects on his mental health 'of being held on his own in a remote location under a high security regime'. Among others the CPT remarked: 'Of course, it is also of crucial importance, from a number of standpoints, that Mr Öcalan be guaranteed *adequate access to a lawyer*. However, the CPT does not intend to pursue this matter, given that the European Court of Human Rights has adopted interim measures on the subject'.[61]

A few days after the State's submission, counsel for the petitioner pointed out that their client was still in 'almost complete isolation'.[62] On the exhaustion of domestic remedies counsel pointed out that there was no obligation to seek remedies that are inadequate or ineffective and they referred to the maximum security measures taken against him, including his incommunicado detention.[63] They also referred to earlier judgment by the ECtHR that trial by the Turkish State Security Court was not in conformity with the impartiality requirement of Article 6 ECHR. Moreover, counsel added that the Court's provisional measures regarding fair trial and access to counsel, taken a week previously, had had 'no positive effect on the proceedings'.[64]

Later that month the ECtHR responded by following up on its earlier provisional measure. It requested further information on its implementation and referred specifically to the request in the last paragraph of its provisional measures to keep it informed 'of all measures taken by the authorities to implement the above request'. It asked questions on all aspects of its provisional measures. Among others it wished to know how frequently his lawyers were 'able to visit him and under what conditions of privacy', to what extent military personnel were involved in the prison visits, 'what steps have been taken by the authorities to ensure that the applicant is not hindered in the effective exercise of the right of individual petition' to the ECtHR. It also questioned whether he had been 'permitted to correspond with his lawyers representing him in these proceedings,' and, if so, under what conditions' Had he 'been free to receive visits' from his lawyers in this respect? Finally, the Court wished to know whether the petitioner would be tried before the State Security Court and, if so, what would be the composition of this court.[65] It appears that the spe-

---

[60] UN Special Rapporteur on Torture, Press release of 16 February 1999.

[61] Visit to Turkey by the European Committee for the Prevention of Torture and Inhuman or Degrading Treatment or Punishment (CPT) from 27 February to 3 March 1999, letter of 22 March 1999, <http://www.cpt.coe.int/documents/tur/1999-05-04-eng.htm#APPENDIX> (consulted 6 October 2006).

[62] He had only been able to see his domestic counsel on 25 February (ten days after his arrest) and on 11 March 1999. The only other contact with the outside world had been a visit by a delegation of the European Committee for the Prevention of Torture and Inhuman or Degrading Treatment of Punishment.

[63] They reminded the Court that the two visits by domestic counsel were very brief. The first lasted only 20 minutes and counsel were only allowed to discuss their client's general health situations. A judge and two masked military were present. The second visit could not take place in private either.

[64] Submission by counsel of 12 March 1999 (on file with the author).

[65] ECtHR Letter Registrar First Section to the State, 23 March 1999 (on file with the author). Subsequently the ECtHR also used provisional measures to halt the execution of the death

cific questions all related to the petitioner's right to a fair trial in the context of the possible imposition of the death penalty and the Court's earlier experience with the proceedings before the State
Security Court.

As noted, this is not the only occasion at which the ECtHR used provisional measures to ensure access of a detained petitioner to his lawyer.[66] In *Shtukaturov* v. *Russia* (2008), for instance,
the petitioner was confined in a psychiatric hospital against his will. In March 2006 the President
of the Chamber dealing with his case decided to invoke Rule 39.[67] The judgment on the merits
provides fairly specific information on what was required of the State.[68] The Government 'was
directed to organise, by appropriate means, a meeting between the applicant and his lawyer. That
meeting could take place in the presence of the personnel of the hospital where the applicant was
detained, but outside their hearing. The lawyer was to be provided with the necessary time and
facilities to consult with the applicant and help him in preparing the application before the European Court. The Russian Government was also requested not to prevent the lawyer from having
such meeting with his client at regular intervals in future. The lawyer, in his turn, was obliged to
be cooperative and comply with reasonable requirements of the hospital regulations'.[69]

3 RELATION BETWEEN PROVISIONAL MEASURES TO ENSURE PROCEDURAL RIGHTS AND THE EXPECTED DECISION ON THE MERITS

3.1 Introduction

The foregoing shows that the few instances in which the adjudicators have taken provisional
measures to ascertain the legal status of detainees and ensure their access to court and counsel all
somehow relate to the right to life and the prohibition of torture and cruel treatment.

In fact they concern rights auxiliary to the right to life and the prohibition of cruel treatment. Were the above-mentioned provisional measures appropriate given the likelihood of success on the merits? One question in this respect is whether the adjudicators have determined, on
the merits, whether procedural rights relating to the right to life and the prohibition of torture and
cruel treatment have a special status in the human rights systems. Another question arose in the

---

sentence imposed on Öcalan, see Press Release 683 of 30 November 1999 and Chapter III
(Halting executions).

[66] See also ECtHR *Shamayev et al.* v. *Georgia and Russia*, 12 April 2005 (Rule 39 of 17 June
2003 for Russia to grant unhindered access by counsel to the extradited petitioners,
especially for the preparation of the hearing).

[67] ECtHR (Grand Chamber) *Shtukaturov* v. *Russia*, Judgment of 27 March 2008, §4.

[68] Generally on the specificity of provisional measures see Chapter XIII (Protection).

[69] ECtHR (Grand Chamber) *Shtukaturov* v. *Russia*, 27 March 2008, §33. Yet the Chief Doctor of
the hospital where the petitioner was detained informed the petitioner's lawyer 'that he did not
regard the Court's decision on interim measures as binding. Furthermore, the applicant's
mother objected to the meeting between the applicant and the lawyer', §35. Initially a domestic court
declared that the ban on meetings between the petitioner and his lawyer was unlawful given the
provisional measures by the ECtHR, §36, but this decision was reversed on appeal (that court
found that the lawyer had not concluded an agreement with the applicant's mother, while she and
not the petitioner was entitled to act on behalf of the petitioner in all legal transactions), §39. The
petitioner was discharged from hospital on the same day and therefore able to meet with his
lawyer and able to pursue the case before the ECtHR. See generally Chapter XVII on official
State responses.

context of the detention of so-called 'unlawful combatants' at Guantanamo Bay: the extra-territorial responsibility of States.[70]

3.2 Status of auxiliary rights

During armed conflicts humanitarian law is particularly relevant in the interpretation of applicable human rights norms. The CIDH has pointed out that human rights law remains applicable and that no derogation is allowed from certain of these rights, including the right to due process of law.[71] The UN Special Rapporteur on Torture has referred to incommunicado detention as the most important determining factor for risk of torture.[72] He has emphasized that basic legal safeguards such as habeas corpus and access to a lawyer within 24 hours of the detention as well as the right to inform a family member or friend of the detention 'ensure his or her humane treatment while in detention'.[73] Indeed prompt and effective access of persons deprived of their liberty to 'a judicial or other competent authority' is a 'key safeguard to prevent incidents of torture or other forms of ill-treatment'.[74] The right to be brought before a court and the right to counsel may serve as safe-guards to prevent irreparable harm to persons.

The UN Commission on Human Rights has pointed out that prolonged incommunicado de-tention 'may facilitate the perpetration of torture and can in itself constitute a form of cruel, in-human or degrading treatment or even torture'.[75]

The UN Working Group on Enforced and Involuntary Disappearances has confirmed the relevance of access to court and counsel in order to prevent disappearances.[76] In particular it pointed out that 'any detention which is prolonged unreasonably or where the detainee is not charged so that he can be brought before a court is a violation of the Declaration'. Given the object and purpose of Art. 3 Declaration 'the period in question should be as brief as possible, i.e., not more than a few days, as this is the only conceivable interpretation of "promptly after deten-tion"'.[77]

The HRC subsequently confirmed this approach in its General Comment on states of emer-gency (2001) and emphasised that 'explicitly non-derogable rights' such as the right to life and the prohibition of cruel treatment 'must be secured by procedural guarantees, including, often, judicial guarantees'. It also gave examples of provisions (or elements thereof) that are not listed in Article 4(2) ICCPR, but nevertheless cannot be derogated from. It pointed out that 'certain ele-ments of the right to a fair trial are explicitly guaranteed under international humanitarian law during armed conflict' and that it found 'no justification for derogation from these guarantees during other emergency situations'. The principles of legality and the rule of law required that

---

[70] This issue is briefly referred to in this chapter and then further discussed in Chapter XIV (Jurisdiction).

[71] CIDH *Coard et al.* v. *US*, 29 September 1999 (on the intervention in Grenada), §§39, 55 and 59.

[72] See also UN Special Rapporteur on Torture (Nigel Rodley), report to the General Assembly, A/54/426, §42.

[73] UN Special Rapporteur on Torture (Theo van Boven), report to the General Assembly A/57/173, 2 July 2002, §18. See generally §§7-18, esp. 16.

[74] UN Special Rapporteur on Torture (Theo van Boven), Report to the Commission on Human Rights, E/CN.4/2004/56, 23 December 2003, §39.

[75] See e.g. Res. 2005/39, 19 April 2005, §9.

[76] See e.g. E/CN.4/1997/34, 13 December 1996, §§26 and 28.

[77] E/CN.4/1997/34,13 December 1996, §29. The international responsibility of States under Article 3 Declaration on the Protection of All Persons from Enforced Disappearance 'arises not only when acts of enforced disappearance occur, but also when there is a lack of appropriate action to prevent or terminate such acts', E/CN.4/1995/38,15 January 1996, §53.

such fundamental elements of fair trial must be respected during a state of emergency. In particular it referred to the right to take proceedings before a court to enable the court to decide without delay on the lawfulness of detention.[78]

The HRC has noted that it is 'inherent in the protection of rights explicitly recognised as non-derogable' under the ICCPR that they 'must be secured by procedural guarantees'. This means, for instance, that 'the right to take proceedings before a court to enable the court to decide without delay on the lawfulness of detention' is a right accessory to the protection of the right to life and the prohibition of cruel treatment and torture. In that sense this is in itself a right that could not be derogated from even in times of emergency. The Committee has specifically noted that even during a state of emergency any trial leading to the imposition of the death penalty 'must conform to the provisions of the Covenant, including all the requirements of articles 14 and 15'.[79] It had also pointed out, elsewhere, that it 'is satisfied that States parties generally understand that the right to habeas corpus and *amparo* should not be limited in situations of emergency'. It considers that the remedies of Article 9(3) and (4) ICCPR, read together with Article 2 'are inherent in the Covenant as a whole'.[80]

In 2003 the UN Working Group on Arbitrary Detention published a legal opinion regarding the deprivation of liberty specifically of persons detained in Guantanamo Bay. It had received many communications alleging the arbitrary character of their detention. It concluded that 'so long as a "competent tribunal" has not declared whether the status of prisoner of war may be considered applicable or not, the persons detained in Guantanamo Bay provisionally enjoy the guarantees stipulated in articles 105 and 106 of the third Geneva Convention'. Moreover, 'should such a court issue a ruling on the matter' in which it would invalidate the provisional prisoner of war status, Articles 9 and 14 ICCPR would remain applicable.[81]

The situation of the detainees at Guantanamo, as well as that of those detained incommunicado for extended periods elsewhere, illustrates the interrelationship between procedural rights and the prohibition of torture and cruel treatment. In its follow up to its initial precautionary measures on behalf of the Guantanamo detainees the CIDH even expressly included the obligation of non-refoulement[82] as well as the obligation to investigate torture allegations,[83] both directly involving the right to life and the prohibition of torture and cruel treatment.

Article XXV of the American Declaration stipulates, among others, that each person deprived of his liberty 'has the right to have the legality of his detention ascertained without delay by a court, and the right to be tried without undue delay or, otherwise, to be released. He also had the right to humane treatment during the time he is in custody'. In the Inter-American system the importance of procedural rights to protect the right to life and personal integrity is already evident in Article 27(2) ACHR, enumerating a list of non-derogable rights and adding that no suspension of 'the judicial guarantees essential for the protection of such rights' is authorised either. More-

---

[78] General Comment 29 on states of emergency (Article 4), 4 July 2001, §§15-16. See also General Comment 24 on reservations, 4 November 1994, §11. See generally on non-derogable rights and states of emergency e.g. Seiderman (2001).

[79] HRC General Comment No. 29 on states of emergency (Article 4), CCPR/C/21/Rev.1/Add.11, 31 August 2001, §§11 and 15. See also the joint report on Guantanamo by the UN Special mechanisms, E/CN.4/2006/120, 15 February 2006, §14, confirming this interpretation.

[80] HRC Recommendation to the Sub-Commission on Prevention of Discrimination and Protection of Minorities about a draft third optional protocol to the ICCPR, A/49/40, I, Annex XI, §2 (considering such protocol unnecessary).

[81] Report UN Working Group on Arbitrary Detention, E/CN.4/2003/8, 16 December 2002, §64. See also on the risk of torture and cruel treatment in secret detention: Report of the UN Working Group on Arbitrary Detention, E/CN.4/2006/7, 12 December 2005, §§56-57.

[82] See also Chapter V (Non-refoulement).

[83] See also Chapter VII (Detention).

over, before the HRC published the General Comment on states of emergency mentioned above, the Inter-American Court had already published its Advisory Opinions on habeas corpus in emergency situations and on judicial guarantees in states of emergency. In these Opinions it stressed the importance of judicial guarantees (such as access to court and counsel) in order to protect non-derogable rights.[84] Habeas corpus, for instance, the Court has noted, 'performed a vital role in ensuring that a person's life and physical integrity are respected, in preventing his disappearance or the keeping of his whereabouts secret and in protecting him against torture or cruel, inhumane, or degrading punishment or treatment'.[85] "In a democratic society, the rights and freedoms inherent in the human person, the guarantees applicable to them and the rule of law form a triad. Each component thereof defines itself, complements and depends on the others for its meaning".[86] '[T]he legal remedies guaranteed in Articles 7 (6) and 25(1) of the Convention may not be suspended because they are judicial guarantees essential for the protection of the rights and freedoms whose suspension Article 27(2) prohibits'.[87] It has confirmed that 'the "essential" judicial guarantees which are not subject to derogation, according to Article 27(2) of the Convention, include *habeas corpus* (Art. 7(6)), amparo, and any other effective remedy before judges or competent tribunals (Art. 25(1)), which is designed to guarantee the respect of the rights and freedoms whose suspension is not authorized by the Convention'.[88]

In their decisions on individual cases the IACHR and the CIDH have confirmed the importance of judicial review for the protection of fundamental rights, also when national security may be at stake.[89] In its precautionary measures on behalf of the 'unlawful combatants' at Guantanamo Bay the Commission specifically referred to the Inter-American Court's judgment in *Castillo Paéz* (1997) discussing the purpose of habeas corpus as 'not only to guarantee personal liberty and humane treatment, but also to prevent disappearance or failure to determine the place of detention, and, ultimately, to ensure the right to life'.[90] Among others it referred to information raising 'serious possibilities that detainees may have been subjected to treatment that constitutes

---

[84] IACHR Advisory Opinion OC-8/87, *Habeas Corpus in Emergency Situations* (Articles 27(2) and 7(6) ACHR), 30 January 1987 and OC-9/87, *Judicial Guarantees in States of Emergency* (Articles 27(2), 25 and 8 ACHR), 6 October 1987.

[85] IACHR Advisory Opinion OC-8/87, *Habeas Corpus in Emergency Situations* (Articles 27(2) and 7(6) ACHR), 30 January 1987, §35.

[86] IACHR Advisory Opinion OC-8/87, *Habeas Corpus in Emergency Situations* (Articles 27(2) and 7(6) ACHR), 30 January 1987, §26.

[87] IACHR Advisory Opinion OC-8/87, *Habeas Corpus in Emergency Situations* (Articles 27(2) and 7(6) ACHR), 30 January 1987, §44.

[88] IACHR OC-9/87, *Judicial Guarantees in States of Emergency* (Articles 27(2), 25 and 8 ACHR), 6 October 1987, §41. On non-derogable rights and provisional measures, see also Conclusion part II.

[89] See e.g. IACHR *Castillo Petruzzi* v. *Peru*, 30 May 1999 ("Clearly, the proceedings in this case did not fulfill the minimum requirements of "due process of law", which is the very essence of the judicial guarantees established under the Convention. Failure to fulfill the requirements of due process renders the proceedings invalid", §221) and CIDH *Coard* v. *US*, 29 September 1999, §§54-55, esp. §55: "The requirement that detention not be left to the sole discretion of the state agent(s) responsible for carrying it out is so fundamental that it cannot be overlooked in any context. The terms of the American Declaration and of applicable humanitarian law are largely in accord in this regard. Article 78 of the Fourth Geneva Convention provides a recourse which, implemented according to its object and purpose, is generally consistent with the supervisory control required under Article XXV of the American Declaration. Supervisory control over detention is an essential safeguard, because it provides effective assurance that the detainee is not exclusively at the mercy of the detaining authority. This is an essential rationale of the right to *habeas corpus*, a protection which is not susceptible to abrogation".

[90] IACHR *Castillo Paéz* (*Peru*), Judgment of 3 November 1997, §83.

torture or other cruel, inhuman or degrading treatment or punishment, including beatings, sleep deprivation, exposure to extreme temperatures, sensory deprivation and prolonged isolation'.[91]

The ECtHR has equally emphasized the importance of access to habeas corpus and counsel in order to protect basic rights against abuse also in such cases.[92] The same applies to the African Commission. In the case mentioned in section 2, in which it had taken provisional measures on behalf of 11 persons detained incommunicado in Eritrea, it eventually found violations on the merits of, among others, the right to liberty and security of person (Article 6 ACHPR) and of access to court and due process (Article 7 ACHPR). The Commission pointed out specifically that while Art. 6 as such was not an absolute right, in this case the detainees were held incommunicado with no access to their lawyers or families. "Their whereabouts are unknown, putting their fate under the exclusive control of the Respondent State". The Commission followed up on and clarified its provisional measures by noting that they were meant to 'ensure that the 11 persons are removed from secret detention and brought before the courts'.

> "Incommunicado detention is a gross human rights violation that can lead to other violations such as torture or ill-treatment or interrogation without due process safeguards. Of itself, prolonged incommunicado detention and/or solitary confinement could be held to be a form of cruel, inhuman or degrading punishment and treatment. The African Commission is of the view that all detentions must be subject to basic human right standards. There should be no secret detentions and States must disclose the fact that somebody is being detained as well as the place of detention. Furthermore, every detained person must have prompt access to a lawyer and to their families and their rights with regards to physical and mental health must be protected as well as entitlement to proper conditions of detention".[93]

The African Commission pointed out that the eleven persons were detained because of their political beliefs and held in secret detention without any access to the courts, lawyer or family, 'in blatant violation of their rights to liberty and recourse to fair trial'.[94] It urged Eritrea to order their immediate release. Thus this case has shown a gradual specificity of the Commission's provisional measures, from 'intervening' on behalf of the detainees to urging either to bring them

---

[91] CIDH *Guantanamo Bay* case, Precautionary measures of 29 July 2004, p. 2, referring among others to the defense department memo on 'Counter-resistance techniques' prepared by Pentagon general counsel William J. Hayes II and approved by the US secretary of defense on 2 December 200, available at <www.nimj.org>.

[92] In ECtHR *Brannigan and McBride* v. *UK*, 25 May 1993, the ECtHR did not find a violation of Article 5 ECHR because it considered that the UK had indeed fulfilled the basic safeguards of access to counsel and *habeas corpus*, §§61-65. On the other hand, in *Aksoy* v. *Turkey* the Court pointed out that 'the denial of access to a lawyer, doctor, relative or friend and the absence of any realistic possibility of being brought before a court to test the legality of the detention meant that he was left completely at the mercy of those holding him'. It took 'account of the unquestionably serious problem of terrorism in South-East Turkey and the difficulties faced by the State in taking effective measures against it. However, it is not persuaded that the exigencies of the situation necessitated the holding of the applicant on suspicion of involvement in terrorist offences for fourteen days or more in incommunicado detention without access to a judge or other judicial officer'. *Aksoy* v. *Turkey,* 18 December 1996, §§82-84. In general the Court has stressed that '[n]ational authorities cannot do away with effective control of lawfulness of detention by the domestic courts whenever they choose to assert that national security and terrorism are involved' see *Al-Nashif* v. *Bulgaria*, 30 May 2002, §94 referring to *Chahal* v. *UK*, 15 November 1996.

[93] African Commission *Liesbeth Zegveld and Mussie Ephrem* v. *Eritrea*, November 2003, §55, referring to *Constitutional Rights Project and Civil Liberties Organisation* v. *Nigeria*, consolidated communication 143/95 and 150/96.

[94] African Commission *Liesbeth Zegveld and Mussie Ephrem* v. *Eritrea*, November 2003, §57.

before a court or to release them. On the merits this culminated in the finding of a range of violations and the Commission's emphasis on their immediate release. Its awareness of the relation between access to counsel and court on the one hand and torture, ill-treatment and disappearances on the other, is apparent from the above statement and may be assumed to underlie its use of provisional measures in this type of cases.[95]

3.3 Effective control

The other question involving the case law on the merits that has gained particular significance in the context of procedural rights, although it obviously applies in other contexts as well, is that of the extraterritorial applicability of human rights treaties.[96] The use of provisional measures would be inappropriate if the adjudicators would generally decline to examine such cases on the merits. Do States have responsibility for the acts and omissions of their agents outside their own sovereign territory? This question has gained increasing significance in the context of counter terrorism activities of States, such as extraordinary renditions and running (secret) detention centres, outside their own territory.[97] The CIDH has taken provisional measures directed against a State operating outside its own territory. Article 1 ACHR refers to 'all persons subject to their jurisdiction. The American Declaration does not specifically discuss jurisdiction *ratione loci*. The Inter-American Commission has determined that OAS member States indeed have obligations under the Declaration any time a person is in their jurisdiction or under their control, even if the authorities holding this person are active on territory not their own.[98]

The ICJ has pointed out that 'physical control of a territory, and not sovereignty or legitimacy of title, is the basis for State liability for acts affecting other States'.[99] Article 1 of the Optional Protocol (OP) to the ICCPR refers to 'individual subject to its jurisdiction'. Article 2(1) ICCPR requires a State party to respect and ensure the rights laid down in the ICCPR refers to 'all individuals within its territory and subject to its jurisdiction'. Already in 1981 the HRC had interpreted Article 2(1) such that the ICCPR applies to all persons within s State's territory *and* to all

---

[95] See also African Commission *Civil Liberties Organisation* v. *Nigeria*, (2000) AHRLR 243 (ACHPR 1999), §26: "While being held in a military detention camp is not necessarily inhuman, there is the obvious danger that normal safeguards on the treatment of prisoners will be lacking. Being deprived of access to one's lawyer, even after trial and conviction, is a violation of article 7(1)(c)".

[96] See on the extraterritorial application of human rights treaties Coomans/Kamminga (2004). See generally on jurisdiction Chapter XIV.

[97] See also Chapter V (Non-refoulement).

[98] See e.g. *Saldaño* v. *Argentina*, 11 March 1999 (inadm.), §§15-20, in particular §17: "The Commission does not believe, however, that the term "jurisdiction" in the sense of Article 1(1) is limited to or merely coextensive with national territory. Rather, the Commission is of the view that a state party to the American Convention may be responsible under certain circumstances for the acts and omissions of its agents which produce effects or are undertaken outside that state's own territory". See also *Coard et al.* v. *US*, 29 September 1999, §97. See further Cerna (2004 and 2006) and Cassel (2004). The ACHPR does not specifically refer to the scope of State obligations in this respect.

[99] ICJ *Legal Consequences for States of the Continued Presence of South Africa in Namibia (South West Africa) Notwithstanding Security Council Resolution 276 (1970)*, Advisory Opinion of 26 January 1971, §118.

persons subject to their jurisdiction. In other words, it recognised the extraterritorial applicability in its case law.[100]

In light of the above it is suggested that when dealing with a request for provisional measures to the effect that a State should act or refrain from acting in order to prevent irreparable harm outside of its own territory the main criterion should be whether the State exercises *prima facie* control with regard to the rights of the persons involved.[101]

4 CONCLUSION

As noted in Chapter VI, disappearances are still a serious human rights issue, also in the context of the 'war on terror' launched after the 9/11 terrorist attacks in the US (2001).[102] It was argued in that chapter that in light of recent reports of such disappearances petitioners could bring complaints before the ECtHR against Council of Europe States in which disappeared persons were last seen or on the basis of reports about secret detention centres on their territory.[103] This could include requests for provisional measures to intervene urgently to clarify the whereabouts and circumstances of the detainees.

Incommunicado detention, prolonged solitary confinement without access to court and counsel are circumstances conducive to torture, ill treatment and disappearances.[104] The underlying rationale for taking provisional measures to ensure access to counsel and court, exactly in a context of incommunicado detention, is indeed the awareness of risk to life and personal integrity. Nevertheless, with regard to the Guantanamo Bay detainees the CIDH did not at first specifically refer to the threat of ill-treatment. It only did so when information became available on the treatment of the detainees and when the general awareness of the media was growing regarding specific allegations of ill-treatment of detainees under the control of US authorities. It then also

---

[100] See e.g. HRC *Celiberti de Casariego* v. *Uruguay*, 29 July 1981 and *Lopez Burgos* (*submitted by his wife Delia Saldias de Lopez*) v. *Uruguay*, 29 July 1981.

[101] See also Gondek (2005); Scheinin (2004b) and Lawson (2004). See further the discussion in Chapter XIV (Jurisdiction).

[102] See e.g. Paust (2004b), pp. 79-96. See further Berman/Clark (1982). See also the discussion on secret detention centres, e.g. the Marty report presented on behalf of the Parliamentary Assembly of the Council of Europe, Committee on Legal Affairs and Human Rights, Document 10957 and Add.; as well as AS (2006) CR 17, 27 June 2006; Res. 1507 (2006), 27 June 2006 and Res. 1754 (2006), 27 June 2006; Amnesty International, *Below the radar: secret flights to torture and disappearance*, 5 April 2006, AI Index: AMR 51/051/2006; Amnesty International, *Partners in crime: Europe's role in US renditions*, 14 June 2006, AI Index: EUR 01/008/2006; Amnesty International, *Secret detention in CIA 'Black Sites'*, 8 November 2005, AI Index: AMR 51/177/2005; Amnesty International, *USA: Torture and secret detention testimony of the 'disappeared' in the 'war on terror'*, 4 August 2005, AI Index: AMR 51/108/2005; Amnesty International urgent action regarding the possible 'disappearance' of Canadian national Maher Arar, 21 October 2002, AI Index: AMR 51/159/2002 and subsequent actions; Human Rights Watch, *The United States' Disappeared; the CIA's long-term ghost detainees'*, a Human Rights Watch briefing paper, October 2004. The issue discussed here is obviously related to those discussed in the chapters on non-refoulement (Chapter V, in particular its discussion of 'extraordinary renditions'), treatment in detention (Chapter VII) and jurisdiction (Chapter XIV).

[103] See also the references in the Introduction to this Chapter. See further Chapter IV (Non-refoulement) on extraordinary renditions. At the same time complaints may be brought before the Inter-American Commission against the US. See further Chapter XIV on jurisdiction and admissibility.

[104] See Van Boven (2006), pp. 92-93. In general see also Boerefijn (2005b), pp. 240-258.

requested information on the location of post 9-11 detainees detained inside and outside of US territory.

Generally speaking the case law on extraterritorial application of human rights obligations suggests that provisional measures could be taken vis-à-vis any State Party with the authority and control over persons.[105] The case law by the three regional adjudicators and by the HRC shows that procedural rights relating to the right to life and personal integrity have a special status in the human rights systems, warranting the use of provisional measures. Indeed this case law, as well as the official statements by UN authorities, suggests that provisional measures to ensure access to counsel and legal recourse is essential in cases of incommunicado detention. Legal protection in the form of access to Court and counsel could help guard against torture, ill-treatment, disappearances and extra-judicial executions. Awaiting the information on ill treatment in such cases is inappropriate given the general knowledge that persons without access to counsel and without legal recourse are by definition particularly at risk.

---

[105]   Yet see further Chapter XIV (Jurisdiction).

CHAPTER IX
PROTECTING AGAINST DEATH THREATS AND HARASSMENT

1   INTRODUCTION

The main problem the Inter-American human rights system has to deal with is that of the intimidation, assault and murder of human rights defenders, witnesses, journalists and others. The Inter-American Commission and Court were the first of the human rights adjudicators to use provisional measures to halt death threats and harassment. They have developed the most extensive practice in this regard. In fact, most of their provisional measures deal with this problem.

Yet the problem of death threats and harassment is not limited to the Americas, but relates to all regions of the world. Indeed, the two other regional adjudicators, the African Commission and the ECtHR, as well as the three relevant international adjudicators, the HRC, CAT and CEDAW, have also used provisional measures at least once to protect against death threats and harassment.

This Chapter discusses the practice of the adjudicators in this respect, focussing on the Inter-American system. Chapter XIII (Protection) focuses on the specific measures of protection that have been ordered to be taken against death threats and harassment, including the obligation to investigate and prosecute.[1]

The persons threatened may be involved in cases pending before the adjudicators, or in attempts at investigating human rights violations before domestic courts. They may receive threats because they are involved as victims, as family members of murder victims or disappeared persons, as witnesses or as counsel, prosecutor or judge.

They may also receive threats as a reprisal for their work as a human rights defender.[2] According to international officials and NGOs 'armed forces and their paramilitary allies have frequently labelled the activities of human rights defenders as subversive, in an attempt to discredit their work and present them as legitimate targets in the counterinsurgency war'.[3]

In 2002 the President of the Inter-American Commission pointed out:

> "Human rights defenders and the organizations for which many of them work play a crucial role in litigation of human rights cases and in the process of civil society scrutiny of democratic institutions. The Commission calls for full protection of the work they do".[4]

---

[1]   This also includes references to case law on the merits relating to this obligation. See Chapter XIII (Protection).

[2]   Some witnesses and human rights defenders become the victims of disappearances (see Chapter VI). Some are harassed but their life and dignity is not at risk. Rather than direct threats to their lives or physical integrity, witnesses and human rights defenders may also receive threats of, for instance, deportation, as a reprisal for their activities. See Chapter XI (Mass expulsion).

[3]   The quote is from Amnesty International, 'Human rights defenders' offices close in climate of terror', AI index: AMR 23/19/99, 19 February 1999.

[4]   Address by Dr. Juan E. Méndez, President of the Inter-American Commission on Human Rights, upon presenting the IACHR Annual Report for 2001 to the Committee on Juridical and Political Affairs of the Permanent Council of the OAS, 30 April 2002, <www.cidh.org/discursos/04.30.02.eng.htm> (consulted 20 January 2006). See also Chapter XIII

2 THE PRACTICE OF THE ADJUDICATORS TO TAKE PROVISIONAL MEASURES TO HALT DEATH THREATS AND HARASSMENT

2.1 Introduction

As noted, most of the practice of using provisional measures to protect persons against death threats and harassment relates to the Inter-American Commission and Court.[5] This Chapter first addresses their practice. It subsequently briefly refers to the practice of the other adjudicators, in chronological order.

The Inter-American Court has referred not only to its authority, but to its duty to prevent irreparable harm to persons. It considered '[t]hat the case known as the Blake Case is presently before the Court, and it is the duty of this Court to avoid irreparable harm to persons, which is understood to include guarding the complete security of witnesses and their relatives and determining whether the measures adopted by the Government have been sufficient'.[6]

The issue of threats may arise in relation to persons in detention (both political detainees and persons convicted of common crime) as well as outside the context of detention.[7] Threats may involve not only the alleged victim, but also family members, attorneys or other people connected in some manner to the alleged victim.

Persons may be threatened directly, for instance because of their work as a human rights defender. In such cases the adjudicator may open a case bringing a claim that in itself concerns death threats and harassment (section 2.3). In other cases the threats to life and personal integrity may take place in the context of another complaint already pending (section 2.2).

2.2 Protecting persons involved in international human rights adjudication

2.2.1 Introduction

Alleged victims, their family, witnesses, attorneys, prosecutors and judges involved in the examination of a specific human rights violation before a domestic court or as part of a case pending before an international tribunal may face death threats and harassment. This section focuses on the Inter-American practice. As noted, it is mainly in the Inter-American system that provisional measures have been used in this context. It also refers to the practice of the other adjudicators.

(Protection). See in general on human rights defenders, e.g. the Declaration on the Rights and Responsibility of Individuals, Groups and Organs of Society to Promote and Protect Universally recognized Human Rights and Fundamental Freedoms. A/RES/53/144, Resolution of 8 March 1999 (text adopted 9 December 1998). Article 12 of this Declaration stipulates that States must ensure protection of human rights defenders against violence and threats. In August 2000 a Special Representative of the UN Secretary General on Human Rights Defenders was appointed. See e.g. her report E/CN.4/2005/101, 13 December 2004. On protecting human rights defenders see further e.g. Hallo de Wolf (2002) and Wiseberg (1991).

[5] See e.g. IACHR Matter of *Adrián Meléndez Quijano et al.* (El Salvador), Order of 12 May 2007; Case of *19 Tradesmen* (Colombia), Order of 12 May 2007; Matter of *Ramírez Hinostroza et al.* (Peru), Order of 17 May 2007; Matter of *Carlos Nieto Palma et al.* (Venezuela), Order of 3 July 2007; Case of *Gutiérrez Soler* (Colombia), Order of 27 November 2007; Matter of *Guerrero Gallucci and Martínez Barrios* (Venezuela), Order of 29 November 2007.

[6] IACHR *Blake* case, Order of 22 September 1995, 5th 'Considering' clause.

[7] See also Chapter VI (Detention).

2.2.2 Inter-American Commission and Court

Already in the Honduran cases, the first three cases examined by the Inter-American Court it had to deal with death threats against witnesses that had testified before it, or had been called to do so. One witness who had testified before the Court in September 1987, as well as one person who had been summoned to appear, were assassinated. In order to prevent further killings in November 1987 the President of the Court sent a letter calling on Honduras to adopt the necessary measures to guarantee the life and property of two persons who had testified at the Court's hearings. He did not have 'sufficient elements of proof to be sure of who or what entities are responsible for these acts', but he did request Honduras to take the necessary protective measures to guarantee the physical security and property of the two witnesses in accordance with its obligations under the ACHR. He also requested protective measures for the Committee for the Defence of Human Rights in Honduras. He warned the State that if the 'abnormal situation' would continue he would, after prior consultation with the Permanent Commission of the Court, call the full Court to a meeting in Washington where the General Assembly of the OAS was holding its session.

It is clear that the reference to the General Assembly meeting was meant as ammunition to back up his letter. The President also explained that he was submitting the original letter personally to the Ambassador of Honduras in Washington. The Agent of Honduras before the Court would receive a copy by fax.[8]

In January 1988 the full Court pointed out that the lives of some of the witnesses who testified in these three cases were being threatened exactly because they gave such testimony. In this respect, it referred to the notes sent to Honduras by the President and the Secretariat of the Court in November and December 1987 respectively. It strongly condemned the two murders:

> "The physical elimination of actual or possible witnesses constitutes a savage, primitive, inhuman and reprehensible act which deeply offends the American conscience and reflects a total disregard for the values that are [sic] essence of the inter-American system".[9]

It ordered Honduras to 'adopt, without delay, such measures as necessary to prevent further infringements on the basic rights of those who have appeared or have been summoned to do so before this Court' in the Honduran cases. It also ordered the State to 'employ all means within its power to investigate these reprehensible crimes, to identify the perpetrators and impose the punishment provided for by the domestic law of Honduras'. Thus, from the start the Court has included in its Orders for provisional measures the obligation to investigate crimes, identify the perpetrators and punish them.[10]

---

[8]   IACHR *Velásquez Rodríguez, Fairén Garbi and Solís Corrales, and Godínez Cruz* Cases (Honduras), Letter by the President on behalf of witnesses Jiménez-Puerto and Custodio López, 6 November 1987. Two weeks later the Secretariat, upon instruction of the President, requested Honduras once more to take the necessary measures to guarantee the life, personal integrity and property of the witnesses. It noted that 'this afternoon this Secretariat has received a complaint regarding the preparation of an attempt on the life of Dr. Ramón Custodio López, President of the Committee for the Defence of Human Rights in Honduras' (CODEH). *Velásquez Rodríguez, Fairén Garbi and Solís Corrales, and Godínez Cruz* Cases (Honduras), Letter Secretariat on behalf of witness Ramón Custodio López, 18 December 1987. See also Chapter XVIII (Follow-up).

[9]   *Velásquez Rodríguez, Fairén Garbi and Solís Corrales, and Godínez Cruz* Cases (Honduras), Order for provisional measures, 15 January 1988. See also section 3 of this Chapter on the relationship with the merits.

[10]   See further Chapter XIII (Protection).

The use of provisional measures to protect witnesses in cases pending before the Court has not been limited to these early cases. In the *Bámaca Velásquez* case, for instance, a witness was also receiving threats after he had testified before the Inter-American Court. In 1998 the Court ordered provisional measures on his behalf and on behalf of his family. It subsequently decided to maintain and expand these measures as they were still necessary during the phase of supervising the implementation of the judgement on reparations.[11]

Another case in which the Court ordered a State to protect the life and integrity of a witness and his family was the *Paniagua Morales* case ('the white panel truck case'). In January 1998 three unknown persons had kidnapped and violently beaten the son of the victim in this case. He had been summoned to give testimony to the Inter-American Court during a hearing on the merits of that case. Upon receipt of information that the security of the beneficiaries had improved the Court lifted its provisional measures.[12]

As discussed in Chapter II, upon request of the Commission the Inter-American Court can also order provisional measures in cases not yet pending before it. In 1990, for instance, it ordered Peru to take provisional measures on behalf of a journalist who had survived an attack as well as witnesses of the attack in a case that was pending before the Commission.[13]

Since 1994 the Court had been involved in the *Colotenango* case. Its Orders for provisional measures in this case against Guatemala aimed to protect witnesses of an armed attack killing several people in a demonstration as well as their family members and the family of the victims and the attorneys. In 2007 it decided to lift its provisional measures in this case.[14]

In November 1995 the Commission took precautionary measures on behalf of seven members of the Civic Human Rights Committee of Meta (Colombia). Nevertheless, some of them continued to receive threats. In October 1996 one of them, Mr. Giraldo, was murdered. In light of these events, the Commission requested the Court to take provisional measures on behalf of three of his family members as well as three members of the Civic Committee. The Court did so.[15]

On several occasions the Inter-American Commission and Court have had to intervene in the context of the *Aguas Blancas massacre*. This massacre took place on 29 June 1995 in the state

---

[11] IACHR *Bámaca Velásquez* (Guatemala), Orders of 29 August 1998, 5 September 2001, 21 February 2003, 20 November 2003 and 11 March 2005.

[12] IACHR *Paniagua Morales* (*'White van'*) (Guatemala), Order of 19 June 1998; Order of 27 November 1998 lifting the provisional measures.

[13] IACHR *Bustíos-Rojas* v. *Peru*, Order of 8 August 1990, followed up by Order of 17 January 1991.

[14] The *matter of Colotenango* (Guatemala), Order of 12 July 2007 (lifting the provisional measures ordered by it on 22 June and 1 December 1994, 19 September 1997, 2 February 2000 and 5 September 2001; and clarifying that this lifting of the provisional measures did not mean that the State had complied fully with its Convention obligations described in Report No. 19/97 of the Inter-American Commission, or that the State was released from its obligation to continue with the respective investigations in the domestic jurisdiction to identify and, if applicable, punish those responsible for the facts, and that the Inter-American Commission was responsible for verifying effective compliance with these obligations).

[15] Subsequently the Court held a public hearing on the provisional measures. Annual Report 1997, Chapter IIIa under 'Colombia'. It expanded them several times and also lifted them for some beneficiaries. On 30 September 1999, for instance, the Court issued an order for provisional measures requiring Colombia to maintain the measures necessary to protect the lives and physical safety of Sister Noemy Palencia, upon her return to Meta and of Mariela de Giraldo and her two children as well as of Ms. Rey. It also required Colombia to investigate the denounced facts, which gave rise to the Court's provisional measures, to inform the Court about the results of this investigation, to discover those responsible and punish them. Later it maintained the provisional measures on behalf of Mrs. Mariela de Giraldo and her two daughters as well as for one other person. See also Chapter XIII (Protection).

of Guerrero in Mexico. The police had stopped members of the Organization Campesina de la Sierra Sur (OCSS) who were on their way to take part in protest against the local authorities. Seventeen peasants ('campesinos') died and 22 were wounded by gunfire. Only two of the policemen were injured.[16] In 1996 the Inter-American Commission asked Mexico to protect the life and personal integrity of several witnesses and their family members.[17] In October 1998 it requested protection on behalf of Bernardo Vásquez and eight other members of OCSS. Between June 1996 and 'the date of the request' 35 members were assassinated and the Government had branded the organisation as 'subversive'. Reportedly one person, under torture, had implicated the involvement of Rocío Mesino in the insurgent People's Revolutionary Army.[18] As a result of her statement the Mesino family had been harassed and physically attacked. The organisation's leader Mr. Vásquez Juárez was assassinated in July 1998. Previously he had received several death threats from the judicial police. Other members of the organisation had testified about human rights violations before an Amnesty International delegation and were beaten afterwards. Moreover, Mexico had refused to comply with the Inter-American Commission's Report on the merits in the *Aguas Blancas massacre* case. In light of all this the petitioner requested protection 'for the lives and physical integrity of the various members of the OCSS and investigation and punishment of the violations reported, including the death of Vásquez Juárez.[19]

A few years later, in July 2001, the Commission took precautionary measures on behalf of another survivor who had received threats because of his activities aimed at securing justice in the *Aguas Blancas* case. For seven survivors of the massacre, still bearing physical and psychological scars from the massacre, the precautionary measures sought medical attention.[20]

In its Order of August 2000, in the *Haitian* case, the Court pointed out, in reference to Article 1(1) ACHR, the responsibility of the Dominican Republic to adopt security measures to protect all persons subject to its jurisdiction. Two witnesses had testified before the Court about the Commission's request for provisional measures to halt deportation in the *Haitian* case and subsequently received threats.[21] During the hearing itself the Commission had already pointed out that it believed that the witnesses who appeared at the public hearing were 'justifiably fearful' and 'the interrogation by the State at said hearing did not help dissipate their fear'. One of the witnesses was working with approximately seven small communities or 'bateyes' without utilities or basic services. She 'indicated that there are legislators and Government representatives who asked, through the media, that she be arrested, investigated and expelled; her children and family have been similarly terrorized'. The Court noted, as it had done in other such cases, that this responsibility was 'still more evident in relationship to those who may be bound by proceedings before the supervising organs of the American Convention'.[22] On the basis of the affirmations by the witnesses themselves, during the public hearing, and on the basis of the Commission's submissions, the Court found that the two witnesses could, as a consequence of their testimony, become the victims of reprisals. This made it necessary to adopt provisional measures in order to prevent irreparable harm to their lives and physical integrity. It pointed out its practice to protect, by way of provisional measures, witnesses who have testified before it and it ordered the Dominican

---

16   CIDH *Aguas Blancas* case, 11.520. The Network of National Civil Organizations 'All rights for everyone' and the Democratic Revolution Party brought the case before the Commission. CEJIL joined later as co-petitioner.

17   CIDH Annual Report, 1996, 14 March 1997, §4a.

18   She had been arrested in June 1998, during the events of El Charco.

19   CIDH Annual Report 1998, §45.

20   On this type of precautionary measures see XII (Other situations).

21   See also Chapter XI (Halting mass expulsion). The case itself was still pending before the Commission.

22   IACHR *Haitians and Dominicans of Haitian Origin in the Dominican Republic*, Order for provisional measures, 18 August 2000.

Republic to 'adopt, forthwith, whatever measures are necessary to protect their lives and personal integrity'.[23]

2.2.3 African system

Aware of the requirements inherent in the right to life and the prohibition of cruel treatment, if not of the practice of the Inter-American Commission and Court in this respect, the African Commission, or its Secretariat, has also intervened to prevent irreparable harm to petitioners or alleged victims in the context of death threats and harassment.

In September 1994 the Commission called on the government of Togo 'to take the necessary measures to prevent irreparable prejudice to Corporal Bikagni'. Two years before, upon his arrest, the petitioner had submitted a complaint on behalf of this Corporal, alleging that he had been tortured and maltreated.[24] The Commission did not indicate the type of information it received subsequently, triggering its use of provisional measures. It may well be that he was being threatened with regard to his complaint about torture. It is also possible that he was in need of medical attention. In 1994 the Secretariat of the Commission also intervened in *Association pour*

---

23   IACHR *Haitians and Dominicans of Haitian Origin in the Dominican Republic*, Order for provisional measures, 18 August 2000. By Order of 26 May 2001 it reiterated that the State was to 'adopt special measures to protect the life and physical integrity of Father Pedro Ruquoy and Solange Pierre'. By Order of the President of 5 October 2005 and the Court's Order of 2 February 2006 the State was to 'adopt such measures as may be necessary to protect the life and personal integrity of Benito Tide-Méndez, Antonio Sension, Andrea Alezy, Janty Fils-Aime, William Medina-Ferreras, Rafaelito Pérez-Charles, Berson Gelim, Father Pedro Ruquoy, Solain Pie or Solain Pierre or Solange Pierre and her four children'. The Court considered 'as regards the background information submitted by the representatives in the instant case, as well as the observations submitted by the Commission, it is *prima facie* evident that the lives and personal integrity of Ms. Solain Pie or Solain Pierre or Solange Pierre's four children are under threat', Order of 2 February 2006, 15th 'Considering' clause. It pointed out that 'the Commission and the representatives have informed the Court that the threats and harassment suffered by Ms. Solain Pie or Solain Pierre or Solange Pierre and her four children have forced them to leave the Dominican Republic, by reason of which this Tribunal deems it necessary that the State create due conditions for those people to return to their home'. In this respect it referred to previous occasions where it had ordered such measures (*Matter of the Communities of Jiguamiandó and Curbaradó*, Order of 6 March 2003, 10th 'Considering' clause; *Matter of the Peace Community of San José de Apartadó*, Order of 24 November 2000, 8th 'Considering' clause and *Matter of Giraldo-Cardona*, Order of 5 February 1997, 5th 'Considering' clause). It stressed that the State was to 'ensure that said beneficiaries of measures do not face any threats or other sources of fear that may prevent them from continuing to live in their habitual places of residence', 17th 'Considering' clause. Even though the beneficiaries were 'not in the Dominican Republic at present, the State must maintain the measures adopted in their favor with a view to making them effective when said beneficiaries return to their country', 18th 'Considering' clause. With regard to Father Ruquoy, who had left the country out of fear for his life and personal security, after having lived there for 30 years, it pointed out that he was a beneficiary of the Court's provisional measures and 'the State must offer whatever conditions are necessary so that, should Father Ruquoy return to the Dominican Republic, he can remain within Dominican territory and have his life and personal integrity duly protected', 19th 'Considering' clause.

24   ACHPR *Degli (on behalf of Corporal N. Bikagni), Union Interafricaine des Droits de l'Homme, International Commission of Jurists* v. *Togo*, March 1995. The official decision does not refer to the provisional measures. See e.g. <http://dcregistry.com/users/ACHPR/index3.html> (consulted 20 October 2005) for the initial decision of March 1995 that does refer to the provisional measure.

la Défense des Droits de l'Homme et des Libertés v. *Djibouti* (2000). The petitioner was an NGO from Djibouti complaining of a series of human rights abuses against members of the Afar ethnic group. It referred to 26 people who had been jailed without trial, tortured or executed.[25] No specific information is available on the background of the provisional measures, but given the fact that they aimed to avoid 'irreparable prejudice to the complainant or the victims' it may be assumed that the petitioners and/or the alleged victims were receiving threats because of their complaints about these violations.[26]

2.2.4 CAT

The three relevant *international* systems have all used provisional measures at least once to deal with the situation of death threats and harassment.

In *B.M'.B.* v. *Tunisia* the petitioner had informed CAT that witnesses had been detained and questioned by Tunisian authorities in connection with the petition before the Committee. Moreover, members of the petitioner's and of the victim's families had allegedly been subjected to intimidation.[27] In April 1994 CAT took provisional measures 'to ensure that no harm is done to the author's family, the alleged victim's family or the witnesses and their families'.[28] The petitioner, who himself was staying in France, had requested such measures to protect the 'physical, moral and economic security' of his family and the other persons threatened.[29] CAT later declared the case inadmissible because the petitioner had not submitted sufficient proof to establish his authority to act on behalf of the victim. At the same time it maintained its provisional measures.[30]

2.2.5 HRC

In January and February 2004 the HRC used provisional measures on behalf of Michael Anthony Fernando, who was being threatened in the context of a case pending before the HRC. The Committee requested Sri Lanka 'to adopt all necessary measures to protect the life, safety and personal integrity of the author and his family members, so as to avoid irreparable damage to them'.[31]

The original petition related to arbitrary detention and torture.[32] The petitioner was released in October 2003 when the case was still pending before the HRC. It discussed his case during its

---

[25]   These violations were committed by government troops in areas of fighting with the Front pour la Restauration de l'Unité et de la Démocratie, an organisation drawing its support mainly from the Afar ethnic group.

[26]   Upon confirmation by the petitioner, in March 2000, that it wished to withdraw the complaint because a friendly settlement had been reached, the African Commission decided to close the case, *Association pour la Défense des Droits de l'Homme et des Libertés* v. *Djibouti*, May 2000 (closure). See the informal publication of cases at: <http://dcregistry.com/users/ACHPR/index3.html>.

[27]   See CAT *B.M'B* v. *Tunisia*, 5 May 1994, §2.6.

[28]   Id., §5(c).

[29]   Id., §2.4.

[30]   See further Chapter XIV (Jurisdiction and admissibility).

[31]   HRC *Anthony Michael Fernando* v. *Sri Lanka*, 31 March 2005, §§5.1-5.8. Provisional measures of 9 January and 13 February 2004.

[32]   The petitioner was sentenced in February 2003 and released in October of that year. The petitioner had been detained for contempt of court after he challenged a controversial Chief Justice of the Supreme Court of Sri Lanka. The Asian Human Rights Commission, an NGO, undertook a combination of actions including an online petition, urgent appeals and press releases and a petition filed with the HRC. It has made available an excerpt from the submission. The Asian Human Rights Commission is a regional non-governmental organisation monitoring and lobbying human rights issues in Asia. It was founded in 1984 and is based in Hong Kong. The

public October-November session. It did so in the context of the reporting procedure of Art. 40 ICCPR. He himself was present in the NGO delegation.[33]

The Committee's Concluding Observations on Sri Lanka (2003) noted with concern reports that victims of human rights violations are reluctant to bring complaints because of intimidation and threats. The State 'should ensure in particular that allegations of crimes committed by State

---

members of its Board of Directors are from Hong Kong, the Philippines, Japan, South Korea and Sri Lanka. Its Advisory Board also includes members from India, Pakistan and Cambodia. See www.ahrchk.net. The Asian Legal Resource Centre is a sister group of the Asian Human Rights Commission. In its initial submission (June 2003) the Asian Human Rights Commission already requested the Committee to use provisional measures, in this case to release the petitioner 'pending a full impartial and independent hearing into the alleged contempt'. It noted the petitioner's 'frail state of health and already substantial period of imprisonment-during which he suffered deterioration of his mental health due to imprisonment and degrading treatment'. In that light early release would be the most appropriate remedy. The HRC did not heed to this request for provisional measures. See <www.ahrchk.net and www.hrschool.org> (consulted on 5 August 2004). See also HRC *Anthony Michael Fernando* v. *Sri Lanka*, 31 March 2005, §1.2. It submitted that the petitioner had been hospitalised and, upon his return to the prison, on 10 February 2003, 'he was assaulted several times, specifically between 2 and 5 p.m., when he was beaten by prison guards outside the prison on the road'. "He was then pushed into a police van where he was kicked repeatedly on the back causing damage to his spinal cord. On his arrival in prison, the Applicant was taken on a stretcher and left to lie near a putrid toilet. He was then stripped naked and left to lie near the toilet for a further 24 hours. Following this sequence of events, the Applicant began to urinate blood and was returned to the hospital in a van". Human Rights Correspondence School, a project of the Asian Human Rights Commission, lesson series 33 on Fernando's complaint to the HRC, 8 April 2004, <www.hrschool.org> (consulted on 5 August 2004). The teaching modules of the internet correspondence school initiated by the above NGO also include a general introduction on filing a complaint with the UN treaty based human rights mechanisms. This introduction also refers to 'special circumstances of urgency or sensitivity'. It notes, referring to provisional measures: 'typically, such requests are issued to prevent actions that cannot later be undone, for example implementing a death sentence or the deportation of an individual facing the risk of ill treatment and/or torture'. "If you wish the Committee to consider a request for interim measures, it is advisable to state this explicitly in your complaint, with reasons for why you consider such action to be necessary". The claims based on Articles 7 (torture on) and 10(1) (conditions of detention) ICCPR were declared inadmissible as a case was still pending before the Supreme Court. *Anthony Michael Emmanuel Fernando* v. *Sri Lanka*, 21 March 2005, §8.2. The HRC did find the State responsible for arbitrary detention contrary to Art. 9 ICCPR, §9.2. Reportedly, in May 2008 the Supreme Court found two prison guards responsible for the violation of Fernando's rights with respect to the pending torture claim, see Asian Human Rights Commission, 'Sri Lanka: SC holds prison officers to have committed torture on Tony Fernando', 15 May 2008, <http://www.universalpeoplesforum.org/news_local/ ahrchk.net_20080606.htm> (consulted 8 August 2008). The same source also reports that the State would not implement the HRC decision and grant compensation to Tony Fernando because of a previous Supreme Court case (the Singarasa case) holding that HRC decisions have no binding effect within Sri Lanka. For that case: Supreme Court of Sri Lanka, *Singarasa* case, 15 September 2006, <http://www.srilankahr.net/pdf/sc_judgement1.pdf> (last consulted 8 August 2008). The HRC decision in *Nallaratnam Singarasa* v. *Sri Lanka* was of 21 July 2004. See also Asian Human Rights Commission, 'Sri Lanka: The recent judgement of the Supreme Court on the Singarasa case is an attack on the sovereignty of the people', 20 September 2006, <www.ahrchk.net/statements/mainfile.php/2006statements/739/> (consulted 8 Augustus 2008).

[33]   HRC Concluding Observations with regard to the report of Sri Lanka, 6 November 2003, CCPR/CO/79/LKA, 1 December 2003.

security forces, especially allegations of torture, abduction and illegal confinement, are investigated promptly and effectively with a view to prosecuting perpetrators'.[34]

Yet upon his return to Sri Lanka the petitioner received threats. He submitted to the HRC that on 24 November 2003, at 9:35 a.m., an unknown person had called his mother and made death threats against him, demanding he withdraw his three complaints (two domestic with regard to his torture and one to the HRC). That same day, at 10:27 a.m. an unidentified person visited the premises of the Ravaya newspaper that had interviewed the petitioner before and had reported on issues involving the independence of the judiciary. This person threatened the reporter and the editor and demanded that they cease publishing further news on the petitioner. The newspaper reported these threats in its weekend edition. On 28 and 30 November a person visited his parents house again threatening to kill him. This person had left before the police arrived. On 4 December 2003 the petitioner informed the HRC that the two prison officers implicated in his torture complaint had been reinstated. 'As a result, the author lives in daily fear for his life as well as for the life and safety of his wife, his son and his parents. In spite of his complaint to the authorities, he has not, to date, received any protection from the police and is unaware of what action has been taken to investigate the threats against himself and his family'. He recalled that he had received death threats in prison as well. He referred to the Committee's Views in *Delgado Paez* v. *Colombia*, that the State was obliged to investigate death threats and protect the victims. Early January 2004 the Committee's Special Rapporteur requested the State party 'to adopt all necessary measures to protect the life, safety and personal integrity of the author and his family, so as to avoid irreparable damage to them'.[35]

It does not appear that the State acted on this provisional measure. In any case, on 3 February 2004 the petitioner submitted that 'on the morning of 2 February 2004, he had been subjected to an attack by an unknown assailant who sprayed chloroform in his face. A van pulled up close by during the attack, and the author believes that it was going to be used to kidnap him. He managed to escape and was taken to hospital. Had he not escaped, he would have been the victim of an assassination or disappearance'. In response on 13 February 2004 'the Committee, through its Special Rapporteur on New Communications' reiterated its previous provisional measures.[36]

---

[34]   HRC Concluding Observations with regard to the report of Sri Lanka, 6 November 2003, CCPR/CO/79/LKA, 1 December 2003. The NGO's urgent appeal of 1 December 2003 also referred to the Concluding Observations (2003) that Sri Lanka 'should diligently enquire into all cases of suspected intimidation of witnesses and establish a witness protection program in order to put an end to the climate of fear that plagues the investigation and prosecution of such cases'. Asian Human Rights Commission, Update on urgent appeal, Michael Anthony Fernando receives death threats, 1 December 2003, <www.ahrchk.net> (consulted on 5 August 2004).

[35]   HRC *Anthony Michael Fernando* v. *Sri Lanka*, 31 March 2005, §5.1-5.5. He explained that he had reviewed the petitioner's request for provisional measures in light of 'the urgency of this matter'. He noted that this request related 'to various alleged death threats against the author and his family, by reason of the author's communication to the Human Rights Committee'. Provisional measure of 9 January 2004 (1189/2003). The Asian Human Rights Commission reproduced part of the Special Rapporteur's letter to the petitioner informing him of this decision. See Human Rights Correspondence School, a project of the Asian Human Rights Commission, lesson series 33, p. 3, 14 April 2004, <www.hrschool.org> (consulted on 5 August 2004).

[36]   HRC *Anthony Michael Fernando* v. *Sri Lanka*, 31 March 2005, §5.6. Eventually the HRC found that Fernando had been detained arbitrarily in violation of Article 9 ICCPR. It devoted a paragraph to its use of provisional measures, but did not return to this issue in its decision on the merits. The State party had responded to the second provisional measure the next month by submitting 'that the Attorney General's Department directed the police to investigate the alleged attack and to take measures necessary to ensure his safety. The police recorded his statement in which he was unable to either name the suspects or to provide the police with the number of the vehicle that the alleged assailants had traveled in. The investigations remain in progress and steps

In a case involving claims of incommunicado detention, ill-treatment and adverse detention conditions, in November 2005 the Special Rapporteur 'drew the State party's attention to the right to submit individual communications to the Committee, under the Optional Protocol to the Covenant, and recalled that an individual and his relatives should not be subjected to intimidation for having submitted a communication to the Committee'.[37] It is not specified whether this intervention was based on the Rule on provisional measures, but it could in any case be classified as an informal provisional measure. Nevertheless the Committee does not discuss what triggered this intervention nor what particular measures the State should take to ensure the right of petition. On the merits, finding violations of Articles 7, 9 and 10 ICCPR, there is no reference to the acts of intimidation that triggered the intervention.

In a case brought on behalf of 'X' against Serbia in 2005 the petitioner, Humanitarian Law Center, had requested provisional measures 'to urge the State party to offer protection to the witnesses named in the complaint, to encourage the State party to prevent further interaction between the perpetrators of the sexual abuse and the victim, and to urge the State party to provide to the victim adequate counseling and continued supervision, as may be necessary'.[38] The Special Rapporteur rejected these requests.[39] The Committee subsequently declared the case inadmissible for lack of standing by the Humanitarian Law Center to act on his behalf, while expressing grave concern for the welfare of the child in question.[40]

The decision not to use provisional measures may be based on the Rapporteur's estimation that the case would be declared inadmissible for lack of standing. If so, this shows a clear distinction with CAT, which used provisional measures in a case, mentioned above, that also related to

---

will be taken to inform the author of the outcome'. It stated that it would take appropriate action 'if the investigations reveal credible evidence that the threats were caused by any person with a view to subverting the course of justice'. See *Anthony Michael Fernando* v. *Sri Lanka*, 31 March 2005, §5.7. The Committee concluded by noting, with regard to the petitioner's safety, 'a police patrol book had been placed at his residence and police patrol have been directed to visit his residence day and night and to record their visits in the police patrol book. In addition to this, his residence is kept under surveillance by plain-cloth policemen'. There was 'no evidence to conclude that the author received threats to his life because of his communication to the Human Rights Committee'. See *Anthony Michael Fernando* v. *Sri Lanka*, 31 March 2005, §5.8.

[37] HRC *Sid Ahmed Aber* v. *Algeria*, 13 July 2007, §1.2.

[38] HRC *Humanitarian Law Center* v. *Serbia*, 26 March 2007 (inadm.), §1.2.

[39] Ibid. (decision of 31 January 2005).

[40] It noted that the child was 12 at the time of the petition to the HRC and thus likely to be able to give his consent. The petitioner had pointed out that consent from the child, his legal guardian or his parents could not be obtained 'because all are under the influence of the alleged perpetrators of the sexual abuse'. See §6.6. The Committee found that 'In the absence of express authorisation, the author should provide evidence that it has a sufficiently close relationship with the child to justify it acting without such authorisation'. The Humanitarian Law Center ceased to represent the child in the domestic proceedings in August 2003 and had not been in contact with him, his guardian or his parents. "In such circumstances, the Committee cannot even assume that the child does not object, let alone consent, to the author proceeding with a communication to the Committee. Consequently, not withstanding that the Committee is gravely disturbed by the evidence in this case, it is precluded by the provisions of the Optional Protocol from considering the matter since the author has not shown that it may act on the victim's behalf in submitting this communication". §6.7. The evidence submitted related to a ten year old Roma boy who had been sexually abused by five men in a bar. Initially a complaint was brought against the men. The victim was represented by the Humanitarian Law Center. Later the victim changed his testimony and the prosecutor dropped the charges. Several witnesses, including the public health nurse that had persuaded the boy to report the incident to the police, had received threats. Others, including the boy's parents, were also offered bribes.

insufficient authorization, although admittedly in different circumstances. CAT even maintained these provisional measures after it declared the case inadmissible.[41] What remains clear, however, is the Committee's position, confirmed in 2008, that it follows from Article 1 OP that States parties 'are obliged not to hinder access to the Committee and to prevent any retaliatory measures against any person who has addressed a communication to the Committee'.[42] In order to help ensure the right to life and the prohibition of cruel treatment, as well as this obligation, the use of provisional measures can no longer be excluded.

2.2.6 ECtHR

It is only haltingly that the ECtHR has followed the approach of the other human rights adjudicators. It did so in June 2004 in *Bitiyeva and X* v. *Russia* (2007). The first petitioner in this case had complained under Articles 3 and 5 ECHR about her ill-treatment and illegal detention in January and February 2000. Yet in May 2003, while the case was pending, she was killed in her house by unidentified gunmen along with three other members of her family. The second petitioner, who is the daughter of the first petitioner, expressed her wish to pursue the petition and complained in her own name under Articles 2, 3, 13 and 34 ECHR about the death of her family members, the lack of effective remedies and hindrance of the right of individual petition.[43] She discussed various occurrences of threats and intimidation and explained that she 'felt intimidated and feared for her safety, security and life'.[44] Subsequently the Court used provisional measures. It 'requested the Russian Government to take all measures to ensure that there was no hindrance in any way of the effective exercise of the second applicant's right of individual petition as provided by Article 34 of the Convention'.[45] Again the Court does not make explicit the link between the right of individual petition (Article 34) and protecting the right to life (Article 2) and personal integrity (Article 3) pending the proceedings. Nevertheless in practice it is the first time it has clearly intervened in a case involving claims of death threats and harassment.[46] Obviously this is just a first step, as no indication is yet provided on what form this protection should take.[47]

---

[41]   In general on the relevance of jurisdiction on the merits and admissibility see Chapter XIV. On representation see also Chapter XIII (Protection), section 4.4.

[42]   HRC General Comment 33, CCPR/C/GC/33, 5 November 2008 (Advance unedited version), §4.

[43]   ECtHR *Bitiyeva and X* v. *Russia*, Judgment of 21 June 2007 (first section), §3.

[44]   Id., §§59-62.

[45]   Id., §63. Without further information this paragraph adds that the provisional measure was lifted on 20 October 2005.

[46]   In its findings on the merits the Court did not return to its provisional measures. It found that there was 'no direct evidence to support the second applicant's assertion that the killings of the first applicant and of her family members were related to her application to the Court. A breach of Article 34 cannot be found on a mere supposition'. It did recognise, however, 'that the brutal and unresolved killing of the first applicant after she had lodged a complaint in Strasbourg alleging serious human-rights violations by State agents would have inevitably had a "chilling effect" on other current and prospective applicants to the Court, especially for the residents of Chechnya. It can only express its deepest regret and disappointment that there has been no effective investigation which could have elucidated the circumstances of the first applicant's killing (see paragraphs 144-151 above). However, it does not consider that it should make a separate finding of a breach of the respondent State's obligations under Article 34 in this respect, having already found a double violation of Article 2 and of Article 13'. ECtHR *Bitiyeva and X* v. *Russia*, Judgment of 21 June 2007 (first section), §164. It also considered that it did 'not have sufficient material before it to conclude that the respondent Government have breached their obligations under Article 34 by putting undue pressure on the second applicant in order to dissuade her from pursuing her application to the Court'. See §167, as discussed in §§165-166. See also the comment by the rapporteur of the Parliamentary Assembly of the Council of Europe

In August 2008 the ECtHR used provisional measures in the context of the armed action in Georgia that month. Georgia had requested the Court to order provisional measures against Russia. The President of the Court called upon 'both the High Contracting Parties concerned to comply with their engagements under the Convention particularly in respect of Articles 2 and 3 of the Convention'.[48] Georgia had brought the inter-State complaint against Russia and, as the ICJ does in such cases, the Court called upon both Russia and Georgia to comply with their international obligations.[49]

---

on this case suggesting that the Court could have found a violation of Article 34 for failing to carry out a proper investigation, Doc. 11183 Addendum, 1 October 2007, §14.

[47] See further on the specificity of provisional measures Chapter XIII (Protection), section 3. See also Council of Europe Parliamentary Assembly Resolution 1571 (2007), calling on the Member States to 'take positive measures to protect applicants, their lawyers or family members from reprisals by individuals or groups including, where appropriate, allowing applicants to participate in witness protection programmes, providing them with special police protection or granting threatened individuals and their families temporary protection or political asylum in an unbureaucratic manner', §17.2 and 'thoroughly investigate all cases of alleged crimes against applicants, their lawyers or family members and to take robust action to prosecute and punish the perpetrators and instigators of such acts so as to send out a clear message that such action will not be tolerated by the authorities' §17.3 and noting 'that member states' co-operation with the European Court of Human Rights would benefit if the Court were to continue to develop its case law to ensure full implementation of the member states' duty to co-operate with the Court, in particular by: taking appropriate interim measures, including new types thereof, such as ordering police protection or relocation of threatened individuals and their families', §18.1.

[48] ECtHR Press release issued by the Registrar, 'European Court of Human Rights grants request for interim measures', 12 August 2008. The press release noted that 'on 11 August 2008 the Georgian Government requested the Court to indicate to the Government of the Russian Federation interim measures to the effect that the Russian Government should "refrain from taking any measures which may threaten the life or state of health of the civilian population and to allow the Georgian emergency forces to carry out all the necessary measures in order to provide assistance to the remaining injured civilian population and soldiers via humanitarian corridor". It also pointed out that '(t)he Agent of the Georgian Government informed the Court that this request was made in the context of an application directed against the Russian Federation alleging violations of Articles 2 (right to life) and 3 (prohibition of inhuman and degrading treatment) of the European Convention on Human Rights and Article 1 of Protocol No. 1 (protection of property) to the Convention'.

[49] See also Chapter I on a request for provisional measures brought by Georgia before the ICJ around the same time, in the context of an application based on violations by Russia of CERD. The ICJ ordered a similar provisional measure: *Application of the International Convention on the Elimination of Racial Discrimination (Georgia v. Russian Federation)*, 15 October 2008. As to the use of provisional measures by human rights adjudicators in inter-State cases, the EComHR had previously used provisional measures to halt the execution of death sentences in two inter-State cases, see EComHR *Application of the ECHR to the Island of Cyprus (Greece v. UK)*, 26 September 1958 (Article 31 report), p. 34 and Partial Decision of the Commission as to the admissibility of the application, *The Second Greek case (Denmark, Norway and Sweden v. Greece)*, 5 October 1970, §11. In another inter-State case, *Ireland v. UK*, the EComHR refused a request by Ireland for the UK to postpone its five interrogation techniques. See further Chapter VII (Detention).

2.3 Protecting persons bringing a claim regarding death threats and harassment

2.3.1 Introduction

As discussed in the previous subsection, the Inter-American Commission and Court have regularly taken provisional measures to protect persons (such as alleged victims or witnesses) involved in the proceedings before them. In addition they have built up an extensive practice of taking provisional measures on behalf of persons who were not already involved in a pending case. In response to petitions specifically relating to death threats and requesting provisional measures at the same time, they have taken provisional or precautionary measures immediately. This subsection will give examples in order to sketch a picture of the types of cases concerned.

2.3.2 Persons involved in domestic (human rights) investigations

Witnesses, attorneys and judges involved in local investigations or trials or otherwise perceived as a threat by local police or militias are often subjected to death threats and harassment. Even members of the military may receive threats, particularly when their (former) colleagues or their 'associates' (e.g. paramilitary groups) consider them whistleblowers who have 'ratted' on them.[50] Prison guards may also harass prisoners because they gave information to human rights defenders, both in retaliation and as a warning never to provide such information again.[51]

The Commission has dealt with a greater number of urgent cases than the Court. It has taken precautionary measures, for instance, on behalf of an ex-member of the police who had participated in a military operation during which several persons were extra-judicially executed. His testimony could implicate those who had taken part in these actions.[52]

---

[50] In 1997 the Commission took precautionary measures requesting Paraguay to take the necessary measures to guarantee the life and physical integrity of a Major and his family. He had allegedly received threats for testifying before a Special Military Tribunal. CIDH Annual Report 1998, §47.

[51] On 4 March 1999 the Commission requested Mexico to take protective measures on behalf of a prisoner who had been beaten brutally. The prison concerned was the Nuevo León Social Rehabilitation Centre. Other prisoners had been beaten as well. Apparently, these beatings took place as a result of their meeting with representatives of Citizens Support of Human Rights (CADHAC). Allegedly these representatives had also been harassed. Two weeks later Mexico informed the Commission of the measures it had adopted. Mexico had arranged for the intervention of the State Human Rights Commission of Nuevo León and of that state's government secretariat. CIDH Annual Report 1999, Chapter III C.1, §42.

[52] The Commission does not indicate whether this testimony would be given as part of a case pending before it or of a case pending before a national court. It is clear, however, that he himself, or an NGO petitioner on his behalf, had brought a case before the Commission. Precautionary measure of 28 February 1996. It appears that he wanted to rejoin the National Police, hence the complaint before the Commission, registered as case 11.237, may have been about his dismissal because he had blown the whistle about this military operation. In the meantime, apparently, he and his family were being threatened. Colombia informed the Commission of a meeting between an official of the Presidential Advisory Board for Human Rights, the beneficiary and a representative of the Colombian Commission of Jurists in order to analyse and study possible measures to be taken. Later, the claimant informed the Commission of his wish 'not to avail himself of any special protection plan and to rejoin the National Police or to join National Bureau of Investigation'. In September 1996 the State reported on the concrete measures it had taken on behalf of the beneficiary. CIDH Annual Report 1996, 14 March 1997, §4a.

Family members of persons who have been assassinated are in a vulnerable position as well, especially when they seek the investigation of such murder.[53] Attorneys are also in a particularly vulnerable position. In June 1999 the Commission used precautionary measures on behalf of an attorney and a public prosecutor, both of the Brazilian state of Espíritu Santo. The attorney was a human rights defender and a key witness in corruption cases. He and the public prosecutor had received serious death threats from a paramilitary organisation.[54]

Judges and prosecutors trying to deal with human rights cases domestically are equally subjected to threats as well. In March 2001 the Commission took precautionary measures on behalf of the President of the Constitutional Court of Guatemala. Unknown persons had fired shots at her home, causing material damage to it. Previously she had received death threats.[55]

In August 2001 the Commission took precautionary measures on behalf of eight members of the National Human Rights Unit of the Colombian Attorney General's office and their families. They had begun a judicial investigation of a General 'in connection with the alleged creation and support of private vigilante groups during his tenure as the commander of the army's XVII brigade in the Urabá region of Antioquia'.[56] As part of this investigation the home of this General was searched and he himself was arrested. Immediately, in retaliation, criminal and disciplinary proceedings were ordered against six members of the Human Rights Unit and two others were asked to resign. One of them was requested to resign as the head of the Anticorruption Unit. The General whose activities they were investigating was released at once. The Commission requested Colombia to protect the lives of the eight persons, to agree with them on the type of security measures to be arranged and to refrain from taking any reprisal against them for simply performing their duties as prosecutors.[57]

Even a former warden requested the protection of the Commission, which in July 2001, took precautionary measures on behalf of a man who had been the warden of La Picota penitentiary in Bogotá in Colombia. At his home he had received death threats by telephone. Persons unknown to him, but claiming to be members of the Calima Block of the United Self-Defence Forces of Colombia (AUC) and other persons claiming to be members of the AUC of South Cesar and Santander had made these threats. At the same time unidentified persons riding motorcycles were constantly following him.[58]

Several people also received threats in the context of the investigation of the murder of Bishop Gerardi in Guatemala. The Bishop had been active in the Interdiocesan Historical Memory Recovery Project (REMHI). He was murdered in April 1998 following the publication of its final report 'Guatemala: nunca mas'. The next year an attorney was targeted who had been working with monsignor Gerardi. In April 1999, on the first anniversary of Gerardi's murder, three

---

[53]   See e.g. the precautionary measures of 30 January 2001 on behalf of Gloria Gaitán Jaramillo (Colombia). Through the so-called 'National and International Truth Tribunal Campaign' she was trying to further the investigation into the assassination of her father. According to the available information she was harassed and persecuted because of this both at home and at her workplace. CIDH Annual Report 2000, §26 and Annual Report 2001, Chapter III (a), §13.

[54]   The organization Scuderie Le Coq, Case 12.003. On 7 September 1999 the Commission reiterated its request to Brazil to protect them. CIDH Annual Report 1999, Chapter III C.1, §13.

[55]   CIDH Annual Report 2001, Chapter III (a), §31. See also, e.g. the precautionary measures of 5 July 2001 to protect the judicial magistrate in charge of the investigation into the murder of journalist Jean Dominique, Annual Report 2001, Chapter III (a), §37. See also Chapter XIII (Protection).

[56]   It concerned General Rito Alejo del Río Rojas (ret.).

[57]   CIDH Annual Report 2001, Chapter III (a), §20. See also Chapter XIII (Protection).

[58]   Annual Report 2001, Chapter III (a), §19. Colombia was requested to take the necessary steps to protect his life and person, to agree with him on security measures and to investigate the source of the threats.

unidentified armed persons violently entered the attorney's home, searched his house, threatened one of his daughters and assaulted his housekeeper. The attackers stated that they brought the attorney a message consisting of 'a slab of concrete and stone'. The Commission took precautionary measures that same day. Later that month Guatemala reported to the Commission that it had deployed uniformed personnel keeping a constant watch on his residence. The Commission received information on this situation 'until the persons concerned left the country'.[59] Although it is clear that Guatemala granted some form of protection, the fact that the attorney and his family left the country may indicate that they considered this protection insufficient.[60] The special prosecutor and the deputy prosecutor investigating Gerardi's murder were threatened as well. In September 1999 the Commission granted precautionary measures on their behalf. Guatemala provided them with personal security and a police patrol was ordered to guard their homes. Subsequently, the special prosecutor resigned and went with his family to the US in voluntary exile.[61] In June 2001 the Commission once more took precautionary measures to protect persons involved in the investigation of Bishop Gerardi's murder. The measures were specifically intended for two persons, one of whom was the coordinator of military affairs at the Myrna Mack Foundation. He had received death threats aimed at keeping him from taking the witness stand in the judicial investigation of Gerardi's murder. Subsequently, Guatemala informed the Commission of the security measures offered: uniformed police officers 'would mount permanent patrols around the perimeter of his home and the Mack Foundation's headquarters'.[62]

2.3.3 Human rights defenders generally

Apart from the group of witnesses and others involved in one specific case many people are also at risk simply because of their participation in human rights work generally. The Commission has taken a considerable number of precautionary measures on behalf of these human rights defenders and the Court has taken provisional measures as well.[63]

As with regard to the aforementioned situation, involving human rights litigation, some examples are given to indicate the range of situations involving human rights defenders. In November 1994 the Commission took precautionary measures on behalf of a forensic anthropologist in charge of exhumations in the clandestine cemeteries found in the Rabinal region of Guatemala.[64] In March 1996 the Commission requested Mexico to protect the life, physical integrity and personal safety of a Mexican human rights defender who was attacked and threatened for visiting a municipal jail to verify complaints by family members of prisoners. The attackers accused her of 'defending delinquents and obstructing police work'.[65] The Commission had also intervened on behalf of a lawyer, her three sons and four co-workers focussing on the rights of women and children in Petén (Guatemala).[66]

---

[59] CIDH Annual Report 1999, Chapter III.C.1, §34.

[60] About the official State responses see Chapter XVII.

[61] CIDH Annual Report 1999, Chapter III.C.1, §35.

[62] CIDH Annual Report 2001, Chapter III (a), §32. The Commission does not specify the circumstances of the threats against the other beneficiary of its precautionary measures or any action undertaken by the State to protect her.

[63] Sometimes these human rights defenders are themselves attorneys involved in specific human rights litigation, as discussed under the previous heading.

[64] The threats continued in 1995. Afterwards, they ceased and at the request of the victims CEJIL requested the Commission to close the case in April 1996. CEJIL case docket 1997.

[65] CIDH Annual report 1996, 14 March 1997, §4a.

[66] CIDH Annual Report 1996, 14 March 1996, Chapter II, §4a (cont.). She was the director of the legal office IXCHEL, involved in human rights and environmental law. On 12 September 1996 Guatemala informed the Commission of the steps it was taking to protect the beneficiaries.

In 2001 the Commission undertook action on behalf of a human rights defender who had publicly denounced acts of harassment intended to terrorise the community of Cuarto Pueblo, Guatemala. Witnesses in a suit against the military for the crime of genocide, crimes against humanity and war crimes (committed between 1982 and 1986) had been harassed in particular.[67] An academic researcher in Guatemala had received threats as well. In 2001 the Commission intervened upon receipt of information about a series of threatening and intimidating acts related to her professional activities. As a historian and social researcher for the Association for the Advancement of Social Science in Guatemala she had completed a study 'on how local power structures showed ties among local elite, the armed forces, and individuals who served as military commissioners and members of civil self-defence patrols during the country's armed conflict'.[68]

Criticism of corruption can equally be life threatening. The Commission requested Ecuador to protect the former director of its State Printing Press as well as a former and a current member of the Congress of Guatemala and their families. They had publicly denounced 'the alleged use by the Guatemalan vice-president of the national printing press to print 20,000 posters and 500,000 handbills bearing accusations and slanderous comments of the president of the Guatemalan Chamber of Commerce, which were later distributed anonymously in the nation's capital and other cities'. The aforementioned director of the State Printing Press was asked to resign and later received a series of serious death threats forcing her to flee Guatemala. The other two persons also received death threats and were harassed. Subsequently Guatemala informed the Commission that it had provided the member of Congress with personal security. The director general of the National Civilian Police had assigned two officers and a vehicle to protect her.[69]

Several human rights defenders in Brazil had denounced the activities of members of the civil police known as the 'Golden Boys' in the North of the state of Rio de Janeiro. As a result a death squad composed of members of this group was threatening them. In December 1996 the Commission took precautionary measures on their behalf.[70]

In 1994 ten members of the Political Prisoners Solidarity Committee (CSPP) in Colombia began receiving a series of death threats from members of local paramilitary groups. These groups promised that they would execute 'the lawyers who worked for the guerrilla force'.[71]

In August of that year a paramilitary organisation[72] issued a press statement that it would execute lawyers who were 'defender of the interest of guerrilla's' in the city of Cúcuta. Subsequently, paramilitary groups, apparently acting with the approval of members of security forces, were threatening members of the CSPP. One of the beneficiaries was working as human rights defender in the city of Popoyán in the Cauca region in Colombia. She had participated in procedures pursued by a lawyers association, including a lawsuit dealing with the massacres at Los Uvos.[73] She had been the victim of many acts of violence, which had increased since June 1995.

---

[67] Annual Report 2001, Chapter III (a), §33. It concerned the president and legal representative of the Ixcán Human Rights Association in the community of La Unión Cuarto Pueblo and of the Association for Justice and Reconciliation. Apparently an individual armed with a sharp bladed weapon had attacked him nine days previously. He was wounded with a stiletto knife that cut through his left arm and caused him serious bleeding. He had previously told the Justice of the Peace in Ixcán that he had received death threats because of his activities as a human rights defender.

[68] CIDH Annual Report 2001, Chapter III (a), §34.

[69] Id., §35.

[70] CIDH Annual Report 1996, 14 March 1996, Chapter II, §4a (cont.).

[71] CIDH Case Rafael Lozano Garza, et al.

[72] The COLSINGUE ('Colombia sin guerrilleros').

[73] See José Alvear Restrepo Lawyers Association (CCA), case 11.020.

Apparently, the threats against her were part of a greater pattern of intimidating acts against human rights defenders who had some relation with the CSPP.[74]

In February 1996 the Commission took precautionary measures to protect six members of the Cúcuta branch of the CSPP whose lives and personal integrity were at risk. It also requested Colombia to protect two attorneys who had received threatening and intimidating calls for defending political prisoners. The Commission asked the State as well to protect an official of the city of Popayán in the Cauca region. She was responsible for processing claims and providing humanitarian assistance to political detainees, as a result of which she was subjected to constant harassment and threats against her life and personal integrity.[75] This example illustrates that officials can be subjected to threats as well.[76]

Members of the clergy may also receive threats because of their human rights work. In July 1997 the Commission took precautionary measures on behalf of the pastor of Caldon in the Cauca region (Colombia). He had conducted the funeral rites for three persons who were killed in a local battle between guerrilla forces and the army. One of the persons killed was a guerrilla fighter. Afterwards, the Archbishop of Popayan received a letter from the Cauca police force, accusing the pastor of Caldon of collaboration with the guerrilla fighters. A clergyman who worked with the pastor was kidnapped. Upon his release he was told to give the pastor a message warning him to leave the area.[77]

A paramilitary group went to the headquarters of the Casa de la Mujer in Puerto Wilches and threatened the life of its coordinator. Together with the members of Peace Brigades International the Organización Femenina Popular, headquartered in Barrancabermeja, lodged a complaint with the domestic authorities. Following this, the paramilitary group sent a message stating that the international presence would not last forever, while the women would remain in the town and would therefore 'suffer the consequences'. A few days later the Commission requested Colombia to take steps to protect the life and physical integrity of the members of the Organización Femenina Popular.[78]

In its discussion of Colombia in 1999 the Commission expressed its concern that certain State officials were making declarations suggesting that members of human rights organisations 'acted improperly or unlawfully'. The State officials who did this most often were those belonging to the security forces. It recommended Colombia to 'clarify unequivocally to public opinion that the work of non-governmental human rights organizations in Colombia is legitimate and important'. The Commission pointed out that in April 1999 General Bravo Silva referred to human rights organisations as 'international terrorists'. This statement was not clarified until September 1999 when the Office of the President issued a Circular ordering public servants to refrain from:

> "(a) questioning the legitimacy of the human rights organizations and their members, (b) making statements that discredit, harass, or incite harassment against those organizations and (c) issuing public or private statements that stigmatize the work of such organizations".

---

[74] In April 1995 one of these human rights defenders, Mr. Ortiz Prieto, had disappeared and another, Mr. Barriga Vergel, was assassinated on 15 June 1995. CEJIL case docket 1997. On 24 June 1995 the CSPP received another threatening phone call. Before hanging up, the caller played sounds of machine-gun fire. In this case as well, the CCA, America's Watch and CEJIL requested the Commission to issue precautionary measures on 27 July 1995 and the Commission did so on 20 February 1996.

[75] CIDH Annual Report 1996, 14 March 1997, §4a.

[76] Some other examples are given at the end of this section.

[77] CIDH Case 11744. Precautionary measures for Fr. Ezio Roattino Bernardi.

[78] CIDH Annual Report 2000, §19.

While the Commission considered this to be a positive measure, it noted that recent events did cast serious doubt on the government's willingness to implement its own directive. It pointed out that the 'continual exposure to threats and accusations and assassination attempts' had forced these human rights defenders into internal displacement. It had even forced them 'to leave the country and their valuable work'. Apparently, in regions such as Antioquia by 1999 there were no longer human rights defenders permanently based in small municipalities, as they had been left unprotected in the face of the paramilitary presence. The civilian or Police authorities had failed to act.[79]

The Inter-American Court has ordered provisional measures for the protection of human rights defenders as well. In July 1991 the President of the Court ordered Guatemala to take urgent measures in the *Chunimá* case. He ordered Guatemala to 'adopt without delay all necessary measures to protect the right to life and the physical integrity' of 14 persons listed by name, 'in strict compliance with its obligation to respect and guarantee human rights under Article 1(1) of the Convention'.[80] The persons threatened were members of an indigenous human rights organisation. The case itself was pending before the Commission, which had requested the Court to take provisional measures based on the following.

The petitioners had urged the Commission to seek the Court's provisional measures because the human rights defenders from the village of Chunimá were exposed to grave and continuous danger. In the last nine months alone five of them had been killed and one had been seriously wounded. They named the two leaders of the civil patrols as the sources of the threats and killings.[81] They noted that on two occasions the police had travelled to the village in an attempt to execute the arrest warrants of the perpetrators. The first time a very large group of armed patrollers confronted them, detained them for two hours and let them leave only 'after extracting a promise from the police that they would never come to Chunimá again'. Their second attempt failed as well. The petitioners also mentioned several other incidents of threats and assaults. Some people, moreover, had distributed anonymous flyers in the village calling CERJ a guerrilla front. CERJ was one of the two human rights organisations whose members were being threatened. The flyers also named residents of the village who belonged to that organisation. The fourteen people

---

[79] CIDH Annual Report 1999, Chapter V – Colombia, §120.

[80] IACHR *Chunimá* v. *Guatemala*, Order of the President of 15 July 1991.

[81] Before the Commission the petitioners had noted that five men in civilian clothes but driving a blue pick-up truck 'known to belong to the army', had abducted a human rights activist in October 1990. The human rights activist was associated with the Mutual Support Group (GAM) and the Consejo de Comunidades Etnicas Runujel Junám/Council of ethnic communities 'we are all equal' (CERJ). It gave the name of the local civil patrol chief who allegedly had shown these five men where the victim was waiting for a bus. This chief of the local civil patrol had previously threatened the life of this activist. On 10 December 1990, in the Guatemala City bus terminal, two masked gunmen shot dead another human rights activist from the community of Chunimá. Before his murder he had been under surveillance by the civil patrols commanded by the above mentioned chief. While a district court judge had issued a warrant for the arrest of this chief in relation to the previous abduction and murder, the police did not carry out the arrest. The petition further noted that the above civil patrol leader, together with another leader, also mentioned by name, and accompanied by four men that could not be identified, shot three other human rights activists from Chunimá. Two of them were killed and one was left seriously injured. One of the persons killed and the man who was seriously injured had been witnesses to the abduction of 6 October 1990. Following their testimony the district court judge had ordered the arrest of the civil patrol leader in Chunimá. The day after they had been shot, the justice of the peace in Chichicastenango ordered the arrest of the above civil patrol leader. Again, the police did not carry out this order. In March 1991 an attorney for the Human Rights Ombudsman of Guatemala took the initiative to evacuate 15 family members of the remaining victim from Chunimá to the office of their human rights organisation in Santa Cruz del Quiché.

for whom the Commission requested the Court's provisional measures included one of the witnesses to the abduction of the human rights activist who was later murdered. Subsequently, this witness had been shot himself and he is now paralysed. During this shooting he had seen the civil patrols murder his father and brother. He and his surviving family members had fled to the office of CERJ.

Another early example dates from April 1996 when the President of the Court issued an order for urgent measures on behalf of Father Vogt, a Catholic priest, who had been harassed and persecuted because of his pastoral work. There had been several death threats and attempts on his life and 'a series of false accusations linking him to offences such as sedition and deforestation'. Thus, Guatemala should 'adopt forthwith' the necessary measures to protect his life and integrity, to investigate the events and punish those responsible. In June 1996 the Court ratified the President's order.[82]

2.3.4 Peace Community

One of the most striking situations of death threats and harassment is that of the *Peace Community of San José de Apartadó* v. *Colombia*.[83] Apart from the particular situation warranting provisional measures, the *Peace Community* case highlights two important aspects of these measures in the Inter-American system: the protective measures required (their specific substance) and the evolution in the approach to their beneficiaries.[84] It is also an example with regard to a State in which the situations the Court faces involve internal armed conflicts. These are difficult to deal with in the context of individual adjudication alone.[85]

The situation warranting provisional measures involved a group of peasants and other civilians who started the Peace Community in 1997, in an effort to isolate themselves from the armed conflict. The Community consists of approximately 1200 civilians and is located in the region of Urabá in the state of Antioquia in Colombia, a region suffering under intensive armed conflict between the FARC on the one hand and military and paramilitary groups on the other. The Community is based on humanitarian principles and collective neutrality, including neutrality vis-à-vis all armed actors and no direct or indirect participation in the war. Its members have pledged not to carry arms and to refrain from offering or manipulating information in favour of any of the armed actors. The Community is ruled by an internal council of eight peasants. The members of the Community elect them democratically for a three-year term.

Despite all this, or maybe because of it, since its origin in 1997 this Community has been subjected to constant paramilitary violence and stigmatisation. The paramilitaries have pointed out inhabitants of the Community as guerrillas or as people helping the guerrillas, for instance by providing them with food. Three months after the Community was created, the paramilitaries

---

[82]   A year and four months later the Commission requested the Court to withdraw the provisional measures. It noted that the threats and harassment had diminished considerably as a result of the provisional measures and that they were not necessary anymore. By order of 11 November 1997 the Court decided indeed to close the provisional measures, *Vogt* case, Order of 11 November 1997, Compendium July 1996-June 2000, p. 425.

[83]   IACHR *Peace Community of San José de Apartadó* v. *Colombia*, Orders of 9 October 2000 (President), 24 November 2000, 18 June 2002, 17 November 2004, Order of 15 March 2005, Order of 2 February 2006, 17 December 2007 (President), 6 February 2008. The case itself was pending before the Commission as case 12.325. See Chapter II about the relationship between the Commission and the Court.

[84]   See Chapter XIII (Protection).

[85]   See also Chapter XVII (Official responses).

established a roadblock between San José and Apartadó and detained people travelling there.[86] This roadblock was four minutes away from the army base. The paramilitaries had limited the free passage of food and made lists of people that later appeared in the hands of other paramilitaries who assassinated them. Initially, the paramilitaries only selectively killed people, but this changed later. Between the creation of the Community early 1997 and December 1997, when the Commission first decided to take precautionary measures, 43 of the Community's members had been murdered.[87]

The Commission requested that precautionary measures be adopted for the members of the Community and for the mayor of Apartado and her family. During her term of office she had criticised both the activities of the guerrillas and those of the paramilitary groups supporting the army.[88] The Inter-American Commission has been involved in the case since the end of 1997 and has maintained and expanded its precautionary measures several times. In June 1998, for instance, it requested Colombia to adopt precautionary measures on behalf of a member of the Missionary Team of the Intercongregational Commission for Justice and Peace accompanying the peace community. He had received threats from members of the National Army in Carepa, Urabá.[89]

The Commission's precautionary measures proved insufficient and in October 2000 it decided to appeal to the Inter-American Court for provisional measures. In its petition it pointed out the liability of the members of the Colombian army for the violence and harassment by paramilitary groups. It informed the Court that it had been notified of the murders of 47 of the members of the Community within a nine-month period.

In light of the seriousness of the situation the Court detailed some of the facts presented by the Commission in its request for provisional measures. It concerns 21 incidents over a period of almost three years. In relation to the level of responsibility of the State and the type of measures it should take to protect people under threat, it is important to clarify who are normally the perpetrators of the threats and violent acts committed against the Community.[90] It appears that paramilitary groups ('autodefensas') and one division of the Army were often involved. With regard to eight of the first nine attacks, which took place between December 1997 and April 1998, members of the 17th Brigade of the National Army reportedly were the perpetrators. About the subsequent events, from April 1999 until September 2000, villagers spoke of military, paramilitary or, more generally, armed men.[91] In one case even the local authorities themselves alleged that the crime was committed by paramilitaries. In another case paramilitaries had forced a member of the Community to get off a public bus. His body was later found in Finca El Bajo. Lying next to him was the body of a woman 'who had also been detained in the same paramilitary reserve'. According to the Commission she was a guerrilla. She had been wounded and members of the International Committee of the Red Cross (ICRC) had been evacuating her when three men of the paramilitary organisation Autodefensas Unidas de Colombia (AUC) intercepted their vehicle. The ICRC delegates had tried to negotiate with them for an hour in an attempt to safeguard her life,

---

86   IACHR *Peace Community of San José de Apartadó* case (Colombia), Order for provisional measures, 24 November 2000. The Spanish text speaks of a 'retén', which in the context seems to be a roadblock where people are being detained.

87   On 12 December 1997 two Community members disappeared at a short distance from the military base of the 17th Brigade on the road leading to the village of San José de Apartado. Five days later the Commission took its precautionary measures.

88   As a result she had been the target of threats and harassment and after her term of office ended the danger to her life and personal integrity grew even worse. CIDH Annual Report 1999, Chapter 3.C.1, §26.

89   CIDH Annual Report 1998, §20.

90   See further Chapter XIII (Protection).

91   IACHR *Peace Community of San José de Apartadó* case (Colombia), Order for provisional measures, 24 November 2000.

but despite their opposition the AUC took her out of the vehicle and forced the delegates to leave. In yet another instance a group of about twenty hooded men assassinated six members of the Community and burned the community centre, also destroying its telephone connection. The 17th Brigade may have been involved in this attack. In any case, the next day members of this Brigade, together with paramilitaries, forced themselves into a house, plundered it and threatened the inhabitant as well as the entire Community.

During this period many members of the Community were murdered, some disappeared and several people were injured. People were attacked in their houses, the community centre and while travelling by public transportation. The last incident before the Commission decided to petition the Inter-American Court took place in September 2000 when six armed men forced themselves into a house and kidnapped three persons who were later assassinated.[92] Early November 2000 the President of the Court ordered urgent measures on behalf of all persons specifically named by the Commission. Later that month the full Court decided to order provisional measures on behalf of all members of the Community, also those it could not specify by name.[93] The Court expanded its provisional measures several times, following the Commission's information on new violent acts.[94]

2.3.5 Union leaders

Yet another popular target-group for threats and attacks are trade unionists. In March 1996 the Commission requested Guatemala to take precautionary measures to protect two persons working for the Union of Bank Workers in Guatemala had received serious death threats in connection

---

[92] In October 2000 the Commission requested the Court to order provisional measures to protect the lives and personal integrity of the members of this peace community, *Peace Community of San José de Apartadó* case (Colombia), Order for provisional measures, 24 November 2000.

[93] See further Chapter XIII (Protection), section 4 on beneficiaries. During the hearing of November 2000 the Commission clarified that there had been several massacres. Since the massacre of 19 February 2000 the Community had requested the involvement of the Vice-Presidency of Colombia. They had a meeting a month later in which the Community proposed a series of measures that were not followed up. A return of inhabitants was nevertheless prepared and another massacre took place on 8 July 2000. In the afternoon some hooded people entered the Community and killed six peasants who, according to medical reports, were shot forty times each. *Peace Community of San José de Apartadó* case (Colombia), Order for provisional measures, 24 November 2000.

[94] The Commission had presented 23 incidents that took place between 15 December 2001 and 18 June 2002, the very day on which the Court indeed expanded its provisional measures. Again, the perpetrators were described as soldiers and paramilitaries. To give a specific example of a situation where there may be a link between the paramilitary and the military, on 15 December 2001 three armed men assassinated a member of the Community in the centre of the town of San José de Apartadó and then left for the road leading from Apartadó to San José. At the time, the military were based three minutes from the place where the armed men entered the village. Twice the information of the Commission mentioned one particular member of the paramilitary, known under the name 'Torolo', who had previously been recognised as a participant in the massacre that took place on 8 July 2000. *Peace Community of San José de Apartadó* case (Colombia), Order for provisional measures, 18 June 2002. There is one occasion where the presence of the military actually seems to have prevented a paramilitary group from murdering someone. Paramilitaries had detained thirteen inhabitants of Apartadó, who were on their way to San José, and had accused them of being guerrillas. They threatened to kill them. They interrogated them about their identities and registered their personal information. When they were beating one of them and it looked like they were going to kill him, an army truck appeared and the paramilitaries withdrew.

with their union work. Some days later, however, one of the two beneficiaries was kidnapped and tortured. In response, the Commission reiterated its request. In May 1996 Guatemala stated that after the kidnapping it had taken protective measures.[95]

In March 1997 heavily armed men in uniforms attacked a car carrying the staff, including Alberto Jaramillo, the President of the Consorcio Porce II Workers Union in Colombia. The uniformed men checked a list they were carrying, identified Alberto Jaramillo and told him to get out. He was later assassinated. Afterwards, groups of armed men in uniform appeared several times at the house of Sergio Jaramillo, the co-founder and former secretary of the Consorcio Porce II Workers Union in Amalfi, Antioquia. In April 1997 the Commission took precautionary measures on his behalf and on behalf of his family.[96]

Mr. Tovar, a member of the Executive Committee of the Unified Workers Central in Colombia had received death threats because of its work as a trade union leader.[97] The Commission requested precautionary measures on his behalf in November 1997. In January 1998 he left Colombia and the Commission shelved its precautionary measures.[98] Upon his return he again received threats. These coincided with the assassination of the Vice-President of the Unified Workers Central, Jorge Ortega. In October 1998 the Commission requested Colombia to reactivate the precautionary measures it had adopted previously to protect the lives and physical integrity of Mr. Tovar and his family.[99]

In June 2000 the Commission requested Colombia to take steps to protect the lives and physical integrity of the leaders of four unions.[100] The next month the Commission decided to expand the precautionary measures. It decided to include as a beneficiary of the precautionary measure someone who was detained by a group of uniformed men with long weapons who said they were members of the Autodefensas Unidas de Colombia. He had since disappeared. The expansion of the precautionary measures also included as a beneficiary a prosecuting attorney with the Union of Municipal Workers of Bugalagrande. His name appeared on a list of the paramilitary group operating in the centre of the Department of Valle, together with another union leader who was recently extra-judicially executed.[101]

2.3.6 Persons involved in land disputes and indigenous communities

Indigenous communities seem to be singularly vulnerable. Not only their cultures and traditional way of life are at risk,[102] but also the lives and physical integrity of many of their members. They

---

95   CIDH Annual Report 1996, 14 March 1997, §4a.

96   The Commission does not refer to a case number. Apparently, at the time this matter had not been processed as a Case.

97   On 14 June 1994, at the transport terminal in Bogotá, he was thrown by force into a car carrying four persons, probably members of intelligence and security agencies. Later, he was set free. In August 1995, however, he received an anonymous death threat and in May 1997 he was attacked. In late September 1997, upon his return from a trip abroad, he received new threats.

98   CIDH Annual Report 1997, February 17 1998.

99   CIDH Annual Report 1998, §21.

100   The unions involved were Municipal Utility Workers Union of Cali-SINTRAEMCALI, the National Union of University Workers and Employees of Colombia (Cali-division), 'Central Unitaria de Trabajadores Sub-directiva Valle del Cauca' and the Union of the Department of Valle del Cauca. The Commission notes that the available information indicated that the leaders of these unions were in imminent danger because the civil and military authorities in the Department of Valle del Cauca were constantly plotting against them and accusing them of being guerrillas, terrorists or sympathisers with insurgent groups.

101   CIDH Annual Report 2000, §21.

102   See also Chapter X (Culture and religion).

may receive threats from the military or the police, from paramilitary groups, large landowners or others.[103]

Many different groups and individuals in Colombia, including campesinos, have been declared 'military targets'.[104] Moreover, the aforementioned large landowners do not only form a threat to indigenous groups but to small peasants and farm-workers as well. Often there are various linkages between security forces, paramilitaries and landowners, which may help explain the impunity for human rights violations perpetrated by these actors. In a few cases in which persons were threatened NGOs resorted to the Inter-American Commission to intervene.[105]

---

[103] Since the beginning of 1996 members of the Nahuatl, Lenca and Mayan Nations in El Salvador had suffered many threats against their lives and physical well-being. The Commission took precautionary measures on behalf of the directors of the National Association of the Indigenous Peoples of El Salvador (ANIS), who had been continuously harassed and assaulted. Some of them had been forced into exile. CEJIL case docket 1997 (precautionary measure undated). ANIS and CEJIL had requested the measures in particular for the head of ANIS, who is the spiritual chief of the Nahuatl, Lenca and Mayan Nations. In March 1998 the Commission requested the Court to protect the lives and integrity of the members of the Zenú Indigenous Community in Colombia. Previously the Commission took precautionary measures on behalf of the Zenú community in June 1996. The previous month paramilitary groups in the San Andrés de Sotavento shelter, in the region of Córdoba, had murdered one of their leaders. Later that month, the Secretary of the Town Council of San Andrés was murdered as well and pamphlets were distributed threatening the indigenous leaders. Annual Report 1996, 14 March 1996, Chapter II, § 4a (cont.). In January 1998 it took precautionary measures for the protection of Maximiliano Campo and eleven other leaders of the Paez indigenous community (Colombia) who were also involved in the *Caloto* case pending before it. Case 11.101, Annual Report 1997, February 17, 1998. On 28 and 29 December 1997 members of a paramilitary force murdered six persons in the area of the Paez indigenous community with lands in Caloto and other parts of northern Cauca in Colombia. Even the official police report mentioned that a paramilitary group was seen in the area of the murders. The precautionary measure was of 7 January 1998. It is mentioned again in the 1998 Annual Report, §17. Paramilitary groups operating in the area had threatened them. The provisional measures requested related to the case *Clemente Teherán et al.* In March 1998 the President of the Court indeed decided to intervene and in June 1998 the full Court ratified this decision in its Order for provisional measures to protect the lives and personal integrity of 22 persons in this community. IACHR *Clemente Teherán et al (indigenous community Zenú)* v. *Colombia*, Orders of 19 June 1998, 29 January 1999, 12 August 2000. The Court lifted its provisional measures by Order of 1 December 2003.

[104] See e.g. precautionary measure of 1 November 2000 to protect the life and physical integrity of the members of the Associación Campesina del Valle del Río Simitarra. Paramilitary groups in the region had declared them military targets and they had been subjected to systematic threats and fatal attacks on their leaders. In 1999 Colombia had already taken measures on behalf of the spokespersons for the campesino exodus from southern Bolívar. Annual Report 2000, §23.

[105] In December 1995 the Commission took precautionary measures in order to protect the lives and physical integrity of the members of a union of indigenous communities (Union of Indigenous Communities of the Northern Zone of Isthmus (UCIZONI), in Mexico who had been threatened and harassed because of land-ownership conflicts. It had defended peasants and farm workers ('Campesinos') in disputes about land in the state of Oaxaca. The conflicts were between villages in Aroyo Tejon and Mazatlan on the one hand and landowners on the other. In its Annual Report the Commission published the names of these landowners: Fuentes and Raymundo. The Commission also noted that the President of the Commission on Justice and Human Rights of UCIZONI had reported that he had repeatedly received telephone calls threatening his life. Annual Report 1996, 14 March 1997, §4a. In connection with land disputes between the indigenous population of Honduras, the Garífuna. Group of Afro-Caribbean descent, speaking Igñeri, a combination of Arahuaco, French, Swahili and Bantu. and certain Honduran

With regard to some situations in which the Commission took precautionary measures information is available in the decision on the merits. In 1999, for instance, the Commission found violations of the right to life, humane treatment, fair trial and judicial protection in a case involving impunity against murder and assaults by large landowners in Brazil against landless peasants, rural workers and their union leaders. It found violations against specific persons, but noted about the 'setting of the violence' that there had been 190 murders of peasants in the Xinguara district (Southern Pará) since 1990 and that a sentence had been handed down for only one of these murders. It concluded that there was 'a campaign of violent and illegal action to silence or murder those who support the occupiers of lands and those who assert the legal rights of the rural workers'.[106] The Commission considered that 'this campaign has been abetted directly by police officers, who by act and omission fail to take the action required to impose order and the rule of law'.[107] When discussing the right to a fair trial and judicial protection (Arts 8 and 25 ACHR) it specifically noted that the victims had to push their domestic complaints forward in the face of 'frequent delays and inaction' as well as persecution and threats. It noted that this even triggered its use of precautionary measures.[108]

2.3.7 Refugees and internally displaced persons

Threats may cause people to become internally displaced or to flee to other countries. This, in turn, makes them particularly vulnerable for other threats. Refugees, moreover, also risk refoulement.[109] Several members of a displaced community in the region of Turbo in Colombia were murdered in 1997. Some of them had taken refuge in the municipal sports stadium and in special shelters. Subsequently, two armed individuals, who were identified as paramilitary, entered the sports stadium looking for one of them. Another paramilitary person was seen inspecting one of the shelters.[110] Within a few days the Commission took precautionary measures.[111]

2.3.8 Detainees

In December 1997 the Commission took precautionary measures on behalf of a detainee and his family. He was threatened because he had provided the authorities with information on presumed connections between paramilitary groups and officials of the Colombian military.[112] The Commission and Court have used the tool of provisional measures to request States to improve

---

landowners, both the former mayor of the Garífuna community in the municipality of Limón, in the Colón region, and the ex-President of the Fraternal Black Organisation had been gravely harassed and intimidated. In May 1999 the Commission requested Honduras to take the necessary measures to safeguard their lives and personal integrity. CIDH Annual Report 1999, Chapter 3.C.1, §38.

[106] CIDH *Newton Coutinho Mendes et al.* v. *Brazil,* 13 April 1999 (merits), §98.

[107] Id., §99.

[108] Id., §111. See further Chapters XIII (Protection), XVI (Legal Status) and XVII (Official responses).

[109] An example of threats against refugees is the precautionary measure of 12 March 2001, in the Camacho case, to protect the right to life and physical integrity of a group of Colombian refugees in Colombia, Annual Report 2001, §61. About the threat of refoulement see Chapter V (Non-refoulement).

[110] The shelter was called 'Unidos Retornaremos' (united we will return). Annual Report 1997, February 17, 1998.

[111] Annual Report 1999, Chapter III.C.1, §26.

[112] CIDH *José Alirio Arcila Vasquez and family* v. *Colombia,* precautionary measures of 17 December 1997. See also Chapter XIII (Protection).

detention situations or provide access to medication,[113] but also in the context of threats against the lives and physical integrity of detainees.[114]

2.3.9 Journalists

Clearly, perpetrators of human rights violations or corruption have no fondness for journalists who expose them. While their distaste for such journalists may result in the curtailment of their freedom of expression, something for which the Commission and Court have used precautionary measures as well,[115] it may also lead to threats to their lives and physical integrity.[116]

Two journalists in Colombia had published an article in which they accused a group called CONVIVIR of having committed certain abuses in Medellin. After the publication of their second article on this subject, a bomb destroyed the offices of the CONVIVIR group in Medellin. Following this, both journalists received telephone threats blaming them for having caused the bombing. As a result they were forced to stay in hiding. In July 1997 the Commission took precautionary measures on their behalf.[117]

In another Colombian case a journalist for 'El Espectador' received a telephone-call from someone with the nickname 'el Panadero' who 'expressed interest in having a journalistic piece done on the paramilitaries' version of the outbreak of violence on 27 April 2000 in the National Model Prison of Bogotá. At the door of the facilities the journalist was approached, 'surrounded, sedated, and driven to a nearby house where several individuals gagged and beat her and sub-

---

[113] See also Chapter VII (Detention).

[114] See also section 2.5.2, Chapter VII (Detention) on separating minors and adults. In May 2000, for instance, the Commission requested Colombia to take steps to protect the life and physical integrity of political prisoners threatened by paramilitary prisoners wearing 'Autodefencas Unidas de Colombia' (AUC) bracelets. The measures of 11 May 2000 were on behalf of the prisoners detained in buildings 1 and 2 of the National Model Prison in Bogotá. Based on the information available at the time on the precautionary measure, on 27 April 2000 prisoners belonging to paramilitary groups, who were detained in cell block 5, violently attacked the prisoners in cell block 4. They killed 47 inmates and injured 17 others. According to the petitioners several prisoners from cellblocks 3 and 5 were patrolling the facilities carrying long-range weapons and making threats against political prisoners. Annual Report 2000, §17. Elsewhere the Commission refers to the killing of 25 detainees (Annual Report 2000, Chapter IV, §93). See also Chapter XVII (Official responses).

[115] See Chapter XII (Other situations), section 3.4.

[116] On 26 May 2000, for instance, the Commission took precautionary measures on behalf of a journalist in Peru. Apparently national intelligence service agents had entered the office of the newspaper where he worked and tortured him in order to obtain certain videos from him. He was hospitalised for cuts on his left arm. On 14 July 2000 the State informed the Commission that it could not comply with the precautionary measures as the journalist in question had left Peru on 31 May 2000, Annual Report 2000, §44. In November 2001 the Commission took precautionary measures of four journalists in Colombia. According to information received by the Special Rapporteur for Freedom of Expression, the Southern Liberators Block of the AUC had threatened them. This included an AUC communiqué urging them to renounce their professions within 48 hours or they would be executed. The beneficiaries were the editor of the newspaper 'Diario Sur', a reporter for the weekly 'VOZ' who was also a peace commissioner for the region of Nariño, a reporter for the RCN newscast and a cameraman for 'Caracol Televisión', Annual Report 2001, Chapter III (a), §24.

[117] Apparently this matter was not yet transferred as a case.

jected her to degrading treatment'. In June 2000, the Commission requested Colombia to take steps to protect her life and physical integrity as well as those of two other editors.[118]

2.3.10 Politicians and government officials

Politicians and government officials may also receive threats. They may be the victims of rivalry between colleagues or political parties, or they may put themselves in danger by actually trying to find resolutions for violent situations, by exposing corruption or by taking seriously their work at a human rights division of their government.[119]

In April 2000 the Commission took precautionary measures requesting Brazil to protect the state police auditor of São Paulo and his family. The Archbishop Emeritus of São Paulo had approached the Commission with a request for such measures. The state police auditor had received threats, 'presumably because of his activities monitoring police conduct'. The State reported that it had granted the precautionary measures.[120]

One precautionary measure directed at Nicaragua is particularly interesting because the President himself seems to have been involved. In February 1999 the Commission requested Nicaragua to protect the lives and physical integrity of three persons who had received threats relating to activities undertaken as part of their professional duties in the General Department for Integrity in Public Service of the Office of the Comptroller-General of Nicaragua. According to the information presented by the petitioner, it was President Alemán himself who had threatened one of the victims, the Comptroller.[121] A few years earlier the Inter-American Court had ordered provisional measures on behalf of Alemán, who was then a presidential candidate. There had been an attempt at his life, which killed one of his bodyguards and injured several persons.[122]

In March 2001 the Commission took precautionary measures on behalf of a public prosecutor on Colombia's specialised judicial circuit and on behalf of her family. For security reasons they had relocated outside the country. The petitioners had pointed out that Colombia had denied an extension of her leave of absence. As a result, and despite the security concerns, she was forced to return to Colombia immediately. The Commission requested Colombia to guarantee the right to life and person of this prosecutor and her family. Colombia 'undertook a series of measures that concluded satisfactorily for the parties'.[123]

The Commission also uses country reports as a tool for human rights protection. These reports, in turn, provide a more in depth context of the violations in specific countries. In its discus-

---

[118] The peace editor and the judicial editor of 'El Espectador'. On 19 June 2000, the Commission requested Colombia to expand the precautionary measures to include a journalist working for 'NTC Noticias'. She had received threats similar to those of her colleagues. Annual Report 2000, §20.

[119] In September 1994, for instance, the Commission requested Colombia to adopt protective measures on behalf of one of its own government officials, the delegated Attorney General for Human Rights of supporting the guerrilla forces. A member of Congress had accused him of supporting the guerrilla forces, Annual Report 1997, (*Hernando Valencia Villa* case). In March 1996 the Commission took precautionary measures on behalf of four members of the Guatemalan National Democratic Front, who were elected to the Congress. Later it reiterated them and extended the measures to include their families. In May 1996 Guatemala responded that it was taking measures to protect the persons involved, CIDH Annual Report 1996, 14 March 1996, Chapter II, § 4a (cont.).

[120] CIDH Annual Report 2000, §13.

[121] See also Chapter XVII (Official responses).

[122] IACHR *Alemán Lacayo* v. *Nicaragua*, Order of 2 February 1996.

[123] CIDH Annual Report 2001, Chapter III (a), §15. Generally about the attitudes of States see Chapter XVII.

sion of the human rights situation in Colombia, for instance, it specifically pointed out that the persons threatened and attacked also included public employees. It mentioned the example of the 'members of the Human Rights Unit of the Office of the Prosecutor-General who are constantly threatened, as well as the municipal ombudsmen ('personeros'), who are involved in human rights-related tasks at the local level'.[124]

The Commission noted that it had received 'numerous requests' for precautionary measures on behalf of 'human rights defenders, members of civil society organizations, and even State employees, such as municipal ombudsmen (*personeros*) who are subject to threats, assassination attempts, and/or accused of collaboration with one or another of the parties to the armed conflict'. It stated that it had 'responded to these urgent calls in the manner that it deemed appropriate'.[125]

The second commander of the Colombian national army had given a statement implicating public employees. He gave this statement during a forum in Miami, Florida organised by the Cuban-American Foundation on Tradition, Family and Property:

> "And, finally, what poses greater limitations for us is defending us from the infiltrators of the subversion in the Office of the Prosecutor-General, the Office of the Human Rights Ombudsman, and the Office of the Procurator-General backed by some international organizations that cause us very much harm...the non-governmental human rights organizations, misinformed or infiltrated, are as dangerous as the guerrillas themselves".[126]

In response both the Prosecutor-General and the Procurator-General publicly warned that these remarks endangered the lives of the members of their institutions.[127] The Commission noted that such accusations against public employees and members of NGOs and the failure of the government to unequivocally reject these statements put the people referred to in serious danger. The government needed to adopt 'specific and effective measures to punish those who practically depict people who work for justice and human rights as enemies of the State'.[128]

2.3.11 CEDAW and domestic violence

Thus far the only time an adjudicator other than the Inter-American Commission and Court has used a provisional measure to protect against threats in a case in which the claim itself also aimed at protection was in October 2003. That month CEDAW used provisional measures for the first time as part of its newly established individual complaint procedure. It requested Hungary to take measures to protect the petitioner against threats by her former common law husband. The petitioner, who was not represented by counsel, had urgently requested it 'to save her life, which she feels is threatened by her violent former partner'.[129]

---

[124] CIDH Annual Report 1999, Chapter V – Columbia, §105.

[125] Id., §118. The Commission took note of the fact that Colombia had handed down indictments in murder cases of five persons including Mr. Valle Jaramillo. It pointed out, however, that seven members of the 'Comité Técnico de Investigaciones' of the Human Rights Unit in the Office of the Prosecutor-General had been assassinated. The Commission also noted that it had learned that more than 100 prosecutors were being threatened and some had had to leave Colombia. Annual Report 1999, Chapter V – Colombia, §121.

[126] Id., §110.

[127] Id., §111.

[128] Id., §§113-114. See also Chapter XIII (Protection).

[129] CEDAW *A.T.* v. *Hungary*, 26 January 2005, §4.1.

**3   RELATION BETWEEN PROVISIONAL MEASURES TO HALT DEATH THREATS
AND HARASSMENT AND THE EXPECTED DECISION ON THE MERITS**

3.1   Introduction

Human rights adjudicators have emphasized the importance for States of implementing their positive obligations under the respective treaties to protect the right to life, the prohibition of cruel treatment and torture and the right to personal security. States that do not protect persons under their jurisdiction against death threats and harassment fail to 'ensure' the fundamental rights involved.[130] Obviously threats to persons who have resorted to an international adjudicator also hinder the right of individual petition under the respective treaties.[131]

Article 2 ICCPR refers to an undertaking to respect and ensure all rights in the Covenant. Similar to the previous Chapters the other relevant provisions are the right to life (Article 6), the prohibition of torture and cruel treatment (Article 7) and Article 9 (the right to security).[132] Article 2 ICAT stipulates that States 'shall take effective legislative, administrative, judicial or other measures to prevent acts of torture in any territory under its jurisdiction'. Article 13 entails the obligation to ensure the right to complain to the competent authorities with allegations of torture. Moreover, '(s)teps shall be taken to ensure that the complainant and witnesses are protected against all ill-treatment or intimidation as a consequence of his complaint or any evidence given'. Based on Article 16 ICAT States shall 'undertake to prevent in any territory under its jurisdiction other acts of cruel, inhuman or degrading treatment or punishment which do not amount to torture as defined in article 1, when such acts are committed by or at the instigation of or with the con-

---

[130]   This issue is relevant in the context of provisional measures, judgments on the merits as well as judgments on reparation. See further Chapter XIII (Protection).

[131]   See 1ˢᵗ Optional Protocol to the ICCPR; Article 22 ICAT; Article 14 ICERD; Optional Protocol to the CEDAW; Article 45(2) ACHPR; Article 44 ACHR; Article 34 ECHR and Article VIII(1) Annex 6 Dayton Peace Agreement. For special attention to victims and witnesses see also the law and practice of the Yugoslavia and Rwanda Tribunals and the International Criminal Court. On protection of witnesses before the Rwanda Tribunal see e.g. Lagrange (2003). See also Article 20 Statute ICTY: 'due regard for the protection of victims and witnesses'; Article 22 'protection of victims and witnesses'. Moreover, Rule 69 (B) Rules of Procedure and Evidence stipulates: "In the determination of protective measures for victims and witnesses, the Trial Chamber may consult the Victims and Witnesses Section". Rule 75 (A), finally, provides: "A Judge or a Chamber may, *proprio motu* or at the request of either party, or of the victim or witness concerned, or of the Victims and Witnesses Section, order appropriate measures for the privacy and protection of witnesses, provided that the measures are consistent with the rights of the accused".

[132]   Chapter VII already discussed the positive obligations of States vis-à-vis detainees. The HRC has pointed out 'the positive obligations on States parties to ensure Covenant rights will only be fully discharged if individuals are protected by the State, not just against violation of Covenant rights by its agents, but also against acts committed by private persons or entities that would impair the enjoyment of Covenant rights insofar as they are amenable to application between private persons or entities. Thus, failure to ensure Covenant rights, as required by Article 2, may 'give rise to violations by States Parties of those rights, as a result of States Parties' permitting or failing to take appropriate measures or to exercise due diligence to prevent, punish, investigate or redress the harm caused by such acts by private persons or entities'. HRC General Comment 31, 29 March 2004, §8. Already in 1992, the HRC noted that Article 7 covers acts committed by private individuals, implying a duty for States to take appropriate measures to protect persons against such acts. HRC General Comment 20 [44] on torture, cruel, inhuman or degrading treatment or punishment (Article 7), 3 April 1992.

sent or acquiescence of a public official or other person acting in an official capacity'. Article 4 ICERD obliges States to take immediate and positive measures against incitement of racial hatred. Article 5(b) lays down the security of the person including the protection from violence or bodily harm and Article 6 ICERD refers to the undertaking to ensure effective protection and remedies including reparation and satisfaction.

In its General Recommendation on violence against women the CEDAW pointed out that 'the definition of discrimination includes gender-based violence' and that 'gender-based violence may breach specific provisions of the Convention, regardless of whether those provisions expressly mention violence'. It also stated that 'discrimination under the Convention is not restricted to action by or on behalf of Governments'.

> "Under general international law and specific human rights covenants, States may also be responsible for private acts if they fail to act with due diligence to prevent violations of rights or to investigate and punish acts of violence, and for providing compensation".[133]

In the first case it dealt with since the entry into force of the Optional Protocol instituting an individual complaint proceeding the CEDAW found violations of Articles 2(a), (b) and (e), 5 and 16 for failure to protect the petitioner against domestic violence.[134] These articles address the positive obligations of States to ensure equality and eliminate discrimination against women.

In the regional systems positive obligations have equally been recognized. Sometimes they have been emphasized in the context of human rights activities other than those directly dealing with individual complaint. Both the African and the Inter-American Commission, for instance, have a Special Rapporteur dealing with the rights of human rights defenders and expressing particular concern when their right to life and personal integrity are under threat.[135]

The Inter-American Court has derived from Articles 4 (right to life) and 5 (humane treatment) together with Articles 1(1) (obligation to respect rights) and 2 ACHR (domestic legal effects) the obligation of States not only to refrain from threatening people but also to actively protect them against threats by others.[136] This includes the duty to investigate prior violence and

---

[133] CEDAW General Recommendation 19 on violence against women, 29 January 1992, §9.

[134] CEDAW *A.T.* v. *Hungary*, 26 January 2005. See also Boerefijn (2005a), pp. 470-480 and, more generally, Boerefijn (2005c), pp. 35-57.

[135] See e.g. Special Rapporteur of the African Commission on Human and Peoples' Rights (ACHPR) on Human Rights Defenders in Africa Me. Reine Alapini-Gansou, Press release on the situation in Cameroon, 7 April 2008 (expressing concern regarding the case of Mrs. Madeleine Afité, president of la Maison des droits de l'Homme du Cameroun (MDHC) 'who has been threatened to death on several occasions these days. Her car was also ransacked during the night of 5 to 6 March, 2008 for having denounced, notably to the international media, human rights violations'). The Inter-American Commission has a Special Unit on human Rights Defenders. The Parliamentary Assembly of the Council of Europe has also paid attention to the issue of death threats and harassment in the context of the ECHr. See Resolution 1571 (2007) on the member States'duty to cooperate with the ECtHR, as well as its Recommendation 1809 and the report by Rapporteur Christos Ourourides, Committee on Legal Affairs and Human Rights, Doc. 11183, 9 February 2007 and Addendum of 1 October 2007. For case law by the African Commission generally acknowledging the positive obligations of States, see e.g. ACHPR *Legal Resource Foundation* v. *Zambia*, 2001 (positive obligations based on Article 1 ACHPR); *Social and Economic Rights Action Center for Economic and Social Rights* (*SERAC*) v. *Nigeria*, 6 June 2001 (positive obligations based on the rights themselves); *Purohit and Moore* v. *The Gambia*, 2003 (obligation to respect and ensure, but taking into account resources); and the ongoing case (July 2008) *Association of Victims of Political Violence & Interights* v. *Cameroon*.

[136] See e.g. IACHR *Velásquez Rodríguez* v. *Honduras*, judgement of 29 July 1998, §§172-175 and *Godínez Cruz* v. *Honduras,* 20 January 1989, §186.

threats and to prosecute and punish the perpetrators.[137] If the threats have resulted in internal displacement the freedom of movement comes into play.[138] If the victims of such displacement are indigenous peoples, their relation to their ancestral ground play a role as well.[139] Given the background of many threats the freedom of expression and association and the special recognition of human rights defenders are often emphasized. Journalists, human rights defenders, trade unionists and others threatened and harassed for their activities have the right to continue these activities unhindered.[140]

The ECtHR only deals with civil and political rights, but these have been interpreted to include positive obligations.[141] This is particularly relevant with regard to Articles 2 (right to life), 3 (prohibition of ill-treatment and torture) and 8 (private life) in conjunction with Article 1 (ensuring the rights). The Bosnia Chamber has equally confirmed that Article 1 ECHR (to 'secure' the rights and freedoms in the Convention) also entails positive obligations to protect those rights.[142]

This section deals with case law in the various systems involving the above provisions that could shed light the relation between provisional measures to halt death threats and the expected decision on the merits.

3.2 Inter-American system

A case in which the Inter-American Commission took precautionary measures to protect minors in detention illustrates that bringing a claim before the Commission may make an NGO vulnerable for retaliation. In 1996 the petitioners reported that the members of the Honduran section of Casa Alianza had been intimidated and harassed. High-ranking government officials had threatened to deprive the organisation of its legal status and to deport Bruce Harris and other members of the organisation who were called 'dangerous aliens' whose purpose it was to slander Honduras.[143] They also alleged that the President of the Honduran Bar Association had threatened

---

[137] See e.g. President IACHR, *Velásquez Rodríguez, Fairén Garbi and Solís Corrales, and Godínez Cruz* Cases (Honduras), Letter President on behalf of witnesses Jiménez-Puerto and Custodio López, 6 November 1987. This was conformed In the judgements on the merits, see e.g. *Velásquez Rodríguez* v. *Honduras*, judgement of 29 July 1998, §188. See further on the obligation to investigate, prosecute and punish as the main reason to take provisional measures Chapter XII (Other situations, section 2.7 on preventing impunity) and as a specific method of protection against death threats Chapter XIII (Protection).

[138] See also Chapter XIII (Protection).

[139] About protecting cultural survival see Chapters X (Cultural and religious rights) and XIII (Protection).

[140] See also Chapter XIII (Protection). About provisional measures ordered mainly to protect freedom of expression see Chapter XII (Other situations).

[141] See e.g. Mowbray (2004); Van der Velde (2002); Vlemminx (2002); Lawson (1995) and Forder (1992). See further Chapter XIII on the protective measures required. The Council of Europe also introduced the European Social Charter and its Protocols (including a collective complaint system).

[142] See e.g. Bosnia Chamber *Matanović et al.* v. *Republika Srpska*, 6 August 1997, §56.

[143] CIDH *Minors in detention* v. *Honduras*, 10 March 1999, §46. The petitioners included the following newspaper articles with their communication: *El Heraldo*, 'Casa Alianza seeks publicity', 6 October 1996; *La Tribuna*, 'Casa Alianza's legal status will be revoked if it keeps up its complaints', 10 October 1996; *La Prensa*, 'Private Development Organization determined to slander Honduras', 11 October 1996 (p. 4A); *El Nuevo Día*, 'Slandering Honduras is no way to resolve the juvenile problem', 12 October 1996 (p. 14); *La Prensa*, 'Casa Alianza acting recklessly', 14 October 1996 (p. 20A); *El Heraldo*, 'Slander, says Sosa Coella: The Director of Casa Alianza should be deported', 10 October 1996.

to revoke the membership of the legal counsel of Casa Alianza in Honduras. As discussed in the previous section in such cases it may become necessary to take protective measures to protect these persons against threats as well. This section refers to the case law on the merits with regard to the obligation of States to protect persons against death threats and harassment. It illustrates how both international and regional adjudicators have interpreted the provisions on the right to life and security and the prohibition of cruel treatment to encompass a positive obligation of the State to protect individuals against threats by private individuals and paramilitaries as well.

3.3 HRC

In *Delgado Páez* v. *Colombia* (1990) the HRC referred to the obligation under Article 9(1) to protect the liberty and security of non-detained persons.[144] It pointed out that there was 'no evidence that it was intended to narrow the concept of the right to security only to situations of formal deprivation of liberty'.

> "It cannot be the case that, as a matter of law, States can ignore known threats to the life of persons under their jurisdiction, just because that (sic) he or she is not arrested or otherwise detained. States parties are under an obligation to take reasonable and appropriate measures to protect them. An interpretation of article 9 which would allow a State party to ignore threats to the personal security of non-detained persons within its jurisdiction would render totally ineffective the guarantees of the Covenant".[145]

An interpretation of Article 9(1) limited to the context of arrest and detention would render ineffective the guarantees of the ICCPR.

In its decision on the merits in *Tshishimbi* v. *Zaire* (1996)[146] the HRC referred to its prior jurisprudence that Article 9(1) also included protection against 'threats made by persons in authority to the personal liberty and security of non-detained individuals within the State party's jurisdiction'. After having found violations of Articles 9(1) and 7 ICCPR it urged the State to thoroughly investigate the circumstances of the abduction and detention and to bring to justice those responsible. As it usually does, the HRC also referred to the obligation to ensure that similar violations do not occur in the future. The investigation and prosecution required could be seen both as a form of redress for the victims and as a means to ensure that similar violations do not occur in the future, taking a firm stance against impunity.[147]

---

[144]   HRC *Delgado Páez* v. *Colombia*, 12 July 1990. The petitioner in this case was a teacher of religion and ethics at a secondary school in Leticia, Colombia. As an advocate of 'liberation theology' his social views differed from those of the man who was the Apostolic Prefect of Leticia at the time the author and alleged victim worked there as a teacher. Among others, the author alleged to have received anonymous phone calls at his residence in Bogotá threatening him with death if he returned to Leticia and did not withdraw his complaint against the Prefect and the education authorities. He received death threats as well at the teachers' residence in Leticia. He reported these to the military authorities in Leticia, the teachers union, the Ministry of Education and the President of Colombia. On 2 May 1986 unknown killers shot to death a colleague, Ms. Rubiela Valencia, outside the teachers' residence. The author himself was attacked five days later in the city of Bogotá. Fearing for his life he left the country and obtained political asylum in France in June 1986.

[145]   HRC *Delgado Páez* v. *Colombia*, 12 July 1990. See also Nowak (1993), p. 163.

[146]   HRC *Tshishimbi* v. *Zaire*, 25 March 1996.

[147]   See also Chapter XIII (Protection).

Other cases against, among others, Zambia, Angola and Equatorial Guinea have confirmed this.[148] In the reparations paragraph in *Bahamonde* v. *Equitorial Guinea* (1993) the HRC urged the State to guarantee the security of the victim. The petitioner had contended that he 'was subjected to harassment, intimidation and threats by prominent politicians and their respective services on a number of occasions'. Observing that the State party had dismissed this claim in general terms without addressing his 'well-substantiated allegations', the HRC concluded that the State had failed to ensure his right to security of person. The petitioner had fled the country for Spain in 1991 and he claimed that since his departure he had received death threats. He claimed that 'the security services of Equatorial Guinea have received the order to eliminate him, if necessary in Spain'.[149] The HRC did not specify its call to guarantee the security of the victim. It could mean either to guarantee his security if he were to return or to guarantee his security in Spain.

It is clear, however, that the HRC considers the State to have extra-territorial obligations, in the sense that Article 2 ICCPR cannot be interpreted in such a way that a State simply may not violate the Covenant on its own territory, but that it is free to do so on the territory of another State.[150] In *Dias* v. *Angola* (2000) the HRC referred to the obligation to 'take adequate measures to protect his personal security from threats of any kind'.[151] Several months later, in *Chongwe* v. *Zambia* (2000) the HRC was more specific, in referring to the obligation, under Article 2(3)(a), to 'take adequate measures to protect his personal security and life from threats of any kind'. Not only did it refer to 'life' as well as to 'security', but it also urged the State 'to carry out independent investigations of the shooting incident, and to expedite criminal proceedings against the persons responsible for the shooting'.[152] Like Mr. Bahamonde, Mr. Chongwe had fled the addressee State, but the Committee simply pointed out that this State was obliged to take adequate measures to protect his personal security and life from threats of any kind without specifying the territorial ramifications.[153]

In *Dias* v. *Angola* (2000) the HRC also referred to the obligation 'to take adequate measures to protect his personal security from threats of any kind'. Mr. Dias had submitted his complaint

---

[148] See e.g. HRC *Bwalya* v. *Zambia*, 14 July 1993; *Bahamonde* v. *Equitorial Guinea*, 20 October 1993; *Chongwe* v. *Zambia*, 25 October 2000; *Dias* v. *Angola*, 20 March 2000 and *Jiménez Vaca* v. *Colombia*, 25 March 2002.

[149] HRC *Bahamonde* v. *Equitorial Guinea*, 20 October 1993.

[150] HRC *Sergio Ruben Lopez Burgos* (*submitted by his wife Delia Saldias de Lopez*) v. *Uruguay*, 29 July 1981 and *Celiberti de Casariego* v. *Uruguay*, 29 July 1981. The State party informed the HRC by note of 31 October 1991 that Mr. Lopez Burgos had filed a request for compensation and that the sum of $ 200.000 had been awarded to him on 21 November 1990, to be paid in four instalments. At this date the State also informed the Committee that Mrs. Celiberti had presented a claim that was under review and that she was elected to the Council of Montevideo on 26 November 1989. See follow-up report CCPR/C/45/R.6. On extra-territorial obligations, see also Chapter V (Non-refoulement)

[151] HRC *Dias* v. *Angola*, 20 March 2000.

[152] Moreover, it pointed out that the remedy should include 'damages' to the victim 'if the outcome of the criminal proceedings reveals that persons acting in an official capacity were responsible for the shooting and hurting of the author'. HRC *Chongwe* v. *Zambia*, 25 October 2000. Mr. Chongwe was an advocate and the chairman of a 13-party opposition alliance. He claimed that Dr. Kaunda, the former President, and himself were shot at and wounded by the police on 23 August 1997. He also included a Human Rights Watch report confirming the shooting and quoting witness statements and medical reports. The HRC found that the State had failed to protect the petitioner's right to life and security of person.

[153] While in certain cases (e.g. occupation) a State does have positive obligations when it acts extraterritorially, it might be far-fetched to require each State also to provide protection against death threats occurring outside of their own jurisdiction. On extraterritorial application of human rights treaties see also Chapter XIV (Jurisdiction).

from Portugal. In this case the Committee specifically noted that he had been unable to enter Angola due to the threats against him.[154] Still, it did not discuss the territorial scope of the obligation to protect the victim against threats nor did it point out the State's obligation to ensure his safe return to Angola. Only in *Jiménez Vaca* v. *Colombia* (2002) did the HRC point out that the State was obliged 'to take appropriate measures to protect his security of person and his life so as to allow him to return to the country'. In this case it also urged the State 'to carry out an independent inquiry into the attempt on his life and to expedite the criminal proceedings against those responsible for it'. On the other hand, it seemed more cautious with regard to the assurances of non-repetition. Rather than the usual reference to the obligation to take measures to prevent similar violations in the future, it referred to the obligation 'to try to prevent' such violations.[155] Chapter XII on the relationship between the protection required in provisional measures and in decisions on reparation more closely discusses the Committee's decisions on reparations in cases involving threats and the indications these may give for the use of provisional measures pending the proceedings.

An early case, dating from 1977, involving a claim that family members were being persecuted, is that of Zairian citizen Mbenge who submitted a communication on behalf of members of his family and persons in their employ as well as on behalf of himself.[156] In his initial letter he complained of 'systematic persecution' of his family by the Government of Zaire (Congo). He submitted his complaint from Belgium where he was residing as a political refugee. He alleged that his family was being persecuted because of his political views. He pointed out that he had learned through the press that he had been sentenced to death in September 1977 for supposedly having participated in the invasion of the province of Shaba (formerly known as Katanga). He claimed that President Mobutu had sought in vain to have him extradited from Belgium. Instead, the Government arrested several members of his family as well as business associates who might give information on his whereabouts.[157] On the merits the Committee found a violation of Article 9 (right to security of person). Neither this decision nor the file shows specific intervention by the Committee pending the proceedings before it.[158]

---

[154] HRC *Dias* v. *Angola*, 20 March 2000.

[155] HRC *Jiménez Vaca* v. *Colombia*, 25 March 2002. Mr. Jiménez Vaca was a practising trial lawyer in the city of Medellín and in the region of Urabá. For his work he was based in the municipality of Turbo. In the region he was the legal advisor to several trade unions and organisations of peasants, including for Sintagro in Antioquia. From 1980 until his flight to the UK in 1988 he was harassed. Several times he asked the authorities for protection. On 26 August 1985 several households received pamphlets asking "are you a member of Sintagro? Doesn't it bother you to belong to a group of hired assassins and murderers of the people, drug bandits led by Argemiro Correa, Asdrúbal Jiménez and Fabio Villa?" Later on one of his brothers disappeared and another was murdered. On 4 April 1988 he was shot at when driving in a taxi in Bogotá. After 5 days in a hospital he was transferred to another hospital for security reasons. He stayed there until he was well enough to travel to the UK. He had identified members of the fourth and tenth army brigades 'as possibly being responsible for the harassment and death threats to which he was subjected'.

[156] HRC *Daniel Monguya Mbenge* v. *Zaire*, 25 March 1983.

[157] His younger brother and his father-in-law were arrested in September 1977. Business relation Mozola, a pharmacist, as well as the family driver (no name provided) were also arrested the same day. Six days later he submitted his case before the HRC.

[158] Eventually the HRC decided that the petitioner was justified to act on behalf of his brothers and father-in-law by reason of close family connection. In July 1980 it discontinued consideration of the case to the extent it related to his brother Simon and his father-in-law since it appeared that they 'would now be in a position to act on their own behalf'. Regarding his younger brother the Committee based its assessment on the undisputed fact that he was arrested in order to force him to disclose the whereabouts of his brother Simon and that he was not released from detention until late in 1978 or early in 1979. The HRC found a violation of Article 9 ICCPR. With respect

Early cases hinting at harassment of counsel are those involving Maître Hammel in Madagascar. In February 1982 his law offices had been searched and he was taken away by officers of the 'political police' and held in a basement cell. He noted that he was informed that he 'was suspected of being an international spy' in view of his contacts and communications with Amnesty International and the HRC since, 'according to the Malagasy political police, those contacts constituted a crime of international espionage'. After 19 years as a member of the Madagascar Bar he was expelled as a French national and had two hours to pack at his home. The State party informed the HRC, in January 1987, of the decision of the Supreme Court of Madagascar on his case, of August 1986. In this decision the court considered that the Minister of the Interior had been correct in expelling him 'insofar as his continued presence in Madagascar would have disturbed public order and security'. The court pointed out that it was 'apparent from the investigation that Mr. Eric Hammel, making use both of his status as a corresponding member of Amnesty International and of the Human Rights Committee [sic] at Geneva, and as a Barrister, of his own free will took the liberty of discrediting Madagascar by making assertions of such gravity that they should have been upheld by irrefutable evidence'. In a case Mr. Hammel submitted on behalf of himself, the HRC found violations of Article 9(4) because he had been unable to challenge his arrest. It found a violation of Article 13 because he had not been allowed to submit reasons against his expulsion and to have his case reviewed by a competent authority while there were no compelling reasons of national security. It also noted with concern that the decision to expel him 'would appear to have been linked to the fact he had represented persons before the Human Rights Committee'. 'Were that to be the case, the Committee observes that it would be both untenable and incompatible with the spirit' of the ICCPR and its OP.[159]

In March 1981 the HRC strongly urged the State to provide detailed information about the access of Dave Marais to Maître Hammel, counsel for the alleged victim, and to ensure that they could effectively communicate. In May 1981 Maître Hammel informed the Committee that, 'as a consequence of his enquiry into his client's state of health through the examining magistrate' he 'was charged at the instance of the Attorney General with spreading false rumours'. He also stated that the political police had questioned him on two occasions.[160] In February 1982 Maître Hammel informed the Committee of his expulsion. In this context he referred to an officers' plot of the previous month and pointed out that the political police had seized part of his dossier on the *Marais* case.[161] Hammel claimed that his expulsion was also related to his involvement in representing a politician, Monja Jaona, following an arrest. Later Hammel represented Jaona before the HRC with regard to yet another arrest.[162] The situation sketched above illustrates that the HRC has faced situations in which access to counsel was limited partly through interference with his activities. Indeed, the HRC intervened pending *Marais* to ensure access to counsel.[163] Obviously this implied that the State should not hinder counsel in his defence. Nevertheless, the HRC did not intervene specifically to protect counsel against harassment.

---

to the petitioner himself it found a violation of Article 6(2) because he had been sentenced to death twice in circumstances contrary to the provisions of the Covenant and of Article 14(3)(a)(b)(d) and (e).

[159] HRC *Eric Hammel* v. *Madagascar*, 3 April 1987.
[160] See also Chapter VIII on ensuring procedural rights to protect the right to life and personal integrity, discussing the Committee's informal provisional measure to ensure access to counsel.
[161] HRC *Dave Marais* v. *Madagascar*, 24 March 1984. See also *John Wight* v. *Madagascar*, 1 April 1985.The first month of his representation of John Wight Maître Hammel was still in Madagascar.
[162] HRC *Monja Jaona* v. *Madagascar*, 1 April 1985.
[163] See Chapter VIII (Ensuring procedural rights).

In her first communication in *Teti Izquierdo* v. *Uruguay* (1982)[164] the petitioner mentioned continued death threats against her husband, detained in Uruguay. The HRC did not respond to this information. Only three months later, in October 1980, when she informed it of his disappearance, it took action and requested to be informed about his health and whereabouts. It is possible that an earlier intervention would have been more effective.

Bautista de Arellana v. *Colombia* (1995)[165] is particularly relevant in the context of the protection against threats. The case had been submitted by a Colombian lawyer residing in Brussels who was instructed by the family of a Colombian citizen who disappeared in August 1987 and whose body was subsequently discovered. When the lawyer submitted the complaint, in June 1993, he also noted that the family of the disappeared person and himself 'have received death threats and are subject to intimidation, because of their insistence in pursuing the case'.[166] Counsel pointed out that the authorities promoted the alleged perpetrator to Brigadier General and, in August 1995, awarded him an Order for Military Merit. Finally, he referred to an incident that same month when the alleged victim's family, together with members of the Association of Relatives of Disappeared Prisoners (ASFADDES), met in a popular restaurant in Bogotá for a demonstration on the occasion of the eighth anniversary of Nydia Bautista's disappearance.

> "Soon after their arrival, an individual in civilian clothes entered the restaurant and occupied a table next to theirs. All those present identified Brigadier General Velandia Hurtado (the alleged perpetrator, ER), who continued to monitor the group throughout the meeting. The presence of Mr. Velandia Hurtado, who otherwise commands the Third Army Brigade in Cali, on those particular premises on that particular day, is considered to be yet another instance of intimidation of Nydia Bautista's family".[167]

Pending the proceedings the HRC could have used provisional measures to protect her family members.[168]

---

[164] HRC *Teti Izquierdo* v. *Uruguay*, 1 April 1982.

[165] HRC *Bautista de Arellana* v. *Colombia*, 27 October 1995.

[166] The State explained the disciplinary proceedings that were taking place. It mentioned that the Division of Special Investigations took up the case again after the victim's body had been found. In February 1991 it heard the testimony of Mr. Garzón Garzón, who was then a member of the National Army. It noted that his testimony could 'never be corroborated' and his whereabouts were 'currently unknown'. The HRC pointed out that the file revealed that this witness 'requested special police protection for himself and his family after giving his testimony'. Later, in June 1995, a domestic court attached full credibility to his testimony about the disappearance of Ms. Bautista de Arellana. The National Delegate for Human Rights had also given full credit to this testimony by resolution of July 1995. In a later submission to the HRC counsel expressed concern for the National Delegate's physical integrity and referred to 'recent reports about further instances of intimidation of Nydia Bautista's sister (the sister of the alleged victim, ER) by agents of the military's intelligence service'. By note of 27 July 1995 counsel added that the family of the alleged victim, in particular his sister, continued to be subjected to intimidation and harassment. He also pointed out that the family's first lawyer had disappeared in Bogotá on 4 July 1990. About the latter's disappearance see CIDH *Dr. A. de Jesus Pedraza Becerra* v. *Colombia*, 25 September 1992.

[167] HRC *Bautista de Arellana* v. *Colombia*, 27 October 1995.

[168] See also Chapter XIII (Protection). Another example involving threats is that of *Vicente Barzana Yutronic (on his own behalf and on behalf of his two sons)* v. *Chile*, 23 July 1999 (inadm.). The complaint referred to death threats to the petitioner's family allegedly because of his human rights activities and his Croatian origin. He claimed that his sons had been arbitrarily detained and tortured in May 1994, but gave no specific examples of threats that took place following his initial submission of 8 July 1996. Hence, it makes sense that on 14 February 1997 the case was

The same applies to the case of *Jayawardena* v. *Sri Lanka* (2002). The complaint concerned death threats and between the initial submission, when the petitioner was an opposition member of parliament and December 2001, when his party obtained a majority and he became a minister in the new government, he informed the HRC by fax of a range of threats against him. On the merits the HRC found, among others, that the failure to investigate these death threats violated his right of security of person under Art. 9(1) ICCPR. No information is available on explicit requests by the petitioner for provisional measures, not of any informal action by the HRC in this regard.[169]

3.4   HRC and death threats on death row

In cases involving death threats on death row the HRC often specifically recommends, as part of the remedy, the humane treatment of the petitioner in detention.[170] There are several cases in which the submissions of petitioners on death row referred to death threats and harassment.

In one case the petitioners were beaten unconscious. The beatings resulted in a fractured arm and other injuries. They were then left without medical attention for almost a day and one of the petitioners was later warned against further pursuing his complaint to the judicial authorities.[171]

In another case the petitioner had complained that warders allegedly told death row inmates that 'since the State party was not prepared to hang them' they would think of 'other ways of decreasing the death row population'. He submitted that 'the warders (...) are taunting with death threats and some of them keep on telling me that they are the ones who will be taking me to the gallows and what size rope will fit my neck and how much weight it will take to take my head off my body'.[172] He claimed that since the death of one of his co-defendants, who died as a result of the violence, warders had repeatedly threatened him with death and that 'the amount of threats increased after those responsible for the death of three inmates were indicted'. The HRC noted that the petitioner had described the events in detail and the State party had not refuted these claims. The State had not informed the Committee 'whether the threats and ill-treatment to which the author himself allegedly was, and *remains*, subjected, are also under investigation' (italics ER).[173]

---

only transmitted under Rule 91 (current Rule 97). Later the case was declared inadmissible, also in relation to the claims on behalf of his sons, because there was nothing in the materials before the HRC to suggest that the sons had authorized their father to represent them.

[169]   HRC *Jayawardena* v. *Sri Lanka*, 22 July 2002. Other cases, such as *Afuson Njaru* v. *Cameroon*, 19 March 2007 also dealt with death threats and harassment, but apparently these were no longer ongoing when the case was submitted to the HRC. Nevertheless on the merits the HRC found that an effective remedy also entailed the obligation of the State to take effective measures to ensure that the petitioner 'is protected from threats and/or intimidation from members of the security forces', §8. Before the case was submitted to the HRC the UN Special Rapporteur against torture had already referred toone of the attacks against the petitioner in his report of his visit to Cameroon, 11 November 1999, Annex II, §37.

[170]   See further Chapters III (Executions), VII (Detention) and XIII (Protection).

[171]   In its decision on the merits the Committee determined that this was an aggravating factor. HRC *Randolph Barrett and Clyde Sutcliffe* v. *Jamaica*, 30 March 1992.

[172]   *Dwayne Hylton* v. *Jamaica*, 8 July 1994. The HRC noted also the allegation that prison warders had severely beaten him during a search.

[173]   "In the absence of further information on such investigations, and taking into account that such investigations as have been undertaken do not appear to have been concluded four and a half years after the events, due weight must be given to the author's allegations to the extent that they

In the third example the petitioner had submitted that warders had beaten to death another inmate in front of his cell. The day after this beating they returned and maltreated him as well. He suffered a kidney injury but was left in his cell for four days before he was brought to a hospital.[174] The State party did not accept that death row inmates were generally afraid to notify the authorities of instances of ill treatment. In its admissibility decision the Committee simply regretted that the State had not provided it with information about the results of the investigation it had announced.[175] Claims do not all concern threats by authorities. They may also relate to failure to protect against threats by fellow inmates.[176]

In all cases involving claims of ill treatment, beatings and death threats upon conviction the HRC expects the State to investigate the situation and inform it accordingly. Lacking this and in the face of detailed descriptions by the petitioner it gives due weight to the latter's allegations.[177] After all, the claims could not have been dealt with during the trial (in which case the HRC normally defers to the findings of domestic courts) because the allegations related to events subsequent to conviction. The HRC did use provisional measures in these cases but not to deal with the threats. It only used them to halt the execution of the petitioners. Nevertheless, in its findings it recommended the State to cease their continuing ill treatment.[178]

---

have been substantiated". HRC *Dwayne Hylton* v. *Jamaica*, 8 July 1994; note the other case *Dwayne Hylton* v. *Jamaica*, 16 July 1996. See also *Garfield Peart and Andrew Peart* v. *Jamaica*, 19 July 1995 and *Anthony Leehong* v. *Jamaica*, 13 July 1999.

[174] HRC *Ian Chung* v. *Jamaica*, 9 April 1998. He had complained about this treatment to the Parliamentary Ombudsman. Later his counsel had requested information from the Ombudsman's Office about these complaints, but with no results.

[175] Subsequently, the State party contended that its investigation had not substantiated the allegation of ill treatment by warders on death row. The HRC noted that the State party had not indicated who had investigated the claim, when it was investigated and whether a formal report was issued on the results of these investigations. The HRC also noted that the petitioner had given a detailed account of the beatings. It reminded Jamaica of its obligation under the OP to properly investigate allegations of violations of the Covenant and forward the outcome of the investigations to the Committee in detail and without undue delay. It found violations of Articles 7 and 10(1). *Ian Chung* v. *Jamaica*, 9 April 1998. See also *Lennon Stephens* v. *Jamaica*, 18 October 1995.

[176] See e.g. HRC *Silbert Daley* v. *Jamaica*, 31 July 1998.

[177] In March 1993, for example, the HRC declared admissible the case of *Garfield and Andrew Peart* v. *Jamaica*, 19 July 1995. Subsequently the alleged victims reported ill treatment and threats and they claimed they did not receive medical treatment. In relation to the claim that warders had beaten Andrew Peart with a metal detector on 4 May 1993, counsel submitted that afterwards he was passing blood in his urine and also suffered from shoulder injuries. He did not, however, receive medical treatment. He further stated that following this incident his client was locked in his cell without water until three days later. Counsel also submitted that Andrew Peart had been receiving death threats from warders, 'allegedly because he testified against one of them before the Court after the death of an inmate in 1989'. The State party submitted that Garfield Peart's communication in relation to the way he was treated in prison was inadmissible because of failure to exhaust domestic remedies. The Committee noted that the petitioner had complained to the acting Superintendent, that his counsel had made a complaint to the Commissioner of Police and was subsequently informed that the complaint was referred to the Commission of Correctional Services for appropriate action. "In the circumstances, the Committee considers that the author and his counsel have shown due diligence in the pursuit of domestic remedies and that there is no reason to review the Committee's decision on admissibility". On the merits the HRC found violations of Articles 7 and 10(1) because of the assaults against both petitioners and the death threats against one of them.

[178] See e.g. HRC *Willard Collins* v. *Jamaica*, 1 November 1991.

The case of *Rickly Burrell* v. *Jamaica* (1996)[179] is illustrative of situations of ongoing threats. The HRC had used provisional measures only to halt the petitioner's execution.[180] Six months after his initial submission he was killed during a prison incident. With regard to the threats and ill treatment his counsel claimed violations of Articles 7 and 10. The petitioner's violent death, he claimed, constituted a violation of Article 6(1).[181] He submitted that there was a *prima facie* case that the authorities had arbitrarily deprived the petitioner of his life. In view of the evidence the burden of proof was now on the State, which had sole access to the most significant information, such as the autopsy reports.[182] Counsel also referred to a letter received from an inmate stating that a warder had previously threatened Mr. Burrell with death. Apparently, Burrell had been convicted of having murdered a relative of this warder. Following the threats the petitioner had lodged a complaint with the Superintendent. According to the above inmate's letter it was this warder who started the incident and it was him who shot the petitioner in his cell. Counsel also referred to other letters of inmates equally alleging the involvement of this warder.[183]

---

[179] HRC *Rickly Burrell* (*submitted by Phillip Leach*) v. *Jamaica*, 18 July 1996. After Burrell had been killed the HRC accepted that his counsel would maintain the communication. Upon consultation with the victim's family, the Jamaica Council for Human Rights had instructed counsel to do so.

[180] Note verbale to the Minister of Foreign Affairs and Foreign Trade of 9 June 1993 (on file with the author). See also HRC *Bakhrom Khomidov* (*submitted by his mother Saodat Khomidova*) v. *Tajikistan*, 29 July 2004. In this case Special Rapporteur used provisional measures in September 2002 to halt the execution of the petitioner's son. In March 2004 she re-iterated that investigators had beaten her son, but she had filed no complaint with the authorities 'as she was afraid that they would further harm her son or would execute him'.

[181] He referred to HRC *Guerrero* v. *Colombia*, 31 March 1982 and *Baboeram* v. *Suriname*, 4 April 1985.

[182] HRC *Rickly Burrell* (*submitted by Phillip Leach*) v. *Jamaica*, 18 July 1996, §3.4. Counsel referred to a press release by Amnesty International reporting the killing of four death row prisoners. While reports indicated that they were shot dead after they had tried to take prison guards hostage, some prisoners had been receiving death threats from prison personnel prior to the incident, because they had complained about ill treatment. Counsel wrote to the Parliamentary Ombudsman and to the Superintendent of St. Catherine's prison about the incident and the preceding threats. He received no reply. In January 1994 Amnesty International published a report about the killings. Among others, it noted that the injuries of the guards appeared to have been minor and that none of them were hospitalised. Eyewitnesses among the prisoners had stated that the four prisoners had been shot in their cells 'when they no longer posed a threat to the warders'. They also claimed that 'because of the confined space, it is difficult to see how prisoners could have been shot without injuring the warders, if they were still being held hostage'. Counsel stated that 'at least three of the warders named by prisoners as having been involved in the shootings have been named repeatedly in other allegations involving threats or maltreatment involving prisoners on death row'. No report had been made available about the incident. Counsel also contended that complaints about the many incidents of excessive violence by prison warders were not adequately dealt with. Instead, prisoners complaining about ill treatment were subjected to threats by warders.

[183] Counsel claimed that the warders had not been trained in restraint techniques and the use of different levels of force. The incidents, he argued, showed that there was no clear chain of command and that 'if the warders had received proper training in control and restraint techniques, they might not have panicked and shot Mr. Burrell and three other inmates'. Among others, the State party submitted that while none of the warders were hospitalised, 'two of them were rendered unfit for work for two months, as a result of the injuries received'. The State party concluded: "Like Burrell, none of these four warders was involved in the commencement of the altercation, but became victims. For Burrell, it was fatal". The HRC regretted that the State had made available neither the autopsy report nor the results of the coroner's inquest. It observed that

Thus, counsel had pointed out that Burrell had been particularly at risk from physical attack and had been seriously threatened and abused prior to his death.[184] Indeed the HRC found a violation of Article 6(1) for failure to take effective measures to protect the victim's life.

If a petitioner informs the HRC about threats such as those mentioned here, it would indeed be appropriate to intervene by means of provisional measures. It could take a gradual approach in this respect, first taking informal provisional measures. As discussed in section 3, the HRC has already formally taken provisional measures to protect against threats. This is in agreement with its approach on the merits to positive obligations to protect the right to life, the prohibition of cruel treatment and torture and the right of personal security.

3.5   CAT

In *Dzemajl et al* v. *Yugoslavia* (2002) CAT considered that, in the circumstances, the burning and destruction of houses constituted acts of cruel, inhuman or degrading treatment or punishment. The nature of these acts was 'further aggravated by the fact that some of the complainants were still hidden in the settlement when the houses were burnt and destroyed, the particular vulnerability of the alleged victims and the fact that the acts were committed with a significant level of racial discrimination'. It pointed out that while the acts were not committed by public officials themselves 'they were committed with their acquiescence' and constituted a violation of Article 16(1) ICAT. CAT also specifically referred to the positive obligations flowing from this provision.[185] *B'M.B* v. *Tunisia* involved a complaint about Articles 2, 11-14 ICAT, but CAT used provisional measures to protect the petitioner's family and the family of the alleged victim and witnesses against death threats and harassment. In its decision declaring the case inadmissible it repeated its request 'to ensure that no harm is done to the author's family, the alleged victim's family or the witnesses and their families'. This seems to be based on the acknowledgment that States have positive obligations under Articles 5(a) and 16 to protect persons somehow related to the case.

3.6   CEDAW

In *A.T.* v. *Hungary* (2005) the CEDAW concluded that 'the obligations of the State party set out in article 2 (a), (b) and (e) of the Convention extend to the prevention of and protection from violence against women, which obligations in the present case remain unfulfilled and constitute a violation of the author's human rights and fundamental freedoms, particularly her right to security of person'.[186] Among others, it pointed out that Articles 5(a) and 16 had been violated, because the petitioner 'could not have asked for a restraining or protection order since neither option

---

the report submitted by the State party acknowledged that the victim's death 'was the unfortunate result of confusion on the side of the warders, who panicked when seeing some of their colleagues being threatened by the inmates'. It also noted that the shooting continued after the warders were rescued.

[184]   In this light counsel had noted that the HRC had previously decided that a State party could be responsible 'either by act or omission' for not taking adequate measures to protect against such threats. See his submission of 14 February 1994 (on file with the author), referring to HRC *Dermit Barbato (submitted by Mr. Gilmet Dermit on behalf of his cousins)* v. *Uruguay*, 21 October 1982.

[185]   CAT *Dzemajl et al* v. *Yugoslavia*, 21 November 2002, §§9.2 and 9.6.

[186]   CEDAW *A.T.* v. *Hungary*, 26 January 2005, §9.3.

currently exists in the State party'. She had been 'unable to flee to a shelter because none are equipped to accept her together with her children, one of whom is fully disabled'.[187]

3.7   Inter-American Commission and Court

The Inter-American Court has pointed out in its provisional measures that the State should take effective measures to investigate and punish the perpetrators, 'as a key element of its protective duty'.[188] In *Velásquez Rodríguez* (1988) it stressed that 'under international law a State is responsible for the acts of its agents undertaken in their official capacity and for their omissions, even when those agents act outside the sphere of their authority or violate internal law'.[189] The Court had found that 'in principle, any violation of rights recognized by the Convention carried out by an act of public authority or by persons who use their position of authority is imputable to the State'.[190]

> "The State has a legal duty to take reasonable steps to prevent human rights violations and to use the means at its disposal to carry out a serious investigation of violations committed within its jurisdiction, to identify those responsible, to impose the appropriate punishment and to ensure the victim adequate compensation".[191]

It is 'obligated to investigate every situation involving a violation of the rights protected by the Convention'. After all, 'if the State apparatus acts in such a way that the violation goes unpunished and the victim's full enjoyment of such rights is not restored as soon as possible, the State has failed to comply with its duty to ensure the free and full exercise of those rights to the persons within its jurisdiction'. "The same is true when the State allows private persons or groups to act freely and with impunity to the detriment of the rights recognized by the Convention".[192]

In its judgments on the merits and on reparations the Inter-American Court often refers to the obligation to prevent, to investigate and to punish.[193] It has pointed out that it mentions this obligation in the judgment on the merits because the obligation to guarantee and ensure the effective exercise of the rights in the ACHR is different from and independent of the obligation to make reparation. This means that the State is obliged to investigate the facts and punish those responsible even if the victim or his next of kin would decide to waive the measures of reparation.[194] Otherwise it would fail to comply with its general obligation to 'ensure the free and full exercise' of the rights under the ACHR.[195]

---

[187]   Id., §9.4. More closely on this case see Boerefijn (2005a), pp. 470-480. See also IACHR pending case *Cotton Field* (*Ramos Monárrez et al.*) v. *Mexico*, lodged by the Commission on 4 November 2007 concerning the joint cases Nos. 12,496, 12,497 and 12,498, *the Cotton Field: Claudia Ivette González, Esmeralda Herrera Monreal and Laura Berenice Ramos Monárrez* (involving an alleged pattern of gender violence that had led to the murder of hundreds of women and girls).

[188]   IACHR *Giraldo Cardona* case (Colombia), Order for provisional measures (on behalf of members of the Civic Human Rights Committee of Meta), 19 June 1998.

[189]   IACHR *Velásquez Rodríguez*, Judgment of 29 July 1988, §170.

[190]   Id., §172.

[191]   Id., §174.

[192]   Id., §176.

[193]   See e.g. Medina-Quiroga/Nash Rojas (2007), pp. 19-29.

[194]   See, e.g. IACHR *Garrido and Baigorria*, judgment on reparations of 27 August 1998, §72.

[195]   See e.g. IACHR *Bámaca Velásquez*, judgment of 25 November 2000, §129 and *Paniagua Morales et al*, judgment of 8 March 1998, §178 (and sixth operative paragraph).

At the same time the Court has expressed an awareness of the difficulties of investigation in certain circumstances. It pointed out:

"The duty to investigate, like the duty to prevent, is not breached merely because the investigation does not produce a satisfactory result. Nevertheless, it must be undertaken in a serious manner and not as a mere formality preordained to be ineffective. An investigation must have an objective and be assumed by the State as its own legal duty, not as a step taken by private interests that depends upon the initiative of the victim or his family or upon their offer of proof, without an effective search for the truth by the government. This is true regardless of what agent is eventually found responsible for the violation. Where the acts of private parties that violate the Convention are not seriously investigated, those parties are aided in a sense by the government, thereby making the State responsible on the international plane".[196]

The Inter-American Commission and Court regularly refer to the aforementioned judgment in *Velásquez Rodríguez* (1988). In its final decision in the *Minors in detention* v. *Honduras* case, for instance, the Commission noted that:

"[that the] insinuation that persons who, for any reason, have recourse to the inter-American system for protection of human rights are disloyal to their country is unacceptable and cannot constitute a basis for any penalty or negative consequence. Human rights are higher values that 'are not derived from the fact that (an individual) is a national of a certain state, but are based upon attributes of human personality' (American Declaration of the Rights and Duties of Man, Whereas clauses, and American Convention, Preamble)".

The Commission considered that any act of intimidation or threat against the petitioners must be duly investigated and punished.[197] The protective duty of the Commission and Court explains the use of provisional measures to protect persons against threats recognized already in *Velasquez Rodriguez* (1988). This is based on the positive obligation of States to prevent attacks on life and dignity, among others by investigating and prosecuting past acts.

In June 1997 the Commission took precautionary measures in the case of *García Prieto et al.* so as to protect several persons against death threats and harassment. Almost ten years later, in September 2006, it requested the Court to order provisional measures. The Court did so that month and in January 2007.[198] At the end of 2007 it found violations on the merits, including a failure to comply with the obligation to investigate the threats and harassment endured. It found 'a lack of diligence by the police and prosecutorial authorities' in the conduct of the investigations. This had 'impeded the determination of the facts and the identification, trial, and possible punishment of the perpetrators responsible for the threats and harassment directed at some members of the García Prieto Giralt family. Moreover, the lack of an adequate and serious investigation has permitted that such events continue to the present'.[199] It had been proven 'that José Mauricio García Prieto Hirlemann and Gloria Giralt de García Prieto have lived for years, and continue living, with feelings of insecurity, anguish, and powerless due to the lack of an investigation of the events perpetrated against them. The failure to investigate the threats and harassment has affected the personal integrity of Ramón Mauricio García Prieto's parents'.[200] By way of reparation the Court ordered the State to conclude the pending investigations into the murder of Ramón

---

[196]   IACHR *Velásquez Rodríguez*, judgment of 29 July 1988, §177.

[197]   CIDH *Minors in detention* v. *Honduras*, 10 March 1999, §§153-155.

[198]   IACHR *García Prieto family et al.* (El Salvador), Order of 26 September 2006 and Order of 27 January 2007.

[199]   IACHR *Case of García-Prieto et al.* v. *El Salvador*, Judgment of 20 November 2007 (Preliminary Objection, Merits, Reparations, and Costs), §158.

[200]   Id., §159.

Mauricio García Prieto and the threats and harassment; as well as to publish the operative paragraphs of the judgment, and certain specific paragraphs, in the official gazette and in another important national newspaper, and to provide the victims with the psychiatric and psychological care required, free of charge.[201]

3.8   ECtHR

Of the three regional systems the European is the last one in which provisional measures have been used in the context of death threats and harassment, and only quite hesitantly. There are various Member States of the Council of Europe in which problems have arisen involving intimidation and harassment of witnesses, human rights defenders, journalists and others.[202] An example of a case in which the petitioner specifically requested provisional measures against harassment is *Aydin* v. *Turkey* (1997). In this case the petitioner requested the ECtHR to take provisional measures against harassment and intimidation. In particular, State officials should stop contacting the petitioner and her family about the petition. The Court did not take provisional measures, but in its judgment on the merits it did find violations of Articles 3 and 25 (now Article 34) ECHR.[203]

In *Osman* v. *UK* (1998) the ECtHR referred to the positive obligation to protect the right to life (Article 2) and prevent and suppress offences against the person. In 'certain well defined circumstances' this would include an obligation to 'take preventive operational measures to protect an individual whose life is at risk from the criminal acts of another individual'.[204] The Court pointed out that 'it must be established to its satisfaction that the authorities knew or ought to have known at the time of the existence of a real and immediate risk to the life of an identified individual or individuals from the criminal acts of a third party and that they failed to take measures within the scope of their powers which, judged reasonably, might have been expected to avoid that risk'. It classified Article 2 as 'a right fundamental in the scheme of the Convention'. In light of the nature of this article it was sufficient for a petitioner 'to show that the authority did not do all that could be reasonably expected of them to avoid a real and immediate risk to life of which they have or ought to have knowledge'. It also referred to Article 1 and the obligation to 'secure the practical and effective protection' of the rights in the Convention, including Article

---

[201]   "The Court finds that it is necessary to order measures of reparation in order to reduce the mental suffering of José Mauricio García Prieto Hirlemann and Gloria Giralt de García Prieto. To this end, the Court orders the State to provide adequate treatment and medication needed by these individuals, through its public health services, free of charge, for as long as necessary, and given their prior consent and a medical evaluation. When providing the medical, psychological, or psychiatric treatment required, the particular needs and circumstances of each person should be considered, in order to provide the proper treatment". IACHR *Case of García-Prieto et al.* v. *El Salvador*, Judgment of 20 November 2007 (Preliminary Objection, Merits, Reparations, and Costs), §201.

[202]   The following States, for instance, have recognized the competence of the ECtHR: Armenia, Azerbaijan (including Nagorno-Karabakh), BiH, Croatia, Georgia, Moldova (incl. Transdniestria), Romania, Russian Federation (incl. Chechnya and other North Caucasus regions), Serbia and Montenegro, Turkey and Ukraine. Belarus is a candidate for membership of the Council of Europe.

[203]   ECtHR (Grand Chamber) *Aydin* v. *Turkey*, Judgment of 25 September 1997. See also section 4 of this Chapter.

[204]   ECtHR *Osman* v. *UK*, 28 October 1998, §115.

2.[205] The Bosnia Chamber has equally confirmed that Article 1 ECHR (to 'secure' the rights and freedoms in the Convention) also entails positive obligations to protect those rights.[206]

With regard to the right to life the ECtHR recalled that the first sentence of Article 2(1) enjoined the State 'not only to refrain from the intentional and unlawful taking of life, but also to take appropriate steps to safeguard the lives of those within its jurisdiction'.[207] This involved 'a primary duty on the State to secure the right to life by putting in place effective criminal-law provisions to deter the commission of offences against the person, backed up by law-enforcement machinery for the prevention, suppression and punishment of breaches of such provisions. It also extends in appropriate circumstances to a positive obligation on the authorities to take preventive operational measures to protect an individual or individuals whose life is at risk from the criminal acts of another individual'.[208]

The ECtHR has also recognized the positive obligation of States under Article 3. The obligation of States under Article 1 ECHR 'to secure to everyone within their jurisdiction the rights and freedoms defined in the Convention', taken together with Article 3, requires States to 'take measures designed to ensure that individuals within their jurisdiction are not subjected to torture or inhuman or degrading treatment, including such ill-treatment administered by private individuals'.[209] 'State responsibility may therefore be engaged where the framework of law fails to provide adequate protection' or 'where the authorities fail to take reasonable steps to avoid a risk of ill-treatment about which they knew or ought to have known'.[210]

The Court reiterated that Article 3 'enshrines one of the most fundamental values of democratic society. It prohibits in absolute terms torture or inhuman or degrading treatment or punishment'.[211] The preventive measures required 'should provide effective protection, in particular, of children and other vulnerable persons and include reasonable steps to prevent ill-treatment of which the authorities had or ought to have had knowledge'.[212]

Its interpretation of the obligations under Article 8 on the right to family and private life is relevant as well. It has determined that the concept of private life covered the 'physical and moral integrity of the person, including his or her sexual life'.[213] It has pointed out that 'these obligations may involve the adoption of measures designed to secure respect for private life even in the sphere of the relations of individuals between themselves'.[214]

"Sexual abuse is unquestionably an abhorrent type of wrongdoing, with debilitating effects on its victims. Children and other vulnerable individuals are entitled to State protection, in the form

---

[205] Id., §116.
[206] See e.g. Bosnia Chamber *Matanović et al.* v. *Republika Srpska*, 6 August 1997, §56.
[207] See e.g. ECtHR *Mahmut Kaya* v. *Turkey*, 28 March 2000, §85 and *L.C.B.* v. *UK*, 9 June 1998, §36.
[208] See e.g. ECtHR *Mahmut Kaya* v. *Turkey*, 28 March 2000, §85 and *Osman* v. *UK*, 28 October 1998, §115.
[209] See e.g. ECtHR *Mahmut Kaya* v. *Turkey*, 28 March 2000, §115, *A.* v. *UK*, 23 September 1998, §22 and *H.L.R.* v. *France*, 29 April 1997, §40.
[210] See e.g. ECtHR *Mahmut Kaya* v. *Turkey*, 28 March 2000, §115, *A.* v. *UK*, 23 September 1998, §22 and *Osman* v. *UK*, 28 October 1998, §§115-116.
[211] See e.g. ECtHR *Z. et al.* v. *UK*, 10 May 2001, § 73, *Osman* v. *UK*, 28 October 1998, §116 and *A.* v. *UK*, 23 September 1998, §22.
[212] See e.g. ECtHR *Z. et al.* v. *UK*, 10 May 2001, §73, *Osman* v. *UK*, 28 October 1998, §116 and *A.* v. *UK*, 23 September 1998, §22.
[213] ECtHR *X and Y* v. *the Netherlands*, 26 March 1985, §22.
[214] Id., §§22-23. See also *Stubbings* v. *UK*, 22 October 1996, §§61-62.

of effective deterrence, from such grave types of interference with essential aspects of their private lives".[215]

In *Aydin* v. *Turkey* (1996) counsel for the petitioner specifically requested the Commission to take provisional measures (under Rule 36) 'directing the Government to stop all contact by state officials with the applicant and her family concerning her application'. The Commission transmitted the complaint of harassment of the petitioner and her family by the security forces to Turkey for urgent response. Turkey did not respond. Three weeks later the Commission decided not to take provisional measures. Nevertheless it drew the attention of the Government to 'the serious consequences which might arise from intimidation and harassment of an applicant and members of his/her family in connection with an application before the Commission'. Further complaints relating to intimidation and harassment of family members were forwarded to the State, which was reminded of its lack of response to the earlier complaints. Only several weeks later the Government made submissions with regard to the allegations of interfering with the right of individual petition. On the merits the Commission found violations of Articles 3 and 25 (now Article 34), Articles that have particular relevance in the context of provisional measures.[216]

In *Mahmut Kaya* v. *Turkey* (2000) the ECtHR was 'satisfied that Hasan Kaya, as a doctor suspected of aiding and abetting the PKK, was at that time at particular risk of falling victim to an unlawful attack. Moreover, this risk could in the circumstances be regarded as real and immediate'. The 'authorities must be regarded as being aware of this risk'.[217] Thus, the case law of the ECtHR has confirmed the positive obligations of States to protect persons against violence perpetrated by a private party. Both the Court and, in the past, the Commission have regularly dealt with positive obligations.[218] On the other hand, they have only recently used provisional measures for the first time in a context of death threats and harassment, while this was certainly not the first occasion on which (potential) petitioners, or witnesses (and their families), have received such threats.

When the Court is faced with situations such as these, involving ongoing threats, it is indeed appropriate for it to take provisional measures requesting the State to take specific protective measures.[219]

4   CONCLUSION

Throughout the world threats to human rights defenders, and to persons involved in domestic or international judicial proceedings, are a recurring problem. The Inter-American Commission and

---

[215]   ECtHR *X and Y* v. *the Netherlands*, 26 March 1985, §27. See also *Stubbings* v. *UK*, 22 October 1996, §64 and *A.* v. *UK*, 23 September 1998, §22.

[216]   ECHR *Aydin* v. *Turkey*, 7 March 1996 (Article 31 Report). The Commission also found violations of Arts 6 and 13, see partly dissenting opinions Thune and Bratza (joined by Trechsel, Soyer, Schermers and Marxer).

[217]   ECtHR *Mahmut Kaya* v. *Turkey*, 28 March 2000, §§89-91.

[218]   See e.g. the aforementioned ECtHR *Osman* v. *the UK*, 28 October 1998, §116. See also *Mastromatteo* v. *Italy*, 24 October 2002, appl. no. 37703/97, §68; *Z. et al.* v. *the UK*, 10 May 2001, appl. no. 29392/95, §109 and *E. et al.* v. *the UK*, 26 November 2002, §88.

[219]   See Barkhuysen/Van Emmerik/Rieter (2002), p. 87; Rieter (2003b) and the Report by CoE Parliamentary Assembly rapporteur Pourgourides, Doc. 11183, 9 February 2007, §52: "As the binding effect of the Court's interim measures is now recognised, such measures can be used to counter-act unlawful pressure on applicants to the Court, their lawyers, or members of their families. The Court could require respondent states to take positive action to protect applicants, as the Inter-American Commission and Court have done".

Court have extensively made use of provisional measures to protect such persons. Apart from protecting the lives and physical integrity of these human rights defenders, such provisional measures were also meant to ensure that the Court's final decision on the merits would not be prejudiced by one of the parties and to preserve the evidence needed in cases before the Court.

Now that the HRC has been functioning for more than three decades at least in one case it has used provisional measures also to halt death threats and harassment.[220] It is feasible that it will indeed use them in more such cases. In other cases, about which it does not yet have sufficient information, even for purposes of provisional measures, it may continue its use of Rule 91 (current Rule 97) to enquire about the situation of a petitioner, both in order to be able to properly deal with the case and to alert the State about possible concerns by the HRC. This applies as well to situations of death threats on death row, in which (informal) intervention might be warranted.

Next to the HRC, CEDAW and CAT have also used provisional measures to protect persons against death threats and harassment. The African Commission has done so as well. Thus, these adjudicators appear to have reaffirmed the extensive practice of the Inter-American Commission and Court with regard to this issue. They may be expected to continue using provisional measures to protect persons against death threats while a case is pending before them. Like the new African Court, all these adjudicators may draw inspiration from the practice of the Inter-American Commission and Court and consolidate their own practices in this respect.

It is only the ECtHR that is lagging behind. Given its case law on the merits (its emphasis on positive obligations and the particular importance attached to the right of petition and the prohibition of cruel treatment) and in light of the death threats against human rights defenders, witnesses and others in various Member States of the Council of Europe, a robust decision by the European Court to use provisional measures in this context would be a logical and appropriate next step.

---

[220]   In 2003 Scheinin considered it more likely that the HRC would decide to request a State to halt an immediate forced eviction with racist motives (Articles 26, 23, 17 ICCPR) than to request it to take positive action to protect against a threat to life. Scheinin, Geneva, April 2003.

CHAPTER X
PROTECTING (INDIGENOUS) CULTURAL AND RELIGIOUS RIGHTS

1   INTRODUCTION

The HRC, the Inter-American Commission and Court and the Bosnia Chamber have used provisional measures to halt certain actions or (industrial) developments that could cause irreparable harm to the (indigenous) culture or religion of certain groups.

In this context the question arises what types of actions or developments would result in irreparable harm to the culture and religion of these groups. A related issue to be addressed in this respect is which rights have been invoked by petitioners or *proprio motu* by the adjudicators in order to help stop these developments. It is also important to note on behalf of which groups the adjudicators have used provisional measures.

This chapter first discusses the practice of the human rights adjudicators in urgently dealing with cases involving indigenous culture. Then it explores how this practice relates to their case law on the merits and whether a finding of a violation is likely in this respect. Among others it deals with the question what type of cultural and religious rights have been protected by provisional measures, on behalf of whom and why.[1] In conclusion it also asks whether the practice of the HRC, the Inter-American Commission and Court and the Bosnia Chamber with regard to the use of provisional measures in cases involving culture is confirmed by the approach taken in the UN Declaration on the Rights of Indigenous Peoples (2007).

2   THE PRACTICE OF THE ADJUDICATORS TO TAKE PROVISIONAL MEASURES TO PROTECT CULTURAL OR RELIGIOUS RIGHTS

2.1   Introduction

This chapter discusses the practice of the HRC, the Inter-American Commission and Court, the African Commission and the Bosnia Chamber with regard to provisional measures to protect cultural or religious rights.

2.2   HRC

In some cases the HRC has used provisional measures to protect cultural rights. While its practice in this regard is not yet extensive, these cases merit close examination because they clarify the concept of provisional measures. They relate to land rights of (members of) indigenous groups and the collective aspects of the right to culture.

The first time it used provisional measures was in *Lubicon Lake Band* v. *Canada* (1990).[2] The petitioner had claimed that the land of the Lubicon Lake Band, approximately 10,000 square

---

[1]   See also Chapter XIII (Protection), section 4 (Beneficiaries).
[2]   HRC *Bernard Ominayak, Chief of the Lubicon Lake Band* v. *Canada*, 26 March 1990.

kilometres, had been expropriated for commercial purposes (oil and gas exploration) and de-stroyed. He claimed that 'the rapid destruction of the Band's economic base and original way of life had already caused irreparable injury'.[3] The State party, on the other hand, maintained that 'continued resource development would not cause irreparable injury to the traditional way of life of the Band'.[4] Three years and five months after the initial submission, the HRC declared the case admissible in so far as it might raise issues under Article 27 ICCPR (minority rights, cultural rights) or under other articles. At the same time it requested Canada to take provisional measures to avoid irreparable damage to Chief Ominayak and other members of the Lubicon Lake Band.[5] In its summary of the submissions the HRC explained that it used provisional measures '(i)n view of the seriousness of the author's allegations that the Lubicon Lake Band was on the verge of extinction'.[6]

Subsequently it simply renewed its original call for provisional measures, without com-menting on the non-compliance.[7] On the merits it found violations and recommended an unclear remedy.[8] Even if it had eventually recommended a remedy seeking a permanent or interim injunc-tion, such recommendation would to some extent have been too late because it was tardy in using provisional measures in the first place and because the State did not appear to respect them once they had been taken. Pending the case the HRC could have monitored compliance more actively.

The HRC did deal with the case as part of its mechanism for follow-up on Views. It re-quested Canada to provide 'any relevant information on measures taken to implement the remedy offered by the State party'.[9] A member of federal parliament submitted a letter to the Special Rapporteur for Follow-up on Views, emphasising that the violations of Article 27 ICCPR were indeed continuing. He also noted that the Committee's View was 'frequently misrepresented by Canadian government officials'. He requested the Rapporteur to urge the State to 'abandon its "take-it-or-leave-it" offer made to the Lubicon on January 24, 1989 – an offer which demonstra-bly has not proved to be a remedy – and instead begin negotiations on adequate economic devel-opment provisions and compensation'.[10]

In its Concluding Observations under the reporting procedure (Article 40 ICCPR) of April 2006 the HRC expressed concern 'that land claim negotiations between the Government of Can-ada and the Lubicon Lake Band are currently at an impasse'. It was also 'concerned about infor-

---

[3]   Id., §29.1.

[4]   Id., §29.2.

[5]   Earlier, it had only requested information under Rule 91 (on 16 October 1984 according to the text, on 9 November 1984 according to the cover page) and additional information by interim decision of 10 April 1986. See also Chapter II on timeliness.

[6]   HRC *Lubicon Lake Band* v. *Canada*, 26 March 1990, §29.3.

[7]   Id., §25.

[8]   See further Chapter XIII (Protection).

[9]   Canada responded almost a year later by stating: "As the Committee is aware, that remedy consisted of a comprehensive package of benefits and programs valued at $45 million (non-inclusive of the value of land, mineral rights, or possible provincial contributions) and a 95 square mile reserve". It pointed out that meetings with the Band were terminated because of its demand 'for additional compensation of at least $170 million'. It noted that 'the Government's offer has remained and continues to remain open for acceptance'. It also announced a negotiated settlement with the Woodland Cree Band similar to the 1989 offer to the Lubicon Lake Band and pointed out that both Bands 'have the same rights under Treaty 8 and are of similar size'. According to Canada the Woodland Cree Band now included about 185 former members of the Lubicon Lake Band. Response of the permanent mission of Canada of 25 November 1991 to the follow-up request of 12 February 1991 (on file with the author).

[10]   Letter by Ross Harvey (MP, Canada) to the Special Rapporteur for Follow-up on Views, 28 November 1991 (on file with the author and also available at: <nativenet.uthscsa.edu/archive/nl/91d/0189.html>, consulted 13 March 2003).

mation that the land of the band continues to be compromised by logging and large-scale oil and gas extraction, and regrets that the State party has not provided information on this specific issue (arts. 1 and 27)'. It recommended that State 'to make every effort to resume negotiations' in order to find 'a solution which respects the rights of the Band under the Covenant, as already found by the Committee'. "It should consult with the band before granting licences for economic exploitation of the disputed land, and ensure that in no case such exploitation jeopardizes the rights recognized under the Covenant".[11] In 2006 the UN Committee on Economic, Social and Cultural Rights specifically addressed the case of the Lubicon Lake Band in its Concluding Observations on Canada's compliance with the Covenant on Economic, Social and Cultural Rights. It recommended 'strongly' that Canada 'resume negotiations with the Lubicon Lake Band, with a view to finding a solution to the claims of the Band that ensures the enjoyment of their rights under the Covenant'. "The Committee also strongly recommends the State party to conduct effective consultation with the Band prior to the grant of licences for economic purposes in the disputed land, and to ensure that such activities do not jeopardize the rights recognized under the Covenant".[12]

Apart from the provisional measures in the *Lubicon* case, the other provisional measures to protect culture involved the Sami in Finland.[13] It was in *Sara et al.* v. *Finland* (inadm. 1994) that the HRC used provisional measures for the second time in order to protect culture.[14] The State denied that there was a causal link between the measures of protection requested by the petitioners and the object of the communication itself.[15] Apparently it argued that this was the reason why provisional measures should not be taken. Quite apart from the question whether it is appropriate in human rights adjudication to be strict about the relationship between the rights claimed and the request for provisional measures, it is clear that in this case the material object of the petitioners' complaint was the threat to their traditional economic and cultural rights caused by logging and road construction activities in certain reindeer husbandry areas. The HRC found that the material object of the complaint *was* related to the request for provisional measures.[16]

In this case the petitioners feared, at the time of initial submission in 1990, that large-scale logging activities were imminent in the areas used by them for reindeer breeding. They noted that two road construction projects into the petitioners' herding areas had been started without prior consultation.[17] When the HRC initially declared the case admissible in 1991, it indeed used provisional measures.[18] In 1994, however, it set aside this decision, including the provisional measures,

---

[11] HRC Concluding Observations (Canada), CCPR/C/CAN/CO/5, 20 April 2006, §9.

[12] CESCR Concluding Observations (Canada), E/C.12/CAN/CO/4; E/C.12/CAN/CO/5, 22 May 2006, §38.

[13] See Donders (2002), pp. 301-326 about the Sami as an indigenous people and their cultural identity and rights, with a focus on the Sami in Norway, Sweden and Finland.

[14] HRC *Sara et al.* v. *Finland*, 23 March 1994 (inadm.).

[15] The State argued that the Board's authority to approve logging activities in areas other than those designated as protected wilderness, such as the residual area outside the Hammastunturi Wilderness, was not derived from the Wilderness Act. "Accordingly, the State party denies that there is a causal link between the measures of protection requested by the authors and the object of the communication itself, which only concerns enactment and implementation of the Wilderness Act". However, the HRC noted that the continuation of road construction in the residual area could indeed be causally linked to the entry into force of the Wilderness Act.

[16] For purposes of admissibility the petitioners had sufficiently substantiated that this could raise issues under Article 27.

[17] See also Chapter XIII (Protection) on consultation and representation.

[18] The cover page does not mention provisional measures, but it appears from the text that the petitioners requested them. On 9 July 1991 when it declared the case admissible the Committee requested Finland to 'adopt such measures as appropriate to prevent irreparable damage to the authors'.

and declared the case inadmissible for non-exhaustion of domestic remedies. Subsequently, by the time the petitioners could submit a new complaint to the HRC, the logging they had aimed to prevent with their first submission had already taken place. In the follow-up case, moreover, the HRC felt it was unable to draw conclusions on the basis of the evidence before it.[19]

In *Jouni Länsman v. Finland* (*Länsman II*, 1996) the HRC used provisional measures for the third time in a case involving indigenous culture.[20] However, it later decided to set aside this decision. The four petitioners were all members of the Muotkatunturi Herdsmen's Committee. The HRC had denied a request for provisional measures in an earlier case (*Länsman I*) as being premature.[21] The petitioners pointed out that about 40 percent of the total number of reindeer owned by the Herdsmen's Committee grazed on the disputed lands during winter. The old untouched forests in the area are covered with lichen, which is very important 'due to its suitability as food for young calves and its utility as emergency food for elder reindeer during extreme weather conditions'.[22] The petitioners relied on the Committee's previous reference to minor infringements on the one hand and a denial of the right to culture on the other.[23] They relied upon the incremental approach to violations of Article 27 ICCPR that the HRC had acknowledged already in *Lubicon*. According to this approach a series of infringements would at some point in time result in a denial of Article 27 ICCPR. They argued that the impending infringement in this case would in fact trigger this denial. In order to prevent this, they requested provisional measures.

The HRC requested the State 'to refrain from adopting measures which would cause irreparable harm to the environment which the authors claim is vital to their culture and livelihood'.[24] This indicates a new phrasing of its provisional measures compared to earlier occasions. In *Lubicon* the HRC requested Canada to avoid irreparable damage to Chief Ominayak and other members of the Lubicon Lake Band. It did explain that it used provisional measures because of the seriousness of the allegations in that the Band was on the verge of extinction, but it did not yet

---

[19] See HRC *Anni Äärelä and Jouni Näkkäläjärvi v. Finland*, 24 October 2001. In this case the HRC did find violations of Art. 14 (fair trial) and considered that the State party was 'under an obligation to restitute to the petitioners that proportion of the costs award already recovered and to refrain from seeking execution of any further portion of the award'. It also considered that since the decision of the Court of Appeal was tainted by a substantive violation of fair trial provisions (equality of arms), the State was under an obligation to reconsider the petitioners' claims. See also *Jarle Jonassen and members of the Riast/Hylling reindeer herding district v. Norway*, 25 October 2002 (inadm.).

[20] HRC *Jouni E. Länsman et al. v. Finland* (*Länsmann II*), 30 October 1996.

[21] See section 3 discussing *Ilmari Länsman v. Finland* (*Länsman I*), 26 October 1994.

[22] HRC *Länsman II*, 30 October 1996, §2.4. They also pointed out that Sami reindeer Herdsmen in Finland had difficulties competing with their Swedish counterparts because Sweden subsidised the production of reindeer meat. Apart from that, traditional Sami reindeer Herdsmen in the north of Finland using nature based Sami methods, had difficulties competing with reindeer meat producers in the south who use fencing and feeding with hay.

[23] See the discussion in *Ilmari Länsman v. Finland* (*Länsman I*), 26 October 1994, §§9.4-9.8. In its subsequent case law the HRC indeed confirmed its approach that not every interference can be regarded as a denial. In *Länsman II*, 30 October 1996, the formulation was that the logging had to be of such proportions as to deny the petitioners' rights to enjoy their culture 'in that area'. In *Äärelä and Näkkäläjärvi v. Finland*, 24 October 2001 it used the term 'threshold' and referred to its practice to enquire whether the interference in the reindeer husbandry was so substantial that it failed to properly protect the right of the petitioners to enjoy their culture. In *Apirana Mahuika v. New Zealand*, 27 October 2000 and *Länsman I* the HRC pointed out specifically that measures with a certain limited impact on the way of life of persons belonging to a minority would not necessarily amount to a denial of the right under Article 27 ICCPR.

[24] HRC *Länsman II*, 30 October 1996, §4.1.

take the two step approach 'risk to environment-risk to culture' taken in *Länsman II*. In *Sara et al.* v. *Finland* (1994) it requested the State to adopt the appropriate measures to prevent irreparable harm to the petitioners.[25] This could be seen as a more traditional approach, as the phrasing did not show an awareness of the collective aspects of the case.[26] In *Länsman II*, however, the HRC not only showed an awareness of the collective aspects of its provisional measure but it noted specifically that the State should refrain from adopting measures that *would cause irreparable harm to the environment*. Only following this it referred to the petitioners rather than the environment, by noting that they claimed that this environment was *vital to their culture and livelihood*. This new two step phrasing shows an awareness of the special relation between indigenous peoples and their lands.

Another new approach taken in *Länsman II* relates to the Special Rapporteur's request to the State party to inform him 'if it contended that the request for interim protection was not appropriate in the circumstances of the case' and, if so, to give reasons for this contention. He would then 'reconsider the appropriateness of maintaining the request under rule 86'.[27]

In response the State argued that provisional measures 'should be issued restrictively, and only in serious cases of human rights violations where the possibility of irreparable damage is real, e.g. when the life or physical integrity of the victim is at stake'. It did not consider that this case revealed circumstances pointing to the possibility of such irreparable damage.[28] It noted that the present logging area was only a small portion of the relevant State owned forests and that it had negotiated with the Muotkatunturi Reindeer Husbandry Herdsmen's Association to which the petitioners also belonged.[29] The State noted as well that Rule 86 (current Rule 92) only referred to avoiding irreparable damage to the victim of the alleged violation and stated: "Clearly enough, it does not cover measures having 'otherwise long-lasting damage' referred to by the authors in their communication".[30]

---

[25] HRC *Sara et al.* v. *Finland*, 23 March 1994 (inadm.).

[26] Id. Of course this does not mean that the Rapporteur was not aware of these aspects. See also the reference to this case in Kamminga (1996), p. 171 and p. 183.

[27] HRC *Länsman II*, 30 October 1996, §4.1. It transpires from the Note Verbale to the State that he requested it to inform him of its reasons to contest the appropriateness 'as soon as circumstances permit'. Note verbale to the State party of 15 November 1995 (on file with the author). In the letter of the same date to counsel the HRC simply noted: 'under rule 86, the State party has been requested to provide information on the alleged irreparable harm caused by logging to the author as early as possible'. Letter to the petitioner of 15 November 1995 (on file with the author).

[28] In its submission dated 20 December 1995 but submitted on 15 December (on file with the author) it was phrased as follows: "The Government therefore regards the Committee's request as inappropriate in the current circumstances, and is of the opinion that the Committee should set aside its request for interim measures".

[29] See also section 3 of this chapter (the heading on consultation) and Chapter XIII (Protection), section 4.4 on representation.

[30] Submission by the Permanent Mission of Finland in Geneva dated 20 December 1995, but submitted on 15 December (on file with the author).

Subsequently the HRC revoked its provisional measures.[31] While it did not explain this decision, one may assume that it agreed with the State party's interpretation of irreparable harm.[32] Indeed in the text of its admissibility decision of March 1996 (unpublished) the HRC noted that it had set aside its provisional measure 'in the light of the State party's observations of 15 December 1995 and its pledge to reduce current logging activities in the area specified in the communication'.[33] In their subsequent submission the petitioners welcomed the Committee's decision to declare the case admissible. They did not refer to its decision to set aside its provisional measure, possibly for strategic reasons.[34]

In 1996 the HRC found that the completed logging of around 250 hectares and the proposed logging of a further 250 hectares in the Angeli area did not constitute a violation of Article 27 ICCPR. On the basis of the information then before it the HRC concluded that the approved logging would not be on a scale threatening 'the survival of reindeer husbandry'. It did point out that if faced with evidence that the effects of the logging 'were more serious than foreseen at present' or new logging plans were to be approved on a larger scale, this could trigger a violation of Article 27. After all, 'though different activities in themselves may not constitute a violation of this article, such activities, taken together, may erode the rights of Sami people to enjoy their own culture'.[35]

Despite the fact that it found no violation in this case, the provisional measures taken pending the proceedings made sense as they aimed at preventing irreparable harm to the cultural survival of an indigenous group. As a practical matter they may have served a purpose in triggering the State's efforts to seriously consider the arguments made by the petitioners. They may also have contributed to the State's decision at least to decrease the amount of logging with 25 percent until the final view.[36]

In November 2000 Jouni and Eino Länsman submitted a new petition. Two years later the chairperson of the HRC used provisional measures requesting the State to 'refrain from conducting logging activities that would affect the exercise by Mr. Jouni Länsman and others of reindeer husbandry in the Angeli area, while their case is under consideration by the Committee'.[37] In April 2003 it declared the case admissible,[38] but another two years later it found that the logging

---

[31] Among others, the petitioners noted that 'for the authors of the communication the harm is in any case irreparable, since the lands in question cannot be used as winter herding lands in their lifetime'. They then pointed out that the local Sami had already experienced the first adverse effect of the logging namely that 'the reindeer cannot just be released to the winter herding lands from the round-up place just north of the logging area but must be brought to specific places'. "This causes a lot of extra work. Within the next months it will be seen whether the reindeer will find enough to eat in the remaining winter herding lands". The HRC considered that the logging activities approved for the future would be such that 'while resulting in additional work and extra expenses for the authors and other reindeer herdsmen' it 'does not appear to threaten the survival of reindeer husbandry', *Länsman II*, §10.6.

[32] See also Chapter XV on assessment of risk.

[33] HRC *Jouni E. Länsman et al.* v. *Finland*, 14 March 1996 (unpublished admissibility decision, on file with the author).

[34] The petitioners' submission of 20 May 1996 (on file with the author).

[35] HRC *Jouni E. Länsman et al.* v. *Finland* (*Länsman II*), 30 October 1996, §10.7.

[36] See further Chapter XVII on the official responses of addressee States.

[37] HRC *Jouni Länsman, Eino Länsman and the Muotkatunturi Herdsmen's Committee* v. *Finland*, 17 March 2005 (*Länsman III*), §1.2. In this case it was the Chairperson rather than the Special Rapporteur that took the decision on behalf of the Committee. Special Rapporteur Scheinin had been involved in bringing the previous Sami cases before the HRC. Moreover, the HRC adheres to the rule that Committee members do not take part in decisions involving their own State.

[38] The HRC noted that legal persons such as the Herdsmen's Committee had no standing and this part of the petition was inadmissible under Article 1 OP.

carried out had 'not been shown to be serious enough as to amount to a denial' of the petitioners' right to enjoy their own culture in community with other members of their group under Article 27 ICCPR.[39] Relevant with regard to the provisional measure may be the Committee's statement, in its decision on the merits, that it was not necessary to consider the negative effect of the proposed logging in the area as the State had committed 'not to proceed to logging' in the Kippalrova area.[40]

2.3   Inter-American Commission

Members of indigenous groups are often threatened and attacked. In such cases the Inter-American Commission has taken precautionary measures to protect their lives and physical integrity.[41] Apart from this, similar to the HRC it has also taken some precautionary measures exactly to prevent irreparable harm to indigenous culture. The Commission's precautionary measures in cultural cases equally have a collective component. The beneficiaries include not only each and every individual member of the indigenous group involved, but also the group as such.

In 1993 the Commission took precautionary measures for the first time in the case of *Mary and Carrie Dann* v. *US*. The US did not respond to this request. The petitioners were two members of the Indian Law Resource Center. They claimed that the sisters Dann, who were members and spokespersons for the Dann Band of the Western Shoshone Nation, had asserted Western Shoshone aboriginal title and treaty right for their lands in Nevada and that their ancestors had used and occupied these lands 'since time immemorial'.[42] The petitioners also claimed that the sisters' family ranch was their sole means of support and that their needs were met by the sale of their livestock, goods and produce. They argued that the US had violated the rights of the sisters by confiscating the land 'through the use of a grossly unfair procedure that "extinguished" the Indian title to the land for a few cents per acre'.[43] In August 1993 the petitioners had informed the Inter-American Commission that the US Bureau of Land Management intended to confiscate all livestock found on the lands where generations of Danns have grazed their livestock. They requested the Commission to take precautionary measures, as they feared that the US would sell the livestock of the Danns and of the Western Shoshone National Council that were grazing on these lands. In response the Commission requested the US to 'stay its intention to impound all livestock

---

[39]   HRC *Jouni Länsman, Eino Länsman and the Muotkatunturi Herdsmen's Committee* v. *Finland*, 17 March 2005, §10.

[40]   HRC *Jouni Länsman, Eino Länsman and the Muotkatunturi Herdsmen's Committee* v. *Finland*, 17 March 2005, §9.3. Subsequent to the use of provisional measures, in October 2001, Finland informed the HRC that it refrained from conducting logging activities in the Angeli area' (the area as defined in the Committee's previous View) 'that would affect the exercise by the individual authors' reindeer husbandry while their communication is under consideration by the Committee'.

[41]   See generally Chapter IX (Death threats).

[42]   CIDH *Mary and Carrie Dann* v. *United States*, 27 December 2002, §38.

[43]   CIDH *Mary and Carrie Dann* v. *United States*, 27 September 1999 (adm.), §7. In the domestic proceedings it was determined that they had lost their lands through 'gradual encroachment'. Before the CIDH the Danns pointed out that they had never left their lands and that there were no white settlers on it. In one newspaper article Carrie Dann is quoted questioning whether 'gradual encroachment' is a valid component of American law: "I certainly don't want people saying 'I gradually encroached on you, and took your rights away'. Either I am a human being or I am not a human being": J. Mullins, 'Oh really? Groups endorse plan to end public lands grazing', Elko Daily Free Press, 1 March 2002, posted in a collection of media accounts on the Dann sisters at <www.angelfire.com/nv2/wells/danns.html> (consulted 15 December 2006).

belonging to the Danns until this case has been resolved'.[44] The Commission had to reiterate its precautionary measures several times. In June 1999, for instance, the Commission requested the US to take appropriate measures in this case 'to stay the efforts of the Bureau of Land Management to impound their livestock, until the Commission had the opportunity to fully investigate the claims raised in the petition'.[45] Almost ten years after its first precautionary measures in this case, in 2002, it found that the State had 'failed to ensure the Danns' right to property under conditions of equality contrary to Articles II, XVIII and XXIII of the American Declaration in connection with their claims to property rights in the Western Shoshone ancestral lands'.[46]

More recently the Inter-American Commission has also dealt with urgent indigenous cases involving States such as Belize, Paraguay and Nicaragua. The famous judgment of the Inter-American Court in the *Awas Tingni* case against Nicaragua started at the Commission level with a precautionary measure 'for the purpose of suspending the concession given by the government to the SOLCARSA Company to carry out forestry work on the lands of the Awas Tingni Indigenous Community'.[47]

With regard to Belize it granted precautionary measures on behalf of the Maya Indigenous Communities and their members in October 2000.[48] It requested Belize to 'take the necessary steps to suspend all permits, licences, and concessions allowing for the drilling of oil and any other tapping of natural resources on lands used and occupied by the Maya Communities in the District of Toledo, in order to investigate the allegations in this case'.[49] In its report on the merits the Commission specified that it requested these measures 'until the Commission had the opportunity to investigate the substantive claims raised in the case'.[50]

Another famous case that later went to the Inter-American Court (which did not use provisional measures) is that of the *Yakye Axa*. In August 2001 a criminal court judge had ordered the removal of the homes of members of the Enxet speaking Yakye Axa Indigenous Community in Paraguay. Under dire circumstances this community had been occupying a strip of land along a highway opposite the lands they claimed as part of their traditional habitat. In September 2001 the Commission took precautionary measures on their behalf in order to halt this removal.[51]

This case shows that the Commission can be elaborate in its precautionary measures. It specifies the relevant rights (e.g. property, freedom of movement, physical, mental and moral integrity), as well as the positive obligations of the State.[52] It noted that the beneficiaries were in

---

[44] CIDH *Mary and Carrie Dann* v. *United States*, 27 September 1999 (adm.), §14.

[45] CIDH *Mary and Carrie Dann* v. *United States*, 27 September 1999 (adm.), §44 and Annual Report 1999, Chapter III, C.1. §67.

[46] CIDH *Mary and Carrie Dann* v. *United States*, 27 December 2002, §5.

[47] CIDH *Awas Tingni* v. *Nicaragua*, case 11.577, Annual Report 1997, Chapter III. Further on this case see infra in this chapter.

[48] CIDH *Maya Indigenous Communities* v. *Belize*, case 12.053. Annual Report 2000, §11 refers to precautionary measures of 5 October 2000. See also *Maya Indigenous Communities* v. *Belize*, 12 October 2004, §8 (noting that it adopted the admissibility report and its decision to take precautionary measures on the same date). The admissibility report refers in §43 to precautionary measures of 28 October 1999 (not mentioned in the Annual Report 1999). The petition involved Mopan and Ke'kchi Maya people of the Toledo District of Soutern Belize, represented by the Toledo Maya Council.

[49] CIDH Annual Report 2000, §11. Belize did not respond.

[50] CIDH *Maya Indigenous Communities* v. *Belize*, report 40/04, 12 October 2004, §8.

[51] CIDH *Yakye Axa Indigenous Community* v. *Paraguay*, Annual Report 2001, Chapter III (a), C. 1, §49.

[52] More generally on positive and negative obligations and the specificity of provisional measures see Chapter XIII (Protection).

'an extremely needy situation, because of their inadequate access to food supplies and health care'. Paraguay was to take the following measures:

> "(1) To suspend the enforcement of any court or administrative order involving the eviction and/or removal of the homes of the Yakye Axa indigenous community and of its members.
> (2) To refrain from all other actions and undertakings affecting the right to property, free transit, and residence of the Yakye Axa indigenous community and its members.
> (3) To take all steps necessary to ensure the life and physical, mental, and moral integrity of the members of the Yakye Axa indigenous community".[53]

The Commission did not specifically refer to prevention of irreparable harm to culture, but this purpose seemed an underlying rationale for its precautionary measures in this case. The indigenous community itself was the beneficiary of the measures, together with its individual members. In that respect the Commission did interpret the right to property, free transit and residence in light of a (collective) right to cultural identity.

Another aspect that played a role here was the utterly inadequate access to food supplies, safe water and health care.[54] Thus the Commission also requested the State to take all necessary steps to ensure the lives and personal integrity of the members of this community. While the reference to life and personal integrity is customary in its precautionary measures, in this case the Commission equally stressed the importance of ensuring the mental and moral integrity of the members of the indigenous community. The wider reference here suggests that the Commission is sensitive to the (individual) right to cultural identity. A failure to respect this right would result in a failure to ensure the mental and moral integrity of persons.

In other words, on the basis of the Commission's precautionary measures the State cannot allow the forcible removal of the members of this community to a place where, while they would have access to food supplies and health care, this would in fact mean a removal from their traditional habitat.

In a case involving the *Bio-Bio River of the Pehuenches* against *Chile* (friendly settlement 2004)[55] the petitioners had requested precautionary measures in order to prevent a company from flooding the lands occupied by the alleged victims, as part of the construction of the dam for the Ralco Hydroelectric Plant Project.[56] The Commission initially, in December 2002, requested Chile, 'bearing in mind the nature of the matter... [to] refrain from taking any steps that might alter the *status quo* in the matter, until the organs of the inter-American system of human rights have adopted a final decision'.[57] For the purposes of this book this request may be qualified as an informal provisional measure. By 2002 the Commission generally was more specific in its use of (formal) precautionary measures and it was not surprising that Chile immediately asked for clarification about the content of this request. It asked the Commission to 'explain precisely the con-

---

[53] CIDH *Yakye Axa Indigenous Community* v. *Paraguay*, Annual Report 2001, Chapter III (a), C. 1, §49.

[54] In Press Release 23/99 the CIDH noted that during its 1999 on-site visit it spoke with the Yakye Axa and the Sawhoyamaxa and 'was able to see the deplorable situation of these peoples, who live alongside the national highway, without services of any kind, waiting for the authorities to allocate them the land they need'. It added that it appreciated the importance of a Presidential Decree dating from earlier that year that declared the two indigenous communities to be in a 'state of emergency' given the 'extreme conditions' they were facing. The Decree had ordered the 'immediate provision of medical and nutritional assistance, but apparently the measures required had not yet been adopted.

[55] CIDH *Mercedes Julia Huenteao Beroiza et al.*, 11 March 2004 (friendly settlement). See also <http://www.ciel.org/Hre/hrecomponent2.html>.

[56] CIDH *Mercedes Julia Huenteao Beroiza et al.*, 11 March 2004 (friendly settlement), §2.

[57] Id., §5.

tent and scope of the request made to the State'.[58] The Commission responded that 'the purpose of the request made to the State of Chile is to ensure that the decisions of the organs of the inter-American system of human rights are not rendered meaningless efforts to protect the human person. Accordingly, the State should refrain from any act that might broaden or exacerbate the dispute and impair the effectiveness of any decision that the Commission might potentially adopt'.[59] Several months later the petitioners renewed their request for precautionary measures 'based on the alleged disregard of the request made by the IACHR to the State to maintain the *status quo*'.[60] The next day the Commission 'granted the requested precautionary measures' (this time formally) and requested the State to '(r)efrain from taking any steps that might alter the *status quo* in the matter, until the organs of the inter-American system of human rights have adopted a final decision on the case, in particular, avoiding or suspending any judicial or administrative action that entails eviction of the petitioners from their ancestral lands'.[61]

Another example involves the *Pueblo Indígena de Sarayaku*. They were granted legal title to their territory in 1992, but Ecuador reserved the right to the subsoil resources. Supported by the Ecuadorian Center for Economic and Social Rights (CDES) the Sarayaku petitioned the Commission fearing negative environmental impact such as pollution, deforestation and threats to the biodiversity of the area. They did not wish companies to access their lands for oil extraction.[62] In May 2003 the Commission decided to take precautionary measures.[63] Later it decided to request the Court to order provisional measures. The Court indeed did so in order to guarantee not just their physical integrity but also their special relation with their territory.[64]

In the *Kankuamo* case the Commission had equally requested the Court to order provisional measures not just to protect the life and personal integrity of all members of the Kankuamo community, but also the cultural identity of the Community as a whole and its special relation to its ancestral grounds.[65] In fact the Court only heeded to part of the Commission's request, although it did add that the protective measures should respect the freedom of movement of the Community members. It observed that all members of this indigenous people were equally at risk of attacks against their personal integrity and life, exactly for belonging to the Kankuamo. Moreover, and this is relevant in the context of their attachment to the lands, they were all at risk of being forcibly displaced. Thus it was necessary for the State to ensure that the beneficiaries of the provisional measures would be able to continue living at their customary place of residence and that the necessary conditions were created so that those members that had already suffered forced displacement would be able to return.[66] The State should also protect them against attacks by third parties.[67]

Many of the cases dealt with in the Inter-American system involved threats and harassment of indigenous peoples.[68] The provisional measures protecting against death threats often include

---

[58] On the specificity of provisional measures generally see Chapter XIII (Protection).

[59] CIDH *Mercedes Julia Huenteao Beroiza et al.*, 11 March 2004 (friendly settlement), §6.

[60] Id., §15.

[61] Id., §15.

[62] They also feared that the building of roads for the purpose of oil extraction would lead to increased access by other companies and individuals.

[63] Precautionary measures of 5 May 2003, referred to in IACHR *Caso Pueblo Indígena de Sarayaku*, Order of 17 June 2005, 'Having seen' clause 2h.

[64] IACHR *Caso Pueblo Indígena de Sarayaku* (Ecuador), Orders of 6 July 2004 and 17 June 2005.

[65] IACHR *Caso Pueblo Indígena Kankuamo* (Colombia), Order of 5 July 2004, 2nd 'Having seen' ('Vistos') clause.

[66] Id., 9th and 10th 'Considering' clauses.

[67] Id., 11th 'Considering' clause.

[68] See Chapter IX (Threats).

instructions to protect against internal displacement.[69] The adverse effect of uprooting people has a particularly pervasive impact on indigenous peoples, because of their particular cultural and spiritual ties to their ancestral lands. Moreover, in many cases the forced eviction is closely related to third party interest in the economic exploitation of indigenous lands. In this light the Court could have added, as suggested by the Commission, a reference to the special relation to the ancestral grounds.

2.4 Inter-American Court

In its abovementioned Order of protection against death threats and internal displacement in the *Kankuamo* case the Court did not explicitly refer to the special relation of indigenous peoples to their lands,[70] but in September 2002 the Inter-American Court ordered provisional measures specifically with the aim to protect indigenous culture. It did so in the context of the *Awas Tingni* case.

Its Order is remarkable for at least three reasons. It was the first time the Court ordered such provisional measures in order to protect indigenous culture as such. Secondly, the timing of the provisional measures is noteworthy: they were ordered *after* the Court had published its Judgment on the merits and reparations. The Court has observed that, under Article 63(2) ACHR, it may adopt provisional measures 'in matters it has under consideration'.[71] "Said measures can also be applied during the stage in which compliance with the judgment is overseen'.[72] It added that 'in the instant case it is probable that irreparable damage will occur'. This would 'preclude faithful and full compliance with the judgment on the merits and reparations'.[73] The third aspect making the Court's order remarkable is that it was not the Commission but the representatives of the Mayagna (Sumo) Awas Tingni that had appealed to the Court.[74]

The Inter-American Court considered that the victims had demonstrated 'the existence of a situation of extreme gravity and urgency regarding the property of the Mayagna Community,

---

[69]   See generally Chapter XIII (Protection).

[70]   IACHR *Caso Pueblo Indígena Kankuamo* v. *Colombia*, Order of 5 July 2004. See also its Order of 30 January 2007.

[71]   See e.g. IACHR Order for provisional measures (requested by the representatives of the victims), *Mayagna (Sumo) Awas Tingni Community* v. *Nicaragua*, 6 September 2002, 2nd 'Considering' clause.

[72]   IACHR Order for provisional measures (requested by the representatives of the victims), *Mayagna (Sumo) Awas Tingni Community* v. *Nicaragua*, 6 September 2002, 9th 'Considering' clause, referring to an earlier occasion on which it had used provisional measures subsequent to its Judgment namely in *Loayza Tamayo*, Order of the president of 13 December 2000 and of the Court of 3 February 2001.

[73]   Ibid.

[74]   As of June 2001, when the Court's new Rules of Procedure became applicable, the victim (or the petitioner) is able to present arguments and claims independently, once the Commission (or the State) has brought a case before the Court: Article 23 (Participation of the Alleged Victims) Rules of Procedure December 2000, with amendments that entered into force January 2003: "1. When the application has been admitted, the alleged victims, their next of kin or their duly accredited representatives may submit their pleadings, motions and evidence, autonomously, throughout the proceedings. 2. When there are several alleged victims, next of kin or duly accredited representatives, they shall designate a common intervenor who shall be the only person authorized to present pleadings, motions and evidence during the proceedings, including the public hearings. 3. In case of disagreement, the Court shall make the appropriate ruling".

including the resources therein, which are the basis for their subsistence, culture, and traditions'.[75] In other words, threats against the property and resources of indigenous peoples may in certain cases warrant the use of provisional measures because of they are essential to the 'subsistence, culture, and traditions' of these peoples.

The Inter-American Court publishes and motivates its provisional measures, often referring to previous case law. Here it could simply draw on its findings on the merits and reparation in the case itself. After all it ordered these measures subsequent to delivering its Judgment. It noted its observation in this judgment that 'a communitarian tradition regarding a communal form of collective property of the land'. It quoted: 'Indigenous groups, by the fact of their very existence, have the right to live freely in their own territory; the close ties of indigenous people with the land must be recognized and understood as the fundamental basis of their cultures, their spiritual life, their integrity and their economic survival'.[76]

Not only did it invoke its Judgment on behalf of the Awas Tingni, but it also referred more generally to a finding on the right to life in another case. This indicates that the Court found it necessary to explain its expansion of the use of provisional measures from cases involving the individual right to life and personal integrity to cases involving cultural survival. It quoted from its Judgment in the *Street Children* case (1999): "In essence the fundamental right to life includes, not only the right of every human being not to be deprived of his life arbitrarily, but also the right that he will not be prevented from having access to the conditions that guarantee a dignified existence".[77]

The Court observed that Nicaragua had reached an agreement with the community to provisionally recognize its land rights, but had failed to implement it. Thus it was 'necessary to protect the geographical area where the members of the (...) Community live and conduct their activities'.[78] It decided to order the State to adopt 'without delay, whatever measures are necessary to protect the use and enjoyment of property of lands belonging to the Mayagna Awas Tingni Community, and of natural resources existing on those lands, specifically those measures geared toward avoiding immediate and irreparable damage resulting from activities of third parties who have established themselves inside the territory of the Community or who exploit the natural resources that exist within it, until the definitive delimitation, demarcation and titling ordered by the Court are carried out'. In addition, it added its – by now customary – order 'to allow the applicants to participate in planning and implementation of those measures and, in general, to keep them informed'. It also expanded its reference to action against impunity from its provisional measures ordering the State to protect persons against death threats and harassment to the different situation of ensuring cultural survival: 'to investigate the facts set forth in the claim that gave rise to the current measures, so as to discover and punish those responsible'.[79]

In sum, the Court clearly established that the situation was extremely grave as the subsistence, culture and traditions of an indigenous people were at risk. It is significant in this respect that it quotes from judgments referring to 'survival' and the right to life as including the right to a dignified existence.[80] It noted that 'in the instant case it is probable that irreparable damage will

---

[75] IACHR *Mayagna (Sumo) Awas Tingni Community* v. *Nicaragua*, Order of 6 September 2002 (requested by the representatives of the victims), 6th 'Considering' clause.

[76] Id., 7th 'Considering' clause, quoting *Mayagna (Sumo) Awas Tingni Community* v. *Nicaragua*, Judgment of 31 August 2001, §149.

[77] IACHR *Mayagna (Sumo) Awas Tingni Community* v. *Nicaragua*, Order of 6 September 2002, 8th 'Considering' clause, quoting from *Villagrán Morales et al.* (*'Street Children'* case) v. *Guatemala*, 19 November 1999, §144.

[78] IACHR *Mayagna (Sumo) Awas Tingni Community* v. *Nicaragua*, Order of 6 September 2002, 10th 'Considering' clause.

[79] Id., decisional clauses 1-3.

[80] Id., 7th and 8th 'Considering' clause.

occur that it will preclude faithful and full compliance with the judgment on the merits and reparations in the case of the Mayagna Community'.[81]

In 2007 the Court lifted the provisional measures. It considered that 'now that more than five years have elapsed since the adoption of the provisional measures, the Court has assessed the different State reports and the observations of the representatives and the Commission concerning the measures adopted to protect the ownership of the ancestral lands of the members of the Awas Tigni Community, and observes that the information provided is closely related to compliance with the judgment' of 31 August 2001.[82] Hence it decided to lift the provisional measures but continue monitoring compliance with the judgment.

A few years after the Court's order for provisional measures in Awas Tingni the Court's again used provisional measures specifically aimed at the protection of cultural identity. In July 2004, in its Order in *Pueblo Indígena de Sarayaku* v. *Ecuador* the State not only was to guarantee the lives and personal integrity of the Sarayaku, but also their freedom of movement.[83] In its subsequent Order of June 2005 it added that the State should also immediately take the necessary measures to ensure that the Sarayaku can make use of the natural resources where they reside and to protect their lives and personal integrity against the activities of third parties exploiting the natural resources, especially against explosive devices. It should guarantee the freedom of movement of the indigenous peoples, in particular on the River Borbonanza. It should maintain the airstrip on the territory in order to maintain their means of transport. Very relevant with regard to the group of beneficiaries is the obligation directed to the state to inform the neighbouring indigenous communities about the meaning and scope of the provisional measures, vis-à-vis the State as well as particular third parties, in order to create an atmosphere conducive to living together in peace.[84]

2.5   African Commission

In June 2004 the African Commission decided to take provisional measures on behalf of the pastoralist Endorois community in Kenya. It urged Kenya 'to take immediate steps to ensure that no further issuance of mining concessions or transfers of parts to the land occurred prior to the case being concluded'[85] Minority Rights Group International (MRG) and the Centre for Minority Rights Development (CEMIRIDE) had requested these measures a year previously, in light of 'imminent mining activities that would cause irreversible damage to Endorois traditional land'.[86] They had been divided and displaced from their traditional lands and now lived 'in a number of locations on the periphery of the reserve, being forced from fertile lands to semi-arid areas'. The priority of the Endorois' is the restitution of their land. The petitioners argued that the Resolution on the Rights of Indigenous Populations/Communities in Africa, adopted in 2003, offered he

---

[81]   Id., 9th 'Considering' clause.

[82]   IACHR *Mayagna (Sumo) Awas Tingni Community* v. *Nicaragua*, Order of 6 September 2002, Order of 26 November 2007, 10th 'Considering' clause.

[83]   IACHR *Matter of Pueblo Indígena de Sarayaku* (Ecuador), Order of 6 July 2004.

[84]   IACHR *Matter of Pueblo Indígena de Sarayaku* (Ecuador), Order of 17 June 2005, 1st Decisional clause.

[85]   As announced by Minority Rights Group, one of the petitioners, 'African Commission urged to toughen stance on state non-compliance', 24 January 2005.

[86]   Minority Rights Group News release 'Commission to consider Kenya pastoralist case following urgent appeal to state, 8 November 2004, <http://www.minorityrights.org/news_detail.asp?ID=316> (accessed on 4 December 2006).

Commission 'a valuable basis upon which to extend its understanding and treatment of indigenous and collective rights, including economic, social and cultural rights'.[87]

> "The Endorois people's health, livelihood, religion and culture are all intimately connected with their traditional land, as grazing lands, sacred religious sites and plants used for traditional medicine are all situated around the shores of Lake Bogoria. By forcing the community to move, not only were the Community's property rights violated, but spiritual, cultural and economic ties to the land were severed".[88]

Reportedly, 'in June 2006, local officials tested Endorois' drinking water sources and found they were poisonously contaminated as a result of ruby mining. Mining has now stopped until the case is resolved'.[89]

The eventual decision on the merits may indicate the provisions of the African Charter that have played a role in the use of provisional measures.[90] The fact that the African Commission

---

[87] Ibid.

[88] Ibid. In November 2004 the District Commissioner of the Lake Bogoria area had summoned the Endorois 'to seek their approval to go forth with mining activities, which they unanimously refused. Two days later mining equipment arrived. In response the Endorois 'gathered to block the road and police forces were sent to the scene where some community members were detained'. "The Chairperson of the Endorois Welfare Council subsequently received a letter requiring his resignation as head teacher of a state school". Minority Rights Group News release 'African Commission urged to toughen stance on state non-compliance', 24 January 2005, <http://www.minorityrights.org/news_detail.asp?ID=342> (accessed on 11 January 2007).

[89] See Minority Rights Group webpage <http://www.minorityrights.org/6779/trouble-in-paradise/the-facts.html> (accessed 22 November 2008). The UN Special Rapporteur on the situation of human rights and fundamental freedoms of indigenous peoples, Rodolfo Stavenhagen, in his Mission to Kenya report, noted that the Government 'should aim at a friendly settlement in the case of the Endorois before ACHPR, leading to the establishment of a system of co-management between the authorities and the local communities in the Lake Bogoria Game Reserve', A/HRC/4/32/Add.3, 26 February 2007, §108.

[90] In their submission the petitioners had invoked the free practice of religion (Article 8 ACHPR), the right to property (Article 14), to enjoy the best attainable standard of physical and mental health (Article 16) and the right to freely take part in the cultural life of the community (Article 17(2)). They also invoked rights that are very specific to the African Charter emphasizing issues of development and the collective dimension of human rights, such as the right of all peoples to exist (Article 20(1): "All peoples shall have the right to existence. They shall have the unquestionable and inalienable right to self-determination. They shall freely determine their political status and shall pursue their economic and social development according to the policy they have freely chosen"). Another right invoked by the Endorois was that of all peoples to freely dispose of their wealth and natural resources (Article 21: "1. All peoples shall freely dispose of their wealth and natural resources. This right shall be exercised in the exclusive interest of the people. In no case shall a people be deprived of it. 2. In case of spoliation the dispossessed people shall have the right to the lawful recovery of its property as well as to an adequate compensation. 3. The free disposal of wealth and natural resources shall be exercised without prejudice to the obligation of promoting international economic cooperation based on mutual respect, equitable exchange and the principles of international law. (…) 5. States parties to the present Charter shall undertake to eliminate all forms of foreign economic exploitation particularly that practiced by international monopolies so as to enable their peoples to fully benefit from the advantages derived from their national resources"). Finally, they invoked Article 22(1), which speaks of development and identity: "All peoples shall have the right to their economic, social and cultural development with due regard to their freedom and identity and in the equal enjoyment of the common heritage of mankind".

used provisional measures in this land rights case submitted by the Endorois of Kenya shows an awareness of cultural identity of groups within States that may subsequently be reflected in the decision on the merits in this case.[91]

2.6 Bosnia Human Rights Chamber and cultural/religious survival

The Bosnia Chamber, with its special nature stemming from the Dayton Peace Agreement, obviously operated in a special context of ethnic/religious conflict. It has taken provisional measures involving the rights of religious minorities, ordering the authorities to desist from implementing a local order to exhume the body of the petitioner's deceased wife from a Muslim cemetery; and more generally to protect religious sites and to allow the burial of deceased persons.

The first years of its existence the Chamber was hesitant to intervene pending the proceedings in order to protect Islamic sites.[92] Yet it eventually decided to use them. It did so in July 1998, three months after it had last refused them in the same case involving the events subsequent to the destruction of 15 mosques in Banja Luka. Upon a request by the respondent Party to postpone the proceedings the Chamber indeed decided to postpone the public hearing. At the same time it used provisional measures ordering the respondent Party 'to take all necessary action to refrain from the construction of buildings or objects of any nature on the sites of the mosques and on the cemeteries and other Islamic sites indicated in the application, and not to permit any such construction by any other institution or person, whether public or private'. Furthermore, it was ordered 'to refrain from the destruction or removal of any object remaining on the sites of the mosques and on the cemeteries and other Islamic sites indicated in the application, and not to permit any such destruction or removal by any other institution, whether public or private'.[93] The substance of this provisional measure of July 1998 corresponds remarkably to part of the decision on reparation subsequently ordered, upon the Chamber's finding of violations of the right to peaceful enjoyment of possessions and the freedom of religion, as well as of the prohibition of discrimination regarding these rights.[94]

---

[91] See in general about this case Morel (2004). According to one of the petitioners this decision is expected for the end of 2008. See Minority Rights Group webpage <http://www.minorityrights.org/6779/trouble-in-paradise/the-facts.html> (accessed 22 November 2008). The UN Special Rapporteur on the situation of human rights and fundamental freedoms of indigenous peoples, Rodolfo Stavenhagen, in his Mission to Kenya report, noted that the Government 'should aim at a friendly settlement in the case of the Endorois before ACHPR, leading to the establishment of a system of co-management between the authorities and the local communities in the Lake Bogoria Game Reserve', A/HRC/4/32/Add.3, 26 February 2007, §108.

[92] See Bosnia Chamber *Islamic Community in Bosnia and Herzegovina* v. *Republika Srpska*, 11 June 1999, referring to decisions to refuse provisional measures of 12 October 1996, 10 October 1997 (asking the office of the High Representative, UNESCO and the Commission to preserve National Monuments to submit any relevant information in their possession and requesting the Human Rights ombudsperson to investigate certain of the allegations) and 4 April 1998, §§4, 6 and 9.

[93] Bosnia Chamber *Islamic Community in Bosnia and Herzegovina* (*Banja Luka mosques*) v. *Republika Srpska*, 11 June 1999, §12. See Chapter II on the special nature of the Bosnia Chamber and the three possible addressees of its Orders for provisional measures. In practice Republika Srpska has been the addressee in the religious cases discussed here.

[94] Bosnia Chamber *Islamic Community in Bosnia and Herzegovina* v. *Republika Srpska* (*Banja Luka mosques*), 11 June 1999, §212. More generally on the relation to reparation see Chapter XIII (Protection).

That same month the Chamber also used provisional measures in response to the situation Mr Mahmutović found himself in. In July 1998 he was ordered 'to exhume, at his own expense, his late wife from the Town Cemetery, and to move her remains "to the new town cemetery located in the eastern part of town" within 15 days receipt of the decision'.[95] At the same time he was obliged 'to request the Municipal Sanitary Inspection for permission to exhume his late wife'.[96] He petitioned the Chamber, which ordered Republika Srpska to 'desist from' implementing the domestic order for exhumation.[97]

Subsequently, in December 1999, in the context of a petition submitted by the Islamic Community in Bosnia, the Chamber ordered Republika Srpska more generally not to forbid or interfere with any burials in this cemetery 'carried out by or with the authority of the applicant'.[98] It did so following information that the authorities had issued a decision prohibiting the burial of Mrs Behija Zec in the Muslim Cemetery in Prnjavor.[99] This provisional measure did not immediately generate the result required. At the end of that month Mrs Alema Mešić died. She had reserved and paid for a parcel in the Muslim Town Cemetery since 1971. The Islamic Community of Prnjavor requested permission to bury her and informed the International Police Task Force (IPTF) station in Prnjavor. When her son was digging his mother's grave the next day the Municipal Inspector of Prnjavor appeared with a policeman. They made a report of the incident and ordered the deceased son to cover up the grave again. The representatives of the Islamic Community 'reminded the Municipal authorities of the Chamber's recent order forbidding any interference with burials at the Muslim Town Cemetery'. The Municipal Inspector 'replied that the Chamber's order was not binding'. "Finally, after several hours of negotiations with the Islamic Community, the municipal authorities and IPTF, the burial of Mrs Alema Mešić was performed at the Muslim Town Cemetery".[100]

The Chamber used provisional measures in various other cases as well.[101] In one case it ordered Srpska to 'take all necessary steps to prevent the christening/consecration' of 'or any per-

---

[95]   See Bosnia Chamber *Mahmutović* v. *Republika Srpska*, 8 October 1999, §23. This new town cemetery did not yet exist (information OSCE field office in Doboj), §6. See also §13.

[96]   Bosnia Chamber *Mahmutović* v. *Republika Srpska*, 8 October 1999, §23.

[97]   Id., §4.

[98]   Bosnia Chamber *Islamic Community in BiH* v. *Republika Srpska* (*Muslim Town Cemetery in Prnjavor*), 11 January 2000. The Chamber specified the cemetery by indicating its location 'at cadastral lot k.č. 741/1 k.o. in Prnjavor'. Since initially there had not been 'any individual threat of exhumation or interference with burials the Chamber at first refused to order the provisional measures requested, §4.

[99]   Id., §9.

[100] Id., §33.

[101] See e.g. Bosnia Chamber *Islamic Community in BiH* (*former mosque sites in Zvornik*) v. *Republika Srpska*, 9 November 2000, provisional measures of 10 July 1999 and 21 October 1999 and further Order of 7 July 2000, maintained by decision of 11 October 2000, §§2-7 and *The Islamic Community in BiH* (*former Atik Mosque, Bijeljina*) v. *Republika Srpska*, 6 December 2000, provisional measure of 10 July 1999 and further Order to protect site Atik Mosque of 7 July 2000. See also *The Islamic Community in BiH* (*Jakeš Cemetery*) v. *Republika Srpska*, 8 October 2001, §6 in which the Chamber ordered provisional measures to the effect that the respondent Party was to 'take all necessary steps to make sure that no burial takes place without the consent of the applicant at the *Jakeš Cemetery* (…) and to prevent any other disturbance of the above cemetery, particularly the exhumation of human remains and damage to funerary monuments or their removal'. 'By its express terms this order remains in force until the Chamber delivers its final decision in the case, unless it is withdrawn at an earlier stage of the proceedings". On the merits the Chamber recalled, at §47, 'the tradition in Bosnia and Herzegovina to maintain separate burial grounds according to religion. Given this tradition and bearing in mind the prevailing circumstances in the country, the chamber finds the unauthorized

formance of any Orthodox ceremony' on the Muslim cemetery of the petitioner's family in Rataj.[102] This family had buried their family members there for several centuries.[103]

The petitioner had complained that the family graves had been disturbed, tombstones had been destroyed, the surrounding fence and gate to the cemetery had repeatedly been torn down and in 2002 an Orthodox cross was engraved into an important stone in the centre of the cemetery. In this regard he had also requested the Chamber to issue an order for the authorities to remove the engraved Orthodox cross. The Bosnia Chamber had rejected this part of the request for provisional measures. It also rejected the request insofar as it was directed against Bosnia and Herzegovina as well as against Republika Srpska.[104] Subsequently, upon a finding of violations on the merits, it did order Republika Srpska 'to ensure that the competent enterprise properly fences in, cleans and maintains the Rataj Muslim graveyard' and 'to take all necessary steps to prevent the Serb Orthodox Church from carrying out any further activities on the Rataj Muslim graveyard'.[105] In other words, upon finding violations, in its decision on reparation it confirmed the provisional measures previously taken.[106] Moreover, it added the obligation to clean, maintain and fence in the Muslim graveyard, which includes the removal of products of vandalism, arguably also in the form of symbols engraved in order to revive the heritage of the Serb Orthodox church. After all, the Chamber had by now found on the merits that the petitioner had been discriminated against in his right to freedom of religion and the enjoyment of the right to respect for private and family life. It had specifically considered that the 'obligation to create conditions conducive to the return of persons expelled during the armed conflict because of the their religion' placed a particular burden on the parties to the Dayton Peace Agreement and its Annexes, 'to ensure that returnees will be met with full respect for their religious beliefs and practices, including full respect for the sites that are connected to the manifestation of religious beliefs, such as graveyards'.[107]

Regarding the planned orthodox religious activities at the Čengić family Muslim graveyard, specifically the liturgy, planned in August 2002, that triggered the petition, the Chamber noted that the authorities 'did not take any action to prevent this liturgy from taking place, nor have they

---

burial on non-Muslims in an exclusively Muslim cemetery to be unjustifiable and provocative'. The Chamber has also ordered the respondent Party, 'as a provisional measures, to prevent the implementation' of certain procedural decisions allocating the site of the Kizlaragina mosque, destroyed in 1992, to a private contractor for the construction of business premises: *Islamic Community in BiH (Mrkonjić Grad)* v. *Republika Srpska*, 22 December 2003, §4.

[102] Bosnia Chamber *Čengić* v. *BiH and Srpska*, 5 September 2003, §3.
[103] Id., §18.
[104] Id., §3.
[105] Id., §§125-126.
[106] In general on the relation between provisional measures and reparation see Chapter XIII. The petitioner had stated that there was a continued threat of an interference concerning the 'consecration-christening' of the central stone that has not been entirely removed by the Chamber's order for provisional measures' Bosnia Chamber *Čengić* v. *BiH and Srpska*, 5 September 2003, §108.
[107] Ibid. On the question whether the difference in treatment was justified in that there was a reasonable relationship of proportionality between the means employed and the aims sought to be realised, the Chamber pointed out that it could not disregard the dramatic events that took place in the municipality in question. It referred to an ICTY Trial Chamber judgment noting that 'only about ten Muslims remained at the end of the conflict'. In 1991 there were still more than 20.000 Muslim inhabitants. Bosnia Chamber *Čengić* v. *BiH and Srpska*, 5 September 2003, §117.

expressed the opinion that it should be prevented'. The Chamber observes that the liturgy was in fact only prevented because of its own Order for provisional measures.[108]

3 RELATION BETWEEN PROVISIONAL MEASURES TO PROTECT CULTURAL AND RELIGIOUS RIGHTS AND THE EXPECTED DECISION ON THE MERITS

3.1 Introduction

As discussed, it was in *Sara et al.* v. *Finland* (inadm. 1994) that the HRC used provisional measures for the second time in order to protect indigenous culture, the first time being on behalf of the Lubicon Lake Band.[109] In *Sara* the State denied that there was a causal link between the measures of protection requested by the petitioners and the object of the communication itself. Apparently it argued that this was the reason why provisional measures should not be taken. Quite apart from the question whether it is appropriate in human rights adjudication to be strict about the relationship between the rights claimed and the request for provisional measures, it is clear that in this case the material object of the petitioners' complaint was the threat to their traditional economic and cultural rights caused by logging and road construction activities in certain reindeer husbandry areas. Indeed the HRC found that the material object of the complaint *was* related to the request for provisional measures.[110]

In practice the provisional measures by the HRC, the Inter-American Commission and Court and the African Commission related to claims about *indigenous* culture. Moreover, when the Bosnia Chamber used provisional measures in cases involving religion they in fact aimed at protecting the spiritual survival of a group with an important link and long history to the area as well.

The HRC has used provisional measures only in certain of those cases where the petitioner claimed a violation of Article 27 ICCPR.[111] Still the issues involved are normally interrelated and it is important to keep the other rights in mind as they may have an impact on the Committee's decision to take provisional measures to protect indigenous culture. Rights in the Covenant that could be relevant for the protection of indigenous culture are the right to self-determination (Article 1 ICCPR), the right to respect for privacy, family or home (Article 17 ICCPR), the freedom of religion (Article 18 ICCPR), the protection of the family (Article 23 ICCPR), the rights of the child (Article 24 ICCPR), the right to participate in public affairs (Article 25 ICCPR) and the right of minorities to enjoy their own culture (Article 27 ICCPR).

---

[108] Id., §96. More generally on the official responses of States to provisional measures see Chapter XVI.

[109] HRC *O. Sara et al.* v. *Finland*, 23 March 1994 (inadm.).

[110] The State had argued that the Board's authority to approve logging activities in areas other than those designated as protected wilderness, such as the residual area outside the Hammastunturi Wilderness, was not derived from the Wilderness Act. "Accordingly, the State party denies that there is a causal link between the measures of protection requested by the authors and the object of the communication itself, which only concerns enactment and implementation of the Wilderness Act". However, the HRC noted that the continuation of road construction in the residual area could indeed be causally linked to the entry into force of the Wilderness Act. For purposes of admissibility the petitioners had sufficiently substantiated that this could raise issues under Article 27.

[111] See in general about the protection of minorities Nowak (1993), pp. 480-505; Meijknecht (2001) and Donders (2002). See about the interdependence of various Covenant rights in relation to indigenous peoples Scheinin (2000).

In 2007 the General Assembly adopted the UN Declaration on the Rights of Indigenous Peoples, which stresses the importance of land rights and reaffirms the need for special protection of and informed consent by indigenous peoples.[112] Yet the provisional measures discussed in this chapter were all taken before that time, when the international legal setting already included, among others, a general recognition of the right to self-determination,[113] ILO-Convention 169 concerning Indigenous and Tribal Peoples in Independent Countries,[114] the World Bank Operational Directive on Indigenous people (1991) and various drafts of the abovementioned Declaration.[115] Obviously the UN Convention on the Elimination of Racial Discrimination (CERD) is also relevant in the context of indigenous and minority rights.

Indigenous groups and minorities have equally resorted to the three regional systems with complaints involving their right to culture and religion. The case of the *Endorois*, in which the African Commission took provisional measures, was the first time that this Commission would consider the merits of an indigenous land rights case.[116] The Inter-American Commission regularly pays attention to the protection of indigenous culture.[117] Like the HRC it has done so in the context of country reports as well as individual complaints and its concerns are often similar to those of the HRC. Yet under the ICCPR the States themselves submit the reports and the HRC simply discusses them in a public hearing and publishes Concluding Observations. The Inter-American Commission, on the other hand, often prepares reports itself, on the basis of fact-finding missions. Moreover the American Convention does not include a 'victim requirement', which renders the Inter-American Commission 'accessible to almost anyone concerned with the fate of indigenous groups in the Americas'.[118] Despite the inevitable lack of expertise by international adjudicators regarding indigenous land rights, the Inter-American Commission has shown awareness of the importance of safeguarding the cultural integrity of indigenous peoples. This awareness may underlie its use of precautionary measures in cultural cases. The same applies to the provisional measures by the Inter-American Court.

The provisional measures involving culture taken in the Inter-American and African systems were decided in the context of claims based on culture, property and non-discrimination and those taken by the Bosnia Chamber involved religion, property and non-discrimination claims. This section discusses the relevance of the case law on the merits in order to explain the practice of the adjudicators, taking the case law of the HRC as a point of reference. It pays particular attention to the topics of self-determination, land rights/collective rights, the moment of infringement on land rights, the special status of (indigenous) culture, consultation and impact assessment.

---

112 A/RES/61/295, 13 September 2007.

113 See e.g. Article 1(2) UN Charter, Article 1 ICCPR and Article 1 UN Convention on Economic, Social and Cultural Rights.

114 Adopted 27 June 1989 and entered into force 27 June 1989.

115 See generally on indigenous rights, group rights, minority rights and/or cultural and environmental rights e.g. Anaya (1996); Pritchard (1998); Henrard (2000); Scheinin (2000); Alston (2001); Donders (2002); Rivera-Salgado (2005). See also the reports of the UN Working Group on Indigenous Populations, the reports by UN Sub-Commission Rapporteur Irene Daes and UN Special Rapporteurs on the Human Rights of Indigenous People Rodolfo Stavenhagen and James Anaya.

116 Minority Rights Group News release 'Commission to consider Kenya pastoralist case following urgent appeal to state, 8 November 2004, <http://www.minorityrights.org/news_detail. asp?ID=316> (accessed on 4 December 2006). In general see also Thornberry (2002), pp. 244-264.

117 For a more general discussion see e.g. Thornberry (2002), pp. 265-289 and Hannum (1998), pp. 323-344.

118 Meijknecht (2001), p. 198. See also Chapter XIII (Protection), on the group of beneficiaries.

3.2 Self-determination

As Cançado Trindade noted, already in its Advisory Opinion on the *Western Sahara* (1975), the ICJ referred to the cultural practices of the nomad populations and affirmed their right to self-determination.[119] Yet a recurring problem in cases involving indigenous peoples and threats to the natural habitat is the fact that the HRC does not consider the right to self-determination (Article 1 ICCPR) part of the individual complaint procedure under the OP. The HRC discussed the issue in *Lubicon Lake Band* v. *Canada* (1990), which is also the first case in which it used provisional measures to protect an indigenous culture. Because Article 1 ICCPR deals with rights conferred upon peoples as such, under the OP the petitioner, as an individual, could not claim to be a victim of a violation of these rights.[120] The question whether the Lubicon Lake Band constituted a 'people' was not an issue to be addressed under the OP, because the rights that could be claimed under this treaty were the individual rights set out in Articles 6 to 27 ICCPR. Nevertheless, collective submissions by groups of individuals claiming to be similarly affected were indeed possible. The HRC pointed out that there was no doubt that many of the claims presented raised issues under Article 27 and that this article included 'the right of persons, in community with others, to engage in economic and social activities which are part of the culture of the community to which they belong'.[121] In other words, it introduced the article *proprio motu* as an alternative to the petitioner's Article 1 claim. This approach of the HRC towards self-determination in the individual complaint procedure helps explain its use of provisional measures to protect indigenous culture.

The concept of self-determination is relevant in dealing with the question of the identity and interests of the beneficiaries of the Committee's provisional measures. Collective aspects of the right to culture (Article 27 ICCPR) play an important role in the use of provisional measures. The discussion on these collective aspects has mainly come up in relation to threats to the natural habitat. Possibly this has been done in order to compensate for the fact that the HRC has not considered the right to self-determination (Article 1 ICCPR) under the OP. It shows the Committee's awareness of the special position of indigenous peoples and the fact that they have no recourse to the HRC except through complaints by individual members of the group. In the *Lubicon*

---

[119] IACHR *Bámaca Velásquez* v. *Guatemala*, 25 November 2000, Separate Opinion Cançado Trindade, §13, referring to ICJ Advisory Opinion on the *Western Sahara*, 16 October 1975, §87.

[120] HRC *Bernard Ominayak, Chief of the Lubicon Lake Band* v. *Canada*, 26 March 1990, §13.3. In later cases, however, the HRC did point out that 'the provisions of article 1 may be relevant in the interpretation of other rights protected by the Covenant, in particular articles 25, 26 and 27'. *Diergaardt et al.* v. *Namibia*, 25 July 2000, §10.3. In his concurring opinion Scheinin pointed out that this *obiter* statement represented 'a proper recognition of the interdependence between the various rights protected by the Covenant, including article 1'. In this case he agreed with the HRC that the petitioners had failed to substantiate their claim under Article 25 ICCPR, but he considered that it had unnecessarily emphasized the individual nature of participation rights under this article. He noted that 'there are situations where article 25 calls for special arrangements for rights of participation to be enjoyed by members of minorities and, in particular, indigenous peoples'. "When such a situation arises, it is not sufficient under article 25 to afford individual members of such communities the individual right to vote in general elections. Some forms of local, regional or cultural autonomy may be called for in order to comply with the requirement of effective rights of participation". See further *Apirana Mahuika et al.* v. *New Zealand*, 27 October 2000 and *Marie-Hélène Gillot et al.* v. *France*, 15 July 2002. See also General Comment 12 on Article 1 ICCPR (1984), HRI/GEN/1/Rev. 6, pp. 134-135 and General Comment 23, 8 April 1994, CCPR/C/21/Rev.1/Add.5 (summarizing the Committee's case law on Article 27) and Nowak (1993), pp. 480-505 discussing the meaning of Article 27, including the *travaux préparatoires*.

[121] See HRC *Bernard Ominayak, Chief of the Lubicon Lake Band* v. *Canada*, 26 March 1990, §32.1 and §32.2. See also the Committee's General Comment 23 on Article 27, 8 April 1994.

Lake Band case the HRC implied that Article 27 aims at ensuring *survival* of the cultural, religious and social identity of minorities.[122] Nevertheless, Article 27 ICCPR only partially addresses the problems indigenous peoples face.[123] This seems to apply equally to the provisions of regional human rights treaties invoked by indigenous peoples. In other words, 'Indigenous peoples rely on human rights mechanisms for lack of a better option'. Such mechanisms 'can monitor and curb excessive State behaviour, but they cannot decide on a transfer of authority'.[124]

3.3   Land rights and collective aspects of the right to culture[125]

To understand the purpose of the provisional measures it is important to pay attention to the collective aspects of minority rights and the right to culture, especially read in light of the right to self-determination. Thus far the adjudicators have only used provisional measures to protect the *collective* aspects of the right to culture, as claimed by individual petitioners and not the individual aspects of this right in relation to exclusion. Given the nature of the individual complaint systems, technically both claims relating to threats to the natural habitat as such and claims relating to exclusion from an indigenous group involve the individual right to live as members of an indigenous group taking part in indigenous culture. Yet in fact the provisional measures have related only to issues of land rights.[126]

Awareness of the special position of indigenous peoples may explain why adjudicators sometimes emphasise collective aspects of land rights and use provisional measures in this context. The preservation of the connection between indigenous peoples and their lands is fundamen-

---

[122]   See the Committee's reference to Art. 27 in its admissibility decision and its explanation that it had taken provisional measures 'in view of the seriousness of the author's allegations that the Lubicon Lake Band was at the verge of extinction', *Lubicon Lake Band* v. *Canada*, 26 March 1990, §29.3.

[123]   Nowak observes that the specific formulation of Article 27 might seem unsatisfactory, 'measured against the demands for comprehensive collective protection of minorities', Nowak (1993), p. 483. Schmidt points out that the Committee's 'judicial self-restraint, which shuts the door on the examination of claims based on Article 1', was 'open to legal criticism' although 'wise from a political point of view', Schmidt (1997), p. 340. See further Huff (1999), p. 187 who notes that the Committee's position is 'untenable' in light of the plain language of Article 1 OP recognizing the Committee's competence to address communications brought by individuals concerning violations of any of the provisions of the ICCPR. Meijknecht notes that 'the HRC, by "translating" the collective claim into a claim under Article 27 ICCPR, basically reduces the claim to individual proportions'. Meijknecht (2000), p. 190. For the discussion on individual versus collective rights see pp. 184-189. De Feyter compares the right to self-determination to the right to development for indigenous peoples. He concludes from the case of the Lubicon Lake Band: "Human rights mechanisms are an awkward forum for dealing with indigenous attempts at taking control of their own destiny". De Feyter (2001), p. 153. This is so because their claims 'go beyond what human rights treaties can achieve' and relate to 'who should exercise decision making power on development'.

[124]   De Feyter (2001), p. 153. The claim of the Band, he notes, was 'not about the individual rights of Chief Ominayak, but about the collective right of the Band to decide on its own development'. "The claim needs to be transformed into an individual claim because the international human rights forum where it is presented so requires". De Feyter (2001), p. 154.

[125]   For a general overview see e.g. Anaya/Williams (2001).

[126]   See similarly CERD General Recommendation XXIII (51) concerning indigenous peoples (August 18, 1997) (calling upon states parties to the UN Convention on the Elimination of Racial Discrimination to 'recognize and protect the rights of indigenous peoples to own, develop, control and use their communal lands, territories and resources').

tal to the effective realization of the human rights of indigenous peoples 'and therefore warrants special measures of protection'.[127]

Article 27 ICCPR has been invoked and applied in or with regard to a wide range of States throughout the world, in the context of indigenous peoples. The interpretation of this provision by the Committee supervising this treaty is thus of special interest, particularly regarding its individual and collective aspects. As noted, under the ICCPR another explanation, related to the above, for the emphasis on collective aspects may be that indigenous peoples as such have no recourse to the HRC. The Committee's special attention to complaints by individual members of indigenous groups if these members seem to represent the interests of the collectivity, rather than 'simply' claim their individual right not to be excluded from the indigenous group, may partly be explained by its wish to compensate for this procedural hurdle.[128]

In *Länsman II* the HRC indicated that the cumulative effect of certain infringements could eventually constitute a violation of Article 27.

> "Even though in the present communication the Committee has reached the conclusion that the facts of the case do not reveal a violation of the rights of the authors, the Committee deems it important to point out that the State party must bear in mind when taking steps affecting the right under article 27, that though different activities in themselves may not constitute a violation of this article, such activities, taken together, may erode the rights of Sami people to enjoy their own culture".[129]

Scheinin has pointed out that *Länsman II* was based, at least in part, 'on assessing the logging project on a *quantitative* scale'.[130] He noted that the State party relied heavily on this argument, but that it did not do full justice to the petitioners' case 'who had emphasised the *strategic* (qualitative) importance of the specific forest lands in question' (italics in original). With regard to the sustainability test used by the HRC he notes that incremental developments related to land use could have the effect of eroding the economic basis for an indigenous community's 'traditional or otherwise typical means of livelihood' and thereby amount to a denial of the rights in Article 27.[131]

---

[127] See CIDH *Mary and Carrie Dann* v. *US*, 27 December 2002, §128. Article 13 of ILO Convention 169 concerning Indigenous and Tribal Peoples also stipulates that States 'shall respect the special importance for the cultures and spiritual values of the peoples concerned of their relationship with the lands or territories (…) and in particular the collective aspects of this relationship'.

[128] In relation to 'other' minorities Art. 1 ICCPR does not seem to apply to the same extent, even though these minorities do not have recourse to the HRC either, except in an individual capacity. See also the discussion of consultation and representation in Chapter XIII (Protection). It has been suggested that it is very problematic to define 'indigenous peoples' as a distinctive legal category or 'a global abstraction capable of working across different types of society with intricate identity politics and rapid cultural and economic change'. See e.g. Kingsbury (2001), p. 245. The UN Declaration on Indigenous Peoples, adopted by the General Assembly on 13 September 2007, A/RES/61/295, does not provide a definition either. See in general about the discussion on the definition of minorities and indigenous peoples: Meijknecht (2001), Chapters III (in particular pp. 115-118) and IV; Donders (2002), pp 169-171 and pp. 204-205; Thornberry (2002), pp. 33-60 and Kingsbury (2001), §§II (Minorities) and V (Indigenous peoples).

[129] HRC *Länsman II* v. *Finland*, 30 October 1996, §10.7.

[130] Scheinin (2000), pp. 170-171.

[131] Ibid. The European Commission on Human Rights has taken a similar approach in the *Alta Dam* case. It considered that the interference with the private life and traditional activities of the Sami caused by the building of a water dam and a hydro-electric power station, was limited to the loss

Article 27 ICCPR does not refer explicitly to the individual right to culture. In this respect it is different from Article 18 ICCPR, which refers to the exercise of the right to religion individually or in community with others. While the absence of a reference to 'individually' may imply that the collective aspect in the right to culture (Article 27 ICCPR) is stronger than in the right to religion (Article 18 ICCPR), Article 27 is still an individual right. Hence it seems reasonable to assume that the recognition of a collective dimension of the right to culture is meant to enhance the quality of the enjoyment of the individual right. In practice, however, the emphasis on this collective dimension, through the quantitative approach, seems to favour a collective right to culture over an individual right, by simply aiming at guaranteeing that some people may be able to maintain this culture. In *Lovelace* v. *Canada* (1981)[132] the HRC put an emphasis on the rights of the individual, while the later case of *Kitok* v. *Sweden* (1988)[133] gave priority to 'the group interest in cultural survival'.[134] In this case the HRC noted that Kitok had 'always retained some links with the Sami community, always living on Sami lands and seeking to return to full-time reindeer farming as soon as it became financially possible, in his particular circumstances, for him to do so'.[135] Nevertheless, it becomes apparent from this case that if the State can show that infringements of individual rights were necessary for the 'continued viability and welfare of the minority as a whole' the HRC lets them pass. What seems to have played a role is the State's argument that Kitok could enjoy the same rights in practice.[136] This is not fully convincing since part of being able to enjoy your culture as member of an indigenous group is the knowledge that

---

of a piece of land that was comparatively small. See EComHR *G. and E.* v. *Norway*, 3 October 1993.

[132] HRC *Sandra Lovelace* v. *Canada*, 30 July 1981. Following publication of this View the State explained the process in which it tried to consult Indian people and at the same time amend the discriminatory provisions as a matter of urgency. See Response of Canada to the Views of the Human Rights Committee, 6 June 1983, *Sandra Lovelace* v. *Canada*, 30 July 1981. As becomes apparent in the discussion of *R.L. and 16 other members of the Whispering Pine Band* v. *Canada*, 5 November 1991, the eventual amendment of the law by Canada did not receive overall approval.

[133] HRC *Ivan Kitok* v. *Sweden*, 27 July 1988.

[134] Anaya (1996), p. 101. The State had acknowledged that the non-reindeer herding Sami had no special rights under the present law. "These other Sami have found it more difficult to maintain their Sami identity and many of them are today assimilated into Swedish society. Indeed, the majority of this group does not even live within the area where reindeer herding Sami live". *Kitok* v. *Sweden*, 27 July 1988, §4.2. The petitioner pointed out: "It is characteristic that the 1964 Royal Committee wanted to call the Lapp village 'reindeer village' (renby) and wanted to make the renby an entirely economic association with increasing voting power for the big reindeer owners. This had also been achieved in the present sameby, where members get a new vote for every extra 100 reindeer. It is because of this organisation of the voting power that Ivan Kitok was not admitted into his fatherland Sörkaitum Lappby". *Kitok*, §5.3.

[135] HRC *Kitok* v. *Sweden*, 27 July 1988, §9.7.

[136] Kingsbury (2001), p. 213 puts it as follows: "In so far as the Sameby policy (...) was a response to the crisis in the long-term viability of reindeer-herding lifestyle and culture, however, the Swedish state was implicated much more fundamentally in not securing sufficient land, pasturage, and support for the Sami culture, yet the Committee became more hesitant to intervene. This paradox structures the result in the case, a very uneasy compromise in which no violation of the ICCPR is found because Kitok was in fact being permitted, although not as of right, to herd reindeer, and nothing is said about the systemic assimilationist effects of the diminishing resource base or other aspects of historic Swedish state policy". See also Thornberry (2002), pp. 159-160 and Simon (1997), p. 160, the latter emphasising the importance of assessing 'the broader harms affecting all Sami'.

the other members still recognise you as belonging to their group. If you are excluded this does not enhance your enjoyment.

In short, while procedurally only individuals can claim a violation of Article 27 under the OP, materially the collective aspects of Article 27 have priority.[137] The article is directed towards 'ensuring the survival and continued development of the cultural, religious and social identity of the minorities concerned, thus enriching the fabric of society as a whole'.[138] Thus, by referring to the aim of ensuring *survival* of the cultural, religious and social identity of minorities, this statement confirms the importance the HRC attaches to the collective aspects of Article 27.

A few cases involving culture may assist in clarifying the outer limits of provisional measures exactly because the measures were *not* used.[139] In *Diergaardt et al.* v. *Namibia* (2000), for

---

[137] See also Meijknecht (2001), pp. 131-139. She raises the question whether it is the individual's, the group's or the culture's existence needing protection and notes that Article 27 is basically formulated as a right bestowed upon the individual. She considers that 'the construction as applied in Article 27 suggests that the tension between the individual and the collectivity can be avoided by denying a legal status and rights to the collectivity, and by attributing rights exclusively to individuals'. The formulation 'in community with other members of their group', she acknowledges, 'suggests some sort of compromise between the individual and collective approach', but this, she points out, 'does not change the fact that the rights in question are bestowed upon individuals'. Certainly, from the perspective of the international personality of indigenous peoples Article 27 denies legal status to the collectivity. In its *interpretation* of the article, however, the HRC seems to attach rights to collectivities at the cost of the individual. General Comment 23 of the HRC points out that while Article 27 ICCPR is expressed in negative terms, a right still exists that 'shall not be denied'. In fact this means that State parties are under an obligation to *ensure* that the exercise of this right is protected. "Positive measures of protection are, therefore, required not only against the acts of the State party itself, whether through its legislative, judicial or administrative authorities, but also against the acts of other persons within the State party". General Comment 23 on Article 27, 8 April 1994, §6.1 (1994). See Crawford (2001), p. 23 for a strictly textual interpretation.

[138] HRC General Comment 23 on Article 27, 8 April 1994, §9.

[139] In HRC *R.L. and 16 other members of the Whispering Pine Band* v. *Canada*, 5 November 1991, for instance, the HRC specifically noted its refusal to use provisional measures. Like *Sandra Lovelace* v. *Canada*, 30 July 1981 and *Ivan Kitok* v. *Sweden*, 27 July 1988 this case related to the issue of exclusion from a cultural group. The petitioners argued that new legislation would have an increasingly negative effect on their families. To avoid the termination of family lines through the implementation of this legislation, the Band would have to arrange all future marriages of Band members with members of other Bands. This, they argued, forced them 'to choose between gradually losing their legal rights and reserve land,' on the one hand and 'depriving their children of personal freedom and privacy' on the other. This, they argued, forced them 'to choose between gradually losing their legal rights and reserve land', on the one hand and 'depriving their children of personal freedom and privacy' on the other. They sought 'immediate measures to preserve the status quo pendente lite' and requested the HRC to use provisional measures and urge the State party 'to refrain from making any additions to or deletions from the Band List of the Whispering Pines Indian Band, except as may be necessary to ensure that every direct descendant of the petitioners is included for the time being as a member of the Band'. HRC *R.L. and 16 other members of the Whispering Pine Band* v. *Canada*, 5 November 1991, §3.9. Among others, the State party noted that it had considered the membership rules as suggested by the Band were 'not acceptable because they excluded certain specified groups, such as women who lost their entitlement to Band membership as a result of marriage to non-Indians, their minor children, and others'. The HRC did not use provisional measures and declared the case inadmissible for non-exhaustion of domestic remedies. One could speak of harm to specific children in that they might grow up with the knowledge that they could only protect the land and cultural rights of their children by finding a registered Indian to marry. Apparently, following the *Lovelace* case the

instance, counsel requested provisional measures to the effect that 'no expropriation, buying or selling of the community land take place, that no rent be collected from tenants and that no herds be prevented from grazing on the community land while the communication is under considera-tion by the Committee'.[140] The Rapporteur refused this request. The discussion on the merits indicates that the HRC did not consider that the petitioners had established a cultural relationship to the lands in question.[141] While the Rapporteur did not motivate his refusal to use provisional measures, given the decision on the merits it is likely that he equally concluded, from the initial complaint, that there was insufficient evidence rendering necessary the use of provisional meas-ures to prevent irreparable harm to the culture of the petitioners, threatening the very existence.

In *Hopu and Bessert* v. *France* (1997)[142] provisional measures were not, but, it is argued, *could* have been used. The petitioners had attempted to halt the building of a hotel on an indige-nous burial site. They were both ethnic Polynesians living in Tahiti, French Polynesia and the descendants of the owners of a land tract of about 4.5 hectares called Tetaitapu. They argued that their ancestors were dispossessed of their property in 1961. In 1990 a company was seeking to initiate construction work on a luxury hotel complex on the site as soon as possible. In protest the petitioners and other descendants of the owners peacefully occupied the site in 1992. They con-tended that 'the land and the lagoon bordering it represent an important place in their history, their culture and their life' and added that 'the land encompasses the site of a pre-European burial ground and that the lagoon remains a traditional fishing ground and provides the means of subsis-tence for some thirty families living next to the lagoon'. They pointed out that their expulsion from the land was imminent. In that light the HRC could have used provisional measures, but apparently it did not.[143]

HRC did express concern about 'ongoing discrimination against aboriginal women'. In its Concluding Observations to Canada's Fourth Periodic Report it noted that the amendment to the Indian Act 'affects only the woman and her children, not subsequent generations, which may still be denied membership in the Community', CCPR/C/79/Add.105, §19. In 2006 the HRC observed in its Concluding Observations 'that balancing collective and individual interests on reserves to the sole detriment of women is not compatible with the Covenant' (Articles 2, 3, 26 and 27). CCPR/C/CAN/CO/5, 20 April 2006, §22. Still, this is not the type of situation that would warrant provisional measures by the Committee because the legislation and acts of implementation would have results that could indeed be reversed. Measures that are reversible cannot be irreparable.

[140] HRC *J.G.A. Diergaardt (late Captain of the Rehoboth Baster Community) et al.* v. *Namibia*, 25 July 2000, §3.7.

[141] It found that there had been no violation of Article 27. "This conclusion is based on Committee's assessment of the relationship between the authors' way of life and the lands covered by their claims. Although the link of the Rehoboth Community to the lands in question dates back some 125 years, it is not the result of a relationship that would have given rise to a distinctive culture. Furthermore, although the Rehoboth Community bears distinctive properties as to the historical forms of self-government, the authors have failed to demonstrate how these factors would be based on their way of raising cattle". *Diergaardt et al.* v. *Namibia*, 25 July 2000, §10.6. The concurring opinion of Evatt and Medina Quiroga more closely addresses the question when land rights may be based on Article 27 ICCPR. They point out that the claim did not draw the protection of this article because it was essentially economic rather than cultural. They note that the petitioners had 'defined their culture almost solely in terms of economic activity of grazing cattle'. "They cannot show that they enjoy a distinct culture which is intimately bound up with or dependent on the use of these particular lands, to which they moved a little over a century ago, or that the diminution of their access to the lands has undermined any such culture".

[142] HRC *Hopu and Bessert* v. *France*, 29 July 1997.

[143] The View was published during the period the HRC did not mention the use of provisional measures. Unfortunately, in March/April 2003 and August 2003 the file of this case was not available in Geneva. It appears from telephone contacts between F. de Vries and counsel for the

The most important legal issue arising from *Hopu and Bessert* (1997) is the question whether and how the HRC may use provisional measures to protect the culture of indigenous peoples when Article 27 ICCPR cannot be invoked. Upon accession to the ICCPR France declared that in light of its constitution Article 27 ICCPR was not applicable.[144] In a previous case dating from 1989 the HRC determined that the French 'declaration' was in fact a reservation.[145]

---

petitioners Lestourneaud (Thonon) and Roux (Montpellier) on 11 November 2003 that provisional measures had not been taken. Avocat Roux confirmed this by letter of 10 December 2003 (on file with the author).

[144] No other States parties objected to this declaration, although the Federal Republic of Germany declared that it interpreted the French declaration to mean that the French constitution already fully guaranteed the individual rights protected by Article 27. CCPR/C/2/Rev. 3 as referred to in Nowak (1993), p. 486. Horn (1988), p. 238 points out that 'reservations and declarations form completely distinct categories of acts due to their different functions'. "A reservation affects the norm- an interpretative declaration operates on the norm's formulation; their objects are distinct". Lijnzaad (1994), p. 61 notes: "The interpretative declaration is an opinion as to how a provision ought to be understood. It is nothing more than a unilateral statement addressed to other states parties and to possible supervisory organs. While the declaration itself has no direct legal effect, either for its author or the other states parties, its aim is obviously to arouse support for the interpretation proposed". She acknowledges, however, that the distinctions are not always as clear as that. Sometimes the purpose of the State is to condition its acceptance of the treaty not only with its reservations but also with its declarations. Scholars have made a distinction between 'qualified interpretative declarations' and 'mere interpretative declarations'. In relation to the first, once an authoritative determination is made about the meaning of a provision and this interpretation conflicts with the declaration, the declaration turns into a reservation (see references in Lijnzaad (1995), pp. 61-62). She also refers to the judgment of the European Court on Human Rights in the case *Belilos* v. *Switzerland*, 29 April 1988. In light of, among others, the lack of transparency in the distinction of the two types of interpretative declarations suggested, Lijnzaad argues that declarations should not have the legal effect of a reservation. "Basically a declaration cannot exclude or restrict the legal effect of provisions of the treaty. It should be understood that in cases where a state wishes to exclude or restrict the legal effects of a treaty, an interpretative declaration cannot be used". (Lijnzaad (1995), p. 65).

[145] See HRC *M.K.* v. *France*, 8 November 1989 (inadm.) and *T.K.* v. *France*, 8 November 1989 (inadm.). It referred to Article 2(1)(d) of the Vienna Convention on the Law of Treaties. It is doubtful, however, whether it should be the State's assumed intent rather than the text of the declaration that should be determinative. The text seems to simply observe that the State considered Article 27 irrelevant or inapplicable because the French Constitution provides equality of all citizens before the law without distinction as to origin, race or religion. In French doctrine the latter means that distinctions between citizens on the basis of origin, race or religion are prohibited which, in turn, means that there are no minorities in France. This is also what Higgins pointed out in her dissenting opinion on this issue in 1989. She considered the French notification of Article 27 a declaration and not a reservation. She emphasised that France had submitted both reservations and interpretative declarations when it ratified the Covenant in January 1982. In that light there was 'no reason to suppose that the contrast in use, in different paragraphs, of the phrase 'reservation' and 'declaration' was not entirely deliberate, with its legal consequence well understood by the Government of the Republic'. Given this distinction it was 'ultimately for the Committee to see if the interpretation of the French Government accords with its own'. The HRC had emphasised that the existence of minorities in no way constituted an admission of discrimination. The existence of minorities in the sense of Article 27, she noted in reference to HRC statements, was a factual matter. In its Concluding Observations to the French report, CCPR/C/79/Add. 80, §24 the HRC concluded that it was unable to agree that France was a country in which there are no minorities. It pointed out that 'the mere fact that equal rights are granted to all individuals and that all individuals are equal before the law does not preclude the

Scheinin has pointed out that even if this were correct, in light of the Committee's General Comment this 'reservation' could be considered contrary to the object and the purpose of the Convention.[146] Yet in its admissibility decision (1994) the HRC confirmed its previous case law that the French 'declaration' on Article 27 operated as a reservation. This meant it could not consider complaints against France under that article. Instead it would consider the claim under Articles 14, 17 and 23 ICCPR (family life and privacy).[147]

Apart from the fact that the ICCPR includes a specific article on the right to culture while the ECHR does not, Article 8 ECHR refers to the right of everyone to respect for his 'private and family life'. Article 17 ICCPR prohibits arbitrary or unlawful interference with one's privacy, family, home or correspondence. Article 8 ECHR may thus have a wider scope of application. Indeed, prior to the HRC in *Hopu* the European Commission on Human Rights already acknowledged the possibility of applying the right of private and family life and the home (Art. 8 ECHR) in relation to threats to indigenous land. In *G. and E.* v. *Norway* (1993),[148] it noted 'a minority group is, in principle, entitled to claim the right to respect for the particular life style it may lead as being "private life", "family life" or "home"'.[149]

The Bosnia Chamber has also accepted that the authorities' order for the exhumation of the petitioner's late wife from the family plot was so closely related to his private and family life that it came within the ambit of Article 8 ECHR.[150] Moreover, in another case, in which it referred as

---

existence in fact of minorities in a country'. As Thornberry (2002), p. 154 notes 'to conclude otherwise would be to accept the argument that a group is created by the prejudices of others-including prejudicial legislation-and that a State has sole authority to make decisions on group existence'.

[146] Scheinin (2000), p. 218, referring to the General Comment 24 on reservations to the ICCPR or the Optional Protocols, 4 November 1994. One might add that denying the existence of minorities could result in a denial of the right to equality in the sense that this right encompasses the right to be different and to express this difference in community with others. It also noteworthy that the HRC pointed out in its General Comment 23 on the right to culture (Article 27), 6 April 1994, the HRC pointed out that '(s)ome States parties who claimed that they do not discriminate on grounds of ethnicity, language or religion, wrongly contend, on that basis alone, that they have no minorities', §4.

[147] Five members of the HRC considered that it should have declared admissible the Article 27 claim in *Hopu*. Rather than arguing to overrule the aforementioned 1989 decision on the French declaration, they made a distinction between the applicability of the French declaration in metropolitan France and in overseas territories. Apparently during the discussion they attempted to re-open the issue of admissibility of the claim. They noted that, after the Committee's decision not to do so, 'we are able to associate ourselves with the Committee's views on the remaining aspects of the communication'. Partly dissenting opinion by Evatt, Medina Quiroga, Pocar, Scheinin and Yalden in *Hopu and Bessert* v. *France*, 29 July 1997. Yet the HRC did not re-open the discussion on the admissibility of the Article 27 claim because the Committee's earlier decision in this respect had been phrased in general terms. It could have considered that it had been the *State party* that had requested a review of the earlier admissibility decision and that this re-opened not only the discussion of those claims declared admissible but also of those declared inadmissible. After all the HRC did in fact amend its admissibility decision to include a claim based on Article 26 ICCPR.

[148] EComHR *G. and E.* v. *Norway*, 3 October 1993, p. 35.

[149] Ibid. It did not find a violation, however, as it considered that the building of a water dam and a hydro-electric power station, while it did interfere with the private life and traditional activities of the Sami, was justified, among others, in the interest of the economic well-being of the country (p. 36). The Commission took a quantitative approach, finding that the interference was limited to the loss of a piece of land that was comparatively small.

[150] Bosnia Chamber *Mahmutović* v. *Republika Srpska*, 8 October 1999, §84.

well to the HRC's decision in *Hopu*, it considered that the petitioner's complaint equally fell within the ambit of Article 8, considering that the graveyard in question had been the graveyard of his family for many generations and that his mother was buried there in 1991.[151]

The petitioners in *Hopu* had claimed that the construction of the hotel complex would 'destroy their ancestral burial grounds, which represent an important place in their history, culture and life, would arbitrarily interfere with their privacy and their family life, in violation of articles 17 and 23'.[152] The HRC indeed concluded that the construction of a hotel complex on their ancestral burial grounds interfered with their right to family life and privacy. Nothing in the information before it showed that the State party duly took into account the importance of the burial grounds for the petitioners when it decided to lease the site. The State had not shown that the interference with the petitioners' rights was reasonable in the circumstances and the petitioners were entitled to an appropriate remedy.[153] The Committee did not refer to the complaint on the threat to their traditional means of subsistence. Clearly this could not be linked to the right to family life and privacy, but only to the inapplicable Article 27 ICCPR.

Both the dissenting opinion on the inadmissibility of the Article 27 claim and the dissenting opinion on the finding of a violation of Articles 17 and 23 seem to consider that, had the Committee been able to deal with the Article 27 claim, it would have found a violation. It is clear that building a hotel complex on the ancestral burial grounds of the petitioners would be a threat to the existence and cultural integrity of the ethnic Polynesians.

Nevertheless, the Committee members differed in their view on the existence of a violation of Articles 17 and 23 ICCPR. The four dissenters who would *not* have found a violation of those articles noted that 'even when the term "family" is extended, it does have a discrete meaning'.[154] The petitioners had 'provided no evidence that the burial ground is one that is connected to their family, rather than to the whole of the indigenous population in the area'.[155] The values to be protected were not family or privacy but cultural values. They shared the concern for these values, but repeated that they were protected under Article 27 and not 17 or 23 ICCPR. In relation to the notion of privacy they pointed out that it 'revolves around protection of those aspects of a person's life, or relationships with others, which one chooses to keep from the public eye, or from outside intrusion'.[156] Interference with participation and public worship or cultural activities that play important roles in the identities of persons in different societies, they noted, may indeed cause violations of Articles 18 (freedom of religion) and 27 ICCPR. It would be interesting, in that sense, to know what position the dissenters would have taken had the petitioners claimed a violation of the freedom of religion (Article 18).[157] The four dissenters in *Hopu* regretted that the

---

[151] Bosnia Chamber *Čengić* v. *BiH and Srpska*, 5 September 2003, §103.

[152] HRC *Hopu and Bessert* v. *France*, 29 July 1997, §10.3.

[153] The Committee did not specify what this remedy would entail. The State was under an obligation to protect their rights effectively and to ensure that similar violations did not occur in the future.

[154] HRC *Hopu and Bessert* v. *France*, 29 July 1997, dissenting opinion Buergenthal, Kretzmer, Ando and Colville.

[155] Ibid.

[156] But see HRC *Coeriel and Aurik* v. *the Netherlands*, 31 October 1994. In this case the HRC considered that 'the notion of privacy refers to the sphere of a person's life in which he or she can freely express his or her identity, be it by entering into relationship with others or alone'. It considered that 'a person's surname constitutes an important component of one's identity', §10.2. This meant that the privacy rights in Article 17 included the protection against arbitrary or unlawful interference with the right to choose and change one's own name. This shows that the HRC also considers part of the right to privacy those expressions of identity which one does *not* choose to keep from the public eye.

[157] In HRC *Vakoumé and 28 other persons* v. *France*, 31 October 2000 (inadm.) the petitioners indeed did so. However, the HRC declared this case inadmissible for non-exhaustion.

Committee was prevented from applying Article 27. They expressed their concern with 'the fail-ure of the State party to respect a site that has obvious importance in the cultural heritage of the indigenous population of French Polynesia'. Yet they believed, 'that this concern does not justify distorting the meaning of the terms family and privacy beyond their ordinary and generally ac-cepted meaning'.[158] Nevertheless, the majority in *Hopu and Bessert* considered that Arts 17 and 23 ICCPR had indeed been violated.

It is important to examine whether provisional measures could be used in similar situations if the HRC maintains its approach towards the French declaration. In *Vakoumé* v. *France* (inadm. 2000)[159] a company had similarly begun construction of a hotel complex. The 29 petitioners were members of the Touété tribe on the Isle of Pines in Southern New Caledonia. They claimed that 'the site on which the complex was built was one of special significance for their history, culture and life'. The Rapporteur did not use provisional measures, most likely because the complex had already (partially) been built when the petitioners submitted their complaint.[160] He may have considered it too far reaching to request restoration of the status quo, as part of provisional meas-ures, rather than as part of a decision on reparations.[161]

The petitioners, on the other hand, are likely to have hoped that the HRC would request the State, pending the proceedings, to demolish the hotel and restore the *status quo*. While it is indeed possible to order the return to the situation *quo ante* as part of a provisional measure, this nor-mally concerns the freedom or the legal status of an individual. In a complex situation involving economic constructions and the right to cultural survival, it is preferable to reserve such recom-mendations for the final determination of the case. Moreover, to the extent demolition of the hotel would redress the violation (an would be considered as a possible form of reparation), the request for provisional measures concerned a situation that was reversible.[162]

Another reason for not using provisional measures upon receipt of the initial complaint may have been the French declaration on Article 27 ICCPR, as discussed in *Hopu and Bessert*. The petitioners claimed violations of Articles 17(1), 18 and 23(1) ICCPR instead. In so far as they based their complaint on interference of their privacy and family life, similar issues arose as in *Hopu and Bessert*. In relation to Articles 17(1) and 23 they declared that the 'Baie d'Oro is an important part of their natural, historical and cultural heritage. Ancestral burial grounds are to be found on the site, which is also the source of legends forming part of the heritage and collective

---

[158] HRC *Hopu and Bessert* v. *France*, 29 July 1997, dissenting opinion Buergenthal, Kretzmer, Ando and Colville.

[159] HRC *Vakoumé and 28 other persons* v. *France*, 31 October 2000 (inadm.).

[160] The View only mentions the petitioners' request for provisional measures and the fact that the Special Rapporteur did not grant these. It does not indicate when and how he responded to this request.

[161] The initial submission was of March 1998, when the company involved had already begun construction of the hotel complex. The complex was inaugurated in November 1998 and has since been operational. The View does not indicate when the Rapporteur registered the case. This means it is not clear whether he did so when the complex had not yet been completed or when it already had.

[162] In a way, the request for provisional measures may have been too late. At the same time, the HRC indicated that the complaint itself was too early because domestic remedies had not been exhausted. It may be, therefore, that the Rapporteur would not have used provisional measures either if they had been in time to halt construction of the hotel. In light of the inadmissibility decision, the Rapporteur may have reasoned that the domestic proceedings did have suspensive effect even though they did not in fact halt this construction. Such reasoning, however, would not be convincing in all cases because the *procedural possibility* of suspensive effect does not guarantee that a domestic court interprets the risk of irreparable harm in the way required by the ICCPR.

memory of the Isle of Pines'.[163] The difference with *Hopu* is, however, that the petitioners also claimed interference with their freedom to manifest their religion or beliefs in worship (Article 18). Indeed the HRC could have resorted to Article 18 in this case, with the advantage that a more obvious link might be established (with some specification) between the protection of sacred indigenous burial sites and the right to have and manifest one's religion in community with others, than the link between the protection of these sites and the right to family life and privacy.[164] The collective aspect of this right, moreover, can also be found in the text of the article.[165] The petitioners had claimed that they 'like all Melanesians, live in a natural environment founded on a network of ties to their parents, their families and their dead. Veneration of the dead is a manifestation of religion and tradition inherent in their lifestyle, beliefs and culture'.[166] Yet the View referred to the petitioners' request for the use of provisional measures without mentioning their resort to Article 18 ICCPR. It is possible that the petitioners invoked this article only at a later stage and the HRC did not consider it.[167] In any case the HRC only noted that the petitioners

---

[163] HRC *Vakoumé and 28 other persons* v. *France*, 31 October 2000 (inadm.), §3.4.

[164] The UN and Inter-American draft declarations on indigenous peoples reaffirm, as Kingsbury phrases it, 'historically-grounded and culturally grounded entitlements and responsibilities with regard to natural resources, religious sites, and spiritual or guardianship relationships with particular land, water, mountains, etc.; (...) duties in relation to ancestors and future generations; continuance of certain kinds of economic practices; and perhaps entitlements and responsibilities in relation to traditional knowledge'. Kingsbury (2001), pp. 239-240. Articles 18 and 27 could assist in protecting religious sites and duties in relation to ancestors, for instance. However, Article 27 is the only article in the Covenant that could be of use to protect certain kinds of *economic* practices.

[165] Nowak notes that this article expressly emphasises this right as both an individual and collective right ('individually or in community with others') while Article 27 does not include a reference to 'individually'. "This means that individual enjoyment of a minority culture, individual profession to the religion of a minority and the individual use of a minority language are not protected". The individual right, he considers, is that of enforcement of the collective right. This statement may be correct at least with regard to the Committee's use of provisional measures. Nowak (1993), p. 499.

[166] HRC *Vakoumé and 28 other persons* v. *France*, 31 October 2000 (inadm.), §3.6.

[167] Yet another reason why the Rapporteur may have decided not to use provisional measures, once he had already decided to await the State party's comments, may be lack of *prima facie* evidence of irreparable harm. The State party only responded in December 1998, when the hotel complex was already in operation. It considered that the case should be declared inadmissible for non-exhaustion of domestic remedies. The petitioners responded in April 1999. They pointed out that all domestic remedies they had invoked to prevent construction and inauguration of the hotel complex had proved ineffective and futile. One of the decisions the HRC referred to in its description of the domestic proceedings is that of the Nouméa Administrative Tribunal of 4 June 1998 authorising the work to continue. It found that the construction did not violate the rights of the petitioners under the ICCPR 'because it had not been proved that the hotel was to be placed on a site where ancestral tombs were located and because the representatives of the tribe had given their consent for the construction'. Under the heading 'facts and proceedings as they emerge from statements by the authors and from the evidence submitted' the HRC noted that the representatives of the Touété tribe participated in the project for the creation of the hotel complex, except for the 29 petitioners. The South Province of New Caledonia would provide the tribe for a 66 percent holding in the company owning the prospective complex. The representatives (with the exception of the petitioners) provided the company with the usufruct, for a period of 25 years, of the land needed for the construction. The petitioners did not take part in this agreement and claimed to have rights to the plots of land in question. Hypothetically the issue of consultation, representation and participation could have played a role in the decision not to use provisional measures, to the extent that the information raised some doubts about the

claimed 'that the site on which the complex was built was one of special significance for their history, culture and life'.[168]

In relation to both *Hopu* and *Vakoumé* the question arises whether, when Article 27 ICCPR does not apply because of a 'reservation', provisional measures clearly aiming at preventing irreparable harm to the cultural integrity of a group could be linked to the right to family life and privacy (Article 23) rather than to the group's right to enjoy its own culture under Article 27. Even if 'family' and 'privacy' are interpreted in the context of the petitioners' culture, as they should in light of different cultural notions about these concepts, the *texts* of these articles still relate to an individual right and not the right of a group. The dissenters in *Hopu* may be correct in noting that the petitioners had failed to provide sufficient information to justify a finding of a violation of the right to family.[169] This could be different if the petitioners had specified why in their culture the concept of 'family' included the ancestors of their ethnic or cultural group. In other words, why it was important not only to respect their ancestral burial grounds as part of their culture but also as part of their family life.[170] Kingsbury notes that the Committee did 'not specify the analytical structure and limits of the concepts' on which it relied. He gives a 'speculative explanation of the Committee's unarticulated premises', namely that it 'was drawing sustenance from the developing international commitment to rights of indigenous peoples'.[171] He also draws attention to 'the wider problem for the Committee of whether to enunciate only standards capable of global application or to try to nudge some governments in a positive direction where

---

wishes of the larger group of beneficiaries relevant in this type of provisional measure involving rights with collective aspects. However, any doubts about the location of ancestral tombs could have been addressed with further questions. See further Chapter XIII, section 4 on representation and consultation and Chapter XV on assessment of risk. The HRC declared the case inadmissible for non-exhaustion of domestic remedies. The petitioners had not awaited the outcome of the appeal and the Committee could not accept 'counsel's contention that given that the construction has already been completed, the courts would no longer be able to guarantee an appropriate remedy'. It noted that review of its decision was possible upon receipt of a written request containing information to the effect that the reasons for inadmissibility no longer applied.

[168] HRC *Vakoumé and 28 other persons* v. *France*, 31 October 2000 (inadm.), §3.2.

[169] Scheinin (2000) takes a more positive attitude towards the decision in *Hopu*. He discusses various aspects of the case in pp. 217-222. See also Donders (2001), pp. 187-188, observing that Article 27 would have been the most appropriate provision, while the use of Articles 17 and 23 'may appear to be far less tenable'. Nevertheless, now that Article 27 was declared inadmissible it was important to find a 'creative solution' so that 'France could not avoid dealing with cases concerning cultural aspects of minority rights'. "Such an approach is allowed considering the cohesion of human rights, especially in relation to the protection of cultural identity". See in general Chapter VII of her book and, in particular, pp. 340-341 discussing the emergence of cultural identity as a principle of human rights law, referring to a 'freedom of cultural identity' reflecting a 'more dynamic approach' and implying 'the right to change cultural identity'.

[170] One might think of a situation in which clan names are personal genealogical names that are used as lineage and family names and that are sometimes counted and memorised for up to sixty generations. Among Hani and Akha, for instance, it is reported that such a system underlines the alliance of transfer of knowledge and is necessary for their survival. The ancestors' service and the complicated customary rules related to it is considered 'the ideology and the backbone of the ethnic alliance system'. They honour their ancestors nine to twelve times each year in ceremonies marking important occasions. Each family in the village performs these ceremonies in honour of its 'line of life'. In such context one could envisage that the concept of family in itself would be such as to include all the ancestors in this line and still have a discrete meaning. See e.g. the information provided at <www.hani-akha.org> (consulted 2 November 2002).

[171] Kingsbury (2001), p. 242.

the local political and legal climate is receptive'. He considers that it had pursued the latter strategy in this case 'with some success'.[172]

While the petitioners necessarily were individuals (to satisfy the requirements of the OP) it is clear that the provisional measures used in cases involving indigenous culture have aimed at preserving the collective aspects of their rights. It turns out, however, that in *Hopu* the HRC found a violation of an article in which the collective aspect does not prevail. Still it would have made sense for the Rapporteur to use provisional measures in this case. After all, at the time of his decision on provisional measures he could not have known that the HRC would decide not to deal with Articles 27 or 18 ICCPR.[173]

From the decision in *Hopu* onwards the use of provisional measures in similar circumstances (only involving Articles 23 claims) would be less opportune, as long as there is no prospect of the Committee changing its attitude towards the French declaration about Article 27. This could only be different if, for instance, the HRC considers that the cultural integrity of ethnic Polynesians as an indigenous people is subsumed in the concept of family and privacy to the extent that the rights to family life and privacy are not individual rights alone. If, moreover, the HRC considers that provisional measures protecting the very existence of individuals or groups should not only be used to prevent irreparable harm to life (Article 6), personal integrity (Article 7) or the cultural survival of an indigenous group (Article 27) but also to prevent irreversible situations in relation to other rights, this could equally explain its use of provisional measures in new cases against France involving cultural issues.[174] In that case the HRC should specify this.

The UN Committee on the Elimination of Racial Discrimination (CERD) has confirmed the importance of the relation of indigenous peoples with their lands. It has especially called upon States parties to the Convention on the Elimination of Racial Discrimination 'to recognize and protect the rights of indigenous peoples to own, develop, control and use their communal lands, territories and resources and, where they have been deprived of their lands and territories traditionally owned pr otherwise inhabited or used without their free and informed consent, to take steps to return those lands and territories'.[175]

The Inter-American Commission and Court have been increasingly specific on the collective rights of indigenous peoples.[176] In the early 1990s several organizations petitioned the CIDH on behalf of the Haorani people.[177] They asserted an imminent threat because oil exploitation

---

[172]   Id., p. 243. According to counsel in *Hopu and Bessert* the French government had not been that receptive, see Chapter XVII on the official responses by addressee States.

[173]   See Chapter XIV on the relationship with admissibility and jurisdiction on the merits.

[174]   This is further discussed in Chapter XII (Other situations) and Conclusion Part II.

[175]   CERD General Recommendation XXIII on the rights of indigenous peoples, A/52/18, annex V, §5 (adding that this right to restitution should only be substituted by the right to just, fair and prompt compensation only when such restitution factually is impossible. In that case the compensation 'should as far as possible take the form of lands and territories').

[176]   Already in 1973 the Inter-American Commission, dealing with a petition on behalf of the Aché people in Paraguay (case 1802), discussed the issue of the refusal to recognize collectively owned lands and other rights 'of a clearly collective nature'. In the Miskitos case against Nicaragua the Commission confirmed the collective right of the Miskitos to determine the form of ownership and use of their ancestral lands. In 1985 the Commission recognized the collective rights of the Yamomami and recommended Brazil, among others, to demarcate their lands. On these cases see CIDH 'The human rights situation of the indigenous people in the Americas', OEA/Ser.L/V/II.108, Doc. 62, 20 October 2000, Chapter III (6A).

[177]   The petition, dated 1 June 1990, was filed by the Confederación de Nacionalidades Indígenas de la Amazonía Ecuatoriana (CONFENIAE) on behalf of the Huaorani People. Hearings on the petition were held on 20 September 1991 and 4 October 1993. The Organización de la Nacionalidad Huaorani de la Amazonia Ecuatoriana (ONHAE) became a co-petitioner in September of 1992.

activities within their traditional lands would irreparably harm them, threatening their physical and cultural survival. It was this petition that prompted the Commission's visit to Ecuador in 1997. In its report of this visit the Commission refers several times to the importance of ensuring cultural survival. It observed that for indigenous peoples the 'continued utilization of traditional systems for the control and use of territory are essential to their survival, as well as to their individual and collective well-being'.[178]

In the more recent case of the *Dann Sisters* v. *US* (2002) the Inter-American Commission pointed out on the merits that 'the provisions of the American Declaration should be interpreted and applied (...) with due regard to the particular principles of international human rights law governing the individual and collective interests of indigenous peoples'.[179] Thus States must take special measures to ensure recognition of the particular and collective interest of indigenous people in the use of their traditional lands and resources.[180]

In this case, in which it had previously used precautionary measures, it found on the merits that the US had failed to ensure the right to property of the Danns under conditions of equality. They should be provided with an effective remedy 'in a manner that considers both the collective and individual nature of the property rights that the Danns may claim in the Western Shoshone ancestral lands' "The process must also allow for [their] full and informed participation in the determination of their claims'.[181]

In a case involving the Mopan and Ke'kchi Maya people of the Toledo District of Southern Belize the Commission also dealt with claims regarding certain lands and natural resources. The Commission noted the development in international human rights law that indigenous human rights 'are frequently exercised and enjoyed by indigenous communities in a collective manner, in the sense that they can only be properly ensured through their guarantee to an indigenous people as a whole'. In the context of the right to property, which 'has been recognized as one of the rights having such a collective aspect',[182] the Commission has noted that 'the organs of the Inter-American human rights system have acknowledged that indigenous peoples enjoy a particular relationship with the lands and resources traditionally occupied and used by them'.[183] Through this relationship 'those lands and resources are considered to be owned and enjoyed by the in-

---

[178] Report on the Situation of Human Rights in Ecuador, Chapter IX, Human rights issues of special relevance for the indigenous inhabitants of the country, OEA/Ser.L/V/II.96, Doc. 10 rev. 1, 24 April 1997. UN sub-commission Rapporteur Daes has pointed out: 'The very survival of indigenous peoples is at risk owing to the continuing threats to their lands, territories and resources'. Final working paper prepared by the Special Rapporteur, Mrs. Erica-Irene A. Daes, Indigenous peoples and their relationship to land, E/CN.4/Sub.2/2001/21, 11 June 2001, §119.

[179] CIDH *Mary and Carrie Dann* v. *US*, 27 December 2002, §131, referring, among others, to 'legal recognition of their varied and specific forms and modalities of their control, ownership, use and enjoyment of territories and property' and emphasizing mutual consent.

[180] Relevant provisions of the American Declaration in this respect include Article II (the right to equality under the law), Article XVIII (the right to a fair trial), and Article XXIII (the right to property). The Commission also referred to Article XVIII Draft American Declaration on the Rights of indigenous Peoples, stipulating the protection of traditional forms of ownership, the right to land and resources and, more generally, cultural survival. It noted that this Declaration had not yet been approved by the OAS General Assembly, but that 'the basic principles reflected in many of the provisions of the Declaration, including aspects of Article XVIII, reflect general international principles developing out of and applicable inside and outside of the inter-American system and to this extent are properly considered in interpreting and applying the provisions of the American Declaration in the context of indigenous peoples'. CIDH *Mary and Carrie Dann* v. *US*, 27 December 2002, §129.

[181] CIDH *Mary and Carrie Dann* v. *US*, 27 December 2002, §§171-173.

[182] CIDH *Maya Indigenous Communities of the Toledo District* (Belize), 12 October 2004, §113.

[183] Id., §114.

digenous community as a whole and according to which the use and enjoyment of the land and its resources are integral components of the physical and cultural survival of the indigenous communities and the effective realization of their human rights more broadly' (footnotes omitted).[184] The Commission also noted that it has stressed the need for States to protect the rights of indigenous peoples to their ancestral territories not only in its decisions on the merits in individual cases, but also in its reports on the general situation of human rights in the OAS members States and in its use of precautionary measures.[185] The right to property under the American Declaration, it has pointed out, 'must be interpreted and applied in the context of indigenous communities with due consideration of principles relating to the protection of traditional forms of ownership and cultural survival and rights to land, territories and resources'.[186]

The Inter-American Court has equally developed a broad concept of property (under Article 21 ACHR), mindful of the communal ownership by indigenous groups. In the landmark case *Awas Tingni* (2001), which was decided before the Commission's decision on the merits in the aforementioned Belize case, it determined that Article 21 ACHR also protects 'the rights of members of the indigenous communities within the framework of communal property'.[187] "As a result of customary practices, possession of land should suffice for indigenous communities lacking real title to property of the land to obtain official recognition of that property, and for consequent registration".[188]

It specifically elaborated on the close ties between indigenous peoples and their lands:

> "Among indigenous peoples there is a communitarian tradition regarding a communal form of collective property of the land, in the sense that ownership of the land is not centred on an individual but rather on the group and its community. Indigenous groups, by the fact of their very existence, have the right to live freely in their own territory; the close ties of indigenous people with the land must be recognized and understood to have one basis of their cultures, their spiritual life, their integrity, and their economic survival. For indigenous communities, relations to the land are not merely a matter of possession and production but a material and spiritual element which they must fully enjoy, even to preserve their cultural legacy and transmit it to future generations".[189]

It concluded that the State must 'carry out the delimitation, demarcation, and titling of the territory belonging to the Community'. Lack thereof had created a 'climate of constant uncertainty among the members of the Awas Tingni Community, insofar as they do not know for certain how far their communal property extends geographically and, therefore, they do not know until where they can freely use and enjoy their respective property'.[190] Until this delimitation the State should abstain from actions 'that might lead the agents of the State itself, or third parties acting with its acquiescence or its tolerance, to affect the existence, value, use of enjoyment of the property located in the geographical area where the members of the Community live and carry out their activities'.[191] In *Moiwana Village* v. *Suriname* (2005) the Court also found that the State was to adopt measures to ensure their property rights, including 'the creation of an effective mechanism for the delimitation, demarcation and titling' of these traditional territories. The remains of the community members killed in November 1986 were to be delivered to the surviving community

---

[184]   Id., §114.
[185]   Id., §115.
[186]   Id., §115.
[187]   IACHR *Awas Tingni* v. *Nicaragua*, 31 August 2001, §148.
[188]   Id., §151.
[189]   Id., §149.
[190]   Id., §153.
[191]   Ibid.

members.[192] Among others this case is interesting as it concerns not an indigenous people, strictly speaking, as being indigenous to the region, but a community that settled in Moiwana in the 19th century and developed a 'profound and all-encompassing relationship to their ancestral lands'.[193]

In *Yakye Axa Indigenous Community* v. *Paraguay* (2005) the Court specifically noted that not just the 'right to community property of the indigenous communities over their traditional territories' but also over the 'natural resources linked to their culture' in fact correlated with the term 'goods' in Article 21 ACHR.[194] The Court concluded that the State had failed to guarantee the rights of the members of the Community to common property, which had affected their right to a dignified life, as they were unable to gain access to their traditional means of subsistence, the use of natural resources necessary to obtain clean water and for the practice of traditional medicine.[195] Among others the Court paid attention to the position of persons of age suffering from chronic diseases and the obligation of States to alleviate suffering. It noted that among the Yakye Axa mainly the elderly have the task to tell the stories and pass on the culture to the younger generations.[196] This indicates an awareness of the importance of cultural practices and the obligation to ensure cultural survival.The majority considered the State was not responsible for the death of 16 members of the Yakye Axa community.[197] Yet it did find that the State had violated Article 4(1) with respect to the surviving community members. It ordered a range of reparations, including a public act acknowledging responsibility,[198] the demarcation of their traditional land and, in the meantime, provision of the basic services necessary for a life in dignity.[199]

The next year the Court dealt with the case of the *Sawhoyamaxa* (2006), an indigenous group in circumstances largely similar to those of the Yakye Axa. The Court found that their right to property, life, personal integrity and legal personality had been violated. It held the State responsible for failure to prevent the deaths of 19 children and one adult.[200] In addition to forms of reparation similar to those ordered in Yakye Axa the Court also ordered to put in place a program of registration and documentation.[201]

It has been noted that cultural identity can be seen as a component or aggregate of the right to life proper.[202] For indigenous peoples this is closely related to their ancestral lands. When they

---

[192] IACHR *Moiwana Village* v. *Suriname,* 15 June 2005. Among others the Court had found that the State had violated the freedom of movement and residence of the community members (Article 22 ACHR) and the right to property (Article 21) in relation to the traditional territories from which they were expelled. Generally on this case see Martin (2006).

[193] IACHR *Moiwana Village* v. *Suriname,* 15 June 2005, §132.

[194] IACHR *Comunidad Indígena Yakye Axa* v. *Paraguay*, Order of 16 June 2005, §§137 and 154. In this case the CIDH had used precautionary measures in September 2001. In March 2003 the Commission had submitted this case, in which it had used precautionary measures, to the Inter-American Court. It noted that the Community's territorial claims had been under litigation since 1993. It had been 'impossible for the community and its members to assert ownership and possession of their territory'. "As a result of the situation, the community has been kept in a situation of nutritional, medical and sanitary deprivation that poses a constant threat to the survival of its members and the integrity of the community". CIDH Press release 30/03, October 2003, §15.

[195] IACHR *Comunidad Indígena Yakye Axa* v. *Paraguay*, 16 June 2005, §168.

[196] Id., §175.

[197] Id., §177. See also the dissents by Judges Abreu Burelli, Cançado Trindade and Ventura Robles.

[198] IACHR *Comunidad Indígena Yakye Axa* v. *Paraguay*, 16 June 2005, §226 (specifying the accessibility and reach of the public event).

[199] Id., §221. See also 6 February 2006 (Interpretation of judgment).

[200] IACHR *Comunidad Indígena Sawhoyamaxa* v. *Paraguay*, 29 March 2006, §178. See also the individual opinions of judges Ventura Robles and Cançado Trindade.

[201] IACHR *Comunidad Indígena Sawhoyamaxa* v. *Paraguay*, 29 March 2006.

[202] Id., Individual Opinion Judge Cançado Trindade, §4.

are forcibly displaced, and thereby uprooted from these lands, this seriously affects their cultural identity and ultimately their right to life in the broad sense.[203] The definite transfer of the communal lands 'is a question of survival of the cultural identity of the members of such Community'.[204]

The African Commission has also dealt with cases involving indigenous peoples, but rather than to cultural identity it has referred to the (collective) right to health, food and housing. Nevertheless its emphasis on the problems created by forced eviction is in fact particularly relevant in the case of indigenous peoples. In the context of the Ogoni people it has discussed environmental degradation and health problems resulting from the contamination of the environment by oil developments. It has pointed out that Nigeria had clearly violated the legal protection against forced eviction, harassment and other threats. This right to be protected was 'enjoyed by the Ogonis as a collective right'.[205] "The survival of the Ogonis depended on their land and farms that were destroyed by the direct involvement of the Government". This impacted not just individual members of the Ogoni, but the life of the 'Ogoni Community as a whole'.[206]

While the provisions of the African Charter invoked in the Endorois case,[207] discussed under section 2, originally may have been intended as equating 'States' and 'peoples' and various governments still take the approach that there are no separate indigenous peoples within African States, the above *Ogoni* case, the recent special attention by the Commission in its non-litigious activities, such as the introduction of a Working group on Indigenous Populations/

---

[203] Ibid., §28.

[204] IACHR *Comunidad Indígena Yakye Axa* v. *Paraguay*, 16 June 2005, §221. See also 6 February 2006 (Interpretation of judgment), Individual Opinion Judge Cançado Trindade, §8.

[205] ACHPR *The Social and Economic Rights Action Center and the Center for Economic and Social Rights* v. *Nigeria* (Ogoni case), October 2001, §63. Specifically it pointed out that the pollution and environmental degradation had reached a level 'humanly unacceptable', which had made 'living in the Ogoni land a nightmare'. In general about this case see Coomans (2003).

[206] ACHPR *The Social and Economic Rights Action Center and the Center for Economic and Social Rights* v. *Nigeria* (Ogoni case), October 2001, §67. The Commission noted that it conducted a mission to Nigeria in March 1997 'and witnessed first hand the deplorable situation in Ogoni land including the environmental degradation'. On this case see also e.g. Coomans (2003). The Commission acknowledged that multinational corporations may constitute a potentially positive force for development as long as the State and the people concerned are aware of 'the common good and the sacred rights of individuals and communities'. ACHPR *The Social and Economic Rights Action Center and the Center for Economic and Social Rights* v. *Nigeria* (Ogoni case), October 2001, §69. It found Nigeria in violation of a range of rights laid down in the African Charter on Human and Peoples' Rights.[206] It listed actions and abstentions that would help 'ensure protection of the environment, health and livelihood of the people of Ogoniland'. These included 'stopping all attacks on Ogoni communities and leaders by the Rivers State Internal Securities Task Force and permitting citizens and independent investigators free access to the territory' and conducting investigations into human rights violations. Adequate compensation should include 'relief and resettlement assistance to victims of government sponsored raids,' and a 'comprehensive cleanup of lands and rivers damaged by oil operations'. ACHPR *The Social and Economic Rights Action Center and the Center for Economic and Social Rights* v. *Nigeria* (Ogoni case), 27 October 2001.

[207] In their submission the petitioners had invoked the free practice of religion (Article 8 ACHPR), the right to property (Article 14), to enjoy the best attainable standard of physical and mental health (Article 16) and the right to freely take part in the cultural life of the community (Article 17(2)), the right of all peoples to exist (Article 20(1)), the right of all peoples to freely dispose of their wealth and natural resources (Article 21) and Article 22(1) on development and identity.

Communities,[208] and the provisional measures in the Endorois case all indicate that the African Commission itself now considers that indigenous peoples within States may themselves claim group rights. Moreover, considering the right to freely take part in the cultural life of the community and the right of all peoples to exist it becomes clear that 'the right to enjoy one's culture cannot be enjoyed if the group no longer exists'.[209] This again points at the importance of cultural survival.

In the context of the Bosnia Chamber's provisional measures it is not surprising that the petitions invoked freedom of religion in Article 9 ECHR,[210] combined with the prohibition of discrimination. Another relevant article is Article 8 ECHR on the right to privacy and family life. Article 27 ICCPR was not specifically invoked, although the Framework Agreement also refers to the ICCPR.

In a case concerning the aftermath of the destruction of the three mosques in Zvornik, in which the Chamber had used provisional measures several times, on the merits it noted that the right to religion includes the right to create a space for practicing it.[211] It also noted that the prohibition of discrimination is a central objective of the framework Agreement 'to which it must attach particular importance'.[212]

---

[208] Triggered, among others, by the Arusha resolutions adopted by indigenous peoples from East, Central and Southern Africa, January 1998, posted at the website of the International Work Group for indigenous Affairs, <www.iwgi.org/sw579.asp>.

[209] Murray/Wheatley (2003), p. 222.

[210] The Chamber has quoted the ECtHR's qualification of the freedom protected in Article 9 ECHR: "It is, in its religious dimension, one of the most vital elements that go to make up the identity of believers and their conception of life, but it is also a precious asset for atheists, agnostics, sceptics and the unconcerned. The pluralism indissociable from a democratic society, which has been dearly won over the centuries, depends on it". Bosnia Chamber *Islamic Community in BiH* v. *Republika Srpska*, 9 November 2000, §80 quoting ECtHR *Kokkinakis* v. *Greece*, 25 May 1993, §31.

[211] Bosnia Chamber *Islamic Community in BiH* v. *Republika Srpska*, 9 November 2000, §86, referring to the case of the *Banja Luka Mosques*, 11 June 1999, §182.

[212] It was 'appropriate to have particular regard to the importance of preventing – and if necessary, stopping – discrimination on religious and ethnic grounds in order to enable refugees and displaced persons to return safely to their homes of origin'. Bosnia Chamber *Islamic Community in BiH* v. *Republika Srpska*, 9 November 2000, §96. See generally Chapter XI on halting mass expulsion and forced eviction. As a form of reparation it ordered, among others, the respondent Party to allocate a suitable and centrally located building site to replace one of the destroyed Mosques, to remove all market stands and a car park from the site of another destroyed mosque and grant the necessary permit for its reconstruction 'at the location at which it previously existed' and, in order to replace the third former mosque, a building site in its vicinity. All of this should be done 'in consultation with the Islamic Community, and for its use only'. Bosnia Chamber *Islamic Community in BiH* v. *Republika Srpska*, 9 November 2000, §§124 and 120-122. More generally on the protection required by provisional measures and their relation with reparation see Chapter XIII (Protection). In the previous case involving Banja Luka (1999) the Chamber ordered Republika Srpska, among others, to allow the petitioner to erect fences around the sites of the 15 destroyed mosques, to refrain from building on the sites, cemeteries, etc. and to swiftly grant them the necessary permits to reconstruct 7 of the mosques at the site where they previously existed. In another case Republika Srpska had ignored the Chamber's provisional measures and allowed construction of a bank on the site of the destroyed Atik mosque in Bijeljina. Upon the finding of various violations, the Chamber ordered reparation to the effect that the Islamic Community should be granted the necessary permits for the reconstruction of the five mosques and that business facilities were to be removed from these sites. Bosnia Chamber

3.4 Moment of infringement-moment of irreparability

In order to clarify the cases in which the HRC used provisional measures in cases involving cultural rights it is important to refer to the Committee's substantive discussion in *Länsman I* (inadm. 1994). In this case, involving the Angeli area, the HRC used a specific test to examine whether activities amounted to a denial of cultural rights. Pending the case it had considered the use of provisional measures to be premature.[213] It recalled its decision in *Kitok* v. *Sweden* (1988) that 'economic activities may come within the ambit of article 27, if they are an essential element of the culture of an ethnic community'.[214] It then pointed out that the right to enjoy one's culture could not be determined *in abstracto* but was to be placed in context. It observed that, contrary to the State party's submission, the article did not just protect the *traditional* means of livelihood of national minorities.[215] The Committee also confirmed that Mt. Riutusvaara 'continues to have a spiritual significance relevant to their culture'.[216] Nevertheless, it considered that economic activities with a limited impact would not necessarily amount to a denial of the right to culture.

The HRC used the following test: whether the impact of the (economic) activities is so substantial that it effectively denies the petitioners the right to enjoy their cultural rights.[217] While it did not find a violation of Article 27, it did point out that in order to comply with this article

---

The Islamic Community in BiH (former Atik Mosque, Bijeljina) v. *Republika Srpska*, 6 December 2000, provisional measure of 10 July 1999 and further Order of 7 July 2000 to protect the site of Atik Mosque.

[213] HRC *Ilmari Länsman* v. *Finland*, 26 October 1994 (inadm.). See further Chapter XIV (Jurisdiction and admissibility). The HRC phrased the issue to be determined on the merits as follows: 'Whether quarrying on the flank of Mt. Etelä-Riutusvaara, in the amount that has taken place until the present time or in the amount that would be permissible under the permit issued to the company which has expressed its intention to extract stone from the mountain (i.e. up to a total of 5000 cubic metres) would violate the authors' rights under article 27 of the Covenant'.

[214] HRC *Ivan Kitok* v. *Sweden*, 27 July 1988, §9.2. See also the discussion under section 3. In General Comment 23 on Article 27 (1994) the HRC refers also to traditional activities such as hunting and fishing, §7.

[215] "Therefore, that the authors may have adapted their methods of reindeer herding over the years and practice it with the help of modern technology does not prevent them from invoking article 27 of the Covenant". *Ilmari Länsman* v. *Finland*, 26 October 1994 (inadm.), §9.3. In other words the HRC explained that the right to enjoy one's culture is not static because this culture itself is not static and cannot be frozen into a specific time capsule. See also Scheinin (2000), p. 169, Meijknecht (2001), p. 96 and Donders (2002), p. 333.

[216] HRC *Ilmari Länsman* v. *Finland*, 26 October 1994 (inadm.), §9.3.

[217] It also specifically dismissed the State's reliance on a margin of appreciation, such as typically used by the ECtHR. It pointed out that the scope of the State's freedom to encourage development or allow economic activities by enterprises was 'not to be assessed by reference to a margin of appreciation, but by reference to the obligations it has undertaken in article 27'. Still, it showed deference to the State and it did not find a violation of Article 27. Schmidt (1997), p. 338 points out that in fact the HRC did allow the State a certain margin of appreciation. He notes that the Committee 'had to balance the applicants' interests against general economic interests advanced by the Finnish government'. "In both decisions the Committee implicitly granted the state party what amounted to a margin of appreciation in determining whether the applicants' interests had been sufficiently protected, and concluded that their rights had not been violated." Yet, the HRC was unwilling to succumb to the State's arguments about the general economic development. Scheinin (2000), p. 169 points out that the HRC took 'a very cautious position to arguments related to general economic development and well being'. He notes the reference in *Kitok* to the well being of the Sami minority rather than of the country as a whole. Hence the Committee does give the State considerable leeway when it argues measures are infringing upon individual rights in the interest of the Sami collectivity.

economic activities must be 'carried out in a way that the authors continue to benefit from reindeer husbandry'.[218] It also emphasized that if the State were to approve mining activities in the Angeli area on a large scale and if companies with exploitation permits would significantly expand their activities this could in fact constitute a violation of Article 27. The State had a duty to bear this in mind 'when either extending contracts or granting new ones'.[219]

In relation to the future logging activities, in *Länsman II* the HRC made a remark clarifying its test for finding a violation of the petitioners' right to enjoy their own culture. It observed that logging had been approved 'on a scale which, while resulting in additional work and expenses for the authors and other reindeer herdsmen, does not appear to threaten the survival of reindeer husbandry'.[220] This suggests that a threat to the *survival* of such husbandry would indeed result in a denial of the right to culture. This, in turn, may mean that in Article 27 cases involving infringements on the natural habitat the HRC would only find a violation if there were a threat of irreparable harm (or such harm had already occurred), but not if harm other than irreparable harm would occur. Indeed, in relation to the collective aspects of Article 27 the HRC has only found a violation in cases in which it had previously considered that further actions would result in irreparable harm to indigenous peoples (rather than minorities). While in other situations involving other rights (without collective aspects) it might find violations of a less serious nature for which it would require compensation, thus far it has never done so with regard to collective aspects. In other words, in such cases the HRC is only likely to find a violation in cases in which, at an earlier stage, provisional measures were (or would have been) warranted as well. As we have seen, however, even in cases in which it did use provisional measures, subsequently, on the merits, it did not often find a violation. The HRC has not yet addressed the question when subsequent exploitation of the lands would result in a violation and when such violation would be irreparable.[221]

3.5 Collective rights and human dignity: special status right to culture of indigenous peoples

Apart from the emphasis on the collective aspects of the right to culture, the special status of indigenous peoples and their right to culture may equally help explain the use of provisional measures by some of the adjudicators. For the HRC this has become apparent in its reference to Article 27 ICCPR in its discussion on reservations and non-derogable rights. The HRC underlined the condition of non-discrimination in Article 4(1) ICCPR (on states of emergency and non-derogable rights) and pointed out that there were elements in Article 27 ICCPR that must be respected in all circumstances, exactly because of their fundamental nature.

Article 27 ICCPR is not listed as one of the non-derogable rights in Article 4 ICCPR, but the HRC has referred to this provision as containing 'rights of profound importance'.[222] Moreover, it has noted that some elements of provisions not explicitly listed as non-derogable in Arti-

---

[218] HRC *Ilmari Länsman* v. *Finland*, 26 October 1994 (inadm.), §9.8.

[219] Ibid.

[220] HRC *Länsman II*, 30 October 1996, §10.6.

[221] The CERD has equally confirmed that measures in relation to the status, use and occupation of traditional lands 'may cumulatively lead to irreparable harm' to the indigenous communities involved. CERD Early warning and urgent action procedure decision 1 (68), February-March 2006, §4.

[222] See HRC General Comment 24 on reservations to the ICCPR or the Optional Protocols, 4 November 1994, CCPR/C/21/Rev. 1/Add. 6, §10.

cle 4(2) cannot be derogated from either. In that context it also referred to elements contained in Article 27.[223]

As Anaya points out the HRC has 'acknowledged the importance of lands and resources to the survival of indigenous cultures', which implies an acknowledgement of the importance of indigenous self-determination.[224] In its discussion of State reports the HRC can be more flexible than in the individual complaint procedure. Among others, it specifically requests information about compliance with the right to self-determination (Article 1 ICCPR).[225] It has noted that a reservation to Article 1 would be incompatible with the object and purpose of the Covenant.[226]

The UN Committee on the Elimination of Racial Discrimination (CERD) discusses the rights of indigenous peoples within the general framework of the International Covenant on the Elimination of Racial Discrimination (ICERD) and the norm of non-discrimination. It has 'effectively promoted the integrity and survival of indigenous groups'.[227] Its General Recommendation on the rights of indigenous peoples indicates the special status of the indigenous right to culture, including the right to control and use of their communal lands and resources.[228] Meanwhile, the possibility of CERD taking provisional measures for the first time and doing so in relation to land rights and indigenous culture cannot be ruled out.[229]

---

[223] HRC General Comment 29 on states of emergency (Article 4), 24 July 2001, § 13(c).

[224] Anaya (1996), p. 104.

[225] See e.g. the discussion in Kingsbury (2001), pp. 206 and pp. 228-229. About the reporting procedure of the Committee in general see Boerefijn (1999). An example is the concern expressed by the HRC that the dam projects on the Biobio River in Chile 'might affect the way of life and the rights of persons belonging to the Mapuche and other indigenous communities'. Concluding Observations of the HRC in relation to Chile, CCPR/C/79/Add.104 (1999) as referred to by Kingsbury (2001), p. 206. According to Schmidt the incremental approach of the periodic State reporting mechanism 'tends to yield positive results' for the promotion of indigenous peoples' rights. Schmidt (1997), p. 339. Other issues the HRC has emphasised under the reporting mechanism are the importance of land demarcation and the protection of cultural identity against developments such as oil drilling and their collateral effects. See e.g. references in Thornberry (2002), p. 164. The Inter-American Commission on Human Rights intervened in relation to the above situation involving the Bio-Bio river, using precautionary measures: *Mercedes Julia Huenteao Beroiza et al.* v. *Chile*, 11 March 2004 (friendly settlement), §§5, 6 and 15.

[226] See HRC General Comment 24 on reservations to the ICCPR or the Optional Protocols, 4 November 1994, CCPR/C/21/Rev. 1/Add. 6, §9. In 2006, in its Concluding Observations to the US report on its compliance with the ICCPR (2006) the HRC also pointed out that the 'State party should review its policy towards indigenous peoples as regards the extinguishment of aboriginal rights on the basis of the plenary power of Congress regarding Indian affairs and grant them the same degree of judicial protection that is available to the non-indigenous population'. HRC Concluding Observations to the US report, 2006

[227] Anaya (1996), p. 157.

[228] CERD General Recommendation XXIII on the rights of indigenous peoples, 1997, A/52/18, annex V.

[229] More generally authors have advocated increased use by indigenous peoples of the individual petition system under the ICERD, see e.g. Anaya (1996), p. 157 and Dommen (1998), p. 13, pointing out that road and bridge construction projects on lands traditionally belonging to the Wichi, Chorote, Nivakle, Toba and Tapiete communities in Northern Argentina could all be brought before CERD, claiming that their traditional ways of life are threatened because they do not have official title to their lands. Dommen argues that the 'impacts of environmental harm often fall hardest on individuals or groups suffering discrimination, thus a case brought to CERD regarding environmental discrimination would likely succeed', p. 23.

It has also taken the historic step to invoke its Early Warning and Urgent Action Procedure on behalf of the abovementioned Western Shoshone peoples who had been unable to resort to the individual complaint procedure under ICERD as the US has not deposited a declaration under Article 14 ICERD.[230] The Committee pointed out that the procedure was 'clearly distinct from the communication procedure' under Article 14. "Furthermore, the nature and urgency of the issue examined in this decision go well beyond the limits of the communication procedure".[231]

Its decision to invoke the Urgent Action procedure not only indicates a recognition of the special position of indigenous peoples in international law, but also follows up on a decision on the merits by the Inter-American Commission on Human Rights involving specific members of the Western Shoshone, confirming the Commission's approach to land rights.

CERD was concerned by the State's position that the Western Shoshone's 'legal rights to ancestral lands have been extinguished through gradual encroachment, notwithstanding the fact that the Western Shoshone peoples have reportedly continued to use and occupy the lands and their natural resources in accordance with their traditional land tenure patterns'. Moreover, this position was made on the basis of processes before the former Indian Claims Commission that, and here CERD quoted from the *Dann Sisters* case by the Inter-American Commission (2002), 'did not comply with contemporary human rights norms, principles and standards that govern determination of indigenous property interests'.[232]

CERD also referred to '(t)he reported resumption of underground nuclear testing on Western Shoshone ancestral lands' and the lack of consultation, combined with the reported intimidation and harassment 'through the imposition of grazing fees, trespass and collection notices, impounding of horse and livestock, restrictions on hunting, fishing and gathering, as well as arrests, which gravely disturb the enjoyment of their ancestral lands'.[233] Among others it urged the State to freeze any plan to privatize their lands, abstain from activities in relation to their natural resources and stop imposing grazing fees etc. until a final settlement was duly reached.[234]

---

[230]   CERD Early Warning and Urgent Action Procedure, Decision 1 (68). This is not the first time CERD intervened on information that a State was disregarding its previous recommendations and that indigenous peoples were facing irreparable harm, see e.g. in response to a draft mining Act approved by the Council of Ministers of Suriname, but addressing a range of issues involving notification, prior agreement or informed consent, Decision 1 (67), CERD/C/DEC/SUR/2, 18 August 2005.

[231]   CERD Early Warning and Urgent Action Procedure, Decision 1 (68), §4. It expressed concern about the lack of action taken by the State upon its 2001 Concluding Observations, in which it had already paid attention to the situation of the Shoshone. CERD Concluding Observations on the US report, A/56/18, 13 August 2001, §400. "Although these are indeed long-standing issues, as stressed by the State party in its letter, they warrant immediate and effective action from the State party". CERD Early Warning and Urgent Action Procedure, Decision 1 (68), §5. In the background of this decision is the State's failure to respond to a list of questions, including questions relating to the situation of the Shoshone, sent by the Committee in August 2005 in the context of the State's periodic reporting obligation (the report had been due in November 2003).

[232]   CERD Early Warning and Urgent Action Procedure, Decision 1 (68), §6, quoting from *Mary and Carrie Dann* v. *US*, 27 December 2002. It expressed particular concern about reported legislative efforts to privatize the ancestral lands 'for transfer to multinational extractive industries and energy developers'; destructive activities conducted or planned ' on areas of spiritual and cultural significance to the Western Shoshone peoples, who are denied access to, and use of, such areas'. It noted the 'reinvigorated federal efforts to open a nuclear waste repository at the Yucca Mountain; the alleged use of explosives and open pit gold mining activities on Mount Tenabo and Horse Canyon; and the alleged issuance of geothermal energy leases at, or near, hot springs'.

[233]   CERD Early Warning and Urgent Action Procedure, Decision 1 (68), §7.

[234]   Id., §§9-10.

The special status of the indigenous peoples' right to culture, or at least the particular vulnerability of indigenous peoples to human rights violations, is also confirmed by the institution of the UN Special Rapporteur on the situation of human rights of indigenous people.[235] As noted, in 2007 the UN General Assembly adopted the Declaration on the Rights of Indigenous Peoples. Over the years many drafts had circulated, which had already served either as overviews of the developments in the law or otherwise to inspire the case law and the practice of various international bodies.[236] In addition, in the Inter-American system a draft declaration on the rights of indigenous peoples has also played an important role in the development of awareness of the importance of indigenous rights. Moreover, both the Inter-American Commission and the African Commission have introduced Rapporteurs on the rights of Indigenous Peoples as well. Within the European (and Eurasian) region indigenous peoples may resort to the international treaties (ICCPR or CERD), to the Framework Convention for the Protection of National Minorities and the general opinions of its Advisory Committee[237] or to the OSCE High Commissioner on National Minorities. Finally, the Inter-American Court has shown particular sensitivity to indigenous culture in its judgment on reparations.[238]

---

[235]　See Resolution 2001/57 of the UN Commission on Human Rights (2001), confirmed by Resolution 6/12 of the UN Human Rights Council (2007). The first Rapporteur was Rodolfo Stavenhagen; the second Rapporteur, since May 2008, is James Anaya.

[236]　For a brief overview of the Declaration see e.g. Anaya/Wiessner (2007).

[237]　In 2000 the Advisory Committee on the Framework Convention for the Protection of National Minorities made the following observation regarding the Sami in Finland: "Given the importance of reindeer herding, fishing and hunting to the Sami as an indigenous people, the issue of land rights in the Sami Homeland is of central relevance to the protection of Sami culture and their identity. Therefore, the Advisory Committee expresses the wish that the existing dispute over land rights in this area be resolved as expeditiously as possible in a manner that will contribute to the protection of the culture of the Sami without interfering with the rights of the non-Sami population. The Advisory Committee is of the opinion that the central role of the Sami Parliament should be maintained in this process and adequate resources should be secured for the Sami Parliament to carry out its tasks in this sphere. The Advisory Committee further emphasises that, while the issue of land rights is being reviewed, the existing practices relating to the use of the land at issue should be carried out in a manner that does not threaten the maintenance or development of Sami culture or the preservation of their identity. This concerns, *inter alia*, logging operations administered by the National Board of Forestry". Advisory Committee on the Framework Convention for the Protection of National Minorities, First Opinion on Finland, 22 September 2000, ACFC/INF/OP/I(2001)002, §22. Six years later the Committee expressed particular concern about reports that logging and other activities State Forest Administration 'are in some cases carried out without adequate attention being paid to the maintenance and development of reindeer herding or other aspects of Sami culture, and in a manner that does not sufficiently accommodate the views of the Sami Parliament'. "While acknowledging the importance of forestry to the economy of the municipalities in the Sami Homeland and while being aware that also some Sami are employed in this sector, the Advisory Committee stresses that there is a clear obligation to pursue logging and other related economic activities in a manner that protects the right of the Sami, as an indigenous people, to develop reindeer herding and other elements of their culture. In this context, the Advisory Committee notes with regret that the specific status of Sami as the only constitutionally recognised indigenous people of Finland seems not to be fully comprehended throughout the State Forest Administration staff". Advisory Committee on the Framework Convention for the Protection of National Minorities, Second Opinion on Finland, 2 March 2006, ACFC/OP/II(2006)003, published 20 April 2006, §55.

[238]　See e.g. IACHR *Aloeboetoe et al.* (Suriname), 10 September 1993; *Bámaca Velásquez*, 22 February 2002; *Massacre at Plan de Sánchez* (Guatemala), 19 November 2004, *Moiwana Community* (Suriname), 15 June 2005.

The Inter-American Commission applies not just Inter-American but also international norms in relation to indigenous peoples, including Article 27 ICCPR, in particular when it proposes solutions.[239] Already in 1985 it interpreted Article 27 ICCPR when it recommended Brazil to demarcate and secure the lands of the Yanomami. It referred to the recognition in international law of the right of ethnic groups to special protection 'for all those characteristics necessary for the preservation of their cultural identity'.[240] In another case it pointed out that preservation of the cultural identity of an indigenous group should extend to 'the aspects linked to productive organization, which includes, among other things, the issue of ancestral and communal lands'.[241] The Commission has held this norm 'to cover all aspects of an indigenous group's survival as a distinct culture, understanding culture to include economic or political institutions, land use patterns, as well as language and religious practices'.[242]

As Anaya and Williams concluded in 2001, 'rights to lands and resources are property rights that are prerequisites for the physical and cultural survival of indigenous communities, and they are protected by the American Declaration, the American Convention, and other international human rights instruments, such as the Convention of the Elimination of All Forms of Racial Discrimination and the Covenant on Civil and Political Rights'.[243]

The step is not that great from protecting land rights of indigenous peoples to protecting the right of peoples that have been subjected to ethnic cleansing to respect for their religious sites.

In the *Mahmutović* case the Chamber had first used provisional measures to 'desist from' implementing the domestic order for the exhumation of his wife from the Muslim cemetery closed by Republica Srpska.[244] On the merits it found that Mr Mahmutović had been discriminated against in the enjoyment of his right to private and family life and freedom of religion. It noted that the ordinance to close the cemetery 'affected only the Muslim Cemetery and not the Orthodox or Catholic cemeteries situated nearby'.[245] The respondent party had never provided a reason for the closure. It found that the only plausible explanation of the 1994 ordinance prohibiting burials at the Muslim Town Cemetery 'was to contribute to the elimination of all traces of the Muslim population from the town centre of Prnjavor'.[246] As part of its decision on the merits it ordered the respondent Party 'to refrain from any steps to remove the remains of Mrs Mahmutović from her place of burial'. In other words the protective measures required as a provisional measure are very similar to those required upon the finding of a violation, except that in the latter case the requirement is more precise.

In another case the Chamber found on the merits that the continued enforcement of a 1994 ordinance putting the Muslim Town Cemetery out of use and prohibiting further burials constituted 'discrimination against the Islamic Community and the Muslim population of Prnjavor in the enjoyment of their right to freely practice religious beliefs'. 'The Chamber therefore deems it appropriate to order the respondent Party to revoke the ordinance' and 'to desist from any further steps of enforcement, such as prohibiting burials at that cemetery or ordering the exhumation of

---

[239]   See e.g. the references by Anaya (1996), pp. 168-169 and p. 182.

[240]   CIDH *Yanomami* case (v. *Brazil*), 5 March 1985 (brought on behalf of a large group of Yanomami, recommending the adoption of preventive health measures, the demarcation and delimitation of their land, educational programs, etc., all to be carried out in consultation with the peoples involved and advised by medical staff, anthropologists and other experts).

[241]   See CIDH *Miskito report relating to Nicaragua*, 16 May 1984 (resolution regarding friendly settlement).

[242]   See Anaya (1996), p. 100.

[243]   Anaya/Williams (2001), p. 53.

[244]   Bosnia Chamber *Mahmutović* v. *Republika Srpska*, 8 October 1999, §4.

[245]   Id., §89.

[246]   Ibid.

the remains of persons buried there'.[247] Pending the proceedings the Chamber had initially refused to order a provisional measure because there had initially not been any individual threat of
exhumation or interference with burials in Prnjavor. Following a domestic decision prohibiting a
specific burial, the Chamber did order provisional measures prohibiting the Municipal authorities
from obstructing further burials.[248] Again there is a clear correlation between the protection required pending the proceedings and in the decision on the merits, where in the latter is simply
more broadly worded.

3.6   Consultation of indigenous peoples and impact assessment

The requirements of notification and consultation, often mentioned in the context of environmental law, also have their counterparts in the jurisprudence of the HRC in relation to indigenous
peoples.[249] Clearly domestic decisions made on the basis of proper consultation gain legitimacy,
as is also recognized, at least theoretically, in non-human rights fora.[250] In its Concluding Observations to State reports, the HRC has recommended States with indigenous populations to 'take
further steps to secure the rights of all indigenous peoples, under articles 1 and 27 of the Covenant, so as to give them greater influence in decision-making affecting their natural environment
and their means of subsistence as well as their own culture'.[251] The substantive law on consultation, as interpreted by the human rights adjudicators, could be relevant in the context of future
decisions about provisional measures, including the group of beneficiaries.

The HRC has developed a two-part test for examining violations of Article 27 in relation to
land use: on the one hand consultation and on the other economic sustainability.[252] In its General
Comment on Article 27 the HRC referred to the positive requirement to take measures to 'ensure
the effective participation of members of minority communities in decisions which affect

---

[247]   Bosnia Chamber *Islamic Community in BiH* v. *Republika Srpska* (*Muslim Town Cemetery in
Prnjavor*), 11 January 2000, §211 (dissenting opinion by Republika Srpska members Popović
and Pajić).

[248]   Id., §§9 and 10.

[249]   Environmental impact assessment requires consultation of those persons directly affected by
certain economic developments such as the construction of a dam. Environmental law
acknowledges the role of indigenous peoples in particular, at least in theory. Principle 22 of the
Rio Declaration, for instance, notes: "Indigenous people and their communities, and other local
communities, have a vital role in environmental management and development because of their
knowledge and traditional practices. States should recognise and duly support their identity,
culture and interests and enable their effective participation in the achievement of sustainable
development." The Rio Declaration on Environment and Development, Rio de Janeiro, 3-14 June
1992.

[250]   In its Operational Directive on indigenous peoples the World Bank has adopted the rule that Bank
staff is required to identify the impact of proposed projects on indigenous peoples. World Bank
officers must identify the indigenous peoples involved 'through direct consultation'. Operational
Directive 4.20 of June 1990, § 8, see World Bank Operation Manual at <www.worldbank.org>.
The World Bank started its first environmental impact assessment in 1992 as part of its decision
making on funding the Sardar Sarovar hydro-electric dam in North-West India. The government
proposing a project should show that indigenous people have 'participated meaningfully in the
development of the plan', particularly in relation to land access and use. The burden of proof is
on the State showing there was adequate consultation of indigenous peoples. See about
Operational Directive 4.20: De Feyter (2001), pp. 164-167.

[251]   HRC Concluding Observations to the US report, 27 July 2006, CCPR/C/USA/CO, §37.

[252]   Scheinin (2000), p. 168, referring to the above Sami cases. See also HRC *Apirana Mahuika* v.
New Zealand, 27 October 2000.

them'.[253] Apparently, in the face of disputes about the facts relating to the cultural survival of the group and the expected risk to economic sustainability, it finds no violation if it believes the group in question has been sufficiently consulted.[254] With regard to consultation the HRC noted, in *Länsman II* (1996), that it was uncontested that the Muotkatunturi Herdsmen's Committee had been consulted 'in the process of drawing up the logging plans' and that it 'did not react negatively to the plans for logging'.[255]

> "That this consultation process was unsatisfactory for the authors and was capable of greater interaction does not alter the Committee's assessment. It transpires that the State party's authorities did go through the process of weighing the authors' interests and the general economic interests in the area specified in the complaint when deciding on the most appropriate measures of forestry management, i.e. logging methods, choice of logging areas and construction of roads in these areas".[256]

---

253 HRC General Comment 23 on Article 27, 8 April 1994, §7.

254 The *second Mikmaq* case (1991) dealt with the issue of consultation. See HRC *Grand Chief Donald Marshall et al.* v. *Canada*, 4 November 1991. The complaint was submitted in 1986, two years after the HRC declared the *first Mikmaq* case, *A.D. (on behalf of the Mikmaq Tribal Society)* v. *Canada*, inadmissible on 29 July 1984. This time A.D. had managed to involve the Grand Chief in the complaint. Grand Chief Donald Marshall, Grand Captain Alexander Denny and Advisor Simon Marshall submitted the complaint as officers of the Grand Council of the Mikmaq tribal society. The HRC gave considerable leeway to the State in its interpretation of the right to take part in the conduct of public affairs. It found that the State party's failure to invite representatives of the Mikmaq Tribal Society to the constitutional conferences on aboriginal matters did not violate Article 25(a) ICCPR. Scheinin (2000), p. 164 notes that the 'view taken by the HRC suggests that no far-reaching standards can be derived from Art. 25 as regards specific arrangements for autonomy or self-government by minorities or indigenous peoples'. In later cases, however, the HRC did point out that 'the provisions of article 1 may be relevant in the interpretation of other rights protected by the Covenant, in particular articles 25, 26 and 27'. See e.g. *Diergaardt et al.* v. *Namibia*, 25 July 2000, §10.3. See in general about consultation: De Feyter (2001), pp. 157-171 and Anaya (1996), Chapter 5.

255 HRC *Länsman II*, 30 October 1996, §10.5.

256 Ibid. Among others, the State had pointed out that the records of the Inari District Court showed that during the extraordinary meeting between the Central Forestry Board and the Muotkatunturi Herdsmen's Committee of 16 July 1993 two opinions were presented: one in support of and one against the petitioners. According to the State the Herdsmen's Committee did not make statements directed against the Central Forestry Board (§6.1). It noted that it had had continuous negotiation links with the Herdsmen's Committee 'in a framework in which interests of forestry and reindeer husbandry are reconciled'. The 'experiences with this negotiation process have been good' (§6.12). The petitioners, on the other hand, asserted that 'there had been no negotiation process and no real consultation of the local Sami when the State forest authority prepared its logging plans'. "At most, the Chairman of the Muotkatunturi Herdsmen's Committee was informed of the logging plans." They also quoted the resolution adopted by the Sami Parliament of 16 December 1995, after it had discussed the experiences with the consultation in relation to the logging plans. Among others this resolution noted that it is 'the opinion of the Sami Parliament that the present consultation system between the Central Forestry Board and reindeer management does not function in a satisfactory way'. The petitioners contended that 'what the State party refers to as "negotiations" with local reindeer herdsmen amounts to little more than invitations extended to the chairmen of the herdsmen's committees to annual forestry board's meetings, during which they are informed of short-term logging plans'. They emphasised that this process involved no real consultation of the Sami (§§7.8 and 7.9). Scheinin (2000), p. 272 notes that '(g)uidance for a more thorough analysis of the requirement of effective participation can be

The discussion in *Länsman II* shows the importance the HRC attaches to the State's opinion that it consulted the petitioners. The State used this consultation as one of the arguments to convince the Committee to set aside its provisional measures. It noted that it had negotiated with the larger association to which the petitioners' Herdsmen Committee belonged, suggesting that consultation should already play a role at the provisional measures stage. The State argued, in addition, that provisional measures only aimed at avoiding irreparable harm to the victim of the alleged violation and did not cover measures resulting in otherwise long-lasting damage.[257]

In the *Maya Indigenous Communities of the Toledo district* case (2004) the Inter-American Commission observed that 'the requirement that states undertake effective and fully informed consultations with indigenous communities regarding acts or decisions that may affect their traditional territories' was 'one of the central elements to the protection of indigenous property rights'.[258] Articles XVIII and XXIII American Declaration 'specially oblige a member state to ensure that any determination of the extent to which indigenous claimants maintain interests in the lands to which they have traditionally held title and have occupied and used is based upon a process of fully informed consent on the part of the indigenous community as a whole'. "This requires, at a minimum, that all of the members of the community are fully and accurately informed of the nature and consequences of the process and provided with an effective opportunity to participate individually or as collectives". The Commission has pointed out that this also applies to other State decisions 'such as the granting of concessions to exploit the natural resources of indigenous territories'. After all, such decisions will also have an impact on indigenous lands and their communities.[259]

One could argue that if the State cannot show meaningful participation this may indeed be an additional reason to resort to provisional measures. At the same time, however, information about some forms of participation should not be a determining factor for *not* using provisional measures at some point during the proceedings.

As noted, in *Länsman II* the HRC responded by setting aside its provisional measures. In future cases it may have to analyse more in depth what constitutes appropriate consultation. Otherwise it will not be able to deal effectively with those cases in which consultation of the indigenous peoples and environmental impact assessments are little more than window dressing.

The Inter-American Commission has equally emphasized the importance of consultation. It has recommended, for instance, that Colombia would carry out the process of consultation with the indigenous communities *before* it authorised the exploitation of natural resources on their lands and not afterwards. Such exploitation of resources should 'not cause irreparable harm to the identity or religious, economic, or cultural rights of the indigenous communities'.[260]

In addition to consultation the use of impact assessments may also be relevant in the decision to order provisional measures. In the context of the aforementioned *Ogoni* case involving environmental degradation and health problems resulting from the contamination of the environ-

---

sought from domestic jurisdiction, e.g. the *Delgamuukw* case'. This case established that in determining aboriginal land rights the cultural importance of lands and resources must be taken into account. See *British Columbia* v. *Delgamuukw*, [1997] 3 S.C.R. 1010. About the Committee's lenient assessment of the effectiveness of the participation in this case, see also De Feyter (2001), p. 157.

[257] HRC *Länsman II*, 14 March 1996, §§4.6 (Negotiation) and 4.4 (Irreparable harm). In fact the Committee's emphasis on consultation and representation seems inspired by ILO Convention 169. Meanwhile the emphasis is now not just on 'informed consent' but also on 'control'. See e.g. UN Declaration on Indigenous Peoples, adopted by the General Assembly on 13 September 2007, A/RES/61/295preamble, Articles 12(1), 14(1), 26(2) and 31(1).

[258] CIDH *Maya Indigenous Communities of the Toledo district* (Belize), 12 October 2004, §142.

[259] Ibid.

[260] CIDH Annual Report 1999, Chapter V – Colombia, §148.

ment the African Commission has also emphasised the importance of 'environmental and social impact assessment' and meaningful access to information on health and environmental risks and 'to regulatory and decision-making bodies to communities likely to be affected by oil operations'.[261]

4   CONCLUSION

The rights invoked by the adjudicators in their use of provisional measures in cases involving culture are minority rights, the right to culture, the right to religion and the right to property read in spiritual rather than financial terms. Several adjudicators have used provisional measures to protect collective aspects of these rights where they considered that (industrial) developments would cause irreparable harm to the collective enjoyment by indigenous peoples of their culture. In the context of the Dayton Peace Accord the Bosnia Chamber has used provisional measures in cases involving religious and property rights, individual dignity and pervasive discrimination. These cases also include a collective element.

It has been suggested that a General Comment on indigenous peoples' rights drafted and presented by the UN treaty bodies jointly would both enhance the rights of indigenous peoples in the UN system and assist the UN specialised agencies and multilateral institutions, such as the World Bank, when their activities may affect the rights of indigenous peoples.[262] Meanwhile various UN treaty bodies and regional adjudicators have dealt with the above rights in the context of indigenous peoples and persecuted minorities. Moreover, the UN General Assembly has adopted the Declaration on the Rights of Indigenous Peoples (2007), which could also help enhance the rights of indigenous peoples by providing an authoritative overview of core rights. After all 'there is substantial movement toward a convergence of international opinion on the content of indigenous peoples' rights, including rights over lands and natural resources'.[263] In fact the text of this UN Declaration confirms and validates the practice of the human rights adjudicators with regard to the use of provisional measures in cases involving indigenous culture.

This is the case in particular for the Inter-American Commission and Court, which have enhanced indigenous rights in the doctrine and also in practice both in their provisional measures and in their decisions on the merits, as well as in country reports. The concepts of survival and participation applied in the Inter-American system are reflected in the Declaration. The UN Declaration speaks of minimum standards for the survival, dignity and well-being of indigenous peoples.[264] Its Preamble affirms the collective rights possessed by indigenous peoples that are indispensable for their existence and well-being. The Declaration also emphasises the importance of participation and the *consent* of the indigenous peoples affected[265] and the special relationship between indigenous peoples and their lands.[266] It points out the positive obligations of States and the right to reparation for wrongs committed against indigenous peoples.[267]

---

[261]   ACHPR *The Social and Economic Rights Action Center and the Center for Economic and Social Rights* v. *Nigeria* (Ogoni case), 27 October 2001.

[262]   Asian Centre for Human Rights (an NGO based in New Delhi), ACHR features, strengthening the UN treaty bodies, index: ACHRF/2004, <www.achrweb.org> (consulted on 5 August 2004).

[263]   Anaya/Williams (2001), p. 54.

[264]   The rights recognized in the Declaration 'constitute the minimum standards for the survival, dignity and well-being of the indigenous peoples of the world' (Article 43).

[265]   See Article 41 (on participation) and, on (informed) consent, Articles 10, 11(2), 19, 28, 29(2) and 32(2).

[266]   See e.g. Articles 25 and 26. Indigenous peoples 'have the right to maintain and strengthen their distinctive spiritual relationship with their traditionally owned or otherwise occupied and used lands, territories, waters and coastal seas and other resources and to uphold their responsibilities

The text of the UN Declaration might also trigger a more pro-active approach by the HRC. Thus far the HRC decisions on the cultural rights of indigenous peoples have been unsatisfactory from both an individual and a collective rights perspective. Indigenous groups cannot, as such, claim the collective right to self-determination under the OP. Neither does the Committee's approach necessarily do justice to the rights of individual self-identified members of indigenous groups. This may be on the assumption that an individual member of an indigenous group would find sufficient satisfaction in the knowledge that some segment of the indigenous group would be able to continue its traditional activities, thereby maintaining the existence of its culture, even though the individual member would no longer be able to participate in it.[268] Thus it appears that within the constraints of the ICCPR and the OP the Committee cannot offer sufficient solace to indigenous peoples.

Still, on the basis of the case law it developed, including the *Lubicon Lake Band* case, it could do more than it has thus far. In a similar case it could intervene earlier in the proceedings by using provisional measures and motivate them on the basis of its previous case law on irreparable harm. Subsequently, it could monitor compliance. If in the discussion on the merits the HRC confirms the *prima facie* evidence of (threats of) irreparable harm and finds violations, it could carefully draft in its decision how these should be prevented or halted permanently or, to the extent that certain acts or omissions have already become irreversible, what measures of compensation should be taken that would protect cultural survival.

Although the decisions by the HRC in these cases have not prevented the actions they aimed to prevent, neither through provisional measures pending the proceedings, nor (in the *Lubicon Lake Band* and *Hopu and Bessert* cases) in the final decision, the concepts developed in these cases may have a protective impact in the long run, including a more effective use of provisional measures by the HRC itself. After all, its approach already is incremental. While its case law in relation to Article 27 may not have brought concrete relief to the indigenous peoples on whose behalf the petitioners were acting, it has confirmed several principles that can be useful to support these peoples domestically. An example is the Committee's statement that an accumulation of infringements could result in the denial of the right to culture even if one infringement examined in isolation would not violate this right. Another example is its confirmation of the dynamic nature of the culture of indigenous groups.

Provisional measures could aim at halting industrial developments until the adjudicator considers that an appropriate environmental impact assessment has taken place, during which the indigenous groups affected have been consulted. The adjudicator could assist in this process, inspired by successful national agreements between indigenous peoples and State and provincial authorities about environmental impact assessment. This approach may broker better results for

---

to future generations in this regard' (Article 25). They have the right to these lands and resources. They have the right to own, use, develop and control them and States shall give legal recognition and protection to these lands, territories and resources. "Such recognition shall be conducted with due respect to the customs, traditions and land tenure systems of the indigenous peoples concerned" (Article 26).

[267] Article 8 stipulates, among others, that States shall provide effective mechanisms to prevent and redress 'any action which has the aim or effect of depriving them of their integrity as distinct peoples, or of their cultural values or ethnic identities'; 'any action which has the aim or effect of dispossessing them of their lands, territories or resources' and 'any form of forced population transfer which has the aim or effect of violating or undermining any of their rights'. Article 20 points out that that indigenous peoples deprived of their means of subsistence and development are entitled to just and fair redress. Article 28 notes that if restitution is not possible, a just, fair and equitable compensation 'shall take the form of lands, territories and resources equal in quality, size and legal status or of monetary compensation or other appropriate redress'.

[268] See e.g. HRC *Ivan Kitok* v. *Sweden*, 27 July 1988.

the indigenous communities concerned than the approach taken by the HRC thus far. The Optional Protocol to the ICCPR and the Committee's Rules of Procedure, for instance, do not rule out possibilities for (informal) mediation and forging a friendly settlement. Its decisions may then become more practically relevant. This approach may be possible even through long-distance paper proceedings, although clearly it would be easier to realise in a regional system making use of on-site visits and hearings, as has become clear from the practice of the Inter-American Commission.[269]

One of the problems to be dealt with by adjudicators that take a quantitative (rather than qualitative) approach to infringements on land rights is how to determine the actual moment at which an accumulation of (industrial) activities triggers a human rights violation. Moreover, if such moment can be determined, does prevention of such a violation warrant the use of provisional measures? It is suggested that in certain circumstances involving threats to indigenous culture human rights adjudicators could and should take provisional measures at once. This would be so if the petitioners can show that exploitation or other economic developments are about to take place that could result in irreparable harm *and* there is some indication that those persons directly affected have not been consulted or the State has not performed an environmental impact assessment, taking into account cultural integrity and sustainability. Upon receipt of information to the contrary the adjudicator could decide to not to maintain its provisional measure.

Because indigenous peoples have acquired a special position in international law, warranting protection against threats to their cultural survival, the prevention of irreparable harm to persons must take into account the collective aspects of the rights involved. The use of provisional measures to halt destruction of indigenous culture could be explained by this special position of indigenous peoples and the inappropriateness, in the face of threats to their very existence, of forms of reparation limited to financial compensation.

Another UN treaty body has also taken a pro-active turn. CERD has invoked its Early Warning and Urgent Action Procedure in order to be able to speak out on behalf of an indigenous group that was unable to formally resort to the individual complaint procedure. In this context it also referred to the State's non-compliance with the decision of a regional human rights adjudicator. This is an illustration of the increasing cross-fertilization, and indeed 'cross-follow-up', between the various adjudicators.[270]

The context of the hybrid Bosnia Chamber is different from that of the (other) international adjudicators, but its provisional measures have been used to help prevent the further eradication of the Muslim religious presence from the region where they have long had their roots. In the context of Bosnia the Orders to respect Muslim sites, including cemeteries, seem particularly appropriate as they aim to address serious and pervasive discrimination relating, moreover, to issues involving respect for religion, for the dead and their community as well as to access to religious sites and protection against erasing them from the history of the region, all affecting to the core the dignity of the group at issue.

The use of provisional measures when the cultural/religious survival of an indigenous people, or of a group that has been subjected to ethnic cleansing, is at stake could be seen as belonging to the category of provisional measures used to prevent irreparable harm to persons, their existence as peoples and their cultural survival.

Given the practice of the Inter-American Commission and Court, the African Commission and the HRC and, in a different context, the Bosnia Chamber the concept of provisional measures in international human rights adjudication no longer relates just to the prevention of irreparable

---

[269]   See in general Chapter II (Systems), section 4.

[270]   Another example is the aforementioned remarks on the situation of the Lubicon Lake Band (Canada) in the Concluding Observations by the UN Committee on Economic, Social and Cultural Rights. More generally on follow-up see Chapter XVIII and on cross-fertilization see Chapter II.

harm to individual life and personal integrity, but also encompasses the survival of indigenous culture as well as the culture of minorities that have recently suffered extreme violence and struggle to survive as a people in a context of pervasive discrimination. Thus the provisional measures of the human rights adjudicators now also aim to prevent irreparable harm to the cultural survival of a people rather than only to the life of an individual person.[271]

---

[271] Given the special background and context of the practice developed by the Bosnia Chamber, on the one hand, and the focus on indigenous peoples by the other adjudicators, on the other hand, it remains to be seen what will be the consequence of this development for minority rights in general.

CHAPTER XI
HALTING MASS OR ARBITRARY EXPULSION AND FORCED EVICTION

1   INTRODUCTION

Different from the Inter-American Commission, the Inter-American Court has not yet dealt with the issue of non-refoulement.[1] This Court has, however, confirmed the Inter-American Commission's practice to intervene urgently in situations of arbitrary or mass expulsion. In other words, the Inter-American Commission and Court have used provisional measures in the context of mass expulsion. Moreover, the Bosnia Human Rights Chamber has dealt extensively with the issue of forced eviction and has sometimes used provisional measures in this context as well. This means that the Inter-American Commission and Court and the Bosnia Chamber have ordered provisional measures in situations not directly involving threats to life and personal integrity or cultural survival. This section refers to relevant cases in order to illustrate this practice.

Mass expulsion and forced eviction may also be part of a wider range of threats and harassment against the life and physical integrity of the persons involved and sometimes also against the cultural survival of an indigenous people.[2] In such cases the adjudicator may specify the provisional measures ordered to protect against such threats to make sure that the State does not 'ensure' this protection through internal displacement. Instead, as part of the provisional measures to protect their lives and personal integrity, the State must also protect them against forced displacement.[3]

Provisional measures to protect against mass or arbitrary expulsion have been used predominantly in the Inter-American system, although one example can be given involving the African system and even the possibility of use in the European system cannot be ruled out.[4] Provisional measures to protect against forced eviction have been ordered in the Bosnian system created under the Dayton Peace Agreement. These instances in which provisional measures were ordered seem particularly adapted to the local situation. Nevertheless, the practice of the adjudicators does indicate a particular kind of provisional measure, ordered in a context of endemic and widespread discrimination. This warrants discussion in a separate chapter.[5]

In addition there is another atypical, but related, situation in which one adjudicator has used provisional measures, namely in order to ensure access to education. It was decided to discuss this

---

[1]   See Chapter V (Non-refoulement).

[2]   On provisional measures to protect against death threats and harassment see Chapter IX (Threats). On cultural survival see Chapter X.

[3]   More generally on the protection required as part of provisional measures see Chapter XIII (Protection).

[4]   With regard to the ICCPR Special Rapporteur Scheinin considered it more likely that he would decide to request a State to halt an immediate forced eviction with racist motives (Articles 26, 23, 17) than to request it to take positive action to protect against a threat to life. Scheinin, Geneva, April 2003. In fact he later did use provisional measures on behalf of a person who had been harassed and threatened, see Chapter IX (Death threats and harassment).

[5]   There is also a clear relation with the previous chapter on provisional measures to protect cultural and religious rights, especially in the context of forced eviction of indigenous peoples from their lands or destruction of, and discrimination in the access to, religious sites.

situation in this Chapter rather than in Chapter XI because it involves another aspect of the *Haitian* case discussed below and has in common the underlying endemic situation of discrimination.

2 THE PRACTICE OF THE ADJUDICATORS TO TAKE PROVISIONAL MEASURES TO HALT MASS OR ARBITRARY EXPULSION AND FORCED EVICTION

2.1 Introduction

This section first discusses the practice developed in the Inter-American system to halt arbitrary or mass expulsion and the related provisional measure to ensure access to education. It then briefly refers to the approach in the African and European systems, concluding with the specific practice developed by the Bosnia Camber to halt forced eviction.

2.2 The Inter-American system

In the landmark Order for provisional measures in the matter[6] of *Haitians and Dominicans of Haitian Origin in the Dominican Republic* (2000)[7] the Inter-American Court dealt with the issue of arbitrary and mass expulsion and the question whether this required urgent intervention.

In November 1999 the Inter-American Commission decided to take a precautionary measure on behalf of a group of Haitians and Haitian-origin Dominican people who were at risk of being expelled or deported collectively by the Dominican Republic. It requested the State to halt these mass expulsions or, at least, 'in the event that they would continue to be made' that this would be done in conformity with the requirements of due process.[8] Six months later it decided to appeal to the Court for provisional measures and while the Court did not accept the Commission's request to cover an unnamed number of people with its protective order (at least not in this case),[9] as to subject matter it did expand its use of provisional measures to a broader range of cases. The Court not only ordered the government to protect the right to life, but also the right to family unification and the free movement of certain people. This was the first time the Inter-American Commission persuaded the full Court to go beyond the protection of the rights of physical integrity and life in its use of provisional measures.[10]

Commissioner Mendez believes that one of the reasons the Commission achieved this was the fact that it had previously taken its own precautionary measures. During the hearing before the Court the Dominican Republic repeatedly asked why they were called to the Court. The Commission answered that it had requested the State to do something about the situation six months previously and that the State had not even responded. In other words, the Commission had no choice

---

[6] The Court refers to it as 'matter' rather than 'case' because the case itself was still pending before the Commission and the Court was only dealing with the Commission's request for provisional measures.

[7] IACHR *Haitians and Dominicans of Haitian Origin in the Dominican Republic* (Dominican Republic), Order of 18 August 2000.

[8] IACHR *Haitians and Dominicans of Haitian Origin in the Dominican Republic* (Dominican Republic), Order of 18 August 2000, second 'Having seen' clause.

[9] See further on the group of beneficiaries Chapter XIII (Protection).

[10] On the possibility of the President of the Inter-American Court to take urgent measures until the full Court would convene to discuss the request for provisional measures, see Chapter II (Systems). See further Chapter XII (Other situations), referring to a few cases in which the President of the Court took urgent measures.

but to go to the Court about this issue.[11] It explained that despite its precautionary measures there had 'been no change in the practice of the Dominican authorities of deporting and expelling Haitians and Haitian-origin Dominicans'.[12] It also noted that '(t)his practice, which is carried out arbitrarily, in summary fashion, and without guarantees, continues to be aimed against individuals whose skin color is "black". Because of the fact that they are black, they are suspected to be Haitian; it is then presumed that if they are Haitian they are illegally in the country and are therefore expelled'.[13] Ten days after the hearing the Court ordered provisional measures for the first time, on behalf of five of the seven persons specifically mentioned.[14] The Court considered that the events presented by the Commission *prima facie* showed a 'situation of extreme gravity and urgency as to the rights to life, personal integrity, special protection for children in the family, and to residence and movement' for the persons identified by the Commission.[15]

The Commission had noted that 'neither the text nor the spirit of Article 63(2) of the American Convention establish an impossibility or restriction as to whether the irreparable damage should be against life, integrity or any other right. There is, therefore, the need to recognize that other rights protected by the Convention should be subject to a protection similar to the protection thus far afforded life and personal integrity'.[16] This statement is not sufficiently clear. A *need* to recognise that rights other than life and personal integrity should receive a similar protection does not necessarily follow from the fact that text and spirit of Article 63(2) do not rule out such an interpretation. The Court, however, indeed ordered provisional measures to halt arbitrary expulsion. It may have combined the fact that Article 63(2) does not rule out such an interpretation with the seriousness of the situation, creating a need to use provisional measures also in a situation of arbitrary expulsion.

In short, in its Orders of August and November 2000 and May 2001 the Court expected the State to respect the lives and personal integrity of the several alleged victims, as well as two witnesses, but also to prevent the expulsion of three of them and allow the immediate return of three others who had already been expelled in an arbitrary manner. In addition, the State should facilitate the family unification of some of the alleged victims and in particular assist one of them in finding his family either in the Dominican Republic or in Haiti. The State should also provide detailed information on the situation of the inhabitants of the *bateyes* who could be subjected to forced repatriation.[17] In its provisional measure of May 2001 the Court confirmed its previous orders and added that all the beneficiaries should receive a document of 'safe passage' and the relevant authorities should be informed of the fact that they were protected by these provisional measures. Finally, the State and the Inter-American Commission should take all necessary meas-

---

[11] Interview of author with Commissioner Juan Mendez, Washington D.C., 17 October 2001.

[12] IACHR *Haitians and Dominicans of Haitian Origin in the Dominican Republic* (Dominican Republic), Order of 18 August 2000.

[13] Id. In its brief of 30 May 2000 the Commission mentioned that it had issued precautionary measures on 22 rather than 21 November 1999.

[14] It did not yet include the other two persons for lack of evidence. About evidentiary requirements see Chapter XV (Immediacy and risk).

[15] IACHR *Haitians and Dominicans of Haitian Origin in the Dominican Republic* (Dominican Republic), Order of 18 August 2000, 9th 'Considering' clause. The Commission had identified these persons in its Addendum of 13 June 2000.

[16] IACHR *Haitians and Dominicans of Haitian Origin in the Dominican Republic* (Dominican Republic), Order of 18 August 2000, 'Having seen' clause 11d.

[17] IACHR *Haitians and Dominicans of Haitian Origin in the Dominican Republic* (Dominican Republic), Orders of 18 August 2000 and 12 November 2000. The latter reference to a larger group at risk is the only concession by the Court vis-à-vis the Commission's request to protect a larger group of unnamed persons. See further Chapter XIII (Protection) and its section on the group of beneficiaries.

ures, before the end of June 2001, to create an appropriate mechanism for the coordination of and supervision over the implementation of the provisional measures.[18] Eventually, in March 2002, the State provided the documents of 'safe passage' and met with the representatives of the Commission and the petitioners to create a supervisory committee for the implementation of the provisional measures.[19]

Yet subsequently the Court received reports that the authorities had destroyed some of the 'safe conducts' and that the children of one of the witnesses were being threatened. Out of fear they left their country. The other witness, Father Ruquoy, had also left the country out of fear for his life, after having lived there for 30 years. Moreover, the Supreme Court had declared unconstitutional the agreement ('Acta de Entendimiento') between the representatives of the State, the Commission and the petitioners regarding the implementation of the provisional measures.

In February 2006 the Court ordered, once more, the protection of the lives and personal integrity of the petitioners and witnesses, especially of the one witness and her four children. The State should ensure the necessary conditions for their return to their place of residence in the Dominican Republic.[20] The Court repeated the substance of its previous Orders and pointed out that the State must ('debe') implement these.[21] This related not just to the order to protect the lives and personal integrity of the beneficiaries, but also to the order to prevent their deportation.[22] For the time being it maintained the provisional measures on behalf of father Ruquoy, even though he had left the country. The State should offer the necessary conditions of safety in case he would decide to return.[23]

The Court further noted the importance of the 'safe passage' documents to protect the lives and personal integrity of the beneficiaries but also prevent their deportation. Thus it expressed concern about the destruction of the 'safe passage' documents of two of the beneficiaries. The State should investigate the facts that led to the burning of these documents and it was to replace them as soon as possible.[24] It also observed that, after the judgment by the Constitutional Court, the State had not yet informed it on the institution of a new and appropriate mechanism for the implementation of the provisional measures.[25]

It pointed out that the State was also required to protect the beneficiaries against threats by third parties, unrelated to the State.[26] Further it stressed that Article 63(2) ACHR made it obligatory on the Addressee State to implement the provisional measures ordered by the Court, just like

---

[18]   IACHR *Haitians and Dominicans of Haitian Origin in the Dominican Republic* (Dominican Republic), Order of 26 May 2001. The content of the Orders is more specific and pressing, yet some of the language used initially appears less obligatory: while the previous two Orders used the term 'requerir'/require, this Order used the term 'solicitar'/seek.

[19]   See Acta de Entendimiento, 19 March 2002, reproduced at the website of the National Coalition for Haitian Rights, one of the petitioners: <www.nchr.org/dr/iachr_entendimiento.htm> (consulted 21 February 2007).

[20]   IACHR *Haitians and Dominicans of Haitian Origin in the Dominican Republic* (Dominican Republic), Order of 2 February 2006, 'Decisional' clauses 2 and 3.

[21]   Id., 9th 'Considering' clause.

[22]   Id., 21st 'Considering' clause.

[23]   Id., 'Considering' clause 19. It added that the Commission and the representatives should keep the Court informed of his situation so that it could evaluate whether these measures should be maintained.

[24]   Id., 13th 'Considering' clause.

[25]   Id., 14th 'Considering' clause.

[26]   Id., 'Considerando' ochendo, referring to its provisional measures in the *Eloisa Barrios et al.* case, Order of 22 September 2005, 'Considerando' séptimo and *Eloisa Barrios et al.* case, Order of 29 June 2005, 'Considerando' octavo and Case of *Penitenciarías de Mendoza*, Order of 18 June 2005, 'Considerando' cuarto.

the basic principle of state responsibility that States must comply with their treaty obligations in good faith.[27] In addition the State was required to create the necessary mechanism to plan and implement the provisional measures.[28]

President Cançado Trindade had attached a Concurring Opinion to the Court's Order of 18 August 2000, its first provisional measures involving arbitrary expulsion. He discussed the legal nature of provisional measures for human rights, pointing out that in order to deal with the tragedy of displacement and uprooted people and the consequent alienation, the emphasis must be on prevention. The use of provisional measures in those situations was a good example of this preventive approach. He referred to an 'intertemporal dimension'[29] that manifests itself in the application of provisional measures as well as in the phenomenon of uprooted people. Moreover, the indivisibility of all human rights was equally clear in the above phenomenon as well as in the application of provisional measures.[30] He argued that there were no legal or epistemological impediments against using provisional measures with regard to rights other than the fundamental right to life and personal integrity. As long as the two requirements of 'extreme gravity and urgency' and prevention of 'irreparable damage to persons' in Article 63(2) ACHR were met, it would be possible, he argued, to order provisional measures with regard to all rights in the Convention, because they are all interrelated.[31] The extreme complexity of the problem of uprooted people caused the extension of the application of provisional measures from the right to life and personal integrity to the right to personal liberty, the right to special protection of children and family and the freedom of movement and residence (Articles 7, 9 and 22 ACHR). He pointed out that this was the first time in the history of the Court that it had used provisional measures this way. It had done this because, in light of its evolutive jurisprudence, it was aware of the need to develop new ways of protection inspired by the reality and intensity of the human suffering involved.[32]

According to Cançado Trindade the Court's Order revealed that the concept 'project of life' was also relevant in the field of provisional measures, just as it had surfaced in its Judgment on reparations in the case of *Loayza Tamayo*[33] and its Judgment on the merits in the case of the *Street children* killed in Guatemala.[34] Provisional measures had their historical roots in domestic

---

[27]   IACHR *Haitians and Dominicans of Haitian Origin in the Dominican Republic* (Dominican Republic), Order of 2 February 2006, 'Considerando' ochendo.

[28]   Id., Resolutory point 4 and 'Considering' clause 9(j).

[29]   IACHR *Haitians and Dominicans of Haitian Origin in the Dominican Republic* (Dominican Republic), Order of 18 August 2000, Concurring Opinion Judge Cançado Trindade, §13. In this context this notion is used to refer to the continuity between generations of people, ancestors and descendants and the consequent need to take preventive action to protect this continuity.

[30]   Id., Concurring Opinion Judge Cançado Trindade, §14.

[31]   Id., Concurring Opinion Judge Cançado Trindade, §§13-14.

[32]   Id., Concurring Opinion Judge Cançado Trindade, §15.

[33]   IACHR *Loayza Tamayo* (Peru), 27 November 1998 (Reparations), §§147-148. The Court has referred to the project of life as 'akin to the concept of personal fulfilment, which in turn is based on the options that an individual may have for leading his life and achieving the goal that he sets for himself'. See §148.

[34]   IACHR *Villagrán Morales et al.* (the *'Street Children Case'* v. *Guatemala*), Judgment of 19 November 1999, referring to the rights of 'at-risk children', and the failure of States to 'prevent them from living in misery, thus depriving them of the minimum conditions for a dignified life and preventing them from the "full and harmonious development of their personality", as referred to in the preamble to the Children's Convention, 'even though every child has the right to harbor a project of life that should be tended and encouraged by the public authorities so that it may develop this project for its personal benefit and that of the society to which it belongs', §191. See also the Concurring Opinion of Cançado Trindade and Abreu Burelli. Cançado Trindade also attached a Concurring opinion to the Court's Judgment on Reparations in this case, 26 May 2001,

legal proceedings and were originally conceived to safeguard the efficiency of the adjudicatory function. Gradually, the autonomy of this precautionary action was confirmed at the international level in both the arbitral and judicial practice. Yet with this transfer to the level of public international law, the rationale of provisional measures did not change substantively. Provisional measures continued to aim at preserving the rights claimed by the parties and the integrity of the eventual decision on the merits. The change in the object of provisional measures only arose with the emergence of the international law of human rights.[35] With the transfer from the realm of the traditional contentious proceedings between States to that of international human rights law, the protective function of provisional measures was enhanced, in order to protect the substantive rights of human beings themselves. The Order in *Haitians in the Dominican Republic*, he noted, consolidated this gradual evolution.[36] He pointed out that the Court's approach was innovative yet prudent. It had recognised the great complexity of the problem and had taken care that it would not prejudge the merits of the case pending before the Commission, in particular with regard to the question of due process of law. Its Order contributed to the characterisation of the concept 'tutelar' (protect), more than simply 'cautelar' (prevent), of provisional measures in the realm of human rights.[37] He pointed out that the law evolves in order to attend to social necessities and in recognition of the values underlying the norms.[38]

In its subsequent Orders, including in the *Haitian* case, the full Court has confirmed the above approach. Indeed in the *Haitian* case the Court considered, in its Order of May 2001, that under national legal systems the purpose of provisional measures is 'to preserve the rights of the parties to a dispute, ensuring that the future judgment on merits will not be prejudiced by their actions pendente lite', but that 'the purpose of provisional measures in international human rights law goes further, because, in addition to their essentially preventive nature, they effectively protect fundamental rights, since they seek to avoid irreparable damage to persons'.[39] In other words the Court confirmed that, in human rights law, the concept of provisional measures is evolving from the traditional preventive function to a more encompassing protective function.

Apart from ordering precautionary and provisional measures to halt arbitrary expulsion, the Inter-American Commission and Court have also dealt with the issue of citizenship registration and access to education of children of Haitian descent born in the Dominican Republic. The Court has done so in a judgment on the merits that will be discussed in section 3, while the Commission has even intervened pending the proceedings, ordering precautionary measures in August 1999 in order to ensure access to primary school for the child Violeta Bosica. It did so in addition to ordering precautionary measures to halt her deportation as well as that of the other alleged victim. The petitioners had claimed that the State had denied Violeta Bosica her Dominican nationality despite the fact that the Constitution established the principle of *ius soli* and she had indeed been born in the Dominican Republic. Many children of Haitian descent who were born in the Domini-

---

in which he invoked the project of life, §§21 and 33. See further *Cantoral Benavides*, 3 December 2001 (Reparations): "The pain and suffering that those events inflicted upon him prevented the victim from fulfilling his vocation, aspirations and potential, particularly with regard to his preparation for his chosen career and his work as a professional. All this was highly detrimental to his "life project"", §60. See also Concurring Opinion Judge Cançado Trindade, §§8, 10, 12-13. See also Chapter VII (Detention), section 3 and Chapter XII (Other situations), sections 2.5 (Preservation of IVF embryos) and 2.6 (Arbitrary detention).

[35] IACHR *Haitians and Dominicans of Haitian Origin in the Dominican Republic* (Dominican Republic), Order of 18 August 2000, Concurring Opinion Judge Cançado Trindade, §17.

[36] Id., §18.

[37] Id., §23.

[38] Id., §24.

[39] IACHR *Haitians and Dominicans of Haitian Origin in the Dominican Republic*, Order of 26 May 2001, 7th 'Considering' clause.

can Republic and would, therefore, have the right to Dominican nationality, have been denied this right. Apparently this also means that they are deprived of their right to attend school. A case was brought on behalf of Violeta Bosica, 4th grader at the time, as well as on behalf of Dilcia Yean, who was still a toddler. The case was originally submitted in October 1998, the year Violeta Bosica was denied access to her school. For the school year 1998-1999 she decided to enrol in adult evening classes instead. It was only in April 1999 that the Commission received an amended petition that included a request for precautionary measures and only in June 1999 this petition was submitted in Spanish, as requested by the respondent State. In August 1999 the Commission indeed requested the State to adopt precautionary measures on behalf of both children to grant them 'forthwith the necessary guarantees to avoid them being expelled from Dominican territory and so that Violeta Bosica (sic) m[ight] continue attending school regularly, and receiving the education offered to all other Dominican children'.[40] The formulation shows that the Commission asserted her Dominican nationality already at this stage. In fact there was no need to do so as by 1999 the right to access to primary education had already been established as being inherent in each child, independent of its nationality.[41] The State responded within three days, requesting the Commission's rationale for using these precautionary measures at this stage of the proceedings 'and not previously or subsequently'. It also inquired about 'any new facts that justified this request'.[42] In its response the Commission simply noted that its request referred to a situation that met 'the requirements of truth and urgency, and the need to prevent irreparable harm to persons'.[43] Subsequently the State pointed out that it would never repatriate a Haitian citizen who was in the country legally, 'or according to any of the conditions that have been established in accepting illegal immigrants, [such as] individuals who have been in the country for a long time, or who are related to Dominican nationals'. It noted that the Directorate General of Migration had emphasised that both children 'should not be repatriated while the procedure of verifying the legitimacy of their arguments was underway'.[44] Violeta Bosica was allowed access to primary school education. Although these precautionary measures seem to have been successful for one girl, there are apparently many other children deprived of primary education in the Dominican Republic.[45]

2.3   African Commission

In the context of a claim of arbitrary expulsion the African Commission has ordered Zambia to allow the return of one of the alleged victims to his home country and to allow the body of the other alleged victim, who had died upon expulsion, to be returned for burial.[46]

---

[40]   IACHR *Yean and Bosico children* v. *Dominican Republic*, 8 September 2005, §8 (including comments from the original).

[41]   See further section 3 of this Chapter.

[42]   IACHR *Yean and Bosico children* v. *Dominican Republic*, 8 September 2005, §9.

[43]   Id., §9.

[44]   Id., §11.

[45]   See further in section 3.

[46]   ACHPR *Amnesty International* v. *Zambia* (on behalf of William Banda and John Chinula), 5 May 1999 (merits), referring to the Commission's decision, at its 23rd session, to order provisional measures. The Commission informed the State on 19 July 1998. It sent a reminder on 17 November 1998, §§17-19.

2.4 ECtHR

In October 1999 the ECtHR used provisional measures in a case in which the petitioner had invoked both the prohibition of cruel treatment in Article 3 ECHR and the prohibition of collective expulsion in Article 4 of Protocol 4 to the ECHR in order to halt the collective expulsion of a group of 74 Roma from Belgium to Slovakia. It is not clear whether the Court ordered provisional measures simply because Art. 3 had been invoked or also in order to prevent a violation of the prohibition of collective expulsion under Article 4 Protocol 4 as such. What is clear is that the petitioner requested it to apply its Rule on provisional measures, or in the alternative, its Rule on prioritizing cases. Moreover, along with its provisional measures, the Court specifically requested information on whether the State had examined the risk of inhuman or degrading treatment in Slovakia. Subsequently, when the Court found a violation of Article 4 Protocol 4, in conjunction with Article 13 ECHR, it did not devote any discussion to its provisional measures and the fact that Belgium had ignored them.[47] In other words the practice of the ECtHR does not yet show an expansion of its use of provisional measures to include cases of arbitrary expulsion, yet it does not deny the possibility either. Contrary to the Bosnia Chamber it does not use provisional measures in the context of forced eviction.

2.5 Bosnia Chamber

Between November 1996 and December 2001 the Bosnia Chamber regularly ordered provisional measures to halt forced evictions. In fact this is the situation in which it used provisional measures most often.[48] After all, under the Dayton Peace Accord it had a particular role in dealing with situations involving discrimination. Yet the fact that so many requests for provisional measures were successful triggered almost automatic requests for them with each petition. Moreover, the Chamber was faced more and more with petitions by individuals requesting the Chamber to order provisional measures on their behalf, even though the eviction order had been brought so as to enable the return to their homes by the persons who had originally lived there, but had fled or been forcibly displaced.[49] In response, while it still often granted them, as of July 1998 the Chamber began to deny the majority of the requests to halt such evictions.[50]

The Chamber has also ordered provisional measures in cases that are not typical of the post war situation in Bosnia, but that have also arisen in other places throughout the world, involving

---

[47] In its decision on admissibility the ECtHR simply echoed *Cruz Varas et al.* v. *Sweden*, 20 March 1991, stating that its provisional measures were not legally binding, *Conka* v. *Belgium*, 13 March 2001 (adm.), §11. It was only in *Mamatkulov* ((Grand Chamber) *Mamatkulov and Askarov* v. *Turkey*, 15 December 2004) that the Court found that its provisional measures are legally binding. See further Chapter XVI (Legal status). See generally on the official State responses Chapter XVII and, on the follow-up by the adjudicator, Chapter XVIII.

[48] During this period the Chamber ordered such provisional measures in more than 30 cases, most of them against Republika Srpska.

[49] Interview by author with Jacob Möller, Geneva, October 1998.

[50] In 1999, for instance, it denied more than 33 requests for provisional measures in eviction cases, while during that year it does not appear to have ordered provisional measures to halt forced eviction. See e.g. Bosnia Chamber *Aiša Tufekčić* v. *Federation BiH*, 6 December 2001 (adm.). While initially, in 2000, provisional measures were ordered in this case, the Chamber subsequently rejected a request for extension by the Citizens' Association for the Protection of Human Rights of Temporary Occupants of Abandoned Apartments in the Federation of BiH. In *Ristić* v. *Srpska*, 4 September 2000 the Chamber initially used provisional measures, but subsequently found that the petitioner himself was an illegal occupant and the case was declared admissible. See also *S.K.* v. *Srpska*, 14 May 1999.

industrial developments threatening to displace persons. In 2000 it ordered such measures in the case *Dautbegović and 51 other villagers from Duge* v. *Fed. BiH* (2001), after the petitioners had alleged that the planned construction of a hydroelectric plant near their village threatened their livelihood and homes.[51]

3 RELATION BETWEEN PROVISIONAL MEASURES TO HALT MASS OR ARBITRARY EXPULSION AND FORCED EVICTION AND THE EXPECTED DECISION ON THE MERITS

3.1 Introduction

As noted in the previous chapters, e.g. on protection against threats and on the right of indigenous peoples to respect for their culture, provisional measures often involve several rights that are interrelated. In the context of complaints regarding threats to the right to life, personal integrity and/or cultural survival, people sometimes face arbitrary expulsion, forced evictions and internal displacement.

What distinguishes the cases discussed in this chapter, in which provisional measures were used, is the arbitrary nature of the expulsion or eviction, without any meaningful review, as well as the dominance of the element of unequal treatment and discrimination. Already in 1935 the Permanent Court of International Justice noted that 'there would be no true equality between a majority and a minority if the latter were deprived of its own institutions, and were consequently compelled to renounce that which constitutes the very essence of its being as a minority'.[52] This statement may serve as a point of reference in discussing provisional measures dealing with the issue of discrimination, such as those of the Bosnia Chamber involving forced evictions and the precautionary and provisional measures in the Inter-American system involving arbitrary or mass expulsion.

The fact that various treaties prohibit, and a range of supervisory bodies emphasises, the seriousness of forced eviction and mass expulsion,[53] especially in the context of discrimination, lends support to the practice of the above adjudicators in using provisional measures to halt certain cases of mass or arbitrary expulsion and forced eviction.

Article 2(1)(a) ICERD stipulates that States are to refrain from racial discrimination and ensure that public authorities and institutions refrain from racial discrimination. Article 5 ICERD speaks of, among others, the right to security of the person including the protection from violence or bodily harm, but also the right to housing, health care and education. Article 6 ICERD is an undertaking to ensure effective protection and remedies including reparation and satisfaction. The Committee supervising the ICERD has instituted an Early-Warning and Urgent Action procedure in order to deal with particularly urgent cases,[54] but it has never invoked its Rule on provisional measures.

The HRC has pointed out that States may not invoke a declaration of a state of emergency, made pursuant to Article 4(1) ICCPR, as a justification to engage in propaganda for war, or in

---

[51] Bosnia Chamber *Dautbegović and 51 Other Villagers from Duge* v. *Federation BiH*, 2 July 2001. In 2000 the Chamber had ordered provisional measures. In reaction the businessmen planning construction of the plant requested provisional measures as well. The Chamber rejected these. See *Drago Lukenda and Miroljub Bevanda* v. *Federation BiH*, 5 July 2001 (inadm.). See also Chapter XIII (Protection), section 4 on the beneficairies.

[52] PCIJ *Minority schools in Albania*, Advisory Opinion of 6 April 1935, p. 17.

[53] See in general on the issue of mass expulsion in international law Henckaerts (1995).

[54] See Van Boven (1998).

advocacy of national, racial or religious hatred that would constitute incitement to discrimination, hostility or violence, contrary to Article 20 ICCPR.[55] This emphasis on Article 20 could also be relevant with regard to the substance of possible provisional measures to halt mass expulsion or systematic forced eviction and internal displacement of certain ethnic or religious groups, to the extent that a State may be ordered to publicly explain that persons are being protected by provisional measures and that discrimination and threats against them will not be tolerated.[56]

The IACHR has noted that 'the principle of equality and non-discrimination is fundamental for the safeguard of human rights in both international law and domestic law' and that 'the fundamental principle of equality and non-discrimination forms part of general international law' and '(a)t the current stage of the development of international law, the fundamental principle of equality and non-discrimination has entered the domain of jus cogens'.[57]

This chapter deals with case law on mass and arbitrary expulsion on the one hand and forced eviction on the other.

3.2 Mass and arbitrary expulsion

A still infamous case of mass expulsion is that by Uganda under Idi Amin, collectively expelling large groups of Asians. As Lillich has noted, this expulsion 'in and of itself violated the UN Charter because it was racially discriminatory in nature'.[58] Article 22 International Convention on the Protection of the Rights of All Migrant Workers and Members of Their Families (1990) prohibits measures of collective expulsion and determines that each case of expulsion should be 'examined and decided individually' and in accordance with the law.[59]

Are the human rights adjudicators likely to find violations on the merits of the specific rights claimed in the cases in which provisional measures have been used? The HRC has pointed out that Article 13 ICCPR 'entitles each alien to a decision in his own case' and that the obligations under this article would therefore 'not be satisfied with laws or decisions providing for collective or mass expulsions'.[60]

In its Concluding Comments to the State report by the Dominican Republic the HRC expressed grave concern 'at the continuing reports of mass expulsions of ethnic Haitians, even when

---

[55] HRC General Comment 29 on states of emergency (Article 4 ICCPR), 24 July 2001, §13.

[56] This is obviously relevant in the context of provisional measures to protect against death threats and harassment, see Chapter VII. See also Article 4 ICERD.

[57] IACHR Advisory Opinion 18(3) on the *Juridical Condition and Rights of the Undocumented Migrants*, 17 September 2003, §173(3) and (4).

[58] Lillich/Hannum (1995), p. 65, referring to Article 55 (c) UN Charter, the Universal Declaration and the Restatement (3rd) of the Foreign Relations Law of the US (1987).

[59] As of 18 July 2007 this treaty was ratified by 35 States (<www.ohchr.org>, accessed 18 May 2008).

[60] It also referred to the right to submit reasons against expulsion and to have the decision reviewed by the competent authority and emphasized that '(d)iscrimination may not be made between categories of aliens in the application of article 13'. HRC General Comment 15(27) on the position of aliens, 22 July 1986, §10. In 1990 it found the Dominican Republic in violation of Article 13 ICCPR because the extradition of Paul Giry was not seen to have been performed according to law and he had not been granted an opportunity to contest it. HRC *Giry* v. *Dominican Republic*, 20 July 1990. In an individual opinion four members of the Committee noted that had there been an administrative decision, this case would have come under Article 13, but as there was not, the case was to be discussed under Articles 9 and 12 ICCPR. They would have found violations of these provisions. Individual Opinion Chanet, Aguilar Urbina, Ando and Wennergren.

such persons are nationals of the Dominican Republic'. It held 'mass expulsions of non-nationals to be in breach of the Covenant since no account is taken of the situation of individuals for whom the Dominican Republic is their own country', in light of Article 12(4) ICCPR, 'nor of cases where expulsion may be contrary to article 7 given the risk of subsequent cruel, inhuman or degrading treatment, nor yet of cases where the legality of an individual's presence in the country is in dispute and must be settled in proceedings that satisfy the requirements of article 13'.[61]

Article 12(5) ACHPR stipulates that 'the mass expulsion of non-nationals shall be prohibited. Mass expulsion shall be that which is aimed at national, racial, ethnic or religious groups'.[62] Subsequent to the mass expulsion from Zambia of 517 East Africans, during two days in February 1992, a case was submitted to the African Commission on their behalf. The expulsion had already taken place and no provisional measures were requested. The Commission found that they were 'arrested and assembled over time, with a view to their eventual expulsion. The deportees were kept in a camp during this time, not even an ordinary prison, and it was impossible for them to contact their lawyers'.[63]

Mass expulsions constitute a violation of human rights whether on the basis of nationality, religion, ethnic, racial, or other considerations and independent of the challenges faced by many African countries.[64] The expulsion of West African nationals from Angola, in 1996, violated Articles 7 and 12(4) ACHPR as they were not allowed to challenge their expulsion. Article 12(5) was violated as well, because they had been expelled based on their nationality.[65] In the case of John Modise, who was deported from Botswana to South Africa after he had started an opposition party, the Commission found, among others, a denial of equal protection before the law and of the respect for each individual's legal status.[66] This had 'greatly jeopardised' his freedom of movement and infringed upon his right to leave and to return to his country.[67]

The case of *Malawi African Association et al.* v. *Mauritania* (2000) illustrates that mass expulsion, forced eviction and the destruction of property often go hand in hand with endemic discrimination.[68] Among others, the African Commission found that '(e)victing Black Mauritanians from their houses and depriving them of their Mauritanian citizenship' constituted a violation of

---

61   HRC Concluding Observations, CCPR/CO/71/DOM, 26 April 2001, §16.

62   In ACHPR *Organisation Mondiale Contre La Torture* v. *Rwanda,* October 1996 the African Commission found a violation of this provision with regard to the expulsion of groups of Burundian refugees. Article 12(4), prohibiting the arbitrary expulsion of asylum seekers, was also found to have been violated, as well as Article 7(1) ACHPR because of their expulsion from Rwanda without giving them the opportunity to be heard by the national judicial authorities.

63   ACHPR *Rencontre Africaine pour la defence des droits de l'homme* v. *Zambia*, October 1997, §28. It found violations of Articles 2, 7(1)(a) and 12(5) ACHPR.

64   ACHPR *Federation Internationale des Ligues des Droits de l'Homme* v. *Angola*, 11 November 1997, §§13 and 16.

65   Id., §14. The African Commission has pointed out that '(w)hile the decision as to who is permitted to remain in a country is a function of the competent authorities of that country, this decision should always be made according to careful and just legal procedures, and with due regard to the acceptable international norms and standards'. ACHPR *John K. Modise* v. *Botswana*, October/November 2000, §83.

66   ACHPR *John K. Modise* v. *Botswana*, October/November 2000, §88.

67   Id., §93.

68   This was a case combining a range of complaints, including torture and cruel treatment in detention as well as slavery like practices. In the latter context the Commission found that 'there was a violation of article 5 of the Charter due to practices analogous to slavery' and emphasised 'that unremunerated work is tantamount to a violation of the right to respect for the dignity inherent in the human being'. It also considered that the conditions to which the descendants of slaves are subjected clearly constitute exploitation and degradation of man', ACHPR *Malawi African Association et al.* v. *Mauritania*, 11 May 2000, §135.

Article 12(1) ACHPR.[69] 'The confiscation and looting of the property of black Mauritanians and the expropriation or destruction of their land and houses before forcing them to go abroad' constituted a violation of the right to property (Article 14 ACHPR).[70] Among others the Commission recommended the new government of Mauritania to 'take diligent measures to replace the national identity documents of those Mauritanian citizens, which were taken from them at the time of their expulsion and ensure their return without delay to Mauritania as well as the restitution of the belongings looted from them at the time of the said expulsion'.[71]

In July 1998 the African Commission had used provisional measures ordering the return of one alleged victim to his home country as well as the return the body of the other alleged victim, who had since died. On the merits it confirmed this as definite obligations.[72] Pending the proceedings of *Amnesty International* v. *Zambia* (1999) the Commission had used provisional measures to ensure the return of Mr Banda and the burial of Mr Chinula (who had died in Malawi). On the merits the Commission found that Zambia had violated Articles 7 and 12(4) ACHPR with regard to Mr Banda, who had unsuccessfully challenged his deportation in the Zambian courts, but was denied access to the administrative proceedings.[73] Mr. Chinula was not allowed to challenge his deportation at all. He was forcibly deported and when he tried to return to Zambia in order to challenge his expulsion he was threatened with imprisonment.[74] The African Commission found a violation of Article 7 ACHPR.[75] It also noted that it had previously used provisional measures and repeated them in substance by stating that 'Zambia must be required to allow the return of William Steven Banda with a view to making application for citizenship by naturalisation'.[76] It added that the family of John Lyson Chinula, who died in Malawi, was 'requesting the return of his body for burial in Zambia. The Government of Zambia should be required to grant that wish'.[77]

In 2002 the ECtHR held that the expulsion of 74 Roma from Belgium to Slovakia constituted a violation of Art. 4 Protocol 4, on the prohibition of collective expulsion, in conjunction with Article 13 ECHR.[78] The procedure had provided insufficient guarantees to ensure that the personal circumstances of each of those concerned would be taken into account 'genuinely and individually'.[79] Moreover, petitioners could not depend on the suspensive effect of domestic proceedings, contrary to Article 13 ECHR.[80] As noted, the Court had ordered provisional measures in this case, but they were not respected and it is not clear whether the Court decided to order them given the Article 3 claim or in light of the collective nature of the impending expulsion.

As discussed, the Inter-American Court has confirmed the Inter-American Commission's approach to urgent situations of arbitrary or mass expulsion. Thus, it has ordered provisional measures in situations not directly involving threats to life and physical integrity. The situation

---

[69]   ACHPR *Malawi African Association et al.* v. *Mauritania*, 11 May 2000, §126.

[70]   Id., §128.

[71]   Id., Concluding part, following §142.

[72]   ACHPR *Amnesty International (on behalf of William Banda and John Chinula)* v. *Zambia*, 5 May 1999.

[73]   Id., §§7 and 44.

[74]   Id., §§7 and 11.

[75]   Id., §46. The Commission noted that the claw-back clauses such as Article 2(2) must not be interpreted contrary to the principles of the Charter and that rules of natural justice must apply, §50.

[76]   Id., §47.

[77]   Id., §48.

[78]   ECtHR *Conka* v. *Belgium*, 5 February 2002.

[79]   Id., §63.

[80]   Id., §§78-83.

clearly related to human rights violations that were more serious than 'simple' mass expulsion.[81] It involved racial discrimination as well. Moreover it concerned a range of rights including the right to access to primary education and other children's rights.

The Inter-American Court specifically referred to statements by UN bodies[82] in its discussion of the case of the *Yean and Bosico children* (2005), including the forms of reparation required on their behalf.[83] The mothers of Dilcia Yean and Violeta Bosica were Dominican and

---

[81]   In his Concurring Opinion to the Order for provisional measures in the *Haitian* case Cançado Trindade sketched the general context of mass expulsion cases, by paying attention to the phenomenon of uprooted people and the state responsibility triggered in this regard. He pointed out that this issue must be treated not in light of state sovereignty but as a truly global problem bearing in mind the *erga omnes* obligations of protection. Since the phenomenon of uprooted people is of a global character, States cannot shirk their responsibility and continue applying criteria based on their internal legal order alone. IACHR *Haitians and Dominicans of Haitian Origin in the Dominican Republic* (Dominican Republic), Order of 18 August 2000, Concurring Opinion Judge Cançado Trindade, §§10-11. They must take into account the consequences of the norms and public policies they adopt in relation to the issue of migration and, in particular, the procedures of deportation and expulsion, id. §12. He emphasized the grave consequences of separating persons from their roots. The connection with their roots is necessary to maintain their spiritual legacy and to keep open channels of communication between the living and the dead. IACHR *Haitians and Dominicans of Haitian Origin in the Dominican Republic* (Dominican Republic), Order of 18 August 2000, Concurring Opinion Judge Cançado Trindade, §5. He noted that uprooting people causes them to lose touch with daily life and their mother tongue as a way to express their ideas and feelings as well as with their work that gives everyone a sense of life and of being useful. By losing their own way to communicate with the outside world, they also lose the possibility of developing a 'project of life'. IACHR *Haitians and Dominicans of Haitian Origin in the Dominican Republic* (Dominican Republic), Order of 18 August 2000, Concurring Opinion Judge Cançado Trindade, §6. On the concept of 'project of life' see also Chapter XII (Other situations). While the roots involved in this case seem less deep than those involving ancestral lands, this remark shows a more general awareness of the problem of displacement. The reference indicates a correlation with the Court's statements on indigenous peoples and their ancestral grounds as well as with those on the importance in general of being able to bury the dead. See respectively IACHR *Mayagna (Sumo) Awas Tingni Community* case, 31 August 2001; *Bámaca Velásquez* case, 22 February 2002 (Reparations); *Villagrán Morales et al. (the 'Street Children Case')*, 26 May 2001 (Reparations). See also African Commission *Amnesty International* v. *Zambia*, 5 May 1999 (on behalf of William Banda and John Chinula). According to Cançado Trindade today answers must be found to the new demands for protection even if they are not literally contemplated in the international human rights instruments. IACHR *Haitians and Dominicans of Haitian Origin in the Dominican Republic* (Dominican Republic), Order of 18 August 2000, Concurring Opinion Judge Cançado Trindade, §7.

[82]   Committee on the Rights of the Child CRC/C/15/Add.150, 21 February 2001.

[83]   IACHR *Yean and Bosico children* v. *Dominican Republic*, 8 September 2005, §237. The Court also invoked its Advisory Opinion 17 on the Juridical Status and Human Rights of the Child, 28 August 2002 and Advisory Opinion 18 on the Juridical Status and Rights of Undocumented Migrants, 17 September 2003. In 1997 the ESC Committee specifically dealt with the plight of Haitian workers in the Dominican Republic. It noted 'that approximately 500,000-600,000 Haitian illegal workers reside in the Dominican Republic, some of them for one or two generations, without any legal status and any protection of their economic, social and cultural rights. In this respect, the Committee is particularly concerned about the situation of the children who, due to the restrictive interpretation of article 11 of the Constitution by the authorities, do not receive Dominican nationality on the grounds that they are children born of foreigners in transit. These children are thus denied their most basic social rights, such as the rights to education and health care'. ESC-Committee E/C.12/1/Add.16, 12 December 1997, §17. Among others it

their fathers Haitian. The two children remained stateless for more than four years despite the fact that in the Dominican Republic *ius soli* applies, meaning that persons born there have the right to Dominican nationality.[84] They are just two of a great many children whose birth registration was made impossible. In this context the Dominican Republic has used the argument that the Haitian workers are within its jurisdiction 'in transit' and therefore its normal rule on *ius soli* does not apply.[85]

---

recommended 'that the principle of *jus soli* under article 11 of the Constitution be applied to the children of Haitian residents without delay'. ESC-Committee E/C.12/1/Add.16, 12 December 1997, §34. It also expressed concern about the inadequate living conditions in the *bateyes*. ESC-Committee E/C.12/1/Add.16, 12 December 1997, §18, also referring to its previous report: E/C.12/1/Add.6, §13. It urged the State to adopt positive measures to improve the living conditions. "To this end, the Committee recommends that the legal status of the *bateyes* be modified and their relationships with municipalities be improved, and that sugar cane companies be required to provide inhabitants of the *bateyes* with basic facilities, such as water and electricity, and with health and social services". ESC-Committee E/C.12/1/Add.16, 12 December 1997, §34. CERD has equally recommended the Dominican Republic to 'take urgent measures to ensure the enjoyment by persons of Haitian origin of their economic, social and cultural rights without discrimination. Efforts should be made, in particular, to improve their living conditions in the bateyes (shanty towns)'. CERD Concluding Observations CERD/C/304/Add.74, 26 August 1999, §11. In addition, CEDAW has expressed concern over the discriminatory character of the definition of nationality and the effects on Dominican women and girls of Haitian origin, who were among the most vulnerable groups in the State. In particular, this definition obstructed their access to education and other basic services. CEDAW Concluding Observations on the report of the Dominican Republic, 26 July 2004, §§33-34.

[84] It was only in September 2001 that birth certificates, and, consequently, Dominican nationality, were granted to both children. IACHR *Yean and Bosico children* v. *Dominican Republic*, 8 September 2005, §147. In its Concluding Comments to the State report by the Dominican Republic the HRC paid attention to a range of human rights issues that are also relevant in the context of the provisional measures ordered in the Inter-American system. These issues include the living and working conditions in the *bateyes* (see e.g. the direct contact mission by the ILO Committee of Experts, January 1991, on the situation of Haitian workers on sugar plantations. See CEACR General Report, §60. See also CEACR individual observation on Convention 111, 2004). Other issues were the difficulties for children born in the Republic to get registered and the mass expulsion of Haitians and Dominicans with Haitian background. The HRC noted that 'failure to protect Haitians living or working in the Dominican Republic from serious human rights abuses such as forced labour and cruel, inhuman or degrading treatment' and expressed 'concern over the living and working conditions of Haitian workers and the tolerated practices that restrict their freedom of movement'. HRC Concluding Observations of CCPR/CO/71/DOM, 26 April 2001, §17. "The State party should give priority to addressing the issue of the working and living conditions of Haitian workers, and ensure that those workers can take advantage of the rights and safeguards laid down in articles 8, 17 and 22 of the Covenant". HRC Concluding Observations of CCPR/CO/71/DOM, 26 April 2001, §17. It also expressed concern 'at the abuse of the legal notion of "transient aliens". According to information in its possession, such persons may be born in the Dominican Republic to parents who were also born there but are still not considered to be nationals of the Dominican Republic'. It pointed out that "The State party should regulate the situation of everyone living in the country and grant the rights recognized by article 12 of the Covenant". HRC Concluding Observations of CCPR/CO/71/DOM, 26 April 2001, §18.

[85] The UN Committee on the Rights of the Child has paid particular attention to the birth registration of children in the Dominican Republic. A large percentage were still not registered and not provided with identity cards. As a result these children, particularly children of Haitian origin or belonging to Haitian migrant families, 'have not been able to enjoy fully their rights,

The Court pointed out that the right to a nationality (Article 20 ACHR) was a fundamental human right that could not be derogated from in times of emergency (Article 27 ACHR). It understood nationality as 'a juridical expression of a social fact that connects an individual to a State'.[86] This allowed 'the individual to acquire and exercise rights and obligations inherent in membership in a political community'.[87] International law had evolved so as to limit the discretional authority of States, 'on the one hand, by their obligation to provide individuals with the equal and effective protection of the law and, on the other hand, by their obligation to prevent, avoid and reduce statelessness'.[88] The Court referred to 'the peremptory legal principle of the equal and effective protection of the law and non-discrimination'.[89] It observed that 'the obligation to respect and ensure the principle of the right to equal protection and non-discrimination is irrespective of a person's migratory status in a State'.[90] Moreover, 'to consider that a person is in transit, irrespective of the classification used,' the State must respect a reasonable temporal limit and understand that a foreigner who develops connections in a State cannot be equated to a person in transit'.[91] Finally, 'under no circumstances, could the State have applied the exception referring to the children of a person in transit to the Yean and Bosico children, because the mothers of the alleged victims are Dominican and the children were born in the Dominican Republic'.[92]

Among others, it found that the State had applied different and more difficult requirements than was the norm. Thus it had 'acted arbitrarily, without using reasonable and objective criteria, and in a way that was contrary to the superior interest of the child'. This constituted discriminatory treatment, placing the children outside the State's juridical system and keeping them stateless. They were brought in a situation of 'extreme vulnerability'.[93] "Bearing in mind that the alleged victims were children, the Court considers that the vulnerability arising from statelessness affected the free development of their personalities, since it impeded access to their rights and to the special protection to which they are entitled".[94] In addition, 'the discriminatory treatment imposed' on them was 'situated within the context of the vulnerable situation of the Haitian population and Dominicans of Haitian origin in the Dominican Republic'.[95]

The failure to recognize persons' juridical personality harmed their human dignity.[96] The Court also discussed that Violeta Bosico had been prevented from attending day school during one school year. It observed that the fact that she was forced to study at evening school 'exacerbated her situation of vulnerability, because she did not receive the special protection, due to her

---

[86] such as to access to health care and education' and the State should increase its measures to ensure their immediate registration. See e.g. Committee on the Rights of the Child CRC/C/15/Add.150, 21 February 2001, §§26-27, referring to Article 7 Children's Convention. It expressed concern at 'various forms of discrimination and exclusion which still affect the right to education of certain groups of children, such as pregnant adolescents, unregistered children, children with disabilities and children of Haitian origin born in the State party's territory or belonging to Haitian migrant families, reflecting insufficient attention to article 29 of the Convention'. Committee on the Rights of the Child CRC/C/15/Add.150, 21 February 2001, §41.

[86] IACHR *Yean and Bosico children* v. *Dominican Republic*, 8 September 2005, §136, referring to ICJ *Nottebohm* (*Liechtenstein* v. *Guatemala*) 2nd phase, 6 April 1955, p. 23.

[87] IACHR *Yean and Bosico children* v. *Dominican Republic*, 8 September 2005, §137.

[88] Id., §140.

[89] Id., §141.

[90] Id., §155.

[91] Id., §157.

[92] Id., §158.

[93] Id., §166.

[94] Id., §167.

[95] Id., §168.

[96] Id., §179.

as a child, of attending school during appropriate hours together with children of her own age, instead of with adults'.[97] She should have attended day school 'together with her peers, owing to her age, aptitudes and the appropriate curriculum and level of difficulty. This situation caused the child uncertainty and anxiety'.[98] The Court noted that the child's right to special protection, laid down in Article 19 ACHR and interpreted in light of the Children's Convention and the Protocol of San Salvador, meant that 'the State must provide free primary education to all children in an appropriate environment and in the conditions necessary to ensure their full intellectual development'.[99]

The African Commission has also dealt with the issue of access to education. In one case it found that the closure of secondary schools and universities for two years was a violation of Article 17 ACHPR on the right to education.[100] It is unlikely that the Commission would use provisional measures in this case, unless the access was hindered just for certain groups. Yet it may consider a case like this to be urgent and accelerate its proceedings, especially when it involves access to primary school education.

In the *Yean and Bosico children* case the Inter-American Court referred to the vulnerability, suffering and uncertainty of the children, but decided to take this into account not in the context of finding a violation of the right to humane treatment, but rather when establishing the pertinent reparations.[101] In other words, with regard to the two children the Court acknowledges a link with the prohibition of cruel treatment, but deals with it not in its finding on the merits, but in determining the appropriate form of remedy.[102] With regard to their next of kin the Court did find a violation of the right to humane treatment. The situation of vulnerability the children were in also caused their mothers and sister uncertainty and insecurity, among others because of 'the very real fear that they could be expelled from the Dominican Republic'.[103]

The case law on the merits of the African Commission has made a link between arbitrary expulsion and cruel treatment. In *Modise* v. *Botswana* (2000) it found that John Modise, after his deportation from Botswana, had never been accepted in South Africa as a citizen and had 'suffered the fate of being deported four times'. He had been forced 'to live for eight years in the "homeland" of Bophuthatswana, and then for another seven years in "No Man's Land", a border strip between the former South African Homeland of Bophuthatswana and Botswana' from which he was later deported back to Botswana.[104] In this context the Commission pointed out that '(d)eportation or expulsion has serious implications on other fundamental rights of the victim, and in some instances, the relatives'.[105] Modise had argued that 'his incessant deportation, constant threats of deportation and the accompanying disastrous consequences constitute a violation of Article 5 of the Charter' and the Commission indeed found that he had been exposed to 'personal suffering and indignity in violation of the right to freedom from cruel, inhuman or degrading

---

[97]   Id., §185.

[98]   IACHR *Yean and Bosico children* v. *Dominican Republic*, 8 September 2005, §225.

[99]   Id., §185. See also §244. It appears that the foreign minister of the Dominican Republic, at a General Assembly meeting of the OAS in June 2006, has announced that the State will comply with the Court's ruling in the *Yean and Bosico* case. See Minority Rights Group, Public letter to President Leonel Fernández, 1 October 2006 at: <www.minorityrights.org/media_centre/media_comment/media_centre_letter_do> (consulted 11 January 2007).

[100] ACHPR *Free Legal Assistance Group* v. *Zaire*, October 1995, §48.

[101] IACHR *Yean and Bosico children* v. *Dominican Republic*, 8 September 2005, §204.

[102] See Chapter XIII (Protection) on the relation between the protection required as part of provisional measures and as part of a judgment on reparations.

[103] IACHR *Yean and Bosico children* v. *Dominican Republic*, 8 September 2005, §§205-206.

[104] ACHPR *John K. Modise* v. *Botswana*, October/November 2000, §87.

[105] Id., §90.

treatment guaranteed under Article 5 of the Charter'.[106] In the abovementioned *Banda and Chinula* case the Commission confirmed this approach. It pointed out that by forcing them 'to live as stateless persons under degrading conditions, the government of Zambia has deprived them of their family and is depriving their families of the men's support, and this constitutes a violation of the dignity of a human being'.[107]

The adjudicators that have dealt with the issue of arbitrary or mass expulsion have expressed themselves strongly on the prohibition of discrimination. The available case law also shows an awareness of the impact of discrimination on personal dignity and have made a link, one way or other, to the prohibition of cruel treatment. Finally, on the merits the particularly vulnerable position of children has been stressed. This case law on the merits would appear to support the use of provisional measures in certain cases of arbitrary or mass expulsion.

3.3 Forced eviction

The issue of forced evictions has 'reached the international human rights agenda because it is considered a practice that does grave and disastrous harm to the basic civil, political, economic, social and cultural rights of large numbers of people, both individual persons and collectivities'.[108] Are the adjudicators likely to find violations on the merits in the type of cases in which the Bosnia Chamber has used provisional measures to halt forced eviction?

Several monitoring bodies that have not dealt with individual complaints have nevertheless dealt with the issue of forced eviction in a manner that indicates the importance attached to this issue. The Committee supervising the International Convention on Economic, Social and Cultural Rights (ESC Committee) has sometimes reacted to planned evictions, or evictions that have already taken place, outside the context of the consideration of a State report. In 1991 the Committee asked the Dominican Republic (in a general context involving housing, not specifically related to persons of Haitian descent) to 'suspend any actions which are not in clearly in conformity with the provisions of the Covenant' and to provide it with additional information 'as a matter of urgency'.[109] The country report of the Dominican Republic was not on the Committee's agenda during that session, indicating a special initiative on the part of the Committee. That same year the Committee also prepared a General Comment on the right to adequate housing (Article 11 (1) ICESCR).[110] A few years later it devoted a General Comment specifically to the issue of forced eviction, in which it defined this phenomenon as 'the permanent or temporary removal against their will of individuals, families and/or communities from the homes and/or land which they occupy, without the provision of, and access to, appropriate forms of legal or other protection'.[111]

---

[106]   Id., §91.

[107]   ACHPR *Amnesty International* v. *Zambia*, 5 May 1999, §58.

[108]   UN study on the right to restitution, compensation and rehabilitation, final report by Special Rapporteur Van Boven, E/CN.4/Sub.2/1993/18, §21. Particularly on the impact on women, see Westendorp (2008).

[109]   ESC-Committee E/C.12/1991/4, §330.

[110]   ESC-Committee General Comment 4 on the right to adequate housing, 13 December 1991.

[111]   ESC-Committee General Comment 7 on the right to adequate housing: forced evictions, 20 May 1997, §4. Other examples are CERD, which has emphasized the right of all refugees and displaced persons freely to return to their homes of origin under conditions of safety. States parties are obliged to ensure that the return of such persons is voluntary (CERD General Recommendation XXII (49)) and the UN Sub-Commission on Human Rights, which in 2005 adopted 'Principles on housing and property restitution for refugees and displaced persons'. See final report Special Rapporteur Pinheiro, E/CN.4/Sub.2/2005/17. In HRC *Dahanayake and 41 others* v. *Sri Lanka*, 25 July 2006 (inadm.), it is noted that two requests by the petitioners for

The African Commission has also shown awareness of the interrelated nature of the rights protected in the Charter. In the *Ogoni* case (2001) it discussed the right to adequate housing of members of the Ogoni community under Articless 14 (right to property) and 18(1) (family life) ACHPR and pointed out that 'when housing is destroyed, property, health, and family life are adversely affected'. Thus, 'the combined effect of Articles 14, 16 and 18(1) reads into the Charter a right to shelter or housing which the Nigerian Government has apparently violated'.[112] It also referred to its obligation to prevent the violation of the right to housing by third parties. It explained that 'the right to shelter even goes further than a roof over ones head. It extends to embody the individual's right to be let alone and to live in peace – whether under a roof or not'.[113] It pointed out that the 'particular violation by the Nigerian Government of the right to adequate housing as implicitly protected in the Charter' also encompassed the right to protection against forced evictions.[114] It noted that it drew inspiration from the definition of the term 'forced evictions' by the UN Committee on Economic Social and Cultural Rights.[115] The African Commission also referred to an earlier General Comment by the UN Committee, stating that 'all persons should possess a degree of security of tenure which guarantees legal protection against forced eviction, harassment and other threats'.[116] The African Commission concluded that the conduct of the Nigerian government clearly demonstrated a violation of this right enjoyed by the Ogonis 'as a collective right'.[117]

The European system takes a more individualistic approach, but has nevertheless dealt with the issue of forced eviction. It has mainly done so in the context of Article 8(1) ECHR, referring to respect for private and family life and home, and Article 1 of Protocol No. 1, stipulating the right to peaceful enjoyment of possessions. In various cases the ECtHR has found that security forces deliberately destroyed the homes and property of certain petitioners, depriving them of their livelihood and forcing them to leave their villages.[118]

While mass expulsion is always based on a specific decision by the State, a pattern of forced evictions may also be based on decisions by private parties against which the State fails to act. Whether the responsibility of the State (or entity) is based on an act or omission, the underlying cause is often racial or religious discrimination resulting in ethnic cleansing of (certain parts of) a State. This is obvious in the cases dealt with by the Bosnia Chamber under the Dayton Peace Accord. The Chamber refers extensively to the case law of the European Commission and Court regarding forced eviction. Yet the context of the Chamber's cases also indicates the rationale for its use of provisional measures. It has dealt with many cases brought by persons who had been forcibly evicted or had fled in light of the general situation of ethnic cleansing. They subsequently faced various obstacles in trying to re-obtain their property. In some cases the authorities had

---

provisional measures to the effect that the State should refrain from evicting them and their families from their land and homes or 'involuntarily resettling' then, were denied by the special Rapporteur, §1.2.

[112] ACHPR *The Social and Economic Rights Action Center and the Center for Economic and Social Rights* v. *Nigeria* (Ogoni case), 27 October 2001, §63.

[113] Id., §64.

[114] Id., §66.

[115] Ibid., referring to ESC-Committee General Comment 7 on the right to adequate housing: forced evictions (Article 11(1) ICESCR), 20 May 1997.

[116] ACHPR *The Social and Economic Rights Action Center and the Center for Economic and Social Rights* v. *Nigeria* (Ogoni case), 27 October 2001, §66, referring to ESC-Committee General Comment 4 on the right to adequate housing, 13 December 1991, §8(a).

[117] ACHPR *The Social and Economic Rights Action Center and the Center for Economic and Social Rights* v. *Nigeria* (Ogoni case), 27 October 2001, §66.

[118] See e.g. ECtHR *Akdivar et al.* v. *Turkey*, 16 September 1996, *Selçuk and Asker* v. *Turkey*, 24 April 1998, *Bilgin* v. *Turkey*, 16 November 2000 and *Dulaş* v. *Turkey*, 30 January 2001.

failed to enforce domestic court orders and had failed to protect against third parties.[119] In many cases the Chamber found that pre-war owners or occupants were still not enabled to return to their houses, constituting continuing violations of the right to their home and property.[120] In other cases the Chamber has pointed out that the 'threatened eviction of a person from their home constitutes an "interference by a public authority" with the exercise of the right to respect for the home'.[121] In such cases there appears to be a clear link between the substantive law on the merits and the provisional measures taken pending the proceedings.

The ECtHR itself has not used provisional measures to halt forced eviction. Yet its case law on the merits recognizes the serious nature of ethnic discrimination. In *Moldovan et al.* v. *Romania* (2005) the ECtHR found that 'police officers were involved in the organised action of burning the houses' of the petitioners (all Roma) and later 'tried to cover up the incident'. The petitioners, 'having been hounded from their village and homes' had to live 'and some of them still live, in crowded and improper conditions – cellars, hen-houses, stables, etc. – and frequently changed address, moving in with friends or family in extremely overcrowded conditions'.[122] While the incident itself took place before Romania became a Party, in light of 'the direct repercussions of the acts of State agents' on the petitioners the Court considered that the responsibility of the Government was engaged with regard to their subsequent living conditions.[123] There was no doubt in this case that these conditions fell within the scope of 'their right to respect for family and private life, as well as their homes', making Article 8 ECHR clearly applicable.[124]

Yet the Court did not 'just' find a violation of Article 8, but also of Article 3 ECHR. It noted that in previous cases it had deemed treatment to be 'degrading' within the meaning of Article 3 ECHR, because it was such as to arouse in the victims feelings of fear, anguish and inferiority capable of humiliating and debasing them.[125] In this respect it would examine whether the object of a particular form of treatment 'is to humiliate and debase the person concerned and whether, as far as the consequences are concerned, it adversely affected his or her personality'.[126] Nevertheless 'the absence of any such purpose cannot conclusively rule out a finding of a violation' of Article 3.[127] It considered that the petitioners' 'living conditions in the last ten years, in particular the severely overcrowded and unsanitary environment and its detrimental effect on the applicants' health and well-being, combined with the length of the period during which the applicants have had to live in such conditions and the general attitude of the authorities, must have caused them considerable mental suffering, thus diminishing their human dignity and arousing in

---

[119] See e.g. Bosnia Chamber *M.J.* v. *Srpska*, 7 November 1997.

[120] One category of cases was based on legislation on so-called 'abandoned property'. In various cases the Chamber found violations of the right to respect for the home and possessions, see further Neussl (1999).

[121] See e.g. Bosnia Chamber *Turčinović* v. *Fed. B&H*, 11 March 1998, §20 and *Nada Blagojević* v. *Srpska*, 11 June 1999, §49. Another category of cases in which the Chamber has also used provisional measures concerned the so-called 'JNA cases' involving a Decree annulling contracts in which persons had bought apartments from the Yugoslav National army (JNA). The Chamber found that the owners' right to their property had been violated, see e.g. *Medan et al.* v. *State and Fed. B&H*, 7 November 1997 and *Kalinčević* v. *B&H and Fed. B&H*, 11 March 1998 (provisional measures of 12 December 1996 and order on the merits not to evict the victim from the apartment).

[122] ECtHR *Moldovan et al.* v. *Romania*, 12 July 2005, §103.

[123] Id., §104.

[124] Id., §105.

[125] See e.g. ECtHR *Kudla* v. *Poland*, 26 October 2000 (Grand Chamber), §92.

[126] See e.g. ECtHR *Raninen* v. *Finland*, 16 December 1997, §55.

[127] ECtHR *Moldovan et al.* v. *Romania*, 12 July 2005, §101, referring to *Peers* v. *Greece*, 19 April 2001, §74.

them such feelings as to cause humiliation and debasement'.[128] It added that the remarks concerning the honesty and way of life of the petitioners, made by some public authorities, 'in the absence of any substantiation', appeared to be 'purely discriminatory'.[129]

The Court reiterated that discrimination based on race could 'of itself amount to degrading treatment within the meaning of Article 3 of the Convention'.[130] Such discriminatory remarks 'should therefore be taken into account as an aggravating factor in the examination' of the complaint under Article 3 ECHR.[131] In conclusion, the ECtHR found that the 'living conditions and the racial discrimination to which they have been publicly subjected by the way in which their grievances were dealt with by the various authorities' constituted 'an interference with their human dignity which, in the special circumstances of this case, amounted to "degrading treatment" within the meaning of Article 3 of the Convention'.[132]

Similarly, in certain circumstances the burning and destruction of houses itself constitutes acts of cruel, inhuman or degrading treatment or punishment. A few years before the ECtHR judgment in *Moldovan* (which for reasons of jurisdiction *ratione temporis* could only relate to the situation subsequent to the burning of houses), the UN Committee against Torture already pointed this out in *Hajrizi Dzemajl et al.* v. *Yugoslavia* (2002). This case was brought on behalf of 65 persons of Romani origin, nationals of Yugoslavia, who had been driven out of their homes while their property was completely destroyed. After the first weeks of hiding they have since continued to live 'in abject poverty, makeshift shelters or abandoned houses'.[133]

CAT added to its statement that the burning of their houses constituted acts of cruel treatment that the 'nature of these acts is further aggravated by the fact that some of the complainants were still hidden in the settlement when the houses were burnt and destroyed, the particular vulnerability of the alleged victims and the fact that the acts were committed with a significant level of racial motivation'. It also emphasized the positive obligations of the State, considering that the complainants had 'sufficiently demonstrated that the police (public officials), although they had been informed of the immediate risk that the complainants were facing and had been present at the scene of the events, did not take any appropriate steps in order to protect the complainants, thus implying "acquiescence" in the sense of article 16 of the Convention'.[134] It found that the State had failed to observe its obligations under this article 'by failing to enable the complainants to obtain redress and to provide them with fair and adequate compensation'.[135]

4   CONCLUSION

The practice of the Bosnia Chamber to halt forced eviction in certain cases is closely related to its function under the Dayton Peace Accord and must be explained in the context of the recent history of ethnic cleansing, along with religious and ethnic discrimination that had become endemic, as well as the particular hybrid nature of the Human Rights Chamber, both constitutional and

---

[128]   ECtHR *Moldovan et al.* v. *Romania*, 12 July 2005, §110.

[129]   Id., §111.

[130]   Id., §111, referring to EComHR *East African Asians* v. *UK*, 14 December 1973, p. 62. In fact in that case the European Commission noted that, depending on the circumstances, this might 'constitute a special affront to human dignity', §207. It found that the UK immigration legislation constituted an interference with the human dignity of the petitioners that, in the circumstances, amounted to 'degrading treatment' forbidden under Article 3 ECHR, §208.

[131]   ECtHR *Moldovan et al.* v. *Romania*, 12 July 2005, §111.

[132]   Id., §113.

[133]   CAT *Hajrizi Dzemajl et al.* v. *Yugoslavia*, 21 November 2002, §2.27.

[134]   Id., §9.2.

[135]   Id., §9.6.

international. At the same time, while the other adjudicators have not used provisional measures to halt forced eviction, their condemnation of the phenomenon of forced eviction on the merits to a great extent converges with the approach of the Chamber. It cannot be ruled out that other adjudicators, faced with a similar set of circumstances, will use provisional measures to halt forced eviction even if their nature is regional or international rather than 'hybrid'.

The extension, in the Inter-American system, of the use of provisional measures to situations of arbitrary expulsion may be based on an extensive interpretation of the requirements of protection of personal integrity or on an extension of the application of Article 63(2) ACHR preventing irreparable harm to other rights than the right to life and personal integrity. In both cases the extension, as the Court puts it, is a confirmation that in human rights law the concept of provisional measures is evolving from the traditional preventive function to a more encompassing protective function.[136] In the *Haitian* case groups of people found themselves in desperate situations without legal protection and separated from their families. In this light the urgent intervention could be seen as aiming at preventing irreparable harm to human dignity and – as such – bearing some relationship with the prohibition of cruel treatment in Article 5 ACHR.

The African Commission has made a link between the uncertain situations that have often resulted from arbitrary expulsion on the one hand and cruel treatment on the other. The Inter-American Commission and Court have considered that the inability to register children and the uncertainty resulting from it might constitute cruel treatment. Moreover, both in the European system and in the system developed under the ICAT discrimination can play a role in the determination that certain acts or omissions resulted in cruel treatment in violation of international obligations.

The findings on the merits by these adjudicators, which elucidate the fact that arbitrary or mass expulsion and forced eviction can result in particular harm to children and may constitute cruel treatment, might therefore help justify a movement of this type of provisional measures towards the common core.[137]

---

[136] See e.g. IACHR *Haitians and Dominicans of Haitian Origin in the Dominican Republic*, Order of 26 May 2001, 7th 'Considering' clause.

[137] See the Conclusion to Part II of this book.

CHAPTER XII
PROVISIONAL MEASURES IN OTHER SITUATIONS

1   INTRODUCTION

The previous chapters have discussed situations in which provisional measures have been used by more than one adjudicator. It appears that these situations mostly involve threats to rights that the various human rights adjudicators have considered particularly crucial for the protection of life and personal integrity.

The Conclusion to Part II will more closely discuss the common core of the concept of provisional measures as used by the human rights adjudicators and will argue that this common core involves the prevention of irreparable harm to *persons*.[1]

Yet the concept of provisional measures must be clarified also by examining its outer limits. In some situations provisional measures have been used in one system only. In addition there have been several situations in which petitioners requested provisional measures to no avail. Some of these cases may nevertheless belong to the common core, but most of them are more likely to help determine the outer limits of the concept. This chapter provides some examples of atypical provisional measures and of failed requests for provisional measures by petitioners.[2] It appears that most of these examples may be situated on a continuum between 'towards the common core' and 'towards the outer limits' (section 2), while some of the examples are clearly *beyond* the outer limits of the concept (section 3).

As noted in the Introduction to Part II, one of the assumptions underlying this book is that the use of provisional measures to prevent *reversible* harm is beyond the outer limits of the concept of provisional measures. On the other hand, their use to prevent harm that is not only irreversible, but also irreparable is more likely to fall within the common core of the concept. The 'in-between' cases involve irreversible harm to the claim or the procedure rather than to persons. When it concerns harm to the claim or the procedure, but not to life and physical integrity, the term *irreversible* harm is used.

2   TOWARDS THE COMMON CORE OR TOWARDS THE OUTER LIMITS?

2.1   Introduction

Most human rights adjudicators have used provisional measures at least in one or two atypical situations. These range from halting the destruction of a painting to safeguarding documentary evidence. Sometimes a broader interpretation is given to the right to life involving a dignified life in which the fundamental right to life also means the right not to be prevented from 'having ac-

---

[1]   As well as groups in some cases, see particularly Chapter X on indigenous peoples and the discussion in the Conclusion to Part II, section 2.3.

[2]   It must be born in mind, however, that most adjudicators do not systematically publish information on failed requests. Thus, while the examples discussed may help clarify the outer limits of the concept, they are not necessarily representative of the range of situations in which a petitioner's request has failed.

cess to the conditions that guarantee a dignified existence',[3] including the so-called 'project of life' of the beneficiaries.[4] Indeed it is assumed that cases affecting a person's life in such manner may be situated more closely towards the common core, even if most (or all) adjudicators may not yet be ready to order provisional measures in that specific situation. That fact, however, does indicate that there is insufficient evidence to consider these cases as already falling within the common core.

---

[3] IACHR *Villagrán Morales et al.* (*the 'Street Children Case'* v. *Guatemala*), Judgment of 19 November 1999, §144. See also IACHR Advisory Opinion 17 on the Juridical Condition and Human Rights of the Child, 28 August 2002, §§80 and 84 (referring to the obligations of the State to provide the necessary means for life to develop under decent conditions and stressing in this respect the importance of the right to education).

[4] This concept was referred to by the Commission as 'life plan' and by the Inter-American Court as 'project of life', or the first time in *Loayza Tamayo* (Peru), 27 November 1998 (Reparations). This Court discussed it as 'akin to the concept of personal fulfilment, which in turn is based on the options that an individual may have for leading his life and achieving the goal that he sets for himself', §148. See also IACHR *Villagrán Morales et al.* (*the 'Street Children Case'* v. *Guatemala*), Judgment of 19 November 1999, confirming that 'every child has the right to harbor a project of life that should be tended and encouraged by the public authorities so that it may develop this project for its personal benefit and that of the society to which it belongs', §191. The representatives of the victims' next of kin in the *Street Children* case had pointed out that the right to life in the ACHR has an autonomous value and the concept is 'superimposed on what the Commission calls the life plan', §85. The Commission had indicated that 'the five youths were deprived of the basic measures of safety and protection that the State should have provided to them as at-risk children, and also the opportunity to develop and live with dignity. Furthermore, the State did not respond to the systematic abuses perpetrated against them'. It considered that the 'elimination and reduction of the life plans of these youths has objectively restricted their freedom and constitutes the loss of a valuable possession', §86. Cynically, the State had proposed that 'the precarious situation of the victims makes it highly probable that they did not have a life plan to put into practice'. It requested the Court to reject the Commission's request to establish separate financial reparations for this concept. It accepted its responsibility in this case 'as regards to general failure to adopt effective policies to avoid having a street children problem' but pointed out that 'the victims' next of kin also bear responsibility in this respect, because they did not fulfil their basic functions', §87. In making its calculation for non-pecuniary damage, the Court noted, it had also 'borne in mind the overall adverse conditions of abandonment endured by the five street children, who were in a high-risk situation and without any protection as regards their future', §§88 and 90. In reference to the UN Convention on the Rights of the Child it established the content and scope of the 'measures of protection' mentioned in Art. 19 ACHR (rights of the child). It emphasised 'non-discrimination, special assistance for children deprived of their family environment, the guarantee of survival and development of the child, the right to an adequate standard of living, and the social rehabilitation of all children who are abandoned or exploited'. It was clear, the Court pointed out, that these rights had been violated by the acts perpetrated against the victims in this case, 'in which State agents were involved', §196. See further *Cantoral Benavides*, 3 December 2001 (Reparations): "The pain and suffering that those events inflicted upon him prevented the victim from fulfilling his vocation, aspirations and potential, particularly with regard to his preparation for his chosen career and his work as a professional. All this was highly detrimental to his 'life project'", §60. Cançado Trindade has invoked the notion also in the context of provisional measures: IACHR *Haitians and Dominicans of Haitian Origin in the Dominican Republic* (Dominican Republic), Order of 18 August 2000, Concurring Opinion Judge Cançado Trindade, §17. See further *infra* sections 2.5 (Preservation of IVF embryos) and 2.6 (Arbitrary detention) of this Chapter. See also Chapter VII (Detention), section 3 and Chapter XI (Mass expulsion), section 2 and the Conclusion to Part II, section 3.2.

Other atypical cases may not (directly) involve a person's basic existence and integrity, but may nevertheless make sense within a given human rights system. This may be the case given the specific function assigned to the adjudicator or the specific aim of the treaty supervised by it. After all provisional measures have also been used simply to prevent irreversible harm to the claim or procedure, albeit not irreparable harm to persons. Such measures fall within the outer limits, but not within the common core.

2.2 Providing assistance in life threatening situations or situations violating personal integrity

2.2.1 Introduction

The Inter-American Commission has regularly used precautionary measures to provide medical assistance against life threatening illness outside the context of detention, as well as in the context of the right to reparation for previous wrongs and to provide humanitarian support. At least on one occasion the European Commission on Human Rights used provisional measures in response to a situation in which a State had put a group of individuals into an adverse humanitarian situation involving lack of basic facilities.[5] The Bosnia Chamber has also done so at least once. Thus far, the HRC has not used provisional measures in medical assistance cases outside the detention context.[6] This section discusses the limited European and the more extensive Inter-American practice.

2.2.2 Practice of the European Commission on Human Rights

As noted, there is one example of a provisional measure by the European Commission on Human Rights in which it intervened on behalf of 53 persons who had been denied access to Spain and were staying on no-man's land in adverse conditions involving lack of water, medication, sanitary facilities. The Commission used provisional measures in July 1992, asking Spain to take measures preventing irreparable harm. Spain responded two days later informing the Commission that it had allowed several organisations to provide relief. Four days later it allowed the entrance of the beneficiaries for humanitarian reasons. While this was just a single case and it involved the impact of a refusal by the State to allow entrance, thus seeming to be linked to non-refoulement,[7]

---

[5] See also Chapter IX (Threats), section 2.2, referring to the ECtHR's provisional measures of 12 August 2008 vis-à-vis Russia and Georgia calling on 'both the High Contracting Parties concerned to comply with their engagements under the Convention, particularly in respect of Articles 2 and 3 of the Convention'. Georgia had requested the Court to order provisional measures to the effect that Russia should 'refrain from taking any measures which may threaten the life or state of health of the civilian population and to allow the Georgian emergency forces to carry out all necessary measures in order to provide assistance to the remaining injured civilian population and soldiers via humanitarian corridor'. Press release 581 of 12 August 2008.

[6] See HRC *W.* v. *New Zealand*, initial submission of 2 October 1997; transmission under Rule 91 on 15 October 1997. In this case the petitioner had requested the HRC to use provisional measures to request the State to make available kidney dialysis so as to prevent irreparable harm. The HRC did not do so and eventually the case was discontinued, at the 66th session (1999), after the petitioner died.

[7] See Chapter V (Non-refoulement).

at least it indicates that a former body of the European human rights system at one point saw fit to intervene in a situation involving dire social and economic conditions of life.[8]

2.2.3 Practice of the Bosnia Chamber

At least once the Bosnia Chamber has ordered provisional measures to protect the beneficiaries' health by improving the heating and sanitary conditions in a refugee camp. It also requested the addressee parties (the federal government and the constituent state of B&H) to consider urgently their transfer to 'more suitable premises'.[9] Subsequently the federal authorities transferred the refugees to newly built facilities.[10]

2.2.4 Practice of the Inter-American Commission to ensure HIV medication outside of the detention context

Between early 2000 and early 2004 the Inter-American Commission intervened several times (on at least twelve different occasions), requesting the State to ensure medication for persons carrying the HIV virus. Together this involved more than 190 beneficiaries. This section discusses the first of these cases.

In February 2000 the Inter-American Commission took the first such precautionary measure. It did so on behalf of 27 members of the Asociación Atlacatl carrying the AIDS virus. They had claimed that their rights to life and health were in great danger and that they needed to be able to access the medication necessary for treatment. More than four months previously the Commission had already requested information from El Salvador about the situation. Since then, ten members of the Association had died. In its precautionary measure the Commission requested El Salvador to provide the necessary treatment and anti-retroviral medication to prevent the deaths of the 27 persons, 'as well as the necessary hospital, pharmacological and nutritional care needed to strengthen their immune systems and prevent the development of infections'.[11]

The petitioners had alleged, among others, that El Salvador violated the right to life, health and well-being of the victims by not providing them with the medication they needed to prevent them from dying and to improve their quality of life. They attributed the situation of these 27 persons to negligence on the part of the State and maintained that this constituted cruel, inhuman and degrading treatment.[12]

---

[8] See EComHR *B. M. and 51 others* v. *Spain*, struck out 11 September 1992, following resolution of the case.

[9] Bosnia Chamber *Dyke Hasanaj et al.* (*11 adults and 27 children*) v. *B&H and Fed. B&H*, 16 April 1999, §4 (provisional measure of 4 December 1998).

[10] Id., §9.

[11] The request for precautionary measures was as follows: "[W]ithout prejudice to other actions that your Government deems necessary, the Commission holds the view that urgent measures should be adopted in order to provide the medical care capable of safe-guarding the life and health of Jorge Odir Miranda Cortéz and the other persons listed above. In particular, the IACHR asks that your Government provides the anti-retroviral treatment and medication necessary to avoid the death of the aforementioned persons, as well as the hospital, pharmacological, and nutritional care needed to strengthen their immune systems and to prevent the development of diseases and infections". CIDH *Jorge Odir Miranda Cortez et al.* v. *El Salvador*, 7 March 2001 (adm.). Precautionary measure of 29 February 2000 (See its footnote 2).

[12] CIDH *Jorge Odir Miranda Cortez et al.* v. *El Salvador*, 7 March 2001 (adm.), §24.

In January 2001 the petitioners maintained that El Salvador was refusing to purchase 'the triple therapy and other medications that prevent death and improve the quality of life of persons living with HIV/AIDS'.[13] They stated:

> "The right to life encompasses much more than not dying as a result of action or negligence attributable to the State, in accordance with the rules of international law. The right to life, in that broader sense, presupposes, *inter alia*, that a person lives under conditions that are conducive to his well being".[14]

In other words, they argued that the State had failed to guarantee the alleged victims 'the quality of life that allows them to achieve well being'.[15] According to the petitioners the State's negligent acts 'can also place or allow a group of persons to be placed in cruel, inhumane, or degrading conditions'.[16]

> "The State should conduct all acts and omissions [sic] that are necessary to improve health, leading to the highest level of physical, mental, and social well being through the use of modern advances and scientific medical discoveries. The Salvadoran State cannot therefore fail to purchase and administer anti-retroviral treatments to persons living with HIV/AIDS for budgetary reasons if it did not seek and implement, sometime earlier, reasonable financial adjustments to permit their purchase and administration".[17]

In March 2001, when the Commission adopted its admissibility report, three of the alleged victims mentioned in the petition had died. In its admissibility decision the Commission stated that it would determine during the merits phase whether the alleged facts, if found, violated Articles 2 (duty of implementation), 24 (equal protection of the law), 25 (judicial protection) and 26 (economic, social and cultural rights) ACHR. In its interpretation of these articles it would take into account the provisions related to health.[18] It also deferred to the merits stage of the case the discussion of admissibility of the claims with regard to the right to life and humane treatment. It believed that these claims were secondary in nature and contingent on the conclusions the Commission would reach on the merits of the other claims already declared admissible.[19]

Shortly after the Commission's admissibility decision the Supreme Court of El Salvador finally ordered the State to provide Odir Miranda with antiretroviral treatment. A UNAIDS report

---

13   Ibid.
14   Ibid.
15   Ibid.
16   Id., §25. Moreover, they alleged that the State had violated the victims' right to health in Article XI of the American Declaration and Article 10 of the Protocol of San Salvador as well as the social rights laid down in Article 26 of the American Convention. According to them, it is possible to infer an 'immediate legal obligation' from the aforementioned instruments.
17   Id., §26.
18   The Commission considered itself competent to examine the merits of the case. It did note, however, that it was not competent *ratione materiae* to determine, through the system of individual petitions, violations of Art. 10 (right to health) of the Protocol of San Salvador. Under this instrument the Commission may deal with individual complaints about violations of trade union rights (Article 8 (1) (a) and the right to education (Article 13) only. At the same time, it could of course 'consider this Protocol in the interpretation of other applicable provisions, in light of the provisions of Articles 26 and 29 of the American Convention'. CIDH *Jorge Odir Miranda Cortez et al.* v. *El Salvador*, 7 March 2001 (adm.), §36.
19   CIDH *Jorge Odir Miranda Cortez et al.* v. *El Salvador*, 7 March 2001 (adm.), §46.

considers that this decision was 'presumably prompted by the Inter-American Commission's criticism'.[20]

In a press release a Costa Rica based organisation supporting the petitioners noted that the Commission's precautionary measure could become a precedent for persons living with AIDS in other Latin American States.[21] Indeed, subsequently the Commission also resorted to precautionary measures in various similar cases.[22] One of them was on behalf of three persons with HIV/Aids in Chile. They had contacted the Commission because 'they believed their right to life and health was in serious danger'. In November 2001 the Commission informed Chile that these three persons 'urgently needed basic assistance from state institutions in order to secure the drugs needed for their treatment'. It requested Chile to 'ensure them access to the medicines needed for their survival and to medical examinations for the regular monitoring of their health conditions'. The State responded two weeks later describing the 'preliminary steps' taken at the Ministry of Health. It reported that the persons involved were receiving medication and undergoing examinations so that the State's services could monitor their health conditions.[23]

In another case the Commission used precautionary measures 'on behalf of the 39 persons named since they had not been dispensed appropriate medication by the Guatemalan public health system'.[24] It subsequently declared admissible the complaints based on Article 4 (right to life), and Article 25 ACHR (judicial protection).[25] Thus in this case it did not consider the right to life 'secondary in nature'.

2.2.5 Practice of the Inter-American Commission to call for the provision of humanitarian support

There are several, quite diverse, situations in which the Commission has intervened pending the proceedings because of the dire living conditions of the alleged victims.

---

[20] UNAIDS, Joint UN programme on HIV/AIDS, March 2006, p. 71.

[21] See Aguabuena Asociación de Derechos Humanos, 'La Comisión Interamericana De Derechos Humanos Ordena A El Salvador Que Suministre Medicamentos Contra El Hiv', 1 March 2000, <http://www.aguabuena.org/articulos/salvador.html> (consulted 15 June 2007).

[22] See e.g. CIDH Annual Report 2001, §12; Annual Report 2002, §§13, 42, 51, 53, 58, 64, 71, 74 and Annual Report 2003, §61, involving (apart from El Salvador), Chile, Bolivia, Colombia, Dominican Republic, Ecuador, Guatemala, Honduras, Mexico and Peru. See also CIDH *Luis Rolando Cuscul Pivaral and 38 others* (*persons living with HIV/AIDS*) v. *Guatemala*, 7 March 2005 (adm.) (petition and request for precautionary measures of 26 August 2003; request by Commission for additional information on some of the petitioners and their state of health of 3 October 2003; response of 9 October 2003 that given the petitioners' whereabouts they would need time to gather the information; the petitioners provided this information on 13 April 2004 ('except for certain tests like the determination of viral load which were deemed too expensive'); on 21 April 2004 the Commission formally forwarded the petition to the State and granted the precautionary measures on behalf of the 39 persons named 'since they had not been dispensed appropriate medication by the Guatemalan health system', §§5 and 7; apparently the Commission had previously used precautionary measures already on behalf of 12 of them, §1).

[23] CIDH Annual Report 2001, Chapter III (a), §12.

[24] The petitioners had requested precautionary measures on behalf of the presumed victims already in August 2003. 'Given the victims' whereabouts' (this explanation is not specified in the case report) it was difficult to gather the information on their state of health and the Commission only decided to grant precautionary measures in April 2004. CIDH *Luis Rolando Cuscul Pivaral et al.* v. *Guatemala*, 7 March 2005 (adm.), §7.

[25] CIDH *Luis Rolando Cuscul Pivaral et al.* v. *Guatemala*, 7 March 2005 (adm.).

In July 2001 the Commission granted precautionary measures on behalf of the survivors of the Aguas Blancas massacre in Mexico.[26] While the Commission sought protection against threats for one of them, for seven survivors 'who still bear physical and psychological scars from the massacre', it sought medical attention. Within two weeks Mexico 'reported on the measures adopted in compliance with the [Commission's] request, which included contacting each of the protected persons, providing access to health centers in the state of Guerrero, and holding meetings to resolve the problems that have been identified'.[27] Obviously this case bears a relation with the State's obligation to provide reparation for past violations as well.[28]

In March 2004 the Commission decided to take precautionary measures on behalf of 63 children and more than 50 adults in the so-called 'Bello diversion' situation in Colombia. The beneficiaries were victims of internal displacement within the city. They had been forcibly evicted 'under conditions that jeopardized their health and personal safety'.[29] The Commission requested Colombia to guarantee 'adequate accommodations and the necessary conditions for the subsistence' of the persons identified.[30] The State should also 'report on the actions adopted to clarify the abuse of force that may have been exercised against the beneficiaries'.[31] Almost half a year later the Commission decided to lift the measures, 'after receiving information provided by the parties on a series of agreements between the State, the beneficiaries and the petitioners'.[32]

That same year the Commission took precautionary measures to protect the life and personal safety of the members of the Community of San Mateo de Huanchor, comprising of more than 5,000 families. The Commission noted that the available information indicated that the 'deposits from an open-air mine in the vicinity of the Rimac River' would severely affect the 'living conditions, health, food, farming and livestock' of these indigenous campesino families. Environmental studies conducted by the Ministry of Health concluded 'that the cumulative power and

---

[26] In June 1995 17 men, members of a Campesinos organisation, had been executed extra judicially in the state of Guerrero, Mexico. See e.g. CIDH *Tomas Porfirio Rondin* v. *Mexico*, 18 February 1998.

[27] In September 2001 'the State reported that a meeting had taken place in Chilpancingo, Guerrero, between the victims and several state and federal officials. This meeting agreed on several issues relating to medical attention, the patients' traveling and accommodation expenses, specialized treatment, and drugs and medical equipment as indicated by their needs'. Annual Report 2001, §40.

[28] See also Chapter XIII (Protection).

[29] CIDH Annual Report 2004, §16.

[30] Ibid.

[31] Ibid.

[32] Ibid. In its Annual Report 2006 the Commission appears to discuss this case, even though it refers to its precautionary measures as adopted in October 2004, rather than 5 March 2004 (lifted on 25 August 2004). It mentions the housing plan formulated by the State, which had allowed the Commission to lift its precautionary measures 'on behalf of a number of families left homeless and displaced in the city of Medellin, who were forcibly evicted in spite of the existence of a judicial order that defined the specific, non-violent circumstances in which they could be moved from the so-called "Bello or river diversion"'. The Commission took new precautionary measures in a situation falling 'within the framework' of the previous because the aforementioned housing plan had apparently excluded nine of the families, 'because they had been displaced from within the city, and they therefore returned to the Bello or river diversion'. These nine families had been subjected to threats from groups of paramilitaries. Apart from adopting the necessary measures to protect the life and integrity of the leader of this community of nine families, as well as that of his wife and children, the state was also requested to 'provide information on the situation of the nine affected families who were beneficiaries of precautionary measure 784-04 *64 Children and 50 Adults in the Bello Diversion*', Annual Report 2006, §15 (precautionary measure on behalf of *Eduardo César Ariza Ulloque et al.* v. *Colombia* of 23 March 2006).

chronic effect of arsenic, lead, and cadmium in the deposits generated a high risk of exposure for the communities of the zone; that environmental pollution is affecting the health of the dwellers of the communities; and that children are suffering from very high levels of lead concentration in their blood'. The Commission did not specify how Peru should protect the life and personal safety of the beneficiaries, but it added that 'likewise' the State should 'implement a health assistance and care program for the population, particularly for children, to identify the persons who might have been affected by the consequences of the pollution and provide the relevant medical care; and to begin transferring the deposits in accordance with the best technical conditions as determined by the relevant environmental impact study'.[33]

In the context of murders, death threats, disappearances and stigmatization of 35 displaced families living in various districts of the city of Villavicencio (Colombia), the Commission not just requested Colombia to take the necessary measures to guarantee the life and physical integrity of the people involved, but added that persons with the status of internally displaced persons must be provided with 'the humanitarian assistance required, in the light of the Governing Principles of Internal Displacements and domestic law'. In this particular case it referred to information that the families were 'living in misery and/or marginal conditions and under the control of the same paramilitary-type structures that led to their displacement from the municipality of Castillo, on the border of the former zone of détente'.[34]

Thus the Commission's precautionary measures have sometimes aimed to provide urgent medical or other support and improvement of living conditions for victims of massacres, for victims of forced displacement (in reference to the Governing Principles) and for victims of environmental pollution. They often involve rights that are interrelated. A precautionary measure, for instance, may also have the composite purpose to protect against death threats and harassment, to ensure cultural survival *and*, as the Commission stressed in its precautionary measure on behalf of the Wiwa People (Colombia), 'to provide humanitarian assistance to the victims of the displacements and food crises, in particular the indigenous people's minor children'.[35]

2.2.6 Conclusion

The Inter-American Commission, as discussed above, makes a very interesting use of precautionary measures in these cases as they clearly deal with prevention of irreparable harm to persons, but in the context of positive obligations of the government outside the contexts of detention or

---

[33]   CIDH Annual Report 2004, §44. See also section 2.5 on protection against nuclear radiation; Chapter XIII (Protection) on the specificity of the provisional measures and the group of beneficiaries and Chapter XV (Immediacy and risk), including the reference to the use of environmental impact assessment.

[34]   CIDH Annual Report 2004, §21.

[35]   In this precautionary measure, taken on behalf of the members of the Wiwa People of the Sierra Nevada, Colombia was also asked 'to agree on collective protection measures, including the presence of a community defender, with the beneficiaries, through their representative organizations'. The Commission mentioned two specific organizations, Annual Report 2005, §14. See also the Commission's precautionary measures of 12 October 2004 on behalf of the Kelyenmagategma Indigenous Community of the Enxet People. They had been forcibly displaced from their ancestral land by individuals who destroyed their homes and working tools. The petitioners had alleged that they were now living in 'deplorable conditions' and that their personal safety was 'in imminent danger'. The Commission requested Paraguay not just to adopt the necessary measures to protect their lives and physical integrity, but also 'to provide humanitarian support to the displaced persons and guarantee their prompt return to their ancestral land'. Annual Report 2004, §41. See further Chapter X (Cultural rights) and Chapter XIII (Protection), section 4.4 (group of beneficiaries).

protection against death threats. While it may take considerable time before the other adjudicators follow suit in using provisional measures to improve social and economic conditions of life that are life threatening or amount to cruel treatment, for the Inter-American Commission the practice now seems firmly established.[36] This practice clearly is within the outer limits of the concept of provisional measures aiming to prevent irreversible harm to the claim. In addition, the harm in question constitutes irreparable harm to persons. Thus the Commission's practice is leaning closely towards the common core.

Moreover, on the *merits* other adjudicators have recognized the positive obligations of States in the context of basic rights such as the right to life and the prohibition of cruel treatment.[37] The African Charter on Human and Peoples' Rights, for instance, refers to economic, social and cultural rights as rights that may be legally enforceable. In a case against Zaire (Congo) the African Commission found that failure by a State to provide basic services such as safe drinking water, electricity and medication was a violation of the right to health in Article 16 ACHPR.[38] While the adjudicators may have qualms to intervene in such cases already pending the proceedings, for fear of entering into the policy choices of States, once several adjudicators have developed a practice first on the merits and subsequently pending the proceedings (for instance by just asking the State to take measures to prevent irreparable harm to persons, but leaving the State free in choosing the necessary measures), this type of provisional measure could be considered part of the common core not just theoretically, but in practice as well.

2.3 Protecting the physical or mental integrity of minors

2.3.1 Introduction

Outside of the context of detention, refoulement and mass expulsion adjudicators have also been faced with the urgent needs of children.[39] The European Court likely faces its share of child custody cases in which risk of harm to the child is at issue.[40] Yet this section discusses a few occasions in which provisional measures were used in the Inter-American system, involving children of disappeared parents and involving positive obligations to protect against child abuse and take remedial measures. It also refers to the practice of the HRC. After all, the latter has emphasized that the accessible and effective remedies required in Article 2(1) ICCPR 'should be appropriately adapted so as to take account of the special vulnerability of certain categories of persons, including in particular children'.[41]

---

[36] The Commission appears to take into account, implicitly the specific situation in countries such as Colombia, El Salvador, etc. when taking such precautionary measures.

[37] See e.g. IACHR *Yakye Axa Indigenous Community* v. *Paraguay*, Judgment of 17 June 2005. More generally on positive obligations see also e.g. Chapters VII (Detention) and IX (Threats).

[38] ACHPR *Free Legal Assistance group, and others* v. *Zaire* (1995), §47. For the African Commission's provisional measures in the context of culture and land rights, see the case of the Endorois referred to in Chapter X (Culture). More generally on basic social and economic rights see e.g. Coomans (2003).

[39] See the Chapters VII, V and XI respectively.

[40] See e.g. ECtHR *Williams* v. *Germany*, Judgment of 12 September 2002 (struck out) involving a refusal by the Court to take provisional measures to halt the return of a child to its father in the US, but with a priority decision under Rule 41.

[41] HRC General Comment on Article 2 ICCPR, §15.

2.3.2 Children of disappeared parents

On one occasion the Inter-American Court has used provisional measures in the context of identity, guardianship, visiting rights and access of grandmothers of the disappeared to their grandchildren.

In 1993 the President of the Court ordered Argentina to adopt, without delay, the necessary measures to protect the psychological well-being of two minors to avoid (any further) irreparable harm. This was a very difficult case relating to children of disappeared parents. They had been brought up by their kidnappers and initially were not aware that these were not their true parents. Of course, in such case the irreparable harm had already been done a long time ago but, at the same time, the harm was increasing each day the situation continued.[42] Yet there could be some such situations where the children involved may be harmed even more by having to move to their biological parents or grandparents. In this particular case, the full Court did not need to ratify the President's decision because Argentina had reported that the minors were brought in the custody of their biological family.[43]

One HRC case relates to the rights of a child of disappeared persons to act against visiting rights of a former caretaker who was complicit in covering up her parents' abduction.[44] In 1984 the petitioner found her granddaughter, who was then residing in the house of a nurse (S.S.) who claimed that she had taken care of the child since her birth. In January 1989 the petitioner received provisional guardianship of her granddaughter, but in September 1989 the nurse was granted visiting rights. The Supreme Court held that the petitioner had no standing in the proceedings about guardianship because only the parents and legal guardians have standing. By the end of September 1989 the petitioner requested the Court to order a discontinuance of the visits, basing herself on the psychiatric reports on the effects of the visits on her granddaughter. Her legal action in this respect was equally dismissed for lack of standing.[45] The unwanted visits were continuing in the Spring of 1991. Eventually the visiting rights were terminated in 1991, without intervention by the HRC. In 1995 the HRC found 'that the protection of children stipulated in article 24 of the

---

[42] As Buergenthal (1994), p. 79 notes, there is no doubt that the mental harm being caused here falls within the scope of Article 63(2) ACHR. "The more difficult issue, however, is whether, given all the time that has already elapsed, the Commission should not first have decided the claim and then referred the entire case to the Court instead of invoking the Article 63(2) procedure".

[43] See IACHR *Reggiardo Tolosa* (Argentina), Order of the President, 19 November 1993. Thus, the Court decided that there was no longer a need to order the provisional measures requested by the Commission, Order of 19 January 1994.

[44] HRC *Darwinia Rosa Mónaco de Galliccho and her granddaughter Ximena Vicario* v. *Argentina*, 3 April 1995. At the time of the submission the petitioner's granddaughter was 14 years old. In February 1977, when she was nine months old, she was taken with her mother to the headquarters of the federal police in Buenos Aires. The next day her father was arrested as well. Both her parents subsequently disappeared.

[45] She submitted that further appeals in civil proceedings would be unjustifiably prolonged to the extent that her granddaughter would likely reach the age of legal competence by the time of final decision. Her initial submission was on 2 April 1990. The Special Rapporteur transmitted the case to the State party on 24 August 1990, four months after the initial submission. In her later comments she pointed out that by the spring of 1991 the criminal proceedings about the disappearance had been pending at first instance for more than six years. The psychological state of her granddaughter had deteriorated 'to such an extent that, on an unspecified date, a judge denied S.S. the month of summer vacation with Ximena Vicario she had requested'. He did authorise her to spend a week with the petitioner's granddaughter in April 1991. The petitioner claimed that the civil proceedings would be unjustifiably prolonged.

Covenant required the State party to take affirmative action to grant Ms. Vicario prompt and effective relief from her predicament'.[46]

Generally speaking the HRC may not be in the most favourable position to assess the best interests of the child in this type of situation (simply because of the absence of hearings and the lack of geographical proximity), but in the face of convincing and consistent expert reports about the situation of a child, together with a declaration of intent (depending on age) of the child on the one hand and consistent actions or omissions by the State contrary to his or her interests on the other hand, the HRC might indeed consider using provisional measures to prevent irreparable harm in such cases.

Since the situation was ongoing, another question arises, namely at what point interference is necessary in order to prevent or put a stop to irreparable harm. Ongoing violations have a cumulative effect. At what point does this result in irreparable harm?[47] In light of the different developmental stages and special vulnerability it is clear that for a child action or omissions could have irreparable consequences much sooner than for an adult.[48] Article 24 ICCPR already acknowledges this by stipulating that every child shall have the right to 'such measures of protection as are required by his status as a minor on the part of his family, society and the State'. In its General Comment to this article the HRC points out that children must benefit from all rights in the Covenant, not only Article 24 and emphasises, in the context of cultural rights, that States should take every possible measure on behalf of children 'to foster the development of their personality'.[49]

---

[46] The HRC found that the initial denial of standing of her grandmother effectively left Ximena Vicario without adequate representation. This way she was deprived of the protection to which she was entitled as a minor, in violation of Article 24 ICCPR. The HRC pointed out that it was evident that the 'abduction of Ximena Vicario, the falsification of her birth certificate and her adoption by S.S. entailed numerous acts of arbitrary and unlawful interference with their privacy and family life' in violation of Articles 17, 23(1), 24(1) and (2) ICCPR. It noted, however, that these acts occurred prior to entry into force of the ICCPR and its OP in November 1986. It then proceeded to examine whether there existed continuing effects of those violations, which in themselves constituted violations of the ICCPR. The HRC observed that the various judicial proceedings extended for more than 10 years. In the meantime the granddaughter, who was 7 years old when found, turned 18 in 1994. Her legal identity as Ximena Vicario was officially recognised only in 1993, when she was 17 years old. "Bearing in mind the suffering already endured by Ms. Vicario, who lost both of her parents under tragic circumstances imputable to State party, the Committee finds that the special measures required under article 24, paragraph 1, of the Covenant were not expeditiously applied by Argentina, and that the failure to recognise the standing of Mrs. Monaco in the guardianship and visitation proceedings and the delay in legally establishing Ms. Vicario's real name and issuing identity papers also entailed the violation of article 24, paragraph 2, of the Covenant, which is designed to promote recognition of the child's legal personality".

[47] See also section 2.6 of this chapter and Chapter X (Culture), section 3.

[48] See e.g. Willems (1998).

[49] The ICCPR refers to the family, society and the State as the responsible parties guaranteeing children the necessary protection. "Although the Covenant does not indicate how such responsibility is to be apportioned, it is primarily incumbent on the family, which is interpreted broadly to include all persons composing it in the society of the State party concerned, and particularly on the parents, to create conditions to promote the harmonious development of the child's personality and his enjoyment of the rights recognised in the Covenant". Article 24(4) provides that every child has the right to be registered immediately after birth and to have a name. The HRC considers that this is closely linked to the right to special measures of protection and is designed to promote recognition of the child's legal personality. Its main purpose is to 'reduce the danger of abduction, sale of or traffic in children, or of other types of treatment that

As discussed, the Inter-American Court has once intervened urgently in a situation in which the child was in the custody of adoptive parents after her biological parents had been disappeared and in which her grandmother had been unable to establish guardianship.[50] This is an extremely painful situation and it is difficult to assess how the mental integrity of the children of disappeared parents is ensured best.

While it may indeed be possible to use provisional measures in such a case, it is vital in such circumstances to assess the wishes of the children involved, as a transfer of custody may in fact equally result in irreparable harm to children, if they consider their caretakers as their parents. Apart from the fact that these cases involve the rights of grandparents and other family to establish contact with their grandchildren, who grew up among strangers following the disappearance of their parents, they may also involve the rights of minors indicating a preference for not knowing about their real family, least of all being forced to live with them. In this respect the question whether the people who raised them have in fact been complicit in the disappearance of their parents, by act or omission, is a relevant consideration as well.

2.3.3 Children who have suffered abuse from their parents or caretakers

An interesting case unrelated to a past of disappearances, but more generally involving the positive obligations of the State to protect the physical and mental integrity of children against harm by third parties is that of a five-year-old child in Nicaragua on whose behalf the Inter-American Commission took precautionary measures in 2001. According to the complaint her father had raped her. The petitioners stated that her physical and mental integrity were at risk for the following reasons: her mother refused to believe her relatives' accusations about her husband, she had suspended the psychological treatment recommended by specialists and she had taken the child to prison to visit her father, 'thus causing her emotional problems'.[51] In September 2001 the Commission asked Nicaragua to adopt protective measures on her behalf.

In a different situation, but also involving the positive obligations of the State, in September 2003 the Commission granted precautionary measures on behalf of a seven-year-old to the effect that the State should adopt the necessary measures, 'including specialized medical treatment', in order to protect his 'physical, psychological, and moral health'.[52] In its Annual Report the Commission noted regarding these precautionary measures that the information available indicated that Michael Roberts[53] had been 'a victim of sexual abuse while at children's homes under the Department of Children and Family Services of Jamaica's Ministry of Health, and that even after the abuse was detected, he was the victim of omissions and negligence for lack of adequate treat-

---

are incompatible with the enjoyment of the rights provided for in the Covenant'. HRC General Comment no. 17 on Article 24, 5 April 1989.

[50] IACHR *Reggiardo Tolosa* (Argentina), Order of the President of 19 November 1993 and Order of the Court of 19 January 1994.

[51] CIDH Annual Report 2001, §47. In an interview by the author with the late Henry Schermers, member of the European Commission on Human Rights, the latter indicated that he would consider feasible the intervention of the Commission in ongoing child abuse cases, if the State concerned failed to take action to prevent further harm, interview of 3 March 1998 (on file with the author).

[52] Before taking precautionary measures the Commission first sought information from the State with regard to the situation of the child.

[53] For the purposes of the proceedings the child was referred to as 'Michael Roberts. The Commission noted that his real name would be kept under seal to protect his identity.

ment'.[54] The State responded to the measures with the statement 'that the beneficiary was receiving specialized medical treatment' and 'asked that the precautionary measures be lifted'.[55] In November of that year the Commission reaffirmed the precautionary measures 'and requested additional information on the medical condition of the beneficiary, and the treatment he was receiving'.[56]

Another form of abuse flows from illegal adoption procedures. The Commission also intervened in such a context, on behalf of 26 children in the process of being adopted. The Commission asked Guatemala to define the conditions and the place where the beneficiaries could be found, and to report on their legal and family status and on the measures it would be taking to protect them.[57]

2.3.4 Conclusion

In situations involving children, adjudicators might use provisional measures in contexts in which they would not on behalf of adults. This is because some situations are likely to impact on the development and thus the life and personal integrity of the child involved.[58]

Yet in the above case by the HRC relating to visiting rights no provisional measures had been taken. In this case the child involved had clearly indicated a wish to live with her real family and carry her real name. As confirmed by psychological reports, the continued encounters with her former caretaker had a negative impact on her.

What is clear in all cases involving minors is that for provisional measures truly to protect the beneficiary there should be sufficient evidence of the psychological impact on the child of continued encounters with certain caretakers or parental figures and, taking into account developmental stages, there should also be sufficient evidence of the will expressed by the child itself, e.g. in an interview with an independent psychologist.

2.4 Protection against nuclear radiation

The ICJ, but also the HRC and the European Commission on Human Rights have been faced with requests for provisional measures to halt nuclear tests. The ICJ dealt with the issue in the Nuclear Test cases (1973-1974).[59] It used provisional measures in June 1973, ordering France to avoid

---

[54] The Commission added that the 'diagnosis in the record' indicated that Michael Roberts 'suffers from post-traumatic stress disorder and that the absence of adequate medical treatment tends to give rise to behavior such as sexual aggression directed at other children'.

[55] CIDH Annual Report 2003, §55.

[56] Ibid.

[57] CIDH Annual Report 2007, 33 ("The persons requesting the measures allege that the adoption procedures are irregular, and that the children are being housed in private homes without judicial authorization and in violation of the law. It is also indicated that there is no information on the conditions in which the children were separated from their biological parents, and that adoption procedures are being carried out through civil-law notary proceedings without the supervision of the competent authorities").

[58] See e.g. Willems (1998).

[59] ICJ *Nuclear Test Cases* (*New Zealand* v. *France* and *Australia* v. *France*), Orders for provisional measures of 22 June 1973. In Judgments of 20 December 1974 the ICJ found that the applications by the two States, dating from 9 May 1973, no longer had any object. Their aim had been achieved in as much as France had announced its intention not to carry out further atmospheric nuclear tests now that it had completed the 1974 series. The ICJ considered that France was held to adhere to its unilateral declaration in good faith.

535

nuclear tests causing a radioactive fall-out on Australian or New Zealand territory. Nevertheless, France carried out a series of atmospheric nuclear tests in 1974.[60]

Different from the ICJ none of the human rights adjudicators has used provisional measures either to halt nuclear tests or to take positive measures to protect persons against nuclear radiation. Thus far petitioners have unsuccessfully requested the HRC and the European Commission to order provisional measures to halt nuclear tests. In *Bordes and Temeharo* v. *France* (1996) the petitioners were French citizens residing in Papeete, Tahiti, French Polynesia.[61] In June 1995 President Chirac announced the intent to conduct a series of underground nuclear tests in the South Pacific on the atolls of Mururoa and Fangataufa. The petitioners claimed that these tests would threaten their right to life (Article 6 ICCPR) and their right not to be subjected to arbitrary interference with their privacy and family life (Article 17 ICCPR).[62] They requested the HRC to use provisional measures. The HRC decided not to grant the protection requested. It may be concluded from the unusual fact that it mentions that it discussed the request for provisional measures during two consecutive sessions, that the refusal to order provisional measures had been a difficult decision.[63] Between 5 September 1995 and the beginning of 1996 the French authorities carried out six underground nuclear tests. In July 1996 the HRC declared the case inadmissible because the petitioners did not satisfy the victim requirement. The question arises whether the Committee's reason not to use provisional measures was the fact that it already anticipated this,[64] or was more generally based on its reluctance to get involved in such a highly politicised issue. It had previously noted, in a different case, that the individual complaint procedure was not meant for public policy discussions on issues such as nuclear weapons.[65]

In a case brought before the European Commission on Human Rights in order to prevent the same tests in the South Pacific, the Commission similarly denied the request for provisional measures and subsequently declared the case inadmissible (December 1995).[66] As noted, the tests had already taken place by that time.

The President of the Commission had rejected two consecutive requests for provisional measures to the effect that the State should be requested not to proceed with the renewed nuclear tests.[67] The subsequent request was rejected by the Commission as a whole, during its session in

---

[60]   See Chapter I.

[61]   HRC *Vaihere Bordes and John Temeharo* v. *France*, 22 July 1996. Initially Tauira also took part in the complaint, but later he withdrew his participation because of his involvement in a case pending before the European Commission on Human Rights, also discussed in this section.

[62]   See also Chapter XV (Immediacy and risk).

[63]   HRC *Vaihere Bordes and John Temeharo* v. *France*, 22 July 1996 (inadm.), § 1-2.3 (discussion on provisional measures during the 54th and the 55th sessions).

[64]   See Chapter XV (Immediacy and risk).

[65]   See e.g. HRC *E.W. and others* v. *the Netherlands*, 8 April 1993 (inadm.). It recalled its second General Comment on Article 6, in which it noted that 'the designing, testing, manufacture, possession and deployment of nuclear weapons are among the greatest threats to the right to life which confront mankind today', §6.2. At the same time it considered 'that the procedure laid down in the Optional Protocol was not designed for conducting public debate over matters of public policy, such as support for disarmament and issues concerning nuclear and other weapons of mass destruction'. It declared the case inadmissible as 'at the relevant period of time', the situation did not 'place the authors in the position to claim to be victims whose right to life was then violated or under imminent prospect of violation', §6.4.

[66]   EComHR *Tauira et al.* v. *France*, 4 December 1995 (inadm.).

[67]   Requests of 8 and 17 August, rejected by the President on 10 and 21 August, respectively, EComHR *Tauira et al.* v. *France*, 4 December 1995 (inadm.), under 'Procedure devant la Commission'.

September 1995. At that time it did decide to grant the case priority under Rule 33 of its Rules of Procedure.[68]

When it declared the case inadmissible it noted, among others, that simply invoking risks inherent in the use of nuclear energy, whether used for military or for civil purposes, was insufficient for making a showing that the petitioners would become victims of a violation of the Convention and thereby fulfilled the victim requirement. It pointed out that a great many human activities generated risk. The petitioners had failed to substantiate that the likelihood of risk of harm, despite the sufficient precautions ('précautions suffisantes') taken by the authorities, would be such as to constitute a violation of the Convention. Moreover, the Commission considered that the consequences of the action were too remote.[69]

In order to understand the Commission's decision not to use provisional measures pending the proceedings it may be useful to examine part of the State's arguments, which involved a reference to the concept of irreparable harm. It had argued, among others, that the decision to resume nuclear tests was not an act, like extradition or expulsion,[70] that would as such and necessarily result in a violation of the Convention. In fact, it argued, the implementation of the decision did not itself constitute a violation, but the violations lay only in the consequences that the petitioners attributed to it, namely a pollution of the environment harming the population. It also argued that the domestic remedies had not yet been exhausted as there would be several such remedies once actual damage were shown. The State then noted that the petitioners' argument that this would be too late was based on the mistaken idea that nuclear tests would necessarily result in irreparable harm ('un préjudice irréparable').[71]

The findings by the Commission itself indicate its difficulty in grappling with the scientific claims asserted by both parties. It pointed out that it was only exceptionally that the victim requirement was fulfilled when it concerned a future risk and that the petitioners had failed to provide sufficient evidence showing that this exception was applicable here. The Commission did not consider it opportune to decide on the scientific validity of the various expert reports, particularly

---

[68] Decision of 5 September 1995 on the renewed request by the petitioners of 31 August 1995, EComHR *Tauira et al.* v. *France*, 4 December 1995 (inadm.), under 'Procedure devant la Commission'.

[69] EComHR *Tauira et al.* v. *France*, 4 December 1995 (inadm.), §2 (¶29). The Commission considered that accidents could always happen, but the petitioners could not show that France had failed to take all necessary measures to prevent such an accident, (¶30). There was such controversy among scientists as to the question whether the tests would fracture the atolls, that the petitioners could not base themselves on this 'hypothetical fracturing' for the purpose of proving they met the victim requirement (¶31). It was not contested that in the past the atmospheric tests had resulted in radioactive contamination, but what was contested was the level of contamination and the consequences for the environment in general and for the health of the population in particular. In any case the Commission considered that the petitioners had furnished insufficient information on their work at Mururoa in the past, that could have exposed them to the radiation (¶32). Moreover, apart from the fact that the petition was directed against the June 1995 decision to resume the tests halted in 1992 and not at the previous period, the petitioners had failed to submit information on their state of health (¶33). Regarding the risk of contamination of the food chain, including the consumption of migratory fish (that would be contaminated at the sites, more than 1000 km from the residence of the petitioners), the Commission considered that the petitioners had provided insufficient evidence for it to conclude that they could be victims of a violation of the Convention, as the resumption of the tests would presently have repercussions that would be too remote for this resumption to be considered an act that would directly affect their personal situation (¶35).

[70] To a State where the petitioner would face a real risk of ill treatment.

[71] EComHR *Tauira et al.* v. *France*, 4 December 1995 (inadm.), §2 (¶4).

as the experts themselves expressed differing views. The Commission's decision does not refer to the precautionary principle and it would appear that the petitioners had not invoked it.[72]

In *Athanassoglou et al.* v. *Switzerland* (2000) the ECtHR (Grand Chamber) had decided, by sixteen votes with one abstention, not to take provisional measures to halt resumption of the operation of a nuclear power plant. It subsequently found on the merits that the rights claimed (Article 6 on the right to a fair trial and Article 13 ECHR on the right to an effective remedy) were not applicable. The petitioners had claimed that they had no access to court and no effective remedy under domestic law to enable them to complain of a violation of their right to life (Article 2) and of a violation of their right to respect for physical integrity. In the latter context they invoked Article 8 (privacy and family life). The Court found that the connection between the domestic procedure about the extension of the operation of the power plant 'and the domestic-law rights to protection of life, physical integrity and property' invoked by the petitioners 'was too tenuous and remote to attract the application of Article 6 § 1'.[73] Equally, the petitioners did not have an arguable claim of violations of Articles 2 and 8 in relation to the domestic law decision in question and, consequently, no entitlement to a remedy under Article 13.[74] The Court, and previously the Commission, did not directly examine Articles 2 and 8 ECHR. The request for provisional measures, on the other hand, clearly related to life and physical integrity rather than just access to court and the right to an effective remedy. An argument could be made that halting resumption of the operation of the nuclear power plant would be the only way to ensure the right to an effective remedy invoked in the petition. A domestic remedy that could not achieve the aim for which it was invoked could not be considered effective. Yet on the merits the majority of the Court considered that the petitioners resorted to a domestic remedy that was not sufficiently related to the right to life and respect for the home. The question arises to what extent this was or should have been clear already at the stage of provisional measures. After all, five members of the Court had considered that the petitioners' claims domestically had been arguable and that Arts 6 and 13 were indeed applicable.[75]

Exceptionally, the Judgment indicates that the decision not to take provisional measures was made 'by sixteen votes with one abstention'.[76] What it does not indicate is the reasoning for this decision. It is possible that some judges did not see a sufficient link with Article 2 because the

---

[72]   Id., §2 (¶11) indicates that the petitioners argued that they had had been refused access to information in light of military secrets and they had been refused access to medical dossiers. A reference was also made to the Rio Declaration, but apparently without specifically invoking the precautionary principle (¶14).

[73]   ECtHR *Athanassoglou et al.* v. *Switzerland*, 6 April 2000, §59.

[74]   Five members dissented. In passing they also said something about risk that may explain why the Grand Chamber had decided not to take provisional measures: "One might of course question whether it is impossible to establish that the danger exists to the requisite degree. For example, it is virtually impossible to prove imminent danger in the case of inherently dangerous installations: the catastrophes that have happened in a number of countries were obviously unforeseeable or, in any event, unforeseen". See ECtHR *Athanassoglou et al.* v. *Switzerland,* 6 April 2000, joint dissenting opinion Costa, Tulkens, Fischbach, Casadevall and Maruste.

[75]   ECtHR *Athanassoglou et al.* v. *Switzerland,* 6 April 2000, joint dissenting opinion Costa, Tulkens, Fischbach, Casadevall and Maruste. They considered that the 'nature of administrative decisions to grant or refuse applications for licences to operate nuclear power plants does not mean that they should be exempt from judicial review; on the contrary, the dangers presented to the environment and the population by such installations make it, if anything, more necessary for such decisions to be subject to review by an independent and impartial tribunal an adversarial proceedings aided, of course, by expert evidence'.

[76]   ECtHR *Athanassoglou et al.* v. *Switzerland,* 6 April 2000, §7. Moreover, usually it is the President rather than the full (Grand) Chamber who decides on the use of provisional measures, see Chapter II (Systems), but in this case it was the Grand Chamber.

petition was based on Articles 6 and 13 ECHR. It is also possible that they considered that if there were a link they would still not be able to prove 'a specific and imminent danger in their personal regard'.[77]

The HRC has also dealt with a case involving storage of radioactive waste near residential areas. The petitioner had requested the Committee 'to consider the matter and to urge the Canadian Government to remove all radioactive waste from Port Hope to a permanent, properly managed, dumpsite away from human habitation'.[78] The HRC transmitted the case to the State party more than three months later. It did not use (informal) provisional measures. Almost a year later it did request information from the State as to how the residents were assisted in the clearance process,[79] but upon receipt of the State's responses in this respect it declared the complaint inadmissible for non-exhaustion of domestic remedies.[80]

These cases indicate that, thus far, the human rights adjudicators have not used provisional measures to halt nuclear tests or to order a State to take positive measures to protect residents against nuclear radiation. This may be explained by the political sensitivity of the subject matter, the conviction that it is a policy issue and the related difficulty in fulfilling the 'victim requirement'. Conflicting scientific evidence in particular appears to be a serious stumbling block for

---

[77] ECtHR *Athanassoglou et al.* v. *Switzerland,* 6 April 2000, §52. After all, the Court eventually observed that the petitioners were rather alleging 'a general danger in relation to all nuclear power plants'. '(M)any of the grounds they relied on related to safety, environmental and technical features inherent in the use of nuclear energy', §52. Thus they were 'seeking to derive' from Art. 6(1) ECHR 'a remedy to contest the very principle of the use of nuclear energy', §53. The Court considered that 'how best to regulate the use of nuclear power is a policy decision for each Contracting State to take according to its democratic processes', §54. See also Chapter XII (Protection), discussing the beneficiaries of provisional measures. The dissenters considered that the fact 'that popular initiatives have enabled the public democratically to declare itself in favour of the State nuclear programme does not to our mind mean that a concrete judicial review would be devoid of purpose'. It is nevertheless possible that the dissenters did vote against the use of provisional measures, as did those in the majority, in order to avoid an *actio popularis*. Another explanation may be their doubts about the urgency and risk involved. See Chapter XV (Immediacy and Risk).

[78] HRC *E.H.P.* v. *Canada*, 27 October 1982 (inadm.), §2.

[79] Id., §6.

[80] Id. The petitioner had submitted the complaint in April 1980, on her own behalf and, 'as Chairman of the Port Hope Environmental Group, on behalf of present and future generations of Port Hope, Ontario, Canada, including 129 Port Hope residents who have specifically authorised the author to act on their behalf', §1.1. The HRC treated the petitioner's reference to 'future generations' as 'an expression of concern purporting to put into due perspective the importance of the matter raised in the communication', §8(a). Port Hope was a town of about 10,000 inhabitants. In 1975 large-scale pollution of their houses and other buildings was discovered. About 200,000 tons of radioactive waste remained in this town. During the cleaning process the waste was stored in eight 'temporary' disposal sites near or directly beside residences. One of them was approximately 100 yards from the public swimming pool. Some of these 'temporary' disposal sites were still in existence more than thirty years after they were licensed. Pending the case the HRC had asked the State party whether the federal government was in a position to assure the HRC that it would give the necessary assistance if the owners of the sites were otherwise unable to heed to an injunction to the effect that they should clear the sites. Canada responded that resolving the problem was 'a matter which necessarily involves delay due to certain practical and technical considerations', §7. If the petitioner was unwilling to accept such delay, 'inherent in resolving the problem, she could seek injunctive relief against the owners of the sites'. It also referred to other possibilities for domestic recourse. On the basis of the State's responses the HRC declared the case inadmissible for non-exhaustion of domestic remedies.

them to decide on a nexus between an act or omission and a risk to life.[81] Yet a precedent is already available in general international law in the form of the ICJ's provisional measures in the aforementioned case by Australia and New Zealand against France. Moreover, exposure to risk of nuclear radiation potentially concerns preventing irreparable harm to persons, involving their very survival, which conceptually would be situated more towards the common core than towards the outer limits of the concept. If a practice were to develop in which human rights adjudicators would regard the issue as one involving human rights and in which they would start to order provisional measures, the type of provisional measure involved would indeed fall within the common core.

2.5   Preservation of IVF embryos

There is one occasion on which one of the human rights adjudicators, the European Court of Human Rights, used provisional measures in order to prevent the destruction of several embryos created through the harvesting of eggs and their fertilization in vitro.

In February 2005 the ECtHR indicated to the UK that 'it was desirable, in the interests of the proper conduct of the proceedings that the Government take appropriate measures to ensure that the embryos were preserved until the Court had completed the examination of the case'.[82]

For medical reasons (the removal of ovaries because of tumours) the petitioner had been told to wait two years before attempting to implant any of the embryos in her uterus. Meanwhile the relationship with her partner, with whom she had created the embryos, had broken down and her former partner informed the clinic involved of his wish for the embryos to be destroyed. The petitioner argued that the particular domestic legislation invoked by her ex partner prevented her 'from using the embryos she and J had created together, and thus, given her particular circumstances, from ever having a child to whom she is genetically related'.[83]

While it was at first the President of the Chamber instituted to deal with the case that had ordered the provisional measures (and decided that the case should be given priority treatment), four months later the full Chamber confirmed these measures.[84]

On the merits the Court held that there had been no violation of Article 2 (life), Article 8 (respect for private life)[85] and Article 14 (non-discrimination) in conjunction with Article 8 ECHR. Yet it decided to maintain its provisional measures until such time as the judgment would become final, or until further order.[86] Indeed, the petitioner requested referral of the case to the Grand Chamber. A panel of the Grand Chamber granted this request in July 2006 and on that day the President of the Court decided to prolong the provisional measures.[87] On the merits the Grand Chamber's decision was similar to the above decision by the Chamber.[88] This meant that eventually the petitioner was unable to prevent destruction of the embryos.

This was the first time that the ECtHR, or any human rights adjudicator, dealt with a case such as this and given the irreversible nature of the destruction of the embryos the use of provisional measures was within the outer limits of the concept.

---

[81]   See further Chapter I (ICJ), section 5.3.3 and Chapter XV (Immediacy and risk).

[82]   ECtHR *Evans* v. *UK*, 7 March 2006, §3. See also ECtHR (Grand Chamber) *Evans* v. *UK*, 10 April 2007, §5.

[83]   ECtHR (Grand Chamber) *Evans* v. *UK*, 10 April 2007, §72.

[84]   ECtHR *Evans* v. *UK*, 7 March 2006, §4.

[85]   See dissenting opinion of judges Traja and Mijović.

[86]   ECtHR *Evans* v. *UK*, 7 March 2006, §77, fifth declaratory clause.

[87]   ECtHR (Grand Chamber) *Evans* v. *UK,* 10 April 2007, §7.

[88]   See also the joint dissenting opinion of Judges Túrmen, Tsatsa-Nikolovska, Spielman and Ziemele.

Moreover, given that the private life argument may make feasible an argument based on personal integrity and the so-called 'project of life',[89] as to underlying rationale this case may be situated more closely towards the common core of the concept than towards the outer limits. Yet there is no practice by the other adjudicators and given the judgment on the merits it is unlikely that the ECtHR will deal with a similar case in the near future. In addition, in this case the 'project of life' argument would apply in some measure to the petitioner's partner as well,[90] indeed making it a situation that may at present be more appropriately dealt with by each European State individually, as the Court considered with its reference to the margin of appreciation.[91]

2.6   Releasing from (prolonged) arbitrary detention

2.6.1   Introduction

There are a few cases in which international adjudicators have dealt with requests by petitioners for provisional measures aimed at someone's release from arbitrary detention or at preventing an arbitrary detention altogether. In yet fewer cases adjudicators have actually ordered such measures.

As discussed in Chapter I, in the *Hostages* case the ICJ had ordered provisional measures to the effect that Iran should make sure that the persons taken hostage in the US Consulate in Tehran would be released. While its findings on the merits were based on the law of diplomatic and consular relations and specifically concerned the detention of internationally protected persons the ICJ noted more generally:

> "Wrongfully to deprive human beings of their freedom and to subject them to physical restraint in conditions of hardship is in itself manifestly incompatible with the principles of the Charter of the United Nations, as well as with the fundamental principles enunciated in the Universal Declaration of Human Rights".[92]

The importance attached by the international community to protection against arbitrary detention is apparent from the institution in 1991 of the UN Working Group on Arbitrary Detention, which constituted the fourth UN thematic mechanism.[93] This Working Group has developed a practice

---

[89]   On the concept of 'project of life' see section 2.1 of this Chapter and references therein.

[90]   His life plan might have been affected by becoming a father, even uninvolved, of a child with whose mother he no longer is in a relationship. Yet this would appear to impact his project of life to a lesser extent, taking into account the impact on him of becoming an (uninvolved) father of a child to which he was genetically related, on the one hand, at this point in his life, and the impact of destroying the embryos on her project of life, on the other hand, given that this was her only chance of becoming a parent of a child to which she was genetically related.

[91]   Yet see the criticisms against this approach, e.g. Forder/Wittingham (2006), pp. 863-880; Brems (2006), pp. 428-442 and Bomhoff/Zucca (2006), pp. 431-440 commenting the judgment of 7 March 2006.

[92]   ICJ *US Diplomatic and Consular Staff in Tehran* (*US* v. *Iran*) (*Hostages* case), Judgment of 24 May 1980, §91. See further Chapter I, section 3.3.3.

[93]   Following the Working Group on Disappearances and the two Special Rapporteurs, one against torture and inhuman treatment and the other against summary and arbitrary executions. In addition, the Restatement (Third) of the Foreign Relations Law of the United States, §702, dating from 1985, mentions the prohibition of prolonged arbitrary detention as a peremptory rule of international law.

of resorting to an urgent action procedure, which it has referred to as necessarily exceptional in principle and summary in method.[94]

As noted, some human rights adjudicators have used provisional measures because of the alleged arbitrary nature of a detention as well. These measures could aim either at the prevention of detention in the first place, or at the release of detainees pending the proceedings. If the beneficiaries of these provisional measures are facing a clear threat to their lives or personal integrity the measures clearly belong to the common core.[95] If the situations in which these provisional measures are used do not involve direct threats of ill-treatment and direct risks to life the question arises whether they belong to the common core of the concept of provisional measures or even whether they belong within the outer limits.

2.6.2 Practice in the Inter-American system

The Inter-American Commission has used precautionary measures several times in order to intervene in a situation of arbitrary detention. The Inter-American Court may have done so once, although it continued to stress the life and safety of the beneficiary rather than his release. In general the Court has not been keen on using provisional measures in this context.

In January 1993 it explicitly refused a request for provisional measures. This was in response to a request by the Inter-American Commission on behalf of Carlos Chipoco, a 'human rights activist' who had 'taken part in the *Neira Alegría et al.* and in the *Cayara* case'.[96] The Commission argued that should he return to Peru and be arrested he could face a prison sentence of more than 20 years, lose his nationality and be held in the same detention place as the 'leaders and activists of the terrorist groups whose acts he has publicly condemned, which would constitute a grave threat to his right to life and integrity of the person which are recognized by the Convention'. It considered that the Peruvian Government wanted to 'punish, penalize and intimidate those who utilize international procedures and courts for the protection of human rights'.[97] The

---

[94]   It was in 1993 that it decided on 'Criteria to resort to the "urgent action" procedure'. It considered that apart from its normal reason for using this procedure, namely 'where there are sufficiently reliable allegations that a person is being detained arbitrarily and that the continuation of the detention constitutes a serious danger to the person's health or even life', it could *also* use this procedure 'where the detention may not constitute a danger to the person's health or life, but where the particular circumstances of the situation warrant urgent action'. It noted that in this case the Chairman must secure the agreement of two other members of the Working Group. See UN Working Group on Arbitrary Detention Deliberation 03 under D. Its Revised Methods of work, which are reproduced in Fact Sheet No. 26 on the Working Group on Arbitrary Detention, Annex IV (undated), discuss the Urgent Action Procedure in §IV: "A procedure known as "urgent action" may be resorted to in the following cases: (a) In cases in which there are sufficiently reliable allegations that a person is being arbitrarily deprived of his liberty and that the continuation of such deprivation constitutes a serious threat to that person's health or even to his life; (b) In cases in which, even if no such threat is alleged to exist, there are particular circumstances that warrant an urgent action. (c) The Chairman, or in his absence the Vice Chairman, shall transmit the appeal by the most rapid means to the Minister for Foreign Affairs of the country concerned". See E/CN.4/1993/24, 12 January 1993.

[95]   See also Chapter VII (Health in detention).

[96]   IACHR *Chipoco* case, President's Order denying provisional measures of 14 December 1992, 4th 'Having seen' clause.

[97]   Id., 6th 'Having seen' clause. Peru had filed criminal charges against him and other Peruvians residing abroad 'for allegedly committing the crime of justification of terrorism against the state', 3rd 'Having seen' clause. Among others he was charged with activities in the US 'in support of subversion' such as 'maintaining contacts with human rights organizations, with false information, in which they denigrate the Armed Forces and the Police and other State institutions

Commission, which had yet to decide on the merits in this case, requested the Court's provisional measures.[98]

What made the situation urgent, according to the Commission, was the need to avoid that an he would be indicted 'without an exhaustive investigation and without having afforded the accused or his representatives an opportunity to prepare his defense'.[99] This, in the argument of the Commission, would violate the right to a fair trial (Article 8 ACHR) and also constitute a violation of the right to humane treatment (Article 5), freedom of thought and expression (Article 13) and the general obligation to respect rights (Article 1(1), as well as the possibility to resort to the Commission and Court.[100]

The Court decided it was 'inappropriate at this time' for it to order provisional measures.[101] It considered that the case concerned 'a matter which is not presently before the Court, but rather before the Commission, and the latter has not submitted information to the Court sufficient to support the adoption of such measures, which requires the Commission to have gathered preliminary evidence to support a presumption of the truth of the allegations and of a situation whose grave seriousness and urgency could cause irreparable harm to persons.[102] In other words, before ordering provisional measures, or apparently even before holding a hearing on the request for provisional measures, the Court required more evidence both on the facts alleged and on the possibility that the situation could cause irreparable harm to persons.[103]

Juan Mendez, who at the time was litigating this case as an attorney at Human Rights Watch,[104] mentions that the petitioners had alleged that Chipoco's liberty was at stake, not his life or physical integrity.[105] This, together with the fact that Mr. Chipoco was still present in the US, may also help explain the Court's refusal to order provisional measures.[106]

A few years later the Court dealt with another request by the Commission involving arbitrary detention. In 1996 the President of the Court did take urgent measures to the effect that Ecuador was to adopt forthwith the measures necessary 'to effectively ensure the physical and

---

related to the struggle against subversion', see 3rd 'Having seen' clause. The Commission's request added that he had condemned the terrorist acts carried out by the Shining Path and MRTA and 'has been critical of the acts of rebels as well as those of the Peruvian Government'. Id., 4th 'Having seen' clause.

[98] See Article 63(2) ACHR, last sentence. See further Chapter II (Systems). The request was to the effect that Peru would 'establish as soon as possible the veracity of the allegations' and if they 'are found to be true, that it carry out an exhaustive investigation, specify the acts on which the charge of justification of terrorism is based, and disclose the evidence against Mr. Chipoco, prior to taking any penal actions against him'. Moreover, at all stages of the proceedings Peru was to guarantee him 'the full exercise of his human rights and, in particular, the right to due process and personal security, should he be deprived of his personal liberty, and taking into account the danger to which he would be exposed wherever he might be held'. Finally, Peru should 'guarantee the right to recur to the American system for the protection of human rights', see IACHR *Chipoco* case, President's Order denying provisional measures of 14 December 1992, 1st 'Having seen' clause.

[99] IACHR *Chipoco* case Order of 27 January 1993 denying provisional measures, 4th 'Considering' clause.

[100] IACHR *Chipoco* case, Order denying provisional measures of 14 December 1992, 7th 'Having seen' clause

[101] IACHR *Chipoco* case Order of 27 January 1993 denying provisional measures, 1st 'Resolving' clause.

[102] Id., 2nd 'Whereas' clause.

[103] On evidentiary issues see also Chapter XV.

[104] Subsequently he became a member of the Inter-American Commission.

[105] Interview of author with Juan Mendez, Washington DC, 17 October 2001.

[106] Id.

moral integrity of Mr. Rafael Iván Suárez-Rosero, so that any provisional measures that the Inter-American Court may take can have the requisite effect'.[107] Yet he did not heed to the Commission's request to seek from Ecuador such provisional measures as were 'necessary to ensure that Mr. Iván Suárez-Rosero is immediately released pending continuation of the procedures'.[108] The Commission had stated that his situation was 'extremely grave, inasmuch as it may cause him irreparable damage' as he had been 'held in preventive detention for a longer period than he would have served had he been tried and convicted'.[109] The President decided not to take these urgent measures, which, he noted, implied 'anticipation of certain effects that would be produced by the judgment on the merits which this Court may deliver'.[110] He observed that the Commission had found on the merits that the imprisonment of the alleged victim was contrary to the ACHR In that sense the measures requested were 'precautionary measures described in legal writings as partially restitutive or anticipatory and which the court cannot prescribe without first hearing the adversary, in this case the Government of Ecuador'.[111] One requisite for provisional measures was 'a preliminary analysis of the situation that necessitates the order for provisional measures'.[112] The President pointed out that he was only authorized to order urgent measures. It was 'for the Court at its next session to decide on the appropriateness of the anticipatory provisional measures sought by the Commission, which can only be granted after the Government concerned has been heard'.[113] This means he did not rule out 'anticipatory provisional measures' as such, but just his *own* authority to order urgent measures to this effect.[114] The Court itself did not deal with this issue. It observed that the reasons for the President to order urgent measures had ceased to exist with the release of the beneficiary and the fact that the Commission had noted that 'there was currently no risk to the safety of Mr. Suárez-Rosero and his family'.[115]

In the case of *Cesti-Hurtado* the Inter-American Commission did take precautionary measures, but the Inter-American Court refused to order provisional measures. In February 1997 Mr. Cesti-Hurtado was detained in the Simón Bolívar barracks in Peru. He was tried by military courts despite an order by a domestic court for his release issued in a habeas corpus ruling. In April the Inter-American Commission on Human Rights took precautionary measures and requested Peru to report within 30 days 'on whether it had completely complied with the order of habeas corpus [and] which measures [would be] adopted'.[116] "Furthermore, it requested the State to submit information on the medical attention that Gustavo Adolfo Cesti Hurtado had received.[117] In May Peru responded by arguing that its military courts had jurisdiction and that the seven year sentence imposed on Mr Cesti-Hurtado was justified. Subsequently the Commission requested the Court to order Peru to comply with the domestic habeas corpus ruling.

---

[107] IACHR *Suárez-Rosero* (Ecuador), Order of 12 April 1996 (President). Later that same month the President expanded the urgent measures to include the family members of the detainee, Order of 24 April 1996 (President).

[108] IACHR *Suárez-Rosero* (Ecuador), Order of 12 April 1996 (President), 4th 'Considering' clause.

[109] Ibid.

[110] IACHR *Suárez-Rosero* (Ecuador), Order of 12 April 1996 (President), 6th 'Considering' clause.

[111] Ibid.

[112] Ibid.

[113] IACHR *Suárez-Rosero* (Ecuador), Order of 12 April 1996 (President), 8th 'Considering' clause.

[114] See also Chapter II (Systems), section 4.3 on the urgent measures by the President before the Court has convened to decide on provisional measures.

[115] IACHR *Suárez-Rosero* (Ecuador), Order of 28 June 1996, 2nd and 3rd 'Considering' clause.

[116] CIDH *Cesti Hurtado* (Peru) precautionary measures of 25 April 1997, referred to in IACHR Order of 29 July 1997, 'Having Seen' clause 2(i).

[117] CIDH *Cesti Hurtado* (Peru) precautionary measure of 25 April 1997, referred to in IACHR Judgment of 29 September 1999, §7.

As the Court was not sitting at the time, the President had to provide an initial response. He did not grant this specific request by the Commission but instead took urgent measures *proprio motu* with the aim to protect his health.[118] The Court confirmed this by ordering provisional measures *proprio motu* in order to protect his health.[119] It equally noted that 'the facts and circumstances raised by the Commission' implied that there was a 'direct link' between the Commission's request for his release, in compliance with the order of habeas corpus issued by the domestic court and the very merits of the case placed before the Inter-American Commission. This matter was 'for the Commission to decide at this stage' and '(t)o accept the request of the Commission would mean that the Court could advance criteria on the merits of a case which is not before it yet'.[120]

Eventually this case was completed by the Commission and brought before the Court. Referring, among others, to the refusal of the military authorities to obey and execute the legitimate order of domestic court, the Inter-American Court determined that his right to personal liberty had indeed been violated.[121] Several years later the President of the Inter-American Court again denied a request by the representative of the victim for provisional measures on his behalf.[122] He noted that at the stage of provisional measures the merits should not be examined unless strictly related to the extreme gravity, urgency and the need to prevent irreparable harm to persons.[123] He noted that it was not the type of situation that would warrant provisional measures. Instead it related to the supervision of compliance with the Court's judgment in this case.[124] Indeed the Court subsequently did deal with this issue in an order on the State's non-compliance.[125]

The above cases indicate that the Inter-American Commission has taken a more liberal approach to the use of provisional measures in these circumstances than the Inter-American Court.[126] It was in the case of General Gallardo that the Court was persuaded to intervene pending the procedure to order a halt to a prolonged arbitrary detention. In November 2001 the Commission had already taken precautionary measures in this case.[127] General Gallardo, who had criti-

---

[118]   IACHR *Cesti Hurtado* (Peru), Order of the President of 29 July 1997, 5th and 6th 'Considering' clauses.

[119]   See further Chapter VII (Detention).

[120]   IACHR *Cesti Hurtado* (Peru), Order of 11 September 1997, 5th 'Considering' clause.

[121]   IACHR *Cesti Hurtado* (Peru), Judgment on the merits of 29 September 1999. See further the judgment on reparations of 31 May 2001 and on the request for interpretation of 27 November 2001 (regarding the indemnities due to Mr Cesti)

[122]   IACHR *Cesti Hurtado* v. *Peru*, Order of the President of 21 December 2005 (denying provisional measures).

[123]   IACHR *Cesti Hurtado* v. *Peru*, Order of the President of 21 December 2005, 5th 'Considering' clause. See also *Jorge Castañeda Gutman,* Order of 25 November 2005, 8th 'Considering' clause and *James and Others (Trinidad and Tobago),* Order of 29 August 1998, 6th 'Considering' clause.

[124]   ACHR *Cesti Hurtado* v. *Peru*, Order of the President of 21 December 2005, 6th 'Considering' clause.

[125]   ACHR *Cesti Hurtado* v. *Peru*, Resolution of 22 September 2006.

[126]   This does not mean that it always uses precautionary measures. See e.g. IACHR *Figueredo Planchart* v. *Venezuela*, 13 April 2000. The petitioner had requested the Commission to order precautionary measures to the effect that the execution of his arrest warrant should be suspended so as to avert irreparable injury to his 'physical and moral integrity' and to allow him to 'come forward at liberty, subject to due assurances and guarantees, to exercise his right of defense in the proceedings against him', §24. At the same time he also requested the Commission to appeal to the Court for provisional measures, §25-27.

[127]   CIDH *Gallardo* v. *Mexico*, precautionary measures of 2 November 2001, Annual Report 2001, §43. The substance of the precautionary measures was as follows: 'measures to protect Gen.

cised corruption and human rights violations by the Mexican Army, remained in prison in spite of the Commission's specific recommendations in its decision on the merits with regard to his case, determining violations of the ACHR.[128] In its Annual Report the Commission subsequently noted that the gravity and urgency of this case arose from the ongoing violations faced by General Gallardo in jail: 'the harassment he receives from the prison authorities and a series of threats and incidents involving him and his family that have never been fully cleared up'.[129] The State did not respect the Commission's precautionary measures and the Commission requested the Court to order provisional measures. As noted, this time, and different from the previous cases, the President of the Inter-American Court indeed decided to take urgent measures, in anticipation of the Court's provisional measures.[130] The Commission had requested these measures to avoid irreparable damage to the life, and the physical, psychological and moral well-being' of the General 'and also to his freedom of expression related to his life'. The provisional measures were also requested to prevent irreparable harm to the psychological and moral well-being of his wife and children. Regarding his eight year old daughter the Commission requested the Court to adopt 'special protection measures to safeguard her safety'. In other words, it argued that Gallardo's continued detention was also harming his family. Moreover, it is clear from the reference to harm 'to his freedom of expression related to his life' that the freedom of expression was an important incentive for the Commission's decision to request provisional measures. This is underlined by its statement that another purpose of the measures is to 'avoid irreparable damage to the right of Mexican society as a whole to receive information freely'.[131] Two days later the President of the Court, 'after having consulted all the judges of the Inter-American Court', decided to order urgent measures calling on the State to adopt without delay all necessary measures to protect Gallardo's life and safety.[132]

While the text of the urgent measures is conventional in referring to life and safety, the decision to order them appears to be based on the fact that his detention was illegal and part of a continuing pattern of harassment. In its submission the Commission had argued that he was 'submitted to numerous acts of harassment, because the prison authorities denied him the right to receive visits on several occasions, in an apparently arbitrary manner, and he had been subjected to sudden transfers without any explanation'. His right to life was threatened by his 'de facto detention'. This continued detention 'did not permit safeguarding his life and physical well-being, or that of the members of his family'. "In these conditions, the liberation of general Gallardo is a

---

Gallardo's life, person, and liberty, along with guarantees to enable his family and representatives to visit the facility where he is being held'.

[128] CIDH *Gallardo Rodríguez* v. *Mexico*, 15 October 1996, in which it found that 'through the detention and continuous submission of General José Francisco Gallardo to 16 preliminary inquiries and 8 criminal cases without a reasonable and justifiable purpose, the Government of Mexico has failed to discharge its obligation to respect and guarantee the rights to personal integrity, legal guarantees, honor and dignity, and legal protection of Brigadier General José Francisco Gallardo Rodríguez, according to articles 5, 7, 8, 11 and 25 of the American Convention, for the repeated acts that have taken place in Mexico since 1988', §115. Among others, he 'should be set at liberty immediately', §116.

[129] CIDH *Gallardo* v. *Mexico*, precautionary measures of 2 November 2001, Annual Report 2001, §43. See also, e.g., Amnesty International, Silencing dissent, An update on General Gallardo, 9 November 2001, AI Index: AMR 41/037/2001.

[130] See Chapter II, section 4.3 on the urgent measures by the President before the Court has convened to decide on provisional measures.

[131] IACHR *Gallardo Rodríguez* v. *Mexico*, Order of 18 February 2002, 1st 'Having seen' clause. See also Order of 23 January 2002.

[132] IACHR *Gallardo Rodríguez* v. *Mexico*, Order of the President of 20 December 2001, 1st 'Resuelve' clause.

sine qua non condition to avoid the occurrence of the irreparable damage that threatens them". With regard to the claim that the 'de facto detention' also 'generated irreparable damage to his freedom of expression in relation to his life' the Commission had noted that it 'prevented him from fully expounding his version of the campaign of harassment to which he has been subjected and freely expressing his opinions about the acts which he considers constitute an abuse of authority within the Mexican army'.[133]

Thus, the facts of the case indicate a concern regarding the effects of continued arbitrary detention on the detainee, his family and the freedom of expression at large, rather than indications of immediate health problems or death threats that would traditionally warrant the use of provisional measures.[134] This is also born out by the witnesses proposed by the Commission, whom the Court planned to hear at a public hearing on 19 January 2002. Two of the witnesses were well-known authors planning to make a statement on the right of both General Gallardo and 'the population of Mexico' to 'seek, receive and disseminate information and opinions about the case'.[135] Indeed, the State understood the underlying intention of the urgent measures. It informed the Court, a few weeks before the planned hearing on the actual use of provisional measures, that it had reduced the General's sentence and had released him. It also noted that he was 'protected 24 hours by an escort'.[136]

Subsequently the Commission withdrew its request for provisional measures and requested a cancellation of the hearing. The President did the latter, but decided to maintain the urgent measures to protect Gallardo's life and safety.[137] As in previous cases, he noted that in human rights law provisional measures do not just have a preventive nature, preserving 'a juridical situation', but that they are 'fundamentally protective, because they protect human rights'. When the basic requisites of extreme gravity and urgency and the prevention of irreparable harm to persons are present, provisional measures become a 'real jurisdictional guarantee of a preventive nature'.[138] Subsequently, the full Court confirmed 'all the terms of the orders of the President'.[139] In its Order of 11 July 2007 the Court discontinued its provisional measures. It noted that the petitioners had submitted, in February 2004, that Gallardo had been threatened by telephone the previous month.[140] It noted, however, that since that time the situation had been stable.[141] The State had pointed out that 'in the last five years the State has adopted measures to protect Mr. Gallardo Rodríguez, among them: security detail provided by federal authorities, an official vehicle with two agents at the beneficiary's home, and a protection service consisting of police patrol-

---

[133]   IACHR *Gallardo Rodríguez* v. *Mexico*, Order of 18 February 2002, 1st 'Having seen' clause a) to i).

[134]   See Chapter VII (Detention situations) and IX (Death threats).

[135]   See e.g. IACHR *Gallardo Rodríguez* v. *Mexico*, Order of the President of 14 February 2002, 3rd 'Having Seen' clause, referring to the President's order of 23 January 2002. In fact the President had already called these witnesses in his Order for urgent measures of 23 January 2002, 1st 'Resuelve' clause. The authors were Hernán Lara Zavala and Homero Aridjis (involved in International PEN).

[136]   The escort was composed of agents of the Ministry of Public Security and the Federal preventive police. See brief of 8 February 2002, referred to in IACHR *Gallardo Rodríguez* v. *Mexico*, Order of 18 February 2002, 4th 'Having Seen' clause. See also CIDH Press Release 3/02, 'IACHR welcomes freeing of General Gallardo in Mexico', 12 February 2002. See generally Chapter XVII (Official responses).

[137]   IACHR *Gallardo Rodríguez* v. *Mexico*, Order of the President of 14 February 2002.

[138]   Id., 5th 'Considering' clause.

[139]   IACHR *Gallardo Rodríguez* v. *Mexico*, Order of 18 February 2002, 1st 'Decisional' clause.

[140]   IACHR *Gallardo Rodríguez* v. *Mexico*, Order of 11 July 2007, 3rd 'Considering' clause.

[141]   Id., 4th 'Considering' clause.

ling and 24-hour emergency telephone numbers'.[142] The petitioners had argued that he would only be safe once investigations into the threats had been completed and those responsible identified.[143] The Court considered that the statements of the representatives 'regarding the fact that there are still judicial processes currently pending', did not constitute circumstances of extreme gravity and urgency that called for the continuance of the provisional measures.[144] It added that 'the above does not prevent the State from continuing with the corresponding investigations within the domestic jurisdiction to identify and, if it is the case, to punish those responsible for the threats suffered by Mr. Gallardo Rodríguez'.[145]

This was a case that involved respect for the Inter-American system, freedom of speech, impunity and arbitrary detention. The detention, implicitly, seemed to have been recognised as arbitrary by the then newly elected Government of Mexico, at least to the extent that it had indicated it would comply with the Commission's reports. Nevertheless, General Gallardo was not released but instead remained subjected to prolonged arbitrary detention. Not just civil society (e.g. International PEN and Amnesty International, which adopted him as a prisoner of conscience), but also the Inter-American Commission and the UN Working Group on Arbitrary Detention[146] had denounced the arbitrariness of his detention. It also constituted a threat to freedom of expression. Moreover, after its recognition of the compulsory jurisdiction of the Inter-American Court, the Government had committed itself – *in abstracto* – to implement the Commission report, but in fact Gallardo remained in detention.[147]

To the extent that the Court's Order was made to intervene in a situation of arbitrary detention, it could be argued that it is exactly the recognised arbitrariness, in combination with the lack of actual redress (even the opposite: a continued detention), that could explain the use of provisional measures to put a stop to this continuing violation. This could help restore, as much as possible, the status quo ante, before a further irreparable harm was done to the project of life of the General and his family.[148]

While the Court does not expressly call for release but instead simply calls for respect for the safety of the General and his family, this case could nevertheless be seen as an example of a

---

[142]   Id.. 9th 'Considering' clause.

[143]   Id., 6th 'Considering' clause.

[144]   Id., 11th 'Considering' clause.

[145]   Id., 12th 'Considering' clause.

[146]   The Working Group on Arbitrary Detention had determined that his detention was arbitrary and related to a violation of, among others, freedom of speech. In the decision it is not mentioned whether it used its urgent appeal procedure, Opinion 28/1998, E/CN.4/2000/4/Add.1, p. 17 and p. 18.

[147]   The Inter-American Commission's determination of arbitrariness in General Gallardo's case was a fact prior to Mexico's recognition of the competence of the Court. Mexico had only recognised the Court's competence for facts subsequent to this recognition. Thus, at the time of the Commission's determination of the arbitrariness of the detention of the General and its recommendation for release, the Commission was the ultimate authority in the Inter-American system. The new Government, on the other hand, has reopened the Commission cases that had been 'closed' by the previous Government. It might be argued that, therefore, they constituted 'new facts' falling within the competence of the Court. In particular, the fact that the Government had committed itself to comply with these Commission cases was an acknowledgement of its obligation to comply with the Inter-American Human Rights system, and in particular the Convention, in good faith and, in the case of the General, it may imply an admission of the arbitrariness of his detention. Continuing such detention clearly constitutes a lack of respect by certain sectors of government for the commitments undertaken under the Convention. It may mean that the Commission needs to open the case anew so that the Court can subsequently examine it. Consequently, all this time the arbitrary detention is being prolonged.

[148]   On the concept of 'project of life' see section 2.1 of this Chapter and references therein.

case in which de facto the Court intervened in a situation of arbitrary detention that also implicated the right to 'seek, receive, and impart information and ideas' (Article 13(1) ACHR). With all of this it must be kept in mind though that the Court used its provisional measures based on its traditional argument of protection against threats and it was on this basis also that it maintained its provisional measures upon Gallardo's release until 2007.

In 2003 the Commission took precautionary measures on behalf of another General, who was claimed to have been arbitrarily deprived of his liberty two weeks previously, this time in Venezuela. It was alleged that the officers who carried out his arrest and detention 'did not show any judicial or other warrant, did not provide information on the reasons for the detention, nor did they indicate which authority had ordered the detention'. Moreover the next day a domestic judge had ordered his release. Through its precautionary measure the Commission asked Venezuela 'to implement immediately the habeas corpus order on behalf of Gen. Alfonso Martínez, and to guarantee him, adopting the pertinent security measures, his personal security and that of his family, and the exercise of his civil and political rights'.[149]

2.6.3 Practice in the African system

In October 2002 the African Commission took a provisional measure on behalf of journalists detained without charge in Liberia. The nature of this provisional measure was not specified.[150]

The decision on the merits does not provide sufficient information to infer any specific approach of the Commission in this regard, e.g. in light of the health situation. The Commission may have intervened urgently simply because of a general concern about the use of detention without charge in order to hinder the freedom of expression.

2.6.4 Practice by the EComHR

In several early cases the European Commission refused to take provisional measures to secure the provisional release of a petitioner on account of poor health.[151] Yet this may have been due to

---

[149] CIDH *Gen. Rafael Alfonso Martínez* v. *Venezuela*, Annual Report 2003, §65.

[150] African Commission *Samuel Kofi Woods, II and Kabineh M. Ja'neh* v. *Liberia*, November 2001 (provisional measure of 23 October 2002; this may have been an informal rather than a formal provisional measure). See also Chapter VIII (Procedure).

[151] See EComHR *X* v. *Germany* (FRG), 22 March 1958 (inadm.) (297/57). The petitioner, a commercial representative, was arrested and placed in preventive detention on 22 May 1957 for holding a leading position in a 'clandestine association' (the German Communist Party, which was declared unconstitutional in 1956), Yearbook of the European Convention on Human Rights Vol. 2, 1958-59, Martinus Nijhoff, The Hague 1960, pp. 204 and 206. In his second appeal against his detention before the national courts he requested, among others, 'his provisional release at least on account of his poor state of health'. Before the Commission, violation of the Articles 5, 6, 7, 8, 9, 10, 11, 13 and 14 ECHR were alleged. The petitioner had asked the Commission to declare his application admissible 'and to intervene with the authorities of the Federal Republic of Germany on his behalf in order to secure his immediate release' "Whereas the Convention does not contain any such obligations binding upon the High Contracting Parties as invoked by the Applicant; whereas, moreover, the Convention does not contain any provision giving the Commission competence to order provisional measures; whereas it therefore appears that the application is in this respect incompatible with the provisions of the Convention; whereas it should, in pursuance of Article 27, paragraph 2, of the Convention, accordingly be rejected". See Yearbook 2 (1960), p. 212.

the Commission's weariness, at the time, about its competence to order provisional measures in the first place, rather than to this specific request to order the release of a detainee.[152]

2.6.5 Practice by the Bosnia Chamber

In October 2001 the Bosnia Chamber ordered provisional measures to prevent resort to compulsory pre-trial detention. The petitioners had argued that 'many citizens had spent several years in detention before being finally released with no charges filed against them'.[153] The Order would remain in force for several days and was not extended, as the State had responded the next day that it would respect it 'completely'[154] and the disputed legislation was subsequently repealed as well.[155] This indicates an approach by the Chamber that is aimed more at preventing undue hardship to persons, or irreparable harm to the Article 5 claim.[156] By respecting the Chamber's provisional measures, the respondent had in fact made the Article 5 claim redundant since as a result the petitioners were never subjected to detention under the old legislation.

In a previous case, in July 1997, it had denied a request for provisional measures for the release of a petitioner.[157] While it appears from the case that the petitioner was in poor health, the request for provisional measures may in fact relate to the claim of illegal detention.[158] In its deci-

---

[152]   See for a refusal to take provisional measures in early cases e.g. *X.* v. *FRG*, 297/57, 22 March 1958 (inadm.), Yearbook 2, pp. 204-214; in 1963, a petitioner sought the quashing of a sentence and the cessation of certain measures pending the case. In this case the Commission equally considered that it was 'not empowered to order protective measures', but could only 'suggest' such measures. Moreover, it considered that the fact that it was dealing with the case did not have suspensive effect at the domestic level. It noted that 'far from obliging national courts to wait for the Commission to complete its work before they complete theirs, the Convention, in principle, provides for the opposite solution (Article 26) and assigns a mainly subsidiary role to the collective guarantee machinery set up by it'. See *X and Y* v. *Belgium* (1420/62, 1477/62, 1478/62), 18 December 1963, Yearbook 2, p. 626. Finally, in *Wemhoff* v. *Germany*, 1 April 1966, the petitioner had requested the Commission to order his release from prison. In February 1965, however, the plenary Commission considered that 'it results from Article 19 of the Convention that the task of the Commission is to 'ensure the observance of the engagements undertaken by the High Contracting Parties' in the Convention; whereas, however, the Convention does not contain any provision giving the Commission competence to order provisional measures in the exercise of its functions under Article 19'. Thus, it added that it had 'no competence to order the Applicant's release from prison as requested by him; whereas, furthermore, the Commission does not consider it appropriate in the circumstances to take any other steps in this connection' *Wemhoff* v. *Germany*, 1 April 1966, pp. 118-121. Again, the reference did not relate to the contents of the request.

[153]   Bosnia Chamber *Ivo Lozančić et al.* v. *Federation BiH*, 8 March 2002, (inadm.), §§14-15.

[154]   Id., §16.

[155]   This was done by the High Representative. Bosnia Chamber *Ivo Lozančić et al.* v. *Federation BiH*, 8 March 2002, (inadm.), §§17.

[156]   There are also several cases in which the Chamber has refused requests for release or suspension of execution of a sentence, often in the context of an alleged arbitrary detention. See e.g. *Milorad Marčeta* v. *The Federation of Bosnia and Herzegovina*, 3 April 1998; *Novo Bencuz* v. *Republika Srpska*, 8 February 2000 (inadm.); *Edin Garplija* v. *Federation BiH*, 9 April 2002; *Jasmin Šljivo* v. *Republika Srpska*, 9 February 2001 (inadm.); *M.A.* v. *Federation BiH*, 7 March 2001 (inadm.) and *Ibrahim Makić* v. *Federation BiH*, 9 November 2001 (inadm.).

[157]   Bosnia Chamber *Milorad Marceta* v. *Fed. B&H*, 3 April 1998, §3.

[158]   In this case representatives of the United Nations High Commissioner for Refugees had learned that the petitioner had been arrested. It had informed his family and the Ombudsperson. His

sion on the merits the Chamber noted its refusal to order provisional measures and added that it did so 'on the basis of the information then available to it'.[159] A month later the Deputy Prosecutor of the International Criminal Tribunal for the Former Yugoslavia (ICTY) stated that 'the evidence was insufficient by international standards to provide reasonable grounds for believing that the applicant had committed a serious violation of international humanitarian law'.[160] Subsequently Senior Deputy High Representative for Bosnia 'stated in strong terms that a serious violation of human rights and breach of the Rome Agreement had occurred'.[161] He called for the release of the petitioner and stated that he 'was referring the case to the Ombudsperson since such a gross human rights abuse could not be remedied simply by [his] release'.[162] The next day the Cantonal Court in Bihać was informed of the decision of the Prosecutor of the ICTY and the petitioner was released that same day.[163] It is very well possible that the Bosnia Chamber would have used provisional measures for the release of the petitioner if it had had more information.[164]

2.6.6 Conclusion

If provisional measures are to be used in the context of an arbitrary detention, somehow it must be established *at which point* the situation of this detention starts to be urgent and why irreparable harm is threatened. Otherwise provisional measures should only be used in situations where the prison conditions and the individual conditions of the person involved require it and then it would concern a traditional reason for using a provisional measure: preventing irreparable harm to life and physical integrity (e.g. prolonged incommunicado detention, threat of disappearance, threat of torture).[165]

At the same time it is suggested that with regard to minors a credible case of arbitrary detention could indeed warrant the use of provisional measures to the effect that they should be released. If, for instance, the CIDH had had *prima facie* evidence of such arbitrariness in the case of the *Honduran minors* discussed in Chapter VII, on halting cruel treatment in detention, it could have used precautionary measures to demand their release pending the case.[166] After all, in its discussion of the legal framework of the right to personal liberty in this case it noted that '[t]here is a clear tendency in international human rights law to afford greater protection to minors than to adults'.[167]

---

family then engaged a lawyer, who lodged a petition with the Ombudsperson. In June of that year the latter referred the case to the Chamber.

[159]   Bosnia Chamber *Milorad Marčeta v. Fed.BiH*, 3 April 1998, §3.

[160]   Id., §30.

[161]   Id., §31.

[162]   Id., §31.

[163]   Id., §34.

[164]   About the information required for the Chamber to take provisional measures see also Chapter XV (Immediacy and risk).

[165]   The protection required in most such cases would not necessarily have to be 'release' but rather to provide protection, medicine, access, etc. See in general about the protection required Chapter XIII (Protection).

[166]   In the actual case the Inter-American Commission noted in its final report that there was insufficient evidence with regard to the particular minors participating in the complaint. With regard to the study of the Office of the National Human Rights Commissioner about the reasons for incarceration of 84 juveniles in the Jalteva prison, the Commission considered that it had not been proved that the specific minors referred to by the parties had been detained for motives of vagrancy, for their own protection, because they were abandoned, or because they were orphans.

[167]   CIDH *Minors in detention case* (Honduras), case 11.491, Report on the merits 41/99, 10 March 1999, §113. In this case the CIDH had concluded that a violation of Article 7(2) ACHR had not been proved, §120. In an obiter, however, it pointed out the legal framework with regard to

While some adjudicators have used provisional measures that appear to aim at preventing arbitrary detention, only the Inter-American Commission has done so more than once and it is too early, given the dearth of information, to argue that a practice has developed in more than one system. Traditionally provisional measures have only been used in detention cases when there was a threat of torture or cruel treatment. Thus, the question must be addressed, in cases not involving children in detention, *at which point* in time the situation of an arbitrary detention starts to be urgent and why irreparable harm is threatened. This can only be done on a case by case basis.

The Inter-American Commission, with its wide protective mandate, and the Bosnia Chamber, with its almost 'constitutional' mandate (on a temporary basis), based on the specific post-war Bosnian situation, have extended this traditional approach at least once to the very limited group of cases of *prima facie* arbitrary detention in combination with another situation of gravity (such as continued detention despite Government 'admission' of arbitrariness). A similar approach is taken by the UN Working Group on Arbitrary Detention, which uses the tool of urgent actions in such cases.[168] Moreover, as to the merits the approach of all human rights adjudicators has indeed converged, showing a clear aversion to the practice of arbitrary detention.

Prolonged arbitrary detention is seen as a particularly serious violation of customary law.[169] Yet it may be argued that arbitrary detention is a situation that is reversible and therefore the use of provisional measures to halt or prevent such detention would be situated beyond the outer limits of the concept. Nevertheless there are several examples of provisional measures ordered in these circumstances. The question arises how their use can be explained.

One situation this section singles out is that where an international adjudicator examines a case involving a detention situation that has already been determined to constitute arbitrary detention (for instance as a punishment for the exercise of the freedom of expression), either in a previous decision by this adjudicator, or by another international adjudicator.

When a judgment on the merits or reparations has ordered the release of a detainee, each day he or she continues to be detained may be argued to result in additional irreversible harm to the *system* of human rights protection. Yet provisional measures do not appear to be the most appropriate tool to prevent such harm. In fact most adjudicators have created follow-up mechanisms that could appropriately be used to emphasize the need for compliance.

On the other hand, there is another situation in which the use of provisional measures to prevent irreparable harm to the procedure does appear particularly appropriate. This is when a

---

Article 7: "The Commission considers that the practice of incarcerating a minor not because he committed a criminalized offence but simply because he was abandoned by society or was at risk, or is an orphan or a vagrant, poses a grave threat to Honduran children. The State cannot deprive of their freedom children who have committed no crime, without incurring international responsibility for the violation of their personal liberty (Art. 7 of the Convention)", §109. The fact that it concerns minors may lead to the conclusion that the 'grave threat' mentioned here would necessitate precautionary measures to prevent irreparable harm to these children, even if detained in special juvenile facilities. "Minors cannot be punished because they are at risk, that is to say, that (sic) because they need to work to earn a living, or because they have no home and thus have to live on the streets. Far from punishing minors for their supposed vagrancy, the State has a duty to prevent and rehabilitate and an obligation to provide them with adequate means for growth and self-fulfilment", §110. See also IACHR Advisory Opinion on *judicial status and human rights of the child*, 28 August 2002.

[168] While insufficient information is available on the approach of the African Commission in this respect, its role could be or become similar to that of the Inter-American Commission: protective, mediatory and rather informal.

[169] See e.g. the statement of the ICJ quoted in the beginning of this section, as well as the decision to institute a UN Working Group on Arbitrary Detention and the reference in the US Restatement of the law (third).

person is faced with detention as a result of participation in the individual petition system, either as a petitioner or as a witness. Outside of the latter context the use of provisional measures against the predetermined arbitrary detention of a person because ignoring previous decisions by the adjudicators would result in irreversible harm to the *system* is not convincing.

A second, rather far-reaching, argument for the use of provisional measures to halt a person's detention in such cases would be that each day a detainee is unlawfully kept in detention she is hindered in the further development of her project of life. Particularly when this detention is prolonged it may have an irreparable impact on the life plans (blocking the capacity to make arrangements for livelihood and life experiences including study, work, family planning, etc.) of the person in question. This may trigger right to life issues in the broader sense of the term, combining life and personal integrity rights and encompassing the right not to be deprived of a dignified life. Provisional measures are then aimed at ensuring to some extent the continuance, in an adapted form, of the detained person's original life plans.[170]

Yet in order to uphold their authority and effectiveness it is important that provisional measures remain exceptional. Clearly the use of provisional measures for the release of persons in *contested* detention (without any health risks) does not fall within the common core of the concept of provisional measures in international human rights adjudication. Many petitioners may claim the reason for their detention is arbitrary or their trial was so unfair as to render their detention arbitrary. Generally speaking, there is no convincing practice supporting the use of provisional measures in this type of circumstance.

In the *Gallardo* case, on the other hand, there was a situation of established prolonged arbitrary detention, both the General himself and his family had been harassed, and the continued detention could result in irreparable harm to their project of life. In that sense the Court's provisional measures could still be seen as somewhat belonging to the traditional group of provisional measures.

While protection against arbitrary detention and supervision of compliance with its judgments are both eminently important, the use of provisional measures to ensure this generally speaking is not warranted. This is different when the rights at stake also involve the basic existence of persons. There may be situations when this existence is at stake because of a prolonged and continuing arbitrary detention as well as clear indications of irreparable harm to the project of life.

2.7 Preventing impunity

2.7.1 Introduction

On one occasion the Committee against Torture has used an atypical provisional measure specifically in order to prevent impunity.[171] It did so in light of the obligation in the Convention against Torture to either prosecute or extradite persons suspected of having perpetrated torture. Thus, this provisional measure was not taken as part of provisional measures against death threats and harassment, but in order to ensure compliance with specific provisions of the Convention

---

[170] On the concept of 'project of life' see section 2.1 of this Chapter and references therein. Apart from stopping the original life plan from being blighted further and ensuring the conditions to pursue the initial life plan as much as possible, another purpose of provisional measures may be ensuring the conditions for a new project of life: planning a liveable life, or even having the option in the first place to plan a life.

[171] It normally takes provisional measures in non-refoulement cases, see Chapters V (Non-refoulement) and XV (Immediacy and risk).

against Torture.[172] As compared to other provisional measures, considerable information is available on the provisional measure and its aftermath, which will be referred to in this section. This serves to illustrate how this provisional measure has been taken to prevent irreversible harm to the claim.

2.7.2 Practice

In 1999 a Chadian NGO,[173] 'with the Pinochet precedent in mind', requested Human Rights Watch to assist it in bringing the former President of Chad, in exile in Senegal, to justice in that country.[174] Habré ruled Chad from 1982 until the end of 1990. He then fled to Senegal. In the early 1990s a Chadian truth commission published a report on the responsibility of Habré's government for 40,000 murders as well as for the systematic use of torture.

In January 2000 seven victims from Chad, acting as private plaintiffs, together with another Chadian NGO,[175] provided a Senegalese court with details of 97 cases of political killings, 142 cases of torture and 100 disappearances committed during 1982-1990 by police forces instructed by Habré. A coalition of NGOs was formed to support the victims.[176] Among others, the victims had asserted that the UN Convention against Torture obliged Senegal to either prosecute or extradite alleged torturers present in its territory. The next month the Senegalese judge in question indicted Habré on torture charges and placed him under house arrest. In July 2000 the Court of Appeals dismissed these charges, considering that Senegalese courts had no jurisdiction over torture committed outside the territory of Senegal and against non-nationals. The Cour de Cassation (court of final appeals) upheld this decision in March 2001.[177] In the meantime, another group of victims had filed a case against Habré in Belgium. They were supported by the same coalition.

In April 2001 the President of Senegal publicly declared that he had given the former dictator one month to leave Senegal. Assisted by Reed Brody of Human Rights Watch, Suleymane Guengueng[178] and six others resorted to CAT in order to ensure the principle that perpetrators of torture must be either prosecuted or extradited: *aut dedere aut iudicare*. They also requested provisional measures. They were afraid 'that Habré would move to a country out of reach of an

---

[172] While it is difficult to disentangle these obligations, an attempt is made to discuss the general obligation in this section and the obligation as part of protection against death threats in Chapter IX and Chapter XIII (Protection).

[173] The Chadian Association for the Promotion and Defence of Human Rights (ATPDH).

[174] See e.g. Human Rights Watch, 'The case against Hissène Habré, an 'African Pinochet', May 2006, <www.hrw.org> (consulted 16 May 2006).

[175] The Chadian Association of Victims of Political Repression and Crime (AVCRP).

[176] It consists of human rights groups from Chad: the Chadian Association of Victims of Political Repression and Crime (AVCRP), the ATPDH and the Chadian League for Human Rights (LTDH), the African Assembly for the Defence of Human Rights (RADDHO) and the National Organisation for Human Rights, both based in Senegal, Agir Ensemble pour les Droits de l'Homme and the International Federation of Human Rights Leagues (FIDH), both based in France and Interights (UK).

[177] See e.g. Human Rights Watch, United Nations asks Senegal to hold ex-Chad dictator, victory for Hissène Habré's victims, 23 April 2001, <www.hrw.org> (consulted on 10 April 2003).

[178] Guengueng is one of the founders of the AVCRP. Human Rights Watch reports that he almost died of dengue fever during two years of mistreatment in prisons in Chad. HRW, Senegalese President urged to aid rights prosecution, 27 June 2001, <www.hrw.org> (consulted 10 April 2003).

extradition request or a final U.N. ruling and asked the Committee to issue an interim ruling to preserve their ability to bring him to justice'.[179]

The complaint before CAT claimed violations of Article 5(2) ICAT (failure to establish jurisdiction over the crime of torture committed abroad in cases where the alleged offender is present on the State's territory) and Article 7 ICAT (failure to prosecute or extradite the alleged offender).[180] As primary forms of remedy for these violations the victims asked the Committee to recommend Senegal to amend its legislation to establish jurisdiction over the crime of torture committed abroad in cases where the alleged offender is present on its territory, in conformity with Article 5(2) and to either extradite Habré or submit his case to the competent authorities in Senegal for the purpose of prosecution, as required by Article 7. At the same time the petitioners also asked the Committee to take provisional measures in order to prevent Habré from leaving Senegal except pursuant to an extradition demand. They first discussed the risk of irreparable harm and then the issue of urgency. On the risk of irreparable harm the complaint pointed out:

> "If Hissène Habré leaves Senegal, the authors will suffer irreparable harm because there will likely be no possibility to bring the man responsible for their torture, Hissène Habré, to justice, and there will thus be no means of remedying the violation of Article 7 which they have suffered. Indeed, Senegal would incur supplemental violation of the Convention by letting Habré flee. Having initiated the prosecution of Habré, the author/plaintiffs have a right to see Habré extradited or prosecuted under Article 7. The victims' right to bring Habré to justice is implicit in their right to a remedy, their right to compensation and their right to reparations, and has been recognized by U.N. rapporteurs such as Joinet and van Boven".[181]

The complaint then continued with an explanation of the urgency of the matter, referring to the fact that in early April President Wade had declared publicly that he had given Habré one month to leave Senegal. The petitioners did not know when the President had notified Habré about this. They also explained that other victims of Habré had opened criminal proceedings in Belgium 'and the authors are concerned that any request for extradition by Belgium, as well as any relief recommended by the Committee against Torture (in particular the prosecution or extradition of Habré pursuant to Article 7), would be frustrated if Habré had already left Senegal'.[182]

In response, CAT took a provisional measure that same month. It requested the State not to expel Habré and to take all necessary measures to prevent him from leaving Senegalese territory in any way other than through an extradition proceeding (the principle *aut dedere aut iudicare*).[183]

---

[179] Human Rights Watch, United Nations asks Senegal to hold ex-Chad dictator, victory for Hissène Habré's victims, 23 April 2001, <www.hrw.org> (consulted on 10 April 2003).

[180] The complaint referred to the concern expressed jointly by the UN Special Rapporteur on the Independence of Judges and Lawyers and the UN Special Rapporteur against Torture about the circumstances surrounding the dismissal of the charges against Habré by the Court of Appeals. The Rapporteurs had reminded Senegal of its obligations under the UN Convention against Torture.

[181] Letter to the United Nations Committee against Torture, 18 April 2001, <http://www.hrw.org/french/themes/habre-cat2.html> (consulted 14 June 2007).

[182] Letter to the United Nations Committee against Torture, 18 April 2001, <http://www.hrw.org/french/themes/habre-cat2.html> (consulted 14 June 2007). See in general about imminence Chapter XV (Immediacy and risk).

[183] It sent a note verbale to this effect to the Government of Senegal, on the basis of its Rule 108(9), and in so far as the conditions for requesting provisional measures existed: 'en vertu de l'article 108, paragraphe 9, de son règlement d'ordre intérieur et dans la mesure où les conditions pour demander des mesures provisionnelles sont remplies, le Comité prie l'Etat partie de ne pas expulser Mr. Hissène Habré et de prendre toutes les mesures nécessaires pour empêcher que Mr. Hissène Habré quitte le territoire du Sénégal autrement qu'en vertu d'une procédure

Reed Brody of HRW pointed out that 'this ruling' (the decision to take a provisional measure) was 'a great victory for Habré's thousands of victims'.[184] His organisation noted that 'States usually comply with its [the Committee's] decisions, and Senegal is expected to do so'.[185] As discussed in Part IV to this book (Responses) various actors subsequently played a role in reinforcing compliance with the provisional measures by the State.

In May 2006 CAT published its decision on the merits. It noted that its consideration 'had been delayed at the explicit wish of the parties because of judicial proceedings pending in Belgium for the extradition of Hissène Habré'.[186] It found violations of Articles 5(2) and 7 ICAT. Senegal was indeed obliged to prosecute Habré 'for alleged acts of torture unless it could show that there was not sufficient evidence to prosecute, at least at the time when the complainants submitted their complaint in January 2000'.[187] In addition, since 19 September 2005, when Belgium made a formal extradition request, the State party 'had the choice of proceeding with extradition if it decided not to submit the case to its own judicial authorities for the purpose of prosecuting' him.[188] By refusing to comply with this extradition request the State party had 'again failed to perform its obligations under article 7 of the Convention'.[189] Under Article 5(2) Senegal was obliged to take the necessary measures, including legislative, to establish jurisdiction and under Article 7 it was obliged to submit the case 'to its competent authorities for the purpose of prosecution or, failing that, since Belgium has made an extradition request, to comply with that request, or, should the case arise, with any other extradition request made by another State, in accordance with the Convention'.[190] The Committee referred to its provisional measure as a request not to expel Habré as well as 'to take all necessary measures to prevent him from leaving

---

d'extradition'. At the end of that month the Secretariat of CAT also informed the petitioner of the registration of the complaint and the provisional measure requesting the State 'not to expel Mr. Hissene Habré an to take all necessary measures to prevent Mr. Hissène Habré from leaving the territory of Senegal except pursuant to an extradition demand, while the communication is under examination by the Committee'. Letter of 27 April 2001, posted on the internet site of Human Rights Watch, <www.hrw.org> (consulted on 10 April 2003).

[184] Human Rights Watch, 'United Nations asks Senegal to hold ex-Chad dictator', press release of 23 April 2001, <http://hrw.org/english/docs/2001/04/23/senega161.htm> (consulted 14 June 2001). According the Human Rights Watch the 'abrupt decision' of the Senegalese President that Habré should leave Senegal within a month 'was a tribute to the victims' efforts'. At the same time it 'raised the possibility that Habré would go to a country out of justice's reach'. This was why the victims appealed to CAT and why the latter indeed decided to take provisional measures. Human Rights Watch, The case against Hissène Habré, an 'African Pinochet', May 2006, <www.hrw.org> (consulted on 16 May 2006). See also Kirgis (2000/2001).

[185] Human Rights Watch, 'United Nations asks Senegal to hold ex-Chad dictator', press release of 23 April 2001, <http://hrw.org/english/docs/2001/04/23/senega161.htm> (consulted 14 June 2001). Senegalese lawyer and President of the Fédération de droits de l'homme (FIDH), Sidiki Kaba, was quoted stating that 'this decision is based on the principle that Senegal is obliged to prosecute or extradite alleged torturers like Hissène Habré'. A representative of the African Assembly for the Defence of Human Rights (RADDHO) considered it unlikely that Senegal would ignore the provisional measure and allow Habré to escape justice. The Chadian victims themselves felt supported by the decision and one of the victims involved in the complaint, Mr. Guengueng stated: "The United Nations has heard our pleas". Human Rights Watch, 'United Nations asks Senegal to hold ex-Chad dictator', press release of 23 April 2001 <http://hrw.org/english/docs/2001/04/23/senega161.htm> (consulted 14 June 2001).

[186] CAT Guengueng et al. v. Senegal, 17 May 2006, §9.1.

[187] Id., §9.8.

[188] Id., §9.10.

[189] Id., §9.11.

[190] Id., §10.

the territory other than under an extradition procedure'. It noted that Senegal had 'acceded to this request'.[191]

Subsequently the abovementioned Committee of Eminent African Jurists set up by the African Union issued its report recommending his prosecution in Senegal. Indeed, in July 2006 the African Union's Assembly followed this recommendation and called on Senegal to prosecute him 'in the name of Africa'. Senegal responded that it would do so.[192]

2.7.3 Conclusion

This section specifically discussed a provisional measure taken by CAT in order to prevent a violation by the State of its obligation under Articles 5 and 7 ICAT to act against impunity.

The obligation to prosecute and punish as part of provisional measures against death threats clearly aims at preventing irreparable harm to persons. The provisional measure in the Habré case, on the other hand, aims to ensure a core provision of the Convention against Torture in light of the general obligation to act against impunity. Thus, it aims to prevent irreversible harm to the *claim* under these articles and, seen more widely, to the system of protection created with this Convention.

The events subsequent to the Committee's provisional measures revealed a complex web of interactions between various actors concerned with the implementation of Articles 5(2) and 7 ICAT.

Requiring States to establish jurisdiction over the crime of torture committed abroad and to extradite or prosecute perpetrators of torture, Articles 5 and 7 ICAT may be considered essential for the implementation of the general obligation to prevent torture. They have been inserted to deal with situations in which the State where the torture took place is unwilling or unable to prosecute the alleged perpetrator so that prosecution should take place in another jurisdiction in order to prevent impunity or, alternatively, to prevent impunity in cases where the alleged perpetrator may run a risk to be tortured or receive the death penalty in the State the requesting his extradition.

While the provisional measure taken by CAT does not directly prevent irreparable harm to the life and personal integrity of specific individuals, it certainly makes sense in the specific context of the Convention against Torture. If Habré would have left Senegal this State could not have made him return in order to satisfy its obligation to extradite or prosecute. In that sense the situation would have been irreversible. Given that at least the situation would result in irreversible harm to the claim, the provisional measures did not stretch beyond the outer limits. After all, once the suspect is no longer present on its territory, a State's chance of implementing this obligation becomes almost nil.

Without the provisional measures it is unlikely that the Committee's finding on the merits would have provoked the African Union to become actively involved in the situation.

The question arises whether the use of such provisional measures is likely in the other systems too. While lacking the abovementioned specific provisions on the prosecution or extradition of torture suspects, the HRC, Inter-American Commission and Court and ECtHR have neverthe-

---

[191] Id., §1.3.

[192] See the African Union's decision of 2 July 2006, Assembly /Au/3 (Vii), reproduced at <http://www.hrw.org/english/docs/2006/08/02/chad13897.htm> (consulted 14 may 2007). See also Lekha Sriram (2006) and the report by UN Special Rapporteur on torture Manfred Nowak, A/HRC/4/33, 15 January 2007, §§ 43-45. For subsequent events see e.g. Human Rights Watch, 'Senegal: New law will permit Habré's trial', 2 February 2007; 'Senegal: EU parliament calls for support of Hissène Habré trial, Senegal should present reasonable plan to prosecute Chad's ex-dictator', 26 April 2007 and Press release by UN High Commissioner for Human Rights Louise Arbour, 'Senegal constitutional change paves way for Habré trial', 11 April 2008.

less developed case law involving the obligation to investigate human rights violations and bring to justice the perpetrators. They have done so on the basis of the positive obligations of States to prevent threats to and attacks on the right to life and the prohibition of cruel treatment. Obviously the obligation to investigate extreme human rights violations and bring to justice the perpetrators, in order to prevent (further) violations of the rights of *specific* persons (right to life and right not to be subjected to torture and cruel treatment) is closely related to the obligation to act against impunity in the *general* interest of preventing further violations and in order to achieve some form of closure for the victims and society as a whole. Impunity often causes further threats against witnesses, petitioners or others. Thus, the Inter-American Court generally requires investigation and prosecution as part of both its provisional measures and of its judgments on merits and reparations. In the first case it is meant as a concrete protective measure, in the second as a concrete step in implementing the obligation of non-repetition. Yet the provisional measures taken in the inter-American system that refer to the obligation to investigate and prosecute differ from the provisional measure by CAT discussed in this section. The former cases involved the need to investigate and prosecute those responsible for direct threats in order to prevent their continuation.[193]

This section, however, discussed a provisional measure taken by CAT in order to prevent impunity in *general*. It was based directly on unique treaty provisions (Articles 5(2) and 7 ICAT), requiring States to establish jurisdiction over the crime of torture committed abroad and to extradite or prosecute perpetrators of torture. Judge Cançado Trindade refers to it as 'the right to the realization of justice'.[194] He notes that only this 'can *alleviate* the suffering of victims caused by the irreparable damage of torture'.[195] He also points out that '(i)n the context of impunity, urgency increase, rather than decreases, with the passing of time'.[196]

This was an obligation aimed at the general prevention of torture, but not specifically related to the existence of ongoing threats to particular persons. It is within the outer limits, but does not (directly) involve preventing irreparable harm to persons. In this light it seems unlikely that the other human rights adjudicators, with a more general mandate, will also order such provisional measures in isolation, separately from the need to protect persons against specific death threats.[197]

2.8 Protecting the independence of the judiciary in the context of harassment

2.8.1 Introduction

There is one situation in which the Inter-American Court ordered provisional measures that appear to be motivated partly by a desire to protect the independence of the judiciary. It does not

---

[193] See Chapter IX on provisional measures to protect against death threats and harassment and Chapter XIII (Protection) on the general reference of these measures to the State's obligation to investigate and prosecute.

[194] ICJ *Questions relating to the obligation to prosecute or extradite (Belgium v. Senegal)*, Order of 28 May 2009, dissenting opinion by Judge Cançado Trindade, §55.

[195] Id., §75.

[196] Id., §59.

[197] Obviously, the ICJ, when faced with a complaint based specifically on a State's non-compliance with these provisions in ICAT, could indeed order provisional measures, as the ICJ pointed out in its Order denying the request for provisional measures in *Questions relating to the obligation to prosecute or extradite (Belgium v. Senegal)*, Order of 28 May 2009. The ICJ noted that the rights asserted appeared plausible but denied the request for other reasons.

appear that other adjudicators have used provisional measures in order to protect the independence of the judiciary, but in a similar set of circumstances it cannot be ruled out.

More specifically, the provisional measures were taken in the context of the constitutional crisis in Peru under Fujimori. They *could* be argued to belong to the category of protection against death threats and harassment. The petitioner, an impeached justice of the Constitutional Court, and her family were being harassed and other justices, including the President of the Constitutional Court, had been physically attacked.

Indeed the Inter-American Court used the traditional phrase to 'ensure the physical, psychological and moral integrity' to motivate its use of provisional measures. In other words, in the text of its Order for provisional measures it did not really move away from its practice of ordering such measures to prevent irreparable harm to the life of the beneficiary and to his or her personal integrity. Yet given the apparent additional rationale of protecting the independence of the judiciary, this section sets out this case in more detail in order to examine whether the provisional measures aimed at preventing irreversible harm to the claim and whether they aimed to protect persons against irreparable harm.[198]

2.8.2 The practice in the Inter-American system

Fujimori had been elected President in 1990. However, two years later he dissolved the Constitutional Court, as well as Congress. The next year a new Constitution was adopted and in 1996 a new Constitutional Court was appointed. That same year legislation was adopted that appeared to make Fujimori eligible for re-election for a third consecutive term of office. This legislation was appealed to the new Constitutional Court, which was divided on the issue. Five of the seven judges voted in favour of a draft judgment to the effect that the legislation did not apply to Fujimori's situation. Such judgment would prevent him from running for re-election. Subsequently one of the two pro-Fujimori judges unlawfully took the draft from a file and, as he later confessed, delivered it to the police and the press. This triggered an 'official campaign to pressure the five justices'.[199] Two of the justices originally in the majority called for a new vote and eventually only three of the five justices confirmed their original vote. The other four justices abstained. As it was a ruling on the inapplicability of legislation to a given situation, rather than on the constitutionality of the legislation, the Organic Law on the Constitutional Court determined that the vote could be taken by simple majority. This meant that, despite the campaign directed at the justices to prevent this conclusion, Fujimori was ineligible to run for re-election. In response the legislature took various actions against the three judges, culminating in their impeachment. They were subjected to various forms of harassment as well, in the context of which one of the justices, Delia Revoredo Marsano, sought and received asylum at the Costa Rican embassy.

---

[198]   The case includes other factors as well that are relevant to the discussion of the concept of provisional measures. It shows the importance attached to the concept of provisional measures in the Inter-American system. It was the first case in which the Inter-American Court ordered them based on a direct request by the petitioner in a case pending before it, rather than a request by the Commission. Moreover, it is one of the instances in which the Court specifically determined on the merits that it would only close the case once it considered that the State has complied with its judgments on the merits and reparations. See further Chapter XVI (Jurisdiction and admissibility) and XVIII (Follow-up). Indeed its judgment on the merits was of January 2001 and its provisional measures were only lifted in March of that year. Only then the case was closed. Finally, it was just after the submission of this case to the Inter-American Court that Peru withdrew its recognition of the Court's competence. On the Court's jurisdiction see also Chapter XVI (Jurisdiction and admissibility).

[199]   CIDH country report on Peru, 2 June 2000, Chapter II, §60.

The subsequent response to the involvement of the Inter-American system illustrates the importance attached to the issue in Peru.[200] In July 1999 Peru simply decided to withdraw its recognition of the Court's contentious jurisdiction 'with immediate effect'.[201] Yet in September 1999 the Inter-American Court found that it was competent to deal with the case.[202]

In April 2000 Mrs Revoredo Marsano, one of the impeached justices, approached the Court directly (rather than going through the Commission first) requesting the use of provisional measures to the effect that Peru should abstain from harassing her and her husband 'while the proceeding on the reinstatement of the Constitutional Court justices is being heard'. This harassment was manifested in the 'control and manipulation of judges and courts'.[203]

As the Court was not in session, its President initially dealt with the request. He decided to order urgent measures *ex officio* (not requested by the Commission) to ensure Delia Revoredo's 'physical, psychological and moral integrity'. In addition, he requested both the State and the Commission to provide the Court with detailed information on her situation. As noted, the language used in the Order was nothing out of the ordinary. What is significant is the fact that the President called for urgent measures. This was subsequently confirmed with provisional measures by the full Court, *ex officio* and in response to a very specific request involving harassment not against the life of the petitioner but against judicial independence. More precisely, the petitioner had asked for the suspension of the judicial proceedings filed against her for 'the alleged crimes of misappropriation, fraud and crime against the authority to attest documents'.[204] She had also requested that the company owned by her husband and herself to be allowed the legal recourse of appealing against an adverse arbitration award.[205] It is clear that the Court did not heed these specific requests. Instead it used the more traditional phrase 'to ensure the physical, psychological and moral integrity'. Yet that at that time there were no clear threats against the life of the petitioner, otherwise they would have been mentioned. The fact that the Court nevertheless ordered provisional measures indicates its serious concern with the situation in Peru at the time.

---

[200] See further Human Rights Watch, "Torture and Political Persecution in Peru", A Human Rights Watch/Americas Division Short Report, Vol. 9, No. 4(B), December 1997. See also section 3.4 of this chapter referring to the threats to the freedom of expression during the Fujimori regime, in particular the case of *Ivcher Bronstein*. In addition see the report of the UN Special Rapporteur, Cumaraswamy, on the independence of judges and lawyers, in an addendum regarding his mission to Peru (September 1996), expressing his concern 'as to whether the action of Congress in this matter has violated the principle of judicial immunity for decisions made in the exercise of judicial functions', E/CN.4/1998/39/Add.1, 19 February 1998, section III. Also see HRC Concluding Observations (Peru), 3 November 2000, §§10 and 14.

[201] The Inter-American Commission brought the case before the Court on 2 July 1999 and the Minister of Foreign Affairs of Peru received official notice of the case on 14 July. Two days later Peru returned all the paper work concerning the case to the Inter-American Court and delivered a note to its Secretariat informing it that it had withdrawn its recognition of the Court's contentious jurisdiction 'with immediate effect' as of 9 July 1999. This was the date on which it had deposited a declaration to this effect with the OAS Secretariat. It stated that this applied 'to all cases in which Peru has not answered the application filed with the Court'. IACHR *Constitutional Court* case (*Manuel Aguirre Roca, Guillermo Rey Terry, and Delia Revoredo de Mur* v. *Peru*), judgment of 24 September 1999 (Competence), §23.

[202] IACHR *Constitutional Court* case, judgment of 24 September 1999 (Competence). See further Chapter XIV (Jurisdiction).

[203] IACHR *Constitutional Court* case, Order of 14 March 2001, 1st 'Having Seen' clause.

[204] IACHR *Constitutional Court* case, Order of 14 August 2000, 2nd 'Having seen' clause.

[205] See IACHR *Constitutional Court* case, President's Order for urgent measures, 7 April 2000 and Order for provisional measures of 14 August 2000, confirming the President's Order 'in all of its aspects', adding that this was 'in order to prevent her from suffering irreparable damage', 1st 'Decisional' clause.

Then the situation took an interesting turn. In September 2000 a video showing Vladimiro Montesinos, the President's advisor and *de facto* head of the National Intelligence Service,[206] handing cash to legislators was broadcast and a corruption scandal unfolded. In November Fujimori and Montesinos fled Peru and a transitional government was installed.

In January 2001 the Court found on the merits that the right to due process (Article 8 ACHR) and adequate judicial recourse (Article 25 ACHR) of the three justices had been violated. It stressed the importance of judicial independence for the rule of law and the added importance of the independence of Justices of a constitutional court, 'owing to the nature of the matters submitted to their consideration'.[207] One of the main purposes of the separation of powers is indeed the protection of judicial independence.[208] The Court also referred to case law by the European Court on the importance of guarantees for judges against external pressure[209] and it invoked the United Nations Basic Principles on the Independence of the Judiciary.[210]

A few days after the publication of the judgment the Commission stated that despite the political change in Peru the provisional measures should be maintained, as the 'precautionary measures corresponding to the legal proceedings filed against [her] have still not been executed'.[211] At the end of that month the State informed the Court that it had 'executed the necessary actions' to comply both with the Court's judgment and with its provisional measures. It stated that it had also taken steps to eliminate the political manipulation of the judiciary, which had 'created favorable conditions for deciding the cases that are being processed'. On 17 November the Congress had reinstated the three justices and, the day before it approached the Inter-American Court, the State had also held a meeting with Delia Revoredo 'to co-ordinate compliance with the judgment on the merits'.[212]

The Court decided to lift its provisional measures and to close the file. It pointed out that provisional measures 'have an exceptional nature and are therefore ordered having regard to the need for protection and, once ordered, they must be maintained' as long as the criteria in Article 63(2) ACHR apply.[213] It noted the changes that had occurred in Peru and the developments in the *Constitutional Court* case, in particular Mrs. Revoredo's reinstatement as a justice. Thus 'the reasons that caused this Court to order provisional measures (..) have terminated', since the cir-

---

[206] In a talk in 2005 Justice Revoredo commented on the role of Montesinos during the Fujimori reign. "Justice Revoredo also recalled the "cell-phone" votes, where Fujimori's secretive security chief Vladimiro Montesinos would call members of congress moments before an issue was to be decided and tell them how to vote. The dismantling of the legal and legislative system was so intricately orchestrated that it was not apparent to anyone, not even those recruited by Fujimori, exactly how the laws were being manipulated to favor Fujimori". See Veronica Herrera, 'Fujimori's Quiet Coup d'Etat and the Restoration of Peru's Constitutional Court', 24 January 2005, report of talk by Justice Delia Revoredo Marsano, co-sponsored by the Center for Latin American Studies and Boalt Hall School of Law, University of California, <http://socrates.berkeley.edu:7001/Events/spring2005/01-24-05-revoredo/index.html> (consulted 10 June 2007).

[207] IACHR *Constitutional Court* case, 31 January 2001 (merits), §73.

[208] Id., §75.

[209] Id., §7, referring to the appointment process (e.g. ECtHR *Langborger,* 27 January 1989, §32); the importance of a fixed term position (see e.g. *Le Compte, Van Leuven and De Meyere,* 23 June 1981, §55; and of guarantees against external pressure (see also, e.g. *Piersack,* 1 October 1982, §27).

[210] Adopted by the Seventh United Nations Congress on the Prevention of Crime and the Treatment of Offenders, Milan 26 August-6 September 1985, and confirmed by the General Assembly in its resolutions 40/32, 29 November 1985 and 40/146, 13 December 1985.

[211] IACHR *Constitutional Court* case, Order of 14 March 2001, 5th 'Having Seen' clause.

[212] Id., 6th 'Having Seen' clause.

[213] Id., 3rd 'Considering' clause.

cumstances of 'extreme gravity and urgency' and the probability of irreparable harm, as required by Article 63(2) ACHR, no longer existed. What is relevant to its approach to the concept of provisional measures is that the Court specifically considered that the Commission's argument that legal proceedings were still pending did 'not bear any relation to the purpose of the provisional measures adopted by the Court' in August 2000, 'in its first operative paragraph; moreover, they do not constitute circumstances of extreme gravity and urgency that would warrant maintaining the actual provisional measures'.[214] In other words, Mrs Revoredo's reinstatement had occurred subsequent to the Commission's submission and seems to have been the most important reason for the Court to lift its provisional measures. Its main concern now was to emphasize the exceptional nature of its provisional measures. Yet this case indicates that in the context of Fujimori's reign the Court *had* considered the legal harassment of a petitioner and her continued impeachment as a justice to be a circumstance of extreme gravity and urgency.

2.8.3 Conclusion

Lack of judicial independence in one individual case generally speaking can be reversed,[215] but the same is not the case when there is a climate of fear and corruption of the judiciary. As the Court's provisional measures were ordered in such a context, they may be considered to be aimed at the prevention of irreversible harm to the claim. In that sense such provisional measures are within the outer limits of the concept. Moreover, to the extent that the legal harassment complained of is likely to lead to other types of harassment and threats as well, the provisional measures aim to prevent irreparable harm to persons. As the case was brought in a context in which death threats and attacks had taken place, the likelihood of irreparable harm to persons was not remote. Given the context and wording of the provisional measures in this case, they may be argued to fall within the common core of the concept as well.

2.9   Preserving evidence

2.9.1 Introduction

The former European Commission appears to have used provisional measures at least once to safeguard evidentiary material. It invoked the rule on provisional measures in a case *after* the deaths of the petitioners. This case may serve as an example where a human rights adjudicator has used provisional measures in order to prevent irreversible harm to the procedure, but not irreparable harm to persons.[216]

The chapter on the development of the concept of provisional measures by the ICJ (Chapter I), referred to irreparable harm to the claim, to the proceedings or to persons. In this chapter a distinction is made between irreparable and irreversible harm. As noted, when it concerns harm to the claim or the procedure, but not to life and physical integrity, the term *irreversible* harm is used.[217]

---

[214]   Id., 4th 'Considering' clause.

[215]   Unless, e.g. the death penalty is imposed, see Chapter III (Executions).

[216]   A situation in which the irreparable harm to persons is not directly related to the rights claimed in the case pending before the adjudicator but rather to harm to the proceedings is that of death threats and harassment to witnesses in the case. In such situation there is irreparable harm to persons as well. See Chapter IX (Threats).

[217]   See the Introduction to Part II.

2.9.2 Practice

In *Ensslin, Baader, Raspe* v. *Germany* (1978) the petitioners before the European Commission claimed that they were subject to exceptional conditions of detention, in particular prolonged isolation, 'causing them to undergo considerable physical, psychological and mental suffering'.[218] In October 1977 the Commission decided to postpone its examination of the complaint 'by reason of the circumstances obtaining at that time'.[219] A few days later, however, the petitioners were found dead. The President of the Commission immediately informed the government, 'under Rules 36, 14 and 28 of the Rules of Procedure', that 'he thought it desirable, in the interests of the proper conduct of the proceedings, that a Commission's delegation should be enabled to visit Stuttgart-Stammheim prison and make any observations which might prove necessary in order to establish the facts'.[220] Rule 36 was the Commission's Rule on provisional measures. With the Government's agreement, two delegates of the Commission travelled to Stuttgart on 19 and 20 October 1977. The Commission's provisional measures were taken following the deaths of the petitioners on 17 October. They do not involve intervention in detention situations, since the petitioners were already dead. The fact that the Commission invoked Rule 36 (together with Rules 14 and 28) may be explained here by the Commission's aim to safeguard the evidence in the interest of the proceedings pending before it.[221]

In this respect it referred to the observations by the delegates of the Commission when they inspected the cells of the petitioners on 19 and 20 October.[222] It also noted that while it was to examine in particular the complaint of sensory and social isolation, and while the circumstances of the deaths of the petitioners were 'not in themselves the subject of the application', the question did arise whether their deaths may have been 'the consequence of the treatment of which they complained'.[223] Yet it concluded that there was 'no objective indication along those lines'.[224] Subsequently the Commission found the claim of violations of Articles 3 and 6 ECHR manifestly ill-founded and the case was declared inadmissible.

As has been pointed out elsewhere, in a similar situation the Court is now more likely to re-sort to the possibility to ask the State for clarifications, or would carry out an on-site investigation, both under different rules,[225] rather than using provisional measures in this context.[226]

2.9.3 Conclusion

The text of the Rules on provisional measures used by the European Court of Human Rights, the former European Commission on Human Rights and the Bosnia Chamber, which are virtually

---

[218] EComHR *Ennslin, Baader and Raspe* v. *FRG*, 8 July 1978 (inadm.), §42.
[219] Id., §44.
[220] Id., §44.
[221] The Commission may have deemed it advisable to show an immediate response especially because just prior to the deaths of the petitioners it had decided to postpone the proceedings, with a rather cryptic justification. It is also possible that the initiative in fact came from the government. In any case, the Commission's decision presents it as the initiative of its President to invoke Rule 36.
[222] According to the delegates the cells 'were well-lit by windows which could be opened from inside; the walls were largely covered with books and posters. The cells were not sound-proofed either from the inside or from the outside: two persons confined on opposite sides of the central corridor could talk to each other by raising their voices', EComHR *Ennslin, Baader, Raspe* v. *FRG*, 8 July 1978 (inadm.), §6.
[223] EComHR *Ennslin, Baader, Raspe* v. *FRG*, 8 July 1978 (inadm.), §11.
[224] Id., §12.
[225] See Rules 54(2a) and 42(2) respectively.
[226] See Haeck/Burbano Herrera/Zwaak (2008), p. 44.

identical, is of particular interest in the context of preventing irreversible harm to the claim and of the proceedings. Different from the provisions of the other human rights adjudicators on provisional measures it does not refer to preventing irreparable harm, but just to 'any interim measure which it considers should be adopted in the interests of the parties or of the proper conduct of the proceedings before it'.[227] In the above case the use of provisional measures could be justified as in the interest of the 'proper conduct of the proceedings before it'. Provisional measures to prevent irreversible harm to the proceedings pending before the human rights adjudicator could be within the outer limits of the concept. Yet they would require a more convincing case than that before the European Commission in this instance. Nevertheless, given the specific function assigned to the European Commission (as well as the Court) and given the text of the Rule on provisional measures employed in the European system, its invocation of the Rule on provisional measures to prevent irreparable harm to the procedure could certainly be justified.

2.10 Halting the destruction of a work of art

The HRC has used provisional measures in one exceptional case involving the threatened destruction of a painting critical of the South Korean government. In *Hak-Chul Shin* v. *Republic of South Korea* (2004) the artist was accused of supporting the North Korean government with this painting. He had been arrested in August 1998 and his painting was seized and allegedly damaged by careless handling. The proceedings against him were concluded in November 1999, confirming his conviction, following the finding that the picture was an 'enemy-benefiting expression'. The painting 'was thus ready for destruction following its earlier seizure'.[228]

Counsel for the petitioner submitted his case to the HRC several months later and the Special Rapporteur used a provisional measure requesting the State, while the case was pending before the HRC, not to destroy the painting for which the petitioner had been convicted.[229] On the merits the HRC found that the painting's confiscation and the conviction of the petitioner violated his right to freedom of expression. The State was to provide him with an effective remedy, including compensation for and annulment of his conviction and payment of legal costs. Moreover, because it had not shown that any infringement on the petitioner's freedom of expression, 'as expressed through the painting' is justified, 'it should return the painting to him in its original condition, bearing any necessary expenses incurred thereby'.[230] Clearly, if the painting had been destroyed this remedy would have been impossible. In that sense the provisional measures aimed to prevent irreversible harm to the claim and may thus be situated within the outer limits. Yet it does not concern irreparable harm to persons involving the right to life and the prohibition or torture and ill-treatment. Currently it does not fall within the common core of the concept of provisional measures in human rights adjudication.

---

[227] See Rule 39 of the current Rules of Court, but also Rule 36 of the former Commission and Rule 36 of the Bosnia Chamber.

[228] HRC *Hak-Chul Shin* v. *South Korea*, 16 March 2004, §2.4.

[229] The petitioner contended that his painting 'depicts his dream of peaceful unification and democratisation of his country based on his experience of rural life from his children'. Among others he sought an 'unconditional and immediate return of the painting in its present condition' and a repeal or suspension of Article 7 of the National Security Law, Id., §3.7. In December 2001 the State party responded that it could not commit itself to such a suspension or repeal. Among others it argued that the case was inadmissible because the judicial proceedings had been consistent with the ICCPR, Id., §4.2.

[230] HRC *Hak-Chul Shin* v. *South Korea*, 16 March 2004, §9.

2.11 Securing political rights

2.11.1 Introduction

There have been a few situations, before the Bosnia Chamber and in the Inter-American system, in which petitioners requested the use of provisional measures in order to secure political rights. It is clear, however, that the European Court does not appreciate receiving requests for provisional measures in the context of political rights. In 2007 its Registrar published a press release entitled 'Inappropriate use of interim measures procedure' in which it was noted that the Court within a few days the Court had received 'a large number of requests' for the Court to adopt provisional measures 'in respect of the French Government's decision not to organise a referendum on the European Union Lisbon Treaty'. Yet 'as a matter of consistent practice', it only uses its power to adopt provisional measures 'where the applicant is at an established risk of imminent and irreparable harm. This typically involves allegations of exposure to ill-treatment in breach of Article 3 (prohibition of torture and inhuman and degrading treatment) of the European Convention on Human Rights and the most common example is where the applicant is on the point of expulsion to a country where he or she will be at risk of such treatment or indeed face a life-threatening situation (raising issues under Article 2 of the Convention – the right to life)'.[231]

Some figures were provided as general background:

> "In 2007 the Court has received approximately 1,060 requests for interim measures and granted 252 of them. The Court has, however, never granted a request for interim measures in circumstances such as the refusal by a government to hold a referendum which falls far outside the usual ambit of this procedure. The recent requests, which appear to be part of an orchestrated campaign, have no chance whatsoever of success and serve solely to take up time which could be spent on more urgent matters in respect of which the Court might be called upon to issue an interim measure. The Court has currently some 100,000 applications pending before it".[232]

Clearly this type of situation does not deal with irreparable harm to persons. Moreover, the claim itself does not appear pressing from an ECHR perspective.[233] This section briefly discusses the Inter-American practice and the practice of the Bosnia Chamber.

2.11.2 Practice of the Bosnia Chamber

In 1998 the Bosnia Chamber ordered provisional measures to secure ballot papers of out-of-country voters for elections taking place in Srpska.[234] It subsequently withdrew its Order, but this was

---

[231] ECtHR Press release issued by the Registrar, 'Inappropriate use of interim measures procedure', 21 December 2007.

[232] Ibid.

[233] For a claim that was considered more serious by the Court see Information Note 18 (May 2000) regarding *Commitato Promotore Referendum Antiproporzionale* (del 21/5/2000), *Commitato Promotore Referendum Maggioritario* (del 18/4/1999) v. *Italy*, where the Court refused to take provisional measures ordering a State to take the necessary measures to alter electoral rules, but where it did decide to treat the case with priority under Rule 41 (decision of 27 April 2000). See also Press Release 555 issued by the Registrar, 'Information concerning an application lodged against Turkey', 28 July 2008, referring to the Court's decision not to adopt a provisional measure under Rule 39 to prevent the Turkish Constitutional Court from ordering the dissolution of the Justice and Development Party AKP. The Court had also rejected the requests for urgent notification and granting priority (Rules 40 and 41).

because it determined it had no competence to deal with the case *ratione personae*.[235] Neverthe-less, this indicates that had the State BiH and Republika Srpska, rather than the OSCE, been responsible for the actions complained of, the Chamber would have maintained its Order. Thus, in this national but internationalized hybrid and transitional post-war system provisional measures have been used in the context of political rights (free elections).

In another case the Chamber denied a request for provisional measures to secure participation in the local elections by certain members of the Serb Radical Party. The petitioners had requested the Chamber to order Bosnia and Herzegovina to take all necessary steps to withdraw a specific Article of the Rules and Regulations of the OSCE Provisional Election Commission 'or to suspend the election proceedings until a final decision was reached'.[236] The Election Commission had required the party to replace three leaders and register itself under a new name. As the party had failed to do so, it had not met the requirements for registration.

Like in the previous case the Chamber subsequently declared the case inadmissible *ratione personae* since the General Framework Agreement did not provide for the intervention of the respondent Party in the conduct of the elections. 'Accordingly', the contested actions were 'not such' as would be 'within the responsibility of the respondent Party'.[237] The Chamber's previous refusal to order provisional measures may be due to its prima facie lack of jurisdiction to deal with the case, which was the more evident as it had already dealt with such a case before. On the other hand, the context of these cases is very different. The first dealt with a situation in which predominantly Bosniak out-of-country voters were prevented to vote in the Srpska elections and the second dealt with disgruntled Serb nationalists wishing to take part in the elections on their own terms, contrary to the principles of the Framework Agreement.

2.11.3 Inter-American practice

In November 2000 the Inter-American Commission 'granted general precautionary measures on behalf of persons affected by detention resulting from the electoral process in Haiti' and on behalf of three persons in particular. It requested Haiti to take the necessary measures:

> "To respect and ensure the full and free exercise of the following rights: freedom of conscience, thought, and expression and the right to assembly, association, free movement, and residence, political rights, and due process".[238]

The Commission noted that, according to the information received, members of the government, government security forces or private agents tolerated or motivated by such public officials, had persecuted and threatened several political opponents. This included acts of violence.[239] The protective measures required, however, apparently did not relate to protection of life and physical integrity but to several political and other rights. Also, the Commission called these 'general precautionary measures'.[240] It seems that the purpose of the precautionary measure in this case was to prevent irreparable harm to rights such as the freedom of expression in the context of the

---

[234] Bosnia Chamber *Adnan Suljanović, Edita Čišić and Asim Lelić* v. *State BiH and Republika Srpska*, 14 May 1998, (inadm.), §12.

[235] Id., §44 (provisional measures 'no longer appropriate'). On provisional measures and jurisdiction see further Chapter XVI (Jurisdiction and admissibility).

[236] Bosnia Chamber *Srpska Radikalna Stranka* v. *State BiH*, 8 December 2000 (inadm.), §6.

[237] Id., §§12-13.

[238] CIDH *Political Opponents* v. *Haiti*, precautionary measure of 13 November 2000), Annual Report 2000, §36.

[239] Ibid.

[240] Ibid.

electoral process. In that case it may be that the rationale for such measures is that violations of aforementioned political rights could not be repaired by allowing such freedoms again after the elections, or by monetary damages. After all such violations may negatively influence the results of the elections themselves.

In October 2005 the Commission had used precautionary measures on behalf of Jorge Castañeda Gutman (Mexico). He could not be registered at an independent political candidate as the domestic rules on elections provided that only political parties could request the registration of candidates 'for popularly elected offices'. According to the Commission 'this situation could lead to irreparable damage to the exercise of political rights'. Thus it requested the government to allow his provisional registration as a political candidate.[241] Yet it could be argued that these measures have the character of summary proceedings rather than provisional measures to prevent irreversible harm to the claim. Indeed, when the Commission subsequently requested the Court to order provisional measures, the Court denied this request.[242] It observed that the case was still pending before the Commission. In this case ordering such measures would anticipate a discussion on the merits of a case that was not yet pending before the Court.[243] It dismissed the request as inadmissible because it could not rule on the presence of a cognizable claim, unless it would have a direct bearing with the extreme gravity, urgency and necessity to prevent irreparable harm to persons.[244] The request was not of the type warranting provisional measures.[245] Other legal claims could only be brought before the Court in the context of contentious cases pending before it, or in request for Consultative Opinions.[246]

The Judges Cançado Trindade and Ventura Robles would have preferred this decision to have been taken after a public hearing, discussing the scope of orders for provisional measures.[247] They would have had many questions to ask of the legal representatives and the Commission. They noted that in this case the Commission requested the Court's provisional measures before it had even decided on the admissibility of the case pending before it. This was in sharp contrast with the many cases involving risk of irreparable harm to the life and personal integrity of persons in which it first maintained its own precautionary measures for a considerable time before resorting to the Court.[248] In many cases it maintained its precautionary measures despite successive violations of fundamental rights such as the right to life and personal integrity by the addressee State.[249] There was an apparent lack of clear criteria applied by the Commission in its decision whether to request the Court's provisional measures.[250] Why was the Commission so quick, they wished to know, in requesting the Court's provisional measures in an election dispute in Mexico that was still pending before it, while on the other hand it waited more than five years before requesting the Court's provisional measures in the case of the detention circumstances at the

---

[241]   CIDH Annual Report 2005, *Jorge Castañeda Gutman* (Mexico), §32.

[242]   IACHR *Jorge Castañeda Gutman* (Mexico), Order of 25 November 2005 denying a request for provisional measures.

[243]   Id., 4th and 9th 'Considering' clauses.

[244]   Id., 8th 'Considering' clause.

[245]   Id., 9th 'Considering' clause.

[246]   Id., 8th 'Considering' clause.

[247]   Id., Voto razonado conunto de los juezes A.A. Cançado Trindade y M.E. Ventura Robles, §1. The two judges also observed that the Court had dismissed certain observations sent by the State *proprio motu* because it had not requested them, see §2.

[248]   Id., Voto razonado conunto de los juezes A.A. Cançado Trindade y M.E. Ventura Robles, §3.

[249]   Id., Voto razonado conunto de los juezes A.A. Cançado Trindade y M.E. Ventura Robles, §8.

[250]   Id., Voto razonado conunto de los juezes A.A. Cançado Trindade y M.E. Ventura Robles, §§4 and 8.

FEBEM detention center,[251] which had already caused the deaths of children and adolescents? In that case, concerning a true human tragedy, it had in vain maintained its own precautionary measures and only resorted to the Court because of the initiatives taken by the representatives of the beneficiaries.[252]

The two judges also noted that this was not the first time that the Commission had attempted to resolve the merits of a contentious case through a request for provisional measures. They referred to another case in which it had attempted thus to resolve a situation involving the electoral process of a State.[253] In addition they referred to the *Chipoco* case (Peru) as 'another example of such trivialization'. In this case the Court had denied the Commission's request for provisional measures 'to protect the freedom of expression' of Mr Chipoco, for lack of sufficient information.[254]

2.11.4 Conclusion

It depends on the context how 'irreversible' hindrance of political rights would be. The result of blocking political access of minorities in a context of pervasive discrimination,[255] or of blocking such access to political opponents, in a context of widespread political persecution, could be argued to be irreversible in the long run. Yet blocking candidacy for political elections in one single instance is unlikely to be considered irreversible.[256] The criterion could be whether the hindrance has a considerable and pervasive impact on society as a whole, rather than on an individual. In such case provisional measures may still be within the outer limits of the concept, but in the other cases they move beyond these limits.

3   BEYOND THE OUTER LIMITS?

3.1   Introduction

There are situations in which petitioners have requested provisional measures where their use clearly would be beyond the outer limits of the concept. An example dealt with by the HRC is *B.L.* v. *Australia* (1996). The petitioner alleged that the legal system and legal profession were corrupt and that the State party was responsible for tolerating it.[257] She requested 'interim protection' by the HRC. Among others, she considered that it had the obligation to warn members of the international community that Australia did not provide equality before the law and that the law

---

[251] See IACHR *Case of the children and adolescents deprived of their liberty in the 'Complexo do Tatuapé' of FEBEM* (Brazil), Orders of 17 and 30 November 2005. See further Chapter VI (Detention).

[252] IACHR *Jorge Castañeda Gutman* (Mexico), Order of 25 November 2005, Voto razonado conunto de los juezes A.A. Cançado Trindade y M.E. Ventura Robles, §5.

[253] Id., Voto razonado conunto de los juezes A.A. Cançado Trindade y M.E. Ventura Robles, §7 referring to *Delgado Parker* (Peru).

[254] See *Chipoco* case, denial of provisional measures of 27 January 1993 (and previously denial by the President of 14 December 1992). See also section 2.6 of this Chapter.

[255] See also the Inter-American Court's judgment on the merits IACHR *Yatama* v. *Nicaragua*, 23 June 2005, in which an indigenous party was excluded from the elections. Among others the Court found violations of Articles 8 and 25 ACHR. See e.g. §248 and §259.

[256] Of course the individual candidate's plans would be hindered, but he could run for elections at a later point.

[257] HRC *B.L.* v. *Australia*, 8 November 1996.

did not protect overseas investments in Australia. In reference to the Committee's statement in *Stewart* v. *Canada*,[258] a case discussed in section 3.2, the Secretariat advised her that no provisional measures could be used in her case.[259] Indeed, if she had had a case in the first place, compensation would have been an adequate remedy for the violation found. This clearly shows a basic requirement of provisional measures, namely that the violation should be prevented because any compensation would be inadequate.

The HRC does not generally refer to failed requests for provisional measures. The above example was found in the case files in Geneva during a research visit in October 1998 and it may be assumed to represent a range of cases which the petitioners considered urgent, but the HRC did not.[260] The Inter-American Court has recorded a few instances in which it refused to order provisional measures.[261] Moreover, the Bosnia Chamber routinely included a reference to its refusal to order provisional measures in its decisions on merits and inadmissibility. Most of them related to forced evictions and some to issues such as reinstatement of officials, payment of pensions, and other financial issues.

There have also been cases in which adjudicators *have* used provisional measures that appear to be beyond the outer limits of the concept. This section singles out a few of them as well.

3.2 Halting deportation in 'family life type' cases (not involving non-refoulement)

Once in a while the ECtHR has used provisional measures in cases pending under Article 8 ECHR on the right to family life, rather than (also) on Article 3 ECHR on the prohibition of cruel treatment.[262] On one occasion the HRC has used provisional measures to halt deportation in a case involving a lawful alien facing a deportation order. In other words this was not a non-refoulement case involving a real risk of ill treatment or the imposition of the death penalty in the receiving State. While this case seems an exception not just vis-à-vis the other adjudicators, but

---

[258] See e.g. submissions by the petitioner of 17 December 1994, 21 and 29 January 1995, 13 and 25 February 1995 and letter by the Secretariat to the petitioner of 7 February 1995, *B.L.* v. *Australia*, 8 November 1996 (inadm.) (on file with the author).

[259] At the same time it requested her to substantiate her claim so that the case could be brought to the attention of the Special Rapporteur in due time. Subsequently, in a two-page decision, the HRC declared the case inadmissible. It observed that the petitioner had not substantiated the claim. The allegations remained sweeping and did not in any way reveal how her rights might have been violated. HRC *B.L.* v. *Australia*, 8 November 1996 (inadm.).

[260] An example of a failed request to which it *did* refer is in HRC *Walter Obodzinsky* v. *Canada*, 19 March 2007 (petitioner, a war criminal, had sought a stay of his citizenship revocation proceedings, which was rejected by the Special Rapporteur on 7 October 2007, §1.2). Another example involves a right to privacy claim (Article 17 ICCPR) in which the petitioner had requested the Committee's provisional measures to the effect that it ask the State 'not to subject her to any non-consensual medical or psychiatric examination, or the threat thereof, before the Committee has considered her case', §3.9. In July 2006 the petitioner was informed by the Secretariat that the Rapporteur had decided not to take the provisional measures requested, §1.2. On the merits the HRC did find a violation of Article 17 as the interference with the privacy of the petitioner was unreasonable in the circumstances. See HRC *M.G.* v. *Germany*, 23 July 2008.

[261] These are discussed in this chapter. The European Commission initially occasionally noted, in the context of specific cases, that it had no power to use provisional measures. See e.g. Chapters II (Systems) and XVI (Legal status).

[262] See e.g. ECtHR *Hamidovic* v. *Italy*, No. 31956/05 and *Useinov* v. *the Netherlands*, No. 61292/00, both referred to in Annual Report 2005 of the Third Section, p. 10.

also for the HRC itself, it is worth discussing as it provides a rationale for its use of provisional measures. Moreover, the case may serve to show the outer limits of the concept.

Stewart v. *Canada* (1996)[263] dealt with a British citizen who had lived in Canada since he was seven years old and was now facing deportation to the UK.[264] In April 1993 the Rapporteur used provisional measures and almost a year later the HRC confirmed this in its admissibility decision.[265] Among others, the petitioner had argued that his deportation would amount to cruel, inhuman and degrading treatment within the meaning of Article 7.[266] He had pointed out that the prison terms he served for various convictions already constituted adequate punishment, that his criminal record did not reveal that he was a danger to public safety, that he had lived in Canada since the age of seven and that his deportation would effectively and permanently sever all his ties in Canada. On the other hand, Canada considered that there were no 'special or compelling circumstances in the case that would appear to cause irreparable harm', although he would 'undoubtedly suffer personal inconvenience'. It noted that it was not deporting the petitioner to a country 'where his safety or life would be in jeopardy'. It also noted that he 'would not be barred once and for all from readmission to Canada'.[267] About the use of provisional measures in general Canada submitted that the Committee 'should not impose a general rule on States parties to sus-

---

[263] HRC *Stewart* v. *Canada*, 1 November 1996 (while the information on the use of provisional measures is not provided on the cover page, §§2.7, 4.1-4.5, 7.7 discuss the issue). The cover page of the *admissibility* decision does refer to provisional measures of 24 April 1993 (§4.1 of the View refers to 26 April 1993); admissibility decision of 18 March 1994, CCPR/C/50/D/538/1993, 3 May 1994 (unpublished document on file with the author).

[264] The petitioner was living together with his mother and younger brother. His mother was in poor health and his brother was mentally disabled and suffering from chronic epilepsy. Apart from his older brother, who had been deported to the UK the previous year, all his relatives lived in Canada. He had two young children, who were living with their mother. Between September 1978 and May 1991 he was convicted on 42 occasions mostly for petty offences and traffic offences, although one was for assault with bodily harm. His counsel noted that most of her client's convictions were attributable to his substance abuse problems, in particular alcoholism. For the last two years and four months he had participated in rehabilitation programs and remained alcohol-free, with the exception of one relapse.

[265] As discussed in Chapter II of this book, in between sessions it is the Special Rapporteur appointed by the HRC from among its members, who decides on how to proceed with new cases. This includes decision-making on the use of provisional measures.

[266] The petitioner claimed violation of Articles 7, 9, 12, 13, 17 and 23 ICCPR. With regard to Article 7 the HRC should determine on the merits the question 'whether the permanent separation of an individual from his/her family and/or close relatives and the effective banishment of a person from the only country he ever knew and in which he grew up may amount to cruel, inhuman and degrading treatment'. He submitted that Article 12(4) was applicable to his situation because for all practical purposes Canada was his own country and his deportation would result in 'an absolute statutory bar from re-entering Canada'. Article 12(4) stipulates: "No one shall be arbitrarily deprived of the right to enter his own country". He pointed out that Article 12(4) used the phrase 'his own country' rather than country of nationality or country of birth. With regard to Article 9 he noted that there was no indication that the concept of liberty only encompassed physical freedom. Article 12 recognized liberty in a broader sense as well. He believed that his deportation would violate 'his liberty of movement within Canada and within his community', §3.5.

[267] Canada pointed out, moreover, that 'although the author's social ties with his family may be affected, his complaint makes it clear that his family has no financial or other objective dependence on him: the author does not contribute financially to his brother, has not maintained contact with his father for seven or eight years and, after the divorce from his wife in 1989, apparently has not maintained any contact with his wife or children'.

pend measures or decisions at a domestic level unless there are special circumstances where such a measure or decision might conflict with the effective exercise of the author's right of petition'.[268] In relation to deportation in particular it considered that '(t)he fact that a complaint has been filed with the Committee should not automatically imply that the State party is restricted in its power to implement a deportation decision'.[269] According to Canada 'considerations of state security and public policy must be considered prior to imposing restraints on a State party to implement a decision lawfully taken'.[270] It therefore requested the HRC 'to clarify the criteria at the basis of the Special Rapporteur's decision to call for interim measures of protection and to consider withdrawing the request for interim protection under rule 86'.[271]

Counsel emphasised that the test of what may constitute 'irreparable harm' to the petitioner should be considered by reference to the Committee's own criteria and not those developed by Canadian courts. In Canada, she submitted, the test for irreparable harm in relation to the right to family life had become 'one of almost exclusive financial dependency'. She had resorted to the HRC 'precisely because Canadian courts, including the Immigration Appeal Division, do not recognise family interests beyond financial dependency of family members'.[272] This test was, in fact, the issue before the HRC. It would, therefore, 'defeat the effectiveness of any order the Committee might make in the author's favour in the future if the rule 86 request were to be cancelled now'.[273] It would be unjustified, moreover, 'to apply a "balance of convenience" test in determining whether or not to invoke rule 86, as this test is inappropriate where fundamental human rights are at issue'.[274]

In March 1994 the HRC (in full session) maintained the Rapporteur's provisional measures. As part of its admissibility decision the Committee 'noted' Canada's request to clarify the criteria for using provisional measures and its request for the withdrawal of the provisional measures in this case.[275] It observed that 'what may constitute "irreparable damage" to the victim within the meaning of rule 86 cannot be determined generally'. It did clarify, to some extent, what it considered essential:

"The essential criterion is indeed the irreversibility of the consequences, in the sense of the inability of the author to secure his rights, should there later be a finding of a violation of the

---

[268] HRC *Stewart* v. *Canada*, 1 November 1996, §4.3.

[269] Ibid.

[270] Ibid., §4.3.

[271] About the issue of the official State responses see Chapter XVII.

[272] HRC *Stewart* v. *Canada*, 1 November 1996, §4.5.

[273] Ibid. 'Rule 86' refers to the rule on provisional measures.

[274] Ibid. As part of its arguments on admissibility the State pointed out, once more, that its decision to deport the petitioner was 'justified by the facts of the case and by Canada's duty to enforce public interest statutes and to protect society. Canadian courts have held that the most important objective for a government is to protect the security of its nationals'. The State noted the immigration authorities had taken into account humanitarian and compassionate grounds, including family considerations, and balanced these against Canada's duty to protect society and 'properly enforce public interest statutes', §5.7. According to counsel the humanitarian and compassionate discretion of the Minister did not provide an effective mechanism to ensure that family interests were balanced against other interests. She also dismissed as 'patently wrong' the argument by Canada 'that the Court, upon application for judicial review of a deportation order, may balance the hardship caused by removal against the public interest', §6.4. She pointed out that the court had repeatedly explained that it is limited to strict judicial review and cannot balance these interests.

[275] HRC *Stewart* v. *Canada*, 1 November 1996, §7.7.

Chapter XII

Covenant on the merits. The Committee may decide, in any given case, not to issue a request under rule 86 where it believes that compensation would be an adequate remedy".[276]

Applying this criterion to the specific situation of deportation cases, the HRC explained that it required information on the ability of the petitioner 'to return, should there be a finding in his favour on the merits'.[277] In fact it maintained the provisional measure while it declared inadmissible the complaint that the separation from his family would amount to cruel and inhuman treatment in violation of Article 7 ICCPR.[278] This article is often invoked in the context of provisional measures. Thus the HRC must have maintained its provisional measures on the basis of the remaining claims of Articles 12(4), on the right to enter his 'own country', 17 and 23 ICCPR (family life).

Canada's reference to the petitioner's right of petition indicates that it considers that the Committee's use of provisional measures is justified at least in order to guarantee this right. The HRC itself did not explicitly refer to the right of petition.[279]

The State's first argument against the provisional measure had been that the petitioner would not be returned to a country where his safety or life would be in jeopardy and that, 'furthermore, he would not be barred once and for all from readmission to Canada'.[280] It is clear from the Committee's decision not to withdraw its provisional measure, that the HRC required more information before it was convinced of the possibility for the petitioner to return to Canada to visit his family.

The State party's second argument was that his family had 'no financial or other objective dependence' on him, although his social ties with the family may be affected. Thus, it considered that there were no special compelling circumstances in the case that would appear to cause irreparable harm in that respect either.[281] In the context of its decision not to withdraw its provisional measures, the Committee did not specifically address this argument. At a later stage, however, in its decision on the merits, it did attach importance to it.

In February 1995 the State considered, once more, that the deportation would not operate as an 'absolute bar' to re-entry into Canada. This time, this remark probably is a direct, albeit not very precise, response to the Committee's statement relating to the ability of the petitioner to return to Canada.[282]

---

[276] Ibid.

[277] Ibid.

[278] It considered that the petitioner had not substantiated his claim that deportation to the UK and separation from his family would amount to cruel and inhuman treatment or violate his right to liberty and security of person. As it was not apparent that the State's decision to deport him was reached arbitrarily, it also declared inadmissible the Article 13 (procedural rights of lawful aliens) claim for failure to substantiate.

[279] There is, however, a clear link between on the one hand the right of petition and on the other the Committee's discussion of irreparable harm to the victim, the petitioner's inability to secure his rights and the possible findings on the merits.

[280] HRC *Stewart* v. *Canada*, 1 November 1996, §4.2.

[281] Ibid.

[282] Subsequently counsel pointed out that the petitioner would 'face serious obstacles in gaining readmission to Canada as a permanent resident and would have to meet the selection standards for admission to qualify as an independent immigrant, taking into account his occupational skills, education and experience', id. §10.2. In any case, he would be barred from readmission as a permanent resident unless he was pardoned from his prior criminal convictions. Counsel also stressed the 'emotionally supportive relationship' with his mother and brother. She argued that the domestic court's emphasis on the financial aspect of the family relationship did not take into account the emotional family bond.

Possibly, the decision on the merits in *Stewart* is based on a sense of realism: the HRC did not want the consequences of finding a violation, which could be that an extensive range of deportation situations would result in cruel treatment. In the meantime, when the provisional measures had been in place for three years and seven months, the HRC found on the merits that Articles 12(4), 17 and 23 ICCPR had not been violated.[283]

In this case the Special Rapporteur evidently had not considered compensation to be an adequate remedy in the event that the HRC would later find a violation of the Covenant on the merits.[284] The full Committee confirmed this by deciding not to withdraw its provisional measures.

Thus far this is the only case in which the HRC has taken such an extensive approach in its use of provisional measures in deportation cases. The explanation it provided does not rule out that it would use them again in other cases not involving non-refoulement. This may mean that the HRC does not limit its use of provisional measures to halt deportation, expulsion or extradition to cases in which the petitioner is being returned to a country where his safety or life would be in jeopardy. In that case it does not limit their use to the prohibition of cruel treatment either. In other words, there may be circumstances other than a threat to safety or life in the receiving State or a separation from the family *as cruel treatment* that the Committee considers to be able to cause irreparable harm.[285]

As a practical matter, this means that in this case the HRC disagreed with the State's argument that there were no special or compelling circumstances that would appear to cause irreparable harm, although the petitioner 'would undoubtedly suffer personal inconvenience'.[286] The HRC's statement implies that before it could withdraw its request it would have to be certain that the petitioner would indeed be able to return to Canada, should there be a finding in his favour on the merits. In other words, in this type of deportation case the HRC may decide to use provisional measures when it considers that, should it later find a violation of the Covenant, the petitioner would be unable to secure his rights, in this case to live in the country in which he grew up and to stay in touch with his family. Interpreting the Committee's general statement about its provisional measures, they aim at postponing *irreversible* consequences until the Committee has been able to determine, on the merits, whether these would result in 'irreparable harm' to the *claim*.[287]

Nevertheless, the HRC may have been proclaiming a general rule to explain its use of provisional measures in this case without actually adhering to that rule in practice. After all, in subsequent cases on the rights of lawful aliens who had considered a State as their own for a considerable number of years and who often had no links with their country of nationality, the HRC did

---

[283]   While several members of the HRC would have preferred a less restrictive interpretation of 'own country' in Article 12(4) and would have found violations of Articles 12 and 13, the majority did not. See the dissents by Evatt, Medina Quiroga, Francis, Chanet, Prado Vallejo and Bhagwati. Bhagwati considered that the Committee's narrow interpretation left without any protection 'people who have forged close links with a country not only through long residence but having regard to various other factors, who have adopted a country as their own, who have come to regard a country as their home country'.

[284]   See also Chapter XIII on the relationship with forms of reparation.

[285]   See also the conclusion to this Chapter arguing that the Committee's provisional measures should indeed be limited to situations causing irreparable harm to persons.

[286]   HRC *Stewart* v. *Canada*, 1 November 1996, §4.2.

[287]   After all, the HRC speaks of the 'irreversibility of the consequences', in the sense of the petitioner's inability to secure his rights, 'should there later be a finding of a violation of the covenant on the merits'. Moreover, it would only take provisional measures when it believes that compensation would be an inadequate remedy, see HRC *Stewart* v. *Canada*, 1 November 1996, §7.7.

not use provisional measures.[288] While several of these cases were subsequently discontinued, *Canepa* v. *Canada* (1997) was decided on the merits. Like the discontinued cases, *Canepa* dealt with issues similar to those raised in *Stewart* v. *Canada* (1996) and again no violations were found. In fact the main difference between the two cases seems to be that the Committee used provisional measures in *Stewart* but not in *Canepa*.[289]

---

[288] See e.g. HRC *Canepa* v. *Canada* (1997), *J.P.A.F.* v. *Canada* (disc. 1998), *L.* v. *Canada*, and *A.B.* v. *Canada* (disc. 1998). With regard to the latter case counsel submitted a claim on behalf of an Italian citizen who had been living in Canada for more than 30 years, since the age of six. His parents and brother were living in Canada and he had no real connections with Italy. Between 1975 and 1992 he was convicted of various crimes, which according to his counsel were mostly attributable to alcoholism and drug addiction. She pointed out that if the petitioner would be deported he would be barred from readmission to Canada. Counsel claimed deportation would interfere with his liberty of movement and with Articles 17 and 23(1) (protection of the family). She also made the argument that enforcement of the deportation order would result in cruel treatment under Article 7 ICCPR. This argument was based on the separate opinion of Judge de Meyer of the ECtHR in *Beldjoudi* v. *France*, Judgment of 26 February 1992, stating that the removal of an applicant from his country of residence and the severance of the ties with his wife and family would amount to inhuman treatment. Counsel pointed out that the deportation order could now be enforced at any point in time and she requested the use of Rule 86. She pointed out that the consequences of deportation were irreversible and 'should there later be a finding of a violation of rights under the Covenant on the merits', he would be 'unable to secure his rights'. The Special Rapporteur decided not to use provisional measures. The petitioner was deported as scheduled and eventually the Rapporteur transmitted the case under Rule 91. Note verbale to the permanent representative of Canada of 3 March 1995 in *A.B.* v. *Canada* (622/1995) (on file with the author). At the end of 1995 counsel notified the HRC that she was no longer retained to continue as counsel for this matter. In August 1998 the HRC informed the petitioner's parents that it had decided to discontinue examination of the case, taking into account that it had received no correspondence since 1995. Letter to the petitioner's parents of 13 August 1998 in *A.B.* v. *Canada* (622/1995) (on file with the author). Different from cases such as *P.L.-B.* v. *Canada* (where the reason provisional measures were not used probably related to time constraints) in this case there seems to have been a clear decision not to use provisional measures.

[289] HRC *Giosue Canepa* v. *Canada*, 3 April 1997. Counsel's requests for provisional measures in *Canepa* v. *Canada* (1997), *J.P.A.F.* v. *Canada* (disc. 1998), *L.* v. *Canada*, and *A.B.* v. *Canada* (disc. 1998) were made in 1994, shortly after the Committee's admissibility decision in *Stewart* approving of the Rapporteur's provisional measures in that case. In 1993 counsel for Canepa and Stewart had asked the HRC to deal with the cases jointly since they raised 'identical issues'. Initial submission of 16 April 1993 in *Canepa* v. *Canada* (558/1993) (on file with the author). The HRC did not do so. The State, on the other hand, had requested the Committee, in November 1995, to examine the above three cases before formulating its Views in *Stewart*, because it considered the four cases raised similar legal issues while the factual situations were significantly different. It believed that the Committee's consideration of each of those cases would be facilitated if it would be familiar with the range of circumstances presented by them. It did not refer to *Canepa*. Letter by the State to the HRC, 1 November 1995 in relation to 538/1993 (*Stewart*) and 620-622/1995 (on file with the author). After 'due consideration' the HRC decided it would nevertheless be appropriate to proceed with the examination of the merits in *Stewart* at its forthcoming session in April 1996, rather than to put this on hold until it would have been able to examine the admissibility of the other three cases. It noted that the State could submit additional information about the different circumstances mentioned by it in order to facilitate the Committee's task. Letter by the Chairman of the HRC to the Deputy Permanent Representative of Canada, 3 November 1995 in relation to 538/1993 and 620-622/1995 (on file with the author). Counsel in *J.P.A.F.* v. *Canada*, 13 August 1998 (disc.) (on file with the author) worked at the same law firm that was dealing with *Stewart* and *Canepa*. The petitioner was convicted of a

As the situations in these cases were similar to *Stewart* and the same Rapporteur dealt with the requests for provisional measures, it may be assumed either that the Secretariat had not been able to contact her in time or the Committee had discussed the issue and decided no longer to use provisional measures in this context. After all it did not involve a real risk of torture or inhuman treatment in the receiving State.

In *Winata and So Lan Li* v. *Australia* (2001)[290] the HRC determined that the removal by the State party of the petitioners would result in a violation of Article 17 (prohibition of interference with privacy, family etc.), Article 23(1) (protection of the family) and Article 24(1) (protection of children).[291] Inspired by this decision counsel have requested the use of provisional measures in

---

series of criminal offences 'largely stemming from an alcohol abuse problem and a very physically abusive childhood'. On 5 July 1994 he was transferred to a facility for immigration detention for deportation to Portugal. Counsel submitted a case on his behalf a week later. She considered that provisional measures should be used because the petitioner had been in Canada since he was nine years old. He was unfamiliar with Portugal and would experience numerous difficulties there. His entire immediate family was in Canada. He was emotionally dependent on his mother and five sisters and had a solid relationship with his wife with whom he had been married for almost thirteen years. He had two sons, thirteen and five years old. In counsel's opinion the petitioner's 'only hope of avoiding a relapse' in his struggle against his alcohol addiction was 'through family support and ongoing treatment'. She noted that Canada seemed to be unwilling to give a guarantee that it would permit a return to Canada should there later be a finding of a violation of the Covenant on the merits. Her argument was based on the admissibility decision in *Stewart*, stipulating that 'the essential criterion for a consideration of action taken under Rule 86 was the irreversibility of the consequences, in the sense of the inability of a person to secure his rights, should there later be a finding of a violation'. Apart from the risk of harm to the petitioner she also referred to the harm to his children. In October 1994 counsel informed the HRC of the negative decision of the Appeal Division, upholding the deportation order. She expected that her client would be removed in a week. She urged the HRC to consider the request for provisional measures. It appears from the file that the Special Rapporteur decided not to use them. Submission of 3 October 1994 in *J.P.A.F.* v. *Canada* (on file with the author).

290   HRC *Hendrick Winata and So Lan Li* v. *Australia*, 26 July 2001.

291   It noted that 'the mere fact that one member of a family is *entitled* to remain in the territory of a State party does not necessarily mean that requiring other members of the family to leave involves such interference' (§7.1). Nevertheless it considered that in this case there was an 'interference' with the family because 'substantial changes to long-settled family life would follow' from the decision of the State party 'to deport two parents and to compel the family to choose whether a 13-year old child, who has attained citizenship of the State party after living there 10 years, either remains alone in the State party or accompanies his parents'. Accordingly, the HRC was to determine whether this interference would be arbitrary and contrary to Article 17. It noted that given the fact that the petitioners' son had grown up in Australia from his birth thirteen years ago, it was 'incumbent on the State party to demonstrate additional factors justifying the removal of both parents that go beyond a simple enforcement of its immigration law in order to avoid a characterisation of arbitrariness'. It found a violation of Article 17(1) in conjunction with Article 23 in respect of all alleged victims and an additional violation of Article 24(1) in relation to Barry Winata 'due to a failure to provide him with the necessary measures of protection as a minor' (§§7.2 and 7.3). Under Article 2(3)(a) the State party was under an obligation to provide an effective remedy 'including refraining from removing the authors from Australia before they have had an opportunity to have their application for parent visas examined with due consideration given to the protection required by Barry Winata's status as a minor'. It did not further discuss Article 24. *Hendrick Winata and So Lan Li* v. *Australia*, 26 July 2001, §9. Bhagwati, Khalil, Kretzmer and Yalden dissented with regard to the findings of a violation under Articles 17 and 23. See also Burchill (2003) discussing the problematic aspects of this case, especially regarding the attitude of the partents and the 'right to live wherever you want'.

several '*Winata*-type claims', based on Article 24(1) ICCPR, the protection of minors. They involved deportation cases in which petitioners were facing the choice between, on the one hand, uprooting their child and taking him along on their forced return or, on the other hand, leaving him alone in the country he grew up in. The Special Rapporteur, however, has refused to use provisional measures in these cases.[292] Thus, while *Winata* type cases concern children, and a finding on the merits already is available, the Special Rapporteur is not inclined to use provisional measures. This is a clear indication that the HRC has become stricter than it was while the *Stewart* case was pending.

Especially in light of the Committee's refusal to take provisional measures in this situation involving children, its use of provisional measures in the *Stewart* case, to halt expulsion in the context of a complaint on the rights of aliens (not involving non-refoulement), is likely a one time occurrence. After all facing being uprooted or being separated from their parents is more likely to have irreparable consequences for *children*, given their developmental needs, than forced removal would have for adults. In this light it may be assumed that the general rule on provisional measures as proclaimed by the HRC in *Stewart* does not apply across the board or, in any case, should be interpreted restrictively. Despite the obvious hardship that an expulsion such as that of Stewart may cause, it does not constitute irreparable harm to the life and personal integrity of the intended beneficiary. In fact on a continuum of situations in which provisional measures have been used, this case could be situated not altogether beyond the outer limits, as indeed in practice once deported it would be difficult to reverse the situation, but nevertheless just inside the outer limits, tending towards its edge.

Thus, provisional measures used in deportation cases not specifically involving Article 7 ICCPR could be situated within or beyond the outer limits of the concept, depending on the facts of the case. The use of provisional measures in situations involving Articles 12 and 13 claims would only be within the outer limits of the concept if their expulsion would be irreversible. In such case there might be irreversible harm to the claim. In all other cases provisional measures would be beyond the outer limits of the concept.

On the other hand, when children are involved, in light of the child's developing life, situations are less easily reversible *and* these irreversible situations may also result in irreparable harm to persons. If provisional measures were to be taken in such a context, they would in fact not just be within the outer limits of the concept, but could be situated more closely towards the common core. If several human rights adjudicators would develop a practice to use provisional measures in certain irreversible situations involving children, in order to prevent irreparable harm to persons, this practice would indeed fall within the common core of the concept.[293]

---

[292] Interview by author with Martin Scheinin, Geneva, April 2003. Scheinin mentioned two or three '*Winata*' type situations involving family life in which he refused to use provisional measures because the government act would not be irreversible but just inconvenient.

[293] In this respect the adjudicators might also turn to the Children's Convention for inspiration with regard to the irreversibility and irreparability of certain situations when involving children.

3.3 Protecting freedom of expression and access to information (without threats to life and physical integrity)

3.3.1 Introduction

The Inter-American Commission and Court (and the African Commission)[294] have used provisional measures in cases involving freedom of expression and access to information also when there was no actual threat to the life and personal integrity of the beneficiaries.[295] In this respect it is worth noting that the Inter-American Commission attaches particular importance to the freedom of expression and in 1997 it instituted the permanent office of the Special Rapporteur for Freedom of Expression, 'with its own functional and budgetary independence'.[296] As one of the duties and mandates of the Office it named 'immediately informing the Commission of urgent situations that merit the Commission requesting the adoption of precautionary measures or provisional measures that the Commission may request of the Inter-American Court, to prevent grave and irreparable harm to human rights'.[297] Several press organisations are actively lobbying the various organs of the OAS including the Inter-American Commission.[298] The OAS Heads of State and Government have supported and ratified the mandate of the Rapporteur.[299]

The Rapporteur brings cases to the attention of the Commission so that it will take precautionary measures to protect the lives and physical integrity of journalists. In fact in 2006 he implemented a system for daily monitoring in which the Office contacts journalists that are receiving threats and informs them of the possibility of seeking precautionary measures from the Commission 'to protect their lives and personal integrity'.[300] Yet apart from actively pursuing these situations, the Rapporteur also brings cases to the Commission's attention where journalists'

---

[294] See ACHPR *Open Society Justice Initiative (on behalf of Njawe Noumeni)* v. *Cameroon*, provisional measures of 15 July 2004 to 'ensure that no irreparable damage is done to the equipment of Radio Freedom FM', §12, case discontinued in May 2006 upon an amicable settlement.

[295] For provisional measures to protect freedom of expression as well as the right to life and physical integrity see Chapter IX (Threats). See also Chapter XIII (Protection).

[296] See e.g. Report of the Office of the Special Rapporteur for Freedom of Expression Dr. Ignacio Alvarez, OEA/Ser.L/V/II.127, Doc.4, 3 March 2007, p. 5. In general see Thompson (1996), pp. 231-254.

[297] Id., p. 6.

[298] The Special Rapporteur on Freedom of Expression is financed by US media, for instance the Washington Post special fund and by La Sociedad Interamericana de Prensa (SIP). In 1999 SIP had started an extensive campaign to amend internal legislation in the Americas in order to abolish *desacato* (crimes against the honour). See also Inter-American Press Organization (IAPA), www.sipiapa.org. See further Report of the Office of the Special Rapporteur for Freedom of Expression Dr. Ignacio Alvarez, OEA/Ser.L/V/II.127, Doc.4, 3 March 2007, p. 3 referring to the firm support of the sectors with which the Office interacts, including journalists and media. In 2006 the Office also organized seminars to train journalists in the use of the Inter-American system, p. 2.

[299] See e.g. the references to the second and third Summit of the Americas in Report of the Office of the Special Rapporteur for Freedom of Expression Dr. Ignacio Alvarez, OEA/Ser.L/V/II.127, Doc.4, 3 March 2007, p. 4 and pp. 6-7. See also E. Green, US Info staff writer, 'United States Emphasizes Importance of Protecting Press Freedom, New report from Organization of American States details threats to journalists', 13 April 2007, <http://usinfo.state.gov/xarchives/display. html?p=washfile-english&y=2007&m=April&x=20070413160048lxeneerg6.847781e-02> (consulted 14 June 2007).

[300] See e.g. Report of the Office of the Special Rapporteur for Freedom of Expression Dr. Ignacio Alvarez, OEA/Ser.L/V/II.127, Doc.4, 3 March 2007, pp. 1-2.

freedom of expression is at stake, but their lives and physical integrity are not under threat. He specifies that these measures 'were adopted to make possible the full exercise of the freedom of expression and to protect journalists'.[301]

3.3.2 Inter-American practice

In 1995 CEJIL, the main NGO in the Inter-American system of human rights protection, requested the Commission to take precautionary measures directly for the protection of freedom of expression. At that time the Commission was not inclined to do so.[302]

Two years later it did, in the case of *Ivcher Bronstein*. The latter was born in Israel but had been a Peruvian citizen since 1984. He was the president and majority shareholder of Channel 2, which disseminated news on torture and other human rights violations and on the multimillion dollar payments to Mr Montesinos, President Fujimori's right hand man. In April 1997 Peru arbitrarily stripped Ivcher Bronstein of his citizenship. Following this, his position as president of this television station was revoked and his shareholder rights were suspended. Moreover, judicial action was brought against him, his wife and two daughters, his employees and his attorneys. The intended purpose was to remove him from editorial control of the TV channel and to abridge his freedom of expression, which he was exercising through reports on corruption and serious human rights violations. In July 1997 the Commission took precautionary measures on his behalf for the first time in order 'to prevent the victim from being stripped of his nationality, so that he might be regarded as a citizen in the legal action he has brought, thereby avoiding irreparable harm to him'.[303] The State had protested this request arguing that its domestic law provided sufficient remedies. Even if he were to win the cases brought before the domestic courts, the damages he already sustained were 'of enormous magnitude and would be very difficult to redress in full'. These damages were 'aggravated day by day' and required a 'simple and effective remedy'. "For that reason, the Commission, without prejudging the facts but applying the maxim that requires it to opt for the interpretation of the law that best protects human rights, agreed to seek precautionary measures for Mr. Ivcher".[304]

In its admissibility decision the Commission observed that the petitioner's 'present situation is extremely disturbing, as he appears to have suffered virtually irreparable damage'.[305]

The domestic remedies had been 'neither swift nor effective in preventing harm of such severity'. "This harm becomes greater with the passage of time, given the nature of the rights involved (...). The fact that harm has materialized in the interim, before the domestic courts handed down a final ruling on the applications filed seeking writs of amparo, demonstrates how slow and ineffective the remedies in this case have been, and gives the Commission grounds to declare the case admissible".[306]

The Commission found that the State's refusal to heed to the Commission's precautionary measures and the delay in the domestic proceedings placed him in a defenceless position 'and have thus far been ineffective in avoiding harm to the victim, although eventually everything

---

[301] Id., p. 5.

[302] Interview by author with Viviana Krsticevic, Executive Director CEJIL, Washington, D.C., 10 October 2001.

[303] CIDH *Baruch Ivcher Bronstein* v. *Peru*, 3 March 1998 (adm.), §57. See also §27.

[304] Id., §56.

[305] Id., §57.

[306] Id., §60.

might well be settled and any wrong done by the regular courts might eventually be fully righted'. It observed that this could happen with the decision of the constitutional court.[307]

In August 1997 the Commission took precautionary measures on behalf of Gorriti Ellenbogen, a Peruvian journalist and the associate director of the Panama's newspaper 'La Prensa'. It requested Panama to 'suspend his imminent expulsion and enable him to continue exercising his profession as a journalist'.[308] In June 1999 it took precautionary measures on behalf of two persons who were under a detention order in relation to the publication of the 'Black Book of Chilean Justice' by journalist Alejandra Matus. A month later the Commission amplified its measures to extend to the journalist. It requested guarantees for her security and physical integrity as well as for her right to freedom of expression and her intellectual property rights.[309] Moreover, in November 1999 the Commission took precautionary measures on behalf of another Peruvian journalist.[310] Allegedly, security agents had committed repeated acts of persecution against him. The Commission pointed out that the measures it requested Peru to adopt 'were based on the need to enable Mr. Gonzáles Arica to fully exercise his freedom of expression'.[311] In other words, the emphasis was on his freedom of expression rather than his life and physical integrity.

In March 2000 the Commission took precautionary measures requesting Peru to respect the press freedom and freedom of expression of Mr. Delgado Parker.[312] Apparently, the authorities had stripped him of control of the television chain 'Global Network' and confiscated the broadcasting equipment of his radio station 'Radio 1160'.[313] In December 2000 Peru reported to the Commission that it had complied with its request.[314] The precise substance of the precautionary measures is not clear, but presumably they dealt with returning the television station to his control and also returning the radio broadcasting equipment.[315]

In July 2000 the Commission took precautionary measures on behalf of the director of the newspaper 'El Siglo' in Panama. He had been detained for violation of the defamation laws ('desacato'). A critical article in his newspaper had potentially implicated the Attorney General in illegal acts. The Commission requested the State to nullify the arrest warrant and guarantee his right to physical integrity and freedom of expression.[316]

It also took precautionary measures on behalf of a journalist in Honduras. It asked his State to 'prevent the risks he is facing from materialising, based on information presented to the Commission, and to guarantee his unrestricted ability to work as a journalist in Honduras'.[317]

In February 2001 the Commission took precautionary measures on behalf of a Venezuelan journalist, director of the weekly 'La Razón'. The Commission indicated that he was 'at grave

---

[307]   Id., §59. On the merits, 9 December 1998, the Commission found, among others, that he had been arbitrarily deprived of his nationality, contrary to Article 20(3), so as to suppress his freedom of expression.

[308]   CIDH *Gorriti Ellenbogen* v. *Panama*, Annual Report 1997.

[309]   CIDH Annual Report 1999, §15.

[310]   Id., §50.

[311]   Ibid.

[312]   CIDH *Delgado Parker*, 12.262, precautionary measures of 10 March 2000, Annual Report 2000, Chapter III, C.1., §42.

[313]   CIDH Annual Report 2000, §42.

[314]   Ibid., §42.

[315]   About the specific protection required as part of provisional measures, see also Chapter XIII (Protection).

[316]   CIDH Annual Report 2000, §41.

[317]   Id., §37.

risk and requested that the affronts on the journalist's freedom of expression be stopped and, as a result, the censorship measures against him be lifted, including those on La Razón'.[318]

The aforementioned *Ivcher Bronstein* case, dealt with by the Commission, was subsequently brought before the Court. In 2000 the Court ordered provisional measures as well, on behalf of Ivcher Bronstein, his wife, daughters and several others 'in order to ensure their physical, psychological and moral integrity and right to judicial guarantees'.[319] The Court noted that 'the purpose of Provisional Measures in international human rights law is broader since, in addition to their essentially preventive character, they protect effectively basic rights inasmuch as they seek to avoid irreparable damage to persons'.[320] While most of the text of the motivation given is not that exceptional (physical, psychological and moral integrity), again it is clear here that the provisional measures were ordered against a background of increasing concern about the freedom of expression and the situation in Peru in general. After the Court found for Ivcher Bronstein on the merits, it maintained the case,[321] including the provisional measures, until its implementation by Peru.[322]

A second situation in which the Inter-American Court has used provisional measures is to delete the registration of a journalist and a representative of a newspaper from the criminal records. In the context of freedom of expression and the phenomenon of 'desacato' (so-called crimes against the honour) the Court has ordered provisional measures in the *La Nacion* case against Costa Rica. Previously, in March 2001, the Commission itself had adopted precautionary measures on behalf of journalist Mauricio Herrera Ulloa and Fernán Vargas Rohrmoser, the legal representative of *La Nación*, the main Costa Rican newspaper. Mr Herrera had reported information previously published in the Belgian newspaper *De Morgen* questioning the activities of a former Costa Rican ambassador. Subsequently, this journalist was criminally convicted for the pain and suffering allegedly caused by this publication. The Supreme Court of Costa Rica upheld his conviction. The Commission requested Costa Rica to suspend execution of his sentence in order to give it time 'to conduct a full investigation of the allegations raised in the petition, on the grounds that executing it before the Commission investigated the case would cause irreparable

---

[318]   Id., §57 (Case 11.762). The journalist had submitted information on this case on November 1999. The president of the country's largest insurance company had sued him because his newspaper had identified this man as having funded the political campaign of President Chávez. It had accused the insurance company of benefiting from state insurance contracts. A trial judge had subsequently ordered the arrest of the journalist and placed a ban on references to the president of this insurance company. In 2001 another trial judge ordered an arrest warrant 'ignoring the Commission's request for precautionary measures'. Annual Report 2001, Chapter III (a), §60.

[319]   IACHR *Baruch Ivcher Bronstein v. Peru*, Order of 21 November 2000. See also the Order of 23 November 2001 expanding the provisional measures.

[320]   IACHR *Baruch Ivcher Bronstein v. Peru*, Order of 21 November 2000, 9th 'Considering Clause'.

[321]   See Chapter XIV (Jurisdiction) and XVIII (Follow-up) on the practice of the Court to maintain a case that has been decided on the merits and reparations until it has been implemented.

[322]   IACHR *Baruch Ivcher Bronstein v. Peru*, Judgment of 6 February 2001 and Order of 14 March 2001 lifting the provisional measures: "That the changes that have occurred in Peru, the willingness of the State to respect the recommendations formulated by the Commission in its Report No. 94/98, the developments in the Ivcher Bronstein case, particularly the Ivcher family's return to Peru, the cancelling of the arrest warrants against them, the reinstatement of Mr. Ivcher as shareholder and chairman of the board of *Compañía Latinoamericana de Radiodifusión S.A.*, the company that operates Peruvian television's Channel 2, and also other relevant information submitted by the parties, lead this Court to conclude that the justification of "extreme gravity and urgency" and the probability of irreparable damage required by Article 63.2 of the Convention, which led to provisional measures being ordered in the instant case, no longer exist". Order of 14 March 2001 lifting the provisional measures, 4th 'Considering' clause.

harm to Messrs. Herrera and Vargas'.[323] The Commission pointed out that it based itself on a recommendation from the OAS Special Rapporteur for Freedom of Expression.[324] It noted that it took these measures 'in light of the information submitted by the petitioners indicating that these individuals' right to free expression required immediate protection in order to avoid irreparable harm'. Apart from the request to suspend execution of the sentence, the precautionary measures included as well a request 'to refrain from any act tending toward the inclusion of the journalist Herrera in the Costa Rican Judicial Register of Criminals' and 'to refrain from any act or action affecting the right of free expression of the aforesaid journalist or of the newspaper *La Nación*'. La Nación published the complete text of the precautionary measures. They consisted of a letter by the Executive Secretary of the Commission, to the Minister of Foreign Affairs of Costa Rica referring to the rule on precautionary measures in its Rules of Procedure as well as of a recommendation of the OAS Special Rapporteur for the Freedom of Expression.[325] According to the Commission the denounced facts could result in 'irreparable harm' to the human rights of journalist Herrera Ulloa and Mr. Vargas Rohrmoser, representative of the newspaper. It pointed out that in its interpretation of Article 13 ACHR (freedom of expression) limiting the freedom of expression would result in irreparable harm.[326] It emphasised that the article corresponds to a broad concept of freedom of expression and autonomy of persons. The respect for the freedom of expression, it noted, was the instrument for the free interchange of ideas and functioned as a fortifier of democratic processes so as to provide a basic instrument for informed participation. The article's object is to protect and promote access to information, ideas and expression and, thus, to fortify the functioning of a pluralist democracy. The Commission pointed out that it has said before that the use of powers to limit the expression of ideas lends itself to abuse and that subduing unpopular ideas or criticism would restrict the debate fundamental for the effective functioning of the democratic institutions. It emphasised that penalising expressions directed at public functionaries in such a way was a disproportionate punishment in light of the importance of freedom of expression and information in a democratic system. Limiting the free flow of ideas, as long as they do not incite violence, is incompatible with the freedom of expression and the basic principles sustaining pluralistic and democratic societies. The Commission distinguished between the individual and the social dimension of the freedom of expression[327] and pointed out that the denounced facts would constitute irreparable harm both to the individual freedom of expression of the two beneficiaries and to the citizens of Costa Rica who find themselves deprived of access to information about the activities of public functionaries. At the end of its letter, after describing the specific type of measures required of the State,[328] it explained that the precautionary measures were aimed at preventing the materialisation of the risks facing the two beneficiaries.[329] Thus, CEJIL pointed out that the Commission had taken precautionary measures to prevent 'irreparable harm' to the freedom of expression of the journalist and newspaper and of the citizens of Costa

---

[323] CIDH *La Nación*, Annual Report 2000, §28.

[324] See also Chapter II, section 4.3 referring to the role of this Rapporteur.

[325] In 2001 this Special Rapporteur, Santiago A. Canton, became the new Executive Secretary of the Commission.

[326] In the Spanish text it says '*ha interpretado como "daño irreparable" el cercenamiento de medidas que limiten la libertad de expresión*'.

[327] It did not use the phrase '*état de droit*' but appears to be referring to it.

[328] Note that the Commission's precautionary measures in Spanish apparently use the term 'requerir' ('*la Comisión requiere al Estado...*') which appears to refer to 'necessitate' or 'require', while the Commission's precautionary measures in English use the term 'request'.

[329] Letter of Jorge E. Taiana, Executive Secretary of the Commission, to the Minister of Foreign Affairs of Costa Rica, Roberto Rojas L., as published in *La Nación*, titled 'Evitar "daños irreparables", 2 March 2001, <www.nacion.com> (consulted 8 May 2002).

Rica who would otherwise be deprived of access of information about the activities of public functionaries.[330]

It is not clear from the information provided by the Commission what would be the irreparable harm caused. The journalist's criminal conviction included an order to pay a fine. A civil suit for damages was also admitted. The journalist and the newspaper company were held jointly liable. The measures did not prevent the public from being informed as they were taken *ex post facto*. Thus, it is not censorship as such.

This means that the precautionary measures aim at the general risk of inability of journalists to inform the public, including the risk of self-censorship. Only if the prosecution took place in a general context of harassment and intimidation and amounted to cutting off public access to information it could properly be considered as causing harm that is irreversible. Provisional measures to prevent such irreversible harm to the claim could be within the outer limits of the concept as used in the Inter-American system.

Apart from using its own precautionary measures that month, in March 2001 the Commission also petitioned the Court to order provisional measures to safeguard the freedom of expression of Mr. Herrera Ulloa and Mr. Vargas Rohrmoser. Costa Rica had not complied with its precautionary measures taken earlier that month. In September 2001 the Court ordered Costa Rica to adopt, without delay, 'those measures deemed necessary to nullify [their] registration in the Judicial Registry of Criminal Offenders until the case was definitively resolved by the bodies of the inter-American human rights system'. It also ordered Costa Rica to stay the order to publish the operative provisions of the guilty verdict in the newspaper *La Nacion* as well as to stay the order to establish an online 'link' in the digital version of *La Nacion* between the operative part of the verdict and the articles that were the subject of the domestic complaint in the first place.[331] A month later Costa Rica informed the Court of its decision indeed to stay the execution of the criminal verdict against the journalist, as well as his registration in the Judicial Registry of Criminal Offenders, but in November 2001 the Commission informed the Court that 'in flagrant disregard for the provisional measures the Court had agreed upon' there was now an affidavit certifying that Mr. Herrera was nevertheless registered in the judicial registry.

In the matter of *La Nación*, brought by the Commission to the Court, the provisional measure by the Court only indirectly dealt with the freedom of speech. It mainly ordered Costa Rica to prevent irreparable harm to the good name of the journalist involved. It does not appear that the Court has confirmed this approach in other cases. Several years later, for instance, it noted that attacks against the honour and good name do not constitute a situation of extreme gravity and urgency.[332] The development made by the Court is also illustrated in the Court's provisional measures regarding the matter of *Luisiana Ríos et al.* At various points in time the Court has put a different emphasis on freedom of expression in its provisional measures. The Commission had requested the Court to order Venezuela also to protect the freedom of expression of the five employees of Radio Caracas Televisión (RCTV), but in 2002 the Court only issued its usual order for the State to adopt all necessary measures to protect their life and personal integrity.[333] Then in November 2003 it also referred to the freedom of expression of the journalists, but in subsequent Orders it did not repeat this,[334] until 2005 when it issued a strongly worded Order for provisional

---

[330]   La Competencia de la CIDH, comunicado del Centro por la Justicia y el Derecho Internacional (CEJIL), in *La Nacion*, 5 April 2001, <www.nacion.com> (consulted 2 April 2002).

[331]   IACHR *La Nación*, Order of 7 September 2001, 2nd 'Decisional' clause.

[332]   IACHR *Miguel Castro Castro Prison* (Peru), Order of 30 January 2007 (denying a request for provisional measures), 13th 'Considering' clause.

[333]   IACHR *Luisiana Ríos et al.*, Orders of 27 November 2002 and 20 February 2003.

[334]   IACHR *Luisiana Ríos et al.*, Order of 21 November 2003. Orders of 2 December 2003; 4 May 2004; 27 July 2004 (President); 8 September 2004 (following up, emphasizing the obligation to comply with the provisional measures).

measures, among others to take measures to protect the life, personal integrity and freedom of expression of all news media people of RCTV. As part of this provisional measure the Court stressed the importance of the freedom of expression for a democratic society, noting, among others, that a society that is not well-informed is not truly free.[335] Since that time the Court has explicitly pointed out that in the previous Orders it decided on the 'protection of freedom of expression in direct relation to the danger to life and personal integrity as a result of the alleged threats and harassment to which the beneficiaries of the measures were being subjected'. Yet it denied a request for an expansion of these Orders aimed separately at the protection of freedom of expression without such threats. It considered it was not appropriate to order the adoption of the measures requested 'in this case' because it was 'not possible to determine *fumus boni iuris* without making a ruling on the merits of the matter in question, which would imply an assessment of whether the facts alleged by the representatives are in conformity with the American Convention. A decision on merits is made in a judgement delivered in the course of the proceedings on a contentious case lodged before the Court, and not while processing provisional measures. The adoption of the requested measures could imply an incidental prior judgment, with the subsequent establishment of some of the facts and their respective consequences, and these are the object of the principal dispute in the case lodged before the Court'.[336]

3.3.3 Conclusion

It is mainly in the Inter-American system that provisional measures have been used to protect the freedom of expression and the public's access to information, although information is available with regard to the African Commission as well.[337] In practice the activities of the Rapporteur, together with those of press organisations, and the institutional support by the OAS for the issue

---

[335]   IACHR *Luisiana Ríos et al.*, Order of 12 September 2005, 8th 'Considering' clause, referring, among others, to its *Herrera Ulloa* judgment of 2 July 2004, §112, its previous Order for provisional measures in *Luisiana Rios et al*, 8 September 2004, 9th 'Considering' clause and its early Advisory Opinion Compulsory Membership in an Association Prescribed by Law for the Practice of Journalism (Articles 13 and 29 American Convention on Human Rights). Advisory Opinion OC-5/85, 13 November 1985, §70.

[336]   IACHR *Luisiana Ríos et al.*, Order of 3 July 2007 (maintaining the previous Orders, but rejecting a request for expansion), 10th 'Considering' clause, referring to *Matter of Castañeda Gutman* (*Mexico*), Order of 25 November 2005, 6th 'Considering' clause. The commission has since referred to 'the precedent set by the Inter-American Court in the *La Nación* case, in which an order was issued requiring that execution of a judicial sentence be suspended', see CIDH Annual Report 2005, §33, in the context of its own precautionary measures asking Panama to suspend execution of the order for the arrest of a person for failure to pay a fine for slander and defamation for publicly reporting that the attorney general's office had tapped, recorded and published his telephone calls.

[337]   See also the HRC's provisional measures to prevent the destruction of a painting, section 2.11. Outside of the Americas importance has also been attached to the freedom of expression, but only in case law on the merits, or by instituting special mechanisms. See e.g. the African Commission's Special Rapporteur on the Freedom of Expression, the UN Special Rapporteur on the Freedom of Expression and the OSCE Representative on the freedom of the media. For case law on the merits see e.g. IACHR Case of *Herrera Ulloa*, 2 July 2004, §113; Case of *Ivcher Bronstein*, 6 February 2001, §152; Case of *"The Last Temptation of Christ"* (*Olmedo Bustos et al.*), 5 February 2001, §69; and ECtHR see e.g. *Scharsach and News Verlagsgesellschaft* v. *Austria,* 13 November 2003, §29; *Otto-Preminger-Institut* v. *Austria*, 20 September 1994, §49; *The Sunday Times* v. *United Kingdom*, 29 March 1979, §65; *Handyside* v. *United Kingdom*, 7 December 1976, §49.

of freedom of expression, may have played a role in the choice by the Inter-American Commission to expand the scope of its use of precautionary measures.

Not only does the American Convention on Human Rights contain a provision on provisional measures, but this provision explicitly refers to irreparable damage to *persons*. Thus, it specifies the type of 'irreparable harm' warranting provisional measures. Nevertheless, the Inter-American Court has not always used provisional measures with the limited aim of preventing such harm to persons. In the case of the *La Nación Newspaper*, for instance, it used them to prevent 'irreparable harm' to the good name of journalists by ordering the State to take their name from the register of delinquents.

The Court paid lip service to the basic requirements of extreme gravity and urgency and the prevention of irreparable damage to persons, mentioned in Article 63(2) ACHR. Yet in fact this provisional measure was aimed at ensuring freedom of expression by taking away inhibiting factors. Even if entry in this register could be said to be irreversible (which clearly it was not) it would result in irreversible harm to the *claim*, not to persons.

On its website the Commission refers to its requests to the Court to order provisional measures in urgent cases involving 'danger to persons'. On the other hand, when it refers to its function to request 'precautionary measures' it specifies these measures as aimed 'to avoid serious and irreparable harm to human rights in urgent cases'.[338] This phrase appears to include irreversible harm to the claim, rather than just irreparable harm to persons. Indeed, different from the provisional measures by the Court, given the functions of the Commission it is feasible that its precautionary measures are used more flexibly.

Despite the fact that the domestic law and practice of various States regarding *desacato* is clearly problematic, and the Inter-American Court has found violations on the merits, the latter's provisional measures in the *La Nación* case seem to be beyond the outer limits of the concept.[339]

3.4 Halting the judicial seizure of assets or other financial measures

In the European and Inter-American systems the question whether or not to use provisional measures to halt financial measures has come up not just in cases declared inadmissible *ratione materiae*[340] but also in more 'serious' cases.

---

[338] See <http://www.cidh.org/what.htm> (consulted 7 June 2007).

[339] Indeed, concerns have been expressed that the use of provisional measures to protect the freedom of expression may be the opening of Pandora's box. Interview of December 2001 by author with Victor Rodriguez, former staff member Court, in December 2001 a senior research fellow at the International Human Rights Law Institute of DePaul University. Still, in its Order in the *La Nación* case the Court apparently considered that 'the basic requirements of extreme gravity and urgency and the prevention of irreparable damage to persons' were met. It was also in this Order that it noted that the nature of provisional measures in international human rights law is not only 'preventative' but 'fundamentally protective'. Provisional measures are preventive 'in the sense that they preserve a juridical situation'. They are protective as well because they 'protect human rights'. It noted that 'provided the basic requirements of extreme gravity and urgency and the prevention of irreparable damage to persons are met, provisional measures become a genuine jurisdictional guarantee of a preventive nature'. In other words, the Court seems to consider that the protective nature of provisional measures in international human rights law is expressed by the fact that they have become a 'genuine jurisdictional guarantee of a preventive nature', Order of 6 December 2001, 4th 'Considering' clause.

[340] See e.g. ECtHR *Izquierdo Galbis* v. *Spain*, 20 May 2003 (inadm.), where a provisional measures requested by the petitioner on 23 March 2001 was not adopted.

The first example is from the European Court. In the summer of 1984, the case *Bönisch* v. *Austria* (1985) was referred to the ECtHR and in the autumn of that year the petitioner requested the Court to recommend the Government to suspend the execution of fines imposed on him in Austria until delivery of the Court's judgment. The petitioner had argued that even if he would be awarded compensation later (under Article 50), he would already have paid his debts and his means of existence would already have been endangered. The State responded that it had no observations on the petitioner's request.

The next month the President of the Court 'took the view that recovery of the fines in question did not constitute a serious and irreparable measure', but nevertheless, 'acting through the Registrar and without prejudice to the Court's ultimate decision on the merits of the case', he 'expressed the wish that the Austrian authorities should consider the possibility of suspending execution'.[341] In January 1985 Austria notified the Registrar 'that this wish had been brought to the attention of the responsible authorities'.[342] While the petitioner's request was made under the Court's rule on provisional measures, it is clear from the President's formulation (not 'serious and irreparable') that his request to the State was not a provisional measure. Despite the text of the European rule on provisional measures, which does not refer to irreparable harm, such harm appears to be the criterion used also in 1985.

The Inter-American Commission appears to have used its precautionary measures at least once in a financial context. The first precautionary measure mentioned in the Inter-American Commission's Annual Report of 1997 clearly does not deal with the prevention of irreparable harm to life and personal integrity. It consisted of postponement of the judicial seizure of the assets of the petitioner, while a friendly settlement procedure was ongoing between him and Argentina. The Commission mentioned that, from 1972 on, the petitioner, Mr. Jose Maria Cantos, had been stripped of a large number of commercial documents. He claimed that State and provincial officials had caused him economic losses and duress for which he sought restitution and indemnity.[343] Now judicial seizure of his assets was threatened based on the judgement of costs, following ten years of processing the case in the Supreme Court of Justice of Argentina. The Commission took precautionary measures in March 1997.

It is not clear why judicial seizure of his assets would result in irreparable harm. In fact, any damage would be reparable at a later stage by returning the money to him. It would be interesting to know why the Commission used precautionary measures here. Did it believe that, in the circumstances of that particular case, the seizure of his assets would cause irreparable harm to his livelihood and, thus, his life?[344]

---

341 ECtHR *Bönisch* v. *Austria*, 6 May 1985, §6.

342 Ibid. The Court found that there had been no equality of arms with regard to the treatment of witnesses, in violation of Article 6(1) ECHR.

343 CIDH *Jose Maria Cantos* v. *Argentina*, case 11.636, Annual Report 1997. CEJIL notes in its case docket of 1997 that Mr. Cantos was detained without cause on 40 occasions and subjected to other forms of intimidation. It presented this case before the Commission in June 1996 'as an example of an individual's lack of access to the judicial process in Argentina'. According to CEJIL he was in danger of having to declare bankruptcy, CEJIL case docket 1997. It seems that CEJIL and the Commission consider this as the irreparable harm that was to be prevented. See also the reference to the Commission's precautionary measures of 11 March 1997 in IACHR *Cantos* v. *Argentina*, Judgment of 28 November 2002, §3.

344 The case was subsequently brought before the Inter-American Court, which found violations of Articles 8(1) and 25 ACHR and ordered the State to abstain from any further financial measures against Mr Campos and to cover the costs of the various proceedings. See IACHR *Cantos* v. *Argentina*, 28 November 2002.

4 CONCLUSION

This chapter gave some examples of atypical use of provisional measures and of failed requests for provisional measures made by petitioners. It presented these examples as gravitating between common core, outer limits and beyond. It distinguished between provisional measures that are within and those that are beyond the outer limits of the concept.

In my view the regional courts and the HRC should reserve their provisional measures mainly for situations where life and physical or psychological integrity are at stake. This way, the authority and effectiveness of provisional measures is likely to be better upheld. Extensively using provisional measures to intervene in pending cases dealing with other rights would inevitably make the use of provisional measures less exceptional and more routine. This could also lead to diminished compliance. The Conclusion to Part II (purpose) further discusses the common core of the concept of provisional measures and how this relates to preventing irreparable harm to persons.

Provisional measures by the Inter-American Commission, the African Commission and the Bosnia Chamber are sometimes used in a context slightly different from those of the other adjudicators. Given their different functions (next to the adjudicatory function also monitoring or State reports, or preparing country or thematic reports, organizing on-site visits, informal meetings, promotional activities and issuing press releases) and regional nature the Inter-American and African *Commission* are more closely in touch with the petitioners and potentially more aware of the local situations in which the victims and the beneficiaries of their provisional measures must operate.[345] Thus these adjudicators may be better able to adapt their use of provisional measures to the exigencies of the situation.

Because of its more constitutional and local '*sui generis*' position, a similar reasoning could apply to the Bosnia Chamber.[346] Moreover, a greater flexibility in the use of provisional measures would be warranted because the Chamber was explicitly mandated to order provisional measures and this mandate was not limited to irreparable harm to *persons*. Yet exactly because it was an adjudicator of final instance, with a near constitutional status to live up to, this flexibility should not extend to the use of provisional measures beyond the outer limits, in other words, provisional measures that do not even aim at the prevention of *irreversible* harm to the claim.

In this chapter the examples discussed were situated either on a continuum between 'towards the common core' and 'towards the outer limits', as discussed in section 2, or possibly *beyond* the outer limits of the concept, as discussed in section 3. Those provisional measures situated more closely towards the common core should therefore be seen as most convincing and authoritative.

Not just the rights invoked are relevant in this respect, but also the persons involved. Indeed the HRC has stressed that the accessible and effective remedies required in Article 2(1) ICCPR

---

[345] Previously this was also the case, to some extent, with the European Commission on Human Rights.

[346] See also the advice of the Venice Commission regarding the merger of the temporary Bosnia Chamber (whose case law is referred to in this book) and the Constitutional Court of Bosnia and Herzegovina, which discussed the need for the Constitutional Court to apply provisional measures in a similar manner as the Bosnia Chamber: 'it must be avoided that the broad protection accorded by means of provisional measures be diminished by the application, by the Constitutional Court, of criteria which may turn out to be more restrictive and thus less functional'. European Commission for Democracy Through Law (Venice Commission), Report of the Working Group on the Merger of the Human Rights Chamber and the Constitutional Court of Bosnia and Herzegovina, Sarajevo, Strasbourg, December 1999-June 2000, 16 June 2000, Restricted CDL (2000) 47 fin, §47, <http://www.venice.coe.int/docs/2000/CDL(2000)047 fine.asp> (consulted 22 June 2007).

'should be appropriately adapted so as to take account of the special vulnerability of certain categories of persons, including in particular children'.[347] More specifically, the protection of children's rights may warrant the adjudicators' early intervention because a violation of their rights is more likely to cause irreparable harm than the violation of the same rights, for instance the right to respect for family life, would cause adults. In that sense, even a temporary separation from his or her parents, for instance through deportation, could cause a child irreparable harm. In fact, this harm could be such as to impact on the development and thus the life and personal integrity of the child involved. Provisional measures used in this context therefore fit within the rationale of provisional measures that all human rights adjudicators seem to have in common.

In other cases, however, not involving children, a violation of the right to family life, freedom of expression, liberty, etc. in itself normally is not irreversible, let alone irreparable in the same sense as a violation of the right to life and personal integrity.

For the sake of argument and presentation this book refers to a common practice when more than one adjudicator has clearly used provisional measures in the circumstances at hand. Together with a common rationale this would bring such provisional measures within the common core of the concept, as discussed in the previous chapters.

Those provisional measures referred to as beyond the outer limits, because the harm they aim to prevent in fact is not irreversible, are in fact inappropriate. This inappropriateness does vary depending on the nature of the tasks of the adjudicator. The Inter-American Commission appears to have developed a practice in which it sometimes uses precautionary measures more loosely in order to publicly intervene and exert pressure pending the proceedings. This way it shows that it attaches particular importance to an issue such as the freedom of expression. Strictly speaking this type of precautionary measures often is beyond the outer limits of the concept of provisional measures.

It is true that when it comes to the African and Inter-American Commission their flexibility is one of their main assets. It could be argued that, given the context of their other, non-adjudicatory, functions, and the presence of a higher adjudicatory body, the need for them to act within the outer limits of the concept of provisional measures is less pressing, so long as the decision-making is sufficiently transparent. Yet the fact that they also prepare country and thematic reports and take promotional and diplomatic action could help inform their decision-making in individual cases, but it should not make this decision-making process and its outcome less 'judicial'. Their flexibility lies in resorting to their reporting function both to reinforce their adjudicatory function and for more general promotional and advisory action.

Thus, while they perform their adjudicatory function they should in fact apply the judicial tool of provisional measures in a manner that is convincing and does not move beyond the outer limits of the concept. This applies all the more for the regional courts and the international adjudicators as judicial bodies of final instance. For them to follow the practice of the Inter-American Commission of sometimes moving beyond the outer limits of the concept would dilute the authority of their provisional measures.

---

[347]   HRC General Comment on Article 2 ICCPR, §15.

1 INTRODUCTION

The previous chapters discussed a range of situations in which human rights adjudicators have used provisional measures and the relation of these measures with the eventual decision on the merits. It appears from the examples discussed that the protection required by provisional measures may take various forms.

This chapter deals first with the question whether provisional measures require action or abstention (section 2) and whether, in the former situation, they are phrased in general terms or specify the exact measures to be taken by the State (section 3). In addition this chapter deals specifically with the approach of the various adjudicators to the beneficiaries and addressees of their provisional measures (section 4).

Finally, in order to properly understand the purpose and scope of provisional measures in human rights adjudication, this chapter also examines how the preventive measures required at the provisional measures stage relate to the measures required upon a finding of a violation, particularly in the form of cessation and reparation (section 5).

With regard to the issues of specificity and the group of beneficiaries, the focus is on the practice of the Inter-American Commission and Court, which provides more insights than that of the other human rights adjudicators. With regard to the relation to reparation the focus is on the somewhat problematic practice of the HRC in this respect.

2 ACTION OR ABSTENTION: POSITIVE OBLIGATIONS IN ORDERS FOR PROVISIONAL MEASURES

2.1 Introduction

At first sight the protection requested in provisional measures would seem exclusively negative: to refrain from torture, execution or threats to life. In fact, however, States must take at least some positive action in order to implement such an Order for provisional measures. We have seen this already in the practice of the ICJ and even of its predecessor, which at one point ordered China to provide 'effective protection' to Belgian citizens.[1] The ICJ's Order to halt an execution in the *LaGrand* case (*Germany* v. *US*) was more explicit in this respect in light of the US response to the earlier Order on behalf of Breard. It specified that the federal State must ensure that its constituent parts comply as well.[2]

---

[1]   PCIJ *Sino-Belgian* case, Order of the President of 8 January 1927. See Chapter I (ICJ).

[2]   ICJ *LaGrand* (*Germany* v. *US*), Order of 3 March 1999. See Chapter I (ICJ). See also ICJ *Questions relating to the Obligation to Prosecute or Extradite* (*Belgium* v. *Senegal*), Order of 28 May 2009, Dissenting opinion of Judge Cançado Trindade, §53 ("The urgency of a situation can bedetermined by reference to action as well as omission").

While it is established in all human rights systems that States must make expenditures in order to fulfil their human rights obligations, including those relating to the right to life and the prohibition of torture, it is mainly in the Inter-American system that this aspect has been introduced in provisional measures as well. Only requiring negative measures, such as halting the execution of a death sentence, as part of an order for provisional measures, may in fact make insufficient use of this tool. This section first discusses how even negatively phrased provisional measures may require positive action. Then it refers to how the human rights adjudicators have dealt with positive obligations in their decisions on the merits. Finally it notes how in the Inter-American system an extensive practice has developed of ordering provisional measures that require positive action too, a practice which appears to be cautiously followed by other human rights adjudicators as well.

2.2   Positive obligations implied in orders to abstain from acting

Even a negatively phrased Order without any directions on implementation requires some positive action, for instance to inform governors, local authorities, courts and the management of prisons. This also implies the use of resources. If the State in question fails to take such positive action, the adjudicator may subsequently specify the action required more closely.

Thus in practice many provisional measures require a State to refrain from certain action. At the same time even such abstention from, for instance, executing a death sentence, corporal punishment or expulsion may imply some obligations to act as well.[3]

2.3   Positive obligations on the merits

In their decisions on the merits the various human rights adjudicators have recognized that certain rights have been violated because of omissions by the State. All adjudicators discussed have found violations of the right to life and the prohibition of torture or cruel treatment for failure to take preventive measures.[4] Thus their case law on the merits does not form an obstacle but indeed supports the use of provisional measures requiring positive action pending the proceedings.

Both in the European and in the Inter-American jurisprudence it is possible to speak of a continuum between negative and positive obligations under the right to life and the prohibition of torture. The ECtHR has also considered that a positive obligation arises when the authorities 'knew or ought to have known', about 'a real and immediate risk to the life of an identified individual or individuals from the criminal acts of a third party'. States should take measures 'within the scope of their powers which, judged reasonably, might have been expected to avoid that risk'.[5]

---

3   See Chapters III-V, respectively.

4   The HRC, for instance, has found violations of the right to life (Article 6 ICCPR), the prohibition of torture and inhuman or degrading treatment (Article 7), the obligation to treat detainees humanely (Article 10) and the obligation to protect their security (Article 9) because of an omission by the State and has recommended positive measures to remedy such violations. See particularly Chapters VI (Disappearances), VII (Health in detention), IX (Death threats), X (Culture) and XI (Mass expulsion).

5   See e.g. ECtHR *Mahmut Kaya* v. *Turkey*, 28 March 2000, §86 and *Osman* v. *UK*, 28 October 1998, §116: "For the Court, and having regard to the nature of the right protected by Article 2, a right fundamental in the scheme of the Convention, it is sufficient for an applicant to show that the authorities did not do all that could be reasonably expected of them to avoid a real and

2.4   Explicit positive obligations in provisional measures

In the Inter-American system the continuum between positive and negative obligations is not just reflected in the Judgments on the merits and reparations, but also in the substance of the provisional measures. Judgments on the merits and reparations may require expenditures, but provisional measures may too. Especially in the Inter-American system, but also in some of the others, provisional measures have been ordered in which the State clearly was to act rather than to refrain from acting. The Inter-American Court has required a State, as part of a provisional measure, to allow a person's return.[6] The European Commission has done so too, but in the particular circumstance in which previous provisional measures to halt their expulsion had been ignored. Following Sweden's expulsion of Cruz Varas to Chile and Mansi to Jordan, in contravention of the Commission's provisional measures, the Commission took new provisional measures for Sweden to enable them to return as soon as possible.[7]

As noted, it is not always easy to distinguish between positive and negative obligations. There is at least one case in which the European Commission implicitly requested a State to take positive measures. In September 1992 Spain had sent a group of 53 African refugees across the border, but Morocco refused their entry. They were waiting on no man's land in the burning sun, without water, shelter or sanitation. In a provisional measure the European Commission indicated the desirability of Spain taking the necessary measures to prevent treatment of the petitioners that could be contrary to Article 3 ECHR.[8] While the Commission did not specify the manner in which the State should take the necessary measures, both immediate provision of water, shelter and sanitation and allowing immediate access to Spanish territory would require positive action rather than abstention. This also illustrates that the obligation to take a positive measure may also be phrased in general terms and does not necessarily have to be specific.[9]

The Inter-American Commission, moreover, has used precautionary measures ordering States to provide HIV medication.[10] Examples of positive action required in provisional measures

---

immediate risk to life of which they have or ought to have knowledge". See also *Z. et al.* v. *UK*, 10 May 2001, §121. When there is a credible assertion that authorities have treated someone in violation of Article 3, the State has the obligation to investigate this, see e.g. *Labita* v. *Italy*, 6 April 2000. In other cases public authorities have specific obligations, involving persons in a vulnerable situation, to investigate a situation before taking certain action. *Keenan* v. *UK*, 3 April 2001, discusses the example of a psychotic detainee who was put in solitary confinement and was found dead the next day, judgment of. Clearly the obligation to investigate a situation before taking any action applies as well in the face of an impending expulsion when the person involved claims a real risk of torture in the receiving State, see *Jabari* v. *Turkey*, 11 July 2000. See generally for the ECtHR approach to positive measures in the context of private life, freedom of expression and the margin of appreciation, e.g. *X and Y* v. *the Netherlands*, 26 March 1985; *Plattform 'Artze für das Leben'* v. *Austria*, 21 June 1988; *Powell and Rayner* v. *UK*, 21 February 1990; *Keegan* v. *Ireland*, 26 May 1994; *Stubbings* v. *UK*, 22 October 1996; *Özgür Gündem* v. *Turkey*, 16 March 2000 and *Von Hannover* v. *Germany*, 24 June 2004. For an analysis see e.g. Vlemmincx (2002) and Mowbray (2004).

6   See Chapter XI (Mass expulsion).

7   EComHR provisional measure of 19 October 1989 in *Mansi* v. *Sweden*, 9 March 1990 (struck out) and 7 December 1989 (adm.). Provisional measures of 9 November 1989 and 7 December 1989 in *Cruz Varas et al.* v. *Sweden*, judgment of 20 March 1991.

8   EComHR *B., M. and 51 others* v. *Spain*, 11 September 1992.

9   See also section 3 on the specificity of provisional measures requiring positive action.

10   See Chapter XII (Other situations).

taken by other adjudicators as well are to *ensure* access to medication in detention and to *ascertain* the whereabouts of alleged victims.[11]

There have equally been several informal provisional measures requesting *information* about the health, whereabouts or access to counsel of the alleged victim.[12] Obviously in such cases the State had to take positive action in order to provide such information. At the same time the adjudicator may have hoped this would encourage the State to take positive measures to protect the health and safety of the detainee.

The Inter-American Commission and Court have gone a step further in their use of provisional measures. In the first case before it the Court ordered provisional measures to protect witnesses against threats, something obviously requiring positive measures. By now the Commission and Court have built an extensive practice in this respect.[13] On a regular basis they order States to take positive action to protect persons (both alleged victims and witnesses) against death threats and harassment. In fact most of their provisional measures involve protection against death threats and thus require such action.

Recently, the HRC also used provisional measures to protect someone against death threats and harassment.[14] More generally, the HRC has noted that the legal obligation under Article 2(1) ICCPR is both negative and positive in nature. This provision also underlies the Committee's use of provisional measures.[15]

In its first provisional measure CEDAW asked a State to protect the petitioner against threats by her former partner.[16] The African Commission, CAT and CEDAW have used provisional measures with this aim as well. The ECtHR, however, has not yet done so.[17] It was argued in Chapter IX (Threats) that all human rights adjudicators should be able to use provisional measures to order the State to take positive measures pending the proceedings in order to prevent irreparable harm to persons. After all, in cases involving life and personal integrity, appropriate redress is no longer possible after the harm has occurred.

In view of the fact that States are expected to devise adequate policies, make expenditures and prioritise in order to meet their obligations under human rights treaties, the use of provisional measures to prevent attacks against persons has been a logical step, taken clearly in the Inter-American system, but to a certain extent in most other human rights systems as well. In particular,

---

[11] See e.g. Bosnia Chamber *Matanović et al.* v. *Republika Srpska*, 6 August 1997, §63, discussed in Chapter VII on disappearances. In this case the Bosnia Chamber used provisional measures 'immediately to take all necessary steps to ascertain the whereabouts or fate of the applicants and to secure their release if still alive'. It left open 'the possibility of ordering further steps to be taken by the respondent Party as may appear appropriate in the future'. More closely see Chapters VII (Health care in detention) and VI (Disappearances).

[12] See Chapters VII (Health care in detention), VI (Disappearances) and VIII (Procedural rights).

[13] This includes positive obligations of the State to protect against acts of third parties as well, e.g. IACHR *Caso de las Comunidades del Jiguamiandó y del Curbaradó*, Order of 15 March 2005, 7th 'Considering' clause; case of the *Peace community of San José de Apartadó*, Order of 15 March 2005, 7th 'Considering' clause and *Case of las penitenciarías de Mendoza*, Order of 22 November 2004, 13th 'Considering' clause. See further Chapter IX (Threats).

[14] See Chapter IX (Threats).

[15] HRC General Comment on Article 2 ICCPR, 29 March 2004, §6.

[16] CEDAW *A.T.* v. *Hungary*, 26 January 2005 (provisional measures of 20 October 2003). In this case CEDAW found violations of Article 2(a), (b) and (e), Article 5 and Article 16. With regard to the petitioner the State was to take 'immediate and effective measures' to guarantee her physical and mental integrity and that of her family. It should also ensure that she was 'given a safe home in which to live with her children, receives appropriate child support and legal assistance as well as reparation proportionate to the physical and mental harm undergone and to the gravity of the violations of her rights', §9.6 under I.

[17] See Chapter IX (Threats).

preventive measures must be taken to protect the right to life and the prohibition of cruel treatment, which have a special place in the human rights treaties.

With regard to detention situations, death threats and disappearances provisional measures generally order to put a stop to an already continuing situation. Thus, while substantively provisional measures may aim at preserving the status quo, in some cases they may even aim at changing it. After all when someone is being threatened over a long period of time a provisional measure could be seen as aiming at changing the status quo, but also as returning to the previous position in which there were no threats (the *status quo ante*). In the interest of the proceedings there may also be a need to maintain the status quo or return to the status quo ante in order to prevent (further) irreparable harm to the witnesses of a violation or to family or counsel of the petitioner or even to human rights defenders in general.

2.5   Conclusion

In sum, in certain contexts involving threats to life or personal integrity, provisional measures have required States to take positive measures as well as measures to refrain from undertaking certain action.[18] Qualifying an obligation as one of action or abstention sometimes depends on the way it is put: using the word 'respect', for instance, seems to point at a duty to refrain from acting while in reality it may encompass an obligation to take positive action as well.

Often there is a continuum between positive and negative obligations as part of the measures that must be undertaken in order to comply with provisional measures. The key is the prevention of irreparable harm. As has been done in the Inter-American system, in the other systems any possible positive measures required could equally be mentioned incrementally.

States must make expenditures in order to fulfil their human rights obligations. Indeed, in decisions on the merits the adjudicators have established that States are not only obliged to refrain from certain action, but must also guarantee, by positive measures, that others do not violate these rights, especially if there is some relationship with the State in the sense of acquiescence or (indirect) involvement. It is therefore not far-fetched for adjudicators to use provisional measures requiring a State to protect persons against death threats and harassment pending the case.

At first sight the obligation to refrain from action seems less invasive to the State than is taking provisional measures that require positive action. Nevertheless, exactly because of this continuum and in light of the importance attached to the rights involved, provisional measures requiring positive action are sometimes essential to guarantee the right to life and the prohibition of cruel treatment and torture. Protection against death threats involves the right to life and protection of physical integrity. They are core rights whose violation causes irreparable harm to persons. Such violations must therefore be prevented even if this entails that the State must take positive measures pending the proceedings.

Provisional measures may be warranted to put a stop to ongoing violations, through positive measures, exactly because continuing violations increase the irreparable harm already incurred. As noted, sometimes this even requires return to the previous situation (*status quo ante*). If this is the only way to halt further irreparable harm to personal integrity in the context of the prohibition of cruel treatment or torture, provisional measures should in fact require this. In other circumstances such return to the previous situation would be too far reaching as part of positive measures required pending the proceedings. For instance, if return to the status quo ante would mean the demolition of buildings constructed against the protests of indigenous people, it would be more appropriate to require this following the finding of a violation, as part of the decision on

---

[18]   See also Nørgaard (1994), p. 184 and Garry (2001), p. 404, noting that provisional measures may be either of a 'prohibitive' or of a 'proactive' nature.

reparations.[19] On the other hand, if the adjudicator has already used provisional measures to *halt* the construction of these buildings but the State ignores these and the building is nevertheless constructed, legally it could be appropriate to require return to the status quo ante already pending the proceedings rather than as a form of reparation only. Nevertheless, even in such circumstances adjudicators are unlikely to require this type of restoration of the *status quo* pending the proceedings, if only because financial consequences would be considerable, especially if the adjudicator would later conclude that there had been no violation other than the disruption of the provisional measure.[20]

An element of positive action is present in most provisional measures and should in fact be made explicit in cases involving ongoing situations such as adverse detention conditions, recent disappearances and death threats.

3   THE SPECIFICITY OF PROVISIONAL MEASURES

3.1   Introduction

As already became evident in international case law not exclusively dealing with human rights, the duty to cooperate is of fundamental importance, for instance in relation to the environment. This duty underlies orders for provisional measures, but sometimes these measures explicitly refer to this duty as well.[21] We will see something similar in the context of the Inter-American human rights system in particular. In addition, as ICJ Judge Shahabuddeen has pointed out, provisional measures 'should be framed in self-executing terms, in the sense that [they] should contain all the legal elements required for [their] interpretation and application'.[22] Again, we will see that such specificity is found in the Inter-American system in particular.

The question of the differences in the specificity of the measures required obviously is closely linked to that of the previous section involving the obligation to act. These differences are particularly relevant for provisional measures to protect against threats and harassment.[23] Already in 1927 the PCIJ ordered China to provide 'effective protection' to Belgian nationals, among others by accompanying any Belgian requiring such protection 'in safety to the nearest Belgian consulate'.[24] As we will see, especially in the Inter-American system provisional measures have sometimes acquired a similar specificity.

In the *Frontier Dispute* case (1986) the ICJ ordered the withdrawal of the armed forces of both parties, the terms of which should be determined by agreement between them. Only if the states would fail to reach such agreement, the ICJ would step in once more. Again we will find similarities in approach in the practice developed by the Inter-American Court ordering the State to agree with the beneficiaries on the specific protection required. At the same time this Court obviously takes into account the special vulnerability of the individual vis-à-vis the State.

---

[19]   This example is inspired on the factual situation in HRC *Hopu and Bessert* v. *France*, 29 July 1997. See Chapter X (Culture).

[20]   See e.g. ICJ *Passage through the Great Belt* case (*Finland* v. *Denmark*), Order of 29 July 1991, §31 as discussed in Chapter I (ICJ), section 3.6.

[21]   See e.g. ITLOS *MOX plant case* (*Ireland* v. *UK*), Order of 3 December 2001. See Chapter I (ICJ and ITLOS), section 3.7.2. See also Chapters XV (Immediacy and risk) and XVIII (Follow up).

[22]   Declaration of Judge Shahabuddeen attached to the ICJ Order for provisional measures in *Cameroon* v. *Nigeria*, 15 March 1996. See further Chapter I (ICJ).

[23]   Obviously this Chapter should be read in close conjunction with Chapters III to XII on the situations in which provisional measures have been used.

[24]   PCIJ *Sino-Belgian* case, Order of the President of 8 January 1927. See Chapter I (ICJ).

We have also seen that the ICJ has the authority to order provisional measures *proprio motu* and that it routinely modifies the substance of the provisional measures as requested by one State in order to accommodate the interest of the other State, as well as in the general interest of preventing the escalation of a conflict or irreparable harm to human beings squashed in the middle.[25] Human rights adjudicators equally have the authority to order provisional measures *proprio motu*, as well as modify the terms of the provisional measures requested by the petitioner.

Sometimes human rights adjudicators only point out that States must protect certain persons or groups.[26] At other times they indicate more concretely the protective measures that States should undertake. As noted, all adjudicators have used provisional measures of a rather general nature, simply ordering the State to refrain from acting in a certain manner or to act exactly in order to achieve a certain result (e.g. protection against threats). At times adjudicators have specified certain of the positive measures required. This could relate, for instance, to providing *information* about an alleged victim's state of health or to access to medication. This specification could also relate to specific measures protecting against threats, including investigation and prosecution of previous threats.

Leaving the choice of implementation to the State generally is the initial approach of the human rights adjudicators. In light of the attitudes of addressee States provisional measures may become increasingly more specific. Generally speaking the HRC and CAT do not specify their provisional measures. On the other hand, already in its first provisional measure the CEDAW specified that the measures to be taken by the State should be 'immediate', 'appropriate', 'concrete' and 'preventive'.[27] The African Commission does not specify its provisional measures either, at least no specific information is available with regard to their contents.[28] Mugwanya points out that, thus far, these measures 'have not been sufficiently elaborate' or 'specific'.[29] In comparison to the Inter-American Commission and Court the ECtHR does not generally specify the specific steps to be taken as part of its provisional measures.[30] Traditionally the European Court has been cautious in its directions, even at the merits stage, possibly still out of fear for being considered 'intrusive'.[31] Various reasons are possible for the Court to increasingly specify

---

[25]   See Chapter I (ICJ).

[26]   The next section deals with the (group of) beneficiaries.

[27]   CEDAW *A.T.* v. *Hungary*, 26 January 2005, §4.2.

[28]   See also Chapter II (Systems).

[29]   Mugwanya (2003), pp. 376-377, referring to ACHPR *Degli* v. *Togo*, March 1995 (17th session) and *Ken Saro Wiwa* v. *Nigeria*, 31 October 1998.

[30]   It does appear to do so on occasion, but it takes a very gradual approach. An example where it apparently became increasingly specific is provided by the NGO St. Petersburg International Collegium of Advocates (London office). It notes that the ECtHR had intervened several times on behalf of Alkesanyan who had contracted HIV/AIDS and was being denied medical treatment in detention. Allegedly, on 28 November 2007 it requested his immediate in-patient treatment in a specialized AIDS hospital; on 5 December it reiterated its provisional measure, indicating it must be implemented before 10 December of that year and requesting a response to the petitioner's allegation that he is being pressured to give false testimony in exchange for release for medical treatment; on 11 December 2007 it asked what efforts Russia had undertaken to secure his transfer to a specialized clinic; and on 21 December 2007 it warned Russia that if the petitioner's health would deteriorate or he would die in detention, 'it may find Russia responsible' for a violation of his right to life and the right not to be subjected to inhuman and degrading treatment. It extended its provisional measure and 'requires the creation of a bipartisan medical commission of doctors' appointed by the petitioner and the State together in order to 'assess his medical condition and prepare a plan for his treatment'. See <www.mka-london.co.uk/timeline.asp> (consulted 23 September 2008).

[31]   See further section 5.3 of this Chapter. This may also be related to a specific perception of the 'non-activist' role of an adjudicator. The sensitivity for a specified manner of implementation,

the obligations of States. The Court is dealing more and more with extreme situations of gross human rights violations. In addition the Court may hope that an increased specificity will assist States in implementing their obligations under the ECHR, both pending the case and upon the finding of a violation on the merits.[32] Both old and new members of the Council of Europe have an interest in this. Moreover, the overburdened Court clearly has, in order to avoid the need to deal with repeated complaints.[33]

In order to clarify the ways in which an international adjudicator could (incrementally) specify its provisional measures, this section draws from the rich practice developed in the Inter-American system. General orders are flexible and leave greater discretion to the State with regard to their implementation. Yet in the experience of the Inter-American Commission and Court they have appeared to be less appropriate in cases involving risks to life and personal integrity.

Before discussing whether it is necessary for human rights adjudicators to specify their provisional measures, first another issue is addressed involving cautious phrasing in provisional measures in unprecedented cases.

---

perceiving this as an 'imposition', applies mainly to European States. In *Ilascu et al.* v. *Moldova and Russia*, 8 July 2004, the ECtHR (Grand Chamber) noted: "Although it is not for the Court to indicate which measures the authorities should take in order to comply with their obligations most effectively, it must verify that the measures actually taken were appropriate and sufficient in the present case. When faced with a partial or total failure to act, the Court's task is to determine to what extent a minimum effort was nevertheless possible and whether it should have been made. Determining that question is especially necessary in cases concerning an alleged infringement of absolute rights such as those guaranteed by Articles 2 and 3 of the Convention". ECtHR *Ilascu et al.* v. *Moldova and Russia*, 8 July 2004, §334. See generally e.g. Van Kempen (2003), pp. 92-101. Yet the ECtHR is more specific about the obligations of States when it has found a violation of the right to life. In *Kaya* (2000) it reiterated with regard to the alleged inadequacy of the investigation, 'that the obligation to protect life under Article 2 of the Convention, read in conjunction with the State's general duty under Article 1 of the Convention "to secure to everyone within [its] jurisdiction the rights and freedoms defined in [the] Convention", requires by implication that there should be some form of effective official investigation when individuals have been killed as a result of the use of force', ECtHR *Mahmut Kaya* v. *Turkey*, 28 March 2000, §102 also referring to *McCann and Others* v. *UK*, 27 September 1995, §161. See also *Assanidze* v. *Georgia*, 8 April 2004 (ordering the petitioner's immediate release). Moreover, the Court is becoming more aware of the possibility to specify the necessary changes in law and practice in its judgments on the merits (see e.g. Minutes of meeting between Court and organizations representing applicants and/or intervening as third parties, 10 April 2006, p. 3). For an example see *Dybeku* v. *Albania*, 18 December 2007, §64 ('the Court considers that in view of its findings in the present case, the necessary measures should be taken as a matter of urgency in order to secure appropriate conditions of detention and adequate medical treatment, in particular, for prisoners, like the applicant, who need special care owing to their state of health').

[32] For an example of such specificity ECtHR *Shtukaturov* v. *Russia*, 27 March 2008, §33 where the provisional measures were as follows: "the respondent government was directed to organize, by appropriate means, a meeting between the applicant and his lawyer. That meeting could take place in the presence of the personnel of the hospital where the applicant was detained, but outside their hearing. The lawyer was to be provided with the necessary time and facilities to consult with the applicant and help him in preparing the application before the European Court. The Russian Government was also requested not to prevent the lawyer from having such meeting with his client at regular intervals in the future. The lawyer, in turn, was obliged to be cooperative and comply with reasonable requirements of the hospital regulations".

[33] See also Rieter (2007), p. 974.

3.2 Cautious phrasing and lack of precedent

The specific terminology used in provisional measures may not only help clarify the nature of the State's obligations, but also indicate the doubts the adjudicator has regarding the appropriateness of the use of provisional measures. This may be illustrated by a provisional measure ordered by the HRC. In *Weiss* v. *Austria* (2003), involving a life sentence in the U.S., the petitioner had argued that he would risk irreparable harm.[34] In response, the Rapporteur did not request the State to halt the extradition until the Committee had been able to examine the case. Instead he requested to halt the extradition until it 'had received and addressed the State party's submission on whether there was a risk of irreparable harm to the author, as alleged by counsel'. In other words, rather than assuming a risk of irreparable harm until it had been able to make a final determination it requested the State to explain why it considered the extradition would not result in irreparable harm. This variation in the substance of the request for provisional measures indicates a special limited duration of its provisional measures. It also makes explicit the shift in the burden of proof that takes place from the petitioner to the State, once the adjudicator has decided to take provisional measures. At that point it is the State that has to show that there is no risk. Once the HRC considers that the State has met this burden it will withdraw the provisional measure.[35]

According to Naldi the Committee's phrasing of its provisional measures in *Weiss* v. *Austria* indicates that 'irreparable harm is no longer a condition precedent for the granting of interim measures' and that those provisional measures 'that are issued while the Committee considers whether they are justified are similarly considered binding'. This, he notes, broadens 'the protective scope' of provisional measures.[36] The phrasing in this case indeed is new, but in fact the HRC has also taken provisional measures in earlier cases, which it withdrew or decided not to prolong in the face of information provided by the Government. While in some cases this may have been new information, for instance the fact that a residence permit has been granted or a death sentence commuted, in other cases the information provided by the Government may simply have convinced the Rapporteur that there was no real risk of irreparable harm. At the provisional measures stage the Rapporteur does not have to be certain about such a risk in any case. In that sense the approach taken in *Weiss* simply draws attention to the fact that the Rapporteur has rather more doubts than usual about the risk of irreparable harm.[37]

In *Länsman II* the Rapporteur equally was rather cautious in the phrasing of the provisional measures involving a complaint by Sami in Finland aimed at the protection of the environment constituting their cultural habitat.[38] In both cases no firmly established case law was available yet about the use of provisional measures in the circumstances. In *Länsman II* there was one precedent, *Lubicon* v. *Canada*, in which the HRC had previously used provisional measures in the context of cultural survival. In *Weiss* v. *Austria* there was no precedent of a provisional measure to halt extradition because of a real risk of a life sentence. The cautious phrasing in both cases may be attributed exactly to the lack of precedent with regard to the purpose of provisional measures, rather than to doubts about the assessment of risk.

---

[34]   HRC *Sholam Weiss* v. *Austria*, 3 April 2003.
[35]   See further Chapter XV (Immediacy and risk).
[36]   Naldi (2004), p. 450. On the legal status of provisional measures see Chapter XVI.
[37]   See Chapter XV (Immediacy and risk).
[38]   See Chapter X (Culture).

3.3 Specific requirements found in orders for provisional measures

3.3.1 Introduction

This section examines the specificity of provisional measures. The discussion of specific requirements first provides examples presented by issue area. The examples range from provisional measures halting executions to those (partly) aimed at protecting freedom of expression or a combination of rights. Subsequently this section deals with one particular requirement found in provisional measures ordered in the context of ongoing situations such as death threats: the obligation to investigate, prosecute and punish. Then the incremental approach to specificity is discussed that is taken by the Inter-American Court in cases of death threats and harassment, with the *Peace Community* case as a point of departure. Again this illustrates that often a range of interrelated rights is involved and again it illustrates the importance of investigation and prosecution of death threats and harassment.

Finally this section examines the obligation implicit in all provisional measures, and made explicit in the Inter-American system, to provide information on their implementation and more generally to cooperate with the adjudicator.

3.3.2 Concrete provisional measures in various issue areas

3.3.2.1 HALTING EXECUTIONS

In 1993 the Inter-American Commission requested 'that the Governor of Texas and the State ensure that the death sentence not be carried out on Mr. Sankofa, for humanitarian reasons and to avoid irreparable harm'. It specifically called upon the US 'to take the necessary measures to ensure that Mr. Sankofa was afforded a hearing before the Texas Board of Pardons and Paroles'. The protective measures as requested are interesting because they are more specific than just requesting a stay of execution. They show an awareness of the specific circumstances in Texas.[39]

3.3.2.2 PROTECTING THE LIFE AND PERSONAL INTEGRITY OF RECENTLY DISAPPEARED PERSONS

In December 2001 the Inter-American Commission took precautionary measures to determine the whereabouts of two persons from the region of Antioquia and to protect their lives and persons. They were last seen three weeks before at a Medellín metropolitan police checkpoint. In its Annual Report the Commission notes that it 'undertook a series of steps toward clearing up this situation during its on-site visit' of 7 to 13 December. Apparently these steps had not been sufficiently effective as five days later the Commission resorted to the formal issuance of precautionary measures. As part of these measures it also asked Colombia to 'launch a prompt and effective investigation using the urgent search mechanism established by Law 589/2000'.[40]

---

[39] CIDH *Gary T. Graham, now known as Shaka Sankofa* v. *US*, 15 June 2000 (adm.). The petitioners had asked the Commission, on 4 October, to request the State to 'ensure that Mr. Sankofa was afforded a fair hearing' before this Board. In Texas, this Board was in the habit of deciding on clemency on the basis of just a telephone conference. No hearing would take place and no clemency would be granted. The petitioners had also asked the Commission to request that the State would 'urge the Board to recommend that he be pardoned of the capital offence of which he was convicted'.

[40] CIDH Annual Report 2001, §26.

In July 2001 the Commission took precautionary measures on behalf of someone who had been violently detained, without a warrant, in June 2001. His family had witnessed how agents of the judicial police of the state of Guerrero had abducted him in an operation involving several vehicles also marked as belonging to this police force. They had filed complaints with the Attorney General of that state, who apparently did not take effective steps to locate him. Upon the petitioners' request the Commission's precautionary measures included intervention by the *federal* Attorney General because they suspected complicity between the kidnappers and the public prosecution service of Guerrero.[41]

3.3.2.3 PROTECTING THE LIFE AND PERSONAL INTEGRITY OF DETAINEES

Also in the context of detention the Inter-American Court is increasingly specific in its use of provisional measures.[42] The case of Elena Loayza Tamayo serves as an example of the possible specificity of provisional measures in detention cases. The Court requested Peru to adopt all necessary measures to 'effectively ensure her physical, psychological and moral integrity'.[43] The Commission had been even more specific in its request to the Court, requesting the end of the solitary confinement and incommunicado detention imposed on her and the return to 'Pavilion 'A' of the Chorrillos Women's Maximum Security Penitentiary in the same conditions in which she had been held prior to her transfer'.[44] The Court subsequently did specify its previous measures by ordering Peru to modify her prison conditions, in particular with regard to her solitary confinement, and provide her with medical treatment.[45]

In September 1997 it issued its judgment on the merits, finding violations of Articles 5 (personal integrity), 7 (liberty) and 8 (judicial guarantees), ordering her release.[46] She was released the next month. Subsequently the Court lifted its provisional measures.[47] In 1998 it ordered Peru to take several measures of reparation.[48] Yet these were not implemented and Ms Loayza continued to live in destitute conditions. Moreover, a June 1999 judgment by the Supreme Court of Peru 'overturned' the judgment of the Inter-American Court, threatening her renewed detention.[49] She

---

41   In November the Commission extended its precautionary measures to cover the wife of the disappeared man who was in grave danger because of her search and a former officer of the judicial police in Guerrero who was under arrest and whose life was being threatened if he continued to make allegations about the involvement of judicial police officers and their superiors in kidnappings. CIDH Annual Report 2001, §39.

42   See e.g. IACHR *Las penitentiarías de Mendoza* v. *Argentina,* Order of 22 November 2004, expanded several times, e.g. 30 March 2006 (including the individual votes of García Sayán, García Ramírez and Cançado Trindade); *Case of the children and adolescents deprived of liberty at the 'Complexo do Tatuapé' of FEBEM,* Order of 30 November 2005 (including the individual votes of García Ramírez and Cançado Trindade). See also Order of 4 July 2006; and *Cárcel de Urso Branco* case (Brazil), Order of 21 September 2005 (including the individual opinions of García Ramírez and Cançado Trindade).

43   IACHR *Loayza Tamayo* v. *Peru,* Urgent measures of 12 June 1996 and Order of 2 July 1996.

44   IACHR *Loayza Tamayo* v. *Peru,* Order of 2 July 1996, §4.

45   IACHR *Loayza Tamayo* v. *Peru,* Order of 13 September 1996.

46   IACHR *Loayza Tamayo* v. *Peru,* 17 September 1997 (merits).

47   IACHR *Loayza Tamayo* v. *Peru,* Order of 11 November 1997.

48   IACHR *Loayza Tamayo* v. *Peru,* 27 November 1998 (reparations).

49   See also IACHR *Loayza Tamayo* v. *Peru,* 17 November 1999 (execution of judgment) and letter of 12 November 2000 of the Inter-American Court, 'signed by all of the Judges, addressed to the Secretary General of the Organization of American States, where its was stated, inter alia, that compliance by the State "has particular effects in the case of Ms. Loayza-Tamayo who, according to truthful information received by the Court, is going through serious economic and health

went into exile in Chile, where she received some medical support by an NGO that itself was lacking adequate means. Because of her physical and emotional condition she was unable to find an adequate and more permanent job. The petitioners requested renewed provisional measures, arguing that her 'life project' had been damaged, and 'the conduct of the State, to date,' had prevented her from having 'the minimum of a dignified life'. In addition her right to health was 'seriously violated and diminished'.[50]

Arguing that in this case the power to order provisional measures implied 'to look after the personal integrity of Ms. Loayza-Tamayo',[51] the President of the Court noted that the information submitted in this case showed *prima facie* a threat to her integrity.[52] He deemed 'necessary for the State to ensure Ms. Loayza-Tamayo the security conditions necessary for her to return to her country without fearing consequences on her physical, psychic, and emotional integrity.[53] He adopted urgent measures on her behalf calling on Peru to 'adopt, without delay, all necessary measures to effectively ensure the return to her country (…), and also her physical, mental and moral integrity, so that any provisional measures that the Inter-American Court of Human Rights may decide to order in this case may have the pertinent effects'.[54] In February 2001 the Court confirmed this decision.[55] In January 2001 the new government of Peru, installed after Fujimori had fled the country, had noted that there was no arrest warrant against Ms Tamayo. It had expressed its 'willingness to grant the said citizen the necessary guarantees and measures that her physical safety, mental health and moral integrity will not be harmed'. It also pointed out that it was taking the 'pertinent measures' to comply with the Court's judgment in her case.[56] While, given the Court's Order of February 2001, it was not immediately convinced by these arguments,

---

difficulties that could be palliated, at least in part, by the compliance of the respective judgement". In said letter, the Court requested the Secretary General to submit the [...] communication "as soon as possible to the Permanent Council, and later, to the General Assembly of the Organization"', IACHR Loayza Tamayo (Peru), Order of 13 December 2000, 4th 'Having seen' clause.

[50] IACHR *Loayza Tamayo* v. *Peru*, Urgent measures of 13 December 2000, 1st 'Having seen' clause. They requested specifically to 'urgently adopt every provisional measure' for the teacher María Elena Loayza-Tamayo, to recover the sum of money decided by the Court as a fair indemnification, together with fair interests in arrears, and all other material and moral damages related to the violations resulting from the failure of Peru to comply with the decision on indemnifications, that will allow her to leave the condition of misery she is now living in, to cease being a cuasi beggar and to begin enjoying a 'dignified life'; [for her] to be able to develop a new (though limited) life project, beginning a new professional formation abroad that would be within her reach, while her situation of insecurity in Peru persists; [for her] to be able to take adequate care of her health; [and for her] to support directly and personally the needs of her children, after suffering the humiliation of having them under the care of the grandparents and aunts'.

[51] IACHR *Loayza Tamayo,* Urgent measures of 13 December 2000, 6th 'Having seen' clause.

[52] IACHR *Loayza Tamayo,* Urgent measures of 13 December 2000, 7th 'Having seen' clause.

[53] IACHR *Loayza Tamayo,* Urgent measures of 13 December 2000, 12th 'Having seen' clause, referring to *Peace Community San José de Apartadó,* Order of 24 November 2000, 8th 'Considering' clause and 5th and 6th 'Resolution' clauses; *Haitians and Haitian-Origin Dominicans in the Dominican Republic,* Order of 18 August 2000, 4th 'Resolution' paragraph; *Alvarez et al.,* Order of 21 January 1998, 4th 'Resolution' paragraph; *Giraldo Cardona,* Order of 5 February 1997, 5th 'Considering' clause; *Giraldo Cardona,* Urgent measures of 28 October 1996, 2nd 'Resolution' paragraph and *Colotenango,* Order of 22 June 1994, 2nd 'Resolution' paragraph.

[54] IACHR *Loayza Tamayo* v. *Peru,* Urgent measures of 13 December 2000.

[55] IACHR *Loayza Tamayo* v. *Peru,* Order of 3 February 2001.

[56] IACHR *Loayza Tamayo* v. *Peru,* Order of 3 February 2001, 7th 'Having seen' clause.

in August 2001, on request of the Commission and the State, it did decide to lift the provisional measures. The situation of the beneficiary was no longer extremely serious and urgent to such an extent as to require provisional measures.[57]

Since this case the Court has regularly dealt with urgent detention cases.[58] The Court has also increasingly specified what it means with the State's reporting obligations.[59] For instance, it has explained that it was essential that the adoption of the priority measures indicated in the Order should be reflected in reports that described concrete results based on the specific needs for protection of the beneficiaries of the measures. It has added that in this respect the supervisory role of the Inter-American Commission was particularly important in order to monitor the implementation of the measures ordered adequately and effectively.[60]

It has equally reiterated that the State should take the relevant steps to ensure that the measures of protection were planned and implemented with the participation of the representatives of the beneficiaries of the measures and, in general, keep them informed of progress in implementation. This also meant that the State must facilitate the entry by the representatives of the beneficiaries of the measures into the detention facility. It must also facilitate communications between the representatives and the young detainees. These communications must be conducted in the most confidential manner possible so as to avoid intimidating the youngsters. The Court has

---

[57] IACHR *Loayza Tamayo* v. *Peru*, Order of 28 August 2001. The State had argued that provisional measures were reserved for extremely urgent situations where the beneficiary was facing irreparable harm and that this was not the case here (3rd 'Having seen' clause). The Court agreed, emphasizing that provisional measures are exceptional in character.

[58] See e.g. IACHR *Matter of the Penitentiary Center of the Central Occidental Region (Uribana Prison)* (Venezuela), Order of 2 February 2007 (e.g. measures must be implemented immediately to avoid the loss of life or harm the physical, mental and moral integrity of all those deprived of liberty in the Uribana Prison, of those who may enter the penitentiary center as prisoners, and also of those who work there and who enter the prison as visitors *and* more long-term measures aimed at, e.g. the reduction of overcrowding and the separation of male and female inmates); *Matter of Urso Branco prison* (Brazil), Orders of 2 May 2008, 21 September 2005, 7 July 2004, 22 April 2004, 29 August 2002 and 18 June 2002; *Matter of the Mendoza prisons* (Argentina), 27 November 2007, 30 March 2006 (particularly, to eliminate the risk of violent death and the inadequate internal security and monitoring conditions in the prisons), 18 June 2005, 22 November 2004; *Matter of the persons imprisoned in the "Dr. Sebastião Martins Silveira" Penitentiary in Araraquara São Paulo* (Brazil), Order of the President of 10 June 2008; Order of 30 September 2006; *Matter of Children Deprived of Liberty in the "Complexo do Tatuapé" of FEBEM* (Brazil), Order of President 10 June 2008, Orders of 3 July 2007, 4 July 2006, 30 November 2005 and 17 November 2005; *Matter of Yare I and Yare II Capital Region Penitentiary Center* (Venezuela), Orders of 30 November 2007 and 30 March 2006; *Matter of Capital El Rodeo I & El Rodeo II Judicial Confinement Center*, Order of 8 February 2008; *Matter of Monagas Judicial Confinement Center ('La Pica')* (Venezuela), Order of 3 July 2007 (e.g., as a more long-term measure, the confiscation of weapons and provide the necessary medical care), and 9 February 2006; *Case of the Miguel Castro-Castro Prison* v. *Peru*, Orders of 29 January 2008 and 30 January 2007 (dismissing the requests by the petitioners).

[59] This is relevant as a measure of follow-up. Generally on follow-up by the adjudicators, see Chapter XVIII.

[60] IACHR *Matter of the Mendoza Prisons* (Argentina), Order of 27 November 2007. See also *Matter of the Yare I and Yare II Capital Region Penitentiary Center (Yare Prison)* (Venezuela), Order of 30 November 2007 (to request the State to report on the availability of means and mechanisms whereby the persons deprived of liberty in the Capital Region Penitentiary Center Yare I and Yare II (Yare Prison) can obtain information on their rights and formulate petitions or complaints in this regard).

equally stressed the obligation to send it an updated list of all the young people residing in the detention facility.[61]

In a follow up provisional measure the Court has even specified that those beneficiaries who would be or had been transferred to another detention center subsequent to the Court's earlier provisional measures, continued under the protection of the Court's provisional measures. Their next of kin were to be informed of these transfers and the State was to avoid unduly violent acts by State officers, particularly during those transfers. It was also to make sure that the beneficiary was not exposed to overcrowded detention conditions upon transfer, that convicted prisoners and pre-trial detainees were not detained together, that access to medical staff was provided and that the right of access to defense counsel and next of kin was respected.[62]

Yet the Inter-American Court now distinguishes between the more long-term measures required in the context of detention and the *immediate* measures required to prevent violations of the right to life and the prohibition of cruel treatment. In this respect in a separate opinion Judge García Ramírez pointed out the difference between the material and temporal scope and nature of provisional measures on the one hand and of judgments of the Court on the other. The more long-term measures (often requiring legal reforms and reorganisation) are matters to be examined on the merits rather than in the context of provisional measures.[63] Judge García Ramírez drew attention to the fact that multiple, complex and persistent measures were necessary to deal with structural problems in the short, medium and long run.[64] At the same time, of course, the Court has stressed that while the State makes the appropriate adjustments to deal with the structural problems, the detainees affected by the existing flaws must be protected by provisional measures if their condition is of extreme gravity and urgency.[65] In a subsequent matter involving detention the Court itself observed that the improvement and correction of the situation in the detention center Urso Branco constituted a process that required the State to take measures in the short, medium and long run to deal with the structural problems affecting the detainees. The duty to adopt such measures derived from the general obligation to respect and guarantee their rights. The compatibility of the measures taken by the State with the Inter-American standards must be examined at the appropriate moment, at the stage of the examination of the *merits*. Meanwhile, as part of the *provisional measures*, the state was to concretely eradicate the risk of violent deaths and attacks against the personal integrity.[66] Yet a detailed analysis of the compatibility of the detention conditions with the ACHR was to be made on the merits of the case, which was still pending before the Commission.[67] In this respect, in the face of allegations of inhuman detention conditions, it was the Commission that should take the measures it considered pertinent, based on its own functions.[68]

At the same time the Court has pointed out that its competence to order provisional measures is not necessarily limited by the existence of a case relating to measures pending before the

---

[61]   See e.g. IACHR *Matter of the Children and Adolescents Deprived of Liberty in the "Tatuapé Complex" of the CASA Foundation* (Brazil), Order of 3 July 2007.

[62]   IACHR *Matter of the persons imprisoned in the "Dr. Sebastião Martins Silveira" Penitentiary in Araraquara, São Paulo* (Brazil), Order of 30 September 2006, 21st-24th 'Considering' clauses.

[63]   IACHR *Matter of Capital El Rodeo I and El Rodeo II Judicial Confinement Center*, 8 February 2008, Separate opinion Judge García Ramírez (joined by Judge Medina Quiroga), §§18 and 19.

[64]   IACHR *Matter of Capital El Rodeo I and El Rodeo II Judicial Confinement Center*, 8 February 2008, Separate opinion Judge García Ramírez (joined by Judge Medina Quiroga), §20.

[65]   IACHR *Matter of Capital El Rodeo I and El Rodeo II Judicial Confinement Center*, 8 February 2008, 14th 'Considering' clause.

[66]   IACHR *Asunto de la Cárcel de Urso Branco* (Brasil), Resolución de 2 de mayo de 2008, 20th 'Considering' clause.

[67]   Id., 21st 'Considering' clause.

[68]   Id., 22nd 'Considering' clause.

Commission, as in certain circumstances, in light of the rights at stake, the Court has recognized that its provisional measures do not just have a preventive, but in fact have a truly protective character.[69] Nevertheless, in the context of these measures the Court may only consider arguments that relate strictly and directly to the extreme gravity that is required for the use of provisional measures.[70] In a situation where the Court must decide whether its provisional measures previously ordered, must be maintained, it must examine whether the situation of extreme gravity persists or whether new circumstances that are equally grave merit the maintenance of the provisional measures. Any other claim can only be brought to the Court's attention through the corresponding contentious proceedings.[71]

It is noteworthy that in the matter that triggered these statements the State had argued many structural steps that it had undertaken. It had hired new prison staff, prison populations had decreased and prison cells that were previously connected had been repaired so that aggression between detainees was limited. Moreover the administration of Urso Branco prison had a policy of eliminating all violence, while the sanctions against detainees were limited to prohibiting visits.[72] Yet the Commission argued that the measures had not been sufficient to guarantee the lives and integrity of the detainees and the petitioners noted, among others, that by the end of 2006 the State had substituted its laisser faire policy for an new repressive policy that included the use of torture in order to guarantee control over the detention centre. Among others, within six months, four directors had been fired for committing or allowing torture.[73] The Court concluded that the continued attacks and killings indicated the persistence of a situation of extreme gravity and urgency and the recent allegations of torture by state agents represented an aggravation of the imminent risk to life and personal integrity of the detainees.[74] The State had not provided information on concrete measures to put a stop to the killings and deal with the allegations of torture. It had limited itself to offering information on hiring new personnel and improving the detention conditions.[75] It observed that the fact that Brazil is a federal state cannot serve as an excuse for non-compliance. The Court found that there had been no major improvement during the six years of provisional measures and it specifically took note of the request by the petitioners at the internal level for the federal government to intervene in the detention system of the constitutive state Rondônia.[76] In the circumstances the measures to be adopted by Brazil must include some directly aimed to protect the right to life and integrity of the detainees, both in their relations amongst themselves and between them and the State agents. In particular the State was to take immediate measures necessary to eradicate concretely the risks of violent killings and grave attacks against personal integrity, making sure that its agents do not commit unjustified acts against the life and integrity of detainees and prohibiting, in all circumstances, the practice of torture. The measures were to include a confiscation of weapons and the maintenance of state control in a manner that fully respected the human rights of the detainees.[77] In other words, in the face of the continuing grave situation the Court specified its provisional measures and, in passing, also reminded the State of a request by the petitioners to intervene in the detention system of a constituent state.

None of the adjudicators have used provisional measures regularly to secure release, halt the execution of a detention order, halt re-imprisonment or arrange a prison transfer in light of the

---

69   Id., 4th 'Considering' clause.
70   Id., 5th 'Considering' clause.
71   Id., 5th 'Considering' clause.
72   Id., 7th 'Considering' clause.
73   Id., 8th 'Considering' clause.
74   Id., 10th 'Considering' clause.
75   Id., 12th 'Considering' clause.
76   Id., 14th 'Considering' clause.
77   Id., 15th 'Considering' clause.

petitioner's state of health. The HRC nevertheless has done so at least once.[78] Moreover, the ECtHR has recently done so on behalf of several persons alleging to be suffering serious health problems as a result of a prolonged hunger strike.[79]

In the Inter-American system the transfer of detainees has also been suggested or even ordered explicitly. A fire had broken out in a juvenile detention centre in Paraguay, killing nine minors protesting the detention conditions. Subsequently 125 minors were transferred to another facility, but this did not meet the minimum standards for the protection of minors either. In addition the authorities sent the other 130 minors to different parts of the country and placed them in prisons together with adults, in overcrowded cells.[80] The relocation of these minors to distant prisons aggravated their critical situation and made family visits impossible. In its precautionary measure of August 2001 the Commission very specifically requested that:

> "(1) The minors be immediately transferred to the Itaguá Education Center. (2) The physical, mental, and moral integrity of the minors be ensured and, in particular, that minors and adults be kept completely separate during the temporary relocation of the young inmates in the aforesaid facilities. (3) Access to the minors by their legal counsel and family visitors be granted. (4) The circumstances that gave rise to these measures be investigated, in particular, those that led to the death of Benito Augusto Moreno (or Augusto Benitez), and that the perpetrators thereof be punished".[81]

Yet the Inter-American Court has also indicated certain limits to its protective task. In the context of a request to amplify a pre-existing Order by the Inter-American Court for provisional measures on behalf of the detainees of Mendoza, which the President of the Court denied, he quoted extensively from judgments and orders by Argentina's domestic courts aimed at the implementation of the State's human rights obligations and explicitly referring to the previous Order of the Inter-American Court.[82] In this respect he specifically referred to the principle of subsidiarity 'that informs the Inter-American human rights system'. This meant that provisional measures would be used only in cases of extreme gravity and urgency when the normally existing guarantees available in the State are insufficient or ineffective and the authorities will not or cannot make them prevail.[83] The full Court confirmed this approach, noting among others that

---

[78]   See e.g. HRC *V.* v. *Spain*, 495/1992 (disc. 1995), provisional measures of 22 May 1992. The telegram to the Ministry of Justice contained more information than the official Note Verbale to the Permanent Representative, but probably the other information could be found in the annexes to the Note Verbale (on file with the author).

[79]   See e.g. ECtHR *Yildiz* v. *Turkey*, 20 October 2005.

[80]   Only in the San Juan Bautista and Emboscada facilities were they placed in separate children's blocks.

[81]   CIDH Annual Report 2001, §48. See also the subsequent judgment of the Court: IACHR *"Instituto de Reeducación del Menor"* (Paraguay), Judgment of 2 September 2004.

[82]   IACHR *Las Penitenciarias de Mendoza* (Argentina), President's Order of 22 August 2007 (maintaining the existing provisional measures, but refusing to amplify them), 11-13th 'Considering' clause. See e.g. Corte Suprema de Justicia de la Nación, 13 February 2007 (*"como custodio que es de las garantías constitucionales, y en atención a la falta de resultados obtenidos con relación a la orden dada por la Corte Interamericana de Derechos Humanos, se ve en la ineludible obligación de, intimar al Estado Nacional a que en el plazo de veinte días adopte las medidas que pongan fin a la situación que se vive en las unidades carcelarias de la Provincia de Mendoza, y de tomar las medidas que se indicarán en las parte dispositiva de esta sentencia"*).

[83]   IACHR *Las Penitenciarias de Mendoza* (Argentina), President's Order of 22 August 2007 (maintaining the existing provisional measures, but refusing to amplify them), 14th 'Considering' clause'. See also *Matter of Yare I and Yare II Capital Region Penitentiary Center* (Venezuela), Order of 8 February 2008, 15th 'Considering' clause.

overcrowding was one of the situations that had generated its previous Order for provisional measures and that Argentina had constructed a new detention centre and transferred detainees to this centre exactly to deal with this issue of overcrowding. As no facts had been brought to the Court's attention implying a situation of extreme urgency and gravity for the life and integrity of the people held in that ne centre, the Court decided not to extend its provisional measures. It did remind the State, however, of its general obligations under Article 1(1) ACHR, in particular in the context of detention.[84]

3.3.2.4 PREVENTING EXPULSION OR EXTRADITION

In November 2002 the Bosnia Chamber ordered provisional measures for the respondent Parties 'to take all necessary steps to prevent the applicants from being taken out of the territory of Bosnia and Herzegovina by the use of force'.[85] They were nevertheless handed over to the US authorities and transferred to Guantanamo Bay. In response, in its decision on the merits and reparation the Chamber was very precise on the measures required of the respondent Parties. The Chamber ordered Bosnia and Herzegovina to 'use diplomatic channels' in order to protect their basic rights. In particular it ordered the State to 'take all possible steps to establish contacts with the applicants and provide them with consular support'. Equally Bosnia was ordered to take all possible steps to prevent imposition and execution of the death penalty, including seeking, ex post facto, assurances of the US authorities, 'via diplomatic contacts', that the death penalty would not be imposed.[86] In addition, both respondent Parties (not only BiH but also the constituent State Fed.BiH, each bearing half of the costs) were ordered to retain lawyers 'authorised and admitted to practice in the relevant jurisdictions and before the relevant courts, tribunals and other authoritative bodies in order to take all necessary action to protect the applicants' rights while in US custody and in case of possible military, criminal or other proceedings involving the applicants'.[87] This very precise order already indicates a relation between provisional measures and reparation, a link further explored in section 4 of this chapter. The increased precision also serves as a form of follow-up for earlier non-compliance.[88]

3.3.2.5 PHYSICAL PROTECTION AGAINST DEATH THREATS[89]

The Inter-American Commission has brokered specific agreements between the beneficiaries (and/or their representatives)[90] and the State such as installing armoured glass or a telephone connection and providing bodyguards to human rights defenders. In the context of death threats by one group of detainees against another the Commission obtained a promise by Colombia to build a 'separating partition' in the prison.[91]

---

[84] IACHR *Matter of the Mendoza Prisons*, Order of 27 November 2007, 9th and 10th 'Considering' clauses.

[85] Bosnia Chamber *Boudellaa, Lakhdar, Nechle and Lahmar* v. *BiH and Fed.BiH*, 11 October 2002 (adm. & merits), §5.

[86] Id., §330.

[87] Id., §331.

[88] On follow up see Chapter XVIII.

[89] See also section 3.3.3.

[90] See also section 4 (beneficiaries).

[91] CIDH Annual Report 2001, Chapter IV, §16 and Press release 33/01 'Inter-American Commission on Human Rights concludes its visit to the Republic of Colombia', 13 December 2001, §18.

As part of the protective measures required of a State sometimes physical protection is warranted. The beneficiaries of such measures, however, do not necessarily feel protected by the members of the police or military proposed. The Commission now includes in its precautionary measures references to the obligation of the State to agree with the beneficiaries about the precise substance of the protective measures. In this respect it is not surprising that organisations like Peace Brigades International (PBI) are sometimes proposed to provide protection.[92] This organisation has built up credibility in certain areas of, for instance, Mexico. The type of protection provided, however, is that of providing an unarmed international presence, peacefully and continuously accompanying persons threatened. Normally persons threatened seem to either contact non-governmental organisations such as PBI, or the Commission requesting it to take precautionary measures. If the Commission does so, it points out to the State concerned its obligation to provide protection against threats. In such cases one often thinks of providing armed protection as well as investigation of the threats and prosecution of the perpetrators. More and more often, however, the protective measures suggested include providing mobile phones, closed-circuit TV systems etc.[93] The beneficiaries of precautionary measures sometimes do not trust the (local) police but they do trust a certain division within the army, or the other way around. In other situations they do not trust any armed public officials. In such case the State and the beneficiaries are forced to find alternatives. They may make a list of persons mutually trusted. The State may have to train these persons and provide them with weapons.

In other cases, where international accompanying organisations such as PBI are involved, who do not carry arms, the State may have to provide them with facilities or cover their expenses. It may also be that the State has offered some form of armed protection that is accepted by the beneficiaries as long as an unarmed international organisation can be present to monitor this as well.

In 1996 the Commission suggested, for instance, that the Court would order the State to give the relatives of a presidential candidate who was receiving threats, 'the name and telephone number of a person in a position of authority in the Government who will be responsible for providing him with protection should it become necessary' and provide him with an 'armoured car' so that he could travel the entire national territory.[94]

In *Newton Coutinho Mendes et al.* v. *Brazil* (1997) the Commission initially asked for each individual name included on a specific list of persons targeted by death squads. It only took precautionary measures on behalf of Father Ricardo Rezende. He had left the region due to the threats against him, but he was planning to return.[95] With regard to the names of the other intended beneficiaries the petitioner responded that 'local police knew whose names were on the list', but 'the petitioner had not gained access to most of the names of the persons threatened due to the complicity of the police with the criminals'.[96] Subsequently the Commission did take pre-

---

[92] See e.g. CIDH *Teodoro Cabrera García and Rodolfo Montiel Flores* v. *Mexico*, 27 February 2004 (adm.), §7. In April 2002 the Commission allowed the measures to expire when it did not hear anymore from either the beneficiaries or the State. See §8. See also Annual Report 2001, Chapter III (a), §44.

[93] See e.g. CIDH Annual Report 2001, Chapter III (a), §45, referring to precautionary measures of November 2001 on behalf of two members of the Zapotec indigenous people in Mexico to provide them 'with vehicles, mobile telephones, and closed-circuit TV systems'.

[94] Communication of 2 February 1996 quoted in IACHR *Alemán Lacayo* v. *Nicaragua*, Order of 2 February 1996, 2nd 'Having seen' clause.

[95] CIDH *Newton Coutinho Mendes et al.* v. *Brazil*, 1 October 1997 (adm.); precautionary measures of 20 March 1996, §§50-51.

[96] CIDH *Newton Coutinho Mendes et al.* v. *Brazil*, 1 October 1997 (adm.); precautionary measures of 20 March 1996, §§14 and 57.

cautionary measures on behalf of all persons.[97] It requested 'more specifically that: (a) the agents entrusted with protecting the persons threatened by the "Xinguara list", including Father Ricardo Rezende, be trained in the use of firearms, and that they be adequately armed so as to guarantee effective protection for the persons threatened; (b) the individuals for whom preventive arrest warrants have been issued be detained; (c) the persons responsible be tried and punished; and, (d) the actions taken in this respect be reported'.[98] When it reiterated its request the next month, it added the names of six persons whom the State should detain, as their arrest had been ordered for their involvement in the murders and death threats. Even more specifically, the Commission added that if the involvement of the Pará civilian police in the escape of one of the suspects was confirmed, the protection of the widow of one of the persons murdered should be provided by *another* police force.[99]

An issue that is relevant as well is the geographic scope of the protection in death threat cases. It is insufficient for the State to provide protection only at the home of the beneficiary. In its follow-up order in *Blake*, for instance, the Court specified that protection should be provided to the beneficiaries also when they ventured outside of their homes.[100]

3.3.2.6 PROTECTION AGAINST MASS EXPULSION

In the *Haitian* case (2000) the Inter-American Commission had requested several concrete measures of protection on behalf of the group as a whole.[101] It argued that the expulsions and deportations placed at risk the life and physical integrity of those deported as well as of the family members who had been separated from them, 'especially children under age who are left abandoned'.[102] It requested the Court to order the State to establish procedures distinguishing 'cases where deportation is not applicable, from cases where it is applicable'. In any such case of applicability the State must strictly observe due process 'including a minimum term for notification, access to family members, adequate hearings, and decisions adopted lawfully by the competent authorities'.[103] In any case, the State must make decisions on deportations with regard to the intended group of beneficiaries on an individual basis.

Later it also urged the Court to order provisional measures on behalf of seven specific persons. These measures were to permit their immediate return from Haiti to the Dominican Republic or, in the alternative, protect them from any 'detention or deportation action based on racial or national origin, or on the suspicion that they are not full-fledged citizens'.[104]

In addition it requested the Court to urge the State more generally 'to establish adequate procedures for the detention and determination of measures for the deportation of deportable aliens, including the holding of hearings to prove the right that the person may have to remain on

---

[97] CIDH *Newton Coutinho Mendes et al.* v. *Brazil*, 1 October 1997 (adm.); precautionary measures of 17 February 1995, §59. See also section 5 of this chapter.

[98] CIDH *Newton Coutinho Mendes et al.* v. *Brazil*, 1 October 1997 (adm.); precautionary measures of 17 February 1995, §59.

[99] CIDH *Newton Coutinho Mendes et al.* v. *Brazil*, 1 October 1997 (adm.); precautionary measures of 23 April 1996, §61. See also the follow up precautionary measures of 1 August 1996.

[100] IACHR *Blake* (Guatemala), Order of 18 April 1997. See further section 3.3.3.

[101] See also section 5 of this Chapter (Beneficiaries).

[102] IACHR *Haitians and Dominicans of Haitian Origin in the Dominican Republic* (Dominican Republic), Order of 18 August 2000, 2nd 'Having seen' clause.

[103] Id., 2nd 'Having seen' clause.

[104] Id., 3rd 'Having seen' clause.

Dominican soil or, in its defect, to communicate with their families and employers, in order to normalize the collection of salaries and the protection of their property and personal effects'.[105]

The Court did not order the exact provisional measures the Commission had requested. It did not take over the Commission's emphasis on due process and it did not refer to the possible racist motivation behind the arbitrary expulsions.[106] It did require the State to abstain from deporting specific persons. With regard to two others it required the State to allow their immediate return to the Dominican Republic. This reaffirmed the Commission's precedent with regard to its own precautionary measures in this respect.[107]

Moreover, the Court required the State to permit 'within the shortest possible time, the family reunification' of one person whose wife and minor children had already been deported. The State was also to collaborate with him in order 'to obtain information on the whereabouts of his next of kin either in Haiti or the Dominican Republic'.[108]

With regard to two persons on whose behalf the Commission had requested the Court's intervention, the Court initially considered that it had insufficient information, in light of the diverging statements of the Commission and the State about them. Thus, the Court required the Commission to 'urgently report in detail' about their current situation. It required the State, moreover, to investigate the situation of these two persons so as to expedite the Commission's examination of their situations.[109] Here the protective measures required (investigation of the situation) are connected to the Court's evidentiary requirements for accepting persons as beneficiaries of its protective Order. By September 2000 the President required the State to protect these two persons as well. As requested by the Commission the State was to refrain from deporting one of them and to allow the immediate return of the other, 'even making it possible for him to meet with his son'.[110] Two months later the full Court confirmed this.[111]

In May 2001 the Court ordered the Dominican Republic, in compliance with its previous Orders, to refrain from deporting or expelling three of the beneficiaries, to allow the immediate return of three other persons and to allow, as soon as possible, the reunification of a family. The Court requested the State to collaborate with one of the beneficiaries, a father and husband, to obtain information about the whereabouts of his family, either in Haiti or in the Dominican Republic. It specified its previous Orders by requiring the State 'to notify the competent authorities in writing' of the names of six beneficiaries of the provisional measures to prevent them from being deported or expelled from the Dominican Republic.[112] The Commission had also suggested that a 'special document' should be given to them, indicating that they were subject to interna-

---

[105]   Id., 3rd 'Having seen' clause.

[106]   In his Concurring Opinion Judge Cançado Trindade considered that the Court had taken care that it would not prejudge the merits of the case pending before the Commission, in particular with regard to the question of due process of law. This may mean he considers that ordering a State to observe principles of due process of law would prejudge the merits.

[107]   Part of the Court's provisional measures simply dealt with the protection of two witnesses who had testified before the Court about the need to order provisional measures to halt arbitrary expulsion. After their testimony they received several threats. This triggered the Court's already established use of provisional measures to protect witnesses.

[108]   IACHR *Haitians and Dominicans of Haitian Origin in the Dominican Republic*, Order for provisional measures, 18 August 2000, 5th and 6th decisional clauses.

[109]   Id., 2nd 'Decisional' clause. See also Chapter XV (Immediacy and risk).

[110]   President IACHR *Haitians and Dominicans of Haitian Origin in the Dominican Republic*, Decision of 14 September 2000, 3rd 'Decisional' clause.

[111]   IACHR *Haitians and Dominicans of Haitian Origin in the Dominican Republic*, Order of 12 November 2000, 3rd 'Decisional' clause.

[112]   IACHR *Haitians and Dominicans of Haitian Origin in the Dominican Republic*, Order of 26 May 2001, 4th 'Decisional' clause.

tional protection.[113] Indeed, the Court ordered the State to grant these six persons identification documents that would indicate that they were the beneficiaries of the Court's provisional measures.[114] It ordered the State to continue following up on the investigations with regard to the situations of the beneficiaries and it requested both the State and the Commission to 'take the necessary steps to create appropriate mechanisms to coordinate and monitor' the measures ordered within a month.[115]

In this case the Commission and Court operated in a continuum, ordering both an abstention from deporting and the immediate return of those already deported. They also emphasised the importance of family reunification, although the Commission put more emphasis on protecting the rights of children and preventing the separation of families. On the Commission's request, the Court ordered the State to grant the beneficiaries identification documents indicating their status as beneficiaries of the Court's provisional measures. It ordered the State and the Commission to follow up the situation as well.

3.3.2.7 PROTECTING FREEDOM OF EXPRESSION

In *Ivcher Bronstein* v. *Peru*, the Commission requested Peru to 'refrain from taking or executing any action or measure that would worsen his situation, including his capture by Interpol' while his case was pending before it.[116] The Court ordered provisional measures as well, but these were generally phrased, referring to the prevention of irreparable harm to his life, personal integrity, but also the right to judicial guarantees.[117]

The Commission's precautionary measure on behalf of a journalist and director of a weekly magazine in Venezuela included a request to lift the 'previous censorship measures' against the journalist and the magazine, to guarantee the full exercise of the journalist's right to defend himself and to ensure his exercise of his personal freedom, freedom of expression and the right to due process of law.[118]

3.3.2.8 PROTECTING A RANGE OF RIGHTS

In July 2001 the Commission requested Haiti to protect the judicial magistrate in charge of the investigation into the murder of journalist Jean Dominique on 3 April 2000.[119] Two earlier judges had also received threats and subsequently withdrew from the investigation. In light of 'the lack of adequate protective measures' he felt forced to withdraw from the case as well. The government, however, did not accept his withdrawal. The Commission noted that, 'with the beneficiary's agreement', it requested Haiti to adopt the following measures:

> "(1) Immediate adoption of all measures necessary to protect their life and personal integrity of Mr. Claudy Gassant; (2) Adoption of all measures necessary to ensure the exercise of his right

---

[113]   Id., 5th and 9th 'Having seen' clauses.
[114]   Id., 4th 'Decisional' clause.
[115]   Id., 5th 'Decisional' clause.
[116]   CIDH Annual Report 1998, §48.
[117]   IACHR *Baruch Ivcher Bronstein* v. *Peru*, Order of 21 November 2000. See further Chapter XII (Other situations), section 3.3.
[118]   CIDH Report of the Special Rapporteur for Freedom of Expression, Chapter V, §§23-25, in Annual Report of the Inter-American Commission 2001, Volume II. See also Chapter XII (Other situations).
[119]   CIDH Annual Report 2001, Chapter III (a), §37.

to investigate, receive, and disseminate information with respect to the investigation of the facts surrounding the death of the journalist Jean Dominique, pursuant to the provisions of Art. 13 of the American Convention on Human Rights and the second principle of the Declaration of Principles on Freedom of Expression".[120]

Apart from the express reference to the beneficiary's agreement with the precautionary measures[121] the protective measures required are themselves remarkable. The Commission requested the State to adopt measures not only to protect the life and personal integrity of the judge but also to ensure the exercise of his right to investigate as well as receive and disseminate information with respect to the investigation of the death of said journalist. In other words, the precautionary measure seems to combine the aim of protecting the life and integrity of persons threatened with the aims of protecting judicial independence and preventing impunity in *another* case by enabling a judge to properly perform his function. In a sense this is comparable to some other precautionary measures taken by the Commission in which it specified that measures to protect persons, in practice human rights defenders or family members of victims, were not to limit the freedom of movement of the beneficiaries. In other words, they should be able to continue their activities. The reason why the Commission was so specific in this case may have been the fact that the judge was involved in the investigation of the murder of a journalist, freedom of expression being a particular interest of the Commission and the OAS.[122]

Equally, the Commission has shown its awareness of the interrelated nature of certain rights in the case of the *Yakye Axa indigenous community*. When it took precautionary measures on behalf of this Community in Paraguay the Inter-American Commission noted that they were in 'an extremely needy situation, because of their inadequate access to food supplies and health care'. It requested Paraguay to take the following measures:

"(1) To suspend the enforcement of any court or administrative order involving the eviction and/or removal of the homes of the Yakye Axa indigenous community and of its members.
(2) To refrain from all other actions and undertakings affecting the right to property, free transit, and residence of the Yakye Axa indigenous community and its members.
(3) To take all steps necessary to ensure the life and physical, mental, and moral integrity of the members of the Yakye Axa indigenous community".[123]

Thus the Commission was aware that access to food and healthcare alone would not be sufficient because it might ensure their life and physical integrity, but not their mental and moral integrity. In other words, it took into account the right to cultural integrity and indicated that the State

---

[120] Ibid.

[121] See Chapter XIII.

[122] In fact, the OAS Special Rapporteur for Freedom of Expression mentions this case in his Annual Report as one of the four cases involving the freedom of expression in which the Commission took precautionary measures. He gave some additional information on this case, noting that the judge involved had 'conducted a series of investigation of political leaders and other Haitian citizens, in spite of having received direct death threats'. He also added that the assassination plot of 8 June was not only directed against this judge but also against a Senator 'who had been demanding justice since the death of the journalist Jean Dominique'. Apparently, the Commission's precautionary measures did not extend to this Senator. The Rapporteur also specified that the 'absence of effective protective measures to ensure the personal safety of Judge Gassant has led him to leave the country'. Report of the Special Rapporteur of Freedom of Expression, Chapter V, §22, in Annual Report 2001. Whatever action Haiti had undertaken to protect him, apparently it was insufficient. The fact that the Rapporteur and not the Commission itself provides this information may show that he has been closely involved in this case.

[123] CIDH case 12.313, Annual Report 2001, Chapter III (a), C.1, §49.

should not force members of the Community to move to another area away from their traditional territories, even if they would have better access to food and medical care. Instead, pending the case it should ensure access to food and healthcare on their traditional territories.[124]

3.3.3 An incremental approach to specificity: the Peace Community and death threats and harassment

3.3.3.1 INTRODUCTION

Generally the Inter-American Commission's precautionary measures are more specific than the provisional measures of the Inter-American Court. This applies even more clearly to the earlier cases. In *Chunimá* (1991) the Commission had requested the Court to order provisional measures protecting a list of witnesses, relatives, human rights activists and judges. It had also requested it to order Guatemala to 'inform the human rights organizations affected of the name and phone-number of a civilian official in the government who will be responsible for providing them with protection should the need arise'.[125] Moreover, Guatemala should effectively ensure the return of human rights activists to their homes in Chunimá. It should carry out the arrest warrants issued against the members of the civil patrol of this village, who are the main suspects. Finally, the highest authorities in the government should 'make a public declaration to be published in the major media establishment in the country recognising the legitimacy of the work of human rights monitors in Guatemala and acknowledging that their activities are protected not only by the American Convention on Human Rights, but also by the Constitution of the Republic of Guatemala'.[126]

The President of the Inter-American Court indeed ordered Guatemala to take 'all necessary measures' to protect the right to life and physical integrity of the fourteen persons.[127] The Court later confirmed this.[128] It did not indicate precisely what type of measures Guatemala was expected to take to protect each of the fourteen persons involved. Thus, the Court's provisional measures were of a more general nature. Yet it did emphasize that the *State* should indeed 'promptly specify' what measures have been taken to protect each of the beneficiaries.[129]

The specificity of provisional measures has increased since, to include 'the granting of a permanent escort at the domicile of each one of the beneficiaries', as well as of the premises of a human rights institute of a university, and a specification that the 'security personnel assigned be given special training and adequate equipment' and that the aforementioned 'escorts should not belong to the law enforcement forces that, pursuant to the beneficiaries' statements, might be involved in the events reported'.[130]

---

[124]   In its Judgment of 17 June 2005 the Court ordered the State to take all necessary steps to ensure the life and physical, mental, and moral integrity of its members.

[125]   IACHR *Chunimá* case (Guatemala), Order of 15 July 1991 (President), 3rd 'Having seen' clause.

[126]   Id., 3rd and 4th 'Having seen' clauses.

[127]   Id.

[128]   IACHR *Chunimá* case (Guatemala), Order of 1 August 1991.

[129]   Id., 2nd 'Decisional' clause. The order specified that the provisional measures would be in force until 3 December 1991. Apparently, in December 1991 the Commission requested the Court to re-establish the provisional measures, but the Court did not do so. IACHR *Chunimá* case. Letter of the President of the Inter-American Court of Human Rights addressed to the Executive Secretary of the Inter-American Commission on Human Rights, 14 January 1992, Compendium 1987-1996, p. 49.

[130]   IACHR *García Prieto family et al.* (El Salvador), Order of 26 September 2006, 11th 'Considering' clause. Protective measures must be provided diligently and effectively and must

Rather than discussing a large range of cases that provide extensive information on the specific action required of the State to protect persons against death threats, and different approaches by the Commission and Court in this respect, this section focuses on the *Peace Community* case dealt with by the Inter-American Court. This case is illustrative of the provisional measures ordered in the Inter-American system with their awareness of the interrelationship between various rights. In the *Peace Community* case the Commission's requests to the Court for provisional measures were very precise not only about the specific *action* required but also about the *manner* in which it wished the State to implement provisional measures. An examination of the views of the Commission and the State in this case also shows that the dialogue between these two parties has gone into considerable detail. The Commission's requests included: preventing forced displacement; guaranteeing a safe return home; confronting the paramilitary; investigating threats and violence, prosecuting and punishing; severing existing links between (local) authorities and paramilitary groups; forbidding local authorities to make statements that could trigger violence and threats, instead formally recognising and publicly supporting the beneficiaries; political coordination and early warning; practical measures for physical protection; ensuring that the beneficiaries can travel freely and ensuring the free transport of goods to and from the Community.

In order to clarify the protective measures required to satisfy the overall requirement of protecting persons against threats, the discussion is subdivided into several different requirements, as they have been suggested by the Commission and sometimes ordered by the Court. The Court's consecutive Orders in the *Peace Community* case show that, when the adverse situation persists, the Court may order more of the measures requested by the Commission in each subsequent Order. Where relevant reference is also made to provisional measures ordered in other cases.

3.3.3.2 PREVENTING FORCED DISPLACEMENT

Due to the violence committed against them, the members of the Peace Community had been displaced to other parts of the country. The Commission had expressed concern about a group of inhabitants of the Municipality of Apartadó who chose their right not to be forcibly displaced from their place of origin.[131] The Commission suggested the State would take the necessary action

---

be planned and implemented with the participation of the beneficiaries of the measures or their representatives. IACHR Matter of *Ramírez Hinostroza et al.* (Peru), Order of 17 May 2007. Sometimes 'diligently and effectively' is further qualified by a reference to who should provide the protective measures: 'by adequately trained and qualified personnel who do not form part of the security units that have been denounced by the beneficiary'. IACHR Matter of *Guerrero Gallucci and Martínez Barrios* (Venezuela), Order of 29 November 2007. Sometimes the Order refers to the protection of the life and personal integrity of some of the beneficiaries and adds 'personal liberty' with regard to others. See e.g. IACHR Case of *Gutiérrez Soler* (Colombia), Order of 27 November 2007 and *Matter of Carlos Nieto Palma et al.* (Venezuela), Order of 3 July 2007.

131 The original Spanish text provides: '*un grupo de habitantes del Municipio de Apartadó optó por ejercer su derecho a no desplazarse de su lugar de origen, derecho reconocido en el Derecho Internacional y plasmado en los principos rectores del desplazamiento interno recogidos por el representante del Secretario General de la Naciones Unidas para los desplazados internos*'. The English translation speaks of a group of inhabitants of the Municipality of Apartadó which 'chose to exercise their right not to move to their place of origin, which is a right recognized in International Law and stipulated in the governing principles of the internal moving collected by the representative of the Secretary General of the United Nations for internal movings'. In the context (see also the reference to the representative of the UN Secretary General on the issue of forced displacement) it is more likely that the inhabitants in question refused to be forcibly

guaranteeing that the people of the Community could continue living in their homes or could return to them. It must offer them 'the guarantee that they will not be persecuted or threatened by the State's agents or by people acting with their acquiescence or by particular individuals'.[132]

Meanwhile, the State had made available to the Court several documents aiming to show its commitment to fight forced displacement.[133] In November 2000, following the hearing and the examination of the written materials, the Court ordered several measures to be taken by the State to prevent displacement and enable displaced persons to return safely. It required the State to guarantee that the beneficiaries of its provisional measures would be able to continue to live in their normal place of residence and to enable those persons who had been forced to leave to return to their homes in San José de Apartadó.[134] In other words, in cases involving death threats the Court has taken over the Commission's request to specifically order protection against forced displacement and guaranteeing safe return for those persons already displaced. Thus it specified that it is insufficient if the State 'protects' persons against death threats by 'ensuring' their protection away from their homes. It explicitly referred to the prevention of displacement.[135]

3.3.3.3 CONFRONTING THE PARAMILITARIES

The Court did not specifically address another request by the Commission, namely to require the State to take the necessary measures to 'repel and neutralise' the paramilitary groups active in the region. The Commission had pointed out that one of the factors explaining the violence against the Community was the presence of paramilitary groups operating in the area freely and openly. Because of their close link with agents of the Colombian State, these paramilitaries had been the main source of hostile acts against the Community. The State should arrange for vigilance in the area surrounding the Community and carry out, in particular, effective operations to repress the

---

displaced from the Municipality of Apartadó, IACHR *Peace Community of San José de Apartadó* case (Colombia), Order for provisional measures, 24 November 2000.

[132] IACHR *Peace Community of San José de Apartadó* case (Colombia), Order for provisional measures, 24 November 2000.

[133] This included its Law 589 of 2000 and a teaching course for members of the public security force in the region of Urabá about the prevention of forced displacement and the protection of forcibly displaced persons (July 2000). Other examples were a workshop on human rights, international humanitarian law and forced displacement (August 2000) as well as a training workshop for instructors of the 17th Brigade of the national army in October 2000. It must be recalled that the 17th Brigade was implicated in violent acts perpetrated against members of the Community. See generally Chapter XVII (Official responses).

[134] IACHR *Peace Community of San José de Apartadó* case (Colombia), Order of 24 November 2000. See also Order of 18 June 2002. The Court referred to its earlier provisional measures in the case of *Giraldo Cardona*, Orders of 28 October 1996 (the President's urgent measures) and 5 February 1997. It also referred to the *Colotenango* case, Order of 22 June 1994.

[135] Obviously the wishes of the beneficiaries are what matters. Thus, in May 1999 the Commission issued precautionary measures asking Argentina to relocate a witness and his family to a safe place and investigate the facts alleged so as to determine who was responsible for the injuries and threats received. The petitioners later requested the maintenance of the precautionary measures because the State had made very little progress in its investigation. Moreover, the arrangements, it had made for relocation to a safe place had been temporary. See Annual Report 1999, Chapter III C.1, §8. Luzia Canuto was the daughter of an agricultural labour union leader who was assassinated. She was a plaintiff and witness in the trial of those responsible for her father's death. In March 1998 the Commission requested Brazil to take precautionary measures to protect her and, in particular, to halt her involuntary transfer to a place where she would have to teach in an area that was especially dangerous for her. Annual Report 1998, §12.

actions of paramilitary groups and to order the agents of the State not to collaborate with these groups. Instead, the Commission had emphasised, the State was expected to order its agents to protect the Community and to refrain from performing acts or making statements that would stigmatise and endanger the Community.[136] The Court did not refer either to the need to cut links between the State and paramilitary groups. During the public hearing the representatives of the State had argued that there was no civil war in Colombia because there was no popular support for the actors.[137] They denied accusations that its agents acquiesced in the activities of such groups or that they failed to take action against them.[138] At the same time they noted that the State was intent on putting an end to any commitment or link that may exist between the public security forces (army and police) and the paramilitaries. In order to achieve this, it intended to provide workshops for alternative dispute settlement and to review the justice-related work already under-taken in the Community, while respecting the Community's own mechanisms of supervision.[139]

In another case, in October 2000, the Commission had used precautionary measures requesting Colombia to take steps to protect the life and physical integrity of the management and workers at the regional Committee for the Protection of Human Rights in Magdalena Medio (CREDHOS). It very specifically requested Colombia to report on measures taken to '(a) shed light on the serious complaints of law enforcement's tolerance or sponsorship of paramilitary groups stationed in Barrancabermeja and Yondó; and (b) guarantee that law enforcement complies with its legal functions and does not tolerate or sponsor paramilitary groups operating in the area'.[140]

3.3.3.4 OFFICIAL RECOGNITION OF HUMAN RIGHTS DEFENDERS

One important example of a protective measure is the formal recognition by government authorities of the legitimacy and importance of the work of human rights defenders and others, as well as the recognition of peace communities. During the hearing the Commission requested the Court to order the State to issue a presidential directive expressly recognising the legality and legitimacy of the Community and expressing the State's support as well as its respect for the national and international organisations accompanying the Community.[141] This probably was a reference to organisations such as Peace Brigades International and the Human Rights Accompaniment volun-

---

[136] IACHR *Peace Community of San José de Apartadó* case (Colombia), Order of 24 November 2000 (Commission request during hearing).

[137] On the other hand, they acknowledged that armed non-state actors had indeed caused confrontations. The State was taking efforts to fight them. It shared the same purposes of peace as the Peace Community and did not subscribe to the accusations that there was a relationship between the State and paramilitaries or illegal groups of armed actors.

[138] IACHR *Peace Community of San José de Apartadó* case (Colombia), Order of 24 November 2000 (statement by the representative of Colombia).

[139] IACHR *Peace Community of San José de Apartadó* case (Colombia), Order of 24 November 2000. See also Chapter XVII (Official responses).

[140] CIDH Annual Report 2000, §22. A course called 'Forum for Life and Human Rights' had been held in Barrancabermeja. State representatives and human rights defenders participated. Several of the human rights defenders were working with CREDHOS. This organisation has its headquarters in Barrancabermeja. When they were taking part in the aforementioned course they apparently found copies of a 'condolence card' making death threats against members of the organisation.

[141] IACHR *Peace Community of San José de Apartadó* case (Colombia), Order for provisional measures, 24 November 2000.

teers of the US based Fellowship of Reconciliation. In its Order of November 2000 the Court did not heed to this specific request.

In its later reports the Commission again emphasised the need to give the Community the necessary support in the eyes of public opinion and in the eyes of the security forces operating locally. After all, the latter were responsible for their safety.[142]

3.3.3.5 PRACTICAL MEASURES FOR PHYSICAL PROTECTION

The Court did not specify the practical measures that should be taken by the State in order to implement its provisional measure and ensure the physical protection of the beneficiaries. The Commission had suggested several concrete measures. In particular, it expected the State to strengthen its preventive and protective measures 'in compliance with the commitments assumed by the Red de Solidaridad Social'.[143] These measures would include supplying short wave radios to San José de Apartadó and other dwellings[144] to which displaced persons had returned, installing reflectors to light the surroundings of the urban central area; providing exterior lighting of both this area and that of La Unión; installation of an alarm system; repairs of the roads between San José and Apartadó and repair of the telephone system between the municipality and the smaller dwellings.[145]

3.3.3.6 PROTECTING FREE PASSAGE

In its first submission to the Court, the Commission already referred to the roadblock between Apartadó and San José. Inhabitants and others were accused of providing the guerrillas with food. The submission referred to paramilitaries entering vehicles in which Community members were travelling. Furthermore, on 11 and 14 November 2000, a month after the President of the Court ordered the State to take urgent measures on behalf of 193 members of the Community, some armed civilians boarded a bus travelling from Apartadó to San José. They forced it to alter its course. They also made the passengers get off the bus and show their identification, verifying whether they were on a list. They took all the food that the passengers were carrying.[146]

Following the Court's Order of 24 November 2000, which did not specifically address this problem, the Commission submitted several reports informing the Court of various violent acts and threats that subsequently occurred in the Community. According to the Commission these acts affected not only the members of the Community as beneficiaries of the measures but also various other persons providing services to the Community.

---

[142]   IACHR *Peace Community of San José de Apartadó* case (Colombia), Order for provisional measures, 18 June 2002. The Commission had also requested the Court to order the State to reinforce the political mechanisms of protection, which could help restore the confidence between the Community and the local authorities: IACHR *Peace Community of San José de Apartadó* case (Colombia), Orders for provisional measures, 24 November 2000.

[143]   This is a network for social solidarity.

[144]   The English translation of the Order mentions 'trails'. Presumably, these trails ('las veredas') also refer to the dwellings along these trails. In other places, the Spanish text mentions 'la Vereda la Unión' suggesting again that 'la vereda' refers to a location and not just a route.

[145]   IACHR *Peace Community of San José de Apartadó* case (Colombia), Orders for provisional measures, 24 November 2000.

[146]   *Peace Community of San José de Apartadó* case (Colombia), Order for provisional measures, 24 November 2000.

In its second Order, of June 2002, the Court did order the State to guarantee the necessary security conditions on the route between Apartadó and San José de Apartadó as well as in the transportation terminal of Apartadó and in Tierra Amarilla. This protection was to ensure that public transportation would not be subjected to new acts of violence. At the same time this should ensure that the Community members would be able to effectively use transport and receive supplies on a permanent basis.[147]

As noted, the problems of armed attacks during public transport and of confiscation of food were already clear from the Commission's first request for provisional measures, even though it did not ask for measures specifically dealing with those two problems.

In its first request the Commission had also mentioned the involvement of groups accompanying the members of the Community. It had requested the Court to order the State to issue a Presidential Directive expressing the State's support and respect for the national and international organisations accompanying the Community. The Court's Order of 24 November 2000, however, did not contain such a requirement. In its next Order, of 18 June 2002, the Court did require the protection of everyone providing services to the members of the community. This could also encompass the protection of unarmed (international) groups accompanying Community members for their protection.

3.3.3.7 INVESTIGATION AND PROSECUTION

The Commission stressed the importance of acting against impunity, remarking that it was necessary to adopt more effective measures to investigate the serious acts of violence and intimidation committed against members of the Community and to prosecute and punish those responsible, as this was 'an essential part of the process of control and elimination of the violence'. It asked the Court to order the dismissal or suspension those State agents with respect to whom there was serious evidence of complicity with paramilitary groups. It specifically mentioned the need to investigate and punish the members of the 17th Brigade Army as well as the police of Urabá involved in the violent acts. These investigations should take place before courts of ordinary jurisdiction. The investigations under military jurisdiction should be suspended. The Commission also emphasised that in order to ensure the effectiveness of the investigations, they should not be treated in a fragmented way as if they were 83 different acts of violence, but they should be accumulated. This request by the Commission again shows that it has become very precise about the type of protection it would like the Court to order. Nevertheless, as we will see, the Court usually does not order measures as precise as that.

The Court did order Colombia to investigate the facts that had prompted the adoption of the provisional measures, in order to identify those responsible and impose the corresponding sanctions. It also ordered the State to inform the Court about the situation of the beneficiaries of this Order.[148] It neither specified that the investigation and prosecution should take place under ordinary jurisdiction, rather than military, nor that the investigations should be taken together rather than be dealt with in a fragmentary way.

In the context of provisional measures ordering a State to protect persons against death threats and harassment, the Inter-American Commission and Court generally point out in their provisional measures that the State should take effective measures to investigate and punish the

---

[147]   *Peace Community of San José de Apartadó* case (Colombia), Order for provisional measures, 18 June 2002, 5th 'Decisional' clause.

[148]   IACHR *Peace Community of San José de Apartadó* case (Colombia), Order of 24 November 2000. According to the English translation Colombia was required 'to inform the people indicated in the above operative paragraphs about this situation'. The Spanish text provides: 'informe sobre la situación de las personas indicadas en los puntos resolutivos anteriores'.

perpetrators, 'as a key element of its protective duty'.[149] Yet at the stage of provisional measures the Court no longer monitors compliance with this requirement. Instead it reserves this for the merits of the case.[150]

In the face of specific death threats the Commission has sometimes been very specific in the protective measures required in this respect. In a case against Brazil it specified in its precautionary measures, among others, that 'the agents entrusted with protecting the persons threatened by the "Xinguara list", including Father Ricardo Rezende, be trained in the use of firearms, and that they be adequately armed so as to guarantee effective protection for the persons threatened' and that 'the persons responsible be tried and punished'.[151] It also requested that 'if the involvement of the civilian police in the escape of Wanderley Borges de Mendonça is confirmed', the protection to be provided to one of the beneficiaries should be by a police force other than the civilian police implicated in the escape.[152] Moreover, once it was informed of the name of one of the Civilian Police officers involved in the escape, the Commission noted that the State should also adopt urgent measures to detain, try, and punish him.[153]

3.3.3.8 RESPECT OTHER RIGHTS

For the Court's provisional measures to have proper effect the conditions of implementation are crucial. The Court itself has indicated the importance of mutual agreement between the beneficiaries and the State on the necessary protective measures. Equally, it has emphasised the importance of keeping the beneficiaries informed and respecting their dignity or the nature of the group, respecting the freedom of movement, information and expression of the beneficiaries and of ensuring that the protective measures do not hinder their normal activities (e.g. as human rights defenders).

In the *Peace Community* case the Commission had specified its request by stating that the Community members, the petitioners and Colombia must mutually agree on the substance of the protective measures.[154] It had also stressed the importance of considering the compatibility of the protective measures offered by the State with the collective neutrality and humanitarian principles on which the Peace Community was founded.[155]

The difference in specificity between the Commission's and the Court's approach is also illustrated in the *Giraldo Cardona* case. In this case many of the members of the Meta Human Rights Civic Committee had been killed, had been forced to flee or otherwise to halt their activities. Eventually there were hardly any members left in Meta. As part of an order for provisional measures the Court pointed out that Colombia had to provide information on the efforts made to reopen this organization's Office.[156]

---

[149]   See e.g. IACHR *Giraldo Cardona* case (Colombia), Order for provisional measures (on behalf of members of the Civic Human Rights Committee of Meta), 19 June 1998, 4th 'Decisional' clause.

[150]   See IACHR *Cárcel de Urso Branco* (Brasil), Order of 2 May 2008, 26th 'Considering' clause. See also *Asunto de los niños y adolescentes privados de libertad en el "Complexo do Tatuapé" de la Fundação CASA* (Brasil), Order of 3 July 2007, 16th 'Considering' clause.

[151]   CIDH *Newton Coutinho Mendes et al. v. Brazil*, 1 October 1997, §59.

[152]   Id., §61.

[153]   Id., §62. See section 5.4 on the more cautious approach by the Court, distinguishing between obligations to act against impunity pending the proceedings and in judgments on reparation.

[154]   IACHR *Peace Community of San José de Apartadó* case (Colombia), Order of 24 November 2000.

[155]   Id., 3rd 'Having seen' clause.

[156]   IACHR *Giraldo Cardona*, Order of 30 September 1999, 3rd 'Decisional' clause.

3.3.4 The obligation of the State and the Inter-American Commission to provide information

Apart from requiring the State to 'take all measures necessary' to preserve the lives and physical integrity of the beneficiaries, the Court's Orders also require the State to inform it on the measures taken. The Court often calls this an 'urgent communication' by the State. At certain intervals thereafter, the State is expected to send in follow-up reports. If the full Court has not yet decided on the Commission's request for provisional measures or their amplification, the President's Orders require the State to submit its observations on such request. This way, the Court can take into account the views of both parties about the urgency and the risk of irreparable harm.

The Orders of the President and the Court itself are not only addressed to the State but also to the Commission. The Court requires the Commission to present its observations on the State's urgent communications and follow-up reports. The State and the Commission must send in these reports within certain time limits. After submission of the first report, the Court generally allots them more time for the submission of follow-up reports.[157]

States used to send very general information in response to provisional measures. In response to this, the provisional measures ordered in the Inter-American system are now more detailed.

The specific information the Court requires from the State concerns 'the status of the cases of all the persons protected by the Provisional Measures' or 'detailed information concerning the proceedings' of a specific person. As part of its follow-up the Court urges the State to continue to report, usually every two months, 'on the status of the appeals and scheduled executions' of the persons concerned. With regard to the initial report, the precise time limits depend on the proximity of an execution date. The Court also urges the State and the Commission to inform it immediately of 'any significant developments concerning the circumstances' of the cases of the beneficiaries. It may summon the parties to a public hearing as well.[158]

In his first Order to halt executions the President of the IACHR required the State to inform the Court, by a certain date, on the measures taken in compliance with his Order and to give the Court its views on the provisional measures requested by the Commission.[159] The Court received the State's observations exactly on the deadline. In these observations it 'gave the reasons why, in its opinion, the execution of the alleged victims could not be stayed'.[160]

In a provisional measure to halt an execution by Trinidad, scheduled early the next morning, the President ordered the State to inform it, that same day, on the measures taken in compliance with the Order. It also required the Commission to present its observations on the urgent communication submitted by the State within two days of its receipt.[161] As the execution would take place the next day it is clear why the President wished immediately to receive information on compliance with his Order. In this respect he may have adapted the deadline for the Commission as well, in order to conform more closely to the time limits required of the State. Normally the

---

[157] Follow-up reports normally are expected every two months and the Commission must comment on them within six weeks of their receipt. See also section 4 of this Chapter (Beneficiaries).

[158] See also Chapter XVIII (Follow-up).

[159] IACHR *James, Briggs, Noel, Garcia and Bethel* cases, Order of 27 May 1998 (President).

[160] The Court confirmed the President's urgent measures and not only ordered the State to take all necessary measures to preserve the life and physical integrity of the six persons, but also to submit a report, by the end of the month, on the measures taken in compliance with the Order. It required the Commission to submit its observations on that report within two weeks of its receipt. *James, Briggs, Noel, Garcia and Bethel* cases, Order of 14 June 1998. As the Court's session took place from 8 to 19 June, one may assume that there were no indications that Trinidad would proceed with the execution during the first half of that month.

[161] IACHR *James et al.* cases, Order of 29 June 1998 (President).

Commission's deadline is within two weeks of receipt of the State's first report.[162] He required the State to submit an urgent communication by 20 May 1999 on the measures taken to comply with the Court's Order. In fact, its next session would be held from 24 May to 4 June. This may explain why the Court ordered Trinidad to submit an urgent communication within nine days rather than the usual fifteen, as normally required, in cases in which there is no immediate execution date. This way the Court's staff could still process the information in time to be included for discussion during the Court's session. In its communication the Commission also mentioned the fact that the State's denunciation of the Convention would become effective on 26 May 1999. Possibly, the Court wanted to make sure that Trinidad would submit the information before 26 May because it expected a decreasing likelihood of compliance beyond this date.[163] In fact, Trinidad responded on 19 May 1999 claiming that the provisional measures requested by the Commission concerned matters falling within the reservation Trinidad made in recognising the compulsory jurisdiction of the Court.[164]

3.4 Conclusion on the specificity of provisional measures

As the practice of the Inter-American Commission and Court shows, provisional measures must indeed be sufficiently specific, especially in relation to protection against threats.[165] The Commission and Court started with general orders, indicating what should be the end result.[166] Over the years they built up a practice of greater specificity that they now apply generally. The level of specificity is based on previous experiences in the system and with the State in question. Initially the measures must leave room for flexibility, as long as the beneficiaries are consulted about the protective measures. When there is a chain of provisional measures relating to one case, they may become increasingly specific in a follow-up to previous State (in-)action.

Faced with the realities in many countries in the Americas the Inter-American Commission and Court became more resourceful in their ways to deal with evasive State practices. In response to initial abuse by States of their more generally phrased provisional measures they became more specific in their provisional measures. States had informed the Court, for instance, that they had increased police surveillance in the neighbourhood of the beneficiaries of the Court's Order. However, the beneficiaries, rather than feel protected by this measure, became more afraid because the police division involved was in fact closely linked to the paramilitary group posing the threats. In cases involving threats resulting in internal displacement of persons, a State would argue something like: 'well, where they are now they are safe'. This meant that the Commission and Court had to be more precise and require the State to 'enable them to return home and be safe' rather than just 'be safe'.[167]

Based on the experiences of the Commission, the Court started to include in its Orders a reference to the obligation of the State to meet with the beneficiaries, their representatives and

---

[162] On timing see also Chapter II (Systems).

[163] IACHR *James et al.* case, Urgent measures of 11 May 1999.

[164] IACHR *James et al.* case, Order of 25 May 1999. See also Chapter XIV (Jurisdiction).

[165] Already in 1994 Buergenthal, p. 94, pointed out the importance of specificity, at the same time considering that the 'remedy sought' should also be 'narrow in scope', because 'the broader the request the more difficult it will be for the Commission or the Court to monitor compliance'.

[166] This brings to mind the old distinction between obligations of conduct and result. Sepúlveda (2003), pp. 184-196 discusses these concepts and rightly criticizes the use of this distinction. Clearly in the context of defining human rights obligations it is unhelpful. While it may not create additional difficulties in the context of the specificity of provisional measures, the distinction does not seem to provide great additional value either.

[167] See e.g. the discussion of the *Peace Community* case in section 3.3.3.

representatives of the Commission in order to agree on specific protective measures that could be agreeable to all parties. The authorities in States such as Guatemala and Colombia have grown accustomed to the directive approach taken in the Court's Orders. In fact generally speaking they do not appear to find fault with this approach, possibly also because the provisional measures concern the most basic of rights: the right to life and the prohibition of torture and cruel treatment. The practice of the Commission and Court in this respect is now well established and is used vis-à-vis other States as well.

Especially when there is a chain of provisional measures relating to one case, it appears that the substance of the Order becomes increasingly specific. Often new Orders confirm and build on agreements made between the Commission, the State and the (representatives of the) beneficiaries.

These specific Orders could include the building of a protective wall between one division of a prison and another in order to prevent violence between the prison wing detaining the para-militaries and the wing detaining opposing rebels. They could also include the obligation to finance bodyguards for human rights defenders, leaders of indigenous groups, trade unionists or religious leaders who are being threatened and attacked by paramilitary groups. Other examples are the obligation to repair a telephone connection to a remote area where a peace community is located or to install armoured glass in the offices of a human rights organisation. All these measures require the use of resources and at the same time they must be taken on an urgent basis.

Both the Inter-American Commission and the Court have taken an incremental approach, specifying more and more the exact measures required to achieve the necessary protection against death threats and harassment. Their specificity is increased particularly in response to previous State (in-)action. Especially the Commission is now very precise on what it wants a State to do. The Court still makes room for flexibility. By referring, for instance, to the possibility of reporting on alternative measures, it allows the State to take a different approach so long as it does prevent irreparable harm. Moreover, even now, the Court often simply directs the State to reach an agreement with the Commission and the petitioners on the specific measures to be taken.[168] This way it provides pressure and follow-up, but the concrete solution can be prepared by the State, as long as certain conditions are fulfilled. In this respect it has also explicitly referred to the principle of subsidiarity.[169]

While the Inter-American Court has not detailed the measures required to the same extent as the Commission, it always requires the State to consult with the representatives of the beneficiaries and of the Commission about the specific protective measures necessary. This way some of the specific measures proposed by the Commission are discussed again during the implementation phase of the provisional measures. After all, the Commission proposed these measures based on the concrete information about and requests by the beneficiaries.[170]

---

[168] Note, however, the scepticism expressed by Judge Cançado Trindade in his individual opinion to IACHR *Las penitentiarías de Mendoza* v. *Argentina,* Order of 30 March 2006: with regard to attempts to 'look for a "negotiation" or "conciliation" between the "parties" in a summary proceeding in connection with the extreme gravity and urgency as is the case of provisional measures of protection. The Inter-American Court is not a "conciliation body", and must act as the international court it is, with even more power in cases of provisional measures of protection'), §16, noting that the participants, including the State, agreed on the need for a 'clear and firm order of the Court'.

[169] IACHR *Las Penitentiarías de Mendoza* (Argentina), President's Order of 22 August 2007 (maintaining the existing provisional measures, but refusing to amplify them), 14th 'Considering' clause.

[170] See also section 5 of this Chapter (Beneficiaries).

Thus, in the Inter-American system the provisional measures have become increasingly specific, partly in light of the experiences of the Commission and Court with certain States.[171] In fact they provide insight into the ways States could or must protect persons under their jurisdiction against threats by paramilitary groups or other groups operating with the acquiescence of (certain factions of) the army, the police, or other authorities. They show that protection against threats means that the State must protect the beneficiaries in the area in which they live and work, rather than banishing them to 'safe areas', claiming that this would absolve it from taking protective measures. Providing effective protection against death threats is not divorced from other human rights obligations, which means that States must assist internally displaced persons to return safely and allow human rights defenders or journalists to continue the activities that had triggered the threats in the first place.[172] In other words, the State's obligations vis-à-vis the persons under threat do not just relate to the right to life and the prohibition of torture and ill-treatment (even though this was the reason for asking provisional measures), but also involve respect for the cultural heritage of the persons threatened, their privacy, freedom of movement and expression and their access to basic resources. Moreover, the measures undertaken by the State should enable the beneficiaries to continue their activities as human rights defenders, journalists, etc. and should help protect against internal displacement.

Another specification introduced by the Inter-American Commission and Court is that the State is to report on the specific measures of protection and, as noted, that the representatives of the beneficiaries and the Commission should agree on these measures.[173] Finally, all provisional measures aiming to protect against death threats and harassment have specified the requirement of investigation and the punishment of those responsible.[174]

Often provisional measures indicate the required result, such as to refrain from executing a death sentence or to protect persons against threats. Sometimes they are also more precise as to how the State should achieve this result, or at least they rule out certain activities that do not qualify as compliance.

In the other systems it may be wise to follow the incremental approach taken by the Inter-American Court. The more information adjudicators have, the more precise they can be about the substance of the Orders for provisional measures. Collecting and interpreting information may be assumed to be easier in a regional than in a universal system. Indeed the specific nature of the Inter-American Commission's precautionary measures may also be explained by its range of functions, visiting States, negotiating with governments and petitioners and acting as an intermediary between the petitioners and the Court. In the Inter-American system specific information may relate to the links between paramilitary groups, such as the Colombian self-defence units, and the police, military or other government authorities. It is assumed that international (rather than regional) adjudicators should also incrementally specify their provisional measures, so as to provide clarity to States as to what is expected of them, but they should do so even more gradually. This gradual approach is warranted exactly because of the less cohesive nature of an international as opposed to a regional monitoring system and the diminished possibility of collecting and interpreting information. Another aspect that might play a role is the sensitivity of some States

---

[171] This applies in particular to their provisional measures ordering States such as Guatemala and Colombia to protect persons against death threats and harassment, but see also the increasingly specific precautionary measures by the CIDH in the case of the 'unlawful combatants' at Guantanamo Bay, directed at the US: 12 March 2002, 23 July 2002, 18 March 2003, 29 July 2004 and 28 October 2005.

[172] See Chapter IX (Threats).

[173] See section 4 of this chapter on the beneficiaries of provisional measures.

[174] See Chapter IX (Threats). See also section 5 of this Chapter, dealing with the relation to reparation.

and the way these States would base their disagreement with certain provisional measures on regional doctrine, or insist on sovereignty over protection of human rights.

In fact States basing their objections on regional doctrine may predominantly be European. The subsidiarity principle, the principle of trust and the margin of appreciation seem rather specific to the European system,[175] although mention has been made of the principle of subsidiarity that 'informs the Inter-American human rights system' as well.[176]

It could be argued that the Inter-American system simply is more expansive and specific in its use of provisional measures because the more extreme violations involved require a more extreme response. In the Americas there appears to be a closer link than in Europe between 'situations' and 'cases' and between collectivities and individuals. In addition, in relation to states of emergency some of the States most often addressed with provisional measures are disrupted anyway. A case in point is Colombia which, with regard to certain areas and in some respects, almost is a failing State. Yet it should be added, on the one hand, that Colombia, for instance, is an established constitutional democracy (with a functioning judicial system including a rather liberal constitutional court) and on the other hand that many European States currently appear to require specific explanations as well on what measures they should take to implement the provisional measures of the ECtHR. This applies not just to the new member States of the Council of Europe, but also to States that have considerable experience with the Strasbourg system. After all, for provisional measures to serve their purpose, the primary concern should be the prevention of irreparable harm to persons. The right to life and the prohibition of torture and cruel treatment may be compromised in the context of the concerted activities against immigration and the so-called 'war on terror'. To the extent these activities lead to a greater tendency to evade the purpose of generally phrased provisional measures, an increased specificity of their terms would be warranted.[177]

The discussion on subsidiarity (and on the related margin of appreciation in the interpretation of treaty obligations) is more important in some systems than in others and plays out differently in each system.[178] In fact the theory of margin of appreciation and, to some extent, that of subsidiarity has been invoked mainly in the European system.[179] According to staff at the Secretariat of the Inter-American Commission the theory of obligation of conduct and result equally is more European. European States may be more sensitive to being allowed the flexibility to determine how they will protect persons. Nevertheless, this may be relevant with regard to provisional measures that are leaning more closely towards the outer limits of the concept. Especially with regard to core rights the provisional measures taken by the other human rights adjudicators should at least give some direction of what the State is expected to do or to abstain from in order to prevent irreparable harm to persons.[180]

---

[175] In the Inter-American system the Commission and Court may be more directive without risking negative State responses. Still, they were not directive from the start.

[176] IACHR *Las Penitentiarias de Mendoza* (Argentina), President's Order of 22 August 2007 (maintaining the existing provisional measures, but refusing to amplify them), 14th 'Considering' clause.

[177] See also Chapter XVII (Official responses) and XVIII (Follow up).

[178] See e.g. Carozza (2003) and Petzold (1993).

[179] Carozza (2003) argues that the principle of subsidiarity applies both internationally and regionally and is not limited to the European system. The President of the IACHR appears to agree: IACHR *Las Penitentiarias de Mendoza* (Argentina), President's Order of 22 August 2007 (maintaining the existing provisional measures, but refusing to amplify them), 14th 'Considering' clause.

[180] More in general there appears to be a tendency in the European system now as well to make decisions more specific, allowing the State to have more clarity of what changes are required

4 THE BENEFICIARIES AND ADDRESSEES OF PROVISIONAL MEASURES

4.1 Introduction

Beneficiaries of provisional measures are individuals or groups whose immediate protection is the direct concern of the adjudicator. In that sense they always involve persons or groups in a vulnerable position vis-à-vis those in power. In this book beneficiaries are dealt with as rights-bearers, not as objects of charity.

In *Alemán Lacayo* (1996) the Inter-American Court initially ordered provisional measures, but subsequently it heeded to the Commission's request to lift them, because the beneficiary had become the president of Nicaragua. This made it 'inappropriate for an international body to adopt provisional measures to be instituted by a government on behalf of its own Head of State'.[181] It is interesting to see how subsequently the Commission used precautionary measures, to be implemented by the State, represented by President Aleman, to protect persons against threats that they claimed originated from the President.[182] Here over time a transformation took place from beneficiary to addressee of provisional (precautionary) measures. While this section focuses on the (group of) beneficiaries of provisional measures, it will also briefly deal with the addressees of these measures. This is an issue that may play out differently in the various systems. The ICJ as an inter-State adjudicator obviously has to take into account the interests of the addressee State as well as the complaining state, in the formulation of its provisional measures. The human rights systems are vertical systems, involving an individual or group on the one hand and a State party to a human rights treaty on the other. Do the human rights adjudicators also take into account the interests of the addressee States in their use of provisional measures?

Under the Dayton Peace accord the complaints before the Bosnia Chamber could be brought against three different state entities (Bosnia Herzegovina as a whole and the constituent States Bosnia en Republika Srpska). In addition, there are some systems in which provisional measures have addressed others than the respondent States. The Inter-American Court addresses the Inter-American Commission to negotiate with representatives of the State and the beneficiaries and report back to the Court on the implementation of the provisional measures, within certain time limits. In the European system the rule on provisional measures has occasionally been invoked to address the petitioner. These issues are discussed in this section.

An aspect of provisional measures that can be found already in provisional measures ordered by ITLOS and the ICJ, is the awareness of an overarching general interest to be protected. For ITLOS the protection of the (marine) environment is such a general interest and for the ICJ, for instance, the prevention of extension or aggravation of the dispute. While taken in response to a request by a party to the conflict, here one may speak of protection of the general interest, next to the specific interests of the States in question.

Both in the border conflicts, in which the ICJ paid attention to the population of a border area, and in cases brought before the ICJ explicitly invoking human rights, the Court appeared to have in mind a large, definite group of beneficiaries, but without names of individuals being

---

domestically, see e.g. Response by President Wildhaber to a remark by a representative of the Irish Human Rights Commission, Minutes of meeting between Court and organisations representing applicants and/or intervening as third parties, 10 April 2006, Strasbourg, p. 3, <http://unionedirittiumani.it/AutoGest/NewsFiles/incontro%20Corte%20ONG.pdf>. This could be the result of an incremental development in the attitude of the ECtHR as well, both as it is more frequently dealing with situations involving gross human rights violations and because States generally appear to prefer greater precision in what is required of them.

[181] IACHR *Alemán Lacayo* (Nicaragua), Order of 6 February 1997, 3rd 'Considering' clause.
[182] CIDH Annual report 1999, Chapter 3., C.1, §46.

listed.[183] From the human rights adjudicators it is in particular the Inter-American Court that has struggled with the level of specificity of the group of beneficiaries that is required for the use of provisional measures.

Preventing irreparable harm to persons may include preventing harm to the alleged victim (and to the rights claimed) as well as to persons other than the alleged victim. In the latter case provisional measures may relate to the integrity of the proceedings on the one hand and on the other hand to the right to life and dignity of the other persons, such as witnesses, family or counsel.[184]

Awareness of the role of the beneficiaries of provisional measures is particularly relevant in the context of adjudication in which the *petitioner* and the alleged victim are not the same. The beneficiary of the provisional measure does not always coincide with the alleged victim. Instead the beneficiary may be a witness in the case of the alleged victim, receiving threats. In both cases it is necessary to establish whether the beneficiaries indeed wish a certain provisional measure to be taken.

Even if a *de iure* representation is not necessary, it is still important to establish whether the petitioners substantively represent the persons on whose behalf they claim to be acting. When the petitioner is one of the alleged victims, claiming to represent a large group, it is important to find out whether this claim is justified. With regard to representation of the beneficiaries this section addresses in particular the issue of representation of indigenous peoples.

A related issue is that of consultation. Consultation is important in order to establish that the beneficiaries really want the provisional measures requested. In this light the question arises not only whether the NGO[185] consulted the beneficiaries before it requested provisional measures, but also whether the adjudicator consulted with the beneficiaries when drafting its provisional measures and whether the State consulted with them in its implementation of these measures.[186]

Apart from the issues of representation and consultation, this section deals with the issue of individualisation. Sometimes provisional measures aim to protect large groups of persons, where no names can be provided for each and every individual beneficiary. It is not always clear whether they must be individualised, what are the advantages and risks of providing the names of the beneficiaries and what is the approach of adjudicators towards *actio popularis*.

4.2 The relation between beneficiaries, petitioners and addressees

4.2.1 Petitioners and victims

It has been noted that in light of the emergence of *erga omnes* obligations the human being is the ultimate subject of the rights of protection, the so called *titulaire*.[187] The procedural rules with

---

183 See Chapter I.

184 See also Chapter IX (Threats).

185 See section 4.2 on NGOs as petitioners in the Inter-American and African systems, where there is no 'victim requirement'.

186 In addition, the criterion of consultation seems to play a role in the decision making on the use of provisional measures by at least one adjudicator to the extent that when indigenous peoples have been consulted domestically regarding industrial developments the HRC seems less likely to use provisional measures, see further Chapter X (Protecting (indigenous) cultural and religious rights).

187 See IACHR *Blake* v. *Guatemala*, Judgment on reparations of 22 January 1999, Separate Opinion Judge Cançado Trindade, §29. In its Order of 18 June 2002 in the *Peace Community* case the Inter-American Court discussed the issue of *erga omnes* obligations of protection. State Parties have the obligation, *erga omnes,* to provide protection to everyone under their jurisdiction in

regard to the submission of petitions in general are important in order to understand the specific practices of the adjudicators with regard to provisional measures. In the international systems of the UN treaty bodies and in the European system the so-called 'victim requirement' applies, meaning that the petitioner must be the alleged victim of the violation claimed. This is different in the Inter-American and African systems. NGOs that are not themselves the victims of the violations claimed may submit petitions in these systems. Their '*actio popularis*' standing can be inferred from the respective treaty provisions that do not refer to any victim requirement. Article 44 of the American Convention (ACHR) stipulates:

> "Any person or group of persons, or any nongovernmental entity legally recognised in one or more member states of the Organization, may lodge petitions with the Commission containing denunciations or complaints of violation of this Convention by a State Party".

Article 55 of the African Charter on Human and Peoples' Rights (ACHPR) speaks of 'communications other than those of States parties', which has been interpreted to mean that individuals and organizations may communicate to the African Commission alleging that a State party has violated one or more of the rights in the Charter. Article 5 Protocol to the ACHPR on the establishment of an African Court on Human and Peoples' Rights (1998) entitles the African Commission and the States involved to submit cases to the Court. It adds, however, that 'the Court may entitle relevant Non Governmental organizations (NGOs) with observer status before the Commission, and individuals to institute cases directly before it, in accordance with article 34 (6) of this Protocol'.[188] With regard to accepting representatives of an NGO or individuals without legal qualifications it has been noted that the African Court 'should display flexibility in order to take account of the lack of material resources from which a sizeable portion of the populations of the African continent still suffers. This solution would also enable the Court to avoid being burdened with requests for free legal aid, which possibility is provided for by the Protocol'.[189] Art 30 of the Protocol on the African Court of Justice and Human Rights (2008) refers to 'relevant Non-Governmental Organizations accredited to the African Union or to its organs'.

---

order to effectively guarantee the rights set forth in the Convention. According to the Court, the State has this obligation not only with regard to direct threats by official functionaries but also in relation to acts perpetrated by third parties, including irregular armed groups. It observed that, because of the special characteristics of the case and the overall conditions of the armed conflict in Colombia, and in light of the Convention and international humanitarian law, it was necessary to extend the protection of the right to life and personal integrity through the use of provisional measures. This extension was necessary to protect not only all members of the Peace Community but also those people who were connected to this Community by way of the services they provided. IACHR *Peace Community of San José de Apartadó* case (Colombia), Order for provisional measures, 18 June 2002. A few years before, in 2000, the State's representatives had acknowledged the important antecedents of international law upholding the provisional measures as well as their collective nature. IACHR *Peace Community of San José de Apartadó* case (Colombia), Order for provisional measures, 24 November 2000. In the original text: '*Estas medidas adoptadas con su carácter colectivo, están sustentadas en importantes antecedentes del derecho internacional*'. On the official responses by States see Chapter XVII.

[188] Article 34(6) stipulates: "At the time of the ratification of this Protocol or any time thereafter, the State shall make a declaration accepting the competence of the Court to receive cases under article 5 (3) of this Protocol. The Court shall not receive any petition under article 5 (3) involving a State Party which has not made such a declaration".

[189] Ouguergouz (2003), p. 737. This reference to free legal aid was not meant to apply as of right, but as an option for the Court, if it 'were to be given the budgetary resources required', p. 738.

4.2.2 Individuals or groups

Another issue that arises is whether only individuals or also groups can submit a petition. Before the HRC generally only individuals can do so.[190] The same applies to CAT.[191] NGOs cannot bring a claim, unless each member submits such a claim on a personal basis. Under Article 14 ICERD and Article 2 Protocol to the CEDAW there is a possibility to bring a complaint on behalf of a *group* of individuals as well. Under Article 34 ECHR the ECtHR may deal not just with petitions by individuals, but also by groups of individuals or by NGOs, *as long as* they themselves claim to be the victim of a violation of any of the rights in the Convention. The Inter-American Commission and Court and the African Commission have all accepted claims involving groups of alleged victims as well as individual victims. As noted, these petitions are being brought either by the alleged victims or by petitioners who are not themselves the alleged victims.

In the *Blake* case (Guatemala)[192] the Inter-American Court draws attention to a related matter, stressing the authority of the Commission to refer *proprio motu* to an additional deceased victim, if his family members show no interest. The Court regretted that the Commission had failed to make use of this authority in this case. It observed that 'there were two people who disappeared in the same circumstances, Mr. Nicholas Blake and Mr. Griffith Davis'.

> "Given that the remains of two people were found and that those of Mr. Griffith Davis were identified before Mr. Nicholas Blake's, the Court is surprised that the Commission did not use its authority to include Mr. Griffith Davis as an alleged victim in the application. Moreover, at the public hearing held before this Court on April 17, 1997, the Commission, in reply to a question from Judge Cançado Trindade, merely declared that Mr. Griffith Davis' relatives had not shown any interest in bringing an action before the Commission. Since the Commission did not use the authority established in Article 26(2) of its Rules of Procedure which enabled it to act *motu proprio* on the basis of any available information, even without an explicit petition by Mr. Griffith Davis' relatives, the Court concludes that it may rule only on the events that occurred in connection with Mr. Nicholas Blake".[193]

Yet another issue relates to representation. Before the HRC a petitioner may only submit a claim on behalf of a victim when the victim is a family member who has been disappeared, detained incommunicado or killed.[194] The Rules of Procedure of CEDAW are a little less strict. Under Art. 2 of the Optional Protocol the CEDAW may examine petitions without explicit consent by the alleged victim, if the petitioner can justify this.[195] Its Rule 68 specifies that the petitioner should provide her reasons for this in writing. There is no mention of an obligation that the author of the petition must have a family relationship with the alleged victim(s).

---

[190] The HRC can examine a complaint by a group if the individuals involved are similarly situated and the petitioner properly represents them. See e.g. *D.F.* v. *Sweden*, 26 March 1998 (inadm.). As noted, in cases involving indigenous culture the HRC has taken provisional measures on behalf of groups, see e.g. *Bernard Ominayak, Chief of the Lubicon Lake Band* v. *Canada*, 26 March 1990.

[191] See Article 22(1) ICAT: 'from or on behalf of individuals'.

[192] Certain witnesses in this case were the beneficiaries of provisional measures.

[193] IACHR *Blake* case (Guatemala), Judgment of 24 January 1998, §85.

[194] See e.g. the examples in Zwart (1994), pp. 72-77 and McGoldrick (1994), pp.170-172. Under the Rules of Procedure of ICERD and ICAT, family members can also submit a complaint on behalf of victims. For an interpretation by CAT see e.g. *B.M'.B* v. *Tunisia*, 5 May 1994 (inadm.).

[195] This Article points out that when a petition 'is submitted on behalf of individuals or groups of individuals this shall be with their consent unless the author can justify acting on their behalf without such consent'.

As noted, in the Inter-American and African systems NGOs have a specific role.[196] They can be the petitioners in cases without having to fulfil the victim requirement necessary for the UN treaties and the ECHR. Without this it is likely that the majority of cases that have in fact been brought before the African and Inter-American Commissions would not have been brought. Without the ability to bring individual petitions, regional or international NGOs can assist individuals and groups that are being harassed and may have difficulty accessing the adjudicators on their own. This way these regional and international NGOs are able to perform their function of helping protect members of local NGOs, especially human rights defenders.[197] Thus petitioners are often NGOs representing the victim, rather than the victims themselves. Especially useful is the fact that, in the Inter-American system, for an NGO to be accepted as a petitioner, it needs to be recognised in just one OAS Member State.[198]

In the Inter-American human rights system the Center for Justice and International Law (CEJIL) is the petitioner in a great majority of cases.[199] The downside obviously is that the position of one NGO may become too dominant. No matter the quality and sincerity of such organization, it is generally preferable for victims to be able to choose among a number of NGOs to effectively represent them. In addition transparency and media interest is particularly important to help counter any complacency that might otherwise occur.

A more specific question is who has standing to request the Inter-American Commission or Court to take provisional measures. In general, the petitioners request the Commission to take precautionary measures. In cases still pending before the Commission, it is the Commission that requests the Court to order provisional measures.[200] It appears, however, that in freedom of speech cases, the OAS Special Rapporteur for Freedom of Expression and the journalists' organisations funding his Office are actively involved as well.[201]

The Inter-American Commission and Court may also take urgent action *proprio motu*.[202] In the *Constitutional Court* case against Peru, that was pending before the Court rather than the Commission, the President indeed adopted urgent measures that were not requested by the Commission.[203] He did this *ex officio* after one of the alleged victims sent information to the Court.[204]

---

[196] See also, e.g. Grossman (1992), pp. 363-389.

[197] The importance of the protection of human rights defenders is further emphasized in the more recent UN principles on the protection of human rights defenders. See further Chapter IX (Protecting against death threats and harassment). About the Declaration see Hallo de Wolf (2002).

[198] In general on the evolving status of NGOs in international law, see e.g. Kamminga (20020, pp. 387-406.

[199] CEJIL has several offices including its headquarters in Washington D.C., the seat of the Commission, and an office in San José, Costa Rica, the seat of the Court. Through its proximity to both the Commission and the Court it is able to attend hearings and maintain a close relationship with the Secretariats of both bodies. Hence, individual victims and local human rights groups very often depend on CEJIL to bring individual complaints before the Commission.

[200] See Chapter II (Systems).

[201] See the report of the Office of the Special Rapporteur attached to the CIDH Annual Reports.

[202] See Chapter II (Systems).

[203] IACHR *Constitutional Court* (Peru), Urgent measures of 7 April 2000 (President).

[204] "4. That, from these provisions [Art. 63(2) ACHR and Rules 25(1) and (4)], it is evident that the Court, or, when appropriate, its President, may act de oficio in cases of extreme gravity and urgency to avoid irreparable damage to persons. The Court has already done so previously (Order of January 15, 1988, Provisional Measures in the Velásquez Rodríguez, Fairén Garbi and Solís Corrales, and Godínez Cruz cases, fourth and fifth preambular paragraphs). As the Court is not sitting, the President is authorized to adopt urgent measures de oficio in such cases of extreme gravity and urgency to avoid irreparable damages to persons". IACHR *Constitutional Court*

Later, during the hearing, the Commission backed up this request. The full Court confirmed the President's urgent measure as an official provisional measure.[205]

In the summer of 2001 the Inter-American Commission requested the Inter-American Court to interpret its Rules of Procedure specifically with regard to provisional measures and the role of the victims before the Court.[206] Pursuant to Article 63(2) ACHR and Articles 23(1) and 25 of the Court's Rules of Procedure the Court decided the following:

> "1. The Court will admit and hear autonomous requests, arguments, and evidence from the beneficiaries of provisional measures which it adopts in cases where the application has been presented before it; this will however, not exempt the Commission from its obligation under the Convention to provide the Court, at its request, with all the relevant information. 2. Only the Inter-American Commission on Human Rights is authorised to provide information to the Inter-American Court of Human Rights during the processing of measures ordered by the Court in cases where no application is pending before it".[207]

Subsequently the Court included the following in Article 25 of its Rules of Procedure: "In contentious cases already submitted to the Court, the victims or alleged victims, their next of kin, or their duly accredited representatives, may present a request for provisional measures directly to the Court".[208] It also added a new Article 23 to the effect that '(w)hen the application has been admitted, the alleged victims, their next of kin or their duly accredited representatives may submit their pleadings, motions and evidence, autonomously, throughout the proceeding'.[209] This constitutes a general norm applicable both to ordinary proceedings in contentious cases and to provisional measures. It affords victims the opportunity to autonomously submit their requests, arguments and evidence once the Court has admitted the application.

The beneficiaries in cases that are pending before the Commission still cannot go directly to Court to request provisional measures or a change in provisional measures already ordered. They need to convince the Commission to approach the Court on their behalf.[210] The beneficiaries of provisional measures in cases that are already before the Court, on the other hand, may now approach the Court themselves.

(Peru), Urgent measures of 7 April 2000 (President). He did so after consultation with all the other judges.

[205] IACHR *Constitutional Court* (Peru), Order of 14 August 2000.

[206] The Commission requested this in its submissions of 16 and 26 July and 1 and 9 August 2001, in relation to the Court's provisional measures in the cases of *Haitians and Dominicans of Haitian Origin in the Dominican Republic, Digna Ochoa and Placido et al., Colotenango* and *Bámaca Velásquez*.

[207] IACHR Order on the issue of provisional measures, 29 August 2001.

[208] Rules of Procedure approved by the Court during its XLIX Ordinary Period of Sessions, held from 16 to 25 November 2000, and partially reformed by the Court during its LXI Ordinary Period of Sessions, held from 20 November to 4 December 2003.

[209] Rules of Procedure approved by the Court during its XLIX Ordinary Period of Sessions, held from 16 to 25 November 2000, and partially reformed by the Court during its LXI Ordinary Period of Sessions, held from 20 November to 4 December 2003.

[210] Judge Cançado Trindade has proposed an amendment to Art. 61(1) ACHR to the effect that with regard to a case not yet submitted to its consideration, the Court may order provisional measures not only at the request of the Commission, but also of the alleged potential victims. IACHR *Matter of the persons imprisoned in the "Dr. Sebastião Martins Silveira" Penitentiary in Araraquara, São Paulo* (Brazil), Order of 30 September 2006, Separate Opinion Judge Cançado Trindade, §31.

4.2.3 Addressees

The issue of the addressees of the provisional measures ordered by the adjudicators also deserves attention. As a general rule the addressees are the States against which a petition has been filed, but in the context of the provisional measures by the Bosnia Chamber the addressees are also (and more often) the constituent entities Republika Srpska and Fed. BiH, rather than just the State of BiH. The ECtHR has sometimes addressed more than one State party with a request to take provisional measures.[211]

The HRC generally addresses the State channelled through its diplomatic mission in Geneva, but in light of certain negative experiences in this regard it has also (informally) sent the information on its decision to take provisional measures to a government minister, prison warden or the judiciary.[212] The ECtHR has equally been known to send its messages directly to the Agent for the Government at the Ministry of Foreign Affairs and only copied them to the permanent representative in Strasbourg. Similarly the Inter-American Commission has sometimes directed itself not only to the US but also to the Governors of constituent states, as it did in 1993 when it approached the Governor of Texas in order to halt the execution of Gary Graham, aka Shaka Sankofa.[213] Obviously this must be seen as extra step in order to assist a State with a federal system in the implementation of its obligations. Article 29 Vienna Convention on the Law of Treaties stipulates that a treaty is binding upon each party in respect of its entire territory and this applies to the OAS Charter as well, meaning that a State is also responsible for its constituent parts (such as states making up a federation).[214]

In the Inter-American system one can speak of the Inter-American Commission as a secondary addressee of the Court's provisional measures in the sense that the Inter-American Court orders it to monitor compliance and to send its observations to the Court within a certain time period.

Moreover, as discussed, the Inter-American Commission and Court often specify to some extent the measures required, including references to the need to contact different (regional) branches of government.[215]

The Inter-American Commission has more flexibility than the Court in its decision-making with regard to urgent cases. It may even take some action vis-à-vis groups that are not the addressees proper of its precautionary measures. Faced with extreme human rights violations by insurgents and other non-state actors, it issues press releases condemning their acts and pointing

---

[211] See e.g. ECtHR *Shamayev and 12 others* v. *Georgia and Russia*, 1 July 2003 (provisional measure of 4 October 2002 addressed to Georgia and of 17 June 2003 addressed to Russia).

[212] For these negative experiences see also Chapter II (Systems).

[213] CIDH *Gary T. Graham, now known as Shaka Sankofa* v. *US*, 15 June 2000 (adm.). This was not only so in October 1993 but already in April, when the Commission sent its first note to the Governor requesting a stay. On this case see also Chapter III (Halting executions) and Chapter XVII (Official responses).

[214] As confirmed also by the US, see e.g. ICJ Request for interpretation of the Judgment of 31 March 2004 in the case concerning Avena and other Mexican nationals (*Mexico* v. *US*), Order for provisional measures of 16 July 2008, §42.

[215] The ICJ has also pointed out the obligations of the Addressee by specifying that the Respondent State should transmit the Court's order to its constituent parts, such as the Governor of Arizona in *LaGrand*. ICJ *LaGrand* case (*Germany* v. *US*), Order of 3 March 1999, §28.

out their obligation to respect humanitarian law.[216] Its precautionary measures proper, however, are addressed to OAS member States only.

4.2.4 The petitioner as addressee

The European Court has pointed out: "In most cases, measures are indicated to the respondent Government, although there is nothing to stop the Court from indicating measures to applicants".[217]

In this respect it has adopted the approach of the former European Commission. In *Altun* v. *Germany* (1983) the European Commission had taken provisional measures to halt the extradition of the petitioner, but also informed the petitioner himself 'in accordance with Rule 36 of the Rules of Procedure, that it was desirable in the interests of the parties and the normal conduct of the proceedings that, if he was released, he should remain at the disposal of the German authorities pending the decision which the Commission might make at its session commencing 2 May 1983'.[218] In other words Germany could not keep him in detention any longer without breaking its domestic laws; hence the Commission's 'indication' for the petitioner not to abscond. The petitioner did not and reported to the police as required. Subsequently the Commission was convinced by the State that a provisional measure to halt his extradition was no longer necessary given certain assurances offered by the requesting State. At the start of a court hearing on his extradition the petitioner killed himself.[219]

The petitioner has also been addressed as part of a decision based on the rule on provisional measures in order to stop a hunger strike.[220] In the context of complaints about detention situations or lack of access to medical treatment in detention, petitioners have requested provisional

---

[216]   An example is: CIDH press release 'IACHR urges the FARC to free Corporal José Norberto Pérez', 31/01, 3 December 2001, appealing to FARC to free this corporal for humanitarian reasons so that his son, who was in a very advanced stage of cancer, could still see him.

[217]   ECtHR Grand Chamber, *Mamatkulov and Askarov* v. *Turkey*, 15 December 2004, §105 the Court referred to *Ilaşcu and others* v. *Moldova and Russia*, 8 July 2004, §11 ("On 15 January 2004 the President decided to urge Mr Ivanţoc under Rule 39 to call off his hunger strike. On 24 January 2004 Mr Ivanţoc's representative informed the Court that his client had ended his hunger strike on 15 January 2004"). In this case a provisional measure was addressed to the State first, see §10 ("On 12 January 2004 the President of the Grand Chamber decided to invite the respondent Governments under Rule 39 to take all necessary steps to ensure that Mr Ivanţoc, who had been on hunger strike since 28 December 2003, was detained in conditions which were consistent with respect for his rights under the Convention. The parties were invited, in accordance with Rule 24 §2 (a), to provide information about the implementation of the interim measures requested. Mr Ivanţoc's representative, Mr V. Gribincea, and the Moldovan Government provided the Court with the information requested in letters dated 24 and 26 January 2004 respectively"). See also Chapter VII (Detention), section 2.5.4 (Protecting detainees on a hunger strike) and Chapter XV (Immediacy and risk), section 3.2.5 on health in detention and assessment of risk.

[218]   EComHR *Altun* v. *Germany*, 3 May 1983 (adm.), §8.

[219]   See also Chapter XV (Immediacy and risk), section 3.3.

[220]   See e.g. EComHR *S., R., A. and C.* v. *Portugal*, 15 March 1984 (inadm.); *Vakalis* v. *Greece* (petitioner was in deteriorating health resulting from hunger strike; the provisional measure of 3 April 1992 did not aim for his release, but indeed aimed at addressing the situation, it was directed to the petitioner as well as to the State), 15 January 1993 (struck from the role upon release) and *Ilijkov* v. *Bulgaria* (complaint about continued pre-trial detention and the conditions in which he was force-fed; provisional measure of 20 October 1997 only to the petitioner to stop his hunger strike; Article 31 Report of 29 October 1998; Judgment of 26 July 2001). See also the aforementioned ECtHR *Ilaşcu and others* v. *Moldova and Russia*, 8 July 2004, §11 and *Rodić et al.* v. *Bosnia and Herzegovina*, 27 May 2008. See further Zwart (1994), p. 34.

measures. In some cases this request boomeranged and the petitioner himself was addressed by the Commission or Court and advised to put a stop to his hunger strike. This has been interpreted as a condition for the further examination of the case.[221] On the one hand, it makes sense for adjudicators to suggest to petitioners that if they choose recourse to an international adjudicator, and this adjudicator intervenes urgently in order to ensure that no irreparable harm occurs, they should not continue their hunger strike in the meantime. On the other hand, in my view it is not appropriate to suggest to the petitioner that stopping this hunger strike is a prerequisite for examining the case and that he, rather than the State, should apply provisional measures.[222] Given the difference in what is at stake, as well as the more vulnerable procedural position of the petitioner, the practice developed by the European Commission and apparently accepted by the Court is puzzling.[223]

The reason why this practice was introduced in the European system, but not in the other systems, may be that in the European system the text of the Rule on provisional measures is different, referring to the interests of the parties and the proceedings, rather than the prevention of irreparable harm to persons. Yet in practice the European Court also applies the criterion of preventing irreparable harm.

Of course de facto a hunger strike often results in irreparable harm as well and, as noted, an adjudicator may have good reason to indicate to the petitioner that apart from using provisional measures addressed to the State in order to improve his detention situation, etc., it is also requesting the petitioner to put a stop to his hunger strike so that the case could be properly examined and concluded.[224] Yet it does not seem appropriate to do this on the basis of the rule on provisional measures. Instead the Court could refer to the duty to cooperate, which includes taking 'such action within their power as the Court considers necessary for the appropriate administration of justice' (Rule 44A ECtHR Rules of Court). In case of failure to comply with an order of the Court concerning the conduct of the proceedings the President of the Chamber may take any steps he or she considers appropriate (Rule 44B). Where a party fails to participate effectively in the proceedings, the Court may draw such inferences as it deems appropriate (Rule 44C).

---

[221] See Zwart (1994), p. 34.

[222] Yet the Court uses the term 'invites' in this context. See ECtHR *Rodić et al.* v. *Bosnia and Herzegovina*, 27 May 2008, §4 where on 24 June one of the petitioners and on 29 June 2005 the other three were 'invited' under Rule 39 to end their hunger strike; they did so on 1 July 2005; on 13 September 2005 the case was granted priority under Rule 41. There have also been cases in which petitioners were on hunger strike but the Court did not use a provisional measure against them nor against the State, see ECtHR Lorsé case 52750/99 (*Lorsé et al.* v. *the Netherlands*), initial application, 19 November 1999, request for provisional measures (cover page and p. 16, referring to a hunger strike since 15 November 1996 (on file with the author). Only the partial inadm. decision refers to the hunger strike, in the description of the facts, referring to 17 rather than 15 November. For the judgment on the merits see *Lorsé et al.* v. *the Netherlands*, 4 February 2003. With regard to the Bosnia Chamber the Berg Handbook (1999), p. 10 notes that the Chamber's Rule 36 on provisional measures may also be applied on the Chamber's own motion. It then adds that an 'injunction could also be issued against an applicant'. It does not give examples in which the Chamber had done so. It is not clear whether the Chamber formally decided that it could do so, or whether the author of the handbook, legal secretary of the ECtHR and legal officer of the former European Commission, has assumed this based on the fact that the Chamber has taken over many rules and practices of the Strasbourg bodies. In a footnote the Handbook refers to the practice of the former European Commission to recommend petitioners to stop their hunger strike.

[223] See also, e.g., Rieter (2007), p. 974.

[224] See e.g. ECommHR *Bhuyian* v. *Sweden*, 14 September 1995 (inadm.). Request of 14 September 1995 to stop hunger strike and suicide attempts pending the case, but also to the State to provisionally suspend the expulsion.

The procedural responsibility of the petitioner may play a role in the decision-making on the use of provisional measures. The petitioners' negligence may have consequences for the progress of the case.[225] If the beneficiaries differ from the petitioners, the petitioners have the responsibility to consult them and obtain their cooperation. In the Inter-American system petitioners in cases already pending before the Court have now procedural responsibility because they deal directly with the Court without the Commission serving as an intermediary. If potential beneficiaries contact the Court in the context of a case pending before it and they are not the petitioners and not even the alleged victims, these beneficiaries have now acquired procedural rights as well, with the consequent responsibilities. Yet this does not mean that the Court's provisional measures could be directed at them. Indeed the Inter-American Commission and Court have never done so. At most they could request information or other forms of cooperation (such as postponing a hunger strike) so that they could perform their function by ordering provisional measures that would indeed have a chance to prevent irreparable harm to persons.

4.2.5 Rights of addressees

As discussed with regard to the inter-State cases dealt with by the ICJ, that Court's Orders for provisional measures often are less far reaching than the original request by (one of) the parties and the ICJ often takes into account the rights of the respondent as well.[226] While this applies more to inter-State cases not involving the rights of individuals, the statement that, given the interests of the addressee State, provisional measures should not accomplish more than necessary to prevent the irreparable harm,[227] appears to hold true for provisional measures by the human rights adjudicators as well. While the main criterion is the protection against irreparable harm, meaning that the means to be chosen must be truly protective against such harm, if there are several options to achieve this, the option that is least invasive to the general interest should be chosen.

Sometimes adjudicators have been very accommodating to the State. In *Länsman II* the HRC used provisional measures before it declared the case admissible, but it almost invited the State to object by suggesting the possibility that it would reconsider its use of provisional meas-

---

[225]   See e.g. ECtHR *Hun* v. *Turkey*, 10 November 2005 (struck out). The petitioner had been invited under Rule 39 to respect its provisional measures in that she was to provide a medical report ordered by the committee of experts appointed by the ECtHR. She had responded that she had been unable to obtain this because of administrative difficulties, §35. Nevertheless, since then the petitioner had still failed to provide these reports and the Court was not convinced of these difficulties. It noted that she had not attempted to obtain the documents from another hospital either and that the government's explanations were more convincing. Moreover, it commended the exemplary cooperation of the State with the Court's provisional measures in this context (noting that even in this case, where at some point the petitioner had been arrested despite the Court's provisional measures to the State to halt her re-imprisonment, she had been released at once when the authorities realized their mistake, see also §§23-24), contrasting this with the failure of the petitioner to do the same, §§36 and 37. To be sure, the petitioner had initially complied with the provisional measures directed to her, by presenting herself for examination by the medical expert mission appointed by the ECtHR. Yet these experts had recommended a neurological examination before they could examine her condition. When almost 7 months later the Court had still not received the report requested of such examination, it decided to lift the provisional measures directed to the State halting her re-imprisonment. This withdrawal (as well as the subsequent striking out of the case) appears to be a reasonable response to the petitioner's procedural attitude.

[226]   See Chapter I (ICJ).

[227]   See e.g. Merrills (1995), p. 100.

ures if the State party disagreed.[228] This was a new approach to the presentation of its provisional measures.[229] CAT even has included in its Rules a specific reference to the possibility for the State to request withdrawal of the provisional measures.[230] It is to be expected, however, that States disagreeing with the use of provisional measures in a given case would protest their use in any case, also without invitation. CAT has observed 'that its procedures are sufficiently flexible and its powers sufficiently broad to prevent an abuse of process in a particular case', which would protect the rights of the addressee States as well.[231]

States have sometimes argued that their rights should be protected beyond ensuring procedural fairness, by stating that the rights and interests of the parties should be balanced, invoking principles such as 'balance of convenience'.[232]

Yet as further discussed in the Conclusion to Part II international human rights adjudicators generally take provisional measures in only a very limited range of cases involving rights that are

---

[228] HRC *Jouni E. Länsman et al.* v. *Finland*, 30 October 1996 (initial submission of 28 August 1995, Rule 86/91 of 15 November 1995); decision of 14 March 1996 to set aside its provisional measures (together with admissibility declaration).

[229] Apart from referring to the possibility of reconsideration already in the Note Verbale, with the provisional measure, sent to the State or even already in the Rules of Procedure, there are also other ways to accommodate the State. In the same *Länsman II* case, in early December 1995 the petitioners informed the HRC, by urgent message, that a division of the Central Forestry Board had started logging at the end of November, despite the Committee's provisional measure taken two weeks previously. This logging was scheduled to continue until the end of March 1996. The petitioners requested a reiteration of the provisional measure so that the State party would discontinue logging immediately. See §4.2 of *Jouni E. Länsman et al.* v. *Finland*, (Länsman II), 30 October 1996. Clearly, the Central Forestry Board should have known about the Committee's provisional measures of 15 November 1995. The urgent request for provisional measures specified that the local branch of the Board was aware of the Rule 86 request before it started the logging. "Some kind of a meeting or consultation between the branch and the Foreign Ministry took place, apparently on Friday 24 November, some days before the logging was started". Fax of the petitioner of 8 December 1995 (on file with the author). In *Länsman I, Ilmari Länsman* v. *Finland*, 26 October 1994, the HRC did not use provisional measures because it considered they would be premature. It is the only case involving culture in which the HRC motivated its refusal to use them. Yet the HRC did not reiterate the provisional measures it had initially ordered, despite the request by the petitioners. Apparently, in December 1995 a negotiation took place between the parties, during which a solution was actively sought. The Finnish Foreign Ministry had also indicated that it would respond to the Committee's provisional measures and concede admissibility in the next week and would then indicate whether it might stop or scale down logging. Note of the Secretariat of 8 December 1995 (on file with the author). In this context the Rapporteur may have decided that it would serve little purpose to use provisional measures for the second time before he had seen the reply promised by the State. In fact, the question whether to maintain the first Rule 86 request was put before the Committee's Working Group and decided in the negative on 14 March 1996. A month after the Committee had indicated provisional measures and more than two weeks after logging had been resumed, the State party indeed submitted its formal response. The State considered that the provisional measures were inappropriate in the circumstances of the case and requested the HRC to set them aside. Nevertheless, it undertook 'not to elaborate further logging plans in the area in question, and to decrease the current amount of logging by 25 percent, while awaiting the Committee's final decision' (on file with the author).

[230] See also Chapter XV (Immediacy and risk).

[231] CAT *Ahmed Hussein Mustafa Kamil Agiza* v. *Sweden*, 20 May 2005, §13.10.

[232] See e.g. Ontario Court of Appeal, *Ahani* v. *Canada*, 8 February 2002, dissenting opinion of Rosenberg, §107.

absolute. In such cases the balance of convenience no longer applies.[233] This principle should apply in relations between equal parties and is therefore more suitable for proceedings not involving a threat to the very existence of a person or indigenous peoples. Balancing the interest of the petitioner with those of the State (or 'the general interest') normally is inappropriate in relation to those rights singled out in the treaties for their fundamental nature, not allowing for derogation even in times of emergency.

4.2.6 Indirect beneficiaries

While provisional measures only bind the addressee vis-à-vis the direct beneficiaries, they could also have an effect beyond the particular case. Other potential beneficiaries could refer to these provisional measures. While a provisional measure does not concern an 'examination' of the case, persons similarly situated to the beneficiary *could* refer domestically to the provisional measures by an international or regional adjudicator. This applies to persons claiming the same rights before domestic decision makers. They would then have to use this to underscore their own claim, as an indication of the risk perceived by this adjudicator in similar situations of urgency. If the provisional measure concerns halting an expulsion of certain persons to a certain State (e.g. in a situation of civil war) counsel for other persons similarly situated and risking expulsion to that same State could argue that it would be a pro-active good faith application of the treaty to halt these other expulsions as well, pending determination of the proceeding in which the provisional measures were used. This would also be in accordance with the rationale of the rule on exhaustion of domestic remedies. Moreover the State would prevent recourse to international proceedings by these other persons as well as the ensuing embarrassment of more provisional measures of a similar nature. Of course such an argument would apply only if the persons involved were truly similarly situated.[234]

4.3   Consent, consultation and representation

4.3.1 Introduction

It is inherent in the function of human rights adjudicators to take into account in particular the perspectives of the powerless. How well they can perform their function depends to a large extent on how the case is presented before them, in other words, on the power of the narrative. Yet in a sense those that are able to get across a powerful narrative are not among the most powerless and it is only to be hoped that the judicial follow-up to their stories will ultimately have an impact on the most powerless as well, or in jargon, 'empower' them. In any case, the question of who is represented by whom, and how, is quite relevant as well, not just in that this may influence whether an adjudicator decides to order provisional measures, but also the contents of these provisional measures and the scope of the group requiring protection.

In a strict inter-State approach, in which the individual is not much more than a pawn in the hands of the conflicting Parties, provisional measures function in a different way than they do as part of human rights adjudication proper. This becomes clear particularly in the context of the role of the beneficiary. Traditionally, there is no obligation to consult with the beneficiaries to see whether they consent to the provisional measures and, if so, how they consider they would best be protected. Yet in the Inter-American human rights system a practice has been developed in which

---

[233]   If human rights adjudicators take provisional measures in a wider range of cases the balance of convenience may apply.

[234]   See e.g. the ECtHR and cases against the Netherlands involving non-refoulement to regions in Somalia, discussed in Chapter II (Systems) and XVII (Official responses).

such consultation serves as a focal point. Given the purpose of preventing irreparable harm to persons, for instance in the face of death threats, such consultation is particularly warranted. Moreover, in the Inter-American and African systems the petitioners often are not the victims, let alone the beneficiaries of the provisional measures, which makes consultation all the more important.

Under the ICCPR the issue of consultation has mainly surfaced in the context of provisional measures to protect indigenous culture. In other words, in the practice of the HRC it is important when dealing with the issue of collective rights. This section first deals with the issue of consent, particularly in the context of provisional measures to protect against death threats. It then examines the issues of consultation and representation, focussing on the rights of collectivities, in particular indigenous cultures.

4.3.2 Beneficiaries and their consent

In cases involving multiple beneficiaries it is especially important to establish that the petitioner does not misrepresent the interests of the beneficiaries.[235] This means that the issue of representation and consent, which often arises in relation to the alleged victim(s), also has relevance with regard to the potential beneficiaries.[236]

In *Sands* v. *UK* (1981) the petitioner had requested the European Commission to intervene urgently on behalf of her brother who was on hunger-strike. As his life was at stake the Commission invoked Rule 36 on provisional measures. Under this Rule it expressed a wish to visit the petitioner's brother to enquire whether he indeed intended to make the petition. In other words this was a special type of provisional measure. While it involved a risk of irreparable harm to persons the Commission still wished to be sure that the person at risk agreed with the involvement of the Commission. It struck out the case once it had ascertained during its on site visit, triggered by its provisional measures, that the petitioner's brother did not intend to make the petition.[237]

Checking whether the beneficiary really wants the provisional measures also includes taking into account that the beneficiary may sometimes only withdraw a request for precautionary measures exactly because of intimidation. In the *Blake* case the Inter-American Commission had requested the Court to order provisional measures on behalf of certain people, including Justo Victoriano Martínez-Morales. He was 'a key witness in the Blake Case' because of 'his investigation of the circumstances that led to Mr. Nicholas Blake's abduction and disappearance'. The President of the Court indeed ordered these measures, pending discussion by the full Court. The

---

[235] See also subsection 4.4.4 of this Chapter on identification and representation.

[236] On this issue in relation to the alleged victims see e.g. Mutua (2004), pp. 191-215; Juma (2004), pp. 235-271; and Nmehielle (2001), pp. 309-324.

[237] ECHR *Marcella Sands and Robert Sands* v. *the UK*, 14 October 1981 (struck out). Bobby Sands did express a willingness 'to see the Delegates in the presence of three persons previously named by him in a press statement which had been issued in his name'. "After further consultations the Delegates decided that in the circumstances it was not possible to see and confer with Mr Sands and accordingly no meeting took place". According to a statement by the Republican Prisoners in the H-Blocks, at the end of the second hunger strike, Marcella Sands had acted on the advice of the Premier of the Republic of Ireland, convincing her that the intervention of the European Commission could solve the issue. After the Delegation of the European Commission had left without meeting Sands and the people he had proposed, Bobby Sands released a statement attacking the Premier for 'unscrupulously exploiting his family's anxiety to cover his own inactivity'. Bobby Sands died from the effects of his hunger-strike on 5 May 1981. Later the other prisoners decided to end the hunger strike, 'faced with the reality of sustained family intervention', see <larkspirit.com/hungerstrikes/81statement_end.html> (consulted 8 September 2005).

State responded, among others, that Mr Victoriano Martínez himself 'had denied being subjected to threats or attacks against his person or his family and would not agree to any personal safety measures. Because of this refusal, the National Police of Huehuetenango offered to guard his residence with a night patrol after 8 p.m., to which he agreed'.[238] Subsequently the Commission 'reiterated that a case of extreme urgency did exist for the aforementioned reasons, and that the threats extended' to his family.[239] The Court ratified the President's Order and requested the State to maintain the provisional measures on behalf of the five persons involved.[240] More than 1,5 year later Mr Victoriano Martínez-Morales testified at the public hearing on the merits of the *Blake* case. He 'said that he feared for his and his family's life and physical safety and that he was only protected at his place of residence'.[241] The Court responded to this by requiring the State 'to provide those measures to the persons in whose favor they were adopted, not only while they are in their homes but also when they are away from them'. It decided to maintain the provisional measures so long as the circumstances of extreme gravity still existed.[242]

In the *Paniagua* case the fifteen year old son of one of the victims had testified at the public hearings on Reparations of the Inter-American Court in August 2000. Subsequently he was threatened. The Inter-American Commission informed the Court of the situation but did not request it to take provisional measures. The Court, though, took provisional measures *proprio motu*.[243] It turned out, however, that the beneficiary felt that the Court's order might work counterproductive. Thus, the petitioner wanted the provisional measures lifted. The Commission requested the Court to lift its provisional measures and the Court did so.[244]

4.3.3 Consultation

As discussed, the letters by the Inter-American Commission to the State have become more specific[245] in its awareness of the importance of consultation between the State and the petitioner about the implementation of its precautionary measures. In its letters to governments it now notes that precautionary measures must be implemented in consultation with the interested parties and their representatives.[246] The Inter-American Court takes a similar approach.

---

[238] IACHR *Blake* case (Guatemala), Judgment of 24 January 1998, §38.

[239] Id., §39.

[240] Id., §40.

[241] Id., §41.

[242] Id., §42.

[243] IACHR *Paniagua Morales et al.* case, Order of 29 January 2001.

[244] Id., noting, in the 5th 'Having seen' clause, the submission by the State that the harassment experienced by the beneficiary 'was due "to personal problems with a gang of hoodlums" and that the State was providing the minor with protection to and from the high school where he was a student' and referring, in the 6th clause, to the 'letter from the representative of the individual under protection (…) wherein the representative requests that the measures ordered by the Court be lifted'; finally mentioning the note by the Commission in which it agreed that 'the provisional measures ordered for the minor should be lifted'(7th 'Having seen' clause). The Court also pointed out, in its 4th 'Considering' clause, that the Commission would 'continue to monitor the situation and, if need be, provide pertinent information'.

[245] See section 3 of this Chapter.

[246] States, especially those that are often the addressees of provisonal measures, have now become accustomed to this type of provisional measures. This has not always been the case. According to Charles Moyer, Inter-American Institute of Human Rights, formerly Secretary of the Court and Commission, interview of December 2001, at least in the type of cases that he had dealt with in the ten years he worked at the Commission and the other ten years he worked at the Court, States would have been too antagonistic to sit around the table and discuss matters.

In the context of the Inter-American (and African) system we may assume that the petitioners representing the victims, also represent witnesses and other people involved in the case domestically (such as counsel, prosecutor or judge in domestic proceedings) when they are subjected to threats. In this context the interested parties ('*los interesados*') that must be consulted are all the beneficiaries of these precautionary measures.

In its Annual Reports the Inter-American Commission sometimes explicitly notes that the measures requested should be taken 'with the beneficiary's agreement',[247] or that a State is expected to investigate the threats and agree with the *petitioners* on security measures.[248] Yet if it does not mention in its Annual Report the even more obvious need for an agreement with the actual *beneficiary*, rather than the petitioner, this does not necessarily mean that the Commission did not require such agreement.

In the *Peace Community* case the Inter-American Court ordered the State to allow the participation of the petitioners in planning and implementing and, in general, to keep them informed about the progress in the implementation of the Court's provisional measures. Likewise, the State was to continue allowing the beneficiaries or their representatives to participate in the planning and implementation of the measures and, in general, to keep them informed about all developments.[249]

In August 1998 the Court took provisional measures again in the context of *Alvarez et al.* (Colombia), on behalf of an attorney and his family. He had been threatened because he was representing the families of detainees and missing persons in several criminal cases and suits for compensation. It requested Colombia to effectively investigate the alleged acts in order to determine the perpetrators and punish them. It requested the Commission to 'urge the beneficiaries of the provisional measures adopted by the Inter-American Court of Human Rights in the matter to cooperate with the State of Colombia in order to enable the latter to more effectively adopt the necessary security measures'.[250]

4.3.4 Representation and collective rights

Many of the rights in the ICCPR may be enjoyed in community with others.[251] The HRC has noted that Article 1 OP restricts its competence to dealing with individual complaints, but that this 'does not prevent such individuals from claiming that actions or omissions that concern legal persons and similar entities amount to a violation of their own rights'.[252]

Regarding the relationship between petitioners and beneficiaries it is important to note that while the HRC does not accept the group itself as a petitioner (although it came close in the *Lubi-*

---

[247] CIDH precautionary measures of 5 July 2001 to protect the judicial magistrate in charge of the investigation into the murder of journalist Jean Dominique, Annual Report 2001, Chapter III (a), §37.

[248] A security cooperative in Colombia had been threatening a trade union leader. This group had earlier claimed responsibility for several killings and for attacks on union leaders, Annual Report 2001, Chapter III (a), §22.

[249] IACHR *Peace Community of San José de Apartadó* case (Colombia), Order for provisional measures, 18 June 2002.

[250] IACHR *Álvarez et al.*(Colombia), Order of 29 August 1998, 5th 'Decisional clause'. See also the even stronger expression in the 6th 'Considering' clause: 'The beneficiaries of the provisional measures adopted by the Court in the instant case have the obligation to cooperate with the State so that the latter might more effectively adopt the necessary security measures'.

[251] See Chapter X (Culture). See also e.g. Coomans (2003), pp. 749-760; Martin (2006), pp. 491-504 and Murray and Wheatley (2003), pp. 213-236.

[252] HRC General Comment on Article 2 ICCPR, the nature of the general legal obligation imposed on States parties to the Covenant, 21 April 2004, §9.

con case), it certainly takes into account group aspects when it uses provisional measures involving the protection of indigenous culture. This was already the case in *Lubicon*, but it was confirmed in subsequent cases. In *Lubicon* the petitioner was Chief Ominayak but the HRC specifically made the Band members beneficiaries of the provisional measures, next to Chief Ominayak. It explained that it used provisional measures in light of the seriousness of the allegations 'that the Lubicon Lake Band was at the verge of extinction'.[253]

In its arguments on admissibility in *Länsman III* the HRC declared inadmissible the complaint in so far as it related to the Herdsmen's Committee and/or its constituent members other than Jouni and Eino Länsman. It noted that there was no indication that individual members had authorised the Herdsmen's Committee to bring a claim on their behalf or that Jouni and/or Eino Länsman were authorised to act on behalf of the Herdsmen's Committee and its members. Yet the provisional measure taken in this case had specified Jouni Länsman et al. as the beneficiaries, which could still include the Herdsmen's Committee. After all, previously the Committee had only taken provisional measures in Article 27 ICCPR cases in which the collective aspects were predominant.[254]

When dealing with the question of the identity and interests of the beneficiaries of the provisional measures used by the HRC to protect indigenous culture it is important to keep in mind the discussion about self-determination. If collective aspects play an important role in the enforcement of individual rights, the issue of who represents a group in international fora is relevant in order to clarify the possible group of beneficiaries of provisional measures.[255] It is not clear, however, to what extent considerations about representation and consultation indeed already play a role in the decision whether or not to take provisional measures in cases involving culture.[256]

Clearly, if the aim is to prevent irreparable harm to an indigenous group the victim-petitioner must be seen to represent the interests of its members. Also, the provisional measures required should not be such as to cause irreparable harm to other indigenous groups in the area. Irreparable harm, however, is not likely to result from a request to postpone industrial activities threatening the natural habitat. The fact that the interests of other indigenous groups could eventually justify certain infringements of the rights of the petitioners does not mean that the HRC could not take provisional measures protecting these rights pending the proceedings.[257] In other

---

[253] HRC *Lubicon Lake Band*, 26 March 1990, §29.2.

[254] See Chapter X (Culture).

[255] The *first Mikmaq* case (1984), HRC *A.D.* v. *Canada* (1st Mikmaq case), 29 July 1984 (inadm.) relates to representation. See generally about representation Meijknecht (2001), pp. 103-120 and p. 189. The Committee observed that the petitioner had not proven that he was authorised to act as a representative of the Mikmaq and the HRC declared the case inadmissible. Furthermore, he had failed to advance relevant facts supporting the claim that he was personally a victim. One member of the Committee pointed out that it should also have dealt with the fundamental question whether the right to self-determination in Article 1 could be dealt with under the OP. Individual opinion by Roger Errera in *A.D.* v. *Canada*, 29 July 1984 (inadm.).

[256] See about the requirement to be personally affected, requirements for other members of a group to be similarly affected, the possibility to submit a communication collectively and the role of the representative Meijknecht (2001), pp. 184-190. About the international legal capacity, international subjectivity and *ius standi* of indigenous peoples in general see Meijknecht (2001), Chapters 3-5.

[257] In this case the State had pointed out that there were competing claims from 'several other native communities in the area', but the Band accused Canada of having sent agents to the area immediately surrounding the traditional Lubicon territory in order to induce native individuals to strike their own private deals with the federal government. HRC *Lubicon Lake Band*, 26 March 1990, §5.7. In the discussion following the Committee's interlocutory decision of July 1989, requesting information and repeating its provisional measures, the petitioner submitted that the State party had further violated Articles 1, 26 and 27 ICCPR by creating the 'Woodland Cree

words, competing interests should generally not prevent the use of this type of provisional measures. On the other hand, by arguing or implying that other indigenous groups or other members of the same group have differing views about the risk of irreparable harm to the natural habitat a State could try to convince the Committee not to take provisional measures or to withdraw those measures already taken.[258]

In any case, it is not clear whether or to what extent the State's argument about conflicting interests of indigenous groups, or the lack of clarity in general about the factual situation, played a role in the HRC's eventual decision in *Lubicon* on the reparation required, with its ambiguous wording and consequent reflection on the purpose of its provisional measures in future cases.[259]

Discord among potential beneficiaries of the Committee's provisional measures could be relevant to the Committee's assessment whether such measures are warranted.[260]

Band' in an alleged attempt to 'fabricate' a competing claim to traditional Lubicon lands. He pointed out that the federal government had supported the new Band both financially and legally, 'recognising it "with unprecedented dispatch", thereby bypassing more than 70 other groups, including six different homogenous Cree communities in northern Alberta that had been awaiting recognition as Bands for over 50 years', §27.5. The Lubicon Lake Band received support from the Assembly of First Nations and others. On 7 November 1989 the National Chief of the Assembly of First Nations sent a letter to the Prime Minister of Canada, pointing out that the Lubicon Lake Nation had been waiting for more than 50 years for 'an acknowledgment of their rights to their unceded, traditional lands'. In this letter he expressed concern about apparent tampering with Band membership lists. In January 1990 the Mohawk Council of Kahnawake considered it 'extremely prejudicial' that the authorities created the Woodland Cree Band 'in the face of long standing, unresolved negotiations over the Lubicon Lake Indian Nation unceded territory and compensation'. He expressed concern that this 'divide and conquer tactic' would be used elsewhere too when the authorities would consider the negotiation process with existing Bands unsatisfactory. On 8 March 1990 the Grand Council of Treaty 8 Nations passed a resolution strongly supporting the Lubicon Lake Nation 'and its inherent jurisdiction to determine its own membership and to the ownership of the Lands and Resources in its Traditional Territory'. It condemned the actions of the Canadian government, seeking 'to undermine the rights and jurisdiction of the Lubicon Lake Nation by the creation of the Woodland Cree Band' and resolved not to recognize the Woodland Cree Band. On 20 March 1990 the Chief of the Assembly of First Nations addressed the Prime Minister once more. He also sent copies of this letter to several addresses, including the HRC. See <nativenet.uthscsa.edu/archive/nl/91d/0071.html> (accessed on 23 August 2003) The HRC did not refer to this, but dismissed as an abuse of the right of submission under Article 3 OP the Lubicon Lake Band's allegations 'that the State party has conspired to create an artificial band, the Woodland Cree Band, said to have competing claims to traditional Lubicon land'. See HRC *Lubicon Lake Band*, 26 March 1990, §32.3. On 22 December 1990 the *Edmonton Journal* published an editorial in which it noted that it was time for a Lubicon deal. It pointed out that Bands with legal status under the Indian Act had submitted 578 specific claims since 1973, only 205 of which had been either rejected or resolved. It noted that according to the Assembly of First Nations only 44 claims had been 'settled to mutual satisfaction in the past 17 years'. The editorial noted the 'cynical motivation behind Ottawa's generosity to the Woodland Cree in Northern Alberta' and pointed out that the authorities hoped that the Lubicon Lake band would now give in and 'stop claiming compensation for millions of dollars in resource revenue pumped from their own land for years without their permission'. Republished on <nativenet.uthscsa.edu/archive/nl/91d/0071.html> (accessed on 23 August 2003).

[258] On the assessment of material urgency for the use of provisional measures see Chapter XV.

[259] See Chapter X (Indigenous culture) and section 5 of this chapter, on the relationship between provisional measures and reparation.

[260] The issue of conflicting rights also surfaced briefly in *Länsman II* when a group of Sami other than the petitioners addressed the Committee, disagreeing with them. HRC *Länsman II*, 30

In *Sara et al.* v. *Finland* (inadm. 1994)[261] the addressee State had also referred to conflicting positions by reindeer herdsmen. By doing this it equally may have been suggesting disagreement between the beneficiaries about the risk of irreparable harm to the environment.[262] The petitioners pointed out that their rights under Article 27 ICCPR should not be denied just because they had not been able to maintain all traditional methods of reindeer herding.[263] Equally, they noted that not all herdsmen in Finland were in fact Sami. This could put into perspective the supposed disagreement among the beneficiaries.

The question also arises whether only the petitioners are the beneficiaries of the provisional measures, whether all the members of the two Sami Herdsmen Committees are or all Finnish Sami.

Equally the question arises whether the rights of the non-Sami Herdsmen, who clearly are no beneficiaries of the provisional measures, should play a role in the Committee's decision to take or maintain provisional measures. In *Sara*, for instance, the State pointed out that the Wilderness Act was based on a 'philosophy of co-existence of reindeer herding and forest economy'. Referring to the unemployment figures in Finnish Lapland it noted:

"While the Government fully took into account the requirements of article 27 of the Covenant, it could not ignore the economic and social rights of that part of the population whose subsistence depends on logging activities".[264]

Another concept that has entered the equation is that of the economic well-being of the State's population in general.[265] In *Länsman I* the HRC pointed out that a 'State may understandably

---

October 1996, §4.3. After the HRC had taken provisional measures, a group of Sami Forestry officials from the Inari area, earning their living from forestry and wood economy, submitted that reindeer husbandry and forestry could be practised simultaneously with reindeer herding. They pointed out that when forestry activities would be forbidden in the area, 'Sami groups practising two different professions would be subject to unequal treatment', ibid. In response the petitioners stated that the local branch of the Central Forestry Board had apparently organized a small group of its employees of Sami ethnic origin to approach the Committee for the purpose of expressing concern for their employment.

[261] HRC *Sara et al.* v. *Finland*, 23 March 1994 (inadm.).

[262] The State had noted that other herdsmen had in fact requested preservative logging, arguing that this would be to the advantage of the lichen and would sustain the tree population. It also referred to the Association of Herdsmen's Committees, which had noted that 'the income derived from logging is essential for securing the herdsmen's livelihood and, furthermore, forestry jobs are essential to forest workers and those Sami herdsmen who work in the forests apart from breeding reindeer'.

[263] "While Finnish Sami have not been able to maintain all traditional methods of reindeer herding, their practice still is a distinct Sami form of reindeer herding, carried out in community with other members to the group and prescribed by the natural habitat. Snow scooters have not destroyed this form of nomadic reindeer herding. Other than in Sweden and Norway, Finland allows reindeer herding for others than Samis; thus, the southern parts of the country are used by herdsmen's committees which now largely resort to fencing and artificial feeding". HRC *Sara et al.* v. *Finland*, 23 March 1994 (inadm.), §7.4.

[264] HRC *Sara et al.* v. *Finland*, 23 March 1994 (inadm.), §4.6.

[265] States have tried to convince the HRC that economic and social rights of the general population could justify transgressions upon the cultural rights of indigenous peoples. The European Commission on Human Rights indeed acknowledged as a justification for infringements on the right to respect for the particular life style of the Sami the interest of the economic well being of the country as a whole. See *G. and E.* v. *Norway* (inadm. 1993). The Commission noted 'a minority group is, in principle, entitled to claim the right to respect for the particular life style it

wish to encourage development or allow economic activity by enterprises' but the 'scope of its freedom to do so is not to be assessed by reference to a margin of appreciation'.[266] Rather, the scope of this freedom must be assessed by reference to its obligations in Art. 27 ICCPR. Still, the HRC pointed out that measures with 'a certain limited impact' will not necessarily amount to a denial of this article.[267] Schmidt notes that the HRC 'had to balance the applicants' interests against general economic interests advanced by the Finnish Government'. Thus it 'implicitly granted the state party what amounted to a margin of appreciation' in determining whether their rights had been protected sufficiently.[268] On the other hand, Scheinin notes the Committee's decision in *Kitok* in which the HRC 'referred to the well-being of the Sami minority, not to the economic well-being of the country as a whole'.[269] Hence, he considers that the HRC has been willing to accept justifications for infringements on the right of an individual member of an indigenous group to enjoy his own culture if they aim at protecting the indigenous group as a whole, rather than if based on arguments about the interests of the general population. When taking Scheinin's interpretation regarding the Committee's decisions on the merits it seems unlikely that arguments about social and economic rights of the general population will play a role in its decisions on provisional measures. In any case, the HRC could more appropriately consider general interests in the reporting procedure under Article 40 ICCPR.[270]

---

may lead as being "private life", "family life" or "home"' (p. 35). It was also 'prepared to accept' that the consequences for the petitioners arising from the construction of a hydro-electric plant did interfere with their private life and traditional activities 'as a minority, who move their herds and deer around over a considerable distance'. Yet this interference was limited to a 'comparatively small area'. Thus the Commission seemed to imply that the extent of the interference was insufficient for purposes of Article 8(1) ECHR. Nevertheless it continued by stating that it did not ascertain 'the exact extent and nature of the interference' under Article 8(1), but considered that such interference could in any case 'reasonably be considered as being justified' under Article 8(2) ECHR, among others 'in the interest of the economic well-being of the country' (p. 36). Following this substantive discussion it declared this part of the petition inadmissible as manifestly ill-founded.

[266] HRC *Ilmari Länsman et al.* v. *Finland*, 26 October 1994, §9.4.

[267] Ibid.

[268] Schmidt (1997), p. 338.

[269] See Scheinin (2001), p. 169.

[270] An interesting case dealt with by the Bosnia Chamber is *Lukenda and Bevanda* v. *Fed. B&H*, 5 July 2001 (inadm.). Petitioners in this case sought the Chamber's withdrawal of the provisional measures it had ordered in another case, *Dautbegović and 51 other villagers from the village of Duge* v. *Fed. B&H*, 6 July 2001. These provisional measures required the respondent party 'to take all necessary measures to ensure that the construction works on the planned hydro-electric power plant near the village of Duge be stopped', §3. The petitioners requested 'as a provisional measure' that the Chamber withdraw this provisional measure, as they wished to continue construction of their power plant. The Chamber decided instead to extend its provisional measures in *Dautbegović* until it would adopt its final decision in that case or withdraw the order, §5. The case submitted by Lukenda and Bevanda was subsequently declared inadmissible as manifestly ill-founded: the approval and permits for the construction of the power plant 'on a site protected as an asset of natural heritage' were not issued in accordance with law, §107.

4.4 Extending the group of beneficiaries, identification and representation

4.4.1 Introduction

As noted, the beneficiaries of provisional measures in a given case do not necessarily coincide with the alleged victim. Moreover, they may also be a *group* of beneficiaries rather than just one or two persons. The issue of larger groups of beneficiaries has arisen mostly in three types of cases: death threats and harassment, mass expulsion and survival of indigenous groups.[271] Often, in consecutive provisional measures, the group of beneficiaries is extended. At times it is difficult to provide the names of all intended beneficiaries. Yet especially if this is not possible, the question arises to what extent they consider themselves to be represented by the petitioners.

This section first deals with extension of the group in general, then focuses on the question whether each person to be protected must be identified by name, whether provisional measures could play a role in early warning mechanisms, and finally it gives an example where, in a case in which not all of them were identified by name, some of them brought a motion for self-representation.

4.4.2 Extending the group of beneficiaries

Usually the HRC has used provisional measures on behalf of an individual or, if the complaint was filed by a group of persons, on behalf of all persons. Only in some cases dealing with the right to culture the group of beneficiaries encompassed in fact a larger group of persons than just those mentioned by name in the application. In the other systems provisional measures have sometimes benefited others than the individual victim as well.

The Inter-American Court's first provisional measures halting executions aimed to protect five persons whose cases were pending before the Inter-American Commission. Subsequently, it amplified its provisional measures from five to 41 beneficiaries.[272] In the Inter-American system the list of beneficiaries is regularly extended to include new persons, most often in cases involv-

---

[271] See Chapters IX (Threats); XI (Mass expulsion) and X (Culture).

[272] IACHR *James et al.* cases, Orders of 25 October 2001 and 26 November 2001 (President). For previous Orders see *James et al.* cases, Orders of 29 June 1998 and 13 July 1998 (President); *James, Briggs, Noel, Garcia and Bethel* cases, Order of 22 July 1998. *James et al.* cases, Order of 29 August 1998. *James et al.* cases, Order of 11 May 1999 (President) and Order of 25 May 1999. *James et al.* cases, Order for provisional measures, 27 May 1999. *James et al.* cases, Order of the President for urgent measures, 19 June 1999 and Order for provisional measures, 25 September 1999. Trinidad executed two of them: Joey Ramiah and Anthony Briggs. Initially, as noted before, the cases of these beneficiaries were still pending before the Commission when the Court ordered provisional measures. Later, the Commission brought before the Court the three cases *Hilaire, Constantine et al.* and *Benjamin et al.* IACHR *Hilaire v. Trinidad and Tobago* case, judgment of 1 September 2001 (preliminary objections); *Constantine et al.* v. *Trinidad and Tobago*, judgment of 1 September 2001 (preliminary objections); *Benjamin et al.* v. *Trinidad and Tobago* case, judgment of 1 September 2001 preliminary objections. Together these cases dealt with 32 persons. All beneficiaries, however, were protected under the same Order for provisional measures. Of the five beneficiaries of the first Order for provisional measures, only two were included in the *Hilaire, Constantine and Benjamin et al. v. Trinidad and Tobago* Judgment. One of the persons not included was the aforementioned Anthony Briggs. The other two were Anderson Noel and Christopher Bethel. In its Judgment, moreover, the Court did not deal with the cases of three more persons who were included as beneficiaries since the Court's Order of 25 May 1999: Kevin Dial, Andrew Dottin and Anthony Johnson.

ing threats.[273] Indeed, in its Annual Reports the Inter-American Commission emphasises that the number of precautionary measures is not the same as the number of persons protected by them. The Commission grants many precautionary measures aimed at protecting several individuals or even 'a group of persons who cannot be counted, such as entire populations or communities'.[274] As Judge Cançado Trindade pointed out, the Inter-American Court's provisional measures have covered almost 12,000 persons and even the members of whole communities. Thereby they have become a true preventive judicial guarantee.[275]

As noted, a distinct feature of the provisional measures in the Inter-American system is that the beneficiaries are not only the direct victims[276] and their family in a pending case before the Inter-American Commission or Court, but also witnesses, counsel and others. Many of the persons abducted, disappeared or murdered had received threats previously. Moreover, the Court was faced with information of threats to witnesses and others involved in cases pending before it (or before the Commission). In response to this situation the Court decided to expand the scope of beneficiaries for the provisional measures from alleged victims and their family alone, to witnesses, counsel and others involved. Later the scope became even wider. Witnesses in a case pending before a local judge, human rights defenders, persons visiting the premises of a human rights organisation, etc. may become the beneficiary of a precautionary or provisional measure as well.[277]

In the European system at times provisional measures have also been used on behalf of larger groups of persons. In *Becker* v. *Denmark* (1976) the petitioner was the director of an organisation called Project Children's Protection and Security International. His petition concerned 'the alleged violation of the Convention by the Danish Government in the envisaged repatriation of 199 Vietnamese children'. The European Commission indeed used provisional measures on behalf of this large group of beneficiaries.[278]

In *Islamic Community in BiH* v. *Republika Srpska* (*Muslim Town Cemetery in Prnjavor*) the Bosnia Chamber initially refused to take provisional measures in the absence of individual threats of exhumation or interference with burials. In the face of a specific domestic decision prohibiting a burial the Chamber did order provisional measures. Apparently it phrased them more generally,

---

[273] See e.g. IACHR *Alvarez et al.* case (Colombia), Orders of the President of 22 July 1997 and subsequent Orders by the Court, such as that of 8 February 2008. The measures included the provision of a cell phone and a security camera.

[274] See e.g. CIDH Annual Report, 2000, §8.

[275] See e.g. IACHR *Matter of the persons imprisoned in the "Dr. Sebastião Martins Silveira" Penitentiary in Araraquara, São Paulo* (Brazil), Order of 30 September 2006, individual opinion Judge Cançado Trindade, §4. This includes about 6,000 beneficiaries in the *Matter of Pueblo indígena de Kankuamo* (Colombia), more than 1,200 in the *Matter of the Peace Community of San José de Apartadó* (Colombia); more than 2,000 in the *Matter of the Communities of Jiguamiandó and Curbaradó* (Colombia), almost 900 in the *Matter of Urso Branco Prison* (Brazil) and about 1,200 in the *Matter of Pueblo indígena de Sarayaku* (Ecuador).

[276] In practice, the petitioner normally is an international NGO, representing the victims and any other beneficiary of the provisional measure.

[277] See also e.g. *Matter of the Yare I and Yare II Capital Region Penitentiary Center (Yare Prison)* (Venezuela), Order of 30 March 2006 (also on behalf of those persons who may, *in the future*, enter the prison as inmates, as well as those who work there, and those who enter as visitors) and IACHR *Asunto de la Cárcel de Urso Branco* (Brasil), Resolución de 2 de mayo de 2008 (including the protection of the life and personal integrity of visitors and security agents; and the obligation of the State to provide an up-to-date list of those who had been killed).

[278] EComHR *Becker* v. *Denmark*, 3 October 1975 (inadm.), D&R 4, p. 215. See also e.g. EComHR *B., M. and 51 others* v. *Spain*, 11 September 1992 involving 53 refugees waiting on no man's land in the burning sun, without water, shelter or sanitation.

to apply not only to that specific burial, but instead ordering Srpska to prohibit the Municipal authorities of Prnjavor from obstructing further burials at the Muslim Town Cemetery.[279]

Sometimes provisional measures have also benefited a larger group than the beneficiaries referred to. The provisional measures by the ECtHR ordering the Netherlands to halt the expulsion of a Somalian asylum-seeker serve as an example.[280] In order to make sure that the Secretary of State on migration issues understood that the European Court's decision also applied to other asylum seekers similarly situated, the Court exceptionally[281] included an explanatory sentence to that effect as well. This was done in order to prevent a flood of cases being brought before the Court in Strasbourg. In a way the other, similarly situated, Somalian asylum seekers could be seen as de facto beneficiaries of the Court's provisional measures.[282]

If the provisional measure concerns halting an expulsion of certain persons to a certain State (e.g. in a situation of civil war) counsel for other persons similarly situated and risking expulsion to that same State could argue that it would be a pro-active good faith application of the treaty to halt these other expulsions as well, pending determination of the proceeding in which the provisional measures were used. This would also be in accordance with the rationale of the rule on exhaustion of domestic remedies and the idea of the subsidiary nature of international supervision. Moreover the State would prevent recourse to international proceedings by these other persons as well as the ensuing embarrassment of more provisional measures of a similar nature. Of course such argument would apply only if the persons involved were truly similarly situated.

While a provisional measure does not concern an 'examination' of the case, persons similarly situated *could* refer domestically to the provisional measures by an international or regional adjudicator.[283]

Sometimes groups are in urgent need of protection, but the use of provisional measures is not an option. As part of the reporting procedure under Article 40 ICCPR, the HRC has started to identify in its Concluding Observations certain urgent issues requiring follow-up. It has also decided to appoint one of its members as a Special Rapporteur on the follow-up of Concluding Observations.[284] Thus, the Special Rapporteur on the follow-up of Views now has its counterpart vis-à-vis the reporting procedure. Some of the issues the Rapporteur on Concluding Observations may have to deal with could relate to individuals in urgent situations. These situations may be comparable to those necessitating provisional measures as part of the individual complaint proce-

---

[279] Bosnia Chamber *Islamic Community in BiH* v. *Republika Srpska* (*Muslim Town Cemetery in Prnjavor*), 11 January 2000.

[280] See President ECtHR, Note Verbale with provisional measure, 3 May 2004, in case 15243/04, published in the Dutch journal JV 226 (*Jurisprudentie Vreemdelingenrecht*). See further Rieter (2005a) and (2006).

[281] See Chapter II (Systems), section 8.2 on the issue of transparency of information.

[282] See also ECtHR judgment *NA.* v. *UK*, 17 July 2008, which concerned even a greater number of cases involving imminent expulsion to Sri Lanka. The judgment referred to the unwillingness by the UK to take a general measure halting the expulsion of Tamils to Sri Lanka, resulting in the Court's being forced to order provisional measures 342 times in individual cases submitted by petitioners at risk of being deported from the UK to Sri Lanka, §§21-22.

[283] See further Rieter (2005a) and (2006). See also IACHR *Communities of the Jiguamiandó and of the Curbaradó*, Order of 6 March 2003, Concurring Opinion Judge Cançado Trindade, §4 ('the protection of human rights determined by the American Convention, to be effective, comprises not only the relations between the individuals and the public power, but also their relations with third parties (...). This reveals the new dimensions of the international protection of human rights, as well as the great potential of the existing mechanisms of protection, – such as that of the American Convention, – set in motion in order to protect collectively the members of a whole community, even though the basis of action is the breach – or the probability or imminence of breach – of individual rights').

[284] See further Chapter XVIII (Follow up)

dure. It is likely that these situations would often concern the plight of certain groups, in other words that the group of beneficiaries of this follow-up would be larger and have a more collective dimension than the group of beneficiaries of the Committee's provisional measures. The urgent situations may also concern threats to rights for the protection of which the HRC does not use provisional measures. The urgent issues approach is a useful complementary approach for those situations where provisional measures are unsuitable (e.g. involving virtually the whole population of a large area) or simply not an option because the State in question did not recognise the individual complaint procedure under the Covenant.[285]

4.4.3 Early warning

Early warning systems and other preventive mechanisms aim to protect large groups of people, while provisional measures normally concern smaller groups.[286] In that respect the approach of the Inter-American Court, using provisional measures involving large groups of beneficiaries, deserves more attention by other human rights adjudicators. Of course the role of the Inter-American Commission with its combined function of investigator, adjudicator, mediator and petitioner, is very important in this respect. Because of, among others, its country visits it is more familiar with specific country situations and able to provide concrete suggestions for the use and implementation of provisional measures to protect groups of persons against threats. It is able to negotiate with representatives of the beneficiaries and the State. For other, especially for global, adjudicators acquiring the relevant knowledge of the situation may be more difficult. Nevertheless, they could also be inventive in creating mechanisms for negotiation about the implementation of such provisional measures. Maybe international adjudicators could informally contact UN Special Rapporteurs of the Human Rights Council in certain States to provide good offices for the negotiation of protective measures between the beneficiaries and State authorities. In some cases they could even provide suggestions and act as a mediator. If country visits and hearings are not possible, regional adjudicators could also suggest the good offices of organisations trusted by both the beneficiaries and the State. An example of such an organisation could be the OSCE. In some respects organisations such as the OSCE or the European prison visiting committee under the European Convention against Torture already perform the function of intervening against threats to life and personal integrity. Nevertheless, the latter Committee mostly only intervenes in specific cases if it happens to be visiting detention centre concerned.

4.4.4 Individual identification of each beneficiary?

4.4.4.1 INTRODUCTION

In the Inter-American system the group of beneficiaries sometimes even involves unnamed individuals. It may be difficult to access all persons at risk or obtain all official information.[287]

---

[285] On serious and mass violations in general, see e.g. Medina Quiroga (1988) and Murray (1999), pp. 109-133.

[286] With regard to high and low intensity conflicts and violent political conflicts in States that have ratified individual complaint proceedings, frequent use of provisional measures may be an indicator for early warning as well as a form of early intervention in specific cases. Yet in practice the step from early warning to early action often proves to be difficult with regard to large groups under threat. See e.g. Grünfeld/Huijboom (2007) and Grünfeld (2000), pp. 131-143.

[287] See e.g. the exchange of information between the Court and the State relating to the death of one of the beneficiaries in IACHR *Blake* case, Order of 6 June 2003: "Justo Victoriano Martínez

The Commission and Court have sometimes ordered a State to protect a specific group as such rather than just those members of the group mentioned by name. In a mass expulsion case in 2000 the inter-American Court still refused to do so, but later that year, in a case involving death threats to all members of a 'peace community' it did grant an Order on behalf of unnamed persons.[288]

4.4.4.2 MASS EXPULSION

In the case of *Haitians and Dominicans of Haitian Origin in the Dominican Republic (Haitian case, 2000)* the Inter-American Commission requested the Court to order the State to suspend the massive expulsions and deportations both of legal and non-documented Haitian workers and of legal and non-documented Dominicans of Haitian origin living in the Dominican Republic. It had 'acquired knowledge of the identity of some of the alleged victims, who had given their approval to being named in the context of the request'.[289] It described some of the specific circumstances of the seven persons it could specifically name, urging the Court to order provisional measures that would permit their immediate return from Haiti to the Dominican Republic or, when they were still in the Dominican Republic, protect them from any 'detention or deportation action based on racial or national origin, or on the suspicion that they are not full-fledged citizens'.[290] The Court indeed ordered provisional measures on behalf of the seven persons specifically named.

The Commission also asked the Court to protect a group of persons not identified by name. It pointed out that it could not get access to these persons. It explained that the State's practice made it impossible to distinguish between individual group members, making all of them targets of mass expulsion. In addition, members of the group were afraid to come forward individually. The Commission also argued that the Inter-American human rights system simply was not equipped to process individual complaints of each member, even if they could be reached and would not be afraid to come forward individually.[291] As a result the Commission suggested some sort of *actio popularis* instead.

The State protested that it was necessary to reveal the identity of those persons in danger of suffering irreparable harm in order for it to take provisional measures. It emphasised that provi-

---

Morales, Justo Víctor Martínez Morales and Justo Víctor Morales Martínez" identify one and the same person, who was a beneficiary of provisional measures, §13.

[288] For a different approach, see e.g. ECtHR *Athanassoglou et al.* v. *Switzerland* (2000) the petitioners had requested the ECtHR to take provisional measures to halt the resumption of a nuclear power plant. The Court decided not to do so. While it did not indicate its reasons, the *actio popularis* nature of the petition may have played a role. The Court subsequently found that Articles 6 and 13 ECHR were not applicable. See Chapter XII (Other situations). In passing it also noted that the petitioners had not been able to 'demonstrate a serious, specific and imminent danger in their personal regard'. ECtHR *Athanassoglou et al.* v. *Switzerland,* 6 April 2000, §§52 and 54. The admissibility report of the Commission was called *Greenpeace Schweiz et al.* v. *Switzerland.* In its judgment on the merits the ECtHR has pointed out that the positive obligation of States to protect the right to life relates to situations in which the authorities were aware, or should have been aware, of a real risk to the life of an *identified* individual or individuals. See e.g. ECtHR *Mahmut Kaya* v. *Turkey,* 28 March 2000, §86 and *Osman* v. *UK,* 28 October 1998, §116.

[289] IACHR *Haitians and Dominicans of Haitian Origin in the Dominican Republic* (Dominican Republic), Order of 18 August 2000, 3rd 'Having seen' clause.

[290] Ibid.

[291] Id., 'Having seen' clause 11c.

sional measures on behalf of nameless persons would hinder its right to protect its border and control the legal status of its inhabitants.[292]

The Court decided not to order provisional measures to protect 'generically those in a given situation or those who are affected by certain measures'.[293] It deemed 'it indispensable to identify individually the persons in danger of suffering irreparable damage, for which reason it is not feasible to order provisional measures without specific names, for protecting generically those in a given situation or those who are affected by certain measures: however, it is possible to protect the individualized members of a community'.[294] At the same time it did decide to order both the State and the Commission to provide it with 'detailed information on the situation of members of the border communities or "bateyes" who could be subject to forced repatriations, deportations or expulsions'.[295]

---

[292] During the hearing of August 2000 the State responded that it was necessary to identify the persons on whose behalf provisional measures were being requested. It continued as follows: 'however, the Dominican Republic is in the best disposition to study any individual case where the violation of rights is alleged', IACHR case of *Haitians and Haitian-origin Dominicans in the Dominican Republic*, Order of 18 August 2000, 'Having seen' clause 12e. In the brief it submitted after the public hearing of 8 August 2000 the State alleged that 'the identity of those persons who are in danger of suffering irreparable damage must be revealed for the adoption of provisional measures; measures adopted in relationship to nameless persons would only hinder the Dominican State's right to protect its border and control the legal status of the persons who enter into its territory and live in it'. The Commission objected to the brief submitted by the State upon the closing of the public hearing. In response to a question by the President of the Court posed during the public hearing, the Commission indicated that its request for provisional measures in this case was an *actio popularis*, 15th "Having seen' clause.

[293] IACHR *Haitians and Dominicans of Haitian Origin in the Dominican Republic* (Dominican Republic), Order of 18 August 2000, 8th 'Considering' clause.

[294] The IACHR referred to its Orders in *Álvarez et al.*, 21 January 1998, *Clemente Teherán et al.*, 19 June 1998, *Digna Ochoa and Plácido et al.*, 17 November 1999.

[295] IACHR *Haitians and Dominicans of Haitian Origin in the Dominican Republic*, Order of 18 August 2000. In its response to the Court's Order to inform it about the situation of people living in 'bateyes' at the border area, the Dominican Republic noted that there were 'bateyes' only in Barahona on the border between the Dominican Republic and Haiti. The community was for seventy percent Dominican. Thirty percent was contracted and came to the Dominican Republic during the sugar cane harvest. The State did not clarify the actual situation of this Community. In his concurring opinion Cançado Trindade referred to the 'undetermined' character of the community and distinguished this from a community or group whose members can be individualised. In this case, he noted, taking an *actio popularis* approach would have risked to 'disfigure the character of provisional measures of protection, in their present stage of historical evolution'. Concurring Opinion Judge Cançado Trindade, §§21-22. He emphasised that the Court needed to individualise the beneficiaries but that it kept an open eye for the context warranting the provisional measures. It also required the State to send it detailed information about the situation of the communities or 'bateyes' at the border. Concurring Opinion Judge Cançado Trindade, *Haitians and Dominicans of Haitian Origin in the Dominican Republic*, Order of 18 August 2000, §22. He furthermore expressed the hope that the measures the Dominican Republic would take to implement the individualised provisional measures of the Court would benefit all the other persons, who were not mentioned by name in the Commission's petition, but who found themselves in the same situation of vulnerability and risk, §24. On the growing emphasis on *actio popularis* in international human rights adjudication, see also the African Commission in the *Ogoni* case: *Social and Economic Rights Action Center for Economic and Social Rights v. Nigeria*, 6 June 2001, §51: "The Commission thanks the two human rights NGOs who brought

4.4.4.3 PROTECTION OF PEACE COMMUNITY

As noted, the Inter-American Court took an altogether different approach later that year. The *Peace Community* case is instructive for the Inter-American Court's approach to the group of beneficiaries of provisional measures. In his Order for urgent measures on behalf of specific members of the Peace Community the President pointed out the more general duty of the States Parties, under Article 1(1) ACHR, to respect the rights and freedoms recognised in the Convention and to guarantee their free and full exercise for every person under their jurisdiction, including the inhabitants of the Peace Community of San José de Apartadó. Apart from the persons specifically named he expected the State's protective measures to benefit other people of the same Community as well, who may be in a similar situation of vulnerability and risk.[296]

During the public hearing of 16 November 2000 the Commission had argued in favour of expanding the protection of the Court's provisional measures from the specific group of beneficiaries in the President's Order for urgent measures to all members of the Peace Community. The Commission explained its effort to register names of members of the Community in its request for provisional measures. This resulted in a list of 193 people,[297] but this list was not complete because 'the great majority of the members of the Community fear stigmatization and violence resulting from such stigmatization, and this is the only reason for which they did not authorize to make their names known'.[298] The Commission referred to elements allowing for the identification of the members of the Community in a collective manner. It first mentioned the geographic element: the Community was located in a determined place, in the Municipality of Apartadó, formed by 32 surrounding dwellings, such as La Vereda la Unión, where the people identified in the President's Order came from. The other element it mentioned was the fact that belonging to this Community implied adherence to a series of norms and bylaws as well as a system of representation. Its members even identified themselves with an identification card.[299] The Commission argued that it was suitable to consider the Community in question as a collective entity because the fundamental individual rights of each member were at stake, such as the right to life and personal integrity.[300]

To counter any arguments about the inability of the State to verify whom it needed to protect, the Commission pointed out that, during the three years in which it maintained its precautionary measures, which had been of a similar nature, the State did not allege 'having had problems to identify the people it had to protect'.

---

the matter under its purview: the Social and Economic Rights Action Center (Nigeria) and the Center for Economic and Social Rights (USA). Such is a demonstration of the usefulness to the Commission and individuals of *actio popularis*, which is wisely allowed under the African Charter".

[296] IACHR *Peace Community of San José de Apartadó* case (Colombia), Order of 9 October 2000 (President).

[297] The Court refers to 189 people, but lists 193 persons.

[298] IACHR *Peace Community of San José de Apartadó* case (Colombia), Order of 24 November 2000.

[299] There were also people in the Community who, although not formally identified with this card, were living there and were guided by the Community's principles and wished to become members. For the purpose of the provisional measures the Commission indicated that these people must be considered as members of the Community as well.

[300] IACHR *Peace Community of San José de Apartadó* case (Colombia), Order of 24 November 2000. The Spanish text is as follows: '*En el presente caso es conveniente definir a la Comunidad de Paz de San José de Apartadó colectivamente, porque se trata de una afectación de derechos individuales fundamentales, como la vida y la integridad personal*'.

"The Commission is convinced that the State understands the collective dimension of the problem, knows which people to protect, understands the geographic limits and the element of belonging to the Community, as well as the functioning mechanisms".[301]

In November 2000 the Court decided indeed to extend the group of beneficiaries. In its considerations, it referred to the State's report and its arguments during the public hearing. It also attached importance to the Commission's statement that many members of the Community did not wish to be identified for fear of reprisals. It differentiated this case from its earlier Order in the case of *Haitians and Dominicans of Haitian origin*. In the latter case it had 'considered indispensable to individualize the people who are in danger of suffering irreparable harm in order to provide them with protective measures'. The *Peace Community* case, on the other hand, had special characteristics.

"Indeed, the Community of Paz de San José de Apartadó, formed according to the Commission by about 1200 people, constitutes an organized community located in a determined geographic place, whose members can be identified and individualized and who, due to the fact of belonging to said community, all its members are in a situation of similar risk of suffering acts of aggression against their personal integrity and lives".[302]

Thus the Court considered that it was not only suitable to order provisional measures on behalf of the people already protected by the President's urgent measures of 9 October 2000 but also, for the reasons presented in the public hearing 'to expand them so that they cover all of the members of the aforementioned Community'. Consequently, it first ratified the President's Order 'in all its terms' and then expanded these measures by ordering the State 'to extend, forthwith, any measures as may be necessary to protect the lives and personal integrity of all of the other members of the Community of Paz de San José de Apartadó'.[303]

Judges Abreu Burelli and García Ramírez more closely discussed the issue of beneficiaries in their concurring opinion. They acknowledged that in the majority of cases it is indeed possible to identify individually the potential victims of the violation the provisional measure aims to protect. Yet there are cases where such precise individualisation proves difficult, at least initially. The real and imminent threat might be a threat against a great number of people who find themselves in more or less similar circumstances, putting them at risk. In such situations their protection is necessary even though it is not yet possible to individualise the subjects of the provisional protection by name. Such provisional protection, after all, always and by definition is an urgent protection.[304]

"To delay action until those exposed to that threat of grave and irreparable harm to legally protected interests – embodied in rights – can be individually identified would be to run the risk that the harm would materialize before the Court could intervene to prevent it, even though it had already established that the threat was not only possible but also probable and imminent. Thus, a surmountable technicality would prevent the Court from acting swiftly to fulfil its true mandate: to use the shield of its jurisdictional power to protect threatened rights. It would be

---

[301] IACHR *Peace Community of San José de Apartadó* case (Colombia), Order of 24 November 2000.
[302] Id., 7th 'Considering' clause.
[303] Id., 3rd 'Decisional' clause.
[304] Id., Concurring Opinion of Judge Abreu Burelli and García Ramírez.

hard to make the case that that kind of judicial restraint was consistent with the Inter-American Court's essential mission of protecting human rights".[305]

They considered the situation similar to that of 'diffuse interests': a group of people with various backgrounds shares a determined interest, legally relevant, that requires public protection. Yet, none of these subjects can be considered holder of a subjective right with regard to the right they invoke, nor can they attribute to themselves such entitlement in a way that would exclude the other subjects who find themselves in the same situation. In those circumstances anyone of them could resort to the relevant legal body and request the adoption of measures that would preserve the common interest of the group. In such case one would speak of an *actio popularis* or class action.[306] The situation may indeed be similar to the example given by the two judges, but it is certainly not the same. After all, each inhabitant of the Community of San José de Apartadó who is threatened definitely could be considered the holder of subjective rights. The difference is that not all of them have individually claimed this before the Inter-American Court.

The two judges referred to the Court's Order in the case of the *Haitians and Dominicans of Haitian Origin in the Dominican Republic* in which it considered that it was indispensable to individualise the persons at risk and that it would not be feasible to order provisional measures without mentioning the names of the beneficiaries (*'de manera innominada'*) simply in order to protect *generically* all people who could find themselves in a certain situation or could be affected by certain measures because the provisional measures could now protect a group of people with various backgrounds, without individualising them in advance. The judges pointed out that the *Peace Community* case went much further. Based on the protective criterion it was a reasonable extension of the scope of provisional measures to a larger group of beneficiaries in a way that fit in well with their preventive purpose. In its new approach, the Court's determination whether someone belongs to the group of victims who are to be beneficiaries of its provisional measures is not based on the knowledge and the precise manifestation of each individual by name, but on objective criteria -taking into account their links to the group in question and the risks involved- that would permit individualisation of the beneficiaries at the moment of implementation of the measures. In other words, the aim is to cover the risk run by all inhabitants of a community and not only, as normally is the case, the risk run by some individuals.[307]

4.4.4.4 MORE GENERALISED PROVISIONAL MEASURES

On several occasions since this case the Court has used a more general provisional measure where not all the beneficiaries are mentioned by name. As has been noted, this type of provisional measures may involve ethnic groups, a group of workers or members involved in a peace community 'linked by a common geography, which could change, and certain common decisions which were the source of the risks to individual and collective interests'.[308] Such situations reveal 'a common-

---

[305]   Concurring Opinion by Judge García-Ramírez in IACHR *Matter of Pueblo Indígena de Sarayaku*, Order of 6 July 2004, §5.

[306]   Concurring Opinion of Judge Abreu Burelli and García Ramírez, *Peace Community of San José de Apartadó* case (Colombia), Order of 24 November 2000.

[307]   The two judges also emphasised the need to take into account that, in the circumstances of this case, the victims did not want to provide their names because this might make them even more vulnerable. Concurring Opinion of Judge Abreu Burelli and García Ramírez, *Peace Community of San José de Apartadó* case (Colombia), Order of 24 November 2000.

[308]   Concurring Opinion by Judge García-Ramírez on IACHR *Matter of Pueblo Indígena de Sarayaku*, Order of 6 July 2004, §§8-9.

ality of situation, which implies, in this case, a commonality of danger'.[309] To give a few examples, when Maria Eugenia Cárdenas and her family were being threatened she was asked to identify her relatives but she did not want to name them for fear this might actually put them even more at risk. The Court then decided just to refer to Ms. Cárdenas 'and her next of kin'.[310] Yet in the context of the same case it did point out that 'in order to ensure an effective protection of the next of kin of Francisco García, it is advisable that they should be duly identified before the State by the Inter-American Commission'.[311]

While most of the beneficiaries of the Court are still individualized, a substantial portion is not. In 2006, for instance, 21% of the beneficiaries of the Court's provisional measures were 'natural persons, not individualized, members of a group' and 80% concerned 'natural persons individualized'.[312]

In sum, the Inter-American Commission's precautionary measures on behalf of human rights defenders and others have become more specific and include an obligation of the State to consult with the beneficiaries. This specificity was necessary to make effective the precautionary measure. At the same time it turned out that, in the interest of the persons who were being threatened, it was sometimes necessary to be less specific about the names of the beneficiaries. While in the past, mentioning the names of the persons to be protected in the precautionary measure often was a guarantee for their safety and while often this is still the case, in some cases the beneficiaries prefer not to be mentioned by name for fear of pointing attention to themselves in a way that would in fact worsen their situation. In other cases the beneficiaries are now less specifically listed because they are an entire community or another group, such as everyone visiting the premises of a certain human rights organisation.

Indeed, the Commission has pointed out that its precautionary measures can protect 'either one person or an unquantifiable group of persons, often covering entire populations or communities'.[313]

In the first case in which the Inter-American Commission took precautionary measures to ensure access to HIV medication the petitioning NGO had requested the Commission to name only one of the persons involved and not to disclose the names of the other 26 victims. The Commission respected this request and noted in its report that El Salvador was informed of the names and that they are on file at the Secretariat of the Commission.[314]

---

[309] Id., §9.

[310] See e.g. IACHR *Alvarez et al.* v. *Colombia*, Order of 13 May 2001, 1st 'Decisional' clause.

[311] Id., 8th 'Considering' clause.

[312] See IACHR Annual Report 2006, part IV Statistics of the Court, p. 93. See also its statistics for 2005, referring to 20%, Annual Report 2005, p. 76. For examples other than the matter of the *Peace Community*, see e.g. *Matter of Capital El Rodeo I and El Rodeo II Judicial Confinement Center*, Order of 8 February 2008, 21st 'Considering' clause and references therein relating to (indigenous) peoples and detainees. In this case the Court noted that 'the possible beneficiaries are identifiable since they are people who are confined or could be admitted as inmates in the future'.

[313] CIDH Annual Report, 2001, Chapter III (a), §10 (discussing the Haitian case). In June 2001 the Commission took precautionary measures on behalf of nine named persons and 'other members of the Embera Katio indigenous community of Alto Sinú' who had been abducted from the community's main town and the neighbouring areas. It asked Colombia to take the necessary steps to clarify the whereabouts of the persons who had been abducted and to protect their lives and persons. On behalf of the other members of that indigenous community, who had not yet been abducted but who were working in collaboration with the petitioners, the Commission took precautionary measures as well. The Commission also requested Colombia to investigate, judge and punish those responsible for the attacks against the indigenous community. Annual Report 2001, §17.

[314] CIDH *Jorge Odir Miranda Cortéz et al* v. *El Salvador*, 7 March 2001 (adm.).

In *Newton Coutinho Mendes et al.* v. *Brazil* (adm. 1997) the petitioners had alleged that a death squad formed by large ranchers had been murdering 'persons involved in or suspected of being involved in land occupations in the region'. The Commission also received information 'that these persons were alleged to be part of a "list of persons marked for death", known as the "Xinguara list", drawn up by those large ranchers, and including the names of dozens of persons'.[315] The petitioners requested precautionary measures on behalf of everyone on this list. Initially the Commission 'asked the petitioner to provide the name of all the members of the "Xinguara list", so that the Commission could request that the precautionary measures be extended to all the persons threatened, not only Father Ricardo Rezende'.[316] The petitioner provided additional information as as to 'the "Xinguara list", petitioner reported that the list was found at the Fazenda Nazaré and that the local police knew whose names were on the list. Even so, the petitioner had not gained access to most of the names of the persons threatened due to the complicity of the police with the criminals'.[317] Moreover, 'the persons against whom the judge of Xinguara had issued arrest warrants were free' and 'this was due to the irregular acts of the civilian and military police'.[318] On this basis the Commission decided to expand its precautionary measures to include everyone on the list, without requiring all names.[319]

In detention cases the Court has also included all detainees, visitors and employees in its protective Orders. It has ordered provisional measures, for instance, in a matter pending before the Commission, where 'the potential beneficiaries are identifiable, as they are persons held in prison, who might be held in prison in the future, or who enter the prison either in the course of their normal business or occasionally, either as officers or as visitors'.[320] In this respect the fact that some beneficiaries are subsequently transferred to other detention facilities does not take away their status as a beneficiary. The State is still responsible for their custody and they are still identifiable.[321]

In short, as Cançado Trindade has pointed out, in the last decade provisional measures have assumed considerable importance. About 12.000 persons in Latin America and the Caribbean,

---

[315] CIDH *Newton Coutinho Mendes et al.* v. *Brazil*, 1 October 1997, §2.

[316] Id., §56.

[317] Id., §57.

[318] Id., §58.

[319] Id., §59.

[320] See IACHR *Matter of the Penitentiary Center of the Central Occidental Region* (Uribana Prison) (Venezuela), Order of 2 February 2007, 6th 'Considering' clause. See also, e.g. *Matter of Yare I and Yare II Capital Region Penitentiary Center,* Order of 30 March 2006, 8th 'Considering' clause; *Matter of Children Deprived of Liberty in the "Complexo do Tatuapé" of FEBEM,* Order of 30 November 2005, 6th 'Considering' clause (and concurring opinions by García-Ramírez and Cançado Trindade); *Matter of Mendoza Prisons,* Order of 22 November 2004, 13th 'Considering' clause and *Matter of Monagas Judicial Confinement Center (*"La Pica"*),* Order of 6 July 2004, 8th 'Considering' clause. In a case against Honduras the petitioners observed that the State had not provided exact figures on the number of juveniles held in adult penal institutions, but according to the Office of the National Human Rights Commissioner this concerned 201 juveniles. They referred to a study that same year by the Human Rights Commissioner reporting that of the 84 juveniles held in the Jalteva prison, 50 were held for vagrancy, 15 for sniffing resistol and the others for taking drugs, including marijuana, 'for their own protection' and 'for being orphans'. CIDH *Minors in detention* v. *Honduras,* 10 March 1999 (merits), §17.

[321] IACHR *Matter of the persons imprisoned in the "Dr. Sebastião Martins Silveira" Penitentiary in Araraquara, São Paulo* (Brazil), Order of 30 September 2006, 10th 'Considering' clause ('the beneficiaries of the measures are identifiable and are those persons detained at the Araraquara Penitentiary for whose benefit the adoption of the protective measures was ordered on July 28, 2006, without regard to the fact that they have been referred to some other penitentiary, since the State is still responsible for their custody').

including the members of whole communities, are covered by the Court's provisional measures.[322]

4.4.5 Identification and representation

In its provisional measures in the case of the *Communities of the Jiguamiandó and the Curbaradó* (2003) the Court considered that it was 'appropriate to order provisional measures of protection for the members of the communities composed of the Community Council of the Jiguamiandó and the families of the Curbaradó that encompass all the members of the said communities'. It noted that 'it is evident that the communities comprising the Community Council of the Jiguamiandó and the families of the Curbaradó, made up of approximately 2,125 persons, forming 515 families, constitute an organized community, situated in a specific geographical location in the municipality of Carmen del Darién, Department of Chocó, whose members can be identified and specified and who, because they form part of the said community, are all in a situation of equal risk of suffering acts of aggression against their safety and lives, as well as being forcibly displaced from their territory, a situation that prevents them from exploiting the natural resources necessary for their subsistence'.[323]

The subsequent developments in this case show how identification and representation can be interrelated. Several years after the initial Order, the representative of the 32 families of Puerto Lleras and Pueblo Nuevo of Jiguamiandó river basin, and the representative of the 177 families of the Community Council of Curbaradó had rejected and challenged the representation by the NGO petitioning this case[324] 'and they requested to be granted the same guarantees provided to other displaced groups to access the "humanitarian zones" represented by such organization and direct communication with the State to agree on measures to their benefit. In that regard, the State informed the Court that it had received various petitions from those who claim to represent said

---

[322] IACHR *Las penitentiarías de Mendoza* v. *Argentina,* Order of 30 March 2006, Individual Opinion of Judge Cançado Trindade §7. He noted that just in *the Matter of the Pueblo Ingídena Kankuamo* (Colombia) there were 6,000 beneficiaries; in the *Matter of the Community of San José de Apartadó* (Colombia) the number of beneficiaries was more than 1,200; in the *Matter of the Communities of Jiguamiandó and Curbaradó* (Colombia) the number of beneficiaries exceeded 2,000; in the *Matter of Urso Branco* (Brazil), almost 900 inmates were the beneficiaries; in the *Matter of the Pueblo Indígena Sarayaku* (Ecuador), there were approximately 1,200 beneficiaries.

[323] IACHR *Communities of the Jiguamiandó and the Curbaradó,* Order of 6 March 2003, 9th 'Considering' clause. In their Concurring opinion in this case Sergio García-Ramírez and Alirio Abreu-Burelli referred to their earlier statement that 'membership of the group of potential victims who benefit from the measures is not based on the precise identification and indication of each individual by name, but according to objective criteria – based on the linkage of membership and the observed risks – which will permit the beneficiaries to be specified when the measures are implemented. The intention is to encompass the danger faced by the members of a community, not merely a few individuals, as is generally the case. It is also necessary to take into account that one of the elements of this case, which could characterize other cases, is that the potential victims choose not to provide their names, owing to the very real risk that this identification might increase their exposure to the irreparable damage that we are trying to prevent'. They were 'pleased to observe that this criterion, accepted for the first time in the said Order corresponding to the Peace Community of San José de Apartadó, is the one that prevails today in the Court's jurisprudence, as can be observed in the measures adopted for the Communities of the Jiguamiandó and the Curbaradó. In this case, the measures encompass a group of identifiable persons who, because they form part of a community, are in a situation of grave risk'.

[324] The Inter-Ecclesiastical Justice and Peace Commission.

families in order to have their representation recognized. In this sense, the Court was requested to indicate the name of the individual beneficiaries of these provisional measures to allow proper implementation thereof'.[325]

The Court called a hearing specifically on this issue, and at the end of this hearing it found that 'the universe of individuals who at this time form part of the beneficiary communities cannot be accurately identified or established'.[326] It held:

> "The criteria submitted by the Commission in its request for provisional measures are indeed insufficient for that purpose. Particularly, at this time the geographical standards for the group of individuals who allegedly benefit from these provisional measures are not clear enough".[327]

It pointed out that the Commission should specify 'to the Court what is the universe of individuals who benefit from these provisional measures, which were adopted at their request'.[328] "To that effect, the Commission must indicate specific criteria to determine and identify the beneficiaries of these measures as a group". Meanwhile, however, the existing provisional measures remained in force.[329]

4.5 Conclusion on beneficiaries and addressees of provisional measures

In order to truly examine the protection offered by provisional measures it must be clear who is included as a beneficiary and whether and how the beneficiaries have been consulted about the measures. While it does not appear appropriate to address an order for provisional measures to the alleged victim instead of to the State, as the European Court has done in hunger strike cases, it is important to make sure that the State's positions and arguments are duly taken into account. In order to uphold the legitimacy of provisional measures it is vital to adhere to principles of procedural fairness.

Both as to purpose and as to substance the provisional measures should be consistent with similar measures already taken in order to increase their credibility and avoid discriminatory application vis-à-vis various beneficiaries and addressees. Comparable situations should be treated similarly and different situations should be treated differently.

The criterion of 'balance of convenience', used by international adjudicators (in cases not involving human rights) and also by some domestic courts, is inappropriate in human rights cases. Only if there is evidence of dispute between (potential) beneficiaries about the required substance of provisional measures this criterion could play a role. In other words, in the face of irreparable harm to persons adjudicators should not balance the rights of the intended beneficiaries with the general interest. In urgent cases involving indigenous culture, for instance, the interest of the

---

[325] IACHR *Asunto comunidades del Jiguamiandó y del Curbaradó* (Colombia), Order of 5 February 2008, 4th 'Whereas' clause.

[326] Id., 15th 'Considering' clause.

[327] Ibid.

[328] Ibid.

[329] IACHR *Asunto comunidades del Jiguamiandó y del Curbaradó* (Colombia), Order of 5 February 2008, 16th 'Considering' clause ("Not withstanding the above and until the Court renders a decision, the measures already adopted by the Court in its Order of March 6, 2003 (*Operating Paragraph 1*) remain fully in force and the subsequent Orders of November 17, 2004, March 15, 2005, and February 7, 2006 (*supra* 'Having seen' clauses 1 and 2) reinforce the obligation of the State to promptly adopt any measures necessary to protect the life and personal integrity "[o]f all members of the communities formed by the Community Council of Jiguamiandó and Curbaradó families").

economic well being of the country as a whole should not play a role in denying provisional measures. Arguments about rights of the general population could more appropriately be considered in reporting procedures (if available) or as arguments at the merits stage.

As noted in Chapter X, when the right to culture of indigenous peoples is at stake their right to self-determination must be taken into account. This right is also relevant in order to determine who should be the beneficiaries of provisional measures to protect cultural survival. If alleged victims request an adjudicator to use provisional measures in order to protect collective aspects of their rights the adjudicator must have prima facie evidence that this will indeed be to the benefit of the group involved. The petitioners do not necessarily need to show formal representation of all beneficiaries. On the other hand, if the aim is to prevent irreparable harm to an indigenous group the alleged victim must be seen to represent the interests of the members of this group. The provisional measures required should not be such as to cause irreparable harm to other indigenous groups in the area. Such harm, however, is not likely to result from a request to postpone industrial activities threatening the natural habitat. The fact that the interests of other indigenous groups could eventually justify certain infringements of the rights of the victims does not mean that the adjudicator could not take provisional measures protecting these rights pending the proceedings. In other words, in the face of *prima facie* evidence of irreparable harm competing interests should generally not prevent the use of this type of provisional measures. On the other hand, by arguing or implying that other indigenous groups or other members of the same group have differing views about the risk of irreparable harm to the natural habitat a State could try to convince the adjudicator not to take provisional measures or to withdraw those measures already taken. This relates to the question of the evidentiary requirements for the use of provisional measures. Nevertheless, while the adjudicator may wish to balance the interests of different indigenous groups with regard to certain lands, normally this would not be necessary at the stage of provisional measures exactly because such measures mainly aim at halting certain developments pending the proceedings.

Apart from the question of the *interests* of the beneficiaries of provisional measures, the question has arisen of how to establish their *identity*. This applies in particular to situations of death threats and harassment and mass expulsion. The requirement that the beneficiaries must agree with the provisional measures applies particularly in cases in which they are indeed identified by name. Clearly, if they do not wish such identification it should not be forced upon them. Sometimes identifying a person who is being threatened will assist in this person's protection by giving him or her a name and a face.[330] In other cases beneficiaries might wish to remain anonymous exactly for fear that threats may increase even more if they are publicly identified for their involvement in an international procedure.

Thornberry has noted:

> "Instead of defining beneficiaries and then allocating rights, international law has often proceeded the other way round. Rights have been set out and continue to be developed in such a way that the contours of the communities appropriating them become clearer".[331]

While the statement was made with respect to rights on the *merits* in cases involving culture, it seems applicable even more to the beneficiaries of provisional measures in such cases.

The majority of persons referred to as the beneficiaries of provisional measures are to be protected against death threats and harassment. In some situations all persons visiting the premises of an NGO are subject to threats. In such cases the practice of using provisional measures to protect all of them is appropriate. If only the members of the organisation working there would be granted protection the NGO would not be able to function properly because all other persons

---

[330] More generally on the importance of 'naming names' see e.g. Bronkhorst (1998), pp. 457-474.
[331] Thornberry (2002), p. 52.

visiting the premises to request its assistance, to deliver goods or run errands would still receive threats and risk their lives. While they are not identified by name, the beneficiaries of the required protective measures are clear to the State.

Sometimes beneficiaries may live in remote areas or be otherwise difficult to reach. In such cases it should not be required to establish written consent of each beneficiary, as long as there are indications that they are likely to agree and as long as there are no indications of disagreement.

Finally, the wider impact of provisional measures deserves attention. A good faith implementation of the obligations under the human rights treaty warrants a pro-active stance of the State to ensure the underlying rationale to a provisional measure is being met. When there are indications that this rationale would require a halt, for instance, to the expulsion of others than the specific beneficiary as well, measures would be warranted in order to arrange matters domestically to this effect so that recourse to the international adjudicator by all others similarly situated is no longer necessary.

5   THE RELATION TO CESSATION, ASSURANCES OF NON-REPETITION AND REPARATION

5.1   Introduction

The petitioner has the right to a procedural remedy and, already pending the proceedings, the substantive right to respect for his life and personal integrity. The adjudicator has the authority to use provisional measures. The State not only has the duty to provide for effective remedies and reparation, but also to prevent human rights violations, pending the proceedings as well as upon the conclusion of these proceedings. This obligation to prevent applies in particular to core rights such as the right to life and the prohibition of torture and cruel treatment.[332]

This section deals with the relation between the substance of provisional measures and of the legal consequences of a failure to comply with obligations under human rights treaties, such as cessation, assurances of non-repetition and forms of reparation.

The underlying argument in the previous chapters, on the various situations in which human rights adjudicators have used provisional measures, was that if there were no likelihood of finding a violation on the merits, given the applicable substantive law, the use of provisional measures pending the case would be inappropriate.[333]

It is argued that a similar approach should be taken as well for the relation between the substance of orders for provisional measures and of orders for reparation or other statements regarding the obligations of the State upon a finding of violation. If the adjudicator is unlikely to order certain measures, such as non-refoulement, following such a finding, it makes little sense to order

---

[332]   See in general, e.g. Shelton (2005a). See also Wellens (2002) noting that '(t)he basic imperative of human rights protection underpinning this network of regional and universal instruments and regimes irreversibly permeates almost every single aspect of the way states conduct their internal and external affairs', p. 15; 'the guarantee of effective legal protection must be considered a general principle of law', p. 16.

[333]   As always a delicate balance must be achieved with the aim not to prejudge the merits. See also Chapter I (ICJ), section 3.6. In particular provisional measures may not prejudge those aspects of the merits that are unrelated to preventing irreparable harm, but it is inevitable that with regard to preventing such harm there is some relation with the merits. See further Chapter XV (Immediacy and risk), as it is argued that the issue of prejudgment is relevant especially in the context of assessment of risk (evidentiary matters).

provisional measures to that effect pending the proceedings.[334] Thus it is submitted that the existing and expected case law on cessation, non-repetition and reparation (restitution) is relevant when deciding on the use of provisional measures.

As discussed in Chapter I, it has been pointed out in the context of the ICJ and its predecessor that provisional measures aim to prevent pre-emption of any meaningful reparation by the respondent State, such as in situations where pecuniary redress would be inadequate.[335] Obviously in its judgments the human rights adjudicator must be able to provide the relief requested as well.

In *Gabcikovo-Nagymaros* (1997) the ICJ pointed out that it was 'mindful that, in the field of environmental protection, vigilance and prevention are required on account of the often irreversible character of damage to the environment and of the limitations inherent in the very mechanism of reparation of this type of damage'.[336]

In human rights cases a similar approach applies, in which the statement could be that in the field of human rights vigilance and prevention are required on account of the often irreversible and irreparable character of harm to persons and of the limitations inherent in the very mechanism of reparation of this type of harm. This section aims to explain why.

In human rights adjudication the substance of provisional measures shares a striking resemblance with that found in friendly settlement agreements, in statements on the obligations of the State upon a finding of violation, and in judgments on reparations. The reason may be that they all aim at preventing further irreparable harm.

Sometimes a distinction is made between promotional, reactive and preventive human rights mechanisms. Judicial systems are generally seen as reactive in nature. Of course the reparation required may be forward looking and in that sense preventive. Yet the provisional measures, as taken by the human rights adjudicators, are inherently preventive. Even if they aim at *halting* ongoing rather than new violations they may be *partly* reactive, but still are predominantly preventive.

Indeed provisional measures aim at prevention while reparation aims at redress. Thus, at first sight they are relevant before and after the fact, respectively. In reality, however, particularly in relation to irreparable harm, an adjudicator may find on the merits that the most appropriate form of redress is for this harm not to occur. In its implementation the required measure may be a permanent injunction. In that sense both provisional measures and the obligation to prevent upon the finding that a violation would otherwise (continue to) occur, as well as forms of reparation are relevant *before* the fact. The substance and ultimate aim are the same: preventing irreparable harm to persons. It is their function that is different. A finding on the merits that a certain event must be prevented is a determination that not preventing this would constitute a violation resulting in irreparable harm to persons. A provisional measure, on the other hand, serves to prevent acts or omissions by the State that would make impossible such a finding. If the adjudicator determines in its decision on the merits that there is insufficient evidence for such a finding, the State is allowed to proceed with its previous course of (in)action. If it does find a violation, true reparation would hardly be available if the irreparable harm to the person has already occurred pending the proceedings.

Thus, alleged victims have the right to a remedy in the sense that they should be able to initiate a meaningful procedure. The adjudicators may then use provisional measures pending this procedure in order to ensure the effectiveness of the procedure. Ensuring this effectiveness means

---

[334] See further the Conclusion to Part II.
[335] See e.g. Dumbault (1932), p. 165.
[336] ICJ *Case concerning the Gabcikovo-Nagymaros project* (*Hungary* v. *Slovakia*), 25 September 1997, §140. At the same time it did not apply the precautionary principle (see section 4.3.5 of Chapter I). Moreover, it did not use provisional measures (which were ruled out by the Parties now that they had brought the case before the ICJ by an Agreement excluding the possibility to request provisional measures). In addition it did not discuss the issue of 'ecological necessity'.

in particular that a meaningful outcome such as cessation, assurances of non-repetition and specific forms of reparation must not be made impossible already pending the case.[337]

This section first refers to the relevant law and practice of human rights adjudicators regarding the correlation between orders for provisional measures and judgments on the merits and reparation. It then refers to the relation between cessation, non-repetition and reparation. Subsequently it singles out specific issues – other than halting executions, which will be discussed separately – in which continuity between prevention and reparation may be observed. In the context of protection against death threats it refers separately to the obligation to investigate, prosecute and punish. Finally, based on a discussion of the case law on the death penalty developed by the HRC and the Inter-American Court, the argument is made that human rights adjudicators should pay particular attention to the relation between provisional measures on the one hand and on cessation and reparation on the other.

5.2   Provisional measures and reparation

Section 3 discussed the specificity not of reparation but of provisional measures. Obviously, if the adjudicator is precise about the protective measures required pending the proceedings, it should also, following a finding on the merits, give a precise indication of the expected form of reparation.

The HRC and, more specifically, the Inter-American Commission and Court have paid particular attention to the issue of reparations.[338] Yet the HRC has done so inconsistently and, at least until 2003, without consideration for the relationship between provisional measures and reparation. With its General Comment (2004) on Article 2 ICCPR (the right to an effective remedy) the HRC finally acknowledged the relationship between provisional measures and reparation.[339]

The European Court has only incidentally referred to forms of reparation other than those involving financial compensation or even just the finding of a violation in itself.[340] Even in cases dealing with extreme violations comparable to those dealt with by the Inter-American Court, the European Court has maintained that it 'will not make consequential orders or declaratory state-

---

[337]   Where possible this book refers to the term 'reparation' when dealing with substantive forms of reparation. Nevertheless, some adjudicators use the term 'remedies' both for procedural recourse and for these substantive forms of reparation.

[338]   Lawson (1999) refers to the 'non-binding' character of the HRC's Views and speculates that it is this character that may have stimulated it to be very concrete in its recommendations. Yet this does not necessarily serve to explain this approach in light of the fact that the Inter-American Court does this as well. Moreover, the HRC emphasises the obligation to comply with its decisions in good faith, defying the 'non-binding character' that has traditionally been ascribed to it. See also Chapter XVI (Legal status).

[339]   See further sections 3.1 and 5.6 of this Chapter.

[340]   E.g. in ECtHR *Hentrich* v. *France*, 22 September 1994, §71, the Court considered 'the best form of redress would in principle be to return the land. Failing that, the calculation of pecuniary damage must be based on the current market value of the land'. In this case it postponed a decision under Article 50. In that decision, of 3 July 1995, the Court simply ordered monetary damages, noting that the State had pointed out that it 'could not, as its national law currently stood, take the measure recommended by the Court. Having become part of the private property of the State, the "pre-empted" land was subject to the provisions of the Code of State Property and it was impracticable to transfer it, let alone without requiring any payment', §10. See also *Clooth* v. *Belgium*, 12 September 1991. Generally see e.g. Van Emmerik (1997) and Van Kempen (2003).

ments in this regard'.[341] Yet the text of the ECHR does not force the Court to take such a limited approach.[342]

The African Commission and the Bosnia Chamber have been more specific in their approaches. Strangely, Article XI (1(b)) of Annex 6 to the Dayton Accord stipulates that the Bosnia Chamber shall determine what steps the respondent Party shall take to remedy a breach, 'including orders to cease and desist, monetary relief (…) and provisional measures'. While this illustrates how closely related orders for protective measures pending the proceedings really are to such orders as part of judgments on reparation, traditionally the term 'provisional measures' is reserved for measures required pending the proceedings.[343]

Of all applicable human rights treaties the American Convention best reflects the correlation between provisional measures and reparation.[344] Article 63 ACHR unites the two concepts in one provision. Article 63(1) stipulates:

> "If the Court finds that there has been a violation of a right or freedom protected by this Convention, the Court shall rule that the injured party be ensured the enjoyment of his right or freedom that was violated. It shall also rule, if appropriate, that the consequences of the measure or situation that constituted the breach of such right or freedom be remedied and that fair compensation be paid to the injured party".

Article 63(2) provides:

> "In cases of extreme gravity and urgency, and when necessary to avoid irreparable damage to persons, the Court shall adopt such provisional measures as it deems pertinent in matters it has under consideration. With respect to a case not yet submitted to the Court, it may act at the request of the Commission".

The Inter-American Court confirmed this relationship in *James and others* (2001).[345] In fact the decisions of the Inter-American Commission and Court show that, throughout a single proceeding, positive obligations may be required at various stages (provisional measures, merits and reparation). This is due to the underlying purpose that cessation, non-repetition and reparation have in common, as discussed in section 5.3.

---

341 ECtHR *Akdivar and others* v. *Turkey*, 1 April 1998 (compensation), §47.

342 See e.g. Van Emmerik (1997) and Lawson (1999), p. 85.

343 In the Inter-American system provisional measures are sometimes maintained until after the Court's judgment on the merits, and often even until after its judgment on reparations. In these cases the Court points out that the case will only be closed once the judgment on reparations has been implemented and there is no complete implementation as long as petitioners or witnesses are still being threatened and harassed. See also Chapter XIV (Jurisdiction and admissibility).

344 Article 27 of the 1998 Protocol on the African Court of Human and Peoples' Rights makes a similar link, but the 2008 Protocol on the Statute of the African Court of Justice and Human Rights does not. Instead its Article 28 on the jurisdiction of the Court, provides under (h) the jurisdiction over disputes relating to 'the nature or extent of the reparation to be made for the breach of an international obligation'. In addition, Article 45, entitled 'Compensation', but referring to a greater range of reparations, stipulates: "Without prejudice to its competence to rule on issues of compensation at the request of a party by virtue of paragraph 1(h), of Article 28 of the present Statute, the Court may, if it considers that there was a violation of a human or peoples' right, order any appropriate measures in order to remedy the situation, including granting fair compensation".

345 IACHR *James et al.* v. *Trinidad & Tobago*, Order of 26 November 2001, 12th 'Considering' clause.

5.3 Provisional measures and cessation, non-repetition, reparation: a unison of purpose

The ILC Articles on State Responsibility have laid down secondary rules to be invoked by (injured) States against States that have committed an internationally wrongful act. Such responsibility is triggered when an act or omission is attributable to the State and constitutes a breach of an international obligation of the State, including a human rights obligation. Indeed the underlying concepts and principles in the ILC Articles are also relevant to the relation between individuals and States, as apparent from the case law developed by the various human rights adjudicators.[346] Thus the Basic Principles and Guidelines on the Right to a Remedy and Reparation for Victims of Gross Violations of International Human Rights Law and Serious Violations of International Humanitarian Law (2006)[347] have been based, where appropriate, on the ILC Articles.[348] This section deals with the contents of decisions on the merits and reparation. In the next sections the parallel with provisional measures is explored.

Strictly speaking assurances of non-repetition are not individual forms of reparation, but constitute more general obligations. Cessation and satisfaction are equally measures more generally owed, yet they obviously have special significance to the specific victims. These obligations arise upon a finding of a violation, but prior to additional statements on reparation.[349] This chapter takes into account the relation of such obligations with obligations based on provisional measures. The substance, for instance, of guarantees of non-repetition may coincide with the protection required in provisional measures.

Part of the general responsibility of States that have committed an internationally wrongful act is that they must 'continue' to perform the obligation breached (Article 29 ILC Articles on State Responsibility, 2001). In practice this means that they must *resume* performance of the obligation. If the internationally wrongful act is continuing, the responsible State is obliged to cease it (Article 30 (a) ILC Articles). This is relevant in the context of any continuing human rights violation. Sometimes it is necessary pending the proceedings to use provisional measures

---

[346] See e.g. Van Boven Study concerning the right to restitution, compensation and rehabilitation for victims of gross violations of human rights and fundamental freedoms, Final Report, E/CN.4/Sub.2/1993/8, 2 July 1993; revised version E/CN.4/Sub.2/1996/17, 24 May 1996 and E/CN.4/1997/104, 16 January 1997; independent expert to prepare a revised version of the Principles and Guidelines, Bassiouni, reports E/CN.4/1999/65 and E/CN.4/2000/62; Shelton (2005); De Feyter/Parmentier/Bossuyt/Lemmens (2005); Gumedze (2003); Van Boven (2001b); Van Boven (1999); Klein 1999 and Tomuschat (1999).

[347] Basic principles and Guidelines on the Right to a Remedy and Reparation for Victims of Gross Violations of International Law and Serious Violations of International Humanitarian Law, GA Resolution, 16 December 2005. See also Article 24 jo. 30 & 31 International Convention for the Protection of all Persons against Enforced Disappearances and the Declaration of Basic Principles of Justice for victims of Crime and Abuse of Power, Adopted by General Assembly resolution 40/34, 29 November 1985.

[348] For a different view see Germany's position that the Basic Principles 'erroneously sought to apply the principles of State responsibility to relationships between States and individuals'. See also d'Argent (2005). Yet see Van Boven's appropriate criticism of the German position, Van Boven (2007), pp. 729-730. See further, e.g. Shelton (2005), pp. 28-29.

[349] See also Report of the Independent Expert to update the Set of Principles to combat impunity, Orentlicher, E/CN.4/2005/102, 18 February 2005, under D. See in particular footnote 76 at p. 28; for the revised text of the Principles see E/CN.4/2005/102/Add.1, 8 February 2005, principle 35. See also Commission resolution 2005/81. See further Van Boven (2007), p. 735 confirming this distinction. Orentlicher also points out that 'the right to restitution, compensation and rehabilitation does not pertain solely to "individual measures", nor are measures of satisfaction appropriate only as "general measures".

exactly in order to make sure that an alleged act that is likely to be internationally wrongful is ceased immediately or in order to ensure the continued performance of an obligation, e.g. in the context of ongoing detention and access to health care.

States have the duty to organise their government apparatus so that they are capable of ensuring full enjoyment of human rights. As a consequence of this obligation they must prevent violations. To the extent violations have nevertheless taken place they must use all means at their disposal to investigate the facts and punish the perpetrators.[350]

The Inter-American Court has often emphasised the positive obligation to investigate death threats and harassment and prosecute those responsible. It considers these measures against impunity necessary in three phases of the proceedings: in the judgments on the merits,[351] in the judgments on reparations and also as part of its provisional measures.

In the judgment on the merits this is necessary because the obligation to guarantee and ensure the effective exercise of the rights in the ACHR is 'independent of and different from the obligation to make reparation'.[352] This means that the State is obliged to investigate the facts and punish those responsible even if the victim or his next of kin would decide to waive the measures of reparation.[353] Otherwise it would fail to comply with its general obligation to 'ensure the free and full exercise' of the rights under the ACHR.[354]

In its judgments on reparations the Court often reiterates the obligation to investigate the facts and identify and punish the perpetrators. From its first cases the Court has emphasised the importance for the next of kin of the victims of their right to know what happened.[355] Equally, they have a right to know the identity of the perpetrators. The State had the duty to properly investigate the facts and punish those responsible.[356]

---

[350] In general see Independent study on best practices, including recommendations, to assist states in strengthening their domestic capacity to combat all aspects of impunity, by Diane Orentlicher, E/CN.4/2004/88, 27 February 2004; Updated Set of principles, E/CN.4/2005/102/Add.1, 8 February 2005 and E/CN.4/2005/102, 18 February 2005.

[351] See e.g. IACHR *Velásquez Rodríguez*, 19 July 1988 discussing the merits: "The State has a legal duty to take reasonable steps to prevent human rights violations and to use the means at its disposal to carry out a serious investigation of violations committed within its jurisdiction, to identify those responsible, to impose the appropriate punishment and to ensure the victim adequate compensation", §174. "The State is obligated to investigate every situation involving a violation of the rights protected by the Convention. If the State apparatus acts in such a way that the violation goes unpunished and the victim's full enjoyment of such rights is not restored as soon as possible, the State has failed to comply with its duty to ensure the free and full exercise of those rights to the persons within its jurisdiction. The same is true when the State allows private persons or groups to act freely and with impunity to the detriment of the rights recognized by the Convention", §176 and "The duty to investigate facts of this type continues as long as there is uncertainty about the fate of the person who has disappeared. Even in the hypothetical case that those individually responsible for crimes of this type cannot be legally punished under certain circumstances, the State is obligated to use the means at its disposal to inform the relatives of the fate of the victims and, if they have been killed, the location of their remains", §181.

[352] IACHR *Garrido and Baigorria*, 27 August 1998 (Reparations), §72.

[353] See e.g. IACHR *Garrido and Baigorria*, 27 August 1998 (reparations), §72.

[354] See e.g. IACHR *Bámaca Velásquez*, judgment of 25 November 2000 (merits), §129; *Garrido and Baigorria*, judgment of 27 August 1998 (reparations), §73 and *Paniagua Morales et al*, judgment of 8 March 1998, §178.

[355] See e.g. IACHR *Velásquez Rodríguez*, 29 July 1988 (merits), §181; *Godínez Cruz*, 20 January 1989 (merits), §191 and *Aloeboetoe et al.*, 10 September 1993 (reparation), §109.

[356] See e.g. IACHR *El Amparo*, judgment of 14 September 1996 (reparation), §61; *Blake,* 22 January 1999 (reparations), §65 and *Suárez Rosero*, 20 January 1999 (reparations), §§79-80, pointing out

The Court has defined impunity as the 'total lack of investigation, prosecution, capture, trial and conviction of those responsible for violations of the rights protected by the American Convention'. In this respect 'the State has the obligation to use all the legal means at its disposal to combat that situation, since impunity fosters chronic recidivism of human rights violations, and total defenselessness of victims and their relatives'.[357]

State responsibility also entails that the responsible State offers assurances and guarantees of non-repetition, that is, 'if circumstances so require' (Article 30 (b) ILC Articles). In cases, for instance, of continuing harassment of human rights defenders, circumstances may certainly require the State to offer them such guarantees. In fact, as we have seen, on the merits various adjudicators have referred to the obligation to investigate the facts and punish the perpetrators.[358] At the same time the aforementioned Basic Principles eventually did not refer to this when they discussed guarantees of non-repetition. Instead they refer to, among others, strengthening the independence of the judiciary, ensuring 'effective civilian control of military and security forces' and one more directly preventive measure, namely 'Protecting persons in the legal, medical and health-care professions, the media and other related professions, and human rights defenders'. In addition the Basic Principles note that the measures listed are not exhaustive ('should include') and that they 'will also contribute to prevention'.[359]

While cessation obviously is a direct consequence of the finding of a violation and is an obligation that applies collectively as well, the Basic Principles also refer to 'effective measures aimed at the cessation of continuing violations as a form of satisfaction to the victim.[360]

In human rights law it appears that not just decisions on provisional measures, but also decisions on the merits and reparation focus on prevention and, ultimately, protection. This is confirmed by the Basic Principles, which point out that the obligation to 'respect, ensure respect for and implement' international human rights law includes the duty to take appropriate measures to *prevent* violations. They add that this obligation includes as well the duty to investigate violations and take appropriate action against the perpetrators, provide equal access to justice for alleged victims and provide effective remedies to victims, including reparation. In other words, according to the Principles the scope of the obligation to respect, ensure respect for and implement human rights law encompasses the duty to prevent, investigate, provide a remedy and provide reparation. As we will see, in fact these obligations are interrelated.

In 1993 UN Special Rapporteur Van Boven, appointed to deal with the issue of reparations, stressed that gross human rights violations are by their nature irreparable. Any form of reparation

---

this is already an obligation on the merits, not just on reparations, referring to its judgment on the merits in this case of 12 November 1997, 6th operative paragraph.

[357] IACHR *Paniagua Morales et al,* judgment of 8 March 1998 (merits), §173. It has also found certain amnesty laws to be incompatible with the ACHR and therefore lacking legal effect. *Barrios Altos* v. *Peru,* judgment of 14 March 2001 (merits).

[358] See e.g. IACHR *Asunto de la Cárcel de Urso Branco* (Brasil), Resolución de 2 de mayo de 2008, 25th 'Considering' clause, specifically noting that the investigation of the facts and the eventual punishment of those responsible is a fundamental measure in order to ensure non-repetition.

[359] Basic Principles, §23.

[360] Basic Principles, §22(a). As noted, in her report Orentlicher correctly distinguishes between reparation, satisfaction, cessation and assurances. See e.g. Independent study on best practices, including recommendations, to assist states in strengthening their domestic capacity to combat all aspects of impunity, by Diane Orentlicher, Updated Set of principles, E/CN.4/2005/102/Add.1, 8 February 2005 and E/CN.4/2005/102, 18 February 2005, under D. See in particular footnote 76 at p. 28; for the revised text of the Principles see E/CN.4/2005/102/Add.1, 8 February 2005, principle 35. See also Van Boven (2007) agreeing with that approach.

would inevitably fail to be proportionate to the harm suffered.[361] Indeed, prevention of further such harm is the most appropriate action required of the State. With regard to the original victim this prevention could consist of halting continued harassment or ongoing adverse detention situations, etc. With regard to those related to persons killed, this could mean preventing *more* killings perpetrated by the same group of persons.[362]

The Basic Principles have confirmed the developments in international law specifically dealing with the relationship between individuals and States. At the same time they are necessarily more specific in their attention to the needs of individuals rather than States. This is illustrated, among others, by the fact that next to the customary restitution and compensation, as laid down also in the ILC Articles,[363] in the Basic Principles from the outset rehabilitation was named as a form of reparation as well.

The Basic Principles refer to the duty to *prevent* not just in the section on the scope of the obligation to respect and ensure respect for human rights law.[364] Also in the context of the *treatment* of victims they note that 'appropriate measures should be taken to ensure their safety, physical and psychological well-being and privacy'.[365] In addition, when discussing *access* to justice for victims they refer to the obligation to 'ensure their safety from intimidation and retaliation, as well as that of their families and witnesses, before, during and after judicial, administrative, or other proceedings that affect the interests of victims'.[366]

The whole point of using provisional measures is that the irreparable harm threatened should be *prevented*. If these measures are subsequently ignored by the State, the adjudicator should comment on this in strongly worded terms. It should follow this up by ordering reparation to the effect of assuring non-repetition so that at least other persons would not suffer the same fate.[367] Moreover, if a person has been tortured, the adjudicator should order reparations to the effect that the State would arrange for medical and psychological treatment[368] and an official public apology.[369]

---

[361] See Study concerning the right to restitution, compensation and rehabilitation for victims of gross violations of human rights and fundamental freedoms, Final Report submitted by Theo van Boven, Special Rapporteur, E/CN.4/Sub.2/1993/45/8, 2 July 1993, §131. See also Revised set of basic principles and guidelines on the right to reparation for victims of gross violations of human rights and humanitarian law prepared by Mr. Theo van Boven pursuant to Sub-Commission decision 1995/117, U.N. Doc. E/CN.4/Sub.2/1996/17, 24 May 1996.

[362] In 1998 the then Commission on Human Rights appointed independent expert Bassiouni who continued examination of the issue. Bassiouni eventually submitted the Van Boven/Bassouni Guidelines to the Commission, which adopted them in 2005. They were subsequently adopted by the General Assembly in December 2005. With regard to the obligations of the State the final version refers to 'should' rather than 'shall'. Yet the Preamble emphasizes that the Principles and Guidelines did not entail new obligations but instead identified 'mechanisms, modalities, procedures and methods for the implementation of existing legal obligations'. Thus it would have made sense to use the term 'shall', rather than 'should' to refer to the existing obligations of States.

[363] According to Article 31 ILC Articles the responsible State is obliged to 'make full reparation for the injury caused by the internationally wrongful act' and restitution, compensation and satisfaction are named as forms of reparation (Article 34 ILC Articles).

[364] Basic Principles, §3(a).

[365] Basic Principles, §10.

[366] Basic Principles, §12(b). The operative term used here is 'should', but, as noted, shall or must would reflect more appropriately the law as developed by the human rights adjudicators.

[367] See also Chapter XVIII (Follow-up).

[368] Rehabilitation, Basic Principles, §21, and to the extent costs have already been made, also compensation, Basic Principles, §20(e).

[369] Satisfaction, see §22(e).

Apart from the traditional remedy of payment of compensation to victims or their family, the Inter-American Court also mentions more concrete forms of reparation such as the obligation to prevent and investigate human rights violations and to punish perpetrators.[370] The obligations are often even more precise: to identify the remains of the victims and surrender them to their families; to declare domestic proceedings invalid; to order that victims are guaranteed a new trial or to take measures to reform domestic legal provisions. Another form of reparation the Court has required is to reopen a school, to attach a commemorative plaque to a public building or to name a street or a school after the victims.[371]

The Inter-American Court has also referred to the obligation to declare domestic proceedings invalid, to order a new trial for the victims or to release someone. More generally it has ordered States to take measures to reform domestic legal provisions.[372]

In *Bámaca Velásquez* (2000) the IACHR had found Guatemala responsible for Bámaca's disappearance, torture and death. On the merits the Court stated: "In view of the nature of the instant case, although the Court is unable to order that the injured parties should be guaranteed the enjoyment of the rights and liberties violated, by means of the *restitutio in integrum*, it must, instead, order the reparation of the consequences of the violation of the rights mentioned and, consequently, the establishment of fair compensation. The amounts and form of this will be determined during the reparations stage".[373]

Two important rights of the family members of disappeared persons are the right to the truth and respect for the link between the living and the dead.[374] With regard to the right to truth Judge Cançado Trindade pointed out that in light of the State's obligation to cease the violations of human rights, ensuring this right is in fact 'essential to the struggle against impunity' and 'is ineluctably linked to the very *realization* of justice, and to the guarantee of non-repetition of those violations'.[375]

A very important obligation the Court has referred to in recent judgments on reparations is to locate bodies, to identify the remains of victims and surrender the remains to the families. In

---

[370]   To this extent, its approach is similar to that of the HRC, but not to that of the ECtHR, which – so far – has been rather conservative in this area. See e.g. Van Emmerik (1997) and Van Kempen (2003). See §22, Basic principles on satisfaction, subsection (f) (and Part II, sections 4 and 5 when dealing with gross violations that constitutes crimes under international law).

[371]   See e.g. IACHR *Aloeboetoe et al.* v. *Suriname*, Judgment of 10 September 1993 (reparation); The *Street Children'* case (*Villagrán Morales et al.* v. *Guatemala*), judgment of 26 May 2001 (reparations).

[372]   At the same time it is not always in a position to identify the exact legislative, administrative or other measures to be implemented in the internal legislation of a State. In the case of the *Street Children*, for instance, it did emphasise the obligation of the State, at the reparations stage, to adopt the necessary legislative or other measures in compliance with Article 2 ACHR, even though it had not found a violation of Article 2 in the judgment on the merits. It considered that the State must take the necessary measures to adapt its legislation to Article 19 ACHR (rights of the child to the measures of protection required by his condition as a minor) in order to ensure non-repetition of the violations. The representatives of the victims' next of kin and the Commission had requested the Court to order the State to derogate from the 1979 Minors Code or to bring into force the Children and Youth Code adopted by the Guatemalan Congress in 1996 and the 1997 plan of action for street children. The Court, however, pointed out it could not establish the exact nature of the implementation measures. IACHR *'The Street Children'* case (*Villagrán Morales et al.* v. *Guatemala*), 26 May 2001 (reparations), §98.

[373]   IACHR *Bámaca Velásquez* v. *Guatemala*, 25 November 2000, §228.

[374]   More closely on the latter see Separate Opinion Cançado Trindade in *Bámaca Velásquez*, 25 November 2000 (merits).

[375]   IACHR *Bámaca Velásquez* v. *Guatemala*, 25 November 2000, Separate Opinion Cançado Trindade, §32.

the *Street Children* case (2001) the Court stated that Guatemala should 'adopt the necessary measures to transfer the mortal remains' of Henry Giovanni Contreras 'to the place chosen by his next of kin, without any cost to them, so as to satisfy the desire of the family to give them appropriate burial, according to their religious beliefs and customs'.[376]

The ILC Articles refer to the obligation to give satisfaction insofar as the injury caused 'cannot be made good by restitution or compensation'. It may 'consist in an acknowledgment of the breach, an expression of regret, a formal apology or another appropriate modality' (ILC Article 37).

A form of satisfaction mentioned in the Basic Principles is the search for the whereabouts of the disappeared and the identities of the children abducted. As discussed in Chapter VI, in disappearance cases provisional measures may be used pending the proceedings. After all when a person has recently been disappeared the likelihood of finding this person alive is greater pending the proceedings than upon their conclusion. Provisional measures prompting a State to find a person alive could thus help ensure the least serious consequences of a breach of State responsibility. The Basic Principles note that even when the victims have already been killed satisfaction should still consist of a search for their bodies as well as 'assistance in the recovery, identification and reburial of the bodies in accordance with the expressed or presumed wish of the victims, or the cultural practices of the families and communities'.[377] Circumstances are feasible in which such measures may be required of the State already pending the proceedings, in order to prevent further harm to those left behind.

Among others, in the *Street Children* case (2001) the Inter-American Court discussed how to deal with those harmful effects of the violations that could not be assessed in monetary terms. It noted that this may include the suffering and distress caused to the direct victims and their next of kin and 'the impairment of values that are highly significant to them'.[378] It was not possible to assign a precise monetary equivalent to the harm. Providing compensation could be done in two ways. The first would be to nevertheless determine a sum of money to be paid, or the assignment of goods or services. A second way would be 'the execution of acts or works of a public nature or repercussion, which have effects such as recovering the memory of the victims, re-establishing their reputation, consoling their next of kin or transmitting a message of official condemnation of the human rights violations in question and commitment to the efforts to ensure that they do not happen again'.[379] In other words, these measures could return some sense of dignity to the victims and their next of kin as well as constitute a preventive measure of a general nature.[380]

---

[376]   IACHR *Street Children* case, 26 May 2001 (Reparations), §102.

[377]   Basic Principles, §22(c).

[378]   IACHR '*The Street Children*' case (*Villagrán Morales et al.* v. *Guatemala*), 26 May 2001 (reparations), §84.

[379]   IACHR '*The Street Children*' case (*Villagrán Morales et al.* v. *Guatemala*), 26 May 2001 (reparations), §84.

[380]   Another example from the same case is the Court's order to 'designate an educational center with a name allusive to the young victims in this case and to place in this center a plaque' with their names on it. This would 'contribute to raising awareness in order to avoid the repetition of harmful acts such as those that occurred in the instant case and will keep the memory of the victims alive'. IACHR *Street Children* case (*Villagrán Morales et al.* v. *Guatemala*), 26 May 2001 (reparations), §103, referring to the names of victims: Henry Giovanni Contreras, Federico Clemente Figueroa Túnchez, Julio Roberto Caal Sandoval, Jovito Josué Juárez Cifuentes and Anstraun Aman Villagrán Morales. The Court also reiterated the obligation to investigate, identify and punish those responsible (§101). See also *Benavides Ceballos*, judgment of 19 June 1998, §§48.5 and 55 and *Aloeboetoe et al.* case, Judgment of 10 September 1993 (reparations), §96. Finally see IACHR *Plan de Sánchez massacre* case (Guatemala), 19 November 2004 (reparations), §§110-111.

In the Basic Principles the right to the truth and the obligation to prosecute and punish perpetrators are not mentioned as examples of guarantees of non-repetition. Instead 'verification of the facts and full and public disclosure of the truth' and 'judicial and administrative sanctions against persons liable for the violations' are mentioned under 'satisfaction'.[381] Public apologies, commemorations and tributes to the victims as well as an official declaration or judicial decision 'restoring the dignity, the reputation and the rights of the victim and of persons closely connected to the victim' are such measures of satisfaction.[382] When provisional measures ordering States to protect persons against death threats are implemented, among others, through an official declaration by the State to the effect that certain people are *not* enemies of the State and that threats against them will be investigated and punished, this could almost be seen as a temporary counterpart of the aforementioned forms of reparation.

In other words, making a public apology and providing for public commemorations has a dual function as well: on the one hand recognition, satisfaction and rehabilitation and on the other hand prevention. Thus, pending the proceedings the State may be required to publicly acknowledge the legitimacy of the activities of human rights defenders, journalists and others under threat. In such cases the public statement is meant to prevent *specific* harm. Indeed, at the stage of provisional measures public apologies or at least public statements condemning rather than condoning or supporting threats and harassments would be warranted as well. The public statement required at the reparations stage in its presentation simply is more permanent and official rather than transitory and its purpose is to ensure satisfaction and general, rather than specific, prevention. Each stage of the proceedings is aimed both at prevention and at reparation.

5.4   A continuum of protection

5.4.1 Introduction

A few examples are given, from different issue areas, in order to illustrate the continuum between the substance of provisional measures on the one hand and cessation, assurances and reparation on the other hand. Whether pending the proceedings or upon a finding of a violation on the merits, States have the obligation to prevent irreparable harm to persons by taking measures of protection that may substantively coincide even though the function of these measures differs depending on whether they are required pending the proceedings or upon the finding of a violation.

5.4.2 Halting corporal punishment and the expected obligations on the merits

As discussed in Chapter IV it appears that all adjudicators, including those that have not been faced with requests for provisional measures, have found corporal punishment in violation of the prohibition of cruel treatment. As discussed, the HRC and the Inter-American Commission are the only adjudicators that have used provisional measures to halt execution of corporal punishment. In *Osbourne* v. *Jamaica* (2000) the HRC pointed out that the State party was obliged, under Art. 2(3)(a) ICCPR, to provide the petitioner with an effective remedy and it 'should compensate him for the violation'. It was also obliged to refrain from carrying out the sentence and it 'should ensure that similar violations do not occur in the future by repealing the legislative provisions that

---

[381]   It adds in this context that this disclosure should not cause further harm or threaten the safety of the victim, the victim's family, witnesses or persons who have intervened to either assist the victim or to prevent the occurrence of further violations. See Basic Principles, §22(a) and (f).

[382]   See Basic Principles, §22(d), (e) and (g).

allow for corporal punishment'.[383] The Committee uses the term 'obligation' of the State when it speaks of the right to a remedy and the duty to abstain from carrying out the sentence of corporal punishment. It uses exhortatory language ('should') when it specifies the remedy, although 'compensation' still is not very specific. It also uses the term 'should' in the context of the obligation to ensure that similar violations do not occur in the future, but since this is in fact an obligation under general international law it may be assumed that the exhortation lies in the second half of the sentence: the HRC considers that the best way to ensure that similar violations do not occur in the future would be to repeal the legislative provisions allowing corporal punishment. It is noteworthy that when the HRC published its decision on the merits, the Court of Appeal of Jamaica had already determined two years previously that the legislation on corporal punishment was unconstitutional.[384]

In corporal punishment cases the substance of the provisional measure and of the measures required following the finding of a violation partially coincide because both require the State to refrain from carrying out the sentence of corporal punishment. The substance of the provisional measure, namely that the State should halt its execution, would therefore have an indeterminate applicability. What is called provisional is in fact already permanent. In other words, on the basis of previous case law we already know before the final determination that the State will be required to respect the substance of the Committee's provisional measures *beyond* the duration of the case before the HRC. Thus, because of the unequivocal pre-existing case law on the merits this provisional measure is similar to an instant judgment on one particular issue. If the execution of a sentence of corporal punishment is indeed impending, the authorities must halt it not only pending the case before the HRC, but *beyond* this period as well.

The risk of execution of corporal punishment does not have to constitute the main claim. If there is a reference to such punishment in the complaint, the HRC can include it in the claims *proprio motu* and if the sentence has not yet been executed the Committee can use provisional measures to prevent irreparable harm. After all, it would find a violation of Art.7 ICCPR for any sentence of corporal punishment and would point out the State party's obligation not to carry out such a sentence. It would be reasonable to expect the HRC's *proprio motu* use of provisional measures in any new case similar to that in *Matthews* (1998).[385] Yet it did not do so in *Sooklal* (2001).[386] In this case it was not the petitioner who had raised a complaint with regard to the corporal punishment imposed on him, but the HRC itself had raised the issue *proprio motu*. It had also pointed out, in its paragraph on reparations, that the State was under an obligation not to carry out the sentence. The facts of the case were similar to those of *Matthews*, but the case law had since developed, in particular with regard to reparations. Moreover, the HRC had already used provisional measures twice in cases specifically complaining about corporal punishment. Nevertheless, the Committee did not use provisional measures *proprio motu* in *Sooklal*. The HRC could have used provisional measures in this case, because there was a relation with the decision

---

[383] HRC *Osbourne* v. *Jamaica*, 15 March 2000.

[384] See also HRC *Higginson* v. *Jamaica*, 28 March 2002. The Committee found that the State party was 'under an obligation to provide the author with an effective remedy, including refraining from carrying out the sentence of whipping upon the author or providing appropriate compensation if the sentence has been carried out'. Once more it noted that Jamaica 'should ensure that similar violations do not occur in the future by repealing the legislative provisions that allow for corporal punishment'.

[385] HRC *Matthews* v. *Trinidad and Tobago*, 31 March 1998. See also Chapter XIV on admissibility and jurisdiction.

[386] HRC *Boodlal Sooklal* v. *Trinidad and Tobago*, 25 October 2001.

on the merits. Provisional measures would not require more than the eventual decision would and these measures would ultimately prevent irreparable harm to persons.[387]

5.4.3 Halting expulsion and extradition and the expected obligations on the merits

Most human adjudicators have used provisional measures to halt expulsion and extradition, but the case law of the HRC provides information on the expected obligations on the merits. In light of its previous case law counsel in *Judge* v. *Canada* (2003) had not brought a claim based on the failure to obtain assurances against the death penalty.[388] Nevertheless, after it had declared inadmissible the original claims the HRC raised this issue *proprio motu*. Ando disagreed with this approach. He considered it 'illogical' for the HRC to declare inadmissible the original complaints under Articles 6, 7, 10 and 14(5) ICCPR but at the same time to state that the communication raised issues under Articles 6, 7 and 2. He felt that a mere reference to 'the seriousness of these questions' did not suffice and that the HRC should have specified how these 'apparent contradictions' were to be solved.[389] In fact it is standard practice of the HRC to indicate which provisions apply to the issues raised. As in the death penalty cases previously discussed the fact that the HRC did introduce this aspect *proprio motu* may indicate that even if there is no claim of Article 14 provisional measures could be used, because the HRC itself could find that the complaint raises issues under Article 14 and/or Article 6 ICCPR.

In *Ahani* (2004) the Committee found that Canada had violated Articles 9(4) and 13 in conjunction with Article 7, as well as the OP as such, by deporting the petitioner before the Committee's determination of his claim and in contravention of its provisional measures. With regard to the obligation to provide the petitioner with an effective remedy it pointed out that the State was obliged '(a) to make reparation to the author if it comes to light that torture was in fact suffered subsequent to deportation, and (b) to take such steps as may be appropriate to ensure that the author is not, in the future, subjected to torture as a result of the events of his presence in, and removal from, the State party'. It also pointed out that Canada was under an obligation 'to avoid similar violations in the future, including by taking appropriate steps to ensure that the Committee's requests for interim measures of protection will be respected'.[390]

In other words, by its nature the violation of the provisional measure could not be made good anymore through full reparation. In this light the HRC points out the obligation to guarantee non-repetition of this violation in future cases, as well as, vis-à-vis Ahani, the obligation to take those preventive measures that were still possible. These are requirements on the merits, which are not specified, but they may include demarches, monitoring and embassy visits. In the event that Ahani is indeed tortured, Canada is required to 'make reparation'. This is not specified either, but since return to the pre-existing situation would not be possible, one might imagine something

---

[387] Since most international and regional adjudicators have declared (and those that have not dealt with it would be likely to declare) (judicial) corporal punishment a violation of the prohibition of cruel treatment there is a clear correlation between the eventual obligations (if sufficient evidence is available that the sentence has indeed been pronounced) and the provisional measure.

[388] HRC *Judge* v. *Canada*, 5 August 2003. For the previous case law see *Kindler* v. *Canada*, 30 July 1993; *Chitat Ng* v. *Canada*, 5 November 1993 and *Cox* v. *Canada*, 31 October 1994.

[389] HRC *Judge* v. *Canada*, 5 August 2003. Ando referred to the Committee's conclusion in §7.8. In fact the Committee noted that 'the facts before it raised two issues under the Covenant that were admissible and should be considered on the merits'. After posing these questions it concluded that, 'given the seriousness of these questions, the parties should be afforded the opportunity to comment on them before the Committee expressed its Views on the merits', §7.8.

[390] HRC *Mansour Ahani* v. *Canada*, 29 March 2004, §12.

like facilitating his return to Canada, or at least his departure from Iran and his treatment in a medical facility specialised in treating torture victims, a public apology and a financial remedy.

In non-refoulement cases, provisional measures to halt an expulsion or extradition on the one hand and a decision on the merits determining that such removal would constitute a violation on the other simply build on each other. The permanent injunction would be pointless without the interim injunction.

5.4.4   Health and whereabouts and the expected obligations on the merits

Claims by or on behalf of persons in detention that are based on violations of the prohibition of torture or cruel treatment *after trial* often relate to *continuing* violations, meaning that part of the remedy should be to put a stop to these violations. In order to prevent irreparable harm ongoing ill treatment should be dealt with as soon as possible pending the proceedings.

In its General Comment on Article 2 the HRC noted that 'cessation of an ongoing violation is an essential element of the right to an effective remedy'.[391] Both its early and its more recent practice recognize the importance of intervening in such continuing violations pending the proceedings, when a determination on the merits about the existence of such violations has not yet been made. Such provisional measures aim at halting the continuation of acts or omissions that (could) constitute a violation. At the same time the HRC also refers to the obligation of States to try to repair 'at the earliest possible opportunity' any harm already caused. It "takes the view that 'the right to an effective remedy may in certain circumstances require States Parties to provide for and implement provisional or interim measures to avoid continuing violations and to endeavour to repair at the earliest possible opportunity any harm that may have been caused by such violations'.[392] In other words, the State is required to redress possible violations causing irreparable harm already pending the proceedings, not only by halting certain actions, but also by repairing violations already caused.

Most ongoing detention cases dealt with by the HRC that show the relationship between the informal provisional measure taken pending the proceedings and the remedy eventually recommended are from the early 1980s. In *Altesor* v. *Uruguay* (1982) the Committee's decision on the merits also specifically referred to the victim's health: 'the State party should also ensure that Alberto Altesor receives all necessary medical care'.[393] On two previous occasions pending the proceedings the HRC had inquired about the health of the victim as well. Indeed the positive obligations mentioned in the Committee's decisions on the merits clearly had their counterpart in its request, pending the proceedings, to inform it of the state of health of the alleged victim and/or to ensure the necessary medical treatment.[394]

---

[391]   HRC General Comment on Article 2 ICCPR, §15.

[392]   Id., §19.

[393]   HRC *Altesor* v. *Uruguay*, 29 March 1982. The HRC found that the victim had been held incommunicado for several months and had been denied the right to habeas corpus. The State party was under an obligation to provide him with effective remedies, including compensation and to take steps to ensure that similar violations did not occur in the future.

[394]   See e.g. HRC *Teti Izquierdo* v. *Uruguay*, 1 April 1982 or *Pietraroia* v. *Uruguay*, 27 March 1981. In *Oxandabarat Scarrone* v. *Uruguay* (1983) the HRC had repeatedly requested the State to provide specific information about the alleged victim's state of health and the medical treatment given to him. The State eventually responded to this request with some specific information about treatment he received in December 1981 and the general statement that he was kept under examination and that his latest general examination (no date provided) found him in good health. It also mentioned two specific medications he was receiving. The HRC considered that the information before it did not justify a finding of a violation of Article 10(1) with respect to the detainee's state of health. It did find a violation of Article 14. The State was obliged to provide

Pending the proceedings in *El Megreisi* v. *Libya* (1994) the HRC had enquired about the whereabouts and health of the alleged victim. On the merits it found violations of Articles 9, 7 and 10(1).[395] The HRC urged the State party to take effective measures to secure his immediate release. Pending the proceedings it had used informal provisional measures that were clearly related to the claims on the merits. Situations of incommunicado detention in an unknown location often result in irreparable harm such as torture or death. If the State would have indicated his whereabouts, would have ensured access to health care and lifted his incommunicado detention pending the proceedings, the violations in this respect would have been less serious. Moreover, the remedy of release would obviously be impossible after the death of the victim.

5.4.5 Death threats and harassment and the expected obligations on the merits

The traditionally most important form of reparation, *restitutio in integrum*, combined with another traditional obligation, namely assurances of non-repetition, could be a rationale for using provisional measures pending proceedings in human rights cases, requesting a State to protect persons against threats.

In its decision on the merits the HRC has referred to the duty to investigate and prosecute human rights violations.[396] In *Bautista de Arellana* v. *Colombia* (1995) the HRC found violations of Articles 6(1), 7 and 9(1) ICCPR. It determined that the State was 'under an obligation to provide the family of Nydia Bautista with an appropriate remedy, which should include damages and an appropriate protection of members of N. Bautista's family from harassment'. It also urged the

---

     the victim with effective remedies 'and, in particular, to ensure that he continues to receive all necessary medical care and to transmit a copy of these views to him'. This shows that the HRC may use informal provisional measures to enquire about the health of an alleged victim pending the proceedings, as well as recommend continued access to medical care, but at the same time fail to find a violation of the right to humane treatment in Article 10. HRC *Oxandabarat Scarrone* v. *Uruguay*, 4 November 1983. By note of 31 October 1991 the State party informed the HRC that under Article 10 of the amnesty law of 8 March 1985 the petitioner was released on 10 March 1985. It is also possible that the Committee first requests the State to ensure medical treatment pending the proceedings, but in its decision on the merits, finding a violation of Article 10, does not specifically refer to the obligation to ensure medical treatment. If it points out that the State is under a particular obligation to ensure that the victim is treated with humanity, the obligation to ensure medical treatment may be interpreted as implicit in that obligation. HRC *Manera Lluberas* v. *Uruguay*, 6 April 1984. By note of 31 October 1991 the State party informed the HRC that the petitioner was released on 14 March 1985, under the amnesty law of 8 March 1985 (on file with the author).

[395] It noted that the petitioner's brother had been 'detained incommunicado for more than three years, until April 1992, when he was allowed a visit by his wife, and that after that date he has again been detained incommunicado and in a secret location'. By being 'subjected to prolonged incommunicado detention in an unknown location', he was 'the victim of torture and cruel and inhuman treatment'. HRC *Mohammed Bashir El-Megreisi* (*submitted by his brother Youssef El-Megreisi*) v. *Libya*, 23 March 1994.

[396] Initially it argued that Article 2 ICCPR constituted a general undertaking by States, which individuals could not invoke in isolation. See e.g. *H.G.B. and S.P.* v. *Trinidad and Tobago*, 3 November 1989 (inadm.). The right to a remedy arose only after a violation of a Covenant right had been established. See e.g. *R.A.V.N. et al* v. *Argentina*, 26 March 1990 (inadm.). This originally meant that it did not refer to this article when it took preventive measures such as indicating provisional measures. Recently, it has indeed recognised the relationship between provisional measures and Article 2 ICCPR. General Comment 31 on the nature of the general legal obligation imposed on States parties to the Covenant (Article 2), 29 March 2004.

State to 'expedite the criminal proceedings leading to the prompt prosecution and conviction of the persons responsible for the abduction, torture and death of Nydia Bautista'. Finally, it reminded the State again of its obligation to ensure that similar events would not occur in the future.[397]

Decisions on the obligation to provide reparation generally include a reference to the obligation to investigate the facts complained of and arrest and try the alleged perpetrator. In the Inter-American system, however, the Commission and Court also order States to investigate and punish perpetrators as part of their precautionary and provisional measures.[398] It is clear that they do this because such measures are necessary to prevent further threats and acts of harassment. Yet the Court will not consider the effectiveness of those investigations that have been realized nor the alleged negligence of the State with regard to these investigations, since it had not yet found a violation in this respect.[399]

The Inter-American Court has pointed out that 'the Government has the obligation to prevent violations of human rights and to investigate the events that led to this request for provisional measures in order to identify those responsible and punish them appropriately so as to prevent any recurrence of the events'.[400] This aim of preventing any recurrence explains the emphasis on investigation, identification and punishment as necessary ingredients in its Orders for provisional measures. Effective measures to investigate the events and, where appropriate, punish the perpetrators were 'a vital aspect' of the State's protective duty. It 'must be assumed by the State as a legal duty and not merely as a formality'.[401]

Equally, the Commission has noted that the obligation to *investigate* the threats is part of its precautionary measures, in order to 'investigate the source of the threats in order to put an end to the harassment of the persons protected by the precautionary measures'.[402]

The recurrence of the obligation in all phases of the proceedings indicates that in order to prevent irreparable harm to persons measures against impunity are necessary not only in the context of decisions on the merits (the obligation to guarantee the effective exercise of the rights in the Convention) and on reparation (the right to reparation), but also as part of provisional measures pending the proceedings (to ensure respect for the rights and in order to prevent their violation).

At the provisional measures stage investigation and prosecution are meant to put a stop to concrete and continuing threats. In the context of judgments on the merits on the right to life and the prohibition of torture and cruel treatment action against impunity (finding the truth and prosecuting those responsible) follows directly from the guarantee of non repetition. Article 1(1) ACHR requires investigation and prosecution in order to guarantee the right to life and the prohibition of cruel treatment.[403]

---

[397] HRC *Bautista de Arellana* v. *Colombia*, 27 October 1995.

[398] See Chapter IX (Threats).

[399] See IACHR *Cárcel de Urso Branco* (Brasil), Order of 2 May 2008, 26th 'Considering' clause. See also *Asunto de los niños y adolescentes privados de libertad en el "Complexo do Tatuapé" de la Fundação CASA* (Brasil), Order of 3 July 2007, 16th 'Considering' clause.

[400] IACHR *Vogt* case, Order of 12 April 1996 (President), 6th 'Considering' clause, referred to in Order of 27 June 1996, 3rd 'Having seen' clause.

[401] IACHR *Vogt* case, Order of 27 June 1996, 5th and 6th 'Considering' clauses.

[402] CIDH Annual Report 2001, Chapter III (a), §18, precautionary measure of June 2001 on behalf of chemistry students who had been declared 'military targets' by the paramilitary group Autodefensas Unidas de Colombia (AUC).

[403] See e.g. CIDH *Damion Thomas* v. *Jamaica*, 4 April 2001 (merits), §45 (establishing that Article 1(1) ACHR, obligating the State to ensure the free and full exercise of the rights and freedoms in the Convention to all persons subject to its jurisdiction, requires the State 'to organize the governmental apparatus and, in general, all the structures through which public power is

Pending the proceedings a provisional measure requiring investigation of death threats and harassment, prosecution and punishment of the perpetrators (as has been seen in the Inter-American system) may serve to prevent further attacks on the life and personal integrity of the beneficiary. At the stage of judgments on reparations action against impunity may be required to achieve reparation for specific individuals: the right to the truth, restoring some measure of dignity, removing fear and recognition of suffering. In other words, action against impunity at this stage aims at recognition, satisfaction and rehabilitation. The action required in all these cases is the same: investigation and prosecution. Its purpose in judgments on reparation encompasses more. As part of the decision on reparations, such investigation, prosecution and punishment, although it serves as a form of satisfaction, dignifying the victims, it may equally be forward looking (as a guarantee of non-repetition).[404]

Thus for the Inter-American Court the specific order to investigate and punish violations has been found both as part of the Court's judgment and as part of its provisional measures to protect persons against death threats and harassment. In the latter case, though, as part of provisional measures the obligation to 'investigate and prosecute' solely aims at preventing further threats, while the obligation to 'investigate and prosecute' as a form of reparation aims not only at prevention of further violations but also at assigning some moral satisfaction.

As noted, the Court has pointed out that the duty to investigate as part of provisional measures is meant to guarantee the right to life and personal integrity, while it will not consider the effectiveness of those investigations that have been realized nor the alleged negligence of the State with regard to these investigations, since it had not yet found a violation in this respect.[405] In other words, in its provisional measures the Court suggests investigation and prosecution as a means of protection against death threats pending the proceedings, but evidently it cannot judge on this issue as part of its follow up on ongoing provisional measures other than to reassert the State's obligation to protect the beneficiaries and again suggest the measures that should be taken in this regard.

There is also another context in which provisional measures have been used addressing the issue of impunity. While in the Inter-American system, the obligation to investigate and prosecute has been referred to in provisional measures aimed at protecting persons against death threats and harassment, in light of its particular function the CAT has very specifically used provisional measures based on the State's obligation either to extradite or prosecute someone suspected of having perpetrated torture.[406]

5.4.6 Cultural survival and the expected obligations on the merits

The provisional measures ordered in the Inter-American system and by the Bosnia Chamber in order to ensure the cultural survival of a group appear justified by their general case law on the obligations on the merits, including reparation in cultural cases. Upon the finding of a violation, the obligations appear to make permanent what was ordered provisionally pending the proceed-

---

exercised, so that they are capable of juridically ensuring the free and full enjoyment of human rights'. Flowing from these obligations 'are correspondent duties to prevent, investigate and punish any violation of the rights recognized in the Convention'.

[404] Yet the official State response to this part of the Orders for provisional measures generally is not or insufficiently implemented by the respondent State. See generally Chapter XVII (Official responses).

[405] See IACHR *Cárcel de Urso Branco* (Brasil), Order of 2 May 2008, 26th 'Considering' clause. See also *Asunto de los niños y adolescentes privados de libertad en el "Complexo do Tatuapé" de la Fundação CASA* (Brasil), Order of 3 July 2007, 16th 'Considering' clause.

[406] See Chapter XII (Other situations), section 2.7.

ings.[407] Obviously this is only possible if the provisional measures are indeed respected. A Bosnia Chamber case concerning the site of the Kizlaragina mosque is a case in point. In October 2001 the Chamber had used provisional measures to prevent the implementation of certain procedural decisions that would allocate the site of this mosque, which had been destroyed in 1992, to a private contractor for the construction of business premises. Nevertheless business premises had meanwhile been constructed. Apparently permission to build these premises 'was obtained unlawfully and without the prior consent or knowledge of the Islamic Community'.[408] Thus, subsequently the petitioner sought permission to rebuild the mosque and to remove these business premises. Yet the Chamber decided not to order demolition of the business premises and restitution of one plot adjacent to that of the destroyed mosque.[409] It did order the respondent Party to ensure that the ownership of the plot where the mosque stood until 1992 'shall be legally transferred to the Islamic community and it shall be permitted to fence in the perimeter of the plot without any further obstruction or hindrance'.[410] In addition, 'all temporary facilities (if any remain)' were ordered to be removed and the site was ordered to be cleaned of all refuse.[411]

The Chamber pointed out that the present case revealed 'a particularly serious form of discrimination (...) that seemed 'to be aimed at humiliating the applicant and thereby disrupting the process of return in the Municipality' in question.[412] The Chamber noted 'the difficulties inherent in the determination of an adequate monetary compensation for this kind of violation'. It recalled in particular that 'the business premises were constructed on the site of a Muslim cemetery without exhuming the graves and that a representative of the respondent Party attempted to justify this by saying that they were 'non-functional' graves and that no one had in fact been buried there for 50 years'.[413] Whichever amount of compensation it would award for non-pecuniary damage, it

---

[407] See Chapter X (Cultural and religious rights).

[408] Bosnia Chamber *Islamic Community in BiH* (*Mrkonjić Grad*) v. *Republika Srpska*, 22 December 2003, §161. In fact the Chamber notes that "It is not known whether the construction of the business premises was concluded at this stage. However, by failing to inform the Chamber that the construction (...) had already been commenced or concluded, the respondent Party failed to implement the order as directed by the Chamber". Bosnia Chamber *Islamic Community in BiH* (*Mrkonjić Grad*) v. *Republika Srpska*, §160. The petitioner had requested provisional measures in July 2001.

[409] Among others it noted that there was sufficient space on which to reconstruct the mosque. It added that it was 'not in a position to evaluate whether the restoration of the Kizlagarina mosque complex as a cultural landmark requires the business premises to be removed', §168.

[410] Bosnia Chamber *Islamic Community in BiH* (*Mrkonjić Grad*) v. *Republika Srpska*, §165.

[411] Id., §164. With regard to the upper part of the mosque site it considered it could not 'now order the respondent party to bear the financial burden' of the reconstruction of the mosque because its competence was limited *ratione temporis* (the destruction of the Mosque occurred before 14 December 1995). Neither would it order the respondent party to grant the petitioner a permit to reconstruct the mosque, because it had previously concluded that the petitioner had not yet exhausted domestic resources in this respect. Yet it did order Republika Srpska 'to consider any future requests by the applicant for reconstruction (...) in good faith and to grant permission without unreasonable conditions'. See Bosnia Chamber *Islamic Community in BiH* (*Mrkonjić Grad*) v. *Republika Srpska*, §163.

[412] Id., §174.

[413] Id., §173. The Chamber concluded that the respondent Party 'targets the applicant as a religious community, because of its religion'. Id., §151. The conduct of the authorities showed 'utter neglect of the religious feelings of the Muslim community that had been burying its dead at the cemetery of the mosque compound (...) over the last few centuries'. The organs of the respondent Party 'took no steps at all to exhume the graves prior to permitting the construction of business premises on the same plot'. Id., §152. The Chamber found that the authorities in Mrkonjić Grad had subjected the petitioner to 'specifically poor treatment, not only if compared

would 'not fully remedy the applicant's complaints and return the previous status quo'.[414] This remark illustrates the importance of provisional measures in order to prevent such a situation.

The relation between provisional measures and subsequent obligations on the merits and reparation appears less straightforward for the HRC than for the Inter-American Commission and Court and the Bosnia Chamber, because of a lack of clarity in some of its case law on the merits.[415]

The *Lubicon Lake Band* case (1990) is instructive in this regard.[416] In this case the HRC confirmed the admissibility of the case just before it found a violation and suggested an unspecified remedy. The HRC published its final View two years after the interlocutory decision reiterating its provisional measure. While it devoted 28 pages to the complicated issue of admissibility in this case, it used only one page for a discussion of the merits. The HRC stated that both historical inequities, 'to which the State party refers' and 'certain more recent developments' were threatening the way of life and culture of the Lubicon Lake Band in violation of Article 27. It concluded that the 'State party proposes to rectify the situation by a remedy that the Committee deems appropriate within the meaning of article 2 of the Covenant'.[417] It is not clear what was the remedy deemed appropriate by the HRC. Apparently it considered sufficient the remedy already proposed by the State.

Chief Ominayak had pointed out that his reason to resort to the HRC had been to request it to assist the Band in 'attempting to convince' the State that the oil and gas development was seriously threatening the existence of the Band and that Canada was responsible for this situation. He stated that without the preservation of the status quo a final judgment on the merits would be ineffective. The only effective remedy would be to seek an interim injunction. Without it a final judgment could never 'restore the way of life, livelihood and means of subsistence' of the Band. The Committee's provisional measures could be seen as seeking such an interim injunction. Yet because of the lack of precision in the remedy the HRC recommended eventually, the Commit-

---

to the Serb Orthodox Church, but to the citizenry in general'. It considered the actions of the authorities 'to amount to a clinical attempt to "cleanse" the Mrkonjić Grad area of all traces of Muslim presence'.

[414] Id., §174.

[415] In a few cases the HRC initially used provisional measures because cultural survival of the indigenous group to which the petitioner belonged might be at stake if the State would continue its activities. In relation to the future logging activities in *Länsman II* the HRC made a remark clarifying its test for finding a violation of the petitioners' right to enjoy their own culture. It observed that logging had been approved 'on a scale which, while resulting in additional work and expenses for the authors and other reindeer herdsmen, does not appear to threaten the survival of reindeer husbandry'. This indicates that only a threat to the *survival* of such husbandry would result in a denial of the right to culture. This, in turn, may mean that in Art. 27 cases involving infringements on the natural habitat, on the merits the HRC would only find a violation if there was a threat of irreparable harm (or such harm had already occurred), but not if harm other than irreparable harm would occur. Indeed, in relation to the collective aspects of Article 27 the HRC has only found a violation in cases in which it considered that further actions would result in irreparable harm. While in other situations involving other rights (without collective aspects) it might find violations of a less serious nature for which it would require compensation, thus far it has never done so with regard to collective aspects.

[416] HRC *Bernard Ominayak, Chief of the Lubicon Lake Band* v. *Canada*, 26 March 1990.

[417] Ando expressed some doubts about 'the categorical statement that recent developments have threatened the life of the Lubicon Lake Band and constitute a violation of article 27', emphasising the importance of economic development for the society as a whole.

tee's decision on the merits could not be seen as seeking a permanent or even an interim injunction.[418]

Most scholars qualify as ineffective the role of the HRC in the specific situation of the Lubicon.[419] They are generally more positive about its *theoretical* contribution to the protection of indigenous peoples, but with regard to the rights of the victims in question they criticise the Committee's vague formulation of the required remedy.[420] Schmidt observes that the Committee's rationale was 'circuitous'.[421] Anaya notes that 'by not providing more guidance on the remedy issue, the committee left it subject to continuing controversy within Canada's internal processes in which the Canadian government had the upper hand'. "Thus, however path-breaking the committee's decision in the Lubicon case is in other respects, its effectiveness in that very case was undermined".[422] He considers that the Committee's deferential stance could be explained on the basis of the presumption of non-interference. Anaya argues that situations involving 'indigenous peoples facing entrenched historical inequities' required more active involvement by the HRC, also in respect of the appropriate remedies. He suggests that it should offer 'good offices to promote or mediate dialogue toward agreement on remedies'.[423]

De Feyter observes that the 'decisional paragraph of *Lubicon Lake Band* is extremely short'. "One may safely speculate that it is as long as the agreement among the majority of the Committee members".[424] This is confirmed by Schmidt who refers to the Lubicon Lake Band case as one that 'has been criticised as having fallen victim of the search for consensus'.[425]

---

[418]   The HRC has sometimes been more flexible in its Concluding Observations as part of the State reporting procedure. Possibly it feels less inhibited in its review of State reports than in its role of adjudicator. In 1999 it recommended 'that Canada's policy of requiring extinguishment of inherent or aboriginal rights be abolished because it violates Canada's human rights obligations under the ICCPR'. HRC Concluding Observations in relation to Canada, 7 April 1999, §8. It urged Canada to take 'decisive and urgent action' in order to fully implement the recommendations of the Royal Commission on Aboriginal Peoples, instituted by the Canadian government. Ibid. In 1996 this Royal Commission had noted that 'the actual reserve or community land base' of aboriginal people in Canada had shrunk by almost two third since 1867. "Aboriginal nations need much more territory to become economically, culturally and politically self-sufficient. If they cannot obtain a greater share of the lands and resources in this country, their institutions of self-government will fail". Ibid., quoting the 1996 recommendations of the Royal Commission on Aboriginal Peoples. The Royal Commission also noted that adequate lands and resources were necessary and without them 'they will be pushed to the edge of economic, cultural and political extinction'. Final Report of the Royal Commission on Aboriginal Peoples, 1996, CD-ROM version, record 8380 as cited in Amnesty International, 'Time is wasting', April 2003, p. 6. This general remark seems to apply to the *Lubicon* case as well and supports the reasoning behind the Committee's use of provisional measures in this case. After all, the HRC had noted that it used provisional measures '(i)n view of the seriousness of the author's allegations that the Lubicon Lake Band was at the verge of extinction'. HRC *Lubicon Lake Band*, 26 March 1990, §29.3.

[419]   An exception is De Zayas (2001), p. 113. "It is the author's conviction, that the negotiations that took place during the Committee's examination of the case ultimately contributed to some very interesting proposals and programs by the Canadian Government".

[420]   See Scheinin (2001), p. 166 and Anaya (1996), p. 165. On official responses and follow up in general see Chapters XVI and XVII.

[421]   Schmidt (1997), p. 340.

[422]   Anaya (1996), p. 166.

[423]   Ibid. See e.g. Opsahl (1992), p. 427, about the mandate and legal capacity to offer good offices and mediate dialogue.

[424]   De Feyter (2001), p. 156. De Feyter also notes that the HRC takes with one hand what it gave with the other. "Yes, there was a violation of Article 27 ICCPR, given 'historical inequities and

The fact that it declared the case admissible shows it still believed that a decision by a *domestic court* would be ineffective. However, in its decision on the merits it also seemed to suggest a remedy opting for the financial damages offered by the State, together with a certain demarcation of land, both of which the Band had rejected as unacceptable. Moreover the HRC did not follow up on its previous provisional measures.[426] If it indeed considers that only compensation is warranted in cases such as these, and nothing more, its use of provisional measures would be questionable.[427]

---

more recent developments', but No the Band could not stop the corporate exploitation of its territories, as long as the Canadian government provided sufficient compensation. The compensation already offered by the Canadian government, i.e. the reservation of an area of land and an amount of money, was sufficient, regardless of the Band refusal to accept the offer (footnote omitted)". De Feyter (2001), p. 156.

[425] Schmidt (1992), pp. 656-657. He noted about consensual procedures that 'as it is sufficient for one expert to oppose strongly a draft text otherwise acceptable to all the others, the search for consensus not only necessitates protracted consultations about a compromise text, it has also occasionally resulted in final decisions in which the close observer will find it difficult to follow the thread, or the logic of the legal argument'. See also on this issue Evatt (1998), p. 103, noting that the 'need to reach agreement means that the texts of the Committee's decisions are at times truncated and hard to understand'. Huff considers that the decision was positive to the extent that it could be interpreted 'as holding that the hunting and trapping culture of the Lubicon Cree constitutes an economic and social activity protected under Article 27'. Thus, 'environmentally based cultures can find some protection under the covenant'. Huff (1999), p. 188. He points out, however, that the Committee's decision 'approved of the very remedy rejected in 1989 by the Lubicon as guaranteeing a future of welfare dependence'. Huff (1999), p. 186. He specified the remedy the HRC could have suggested: "Theoretically, the HRC could have recommended that Canada take steps to encourage corporate withdrawal from Lubicon land. Such a recommendation would have been a strong affirmation of the basic link between degradation of the environment and resultant human rights abuses. It would have recognised that the only way to remedy such abuses is to restore the environment. However, any practical effect the HRC decision may have had was rendered moot by the HRC's actual recommended remedy: a small reserve and monetary resources for infrastructure development. This remedy does not provide for any reassertion of significant Lubicon control and thus seems to contemplate a future dependent upon federal welfare". Huff (1999), pp. 188-189.

[426] See Chapter XVIII (Follow-up). See also Chapter X (Culture).

[427] In a letter expressing the Band's discontent with the Committee's View Chief Ominayak pointed out that the Canadian Government 'initiated a major anti-Lubicon propaganda campaign claiming, among other things, that "the Human Rights Committee found the (take-it-or-leave-it) offer which Canada made to the (Lubicon people) is fair and reasonable and would meet any obligation Canada has under the International Covenant on Civil and Political Rights"'. Letter of 19 December 1991 to the HRC, on file with the author. This letter has also been posted on <nativenet.uthscsa.edu/archive/nl/9201/0028.html> (consulted on 13 March 2003). The sustainability test refers to the requirement of economic sustainability of the traditional way of life of indigenous peoples. After discussing this requirement of economic sustainability of the traditional way of life Scheinin has pointed out what *should* be the adequate remedy for a violation of Art. 27. He emphasised that it 'must be the termination of the interference, accompanied by a restitution of the conditions of the specific way of life'. Such a remedy 'should be compatible with the object of preserving and developing the specific way of life pursued by the community in question'. "The sustainability test requires that the form and modalities of compensation or other remedies for a violation of indigenous rights under Article 27 must be such as to serve the continued viability of the distinctive culture in question". He notes that the remedy could still 'partly be in the form of pecuniary compensation in cases where the economic hardship caused to the sustainability of the traditional economic activities cannot fully be

Thus far, this is the only provisional measure in an indigenous culture case in which the HRC later found a violation. It is unfortunate, however, that the protective measures it recommended on the merits do not seem to correspond with the aim of the provisional measures used pending the proceedings.

If the HRC indeed maintains its limited concept of measures required on the merits, taking the approach that only compensation is warranted and nothing more, its use of provisional measures in such cases is questionable.[428] There should be a correlation between the measures required pending and concluding the procedure. If the HRC would never refer to the obligation to permanently halt certain destructive developments, provisional measures that would require a temporary halt to such developments would not be of much use. In fact the provisional measures would then go further than the eventual obligations on the merits.[429]

Indeed, a form of reparation aimed at restoring the situation as much as possible or at least at preventing further degradation would fit in well with the Committee's present approach to reparation as referred to in the 2004 General Comment. It would also justify the type of provisional measure taken pending the proceedings.[430]

[footnote] restituted through measures that seek to restore the natural environment'. Scheinin (2001), p. 171. This illustrates the need for provisional measures pending the proceedings, to prevent such harm to the natural environment in the first place.

[428] In a letter expressing the Band's discontent with the Committee's View Chief Ominayak pointed out that the Canadian Government 'initiated a major anti-Lubicon propaganda campaign claiming, among other things, that "the Human Rights Committee found the (take-it-or-leave-it) offer which Canada made to the (Lubicon people) is fair and reasonable and would meet any obligation Canada has under the International Covenant on Civil and Political Rights"'. Letter of 19 December 1991 to the HRC, on file with the author. This letter was also posted on <nativenet.uthscsa.edu/archive/nl/9201/0028.html> (consulted on 13 March 2003).

[429] The HRC has sometimes been more flexible in its Concluding Observations as part of the State reporting procedure. Possibly it feels less inhibited in its review of State reports than in its role of adjudicator. In 1999 it recommended 'that Canada's policy of requiring extinguishment of inherent or aboriginal rights be abolished because it violates Canada's human rights obligations under the ICCPR'. HRC Concluding Observations in relation to Canada, 7 April 1999, §8. It urged Canada to take 'decisive and urgent action' in order to fully implement the recommendations of the Royal Commission on Aboriginal Peoples, instituted by the Canadian government. Ibid. In 1996 this Royal Commission had noted that 'the actual reserve or community land base' of aboriginal people in Canada had shrunk by almost two third since 1867. "Aboriginal nations need much more territory to become economically, culturally and politically self-sufficient. If they cannot obtain a greater share of the lands and resources in this country, their institutions of self-government will fail". Ibid., quoting the 1996 recommendations of the Royal Commission on Aboriginal Peoples. The Royal Commission also noted that adequate lands and resources were necessary and without them 'they will be pushed to the edge of economic, cultural and political extinction'. Final Report of the Royal Commission on Aboriginal Peoples, 1996, CD-ROM version, record 8380 as cited in Amnesty International, 'Time is wasting', April 2003, p. 6. This general remark seems to apply to the aforementioned *Lubicon* case as well and supports the reasoning behind the Committee's use of provisional measures in this case. After all, the HRC had noted that it used provisional measures '(i)n view of the seriousness of the author's allegations that the Lubicon Lake Band was at the verge of extinction'. HRC *Lubicon Lake Band*, 26 March 1990, §29.3.

[430] In the other situation in which the HRC clearly found a violation of the right to culture, although read into the right to family life and privacy (because of the French declaration to Article 27 ICCPR) it recommended an 'appropriate remedy'. In this case, *Hopu and Bessert*, the Committee noted that the State party was required to protect the petitioners' rights effectively and to ensure

5.4.7 Halt interrogation techniques and the expected obligations on the merits

In *Ireland* v. *UK* (1972) the European Commission considered that it could not meet the specific request for provisional measures made by Ireland. It did not address an argument raised by this State with regard to the right to an adequate remedy. In its original submission, Ireland pointed out that in domestic law the only remedy for violations of Article 3 ECHR would be the right to claim monetary damages. Such a remedy was insufficient, inadequate, and ineffective.[431] In its decision on the merits the Commission did find that the combined use of the five techniques in the cases before it constituted a practice of inhuman treatment and torture. Given the finding of both Commission and Court that these techniques constituted a violation of Article 3[432] and in light of the evolution in the practice of using provisional measures it may be expected that the present Court would in fact use provisional measures to halt continued use of such techniques pending the proceedings before it.[433]

Certain acts about to be committed are analogous to others that have already been found to violate the prohibition of torture or cruel treatment. It is submitted that in such cases the Court would be justified in using provisional measures also to halt such actions that it has not previously determined to be in violation of Article 3 ECHR. An example would be an interrogation method that appears to satisfy the criteria for illegal methods established in previous jurisprudence.

5.5 Halting executions and the expected obligations on the merits and reparations

5.5.1 Introduction

When it finds violations, the HRC always refers to the obligation to provide victims with an 'effective remedy, including compensation' and to the obligation 'to ensure that similar violations do not occur in the future'. These forms of reparation are compatible with those under traditional international law (e.g. assurances of non-repetition). It also suggests measures such as commutation (in death penalty cases) or even release. Other possibilities are a retrial respecting the principles of Article 14 ICCPR, investigation of the killing, torture or disappearance and prosecution of those responsible could fall under the traditional *restitutio in integrum* (restitution in kind), while the investigation and prosecution would at the same time also qualify as concrete assurances of non-repetition. Sometimes the wording 'an appropriate remedy, *including*' is used, sometimes 'an

---

       that similar violations did not occur in the future. Yet it did not specifically point out that this meant that the State was required, for instance, to put a stop to the completion of the hotel complex.

[431] EComHR *Ireland* v. *UK*, 5310/71, Yearbook 23 (1972), p. 100. It noted 'the only purported remedy available to a person subjected to the aforesaid treatment constituting a breach of Art. 3 of the Convention, within the domestic law of the respondent Government, is, in the case where the tort of assault has occurred, the right to claim monetary damages. Such a remedy is not an effective remedy, nor is it a sufficient or adequate remedy for the acts referred in this submission to the Commission, and constituting breaches of Art. 3 of the Convention. Further, in cases where no such tort or assault has occurred not even this purported remedy exists'.

[432] For the ECtHR judgment finding a violation of the prohibition of inhuman and degrading treatment see *Ireland* v. *UK*, 18 January 1978. The finding of a practice of inhuman and degrading treatment was sixteen votes to one, and the finding that it did not constitute a practice of torture was thirteen to four.

[433] In addition, of course, the Court's Art. 3 jurisprudence has evolved as well. See e.g. *Selmouni* v. *France*, 28 July 1999.

appropriate remedy *entailing* (...)' When the word 'including' is used, this is a minimum and more is warranted.

In *Bradshaw* v. *Barbados* (1994) the HRC referred to avoiding 'irreparable damage to the victim of the alleged violation'. This is an indication that the HRC aims to prevent irreparable harm to persons and that this harm is related to the alleged violation.[434]

In this section the focus is on the Committee's decision on cessation, assurances and reparation specifically in death penalty cases. Because of the assumption that provisional measures and such decisions are substantively interrelated, an examination of decisions by the HRC may shed light on the concept of provisional measures. As noted, its decisions on the merits, also indicating the remedy necessary to redress the violation, constitute practically the only public sources on its use of provisional measures.[435]

Pending the proceedings provisional measures aim to prevent the State from creating the impossibility of providing a remedy in case a violation will be found. The general legal obligations undertaken by States parties are closely related to the need to provide effective remedies in the event of a breach. In turn, the use of provisional measures in domestic proceedings and by the HRC itself is closely related to the right to an effective remedy.

At the same time, this section discusses how the Committee's decisions on cessation, assurances and reparation in death penalty cases have not necessarily clarified its attitude towards the concept of provisional measures. Yet in 2004 the Committee published a General Comment on Article 2 ICCPR, which did confirm the relation between provisional measures and reparation. Finally this section refers to the practice developed in this respect in the Inter-American system.

5.5.2 The rationale of the Committee's approach until its General Comment (2004)

Given the purpose of provisional measures the most important criterion for using them should not be the *prima facie* evidence of a violation, but the Rapporteur's expectation of the obligations the Committee would refer to or the form of reparation it would recommend *if* it would find a violation.

Initially the situation was clear. In 1989, in the first death penalty case it determined on the merits, the HRC found that the petitioners were entitled to a remedy 'the necessary prerequisite in the particular circumstances is the commutation of the sentence'.[436] Different from later Views,

---

[434] HRC *Peter Bradshaw* v. *Barbados*, 19 July 1994 (inadm.), §§2.9, 2.10, 4.2, 5.3; see also *Denzil Roberts* v. *Barbados*, 19 July 1994, §2.6, 2.7, 6.3.

[435] See Chapter II (Systems).

[436] HRC *Earl Pratt and Ivan Morgan* v. *Jamaica*, 6 April 1989. It found that the petitioners had been unable to appeal to the JCPC in the absence of a written judgment of the Court of Appeal. It also found a violation of Article 7 because of the delay of almost twenty hours from the time the stay of execution was granted to the time they were removed from their death cell. They were notified of the stay of execution only 45 minutes before the execution was originally scheduled. The authorities indeed commuted the sentence of Pratt and Morgan following the JCPC decision in their case. Ivan Morgan died on 28 April 1995. On this day an inmate sent a letter to the HRC informing it that Morgan was found dead in his cell that morning. He pointed out that Morgan had suffered a long illness and that he considered an autopsy should be done. He referred to stomach pain, an ulcer and 'insanity'. He questioned why he was in a cell and not in hospital. He argued that Morgan died because of Government negligence. If he had been placed under medical observation his quick medical deterioration would have been detected. He noted that an autopsy could not bring back Morgan's life, 'but we can find out if there was negligence on the part of the Government in order that such a crisis doesn't repeat itself on another prisoner'. Letter by an inmate in relation to Morgan's death, 28 April 1995 (on file with the author). The Jamaica

the Committee did not imply that only Article 14 violations result in a violation of Article 6. On the contrary, it stated that the death penalty 'should not be imposed in circumstances where there have been violations by the State party of *any of its obligations* under the Covenant' (emphasis added). It also explained that the necessary prerequisite in the particular circumstances was the commutation of the sentence.

Yet subsequently the HRC came to distinguish between death penalty cases involving fair trial claims and those without such claims. In death penalty cases where a violation of Article 14 (fair trial) and hence Article 6 (right to life) was found the HRC normally referred to 'remedies' ranging from release to commutation.[437] But when it found violations of other provisions it did not specify, as a prerequisite, that the petitioner should remain alive in order to enjoy the reparation to which he was entitled.

With regard to Article 14 the case *Ashby* v. *Trinidad and Tobago* (2002) is particularly noteworthy. In this case the petitioner had been executed despite the Committee's provisional measure. The HRC pointed out:

Council for Human Rights sent several letters to the Commissioner of Corrections, the Department of Correctional Services and the Commissioner of Police, requesting copies of the medical and autopsy reports. Several newspapers also reported that Morgan may not have been admitted in the hospital because of insufficient availability of guards. Letters of 28 April, 4 May and 29 May 1995; 'Dead inmate suffered from depression', *the Jamaica Herald*, 3 May 1995; 'Why was Morgan not admitted to hospital?-JCHR', *the Daily Observer*, 2 May 1995; 'Morgan said ill, depressed before his death', *the Sunday Gleaner*, 30 April 1995 and Eulalee Thompson, 'Doctors shunning prisons', *the Gleaner*, 11 and 12 April 1995 (on file with the author).

[437] 'In capital punishment cases, the obligation of States parties to observe rigorously all the guarantees for a fair trial set out in Art. 14 of the Covenant admits of no exception'. See e.g. HRC *Paul Kelly* v. *Jamaica*, 8 April 1991; *Aston Little* v. *Jamaica*, 1 November 1991; *Raphael Henry* v. *Jamaica*, 1 November 1991; *Leaford Smith* v. *Jamaica*, 31 March 1993 and *Lenford Hamilton* v. *Jamaica*, 21 March 1994; *Garfield and Andrew Peart* v. *Jamaica*, 19 July 1995; *Abdool Saleem Yasseen and Noel Thomas* v. *Republic of Guyana*, 30 March 1998; *Tony Jones* v. *Jamaica*, 6 April 1998; *Victor Domukovsky, Zaza Tsiklauri, Petre Gelbakhiani and Irakli Dokvadze* v. *Georgia*, 6 April 1998; *Irving Phillip* v. *Trinidad and Tobago*, 20 October 1998. The case *Smith and Stewart* v. *Jamaica*, 8 April 1999 illustrates the distinction the HRC appears to make between the need for reparation for a violation of Article 14 and reparation for other violations. In the case of Stewart the HRC found a violation of Articles 7 and 10(1) ICCPR, but in the case of Smith a violation of Article 14(3)(d). The effective remedy included compensation for both of them and release for Smith. *Errol Smith and Oval Stewart* v. *Jamaica*, 8 April 1999 (no provisional measures because their death sentences were already commuted prior to their initial communication). See also HRC *Daniel Pinto* v. *Trinidad and Tobago*, 20 July 1990. In this case the HRC had found violations of Articles 14(3)(d) and 6. Subsequently, he was not released, contrary to the recommendation of the HRC in 1990. Instead, in November 1992 his death sentence was commuted to life imprisonment with hard labour. He submitted a new case that year, on which the HRC decided in 1996. The HRC pointed out that 'to convey to the author that the prerogative of mercy would not be exercised and his early release denied because of his human rights complaints reveals a lack of humanity and amounts to treatment that fails to respect the author's dignity, in violation of article 10, paragraph 1'. *Daniel Pinto* v. *Trinidad and Tobago*, 16 July 1996, §§8.2-8.3. In this respect the HRC made a distinction between the specific entitlements of the petitioner on the one hand and the State's treaty obligation to implement its earlier View on the other. With regard to this case the petitioner was entitled to an appropriate remedy for the violation of Article 10. At the same time the State had a treaty obligation to implement its earlier View. In this light the HRC called upon it to release Pinto. As of 1995 the HRC introduced new phrases such as 'consider early release' or 're-trial' instead of release.

"Under article 2, paragraph 3, of the Covenant, Mr. Ashby would have been entitled to an effective remedy including, first and foremost, the preservation of his life. Adequate compensation must be granted to his surviving family".[438]

Yet in relation to death penalty cases where it found violations of Articles 7 (prohibition of torture and cruel treatment), 9 (right to habeas corpus, etc.) and 10 (right to humane treatment) it simply noted that 'an appropriate remedy' was required without specifying that this implied that the petitioner should remain alive.[439] Consequently, the State itself would not be inclined to consider this a prerequisite.

It is clear that in Article 14 cases (fair trial) without the provisional measure the required action on the merits, ranging from release to commutation, would have been made impossible. This explains as well why the HRC used provisional measures in such cases that were later found inadmissible or in which it found no violations.[440] It explains equally cases where Articles 14 and 7 were claimed, but where the HRC later found a violation of Article 7 only.[441] This case law

---

[438]   HRC *Glenn Ashby* v. *Trinidad and Tobago*, 21 March 2002. See also Chapter XVII (Official responses).

[439]   In cases in which the HRC found violations of Articles 7 and 10 it simply recommended an 'effective remedy'. The same applies to a case involving a finding of a violation of Article 9: HRC *Peter Grant* v. *Jamaica*, 22 March 1996; *Michael Freemantle* v. *Jamaica*, 24 March 2000 (commuted on an unspecified date) related to a violation of Article 9(3) as well, but in this case the HRC had also found violations of Articles 7 and 10(1)). Klein attached an individual opinion. He noted in relation to the remedy that the Committee should have expressly spelled out that apart from other possible appropriate remedies the petitioner was entitled to compensation according to Article 9(5) ICCPR.

[440]   Some of the petitioners specifically invoked Article 14 but the HRC eventually did not find a violation of that article. See e.g. HRC *Willard Collins* v. *Jamaica*, 1 November 1991. See also *Peter Blaine* v. *Jamaica*, 17 July 1994. In some cases the HRC did specify the remedy to a certain extent. In *Hylton* v. *Jamaica* (1994) the HRC found violations of Articles 7 and 10(1). At the time of the View the victim was awaiting execution. He was also receiving threats. On death threats see Chapter IX. The Committee pointed out that Jamaica was under an obligation to take effective measures to remedy the violations suffered, including the award of appropriate compensation, and 'to ensure that similar violations do not occur in the future'. "In particular, the State party is requested to complete the investigations into the threats and the ill-treatment to which Mr. Hylton has been subjected, and to punish those who are held to be responsible for his treatment". In other words, in this case the HRC does specify part of the remedy, but this specification does not imply that the State should preserve the life of the petitioner in the context of the death penalty. The conflicting language about the remedy that is required is worth noting: an 'obligation' to take effective measures, including an 'obligation' to award appropriate compensation and an 'obligation' to ensure that similar violations do not occur in the future. The Committee then specifies these obligations stating that, in particular, and now one would expect another obligatory term, the State party is 'requested' to complete the investigations and to punish those responsible. In other words the State party has an 'obligation' to award compensation and to ensure non-occurrence of similar violations and, *in particular*, it is 'requested' to investigate the occurrences and punish those found responsible. In *Linton* v. *Jamaica* (1992) the HRC found no violation of Article 14(1), but it did find violations of Articles 7 and 10(1). The State party was urged to take effective steps to investigate the ill treatment of the petitioner and to prosecute any persons that could be responsible and to grant the petitioner compensation. The HRC did not specify the remedy to include commutation. Again, this meant that the State would have the way clear for execution. *Carlton Linton* v. *Jamaica*, 22 October 1992.

[441]   See e.g. HRC *Dennie Chaplin* v. *Jamaica*, 2 November 1995; *Junior Leslie* v. *Jamaica*, 31 July 1998 (later commuted); *Barrington Campbell* v. *Jamaica*, 20 October 1998; *Anthony Leehong* v.

does not explain, however, the use of provisional measures in cases where the petitioners had claimed a violation of Articles 7, 9 and/or 10(1) but not of Article 14.[442] In such cases it recom-

---

Jamaica, 13 July 1999; death sentence was reclassified as non-capital in November 1994); *Michael Freemantle* v. *Jamaica*, 24 March 2000 and *Michael Robinson* v. *Jamaica*, 29 March 2000 (commutation in 1997). In some cases the HRC did declare admissible these Article 14 claims, although eventually it did not find a violation. See e.g. HRC *Ian Chung* v. *Jamaica*, 9 April 1998. In other words, given the *possibility* of a finding of a violation of Article 6 (right to life) because of a finding of a violation of Article 14 (fair trial), the use of provisional measures pending the proceedings was clearly justified. In addition, as the State often subsequently commuted the death sentences, the fact that the HRC did not refer to commutation, retrial or release does not *necessarily* imply that it would have failed to do so in cases in which the petitioners were still awaiting execution. In one case it seems that the HRC considered Article 14 *proprio motu* and decided not to declare it inadmissible *ratione materiae* to allow the possibility of a finding of a violation requiring commutation under its case law. At the same time the possibility of such finding seemed remote from the beginning. In *Barrett and Sutcliffe* v. *Jamaica* (1992) the petitioner only invoked Articles 7 and 10 but the HRC considered that the complaint also related to Article 14 ICCPR. The role this inclusion played pending the proceedings before the HRC was as follows. The HRC obliquely noted that 'although counsel only invokes a violation of article 7 of the International Covenant of Civil and Political Rights, it transpires from some of the submissions that they also allege violations of article 14'. In 1989 it declared the communications admissible because the pursuit of domestic remedies had been unreasonably prolonged. It did not examine the claims *ratione materiae* for purposes of admissibility. Following this, it requested additional information from the State party in relation to the allegations under Articles 7 and 10, but not Article 14. On the merits, the HRC considered the Article 14 claim and noted that the petitioners had not corroborated the allegations that their identification parade was unfair, that the preparations for Barrett's defence were inadequate and that Sutcliffe had been denied access to counsel before his formal indictment. Hence it did not find a violation of Article 14 ICCPR, considering that counsel had not put forward any claims under that article. HRC *Randolph Barrett and Clyde Sutcliffe* v. *Jamaica*, 30 March 1992 (on 16 May 1995 his sentence was commuted to life imprisonment). Eventually, the HRC found a violation of Articles 7 and 10(1) in respect of the beatings and injuries suffered by one of the petitioners. Again this required 'an appropriate remedy' without specification as to commutation. With this the HRC removed the obstacle to the execution of the petitioners. This seems strange because the petitioner is unlikely to enjoy any remedy upon his execution. In this light the wording used seems hardly appropriate. In HRC *Balkissoon Soogrim* v. *Trinidad and Tobago*, 8 April 1993, the petitioner was awaiting execution and the claim included Article 14. Initially, all claims were declared admissible, but upon review the HRC limited this to those based on Articles 7 and 10. Apparently it *maintained* its provisional measure. Following this, it found violations of Articles 7 and 10(1). The petitioner was 'entitled to a remedy, including appropriate compensation'. The View does not refer to the use of provisional measures, but its use appears from the file. The petitioner was still awaiting execution at the time of publication of the View. Only subsequently his sentence was commuted to life imprisonment. This was done in light of the JCPC judgment in *Pratt and Morgan* (letter of 18 February 1994 by the Permanent Mission, on file with the author).

[442] In several cases in which petitioners *were* still awaiting execution the HRC found violations of Articles 7 and 10 for which it simply noted that 'an appropriate remedy' was required. It did not specify that it was a prerequisite to the enjoyment of any type of reparation not to execute the persons involved. In the approach of the State concerned (Jamaica) the fact that the HRC did not mention commutation as part of the remedy meant that its View did not block the execution of the victims. All the same, pending the proceedings the Committee had used provisional measures to halt their execution. In HRC *Dwayne Hylton* v. *Jamaica* and *Ramcharan Bickaroo* v. *Trinidad and Tobago* the claim only involved Articles 7 and 10. Nevertheless, in 1993 and 1994 the

mends 'an appropriate remedy' without specification, which the addressee State may interpret as a licence to kill the petitioner. In other words, in such cases the rationale of the use of provisional measures must lie elsewhere. It may be that the Committee always uses provisional measures when an execution is threatened, without relating this decision to the possible findings of a violation and without looking at the possible remedy in such cases. This could be argued to be in line with its customary statement at the end of its communications (Notes Verbales) to the State referring to provisional measures, that an 'expression of its views on interim measures does not imply a determination on the merits of the communication'. On the other hand, if the Committee would link the provisional measure to the possible remedy, this would still not imply a determination on the merits of the communication, since there are also many Article 14 cases where the HRC took a provisional measure but eventually did not find a violation.[443]

The argument has been made that the HRC uses provisional measures in cases not mentioning Article 14 claims because a discussion on this article was raised *proprio motu* in discussions within the Committee but eventually dropped. This discussion was simply not mentioned in the decision on the merits.[444] This explanation seems strained as this discussion obviously is not part of the material before the Special Rapporteur on New Communications taking a decision on the use of provisional measures.[445]

It seems more likely that some Rapporteurs, especially abolitionists, tended to always use provisional measures, even if they did not expect the determination of a violation nor a finding that the remedy for a violation would include commutation. They may have decided to take provisional measures automatically in all death penalty cases.

In my view this would constitute an inappropriate use of this tool. The Special Rapporteur faces the choice to decide whether or not provisional measures are warranted given the Committee's case law on the State obligations upon a finding of a violation in death penalty cases, or the

---

Committee did take provisional measures in these cases. By this time its case law about the relationships between violation of Article 14 and commutation or release on the one hand and Articles 7 and 10 and an unspecified remedy on the other was already evolving. Given the fact that not only the findings, but also the claim involved Arts 7 and 10 alone, it is not clear why the HRC took provisional measures. After all, it must have been clear that any eventual remedy would not specify that the petitioner should remain alive. See *Dwayne Hylton* v. *Jamaica*, 16 July 1996, (provisional measure of 28 November 1994, death sentence commuted in 1995 by the Governor General upon advice of the Jamaican Privy Council; no violation Article 14) and *Ramcharan Bickaroo* v. *Trinidad and Tobago*, 29 October 1997 (provisional measure (no date); subsequent to his submission of 5 October 1993 his death sentence was commuted to life imprisonment by the President of Trinidad and Tobago on 31 December 1993, following the judgment of the JCPC of 2 November 1993 in the case of *Pratt and Morgan* v. *Attorney General of Jamaica*; no violation found). See also HRC *A. H.* v. *Trinidad and Tobago*, 31 October 1990 (inadm.).

[443] See also Chapter I, section 3.5 discussing prejudgment.

[444] Suggestion by Sir Nigel Rodley, Geneva, April 2003. In this respect HRC *Randolph Barrett and Clyde Sutcliffe* v. *Jamaica*, 30 March 1992, discussed in Chapter III (Executions) may serve as an example. Indeed the *proprio motu* inclusion of Article 14 in the initial discussion of *Randolph Barrett and Clyde Sutcliffe* v. *Jamaica*, 2 March 1992 justified the use of provisional measures ex post, whether this inclusion was intended as such or not. After all in this case the reference to Art. 14 was published in the decision on the merits.

[445] The Special Rapporteur normally decides to transmit a case and use provisional measures on the basis of a case summary prepared by the Secretariat. This summary generally refers to the claims introduced by the petitioner. The fact that later in the proceedings members of the Committee, or the Rapporteur assigned particularly to that case, decide to introduce Article 14 into the discussion *proprio motu* does not necessarily have a bearing on the Special Rapporteur's use of provisional measures earlier on.

likelihood of a change in its case law. Of course it would be tragic if the jurisprudence would indeed change and the petitioner who triggered this has already been executed by then. In this respect, it seems that the Special Rapporteur usually takes the approach of 'better be safe than sorry'. Nevertheless if he would decide to take provisional measures based on his belief that the Committee's jurisprudence should change, in a situation where this is very unlikely, this may not be a wise approach.

In practice the number of cases in which provisional measures were used when there was no Article 14 claim is limited, but generally speaking it would not enhance the goodwill of the addressee State if provisional measures would routinely be used also in cases where in the end the Committee does not recommend commutation of the sentence. More importantly, the Committee's role should not be to postpone death and prolong suffering until it publishes a finding on the merits that will require an unspecified form of reparation, but *not* commutation. A clear distinction should be made between taking provisional measures on the one hand and trying to change the Human Rights Committee's jurisprudence on the other. Provisional measures should not be used as statements in a quest to bring about such changes.[446]

Until the HRC is willing to clearly decide that violations of Arts 7 and 10(1) require commutation just as much as violations of Article 14, it is indeed necessary, for purposes of provisional measures, for the petitioner to claim a violation of Article 14.

The situation would be different if the HRC would either clearly establish that any finding of a violation in a death penalty case required an appropriate remedy the prerequisite for which would be that the petitioner would be allowed to remain alive.

In the alternative, it would be different if the HRC would clearly indicate that it uses provisional measures in all death penalty cases in order to guarantee the integrity of the OP by ensuring that both parties to the conflict can properly present their claims. After all, it is a plausible argument that it would never be acceptable to execute someone pending a case because that would cause irreparable harm to the proceedings under the OP. Once executed, the possible vindication of his rights would be of limited importance to the petitioner. Another purpose of provisional measures to halt execution could thus be to serve the interests of the proceedings before the Committee. If the petitioner is executed during the course of the proceedings of the Committee it would be difficult to properly hear both sides in a balanced examination (*audiatur et alteram pars*). In other words, it would obstruct equality of arms and, therefore, the proper examination of the case. If this specific reason for the use of provisional measures applies, however, the HRC should make it clear from the outset. In any case this may be easier to argue in cases already pending before the Committee rather than in those declared inadmissible but open to review, such as *A.H.* v. *Trinidad and Tobago*.[447] Nevertheless, the HRC could have justified its decision to *maintain* provisional measures with the argument of protecting the integrity of the ICCPR and the OP. After all executing petitioners immediately upon exhaustion of domestic remedies would prevent them from taking up their right to resort to the OP. This way the State would evade its obligations under the Covenant and the OP. Nevertheless, preventing irreparable harm to the procedure only seems a rather artificial explanation for the use of provisional measures in a death penalty case.

The most appropriate would be a clear decision on obligations on the merits and reparation in death penalty cases. In cases in which a violation of the right to life had been found reparation may consist of life as a right or of life as a remedy. Life as a *right* refers to the 'continued enjoyment' of this right. This would be required in the context of a finding of a violation of Article 14 ICCPR. Life as a *form of reparation* refers to the specific situation of a person sentenced to death, who has been the victim of torture or ill treatment in violation of Articles 7 and 10 ICCPR. In this

---

[446] Of course, if the HRC explicitly uses provisional measures in the interest of the proceedings, it does make sense to use them in Articles 7, 9, or 10 cases as well.

[447] HRC *A. H.* v. *Trinidad and Tobago*, 31 October 1990 (inadm.).

light it is argued that full rehabilitation requires commutation of the death sentence since enjoyment of other forms of compensation becomes impossible if the person is executed. In other words, life is a precondition for the enjoyment of an adequate form of reparation.

Linked to the idea that life is a precondition to the enjoyment of any remedy, provisional measures are essential as well. Such measures halting the execution of a death sentence are crucial to ensure the commutation as a form of reparation in these circumstances, whether they preserve a right in itself or preserve instead the possibility for reparation for other violations. Without them the eventual determination of the case would be deprived of any sense. Obviously a return to the previous situation is not possible once the execution has already taken place.

Thus far the HRC has not taken the above approach to life as a form of – or precondition to the enjoyment of any form of – reparation. The case law of the HRC seems to point to the conclusion that only when an execution would result in a *new* violation, the remedy is commutation or release. In other words, the 'appropriate remedy, including commutation' is not so much a remedy for a past violation, but rather the action required for preventing a new violation (related to this past violation).

Yet pending the proceedings the HRC has used provisional measures even in cases in which Article 14 was not claimed, although it knew that if it would find violations the petitioner would nevertheless be executed, due to its approach towards reparation in Articles 7 and 10 cases.[448] This means that the use of provisional measures in those cases made little sense because in its final decision the Committee would not recommend the State to continue to prevent irreparable harm to the person.

There are, however, indications of a change in the approach of the Committee in that it has spoken of commutation in relation to Articles 7 and 10 as well, although in these cases it did not refer to an *entitlement* to the preservation of their life, but simply *recommended* commutation.[449] The individual opinions of one member of the Committee may be a precursor to a possible change in the Committee's approach on the issue of reparation: 'when a person has been sentenced to death in violation of the Covenant or treated contrary to the provisions of the Covenant while awaiting execution, the remedy should include an irreversible decision not to implement the death

---

[448]   See e.g. HRC *A. H.* v. *Trinidad and Tobago*, 31 October 1990 (inadm.); *Dwayne Hylton* v. *Jamaica*, 16 July 1996 and *Ramcharan Bickaroo* v. *Trinidad and Tobago*, 29 October 1997. In *A. H.* v. *Trinidad and Tobago*, 31 October 1990 (inadm.) the HRC declared a petition inadmissible based on non-exhaustion, with the possibility to deal with it again upon exhaustion. The petitioner could request a review of the inadmissibility decision once he had completed domestic remedies. However, the claims under Article 14 did not raise *prima facie* issues under Article 14 or they were insufficiently substantiated. It decided to maintain the provisional measure pending review of admissibility, upon exhaustion of domestic remedies for the Article 10 claim. Yet this may be explained by the fact that in 1990 the HRC had not yet determined the type of reparation required for ill treatment of persons sentenced to death. Its members may have assumed that the prerequisite for any 'appropriate remedy' was commutation. In the alternative, its use of provisional measures could also mean that it made no connection between provisional and remedial measures and simply aimed to prevent, for the time being, irreparable harm to the person involved even if its jurisprudence did not allow it to recommend preventing such harm as part of its decision on the merits.

[449]   See HRC *Stephens* v. *Jamaica*, 18 October 1995 (further consideration by Parole Board); *Nicholas Henry* v. *Jamaica*, 20 October 1998 (consideration for early release). See also *Brown* v. *Jamaica*, 23 March 1999 and *R. S.* v. *Trinidad and Tobago*, 2 April 2002 (appropriate remedy for violations of Articles 7 and 10(1) were appropriate medical and psychiatric care and improvement of conditions of detention in accordance with Article 10 or release. Had the petitioner still been under sentence of death, the reference to release may be expected to have implied commutation).

penalty'.[450] The preservation of life was required under the entitlement to an effective remedy under Article 2(3) ICCPR.[451]

Moreover, in 2004 the HRC acknowledged, in its General Comment on Article 2, that provisional measures and the right to a remedy (including the right to reparation) are related.[452] One might expect that it will continue in this direction and recommend commutation in relation to violations other than those of Article 14. In fact, now that it has acknowledged a relationship between provisional measures and the remedy it should consider the preservation of life a prerequisite for the enjoyment of *any* form of reparation for a violation of the ICCPR.

5.5.3 HRC General Comment on the right to an effective remedy (Art. 2 ICCPR)

In 2004, in its General Comment on Article 2 ICCPR, the HRC finally confirmed the relationship between the right to 'an effective remedy' and the use of provisional measures.[453] The fact that the HRC has now specifically acknowledged the relation with the eventual form of reparation will likely improve its practice of using provisional measures and indicating the obligations required, at least in death penalty cases.[454]

In its General Comment the Committee noted that the legal obligation of States under Article 2(1), the obligation to respect and ensure the rights recognised by the Covenant, is both nega-

---

[450] Individual opinion HRC member Scheinin, *Deon Mc Taggart* v. *Jamaica*, 31 March 1998. See also his individual opinions in *Neville Lewis* v. *Jamaica*, 17 July 1997 and *Terrence Sahadeo* v. *Guyana*, 1 November 2001.

[451] Individual opinion HRC member Scheinin *Deon Mc Taggart* v. *Jamaica*, 31 March 1998 and *Terrence Sahadeo* v. *Guyana*, 1 November 2001.

[452] See the next heading.

[453] HRC General Comment 31 on Article 2 ICCPR: the nature of the general legal obligation imposed on States parties to the Covenant, 29 March 2004, §19. In 1977 Committee member Opsahl already made a connection with Article 2. During the initial discussion on the Rules of Procedure Committee member Movchan (USSR) did not agree with 'the provisions contained in rule 86' (the Rule on provisional measures) because they went 'beyond the scope' of the OP. Opsahl responded to this by stating that they should consider the question of provisional measures to avoid irreparable harm 'in the context of the Covenant and the Optional Protocol as a whole'. The suggestion that the procedure provided for in Rule 86 was outside the scope of the Covenant was 'unacceptable' in light of the States parties' undertaking in Article 2(2) ICCPR. Summary records of the meetings of the first session, thirteenth meeting, 29 March 1977 and seventeenth meeting, 31 March 1977, Yearbook of the HRC 1977-1978, Vol. I, CCPR/1, pp. 44-46 and 54. Moreover, in 1996, during the public meeting convened following the execution of Glenn Ashby, Committee member Evatt emphasised the obligation of the State to ensure an effective remedy for any person whose rights have been violated (Article 2 ICCPR). By executing a petitioner, she noted, a State fails to guarantee this right. Committee member Higgins equally referred to Article 2(3)(a) and the undertaking by the State to ensure an effective remedy. "In the present case, Mr. Ashby had been executed, and the Committee had been prevented from determining whether the State party had violated the provisions of the Covenant. Given those two facts, the Committee could justifiably conclude on the merits that Mr. Ashby had not had any remedy. It was precisely to avoid a situation of that sort that the Committee had adopted rule 86". Summary Record of the 1352nd meeting: Trinidad and Tobago, 26 July 1994, CCPR/C/SR.1352, 31 July 1996, §§15 and 24.

[454] As discussed in section 4.6.2 its case law until this General Comment was lacking in clarity on the relation between the two concepts.

tive and positive in nature.[455] Under Article 2(2) States must 'take the necessary steps to give effect to the Covenant rights in the domestic order'.[456] This 'provides the overarching framework within which the rights specified in the Covenant are to be promoted and protected'.[457] Article 2(3) ICCPR requires that individuals have accessible and effective remedies to vindicate their Covenant rights.[458] In order to comply with the obligation to provide an effective remedy, an obligation 'central to the efficacy' of Article 2(3), States must make reparation to victims.[459] Apart from the explicit reparation required by Articles 9(5) and 14(6) ICCPR the HRC 'considers that the Covenant generally entails appropriate compensation'.[460] It notes that 'where appropriate reparation can involve restitution, rehabilitation and measures of satisfaction, such as public apologies, public memorials, guarantees of non-repetition and changes in relevant laws and practices, as well as bringing to justice the perpetrators of human rights violations'.[461]

Moreover, the obligation of non-repetition is integral to Article 2. Without this the purposes of the Covenant would be defeated. This is why the HRC often emphasises, in its decisions on the merits, the need to take measures to avoid a recurrence of the violation. This reminder on avoiding a recurrence goes 'beyond a victim-specific remedy' and may require changes in the laws of practices of the State in question to ensure that a similar violation does not recur with regard to other possible victims.[462]

Obviously a reservation to the obligation to respect and ensure the rights in the ICCPR on a non-discriminatory basis would be unacceptable. Equally it would be unacceptable to indicate, through a reservation to Article 2(3) ICCPR, the intent to provide no remedies for human rights violations. After all, 'guarantees such as these are an integral part of the structure of the Covenant and underpin its efficacy'.[463]

The use of provisional measures by the HRC is based on the right to an effective remedy as well. The HRC pointed out that 'in certain circumstances' the right to an effective remedy may require States parties 'to provide for and implement provisional or interim measures to avoid continuing violations and to endeavour to repair at the earliest possible opportunity any harm that may have been caused by such violations'.[464] It added that the use of provisional measures in *domestic* proceedings is equally based on the right to an effective remedy. The phrase 'provide for' provisional measures, used in the General Comment on Article 2 ICCPR, seems to refer to taking such measures on the basis of domestic law without instigation by the HRC, and the term 'implement' seems to refer to those provisional measures indicated by the HRC.

In sum, it is argued that a provisional measure cannot go further than the eventual form of reparation could. Upon finding a violation the obligation on the merits or form of reparation required should continue to prevent irreparable harm to persons. If the eventual obligation signifies less than the preservation of life the provisional measures used pending the proceedings do

---

[455] HRC General Comment on Article 2 ICCPR, the nature of the general legal obligation imposed on States parties to the Covenant, 29 March 2004, §6 (negative in the sense of 'refraining from').

[456] Id., §13.

[457] Id., §5.

[458] Id., §15.

[459] Id., §16.

[460] Ibid.

[461] Ibid.

[462] HRC General Comment on Article 2 ICCPR, §17.

[463] See HRC General Comment 24 on reservations to the ICCPR or the Optional Protocols, 4 November 1994, §§9 and 11, as confirmed in General Comment 31 on Article 2 ICCPR, 29 March 2004, §5.

[464] HRC General Comment 31 on Article 2 ICCPR: the nature of the general legal obligation imposed on States parties to the Covenant, 29 March 2004, §19.

not truly prevent irreparable harm to persons. They could only be said to prevent harm to the procedure.

In my view the HRC should follow the course it seems to have set by recommending commutation in all future death penalty cases finding a violation of any of the articles of the ICCPR. In fact, this would simply confirm what it already set out in *Pratt and Morgan* v. *Jamaica* (1989).[465] This way there would be a relation between the provisional measures and the eventual reparation required so that provisional measures would truly serve to protect against irreparable harm to persons.

5.5.4 The Inter-American practice regarding obligations on the merits and reparation in death penalty cases

The Inter-American Commission has been very precise in its motivation of its precautionary measures. "It based its request on the fact that if the State were to execute (...) before such an assessment, any later decision of the Commission would be ineffective in providing potential remedies and that this would cause him irreparable harm".[466]

The motivation used here seems to be implicit in all its requests to stay an execution. This is interesting because this statement implies, in my view correctly, that whenever the Commission would find a violation, the remedy provided would be ineffective if the State would still be allowed to execute the petitioner. As discussed, the HRC seems to have thought differently, at least for a considerable period, as in some cases it recommended 'an effective remedy, including commutation' while in other cases it merely recommended 'an effective remedy', knowing that in such cases the State would proceed with the execution.

In 2001 the Inter-American Commission clarified its use of precautionary measures by pointing out that an execution would make ineffective any eventual decision 'in terms of future compensation and [the prisoner] would suffer irreparable harm'.[467] In requesting the Court to order provisional measures the Inter-American Commission also argued that 'the execution of the alleged victims prior to the completion of these processes would render any eventual recommendations or judgments moot in terms of the efficacy of potential remedies, such as commutation of their death sentences'.[468]

In practice, apart from commutation, in some cases the Commission went further in its petitions on the merits, requesting the Court to order a re-trial in accordance with due process or, if that were not possible, release.[469] It has noted that, to the extent possible, the State must reestablish 'the status quo ante which in the present case could be achieved by commuting the

---

[465] HRC *Earl Pratt and Ivan Morgan* v. *Jamaica*, 6 April 1989.

[466] See e.g. CIDH Annual Report 2000, §§45-46.

[467] See e.g. CIDH Arnold Ramlogan, Case P12.355, 22 January 2001; Beemal Ramnarace, Case P12.377, 19 April 2001; Takoor Ramcharan, Case P0197/2001, 11 May 2001; Alladin Mohamed, Case P0842/2001, 18 December 2001. In *Roodal* v. *Trinidad and Tobago*, 10 October 2001 (adm.) the Commission noted that it used precautionary measures 'contemporaneously with the transmission of the pertinent parts' of his petition, on 13 November 2000. It noted that this request was made on the basis that if the State were to execute him before the Commission had had the opportunity to examine his case 'any eventual decision would be rendered moot in terms of available remedies' and he would suffer irreparable harm. In none of these cases did the State respond. CIDH Annual Report 2001, §§52-55.

[468] IACHR *Boyce and Joseph* v. *Barbados*, 25 November 2004, 3rd 'Having seen' clause.

[469] See e.g. IACHR *Benjamin et al.*, 1 September 2001 (preliminary objections), §14B.

complainant's death sentence and adjusting the domestic law of Trinidad and Tobago accordingly'.[470]

While the Commission was still dealing with the cases on the merits it had already requested the Court to order provisional measures. In August 1998 the Court indeed ordered such measures to halt their executions.[471] In its reports about the cases of the eight persons discussed in the Court's Order of August 1998 the State argued that it had followed due process and that 'the Commission would still have other options available to compensate any violations it finds subsequent to an execution'.[472] Apparently the State does not subscribe to the traditional approach to the right to reparation. This traditional approach has a marked preference for *restitutio in integrum*. Instead the State believed it could go ahead with an execution pending the proceedings before the Commission. It argued that even when the Commission would find that the State had violated the Convention – something the Commission had in fact done already in the case Briggs – it would be sufficient to award monetary damages or other forms of compensation, *following* the execution.

In 2002 the Inter-American Court found violations in the death penalty cases that were brought before it by the Commission to deal with on the merits[473] and it decided on a variety of reparations. It referred to its earlier jurisprudence that Article 63(1) ACHR is the codification of a rule of customary law constituting 'one of the fundamental principles of contemporary international law on State responsibility'.[474] When the State is responsible for an illicit act, it has an immediate responsibility for the breach of the international norm involved, 'together with the subsequent duty to make reparations and put an end to the consequences of said violation'.[475] It emphasised that such reparation required full restitution (*restitutio in integrum*), whenever possible, consisting of 'restoring the situation that existed before the violation occurred'.[476] The Court also pointed out that a violating State cannot invoke provisions of its domestic law to modify or

---

[470] IACHR *Benjamin et al.*, 1 September 2001 (preliminary objections), §14C. See also IACHR *Hilaire, Constantine & Benjamin et al.*, 21 June 2002 (merits & reparations), Operative paragraphs 8-11, in particular 11: 'the State should abstain from executing, in all cases, regardless of the results of the new trials'. With regard to the case of Joey Ramiah, who had been executed despite the Court's provisional measure, the Commission noted that this was no longer possible and that the consequences of the violations must be remedied by other means. In his case the Commission petitioned the Court to order the State to provide adequate compensation to his next of kin.

[471] The Commission can request the Court's intervention in such cases, based on Article 63(2) ACHR. See Chapter II (Systems). See further Chapters III (Executions) and XVII (Official responses).

[472] IACHR *James et al.* cases, Order of 29 August 1998 (reports of 5 June, 30 June, 29 June, 8 July, 15 July and 28 July 1998).

[473] Violations of Articles 4(1), 4(2), 4(6), 5(1), 5(2), 7(5), 8, and 25.

[474] IACHR *Hilaire, Constantine and Benjamin et al. v. Trinidad and Tobago*, Judgment of 21 June 2002, §202.

[475] Ibid., referring to *Cantoral Benavides* case, Judgment of 3 December 2001 (reparations), §40, *Cesti Hurtado* case, Judgment of 31 May 2001 (reparations), §35, *Villagrán Morales et al.* (*'Street Children'* case), Judgment of 26 May 2001 (reparations), §62.

[476] "When this is not possible, as in the present Case, it is the task of this international Tribunal to order the adoption of a series of measures that, in addition to guaranteeing respect for the rights violated, ensure that the damage resulting from the infractions is repaired, and order the payment of an indemnity as compensation for the harm caused in that case". IACHR *Hilaire, Constantine and Benjamin et al. v. Trinidad and Tobago*, Judgment of 21 June 2002, §203, referring to *Cantoral Benavides* case, Judgment of 3 December 2001 (reparations), §41, *Durand and Ugarte*, Judgment of 3 December 2001 (reparations), §25 and *Barrios Altos*, Judgment of 30 November 2001 (reparations), §25.

ignore altogether its obligation to make reparations. This obligation 'is regulated in all its aspects (scope, nature, modalities, and designation of beneficiaries) by international law'.[477] 'Reparations,' it noted, 'consist of those measures necessary to make the effects of the violations committed disappear'.[478]

Following these general remarks about reparation, the Court ordered the State to abstain from applying its law dating from 1925 that made the death penalty mandatory for all cases of murder irrespective of the individual circumstances.[479] It determined that in the cases of the 31 petitioners that were still alive, the State was to order a retrial applying the new criminal legislation resulting from the reform of the law of 1925. The Advisory Committee on the Power of Pardon was to resubmit the cases of the victims to the executive authority competent to render a decision in the mercy procedure. Implementing these obligations, however, was not sufficient. In the exercise of the authority conferred upon it by Article 63(1) ACHR it held 'on the grounds of equity, that the State, regardless of the outcome of the new trials (...) and independently of whether the new trials are actually carried out, should refrain from executing' the 31 persons involved.[480]

---

[477] IACHR *Hilaire, Constantine and Benjamin et al.* v. *Trinidad and Tobago*, Judgment of 21 June 2002, §203, referring to *Cantoral Benavides*, Judgment of 3 December 2000 (reparations), §41, *Cesti Hurtado*, Judgment of 30 May 2001 (reparations), §35 and *Villagrán Morales et al.* ('Street Children' case), Judgment of 26 May 2001 (reparations), §61.

[478] IACHR *Hilaire, Constantine and Benjamin et al.* v. *Trinidad and Tobago*, Judgment of 21 June 2002, §205, referring to *Cantoral Benavides*, Judgment of 3 December 2000 (reparations), §36, *Cesti Hurtado*, Judgment of 30 May 2001 (reparations), §36 and *Villagrán Morales et al.* ('Street Children' case), Judgment of 26 May 2001 (reparations), §63. Another general form of reparation was the obligation to improve the conditions of detention. The Court considered it pertinent and necessary to direct the State to bring its prison conditions in line with international human rights law. IACHR *Hilaire, Constantine and Benjamin et al.* v. *Trinidad and Tobago*, Judgment of 21 June 2002, §217.

[479] Because of its finding that the way in which the crime of murder was penalised in the Offences Against the Person Act was 'in and of itself' a violation of the ACHR, the Court held that the State should refrain from future application of this Act and, 'within a reasonable time, bring the law into compliance with the American Convention and other international human rights norms, in accordance with Article 2, so that the respect and enjoyment of the rights to life, personal integrity, a fair trial and due process embodied in the Convention are guaranteed'. The Court was indeed very precise in its directions, establishing that 'the legislative reforms contemplated should include the introduction of different categories (criminal classes) of murder, in keeping with the wide range of differences in the gravity of the act, so as to take into account the particular circumstances of both the crime and the offender'. It also specified that the State should introduce a 'system of graduated levels' ensuring 'that the severity of the punishment is commensurate with the gravity of the act and the criminal culpability of the accused'. It pointed out that this form of reparation was 'consistent with the position which this Court has taken in the past'. IACHR *Hilaire, Constantine and Benjamin et al.* v. *Trinidad and Tobago*, Judgment of 21 June 2002, §213.

[480] IACHR *Hilaire, Constantine and Benjamin et al.* v. *Trinidad and Tobago*, Judgment of 21 June 2002, §215. In his Concurring Opinion Judge de Roux-Rengifo pointed out that while these 31 persons had not yet been deprived of their lives, Article 4(2) had nevertheless been violated because of the application of a domestic law that led to the imposition of the death penalty for crimes that do not fall into the category of 'most serious'. The Court had 'abstained from evaluating the possibility that some of those condemned to death could have committed crimes which are considered "most serious," because the aforementioned law has been applied to all of them, and this necessitates, without question, a declaration of a violation of Article 2 of the

5.5.5 Conclusion on halting executions and the expected obligations on the merits and reparation

The Inter-American Commission has made explicit its motivation for precautionary measures to halt an execution by pointing out that if the State were to execute the petitioner before an assessment on the merits could take place, any later decision of the Commission would be 'ineffective in providing potential remedies and that this would cause him irreparable harm'.[481] In addition the Inter-American Court has made clear that once a violation has been found, the obligations of the State include as a minimum a 'permanent injunction' against the execution of the victims.[482]

The HRC has been less clear in its case law on this issue. In cases involving a finding of a violation of the right to a fair trial (Article 14 ICCPR), and thereby a violation of the right to life (Article 6 ICCPR), it always indicates that the State party is under an obligation to provide the victim with an effective remedy, 'including commutation'. Yet in the past, in its decisions on the merits, it has failed to refer to the obligation not to execute the victims of violations of the ICCPR not involving Article 6.

An unequivocal statement by the HRC that the pre-requisite of any form of compensation for any type of violation of the ICCPR is that the petitioner remains alive, would provide a convincing rationale for the use of provisional measures in all death penalty cases.[483] An execution would then deprive the petitioner of the most essential form of reparation and would result in irreparable harm to persons.

5.6 Conclusion on the relation of provisional measures to cessation, assurances of non-repetition and reparations

As discussed more closely in the Conclusion to this Part (Part II Purpose) the harm to be prevented pending the proceedings and subsequent to the finding of a violation should be harm to persons rather than just harm to the claim.

Convention'. Concurring Opinion of Judge de Roux-Rengifo, IACHR *Hilaire, Constantine and Benjamin et al.* v. *Trinidad and Tobago*, Judgment of 21 June 2002. By way of reparation for immaterial harm, the Court ordered Trinidad to pay the widow of Joey Ramiah $50,000 USD to support her in bringing up their son and assist in his education. It also ordered the State to pay his mother $10,000 USD. In addition, as reimbursement for the expenses incurred in bringing the case before the Court, the State had to pay the representatives of the victims the sum of $13,000 USD. Furthermore the Court referred to earlier jurisprudence on the general obligations of the State under Article 2 ACHR. These obligations include the adoption of measures to suppress laws and practices in violation of the Convention and the adoption of laws to effectively protect its guarantees. Under customary international law States must introduce the necessary modifications to their domestic law to ensure compliance with the obligations assumed under the human rights treaties they ratified. This general obligation, laid down in Article 2 ACHR, implies that the measures of domestic law must be effective: the principle of *effet utile*. IACHR *Hilaire, Constantine and Benjamin et al.* v. *Trinidad and Tobago*, Judgment of 21 June 2002, §213, referring to '*The Last Temptation of Christ*' case (*Olmedo Bustos et al.*), Judgment of 5 February 2000, §§85 and 87.

[481] See e.g. CIDH Annual Report 2000, §§45-46.

[482] IACHR *Hilaire, Constantine and Benjamin et al.* v. *Trinidad and Tobago*, Judgment of 21 June 2002, §215.

[483] This would then be independent of the question whether an execution would constitute a further violation of the right to life in Article 6 ICCPR because of a violation of the right to a fair trial in Article 14 ICCPR.

In human rights cases provisional measures could be used also to prevent irreparable harm to rights *collateral* to the claim, as long as these rights involve the right to life and the prohibition of cruel treatment. This would be the case when the provisional measures are ordered to protect the witnesses in a case, rather than the alleged victims. An example of a case of provisional measures protecting rights collateral to the claim, but involving the alleged victim rather than other beneficiaries would be when someone appeals to an adjudicator claiming to be the victim of an arbitrary detention, and meanwhile there is reason to fear ill treatment. Pending the determination of the issue whether or not this detention is arbitrary, the adjudicator may indicate to the State concerned that it should take the provisional measure of preventing, or ending, the alleged ill treatment. Here the specific measure requested is not provisional in the sense that such ill treatment may be resumed after determination of the legal question, but it is in the sense that it is a form of collateral protection applicable while the case is pending.

In other situations the *claim* pending before the international adjudicator relates to the threat itself of irreparable harm to life and physical integrity. This is often so in the Inter-American cases involving threats to human rights defenders. In such cases the provisional measures may still be collateral to the claim if they also aim to protect persons other than the alleged victims.

The claim itself could also involve something else, but family members of the alleged victims, witnesses or others are receiving death threats. In such cases persons *other* than the alleged victim(s) involved in the main claim risk irreparable harm. These persons are being threatened because they are somehow related to the alleged victim, for instance as family members or co-workers or as witnesses, judges or counsel in the international or domestic proceedings.[484] In these cases too the provisional measure should not go further than the eventual form of reparation could. The difference is that the eventual remedy is hypothetical in the sense that it relates to violations perpetrated against persons other than the alleged victim(s). In other words, the criterion is irreparable harm to persons rather than the link between the object of the complaint and the provisional measures. Still, there must be a relationship between what form of reparation the adjudicator *could* have suggested on the merits, had the main claim been about the right to life and the prohibition of cruel treatment of these persons. They should be protected against irreparable harm to their life and personal integrity pending the proceedings in the case of the alleged victim, exactly because they are being threatened in relation to that case. In order to obtain an eventual (financial) remedy, however, as part of a judgment on the merits, these persons must institute their own proceedings. In sum, what the petitioner needs to show, for purposes of provisional measures, is the threat of irreparable harm to persons and the relationship of these persons to the alleged victim. The adjudicator needs to take into account also whether the provisional measures would go no further than the eventual remedy would have, if the persons involved had been the alleged victims.

Yet being overly strict about the relationship between the main claim and the request for provisional measures is inappropriate in the context of irreparable harm to persons. Of course the adjudicator could continue to use provisional measures without hinting at the rights involved. It is possible that it does not relate its concept of irreparable harm to specific articles of the applicable treaty, but uses independent concepts of life, dignity and personal integrity, all part of the underlying rationale of protecting the existence of individuals and indigenous peoples. Yet in order to enhance transparency and the authority of their provisional measures it would be useful if the adjudicators would indicate the rights involved.

The link between halting an execution pending a case and ordering commutation or a new trial as part of the decision on the merits so as to prevent a violation of the right to life is evident. With regard to ordering a State to protect a person against threats, the aim of the Court's authority seems to be identical in provisional measures and judgments on the merits and reparations. The

---

[484]   See also section 4 on the group of beneficiaries.

specific order to investigate and punish violations can also be found both as part of the Court's judgment and as part of its provisional measures. In this case, though, as part of provisional measures 'investigate and prosecute' solely aim at preventing further threats, while 'investigate and prosecute' as a form of reparation aims not only at prevention of further violations but also as a form of moral satisfaction. Possibly, the drafters of the American Convention had already foreseen this, as they put in the same article both the power to order provisional measures and the power to order reparation (Article 63 ACHR). The 1998 Protocol to the African Charter, establishing an African Court of Human and Peoples' Rights, was inspired by this provision and equally combines provisional measures and reparation in one provision (Article 27 of the 1998 Protocol). Unfortunately this direct relationship is lost in the Protocol on the African Court of Justice and Human Rights (2008), which refers to reparation in a separate provision.

Indeed there should be a correlation between the measures required pending and concluding the procedure. In the context of the right to culture, for instance, if the HRC would never refer to cessation, such as a permanent halt to certain destructive developments, then provisional measures that would require a temporary halt to such developments would not be of much use. In fact the provisional measures would then go further than the eventual action or abstention required.[485] If a violation is indeed found, the subsequent obligations, including reparation, should correspond to the provisional measures earlier taken. An obligation aimed at restoring the situation as much as possible or at least at preventing further degradation would justify the type of provisional measure taken pending the proceedings.

The State must provide for cessation and assurances of non-repetition, thereby preventing irreparable harm to persons that would otherwise constitute a further violation of the human rights treaty. It must also provide for exactly the form of reparation indicated in so far as this represents the most essential form of reparation (e.g. the prerequisite for the enjoyment of any form of compensation).[486]

Provisional measures have several different general purposes. One would be to enable the adjudicator to make a determination on the merits that makes sense in light of the human rights treaty. This is the case, for instance, when the aim of the claim is to prevent a violation of the right to life. This purpose would be applicable in cases where a human rights claim includes cessation or a request for restitution in kind such as a retrial in conformity with the right to a fair trial. An adjudicator could use provisional measures in all cases to prevent that an impending act by the government concerned (or its omission in relation to impending acts by third parties), which would result in the death of the petitioner, would make fulfilment of that claim impossible. Another aim of a claim could be that the adjudicator would declare that commutation of the death penalty would be warranted *as a remedy* for a past violation, rather than in order to *prevent* a new violation. In both cases (life as a right and life as a remedy) the general purpose of the provisional measure is to safeguard a final determination that makes sense in the light of the human rights treaty.

---

485 See e.g. the discussion of HRC *Lubicon Lake Band*, 26 March 1990 in Chapter X (Culture).

486 If the remedy is more compensatory than aimed at prevention of a further violation, any specific directions of the HRC must be considered seriously, but are not necessarily binding. Nevertheless the State should not act such as to make impossible the petitioner's enjoyment of some form of compensation. It is argued that this means that at least the precondition must be fulfilled that the victim is alive to enjoy the compensation awarded. On the legal status of provisional measures see Chapter XVI.

6   CONCLUSION: PROTECTING THE BENEFICIARY AGAINST IRREPARABLE HARM

This chapter discussed several issues involving protection. The first three were the type and specificity of the protective measures and the group of beneficiaries and addressees. The last issue involved the link between the protection required as part of provisional measures and the protection required on the merits (cessation, assurances of non-repetition) and as part of a judgment on reparation.

Human rights adjudicators have all used provisional measures so as to prevent irreparable harm to persons pending the proceedings. Yet the protection required in provisional measures takes various forms. An element of positive action is present in most provisional measures and should be made explicit in cases involving ongoing situations such as adverse detention conditions, recent disappearances and death threats. Protection against death threats involves the right to life and protection of personall integrity. They are core rights whose violation causes irreparable harm to persons. Such violations must therefore be prevented even if this entails that the State must take positive measures pending the proceedings.

Compared to the European and African systems (and the Geneva systems) the Inter-American system appears to be more responsive to the particular situations it faces. Often provisional measures indicate the required result, such as to refrain from executing a death sentence or to protect persons against threats. Sometimes they are also more precise as to how the State should achieve this result, or at least they rule out certain activities that do not qualify as compliance. Thus, in the Inter-American system the provisional measures have become increasingly specific, partly in light of the experiences of the Commission and Court with certain States. In fact they provide insight into the ways States could or must protect persons under their jurisdiction against threats by paramilitary groups or other groups operating with the acquiescence of (certain factions of) the army, the police, or other authorities. They show that protection against threats means that the State must protect the beneficiaries in the area in which they live and work, rather than banishing them to 'safe areas', claiming that this would absolve it from taking protective measures. Providing effective protection against death threats is not divorced from other human rights obligations, which means that States must assist internally displaced persons to return safely and allow human rights defenders or journalists to continue the activities that had triggered the threats in the first place. Generally speaking the States involved do not appear to find fault with this approach, possibly also because at the core the provisional measures concern the most basic of rights: the right to life and the prohibition of torture and cruel treatment.

Similarly to the practice in the Inter-American system it is argued that international adjudicators should also incrementally specify their provisional measures, so as to provide clarity to States on what is expected of them, but they should do so even more gradually than the regional systems. This gradual approach is warranted exactly because of the less cohesive nature of an international as opposed to a regional monitoring system and the diminished possibility of collecting and interpreting information. Another aspect that might play a role is the sensitivity of some States and the way these States would base their disagreement with certain provisional measures on regional doctrine, or insist on sovereignty over protection of human rights. The discussion on subsidiarity (and on the related margin of appreciation in the interpretation of treaty obligations) is more important in some systems than in others and plays out differently in each system. Especially with regard to core rights the provisional measures taken by the other human rights adjudicators could at least give some direction to an adjudicator regarding what the State is expected to do or to abstain from doing in order to prevent irreparable harm to persons.

Apart from the type (action or abstention) and specificity of provisional measures, in order to truly ensure the protective nature of provisional measures it must be clear who is included as a beneficiary, even if not mentioned by name, and whether and how the beneficiaries have been consulted about the measures intended to protect them.

In the European system the tables have sometimes been turned by addressing the alleged victim under the Rule on provisional measures. It does not appear appropriate to address an order for provisional measures to the alleged victim instead of to the State.

Both as to purpose and as to substance the provisional measures should be consistent with similar measures already taken in order to increase their credibility and avoid discriminatory application vis-à-vis various beneficiaries and addressees. Yet in the face of irreparable harm to persons adjudicators should not balance the basic rights of the intended beneficiaries with the general interest. At the same time, in order to uphold the legitimacy of provisional measures it is vital to adhere to principles of procedural fairness. In this regard it is important to make sure that the State's positions and arguments are duly taken into account.

In case of a group of beneficiaries, is there a need for the beneficiaries of provisional measures to be mentioned individually? The practice developed in the Inter-American system of using provisional measures to protect the members of a defined community, or people working at human rights organisations, as well as all other persons visiting the premises is appropriate. While they are not identified by name, the beneficiaries of the required protective measures are clear to the State.

Sometimes beneficiaries may live in remote areas or be otherwise difficult to reach. In such cases it should not be required to establish written consent of each beneficiary, as long as there are indications that they are likely to agree and as long as there are no (subsequent) indications of disagreement. While consultation of the beneficiaries proves to be difficult at times, the Inter-American Commission and Court do appear to strive for it, more than the other adjudicators.

The wider impact of provisional measures also deserves attention. A good faith implementation of the obligations under the human rights treaty warrants a pro-active stance of the State to ensure the underlying rationale to a provisional measure is being met. This may include general measures that protect others in a situation similar to that of the specific beneficiary.

The final issue discussed in this chapter was the link between the protection required as part of provisional measures and the protection required on the merits (cessation, assurances of non-repetition) and as part of a judgment on reparation. The general purpose of the provisional measure is to safeguard a final determination that makes sense in the light of the human rights treaty. Therefore there should be a correlation between the measures required pending and concluding the procedure, in case a violation is indeed found. Without such correlation the question arises whether the object of the provisional measure was simply to postpone the suffering until after the expected finding. This would be an unsatisfactory approach to the concept of provisional measures.

An obligation aimed at restoring the situation as much as possible or at least at preventing further degradation would justify the type of provisional measure taken pending the proceedings to prevent irreparable harm to persons.

It is argued that this would apply as well to situations in which the alleged victim and the beneficiary do not coincide. As noted, persons who are not the alleged victims may still receive protection as beneficiaries of provisional measures, for instance because they are receiving threats as witnesses in this case. What the petitioner needs to show, for purposes of such provisional measures, is the threat of irreparable harm to persons and the relationship of these persons to the alleged victim. In order to make sure that the action or abstention required of the State remains credible, the petitioner also needs to show that the provisional measures would go no further than the eventual remedy would have, if the persons involved had been the alleged victims. Yet in order to obtain an eventual (financial) remedy as part of a judgment on the merits, persons other than the alleged victims must institute their own proceedings.

Both in provisional measures and on the merits the ultimate aim is to prevent irreparable harm to persons. The substance of the protection required is often similar as well. What is different is the function of the protection required: at the provisional measures stage reference is made to this protection in order to ensure the possibility of an effective decision on the merits *in case* a violation is found on the merits. At the merits stage, on the other hand, reference is made to this protection because it is indeed necessary in order to prevent irreparable harm to persons.

CONCLUSION

1   INTRODUCTION

It is not always evident from the case law how the human rights adjudicators perceive the purpose of provisional measures. After all, apart from the Inter-American Court and, to some extent, the Inter-American Commission, they normally do not motivate their use of these measures. Outside of the Inter-American context jurisprudence on *why* provisional measures were or were not used in a given case is hardly available at all. Because the adjudicators do not motivate their provisional measures they are also unclear about the question under which provision they take them.[1] If they indeed take provisional measures on the basis of a theory, they do not indicate this to the State or the petitioners.

Is their rationale for the use of provisional measures similar to that of the ICJ? To the extent that their provisional measures aim to ensure a meaningful outcome of the case before the adjudicator the answer has to be in the affirmative. In death penalty cases, for instance, a meaningful outcome of a case is not ensured when one of the parties (i.e. the State party) inflicts irreparable harm on either the person of the petitioner, or on the fairness of the procedure.

Three requirements for the use of provisional measures that have been mentioned in the various human rights systems are risk, immediacy and irreparable harm. Of those, irreparable harm is indicative of the purpose of provisional measures and were discussed in this Part, while immediacy and risk are indicative of urgency and therefore are discussed in Part III, Chapter XV. Apart from the European system, all human rights systems specifically refer to the prevention of irreparable harm. The European system, on the other hand, provides for a very general rule on provisional measures, similar to that in the ICJ Statute, referring to the interests of the parties. Different from the ICJ Statute the Rule also mentions, as an alternative, the interests of the 'proper conduct' of the proceedings before it. Yet in practice the ECtHR uses the criterion of preventing irreparable harm just like other human rights adjudicators do.

Only in the Inter-American system there are some specific statements about the purpose of provisional measures. In his Order for urgent measures in the *Peace Community* case, for instance, the President of the Inter-American Court pointed out that in national legal systems the purpose of provisional measures generally is to preserve the rights of the parties in a dispute. This would guarantee that any future decision on the merits would not be harmed by their actions *pendente lite*. In international human rights law, on the other hand, the purpose of provisional measures went beyond this because, next to their essentially preventive character, they effectively protect fundamental rights to the extent that they prevent irreparable harm to persons.[2] The Court repeated this when it confirmed the President's Order.[3]

Apparently the President and the full Court distinguish between the more traditional preventive character of provisional measures on the one hand and the newer protective nature on the

---

[1]   They may even consider that provisional measures are not necessarily related to specific rights.

[2]   IACHR *Peace Community of San José de Apartadó* case (Colombia), Order of 9 October 2000 (President).

[3]   IACHR *Peace Community of San José de Apartadó* case (Colombia), Order of 24 November 2000.

other. At the same time this protection takes place in order to prevent 'irreparable harm'. In other words, the main difference seems to relate to the type of obligation. With the term 'prevention' the President seems to refer to the negative obligation of 'refraining from action' and with the term 'protection' to positive obligations as well.

From the practice of the various adjudicators other than in the Inter-American system it is not always apparent to whom or what the harm is irreparable. The various human rights bodies have only haphazardly offered clues as to how they define irreparable harm. Thus, while in most complaints it is not so difficult to establish the immediacy (or imminence) of the risk,[4] the examination of the practice of the human rights adjudicators shows that their use of the concept of irreparable harm is not always clear.

One criterion did appear in the case law. This is the requirement that for provisional measures to be used an act or omission should have irreversible consequences. While this is not further explained, examples are easily imaginable. In fact, irreversible means that *restitutio in integrum* would be impossible.

Moreover, in practice the general attitude of the human rights adjudicators seems to be that provisional measures are meant to be exceptional.[5] The ECtHR, for instance, has pointed out that the grounds on which it applies provisional measures are not set out in the Rules of Court. Instead the Court has determined these in its case law. Just like the European Commission did prior to the entry into force of Protocol 11 (1998), the Court only applies provisional measures 'in restricted circumstances' or 'limited spheres'.[6] There must be an imminent risk of irreparable damage.

> "While there is no specific provision in the Convention concerning the domains in which Rule 39 will apply, requests for its application usually concern the right to life (Article 2), the right not to be subjected to torture or inhuman treatment (Article 3) and, exceptionally the right to respect for private and family life (Article 8) or other rights guaranteed by the Convention. The vast majority of cases in which interim measures have been indicated concern deportation and extradition proceedings".[7]

The ECtHR has considered that 'in the light of the general principles of international law, the law of treaties and international case-law, the interpretation of the scope of interim measures cannot be dissociated from the proceedings to which they relate or the decision on the merits they seek to protect'.[8] This statement about the scope of provisional measures is significant. It shows that the ECtHR now recognises as well that in the context of such measures procedural and substantive law meet.

In *Mamatkulov* (2005) the ECtHR observed that 'the ICJ, the Inter-American Court of Human Rights, the Human Rights Committee and the Committee against Torture of the United Nations, although operating under different treaty provisions to those of the Court, have confirmed in their reasoning in recent decisions that the preservation of the asserted rights of the parties in the face of the risk of irreparable damage represents an essential objective of interim measures in international law. Indeed it can be said that, whatever the legal system in question,

---

[4]   See Chapter XV (Immediacy and risk).

[5]   See also Garry (2001), p. 410, discussing the European system: "As the Commission and Court have had to rely on the good faith of the Member State in complying with the interim order, they have issued them only in extreme cases where there is an 'apparent real and imminent risk of irreparable harm'".

[6]   ECtHR Grand Chamber *Mamatkulov and Askarov v. Turkey*, 4 February 2005, §§103-104.

[7]   Id., §104.

[8]   Id., §123.

the proper administration of justice requires that no irreparable action be taken while proceedings are pending'.[9]

As noted in the Introduction to this part of the book (Part II), irreparable harm to persons may be interpreted in various ways. A distinction could be made between three interrelated types of irreparable harm: to the claim, to the procedure and to persons. To prevent harm to the claim provisional measures could be taken in a wide range of cases. After all, preventing such harm could relate to any claim under the human rights treaty involved, as long as the consequences would be irreversible. Provisional measures to prevent harm to the procedure are hardly ever taken in isolation. Generally there also is a risk of harm to the claim or to persons.[10]

Human rights adjudicators generally take a dynamic approach, acutely aware of the vulnerable position of the individual vis-à-vis the State. Yet with regard to the range of situations in which provisional measures have been taken often their practice seems to be more limited than that of international adjudicators not focusing on human rights. This may be due to their exercise of adjudicatory caution based on the idea that if the constitutive document instituting an individual complaint procedure does not explicitly refer to the authority to use provisional measures it may be wise to start out using them only in the most serious of circumstances.

It is argued that in order to make the system of interim protection work it is necessary to draw the line somewhere. Part II of this book and in particular this Conclusion, aims to provide a conceptual motivation on where to draw the line. This conclusion to Part II addresses the question whether provisional measures to prevent irreparable harm involve *any* type of human rights violation (harm to the claim only) or only particularly fundamental rights (harm to the claim as well as to persons). A related question is whether a provisional measure to prevent harm to the proceedings is ultimately linked to harm to the claim or to harm to persons and whether the protective measures required coincide with those that may be required on the merits and reparation.

2 COMMON CORE AND OUTER LIMITS OF THE CONCEPT

2.1 Introduction

This book distinguishes between the wider category of provisional measures to prevent irreversible harm to the claim or procedure and the more limited category, which forms part of it, of provisional measures to prevent or halt irreparable harm to persons. As discussed below, it is argued that the latter provisional measures belong to the common core, while provisional measures that do not aim to prevent *irreparable* harm to persons, but nevertheless do aim to prevent *irreversible* harm to the claim or procedure, are still within the outer limits of the concept.

All human rights adjudicators have used provisional measures to protect against irreparable harm to persons involving the right to life and the prohibition of torture and cruel treatment. Most of them have done so to halt the execution of death sentences, to halt expulsion or extradition in the context of non-refoulement and to protect against death threats and harassment. There have been several other situations in which provisional measures have been used in one system or another. These range from cultural survival and the destruction of a painting to the payment of a fine. In the previous chapters an attempt was made to find the rationale for the use of provisional measures in all these situations.

---

[9]   Id., §124.

[10]   See EComHR *Ennslin, Baader and Raspe* v. *FRG*, 8 July 1978 (inadm.), §44 for an example of provisional measures to preserve the evidence. In that sense they were clearly aimed at preventing harm to the procedure. Still, any harm to the procedure would somehow cause harm to the rights claimed as well. See also Chapter XII (Other situations), section 2.9.

After a more general discussion of the common core of the concept of provisional measures, as it relates to the purpose, this section deals with the right to life and the prohibition of cruel treatment. It subsequently focuses on two situations in which provisional measures could be used, one involving the rights of indigenous peoples and religious minorities and one involving mass expulsion and internal displacement. The first situation, about indigenous culture and religious minorities, already has an established practice in the Inter-American and African systems, in the international Optional Protocol system and in the practice of the Bosnia Chamber.[11] The other situation relates to provisional measures involving protection against mass expulsion, introduced by the Inter-American Commission and Court.[12] It is proposed that provisional measures are indeed feasible in such situations. The last part of section 2 addresses other situations in which provisional measures have been used and attempts to determine the underlying rationale for this use. This culminates in a discussion of the outer limits of the concept.

2.2   Common core: preventing irreparable harm to persons

2.2.1 Introduction

It seems that a convergence has taken place in the approaches of adjudicators dealing with comparable obligations, making possible the identification of a common core. This is not surprising given the similarities in the object and purpose of the various human rights treaties and their emphasis on the imperative character of certain rights. It is suggested that provisional measures are based on underlying rationales that are equally similar, although normally not explicitly discussed by the human rights adjudicators.[13]

In some situations provisional measures have not just been used by one regional adjudicator, but also by the HRC, as the only international adjudicator monitoring a general human rights treaty. For lack of explanation by the adjudicators themselves about their use of provisional measures, assumptions about the rationale of the measures must be made on the basis of the adjudicators' decisions on the merits. If several adjudicators have in common certain reasoning on the merits in situations in which they previously used provisional measures, it is assumed that these situations have now come to belong to the common core of the concept of provisional measures in human rights adjudication. At present the core that the approaches of all adjudicators have in common is the protection of persons against irreparable harm to their lives and personal integrity. Sections 2.2.3 and 2.2.4 also discuss what could be the rationale for the expansions by the various adjudicators of the use of provisional measures within the framework of protecting existence itself. It suggests two expansions found in one or two systems that would also be feasible in other human rights systems.

Certain principles seem to underlie the practice of all human rights adjudicators with regard to provisional measures. In human rights cases involving an individual and a State party, the power is concentrated in the State party, triggering obligations of action and abstention. Provisional measures, therefore, should either serve to shield the individual against abuse of power by the State resulting in irreparable harm or should serve to invoke the core obligations of the State

---

11   See Chapter X (Culture).

12   See Chapter XII (Mass expulsion).

13   Yet see the opinion recently expressed by Judge Cançado Trindade that the 'absolute and peremptory prohibition in any circumstances whatsoever', of torture and other atrocities, 'a prohibition of jus cogens – in contemporary international law' has ' a direct bearing on the issue of the indication of provisional measures'. ICJ *Questions relating to the Obligation to Prosecute or Extradite (Belgium* v. *Senegal)*, Order of 28 May 2009, Dissenting Opinion Judge Cançado Trindade, §49.

to protect individuals against irreparable harm caused by other individuals or entities. Thus, the purpose of provisional measures normally is not 'in the interest of the parties' in the same way as cases before the ICJ, which concern conflicts between States. This is mainly relevant in the face of arguments such as 'balance of convenience' that are applicable more in relations between equal parties. At the same time the practice of the human rights adjudicators with regard to the purpose of provisional measures seems to be more limited than that of the ICJ. Indeed, if they would take provisional measures in *all* cases involving irreparable harm to the claim this might diminish the importance of provisional measures. It also might lessen the persuasive force of the follow-up by adjudicators in cases of non-compliance.[14]

One could argue that any harm to the claim in human rights cases results in irreparable harm to the victims of human rights violations or to other persons involved. After all, human rights violations are, as such, attacks on personal integrity. Such attacks should be prevented if the result would be irreversible. In that sense harm to the claim and harm to persons coincide. On the other hand, the specific references in the texts of the treaties or rules of procedure to harm to the victim or to persons and to 'irreparable' rather than 'irreversible' harm could refer to a more limited category of extreme human rights violations. This would be violations for which reparation by financial compensation would be particularly inappropriate, rather than simply irreversible harm to all claims.

Immediacy[15] and irreversibility always play a role. In addition, in order to remain authoritative, provisional measures must be taken in exceptional cases only.[16] Clearly, provisional measures should be taken to prevent irreversible situations in the sense that measures that are reversible cannot be irreparable. If legislation and acts of implementation would have results that could indeed be reversed, they do not trigger irreparable harm. Thus, irreversibility is a threshold criterion for the use of provisional measures. At the same time measures that are irreversible are not necessarily irreparable. The term 'irreparable' connotes a relationship with the concept of reparation. Not only would *restitutio in integrum* be impossible without provisional measures (irreversibility), but forms of reparation other than *restitutio in integrum* would be unacceptable. They will be manifestly inadequate exactly because the consequences of the violation are so serious as to be incapable of being erased. A decision by a State to allow a certain act or omission when the adjudicator has indicated that prevention is the only appropriate remedy, constitutes a grave violation of international law.[17]

Indeed, the references in the applicable text to irreparable harm to the victims of the alleged violations, and even more so the references to irreparable harm to persons, combined with the exceptional nature of provisional measures, argue for an approach that initially is limited to preserving the most fundamental rights. Violations of rights causing irreparable harm must be prevented since a return to the *status quo ante* is impossible after the irreversible has taken place, while the nature of the harm implies that such violations can never be repaired by forms of reparation other than *restitutio in integrum*. In human rights cases the relevance of this traditional reason for using provisional measures is particularly striking.

In several systems, including that of the ICCPR, the reference to provisional measures is only made in the rules of procedure but not in the constituent text. Although the power to use provisional measures is derived from the inherent function of adjudicators, in light of an effective

---

[14] On follow up by the adjudicators see Chapter XVIII.

[15] See Chapter XV (Immediacy and risk).

[16] See also e.g. Buergenthal (1994), p. 93.

[17] If such violation nevertheless takes place, other measures, including forms of reparation, – however inadequate – are still warranted. At least public statements of acknowledgement, validation of the victims, investigation and prosecution of the perpetrators and, more generally, assurances of non-repetition would help prevent similar violations as well as restore some measure of dignity to the survivors. See Chapter XIII (Protection).

right of individual complaint, they seem to invoke them mainly in the context of rights singled out in the treaty for their particularly fundamental nature. Indeed, the references to irreparable harm to the victims of the alleged violations in the treaties or rules of procedure, and even more so the references to irreparable harm to *persons* argue for an approach that initially is limited to preserving the most fundamental rights. This approach is confirmed by the statements by human rights adjudicators about the exceptional nature of provisional measures, probably in order to ensure that they remain authoritative. They have distinguished certain rights on the basis of their fundamental nature and it is in the context of these rights that *all* human rights adjudicators have used provisional measures.

Hence, under general international law provisional measures may be taken in a wide range of cases. Yet the minimum level approach proposed in this book, with regard to provisional measures in human rights cases that are not based on an explicit treaty provision, is based on the premise that provisional measures should remain exceptional. In other words, in light of the fact that several adjudicatory systems do not include an explicit reference to provisional measures, it is proposed that at least in universal systems of adjudication provisional measures should only involve rights essential for the very existence of persons and of indigenous peoples.

Adjudicators have referred to core rights that are so fundamental that States may not make reservations because this would be contrary to the object and purpose of the treaty. They have also referred to core rights that may not be derogated from even in times of emergency. The provisions on non-derogable rights specifically included in most human rights treaties, or referred to in the jurisprudence of the adjudicators, give some indication of the rights recognised for their fundamental nature within the relevant treaties.[18] Judge of the Inter-American Court Cançado Trindade has referred to 'the formation of a universal nucleus of non-derogable fundamental rights' and a 'true international regime against torture, forced disappearances of persons, and summary, extra-legal and arbitrary executions'.[19]

---

[18]   The ECHR was concluded before the ICCPR and includes the most limited list of non-derogable rights. The ACHR, on the other hand, was concluded after the ICCPR and provides a more extensive list of such rights. The ACHPR does not include a provision on states of emergency with a list of non-derogable rights. Article 15 ECHR refers to the right to life, the prohibition of torture or inhuman or degrading treatment or punishment, the prohibition of slavery or servitude and freedom from *ex post facto* laws. Article 4 ICCPR refers to the same rights but adds the prohibition of imprisonment on the ground of inability to fulfil a contractual obligation, the right to recognition as a person before the law and the freedom of thought, conscience and religion, including the right to manifest religion or belief. Except for the prohibition of imprisonment on the ground of inability to fulfil a contractual obligation, Article 27 ACHR equally refers to the foregoing rights. Moreover, it adds the rights of the family, the right to a name, the rights of the child, the right to a nationality, the right to participate in government and 'the judicial guarantees essential for the protection of such rights'. See generally on the human rights dimension of hierarchy in international law e.g. Seiderman (2001). See also Orakhelashvili (2006). This book does not deal with the prohibition of slavery for lack of practice by the adjudicators of dealing with such cases and using provisional measures. In HRC *Dissanayake, Mudiyanselage Sumanaweera Banda* v. *Sri Lanka*, 22 July 2008, the petitioner had requested provisional measures to the effect that he be granted respite from the execution of the sentence of hard labour. In March 2005 the Special Rapporteur denied this request 'on the ground that working in a print shop did not appear to come within the terms of article 8, paragraph 3(b)', §1.2.

[19]   IACHR *Bámaca Velásquez* v. *Guatemala*, 25 November 2000, Separate Opinion Cançado Trindade, §§25 and 26. He concludes: "All this points to the prevalence of the safeguard of the non-derogable rights in any circumstances (in times of peace as well as of armed conflict). The normative and interpretative convergences between the International Law of Human Rights and International Humanitarian Law (...) contribute to place those non-derogable rights, – starting with the fundamental right to life itself, – definitively in the domain of *jus cogens*", §27. See also

This book draws on the ICCPR in order to determine a minimum level approach. The rights recognised under the ICCPR for their particularly fundamental character are also recognised as such under the ACHR. The latter treaty is even more extensive in its recognition of non-derogable rights than the ICCPR. The African Charter (ACHPR) does not provide for derogation in times of emergency.[20] While the ECHR is more limited with regard to non-derogable rights than the other treaties, all State parties to it have also recognised the ICCPR. Moreover, the ECHR itself recognises in Article 53 that no provision in the treaty will be interpreted to limit fundamental rights recognised in any other treaty ratified by the member States. The ICCPR is the treaty most generally applicable and all State parties to regional human rights treaties, apart from the Comores, have also ratified the ICCPR.[21] Thus, it makes sense to use the universal system and its approach to rights of a particularly fundamental nature as a point of departure.[22]

Thus in this book the ICCPR is taken as a model for the discussion of rights recognised for their fundamental character. The HRC has stated that while it is not its function to review State parties' conduct under other treaties,[23] it does have the competence to take these other international obligations into account when it considers whether the ICCPR allows the State to derogate from specific provisions.[24] In order to clarify the underlying rationale for the use of provisional measures by the HRC its General Comments often provide more information than the case law on the merits. The Committee considers that provisions representing 'customary international law (and *a fortiori* when they have the character of peremptory norms) may not be the subject of reservations'. While it does not distinguish between the norms of customary law and norms of *ius cogens* it has listed certain rights that may not be subjected to reservations because this would be contrary to the object and purpose of the Covenant. In other words, it singles out these norms for their particularly fundamental nature. The HRC has called the right to life the 'most essential' right in the ICCPR[25] or, more generally, the 'most fundamental' right.[26] Moreover, it has referred to the right to be free from torture as 'one of the highest values protected by the Covenant'.[27]

CIDH *Guantanamo Bay*, Precautionary measure of 12 March 2002, p. 3 noting that human rights and humanitarian law may complement and reinforce each other 'sharing as they do a common nucleus of non-derogable rights and a common purpose of promoting human life and dignity'. See further e.g Van Boven (2006), p. 95.

[20] See e.g. ACHPR *Commission Nationale des Droits de l'Homme et des Libertés* v. *Chad*, October 1995: "The African Charter, unlike other human rights instruments, does not allow for States parties to derogate from their treaty obligations during emergency situations. Thus, even a civil war in Chad cannot be used as an excuse by the State violating or permitting violations of rights in the African Charter", §21. On the other hand, the text of the Charter does confront the Convention organs with the problem of the so-called claw-back or limitation clauses. Yet the Commission has pointed out: "The reasons for possible limitations must be founded in a legitimate state interest and the evils of limitations of rights must be strictly proportionate with and absolutely necessary for the advantages which are to be obtained. Even more important, a limitation may never have as a consequence that the right itself becomes illusory". *Media Rights Agenda and Others* v. *Nigeria*, 31 October 1998, §§69-70. Generally see Naldi (2000).

[21] Moreover, the Comores signed the ICCPR in September 2008.

[22] See section 2 of the Introduction.

[23] This is different from the African Court and the Inter-American Commission. Moreover, the Inter-American Court can review the conduct of State parties under other treaties as part of its advisory function.

[24] See HRC General Comment 29 on states of emergency (Article 4), 24 July 2001, §10.

[25] See e.g. HRC *Ng* v. *Canada*, 5 November 1993, §14.1.

[26] See e.g. HRC *Judge* v. *Canada*, 5 August 2003.

[27] HRC *Mansour Ahani* v. *Canada*, 29 March 2004. See also e.g. ACHPR *Zimbabwean Human Rights NGO Forum* v. *Zimbabwe*, May 2006, §86 (referring to the right to life as 'the fulcrum of all other rights').

Even if not all rights mentioned in Article 4 ICCPR as non-derogable are argued to have been included because of their particularly fundamental nature,[28] nevertheless the non-derogable rights enumerated in Article 4 ICCPR could be seen 'partly as recognition of the peremptory nature of some fundamental rights ensured in treaty form in the Covenant (e.g., Articles 6 and 7)'.[29] In this respect Article 8 on the prohibition of slavery, slave trade and servitude could be added. This right is enumerated as a recognition of its peremptory nature, just as Articles 6 and 7 on the right to life and the prohibition of cruel treatment and torture. Thus far, provisional measures have not yet been used in the context of (modern) slavery, but this would be feasible if a State that could be held (partly) responsible has in fact recognised an international individual complaint procedure.

The HRC has pointed out that Article 4(1) 'requires that no measure derogating from the provisions of the Covenant may be inconsistent with the State party's other obligations under international law, particularly the rules of international humanitarian law'. In this respect it also refers to Article 5(2) stipulating that the ICCPR cannot be used to justify restrictions upon or derogations from fundamental rights recognised in other legal instruments 'on the pretext that the Covenant does not recognise such rights or that it recognises them to a lesser extent'. The HRC is competent to take into account a State party's other international obligations when it considers whether a State may derogate from specific provisions of the ICCPR. It notes that States parties 'should duly take into account the developments within international law as to human rights standards applicable in emergency situations'.[30]

---

[28] The HRC acknowledges that some articles are mentioned as non-derogable 'because it can never become necessary to derogate from these rights during a state of emergency (e.g., articles 11 and 18)'. See General Comment 29 on states of emergency (Article 4), 24 July 2001, §11. Article 11 concerns the prohibition of imprisonment because of inability to fulfil a contractual obligation and Article 18 concerns the freedom of thought, conscience and religion. Because of the different purpose of the non-derogatory character assigned to them they do not qualify as rights to be protected by provisional measures to the same extent as the right to life, the prohibition of cruel, torture and slavery, made non-derogable in light of their inherent priority character. The two remaining non-derogable rights listed in the ICCPR are Article 15, laying down the principle of legality in the field of criminal law and Article 16 on the recognition of everyone as a person before the law. Equally it cannot become necessary to derogate from these rights during a state of emergency, which may be a reason for their inclusion in the list of non-derogable rights. On the other hand, Article 15 also seems particularly fundamental in relation to the right to life and Art. 16 both in relation to the right to life and the prohibition of cruel treatment and torture. With regard to Article 15 the HRC itself indicated this when it mentioned it in the context of the discussion of the procedural guarantees necessary to protect the right to life. See General Comment 29 on states of emergency (Article 4), 24 July 2001, §§11 and 15 (obviously referring to Article 14 as well).

[29] See HRC General Comment 29 on states of emergency (Article 4), 24 July 2001, §11.

[30] Id., §§9 and 10. Among others it referred to the ILA Paris Minimum Standards of Human Rights Norms in a State of Emergency, 1984; the Siracusa Principles on the Limitation and Derogation Provisions in the ICCPR, the final report of Despouy, Special Rapporteur of the Sub-Commission on human rights and states of emergency, E/CN.4/sub.2/1997/19 and Add.1; the Guiding Principles on Internal Displacement, E/CN.4/1998/53/Add.2; the Turku (Åbo) Declaration of Minimum Humanitarian Standards (1990), E/CN.4/1995/116; and reports of the Secretary General to the Commission on Human Rights on fundamental standards of humanity, see e.g. E/CN.4/2001/91. The codification of crimes against humanity in the Rome Statute of the International Criminal Court is relevant in the interpretation of Article 4 ICCPR. The fact that certain human rights violations are defined as such crimes underscores the priority character of these rights. The Committee pointed out, among others, that Article 7 of the Rome Statute, on crimes against humanity, not only covers practices relating to Articles 6, 7 and 8 ICCPR but also

The question arises whether the ICCPR contains other rights of a particularly fundamental nature that are not enumerated in Article 4. The HRC has indeed singled out additional rights as well. It pointed out that 'the category of peremptory norms extends beyond the list of non-derogable provisions' of Article 4(2) ICCPR. States may not invoke this article as a justification for acting in violation of humanitarian law or *ius cogens*, 'for instance by taking hostages, by imposing collective punishments, through arbitrary deprivations of liberty or by deviating from fundamental principles of fair trial, including the presumption of innocence'.[31]

The HRC has mentioned some 'illustrative' examples of elements of rights not enumerated in Article 4(2) on safeguards during times of emergency that still could not be made subject to lawful derogation under that article. For instance, the fundamental obligation to provide an effective remedy for violations of the ICCPR 'constitutes a treaty obligation inherent in the Covenant as a whole'. This obligation should also be respected during states of emergency. This remark may be seen as indicative for the importance of the concept of provisional measures as well.[32]

In short, the HRC has argued that several of the non-derogable rights enumerated as such in the ICCPR, as well as certain other rights that have come to be seen as non-derogable, have been distinguished as such because of their particularly fundamental nature. The other adjudicators do not contradict this approach or they confirm it. They distinguish similar rights on the basis of their particularly fundamental nature: the right to life, the prohibition of cruel treatment and torture, slavery and discrimination, certain rights of indigenous peoples and the (procedural) rights necessary to ensure these rights.

It is suggested that in order to meet the criterion of exceptionality the common core of provisional measures is limited to these rights. It aims at protecting the very existence (in dignity) of persons and indigenous peoples. The subsequent subsections on protecting the right to life and preventing torture and cruel treatment on the one hand and protecting cultural survival on the other discuss this more closely.

2.2.2 Protecting the right to life and preventing torture and cruel treatment

Provisional measures to protect the right to life and prevent cruel treatment and torture may be illustrated by the following examples. The most obvious situation is that involving the death penalty.[33] If a petitioner is facing execution the adjudicator uses a provisional measure to halt this. Clearly, execution would result in irreparable harm to persons. Another example is the use of provisional measures to halt expulsions or extraditions in the context of non-refoulement. If such forms of removal relate to a real risk to the life of the alleged victim or of torture or cruel treatment in the receiving or requesting State this would then trigger the responsibility of the sending State. Thus pending the proceedings provisional measures are used to prevent irreparable harm.[34]

There are other situations as well in which provisional measures have been used to prevent irreparable harm to persons: lack of medical attention to detainees, disappearances and incommunicado detention. These situations all relate to personal security. In the case of incommunicado detention provisional measures are warranted when there is a risk of irreparable harm to the person in question due to lack of access to court and counsel. After all the right to personal security is closely related to the right to life and the prohibition of cruel treatment and torture. In a way the right to personal security, together with the purpose of preventing disappearances, explains the

---

[31] those relating to Articles 9, 12, 26 and 27. HRC General Comment 29 on states of emergency (Article 4), 24 July 2001, §12 (footnote 7).

[32] HRC General Comment 29 on states of emergency (Article 4), 24 July 2001, §11.

[33] See Chapters XIII (Protection) and XVI (Legal status).

See also Harrington (2003), p. 86 pointing out about the HRC that it, 'by definition' only uses provisional measures 'when there is a risk of irreparable harm to an individual's life or limb'.

[34] About assessment of material urgency see Chapter XV (Immediacy and risk).

importance of the right to access to court and counsel.[35] It is submitted that the few provisional measures that have been taken to ensure access to court and counsel may indeed be justified because these rights are accessory to the protection against ill-treatment and torture and against threats to life. The HRC has referred to the right of all persons deprived of their liberty to be treated with humanity and respect for their inherent dignity (Article 10) as expressing a norm of general international law not subject to derogation. It noted that this was supported by the close connection between Articles 7 and 10 and by the reference to the inherent dignity of the human person in the preamble to the ICCPR.[36] It also referred to the absolute nature of the prohibition of taking hostages, abducting people or unacknowledged detention.[37]

The right to personal security comes into play in relation to threats to life and integrity outside of the detention context. Not only the right to personal security but also the right to life and the prohibition of cruel treatment and torture imply positive obligations. Chapter XIII on the protective measures required more closely discussed this aspect of provisional measures.

On the basis of established jurisprudence on positive obligations in the context of detention, arguments based on resource limitations are not accepted. All human rights adjudicators have used or could use provisional measures to ensure access to health care in detention. On the other hand, sometimes there is a threat of irreparable harm to the health or even the lives of persons not in detention, because they have no access to basic services, such as HIV medication. Provisional measures to order such access could then assist in halting cruel treatment and preventing deaths. In a regional system involving States in circumstances that are more or less similar as well as a monitoring system including the possibility of conducting on site visits, negotiations and hearings, an adjudicator may be bolder in taking an incremental approach than in an international system. A regional adjudicator could, as the Inter-American Commission has done, at some point order a State to make available such services. In an international system, on the other hand, it may not yet be feasible to require such a reallocation of resources already pending the proceedings. Nevertheless, international adjudicators might indeed intervene pending the proceedings when there is evidence of widespread discrimination excluding persons from basic services and thereby exacerbating illnesses and even causing deaths, while these services are indeed available for other segments of the population. An obvious example is blocking access to food aid to certain ethnic groups.[38] In such cases (as in others) provisional measures certainly are not a cure-all remedy.[39]

---

[35] See also Chapter VIII on procedural rights to protect the right to life and prevent cruel treatment and torture.

[36] See HRC General Comment 29 on states of emergency (Article 4), 24 July 2001, § 13(a). In the three regional systems the right to humane treatment in detention is indeed part of the prohibition of inhuman or degrading treatment and torture or is mentioned as part of a provision that, as such, is non-derogable (see Article 5(2) ACHR: 'All persons deprived of their liberty shall be treated with respect of the inherent decency of the person', see also Articles 3 ECHR and 5 ACHPR.

[37] HRC General Comment 29 on states of emergency (Article 4), 24 July 2001, §13(b).

[38] See e.g. HRC General Comment 6 on Article 6 ICCPR, 30 April 1982, §5 on infant mortality and the right to life and several reports by UN thematic Rapporteurs of the Commission and sub-Commission and the current Human Rights Council. In April 2008 the UN Working Group on the Optional Protocol International Covenant on Economic, Social and Cultural Rights adopted by consensus a draft for an Optional Protocol to this Covenant and sent it for consideration to the Human Rights Council. This draft also includes an Art. 5 on interim measures, which refers to the discretion of the supervisory committee to 'transmit to the State Party concerned for its urgent consideration a request that the State Party take such interim measures as may be necessary in exceptional circumstances to avoid possible irreparable damage to the victim or victims of the alleged violations'. If there would be an individual complaint system to the International Covenant on Economic, Social and Cultural Rights the adjudicator should certainly be able to use provisional measures in relation to discrimination in access to adequate water, food and shelter causing irreparable harm. However, given the core content of the right to an adequate standard of

Nevertheless, in some situations a very focused and well-motivated provisional measure could assist their representatives in their endeavours to change the situation. Still, some situations may be so complex and politicised that international adjudicators would prefer not to get involved. We have seen this in relation to complaints about nuclear tests before various international adjudicators.

The prohibition of torture, from which the principle of non-refoulement is derived, is a peremptory norm of international law or *ius cogens*.[40] As long as the adjudicator would be likely to find a violation on the merits of the prohibition of cruel treatment and torture, irreparable harm to persons refers not only to harm to physical integrity, but also to psychological and moral integrity.[41] The risk of the latter category of irreparable harm may vary depending on the vulnerability of the persons involved. This is also the rationale of, for instance, the rule that minors in detention should be separated from (unrelated) adults. Because of the risk of irreparable harm to a minor detained together with adults an international adjudicator would be justified in using provisional measures ordering a State to detain this minor in a safer environment.[42] Similarly, in some situations an adjudicator could use provisional measures to halt a deportation if the receiving State would be unable to provide the requisite care for persons with a serious handicap, life-threatening (or even terminal) illnesses or for unaccompanied children. Certain acts or omissions, moreover,

---

living (Article 11 ICESCR) and the right to health (Article 12), in specific circumstances the use of provisional measures may be warranted to prevent irreparable harm to the life and physical integrity of persons, also without obvious indications of discrimination. In such cases petitioners should present a prima facie case of misallocation of resources and of policy decisions insufficiently taking into account risks of irreparable harm to persons. It is also feasible that the adjudicator would use provisional measures on behalf of children who are being denied access to primary education. To a certain extent this right is auxiliary to the aforementioned articles just like the right of a detainee to access to court and counsel is auxiliary to the right to life and the prohibition of cruel treatment. In certain cases respect for these rights could help prevent irreparable harm to persons, although the connection in time is more remote. Moreover, for children realisation of their right to education is necessary for the full development of their personality (see Article 13). See further on these issues the General Comments of the Committee on Economic, Social and Cultural Rights, as authoritative statements regarding the minimum norms in the Convention. If the approach would be taken that the implied power to use provisional measures is triggered not only to prevent irreparable harm to persons but to prevent such harm to all claims (an approach not advocated in this book), for this treaty another example would be the use of provisional measures to protect the right to benefit from the protection of the moral and material interests resulting from one's own scientific, literary or artistic productions (Article 15(1)(c) ICESCR). Of course this applies only if the petitioner could show that a violation would be irreversible.

39   See e.g. Chapter XVII (Official responses).

40   See e.g. ICTY *Prosecutor* v. *Furundzija*, case IT-95-17/I-T, 10 December 1998, 38 ILM 317 (1999), §§144-154; *Prosecutor* v. *Delacic and Others*, case IT-96-21-T, 16 November 1998, §454; *Prosecutor* v. *Kunarac*, cases IT-96-23-T and IT-96-23/1, §466; ECtHR *Case of Al-Adsani* v. *the United Kingdom*, Judgment of 21 November 2001, §61; HRC General Comment 29 (under 11); IACHR *Cantoral Benavides* v. *Peru*, Judgment of 18 August 2000 and *Maritza Urrutia* v. *Guatemala*, Judgment of 27 November 2003 ('The absolute prohibition of torture, in all its forms, is now part of international jus cogens', §92); Cartagena Declaration, Conclusion 5, which calls the non-refoulement principle itself a rule of *ius cogens*; see also e.g. O'Boyle (1977) p. 687; Burgers/Danelius (1988), p. 12; Verdross/Simma (1984), p. 819; Bassiouni (1996), p. 68; Alleweldt (1996), p. 1; Seiderman (2001), p. 275 and Smeulers (2002), p. 87.

41   Generally on psychological torture see e.g, IACHR *Maritza Urrutia* v. *Guatemala*, Judgment of 27 November 2003, §89.

42   See Chapter VII (Detention).

are more likely to cause irreparable harm in cases involving children exactly because they could irreparably harm their development. These acts or omissions could therefore constitute cruel treatment even though they would not necessarily be qualified as such if the victims were older than eighteen.

A very serious problem involving the right to life and the prohibition of cruel treatment is that of death threats against witnesses, family members, human rights defenders and others. Intervention against death threats both inside and outside of the detention context would also prevent irreparable harm to persons. The Inter-American Commission and Court have used provisional measures requesting States to ensure protection many times. The other human rights adjudicators have also done so by now. In their case law on the merits all adjudicators have in common an underlying principle that States have positive obligations to ensure respect for personal security, the right to life and the prohibition of torture and cruel treatment. Moreover, threats against human rights defenders, lawyers, journalists and witnesses take place with impunity in all regions of the world. Thus, it may be expected that the above adjudicators will increase their use of provisional measures in this respect. The ECtHR as well could respond to threats on an incremental basis, starting with a convincing case of a petitioner who is threatened because of his complaint, or of threats to witnesses (of an event about which the petitioner complains), preferably involving a State that is known for its failure to prevent threats in other cases. At first such intervention could even take place informally. It would be an intervention to suggest looking into the situation, informing the State of the adjudicator's awareness and at the same time reminding the State of the fact that if it knows about a threat and does nothing about it, it violates the right to security of person and often the right to life or the prohibition of cruel treatment as well. All these situations involve the right to life or the prohibition of cruel treatment and torture. In such situations the risk of irreparable harm to persons should trigger the use of provisional measures.

2.2.3 Protecting cultural survival

About the protection of the rights of persons belonging to minorities the HRC has noted that there were elements that must be respected in all circumstances. It noted that this was reflected not only in the prohibition of genocide but also in the inclusion of a non-discrimination clause of Article 4(1) and in the non-derogable nature of Article 18 ICCPR.[43] In addition, in the context of other rights, such as the right not to be discriminated against, minority rights must be protected also during states of emergency exactly because of their particularly fundamental nature. Related to the non-discrimination clause is Article 20 stipulating that State parties cannot invoke a state of emergency to justify incitement to discrimination, hostility or violence. The HRC determined that this prohibition has a peremptory nature under the ICCPR.[44]

Another peremptory right mentioned by the HRC is the protection against forced displacement 'by expulsion or other coercive means from the area in which the persons concerned are lawfully present'. The Committee has pointed out that the Rome Statute of the ICC also confirms that such deportation or forcible transfer of population constitutes a crime against humanity.[45] As a norm recognised by the HRC for its fundamental nature, the use of provisional measures to prevent or halt violations of this right could be warranted.

The right to life and the prohibition of torture and cruel treatment clearly necessitate the use of provisional measures because violations result in irreparable harm to persons threatening their very existence. What about the situation of a *group* threatened in its very existence, even if the lives of the individual members are not threatened? As discussed, several adjudicators have indeed used provisional measures in cases involving indigenous culture (Chapter X). If international

---

43   HRC General Comment 29 on states of emergency (Article 4), 24 July 2001, §13(c).
44   Id., §13(e).
45   Id., §13(d).

adjudicators should only use provisional measures to prevent irreparable harm to persons, the violation of the right claimed would not only have to be irreversible and result in irreparable harm to the rights claimed, but it should also be established that such a violation would result in irreparable harm to the (group of) persons involved. In the face of threats to the natural habitat, one question would be that of irreversibility and the assessment of risk.[46] Another question would be whether there was a risk of irreversible harm to possible claims of individuals as part of a group. Finally, the question would have to be dealt with whether this would also result in harm to the person's life and physical integrity, as seems to be the implicit criterion in most provisional measures, or whether that criterion has been expanded to encompass irreparable harm to the survival of an indigenous group as well.[47]

If it would be required to establish that the threats to the natural habitat or otherwise to the cultural survival of an indigenous group would cause harm to the person's life and integrity, it would be necessary to specify that personal integrity means not only physical but also mental integrity and that this would include sense of identity. Donders has described cultural identity as a broad and dynamic concept with both an individual and a collective dimension. She has noted that 'the suppression or limitation of the development and expression of cultural identity can make people feel alienated, which seriously affects their human dignity'.[48] Indeed, in that sense the concept of cultural identity is related to that of physical, psychological and moral integrity. Thus one could argue that the interest of survival as an indigenous group could be subsumed under an expanded interpretation of the right to life and the prohibition of cruel treatment to include collective aspects of these rights for members of indigenous groups. Nevertheless, while the concepts are clearly related, the prohibition of cruel treatment would lose its independent meaning if it included not only the concepts of physical, psychological and moral integrity, but also that of cultural integrity (as the counterpart of cultural identity).[49] The use of provisional measures in cases involving threats to culture should not be subsumed under the limited category of preventing cruel treatment.

Given the special position of indigenous peoples, however, adjudicators may consider using provisional measures not only in the face of threats to personal integrity and life, but in the face of threats to the cultural survival of an indigenous people as well.[50] This could mean that they would

---

[46] See Chapter XV (Immediacy and risk).

[47] Yet another question is what is an indigenous group. It has been suggested that it is very problematic to define 'indigenous peoples' as a distinctive legal category or 'a global abstraction capable of working across different types of society with intricate identity politics and rapid cultural and economic change'. See e.g. Kingsbury (2001), p. 245. See in general about the discussion on the definition of minorities and indigenous peoples: Meijknecht (2001), Chapters III (in particular pp. 115-118) and IV; Donders (2002), pp 169-171 and pp. 204-205; and Thornberry (2002), pp. 33-60.

[48] Donders (2002), pp. 327-328. She noted: "Cultural identity is an important value for communities and individuals, since it concerns their belonging, their 'roots', way of thinking, feeling and acting. Most people consider their cultural identity as essential to their life, and value the choice they have made to belong to a certain cultural community because these communities give them valuable life options".

[49] Obviously certain measures involving religious or cultural issues *would* indeed constitute cruel or degrading treatment, such as forcing devout Muslims to eat pork or devout Hindus to eat beef. Destruction of the natural habitat or of sites of cultural importance, on the other hand, relates to collective rights and is covered by Articles 1 and 27 rather than 7 and 10 ICCPR.

[50] See e.g. ILO Convention 169 affirming, as Anaya (1996), p. 106 puts it, 'that indigenous peoples as groups are entitled to a continuing relationship with lands and natural resources according to traditional patterns of use or occupancy'. See e.g. Articles 13(1) and 14(1) of this Convention. See also Agenda 21 (Chapter 26) of the UN Conference on Environment and Development, Rio de Janeiro, 13 June 1992, A/CONF.151/26 (Vol. 3), Annex 2 (1992), Operational Directive 4.20

use provisional measures in the context of the right to life, the prohibition of torture and cruel treatment *and* of the right to culture. The special position of indigenous peoples and the importance of collective aspects of the right to culture may be explained by various factors. In domestic law land rights have regularly been dealt with on the basis of property rights. Yet it is often difficult for indigenous peoples to prove ownership and this approach does not take into account traditional occupancy. Moreover, domestic law in relation to property often considers financial compensation an appropriate remedy for expropriation. In relation to indigenous peoples, however, an appropriate remedy should take into account their cultural integrity and survival. Their very existence may be at stake. In other words, 'the requirement to provide meaningful redress for indigenous land claims implies an obligation on the part of states to provide remedies that include for indigenous peoples the option of regaining lands and access to natural resources'.[51] Acts precluding this option would be irreversible and, in the sense that financial compensation alone would not constitute meaningful redress, would be irreparable as well. Pending the proceedings provisional measures could prevent such irreparable harm.

There have been two types of claims about the right to culture in which petitioners have asked provisional measures: those relating to threats to the natural habitat and, for instance, religious sites on the one hand and those relating to exclusion from an indigenous group on the other. Only in the first type of cases have adjudicators used provisional measures.[52] Given the nature of the individual complaint system, technically both types of claims involve the individual right to live as members of an indigenous group taking part in indigenous culture. An important aspect of the right to culture relates to the dignity of an individual self-identified member of a minority or indigenous people as opposed to the rights of the members of the group collectively. This is an individual right to respect for this person's cultural identity. Often this right is materially related to the right to equality and non-discrimination. Nevertheless, the consequences of a violation in this context normally are not irreversible in the sense that it *is* possible to reverse a decision to exclude a person from a group. While the harm that is done in the meantime can be serious, this equally applies to other reversible decisions resulting in a violation of a human rights treaty. Detention of a person who later turned out to be innocent is but one example.[53]

Hence, rather than to protect the individual aspects of the right to culture in relation to exclusion adjudicators have only used provisional measures to protect the collective aspects, as claimed by individual victims. The reason for this is that the irreparable consequences relate exactly to the collective and not to the individual aspects of the right to culture.

The question arises whether and how this use of provisional measures fits one of the types of irreparable harm to be prevented. Once the criteria of immediacy and irreversibility are fulfilled this type of provisional measure may be seen to belong clearly to the broader second category of preventing irreversible harm to the rights claimed. It also comes quite close to the category of preventing irreparable harm to persons. In this particular context 'persons' may refer as well to a group or collectivity as such. 'Survival' may refer not only to the right to life but also to the survival of a culture. After all, indigenous peoples have a special position in substantive international law, but no satisfactory recourse to implement their rights. If their cultural survival is at

---

of the World Bank (1991) and the UN Declaration on the Rights of Indigenous Peoples adopted by the General Assembly in 2007. The rights recognized in the Declaration 'constitute the minimum standards for the survival, dignity and well-being of the indigenous peoples of the world' (Article 43).

[51] Anaya (1996), p. 107.

[52] See Chapter X (Culture).

[53] In some instances arbitrary detention can be so closely related to the risk of torture or disappearances that intervention in the form of provisional measures could be warranted, see Chapters VIII (Procedural rights) and XII (Other situations).

stake this is a convincing reason to take into account the *collective* aspects of rights claimed by members of indigenous groups, through individual complaint systems.

An example of a very important right for indigenous peoples is the right to self-determination. If individual complaint systems do not allow claims based directly on this right (as is the case with the ICCPR), other rights relevant to indigenous peoples must be read in light of the concept of self-determination, emphasising also the collective aspects of these rights. In this respect the right to culture (as laid down or implied in human rights treaties) is, as Nowak has put it, the individual right to enforcement of the collective right.[54] Indeed, procedurally only individuals can claim to be the victim of a violation, but substantively the HRC gives priority to the collective aspects of the right to culture.[55] This certainly applies to the use of provisional measures in cases involving culture. Another reason why adjudicators may be inclined to use provisional measures to prevent irreparable harm to indigenous culture, apart from the special position of indigenous peoples, is that such measures may at the same time prevent environmental degradation. The ICJ itself has pointed out that 'the environment is not an abstraction but represents the living space, the quality of life and the very health of human beings, including generations unborn'.[56] The ITLOS, to give an example of an adjudicator specifically dealing with the law of the sea, has the authority to use provisional measures to preserve the respective rights of the parties to the dispute, but also to prevent *serious harm* to the marine environment (Article 290 UNCLOS).[57] The human rights adjudicators have sometimes addressed environmental issues in the context of the right to life and the prohibition of cruel treatment or in context of the right to family life, but these issues may also play a role in their decision-making in cases involving indigenous culture.

In light of the right to self-determination and the inability for indigenous groups to otherwise receive protection against threats to their cultural survival and in light of the principle of environmental protection, the criterion of irreparable harm to persons could be extended to include irreparable harm to indigenous groups. Not only would some threats to the collective aspects of the right to culture have irreversible consequences but, given the seriousness of the harm, any financial remedy would clearly be inappropriate because the indigenous group would not exist as such anymore. The only appropriate remedy would be halting the industrial activities that may constitute a violation and putting a stop to violations already determined, that threaten the survival of the group.

The HRC has pointed out that States may not make reservations to the freedom of religion or to the right of minorities to enjoy their own culture and profess their own religion.[58] As noted it has also pointed out that 'the international protection of the rights of persons belonging to minori-

---

[54]   See Nowak (1993), p. 499. Nowak pointed this out in the context of Article 27 ICCPR and made an analogy with the freedom of religion of Article 18(1).

[55]   See Chapter X (Culture). Meijknecht (2001), pp. 131-139, focusing on the ICCPR, raises the question whether it is the individual's, the group's or the culture's existence needing protection. She notes that Article 27 is basically formulated as a right bestowed upon the individual. She considers that 'the construction as applied in Article 27 suggests that the tension between the individual and the collectivity can be avoided by denying a legal status and rights to the collectivity, and by attributing rights exclusively to individuals'. The formulation 'in community with other members of their group', she acknowledges, 'suggests some sort of compromise between the individual and collective approach', but this, she points out, 'does not change the fact that the rights in question are bestowed upon individuals'. Certainly, from the perspective of the international personality of indigenous peoples Article 27 denies legal status to the collectivity. In its *interpretation* of the article, however, the HRC seems to attach rights to collectivities at the cost of the individual.

[56]   ICJ, Advisory Opinion on the *Legality of the threat or use of nuclear weapons*, 8 July 1996, §29.

[57]   See Chapter I.

[58]   HRC General Comment 24 on reservations, 4 November 1994, §8.

ties includes elements that must be respected in all circumstances'.[59] Provisional measures to protect the existence of indigenous peoples have been used in (sub-)regional contexts as well as under the ICCPR, the only international complaint system involving a range of human rights. It is argued that they could be used in all systems.[60] This type of provisional measure can be considered an expansion of the common core of the concept of provisional measures in human rights cases.

Most provisions in human rights treaties refer to one individual only, although they assume, of course, the interaction with other people. Next to the right to culture there are some other rights that clearly belong to a group as well as to the individuals making up this group, even though under most treaties only individual victims are able to claim these rights.[61] These are religious rights, the right of peaceful assembly and the right to freedom of association (including the right to form and join trade unions). Still, it is mainly with regard to the collective aspects of the right to *culture* that provisional measures could serve a purpose in preventing irreparable harm, exactly because what is at stake is the existence itself of an indigenous group and its cultural integrity.

At present the use of provisional measures to protect collective rights should be limited to protecting indigenous culture.[62] Violation of the other more or less collective rights normally is not irreversible and, even if such a violation would be irreversible, this would not be of a similar magnitude as destruction of the natural habitat threatening the existence of an indigenous group. Even if State authorities would close a trade union and prohibit its members to form a new one, for instance, this action may have long-term pervasive effects but is still reversible. As part of a judgment finding a violation the adjudicator may indicate that the trade union should be restored and its assets returned. Often, of course, other acts related to the closure of such trade union, taking place pending a case, are indeed irreparable. Obvious examples are the murder and ill treatment of trade unionists.

Desecration of a religious site would be different from acts prohibiting the freedom of religion or peaceful assembly in that this would not only raise the collective aspect of the right but such act is not fully reversible either. This situation could fall under both the right to culture and the right to religious expression. Possibly, particularly if the treaty involved does not contain a provision on the right to culture, or this provision does not apply, petitioners may invoke the right to religion and the adjudicator may equally decide to use provisional measures to protect against threats to cultural survival that can be shown to be related to the right to religion.

As noted, acts resulting in violations of individual rights to access, in the face of exclusion, normally can be reversed. If there is a threat to the collective aspects of the right to culture, however, this may often be irreversible because the acts to be halted threaten to encroach on the envi-

---

59 HRC General Comment 29 on states of emergency (Article 4), 24 July 2001, §13(c).

60 This could be so as long as these systems cover a range of rights including, explicitly or implicitly, cultural rights.

61 An exception is the collective complaint procedure for the European Social Charter. This Charter, however, does not include a right to culture nor a possibility for provisional measures. In the Inter-American system the petitioners may be the NGOs acting on behalf of victims. They do not need to be victims themselves. Nevertheless they have to indicate clearly the group of beneficiaries involved. Chapter XIII (Protection), section 4 on the group of beneficiaries.

62 Possibly in a specific system the context allows the adjudicator to go further than this. As discussed in Chapter X, in the context of the post-conflict situation in Bosnia the provisional measures ordered by the Bosnia Chamber under the Dayton Peace Agreement to respect Muslim sites, including cemeteries, seem particularly appropriate. They aim to address serious and pervasive discrimination relating, moreover, to issues involving respect for religion, for the dead and their community as well as to access to religious sites and protection against deletion of a suppressed group from the history of the region, all affecting to the core the dignity of the group at issue.

ronment and, thereby, the natural habitat of certain indigenous peoples. In such cases the first question is whether the act would have an irreversible impact on the environment and the second whether this would result in irreparable harm to the culture of an indigenous group because this group depends on this environment for its culture and livelihood. Other acts might not be related to the natural environment but would equally be irreversible as well as irreparable. An example would be the destruction and desecration of an ancient burial site or of a work of art essential to the culture of an indigenous people.

Halting the destruction of works of art essential to the culture of an indigenous people may at the same time protect cultural heritage in general. An example would be if a State plans to allow the destruction of a Maya site. On the other hand, human rights adjudicators cannot use provisional measures solely to protect the cultural heritage of mankind if there is no specific link between the alleged victim and the culture of an indigenous group.[63] In any case, other organisations, such as UNESCO, would be better suited to deal with situations of large-scale threats to cultural heritage. Moreover, even if the States involved have ratified an individual complaint procedure and the petition would not constitute *actio popularis*, such threats often take place during civil wars or when there is no central government to be contacted. Even if the adjudicator could take into account international humanitarian law it would not be easy to establish state responsibility.

Another situation that conceivably concerns culture is the threat that a painting will be destroyed. Again, except when this painting would be shown to be essential to an indigenous group, this would either concern the common heritage of mankind (an example could be a government plan to paint over Van Gogh's Sunflowers) or it would concern freedom of expression. In the first case the above comment on the specific link to the alleged victim would apply and in the second the victim would be the artist. The result would be irreversible even if a photograph had been made of the original painting. Clearly it would cause irreparable harm to the rights claimed (freedom of expression). It would also violate the artist's personal dignity in the broad sense of the term. Nevertheless, lacking a specific treaty provision on provisional measures to the contrary, in an international human rights system such situation should not trigger the use of provisional measures because the category of irreparable harm to survival or personal integrity, in the more limited sense, would not apply.[64]

2.2.4 Protecting against mass expulsion, internal displacement and forced eviction

The Inter-American Commission and Court have used provisional measures to intervene in a situation of mass-expulsion.[65] The Bosnia Chamber has sometimes intervened to halt forced eviction.[66] The question is whether these situations could qualify as part of the common core proposed for the use of provisional measures in international human rights adjudication.

In some contexts provisional measures may indeed assist in alleviating the situation even of potentially large groups of people.[67] Presently, it is already clear that not only the right to life and the prohibition of cruel treatment are rights singled out in each treaty for their exceptional nature, but the prohibition of racial discrimination is as well. Moreover, it is one of the few human rights

---

[63] Hypothetically an inter-State complaint would be possible but, thus far, this procedure has been used very rarely and only in the European system have provisional measures been used in this context.

[64] See further section 2.3 of this Conclusion on provisional measures within the outer limits of the concept, but not within the common core.

[65] See Chapter XI (Mass expulsion).

[66] Ibid.

[67] See Chapter XIII (Protection), section 4 (beneficiaries).

specifically mentioned in the UN Charter and referred to by the ICJ for its character *erga omnes*.[68] Under Article 4(1) ICCPR derogations may only be justified on condition that they 'do not involve discrimination solely on the ground of race, colour, sex, language, religion or social origin'. The HRC has noted that while Article 26 and other rights related to non-discrimination have not been listed specifically among the non-derogable provisions in Article 4(2) ICCPR 'there are elements or dimensions of the right to non-discrimination that cannot be derogated from in any circumstances'.[69]

In this light, international adjudicators might be justified in using provisional measures to order the halting of mass expulsion and internal displacement, especially because the victims are being expelled or displaced on a discriminatory basis and are often threatened and harassed in the process as well. Moreover, there are often children involved and for them the context of mass expulsion or displacement may be particularly traumatic.[70] Finally, apart from the discrimination and the traumatic effects on children, it is also unlikely that large groups of persons, after it is determined that they have been arbitrarily expelled, will be allowed to return. The State is less likely to allow the return of all persons arbitrarily expelled than just the return of some individuals. Thus the issue of irreversibility becomes relevant as well. Mass expulsion (and internal displacement) must be prevented exactly because the causes may be endemic (e.g. based on religious or ethnic grounds) and the consequences may be extremely long-lasting for a large group of people.

Given the hardships suffered by the victims of mass or arbitrary expulsion and forced eviction and the interrelatedness between the rights at stake, including the particular impact on the basic rights of children, and in light of the special responsibility of the adjudicators involved to address the prohibition of discrimination, this type of provisional measure is clearly moving towards the common core. There are some cases where the human hardship involved would be particularly abrasive and where appropriate redress would be impossible. There are some cases where it will be impossible to appropriately redress the situation after the fact, justifying a shift to the common core given the seriousness of the harm resulting from the combination of pervasive discrimination and mass expulsion or internal displacement. This applies in particular when a range of interrelated rights is involved, and especially the rights of children.[71] Thus, if the Inter-American Commission and Court were to expand their practice in this respect and more adjudicators were to start following their lead, together with the precedent of the Bosnia Chamber's provisional measures in forced eviction cases, this might indeed lead to an expansion of the common core. Similarly, it is possible that the human rights adjudicators would determine that certain kinds of treatment (such as rounding up persons in vans and dumping them across borders in unknown territory without due process or without allowing them to contact their families; or refusal to register a birth, and a denial to access primary education as well as a constant threat of expulsion) triggered by racist motives, would have such an impact of humiliation that they would come down to cruel, inhuman or degrading treatment.[72] If the case law of the adjudicators were to

---

[68] See e.g. Article 1(3) UN Charter (a purpose of the UN is to achieve international cooperation in promoting and encouraging respect for human rights 'for all without distinction as to race, sex, language or religion'). See also Articles 13(1)(b) and 55(c); and ICJ *Barcelona Traction* case (*Belgium* v. *Spain*), second phase, ICJ reports 1970, 3 §§33-34 referring to 'basic rights of the human person' as obligations *erga omnes* (concerns of all States), mentioning as examples the protection from slavery, racial discrimination and genocide.

[69] See HRC General Comment 29 on states of emergency (Article 4), 24 July 2001, §8.

[70] Being in a process of development that may irreparably stunted as a result of the mass eviction.

[71] In many cases persons are also being threatened and harassed, see Chapters IX (Death threats) and XIII (Protection).

[72] See e.g. CAT *Hajrizi Dzemajl et al.* v. *Yugoslavia*, 21 November 2002 and ECtHR *Moldovan et al.* v. *Romania*, 12 July 2005, discussed in Chapter XI (Mass expulsion).

converge in this respect, provisional measures to halt mass expulsion or forced eviction in such circumstances would belong to the common core simply by virtue of preventing such treatment.

In other words there is an accumulation of reasons (the interrelated rights at stake, the hardship on particularly vulnerable groups, the impact on the rights of groups uprooted and forcibly removed across the region, the possible evolution of the case law on racist acts constituting cruel treatment) why the common core of provisional measures in international human rights adjudication may be shifting to include ordering a halt to certain situations of mass expulsion or forced eviction.

Nevertheless, apart from the conceptual issue there is also the practical difficulty that international adjudicators may not be able to collect sufficient information to assist the potential beneficiaries with provisional measures that are sufficiently focused. Thus, while the use of provisional measures in cases of mass expulsion and internal displacement may be justified normatively, in practice such use of provisional measures does not seem to be immediately possible. If at all, in an international system such provisional measures might only be used incrementally on the basis of clearly established case law on the merits as well as an ongoing exchange of thoughts with the particular State in question and the alleged victims. Regional systems with a monitoring presence or at least the capacity of making country visits and organising hearings may have a better chance in this respect.[73] Nevertheless, rather than using provisional measures directly on this issue, international adjudicators may in any case specify their provisional measures taken in the context of protection against death threats and harassment by indicating that displaced persons should be allowed to return.

2.3   Outer limits: preventing irreversible harm to the claim or procedure

It appears from the foregoing that the common core of provisional measures in human rights adjudication is the protection of the very existence of persons and groups. Yet it is possible that some adjudicators consider that in the context of their own system their protective role implies the use of provisional measures in a less limited set of circumstances than only to protect survival and physical integrity. If so, it should be possible to identify the rationale of these measures. One rationale could be that the use of provisional measures should be extended to prevent irreversible harm to the rights claimed and to the eventual forms of reparation rather than to prevent irreparable harm to persons as discussed above. As noted, this is a broader category preventing all irreversible harm. An example would be that of halting the destruction of a work of art as a form of freedom of expression. The HRC has used provisional measures once exactly for this purpose.[74] In addition it has used provisional measures in a family life case involving deportation by a State of someone who had lived in that State since childhood.[75] In this case the HRC argued that the consequences of deportation were irreversible. This means that the case fits into the category of preventing irreversible harm to the *claim*. On the other hand, in later cases involving family life the HRC noted that, if it would find a violation, it could still order the return of victim. Thus, while the likelihood that this would indeed happen seems remote, clearly the situation is not as irreversible as irreparable harm to *persons* (e.g. execution and cruel treatment) or irreparable harm to the *claim* (e.g. the destruction of a work of art). The aim of the provisional measure in this case seems to be to prevent 'undue hardship' to the person rather than to prevent 'irreparable harm' to either the person or the claim. An attempt *could* be made to fit this measure in the third category of preventing irreversible harm, namely harm to the procedure. In my view, however, provisional

---

[73]   See Introduction and Chapter II.
[74]   See Chapter XII (Other situations), section 2.10.
[75]   See Chapter XII (Other situations), section 3.2.

measures should not be used to prevent irreversible harm to the procedure in all situations, but mainly as a collateral purpose in death penalty and non-refoulement cases involving claims relating to the prohibition of torture and cruel treatment or the right to life. After all, once a person has been deported to a State in which there is a fear for his physical integrity and even his life, the State has not only hindered the right of individual complaint and the proceedings under the treaty in question, but also exposed him to a real risk of violations of the right to life and personal integrity. Both dangers are closely interrelated because the individual complaint procedures were initiated to prevent irreparable harm to persons at minimum and to allow the petitioner to present evidence and substantiate claims of a real risk of such harm. If he would be returned nevertheless, he would not only risk irreparable harm. The return would also hinder the chance of contacting him. In fact the chance of completing the proceedings under the relevant treaty in an appropriate manner would be even slimmer than in deportation cases involving family life.

The use of provisional measures to refrain from action causing undue hardship rather than irreparable harm seems less appropriate in a universal system, at least until such use has been firmly established in more than one regional system. Especially in a universal system lacking sufficient cohesion, a more cautious approach may be warranted in which provisional measures must remain exceptional, clearly aiming at the prevention of irreparable harm to persons or procedure. In regional systems, on the other hand, tighter links between States may lead to a higher degree of pressure to comply even with provisional measures in less serious situations.

As discussed in Chapter I, scholars have discerned a so-called 'humanization' of international law.

There seems to be a convergence, rather than divergence of jurisprudence on provisional measures that ties in with this humanization. This may be explained even if the adjudicators are not aware of each other's jurisprudence, simply by the fact that all the human rights adjudicators examined in this book are dealing with similar treaty provisions, for instance on the right to life and the prohibition of torture and cruel treatment and on the right of individual petition. It could also be explained exactly by this awareness of each other's jurisprudence, sometimes evident from conscious cross-referencing of jurisprudence, as was seen in the ECtHR judgment in *Mamatkulov*.[76]

At the same time some provisional measures seem typical to a certain region. The most particular adjudicator dealt with in this book, the Bosnia Human Rights Chamber, may serve as an example. The Bosnia Chamber was a hybrid and non-permanent body that may be assumed to have been rather specific in its approaches to provisional measures, closely adapting its practice to the exigencies of the post-war situation in Bosnia and Herzegovina. The Chamber had to deal with the aftermath of a four year war with ethnic cleansing and discriminatory practices that were still pervasive after the war. It had to deal with only three addressees (the State of BiH and its constituent parts: the Federation of BiH and the Republica Srpska), all from the same geographical region. The Secretariat of the Chamber was based in the area concerned and the Chamber held its sessions there. Although it was a *sui generis* body rather than a constitutional court, its case law clearly is – and should be – more context-specific than that of an international adjudicator like the HRC.

Apart from the Bosnia Chamber as a *sui generis* adjudicator, on the one hand, and the HRC as the international human rights adjudicator operating with regard to the widest range of human rights, on the other hand, there are also the regional systems. In the context of the Inter-American system it is noteworthy that according to some (former) Judges of the Inter-American Court provisional measures can apply to all rights.[77] Moreover, the requirements for precautionary meas-

---

[76]   About the latter see also Pasqualucci (2005).

[77]   See e.g. IACHR *Matter of Capital El Rodeo I and El Rodeo II Judicial Confinement Center*, Order of 8 February 2008, Separate Opinion Judge García Ramírez, §12 and Cançado Trindade (2003), p. 165, as well as in his Introduction to the third volume of the Court's provisional

ures by the Inter-American Commission are less rigorous and less regulated than those for the provisional measures of the Inter-American Court. Until 1999 the Court only acted when personal security was involved while the Commission acted upon all the rights of the Convention. The Commission's criterion has always been that there was some urgency, some imminent danger. The informal beginnings of the Commission's practice may explain this.[78] In light of the Commission's other activities, such as taking part in country visits and drafting country reports, moreover, the Commission has more of a hands-on experience of the actual human rights situations in the Americas. This may also explain its more flexible use of precautionary measures.

Commissioner Juan Mendez had noted that the practice of the Commission with regard to precautionary measures started with disappearances, but it was never limited to that. Moreover, there was never a time in which the Commission limited itself to taking precautionary measures to situations where life and limb were threatened. There have been cases, for instance, in which the Commission took precautionary measures when someone was under an arrest warrant and was to be detained at any time. Under the new Rules of Procedure the Commission has crystallized its practice over a long period of time. Mendez stated that they have made very broad the possibility to take precautionary measures. This would be basically in any situation that needs immediate attention according to the Commission. Its criterion is that when there is no harm in waiting to resolve the issue at the merits stage, then it will not intervene, but otherwise it will.[79] According to Mendez any right threatened by an immediate violation or irreparable harm may warrant a precautionary measure, but it would have to be a right spelled out under the Convention or the Declaration. For instance, a threat to the 'project of life' by definition deals with a situation that is prolonged, such as prolonged administrative detention and, he considers, by definition something that is urgent is not very prolonged. Although he finds it difficult to imagine when the 'project of life' issue would come up in the context of precautionary measures, he notes, there is no reason to say it should not. Generally, however, if it would come up this would be at the stage of reparations, not at the stage of provisional measures or even precautionary measures.[80] It must be borne in mind, though, that provisional measures have in fact been used in ongoing cases, e.g. involving detention situations or death threats, meaning it is not necessarily contradictory for the project of life to play a role.[81]

The criterion that the right must be 'spelled out' under the American Convention or the Declaration before the Commission may take precautionary measures, paradoxical as it may sound, must not be taken literally. After all, the first precautionary measures almost all dealt with recent disappearances in which a composite of articles is applicable. Of course it is true that these articles, such as the right to life, in themselves are indeed very clearly spelled out under both the Convention and the Declaration. In my view it is not entirely impossible to use project of life argument in the context of provisional measures, although in the first instance it might sound contradictory, as this is a thing that can only take place over a long stretch of time. At the same time, if it is clear that certain illegal acts or abstentions result in obstacles to the project of life and possible irreparable harm to it, it makes more sense to intervene timely than just to pronounce on reparations (including compensation) afterwards. I believe this could also be the case in situations

---

measures, §21 and interview by author with President Cançado Trindade, San José, Costa Rica, November/December 2001. But see Buergenthal (1994), p. 77 referring to the wording and the legislative history of Article 63(2), noting that these ' make clear that its sole purpose is to protect human beings against the loss of life or extreme physical or mental abuse when there is a very strong likelihood that they are in imminent danger and there exists a corresponding urgency for protective action'.

[78] Interview by author with Commissioner Juan Mendez, Washington D.C., 17 October 2001.

[79] Id.

[80] Id.

[81] On the project of life see also Chapter XII (Other situations), section 2.1.

where *access* to a project of life (to even think about embarking on such a project) is blocked.[82] In other words, in particular cases in which government action can create this access, provisional measures might order a government to actually do so. Thus in some specific cases provisional measures could indeed be used in economic and social rights cases, especially in relation to children.

Formally the Inter-American Court has continued to adhere to the exceptional nature of provisional measures, but it is doubtful whether it has always adhered to this principle in practice. If the Court only orders provisional measures in exceptional cases, it is difficult to understand why it also does so to protect someone's good name, especially since an incorrect registration in the criminal records can be repaired. It is unlikely that the good name of a journalist will suffer irreparable harm from a temporary registration in such records for having published an article. The same applies to several of the precautionary measures taken by the Commission in freedom of expression cases, possibly with the exception of curtailment of freedom of expression previous to, or during, an election period.[83] In any case, even when it is possible to establish that these rights would be irreversibly harmed without the Commission's or the Court's intervention, it concerns rights other than the right to life and dignity. If the Commission and the Court emphasize the factor of urgency rather than that of irreparable harm, this would be an evolutive interpretation of the Convention requiring clear motivation.

The more adverse the impact of certain measures is likely to be on the well-being of people, facing a situation that would be intolerable, the more reason adjudicators have for the use of provisional measures pending the proceedings, particularly if the task of the adjudicator specifically relates to this issue or if the problem in question is endemic in that region.

The use of provisional measures as taken by just one adjudicator, for instance by the Inter-American Commission and Court to protect freedom of expression, can often be explained in the context of problems occurring in a specific region or because of opportunities arising in that region (e.g. a powerful lobby of press agencies, the special respect an adjudicator commands in a given State at a given moment, the scope of the provision on provisional measures in the applicable treaty or Rule of Procedure) or simply because they are based on the provisions of a specialised treaty (e.g. those of CEDAW or ICAT). Such measures may presently be within the outer limits of the concept but beyond the common core because they do not deal with preventing irreparable harm to persons.

In some cases the provisional measures seem to have been taken in error. The concept of provisional measures in human rights adjudication does not allow for the use in situations in which a violation could later be repaired through financial measures alone. For instance, using provisional measures to postpone payment of a fine is beyond the outer limits of the concept. Thus in some situations the use of provisional measures is inappropriate, as they aim to prevent harm that would mostly be reversible. An example could be a single action hindering the freedom of expression or the independence of the judiciary. Yet in a climate of harassment against journalists or the judiciary, it is no longer possible to speak of reversible harm to the claim. In such a context it could be appropriate for regional adjudicators to order provisional measures to prevent irreversible harm to the claim. Moreover, such a climate of harassment would probably involve death threats and harassment against the personal integrity of the intended beneficiaries as well, bringing the provisional measures within the common core of the concept to the extent that they aim to protect the life and personal dignity of the person involved, while also specifying that this person should be able to continue his or her activities (journalist, judge, witness, human rights defender, etc.).

---

[82]   Such as in the case of street children, see Chapter XII (Other situations), section 2.1.

[83]   See Chapter XII (Other situations), section 3.3.

For the time being it may be a bridge too far for a supervisory body to an international treaty without a specific treaty provision on provisional measures to expand the use of provisional measures to issues other than those involving the survival and physical integrity of persons. This does not mean it is impossible conceptually, or that it is not important from the perspective of the individuals involved, but just that it may not be very wise from the perspective of expected compliance. Use of provisional measures with regard to any type of irreversible harm to the claim would be better suited in a regional or even in a constitutional approach by a hybrid court such as the Bosnia Chamber. Yet at some point in the future, once it has been firmly established by regional bodies, the international adjudicator might consider similar expansions.

3   PROTECTIVE MEASURES, MERITS AND REPARATION

An element of positive action is present in most provisional measures and should be made explicit in cases involving ongoing situations such as adverse detention conditions, recent disappearances and death threats. The discussion on subsidiarity plays out differently in each system but, like the Inter-American Commission and Court, the other human rights adjudicators should also incrementally specify their provisional measures, so as to provide clarity to States on what is expected of them, especially with regard to core rights. This way States have at least some direction of what they are expected to do or to abstain from doing in order to prevent irreparable harm to persons.

The European Commission and Court have directed provisional measures to petitioners who were on hunger strike to protest against adverse prison conditions, lack of access to medication or arbitrary detention. None of the other adjudicators have used provisional measures to the effect that petitioners should stop a hunger strike. Here, again, the question arises whether the aim of preventing irreparable harm to persons is independent of the claim or related to the claim. If related to the claim, it would be inappropriate for the adjudicator to turn around and direct a provisional measure to the petitioner. Nevertheless, this is what the European Commission and Court did. In these circumstances they took provisional measures *proprio motu* directed against the petitioner rather than against the State. They took a very traditional approach of using provisional measures 'in the interests of the parties'. They appear to lean towards preventing irreparable harm to the procedure. While this clearly agrees with the text of the Rules of Procedure, in a dynamic and purposive approach it seems contrary to the Convention to assume that both parties are on equal footing. In human rights cases involving an individual and a State party the power is concentrated in the latter. Provisional measures, therefore, should serve to shield the threatened individual or group against abuse of power by the State or make the State act against abuse of power by others.[84]

It is argued that the Inter-American practice of using provisional measures not just to protect persons mentioned by name, but also to protect the members of a defined community, or people working at human rights organisations, as well as all other persons visiting the premises is indeed appropriate. While they are not identified by name, the beneficiaries of the required protective measures are clear to the State. Obviously there must be no indications of disagreement by beneficiaries with their inclusion in an order for provisional measures. Moreover, provisional measures may even protect a larger group than that mentioned in the provisional measures. After all a good faith implementation of the obligations under the relevant human rights treaty warrants a pro-active stance of the State to ensure that the underlying rationale to a provisional measure is being met.

---

[84]   See Chapter XIII (Protection), section 4.

Sometimes petitioners may have as their main aim to obtain a provisional measure rather than a decision on the merits. In the context of the ICJ this has occasionally been criticised.[85] Even if this tendency may be criticized vis-à-vis States, in human rights cases the situation is different, especially if the purpose of the main claim coincides with the purpose of the provisional measures, both aiming at preventing irreparable harm to persons. In the practice of the human rights adjudicators the use of provisional measures may trigger a State's attempt to solve the issue, sometimes making it possible to strike out the case.

Also if the purpose of provisional measures is to prevent irreparable harm to persons rather than to the claim, when using provisional measures the adjudicator should refer to the rights involved. It is possible that some adjudicators have used independent concepts of life, dignity and personal integrity without relating the concept of irreparable harm to specific articles of the relevant treaty. In view of the fact, however, that they may have to declare subsequently, on the basis of previous case law, that there was no violation, the question arises whether the object of the provisional measures was simply to postpone the suffering until after the expected finding. This would be an unsatisfactory approach to the concept of provisional measures. After all, if it would not be possible to achieve a similar result as part of the merits (and reparation) phase, achieving it temporarily, as part of provisional measures, would serve no purpose in the long run. Provisional measures should go no further than the eventual obligation could.

When dealing with a request for provisional measures the Inter-American Court equally notes that the case is only before it for the purpose of provisional measures. A decision to order such measures, or the President's decision to request urgent measures, does not imply a decision on the merits of the dispute between the petitioners and the State.[86] By adopting urgent measures, for instance, the President was simply guaranteeing the Court's ability to exercise faithfully its conventional mandate.[87] As noted, if in a request by petitioners for provisional measures the facts complained of relate to other aspects of the main case, not directly constituting a situation of urgency, the adjudicator will declare (this part of) the request for provisional measures inadmissible. The Inter-American Court has emphasized that it may not examine 'any arguments other than those which are directly and strictly related to situations of extreme gravity and urgency which require the adoption of protection measures to avoid irreparable damage to persons. Any other arguments or facts may only be examined and determined by the Court when considering the merits of contentious cases brought before the Court'.[88]

Apart from the usual statement that the decision on provisional measures does not prejudge the merits, specific practice of the other adjudicators, such as the HRC, with regard to the approach to the issue of prejudgment in the use of provisional measures currently is unavailable. Undoubtedly they have considered the issue in their decision-making, but generally they have not publicly elaborated on it.

The remark by Judge Gros, in his dissent to the Order for provisional measures in the *Nuclear Test* (1973) cases, that it is contrary to the nature of interlocutory proceedings if they enable the dispute to be disposed of, may already be disputed in the context of the ICJ's judgments and provisional measures.[89] At any rate it does not apply to human rights cases. The protective function of provisional measures to prevent irreparable harm to persons often coincides so much with

---

[85] See Mani (1973), p. 262 and Sztucki (1983), p. 260.

[86] See e.g. IACHR *Peace Community of San José de Apartadó* case (Colombia), Order of 24 November 2000.

[87] See e.g. IACHR *James and others*, Orders of 27 May, 29 June, 13 and 22 July 1998, 11 May and 19 June 1999.

[88] IACHR *Matter of Adrián Meléndez-Quijano et al* (El Salvador), Order of 26 November 2007, 9th 'Considering' clause, referring to various cases including *Matter of Luisiana Rios et al.* (Venezuela), Order of 3 July 2007, 9th 'Considering' clause.

[89] See Chapter I (ICJ).

the protection required if the claim on the merits is granted that these measures cannot be seen simply as 'an accessory element' of the dispute. This is shown in the practice of several human rights adjudicators, for instance because provisional measures caused the State to seek a solution and resulted in the withdrawal of cases and in the decision to strike them from the list of pending cases.

The authority to order provisional measures and the authority to order action or abstention on the merits, as well as reparations are closely related. In some cases it would be particularly unacceptable to await the harm and then award pecuniary damages. Prevention (or putting a halt to ongoing violations) would be the only appropriate measure exactly because the harm is irreparable. Clearly, any form of financial compensation would be insufficient in relation to the harm done. In such cases the reason for using provisional measures would be so pressing that States would normally feel especially embarrassed to ignore them.

The link between halting an execution pending the proceedings and ordering commutation or a new trial as part of the decision on the merits is evident. With regard to ordering a State to protect a person against threats, the aim seems to be identical in provisional measures and on the merits. Thus if in the final determination of the case the HRC does not recommend at least the preservation of the life of the victim it seems that its provisional measures to prevent harm to persons serve little purpose. In other words, the aim of preventing harm to the claim and ensuring an adequate remedy is a prerequisite to preventing harm to the person.[90]

While the ICJ's power to use provisional measures normally must maintain its 'proper subordination to the main judgment',[91] this is different in cases involving irreparable harm to persons. Clearly, because they aim at preventing such harm they must be in accordance with the pre-existing jurisprudence on the right to life, the prohibition of cruel treatment, the right to culture of indigenous peoples and the prohibition of mass expulsion and internal displacement on ethnic grounds.

At the same time, the protective measures required cannot go further in substance than an eventual decision on the merits and reparations would. This means that decisions on provisional measures already give an indication on substantive law. The 'rule' of non-anticipation by the adjudicator (rather than the parties) of the decision on the merits simply is a corollary to the customary statement that a decision to take provisional measures does not prejudice the eventual legal determination of the main conflict. The requirement not to prejudice the eventual legal determination, it is argued, is related to the assessment of risk.[92]

Often it is already established that *if* an adjudicator finds sufficient evidence (on the merits stage) it will find a violation. Sometimes, however, the adjudicator has not yet dealt with the meaning of a certain provision in the situation at hand, or there are clear indications that it may change its case law. On occasion provisional measures have been taken pending the proceedings in such cases.[93] This might be seen as anticipating the eventual determination. Yet, in light of the risk of irreparable harm to persons, in human rights cases such risk of anticipation should not

---

[90]   See Chapter XIII (Protection).
[91]   Merrills (1995), p. 106.
[92]   See further Chapter XV (Immediacy and risk).
[93]   See e.g. in corporal punishment cases (Chapter IV) non-refoulement cases involving lack of proper care (Chapter V) and in cases involving indigenous culture (Chapter X). See also e.g. the use of provisional measures to halt destruction of IVF embryos and the subsequent decision on the merits finding that such destruction would not result in a violation of the Convention, Chapter XII (Other situations), section 2.5.

hinder the use of provisional measures.[94] What is important is that upon final determination the adjudicator is not led by the fact that pending the proceedings provisional measures were taken.[95]

Violations of rights causing irreparable harm must be prevented since a return to the *status quo ante* is impossible after the irreversible has taken place (irreversibility), while the nature of the harm implies that such violations can never be repaired by financial compensation (irreparability). In human rights cases the relevance of this traditional reason for using provisional measures is particularly striking.

In a case where one party (the State) threatens to execute a death sentence imposed on the other party and that party claims that this would violate his *right to life*, an execution before the case is finally determined would amount to an irrevocable anticipation of the adjudicator's decision by the State party. This action would make impossible the fulfilment of the requirements claimed on the merits. These requirements would have constituted, first and foremost, the prevention of a further violation of the right to life. Next to cases in which there is precedent for the measures claimed on the merits, there may also be cases in which case law on the specific remedy claimed is not yet available. In some of these cases execution of the petitioner may inflict irreparable harm as well. In all such situations provisional measures have been used to prevent irreparable harm to persons.

A similar approach applies to the prevention of corporal punishment and of refoulement. Intervention in cases of disappearances or in detention situations involving lack of access to medical treatment equally prevents irreparable harm to persons. At the same time the intervention is justified by the fact that, once a violation is found, adjudicators have indicated the action or abstention required on the merits and recommended forms of reparation corresponding to the protective measures required pending the proceedings. Evidently, without the provisional measures there could be no appropriate decision on the merits nor form of reparation.

Adjudicators often deem warranted remedies for violations that have already taken place, in addition to those preventing (further) violations. In death penalty cases it would also be an option to use provisional measures to halt an execution because the victim could not enjoy the requested form of reparation, once executed, even if such reparation in itself does not refer to release or commutation, but to an unspecified (and possibly only monetary) remedy. Nevertheless, if the case law indicates that a remedy such as commutation is never recommended in relation to certain findings, the State itself is unlikely on its own motion to consider life a prerequisite for the enjoyment of any form of reparation. This already indicates that there are death penalty cases in which provisional measures eventually would *not* help prevent irreparable harm to persons because a link with the eventual obligations on the merits and reparation is lacking.

In death penalty cases an adjudicator should not use provisional measures simply to express an abolitionist stance in cases where he or she could expect the adjudicator would *not* recommend commutation. Provisional measures used in such circumstances do not truly prevent irreparable harm to persons because the eventual measures on the merits will not. Of course there is still a rationale to the use of provisional measures in such cases, namely to prevent irreversible harm to the procedure. The execution of the petitioner pending the proceedings hinders irreversibly the right of individual complaint. Such an execution causes irreversible harm to the fairness of the proceedings before the adjudicator and, thereby, the integrity of the individual complaint procedure under the treaty in question. Clearly, when one party in a conflict kills the other party during

---

[94]   Thus in my view the ECtHR could have used provisional measures in *Ireland* v. *UK*, Judgment of 18 January 1978, as discussed in Chapter VII (Detention), section 2.2.

[95]   See also Chapter III (Executions), section 3.2 on prejudgment and see Chapter XV (Immediacy and risk) and XVIII (Follow-up). It should be the other way around: at the provisional measures stage the adjudicator should take into account the likelihood of finding a violation that would require an action or abstention necessitating a similar action or abstention already pending the proceedings.

the course of legal proceedings instituted in order to settle their conflict, that party, rather than the adjudicator, settles the conflict. Such a course of action, moreover, is not conducive to the principle of equality of arms. This principle is a prerequisite to any legal proceedings aiming at being fair. The HRC, for instance, attaches great importance to it. This is evident both from its references to this principle in the examination of cases and from its own emphasis on the importance of making all information available to the State and the petitioner, giving both of them the opportunity to reply to each other's submissions and deciding the case on the basis of all the information before it, often sending reminders to the parties for more information. Execution of the petitioner by the State party is the ultimate example of inequality of arms. This form of irreversible harm to the proceedings is so serious that the use of provisional measures to prevent it could be justified even if there is no clear link with an eventual requirement on the merits preserving the life of the victim. Nevertheless, this approach is less satisfactory from the perspective of logic and the right to life than, for instance, in the case law of the HRC, the improvement and specification of references to 'an appropriate remedy' would be, by including to preservation of the life of the victim. The latter would ensure a correlation between the provisional measure and the eventual obligations on the merits and forms of reparation. In this approach the provisional measures would serve to prevent irreparable harm to persons.

Even if the purpose of provisional measures is to prevent irreparable harm to persons rather than simply irreversible harm to the claim, when using provisional measures the adjudicator should indeed refer to the rights involved. It is possible that some adjudicators have used independent concepts of life, dignity and personal integrity without relating the concept of irreparable harm to specific articles of the relevant treaty. In view of the fact, however, that they may have to declare subsequently, on the basis of previous case law, that there was no violation, or that there was, but no action or abstention is required to prevent irreparable harm to persons at the merits stage, the question arises whether the object of the provisional measures was simply to postpone the suffering until after the expected finding. In order to prevent this, provisional measures should go no further than what could be required on the merits. If the provisional measures aim to ensure that a possible judgment on the merits will not be pre-empted, it should be established that the result hoped for, in the judgment on the merits, by the party requesting the provisional measures is at least feasible. In other words, if it is not feasible that the adjudicator would determine an outcome anywhere close to that hoped by the party requesting the provisional measure, pending the proceedings the adjudicator should not use it in the form requested. This simply requires a very initial prima facie assessment of feasibility.

In human rights cases provisional measures could be used also to prevent irreparable harm to rights collateral to the claim, if these rights involve the right to life and the prohibition of cruel treatment. After all, apart from direct complaints about death threats and harassment the issue of threats can also be collateral to the original claim. In such cases *other* persons than the alleged victim(s) involved in the main claim are at risk of irreparable harm. These persons are being threatened because they are somehow related to the alleged victim, for instance as family members or co-workers or as witnesses, judges or counsel in the international or domestic proceedings. In these cases too the provisional measure should not go further than the eventual decision on the merits could. The difference is that the latter is hypothetical in the sense that it relates to violations perpetrated against persons other than the alleged victim(s). In other words, the criterion is irreparable harm to persons rather than the link between the object of the complaint and the provisional measures. Still, there must be a relationship between what decision on the merits (prevention, non-repetition, reparation) the adjudicator *could* have suggested on the merits had the complaint itself been about the death threats. Thus, what the petitioner needs to show, for purposes of provisional measures, is the threat of irreparable harm to persons and the relationship of these persons to the alleged victim. It is also useful to show that violations have been found in similar cases in the past and that the provisional measures would go no further than the eventual decision on the merits would have, if the persons involved would have been the alleged victims.

In sum, human rights adjudicators should use provisional measures in cases in which they consider, *prima facie*, that the petitioners have shown not only immediacy of the harm and irreversibility of the act or omission[96] but also the risk of irreparable harm to persons, including in ongoing situations. The latter should normally be established by a two-prong test of (1) irreparable harm to persons and (2) irreversible harm to the rights claimed, including the possibility of reparation.

Only if persons other than the alleged victim(s) are risking irreparable harm the situation is different. Then the third type of irreversible harm, harm to the procedure, may play a role as well. This is the case when witnesses, counsel or family members of the alleged victim are harassed and receive death threats. In such cases there is *no* need to establish a relationship with the main claim. Here the test is (1) irreparable harm to persons and (2) irreversible harm to the integrity of the complaint procedure.[97] In relation to the purpose of provisional measures this is the core common to all international and regional human rights systems. This again illustrates the interrelated nature of procedural and substantive aspects of the concept of provisional measures.

4 CONCLUSION

Under universal treaties provisional measures are normally reserved for the prevention of irreparable harm to persons. Such provisional measures are taken in a limited set of circumstances, mainly involving claims about the right to life and the prohibition of cruel treatment. This constitutes the core common to provisional measures used by international adjudicators in human rights cases. Sometimes it concerns irreparable harm to the environment if this would result in irreparable harm to the cultural life or the psychological existence of an indigenous group (or of a persecuted minority). Thus, presently provisional measures to prevent irreparable harm to persons relate to ensuring survival of persons (and groups) and personal integrity.

Adjudicators in human rights cases have taken most provisional measures in relation to the right to life and the prohibition of cruel treatment and torture. These fundamental rights are considered non-derogable in all treaties under examination exactly because their violation, even during a state of emergency, would defeat the whole purpose of the treaty. The exceptional nature of these non-derogable rights is also confirmed by the fact that their violation may constitute a crime against humanity. In that sense there *is* a hierarchy in international human rights law.[98]

Even if the treaty in question does not explicitly provide for the use of provisional measures, the duty to protect against threats to life and personal integrity requires the State to take positive measures also pending international proceedings. The right to personal security, the right to life and the prohibition of cruel treatment and torture imply positive obligations. In that light, rather than abstention alone, provisional measures should imply action as well. An obvious exam-

---

[96] See Chapter XV (Immediacy and risk) and Chapter XIII (Protection: prevention and reparation).

[97] In addition, as noted, preventing irreparable harm to the proceedings (the integrity of the complaint procedure) could be seen as a collateral purpose in death penalty and non-refoulement cases. The execution of a petitioner, for instance, pending the proceedings causes irreparable harm to the fairness of the proceedings before the adjudicator and, thereby, the integrity of the individual complaint procedure under the treaty in question.

[98] The HRC has noted that 'while there is no hierarchy of importance of rights under the Covenant, the operation of certain rights may not be suspended, even in times of national emergency'. "This underlines the great importance of non-derogable rights". General Comment 24 on reservations, 4 November 1994, §10. In this context it refers to peremptory norms and to rules of customary international law in general. See also its General Comment 29 on states of emergency, 24 July 2001. See in general about this issue Seiderman (2001). See also Simma (1995), p. 230.

ple is a provisional measure to prevent irreparable harm to persons by protecting them against death threats and harassment.

Irreparable harm to persons refers not only to harm to physical integrity, but also to psychological and moral integrity, as long as the adjudicator would be likely to find a violation on the merits of the prohibition of cruel treatment and torture. Moreover, as noted, the risk of irreparable harm may vary depending on the vulnerability of the persons involved. It is submitted that the few provisional measures that have been taken to ensure access to court and counsel are equally justified because in the context in which they were used these rights were accessory to the protection against ill treatment and torture and against threats to life.[99]

The example of the Inter-American Commission and Court to protect alleged victims, witnesses and other persons against death threats has been followed by most other adjudicators. While these have not yet built an extensive practice in this regard, their decision to intervene in these circumstances may be explained by the importance attached in all human rights systems to preventing irreparable harm to life and physical integrity.[100] At some point it may be expected that the ECtHR will use provisional measures in situations of death threats and harassment more robustly as well.

The right to life and the prohibition of torture and cruel treatment clearly necessitate the use of provisional measures because violations result in irreparable harm to persons threatening their very existence. Yet there are situations not involving the right to life and the prohibition of cruel treatment and torture in which human rights adjudicators have used provisional measures that have by now become part of the common core. Adjudicators have considered using provisional measures not only in the face of threats to personal integrity and life, but in the face of threats to the cultural survival of an indigenous people as well. This may be explained by the special position of indigenous peoples and other minorities in a particularly vulnerable position. After all, an appropriate obligation on the merits or form of reparation for violations of the right to culture and religion should take into account cultural integrity and survival. Financial compensation alone would not constitute meaningful redress because the very existence as a people may be at stake. Pending the proceedings provisional measures could prevent such irreparable harm, but at present their use to protect collective rights has been limited to protecting indigenous culture.[101]

Irreparable harm results from the violation of rights crucial to a person's or a group's basic existence or crucial to a person's dignity.[102] In some contexts provisional measures may assist in alleviating the situation even of potentially large groups of people. Combined with pervasive discrimination, mass expulsion or internal displacement may indeed be so serious as to constitute not just undue hardship, but irreparable harm to the very existence of people. Such harm must be prevented rather than only redressed following the mass expulsion or displacement. Mass expulsion (and internal displacement) must be prevented exactly because the causes may be endemic (e.g. based on religious or ethnic grounds) and the consequences may have extremely long-term effects for a large group of people. The protection against forced displacement 'by expulsion or other coercive means from the area in which the persons concerned are lawfully present' is another norm recognised by the HRC for its fundamental nature.[103] The use of provisional measures to prevent or halt such violations could be warranted although at the same time international

---

[99]   See Chapter VIII (Procedure).
[100] See Chapter IX (Threats).
[101] See Chapter X (Culture).
[102] Of course the terms 'basic existence' and dignity as used here, are themselves open to interpretation and one may wonder what aspects of the right to 'live' are included, apart from the right to 'life' per se. This includes the very initial discussion in the Inter-American system on the concept of 'project of life', see Chapter XII (Other situations), section 2.1.
[103] See Chapter XI (Mass expulsion).

adjudicators may not be able to collect enough information to assist the potential beneficiaries with provisional measures that are sufficiently focused.

It is argued that particularly in systems not providing for them in the text of the constitutive document, provisional measures should remain exceptional.[104] If the authority of human rights adjudicators to use provisional measures is not based on the constituent document but derived from their function (and based on the rules of procedure),[105] the importance of preventing irreparable harm requires that they are limited to situations threatening the very existence of persons. They should not be used to prevent human rights violations that 'simply' cause undue hardship rather than irreparable harm. This is not because this would not be possible conceptually, but because it risks devaluating the system, especially if used abruptly and without sufficient explanation and discussion.

Still the rule that provisional measures are only to be used to prevent irreparable harm to persons should be applied with a certain measure of flexibility, taking into account, for instance, the developmental rights of children and their ensuing special right for protection. If the beneficiary is a young child one might indeed speak of prevention of irreparable harm to persons in some cases that would otherwise cause undue hardship short of irreparable harm.[106]

In any case in order for provisional measures to remain exceptional any expansion of their use should only involve other rights essential for the very existence of persons and indigenous peoples. As noted, these rights may coincide with rights recognised for their particular fundamental nature within the treaty.

When provisional measures presently belong to the common core the adjudicator may be expected to use them, whether the system is regional or international, and whether it is based on an explicit treaty provision on provisional measures or not. On the other hand, when provisional measure do not belong to the common core adjudicators could still decide to take them, so long as their aim and the protection required are not beyond the outer limits of the concept. Whether such use of provisional measures is advisable would depend on the context. One relevant factor is the international, regional or 'constitutional' nature of the complaint system. Regional systems with a monitoring presence or at least the capacity of making country visits and organising hearings are likely to have a better chance to collect sufficient information and focus the provisional measures on the specific needs. This applies even more to the provisional measures of more 'constitutional' or hybrid adjudicators, such as the Bosnia Chamber. Another relevant factor is whether the adjudicator was introduced in order to deal with a range of rights (HRC, CIDH, IACHR, EComHR, ECtHR, Bosnia Chamber) or with one issue in particular (CAT, CEDAW, CERD).[107] In general, a useful approach for all adjudicators would be to expand their use of provisional measures, as much as possible, on an incremental basis connected to pre-existing notions and practices.

---

[104]   For a different approach, see e.g. Haeck/Burbano Herrera/Zwaak (2003), pp. 60-61.
[105]   See further Chapter XVI (Legal status).
[106]   See also Chapter XII (Other situations).
[107]   See also Chapter II (Systems).

PART III

IMPACT OF THE IRREPARABLE
NATURE OF THE HARM

INTRODUCTION

Part III examines the consequences that flow from the conclusions drawn in Part II on the common core and outer limits of provisional measures in relation to their purpose. In other words, has the irreparable nature of the harm risked to persons, involving their very existence and personal integrity, had an impact on the approach by the adjudicators with regard to other aspects of the concept of provisional measures?

Chapter XIV deals with the relationship of provisional measures in human rights adjudication with jurisdiction and admissibility on the merits. Chapter XV examines the issue of immediacy or temporal urgency on the one hand and risk or material urgency on the other. Chapter XVI is devoted to the legal status of provisional measures.

1   INTRODUCTION

There has only been one case in which the ICJ used provisional measures because it considered it had *prima facie* jurisdiction on the merits, but in which it subsequently determined – during the stage of preliminary objections – that it lacked such jurisdiction.[1] In the practice of the human rights adjudicators provisional measures have been used more often in cases later declared inadmissible. It appears that the adjudicators have taken a more flexible approach, taking into account the irreparable nature of the harm faced by the petitioners and the inequality between the parties. There are even cases in which the HRC has maintained provisional measures beyond declaration of inadmissibility. The IACHR, moreover, has used them after having made a finding on the merits and reparation.

This chapter discusses the relevance of the criteria for admissibility and jurisdiction on the merits for the decisions of the respective human rights adjudicators on provisional measures.[2]

The adjudicator clearly has no competence to use provisional measures if the Addressee State has not ratified the individual complaint procedure, because in such cases the adjudicator clearly has no jurisdiction. Yet other questions are not that easily answered. What, for instance, is the role of reservations to the individual complaint procedure, or of reservations to the rights on which the request for provisional measures is based? In the context of provisional measures, have human rights adjudicators treated reservations to their jurisdiction on the merits the same way as the ICJ has?

While admissibility and jurisdiction are two distinct concepts, inadmissibility is one factor depriving the adjudicator of jurisdiction to deal with a case. In human rights cases the issue of *prima facie* admissibility of the claim is important, including the relationship between the obligation to exhaust domestic remedies and their suspensive effect. Human rights adjudicators have often declared inadmissible cases in which they previously used provisional measures. The question arises what is the relationship between provisional measures and inadmissibility in these cases. At the same time decisions by adjudicators declaring claims admissible or inadmissible do not provide many clues about their approach to expected (lack of) jurisdiction or (in)admissibility and the use of provisional measures. In addition, to fully understand the approach of the adjudicators it would be necessary to have a record of cases in which they refused to use provisional measures. Such information, however, is not available. Nevertheless, an attempt is made to derive information from the admissibility decisions in cases in which adjudicators have used provisional measures. The practice of the HRC serves as a point of departure.

First this chapter refers to jurisdiction and provisional measures, with a focus on the significance of reservations for the use of provisional measures and on the use of provisional measures beyond inadmissibility or beyond judgments on the merits or reparation (section 2). Following

---

[1]   ICJ *Anglo-Iranian Oil Co.*, Order of 5 July 1951. See also Chapter I.

[2]   This relates to admissibility of the case in order to be able to deal with it on the merits, as distinct from the admissibility of the petitioner's provisional measures request itself. Chapter II referred to the competence of the respective human rights adjudicators to use provisional measures.

this, it refers to admissibility and provisional measures, focussing on the issue of exhaustion of domestic remedies (section 3).

2   JURISDICTION AND PROVISIONAL MEASURES

2.1   Introduction

When dealing with requests for provisional measures in cases where the State contests the adjudicator's jurisdiction to deal with the case on the merits, the irreparable nature of the harm faced by the petitioners should be taken into account.

Indeed the human rights adjudicators appear to have done so. This is most clearly the case with the Inter-American Court in its practice of ordering provisional measures to protect against death threats. In the *Peace Community* case, for instance, the Court simply referred to the fact that Colombia is a State Party and has recognised the competence of the Court. Following this, it reproduced the texts of Article 63(2) ACHR and Article 25(1) Rules of Procedure, both on the competence to order provisional measures.[3] While the Court did not specify why this meant that it need to examine jurisdiction on the merits, in their concurring opinion judges Abreu Burelli and García Ramírez noted that the text of the Convention itself, in Article 63(2) ACHR, justified the Court's anticipation of its normal jurisdiction, at the request of the Commission, in order to provide adequate and immediate protection ('amparo') to persons. In this light they noted that the Convention only requires fulfilment of certain objective conditions for the adoption of provisional measures: one being extreme gravity and urgency because of possible harm to fundamental rights and the other the imminence of such harm. Article 63(2) does not have other requirements that could delay or impede the Court's decision to take such measures and, thereby, put at grave risk the human rights it aims to protect.[4]

In some cases other adjudicators also appear to have taken into account the irreparable nature of the harm faced by the petitioners. Before determining whether it had jurisdiction on the merits (*ratione temporis*), for instance, the Bosnia Chamber used provisional measures not to interfere with any burials in the Muslim Town Cemetery of Prnjavor carried out by or with the authority of the Islamic Community.[5]

This section deals with some other cases involving provisional measures and contested jurisdiction, in particular involving doubts with regard to the addressee of the provisional measures,

---

[3]   IACHR *Peace Community of San José de Apartadó* case (Colombia), Orders of 24 November 2000 and 18 June 2002.

[4]   IACHR Concurring Opinion of Judges Abreu Burelli and García Ramírez, *Peace Community of San José de Apartadó* case (Colombia), Orders for provisional measures, 24 November 2000, §2.

[5]   The Chamber subsequently discussed whether it had jurisdiction *ratione temporis* to examine the complaint about discrimination in the enjoyment of the freedom of religion. The domestic ordinance providing for the closure of the Cemetery was taken prior to entry into force of the Framework Agreement, which does not have retroactive effect. Nevertheless, in this case the ordinance formed the legal basis for the decision prohibiting the burial that was taken after the entry into force of the Agreement. This decision affected the members of the Islamic Community in Prnjavor because it gave rise to a continuing prohibition to bury their dead in the Cemetery. The Chamber noted that 'in considering whether the decisions affecting the applicant were discriminatory' it was relevant to consider the ordinance providing for the closure of the Muslim Town Cemetery as well. Bosnia Chamber *The Islamic Community in Bosnia and Herzegovina* v. *Republika Srpska*, 11 January 2000 (adm. & merits).

including the issue of extraterritoriality, reservations, and the use of provisional measures beyond inadmissibility or beyond judgments on the merits and reparation.

Most discussion involves the jurisdiction of adjudicators to deal with cases in the face of reservations made by States to substantive or procedural treaty obligations.

2.2 Addressees and extraterritoriality

As in the aforementioned case involving interference with burials, in an elections case the Bosnia Chamber also ordered provisional measures in a borderline case of prima facie lack of jurisdiction. Yet while this was a serious case, it did not involve irreparable harm to persons in the sense of (cultural) survival. In March 1998 the President of the Chamber ordered the State BiH and Republika Srpska to secure the ballot papers for the 1997 Elections to the National Assembly of the Republika Srpska.[6] She also directed the Registrar of the Chamber to transmit copies of the decision to the Office of the High Representative and the Organisation of Security and Co-operation in Europe (OSCE). In fact the OSCE seemed to be the true addressee of the provisional measures and the case was later declared inadmissible for lack of jurisdiction *ratione personae*.[7] When the addressee of an order for provisional measures clearly is not a party to the treaty in-

---

[6] These were specified as those ballot papers received in Vienna before 5 December 1997, but posted after 24 November 1997.

[7] The complaint related to the fact that the votes of the petitioners were not counted as valid 'due to the failure of the procedures adopted by the OSCE in relation to the administration of out-of-country voting' of the Provisional Election Commission (the "PEC"). This Commission was established under Article III of Annex 3 to the General Framework Agreement. Previously the Ombudsperson had indicated to the respondent parties that it was desirable to ensure that these ballots were safeguarded. She had done so on 11 December 1997, under Rule 16 of her Rules of Procedure. Later she adopted a report concluding that there had been a violation of Art. 3 of Protocol 1 ECHR and that the respondent Parties 'although not directly involved in the organisation of the elections at issue … (were) responsible therefor [sic] under Annex 3 to the (General Framework Agreement)'. The fact that the Chamber did use provisional measures may indicate that at the stage of provisional measures it does not closely examine its jurisdiction on the merits. In its subsequent decision on admissibility the Chamber stated at the outset that 'any actions taken by the OSCE are, as such, outside the competence of the Chamber *ratione personae*', §36. It then examined whether this applied as well to its actions 'in pursuance of its role under Annex 3', §36. It pointed out that the actions of neither the High Representative nor the International Police Task Force were subject to any review with regard to how they carried out their functions under the General Framework Agreement. Equally, 'the nature of the functions carried out by the OSCE under Annex 3, which in substance is the management of elections in Bosnia and Herzegovina is not such as to be subject to review, except as specifically provided for in Annex 3', §41. The Agreement did 'not provide for the intervention of either respondent Party in the conduct of the elections'. The Chamber found that a breach of the rights of the petitioners under Article 3 of Protocol 1 ECHR (free elections) may have occurred but that 'the impugned acts to not come within the responsibility of the respondent Parties' and were outside the competence of the Chamber. It declared the petition inadmissible and considered that the order for provisional measures was no longer appropriate and should be withdrawn. Bosnia Chamber *Adnan Suljanović, Edita Čišić and Asim Lelić* v. *State BiH and Republika Srpska*, 14 May 1998, (inadm.). See also Bosnia Chamber *Srpska Radikalna Stranka* v. *State BiH*, 8 December 2000 (inadm.), §§12-13 (provisional measures refused, §6).

voked, ordering provisional measures would be inappropriate.[8] Yet when there are doubts as to state responsibility, jurisdiction *ratione personae* and *loci*, it would indeed be appropriate to order provisional measures, taking the risk of a later finding of a lack of jurisdiction rather than that of irreparable harm to persons.

On occasion issues regarding the jurisdiction of States to deal with cases involving actions of their agents extraterritorially have come up at the stage of provisional measures. Given the range of counter-terrorism measures applied worldwide, the number of requests for provisional measures in this context is likely to increase.

In the range of precautionary measures taken by the Inter-American Commission on behalf of the persons detained by the US at Guantanamo Bay (Cuba), the Commission was able to refer to its previous case law on the merits regarding the extraterritorial application of the human rights obligations under the American Declaration, as part of the OAS Charter, and under the ACHR.[9] The main criterion is that the detainees are under the 'authority and control' of US agents.[10] The Inter-American Commission was not alone in taking this approach on the merits. The HRC has emphasized the responsibility of States for actions of their agents outside of their borders since the early 1980s.[11] The ICJ has confirmed this case law.[12]

In its General Comment on Article 2 ICCPR, dating from 2003, the HRC takes a rather extensive approach to extraterritorial application. After confirming that Article 2(1) ICCPR requires a State party to respect and ensure the rights laid down in the ICCPR 'to anyone within the power or effective control of that State Party, even if not situated within the territory of the State Party', it stated:

> "This principle also applies to those within the power or effective control of the forces of a State Party acting outside its territory, regardless of the circumstances in which such power or

---

[8] See e.g. the requests for provisional measures denied by the Bosnia Chamber in *Čavić* v. *B&H*, 18 December 1998 (inadm.), §13 (the request for provisional measures by the petitioner concerned invalidation of the decision by the High Representative in B&H, Carlos Westendorp, based on the Dayton Peace Agreement and various UN Security Council resolutions, to remove the petitioner as a member of the newly elected National Assembly of the Republika Srpska and barring him indefinitely from holding further official positions in B&H; the case was subsequently declared inadmissible for lack of jurisdiction *ratione personae*); see also Bosnia Chamber *Municipal Council of the Municipality South-West Mostar* v. *the High Representative*, 9 March 2000 (inadm.), §§5-6 (the petitioner had requested the Chamber to order a provisional measure annulling the decision of the Acting Head of a regional office of the High Representative to instantly replace the Head of a Housing Commission (and subsequently the Head of the Municipality itself for failure to carry out this order) for obstructing the return of displaced persons; this case was subsequently decaled inadmissible for obvious lack of jurisdiction *ratione personae*).

[9] CIDH Detainees at *Guantanamo Bay*, precautionary measures of 12 March and 23 July 2002; 18 March 2003; 29 July 2004 and 28 October 2005.

[10] See e.g., CIDH *Coard et al.* v. *US*, 29 September 1999. See further Medina Quiroga (2005), pp. 12-14.

[11] HRC *López Burgos* v. *Uruguay*, 29 July 1981 and *Celiberti de Casariego* v. *Uruguay*, 29 July 1981.

[12] See ICJ *Legal consequences of the construction of a wall in the occupied Palestinian territory* (Advisory Opinion), 9 July 2004, holding that the ICCPR is applicable in respect of 'acts done' by a State in the exercise of its jurisdiction outside its own territory, §§107-113 and *Armed Activities on the Territory of the Congo* (*Congo* v. *Uganda*), judgment of 19 December 2005, §§178-180 and 216-217.

effective control was obtained, such as forces constituting a national contingent of a State Party assigned to an international peace-keeping or peace-enforcement operation".[13]

This extensive approach on the merits may mean that the Committee is willing to order provisional measures with regard to any situation claimed to involve such power and control.

As suggested by Scheinin 'the correct approach in the ICCPR is based on the universal nature of human rights, irrespective of whether the country where the alleged extraterritorial violations occur is a party to the ICCPR'.[14] Indeed in 2004 the ICJ also considered that the ICCPR was 'applicable in respect of acts done by a State in the exercise of its jurisdiction outside its own territory'.[15] It referred to the object and purpose of the ICCPR, the constant practice of the HRC (invoking its case law and quoting from its Concluding Observations) and the *travaux* of the ICCPR.[16]

The European Court takes a more cautious approach. Its initial case law[17] appeared similar to that of the Inter-American Commission and the HRC, but then, in *Bankovic*, it introduced the controversial concept of the 'espace juridique' of the ECHR.[18] In effect this resulted in excluding from monitoring by the ECtHR any action by agents from European States undertaken outside the territory of States making up the Council of Europe. Nevertheless, subsequent cases appear to argue away this concept.[19] In November 2004, for instance, the Court published its judgment in *Issa* v. *Turkey* (2004), in which it considered that Turkey could be answerable under the Convention for its actions in Iraq, despite *Bankovic*.[20]

---

[13] HRC General Comment 31 on Article 2 ICCPR, the nature of the general legal obligation imposed on States parties to the Covenant, 21 April 2004, §10. See also HRC Concluding Observations to US report, CCPR/C/USA/CO/3, 15 September 2006 and CAT Concluding Observations to US report, CAT/C/USA/CO/2, 25 July 2006.

[14] Scheinin (2004b), p. 77.

[15] ICJ *Legal consequences of the construction of a wall in the occupied Palestinian territory*, Advisory Opinion of 9 July 2004, §111.

[16] Id., §§109-110. See also ICJ *Armed Activities on the Territory of the Congo* (*Congo* v. *Uganda*), judgment of 19 December 2005, §§179-180 and ICJ Case concerning the application of the International Convention on the Elimination of All Forms of Racial Discrimination (Georgia v. Russia), Order for provisional measures of 15 October 2008, §109. Article 2 ICAT refers to the responsibility of a State 'in any territory under its jurisdiction'. Article 3 of the Declaration on the Protection of All Persons from Enforced Disappearance stipulates that 'each State shall take effective legislative, administrative, judicial or other measures to prevent and terminate acts of enforced disappearance in any territory under its jurisdiction'. The UN Working Group on Enforced Disappearances has emphasized that this provision calls for action by States 'in any territory' under their jurisdiction. E/CN.4/1995/38, 15 January 1996, §49.

[17] ECtHR *Cyprus* v. *Turkey*, 10 May 2001 and *Loizidou* v. *Turkey*, 23 March 1995.

[18] ECtHR *Bankovic et al* v. *Belgium and 16 other States*, 12 December 2001 (inadm.). For a criticism see e.g. Lawson (2004), pp. 83-123. For a different perspective see O'Boyle (2004), pp. 125-139 and Caflisch/Cançado Trindade (2004), p. 36.

[19] In fact the reason for declaring *Bankovic* inadmissible may have been more the factual situation of high altitude bombing rather than the fact that Serbia was not within the 'legal space' of the Convention.

[20] ECtHR *Issa* v. *Turkey*, 16 November 2004; see also, e.g., *Ilaşcu and Others* v. *Moldova and Russia*, 8 July 2004. It turns out that, after all, in light of the criterion of effective control the Court finds important the type of action (e.g. high altitude bombing does not bring the victims 'within the jurisdiction', as opposed to arresting or detaining a person). See e.g. *Öcalan* v. *Turkey*, 12 May 2005; see also *Pad et al.* v. *Turkey*, 28 June 2007 (inadm. for non exhaustion) ("Accordingly, a State may be held accountable for violations of the Convention rights and

At the time when lawyers requested the Court to order provisional measures on behalf of Saddam Hussein, however, the Court had not yet decided these cases. In June 2004 lawyers acting on behalf of Saddam Hussein asked the ECtHR 'to permanently prohibit the United Kingdom from facilitating, allowing for, acquiescing in, or in any other form whatsoever effectively participating, through an act or omission, in the transfer of the applicant to the custody of the Iraqi Interim Government unless and until the Iraqi Interim Government has provided adequate assurances that the applicant will not be subject to the death penalty'.[21] They relied on Articles 2 and 3 ECHR and on Protocols 6 (abolition in times of peace) and 13 (abolition in all circumstances) to the Convention, arguing that the UK 'has an obligation to ensure individuals are not subject to the death penalty and therefore not to surrender legal or physical custody of individuals to a country or jurisdiction where they would face such consequences and other breaches of the Convention'. The ECtHR decided not to grant this request.[22] Press agency Reuters, observing that the decision was not motivated,[23] noted that a spokesperson for the Court had indicated to it that it only takes provisional measures if it is convinced that there is a risk of physical harm that is very important, irreversible and imminent.[24] Obviously in earlier cases the Court already considered the death penalty to involve both important and irreversible harm. Thus it is unclear in this case what was the exact reason for the European Court not to order provisional measures.[25] The fact that it denied the request *could* be attributed to the fact that, five months before its decision in *Issa*, it still considered that Iraq was not within the 'espace juridique' of the ECHR and therefore prima facie it had no jurisdiction to order provisional measures. In 2006 it declared the *Hussein* case inadmissible, not based on an 'espace juridique' argument, but because it considered that the US and not the UK had control over Saddam Hussein for the purpose of handing him over.[26]

The later case of *Behrami and Behrami* v. *France* (2007) was not declared inadmissible based on an 'espace juridique' argument either. The Court did exclude actions undertaken extra-territorially as part of a collective action *and* authorized under Chapter VII of the UN Charter,

---

freedoms of persons who are in the territory of another State which does not necessarily fall within the legal space of the Contracting States, but who are found to be under the former State's authority and control through its agents operating – whether lawfully or unlawfully – in the latter State", §53) and *Isaak et al.* v. *Turkey*, 28 September 2006 (adm.) ('even if the acts complained of took place in the neutral UN buffer zone, the Court considers that the deceased was under the authority and/or effective control of the respondent State through its agents', §2(b) (ii), also confirming the HRC and CIDH case law under 2(b) (1), General principles). On *Issa* see also e.g. Leach (2005) and Mole (2005).

21 ECtHR Press Release 337, 'European Court of Human Rights rejects requests for interim measures by Saddam Hussein', 30 June 2004.

22 Ibid.

23 See also Chapter II, section 8.3.

24 See Reuters, 'Conseil de l'Europe: pas de "mesures provisoires" pour Saddam Hussein', 30 June 2004 *('n'impose à un État des «mesures provisoires», en vertu de l'article 39 de son règlement, que lorsqu'elle est «convaincu qu'il y a un risque de préjudice physique très important, irrémédiable et imminent»')*, posted on <www.peinedemort.org> (accessed on 13 August 2004).

25 See also Chapter V (Expulsion), speculating on the possibility that the ECtHR wrongly assumed that the moratorium on the death penalty would not be lifted. In that respect the Court could have considered that Hussein was not facing irreversible harm (at least not imminently). In fact the moratorium was lifted, and Saddam Hussein was sentenced to death and executed. Political reasons may have played some role as well, because of the person involved, or for policy reasons, fearing a flood of new submissions regarding extraordinary renditions, although the latter seems too cynical, despite the heavy case load the Court is dealing with.

26 ECtHR *Saddam Hussein* v. *Albania, UK et al.*, 14 March 2006 (inadm.).

reminding States of the best way to act extraterritorially without effective monitoring by the European Court.[27]

As noted in Chapter V,[28] the ECtHR has now used provisional measures vis-à-vis a State operating outside the Council of Europe, e.g. to halt transfer of detainees by UK authorities in Iraq to the Iraqi authorities.[29]

In the face of a practice, developed by several States after the September 11th 2001 terrorist attacks, of making use of so-called extraordinary renditions, and the factual activities of States outside their own borders, for instance in the context of international organisations, a more coherent approach by the ECtHR towards extraterritorial application of the ECHR to the acts of Council of Europe member States, taking into account relevant case law developed by other international adjudicators, is indeed particularly warranted.[30] This may also be helpful in the Court's treatment of requests for provisional measures ordering States to act or refrain from acting outside their borders and in addressing misunderstandings by domestic courts in this respect.[31]

---

[27] ECtHR *Behrami and Behrami* v. *France*, 2 May 2007. Children were playing outside when a cluster bomb detonated that had been dropped by NATO during the Kosovo war, leaving one child dead and another crippled. Their family complained against France, whose local KFOR troops were aware of the cluster bombs, but had not marked the area. The ECtHR declared the case inadmissible. The international presence mandated by a binding UN Security Council decision has effective control over Kosovo. The UN had 'ultimate authority and control' over KFOR even though NATO had operational control and in fact the Troop Contributing Nations had a great level of autonomy. The ECtHR did not explain why it did not use the criterion of 'effective control' in Article 5 of the 2004 ILC Draft Articles on the Responsibility of International Organisations, but instead introduced a criterion of 'ultimate' authority and control. In any case it found that the Convention could not be interpreted in a manner that would subject the acts and omissions of Contracting Parties to the scrutiny of the Court in this case because that could interfere with the fulfillment of the UN's key mission to secure international peace and security. Operations under Chapter VII UN Charter were fundamental to this mission and they relied for their effectiveness on support from member States. For a discussion of this case, see e.g. Bulterman (2007) and Lawson (2008). Distinguishing this case from the situation in Iraq, see e.g. *House of Lords R* (*Al-Jedda*) v. *Secretary of State for Defence*, 12 December 2007, [2007] UKHL 58.

[28] See Chapter V (Non-refoulement), section 3.4.

[29] Provisional measures in case of *Faisal al-Saadoon and Khalef Mufdhi* v. *UK*, 30 December 2008 (by the Acting President of the Fourth Section). A scan of the ECtHR letter to counsel confirming its use of provisional measures was posted at <http://humanrightsdoctorate.blogspot.com/2009/01/uk-breaches-provisional-measures.html>; the measure was ignored by the UK in reference to a decision of a domestic court. See further Chapter XVII (Official responses).

[30] For an excellent analysis see further Gondek (2005), pp. 349-387 as well as Cerone (2006) and Cerna (2006). For a discussion of extraterritorial application of various human rights treaties see Coomans/Kamminga (2004).

[31] See e.g. the UK Court of Appeal decision in the above *Faisal al-Saadoon and Khalef Mufdhi* v. *UK* case: *R* (*Al-Saadoon*) v. *Secretary of State for Defence*, [2009] EWCA Civ 7, appeal dismissed on 30 December 2008, motivated and published on 21 January 2009, <http://www.bailii.org/ew/cases/EWCA/Civ/2009/7.html>.

2.3 Reservations and denunciation and provisional measures halting executions

2.3.1 Introduction

Both the HRC and the Inter-American Court have had to deal with the withdrawal of Trinidad and Tobago from the OP and the ACHR, respectively. This triggered issues relating to the compatibility of reservations, the jurisdiction of the adjudicators *ratione temporis* and the question whether a case that was pending before the Inter-American Commission could already be registered (and provisional measures be granted) by the HRC.[32] This section deals with the case law developed by the HRC and the Inter-American Court in this respect. Their approach is set off against that of the ICJ.

2.3.2 HRC

In *Bethel* v. *Trinidad and Tobago* (1999)[33] the petitioner had petitioned the Inter-American Commission, 'in accordance with the guidelines issued by the State party in October 1997, which set out a strict timetable to be adhered to by applicants'. The petitioner had instructed his counsel to submit the case to the HRC as well, in case his petition to the IACHR would be unsuccessful. In May 1998, however, Trinidad denounced the OP. It re-acceded with the following reservation:

> "The Human Rights Committee shall not be competent to receive and consider any communications relating to any prisoner who is under sentence of death in respect of any matter relating to his prosecution, his detention, his trial, his conviction, his sentence or the carrying out of the death sentence on him and any matter connected herewith".[34]

Trinidad issued new 'instructions' as well about the time periods that should apply to petitions in relation to prisoners sentenced to death between the date of denunciation (26 May 1998) and the date on which the denunciation would become effective (26 August 1998). Counsel considered that the petitioner would not be able to present a communication to the HRC after 26 August 1998 when the State's re-accession to the OP would become effective with a reservation excluding death row inmates from the right of petition. By the time the Inter-American Commission would adopt its decision the denunciation of the OP by Trinidad and Tobago would have become effective.[35] Yet the petitioner had had a reasonable expectation to pursue his right of access to the HRC since October 1997. He claimed that the State party's denunciation constituted a breach of Article 1 OP and Article 26 ICCPR. At the same time he requested the HRC to already register the case in order to guarantee his right to petition if his application to the Inter-American Commission would be rejected.

According to the State party the petitioner had the choice between submitting an application to the IACHR or to the HRC. It argued that splitting petitions between two human rights bodies was an abuse of the right of submission. It considered that the HRC 'should not condone a situa-

---

[32] While the latter is an issue involving other grounds for inadmissibility ('same matter') discussed in section 3, it is so closely linked to the others that it is discussed here.

[33] HRC *Christopher Bethel* v. *Trinidad and Tobago*, 31 March 1999.

[34] As reproduced in e.g. A/53/40, Chapter I and *Christopher Bethel* v. *Trinidad and Tobago*, 31 March 1999, §2.3.

[35] HRC *Christopher Bethel* v. *Trinidad and Tobago*, 31 March 1999.

tion where a petitioner seeks to submit some complaints to the IACHR and reserves others for the Committee'.[36]

Surprisingly, the HRC considered that the right of access to the HRC is not a right protected by the Covenant and declared the case inadmissible. This is puzzling since the HRC could have argued *proprio motu* that the reservation attached to the re-accession violated the object and purpose of the individual complaints procedure under the Optional Protocol and the object and purpose of the Covenant itself, including the principle of non-discrimination of Article 26.[37]

In any case before declaring the case inadmissible the HRC had used provisional measures in *Bethel*. On this issue Pocar and Scheinin attached a concurring opinion. They considered that the HRC should have declared the case inadmissible not because the right of access to the HRC is not a right protected by the Covenant, but instead for non-exhaustion of domestic remedies. They referred to the practice of upholding the request for provisional measures cases of non-exhaustion in light of the possibility of review. They noted that the Committee's provisional measures should have been upheld and 'the inadmissibility decision should have been made subject to a possibility of review when the obstacle for inadmissibility has been removed'.[38]

They pointed out that the HRC had stated its position about the reservation in the Annual Report to the effect that it would 'deal with the validity and legal effect of the reservation by Trinidad and Tobago in due course and in the concrete context of such individual cases related to the death penalty that have been submitted after 26 August 1998'.[39] They emphasised that the reservation in question could 'not be seen to bar, in abstracto, access by the author or any other prisoner under the sentence of death, to the Committee in its functions under the Optional Protocol'.[40]

In their discussion in *Bethel* Scheinin and Pocar anticipated the Committee's decision in *Kennedy* v. *Trinidad and Tobago* (2002).[41] This decision is directly relevant to the question about the relationship between the general jurisdiction of the HRC to deal with complaints and its jurisdiction to take provisional measures.[42] The Committee considered that the aforementioned reser-

---

[36] Id., §6.2.

[37] Later, in HRC *Kennedy* v. *Trinidad and Tobago* (2002), the HRC did so. HRC *Rawle Kennedy* v. *Trinidad and Tobago*, 26 March 2002 (merits) and public admissibility decision of 2 November 1999, see *infra*.

[38] Concurring opinion Pocar and Scheinin in HRC *Christopher Bethel* v. *Trinidad and Tobago*, 31 March 1999. "This course of action would have made it clear to the author, his counsel and the State party that the State party's withdrawal and re-accession accompanied by reservation, of the Optional Protocol, dated 26 May 1998 and effective 26 August 1998, does not constitute an obstacle for the future consideration of the author's case by the Committee".

[39] Concurring opinion Pocar and Scheinin. In HRC *Christopher Bethel* v. *Trinidad and Tobago*, 31 March 1999.

[40] Ibid. This statement is also the only reference to the fact that the Special Rapporteur had used provisional measures earlier in the proceedings. In fact his counsel had requested this as part of the initial submission and the Rapporteur had transmitted the case and used provisional measures on 17 September 1998 (on file with the author).

[41] HRC *Rawle Kennedy* v. *Trinidad and Tobago*, 26 March 2002.

[42] Almost three months after the Committee's provisional measures in this case the State replied, referring to the new reservation attached to its accession to the OP of 26 May 1998. It pointed out that the HRC was not competent to consider the petitioner's communication and it considered that the HRC had 'exceeded its jurisdiction by registering the communication and purporting to impose interim measures'. Thus, its 'actions in respect of this communication were void and of no binding effect', HRC *Rawle Kennedy* v. *Trinidad and Tobago*, 26 March 2002, §4.2. The petitioner referred to the general principle of international law that 'the body to whose

vation to the OP could not be deemed compatible with the object and the purpose of the Protocol and declared the case admissible despite the fact that it was submitted after Trinidad's denunciation became effective.[43] Four members dissented because they considered that the communication was inadmissible.[44] Nevertheless they did agree that it had been within the Committee's compe-

---

jurisdiction a purported reservation is addressed decides on the validity and effect of that reservation', HRC *Rawle Kennedy* v. *Trinidad and Tobago*, 26 March 2002, §5.

[43] Because of the importance of the issue the HRC decided to make public this admissibility decision. HRC *Rawle Kennedy* v. *Trinidad and Tobago*, admissibility decision of 2 November 1999. One member, Henkin (US), attached a concurring opinion simply pointing out that he concurred with the result.

[44] The dissenters pointed out the difficulties for the State party, given constitutional restraints. Even if the HRC would later find no violation, they noted, the State party may be prevented from carrying out the sentence. It is not clear whether this remark applies only to those cases in which the HRC has taken provisional measures or whether they already anticipated the later decision, in HRC *Dante Piandiong, Jesus Morallos and Archie Bulan (deceased)* v. *the Philippines*, 19 October 2000, that the fact itself that a case is pending before the HRC implies that the State must not execute the petitioner. See Chapter XVI on legal status. They also pointed out that if they had accepted the majority's view that the reservation was invalid they 'would have had to hold that Trinidad and Tobago is not a party to the Optional Protocol'. This would, they pointed out, equally make the communication inadmissible. Individual opinion Ando, Bhagwati, Klein and Kretzmer in HRC *Rawle Kennedy* v. *Trinidad and Tobago*, admissibility decision of 2 November 1999, §17. In an individual opinion attached to the final View Ando, Klein and Kretzmer referred to their dissenting opinion to the admissibility decision in this case: "Our view was not accepted by the Committee, which held that it was competent to consider the communication. We respect the Committee's view as to its competence and so have joined in the consideration on the merits". Individual opinion Ando, Klein and Kretzmer (this time not joined by Bhagwati), HRC *Rawle Kennedy* v. *Trinidad and Tobago*, 26 March 2002. In *Xavier Evans* v. *Trinidad and Tobago*, 21 March 2003, Wedgwood, who has been the US member of the HRC subsequent to Henkin's retirement, attached an individual opinion in order to express her view about this issue. She dissented to the admissibility of this case, referring to the opinion of Ando, Klein and Kretzmer in *Kennedy*. Wedgwood also considered that 'the failure of the State party to cooperate with the Committee in the examination of the merits in this case and in the earlier case of *Kennedy* v. *Trinidad and Tobago* may bear some relation to the disregard of this reservation'. While this may indeed partially explain the attitude of the State (although the State already failed to co-operate in many cases previous to the HRC decision in *Kennedy*), it seems that Wedgwood considers this attitude justified. The petitioner's death sentence had been commuted in 1994, several years before his initial submission of 16 November 1999. According to Wedgwood this did 'not evidently displace the effect of the reservation'. If one considers, like Wedgwood, that the HRC should respect State party reservations, even when contrary to object and purpose, it is still not evident that the reservation in question would apply to the petitioner. The reservation declared the HRC incompetent 'to receive and consider communications relating to any prisoner who is under sentence of death in respect of any matter relating to his prosecution, his detention, his trial, his conviction, his sentence or the carrying out of the death sentence on him and any matter connected herewith'. This formulation included a large group of persons, but it did not say 'any person who is *or was* under sentence of death'. After all, Evans was no longer under sentence of death when he submitted his complaint. The HRC had previously discussed the issue of reservations in a General Comment that had triggered criticism from a few States. HRC General Comment 24 on reservations to the ICCPR or the Optional Protocols, 4 November 1994. Clearly, under both customary international law and the Vienna Convention on the Law of Treaties States parties are entitled to make reservations, but only if they are not contrary to the object and purpose of the treaty in question. This, however, was not the dispute that arose following the

tence to register the communication and take provisional measures 'so as to allow the Committee to consider whether the State party's reservation to the Optional Protocol makes the communication inadmissible'.[45] This, once more, underlines that all Committee members consider that there is no need to determine jurisdiction before using provisional measures.

In *R. S.* v. *Trinidad and Tobago* (2002)[46] the HRC confirmed its majority View in *Kennedy* that Trinidad's reservation was incompatible with the objective of the OP and complaints by death row inmates were admissible. In other words it was not precluded from considering the case. Trinidad has now fully withdrawn from the OP,[47] but in cases involving, for instance, Guyana, which has attached the same reservation to its re-accession,[48] or Tajikistan, a resumption of

---

issuance of the General Comment. Some States made objections relating to the question whether supervisory committees to human rights treaties may not only determine whether a reservation is contrary to the object and purpose of the treaty they supervise, but also the consequences of such a reservation, such as severability. ILC Rapporteur Pellet has also referred to this Comment as 'controversial', Report of the International Law Commission on the work of its 48th session, 2 May-26 July 1996, §116. See Observations by France, 4 *International Human Rights Report* 6 (1997); Observations by the UK 3 *International Human Rights Report* 262 (2006); Observations by the US 3 *International Human Rights Report* 265 (2006). For an analysis of the discussion see e.g. Redgwell (1997), pp. 390-412; Goodman (2002), pp. 531-560; Higgins (2007), p. 747; Kamminga (2008), §3.2 and Ziemele (2004) and the contributions therein (see in particular Scheinin, pp. 41-58, also explaining, at pp. 50-51, why dissenting opinions generally are less complete in their argumentation than the HRC majority view or concurring opinions).

[45] HRC *Rawle Kennedy* v. *Trinidad and Tobago*, admissibility decision of 2 November 1999, dissenting opinion by Ando (Japan), Bhagwati (India), Klein (Germany) and Kretzmer (Israel).

[46] HRC *R. S.* v. *Trinidad and Tobago*, 2 April 2002.

[47] It withdrew on 27 March 2000. This became effective on 27 June 2000.

[48] Guyana denounced the OP on 5 January 1999 and re-acceded to it on the same date with a reservation related to the competence of the Committee to examine death penalty cases. This reservation became effective on 5 April 1999. Subsequent to this date the HRC used provisional measures several times in order to halt an execution. Yet in these cases the initial submission was made before the date on which the reservation became effective and rather than referring to the incompatibility of the reservation and its severability, the HRC simply noted that the initial submission predated this reservation. See e.g. *Hazerat Hussain and Sumintra Singh* v. *Guyana*, 25 October 2005 (initial submission of 16 March 1999 and provisional measure of 22 April 1999); *Smartt* v. *Guyana*, 6 July 2004 (initial submission on 28 March 1999; provisional measure on 28 April 1999); *Deolall* v. *Guyana*, 1 November 2004 (initial submission of 5 January 1999; provisional measures of 7 February 2000. In §4.5 the Committee explicitly discusses admissibility in this respect: "The Committee notes that the communication was submitted prior to Guyana's denunciation of the Optional Protocol on 5 January 1999 and its re-accession to it with a reservation related to the competence of the Committee to examine death penalty cases. It concludes therefore that its jurisdiction is not affected by this denunciation. The Committee can find no reasons to consider this communication inadmissible and proceeds to a consideration of the merits"); *Lawrence Chan* v. *Guyana*, 31 October 2005 (initial submission of 15 September 1998; provisional measures of 7 February 2000; in her individual opinion Wedgwood considered that the HRC had 'assumed in this matter that it is the date of an author's initial submission of a communication, rather than the date of its formal registration and transmission to the state party for reply, that is the decisive date for judging admissibility *ratione temporis*'. After referring to some previous case law she notes that '(t)hough this is a debatable conclusion, within reasonable limits, I am willing to accept the Committee's view'); See also *Raymond Persaud and Rampersaud* v. *Guyana*, 21 March 2006 (in this case the provisional measures were prior to the re-accession with reservation, on 9 April 1998; 'On 16 or 17 July 1998, warrants of execution

the old practice of maintaining provisional measures in the face of non-exhaustion, as suggested by Pocar and Scheinin, would seem warranted.[49]

2.3.3 IACHR

As noted, Trinidad also withdrew from the ACHR. The Inter-American Court was faced with two issues, the incompatibility of this State's previous reservations to the ACHR and the applicability of the Convention *ratione temporis* given the withdrawal.

When this Court orders provisional measures, the State's recognition of its jurisdiction is the first issue it deals with. The first Order of the Inter-American Court for provisional measures to halt an execution (June 1998) mentioned that Trinidad and Tobago had been a State Party to the ACHR since May 1991 and had accepted the Court's jurisdiction. In addition it noted that this jurisdiction extended to the application of Article 63(2), the article on provisional measures. It pointed out that the Court's jurisdiction as such was based on Article 62(3) ACHR, stipulating that it was empowered to hear 'all cases concerning the interpretation and application' of the provisions of the Convention.[50] In its subsequent provisional measures the Court continued to refer to the fact that Trinidad had been a State Party from 28 May 1998 until 26 May 1999.[51]

Particularly interesting is its decision to order provisional measures requested *after* Trinidad's denunciation of the Convention became effective. It argued that the denunciation did not release the State from its obligations with respect to acts occurring prior to the effective date of denunciation. It pointed this out not only in its decision on preliminary objections,[52] but also in its provisional measures. In an Order for provisional measures issued the day before the denunciation became effective the Court stated that 'pursuant to Article 78(2) of the American Convention, the denunciation does not have the effect of releasing the State from its obligations with respect to acts occurring prior to the effective date of denunciation which may constitute a violation of the said Convention'.[53]

---

were mistakenly issued and read to the authors, because the Office of the President had not been notified that interim measures had been granted by the Committee. The warrants were withdrawn and the authors subsequently received letters of apology for the mistake' (§2.2)".

[49] See also section 3.4 of this Chapter.

[50] IACHR *James, Briggs, Noel, Garcia and Bethel*, Order of 14 June 1998, 1st 'Considering' clause.

[51] See IACHR *James et al.*, Order for provisional measures, 26 November 2001. For other references to the fact that Trinidad had accepted the jurisdiction of the Court see e.g. 25 May 1999, 27 May 1999 and 25 September 1999. Trinidad's withdrawal of 26 May 1998 became effective on 26 May 1999.

[52] See the three IACHR Judgments of 1 September 2001 in the cases of *Hilaire, Constantine and Benjamin et al.* v. *Trinidad and Tobago*, as discussed *infra*.

[53] See e.g. IACHR *James et al.*, Order of 27 May 1999, 3rd 'Considering' clause. Subsequently the Commission noted that it had received two additional petitions on the day before Trinidad's denunciation would become effective. It requested the Court to include the petitioners as new beneficiaries in the *James et al.* Order. It argued that the State's denunciation of the Convention 'should not be considered to affect the jurisdiction of either the Court or the Commission to entertain these matters', §5e. The President and later the Court itself ordered their inclusion in the provisional measures, simply noting again that the denunciation did not release the State from its obligations with respect to acts that occurred prior to the effective date of denunciation. See IACHR *James et al.*, Order of the President for urgent measures, 19 June 1999. The President subsequently amplified the provisional measures also with regard to five petitions the Commission received between November 2000 and April 2001, in other words *after* the denunciation became effective. In this case the Commission had argued as well that the State's

The Court has clearly stated that Trinidad's denunciation of the Convention 'does not affect the jurisdiction of either the Court or the Commission to consider the alleged acts, occurring in whole or in part, before May 26, 1999, the day in which the State's denunciation of the Convention entered into force'.[54] This applied even though the *petitions* were received after that date.[55] Clearly, if the Court is still able to deal with the petition on the merits at a later stage there is no doubt either that it can order provisional measures in the meantime.

An examination of Trinidad's attitude may shed light on some of the Court's criteria vis-à-vis its jurisdiction but also on the State's insistent strive to free itself from the Court's supervision.[56] In its follow-up reports Trinidad expressed jurisdictional objections against the Court's Orders for provisional measures. These were the same objections subsequently expressed during the preliminary objections phase of the *Hilaire, Constantine et al.* and *Benjamin et al.* cases. It referred to its reservation to the ACHR with regard to its recognition of the Court's compulsory jurisdiction under Article 62. According to this reservation its recognition was applicable 'only to such extent' that it was 'consistent with the relevant sections of the Constitution of the Republic of Trinidad and Tobago; and provided that any judgment does not infringe, create or abolish any existing rights or duties of any private citizens'.[57]

The State claimed that the provisional measures requested by the Commission concerned matters falling within its reservation. Thus, it did not recognise the Court's jurisdiction and considered the Orders *'ultra vires* and void'.[58] Evidently, the Court did not agree as it ratified the President's Order. Apart from the linguistically puzzling matter how a judgment can create *existing* rights, the question arises whether Trinidad's reservation to the provision on the Court's compulsory jurisdiction is permissible in light of the Convention's object and purpose. The Court did not discuss this issue in its Order for provisional measures but subsequently, in its Judgments on preliminary objections, it determined that the State's declaration (that its recognition is only valid to the extent that it is consistent with the relevant sections of Trinidad's Constitution) can lead to numerous interpretations but that it 'cannot be given a scope that would impede this Tribunal's ability to judge whether the State had or had not violated a provision of the Convention'.[59] With regard to the second part of Trinidad's 'purported restriction' aimed at limiting the Court's compulsory jurisdiction to judgments that do not 'infringe, create or abolish any existing rights or duties of any private citizen' it pointed out that, while the precise meaning of this condition was unclear, without a doubt it could not be utilized for the purpose of suppressing 'the jurisdiction of the Court to hear and decide an application related to an alleged violation of the State's conventional obligations'.[60]

---

denunciation 'should not be considered to affect the jurisdiction of either the Court or the Commission to entertain these matters, for the events complained of in the petitions are alleged to have occurred in whole or in part prior to May 26, 1999', IACHR *James et al.*, Order of 26 November 2001, 'Having seen' clause 4a. In reference to the Commission's statements, the President confirmed that 'pursuant to Article 78(2) of the American Convention, the denunciation does not have the effect of releasing the State from its obligations with respect to acts occurring, in whole or in part, prior to the effective date of denunciation, which may constitute a violation of the said Convention'. IACHR *James et al.*, Order of 26 November 2001, 3rd 'Considering' clause.

[54] IACHR *James et al.*, Order of 25 May 1999.

[55] IACHR *James et al.*, Order of 26 November 2001.

[56] See generally on official State responses Chapter XVII.

[57] IACHR *James et al.*, Order of 29 August 1998. See also Chapter XVII (Official responses).

[58] See IACHR *James et al.*, Order of 25 May 1999 (submission of the State of 19 May 1999).

[59] IACHR *Constantine et al.* v. *Trinidad and Tobago*, 1 September 2001 (Preliminary Objections), §77.

[60] Id., §77.

According to Trinidad the Convention permits States to accept the Court's jurisdiction un-der Article 62 subject to restrictions. It considered that such restriction did not affect the enjoy-ment of the rights in the Convention. Because its reservation did not deny the exercise of any of the rights in the ACHR, it could be considered compatible with its object and purpose. The State contended that 'in accordance with universally recognized principles of International Law, the exercise of the jurisdiction by an international court with respect to a State is not a right but a privilege only exercisable with the express consent of the State'. In the event that the Court would nevertheless declare Trinidad reservation incompatible with the Convention's object and purpose, Trinidad put forward, 'the effect of such a determination would be to render the State's declara-tion accepting the Court's compulsory jurisdiction null and void *ab initio*'.[61]

> "If the 'reservations' of the State were, for any reason, considered invalid, it would not mean that the State declared its unlimited acceptance of the compulsory jurisdiction of the Court. On the contrary, it is clear that the State never intended to accept, in its totality, the jurisdiction of the Court. If the 'reservation' is invalid, then the declaration was invalid, and the State never made a declaration".[62]

The Inter-American Commission, on the other hand, argued that the State's reservation should be considered invalid because it was impossible to determine its exact nature and scope. It referred to the UN Human Rights Committee's statement that reservations to human rights trea-ties must be specific and transparent. The Commission pointed out that the reservation was not permitted because it was contrary to the Convention's object and purpose as well as to general principles of international law. The State's interpretation limited the ability of the Court to inter-pret and apply the Convention in cases against Trinidad because it would only be able to apply the Convention rights 'to the extent that such rights are protected in the State's Constitution'.[63] Thus, the State's position ignored the fact that it was the responsibility of the Court and not of the State to determine whether domestic laws were consistent with the Convention. The State interpreted its declaration in such a way that the Court would be prevented from considering the specific aspects of the 'mandatory death penalty'. Such interpretation 'would effectively permit the State to violate the Convention with respect to the alleged victims in this case', in contravention of Article 29(a) ACHR.[64] The Commission underlined the importance of a purposive interpretation in human rights cases in which the human rights systems would be strengthened rather than weakened. In that light:

> "Severing the impugned term from the State's declaration of acceptance, instead of annulling the declaration *in toto*, serves to guarantee the fundamental human rights of the alleged victims and those of individuals in similar situations who would not otherwise have effective domestic remedies of protection".[65]

---

[61] Id., §48.

[62] Id., §51. This statement obviously indicates the attitude of Trinidad and Tobago vis-à-vis the Court's provisional measures in this case. See further on the attitudes of addressee States Chapter XVII.

[63] Id., §54.

[64] Id., §63.

[65] Id., §66.

It suggested that the Court could follow the reasoning of the ECtHR in *Loizidou* v. *Turkey*, 'which declared that *ratione loci* restrictions could be severed from the declaration of acceptance leaving intact the acceptance of the optional clauses'.[66]

One common feature in the approach of the human rights adjudicators to this issue is their emphasis on arguments about the object and purpose of human rights treaties as instruments of public order and collective enforcement. In *Loizidou*, for instance, the ECtHR stated that the European Convention is a constitutional instrument of the European public order.[67] It noted that the Convention comprised 'more than mere reciprocal engagements between contracting states. It creates over and above a network of mutual, bilateral undertakings, objective obligations, which, in the words of the Preamble (of the ECHR) benefit from a collective enforcement'.[68] Equally, with regard to the ACHR the Inter-American Court has considered that recognition of its binding jurisdiction 'is an ironclad clause to which there can be no limitations except those expressly provided for in Article 62(1) of the American Convention. Because the clause is so fundamental to the operation of the Convention's system of protection, it cannot be at the mercy of limitations not already stipulated but invoked by States Parties for internal reasons'.[69]

"The States Parties to the Convention must guarantee compliance with its provisions and its effects (*effet utile*) within their own domestic laws. This principle applies not only to the substantive provisions of human rights treaties (in other words, the clauses on the protected rights), but also to the procedural provisions, such as the one concerning recognition of the Tribunal's contentious jurisdiction (footnote omitted). That clause, essential to the efficacy of the mechanism of international protection, must be interpreted and applied in such a way that the guarantee that it establishes is truly practical and effective, given the special nature of human rights treaties (..) and their collective enforcement".[70]

The case law of the human rights adjudicators appears to indicate that once a State has pre-committed itself to human rights obligations and supervisory mechanisms, it cannot easily move backwards anymore. From the moment a State has accepted the Court's compulsory jurisdiction, this jurisdiction had become an *intrinsic* component of the guarantees available to individuals in that State.

The Inter-American Court has pointed out, among others in *Benjamin et al.* v. *Trinidad and Tobago* (2001), that the restrictions included in the instrument of acceptance, in the terms proposed by the State, would lead to a situation where the Court would have the Inter-American Convention only as a subsidiary parameter of reference and the Constitution of the State as the first parameter. This would result in a fragmentation of the international legal order for the protec-

---

[66] Id., §68.

[67] ECtHR *Loizidou* v. *Turkey*, judgment of 23 March 1995. See also. e.g. Oellers-Frahm (2001b), pp. 82-83.

[68] ECtHR *Ireland* v. *UK*, judgment of 18 January 1978, §239. In general on the movement of the ECtHr towards an approach that is more conducive to an effective protection of human rights and the fact that this also applies to the analysis of the notion of jurisdiction, Cohen-Jonathan (2005c).

[69] IACHR *Constitutional Court* case (Peru) 24 September 1999 (Competence), §35; *Ivcher Bronstein*, Judgment of 24 September 1999 (Competence), §36; see also *Blake* v. *Guatemala* (Reparations), Judgment of 22 January 1999, Concurring Opinion of Judge A.A. Cançado Trindade, §§23 and 27-28.

[70] IACHR *Constitutional Court* case (Peru) 24 September 1999 (competence), §36.

tion of human rights and make illusory the object and purpose of the Convention.[71] This was manifestly incompatible with the object and purpose of the Convention as a whole.[72]

It has noted that 'as with any court or tribunal' it has the inherent authority to determine the scope of its own competence. It emphasised that it 'must give an interpretation to the declaration of the State, as a whole, that is in accordance with the canons and practice of International Law in general, and with International Human Rights Law specifically'.[73] In this respect the balance should be tipped by the law awarding the greatest degree of protection to the human beings under its guardianship'.[74] This prerogative it could not abdicate, 'as it is a duty that the American Convention imposes upon it, requiring it to exercise its functions in accordance with Article 62(3) thereof'.[75] Like the HRC, the ECtHR and Inter-American Commission, it opted for a severability approach.[76]

With regard to interpretation methods and its jurisdictional role the Inter-American Court has noted:

> "Interpreting the Convention in accordance with its object and purpose the Court must act in a manner that preserves the integrity of the mechanism provided for in Article 62(1) of the Convention. It would be unacceptable to subordinate said mechanism to restrictions that would render the system for protection of human rights established in the Convention, and, as a result, the Court's jurisdictional role, inoperative".[77]

It also mentioned its earlier jurisprudence on the principle of *effet utile* that applied not only to the substantive provisions of human rights treaties but to their procedural provisions as well. In that light, the provision concerning recognition of the Court's contentious jurisdiction, a provision 'essential to the efficacy of the mechanism of international protection', was to be 'interpreted and applied in such a way that the guarantee it establishes is truly practical and effective, given the special nature of human rights treaties and their collective enforcement'.[78]

2.3.4 Distinguishing the ICJ approach to jurisdiction

It is clear that allegations of lack of competence on the merits do play a role in the considerations of adjudicators faced with a request for provisional measures. At the same time it is noteworthy that in their determination of prima facie jurisdiction at the stage of provisional measures the human rights adjudicators have taken into account the irreparable harm faced by the petitioners. The HRC's provisional measures in *Kennedy* (1999) provide a clear example. While some of the

---

[71] IACHR Judgment of *Benjamin et al.* v. *Trinidad and Tobago* (competence), 1 September 2001, §84. See also the cases *Hilaire et al.* and *Constantine et al.* of the same date.

[72] Id., §79.

[73] IACHR *Constantine et al.* v. *Trinidad and Tobago*, 1 September 2001 (Preliminary Objections), §70.

[74] Id., §70.

[75] Id., §71.

[76] See also, e.g., IACHR *Caesar* v. *Trinidad & Tobago*, 11 March 2005, Concurring Opinion of Judge A.A. Cançado Trindade, §§21-46, with a literature overview with regard to reservations and stressing the convergence of approaches by the supervisory bodies on the one hand, and the fragmentation resulting from the traditional approach based on the Vienna Convention on the Law of Treaties, on the other.

[77] Id., §73.

[78] Id., §74, referring to *Constitutional Court* case, Judgment of 24 September 1999 (Competence), §36 and *Ivcher Bronstein* case, Judgment of 24 September 1999 (Competence), §37.

Committee members dissented as to the jurisdiction of the Committee to deal with the case –because they did not believe that incompatible reservations could be severed from the ratification –, they specifically pointed out that they did agree with the prior decision to take provisional measures.[79]

Even if the ICJ is less likely than human rights adjudicators to order provisional measures in the face of doubts about its jurisdiction, there are indications that some members of the Court are open to the severability approach of the human rights adjudicators, as an appropriate development of international law when dealing with fundamental human rights.[80] If the ICJ's approach to this issue would be likely to change, it is possible that it would order provisional measures despite reservations to compromissory clauses in treaties involving human rights.

As Judge Cançado Trindade has pointed out, the case law of the Inter-American Court had 'discarded an analogy with the permissive practice of the States' under Art. 36(2) ICJ Statute (the optional clause of the ICJ's compulsory jurisdiction).[81] After all, while the optional clauses recognising the compulsory jurisdiction of the Inter-American Court and the ECtHR (before Protocol 11) were inspired on the optional clause of the ICJ, these adjudicators had interpreted the 'rationale of the application of the optional clause (...) in a fundamentally distinct way'.[82] In light of their protective function of these human rights courts, he noted, they have taken a human rights perspective, where 'considerations of *ordre public*' prevail over the traditional State voluntarism. In this context States cannot count on the same level of discretion they have reserved for themselves in the traditional context of the purely interstate contentious proceedings.[83] After all human rights treaties are aimed at 'the accomplishment of a common goal, superior to the individual interests of each Contracting party'.[84] In fact, he noted, even at the purely inter-State level the optional clause of the compulsory jurisdiction has become dated. The ICJ is now faced with an arrangement from the 1920s that became stratified by the decision to copy it from the PCIJ to the

---

[79]   HRC *Kennedy* v. *Trinidad and Tobago*, admissibility decision of 2 November 1999, dissenting opinion by Ando (Japan), Bhagwati (India), Klein (Germany) and Kretzmer (Israel).

[80]   See Chapter I (ICJ) and the individual opinion in ICJ *Armed Activities on the Territory of the Congo* (new application: 2002) (*Congo* v. *Rwanda*), Judgment on jurisdiction of the Court and admissibility of the application of 3 February 2006, Separate Opinion Judges Higgins, Kooijmans, Elaraby, Owada and Simma, e.g. §16: "The practice of such bodies is not to be viewed as 'making an exception' to the law as determined in 1951 by the International Court; we take the view that it is rather a development to cover what the Court was never asked at that time, and to address new issues that have arisen subsequently".

[81]   IACHR Judgment on preliminary objections in *Constantine et al.* v. *Trinidad and Tobago*, 1 September 2001, Separate Opinion of judge Cançado Trindade, §3, referring to *Constitutional Court* and *Ivcher Bronstein*.

[82]   Id. §4.

[83]   Id., §20. In addition, he noted, States cannot sustain the argument that that which is not prohibited is permitted. This approach, he stated, would be equal to the traditional and outdated attitude of *laissez faire*, characteristic of an international legal order fragmented by subjective State voluntarism. In legal history such voluntarism inevitably favoured the most powerful. Thus in the field of human rights it is the reverse logic that must prevail: what is not permitted is prohibited, §24. Cançado Trindade stressed the importance of the nature of the treaty involved when considering the meaning and scope of a statement of acceptance of an optional clause laying down compulsory jurisdiction. This nature, he wrote, corresponds to the second element forming the general rule of interpretation of treaties (Article 31 Vienna Convention on the Law of Treaties): context, §31.

[84]   Id., §4. See also ECtHR *Loizidou* v. *Turkey*, 23 March 1995 (preliminary objections), §70, referring to a system of collective enforcement of human rights.

ICJ Statute, yet international law as such has gradually evolved away from traditional State volun-tarism.[85] He noted that obviously the 'distorted and incongruous practice' developed under Article 36(2) of the ICJ Statute cannot be taken as an example or model to be followed by States parties to human rights treaties with regard to the extent of their jurisdictional basis.[86]

In this respect the question arises of the relevance to the ICJ of the practice of human rights adjudicators to use provisional measures also in the face of objections with regard to their juris-diction (e.g. based on a State's reservations). While the ICJ seems to have been inspired by the developments in international human rights law that have taken place in the last decades and should indeed consult the jurisprudence of human rights adjudicators if it is dealing with requests for provisional measures, it is arguable that, given Article 36(2) ICJ Statute, the developments with regard to jurisdiction cannot easily be transferred to the jurisprudence of the ICJ. Nevertheless, especially with regard to its jurisdiction based on the compromissory clauses in human rights-related treaties (such as the legality of reservations to the compromissory clause in the Genocide Convention), it could certainly draw inspiration from the developments in human rights jurisprudence, away from state voluntarism.[87] This would be warranted by the *effet utile* of these treaties.[88]

Like the power to decide on contested jurisdiction, the power to use provisional measures equally is essential to the efficacy of the system of international protection. The two are interrelated and both require an interpretation taking into account the *effet utile* of the treaty system.[89] For the use of provisional measures the *prima facie* jurisdiction of the Court is sufficient.

2.4 The Inter-American Court's jurisdiction to maintain provisional measures in matters that will never be brought to it on the merits

The Inter-American Court, like the other adjudicators, often points out that its use of provisional measures does not imply a prejudgment on the merits, but rather is based on the State's proce-dural obligations under the Convention. This remark could be relevant to explain the use of provi-sional measures in cases with which – at a later stage – the Court will not be able to deal. An argument based on the *separate* jurisdiction of Article 63(2) ACHR could apply to cases that the Commission failed to bring before the Court in time for it to deal with them on the merits. The Court could be considered to have jurisdiction because the State's procedural obligations are not limited to the proceedings on Preliminary Objections, merits and reparation but are also based on the Court's provisional measures ordered under Article 63(2) ACHR.

In this respect a particularly striking issue that the Inter-American Court has had to deal with was the execution by Trinidad and Tobago of Mr. Briggs. In its Order of 25 May 1999 the

---

85   IACHR Judgment on preliminary objections in *Constantine et al.* v. *Trinidad and Tobago*, 1 September 2001, Separate Opinion of judge Cançado Trindade, §13.
86   Id., §12.
87   See also Chapter I (ICJ), section 4, under the heading 'The development of international law and Article IX Genocide Convention as a jurisdictional basis for provisional measures'.
88   On *effet utile*/the principle of effectiveness see e.g. ECtHR *Soering* v. *UK*, 7 July 1989, §87; *Loizidou* v. *Turkey*, 23 March 1995 (preliminary objections), §70; *Mamatkulov* v. *Turkey*, 4 February 2005 (Grand Chamber), §123; and IACHR *Constitutional Court* case, September 1999, (judgment on competence), §23. These cases make clear that the ECtHR and IACHR also apply this principle to the interpretation of standards generally referred to as 'procedural'. This is not surprising as substantive and procedural human rights law cannot be artificially separated, see also Chapter XVI (Legal status).
89   See also Chapter XVI (Legal status).

Court decided to maintain the provisional measures ordered on behalf of Mr. Briggs 'until such time as the Court, having previously considered the reports concerning the present status of his Case, issues a decision on this matter'.[90] The Commission had previously requested the Court to order provisional measures on his behalf and the Court had done so. In the meantime, the Commission had issued a final report in his case, but had failed to bring the case itself before the Court.[91]

In response, Trinidad had argued that the Court had no longer any competence to maintain the provisional measures.[92]

In the aforementioned Order the Court refuted this argument and maintained the measures. It did not specify, however, their duration other than 'until such time as the Court (...) issues a decision on this matter'.[93] For lack of explanation in the Order itself, it is necessary to resort to the concurring opinions dealing with the issue. Judge Cançado Trindade pointed out that the Court only had a few hours to decide on the subject but that, in his understanding, its decision contributed to 'the fulfilment of the object and purpose' of the ACHR, preserved 'the integrity of the mechanism of supervision' of the Convention and reflected 'the juridical nature of the provisional measures of protection, complying with the basic and indispensable requisite of juridical security'.[94] With regard to the competence of the Court he pointed out that the subject fell under its jurisdiction from the moment the Court received the Commission's initial request for provisional measures.

"The fact that, subsequent to its request, the Commission came to adopt, in the specific case pertaining to Mr. Anthony Briggs, the Reports under Articles 50 and 51, respectively, of the

---

[90]   IACHR *James et al.*, Order for provisional measures, 25 May 1999.

[91]   The Commission had brought the case, which was then still pending before it, before the Court for the purpose of obtaining provisional measures of protection. It had found a violation of Article 7(5) ACHR because Trinidad failed to bring the petitioner to trial within a reasonable time. Briggs had been in pre-trial detention for three years and three months. The Commission recommended the State to compensate him and give consideration to his early release or commutation of the sentence. It did not bring this case before the Court to deal with it on the merits within the period of three months from the date of the transmittal to the State. Instead, it published its opinions and conclusions in this matter. CIDH *Anthony Briggs* v. *Trinidad and Tobago*, 15 April 1999. (One interesting response by the State was the following: "As regards the possible breach of Article 6(6), it is submitted that the punishment to be inflicted on the petitioner under the laws of Trinidad and Tobago does not consist of deprivation of liberty, but death by hanging. Accordingly, the reform and social readaptation of the petitioner is irrelevant at this time"). Later the Commission affirmed its report and made it public (15 April 1999). The next day Trinidad rejected the Commission's recommendations and declared that 'the law should take its course'. IACHR *James et al.*, Order for provisional measures, 25 May 1999, 'Considering' clause 1(f).

[92]   Early February 1999 Trinidad requested the Court to 'confirm' that its Order of August 1998 was 'discharged in so far as it relates to [him]'. IACHR *James et al.*, Communication of the State of 5 February 1999 in: Order for provisional measures, 25 May 1999, 'Considering' clause 1(d). A month later the State requested the Court once more to confirm that its Order for provisional measures with regard to Mr. Briggs was now discharged.

[93]   Judge De Roux Rengifo attached a concurring opinion to the Order referring to the problem of duration but not fully addressing it: he spoke of a 'reasonable length of time'. IACHR *James et al.*, Concurring Opinion of Judge De Roux Rengifo, Order for provisional measures, 25 May 1999.

[94]   Presumably this is a reference to legal certainty for the petitioner, as the vulnerable party in human rights adjudication.

American Convention, does not mean that the examination of the case is already concluded under the inter-American system of protection of human rights".[95]

He pointed out that while the Commission had concluded its examination of the case, the matter remained pending under the jurisdiction of the Court, 'as the supreme organ of interpretation and application of the American Convention'.[96] This understanding, he wrote, found support in the Court's Order of August 1998 to take all necessary measures to preserve the life and physical integrity of, among others, Mr. Briggs, so as 'not to hinder the processing of their cases before the inter-American system'.[97] In other words the Court did not refer to the Commission alone, but to 'the inter-American system' as a whole. The case must be pending before the Commission for it to be able to request the Court to order provisional measures, but this requirement only applies with regard to the moment triggering the Court's jurisdiction. Once set in motion it 'cannot be affected in any way by the subsequent conduct or action by the parties (in contentious matter), or of the requesting State or organ (in advisory matter), or of the Commission as the organ requesting provisional measures of protection'.[98]

He pointed out that nothing in Article 63(2) ACHR made the consideration of the subject by the Court dependent on the proceedings before the Commission. A contrary interpretation would make the Court's power to continue considering a given matter, in which it was competent to supervise its own provisional measures, conditional upon the subsequent conduct of the organ requesting such measures, in this case the Commission.[99] The Court's inherent power to determine the extent of its own competence applied to its advisory and contentious jurisdiction as well as to its competence to order provisional measures. He reiterated that the Inter-American Court is guardian and master of its own jurisdiction and the American Convention has given it an important role in the construction of an Inter-American *ordre public* for the protection of human rights.[100]

Judge De Roux Rengifo added the following arguments in support of the Court's decision to 'maintain, for at least a reasonable length of time, the provisional measures ordered on behalf of Anthony Briggs'.[101] Pointing out that the circumstances of the Briggs case were unique, he referred to the fact that the Commission had already submitted the 'reports to which articles 50 and 51 of the American Convention on Human Rights refer'. 'One would have thought', he said, 'that provisional measures would have become superfluous once the reports in question were issued', in particular the Article 51 Report.

> "But matters are not so simple. Were the Court to call for the measures to be lifted immediately, it would be disregarding the absolutes that follow from a full and balanced interpretation of the provisions of chapters VI, VII and VIII of the Pact of San José, which define the structure of the inter-American system for the protection of human rights and legislate the membership and functions of the organs of that system, which must work in tandem to accomplish the system's

---

[95] IACHR *James et al.*, Order for provisional measures, 25 May 1999, Concurring Opinion of Judge Cançado Trindade, §3.
[96] Id., §4.
[97] Id., §4., referring to the 2nd 'Decisional' clause.
[98] Id., §5.
[99] Id., §6.
[100] Id., §§7-8.
[101] IACHR *James et al.*, Order for provisional measures, 25 May 1999, Concurring opinion of Judge De Roux Rengifo.

purposes. Had it not prolonged the life of the provisional measures, the Court would have been disregarding the combined scope of articles 50, 51 and 63(2) of the Convention".[102]

He referred to the Court's Judgment in the *Loayza Tamayo* case, holding that if a State ratifies an international treaty, especially on human rights, 'it has the obligation to make every effort to apply the recommendation of a protection organ such as the Inter-American Commission' in accordance with the principle of good faith as laid down in Article 31(1) of the Vienna Convention on the Law of Treaties.[103] This obligation has 'multiple ramifications'.

> "Clearly the State must take a constructive attitude towards those recommendations, carefully and deliberately study the steps and measures it must take to comply with them, find ways to sort out any obstacles that might prevent it from taking the measures in question, and apply the measures to the fullest should the obstacles prove not to be insurmountable".[104]

In this light 'the Court could hardly deny the protection of its provisional measures to anyone whose rights had been protected by express recommendations of the Inter-American Commission, right from the time those recommendations became final'.[105] He then proceeded with the following argument:

> "When articles 50, 51 and 63.2 are read in combination, it becomes clear that the proper course of action is to prolong those measures for a reasonable period, so as to ensure that a timeframe can be established during which the State truly makes "every effort to apply the recommendations [...] of the Inter-American Commission" before any irreparable harm is done (which in the instant case means before Anthony Briggs is executed)".[106]

In light of the concurring opinions attached to the Order of the Court it is possible to interpret the Court's order as follows: by maintaining the provisional measures on behalf of Mr. Briggs, the Court in fact confirms the Commission's approach to follow-up ('seguimiento') of its cases.[107] A case is not closed until it has been complied with. In matters in which the Commission requested the Court to order provisional measures, these measures continue to apply even when the Commission has published an Article 51 Report and has not sent the case to the Court for consideration on the merits. As long as the case was indeed pending before the Commission at the time it requested the Court's provisional measures, the Court maintains its jurisdiction to continue its provisional measures under Article 63(2), despite the fact that the case did not and will not reach it for a determination on the merits. Cançado Trindade explained this by pointing out that once the Court's jurisdiction has been established, it cannot be taken away by acts or omissions of others. De Roux Rengifo added that the case would still be pending until there had been some form of follow-up by the State on the Commission's recommendations, justifying maintenance of provisional measures.

A domestic Court believed differently. The Judicial Committee of the Privy Council (London) considered that the Inter-American Court had no jurisdiction to maintain its provisional

---

[102] Ibid.

[103] IACHR *Loayza Tamayo* case, Judgment of 17 September 1997, §80.

[104] IACHR Concurring Opinion of Judge De Roux Rengifo, *James et al.*, Order for provisional measures, 25 May 1999. See also Chapter XVI (Legal Status).

[105] IACHR *James et al.*, Order for provisional measures, 25 May 1999, Concurring opinion of Judge De Roux Rengifo.

[106] Ibid.

[107] See also Chapter XVII (Official responses).

measures on behalf of Mr. Briggs once the Commission had published its Report on the merits in his case. The Privy Council expressed its expectation that national courts would give 'great weight to the jurisprudence of the Inter-American Court'. At the same time it would be 'abdicating' its duty if it 'were to adopt an interpretation of the Convention', which it considered 'untenable'. In this respect the Judicial Committee considered that the Court had no power to adopt provisional measures once the proceedings were complete. "Once the processing of the case was complete, the order automatically expired". The Commission had made its findings of fact and it had made 'recommendations with which the State has not complied, but it is not bound to do so'. The Commission had failed to bring the case before the Court and there was 'no longer any *lis*'.[108] Lord Nicholls of Birkenhead dissented. He pointed out that by acceding to the Convention the State 'intended to confer benefits on its citizens. The benefits were intended to be real, not illusory. The Inter-American system of human rights was not intended to be a hollow sham or, for those under sentence of death, a cruel charade'. He criticised the State's position that the Inter-American Court had no jurisdiction to make its Order of May 1999 and emphasised that the jurisdiction of the Inter-American Court 'is a matter within the sole jurisdiction of that court'. "Thus, it is not for the courts of the State parties to the Convention to decide the scope of the Inter-American Court's jurisdiction".[109]

During the subsequent proceedings before the Inter-American Court, mainly involving the other persons covered in the provisional measures, Trinidad also gave its position on the execution of Briggs despite the Court's provisional measures. It pointed out that 'after the Commission decided to publish its Article 51 report, there was no matter pending before the Commission, nor any matter pending before the Court, nor any other matter capable of being submitted to the Court'. It concluded its argument with the statement that 'after the Commission so decided, the Court had no power to adopt provisional measures. The Court's purported Order of 25 May 1999 was made without jurisdiction and, therefore, was null'.[110] The Court did not comment any further on the issue of its jurisdiction to maintain its provisional measures in these circumstances. It simply pointed out that under Article 68(1) ACHR States Parties undertake to comply with the judgment of the Court in any case to which they are parties, that they should fully comply with all the provisions of the Convention in good faith and that States must refrain from taking action that may frustrate *restitutio in integrum*.[111]

Yet on subsequent occasions it has interpreted the phrase 'case not yet submitted to the Court' in Article 63(2) ACHR 'to imply, at least, the possibility of bringing the issue that is the subject-matter of the provisional measures to the adjudicatory jurisdiction of the Court'.[112]

Obviously it is the Court itself that determines its own competence, not a State or a domestic Court. The Court has the inherent power to determine the scope of its own competence (*compétence de la compétence/Kompetenz-Kompetenz*) both in its Orders and in its decisions on admissibility, merits and reparation. It is not allowed to subordinate the mechanisms foreseen in the

---

[108] JCPC *Briggs v Cipriani Baptiste (Commissioner of Prisons) and Others (Trinidad and Tobago) [1999] UKPC 45 (28 October 1999)*. See further Chapter XVII (Official responses).

[109] JCPC Dissenting Opinion by Lord Nicholls of Birkenhead, *Briggs v Cipriani Baptiste (Commissioner of Prisons) and Others (Trinidad and Tobago) [1999] UKPC 45 (28 October 1999)*.

[110] IACHR *James et al.*, Order for provisional measures, 16 August 2000, 13th 'Having seen' clause.

[111] Id., 11th 'Considering' clause.

[112] See e.g. IACHR *Matter of García Uribe et al.* (Mexico), Order of 2 February 2006, 3rd 'Considering' clause; *Matter of Capital El Rodeo I & El Rodeo II Judicial Confinement Center* (Venezuela), 8 February 2008, 5th 'Considering' clause and *Tyrone Dacosta Cadogan* (Barbados), Order of the President of 4 November 2008, 4th 'Considering' clause.

ACHR to restrictions that undermine the function of the tribunal and, for that matter, the protective system laid down in the Convention.[113]

In another context the court has also distinguished between on the one hand the preventive nature ('cautelar') of provisional measures in international adversarial cases, aimed at the preservation of the proceedings and at the eventual execution of the decisions on the merits, and on the other hand the protective nature ('tutelar') of its measures.[114] This implies a transformation of its provisional measures into a 'true judicial guarantee' of a preventive nature, 'since they protect human rights inasmuch as they are intended to avoid irreparable harm to persons'.[115] It has pointed out that 'in view of the protective nature of the provisional measures the Tribunal may order such measures even when there is not exactly an adversarial case in the Inter-American system, in situations that, *prima facie*, may result in a serious and urgent impairment of human rights'.[116] This means that the Court must make 'an assessment of the proposed problem, the effectiveness of the State measures regarding the described situation and the degree of lack of protection in which the people requesting the measures would be if such measures are not adopted'. For an appropriate assessment the Court depends for a great deal on the information provided by the Commission. Thus it has pointed out that it is essential that the Commission 'submits a sufficient ground to comprise the already mentioned criteria and that the State fails to show, in a clear and sufficient way, the effectiveness of the specific measures adopted within the domestic jurisdiction'.[117]

In his separate opinion Judge García Ramírez notes that the distinction between the preventive and the protective nature of the Court's provisional measures is more a matter of emphasis and in each case there is both 'a protective (protection of human rights) and cautionary (preservation of the suit at law) purpose'.[118] He points out, correctly that also when the Court orders provisional measures in matters that are still before the Commission there is a preventive as well as a protective function to these provisional measures. After all, they aim to protect 'the suit at law that eventually will be brought before the Court, as well as the effect of the final decision resulting from such case', but apart from that also simply the proceedings before the Commission itself that would become ineffective if faced with violations.[119]

---

[113] See e.g. IACHR *Cases Liliana Ortega et al.; Luisiana Ríos et al.; Luis Uzcátegui; Marta Colomina and Liliana Velásquez* (Venezuela), Order for provisional measures of 4 May 2004, 8th 'Considering' clause, referring e.g. to *Hilaire, Constantine and Benjamin et al.*, Judgment of 21 June 2002, §19.

[114] IACHR *Matter of Capital El Rodeo I and el Rodeo II Judicial Confinement Center*, Order of 8 February 2008, 7th 'Considering' clause (see Spanish text).

[115] See e.g. IACHR *Matter of Capital El Rodeo I and el Rodeo II Judicial Confinement Center*, Order of 8 February 2008, 8th 'Considering' clause (paraphrased part is derived from the Spanish text rather than the translation).

[116] IACHR *Matter of Capital El Rodeo I and el Rodeo II Judicial Confinement Center*, Order of 8 February 2008, 9th 'Considering' clause.

[117] Ibid.

[118] IACHR *Matter of Capital El Rodeo I and el Rodeo II Judicial Confinement Center*, Order of 8 February 2008, separate opinion Judge García Ramírez, §9 (Spanish text, not the translation).

[119] IACHR *Matter of Capital El Rodeo I and el Rodeo II Judicial Confinement Center*, Order of 8 February 2008, separate opinion Judge García Ramírez, §10 (paraphrased text is derived from the Spanish text).

2.5   Use of provisional measures beyond inadmissibility or beyond judgments on the merits and reparation

The HRC has occasionally maintained provisional measures beyond inadmissibility and CAT has done so once too. To start with the latter, in *B. M'B.* v. *Tunisia* CAT took provisional measures in April 1994 'to ensure that no harm is done to the author's family, the alleged victim's family or the witnesses and their families'.[120] It later declared the case inadmissible because the petitioner had not submitted sufficient proof to establish his authority to act on behalf of the victim. At the same time it maintained its provisional measures.

As to the practice of the HRC, in some of its early death penalty cases the HRC maintained provisional measures *beyond* the inadmissibility decision. In the period July 1988 to July 1994 it declared many cases inadmissible, but at the same time referred to the possibility of review.[121] In the meantime it requested the State party not to execute the petitioners before they had had a reasonable time, after completing the effective domestic remedies available to them, to request the Committee to review the previous decision in their case. In general, in these cases provisional measures were used twice, *both* before deciding on admissibility *and* as part of the inadmissibility decision. Those cases about which the HRC specifically noted that they were open to review dealt with exhaustion of local remedies. In such cases the Committee maintained its provisional measures beyond the inadmissibility decision in order to enable the petitioners to re-submit the case upon exhaustion of local remedies.[122]

In total, the HRC maintained its provisional measures following inadmissibility declarations in twenty cases between July 1988 and July 1994. In several of these cases it requested the State

---

[120]   CAT *B. M'B.* v. *Tunisia,* 5 May 1994, §5(c).

[121]   Under Rule 92(2) of the Rules of Procedure.

[122]   In ten cases between July 1988 and July 1990 it maintained the provisional measures by explaining that it could review the inadmissibility decision, under Rule 92(2) of its rules of procedure, 'upon receipt of a written request by or on behalf of the author to the effect that the reasons for inadmissibility no longer apply'. It requested the State, 'taking into account the spirit and purpose' of its Rule on provisional measures, 'not to carry out the death sentence against the author, before he has had reasonable time after completing the effective domestic remedies available to him to request the Committee to review the present decision'. Five inadmissibility decisions of 26 July 1988, one of October 1989 and four of 13 July 1990: HRC *O.W.* v. *Jamaica,* 26 July 1988; *C.J.* v. *Jamaica,* 26 July 1988; *L.C. et al.* v. *Jamaica,* 26 July 1988, annex VIII, section J (pp. 269-271); *L.G.* v. *Jamaica,* 26 July 1988; *L.S.* v. *Jamaica,* 26 July 1988; *A.A.* v. *Jamaica,* 30 October 1989; *L.R. and T.W.* v. *Jamaica,* 13 July 1990; *D.B.* v. *Jamaica,* 13 July 1990; *C.B.* v. *Jamaica,* 13 July 1990 and *N.C.* v. *Jamaica,* 13 July 1990. Four years later it returned to this formulation in the last cases in which it maintained its provisional measures until the petitioner would have had reasonable time, after completing the available remedies, to request the HRC to review its inadmissibility decision. HRC *Denzil Roberts* v. *Barbados,* 19 July 1994 and *Peter Bradshaw* v. *Barbados,* 19 July 1994. Between October 1990 and July 1992 equally maintained its provisional measures in these cases but during this period it simply referred to its provisional measures without reference to the spirit and purpose of Rule 86. HRC *W.W.* v. *Jamaica,* 26 October 1990; *R.M.* v. *Jamaica,* 26 October 1990; *E.B.* v. *Jamaica,* 26 October 1990; *A.H.* v. *Trinidad and Tobago,* 31 October 1990; *D.D.* v. *Jamaica,* 11 April 1991; *M.F.* v. *Jamaica,* 21 October 1991; *M.F.* v. *Jamaica,* 17 July 1992, 335/1988 (not the same author as M.F. in 233/1987) and *R.W.* v. *Jamaica,* 21 July 1992. Apart from this the formulation was the same.

to provide the petitioner with the relevant court documents in order to be able to exhaust domestic remedies.[123]

In three non-exhaustion cases, however, it only pointed out that its decision was open to review, but it did not maintain its provisional measures.[124] The first case was when it declared inadmissible *Guerra and Wallen* v. *Trinidad and Tobago* (1995).[125] It deeply regretted that the State was 'not prepared to give the undertaking requested by the Committee' in its provisional measure, 'apparently because it considers itself bound by the conservatory order issued by the Court of Appeal on 29 April 1994'.[126] The HRC considered that, in fact, 'this situation should have made it easier for the State party to confirm that there would be no obstacles to acceding to the Committee's request; to do so would, in any event, have been compatible with the State party's international obligations'.[127] In view of the fact that the State was not prepared to respect the provisional measures taken pending the case,[128] the HRC could also have maintained them similar to the other non-exhaustion cases.

Equally, it could have done this in *Hylton* v. *Jamaica* (1994).[129] In this case the allegations under Article 14 related to the availability and the effectiveness of counsel. The claim based on Article 14 ICCPR clearly justified the HRC's use of provisional measures.[130] The petitioner had pointed out that he was notified of the date of the appeal and of the fact that a new lawyer had been assigned to him only two weeks before the hearing for his appeal. He claimed he immediately wrote to this lawyer 'explaining that he had never had the opportunity to discuss his case with his previous counsel, and that he would like to meet him prior to the hearing; if not, he would assume that counsel could not, or would not, represent him on appeal'.[131] He did not receive a reply to his enquiries, but later found out that his appeal was dismissed. The HRC considered the complaint inadmissible because domestic remedies had not yet been exhausted. Within a fortnight after declaring the case inadmissible Hylton's petition to the JCPC was dismissed. Apparently, the Committee does not allow the petitioner to resubmit his claim in this respect, as it has done in earlier cases relating to non-exhaustion.

The third example is a case in which the HRC concluded that the delay could be attributed mainly to the petitioner. The Committee declared the case inadmissible for non-exhaustion but did not refer to the possibility of review nor maintained its provisional measures. One might conclude from this example that the HRC is unlikely to maintain its provisional measure beyond the admissibility declaration if the delay is attributable to the petitioner.[132]

Finally, the HRC has also declared cases inadmissible in situations that did not lend themselves to review and did not involve the issue of exhaustion of domestic remedies either. Obviously, in such cases it did not maintain its provisional measures. While it declared one case inadmissible observing that this did not exclude humanitarian measures on behalf of the petitioner,

---

123 See e.g. HRC *L.R. and T.W.* v. *Jamaica*, 13 July 1990; *D.B.* v. *Jamaica*, 13 July 1990; *C.B.* v. *Jamaica*, 13 July 1990; *N.C.* v. *Jamaica*, 13 July 1990; *W.W.* v. *Jamaica*, 26 October 1990; *R.M.* v. *Jamaica*, 26 October 1990; *E.B.* v. *Jamaica*, 26 October 1990 and *D.D.* v. *Jamaica*, 11 April 1991.

124 See e.g. HRC *C.F.* v. *Jamaica*, 28 July 1992 and *Guerra and Wallen* v. *Trinidad and Tobago*, 4 April 1995 (while Wallen had since died, Guerra was still awaiting execution).

125 HRC *Lincoln Guerra and Brian Wallen* v. *Trinidad and Tobago*, 4 April 1995.

126 Id., §6.5.

127 Ibid.

128 See the discussion in Chapter XVII, section 2.2.2.

129 HRC *Dwayne Hylton* v. *Jamaica*, 8 July 1994.

130 See Chapter XIII on forms of reparation.

131 HRC *Dwayne Hylton* v. *Jamaica*, 8 July 1994, §2.5.

132 HRC *N.A.J.* v. *Jamaica*, 26 July 1990.

such as the commutation of his sentence,[133] in the majority of cases it did not add such an observation.[134]

In sum, the HRC maintained its provisional measures *beyond* the decision declaring a case inadmissible for non-exhaustion of domestic remedies in cases in which court documents were missing that were necessary for domestic appeals. Moreover, it did so only for a limited period. In 1993 the HRC decided, in *Collins* v. *Jamaica*,[135] that in the absence of a written judgment from the Court of Appeal there was no reasonable prospect of success for applications to the JCPC. Hence it would no longer declare such cases inadmissible and it could simply maintain its provisional measures as part of its admissibility declaration rather than as part of its inadmissibility declaration.

Five years after it had last maintained provisional measures beyond its inadmissibility decision two members of the HRC suggested recycling this method of upholding the request for provisional measures given the possibility of review.

The Dayton Agreement (Article XI, 1(b) of Annex 6) grants the Bosnia Chamber the power 'to include an order for provisional measures in its final decision on the merits of a case'. As discussed in Chapter II (Systems), at first sight this is a strange provision, because it grants the Chamber the power 'to include an order for provisional measures in its final decision on the merits of a case'. Yet the Chamber seems to have found a way to interpret the provision: "This power might be used to regulate the position of the parties before the decision becomes final and binding, or pending the full implementation of the decision".[136] As noted in Chapter II, it may often be useful pending implementation to follow up on the situation of the victims in order to make sure that nothing happens that could prevent further implementation.[137]

In the Inter-American system the competence of the adjudicator is at issue in a circumstance different from that of maintaining provisional measures beyond inadmissibility in order to make sure that a petitioner is able to renew his petition upon exhaustion. The Inter-American Commission and Court often maintain their provisional measures for a long time, but what is remarkable is that these measures may be maintained, or ordered for the first time, after a judgment on the merits or reparation.[138] This is done to protect persons against death threats. In situations in which the Inter-American Court specifically orders the *maintenance* of provisional measures, it usually notes that the situation of 'extreme gravity and urgency' of the beneficiaries of the provisional

---

[133] See *G. J.* v. *Trinidad and Tobago*, 5 November 1991.

[134] *A.W.* v. *Jamaica*, 8 November 1989; *G.S.* v. *Jamaica*, 8 November 1989; *N.A.J.* v. *Jamaica*, 26 July 1990, (246/1987) (not the same petitioner as N.A.J. in 351/1989); *D.S.* v. *Jamaica*, 11 April 1991, (304/1988) (not the same petitioner as D.S. in 234/1987); *D.S.* v. *Jamaica*, 8 April 1991, (234/1987/Rev.1) (not the same petitioner as D.S. in 304/1988); *N.A.J.* v. *Jamaica*, 6 April 1992, (351/1989) (not the same petitioner as N.A.J. in 246/1987); *E.E.* v. *Jamaica*, 23 October 1992; *N.P.* v. *Jamaica*, 5 April 1993; *R.M.* v. *Trinidad and Tobago*, 29 October 1993; *Errol Simms* v. *Jamaica*, 3 April 1995; *Lloyd Rogers* v. *Jamaica*, 4 April 1995 and *Christopher Bethel* v. *Trinidad and Tobago*, 31 March 1991.

[135] *Trevor Collins* v. *Jamaica*, 25 March 1993.

[136] See Bosnia Chamber Annual Report 2000 (under the heading 'provisional measures').

[137] The Inter-American Court only considers a case closed once the State has fully implemented it. Before such time it may maintain provisional measures, for instance to protect witnesses. See also Chapter XVIII on follow-up.

[138] For the Commission's precautionary measures as part of a decision on the merits see e.g. CIDH *Rudolph Baptiste* v. *Grenada*, 13 April 2000 (merits), §31.

measures is continuing and that this makes 'it imperative to require the State to maintain the provisional measures necessary to preserve their life and physical integrity'.[139]

Normally one would assume that provisional measures are provisional exactly because they are issued pending a case (*pendente lite*) and not after the case has been closed. The Inter-American Court, however, does not consider a case closed until the State has fully implemented its judgment on the merits and its judgement on reparations. Meanwhile such cases are still 'pending'. This again shows the link between the substance of judgments on reparation, the stage of supervision and provisional measures.[140] In other words some of the protection offered in the Inter-American system in the form of provisional measures, is ordered while the case is not yet decided on the merits while other protection is ordered following the finding of a violation. This is so because victims or witnesses in the case in which the Court already issued a judgment may still be exposed to threats, for instance by paramilitary groups.

This approach by the Court, not considering a case closed until it has been implemented, appears to have been developed in light of the rationale behind the system of protection created under the American Convention, in the context of the cases of death threats and harassment that the Commission and Court are faced with and of the lack of actual monitoring by the OAS political organs. Again the Inter-American Court took into account the irreparable nature of the harm faced by the petitioners.

An example showing an extended duration of provisional measures involves a case that was not even pending before the Court. This is the *Colotenango* case. Since 1994 the Court used provisional measures on behalf of Juan Chanay Pablo and others.[141] Meanwhile the Commission had brokered a friendly settlement in 1997.[142] Nevertheless the persons involved were still receiving death threats, indicating that the case before the Commission was not yet closed, and therefore Court's provisional measures were again maintained in 2001.[143]

Yet six year later the Court decided to lift the measures. While doing so it observed that 'on various occasions the State failed to present its reports or did not provide sufficient information, making it difficult for the Court to determine the actual circumstances of the beneficiaries of the measures ordered. This creates a situation of uncertainty that is incompatible with the preventative and protective nature of provisional measures'.[144] Nevertheless, it pointed out, 'after 13 years of having ordered the provisional measures, the main point of controversy in regards to these remains the potential danger to the beneficiaries if the apprehension orders against the former patrol officers, who escaped from prison in April 1999, are not enforced. Furthermore, the reports from the State as well as the comments from the Commission and the representatives have revolved around the investigation into the facts which gave rise to the current provisional measures as well as the effectiveness of the implementation of security measures directed towards the beneficiaries, particularly in regards to the frequency in which foot and vehicle patrols have or have

---

[139] See IACHR *James et al.*, Orders for provisional measures, 16 August 2000 and 24 November 2000. In general, the Commission petitions the Court to order a stay of executions 'until such time as the Commission has had the opportunity to examine end decide these cases pursuant to the Convention and the Commission's Regulations', *James et al.*, Order of 29 August 1998. At other times the Commission specifies this by adding 'and until the situation of extreme gravity and urgency no longer persists in relation to these individuals'. See e.g. *James et al.*, Orders of 27 May 1999 and 25 September 1999.

[140] See Chapter XIII (Protection).

[141] See *Colotenango* case (Guatemala), Orders of 22 June 1994 until 5 September 2001.

[142] CIDH *Juan Chanay Pablo* v. *Guatemala*, 13 March 1997 (Friendly Settlement).

[143] See IACHR *Colotenango* case, Order of 5 September 2001.

[144] Id., 8th 'Considering' clause.

not occurred, in order to protect the boundaries of the community".[145] It considered that the Commission was to monitor this as part of the obligations entered into in the Friendly Settlement agreement brokered by it. The Court did observe that removing the provisional measures did not mean that the State had complied with its obligations under the ACHR.[146]

Thus on the one hand the Court does not consider a case closed until its judgment on reparations has been fully implemented. In this light it has sometimes maintained some of its Orders for provisional measures. This use of provisional measures during the stage of monitoring compliance with its judgments is a significant extension of the traditional concept of provisional measures. On the other hand, more recently it has referred situations that it previously dealt with through provisional measures, to its supervision of compliance procedure, issuing orders on State's compliance with its judgments.[147] Moreover, in the above *Colotenango* case, that never made it to the Court on the merits, after 13 years it decided to lift the provisional measures and refer the petitioners to the Commission for supervision of compliance with the Commission's Report in that case. While doing so it did not say it was changing its approach to its jurisdiction to use provisional measures until after a judgment on the merits or reparation. Its recent practice simply indicates that, in the absence of concrete and recent information on death threats, it will deal with these matters through its procedure on supervision of compliance with judgments instead.[148]

While the practice of the Inter-American Court and the HRC is triggered in different legal contexts (making sure there is no gap in treaty protection between exhaustion and submitting a case; making sure the judgments are fully implemented and meanwhile the petitioners or others involved are not receiving death threats), their underlying rationale appears to be the same. The irreparable nature of the harm to persons triggered an inventive approach to jurisdiction in particular, well-defined, circumstances.

---

[145] Id., 11th 'Considering' clause.

[146] Id., 14th 'Considering' clause.

[147] See e.g. IACHR *Case of Comunidad Indígena Sawhoyamaxa* v. *Paraguay,* Order of 2 February 2007 on supervision of compliance, 9th and 12th 'Considering' clause.

[148] Yet see Order on supervision of compliance of the IACHR cases *Fermín Ramírez* v. *Guatemala* and *Raxcacó Reyes* v. *Guatemala* and on the request to expand the provisional measures in *Raxcacó Reyes y otros*, 9 May 2008, in which the Court does appear to make a strict division; it argues that because Article 62(2) ACHR referred to cases of *prima facie* urgency while the risk of irreparable harm in these cases related to violations that have already been established by judgments of the Court that have *res iudicata* status, the Court did not order provisional measures but it ordered the State simply to comply with its judgment, adding specifications and noting that it would continue to monitor the situation. This reasoning does not apply, of course, to situations where witnesses and others in cases that have already been decided on the merits, or even reparations, are still being threatened. See e.g. IACHR *Bámaca Velásquez* v. *Guatemala*, Order of 27 January 2009, declaring Guatemala's partial compliance with the Judgment on Reparations, declaring to keep open its monitoring process until full compliance is achieved and *maintaining* its provisional measures of 11 March 2005 (Provisional Measures and Monitoring Compliance with Judgment).

3   ADMISSIBILITY AND PROVISIONAL MEASURES

3.1   Introduction

Apart from the lack of jurisdiction on the merits there are other reasons for inadmissibility as well.[149] This section examines whether such inadmissibility criteria hinder the use of provisional measures in human rights adjudication.

When drafting its rules of procedure, the HRC specifically discussed the relation between admissibility of the case on the one hand and the use of provisional measures on the other (section 3.2). The Inter-American Commission sometimes uses provisional measures prior to formally opening a case, which indicates the importance it attaches to preventing irreparable harm, but at the same time may at times have undermined the stature of the measures (section 3.3). The main criterion for admissibility of a case that is relevant in the context of decision-making on the use of provisional measures is that of exhaustion of domestic remedies (section 3.4). Other admissibility criteria that could be relevant at the stage of provisional measures include the question whether the 'same matter' is or has been pending before another adjudicator and the question of compatibility with the treaty (section 3.5).

3.2   The HRC's discussion on the relation between admissibility and provisional measures

While other adjudicators have also dealt with death penalty cases, relevant information with regard to the relation between admissibility of the case and the use of provisional measures in human rights adjudication is mainly found in the practice of the HRC.

Article 5(2) OP stipulates that the HRC shall declare a case inadmissible if domestic remedies have not been exhausted or if the same matter is being examined under another procedure of international investigation or settlement.

During the drafting of the rules of procedure in 1977 the issue came up whether it was necessary to determine the admissibility of the case before using provisional measures. The Rules of Procedure of CERD, the first treaty body established, stipulate that provisional measures may be used *after* a case has been declared admissible. In its current Rules of Procedure, Rule 94(3) still refers to the possibility of provisional measures under the heading 'method of dealing with admissible communications'.[150] Thus far CERD has never used provisional measures. In any case, the requirement may be considered an anomaly.[151] While the proposal for a rule on provisional measures by the HRC was probably inspired by the rules of CERD, it became clear during the discussions in 1977 that several members of the HRC did not wish to copy the admissibility requirement found in CERD's Rules of Procedure.[152] At the same time the HRC decided to leave open this

---

[149]   CAT even explicitly notes in its Annual Reports that it has 'conceptualized the formal and substantive criteria' applied by its Rapporteur when granting or rejecting requests for provisional measures, pointing out that the basic admissibility criteria set out in Article 22 (1)-(5) ICAT must be met, although the requirement of exhaustion can be dispensed with in some circumstances (see section 3.4 of this Chapter). See e.g. CAT Annual Report A/61/44 (2005/2006), §61.

[150]   CERD/C/35/Rev.3, 1 January 1989.

[151]   If at one point CERD would consider using provisional measures it may be expected that it will adapt its Rules in order to make effective use of such measures.

[152]   Sir Vincent Evans (UK) expected that the procedure for determining admissibility would take time and he hoped that the rule on provisional measures (then rule 86) 'would enable the

question. Subsequently it did use provisional measures in advance of declaring a case admissible, as members like Opsahl and Uribe Vargas had proposed. Uribe Vargas had referred to the *purpose* of provisional measures, noting that the text of the rule envisaged 'an exceptional or emergency situation in which irreparable damage to the victim might be involved'.[153] It seems that he argued from the perspective of preventing irreparable harm to persons.[154] In addition, Committee member Opsahl had pointed out that Article 5(2) OP 'did not mean that the Committee should ignore such communications but only that it should not consider them on their merits until the conditions indicated in that article had been met'.[155] In other words, the HRC would be able to use provisional measures in advance of its determination of admissibility. His remark may imply that he considered it possible for the HRC to maintain provisional measures after declaring a case inadmissible.[156]

Committee to deal with urgent matters on a priority basis, inasmuch as the possible need for interim measures might of itself be grounds for urgency'. Opsahl (Norway) believed that provisional measures should not be dependent on an admissibility declaration. He pointed out that the second sentence of the proposal (the requirement to inform the State that the provisional measure did not imply a determination on the admissibility or substantive validity of the claim) already made it clear that provisional measures would not prejudice the determination of admissibility or the validity of a communication. Lallah (Mauritius) suggested the replacement of the words 'substantive validity' with the word 'merits'. He also suggested the replacement of the word 'necessary' with 'desirable'. He noted that '(a) peculiar situation might arise in which a State received no hearing, and he felt that care should be taken to avoid a situation in which views might be expressed without recourse'. It is not fully clear what he meant with this remark, because also without hearings, both Parties subsequently have the opportunity to argue for or against the continuation of the provisional measures. In the sense the State does have recourse. In any case his remark does show that during the drafting of the HRC's Rules of Procedure the issue of hearings already came up in relation to provisional measures. Summary records of the meetings of the first session, 13th meeting, 29 March 1977 and 17th meeting, 31 March 1977, Yearbook of the HRC 1977-1978, Vol. I, CCPR/1, pp. 44-46 and p. 54.

[153] Ibid.
[154] See Conclusion Part II with the conceptual framework proposed in this book, discussing the purpose of provisional measures in human rights adjudication.
[155] Summary records of the meetings of the first session, 13th meeting, 29 March 1977 and 17th meeting, 31 March 1977, Yearbook of the HRC 1977-1978, Vol. I, CCPR/1, pp. 44-46 and p. 54.
[156] Opsahl noted that Uribe Vargas (Colombia) 'had correctly stated the intentions of the Protocol as a whole'. According to Uribe Vargas the HRC should view the rule 'in the light of all the articles of the Protocol rather than just article 5'. The text of the rule envisaged 'an exceptional or emergency situation in which irreparable damage to the victim might be involved'. He considered that a 'human rights committee established to guarantee the implementation of the Universal Declaration of Human Rights could not wait for the implementation of a rule of procedure when humanitarian questions were involved'. Given the context it can be assumed that he meant the ICCPR and not the Universal Declaration. Agreeing after all with Uribe Vargas and Opsahl, Ganji (Iran) considered that there was 'no inconsistency between rule 86 and the Protocol'. In his view the conditions in Article 5(2) made it especially important to have a rule dealing with emergency situations 'involving the possibility of irreparable damage'. He had initially expressed some reservations with respect to the proposed rule 'because it might be incompatible with the conditions for the consideration of a communication by the Committee' under Article 5(2) OP. Sir Vincent Evans suggested that they could leave open the question whether the HRC 'might indicate the need for interim measures, prior to a determination of admissibility'. For that purpose, he proposed to replace the phrase 'at any time' with 'prior to forwarding its final views'. Chairman Mavrommatis (Cyprus) suggested an amended text to incorporate this suggestion.

In any case, from the start the HRC used provisional measures in advance of determining the admissibility of the case. By appointing a Special Rapporteur, first on death penalty cases and later on New Communications, to take provisional measures between sessions it confirmed that there was no need to determine the admissibility of a case.

In 1986 the HRC used provisional measures for the first time in order to halt an execution.[157] It published this decision.[158] The next year it published separately one other provisional measure decision as well.[159] The texts of these decisions already show a relationship between provisional measures and the issue of admissibility. The HRC considered that it needed further factual information, in one case from the State, in the other from the petitioner, before it could examine the question of the admissibility of the case. It pointed out that it was relying on the willingness of the government of the State in question (not identified in the publication) to cooperate with it 'at this early stage in the consideration of the subject-matter'.[160] It requested the State party, under its Rule on provisional measures (at the time Rule 86), not to carry out the death sentence before the HRC had had 'an opportunity to consider further the question of the admissibility' of the case. In its request for information from the petitioner it posed nine specific questions about the conduct of the trial, to be answered under its Rule on the transmission of cases to the State. At least one of the questions clearly related to the issue of admissibility.[161]

In none of its inadmissibility decisions, in which it initially used provisional measures did it say anything about its earlier use of these measures. It simply used them initially and eventually declared the case inadmissible. Yet when inadmissibility is already very clear at an early stage the HRC apparently does not use provisional measures. This applies in particular to situations in which a case is likely to be declared inadmissible for lack of substantiation or failure to bring a claim (Article 2 OP and Rule 90(b) of the Rules of Procedure) or even abuse of the right of petition. Reasons for such inadmissibility include that the case is incompatible with the terms of the treaty or clearly based on incorrect interpretations of its provisions or on facts not within the scope of the treaty.

The HRC (as well as CAT) has tried to expedite proceedings by dealing with admissibility and merits together rather than consecutively. Initially Jamaica, which has long been the main addressee of the provisional measures to halt executions, often contested the Committee's admissibility decisions, usually for non-exhaustion of domestic remedies. The HRC reviewed its decisions, and usually confirmed them. Later, from early 1995 on, Jamaica and Trinidad and Tobago

---

Summary records of the meetings of the first session, 13th meeting, 29 March 1977 and 17th meeting, 31 March 1977, Yearbook of the HRC 1977-1978, Vol. I,CCPR/1, pp. 44-46 and p. 54. This amended text, with some minor changes, was eventually included in the HRC's first Rules of Procedure and is still applicable.

[157] HRC *X* v. *S*, Rule 86/91 decision of 21 July 1986. From the decision on the merits it appears this is *Earl Pratt* v. *Jamaica*.

[158] See its *Selected Decisions* vol. II, under the heading 'interlocutory decisions', CCPR/C/OP/2.

[159] HRC *X.* v. *S.*, Rule 86/91 decision of 13 November 1987. The HRC later declared the communication inadmissible for non-exhaustion of local remedies, *C.J.* v. *Jamaica*, 26 July 1988 (inadm.), but maintained the provisional measure.

[160] HRC *X.* v. *S.*, Rule 86/91 decision of 13 November 1987.

[161] It dealt with the requirement of exhaustion of local remedies. This was the question whether the authorities had offered the petitioner legal aid during his trial and appeal and whether legal aid was now available for petitioning for leave to appeal to the Judicial Committee of the Privy Council (JCPC). Legal aid indeed became one of the main issues in the cases before the HRC during the next few years. The other questions posed also were relevant to the issue of admissibility, to the extent that the answers could clarify compatibility with the provisions of the Covenant.

changed their attitude towards the proceedings before the HRC. Rather than arguing against admissibility and failing to submit comments on the merits, in fact they immediately commented on the merits and requested a joint examination on admissibility and merits in order to expedite the procedure. This way these States could go ahead with an execution before a specific deadline would be triggered that had been set by the domestic case law (developed by the JCPC) on the death row phenomenon causing a violation of the Constitution's prohibition of cruel treatment. Otherwise this deadline would prevent these States permanently from executing the petitioner.[162]

3.3 Provisional measures and opening a case in the Inter-American system

Until May 2001 the Inter-American Commission often used precautionary measures separately from the main case. Some of them were taken independent of a specific case pending before it. If the situation was not solved, the Commission could formally open a case.[163] In August 1997, for instance, the Inter-American Commission requested Paraguay to inform it about the implementation of the precautionary measures it took to protect the lives of two attorneys and a judge who were involved in the case of *Napoleon Ortigoza* pending before it. The Commission explicitly mentioned that it took precautionary measures 'without opening a specific case'.[164] This example, however, was remarkable because the Commission normally did not explicitly note that it did not yet open a case. Moreover, the threats seemed to have been made in relation to a case already pending before the Commission. It would therefore have been possible to treat the precautionary measures as part of the *Napoleon Ortigoza* case until such time when the Commission would

---

[162] Following this change the HRC often decided to consider admissibility and merits together in cases in which the State party had explicitly waived its right to invoke non-exhaustion of domestic remedies and had addressed the merits of the communication. See e.g. HRC *Conroy Levy* v. *Jamaica,* 3 November 1998 and *Clarence Marshall* v. *Jamaica,* 3 November 1998. It would recall Article 4(2) OP, stipulating that the State shall submit its written observations on the merits of a communication within six months of the transmittal of the communication. This period may be shortened in the interests of justice, if the State party so wishes. See e.g. HRC *Clement Francis* v. *Jamaica,* 25 July 1995; *Errol Johnson* v. *Jamaica,* 22 March 1996; *Michael Adams* v. *Jamaica,* 30 October 1996; *Anthony McLeod* v. *Jamaica,* 31 March 1998; *Tony Jones* v. *Jamaica,* 6 April 1998 and *Errol Smith and Oval Stewart* v. *Jamaica,* 8 April 1999. In some cases the HRC decided nevertheless to issue a separate admissibility decision, since the information before it was not sufficient to enable it to adopt a decision on the merits. See e.g. HRC *Clive Johnson* v. *Jamaica,* 20 October 1998 and *Samuel Thomas* v. *Jamaica* (in this case the petitioner had objected to the joint consideration of admissibility and merits because the State party had failed to address all the issues raised in the complaint). In other cases it decided to deal with admissibility and merits together despite the request of the petitioner not to do so, '(a)s both parties have had the full opportunity to comment on each other's merits submissions'. See e.g. HRC *Desmond Taylor* v. *Jamaica,* 2 April 1998. In HRC *Peter Blaine* v. *Jamaica,* 17 July 1997. Scheinin disagreed with such a decision because he considered that the petitioner had not been given the opportunity to comment on the merits. As stipulated in (then) Rule 91(2) of the rules of procedure the situation is now as follows. The HRC examines admissibility and merits together in order to expedite the procedure under the OP. Only in exceptional cases the Committee, the Working Group or the Special Rapporteur on New Communications will initially request the State only to respond to the issue of admissibility.

[163] It did so when, *prima facie,* petitions met the procedural requirements for processing. See e.g. CIDH Annual Report 2000, Chapter III.B (Statistics) under c.

[164] CIDH Annual Report 1997, Chapter III(a).

open a new case. Obviously this would require precautionary measures on behalf of certain beneficiaries initially to be taken in the context of one and subsequently in that of another case.

In cases involving the death penalty, the Inter-American Commission developed the practice of always opening a case and assigning a case number immediately upon receipt of a submission requesting precautionary measures to halt an impending execution. This differed from other matters pending before it where it would also take precautionary measures before actually opening a case and assigning a communication number.

As of May 2001, Rules 26 to 30 of the new Rules of Procedure govern the requirements for opening a case. The Commission processes, through its Executive Secretariat, the petitions that contain all the information required under Rule 28. The Commission provides a form for presenting petitions on human rights violations. It is prepared by its Executive Secretariat and is aimed at assisting victims, their families, civil society organisations and others in presenting a petition. In its instructions accompanying this form the Executive Secretariat points out:

> "In cases where the life or physical integrity of a person or group of persons is in imminent danger despite having approached appropriate domestic authorities, you may submit the pertinent information to the Commission even if information concerning the exhaustion of domestic remedies is not currently available".[165]

With its new Rules of Procedure (2000) the Inter-American Commission aims at integrating the examination of individual complaints under both the ACHR and the Declaration. It must now issue a formal admissibility decision in all petitions transferred to the State. Previously an admissibility declaration was not necessary.[166] At present, only in exceptional circumstances the Commission may open a case but defer its treatment of admissibility until the debate and decisions on the merits.[167] Upon the adoption of the admissibility report[168] the Commission shall register the petition as a case and initiate procedures on the merits.[169] Admissibility requirements are now more specifically listed and this applies to time limits as well.

In other systems it is not necessary to declare a case admissible before ordering provisional measures. The only requirement is *prima facie* admissibility. It is not clear, however, what the Inter-American Court will do in extremely urgent cases because the new Rules seem to require the Commission to declare a case admissible before it can appeal to the Court to order provisional measures. Of course the requirement to declare a case admissible before using precautionary measures does not apply when the situation is so urgent that irreparable harm would otherwise result. Similarly there may be cases where the issue of admissibility is very intricate and the Commission needs the view of both parties before it can decide on it. Meanwhile it should be able to use provisional measures.

---

[165] Form for presenting petitions on human rights violations, <http://www.cidh.org/Basicos/English/Basic24.Petition%20Form.htm> (consulted 8 February 2008).
[166] See on this issue Gómez (2001).
[167] Article 37(3) CIDH Rules of Procedure.
[168] Upon a decision based on Article 37(3) of the CIDH Rules of Procedure.
[169] Article 37(2) CIDH Rules of Procedure.

3.4   Exhaustion of domestic remedies

3.4.1 Introduction

Sometimes States have argued that provisional measures are not appropriate because domestic resources have not yet been exhausted.[170] Indeed the requirement of exhaustion of local remedies[171] may be relevant in the choice to take or maintain provisional measures. The HRC has stated that the mere affirmation by the State party that a remedy exists is not sufficient for it to consider it an effective remedy that needs to be exhausted for purposes of the OP. According to its consistent jurisprudence only those domestic remedies that are effective and available must be exhausted.[172]

The Inter-American Court had already noted in 1989 that:

> "Thus, when certain exceptions to the rule of non-exhaustion of domestic remedies are invoked, such as the ineffectiveness of such remedies or the lack of due process of law, not only is it contended that the victim is under no obligation to pursue such remedies, but, indirectly, the State in question is also charged with a new violation of the obligations assumed under the Convention. Thus, the question of domestic remedies is closely tied to the merits of the case".[173]

This section first discusses the requirement of exhaustion in the context of death threats, the right of habeas corpus and patterns of violations, then in the context of non-refoulement and more generally in light of the absence of legal aid in the domestic proceedings. Subsequently it deals with the approach of the HRC to exhaustion in death penalty cases, as well as the availability of a

---

[170]   The following case before the CIDH serves as an example. In December 1997 Peru sent a response to precautionary measures that had been addressed to it on behalf of members of a human rights organisation and of petitioners who were threatened in a case (case 11.811) pending before the Commission. Peru stated that an investigation into the 'presumed threats noted in the request for precautionary measures' was already underway before the petitioners filed a case with the Commission. It believed it 'inappropriate and inadmissible' for the Commission to take precautionary measures 'that would duplicate in most cases the processing of personal guarantees that petitioners have been seeking in the domestic courts'. CIDH Annual Report 1997, Chapter III(a), under 'Peru'. Adjudicators have also refused to take provisional measures in cases subsequently declared inadmissible for non-exhaustion, see e.g. CAT *L.Z.B. on her own behalf and on behalf of her daughter J.F.Z.* v. *Canada*, 8 November 2007 (inadm.).

[171]   On this requirement in general international law, see e.g. Second report on diplomatic protection, by ILC Special Rapporteur John Dugard, A/CN.4/514, 28 February 2001 (among others noting that the distinction between primary and secondary rules has served its purpose in the field of state responsibility, 'it is a distinction that cannot be too strictly maintained in a study on exhaustion of local remedies in the context of diplomatic protection, as the concept of denial of justice is intimately connected with the exhaustion of remedies rule'.This rule may be seen 'both as a secondary rule, excusing recourse to further remedies (…) or as a primary rule giving rise to international responsibility', §10).

[172]   See e.g. HRC *Clive Smart* v. *Trinidad and Tobago*, 29 July 1998.

[173]   IACHR *Velásquez Rodríguez*, Judgment of 26 June 1987, §91. As Buergenthal (1994), p. 76 has pointed out with regard to the Inter-American Court, '(t)he fact that a case at some stage of the proceedings be determined by the Court to be inadmissible will not affect its power to grant provisional measures so long as it has jurisdiction over the parties. If that were not so, it would make no sense whatsoever to authorize the Court to issuew provisional measure sin cases not yet referred to it which, at stat stage, would *ipso facto* be inadmissible under Article 61(2) of the Convention'.

written judgment for the decision by the HRC to maintain provisional measures beyond admissibility. Finally this section notes the approach of the HRC in cases involving threats to indigenous culture.

3.4.2 Exhaustion and threats

Death threats may also make domestic remedies unavailable and ineffective. In *Neptune* v. *Trinidad and Tobago* (1996), for instance, in March 1995 the HRC declared admissible a claim about degrading conditions of detention 'in the absence of information from the State party about effective domestic remedies available to the author and noting the author's claim that he had been threatened with death for making complaints'.[174] The latter claim was not further discussed. Several years previously, in December 1992, the HRC had used provisional measures in this case. It did so to halt the execution of the death sentence against the petitioner, not to put a stop to the death threats.[175]

A decision to declare a case inadmissible could also have repercussions for the persons who have appeared as witnesses. This triggers the question of what happens to the local investigators, and others who are not themselves the petitioners, when a case has been declared inadmissible while previously the Inter-American Court had used provisional measures on their behalf. Presumably, in a situation like this, the Inter-American Commission would have to open a new case specifically dealing with threats against witnesses or human rights defenders involved in the case at the local level and immediately request the Court to take provisional measures.

3.4.3 Habeas corpus and patterns of violations

The Inter-American Commission has found that swift action is necessary to ensure the effectiveness of the remedy of habeas corpus. There is no need to exhaust petitions for habeas corpus if they are 'powerless to compel the authorities' (a reference to the Court's jurisprudence in the *Honduran* cases)[176] to 'ensure proper protection within a reasonable period of time in order to

---

[174]   HRC *Clyde Neptune* v. *Trinidad and Tobago*, 16 July 1996, §4.4.

[175]   See also Chapter IV on detention situations and death threats and harassment. Zwaak/Haeck (2008), p. 128, have suggested, appropriately, that in the context of severe acts of intimidation apparently aimed at deterring recourse to available domestic remedies, the European Court 'could consider waving the requirement of exhaustion of internal remedies systematically, until the situation in the region has improved'.

[176]   IACHR *Velásquez Rodríguez*, Judgment of 28 July 1988, §§66-68; *Godínez Cruz*, Judgment of 20 January 1989, §§69-71; *Fairén Garbi and Solís Corrales*, Judgment of 15 March 1989, §§91-93 ("A remedy must also be effective – that is, capable of producing the result for which it was designed. Procedural requirements can make the remedy of habeas corpus ineffective: if it is powerless to compel the authorities; if it presents a danger to those who invoke it; or if it is not impartially applied. On the other hand, contrary to the Commission's argument, the mere fact that a domestic remedy does not produce a result favorable to the petitioner does not in and of itself demonstrate the inexistence or exhaustion of all effective domestic remedies. For example, the petitioner may not have invoked the appropriate remedy in a timely fashion. It is a different matter, however, when it is shown that remedies are denied for trivial reasons or without an examination of the merits, or if there is proof of the existence of a practice or policy ordered or tolerated by the government, the effect of which is to impede certain persons from invoking internal remedies that would normally be available to others. In such cases, resort to those remedies becomes a senseless formality. The exceptions of Article 46 (2) would be fully

prevent the consummation or worsening of the human rights violation that was the object of the complaint'.[177] It has equally applied an exception to the rule of exhaustion of local remedies because 'amparo' proceedings had 'not proven effective in responding to the claims of alleged violations of human rights'.[178]

---

applicable in those situations and would discharge the obligation to exhaust internal remedies since they cannot fulfill their objective in that case").

[177] CIDH *Minors in detention* v. *Honduras*, 10 March 1999, §65. As evident already from the *Honduran* cases, the issue of disappearance is relevant as well in the context of exhaustion. The following case is puzzling in its failure to use precautionary measures. In June 1990 CEJIL and CEAPAZ petitioned the Commission on behalf of Mr. Ramos Diego who had disappeared in Peru the previous month. In such case it could have been useful to take precautionary measures as the disappearance was recent. The Commission, however, rejected this petition for failure to exhaust domestic remedies. It is not clear whether the petitioners also had requested the Commission to take precautionary measures in order to be able to locate the disappeared person. In July 1992 CEJIL presented a new complaint and strongly urged the Commission to open a case. Clearly, at this time the disappearance was no longer recent and a precautionary measure would have been futile. The complaint is mentioned in CEJIL case docket 1997. Mr. Ramos had disappeared on 7 May 1990. It was more than two years later, in July 1992, that the Commission opened his case. It subsequently decided to process six disappearance cases together. These cases related to the same region and period, 'were attributed to soldiers, and followed a pattern of behavior indicating a State policy'. The other cases were opened between one month after the disappearance and two years afterwards. The Commission referred to the Court's holding that 'the proper remedy in the case of the forced disappearance of persons would ordinarily be habeas corpus, since those cases require urgent action by the authorities'. IACHR *Velásquez Rodríguez*, 21 July 1988 §65; *Caballero Delgado and Santana*, 21 January 1994 (Preliminary Objections), §64. Habeas corpus is 'the normal means of finding a person presumably detained by the authorities, of ascertaining whether he is legally detained and, given the case, of obtaining his liberty'. IACHR *Caballero Delgado and Santana*, 21 January 1994 (Preliminary Objections), §67. The Commission further referred to the Court's ruling that domestic remedies 'must be capable of producing the results for which they were intended'. *Velásquez Rodríguez*, 21 July 1988, §68. The Commission found that, during the period in question, 'there existed in Peru a practice or policy of disappearances, ordered or tolerated by various Government authorities'. This 'practice rendered writs of habeas corpus completely ineffective in cases of disappearances'. Thus, it was not necessary to attempt this or any other remedy. The exceptions mentioned in Article 46(2) ACHR were fully applicable. CIDH *Juan de la Cruz Núñez Santana et al.* v. *Peru*, 13 April 1999, §57. In this light the Commission's earlier decision to declare the case of Samuel Ramos Diego inadmissible is surprising, especially since the applicable case law of the Court predates this decision. At the time the disappearance was very recent and precautionary measures by the Commission could have served some purpose. As noted, it is not clear whether the Commission took such measures before it rejected the petition. In one of the other six cases the Commission processed the case within a month of the disappearance. It is possible that it took precautionary measures, but the report on the merits does not provide information in this respect. More generally on effective remedies by the Inter-American Court see e.g. Medina Quiroga (2005), pp. 372-380.

[178] See e.g. CIDH *Jorge Odir Miranda Cortez et al.* v. *El Salvador*, Report 29/01, 7 March 2001, §§40-41 ('Almost two years have elapsed since the petition was filed and no final decision has been handed down by the Salvadoran Supreme Court') and §42 ('that in this case, after almost two years, a final ruling has not been handed down regarding the claim of the petitioners in El Salvador, and has determined that an unjustified delay has occurred in terms of domestic remedies'). An example of an issue that was not brought before the Commission exactly because the local NGO, together with CEJIL had been able to resolve the urgent situation is that of the

In the case of the 'unlawful combatants' detained by the US at Guantanamo Bay after 9/11 the CIDH took precautionary measures for the first time early 2002, when the beneficiaries had been detained incommunicado and without charge for several months. Several years later the US argued that there were 'avenues of potential domestic relief' available, which were 'effective and timely'.[179] Thus, it concluded, the case was inadmissible for failure to exhaust domestic remedies.

> "Nevertheless, in a spirit of cooperation, the United States has to date made six numerous lengthy and detailed submission to the Commission and attended every scheduled hearing in this matter. At this point, while into the fourth year of this proceeding, the United States intends to defer further formal participation until the international law requirement of exhaustion of domestic remedies has been fulfilled".[180]

However, the CIDH observed that nearly half of the detainees had not been granted effective access to counsel. It considered that the urgent situation continued to exist and had been exacerbated. It maintained its precautionary measures.[181]

The African Commission has taken an approach that is similar to that of the Inter-American Commission. In situations of gross human rights violations, local remedies (Article 56(5) ACHPR) need not be exhausted. It has even been pointed out that given the absence of effective juridical procedures, in many cases this has resulted in the 'Commission somehow becoming the court of first instance in many of the claims that have come before it, thus negating the whole essence of the local remedies rule'.[182] Thus, it 'has been able, only at the stage of admissibility, to expose realities of the human rights situations in what have hitherto been Africa's foremost dictatorial regimes'.[183] In two arbitrary deportation cases, in which it had equally used provisional measures, the African Commission noted that because of the deportation the petitioner had been prevented from exhausting domestic remedies. It declared the case admissible.[184] In the face of imminent irreparable harm it is likely that the Commission will continue to use provisional measures and subsequently find that the domestic remedies are ineffective.

Another situation in which provisional measures have been used while domestic remedies were not yet exhausted, is in the context of extreme detention conditions or lack of medical treat-

---

village El Hornito in the state of Zulia in Venezuela. For more than 15 years the state petrochemical company 'El Tablazo' had disposed chemical waste in the lake on the edge of which this village was located. This resulted in a contamination of the town and a diminished air quality. This, in turn, affected the health conditions of the inhabitants. PROVEA, Physicians for Human Rights and CEJIL were trying to relocate them, to obtain guaranteed medical attention and redress for the harm suffered. Action at the local level achieved improvement in their situation, CEJIL case docket 1997 (on file with the author)

[179] CIDH *Guantanamo Bay*, Response of the US government of 19 October 2005, pp. 12-13, available at <www.ccr-ny.org> (consulted 20 September 2006).

[180] Ibid.

[181] See CIDH *Guantanamo Bay* case, precautionary measures of 23 July 2002, 18 March 2003, 29 July 2004 and 28 October 2005. CIDH Resolution 1/06 in Press Release 27/06, 'Inter-American Commission urges to close Guantanamo without delay', 28 July 2006, available at <http://www.cidh.org/Comunicados/English/2006/27.06eng.htm> (consulted 6 October 2006). See further Chapter VIII (Ensuring procedural rights) and XVIII (Follow-up).

[182] Onoria (2003), p. 29.

[183] Ibid.

[184] See ACHPR *Amnesty International* (*on behalf of William Banda and John Chinula*) v. *Zambia*, 212/98, 5 May 1999. See also *Modise* v. *Botswana* decided in 1997. See also Chapter XI (Mass or arbitrary expulsion).

ment. The ECtHR, for instance, has used provisional measures and also 'put a question to the parties asking whether there existed within the Georgian prison system an administrative practice consisting of keeping detainees in unsatisfactory conditions, an/or a structural problem underlying the lack of medical treatment in prison. Were this to be the case, the applicant would be exempted from the requirement laid down by Article 35§1 to exhaust domestic remedies for the purposes of his complaints under article 3 of the Convention'.[185]

3.4.4 Exhaustion and suspensive effect in non-refoulement cases

When there is a risk of irreparable harm, in order for a case to be declared admissible there is no need to exhaust domestic remedies without suspensive effect. CAT has been particularly clear on this with regard to the protection against refoulement in Article 3 ICAT.[186]

At the same time, when domestic remedies clearly do not appear to have been exhausted wile their effectiveness has not been challenged, CAT refuses requests for provisional measures.[187] In the European system the approach is similar. Petitioners before the ECtHR must provide copies of all domestic decisions exactly because for provisional measures to be used domestic proceedings must be exhausted. Yet an exception is made when the domestic proceedings do not have suspensive effect. In such cases the Court can indeed use provisional measures.[188]

---

[185] ECtHR *Ghvaladze* v. *Georgia*, 42047/06, provisional measures ('to admit the petitioner to a hospital setting where he could receive the appropriate care') and communicated, Case Law Information Note 100, 30 September 2007, p. 10.

[186] See e.g. CAT *Josu Arkauz Arana* v. *France*, 9 November 1999 (an appeal against the ministerial deportation order issued in respect of the complainant on 13 January 1997 would not have been effective or even possible, since it would not have had a suspensive effect and the deportation measure was enforced immediately following notification thereof, leaving the person concerned no time to seek a remedy. The Committee therefore found that article 22, paragraph 5 (b), did not preclude it from declaring the communication admissible', §6.1); *Iratxe Sorzábal Díaz* v. *France*, 3 May 2005 (an appeal against the ministerial deportation order issued in respect of the complainant on 31 August 1999 but served on the very day of her expulsion, at the same time as the order indicating the country of destination, would not have been effective or even possible, since the deportation measure was enforced immediately following notification thereof, leaving the person concerned no time to seek a remedy, §6.1); and *Nadeem Ahmad Dar* v. *Norway*, 11 May 2007 (the remedies suggested by the State party as effective remedies to be exhausted did not have suspensive effect and the complainant might face irreparable harm if returned to Pakistan and provisional measures were used; petitioner was nevertheless deported to Pakistan, which constituted a violation of Article 22 (individual complaint); this breach was remedied by granting a residence permit for three years upon return to Norway and the issue whether the deportation constituted a violation of Article 3 ICAT had become moot because the petitioner had been able to return to Norway). See also its Annual Reports, e.g. A/61/44, §61. The HRC has taken a similar approach. See e.g. HRC *Simalae Toala et al.* v. *New Zealand*, 2 November 2000, ("It was not apparent to the Committee that any remedies that might still be available to the authors would be effective to prevent their deportation", §6.4). See also HRC *Jagjit Singh Bhullar* v. *Canada*, 31 October 2006 (inadm.) (provisional measures were used pending the proceedings). See also *Ominayak* v. *Canada*, 26 March 1990.

[187] See e.g. CAT *L.Z.B. and her daughter J.F.Z.* v. *Canada*, 8 November 2007 (inadm.).

[188] When a petitioner complains that his removal would expose him to treatment contrary to Article 3 ECHR a remedy that does not suspend execution of his expulsion order is not 'effective' within the meaning of Article 35(1) ECHR and does not have to be used. See e.g. ECtHR *Sultani* c. *France*, 20 September 2007 (provisional measures of 20 December 2005 and 5 January 2006) (see §50: "*Par ailleurs, lorsqu'un individu se plaint de ce que son renvoi l'exposerait à un*

Moreover, the ECtHR has explicitly confirmed that an effective remedy in expulsion cases must include suspensive effect. Lack of such effect results in a violation of Article 13, sometimes combined with Article 3 ECHR.[189] Obviously, prior to an admissibility decision involving a

---

traitement contraire à l'article 3 de la Convention, les recours sans effet suspensif ne peuvent être considérés comme efficaces au sens de l'article 35 §1 de la Convention (voir mutadis mutandis et parmi beaucoup d'autres X. c. Allemagne, no 7216/75, décision de la Commission du 20 mai 1976, Décisions et rapports (DR) 5, p. 137; M. c. France, no 10078/82, décision de la Commission du 13 décembre 1984, DR 41, p. 103)"). For the practice of the former Commission see e.g. EComHR *Barir and Amuur et al.* v. *France*, 18 October 1993, noting that already in the 1980s it had pointed out that petitioners claiming that their expulsion would expose them to a grave danger couild not be expected to exhaust domestic remedise without suspensive effect)partly struck from the list. Its provisional measures were of 27 March 1992. Other examples are EComHR *A.* v. *France*, 27 February 1991 (inadm.), p. 335; *Z.* v. *The Netherlands*, 14 May 1984 and *L.* v. *France*, 10 December 1984 (no provisional measures). In *B.* v. *France*, 22 January 1987 (inadm.). the Commission initially used provisional measures but later concluded that the petitioner did have a national remedy. He could bring an application before the Conseil d'État to set aside the extradition order. It observed 'that an application of this kind may be accompanied by an application for a stay of execution which, although it does not in itself have suspensive effect, is intended to ensure that the administrative court will very speedily conduct an initial examination of the extradition order and, if appropriate, order a stay of execution'. It pointed out that the general practice, as indicated by the Government, was that it refrained from implementing the order until the Conseil d'État has considered the petition. In *Becker* v. *Denmark* (1976) the (former) European Commission had used provisional measures to delay the repatriation of a large group of Vietnamese children. Subsequently there was discussion about whether or not domestic remedies had been exhausted. The State had acknowledged that the available remedy had no suspensive effect, see *Becker* v. *Denmark*, 3 October 1975 (inadm.), Yearbook XIX, p. 228. Thus, the Commission considered that it would not be an effective remedy, see p. 233. See also *Denmark, Norway, Sweden and The Netherlands* v. *Greece* (First Greek case), 24 January 1968, pp. 770-774 with an interesting discussion on admissibility, administrative practice and effective and sufficient remedies.

[189] See e.g. ECtHR *Sultani* v. *France*, 20 September 2007, §50; *Gebremedhin* v. *France*, 16 April 2007, §58; *Conka* v. *Belgium*, 5 February 2002, §83 and *Jabari* v. *Turkey*, 11 July 2000, §50. See also Guideline 5 of the Committee of Ministers "twenty guidelines on forced return", 4 May 2005 ("1. In the removal order, or in the process leading to the removal order, the subject of the removal order shall be afforded an effective remedy before a competent authority or body composed of members who are impartial and who enjoy safeguards of independence. The competent authority or body shall have the power to review the removal order, including the possibility of temporarily suspending its execution. 2. The remedy shall offer the required procedural guarantees and present the following characteristics: – the time-limits for exercising the remedy shall not be unreasonably short; – the remedy shall be accessible, which implies in particular that, where the subject of the removal order does not have sufficient means to pay for necessary legal assistance, he/she should be given it free of charge, in accordance with the relevant national rules regarding legal aid; – where the returnee claims that the removal will result in a violation of his or her human rights as set out in guideline 2.1, the remedy shall provide rigorous scrutiny of such a claim. 3. The exercise of the remedy should have a suspensive effect when the returnee has an arguable claim that he or she would be subjected to treatment contrary to his or her human rights as set out in guideline 2.1. [real risk of being executed, or exposed to torture or inhuman or degrading treatment or punishment; real risk of being killed or subjected to inhuman or degrading treatment by non-state actors, if the authorities of the state of return, parties or organisations controlling the state or a substantial part of the territory of the state, including international organisations, are unable or unwilling to provide appropriate and

State's argument of non-exhaustion of non-suspensive remedies, the human rights adjudicator may use provisional measures.[190]

Moreover, in the European system the practice has developed of informing the Court ahead of time of a request for provisional measures, including the submission of all relevant information, so that the Court may order provisional measures immediately upon exhaustion. The European Court (and previously the Commission) may sometimes itself anticipate exhaustion of domestic remedies by taking provisional measures that are conditional on such exhaustion. It has done so on some occasions when there would be insufficient time for the petitioner to request provisional measures to prevent expulsion or extradition immediately upon exhaustion of domestic remedies.[191]

In *K.C.* v. *Canada* (inadm. 1992) counsel had requested the HRC to use provisional measures because extradition of the petitioner to the US 'would deprive the Committee of its jurisdiction to consider the communication, and the author to properly pursue his communication'.[192] The HRC did use them, but later it declared the complaint inadmissible because of non-exhaustion of domestic remedies. It also specifically set aside the provisional measures earlier indicated. In this respect the inadmissibility decision in this extradition case differs from the aforementioned death penalty cases against Jamaica in which the HRC *maintained* provisional measures beyond the inadmissibility decision, pending exhaustion of local remedies and pending a renewed application to the Committee. The Committee did point out that the petitioner could bring the issue again after exhausting local remedies. The petitioner did this in *Cox* v. *Canada* (1994). It was able to do

---

effective protection; other situations which would, under international law or national legislation, justify the granting of international protection])".

[190] In CIDH *Cheryl Monica Joseph* v. *Canada*, 6 October 1993, the petitioners had unsuccessfully requested the Inter-American Commission to take precautionary measures. They had requested these measures 'in order to avoid irreparable damage to Mrs. Joseph, that she be granted temporary permission to remain in Canada, and that the deportation order be stayed', §II, 2. Later, the Commission declared the case inadmissible for non-exhaustion of domestic remedies. It considered she could have used a domestic procedure that had suspensive effect, but did not do so within the deadline. If there had been special reasons for not having done so in time, a later application would have been possible. She would also have had the right to counsel to represent her in this 'application for leave' to start proceedings against the removal order. While declaring the case inadmissible, the Commission, 'bearing in the mind the humanitarian aspects' of the case, invited Canada 'to give favourable consideration to the possibility of permitting Mrs. Joseph to remain in Canada until the completion of the court actions brought in connection with the estate of her late husband', §31. The Commission did not explain its refusal to take precautionary measures but it may have considered, already at this stage, that the petitioner could have used domestic remedies that would have had suspensive effect. This would suggest that the Commission takes into account prima facie admissibility in its use of precautionary measures. It is also possible, however, that the Commission simply considered that the petitioner's removal to Trinidad prima facie would not cause irreparable harm to her life and physical integrity. The Commission's exhortative remark ('give favourable consideration') when it declared the case itself inadmissible reminds one of certain statements by the Committee on the Elimination of Racial Discrimination. See e.g. CERD *Lacko* v. *Slovakia*, 9 August 2001, although this was not in the context of provisional measures. See also HRC *Hendriks* v. *the Netherlands*, 27 July 1988.

[191] See e.g. EComHR *Yeung Yuk Leung* v. *Portugal*, 27 November 1995. See further Norgaard/Krüger (1988), p. 115, equally referring to the possibility of conditional request by the (then) European Commission under Rule 36 (provisional measures), pending the decision of the domestic authorities or courts.

[192] HRC *K.C.* v. *Canada*, 29 July 1992 (inadm.), §2.5.

so as the State had not extradited him in the meantime.[193] In this case counsel explained why he chose to submit the case and apply for provisional measures prior to discontinuing the domestic appeal:

> "This move was taken because I presumed that a discontinuance of the appeal might result in the immediate extradition of Mr. Cox. It was more prudent to seize the Committee first, and then discontinue the appeal, and I think this precaution was a wise one, because Mr. Cox is still in Canada".[194]

This strategy of counsel seems to be a response to Canada's actions in the previous extradition cases *Kindler* and *Ng* who were both extradited immediately upon the final decision of the domestic court and despite the Committee's provisional measures.[195]

The Committee's use of provisional measures in *E.G.* v. *Canada* (disc. 1997) shows that it aims to take provisional measures that have the potential to be effective.[196] While domestic remedies had not yet been exhausted, counsel had pointed out that the State had extradited fugitives 'within minutes or hours of a judgement by the Supreme Court of Canada, allowing no time for defendants to pursue any domestic or international remedies aimed at obtaining a stay'. For this reason, counsel noted, it was 'imperative' that the HRC would address the issue of provisional measures in advance of the decision of the Supreme Court of Canada on the application for leave to appeal. "(F)ailure to consider the issue of interim measures prior to the Supreme Court of Canada decision will in effect render applicant's recourse to the Human Rights Committee completely illusory and ineffective".[197] She recalled that the HRC used provisional measures subsequent to the decision of the Supreme Court in the abovementioned cases *Kindler* and *Ng*. Yet, Canada extradited these petitioners within a few hours of the judgment.[198] Later, in *Judge* v. *Canada* (2003) the HRC did not have the chance to order provisional measures.[199] In *Bakhtiyari family* v. *Australia* (2003) the Special Rapporteur, in May 2002, adjusted his request to halt the deportation of the children and their mother 'to be conditional on an adverse decision on the application by the High Court'. In other words, if still necessary the provisional measures would apply immediately upon exhaustion of domestic remedies. Later, when the Committee considered the admissibility of the case, it responded to the State's argument of non-exhaustion by referring to its practice to decide on this question 'at the point of the consideration of the communication, not least for the reason that a communication in respect of which domestic remedies had been

---

[193] HRC *Cox* v. *Canada*, 31 October 1994.

[194] Id., §8.1.

[195] See Chapter XVII on the official responses of Addressee States. See also Chapter XV on assessment of temporal urgency.

[196] HRC *E.G.* v. *Canada*, 17 November 1997 (disc.); 738/1997; initial submission 5 January 1997 (received 7 January 1997), provisional measures of 17 January 1997; withdrawal of provisional measures on 28 April 1997; petitioner's request to withdraw the case of 26 May 1997; on 17 November 1997 the HRC informed the petitioner that it had discontinued the case (on file with the author).

[197] HRC *E.G.* v. *Canada*, 17 November 1997 (disc./on file with the author).

[198] Initial submission of 5 January 1997 in HRC *E.G.* v. *Canada* (on file with the author). See also Chapter XV on prompt decision-making and assessment of temporal urgency, discussing the requirement of immediacy.

[199] HRC *Judge* v. *Canada*, 5 August 2003. See Chapter XV on prompt decision-making and assessment of temporal urgency.

exhausted after submission could be immediately resubmitted to the Committee if declared inadmissible for that reason'.[200]

Sometimes the State's non-exhaustion arguments are rather disingenuous. In *Olaechea Cahuas* v. *Spain* (2006) the petitioner was extradited despite a provisional measure ordered by the ECtHR. The State had argued that the case was inadmissible for non-exhaustion of domestic remedies. The Court dismissed this argument as the domestic recourse suggested by the State did not have suspensive effect. In other words the recourse suggested was incapable of halting the extradition, as became clear by the extradition. Thus it could not be regarded as an effective remedy.[201] Indeed it was rather ironic for the State to argue non-exhaustion while it had itself extradited the petitioner in violation of the Court's provisional measures.[202]

In *Weiss* v. *Austria* (2003) the State party had extradited the petitioner in contravention of the HRC's provisional measures and subsequently argued that he had not exhausted domestic remedies. The Committee pointed out that it takes provisional measures because of the possibility of irreparable harm to the victim.

> "In such cases, a remedy which is said to subsist after the event which the interim measures sought to prevent occurred is by definition ineffective, as the irreparable harm cannot be reversed by a subsequent finding in the author's favour by the domestic remedies considering the case. In such cases there remain no effective remedies to be exhausted after the event sought to be prevented by the request for interim measures takes place; specifically, no appropriate remedy is available to the author now detained in the United States should the State party's domestic courts decide in his favour in the proceedings still pending after his extradition".[203]

It is not surprising that adjudicators have expressed themselves emphatically on a State's argument of non-exhaustion after it has deported the petitioner despite a provisional measure. CAT has pointed out that 'when it called for interim measures of protection such as those that would prevent the complainant from being deported to Algeria, it did so because it considered that there was a risk of irreparable harm. In such cases, a remedy which remains pending after the action which interim measures are intended to prevent has taken place is, by definition, pointless because the irreparable harm cannot be averted if the domestic remedy subsequently yields a decision favourable to the complainant: there is no longer any effective remedy to exhaust after the action which interim measures were intended to prevent has taken place. In the present case, the Committee felt no appropriate remedy was available to the complainant now he had been deported to Algeria, even if the domestic courts in the State party were to rule in his favour at the conclusion of proceedings which were still under way after the extradition'.[204] In such case for the

---

[200] HRC *Bakhtiyari family* v. *Australia*, 29 October 2003, §8.2. It observed that the proceedings brought in the High Court had meanwhile been adversely concluded.

[201] ECtHR *Olaechea Cahuas* v. *Spain*, Judgment of 10 August 2006 (5th Section), §35.

[202] See also Bosnia Chamber *Boudellaa et al.* v. *BH and Fed.BH*, 3 September 2002 (adm. and merits), §152 (the domestic appeal of petitioner Lahmar was still pending and the Chamber noted that the execution of the decision to expel him should have been stayed. "The argument made by Bosnia and Herzegovina hence appears not to apply to him as the applicant has exhausted all possible remedies").

[203] HRC *Sholam Weiss* v. *Austria*, 3 April 2003, §8.2.

[204] CAT *Mafhoud Brada* v. *France*, 17 May 2005, §7.7. In this case the petitioner was deported to Algeria on a flight to Algiers on 30 September 2002 and had been missing since, §2.7. CAT also noted that the State party had enforced the order for the deportation of the complainant to Algeria after communicating its comments on the admissibility of the complaint, §7.5. See also CAT *Adel Tebourski* v. *France*, 1 May 2007.

State the consequence of ignoring the adjudicator's provisional measures is that the case is declared admissible because exhaustion is no longer effective. It noted:

> "The essential purpose of the appeal was to prevent the deportation of the complainant to Algeria. In this specific case, enforcing the deportation order rendered the appeal irrelevant by vitiating its intended effect: it was inconceivable that, if the appeal went in the complainant's favour, he would be repatriated to France. In the circumstances, in the Committee's view, the appeal was so intrinsically linked to the purpose of preventing deportation, and hence to the suspension of the deportation order, that it could not be considered an effective remedy if the deportation order was enforced before the appeal concluded".[205]

In other words: returning the petitioner despite the provisional measures 'and before the admissibility of the complaint had been considered made the remedies available to the complainant in France pointless, and the complaint was accordingly admissible'.[206]

Only when a petitioner in a non-refoulement case has not yet been deported, the addressee State can properly prevent him from exposure to irreparable harm to his life or personal integrity in the receiving State. Once the petitioner has been deported the addressee State can only use diplomatic means to gain access to this person in detention and monitor his treatment in order to remedy to some extent, the wrong done.[207] Strictly speaking the question whether exhaustion of domestic remedies is required when the petitioner has already been deported, is unrelated to the (earlier) question of provisional measures. Nevertheless, the statements on the illusory nature of such domestic remedies are relevant exactly because they illustrate the need for respect for provisional measures.

One other issue with regard to non-refoulement involves the consequence of compliance by a State with a provisional measure for the admissibility of a case. Such compliance does not automatically deprive a petitioner of his or her victim status.[208] In other words, a State cannot just argue that a case is inadmissible because it has complied with a provisional measure. Otherwise it could subsequently be tempted to quickly expel the person in question as there is no longer a case pending before the Court.

3.4.5 Absence of legal aid

In 1990 the Inter-American Court issued an Advisory Opinion on the issue of the exhaustion of domestic remedies (Article 46(2) ACHR). It found, in reference to the language of Article 46(2)

---

[205] CAT *Mafhoud Brada* v. *France*, 17 May 2005, §7.8.
[206] Id., §7.9.
[207] See also Chapter XVIII (Follow-up).
[208] See e.g. ECtHR *Gebremedhin* v. *France*, 16 April 2007, noting in §56 that 'a decision or measure favourable to the applicant is not in principle sufficient to deprive him of his status as a victim unless the national authorities have acknowledged, either expressly or in substance, and then afforded redress for, the alleged breach of the Convention. It is quite clear in the instant case that those conditions have not been met in relation to the complaint under Articles 13 and 3 taken together. The fact that the applicant was not removed to Eritrea and was eventually able to enter France to lodge an asylum application appears to have been due to his not being issued with a laissez-passer by the Eritrean embassy and then to the application by the Court of Rule 39. Furthermore, the Court observes in this regard that the administrative authorisation to enter the country and the safe conduct issued on 20 July 2005, and also the decision of the *Conseil d'Etat* of 11 August 2005, referred expressly to Rule 39 and to the interim measure taken in accordance with that provision'.

jo. Articles 1(1), 24 and 8 ACHR, that 'if it can be shown that an indigent needs legal counsel to effectively protect a right which the Convention guarantees and his indigency prevents him from obtaining such counsel, he does not have to exhaust the relevant domestic remedies'.[209] In addition, 'where an individual requires legal representation and a generalized fear in the legal community prevents him from obtaining such representation, the exception set out in Article 46(2)(b) is fully applicable and the individual is exempted from the requirement to exhaust domestic remedies'.[210] It stated that under Article 46(1) ACHR 'and in accordance with general principles of international law', it was for the State asserting non-exhaustion of domestic remedies to prove that such remedies in fact existed and that they had not been exhausted.[211]

In the African system there is an even greater problem with regard to access to legal aid, but in light of the fact – in the absence of a victim requirement – that most petitioners are NGOs, the African Commission has not considered this to excuse non-exhaustion.[212]

The HRC has dealt with the availability of legal aid as well, in particular for constitutional motions by death row inmates. In its considerations of this issue it also took into account the length of proceedings. It pointed out that 'in capital punishment cases, legal aid should not only be made available; it should also enable counsel to prepare his client's defence in circumstances that can ensure justice'.[213] With regard to Jamaica, the Addressee in most early death penalty cases dealt with by the HRC, the absence of legal aid could excuse non-exhaustion of local reme-

---

[209] IACHR Advisory Opinion OC-1190 on *Exceptions to the Exhaustion of Domestic Remedies* (Article 46(1), 46(2) and 46(2)(b) ACHR), 10 August 1990, §31.

[210] Id., §35.

[211] It is only 'once a State Party has shown the existence of domestic remedies for the enforcement of a particular right guaranteed by the Convention' that the burden of proof shifts to the complainant, who must then demonstrate that the exceptions provided for in Article 46(2) are applicable, whether as a result of indigency or because of a generalized fear to take the case among the legal community or any other applicable circumstance. Of course, it must also be shown that the rights in question are guaranteed in the Convention and that legal representation is necessary to assert or enjoy those rights'. See IACHR Advisory Opinion OC-1190 on *Exceptions to the Exhaustion of Domestic Remedies* (Article 46(1), 46(2) and 46(2)(b) ACHR), 10 August 1990, §41. The Inter-American Commission has stressed the importance of access to legal representation for asylum seekers. In its Special Report on Canada (2000) it noted: '(g)iven the nature of the refugee determination process and the interests at stake for the claimant, it is obviously in his or her interest to be represented by competent legal counsel'. Not only in reference to its own doctrine on the exhaustion of domestic remedies, in which it had addressed the question of when legal aid must be provided, but also in reference to the right of access to judicial protection under Article XVIII American Declaration, it pointed out that legal aid is required 'in order to effectively vindicate a fundamental protected right under the American Declaration or the Constitution or laws of the country concerned'. According to the Commission this flowed from the rights to equal protection of the law but even more 'from the principle that rights must be implemented in ways that give them proper effect'. It summarised the issue as follows: "States have an obligation to make the right to judicial protection effective. Distinctions in the availability or coverage of legal aid provided by the provinces which have the effect of depriving claimants requiring such services to ensure their access to judicial protection of fundamental rights necessary [sic] implicate the responsibility of the State". CIDH Canada Report 2000, §127.

[212] See e.g. ACHPR *Africa Legal Aid* v. *the Gambia*, 11 May 2000. Yet there is no victim requirement in the Inter-American system either. In general the African Commission does take a wide interpretation of Article 56(5) ACHPR. On exhaustion see, e.g., Udombana (2003), pp. 1-37.

[213] See e.g. HRC *Willard Collins* v. *Jamaica*, 1 November 1991.

dies not only for constitutional motions to the Supreme (Constitutional) Court, but also for the appeal to the Judicial Committee of the Privy Council (JCPC) in London, the ultimate domestic appeal at the time.[214]

In the period between 1989 and 1991 the HRC was awaiting clarification of the domestic situation in Jamaica and had not yet firmly determined whether a constitutional motion, following the rejection by the JCPC of a petition for leave to appeal, was an effective remedy for purposes of exhaustion. The State party failed to respond to requests for clarifications about constitutional motions before the Supreme (Constitutional) Court.[215] Some death row inmates requested their counsel to withdraw their communication to the HRC and file a constitutional motion instead, possibly on the assumption that a favourable HRC decision would not mean that the State would release them, while a constitutional motion would. They may have assumed it was necessary to withdraw their complaint and first seek such a motion.[216]

Later the domestic situation was clarified and the HRC also established its own position on the issue. It determined that the considerations governing the application of Article 5 (2)(b) OP are the impact of the length of judicial proceedings and the availability of legal aid. There is no need to exhaust domestic remedies that have been unreasonably prolonged,[217] nor to complete

---

[214] See e.g. HRC *Robinson LaVende* v. *Trinidad and Tobago*, 29 October 1997. In this case the HRC not only declared the case admissible but also found violations of Article 14(3)(d) and 14(5) ICCPR because of the denial of legal aid for an appeal to the JCPC.

[215] Section 25(2) of the Constitution of Jamaica stipulates that the Supreme (Constitutional) Court shall *not* deal with such motions if it believes that other means of redress have been available.

[216] Information obtained at Secretariat in Geneva, October 1998. In the case of *Carlton Reid* v. *Jamaica*, 20 July 1990, the HRC not only discussed the prospect of success but also already discussed the availability of legal aid for constitutional motions. In a number of interlocutory decisions the HRC had requested the State party to clarify whether the Supreme (Constitutional) Court had had the opportunity to determine a question that had long been unclear. This was the question whether an appeal to the Court of Appeal and the JCPC constituted 'adequate means of redress' within the meaning of Section 25(2) of the Constitution of Jamaica. The State party had replied that the Supreme Court had not yet done so. Given this reply the HRC declared the case admissible: "Taking into account the State party's clarification, together with the absence of legal aid for filing a motion in the Constitutional Court and the unwillingness of Jamaican counsel to act in this regard without remuneration, the Committee finds that recourse to the Constitutional Court under Section 25 of the Jamaican Constitution is not a remedy available to the author with in the meaning of Art. 5, paragraph 2(b), of the Optional Protocol". It clarified this by referring to the State's acknowledgment that the Supreme Court had not yet determined whether an appeal to the Court of Appeal and the JCPC constituted adequate means of redress under the Jamaican Constitution, thereby blocking recourse to the Supreme Court. The HRC added another reason why recourse to the Constitutional Court was not an available remedy under the OP: the absence of legal aid for filing such a motion and the unwillingness of Jamaican counsel to act pro deo. See also *Michael Sawyers and Michael and Desmond McClean* v. *Jamaica*, 11 April 1991 and *Clifton Wright* v. *Jamaica*, 27 July 1992. In this case Jamaica had challenged the HRC's admissibility findings by stating that its reasoning reflected a 'grave misunderstanding' of the relevant Jamaican law. It referred to its earlier statement that 'the decision of the Committee would render meaningless and nugatory the hard earned constitutional rights of Jamaicans (...) by the failure to distinguish between the right to appeal against the verdict and sentence of the Court in a criminal case, and the 'brand new rights' to apply for constitutional redress granted in 1962'.

[217] See e.g. HRC *Raphael Henry* v. *Jamaica*, 1 November 1991; *Aston Little* v. *Jamaica*, 1 November 1991; *Leroy Simmonds* v. *Jamaica*, 23 October 1992; *Randolph Barrett and Clyde Sutcliffe* v. *Jamaica*, 30 March 1992; *Clifton Wright* v. *Jamaica*, 27 July 1992; *Carlton Linton* v. *Jamaica*, 22 October 1992 and *Lenford Hamilton* v. *Jamaica*, 21 March 1994.

constitutional motions if the petitioner is indigent but the State is unwilling or unable to provide legal aid for filing these motions.[218]

3.4.6 Exhaustion, availability of a written judgment and maintaining provisional measures beyond inadmissibility

As noted in section 2.5, the HRC developed a most remarkable practice with its decisions to *maintain* provisional measures to halt an execution not until, but beyond its inadmissibility decision. In the early 1990s the HRC declared inadmissible several petitions because 'while expressing concern about the unavailability, so far, of relevant court documents in the case' it did not consider that a petition to the JCPC would be 'a priori ineffective'. In other words, it expected the petitioners to exhaust this remedy before resorting to the HRC.[219] Yet the Committee maintained its provisional measures *beyond* the inadmissibility declaration.[220] The only exception was a case in which it considered that the delays could be attributed mainly to the petitioner. In its inadmissibility decision to that case it did not mention the possibility that the decision could be reviewed upon exhaustion of effective domestic remedies.[221]

In *Trevor Collins* v. *Jamaica* (1993)[222] the HRC finally determined that, in the absence of a written judgment it should declare a complaint admissible. It noted that domestic counsel could objectively have assumed that any petition for leave to appeal to the JCPC would have failed on account of the unavailability of a written judgment from the Court of Appeal. Thus, such petition

---

[218]   See e.g. HRC *Willard Collins* v. *Jamaica*, 1 November 1991; *Raphael Henry* v. *Jamaica*, 1 November 1991; *Aston Little* v. *Jamaica*, 1 November 1991; *Leroy Simmonds* v. *Jamaica*, 23 October 1992; *Randolph Barrett and Clyde Sutcliffe* v. *Jamaica*, 30 March 1992; *Clifton Wright* v. *Jamaica*, 27 July 1992; *Carlton Linton* v. *Jamaica*, 22 October 1992; *Lenford Hamilton* v. *Jamaica*, 21 March 1994; *Dwayne Hylton* v. *Jamaica*, 8 July 1994; *Anthony Currie* v. *Jamaica*, 29 March 1994 and *Clive Smart* v. *Trinidad and Tobago*, 29 July 1998.

[219]   See e.g. HRC *E.B.* v. *Jamaica*, 26 October 1990; *A.A.* v. *Jamaica*, 30 October 1989 and *R.M.* v. *Jamaica*, 26 October 1990. Previously, during the last two sessions of 1989 and the first session of 1990 the HRC declared certain petitions admissible because the petitioner's counsel had been unable to obtain copies of the reasoned judgment of the Court of Appeal. Without such judgment a petition for special leave to appeal to the JCPC would objectively have no prospect of success. *Irvine Reynolds* v. *Jamaica*, 8 April 1991 (eventually the HRC found no violations for lack of sufficient evidence); see also *Barrett and Sutcliffe* v. *Jamaica*, 30 March 1992 (determining that, in the absence of legal aid and bearing in mind the delay, recourse to the Supreme (Constitutional) Court was not required; declaring the case admissible, but finding, after examination of the evidence, that the Court of Appeal 'rapidly produced its written judgment and that the ensuing delay in petitioning the Judicial Committee is largely attributable to the authors'; it did find violations of Articles 7 and 10(1)); *M.F.* v. *Jamaica*, 21 October 1991 (on 15 March 1990 the HRC declared the case admissible under Article 14 because in the practice of the JCPC all petitions unsupported by the relevant court documents had been dismissed; this is why the HRC considered 'that if a petition for leave to appeal was to be considered an available and effective remedy, it had to be supported by the judgment from which leave to appeal was sought'). *Paul Kelly* v. *Jamaica*, 8 April 1991 (also a violation of Article 14(3)(c) and 14(5) because of the absence of a written judgment by the Court of Appeal); *Trevor Collins* v. *Jamaica*, 25 March 1993 (also a violation of Article 14(3)(c) and 14(5) because of the absence of a written judgment by the Court of Appeal).

[220]   See e.g. HRC *A.H.* v. *Trinidad and Tobago*, 31 October 1990; *M.F.* v. *Jamaica*, 17 July 1992, and *Peter Bradshaw* v. *Barbados*, 19 July 1994.

[221]   HRC *N.A.J* v. *Jamaica*, 26 July 1990.

[222]   HRC *Trevor Collins* v. *Jamaica*, 25 March 1993.

would not have had a real prospect of success. It was true that the Judicial Committee had heard several petitions concerning Jamaica in the absence of a written judgment of the Court of Appeal, but, on the basis of the information available to the Committee, all of these petitions were dismissed *because* of the absence of such a judgment. Thus it would henceforth declare such complaint admissible. On the merits the HRC determined that the absence of a written judgment by the Court of Appeal constituted a violation of Article 14(3)(c) and 14(5) ICCPR.

Thus it was during the years preceding its eventual determination that the unavailability of a written judgment by the court of appeal would in fact *excuse* non-exhaustion of domestic remedies that the HRC developed a practice of maintaining provisional measures beyond inadmissibility. During these years it used provisional measures both prior to a determination of admissibility, *and* subsequent to a determination of inadmissibility. It did so in order to prevent irreparable harm to persons. Once the Committee's case law was clarified with regard to the unavailability of a written judgment by the domestic court, provisional measures would be used in advance of a determination about the effectiveness of domestic remedies, but no longer beyond a declaration of inadmissibility.

3.4.7 Exhaustion in death penalty cases not relating to the availability of a written judgment

The HRC has considered that a petition to the Governor General for a stay of execution is not a domestic remedy that should be exhausted under the OP.[223] This situation is different with regard to a petition to the Judicial Committee of the Privy Council (JCPC). In *Guerra and Wallen* v. *Trinidad and Tobago* (1995)[224] the Committee had first used provisional measures and then declared the case inadmissible for non-exhaustion of domestic remedies, because a petition for leave

---

[223] HRC *Trevor Ellis* v. *Jamaica*, 28 July 1992. The State had argued that the complaint was inadmissible because the petitioner had not exhausted domestic remedies. It noted that the petitioner 'has petitioned the Governor General for a stay of execution'. It also noted that the JCPC had recommended to the Governor General to grant a stay of execution 'pending the outcome of the representations made on his behalf'. Counsel had pointed out that the State failed to indicate whether the Governor General had indeed adopted the JCPC's recommendation of a stay. It was not clear whether a stay of execution was indeed in force. Counsel also submitted that he had not yet received a reply to his petition to the Governor General, requesting a stay of execution pending the outcome of several similar cases before the JCPC.

[224] HRC *Lincoln Guerra and Brian Wallen* v. *Trinidad and Tobago*. The situation in this case was as follows. An earlier petition for special leave to appeal to the JCPC had been dismissed a few days previously. The initial submission was of 25 March 1994, the day of their planned execution. The Special Rapporteur took provisional measures a month later. In its first submission, 23 June 1994, the State argued that the petitions were inadmissible because the petitioners had also submitted their case to the Inter-American Commission on Human Rights (nr. 11279). On 10 November 1994 counsel informed the HRC, including documentary evidence, that Mr. Guerra had withdrawn his case before the Inter-American Commission, as it was under consideration by the HRC. By submission of 23 June 1994 and 7 September 1994 the State argued non-exhaustion of domestic remedies. In the latter submission it referred to the JCPC's conservatory order of 25 July 1994. Counsel responded that the State's argument was inconsistent with its clearly manifested intention to execute the petitioners 'on merely 17 hours' notice, within three days after the confirmation of their conviction, irrespective of their desire to make representations to the Mercy Committee for commutation of their death sentences, to apply to the courts of Trinidad for relief staying their execution and to apply to the Human Rights Committee'.

to appeal before the JCPC was still pending and the JCPC had ordered a stay of execution.[225] It declared the case inadmissible but pointed out that this decision could be reviewed upon exhaustion. Yet it did not maintain the provisional measures, as it had done in cases involving unavailability of legal documents.[226] This seems to indicate that it is only when non-exhaustion could be attributed to the State's failure to make available legal documents that it maintains its provisional measures beyond its inadmissibility declaration. Nevertheless, in this case the HRC could have maintained its provisional measures as an indication to the State that it should not execute the death sentence of the petitioner immediately upon exhaustion when there is still a possibility of review by the HRC upon exhaustion.

After the State had issued an execution warrant the petitioners had submitted the case to the HRC and the JCPC as well as to the Inter-American Commission on Human Rights. This shows that in urgent cases petitioners may resort to various international and domestic bodies. In my view this does not necessarily conflict with rules on exhaustion of local remedies, on the one hand, and on non-submission of the 'same matter' to different international bodies, on the other hand,[227] as long as this is only done at the early stages of the proceedings, in order to prevent irreparable harm to persons.

In the context of *Bethel* v. *Trinidad and Tobago* (1999)[228] the State referred to the rules on exhaustion and subsidiarity. Among others, it pointed out that domestic remedies had not been pursued and exhausted. The appeal was pending before the Court of Appeal and the remedies available could include 'the power to quash his sentence or to order a retrial'. In its reasoning the State brought up the subsidiarity principle.

> "The competence of the Committee is subsidiary to that of the domestic legal system of the state. For the Committee to be seized of this case while legal proceedings are continuing before the domestic courts of the State party is a direct challenge to the balanced relationship between the international protection of human rights and the domestic jurisdiction of States parties".[229]

Yet the State did not explain how the obligation to exhaust of domestic remedies without suspensive effect would satisfy the subsidiarity criterion. After all, the whole point is that international organisations and adjudicators may not interfere in situations that can adequately be dealt with at

---

[225] One of the petitioners in this case (Wallen) had died four months after the initial submission and one month after the provisional measure. Counsel argued that the State's determination to execute the other petitioner (Guerra), 'irrespective of undetermined violations of the author's constitutional rights or rights under the Covenant', was 'demonstrated by the events surrounding the execution of Glenn Ashby in July 1994' (see also Chapter XVI (Legal status) and Chapter XVII (Official State responses)) after his case had been submitted to the HRC. The HRC concluded, however, that a petition to the JCPC could not be considered ineffective in this case, meaning that domestic remedies had not yet been exhausted. This had not prevented it from using provisional measures initially.

[226] See section 2.4 of this Chapter.

[227] For a case brought first to the Inter-American Commission and then to the HRC, see e.g. HRC *Clifton Wright* v. *Jamaica*, 27 July 1992, §2.8. The case had been submitted to the CIDH on 13 February 1984, registered as no. 9260, hearing of 24 March 1988 and resolution 29/88 of 14 September 1988. On 4 November 1988 Jamaica challenged this resolution. Two months later the case was submitted to the HRC.

[228] HRC *Christopher Bethel* v. *Trinidad and Tobago*, 31 March 1999. Provisional measures of 17 September 1998 (on file with the author).

[229] Further submission of the Government of Trinidad and Tobago of 9 February 1999 in the case of Bethel (830/1998) (on file with the author).

the level of the State. The State should have the first opportunity to remedy alleged violations. Yet if a State would have the ultimate say on what constitutes adequacy this would not reflect subsidiarity, but rather absolute national sovereignty.[230]

The relationship between provisional measures and exhaustion of domestic remedies is illustrated in *Ashby* v. *Trinidad and Tobago* (2002).[231] According to the State the petitioner had not exhausted available domestic remedies for his right to life claim (Article 6 ICCPR). Counsel responded that since the petitioner 'was executed unlawfully while he was pursuing judicial remedies, the State party is estopped from claiming that further remedies remained to be exhausted'.[232] In light of the State's disrespect for its provisional measures, the HRC declared admissible the complaint under Article 6. It was not necessary for counsel first to exhaust domestic remedies in respect of her claim that her client was arbitrarily deprived of his life. It observed the following about this issue:

> "[I]t was to prevent 'irreparable harm' to Mr. Ashby that the Committee's Special Rapporteur issued, on 13 July 1994, a request of a stay of execution pursuant to rule 86 of the rules of procedure; this request was intended to allow Mr. Ashby to complete pending judicial remedies and to enable the Committee to determine the admissibility of Mr. Ashby's communication".[233]

In the context of its admissibility decision the HRC specifically referred to the prevention of irreparable harm to Ashby, in other words, irreparable harm to a person. At the same time it referred to the aim of enabling it to determine admissibility. In this respect it noted that the provisional measure was to ensure and reinforce the suspensive effect of the domestic remedies that were still being pursued.[234]

The Inter-American Commission has included the issue of exhaustion of domestic remedies in its arguments to convince the Inter-American Court to take provisional measures on behalf of alleged victims who had been sentenced to death. It pointed out that the alleged victims had not been able to effectively challenge the compatibility of their death sentences with the rights under the Convention. In other words, effective domestic remedies did not appear to be available.[235] The Court itself, though, has not dealt with this issue in the context of halting executions.

The African Commission has been faced with non-exhaustion arguments with regard to persons who had already been executed. In the *Ken Saro-Wiwa* case it noted that in 'light of the fact that the subjects of the communications are now deceased, it is evident that no domestic remedy can give the complainants the satisfaction they seek'.[236] Indeed this is particularly so because the Commission had used provisional measures that had been ignored. Only when the complaint would have been made by family members *subsequent* rather than prior to the execution, it should have been examined first whether effective domestic remedies were available.[237]

---

[230] On subsidiarity see also Carozza (2003). See further Chapter XVII on the official responses by addressee States.

[231] HRC *Glenn Ashby* v. *Trinidad and Tobago*, 21 March 2002.

[232] Id., §7.4.

[233] Id., §5.7.

[234] Following the HRC's decision on admissibility the State repeated its argument that proceedings were still pending before the domestic courts in relation to Mr. Ashby's execution. See also Chapter XVII on the official responses by Addressee States.

[235] See IACHR *James et al.*, Order of the President for urgent measures, 19 June 1999.

[236] ACHPR *Ken Saro-Wiwa* v. *Nigeria*, October 1998, §77.

[237] See also the above discussion, under the heading 'Exhaustion and suspensive effect in non-refoulement cases', on the disingenuous arguments by some States in non-refoulement cases.

3.4.8 Suspensive effect and cultural survival

In *Sara et al.* v. *Finland* (1994) the HRC had initially used provisional measures to help ensure cultural survival.[238] The case shows that the Committee's provisional measures in cases involving cultural survival no longer apply once the HRC considers domestic remedies have not yet been exhausted. In this case the HRC, which had previously used provisional measures, took the opportunity to expand on its earlier admissibility findings in light of the State's argument that the petitioners could still avail themselves of local remedies in respect of road construction activities in the residual area.[239] It declared the case inadmissible. Different from certain death penalty cases,[240] this also terminated the provisional measure.

The case of the *Lubicon Lake Band* (1990), submitted by Chief Ominayak, shows the relationship between provisional measures, exhaustion of domestic remedies and the question whether such remedies have suspensive effect.[241] The HRC confirmed that if domestic remedies are delayed and have no suspensive effect they cannot prevent irreparable harm. The petitioner claimed that Government officials and representatives of energy corporations were using the domestic political and legal process 'to thwart and delay the Band's actions until, ultimately, the Band becomes incapable of pursuing them, because industrial development at the current rate in the area, accompanied by the destruction of the environmental and economic base of the Band, would make it impossible for the Band to survive as a people for many more years'.[242] Since 1975 the Lubicon had already taken various actions domestically to assert title over their lands and prevent oil and gas developments destroying their cultural and economic basis. These actions included a request for a 'caveat', a declaratory judgement and an interim injunction.[243] More than

---

[238]   See Conclusion Part II.

[239]   HRC *Sara et al.* v. *Finland*, 23 March 1994 (inadm.). It noted that Article 27 ICCPR had seldom been invoked before the local courts, while the Finnish judicial authorities, on the other hand, had become increasingly aware of the domestic relevance of international human rights standards. In this light the doubts of the petitioners about the readiness of domestic courts to deal with claims based on Article 27 ICCPR did not justify their failure to resort to domestic remedies. It did not consider that a recent judgment of the Supreme Administrative Tribunal should be seen as a negative precedent for the adjudication of the case just because it made no reference to Article 27.

[240]   See section 2.4 of this Chapter.

[241]   HRC *Bernard Ominayak, Chief of the Lubicon Lake Band* v. *Canada*, 26 March 1990.

[242]   See HRC *Bernard Ominayak, Chief of the Lubicon Lake Band* v. *Canada*, 26 March 1990, §3.2.

[243]   Chief Ominayak explained that, in 1975, the Band filed a request for a 'caveat' with the appropriate authorities, 'which would give notice to all parties dealing with the caveated land of their assertion of their aboriginal title'. A year later the Attorney General of Alberta requested a postponement of the case pending resolution of a similar case and the provincial Supreme Court granted this application. In 1977, however, an amendment to the Land Title Act was passed, introduced by the Attorney General, precluding the filing of caveats. This amendment was made retroactive to January 1975, predating the caveat filed on behalf of the Lubicon Lake Band. As a result, the Supreme Court's hearings were dismissed as moot. In 1980 members of the Band requested a declaratory judgment of the Federal Court of Canada for the protection of the rights to their land and the use of the natural resources. This Court dismissed the claim against the provincial government and all energy corporations except Petro-Canada. The claim against this one energy corporation and against the federal government still stood. In 1982 the Band requested an interim injunction 'to halt development in the area until issues raised by the Band's land and natural resource claims were settled'. The petitioner noted that the main purpose of the injunction was to prevent the provincial government of Alberta and the oil companies 'from further destroying the traditional hunting and trapping territory of the Lubicon people'. The

a year after initial submission and more than two months after the Supreme Court of Canada refused leave to appeal, Canada responded to the petitioner's submission before the HRC and argued that the legal actions in the federal and provincial court were still pending. It explained that the Band's request for an interim injunction had been dismissed on the basis of previous jurisprudence in which the following criteria had been set out for the use of such injunctions: the issue is serious, without the injunction irreparable harm will be suffered prior to trial and, finally, 'the balance of convenience between the parties favours relief to the applicant'.[244] The dispute was mainly about whether the Band 'could be adequately compensated in damages if it was ultimately successful at trial'. The petitioner explained his reason to resort to the HRC as follows:

> "The Lubicon Lake Band is not requesting a territorial rights decision. Rather, the Band requests only that the Human Rights Committee assist it in attempting to convince the government of Canada that: (a) The Band's existence is seriously threatened by the oil and gas development that has been allowed to proceed unchecked on their traditional hunting grounds and in complete disregard for the human community inhabiting the area; (b) Canada is responsible for the current state of affairs and for co-operating in their resolution in accordance with article 1 of the Optional Protocol to the International Covenant on Civil and Political Rights".[245]

He argued that the only effective remedy in this case was to seek an interim injunction. He noted that 'without the preservation of the status quo, a final judgment on the merits, even if favourable to the Band, would be rendered ineffectual'.[246]

> "[A]ny final judgement recognizing aboriginal rights, or alternatively treaty rights, [could] never restore the way of life, livelihood and means of subsistence of the Band".[247]

In reference to its established case law that only effective and available remedies must be exhausted, the HRC found that there were no effective remedies still available to the Band.[248] It was only at this time, in 1987, that the HRC also used provisional measures to avoid irreparable harm. It did so in light of the seriousness of the claim that the Band was on the verge of extinction.[249]

The fact that the HRC declared the case admissible shows that it did not consider the domestic remedies effective in saving or restoring the 'cultural livelihood' of the Band. It confirmed this following the State's request for a review.[250] This may mean that at the time it still assumed

---

provincial court, however, 'did not render its decision for almost two years, during which time oil and gas development continued, along with rapid destruction of the Band's economic base'. It eventually denied the request. They appealed this decision to the Court of Appeal of Alberta, which dismissed it more than a year later. Finally, the Band requested leave to appeal from the judgment of the Alberta Court of Appeal, but the Supreme Court of Canada refused this in March 1985.

[244] See Supreme Court of Canada *Erickson* v. *Wiggins Adjustments Ltd.* (1980) 6 W.R.R. 188.

[245] HRC *Lubicon Lake Band*, 26 March 1990, §12.

[246] Id., §13.2.

[247] Id., §13.2.

[248] Id., §13.2.

[249] See Chapter X on protecting cultural survival of indigenous peoples.

[250] Wennergren submitted an individual opinion considering the communication inadmissible because of non-exhaustion of domestic remedies. "To my mind, it is not compatible with international law that an international instance consider issues which, concurrently, are pending before a national court". He did not specifically discuss the availability of domestic remedies

that its decision on the merits, if it would find a violation, would at least suggest an effective remedy.[251] In light of the absence of suspensive effect of the domestic proceedings, the use of provisional measures was appropriate.[252] However, they would have been more functional had they been taken earlier in the proceedings.[253] The Committee's decision only to use provisional measures in this case once it declared it admissible, may be explained by the fact that in 1987 it did not yet have an extensive practice with regard to provisional measures, let alone with regard to their use to protect of cultural survival of indigenous peoples.

3.4.9 Conclusion

In sum, the above cases indicate that human rights adjudicators have determined that for the same reason there is no need to fully determine admissibility for the use of provisional measures, there is no need to exhaust domestic remedies that do not have suspensive effect. This reason is the overriding aim of protecting persons against irreparable harm in death penalty, non-refoulement and cultural survival cases.

Given the fact that for the use of provisional measures what is required is, at most, prima facie admissibility, it is obvious that they may be used when domestic remedies clearly have been determined as ineffective in previous cases. In addition provisional measures are sometimes even used when those domestic remedies that *could* be effective are not yet exhausted, but might be at any moment.[254]

3.5 Provisional measures and the likelihood of inadmissibility for reasons other than non-exhaustion

3.5.1 Introduction

To what extent does possible inadmissibility for reasons other than non-exhaustion play a role in the decision of the human rights adjudicator to take provisional measures?[255] This section first refers to the fact that many claims are declared inadmissible as manifestly unfounded and some as an abuse of process. Then it deals with inadmissibility because the same matter has already been

---

[251] with suspensive effect, nor the Committee's previous case law on the effectiveness of domestic remedies.

See further on this case Chapter X (Culture) and Chapter XIII, section 5 on beneficiaries and section 4 on forms of reparation.

[252] They made little sense, however, in light of the remedy suggested immediately upon upholding the admissibility decision. This remedy did not amount to much, as is discussed in Chapter XIII on the relationship between provisional measures and reparation.

[253] See also Chapter XV on immediacy and risk.

[254] See also Chapter II (the sections on promptness in the various systems).

[255] The HRC, for instance, has regularly declared cases inadmissible for incompatibility with the ICCPR. It has also dealt with arguments that petitions were inadmissible as an abuse of the right of submission, for instance in light of consecutive claims by the same petitioner. In addition it has declared cases inadmissible as they cannot claim to be a 'victim' of a violation. Cases involving Article 6 (right to life) and risks to health of environmental pollution are often considered to constitute *actio popularis* and are declared inadmissible as the petitioners cannot show they are or will be victims themselves in the foreseeable future. In such cases the HRC has decided not to use provisional measures. See also Chapter XII (Other situations) and Chapter XV (Immediacy and risk).

dealt with by another international adjudicator ('same matter'). Finally it refers to the Bosnia Chamber's discussion of its jurisdiction *ratione termporis* under the Dayton Peace Agreement.

3.5.2 Manifestly unfounded or an abuse of process?

Many cases are declared inadmissible as manifestly unfounded. In death penalty cases provisional measures have nevertheless been used. An example of an inadmissibility decision for reasons other than non-exhaustion is *R.M.* v. *Trinidad and Tobago* (1993).[256] The HRC declared inadmissible many claims in relation to Art. 14(1), especially when they involve claims of inadequate evaluation of the evidence or inadequate jury instructions by the trial judge.[257]

In *Hylton* v. *Jamaica* (1996) the State had argued that the communication was inadmissible as an abuse of the right of submission (Article 3 OP).[258] The Committee stated that although the petitioner should display due diligence in the presentation of claims, and although 'it is conceivable that the sequential introduction, in the course of consideration of a case, of claims which could have been formulated at the time of the initial submission may constitute an abuse of process, this does not apply if the petitioner of a case whose examination is concluded subsequently raises new claims which he could not have raised in the context of the previous complaint. In the Committee's opinion, issues of res judicata do not arise in the latter hypothesis'.[259] The 'death row phenomenon'-claim brought in the second case was not at issue in the first case.

---

[256] HRC *R.M.* v. *Trinidad and Tobago*, 29 October 1993 (submission of 16 July 1989; provisional measure of 29 January 1990; transmission of 13 August 1991; inadmissible (evaluation of the evidence and jury instructions generally for the domestic courts; insufficient evidence of inadequate time and facilities) (on file with the author). According to the cover page the Special Rapporteur used Rule 91 (on transmission of cases) only, but in fact the previous Rapporteur had already used Rule 86 (provisional measures). The HRC later declared this case inadmissible for failure to substantiate and lack of jurisdiction *ratione materiae.* The State party had raised no objections to the admissibility of the claim. The only matter that remained pending in court was a constitutional motion, filed in July 1986, seeking a 'declaration that should an order for the execution be made', the petitioner 'must be given five days notice'. The State added that it had given assurances not to execute R.M. pending the determination of the motion, although it pointed out that the motion itself was 'unnecessary' because the question had already been solved in the affirmative in another case.

[257] The HRC never intended to function as a so-called 'fourth instance' and in two early inadmissibility decisions (1989) it pointed out that it was for the appellate courts of States parties to evaluate facts and evidence. It was beyond the scope of application of Article 14 for the HRC to review generalised claims of bias or specific jury instructions. Chanet attached individual opinions to these decisions, considering that in this formulation the HRC seemed to take away too much from its task of monitoring compliance with Article 14 (fair trial). HRC *A.W.* v. *Jamaica*, 8 November 1989 and *G.S.* v. *Jamaica*, 8 November 1989. Chanet noted that while it was within the competence of national courts to assess the fairness of the conditions in which a trial takes place, this competence could not exclude that of the HRC in the implementation of the ICCPR. The HRC modified its formulation during the next session in March 1990. Since then the expression has been: "It is not in principle for the Committee to review specific instructions to the jury by a judge in a trial by jury, unless it can be ascertained that the instructions to the jury were clearly arbitrary or amounted to a denial of justice". See e.g. HRC *D.F.* v. *Jamaica*, 26 March 1990 (not a death penalty case; no provisional measures).

[258] HRC *Dwayne Hylton* v. *Jamaica*, 16 July 1996.

[259] Id., §6.3.

"Given that he had been detained on death row for slightly over two years when he submitted his initial complaint, he could not have argued with any reasonable prospect of success that the length of his detention on death row was, at that time, contrary to articles 7 and 10 paragraph 1".[260]

In October 1994, when he submitted his second case, his factual situation had changed.

"In these circumstances, the present complaint does not amount to an abuse of process; nor does the Committee consider that it 'unnecessarily prolongs' the judicial process, as the claim at issue in the present communication has never been adjudicated".[261]

Thus, the communication was declared admissible in so far as it concerned the length of detention on death row. The HRC later dismissed the claim on the merits.[262] In this type of consecutive claim the use of provisional measures would be justifiable. This would be different with regard to a clear case of abuse of process.[263]

3.5.3 Same matter

In some cases the petitioner first petitions to a regional and subsequently to an international adjudicator. In *Wright* v. *Jamaica* (1992) the HRC declared a case admissible because it was no longer under examination by the Inter-American Commission.[264] Just like the IACHR the HRC found that the State had violated the fundamental right to a fair trial.[265]

In the first expulsion case dealt with by the HRC (1978) it did draw the petitioner's attention to the State party's observation that the Inter-American Commission on Human Rights was examining the 'same matter'. It decided 'that it should be explained to the petitioner that this is not a decision on the admissibility of his communication,' but it used provisional measures.[266] This again shows that the HRC is rather safe than sorry initially.

---

[260] Id., §6.4.

[261] Ibid.

[262] Thus far it has virtually always dismissed claims relating to the death row phenomenon either on the merits or already in the admissibility phase. See for two possible exceptions the discussion of the death row phenomenon in Chapter III (Halting executions).

[263] The question arises what would be the use of taking provisional measures to halt an execution pending the case in relation to a death row phenomenon claim alone, if the HRC is intent on maintaining its present approach towards such claims.

[264] HRC *Clifton Wright* v. *Jamaica*, 27 July 1992, §2.8. The case had been submitted to the CIDH on 13 February 1984, registered as no. 9260, hearing of 24 March 1988 and resolution 29/88 of 14 September 1988. On 4 November 1988 Jamaica challenged this resolution. Two months later the case was submitted to the HRC.

[265] It had declared that 'since the conviction and sentence are undermined by the record in this case, and that the appeals process did not permit for a correction, the Government of Jamaica has violated the petitioner's fundamental rights' under Article 25 ACHR. This is a rare case in which the HRC found a violation of Article 14(1) for a denial of justice. See Chapter XV on assessment of risk.

[266] HRC *O.E.* v. *S.*, 26 July 1978. On 27 October 1978 the HRC decided to discontinue consideration of the case. A few weeks previously the petitioner had requested this in light of the submission of the same matter to the Inter-American Commission. *O.E.* v. *S.*, 27 October 1978. See also e.g. HRC *Alzery* v. *Sweden*, 25 October 2006. Yet see also CAT *A.R.A.* v. *Switzerland*, 30 April 2007 (inadm.). The case was declared inadmissible for dealing with the same matter as one before the ECtHR. Previously a request for provisional measures had been denied.

Related to the issue of consecutive claims before the same adjudicator, is the issue of the same matter brought before a different adjudicator. Uruguay had contested the admissibility of several early detention cases before the HRC arguing that the 'same matter' was pending before the Inter-American Commission on Human Rights. It appears that any *prima facie* inadmissibility on this ground did not prevent the HRC from inquiring about the health of the alleged victims. A combination of the urgency involved and the fact that the petitioners could easily remedy any possible inadmissibility by withdrawing the complaint before the Inter-American Commission in advance of any decision by the HRC, could explain this approach.

It is unlikely that the HRC already considered the possible inadmissibility in *Sendic* v. *Uruguay* (1981)[267] when it transmitted the case to the State and requested information on the state of health of Mr. Sendic. After all, it was only *after* Uruguay contested the admissibility of the case that the Committee checked with the Secretariat of the Inter-American Commission whether the 'same matter' might already be pending before that Commission. Upon inquiry the Secretariat of the Inter-American Commission explained that a third party had submitted the case to which the State referred.[268]

By contrast, when the HRC enquired about the health of the alleged victims in *Lafuente Penarrieta et al.* v. *Bolivia* (1987)[269] it had already ascertained that the Inter-American Commission had not registered the same matter. Still, this may be attributed to the fact that, at the time, the HRC could only decide on (informal) provisional measures during sessions, as there was no Special Rapporteur yet.[270] In *Polay Campos* v. *Peru* (1997)[271] the HRC used informal provisional measures only when it declared the case admissible. By that time it had contacted the Inter-American Commission on Human Rights to find out whether the same matter was already pending before another international adjudicator. The Inter-American Commission had registered a case[272] on behalf of Polay Campos but it had no plans to prepare a Report on it within the next 12 months. In this light the HRC considered it was not precluded from considering the case before it. Nevertheless, the reason the Committee did not use (informal) provisional measures before it decided on admissibility is probably due to an oversight rather than based on the view that admissibility must be determined before provisional measures could be used.[273]

3.5.4 Dayton and jurisdiction *ratione temporis*

The Dayton Peace Agreement entered into force on 14 December 1995. The Bosnia Chamber does not have jurisdiction *ratione temporis* over violations prior to that date. It declared admissible several cases involving violations originating before that date but continuing until afterwards. In *Islamic Community in BiH* v. *Republika Srpska* (Muslim Town Cemetery in Prnjavor), for instance, the Chamber first established that the violation was ongoing and it had jurisdiction *ratione temporis* and subsequently took the view that it was 'not necessary to assess whether at

---

[267] HRC *Sendic Antonaccio* (*submitted by his wife Violeta Setelich*) v. *Uruguay*, 28 October 1981.

[268] Later the petitioner also sent the Committee a copy of the request by this third party to the Commission to *discontinue* the case before it 'so as to remove any procedural uncertainties' about the HRC's competence to deal with the case.

[269] HRC *Lafuente Penarrieta, Rodriguez Candia, Ruiz Caceres and Toro Dorado* v. *Bolivia*, 2 November 1987.

[270] See Chapter XV on prompt decision-making and assessment of temporal urgency.

[271] HRC *Polay Campos* (*submitted by his wife Espinoza de Polay*) v. *Peru*, 6 November 1997.

[272] Case 11.048.

[273] It was Committee member Prado Vallejo (Ecuador) who suggested the use of such provisional measures in July 1996, just before the adoption of the admissibility decision. Letter of Prado Vallejo to the Geneva Secretariat, 2 July 1996 (on file with the author).

the time when the alleged violation began, a remedy effective in theory and practice would have been available to the applicant'. It was satisfied that the remedy indicated by the respondent Party was 'currently not available' and had not been available since the entry into force of the Agreement.[274]

In *Matanović* (1997) Nowak pointed out that the fact that most missing persons in Bosnia and Herzegovina disappeared before the entry into force of the Dayton Peace Agreement did not preclude it from considering such cases 'if there is presumptive evidence that they were still held in detention' after the entry into force. He referred to Article 17 (1) of the UN Declaration on the Protection of All Persons from enforced Disappearance stipulating that 'as long as the perpetrators continue to conceal the fate and the whereabouts of persons who have disappeared and these facts remain unclarified' the act of enforced disappearance constitutes a 'continuing offence'.[275]

The Chamber has pointed out that 'evidence of detention prior of the entry into force of the Agreement may well be relevant to the question whether the person concerned has been in custody since'.[276] The weight to be attached to such evidence varies with the circumstances, 'including the length of time which has elapsed since the person concerned was last shown to have been in custody'. Normally 'it would be essential that there should be some other evidence (even circumstantial or presumptive evidence), pointing to the detention having continued after the Agreement came into force, before the Chamber could conclude that the Agreement had been violated'.[277] While doubts on jurisdiction *ratione temporis* may not be an obstacle to the use of provisional measures, at the same time it is clear that it is more likely that disappeared persons will return alive if provisional measures are taken shortly after the disappearance.[278]

3.6 Admissibility criteria and the two kinds of provisional measures in the new Convention against Disappearances

In urgent cases the supervisory committee that will be instituted under the International Convention for the Protection of All Persons from Enforced Disappearance[279] may use either provisional measures proper, with regard to States that have recognized the individual complaint procedure under Article 31,[280] or an alternative type of provisional measure, based on Article 30. This article introduces the possibility for the Committee to intervene upon a request 'by relatives of the disappeared person or their legal representatives, their counsel or any person authorized by them, as well as by any other person having a legitimate interest' that 'a disappeared person should be

---

[274] Bosnia Chamber *Islamic Community in BiH* v. *Republika Srpska* (Muslim Town Cemetery in Prnjavor), 11 January 2000, §93.

[275] Bosnia Chamber *Josip, Božana and Tomislav Matanović* v. *Republika Srpska*, 6 August 1997 (merits), concurring opinion Manfred Nowak, §7.

[276] Bosnia Chamber *Grgić* v. *Republika Srpska*, 5 August 1997, §18.

[277] See Bosnia Chamber *Grgić* v. *Republika Srpska*, 5 August 1997, §18 and *Matanović* v. *Republika Srpska*, 6 August 1997, §32.

[278] See also Chapter VI (Locating and protecting disappeared persons).

[279] Adopted in 2006, but not yet entered into force.

[280] Article 31 provides for an optional individual complaint procedure. Its section 4 stipulates: "4. At any time after the receipt of a communication and before a determination on the merits has been reached, the Committee may transmit to the State Party concerned for its urgent consideration a request that the State Party will take such interim measures as may be necessary to avoid possible irreparable damage to the victims of the alleged violation. Where the Committee exercises its discretion, this does not imply a determination on admissibility or on the merits of the communication".

sought and found'. In fact when it considers that a range of procedural requirements is met, it 'shall request the State Party concerned to provide it with information on the situation of the persons sought, within a time limit set by the Committee'. It appears to be a very circumscribed treaty based 'urgent action'. The procedural requirements are stricter than those applied by the other adjudicators. The reason for including the list of procedural requirements (exhaustion etc.) that are generally relevant mainly for declaring a case admissible, and not already at the state of provisional measures, may be that the States wished to circumscribe the new power of the treaty body introduced in this treaty. After all it can intervene also with regard to States that have not recognized the individual complaint procedure. Nevertheless these requirements are mentioned in the context of the Committee's *obligation* to intervene ('shall'). The Committee could argue that it still has the discretionary power to intervene also in other cases, especially in circumstances in which all other adjudicators, as well as the UN special procedures, consider this warranted.

In any case this strict approach should not be read into Article 31(4) on provisional measures proper. Such interpretation would be a retreat from the practice of the other treaty bodies and contrary to the object and purpose of the treaty, including the reference to 'admissibility' in the sentence in Article 31(4) noting that the use of provisional measures, based on a discretionary power, 'does not imply a determination on admissibility or on the merits of the communication'. Like in the other systems, only when inadmissibility or lack of jurisdiction is evident, provisional measures should be refused.

4   CONCLUSION

What is the standard for assuming the competence to use provisional measures in light of the likelihood of jurisdiction on the merits? The rules discussed in Chapter I on traditional international law seem to apply in human rights cases as well, but in those cases the adjudicator appears more flexible, not requiring prima facie admissibility. Rather, only if the case were *prima facie* *in*admissible an adjudicator would have no competence to use provisional measures.[281] In other words there is no need to determine admissibility and jurisdiction on the merits other than at very first glance.

If the State has not ratified the individual complaint procedure, the adjudicator clearly has no jurisdiction on the merits and therefore no competence to use provisional measures. In other cases, for purposes of provisional measures, the adjudicator is normally assumed to be competent to deal with the case. Generally speaking the human rights adjudicators are not reticent on this issue. The HRC and the Inter-American Court have used provisional measures in cases involving disputed recognition of their authority. They reserved determination of a dispute, e.g. on the significance of certain reservations, to the phase of preliminary objections or admissibility. One case by the HRC involving a dispute about its competence to deal with complaints despite the reservations by the State concerned serves as an example. In that case those members disagreeing with the majority's position that it had such jurisdiction still emphasised that the HRC had nevertheless acted legitimately in using provisional measures.[282] More than the ICJ, human rights adjudicators have confirmed the principle that there is no need to finally establish their jurisdiction before using provisional measures.

---

[281]   The only exception is Rule 94(4) of the CERD Rules of Procedure, discussing the possibility of using provisional measures only with regard to 'admissible communications'.

[282]   See individual opinion Ando, Bhagwati, Klein and Kretzmer in HRC *Rawle Kennedy* v. *Trinidad and Tobago*, admissibility decision of 2 November 1999.

One example in which this principle also applies, or should apply, is in the context of the extraterritorial application of human rights treaties. Most adjudicators, including the ICJ, have recognized that States may have obligations under human rights treaties with regard to acts (and sometimes omissions) by their agents outside of the national borders. Some human rights adjudicators have already been faced with requests for provisional measures in this context and this may increasingly be the case in the future. While the case law is yet to fully crystallize, the adjudicators should not shrink from using provisional measures, if otherwise warranted, simply because they *might* later declare themselves incompetent to deal with such an 'extraterritorial' petition.

As to the duration of provisional measures, human rights adjudicators sometimes indicate that they apply until a given date, until 'further notice' or until a decision on admissibility has been made. In those cases, if there would still be urgency, they will extend the provisional measures just before expiry of the previous date, or upon declaring the case admissible. At other times they note that the provisional measures apply 'pending the case', meaning throughout the proceedings. One remarkable practice of the HRC has been to *maintain* its provisional measures upon declaring the case inadmissible. It did so in death penalty cases where the inadmissibility declaration related to non-exhaustion and was open to review. In its decision it reminded the State, under its Rule on provisional measures, not to execute the petitioner in the period between exhaustion and a renewed petition to the HRC. Thus if it declares a death penalty case inadmissible for non-exhaustion of domestic remedies, it may maintain provisional measures to cover the period between inadmissibility and the resubmission of the case following exhaustion. If the State would execute the petitioner before he would have a chance to renew his submission, this would in fact pre-empt the use provisional measures.[283] In such cases it operates from the perspective that the case is still pending. This shows the importance the HRC attaches to the protective function of its provisional measures to protect against irreparable harm. As compared to the ICJ it seems to have developed a *sui generis* approach to jurisdiction for purposes of provisional measures, based on this protective function. If irreparable harm could otherwise take place it is indeed appropriate for adjudicators dealing with human rights cases to maintain their provisional measures in cases susceptible to review.

The Inter-American Court has determined that, if necessary, its provisional measures remain applicable even beyond its judgment on reparations because it considers cases closed only once they are fully implemented. Therefore it appears to view its jurisdiction as extending until that moment. In a similar vein, the HRC has sometimes followed up its decision on the merits, urgently communicating to the State, in the face of an execution date, that at the very least its findings of a violation meant that the death sentence should not be executed.[284]

With regard to general international law the argument has been made that because provisional measures primarily serve the legal interests of those requesting them, 'the principle of equality of parties before justice requires that the balance be restored by restraint in the practice of granting interim protection and by allowing the benefit of doubt to serve the respondent'.[285] Obviously this argument does not apply in cases involving risk of irreparable harm to persons. In such cases it is clearly not necessary nor warranted, in light of the urgency concerned, to wait

---

[283] See also the discussion in Chapter XVI (Legal status) on the case law of the HRC to the effect that a good faith application of the ICCPR and its Optional Protocol means that States are to halt executions once they are informed that a petition has been brought before the HRC, in other words, already before the HRC has taken provisional measures.

[284] In fact this is a follow-up to its final View, finding a violation of Article 14 and, therefore, Article 6 ICCPR. On the official responses of States and the follow up of provisional measures see Chapters XVII and XVIII.

[285] Sztucki (1983), pp. 258-259.

until jurisdiction and admissibility are fully determined before using provisional measures.[286] Within the conceptual framework proposed in this book, and consonant with the practice of the HRC and Inter-American Court, it is suggested that if the State has withdrawn from the individual complaint procedure and different interpretations are possible about the competence (e.g. *ratione temporis*) of the adjudicator to still deal with the case, this should be examined as part of the decision on preliminary objections or admissibility and not already at the stage of provisional measures. As noted by the ICJ in its Order in the *Nuclear Test* cases (1973) it should be sufficient that there is no *a priori* lack of jurisdiction.[287] As noted, in light of the principle of effective protection against irreparable harm to persons[288] in human rights adjudication there should be no need to determine *prima facie* admissibility. Only if the case were *prima facie inadmissible* an adjudicator would have no competence to use provisional measures. In such cases it could be worthwhile for UN treaty body adjudicators to forward to other appropriate UN bodies or special mechanisms urgent cases for which they have no *prima facie* jurisdiction. In the alternative they could inform the petitioners about other possibilities.

From the analysis of the wider issue of admissibility (not just involving jurisdiction on the merits) in cases in which provisional measures were used, it is clear that at the stage of provisional measures there is no need for full evidence about admissibility. This appears from the fact that the human rights adjudicators use provisional measures before they declare cases (in)admissible. Yet the case law does not explicitly say whether some measure of *prima facie* evidence for admissibility is required for the use of provisional measures. It would not be unreasonable for them to require, in a flexible manner, that the case is not *prima facie inadmissible*, as the ICJ does.

In urgent cases petitioners may resort to various international and domestic adjudicators at the same time. This does not necessarily conflict with rules on exhaustion of local remedies on the one hand and non-submission of the 'same matter' to different international adjudicators on the other hand, as long as this is done only at the early stages of the proceedings, in order to prevent irreparable harm to the persons involved. Subsequently the petitioner needs to withdraw one of the petitions. This means that the other case will not result in inadmissibility and therefore does not affect the possibility to use provisional measures.

If the applicable remedies have no suspensive effect, exhaustion of domestic remedies is not necessary before granting provisional measures. In decisions on admissibility human rights adjudicators have made clear that domestic remedies must only be exhausted to the extent that they have suspensive effect. If they do not have such effect, resort is warranted to an international adjudicator who can also use provisional measures before determining that the domestic remedies indeed lack suspensive effect. After all, it is exactly in situations in which the domestic remedies do not prevent irreparable harm, that provisional measures are warranted. In this approach the international adjudicator would equally have competence to use provisional measures if the domestic proceedings are theoretically capable of halting certain measures, in other words, have suspensive effect, but not in practice – for instance because of a domestic theory of 'balance of convenience', whereby the interest of the petitioner is balanced with those of the State (or 'the general interest'). As noted, this balancing is inappropriate in relation to those rights singled out in the human rights treaties for their fundamental nature, not allowing for derogation even in times of emergency.[289] With such domestic approaches remedies may not have suspensive effect in practice and the use of provisional measures may be warranted. This is not contrary to the text

---

[286] In this respect Rule 94(3) of the CERD Rules of Procedure is an anomaly.
[287] ICJ *Nuclear Tests* case (*New Zealand* v. *France*), Order of 22 June 1973.
[288] See Conclusion Part II and Chapter XVI (Legal status).
[289] See Chapter XIII, section 4 on the beneficiaries of provisional measures.

of the respective provisions on exhaustion, while it corresponds with the principle of effective protection of persons against irreparable harm.[290] In addition, if a complaint is submitted to more than one international adjudicator, provisional measures could initially be requested by the petitioner and used by both adjudicators. The petitioner should subsequently indicate which claim he maintains. Any provisional measures used by the other adjudicator should then be withdrawn. In some instances, if the case would later be declared inadmissible, the petitioner could bring a renewed claim to the other adjudicator.[291]

In general, human rights adjudicators, like other international adjudicators, consider provisional measures terminated upon inadmissibility declaration or final judgment.

Yet they often deal with extreme situations of threats to life and physical integrity. In some cases this warrants an approach to jurisdiction and admissibility that is different from that taken by other adjudicators, dealing with non-human rights cases.

Even without formally maintaining or taking provisional measures, if there is still a threat following final determination, the follow-up proceeding could specifically indicate that the case would only be closed once resolved.[292] At minimum, the adjudicator should commit actively to follow up the final decision not only through regular follow-up proceedings but also through emergency proceedings and press releases. In exceptional cases it could also decide *proprio motu* to ask the petitioner whether she wishes to re-institute a case and take new provisional measures. A final option would be to 'maintain' the provisional measures formally. This last option would be feasible after an adjudicator has built up a considerable practice of using provisional measures aiming to protect witnesses, human rights defenders and others against death threats and harassment, as is the case in the Inter-American system. Provisional measures could then become a tool to some extent operating independently from the main proceedings. Thus far, the Inter-American system, which is the only system maintaining provisional measures even beyond the judgments on the merits or reparations, is also a system that includes a provision on provisional measures in the treaty itself. Different from systems where the authority to use provisional measures is implied, this explicit presence may justify such 'free-standing' provisional measures. Such measures protect against irreparable harm to *persons* by treating a case as pending so long as it has not yet been implemented. On the other hand, if the authority is implicit the irreparable harm to persons must be linked to the case on the merits, either because of irreparable harm to the claim or because of irreparable harm to the procedure. In any case, whether the authority to order provisional measures is implicit or explicit, awareness of the irreparable nature of the harm has been reflected in the case law of the human rights adjudicators.

---

[290] See Conclusion Part II on the purpose of preventing irreparable harm to persons and Chapter XVI on legal status.

[291] This depends on whether the system allows it and the State concerned has not made a reservation to this option.

[292] See also Chapter XVIII (Follow-up).

1   INTRODUCTION

Just like the ICJ human rights adjudicators will abstain from using provisional measures if there is no urgency. This applies to both the immediacy, or imminence, of the risk (temporal urgency) and to the likelihood of the risk (material urgency).[1] This Chapter will discuss both imminence and the likelihood of risk.

The ICJ has pointed out that 'imminence' is synonymous with 'immediacy' or 'proximity' and goes 'far beyond' the concept of 'possibility'.[2] This does not exclude 'that a "peril" in the long term might be held to be "imminent" as soon as it is established, at the relevant point in time, that the realisation of that peril, however far off it might be, is not thereby any less certain and inevitable'.[3] Yet in *Pulp mills on the river Uruguay* (*Argentina* v. *Uruguay*), it denied Argentina's request for provisional measures (2006), among others, for lack of imminence, because 'the threat of any pollution is not imminent as the mills are not expected to be operational' before the summer of 2007 and that of 2008, respectively.[4]

In cases not involving the environment imminence sometimes is easier to pinpoint. When the ICJ ordered provisional measures to halt the execution of the death penalty in *Avena* (2003) it did not do so on behalf of all 52 Mexican nationals on death row in the US, but just on behalf of three of them for whom an execution date was imminent because they had exhausted domestic remedies.[5]

The other aspect of urgency involves the likelihood of risk. Adjudicators do apply some evidentiary requirements for showing risk at the stage of provisional measures. In addition the manner in which they assess the evidence is important for the question whether they will use such measures. The manner in which they assess this evidence has an impact on the timing of provisional measures as well. As seen in Chapter II, this timing, in turn, partly determines the impact the provisional measure will eventually have.

---

[1]   The importance of the value to be protected was discussed in Part II on the purpose of provisional measures. As noted in Chapter I the phrase 'temporal urgency' or 'urgency in the temporal sense' is taken from Judge Treves (ITLOS) who distinguishes between the 'temporal dimension of the requirement of urgency' and the 'qualitative dimension'. See ITLOS Separate Opinion of judge Treves in the *Southern Bluefin Tuna* cases, Order of 27 August 1999.

[2]   ICJ *Gabcikovo-Nagymaros* (*Hungary* v. *Slovakia*), Judgment of 25 September 1997, §54 (no provisional measures because of an agreement between the parties).

[3]   ICJ *Gabcikovo-Nagymaros* (*Hungary* v. *Slovakia*), judgment of 25 September 1997, §54.

[4]   ICJ *Pulp mills on the river Uruguay* (*Argentina* v. *Uruguay*), Order of 13 July 2006 (denying provisional measures, among others because 'the threat of any pollution is not imminent as the mills are not expected to be operational before August 2007 (Orion mill) and June 2008 (CMB mill), §75.

[5]   ICJ *Avena and other Mexican nationals* (*Mexico* v. *US*), Order of 5 February 2003, *Avena and other Mexican nationals* (*Mexico* v. *US*), Judgment of 31 March 2004), §21. On the issue of exhaustion see also Chapter XIV (Jurisdiction and admissibility).

At the stage of provisional measures the adjudicators do not indicate their criteria for assessment of risk. Clarifying their approach with regard to evidentiary requirements on the *merits* is the first step to understanding their approach towards the risk required for the use of *provisional measures*. Very often decisions on the merits in human rights cases turn on evidentiary requirements rather than the legal interpretation of the scope of substantive rights. This applies in particular to cases involving the death penalty, expulsion and extradition and threats to indigenous culture and it is relevant as well in the context of requests for provisional measures. Addressee States often contest provisional measures exactly on factual issues, for instance denying the existence of a 'real risk'.

Adjudicators indeed try to assess risk before they use provisional measures. Without this the credibility and persuasive force of such measures would be limited. Yet do the adjudicators take into account the inequality between the parties and the irreparable nature of the harm faced by the petitioners? Similar to the link between the importance attached to preventing irreparable harm and the issue of jurisdiction and admissibility, discussed in the previous chapter, there appears to be a link between this importance and the issues of temporal urgency and risk.

This chapter first addresses the issue of temporal urgency (section 2). Then it refers to statements on evidentiary requirements found in decisions on the merits, paying attention to some of the pitfalls in the case law of the human rights adjudicators. It is assumed that deciding whether provisional measures are warranted depends on the available information on likelihood of risk at that stage (section 3). It also examines criteria suggested in the context of the precautionary principle to see whether they could be of use to understand assessment of risk in human rights cases (section 4).

2   ASSESSMENT OF TEMPORAL URGENCY

2.1   Introduction

Before human right adjudicators decide to use provisional measures they generally determine whether the material risk, discussed in the next section, is imminent.[6] Do the human rights adjudicators take an approach to temporal urgency that is as strict as that of the ICJ in its refusal to order provisional measures in *Pulp Mills*? Or have they taken a more flexible approach, taking into account the irreparable nature of the harm faced by the petitioners and the inequality between the parties?[7]

2.2   Immediacy in death penalty cases

Provisional measures to halt an execution only serve a purpose when they are used *prior* to an execution date. They should preferably be known to the relevant authorities well in advance of

---

[6]   See also Van Boven (2006), p. 99.

[7]   They did take such a flexible approach with regard to jurisdiction and admissibility, discussed in Chapter XIV. It is important to keep in mind as well that *Pulp Mills* may have depended more on doubts on the irreparable nature of the harm, which was the other reason for the Court's refusal to order provisional measures. See Chapter I on ICJ and ITLOS, as well as Conclusion Part II, on the Purpose of provisional measures in human rights adjudication.

this date. After all, a busy prison phone could result in an execution for someone who just received clemency.[8]

Attitudes have differed within the HRC about the need to use provisional measures if the execution is not imminent.[9] Some members have considered provisional measures should be used in such cases as well, simply as a matter of principle.[10]

In the submission to the HRC in *Yasseen and Thomas* v. *Republic of Guyana* (1998),[11] counsel noted that the petitioners could not be expected to wait until their final claim had been heard before resorting to the HRC. Given the nature of the situation, 'the authors will be pursuing all legal procedures until the very last minute.' If they would wait until their final claim would have been heard they would have to wait 'until a moment dangerously close to their execution before invoking their rights under the International Covenant on Civil and Political Rights'.

[8] NRC Handelsblad, 'executie wegens drukke telefoon', 26 June 1999 (reporting about the failed attempt of the President of the Philippines to cancel an execution, because the telephone lines of the prison were busy). In relation to halting corporal punishment one of the provisional measures decisions was taken within eleven days and the other within a year. In *Osbourne* v. *Jamaica*, 15 March 2000, the complaint was submitted on 12 June 1997 (the case file mentions 6 June which would mean 17 rather than 11 days) and it appears from the files in Geneva that the HRC used provisional measures on 23 June 1997. In *Higginson* v. *Jamaica*, 28 March 2002, the initial submission was on 20 January 1997 while the Special Rapporteur only transmitted its provisional measures decision to the State on 14 January 1998, almost a year later. While the Committee published its View in *Matthews* v. *Trinidad and Tobago*, the first case dealing with corporal punishment, on 31 March 1998, and its first use of provisional measures to halt corporal punishment dates from 23 June 1997 (on behalf of Osbourne) and its second dates from 14 January 1998 (on behalf of Higginson), it is unlikely that it already used provisional measures in *Matthews*. His complaint was of 11 October 1993 and the Committee declared it admissible, also with regard to the corporal punishment issue, two years later. Indeed the file does not indicate the use of provisional measures.

[9] While before 1989 the full Committee decided to use provisional measures on behalf of all petitioners awaiting execution, the first two Special Rapporteurs on New Communications decided to intervene only in the face of an execution date. There was a decrease in the use of provisional measures by the HRC from 1989 until early 1993. This could to some extent be explained by a different attitude of the Committee towards the immediacy of the threat. In many cases the HRC does not indicate the date on which it used provisional measures.

[10] See e.g. interview by author with Special Rapporteur Scheinin, Geneva, April 2003. See the discussion of transparency or obscurity in Chapter II (Systems). While its promptness is unclear in these cases (at least on the basis of publicly available information), the discussion in the View may still provide some information relevant to the issue of urgency and exhaustion of local remedies.

[11] HRC *Abdool Saleem Yasseen and Noel Thomas* v. *Republic of Guyana*, 30 March 1998. On 1 February 1996 a warrant of execution was read to them. The next day they submitted the case to the HRC. That week the HRC used provisional measures and it sent reminders twice (on file with the author). "On Thursday 1 February 1996 at 3:00 p.m., warrants were read to the authors for their execution at 8:00 a.m. on Monday 5 February 1996. The normal practice is for warrants to be read on a Thursday for the execution to take place the following Tuesday. The authors' families were informed of the execution through an anonymous telephone call at 10:00 p.m. on Thursday 1 February". An application for a stay of execution was heard on Saturday 3 February 1996 and a conservatory Order was requested to allow a hearing to take place. This conservatory order was denied but an appeal against this denial was granted to the full Court of Appeal. At this point a seven-day stay of execution was granted. Yasseen and Thomas were informed on 7 February that the Court of Appeal would hear the merits of their case the next day.

Counsel considered it highly unlikely that the particular domestic proceeding (a conservatory motion) would succeed. Yet he did not wish to refrain from taking all possible courses of action in the domestic courts. The HRC did use provisional measures in this case.[12]

Sometimes the Rapporteur may decide not to use provisional measures immediately, exactly because some domestic proceedings are still pending, meaning both that there is no immediate risk of execution and that proceeding with the case before the HRC could result in having to declare the case inadmissible.[13]

There are also some cases in which the Rapporteur waited with the use of provisional measures until an execution date was imminent. These cases do indicate the approach of some Rapporteurs and the importance they attached to fulfilling the criterion of temporal urgency in using provisional measures.[14]

---

[12]   See Chapter XIV on the relationship with admissibility.

[13]   In HRC *Junior Leslie* v. *Jamaica* (564/1993) the initial submission was of 9 October 1993. Transmission under Rule 91 was on 3 December 1993. Yet the Special Rapporteur only used provisional measures on 8 February 1995. It appears from the case file that the Rapporteur may have decided to postpone use of provisional measures until she would receive information that the petitioner was formally classified as a capital offender under a review procedure. By submission of 3 February 1995 counsel informed the HRC that their client's appeal against his classification as a capital offender would be heard on 13 February 1995. "We understand that if that appeal fails (and the Court of Appeal has already given a preliminary indication that it will) then Mr Leslie is in real and immediate danger of a Warrant of Execution being issued and it being carried out before the Committee can consider Mr Leslie's communication on issues of admissibility or on the merits". In that context counsel requested the HRC to take provisional measures. Five days later and five days before the abovementioned hearing, the HRC sent a note verbale to the minister of foreign affairs (with a copy to the Permanent Mission) to that effect (on file with the author). In some cases it is clear why the HRC did not use provisional measures. In HRC *Errol Smith and Oval Stewart* v. *Jamaica*, 8 April 1999 (transmitted under Rule 91 on 15 November 1995), for instance, the petitioners' death sentences were already commuted, not only before registration of the case but also before submission. In other cases the HRC only registered the complaint several months after initial submission when the death sentences had already been commuted. See e.g. HRC *Desmond Amore* v. *Jamaica,* 23 March 1999. In this case provisional measures were not used, but it is not clear from the View or the case file why not. On 17 January 1995 counsel did request provisional measures (on file with the author). Four months later the State commuted the death sentence and only subsequently the HRC transmitted the case to the State. This means that when the Secretariat made the case summary the petitioner was still awaiting execution. See also *McCordie Morrison* v. *Jamaica*, 3 November 1998. The petitioner submitted the case, including an Art. 14 claim, in November 1994, before commutation of his sentence (on file with the author). See also *Adams* v. *Jamaica*, 30 October 1996.

[14]   See e.g. HRC *McCordie Morrison* v. *Jamaica*, 3 November 1998. The initial submission was of 25 November 1994, but the Rapporteur did not use provisional measures in this case, and she transmitted the case a year after initial submission. The fact that the claim included Art. 14 but that the Rapporteur nevertheless did not use provisional measures must mean that she had a reason unrelated to preservation of the eventual form of reparation. She may have considered that execution was not imminent. See also *Victor Francis* v. *Jamaica*, 24 March 1993. This is an unclear case. The Working Group transmitted the complaint in October 1988, but while the claim included Article 14(3)(c) and (5) the HRC did not use provisional measures. Death penalty cases in which the HRC did not use provisional measures may also clarify the Committee's approach. It appears, however, that there is almost no information available about such cases. In HRC *V.B.* v. *Trinidad and Tobago*, 26 July 1993 (inadm.), initially it seemed provisional measures were not

Yet this seems to have changed. After all, following *Piandiong et al.* v. *the Philippines* (2000) States must be aware that they cannot execute a person after they have been informed of a submission to the HRC.[15] In other words, they cannot quickly execute a petitioner in an attempt to avoid a specific request by the Committee to halt the execution pending the proceedings. This means that for future cases States must take into account that the obligation to halt the execution pending the proceedings is triggered once they are informed of the submission of the case rather than once the case is formally registered. It also means that, once a case is pending before the HRC, in death penalty cases a specific request for provisional measures is not necessary (although still desirable as a clear statement by the HRC) because the irreversible nature of capital punishment in itself requires the State to halt an execution.

The HRC has continued to use provisional measures in these cases. Once, prior to *Piandiong*, it even used them in advance of the pronouncement of a death sentence rather than in advance of the execution itself. In *Domukovsky and three others* v. *Georgia* (1998)[16] the HRC used provisional measures when it was not yet clear whether a death sentence would be imposed or not. The case is interesting because the person concerned, Domukovsky, had not yet been sentenced to death when the HRC used provisional measures. Four days later he was sentenced to fourteen years imprisonment. It is the first example of the use of provisional measures already where a death sentence is threatened ('to defer the execution of an eventual death sentence') rather than only in cases where someone has already been sentenced to death.[17] The decision to take provisional measures at this stage may relate to the abolitionist stance of the Rapporteur in question and simply be a statement of principle. It is also possible that she assessed that there was indeed a real risk of imposition of the death penalty that would, in itself, result in irreparable harm

---

used, but if appears from the files that they were in effect used on 25 August 1992 (initial submission of 28 November 1991).

[15] HRC *Dante Piandiong, Jesus Morallos and Archie Bulan* (*deceased*) (*submitted by Alexander Padilla and Ricardo III Sunga*) v. *the Philippines*, 19 October 2000. See also *Anton Bondarenko and Natalia Schedko* (*submitted by the latter on behalf of her deceased son and herself*) v. *Belarus*, 3 April 2003 and *Igor Lyashkovich and Mariya Staselovich* (*submitted by the latter on behalf of her deceased son and herself*) v. *Belarus*, 3 April 2003.

[16] HRC *Victor Domukovsky, Zaza Tsiklauri, Petre Gelbakhiani and Irakli Dokvadze* v. *Georgia*, 6 April 1998.

[17] The HRC used provisional measures on 2 March 1995 on behalf of Domukovsky (only Rule 91 for Tsiklauri). Note verbale transmitting the case and using provisional measures, 2 March 1995. See also fax of 2 March 1995 to Head of State Shevardnadze accompanying the two notes verbales addressed to his government transmitting the cases of Domukovsky and Tsiklauri and noting the provisional measures 'to defer the execution of an eventual death sentence against Mr. Domukovsky, for the period during which the Committee is examining his communication'. On behalf of the other two petitioners the Special Rapporteur took provisional measures a few days after they had been sentenced to death. A separate admissibility decision was made on 5 July 1996. It again referred to provisional measures in relation to Dokvadze and Gelbakhiani. The State party was requested not to carry out the death sentence against them while their communication was under consideration by the Committee (on file with the author). Domukovsky claimed that he and a co-defendant, Gelbakhiani, were kidnapped from Azerbaijan and illegally arrested in April 1993. Domukovsky was sentenced to 14 years imprisonment on 6 March 1995. Gelbakhiani was sentenced to death on 6 March 1995. Dokvadze was arrested on 3 September 1992 and sentenced to death on 6 March 1995. Tsiklauri claimed he was arrested without a warrant on 7 August 1992 and that a warrant was shown to him only a year later. He was sentenced to five years imprisonment on 6 March 1995. By decree of the President of Georgia of 25 July 1997 54 persons were pardoned and their death sentences were replaced by twenty years imprisonment. Gelbakhiani and Dokvadze were among these 54 persons.

even if not executed, e.g. because it was likely to be based on an unfair trial. In the alternative, she could have assessed that there was a real risk that execution would follow soon after imposition of the death penalty. The file shows that the latter may be the case.

All Special Rapporteurs of the HRC have dealt with requests for assistance by death row inmates or with information to the effect that their execution is impending as requests to use provisional measures on their behalf, even if they did not explicitly ask for provisional measures.

In 2003 Special Rapporteur Scheinin indicated that in Eastern European cases he had also used provisional measures already at this stage, although the Committee might not use them in cases involving States that always have long delays.[18] At the same time provisional measures have been used in relation to Zambia, which *de facto* has not executed death row prisoners for a long time.

It seems that two factors play a role: the urgency on the one hand and on the other the principle that the State should at least be informed of the Committee's position that persons sentenced to death and awaiting execution must not be executed pending the proceedings before it. Once a case gets so far as to be registered, the Rapporteur believes it would be 'strange' not to indicate the Committee's position on this point.[19]

The President of the Inter-American Court has also ordered urgent measures in cases in which the precise execution dates were not known, but the executions were planned on an unspecified date the next month.[20] In the case of *Baptiste* the President ordered urgent measures the day after he received the Commission's application, despite the fact that a warrant of execution had not yet been issued.[21] Concern about the State's internal instructions in death penalty cases may explain this sense of urgency.[22] In its Order in *Boyce and Joseph* v. *Barbados* the Court decided to maintain its provisional measures despite the fact that the execution ceased to be imminent because of a temporary stay of execution by the High Court of Barbados.[23] In other words, the Inter-American Court and the HRC have used provisional measures not just in the face of an execution date, but already earlier in the proceedings. This betrays a more flexible approach than that taken by the ICJ, indeed taking into account the inequality between the parties and the irreparable nature of the harm that would be faced once the risk would become immediate.

2.3   Immediacy in expulsion and extradition cases

More than in death penalty cases, in non-refoulement cases the HRC has insisted on the immediacy of the risk. On occasion it has focussed on formal lack of immediacy rather than practical immediacy. In fact the lack of imminence was more apparent than real. Domestic legislation was

---

[18]   Interview by author with Special Rapporteur Scheinin, Geneva, April 2003.

[19]   Id.

[20]   IACHR *James et al.* cases, Order for provisional measures, 29 August 1998.

[21]   Id. (Reference to the Commission's observations of 2, 17 and 30 July 1998).

[22]   There were indications that an execution day was impending because the six month period set forth under the State's internal Instructions for Death Penalty Applications expired on 16 July and the State may give very short notice of an impending execution, even as little as five days. It appears from the Court's summary of the Commission's observations with regard to its requests to amplify the Order with new beneficiaries that it considered the short time frame of only five to seven days between the issuance and reading of an execution warrant and the execution as an impediment to the Court's ability to issue effective provisional measures. It is also possible to explain the swiftness in this case, or the lack thereof in others, in light of the situation at the Secretariat at a given time and by its communication channel with the President.

[23]   IACHR *Boyce and Joseph* v. *Barbados*, Order of 25 November 2004.

such that in practice the petitioner could be expelled at very short notice and might not have sufficient time to petition the HRC again upon receipt of information about the date and time of removal.[24]

In *E.G.* v. *Canada* (disc. 1997)[25] counsel submitted the case before exhaustion of domestic remedies by referring to the fact that in other cases[26] extradition took place 'literally within minutes' of the Supreme Court's ruling and pointed out that the State should not attempt to deny an effective remedy before the HRC.

> "If the Canadian Government is prepared to commit itself to allow a reasonable period of time subsequent to an unfavourable decision of the Supreme Court of Canada in petitioner's case, we will admit that the application is premature".[27]

The next year this argument returned, again with regard to Canada. In a family life case – in which the HRC did not use provisional measures – counsel made an argument involving the assessment of temporal urgency. In *J.P.A.F.* v. *Canada* (disc. 1998)[28] counsel mentioned the manner in which the Immigration Department removed another petitioner 'without any advance notice'.[29] She referred to the publicity surrounding deportation of 'foreign criminals' and noted that, in this light, she fully expected that her client would be removed from Canada as soon as the Immigration Appeal Division had rendered a negative decision, 'likely on only a few hours notice to him, and no advance notice to us as his counsel'. She pointed out that domestic proceedings that could be taken subsequently would have no suspensive effect.[30] She noted that she was not sure whether the Committee could respond to prevent removal before it takes place and that it appeared that it would take some time for a decision on provisional measures to be made. Hence, she requested the HRC to consider the request now 'so that in the event the appeal is denied, your office may be in a position to act immediately, if Rule 86 measures can be invoked'. She requested the HRC to use provisional measures immediately upon her notification to it that her client's appeal had been denied.[31] This is in fact comparable to the approach taken by the

---

24   HRC *Hamid Reza Taghi Khadje* v. *the Netherlands*, 31 October 2006 (inadm.) (very formally concluding that 'no order has in fact been made for his forcible return to Iran. It is not an inevitable consequence of a failed application for asylum that a deportation will take place', §6.3, without taking into account the practice of expelling upon very short notice). Apparently no provisional measures were used pending the proceedings. This case is different from *S.B.* v. *the Netherlands*, 30 March 2005 (nadm.) as in that case the petitioner did not expect to be expelled, §6.2.

25   HRC *E.G.* v. *Canada* (738/1997). Initial submission 5 January 1997 (received 7 January 1997), provisional measures of 17 January 1997; withdrawal of these measures on 28 April 1997; petitioner's request to withdraw the case itself of 26 May 1997. On 17 November 1997 the HRC informed the petitioner that it had discontinued the case (on file with the author).

26   HRC *Kindler* v. *Canada*, 30 July 1993 and *Ng* v. *Canada*, 5 November 1993.

27   Letter by the petitioner in HRC *E.G.* v. *Canada* (738/1997), 21 April 199, disc. on 17 November 1997 (on file with the author).

28   HRC *J.P.A.F.* v. *Canada* (disc. 1998), 620/1995 (on file with the author).

29   This was a reference to HRC *Canepa* v. *Canada*, 3 April 1997.

30   This was the case in particular because apparently they could not use the Committee's admissibility decision in *Stewart* to 'attempt to establish a serious constitutional issue on the matter of family separation'. The decision on the merits in *Stewart* had not yet been published at the time. See further Chapter XII (Other situations).

31   Submission of 12 July 1994 in HRC *J.P.A.F.* v. *Canada* (disc. 1998) (620/1995) (on file with the author). Counsel in *A.B.* v. *Canada* (disc. 1998) referred to the HRC's expression of concern

ECtHR.[32] In other cases involving a threat of immediate refoulement upon exhaustion, the HRC has now used conditional provisional measures before remedies were fully exhausted.[33]

The Committee decided not to use provisional measures in *J.C.A.* v. *Costa Rica* (disc. 2000),[34] probably because of the (lack of) immediacy of the risk.[35] There was no decision yet about a deportation, let alone a deportation date.[36]

---

[32] during the 42nd session about expulsion of aliens in Canada and the lack of suspensive effect of appeals against expulsion or deportation orders. She requested the HRC to take its decision on the use of provisional measures prior to 1 November 1994, which was the date on which the petitioner was scheduled to be deported. In fact she noted that the deportation was scheduled for 17:45 and also provided the address, telephone and fax numbers of the immigration officer responsible for his removal. Submissions of 25 and 26 October 1994 on behalf of *A.B.* v. *Canada* (622/1995) (on file with the author).

In situations where the implementation of an expulsion order is expected immediately upon a decision by domestic court of last instance, petitioners should ask the ECtHR to anticipate on a possible negative decision and prepare a provisional measure in advance. This applies in particular if there is a risk of immediate expulsion after business hours, during the weekend or during French holidays, when there is limited or no presence of relevant staff in Strasbourg. In such cases it would be too late to approach the Court in Strasbourg only upon exhaustion of domestic remedies.

[33] See e.g. HRC *Steven Romans* v. *Canada*, 9 July 2004 or *D. and E. and their two children* v. *Australia*, 11 July 2006 (in the latter case requesting the State, on 12 February 2002, to 'provide information to the Committee, on an urgent basis, of whether the authors are under a real risk of deportation while their communication is being considered by the Committee', adding that it trusts the State 'will not deport the authors before the Committee has received such information and had an opportunity to consider whether the request for interim measures should be granted', §1.2). This could be seen as a more 'procedural' and temporary provisional measure, in fact explicitly asking the State to provide more information and to halt an expulsion until it provides the Rapporteur with information that no irreparable harm would result.

[34] HRC *J.C.A.* v. *Costa Rica* (725/1996), initial submission 26 October 1996, discontinued at 69th session in July 2000 (on file with the author).

[35] This is an example of a case that was later discontinued. Counsel had requested provisional measures in October 1996, in order to halt the Basque petitioner's return to Spain. The representatives of three NGOs submitted a letter to the HRC supporting the request for provisional measures. They referred to the risk to the life and physical and psychological integrity of the petitioner, in particular when considering the use of torture and violence in Spain against persons suspected of links with the ETA. The Rapporteur transmitted the case to the State without using provisional measures. Subsequently counsel repeated his request for provisional measures. Again the Special Rapporteur decided that they were not necessary. In this case the State had contested the admissibility of the complaint. Among others, it pointed out that it aimed to prevent 'a hypothetical and eventual expulsion' and was brought before the Committee with the obvious intention that it would use provisional measures. Until then, there had been no decision of the competent authorities to expel him. The petitioner, noted the State, hoped that the HRC would use provisional measures to prevent an *eventual* decision to expel him. The State argued that the submission constituted an abuse of the right of petition. It pointed out that the petitioner referred to a hypothetical decision and that he asked the Committee to substitute its own actions for those of the Costa Rican authorities. This way the petitioner wished to make sure in advance that the domestic legal bodies would not be able to decree an eventual expulsion. In September 2000 the HRC informed his counsel that it had decided to discontinue its consideration of the case for lack of information. HRC *J.C.A.* v. *Costa Rica* (725/1996), disc.

2.4   Immediacy of the risk in cases involving death threats

The *Chipoco* case is an example of a failed request by the Inter-American Commission to the Inter-American Court to order provisional measures.[37] One may argue that the alleged threat was not imminent because the intended beneficiary was in the US at the time. Chipoco originally was a human rights defender from Peru. He spent several years in the US and during that time he took part in litigation by Human Rights Watch against Peru within the Inter-American human rights system.[38] When he was about to return to Peru, the Fujimori government issued a black list of persons accused of denigrating the honour of the nation by litigating cases before the Inter-American Court of Human Rights. In fact, however, the judiciary was not acting upon this list and no warrant had yet been issued for his arrest. In any case, upon his return he ran for Congress and won a seat and the Government did not dare to jail him.

    Nevertheless, even without a specific (execution or expulsion) date, the situation is imminent once there is evidence of recent threats.[39]

2.5   Immediacy in cases involving indigenous culture

More difficult to pinpoint is the urgency in cases involving threats to indigenous culture. This applies both to temporal urgency, as discussed here, and to risk, as discussed in the next section.

    When does the HRC consider a risk involving indigenous culture to be imminent? What is the role of suspensive effect in domestic proceedings? A case involving culture hinting at the immediacy of the threat is *Sara et al.* v. *Finland* (inadm. 1994).[40] The HRC declared part of the claim inadmissible because the petitioners had not yet been affected by an administrative measure

---

2000 (on file with the author). It is not clear why the petitioner did not resort to the Inter-American Commission in Washington D.C. It may be that counsel expected the HRC to be more forthcoming in its use of provisional measures, but in that case he was disappointed.

[36]   In HRC *Ngoc Si Truong* v. *Canada*, 28 March 2003 (inadm.) the HRC apparently did not use provisional measures either. It appears from a note in the file that the petitioner did not seem to be under immediate threat of deportation and counsel did not request the use of provisional measures. In *Samira Karker on behalf of her husband Salah Karker* v. *France*, 26 October 2000, it is not evident from the text of the View why the HRC used provisional measures. This expulsion did not appear to be imminent. The HRC used provisional measures half a year after the initial submission of 18 September 1998. It appears from the case file that the provisional measure was to halt his expulsion to Tunisia pending the examination of the case. In other words, the Rapporteur decided to use this provisional measure just in case his expulsion would become imminent after all.

[37]   IACHR *Chipoco* (*Peru*), Order of 27 January 1993 (denying a request for provisional measures).

[38]   Carlos Chipoco accompanied the Commission to Court hearings, e.g. as an advisor in the IACHR *Neira Alegria* case (Peru), Judgment of 19 February 1995.

[39]   IACHR Evidence of threats must include examples of *recent* occurrences, see e.g. *Miguel Castro Castro Prison* (Peru), Order of 29 January 2008 (denying a request for provisional measures), 5th 'Considering' clause. (denying the provisional measures requested by the petitioners- a request not supported by the Commission – because the facts complained of were not recent and there was no evidence of a persisting situation endangering the life or personal integrity of the intended beneficiaries and therefore the requirement of 'urgency' was not met, also referring to the Court's previous denial of a request of 30 January 2007)

[40]   HRC *Sara et al.* v. *Finland*, 23 March 1994 (inadm.) (initial submission of 18 December 1990, Rule 91 of 12 February 1991, Rule 86 probably on 9 July 1991 together with initial admissibility decision).

implementing the disputed legislation. At the same time it found a causal link between the continuation of road construction in a certain area and the entry into force of this legislation. It declared the claim admissible in this respect.[41] At this point it also used provisional measures.[42] Yet later it set aside its provisional measures as well as its admissibility decision and declared the case inadmissible because it considered there was no imminent threat.[43] When the petitioners submitted their new complaint the activities had already taken place.[44]

In *Länsman I* the request for provisional measures to halt the quarrying of stone in traditional herding areas failed.[45] The HRC considered that the use of provisional would be premature but that the petitioners retained the right to repeat their request.[46]

---

[41] In HRC *Sara et al.* v. *Finland* (inadm. 1994) the petitioners feared that the Central Forestry Board would 'approve the continuation of road construction or logging by the summer of 1991, or at the latest by early 1992, around the road under construction and therefore within the confines of their herding areas'. According to the State the petitioners had failed to demonstrate how their concerns about irreparable harm 'purportedly resulting from logging in the area designated by them' would translate into actual violations of their rights. It considered 'they are merely afraid of what might occur in the future'. "While they might legitimately fear for the future of the Sami culture, the 'desired feeling of certainty is not as such protected under the Covenant. There must be a concrete executive decision or measure taken under the Wilderness Act', before anyone may claim to be the victim of a violation of his Covenant rights". The HRC observed that the complaint related both to '*expected* logging and road construction activities *within* the Hammastunturi Wilderness and *ongoing* road construction activities in the residual area located *outside* the wilderness'. With regard to the expected activities it considered the claim inadmissible because the petitioners had not yet been affected by an administrative measure implementing the Act.

[42] This was the second time the Committee used provisional measures to halt actions affecting the natural habitat. The first time was in the *Lubicon Lake Band* case, because the domestic appeal still pending was without suspensive effect. HRC *Lubicon Lake Band*, 26 March 1990. See also Chapter XIV (Jurisdiction and admissibility and section 4 of this Chapter (On material urgency).

[43] HRC *Sara* v. *Finland*, 23 March 1994 (inadm.). It did so after receipt of information about a delay until the finalisation of the implementation plan for the disputed activities. The HRC referred to counsel's comment that the petitioners were expecting a delay until 1996 for the finalisation of the Central Forestry Board's implementation plan and understood this 'as an indication that no further activities in the Hammastunturi Wilderness and the residual area will be undertaken by the State party while the authors may pursue further domestic remedies'. In other words, the HRC assumed no immediate threat. The provisional measure was applicable from July 1991 until the inadmissibility decision. It seems that the HRC implicitly reminds the State that it should not undertake further activities while the petitioners are pursuing domestic remedies. After all, an expected delay of activities until finalisation of an implementation plan is not the same as a commitment to suspend activities until domestic remedies have been undertaken and certainly not until the petitioners have been enabled to submit a new complaint to the HRC. The HRC took this as an indication that the State party would not undertake further activities while the petitioners were pursuing domestic remedies. If the HRC had expected the State to take this reminder seriously, it was let down.

[44] The State did in fact undertake further activities. Two of the petitioners submitted a new complaint to the HRC more than three years later, in November 1997. See *Anni Äärelä and Jouni Näkkäläjärvi* v. *Finland*, 24 October 2001. In that case the HRC did not use provisional measures because the events complained of had already occurred.

[45] HRC *Ilmari Länsman* v. *Finland* (*Länsman I*), 26 October 1994.

[46] In another case the request may have been too late, because the acts to be prevented had already proceeded and a request by the HRC – pending the proceedings before it – for the State to return

The Committee considered that the claims under Article 27 had been sufficiently substantiated for purposes of admissibility, but it agreed with the State that the use of provisional measures would be premature at this stage.[47] It pointed out that 'the authors retained the right to address another request under rule 86 to the Committee if there were reasonably justified concerns that quarrying might resume'.[48] The file shows that the petitioners submitted a renewed request for provisional measures in February 1993.[49] As this failed, six months later the petitioners submitted

---

to the *status quo ante* would be too far reaching in the circumstances (viz. *Vakoumé et al.* v. *France*, 31 October 2000 (inadm.)). This first case, *Ilmari Länsman* v. *Finland* (*Länsman I*), 26 October 1994, involving the areas of Angeli and Inari, was initially submitted in June 1992 by 75 members of the Muotkatunturi Herdsmen's Committee and members of the local community of Angeli. They were all reindeer breeders of Sami origin challenging the decision of the Central Forestry Board to sign a contract with a private company. This contract would allow quarrying of stone in an area covering ten hectares on the flank of the mountain Etelä-Riutusvaara. They argued that this contract would 'not only allow the private company to extract stone but also to transport it right through the complex system of reindeer fences to the Angeli-Inari road'. They pointed out that the ownership of lands traditionally used by the Samis was disputed between the State and the Sami community. While they conceded that the economic value of the stone to be quarried was considerable, they emphasised that the village of Angeli was 'the only remaining area in Finland with a homogenous and solid Sami population' and that the 'quarrying and transport of anorthocite would disturb their reindeer herding activities and the complex system of reindeer fences determined by the natural environment'. They also observed that the mountain was a sacred place of the old Sami religion. Together with the initial submission they requested the HRC to adopt provisional measures, as they feared that further quarrying was imminent. The petitioners had seen the precedents of the *Lubicon Lake Band*, with provisional measures in July 1987 and *Sara* with provisional measures in July 1991. See the discussion in §4.2 of the View. The State party had submitted that the request for provisional measures by the petitioners was 'clearly premature' because only test quarrying had been carried out on the contested site.

[47] In fact, in the initial submission the petitioners had pointed out that the private company 'may be unwilling or even financially incapable to make the investments necessary for starting the actual quarrying as long as it does not have a permanent contract with the land owner'. They pointed out that the present contract only allowed for extraction of stone until the end of 1993. "The authors would hope that the Central Forest Board, being an governmental body, does not make a new contract before the Human Rights Committee has had a possibility to consider their communication under the Optional Protocol". Petitioners' submission of 10 June 1992 (on file with the author).

[48] See §6.3 of the View. In the View the HRC specifically discussed the petitioners' request for provisional measures. It noted the State's argument that interim protection under Rule 86 'would be premature, as only limited test quarrying in the area of Mount Etelä-Riutusvaara has been carried out' and it explained its decision not to use provisional measures 'at this juncture'. It appears from the Committee's admissibility decision that the Special Rapporteur transmitted the case under Rule 91 two months after initial submission, on 25 August 1992. See Admissibility decision of 14 October 1993, CCPR/C/49/D/511/1992, 3 November 1993 (on file with the author). In the View it did not address further their statement that even the limited test quarrying carried out already had left 'considerable marks'. The petitioners had alleged that, because of climatic conditions the marks would remain in the landscape for hundreds of years. They also reiterated that the location of the quarry and the road leading up to it were crucial to the activities of the Muotkatunturi Herdsmen's Committee.

[49] They pointed out that the government's contention that no actual quarrying had taken place since the initial submission was incorrect. On an unspecified date in the summer of 1992 the actual quarrying had started and by early September 1992 'the company had taken some 30 cubic metres (approximately 100.000 kilograms) of stone from the quarry and transported it through the

a request for urgent consideration at the October session in order to determine the admissibility of their claim. They explained why they considered the case urgent, referring to 'the fact that the provisional land lease contract for the quarrying company expires at the end of this year and negotiations on a longer land lease contract are at present going on'.[50] It is clear that the petitioners resorted to a request for urgent consideration of the case because their requests for provisional measures had failed. Apart from being the only case in which the HRC motivated its refusal to use provisional measures, *Länsman I* is also the predecessor of the cases *Länsman II* and *III*. In those cases the HRC did use provisional measures.[51]

3   THE LIKELIHOOD OF RISK

3.1   Introduction

The use of provisional measures does not imply a determination on the merits.[52] In *Weiss v. Austria* (2003) the HRC determined that a decision to take provisional measures does not constitute an 'examination' of the case. This already indicates that at this stage the assessment of risk should be considerably less strict that the evidentiary requirements on the merits.[53]

---

reindeer herding area of the authors'. They noted that the present contract was valid only until the end of 1993 and they requested the HRC to recommend, under Rule 86, that the government 'firstly, take appropriate measures to at least temporarily prevent the company from further quarrying within the year 1993, and, secondly, refrain as the landowner from concluding a new contract on land lease with the company as long as the communication is pending before the Committee'. Petitioners' submission of 5 February 1993 (on file with the author).

[50]   In his submission of 31 August 1994 counsel for the petitioners pointed out that the State party had indeed confirmed that the lease contract was valid until the end of 1993. "This implies that no contractual obligations would be breached if the Human Rights Committee were to find that any further quarrying would be unacceptable in the light of article 27". HRC *Ilmari Länsman* v. *Finland*, 26 October 1994, §8.2. "After a new contract is made, the private company in question intends to make considerable investments, including road construction. The authors remind the Committee of the fact that also in the Government submission of 27 October 1992 a position was taken that no urgency was involved as long as there was only a provisional land lease contract". Petitioners' submission of 16 August 1993 (on file with the author).

[51]   HRC *Jouni E. Länsman et al.* v. *Finland*, 30 October 1996 (*Länsman II*) (initial submission of 28 August 1995, provisional measures of 15 November 1995); decision of 14 March 1996 to set aside its provisional measures (together with admissibility declaration). With regard to the immediacy of the threat in *Länsman II* the petitioners noted that the Central Forestry Board had started its activities late October 1994. While the Supreme Court put a stop to this in November 1994, it withdrew the injunction in June 1995. The petitioners noted, moreover, that a representative of the Central Forestry Board had 'recently' stated that logging and road construction would resume before the winter, in October or November 1995 and was therefore imminent. In November 1995 the Rapporteur used provisional measures. On the three *Länsman* cases, see Chapter X (Culture).

[52]   HRC *Lloyd Reece* v. *Jamaica*, admissibility decision of 30 March 1989, CCPR/C/35/D/247/1987, 3 April 1989 (on file with the author). This remark, which has now become customary, was not yet made in the Committee's earlier decisions.

[53]   HRC *Sholam Weiss* v. *Austria*, 3 April 2003, § 3.7. In this case the State claimed that the European Court of Human Rights (ECtHR) had already dealt with the same matter and referred to its reservation to the OP. The HRC noted that Austria's reservation to Article 5(2)(a) OP

Like the ICJ and ITLOS, with regard to the assessment of the likelihood of risk for the use of provisional measures the human rights adjudicators have not developed clear criteria, but a common denominator seems to be that of 'prima facie' evidence. This cannot be defined in the abstract. It depends on the circumstances of the case and the context of the legal system.

Using provisional measures may sometimes be a matter of acting first and asking later. This means adjudicators could withdraw or adapt a provisional measure taken on the basis of the responses and new information provided by both parties. Still, it seems reasonable to assume that cases that would be inadmissible at face value, or in relation to claims (factual situations and interpretation of rights) for which previous case law has never found a violation, would not warrant a provisional measure.

In order to examine how assessment of risk at the stage of provisional measures differs from that at the stage of decisions on the merits, this chapter discusses the practice of the HRC with regard to the death penalty, non-refoulement, health in detention and indigenous culture. In addition some observations are made from the perspective of CAT and the ECtHR with regard to expulsion and extradition cases and some about death threats from the perspective of the Inter-American system.

Have the human rights adjudicators indeed taken an approach to assessment of the likelihood of risk for the use of provisional measures that is more flexible than that of the ICJ and ITLOS, taking into account the irreparable nature of the harm faced by the petitioners and the inequality between the parties?

3.2   The practice of the human rights adjudicators

3.2.1   Introduction

In this section the practice of the adjudicators with regard to assessment of risk for purposes of provisional measures is discussed by way of examples of situations in which provisional measures have been used. In case of corporal punishment, for instance, the petitioner need bring no more evidence for the decision on the merits than the fact that he has been sentenced to corporal punishment and that this sentence has not yet been executed. In most other situations the evidentiary requirements on the merits are much more difficult to meet or an argument must still be made that certain acts or omission indeed constitute a violation, which has already been confirmed in the case of corporal punishment.[54]

---

involved claims submitted to the European Commission on Human Rights. The ECtHR had taken provisional measures but had never examined the case. It had accepted withdrawal before it had even considered the case for admissibility. "Assuming *arguendo* that the reservation does operate in respect of complaints received, in place of the former European Commission, by the European Court of Human Rights, the Committee refers to its jurisprudence that where the European Court has gone beyond making a procedural or technical decision on admissibility, and has made an assessment of the merits on the case, then the complaint has been 'examined' within the terms of the Optional Protocol, or, in this case, the State party's reservation". See §8.3. The HRC referred to *Linderholm* v. *Croatia*, 23 July 1999 (inadm.). In order to accept withdrawal the ECtHR simply needs to decide that this would not be contrary to *ordre publique*. The HRC considered that 'a decision that a case is not of sufficient importance to continue its examination after an applicant's action to withdraw the complaint, does not amount to a real assessment of its substance'. In other words, the complaint had not been 'examined' by the ECtHR and Austria's reservation did not preclude the HRC from considering the claims.

54   See Chapter IV (Halting corporal punishment).

The subsequent sections are presented by type of situation in which the HRC has used provisional measures: death penalty; non-refoulement; detention; death threats; cultural survival and nuclear tests. To the extent that this further clarifies assessment of risk, references are made to the practice of the other adjudicators as well. Before discussing these situations, first the contours are sketched of assessment of risk for the use of provisional measures.

3.2.2 Sketching the contours of the assessment of risk for the use of provisional measures

The contours of the assessment of risk for the use of provisional measures may be sketched in relation to the general approach of the adjudicator to the evidentiary requirements on the merits of cases. The term 'evidentiary requirements' is used here to refer to the criteria to be met in order to prove a case as well as to the standard and burden of proof. These issues are interrelated and normally adjudicators do not clearly distinguish between them. Apart from the issue of evidentiary requirements there is also the issue of how the adjudicators evaluate this evidence: the standard of review.[55]

Thus far academic research has not distinguished between evidentiary requirements during various stages of the proceedings on the merits, at the stage of decision-making on jurisdiction and admissibility and at the stage of decision-making on provisional measures. It is suggested that while it may not be possible to indicate the precise requirements for these different stages of international adjudication, the significance of these stages warrants specific attention. The strictest requirements can be found exactly in relation to the merits. In relation to admissibility the evidentiary requirements are less strict and, given the limited time available for decision-making as well as the serious nature of the harm risked, in relation to provisional measures the adjudicator should be very lenient.

With regard to the serious nature of the harm risked the adjudicators have also acknowledged that the level of scrutiny of *State* acts and omissions must be higher in those cases involving the most extreme violations. The practice of the ECtHR, which is generally more restrictive in this respect than that of the other human rights adjudicators,[56] serves as an example. While in *Bazorkina* v. *Russia* (2006) this Court noted it was 'sensitive to the subsidiary nature of its role' and recognised 'that it must be cautious in taking on the role of a first-instance tribunal of fact, where this is not rendered unavoidable by the circumstances of a particular case', it pointed out that: "Nonetheless, where allegations are made under Articles 2 and 3 of the Convention the Court must apply a particularly thorough scrutiny (...) even if certain domestic proceedings and investigations have already taken place'.[57]

As to the relation between the alleged facts and the rights explicitly claimed, the ECtHR has noted that it is 'master of the characterisation to be given in law to the facts of the case'. It has 'considered of its own motion complaints under Articles or paragraphs not relied on by those appearing before it and even under a provision in respect of which the Commission had declared the complaint to be inadmissible while declaring it admissible under a different one. A complaint is characterised by the facts alleged in it and not merely by the legal grounds or arguments relied on'.[58] In particular it has pointed out: "In the light of the importance of the protection afforded by Article 2, the Court must subject deprivations of life to the most careful scrutiny, taking into

---

[55] This book uses the phrases standard of review as well as level of scrutiny.
[56] See e.g. Chapter VI (Locating and protecting disappeared persons).
[57] ECtHR *Bazorkina* v. *Russia*, 27 July 2006 (1st section) §107.
[58] ECtHR *Akdeniz* v. *Turkey*, 31 May 2005, §88.

considerations not only the actions of State agents but also all the surrounding circumstances".[59] While these remarks were made as part of the assessment on the merits, the argument of the importance of the protection afforded equally applies at the provisional measures stage.

The ECtHR examines Article 3 ECHR cases *proprio motu*, given the absolute nature of the protection offered by that article and in light of the supervisory nature of its task as an international human rights court.[60] If the State does not respond sufficiently, the HRC will equally examine the complaint *proprio motu*. It may use sources of information not provided by the parties,[61] but in practice it hardly ever does so. Even when reading additional claims in the facts as alleged by the petitioners, the human rights adjudicators have often interpreted their mandates to be strictly limited to the examination of the submissions by the parties.[62] Yet it is submitted that at the stage of provisional measures all adjudicators should be able to take into account information derived from publicly available reports by authorities such as UN Special Rapporteurs or by reputable NGOs. Subsequently they must of course ensure that both parties are able to react to this information.[63]

The adjudicators take a flexible approach as to the types of evidence that must be brought by the individual petitioner and if the State party does not respond satisfactorily or not at all the adjudicators may draw negative inferences and take into account circumstantial evidence.[64] After all the State has the duty to cooperate with the adjudicator within the individual complaint procedure established in the respective human rights treaties.[65] Obviously the duty to cooperate is even stronger in situations where the adjudicator depends on information provided by the Parties and cannot conduct *in situ* investigations and hearings, as is the case with, for instance, the HRC.

Yet before ordering provisional measures there is often insufficient time to consult the State. Given the serious nature of the harm risked the adjudicators may already take into account circumstantial evidence and negative inferences even though the State has not yet had a chance to cooperate in this particular case. The negative inferences are then based on previous dealings of the adjudicator with the same State. After the first use of provisional measures the State may provide information prompting the adjudicator to withdraw them.

---

[59] Id., §95.

[60] See ECtHR *Sheekh* v. *the Netherlands*, 11 January 2007, §136: "In respect of materials obtained *proprio motu*, the Court considers that, given the absolute nature of the protection afforded by Article 3, it must be satisfied that the assessment made by the authorities of the Contracting State is adequate and sufficiently supported by domestic materials as well as by materials originating from other reliable and objective sources such as, for instance, other Contracting or non-Contracting States, agencies of the United Nations and reputable non-governmental organisations. In its supervisory task under Article 19 of the Convention, it would be too narrow an approach under Article 3 in cases concerning aliens facing expulsion or extradition if the Court, as an international human rights court, were only to take into account materials made available by the domestic authorities of the Contracting State concerned, without comparing these with materials from other reliable and objective sources". See also e.g. *Ryabikin* v. *Russia*, 19 June 2008, §111.

[61] See Zwart (1994), p. 12.

[62] See also Chapter XIV (Jurisdiction and admissibility).

[63] CEDAW does mention, in Rule 72(2), that it may receive information from UN organisations and bodies through the Secretariat of the Office of the High Commissioner, so long as both parties are offered the opportunity to react to this information.

[64] See e.g. Pasqualucci (2003), pp. 208-210, discussing the Inter-American Court's use of presumptions and circumstantial evidence.

[65] See e.g. IACHR Rules of Procedure (2001), Article 44. See in general on the duty to cooperate e.g. Medina Quiroga (2005), pp. 26-27.

The State generally has the monopoly of power vis-à-vis the individual. In addition it usually also has a monopoly on information, especially in the context of disappearances and torture.[66] Exactly given this unequal situation between the two, both as to the consequences and in light of the possibility to obtain evidence, on the merits the standard of proof in cases between unequal parties should be higher if the initial burden is on the State (e.g. in a criminal trial). It should be lower if the initial burden is on the individual (e.g. in disappearance or torture cases claiming state responsibility). In the latter case the burden shifts from the individual to the State once the individual has made a *prima facie* case. After all the individual claims human rights violations of a very serious nature often involving the right to life and the prohibition of cruel treatment while the consequences for the State if a violation is found would simply involve refraining from acting, providing access, releasing a person, providing compensation, etc. Moreover, the State is able to retrieve and make disappear information and evidence and therefore is in a much stronger position than the individual claiming a human rights violation. In cases involving claims of disappearances, ill treatment in detention, or the risk of cruel treatment or torture in a third State the importance attached to the prohibition of torture and ill-treatment in itself warrants particular scrutiny of the behaviour of the State.

In particular the HRC and the Inter-American Commission and Court have acknowledged the importance of the factual inequality between the parties and the difference in the consequences of finding or not finding a violation on the merits for the petitioner and the State. These factors are all relevant already at the stage of provisional measures.

The standard phrase of the HRC is that the burden of proof 'cannot rest on the author of the communication alone, especially considering that the author and the State party do not always have equal access to the evidence and that frequently the State party alone has access to relevant information'. It then continues with: "It is implicit in article 4(2) of the Optional Protocol that the State party has the duty to investigate in good faith all allegations of the violation of the Covenant made against it and its authorities, and to furnish to the Committee the information available to it".[67] The Inter-American Court has explicitly confirmed this approach.[68]

The Inter-American Commission's doctrine and the Court's jurisprudence both establish that, different from criminal cases, in a situation where one of the parties in a conflict has a monopoly of power and a consequent monopoly on information, the burden of proof shifts to that party (the State). The situation of an individual petitioner in detention is particularly illustrative. As the Commission has noted, inmates are 'defenceless and under the absolute control and in the exclusive custody of the State'.[69] It bases itself on the principle established by the Court that the silence of the State or 'elusive or ambiguous answers on its part' may be interpreted 'as an acknowledgement of the truth of allegations made, so long as the contrary is not indicated by the record or is not compelled as a matter of law'.[70] The Commission may note, for instance, that in a given case 'the State's silence and the lack of diligence in defending itself aside, the evidence still tends to corroborate many of the facts alleged'.[71] It may also point out that the State has supplied no evidence refuting the petitioners' allegations, or that the information it has supplied is incomplete and confined to generalities.[72]

---

[66]   See also e.g. ICJ *Corfu Channel* (*UK* v. *Albania*), 9 April 1949.

[67]   See e.g. HRC *Bleier* v. *Uruguay*, 29 March 1982, §13.3.

[68]   See IACHR *Bámaca Velásquez* (Guatemala), Judgment of 25 November 2000, §153, quoting *Hiber Conteris* (*submitted by Ilda Thomas on behalf of her brother*) v. *Uruguay*, 17 July 1985, §§182-186.

[69]   See e.g. CIDH *Minors in Detention* v. *Honduras*, 10 March 1999, §95.

[70]   See e.g. IACHR *Velásquez Rodríguez* case, Judgment of 29 July 1988, §138.

[71]   CIDH *Minors in Detention* v. *Honduras*, 10 March 1999, §96.

[72]   See e.g. CIDH *Minors in Detention* v. *Honduras*, 10 March 1999, §92.

In urgent actions by UN Special Rapporteurs the procedure is not accusatory but humanitarian and the Rapporteur simply requests the State to take action in case the allegations are true. The Inter-American Commission and the African Commission's function seems to be in between that of a Special Rapporteur and that of a Court or the UN treaty bodies.[73]

Aside from this shift in burden of proof, the Commission also expects a certain standard of proof to be met. It has not defined this standard but it requires, first of all, that petitioners substantiate their claims.[74] Indications for risk include that the information should be sufficiently specific and concrete with regard to the petitioner as well as information about the general human rights situation in the State in question.[75]

Evidence used by the Commission normally includes materials provided by the State and the petitioner, statements taken from witnesses or obtained from documents, records or official publications. It may also include the information collected during an on-site investigation. The Commission has found, with the Court, that press clippings cannot be regarded as documentary evidence *per se*. On the other hand it has referred to the Court's statement that 'many of them contain public and well-known facts which, as such, do not require proof; other are of evidentiary value as has been recognized in international jurisprudence in so far as they reproduce public statements, especially those of high-ranking members (...) of the Government, or even of the Supreme Court of Honduras'.[76]

The Commission considers that press articles have some evidentiary value 'to the extent that they can be used to draw consistent and undisputed conclusions about facts that were public and well known at the time they occurred. These clippings, furthermore, serve to corroborate the evidence submitted with the statements of testimony, and in many cases serve to compensate for the silence and evasive responses of the State which, by themselves, would have been sufficient grounds to presume the alleged facts to be true'.[77]

Ironically, with regard to allegations of future facts in another State all adjudicators show deference to the sending State even in cases involving allegations of a real risk of torture in the receiving State. Further, if the claim involves torture or ill treatment that has already taken place the adjudicators seem to make a difference between cases involving violations that are alleged to have taken place in pre-trial detention and allegations following conviction. In the latter case there usually is no testimony in Court about the violation, which means that the international adjudicator cannot consult a trial transcript. In such case the international adjudicator shows less deference to the State's submissions. On the other hand, if the alleged ill treatment or torture took place during pre-trial detention the adjudicators normally assume that counsel should have brought it up during the trial and if he did, but the court dismissed it, they will normally defer to the decision by the domestic court.

---

[73] In this respect the function of the Working Group on Arbitrary Detention seems to be similar to that of the Inter-American Commission in that it specifically makes use of an accusatory procedure. It is a thematic mechanism that uses a procedure to deal with individual complaints that more closely resembles a judicial procedure than that employed by the other thematic mechanisms.

[74] See also Pasqualucci (2003), p. 213 discussing the flexible approach to the standard of proof taken by the Inter-American Court, depending on the violation to be proved.

[75] This criterion is also used by UN Special Rapporteurs.

[76] CIDH *Minors in Detention* v. *Honduras*, 10 March 1999, §184, referring to IACHR *Velásquez Rodríguez* case, judgment of 29 July 1988, §146. The Court took judicial notice of those facts reported in newspaper clippings that, while they did not constitute documentary evidence, nevertheless contained 'public and well-known facts which, as such, do not require proof'.

[77] CIDH *Minors in Detention* v. *Honduras*, 10 March 1999, §185.

The standard of review depends on the importance accorded to the right. In particularly striking situations involving the right to life and the prohibition of cruel treatment, international adjudicators should apply, to borrow a term from American constitutional law, 'strict scrutiny'.

In *Ahani* v. *Canada* (2004) the HRC observed that 'where one of the highest values protected by the Covenant, namely the right to be free from torture, is at stake, the closest scrutiny should be applied to the fairness of the procedure to determine whether an individual is at a substantial risk of torture'.[78] It emphasised that its provisional measures in this case had highlighted this risk.

This type of cases, in which on the merits the adjudicator uses (or should use) the strictest level of scrutiny, coincides with the type of cases in which provisional measures may be warranted as well.[79] In the face of the serious and irreparable nature of the harm risked by the petitioner, the strict approach must be vis-à-vis the State rather than vis-à-vis the petitioner. In other words, in particular at the stage of provisional measures the nature of the harm risked and the inequality between the parties should be reflected in the manner in which the likelihood of risk is assessed. The question is whether this is indeed the case.

3.2.3 Death penalty cases and assessment of risk

3.2.3.1 INTRODUCTION

This section deals with the evidentiary requirements of the HRC for finding a violation of Article 14 ICCPR and their relevance to its decision on provisional measures.[80] After all it has been pointed out that:

> "In all capital punishment cases considered by the Committee in which the complainant had substantiated his allegations in such a way as to warrant a thorough examination of his case, the Committee, through its Special Rapporteur for New Communications, requested the State party not to execute the petitioner while his case was under consideration by the Committee".[81]

The question arises whether the HRC has indeed used provisional measures in all such cases.

One factor that confirms this statement is the fact that at times HRC Special Rapporteurs have used provisional measures even when they considered that there was insufficient information from the petitioner for purposes of transmitting the case to the State.[82] This indicates that

---

[78] HRC *Mansour Ahani* v. *Canada*, 29 March 2004, §10.6.

[79] See Conclusion Part II on the purpose of provisional measures.

[80] Case law on the death penalty is discussed in Chapters III (Halting executions) and XIII (On the relationship with forms of reparation).

[81] Ando (Japan), the Chairman of the HRC, Summary Record of the 1352nd meeting: Trinidad and Tobago, 26 July 1994 (public meeting held in response to the execution of Glenn Ashby), CCPR/C/SR/1352, 31 July 1996, §3.

[82] Normally Rapporteurs use provisional measures at the same time they transmit the case to the State. Sometimes, however, a Rapporteur initially considered there was insufficient information from the petitioner for purposes of transmitting the case to the State. She would send a Note Verbale to the State only on the basis of the Rule on provisional measures, without mentioning the Rule on the transmittal of cases. Instead, she would request the petitioner, not the State, to provide more information. Rapporteurs have done this on several occasions in which there was an immediate risk of execution. See e.g. HRC *Collins* v. *Jamaica* (356/1989), provisional measures of 25 May 1989; *G.S.* v. *Jamaica* (369/1989), provisional measures of 15 September 1989;

there is no strict assessment of risk for the use of provisional measures. Still, if there were no risk at all the HRC probably would not use them.[83] What is clearly problematic, moreover, is that the HRC very often is not in a position to thoroughly assess certain claims on the merits and consequently does not find a violation. Any executions may then go ahead as planned. Before discussing the suitability of using provisional measures in cases involving such claims, the next subsections first illustrate the HRC's case law on the merits on these claims.

3.2.3.2 RIGHT TO COUNSEL

The quality of counsel in the domestic proceedings is of crucial importance for defendants in capital cases. Counsel before the HRC often notes that 'the legal aid given by the State party is at such a meagre level that it is most often inexperienced counsel who take death row cases'. '(B)ecause of the level of remuneration counsel will almost inevitably reduce the time he spends in preparation of the case'.[84] The criteria developed by the HRC for *ineffective* legal assistance on

---

Lennon Stephens v. *Jamaica* (373/1989), provisional measures of 15 September 1989 and *R.M.* v. *Trinidad and Tobago* (384/1989), provisional measures of 29 January 1990 (all by Rapporteur Higgins). See also *Denzil Robberts* v. *Barbados* (504/1992), provisional measures of 2 July 1992 (by Rapporteur Lallah) and *Zephiniah Hamilton* v. *Jamaica* (616/1995), provisional measures of 31 January 1995 (by Rapporteur Chanet). On 24 July 1991 the Committee adopted revised terms of reference for the mandate of the Special Rapporteur on New Communications. This included 'to issue rule 86 requests, whether coupled with a request under rule 91 or not' and 'to inform the Committee at each session on action taken under rules 86 and 91'. Annex X, Mandate of the Special Rapporteur on New Communications, revised terms of reference adopted at the 1087th meeting, 24 July 1991, A/46/40, 10 October 1991, in: Official Records of the Human Rights Committee 1990/1991, Vol. II, CCPR/10/Add. 1. As noted, at the time Rule 86 was the Rule on provisional measures and Art. 91 was the Rule on the transmittal of cases to the State.

[83] From spring 1987 until summer 1988 (five sessions) the HRC would register all complaints involving the death penalty. Information obtained at Secretariat, Geneva, October 1998. Some of these cases offered very little information at the time of registration. During the first seven sessions dealing with death penalty cases (from early 1987 until March 1989) the HRC registered more than sixty communications involving the death penalty in Jamaica. This research uncovered more than fifty cases in which the HRC used provisional measures to halt an execution during this period. In the other 16 cases the HRC may not have used them because the death sentence was already commuted. It is also possible that they were used, but not mentioned, or that they were used in cases that were later discontinued. By contrast to the large number of death penalty cases registered during the first three years, between April 1989 and January 1991 the newly appointed Special Rapporteur for New Communications only registered 18 such cases. Information obtained at Secretariat, Geneva, October 1998. In this period the HRC took a more cautious approach to the registration of complaints containing little information. Before registering them the Rapporteur asked the Secretariat to request additional information, for instance when it was unclear what steps were taken to exhaust domestic remedies or when the submission did not yet seem to make a *prima facie* case under the ICCPR. Hence, the Rapporteur did not yet authorise the Secretariat to transmit the case to the State under Rule 91 (current Rule 97). She did, on the other hand, authorise it to transmit some cases solely for the purpose of provisional measures. HRC *G.S.* v. *Jamaica*, 369/1989, provisional measures of 15 September 1989; *Lennon Stephens* v. *Jamaica*, 373/1989, provisional measures of 15 September 1989 and *R.M.* v. *Trinidad and Tobago*, 384/1989, provisional measures of 29 January 1990.

[84] HRC *Peter Blaine* v. *Jamaica*, 17 July 1994. Counsel from the London law firm Allan & Overy in *Lewis* v. *Jamaica*, also of 17 July 1997, used the same argument. Peter Blaine and Neville

appeal include: the petitioner was not informed beforehand on who would represent him at the appeal; he was not informed of the date of the hearing; or counsel for the petitioner did not argue the appeal on his behalf without consulting him.[85]

Nevertheless, the HRC usually cannot address the problems arising from poor quality of counsel. The HRC considers that the State party cannot be held accountable for alleged errors made by a defence lawyer 'unless it was or should have been manifest to the judge that the law-yer's behaviour was incompatible with the interests of justice'.[86] It appears, however, that the fact

---

Lewis were co-defendants. Blaine's lawyer was David Stewart of S.J. Berwin and Co. In *Anthony Finn* v. *Jamaica*, 31 July 1998. The State party had observed that, in relation to the allegation of the violation of Article 14 (3)(b), 'it is unfair to hold the State party accountable for the professional conduct of legal aid counsel'. However, it is the State that appoints counsel to cases and that is responsible for very low remuneration. It is interesting that the State uses the term 'unfair' in a situation where it seems evident that many petitioners were sentenced to death, at least partly, due to the inadequacy of their defence at trial. Usually, this inadequacy can no longer be remedied at a later stage. For the HRC this is part of 'counsel's professional judgment' except in a case where counsel's behaviour has been such as to be 'incompatible with the interests of justice'.

[85] See e.g., HRC *Neville Lewis* v. *Jamaica*, 17 July 1997. States must take measures to ensure that counsel, once assigned, provides effective representation in the interests of justice. This includes consulting with, and informing, the accused if he intends to withdraw an appeal or to argue before the appellate instance that the appeal has no merit. See e.g. HRC *Trevor Collins* v. *Jamaica,* 25 March 1993; *Lloyd Grant* v. *Jamaica,* 31 March 1994; *George Graham and Arthur Morrison* v. *Jamaica,* 25 March 1996 and *Silbert Daley* v. *Jamaica*, 31 July 1998. See also Spronken (2001), pp. 447-449. With regard to the right to appeal the HRC is not in a position to question counsel's professional judgment itself that there was no merit to such an appeal.

[86] See e.g., HRC *Beresford Whyte* v. *Jamaica*, 27 July 1998. An example of a questionable attitude by counsel that the HRC was unable to address can be found in *Clive Smart* v. *Trinidad and Tobago,* 29 July 1998. The petitioner had claimed that counsel had failed to properly consult with him in the case before the Court of Appeal. She had not pursued two of the grounds of appeal prepared by a different counsel, had not given the petitioner any explanations and denied him the possibility of clarifying the matter. The State party had contended that there was no merit to this allegation. It submitted an affidavit from the petitioner's counsel in Trinidad and Tobago. Subsequently (at the time of the HRC View) this counsel was sitting on the High Court of Trinidad and Tobago. The latter stated that she 'reviewed all the grounds and adopted and incorporated those with which the law and I were in agreement'. She 'did not explain this decision to Mr. Smart since these were matters exclusively with the purview of an Attorney-at-law. Mr. Smart could make no useful input in respect of such matters'. While the HRC may have been correct in concluding that there had been no violation of Article 14(3)(b) ICCPR, the case does serve as an illustration of the wide range of behaviour that still falls within 'professional judgment'. The Committee does not consider itself in a position to ascertain 'whether the alleged failure of the representatives to call witnesses who might have corroborated the authors' testimonies was a matter of professional judgment or of negligence'. HRC *Michael Sawyers and Michael and Desmond McClean* v. *Jamaica*, 11 April 1991. See also *Byron Young* v. *Jamaica*, 4 November 1997 and *Earl Pratt and Ivan Morgan* v. *Jamaica*, 6 April 1989. It is not explicit in distinguishing between the accountability of States parties in relation to privately retained and assigned counsel but, apparently, it does attach importance to distinguishing between the two. In that respect, it has considered relevant the fact that counsel was *initially* privately retained. In *Michael Sawyers and Michael and Desmond McClean* v. *Jamaica*, 11 April 1991, for instance, it noted that privately retained counsel had represented all three petitioners during trial and the same privately retained counsel had represented two of them on appeal. It also noted that a

---

that on the merits the HRC is unlikely to find violations in this respect has not hindered the use of provisional measures pending the proceedings.

The HRC tolerates many choices with possibly disadvantageous effects for the petitioner as falling within counsel's professional judgment.[87] If counsel made allegations during the trial, and protested occasionally, the HRC normally assumes that the domestic court has properly dealt with the claim.[88] At the same time, if counsel did not protest during trial, this was his professional judgment.

---

different counsel represented Mr. Sawyers. This counsel withdrew before the appeal was concluded. It then noted, between brackets, that instead a legal aid lawyer, a Queen's counsel, was appointed. "Any shortcomings regarding time for consultation and preparation of the defence cannot, therefore, be attributed to the State party". It is not clear whether the period when Mr. Sawyers had a legal aid lawyer had any significance. See also *Abduali Ismatovich Kurbanov* (*submitted by his mother Safarmo Kurbanova*) v. *Tajikistan*, 6 November 2003.

[87] For finding a violation of Article 14(3)(b) (adequate time and facilities to prepare a defence) there must always be a request for an adjournment that was then disallowed by the judge. Generally, the HRC analyses the material before it to find out whether either the petitioner or his counsel complained to the trial judge that the time or facilities were inadequate. If they did not do so the inadequate time and facilities could not be attributed to the State. Alternatively the petitioner must prove that counsel's decisions could not have been based on the exercise of his professional judgment. Sometimes the HRC points out that it could not ascertain whether the domestic court 'actually denied counsel adequate time for the preparation of the defence' or whether defence counsel's failure to call witnesses on behalf of the petitioner was a matter of counsel's professional judgment or the result of intimidation. See e.g. HRC *Raphael Henry* v. *Jamaica*, 1 November 1991 and *Delroy Prince* v. *Jamaica*, 30 March 1992. Normally the HRC considers the choices of counsel to remain within the confines of his professional judgment. Thus, when it seems to have been counsel, and not the State party, who has obstructed the preparation of the defence, it finds no violation of Article 14(3)(b). See e.g. HRC *Christopher Brown* v. *Jamaica*, 23 March 1999 and *Alrick Thomas* v. *Jamaica*, 31 March 1992.

[88] The principle of *equality of arms* is laid down in Article 14(3)(e), although not in express terms. It also underlies other aspects of Article 14. One of the issues discussed under this principle is the examination of witnesses. The HRC does not easily find violations in this respect. On this issue too it generally has faith in counsel's professional judgment. It has determined that Article 14(3)(e) 'protects the equality of arms between the prosecution and the defence in the examination of witnesses, but does not prevent the defence from waiving or not exercising its entitlement to cross-examine a prosecution witness during the trial hearing'. HRC *Glenmore Compass* v. *Jamaica*, 19 October 1993. In the absence of material disclosing whether the petitioner or his counsel complained to the trial judge that potential defence witnesses were subjected to intimidation, the HRC has considered it is 'not in a position to ascertain whether the failure of the defence to call witnesses on the author's behalf was a matter of counsel's professional judgment or the result of intimidation'. HRC *Delroy Prince* v. *Jamaica* 30 March 1992. Only occasionally it has found a violation of Article 14(3)(e). See e.g.HRC *Garfield Peart and Andrew Peart* v. *Jamaica*, 19 July 1995; *Lloyd Grant* v. *Jamaica*, 31 March 1994 and *Anthony McLeod* v. *Jamaica*, 31 March 1998. Claims often relate to counsel's failure to follow instructions, failure to request additional time to prepare the defence, failure to call alibi witnesses or general inexperience and related situations impacting on the principle of equality of arms. In such cases the HRC generally finds no indication that counsel's acts or omissions were not made in the exercise of his professional judgment. The State party normally is not responsible for the actions of counsel.

3.2.3.3 DISPUTES ABOUT FACTS AND EVIDENCE

It is also very difficult for petitioners to prove violations based on disputes about facts and evidence or claims about inadequacy of counsel. They are often facing very serious situations, with fatal consequences, that the HRC nevertheless cannot always address on the merits. The Committee is not a fourth instance of appeal and it normally dismisses such claims.[89] Again the question arises what is the function of provisional measures used in such cases.

The Committee often simply is not in a position to deal with issues arising from problematic jury behaviour and other matters of factual evidence.[90] As long as the judge has brought certain

---

[89] See e.g. HRC *Daniel Pinto* v. *Trinidad and Tobago*, 20 July 1990 (after a discussion on the merits); subsequently it dismissed these claims already in the admissibility phase; *Anthony Finn* v. *Jamaica*, 31 July 1998; *Raphael Henry* v. *Jamaica*, 1 November 1991 and *Beresford Whyte* v. *Jamaica*, 27 July 1998. In his individual opinion in *McTaggart* v. *Jamaica* (1998) Committee member Scheinin discussed the dilemma of how the HRC should deal with the lack of cooperation by some States. HRC *Deon Mc Taggart* v. *Jamaica*, 31 March 1998. In this case the petitioner had submitted substantive documentation but the State had submitted only a reply of a few pages. The HRC declared inadmissible the petitioner's Art. 14(1) claim. The Committee's dilemma, according to Scheinin, was a result of the failure by the State to respond. In such case the Committee must choose either to find violations of the Covenant on the basis of the petitioner's allegations or examine 'the extensive documentation submitted on behalf of the author in order to make an autonomous investigation of the merits of each allegation'. He argued that '[b]oth of these approaches are untenable and bear the risk of errors which, in death penalty cases, may be lethal in the literal meaning of the term'. "The only alternative to these two approaches would be to request additional information and clarifications from the parties, an option the Committee is unwilling to take both because of its extremely scarce resources and because of the fully justified aim of expeditious handling of death penalty cases". He drew attention to an important issue for adjudication: the impact of the manner in which the facts are presented on the actual determination of a case. The narrative presented by the Committee 'appears coherent but represents only a reconstruction of what might have happened at the scene of the crime'. After discussing the reliability of the trial testimony by the only witness who identified the petitioner, he pointed out that '[i]t is obvious to me that the trial testimony by David Morris is unreliable and that the Committee should not have altered the 'narrative' of the events in order to add coherence to the case of the prosecution'. He agreed that it was for the domestic appeals courts to review jury instructions by the judge and the conduct of the trial, but his argument here was that the *prerequisites* of a fair trial had been denied. HRC *Deon Mc Taggart* v. *Jamaica*, 31 March 1998.

[90] See e.g. HRC *Byron Young* v. *Jamaica*, 4 November 1997. See also the case of co-defendant *Samuel Thomas* v. *Jamaica*, 31 March 1999. The third co-defendant was Hixford Morrison, see *Hixford Morrison* v. *Jamaica*, 31 July 1998. Counsel had argued that irregularities in the course of the jury deliberations constituted a violation of Article 14. Two jurors had come forward with sworn affidavits stating that only three of twelve jurors found the man guilty, but it was getting late and the jury foreman was pressuring them so they told him just to do what he wanted. It was argued that the judge had had a responsibility in this because he had pressured for a unanimous verdict and had sent the jury back several times. In *Young* HRC member Bhagwati apparently questioned the reliability of the affidavits in question, because of the immoral character of these two jurors. It is equally possible that these jurors came forward now because they had the courage to admit that they had acted under pressure, while the other jurors who did not come forward have erased this from their memories. The fact still remains of course, as Bhagwati pointed out, that 'jurors cannot be required to disclose which way they voted in the verdict. There is an obligation of confidentiality upon them. The State could not have therefore enquired from the other jurors as to what was their verdict'. In *Thomas* Solari Yrigoyen dissented, taking a position quite different from that of Bhagwati expressed two years previously. He noted that it is the State

issues, such as medical evidence, to the attention of the jury, the fact that the jury chooses to ignore this does not constitute a violation of the right to a fair trial. Neither does the short time the jury takes for deliberations (such as seventeen minutes).[91]

The HRC usually does not sustain complaints about the jury instructions and the attitude of the judge, especially when counsel failed to object during the trial.[92] In one case the petitioner had claimed, among others, that the trial judge fundamentally erred in directing the jury that it was 'safer and better' to convict on the basis of circumstantial evidence. Still, the HRC considered that the material before the Committee did not show that the jury instructions were clearly arbitrary or amounted to a denial of justice.[93] It is generally beyond the Committee's competence to evaluate jury instructions. It normally declares these claims inadmissible.[94] It makes an exception, however, vis-à-vis claims that these instructions were clearly arbitrary or amounted to a denial of justice or that the judge manifestly violated his obligation of impartiality.[95] In such cases, the Committee examines the claim in order to find out whether the jury instructions were indeed

---

party's responsibility to provide for competent, independent and impartial courts of justice established by law to produce a determination of any criminal charge, in accordance with Article 14. He considered that the sworn statements of the two jury members, which were not rebutted by the State party, showed that the foreman acted irregularly by pressuring the members of the jury to deliver a unanimous verdict when nine of them believed that the petitioner was not guilty and only three believed the opposite. The change made in the announcement of the verdict showed that the petitioner did not enjoy the due process accorded by Art. 14 to defendants in criminal cases. "This circumstance is particularly serious in view of the fact that the verdict announced as having been reached by the jury amounts to a death sentence for the convicted person".

[91] See e.g., HRC *Leaford Smith* v. *Jamaica*, 31 March 1993 and *Beresford Whyte* v. *Jamaica*, 27 July 1998.

[92] HRC *Willard Collins* v. *Jamaica*, 1 November 1991 (Chanet, Herndl, Aguilar Urbina and Wennergren would have found a violation of Article 14(1) because of bias of the judge).

[93] HRC *Everton Morrison* v. *Jamaica*, 27 July 1998 and *Clarence Marshall* v. *Jamaica*, 3 November 1998. See also *Trevor Bennett* v. *Jamaica*, 25 March 1999. In this case the Committee referred to the Court of Appeal's review of the judge's instructions, while it had previously noted, under "the facts as submitted by the author" that the Court of Appeal of Jamaica had refused the application for leave to appeal. A refusal of an application for leave to appeal, presumably, is not the same as the review of the appeal itself. If this review did not take place, it is not clear how the Committee could have noted it.

[94] See e.g. HRC *R.M.* v. *Trinidad and Tobago*, 29 October 1993 (inadm.). Like the HRC the Inter-American Commission considers that it is generally for the domestic courts to review the factual evidence in a given case. In *Sankofa* v. *US*, however, it found that the treatment of identification and ballistic evidence amounted to a denial of justice contrary to the fair trial and due process standards of the American Declaration. CIDH *Shaka Sankofa (Gary Graham)* v. *US*, 29 December 2003, §§42-49.

[95] See e.g., HRC *Daniel Pinto* v. *Trinidad and Tobago*, 20 July 1990; *Carlton Reid* v. *Jamaica*, 20 July 1990; *Paul Kelly* v. *Jamaica*, 8 April 1991; *Michael Sawyers and Michael and Desmond McClean* v. *Jamaica*, 11 April 1991; *Aston Little* v. *Jamaica*, 1 November 1991; *Raphael Henry* v. *Jamaica*, 1 November 1991; *Glenford Campbell* v. *Jamaica*, 30 March 1992; *Clifton Wright* v. *Jamaica*, 27 July 1992 (an unusual case in which the HRC found a violation of Article 14(1) for a denial of justice); *George Graham and Arthur Morrison* v. *Jamaica*, 25 March 1996; *Clifford McLawrence* v. *Jamaica*, 18 July 1997; *Byron Young* v. *Jamaica*, 4 November 1997; *Deon Mc Taggart* v. *Jamaica*, 31 March 1998; *Anthony McLeod* v. *Jamaica*, 31 March 1998; *Anthony Finn* v. *Jamaica*, 31 July 1998; *Beresford Whyte* v. *Jamaica*, 27 July 1998; *Dole Chadee et al* v. *Trinidad and Tobago*, 29 July 1998; *Christopher Brown* v. *Jamaica*, 23 March 1999; *Samuel Thomas* v. *Jamaica*, 31 March 1999 and *Mohammed Ajaz and Amir Jamil* v. *Korea*, 13 July 1999.

clearly arbitrary or did indeed amount to a denial of justice or in order to find whether it was indeed demonstrated that the judge manifestly violated his obligation of impartiality.[96] The HRC takes into account information derived not just directly from the facts as stated by either the petitioners or the State party but also from the domestic court's judgments and the trial transcript.[97] Sometimes the result is favourable to the petitioner,[98] but often to the State, because of the Committee's reliance on the facts and evidence as established domestically. The HRC may acknowledge that the allegations and the trial transcript suggest deficiencies in the evidence, but normally it does not consider that this amounts to arbitrariness or a violation of the obligation of impartiality.[99] It usually concludes, on the basis of the trial transcripts, that the conduct of the trial or the

---

[96]   See, e.g., HRC *Carlton Reid* v. *Jamaica*, 20 July 1990. The HRC also found violations of Art. 14(1) in cases against Guyana and Tajikistan. In *Lallman Mulai and Bharatraj Mulai (submitted by their sister Rookmin Mulai)* v. *Republic of Guyana*, 20 July 2004, for instance, it noted that it was 'not in the position to establish that the performance and the conclusions reached by the jury and the foreman in fact reflected partiality and bias' against both petitioners. It appeared that the Court of Appeal did deal with the issue of possible rights. Nevertheless, the court 'did not address that part of the grounds of appeal that related to' the right before the courts, 'on the strength of which the defence might have moved for the trial to be aborted'. In *Abduali Ismatovich Kurbanov (submitted by his mother Safarmo Kurbanova)* v. *Tajikistan*, 6 November 2003. it found a violation because the State had not provided 'any explanation as to why the trial was conducted, at first instance, by the Military Chamber of the Supreme Court'. 'In the absence of any information by the State party to justify a trial before a military court' the trial and death sentence of the petitioner's son, who was a civilian, did not meet the requirements of Article 14(1). In *Gaibullodzhon Ilyasovich Saidov (submitted by his wife Barno Saidova)* v. *Tajikistan*, 8 July 2004 the HRC noted the petitioner's claim that her husband's right to a fair trial was violated, among others 'by the fact that the judge conducted the trial in a biased manner and refused even to consider the revocation of the confessions made by Mr. Saidov during the investigation'. 'No explanation was provided by the State party for the reasons of that situation'. Thus, 'on the strength of the material before it', it found a violation of Article 14(1). With regard to these confessions it is noteworthy that the HRC found that due weight must be given to the claim that the confession had been extracted under torture, since the State had failed to either indicate how the court had investigated these allegations or to provide copies of any medical reports. The Committee found violations of Articles 7 and 14(3)(g) because his conviction was based on a confession obtained under duress. Finally, in *Bakhrom Khomidov (submitted by his mother Saodat Khomidova)* v. *Tajikistan*, 29 July 2004 it found violations of Article 14(1) and (3)(e) and (g). In the absence of any pertinent information by the State party it found that the court did not fulfil its obligation of impartiality and independence. Moreover, the judge denied the request by counsel to call witnesses and to have his client examined by a doctor.

[97]   See e.g. HRC *Anthony Finn* v. *Jamaica*, 31 July 1998. See also *Clarence Marshall* v. *Jamaica*, 3 November 1998.

[98]   For an example see HRC *Collin Smartt (submitted by his mother Daphne Smartt)* v. *Republic of Guyana*, 6 July 2004. In this case the HRC noted *proprio motu*, when it was considering the admissibility of the case, 'that the trial documents submitted by the author reveal that her son was not represented by counsel during the committal hearings'. It also noted with concern 'that, despite three reminders addressed to it, the State party has failed to comment on the communication'. The petitioner was not represented by counsel in her petition to the HRC.

[99]   See e.g. HRC *Anthony McLeod* v. *Jamaica*, 31 March 1998. It does not automatically find a violation if the State party does not contest the claim. It considers the material before it in order to ascertain whether the petitioner has sufficiently substantiated his allegation. If the prosecutor, for instance, successfully challenged the claim in court, the HRC finds itself unable to conclude a violation of Articles 7 and 14(3)(g). See e.g., *Paul Kelly* v. *Jamaica*, 8 April 1991 and *Glenford*

judge's instructions to the jury were not 'clearly arbitrary' and did not amount to a denial of justice, or it concludes that the judge had not manifestly violated his obligation of impartiality.[100]

Maybe if the State plays it procedurally correct at the domestic and international level, there is simply not much international bodies can do about claims of improper jury instructions and similar issues. It would mainly be the NGOs and media that could achieve change if court cases systematically result in irreparable harm to individuals or groups. They could investigate and

---

Campbell v. *Jamaica*, 30 March 1992. Another example is when the judge had examined the claim at the trial during a *voir dire* and found it lacking in substance. See e.g., *Errol Johnson* v. *Jamaica*, 22 March 1996. See also the individual opinions of Solari Irigoyen and Scheinin in *Terrence Sahadeo* (*submitted by his sister Margaret Paul*) v. *Republic of Guyana*, 1 November 2001. Scheinin noted that it appeared from 'the incomplete materials submitted to the Committee that when presenting the evidence related to the credibility of Mr. Sahadeo's testimony that he signed the confession statement under ill treatment, the presiding judge used language that was prejudicial to the defendant. For instance, he referred to Mr. Sahadeo's colour of skin as basis for an inference that ill treatment would have left marks that would have been visible in the medical inspection that took place afterwards, in addition to the bruise on the toe that was recorded. As the court, consequently, did not address the issue of the possible coercion and ill treatment in a proper way in a case that led to the imposition of capital punishment, I find that there has been a violation of articles 7 and 14 of the Covenant'. Moreover, 'the mere fact that no allegation of torture was made in the domestic appeal proceedings can not as such be held against the alleged victim if it is proposed, (…) that such an allegation was in fact made during the actual trial but was neither recorded nor acted upon'. In such case due weight must be given to the allegations, in light of the details given by the petitioner, the unavailability of a trial transcript and the absence of any further explanations from the State party. HRC *Abduali Ismatovich Kurbanov* (*submitted by his mother Safarmo Kurbanova*) v. *Tajikistan*, 6 November 2003.

[100] Even in a case in which the State initially failed to make available the trial transcripts and domestic judgments and later only provided copies of English translations of these judgments, but not the originals nor the trial transcripts, the HRC did not shift the burden of proof to the State. HRC *Mohammed Ajaz and Amir Jamil* v. *Korea*, 13 July 1999. In reply to the Committee's request for the trial transcripts and the judgments in the case, Korea stated that it maintained as a rule "[t]hat it is not allowed to peruse, photocopy and transmit the records of closed cases in order to protect the safety of victims and witnesses and the repute of defendants". Later the State party did provide copies of English translations of the courts' judgments. Apparently the originals were not provided, nor the file transcripts. From these translations, the Committee concluded that it appeared, among others, "that the District Court considered the voluntariness of the statements made by the defendants, but that in the light of the testimonies it found no sustainable reason to doubt the voluntariness of the statements". Thus, the Committee noted that the applicants' claims that the evidence to convict them was insufficient, that they had been tortured in order to force them to confess, and that mistakes occurred in the translations of their statements, were examined by the court of first instance and the court of appeal. Both Courts rejected their claims. The Committee reiterated that it was not for the Committee, but for the courts of States parties, to evaluate the facts and evidence in a specific case, unless it could be ascertained that the evaluation was clearly arbitrary or amounted to a denial of justice. It did regret that the State party did not provide a copy of the trial transcript, for this had prevented the Committee from examining fully the conduct of the trial. However, after consideration of the judgments of the District Court and the High Court, and in particular their evaluation of the claims subsequently made to the Committee, the Committee did not find that those evaluations were arbitrary or amounted to a denial of justice or that the authors had raised before the Committee any issues beyond those so evaluated by the domestic courts. The Committee concluded that none of the articles of the ICCPR had been violated.

report on the question whether there is true equality of arms and whether courts are sufficiently informed and aware of certain issues and not just go through the motions.

Yet the HRC and the Inter-American Commission did not just use provisional measures in cases that, already at that stage, clearly appeared to be arbitrary or amounted to a denial of justice. Many provisional measures used in cases that included claims of an unfair trial in violation of Article 14 ICCPR, but in which the HRC did not find a violation of this article, have performed no function relating to the claim on the merits other than postponing the execution for the sake of postponement.[101] In these cases the Committee found that the facts before it did not disclose any violation of the provisions of the Covenant, that there was insufficient evidence of a violation or that the claim dealt with facts and evidence in a particular case and it was not for the Committee to evaluate these.[102] In other cases the HRC did find violations, but not of Article 14. At the time of submission, it made sense to use provisional measures, as there was a possibility the Committee would conclude a violation of Art. 14 meaning that the remedy would be commutation.[103]

In my view the *type* of violation claimed is more significant for a decision to use provisional measures than the extent of the evidence available at the stage of provisional measures. What should be the most important criterion for using provisional measures is the Rapporteur's expecta-

---

[101] In a few of these cases the death sentence had already been commuted, but in others the petitioners were still awaiting execution. After the finding of no violation the State can execute the petitioner as planned.

[102] HRC *Michael Sawyers and Michael and Desmond McClean* v. *Jamaica* (provisional measures in pre-Rapporteur period); *Irvine Reynolds* v. *Jamaica*, 8 April 1991 (idem). The HRC concluded that there was no violation of Art. 14 'after considering those parts of the judge's instructions that were made available to it'. It seems that in this case the State was rewarded for general unresponsiveness and for providing an incomplete trial transcript; *Dole Chadee et al* v. *Trinidad and Tobago*, 29 July 1998. Scheinin's dissent related to both the prison conditions and the fairness of the trial. The partial dissent of Klein and Kretzmer related to the quality of the water provided in jail. Pocar, who had been the Special Rapporteur deciding on the provisional measure was not present in July 1998 when the Committee decided the case. *Dante Piandiong, Jesus Morallos and Archie Bulan (deceased)* (*submitted by Alexander Padilla and Ricardo III Sunga*) v. *the Philippines*, 19 October 2000. Three persons had been executed while the case was still pending, despite a provisional measure. See Chapter XVII for a discussion of the State party's official responses towards these provisional measures and the response by the HRC. It did point out that the substance of the claim appeared to raise important questions. One of these was 'whether or not the crime for which they were convicted was a most serious crime as stipulated by article 6(2). Another was 'whether the re-introduction of the death penalty in the Philippines is in compliance with the State party's obligations under article 6(1) (2) and (6) of the Covenant'. It considered, however, that it was not in a position to address the issues in this case because neither counsel nor the State had made submissions in this respect. Apparently this was different from the situation in which it considered issues *proprio motu*. In short, it could not make a finding of a violation of any of the articles of the ICCPR. At the same time it reiterated its conclusion that 'the State committed a grave breach of its obligations under the Protocol by putting the alleged victims to death before the Committee had concluded its consideration of the Communication'. Evatt and Medina Quiroga dissented on the issue of fair trial, considering that the alleged defects in the identification parade left serious questions about the fairness of the trial. Chanet considered that the accused should have been provided with a lawyer during the line-up identification. As this was not done, the HRC should have found violations of Articles 14(3)(b) and (d) and 6. Scheinin, finally, considered that the State should have provided legal assistance during the 6-8 months of pre-trial detention.

[103] See Chapter XIII on the relationship with forms of reparation.

tion of the remedy the Committee would recommend *if* it would find a violation.[104] The HRC takes seriously its subsidiary role in the system of human rights protection. It assumes that the domestic courts 'have got it right'. Despite the difficulty of proving violations of Art. 14 there is always a remote possibility that the HRC will find a denial of justice or clear arbitrariness in the court's or jury's handling of the facts and evidence or in the judge's instructions to the jury.

In its case law the HRC has not clarified what are the criteria to assess the risk for the use of provisional measures. It would be virtually impossible for the petitioner to provide information indicating, for instance, a violation of Article 14 ICCPR amounting to a denial of justice, already when he requests the HRC to take provisional measures halting an execution. More than some *prima facie* evidence of a claim should not be required.

As the HRC has not indicated that it requires a certain level of evidence before it would use provisional measures to halt an execution, the Rapporteur correctly uses provisional measures also in all cases involving claims of a violation of Article 14. Given the difficulty in establishing such a violation, combined with the importance of the right to life, it would be unreasonable to require the petitioner to already do so at the stage of provisional measures. Hence, if there is a possibility that the HRC finds a violation, even if remote, the HRC, in my view, is justified in its use of provisional measures to halt an execution.[105]

3.2.4 Non-refoulement cases and assessment of risk

3.2.4.1 INTRODUCTION

Internationally, both the HRC and CAT have dealt with cases involving claims that the expulsion or extradition of the petition would result in a violation of the principle of non-refoulement. In addition, the European system has dealt with the issue of non-refoulement very often as well. An important factor in their case law has been that of the evidentiary requirements for a 'real risk' on the merits.[106]

Certain States, such as Australia and Canada, have put pressure on the individual complaint systems of the ICCPR and the Convention against Torture.[107] At times the supervisory Committees to both treaties may have felt inclined to take a rather limited approach, certainly to the evidentiary requirements on the merits,[108] but also to the use of provisional measures. They may use them more sparingly and in fewer situations than legally might be possible. This is relevant in the context of the type of cases in which provisional measures are used, but particularly in the context of the assessment of evidence.

This section first deals with the assessment of risk by CAT and the HRC. It also examines the approach to assessment of risk in the European system. It singles out the issue of the evidence required for lifting provisional measures and the issue of diplomatic assurances.

---

[104] See Chapter III (Halting executions) and Chapter XIII (Protection) on the relationship with reparation.

[105] This depends of course on the obligations on the merits and forms of reparation required by it, as discussed in Chapter XIII (Protection).

[106] See in general on this issue e.g. Battjes (2006).

[107] Interview of author with HRC Special Rapporteur Martin Scheinin, Maastricht 20 September 2002.

[108] CAT has recalled 'that it is normally for the complainant to present an arguable case and that the risk of torture must be assessed on grounds that go beyond mere theory and suspicion'. *C.A.R.M.* v. *Canada*, 18 May 2007, §8.10; *M.Z.* v. *Sweden*, 12 May 2006, §9.3; *M.A.K.* v. *Germany*, 12 May 2004, §13.5; and *S.L.* v. *Sweden*, 11 May 2001, §6.3.

3.2.4.2 ASSESSMENT OF RISK BY CAT

In 1997 CAT devoted a General Comment on its assessment of risk on the merits. It noted that 'the burden is upon the author to present an arguable case' of a violation of Art. 3 on the merits. This means that 'there must be a factual basis for the author's position sufficient to require a response from the State party'.[109] The 'risk of torture must be assessed on grounds that go beyond mere theory or suspicion. However, the risk does not have to meet the test of being highly probable'.[110] The petitioner must show 'substantial grounds' for his or her belief to be in danger of being tortured and this danger must be 'personal and present'.[111] Pertinent information would include, and the Committee has noted that this list is non-exhaustive, evidence of a consistent pattern of gross, flagrant or mass violations of human rights; the fact that the petitioner has been 'tortured or maltreated by or at the instigation of or with the consent or acquiescence of a public official or other person acting in an official capacity' in the (recent) past; any medical or other independent evidence to support a claim by the petitioner in this respect. CAT would also consider as pertinent information to the effect that the situation has since changed; that the petitioner has 'engaged in political or other activity within or outside the State concerned which would appear to make him/her particularly vulnerable to the risk of being placed in danger of torture were he/she to be expelled, returned or extradited to the State in question'; 'any evidence as to the credibility of the author and any relevant factual inconsistencies in the petitioner's claim.[112] These criteria all appear relevant already at the stage of provisional measures.

In its General Comment CAT noted that 'Bearing in mind that the Committee against Torture is not an appellate, a quasi-judicial or an administrative body, but rather a monitoring body created by the States parties themselves with declaratory powers only, it follows that: (a) Considerable weight will be given, in exercising the Committee's jurisdiction pursuant to article 3 of the Convention, to findings of fact that are made by organs of the State party concerned; but (b) The Committee is not bound by such findings and instead has the power, provided by article 22, paragraph 4, of the Convention, of free assessment of the facts based upon the full set of circumstances in every case".[113]

'Complete accuracy' cannot be expected from victims of torture. Contradictory submissions presented by the petitioner do not necessarily make a complaint unfounded, particularly when it has been shown that the petition suffers form a post traumatic stress syndrome.[114] Yet a complaint involving risk of violation of Article 3 should be detailed sufficiently or there should be sufficient circumstantial evidence for a shift in the burden of proof.[115]

---

[109] CAT General Comment 1 of 21 November 1997 on Communications concerning the return of a person to a State where there may be grounds he would be subjected to torture (Article 3 in the context of Article 22), §5.

[110] Id., §6.

[111] Id., §7.

[112] Id., §8.

[113] Id., §9. See also Bruin (1998), pp. 145-150. A more recent example is *C.T. and K.M.* v. *Sweden*, 17 November 2006.

[114] See e.g. CAT *Alan* v. *Switzerland*, 28 May 1996 and *Tala* v. *Sweden*, 15 November 1996. See also, more recently, *V.L.* v. *Switzerland*, 20 November 2006.

[115] This also includes plausible explanations for and the story of the petitioner's flight, e.g. *S.P.A.* v. *Canada*, 7 November 2006, §7.5 ("the Committee deems that the complainant has not submitted sufficient details or corroborating evidence to shift the burden of proof. In particular, she has not adduced satisfactory evidence or details relating to her detention or escape from detention. Further, she has failed to provide plausible explanations for her failure or inability to provide certain details which would have been of relevance to buttress her case, such as her stay for over

At the admissibility stage the petitioner already must provide evidence indicating that the petition is not manifestly unfounded.[116] On the merits the risk faced by the petition must be 'foreseeable, real and personal'.[117] It is normally for the petitioner 'to present an arguable case'. The risk of torture 'must be assessed on grounds that go beyond mere theory and suspicion'. The risk does not need to meet the test of 'highly probable', but the petitioner must provide 'sufficiently reliable evidence' which would 'justify a shift of the burden of proof to the State party'.[118]

After the first few years dealing with individual complaints CAT became rather strict in its interpretation of what constitutes 'personal risk', although more recently it appears at times to return to a more critical approach to the arguments of the State.[119]

CAT has 'conceptualized the formal and substantive criteria applied by the Rapporteur for new complaints and interim measures in granting or rejecting requests for interim measures of protection'.[120] In this respect it has noted that for the Rapporteur to use provisional measures a petition 'must have a substantial likelihood of success on the merits for it to be concluded that the alleged victim would suffer irreparable harm in the event of his or her deportation'.[121] This statement refers both to evidentiary requirements and to the applicable substantive law.[122]

---

three months in Kermanshah and the names of those who helped her to escape. Finally, the Committee deems that she has failed to provide plausible explanations for her subsequent journey through seven countries, including some asylum countries, prior to finally claiming refugee status in Canada").

[116] See e.g. CAT *I.A.O.* v. *Sweden*, 6 May 1998 (inadm.: no 'substantial grounds').

[117] See e.g. CAT *A.R.* v. *The Netherlands*, 21 November 2003, §7.3 and *S.S. and S.A.* v. *the Netherlands*, 11 May 2001 (no violation).

[118] See e.g. CAT *M.A.K.* v. *Germany*, 12 May 2004, §13.5. CAT is not always consistent in its phrasing, see e.g. *Gamal El Rgeig* v. *Switserland*, 15 November 2006 and *JV* 2006, 160 annotated by Spijkerboer.

[119] In the period covered by its Annual Report 2000 it discussed nine cases involving non-refoulement claims. In one case it found a violation. In the other cases it did not. Five times because it considered there were no 'substantial grounds'; twice because it considered that the risk was limited given the considerable time that had passed; once because the petitioner, who had been expelled pending the proceedings before CAT, in practice was not tortured upon return and once because the complaint was not convincing. In the period covered by its Annual Report 2005 it found violations in four of the nine non-refoulement cases. In the period covered by its Annual Report 2006, on the merits CAT dealt with the issue of non-refoulement nine times. On one occasion it did find a violation of Article 3 but in the other cases it did not. In its Annual Report 2007 (covering the Fall 2006 and Spring 2007 sessions), in 12 non-refoulement cases it found no violation and in seven cases it did find a violation. Its more critical approach is reflected in particular in its discussion of diplomatic assurances, see *infra*.

[120] See CAT Annual Report 2005, §135; Annual Report 2006, §61; Annual Report 2007, §70.

[121] Ibid.

[122] As to the relevance of the latter, see Chapter V (Non-refoulement). Since CAT adapted its practice with regard to provisional measures there was an expectation that more petitioners would resort to the HRC in expulsion cases. Interview by author with HRC Special Rapporteur Martin Scheinin, Maastricht 20 September 2002. By April 2003, however, there was no evidence of this yet. Interview by author with HRC Special Rapporteur Martin Scheinin, Geneva, April 2003. Of the 33 Views referred to in its Annual Report 2006, A/61/44, 1 November 2006, discussing the follow up on CAT's findings of violations 'up to the thirty-fourth session', 21 related to Article 3 (non-refoulement). In 20 of the 21 cases provisional measures were used pending the proceedings. In the one case in which they were not, the removal had taken place before the petitioner could apply to CAT (*Agiza* v. *Sweden*). Until 2003 it took provisional measures more than 80 times. These approximate numbers in themselves also indicate that CAT is considerably

CAT is considerably less strict in its use of provisional measures than it is on the merits. Given the absence of consistent publication of information on the use of provisional measures, including statistics, it is difficult to assess to what extent their use decreased upon the Committee's adoption of guidelines as to the use of provisional measures. In fact it must be kept in mind that both before and after the adoption of these guidelines, there have been occasions on which it refused to take provisional measures in non-refoulement cases, but at the same time it has continued to use them in the majority of cases.[123]

3.2.4.3 ASSESSMENT OF RISK BY THE HRC

The HRC has not discussed the evidence required on the merits, let alone that required at the stage of provisional measures, to the same extent as CAT. Yet it has also dealt with the issue of non-refoulement in expulsion and extradition cases. In fact the question which test to apply to establish real risk is one of the main questions arising on the merits in non-refoulement cases under the ICCPR. This question may be expected to play a role as well at the provisional measures stage.[124]

As discussed in the context of the evidence required for the use of provisional measures to halt the execution of the death penalty, in the practice of the HRC we see that the Rapporteur transmits the case to the State once there is a certain amount of evidence and, possibly, once there are some questions to be posed to the State. It is also at this stage that the Rapporteur normally

---

less strict in its use of provisional measures than it is on the merits. Yet since the introduction of a Rapporteur to deal with requests for provisional measures, the latter would ask the secretariat to make a quick assessment on the substance of the complaint and whether there was prima facie evidence of risk. Reportedly, this resulted in the use of provisional measures in a lower percentage of cases. About 60 to 70 % according to an estimate made at the secretariat in Geneva in October 2003.

[123] See e.g. the following cases in which provisional measures were used, but in which subsequently no violation was found for failure to substantiate: CAT *E.R.K and Y.K.* v. *Sweden* 30 April 2007; *T.A.* v. *Sweden*, 22 November 2007; *Z.K.* v. *Sweden*, 9 May 2008 and *R.K. et al.* v. *Sweden*, 16 May 2008. In one case in which no violation was found on the merits the Rapporteur decided *not* to use provisional measures (decision of 30 January 2007): *M.X.* v. *Switzerland*, 7 May 2008, §1.2. Another case, in which provisional measures *were* used, was subsequently declared inadmissible as the claim did not 'rise to the basic level of substantiation required for purposes of admissibility', see *K.A.* v. *Sweden*, 16 November 2007 (inadm.) §7.2. In this case the Rapporteur added that his request for provisional measures, of 24 November 2006, was made on the basis of the information contained in the petitioner's submissions and could be reviewed at the request of the State in light of information and comments from the State and the petitioner, §1.5. Following this request, on 5 December 2006, the Swedish Migration Board decided to stay the enforcement of the expulsion orders, §1.6. On official responses see Chapter XVII.

[124] As in the other systems, provisional measures have been used in cases in which subsequently no violation was found on the merits, or in cases that were later declared inadmissible as insufficiently substantiated. See e.g. HRC *Daljit Singh* v. *Canada*, 30 March 2006 (inadm.). In this case the Rapporteur had initially used a qualified provisional measure on 5 November 2004, requesting the State not to deport the petitioner 'before it provides the Committee with information as to whether it intends to remove' him to India, and before providing the Committee with its observations on the communication. Following a request for clarification the Committee requested the State, on 9 November 2004, 'not to deport Mr. Daljit Singh to India before the State party has made its observations either on admissibility or the merits of the author's allegations and the Committee has acknowledged receipt'. §1.2.

uses provisional measures, although there are exceptions. There have been instances in which the Rapporteur used provisional measures before he or she ordered the Secretariat to transmit the petitioner's submission to the State for comment. In other words, while the HRC generally seems to use the same criterion for *prima facie* evidence for decisions to transmit the case and for decisions to use provisional measures, there are situations in which material and temporal urgency warrant the use of provisional measures even though the Rapporteur considers that insufficient information is available to transmit the case to the State.

From the perspective of non-refoulement the main difference between extradition and other forms of removal is that it is easier for the alleged victim to show that his *extradition* is likely to expose him to torture or ill treatment than his *expulsion*, exactly because in cases of extradition it is certain he faces detention upon return. This applies even more to the situation in which he is facing a *punishment* in the requesting country that would violate the obligations of the sending country.[125]

The HRC's first expulsion case, dating from 1978, gives some indication of the assessment of risk at the stage of provisional measures. It used provisional measures and decided to inform the petitioner that unless he provided the information requested, within certain time limits, the HRC might conclude that he no longer wished it to continue consideration of the case.[126] Obviously if this failure to provide further information could result in a discontinuation of the case, it could also result in withdrawal of the provisional measures.

In extradition cases the HRC decided that a test of 'necessary and foreseeable' consequences of the removal to the petitioner was to be applied in its decisions on the merits.[127] However, this

---

[125] In connection with a possibly conflicting obligation under an extradition treaty, invoked by Canada, the HRC stated: "A State party to the Covenant is required to ensure that it carries out all its other legal commitments in a manner consistent with the Covenant". HRC *Kindler* v. *Canada*, 30 July 1993, §13.1. See in general about this issue Smeulers (2002), pp. 11-73.

[126] HRC *O.E.* v. *S.*, 26 July 1978.

[127] See e.g. HRC *Ng* v. *Canada*, 5 November 1993, §6.2. It pointed out that the State's duty under Article 2 ICCPR 'would be negated by the handing over of a person to another State (whether a State party to the Covenant or not) where treatment contrary to the Covenant is certain or is the very purpose of the handing over'. As an example, the HRC mentioned that the State party would violate the ICCPR 'if it handed over a person to another State in circumstances in which it was foreseeable that torture would take place'. Given the example, it seems that certainty is not required but rather foreseeability. Accordingly, the 'foreseeability of the consequence would mean that there was a present violation by the State party, even though the consequence would not occur until later on'. With regard to the assessment of risk the HRC recalled the following: "(a) California had sought the author's extradition on charges which, if proven, carry the death penalty; (b) the United States requested Ng's extradition on those capital charges; (c) the extradition warrant documents the existence of a prima facie case against the author; (d) United States prosecutors involved in the case have stated that they would ask for the death penalty to be imposed; and (e) the state of California, when intervening before the Supreme Court of Canada did not disavow the prosecutors' position". *Ng* v. *Canada*, §13.5. Committee member Aguilar Urbina briefly referred to the State's argument that the petitioner could not be considered a victim because the allegations were derived from assumptions about 'possible future events, which may not materialise and which are dependent on the law and actions of the United States'. He pointed out that the 'foreseeability' of a future event referred to the question 'whether, according to common sense, it may happen, in the absence of exceptional events that prevent it from occurring'. At the same time 'necessity' referred to future events that 'will inevitably occur, unless exceptional events prevent it from happening'. He agreed with the views of the majority, finding that the petitioner 'would necessarily and foreseeably be executed'. *Ng* v. *Canada*, dissenting opinion Aguilar Urbina, §5. On the issue of necessary and foreseeable consequences

test may be too difficult to meet for petitioners even in *extradition* cases. In addition, the HRC takes a narrow view of what is 'necessary and foreseeable' and has pointed out that it is not a fourth instance of appeal, meaning that it is not within its competence to review sentences of domestic courts.[128] Generally it does not consider itself competent to review facts and evidence already decided on by domestic courts. This leads exception if the petitioner can show arbitrariness or a 'denial of justice'.[129]

Of course there are cases where a finding of a risk in an extradition case would appear self-evident given the type of information available at that stage, also with a test of 'necessary and foreseeable'. When the prosecutor is seeking the death penalty this indicates a real risk in itself.[130] In light of the practice in the US, the fact that accomplices did not receive the death penalty gives no indication about the fate of the petitioner. Such results depend on the quality of the defence, on what the prosecutor has invested in the domestic case, as well as other circumstances. Obviously in such cases provisional measures have been used.[131]

E.G. v. *Canada* (disc. 1997)[132] is relevant with regard to assessing risk in the context of the credibility of assurances against the death penalty at the stage of the merits as well as provisional measures. At the time the HRC did not consider that Canada was under an obligation to request assurances of the US that the death penalty would not be sought, but in this case Canada apparently did request them. Counsel for the petitioner referred to a report from a Florida newspaper about another person who had been extradited from Canada 'under essentially the same circumstances'.[133] In that case Florida prosecutors had given assurances that the death penalty would not be imposed, but once he was extradited they suggested they were not bound by this undertaking. 'Given the ambivalence of Florida prosecutors' about such undertakings, he noted, there was a real risk that the petitioner would be exposed to the death penalty by electrocution. Moreover, he pointed out that the federal government gave no assurances against the death penalty.[134] Initially

---

Committee member Lallah has considered that it was sufficient that the offence for which the petitioner faced trial in the US in principle carried the death penalty. He was thus facing a charge placing his life in jeopardy. The fact that one petitioner had already been tried and sentenced to death when the HRC adopted its Views, while another had not, made no material defence. *Cox* v. *Canada*, 31 October 1994, dissenting opinion Lallah. See also *Kindler* v. *Canada*, 30 July 1993.

[128] HRC *Ng* v. *Canada*, 5 November 1993, §15.2.

[129] See e.g. HRC *Agabekova* v. *Uzbekistan*, 16 March 2007. For exceptional (death penalty) cases in which it did dispute the approach by the domestic court see e.g. *Clifton Wright* v. *Jamaica*, 27 July 1992; *Mulai* v. *Guyana*, 20 July 2004 and several cases against Tajikistan, e.g. *Khomidova* (*on behalf of her son Khomidov*) v. *Tajikistan*, 29 July 2004.

[130] The group of persons protected under Article 6 ICCPR would otherwise be extremely limited. Only people like Kindler who have already been sentenced to death and have somehow been able to escape from the US to another State would run a 'real risk' of the death penalty upon extradition to the US.

[131] See e.g. the aforementioned HRC cases *Kindler, Ng and Cox* v. *Canada*.

[132] HRC *E.G.* v. *Canada*, 738/1997, disc. 17 November 1997; initial submission 5 January 1997, received 7 January 1997 with newspaper clipping of the Orlando sentinel of 18 September 1996, provisional measures of 17 January 1997; discontinued November 1997, including withdrawal of provisional measures (on file with the author).

[133] Ibid.

[134] HRC *E.G.* v. *Canada*, 738/1997, disc. 17 November 1997, "While it is true that your petitioner is not now charged with a capital offence, this can change simply by increasing the quantity of marijuana in the charge. There is nothing in international extradition law to confirm that this would violate the rule of specialty and extradition treaties, such as the Canada-US treaty, which affirm this rule". While the petitioner was reassured by a comment in the Canadian response

the HRC used provisional measures,[135] but it appears from the file that the State party was keen on their withdrawal and the Rapporteur decided that there was no need to maintain them. He had made his decision 'after careful consideration and upon reflection' and 'on the basis of the assurances obtained by the Canadian Government from United States authorities, to the effect that the death penalty will not be sought against and imposed on' the petitioner.[136]

Sometimes a risk of the death penalty has also played a role in expulsion cases. In *G.T.* v. *Australia* (1997)[137] the petitioner feared he would be arrested upon return to Malaysia and tried for a drug-related crime that carried the death penalty. Pending the proceedings the HRC used provisional measures, but on the merits it found that the death penalty was not a foreseeable and necessary consequence of G.T.'s deportation.[138] Thus Australia was free to expel T. Effectively,

---

stating that 'in other words, Canada is not prepared to consent to the imposition of the death penalty', he noted nevertheless that the signals sent to him directly were far less encouraging. He referred to the Minister's decision of October 1994 that a request for assurances was not necessary and a letter of November 1994 in which Senior Counsel for the Minister 'felt it necessary' to 'reaffirm that Canada did not seek any formal assurances under Article 6 of the *Treaty* in this case'. The petitioner, on the other hand, sought binding assurances by both federal and State authorities that the death penalty would not be imposed. "As things stand, although there is an undertaking from the Florida prosecutor, it does not bind the United States Government because it has not been sought under Article 6 of the treaty. Furthermore, there is no undertaking with respect to the federal charges". Finally, counsel explained that his client 'strongly resents the suggestions of abusive behaviour'. Thus, his client had instructed him to inform both the HRC and the Canadian Government that if the Minister would provide credible assurances against the death penalty the petitioner would formally renounce all remedies within Canada and accept his extradition to the US.

[135]   On 17 January 1997.

[136]   HRC Note verbale by the Special Rapporteur to the Permanent Mission of Canada in *E.G.* v. *Canada* (738/1997), 28 April 1997 (on file with the author). In the letter sent by the Secretariat to counsel it was noted that the Rapporteur was 'satisfied that the Government of Canada has obtained the appropriate assurances from the United States authorities, both at the Federal and at the State level'. Letter by the Secretariat to the petitioner's counsel, 28 April 1997 (on file with the author). In May 1997 the petitioner withdrew his communication before the HRC. "The answers provided by Canada in response to the communication have helped to clarify his legal situation and he feels that the assurances are now sufficient that the death penalty will not be imposed'. Letter by counsel to the HRC, 26 May 1997; In November 1997 the HRC decided to discontinue examination of the case, letter by the Secretariat to counsel informing about the decision, taken at the 61st session, to discontinue the case, 17 November 1997 (on file with the author).

[137]   HRC *Mrs. G.T.* v. *Australia*, 4 November 1997.

[138]   The State had considered that the HRC should use the 'necessary and foreseeable consequence test' also for expulsion cases. It noted that the Committee's 'necessary and foreseeable consequence test' was stricter than the 'real chance test' used by domestic courts and that it placed a higher evidential burden on the petitioner than the test of 'well-founded fear of persecution' under the Refugee Convention. The petitioner was required to demonstrate that a prospective violation could be foreseen and was inevitable and that there was a clear causal link between the decision of the expelling State and a future violation by the receiving State. See HRC *Mrs. G.T.* v. *Australia*, 4 November 1997, §5.8 and the submission by the State on the admissibility and merits in this case, May 1997, submitted on 3 June 1997 (on file with the author). In effect, in this approach the petitioner would hardly ever be able to show such consequence other than in extradition cases. The State argued, moreover, that there was no real risk of prosecution of the petitioner in Malaysia and, in the alternative, there was insufficient

the provisional measure came to an end with its decision on the merits. This case not only indicates that evidentiary requirements on the merits are very strict,[139] but also that for the use of provisional measures the requirements for assessment of risk are not. It is clear that while the HRC considered there was insufficient evidence to find a violation, there was sufficient evidence for it to use provisional measures.[140]

---

evidence that, if prosecuted and convicted, he would be subjected to caning or an 'unreasonable period of detention on death row'. It is clear that it based its reasoning on *Kindler* v. *Canada* and also ignored the fact that, different from Canada, Australia is a party to the Second OP (on the abolition of the death penalty). It referred to information received from its Mission in Kuala Lumpur and noted 'it is the considered view of our interlocutors that there is nothing notably inhumane or unusually harsh about the conditions of those placed in Malaysia's death row'. The petitioner submitted that her husband's family had made inquiries and found that his name was placed on the Malaysian computers for arrest. See §6.6 of the View. Moreover, he had been convicted of importing 240 gram of heroine into Australia and it may be assumed that he had this 'under his control' when he left Malaysia. Malaysia carries the mandatory death penalty in such circumstance.

[139] Three members dissented and argued that in this case there *was* a real risk that the alleged victim would be subjected to the death penalty. They argued that, different from *A.R.J.* v. *Australia* (1997), in this case Malaysia would apply its law, under which the death penalty is mandatory. In fact, this difference meant that Australia had the burden to 'refute the assumption that Malaysian law will be applied' rather than that the petitioner had to prove an intention of the Malaysian authorities to prosecute her husband. In that respect they noted that they 'cannot ascribe much weight to the oral confirmation of the Royal Malaysian Police (...) that they do not institute criminal proceedings for trafficking in drugs against a person returned to Malaysia'. They pointed out that even if Malaysia would not prosecute the petitioner's husband for acts for which he had already been convicted in Australia, it could still prosecute him for possession of drugs in Malaysia or for exporting drugs from Malaysia. "As these acts carry a mandatory death sentence under Malaysian law something stronger than a vague oral confirmation is required to refute the assumption that the Malaysian authorities will indeed enforce their law". The dissenters pointed out that, contrary to the positive evidence Australia had provided in the other case, to the effect that persons in a similar situation had not been charged in Iran, it had only presented negative evidence in this case, to the effect that it knew of no cases of executions of persons in similar circumstances. They considered this evidence to be 'insufficient to refute the assumption that Malaysian law will be applied in T'.s case'. They equally considered insufficient the oral confirmation of the Royal Malaysian Police. For that reason they were 'forced to conclude that there is a real risk that T. will face a death sentence if he is deported to Malaysia', in violation of the State's obligation to ensure his right to life under Article 6 ICCPR. *Mrs. G.T.* v. *Australia*, 4 November 1997. Dissent by Klein and Kretzmer. Scheinin agreed. He also considered that the HRC should have taken a separate decision declaring the case admissible and requesting comments on the merits, at least in relation to Articles 17 and 23. He pointed out that the petitioner had not specified which Covenant articles she invoked, which meant that the merger of admissibility and merits gave Australia the possibility to determine the substantive issues. In his view, the communication raised 'more issues under the Covenant than those to which the State party replied'. In particular, the State had 'failed to address the issue of whether the reasons justifying the deportation of a person who has fully served his criminal sentence and who has already been able to re-establish his family life are weighty enough to legitimize the adverse consequences for the family life of the person and his closest ones'.

[140] A related question is whether this test is a factual test, for instance whether or not the death penalty is a necessary and foreseeable consequence of an extradition or expulsion, or already a test whether or not there has been a violation of the Covenant. Herndl obviously focuses on the

In *Judge* v. *Canada* (2003) the HRC overturned its case law on extradition without assurances against the death penalty.[141] Before 2003 it considered that Canada was allowed to extradite without such assurances. In *Judge* the petitioner had been deported before the HRC could use provisional measures, but its decision on the merits to the effect that assurances against the death penalty must be provided before a petitioner may be extradited, provides a firm basis for the use of provisional measures in new cases.[142] To request provisional measures in order to halt an extradition, petitioners only need to show either that the State did not request assurances or that the assurances provided by the requesting State are insufficient. The expulsion case *A.A.T.* v. *Hungary* (disc. 1994) illustrates that the HRC does expect a certain level of information before it takes provisional measures. In this case it only took them after having received additional information.[143] In the expulsion case *A.R.J.* v. *Australia* (1997)[144] the HRC did use provisional measures, but subsequently, drawing on the information and arguments provided by the State,[145] it resorted to the definition of a 'real risk' it had used earlier in extradition cases (rather than expulsion cases). It considered that such a risk existed when a violation of rights under the Covenant would be a 'necessary and foreseeable consequence' of the deportation.[146] Accordingly, it found no violation, allowing the petitioner's return to Iran.

Ahani v. *Canada* (2004) specifically dealt with the information available to the petitioner in the domestic expulsion proceedings. The original complaint stated that the 'discretion of the Minister of Immigration in directing a person's return to a country may be affected by considerations adverse to human rights concerns, including negative media coverage of a case'.[147] The petitioner added that the Minister's role in the expulsion process was 'neither independent nor impartial' and that instead a tribunal should make such a decision.[148] He noted that he could not rebut the Minister's submissions as he was unaware of their contents. "The absence of any rea-

---

	question whether or not the death penalty will be imposed rather than whether or not this would result in a violation. *Cox* v. *Canada*, 31 October 1994, dissenting opinion Herndl, §§6-8.
141	HRC *Judge* v. *Canada*, 5 August 2003.
142	It may have been influenced by the changed attitude of the Canadian Supreme Court, emphasising aspects relating to the judicial system and wrongful convictions in the requesting State.
143	HRC *A.A.T.* v. *Hungary*, 543/1993 (disc. 1994). The initial communication was of 10 August 1992. Early September 1992 the Secretariat contacted the Special Rapporteur. Later that month the Special Rapporteur requested some additional information. In January 1993 the Secretariat informed the petitioner that the case could now soon be brought to the attention of the Special Rapporteur, but some additional information was still necessary about exhaustion of domestic remedies and contact information for his lawyers (so that they could provide a complete file). Eventually, following some informal interventions, the Rapporteur used provisional measures on 2 June 1993.
144	HRC *A.R.J.* v. *Australia*, 28 July 1997. The HRC used provisional measures on 3 April 1996.
145	The State party, submitting its comments six months after the HRC used provisional measures, argued that the petitioner could not pass the 'necessary and foreseeable consequence' test in this case. A retrial for drug trafficking offences upon expulsion was not 'certain' nor 'the purpose' of returning him to Iran.
146	It is puzzling that the HRC only refers to Art. 6 and not to the Second Optional Protocol, to which Australia is a party. For the use of the 'necessary and foreseeable consequence' criterion see also e.g. HRC *Dawood Khan* v. *Canada*, 25 July 2006, §5.4.
147	HRC *Mansour Ahani* v. *Canada*, 29 March 2004, §3.1.
148	Ibid. See also Smeulers (2002).

sons provided in the decision makes judicial review of the decision against the submissions made to the Minister impossible".[149]

'Recalling its own limited role in the assessment of facts and evidence' the HRC did not discern 'any elements of bad faith, abuse of power or other arbitrariness' on the domestic court record. It also observed that the ICCPR 'does not, as of right, provide for a right of appeal beyond criminal cases'.[150] On the other hand, with respect to the subsequent decision by the Minister that Ahani could be deported the HRC did find violations of the ICCPR. It observed that 'where one of the highest values protected by the Covenant, namely the right to be free from torture, is at stake, the closest scrutiny should be applied to the fairness of the procedure to determine whether an individual is at a substantial risk of torture'. It emphasised that its provisional measures in this case had highlighted this risk.[151]

The Committee pointed out that the Canadian Supreme Court had held in *Suresh*[152] that the process of the Minister's determination of the risk and the balancing with national security grounds 'was faulty for unfairness' because the individual in question 'had not been provided with the full materials on which the Minister based his or her decision and an opportunity to

---

[149] HRC *Mansour Ahani* v. *Canada*, 29 March 2004, §3.2. With regard to the expulsion process followed by the State party counsel noted that the initial security certification was made by two Ministers without any input from the petitioner. The Federal Court hearing only determined whether the Ministers' assessment was reasonable and the Crown evidence was put forward '*in camera* and *ex parte*, without being tested by the court or supported by witnesses'. She argued that 'the conclusion of a national security threat, which was subsequently balanced at the removal stage by one elected official (a Minister) against the risk of harm, was reached by an unfair process'. She pointed out that Canadian security agencies had destroyed their evidence and provided only summaries and that the evidence 'could have been tested as is the case before the Security Intelligence Review Committee, where an independent counsel, cleared on security grounds could call witnesses and cross-examine in secret hearing'. She noted that the basis of the Supreme Court's decision was that the petitioner 'had not made out a *prima facie* risk of torture' but that 'the entire premise of a fair process is that an accurate determination of precisely this question can be made'. Instead, the petitioner only received 'a post-decision judicial review on whether it was "reasonable" to so conclude'. She pointed out that this was 'an inappropriately low standard for a decision that could result in torture or loss of life'. See §§6.2-6.4. She argued that the State was 'in error' with regard to both of its alleged claims 'that (i) he is not at risk of torture, and (ii) even if he were, he may be expelled on the grounds of threat to national security', §3.5. She pointed out that Iran had been monitoring his case and that the details of cooperation and the (confidential) information he provided to the Canadian authorities, and his resistance to deportation could 'very likely constitute treason in Iran', §3.6. With regard to the risk to Ahani she noted that the press had extensively referred to him as a defector and that the Government of Iran was fully aware of the nature of his case. The Supreme Court of Canada had decided that the decision of the minister in Ahani was 'largely fact-based'. "The inquiry into whether Ahani faces a substantial risk of torture involves considerations of the human rights record of the home state, the personal risk faced by the claimant, any assurances that the claimant will not be tortured and their worth and, in that respect, the ability of the home state to control its own security forces, and more. Such issues are largely outside the realm of expertise of reviewing courts and possess a negligible legal dimension. Considerable deference is therefore required". Supreme Court of Canada *Ahani* v. *Canada*, 208 D.L.R. (4th) 57, 2002 SCC 2, §17. See also Macklin (2002) discussing the court's deferential stance.

[150] HRC *Mansour Ahani* v. *Canada*, 29 March 2004, §10.5.

[151] Id., §10.6.

[152] Supreme Court of Canada *Ahani* v. *Canada*, 208 D.L.R. (4th) 57, 2002 SCC 2.

comment in writing thereon' and further because this decision was not reasoned.[153] The Committee considered that the decision by the State not to provide Ahani with the procedural protections deemed necessary in the domestic *Suresh* case, because Ahani 'had not made out a *prima facie* risk of harm', failed to meet the requisite standard of fairness. It observed that the argument was circuitous in that the petitioner 'may have been able to make out the necessary level of risk if in fact he had been allowed to submit reasons on the risk of torture faced by him in the event of removal'.[154] It found a violation of Article 13 in conjunction with Article 7 ICCPR for the failure to provide the petitioner with 'the procedural protections afforded to the plaintiff in *Suresh* on the basis that he had not made out a risk of harm'. After all in Article 13 the State is obliged to allow the petitioner to submit reasons against his removal and to have his 'submissions reviewed by a competent authority, entailing a possibility to comment on the material presented to that authority'.[155] Here risk assessment at the stage of provisional measures was subsequently confirmed on the merits.[156]

---

[153] HRC *Mansour Ahani* v. *Canada*, 29 March 2004, §10.6.

[154] Ibid.

[155] HRC *Mansour Ahani* v. *Canada*, 29 March 2004, §10.8 (Ando dissenting). The HRC considered that because Article 13 'speaks directly to the situation in the present case and incorporates notions of due process also reflected in article 14 of the Covenant', it would be 'inappropriate in terms of the scheme of the Covenant to apply the broader and general provisions of article 14 directly'. See §10.9. In HRC *Byahuranga* v. *Denmark*, 1 November 2004 the HRC took note of the petitioner's 'detailed account as to why he fears to be subjected to ill-treatment at the hands of the Ugandan authorities' and it concluded that he 'made out a *prima facie* case of such a risk', §11.2. It noted that the State party sought to 'refute the alleged risk of treatment contrary to article 7 merely by referring to the outcome of the assessment made by its own authorities, instead of commenting the author's fairly detailed account on why such a risk in his opinion exists', §11.3. In the light of the State party's 'failure to provide substantive arguments' in order 'to rebut the author's allegations', the HRC found that due weight must be given to his detailed account of the existence of a risk of treatment contrary to Article 7. Id., §11.4. Wedgwood and Yalden attached a dissenting opinion pointing out that if the Committee had wished to have the petitioner's full immigration file 'or any other documents within it, it could easily have asked the State party'. "Denmark has been wholly cooperative with the Committee while this complaint was pending, holding in abeyance the author's deportation at the Committee's request, and releasing him on parole to his family". They pointed out that '(a)t a minimum, the Committee should have given the State party an opportunity to provide any additional documents it wished to inspect'.

[156] See also, e.g. HRC *Blanca Lilia Londoño Soto, Oscar Alberto Teran Cano, Maria Hercilia Cano Bedoya, Lina Marcela Teran Londoño, and Lilia Andrea Teran Londoño* v. *Australia*, 1 April 2008 (inadm.), in which the Special Rapporteur denied the petitioners' request for provisional measures on 20 September 2005 and subsequently the Committee declared the Article 7 claim inadmissible for failure to sufficiently substantiate. In this respect the Committee noted the finding by the Refugee Review Tribunal that a real risk could not be established for lack of credibility of the petitioners. In addition the Committee noted that the petitioners had not demonstated the existence of a real risk of being deprived of their life or exposed to torture or cruel treatment.

3.2.4.4 ASSESSMENT OF RISK IN THE EUROPEAN SYSTEM

Much has been written on the assessment of risk in judgments on the merits by the ECtHR in the context of refoulement.[157] In *N.* v. *Finland* (2005), for instance, the Court interviewed the petitioner and witnesses on a fact-finding mission. Eventually it found that the petitioner's return to Congo (DRC) would violate Article 3.[158] As to the general credibility of a petitioner's statements the Court has observed, in *Said* v. *the Netherlands* (2005), that firstly, the statements in this case had been 'consistent', and, secondly, that he had submitted 'persuasive argument to rebut the Government's claim that his account lacked credibility'.[159] In *Salah Sheekh* v. *the Netherlands* (2007) the Court found that the Netherlands could not ensure the safety of a Somali national. Among others, the Dutch government had no way to monitor his treatment upon return.[160]

The Court applies a 'rigorous examination', in which the petitioner, as the Court put it in *Saadi* v. *Italy* (2008), must 'adduce evidence capable of proving' substantial grounds for a real risk of violation of Article 3 through removal. What is interesting is that in it uses the phrase 'capable of proving' rather than 'proving'.[161] Once the petitioner has provided such evidence, the burden shifts to the State. When does the State have the obligation to take away any doubt? In other words: when has the petitioner offered evidence capable of proving that his removal would violate Article 3? According to Spijkerboer this comes down to the 'arguability' criterion used by the Court in the context of admissibility and in its case law on Article 13.[162]

In cases of suspected terrorists or convicted criminals, States have sometimes argued that 'the examination of possible irreparable harm should be a rigorous one, particularly when the individual concerned was found to represent a threat.[163] Yet obviously when there is a real risk, this cannot become less real simply because the person at risk is a convicted criminal or a suspected terrorist.

---

[157] Often referring to the early case ECtHR *Vilvarajah et al* v. *UK*, 30 October 1991.

[158] ECtHR *N.* v. *Finland*, 6 July 2005.

[159] ECtHR *Said* v. *the Netherlands*, 5 July 2005, §51. In addition, in her concurring opinion Judge Thomassen noted that 'a conclusion that an asylum-seeker's account is not credible should (...) be based on a thorough investigation of the facts and be accompanied by adequate reasoning'. She pointed out that this obligation flows directly from Articles 2 and 3 ECHR. She would 'draw a parallel with other procedural aspects which, under the Court's case-law, can be derived from these provisions, such as the obligation to conduct an effective investigation into a homicide or into a credible assertion that someone has been subjected to treatment contrary to Article 3'.

[160] ECtHR *Salah Sheekh* v. *Netherlands*, 11 January 2007, §§46 and 143. See also, e.g., Terlouw (2007); Vermeulen (2007); Woltjer (2007).

[161] ECtHR *Saadi* v. *Italy*, 23 February 2008 (Grand Chamber), §129 (this phrasing may have been inspired by that of the domestic court in this case, see §18). See also e.g. *Ryabikin* v. *Russia*, 19 June 2008, §112, repeating the phrase 'capable of proving', referring to *N.* v. *Finland*, 26 July 2007, §167, which does not yet use this phrase.

[162] Spijkerboer (2008), p. 1015, also noting that this would be in line with ECtHR *Sheekh*, 11 January 2007, §136, with the fact that it will collect evidence *proprio motu* if doubts arise as to the accuracy of the information provided by the State and with the argumentation used by the Court in *Mamatkulov* for the obligations of States under the right of individual complaint to respect the Court's provisional measures (maintain status quo; ensure the object of the complaint; prevent irreparable harm). These are all phrases that are linked to the idea that once the Court is dealing with a serious case, a rigorous examination is warranted and meanwhile the petitioner may not be removed.

[163] See e.g. CAT *T.P.S.* v. *Canada*, 16 May 2000, §§8.5 and 8.3. See also Chapter XVII (Official responses).

NA. v. *UK* (2008) relates to various aspects of establishing risk on the merits that are already relevant also at the stage of provisional measures. One is the Court's practice of assessing the evidence *ex nunc* if the petitioner has not yet been removed. In other words, in such cases 'the relevant time will be that of the proceedings before the Court'.[164] "A full and *ex nunc* assessment is called for as the situation in a country of destination may change in the course of time. Even though the historical position is of interest in so far as it may shed light on the current situation and its likely evolution, it is the present conditions which are decisive and it is therefore necessary to take into account information that has come to light after the final decision taken by the domestic authorities".[165]

The Court has acknowledged circumstances at which risk may be established by providing evidence of group persecution as such without having to show further special distinguishing features. It has noted that it 'has never excluded the possibility that a general situation of violence in a country of destination will be of a sufficient level of intensity as to entail that any removal to it would necessarily breach Article 3 of the Convention'. Yet it 'would adopt such an approach only in the most extreme cases of general violence, where there was a real risk of ill-treatment simply by virtue of an individual being exposed to such violence on return'.[166] It has pointed out:

> "Exceptionally, however, in cases where an applicant alleges that he or she is a member of a group systematically exposed to a practice of ill-treatment, the Court has considered that the protection of Article 3 of the Convention enters into play when the applicant establishes that there are serious reasons to believe in the existence of the practice in question and his or her membership of the group concerned (...).[167] In those circumstances, the Court will not then insist that the applicant show the existence of further special distinguishing features if to do so would render illusory the protection offered by Article 3. This will be determined in light of the applicant's account and the information on the situation in the country of destination in respect of the group in question".[168]

Thus

> "The Court may take account of the general situation of violence in a country when determining whether it should or should not insist on further special distinguishing features. It considers that it is appropriate for it to do so if that general situation makes it more likely that the authorities (or any persons or group of persons where the danger emanates from them) will systematically ill-treat the group in question".[169]

In addition the Court has considered that 'due regard should also be given to the possibility that a number of individual factors may not, when considered separately, constitute a real risk; but when taken cumulatively and when considered in a situation of general violence and heightened security, the same factors may give rise to a real risk'.[170] If the general situation in a country or region,

---

[164] ECtHR *NA.* v. *UK*, 17 July 2008, §112. On this case see Terlouw (2008). See also *Saadi* v. *Italy*, 23 February 2008 (Grand Chamber), §133.

[165] ECtHR *NA.* v. *UK*, 17 July 2008, §112 also referring to *Salah Sheekh*, 11 January 2007, §136.

[166] ECtHR *NA.* v. *UK*, 17 July 2008, §115.

[167] Here the Court refers to *Saadi* v. *Italy*, 23 February 2008 (Grand Chamber), §132.

[168] ECtHR *NA.* v. *UK*, 17 July 2008, §116 referring to *Salah Sheekh*, 11 January 2007, §148.

[169] ECtHR *NA.* v. *UK*, 17 July 2008, §117, among others referring to *Salah Sheekh*, 11 January 2007, §148 and *Saadi* v. *Italy*, 23 February 2008 (Grand Chamber), §§132 and 143. See also *Ryabikin* v. *Russia*, 19 June 2008, §114.

[170] ECtHR *NA.* v. *UK*, 17 July 2008, §130.

systematic violence against certain groups and cumulative individual factors may be determinative on the merits, this clearly is the case at the stage of provisional measures.

The domestic courts normally are positioned closer to the situation and seem better placed to assess personal risk. This is different with regard to the issue of the consistent pattern. On this issue international adjudicators are probably better placed than the State (and its courts) in those situations where the State predominantly bases itself on embassy reports, especially when domestic courts defer to the minister. In fact, while on the merits the risk must be personal, at the stage of provisional measures it may be argued that the consistent pattern is crucial and only when the State can show that there is no specific risk to the petitioner, a provisional measure may be withdrawn.[171]

Important is also the ongoing discussion on the standard of proof. As submitted previously, the use of a standard of proof 'beyond a reasonable doubt' is inappropriate outside of the context of criminal law.[172] It is necessary to establish criminal culpability, but, as Judge Bonello expressed it in one of his dissenting opinions, 'in other fields of judicial enquiry, the standard of proof should be proportionate to the aim which the search for truth pursues: the highest degree of certainty, in criminal matters; a workable degree of probability in others'.[173] Thus, the ECtHR is obliged to establish '(1) on whom the law places the burden of proof, (2) whether any legal presumptions militate in favour of one of the opposing accounts, and (3) "on a balance of probabilities", which of the conflicting versions appears to be more plausible and credible. Proof "beyond reasonable doubt" can, in my view, only claim a spurious standing in 'civil' litigation, like the adversarial proceedings before this Court. In fact, to the best of my knowledge, the Court is the only tribunal in Europe that requires proof 'beyond reasonable doubt' in non criminal matters'.[174]

Expecting those who claim to be victims of torture to prove their allegations "beyond reasonable doubt" places on them a burden that is as impossible to meet as it is unfair to request. Independent observers are not, to my knowledge, usually invited to witness the rack, nor is a transcript of proceedings in triplicate handed over at the end of each session of torture; its victims cower alone in oppressive and painful solitude, while the team of interrogators has almost unlimited means at its disposal to deny the happening of, or their participation in, the gruesome pageant. The solitary victim's complaint is almost invariably confronted with the negation 'corroborated' by many".[175]

In *NA* v. *UK* (2008) the Court also discussed the use of materials, at the merits stage, to establish risk. This discussion may also shed light on the materials it takes into account at the stage of provisional measures, although it may be expected it is less strict there, having less time to await, examine and compare all materials. It noted that it has often attached importance to the information in recent reports by independent human rights NGOs such as Amnesty International, or governmental sources including the US State Department.[176] Criteria for the assessment of such materials include the 'independence, reliability and objectivity' of the source. Thus 'the authority and reputation of the author, the seriousness of the investigations by means of which they were compiled, the consistency of their conclusions and their corroboration by other sources

---

[171]   See also the ECtHR approach in regard to the petitions by Somalians in the Netherlands e.g. in Chapter XIII (Protection), section 4 (beneficiaries).

[172]   See also Chapter VI (Disappearances).

[173]   ECtHR *Sevtap Veznedaroğlu* v. *Turkey*, 11 April 2000, individual partly dissenting opinion Judge Bonello, §12.

[174]   Id., §13.

[175]   Id., §14.

[176]   ECtHR *NA.* v. *UK*, 17 July 2008, §119 referring to *Saadi* v. *Italy*, 23 February 2008 (Grand Chamber), §131.

are all relevant considerations'.[177] The Court also takes into account whether the author of the material has been present in the country in question and what were its reporting capacities. In that respect is observed that States 'through their diplomatic missions and their ability to gather information, will often be able to provide material which may be highly relevant to the Court's assessment of the case before it' and this applies a fortiori to UN agencies 'particularly given their direct access to the authorities of the country of destination as well as their ability to carry out on-site inspections and assessments in a manner which States and non-governmental organisations may not be able to do'.[178]

The question arises how the Court's assessment of risk in judgments on the merits has impacted on its approach to the evidence required for the use of provisional measures. This involves both the types of evidence and the manner in which evidence is being weighed. Time permitting, the President or Acting President of the ECtHR could request more research before taking a decision on the use of provisional measures.[179] Yet time does not often permit. What then does the Court do in the face of the imminent removal of a petitioner and claims of irreparable harm to persons? It has used provisional measures in many cases in which it later found no violation, or which it declared inadmissible.[180] On the other hand, it uses provisional measures in a minority of the situations in which petitioners have requested them.

How did the European Commission on Human Rights deal with evidentiary requirements in urgent non-refoulement cases? In *Lynas* v. *Switzerland* (1976) it already emphasised that it only made use of provisional measures 'in urgent and exceptional circumstances where it appeared at first sight that steps entailing irreversible consequences were about to be taken'.[181] In this case it had taken such measures, but subsequently it declared the case inadmissible as manifestly ill-founded. It did not consider that the 'uncorroborated declarations constitute satisfactory prima facie evidence'.[182] This implies that the Commission did see *prima facie* evidence for taking provisional measures. Subsequently, when deciding on admissibility, it reconsidered its view about *prima facie* evidence and concluded that it was not there.

In the European system a petitioner must show a risk of a violation of the ECHR which *prima facie* would cause irreparable harm. Both the risk of a violation of the Convention and the *prima facie* risk of irreparable harm that this violation would cause must be shown on a lower threshold. The petitioner must indicate a 'probability' of such violation and of the irreparable harm it would cause.[183]

Indeed, a substantial number of cases in which provisional measures were used are subsequently declared inadmissible. This in itself may indicate that the Commission and Court do apply a lower threshold at the provisional measures stage.[184]

---

[177] ECtHR *NA.* v. *UK*, 17 July 2008, §120 referring to *Saadi* v. *Italy*, 23 February 2008 (Grand Chamber), §143.

[178] ECtHR *NA.* v. *UK*, 17 July 2008, §121.

[179] Nørgaard (1994), p. 281.

[180] For a recent case, see e.g. ECtHR *Nnyanzi* v. *UK*, 8 April 2008 (provisional measures of 10 July 2006 and granted priority under Rule 41 on 11 July 2006).

[181] EComHR *Lynas* v. *Switzerland*, 6 October 1976 (inadm.), p. 160.

[182] Id., p. 165.

[183] See Garry (2001), p. 410 referring to her interview with Judge Pellonpää, section IV, Strasbourg 28 June 2000.

[184] See also Garry (2001), p. 410. Buquicchio-de Boer (1998), pp. 229-236 pointed out that 55 percent of all cases in which the Commission ordered provisional measures 'were eventually declared inadmissible'. As Nørgaard (1994), who was President of the Commission from 1981 until 1995, has noted the President of the Court or Commission examines the credibility of the request for provisional measures. In this respect the presentation, at this stage, of information

The former European Commission also often refused to take provisional measures, referring to the short decision-making period and lack of adequate information to meet the threshold test of risk under Article 3 ECHR. The Commission did not wish to cause the delay of a 'legitimate' deportation.[185] In some cases it did decide to depart from its usual time-table and expedite the case.[186] The present Court has also done so under Rule 41 of its Rules of Court.

The Commission and Court have also informed a State that they were considering using provisional measures in cases in which such an approach on its own would already bring about the desired result. These could be called informal provisional measures. The Commission also used informal provisional measures when its Rules of procedure did not yet contain a formal rule on provisional measures.[187]

Invoking Rule 41 on expediting the proceedings, on the other hand, seems more of an intermediate approach to urgency taken if the Court is not willing to use provisional measures but nevertheless considers that there is some urgency involved. The cases involving complaints by terminally ill petitioners about past violations serve as an example. The Commission and Court were not asked to intervene in an ongoing situation, but they decided to accelerate examination of the case so that there would be a decision by the Commission or a judgment by the Court before the death of the petitioner.[188]

According to Buquicchio-de Boer, the Commission and Court take into account 'all the circumstances' of the case, including 'foreseeable consequences' given the country conditions and the 'personal circumstances' of the petitioner.[189] She also notes that certain allegations have been considered 'insufficient to demonstrate risk of a clear violation of Article 3'. As examples she mentions the 'mere belonging to a minority group or opposition movement in the country of destination' and the 'risk of criminal prosecution for refusal to undertake military service or desertion'.[190] Yet judge Pellonpää, member of the Court since 1999, noted in 2000 that at the stage of provisional measures a lower threshold of proof is required and the petitioner does not need 'solid evidence of a direct personal link; general background documents from Amnesty International or UNHCR may at times be sufficient'.[191]

What the Convention organs have considered a *prima facie* case for the use of provisional measures is a prior decision by the Government or the UNHCR to grant the petitioner refugee status. Reasons why the Commission or Court decided not to use provisional measures may be a 'lack of specific background evidence corroborating the specific claim' or 'general lack of credibility in the request'.[192] Garry also mentions a change of conditions in the receiving or requesting State that may equally 'have weight in the decision' not to take provisional measures. Moreover, 'illegal stay in a Member State and failure to pursue rigorously some kind of residence status is another factor'. "Commission of crimes in a Member State and especially recidivism may have negative bearing".[193] This of course is unrelated to the risk of irreparable harm. In other words, it should not, as such, be a factor in the assessment of risk.

---

documenting county conditions or, for instance, medical evidence has played a role in the decision to use provisional measures, p. 284.

[185] For references see e.g. Nørgaard (1994), p. 287.
[186] See Rules 27 and 28 of the Commission's Rules of Procedure.
[187] See Chapter II (Systems).
[188] Ibid.
[189] Buquicchio-de Boer (1998), p. 231. See also Chapter XIII (Protection), section 4 (beneficiaries).
[190] Buquicchio-de Boer (1998), p. 233.
[191] See Garry (2001), p. 411, interview with Judge Pellonpää, section IV, Strasbourg 28 June 2000.
[192] See Garry (2001), p. 411.
[193] Garry (2001), p. 412. As discussed in Chapter II unfortunately most adjudicators do not specifically indicate their criteria for using provisional measures. The reference to Garry is made

The President of the Section follows a 'checklist' for the use of provisional measures, 'looking at such criteria as: grounds of fear; evidence submitted; Convention issue or Article invoked; reasons for leaving home country; whether applicant applied for political asylum and decision made as to it; date of arrival in Member State; decisions by the Member State administrative or judicial bodies on expulsion/extradition of the petitioner; availability of any other domestic authority to stop the impending expulsion/extradition; suspensive effect of domestic remedies; government assurances given by the state to be expelled or deported to; and involvement of UNHCR and decisions made by that body'.[194]

While some of these criteria relate to the purpose of provisional measures (Convention issue or Article invoked)[195] or the relevance of admissibility (exhaustion of domestic remedies and supensive effect),[196] or immediacy of the risk,[197] most of them indeed relate to the assessment of risk.

What is clear is that the Court is not just sparse in its use of provisional measures in that, rather than in a range of situations, it uses them predominantly in non-refoulement cases, but also in that it grants only a small percentage of requests for provisional measures in these non-refoulement cases. It is only in a very small number of non-refoulement cases that the ECtHR orders provisional measures. The Registrar of the Court indicated in a Press Release at the end of 2007 that during that year alone the Court had received 1,060 requests for provisional measures, but it had only granted such request in 252 cases.[198]

While several refusals may be based on frivolous claims involving rights in the context of which the Court has never used provisional measures, to the extent that they relate to non-refoulement claims, the refusal to take provisional measures must be based on an absence of risk. In a concurring opinion Judge Zupančič noted that a provisional measures should be ordered once there is 'a shadow of a doubt'. Then the burden shifts to the State.[199] Given the risk faced by the petitioner it is difficult to disagree with this statement. Yet in light of the fact that most provisional measures requested and most of them granted involve non-refoulement cases, it appears that the Court is rather stricter.

3.2.4.5 THE INTER-AMERICAN COURT AND MASS EXPULSION

The Inter-American Court thus far has not dealt with the issue of non-refoulement. It has dealt with the issue of assessment of risk in the context of a mass expulsion case. It makes a clear dis-

---

because this author drafted a report at the European Court during a two month visit in 2000. During this time she was able to consult with one of the judges and several staff members of the Court. It may be assumed that her remarks about reasons for not taking provisional measures are inspired by conversations with these persons.

[194] Garry (2001), p. 414.

[195] See Part II (Purpose).

[196] See the discussion on exhaustion in Chapter XIV (Jurisdiction and admissibility).

[197] See section 2 of this Chapter on temporal urgency.

[198] Press release issued by the Registrar, 'Inappropriate use of interim measures procedure', 21 December 2007. See also Minutes of Meeting between Court and organisations representing applicants and/or intervening as third parties, 10 April 2006, p. 6, in which it was indicated that in 2005 it only used provisional measures in 49 cases, while it had received requests for such measures in 453 cases.

[199] ECtHR (Grand Chamber), *Saadi v. Italy*, 28 February 2008, concurring opinion Judge Zupančič. Spijkerboer (2008), p. 1015 agrees, although he considers that the criterion 'shadow of a doubt' may be rather too light.

tinction between the proof required for admissibility and merits and the *prima facie* evidence necessary for taking provisional measures. The *Haitian* case illustrates the problems the Inter-American Commission faces when persons find themselves in adverse circumstances in remote areas at the border between two States. If the Commission is unable to contact the victims, it may be unable to convince the Court to take provisional measures.[200]

In reference to the hearing it held on the Inter-American Commission's request for provisional measures in the *Haitian* case the Court pointed out that (at that stage) a State policy of deportations and mass expulsions in violation of the Convention had not been proven, but that the testimonies had enabled it to establish a 'prima facie assumption of the occurrence of cases where individuals are subject to abuse'.[201] The President of the Court considered that 'the standard of prima facie appreciation of a case and the application of presumptions in face of the needs for protection have prompted this Court to order provisional measures at different times'.[202]

---

[200] Particularly if the Court takes the approach that the group of beneficiaries needs to be clearly identifiable, see also Chapter XIII (Protection), section 4 on beneficiaries.

[201] IACHR *Haitians and Dominicans of Haitian Origin in the Dominican Republic*, Order of 18 August 2000, 5th 'Considering' clause. The next month, with regard to five of the seven persons specifically identified by the Commission, the Court's President found sufficient *prima facie* evidence of a situation of extreme gravity and urgency as to the rights to life, personal integrity, special protection for children in the family, and to residence and movement, 4th 'Considering' clause. With regard to the other two persons it postponed their inclusion as beneficiaries, in light of the diverging statements of the Commission and the State about their situation. It required the Commission to 'urgently report in detail' about their situation while it ordered the State to investigate their situation, apparently with less urgency. The Commission explained that one of these two persons was not living in his own community for fear of being deported again without being given the chance to prove his Dominican nationality. He was also afraid for his life because of his complaint to the Commission. Regarding the other person about whom the State had protested that he had not been registered as deported, the Commission noted again that the State did not keep adequate record of its deportations. Based on this information the President ordered the Dominican Republic to refrain from deporting or expelling one of them and to allow the immediate return of the other, making it possible for him to meet with his son. President IACHR *Haitians and Dominicans of Haitian Origin in the Dominican Republic*, Decision on urgent measures, 14 September 2000, 'Decisional' clauses 1-3.

[202] President IACHR *Haitians and Dominicans of Haitian Origin in the Dominican Republic*, Decision on urgent measures, 14 September 2000. The Court's English translation of the original Order in Spanish speaks of circulation, in a literal translation of 'circulación'. In the official English version of Article 22 ACHR this is obviously referred to as 'freedom of movement'. Two months later the Court confirmed the President's expansion of the provisional measure to include these two persons. Once again it considered that the information submitted by the Commission showed *prima facie* a situation of extreme gravity and urgency with regard to 'the rights to life, to humane treatment, to the special protection of the child by its family, and to the freedom of movement and residence of the beneficiaries of these measures'. IACHR *Haitians and Dominicans of Haitian Origin in the Dominican Republic*, Order for provisional measures, 26 May 2001. The Court decided not to order provisional measures on behalf of members of 'bateyes' that were not known by name. See Chapter XIII (Protection), section 4 on beneficiaries. It did include a statement about the necessity of obtaining additional information on the situation of the members of bordering communities or 'bateyes' whose inhabitants, according to the information provided at the public hearing, were subjected to forced repatriations, deportations or expulsions. IACHR *Haitians and Dominicans of Haitian Origin in the Dominican Republic*, Order of 18 August 2000.

Another interesting aspect of this case is the discussion on the witnesses to be summoned to the hearings of the Court dealing with the Commission's request for provisional measures. The Court's first Order responding to the Commission's request for provisional measures to halt arbitrary expulsion in the *Haitian* case was itself not a provisional measure, but it dealt with the Dominican Republic's objections against the Commission's offer of expert witnesses for the *hearing* that would be held on the provisional measures requested.[203] The State had objected that one of them was the Director of an organisation that had been the main source of information for the petitioners and the Commission. It pointed out that she had appeared as a petitioner in another case pending before the Commission and that she was known as an activist on behalf of Haitian immigrants. The Commission had proposed these expert witnesses so that they could provide information on the frequency, form and consequences of the expulsions and deportations. This would 'furnish the Court with elements of special informative value to acquire a better understanding of the context within which the request for provisional measures has been made'.[204] The Court considered that the purpose of the testimonies of the two witnesses proposed by the Commission 'bears no relationship to technical or specialized items with respect to which this Tribunal would request the opinion of experts'.[205] It noted, however, that Art. 44 (1) of its Rules provides that it may 'obtain, on its own motion, any evidence it considers helpful. In particular, it may hear as a witness, expert witness, or in any other capacity, any person whose evidence, statement or opinion it deems to be relevant'.[206] Judging from the information provided by the Commission as well as the State, both persons had worked with the alleged victims and had directly perceived the circumstances in which they were living. For this reason, the Court ordered them to appear before it in their capacity as witnesses. The Court pointed out that 'the fact that a person has a direct interest in the outcome of a proceeding or may have taken part as a petitioner in a case before the Commission, is not a cause for hindrance to deposing before this Court which, in practice, has even admitted statements from the victim and her or his relatives'.[207] The Court also ordered the Dominican Republic to 'facilitate the exit from and entry into its territory' of these witnesses. It noted that the Commission, as the party requesting the production of the evidence, was to pay the costs involved.[208]

---

[203] IACHR *Haitians and Dominicans of Haitian Origin in the Dominican Republic*, Order on the summoning of witnesses, 7 August 2000.

[204] Id., 'Having seen' clause 5b. The State also objected to the other expert witness proposed, stating he was, among others, a founding member of another organisation that had acted on behalf of these immigrants. Thus, it argued, they were no independent technical advisors or experts who could 'offer totally objective and impartial information and opinions'. It referred to Article 49 of the Court's Rules of Procedure (old) and Article 19 of the Court's Statute, 'Having seen' clause 6c.

[205] Id., 2nd 'Considering' clause.

[206] Id., 3rd 'Considering' clause.

[207] The Court referred here to various cases where it had done so: *Loayza-Tamayo* Case. Judgment of 17 September 1997; *Castillo-Páez* Case. Judgment of 3 November 1997; *Suárez-Rosero* Case. Judgment of 12 November 1997; *Blake* Case, Judgment of 24 January 1998; *Paniagua-Morales et al.*, Judgment of 8 March 1998; *Villagrán-Morales et al.*, Judgment of 19 November 1999.

[208] The Court referred to Article 45 of its Rules of Procedure (old). This is an interesting situation because, in fact, the Commission had requested them as expert witnesses but the Court ordered them to appear as witnesses 'on its own motion'. See further Chapter IX (Threats) on subsequent threats against these witnesses and Order for provisional measures on their behalf.

3.2.4.6 DIPLOMATIC ASSURANCES AND LIFTING PROVISIONAL MEASURES

Adjudicators may extend or withdraw their provisional measures.[209] Particularly relevant in the context of evidentiary requirements in non-refoulement cases is CAT's approach to the possibility of lifting its provisional measures. With the introduction of Article 108(6) of its Rules of Procedure it has formalized the general possibility to lift provisional measures. The Special Rapporteur for new complaints and interim measures has also developed 'working methods' regarding the withdrawal of provisional measures. "Where the circumstances suggest that a request for interim measures may be reviewed before the consideration of the merits, a standard sentence is added to the request, stating that the request is made on the basis of the information contained in the complainant's submission and may be reviewed, at the initiative of the State party, in the light of the information and comments received from the State party and any further comments, if any, from the complainant".[210] CAT has noted that some States parties 'have adopted the practice of systematically requesting the Rapporteur to withdraw his request for interim measures of protection'. Yet the Rapporteur 'has taken the position that such requests need only be addressed if based on new information which was not available to him when he took his initial decision on interim measures'.[211]

In its Annual Reports CAT has also expressed its awareness of the concern by 'a number of States parties' that it has used provisional measures 'in too large a number of cases, especially where the complainant's deportation is alleged to be imminent, and that there are insufficient factual elements to warrant a request for interim measures'. It has noted that 'it takes such expressions of concern seriously and is prepared to discuss them with the States parties concerned'. "In this regard it wishes to point out, that in many cases, requests for interim measures are lifted by the Special Rapporteur, on the basis of pertinent State party information".[212] On several occasions CAT has indeed lifted its provisional measures. In *C.A.R.M.* v. *Canada* (2007), for instance, it had used provisional measures in June 2006 and the State had immediately informed it of its compliance. Three months later the State requested the Committee to lift its provisional measures and within a month the special Rapporteur decided to 'suspend' them.[213]

In recent years both the HRC and CAT have stressed that diplomatic assurances as such do not remove the risk of refoulement.[214] UN experts have equally expressed themselves negatively about the use of such assurances.[215]

---

[209] See e.g. HRC *Youni E. Länsman e.a.* v. *Finland*, 30 October 1996.

[210] See e.g. CAT Annual Report 2006, §60.

[211] See e.g. Annual Report 2006, §60. The first time Germany ever received a request for provisional measures by CAT it immediately requested their withdrawal; See e.g. CAT *M.A.K.* v. *Germany*, 12 May 2004, §13.5. The provisional measures was of 11 September 2002 and the motion by Germany to withdraw the provisional measures of 11 November 2002; the Rapporteur decided not to withdraw them, §1.3.

[212] See CAT Annual Report 2006, §62 and Annual Report 2007, §71.

[213] CAT *C.A.R.M.* v. *Canada*, 18 May 2007, §1.3. On the merits CAT found no violation of Article 3 (insufficient substantiation).

[214] See e.g. HRC *Mohammed Alzery* v. *Sweden*, 25 October 2006 and CAT *Ahmed Hussein Mustafa Kamil Agiza* v. *Sweden*, 20 May 2005. See further Van Boven's annotation (2006) of *Agiza*, critically discussing the issue of diplomatic assurances. In this case the Committee considered it appropriate to observe that its decision reflected a number of facts that 'were not available to it when it considered the largely analogous complaint' of *Hanan Attia* v. *Sweden*, 17 November 2003, 'where, in particular, it expressed itself satisfied with the assurances provided', §13.5. CAT confirmed its critical stance on assurances in *Pelit* v. *Azerbaijan*: "While a certain degree of post-expulsion monitoring of the complainant's situation took place, the State party has not supplied

By contrast, the European Commission and Court appear to have been more willing to accept diplomatic assurances, but the case law in this respect generally is less recent. *Altun* v. *Germany* (1984) warrants special attention as an early case dealt with under the ECHR indicating the approach of the former European Commission towards assurances by requesting States in the context of extradition and the impact such assurances may have on its decision to maintain provisional measures.[216] The Commission initially took provisional measures but, following a request by Germany, it decided not to maintain them.[217]

The petitioner, Cemal Altun, had been partly brought up by his elder brother Ahmat Altun. His brother was politically active and, at the time of submission, lived in France with a status of political refugee. The petitioner himself also became politically active and left Turkey after proceedings were instituted against him as one of the founders of a banned student party. He requested political asylum in Germany in 1981. The next year Turkey requested his extradition, initially for incitement to the murder of a Minister, later on charges of harbouring criminals and suppression of evidence in connection with this murder. In February 1983, following court decisions authorizing this, the German Government decided to extradite him. In 1983 Altun petitioned the European Commission, which took provisional measures and subsequently it declared the case

---

the assurances to the Committee in order for the Committee to perform its own independent assessment of their satisfactoriness or otherwise (see its approach in *Agiza* v. *Sweden*), nor did the State party detail with sufficient specificity the monitoring undertaken and the steps taken to ensure that it both was, in fact and in the complainant's perception, objective, impartial and sufficiently trustworthy. In these circumstances, and given that the State party had extradited the complainant notwithstanding that it had initially agreed to comply with the Committee's request for interim measures, the Committee considers that the manner in which the State party handled the complainant's case amounts to a breach of her rights under article 3 of the Convention", *Pelit* v. *Azerbaijan*, 1 May 2007, §11.

[215] See e.g. Special Rapporteur against Torture (Theo van Boven), A/59/324, 1 September 2004, §40 and Special Rapporteur against Torture (Manfred Nowak), E/CN.4/2006/6, 23 December 2005, §§28-33 (pointing out that diplomatic assurances are not legally binding; ' (i)t is therefore unclear why States that violate binding obligations under treaty and customary international law should comply with non-binding assurances'; moreover it is the question whether the authority providing the assurances has the power to enforce them; post-return monitoring mechanisms are no guarantee against torture; the individual has no recourse is the assurances are violated; normally they do not contain any sanctions in case of violation; both sending and receiving State have a common interest in denying that returned persons were subjected to torture; if independent organisations have been identified to undertake monitoring functions under the return agreement, these may experience undue political pressure, especially where one is funded by either the sending or the receiving State; in sum, he argued. ' diplomatic assurances with regard to torture are nothing but attempts to circumvent the absolute prohibition of torture and refoulement'); see also UN Independent Expert on counterterrorism and human rights (Martin Scheinin), E/CN.4/2006/98, 28 December 2005, §56(b); Human Rights Watch, "Empty promises", diplomatic assurances no safeguard against torture, 14 April 2004 and Human Rights Watch, Still at risk: diplomatic assurances no safeguard against torture, April 2005 (Vol. 17, No. 3(D). See further Smeulers/De Vries (2003).

[216] The importance attached by the Commission to the fact that the State of return had recognized the individual complaint system under the ECHR must be kept in mind.

[217] ECommHR *Cemal Kemal Altun* v. *The Federal Republic of Germany*, 3 May 1983 (adm.), §8, p. 228.

admissible.[218] It could not 'rule out immediately the possibility of a violation' of Art. 3. Thus, it had to determine whether there was a 'certain risk of prosecution for political reasons which could lead to an unjustified or disproportionate sentence being passed on the applicant, and, as a result, inhuman treatment'.[219] At this stage of the proceedings it was 'not possible to rule out with sufficient certainty the danger that the criminal proceedings instituted against the applicant have been falsely inspired'.[220] Subsequently the Turkish Embassy assured the Ministry of Foreign Affairs that Turkey would respect the principle of specialty in the event of an extradition. In a message to the Turkish government Germany pointed out that 'assurances that in the event of the applicant's extradition a representative of the German Embassy in Ankara could visit the applicant without supervision at frequent intervals, could be useful for proceedings before the Commission and would be taken into consideration when reaching a decision on the enforcement of the extradition order'.[221] In July Turkey informed Germany 'that it had decided to apply the relevant regulations to enable a representative of the German Embassy in Ankara to visit the applicant in the event of his extradition'.[222]

Meanwhile domestically a decision was made on the request for asylum.[223] It was decided that because of circumstances occurring after his departure from Turkey he could not now be required to return to his country. The media had widely reported his case – even, contrary to normal practice, quoting his full name.[224] The Turkish authorities were aware of this.[225]

In July of 1983 Germany sent the Commission a memorial requesting it to cancel its provisional measures 'on the ground that the Turkish Government had given the Government of the Federal Republic an *assurance* that in the event of the applicant's extradition, the principle of speciality would be observed and that a representative of the German Embassy in Ankara could visit the applicant in prison'. Thus, Germany considered that it had done everything necessary to ensure that the petitioner would not be exposed to treatment contrary to Article 3 of the Convention upon his extradition to Turkey. Germany considered that the visits by an Embassy representative it had promised to arrange would guarantee the petitioner the possibility to pursue his application before the Commission. Its embassy would be able to verify the petitioner's state of health,

---

[218] It also directed provisional measures to Altun himself so that he would not abscond upon release. Id., §8, p. 229. He did not and reported to the police station upon request. There he was detained once more. See also Chapter XIII (Protection), section 4 (beneficiaries and addressees).

[219] EComHR *Cemal Kemal Altun* v. *The Federal Republic of Germany*, 3 May 1983 (adm.), §8, p. 233.

[220] The risk of pressure being used upon him incompatible with Article 3 could not be ruled out. EComHR *Cemal Kemal Altun* v. *The Federal Republic of Germany*, 3 May 1983 (adm.), §10, p. 233.

[221] EComHR *Cemal Kemal Altun* v. *The Federal Republic of Germany*, 7 March 1984 (struck out), §9, p. 4. About the official responses by addressee States with regard to provisional measures see Chapter XVII.

[222] EComHR *Cemal Kemal Altun* v. *The Federal Republic of Germany*, 7 March 1984 (struck out), §9, p. 4.

[223] In June 1983 the Bundesamt für die Anerkennung ausländischer Flüchtlinge (Federal Office for the Recognition of Foreign Refugees) indeed decided to grant him political asylum.

[224] The petitioner himself took no direct part in this publicity.

[225] 7 March 1984 (struck out), §10, p. 5. "The measures that the petitioner must expect in Turkey could at the very least be termed political prosecution. As a result the Federal Office was convinced that in the event of his return to Turkey the petitioner would very probably be the subject of a prosecution relating to the right of asylum (*asylhebliche Verfolgung*)". Id., §18, p. 9.

and discuss any questions of fact or law relating to his application with him. "The fact that the Embassy representative could attend the hearing before the court was an additional guarantee".[226]

In fact, according to Germany 'there was no need in principle to request specific undertakings' since 'the Federal Republic and Turkey are Contracting Parties to the European Convention on Extradition'. It pointed out that it had nevertheless obtained additional guarantees on compliance with the specialty rule, 'at the request of the Commission'. Germany reiterated that 'the fact that the right to asylum was granted did not have a direct bearing on extradition proceedings'. Moreover, it considered that pending interstate cases against Turkey did not prevent extradition either because these cases concerned the internal situation in Turkey 'and not automatically the situation of a presumed criminal under the particular protection of the requested State'.[227]

In response the petitioner considered that the assurances mentioned by the Government were insufficient. "In the past, information given by the ministry of Foreign Affairs concerning the situation in Turkey had been criticised as being contradictory. He referred to a question raised in the Bundestag and to judgments by the administrative Courts and the Federal Constitutional Court".[228] The Commission subsequently decided not to maintain its provisional measures, taking into account the undertaking given by the German Government 'based on assurances given by Turkey, which were intended to safeguard the applicant's position after his extradition to Turkey'.[229]

> "When informing the parties of this decision the Commission noted that it was based on the idea that the discussions envisaged between a representative of the German Embassy in Ankara and the applicant in prison would take place in the absence of third parties. The Commission requested the Government to inform it about the possible execution of the extradition and, in this event, to keep it informed of the applicant's situation as regards his conditions of detention and criminal proceedings".[230]

In August 1983 the petitioner attended a domestic court hearing, which was due to resume on 30 August 1983. On that day the petitioner had been led into the courtroom by the guard. After his handcuffs had been taken off he was seated beside his lawyer and an interpreter, awaiting the entrance of court personnel. Mr Altun then 'rushed over towards an open window and threw himself out. Having fallen from the sixth floor where the courtroom was situated, he died shortly afterwards in an ambulance sent to the spot'.[231]

---

[226] EComHR *Cemal Kemal Altun* v. *The Federal Republic of Germany*, 7 March 1984 (struck out), §18, p. 9.

[227] EComHR *Cemal Kemal Altun* v. *The Federal Republic of Germany*, 7 March 1984 (struck out), §24, p. 12.

[228] EComHR *Cemal Kemal Altun* v. *The Federal Republic of Germany*, 7 March 1984 (struck out), §19.

[229] EComHR *Cemal Kemal Altun* v. *The Federal Republic of Germany*, 7 March 1984 (struck out), §20.

[230] Ibid.

[231] EComHR *Cemal Kemal Altun* v. *The Federal Republic of Germany*, 7 March 1984 (struck out), §10, p. 4. The Commission noted that it was informed by counsel and government representatives on that same day that the petitioner had committed suicide, 'although proceedings relating to his request for asylum were still pending and further discussions between the Federal Ministry of Justice and the applicant's lawyer concerning extradition were in progress'. Germany had pointed out that the petitioner's lawyer must have been assured that his client would not be extradited before he had been able to travel to Turkey in order to consult the criminal files against his client. The Government assumed that the lawyer notified the petitioner of this proposed plan.

The petitioner's brother, Ahmed Altun, then instructed counsel to ask the Commission to pursue the proceedings.[232] He believed continuation of the proceedings was necessary because there was a risk that similar cases might occur, given the formal extradition relations with Turkey.[233] Nevertheless the Commission decided to strike out the case, finding that the decision to extradite the petitioner had lapsed and 'the particular nature' of the complaint could not be transferred to the heirs. It considered that 'the grounds relied on by the applicant's brother to pursue the application in his own name have no direct relation to the subject of the application'. Thus, the Commission considered that the petitioner's brother, 'who was not associated with the application instituting the proceedings', 'cannot now in the circumstances of the case claim to have a sufficient legitimate interest to justify proceeding with an examination of the application on his behalf'.[234]

As one of the reasons for striking out the case following the death of the petitioner the Commission pointed out that the administrative practice of torture and ill-treatment would also be addressed in the pending inter-state applications on the administrative practice of torture in Turkish prisons.[235] This suggests that the Commission did not subscribe to Germany's view that the aforementioned inter-state proceedings were not relevant for the determination of the risks facing the petitioner. Indeed, the State's argument is surprising. The petitioner would have been extradited into exactly that 'internal situation' in Turkey that was the subject of these interstate cases against Turkey. Interstate cases do not discuss the 'internal situation', but the internal human rights situation. People live in this 'internal situation'. In deciding extradition cases it would be especially important, given such internal situation, to examine the particular situation of a 'presumed criminal'.

Yet by deciding to withdraw its provisional measures the Commission apparently attached more importance to the assurances by Turkey than to the fact that the petitioner had been granted asylum in Germany. Germany's argument that the granting of asylum 'did not have a direct bearing' on the extradition proceedings seems rather insufficient. Asylum is granted when the authorities find that there is a well founded fear of persecution. Hence it is not safe for that person to return to his/her country. In their decision they have taken into account the criminal proceedings against him. These proceedings may in fact even have been one of the reasons for believing him to be in danger and granting him asylum. Although, strictly speaking, the decisions are made by different organs with their own responsibilities, surely the fact that someone has been granted asylum has a relevant 'bearing' on his extradition proceedings.

The domestic decision to grant asylum apparently played no role in the Commission's decision. While it is true that domestic proceedings (with regard to arranging a consultation of the case file against the petitioner in Turkey) were still pending, in my view the fact that the petitioner was so desperate about his extradition to Turkey (which he apparently still expected) that

---

[232] In the admissibility decision it was stated that as a child the petitioner was partly brought up by his elder brother Ahmed Altun, after the death of their father; in the report striking out the case it was mentioned that the brother decided to pursue the proceedings after consulting his parents in Turkey, 3 May 1983 (adm.), §23, p. 10.

[233] 'Furthermore, the applicant's family had an interest in counteracting the false information and defamation in the Turkish press following the applicant's death'.

[234] EComHR *Cemal Kemal Altun* v. *The Federal Republic of Germany*, 7 March 1984 (struck out), §31, p. 14.

[235] EComHR *Cemal Kemal Altun* v. *The Federal Republic of Germany*, 7 March 1984 (struck out), §32, p. 15. Indeed, the Commission declared admissible the inter-State case *France, Norway, Denmark, Sweden and the Netherlands* v. *Turkey*, 6 December 1983 (adm.) (relating to the allegation that during the period 12 September 1980 to 1 July 1982 there was an administrative practice of torture or ill-treatment of prisoners in Turkey).

he jumped out of a window of the courthouse would have been cause to maintain the case on the Commission's roll. It could be argued that the deceased petitioner's claims were indeed transferable to his older brother, with whom he had been very close since childhood, in light of the express wish of his brother to continue the case as well as the need to further investigate the Commission's own decision-making with regard to assurances and provisional measures.

Subsequently, in *Chahal* (1996) the European Court expressed some caution with regard to diplomatic assurances. It considered that in the circumstances of that case the State providing the assurances was indeed in good faith but that it did not have sufficient control over the members of the security forces responsible for torture in police custody. Thus, return of the petitioner to that State would be in violation of Art.3 ECHR. Pending the case it had also used provisional measures.[236]

Yet in for instance *Shamayev* (2005), the ECtHR withdrew its provisional measures upon receipt of information provided by the addressee State (Georgia) of some assurances by the receiving State (Russia) with regard to the treatment of the petitioner(s).

> "The Court decided that, in the light of the undertakings given by the Russian authorities, which included guarantees of unhindered access for the applicants to appropriate medical treatment, legal advice and the Court itself, the Rule 39 interim measure could be lifted. The Russian authorities had further undertaken that the applicants would not face capital punishment and that their health and safety would be protected".[237]

The Court had actively sought information both from the State requesting extradition of the petitioners (Russia) and from the State planning to extradite them to the requesting State (Georgia), as both were members of the Council of Europe.

What is remarkable is that already at the stage of provisional measures the European Court let itself be convinced by Russia. It is mainly when provisional measures are initially taken that the standard of proof is lower. Subsequently, once the addressee State has been able to cast doubt on the risk claimed, the burden is on the petitioner to convince the Court to maintain its provisional measures. Yet in this case the Court could have ordered new provisional measures on its own motion. It could have appealed to Russia to report to the Court on the treatment and health of the suspects that had already been extradited to Russia.[238]

On the merits the European Court noted that subsequent to their extradition to Russia, the petitioners were unable to stay in touch with their representatives in the case before the Court.[239] The weight the Court had attached to the assurances by Russia resulted in the withdrawal of the provisional measures and in the extradition. Subsequently the collection of evidence was seriously

---

[236] ECtHR *Chahal* v. *UK*, 15 November 1996.

[237] ECtHR press release of 26 November 2002 in the case *Shamayev and 12 Others* v. *Georgia and Russia*, which was at that point still ongoing.

[238] See further Rieter (2003b).

[239] Their representatives were unable to visit them despite an express indication by the Court that this should be made possible. ECtHR (Second Section) *Chamaïev et autres* c. *Géorgie et Russie*, 12 April 2005, §476. The Court itself had not been allowed to pay a research visit (under Article 38 §1a) either. The Court noted that this refusal by Russia could not be attributed to Georgia. It concluded that it had insufficient information to examine on the merits the claims against Russia, which had hindered the collection of evidence. ECtHR (Second Section) *Chamaïev et autres* c. *Géorgie et Russie*, 12 April 2005, §477.

hindered, but it does not appear that the Court was willing to take this into account in its judgment on the merits.[240]

In *Mamatkulov* (2004) the extradition took place despite the Court's provisional measures and the examination of evidence was on the merits was seriously hindered. Counsel before the ECtHR did not even have access to the petitioners upon their extraction to Uzbekistan. Here it does not appear that the Court was willing to take into account the fact that Turkey had ignored its provisional measures.[241] Again it appears to rely on assurances. At the same time the Court noted that a provisional measure 'means more often than not that the Court does not yet have before it all the relevant evidence it requires to determine whether there is a real risk of treatment proscribed by Article 3 in the country of destination'.[242] This statement does indicate that at the stage of provisional measures a much lower level of evidence is necessary for the assessment of risk at the merits stage.

Possibly the European Court will come to realize, as the UN bodies and experts did before it, that diplomatic assurances are simply unreliable in the context of allegations of torture and human rights adjudicators should not easily rely on them when deciding on the use or maintenance of provisional measures.[243]

3.2.5 Health in detention and assessment of risk

The monopoly of information by the State is particularly relevant with regard to treatment in detention. The HRC may often be able to consult the trial transcripts even if the State in question itself does not provide any information about the claim.[244] Adjudicators such as the HRC normally defers to the approach of the domestic court as found in these transcripts.

Similarly, for complaints about detention situations there is a difference between claims of pre-trial ill treatment and claims of ill treatment of persons already convicted. Dealing with claims

---

[240] Russia had reacted very strongly to the initial provisional measures and the relation between Russia and the Court became very strained. Currently it is still blocking the entry into force of the Protocol aimed at streamlining the Court proceedings, although this may be related also to the subsequent Chechnya cases and the fact that the Court is associated with the decision-making by the Council of Europe political bodies. See also Chapter XVII (Official State responses) and XVIII (Follow-up).

[241] See further Rieter (2003a) on the previous judgment by the first chamber and Rieter (2005b) on the Grand Chamber judgment. On the question how much importance adjudicators should attach on the merits to their decision that, at the stage of provisional measures, there was a real risk, when the State subsequently ignored the provisional measures, see also Chapter XVIII (Follow-up).

[242] ECtHR Grand Chamber *Mamatkulov and Askarov* v. *Turkey*, 15 December 2004, §69.

[243] See also e.g. Letsas (2003), p. 536. For a more critical approach by the Court see e.g. ECtHR *Saadi* v. *Italy*, 28 February 2008, §§147-148 pointing out that diplomatic assurances are not in themselves sufficient to ensure adequate protection where reliable sources have reported practices resorted to or tolerated by the authorities that are manifestly contrary to the principles of the Convention. See also *Ryabikin* v. *Russia*, 19 June 2008, §119 confirming this and, in this case, questioning the assurances from the Prosecutor General of Turkmenistan invoked by Russia. First of all, 'no copy of that letter has been submitted to the Court'. 'In any event, even accepting that such assurances were given', the Court noted that the reports it had previously cited pointed out that 'the authorities of Turkmenistan systematically refused access by international observers to the country, and in particular places of detention. In such circumstances the Court is bound to question the value of the assurances that the applicant would not be subjected to torture, given that there appears to be no objective means of monitoring their fulfilment".

[244] As seen in section 3.2 with regard to the right to fair trial and death penalty cases.

of pre-trial ill treatment, the HRC leans more towards the information contained in national court documents, as these claims supposedly have been dealt with during the trial. Once convicted, on the other hand, usually there are no national court documents on treatment in detention. The detainee often has fewer possibilities for an investigation of ill treatment, threats, lack of medical treatment or adverse prison conditions in general. If in such cases the petitioner has made very precise allegations relating to incidents, '[d]ue weight' should be given to his allegations, 'in the absence of any refutation by the State party'.[245] It is in such cases that the HrC has also used provisional measures.

Vasilskis v. *Uruguay* (1983) illustrates the risk for detainees of talking to representatives of international organisations.[246] The petitioner referred to the treatment of some of the prisoners following the visit of the Special Representative of the UN Secretary General, Mr. Rivas Posada, in January 1982. According to the testimony of the mother of one of the prisoners, they were beaten with clubs, items of their personal property were confiscated and their food was thrown on the floor.[247] The HRC has inquired about the health and whereabouts of political detainees on several occasions.[248]

In *Maleki* v. *Italy* (1999) the petitioner's son, who represented him before the HRC, had complained that his father had a heart condition for which he was not receiving adequate treatment.[249] In this case the HRC did *not* use (informal) provisional measures, possibly because it never considered the issue or otherwise because there was no history of failure to provide medical treatment by the State in question.[250] The State party subsequently submitted 'a comprehensive file' 'showing that Mr. Maleki's medical condition was being closely monitored'.[251]

While it is in the nature of provisional measures that the risk of irreparable harm must be assessed on an urgent basis, requiring a lower standard of proof, it is evident from the Uruguayan cases discussed in Chapter VII, relating to political detainees, that in the 1970s and 80s the HRC was unwilling to use *formal* provisional measures to intervene in ongoing violations.

---

[245] HRC *Michael Freemantle* v. *Jamaica*, 24 March 2000.

[246] HRC *Vasilskis* v. *Uruguay*, 31 March 1983.

[247] This case equally indicates the HRC's approach towards the burden of proof. In its decision on the merits it regretted that it had not received any of the documents requested in its admissibility decision, including copies of the existing medical reports. This indicates a relationship between the Committee's request for information pending the proceedings and the standard and burden of proof it requires for the final determination of the case. With regard to the alleged victim's health, it pointed out that 'the author's precise allegations, which include allegations that her treatment in prison has contributed to her ill-health called for more detailed submissions from the State party'. In reference to earlier case law it pointed out that the burden of proof 'cannot rest alone on the author of the communication, especially considering that the author and the State party do not always have equal access to the evidence and that frequently the State party alone has access to relevant information'. It pointed out that the State party should have furnished the medical reports under Article 4(2) OP and found violations of Articles 7 and 10(1).

[248] See Chapter VII (Health in detention).

[249] HRC *Ali Maleki* v. *Italy*, 15 July 1999.

[250] The petitioner was a 65-year-old Iranian citizen serving a ten-year prison sentence in Italy for drug trafficking. Prior to the initial submission the petitioner had been on a hunger strike to obtain a review of his conviction. The HRC transmitted the case under Rule 91 more than three months after initial submission.

[251] In August 1997 the HRC decided separately on admissibility. While it declared the case admissible it considered that the complaint about lack of medical treatment was insufficiently substantiated. In its View it found a violation of Article 14(1) requiring 'his immediate release or re-trial in his presence'.

The fact that it did not use provisional measures in the face of serious concerns about the health of political detainees may relate to the lack of practice during the initial stages of the Committee's existence rather than to the fact that the violations were ongoing and not simply 'imminent'. On the other hand, during the 1990s and beyond 2000 Rapporteurs equally have used a different type of provisional measure in ongoing cases.[252] Scheinin noted that the previous Rapporteur, Pocar, initiated the practice of using informal provisional measures, which he called 'quasi-interim measures' where the Rapporteur hints at provisional measures but does not formally invoke them. Instead his Note Verbale transmitting the case to the State simply contains a normal Rule 91 (current Rule 97) request for information, but in the last sentence the Rapporteur invites the State Party to provide information on the health of the petitioner.[253] In fact this is similar to the earlier cases involving Uruguay. Scheinin points out that his cautious approach to provisional measures would not prevent him from using them formally, also in health cases. Apparently, the choice between formal and informal measures was determined by the evidence available. As he put it, when there was only an allegation of a threat to the health of a prisoner, he would opt for a 'quasi-interim measure' rather than a formal provisional measure under Rule 86 (current Rule 92).[254]

In December 1992 the President of the Inter-American Court decided not to take urgent measures in the Peruvian Prisons cases.[255] He noted that the Commission itself had taken precautionary measures and also noted the accompanying documentation, but then he pointed out that 'some of those measures cannot properly be considered precautionary and provisional measures' within the meaning of Article 63(2) ACHR, 'given that they refer to the Government's authorization for the Commission to carry out on-site visits to several Peruvian prisons'. He considered that this situation was regulated by Articles 48(2) ACHR and 44(2) of the Commission's Regulations instead. This required the prior consent of the Government, which had not yet been granted, and

---

[252] See also *Weiss* v. *Austria*, 3 April 2003, discussed in Chapter IV, section 2.3, subheading extradition and the risk of life imprisonment.

[253] Interview of author with HRC Special Rapporteur Martin Scheinin, Maastricht 20 September 2002.

[254] Id.

[255] The petition of the Inter-American Commission for provisional measures by the Court in the *Peruvian Prisons case* (Miguel Castro Castro and Santa Mónica in Lima, Cristo Rey in Ica and Yanamayo in Puno) was based on Peru's failure to comply with its precautionary measures of August 1992 on behalf of 'those persons deprived of their liberty for allegedly committing terrorist acts'. The Commission noted that there was 'credible evidence of a grave situation in the Peruvian prisons' posing 'an immediate danger to the right to integrity of the person of those accused and sentenced for terrorism because of the poor conditions in which they are imprisoned'. It had received information that there was a 'high incidence of diseases', loss of weight, overcrowding, isolation, and psychological and emotional problems among male and female prisoners in the prisons concerned. When the prisoners were transferred to those prisons, some of which were 'in very cold zones', they were 'mistreated, insulted, humiliated', some of them were wounded and only had their summer clothing. The prisoners could not receive visits by their relatives and the International Committee of the Red Cross was not authorized to inspect the prisons. The Commission pointed out that all of this lent 'a grave and urgent nature to the situation described'. Subsequently, early December 1992, the Secretariat of the Commission sent additional documentation to the Court containing a complaint. The Commission noted that 'a situation may be developing which could result in the violation of the rights of the women prisoners in the Santa Mónica Prison of Chorrillos, and if true, would increase the seriousness and urgency of the situation being considered by the Members of the Court'. IACHR *Peruvian Prisons* case, Resolution of the President of 14 December 1992, 6th 'Having seen' clause.

which could 'not be remedied by measures ordered by the President'.[256] The President then pointed out: "Insofar as the Commission's request that the Government be asked to take the necessary provisional measures to stop the mistreatment and to provide medical assistance to the inmates of those prisons, the Commission does not provide any evidence regarding the truth of the allegations, which would probably depend on the observations the Commission might make in the visits it wants to carry out in those prisons, or other means of proof, which have not yet been submitted". The President considered it more appropriate for the full Court to decide on the use of the provisional measures requested.[257] In plenary session the Court decided not to order provisional measures. It pointed out that the case concerned a matter not yet before the Court, but still pending before the Commission. The latter had 'not submitted information to the Court sufficient to support' the adoption of provisional measures. This would have required the Commission 'to have gathered preliminary evidence to support a presumption of the truth of the allegations and of a situation whose seriousness and urgency could cause irreparable harm to persons'. Thus the Court considered it inappropriate 'at this time' to adopt the provisional measures requested by the Commission.[258] As Buergenthal has put it, this resulted in a Catch-22 situation since Peru did not allow the Commission to visit the detention centers, which would be necessary in order to collect the evidence required by the Court.[259] He points out that it can be argued 'that in situations where a Government obstructs all legitimate efforts by the Commission to gather evidence relating to allegations of violations of the right to life or physical or metal integrity, the Court might be justified in holding the Commission to a burden of proof that is less stringent than might be the case ordinarily'.[260] The Court should have granted a hearing. Without a hearing, 'and given the pressure of time, the Commission will often find difficult to make the strongest case possible for provisional measures'.[261]

Fact-finding missions require the permission of the State concerned. Such missions have indeed been conducted in a context that would not just assist the adjudicator in its assessment on the merits, but already pending the proceedings with regard to requests for provisional measures. In September 2004, for instance, a delegation of judges of the ECtHR conducted a fact-finding mission in Turkey regarding petitions by about 50 detainees claiming to have developed Wer-

---

[256] IACHR *Peruvian Prisons* case, Resolution of the President of 14 December 1992, 5th 'Considering' clause.

[257] Id., 6th 'Considering' clause.

[258] IACHR *Peruvian Prisons* case, Order of 27 January 1993, 2nd and 3rd 'Whereas' clause.

[259] Buergenthal (1994), p. 80 pointing out that 'to qualify for the Article 63(2) remedy', the Commission 'needed to obtain at least some credible evidence about conditions in these prisons, but it could get that evidence only by means of an investigation which the Government of Peru refused to permit in the proceedings pending before the Commission'. "Moreover, while the Commission might have been able to gather the requisite evidence from witnesses and other sources, it no doubt feared that the long time needed to accomplish this result would greatly increase the probable threat to the lives of the inmates of those prisons". See further e.g. CIDH *Hugo Juarez Cruzat et al.* (*Miguel Castro Castro Prison*) v. *Peru*, 5 March 2001 and CIDH *Polay Campos* v. *Peru*, 10 March 2000 (inadm.). The Court has since dealt with the *Miguel Castro Castro Prison* case on the merits as well, Judgment of 25 November 2006 (referring the provisional measures denied in 1993, §13 and those denied by the President on 3 May 2006, §§67-68).

[260] Buergenthal (1994), p. 81. He refers to the Court's approach on the merits in *Velasquez*, 29 July 1988 and in *Godinez Cruz*, 20 January 1989 and points out that 'of necessity' this approach 'presupposes the existence of at least some evidence to support the Commission's contentions concerning the need for provisional measures'.

[261] Buergenthal (1994), p. 91.

nicke-Korsakoff syndrome in 2001.[262] They argued that their continued detention would be a violation of Articles 2 and 3 ECHR given their state of health.[263] The Court also nominated three medical experts to examine the petitioners.[264]

3.2.6 Death threats and assessment of risk

3.2.6.1 INTRODUCTION

As it is mainly in the Inter-American system that provisional measures have been used to protect against death threats, this section sets out with a more general discussion of the evidentiary requirements applied in this system at the stage of provisional measures. The Inter-American Commission has often taken precautionary measures prior to requesting the Court's intervention. Hence, those matters reaching the Court are examples of cases where the Commission considered its own precautionary measures ineffective.[265] As part of its considerations the Court usually refers to the fact that the State failed to respond to the Commission's precautionary measures.[266] Indeed the Court considers that when the Commission's precautionary measures were ineffective and other threats have taken place since, this triggers a presumption that provisional measures are necessary.[267] This relates to both risk and immediacy.[268]

3.2.6.2 EVIDENTIARY REQUIREMENTS FOR PROVISIONAL MEASURES IN THE INTER-AMERICAN SYSTEM

When it orders provisional measures the Inter-American Court explicitly uses a 'prima facie' norm. When it decides to use provisional measures it generally points out that the Commission's

---

[262] This is described by the Court as a 'brain disorder involving loss of specific brain functions caused by thiamine (B1) deficiency'.

[263] See ECtHR *Balyemez* v. *Turkey*, 32495/03 and 52 other cases.

[264] Press release ECtHR 412, 'Fact-finding mission to Turkey in hunger-strike cases', 6 September 2004, referring to this case and '52 other cases'. A report by the Human Rights Foundation of Turkey, September 2004, notes that the ECtHR delegation examined 54 prisoners at the hospital of Istanbul University. The report specifically named petitioners Yanick, Gençay, Balyemez, Kör, Kuruçay, Gürbüz, Uyan, Yildiz and Hun. With regard to Balyemez it noted that the Court had already taken provisional measures on 5 February 2004 to halt his re-imprisonment. See also provisional measures not to re-imprison in the cases of Hun Kuruçay, Gürbüz, Uyan and Yildiz, all following the fact-finding mission of September 2004, Report Human Rights Foundation of Turkey, <www.tihv.org.tr/report/2004_09/septprison.html>, §4.1. See also Chapter VII (Detention), section 2.5.4 (Protecting detainees on a hunger strike) and Chapter XIII (Protection), section 4.2 on beneficiaries and addressees (under the heading 'the petitioner as addressee').

[265] They are examples because the Commission does not always resort to the Court for provisional measures in such cases. Moreover, in other cases the Commission might not even try its own precautionary measures and immediately resorts to the Court.

[266] See, e.g. IACHR *James, Briggs, Noel, Garcia and Bethel* cases, Order for provisional measures, 14 June 1998, *James et al.* cases, Order of the President for urgent measures, 25 October 2001 and Order for provisional measures, 26 November 2001.

[267] Pasqualucci (2003), p. 297.

[268] See e.g. IACHR *Digna Ochoa et al.* (Mexico), Order of 17 November 1999, 6th 'Considering' clause.

presentations in the case in question 'reveal prima facie a situation of extreme gravity and urgency, rendering it necessary to avoid irreparable damage to the right to life and physical integrity'.[269] Apart from the phrase 'prima facie' the rest of the sentence is derived directly from Article 63(2) ACHR on the use of provisional measures.[270]

While the Inter-American Court is explicit in its use of a *prima facie* norm for the evidence required for the use of provisional measures, it nevertheless is not very clear about the evidentiary standard used at this stage. The same applies for the Inter-American Commission and its precautionary measures. In its new Rules of Procedure the Commission deleted the odd reference in the

---

[269] See e.g. IACHR *Boyce and Joseph* v. *Barbados*, Order of 25 November 2004, 8th 'Considering' clause.

[270] The first time he took urgent measures to halt executions, the President pointed out that the Commission had informed him that it had not yet had the opportunity to examine the complaints. 'Consequently', he noted 'the situation as described by the Commission in its request constitutes a *prima facie* case of extreme gravity and urgency which could result in irreparable damage to persons'. The term 'consequently' is not immediately clear as a link to his previous statement that the Commission had not had the opportunity to examine the complaints. The Spanish version also uses the term 'en consecuencia'. Together, however, with his preceding statement that Trinidad's failure to respond to the Commission's precautionary measures was 'an exceptional circumstance', his remark makes more sense. The State's failure to respond to these precautionary measures may indicate its intent to proceed with the executions. *Prima facie* this constitutes a situation of extreme gravity and urgency, which 'could result' in irreparable harm. IACHR *James, Briggs, Noel, Garcia and Bethel* cases, Order of the President for urgent measures, 27 May 1998. See also *James et al.* case, Orders of the President for urgent measures, 29 June, 13 and 22 July 1998. The criterion of *prima facie* evidence is important for proving both the imminence and the risk of irreparable harm. The Court is clearer in its Order of June 1998 in its approach to evidentiary requirements for provisional measures by indicating that it was on the basis of the information presented by the Commission and the State that it could conclude that a situation of extreme gravity and urgency existed. IACHR *James, Briggs, Noel, Garcia and Bethel* cases, Order for provisional measures, 14 June 1998. It pointed out that, although the Commission had not completed its consideration of the cases, it had advised the Court that '[i]n each case the petitioner made a *prima facie* case alleging that the State violated one or more Articles of the American Convention to the detriment of the defendant'. There are two differences between the formulation of the Court and that of the President. In the first place, the Court refers to the Commission's view that the petitioner made a *prima facie* case of violations of one or more articles of the ACHR. This indicates that while in a case of urgency it is not necessary to determine the case on the merits before ordering provisional measures, there must be *prima facie* evidence of such violations. This means that the evidentiary requirements not only relate to the threat of irreparable harm as such but that in this situation the Commission believes that the Court expects some links with the merits of the case. Different from the Court, the President speaks of a *prima facie* case of extreme gravity without reference to the merits or to the Commission's allegations. In its Order of August 1998 the Court referred to the Commission's statement that it had opened a case after having 'established that the petitioners had presented elements sufficient to meet the requirements of the Convention and its regulations'. The Court also referred to the Commission's statements during the public hearing of the previous day. These statements 'demonstrated the urgency of the situations of the alleged victims, all of whom are still under imminent sentence of death and, therefore, at continued risk of irreparable damage'. Moreover, the Court noted the State's refusal to take part in this hearing. ACHR *James et al.* cases, Order for provisional measures, 16 August 2000.

old Regulations to 'in cases where the denounced facts are true'.[271] At the stage of precautionary measures it would indeed be difficult to expect anything more than *prima facie* credibility of the facts. In addition this would prejudge the merits of the case.[272] It seems that apart from showing *prima facie* evidence of a threat of irreparable harm the petitioner must show the existence, *prima facie*, of an issue under the American Convention (or the American Declaration). Yet obviously he need not show definitely, at that stage, that the denounced facts are 'true'. After all, at the subsequent admissibility stage the Commission 'must conduct a prima facie assessment to determine whether the complaint demonstrates an apparent or potential violation of a right protected by the Convention. This is a summary analysis, which does not imply any prejudgment as to the merits of the dispute'.[273]

The Inter-American Commission's experience with the various country situations, visiting them and preparing country reports continues to provide contextual information that seems to play a role in the Commission's decision making on precautionary measures as well.

From the perspective of the Commission the Court is seen as more legalistic, while the Commission itself is considered a more flexible organ. The Commission takes into account the track record of a human rights organisation bringing a claim. Some organisations may give unreliable information or tend to exaggerate. The information provided by a human rights organisation that is known to be credible and rigorous in terms of its fact-finding and other activities, even if brief, receives serious consideration by the Commission. Generally the Commission prefers to first ask information from the State to find out whether the situation cannot be resolved informally. Only if that is not possible it makes an independent determination on the basis of the evidence and continues dealing with the case. If the Commission receives very little information on an urgent human rights situation, it also takes into account its general knowledge about the human rights situation in that particular country or area as well as the general attitude of that State.

As noted, sometimes the Inter-American Court has refused to take provisional measures due to lack of information. Commissioner Goldman believes that the Court has emphasized the aspect of lack of information too much, possibly in a misplaced deference to the European system. He argues that this lies partly in the different experiences and functions of the Commission and Court, as well as their members. Members of the Court have tended to be constitutional lawyers, experts in criminal procedure, people who had been on the bench in their own country, while members of the Commission tend to have a more practical human rights experience. He considers the Commission to be the barometer of what is 'going on' in society. It is the Commission that starts receiving the complaints, the calls, the faxes and the e-mails.[274]

This section gives some examples of cases involving death threats that may provide some indications as to the approach of the Court with regard to evidentiary requirements.

In August 1991 the Court ratified its President's provisional measures in the *Chunimá* case. The 'possibility for injury' was imminent and called for immediate action by the Court because five people had already been killed and the judges that issued the arrest warrants for the suspects had received death threats and were in hiding.[275]

---

[271] See Article 29(2) of CIDH former Regulations (dating from 1987). Article 25(1) of the CIDH 2001 Rules of Procedure simply uses the criterion 'whenever necessary according to the information available'.

[272] See also Pasqualucci (1993), p. 803 and Pasqualucci (2003), p. 296.

[273] See CIDH *Teodoro Cabrera Garcia and Rodolfo Montiel Flores* v. *Mexico*, 27 February 2004 (adm.), §47.

[274] Interview by the author with Commissioner Robert Goldman, American University, Washington College of Law, 26 September 2001.

[275] Pasqualucci (2003), p. 302.

Yet the Court set out certain requirements that must be met before the Court can adopt provisional measures at the request of the Commission. It pointed out that the reference to 'in cases where the denounced facts are true' in Article 29(2) of the Commission's old Regulations was 'not a question of fully determining the truth of the facts; rather, the Commission must have reasonable basis for assuming them to be true'.[276] It found, however, that the Commission had not fulfilled this requirement because its request 'merely transcribes the facts reported by the petitioner'.[277] The Court also referred to the acknowledgement by Guatemala of an 'internal armed conflict'. "Such a blanket acknowledgement does not imply acceptance that the facts denounced are true; however, it does lead to the presumption that a situation exists which could bring about irreparable damage to persons".[278]

The Court referred to the wording in Article 63(2), indicating 'that we are dealing here with an extraordinary instrument, one which becomes necessary in exceptional circumstances'.[279]

It also pointed out that the request for provisional measures referred to a case 'not yet submitted to the Court'. This meant 'that the Court lacks information regarding the facts and circumstances surrounding the case, which information must be at the disposal of the Commission. The latter must, consequently, transmit such information together with the corresponding petition, in order to provide the Court with the facts necessary to enable it to arrive at a decision'.[280] Despite its critical remarks the Court considered that provisional measures were warranted. In fact the measures taken on behalf of the persons listed in the President's previous order[281] were to be extended, a position, the Court noted, 'with which the Government concurred at the hearing'.[282] The Order remained into effect until December 1991.[283] Subsequently the Commission re-established its own precautionary measures.[284]

---

[276] IACHR *Chunimá* (Guatemala), Order of 1 August 1991, §6a.

[277] Ibid.

[278] Ibid.

[279] IACHR *Chunimá* (Guatemala), Order of 1 August 1991, §6b.

[280] Id., §7. See also IACHR *Colotenango* (Guatemala), Order of 1 February 1996, where the Court hoped the Commission would bring the case itself to the Court, rather than just its request for a prolongation or expansion of provisional measures, stating it 'is incumbent on the Commission to take all necessary steps to examine the possibility of submitting to the jurisdiction of the Court any case in which circumstances of extreme gravity and urgency persist for a prolonged period of time, since the Court is not in possession of sufficient direct knowledge of the facts and of the surrounding circumstances to permit it to come to the most appropriate decision', 5th 'Considering' clause. See also e.g. IACHR *Millacura Llaipén y otros* (Argentina), Order of the President of 21 June 2006.

[281] IACHR *Chunimá* (Guatemala), President's Order for urgent measures of 15 July 1991. In this case the Court stressed the importance of distinguishing between the provisional measures the Court can adopt under Article 63(2) of the Convention and 'the emergency measures that Article 23 (4) of the Rules empowers the President to order the parties in the *interim*, so as to permit any decision that the Court may eventually take to have the appropriate effect; in other words, so that the Court may not find itself facing a *fait accompli*'. IACHR *Chunimá* (Guatemala), Order of 1 August 1991, §5.

[282] IACHR *Chunimá* (Guatemala), Order of 1 August 1991, §8. See also Buergenthal (1994), p. 79 noting that the Court did so 'because the additional facts brought to its attention by the Government at the public hearing strengthened the Commission's allegations'.

[283] IACHR *Chunimá* (Guatemala), Order of 1 August 1991, 1st 'Resolving' clause.

[284] CIDH Annual Report 1991, Chapter IVb. CEJIL notes that in an unprecedented decision, in March 1993, some of the perpetrators of the persecution were convicted and sentenced to prison terms. CEJIL case docket 1997 (in file with the author).

As noted, in its Orders for provisional measures in cases not yet pending before it the Court often refers to the fact that the Commission previously used precautionary measures to no avail. An example is the case of Father *Vogt*. He was threatened in relation to his pastoral work. Before the Court was in session its President ordered 'urgent measures' in April 1996 based, among others, on the consideration that the Commission had taken precautionary measures on three occasions and that these had not had the required effect. This had become 'a special circumstance making it incumbent on the President of the Court to request urgent measures'.[285] He noted in his order for urgent measures of April 1996 that 'the background information presented in this case' effectively constituted 'a *prima facie* case of urgent and grave danger to Father Daniel Vogt's life and the integrity of his person'.[286] By its Order of 27 June 1996 the Court confirmed the President's Order 'finding it to be consistent with the law and the merits of the proceedings'.[287] In later cases the Court simply ratifies orders of the President without such statement. In 1997 the Court lifted its provisional measures in the *Vogt* case because the threats and harassment had diminished considerably as a result of the provisional measures.[288]

In August 1999 the Commission requested Colombia to protect the lives and personal integrity of a spokesman for Cartagena del Chairá in the region of Caquetá. It was alleged that a high-ranking official of the National Army of Colombia had publicly identified him as a spokesman for the guerrillas. Apparently he had been harassed and received threatening telephone calls 'of the type that usually precedes criminal attacks'.[289]

In his decision to order urgent measures in the *Peace Community* case (2000) the President of the Court, Judge Cançado Trindade, considered that the 'records produced by the Commission in its request demonstrate prima facie a situation of extreme seriousness and urgency as to the rights to life and personal integrity' of 193 persons.[290] The Court used a similar phrase but without referring to *prima facie* evidence: 'the Commission has described a situation of extreme seriousness and urgency that conforms to the basis under Article 63(2) of the American Convention' with regard to these named persons.[291]

The President had noted that the Commission had already taken precautionary measures but that these had not been able to stop the serious and continuous violence perpetrated against members of the Community.[292] During the hearing of November 2000 the Commission again referred to the precautionary measures it had used in 1997, in light of more than 40 summary executions and forced disappearances. It emphasised that almost three years later the Community was still under continuous threat and without adequate protection by the government. The last months the violence had increased.

---

[285] IACHR *Vogt* case, Order of 27 June 1996, Compendium 1987-1996, p. 160.

[286] Ibid.

[287] Id., p. 172.

[288] IACHR *Vogt* case, Order of 11 November 1997. Another example is the Court's decision to lift the provisional measures on behalf of four persons in the *Carpio Nicolle* case, Order of 19 June 1998 (case 1011-97). It continued them on behalf of two family members of Carpio Nicolle. Subsequently others were again added in the list of beneficiaries. At the end of 2008 the State again requested the Court to lift the provisional measures. See Order of the President of 18 November 2008 ordering a hearing for the beginning of 2009.

[289] CIDH Annual Report 1999, Chapter 3.C.1, §21.

[290] IACHR *Peace Community of San José de Apartadó* case (Colombia), Order of the President for urgent measures, 9 October 2000, 4th 'Considering' clause.

[291] IACHR *Peace Community of San José de Apartadó* case (Colombia), Order of 24 November 2000, 4th 'Considering' clause.

[292] IACHR *Peace Community of San José de Apartadó* case (Colombia), Order of the President for urgent measures, 9 October 2000, 5th 'Considering' clause.

"In spite of the active accompaniment of organizations such as the Peace Brigades, the interest of the foreign diplomatic representations in Colombia, and the Office of the High Commissioner of the United Nations, and, even, the actions of the Vice-presidency of the Republic, the members of the Community of Paz continue to be 'prisoners of violence' specially from paramilitary groups, and they remain to be without the effective protection of the State's agents".[293]

The Court ratified the President's Order and expanded it to include all members of the Community.[294] They were subsequently maintained and expanded several times.[295]

The Court has dismissed requests for provisional measures 'on grounds of inadmissibility' because it considered it 'not possible to determine, on a *prima facie* basis, that the persons listed by the representative (...) are in a situation of extreme gravity and urgency, or that their lives and personal integrity are threatened and at serious risk'.[296] After all, it pointed out, 'provisional measures may be ordered as long as the background data submitted to the Court provide *prima facie* evidence that there exists a situation of extreme gravity and urgency and that irreparable damage to persons is imminent'.[297]

3.2.6.3 DENYING REQUESTS FOR PROVISIONAL MEASURES

The Inter-American Court has pointed out that 'in a request for provisional measures it is not possible to consider arguments pertaining to issues other than those which relate strictly to the extreme gravity and urgency, and the necessity to avoid irreparable damage to persons'.[298] Otherwise the provisional measures would conflict with the notion of non-anticipation. Hence the Court has sometimes considered that a request by petitioners for provisional measures did 'not refer to a situation of extreme gravity and urgency warranting the adoption of provisional

---

[293] See IACHR *Peace Community of San José de Apartadó* case (Colombia), Order of 24 November 2000, 'Having seen' clause 9b.

[294] IACHR *Peace Community of San José de Apartadó* case (Colombia), Order of 24 November 2000. The Court pointed out that, because of the seriousness of the situation, it gave a detailed description of the facts stated in the Commission's report. It noted that the State did not dispute the facts as described by the Commission, that it had examined the facts and circumstances that served as the basis for the President's Order for urgent measures and ratified this decision because it found it to be in conformity with the law and the merits of the records. See IACHR *Peace Community of San José de Apartadó* case (Colombia), Order of 24 November 2000, 15th 'Considering' clause. The Spanish text speaks of '*por encontrarla ajustada a derecho y al mérito de los autos*'.

[295] See e.g. IACHR *Peace Community of San José de Apartadó* case (Colombia), Order of the President for urgent measures, 9 October 2000, Orders for provisional measures, 24 November 2000 and 18 June 2002.

[296] IACHR Case of *Bueno-Alves* (Argentina), Order of 2 February 2007 (denying request for provisional measures), 5th 'Considering' clause.

[297] IACHR Case of *Bueno-Alves* (Argentina), Order of 2 February 2007 (denying request for provisional measures), 4th 'Considering' clause, referring to various cases including *Case of the 19 Tradesmen*, Order of 4 July 2006, 5th 'Considering' clause.

[298] IACHR *Case of the Miguel Castro-Castro Prison* v. *Peru*, Order denying provisional measures of 29 January 2008, 10th 'Considering' clause. See also *Matter of James et al.* (Trinidad and Tobago), Order of 20 August 1998, 6th 'Considering' clause; *Matter of "Globovisión" Television Station* (Venezuela), Order of 29 January 2008, 10th 'Considering' clause and *Matter of Luisiana Ríos et al.* (Venezuela), Order of 3 July 2007, 9th 'Considering' clause.

measures to avoid irreparable damage to persons pursuant to Article 63(2) of the American Convention on Human Rights'.[299] It explained that it would consider the implications of the facts reported to it 'if appropriate, at the stage, still pending, of oversight of compliance' with its judgment in the case in question.[300]

3.2.6.4 LIFTING PROVISIONAL MEASURES IN CASES OF DEATH THREATS

Petitioners consult with the beneficiaries of precautionary measures and may report to the Commission that the situation 'no longer requires the application of urgent measures'. If the Commission decides to lift then it often observes that it will continue watching over the situation closely and will seek to apply these measures once again if circumstances warrant it.[301]

The Court has also lifted its provisional measures when it considers that a reasonable time had elapsed since the beneficiary had received any threats or intimidation.[302] In *Alemán Lacayo* (1996) the Court ordered provisional measures, noting "That in the instant case, independently of the fact that the merits of the matter are under consideration by the Commission, publicity in both the national and international Press, the death of one of Dr. Alemán-Lacayo's bodyguards, and the injuries sustained by others in his entourage, have invested the events on which the Commission bases its request for provisional measures with a high degree of notoriety and credibility".[303] Subsequently, the Court heeded to the Commission's request to lift the provisional measures. The Commission had noted that "[T]he Nicaraguan people voted on October 20, 1996, to elect its Government. At that election Dr. Arnoldo Alemán-Lacayo was elected President of the Republic and is to assume the country's highest office today. As a consequence, the Inter-American Commission on Human Rights considers that the provisional measures duly ordered by the Honorable Court attained its main purpose".[304] It considered that 'the instant case, in view of Mr. Alemán's election as President of Nicaragua and, taking the Commission's request into account, the situation of "*extreme gravity and urgency*" which prompted the adoption of the provisional measures has ceased to exist, in itself making them no longer necessary'.[305] In fact 'as the beneficiary of the measures is today President of the Republic of Nicaragua, it is inappropriate for an international body to adopt provisional measures to be instituted by a government on behalf of its own Head of State'.[306]

In May 1997 the Commission indicated to the Court that there was no information that the physical integrity of two beneficiaries of the Court's provisional measures in the *Caballero*

---

[299] IACHR *Case of the Miguel Castro-Castro Prison* v. *Peru*, Order denying provisional measures of 29 January 2008, 11th 'Considering' clause.

[300] IACHR *Case of the Miguel Castro-Castro Prison* v. *Peru*, Order denying provisional measures of 29 January 2008, 12th 'Considering' clause. See also *Case of the Miguel Castro-Castro Prison* v. *Peru,* Order of 30 January 2007 (denying a request for provisional measures). See also *Miguel Castro-Castro Prison,* Judgment of 25 November 2006.

[301] See e.g. IACHR *Serech and Saquic,* Order of 19 September 1997, 4th and 6th 'Having seen' clause for a similar statement in the context of cases in which the Court lifted its Order for provisional measures.

[302] See e.g. IACHR *matter of Gallardo Rodríguez* (Mexico), 11 July 2007.

[303] IACHR *Alemán Lacayo* (Nicaragua), Order of 2 February 1996, §7.

[304] IACHR *Alemán Lacayo* (Nicaragua), Order of 6 February 1997, 4th 'Having seen' clause (referring to the Commission's brief of 10 January 1997).

[305] IACHR *Alemán Lacayo* (Nicaragua), Order of 6 February 1997, 2nd 'Considering' clause.

[306] IACHR *Alemán Lacayo* (Nicaragua), Order of 6 February 1997, 3rd 'Considering' clause. On the beneficiaries of provisional measures see also Chapter XIII (Protection), section 4.

Delgado and Santana case continued to be threatened. It pointed out that the personal circumstances of these two persons had fundamentally changed and that one of them was even working as an official in the Administrative Security Department of Colombia. In this light, it was reasonable to lift the provisional measures on their behalf. In June 1999 the Court indeed decided to lift the provisional measures it had ordered for those two persons. It also decided to maintain its provisional measures ordered on behalf of the other three beneficiaries in this case.[307]

In *Clemente Teherán* (2000) the Commission and the State suggested that the Court would lift its provisional measures because the Commission had been unable to get in touch with the indigenous community that had initially reported the violations. At the same time the Commission suggested that the lack of contact was due to fear on the part of the petitioners. The Court refused to lift its provisional measures, arguing that it had not been provided with 'sufficient reasons to indicate that the '*situation of extreme gravity and urgency*' has ceased'.[308] It has been suggested that this decision 'may be frustrating to the Commission, which has limited resources for verifying the situations of petitioners', but is positive 'in that it may serve to minimize State attempts at intimidating petitioners to the Inter-American system to abandoning their petitions'.[309]

In January 1995 the Inter-American Commission had requested Mexico to take precautionary measures on behalf of the Director of the Miguel Agustin Pro Juarez Human Rights Centre (Centro Pro), an attorney and the Technical Director of the National Network of Human Rights Organisations 'Todos los derechos para todos'.[310] If the threats against Centro Pro indeed subsided, this was only temporarily. In September 1999 Centro Pro (PRODH) received three envelopes containing threats against the director and staff of the Centre. On 9 August 1999 unknown persons kidnapped Digna Ochoa, the Centre's attorney. Her kidnappers had taken certain personal items from her including her personal calling cards. One of these cards was later found in one of the envelopes the Centre received containing further threats against them. The Commission decided to take precautionary measures and requested Mexico to adopt specific measures to protect the lives and physical integrity of Digna Ochoa, the Director of Centro Pro and its members. On 21 September 1999 Mexico informed the Commission that its National Human Rights Commission (CNDH) had taken steps to protect the beneficiaries of the precautionary measures. It also noted that the Office of the Attorney General of the Federal District had initiated preliminary investigations of the threats and the kidnapping. Furthermore, it referred to the fact that the Hu-

---

[307] IACHR *Caballero-Delgado and Santana* (Colombia), Order of 3 June 1999. Several years later the State argued that certain remaining provisional measures should be lifted, 'since: i) they have been in force for more than 13 years, and in fact provisional measures should be exceptional in nature; ii) there is no evidence of new threats; iii) domestic law provides for effective mechanisms to protect a person who acts as trade union leader, as in the case of María Nodelia Parra and a person detained in a penitentiary, as in the case of Gonzalo Arias-Alturo'. *Caballero-Delgado and Santana* (Colombia), Order of 6 February 2008, 8th 'Having seen' clause. Yet the Court decided to maintain the provisional measures. It pointed out that it appreciated 'the information provided by the State in the sense that certain protection measures set forth in the domestic legislation could benefit both petitioners'. It considered that 'the State should address in its next report the domestic protection mechanisms that would apply to both beneficiaries. Particularly, the Court is keen on knowing the specific domestic protection measures that could be adopted regarding both beneficiaries; such measures would guarantee a protection level similar to that enjoyed by the beneficiaries of provisional measures contemplated herein'. IACHR *Caballero-Delgado and Santana* (Colombia), Order of 6 February 2008, 13th 'Considering' clause.

[308] IACHR *Clemente Teherán et al.* (Guatemala), Order of 12 August 2000, 7th 'Considering' clause.

[309] Pasqualucci (2003), p. 316. See also Chapter IX (Threats).

[310] CIDH Annual Report 1996, 14 March 1997, Chapter II, section 4a.

man Rights Commission of the Federal District had intervened as well. The Commission notes in its Annual Report of 1999 that the petitioners reported another serious attack against Digna Ochoa that took place within the time period the Commission had set for receiving comments. On 11 November 1999, upon receipt of this information, the Commission decided to request the Inter-American Court to take provisional measures.[311] Provisional measures on behalf of Digna Ochoa remained in place for almost two years. In August 2001 they were lifted at the request of Mexico and without the opposition of the Commission. The State had argued that it was 'an abuse of provisional measures to use them as a *de facto* substitute for prosecuting a case that should have sufficient merit to be heard before the Inter-American Court of Human Rights'.[312] It was reported that Digna Ochoa and her colleagues considered that violence against them 'could not happen in present day Mexico'.[313] Tragically two months later Digna Ochoa was murdered. Immediately the President of the Court ordered new provisional measures on behalf of her colleagues and family. A hearing took place discussing the circumstances, including the earlier decision to lift the provisional measures, after which the Court confirmed the President's measures.[314]

---

[311] CIDH Annual Report 1999, Chapter III C.1, §44.

[312] IACHR *Digna Ochoa et al.* (Mexico), Order of 28 August 2001, 3rd 'Having seen' clause.

[313] IACHR *Miguel Agustín Pro Juárez Human Rights Center et al.* (Mexico), Order of 30 November 2001, 8th 'having seen' clause.

[314] The Court refers to the statements, made at the hearing of 26 November 2001, by the Commission and the State with regard to the previous request to lift the provisional measures. "The statement of one of the Commission's assistants on the factors that she had taken into account when she had agreed that the provisional measures ordered in favor of Digna Ochoa and others should be lifted: "When we took the decision to request that the measures should be lifted, we took various factors into consideration. The first was that the Attorney General had closed the investigation; according to the petitioners, this ended the possibility of terminating the impunity in this series of threats and harassment, at that time. I believe that [it is necessary to express a] public *mea culpa*; we underestimated the sword of Damocles that impunity represented for the physical safety of all of us, [...] the members of the PRODH Center, who agreed that the measures should be lifted, because there was no point in continuing to insist on investigations when the State was not undertaking them and refused to continue with them. The lawyer, Digna Ochoa, manifested her frustration with the ineffectiveness of the administration of justice and also, to a certain extent, her confidence that [...] acts [such as her homicide] could not happen in present day Mexico. I therefore believe that, in these circumstances, we, the representatives of the victims, and the victims themselves made an error in our calculations; we did not believe that impunity was a sword of Damocles and this error led to fatal consequences for ourselves and for our colleagues. We made a mistake owing to our frustration in the face of the response of the administration of justice and of the State of Mexico itself", IACHR *Miguel Agustín Pro Juárez Human Rights Center et al.* (Mexico), Order of 30 November 2001, 8th 'Having seen' clause. "The statement of the State's representative on the factors that had been taken into consideration in order to request that the provisional measures ordered in favor of Digna Ochoa y Plácido and others should be lifted: "the following factors were taken into consideration in the decision to request the lifting of the precautionary measures. First, the absence of complaints of threats by Digna Ochoa or the Miguel Agustín Pro Juárez Human Rights Center. The fact that, for several months, she had not had police protection, when she went to the United States and then returned [...] and there were no complaints or threats, which [...] led us to believe that the climate of intimidation and harassment had ceased. Lastly, the issue of the investigation, and in this case, I am referring to the investigation of the Office of the Attorney General: [...] the response of the Office of the Attorney General was always that there were no elements to continue with the investigation [...]. But, in any case, we felt that the measures had achieved their purpose.

3.2.7 Cultural survival and assessment of risk

On occasion the HRC has dealt with the issue of cultural survival. It appears that the threshold for a violation of Article 27 ICCPR is very high and the difference between provisional measures and the eventual finding on the merits can be found in the assessment of risk. The merits and the provisional measures coincide in the sense that the evaluation by the Rapporteur before provisional measures are used is a miniature of the analysis preceding a decision on the merits. Thus far, the HRC seems to consider that only when the cultural survival of the *group* is at stake it would find a violation.[315]

The HRC practice with regard to provisional measures to protect cultural survival serves to illustrate how the difficulties in assessing the evidence have an impact not just on the decisions on the merits but also on the use of provisional measures. It also shows that the Committee is less inclined to consider on the merits that certain acts would result in irreparable harm to cultural survival. While sometimes it did use provisional measures pending the proceedings, it did so in a manner that was much feebler. It acted much less swiftly and with more circumscription, almost anticipating their subsequent decision to withdraw them.[316] If the adjudicator initially refuses to take provisional measures the petitioner may still be able to convince it at a later stage with new arguments and evidence of risk.[317]

The stricter assessment of the evidence may have been based purely on the type of (conflicting) evidence available. Yet it is also possible that while the HRC has recognized in principle that certain measures may result in irreparable harm to cultural survival, in practice it attaches less importance to preventing this type of harm than to preventing irreparable harm to the life and personal integrity of individuals.[318]

The excessive length of the proceedings in the case involving the *Lubicon Lake Band* (1990) has been explained elsewhere.[319] Yet, assuming that for the use of provisional measures an exhaustive and definitive examination of the evidence is not necessary, the fact that the HRC used provisional measures so late in the proceedings remains puzzling.[320]

Domestically the Band's requests for an interim injunction, a caveat and a declaratory judgment had failed. The domestic court cases clarified the concept of irreparable harm used by

---

Unfortunately, we were mistaken also and we agree with the petitioners that, this time, we cannot allow these facts to happen again, so we have implemented all the measures of protection requested of us. Consequently, we have set up a permanent dialogue with the petitioners, with the human rights defenders and, therefore, we submit ourselves to the Court, the Commission and to public opinion in everything related to these provisional measures", 10th 'Having seen' clause.

[315] See Chapter IX (Culture).

[316] See Chapter IX (Culture) and Chapter XIII (Protection), section 4 (group of beneficiaries).

[317] Sometimes, however, provisional measures are too late by that time, or in any case less effective in preventing irreparable harm.

[318] See Part II on the common core and outer limits of the concept of provisional measures. It appears that while ensuring cultural survival, while now belonging to the common core, nevertheless is not considered as important as ensuring the right to life and personal integrity.

[319] Schmidt (1992), pp. 651-652 has noted that 'the final decision was adopted on the basis of a total of 78 documents, fact sheets and conference room papers submitted by the parties or prepared by the Secretariat, as well as decisions adopted by the Committee'. He observes that the entirely written procedure, without oral hearings or independent fact-finding, had caused 'considerable delays in the consideration of many factually or legally complex communications, since the treaty body concerned was forced to engage in time-consuming exchanges of correspondence with either of the parties before disposing of the necessary information enabling it to adopt a decision'.

[320] See also Chapter II (Systems), discussing prompt intervention.

Canadian courts and the manner in which the evidence was assessed. They employed the criterion of 'balance of convenience'. The Court of Appeal of Alberta considered that interim relief might be warranted if the defendants were attempting to force members of the Band from their dwellings, or to deny them 'access to traditional burial grounds or other special places, or to hunting and trapping areas'. The petitioner argued that the Band had, in fact, 'alleged denial of access to all of these areas, supporting its allegations with photographs of damage and with several uncontested affidavits'.[321]

Thus, the dispute turned on an assessment of the evidence, which was linked to the court's approach to the concept of irreparable harm. The petitioner referred to the definition of irreparable injury by the Court of Appeal, which is an injury for which fair and reasonable redress in a court of law is not possible. To refuse an injunction to prevent such irreparable injury would be a 'denial of justice'.[322] Yet in this case the domestic court did not consider that the balance of convenience favoured relief to the Band. It considered that the Band would suffer no irreparable harm if resource development continued fully.[323]

According to the State this meant that interim injunctions were only used if the issue was serious, if without the injunction irreparable harm would be suffered and if the balance of convenience between the parties favoured relief to the applicant. It suggested that the HRC should take the same approach.[324]

As the domestic appeals that were still pending were without suspensive effect, their non-exhaustion was no obstacle to admissibility before the HRC. Moreover, the adjudicator could use provisional measures before finally determining the admissibility of a claim.[325] However, the HRC took three years and five months to determine that the case was admissible and only then it took provisional measures. At that stage the HRC did assess the evidence for irreparable harm differently from the domestic court and used provisional measures. It did so in light of the seriousness of the claim that the Band was on the verge of extinction.

It would have been preferable had it made the assessment earlier in the proceedings. However, this was the first time the HRC used provisional measures in a case not involving irreparable harm to the life or personal integrity of individuals. At the time the HRC may not have been confident about the appropriateness of their use in the context of threats to the cultural survival of a group. Or possibly the case was so complex that its urgency escaped the attention of the Committee.

Sara et al. v. *Finland* (inadm. 1994) equally illustrates the difficulty of dealing with cases on an urgent basis when the evidence is conflicting.[326] The Committee used provisional measures

---

[321] See HRC *Lubicon Lake Band*, 26 March 1990, §3.7. Ominayak submitted that the Band 'clearly met this test by demonstrating, with uncontested evidence, injury to their livelihood, to their subsistence economy, to their culture and their way of life as a social and political entity'.

[322] HRC *Lubicon Lake Band*, 26 March 1990, §3.8.

[323] Like the lower court, the Court of Appeal of Alberta did consider that the Band's 'claim of aboriginal title to the land presented a serious question of law to be decided at trial,' but that, nevertheless, the Band would 'suffer no irreparable harm if resource development continued fully and that the balance of convenience, therefore, favoured denial of the injunction'. Chief Ominayak stated that the provincial government and the oil companies attempted to convince the Court that the Band had 'no right to any possession of any sort in any part of the subject lands, which, logically, included even their homes'. HRC *Lubicon Lake Band*, 26 March 1990, §3.7.

[324] HRC *Lubicon Lake Band*, 26 March 1990, §§5.3, 5.7 and 21.3.

[325] See also Chapter XIV on admissibility.

[326] HRC *Sara et al.* v. *Finland*, 23 March 1994 (inadm.). The State had contended that the envisaged forestry operations, consisting merely of silvicultural logging, were in fact expected to contribute to the natural development of the forest. It referred to a report for the Ministry of Agriculture and

only when it initially declared the case admissible. This was seven months after initial submission.[327] By contrast, if it had been a death penalty or expulsion case it would probably have used provisional measures prior to declaring the case admissible.[328] Eventually it declared the case inadmissible for non-exhaustion of domestic remedies and did not address the qualitative argument of the petitioner.[329] While clearly the problem of conflicting evidence plays a role in the Committee's late use of provisional measures, it may also simply attach less importance to preventing irreparable harm to cultural survival than to life or personal integrity.

In the case following up the situation in *Sara*, the case of *Äärelä and Näkkäläjärvi v. Finland* (2001), the HRC did not use provisional measures because the events complained of had already taken place.[330] On the merits it found no violation because it was 'unable to conclude'

Forestry by a professor of a Finnish university stating that 'no single forest or land use can on its own fulfil the income and welfare needs of the population' and schemes of multiple use were necessary. This advice seems not to relate to the environmental impact of this type of logging. Instead it is an economic assessment. It also noted that the petitioners could not be considered as 'victims' of a violation of the Covenant. It pointed out that the rationale of the Wilderness Act was in fact to enhance protection of the Sami culture and traditional nature based means of livelihood. The petitioners submitted the reports of two experts 'according to which (a) under certain conditions reindeer are highly dependent on lichen growing on trees; (b) lichen growing on the ground are a primary winter forage for reindeer; (c) old forests are superior to young ones as herding areas; and (d) logging negatively affects nature based methods of reindeer herding'.

[327]   It had transmitted the case in February 1991, two months after initial submission, but at that time it did not yet use provisional measures. *Sara et al. v. Finland*, 23 March 1994 (inadm.).

[328]   See Conclusion Part II (on the purpose of provisional measures).

[329]   The petitioners criticized the State's remark that practicing intensive reindeer husbandry was not incompatible with intensive logging. They noted that this only applied to the modern forms of reindeer herding using artificial feeding, while they used traditional methods for which the old forests in the area were essential. They gave the following example: "The winter 1991-1992 demonstrated how relatively warm winters may threaten traditional herding methods. As a result of alternating periods of temperatures of above and below 0 degree centigrade the snow was, in many parts of Finnish Lapland, covered by a hard layer of ice that prevented the reindeer from getting their nutrition from the ground. In some areas without old forests carrying lichen on their branches, reindeer have been dying from hunger. In this situation, the herding area designated in the communication has been very valuable to the authors". *Sara et al. v. Finland*, 23 March 1994 (inadm.), §7.9.

[330]   HRC *Äärelä and Näkkäläjärvi v. Finland*, 24 October 2001. The petitioners had argued about an area that was the last remaining natural wilderness for the Lappi Herdsmen's Committee and that for the Sallivaara Herdsmen's Committee formed 'one third of its best winter herding areas and is essential for the survival of reindeer in extreme climatic conditions'. Again they argued about the impact on the environment. They pointed out that snow and rainfalls were common in this area and the winter season was approximately one month longer than in other areas. "The climate has a direct impact on the area's environment, in particular the trees (birch and spruce), whose growth is slow; the trees in turn encourage the growth of the two types of lichen that constitute the winter diets for reindeer". They emphasised that 'even partial logging would render the area inhospitable for reindeer breeding for at least a century and possibly irrevocably, since the destruction of the trees would lead to an extension of the marsh, with the resulting change of the nutrition balance of the soil'. They also submitted that the 'silvicultural methods of logging (i.e. environmentally sensitive cutting of forest areas) advocated by the authorities for some parts of the wilderness areas used by the authors would cause possibly irreversible damage to reindeer herding, as the age structure of the forest and the conditions for the lichen growth would change'. They spoke of the strategic significance of certain lands and pointed out that other activities in

whether the logging of trees in the area at issue rose to the threshold it had established earlier, namely whether the interference by the State party was so substantial as to fail to properly protect the right the right of the petitioners to enjoy their culture.[331]

In *Länsman II* (1996) the HRC initially used provisional measures, but later set them aside without explaining why.[332] On the merits the HRC had to determine whether the logging that had already taken place, as well as the logging that had been approved for the future, was 'of such proportions as to deny the authors the right to enjoy their culture' in the area in question. The ensuing discussion turned on evidentiary matters about the consultation process and the impact of logging plans on the one hand and the Committee's deference to the interpretation of domestic courts on the other. Again, the HRC determined that it was 'unable to conclude that the activities carried out as well as approved constitute a denial of the authors' right to enjoy their own culture'. It pointed out that this was the result of a careful consideration of the material placed before it by the parties and that it had duly noted 'that the parties do not agree on the long-term impact of the logging activities already carried out and planned'.[333]

It then deferred to these courts' interpretation of Article 27 in noting that it was 'not in a position to conclude, on the evidence before it, that the impact of logging plans would be such as to amount to a denial of the authors' rights under article 27 or that the finding of the Court of Appeal affirmed by the Supreme Court, misinterpreted and/or misapplied article 27 of the Covenant in the light of the facts before it'.[334] In other words, according to the Committee the logging activities did not appear to threaten the survival of reindeer husbandry.[335]

---

the area, 'including large-scale gold-mining, other mineral mining, large-scale tourism, and the operation of a radar station', had limited the possibilities for herding.

[331] The test the HRC applied was whether interference by the State party in reindeer husbandry, as an essential element of Sami culture, was so substantial that the State had failed to properly protect the right of the petitioners to enjoy their culture. The Committee considered that the requirement of consultation had been fulfilled. The State had indicated that, as required by the Committee's decision in *Jouni Länsman*, the plans had been developed in consultation with reindeer owners. Apart from finding that the requirement of consultation had been fulfilled, the HRC also referred to the partly conflicting expert evidence, which the District Court had assessed differently from the appellate court. It considered that 'it does not have sufficient information before it in order to be able to draw independent conclusions on the factual importance of the area to husbandry and the long-term impact on the sustainability of husbandry, and the consequences under article 27 of the Covenant', HRC *Äärelä and Näkkäläjärvi v. Finland*, 24 October 2001, §7.6.

[332] HRC *Jouni E. Länsman et al. v. Finland*, 30 October 1996. The HRC simply noted the State party's argument that the request for interim measures of protection should be set aside. Hence, from the publicly available information it is not clear on what basis it made this decision. See also Chapter X (Culture).

[333] See also Chapter XIII (Protection), section 4 on the group of beneficiaries, discussing consultation and representation in cases involving indigenous peoples.

[334] See also Schmidt (1997), p. 338.

[335] The State party had indeed solicited deference by the HRC. It had recalled that the claims had been thoroughly examined by the domestic courts. These courts had had before them extensive documentation and Article 27 had been taken into account as well. It submitted that 'the national judge is far better positioned than an international instance to examine the case in all of its aspects'. In this case the petitioners had used an argument loosely based on the precautionary principle, although they did not use this terminology. See Chapter I, section 5.3.3 and section 4 of this Chapter. They submitted that if the government invoked 'the argument that the effects of selective cutting are milder than in the case of clear felling, the only conclusion should be that all further logging in the area in question should be postponed until objective and scientific findings

It considered that, on the basis of the available information, the fact that such traditional reindeer husbandry was an activity of low economic profitability was not 'a result of the encouragement of other economic activities by the State party in area in question, but of other, external, economic factors'.[336] In light of its deference to the State party's arguments and the assessment by the domestic courts of the risks involved, on the merits the Committee could not confirm its earlier assessment of the risks that had resulted in the decision to take provisional measures and it found no violation.[337]

The petitioners noted that the State should support its argument for continuing the logging of trees by objective and scientific findings showing that the forest in the area already logged had indeed recovered. Their argument relies on the precautionary principle.[338]

The HRC did indicate that the cumulative effect of certain infringements could eventually constitute a violation of Article 27.[339] In other words, the question arises at what point one can speak of irreparable harm and use provisional measures. This question applies particularly when the HRC takes a quantitative approach.[340] If it would take a qualitative approach it would sometimes be easier to find that there was a threat of irreparable harm.

This could be so in case of *prima facie* evidence of threats to an area of religious or cultural significance. Establishing the qualitative importance of a certain area (however small) for traditional livelihood would still require specific evidence of the importance of that piece of land to maintain traditional livelihood. Tree logging or oil drilling or other actions could result in irreparable harm also if it involved only a small part of the traditional lands, if these parts are qualitatively essential for the collective as well as individual right to culture.

By contrast, the quantitative approach involves (incremental) threats to such a large area that this would equally make impossible cultural survival. In other words, depending on the ap-

---

show that the forest in the area already logged-the Pyhäjärvi area-has recovered'. See §9.2. The petitioners had emphasised the fact that the past and future logging would exacerbate an already difficult situation. It appears from their submission of 28 August 1995 that they argued that 'the situation of the Sami in Finland, and in the Angeli area in particular, is very difficult already *before* any new interference with their way of life'. Because of this a threshold approach such as that used by the domestic courts would be inappropriate. The domestic courts had ruled that a certain 'threshold' was to be met before adverse effects on traditional minority activities would amount to a 'denial' of Article 27 (on file with the author).

[336] See HRC *Jouni E. Länsman et al.* v. *Finland*, 30 October 1996, §10.6.

[337] See also HRC *Jarle Jonassen and members of the Riast/Hylling reindeer herding district* v. *Norway*, 25 October 2002 (inadm.). The HRC considered that the application of domestic remedies had not been unreasonably prolonged because 'the period of time it has taken for the authors to obtain a remedy, may not be gauged from the time the Samis have litigated grazing rights, but from the time the authors themselves have sought a remedy' (§8.8). This shows again an emphasis on the individual right rather than its collective aspects. Committee members Henkin, Scheinin and Solari Yrigoyen dissented, considering, among others, that instituting expropriation proceedings to secure reindeer herding rights was not at all an effective remedy, that the proceedings were already unreasonably prolonged and that the petitioners would be subjected to legal sanctions if they continued to herd their reindeer in certain traditional areas, while the expropriation proceedings could not address this problem.

[338] See HRC *Jouni E. Länsman et al.* v. *Finland*, 30 October 1996, §9.2. The relevance of the precautionary principle to human rights law is discussed later in this Chapter, in section 4. For a discussion on the precautionary principle in general, see Chapter I, section 5.3.3.

[339] On this substantive issue see further Chapter IX (Culture), section 3, under the heading 'Land rights and collective aspects of the right to culture'.

[340] Here evidentiary and substantive law issues again are clearly interrelated.

proach the petitioners would have to prove either that the specific area is of strategic importance to their culture or that the past and future infringements combined would result in a denial of the right to culture. The Committee's recognition of the cumulative effect of certain infringements should also take into account qualitative aspects to the right to land, next to the quantitative aspects.

The quantitative approach to culture currently taken by the HRC may sometimes give precedence to collective rights over individual rights.[341] Indeed, apart from the quantitative versus qualitative approach, there is also the tension between the collective dimension of the right to culture in Article 27 and the fact that it is an individual right. As discussed in Chapter X, the Committee's use of provisional measures is generally triggered by its awareness of the collective dimension of the right. An individual's 'cultural survival' is considered less important.[342] At the same time the quantitative approach may conflict with the collective right to culture as well exactly because a purely quantitative approach ignores the qualitative aspects of the right to land as part of the right to culture.

The way the HRC deals on the merits with the question whether certain developments would result in a denial of the right to culture is also relevant for its use of provisional measures pending the proceedings. Accepting that the cumulative effect of certain (industrial) developments may be an infringement of the right to culture, raises the question at what moment this infringement is triggered. The evidentiary requirements depend in part on the Committee's answer to questions such as whether only the extent of the measures or also the specific area that is at risk determines the risk of irreparable harm (i.e. the quantitative versus qualitative approach), and whether only the collective right is examined or also the individual right to culture. When a qualitative and individual rights approach is taken, risk of irreparable harm is assumed sooner than when a quantitative and collective approach is taken. In this respect the choice of evidentiary requirements appears based also on the importance attached to the right.[343]

Either the contested measures encroach upon the culture of an indigenous people so much that its survival is at stake or they encroach upon it to a lesser extent. In the first situation this would warrant provisional measures pending the proceedings and, in case of an eventual finding of a violation, a precise indication about the expected form of reparation. In the latter case, however, there may still be a violation (although the HRC has not yet found so), but provisional measures are simply not warranted and an appropriate form of financial compensation or, if possible, a return to the previous situation might be sufficient.[344]

3.2.8 Nuclear tests and assessment of risk

In *Bordes and Temeharo v. France* (1996) the petitioners claimed that the authorities had not been able to show that the underground nuclear tests did not constitute a danger to the health of the inhabitants of the South Pacific and to the environment.[345] They requested the HRC to use

---

[341]   Without the French declaration the HRC would likely have found a violation of Article 27 in *Hopu*. This would have been an example of a finding of a qualitative rather than quantitative encroachment of the right to culture.

[342]   Again see the discussion on the substantive issue of irreparable harm in Chapter X and Conclusion Part II.

[343]   On preventing irreparable harm to cultural survival see Chapter X (Culture) and Conclusion Part II.

[344]   In general on the relation to reparation see Chapter XIII (Protection).

[345]   HRC *Vaihere Bordes and John Temeharo v. France*, 22 July 1996. See also Chapter XII (Other situations). Between September 1995 and early 1996 the French authorities carried out six underground nuclear tests. The State provided a detailed description of the geology of Mururoa

provisional measures and ask France 'not to carry out any nuclear tests until an independent international commission had found that the tests were indeed without risks and did not violate any of the rights protected under the Covenant'.[346] Without calling it such, this seems an appeal to the HRC to take into account the precautionary principle in its use of provisional measures.[347] The HRC decided not to grant the protection requested.[348] Subsequently it declared the case inadmissible because it was not satisfied that the petitioners could claim to be victims within the meaning of Article 1 OP. About the claim that the tests 'will further deteriorate the geological structure of the atolls on which the tests are carried out, further fissurate the limestone caps of the atolls, etc., and thereby increase the likelihood of an accident of catastrophic proportions'[349] it noted that 'this contention is highly controversial even in concerned scientific circles; it is not possible for the Committee to ascertain its validity or correctness'.[350] In other words, it did not

---

and of the techniques developed to conduct the tests. Among others, it argued that the level of radioactivity at Mururoa, following earlier underground tests in the 1970s, was now identical to that at other islands and atolls in the South Pacific and less than that measured in, for instance, metropolitan France, where the emissions resulting from the nuclear accident in Chernobyl, Ukraine (1985) were still clearly measurable. About the risk to the food chain it pointed out that 'all serious scientific studies on the environmental effects of underground nuclear tests have concluded that whatever radioactive elements reach the surface of the lagoon at Mururoa or Fangataufa, are subsequently diluted by the ocean to levels which are perfectly innocuous for the marine fauna and flora and, a fortiori, for human beings'. HRC *Vaihere Bordes and John Temeharo* v. *France*, 22 July 1996, §§3.2-3.5. The State also noted that, in the past, it had granted access to the testing area to several independent commissions of inquiry and that the Lawrence Livermore laboratory (California) and the International Laboratory of Marine Radioactivity in Monaco had confirmed that the monitoring of environmental effects had been serious and of high quality, §§3.2-3.5. The State argued that the petitioners should have requested compensation from the competent authorities 'as the authors essentially invoke the potential risks which the tests entail for the health and the environment'. It is not clear from the State's submission why a request for compensation should be considered a satisfactory alternative in the face of such potential risks. Finally, it argued that the claim was inadmissible *ratione materiae*. It considered that Article 6 ICCPR 'only applies in the event of a real and immediate threat to the right to life, which presents itself with some degree of certainty'. Equally, Article 17 related to a real and effective interference with private or family life and not to 'the risk of a purely hypothetical interference', §3.9. Counsel for the petitioners responded that the risk of adverse effects of the tests already carried out since the initial submission to the HRC was real and serious. She deplored the absence of independent investigation into the impact of the tests already concluded and those that were still programmed. She criticised the lack of transparency in the actions of the French authorities and also noted that even the reports invoked by the State party itself contained passages cautioning about the real danger of escape of radioactive particles from the underground shafts, with the consequent contamination of the atmosphere. Counsel further referred to a report by Médecins sans Frontières, from July 1995, criticising the absence of medical supervision of the population of French Polynesia in the aftermath of the earlier nuclear tests, §§4.1-4.2.

[346] HRC *Vaihere Bordes and John Temeharo* v. *France*, 22 July 1996, §2.3.
[347] On the precautionary principle see section 4 of this Chapter.
[348] It discussed the issue during both the 54th and the 55th sessions. HRC *Vaihere Bordes and John Temeharo* v. *France*, 22 July 1996, §§1-2.3.
[349] HRC *Vaihere Bordes and John Temeharo* v. *France*, 22 July 1996, §5.6.
[350] Ibid.

apply the precautionary principle.[351] In the European system provisional measures have been refused in similar circumstances.[352]

4   THE RELEVANCE OF THE PREVENTIVE AND PRECAUTIONARY APPROACH

4.1   Introduction

With regard to the assessment of risk for the use of provisional measures the human rights adjudicators have not developed clear criteria. Nevertheless, a common denominator seems to be that of 'prima facie' evidence. This cannot be defined in the abstract. It depends on the circumstances of the case and the context of the legal system. The question arises whether the discussion on the preventive and precautionary principle or approach in international environmental law (and EU health law) can be of some assistance in this respect. The precautionary principle is not to be confused with the precautionary measures taken by the Inter-American Commission. The latter are simply provisional measures by another name. The preventive and precautionary principles were discussed in Chapter I in the context of the practice of the ICJ and ITLOS.[353]

In light of the value attached to what is being protected it may be possible to draw an analogy with the precautionary principle or approach with regard to assessment of risk. The umbrella principle 'better be safe than sorry', often referred to in the context of the precautionary approach, is particularly applicable in human rights cases. This warrants a preliminary rather than a full assessment of all available evidence. Yet thus far human rights adjudicators do not seem to have used the precautionary principle in the strict sense.[354]

---

[351]   Nevertheless, it wished to reiterate its observation in its General Comment on the right to life that 'it is evident that the designing, testing, manufacture, possession and deployment of nuclear weapons are among the greatest threats to the right to life which confront mankind today'. Id., §5.9.

[352]   EComHR *Tauira et al.* v. *France*, 4 December 1995 (inadm.).

[353]   See Chapter I (ICJ), section 5.3.3.

[354]   See e.g. the argument of counsel in the aforementioned HRC case involving Sami lands and cultural rights. See also counsel's invocation of the principle in *Brun* v. *France*, 18 October 2006 (inadm.), §3.2. The HRC declared the case inadmissible considering that the petitioner could not be considered a victim as the facts did not show an actual or imminent threat of violation of his right to life and his light to privacy, family and home. See also e.g. ECtHR *Balmer-Schafroth et al.* v. *Switzerland*, 27 June 1997. The Court found that the petitioners had not established 'a direct link between the operating conditions of the power station which were contested by them and their right to protection of their physical integrity, as they failed to show that the operation of Mühleberg power station exposed them personally to a danger that was not only serious but also specific and, above all, imminent. In the absence of such a finding, the effects on the population of the measures which the Federal Council could have ordered to be taken in the instant case therefore remained hypothetical. Consequently, neither the dangers nor the remedies were established with a degree of probability that made the outcome of the proceedings directly decisive within the meaning of the Court's case-law for the right relied on by the applicants. In the Court's view, the connection between the Federal Council's decision and the right invoked by the applicants was too tenuous and remote', §40. The dissenting opinion by Judge Pettiti, joined by Mr Gölcüklü, Mr Walsh, Mr Russo, Mr Valticos, Mr Lopes Rocha and Mr Jambrek, criticized the Court's failure to find a violation of Article 6 ECHR. The Opinion noted that the 'majority appear to have ignored the whole trend of international institutions and public international law towards protecting persons and heritage, as evident in European Union and Council of Europe

As noted in Chapter I the preventive principle applies when a causal relationship can already be established between the act or omission and serious or irreparable harm and when the probability of the risk can be established either quantitatively or qualitatively. The difference with the precautionary principle is that uncontroversial scientific evidence is available. Depending on the value attached to a certain right even evidence of a slight risk could be sufficient to trigger the preventive principle and halt the act or remedy the omission. The preventive approach certainly applies to decisions to take provisional measures in human rights cases if these aim at preventing irreparable harm to persons and the survival of indigenous groups. As discussed in the Conclusion to Part II certain rights are so fundamental that balancing them with other interests is not allowed under the human rights treaties. The evidentiary requirements for triggering a shift in the burden of proof are generally considered to be less strict in relation to risks of irreparable harm to such fundamental rights than in other cases. The preventive principle clearly applies to human right cases because provisional measures aim to prevent human rights violations rather than redress them. The remark of Judge Treves, in the context of the law of the sea (rather than human rights law), that 'a precautionary approach seems to me inherent in the very notion of provisional measures' can be understood in this sense. He noted that it was 'not by chance that in some languages the very concept of "caution" can be found in the terms used to designate provisional measures: for instance, in Italian, *misure cautelari*, in Portuguese, *medidas cautelares*, in Spanish, *medidas cautelares* or *medidas precautorias*'.[355]

This section briefly refers to the relationship between provisional measures and the preventive and precautionary principle or approach. It discusses why the precautionary approach is more relevant in human rights cases than the precautionary principle. It deals with existing criteria for the use of the precautionary principle that could also be useful in the precautionary approach warranted in human rights cases.

4.2   The relationship between provisional measures and the preventive and precautionary approach

Both in environmental law and in human rights law the adjudicator has to assess risks. The adjudicator has to 'cope with uncertainty' in the sense that he has to 'reach decisions even if the available information is not entirely conclusive'.[356] The human rights approach, just like the approach under environmental law, emphasises prevention. In human rights cases risk assessment takes place mainly in relation to complaints by petitioners claiming that they run a 'real risk' of being ill treated or executed upon expulsion and extradition on the one hand and complaints about irreparable harm to indigenous culture on the other. With regard to non-refoulement it is a question of how a person will be treated by the authorities of a third State in the foreseeable future.

---

instruments on the environment, the Rio agreements, UNESCO instruments, the development of the precautionary principle [references omitted] and the principle of conservation of the common heritage (…).Where the protection of persons in the context of the environment and installations posing a threat to human safety is concerned, all States must adhere to those principles'. Judge Pettiti concluded that, together with his colleagues in the minority, he 'would have preferred it to be the judgment of the European Court that caused international law for the protection of the individual to progress in this field by reinforcing the "precautionary principle" and full judicial remedies to protect the rights of individuals against the imprudence of authorities'.

[355]   Separate opinion of Judge Treves, ITLOS, *Southern Bluefin Tuna cases* (*New Zealand* v. *Japan*; *Australia* v. *Japan*), Order of 27 August 1999, §9.

[356]   Kamminga (1996), p. 171.

This is an area of fact-finding in which an adjudicator may feel more at ease than if the dispute relates to scientific facts.

Some scientific evidence relates to past facts and other to future facts or predictions. With regard to the latter the preventive and precautionary principles may sometimes be relevant. In all cases involving scientific evidence adjudicators have to assess and balance the authority and credibility of the evidence and the independence of the experts.

The precautionary principle as originally developed in the context of environmental law relates to the duty of States to take precautionary measures in the face of risks when scientific evidence is lacking or conflicting. It does not as such refer to the authority of international adjudicators to decide on precautionary measures. Given the difference between the roles of States and adjudicators different criteria may apply for the use of the precautionary principle by States and a precautionary approach taken by adjudicators.

It may be assumed that the use by an adjudicator of the precautionary principle as a rationale for the decision to take provisional measures or as a rationale for finding a violation on the merits is less far reaching than the State's discretion to take precaution based on the precautionary principle.

The principle is more established in the context of preventing serious harm to the environment in the face of scientific uncertainty than in the context of preventing health hazards. Yet if faced with a situation of scientific uncertainty the precautionary principle could be relevant to the adjudicator, whether or not it is dictated by a rule of customary international law.[357] It is submitted that an international adjudicator should not be prevented, by lack of full scientific certainty, from imposing provisional measures to halt certain industrial developments threatening cultural survival or to take measures to prevent irreparable harm to persons. Moreover, apart from the direct application of the precautionary principle when deciding on the use of provisional measures, some of the criteria that have been developed for the use of the precautionary principle could also be helpful for the use of provisional measures in situations not involving scientific evidence.

Clearly, a precautionary or preventive approach underlies the use of provisional measures. Yet the precautionary *principle* (in a strict sense) in my view is not 'inherent in the very notion of provisional measures', at least not in human rights cases. In those cases at the merits stage the criterion applied for establishing future facts normally is that of 'real' risk rather than an 'uncertain', 'hypothetical' or 'negligible' risk. Thus, at the merits stage it is necessary to establish (qualitatively) the likelihood of irreparable harm, meaning that the adjudicators do not apply the precautionary principle in the strictest sense. At that stage the threshold is much higher exactly because of the role of the adjudicator, which is different from that of the State. States may decide to take precautionary measures if there is conclusive evidence of a very small risk to human or plant health only. In the face of a very small risk the international adjudicator is unlikely to find a violation in its decision on the merits. Nevertheless, its lowering of the standard *at the provisional measures stage*, not requiring conclusive evidence (of a real risk), clearly is based on a precautionary approach.

On the other hand, there are cases in which the precautionary principle could apply as such.[358]

Counsel, in cases pending before the HRC, has sometimes referred to this principle. They argued that lack of full scientific certainty about (the level of) environmental degradation could not be used as an excuse for allowing exploitation of natural resources.[359]

---

357 See Chapter I, section 6.3.3.
358 See e.g. Cançado Trindade (1992) and Kamminga (1996) discussing the responsiveness of human rights mechanisms to risk and uncertainty.
359 See e.g. HRC *Jouni E. Länsman et al.* v. *Finland*, 30 October 1996, §9.2.

Disputes of fact in which the precautionary principle could be relevant may relate to health risks, threatening irreparable harm to the right to life. In such cases the dispute could concern medical evidence about the impact on health. They could also relate to environmental risks, threatening cultural survival. The disputes may then concern evidence based on environmental sciences about the risk of environmental degradation. With regard to the next step of showing the impact on cultural rights and the way of life of certain groups this could involve depositions and testimonies by the people involved, e.g. indigenous peoples themselves, possibly reinforced by testimonies by anthropologists etc. about the impact of the level of environmental degradation on the traditional way of life and the possibility to maintain a culturally acceptable livelihood.

It could be argued that in human rights cases dealing with a lack of scientific certainty (normally involving environmental harm) adjudicators could apply the precautionary principle as an argument reinforcing the general principle that irreparable harm to persons must be prevented. After all it may not be possible to show the effects of certain actions or omissions immediately. The actions or omissions may relate to the environment or to *long-term* health effects.

Given the nature of the risk (to life or cultural survival) and the required level of protection under the human rights treaty, it seems particularly warranted, in the face of scientific uncertainty, to resort to the precautionary principle in the determination of provisional measures. Scientists may make conflicting predictions about the risk of irreparable harm to the environment or to people's health. Apart from the fact that this does not relate to the foreseeable future but to long-term effects, this type of scientific evidence is even more difficult to assess than that of the risk of ill treatment in a third State. In this respect the precautionary principle may be used as an argument to require certain action to be postponed pending full scientific evidence or, instead, to require the State to act to prevent (further) environmental degradation and risk to health. If human rights adjudicators make use of this principle provisional measures are the practical tools for requiring States to postpone certain industrial activities until more scientific information is available to determine the risk to the environment (or to determine health hazards).

4.3   Criteria for the precautionary approach in human rights cases

In the context of WTO and EU law and policy the question has arisen whether, and if so how, the precautionary principle also applies in relation to the safety of food and feed and the protection of consumer health. In this context the European Commission has published a Communication. It considers that the precautionary principle applies not just to protect the environment, but also to protect consumer's health.

As no clear criteria are available as of yet on the use of provisional measures by human rights adjudicators, let alone on the use of the precautionary principle, it may be useful to examine the aforementioned policy document published in the context of the system of the European Union to see whether some of the criteria for the use of the precautionary principle mentioned could be relevant in the context of human rights adjudication as well. After all, the rationale for both is a precautionary approach. As discussed, the precautionary principle itself does not necessarily apply in the context of human rights adjudication, but the reasons for the use of the precautionary principle and for the use of provisional measures in human rights cases are often similar.[360]

---

[360]   The criteria of the somewhat controversial Commission Communication have been developed specifically in relation to the safety of food and feed. The use of the precautionary principle in this context triggers disputes about protectionism and the impact on import and export. Yet it is one of the few official documents discussing criteria relevant in the application of the precautionary principle. It could be relevant, to some extent, to the discussion of provisional

Even if the European Court of Justice normally simply accepts the State's view that precaution was necessary, the aforementioned Communication does provide some insight in the EU Commission's theoretical approach to the principle. Obviously the criteria are not applicable in exactly the same way in human rights cases. First of all protectionism is not a central issue here. Different from the situation in which States invoke the precautionary principle against import of goods, in human rights cases there is little risk that recourse to the precautionary principle by petitioners (and ultimately the adjudicator) is a disguised form of protectionism. In these cases individuals invoke it against a State to prevent human rights violations that could cause irreparable harm to life or cultural survival.

Moreover, the main criterion for the use of provisional measures is stricter than that often used for recourse to the precautionary principle. The latter principle is invoked in the face of scientific uncertainty about serious or long lasting damage. Provisional measures in human rights cases normally aim to prevent irreparable harm only, rather than all serious or long lasting damage. On the other hand, provisional measures are also used in cases where there is *no* scientific uncertainty, constituting a range of cases that is much more extensive than that in which the precautionary principle applies.

Despite the differences, in situations involving the uses of the precautionary principle, issues often arise that could be relevant in the discussion on the use of provisional measures as well. Indeed some of the criteria the European Commission mentions in its Communication also have relevance in decision-making on provisional measures in human rights cases.

These are the criteria suggested by the Commission: measures based on the precautionary principle should, among others, be 'proportional to the chosen level of protection'; non-discriminatory; 'consistent with similar measures already taken'; 'based on an examination of the potential benefits and costs of action or lack of action'; 'subject to review in the light of new scientific data' and 'capable of assigning responsibility for producing the scientific evidence necessary for a more comprehensive risk assessment'.[361]

In a precautionary approach State decisions for the protection of health or the environment normally are not based on such risks alone but also on other risks that must be balanced. Balancing also takes place with regard to the advantages and disadvantages of 'taking the risk'. These advantages and disadvantages are related to social values and often also to legal obligations. In such cases an essential step to take is to assess whether there is a hierarchy in values and legal obligations. In relation to rights of such a fundamental nature as the right to life and the prohibition of cruel treatment the level of uncertainty of the risk may be quite high while still justifying the use of provisional measures. Moreover, with regard to those rights, balancing with other interests is inappropriate.

Equally, one could argue that if indigenous peoples can make credible that serious harm to the environment would cause irreparable harm to their cultural survival, the level of protection

---

measures in human rights adjudication. In its Communication the European Commission noted that the decision to invoke the precautionary principle is 'a decision exercised where scientific information is insufficient, inconclusive or uncertain and where there are indications that the possible effects on the environment, or human, animal or plant health may be potentially dangerous and inconsistent with the chosen level of protection'.[360] The Communication provides some criteria, but stresses that 'it is for the decision-makers and ultimately the courts to flesh out the principle'. Commission of the European Communities, Communication from the Commission on the precautionary principle, 2 February 2000, COM (2000) 1, p. 10.

361 Commission of the European Communities, Communication from the Commission on the precautionary principle, 2 February 2000, COM (2000) 1, pp. 18-20. For a commentary on these criteria see e.g. Wibisana (2008), discussing as questionable the distinction made between scientific risk assessment and non-scientific risk management, pp. 126-130.

required by the human rights treaties does not allow for balancing with other interests.[362] The chosen level of protection should necessarily be higher in human rights cases involving a real risk of irreparable harm to persons (including harm to cultural survival). Hence, while in these cases the proportionality criterion does apply as well, it applies in an adapted manner. The criterion would be as follows: provisional measures (including those taken on the basis of the precautionary principle) should not accomplish more than necessary to prevent the irreparable harm. In other words while the obligation to prevent irreparable harm to persons comes first the adjudicator must allow the addressee State to implement its obligations in a way that is least invasive to its other vital interests.[363]

Consideration of the potential benefits and costs of action or lack of action could be relevant for determining the type of measure required, for instance, a positive or a negative obligation.[364] Moreover, provisional measures should be consistent with similar measures already taken in order to increase their credibility and avoid discriminatory application vis-à-vis beneficiaries and addressees. Comparable situations should be treated similarly and different situations should be treated differently.[365]

Inequality of arms or lack of scientific evidence may warrant a shift in the burden both on the merits and at the provisional measures stage. The provisional measures by the various human rights adjudicators have always been subject to review and clearly such review should also take into account relevant new scientific data. This could result in a withdrawal of provisional measures. Yet it is proposed that in human rights cases the general rule should be that very early in the proceedings the State proposing to allow a certain (industrial) development has the burden to prove that this would not cause irreparable harm to the cultural survival of indigenous groups. This rule would then also apply in the face of scientific uncertainty. In other words, different from the general rule applied by human rights adjudicators that on the merits the likelihood of irreparable harm must be established, in human rights cases involving the environment (mainly in relation to cultural survival, but also with regard to health risks) the precautionary principle should apply.

According to its Communication the Commission noted that 'the appropriate response in a given situation' is 'the result of a political decision, a function of the risk level that is "acceptable" to the society on which the risk is imposed'.[366] To a certain extent the acceptable level of risk in human rights cases is determined already through adherence to *human rights* treaties. The adjudicators monitoring the compliance of States with their obligations under these treaties have the responsibility to decide whether or not to use provisional measures and whether or not to be guided by the precautionary principle. Nonetheless, the European Commission's emphasis on the level 'acceptable' to 'the society on which the risk is imposed' may be relevant in human rights adjudication as well to the extent that the subjective element, the views of indigenous peoples themselves on the risk to their cultural survival, should be included as a factor in an adjudicator's decision to invoke the precautionary principle.[367]

---

362   See Conclusion Part II of this book, discussing the issue of cultural survival.
363   See also Chapter XIII (Protection), section 4.2 on the rights of the addressee of provisional measures.
364   See Chapter XIII (Protection).
365   See also Chapter II, section 8.2 on publication and motivation of provisional measures.
366   Commission of the European Communities, Communication from the Commission on the precautionary principle, 2 February 2000, COM (2000) 1, p. 16.
367   See also Chapter X (Culture) and Chapter XIII (Protection).

5   CONCLUSION

5.1   Assessment of temporal urgency

Before human right adjudicators decide to use provisional measures they generally determine whether the material risk is *imminent*. For the most part this approach is similar to that of the ICJ. If there is no immediate risk a provisional measure is premature.

In certain death penalty cases an exception has been made to the requirement of immediacy. With regard to some States the adjudicator may have the experience that once a person has been sentenced to death an execution follows soon after exhaustion of domestic remedies. In such cases the promptness requirement is more important than the requirement that a provisional measure is not taken prematurely. This applies similarly to deportation cases. Yet adjudicators sometimes have used provisional measures in death penalty case with no imminent risk of execution, maybe simply to express moral condemnation or because provisional measures are automatically used in all death penalty cases, which generally involve imminent execution dates.

Some adjudicators have also indicated, and this is a useful development given the risk of irreparable harm to persons, that once the State has been informed of a submission involving irreparable harm to life or physical integrity it must refrain from acting to cause such harm even when the adjudicator has not yet had a chance to use provisional measures.

5.2   Assessment of risk

5.2.1   Introduction

While the practice of the adjudicators examined for this book is not straightforward it does appear that on the merits they all use the standard of 'real risk'. For purposes of admissibility many adjudicators look at *prima facie* evidence *ratione materiae*.

At the provisional measures stage, however, there must simply be *prima facie* evidence with regard to that part of the claim involving a risk of irreparable harm to persons. The term *prima facie* must be interpreted in light of the urgency of the situation. At the admissibility stage the adjudicator should not already determine whether there is sufficient evidence to find a violation. He can declare the case inadmissible if there is clearly a lack of substantiation and evidence of inadmissibility *ratione materiae*. Because there is no particular urgency involved at this stage, the requirement of *prima facie* evidence is stricter than at the stage of provisional measures. At the admissibility stage there must be sufficient evidence at first sight (*prima facie*). At the provisional measures stage there must be sufficient evidence at first – and urgent – glimpse. Hence, at the stage of provisional measures the addressee State may already be 'required to answer', by urgently preventing irreparable harm, at a lower level of *prima facie* evidence (*prima prima facie*).

Given the purpose of provisional measures, discussed in the Conclusion to Part II, the risk claimed must be shown to relate to irreparable harm to persons or to indigenous culture. This means that there is no need to assess the evidence in relation to claims involving other rights. At this stage only the aspects of the claim relating to irreparable harm need to be substantiated, not other parts of the claim unrelated to such harm. If the main claim relates to irreparable harm to persons, this claim must be sufficiently substantiated for purposes of provisional measures. If the alleged risk of irreparable harm to persons is collateral to the claim it is not necessary to substantiate the main claim for purposes of provisional measures. It is only necessary to provide information on the risk of irreparable harm to life or personal integrity. If at the admissibility stage the beneficiary is still in need of protection, next to the evidence for purposes of admissibility, the petitioner should again show *prima facie* evidence of irreparable harm in order to convince the adjudicator to maintain provisional measures.

For each human rights system it is important to determine whether the adjudicator is limited to using evidence submitted by the parties or, on the other hand, has wide fact-finding powers. Nevertheless, whatever these powers, the rule of the burden of persuasion always applies.[368] As in general international law, in the field of human rights legal presumptions may cause a shift in this burden. One source of a legal presumption is the principle of effective human rights protection, taking into account that the consequences of a finding normally are more far reaching for the individual petitioner than for the respondent State. Another applicable principle is that of equality of arms and the need to take into account the difficulty for the individual petitioner of obtaining and presenting direct evidence of human rights violations by the State. This principle is related to the duty (of both parties) to cooperate with the adjudicator during the proceedings. Finally the principle of preventing irreparable harm to persons applies, as well as the related precautionary principle (in case of conflicting or insufficient scientific evidence) on environmental degradation. These principles combined may not only cause an early shift of the burden on the merits,[369] but may also justify, at the provisional measures stage, a rather low standard of proof to be met by the person requesting such measures of protection against irreparable harm.

States have sometimes argued that rights and interests should be balanced, invoking principles such as 'balance of convenience'. However, this principle should apply in relations between equal parties and is therefore more suitable to be applied in proceedings not involving a threat to the very existence of a person or to indigenous peoples.

5.2.2 Assessment of risk: right to life and prohibition of torture and cruel treatment

While domestic systems may choose to apply the preventive or protective principle any time there is sufficient evidence to establish some risk (even if negligible), this is not the case for international adjudicators dealing with expulsion and extradition cases. Given the fact that no adjudicator grants all requests for provisional measures by all petitioners claiming a real risk of irreparable harm, it is assumed that the likelihood of the risk must be determined at least to some extent. In fact the criterion most often surfacing is that of 'real risk'. Because provisional measures are only used in very serious situations involving threats of irreparable harm to persons and because quick decision-making is required, it would be sufficient if petitioners were to make a credible case of the possibility of such harm. In this respect *prima facie* evidence of a real risk means a quick assessment of the then available evidence, at face value, finding indications of such a real risk. At the merits stage the adjudicator could then determine whether the risk was indeed real.

---

[368] Kokott (1998), pp. 155-156.

[369] See e.g. ICJ *Corfu Channel* case (*Albania* v. *UK*), 9 April 1949; HRC *Bleier* v. *Uruguay*, 29 March 1982, §13.3 and ECtHR *Salman* v. *Turkey*, Judgment of 27 June 2000, §100 (noting that the Court has generally applied the standard of proof 'beyond reasonable doubt', referring to *Ireland* v. *UK*, 18 January 1978, §161 but that 'such proof may follow from the coexistence of sufficiently strong, clear and concordant inferences or of similar unrebutted presumptions of fact'. It then specifically addressed the monopoly by the State: "Where the events of an issue lie wholly, or in large part, within the exclusive knowledge of the authorities, as in the case of persons within their control in custody, strong presumptions of fact will arise in respect of injuries and death occurring during such detention. Indeed, the burden of proof may be regarded as resting on the authorities to provide a satisfactory and convincing explanation"); see also *Avşar* v. *Turkey*, Judgment of 10 July 2001, §392 repeating the second part of the statement, relating to the monopoly of information by the State.

If the likelihood of the risk is already clearly negligible at the provisional measures stage or cannot be determined at all, provisional measures are not used. The latter situation, in which the probability cannot be determined at all or only at a very low level shows that, while the preventive principle does apply to some extent, the precautionary principle does not.

As noted, it is possible that the standard in relation to past facts differs from that in relation to future facts. Provisional measures only relate to ongoing situations and future facts and the risk of irreparable harm. Nevertheless, often proof of past facts (torture, ill treatment and threats) plays a role in establishing risk. This may relate to risks in the addressee State itself, such as disappearance, death threats and harassment or ill-treatment in detention. Often there is concrete evidence in such cases. For instance, in detention situations medical evidence may be important.

Claims based on the principle of non-refoulement may require a different type of evidence. Human rights adjudicators that have dealt with this issue have referred to 'substantial grounds' of a 'real (and personal) risk'. They have interpreted the requirement of a 'real risk' either strictly (the violation would be a 'necessary and foreseeable consequence' of the extradition or expulsion) or more leniently (the violation would be 'more than a mere possibility').

In expulsion and extradition cases the standard of proof relates to the question of the likelihood of the risk triggering the responsibility of the sending State. *On the merits* there are several factors most adjudicators have referred to as playing a role in determining whether there is a real risk. First of all, the petitioner should *personally* be at risk. A clear indication of risk is previous torture or ill treatment of the petitioner in the State to which he would be returned. While not decisive in itself, a consistent pattern of human rights violations in this State is a relevant factor taken into account by most adjudicators to determine personal risk. Harassment of family or friends in the receiving State and political activities by the petitioner either in the receiving State or in the sending State may also play a role. Different from the merits stage, at the stage of *provisional measures* a consistent pattern of human rights violations in the receiving or the requesting State often is considered sufficient in itself.

The European Court has sometimes attached importance to the fact that the requesting or receiving State has ratified human rights treaties, especially if these include individual complaint proceedings. The argument is that such States must be presumed to be safe and, if not, the returned person could always appeal to an international adjudicator. The other human rights adjudicators do not seem to increase the burden on the petitioner for showing a real risk just because the receiving State is a party to human rights conventions. Their approach is more appropriate given that practice shows that the possibility of individual complaint does not always prevent irreparable harm.[370]

In the past the Committee against Torture appropriately pointed out that if a petitioner has submitted credible evidence that he has been tortured, inconsistencies and contradictory elements in his submissions claiming a real risk of renewed torture or ill treatment upon return should not immediately result in a negative assessment of the risk. As discussed, however, CAT subsequently took a rather restrictive approach, for an extended period hardly ever finding violations in non-refoulement cases.

While in some cases human rights adjudicators may also take into account the general interest, the text of the treaty provision in question should specifically allow this. In the context of non-refoulement it is important to note that the treaty provisions on the prohibition of torture and ill treatment in the various regional and international treaties do *not* allow for this, exactly because this prohibition is absolute. In the determination of whether the petitioner runs a real risk of ill treatment or torture the adjudicator should not allow any balancing with other interests. The standard of proof of a real risk should not be heightened for one specific case simply for policy

---

[370] See e.g. Smeulers/De Vries (2003).

reasons, for instance taking into account the fact that the petitioner is a suspected criminal (or terrorist) and the victims in the requesting State have a right to see him prosecuted there or the sending States wishes to protect its inhabitants.[371] In relation to the right to life and the prohibition of torture or ill treatment, which have been accorded a higher status in international proceedings, this type of balancing is inappropriate in both the main case and at the stage of provisional measures.[372]

Different from cases involving the impact on the environment and health the evidence relating to a real risk in cases about refoulement does not have to be 'scientific' but can be more traditional. In cases involving scientific evidence if a decision-maker cannot pinpoint the probability of a risk of irreparable harm, in the sense of cause and magnitude, he may still take temporary measures on the basis of the precautionary principle. In human rights cases, on the other hand, adjudicators normally apply the same criteria at both stages (merits and provisional measures), indicating the degree of probability required on the merits. Whatever information is available at the provisional measures stage is quickly examined to determine whether such provisional measures are warranted. The difference between the assessment of risk when deciding about the use of provisional measures and the assessment of the risk at the merits stage is simply a matter of degree in the standard of proof and evaluation.

In short, if in expulsion cases nothing can be said about the risk (negligible, small, real or clear and convincing) at the merits stage, not even qualitatively, no violation will be found. The same is relevant when the risk is considered to be small or negligible. This means that the precautionary principle does not apply. On the merits the question is whether there is a real risk. At the provisional measures stage it is whether there is sufficient indication of such a real risk. At the same time the evidentiary standard should certainly be relaxed in non-refoulement cases. In that sense an analogy with the precautionary approach could be made. At the stage of provisional measures it should not be necessary to already show personal risk, as long as there is persuasive evidence of a consistent pattern of gross human rights violations.

5.2.3 Assessment of risk: irreparable harm to indigenous culture

In one field the precautionary principle should indeed apply: that of indigenous culture. Different from non-refoulement cases, in some other cases, such as those involving the natural habitat, there may be conflicting scientific evidence of risk. The adjudicator should use provisional measures if there is some (non-negligible) indication of risk. Adjudicators should be able to consider the use of provisional measures even if the probability of environmental damage (threatening cultural survival) cannot be determined or if the evidence is conflicting. Cases of threats to cultural survival relate to conflicting *scientific* evidence (about causality and probability) exactly because of the argument of the risk of harm to the environment. In my view the international adjudicator could then take into account the precautionary principle, at least in its decision on provisional measures.

Thus, if there is uncertainty because of conflicting evidence (some of which is pointing to a real risk) or if there is inconclusive evidence the precautionary approach, as generally understood under international environmental law, could play a role.

---

371   See e.g. ECtHR *Chahal* v. *UK*, 15 November 1996 and *Saadi* v. *Italy*, 28 February 2008 (Grand Chamber). See further e.g. Smeulers (2002), pp. 130-133 and p. 167; Van den Wyngaert (1990), p. 765; Vermeulen (1989), p. 239 and (1990), p. 331.

372   Also for courts with a general jurisdiction (not limited to human rights), the prohibition of torture and cruel treatment should outweigh other rights or interests. See e.g. Hoge Raad (Dutch Supreme Court) 30 March 1990 *RvdW* 1990, 76, *Nederlandse Jurisprudentie* 1991, no. 249 (*Short* case).

Discussing the case law of the HRC Scheinin has distinguished between a quantitative and strategic approach to infringements on the right to culture. He emphasized the '*strategic* (qualitative) importance of the specific forest lands in question' (italics in the original). If the adjudicator would only assess the industrial developments on a quantitative scale this would not do full justice to some cases brought by indigenous peoples. Still, the quantitative approach is important as well because it recognises that incremental developments with regard to land use could have the effect of eroding the economic basis for an indigenous community's 'traditional or otherwise typical means of livelihood'.[373]

The qualitative-quantitative distinction is more generally applicable to cases involving cultural rights, also in the context of regional systems. It could equally be relevant to the use of provisional measures. The assessment of risk is different depending on whether the approach taken is qualitative or quantitative. Applying Scheinin's distinction between qualitative and quantitative infringements on the right to culture to the concept of provisional measures, it can be established that for both types of infringement *prima facie* evidence is required of threats to an area of religious or cultural significance, but in a qualitative approach the actual threat may be easier to prove because the moment triggering irreparable harm is easier to pinpoint than it is in an incremental approach.

Establishing the qualitative importance of a certain area (however small) for traditional livelihood would also require specific evidence of the importance of that piece of land to maintain traditional livelihood. In a qualitative approach to irreparable harm an adjudicator would look at the impact of industrial developments on sites of particular cultural importance. This would be less difficult to establish in relation to specific religious or cultural sites or objects than with regard to land and traditional livelihood where it would have to relate, for instance, to specific types of vegetation necessary for maintaining traditional livelihood.

The quantitative approach involves an examination of a progressive encroachment on traditional lands. In other words it involves incremental threats to such a large area that this would equally make impossible cultural survival.[374] In that case the questions arise (1) whether the environmental harm would be serious and long lasting[375] and (2) at what point one can speak of irreparable harm to indigenous culture and use provisional measures. In other words, at what point do State activities (or does State inaction) trigger irreparability?

The available practice shows that the HRC thus far has not opted for a qualitative approach.[376]

Even if the situation would be reversible in the long run, it could destroy cultural survival in the meantime. It would be possible to show the impact on the culture of an indigenous group by

---

[373] Scheinin (2001), pp. 170-171.

[374] See also the separate opinion of Judge Treves in ITLOS *Southern Bluefin Tuna* cases (*New Zealand* v. *Japan, Australia* v. *Japan*), Order for provisional measures of 27 August 1999. In his opinion he discussed incremental threats, which he called the 'qualitative urgency' requirement. He considered that this urgency concerned halting 'a trend towards a collapse of the southern bluefin tuna stock'. He noted: "Each step in such deterioration can be seen as 'serious harm' because of its cumulative effects towards the collapse of the stock. There is no controversy that such deterioration has been going on for years. However, as there is scientific uncertainty as to whether the situation of the stock has recently improved, the Tribunal must assess the urgency of the prescription of its measures in the light of prudence and caution".

[375] This is a criterion derived from ITLOS. In my view the criterion is more appropriate than that of irreparable harm to the environment, exactly because the scientific evidence issues trigger the precautionary approach. Only as part of the next step, linking the serious environmental degradation to harm to indigenous culture, the criterion of irreparable harm is applicable again.

[376] See the discussion in Chapter X (Culture).

statements of members of the group (and complemented by anthropological expertise). In order to assess the harm to the environment itself, however, scientific evidence about the probability of the risk could play a role.[377] In this light it is argued that if there is uncertainty about the risk, there is a lower burden of proof to show a *prima facie* case before the burden shifts to the State to show that certain industrial developments will not result in irreparable harm to the environment and consequently to indigenous culture.

In the discussion about the precautionary principle reference is often made to risk assessment. In particular there is disagreement about the level of assessment that must have taken place *before* a decision-maker may invoke the precautionary principle as well as about the level of the risk assessment that must take place *following* the use of the precautionary principle. The requirements of notification and consultation are important for an appropriate use of the precautionary principle in environmental law, but also in environmental impact assessment by for instance the Inspection Panels instituted by the World Bank. These requirements also appear to have their counterparts in the jurisprudence of human rights adjudicators in relation to indigenous peoples. They may indeed come to play a role in the use of provisional measures.

The distinction between the qualitative and the quantitative approach to infringements on human rights, as discussed by Scheinin, clearly is important in the context of risk assessment. International public authorities not specifically dealing with human rights, such as the European Commission of the EU, seem to have acknowledged that risk assessment may also be based (partially) on qualitative rather than quantitative information.[378]

It is suggested that in certain circumstances adjudicators could take provisional measures immediately. This would be so if the petitioners of a complaint can show that the exploitation or economic developments are about to take place and could result in irreparable harm *and* there is some indication that those persons directly affected have not been consulted and/or the State has not performed an environmental impact assessment, taking into account cultural integrity and sustainability. Provisional measures could aim at halting such industrial development until the adjudicator considers that an appropriate environmental impact assessment has taken place, during which the indigenous groups affected have been consulted properly. Inspired by successful national agreements between indigenous peoples and State and provincial authorities on environmental impact assessment, the approach by the HRC may broker better results for the indigenous communities concerned than the approach taken thus far. The adjudicator may then be more informed and its decisions more practically relevant. This approach may be possible even through long-distance paper proceedings, although clearly it would be easier to realise in a regional system making use of on-site visits and hearings.

Of course, if the impact assessment in itself was appropriate but the State ignored any results favourable to the indigenous peoples, this may be a ground for the use of provisional measures as well. Hence, this approach requires a more in-depth analysis of what constitutes appropriate consultation. Without this, the adjudicator would not be able to deal with all cases in which

---

[377]   This issue is discussed in section 4.2.2 on the precautionary principle.

[378]   According to the European Commission the concept of risk assessment in the SPS Agreement 'leaves leeway for interpretation for what could be used as a basis for the precautionary approach'. It considers that the risk assessment on which a temporary measure is based 'may include non-quantifiable data of a factual or qualitative nature and is not uniquely confined to purely quantitative scientific data'. It has noted that the Appellate Body of the WTO had confirmed this in the Growth Hormones case. In this case it 'rejected the panel's initial interpretation that the risk had to be quantitative and had to establish a minimum degree of risk'. Commission of the European Communities, Communication from the Commission on the precautionary principle, 2 February 2000, COM (2000) 1, p. 12.

consultation of the indigenous peoples and environmental impact assessments are little more than window dressing.

5.2.4 Conclusion on the assessment of risk at the stage of provisional measures

5.2.4.1 INTRODUCTION

In the practice of the human rights adjudicators there is indeed a link between the importance attached to preventing irreparable harm and the issue of temporal urgency.[379] While conceptually a similar link would be expected between the importance attached to preventing irreparable harm on the one hand and assessment of risk on the other, in practice this does not always appear to be the case.

For provisional measures in human rights cases the risk to be prevented generally relates to irreparable harm to the life or physical integrity of persons and the cultural survival of indigenous groups. When the alleged risk is imminent quick action is to be preferred over lengthy deliberation about the existence of such risk. In cases where there is friction between lack of information and urgency, the standard of proof may have to be lowered. Given the overriding importance of protecting the very existence of people(s)[380] this applies to the assessment of risk in human rights cases even more than it does to such assessment in other cases.[381] Yet in practice it seems that the human rights adjudicators sometimes take a rather restrictive approach in their use of provisional measures.

Looking at the specific situations in which provisional measures have been used in human rights cases it is evident that they related to future (or ongoing) facts. Nevertheless the level of evidence available may differ considerably. In some cases of ongoing harm very concrete evidence is available already at the stage of provisional measures to show the risk of irreparable harm. In other cases, involving future harm, the adjudicators have to determine at this stage whether there is a 'real risk'.

In all these cases the factors to be taken into account in the decision on the merits coincide with those relevant for an assessment at the stage of provisional measures. The difference lies in the difficulty of proving future facts. In non-refoulement cases involving claims of a risk to life or physical integrity in the receiving or requesting State if someone would be removed to that State, the facts necessary for a risk assessment are often difficult to obtain and are insufficient in themselves: a combination of those facts is usually required.

At the admissibility stage the standard of evidence to be shown by the petitioner is lower than at the merits stage. Among others, there must be *prima facie* evidence of admissibility *ratione materiae*. On the premise that provisional measures may be used in advance of the admissibility declaration the level of evidence required is again lower than that required at the admissibility stage. In other words, the petitioner must be able to show evidence of risk of irreparable harm at very first sight (*prima prima facie*).

Some examples illustrate the various situations in which petitioners have requested the use of provisional measures. With regard to requests for provisional measures to protect persons whose life is threatened concrete evidence of recent threats and harassment could be provided. In the eventual decision on the merits of claims involving death threats and harassment the evidence that must be provided is similar, but more definitive.

---

[379] For a similar conclusion with regard to jurisdiction and admissibility see Chapter XIV.

[380] See Conclusion Part II.

[381] See Chapter I (ICJ and ITLOS).

A situation in which the adjudicators have to attach great importance to circumstantial evidence is that of enforced disappearances.[382] In this case as well the factors taken into account on the merits are equally important in the assessment for the use of provisional measures. With regard to provisional measures, however, the adjudicator will additionally take into account the question whether the alleged disappearance is sufficiently recent to make the use of provisional measures worthwhile.

For provisional measures to put a stop to *ongoing* ill-treatment or ensure access to medical treatment in detention concrete evidence concerning ill-treatment may be provided as well. Again similar criteria of what has to be proved at the merits stage must be met.[383] In relation to requests for provisional measures to halt corporal punishment or the execution of a death sentence it is even possible to provide very concrete evidence of material risk.[384]

In contrast, in expulsion or extradition cases the claims of irreparable harm are more uncertain because they deal with future facts. The criterion to be met on the merits is that there is a real risk of such harm. Here the risk assessment for decision-making on provisional measures equally coincides with the assessment of 'real risk' at the merits stage. Specific factors that may be relevant in this respect are the general human rights situation in the receiving State and, if available at the stage of provisional measures, evidence that petitioners have been ill treated in the receiving State, that they belong to a specific (ethnic) group that is being targeted, that they had been politically active (in the opposition) in the receiving State (or had subsequently been vocal about their State of origin in the sending State).

Particularly in urgent cases, all adjudicators should be able to consult and take into account information derived from publicly available reports by authorities such as UN Special Rapporteurs or by reputable NGOs, even when the parties did not provide it.

5.2.4.2 STANDARD OF PROOF AND SHIFTING THE BURDEN

The question arises to what extent evidence of real risk and *prima facie* evidence of such risk differ or, more generally speaking, whether and how the standard of proof on the merits could be relevant already in the assessment of risk of irreparable harm *pending* the proceedings.

The contours of the assessment of risk for the use of provisional measures may be sketched in relation to the various stages of decision-making. The strictest requirements can be found exactly in relation to the merits. In relation to admissibility the evidentiary requirements are less strict and in relation to provisional measures to prevent irreparable harm to persons the adjudicator should be very lenient.

In the various situations the type of evidence necessary to show a real risk is similar at the merits and provisional measures stages. Thus the *type* of evidence required on the merits coincides with that required for provisional measures. It is only the standard of proof that is lower at the stage of provisional measures.

At the provisional measures stage there must be sufficient evidence at first – and urgent – glimpse. Hence, at the stage of provisional measures the respondent may already be 'required to answer', by urgently preventing irreparable harm, at a lower level of *prima facie* evidence.

A full assessment of the evidence at the merits stage must be stricter than an assessment of risk at the stage of provisional measures. The latter concerns a *prima facie* assessment only. Moreover, this assessment concerns those claims alone that relate to irreparable harm. Hence, the

---

[382] See Chapter VI.
[383] Probably at the merits stage additional evidentiary criteria must be met as well.
[384] Obviously a conviction and execution date equally provide evidence of temporal urgency.

assessment of the evidence pending the case for the purpose of provisional measures does not prejudice the eventual determination of the case.

Of course in all situations referred to (disappearances, threats, treatment in detention, expulsion) the State is in a position to cover up or withhold information. In general this warrants a lowering of the standard of proof required for the petitioner before the burden shifts to the State. Yet the question arises whether the issue of burden of proof is relevant already at the provisional measures stage. In this respect there is a difference between the provisional measures that are taken for the first time in a given case and those that are taken subsequently. Initially, when an adjudicator has to decide urgently on the use of provisional measures, this is often on the basis of an urgent evaluation of the credibility and sufficiency of the information provided by the petitioner alone. Yet when the adjudicator takes a provisional measure and subsequently is called upon to confirm, adapt or withdraw this measure, the burden of proof does play a role similar to that at the merits stage. If the State provides information to the effect that the petitioner is not (or no longer) facing irreparable harm, the petitioner wishing a continuation of the provisional measures, must bring evidence to convince the adjudicator that such continuation is necessary despite the information provided by the State.

5.2.4.3 SCRUTINY AND THE PRECAUTIONARY PRINCIPLE

In decisions on the merits the level of scrutiny applied by the adjudicator to the State's act or omission that is claimed to cause irreparable harm depends on the importance accorded to the right. The strictest level of scrutiny applies in the same type of cases, invoking particularly fundamental rights, in which provisional measures may also be warranted. In a similar vein the evidentiary requirements for triggering a shift in the burden of proof from the petitioner to the State are generally considered to be less strict in relation to risks of irreparable harm to such fundamental rights than in other cases.

One source of legal presumption in treaty interpretation is the principle of effective human rights protection, taking into account that the consequences of a finding normally are more far reaching for the individual petitioner than for the respondent State. Of course the principle of preventing irreparable harm to persons applies.[385] Moreover, in case of conflicting or insufficient scientific evidence the related precautionary principle is relevant.

It is clear that the premise for using provisional measures in human rights cases is similar to the premise on which both the preventive and the precautionary principle are based: better be safe than sorry in the assessment of the risk involved. Thus, some discussion of these principles was thought necessary to assist the argument about the assessment of risk and the use of provisional measures. Normally adjudicators can simply deal with risks the traditional way, not involving scientific evidence. In expulsion or extradition cases the causality between the removal and irreparable harm in the receiving State is not as difficult to establish as is the causality between certain acts or omissions and harm to the environment. It is in the latter situation that the precautionary principle is applicable.

The precautionary *principle* (in the strict sense) in my view is not inherent in the very notion of provisional measures, at least not in human rights cases, because in those cases the criterion applied for establishing future facts normally is that of 'real risk'. This shows that it is necessary to establish (qualitatively) the likelihood of irreparable harm, meaning that the adjudicators do not apply the precautionary principle. Indeed, provisional measures are used in a wider range of cases, not just those involving lack of scientific evidence.

---

[385] See Conclusion Part II.

On the other hand, there are cases in which the principle could apply. Scientists may make conflicting predictions about the risk of irreparable harm to the environment or to health. The precautionary principle may be used as an argument to require certain action to be postponed pending full scientific evidence or, instead, to require the State to act to prevent (further) environmental degradation and risk to health. If human rights adjudicators make use of this principle provisional measures are the practical tools for requiring States to postpone certain industrial activities until more scientific information is available to determine the risk to the environment (or to determine health hazards).

Given the nature of the risk (to life or cultural survival) and the required level of protection under the human rights treaty, it seems particularly warranted, in the face of scientific uncertainty, to resort to the precautionary principle in the determination of provisional measures.

An international adjudicator should be able to examine whether a State is using lack of full scientific certainty of harm as a reason for allowing certain industrial developments or for postponing taking measures to prevent irreparable harm to persons. It could be argued that in human rights cases dealing with a lack of scientific certainty (normally involving environmental harm) adjudicators could apply the precautionary principle as an argument reinforcing the general principle that irreparable harm to persons must be prevented even if the effect of certain actions or omissions will not be shown immediately but relate to the environment or long-term health effects. Different from States invoking the precautionary principle against import of goods, in such cases there is no risk that recourse to the precautionary principle by petitioners (and ultimately the adjudicator) is a disguised form of protectionism. In these cases individuals invoke it against a State to prevent human rights violations that could cause irreparable harm to life or cultural survival.

The main criterion for the use of provisional measures is stricter than that often used for recourse to the precautionary principle. The precautionary principle is invoked in the face of scientific uncertainty about serious or long lasting damage, while provisional measures in human rights cases normally aim to prevent immediate and irreparable harm only, rather than all serious or long lasting damage. At the same time, provisional measures clearly are used also in cases where there is no scientific uncertainty, constituting a range of cases that is much more extensive than that in which the precautionary principle applies. Nevertheless, despite the differences, in situations involving the use of the precautionary principle issues often arise that could be relevant in the discussion on the use of provisional measures as well.

With regard to scientific data the general rule should indeed be that the State proposing to allow, for instance, a certain industrial development has the burden to prove that this would not cause irreparable harm to the cultural survival of indigenous groups. This rule would then also apply in the face of scientific uncertainty. In other words, different from the general rule applied by human rights adjudicators that the likelihood of irreparable harm must be established, in human rights cases involving the environment (mainly in relation to cultural survival, but also with regard to health risks) the precautionary principle should apply. This means that the precautionary principle triggers a shift in the burden of proof from the party alleging irreparable harm to the respondent party.

The chosen level of protection, both at the stage of provisional measures and on the merits, should necessarily be higher in human rights cases involving a real risk of irreparable harm to persons (including harm to cultural survival). To a certain extent the acceptable level of risk in human rights cases is determined already through adherence to human rights treaties. The adjudicators monitoring State compliance with their obligations under these treaties have the responsibility to decide whether or not to use provisional measures and whether or not to invoke the precautionary principle.

As discussed the precautionary principle applies only in the context of doubtful scientific evidence. Yet the preventive principle applies in any case. Thus, conceptually one could argue that in the context of preventing irreparable harm to persons the human rights adjudicators should apply the preventive principle very strictly, already in the face of some slight risk of irreparable harm. Yet in practice they have applied the criterion of 'real risk' both on the merits and, to some extent, already at the stage of provisional measures. Thus, a hypothetical or slight risk is insufficient. This practice, which has manifested itself most clearly in the context of the case law on non-refoulement, may be explained by the awareness by the adjudicators of the fact that using provisional measures in all cases involving claims of a risk of irreparable harm upon expulsion, would make these measures less exceptional and authoritative in the eyes of the States.

5.2.4.4 RISK AND NON-ANTICIPATION

Provisional measures show that adjudicators believe the matter to be so urgent that measures should be taken, although they have not yet been able to evaluate all the evidence and arguments in relation to the main claim. The adjudicator simply tried to assess, on an urgent basis and when the case was pending, all the information available at that point of the risk of irreparable harm to the person involved.

In my view the requirement that provisional measures must not prejudice the eventual legal determination is related to the assessment of risk.[386] If provisional measures are taken this does not mean a violation will eventually be found. This is so exactly because pending the case the adjudicator takes decisions on the basis of urgency, without being able to examine fully the evidence in relation to the main claim.

If the adjudicator did not use provisional measures, eventually it can still find a violation of, for instance, the right to life. If it did use provisional measures it can still declare the case inadmissible or find no violations. With regard to the evidence, in other words, the decision on provisional measures does not predetermine the decision on the merits.[387]

---

[386]   Chapter I discussed the issue of prejudgment and the provisional measures by the ICJ. Chapter II briefly dealt with the approach to this issue by human rights adjudicators.

[387]   The decision-making on provisional measures, being separate from that on admissibility and merits, has rightly been considered not to be part of the 'examination' of the case. See e.g. HRC *Weiss* v. *Austria*, 3 April 2003. If the case is discontinued or struck out (depending on the terminology used by the adjudicator) before consideration of admissibility, it is considered not to have been examined. Another international adjudicator may then deal with it also if a State has precluded examination of cases previously 'examined' by other international adjudicators. See also Chapter XIV (Jurisdiction and Admissibility).

What is important is that upon final determination the adjudicator is not led by the fact that provisional measures were taken pending the proceedings. After all, a full assessment of the evidence at the merits stage must be stricter than an assessment of risk at the provisional measures stage. The latter concerns a *prima facie* assessment only. Moreover, this assessment concerns those claims alone that relate to irreparable harm.[388]

---

[388] This should also be reflected in the motivation of provisional measures that this book argues for, see e.g. Chapter II (Systems).

CHAPTER XVI
THE LEGAL STATUS OF PROVISIONAL
MEASURES IN HUMAN RIGHTS ADJUDICATION

1 INTRODUCTION

In its *LaGrand* judgment (2001) the ICJ finally determined that its provisional measures were legally binding. While the power to 'indicate' them is included in the ICJ Statute, neither the ICJ nor its predecessor, dealing with a similar text, had previously clarified the legal status of these measures. As has been noted, the arguments of ICJ Judges Ajibola and Weeramantry, made years previously,[1] in favour of the binding nature of the measures ordered, were indeed 'particularly persuasive especially in cases where such orders involve matters of life or death such as preventing genocide or stopping expulsions as such acts will obviously cause irreparable damage to the parties and affect the outcome of the case on the merits'.[2] Yet in 2001, when the Court finally clarified the legal status of its provisional measures, it noted that they are legally binding in all cases. In other words its provisional measures are obligatory always, not just when they involve matters of life and death.[3]

While interpreting Article 41 ICJ Statute the ICJ in fact discussed a principle that has been accepted universally.

This chapter deals with the question whether the provisional measures used by human rights adjudicators are legally binding not only when the treaty refers to the authority to use them, but also when the treaty provisions establishing the individual complaint system do *not* explicitly refer to provisional measures. The latter is the case with regard to the provisional measures by the three regional human rights Commissions, the European Court of Human Rights (ECtHR) and three of the four UN supervisory bodies that have dealt with individual petitions.

It is only since 2005 that the ECtHR has developed case law recognizing the binding nature of its provisional measures. The other human rights adjudicators had stressed the binding nature of provisional measures already long before 2005.[4] Yet some States have disputed this. Section 2 deals with the relevant treaty provisions or Rules of Procedure on provisional measures and the development of the case law by the adjudicators with regard to the binding nature of these measures. Section 3 discusses whether principles of treaty interpretation and general principles of law underlie the practice of the adjudicators, related to the awareness by the adjudicators of the irreparable nature of the harm at issue.

---

[1] In their individual opinions to the Order on Bosnia's second request for provisional measures in the *Genocide Convention* case, Order of 13 September 1993. See Chapter I, section 6 on the legal status of provisional measures by the ICJ and ITLOS.

[2] Garry (2001), p. 406.

[3] See Chapter I.

[4] This is discussed in section 2 of the Chapter.

2   THE PRACTICE OF THE ADJUDICATORS WITH REGARD TO THE LEGAL STATUS OF PROVISIONAL MEASURES

2.1   Introduction

This section discusses the practice developed by the human rights adjudicators with regard to the legal status of provisional measures. Next to arguments that may be specific to the treaty system in question, the adjudicators have used arguments that appear to be based more on general principles of law and interpretation.[5]

Sometimes States have made the argument that provisional measures by the HRC are not legally binding because, in their view, the decisions of the HRC on the merits are not legally binding either. As this book does not concern the legal status of decisions on the merits, it does not analyse this issue in detail, but section 2.2 briefly addresses the argument.[6]

The remainder of the section focuses on the relevant case law involving the legal status of provisional measures, also in the absence of a specific treaty provision on this issue. Section 2.3 refers to the treaties that include a reference to provisional measures and discusses the case law of the Inter-American Court. Section 2.4 deals with the treaty systems in which a reference to provisional measures is found in the Rules of Procedure of the adjudicators, but not explicitly in the treaty text.

In their approach to the legal status of provisional measures do the adjudicators take into account the inequality between the parties and the irreparable nature of the harm faced by the petitioners?

2.2   The legal status of decisions on the merits by the HRC and its relevance to the legal status of the Committee's provisional measures

The UN individual complaint systems have followed the approach of ICERD, the first UN human rights treaty introducing an individual complaint procedure, of referring to decisions on the merits

---

[5]   This is further discussed in section 3 of the Chapter

[6]   See e.g. HRC *Anthony Currie* v. *Jamaica*, 29 March 1994; on 22 June 1995 the State responded to the Committee's Views, informing the Special Rapporteur on the follow-up on Views that it had sent them to the Jamaican Privy Council, which had decided 'that in the circumstances of the case it is unable to make a recommendation for release'. The letter did not mention whether the death sentence would at least be commuted. The State gave its view about the legal status of the Committee's decisions on the merits. "While it is clear that the Protocol does not impose any legal obligation on State Parties to implement the Views of the Committee, the Ministry has always acknowledged that there is a duty to give serious consideration to those Views; accordingly, the Views of the Committee have always been submitted to the Privy Council, which is established by the Jamaican Constitution to make recommendations to the Governor General on the exercise of the prerogative of mercy. The Ministry wishes to assure the Committee of its intention to continue to deal in good faith with the Views of the Committee" (on file with the author). See also Chapter XVII (Official responses). States have made similar arguments with regard to the other UN adjudicators and with regard to the former European Commission, the Inter-American and African Commission, but these are not discussed separately here.

as 'views'. The status of decisions on the merits by the regional Commissions have not been referred to as 'judgments' either.[7]

This section singles out for discussion the complaint system under the ICCPR, as the international human rights system discussing the widest range of rights.

During the drafting process of the HRC's Rules of Procedure Committee member Ganji (Iran) noted that '(a) request for interim measures would constitute very strong action on the part of the Committee, considering that ultimately all the Committee could do in connection with a case was to forward its views to the State and the individual concerned'.[8]

When the ICCPR and the Protocol were codified in 1966, the highest obtainable was a supervisory committee whose decisions would be called 'Views'.[9] Nevertheless, given the Commit-

---

[7]　In this respect a brief reminder with regard to the Inter-American Commission may also be useful, especially relating to its decisions on the merits based on the American Declaration. See Chapter II. The CIDH has invoked the Declaration vis-à-vis OAS member States, who have international obligations under the OAS Charter. Based on Article 20 of the Statute of the Inter-American Commission of Human Rights, approved by the OAS General Assembly in October 1979, this Commission monitors compliance with the American Declaration of the Rights and Duties of Man for those States that have not yet ratified the ACHR. The Inter-American Commission's competence to take action and examine individual complaints with respect to member States of the OAS that are not party to the ACHR is based on the OAS Charter and on the practice established by the Commission. The General Assembly's adoption of the Statute of the Commission has confirmed this practice. In an Advisory Opinion of 1989, the Inter-American Court of Human Rights has held that the American Declaration has become a source of international obligations for all member States of the OAS. See IACHR Advisory Opinion OC-10/89, Interpretation of the American Declaration of the Rights and Duties of Man within the Framework of Article 64 of the American Convention of Human Rights, 14 July 1989, Ser. A. No. 10 (1989), §§35-45. See also Separate Opinion Cançado Trindade in *Blake* v. *Guatemala*, judgment of 24 January 1998, §§35 and 36 and, for instance, CIDH *Maya indigenous Communities* v. *Belize* (2004), 12 October 2004, in which the CIDH specified that all OAS members have obligations under the Declaration and are answerable the Commission independent of their ratification of the ACHR. See also e.g. CIDH *James Terry Roach and Jay Pinkerton* v. *US*, 22 September 1987, §§46-49 and *Mary and Carrie Dann* v. *US*, 27 December 2002, §96. See further Tittemore (2006), pp. 382-283.

[8]　HRC Summary records of the meetings of the first session, 13th meeting, 29 March 1977 and 17th meeting, 31 March 1977, Yearbook of the HRC 1977-1978, Vol. I, CCPR/1 pp. 44-46 and p. 54.

[9]　Article 5 OP stipulates, among others, that the HRC shall consider communications in the light of all written information made available to it by the parties, after the individual has exhausted the available domestic remedies. Article 5(4) provides that it 'shall forward its views to the State Party concerned and to the individual'. Originally these Views were not intended to be binding. The Committee itself initially appeared to take this approach until 1988. It seems the majority of the Committee agreed with, or did not notice the statement in the Report that its 'decisions on the merits are non-binding recommendations', Annual Report 1988, A/43/40, 28 September 1988, §645. This old approach towards the function of the HRC and the status of its decisions seems to have found its way even in the third publication of its Selected Decisions (2002). Whole paragraphs of the introduction have been copied from earlier versions. Of course this third volume only covers the period between July 1988 and July 1990. HRC Selected Decisions of the Human Rights Committee under the Optional Protocol, Volume 3 (July 1988-July 1990), CCPR/C/OP/3, p. 8. In 1993 the HRC noted that 'the absence of an explicit provision in the Optional Protocol on enforcement may be considered a major shortcoming in the implementation machinery established by the Covenant'. In this context it still noted that its Views were 'in the nature of recommendations on the basis of which States parties should endeavour to settle the

tee's function and the developments since 1966, its Views have acquired legal authority and, and to some extent can now be regarded as legally binding. Indeed, it is evident from the Committee's practice with regard to follow-up that it expects its Views to be complied with.[10] Also interesting

case in question'. It did point out that States adhere to the OP on a voluntary basis and that 'it is reasonably assumed that they would accept and implement the Committee's recommendations'. Report of the HRC to the General Assembly, A/48/40 (Part I), 7 October 1993, Annex X 'Documents submitted to the Human Rights Committee on the World Conference on Human Rights' under B (Follow-up on Views), §2. Various scholars have taken this approach as well. See e.g. McGoldrick (1994), pp. 202-204 and Tomuschat (2003), p. 181. Naldi considers that the Views 'do not formally have the binding force of a ruling of a court of law but rather a persuasive quasi-legal authority'. Yet he adds that 'an expectation of compliance' nevertheless appears to 'have been engendered where the Committee finds a violation of the Covenant'. Naldi (2004), p. 446. Moreover, it has been argued that the 'opinions on the merits by the treaty bodies are increasingly considered as authoritative expressions and interpretations of the law and accordingly complied with by the large majority of States Parties'. Thus these opinions may assume 'the nature of binding decisions'. "This also applies to the measures States Parties are expected to take as a matter of good faith cooperation in the framework of the treaty protection system'. Van Boven (1995), p. 97. See also e.g. Boerefijn (1999b) and Castan/Joseph/Schultz (2004). In its General Comment 33 (2008) the Committee itself appears rather cautious when it comes down to describing its function, but it does stress the obligations of States to comply. "While the function of the Human Rights Committee in considering individual communications is not, as such, that of a judicial body, the views issued by the Committee under the Optional Protocol exhibit some important characteristics of a judicial decision. They are arrived at in a judicial spirit, including the impartiality and independence of Committee members, the considered interpretation of the language of the Covenant, and the determinative character of the decisions". HRC General Comment 33, CCPR/C/GC/33, 5 November 2008 (Advance unedited version), §11. The Committee's views are an authoritative determination of the State's obligations under the OP and the Covenant and they 'derive their character, and the importance which attaches to them, from the integral role of the Committee under both the Covenant and the Optional Protocol', §13. The character of the Committee's views 'is further determined by the obligation of States parties to act in good faith, both in their participation in the procedures under the Optional Protocol and in relation to the Covenant itself. A duty to cooperate with the Committee arises from an application of the principle of good faith to the observance of all treaty obligations', §15. On the legal status of the findings of the African Commission see e.g. Viljoen/Louw (2004), pp. 1-22; Gumedze (2003), pp. 142-143.

[10] On follow-up to provisional measures see Chapter XVIII. Since 1990 the HRC requests the State, as part of its decision on the merits, to inform it of what action it has taken with regard to the Committee's finding of a violation. It points out that States that have ratified the OP have recognised the competence of the HRC to determine whether or not there has been a violation of the ICCPR. Moreover, under Article 2 ICCPR States have 'undertaken to ensure' to all individuals within their territory and subject to the jurisdiction the rights recognised in the Covenant. They have undertaken to provide an effective and enforceable remedy in case a violation has been established. See e.g. HRC *Roger Judge* v. *Canada*, 5 August 2003. Its wish to receive, within 90 days, information about the measures taken to give effect to its Views equally indicates that the HRC now takes the approach that States are bound to respect its decisions on the merits. It was in 1990 that the HRC created the mandate of a Special Rapporteur for follow-up on Views to monitor the compliance of States parties with its Views. See A/45/40, Vol. II, Annex XI. See also De Zayas (1991) and Schmidt (1992). The HRC further amended its guidelines for the preparation of State party reports under Article 40 ICCPR. In these reports States should provide information on follow-up as well. This information should be provided in addition to the responses as part of the follow-up procedure itself. See Consolidated Guidelines

in the context of its authority to use provisional measures, the HRC has referred to the statement by the International Court of Justice 'that even in the absence of specific enabling powers, an international instance, may act in ways not specifically forbidden, so as to ensure the attainment of its purposes'.[11]

The HRC is not a court, but rather a Committee supervising the ICCPR. Yet States parties are bound to respect the treaties they ratify, in this case the OP and the ICCPR. Despite the mis-guiding name ('Views') given to its decisions at the time, in practice they concern judicial deci-sions determining a legal conflict, by a competent and independent body of experts.[12]

---

for State Reports under the ICCPR, adopted July 1999 and amended October 2000, CCPR/C/66/GUI/Rev. 2, 26 February 2001, Guideline F1. See CCPR/C/5/Rev. 2, 28 April 1995, §5 for the earlier document, with amendments of July 1990, July 1991 and April 1995 (found on <www.pch.gc.ca>, consulted on 21 October 2004). More closely on follow up see Boerefijn (1999), pp. 101-112 and Ghandhi (1998), pp. 343-353.

[11] ICJ *Certain Expenses (of the United Nations)*, Advisory Opinion of 20 July 1962, pp. 150-167 as referred to in Report of the HRC to the General Assembly, A/48/40 (Part I), 7 October 1993, Annex X 'Documents submitted to the Human Rights Committee on the World Conference on Human Rights' under B (Follow-up on Views), §5. During the spring session of 1993 the HRC decided that the information on its follow-up activities 'should in principle be made public', in the interest of the victims and because this could 'serve to enhance the authority of the Views and provide an incentive for States parties to implement them'. For the decision to make the follow-up activities public see CCPR/C/SR.1227/Add. 1. In April 1993 the Chairpersons of the UN human rights treaty bodies also proposed that 'views and recommendations expressed by the treaty bodies in relation to individual communications should be fully respected'. A/CONF.157/PC/62/Add.15, p. 8. The Committee noted that another desirable step would be to call upon States to accept the decisions of the treaty bodies on the merits as binding. It proposed a new paragraph to be added to Article 5 OP to the effect that 'States Parties undertake to comply with the Committee's Views under the Optional Protocol', see Report of the HRC to the General Assembly, A/48/40 (Part I), 7 October 1993, Annex X 'Documents submitted to the Human Rights Committee on the World Conference on Human Rights' under B (Follow-up on Views), §15. It also suggested to give the Special Rapporteurs on the follow-up of Views a fact-finding mandate (§16), to effectively utilise the tool of publicity (it noted that this could be done by including a chapter on follow-up in the Annual Reports of the respective Committees, §17, but did not mention press releases). Moreover, it suggested to extend some form of technical assistance (§18) and, finally, emphasised that the implementation of the follow-up mandate required 'appropriate human and material resources' (§19). In 1994 the Committee adopted a new Rule to its Rules of Procedure to the effect that the Special Rapporteur may 'make such contacts and take such action as appropriate for the due performance of the follow-up mandate'. It also decided to give publicity to its follow-up activities rather than deal with it confidentially, as it had done previously. Since that time it includes a discussion of follow-up activities and lists States that have not provided follow-up information. See also Klerk (2000), pp. 149-159. See Rule 101 for the HRC Special Rapporteur on Follow-up on Views. Since 2002 CAT also has a Rapporteur for Follow-up of decisions on complaints (Rule 114). See also CAT's Rule 112(5). See further CERD Rule 95, of 15 August 2005, §§6-7. The Rules of Procedure of CEDAW provide for the possibility of instituting a special rapporteur or working group (Rule 73), but currently the Committee appoints members each session in order to follow up specific Views.

[12] See also Harrington (2003), p. 65 noting that because of the personal standing of its members 'and their judicial qualities of impartiality, objectivity and restraint' the decisions of the HRC 'acquire persuasive authority'. The HRC decides cases 'in an adjudicative fashion, providing both the state and the individual complainant with an opportunity to fully present their case' and 'later makes a reasoned ruling on the issues in the complaint'. While she considers that the

Such individual complaint procedure, as recognised by the State, must indeed serve a function. Considering the Committee's Views as mere exhortatory remarks would deprive the right of individual complaint of any meaning.[13] Instead, a State party must comply in good faith with its obligations under the OP and under the ICCPR itself and respect the Committee's decisions.

When domestic courts of States that have ratified the ICCPR are dealing with provisions of this treaty, either because the domestic legal system gives them direct effect or because they inform the meaning of domestic legal concepts, they must take into account the decisions and comments of the HRC as the most authoritative interpretation of ICCPR-law.[14] In addition, State parties to the Optional Protocol have voluntarily recognised the right of individual complaint of everyone under their jurisdiction. By having accepted the individual complaint procedure States have recognised the HRC as the adjudicator in a legal conflict between a State and an individual. The obligation of good faith compliance with this procedure implies that the State is internationally bound to respect the contents of the View. State parties have the legal obligation to implement these Views and to redress the violations found by the Committee.[15] The Committee's Views are legal decisions determining a concrete legal conflict. Indeed the practice of the HRC indicates that it considers States legally bound to respect and implement its Views.[16]

Committee's Views 'are not legally binding in the literal sense', she notes that this 'does not mean that they are without legal consequences'. "If the Committee, as the body competent to do so by the terms of the ICCPR, has found a violation, then under article 2 of the ICCPR the state has a legal obligation to provide an effective remedy for that violation". The above is not to say that members of the HRC have always shown impartiality, but indeed the HRC is generally well respected.

[13] In HRC *C.* v. *Australia*, 28 October 2002, §7.3 the HRC considered that the complaint of the petitioner was admissible because those administrative remedies that had not been exhausted could 'not be described as ones which would, in terms of the Optional Protocol, be effective. The reason for this was the Committee's observation that any decision of the Common Wealth Ombudsman and the Human Rights and Equal Opportunity Commission (HREOC) 'would only have had recommendatory rather than binding effect, by which the Executive would, at its discretion, have been free to disregard'. With this statement the HRC also implies that its own decisions under the Optional Protocol are themselves something more than recommendations.

[14] See also e.g. HRC General Comment 33, CCPR/C/GC/33, 5 November 2008 (Advance unedited version), §12.

[15] Under international law, such redress includes the obligation to provide the victim of the violation with an effective remedy. This is also an explicit obligation under the ICCPR, where Article 2(3)(a) provides that each State party undertakes to ensure that any person whose rights or freedoms are violated shall have an effective remedy. See General Comment 31 on the nature of the general legal obligation imposed on States parties to the Covenant (Article 2), 29 March 2004. Moreover, the State party to the OP is under an obligation to ensure that similar violations do not occur in the future. In other words, this is the obligation, under international law, of non-repetition of an act declared to have been in violation of an international rule. See also Chapter XIII (Protection).

[16] As part of its Views finding violations it normally points out that, pursuant to Article 2 ICCPR, the State party has undertaken to ensure to all individuals within its territory or subject to its jurisdiction the rights recognised in the Covenant. The State has undertaken as well to provide an effective and enforceable remedy in case a violation has been established. The HRC also wishes to receive from the State party, within 90 days, information about the measures taken to give effect to the Committee's Views. The Committee also requests the State to publish its Views. See e.g. HRC *Rawle Kennedy* v. *Trinidad and Tobago*, 26 March 2002; *Silbert Daley* v. *Jamaica*, 31 July 1998, and *Anthony McLeod* v. *Jamaica*, 31 March 1998. In relation to cases that were submitted after Jamaica's denunciation of the OP but before this denunciation became effective,

State parties are under an obligation to implement the Views of the Committee, in the sense that they cannot ignore the HRC's determination. At the same time, such violation determined by the Committee creates an entitlement on the part of the victim to an 'effective remedy'. State parties have a certain amount of discretion in deciding the type of reparation or the amount of compensation in cases that do not involve either a continued violation of the Covenant or the threat of a (further) violation of the Covenant.[17]

In human rights adjudication the substance of provisional measures, of friendly settlement agreements, of statements regarding the obligations of the State upon a finding of violation and of judgments on reparations often share a remarkable resemblance.[18] This may be explained by the fact that while their function is different, their ultimate aim is the same: preventing irreparable harm to persons.[19]

It is submitted that States at minimum have direct obligations based on the Committee's Views when preventing irreparable harm is the *aim* of the reparation. Even if some other forms of reparation mentioned in the Committee's decisions on the merits are indeed mere suggestions, the obligation to prevent (further) violations, as determined by the Committee, must be respected at minimum.[20] Without this one cannot speak of good faith compliance with the treaty. In order to ensure that this irreparable harm to persons does not occur already pending the proceedings respect for provisional measures belongs to the minimum of what is required of States parties having recognised the individual complaint system.[21]

---

on 23 January 1998, the HRC customarily noted that in accordance with Article 12(2) of the OP Jamaica was subjected to its continuing jurisdiction. The HRC has stressed that its monitoring role is an 'essential element in the design of the Covenant, which is also directed to securing the enjoyment of the rights'. Thus, reservations purporting to evade this role are incompatible with the object and purpose of the ICCPR. "The Committee's role under the Covenant, whether under article 40 or under the Optional Protocols, necessarily entails interpreting the provisions of the Covenant and the development of a jurisprudence. Accordingly, a reservation that rejects the Committee's competence to interpret the requirements of any provisions of the Covenant would also be contrary to the object and purpose of that treaty". See General Comment 24 on reservations to the ICCPR or the Optional Protocols, 4 November 1994, §11. In its General Comment on Article 2 (2004) the HRC pointed out that States parties are required to give effect to the obligations under the ICCPR in good faith, pursuant to 'the principle articulated in' Art. 26 Vienna Convention on the Law of Treaties (VCLT). Equally, under Article 27 VCLT ('may not invoke the provisions of its internal law as justification for its failure to perform a treaty') the obligations of the ICCPR in general and of Art. 2 in particular are binding on every State party *as a whole*. All branches of Government as well as 'other public or governmental authorities' may be in a position to engage the responsibility of the State party. While it is usually the executive branch that represents the State party internationally, this branch cannot relieve the State from responsibility for actions carried out by other branches of government. The General Comment also reminds States with a federal structure of the terms of Article 50 ICCPR, stipulating that the provisions of this treaty 'shall extend to all parts of federal States without any limitations or exceptions'. HRC General Comment No. 31 on the nature of the general legal obligation imposed on States parties to the Covenant (Article 2), 29 March 2004, §§3-4.

[17] See e.g. HRC *Beresford Whyte* v. *Jamaica*, 27 July 1998.

[18] See Chapter XIII (Protection).

[19] See also Conclusion Part II.

[20] See Chapter XIII (Protection).

[21] See also Harrington (2003), arguing that even if Views are not legally binding, provisional measures are. See also Letsas (2003), p. 537. See further Tomuschat (2003), p. 181, referring to the HRC reasoning to the effect that States are bound to comply with its provisional measures as

2.3   Systems referring to provisional measures in the treaty text

2.3.1   Introduction

This section first refers to the relevant treaty texts specifically dealing with provisional measures and then deals with some pertinent case law by the Inter-American Court indicating that this Court would consider its provisional measures binding even without an explicit reference to its authority to use them in the treaty text.[22]

2.3.2   The treaty texts on provisional measures

Different from the other – older – international human rights treaties with an active individual complaint system,[23] Article 5 of the OP to the Women's Convention explicitly refers to the power to take provisional measures. Yet the text of this provision still is rather weak, only referring to a 'request that the State party take such interim measures as may be necessary to avoid possible irreparable damage to the victim or victims of the alleged violation'.[24] Article 31 of the new International Convention for the Protection of All Persons from Enforced Disappearance[25] provides for an optional individual complaint procedure that includes a similar text.[26]

'indeed sensible'. He notes that it could be argued that its provisional measures could have 'no higher degree of authoritativeness than the final result of a proceeding, which the OP-CCPR classifies as 'views' (Article 5(4), a term which according to general linguistic usage as well as according to current legal terminology designates an act which is not binding', yet on the other hand 'a proceeding which has been instituted and in which the respondent state is obligated to cooperate in good faith, loses its very raison d'être if that state during the course of the proceedings takes measures which settle the matter once and for all, making the subject matter moot'. In this respect he considers that, apart from preserving the alleged rights of the alleged victim, the provisional measures serve to preserve 'in the first place, the integrity of the procedure'. He adds that 'from a teleological viewpoint [the reasoning of the HRC] is persuasive. It is further buttressed by the case law of the ICJ" and, p. 182: 'it should not be overlooked that a powerful argument supporting the argumentation eventually chosen was the concern by the ICJ that legal relief cannot be provided in the form of half-hearted measures. This consideration applies also, and perhaps even a fortiori, to individual complaint procedures. More than states, which generally have other means at their disposal to defend their rights, individuals may be in dire need of a pronouncement of one of the relevant expert bodies in order to preserve the enjoyment of right that allow a life of physical integrity and dignity".

22   Section 2.3.2 also refers to the treaty texts including a provision on provisional measures, but section 2.3.3 only discusses the case law of the Inter-American Court in this respect, as the other adjudicators have not discussed the issue separately.

23   See section 2.4 of this Chapter.

24   "1. At any time after the receipt of a communication and before a determination on the merits has been reached, the Committee may transmit to the State Party concerned for its urgent consideration a request that the State Party take such interim measures as may be necessary to avoid possible irreparable damage to the victim or victims of the alleged violation. 2. Where the Committee exercises its discretion under paragraph 1 of the present article, this does not imply a determination on admissibility or on the merits of the communication".

25   Adopted 20 December 2006, not yet entered into force (by December 2008: 71 signatories and one ratification (Albania)).

26   "4. At any time after the receipt of a communication and before a determination on the merits has been reached, the Committee may transmit to the State Party concerned for its urgent consideration a request that the State Party will take such interim measures as may be necessary

The Inter-American and African Courts and the Bosnia Chamber do have the explicit power to order provisional measures. Article 63(2) ACHR deals with provisional measures to prevent irreparable harm to persons:

> "In cases of extreme gravity and urgency, and when necessary to avoid irreparable damage to persons, the Court shall adopt such provisional measures as it deems pertinent in the matters it has under consideration. With respect to a case not yet submitted to the Court, it may act at the request of the Commission".

It appears from the last sentence that the Commission may request the Court to act with respect to a case not yet submitted to the Court.[27] Obviously the Commission cannot do this in relation to States that have not ratified the ACHR or States that have ratified the Convention but have not accepted the compulsory jurisdiction of the Court.[28]

Buergenthal notes that Article 68(1), which in the English text refers to the undertaking to comply with the Court's judgments, in the other authentic languages refers to the more inclusive term decision and that in fact neither the language nor the legislative history of the Convention is opposed to the conclusion that provisional measures are legally binding. Moreover, and here he points out something that is relevant as well with regard to the other human rights systems, the purpose of Article 63(2) ACHR 'would appear to require that these decisions be deemed to be obligatory'. Given the function of the provisional measures to apply in exceptional circumstances in order to avoid irreparable harm to persons, and given the fact that the Convention is a human

---

to avoid possible irreparable damage to the victims of the alleged violation. Where the Committee exercises its discretion, this does not imply a determination on admissibility or on the merits of the communication". One of the innovative aspects of this treaty is that in urgent cases the supervisory Committee to this treaty may address even States parties that have not recognized the individual complaint procedure under Article 31. Article 30 introduces the possibility for the Committee to intervene upon a request 'by relatives of the disappeared person or their legal representatives, their counsel or any person authorized by them, as well as by any other person having a legitimate interest' that 'a disappeared person should be sought and found'. In fact when it considers that a range of procedural requirements is met, it 'shall request the State Party concerned to provide it with information on the situation of the persons sought, within a time limit set by the Committee'. On the procedural requirements see Chapter XIV (Jurisdiction and admissibility).

[27] The Statute of the Commission provides in Article 19 (c) that the Commission shall have the power 'to request the Inter-American Court of Human Rights to take such provisional measures as it considers appropriate in serious and urgent cases which have not yet been submitted to it for consideration, whenever this becomes necessary to prevent irreparable injury to persons', Statute of the Inter-American Commission on Human Rights, approved by Resolution N1 447 taken by the General Assembly of the OAS at its ninth regular session, held in La Paz, Bolivia, October 1997.

[28] The last sentence ('a case not yet submitted') could also be interpreted to imply that the Commission may only request provisional measures if it will later bring the case before the Court on the merits as well. On the other hand, the inclusion of the word 'yet' may also simply distinguish between cases already pending before the Court and those still pending before the Commission, without implying anything more than an assumption that, at a later stage, the latter will be submitted to the Court as well. In any case, the word does not justify lifting a provisional measure when the Commission has not yet submitted a case to the Court within a certain time frame. See also Chapter XIV (Jurisdiction and admissibility) and Chapter XVI (Official responses).

rights treaty, 'it is difficult to support the proposition that Article 63(2) decisions should not be legally binding'.[29]

Cançado Trindade refers to the 'autonomous legal framework of provisional measures of protection' in which the Inter-American Court's provisional measures, in light of their conventional force, constitute an autonomous legal remedy.[30]

Article 27(2) of the Protocol to the African Charter establishing the African Court on Human and Peoples' Rights provides for this Court's duty to order provisional measures.[31] In the text of the Protocol there is no arrangement similar to that in Article 63(2) ACHR whereby the African Commission would request the Court's provisional measures in cases that can be brought before the Court but at that time are still pending before the Commission.[32] Article 35 of the Protocol on the Statute of the African Court of Justice and Human Rights (2008), merging the aforementioned Court with the African Court of Justice, equally includes an explicit power to order provisional measures.

The Bosnia Chamber, finally, active between 1995 and 2003, under Article X (1) of Annex 6 to the Dayton Peace Agreement also had the explicit power to order provisional measures.[33]

2.3.3 The case law of the Inter-American Court

In its first order for provisional measures in *Velásquez Rodríguez*, in 1988, the Inter-American Court referred to Article 63(2) ACHR as the legal basis for its Order, as well as to Article 23(5) of its Rules of Procedure which provides that it may take provisional measures *ex officio* at any time. In this context the Court also noted the obligation of States Parties under Article 1(1) ACHR to respect and ensure the rights contained in the Convention.

---

[29]   Buergenthal (1994), pp. 86-87.

[30]   See IACHR *Matter of the persons imprisoned in the "Dr. Sebastião Martins Silveira" Penitentiary in Araraquara, São Paulo* (Brazil), Order of 30 September 2006, individual opinion Judge Cançado Trindade, §§24-25. See also IACHR Matter of *Eloísa Barrios et al.* (Venezuela*),* Orders of 25 June 25 and 22 September 2005, Concurring Opinions Judge Cançado Trindade.

[31]   "In cases of extreme gravity and urgency, and when necessary to avoid irreparable harm to persons, the Court shall adopt such provisional measures as it deems necessary".

[32]   See Articles 2 and 8 Protocol to the African Charter on Human and Peoples' Rights.

[33]   "The Chamber shall have the power to order provisional measures, to appoint experts, and to compel the production of witnesses and evidence". Article VIII, 2(f) on the jurisdiction of the Chamber stipulates: "Applications which entail requests for provisional measures shall be reviewed as a matter of priority in order to determine (1) whether they should be accepted and, if so (2) whether high priority for the scheduling of proceedings on the provisional measures request is warranted". See also Article XI (Decisions): "1. Following the conclusion of the proceedings, the Chamber shall promptly issue a decision, which shall address: (a) Whether the facts found indicate a breach by the Party concerned of its obligations under this Agreement; and if so (b) what steps shall be taken by the Party to remedy such breach, including orders to cease and desist, monetary relief (including pecuniary and non-pecuniary injuries), and provisional measures". And Article XII (Rules and Regulations) "The Chamber shall promulgate such rules and regulations, consistent with this Agreement, as may be necessary to carry out its functions, including provisions for preliminary hearings, expedited decisions on provisional measures, decisions by panels of the Chamber, and review of decisions made by any such panels". See also Bosnia Chamber *Boudellaa, Lakhdar, Nechle and Lahmar* v. *BiH and Fed. BiH*, 11 October 2002, §185 and *D.K.* v. *Republika Srpska*, 2 November 1999, §§33-37.

"The States Parties therefore are required to adopt such measures as are necessary to preserve the life and ensure the personal safety of those whose rights might be endangered, or the more so if these threats are linked to their participation in proceeding bearing upon the protection of human rights".[34]

With this the Court seems to imply that even without a provision on provisional measures in the Convention, States have the obligation to comply with the Court's Orders simply on the basis of their human rights obligations in the Convention. As Buergenthal has noted, 'the Court expressly recognized the existence of inherent powers without, however, spelling them out in any detail'.[35]

In its next Order in this case the Court again referred to the basis of its authority to Order provisional measures. Here it did not only refer to Articles 63(2) ACHR and 23 of its Rules of Procedure but also to Articles 33 (on the competence of the Commission and Court) and 62(3) ACHR (the Court's jurisdiction regarding all cases of interpretation and application of the ACHR submitted to it), Articles 1 and 2 of the Court's Statute (on the nature and jurisdiction of the Court)[36] and 'the judicial character of the Court and the powers derived therefrom'.[37]

The reference to its judicial character clearly is a more general argument based on the principle that the ability to order provisional measures is simply part of the adjudicatory function.[38]

In reference to Article 1(1) ACHR the Court has often pointed out the State's responsibility to adopt security measures to protect everyone under its jurisdiction. In the *Peace Community* case the State must do so for all members of the Peace Community.[39]

In their concurring opinion attached to the Court's first Order in the *Peace Community* case, two of the Judges pointed out that provisional measures as laid down in Article 63(2) ACHR are a fundamental part of the effective protection ('tutela') of human rights.[40] They referred to Articles 1(1) and 2 ACHR and emphasised the latter's reference to the duty to adopt *other* measures nec-

---

[34] IACHR *Velásquez Rodríguez, Fairén Garbi/Solís Corrales* and *Godínez Cruz* cases, Order of 15 January 1988, 3rd 'Whereas' clause.

[35] Buergenthal (1994), p. 83.

[36] Article 1 (Nature and Legal Organization): 'The Inter-American Court of Human Rights is an autonomous judicial institution whose purpose is the application and interpretation of the American Convention on Human Rights. The Court exercises its functions in accordance with the provisions of the aforementioned Convention and the present Statute'. Article 2 (Jurisdiction): 'The Court shall exercise adjudicatory and advisory jurisdiction: 1. Its adjudicatory jurisdiction shall be governed by the provisions of Articles 61, 62 and 63 of the Convention, and 2. Its advisory jurisdiction shall be governed by the provisions of Article 64 of the Convention'.

[37] IACHR *Velásquez Rodríguez, Fairén Garbi/Solís Corrales* and *Godínez Cruz* cases Order of 19 January 1988, 1st 'Considering' clause.

[38] See e.g. Buergenthal (1994), pp. 83-84.

[39] The Court continued to note that this duty becomes even more evident with regard to persons involved in proceedings before the supervisory organs of the ACHR. IACHR *Peace Community of San José de Apartadó* case (Colombia), Order for provisional measures, 24 November 2000, with references to *Digna Ochoa y Plácido et al.*, Order for provisional measures, 17 November 1999; *Constitutional Court* case, Order for provisional measures, 14 August 2000.

[40] See IACHR *Peace Community of San José de Apartadó* case (Colombia), Order for provisional measures, 24 November 2000, Concurring Opinion of Judge Abreu Burelli and García Ramírez. They wrote that, apart from the considerations based on the progressive interpretation of Article 63(2) ACHR, the State had the broad duty in each case to respect the rights and freedoms recognised in the Convention. This duty justified actions on the part of the authorities on the one hand and legitimate expectations of individuals on the other.

essary to give effect to the rights in the Convention. Such measures should include urgent protective measures.[41]

The Court's position on state responsibility is that the State is responsible to adopt effective safety measures to protect all the persons who are subject to its jurisdiction and that this obligation is even more evident in relation to those who are involved in proceedings before the supervisory organs of the American Convention.[42]

In Orders to halt an execution the IACHR considers that 'if the State were to execute the alleged victims, this would lead to an irreparable situation, as well as constitute conduct incompatible with the object and purpose of the Convention'.[43]

The Court has emphasised that the principles of effectiveness and good faith are also applicable in the implementation of its provisional measures.[44] In its Orders for provisional measures in *James et al.* v. *Trinidad and Tobago* the Court determined that States 'must fully comply in good faith (*pacta sunt servanda*) with all of the provisions of the Convention, including those relative to the operation of the two supervisory organs of the American Convention; and, that in view of the Convention's fundamental objective of guaranteeing the effective protection of human rights (Articles 1(1), 2, 51 and 63(2)), States Parties must refrain from taking actions that may frustrate the *restitutio in integrum* of the rights of the alleged victims'.[45] This provides a rationale for arguing that States are legally bound to respect the precautionary measures of the Commission as well.

The Court has also added to the equation Article 51 ACHR, on the findings and recommendations of the Commission. In its first Order for provisional measures to halt executions, for instance, it pointed out:

"That States Parties must respect the provisions of the American Convention in good faith (*pacta sunt servanda*), including those that facilitate proceedings before the protective bodies of the Inter-American system and ensure the fulfilment of the goals of those provisions. In view of this, and of the Convention's fundamental objective of guaranteeing the effective protection of

---

[41] Concurring Opinion of Judge Abreu Burelli and García Ramírez, IACHR *Peace Community of San José de Apartadó* case (Colombia), Order of 24 November 2000.

[42] See e.g. IACHR case of *Haitians and Dominicans of Haitian Origin in the Dominican Republic*, Order for provisional measures, 26 May 2001.

[43] See e.g. IACHR *James et al.* Order of 26 November 2001, 12th 'Considering' clause; *Raxcacó et al*, 30 August 2004, 9th 'Considering' clause; *Boyce and Joseph* v. *Barbados*, 25 November 2004, 9th 'Considering' clause; see also the Court's judgment in this case, 20 November 2007, §113; sometimes the phrasing is somewhat more cautious ('as well as possibly constitute conduct incompatible with the object and purpose of the Convention'), *Tyrone Dacosta Cadogan* (Barbados), Order of the President of 4 November 2008, 10th 'Considering' clause.

[44] See e.g. IACHR *James et al.* v. *Trinidad and Tobago*, Order of 26 September 2001, 10th 'Considering' clause. It already stated this in early cases, see e.g. *Caballero-Delgado and Santana* (Colombia), Order of 6 February 2008, 15th, 'Considering' clause: "That pursuant to Article 63(2) of the Convention, the State has a duty to adopt such provisional measures as this Court may order, insofar as the basic principle of the International Responsibility of States, supported by international case law, provides that States must fulfill their treaty obligations in good faith (*pacta sunt servanda*)".

[45] IACHR *James et al.* v. *Trinidad and Tobago*, Order of 21 May 1999, 9th 'Considering' clause. See also Chapter XIII on the relationship with reparation.

human rights (Articles 51 and 63(2)), States Parties must not take any action that will frustrate the *restitutio in integrum* of the rights of the alleged victims".[46]

It confirmed this in its later Orders, in which it not only referred to Articles 51 and 63(2) but also to Articles 1(1) and 2, as laying down obligations related to the fundamental objective of guaranteeing the effective protection of human rights.[47]

The Court has also stressed that in light of the obligations under Article 1(1) ACHR, the State is 'especially bound to guarantee the rights of persons in a risk situation and must advance the investigations necessary to establish the facts and, if it be the case, to punish those responsible', all of this 'regardless of the existence of specific provisional measures'.[48]

In the context of provisional measures the Court has drawn attention to Article 68(1) ACHR as well, with the undertaking of the States Parties 'to comply with the judgment of the Court in any case to which they are parties'.[49] In addition the Court has referred to Article 29 ACHR providing that no provision shall be interpreted as permitting the suppression of the enjoyment or exercise of the rights recognised in the Convention or their restriction to a greater extent than provided for in the Convention. Following this, the Court would point out:

> "That, should the State execute the alleged victims, it would create an irremediable situation and this conduct would be incompatible with the object and purpose of the Convention by disavowing the authority of the Commission and adversely affecting the very essence of the Inter-American system".[50]

Clearly, the rationale for provisional measures is important to understand their legal status. In this respect the Court's reference to *restitutio in integrum* in its death penalty cases is very relevant.[51]

In his Concurring Opinion to the Order of 25 May 1999, judge Cançado Trindade noted that considerations of *ordre public* underlie the 'exercise of the advisory and contentious functions of the Tribunal in general', and extend themselves 'to the provisional measures of protection in particular'. He emphasised that these have a mandatory character: – 'ordered as they are by an international tribunal like the Inter-American Court'.[52] In light of his remarks about *ordre public* and the effective protection of human rights, all provisional measures arguably have a mandatory character, not just those by Courts but also those by the regional Commissions and the Geneva Committees.

---

[46] IACHR *James, Briggs, Noel, Garcia and Bethel* cases, Order for provisional measures, 14 June 1998.

[47] See e.g. IACHR *James et al.* cases, Order for provisional measures, 29 August 1998, 25 May 1999, 27 May 1999, 25 September 1999, 16 August 2000, 24 November 2000 and 26 November 2001.

[48] IACHR *Álvarez et al.* (Colombia), Order of 8 February 2008.

[49] IACHR *James et al.* cases, Order of 16 August 2000 and 24 November 2000.

[50] IACHR *James, Briggs, Noel, Garcia and Bethel* cases, Order of 14 June 1998. Similar statements, always in combination with the reference to Article 29, can be found in later Orders, e.g. 19 August 1998, 25 and 27 May and 25 September 1999. The President's Order for urgent measures of 26 November 2001 refers to Article 29, 'an irremediable situation' and 'incompatible with the object and purpose of the Convention' but it does not proceed with 'by disavowing the authority of the Commission and adversely affecting the very essence of the Inter-American system'.

[51] See further Chapter XIII (Protection).

[52] IACHR James et al. case, Order of 25 May 1999, Concurring Opinion of A.A. Cançado Trindade.

In *Boyce and Joseph* v. *Barbados* the Inter-American Court referred to 'the well-established principles regarding international state responsibility, whereby States are required to comply in good faith with their treaty obligations (*pacta sunt servanda*)'. In this light 'urgent measures ordered by the President of this Tribunal by virtue of the provisions of Article 63(2) of the Convention have an obligatory character. Consequently, Barbados is under the obligation to keep this Tribunal informed regarding the actions it has taken to comply with the Order of the President. The provision of such information is essential in order to permit the Court to evaluate the State's degree of compliance with the said Order'.[53]

The Court responded to the executions of Anthony Briggs and Joey Ramiah by pointing out that the State had a duty to preserve their life and physical integrity pursuant to its Orders for provisional measures. It referred to Article 68(1) ACHR, which provides that States Parties shall undertake to comply with the Court's judgment in any case to which they are parties. As usual, it pointed out that States 'should fully comply in good faith (*pacta sunt servanda*) with all of the provisions of the Convention, including those relative to the operation of the two supervisory organs of the American Convention'. It also pointed out that 'in view of the Convention's fundamental objective of guaranteeing the effective protection of human rights' (Articles 1(1), 2, 51 and 63(2)) 'States Parties must refrain from taking actions that may frustrate the *restitutio in integrum* of the rights of the alleged victims'.[54] This shows the Court's view that the power to order legally binding provisional measures simply answers to the fundamental objective of guaranteeing the effective protection of human rights, even irrespective of a specific reference to provisional measures in the treaty itself.

2.4 Systems referring to provisional measures solely in the Rules of Procedure

2.4.1 Introduction

This section first deals with the relevant rules in the Rules of Procedure laid down by the human rights adjudicators adjudicating complaints based on treaties that do not explicitly refer to the authority to use provisional measures. Then it deals with the pertinent case law on the legal status of provisional measures developed by these adjudicators.

---

[53] IACHR *Boyce and Joseph* v. *Barbados,* 25 November 2004, §6. In the context of provisional measures ordered vis-à-vis Venezuela, the Court also pointed out that while this State is not a party to the VCLT, the international obligation of *pacta sunt servanda* is binding on it as a rule of customary international law. With regard to the Court's provisional measures the addressee States must take all necessary measures to effectively protect the beneficiaries, in conformity with the Court's instructions. This includes the obligation periodically to inform the Court of the implementation measures taken. IACHR *Liliana Ortega et al.; Luisiana Ríos et al.; Luis Uzcátegui; Marta Colomina and Liliana Velásquez* (Venezuela), Order of 4 May 2004, 7th 'Considering' clause. See also e.g. IACHR *Matter of Liliana Ortega et al.* (Venezuela), Order of 14 June 2005, 13th 'Considering' clause. See further Chapter XVII (Official State responses).

[54] IACHR *James et al.* case, Order for provisional measures, 25 September 1999. See also its Orders of 14 June and 29 August 1998, 25 and 27 May 1999, 16 August, 24 November 2000 and 26 November 2001. In the latter the Court noted that States Parties should refrain from taking actions that 'may cause irreparable harm to persons by reason of the gravity of the possible consequences of said acts' rather than from actions that 'may frustrate the *restitutio in integrum* of the rights of the alleged victims'.

2.4.2 Rules of Procedure on provisional measures

Two of the three UN human rights adjudicators that have used provisional measures have done so on the basis of their own Rules of Procedure. The Optional Protocol establishing the right of individual complaint about violations of the ICCPR, for instance, does not contain a specific reference to provisional measures. Instead, the HRC has included a rule on such measures in its Rules of Procedure. Its current Rule 92 (previously Rule 86) stipulates:

> "The Committee may, prior to forwarding its Views on the communication to the State Party concerned, inform that State of its view as to whether provisional measures may be desirable to avoid irreparable damage to the victim of the alleged violation. In doing so, the Committee shall inform the State Party concerned that such expression of its views on provisional measures does not imply a determination on the merits on the communication".[55]

Tomuschat has pointed out that 'it is remarkable that the Committee, notwithstanding the difficult political context within which it was working, was eventually able to hammer out an agreed formula by consensus'. He described this political context as follows:

> "A school of strict constructionists-mostly members from Eastern European countries-was opposed in that debate to a school of broad constructionists-mainly made up of members from Western Europe-who emphasized the need to take into account object and purpose of the Protocol as an instrument to secure effective procedural protection to individual rights".[56]

---

[55] In 1977, during the deliberations on the Rules of Procedure, Tomuschat (Federal Republic of Germany) noted that it was 'clear that the power of any group established by the Committee would be limited to making recommendations'. Summary records of the meetings of the first session, 13th meeting, 29 March 1977 and 17th meeting, 31 March 1977, Yearbook of the HRC 1977-1978, Vol. I, CCPR/1 pp. 44-46 and p. 54. Espersen (Denmark) noted 'it was a commonly accepted notion that bodies had such implied powers as were necessary to enable them to perform their functions in a reasonable manner'. This required a 'stronger formulation of rule 86'. Thus, he proposed to replace the words 'request the State Party concerned to take interim measures' by the words 'forward to the State Party concerned its views as to whether interim measures might be necessary'. Espersen explained that '(s)uch a change would be in conformity with the letter and spirit of the protocol and would ensure that the Committee would have the impact it was intended to have'. It is possible that the other members agreed with this change because the expression 'forward to the State party concerned its Views as to whether interim measures might be necessary' is sufficiently vague to be interpreted as both weaker and stronger than the previously proposed term 'request'. Tomuschat wrote, almost two decades later, that '(t)he compromise finally reached consisted in attenuating the language of the Rule, in particular replacing the word 'request' by a more flexible phrase attuned to the formulation of Article 5(4)'. Tomuschat (1995), p. 625. The only change the Committee made to this part of the provision, at a later stage, was the replacement of the word 'necessary' by the word 'desirable', as suggested by Lallah (Mauritius). Summary records of the meetings of the first session, 13th meeting, 29 March 1977 and 17th meeting, 31 March 1977, Yearbook of the HRC 1977-1978, Vol. I, CCPR/1 pp. 44-46 and p. 54.

[56] Tomuschat (1995), p. 625. Nine Eastern European States were involved in the ICCPR system from the early stages, but none of them had recognised the individual complaint procedure. In 1988 Hungary was the first Eastern European country to ratify the OP. Between 1991 and 2002 more than 20 former communist States became a party to the OP. Four of the first members of the

Rule 92 of its Rules of Procedure (previously Rule 86) refers to the HRC's authority to use provisional measures.[57] Rule 108 of CAT's Rules of Procedure refers to the latter's authority in this respect.[58]

The European Commission on Human Rights was the first international adjudicator that resorted to provisional measures as part of the contentious proceedings pending before it. As discussed in Chapter II, in 1957 the former European Commission used informal provisional measures for the first time, urgently requesting the UK not to execute Nicolaos Sampson until the Commission had been fully informed of the circumstances of the case. The Commission stated it had decided to make this request in order to prevent "any irreparable act".[59] Yet in two less serious cases, decided in 1958 and 1963, the Commission refused to take provisional measures, considering that the Convention did not give it the competence to order them.[60] In 1964 it again took

---

HRC nevertheless came from Eastern Europe. Apart from them five members came from Western Europe and Canada, three from Latin America and six from other regions.

[57] "The Committee may, prior to forwarding its Views on the communication to the State party concerned, inform that State of its Views as to whether interim measures may be desirable to avoid irreparable damage to the victim of the alleged violation. In doing so, the Committee shall inform the State party concerned that such expression of its Views on interim measures does not imply a determination on the merits of the communication".

[58] "1. At any time after the receipt of a complaint, the Committee, a working group, or the Rapporteur(s) for new complaints and interim measures may transmit to the State party concerned, for its urgent consideration, a request that it take such interim measures as the Committee considers necessary to avoid irreparable damage to the victim or victims of alleged violations. 2. Where the Committee, the Working Group, or Rapporteur(s) request(s) interim measures under this rule, the request shall not imply a determination of the admissibility or the merits of the complaint. The State party shall be so informed upon transmittal. 3. Where a request for interim measures is made by the Working Group or Rapporteur(s) under the present rule, the Working Group or Rapporteur(s) should inform the Committee members of the nature of the request and the complaint to which the request relates at the next regular session of the Committee. 4. The Secretary-General shall maintain a list of such requests for interim measures. 5. The Rapporteur for new complaints and interim measures shall also monitor compliance with the Committee's requests for interim measures". CERD was the first UN treaty body introducing provisional measures in its Rules of Procedure. Its Rule 94(3), which has never been used, is phrased as follows: "In the course of its consideration, the Committee may inform the State party of its views on the desirability, because of urgency, of taking interim measures to avoid possible irreparable damage to the person or persons who claim to be victim(s) of the alleged violation. In doing so, the Committee shall inform the State party concerned that such expression of its views on interim measures does not prejudice either its final opinion on the merits of the communication or its eventual suggestions and recommendation".

[59] See EComHR *Application of the ECHR to the Island of Cyprus* (*Greece* v. *United Kingdom*), Article 31 report of the Commission, No. 176/56, 26 September 1958, p. 24. This request was respected, see further Chapter III (Executions).

[60] EComHR *X.* v. *Federal Republic of Germany*, 22 March 1958 ("Whereas the Convention does not contain any such obligations binding upon the High Contracting Parties as invoked by the Applicant; whereas, moreover, the Convention does not contain any provision giving the Commission competence to order provisional measures; whereas it therefore appears that the application is in this respect incompatible with the provisions of the Convention; whereas it should, in pursuance of Article 27, paragraph 2, of the Convention, accordingly be rejected") and *X. and Y.* v. *Belgium*, 18 December 1963 ('whereas the fact that the Commission is dealing with a case does not have suspensive effect and the Commission is not empowered to order protective measures (see the decision on the admissibility of Application No. 297/57, Volume II, page 213);

informal provisional measures, this time to halt an extradition.[61] Since that time an informal practice developed in which the Commission requested – and obtained – the cooperation of Governments in urgent cases pending before the Commission involving extradition or expulsion. In 1974 the Commission decided to formalize its practice of using provisional measures by including a provision on provisional measures in its Rule 36 of its Rules of Procedure.[62] In 1982 the Court did as well. Presently the authority to use provisional measures can be found in Rule 39 of the Court's Rules of Procedure.[63]

As noted, the ACHR explicitly authorizes the Inter-American Court to order provisional measures and it assigns the Inter-American Commission a task in this respect as well. In Article 25 of its Rules of Procedure the Inter-American Commission has introduced a reference to its authority to order its own precautionary measures as well. Vis-à-vis those States that have recognized the Inter-American Court it uses this mechanism when it considers it needs the flexibility of a swift and incremental approach before resorting to the Court. Vis-à-vis those States that have not recognized the Court, or have not even ratified the ACHR, the Commission's precautionary measures are the only mechanism to prevent irreparable harm pending the proceedings before the Commission based on its function of adjudicating petitions under the OAS Charter (as well as under the ACHR for those States that have ratified it, but did not recognize the Court).

The African Charter, finally, does not contain a specific article on provisional measures either. The African Commission has referred to its authority to do so in Rule 111 of its Rules of Procedure.[64] As noted, the Protocol introducing the African Court does refer to provisional measures.

---

whereas, far from obliging national courts to wait for the Commission to complete its work before they complete theirs, the Convention, in principle, provides for the opposite solution (Article 26) and assigns a mainly subsidiary role to the collective guarantee machinery set up by it').

[61] EComHR *X* v. *Austria and Yugoslavia*, 30 June 1964 (inadm.); provisional measure on 14 February 1964. See also *S.B.* v. *FRG*, 19 December 1969 (struck off), provisional measure on 7 January 1965 and 24 April 1965.

[62] Article 36 ECHR (pre-Protocol 11) stating that the Commission shall draw up its own rules of procedure. It did so on 13 December 1974. In its 1993 Rules of Procedure, Rule 36 was phrased as follows: "The Commission, or when it is not in session, the President may indicate to the parties any interim measure the adoption of which seems desirable in the interest of the parties or the proper conduct of the proceedings before it". Revised version as adopted by the Commission on 12 February and 6 May 1993 and entered into force on 28 June 1993.

[63] "1. The Chamber or, where appropriate, its President may, at the request of a party or of any other person concerned, or of its own motion, indicate to the parties any interim measure which it considers should be adopted in the interests of the parties or of the proper conduct of the proceedings before it. 2. Notice of these measures shall be given to the Committee of Ministers. 3. The Chamber may request information from the parties on any matter connected with the implementation of any interim measure it has indicated".

[64] "1. Before making its final views know to the Assembly on the communication [sic], the Commission may inform the State party concerned of its views on the appropriateness of taking provisional measures to avoid irreparable damage being caused to the victim of the alleged violation. In so doing, the Commission shall inform the State party that the expression on its views on the adoption of those provisional measures does not imply a decision on the substance of the communication. 2. The Commission, or when it is not in session, the Chairman, in consultation with other members of the Commission, may indicate to the parties any interim measure, the adoption of which seems desirable in the interest of the parties or the proper conduct

2.4.3   Pertinent case law on the legal status of provisional measures

2.4.3.1   INTRODUCTION

The adjudicators supervising treaties without an express reference to provisional measures in the treaty text consider respect for these measures as a necessary corollary to the obligations under the treaties.

This section deals with the approaches of the various human rights adjudicators in this respect.

2.4.3.2   HRC ON THE LEGAL STATUS OF ITS PROVISIONAL MEASURES

Some States have argued that the Committee's provisional measures are not legally binding because no such specific reference was made in the text of the OP, because the text of the Rule on provisional measures contains exhortatory language ('desirable') or, as noted, because they consider decisions on the merits to be non- binding as well.

On the other hand, the HRC itself has referred to the obligations under the ICCPR and the OP condemning executions, expulsion and extradition in contravention of its provisional measures. Apart from this it has always emphasised certain obligations of States with regard to the complaint proceedings.[65] *Audiatur et alteram pars* includes hearing and informing each party. Procedural equality (Article 14) applies also in cases pending before the HRC under the OP and not only in domestic cases. Lack of procedural equality may be said to cause irreparable harm to the proceedings before the Committee.

Certain general obligations and consequences became apparent early on in the activities of the HRC with regard to cases of political detainees and their health and whereabouts. The ability of detainees to communicate directly with the Committee is a prerequisite for the effective appli-

---

of the proceedings before it. 3. In case of urgency when the Commission is not in session, the Chairman in consultation with other members of the Commission, may take any necessary action on behalf of the Commission. As soon as the Commission is again in session, the Chairman shall report to it on any action taken". Rules of Procedure of 6 October 1995 (<www.achpr.org>). Previously this was Rule 109, Rules of Procedure, 1 February 1988, see Murray/Evans (2001), p. 161.

[65]   It is the Committee that should set the deadlines for the proceedings, not the parties themselves. It is equally for the Committee to decide on the admissibility of a case, not for the Addressee State. The HRC always emphasises that it is implicit in Article 4(2) OP that a State party make available all the information at its disposal. Pending the proceedings Addressee States have several obligations under the OP. Their recognition of the OP implies that they must heed to the procedural orders of the HRC, such as answering questions, sending requested documentation or investigating claims. They must respect the procedure as set by the Committee, including deadlines and admissibility decisions. If they do not, they shall suffer the consequences, as the Committee may decide that due weight must be given to the petitioner's claims in the absence of information from the State party. Of course, the petitioner must also respect the procedure as set by the Committee and similarly suffer the consequences for not doing so. In this light it is self-evident that States are also expected to postpone action if the Committee considers that this action would result in irreparable harm. As the case may be, States may also have to take action to prevent third parties from causing irreparable harm to the alleged victim or to the proceedings before the Committee, if the Committee so indicates.

cation of the OP. Governments have no right to create obstacles to this communication. Such obstacles would, in many cases, render meaningless the individual complaint procedure.[66] This approach by the HRC is important for the procedural position of the parties.

The whereabouts of the person concerned should be known and he or she should be able to communicate with the HRC freely without fear for repercussions. The State's obligation under Article 4(2) OP includes providing information on the state of health of detainees. States that fail to provide information and clarifications, seriously hamper the HRC in discharging its responsibilities under the OP.[67]

States must make available administrative mechanisms 'to give effect to the general obligation to investigate allegations of violations promptly, thoroughly and effectively through independent and impartial bodies'. After all, a 'failure by a State Party to investigate allegations of violations could in and of itself give rise to a separate breach of the Covenant'.[68]

It has been on the occasion of executions of death sentences in defiance of its provisional measures that the HRC has expressed itself most strongly on the rationale of provisional measures and their legal status.[69] Over the years it has taken a stronger position on non-compliance.[70] It now condemns such executions as incompatible with the obligation to respect the Covenant in good faith and with the right of individual communication under the OP.

In *Piandiong* (2000) the HRC referred to the preamble and Article 1 OP and noted that the undertaking to co-operate with the Committee in good faith was implicit in a State's adherence to the OP. It pointed out that denying its provisional measures was incompatible with the obligations of the State not to hinder the Committee's task of examining the communication and determining the case on the merits under Article 5(1) and (4). The HRC pointed out that provisional measures are essential to the Committee's role under the OP.[71] The Committee's reference to the obligation of States not to frustrate it in its consideration of a case may be classified as an obligation not to harm the procedure. Its reference to the obligation not to prevent it to express its Views may be classified as an obligation not to cause irreparable harm to the claim either. In other words, the HRC seems to allude to both rationales for the use of provisional measures.[72]

---

[66] See e.g. HRC *Sendic Antonaccio* (*submitted by his wife Violeta Setelich*) v. *Uruguay*, 28 October 1981.

[67] See e.g. HRC *Dave Marais* v. *Madagascar*, 24 March 1984.

[68] HRC General Comment on the nature of the general legal obligation imposed on States parties to the Covenant (Article 2 ICCPR), 21 April 2004, §15. See further Chapter XIII (Protection).

[69] In the vast majority of death penalty cases States have respected the Committee's provisional measures. On these measures see Chapter III. See further Chapter XVII (Official State responses).

[70] See also Harrington (2003), p. 69 referring to a 'movement towards recognizing the binding nature of interim measures requests' as 'reflected' in the jurisprudence of the HRC. She notes that the Committee 'has taken an increasingly stronger stance' and 'what were once seen as mere "failures to cooperate" are now viewed as violations of a state's very obligations under the ICCPR regime'.

[71] Already HRC *Peter Bradshaw* v. *Barbados*, 19 July 1994 (inadm.), §§2.9, 2.10, 4.2, 5.3; see also *Denzil Roberts* v. *Barbados*, 19 July 1994, §§2.6, 2.7, 6.3 the HRC established that the State party had accepted the legal obligation to make the provisions of the Covenant effective. It was under an obligation to adopt appropriate measures to give legal effect to the Committee's interpretation on the merits, but also to its provisional measures to avoid irreparable harm 'to the victim of the alleged violation' pending the proceedings. Further on the position of the HRC prior to 2000 see Chapter XVIII (Follow-up).

[72] On these rationales, see Conclusion Part II.

The executions rendered examination by the HRC moot and the expression of its Views 'nugatory and futile'. Flouting its provisional measures, 'especially by irreversible measures such as the execution of the alleged victim' undermined the protection of Covenant rights under the OP.[73] This means that the Committee emphasises the importance of provisional measures for the prevention of 'irreversible measures'. Nevertheless, it found no violations of specific articles of the Covenant, only of the State's legal obligations under the OP. It referred to Article 1 OP and to the object and purpose of the OP in general.

In *Piandiong* the HRC also pointed out that even when the HRC has not (yet) acted under Rule 86 the State's obligation to co-operate with the HRC in good faith forbids the State party to execute the petitioners.[74] In other words, in death penalty cases the State party breaches its obligations under the OP when it executes an alleged victim while the petitioner had informed it that he had submitted a case to the HRC. In subsequent Views in relation to Sierra Leone and Trinidad and Tobago the HRC confirmed this approach. At the merits stage in *Ashby* v. *Trinidad and Tobago* (2002) it noted:

> "The behaviour of the State party represents a shocking failure to demonstrate even the most elementary good faith required of a State party to the Covenant and the Optional Protocol".[75]

The State had breached its obligations under the OP 'by proceeding to execute Mr. Ashby before the Committee could conclude its examination of the communication, and the formulation of its Views'. It found it 'particularly inexcusable' that the State had done so after the Committee's use of provisional measures.[76]

When States have failed to comply with its provisional measures, the HRC reserves a separate section of its decision on the merits to deal on this issue. These sections have had headings such as 'State party's failure to respect the Committee's request for interim measures under rule 86',[77] 'Breach of the Optional Protocol'[78] or 'Non respect of the Committee's request for interim measures'.[79]

Not only in death penalty but also in expulsion and extradition cases the HRC has found that States are bound to respect its provisional measures to prevent irreparable harm. It equally found States in breach of the Optional Protocol as well as of Article 2 ICCPR on the right to the

---

[73]   See HRC *Dante Piandiong, Jesus Morallos and Archie Bulan (deceased) (submitted by Alexander Padilla and Ricardo III Sunga)* v. *the Philippines*, 19 October 2000, §§5.1-5.4. See also, e.g., *Mansaraj et al., Gborie et al. and Sesay et al.* v. *Sierra Leone*, 16 July 2001 and *Glenn Ashby* v. *Trinidad and Tobago*, 21 March 2002. See further press release, 'Human Rights Committee deplores the execution of six individuals in Uzbekistan', 24 July 2003. The petitioners who were executed were Muzaffar Mirzaev (case 1170/2003), Shukrat Andasbaev (case 1166/2003), Ulugbek Ashov (case 1165/2003), Ilkhon Babadzhanov and Maksud Ismailov (case 1162/2003), and Azamat Uteev (case 1150/2003). Furthermore see *Barno Saidova* v. *Tajikistan*, 8 July 2004.

[74]   HRC *Dante Piandiong, Jesus Morallos and Archie Bulan (deceased) (submitted by Alexander Padilla and Ricardo III Sunga)* v. *the Philippines*, 19 October 2000.

[75]   HRC *Glenn Ashby* v. *Trinidad and Tobago*, 21 March 2002, §10.9.

[76]   Id., §10.10.

[77]   See HRC *Barno Saidova* v. *Tajikistan*, 8 July 2004, §§4.1-4.4 and *Maryam Khalilova on behalf of her son Validzhon Alievich Khalilov* v. *Tajikistan*, 30 March 2005, §§4.1-4.4.

[78]   HRC *Davlatbibi Shukurova on behalf of her husband Dovud and his brother Sherali Nazriev* v. *Tajikistan*, 16 March 2006, §§6.1.-6.4.

[79]   HRC *Roza Uteeva on behalf of her brother Azamat Uteev* v. *Uzbekistan*, 26 October 2007, §§5.1-5.3. See also *Shevkkhie Tulyaganova* v. *Uzbekistan*, 20 July 2007, §§6.1-6.3.

effective remedy.[80] In *Ahani* v. *Canada* (2004) the HRC pointed out that action by a State party giving rise to a risk of irreparable harm, 'as indicated a priori by the Committee's request for interim measures, must be scrutinized in the strictest light'.[81] The Committee's Rules of Procedure have been adopted in conformity with Article 39 ICCPR and its provisional measures, taken pursuant to Rule 86, are 'essential' to its role under the OP. "Flouting of the Rule, especially by irreversible measures such as the execution of the alleged victim or his/her deportation from a State party to face torture or death in another country, undermines the protection of Covenant rights through the Optional Protocol".[82]

Strangely, the word 'especially' seems to imply that it could also use provisional measures to halt measures that are not irreversible. On the other hand, it specifically refers to provisional measures to halt executions or to such measures to halt expulsion in non-refoulement cases. Such measures in fact aim to halt not only that which is irreversible, but that which is irreparable as well.

In 2004 the Committee confirmed its approach to the obligation under the OP to respect its provisional measures in its General Comment on Article 2 ICCPR. It noted that failure to implement its provisional measures 'should be regarded as incompatible with the obligation to respect in good faith the Covenant, in particular its article 2 and the right of individual communication under the Optional Protocol'.[83] It explicitly refers to the obligation to respect its provisional measures based on Article 2 of the Covenant rather than based only on the Covenant rights through the right of individual communication.[84]

It pointed out that provisional measures may be required in certain circumstances because of the right to an effective remedy. In such cases States parties must 'provide for and implement provisional or interim measures to avoid continuing violations and to endeavour to repair at the earliest possible opportunity any harm that may have been caused by such violations'.[85]

---

[80]   See HRC *Sholam Weiss* v. *Austria*, 3 April 2003, §7.2. See also the arguments of counsel in §§6.3 and 6.4. Some members of the Committee may consider that in extradition and expulsion cases when provisional measures have been ignored it should look at whether irreparable harm indeed followed. In other words, they may belong to the 'after the fact'-school, to which the ECtHR adheres as well. If they believe that for finding a violation they have to take into account what comes later, they may wish to consider this in the determination of the gravity of certain decisions by States to ignore provisional measures. While it may be justified to take into account the most recent situation in cases in which the petitioner has not yet been expelled, it seems inappropriate to do so to justify the fact that the State has ignored the Committee's provisional measures.

[81]   HRC *Mansour Ahani* v. *Canada*, 29 March 2004, §8.1.

[82]   HRC *Mansour Ahani* v. *Canada*, 29 March 2004, §§8.1 and 8.2. See also *Alzery* v. *Sweden*, 25 October 2006, §11.11.

[83]   HRC General Comment 31 on the nature of the general legal obligation imposed on States parties to the Covenant (Article 2), 29 March 2004. It confirmed this in 2008 in its General Comment on the OP. "Failure to implement such interim or provisional measures is incompatible with the obligation to respect in good faith the procedure of individual communication established under the Optional Protocol". HRC General Comment 33, CCPR/C/GC/33, 5 November 2008 (Advance unedited version), §19.

[84]   See Chapter XIII (Protection) the relationship between provisional measures, the rights claimed and the eventual form of reparation. For a confirmation of its approach see also HRC *Barno Saidova* v. *Tajikistan*, 8 July 2004.

[85]   HRC General Comment No. 31 on the nature of the general legal obligation imposed on States parties to the Covenant (Article 2), 29 March 2004, §§19, 17 and 12. It referred to 'the provisional measures indicated by the Committee in cases under the Optional Protocol with a

Authorities other than the HRC have also stressed that States should comply with the Committee's provisional measures. The UN Rapporteur against Torture, for instance, did so in 2003 and 2004[86] and the Deputy UN High Commissioner for Human Rights equally urged respect for the Committee's provisional measures (2003). He emphasised the importance of respecting 'interim measures of protection ordered by Human Rights Treaty Bodies'.[87] With regard to executions of death sentences in violation of the provisional measures by the HRC he spoke of a 'grave breach' of the obligations under both the ICCPR and the OP.[88]

While the case law of the HRC on the obligation to respect its provisional measures to halt irreparable harm seems to be firmly established, this fact has not yet found its way in much of the general literature on the HRC, most of which was published before *Piandiong* (2002) and before the General Comment on Article 2 (2004).[89]

'The traditional view', it has been noted, 'based on a strict legalistic interpretation that considered procedural rules as non-binding, no longer seems adequate'. In this respect 'the Committee has demonstrated leadership' and 'its approach has since been adopted in the jurisprudence of other international human rights organs'.[90] The Committee's approach indeed is consistent with the dynamic treaty interpretation that human rights adjudicators now generally adhere to.[91] The

---

view to avoiding irreparable harm pending the Committee's consideration of a case'. Again, it did not specify whether it meant irreparable harm to persons, the claim or the procedure.

[86] See e.g. UN Special Rapporteur on Torture, mission to Uzbekistan of November-December 2002, E/CN.4/2003/68/Add.2. See also official statement by the Special Rapporteur on Torture, 13 September 2004, referring to the 'interim measures ordered by the Committee and urgent appeals dispatched by United Nations monitoring mechanisms regarding persons whose life and physical integrity may be at risk of imminent and irreparable harm'.

[87] Press release Deputy United Nations High Commissioner for Human Rights Bertrand Ramcharan, 'Deputy Human Rights Chief ends visit to Uzbekistan with call for implementation of official commitments', 14 March 2003.

[88] See e.g. press release Acting High Commissioner for Human Rights Bertrand Ramcharan, 'Acting High Commissioner for Human Rights asks Uzbek government not to carry out death sentences in cases under international appeal', 4 July 2003 and 'Acting High Commissioner for Human Rights deeply concerned at executions in Uzbekistan', 25 July 2003.

[89] McGoldrick (1994), p. 128 considered that they are 'non-binding as a matter of law and depend totally on the cooperation and good faith of the State party concerned'. Robertson and Merrills (1996) noted that although they 'are not binding, they have a moral force', p. 57. Ghandhi (1998) wrote that 'it is clear that the Committee's view on the desirability of interim measures is not binding on the State Party concerned', p. 58. Castan/Joseph/Schultz (2004) do pay attention to the most recent case law, as do Harrington (2003) and Naldi (2004). Harrington considers that while the Views are not binding, the provisional measures are because the individual complaint system would otherwise be 'rendered meaningless'. "By acceding to the *Optional Protocol*, Canada granted individual litigants the right to petition and ultimately to receive a non-binding view from the Human Rights Committee. Notwithstanding any concerns one might have about the inherent weaknesses of a non-binding view, Canada is therefore acting in bad faith with respect to its treaty commitments when it engages in acts that have the effect of preventing or frustrating the consideration of a communication by the Committee and rendering the outcome nugatory". In this context Harrington notes that 'it must be acknowledged that many international instruments adopt language with a diplomatic flavour to avoid offence to the susceptibilities of states,' Harrington (2003), pp. 86 and p. 68 respectively.

[90] Naldi (2004), p. 454.

[91] As provisional measures are central to the Committee's protective function, its 'reasoned justification for its conclusion, commensurate with the "dynamic and evolutive" approach appropriate to human rights treaties, must be considered correct, if only on the utilitarian ground

approach of the HRC towards the legal status of its provisional measures is in accordance with the purpose of the OP and the aim of effective protection of the rights in the ICCPR.

2.4.3.3 THE ATTITUDE OF THE ADJUDICATORS TO FRUSTRATION OF THE RIGHT OF PETITION THROUGH PRE-EMPTION OF THE POSSIBILITY TO REQUEST PROVISIONAL MEASURES

As noted, in the context of the death penalty the HRC has pointed out that the obligation of good faith application of the Covenant and in particular of the right to an effective remedy (Article 2 ICCPR) presumes that a State postpones an execution once it knows (or should reasonably be expected to know) that the petitioner has brought a petition before the HRC, and not only once the HRC has been able to inform the State of its decision to take provisional measures.[92] It is incompatible with the obligations under the OP when the State undertakes action hindering or frustrating the examination of a complaint and rendering futile any subsequent decision on the merits. Such State commits a grave breach of the right of individual petition. This breach is even more serious when this occurs contrary to a provisional measure.[93]

If the State preempts the possibility of invoking Article 22 ICAT and of requesting the Committee to take provisional measures, by expelling the petitioner without giving him a reasonable opportunity to resort to the Committee, before execution of a final decision, this in itself constitutes a breach of the obligations under Article 22 ICAT.[94]

Apart from the HRC, also CAT and the ECtHR have dealt with situations in which the State pre-empted the possibility for the petitioner to resort to the individual petition systems recognized by States under international treaties. They have stressed that the obligation not to do so applies as well in the context of non-refoulement. The petitioner should have a reasonable opportunity of sending a complaint to the Committee or ECtHR before the final decision of domestic authorities is being executed.[95]

2.4.3.4 CAT ON THE LEGAL STATUS OF ITS PROVISIONAL MEASURES

According to CAT ratification of the treaty and recognition of the right of individual petition require a good faith cooperation with the Committee. Respecting its provisional measures is essential for the protection of the beneficiary against irreparable harm. Such harm would deprive the further proceedings of any sense.[96]

---

of seeking to ensure maximum protection for people at risk'. Naldi (2004), p. 454, referring to ECtHR *Wemhoff* v. *Germany*, 27 June 1968 and IACHR, Advisory Opinion, Compulsory membership of journalist association, 13 November 1985.

[92] HRC *Ashby* v. *Trinidad and Tobago*, 21 March 2002; *Shukurova* v. *Tajikistan*, 17 March 2006; *Sultanova* v. *Uzbekistan*, 30 March 2006; *Uteeva* v. *Uzbekistan*, 26 October 2007.

[93] See CAT *Agiza* v. *Sweden*, 20 May 2005 and ECtHR *Al-Moayad* v. *Germany*, 20 February 2007, §125 (acts or omissions aimed to prevent the Court from ordering provisional measures or from timely informing the government of such measures, could be in violation of Article 34 ECHR).

[94] CAT *Agiza* v. *Sweden*, 20 May 2005, §13.9.

[95] As noted, this relates to e.g. CAT *Agiza* v. *Sweden*, 20 May 2005; HRC *Shukurova* v. *Tajikistan*, 17 March 2006; *Sultanova* v. *Uzbekistan*, 30 March 2006; *Uteeva* v. *Uzbekistan*, 26 October 2007; ECtHR *Al-Moayad* v. *Germany*, 20 February 2007.

[96] CAT *Núñez Chipana* v. *Venezuela*, 16 December 1998 and *T.P.S.* v. *Canada*, 16 May 2000.

In *T.P.S.* v. *Canada* Canada ignored a provisional measure. It considered that a request for provisional measures was 'a recommendation to a State to take certain measures, not an order'. "Support for this proposition may be found not only in the word employed ('request') in rule 108, paragraph 9 but also in the European Court of Human Rights decision in *Cruz Varas and others* v. *Sweden*'.[97] CAT responded by expressing deep concern about Canada's deportation of the petitioner to India despite the Committee's provisional measures. It pointed out that Canada had ratified the Convention against Torture and had voluntarily accepted the Committee's competence to consider individual communications (Article 22). It had undertaken to cooperate with it in good faith in applying the procedure. "Compliance with the provisional measures called for by the Committee in cases it considers reasonable is essential in order to protect the person in question from irreparable harm, which could, moreover nullify the end result of the proceedings before the Committee".[98]

CAT has subsequently reinforced this approach.[99] The use of provisional measures is 'vital to the role entrusted to the Committee' under Article 22 ICAT. 'Failure to respect that provision, in particular through such irreparable action as deporting an alleged victim, undermined protection of the rights enshrined in the Convention'.[100]

Moreover the petitioner is 'entitled to rely' on its provisional measures.[101] The expulsion of the petitioner 'in the face of the Committee's request for interim measures nullified the effective exercise of the right to complaint conferred by article 22, and has rendered the Committee's final decision on the merits futile and devoid of object'.[102]

In *Agiza* v. *Sweden* (2005) CAT referred to the procedural assessment of the substantive right not to be subjected to refoulement. It held that the principle of non-refoulement in Article 3 ICAT should be understood to encompass a remedy to prevent its breach.[103] It added that in the

---

[97] CAT *T.P.S.* v. *Canada*, 16 May 2000, §8.2. On ECtHR *Cruz Varas* and its subsequent overturn see *infra*.

[98] CAT *T.P.S.* v. *Canada*, 16 May 2000, §15.6. According to Committee member Camara (Senegal) the Committee's authority to request provisional measures is a 'logical attribute' of its competence based on Art. 22. Ignoring the Committee's provisional measures 'renders Article 22 meaningless'.

[99] By recognizing the right of individual complaint 'States parties implicitly undertook to cooperate with the Committee in good faith by providing it with the means to examine the complaints submitted'. CAT *Mafhoud Brada* v. *France*, 17 May 2005, §6.1.

[100] CAT *Mafhoud Brada* v. *France*, 17 May 2005, §6.2. In *Brada* v. *France* (2005) CAT observed that a domestic appeal was still pending at the time of the expulsion. It added: '(e)ven more decisively' the Committee had indicated provisional measures to stay his execution 'until it had had an opportunity to examine the merits of the case, the Committee having established, through its Special Rapporteur on Interim Measures, that in the present case the complainant had established an arguable risk of irreparable harm'. CAT *Mafhoud Brada* v. *France*, 17 May 2005, §13.3. On assessment of risk see Chapter XV (Immediacy and risk).

[101] CAT *Mafhoud Brada* v. *France*, 17 May 2005, §13.3.

[102] Id., §13.4. See also *Elif Pelit* v. *Azerbaijan*, 1 May 2007, §10.2. In *Brada* In this case it did not find a violation of Article 22 ICAT alone. The State ignored he fact that a domestic case was still pending, it ignored CAT's provisional measures and it argued that the subsequent judgment of the Court of Appeal could not be regarded as 'clearly arbitrary or tantamount to a denial of justice'. CAT noted the finding of the Court of Appeal that the expulsion occurred in breach of Article 3 ECHR and agreed that this finding could not be regarded as 'clearly arbitrary or tantamount to a denial of justice'. It concluded that the expulsion was in breach of Article 3 ICAT. CAT *Mafhoud Brada* v. *France*, 17 May 2005, §13.6.

[103] CAT *Ahmed Hussein Mustafa Kamil Agiza* v. *Sweden*, 20 May 2005, §13.6. See on this case also Van Boven (2006), pp. 746-758.

context of non-refoulement the right to an effective remedy requires 'an opportunity for effective, independent and impartial review of the decision to expel or remove, once that decision is made, when there is a plausible allegation that article 3 issues arise'.[104]

CAT will find a breach of Article 22 based on a conception of 'effective exercise' of the right of individual petition that encompasses more than just access to the Committee. In *Agiza* it pointed out, once more, that by making the declaration under Article 22 ICAT the State 'undertook to confer upon persons within its jurisdiction the right to invoke the complaints jurisdiction of the Committee. That jurisdiction included the power to indicate interim measures, if necessary, to stay the removal and preserve the subject matter of the case pending final decision'. It added that in order 'for this exercise of the right of complaint to be meaningful rather than illusory', the 'individual must have a reasonable period of time before execution of a final decision to consider whether and, if so, in fact, seize the Committee under its article 22 jurisdiction'.[105] In *Dar* v. *Norway* (2007) CAT noted that Article 18 ICAT 'vests it with competence to establish its own rules of procedure, which become inseparable from the Convention to the extent they do not contradict it'. Its Rule 108 on provisional measures was 'specifically intended to give meaning and scope to articles 3 and 22 of the Convention, which otherwise would only offer asylum-seekers invoking a serious risk of torture a merely theoretical protection. By failing to respect the request for interim measures made to it, and to inform the Committee of the deportation of the complainant, the State party committed a breach of its obligations of cooperating in good faith with the Committee, under article 22 of the Convention'.[106] While in this case it did not find a procedural violation of Article 3 ICAT, in *Tebourski* v. *France* (2007) it did find a violation of both Article 22 and Article 3 ICAT. In this case it explicitly linked the right of petition in Article 22 to the substantive rights in Article 3 ICAT. It noted that 'article 3 of the Convention offers absolute protection to anyone in the territory of a State party which has made the declaration under article 22'.[107] By expelling the petitioner to Tunisia 'under the conditions in which it did and for the reasons adduced, thereby presenting the Committee with a fait accompli, the State party not only failed to demonstrate the good faith required of any party to a treaty, but also failed to meet its obligations under articles 3 and 22 of the Convention'.[108] In short, CAT has confirmed that disrespect for provisional measures negates the effective exercise of the right of petition.[109]

2.4.3.5 INTER-AMERICAN COMMISSION ON THE LEGAL STATUS OF ITS PRECAUTIONARY MEASURES

In March 2005 the CIDH issued a resolution in which it emphasized the international obligation of OAS member States to comply with its precautionary measures.[110] In its case law the Commis-

---

[104] CAT *Ahmed Hussein Mustafa Kamil Agiza* v. *Sweden*, 20 May 2005, §13.7. The Committee added: 'that its previous jurisprudence has been consistent with this view of the requirements of article 3, having found an inability to contest an expulsion decision before an independent authority, in that case the courts, to be relevant to a finding of a violation of article 3'.

[105] CAT *Ahmed Hussein Mustafa Kamil Agiza* v. *Sweden*, 20 May 2005, §13.9.

[106] CAT *Nadeem Ahmad Dar* v. *Norway*, 11 May 2007, §16.3. See also *Tebourski* v. *France*, 1 May 2007, §8.6.

[107] CAT *Tebourski* v. *France*, 1 May 2007, §8.4.

[108] CAT *Tebourski* v. *France*, 1 May 2007, §8.7.

[109] CAT *Brada* v. *France*, 17 May 2005; *Agiza* v. *Sweden*, 20 May 2005; *Singh Sogi* v. *Canada*, 16 November 2007; *Pelit* v. *Azerbaijan*, 1 May 2007.

[110] CIDH Resolution 1/05, 8 March 2005, §1.

sion equally stressed that States must comply with its precautionary measures in light of the fundamental role played by these measures in maintaining the effectiveness of the Commission's mandate. It does so in particular in death penalty cases.

In *Beazley* v. *US* (2003), for instance, it reiterated that 'its ability to effectively investigate and determine capital cases has frequently been undermined when states have scheduled and carried out the execution of condemned persons, despite the fact that those individuals have proceedings pending before the Commission'.[111] It pointed out that it uses precautionary measures exactly in order to prevent 'this unacceptable situation'. It emphasized that 'OAS member states, by creating the Commission and mandating it through the OAS Charter and its Statute to promote the observance and protection of human rights of the American peoples, have implicitly undertaken to implement measures of this nature where they are essential to preserving that mandate'.[112]

In its Order for provisional measures in *James et al.* v. *Trinidad and Tobago* the Inter-American Court has pointed out, based on the principles of effectiveness and good faith, that States were to respect not only its Orders for provisional measures but also the Commission's precautionary measures.[113]

The competence of the Inter-American Commission to adopt precautionary measures, as laid down in its rules of procedure, is also based on Articles 33 and 41 ACHR. Article 33 refers to the Commission as one of the competent bodies to monitor compliance with the obligations of States parties to the Convention. Article 41 establishes that the Commission may, in the exercise of its function to defend human rights, formulate recommendations for member States to adopt measures for the protection of human rights in the same way as measures applied to further the obligation to respect such rights.[114]

In the *Vogt* case the Court considered that 'in particular, the Commission has the obligation in every case to take measures to guarantee the life and physical integrity of all persons whose rights may be violated'.[115] Whether this means that it should always immediately request the Court to order provisional measures in cases that can go to the Court and should reserve its precautionary measures for cases that cannot, is not specified. Yet in the past the Court has assumed that the Commission initially takes precautionary measures in all urgent cases.[116]

---

[111] CIDH *Napoleon Beazley* v. *US*, 29 December 2003, §51.

[112] "As the Commission has emphasized on numerous occasions, it is beyond question that the failure of an OAS member state to preserve a condemned prisoner's life pending review of his or her complaint undermines the efficacy of the Commission's process, deprives condemned persons of their right to petition in the inter-American human rights system, and results in serious and irreparable harm to those individuals. For these reasons, the Commission has determined that a member state disregards its fundamental human rights obligations under the OAS Charter and related instruments when it fails to implement precautionary measures issued by the Commission in these circumstances". CIDH *Napoleon Beazley* v. *US*, 29 December 2003, §52, referring to *Juan Raul Garza* v. *United States*, §117 and Fifth Report on the Situation of Human Rights in Guatemala, 6 April 2001, §§71-72.

[113] IACHR *James et al.* v. *Trinidad and Tobago*, Order of 26 September 2001.

[114] See also CEJIL, La Competencia de la CIDH, comunicado del Centro por la Justicia y el Derecho Internacional (CEJIL), in: *La Nacion*, 5 April 2001, <www.nacion.com> (consulted 2 April 2002).

[115] IACHR *Vogt* case, Order of 27 June 1996.

[116] Judge Cançado Trindade argues that the Commission should always refer requests for provisional measures to the Court, without first using its own precautionary measures. He considers that the latter 'lack conventional force'. IACHR *Matter of the persons imprisoned in the "Dr. Sebastião Martins Silveira" Penitentiary in Araraquara, São Paulo* (Brazil), Order of 30 September 2006,

The Commission uses terminology such as 'requests' and its Reports include recommendations. Still, State parties to the American Convention are bound not to violate the rights it contains and have accepted the Commission's role in monitoring this. In any case, the fact that the Commission issues recommendations as to how to remedy a violation, does not detract from the binding character of its precautionary measures. After all there are situations where the Commission is the ultimate interpreter of a State's obligations within the OAS system. It is argued that as part of the latter function, as it is the only adjudicator interpreting and determining a State's obligations under the OAS Charter, its precautionary measures must be respected. Otherwise the individual complaint system developed by the Commission under the OAS Statute and American Declaration, as confirmed by the OAS political bodies, would be deprived of effectiveness exactly in the most pressing cases.[117] The Commission does not distinguish the precautionary measures under the Convention from those made as part of the adjudicatory function assigned to it by the OAS States under the OAS Charter, monitoring compliance with the American Declaration. Indeed it would appear artificial to argue that in the former case they are not legally binding and in the latter they are. Moreover, with regard to its function under the Convention, where the Commission may also request the Court to order provisional measures, if it indeed does so, but before the Court's staff in Costa Rica and the Court itself or its President has had the opportunity to deal with this request, the Commission's precautionary measures are also binding by virtue of the binding nature of the Court's provisional measures themselves. After all the State may not quickly pre-empt any decision by the Court to order provisional measures by taking irreversible action, in the face of the Commission's decision to use precautionary measures and request the Court's provisional measures. Finally, if the Commission fails to request the Court's provisional measures and continues to use its own precautionary measures in a case in which it the State concerned has recognized the competence of the Court to deal with cases, this deserves criticism, but it does not absolve the State from complying in good faith with its obligations under the ACHR, an obligation brought to its attention specifically by the use of precautionary measures.

---

[117] Separate Opinion Judge Cançado Trindade, §30. At the same time he argues for the Court's power to order provisional measures in matters still pending before the Commission when the petitioners, rather than the Commission, request them, in such cases where the Commission does not motivate its denial. Such situation 'legitimizes the potential victims, as subjects of international human rights law, to resort to the Court to seek the granting of these provisional measures; otherwise, there could be a denial of justice at the international level', ibid. Yet it is submitted here that all human rights adjudicators have the inherent power to order provisional measures that are legally binding, unless this is explicitly excluded in their constituent document. The latter is the case with regard to dealing with requests for provisional measures by petitioners rather than the Commission in matters still pending before that Commission. While the Commission indeed must motivate its decisions and must make sure that individuals have access to the highest level of decision-making available within the system, this is unrelated to the lack of explicit conventional basis of its own precautionary measures. Moreover, as argued in this chapter, the absence of an explicit conventional basis does not mean that its precautionary measures, which are after all the only options in cases involving States that have not recognized the competence of the Court, are not legally binding.

See also e.g. Pasqualucci (2005), p. 25.

2.4.3.6 AFRICAN COMMISSION ON THE LEGAL STATUS OF ITS PROVISIONAL MEASURES

The African Commission has pointed out that it was one of its functions to assist States in the implementation of their obligations under the ACHPR. After the execution of Ken Saro-Wiwa the Commission found that Nigeria had violated its obligations under Article 1 ACHPR by 'ignoring its obligations to institute provisional measures'. This article stipulates:

> "The Member States of the Organisation of African Unity parties to the present Charter shall recognise the right, duties and freedoms enshrined in this Charter and shall undertake to adopt legislative or other measures to give effect to them".

The Commission strongly condemned the execution:

> "To have carried out the execution in the face to pleas to the contrary by the Commission and world opinion is something which we pray will never happen again. That it is a violation of the Charter is an understatement".[118]

2.4.3.7 EUROPEAN COMMISSION ON THE LEGAL STATUS OF ITS PROVISIONAL MEASURES

In *Mamatkulov* (2005) the ECtHR Grand Chamber pointed out with regard to the practice of the former Commission: "Even before the provisions regulating the question of interim measures came into force, the Commission had not hesitated to ask respondent Governments for a stay of execution of measures liable to make the application pending before it devoid of purpose".[119] Later the Commission formally included a rule in its Rules of Procedure. Two old cases have some significance to the discussion on the legal status of provisional measures.

In October 1971 the Commission gave precedence to a complaint against eviction. Although it did not use provisional measures the ensuing domestic discussion about the obligation of States to enable the Commission to operate effectively is interesting for understanding the legal status of provisional measures. In the domestic proceedings counsel argued that the eviction of the petitioner should be postponed pending the proceedings before the Commission. He submitted that the eviction would render the Commission's decision ineffective from the outset. In February 1972 the district court determined that the execution of its eviction order of April 1971 should be suspended until December 1972, provided that the petitioner paid compensation to the owner of the house for the use of the house and the settlement of arrears. It considered that Germany was required, under then Article 28, 'to furnish to the Commission all necessary facilities for the effective conduct of the investigation'.[120] The domestic court also considered 'of decisive influence' that the Commission 'must not be prevented by accomplished facts from investigating the

---

[118] IACHPR *International Pen, Constitutional Rights Project and Interights on behalf of Ken Saro-wiwa Jr. and Civil Liberties Organisation* v. *Nigeria*, published in 7 International Human Rights Reports 274 (2000), §115.

[119] ECtHR Grand Chamber *Mamatkulov and Askarov* v. *Turkey*, 15 December 2004, §106.

[120] EComHR *Raupp* v. *FRG*, 5207/71, Decision of 1 June 1972, Collection of Decisions 42, May 1973; *X* v. *FRG*, 5207/71, 13 December 1971, Collection of Decisions 39, June 1972, p. 92: Decision of the District Court of Würzburg of 4 February 1972 (translation by the Council of Europe).

application'.[121] It noted that 'compulsory eviction, and the possible consequences thereof with regard to the debtor's state of health, would render it impossible for the European Commission of Human Rights, thereby faced with accomplished facts, to fulfil the tasks incumbent on it under Article 28 of the Convention'.[122]

In the *first Greek* case, in which it had used provisional measures, the European Commission pointed out that it 'was established under Article 19 of the Convention with the task to ensure, together with the Court, the observance of the engagements undertaken by the High Contracting Parties in the Convention'.[123]

The main cases in which the Commission had to deal with the legal status of provisional measures were those of Mansi and Cruz Varas. It argued that they were legally binding, but the ECtHR subsequently found that they were not. This situation continued for more than ten years until the judgment of the first section and later the Grand Chamber in the case *Mamatkulov*.

Mr. Cruz Varas, faced with an expulsion order, had petitioned the European Commission on Human Rights, claiming his expulsion by Sweden to Chile, at the time still under General Pinochet, would result in the breach of certain articles of the European Convention, most importantly the prohibition of torture, or inhuman or degrading treatment or punishment (Article 3 ECHR). The Commission had used provisional measures, under Rule 36 of its Rules of Procedure, to stay the expulsion until the Convention organs had had a chance to examine the issue. Mr. Cruz Varas was forced to return to Chile notwithstanding this provisional measure.

As the Court put it, Sweden was the first ECHR Contracting State which chose not to respect a provisional measure.[124] In the Commission's view Sweden's behaviour was contrary to

---

[121] EComHR *Raupp* v. *FRG,* 5207/71, Decision of 1 June 1972, Collection of Decisions 42, May 1973; *X* v. *FRG,* 5207/71, 13 December 1971, Collection of Decisions 39, June 1972, p. 93: "The European Convention on Human Rights and the Rules of Procedure of the European Commission of Human Rights do not, like Art. 572(3) of the Code of Civil Procedure, make provision for a temporary order granting a stay of execution of the disputed decision. However, Art. 572(2) of the Code of Civil Procedure is applicable mutatis mutandis; the principle underlying this provision, namely that the decision of a higher authority must not be anticipated, applies equally in respect of an individual application to the European Commission of Human Rights. The Federal Republic of Germany did not oppose the application mutatis mutandis of Art. 572(2) of the Code of Civil Procedure, for the reason that such application mutatis mutandis would, in the result, meet the obligation imposed upon the Federal Republic of Germany under Art. 25(1), in fine of the Convention for the Protection of Human Rights and Fundamental Freedoms".

[122] Subsequently the Commission declared the case inadmissible for abuse of the right of petition. It noted that without good reason the petitioner had failed to comply with the terms of the stay of execution of the eviction order. It observed that her failure to pay compensation was 'not only contrary to repeated assurances previously given by her in the present proceedings; it also disregards the decision of the District Court which was taken under Art. 28(a) in fine of the Convention in order to facilitate the Commission's investigation of the present case'. Thus, it could only conclude that the petitioner was 'taking advantage of the proceedings before the Commission in order to evade her obligation under domestic law to pay compensation for the use of the house concerned', p. 90. It referred to the description by Senior Judge Spies of the District Court of Würzburg: 'she clearly believed that, because of the state of her health, she could live in someone else's house without paying compensation', p. 93.

[123] EComHR *First Greek case, Denmark, Norway, Sweden and the Netherlands* v. *Greece*, 3321-3323/67 and 3344/67, 24 January 1968.

[124] ECtHR *Case of Cruz Varas and Others* v. *Sweden*, Judgment of 20 March 1991, §121. This is not entirely correct. There had been a handful of cases in which there had been problems before, see e.g. EComHR *Lynas* v. *Sweden*, 6 October 1976 and *S.I.G.* v. *the Netherlands*, 10 October 1985 (inadm.). Non-compliance sometimes related to the timing of the provisional measure. For a case

the spirit of the Convention, and to Article 25(1), now Article 34 ECHR, on the right of individual petition in particular. The Court, however, decided that States parties were not bound by the Commission's provisional measures, because no provision in the Convention itself dealt specifically with the issue, and neither Article 25, nor other rules of law could be interpreted as such.

The State had argued that the right of petition had so far been interpreted as exclusively procedural and the Commission's interpretation that it protected petitioners from irreparable harm 'found no support in the wording of the provision or in legal writing'.[125]

The European Commission on Human Rights, by a 12-1 vote, concluded that Cruz Varas' expulsion resulted in a violation of the right of petition. It did not, however, regard the undertaking under that article to imply a general duty to suspend measures domestically or not to enforce domestic decisions in all cases where an individual had lodged an application with the Commission. There could, nevertheless, be special circumstances where the enforcement of a national decision could indeed be in conflict with the effective exercise of the right to petition. In the Commission's opinion this was particularly the case when the enforcement of such a national decision would result in serious and irreparable damage to the petitioner and when the Commission had used provisional measures indicating that it was desirable not to enforce that decision.[126] On the one hand, the Commission stated, an applicant is entitled, to the 'effective exercise' of his right to petition to the Commission, meaning that the Contracting State shall not prevent the Commission from making an effective examination of the application, and, on the other hand, an applicant claiming a violation of Article 3 (prohibition of torture and cruel or degrading treatment or punishment) is entitled to an effective examination of whether the intended extradition or expulsion would indeed be a violation of that article. In these circumstances provisional measures serve the purpose, as the Commission puts it, 'of enabling the Commission, and subsequently the Court or Committee of Ministers, to examine effectively an application and to ensure the effectiveness of the safeguard provided by Article 3'.[127] The deportation, in this case, was contrary to the spirit of the Convention and incompatible the right of petition.[128]

The question could be raised whether the Court would have decided the way it did, had the petitioner, upon return to Chile, indeed been tortured, disappeared or executed. This happened to a Jordanian who was expelled by Sweden and who was tortured upon return in Jordan. In this case a friendly settlement was reached.[129]

---

on non-compliance, if one can say so relating to a very early case, dating from before the introduction of a rule on provisional measures in the Commission's rules of procedure, *X.* v. *Austria and Yugoslavia*, 30 June 1964 (inadm.), where on 10 March 1964 a group of three members of the Commission had informally requested Austria not to return a person to Yugoslavia. After this request failed and the person was extradited, a phone call was made to the Permanent Delegation to inquire about the situation and subsequently, in plenary session, the Commission decided to give precedence to the case and to request details on the extradition.

[125] ECtHR *Case of Cruz Varas and Others* v. *Sweden*, Judgment of 20 March 1991, §92.

[126] Id., §118.

[127] Id., §120.

[128] Id., §122.

[129] EComHR *Mansi* v. *Sweden*, 9 March 1990 (friendly settlement). In this case, like in the case *Cruz Varas*, a provisional measure was used. The case was introduced and registered on 19 October 1989. On that same day the President of the Commission, in accordance with Rule 36, decided to indicate that it was 'desirable in the interest of the parties and the proper conduct of the proceedings before the Commission not to deport the applicant to Jordan until the Commission had had an opportunity to examine the application at its forthcoming session from 6 to 10 November 1989'. The petitioner was nevertheless expelled to Jordan on 21 October 1989. See admissibility decision of 7 December 1990. When the Commission heard this, it decided to

After Mansi's expulsion, contrary to the Commission's provisional measures, Mr Mansi had met with a representative of Amnesty International and a representative of the Swedish embassy at Amman. These reported he had been tortured and had required hospitalization.

The Commission considered that Sweden's failure to comply with the provisional measures of the Commission raised the question whether there had been a violation of Article 25 (1) ECHR (the present Article 34) in conjunction with Article 1 'in view of the special nature of the alleged violation of Article 3 of the Convention'. This question involved issues that, in the Commission's view, justified further examination.[130] In January 1990 the petitioner returned to Sweden. He reached a friendly settlement with the State.[131] Consequently the case was struck out and only in the other case in which Sweden ignored the Commission's provisional measures a decision on the merits was reached. That case was subsequently brought before the Court.

2.4.3.8 ECtHR ON THE LEGAL STATUS OF PROVISIONAL MEASURES

In the aforementioned *Cruz Varas* case, different from the Commission, the Court, by a narrow majority, found that States parties to the ECHR were not legally bound to respect provisional measures.[132] This judgment not only drew a strong dissenting opinion, but also many critical commentaries.[133] At the same time States, even from other continents, have referred to this case to justify non-compliance with provisional measures.[134] Years later, in an admissibility decision in *Conka* (2001) the Court's Third Section simply confirmed *Cruz Varas* without further discussion.[135]

Yet in *Mamatkulov* first the Court's First Section (2003) and later the Grand Chamber (2005) found that under Article 34 ECHR States are obliged to respect its provisional measures.[136] In subsequent cases it explicitly stated that its provisional measures are legally binding.[137]

---

take another provisional measure, namely that the Government of Sweden 'take measures which will enable the applicant to return to Sweden as soon as possible'. Eventually, the question whether the expulsion was in violation of the Articles 3 and 25 remained unresolved, since a friendly settlement was reached. Friendly settlement Report adopted by the Commission on 9 March 1990, pursuant to Article 28(2) ECHR.

[130] EComHR *Mansi* v. *Sweden*, 7 December 1989 (adm.), 'The Law' (2), 5th paragraph.

[131] EComHR *Mansi* v. *Sweden*, 9 March 1990 (friendly settlement).

[132] ECtHR *Cruz Varas* v. *Sweden*, 20 March 1991.

[133] MacDonald, for instance, argued that '(p)arties who submit to the jurisdiction of a court have the implied obligation not to act in such a way as to render the judgment of the court meaningless'. MacDonald (1992), p. 730. See further, e.g. the strongly critical comments by Cohen-Jonathan (1991), pp. 205-209 and Oellers-Frahm (1991), pp. 197-199.

[134] See e.g. CAT *T.P.S.* v. *Canada*, 16 May 2000, §8.2.

[135] ECtHR *Conka* v. *Belgium*, 13 March 2001 (adm.), §11.

[136] See Judgment of the First Section, 6 February 2003. Its finding on Article 34 had been made by six votes to one (with Türmen, the Turkish judge, dissenting). Turkey had requested the case to be referred to the Grand Chamber in April 2003 and a panel of the Grand Chamber decided to accept this request in May 2003. The composition of the Grand Chamber (17 members) was determined according to the provisions of Article 27(2) and (3) ECHR and Rule 24 of the Rules of Court. Mr. Türmen was the only member of the Chamber also participating in the Grand Chamber decision.

[137] ECtHR *Aoulmi* v. *France*, 17 January 2006, §112. See also Rieter (2007) and the discussion below.

While in *Mamatkulov* it only found a violation of Article 34 ECHR (effective exercise of the right of application), the Court did make a link with the 'core rights' under the Convention. It noted that 'there is plausibly asserted to be a risk of irreparable damage to the enjoyment by the applicant of one of the core rights under the Convention'. In such cases 'the object of an interim measure is to maintain the status quo pending the Court's determination of the justification for the measure'. The provisional measure 'goes to the substance of the Convention complaint', 'being intended to ensure the continued existence' of the subject matter. The petitioner seeks the 'preservation of the asserted Convention right before irreparable damage is done to it'. Thus, the ECtHR concluded that the provisional measure is sought by the petitioner and granted by the Court 'in order to facilitate the "effective exercise" of the right of individual petition under Article 34 of the Convention in the sense of preserving the subject-matter of the application when that is judged to be risk of irreparable damage through the acts or omissions of the respondent State'.[138]

2.4.4 The status of provisional measures: Mamatkulov singled out

2.4.4.1 INTRODUCTION

The aforementioned *Mamatkulov* judgment of the Grand Chamber is discussed from three interrelated perspectives: the methods of treaty interpretation, the case law of other adjudicators and the issue of general principles of law. Finally the Court's reasoning for the reversal of *Cruz Varas* (1991) is analysed.

2.4.4.2 MAMATKULOV AND TREATY INTERPRETATION

In its interpretation of Article 34 the ECtHR set out with a reference to the case *Loizidou* (1995):

> "The Court has previously stated that the provision concerning the right of individual application (Article 34, formerly Article 25 of the Convention before Protocol No. 11 came into force) is one of the fundamental guarantees of the effectiveness of the Convention system of human-rights protection. In interpreting such a key provision, the Court must have regard to the special character of the Convention as a treaty for the collective enforcement of human rights and fundamental freedoms. Unlike international treaties of the classic type, the Convention comprises more than mere reciprocal engagements between Contracting States. It creates, over and above a network of mutual, bilateral undertakings, objective obligations which, in the words of the Preamble, benefit from a 'collective enforcement'".[139]

---

138 ECtHR Grand Chamber *Mamatkulov and Askarov* v. *Turkey*, 15 December 2004, §108. While there is no specific provision in the Convention concerning the domains in which Rule 39 will apply, requests for its application usually concern the right to life (Article 2), the right not to be subjected to torture or inhuman treatment (Article 3) and, exceptionally the right to respect for private and family life (Article 8) or other rights guaranteed by the Convention. The vast majority of cases in which interim measures have been indicated concern deportation and extradition proceedings". ECtHR Grand Chamber *Mamatkulov and Askarov* v. *Turkey*, 15 December 2004, §104.

139 ECtHR Grand Chamber *Mamatkulov and Askarov* v. *Turkey*, 15 December 2004, §100, referring to *Loizidou* v. *Turkey*, 23 March 1995 (preliminary objections), §70.

It referred to the object and purpose of the Convention 'as an instrument for the protection of individual human rights'. This required an interpretation and application of its provisions 'so as to make its safeguards practical and effective'.[140] It reiterated that the undertaking not to hinder the effective exercise of the right of individual petition 'precludes any interference with the individual's right to present and pursue his complaint before the Court effectively'. In that context it is 'of the utmost importance for the effective operation of the system of individual application instituted under Article 34 that applicants or potential applicants should be able to communicate freely with the Court without being subjected to any form of pressure from the authorities to withdraw or modify their complaints'. This 'pressure' included 'not only direct coercion and flagrant acts of intimidation against actual or potential applicants, members of their family or their legal representatives, but also other improper indirect acts or contacts designed to dissuade or discourage applicants from pursuing a Convention remedy'.[141]

The Court found that the obligation set out in Article 34 required the Contracting States 'to refrain not only from exerting pressure on applicants, but also from any act or omission which, by destroying or removing the subject-matter of an application, would make it pointless or otherwise prevent the Court from considering it under its normal procedure'.[142] Its next step was to examine whether the extradition hindered the effective exercise of the petitioner's right of application. The Court noted that the petitioners had 'plausibly asserted' that there was a risk of irreparable harm to 'one of the core rights under the Convention'. In such cases 'the object of an interim measure is to maintain the status quo pending the Court's determination of the justification for the measure'. The Grand Chamber found that it 'was prevented from properly assessing whether the applicants were exposed to a real risk of ill-treatment and, if so, from ensuring in this respect a "practical and effective" implementation of the Conventions safeguards, as required by its object and purpose'.[143]

The Court noted that under the Convention system provisional measures, 'as they have consistently been applied in practice' equally 'play a vital role in avoiding irreversible situations that would prevent the Court from properly examining the application and, where appropriate, securing to the applicant the practical and effective benefit of the Convention rights asserted'.

> "Accordingly, in these conditions a failure by a respondent State to comply with interim measures will undermine the effectiveness of the right of individual application guaranteed by Article 34 and the State's formal undertaking in Article 1 to protect the rights and freedoms set forth in the Convention".[144]

The Court's provisional measures 'permit it not only to carry out an effective examination of the application but also to ensure that the protection afforded to the applicant by the Convention is

---

[140]   ECtHR Grand Chamber *Mamatkulov and Askarov* v. *Turkey*, 15 December 2004, §101, adding that any interpretation had to be consistent with 'the general spirit of the Convention, an instrument designed to maintain and promote the ideals and values of a democratic society', see *Soering* v. *UK*, 7 July 1989, §87 and, *mutatis mutandis, Klass and others* v. *Germany*, 6 September 1978, §34.

[141]   ECtHR Grand Chamber *Mamatkulov and Askarov* v. *Turkey*, 15 December 2004, § 102, referring to *Akdivar and others* v. *Turkey*, 16 September 1996, §105; *Aksoy* v. *Turkey*, 18 December 1996, §105; *Kurt* v. *Turkey*, 25 May 1998, § 159 and *Petra* v. *Romania*, 23 September 1998, §43.

[142]   ECtHR Grand Chamber *Mamatkulov and Askarov* v. *Turkey*, 15 December 2004, § 102, referring to *Akdivar and others* v. *Turkey*, 16 September 1996, §105; *Aksoy* v. *Turkey*, 18 December 1996, §105; *Kurt* v. *Turkey*, 25 May 1998, § 159 and *Petra* v. *Romania*, 23 September 1998, §43.

[143]   ECtHR Grand Chamber *Mamatkulov and Askarov* v. *Turkey*, 15 December 2004, §108.

[144]   Id., §125.

effective'.[145] Moreover, its provisional measures enable the Committee of Ministers to supervise the execution of the final judgment and thus the Addressee State 'to discharge its obligation to comply with the final judgment of the Court, which is legally binding by virtue of Article 46 of the Convention'.[146] In other words, provisional measures 'must be examined in the light of the obligations which are imposed on the Contracting States by Articles 1, 34 and 46 of the Convention'.[147]

In this case 'the applicants were hindered in the effective exercise of their right of individual application guaranteed by Article 34 of the Convention, which the applicants' extradition rendered nugatory'.[148] The previous Section Judgment in *Mamatkulov* also used the word nugatory in the same context,[149] a term earlier utilised by the HRC with relation to the importance of respecting its provisional measures.[150] The Grand Chamber found a violation of Article 34 by 14 votes to three.[151]

Judge Cabral Barreto (Portugal) concurred in finding a violation of Article 34 ECHR but he would have wished to maintain *Cruz Varas*.[152] He considered that only 'if a refusal to comply with a request for interim measures has hindered the exercise of the right to application, the conclusion must be that there has been a violation of the obligations arising under Article 34 of the Convention'. This would be different if the applicant has nevertheless been able to exercise the right of petition effectively and the Court has been able to properly examine the case. He mentioned detention cases in particular. In such cases, he noted, 'a person is suffering from an illness in conditions which may come within Article 3 of the Convention and are so bad as to justify interim measures being taken to bring the situation to an end'. He pointed out: "In such cases, the procedural aspects do not come into play".

> "While the government's failure to comply with the Court's request may entail a finding of a violation, even an aggravated violation, of Article 3, it will not give rise to a violation of Article 34 as the applicant has exercised his right of application and the Court duly examined the complaint".

In his view provisional measures may be taken in detention cases, but these would not be legally binding because the procedural aspects of Article 34 do not come into play.[153]

---

[145] ECtHR Grand Chamber *Mamatkulov and Askarov* v. *Turkey*, 15 December 2004, §§125 and 126.

[146] Ibid.

[147] Ibid.

[148] ECtHR Grand Chamber *Mamatkulov and Askarov* v. *Turkey*, 15 December 2004, §127.

[149] ECtHR (First section) *Mamatkulov and Abdurasulovic* v. *Turkey*, 6 February 2003, §109.

[150] HRC *Piandiong* v. *Philippines*, 19 October 2000, §5.2.

[151] Wildhaber, President (Switzerland), Rozakis, Vice-President (Greece), Costa, Vice-President (France), Bratza, Section President (UK), Bonello, (Malta), Palm (Sweden), Tulkens (Belgium), Vajić (Croatia), Hedigan (Ireland), Pellonpää (Finland), Tsatsa-Nikolovska (FRYM), Baka (Hungary) and Pavlovschi (Moldova); Cabral Barreto concurring; Caflisch (Switzerland), Türmen (Turkey) and Kovler (Russia) dissenting.

[152] He disagreed with the reasoning behind this finding of a violation of Article 34. He did not consider that such finding should result automatically any time a State would ignore the Court's provisional measures. He considered that the Court was prevented from according binding force to provisional measures and imposing on the States obligations that they had always declined to accept. Concurring Opinion Judge Cabral Barreto, ECtHR Grand Chamber, *Mamatkulov and Askarov* v. *Turkey*, 15 December 2004.

[153] Another example he gave is when a Contracting State extradites a petitioner to a death penalty State despite the Court's provisional measures. He considered that in such cases the person

Judges Caflisch (Switzerland), Türmen (Turkey) and Kovler (Russia) dissented with regard to the legal status of the Court's provisional measures. Their main conclusion was that the matter was one of legislation rather than judicial action.

> "As neither the constitutive instrument of this court nor general international law allows for holding that interim measures must be complied with by States, the Court cannot decide the contrary and, thereby, impose a new obligation on States Parties. To conclude that this Court is empowered, *de lege lata*, to issue binding provisional measures is *ultra vires*. Such a power may appear desirable; but it is up to the Contracting Parties to supply it".[154]

They noted that while the Court's decision was ambiguous, not referring directly to the legal consequences of provisional measures under Rule 39, 'it can be deduced from paragraph 128 of the Judgment that the majority wishes to attribute binding effect to such measures'. They pointed out that the judgment based the mandatory nature of provisional measures 'essentially' on Article 34 and asserted that this article could not serve as a basis for holding that the Court's provisional measures are binding.

> "There certainly are cases where the Court has all the elements to examine the applicant's complaint despite non-compliance; and there are also cases where the Court applies Rule 39 to the applicant (for instance, in cases of hunger strike) and not to the government".[155]

Moreover, even if the Court could not properly examine the applicant's complaint because of non-compliance with provisional measures, the dissenters would not find a violation of Article 34.[156]

The dissenters noted, first of all, that the text does not refer to provisional measures. Secondly, they saw 'little reason' to rely heavily on the object and purpose of the treaty, as the Court had done by invoking the 'living instrument' doctrine. They pointed out that in *Cruz Varas* the Court had not even expressly invoked the teleological method. They added that 'nothing much has changed between the time at which that judgment was made and now'. They considered that: 'binding interim measures were as desirable then as they are today yet they cannot be justified without an enabling provision in the Convention, the Court's constitutive instrument'.[157]

The dissenters noted that the Court's judgment in *Cruz Varas* referred to the fact that a provision similar to Article 41 ICJ Statute was not included in the Convention despite proposals to

---

extradited is able to present his complaint before the ECtHR 'in better conditions' because he has a lawyer in the State to which he has been extradited. Concurring Opinion Judge Cabral Barreto, ECtHR Grand Chamber, *Mamatkulov and Askarov* v. *Turkey*, 15 December 2004. He put it as follows: "However, the fact that the applicant was represented by a lawyer who worked in the requesting State meant had [sic] permitted useful contact between the applicant and his lawyer and, in a way, helped the applicant to present his complaint in better conditions".

[154] Joint partly Dissenting Opinion judges Caflisch, Türmen and Kovler, ECtHR Grand Chamber, *Mamatkulov and Askarov* v. *Turkey*, 15 December 2004, §25.

[155] On this issue see Chapter XIII (Protection), section 4 on addressees and beneficiaries.

[156] Joint partly Dissenting Opinion judges Caflisch, Türmen and Kovler, ECtHR Grand Chamber, *Mamatkulov and Askarov* v. *Turkey*, 15 December 2004, §2.

[157] Ibid.

that effect.[158] This circumstance was 'certainly not favourable to reading a power to issue binding provisional measures into the Convention'.[159]

Resorting to the analysis in *Cruz Varas* they referred to 'early unsuccessful attempts of Convention organs at adopting recommendations in the matter'.[160] They considered that there was no agreement of the parties regarding the interpretation of the Convention on the issue, as required by Article 31(3) (b) VCLT.[161]

The dissenters in *Mamatkulov* referred to the practice of the ECtHR itself: '[i]n the present case *the Court itself* considered its interim measures to be optional'. "This is evident from the wording of Rule 39, which uses the words 'indicate' and 'should be adopted', as well as from the text of the letter of 18 March 1999 addressed to Turkey, the respondent State".[162]

Finally they pointed out that the Judgment did not address the question whether the Court also considered legally binding its provisional measures in Inter-State cases:

> "[I]f the binding character of interim measures could be derived from the necessity of giving full effect to the right of individual application enshrined in Article 34 of the Convention, what would the situation in inter-State cases be? Would measures indicated in such cases continue to be optional? Or would they be considered binding, by analogy, to give the fullest effect possible to Article 33 (inter-State cases) of the Convention?"[163]

2.4.4.3 EVALUATION OF THE COURT'S TREATY INTERPRETATION

Judge Cabral Barreto seems to take a rather limited and technical approach to Article 34, not taking into account the individual complaint system as such. After all there are more situations than those involving refoulement in which certain violations are impending or ongoing. If a human rights case is pending before it the adjudicator must be able to effectively intervene to prevent irreparable harm to the petitioners. Without this there cannot be an effective system of litiga-

---

158 ECtHR *Cruz Varas* v. *Sweden,* 20 March 1991, §95.

159 ECtHR Grand Chamber *Mamatkulov and Askarov* v. *Turkey,* 15 December 2004, Joint partly dissenting opinion judges Caflisch, Türmen and Kovler, §17.

160 Id., §18, referring to *Cruz Varas* v. *Sweden,* 20 March 1991, §96.

161 They referred to the proposals of the European Commission on Human Rights (DH-PR (94) 2 and DH-PR (94) 4, 31 January 1994), the Court and the Swiss Delegation to include an article on legally binding provisional measures in Protocol 11, proposals that were rejected by the Government experts. They noted that the Committee of Ministers had subsequently also ignored a similar proposal by the Committee on Migration, Refugees and Demography. They referred to Draft Report AS/PR (1997) 2 by the Committee on Migration, Refugees and Demography, revised on 19 February 1997. "This can only mean that the widespread acceptance of the practice in question rests on courtesy, cooperation and convenience, but not an agreed interpretation". ECtHR Grand Chamber, *Mamatkulov and Askarov* v. *Turkey,* 15 December 2004, Joint partly dissenting opinion judges Caflisch, Türmen and Kovler, §19. They added that the Committee of Ministers had not 'seen fit to suggest the introduction of binding provisional measures in Draft Protocol No. 14'. "Again this must have been so because there was no agreement on making such measures compulsory and not because the Committee thought it superfluous to do anything on the assumption that provisional measures *were* binding". Ibid.

162 The dissenters quoted from this letter, emphasising the words *'indiquer'* and *'souhaitable'*. ECtHR Grand Chamber, *Mamatkulov and Askarov* v. *Turkey,* 15 December 2004, Joint partly dissenting opinion judges Caflisch, Türmen and Kovler, §20.

163 Id., §7.

tion securing the protection of human rights. In fact, the Grand Chamber itself makes a link to the claims and reparation that Cabral Barreto overlooks.

The Court's practice of using provisional measures in the context of Article 3 has been extensive.[164] The Court seems to indicate that its provisional measures to maintain the status quo pending the proceedings are essential for the effective exercise of the right of petition only in cases involving 'core rights' and it has specified these as the right to life (Article 2) and the prohibition of torture and cruel treatment (Article 3).

Indeed, ignoring provisional measures may not only result in a violation of Article 34, but in a violation of the right to life and the prohibition of cruel treatment, which have been referred to by the Court as 'core rights'. It would be ironic if the Court's provisional measures to prevent irreparable harm to claims involving such core rights would not be binding because the link with the right of petition would be less obvious.[165]

Thus, while under general international law the object of provisional measures may relate to the maintenance of the status quo in general, the ECtHR did specifically refer to risk of irreparable harm to one of the 'core rights' under the ECHR.[166] In other words, it made a link with the importance of the rights claimed. It may be assumed that it did so exactly because it wished to confirm the obligatory nature of those provisional measures it had used thus far. Article 15 ECHR distinguishes certain rights as non-derogable, including the prohibition of torture and cruel treatment.

The Court has been established 'to ensure the observance of the engagements undertaken by the High Contracting Parties' (Article 19 ECHR). In order to perform this function properly, also in light of the Preamble (e.g. 'securing the universal and effective recognition and observance' of the rights in the Convention) the Court necessarily has the authority, pending adjudication, to order contracting parties to prevent irreparable harm to the life and personal integrity of individuals within their jurisdiction. This preventive authority is implied by its function of ensuring the observance of the human rights obligations undertaken by the States.

Under Rule 39 it could also use provisional measures to prevent irreparable harm to any other claim under the ECHR as well, not involving the right to life and the prohibition of torture or cruel treatment. While ignoring such provisional measures would hinder the right of petition as well, the risks involved would be less serious. Thus far the Court has on the whole abstained from using provisional measures that are entirely unrelated to non-derogable rights.[167] Indeed, as noted, it has stressed its practice of interpreting Rule 39 narrowly, (almost) only using provisional measures in the context of Articles 2 and 3 ECHR, referring to these rights as 'core rights'. Thus the Court is unlikely to argue that only those provisional measures are legally binding that would hinder the right of petition in the limited sense of access to the Court.

---

[164] In particular in non-refoulement cases.

[165] While not explicitly, by the mere fact of having been taken the Court's provisional measures of September 2008 in the inter-State case of *Georgia* v. *Russia*, confirm this. After all, these measures cannot be linked to the case of individual complaint, but they clearly involve core rights. ECtHR Press release issued by the Registrar, 'European Court of Human Rights grants request for interim measures', 12 August 2008.

[166] ECtHR Grand Chamber, *Mamatkulov and Askarov* v. *Turkey*, 15 December 2004, §108.

[167] EComHR *Ennslin, Baader and Raspe* v. *FRG*, 8 July 1978 (inadm.) related to preventing irreparable harm to the procedure in the sense of preserving evidence but in the context of an Article 3 claim. The first provisional measure in the *Öcalan* case concerned access to counsel, but in the context of a death penalty case. Admittedly, private and family life and interference with property rights do not directly relate to non-derogable rights. Nevertheless, these cases seem to be an exception to the rule. See further Chapter XII (Other situations).

The dissenters saw 'little reason' to rely heavily on the object and purpose of the treaty and on the Court's 'living instrument' doctrine. Yet, they did not clarify how this issue differed from others in which the living instrument doctrine did apply. They only pointed out that the matter was not invoked in *Cruz Varas*. As noted, *Cruz Varas* was a close decision and following that judgment the Court often invoked both the living instrument approach and that of *effet utile*. In addition the Court has observed the attitudes of other adjudicators affirming the binding nature of provisional measures equally based on interpretations involving *effet utile*.

With regard to the dissenters' reliance on the wording of the provisional measures taken by the Court in *Mamatkulov*, it must be noted that this is not an approach intended by the words used in this particular case. It is customary to phrase letters to respondent States this way, maybe for diplomatic reasons, although it would indeed be desirable to adapt its wording.[168]

In my view the arguments of the Court must extend to inter-State cases. Admittedly, Article 33 ECHR does not specifically include the undertaking not to hinder the effective exercise of the right of High Contracting Parties to refer alleged breaches of the Convention to the Court. Nevertheless, the undertaking by the Contracting Parties to secure the right to life and the prohibition of torture and inhuman or degrading treatment or punishment to everyone within their jurisdiction, together with the Court's task to adjudicate inter-State cases, argues in favour of the Court's implicit authority to order provisional measures that are indeed legally binding.

2.4.4.4 REFERENCE TO OTHER HUMAN RIGHTS SYSTEMS

The overview of relevant international law and practice provided in the *Mamatkulov* Grand Chamber judgment is almost identical to that in the earlier judgment by the first section. With regard to human rights petition systems in which the constitutive document does not explicitly refer to the power to order provisional measures it discussed the Rule on provisional measures adopted by the HRC as well as its decisions that flouting these measures undermines the protection of Covenant rights through the OP. It quoted extensively from the HRC decision in *Piandiong* (2000). The Grand Chamber also referred to the relevant rule adopted by the Committee against Torture and the latter's decisions that non-compliance could nullify the end result of the proceedings before it. After having discussed these two universal systems of human rights protection, it referred to the ICJ's interpretation of the obligations under Article 41 ICJ Statute, quoting extensively from the *LaGrand* case (2001). Finally, it referred to the relevant Rule of the Inter-American Commission on Human Rights and the provision in the American Convention on the power of the Court to order provisional measures, noting that in *James et al.* v. *Trinidad and Tobago* the Inter-American Court determined that States must refrain from taking actions that may frustrate the *restitutio in integrum* of the rights of the alleged victims (1999).[169] The Court

---

[168] In a report to the General Assembly the Special Rapporteur listed recommendations to States with regard to combating torture. The following remark may be useful in this respect. He pointed out that '(s)ince these recommendations are presented in the language of recommendations, the word 'should' is consistently used'. He stressed, however, that 'it must be understood that whenever these recommendations are directly based on obligations contained in legal instruments, the wording of these recommendations in no way detracts from these obligations''. The reference of the dissenters to the use of Rule 39 vis-à-vis the petitioner is interesting, as it illustrates the problems involved in this practice, as discussed in Chapter XIII (Protection), section 4 on the Addressees of provisional measures. Can the petitioner be found in violation of the Convention? Can the Court refuse to intervene to prevent irreparable harm until the petitioner respects the proceedings? Would continuing a hunger strike constitute contempt of court?

[169] See Chapter XIII (Protection) about the relationship with reparation.

did not mention the African Commission's Statement following the execution of Ken Saro-wiwa.[170]

With regard to human rights petition systems in which the constitutive document does explicitly refer to the power to order provisional measures, the Grand Chamber referred to decisions of the Inter-American Court and the ICJ, but not to the provisions in the Optional Protocol to CEDAW and the Protocol establishing the African Court of Human Rights authorising the CEDAW Committee and the African Court, respectively, to use provisional measures.

The Court acknowledged that it had previously considered that it could not infer the power to order legally binding provisional measures from Article 34 ECHR or from other sources.[171] Then it pointed out that this time it would also have regard to 'general principles of international law and the view expressed on this subject by other international bodies' since its decision in *Cruz Varas*.[172] '[I]n that connection' it reiterated that the ECHR should be interpreted in light of the rules set out in the Vienna Convention on the Law of Treaties (VCLT). It referred to Art. 31(3)(c) VCLT stipulating that account must be taken of 'any relevant rules of international law applicable in the relations between the parties'. It must 'determine the responsibility of the States in accordance with the principles of international law governing this sphere, while taking into account the special nature of the Convention as an instrument of human rights protection'.[173] "Thus, the Convention must be interpreted so far as possible consistently with the other principles of international law of which it forms a part".[174]

It noted that in international legal disputes 'the purpose of interim measures is to preserve the parties' rights, thus enabling the body hearing the dispute to give effect to the consequences which a finding of responsibility following adversarial process will entail'.[175] The Court extensively referred to decisions by other international adjudicators emphasising the importance of provisional measures to ensure the effectiveness of their decision on the merits.

It first noted that different rules apply for each adjudicator and then referred to the case law of the HRC, CAT, the Inter-American Court and the ICJ.

In its *LaGrand* judgment the ICJ referred to 'the basic function of judicial settlement of international disputes by binding decisions'.[176] Apart from the terms of Article 41 ICJ Statute (on provisional measures) when read in their context, it followed from the object and purpose of that Statute 'that the power to indicate provisional measures entails that such measures should be binding, inasmuch as the power in question is based on the necessity, when the circumstances call for it, to safeguard, and to avoid prejudice to, the rights of the parties as determined by the final judgment of the Court'.[177]

The dissenters did not mention the jurisprudence of the HRC and CAT. They simply noted that the earlier case law of the ECtHR did not allow 'reading a rule asserting the binding force of

---

[170] ACHPR *International Pen, Constitutional Rights Project and Interights on behalf of Ken Saro-wiwa Jr. and Civil Liberties Organisation* v. *Nigeria*, 31 October 1998, §115.

[171] ECtHR Grand Chamber, *Mamatkulov and Askarov* v. *Turkey*, 15 December 2004, §109, referring to *Cruz Varas and others* v. *Sweden*, 20 March 1991 and *Conka et al.* v. *Belgium*, 13 March 2001 (partly admissible).

[172] ECtHR Grand Chamber, *Mamatkulov and Askarov* v. *Turkey*, 15 December 2004, §110.

[173] ECtHR Grand Chamber, *Mamatkulov and Askarov* v. *Turkey*, 15 December 2004, §111, referring to *Golder* v. *UK*, 21 February 1975, §29.

[174] ECtHR Grand Chamber, *Mamatkulov and Askarov* v. *Turkey*, 15 December 2004, §111, referring to Grand Chamber, *Al-Adsani* v. *UK*, 21 November 2001, §60. On Article 31(3) (c) VCLT see Chapter II, section 8.

[175] ECtHR Grand Chamber, *Mamatkulov and Askarov* v. *Turkey*, 15 December 2004, §113.

[176] ICJ *LaGrand* (*Germany* v. *US*), Judgment of 27 June 2001, §102.

[177] Ibid.

interim measures into the Convention' and that the ICJ's judgment could not be relied on because the ICJ interpreted a provision of its own constitutive treaty.

The dissenters considered the Court's reliance on the ICJ's judgment in *LaGrand* misguided because the ICJ was called upon to interpret a provision of its own constitutive treaty. In this case there was 'a *close relation* between the enabling treaty provision and the purpose to be reached'.[178]

> "By contrast, no such provision can be found in the European Convention on Human Rights; and neither Article 26(d) of that Convention, empowering the Court to enact rules of procedure, nor Article 34, instituting the right of individual application, is sufficiently connected to the issue under consideration to fill a 'gap' in the Convention by instituting *binding* interim measures *ex nihilo*, thereby imposing on the States Parties to the Convention an obligation without their consent. To put it differently, there is a wide difference between the mere *interpretation* of a treaty and its *amendment*, between the exercise of judicial functions and international law-making".[179]

They also noted that '*Cruz Varas* was confirmed, regarding measures issued by the *Court itself*, in the *Čonka* case, only three months before the *LaGrand* judgment of the ICJ'.[180]

According to the dissenters the judgments *Cruz Varas* and *Čonka* mean 'in essence, that while the Court is entitled to interpret the provisions of the Convention, it may *not* – by way of interpretation or through the enactment of rules of procedure, or both – write *new rules* into the Convention, not even if there is a fairly widespread practice in the desired sense, as long as that practice is not uniform (see Belgium's attitude in *Čonka* or that of Turkey in the present instance), accompanied by a corresponding *opinio juris*'.[181]

Finally, they argued that the meaning attributed by the ICJ to the authority to 'indicate' provisional measures cannot have an impact on the ECtHR as long as the Convention contains no authorisation to 'indicate' them.[182]

2.4.4.5 EVALUATION OF THE DISSENTERS' POSITION ON THE REFERENCE TO THE PRACTICE OF OTHER ADJUDICATORS

It is likely that the European Commission and Court included the possibility to use provisional measures in their rules of procedure because they considered this possibility essential to their function as an adjudicator. It is also likely that they chose the wording of Article 41 ICJ Statute to make a connection with existing law on this issue. In this sense the meaning attributed by the ICJ to its authority to 'indicate' provisional measures certainly can have an impact on the European Court's interpretation.

By referring to uniform practice the dissenters seem to allude here to the development of customary international law without, however, specifying its relevance for the interpretation of the Convention obligations and the function of the Court. At the same time they consider that State practice should be 'uniform'. They consider that the practice is not uniform because both Turkey and Belgium ignored the Court's provisional measures in one case. Yet the ICJ deter-

---

[178] ECtHR Grand Chamber, *Mamatkulov and Askarov* v. *Turkey*, 15 December 2004, Joint partly dissenting opinion judges Caflisch, Türmen and Kovler, §9.

[179] Id., §11.

[180] ECtHR Grand Chamber, *Mamatkulov and Askarov* v. *Turkey*, 15 December 2004, §15.

[181] Id., Joint partly dissenting opinion judges Caflisch, Türmen and Kovler, §7.

[182] Id., §21.

mined in its *Nicaragua* judgment that State practice does not have to be uniform, as long as Contracting States generally comply.[183] Only in the context of customary law that developed within a short time period would it be necessary to show extensive and virtually uniform State practice.[184]

2.4.4.6 MAMATKULOV AND GENERAL PRINCIPLES OF INTERNATIONAL LAW

The ECtHR pointed out that in its examination of the *Mamatkulov* case it would also have regard to 'general principles of international law and the view expressed on this subject by other international bodies' since its decision in *Cruz Varas*.[185] It noted that 'in the light of the general principles of international law, the law of treaties and international case-law, the interpretation of the scope of interim measures cannot be dissociated from the proceedings to which they relate or the decision on the merits they seek to protect'.[186] It referred to Article 31(1) Vienna Convention on the Law of Treaties stipulating that treaties must be interpreted in good faith in the light of their object and purpose 'and also in accordance with the principle of effectiveness'.[187]

In fact while the Court referred to general principles of law it did not specify which particular principles of international law it considered applicable.[188] Yet when looking at the judgment as a whole the Court does recognize a principle of law underlying the case law of the various adjudicators. It observed that the ICJ, the IACHR, the HRC and CAT, while obviously operating under different treaty provisions, all 'have confirmed in their reasoning in recent decisions that the preservation of the asserted rights of the parties in the face of the risk of irreparable damage represents an essential objective of interim measures in international law'.

> "Indeed it can be said that, whatever the legal system in question, the proper administration of justice requires that no irreparable action be taken while proceedings are pending".[189]

Moreover, the Court reiterated the importance of having remedies with suspensive effect in deportation or extradition proceedings.

---

[183] ICJ *Case concerning Military and Paramilitary Activities in and against Nicaragua* (*Nicaragua v. US*), 27 June 1986, §186. The ICJ considered that 'for a rule to be established as customary' the corresponding practice did not have to be 'in absolutely rigorous conformity with the rule'. It deemed it 'sufficient that the conduct of States should, in general, be consistent with such rules, and that instances of State conduct inconsistent with a given rule should generally have been treated as breaches of that rule, not as indications of the recognition of a new rule'. To find a rule of customary international law the traditional approach is to look at *opinio iuris* and practice of States, not adjudicators and it is not clear whether States generally complied because they considered they were legally bound to do so or simply out of comity.

[184] See ICJ *North Sea Continental Shelf* (*Germany v. the Netherlands*), 20 February 1969, §74.

[185] ECtHR Grand Chamber, *Mamatkulov and Askarov v. Turkey*, 15 December 2004, §110.

[186] Id., §123.

[187] Ibid. Note that Article 31(1) Vienna Convention does not specifically refer to the principle of effectiveness. Instead the practice of international adjudicators have understood this as an interpretative principle related to object and purpose.

[188] With regard to the principle of effectiveness it probably meant a principle of treaty interpretation, not of law. See also section 4 of this Chapter.

[189] ECtHR Grand Chamber, *Mamatkulov and Askarov v. Turkey*, 15 December 2004, §124.

"The notion of an effective remedy under Article 13 requires a remedy capable of preventing the execution of measures that are contrary to the Convention and whose effects are potentially irreversible".[190]

It argued that the notion of an effective remedy mentioned in Article 13 ECHR is a principle inherent in the Convention, applicable not only to the domestic proceedings but also to the international proceedings before the ECtHR.

"It is hard to see why this principle of the effectiveness of remedies for the protection of an individual's human rights should not be an inherent Convention requirement in international proceedings before the Court, whereas it applies to proceedings in the domestic legal system".[191]

In that sense the Court appears to argue it is a general principle of law that remedies aiming to protect against (human rights) violations should be effective.[192] Based on this principle, the Court's provisional measures necessarily must be binding. After all, 'under the Convention system, interim measures, as they have consistently been applied in practice' (…) 'play a vital role in avoiding irreversible situations that would prevent the Court from properly examining the application and, where appropriate, securing to the applicant the practical and effective benefit of the Convention rights asserted. Accordingly, in these conditions a failure by a respondent State to comply with interim measures will undermine the effectiveness of the right of individual application guaranteed by Article 34 and the State's formal undertaking in Article 1 to protect the rights and freedoms set forth in the Convention'.[193]

Provisional measures do not only permit the Court 'to carry out an effective examination of the application but also to ensure that the protection afforded to the applicant by the Convention is effective; such indications also subsequently allow the Committee of Ministers to supervise execution of the final judgment. Such measures thus enable the State concerned to discharge its obligation to comply with the final judgment of the Court, which is legally binding by virtue of Article 46 of the Convention'.[194]

The dissenting opinion provides the opportunity to further discuss some relevant issues. The dissenters challenged the argument that in order to meet the object and purpose of the right of individual complaint laid down in Art. 34 it is indispensable to accept the mandatory character of such measures. They considered that while this may be the case domestically, this is not so internationally. They advanced several reasons relevant to the discussion on general principles of international law. One is that 'States are entirely free *to accept or to refuse compulsory jurisdiction* of international courts and, if they do accept it, to limit its scope, for instance by not including rules on the binding character of provisional measures'.[195] They contrast this to the domestic level, 'where the principle of *compulsory jurisdiction* of the courts prevails'.[196]

---

[190] Ibid., referring to *Čonka and others* v. *Belgium*, 5 February 2002, §79.

[191] ECtHR Grand Chamber, *Mamatkulov and Askarov* v. *Turkey*, 15 December 2004, §124.

[192] At the same time it is a general principle of interpretation that the provisions of a treaty should be interpreted so as to ensure their practical and effective implementation.

[193] ECtHR Grand Chamber, *Mamatkulov and Askarov* v. *Turkey*, 15 December 2004, §125.

[194] Ibid.

[195] ECtHR Grand Chamber, *Mamatkulov and Askarov* v. *Turkey*, 15 December 2004, Joint partly dissenting opinion judges Caflisch, Türmen and Kovler, §16. In this respect the dissenters refer to Article 47 (arbitration procedure) of the Washington (World Bank) Convention on the Settlement of Investment Disputes (1965).

[196] Ibid.

Another reason they advanced involves the relationship between Article 34 ECHR and the Court's provisional measures. The majority found that by ignoring its provisional measures the State had hindered the effective exercise of the right of individual complaint. The dissenters point out that '[b]y providing for interim measures and, *a fortiori*, by not vesting them with binding force, the right of individual application is "hindered" in no way; and to say the contrary would stretch the interpretation of Article 34 to a point at which the Court *ceases to interpret* and *assumes legislative functions*'.[197]

They added that the fact that 'this is so is shown by other instruments of dispute settlement: nowhere else have jurisdiction and the right of application been linked to the issuance and the binding force of interim measures'.[198]

In this context they pointed out that the argument in *LaGrand* was based on Article 41 ICJ Statute and its reference to the Court's power to 'indicate' provisional measures. It was not based on Article 35 ICJ Statute, which was 'the approximate equivalent' of Article 34 ECHR. Moreover, Article 63(2) ACHR enabled the Inter-American Court to order provisional measures, but Article 34 ECHR could not serve as a 'reasonable legal basis for drawing a similar conclusion'.[199]

The dissenters considered that 'there may well be a widespread rule on obligatory interim measures on the domestic level, based on the rule of compulsory jurisdiction applicable on that level'. On the other hand, 'that rule does not prevail on the international level, which is why it cannot be applied as such on that level'. "In other words, the principle cannot be transposed to the business of international courts".[200] They concluded as follows:

> "There must, however, be a *customary rule* allowing international courts and tribunals, even in the absence of a treaty provision, to enact Rules of Procedure, a rule which may include the power to *formulate* interim measures. But that rule cannot be taken to include the power to *prescribe* such measures".[201]

2.4.4.7 EVALUATION OF THE DISSENTING OPINION WITH REGARD TO GENERAL PRINCIPLES

It seems that the dissenters recognise a general principle of *domestic* law that provisional measures are legally binding, but that they consider that this cannot be a general principle of *international* law because there is no rule of compulsory jurisdiction at the international level. Still, in my view once States have recognised an international adjudicator, the same principle of effectiveness applies that requires provisional measures to be binding on the domestic level.

In view of the fact that they start out by mentioning not only general principles of law, but also 'general international law', the reference of the dissenters to a 'customary rule' probably relates to customary international law. They consider that international courts and tribunals may

---

[197] Ibid. The third reason why they consider that on the international level the effectiveness argument does not apply is that 'one should not forget that for many years international tribunals such as the Permanent Court of International Justice (1920-1939) and its successor, the ICJ, for most of its existence (1946 to 2001), confined themselves to indicating provisional measures without specifying their binding character'.

[198] Ibid.

[199] Ibid.

[200] ECtHR Grand Chamber Joint partly Dissenting Opinion judges Caflisch, Türmen and Kovler, *Mamatkulov and Askarov* v. *Turkey*, 15 December 2004, §22.

[201] Id., §23.

formulate provisional measures but not to prescribe them. They relate the power to *formulate* such measures to the 'customary rule' allowing adjudicators to enact Rules of Procedure.

The reference by the dissenters to the Washington Convention on the Settlement of Investment Disputes is not entirely clear. They mention this Convention to illustrate that States are free to limit the scope of compulsory jurisdiction by not including rules on the binding character of provisional measures. Article 47 of the Washington Convention on the Settlement of Investment Disputes stipulates:

> "Except as the parties otherwise agree, the Tribunal may, if it considers that the circumstances so require, recommend any provisional measures which should be taken to preserve the respective rights of either party".

The fact, however, that in one treaty States explicitly include the possibility for parties to agree that the Tribunal may *not* use provisional measures does not negate the general principle of the inherent power to use provisional measures in systems of adjudication in which this power is not explicitly excluded. Neither does the fact that the language with regard to provisional measures used in this treaty is rather weak. Moreover, this example is derived from a commercial law treaty, making the comparison with the ECHR less appropriate. After all, the object and purpose of a human rights adjudication system such as that established under the ECHR, even more clearly than an adjudication system such as that established under the ICJ Statute, with general jurisdiction,[202] requires the use of provisional measures to prevent irreparable harm to, at least, life and personal integrity.

The dissenters' reliance on the fact that Article 63(2) ACHR explicitly enables the Court to order provisional measures and on the fact that the ICJ's judgment in *LaGrand* was based on a provision of the ICJ Statute specifically dealing with provisional measures (Article 41 ICJ Statute) does not convince. The fact that these courts obviously also refer to the provisions that specifically relate to provisional measures does not mean that they consider that there is no inherent authority to use binding provisional measures. As discussed, the IACHR has not just referred to Article 63(2) ACHR as the basis for its authority to order provisional measures, but also to Article 62(3) ACHR on reparation, to Article 33 ACHR on the competence of the Commission and Court 'with respect to matters relating to the fulfilment of the commitments' by the States parties as well as to 'the judicial character of the Court and the powers derived therefrom'.[203] It has stressed 'the Convention's fundamental objective of guaranteeing the effective protection of human rights' and pointed out that "States Parties must not take any action that will frustrate the *restitutio in integrum* of the rights of the alleged victims".[204]

In *LaGrand* the ICJ referred to the object and purpose of the ICJ Statute and considered that the power to indicate provisional measures entailed 'that such measures should be binding, inasmuch as the power in question is based on the necessity, when the circumstances call for it, to safeguard, and to avoid prejudice to, the rights of the parties as determined by the final judgment of the Court'.[205] It also referred to the principle 'universally accepted by the international tribunals and likewise laid down in many conventions (...) to the effect that the parties to a case must abstain from any measure capable of exercising a prejudicial effect in regard to the execution of

---

[202] See Chapter I (ICJ).

[203] IACHR *Velásquez Rodríguez, Fairén Garbi, Solís Corrales* and *Godínez Cruz* cases, Order of 19 January 1988, 1st 'Considering' clause.

[204] IACHR *James, Briggs, Noel, Garcia and Bethel*, Order for provisional measures, 14 June 1998.

[205] ICJ *LaGrand (Germany* v. *US)*, Judgment of 27 June 2001, §102.

the decision to be given, and, in general, not allow any step of any kind to be taken which might aggravate or extend the dispute'.[206]

Aside from this general principle that States must refrain from causing prejudice to the 'execution of the decision to be given', the HRC and CAT, to which the ECtHR does refer, and the African Commission, to which it does not refer, have in fact linked jurisdiction, the right of petition to the obligation to respect their provisional measures, focussing on the obligation to ensure respect for the 'core rights' in the treaties. Specifically, the human rights adjudicators have made the link between the importance of the rights to be protected and the binding nature of their provisional measures.

The case law of the ECtHR confirms this. An indication of the importance it attaches to Articles 2 (right to life) and 3 ECHR (prohibition or torture and cruel treatment) is the fact that it has noted that in expulsion and extradition cases it is only with regard to these rights that the obligation under Article 1 ECHR applied to ensure the Convention rights to everyone under their jurisdiction. The far reaching obligation not to expel or extradite is derived from the special nature of these articles, requiring a reading in conjunction with Article 1 ECHR, implying the principle of non-refoulement.[207]

Similarly, it is in the context of the right to life and the prohibition of torture and cruel treatment that effective proceedings before an international adjudicator trigger the inherent power to order legally binding provisional measures. The system of adjudication (both individual complaint and inter-State) is undermined in particular by acts threatening the right to life and the prohibition of torture as shown in the relation between provisional measures and the right to reparation.[208] It is exactly in such cases that States are legally bound to comply with provisional measures because without them the system of individual complaint itself is made nugatory, as the HRC calls it, and restitution in kind would be made impossible.

2.4.4.8 EXPLAINING THE REVERSAL

The ECtHR observed that in *Cruz Varas* it only determined the question whether the European *Commission* had power to order legally binding provisional measures. It noted that former Article 25 applied only to proceedings brought before the Commission, adding that it conferred upon the petitioner a right of a procedural nature distinguishable from the substantive rights in the Convention. "The Court thus confined itself to examining the Commission's power to order interim measures, not its own".[209] The Grand Chamber emphasised that 'unlike the Court and the Committee of Ministers, the Commission had no power to issue a binding decision that a Contracting State had violated the Convention'. "The Commission's task with regard to the merits was of a preliminary nature and its opinion on whether or not there had been a violation of the Convention was not binding".[210]

---

[206]   ICJ *LaGrand* (*Germany* v. *US*), Judgment of 27 June 2001, §103, quoting from PCIJ *Electricity Company of Sofia and Bulgaria*, Order of 5 December 1939, p. 199.

[207]   See Chapter V (Halting expulsion and extradition).

[208]   See Chapter XIII (Protection).

[209]   ECtHR Grand Chamber, *Mamatkulov and Askarov* v. *Turkey*, 15 December 2004, §118.

[210]   Id., §119.

With regard to *Cruz Varas* it stated that '[w]hile the Court is not formally bound to follow its previous judgments, in the interests of legal certainty and foreseeability it should not depart, without good reason, from its own precedents'.[211]

> "However, it is of crucial importance that the Convention is interpreted and applied in a manner which renders its rights practical and effective, not theoretical and illusory. It is a living instrument which must be interpreted in the light of present-day conditions".[212]

In addition, the Court stressed 'that although the Convention right to individual application was originally intended as an optional part of the system of protection, it has over the years become of high importance and is now a key component of the machinery for protecting the rights and freedoms set forth in the Convention'.[213] Moreover, since the entry into force of Protocol 11 'the right of individual application is no longer dependent on a declaration by the Contracting States'.

> "Thus, individuals now enjoy at the international level a real right of action to assert the rights and freedoms to which they are directly entitled under the Convention".[214]

The dissenters extensively quoted from *Cruz Varas* v. *Sweden* (1991) and noted that in *Čonka* v. *Belgium* (2001) the Court confirmed this decision in the context of its own provisional measures. Thus, they pointed out that the majority's interpretation in *Mamatkulov* that *Cruz Varas* concerned only the Commission's power to order provisional measures 'is not very persuasive in the light of the *Čonka* decision, where the Court reiterated the principles set out in *Cruz Varas* with regard to its own jurisdiction'. They considered that there had not been any change since *Čonka* that would justify the 'diametrically opposite conclusion' in *Mamatkulov* and reiterated that the Court 'should not depart, without good reason, from its own precedents'.[215]

2.4.4.9 EVALUATION OF THE COURT'S EXPLANATION OF THE REVERSAL

Indeed the distinction the Court draws between the provisional measures of the Court and those of the Commission, so as to justify the revision of its case law, is not very convincing. Even if the Commission's task with regard to the merits 'was of a preliminary nature' it was the first adjudicator responsible for dealing with individual complaints. If the Contracting States were free to ignore the provisional measures by the Commission, the Court noted, in reference to the ICJ, it would be 'hampered in the exercise of its functions because the respective rights of the parties' to the dispute before it were not preserved.

---

[211] Id., §121, referring to *Tyrer* v. *UK*, 25 April 1978, §31 and *Christine Goodwin* v. *UK*, 11 July 2002, §75. In *Mamatkulov* the Grand Chamber referred to, but did not discuss *Čonka*. ECtHR Grand Chamber, *Mamatkulov and Askarov* v. *Turkey*, 15 December 2004, §120. Two of the seven Judges of the Third Section that decided on admissibility in *Čonka* also took part in the Chamber decision. They were not among the dissenters. For *Čonka* see *Conka et al.* v. *Belgium*, Judgment of 13 March 2001 (partly admissible).

[212] ECtHR Grand Chamber *Mamatkulov and Askarov* v. *Turkey*, 15 December 2004, §121, referring to *Tyrer* v. *UK*, 25 April 1978, §31 and *Christine Goodwin* v. *UK*, 11 July 2002, §75.

[213] ECtHR Grand Chamber, *Mamatkulov and Askarov* v. *Turkey*, 15 December 2004, §122.

[214] Ibid.

[215] ECtHR Grand Chamber, *Mamatkulov and Askarov* v. *Turkey*, 15 December 2004, Joint partly dissenting opinion judges Caflisch, Türmen and Kovler, §6.

Moreover, the arguments with regard to effectiveness and object and purpose invoked by the Grand Chamber, as well as by the various adjudicators it referred to in its judgment, seem to apply also to the Commission's provisional measures and must sound familiar to the members of the Commission and the dissenters in the Court's *Cruz Varas* judgment.

The distinction made between the legal status of the provisional measures by the Commission and the Court is a somewhat artificial attempt to pretend no shift in the case law has taken place. Even if the crucial element of *Cruz Varas* had indeed been the distinction between the Commission and the Court, as the Court seems to argue in *Mamatkulov*, the admissibility decision in *Čonka* v. *Belgium* clearly indicated that, based on *Cruz Varas*, the Court's provisional measures were not legally binding either. *Čonka*, of course, is not a very persuasive precedent, because the Third Section, in a composition of seven Judges deciding on admissibility, did not really discuss and analyse the issue. The fact that it summarily confirmed the controversial judgment in *Cruz Varas*, decided more than ten years previously, with the narrowest of margins, seems more of an oversight than anything else.

In that sense it would have been preferable had the Court explicitly acknowledged its shift from *Cruz Varas* and *Čonka* to *Mamatkulov*.[216]

It did refer to its *general* case law on departing from earlier decisions regarding the interests of legal certainty and foreseeability and 'the orderly development of the Convention case-law' and to equality before the law.[217] Such concerns, however, 'would not prevent the Court from departing from an earlier decision if it was persuaded that there were cogent reasons for doing so. Such a departure might, for example, be warranted in order to ensure that the interpretation of the Convention reflects societal changes and remains in line with present-day conditions'.[218]

> "However, since the Convention is first and foremost a system for the protection of human rights, the Court must have regard to the changing conditions within the respondent State and within Contracting States generally and respond, for example to any evolving convergence as to the standards to be achieved".[219]

In this context the Court has proposed to 'look at the situation within and outside the Contracting State to assess "in the light of present-day conditions" what is now the appropriate interpretation and application of the Convention'.[220]

> "It is of crucial importance that the Convention is interpreted and applied in a manner which renders its rights practical and effective, not theoretical and illusory. A failure by the Court to

---

[216] See also Oellers-Frahm (2003), pp. 692-693 discussing the earlier Chamber decision in *Mamatkulov* (arguing that the positive step made by the Court to strengthen the effectiveness of the ECHR protection system could have been made explicit) and Tams (2003), p. 689 (considering that the Court's approach to precedent was deceptive because in *Mamatkulov* its conclusion was exactly the opposite of that in *Cruz Varas*. The Court's judgment would have been more convincing if it had explicitly acknowledged the change in the jurisprudence).

[217] See e.g. ECtHR *Cossey* v. *UK*, 27 September 1990, §35 (orderly development) and *Chapman* v. *UK*, 18 January 2001, §70, *Goodwin* v. *UK*, 11 July 2002, §74 and *Stafford* v. *UK*, 28 May 2002, §68 (equality before the law).

[218] ECtHR *Cossey* v. *UK*, 27 September 1990, §35. Subsequently the Court used the phrase 'good reason' (rather than 'cogent reasons'). See e.g. *Goodwin* v. *UK*, 11 July 2002, §74.

[219] See e.g. ECtHR *Goodwin* v. *UK*, 11 July 2002, §74, *Stafford* v. *UK*, 28 May 2002, §68 and *Chapman* v. *UK*, 18 January 2001, §70.

[220] See e.g. ECtHR *Goodwin* v. *UK*, 11 July 2002, §75, *Stafford* v. *UK*, 28 May 2002, §69 and references therein.

maintain a dynamic and evolutive approach would risk rendering a bar to reform or improvement".[221]

While the development to which the Court refers, including the now (since Protocol 11) obligatory respect for the right of petition, is indeed significant, the individuals petitioning the Court in the pre-Protocol 11 period equally enjoyed 'a real right of action' to assert their rights under the Convention. The fact that the Contracting State previously had taken the additional step of recognising the competence of the Court does not detract from the obligations of that State. Through its recognition of the competence of the Court the Contracting State had committed itself to preserve the rights claimed pending the proceedings and not to hinder the right of individual application. There was also good reason to now rule on the basis of the effectiveness approach generally used by the Court.

The Court's judgment generally has been welcomed.[222] Indeed, the prohibition of torture was part of the Convention from the outset, as was the idea that the Convention's substantive rights must be effectively ensured. Procedural rights intended to make effective substantive rights, such as the right not to be exposed to torture, must be interpreted so as to do just that. Procedural rights always assume the existence of substantive rights. Article 34 ECHR (and former Article 25 ECHR) refers to the obligation not to hinder the right of petition in any way. The open-ended phrase 'in any way' indicates that the drafters left it to the Court to fill in what this means in practice. Ignoring provisional measures appears to be a very good way to hinder the effective exercise of the right of petition.

The power to take provisional measures may be implied given the function of human rights adjudicators. In line with the principle of effectiveness applied in the interpretation of human rights treaties the binding nature of provisional measures is inherent to the effective exercise of this power.

The power to take such measures can be presumed to be implied in the task of judicial bodies supervising human rights treaties and the principle that these measures must be binding may be inherent in the concept of the protection of human rights. In any case it is implied in the State's recognition of the right of individual petition and of the substantive rights in the Convention.

It is, furthermore, doubtful whether a 'uniform legal rule' is necessary to prove the existence of a general principle. In my view such principle can be derived from national practices on provisional or interlocutory measures. These may be filled in differently in different places, but that only denies its existence as a 'uniform rule', not as a concept or general principle. The concept represented by these measures has been applied in general international law to provide for the possibility of provisional measures in cases of international contention. Provisional measures in national law are legally binding and must be so, in order to perform their judicial function. There is no reason to assume otherwise in international law.

The judgment of the Grand Chamber, in its conclusion, does not refer to the prevention of irreparable harm and does not make an explicit link between Article 34 and Article 3.[223] On the other hand, earlier in the judgment it does refer to the 'core rights' under the Convention, irrepa-

---

[221]   See *Stafford* v. *UK*, 28 May 2002, §68. In fact the Court also used this argument in his decision in *Mamatkulov*, 15 December 2004, §121.

[222]   Discussing the 2003 and/or 2005 judgments see e.g. Letsas (2003), pp. 527-538; Oellers-Frahm (2003), p. 689; Tigroudja (2003), p. 601 (disagreeing); Rieter (2004), pp. 73-87; Cohen-Jonathan (2005b), pp. 283-307; Cohen-Jonathan (2005d); Rieter (2005), pp. 320-324; Vermeulen/de Vries (2005); Barkhuysen (2005); Bruin (2005); Mowbray (2005), pp. 377-386 (somewhat critical).

[223]   See ECtHR Grand Chamber, *Mamatkulov and Askarov* v. *Turkey*, 15 December 2004, §§128-129.

rable damage and the fact that the petitioners in this case were asserting rights under Articles 2 and 3.[224]

2.4.4.10 DEVELOPMENTS SINCE MAMATKULOV

Since Mamatkulov the Court's case law has evolved. In *Olaechea Cahuas* v. *Spain* (2006) the ECtHR noted, referring to a jurisprudential evolution of the relevant principles, that in *Mamatkulov* it had removed itself from its earlier case law on provisional measures (e.g. *Cruz Varas* (1991) and *Conka* (2001)).[225] It recalled that it applied Rule 39 strictly, ordering provisional measures only in a limited range of cases in which there is an imminent risk of irreparable harm.[226] It further noted that in *Shamayev et al.* v. *Georgia and Russia* (2005) it had refined this conclusion with the statement that the fact that it was able to examine the case on the merits did not mean that Article 34 ECHR was not violated.[227] Finally, it referred to *Aoulmi*, in which it stressed that the fact that the obligatory nature of its provisional measures had not yet been made explicit at the time of the expulsion did not detract from the obligations of the State under Article 34. It pointed out that this was the first time that the Court used the adjective 'obligatory' when referring to its provisional measures.[228]

In the cases *Mamatkulov*, *Shamayev* and *Aoulmi* the State had ignored the Court's provisional measures. Moreover, the Court had noted that, in addition, upon the extradition or expulsion of the petitioners their lawyers had lost all contact with their clients. It found violations of Article 34 ECHR. In *Aoulmi*, for instance, the Court first concluded, more generally, that 'the level of protection that the Court was able to afford the rights which he was asserting under Article 3 of the Convention was irreversibly reduced'. It then added that 'the gathering of evidence in support of the applicant's allegations' had 'proved more complex' as his lawyer had 'lost all contact with him since his expulsion'.[229]

Olaechea Cahuas v. *Spain* (2006) can be distinguished from the previous three cases to the extent that counsel was able to stay in touch with the petitioner after he had been extradited in violation of the Court's provisional measures. In this case the ECtHR pointed out that one question that still needed an explicit answer was whether the obligation of States to respect provisional measures was based on the finding *ex post* that the effective exercise of the right of petition was hindered upon removal. The Court considered that there was a clear difference with the previous cases and in that sense it could not conclude that the right to individual petition had been hindered.[230] Nevertheless, this conclusion, based on information received *subsequent* to the use of

---

[224] See ECtHR Grand Chamber, *Mamatkulov and Askarov* v. *Turkey*, 15 December 2004, §108. On this issue see also Tams (2003), p. 688.

[225] ECtHR *Case of Cruz Varas and Others* v. *Sweden*, Judgment of 20 March 1991 and *Conka et al.* v. *Belgium*, Judgment of 13 March 2001 (partly admissible).

[226] ECtHR *Olaechea Cahuas* v. *Spain*, Judgment of 10 August 2006 (5th Section), §72, referring to *Mamatkulov*, §§103-104 and 128.

[227] ECtHR *Olaechea Cahuas* v. *Spain*, Judgment of 10 August 2006, §73.

[228] Id., §74, referring to *Mamatkulov*, §111.

[229] ECtHR *Aoulmi* v. *France*, Judgment of 17 January 2006 (4th Section), §104. See also *Mamatkulov and Askarov*, 15 December 2004, §127; *Shamayev et al.* v. *Georgia and Russia*, Judgment 16 September 2003 (2nd Section) (inadm.), §478 and *Aoulmi*, Judgment of 17 January 2006, §93.

[230] ECtHR *Olaechea Cahuas* v. *Spain*, Judgment of 10 August 2006, §79. The Court expresses it as follows: "En conséquence, il n'est pas possible de conclure à l'existence d'une entrave, dans le sens des affaires précitées, au droit au recours effectif du requérant". In fact it may have meant

provisional measures did not relieve the State from its obligation not to hinder in any way the effective exercise of the right protected by Article 34 ECHR. The ECtHR pointed out that Article 34 ECHR was in fact closely linked to the Rule on provisional measures laid down in Article 39 of its Rules. This Rule enabled the Court to consider whether the petitioner would run a risk of irreparable harm because of an act or omission by the State. It added that, consequently, Rule 39 enabled it to consider whether such act or omission would hinder the effective exercise of the right of petition.[231]

More in particular the Court wished to point out that a provisional measure, by its nature, is provisional. Its necessity is evaluated at one particular moment in time by reason of the existence of a risk that could hinder the effective exercise of the right of petition in Article 34 ECHR. If the State party respects the provisional measure this risk is avoided and a future hindrance of the right of petition is eliminated. On the other hand, if the State does not respect the provisional measure, the risk of the obstruction of the effective exercise of this right continues and subsequent facts, as well as the State's non-compliance itself, determine whether the risk has become a reality or not. Yet even if it has not become a reality, the Court's provisional measure must be considered legally binding. Whether or not Article 34 ECHR is violated cannot depend on the eventual confirmation of the existence of the risk. The fact that a State fails to respect a provisional measure decided by the Court, in light of the existence of a risk, is in itself a grave hindrance, at that particular moment, of the effective exercise of the right of individual petition.[232] This was confirmed and specified in *Paladi* (2007) where the Court pointed out that a *delay* in the implementation of a provisional measure could also constitute a violation of Article 34 ECHR. It is not necessary to provide evidence of actual harm during the period of delay. Evidence of a risk of irreparable harm to one of the 'core Convention rights' is sufficient to trigger state responsibility.[233]

3   PRINCIPLES OF INTERPRETATION AND GENERAL PRINCIPLES OF LAW

The power to order provisional measures has been referred to as an inherent part of the judicial function.[234] In addition, the PCIJ already noted in the *Electricity Company of Sofia in Bulgaria* case (1939) that Article 41 on provisional measures applied the principle 'universally accepted by international tribunals and likewise laid down in many conventions to which Bulgaria has been a party – to the effect that the parties to a case must abstain from any measure capable of exercising a prejudicial effect in regard to the execution of the decision to be given and, in general, not allow any step of any kind to be taken which might aggravate or extend the dispute'.[235]

In both national and international systems for the settlement of legal disputes, the power to use provisional measures is a necessary attribute of the judicial function and the obligation to

---

that the right of petition was not hindered *to the same extent* as the cases mentioned previously. On *Oleachea* see also Woltjer (2006); Rieter (2007) and Haeck/Burbano Herrera/Zwaak (2008).

[231] ECtHR *Olaechea Cahuas* v. *Spain*, Judgment of 10 August 2006, §80, referring to *Mamatkulov*, §108.

[232] ECtHR *Olaechea Cahuas* v. *Spain*, Judgment of 10 August 2006, §81.

[233] ECtHR *Paladi* v. *Moldova*, 10 July 2007. See further Rieter (2007).

[234] Judge Sir Gerald Fitzmaurice, in his Separate Opinion in the ICJ *Northern Cameroons* case, Judgment of 2 December 1963 (preliminary objections), p. 103 noted that it is 'really an inherent jurisdiction, the power to exercise which is a necessary condition of the Court or of any court of law-being able to function at all'. See also Judge Singh in the ICJ *Nuclear Test* cases, Order of 22 June 1973, p. 145 noting that Article 41 reflects an inherent power.

[235] PCIJ *Electricity Company of Sofia and Bulgaria* (*Belgium* v. *Bulgaria*), Order of 5 December 1939, p. 199. See also Chapter I (ICJ).

respect them is necessitated by the effective protection of the right to life and the prohibition of torture and cruel treatment of those making use of the right of petition. After all the principle of effectiveness or *effet utile* is a principle of interpretation of particular relevance in human rights cases.[236] Indeed, such provisional measures by international adjudicators 'must carry some connotation of obligation if they are to fulfil their function of ensuring some efficacy to the final outcome of the proceedings'.[237]

As discussed in Chapter II, it may be assumed that States have recognized supervisory mechanisms to human rights treaties in good faith, meaning that the human rights adjudicators established by these treaties have genuinely been assigned the task of monitoring compliance with, and therefore interpreting, the provisions of the treaty. Thus the practice developed by the human rights adjudicators arguably establishes the agreement of the parties regarding their interpretation, exactly because these adjudicators were created under the treaty in order to interpret it.[238]

As noted, apart from the relevance of the subsequent practice developed by the adjudicators to the interpretation of treaty provisions, 'judicial decisions' also constitute 'subsidiary means for the determination of international law'.[239] These may be domestic or international judicial decisions. The phrase 'judicial decisions' is used, rather than 'court decisions', which potentially includes the decisions made in individual cases by treaty monitoring bodies.[240]

Thus, in light of their special protective function it is argued that human rights adjudicators have the implied power to order binding provisional measures. They are binding through legal interpretation, as the power to use them is necessarily *implied* in the task of bodies supervising human rights treaties and their binding nature is based on a principle *inherent* in the concept of the protection of human rights together with the explicit duty of State parties to co-operate in good faith with the supervisory bodies. Once a State recognizes an individual complaint system it is bound not to frustrate it.[241]

While a general principle of law is a source of law and a general principle of interpretation is a method rather than a source, it is not always easy to distinguish between the two in concrete cases.[242] Both principles of interpretation and principles of law are developed and applied by

---

[236] See e.g. IACHR *Colotenango* (Guatemala), Order of 5 September 2001, 5th 'Considering' clause; ECtHR (First Section) *Mamatkulov and Abdurasulovic v. Turkey*, Judgment of 6 February 2003, §109 and ECtHR (Grand Chamber), *Mamatkulov and Askarov* v. *Turkey*, Judgment adopted on 15 December 2004, published on 4 February 2005.

[237] Harrington (2003), p. 58. See generally Elkind (1981), p. 169, who points out, p. 170, that provisional measures are not merely procedural and that the power to indicate them cannot be equated with the power to fix deadlines, admit counter claims or permit the intervention of third parties. In the context of human rights see e.g. Bernhardt (1994), p. 102. See also Pasqualucci (2005), p. 16 ('The argument that interim measures are essential to the competence granted to quasi-judicial enforcement bodies by the States and that such measures are, therefore, implied in the underlying treaty is compelling and neceaary to the fabric of international law').

[238] Of course States will sometimes argue that adjudicators overstepped their mark and tried to create rather than interpret the law. This is a discussion that cannot be avoided. It means in any case that adjudicators must motivate their findings, with a thorough and coherent legal analysis. See also Mahoney (1990), pp. 57-88, arguing, in the context of the practice of the ECtHR, that judicial activism and judicial self-restraint are two sides of the same coin.

[239] Article 38(1)(d) ICJ Statute.

[240] See further Chapter II (Systems), section 8.

[241] See also Harrington (2003), p. 63.

[242] It is not always self-evident whether, for instance, this functional approach is derived from the general principle of effectiveness as a general principle of law, or whether it is a method of

adjudicators and, in this case, are quite interrelated as to contents (the general principle of law possibly triggering the choice of certain interpretation methods over others). This is why they are discussed together in this section.

The interpretative principle of *effet utile* applies to procedural standards as well, in particular the right of individual complaint and 'the acceptance of the contentious competence of the judiciary organ of protection'.[243] In the context of human rights treaties the principle of *effet utile* creates a presumption that the most protective interpretation is warranted.

General principles of (international) law are used by adjudicators in order to fill gaps left by treaty law and customary law. Some principles are derived directly from the concept of law or from legal logic. Others originate from the domestic law of many States. Examples are *nullum crimen sine poena*, the obligation to compensate for harm caused and procedural protection of criminal defendants. Other general principles of international law are derived directly from (developments in) international law. Examples are the principles of state responsibility, the notion that each violation requires a remedy, which may in turn include *restitutio in integrum* and the jurisdictional principle of *compétence de la compétence*.[244] The principle of good faith application and interpretation of international obligations, for instance, is often seen as the ultimate general principle of law.[245]

Cohen-Jonathan, for instance, has pointed out that any proper administration of justice, whether internal or international, means to safeguard the rights invoked by the parties, and that this is the case with a particular vigilance and rapidity when there is a risk of irreparable harm to fundamental human rights.[246] Ordering provisional measures is a power inherent to the function of each tribunal. This is in fact an expression of a general principle of international law in the sense of Article 38(1) (c) ICJ Statute.[247]

As discussed, human rights adjudicators, alleged victims, NGOs and States appear to have assumed, even if implicitly, the existence of the principle of effective protection to prevent irreparable harm to persons as a fundamental norm around which the human rights system is built.[248]

Several human rights adjudicators have been inspired by each other's case law and have elaborated on and applied norms found in all human rights systems with regard to preventing

---

interpretation in itself. I would argue, however, that it is a general principle of interpretation rather than a general principle of law as a source of law as it is always related to a substantive rule that must be applied such as to have the intended effect. Yet the *reason* for choosing the principle of effectiveness when interpreting the treaty obligations of States may be a general principle of law, as discussed infra..

243 IACHR Judgment on preliminary objections in *Constantine et al.* v. *Trinidad and Tobago*, 1 September 2001, separate opinion of judge A.A. Cançado Trindade, §15.

244 On general principles of (international) law as a source of international law, see e.g. Cheng (1953).

245 See e.g. treaty references in Article 2(2) UN Charter and Article 31 Vienna Convention on the Law of Treaties; see also ICJ *Nuclear Test Cases* (*New Zealand* v. *France*), Judgment of 20 December 1974, §46 (France was expected to live up to its unilateral declaration not to continue atmospheric testing: "Just as the very rule of *pacta sunt servanda* in the law of treaties is based on good faith, so also is the binding character of an international obligation assumed by unilateral declaration") and *Nuclear Test Cases* (*Australia* v. *France*), judgment of 20 December 1974, §49. See ICJ *Border and Transborder Armed Actions* (*Nicaragua* v. *Honduras*), Judgment of 20 December 1988, §94 (the principle of good faith is an underlying principle, always linked to existing obligations).

246 Cohen-Jonathan (2005a), p. 434.

247 Cohen-Jonathan (2005a), p. 433.

248 See Chapter II (Systems).

irreparable harm to persons pending the proceedings before them. Indeed one might consider that this aspect of provisional measures in human rights cases can be seen in the practice of such a range of adjudicators and has obtained such a level of generality over such a period of time that it may indicate a general principle of law.

Thus the obligation to respect provisional measures may be considered to be based on a general principle of law that pending the proceedings irreparable harm should be prevented. It applies even more in the context of complaints about ongoing or impending violations of fundamental human rights. Not just any adjudicator, but morally speaking any actor has to take this principle into account when dealing with urgent situations that threaten to cause irreparable harm to persons.

For a human rights adjudicator to derive the existence of a general principle of international law, it is not State practice but the practice of other international adjudicators that is most relevant. There is a general principle for States not to cause harm to other States and to show due diligence in preventing such harm. It is argued that there is a corollary and even stronger principle of preventing irreparable harm to persons pending international litigation. This principle is based on the practices developed by the human rights adjudicators themselves, to which States had assigned this adjudicatory function. The principle also appears to have become part of the humanization of law that is seen in the approach of the ICJ to the use of provisional measures.[249]

In cases pending before them all human rights adjudicators have used provisional measures to prevent irreparable harm to persons. They used provisional measures in cases involving rights singled out for their particularly fundamental nature. All relevant human rights treaties have done so with the right to life and the prohibition of torture or cruel treatment and they all pay special attention to these rights in their proceedings.[250] The commonality in the practices of the adjudicators appears to be based not just on the interpretative principle of effectiveness, but also on an implicitly recognized general principle of law aimed at the prevention of irreparable harm to persons. In fact this principle of preventing irreparable harm to persons underlies the decision-making of all international adjudicators.

4 CONCLUSION

This Chapter argues that the authority of human rights adjudicators to take binding provisional measures is derived from the core rights singled out in the treaties, in light of the practice developed of attaching particular importance to the protection of personal integrity and (cultural) survival, read together with the right of individual petition.[251] After all, the principles of effectiveness and of the prevention of irreparable harm have been used by the adjudicators, either explicitly or implicitly, when interpreting these provisions. In addition it is submitted that the prevention of irreparable harm is not just a principle of treaty interpretation, but has also developed into a general principle of law, which is, as such, binding on States (Article 38 (1)(c) ICJ Statute).

The human rights adjudicators do have in common an underlying interpretative approach, both with regard to their implied power to use provisional measures and as to the binding nature of provisional measures. In fact one can speak of an 'acquis humanitaire' based on the standards

---

[249] See Chapter I (ICJ).
[250] See Conclusion Part II.
[251] See also Conclusion Part II.

of protection that all human rights adjudicators have in common,[252] which also applies to the legal status of provisional measures.

The text of the treaties must be interpreted in light of their context and object and purpose in a dynamic manner, taking into account that they must be interpreted so as to have effect. The principle of effectiveness flowing from the object and purpose indicates that the adjudicators instituted under these treaties must have the power to use provisional measures.

The ECtHR has considered that 'in the light of the general principles of international law, the law of treaties and international case-law, the interpretation of the scope of interim measures cannot be dissociated from the proceedings to which they relate or the decision on the merits they seek to protect'.[253] This statement about the scope of provisional measures shows that now the ECtHR too recognises that in the context of such measures procedural and substantive law meet. The emphasis on the decision on the merits that provisional measures seek to protect underscores the binding nature of these measures. After all, otherwise States would be allowed to cause irreparable harm to the claim on the merits, and, as the provisional measures generally relate to claims involving the survival and personal integrity, irreparable harm to persons.[254]

By accepting the jurisdiction of an international (including regional) adjudicator a State has committed itself to an international system of adjudication.[255] Just like a domestic system of adjudication, an international system can, in my view, only be effective if the adjudicator has the power to order provisional measures that are legally binding. In this respect the main difference between domestic and international systems of adjudication is the all-inclusive nature of the former on the one hand and the fact that in most international systems States initially are free to accept or reject compulsory jurisdiction. This difference, however, loses much of its significance once a State has accepted the jurisdiction of an adjudicator. Even if a rule on the binding character of provisional measures is not included as such in a treaty text, by accepting the competence of an adjudicator to deal with conflicts between States or between individuals and States the State has accepted the adjudicator's judicial independence and its power to deal with these conflicts effectively. The authority to use binding provisional measures is inherent to effective adjudication.

Even if the treaty in question does not explicitly provide for the use of provisional measures, the duty to protect against threats to survival and personal integrity requires the State to take positive measures also pending international proceedings. If it is the international adjudicator who recommends such positive measures, in the form of provisional measures, respecting them is also required as part of the obligations entered into by the State's recognition of the complaint procedure.

It is argued that the human rights adjudicators have been correct to stress that the *effet utile* of the adjudicator's decision on the merits necessitates respect for the provisional measures indicated by it. If decisions on the merits are not considered legally binding in all respects (such as certain recommendations for reparation), at least the State's recognition of the substantive rights and its recognition of the individual complaint system require a basic level of action and abstention on the part of the State. With regard to the most fundamental rights in the treaty at issue they require at least the protection of the practitioner from irreparable harm, as well as the good faith cooperation with the relevant adjudicator.

---

[252] On the issue of convergence and divergence in general, see Chapter II, section 8. On the common core of the concept of provisional measures, see Conclusion Part II. Simma used the expression acquis humanitaire already in 1995, p. 173.

[253] ECtHR Grand Chamber, *Mamatkulov and Askarov* v. *Turkey*, 15 December 2004, §123.

[254] See also Conclusion Part II on the relation between irreparable harm to the claim and to persons.

[255] See also Pasqualucci (2005), p. 49, noting that provisional measures must be considered binding when issued by both international judicial and quasi-judicial bodies.

An action or omission causing irreparable harm to persons (personal integrity and survival) is an aggravated breach of the human rights treaty. If a State has recognized the right of individual complaint (or inter-State complaint for that matter) and the adjudicator decided to use provisional measures to prevent such harm, ignoring these measures is an aggravated breach of the right of petition as well.

While not an aggravated breach, ignoring *other* provisional measures, which may not (yet) fall within the common core, is also contrary to the obligation to cooperate with the adjudicator in good faith.

Finally, a State may consider that the adjudicator was in error in using provisional measures. Also in such a case the State should respect the measures. In most such cases the State has a different assessment of the risk (urgency), but it is ultimately for the human rights adjudicator to decide on this. In addition, the State's belief that the adjudicator was in error may also be based on a genuine conviction that the risk is not irreversible, meaning that the provisional measures can be situated beyond the outer limits. Even then the State must respect the provisional measures based on its obligations under the system of individual complaint. At the same time the adjudicator must take care not to go beyond the outer limits, also for the sake of the sustainability of the individual petition system.

CONCLUSION

Part III showed that the serious nature of the harm risked has an impact on the approach of the human rights adjudicators to the requirements of *prima facie* admissibility and jurisdiction on the merits (Chapter XIV); on the requirements of immediacy and real risk (Chapter XV) and on the legal status of provisional measures (Chapter XVI).

In addition, when deciding on the use of provisional measures the human rights adjudicators have also taken into account the inequality between the parties. Together with their awareness of the serious nature of the harm risked, this inequality played a role in the more lenient attitude of the human rights adjudicators towards the requirements of *prima facie* admissibility and jurisdiction on the merits and of immediacy and real risk. It does not play a similar role in the discussion on the legal status of provisional measures.

To the extent that cases before the ICJ also involve the rights of individuals, the case law of the human rights adjudicators could be relevant to it as well. Strictly speaking the inequality between the parties is a criterion only applying in the context of individual complaints about human rights violations. Yet the serious nature of the harm risked to persons clearly applies in the inter-State context of the ICJ as well.

PART IV

RESPONSES

INTRODUCTION

This Part deals on the one hand with the official responses by the addressee States to provisional measures and on the other hand with the human rights adjudicators' follow up.

For the clarification and further development of a legal concept of provisional measures as used by the human rights adjudicators, the focus of this book was on the discussion of the common core and outer limits of the concept as applied by the adjudicators with regard to the purpose of these measures (Part II). Subsequently it dealt with the impact of the irreparable nature of the harm on the approach of the adjudicators to requirements of *prima facie* admissibility and jurisdiction, immediacy and real risk at the stage of provisional measures, as well as on the binding nature of these measures (Part III).

Another question with regard to provisional measures in human rights adjudication is whether (and how) they actually work. Yet the question of effectiveness is one of causality and an empirical question that falls outside the scope of this conceptual research. Nevertheless, the adjudicators address the States concerned with decisions on provisional measures with the express purpose of preventing irreparable harm to persons and ensuring the effectiveness of the individual petition system. Therefore it is useful to see what types of responses the addressee States have provided and how the adjudicators (and others) have followed up on (initial) non-compliance. This is what Part IV aims at.

The available case law provides some information on the official responses of addressee States and the follow-up by adjudicators. Chapter XVII gives examples of the former in order to indicate types of reasoning chosen by States to justify their failure to comply vis-à-vis the adjudicators. From the official responses available it is possible to identify various explanations for non-compliance with provisional measures. This is not to say that the reasons forwarded by States are the 'real' reasons. Nor do the reasons forwarded for non-compliance explain why in the majority of cases States have complied with provisional measures. Nevertheless these are the reasons that are publicly available, generally by studying the references to them in the decisions on the merits published by the adjudicators subsequent to any discourse between them and the States with regard to the need for provisional measures.

Chapter XVIII then deals with the related question of how the adjudicators have dealt with non-compliance with their provisional measures. The follow-up by the adjudicators may have an impact on compliance in the long run, not just vis-à-vis the State involved, but also vis-à-vis the other States that have recognized the right of individual petition in the human rights system at issue. In addition, the follow up by adjudicators and others to non-compliance by States provides an additional indication of the importance they attach to preventing irreparable harm to persons.

1   INTRODUCTION

Already in 1995 it was argued that 'inasmuch as interim or provisional measures ordered by worldwide or regional treaty bodies are increasingly based on the expectation and on actual practice of compliance, such measures are becoming an integral part of the human rights legal protection system'.[1]

Compliance with the provisional measures of the ICJ has improved over time, but still is not impressive.[2] Do the responses of addressee States towards the provisional measures by human rights adjudicators differ in this respect? This Chapter deals with the official responses of States to the provisional measures directed against them.

States seem to comply more often with the provisional measures of the human rights adjudicators than with their decisions on the merits.[3] This may be due to the fact that what is required on the merits is permanent and often more detailed and extensive, resulting in more obstacles to a timely implementation than do provisional measures.[4] Yet the general attitude of compliance with provisional measures may also be due to the realization that adjudicators generally take decisions on provisional measures in the most serious situations, in order to prevent irreparable harm to persons.[5] Indeed the adjudicators themselves have been influenced in their decision-making on the use of provisional measures by the nature of the harm risked.[6] The question arises whether compliance by States is also higher with regard to provisional measures aimed at protecting irreparable harm to persons than with regard to other provisional measures.

---

[1]   Van Boven (1995), p. 106.

[2]   See Chapter I (ICJ).

[3]   See also e.g. Rodriguez who points out that States have complied more with provisional measures than with judgments. He qualifies them as a very effective instrument of human rights protection, Interview with Victor Rodriguez, senior research fellow at the International Human Rights Law Institute of DePaul University, former staff member Court, San Jose, Costa Rica, November 2001.

[4]   In the admissibility decision in HRC *Irving Phillip* v. *Trinidad and Tobago*, 20 October 1998, for instance, the HRC specifically expressed its appreciation for the fact that the State had respected its provisional measures. Apparently the State's attitude towards provisional measures was different from its attitude in general. After all, in the decision on the merits the Committee gave its usual remarks about the non-cooperation of the State with the proceedings in general, warranting a shift in the burden of proof from the petitioner to the State.

[5]   With regard to the ECtHR Cohen-Jonathan (2005), p. 782 also notes that the Court's selection of situations in which it would use provisional measures has always been very strict and because of that the States have mostly cooperated with the Court.

[6]   Part III showed that the serious nature of the harm risked, together to some extent with the inequality between the parties, has an impact on the approach taken by the human rights adjudicators to the requirements of *prima facie* admissibility and jurisdiction on the merits; on the requirements of immediacy and real risk and on the legal status of provisional measures.

As discussed, in the concept of provisional measures procedural and substantive law meet. Compliance with provisional measures is based on a process that involves attitudes towards substantive issues as well. For the interpretation of the meaning of the concept of provisional measures a discourse takes place – sometimes consciously, sometimes not – between the various international adjudicators.[7] For the implementation of the provisional measures domestically a discourse appears to take place as well. Internationally, apart from a discourse between the various adjudicators, it is mainly between the parties, on the one hand, and between the adjudicators and the parties, on the other. NGOs, the media, the other human rights adjudicators and authorities appointed within international systems, such as the UN or the Council of Europe, play a role as well. Domestically the discourse is mainly taking place between the parties, including the various branches of government, while media and NGOs play their part as well.

In this discussion not only (or even mainly) the attitudes towards the concept of provisional measures, and thereby to the substantive law at issue, appear to be relevant, but other factors as well. Some domestic decision-makers may indeed personally adhere to the same principles underlying the use of the provisional measures and become convinced by the arguments used by the international adjudicator. It also happens that they were convinced of the need for action or abstention already before the provisional measures were used. In such cases they may use the provisional measure as leverage in the domestic discourse.

Other decision-makers may not be convinced normatively, but may consider that apart from national interest factors advocating against the action or omission required by the provisional measure, there are national interest factors such as fear for the State's international reputation (international embarrassment and loss of prestige) that would warrant compliance nevertheless.

This book takes the approach that States that have recognized individual complaint procedures under human rights treaties have consented to a normative process.[8] This means that further along in the process States should no longer invoke traditional State sovereignty and State voluntarism arguments in order to justify non-compliance with decisions of international adjudicators. The obligation to comply with decisions of these adjudicators is considered a given.

Obviously stating that this obligation exists does not as such effectuate compliance. States may have various reasons to deviate from legal commitments, including arguments that they are in fact not legally bound.[9]

As consistent information on the responses of States is lacking, this Chapter simply provides *examples* of compliance and non-compliance with provisional measures to protect against irreparable harm to the survival and personal integrity (within the common core) on the one hand and provisional measures in miscellaneous cases (within the outer limits) on the other.

The information on the responses by States to provisional measures is derived from the decisions on the merits that refer to them.[10] Occasionally this is supplemented by other information. Obviously this information can do no more than indicate to some extent the compliance of States. An examination of effectiveness would require consistent information about what really happened to the beneficiaries of the provisional measures, together with additional information on causality. This would be within the realm of social science research.

Nevertheless it is assumed that other factors than the legal character of decisions, 'such as the political will and the authority of the organ in question' may often be more important to ex-

---

[7]   See Chapter II (Systems), section 8.
[8]   See generally about State consent to normative process, Hey (2003).
[9]   See also Chapter XVI (Legal status).
[10]   As the Inter-American Commission reserves a special section of its Annual Report to its practice with regard to precautionary measures and the Inter-American Court publishes its orders for provisional measures, references are made to these as well.

plain the responses of the addressee States and some references are made to such information.[11] This chapter simply aims to identify some levels of implementation, taking as example provisional measures to halt executions, as well as to identify some aspects that help explain compliance and non-compliance. If available, references are made to specific responses by adjudicators to justifications for non-compliance given by addressee States.[12]

2 COMPLIANCE

2.1 Introduction

The adjudicators generally note that non-compliance with their provisional measures only occurs occasionally. In *Mamamatkulov* (2004), for instance, the European Court pointed out: "Cases of States failing to comply with indicated measures remain very rare".[13] Yet data on the level and manner of compliance are not generally compiled.

As discussed, generally the Inter-American system provides more information on the practice of the adjudicators with regard to provisional measures than the other systems.[14] This applies as well to the information on compliance by States with these provisional measures.[15] Nevertheless, in the Inter-American system too the nature of the State's reply and the level of compliance often remain unclear.[16] At the same time the Inter-American Commission has noted that States, 'when formally approached' sometimes show 'different levels of responsiveness, diligence and efficiency of the IACHR's requests'.[17]

There are various levels at which States may comply with the provisional measures taken by human rights adjudicators. This section provides some examples, first organised by different types of provisional measures and then in different types of responses.

---

[11]   See Klerk (2000), p. 156. She points out that it 'might be doubted whether compliance with views and judgments is much influenced by the extent to which they are binding'. See also Boerefijn (1999). On the legal status of provisional measures see Chapter XVI.

[12]   Chapter XVII more generally discusses the follow up by adjudicators to non-compliance by States.

[13]   ECtHR Grand Chamber, *Mamatkulov and Askarov* v. *Turkey*, 15 December 2004, §105.

[14]   See Chapter II (Systems).

[15]   See the sections on transparency of information in Chapter II (Systems).

[16]   See e.g. precautionary measures of 11 May 2000, on behalf of Mr. Uribe, a well-known human rights defender and an active member of the 'José Alvear Restrepo' Lawyers Collective. Apparently a military intelligence report identified him as part of the 'ELN support network'. Some persons mentioned in this intelligence report have been extra-judicially executed. Others have been the victims of forced disappearance, arbitrary detention, or constant threats forcing them to move of live in exile. There is no information on the response of the State. Annual Report 2000, §16.

[17]   CIDH Annual Report 1999, Chapter V – Colombia, §118.

2.2   A range of attitudes towards implementation of provisional measures

2.2.1 Introduction

States often prefer to remedy a situation in advance of a decision on the merits. In such cases it may be possible then to discontinue the case or declare it inadmissible.[18] In addition, while in some cases they are so determined to act a certain way that they prefer to act quickly in order actually to prevent an adjudicator from taking provisional measures, in other cases they may wish to a remedy the situation to avoid the embarrassment of a provisional measure. In such situations the staff of the adjudicator may inform the State in question informally of its intention to take formal provisional measures. The State will then act accordingly and a provisional measure will no longer be necessary.[19] This section gives some examples of the range of attitudes towards implementation, starting with State responses to provisional measures to halt the execution of a death sentence. Then the responses to provisional measures to halt expulsion and extradition are discussed, those to measures in the context of detention and disappearances, health care outside the detention context and death threats.

2.2.2 Various responses to provisional measures to halt executions

2.2.2.1 INTRODUCTION

This subsection focuses on the range of attitudes towards provisional measures to halt executions by the HRC, with some discussion of the Inter-American system as well. Some of the provisional measures by the African Commission to halt an execution have been ignored.[20] Those by the Bosnia Chamber,[21] the European Commission[22] and the European Court have been respected.[23]

---

[18]   This is often the case in the European system.

[19]   Several cases of compliance may be explained by factors other than the provisional measures, e.g. by domestic court decisions that did not take into account these measures but nevertheless decided to halt an execution or expulsion.

[20]   ACHPR See *International Pen, Constitutional Rights Project, Interights on behalf of Ken Saro-Wiwa Jr. and Civil Liberties Organisation* v. *Nigeria*, provisional measure somewhere between 2 and 9 November 1995 (secret execution 10 November 1995 and *Interights et al. (on behalf of Mariette Bosch)* v. *Botswana*, provisional measures of 27 March 2001 (execution on 31 March 2001).

[21]   Bosnia Chamber *Sretko Damjanović* v. *Fed. BiH.*, provisional measure of 16 December 1996; *Nail Rizvanović* v. *Fed.BiH*, provisional measure of 2 September 1997 and *Borislav Herak* v. *Fed. BiH*, provisional measure of 10 November 1997.

[22]   In 1957 the UK respected the Commission's informal provisional measures in the *Cyprus* case (*Greece* v. *UK*) not to execute Nicolas Sampson. See EComHR *Application of the European Convention of Human Rights and Fundamental Freedoms to the Island of Cyprus* (*Greece* v. *UK*), report of the Commission, 26 September 1958, §34; in 1970 Greece, under the Colonels' regime, respected the Commission's provisional measures to halt the execution of 34 suspects. Partial Decision of the Commission as to the admissibility of the application, *The Second Greek case* (*Denmark, Norway and Sweden* v. *Greece),* 5 October 1970, §11.

[23]   ECtHR *Öcalan* v. *Turkey*, Judgment of 12 March 2003 (provisional measure of 30 November 1999 respected. See also Grand Chamber Judgment 12 May 2005.

The great majority of the HRC's provisional measures to halt executions have been respected.[24] Only in some cases the Committee's decisions on the merits specifically refer to domestic decisions to stay an execution, possibly in part on the basis of the Committee's provisional
measures. States normally give no reasons for compliance with provisional measures or with
other decisions. It is only when they disagree that they may provide some arguments and that they
may even decide not to comply with them altogether.[25] In light of the foregoing, the most obvious
examples showing the attitude of the State party are cases of blatant disregard for the Committee's provisional measures. Trinidad and Tobago, Guyana, Sierra Leone, the Philippines, Uzbekistan and Tajikistan have executed petitioners despite provisional measures. In response, the HRC
has expressed itself forcefully about the legal obligation of States under the OP to respect its
provisional measures and to halt executions pending the proceedings before it.[26] Jamaica was the
addressee of the majority of provisional measures. This State always respected the Committee's
provisional measures, but it withdrew from the OP in 1997.[27] The responses of States to provi-

---

[24] During the period 1986-2004 information was examined about provisional measures to halt
executions in cases against two Asian States (South Korea and the Philippines), against five
States of the former Soviet Union (Georgia, Belarus, Uzbekistan, Tajikistan and Ukraine) and
two African States (Sierra Leone and Zambia). The remainder of cases were all directed to
Caribbean States: one to St. Vincent and the Grenadines, eight to Guyana, 24 to Trinidad and
Tobago and 112 to Jamaica.

[25] In 1995 Trinidad and Tobago responded to the HRC that it would not respect its provisional
measure because it was already respecting the conservatory order of the Court of Appeal. The
HRC considered 'this situation should have made it easier for the State party to confirm that there
would be no obstacles to acceding to the Committee's request; to do so would, in any event, have
been compatible with the State party's international obligations', HRC *Lincoln Guerra and Brian
Wallen* v. *Trinidad and Tobago*, 4 April 1995, §6.5.

[26] It has been very clear about the seriousness of the breach by these States of their obligations
under the OP and the Covenant itself. It referred in particular to the obligation to cooperate with
it in good faith, the obligation not to hinder its task to examine the case on the merits as well as to
the obligations under Article 2 ICCPR. It has pointed out that the executions rendered
examination by the HRC moot and the expression of its Views 'nugatory and futile'. It also
pointed out that a State should not execute petitioners once it knows they have submitted a case
to the HRC, even when the Committee has not (yet) used provisional measures. See also Chapter
XVI (Legal status) and Chapter XVIII (Follow-up).

[27] It withdrew on 23 October 1997. This became effective on 23 January 1998. Jamaica has always
respected the provisional measures by the Committee, although it did point out that they could
sometimes amount to an indefinite stay of execution and could, therefore, obstruct its
administration of justice. In January 1998 its withdrawal from the OP became effective. It
withdrew exactly because it wished to be able to execute its prisoners within the deadline set by
the JCPC. The withdrawal of Jamaica, followed by that of Trinidad and Tobago and Guyana,
from the individual complaint system has been deplored internationally. The reason for the
withdrawals related to the deadline set by the JCPC combined with the factor public opinion.
Already in June 1994 the Jamaica Council for Human Rights provided the HRC with extracts of
two speeches made to Parliament by the Minister of National Security and Justice, forewarning
the 1997 withdrawal. In the first speech the Minister pointed out that appeals to the UN Human
Rights Committee and to the Inter-American Commission on Human Rights had become the
standard practice for persons sentenced to death whose appeals had been dismissed. "This in
itself constitutes a source of considerable delay since a sentence of death could not be carried out
whilst an appeal to one or other of these bodies is pending. To make matters worse the rules of
these organisations not only permit but actually require that an applicant has to appeal to each of
them in sequence. The proceedings cannot be shortened by simultaneous hearings". The Minister

sional measures to halt executions have varied from explicitly positive, to silence and even blatant disregard. There seems to be a continuum between the above extremes, including granting a stay, conditional compliance (which could partially be attributed to the adjudicators' provisional measures), domestic courts refusing to take into account the adjudication and explicit refusal by State authorities to respect provisional measures, culminating in an execution.

2.2.2.2 EXPLICITLY POSITIVE RESPONSE BY THE STATE

In some cases the State expressly informs the HRC that it will comply with the provisional measures to halt the execution of a death sentence.[28] Of course while the international involvement, including the use of provisional measures, may play a role, this is not necessarily the case. Several cases of compliance with provisional measures halting executions of death sentences may also be attributed to the fact that there is a national policy of putting executions on hold,[29] or on the fact that a domestic court or an executive has decided to commute the death sentence of the petitioner.[30] Six days after using provisional measures to halt the execution of two

---

noted that this had put Jamaica in an 'intolerable situation'. His Ministry and that of Foreign Affairs and Foreign Trade were 'in dialogue with the international organisations to get concrete implementation of the general assurances given to speed up the hearing'. This way they hoped to be able to enforce their 'own laws without depriving the convicts of their right to appeal to these international bodies'. "If a solution is not found, then we will have to take the serious but necessary step of curtailing the rights to appeal to one or other of these two bodies". He noted that the people of Jamaica had been calling for the resumption of hanging and that he wished to assure the public that 'this Government does not intend to abandon our sovereign right to implement our own laws'. "In this country death remains the penalty for capital murder and therefore must be carried out with as much efficiency and effectiveness as any other prescription in the judicial system". The other speech discussed certain steps to be taken to speed up the appellate process in Jamaica, but it also pointed out that there should be a strict time-table of 21 days for appealing to the JCPC in London, followed by a time-limit of 21 days for appeals to international human rights bodies. Letter of the Jamaica Council for Human Rights, 29 June 1994, with extracts of the Minister's speeches (on file with the author).

[28] See e.g. HRC *Matlyuba Khudayberganova on behalf of her son Iskandar Khudayberganov* v. *Uzbekistan*, 24 July 2007, §2.1: on 11 December 2003, the State party replied that the Supreme Court had deferred the execution, pending the Committee's final decision. States may fail to submit any observations on the admissibility or merits of a claim, showing a lack of co-operation generally, but still respond positively to the Committee's provisional measures. See also, e.g., HRC *Bernhard Lubuto* v. *Zambia*, 31 October 1995. The State confirmed that 'pursuant to the Committee's request, the appropriate authorities have been instructed not to carry out the death sentence against the author while his case is before the Committee'.

[29] This may be the case, for instance, with regard to Zambia.

[30] See e.g. HRC *Trevor Ellis* v. *Jamaica*, 28 July 1992; *Karina Arutyunyan on behalf of her brother Arsen Arutyunyan* v. *Uzbekistan*, 29 March 2004, §1.2; *Abdukarim Boimurodov on behalf of son Mustafakul Boimurodov* v. *Tajikistan*, 20 October 2005, §2.7; *Nazira Sirageva on behalf of her son Danis Siragev* v. *Uzbekistan*, 1 November 2005, §1.2; *Nadezhda Agabekova on behalf of her son Valery Agabekov* v. *Uzbekistan*, 16 March 2006, §§1.2 and 4.2; *Larisa Tarasova on behalf of her son Alexander Kornetov* v. *Uzbekistan*, 20 October 2006, §§1.2.

petitioners the HRC received a response by the Chairman of the State Committee for Human Rights and Ethnic Relations of the Republic of Georgia.[31]

> "The State Committee for Human Rights and Ethnic Relations of the Republic of Georgia regards as its obligation to ensure the full enjoyment by the convicted of all the rights that are granted to them by the Georgian legislation and international instruments. We will also do our best to help commute the death penalty to one of imprisonment".[32]

It is not clear what exactly is the function of this State Committee in the system of government in Georgia, but given the fact that the authority to provide the HRC with an official response was delegated to this State Committee, it may be assumed that the State would at least respect the provisional measures by the HRC and stay the execution upon exhaustion of domestic remedies. The State Committee, moreover, also committed itself to strive for a permanent stay of execution in the form of a commutation. Subsequently the Ministry of Foreign Affairs and not the State Committee on Human Rights informed the HRC of the Decree of the President of Georgia of July 1997 pardoning 54 persons and replacing their death sentences by twenty years imprisonment. It pointed out that Gelbakhiani and Dokvadze were among these 54 persons.[33]

An interesting example of a case in which a stay was granted following receipt of provisional measures by the HRC is *Marshall* v. *Jamaica* (1998).[34] In this case London counsel submitted a complaint to the HRC in December 1996. The action by counsel had been triggered by a fax from the Secretary of the Governor-General of Jamaica, stating, among others, that the HRC had not yet registered Marshall's case:

> "[O]ur process for implementing the sentence imposed has commenced and only a request from the U.N. under Rule 86 will stop it, so I would suggest that as a matter of urgency you get your application fully in order so that that office can decide whether a Rule 86 request is merited".

The fax ended with 'D Day is December 12, 1996'. Counsel replied to this fax on the same day, expressing 'extreme surprise', referring to Marshall's initial communication to the HRC of June 1995 and to an agreement with the Jamaican government's solicitors in London that they would await the reclassification process before they would take further steps in Marshall's case. They received a response on the same day, pointing out that other counsel did seem to realize that the reclassification process had been finalized two weeks previously. The Office of the Governor-General referred to the JCPC's remark in *Pratt and Morgan* that 'where nothing is done to pursue remedies it is up to the authorities to issue a writ and galvanize the prisoner and his legal

---

[31] HRC *Victor Domukovsky, Zaza Tsiklauri, Petre Gelbakhiani and Irakli Dokvadze* v. *Georgia*, 6 April 1998. Provisional measures were used on behalf of Gelbakhiani and Dokvadze. Chairman of the State Committee for Human Rights and Ethnic Relations wrote that the convicted 'and other interested persons' had the right to appeal a death sentence. The Chairman of the Collegium of the Supreme Court on Criminal Cases would first examine such complaint. If he would refuse it, the Chairman of the Supreme Court could consider the appeal. The Prosecutor General also had the right to re-examine the case. If the death sentence would still remain in force, the execution would be deferred until the Pardon Commission had examined it. He also noted that Georgia had acceded to the OP in the previous year so that the HRC could examine the case.

[32] Letter by the Chairman of the State Committee for Human Rights and Ethnic Relations, 16 March 1996 (on file with the author).

[33] Letter of the Ministry of Foreign Affairs of 9 September 1997 (on file with the author).

[34] HRC *Clarence Marshall* v. *Jamaica*, 3 November 1998, Note Verbale of 5 December 1996, submission of 4 December 1996 (on file with the author).

representatives into action'. It reminded them that it 'need not have faxed you at all' and pointed out: "We await the views of the U.N. as to whether the application will merit a request under Rule 86".[35] Once it did receive a Note Verbale with a decision on provisional measures, the State informed the Committee that it 'stood down the warrants for the abovementioned persons'.[36]

2.2.2.3 LEVEL OF COMPLIANCE BY TRINIDAD WITH PROVISIONAL MEASURES OF THE INTER-AMERICAN COMMISSION AND COURT

In the death penalty cases pending before the Inter-American Commission States often do not reply to the Commission's precautionary measures requesting a stay of execution. Trinidad, for instance, is not much inclined to comply with the Commission's precautionary measures. It may request for information on the case itself, but fail to reply to the precautionary measure as such. In the case of Mr. Baptiste the State simply informed the Commission again that the Instructions Relating to Applications from Persons under Sentence of Death issued by the Government of Trinidad and Tobago on 13 October 1997 also applied to his application.[37]

From the end of 1998 for Trinidad and Tobago the pattern changed from (semi-)compliance to non-compliance, also with regard to the Court. In its Order of May 1999 the Court notes that the State had not complied with the obligation to submit periodic reports on the status of the appeals and regularly scheduled executions of the beneficiaries of the Court's provisional measures.[38] Only in the second half of 2000 the State showed some willingness again to comply with its reporting obligations.[39]

---

[35] Information letter to the counsel by the State, 3 December 1996 (on file with the author).

[36] In his complaint of 4 December 1996 counsel pointed out that a warrant had been issued for the execution of his client on 12 December 1996. On 4 December the Secretariat had also received an anonymous telegram from Jamaica, possibly sent through information by other inmates: "Keith McKnight and Clarence Marshall are at gallows from 2nd December 1996 please contact relevant authority St. Catherine Dist Prison" (on file with the author). The next morning the Secretariat faxed Special Rapporteur Pocar. That same day, after Pocar had authorized it, the Secretariat sent a Note Verbale to the Minister of Foreign Affairs and Foreign Trade informing the State of the registration of the communication and requesting it to make submissions on the admissibility of the case (under Rule 91) and not to carry out the death sentence (under Rule 86) while the HRC was considering the communication. A copy was sent to the Permanent Mission of Jamaica in Geneva. On 11 December the Secretariat received a fax from the Jamaican Mission that the Office of the Governor-General had informed it that they had received the Committee's faxes in relation to three persons, including Marshall, whose cases were pending before it, and that they 'stood down the warrants for the abovementioned persons'. Note Verbale of 5 December 1996 transmitting the case under Rule 86/91 and fax by Permanent Mission of Jamaica to U.N. Centre for Human Rights, 11 December 1996 (on file with the author).

[37] See IACHR *James et al.* cases, Order for provisional measures, 29 August 1998.

[38] The Court also considered that 'neither the State nor the Commission has informed the Court immediately and sufficiently', as required by its Order of August 1998, 'of any significant developments concerning the circumstances' of the beneficiaries. *James et al.* cases, Order for provisional measures, 25 May 1999. Here the Court also reprimands the Commission, presumably in light of the developments surrounding Mr. Briggs, who was later executed.

[39] In its Order of 26 August 2000 the Court required the State to submit information on or before the end of that month on the circumstances that led to the execution of Joey Ramiah. The State did so on 4 September 2000. The Court also required the Inter-American Commission to submit, by the end of the month, detailed information on the status of the cases of five persons. The

Trinidad and Tobago executed Mr. Briggs, arguing that the Court had no jurisdiction to maintain the provisional measures on his behalf.[40] The Court's other provisional measures to halt executions, used in the *James and Others* case have been considered to be among the most effective of its provisional measures.

With the respect shown by Trinidad for *those* provisional measures, as well as the respect by Jamaica for the provisional measures by the HRC halting executions, note must be made of the withdrawal of these States from the individual complaint system, which has been deplored internationally.[41]

2.2.3 Various responses to provisional measures to halt expulsion and extradition

2.2.3.1 INTRODUCTION

There is little information about the cases in which States complied with provisional measures in non-refoulement cases and about what role these measures played as compared to other factors

---

Commission did so on 31 August 2000. The Court had urged the State as well to report every two months on the status of the appeals and scheduled executions of all the beneficiaries. On 5 September 2000 the State informed the Court that 'pursuant to its Order' it was 'in the course of preparing its bi-monthly report on the status of the appeals and scheduled executions of *James et al.* and it would be forwarding the said report to the Court within the next fourteen days'. While this shows willingness again, on the part of the State, to comply with the Court's Orders, in October 2000 the Secretariat of the Court had to remind the State to submit its report and in November 2000 the Court considered that the State had failed to do so. IACHR *James et al.* cases, Order for provisional measures, 24 November 2000.

[40] The State considered that 'after the Commission decided to publish its Article 51 report, there was no matter pending before the Commission, nor any matter pending before the Court, nor any other matter capable of being submitted to the Court'. It concluded that the Court's 'purported Order of 25 May 1999 was made without jurisdiction and, therefore, was null'. IACHR *James et al.* cases, Order for provisional measures, 16 August 2000, 13th 'Having seen' clause.

[41] Several States protested against the reservation by Trinidad and Tobago. With this reservation it purported to re-accede to the OP. They considered that obligations should not be watered down to such an extent that they become devoid of any meaning. Denmark, Norway and the Netherlands objected on 6 August 1999; Germany on 13 August, Sweden on 17 August, Ireland on 23 August, Spain on 25 August, France on 9 September and Italy on 17 September 1999, www.un.org (consulted on 7 October 2004). Clearly, the persons most likely to wish to make use of the individual complaint procedure have deplored this withdrawal. One death row inmate from Jamaica, for instance, wrote in June 2000: "People in this country, the Government of Jamaica don't know what he did when he withdraw from the United Nations, he just make a mistake, from that he keep on making mistake (...) this country is in a lot of danger at this time. (...) The prison is like a time bomb waiting to go off. Also the Governor General of Jamaica considered the United Nations for human rights recommendation, but they rejected them all. Also they did not let me know that they did this. (...) I went to the condemned cell at the gallows two time now and it was not easy over there. I don't want to go back over this place again. This place will mad any man. (...) At this time we don't have any more appeals to go through, we went through all the bodies. Also the Government of Jamaica is planning to withdraw from the Privy Council very soon. (...) Also please tell me what you think about the Caribbean Court? This Government is planning to carry out hanging in this country. Also most of the peoples of the Caribbean want to see hanging carried out". (on file with the author).

favouring a stay of expulsion or extradition. Most cases in which expulsion or extradition was stayed do not indicate the specific response of the State. It is mainly in the context of non-compliance that some information is available about the attitudes of States towards provisional measures.

This subsection first gives some examples of compliance and non-compliance. Then it discusses three strategies by States unwilling to respect provisional measures: the speed of deportation as a way to pre-empt the use of provisional measures; requesting the adjudicator to withdraw provisional measures and invoking contrary obligations under international law.

2.2.3.2 EXAMPLES OF COMPLIANCE AND NON-COMPLIANCE IN THE EUROPEAN SYSTEM AND UNDER THE ICCPR

Various cases in which the adjudicator took provisional measures are subsequently solved and struck out. It may well be that provisional measures trigger a renewed consideration of a decision to expel someone. Yet States may prefer not to acknowledge this formally. As part of a friendly settlement they tend to emphasize that their decision to allow a petitioner to remain in the country is based on strictly humanitarian reasons rather than a legal obligation under a human rights treaty. Sometimes they add that their decision should not be regarded as a precedent.[42]

Ms. Jabari had appealed against an order of deportation because under Iranian law she would be subject to death by stoning, whipping or flogging. The European Commission used provisional measures to stay the deportation. After Protocol 11 entered into force the Court confirmed the provisional measures, under Rule 39, until further notice. Turkey complied with the provisional measure.[43] In *Taspinar* v. *the Netherlands* (1985) the European Commission had used provisional measures on behalf of a seven year old boy facing expulsion to Turkey. The State respected the provisional measures and subsequently informed the Commission that it no longer objected to his presence in the Netherlands.[44]

Several types of non-compliance may also be observed. Interesting is the case of *Muminov* v. *Russia* (2008). On 24 October 2006 the Court had used provisional measures to prevent his expulsion to Uzbekistan. Later that day he was nevertheless expelled. Apart from the fact that this time the Court did find a violation of Article 3 – contrary to the case of *Mamatkulov* also involving a return to Uzbekistan[45] – in this case there was a lack of clarity about the moment of expulsion and the awareness by the authorities of the Court's provisional measures.[46] The Court's

---

42   See e.g. ECtHR *Tatete* v. *Switzerland*, 6 July 2000 (struck out).

43   ECtHR *Jabari* v. *Turkey*, Judgment of 11 July 2000.

44   EComHR *Taspinar* v. *the Netherlands,* 9 October 1985 (struck out). Yet there have been cases manifesting conflicting approaches within government. In *A.* v. *France* (inadm.1991) the European Commission noted 'that the deportation order was issued by the Prefect of Ain on 4 January 1991, whereas by that time, after an initial decision dated 9 October 1990 and subsequent decisions covering the period up to 18 January 1991, the Commission had decided to apply Rule 36 of its Rules of Procedure and indicated to the Government that it would be desirable in the interests of the parties and the proper conduct of the proceedings not to expel the applicant before it had had time to examine the application in greater detail'. The Commission also notes that the Prefect issued the above-mentioned order despite its use of provisional measures and while the Government had stated that they had decided to comply with the Commission's wishes, *A.* v. *France*, 27 February 1991 (inadm.), pp. 337-338.

45   See Chapter XVIII (Follow-up), section 2.3.3.

46   The Court observed that the parties disagreed as to whether the petitioner had been expelled 'before or after the Russian authorities had learnt about a Rule 39 request, as well as about the

discussion in this respect shows that it is crucial for counsel to inform the Office of the Representative of the relevant State at the European Court, as well as the detention centre or another competent authority of the fact that a request for provisional measures has been made with the Court.[47] Another intriguing aspect related to this case is the fact that apparently subsequently the Director of the Detention Centre for Aliens was convicted for abuse of power for authorising the execution of Muminov's expulsion order while being aware that this order had not become final. The verdict specifically mentioned the fact that as a result of this unlawful action Russia had been unable to comply with the European Court's provisional measure.[48]

There are also occasions in which the State first ignored the adjudicator's provisional measures, but later attempted to remedy the situation. In *Dar* v. *Norway* (2007), in violation of Article 22 ICAT, the State deported the petitioner to Pakistan despite provisional measures. On the merits CAT found that the breach of Article 22 ICAT was remedied by Norway granting him a residence permit for three years upon return. According to the Committee the issue whether deportation constituted a violation of Article 3 ICAT had become moot because complainant had returned to Norway.[49]

With regard to the HRC, in most expulsion and extradition cases States have respected its provisional measures to halt expulsion, extradition or other forms of forced return. Yet there have been cases of non-compliance. Interestingly, one case in which Canada respected a provisional measure related to the right to family life (Articles 17 and 23 ICCPR) rather than to non-refoulement (Articles 6 and 7 ICCPR). The fact that it requested the HRC to clarify its criteria for using provisional measures and to withdraw them in this case because there was no risk of irrepa-

---

actual time of his departure from the territory of Russia'. It confirmed that 'the information concerning the application of Rule 39 in the applicant's case was published on its secure website at 7.17 p.m. (Moscow time) on the same date'. It found that the petitioner 'most likely left the territory of Russia shortly before midnight (Moscow time) on 24 October 2006. The Government did not specify, however, when they had first learnt about the application of Rule 39 in the present case and whether the administration of the detention centre and other competent authorities had been notified of it, if at all', ECtHR *Muminov* v. *Russia*, Judgment of 11 December 2008, §135. It did not exclude the possibility that a State's 'failure to make practical arrangements for receiving and processing information from the Court regarding the examination of a Rule 39 request or the Court's decision to apply it in a given case may raise an issue under Article 34 of the Convention. However, in the present case the Court cannot establish with sufficient certainty that having been put on notice about the Court's decision to apply Rule 39, the respondent Government deliberately omitted to comply with it', §136. A willingness of Russian courts to comply is also shown in *Ryabikin* v. *Russia*, 19 June 2008, (the Kuybyshevskiy district court and the St. Petersburg City Court), see §§84-85. See also *Mostafa et autres* c. *Turquie*, 15 January 2008, §38.

47   The Court noted that it was 'unclear whether the applicant's lawyer – assisted by members of a non-governmental organisation helping asylum-seekers – informed the Office of the Representative of the Russian Federation at the European Court, the detention centre or another competent authority that the applicant had already lodged a request for interim measures under Rule 39 of the Rules of Court'. Accordingly, the Court noted, it could 'not consider that the respondent State was duly informed that a request under Rule 39 had already been made'. 'Against this background, the Court's assessment of the material before it leads it to find that there is an insufficient factual basis for it to conclude that the respondent State deliberately prevented the Court from taking its decision on the applicant's Rule 39 request or notifying it of that decision in a timely manner, in breach of its obligation to cooperate with the Court in good faith', ECtHR *Muminov* v. *Russia*, Judgment of 11 December 2008, §137.

48   ECtHR *Muminov* v. *Russia*, Judgment of 11 December 2008, §44.

49   CAT *Nadeem Ahmad Dar* v. *Norway*, 11 May 2007.

rable harm indicated a wish for a restrictive interpretation of the power to use provisional measures, but at the same time it showed that Canada took this power seriously and was willing to respect the Committee's provisional measures even in this case.[50] The very first case, dating from 1978, involved an unidentified State that apparently respected the provisional measure as well.[51]

In *Weiss* v. *Austria* (2003)[52] the petitioner claimed that a sentence of 845 years imprisonment in the requesting State (US) would constitute a violation of this article. The Special Rapporteur used provisional measures, although they were more cautiously formulated and their maintenance would depend on the response of the State to certain questions. The Administrative Court had also ordered a stay of his extradition. The authorities nevertheless attempted to surrender the petitioner. They only returned him to a detention facility 'after a telephone call by the ranking officer of the airport police to the president of the Administrative Court', in light of the stay granted by the Administrative Court and of the petitioner's poor health. Subsequently, however, the investigating judge of the Vienna Regional Criminal Court ordered the surrender of the petitioner, considering the Administrative Court 'incompetent' to entertain any proceedings or bar the extradition. The State extradited the petitioner to the US on 9 June 2002.[53]

2.2.3.3 PRE-EMPTING THE USE OF PROVISIONAL MEASURES: SPEED OF DEPORTATION

In *Canepa* v. *Canada* (1997) counsel suggested that one reason for the way in which the petitioner was removed, on such short notice, may have been the wish to ensure removal in advance of the Committee's use of provisional measures.[54] She also thought that the State might have depended as well on the expectation that, because of protocol, the Secretariat of the HRC would not be able to contact the State directly when the Canadian Mission in Geneva was closed.[55] The State took issue with these allegations. It noted it was a strong supporter of the HRC and took its international human rights obligations seriously. It considered that the 'facts in this case disclose no impropriety under domestic or international law'. It rejected 'the implications by counsel for Mr. Canepa that it acted in a manner that might frustrate a possible request by the Committee for interim measures'. His removal, it pointed out, did 'in no way' prejudice the consideration of his

---

[50]   HRC *Stewart* v. *Canada*, 1 November 1996. See further Chapter IV. See e.g. *C.* v. *Australia*, 28 October 2002, §4.32. The State 'stayed the deportation in response to the Committee's rule 86 request pending finalization of this matter'. See further *G.T.* v. *Australia*, 4 November 1997, *A.R.J.* v. *Australia*, 28 July 1997, *Baban* v. *Australia*, 6 August 2003 and *Bakhtiyari* v. *Australia*, 29 October 2003, *A.A.T.* v. *Hungary*, (disc.1993) and *Karker* v. *France*, 26 October 2000.

[51]   HRC *O.E.* v. *S.*, 26 July 1978.

[52]   HRC *Sholam Weiss* v. *Austria*, 3 April 2003.

[53]   On 10 May 2002 the ECtHR had used provisional measures. Six days later it decided not to prolong them, 'following representations of the State party', §2.9. See further Chapter V (Non-refoulement). The next day the Constitutional Court issued an injunction to stay the extradition until 23 May 2002. On that day this Court terminated the injunction. The petitioner once more requested the ECtHR to use provisional measures, which it denied. The next day he withdrew his application before the ECtHR. He submitted his case to the HRC, which used provisional measures.

[54]   HRC *Giosue Canepa* v. *Canada*, 3 April 1997. Chapter XVI (Legal status), section 2.4.3 discusses the attitude of the adjudicators to frustration of the right of petition through pre-emption of the possibility to request provisional measures.

[55]   HRC *Giosue Canepa* v. *Canada*, 3 April 1997, Submission by counsel of 7 June 1994 (on file with the author).

case by the Committee, nor 'affect the position that Canada might take' about its determination on the merits. It wished to assure the HRC of its 'full and continued cooperation'.[56] Independent of whether the State party or counsel was correct in this particular case (and independent of whether this case would have been an appropriate candidate for provisional measures),[57] it cannot be excluded that some States may wish to quickly undertake certain action before provisional measures are used aiming at halting such action.

There is at least one case in which the HRC was unable to use provisional measures given the speed of the deportation. This case, *Judge* v. *Canada* (2003), should have been an extradition case. The petitioner had requested a stay until Canada would seek and receive an extradition request from the US. If removed under the bilateral extradition treaty with the US the State could have asked for assurances against execution of the death penalty. However, he was deported on the day he submitted his petition, leaving no opportunity for the HRC to use provisional measures. Counsel pointed out that he was removed within hours after a court decision that was handed down 'late evening'. Subsequently the State argued that the petitioner had not exhausted domestic remedies for his complaint about his deportation to the US. The Committee noted that the State 'had not contested the speed with which the author was deported, after the decision of the Superior Court'. Thus, 'irrespective of whether the author could have appealed his case on the merits' it found that 'it would be unreasonable to expect the author to appeal such a case after his deportation, the very act which was claimed to violate the Covenant'.[58]

2.2.3.4 REQUESTS FOR WITHDRAWAL OF PROVISIONAL MEASURES

In July 1978, in the early expulsion case of *O.E.* v. *S* (disc. 1978) the HRC expressed its appreciation to the Addressee State about the information it provided in response to its request whether it was contemplating the alleged victim's deportation or extradition to country X. Nevertheless, 'pending further consideration of the case', the Committee still considered that the alleged victim should not be handed over or expelled to that country.[59] In two expulsion cases against Australia the State also respected the Committee's provisional measures. About eleven months after it had used them in *A.R.J.* v. *Australia* (1997)[60] the Attorney General of Australia transmitted a letter to the Chairman of the Committee in which he requested the HRC to withdraw the provisional measures, pointing out, among others, that the continued detention of the petitioner was the Committee's responsibility.[61] He noted that the authorities had placed the petitioner under immigration detention in October 1996 and would keep him there 'as long as the Committee had not reached a final decision on his claims'. This remark signifies, on the one hand, the State party's willingness to respect the Committee's provisional measures and stay the return of the petitioner to Iran pending the proceedings. On the other hand it shows the State's disagreement with the

---

[56] HRC *Giosue Canepa* v. *Canada*, 3 April 1997, Submission by the State of 13 June 1994 (on file with the author).

[57] See Conclusion Part II.

[58] HRC *Judge* v. *Canada*, 5 August 2003. §7.6. The petitioner had been removed 'in the early hours of 7 August 1998, before any appeal could be launched'. Previous decision had been 'rendered orally on 6 August 1998, at approximately 20:00'. See §6.4.

[59] HRC *O.E.* v. *S.*, 26 July 1978. In other words, it maintained its provisional measures. Later that year it discontinued the case.

[60] The HRC used provisional measures on 3 April 1996. *A.R.J.* v. *Australia*, 28 July 1997.

[61] He pointed out that 'the author had been convicted of a serious criminal offence, after having entered Australia with the express purpose of committing a crime'. The immigration authorities had 'given his applications full and careful consideration'.

provisional measure, hinting at the argument that the Committee is no fourth instance of appeal and emphasising the importance of its sovereign decision-making on law enforcement and immigration. The State pointed out, moreover, that the petitioner's continued detention was the Committee's responsibility. This indicates that the stay (and continued detention) was indeed triggered by the Committee's provisional measure.[62] The State urged the Committee to give priority to the case. Requesting the HRC to decide on the petitioner's claims on a priority basis is not the same as requesting it to withdraw its provisional measure. It is possible that its primary request was withdrawal and its subsidiary request was giving the case priority. The Attorney General addressed his letter to the Chairman of the Committee, rather than to the Special Rapporteur.[63]

In *G.T.* v. *Australia* (1996)[64] the Geneva Secretariat advised the petitioner to keep the Committee informed of the developments in her husband's case and contact it immediately if he were under imminent threat of deportation.[65] The Australian government submitted its comments on the admissibility and merits of the complaint only much later. This submission mainly dealt with evidentiary requirements, particularly the standard of proof.[66] It requested the HRC to lift its provisional measures. It referred to assurances it had received from the Malaysian government that it would not prosecute its nationals for offences committed overseas.[67]

---

[62] The State had requested the HRC to examine admissibility and merits at the same time. It pointed out that, following his application under the section of the Migration Act, allowing the Minister to grant persons the right to stay in Australia for humanitarian reasons, he had received a further bridging visa until July 1997 and if the Minister had not considered his request by then, he would be eligible for an extension of the visa.

[63] See also the decision of the HRC during its 55th session in 1995 about the competence of the Chairman to decide on provisional measures once the Working Group on Communications had taken up the question of admissibility. The Committee considered Australia's request that same month, during its 59th session. In its View the HRC noted that it gave this request 'careful consideration'. It decided that 'on the balance of the material before it, the request for interim protection should be maintained, and that the admissibility and the merits of the petitioner's case should be considered during the 60th session'. Joining the admissibility and merits was possible under the rules of procedure. The HRC has since decided to take this approach as a general rule, but at the time it may have been a response to the State's request to treat the case on a priority basis. In any case, it expressed its appreciation about the fact that the State had also provided information and observation on the merits, although it was challenging the admissibility. This enabled the Committee to accelerate the proceedings. See further Chapter XIV on the relationship with admissibility and jurisdiction on the merits.

[64] HRC *Mrs. G.T.* v. *Australia*, 4 November 1997.

[65] Letter of the Secretariat to the petitioner of 19 March 1997 in *G.T.* v. *Australia*, 706/1996 (on file with the author).

[66] See Chapter XV (Immediacy and risk).

[67] Malaysia had explained that it may charge a Malaysian national on other offences that he may have committed in Malaysia. Australia added that it had informed the petitioner's husband of these assurances two years previously and that he had responded that this information was 'very comforting and reassuring'. Three months before its request to lift the provisional measures in *G.T.*, Australia had addressed the Committee with a similar request in *A.R.J.* Different from that case, here the View did not inform us of the Committee's reply, if any, to the request. In October 1997 the petitioner requested the HRC to maintain its provisional measures. The petitioner pointed out that her husband committed a criminal offence in Malaysia under legislation providing for the mandatory death penalty for trafficking drugs. She also explained that another inmate in prison wrote his reply to the aforementioned assurances of 1995 and 'that her husband signed the letter thinking it was a thank you letter in general terms'. She noted that his knowledge of English was limited and that he could not read or write it. Australia noted that it had

In one case, *E.G.* v. *Canada* (disc. 1997), counsel for the petitioner noted 'with satisfaction that the Canadian Government has requested the withdrawal of interim protection, because this would appear to indicate that the Canadian Government now accepts the legitimacy of interim measures and, implicitly at least, its obligation to respect the requests of the Committee pursuant to Rule 86'.[68]

2.2.3.5 INVOKING CONTRARY OBLIGATIONS UNDER INTERNATIONAL LAW

Sometimes contrary obligations under international law have been invoked. The UK defended its decision to ignore the provisional measures by the European Court to halt the transfer of two detainees in Iraq from the UK authorities to the Iraqi authorities[69] by reference to a domestic court decision 'and its analysis of the application of the European Convention of Human Rights and the broader requirements of international law', considering that it had 'no lawful option other than transfer to the Iraqi authorities'.[70] Apparently the State had also pointed out that the ECtHR had asked the UK to retain power in Iraq of the two petitioners when the UK had 'no legal power to do so. Compliance with Strasbourg requests would normally be a matter of course but these are exceptional circumstances'.[71]

---

assurances from the government of Malaysia that it would not prosecute the petitioner again 'in connection to the drug trafficking offences for which he was convicted in Australia and that no question of double jeopardy would arise'. In this light Australia considered that the petitioner was 'not at risk of imposition of a capital sentence should he be returned to Malaysia and, consequently, the Rule 86 request should be lifted'. Submission by the State of 3 June 1997 in *G.T.* v. *Australia*, 706/1996 (on file with the author). See about the often doubtful nature of assurances: Human Rights Watch (2004), also making reference to the more recent Concluding Observations of the HRC about the adequacy of assurances and the credibility of post-return monitoring mechanisms, pp. 10-12. On two occasions, one in 1993 and one in 1997 Canada respected the Committee's provisional measures. *Stewart* v. *Canada*, 1 November 1996, 538/1993, Rule 86 of 26 April 1993 and 18 March 1994; *E.G.* v. *Canada*, 17 November 1997 (disc.) 738/1997, Rule 86 of 17 January 1997.

[68] HRC *E.G.* v. *Canada* (738/1997), initial submission 5 January 1997 (received 7 January 1997), Rule 86/91 of 17 January 1997; withdrawal of Rule 86 on 28 April 1997; petitioner's request to withdraw the case of 26 May 1997. On 17 November 1997 the HRC informed the author that it had discontinued the case (on file with the author).

[69] See ECtHR provisional measures of 30 December 2008 by the Acting President of the Fourth Section. A scan of the ECtHR letter to counsel confirming its use of provisional measures was posted at <http://humanrightsdoctorate.blogspot.com/2009/01/uk-breaches-provisional-measures.html>.

[70] See the reference to the State's Letter dated 31 December 2008 from Derek Walton, Agent of the Government of the United Kingdom to Mr T.L. Early, Section Registrar, European Court of Human Rights in: UK House of Commons Joint Committee on Human Rights, Letter by Chair Andrew Dismore MP to the Secretary of State for Defence, 13 January 2009, expressing concern regarding the transfer contrary to the European Court's provisional measures and requesting clarifications, <http://www.parliament.uk/documents/upload/JCHRAlSaadon.pdf>.

[71] See the reference to statements published in the Independent, *Pair accused of murder handed over to Iraqi authorities,* 31 December 2008, in: UK House of Commons Joint Committee on Human Rights, Letter by Chair Andrew Dismore MP to the Secretary of State for Defence, 13 January 2009, expressing concern regarding the transfer contrary to the European Court's provisional measures and requesting clarifications, <http://www.parliament.uk/documents/upload/JCHRAlSaadon.pdf>.

These arguments are faulty. Given the difference in international obligations at stake the 'broader requirements of international law' were those based on the ECHR and the UK should have told the Iraqi authorities that it had 'no lawful option' other than compliance with the Court's provisional measures. Indeed, parliamentary concern was expressed in response to the transfer and the government's justification for it. Detailed information on the provisional measures and the transfer was requested, as well as a 'a more detailed a more detailed explanation of the Government's view that its decision to transfer the applicants is compatible with the right of individual petition secured by Article 34 ECHR, in the light of the interim measures decision of the European Court of Human Rights. In particular: a. Why does the Government consider it was appropriate to ignore the interim measures decision of the European Court on the basis of the UK courts' interpretation of international law, and on the application of the ECHR? b. Does the Government agree that the final interpretation of the Convention and the scope of its application is a matter for the ECHR? If not, please explain the Government's view'.[72]

2.2.4 Various responses to provisional measures to intervene in detention and disappearance cases

2.2.4.1 DISAPPEARANCE CASES

While not much information is available about the Inter-American Commission's intervention in disappearance cases there are indications that these may have some effect, especially when it intervenes shortly after a disappearance.[73]

Colombia established an urgent search mechanism, at least partially in light of its obligations under the ACHR and other human rights treaties.[74] The Commission has in turn invoked this mechanism when it used precautionary measures. On 18 December 2001 the Commission used such measures to determine the whereabouts of two persons from the region of Antioquia and to

---

[72] UK House of Commons Joint Committee on Human Rights, Letter by Chair Andrew Dismore MP to the Secretary of State for Defence, 13 January 2009, expressing concern regarding the transfer contrary to the European Court's provisional measures and requesting clarifications, <http://www.parliament.uk/documents/upload/JCHRAlSaadon.pdf>.

[73] In March 1997, for instance, lawyers collective 'José Alvear Restrepo' in Colombia requested the Commission to take precautionary measures on behalf of one of its lawyers. Members of the National Police in Bogotá had arbitrarily detained him after a demonstration involving professors and students. CEJIL notes that the Commission immediately requested information from the Colombian government with regard to his detention and that he was freed the next day. Case of Mr. Vilalba Vargas, CEJIL case docket 1997. It is not clear whether the Commission simply requested information or indeed formally took precautionary measures. This example involves a specific type of threat to a human rights defender who is detained in unclear circumstances conducive to such disappearance. On 28 January 1999 the Commission was informed that a group of armed civilians had forcefully entered the headquarters of the Popular Training Institute (IPC) in Medellin, Antioquia and had abducted four investigators of the IPC. The Commission immediately took precautionary measures, that same afternoon. It urgently contacted Colombia to take the necessary measures to ascertain the whereabouts of the victims and protect their lives, physical integrity and liberty. Two of them were freed on 11 February and the two others on 19 February 1999. The 'Autodefensas' of Córdoba and Urabá had claimed responsibility for the kidnappings. Annual Report 1999, Chapter III.C.1, §17.

[74] See Law 589/2000, 10 July 2000, criminalizing enforced disappearance, instituting a national search mechanism including an urgent search mechanism.

protect their lives and persons. They were last seen on 27 November 2001 at a Medellín metropolitan police checkpoint. A few days later the two men contacted their families and told them a paramilitary group had abducted them. In its Annual Report the Commission notes that it 'undertook a series of steps toward clearing up this situation during its on-site visit'. This visit had taken place from 7 until 13 December, but apparently these steps had not been sufficiently effective as the Commission resorted to the formal issuance of precautionary measures. As part of these measures it asked Colombia to 'launch a prompt and effective investigation using the urgent search mechanism established by Law 589/2000'.[75] Again, the Commission does not indicate the precise contents of the State reply but it does note that it continued to receive information from the parties with regard to the situation of the protected persons.[76]

2.2.4.2 HEALTH AND SAFETY IN DETENTION

In the early detention cases dealt with by the HRC, involving political prisoners, it appeared that State parties sometimes were more willing to respond to inquiries about health situations than to the claim on the merits relating to arbitrary detention etc. At other times Uruguay, the State most often involved, simply responded by denying admissibility.[77] The responses with regard to the health situation of political detainees ranged from blanket denial to precise information on medi-

---

[75] CIDH Annual Report 2001, §26.

[76] Ibid.

[77] The great majority of detention cases from the 1970s and 1980s relates to Uruguay, which at that time was led by a military junta. Other Latin American States from which such detention cases could have originated only recognized the right of individual complaint after a regime change. Uruguay, on the other hand, had ratified the OP in March 1976. Its military dictatorship lasted from 1973 to 1985. The State argued that the HRC exceeded its authority by dealing with complaints by detainees. In *Sendic*, for instance, the HRC had urged the State to provide information on the health and whereabouts of the petitioner's husband, to transmit all the written material, such as submissions of the parties and the decisions of the HRC in this case to Raúl Sendic himself and allow him to communicate directly with the Committee. The State particularly protested the latter part of this decision, arguing that the HRC had 'absolutely no basis' for its request to give 'a detainee under the jurisdiction of the State party' the opportunity to communicate directly with it. Accepting this decision would 'create a dangerous precedent'. It considered that the HRC had violated 'international instruments such as the Covenant and its Protocol'. Uruguay considered that the provisions in these instruments extended to State parties as subjects of international law. "Thus these international norms, like any agreement of such nature, are applicable to States and not directly to individuals. Consequently, the Committee can hardly claim that this decision extends to any particular individual". The State even went so far as to argue that the Committee's decision violated elementary principles and norms 'and thus indicates that the Committee is undermining its commitments in respect of the course of promoting and defending human rights'. The HRC pointed out that the State's argument was 'devoid of legal foundation' because it had recognised the OP and, thus, the Committee's competence to receive and consider communications from individuals. It pointed out that 'denying individuals who are victims of an alleged violation their right to bring the matter before the Committee is tantamount to denying the mandatory nature of the Optional Protocol'. The ability of detainees to communicate directly with the Committee was, in fact, a prerequisite for the effective application of the OP. Governments had no right to create obstacles to this communication. Such obstacles would, in many cases, render meaningless the individual complaint procedure. HRC *Raul Sendic Antonaccio (submitted by his wife Violeta Setelich)* v. *Uruguay*, 28 October 1981.

cal treatment. Especially in the last two detention cases against Uruguay this State provided detailed information using medical terminology.[78] It is clear that the HRC rewarded this because in these cases it did not find a violation with regard to the alleged victims' health situations and it did not recommend the State to ensure adequate medical treatment.

While the general attitude of Uruguay with regard to the HRC's examination of cases of political prisoners in the 1970s and 1980s was far from cooperative, it is possible that the interest expressed by the HRC about the health of certain detainees has played a role not only in the State's decision to provide information but also in its decision to provide medical care. In any case it is likely that the HRC intended its requests for information at least partially to trigger such reaction and, thereby, to put a halt to continuing violations and prevent further irreparable harm. Of course, the Committee itself has expressly referred to the other reason for requesting information about an alleged victim's state of health: as necessary evidence to determine whether there has been a violation. Between August 1984 and 1 March 1985, when the newly elected government of Uruguay came to power, several people were released and cooperation improved dramatically since that time.

The Inter-American Commission has regularly intervened in detention situations, In August 2001, for instance, it took precautionary measures on behalf of an inmate at a women's penitentiary in Lima. The petitioners in her case had informed the Commission that her health problems included mobile breast lumps.[79] Specialized examinations were necessary to identify their nature and treatment. The Commission requested Peru to immediately provide the medical examinations necessary to protect her health. The State responded that it was providing her with medical attention and administered the medical exams necessary to protect her health.[80]

In 2003, in a case involving psychiatric patients the Commission used precautionary measures in the face of information about female patients having been raped, children held together with adults and two youths that 'were kept for more than four years in solitary confinement in small cells, naked, and without access to the bathrooms'. It asked Paraguay to adopt measures to protect the 'life and physical, mental, and moral integrity' of these two youths as well as the other 458 patients. In response the State noted that two weeks after it received the precautionary measures the President of Paraguay, together with the Minster of Public Health and Social Welfare 'visited the hospital to learn more about the situation. After their visit, action was taken, as the director was replaced and an audit was launched'.[81]

2.2.4.3 IMMIGRATION DETENTION INVOLVING MINORS

The HRC has dealt with immigration detention involving children. In *Bakhtiari family* v. *Australia* (2003)[82] the Rapporteur had requested the State to inform the Committee of the measures it had taken on the basis of the evaluation by Australia's own expert authorities that the children and their mother should have ongoing assessment outside of the Woomera detention centre in order to prevent further acts of self-harm. The State observed that it was closely monitoring the family and that there were individual care and case management plans in place that were regularly reviewed. It considered that release from detention would not be appropriate. 'Its processes had determined

---

[78]   HRC *Estradet Cabreira* v. *Uruguay*, 21 July 1983 and *Manera Lluberas* v. *Uruguay*, 6 April 1984.

[79]   CIDH Annual Report 2001, Chapter III C1, §50.

[80]   Ibid.

[81]   CIDH Annual Report 2003, Chapter III C1, §60.

[82]   HRC *Bakhtiari family* v. *Australia*, 29 October 2003.

that it did not owe protection obligations to Mrs Bakhtiyari and her children'. Moreover, 'the Minister personally considered the case, inter alia in the light of the State party's obligations including the Covenant, and decided that it would not be in the public interest to substitute a more favourable decision'. Finally, the State considered it inappropriate to release the children and their mother when their father's visa was under consideration for cancellation for alleged fraud.[83]

According to the State Article 24(1) ICCPR should not be interpreted as if it were the Convention on the Rights of the Child. Referring to its previous response to 'the Committee's request for information pursuant to Rule 86', it submitted that it had met its obligations with regard to the Bakhtiyari children. It added that 'all staff in detention facilities must advice local child protection authorities if they consider a child is at risk of harm'. Arrangements had been formalised in this respect. Moreover, in light of the concern about their well-being, 'special protective measures were implemented'.[84] Subsequently, however, the children and their parents were released following family court decisions.[85]

---

[83]   See HRC *Bakhtiari family* v. *Australia*, 29 October 2003, §§4.3 and 4.4.

[84]   "An officer has been specifically assigned to monitor the children's participation in educational and recreational activities, and to work with Mrs Bakhtiyari to encourage these ends. Records indicate that the two eldest boys attend school regularly, use computer facilities, play soccer regularly and attend exercise classes. They attend regular pool excursions and enjoy watching television, while Muntazar has actively taught other children cycling. Of the other children, the school-aged girls attend school and participate in recreational activities, including sewing with their mother".

[85]   On 19 June 2003 the Family Court determined that the prolonged detention of children was unlawful. It considered that there was an obligation under the UN Convention on the Rights of the Child to protect minors held in custody. Family Court, *B and B* v. *Minister for Immigration & Multicultural and Indigenous Affairs* [2003] FamCA 451, judgment of 19 June 2003, see www.familycourt.gov.au. It found that its jurisdiction extended to protection against prospective as well as present harm, including by third party. The appeal was initially brought on behalf of two boys aged fourteen and twelve. Their three sisters of eleven, nine and six were later added. In this light all three judges considered that the Court did have jurisdiction to make certain protective orders concerning in immigration detention (including those related to medical and educational facilities). The majority considered that if it was to be determined at trial that the children were being held in detention indefinitely, this would be unlawful. They considered that for the purposes of this case the UN Convention on the Rights of the Child had been incorporated into the Family Law Act by the Family Reform Act of 1995, pursuant to the external affairs power in the Constitution. They also considered that the Migration Act should be interpreted as having been passed subject to Australia's obligations under the Children's Convention or having regard to them. The Court ordered that the case be remitted for rehearing as a matter of urgency. Following this decision several political parties called for the release of the approximately 107 children. The Labor party called upon the Government to immediately move families seeking asylum out of detention and into supervised housing, Agence France-Presse (via ClariNet), 'Release detained families now, opposition urges Australia's Howard', 21 June 2003, quickstart.Clari.net. The Democrats also emphasised this both following and previous to the landmark decision, Australian Democrats Senator Andrew Bartlett, media releases 03/373 and 03/443 of 28 May and 20 June respectively, AusNews, AusIssues.com. Finally, the Greens equally re-emphasised that the 107 children should be released, Australian Greens-Federal leader Senator Bob Brown, media release of 19 June 2003, AusNews, AusIssues.com (consulted 13 August 2003). In July 2003 the State party informed the Committee that Mrs Bakhtiyari and her three daughters 'were currently resident in the Woomera Residential Housing Project, a facility aimed at special needs of women and children'. They were able to leave the house, provided they were escorted by correctional officers. By that time Mr Bakhtiyari was detained as well and the

Again it is unclear what role the Committee may have played. Presumably domestic pressure and, ultimately, the decision of the family court were crucial. Nevertheless, the various international efforts, including the Committee's provisional measures, may have played some role, directly or indirectly in the State's treatment, monitoring and eventual release of the children.[86]

2.2.4.4 SEPARATE MINORS FROM ADULT DETAINEES

To some extent Honduras took seriously the Commission's intervention in the case of the minors detained in adult prisons. A few months after its precautionary measures it informed the Commission of the 'emergency measures taken to resolve the situation'.[87] In October 1996 the Commission took precautionary measures for the protection of the juveniles at the San Pedro Sula Prison. The next month the petitioners informed the Commission that the State had not yet implemented the precautionary measures, that it 'had failed to advise the courts that they were to cease the practice of incarcerating juveniles in adult facilities' and that it 'continued to allow juvenile offenders to be sent to those facilities'.[88] A month later the petitioners reported once more that Honduras had not yet adopted the precautionary measures. It requested the Commission to seek a government report on the concrete measures adopted to assign public defenders to all juveniles and to seek a suspension of the practice of incarcerating juveniles in adult facilities. Three days later, on 26 December 1996, the Commission reiterated the precautionary measures and requested information about their concrete implementation.[89]

2.2.4.5 HOSTILE RESPONSE, BUT SITUATION OF DETAINEE REMEDIED

In April 2001 the Inter-American Commission took precautionary measures on behalf of a prisoner in Cuba. In its Annual Report the Commission quoted from the petitioners' request for precautionary measures that 'his health is delicate because of a tumor on his right lung' and that the prisoner began a hunger strike in February 2001 in demand of medical care. The Commission did not receive a friendly response. The Commission reports that Cuba 'returned the IACHR's document requesting the precautionary measures in an envelope from the Cuban Interests Section in Washington D.C'.. It also reports, however, that it received information that the prisoner was moved to a hospital in Havana where he received specialized treatment. He was then transferred to a prison in that city.[90]

---

two sons remained at the Baxter Immigration Reception and Processing Centre, because they were over the age limit for release into the Residential Housing Project for 'cultural sensitivities and security'. In August 2003 the Full Bench of the Family Court ordered the immediate release of all the children, pending resolution of the final application to the High Court. They were released that very day. More than two months later the HRC published its decision on the merits. Apart from violations of Article 9 (1) and (4), it also found violations of Article 24(1) and, potentially, of Articles 17(1) and 23(1) ICCPR.

86   See also Chapter XVIII (Follow-up).
87   CIDH *Minors in detention* v. *Honduras*, 10 March 1999 (merits), §21.
88   See also Annual Report 1996, 14 March 1997, Chapter II, §4a (cont.).
89   Ibid.
90   CIDH Annual Report 2001, §28. Cuba is in a special situation as it is subjected to human rights monitoring but expelled from the political organs of the OAS. According to the Commission the OAS General Assembly had only suspended the participation of the Cuban Government but not

2.2.5 Responses to provisional measures to ensure access to health care outside the detention context

2.2.5.1 INTRODUCTION

As discussed in chapter XII, on occasion the Inter-American Commission has used provisional measures to ensure access to health care outside the detention context. The question arises how States have responded to such atypical provisional measures.

2.2.5.2 ENSURE ACCESS TO HIV MEDICATION

With regard to one of the new situations in which the Inter-American Commission has introduced the use of precautionary measures, namely to ensure access to medication for persons not in detention, but suffering from a serious illness, there has been some compliance and little outright criticism by the States concerned with regard to the Commission's decision to use the tool of precautionary measures in this context.

The case of El Salvador serves as an example, also of the responsiveness of the Commission to the State showing cooperation. A month after the Commission requested El Salvador to ensure access to HIV medication to prevent the death of 27 persons, the State informed the Commission that the authorities were reviewing their medical files 'in order to evaluate the anti-retroviral therapy and care needed for each case, and that they were seeking abroad the additional funds needed to provide the treatment'.[91] A few months later the Board of Directors of the Social Security Institute of El Salvador authorised the procurement of the triple anti-retroviral therapy for persons who are HIV-positive or have AIDS. From that day on, El Salvador began to provide the requested treatment.[92] Subsequently the Commission continued to request information regarding the State's compliance with the precautionary measures, but it did not heed to the petitioner's request to seek provisional measures from the Court.[93]

---

the obligations of the State. Cuba does not subscribe to the Commission's view that it still has obligations under the OAS Charter.

[91] CIDH Annual Report 1999, Chapter III C.1, §32.

[92] CIDH Annual Report 2000, §30.

[93] In March 2000 the petitioners requested that the Commission would declare that El Salvador had not complied with the precautionary measures. They requested the Commission to seek provisional measures from the Court. In March 2000 the State reported that it had appointed someone at the Office of the Director General for Foreign Policy as the liaison officer for the petitioners in relation to this case. That same month the Commission requested the petitioners to provide it with the names of the alleged victims who had died since it had began processing the case. It also requested specific information with regard to the precautionary measures. In April 2000 the petitioners submitted this information and they asked the Commission again to request the Court to order provisional measures. Four days later they repeated this request. Later that month the Commission transmitted the petitioners' comments to the State and requested more information with regard to compliance with the precautionary measures. In June 2000 the petitioners requested the Commission once more to move the case forward. In June El Salvador submitted the information the Commission had requested. This included 'the list of persons identified in the request for precautionary measures, together with detailed information on medical care, treatment, medical recommendations and other pertinent information'. Commenting on the information provided by the State, the petitioners reiterated their position

In July 2000 the State reported that the Governing Board of the Salvadoran Social Security Institute had decided to authorize the purchase of the triple therapy medication. It mentioned that this was authorized 'for persons who are insured' and reported the establishment of a fund. On 20 July 2000 El Salvador submitted additional information in relation to the treatment received by Mr. Miranda Cortéz. The Commission 'expressed its appreciation for this information and for the action taken by the Salvadoran State within the context of the precautionary measures granted in this case'. Later that month the State submitted additional information on the action undertaken to implement the measures. This included 'strengthening and taking up activities aimed at preventing the transmission of AIDS through education and the promotion of hygiene and preventive health … among the sectors most at risk for this disease' and 'creating a fund aimed at purchasing anti-retroviral medications for the provision of triple therapy to HIV infected persons'.[94]

In December 2000 the Commission decided in so many words not to grant the petitioners' request to seek provisional measures by the Court.

"In making this decision the Inter-American Commission considered the information received from both parties, and evaluated the different actions taken by the Salvadoran State to provide medical treatment not only to the members of the Atlacatl Association but also to other persons infected with HIV/AIDS in that country. These actions had continued even after expiration of the deadline for precautionary measures on August 29, 2000".[95]

---

[94] that it had not complied with the Commission's precautionary measures. They asserted, for instance, that the two alleged victims who died on 5 and 11 May 2000 had not received the treatment from the State 'that would have avoided their deaths'. Again, they requested the Commission to go to the Court for provisional measures. See footnote 3 in CIDH *Jorge Odir Miranda Cortéz et al* v. *El Salvador*, 7 March 2001 (adm.).

In August the petitioners commented on this information, repeated their position on El Salvador's non-compliance with the precautionary measures and their request to seek provisional measures by the Court. In the meantime, the period for the precautionary measures expired on 29 August 2000 and the Commission did not extend the measures. They requested a hearing before the Commission, which took place in October 2000. In November and December 2000 the petitioners again asked the Commission to declare non-compliance and to seek provisional measures by the Court. In December El Salvador provided the Commission with a summary of its activities in order to comply with the precautionary measures.

[95] CIDH *Jorge Odir Miranda Cortéz et al* v. *El Salvador*, 7 March 2001 (adm.), §20. That same month, however, the Commission sent the State a request for information about the medical care and treatment provided to the 24 surviving persons identified in the case. In February 2001 the State informed the Commission that it had provided the anti-retroviral medication to eleven of the 24 persons. It noted that this medication was available to the other persons as well 'subject to the proper medical evaluation'. It had also expanded the provision of the medication to other persons not included in the case. With regard to the exhaustion of domestic remedies and the merits of the case, the State argued that the Commission should construe the information it had provided during the processing of the precautionary measures as the State's response to the petitioners' allegations. "The petitioners have availed themselves of domestic remedies and have at all times, had access to the appropriate entities in the country. We have evidence, which has also been provided to the Commission, pertaining to specialized medical and hospital care, the measures adopted by state institutions, the treatment provided to each patient living with HIV/AIDS, and the budget approved to provide them with the medication requested". Communication from the state, 8 September 2000, 7 March 2001 (adm.), §29. The State also noted that patients who did not yet begin the treatment plan would be notified by telegram to appear at the Social Work Unit of

El Salvador requested the Commission to close the case. It argued that the attention it provided to the alleged victims within the framework of the precautionary measures already demonstrated its compliance with its international commitments.[96]

When declaring the case admissible the Commission noted the following:

> "The IACHR is aware of the fact that the people of El Salvador are in the midst of a very difficult period brought on by a series of natural disasters, which has placed enormous demands on the health authorities and officials. In that context, the Inter-American Commission appreciates the efforts of the Salvadoran authorities to address the needs of persons infected with HIV/AIDS in that country. The supply of anti-retroviral medications has been steadily increasing in recent months, and the state has announced that it will continue to adopt the measures necessary in that regard".[97]

2.2.5.3 ENSURE ACCESS TO HEALTH CARE TO SURVIVORS OF A MASSACRE

Two weeks after the Inter-American Commission had taken precautionary measures in the *Aguas Blancas* case Mexico reported the measures it had taken to comply.[98] These included 'contacting each of the protected persons, providing access to health centres in the state of Guerrero, and holding meetings to resolve the problems that have been identified'. A month later, Mexico reported that a meeting that had taken place between the victims and several state and federal officials. During this meeting agreements were made in relation to medical attention, travelling and accommodation expenses and drugs and medical equipment 'as indicated by their needs'.[99]

2.2.6 Various responses to provisional measures aimed at protecting against death threats

2.2.6.1 INTRODUCTION

It appears from the case law that States are taking the Inter-American Court's provisional measures more and more seriously. States generally do not question the Orders by the Court for provisional measures. They often send a high level delegation to a hearing to argue why the Court should not order such measures.[100]

The situation in which the Court has used provisional measures most often (as has the Commission) is in the context of death threats and harassment. Killings have subsided when whole communities have been covered by an order for provisional measures.

---

the Oncology Hospital of the Salvadoran Social Security Institute. The liaison officer for the case contacted the legal representative of the petitioners on this issue.

[96] CIDH *Jorge Odir Miranda Cortéz et al* v. *El Salvador*, 7 March 2001 (adm.), §3.

[97] Id., §48.

[98] CIDH *Tomás Porfirio Rondin ('Aguas Blancas' case)* v. *Mexico*, 18 February 1998.

[99] CIDH *Floriberto Cruz and another 7 survivors of the massacre in Aguas Blancas, Guerrero* v. *Mexico*, precautionary measures of 17 July 2001, CIDH Annual Report 2001, Chapter III (a), §40.

[100] The Dominican Republic, for instance, in the *Haitians in the Dominican Republic* case, sent a delegation to the Court that included the representatives of all the parties. On this case see Chapter XI (Mass expulsion).

The first time the Inter-American Court ordered provisional measures directing a State to protect persons against death threats was in the famous case *Velásquez Rodríguez*, the first one decided by the Court on the merits. What was interesting in this disappearance case, in which two witnesses had been killed, is that it was the State that first proposed to take certain measures. In its Order of 19 January 1988 the Inter-American Court noted that Honduras had proposed, during the Court hearing, to take measures on its own initiative to investigate and punish those responsible for the murders of the two witnesses. It had announced that it would submit to the Court the findings of the autopsies of the victims. Honduras had also proposed to protect persons under threat, in particular the two persons mentioned before in the letter of the President. Honduras had included in its submission press releases of the Secretariat of its Presidency and of its Inter-Institutional Commission of Human Rights repudiating the assassination and the violence. The Inter-American Court subsequently ordered Honduras to 'adopt concrete measures to make clear that the appearance of an individual before the Inter-American Commission or Court of Human Rights, under conditions authorized by the American Convention and by the rules of procedure of both bodies, is a right enjoyed by every individual and is recognized as such by Honduras as a party to the Convention'.[101]

The Commission has used precautionary measures in many cases and sometimes they appear to be quite effective.[102] Yet in other cases recourse to the Court is necessary. Sometimes the Commission takes a rather long time before actually doing so. In November 1995 the Commission requested Colombia to take precautionary measures on behalf of seven members of the Civic Human Rights Committee of Meta. This Committee exists since 1991 and its members have been subjected to constant threats and attacks since that time. Some have been summarily executed. Mr. Giraldo, however, who was protected by these precautionary measures, was murdered in October 1996. In response, the Commission requested the Court to take provisional measures on behalf of three of his family members as well as three members of the Civic Human Rights Committee of Meta, who had also been the beneficiaries of the Commission's precautionary measures.[103] The Court indeed did so.[104]

---

[101] IACHR *Velásquez Rodríguez, Fairén Garbi/Solís Corrales* and *Godínez Cruz* cases, Order of 19 January 1988, Compendium 1987-1996, pp. 9-11.

[102] For instance, almost a month after the Commission had taken precautionary measures on behalf of the President of the Constitutional Court, Guatemala informed the Commission that it had already deployed two uniformed officers 'to protect the perimeter' of her home before the Commission's precautionary measures. Later it had permanently assigned four plain-clothes officers from the protection and security service of the National Civilian Police to protect her. CIDH Annual Report 2001, Chapter III (a), §31. Another example is that of a journalist in Mexico who had received death threats from members of the judicial police in the state of Sonora. Allegedly, these threats were connected to his investigation into corruption and ties to drug trafficking by the judicial police in that state. In September 1999 the Commission requested Mexico to protect his life and physical integrity. In October 1999 Mexico responded that the National Human Rights Commission communicated with him twice a day. Mexico also informed the Commission that it was investigating the alleged acts. Annual Report 1999, Chapter 3.C.1, §45. In March 2000, the Commission requested Brazil to take precautionary measures on behalf of Catherine Halvey, a human rights defender working with the Human Rights Centre of the Archdiocese of Manaos. She had informed the Commission that, as a result of her activities, she had received several death threats. Brazil replied that it had taken precautionary measures after the six months period. Apparently there was no reason to maintain the measures. CIDH Annual Report 2000, §12.

[103] Case 11.690.

[104] CIDH Annual report 1997, Chapter III (a) under 'Colombia'.

Obviously a State may nominally follow up the Inter-American Commission's suggestions, made either as part of precautionary measures or in the context of State or thematic reports or the Court's provisional measures, without really solving the underlying problems. It cannot be ruled out that in some cases following, or seemingly following, the Commission's suggestions may in fact exacerbate the situation locally.

This subsection will further deal with responses that lack specificity, with the difficulty States have in implementing the obligation to investigate, prosecute and punish, but also with specific measures taken by States in response. Also discussed are the use of provisional measures as leverage by certain members of government to indeed help achieve better protection, State compliance after regime change, the introduction by a State of a formalised protection program and the proactive approach by a State taking voluntary precautionary measures.

2.2.6.2 LACK OF SPECIFICITY IN RESPONSE: WE ARE TAKING 'THE APPROPRIATE STEPS'

Generally States respond to precautionary measures in the context of threats and harassment. Often they could be more specific about the implementation of the measures. They have noted, for instance, that they were 'in the process of implementing' them.[105] Armed civilians allegedly reporting to the Governor of Oaxaca had issued politically motivated death threats against a group of residents of the town of San Miguel Copala.[106] In August the Commission took precautionary measures. One of the beneficiaries was a survivor of an attack by these armed civilians who had been receiving medical treatment in Mexico City and was afraid to return home. Mexico responded that it had identified the perpetrators and issued warrants for their arrest. It added that the Human Rights Commission of Oaxaca state had played a role in solving the matter and that 'all the competent authorities were taking the appropriate steps within their respective areas of influence'. In September, however, the petitioners informed the Commission that the dangerous situation keeping one of the survivors of the ambush from returning to his community still existed.[107] While many less forthcoming responses are possible, the reference to 'taking the appropriate steps' is very vague and given the reaction of the petitioners did not include specific protection allowing this one survivor to return. The statement that it had identified the perpetrators and issued warrants for their arrest would be very positive, if followed by information that the arrest indeed took place and the perpetrators were prevented from continuing their threats. According to the petitioners, however, for at least one survivor the dangerous situation still persisted.

2.2.6.3 INVESTIGATE, PROSECUTE, PUNISH

In general, as noted, the Commission's precautionary measures on behalf of witnesses and human rights defenders seem to be reasonably effective.[108] In the majority of cases the Commission does

---

[105] Response by Guatemala of 11 April 1996 to precautionary measures of 2 March 1996 on behalf of five persons and their families the Commission requested Guatemala to take who had received various death threats. Annual Report 1996, 14 March 1997, §4a.

[106] In July 2001 they had shot several persons in an ambush. Two of them died.

[107] CIDH Annual Report 2001, Chapter III (a), §41.

[108] Early 1998 the President of the Court had adopted urgent measures requesting Guatemala to guarantee the personal integrity of the members of the Vásquez family, involved in the *Paniagua*

not resort to the Court to ask for provisional measures, although this may be due mainly to lack of resources on the part of the Commission. There is one aspect of its precautionary measures, however, that States usually do not respect. This is the obligation to investigate threats and punish those found responsible.[109]

In December 2000 the Commission requested Guatemala to guarantee the life and physical integrity of the President of the Association of Family Members of the Detained and Disappeared of Guatemala (FAMDEGUA).[110] It also requested Guatemala to take effective measures to guarantee the safety of persons visiting or working at the offices of this organisation. Guatemala informed the Commission that the alleged perpetrators had been captured and that it was conducting judicial investigations and providing police protection.[111]

Yet in those cases where there *is* a willingness to investigate and prosecute, the investigator and prosecutor, the witness and even the judges are often being threatened. In the end neither the original attacks, nor the subsequent threats and harassment are properly dealt with. Even when a prosecution results in a conviction, there are cases where the perpetrators escape or are liberated by armed groups and are not captured again, resuming their threats.[112]

States are prepared to enter into detailed negotiations with the beneficiaries and the Commission and take very specific action as suggested by the Commission, but their investigation of death threats, attacks and harassment lags behind dramatically. Prosecuting alleged perpetrators and punishing them when found guilty is a much more sensitive issue than spending resources on protective measures. The rate of compliance with regard to the latter is much higher than with regard to the former. This applies to the Court's provisional measures as well.

In April 2004 Guatemala informed the Court of the place of detention of the man convicted for the murder of Nicolas Blake, who was sentenced to 28 years in prison and would not be released before March 2025.[113] Such detention is obviously an important step in the prevention of irreparable harm. Yet to the extent that the beneficiaries of provisional measures in the *Blake* case had been harassed by other persons, their acts should be investigated as well.

---

[109] *Morales* ('White Van') case, President's urgent measures of 10 February 1998. The Court ratified these in June. Subsequently the security of the beneficiaries improved, and upon suggestion of the Commission, the Court lifted its provisional measures, Order of 28 August 2001.
In the *Carpio-Nicolle* v. *Guatemala* case, for instance, compliance with the concrete recommendations was good but the threats and harassment themselves had not been well investigated. Here the political profile of the family and the nature of the case were very important.

[110] FAMDEGUA is a petitioner in the case of the Dos Erres village massacre pending before the Commission, case 11. 681.

[111] CIDH Annual Report 2000, §33.

[112] In the *Colotenango* case several former civilian patrol members responsible for the murder and other facts dealt with in this case had escaped. The lives and physical integrity of the witnesses remained at risk as a result. The situation in Colotenango is very complicated because of the inter-community battle between members of PAC and non-members. In the circumstances, many believe that all the media attention did not help and neither did the pressure by the UN presence Minugua. The first Order was of 1994 and the orders were finally lifted by Order of 12 July 2007. They were lifted because the main point of contention between the beneficiaries and the State related to the non-implementation of a point agreed on in the friendly settlement in 1997. The Court clarified that lifting the Order did not mean that the State had fully met its obligations under the Convention specified in the Inter-American Commission's Friendly Settlement Report, Juan Pablo Chanay (Guatemala), 13 March 1997 (Friendly Settlement). The State was not released either from its obligation to investigate, identify and, when appropriate, punish.

[113] IACHR *Blake*, Order of 17 November 2004, 10th 'Having seen' clause.

Often protection is partial and an ongoing process requiring continued vigilance on the part of NGOs and the Commission. The result is some compliance but not sufficient to ensure lasting protection. The situation of the *Peace Community* is a case in point.[114] An incredible number of people from this Community have been murdered. The provisional measures ordered by the Inter-American Court have helped achieve some protection to them. In addition the Community has gained international attention. Yet the members of this Community, as well as those persons providing services to them, are still in need of protection and the killings have not been investigated. President Uribe has never been a friend of the Peace Community.

At the same time, from the first Order for provisional measures in this case one may conclude that the government prefers to be perceived as being cooperative. Moreover, it seems that some civil servants, politicians or other officials are more willing to respect the Court's Order than others.

The comments of the State, in its reports or during hearings, may shed some light on its willingness to implement that part of the Court's orders for provisional measures aiming at investigation and prosecution. It pointed out that a Committee of representatives of the Office of the Attorney General, the Office of the General Prosecutor and the Office of the UN High Commissioner for Human Rights visited the local authorities of San José de Apartadó in order to promote investigations of the facts that took place in 1999-2000. This allowed for a formal opening of the investigations into the occurrences of April 1999, with the detention order for one person. The State's representatives made the observation that the actions of the State need to aim at eliminating any trace of impunity and 'render important results in the medium term'.[115]

With regard to its obligation to investigate and prosecute, the State had mentioned several times that it had opened an investigation, that it was in a preliminary stage, or at the stage of collecting evidence. During the hearing, in November 2000, the Commission pointed out that a situation of total impunity was prevailing in spite of the collaboration of the Community with the judicial authorities. Some of the violent acts, moreover, were now being dealt with under the military criminal justice system, specifically by the military judge of the 17th Brigade of the Army dealing with the investigation of criminal offences. It was the 17th Brigade that was mainly implicated in the violent acts against the Community perpetrated by paramilitaries. The State reported that its Defence Ministry had taken measures through the Lower Operating Unit ('la Unidad Operativa Menor'). This included operations in the area and capture of several members of the paramilitary ('Autodefensas') as well as of the armed revolutionary group FARC.

During the November hearing the State's representatives had also noted that the Vice-Presidency's promotion of actions providing physical protection, in collaboration with the local authorities and the Network of Social Solidarity, reaffirmed the State's commitment towards the Community of San José de Apartadó.[116]

---

[114] See also Chapter IX (Threats).

[115] IACHR *Peace Community of San José de Apartadó* case (Colombia), Order of 24 November 2000. In the original text: '*dar frutos importantes a mediano plazo*', 'Having seen' clause 10(g).

[116] The State was fully capable of contributing to and making concrete the implementation of these measures as well as to make progress in its dialogue with the Commission. They also pointed out that the Ministry of the Interior had followed up the developments around the Community since its creation. It had coordinated actions with local authorities and with City Hall in particular. It had provided humanitarian assistance to the displaced persons, which it had coordinated with the Municipality and the Office of the Governor. It had taken measures through the Lower Operating Unit ('*la Unidad Operativa Menor*'). These included controls on the road between Apartadó and San José de Apartadó, as well as orders from the Commanders of the 17th Brigade of the Army to the local units to protect human rights. In all this the State had emphasized the rights of the Peace Community. The Office of the UNHCHR, the Office of the National Ombudsman, the ICRC and

Five days before it was expected to hand in its first implementation report the State held a meeting with representatives of several State organs to analyse the situation of the Community. During this meeting the decision was taken to send to the Community an Inter-Institutional Commission made up of representatives of the Vice Presidency, the Office of the Attorney General and the Office of the General Prosecutor. A week before the Court would hold its public hearing on the Commission's request for provisional measures this delegation would visit the Community.[117]

The State's representatives acknowledged that the Court's provisional measures, with their collective nature, were based on important precedents in international law.[118] They observed that the Court's hearing had allowed them to become more closely aware of all the different views. They also pointed out an additional purpose for the participating institutions: to take initiatives and be spokespersons inside the government so that the required actions would be implemented promptly and completely in the entire country.[119]

During the public hearing the Commission referred to the commitment of the Vice-Presidency of Colombia to allow the Community to ask for help, to resolve emergency situations and prevent violent acts from taking place. Measures to ensure this were now in the process of implementation and 'among them are the supply of short wave radios, repair of the telephone system of the place, repair of the road, and the installations of reflecting lights in the urban central area'.[120] The Commission emphasised these measures would be adopted by mutual agreement between the State, the Members of the Community and the petitioners in order to guarantee their effectiveness as well as compatibility with the Peace Community's commitment to the principle of neutrality. It noted that personnel and armed protection inside the Community itself could endanger this commitment.[121] This relates to the intention expressed by the State to position such people inside the Community.

The State representatives pointed out that the State respected the position of the Peace Community and had worked with the authorities to ensure that they would afford armed protection on the outside of this Community. Nevertheless, the armed forces would be able to enter it if necessary. The State representatives also informed the Court that both the Minister of the Interior and the Office of Human Rights considered that the protection afforded to the Community must be coordinated. It is not clear whether they just meant coordination between the various governmental offices and local authorities or also with the beneficiaries. The State representatives continued with the remark that the State had dealt with petitions through the Network of Social Solidarity and the Ministry had made available a sum of 35 million pesos for a project of workshops intended to relieve tension between the authorities and the Community and to restore confidence between them. They did say, in so many words, that the early warning system promised by the State must be coordinated between the Community and the public security forces in order for it to be effective.[122] They pointed out that the Vice-Presidency had promoted multiple actions on behalf of the Community, including the aforementioned 'installation of light reflectors in the

---

others had also provided training to the troops on human rights and humanitarian law issues. Id., 'Having seen' clause 7(a).

[117] Id., 'Having seen' clause 7(b).

[118] In the original text: '*Estas medidas adoptadas con su carácter colectivo, están sustentadas en importantes antecedentes del derecho internacional*'. Id., 'Having seen' clause 10(h). See also Chapter XIII (Protection), section 4 on beneficiaries.

[119] Id., 'Having seen' clause 7(h).

[120] Id., 'Having seen' clause 9(m), iv.

[121] Ibid.

[122] IACHR *Peace Community of San José de Apartadó* case (Colombia), Order of 24 November 2000, 'Having seen' clause 10(f).

Community of San José and in La Unión, supply of communication radios and improvement of roads'. These were all undertaken in collaboration with the Municipality, the City Hall and the Network of Social Solidarity ('Red de Solidaridad Social').[123] They also repaired the telephone of the town centre of the Community, which was now in operation.[124]

The Order in the *Peace Community* case has been repeated and expanded several times.[125] Early 2008 the Constitutional Court of Colombia ordered the State, among others, to comply with the Orders of the Inter-American Court. A new and potentially far-reaching part of its judgment is its order to provide specific information on the members of the armed forces etc. who were present in an area where massacres took place. The constitutional court also emphasized that the State should take efforts to gain the trust of the beneficiaries of the provisional measures.[126] The Constitutional Court of Colombia has pointed out that part of the Inter-American Court's provisional measures was the requirement to investigate and prosecute. Despite the fact considerable time had passed with regard to several of the killings, still no investigations had been completed. It also pointed out that the fact that the State had ratified the ACHR required all institutions of the State to conduct themselves in accordance with the terms of the Convention, in such a manner that the Inter-American Commission and Court are not required to intervene. It added that the same could be said with regard to the International Criminal Court (ICC). By ratifying the ICC-Statute Colombia had committed itself to do everything possible not to enter into a situation of

---

[123] Id., 'Having seen' clause 10(e).

[124] Id., 'Having seen' clause 7(c).

[125] See e.g. IACHR *Peace Community of San José de Apartadó* case (Colombia), Order of 6 February 2008.

[126] Constitutional Court of Colombia, Sala de Revisión, T-1025/07, decided 3 December 2007, published 22 January 2008. The Constitutional Court concluded that the facts demonstrated that Colombia had failed to comply with its duty to prosecute the violations against the members if the Peace Community. Despite the gravity of the crimes and the fact that many of them had been committed many years back, as of yet there have been no convictions. Many old cases were still at the initial stage of investigation, or the investigation has been suspended. In many other cases no information is available at all on the stage of investigation and yet other cases appear to remain inactive as they have been transferred to other jurisdictions or a verdict has been passed inhibiting further investigation. All of this results in impunity, in violation of the right of the Community members to access to justice and the right to know the truth of what happened, §25. The petitioner in the case before the Constitutional Court had noted that by May 2006 the number of members that were assassinated already reached 175. The Constitutional Court also derived from the information provided to it by the Prosecutor's Office that this Office was investigating more than 100 cases, §25. The Constitutional Court pointed out that in important percentage of the members that had established the Community had now been murdered. This situation was intolerable for a State that had committed itself in its Constitution to the protection of human rights. It added that it had previously established that the precautionary measures of the Inter-American Commission and the provisional measures of the Court were legally binding. This meant that the provisional measures ordered by the Court in this context, on six occasions, obliged the State in a special manner to take the urgent measures necessary to protect the Community. Consequently the Court put together a serious list of requirements for the State to fulfil, including providing specific information on ongoing investigations and investigations that had yet to be initiated. The Office of the Public Prosecutor was to establish a proceeding for accelerating the military investigations so that it could properly start its investigations as well. It indicated how a high level officer was to be responsible for coordinating all proceedings with regard to the killings and harassment of members of the Peace Community and those providing services to them, §27.

being unable or unwilling to investigate and prosecute.[127] This domestic judgment shows international and domestic courts working to remind the State of its human rights obligations under international and domestic law.[128]

2.2.6.4 SPECIFIC MEASURES

In December 2000 the Commission requested Brazil to take precautionary measures on behalf of three Justice Advocates of São Paulo and their family members, as well as sixteen detainees. The last were detained in the Public Prison of Sorocaba in the State of São Paulo. They had received death threats 'presumably linked to the mistreatment and torture taking place in that prison'.[129] The Commission requested Brazil to provide guarantees for the right to life and physical integrity of these persons as well as their ability to testify without fear of reprisal. In response, the State reported that it had transferred the guards involved in the case to administrative positions.[130]

In response to a precautionary measure on behalf of three persons at the General Department for Integrity in Public Service, Nicaragua denied that President Alemán had threatened 'any public official'.[131] It did note, however, that 'in keeping with the measures requested, the protection and personal security had been increased including, in the case of Mr. Anaya, a personal escort service comprised of five persons, protection of his residence and place of work by a uniformed policeman 24 hours a day; and a telephone communications monitoring service, by the Department of Investigation of Personal Security Matters in co-ordination with the Department of Criminal Investigation of the National Police, to process information and investigate threats made against him'.[132]

2.2.6.5 PROVISIONAL MEASURES AS LEVERAGE FOR THOSE INDIVIDUALS WITHIN GOVERNMENT THAT ARE INDEED INTERESTED IN PREVENTING IRREPARABLE HARM

Often the situations in which provisional measures are taken to protect persons against death threats and harassment are extremely complicated and volatile. There may be a partial willingness of a government to comply on the one hand and perpetrators with influential networks (of army, police and other governmental officials) on the other.

---

[127]   Constitutional Court of Colombia, Sala de Revisión, T-1025/07, decided 3 December 2007, published 22 January 2008, §26.

[128]   Ibid. In October 2007, upon invitation by the Colombian government, an ICC delegation visited Colombia. The ICC media Advisory announced that, among others, a meeting would take place with Colombian judges and others 'to discuss relevant justice issues, including the implementation of the law on Justice and peace'., International Criminal Court Media Advisory: ICC Prosecutor visits Colombia', 18 October 2007, at <www.icc-cpi.int/press/pressreleases/282.html> (visited 13 May 2008).

[129]   CIDH Annual Report 2000, §14.

[130]   The Commission does not mention the State's approach, if any, to the protection of the Justice Advocates and their family. CIDH Annual Report 2000, §14.

[131]   It is interesting that Alemán himself, as a presidential candidate had once been under the protection of an Order for provisional measures by the Inter-American Court. See IACHR *Alemán Lacayo* (Nicaragua), Order of 6 February 1997, §4.2.2 and §5.1.

[132]   CIDH Annual report 1999, Chapter 3.C.1, §46.

El Salvador, for instance, in one case reported to the Commission that it had instructed the Director General of the National Civil Police Force to protect the life and personal integrity of the García Prieto family. It had also ordered him to start or continue the investigation of the acts of intimidation against them. Finally it had instructed the Director General to review the out-of-court steps taken by the National Civil Police Force to gather information in the murder case of García Prieto Girald.[133] Nevertheless repeated precautionary measures were necessary as the petitioners continued to receive threats in order to deter their search for justice in the murder case.[134]

In some situations States themselves may find that provisional measures are very useful. This may be the case in certain regions where the provisional measures give them backing to deal with the armed forces.[135] In some cases a government even indicates that it wishes the Court to take provisional measures. States may actually prefer the Court to maintain or reintroduce provisional measures. They may use them as a 'back-up' in their struggle against certain sectors of their own armed forces, police or other governmental agencies.

In its 1997 Annual Report the Commission mentions that it had the opportunity to meet with representatives of the Colombian government to discuss the Court's decision to lift the provisional measures when it handed down its final judgment in the *Caballero Delgado and Santana*

---

[133] Mr García Prieto Girald was murdered in El Salvador in June 1994 in the presence of his wife and son. In October 1996, his family, CEJIL and IDHUCA requested the Commission to take precautionary measures for their protection (case 11.697). In June 1997 the Commission requested El Salvador to adopt precautionary measures safeguarding the life, liberty and personal integrity of three members of his family as well as of the attorneys and witnesses associated with the investigation and trial of those guilty of his death. More than two months later the government of El Salvador reported the above to the Commission. CIDH Annual Report 2001, Chapter III (a), §30.

[134] Subsequently the Commission sent a new request for precautionary measures. The government of El Salvador informed it that it was continuing its attempts to clarify the facts. In January 1998 the State informed the Commission of a meeting that had taken place between the beneficiaries and several authorities and some human rights defenders. The parties involved were the three family members and several public officers, the Director of the National Police Force, a representative of the Office of the Attorney for the Defence of Human Rights and someone from the Human Rights Institute of the José Simeón Cañas Central American University (IDHUCA). During this meeting a discussion took place about several options for the implementation of a security plan to protect the lives and integrity of this family. This security plan was also to protect the witnesses in connection with both the murder of Mr García Prieto Girald and with the acts of intimidation suffered by his family members. In November 2001, however, the Commission again took precautionary measures in connection with this case. It granted these measures on behalf of the parents of the murder victim and their legal advisers from the Human Rights Institute of the José Simeón Cañas Central American University. In its Annual Report 2001 the Commission refers to a preliminary report from El Salvador in which it noted that it had scheduled a meeting between its Attorney General, the family and their representatives for 22 November 2001. In this meeting it planned to reach an agreement on the necessary protection measures. On 5 December 2001 the petitioners 'submitted a series of specific proposals for the Salvadorian authorities to pursue, including appointing a special prosecutor and a special investigator from the National Civilian Police, assigning the García Prieto family and their advisors security guards, details on the equipment needed to protect them, and holding regular meetings with the competent authorities'. CIDH Annual Report 2001, Chapter III (a), §30.

[135] Interview by author with President of the IACHR Cançado Trindade, San José, Costa Rica, November 2001.

case.[136] The Commission notes that the Court's decision to lift these measures 'raised some concerns because of the dangerous situation of several persons as a result of the domestic investigations and tasks that were performed in this case'. Following this meeting, Colombia requested the Court to re-establish the provisional measures. In its Annual Report the Commission points out that this 'constitutes an important precedent that is worthy of following in similar circumstances in the future'.[137] Thus, in March 1997, the State itself proposed a continuation of the provisional measures, 'as long as the risk situation continues, bearing in mind that the internal proceedings are currently being carried out by the investigating authorities [...] The Government of Colombia will inform the Honorable Court when it considers that the situation no longer warrants maintenance of the measures requested, but until then, it trusts that these will be maintained, inasmuch as it is a question of protecting the life and physical integrity of those persons who have given evidence in the proceedings now under way and at those conducted by the Honorable Inter-American Court of Human Rights'. The Court indeed did so.[138]

2.2.6.6 COMPLIANCE AFTER REGIME CHANGE

After Fujimori fled, the situation in Peru changed, even before elections took place. The Court was able to lift provisional measures in three cases, but in February 2001 it had to order them in another case. It ordered Peru to maintain those measures necessary to secure effectively the return of Ms Loayza to her country, guaranteeing her physical, psychological and moral integrity.[139]

The other cases, however, were finally solved. In August 2000, in the case of *Cesti Hurtado*, the Court lifted the provisional measures dating from 1997. His security and that of his family did not appear to be at risk anymore. Thus, the circumstances of extreme gravity and urgency, which had motivated the adoption of the provisional measures, no longer existed.

That same month, in the case of the *Constitutional Tribunal*, the Court still had to ratify the resolution of the President of April 2000 for the protection of Ms Delia Revoredo. Again, in September 2000, the Commission informed the Court that acts of persecution persisted against her with the aim to deprive her of her liberty and her property and to prevent her from being re-instituted as a member of the Constitutional Tribunal.

In February 2001, however, Peru transmitted to the Court the express recognition of its responsibility for the violation of their rights of three magistrates of the Constitutional Tribunal including Delia Revoredo. Peru informed the Court that in November 2000 the seats in the Constitutional Tribunal were returned to those three magistrates. In March 2001 the Court lifted the provisional measures.

In November 2000, the Court had confirmed, and increased the scope of, provisional measures in the case of *Baruch Ivcher*. In February 2001, however, Peru informed the Court that it had annulled the decision to take away his Peruvian nationality. It had accepted the Commission's recommendations of December 1998[140] and Mr Ivcher and his family and others would enjoy the

---

[136] CIDH Annual Report 1997, section III(b). See IACHR *Caballero Delgado and Santana* (Colombia), Order of 31 January 1997 lifting its provisional measures following its judgment on the merits of 8 December 1995 and 29 January 1997.

[137] CIDH Annual Report 1997, section III(b).

[138] IACHR *Caballero Delgado and Santana* (Colombia), Order of 16 April 1997 reinstating its provisional measures. See also the Court's Order of 6 February 2008 maintaining the provisional measures despite the State's request to lift them.

[139] IACHR *Loayza-Tamayo* (Peru), Order of 3 February 2001. See also Order of 28 August 2001, lifting and terminating these provisional measures.

[140] See CIDH Report 94/98 of 9 December 1998.

protection of their physical, psychological and moral integrity as well as their judicial guarantees. Mr Ivcher was able to return to his previous position as shareowner of the news channel. Peru also indicated that it was at the disposition of the Commission to reach an amicable solution. The Court considered that the violations that were the reason for the order of provisional measures had ceased and it lifted the provisional measures.[141]

2.2.6.7 FORMALISED PROTECTION PROGRAM

The case *Jiménez Vaca* v. *Colombia* (2002) by the HRC is important because of its similarity to Colombian cases pending before the Inter-American Commission and Court. It is clear from the State's response that witnesses, members of NGOs and trade unions are often facing threats. In its submission of September 1999 the State explained that it had instituted new protection programs:

> "In the particular case of union leaders, there is now a protection programme for witnesses and threatened persons. Provisions under this programme include an information centre, technical assistance, preventive action, emergency help, the purchase of communications systems, the purchase of vehicles, individual protection and protection for the offices of non-governmental and trade union organizations. Moreover, if the author should decide to return to the country, he would enjoy all the safeguards provided by the authorities and the protections merited in his particular case".[142]

The Commission's Annual Reports also provide information on the attitudes of States with regard to implementation of requirements for immediate protection. In 1999, for instance, the Commission noted that Colombia had informed it that it had strengthened the Program of the Ministry of Interior for the protection of witnesses and persons receiving threats. The Risk Evaluation Committee of the Protection Program processes the requests for protection from human rights defenders and witnesses. With the support of the General-Command of the National Police and if necessary, the Armed Forces and the 'Departamento Administrativo de Seguridad', it co-ordinates the adoption of urgent measures. The Commission, however, notes that the budget for this program was, in American dollars, $250,000, 'which cannot be considered an adequate or realistic amount in light of the high levels of risk these persons face'.[143]

The State also reported that it had extended the terms of Law 418 of 1997 (intending to implement final decisions of the Commission and Court on reparations) and that it had regulated a program for the protection for persons at risk. The State pointed out, moreover, that it General Law Budget included an amount of approximately $ 1,400,000,000 for preventive and protective measures in the field of human rights. This amount was assigned to the Special Administrative Unit for Human Rights of the Ministry of the Interior.[144]

---

[141]   IACHR *Ivcher Bronstein et al.* (Peru), Order of 14 March 2001.
[142]   HRC *Jiménez Vaca* v. *Colombia*, 25 March 2002, §5.4.
[143]   CIDH Annual Report 1999, Chapter V – Colombia, §116.
[144]   Id., §117.

2.2.6.8 TIMELINESS AND SPECIFICITY OF THE STATE'S REPORTING ON IMPLE-MENTATION

The attitude of States could differ when they are approached informally, rather than formally. In the case of Father Vogt (Guatemala) the Government presented its first implementation report on time, but it stated that there was no situation of extreme urgency in the municipality where he lived and that Father Vogt was 'living and moving about in this and other communities and even travelling abroad in all tranquillity'. The Commission observed that his situation, on the contrary, was still one of extreme gravity and urgency and that full compliance with the Orders of the Court was 'of the utmost importance'. The Government presented its second report more than 30 days after its first, one day before the Court hearing, stating that the police department was still providing day and night patrols and that Father Vogt was in communication with the police authorities and with the Pro-Defence Committee of El Estor (the community where he lived). Guatemala also stated that the investigations into the threats and harassments were continuing and the authorities had asked a domestic court to issue a warrant for the arrest of the person accused of making the threats. Guatemala mentioned the name of the alleged perpetrator.[145] In relation to the timeliness of implementation reports of States, it seems that here the Court hearing provided a trigger for the Government to seriously prepare its second report.[146]

2.2.6.9 PROACTIVE MEASURES BY THE STATE: VOLUNTARY PRECAUTIONARY MEASURES

In Ecuador witnesses to a police killing were receiving threats. The Commission was informed that Pedro Baque and his friends had been riding a motorcycle on their way to buy motor-cross equipment when the national police intercepted them. Then they were shot. His two friends died and he was left there, seriously wounded. Following this, he, his family and his attorneys were being threatened so that he would be too scared to offer testimony in court. In June 1999, when the Commission expressed its concern about this situation during a country visit, Ecuador voluntarily adopted precautionary measures to guarantee the life and personal integrity of Pedro Baque, his family and attorneys and to guarantee their access to the courts. On 16 June 1999 the Com-

---

[145] IACHR *Vogt* case, Order of 27 June 1996, Compendium 1987-1996, p. 161.

[146] It appears from the Court's order of 11 November 1997, in which it closed the provisional measures in the case of Father Vogt, that Guatemala had sufficiently respected the Court's order. The Court refers to the Commission's brief of 27 October 1997 requesting the withdrawal of the provisional measures. The Commission informed the Court that the petitioners had informed it that 'owing to the effective and timely intervention of the Honourable Court those threats and direct and specific acts of harassment had abated considerably and [that] Father Vogt [was] conducting his pastoral activity in a normal manner ... [and] that it would be fitting for the Honourable Court to order the withdrawal of the provisional measures presented on behalf of Father Vogt'. It does not discuss Guatemala's compliance with the part of the provisional measures referring to the duty to investigate the threats. The Court does note that the Commission's brief stated that it 'will continue to monitor the situation in connection with its processing of the case and, if the circumstances so warranted, it would once more request that such measures be provided'. IACHR *Vogt* case, Order of 11 November 1997, Compendium July 1996-June 2000, p. 426.

mission ratified these precautionary measures, duly recognising Ecuador for having adopted them on its own initiative.[147]

In November 2001 the Commission took precautionary measures on behalf of two *campesino* environmentalists in Mexico.[148] They had been released from prison on that day. On the same day the Commission received a letter from the Undersecretary for Human Rights and Democracy in which she noted that the Mexican government shared the concern of the petitioners about 'incidents that could cause irreparable harm' to these two persons. When Mexico reported their release it requested the Commission, on its own initiative, to grant precautionary measures on their behalf.[149] Subsequently, when the beneficiaries had made reference to protection by PBI, the State responded that it would offer this organisation 'the necessary facilities' to fulfil their protective task.[150]

3 STATED REASONS FOR NON-COMPLIANCE

3.1 Introduction

Do the responses depend on the types of cases, the substance of the request, the type of State (e.g. federal law States or common law States)? Do they depend on the type, the wording and the frequency of appeals? There are indications that the official responses by States may be explained by various other reasons as well. There are reasons for compliance, from norm-internalization to a wish to 'join the club'; regain prestige etc. There are also reasons from non-compliance. This book gives some examples that indicate reasons for non-compliance that have been officially forwarded by States, such as their view on the legal status of provisional measures.

At the same time the formal reasons for non-compliance may not necessarily be the 'real' reasons. This book refers to some other reasons that *may* be behind such decisions not to comply with certain provisional measures

For the sake of presentation the stated reasons for non-compliance are subdivided into three categories: (1) disagreement with the (temporary) outcome of the normative process (substantive disagreement); (2) the reputation of the adjudicator, the manner in which the provisional measure has been communicated or disagreement with the decision-making process on the provisional measures at issue; and (3) the domestic situation (sometimes stated, sometimes underlying).

Obviously in practice the various categories are interrelated. As justifications for non-compliance, States have, among others, invoked provisions of their internal law, doubted the legal nature of the provisional measures by the adjudicator in question, invoked 'contrary obligations' of international law (such as an extradition treaty) as well as the fact that their domestic courts

---

[147] CIDH Annual Report 1999, Chapter III C.1, §31. In the period covered by the 2000 Annual Report the Commission continued to receive information on these precautionary measures voluntarily granted by Ecuador on 14 June 1999. Annual Report 2000, §29.

[148] They were members of the Ecological Peasant Organisation of the Petatlán Sierra.

[149] See CIDH *Teodoro Cabrera García and Rodolfo Montiel Flores v. Mexico*, 27 February 2004 (adm.), §6 and accompanying footnote.

[150] Id., §7. In the Annual Report 2001, Chapter III (a), §44 the Commission speaks of the State's willingness to provide PBI 'with all possible support' in order to protect the two beneficiaries.

(and another international adjudicator, such as the ECtHR) had already considered the case 'extensively'.[151]

3.2   Disagreement with the (temporary) outcome of the normative process

Sometimes States use a substantive law argument to justify ignoring a provisional measure. Such disagreement on the substantive law has arisen when the State considered that a given situation does not result in a human rights violation. A case in point is the question whether ICCPR and ACHR prohibit application of the mandatory death penalty. The Court of Appeal of Barbados considered with regard to Article 6(2) ICCPR and Article 4(2) ACHR that 'the question of what constitutes a 'most serious crime' for the purpose of those provisions obviously has to be determined in Barbados and nowhere else'.[152]

In the *Mary and Carrie Dann* case involving land rights and cultural identity, the US had not respected the Commission's precautionary measures. It claimed that the petition of the Danns did not involve a human rights violation at all. Instead, it considered, their claims involved 'lengthy litigation over land title and land use questions which have been carefully considered by all three branches of the United States Government'.[153]

In this case the CIDH had taken precautionary measures already in 1993. Three years later, during a hearing in Washington, D.C., the petitioners informed the Commission that in March 1992 the US had impounded and sold 161 horses belonging to the Danns and in November 1992

---

[151]   See e.g. HRC *Sholam Weiss* v. *Austria*, 3 April 2003, §§6.1 and 6.2. The petitioner had pointed out that the treaty obligations were not really conflicting because the extradition treaty itself as well as Austria's own legislation provided for refusal of extradition on human rights grounds. Moreover, even if there had been a conflict, 'mandatory obligations under human rights treaties ought *erga omnes*, including under the Covenant, to take precedence over any interstate treaty obligation'. With regard to the situation of the petitioner following his extradition Austria observed that the US Attorney had applied to the US District Court for a re-sentencing of the petitioner since he was extradited 'on fewer than all the charges for which he was initially sentenced'. 'According to information supplied to the State party' the re-sentencing would provide the petitioner with a full right of appeal against the new sentence as well as the original conviction. It also noted that it would continue to seek information from US authorities 'in an appropriate manner' about the proceedings in the US courts. See §§5.4 and 9.3. In its decision on the merits the HRC found violations of Article 14(1) ICCPR, taken together with Article 2(3) ICCPR, as well as a breach of the State's obligations under the OP by extraditing the petitioner before the HRC could address the risk of irreparable harm. See also the discussion of this case in Chapter V (Non-refoulement). The petitioner had claimed also that he State had violated Article 9(1) by surrendering to the US in breach of the Committee's provisional measures. On 6 August 2003, following the publication of the Committee's decision on the merits, the Permanent Mission of Austria forwarded the Observations of the Government of Austria. It noted that it had complied with the Committee's wish of publication by making the link to the View accessible to everyone on the website of the Constitutional Law Department of the Federal Chancellery. See <www.bka.gv.at/wir_informieren_ueber/grund_menschenrechte.html> (consulted on 10 July 2003). It further considered that 'in order to avoid similar situations in future', it had generally complied with 'the Committee's legal view' because the complaint proceedings in the petitioner's case were pending before the Supreme Court and a decision was expected by September 2003.

[152]   HRC *Bradshaw* v. *Barbados*, 19 July 1994, §4.2.

[153]   CIDH *Mary and Carrie Dann* v. *US*, Report 99/99 of 27 September 1999 (case 11.140), §14 and 19.

it had sold 269 of their horses. According to the petitioners a gold mining company called Oro Nevada Mining Company was claiming the land in question 'under a law that permits mining companies to acquire land belonging to the United States for a token payment'.[154] The precautionary measures were repeated several times as the Bureau had continued with its trespass actions against the Danns and against other members of the Western Shoshone Nation. At one point the State noted: 'out of respect for the Commission, the State Department has initiated an interagency dialogue with the relevant Federal agencies to consider further the Commission's request. In the meantime, however, the United States will not hold in abeyance the normal operation of its laws'.[155] In June 1999 the Commission received another letter by the petitioners that federal officials were continuing trespass actions by issuing additional orders and decisions against the Danns and other Western Shoshone, despite the Commission's precautionary measures.[156] Subsequently the Commission received information that prompted it to reiterate its precautionary measures.[157] As the US have not ratified the ACHR the Commission could not ask the Court to order provisional measures, something it normally does when compliance with its own precautionary measures is less than sufficient.

In the context of the precautionary measures on behalf of the detainees at Guantanamo Bay the US has pointed out that it is not a Party to either the American Convention on Human Rights or any other convention making the Commission competent to consider the application of international humanitarian law. It based its reasoning that the precautionary measures were unnecessary on the argument that the legal status of the detainees was clear. It was a matter of public record, it suggested, that the Guantanamo detainees are not prisoners of war ('POWs') because they 'do not meet the criteria applicable to lawful combatants'. The US further argued that, pursuant to international humanitarian law, States engaged in armed conflict have a right to capture and detain

---

[154]   In February 1998, more than a year after the Commission used precautionary measures, the petitioners once more requested it to take such measures 'to avoid immediate, grave and irreparable harm'. They stated that the Bureau of Land Management had issued, that month, notices declaring that the sisters Dann and other Western Shoshone people were trespassing on lands. It had also issued orders to remove cattle and property and threatened them with fines, imprisonment and confiscation. The petitioners argued that there was an urgent need for precautionary measures 'because this aggressive Government action enhances the threat to the economic and cultural survival of the Danns and other Western Shoshone'. The Commission indeed reiterated its precautionary measure.

[155]   CIDH *Mary and Carrie Dann* v. *US*, 27 September 1999, §40.

[156]   Because of the imminent threat of the impoundment of their cattle without further notice, the Danns initiated discussions with the Bureau. They met on 28 January 1999 and were invited to submit a proposal for an 'interim measures agreement'. They presented such proposal on 28 March 1999, but on 26 May 1999 the Bureau rejected it in 'terms that essentially restate the BLM's [Bureau of Land Management] position, that the Western Shoshone people no longer have rights to their ancestral lands'. *Mary and Carrie Dann* v. *US*, 27 September 1999, §42. Two days later, the Bureau issued a notice of intent to impound any 'unauthorized livestock grazing upon public land'. Again, the petitioners requested the Commission to issue precautionary measures. They stated that this notice 'demonstrated the intention of the United States to deprive them of access to and use of their ancestral lands', see §43.

[157]   The Commission decided to take precautionary measures yet another time. It requested the US to 'take the appropriate measures to stay its intention to impound' the cattle of the Dann sisters, until it had had the opportunity to fully examine the claims. CIDH *Mary and Carrie Dann* v. *US*, 27 September 1999, §44. When it declared the case admissible in September 1999 it decided to maintain in effect the precautionary measures of June 1999. Both the Yomba Shoshone Tribe and the Ely Shoshone Tribe wished to intervene in the case as *amicus curiae*. On the merits see CIDH *Mary and Carrie Dann* v. *US*, 27 December 2002.

enemy combatants whether or not they are POWs. Alternatively, the US claimed that Guantanamo detainees are treated humanely and that they are not facing any "peril or irreparable harm", which would have been a precondition for imposition of provisional measures pursuant to Article 19(c) of the Commission's Statute.[158]

In *Mamatkulov* (2005) the State considered that: "It would be straining the language of Article 3 intolerably to hold that by surrendering a suspect in accordance with the terms of an extradition agreement, the extraditing State had subjected him to the treatment or punishment he received after his conviction and sentence in the receiving State".[159] This would conflict with 'the norms of international judicial process' because 'it would entail adjudication on the internal affairs of foreign States that were not Parties to the Convention'.[160]

In response, the European Court referred to its settled case-law that extradition may give rise to an issue under Article 3, 'where substantial grounds have been shown for believing that the person in question would, if extradited, face a real risk of being subjected to treatment contrary to Article 3 in the receiving country'. "The establishment of such responsibility inevitably involves an assessment of conditions in the requesting country against the standards of Article 3 of the Convention. Nonetheless, there is no question of adjudicating on or establishing the responsibility of the receiving country, whether under general international law, under the Convention or otherwise".[161] It noted that it 'would hardly be compatible with the "common heritage of political traditions, ideals, freedom and the rule of law" to which the Preamble refers, were a Contracting State knowingly to surrender a person to another State where there were substantial grounds for believing that he would be in danger of being subjected to torture or inhuman or degrading treatment or punishment'.[162]

Even when the State does not dispute the adjudicator's interpretation of substantive provisions on the merits, it may still argue that pending the proceedings the harm likely to occur is not irreparable. When the ECtHR used provisional measures requesting Turkey to ensure access to domestic counsel in the *Öcalan* case, the State did not wish to comply because it considered that this measure 'went beyond the scope of the function that these orders are intended to serve'.[163] The Court informed the Committee of Ministers of the Council of Europe of Turkey's refusal to comply.[164]

In October 1987 Canada requested the HRC to review its admissibility decision in the *Lubicon Lake Band* case, arguing that the petitioner had not exhausted domestic remedies and the delays in the judicial proceedings 'were largely attributable to the Band's own inaction'. The State also insisted 'that no irreparable damage to the traditional way of life of the Lubicon Lake Band had occurred and that there was no imminent threat of such harm, and further that both a

---

[158] As phrased by the editorial staff of International Legal Materials in: *International Law In Brief* of the American Society of International Law, 4 June 2002 (the text of the precautionary measures was provided to the ILM office in print form).

[159] ECtHR Grand Chamber, *Mamatkulov and Askarov v. Turkey*, 15 December 2004, §64.

[160] Ibid.

[161] ECtHR Grand Chamber, *Mamatkulov and Askarov v. Turkey*, 15 December 2004, §67.

[162] Id., §68.

[163] ECtHR Information Note 5, April 1999, p. 6. See also Garry (2001), p. 410: "As the Commission and Court have had to rely on the good faith of the Member State in complying with the interim order, they have issued them only in extreme cases where there is an 'apparent real and imminent risk of irreparable harm'". See also CAT *R.T. v. Switzerland*, 24 November 2005.

[164] In general on follow-up see Chapter XVIII.

trial on the merits of the Band's claims and the negotiation process constitute effective and valuable alternatives to the interim relief which the Band had unsuccessfully sought in the courts'.[165]

Canepa was removed before his counsel could request the HRC to take provisional measures. The Committee had done so in the similar case *Stewart*. In *Canepa* the Minister did not agree to counsel's request not to remove her client from Canada pending the case before the HRC. He 'had to take account of the serious nature of the offences' committed by the petitioner and of 'the fact that the removal to Italy would not cause irreparable harm'. His letter confirmed the willingness to 'cooperate fully in the processing of the communication in order to expedite its final resolution'.[166]

3.3 Communication of the provisional measures and disagreement with the decision-making process

3.3.1 Introduction

Compliance with provisional measures may relate to the reputation of the adjudicator, the visibility and specificity of its provisional measures. Specific arguments used by States to justify their non-compliance involve the alleged non-binding nature and procedural issues somehow implying a lack of due process on the part of the adjudicator.[167]

3.3.2 Lack of due process

Several justifications offered for non-compliance relate to the procedure followed by the adjudicator in taking provisional measures. Obviously, also with regard to provisional measures the

---

[165] HRC *Bernard Ominayak, Chief of the Lubicon Lake Band* v. *Canada*, 26 March 1990, §29.4. In *Länsman I, Ilmari Länsman* v. *Finland*, 26 October 1994, the HRC did not use provisional measures because it considered they would be premature. It is the only case involving culture in which the HRC motivated its refusal to use them. This case also gives some indication of Finland's attitude towards situations pending before the Committee. The State party referred to an inspection of the site during which the company representatives had noted that the construction of a proper road was necessary for the profitability of the project. The representative of the Forest District had replied that the Herdsmen's Committee and the company had to negotiate a solution. The State party added that 'the Forestry and Park Service has informed the Government that a decision on a possible new contract with the company will be taken only after the adoption of Views by the Committee in the present case'. This is an interesting addition in the sense that, on the one hand, the Forestry and Park Service (the new translation by the State for the Central Forestry Board) shows an awareness of the case pending before the HRC and the importance of suspending the activities in order not to pre-empt the Committee's decision, and on the other hand the State itself simply mentions this for information but does not itself commit to this effect.

[166] HRC *Giosue Canepa* v. *Canada*, 3 April 1997. Letter of the Department of Justice to counsel faxed 31 May 1994 and faxed to the HRC by counsel on 6 June 1994 (on file with the author). See also section 3.4 of this chapter, referring to the 'danger to the public' argument.

[167] For criticism based on due process arguments see also ICJ *LaGrand* (*Germany* v. *US*), Order of 3 March 1999, Separate Opinion Judge Schwebel and Judgment of 27 June 2001, Dissenting Opinion Judge Buergenthal as referred to in Chapter I (ICJ). Obviously these judges did not argue that a lack of due process would justify non-compliance by States.

parties should have had a fair hearing, if hearings are being held, and their submissions must be shown to have been considered.[168]

At one point in the *Blake* case the State informed the Inter-American Court that it decided to cease to provide safety measures to certain persons as of that date, because the Court had not yet taken a decision on its previous request to lift the provisional measures.[169] The Court specifically responded to this by noting that it 'is not a permanent Court, so that matters submitted to its consideration may only be decided when it is sitting'. When its previous session was held in February/March 2003 the Court 'did not have sufficient information to evaluate the request to lift the provisional measures, because the State, the representatives, and the Commission had not yet transmitted all the requested information'.[170] It pointed out 'provisional measures are exceptional in nature, are adopted in function of the needs for protection and, once adopted, must be maintained while the basic requirements mentioned in the second considering paragraph subsist'.[171] It stressed that 'only the Court has the competence to decide on the continuance or lifting of a provisional measure. Consequently, the provisional measures that it adopts are fully in force and produce their effects until the Court orders that they be lifted'.[172]

In *T.P.S.* v. *Canada* (2000) the State questioned why it had not had an opportunity to have its say on the use of provisional measures now that some time had passed between the petitioner's first request and CAT's decision to take them, 'a few days before his scheduled removal'. Canada pointed out that it had not been given the 'opportunity to comment on these *ex parte* communications with the Committee'.[173] While the HRC did not specifically respond to this statement, the duration of the proceedings, the extensive discussion on admissibility and the outcome of the case make this argument less credible.

In a case involving cultural survival by interlocutory decision the HRC 'invited the State party to submit to the Committee any further explanations or statements relating to the substance of the author's allegations, in addition to its earlier submissions'. At the same time it repeated its provisional measures 'to avoid damage to the author and the members of the Lubicon Lake Band'.[174] In its response to this interlocutory decision the State party asserted that it was 'being denied due process, since the principles of natural justice require that a party be aware of the specific charge and evidence on which the accusations of the author of the communication are based. It claims that since it was never informed of the articles of the Covenant and the evidence in respect of which the communication was declared admissible, the principles of procedural

---

[168] See in general Cassel (2002), p. 886.

[169] IACHR *Blake*, Order of 6 June 2003, 14th 'Having seen' clause, referring to the State's note of 13 May 2003.

[170] Id., 7th 'Considering clause'.

[171] Id., 9th 'Considering clause'. The second considering paragraph refers to the requirements of extreme gravity and urgency, and when necessary to avoid irreparable damage to persons mentioned in Article 63(2) ACHR.

[172] Id., 10th 'Considering clause'.

[173] CAT *T.P.S.* v. *Canada*, 16 May 2000, §8.4 ("The Government of Canada first became aware that the petitioner had submitted a communication, including a request for interim measures, when the author's counsel alluded to the Committee's granting of the request during a discussion with a CIC official on 18 December 1997, three months after the Committee had received the author's communication and request for interim measures. The record before the Committee reveals that the interim measures request was issued, after several appeals by the author's counsel to the Committee, a few days before his scheduled removal").

[174] HRC *Chief Bernard Ominayak and the Lubicon Lake Band* v. *Canada*, 26 March 1990, §25.

fairness have not been respected, and that the federal Government remains prejudiced in its ability to respond to the Band's claim'.[175]

Following the public hearing before the Inter-American Court of 18 August 2000 the Dominican Republic submitted a brief alleging that the Commission 'acted hastily' when it requested provisional measures, as it did not wait for a State reply 'nor did it use the means and mechanisms at its disposal to ascertain the complaint'. According to the Dominican Republic its deportation procedure did in fact ensure due process and a personalised treatment. It pointed out that this procedure consists of three stages: 'detention and identification, investigation and depuration (sic) and, finally, verification and confirmation'.[176] The Court did not specifically deal with this statement nor with the allegation that the Commission 'acted hastily' when it required provisional measures. In fact the Commission had allowed the State six months time to reply to its own precautionary measures before it brought the case before the Court.

Bosnia and Herzegovina considered that the English and Bosnian version of the Order not to hand over the petitioners to US authorities, who were then transferred to Guantanamo Bay, were 'different in a number of decisive details'. It 'assumes from these mistakes that both the President and the Vice President were outside of Sarajevo at the relevant time. Bosnia and Herzegovina considers that in particular cases of such importance, the order should have been issued only after the President or any other judge issuing the order had personal insight into the files, even if that means that the judge must travel to Sarajevo immediately'.[177]

When an adjudicator makes explicit procedures for requesting withdrawal of provisional measures, this does not guarantee that the State will respect them. CAT has observed 'that its procedures are sufficiently flexible and its powers sufficiently broad to prevent an abuse of process in a particular case'.[178] In *Dar* v. *Norway* the State expelled the petitioner to Pakistan despite a provisional measure by CAT that explicitly referred to the possibility of review. Norway informed CAT 'that it refused the Committee's request. However, at no time did it ask the Committee to lift the request'.[179] Half a year later he was allowed to return and was granted a residence permit for three years.[180]

3.3.3 Delays

Apart from arguing to have had insufficient time to respond, States have also argued that provisional measures have caused too much delay.[181] Jamaica, which had a practice of respecting provisional measures to halt the execution of a death sentence, decided to withdraw from the OP to the ICCPR because domestic law obliged it to otherwise commute death sentences. For similar

---

[175]   Id., §26.

[176]   IACHR *Haitians and Dominicans of Haitian Origin in the Dominican Republic* case, Order of 18 August 2000. Indeed, it is not immediately evident how these three stages could ensure due process.

[177]   Bosnia Chamber *Boudellaa, Lakhdar, Nechle and Lahmar* v. *BiH and Fed. BiH*, 11 October 2002, §108.

[178]   CAT *Ahmed Hussein Mustafa Kamil Agiza* v. *Sweden*, 20 May 2005, §13.10.

[179]   CAT *Nadeem Ahmad Dar* v. *Norway*, 11 May 2007, §16.2.

[180]   Id., §§1.2-1.4. The Special Rapporteur then denied a renewed request for provisional measures to prevent his deportation to Pakistan, see §1.5. While the reason is not mentioned, it is obvious that such deportation would not be imminent, see also Chapter XV (Immediacy and risk).

[181]   See e.g. Report of the Special Rapporteur for Freedom of Expression, Chapter V, §§23-25, in Annual Report of the Inter-American Commission 2001, Volume II, referring to precautionary measures of February 2001 on behalf of a journalist and director of a weekly magazine in Venezuela.

reasons Trinidad and Tobago sometimes responded to the HRC by making its compliance conditional on the ability of the HRC to determine a case within the deadline set by the State. In *Smart* v. *Trinidad and Tobago* (1998)[182] the State party had informed the Committee that it would submit its comments on the admissibility of the case in three days. In its submission, two weeks later, the State party did *not* address the admissibility of the communication but informed the Committee that 'to avoid further delays in the case of Mr. Smart, the State party would stay the author's execution for a period of two months only'. The HRC quoted a longer part of the State's submission:

> "1. The Government of Trinidad and Tobago is committed to upholding the rule of law and it would therefore not deny Mr. Smart access to the United Nations Human Rights Committee for the determination of his petition *provided that the process is not abused by the condemned prisoner*. 2. The Government however has a responsibility to ensure that these petitions are determined quickly so as not to frustrate the application of the law. *Any delay or procrastination by the United Nations Human Rights Committee* can have the effect of subverting the sentence of the Court and Constitution of Trinidad and Tobago. 3. The Government therefore requests the petition of Smart be heard and determined within two months of the Government of Trinidad and Tobago submitting its response to the application before the said Committee. 4. During the two month period, the Government will not carry out the death sentence…". (italics E.R.)

In other words, the State accused both the petitioner and the HRC of causing delays. Two weeks later the Committee, which was not in session at the time, replied through its Chairman. His letter reminded the State that it had been 'the State party's own failure to submit comments on the admissibility within the imparted deadline that had caused the delay in the deciding on the case'.[183] The HRC did not respond specifically to the State's remark that it would only stay the execution for two months, but it is clear from its reaction that it considers it should set the deadlines for the proceedings, not the State party.

The State took a similar approach to the proceedings in the Inter-American system. In one of the Orders for provisional measures in the *James* case Trinidad stated that the Inter-American Commission had failed 'to follow the approximately eight months timeframe established by the State for appeals to international bodies'. It noted that the delay constituted cruel and unusual punishment as defined by the State's domestic laws as established by the [JCPC] case of Pratt and

---

[182] HRC *Clive Smart* v. *Trinidad and Tobago*, 29 July 1998.
[183] He informed the Ambassador that the Committee had instructed him 'to express its regret that your Government has, to date, failed to comply with the deadline set for the State party's observations relating to the admissibility' of the case. This meant that the HRC could not consider the case at the session that was then pending. He announced that he intended to take up the case during its next session. Accordingly, he would wish to receive the State's submission on the admissibility of the case within six weeks. He also pointed out that the HRC could only deal with the cases during its sessions and that the UN determined the dates of its three annual sessions. "If a State party does not comply with the deadlines set by the Committee, thereby making it necessary to hold over consideration of a case to subsequent sessions, the full responsibility for the resulting delay and its consequences is with the State party". Request by counsel for use of Rule 86, 11 December 1995; Note Verbale transmitting the case under the Rule 86/91, 18 December 1995; submissions by the State party of 5 and 19 March 1996 and letter by Chairperson Aguilar Urbina of 2 April 1996, all in relation to *Smart* v. *Trinidad and Tobago*, 672/1995 (on file with the author).

Morgan. This 'would *de facto* abolish the death penalty, thereby usurping the legislative functions of the State of Trinidad and Tobago'.[184]

The Commission considered as 'mere policy' the time-frames the State wished to impose on the Court. These timeframes were, moreover, 'inconsistent with the timeframes established by the Statutes and Rules of Procedure of the Commission and the United Nations Human Rights Committee'.[185] The State's Instructions Relating to Applications from Persons under Sentence of Death show that Trinidad wished to impose a timeframe on the Commission (as it has also done vis-à-vis the Human Rights Committee) so that it could comply with domestic case law and still execute its prisoners. In effect this meant Trinidad intended to disregard both its substantive and its procedural obligations under the ACHR.

The Court referred to Trinidad's letters of August 1998 informing the Court that it would not attend the public hearing and that it would not accept any responsibility for the Commission's failure to organise its proceedings with regard to the death penalty cases pending before it within the time limits established by Trinidad. The Court noted that its President had sent Trinidad's Prime Minister a letter indicating the Court's concern about this attitude. It also referred to the State's letter of September 1998 that it would no longer report on this case to the Court or to the Commission.[186] The Court criticised the refusal of the State to recognise the obligatory nature of the Court's decisions in this case and in particular its failure to appear at the Court's hearing and to comply with its obligation to report periodically on the case.

In December 1999 the Commission requested the Bahamas to stay the executions of Mr. Mitchell and Mr. Higgs. On 23 December 1999 the Bahamas wrote to the Commission that the 'government has already waited a considerable time for the receipt of recommendations from the IACHR in respect of Messrs. Higgs and Mitchell and will not further postpone the process of its domestic law'.[187]

In *Olaechea Cahuas* v. *Spain* (2006) Spain had disrespected the ECtHR's provisional measures. After receipt of the Court's provisional measures the State sent the Court a decision by a domestic court confirming the extradition. This action, the Court pointed out in its Judgment on the merits, implied the State's disrespect for the provisional measures. Subsequently, in its submissions to the Court, the State insisted that normally it would respect them, but in this case the petitioner had been so tardy in requesting them that it had not had sufficient time to put in place

---

[184] IACHR *James et al.* cases, Order of 29 August 1998, 'Having seen' clause 5c.

[185] Id., 'Having seen' clause 6c. Judge García Ramírez made some remarks about the issue in his concurring. He took note of the 'statements in the file, in the sense that the State of Trinidad and Tobago is under certain judicially established timeframes to execute the capital punishment'. He observed 'that considerable time remains before these timeframes expire in the cases referred to by these provisional measures, as well as in those provisional measures previously considered by the Court, in which it has ordered the similar measures'. *James et al.* cases, Concurring Vote of Judge Sergio García-Ramírez. It is not clear whether this means that he would have voted differently otherwise or whether the remark was simply to stress that the State cannot use the timeframes argument as an excuse here.

[186] See IACHR *James et al.* cases, Order of 29 August 1998. In a footnote, the CIDH Annual Report referred to the State's note of 5 February 1999 in which it requested the Court to confirm that the provisional measures on behalf of Mr. Briggs had been lifted. At the time of publication of the Court's Annual Report the State had presented none of the periodic reports required in the Court's resolution of 29 August 1998.

[187] CIDH Annual Report 1999, Chapter III.C.1, §11. On 5 January 2000 the Commission repeated its precautionary measures. The petitioners informed the Commission, however, also on 5 January 2000, that the day before Mr. Higgs had committed suicide while shaving. On 23 February 2000 they informed the Commission that Mr. Mitchell had been executed on 6 January 2000.

the necessary measures to prevent the extradition.[188] The petitioner, on the other hand, considered that some two or three hours would have been sufficient to halt the extradition.[189] The ECtHR did not accept the justification offered by the State. When it received the provisional measure the government sent it to the domestic court dealing with the case and subsequently transmitted the latter's negative response back to the ECtHR. It appeared it had sufficient time to implement the provisional measures by ensuring the suspension of the extradition.[190]

3.3.4   Procedural duration: what is provisional?

The Inter-American Commission has now placed limits on the time period in which its precautionary measures are active. After a six months period, for instance, it reviews the measure and determines whether it must be maintained or not. Sometimes the measures are shelved because the situation is still the same and sometimes because the situation is more or less solved. At other times the Commission specifically maintains or renews them. The Court seems to take a similar attitude towards its provisional measures. In theory, it places limits on their duration. It is faced, however, with certain situations of continuing threats where sometimes even the State itself indicates that the court should maintain its provisional measures. The case of Digna Ochoa is a tragic example in which Mexico requested the Court to lift its order for provisional measures, because at a certain point in time 'provisional' is no longer 'provisional'. The Commission informed the Court that the petitioners did not object to the State's request and the Court lifted its provisional measures. Several months later human rights defender Digna Ochoa was murdered.[191] At the Court's hearing of 26 November 2001 on the provisional measures requested by the Commission for the protection of, among others, the members of *Centro Pro* after the murder of Digna Ochoa, a member of the Court asked the petitioners why, prior to this murder, they had agreed to Mexico's request to the Court to lift its provisional measures. One of the members of Centro Pro answered that they did not think the provisional measures made a difference.[192] At the same time, they did attend this hearing to request new provisional measures for their protection.

3.3.5   Disputing the binding nature of provisional measures or the authority to take them

With regard to the HRC, according to the Court of Appeal of Canada 'in signing the Protocol, Canada did not agree to be bound by the final views of the Committee, nor did it even agree that it would stay its own domestic proceedings until the Committee gave its views'. It considered that neither the Committee's Views nor its provisional measures were binding on Canada 'as a matter of international law, much less as a matter of domestic law'. It added that the States parties to the ICCPR and the OP had decided 'as a matter of policy' that they should *not* agree to be bound by the Committee's Views nor 'agree to refrain from taking any action against an individual who had sought the Committee's views until they were known'. They left 'each party state, on a case by case basis, free to accept or reject the Committee's final views, and equally free to accede to or not accede to an interim measures request'.[193]

---

[188]   ECtHR *Olaechea Cahuas* v. *Spain*, Judgment of 10 August 2006 (5th section), §§65 and 69-70.

[189]   Id., §66.

[190]   Id., §70. Generally on the follow up by the adjudicators see Chapter XVIII.

[191]   See further Chapter XV (Immediacy and risk), section 3.2.6.

[192]   Ibid.

[193]   Ontario Court of Appeal *Ahani* v. *Canada*, 8 February 2002, §32.

Different from what might have been expected it was only as an additional argument that the court referred to the wording of the OP and of Rule 86. It considered that this wording, as well as 'the Committee's own pronouncement', 'the opinions of recognised international law scholars' and 'case law' showed that 'the Committee's final views and its interim measures request are not binding or enforceable in international law'.[194] With regard to the wording it noted that both the OP and Rule 86 'used permissive language' ('views') and added that 'neither has an enforcement mechanism'. It further referred to international scholars considering that the HRC 'cannot issue binding decisions'.[195]

The domestic court considered that when Canada ratified the OP (the Court speaks of 'signed') it 'qualified' the right to seek the Committee's Views.[196] In addition, arguing from the non-binding nature of the Committee's Views, the domestic court considered that States parties 'did not agree to await the Committee's views before enforcing their own laws'. "If Canada is free not to accept the Committee's views, it is also free not to accede to an interim measures request".[197]

In *Ahani* v. *Canada* the HRC had used provisional measures to halt an expulsion.[198] A domestic court found that such measures were not legally binding and the petitioner was expelled. The court noted Ahani's argument that, according to Article 26 of the Vienna Convention on the Law of Treaties, States shall perform in good faith the international treaties to which they are a party. Counsel for Ahani had argued that if Canada did not wish to comply with the OP, it should denounce it rather than arbitrarily frustrate the proceedings. The court, however, considered 'on its face the argument that Canada will not be acting in good faith by deporting Ahani now is difficult to support'. "In deporting him, Canada will be enforcing its own laws and the decision of its highest court. It will be doing nothing more than it is entitled to do under the terms of the Protocol".[199] In other words, it considered that Canada 'would have every reason to hold a good faith belief that deporting Ahani now would not breach its obligations under the Covenant' because it had a right to enforce its own laws, these laws also took into account fundamental rights, as interpreted by its Supreme Court, and it was entitled to deport Ahani 'under the terms of the Protocol'. As a side remark the court noted:

---

[194] Id., §35.

[195] It referred to the book by Burgers and Danelius on the Convention against Torture (1988), p. 9, Ghandhi; Bayefsky and Duxbury (2000) (none with page numbers). See Chapter XVI on legal status. It invoked the introduction to the second volume of the Selected Decisions of the HRC, published in 1990. This introduction made a comparison with the European Commission on Human Rights, noting that the decisions on the merits of both bodies are 'non-binding recommendations'. This same introduction also noted that the Committee is 'neither a court nor a body with a quasi-judicial mandate'. Selected Decisions of the Human Rights Committee under the Optional Protocol, Volume 2, (October 1982-April 1988), CCPR/C/OP/2, pp. 1-2. Note that this introduction has changed with the subsequent volumes.

[196] "In any given case, Canada first reserved the right to reject the Committee's views, and second reserved the right to enforce its own laws before the Committee gave its views. In deporting Ahani, Canada is acting consistently with the terms under which it signed the Protocol. It is not denying Ahani procedural fairness or depriving him of any remedy to which he is entitled. Even under the Protocol, Ahani has no right to remain in Canada until the Committee gives its views. He can therefore hardly claim that the principles of fundamental justice give him that right". Ontario Court of Appeal, *Ahani* v. *Canada*, 8 February 2002, §42.

[197] Ontario Court of Appeal *Ahani* v. *Canada*, 8 February 2002, §44.

[198] HRC *Ahani* v. *Canada*, 29 March 2004.

[199] Ontario Court of Appeal *Ahani* v. *Canada*, 8 February 2002, §46.

"If, however, Canada had not acted in good faith, then it may justifiably be open to public criticism. If it falls short of the laudable call of a full commitment to human rights conventions and treaties, other states may take it to task. But the principles of fundamental justice lie in the basic tenets of our legal system. They are found in the domain of the judiciary, the guardian of the justice system. What Ahani complains about is a matter for the court of public or international opinion, not for a court of law".[200]

One of the three judges of the Court of Appeal dissented addressing several of the arguments made in the majority decision in *Ahani*. Justice Rosenberg stressed the obligation in Article 2 ICCPR 'to respect and to ensure to all individuals within its territory and subject to its jurisdiction the rights recognised in the present Covenant'. He observed that this was a binding obligation that Canada had undertaken to perform the obligations in the Covenant in good faith. In reference to its obligations under the Vienna Convention on the Law of Treaties he noted that Canada had also undertaken not to invoke the provisions of its internal law as a justification for a failure to perform.[201] Moreover, it was ultimately the HRC, rather than a domestic court, that has the expertise on the meaning of the obligations in the ICCPR.[202] He considered that 'where the legislation had established a statutory right to review a decision that could affect the security of the person, it is a principle of fundamental justice that the state cannot unreasonably frustrate that right'.[203] He quoted from Lord Millett in the JCPC case of *Thomas* v. *Baptiste* (1999): 'the right to be allowed to complete a current appellate or other legal process without having it rendered nugatory by executive action before it is completed is part of the fundamental concept of due process'.[204] Rosenberg noted that 'this principle of fundamental justice, although derived from a statutory right of review, can be applied by analogy to the process permitted by the Covenant and the Protocol'. This meant that 'individuals within Canada facing a deprivation of their right to life, liberty or security of the person have a right under s.7 of the Charter, within reason, to have their petition reviewed by the Human Rights Committee free from any executive action that would render this review nugatory'.[205]

In *T.P.S.* v. *Canada* (2000) CAT expressed deep concern about Canada's deportation of the petitioner to India despite the Committee's provisional measures. According to Canada a request for provisional measures was 'a recommendation to a State to take certain measures, not an order'. "Support for this proposition may be found not only in the word employed ('request') in rule 108, paragraph 9 but also in the European Court of Human Rights decision in *Cruz Varas and others* v. *Sweden*'.[206] Interestingly, as discussed, based on general principles of law the European Court has since found that its provisional measures are legally binding.[207]

In March 2006 the European Court had used provisional measures ordering Russia to allow a lawyer access to a petitioner who had been committed to a psychiatric hospital against his will.

---

[200] Id., §47.
[201] Id., dissenting opinion of Rosenberg J.A., §70.
[202] He referred to the 'arcane language' of the OP in forwarding its 'views'. He observed that both Canada and its provinces had changed legislation because of the Committee's Views. Rosenberg dissent, §72.
[203] Ontario Court of Appeal, *Ahani* v. *Canada*, 8 February 2002, Rosenberg dissent, §86.
[204] JCPC *Thomas v. Baptiste*, [1999] UKPC 13 (17 March 1999).
[205] Ontario Court of Appeal *Ahani* v. *Canada*, 8 February 2002, Rosenberg dissent, §89.
[206] CAT *T.P.S.* v. *Canada*, 16 May 2000, §8.2. For other examples of State arguments to this effect, see e.g., HRC *Ahani* v. *Canada*, 29 March 2004, §5.3, CAT *Mafhoud Brada* v. *France*, 17 May 2005, §8.2, CAT *Tebourski* v. *France*, 1 May 2007, §§8.6 and 8.7 and CAT *Singh Sogi* v. *Canada*, 16 November 2007, §7.7.
[207] See also Chapter XVI (Legal status) on the ECtHR *Mamatkulov* judgment overruling *Cruz Varas*.

Yet the Chief Doctor of that hospital informed the lawyer that 'he did not regard the Court's decision on interim measures as binding'.[208] Subsequently two domestic court examined the European Court's provisional measures and held that the lawyer should be allowed to meet the petitioner.[209] But the hospital and the petitioner's mother appealed against that decision and a higher court eventually quashed both decisions by the lower courts. Among others it held: "The Russian Federation as a special subject of international relations enjoys immunity from foreign jurisdiction, it is not bound by coercive measures applied by foreign courts and cannot be subjected to such measures ... without its consent. The [domestic] courts have no right to undertake on behalf of the Russian Federation an obligation to comply with the preliminary measures... This can be decided by the executive ... by way of an administrative decision".[210] This Court later also held that 'under Russian law the lawyer could not act on behalf of a client in the absence of an agreement between them'. It argued that the lawyer should have concluded such an agreement with the petitioner's mother rather than with the petitioner himself, as she had the right, under domestic law, to act on his behalf in all legal transactions.[211] On the merits the ECtHR found violations of Article 5 (lawfulness of his confinement in hospital and inability to obtain release), Article 6 with regard to the incapacitation proceedings and Article 8 (private life). Moreover, it found that the State failed to comply with its obligations under Article 34 by hindering petitioner's access to the European court and by not complying with its provisional measure indicated 'in order to remove this hindrance'. Specifically it noted that it was 'struck by the authorities' refusal to comply'.[212] The interpretation by domestic courts that the provisional measure 'was addressed to the Russian State as a whole, but not to any of its bodies in particular' and that 'Russian law did not recognise the binding force 'of the European court's provisional measures, was contrary to the Convention.[213] The same applied to the interpretation that the petitioner could not act without the consent of his mother. Regarding the status of the lawyer, 'it was not for the domestic courts to determine whether or not he was the applicant's representative for the purposes of the proceedings before the Court – it sufficed that the Court regarded him as such'.[214] As to the legal force of a provisional measure, the Court quoted from its 2006 *Aoulmi* judgment and summarised this by stating that a provisional measure is 'binding to the extent that non-compliance with it may lead to a violation under Article 34 of the Convention'. "For the Court, it makes no difference whether it was the State as a whole or any of its bodies which refused to implement an interim measure".[215]

In some cases Trinidad and Tobago conditioned its compliance with the provisional measures on its own estimation of the admissibility of a complaint, arguing that the case was inadmissible for non-exhaustion of domestic remedies and that it was already respecting the stay of execution ordered domestically.[216] In *Ashby* it questioned the competence of the HRC to examine the

---

[208] ECtHR *Shtukaturov* v. *Russia*, 27 March 2008, §34.
[209] Id., §37.
[210] Id., §38. See also sections 3.4.3 (Attitudes of domestic courts) and 3.4.5.3 (Generally negative attitude towards international supervision).
[211] Id., §39.
[212] Id., §142.
[213] Id., §§142-143.
[214] Id., §143.
[215] Id., §144.
[216] HRC *Michael Bullock* v. *Trinidad and Tobago,* 19 July 1995. The HRC observed that it was not for the State party but for the HRC to decide on the admissibility of a communication. It requested the State 'to cooperate fully with the Committee's examination of communications in the future'. Following this, it declared the case inadmissible, not for non-exhaustion of domestic remedies, but because the jury instructions did not show such defects as to render them

communication because it had been submitted at a time when he had not exhausted his domestic remedies. Apparently, the State considered that the HRC could only legitimately use provisional measures after domestic remedies had been exhausted and the petitioner had been executed. The Committee pointed out:

> "The Committee remains deeply disturbed by the State party's argument, being unable to appreciate how at one and the same time the State party could regard it as lawful to execute Mr. Ashby while indicating that he had not exhausted his local remedies. (Any remedies that may have existed cannot now be exhausted by Mr. Ashby)".[217]

The State also disputed the HRC's finding in its public decision that it had failed to comply with its obligations under the OP and the ICCPR:

> "Apart from the fact that the relevant authorities were unaware of the request, the State party is of the view that rule 86 does not permit the Committee to make the request which was made nor does it impose an obligation on the State party to comply with the request".[218]

In the context of an Order for provisional measures by the Inter-American Court Trinidad has argued that 'international organs have a duty to create the necessary machinery to allow a State to comply with its own domestic laws and its constitutional obligations in the field of human rights'.[219] In its Order of August 1998, the Court, on the other hand, pointed out that the function of the supervisory organs of the ACHR 'is to ensure that the provisions of the American Convention are observed and adequately applied by States in their domestic laws, and not, as Trinidad and Tobago has argued, to ensure that State Parties comply with their own domestic laws'.[220]

Following the decisions of domestic courts in Trinidad and the UK, the State had read a warrant of execution to Anthony Briggs. His execution was scheduled for 28 July 1999. On 27 July the Secretariat of the Inter-American Court, on instruction by the President of the Court, reminded the State of the Court's Order of May 1999 *maintaining* its provisional measures on behalf of Anthony Briggs. Despite this, the State executed Mr. Briggs as scheduled. The next day, the State submitted its observations on his execution. As neither the Inter-American Commission nor the State submitted Briggs' petition to the Court, the State argued, the Court's Order for provisional measures of 29 August was 'spent'. It proceeded with the execution.[221]

In several death penalty cases the US took the position that the Inter-American Commission's recommendations were not legally binding. It considered that the Commission's power to

---

manifestly arbitrary or a denial of justice and because it was generally for the appellate courts to review the judge's discretion in relation to the admission of evidence. See further Chapter XIV on admissibility.

[217] See also Chapter XIV on the relationship with admissibility.

[218] HRC *Glenn Ashby* v. *Trinidad and Tobago*, 21 March 2002, §5.6, referring to the Committee's public decision of 26 July 1994.

[219] IACHR *James et al.* cases, Order of 29 August 1998, 'Having seen' clause 5(e).

[220] Id., 10th 'Considering' clause.

[221] IACHR *James et al.* case, Order for provisional measures, 16 August 2000. It noted that the Commission completed its consideration of the case in November 1998 and transmitted the ensuing Article 50 Report to the State. In February 1999 the three-month period allowed under the Convention and the Statute of the Commission for submission of the matter to the Court expired. The Commission adopted its Article 51 Report in March 1999 and published it the next month.

grant precautionary measures did not exist in either the American Convention or the Statute of the Commission and, consequently. Thus its request was a non binding recommendation.[222]

In April 2002 the US responded to the Inter-American Commission's precautionary measures on behalf of the detainees at Guantanamo Bay. It claimed that the Commission acted without basis 'in fact or law' in requesting precautionary measures in this case. It also argued that the Commission did not have the requisite jurisdictional competence to apply international humanitarian law. According to the US it is humanitarian law, and not human rights law, that governs the capture and detention of enemy combatants in armed conflict. It argued that the Commission, 'whose mission ... is to interpret human rights under the [American Declaration of the Rights and Duties of Man],' lacks the jurisdictional competence to interpret and apply humanitarian law. Alternatively, it claimed that the precautionary measures were neither necessary nor appropriate in the case at hand. It argued that the Commission lacked a mandate to request the US to implement precautionary and even if it had the authority to issue them, such measures would not be binding.[223]

In March 2001, in the *La Nación* case, the Costa Rican court dealing with the case published its decision of the previous day rejecting the competence of the Inter-American Commission to dictate precautionary measures with regard to decisions by national courts. Counsel for Herrera and the newspaper 'la Nación' petitioned for a review of this decision, but the court rejected this the next day for lack of 'current interest'.[224] In an Opinion published in 'la Nación' the NGO CEJIL criticised the *Tribunal de Juicio* for having misjudged and ignored the Commission's precautionary measures. It noted that this Tribunal justified its decision on the basis of the assumption that the power to order precautionary measures is not a function of the Commission and, moreover, that its decisions do not have a binding character, which is to say they are a request rather than an order.[225] CEJIL, on the other hand, affirmed that the competence of the Commission to adopt precautionary measures is part of its Rules of Procedure and is founded on Articles 33 and 41 ACHR. CEJIL expressed its surprise at the attitude of the State, considering that the Government had only recently presented a proposal to the General Assembly of the OAS aimed at fortifying the Inter-American Human Rights System by creating a follow-up mechanism for the political organs of the OAS. This mechanism would make effective the reports and recommendation of the Commission and the decisions of the Court. In other words, it pointed out that this contradiction between how the State expressed itself externally and how it acted domestically could put at risk the international image of Costa Rica and the international obligations assumed by it.[226]

---

[222] See e.g. CIDH Annual Report 2001, §56 regarding *Nevius* v. *US*; §57 regarding *Robert Bacon Jr* v. *US*; and §59 regarding *Gerardo Valdez Maltos* v. *US*.

[223] Digest of the US practice in international law 2002, Chapter 6, no. 21. 'U.S. Additional Response to the request for precautionary measures', 15 July 2002, <http://www.state.gov/s/l/38642.htm> (consulted 8 January 2009).

[224] The phrase was: '*por falta de interés actual*', in: Tribunal rechaza pedido de CIDH, Aduce que la Comisión no tiene competencia, *La Nación*, 24 March 2001, <www.nacion.com> (consulted 2 April 2002).

[225] Literally, CEJIL wrote the following: "*El tribunal justificó su decision señalando que dentro de las funciones de este órgano de protección de los derechos humanos no se encuentra la facultad de decretar medidas cautelares y que, además, sus resoluciones no tiene carácter vinculante, es decir, son una requisitoria y no una orden*". See: La Competencia de la CIDH, comunicado del Centro por la Justicia y el Derecho Internacional (CEJIL), in: *La Nación*, 5 April 2001, <www.nacion.com> (consulted 2 April 2002).

[226] La Competencia de la CIDH, comunicado del Centro por la Justicia y el Derecho Internacional (CEJIL), in: *La Nación*, 5 April 2001, <www.nacion.com> (consulted 2 April 2002).

Both the Commission and the CIDH Special Rapporteur for Freedom of Expression note, in their Annual Report for 2001, that Costa Rica's ineffectiveness in protecting the freedom of expression 'combined with the fact that the Costa Rican courts did not carry out the required precautionary measures on a timely basis' forced it to resort to the Inter-American Court, which subsequently adopted provisional measures.[227] Costa Rica informed the Court that 'due to a mistaken interpretation there had been confusion when [his] criminal record was certified'. It added that 'the Department of Judicial Records and Files had already taken the corresponding records to add definitively all the uncertainties surrounding [his] situation' and it guaranteed that 'a similar situation regarding certifications that might be issued in the future would by no means recur'. The Court took note of Costa Rica's report and ordered it to continue to apply the provisional measures, in particular to ensure nullification of the registration in the Judicial Registry of Criminal Offenders.[228] After the Court's provisional measure, the State suspended all action against the journalist and the newspaper. In other words, it did more than the Court had requested. The State may have done this in order to prevent having to pay damages under national law later on, if the Court would eventually find a violation.[229]

3.3.6 Reputation, clear communication, visibility and specificity

The reputation of the adjudicator in the State in question may play a role. States may also argue, by way of justification for non-compliance with provisional measures, that the case law of another adjudicator is different on the issue at hand.[230]

Yasseen and Thomas v. *Guyana* (1998) shows the importance of sending submissions to the correct address.[231] In this case Guyana had mistakenly sent its submission to the UN Special

---

227 CIDH Annual Report 2001, Chapter III (a), §27 and Report of the Special Rapporteur for Freedom of Expression, Chapter V, §21.

228 CIDH Report of the Special Rapporteur for Freedom of Expression, Chapter V, §2 in: Annual Report 2001.

229 On the merits the Inter-American Court found that the contested judgment by the domestic criminal court convicting Herrera Ulloa had the effect of violating his right to freedom of thought and expression. Therefore Costa Rica 'must nullify that judgment and all the measures it ordered, including any involving third parties'. The state was to 'take all necessary judicial, administrative and any other measures to nullify and abolish any and all effects of the November 12, 1999 judgment'. IACHR *Herrera-Ulloa* v. *Costa Rica*, Judgment of 2 July 2004 (merits and reparation), §195. The 'State's obligations vis-à-vis the ordered provisional measures are now replaced by the obligations ordered in the present judgment, effective as of the date of its notification'. Id., §196. With regard to the other claims the court found that its judgment constituted *per se* a form of reparation, except for Mr Herrera Ulloa for whom compensation was to be paid for non-pecuniary damages.

230 Canada (in the context of refoulement) and the US (in the context of access to court for detainees at Guantanamo), for instance, have referred to the 1991 ECtHR judgment *Cruz Varas* where the European Court still considered not legally binding its provisional measures. See e.g. Ontario Court of Appeal *Ahani* v. *Canada*, 8 February 2002, §37 and Digest of the US practice in international law 2002, Chapter 6, no. 21. 'U.S. Additional Response to the request for precautionary measures', 15 July 2002, <http://www.state.gov/s/l/38642.htm> (consulted 8 January 2009).

231 HRC *Abdool Saleem Yasseen and Noel Thomas* v. *Republic of Guyana*, 30 March 1998. The Committee received information from counsel that the Court of Appeal of Guyana had dismissed the petitioners' application. Subsequently, the State party requested an extension of the deadline for submission of observations on admissibility. By contrast, in its View the HRC referred to a

Rapporteur on Summary and Arbitrary Executions instead of to the HRC and subsequently protested with the HRC that it failed to take into account its observations.[232] While this mistake cannot be attributed to the Committee, the incident indicates the importance of open and efficient lines of communication between different departments of the High Commissioner's Secretariat in Geneva. The staff, for instance, servicing the Special Rapporteur on Summary and Arbitrary Executions does have a responsibility in re-channelling communications not meant for it.

Six months after the execution of Glenn Ashby in disregard of the Committee's provisional measures, the State party responded by mentioning that its authorities 'were not aware' of the 'request under rule 86 at the time of Mr. Ashby's execution'.[233]

> "The representative of Trinidad and Tobago at Geneva transmitted a covering memorandum by fax at 16.34 (Geneva time) (10.34 Trinidad time) on 13 July 1994. This memorandum made reference to a note from the Centre for Human Rights. However, the note referred to was not attached to the memorandum. The entire application filed on behalf of Mr. Ashby, together with

---

[232] note in which the State criticised the delays in the proceedings before the HRC. The Committee regretted the lack of co-operation from the State party and rejected this criticism.

The HRC declared the case admissible in July 1997. In August of that year it received a Note Verbale in which Guyana's Minister for Foreign Affairs expressed 'disappointment and distress' about this admissibility decision. The Minister wrote that the Committee had failed to take into account the government's observations of October 1996 on the petitioners' claims. The HRC, however, had not received these observations. "Upon inquiry by the Committee, it transpired that the State party's submission of that date had been addressed to the Special Rapporteur for Summary and Arbitrary Executions of the UN Commission on Human Rights". The confusion may have arisen because in February 1996 the Special Rapporteur on Summary and Arbitrary Executions, Ndiaye, had submitted an urgent appeal to the Minister of Foreign Affairs of Guyana as well, through its Permanent Mission. He had requested the State to refrain from carrying out the execution of Yasseen and Thomas scheduled two days later. Urgent appeal of 8 February 1996 to the Ministry of Foreign Affairs of Guyana by Bacre Waly Ndiaye (on file with the author). After Guyana was informed of this mistake it requested that its observations of 3 October 1996 be incorporated into the case file and that the Committee reconvene to consider the admissibility and the merits of the case. The Committee gave the petitioners' counsel an opportunity to comment on the above observations. It then reconsidered its admissibility decision. It observed, however, that the submission of October 1996 addressed the merits of the complaints rather than the admissibility. The only claim of which the State had challenged the admissibility was the claim that the jury foreman for the last trial, which had taken place in 1992, was related to the wife of the deceased. The State party argued that the petitioners did not raise this claim during the domestic proceedings. Observing that in that respect, in effect, domestic remedies had not been exhausted, the Committee set aside its earlier admissibility decision 'in as much as it relates to this claim'. It saw no grounds to review its admissibility decision in relation to the other claims made by the petitioners. At the same time, the Chairperson pointed out that the mandate of the HRC under the OP is 'distinct and entirely separate' from that of the Commission's Special Rapporteur on Summary and Arbitrary executions. Procedures before both bodies 'may proceed in parallel, but independently of each other'. She also re-iterated the Committee's provisional measures. Letter by the Chairperson of the HRC to the Permanent Representative of Guyana, 22 August 1997 (on file with the author).

[233] HRC *Glenn Ashby* v. *Trinidad and Tobago*, 21 March 2002, §5.1. See also under 'Execution by Trinidad and Tobago: the case Ashby'

the Special Rapporteur's request under rule 86, was received by the Ministry of Foreign Affairs on 18 July 1994, that is, four days after Mr. Ashby's execution".[234]

According to the State the Secretariat staff should have reminded the Permanent Representative of the urgency of the request. Without this, 'he would not in any way have been aware of the extreme urgency with which their request was to be transmitted to the relevant authorities in Trinidad and Tobago. It is not known whether the Committee in fact drew the urgency of the request to the attention of the Permanent Representative'. The HRC responded by writing that urgency *was* duly conveyed to the First Secretary at 16.05 on 13 July and was personally delivered.[235]

In the case of *Rockliff Ross* v. *Guyana* (disc. 1997) the HRC used provisional measures within a day after receipt of the communication. The execution was scheduled on that day. Despite the extensive efforts by the Committee's Secretariat to contact the relevant authorities including the prison director, the petitioner was executed. It is not clear whether the State would have failed to comply as well had the Committee been in a position to issue provisional measures several days in advance of the execution date.[236]

In *Thompson* v. *St. Vincent & the Grenadines* (2000)[237] the HRC received information, a year and seven months after it used provisional measures, that the State had issued an execution warrant. The Special Rapporteur sent an immediate message to the State reminding it of the provisional measure under Rule 86.[238] The State let the HRC know 'that it was not aware of having received the request nor the communication concerned'.

"Following an exchange of correspondence between the Special Rapporteur for New Communications and the State party's representatives, and after a constitutional motion had been presented to the High Court of St. Vincent and the Grenadines, the State party agreed to grant the author a stay of execution in order to allow the Committee to examine his communication".[239]

Bosnia and Herzegovina did not comply with the Bosnia Chamber's Order for provisional measures to halt handing over the petitioners to US forces. Bosnia and Herzegovina alleged that the order had never been delivered to it 'in a proper way'. It argued that 'even if the order was transmitted to the facsimile of the legal service of the Council of Ministers on 17 January 2002, at 6:26 p.m., it could not have complied with the order, because the Council of Ministers, where the Agents are situated, stops working at 5:00 p.m. However, on 18 January 2002, at 9:00 a.m., when the Agents started working the next day, the applicants were already outside of the territory of Bosnia and Herzegovina. Moreover, the regular practice is that the Agents of Bosnia and Herzegovina receive cases and decisions of the Chamber and other materials directly by courier'.[240]

---

[234] HRC *Glenn Ashby* v. *Trinidad and Tobago*, 21 March 2002, §5.1.

[235] See also the references to HRC *Thompson* v. *St. Vincent & the Grenadines*, 18 October 2000 and *Ross* v. *Guyana*, 10 December 1997 (disc.) as discussed in this section under 'Communication and compliance'.

[236] HRC *Rockliff Ross* v. *Guyana*, 10 December 1997 (disc.), (703/1996) (on file with the author).

[237] HRC *Eversley Thompson* v. *St. Vincent & the Grenadines*, 18 October 2000.

[238] While the HRC seems to have received the information three days after the execution was scheduled, it acted immediately and the State granted a stay. This means he had not yet been executed at the time.

[239] HRC *Mr. Eversley Thompson* v. *St. Vincent & the Grenadines*, 18 October 2000.

[240] Bosnia Chamber *Boudellaa, Lakhdar, Nechle and Lahmar* v. *BiH and Fed. BiH*, 11 October 2002, §107. See also e.g. the State's argument in ECtHR *Koughouli* v. *France*, 26 September 2002 (inadm.), that even if the provisional measure had been in time, it would not postpone a

The *visibility* of provisional measures by the supervisory bodies concerned, including their motivation, may have an impact on the willingness of States to respect them.[241] In this context it is also interesting to note that, in its press releases on precautionary measures, the Inter-American Commission has introduced a practice of attaching background information (less than half a page) on its mandate and composition, evidently intended to inform the (US) media.[242] In addition, in particular in the Inter-American system another factor many petitioners and the Commission see as important in improving the effectiveness of precautionary and provisional measures is their specificity.[243]

In almost all cases a decision of non-compliance may be based on a combination of reasons. In the aftermath of the execution of the execution of Glenn Ashby, for instance, the State suggested several reasons for ignoring the Committee's provisional measures: it did not get the request in time, the HRC had no authority under its Rule on provisional measures to make this particular request (because of non-exhaustion) and that this Rule did not impose an obligation to comply with the Committee's provisional measures.[244]

3.4   The domestic situation

3.4.1 Introduction

The lack of knowledge of human rights obligations[245] and the perception that international human rights law is a foreign affairs issue, rather than one of domestic implementation, seems to apply to the three branches of government in various States and is relevant to explain respect and disrespect for provisional measures as well. This section deals with the attitude of domestic courts to international adjudicators, including the issue of incorporation into domestic law (3.3.2); then it gives examples of three types of excuses for non-compliance; the first is a professed inability to comply (3.3.3), the second is a statement denying responsibility (3.3.4); and the third is an outright refusal to comply (3.3.5). The latter may involve an emphasis on public safety or the idea that domestic authorities are less capable or appropriate to deal with the issue than are international adjudicators.

---

decision to expel based simply on a telephone request. In other words, the State apparently insists on receiving all the information before it is prepared to respect the Court's provisional measures.

[241] The availability of persuasive provisional measures may contribute to convincing the State to comply in a particular case, although, as indicated by Viljoen/Louw (2007), pp. 1-34 with regard to the merits decisions of the African Commission, to the extent information was available the more persuasive merits decisions did not necessarily trigger compliance nor did cases of limited reasoning trigger non-compliance. Nevertheless this book considers accessible and persuasive provisional measures as a value in itself that will improve the concept in the long run and is more likely to be of use to non-governmental organisations in order to stir up public opinion than will less persuasive provisional measures. On follow-up by NGOs see section 4 of Chapter XVIII.

[242] See e.g. IACHR calls upon the United States to postpone execution of juvenile offender Alexander Williams, press release 7/02, 19 February 2002. See also Chapter XVIII (Follow-up).

[243] See also Chapter XIII (Protection).

[244] HRC *Ashby* v. *Trinidad & Tobago*, 21 March 2002, §5.6.

[245] In a country report, for instance, the Inter-American Commission recommended a State to take additional measures to 'inform and train relevant officials at all levels, particularly judges and other decision-makers responsible for interpreting and applying the State's human rights obligations, to ensure that they are aware of and understand those obligations under applicable international law'. See CIDH Canada Report 2000, §181.

3.4.2 Attitude of domestic courts towards international adjudicators

As a branch of government, the judiciary plays an important role in the (non-)implementation of international obligations,[246] including provisional measures. Issues like incorporation of international law and the extent of deference to the executive are important in this respect. Sometimes international and national courts are each other's allies.[247] At other times domestic courts have a much more 'internal' outlook on international law, much more in unison with the executive.

Both situations may be observed in the context of provisional measures to halt executions. The Judicial Committee of the Privy Council (JCPC) is a domestic court with jurisdiction in many Caribbean States, although based in London. In *Thomas* v. *Baptiste* (1999) it found that an execution in advance of the completion of proceedings in the Inter-American human rights system would violate domestic constitutional rights.[248] In any case, on the basis of common law a 'general right' could be found 'accorded to all litigants not to have the outcome of any pending appellate or other legal process pre-empted by executive action'.[249] The JCPC considered that the government had made the international proceedings part of the domestic criminal justice system by ratifying treaties providing for individual access to an international adjudicator. This meant that it had at least temporarily extended the scope of the due process clause in its Constitution.[250]

It also pointed out that the constitutional reference to 'protection of the law' entitled the petitioner to complete international complaint procedures. Because the State in question was a party

---

[246] Next to organisations such as Interights, making accessible Commonwealth and international case law on human rights in searchable databases (<http://www.interights.org/database-search/index.htm>; accessed 29 December 2007), commercial initiatives have also been introduced, including the Oxford University Press project coordinated by the University of Amsterdam called International Law in Domestic Courts (ILDC) (<http://ildc.oxfordlawreports.com/public/login>; accessed 29 December 2007), making available a searchable database of domestic case law from more than 60 jurisdictions both in original and in English translation, together with commentaries, regarding various topics of international law, including human rights.

[247] Take, for instance, the Constitutional Court of Colombia.

[248] JCPC *Thomas* v. *Baptiste*, 27 January 1999/17 March 1999 (reasoned). Lord Millett, Lord Browne-Wilkinson and Lord Steyn for the majority and Lord Puff of Chieveley and Lord Hobhouse of Woodborough dissenting. Initially it did not appear open to the relevance of international proceedings. In 1998, in the *Fisher* case, the JCPC determined that the petitioner had no legitimate expectation that the Bahamas would allow for a reasonable amount of time in order to complete the proceedings before the Inter-American Commission on Human Rights. JCPC *Fisher* v. *Minister of Public Safety and Immigration* (*No. 2*), 5 October 1998. The dissenters considered it 'hard to imagine a more obvious denial of human rights than to execute a man, after many months of waiting for the result, while his case is still under legitimate consideration by an international human rights body'. JCPC *Fisher* v. *Minister of Public Safety and Immigration* (*No. 2*), 5 October 1998. Dissenting opinion of Lord Slynn of Hedley and Lord Hope of Craighead, p. 452 E-F. The difference between the *Fisher* case (1998), concerning the Bahamas, and the *Thomas* case (1999), concerning Trinidad and Tobago, is that the Constitution of the Bahamas does not contain a due process clause while the Constitution of Trinidad does. In *Higgs* v. *Minister of National Security* the JCPC concluded that 'the ratio decidendi of *Thomas* v. *Baptiste* is that a due process clause in section 4(a) of the Trinidad and Tobago Constitution gave the Crown power to accept an international jurisdiction as part of the domestic criminal justice system'. JCPC *Higgs* v. *Minister of National Security*, 14 December 1999, p. 245E.

[249] This was confirmed by the due process clause of the Constitution of Trinidad and Tobago, JCPC *Thomas* v. *Baptiste*, 27 January 1999/17 March 1999 (reasoned), p. 23 D-E.

[250] JCPC *Thomas* v. *Baptiste*, 27 January 1999/17 March 1999 (reasoned), p. 23 E-F.

to the ACHR, the ICCPR and (for the cases still pending) the OP, the petitioner could obtain the reports by the Inter-American Commission and the HRC and present them to the Jamaican Privy Council for consideration *before* the latter would deal with his application for mercy. Until it had received and considered those reports the petitioner was entitled to a stay of execution.[251] The JCPC pointed out that the relevant executive body of the State was to consider the reports of international human rights adjudicators. If, after considering such a report, it would decide not to accept its recommendations this executive body was obliged to provide an explanation.[252]

One aspect that is likely to play a great role in the attitudes of domestic courts is the system of implementation of international law in domestic law: where is the domestic system situated on the continuum between monist and dualist? For more dualist systems: has the applicable international treaty been incorporated in domestic legislation and does this legislation take into account the possibility of the international adjudicator taking provisional measures? The JCPC has confirmed a principle that is important in many common law countries, namely that international conventions do not alter domestic law, except in so far as they are incorporated. Nevertheless, it has noted that it is 'sometimes argued that human rights treaties form an exception to this principle'.[253]

Apart from the JCPC's decisions, relevant to various Caribbean States, the domestic courts of individual States have sometimes faced decisions by international adjudicators. Two cases against Barbados show that in 1992 its courts dismissed the legal relevance of the proceedings under the OP.[254] In *Bradshaw* v. *Barbados* (1994) counsel observed that 'the court of first instance refused to grant the author a stay of execution pending the consideration of his communication by the Human Rights Committee, and that it found that the author could not invoke the provisions of the Covenant, that the Covenant was not part of the law of Barbados, and did not bind the Government of Barbados in respect of it citizens'.[255] The Court of Appeal then observed that 'the provisions enabling written representations to the Human Rights Committee, and the procedural and other provisions thereunder, are not part of the law of Barbados' because the State had not enacted legislation to fulfil its treaty obligations under the ICCPR and the OP.[256]

---

[251] JCPC *Lewis* v. *Jamaica*, 12 September 2000, p. 85B-C.

[252] Id., p. 79E/F and 85C.

[253] JCPC *Thomas* v. *Baptiste*, 27 January 1999/17 March 1999 (reasoned), p. 23C.

[254] HRC *Bradshaw* v. *Barbados*, 19 July 1994 and *Denzil Roberts* v. *Barbados*, 19 July 1994. On 23 May 1992 the authorities read Bradshaw a warrant for his execution on 25 May 1992. His counsel filed a constitutional motion and a stay of execution was granted on 24 May 1992. Four months later the court of first instance dismissed the constitutional motion. The Court of Appeal dismissed the appeal six months afterwards. As in the case of Bradshaw, in *Roberts* the HRC did not receive any further information from the State party about the petitioner's constitutional motion since July 1992. On 24 November 1992 counsel informed the HRC that the court of first instance dismissed the constitutional motion on 29 September 1992 but granted a temporary stay of execution for six weeks, until 10 November 1992. The petitioner appealed to the Court of Appeal and applied for a stay of execution pending the hearing of the appeal against the decision of the court of first instance. On 19 November 1992 the Court of Appeal granted a stay of execution.

[255] HRC *Bradshaw* v. *Barbados*, 19 July 1994, §4.2.

[256] Ibid.

The HRC noted with concern the abovementioned remarks of the Court of Appeal of Barbados.[257]

> "By ratifying the Covenant and the Optional Protocol, Barbados has undertaken to fulfil its obligations thereunder and has recognised the Committee's competence to receive and consider communications from individuals subject to its jurisdiction who claim to be victims of a violation by the State party of any of the rights set forth in the Covenant; while the Covenant is not part of the domestic law of Barbados which can be applied directly by the courts, the State party has nevertheless accepted the legal obligation to make the provisions of the Covenant effective. To this extent, it is an obligation for the State party to adopt appropriate measures to give legal effect to the views of the Committee as to the interpretation and application of the Covenant in particular cases arising under the Optional Protocol. This includes the Committee's views under rule 86 of the rules of procedure on the desirability of interim measures of protection, to avoid irreparable damage to the victim of the alleged violation".[258]

The refusal of the State to respect the HRC's provisional measures in *Ahani* is based on the argument of protection of the general public, but also on the approach of domestic courts towards the obligations under the OP. To understand the decision by the Supreme Court of Canada to dismiss Ahani's appeal, it is important to note that while his case originated years before the terrorist attacks on the US of September 11th, the Supreme Court of Canada made a decision on his expulsion after that date.[259] Subsequently counsel resorted to the HRC and its Special Rapporteur used provisional measures to halt his expulsion. When the Minister refused to do so, counsel brought the case before the Ontario Superior Court, which held that 'if there is a right protected by s. 7 of the *Charter* not to have the outcome of any pending appellate or other legal process pre-empted by executive action, this does not extend to an analogous legal process such as a petition to an international body whose advise is not binding domestically'. The OP did not create a 'legitimate expectation not to be deported pending consideration of a communication by the Committee'.[260]
The Court of Appeal for Ontario dismissed Ahani's appeal from this decision by way of Justice Laskin's majority opinion. It considered that the domestic system did not allow for application of international legal obligations and added that the HRC's provisional measures were not legally binding. It acknowledged that Ahani was still a Convention refugee under the definition in the Refugee Convention and noted that it 'must therefore recognize that he still has a well-founded fear of persecution if returned to Iran'. Nevertheless, 'no principle of fundamental justice entitles him to remain in Canada until his communication is considered by the Committee'.[261] Justice

---

[257]   While it declared the case inadmissible for non-exhaustion, the HRC expressed concern about the fact that the State party had issued an execution warrant for May 1992, in spite of the provisional measures by Special Rapporteur Lallah earlier that month. The HRC confirmed these measures.

[258]   HRC *Peter Bradshaw* v. *Barbados*, 19 July 1994 (inadm.), §§2.9, 2.10, 4.2, 5.3; see also *Denzil Roberts* v. *Barbados*, 19 July 1994, §§2.6, 2.7, 6.3. This follow-up and early expression by the HRC of the legal status of its Views and provisional measures dates from July 1994, the month in which another State, Trinidad and Tobago, executed a petitioner in defiance of a provisional measure. Generally on follow up see Chapter XVIII.

[259]   Supreme Court of Canada *Ahani* v. *Canada*, 11 January 2002.

[260]   Ontario Superior Court Justice Michael R. Dambrot, 15 January 2002, as referred to in Ontario Court of Appeal, *Ahani* v. *Canada*, 8 February 2002, §19.

[261]   Ontario Court of Appeal *Ahani* v. *Canada*, 8 February 2002, §27. Ahani had argued that a domestic injunction was necessary 'to preserve an effective remedy in international law'. Surprisingly, he did not refer to the Committee's case law about provisional measures. He did consider 'that the content of procedural fairness is greater the more vital the interest at stake, and that Canada's international human rights commitments are an indicator, even an important

Laskin argued that neither the ICCPR nor the OP was incorporated into Canadian law. This meant that they had no legal effect in Canada. He considered that Ahani could not use the Canadian Charter and its principles of fundamental justice to 'enforce Canada's international commitments in a domestic court'.[262] Laskin did refer to the case law of the JCPC. However, he 'confessed' that he had difficulty understanding the reasoning of that Court in *Thomas* v. *Baptiste* (1999).[263] Instead he preferred the arguments by Lord Goff, dissenting in that case, considering them 'more in line' with Canadian law.[264] He considered that 'this case demonstrates the difference between the proper role of the executive and the proper role of the judiciary'. "Judges are not competent to assess whether Canada is acting in bad faith by rejecting the Committee's interim measures request and instead deporting Ahani immediately".[265]

He considered that the relevant considerations 'lie within the executive's expertise in foreign relations'.

> "Courts have no expertise in these matters, and in my respectful opinion, have no business intruding into them. Canada agreed to sign an international covenant and protocol that was not binding. It chose not to make these instruments part of its domestic law. It is not for the courts, under the guise of procedural fairness, to read in an enforceable constitutional obligation and commit Canada to a process that admittedly could take years, thus frustrating this country's wish to enforce its own laws by deporting a terrorist to a country where he will face at best a minimal risk of harm".[266]

Another doctrine discussed by the domestic court was that of legitimate expectations. Justice Laskin noted that this doctrine was limited. "It is a doctrine of procedural fairness only. It creates no substantive rights". He considered that Ahani tried to use the doctrine of legitimate expectations to impose procedural requirements on Canada rather than on the HRC. He pointed out that procedural fairness normally relates to participatory rights. Apart from this, he stated that 'nothing in Canada's past practice with interim measures requests or in its dealings with Ahani could give rise to a legitimate expectation that it would permit Ahani to remain in the country until the Committee considers his communication'.[267] He emphasised that Canada 'had no consistent practise of acceding to interim measures requests. In some cases it has; in others it has not'. He pointed out in particular that 'in the only other case concerning a terrorist – Tejinder Pal Sing – Canada did not accede to an interim measures request from the United Nations Committee against Torture'. In this case too it concluded that the petitioner's immediate removal was required by 'its international obligation to ensure it did not become a safe haven for terrorists'.[268] He also considered that Ahani was in fact seeking not only procedural fairness but also a substantive right to remain in Canada until the Committee delivered its Views. Rather than explaining why this was a

---

indicator, of the scope of the principles of fundamental justice'. Ontario Court of Appeal *Ahani* v. *Canada*, 8 February 2002, §30.

[262] Ontario Court of Appeal *Ahani* v. *Canada* (*A.G.*) (2002), §31.

[263] JCPC *Thomas* v. *Baptiste*, 27 January 1999/17 March 1999 (reasoned), Lord Millett, Lord Browne-Wilkinson and Lord Steyn for the majority and Lord Goff of Chieveley and Lord Hobhouse of Woodborough dissenting.

[264] Ontario Court of Appeal *Ahani* v. *Canada*, 8 February 2002, §33.

[265] Ibid.

[266] Ontario Court of Appeal *Ahani* v. *Canada*, 8 February 2002, §49. It may be assumed that he meant: 'at worst a minimal risk of harm'. On the role of the judiciary and the executive in extradition cases see Smeulers (2002).

[267] Ontario Court of Appeal *Ahani* v. *Canada*, 8 February 2002, §§59-61.

[268] Id., §62.

substantive right, he only noted that the doctrine of legitimate expectations did not create substantive rights. It referred to the 'substantive right to remain in Canada until the Committee delivers its views, a process that could take years'.[269]

Judge Rosenberg's dissent in *Ahani* discussed the rationale of the domestic principle of incorporation, invoked by the government, that international conventions are not binding unless they have been specifically incorporated into Canadian law. This was to protect Parliament and the people of Canada from executive action. This case, however, related to 'administrative decision-making (as opposed to legislative interpretation)'.[270] It was the government that sought to invoke this 'non binding principle' in order to 'shield the executive from the consequences of its voluntary decision to enter into and therefore be bound by the Covenant and the Protocol'.[271] The 'non-binding principle' of treaty incorporation 'goes only so far as to affirm that the Covenant and the Protocol do not create rights in the appellant that can be enforced in a domestic court'. In this case, however, the applicant 'claims only the limited procedural right to reasonable access to the Committee, upon which the federal government has conferred jurisdiction'. Whatever the nature of this right of review, the government 'should not be entitled to render it practically illusory by returning him to Iran before he has had a reasonable opportunity to access it'. It was indeed 'a principle of fundamental justice that individuals in Canada have fair access to the process in the Protocol'.[272] While he believed that application of the principle is more difficult in the international context 'because of the difficulty for a Canadian court to assess the merits of a communication to the Committee', he noted 'a generally held consensus in Canada that in the human rights context an individual whose security is at stake should within reason be given the opportunity to access remedies at the international level'. This was 'particularly so where the individual seeks access to a body of the stature of the Committee,' with its adjudicative functions.[273] It was a 'simple principle of justice that where there is a right there should be a remedy'.[274] At least in capital cases the JCPC had held that 'states subject to a constitutionally enshrined due process clause may be obliged to await the decision of international bodies such as the Human Rights Committee'.[275] Justice Rosenberg referred to JCPC cases 'simply as an indica-

---

[269] Id., 8 February 2002, §63.

[270] As phrased by Weiser (2004), pp. 136-137, who notes that 'this is not the accepted position in Canada' although the Supreme Court had not yet specifically addressed this issue. Harrington (2003), p. 82, points out that the judge failed to take into account the practical realities of the OP. She suggests that the common law principle that unincorporated international treaties have no domestic legal consequences should not apply in the same extent to treaties creating international complaint procedures.

[271] Ontario Court of Appeal *Ahani* v. *Canada*, 8 February 2002, Rosenberg dissent, §§91-92.

[272] Id., §93.

[273] Id., §94. He points out that Professor Walter Tarnopolsky was a member of the HRC before he was appointed to Supreme Court of Canada. He also refers to the statement by Lord Millett in *Tangiora* v. *Wellington District Legal Services Committee*, [2000] 1 W.L.R. 240 (P.C.), pp. 244-245 that the (non-binding) views of the HRC 'acquire authority from the standing of its members and their judicial qualities of impartiality, objectivity and restraint'.

[274] Ontario Court of Appeal *Ahani* v. *Canada*, 8 February 2002, Rosenberg dissent, §§95-96.

[275] Id., §97. At §98 he quotes the dissenting opinion of Lord Nicholls in *Briggs* v. *Baptiste*, [2000] 2 A.C. 40, §47: "By acceding to the Convention, Trinidad and Tobago intended to confer benefits on its citizens. The benefits were intended to be real, not illusory. The Inter-American system of human rights was not intended to be a hollow sham or, for those under sentence of death, a cruel charade".

tion that countries with legal systems like ours have found that due process requires that individuals be given the opportunity to access these international bodies'.[276]

3.4.3 'Sorry: we can't comply'

3.4.3.1 INTRODUCTION

States have often said that domestic legislation did not allow them to implement provisional measures. They said, for instance: 'we can't find the beneficiaries'. In 2001, in the *Haitian* mass expulsion case the Dominican Republic informed the Court that it still had not been able to locate the two beneficiaries of the Court's second Order for provisional measures.[277] Two more excuses of this kind are discussed in this section.

3.4.3.2 'WE LACK THE AUTHORITY TO TAKE MEASURES'

Almost two months after it had taken precautionary measures in a case against Ecuador, during an on-site visit, member of the Inter-American Commission Marta Altolaguirre received a commitment from the Minister of Defence that he would deploy the personnel needed to enforce the Commission's precautionary measures. The petitioners, however, reported later that measures were never implemented and that 'the Ministry of Defence had told them that it lacked the authority to take such actions'. Thus, the Commission repeated its precautionary measures and asked the government to provide information on the implementation on a monthly basis.[278]

In September 1996 the Inter-American Commission took precautionary measures on behalf of Roberto Girón and Pedro Castillo Mendoza. Guatemala responded two days later, 'sending an explanation as to why it would not implement the measures requested'.[279] In November 1997 the Commission requested Guatemala to take precautionary measures to stay the execution of Manuel Martinez Coronado. His complaint dealt with violations of due process.[280] Guatemala went ahead with the execution despite the precautionary measure. It just stated that its Court system did not provide for the application of such measures to stay the execution of a death sentence. This is significantly different from its responses to precautionary measures involving death threats and harassment.

---

[276] Ontario Court of Appeal *Ahani* v. *Canada*, 8 February 2002, Rosenberg dissent, §99. He considered that the appellant has a procedural right because the executive had ratified the OP. "That right is a narrow one. It does not entitle him to any particular result either from the Human Rights Committee or the government once it receives the views of the Committee". Rosenberg dissent, §113.

[277] It had requested the help of the Network 'Dominican-Haitian Meeting' and had met with them on 27 November 2000. IACHR *Haitians and Dominicans of Haitian Origin in the Dominican Republic*, Order of 26 May 2001.

[278] CIDH Annual Report 2001, Chapter III (a), §29.

[279] CIDH Annual Report 1996, Chapter II, §4a (cont.).

[280] CIDH Annual Report 1997, Chapter III (2a) under the heading 'Guatemala'.

In *Weiss* v. *Austria* (2003) in response to the HRC Chairperson's letter of regret[281] with regard to Austria's decision to ignore the Committee's provisional measures, the State argued that Rule 86 did not oblige States to amend their constitutions to arrange for direct effect. It considered that a Rule 86 request 'does not as such have any binding effect under international law'. It 'cannot override a contrary obligation of international law, that is, an obligation under the extradition treaty between the State party and the United States to surrender a person in circumstances where the necessary prerequisites set out in a treaty were followed'.[282]

On the Order not to hand over the petitioners to US authorities Bosnia and Herzegovina stated that the Bosnia Chamber was 'fully aware' that Bosnia and Herzegovina had 'no authority to give effect to orders by the Chamber': "In its provisional measure the Chamber requested the state of Bosnia and Herzegovina to prevent the applicants to be taken out of Bosnia and Herzegovina by the use of force. The esteemed Chamber, most certainly, should know by now that the state of Bosnia and Herzegovina, in its distinction from its Entities, does not institutionally possess any instrument of force ... and such wording of the order for provisional measures is not enforceable by the state of Bosnia and Herzegovina".[283]

3.4.3.3 'YOU ARE NOT BEING FAIR: WE CANNOT DO THE IMPOSSIBLE'

In the case of the deportation and expulsion of Haitians and Dominicans of Haitian origin, the Dominican Republic argued during the hearing of August 2000 that it is 'obliged to maintain a permanent return and expulsion policy, but it is necessary to point out that the number of persons repatriated does not compensate even remotely for the number of persons who come into the country illegally'. According to the State, the Court's acceptance of the Commission's request for provisional measures 'would be like tying the hands of a State that has been trying for years to make headway in the field of human rights and concerning its immigration problem'.[284] In another context the Inter-American Commission had already pointed out that the 'State has the

---

[281]   In August 2002 the Chairperson of the HRC, by letter to the mission of Austria at the UN, expressed 'great regret' about the extradition in contravention of the request for interim protection. The HRC sought 'a written explanation about the reasons which led to disregard of the Committee's request for interim measures and an explanation of how it intended to secure compliance with such requests in the future'. On the same date the Special Rapporteur on New Communications requested the State 'to monitor closely the situation and treatment of the author subsequent to his extradition, and to make such representations to the Government of the United States that were deemed pertinent to prevent irreparable harm to the author's Covenant rights'. See HRC *Sholam Weiss* v. *Austria*, 3 April 2003, §5.1.

[282]   HRC *Sholam Weiss* v. *Austria*, 3 April 2003, §5.3.

[283]   Bosnia Chamber *Boudellaa, Lakhdar, Nechle and Lahmar* v. *BiH and Fed. BiH*, 11 October 2002, §109. See also ACHPR *Interights* (*on behalf of Husaini et al.*) v. *Nigeria*, April 2005, response by the State to provisional measures of 6 February 2002 assuring the Chairman of the Commission 'that the administration and many Nigerians equally shared his concern' and expressing' optimism that, in the long run, justice would be done and Safiya's life would be spared'. "While noting that the federal government could not unilaterally suspend the *Sharia* penal statutes and decisions which were within the prerogative of the state government in accordance with the Nigerian Constitution, the letter assured the Chairman that the administration would leave no stone unturned in ensuring that th right to life and human dignity of Safiya, and that of all other Nigerians that may be affected in future, were adequately protected", §20.

[284]   IACHR *Haitians and Dominicans of Haitian Origin in the Dominican Republic* case, Order of 18 August 2000.

obligation to keep order and maintain the conditions for ordinary life with the limits of the law. It cannot abdicate its sovereign obligation to provide guarantees, and the fact that a location is distant from the major urban centers is no excuse for shirking that responsibility'.[285]

Sometimes the measures to be taken require considerable resources, in particular in the context of protection against death threats. The protection required could sometimes amount to an internationally triggered domestic witness protection programme, but mostly it just requires allocation of resources such as building a wall, between two warring factions in a prison. Delay in implementation may then be caused by inter-agency ducking and diving about finances.

As noted, in the European system provisional measures have only once been used to protect persons against threats pending the proceedings before it. Yet on the merits the ECtHR has made quite clear that in order to protect life and personal integrity States are expected to take positive certain measures. In *Kaya* v. *Turkey* (2000) the government contended that they could not have provided effective protection against the attacks. The ECtHR was not convinced by this argument.

> "A wide range of preventive measures would have been available to the authorities regarding the activities of their own security forces and those groups allegedly acting under their auspices or with their knowledge".[286]

3.4.4 'Sorry: it is not our responsibility'

3.4.4.1 INTRODUCTION

There have been several occasions when the State has stated it was not responsible for the non-compliance, for instance because it was a private problem between individuals, because it was a problem created by the previous government and, most often, referring to the internal division of responsibilities between the national government and the governments of constitutive states in a federation.

3.4.4.2 THE MATTER IS A 'PRIVATE PROBLEM BETWEEN INDIVIDUALS'

In November 1995 the Inter-American Commission requested Guatemala to take precautionary measures on behalf of an official of the Myrna Mack Foundation and of an organisation of indigenous peoples in Santa Barbara in the Province of Huehuetenango. He had been threatened and attacked by both local militia patrols and military officers. As a result he had been obliged to leave the community. This interfered with his ability to continue his work on behalf of both organisations. Guatemala refused to implement the precautionary measures requested by the Commission. It alleged that 'the matter was a private problem between individuals'.[287] The State has not generally refused to take positive measures because of precautionary measures by the Commission or provisional measures by the Court, indicating that the refusal is based on a disagreement about the facts, not the law.

---

[285] CIDH *Newton Coutinho Mendes et al.* v. *Brazil*, 13 April 1999, §114.

[286] ECtHR *Mahmut Kaya* v. *Turkey*, 28 March 2000, §100: "The Government have not provided any information concerning steps taken by them prior to the Susurluk report to investigate the existence of contra-guerrilla groups and the extent to which State officials were implicated in unlawful killings carried out during this period, with a view to taking appropriate measures of prevention". See further Chapters IX (Threats) and XIII (Protection).

[287] CIDH Annual Report 1996, 14 Mach 1997, §4a.

3.4.4.3 'IT IS THE PREVIOUS GOVERNMENT'S FAULT'

In response to an argument by Honduras that the previous government was responsible for the situation that triggered precautionary measures, the Inter-American Commission has noted that just like a Government cannot justify a violation of state responsibility because it has been committed by a previous Government, it cannot justify non-implementation of precautionary measures on that basis either. After all, the Commission argues, 'the passive subject of the obligations deriving from this provision of the Convention, which for the most part are concrete and automatic, is not the government or any other body that exercises public power but rather the State itself'. It also noted that 'according to the principle of identity or continuity of the State in international law that responsibility subsists independently of any change of government over the course of time and, concretely, between the time of the illegal act that gave rise to the responsibility and the time that it is denounced'.[288]

3.4.4.4 'IMPLEMENTATION IS THE PREROGATIVE OF THE RELEVANT CONSTITU-ENT STATE IN THIS FEDERATION'

With regard to the United States (US) the Inter-American Commission has requested a stay of execution many times. It generally received no response at all,[289] or it is informed that the Government has forwarded the Commission's request to the Governor or the Office of the Attorney General of the constituent State in question.[290] Shaka Sankofa (formerly Gary Graham) was seventeen at the time of the offence for which he was subsequently sentenced to death and there were serious doubts about his guilt. Years later he was nevertheless executed.[291] In January 1999 the Commission requested the US to stay the execution of Sean Sellers. This stay would enable the Commission to 'study the reports of alleged violations of his human rights, since he was a minor when he committed the crime for which he was sentenced to capital punishment, and he was mentally incapacitated'. Despite this request Mr. Sellers was executed as scheduled on 4 February 1999.[292] Stanley Faulder was a Canadian national sentenced to death in violation of the Vienna Convention on Consular Relations and his execution took place under vigorous protests by Can-

---

[288] CIDH *Minors in Detention* case (Honduras), 10 March 1999, §188. The Commission has used a similar argument with regard to the obligations of Cuba since the OAS had suspended the participation of the Government of Cuba, see paragraph 2.1 of this Chapter (ft. 1).

[289] See e.g. CIDH *Zeitvogel* v. *US*, Annual Report 1996, 14 March 1997, Chapter II, §4a (cont.); *Faulder* v. *US*, Annual Report 1999, Chapter III C.1, §66; *Leisure* v. *US*, Annual Report 1999, Chapter III C.1, §68; *Michael Domingues* v. *US*; *Miguel Ángel Flores* v. *US*; *Alexander Williams* v. *US*, Annual Report 2000 §§49, 51, 52.

[290] See e.g. CIDH *Bannister* v. *US*, Annual Report 1997, Chapter III (a); and *Leisure* v. *US*, Annual Report 1999, Chapter III C, §68; In one case, for instance, the State noted 'the U.S. federal government had no involvement with the case prior to the receipt of the Commission's request and that Mr. Thomas had been executed by the state of Virginia on January 10, 2000, after the U.S. Supreme Court refused to grant a stay'. The US sent this note the day after the execution.6 January 2000, *Douglas Christopher Thomas*, Case 12. 240, scheduled for execution in Virginia on 10 January 2000, executed as scheduled according to information sent by the US on 11 January 2000, Annual report 2000, §47.

[291] CIDH *Case of Gary T. Graham, now known as Shaka Sankofa* v. *US*, 15 June 2000 (adm.) and 29 December 2003 (merits).

[292] CIDH Annual Report 1998, Chapter III (a), §23.

ada.[293] The US message appears to be that it bears no responsibility for the actions of its constituent states.

The federal structure may be more an argument of convenience than the real reason for non-compliance. Moreover, in a federal death penalty case it obviously cannot use the argument that the decision to grant a stay is a prerogative of the relevant constituent state.[294] In the context of the Order by the Inter-American Court for provisional measures on behalf of the *detainees of Mendoza*, in March 2007 the Corte Suprema de Justicia of Argentina pointed out that it was a matter of national rather than regional interest in the consequences of compliance or non-compliance with the recommendations and decisions adopted by the Inter-American Commission and Court. The national executive must represent the State internationally and bear responsibility for any wrongs. The matter has left the domestic sphere and regional authorities and courts could not counteract the obligations incurred by the State. It added that this also appeared from the fact that the Inter-American Commission and Court clearly addressed the State and not the Province of Mendoza.[295] Significantly, the Corte Suprema de Justicia de la Nación also quoted from the Inter-American Court's Order of 30 March 2006 to the effect that the State cannot invoke reasons of domestic law as an excuse for not taking firm, concrete and effective action to implement the Order. The State could not justify failure to comply fully with the excuse that the provincial and national authorities were unable to coordinate their activities to prevent the killings and violence that had continued to take place despite the Court's provisional measures.

In international proceedings it is the State that is responsible, independent of its unitary or federal structure.[296]

3.4.5 'We won't comply'

3.4.5.1 INTRODUCTION

As noted, most provisional measures are generally respected, but this chapter discusses the reasons for States that fail to comply with them. On some occasions a State refuses outright to comply with provisional measures because of domestic concerns or a generally negative attitude towards international supervision.

3.4.5.2 DOMESTIC CONCERNS INCLUDING STATE SECURITY AND PUBLIC SAFETY

In *S.I.G.* v. *the Netherlands* (1985) the Netherlands ignored the European Commission's provisional measures arguing that respecting them would bring the government in conflict with its

---

[293] CIDH Annual Report 1999, Chapter III C.1, §66.

[294] See e.g. CIDH *Juan Raúl Garza* v. *US*, 4 April 2001 (adm.), in which the Commission had already issued a Report on the merits. He has been executed on 19 June 2001. See CIDH Annual Report 2000, §48.

[295] Corte Suprema de Justicia de la Nación, 20 March 2007, as quoted by the IACHR *Las Penitentiarias de Mendoza* (Argentina), President's Order of 22 August 2007 (maintaining the existing provisional measures, but refusing to amplify them), 13th 'Considering' clause.

[296] IACHR *Las Penitentiarias de Mendoza* (Argentina), 11th 'Considering' clause, as quoted by the Corte Suprema de Justicia de la Nación, 20 March 2007, as quoted by the IACHR *Las Penitentiarias de Mendoza* (Argentina), President's Order of 22 August 2007 (maintaining the existing provisional measures, but refusing to amplify them), 13th 'Considering' clause. See also Article 27 VCLT.

domestic legislation. There was some follow-up by the Commission in that it reminded the Dutch Government of its established practice with regard to provisional measures.[297]

In the 'immigration context' provisional measures raised 'some particular difficulties' in which occasionally other (non legal) considerations may take precedence.[298] Canada often refers to its obligations under domestic law.[299]

---

[297]   EComHR *S.I.G.* v. *the Netherlands*, 10 October 1985 (inadm.). See also EComHR *S.* v. *the Netherlands*, 5 March 1984 (inadm.) where the Dutch government refused to comply with the Commission's provisional measures. In practice it did not expel the petitioner pending the proceedings in Strasbourg, but the attitude displayed remains puzzling. The State argued, among others, that there had not been a prima facie violation of the ECHR. It argued it had a policy freedom to decide in which cases to comply and referred to the text of the Rule on provisional measures, which uses the verb: 'may indicate'. A Dutch court also concluded that the Netherlands was not obliged to comply: President of the Court in Rotterdam in summary proceedings, 2-4-1984, KG 118. See e.g. the critical comments by Zwart (1985), pp. 65-71.

[298]   See HRC *Ahani* v. *Canada*, 29 March 2004, §5.3. The State 'fully supported the important role mandated to the Committee and would always do its utmost to cooperate with the Committee'. It stated that 'it took its obligations under the Optional Protocol very seriously and that it was in full compliance with them'. Noting that 'alongside its human rights obligations it also has a duty to protect the safety of the Canadian public and to ensure that it does not become a safe haven for terrorists' (§5.2), it considered that requests for provisional measures are 'recommendatory rather than binding' because neither the ICCPR nor the OP provide for them. It pointed out that it nevertheless 'usually responded favourably' to requests for provisional measures. It had seriously considered the instant request 'before concluding in the circumstances of the case, including the finding (upheld by the courts) that he faced a minimum risk of harm in the event of return, that it was unable to delay the deportation'. "The State party pointed out that usually it responds favourably to requests its decision to do so was determined to be legal and consistent with the *Charter* up to the highest judicial level". See §5.3. A word (or several words) seems to be missing in this sentence. It is not clear, moreover, whether it considered the procedure under the OP the 'highest judicial level'. It referred to its constitutional obligations under the Canadian Charter of Rights and Freedoms rather than to its international obligations. In the 'immigration context' provisional measures raised 'some particular difficulties' in which occasionally other (non legal) considerations may take precedence. However, this 'should not be construed as a diminution of the State party's commitment to human rights or the Committee', §5.3. Interestingly, given the fact that it was its decision to return the petitioner contrary to the Committee's provisional measures, Canada argued with regard to the Committee's request to monitor his treatment in Iran that it had 'no jurisdiction' over him and 'was being asked to monitor the situation of a national of another State party on that State party's territory'. Nevertheless, 'in a good faith desire to cooperate with the Committee' it stated that Iranian authorities had advised it on 2 October 2002 that Ahani 'remained in Iran and was well', §5.4. It added that a representative of the Iranian embassy had contacted it at the end of September of that year informing it that the petitioner had called to enquire about three pieces of luggage he had left at the detention centre. According to the State this showed that he did not fear the Iranian government and that the latter was willing to assist him. It also noted that the petitioner visited the Canadian embassy in Iran in October 2002. He did not raise ill treatment issues, but only noted he had difficulty to obtain employment. Canada stated that it had indicated to Iran that it expected it to comply fully with its international human rights obligations. See §5.4. Almost a year later counsel for the petitioner pointed out that she had initially considered that the petitioner had been arrested upon arrival, but not mistreated and subsequently had been released. Later, however, she had repeatedly attempted to call his family and was told that 'he was at another location and/or that he was sick'. She also pointed out that Canadian officials had reported no

Some States have argued that the HRC should consider State security and public policy before it would impose constraints on State parties. Yet these considerations may not determine whether or not there has been a violation of the Covenant. It is only in the context of permissible restrictions that these considerations could play a role. Similar to many other countries in Canada the Minister has a broad discretion in deciding whether or not to extradite someone and under which conditions. The Extradition Treaty between Canada and the US does provide for the possibility of seeking assurances against the death penalty, but in practice the Minister did not consider it necessary to routinely seek assurances in every case in which the death penalty was an issue.

In *Kindler* (1993) Canada submitted on the merits that it shared a 4,800 kilometre unguarded border with the US and that there had been a steadily increasing number of extradition requests from the US. In 1980 there were 29 such requests and by 1992 there were 83.[300] Canada did not specify how many of these involved death penalty cases, but it explained it chose not to seek assurances against the death penalty on a routine basis because it did not wish to become a haven for the most wanted and dangerous criminals from the US. In *Ng* v. *Canada* (1993) counsel for the petitioner pointed out that the increase in extradition requests related to tax offences and other reasons unrelated to dangerous criminals.[301] The State respected the provisional measures in

---

contacts since fall 2002 and neither had Amnesty International been able to obtain further information. See §6.1.

[299] Weiser (2004) argues that 'current judicial approaches do not give full and consistent credence to international obligations undertaken by Canada, nor do they offer sufficient guidance on the effect of international human rights treaties on domestic laws'. (p. 114) 'There appears to be no presumption of conformity' with regard to international obligations unless the court is faced with 'legislation enacted specifically in furtherance of a treaty'. She refers to the statement of the Supreme Court in *Suresh* that 'our concern is not with Canada's international obligations qua obligations'. The court simply looks at international law as evidence of Canada's principles of fundamental justice rather than 'as controlling in itself', p. 133. She offers explanations for Canada's attitude towards international legal obligations. There are few countries, she notes, facing 'as many constitutional obstacles as Canada to the successful integration of domestic and international law'. Apart from the role of the Canadian Charter of Rights and Freedoms and the fact that treaties are not considered self-executing she refers to the fact that treaty ratification is an executive act and 'the extent of Parliamentary scrutiny in the process of treaty adherence is limited', p. 122. The assessment and considerations on which a decision to ratify is based 'remains an internal document and so, non-governmental actors (including courts) face obvious difficulties in trying to identify the international obligations underlying a particular domestic law'. Subsequently there is 'no systematic review' either 'of new legislation for consistency with treaty obligations', pp. 127-128. She points out that recently 'other countries with Westminster-style Governments have taken steps to rectify similar situations', p. 123. In practice federalism is another obstacle. She points out that 'while the *federal* Executive alone is empowered to enter into international treaties, it has no power to implement them in areas of *provincial* jurisdiction'. By contrast, in other federal States 'such as Australia, the federal government retains residual power to legislate a furtherance of a treaty, even where the subject matter typically falls outside federal jurisdiction', p. 124.

[300] In HRC *Ng* v. *Canada*, 5 November 1993 and *Cox* v. *Canada*, 31 October 1994, the State referred to 88 cases by 1992.

[301] Canada and the US had amended the terms of their bilateral treaty in 1991, making taxation offences extraditable and removing ambiguities about the rules of double jeopardy and reciprocity. The increase in extradition requests, she noted, could well be attributable to these amendments. She submitted that at the time of her client's surrender, the applicable article in the treaty had been in place for fifteen years. During this time the Minister of Justice had only made

Cox v. *Canada* (1994), the third extradition case, but in all three cases Canada put forward arguments against extradition with assurances. It considered that only if it had summarily or arbitrarily taken its decision to extradite without assurances the extradition would violate the petitioner's rights. The Committee took specific note of the reasons advanced by the minister of justice, 'in particular, the absence of exceptional circumstances, the availability of due process and of appeal against conviction, and the importance of not providing a safe-haven for those accused of murder'.[302]

---

302   three decisions on whether or not to ask for assurances that the death penalty would not be imposed or executed.

302   HRC *Ng* v. *Canada*, 5 November 1993 §15.5-15.6. In both *Kindler* and *Ng* the State party referred to the United Nations Model Treaty on Extradition, arguing that this treaty allowed for discretion in obtaining assurances against the death penalty. This argument does not convince. The model treaty on extradition, like the bilateral treaty between the US and Canada, is not a human rights treaty and does not aim to be one. It simply provides the option to obtain assurances in order to help solve possible conflicts of participating States' obligations under human rights treaties. In other words, the extradition treaty may provide for discretion, *allowing* a State to obtain assurances, while that State's human rights obligations *oblige* the State to make use of this possibility. In this respect counsel pointed out that 'it is very significant that the existence of the discretion embodied in article 6, in relation to the death penalty, enables the contracting parties to honour both their own domestic constitutions and their international obligations without violating their obligations under the bilateral Extradition Treaty'. See e.g. *Ng* v. *Canada*, 5 November 1993, §11.2. Although unrelated to its task under the OP or the Covenant, in its decision on the merits the HRC added an observation on Canada's obligations under treaties other than the ICCPR, noting that abolition of the death penalty did not release Canada from its obligations under extradition treaties. It considered that only if the decision to extradite without any assurances would have been taken arbitrarily or summarily it would have violated its obligations under Article 6 ICCPR. See e.g. *Cox* v. *Canada*, 31 October 1994. Counsel stressed that Pennsylvania had stated in its extradition application that it was seeking the death penalty. The HRC observed once more that the domestic abolition of capital punishment did not release Canada of its obligations under the extradition treaties. "However, it is in principle to be expected that, when exercising a permitted discretion under an extradition treaty (namely, whether or not to seek assurances that capital punishment will not be imposed) a State which has itself abandoned capital punishment would give serious consideration to its own chosen policy in making its decision. The Committee observes, however, that the State party has indicated that the possibility to seek assurances would normally be exercised where exceptional circumstances existed. Careful consideration was given to this possibility. The Committee notes the reasons given by Canada not to seek assurances in Mr. Cox's case, in particular, the absence of exceptional circumstances, the availability of due process in the State of Pennsylvania, and the importance of not providing a safe haven for those accused of or found guilty of murder". See §16.4. See also *Kindler* v. *Canada*, §14.5 and *Ng* v. *Canada*, §15.5 (in this case the phrasing was slightly different: 'However, it should be expected that'). In the three cases the HRC considered that Canada's decision was not taken arbitrarily or summarily. In other words, while pointing out that States must be 'mindful of the possibilities for the protection of life when exercising their discretion in the application of extradition treaties', the HRC left a wide margin of discretion to the State. This remark is particularly striking firstly because it seems that in this case the HRC takes the approach that the question whether or not there is a violation depends on whether there are conflicting treaty obligations. Secondly, these obligations are not really conflicting because the applicable extradition treaty explicitly provides for the possibility to request assurances. A reason for this approach may be the ambiguity within the Committee about the interpretation of

In a case before its own Supreme Court, ten years after the Committee's decision in *Kindler* and *Ng*, but before its reversal of these cases, the Canadian government argued once more that if it would seek assurances and the US would refuse these it could face the possibility that the respondent might avoid a trial altogether. The Supreme Court replied with the question why the US would prefer not to try them at all if the death penalty could not be imposed. It also noted that in cases where assurances against the death penalty had been asked of the US (by Mexico, by European states and twice by Canada) the US had indeed given them.[303] In this domestic case Canada emphasised once more the need to ensure that Canada would not become a 'safe haven' for dangerous fugitives. However, the Supreme Court argued that there was no evidence that extradition to face life imprisonment without release or parole provided a lesser deterrent to those seeking a 'safe haven' than did the death penalty. "Elimination of a 'safe haven' depends on vigorous law enforcement rather than on infliction of the death penalty by a foreign State after the fugitive has been removed from this country".[304] This domestic law case, decided ten years after the extraditions of Kindler, Ng and Cox, changed Canada's attitude, at least domestically. In a unanimous decision issued in February 2001 the Supreme Court of Canada ruled that Canadian authorities must seek and obtain assurances against the death penalty to States that still impose it. In all but exceptional circumstances this obligation outweighs all other considerations. The decision turns on the increasing awareness of the possibility of error in criminal cases, making the death penalty unacceptable since it is irrevocable. While this new attitude has no direct bearing on the HRC's provisional measures, the Supreme Court of Canada addressed several issues the State had brought up in its arguments before the HRC ten years earlier.

The Court states that it must determine what constitutes the applicable principles of fundamental justice in the extradition context. These principles are derived from "the basic tenets of our legal system".[305] It noted that its *appreciation* of the applicable principles of fundamental justice may have changed since 1991.[306] Its concern about wrongful convictions was probably the most important factor in the Court's change of heart.[307] The recent developments originating in the

---

the obligations under Article 6 for States that have abolished the death penalty. The HRC reversed its case law in 2003. See *Judge* v. *Canada*, 5 August 2003.

[303] Supreme Court of Canada *United States* v. *Burns*, 15 February 2001.

[304] Id.

[305] The question before the Supreme Court was whether ministerial discretion in extradition cases might go so far that it would infringe on the rights and freedoms in the Canadian Constitution. "Although it is generally for the Minister, not the court, to assess the weight of competing considerations in extradition policy, the availability of the death penalty opens up a different dimension. Death penalty cases are uniquely bound up with basic constitutional values and the Court is the guardian of the Constitution".

[306] "While these basic tenets have not changed since 1991 when *Kindler* and *Ng* were decided, their application 10 years later must take note of factual developments in Canada and in relevant foreign jurisdictions".

[307] The Court stated: "The accelerating concern about potential wrongful convictions is a factor of increased weight since Kindler and Ng were decided. The avoidance of conviction and punishment of the innocent has long been in the forefront of 'the basic tenets of our legal system'. The recent and continuing disclosures of wrongful convictions for murder in Canada and the United States provide tragic testimony to the fallibility of the legal system, despite its elaborate safeguards for the protection of the innocent. This history weighs powerfully in the balance against extradition without assurances when fugitives are sought to be tried for murder by a retentionist state, however similar in other respects to our own legal system". The Court devoted several paragraphs on a discussion of wrongful convictions cases in Canada, the US and the UK (§§96-117) and concluded that there was an inherent risk of judicial error in the Anglo-

United States itself, bringing to light so many wrongful convictions, contributed to convince the Supreme Court of Canada that legal systems cannot be infallible, that mistakes are bound to be made even in the best systems with the best lawyers and judges. Apart from this, its arguments included the following:

> "It is final. It is irreversible. Its imposition has been described as arbitrary. Its deterrent value has been doubted. Its implementation necessarily causes psychological and physical suffering. It has been rejected by the Canadian Parliament for offences committed within Canada. Its potential imposition in this case is thus a factor that weighs against extradition without assurances".

The Canadian Supreme Court does not seem to have been influenced by the HRC case law, but rather by developments in the US itself and by international developments in general.[308]

In *T.P.S.* v. *Canada* (2000) the State submitted that 'the examination of possible irreparable harm should be a rigorous one, particularly when the individual concerned was found to represent a danger to the public or, as in the author's case, whose continued presence in the State was determined to be contrary to the public interest'.[309] It then submitted that the authorities had concluded that the risk was minimal 'on the basis of the documentary evidence submitted by the author as well as their own evidence regarding the author's risk upon removal to India'. Finally, it mentioned that a judge of the Federal Court Trial Division had determined that the risk to the author was not sufficient to justify a stay of his removal.[310] It is not clear whether this judge was aware of the involvement of CAT and its provisional measures.

With regard to the State's policy argument based on the obligation under the post-September 11th Security Council resolution, in his dissent to the domestic *Ahani* case Justice Rosenberg pointed out that Canada was 'not harbouring terrorists or setting itself up as a haven for terrorists'. If Canada would nevertheless be concerned that the OP would be used 'as a vehicle to shield terrorists' it could denounce it. "It did not have to ratify the Protocol and many nations, such as the United States of America and the United Kingdom, have not done so".[311] He found it 'difficult to accept that the federal government ratified the treaty because it knew it could not be made to comply with its binding obligations'. "This would undermine the good faith obligation inherent in ratifying treaties". He noted the statements by the government of Canada in 1976 announcing it would ratify the ICCPR and the OP: 'our becoming party to these extremely important human rights instruments will enable us to play a more active role internationally in the human rights field and will moreover strengthen our credibility in urging other states also to become parties and to implement their provisions'.[312] Another official government statement he referred to was that Canada 'accepts the authority of the UN Human Rights Committee to hear com-

---

American system. This discussion included a summary of recent concerns raised within the USA (§§104-111). This inherent risk was clearly an important argument for the Court to change its views.

[308] In turn the HRC's reversal of *Kindler* and *Ng* does appear to be influenced by *Burns*, see *Judge* v. *Canada,* 5 August 2003.

[309] CAT *T.P.S.* v. *Canada,* 16 May 2000, §8.3. Also referring to the '*danger to the public*' argument see the State in CAT *Mafhoud Brada* v. *France,* 17 May 2005, §8.10.

[310] CAT *T.P.S.* v. *Canada,* 16 May 2000, §8.3.

[311] Ontario Court of Appeal, *Ahani* v. *Canada,* 8 February 2002, dissenting opinion of Rosenberg, §101.

[312] Statement by Hon. Allan J. MacEachen (Secretary of State for External Affairs) to the House of Commons, 18 May 1976, as quoted by Rosenberg, §103 in Ontario Court of Appeal, *Ahani* v. *Canada,* 8 February 2002, dissenting opinion of Rosenberg. See also Harrington (2003), p. 56.

plaints' under the OP and that Canada's human rights undertakings strengthen its 'reputation as a guarantor of its citizens' rights and enhance our credentials to urge other governments to respect international standards'.[313]

Responding to the argument that 'the Committee, which is chronically under funded, can take years to reach a decision', he considered that the right of access to the HRC was 'not absolute and the appellant may not have an unconditional right to stay in Canada indefinitely'.[314] He 'would not foreclose the possibility that the government might be able to show that the Committee process will result in such an intolerable delay that the balance of convenience favours deportation'.[315] "I would think, however, that would be an unusual case. Here the domestic procedures have occupied over eight years and the appellant has remained in custody throughout. Canada can hardly complain about some delay at the Committee level when it is a condition of invoking that jurisdiction that all domestic remedies have been exhausted".[316] He remarked, furthermore, that the principle of fundamental justice that the right of access to the HRC includes a stay of expulsion 'may only be enforced in cases where the individual's life, liberty or security of the person interests are implicated, as in the case of a Convention refugee'. "The right to pursue the international remedy is not a means for delaying deportation in less serious cases".[317]

The domestic court clearly confuses legal status and enforcement. The ICJ itself explained that those are two different matters when it noted 'the fact that the court does not itself have the means to ensure the execution of orders (...) is not an argument against the binding nature of such orders'.[318] While the domestic court referred to 'case law' to support its view that provisional

---

[313]   See Ontario Court of Appeal *Ahani* v. *Canada*, 8 February 2002, dissenting opinion of Rosenberg, §103, quoting from Human Rights in Canadian Foreign Policy, at a government internet address that is not accessible anymore. Presently the government provides information entitled 'Canada's Commitment to Human Rights', last updated 9 April 2003, at <www.dfait-maeci.gc.ca/foreign_policy/human-rights/hr3-commit-en.asp> (consulted on 3 August 2004). On this page it states that it takes its international human rights obligations seriously, that it accepts the authority of the UN treaty monitoring Committees to hear complaints 'from Canadian citizens' (this is imprecise because it has recognised this right for 'individuals subject to its jurisdiction') under the OP and the Convention against Torture. "These international mechanisms provide an independent perspective on the state of human rights in Canada, and allow the Canadian government to review laws or policies which may be in conflict with international obligations. This willingness to accept independent, constructive criticism is critical to Canada's credibility, both domestically and internationally. Canada holds itself to the same standard it expects from other countries".

[314]   Ontario Court of Appeal *Ahani* v. *Canada*, 8 February 2002, dissenting opinion of Rosenberg, §§105 and 106.

[315]   The reference to 'balance of convenience' is derived from the domestic test for granting an interlocutory injunction. "That test requires the court first to make a preliminary assessment of the merits of the case to ensure that there is a serious question to be tried. Secondly, the court must determine whether the applicant would suffer irreparable harm if the application were refused. Finally, an assessment must be made as to which of the parties would suffer greater harm from the granting or refusal of the remedy pending a decision on the merits". Ontario Court of Appeal *Ahani* v. *Canada*, 8 February 2002, dissenting opinion of Rosenberg, §107, referring to *RJR-Macdonald Inc.* v. *Canada (Attorney General)* (1994), 111 D.L.R. (4th) 385 (S.C.C.), at 400.

[316]   Ontario Court of Appeal *Ahani* v. *Canada*, 8 February 2002, dissenting opinion of Rosenberg, §110.

[317]   Apart from this, he considered that there could be cases in which the balance of convenience would favour removal 'as where the applicant poses an unacceptable risk to public security even where, as in this case, he or she is being held in custody', Rosenberg dissent, §109.

[318]   See ICJ *LaGrand* (*Germany* v. *US*), 27 June 2001, §107.

measures are not binding, it did not specify this case law, let alone refer to the Committee's consistent decisions actually emphasising the legal obligation to respect provisional measures.[319] Harrington points out that in light of the Committee's strong statements in previous cases on the seriousness of ignoring its provisional measures and given 'the ready availability of this information on the internet', it was 'disturbing' that the domestic court did not mention this line of jurisprudence and even 'more disturbing that Canada continues to simply decline to abide by a rule 86 request rather than, at a minimum, making an application to have the request withdrawn'. "It is also disturbing that Canada routinely accepts the Committee's rules of procedure on relatively minor issues, such as the form and due date for its submissions, but disregards the procedures developed by the Committee for the preservation of an individual's life or physical integrity".[320]

The domestic court took the baffling position that 'the international community has agreed to binding obligations in other treaties', but 'in the Covenant and the Protocol, it made a policy decision to do otherwise'.[321] Mystifying is also the Court's statement that 'both the European Court of Human Rights and the Privy Council have acknowledged that the Committee's views are not binding or enforceable'. It referred to the European Court's judgment in *Cruz Varas*, dealing with the provisional measures in the European system. Obviously the ECtHR would have no competence to pronounce itself on the legal status of the Committee's Views. Thus, the domestic court must have had the intention to draw an analogy between the European system and the system under the OP. In that context it is significant that the ECtHR has since determined that its provisional measures to halt refoulement are legally binding, confirming the approach taken by the HRC and the Committee against Torture.[322]

The domestic court seems to have a rather limited conception of the function of the judiciary in the context of international obligations. Apparently it thought that compliance with international treaties was a political rather than a legal matter. Also the 'political question' doctrine does not necessarily mean that such compliance is not a legal matter. The decision to declare provisional measures non-binding appears to be based on the conviction that it *is* a legal matter.

It is exactly in times of 'real or perceived threat' that the 'responsibility of the judiciary to protect human rights comes under special scrutiny'.[323] It does not seem, however, that the domestic courts considered they had such a responsibility in *Ahani*. The Court also failed to mention CAT's response to Canada's non-compliance in *T.P.S.* v. *Canada*.[324] It places undue deference to

---

[319]　See also Harrington (2003), pp. 83-84. The court also referred to an incorrect observation in the introduction to the Committee's earlier volumes of Selected Decisions. This introduction does not comport with the approach of the HRC itself. In any case an introduction to a bound volume of the Committee's Selected Decisions is not nearly as authoritative as the Committee's Views, Concluding Observations and other official public statements.

[320]　Harrington (2003), p. 72, pp. 83-84.

[321]　See Ontario Court of Appeal *Ahani* v. *Canada*, 8 February 2002, §37.

[322]　ECtHR (first section) *Mamatkulov and Abdurasulovic* v. *Turkey*, 2 February 2003 and Grand Chamber *Mamatkulov and Askarov* v. *Turkey*, 15 December 2004, discussed in Chapter XVI (Legal status). Similarly the US tried to base its argument of the non-binding character of the Inter-American Commission's precautionary measures on the 1991 *Cruz Varas* judgment by the ECtHR, see Digest of the US practice in international law 2002, Chapter 6, no. 21. 'U.S. Additional Response to the request for precautionary measures', 15 July 2002, <http://www.state.gov/s/l/38642.htm> (consulted 8 January 2009).

[323]　See Macklin (2002), p. 15, discussing the domestic *Ahani* and *Suresh* cases.

[324]　See CAT *T.P.S.* v. *Canada*, 16 May 2000. See also Harrington (2003), pp. 85-86.

the executive and starts from the remarkable assumption that the ICCPR and the OP, international treaties ratified by Canada, are not binding.[325]

In his case the length of proceedings was mainly due to the domestic proceedings. Ahani had been in detention fighting his expulsion since June 1993. Only in 2002, upon exhaustion of domestic remedies, he petitioned the HRC.[326]

Harrington concludes that the *Ahani* decision by the Ontario Court of Appeal was 'a most regrettable and undesirable precedent and one that runs counter to the very principles and spirit of international dispute settlement, a phenomenon that now extends beyond interstate disputes to include those between states and individuals where a State has given its consent'.

> "By allowing Canada to disregard requests for interim measures from a body such as the Human Rights Committee, the Ontario Court of Appeal and the Supreme Court of Canada have, in essence, gutted the right of individual petition of all utility, since any subsequent finding of a violation will be impossible to remedy with the individual outside Canada's jurisdiction".[327]

France has also justified ignoring provisional measures by CAT because a petitioner was a 'demonstrably dangerous common criminal' who 'presented a particularly disproportionate risk to public order and the safety of third parties'.[328] CAT itself emphasised that in non-refoulement cases the balancing with the general interest, preferred by many States, is not allowed. In *Adel Tebourski* v. *France* (2007) CAT noted that 'article 3 of the Convention offers absolute protection to anyone in the territory of a State party which has made the declaration under article 22. Once this person alludes to a risk of torture under the conditions laid down in article 3, the State party can no longer cite domestic concerns as grounds for failing in its obligation under the Convention to guarantee protection to anyone in its jurisdiction who fears that he is in serious danger of being tortured if he is returned to another country'.[329] It noted that 'even if the Committee takes into consideration all the comments which the State party has submitted on this communication, the declaration made by the State party under article 22 confers on the Committee alone the power to assess whether the danger invoked is serious or not. The Committee takes into account the State party's assessment of the facts and evidence, but it is the Committee that must ultimately decide whether there is a risk of torture'.[330]

---

[325] Harrington points out that the 'lack of a world policeman does not make a treaty any less binding on a state that has voluntarily agreed to become a party through ratification or accession'. In this context she expresses concern about the domestic court's obviously incorrect 'appreciation of the very nature of international law'. Harrington (2003), p. 83. She adds that the responses by the HRC and the CAT to the State's non-compliance show that the two international adjudicators do not recognize exceptions in the context of terrorism. The wish to deport suspected terrorists 'does not justify downgrading long-standing treaty law commitments in the field of human rights to ineffective exhortations', Harrington (2003), p. 86.

[326] In January and May 2002 the HRC used provisional measures. Canada nevertheless deported Ahani in June 2002. The Committee published its View in March 2004. *Mansour Ahani* v. *Canada*, 29 March 2004.

[327] Harrington (2003), p. 86.

[328] CAT *Mafhoud Brada* v. *France*, 17 May 2005, §8.10.

[329] CAT *Adel Tebourski* v. *France*, 1 May 2007, §8.3. Obviously this response equally indicates the follow up by CAT, see also Chapter XVIII.

[330] CAT *Adel Tebourski* v. *France*, 1 May 2007, §8.3.

3.4.5.3 GENERALLY NEGATIVE ATTITUDE TOWARDS INTERNATIONAL SUPERVISION

3.4.5.3.1 Introduction

In the interest of easing domestic or international pressures a State may respond to provisional measures in a hostile fashion, indifferently or, on the other hand, in a cooperative manner. The role of the media and public opinion may be manifested both ways. It may result in public shaming of the State, triggering compliance, or in pressure on the State *not* to implement provisional measures. The latter may occur in the context of the death penalty and certain asylum cases. In such cases States domestic public opinion often is considered much more important than international public opinion. States may then have a negative attitude towards international supervision, which is also reflected in their response to provisional measures.

In February 2002 the Inter-American Commission used precautionary measures calling on the US to stay the execution of British citizen Mr. Housel, scheduled to be executed in Georgia on 12 March 2002.[331] He was executed as scheduled. An indication of the intransigent attitude of the State with regard to this subject matter is the fact that this was done despite involvement not just by the Inter-American Commission, but also by the U.K. government, the European Union and the Council of Europe, which had all appealed for clemency.[332] This subsection provides some other examples in this respect.

3.4.5.3.2 'No foreign meddling with judicial orders or lawfully imposed sentences'

In its Order of May 1999 the Inter-American Court referred to a note of Trinidad and Tobago of September 1998. In this note Trinidad asserted that 'the Court does not have jurisdiction (…) to take any steps or decide upon any measures that will frustrate the implementation of a lawfully imposed sentence of death in Trinidad and Tobago'. Trinidad also declared that it would not 'be consulting with the Commission or the Court any further in these matters'.[333]

After extraditing a petitioner on whose behalf the HRC had used provisional measures Austria noted that its reason for disrespecting the provisional measures and extraditing the petitioner was that a lower court had blocked the State's compliance. It noted that the Federal Minister of Justice had ordered the Public Prosecutor's Office in Vienna 'to file a request with the investigating judge of the Vienna Regional Criminal Court seeking suspension of the extradition'. However, 'the Court refused to comply with this request, on the basis that Rule 86 of the Committee's

---

[331] Amnesty International, Urgent Action, 4 March 2002, AI Index: AMR 51/043/2002.

[332] Amnesty International, further information on EXTRA 18/02(AMR 51/043/2002, 4 March 2002), AI Index: AMR 51/046/2002, 13 March 2002. See the urgent humanitarian appeal sent on 4 March 2002 by Spain as the current president of the EU together with Denmark, its subsequent president and the European Commission on behalf of the EU to both the Governor of Georgia and to the Chairman of the Georgia Board of Pardons and Paroles. See also the statement of Walter Schwimmer, the Secretary General of the Council of Europe, condemning the decision to refuse clemency in this case, press statement of 12 March 2002, 131a (2002) and the statement of the President of the Parliamentary Assembly of the Council of Europe of 13 March 2002, 137a (2002).

[333] IACHR *James et al.* case, Order of 25 May 1999.

Rules of Procedure may neither invalidate judicial orders nor restrict the jurisdiction of an independent domestic Court'.[334]

3.4.5.3.3 'We don't need outsiders'

After the execution of three petitioners and beneficiaries of the Committee's provisional measures one State party had argued that it was 'highly inappropriate' for counsel to petition the HRC after they had applied for presidential clemency and this application had been rejected.[335] In response the HRC expressed 'grave concern about the State party's explanation for its action' and pointed out:

> "There is nothing in the Optional Protocol that restricts the right of an alleged victim of a violation of his or her right under the Covenant from submitting the communication after a request for clemency or pardon has been rejected, and the State party may not unilaterally impose such a condition that limits both the competence of the Committee and the right of alleged victims to submit communications".[336]

3.4.5.3.4 'Our own system of protection suffices'

States often consider that domestic courts can do the job. In *Weiss* v. *Austria* (2003) the State emphasised 'the extensive consideration' of the petitioner's case by the Austrian courts and the ECtHR, implying that there was no need for the HRC to examine a case like this.[337]

They have also justified ignoring provisional measures by stating that the allegations of the asylum seeker were 'not credible'. Mansi had claimed that his expulsion to Jordan involved a risk that 'he would be detained and tortured in the way he has been tortured before'. Upon his expulsion he also claimed a violation of Articles 1 and 25 (current Article 34) ECHR by Sweden for deporting him despite the provisional measures. The State had submitted that the petitioner had 'changed his story several times'. It considered that his allegations, pending the domestic proceedings in Sweden, that he had suffered torture in Jordan were not credible. Only at a late stage he had mentioned anything about torture. "At the time of the expulsion the Government had available relevant and reliable information about the current situation in Jordan. There was no reason to believe that the applicant would be subjected to treatment contrary to Article 3 of the Convention in Jordan".[338] The Commission examined the question whether, 'at the time of the expulsion, there existed substantial grounds for believing that he faced a real risk of being treated contrary to Article 3 of the Convention in Jordan'. At the stage of admissibility it had carried out a preliminary examination of the issue. It considered that it raised 'questions of fact and law which are of such a complex nature that their determination should depend on an examination of the merits'.[339] Mansi was returned to Jordan contrary to the Commission's provisional measures.

---

[334] See HRC *Sholam Weiss* v. *Austria*, 3 April 2003, §5.2.

[335] HRC *Dante Piandiong, Jesus Morallos and Archie Bulan (deceased) (submitted by Alexander Padilla and Ricardo III Sunga)* v. *the Philippines*, 19 October 2000, §§3.1 and 5.3.

[336] Id., §5.3. Additionally, the HRC noted that the State party had not shown that the course of justice would have been obstructed by acceding to its request for provisional measures.

[337] See HRC *Sholam Weiss* v. *Austria*, 3 April 2003, §5.3.

[338] EComHR *Mansi* v. *Sweden*, 7 December 1989, §1.

[339] Ibid.

There he was subjected to ill treatment upon his return to Jordan, and subsequently needed treatment at the Danish torture rehabilitation centre. The case was closed with a friendly settlement.[340]

In 2000 the Philippines ignored provisional measures by the HRC to halt an execution because it considered that the beneficiaries of the Committee's provisional measures had received a fair trial.[341]

During 1997 alone the Inter-American Commission granted precautionary measures in fourteen death penalty cases with regard to Trinidad and Tobago.[342] In the case of Mr. Ross the Commission received the following response: '(t)his petition duplicates the petition to the Judicial Committee of the Privy Council, and the petitioner seeks to use the Commission as a fourth level of appeal, which is not its function'.[343] In the case of Mr. Thomas Trinidad and Tobago likewise responded that '(t)he petitioner is attempting to use the Commission as a fourth level of appeal' and it added that this is 'only permissible if there has been some denial of justice'. It argued that this could not be the case: '(t)his matter has been presented to the Privy Council, which rejected the appeal. As a result, it is unthinkable that justice was denied'.[344]

The response of Trinidad and Tobago has often been rather blunt: 'There was no denial of justice and Mr. Denny Baptiste was not treated in a cruel and inhuman manner. In addition, legal assistance is available to the poor'.[345]

In its first submission to the Inter-American Court to apply for provisional measures to halt the execution of persons, the Commission pointed out that it had adopted its own precautionary measures, but that Trinidad did not respond. Later, Trinidad alleged that the Commission did not have jurisdiction 'either by its acts or omissions to prevent in any way a sentence, authorized by the Constitution and laws of Trinidad and Tobago and pronounced by a Court of competent jurisdiction, from being carried into effect'. It declared that it was 'at liberty to carry out the death sentences according to its domestic laws'.[346] The State's attitude towards the Commission's decisions was that Article 41 only empowered the Commission to make recommendations. This meant that the Commission could not overturn judgments of domestic courts.[347]

3.4.5.3.5 'Dangerous international law'

Tensions flared up as views on the government policy on detention of immigrants, both pro and contra, were expressed in the press. This was especially so in the context of discussions in the press on the detention of children in Australia. The Bakhtiyari case was often taken as an example. Commenting on the Family Court decision in April 2002 to hear the case of the two Bakhtiyari boys in September, one newspaper qualified this as 'a skewed interpretation of the law'. This is an example of one section of public opinion in Australia. It noted:

---

[340] EComHR *Mansi* v. *Sweden*, 9 March 1990 (Friendly settlement).

[341] HRC *Dante Piandiong, Jesus Morallos and Archie Bulan (deceased) (submitted by Alexander Padilla and Ricardo III Sunga)* v. *the Philippines*, 19 October 2000.

[342] See CIDH Annual Report 1997, Chapter III (2a), under 'Trinidad and Tobago'.

[343] The case of Mr. Ross, response of 23 December 1997, ibid.

[344] The case of Mr. Thomas, response of 15 December 1995, ibid.

[345] The cases of Mr. Hilaire and Mr. Baptiste respectively, ibid.

[346] IACHR *James, Briggs, Noel, Garcia and Bethel* cases, Order of the President for urgent measures, 27 May 1998.

[347] For some very critical comments on the general attitude of Trinidad see e.g. IACHR *Caesar* v. *Trinidad and Tobago*, Judgment of 11 March 2005, individual opinion of Judge Jackman.

"As even Nicholson [family court judge, E.R.] noted in his Cape Town address, international treaties and conventions don't hold much sway under Australian domestic law. That, of course, has not stopped him and other activist judges from relying on so-called international law in their ideologically driven attempts to seek justice – a short hand word for what the law should be according to them. It's easy. These conventions are couched in generous language. Like a horoscope they can mean just about whatever you want them to mean. And so, as law professor Pat Lane said recently, 'the commonwealth Government's innumerable international assurances lie in ambush', waiting to overturn the decisions of domestic democratic bodies".[348]

3.4.5.3.6 'We decide how our country should be run'

In response to international criticism (not just the provisional measures by the HRC, but a range of statements and visits by other UN officials)[349] of its system of mandatory immigration detention, also for children, Australia's Foreign Minister told the Australian parliament: 'We do not run off to the United Nations asking how Australia should be run,' and 'whatever the rights and wrongs of these issues, we will decide them for ourselves, not have bureaucrats in Geneva decide them for us'.[350]

3.4.5.3.7 Conclusion on domestic reasons for non-compliance

Many interrelated factors play a role. The precise reasoning may be blurred. An argument, for instance, that the assessment of risk by domestic courts is better may be based not only on the assumption that international adjudicators are more removed from the facts, but also on the fact that the domestic court took into account the risk to society in its assessment of the risk to the petitioner, while the international adjudicator has pointed out that the international obligation is of such nature that it does not allow for balancing.[351]

Compliance with provisional measures seems to be more difficult in relation to decisions to execute extradition or expulsion orders or even death sentences in a democracy. While the international adjudicator takes provisional measures considering that the petition has brought a valid claim under international law and is facing irreparable harm to life or personal integrity, domestic authorities may decide not to comply in order to satisfy and protect the public. The mobilization of shame customarily referred to as an important means of enforcement of human rights obligations does not apply to the same extent in such cases. There may be a belief among many members of the public, as reported by the media, that human rights only apply to law-abiding citizens, experiencing an urgent need to protect their own safety and not wishing to know exactly how this is being done.[352] It may also be a partial explanation of the attitudes of Trinidad and Tobago and

---

[348] J. Albrechtsen, 'Ideology blurs role of judiciary', The Australian, 21 August 2002, originally posted at <www.theaustralian.com.au>. It may still be found at the website of the Richard Hillman Foundation, in apparent support of her position, <www.rhfinc.org.au/docs/blurs.pdf> (consulted on 4 August 2004).

[349] See Chapter XVIII (Follow-up).

[350] Michael Millett and Michael Bradley, 'Criminals better off than asylum seekers', Sydney Morning Herald, 7 June 2002, <www.smh.com.au> (consulted on 9 April 2003).

[351] See also Conclusion Part II and Chapter XV (Immediacy and risk).

[352] For instance, during the first period Fujimori (Peru) was in power he was popular for being tough on crime and terrorism.

the US.[353] In other cases States might comply in order to avoid media attention, but this obviously is less often the case with regard to halting executions in democracies with a public opinion largely favouring the death penalty or largely suspicious of foreign courts.

4   CONCLUSION

A distinction may be made between responses in which the parties (in particular the State) protest against the (temporary) outcome of the normative process, on the one hand, and against the development of the process as such on the other hand. Explanations for the first type may be derived from the system of implementation in domestic law, specific politics, the role of media, domestic and international NGOs and other international actors.[354] This response may differ depending on the type and specificity of the provisional measure.

Explanations of non-compliance based on the second type, disagreement with the decision-making process of the adjudicator, may relate to the procedures of the adjudicator in general or to specific issues arising in the case, e.g. relating to the principle of *audiatur et altera pars* or the lack of transparency in the decision-making process.

Non-compliance should not necessarily be attributed to the common law system. Equally, non-common law countries such as Austria and Finland have argued that their administrative system did not permit them to implement provisional measures because they did not have the authority to overrule the decision of a domestic court. This is a problem occurring in both common and civil law systems. It may be related more to the fact that in many States international law is not part of domestic law. Thus, one explanation for non-compliance may be that international obligations have not (yet) been incorporated in the domestic system. In addition, compliance may also depend on whether it is a federal State, on the role of the media, of public opinion (as perceived) and on the fact that there will be elections soon.

Apart from the domestic circumstances at the time, some explanatory power for the attitudes of addressee States may lie, for instance, in the perceived authority of the adjudicator among the State parties in general or the attitude of that particular State to international adjudicators in general.

As to the type of provisional measures, what may matter is the controversial nature of the particular subject matter, the required measures of protection (positive or negative, general or detailed) and whether the provisional measure has been accompanied by some explanation.

The paucity of consistent information on State responses does not allow for a clear answer to the question whether States respond more favourably to provisional measures that aim to protect those rights that are commonly considered the most fundamental. Yet the fundamental nature of some of the rights involved does seem to play a role in the follow up by the adjudicators and others, which is discussed in the next chapter.

As Buergenthal has pointed out:

> "The effectiveness of decisions by international human rights tribunals ordering provisional measures depends, in large measure, on their judicious use. They are exceptional measures and should be reserved for exceptional and urgent situations. Most of the time that means that they should be granted very sparingly. Such orders are likely to be disregarded or not fully complied

---

[353]   It has been suggested that the Inter-American Commission and Court sometimes are too keen on publicity. In fact an important factor in non-compliance, for instance in relation to Peru and the US, is the public's inborn fear for personal security. Interview by author with Charles Moyer, San Jose, Costa Rica 2001.

[354]   See also Chapter XVIII (Follow-up).

with by States if they are permitted to be transformed from an exceptional remedy into one more procedural tool to be used against a recalcitrant State. Their effectiveness depends on their exceptional character precisely because that is how they preserve their shock value and corresponding effect on public opinion. Here it must never be forgotten that, in the final analysis, public opinion will determine whether or not the State will comply with the decision".[355]

---

[355] Buergenthal (1994), p. 93.

1 INTRODUCTION

In some cases the ICJ has requested follow-up in its initial Orders for provisional measures involving the fate of human beings.[1] This chapter gives examples of the manner in which the human rights adjudicators have followed up on the implementation of their provisional measures, including the possible consequences attached to non-compliance with provisional measures with regard to findings on admissibility and merits (section 2). Indeed this follow-up by the adjudicators themselves is considered to be a very important factor contributing to the effectiveness of provisional measures: 'securing a vigilant and active follow-up monitoring process', it has been noted, is an important condition for the effectiveness of urgent action procedures.[2]

The public statements made by authorities from various inter-State systems of cooperation (section 3), as well as those made by NGOs (section 4) may help reinforce the follow-up activities performed by the adjudicators themselves.[3]

In addition to indicating a conviction that following up on compliance with provisional measures is important to ensure their effectiveness, the practice of the adjudicators, officials of intergovernmental organisations and NGOs also indicates their awareness of the irreparable nature of the harm at stake.

2 FOLLOW-UP BY THE ADJUDICATORS

2.1 Introduction

With regard to the developments in monitoring compliance with provisional measures this section focuses on the practice of the HRC and the Inter-American Commission and Court. It also gives a few examples from the practice of CAT. Further, some references are made to the follow-up on provisional measures separate from the individual petition procedure, as part of the state reporting procedure (section 2.2).

With regard to the possible consequences of failure to respect provisional measures for deciding on admissibility a few references are made to HRC case law. For such consequences for

---

[1] See further Chapter I (ICJ), section 7.

[2] Van Boven (2005), p. 106. See also Boerefijn (1999b), pp. 101-112 on the general issue of follow-up.

[3] In turn these organisations use the provisional measures decided on by the adjudicators in order to reinforce their own goals of preventing irreparable harm to persons. Obviously critical domestic follow-up on (intended) non-compliance also occurs. See e.g. questions put by members of parliament in the case of *J.R.* v. *the Netherlands*, 124/1998, 19 November 1999 (disc.) as well as the comment by Rieter/Van Boven/ Flinterman (1999) and letter of the Netherlands Advisory Committee for International Affairs of 13 July 1999, as referred to in Böcker (2006), p. 137.

decisions on the merits, the ECtHR judgment in *Mamatkulov* is singled out for discussion (section 2.3).

2.2 Monitoring compliance

2.2.1 Introduction

This section sets out by explaining the gradual approach to follow-up taken by the HRC. It then focuses on its follow-up to its provisional measures to halt executions, on the one hand, and to halt expulsion or extradition, on the other. Subsequently it deals with one method of follow-up; that of sending reminders. Then follow-up by CAT and 'seguimiento' in the Inter-American system is discussed, as well as monitoring in the European system and under the Dayton peace agreement. Finally this chapter briefly refers to the possibility for adjudicators of using the respective State reporting procedures to follow up on provisional measures previously taken under the complaint proceedings.

2.2.2 The gradual approach of the HRC

The HRC has introduced a Special Rapporteur on Follow Up on Views, which indicates the importance it attaches to follow-up in general.[4] Yet since provisional measures apply *pending* a case this Rapporteur does not deal with the follow-up on provisional measures. This is done by the Special Rapporteur on New Communications and Interim Measures as well as by the full Committee. Nevertheless there is a substantive link between the State's obligations at the merits stage and at the provisional measures stage.[5] For instance, the HRC has sometimes followed up its decision on the merits, urgently communicating to the State, in the face of an execution date, that at the very least its findings of a violation meant that the death sentence should not be executed. There is no consistent policy or practice regarding this type of monitoring or follow-up.

The practice of the HRC with regard to follow-up in general, and to follow-up on provisional measures in particular, has developed significantly. In the detention cases of the 1970s and 1980s, in the face of insufficient response, the HRC generally followed up its informal request for provisional measures at periodic intervals,[6] including as part of its admissibility decision. At that stage it sometimes made a stronger request than it had made previously, namely to *ensure* access to medical treatment. At the same time it rewarded any semblance of cooperation by the State by referring to it extensively. As a result, in some of these cases, on the merits it did not refer to the importance of ensuring medical attention.

---

[4]   CAT has equally done so, but CEDAW thus far continues with an ad hoc follow-up procedure. In its report on its 7th session the Working group on Communications under the OP to the CEDAW recommended to continue with an ad hoc follow-up procedure and refrain, 'for the time being' from establishing a permanent mechanism, see its report, in Annex IX to the 2006 Annual Report, A/61/38, §9(c); see also Report of the Working Group on Communications, 26 February 2007, in Sessional/Annual Report of Committee CEDAW/C/2007/111/WGCOP/L.1, §8(e), appointing, ad hoc, two of its members in order to follow up its View in *A.S.* v. *Hungary* (on this case see Chapter IX on protection against threats).

[5]   See also Chapter XIII (Protection).

[6]   See Chapter II (Systems) and Chapter VII (Detention) on the issue of informal provisional measures.

Sendic v. *Uruguay* (1981) serves as an example of follow-up in the context of the early de-tention cases dealt with by the HRC.[7] The State argued, more than two months after the HRC used informal provisional measures, that the case was inadmissible because the same matter had been submitted to the Inter-American Commission on Human Rights. It did not provide any of the information requested by the HRC. A week later the petitioner commented on the State's submis-sion, stating that she had never submitted her husband's case to the Inter-American Commission. She also informed the HRC of the place of detention of her husband that had become known 'thanks to strong international pressure'.[8] When it declared the case admissible the HRC pointed out the State's obligation under Article 4(2) OP and decided that it 'should be requested to furnish the Committee with information on the present state of health of Raúl Sendic Antonaccio, the medical treatment given to him and his exact whereabouts'. It is noteworthy that the Committee again asked about his whereabouts. The petitioner had already provided some information but the HRC had never received any response by the State.[9] The petitioner also asked the HRC 'to take appropriate action with a view to securing her husband's right to submit a communication him-self'.[10] In October 1980 she argued once more that her husband had the right to be informed of the Committee's admissibility decision, taken more than two months previously. Later that same month the HRC noted that in her first submission the petitioner had expressed 'grave concern as to her husband's state of health and the fact that his whereabouts were kept secret'. Taking into account 'the fact that its previous requests for information about the present situation of Raúl Sendic Antonaccio had gone unheeded' and further noting the latest letter by the petitioner, the HRC decided to formally follow up on the situation. It reminded the State of its previous decision requesting 'information about the state of health of Raúl Sendic Antonaccio, the medical treat-ment given to him and his exact whereabouts'. It urged the State 'to provide the information sought without any further delay' and, 'as requested by Violeta Setelich, the State party should be requested to transmit all written material pertaining to the proceedings (submissions of the parties, decisions of the Human Rights Committee) to Raúl Sendic Antonaccio, and that he should be given the opportunity himself to communicate directly with the Committee'.[11]

On the merits the HRC noted 'with deep concern' the State's failure to fulfil its obligations under Article 4(2) OP. It also pointed out that Uruguay had 'completely ignored the Committee's repeated requests' for information about the health and whereabouts of Mr. Sendic. It is unable to fulfil its task if State parties do not provide it with all the relevant information. Knowledge of the state of health of the person concerned is 'essential to the evaluation of an allegation of torture or ill-treatment'. In other words, judging from this remark alone, the emphasis of the Committee's request for information seems actually to have been the need for information and not the need for intervention.[12]

---

[7]   HRC *Sendic Antonaccio* (*submitted by his wife Violeta Setelich*) v. *Uruguay*, 28 October 1981.

[8]   According to the petitioner, Uruguay 'had refrained from giving any information on her husband's state of health because he was kept on an inadequate diet in an underground cell with no fresh air or sunlight and his contacts with the outside world were restricted to a monthly visit that lasted 30 minutes and took place in the presence of armed guards'.

[9]   HRC *Sendic Antonaccio* (*submitted by his wife Violeta Setelich*) v. *Uruguay*, 28 October 1981.

[10]   This shows that already in very early cases the petitioners of a communication emphasised the autonomy of the actual victim under the individual complaint system.

[11]   HRC *Sendic Antonaccio* (*submitted by his wife Violeta Setelich*) v. *Uruguay*, 28 October 1981.

[12]   For an example of follow-up by the HRC in a disappearance case see HRC *Tshishimbi* v. *Zaire*, 25 March 1996. When the HRC declared the case admissible it criticized the lack of cooperation on the part of the State and specifically followed up the Special Rapporteur's provisional measures. In its examination of the merits the HRC once more noted 'with serious concern the total absence of cooperation' by the State party. It referred to the State's obligations under Article

The first time a State ignored the *formal* provisional measures of the HRC, the Committee simply expressed its regret. The case involved halting destruction of the natural habitat. In the *Lubicon Lake Band* case (1990)[13] the HRC did not monitor compliance with its provisional measures other than by sending a renewed request for provisional measures more than a year after it first used them. Even if it had eventually recommended a remedy seeking a permanent or interim injunction, this would have been too late because it was tardy in using provisional measures in the first place and because the State did not appear to respect them once they had been taken. The HRC could have monitored compliance more actively.[14]

The first non-refoulement case in which a State ignored the Committee's provisional measures was *Kindler* v. *Canada* (1993). The HRC found no violations of Articles 6 and 7 but it expressed 'its regret that the State party did not accede to the Special Rapporteur's request under rule 86'.[15] In his dissent Aguilar Urbina specifically commented on the way the petitioner was extradited in disregard for the Special Rapporteur's provisional measures.

> "On ratifying the Optional Protocol, Canada undertook, with the other States Parties, to comply with the procedures followed in connection therewith. In extraditing Mr Kindler without taking into account the Special Rapporteur's request, Canada failed to display the good faith which ought to prevail among the parties to the Protocol and the Covenant".[16]

It was in this context that he considered there had been a violation of Article 26 ICCPR (right to equality). He pointed out that Canada had given 'no explanation as to why the extradition was

---

4(2) OP and pointed out, once more, that the State had failed to react to the Special Rapporteur's provisional measures in May 1993. The Committee pointed out that it had not received any information on the fate of Mr. Tshishimbi at all; see also *Mohammed Bashir El-Megreisi* (*submitted by his brother Youssef El-Megreisi*) v. *Libya*, 23 March 1994. The HRC had requested information on the whereabouts of the alleged victim on several occasions. In its View it noted 'with regret and great concern' the absence of cooperation by the State party and pointed out that it is implicit in Article 4(2) OP and in Rule 91 that the State party must investigate in good faith all the allegations of violations of the Covenant and provide the Committee with the information available to it. An example of follow-up by the Bosnia Chamber is its decision on the merits in *Matanović et al.* v. *Republika Srpska*, 6 August 1997, noting in §5 that it never received a response from Republika Srpska to its requests with regard to the whereabouts of a Roman Catholic priest and his parents, and in §31 that the respondent had not taken part in the proceedings before the Ombudsperson and Chamber until after the case had been declared admissible, stressing the obligation of the Parties to the Agreement to cooperate with the Chamber and the Ombudsperson under Articles X (5) and XIII (4).

13   HRC *Bernard Ominayak, Chief of the Lubicon Lake Band* v. *Canada*, 26 March 1990.

14   In HRC *Jouni E. Länsman et al.* v. *Finland*, 30 October 1996, another case involving a claim of destruction of the natural habitat, the petitioner had requested the Committee to reiterate its provisional measures, but it did not do so. Apparently, in December 1995 a negotiation took place between the parties, in which a solution was actively sought. Note of the Secretariat of 8 December 1995 after speaking with the Finnish Foreign Ministry and counsel to the petitioners (on file with the author).

15   HRC *Kindler* v. *Canada*, 30 July 1993, §17.

16   HRC *Kindler* v. *Canada*, 30 July 1993, dissent Aguilar Urbina, §23. See also his dissent in HRC *Ng* v. *Canada*, 5 November 1993, §12.

carried out so rapidly once it was known that the author had submitted a communication to the Committee'.[17]

> "By its censurable action in failing to observe its obligations to the international community, a State party has prevented the enjoyment of the rights which the author ought to have had as a person under Canadian jurisdiction in relation to the Optional Protocol. In so far as the Optional Protocol forms part of the Canadian legal order, all persons under Canadian jurisdiction enjoy the right to submit communications to the Human Rights Committee so that it may hear their complaints. Since it appears that Mr Kindler was extradited on account of his nationality and in so far as he has been denied the possibility of enjoying its protection in accordance with the Optional Protocol, I find that the State party has also violated article 26 of the Covenant".[18]

Lallah equally pointed out that the very notion of protection required preventive measures, in particular in relation to the right to life, because once a person is deprived of his life 'it cannot be restored to him'.[19]

While in *Ng* v. *Canada* (1993) the HRC expressed its regret that the State had not acceded to its request to stay the petitioner's extradition, it did so only when it decided to join the question of the victim requirement to the consideration of the merits. In *Kindler* it had expressed its regret as part of its discussion on the merits. Since the HRC did find a violation of Article 7 in *Ng*, it could have argued that Canada's extradition despite the Committee's provisional measures was an aggravated violation of Article 7. Instead, it requested Canada 'to make such representations as might still be possible to avoid the imposition of the death penalty' and it appealed to this State to ensure that a similar situation did not arise in the future.[20] It may have considered that the matter was too sensitive to draw attention to it, especially given the heinous crimes Ng was charged with. In fact Aguilar Urbina was the only Committee member to specifically deal with Canada's failure to respect the Committee's provisional measures.[21]

The quality of submissions by petitioner and State may have an impact on the attitude of the adjudicators towards non-compliance by governments and on whether or not they will take provisional measures in the first place. Equally, certain *factual* situations, such as public opinion, may have an impact on the attitude of the adjudicator towards whether it will take provisional measures in certain situations as well as its attitude towards non-compliance. Yet the lack of firm response in these cases by the HRC as a whole may mainly be due to the fact that they were among the first in which it was faced with non-compliance.

---

[17] HRC *Kindler* v. *Canada*, 30 July 1993, dissent Aguilar Urbina, §24.

[18] Ibid.

[19] HRC *Kindler* v. *Canada*, 30 July 1993, dissent Lallah, §3.3. He also suggested that the Canadian act concerned arbitrary deprivation of life under Article 6(1) because 'unequal treatment is in effect meted out to different individuals within the same jurisdiction'. He noted that under Canadian law Canada could not sentence an individual to death through its judicial arm but it did find it possible, through its executive arm, to extradite him to face the real risk of such sentence. He would therefore have found a violation of Article 26 which 'regulates a State party's legislative, executive as well as judicial behaviour'. Chanet also would have found a violation of Article 26.

[20] HRC *Ng.* v. *Canada*. In his dissent Lallah considered that there had been a violation of Articles 6 and 7 and '(e)ven at this stage, Canada should use its best efforts to provide a remedy by making appropriate representations, so as to ensure that, if convicted and sentenced to death, the author would not be executed'.

[21] HRC *Ng.* v. *Canada*, dissenting opinion Aguilar Urbina, §§12-13.

Subsequent to these sensitive extradition cases the HRC did develop a practice of strong condemnation on the basis of the obligations under the OP and the ICCPR, as discussed next.

2.2.3 Follow-up by the HRC on halting executions

As noted, it has been on the occasion of executions of death sentences in defiance of its provisional measures that the HRC has expressed itself most strongly on the rationale of provisional measures and their legal status.[22]

---

[22] In the vast majority of death penalty cases States have respected the Committee's provisional measures. Sometimes execution dates are scheduled even after the HRC has found a violation and recommended commutation. In such cases the HRC has also followed up, but not by using provisional measures, as the Inter-American Court had done. See e.g. HRC *Anthony McLeod* v. *Jamaica*, 31 March 1998. The Special Rapporteur had used provisional measures in January 1997. In March 1998 the HRC adopted its Views in this case, recommending a new appeal or release. Two months later counsel noted that he was still awaiting the Committee's Views and that his client was at risk of execution in June. He inquired when the HRC would make a determination on the merits. It seems he was not yet aware of the aforementioned View. He urgently requested the HRC to reapply provisional measures. Apparently the execution date was postponed to early 1999, when counsel again approached the HRC. This is one example of a case in which the Secretariat had to remind the State of the Committee's Views and of the State's obligation, under Article 2, to provide the victim with an effective remedy rather than with a warrant of execution. Note Verbale transmitting the case under Rule 86/91, 17 January 1997; fax by counsel of 12 and 20 May 1998 and 19 January 1999; faxes by Amnesty International of 19 and 20 January 1999 pointing out that scheduling a warrant of execution 'flies in the face of recommendations' by the HRC and 'would undermine the very international protection of fundamental human rights which petitions to the Committee are designed to provide'; letter by the Secretariat to the Permanent Mission referring to the Views of 31 March 1998 and the State's obligation under Article 2 ICCPR to provide an effective remedy, noting that a warrant of execution had been issued and reiterating its recommendation that the victim should be granted a new appeal hearing or be released, 22 January 1999 (on file with the author). In April 1997 the Special Rapporteur reiterated his earlier request for provisional measures in *Abdool Saleem Yasseen and Noel Thomas* v. *Republic of Guyana*, 30 March 1998. following an urgent submission by their counsel. Six days previously she reported that a government minister had publicly stated that the death sentences against her clients would be carried out in due course. See letter by counsel of 18 April 1997, with an attached newspaper article from the Starbroek news of 16 April 1997; Note Verbale of 24 April 1997 to the Permanent Mission reiterating the Rule 86 request of 7 February 1996 (on file with the author). Subsequently, in March 1998 the HRC found violations of the right to a fair trial and recommended the release of the petitioners. At the end of that year Guyana withdrew from the OP. In September 1999 it announced that it would proceed with the execution of Yasseen and Thomas. Both Amnesty International and the Guyana Human Rights Association took action on their behalf and on 10 September the UN Secretary General sent a Note Verbale to the Attorney General of Guyana (copied to the Permanent Mission in New York) reiterating the Committee's recommendations and urging the State to refrain from carrying out the death sentence. Again he referred to the obligations undertaken by the State under the ICCPR and its Optional Protocol.Amnesty International press release of 10 September 1999, 'Guyana: two men to be hanged after an unfair trial', AI Index: AMR 35/02/1999; letter by Michael McCormack, Co-President of the Guyana Human Rights Association to Secretary General Kofi Annan, with copies to the UN Legal Counsel and the High Commissioner for Human Rights, 12 September 1999; Note Verbale by the UN Secretary General to the Attorney General of Guyana of 10 September 1999. As becomes clear from a letter by the father of Yasseen sent to the UN Development Programme in Guyana on 14 August 2000

Over the years it has taken a stronger position on non-compliance.[23] It now condemns such executions as incompatible with the obligation to respect the Covenant in good faith and with the right of individual communication under the OP.

The day after the execution of Rockliff Ross, in defiance of a provisional measure by the HRC, the Secretariat sent a note to counsel:

> "We profoundly regret having learnt of Mr. Ross' execution on 4 June 1996. By the time of his execution, the case had in fact been registered upon instruction of the Chairman of the Human Rights Committee and been sent to the President of Guyana".

The case was discontinued after the execution since the purpose of the submission had been to prevent the execution and counsel had not submitted any further comments. Aguilar Urbina, the Chairperson of the HRC addressed the Permanent Representative of Guyana in a formal response to the execution. He pointed out that the case had been transmitted before the execution took place, that it included a provisional measure and that the Superintendent of the Prison had also been informed.

> "On 23 July 1996 the Committee discussed the case of Mr. Ross and expressed dismay at his execution on 4 June 1996, in spite of the Committee's request for interim protection. In the name of the Committee and further to its unanimously adopted instructions, I should like to seek prompt written explanations from your Excellency's Government as to the reason for which the Committee's request was not respected. I am at you disposal for any clarifications in the matter".[24]

Trinidad and Tobago executed Glenn Ashby in July 1994 despite the Committee's provisional measure, six days before he would have been eligible for commutation of his sentence under the JCPC's *Pratt and Morgan* rule.[25]

Following the HRC's use of provisional measures the petitioner had written to the Mercy Committee. He had requested the right to be heard before that body, 'stating that the Human Rights Committee was considering his communication and asking that the Mercy Committee await the outcome of the Human Rights Committee's recommendations'. Five days later the Mercy Committee rejected his petition for mercy. On that same day a warrant for execution was read to him, to take place on 14 July 1994 at 6 a.m.[26] The subsequent events show that the assur-

---

(and transmitted to the HRC on 25 August 2000) both were still on death row at that time (on file with the author).

[23] See also Harrington (2003), p. 69 referring to a 'movement towards recognizing the binding nature of interim measures requests' as 'reflected' in the jurisprudence of the HRC. She notes that the Committee 'has taken an increasingly stronger stance' and 'what were once seen as mere "failures to cooperate" are now viewed as violations of a state's very obligations under the ICCPR regime'.

[24] HRC (*The late*) *Rockliff Ross* v. *Guyana*, 10 December 1997 (disc.), (703/1996), letter by Secretariat to counsel, 4 June/15 June 1994; Note Verbale by Chairman Aguilar Urbina to the Permanent Representative of Guyana, 24 July 1994 (on file with the author).

[25] HRC *Glenn Ashby* v. *Trinidad and Tobago*, 21 March 2002.

[26] HRC *Ashby* v. *Trinidad and Tobago*, 21 March 2002, §6.2.

ances by Trinidad to the JCPC that Ashby would not be executed before he had exhausted the available remedies could not be depended upon.[27]

> "At this point, one of Mr. Ashby's lawyers appeared in Court with a written transcript of an order of the Privy Counsel staying the execution. The order had been read to him over the telephone, having been granted at approximately 6:30 a.m. Trinidad and Tobago time (11:30 a.m. London time). Shortly thereafter, it was announced that Mr. Ashby had been hanged at 6:40 a.m.".[28]

The HRC met the day after the execution requesting clarifications on an urgent basis. It invited the State to send an authorised person to provide such clarifications at that session's plenary

---

[27] "The representative of the Attorney-General of Trinidad and Tobago then informed the Privy Council that Mr. Ashby would not be executed until all possibilities of obtaining a stay of execution, including applications to the Court of Appeal in Trinidad and Tobago and the Privy Council, had been exhausted. This was recorded in writing and signed by counsel for Mr. Ashby and counsel for the Attorney-General". HRC *Ashby* v. *Trinidad and Tobago*, 21 March 2002, §6.3. Before the Court of Appeal, however, counsel for the respondents said that the petitioner would nevertheless be hanged at 7 a.m. (noon London time) unless the Court of Appeal granted a conservatory order. "The Court of Appeal then proposed to adjourn until 11 a.m. Trinidad and Tobago time in order to seek clarification of what had taken place before the Privy Council. Lawyers for Mr. Ashby asked for a conservatory order until 11 a.m., noting that the execution had been scheduled for 7 a.m. and that counsel for the respondents had made it clear that Mr. Ashby could not rely on the assurance given to the Privy Council. The Court expressed the view that, in the interim, Mr. Ashby could rely on the assurance given to the Privy Council and declined to make a conservatory order. The Court instead decided to adjourn until 6 a.m. Lawyers for Mr. Ashby applied for an interim conservatory order until 6 a.m. but the Court denied this request. At no time did the lawyers for the State party indicate that the execution was scheduled to take place earlier than 7 a.m". Id. §6.4 on 14 July at 10.30 a.m. London time, the JCPC held a special sitting, preparing a document about the decision-making the previous day. The Registrar immediately faxed this document to the Court of Appeal and to counsel for both sides in Trinidad and Tobago. The JCPC also requested further clarification of the Attorney-General's position. Having received no such clarification, the JCPC ordered a stay of execution at about 11.30 a.m. London time. The Court of Appeal reconvened at approximately the same time, 6.20 a.m. Trinidad and Tobago time. Twenty minutes later counsel again applied to the Court of Appeal for a conservatory order. This Court denied the order, once more emphasising that the petitioner could rely on the assurance given to the JCPC. Id., §6.6. According to the State party the Court of Appeals did not express the view that counsel should rely on the assurances given to the JCPC that Mr. Ashby would not be executed. "Instead, the Court expressed that it was not prepared to do anything until the Judicial Committee of the Privy Council resolved the dispute". Id., §9.8. See also Summary Record of the 1352nd meeting: Trinidad and Tobago, 26 July 1994, CCPR/C/SR.1352, 31 July 1996, §§5-10. During this meeting Committee member Francis (Jamaica) also observed that the Clerk of the Court of Appeals had been asked to attend the meeting at 6 p.m. on 14 July in order to communicate any decision of the Court to the Government. However he did not attend this meeting and appeared only after the execution. He wondered whether or not his absence had been deliberate. He also noted that the order for execution referred to an execution time between 6 a.m. and noon and he would like to know why the petitioner had been executed so early in the morning, §§18-19.

[28] Six days after the execution the Permanent Mission transmitted a copy of an undated media release issued by the advocate-general of Trinidad. According to this press release all the requirements of the law and the Constitution of Trinidad and Tobago had been satisfied.

meeting of the Committee. Moreover, it decided to hold a public meeting on this issue. At this meeting it briefly addressed the information transmitted by the Permanent Mission.

"The Committee studied the said media release and regretted that no replies had been given to its specific question. It noted with concern that the State party had failed to explain why it had not complied with the Committee's request of interim measures of protection, and that nor the proceedings under the Optional Protocol, nor the Committee was mentioned in the media release".[29]

Twelve days after the execution the HRC held a public meeting, on an exceptional basis, and issued a public statement in which it expressed its indignation regarding the State's failure to comply with its provisional measures and strongly urged the State party 'to ensure, by all means at its disposal, that situations similar to that surrounding the execution of Mr. Ashby do not re-cur'.[30] The Committee decided to continue its consideration of the case under the OP.

Normally discussions about individual cases are not public, let alone published. Yet in this situation the Committee decided to make an exception and publish its summary records.[31] In addition it published its discussion in the Annual Report to the General Assembly.[32]

During the meeting the Chairman of the Committee had pointed out that States parties had thus far respected all the Committee's provisional measures to halt executions (in more that 100 cases).[33] Each member of the Committee made an individual statement. All of them strongly regretted the execution, and all of them, except for Francis (Jamaica), argued for a strongly worded response. Aguilar Urbina (Costa Rica), for instance, considered that Trinidad and Tobago had carried out an extrajudicial execution and the Committee should react strongly.[34] El Shafei (Egypt) stressed that the other States parties to the OP should take up the issue of the serious breach by the authorities of Trinidad and Tobago of their obligations.[35] Sadi (Jordan) considered that Mr. Ashby had been the victim of a very grave miscarriage of justice. Following the execution 'there was no hope of being able to remedy any mistakes that might have been committed during his trial'. "The authorities owed the Committee an explanation, but they owed to Mr. Ashby's family even more".[36] Francis (Jamaica) 'particularly regretted' the State's behaviour 'as he himself was from the Caribbean'.[37] Bán (Hungary) 'shared the sorrow and indignation of the other members of the Committee'. The HRC should indeed 'insist on the need to clarify under what circumstances and for what reasons it had taken place'. "That information was very impor-

---

[29] HRC Summary Record of the 1352nd meeting: Trinidad and Tobago, 26 July 1994, CCPR/C/SR.1352, 31 July 1996, §10.

[30] HRC *Ashby* v. *Trinidad and Tobago*, 21 March 2002, §3.4.

[31] HRC Summary Record of the 1352nd meeting: Trinidad and Tobago, 26 July 1994.

[32] See A/49/40, §§410-411. During the special session Higgins had noted that the Committee had decided to adopt a new format for its Annual Report that 'would highlight the cooperation or lack of co-operation by a State party, whether in regard to submission of reports or communications'. In that light the case of Mr. Ashby 'should be given a prominent place in the annual report to be adopted at the end of the current session'. HRC Summary Record of the 1352nd meeting: Trinidad and Tobago, 26 July 1994, §39.

[33] HRC Summary Record of the 1352nd meeting: Trinidad and Tobago, 26 July 1994, §2.

[34] Id., §12.

[35] Id., §31.

[36] Id., §32.

[37] Id., §17.

tant, as it could prevent the recurrence of such incidence". The HRC should continue its investigation and seek assurances of non-repetition.[38]

With regard to Trinidad's media release following the execution, Higgins pointed out that '(t)he media release was in no way a reply to the Committee: it was, quite simply, an insult'. She also expressed her concern about the situation of two other petitioners, Guerra and Wallen, and pointed out that the Committee should press the authorities to comply with the provisional measures in their cases. She pointed out that the State was bound to respect the provisional measures on behalf of Guerra and Wallen and other cases.[39]

Prado Vallejo (Ecuador) equally pointed out: "Others besides Mr. Ashby were awaiting execution in Trinidad and Tobago, and it was to be hoped that the authorities would fulfil their obligations towards them. It was also to be hoped that the State party would understand the gravity of its actions and in future honour its commitments in good faith".[40] He noted that the State 'had not honoured its obligations under the Covenant and the Optional Protocol' and 'committed a flagrant violation of article 6 of the Covenant'.[41]

Pocar (Italy) stated that each State had 'the legal obligation to cooperate with the Committee when it considered communications concerning that State party, and at the very least it must allow it to examine those communications in the most effective possible manner'.

> "That was an obligation which the State party had to fulfil in good faith. As to the Covenant, under article 39, the Committee established its own rules of procedure, and no State party had ever contested any of the provisions of those rules, including rule 86. By ignoring those provisions, Trinidad and Tobago had clearly prevented the Committee from examining the communication of Mr. Ashby in the most effective way".[42]

Higgins (UK) drew particular attention to Article 1 OP and pointed out that the Committee 'was clearly not in a position to consider a communication under the normal procedure if its author was dead'. She noted that 'if the Committee had been able to consider the communication under the usual conditions, it might have concluded that the Covenant had not been violated by the State party'.[43]

> "One thing, however, was certain: Trinidad and Tobago had violated the provisions of both the Covenant and the Optional Protocol. With respect to the Covenant, no matter what the merits of Mr. Ashby's complaint, it was clear that the State party had violated article 6, given that it had ignored the guarantees called for by the Optional Protocol. The State party had also violated that instrument by refusing to cooperate with the Committee, particularly by failing to reply to the questions asked and to cooperate more generally with the Committee's procedure".[44]

Thus Higgins duly noted the link to the seriousness of the harm risked, pointing out that ignoring provisional measures and executing the petitioner pending the proceedings ignoring the Committee's provisional measures, was in itself a violation of Article 6 (right to life), 'no matter what the merits' of the petition.[45] Condemning the execution she proposed that the Committee would

---

[38]   Id., §37.
[39]   Id., §§24-29.
[40]   Id., §33.
[41]   Ibid.
[42]   HRC Summary Record of the 1352nd meeting: Trinidad and Tobago, 26 July 1994, §22.
[43]   Id., §24.
[44]   Id., §27.
[45]   Ibid.

'strongly assert that such incident should be avoided in the future' and that the State 'was bound to grant the Committee's request under rule 86' in other cases.[46]

Wennergren (Sweden) considered that the State had committed 'a flagrant violation of the Committee's rules of procedure'. Nevertheless he considered, different from Higgins, that 'it was only subsequently that the Committee would be able to determine whether or not article 6 of the Covenant had been violated'.[47]

The Chairman proposed the adoption of a text expressing the Committee's deep concern and regret. The 'attitude of the authorities was in flagrant breach of their obligations under the Covenant and the Optional Protocol'. He suggested that the Committee would 'deplore the State party's failure to make available a representative for the meetings at which Mr. Ashby's case would be considered'. The Committee could recall that the State was bound to fulfil its obligations under the Covenant and the OP. It should also 'insist on the need for a favourable reply by the authorities of Trinidad and Tobago' to the provisional measures on behalf of two other petitioners as well.[48] Lallah (Mauritius) supported this proposal and Mavrommatis (Cyprus) said that the Committee should also issue a press release. He agreed that the case should be mentioned in the Annual Report 'but would go even further: that case could be the subject of a special section of the report, given the grave consequences of the State party's failure to cooperate'.[49] Francis considered that the Committee 'should avoid using verbs such as "condemn" and "deplore" in the text to be adopted'. "It was true that the authorities of Trinidad and Tobago had committed irreparable damage, but the Committee should try to use wording that was generally acceptable to its members, and he was in favour of using measured language".[50] The Chairman concluded that the Secretariat would be asked to draft a decision based on his proposal and the suggestions by members of the Committee.[51]

Thus the Committee's position towards the obligation to respect its provisional measures first became clear with its immediate response to the execution of Glenn Ashby in 1994, also showing the position of individual members. Its first decision on the *merits* that fully establishes its position, however, is *Piandiong et al. v. the Philippines* (2000), not *Ashby v. Trinidad* that was only decided on the merits in 2002.[52] The executions rendered examination by the HRC moot and the expression of its Views 'nugatory and futile'. Flouting its provisional measures, 'especially by irreversible measures such as the execution of the alleged victim' undermined the protection of Covenant rights under the OP.[53] To underscore its indignation the HRC has not waited until its decision on the merits, but exceptionally published its Summary Records discussing an individual case (following the execution of Ashby) and on several occasions issued press releases condemning executions.[54]

---

[46]   Id., §29.

[47]   Id., §35.

[48]   Id., §41. This concerned the case of Guerra and Wallen also pending before the HRC.

[49]   Id., §§42-43.

[50]   Id., §44.

[51]   Id., §45.

[52]   HRC *Dante Piandiong, Jesus Morallos and Archie Bulan* v. *the Philippines*, 19 October 2000.

[53]   See *HRC Dante Piandiong, Jesus Morallos and Archie Bulan (deceased) (submitted by Alexander Padilla and Ricardo III Sunga)* v. *the Philippines*, 19 October 2000. See also *Mansaraj et al.; Gborie et al. and Sesay et al.* v. *Sierra Leone*, 16 July 2001 and *Glenn Ashby* v. *Trinidad and Tobago*, 21 March 2002. In addition see *Barno Saidova* v. *Tajikistan*, 8 July 2004.

[54]   See e.g. press release, 'Human Rights Committee deplores the execution of six individuals in Uzbekistan', 24 July 2003. The petitioners who were executed were Muzaffar Mirzaev (case 1170/2003), Shukrat Andasbaev (case 1166/2003), Ulugbek Ashov (case 1165/2003), Ilkhon Babadzhanov and Maksud Ismailov (case 1162/2003), and Azamat Uteev (case 1150/2003).

Thus, by the time it published its decision on the merits in *Ashby* (2002) it had already published *Piandiong* v. *the Philippines* (2000)[55] and the case against Sierra Leone (2001), involving executions that took place subsequent to that of Glenn Ashby.[56] Apart from violations of Article 14(3)(c) and (5) ICCPR (undue delay), the HRC found a violation of Article 6(1) and (2) for carrying out the execution when his sentence was still under challenge. It discussed closely the State's breach of the principle of good faith and the obligations under the OP.

> "[H]aving regard to the fact that the representative of the Attorney-General informed the Privy Council that Mr. Ashby would not be executed until all possibilities of obtaining a stay of execution had been exhausted, the carrying out of Mr. Ashby's sentence notwithstanding that assurance constituted a breach of the principle of good faith which governs all States in their discharge of obligations under international treaties, including the Covenant. The carrying out of the execution of Mr. Ashby when the execution of the sentence was still under challenge constituted a violation of article 6, paragraphs 1 and 2, of the Covenant".[57]

The State had breached its obligations under the OP 'by proceeding to execute Mr. Ashby before the Committee could conclude its examination of the communication, and the formulation of its Views'. It found the State's act 'particularly inexcusable' because the HRC had used provisional measures specifically requesting it to refrain from executing Mr. Ashby pending the determination of the case.

> "The behaviour of the State party represents a shocking failure to demonstrate even the most elementary good faith required of a State party to the Covenant and the Optional Protocol".

When Sierra Leone executed twelve petitioners in spite of the Committee's provisional measures, the HRC expressed 'its indignation' not only through its Permanent Mission in New York but also through the Office of the Secretary General's Special Representative in Freetown. At the same time it referred to the State's obligations under the reporting procedure of Article 40 ICCPR.[58]

Sometimes the HRC also has a meeting with officials of the State party to follow up on an execution.[59]

In *Piandiong* the HRC not only used several paragraphs of its View to stress the serious nature of the violation, it also entered these paragraphs in its Annual Report under the separate heading 'Breach of Optional Protocol obligations'.[60] Harrington points out that by doing so the HRC put all UN member States 'on notice as to the severity with which the body created by states to supervise them now viewed a state's failure to abide by a request for interim measures'.[61]

---

[55] HRC *Dante Piandiong, Jesus Morallos and Archie Bulan* v. *the Philippines*, 19 October 2000.

[56] HRC *Mansaraj et al.; Gborie et al. and Sesay et al.* v. *Sierra Leone*, 16 July 2001.

[57] HRC *Glenn Ashby* v. *Trinidad and Tobago*, 21 March 2002.

[58] HRC Public Decision, 4 November 1998, CCPR/C/64/D/839/1998, 4 November 1998. For the View on the merits, see: HRC *Mansaraj et al.; Gborie et al. and Sesay et al.* v. *Sierra Leone*, 16 July 2001.

[59] Two weeks after the execution of the three petitioners in *Piandiong*, for instance, the Special Rapporteur for New Communications and the Vice-Chairperson met with the representative of the State party. See *Dante Piandiong, Jesus Morallos and Archie Bulan* (*deceased*) (*submitted by Alexander Padilla and Ricardo III Sunga*) v. *the Philippines*, 19 October 2000.

[60] See A/56/40 (2001), §§128-130.

[61] Harrington (2003), p. 72.

2.2.4 Follow-up by the HRC on halting expulsion and extradition

In *Weiss* v. *Austria* (2003) the HRC devoted a separate heading to the State's failure to respect its provisional measures. It found, in the circumstances of the case, that the State breached its obligations under the OP by extraditing the petitioner before the Committee could address his allegation of irreparable harm to his rights under the ICCPR. It specifically noted that it had offered the State the opportunity to convince it that provisional measures were not warranted, but rather than taking this opportunity the State simply ignored the provisional measures and went ahead with the extradition.

> "In particular, the Committee is concerned by the sequence of events in this case in that, rather than requesting interim measures of protection directly upon an assumption that irreversible harm could follow the author's extradition, it first sought, under Rule 86 of its Rules of Procedure, the State party's views on the irreparability of harm. In so doing, the State party could have demonstrated to the Committee that extradition would not result in irreparable harm".[62]

In fact this specification indicated bad faith on the part of the State.

The HRC specifically responded to the State's non-compliance in *Ahani*. In August the Chairperson to the HRC expressed 'great regret' at the deportation, seeking a written explanation about the reasons that led to this disregard for its provisional measures. A few days later the Committee followed up this action through its Special Rapporteur, acting under its Rule on provisional measures, who requested the State 'to monitor closely the situation and treatment of the author subsequent to his deportation to Iran and to make such representations to the Government of the Islamic Republic of Iran that were deemed pertinent in order to prevent violations of the author's rights under articles 6 and 7 of the Covenant'.[63] In its View in the *Ahani* case the HRC reiterated its conclusion that the State breached its obligations under the OP by deporting the petitioner before the Committee's determination of his claim.[64] The State had mainly referred to its obligations under domestic law.[65] At the same time it pointed out that it 'usually responded

---

[62] See HRC *Weiss* v. *Austria*, 3 April 2003, §7.1. See also Chapter XIII (Protection).

[63] See HRC *Mansour Ahani* v. *Canada*, 29 March 2004, §5.1.

[64] Id., §11.

[65] Weiser (2004) argues that 'current judicial approaches do not give full and consistent credence to international obligations undertaken by Canada, nor do they offer sufficient guidance on the effect of international human rights treaties on domestic laws', p. 114. 'There appears to be no presumption of conformity' with regard to international obligations unless the court is faced with 'legislation enacted specifically in furtherance of a treaty'. She refers to the statement of the Supreme Court in *Suresh* that 'our concern is not with Canada's international obligations qua obligations'. The court simply looks at international law as evidence of Canada's principles of fundamental justice rather than 'as controlling in itself', p. 133. She offers explanations for Canada's attitude towards international legal obligations. There are few countries, she notes, facing 'as many constitutional obstacles as Canada to the successful integration of domestic and international law'. Apart from the role of the Canadian Charter of Rights and Freedoms and the fact that treaties are not considered self-executing she refers to the fact that treaty ratification is an executive act and 'the extent of Parliamentary scrutiny in the process of treaty adherence is limited', p. 122. The assessment and considerations on which a decision to ratify is based 'remains an internal document and so, non-governmental actors (including courts) face obvious difficulties in trying to identify the international obligations underlying a particular domestic law'. Subsequently there is 'no systematic review' either 'of new legislation for consistency with treaty obligations', pp. 127-128. She points out that recently 'other countries with Westminster-

favourably' to requests for provisional measures.[66] The HRC stressed that Canada was under an obligation 'to avoid similar violations in the future, including by taking appropriate steps to ensure that the Committee's requests for interim measures of protection will be respected'.[67]

2.2.5 One of the methods of follow-up: sending reminders

In some cases it was also important to confirm to the State that a case was still pending before the HRC. In *Shaw* v. *Jamaica* (1998)[68] counsel wrote to the Committee, on 18 May 1988, that the State had threatened not to further postpone the execution 'unless counsel could intimate,' by 20 May 1988, that he would make an application to the Inter-American Commission of Human Rights.[69] Counsel pointed out: 'Whilst Mr. Shaw's motion is pending before the UN Human Rights Committee, I cannot submit an application to the Inter-American Commission on Human Rights. In the circumstances, it is imperative that the United Nations High Commissioner for Human Rights make strong representations to the Jamaican authorities that Mr. Shaw's matter is still pending before the Human Rights Committee and has been afforded Rule 86 protection'. The HRC often repeats its provisional measures. An example is *Junior Leslie* v. *Jamaica* (1998).[70] In this case there was a real and immediate danger of the petitioner's execution. After all, he was only two months away from having been on death row for five years. Because of the JCPC case law, counsel believed that the Jamaican Government was prioritising Leslie's case with a view to executing him before the period of five years would elapse.[71]

---

style Governments have taken steps to rectify similar situations', p. 123. In practice federalism is another obstacle. She points out that 'while the *federal* Executive alone is empowered to enter into international treaties, it has no power to implement them in areas of *provincial* jurisdiction'. By contrast, in other federal States 'such as Australia, the federal government retains residual power to legislate a furtherance of a treaty, even where the subject matter typically falls outside federal jurisdiction', p. 124. See also Chapter XVII on official responses.

[66] See HRC *Mansour Ahani* v. *Canada*, 29 March 2004, §5.3. In fact until then it had respected the Committee's provisional measures four times and ignored them three times (all in the immigration context). The other time the HRC used provisional measures related to Article 27 ICCPR and indigenous peoples. Canada ignored these as well. See further the discussion in this section on its compliance with the provisional measures by CAT and the Inter-American Commission.

[67] HRC *Mansour Ahani* v. *Canada*, 29 March 2004, §12.

[68] HRC *Steve Shaw* v. *Jamaica*, 2 April 1998.

[69] He enclosed a letter of 15 March 1998 by the Secretary of the Governor General: 'execution will not be further postponed unless intimation in writing is given to the Governor General that an application will be made to the second International Human Rights Body, in this case the Inter American Commission on Human Rights. The intimation must be made by May 20, so you may wish to act accordingly'.

[70] HRC *Junior Leslie* v. *Jamaica*, 31 July 1998.

[71] In this light he requested the HRC to repeat its provisional measures and the HRC did so four days after it received counsel's fax and five days before the scheduled hearing. Another example is *Reece* v. *Jamaica* (disc. 1993): the first Rule 86/91 was transmitted to the State on 25 November 1987 (based on a decision of 12 November 1987); it was repeated as part of the admissibility decision of 30 March 1988, interlocutory decision of 2 November 1989 and letter of 24 March 1992, again to the Ministry of Foreign Affairs, with a copy to the Permanent Mission of Jamaica in Geneva. *Lloyd Reece* v. *Jamaica*, admissibility decision of 30 March 1989; interlocutory decision of 2 November 1999; Letter by the UN Secretariat of 24 March 1992 to the Ministry of Foreign Affairs of Jamaica concerning Lloyd Reece, 247/1987. Eventually the HRC

2.2.6 Follow-up by CAT

In *Brada* v. *France* (2005) CAT used strong wording. It stressed that the State party 'seriously failed' in its obligations under Article 22 ICAT 'because it prevented the Committee from fully examining a complaint relating to a violation of the Convention, rendering action by the Committee futile and its comments worthless'.[72] In *Agiza* v. *Sweden* (2005) it addressed, in passing, one reason that States might forward for ignoring provisional measures.[73] After pointing out that by making the declaration under Article 22 ICAT, recognizing the right of individual petition, a State 'assumes an obligation to cooperate fully with the Committee', it observed that 'its procedures are sufficiently flexible and its powers sufficiently broad to prevent an abuse of process in a particular case'.[74]

Pending the case the Committee, through its Special Rapporteur, follows up by recalling the State's obligation to respect provisional measures and requesting clarifications on the 'current status and whereabouts' of the petitioner extradited in disregard of the Committee's provisional measures.[75] During the Committee's sessions the situation may also be discussed. In this case, for instance, CAT had sent a letter expressing 'grave concern about the manner in which the State party acted in the case' and requesting timely information on her 'current whereabouts and state of well-being'.[76]

After finding a violation of Articles 3 and 22 ICAT in *Tebourski* v. *France* (2007) the Committee wished to be informed, among others, of the steps taken 'to make reparation for the breach of article 3 of the Convention, and to determine, in consultation with the country (also a State party to the Convention) to which he was deported, the complainant's current whereabouts and the state of his well-being'.[77]

In *Dar* v. *Norway* (2007) CAT had used provisional measures in April 2004. Early June Norway informed the Committee that it would not comply, but at the end of that month it added that it would refrain from proceeding with the expulsion to Pakistan until the court of first instance had reviewed the case.[78] In September 2005 he was expelled to Pakistan after all.[79] In its admissibility decision, two months later, CAT observed that 'in ratifying the Convention and voluntarily accepting the Committee's competence under article 22', the State 'undertook to cooperate with it in good faith in applying the procedure'. It pointed out that compliance with the provisional measure called for 'was essential in order to protect the person in question from irreparable harm, which could, moreover, nullify the end result of the proceedings before the

---

discontinued the case after it received a confirmation by the petitioner's counsel that he wished to withdraw his application. Letter from counsel to the UN Secretariat of 28 April 1993 (on file with the author). Yet another example is *Christopher Brown* v. *Jamaica*, 23 March 1999; fax by counsel of 23 December 1998; response by Secretariat of 31 December 1998; faxes by Amnesty International of 19 and 20 January 1999 pointing out that his execution while his petition is pending before the HRC would violate 'the country's international obligations and his rights to a remedy'; fax by counsel of 21 January 1999 and Note Verbale to the State of 22 January 1999 reminding it of the earlier provisional measure (on file with the author).

[72]   CAT *Mafhoud Brada* v. *France*, 17 May 2005, §6.1.

[73]   See Chapter XVII (Official responses), section 3.3.

[74]   CAT *Ahmed Hussein Mustafa Kamil Agiza* v. *Sweden*, 20 May 2005, §13.10.

[75]   CAT *Elif Pelit* v. *Azerbaijan*, 1 May 2007, §8.2.

[76]   Id., §8.4. The State party subsequently did provide updated information and noted that a member of its embassy had had private conversations with her, §§8.19.4.

[77]   CAT *Adel Tebourski* v. *France*, 1 May 2007, §10.

[78]   CAT *Nadeem Ahmad Dar* v. *Norway*, 11 May 2007, §1.2.

[79]   Id., §1.3.

Committee'. It explicitly 'invited' the State 'to comply with the Committee's request for interim measures of protection'.[80] On the merits it found that Norway had remedied the breach of its obligations under Article 22, half a year after the expulsion that CAT's provisional measures had meant to halt, by facilitating the safe return of the petitioner and granting him a residence permit for three years.[81] Thus it appears that the Committee invited remedial action by the State pending the proceedings and when this action was undertaken, rewarded the State by not finding a violation.

2.2.7 'Seguimiento' in the Inter-American system

Reiterating and specifying provisional measures are just two of the methods the adjudicators have in dealing with States that fail to implement the obligations indicated in these measures. The Inter-American Commission, for instance, has several other (more or less resource intensive) tools to deal with non-compliance: on-site visits, country reports, discussion of the non-compliance in its Annual Reports, case law, renewed precautionary measures and requesting the Court to order provisional measures.[82]

The OAS is still politicised and its General Assembly is not inclined to clearly support the Inter-American Commission and Court in their monitoring and follow-up of compliance with State obligations under the Convention and Declaration.[83] In this sense, the Inter-American system differs from the European human rights system. Comparatively speaking, the political bodies of the Council of Europe seem more inclined to support the ECHR both in its political statements and in its financial contribution.

Since 1998 the Commission has established the practice of *seguimiento* or follow-up on its case law. *Seguimiento* is the creation of a follow-up policy after the final decision. This way the Commission tries to monitor the activities of States with regard to its recommendations. Follow-up seems to be one of the better ways to increase effectiveness, both of precautionary and provisional measures and of decisions on the merits.[84] During the stage of *seguimiento* States sometimes reply that they need more time. Sometimes they say that they take it very seriously but chose not to act on the Commission's final report.[85] Normally States do not send the information on their compliance with provisional measures in time. The information they do send usually is very general and rather vague. In response, the Inter-American Commission's decisions on pre-

---

[80]   Id., §6.7 (referring to its established case law in this respect).

[81]   CAT *Nadeem Ahmad Dar* v. *Norway*, 11 May 2007, §§16.4, 17 and 18.

[82]   The African Commission has also sent its urgent appeals in the context of individual complaints, not just to the State concerned, but also to authorities of the African Union. See e.g. ACHPR *Interights (on behalf of Husaini et al.)* v. *Nigeria*, April 2005, provisional measures ('urgent appeal') of 6 February 2002 'to His Excellency Amara Essy of the African Union, respectfully urging him to draw the attention of the President of the Federal Republic of Nigeria to the Commission's request and to positively respond thereof', §14. The next month the Director of the Political Affairs Department of the AU wrote to the Chairman of the African Commission that the Secretary General of the AU had formally taken up the matter, §18. See further §22.

[83]   For some pointed comments and analysis on the failure of the OAS political organs see e.g. IACHR *Caesar* v. *Trinidad and Tobago*, Judgment of 11 March 2005, individual opinion of judge Ventura Robles. In general see Gómez (1998b), pp. 173-197.

[84]   Similar to Article 46 of its new Rules, dealing with the follow-up of compliance with its final reports, Article 25(3) of its Rules confirms the Inter-American Commission's increasing practice to follow up compliance with precautionary measures.

[85]   Interview by author with Juan Mendez, Washington D.C., 17 October 2001.

cautionary measures have now become very detailed so as to invite specific responses with regard to their implementation.

The Inter-American Commission also makes use of press releases stating its grave concern about impending executions ignoring the fact that the case is pending before the Inter-American human rights system. Such an execution would deprive the alleged victim of his 'fundamental right to have his complaint effectively determined by the Commission' and would cause him irreparable harm. It would be incompatible with the international human rights obligations under the OAS Charter and related instruments.[86]

The case of Rudolph Baptiste is interesting because the Inter-American Commission also used the tool of precautionary measures as part of its Report on the merits. On 13 April 2000 the Commission decided to publish its report in this case. One of its recommendations in this report was a request to Grenada to adopt precautionary measures to stay his execution.[87] At the time of the publication of Annual Report 2000 the Commission had not received any reply yet from Grenada.[88] What is interesting here is that, according to the information provided in the Annual Report, the Commission requested precautionary measures as part of its report on the merits in a case that it had not sent to the Court for its consideration, as Grenada has not recognized the competence of the Court. In other words, given the use of precautionary measures, the case is not closed yet, while at the same time it can never go any further.[89]

At the end of April 2000 armed inmates in the Bogotá Model Prison clashed, leaving 25 persons dead and 17 wounded. Subsequently political prisoners continued to be threatened by paramilitary prisoners wearing AUC bracelets. The Commission took precautionary measures on their behalf in May 2000.[90]

"The threats made by paramilitary inmates against political prisoners in that penitentiary materialised in an attack last July with a high toll of deaths and injuries, even though the Commission's precautionary measures were still in effect". During its on-site visit, 7-13 December 2001, at the invitation of the administration of President Pastrana, the Commission visited the facilities at the Model Prison 'to check on compliance with the protective measures it had issued'. During its visit the Commission did not find full compliance, although it appreciated the appointment of a new director and hoped that he would be given 'the appropriate means to fulfill his functions'. It obtained a pledge by the Government to begin to build a separate partition by the end of that month in order to prevent new acts of violence. Both in a press release concluding its

---

[86]   See e.g. CIDH press release 7/02 'IACHR calls upon the United States to postpone execution of juvenile offender Alexander Williams, 19 February 2002. Obviously it has also used press releases to publicly condemn executions that have taken place nevertheless. See e.g. CIDH press release 33/08 'IACHR condemns execution of José Ernesto Medellín', (condemning the execution 'in contempt of' the Commission's precautionary measures and its report on the merits in which it had concluded that the failure to fulfil the obligations under Article 36(1) VCCR did not meet the minimum standards of due process and a fair trial required under Articles XVIII and XXVI of the American Declaration. It reminded the State in its press release that in its report on the merits it had pointed out that if the State executed the victim based on those proceedings, 'it would commit an irreparable violation of his fundamental right to life, protected by Article I of the American Declaration').

[87]   CIDH *Baptiste* v. *Grenada*, 13 April 2000.

[88]   CIDH Annual Report 2000, §31.

[89]   Id., §31.

[90]   Id., §17.

visit and in its Annual Report the Commission emphasized that it would 'continue to closely follow security conditions in the jail and compliance with the precautionary measures'.[91]

The Commission's precautionary measures on behalf of the 9-11 detainees at Guantanamo Bay have been confirmed and expanded several times and eventually the Commission followed this up with a Resolution of July 2006 concluding that the non-compliance had 'resulted in irreparable prejudice to the fundamental rights of the detainees at Guantanamo Bay including the rights to liberty and to humane treatment'. The Resolution urged the US, among others, to close Guantanamo without delay.[92]

Sometimes the Commission issues press releases specifically to reinforce its precautionary measures. At other times it simply reacts to specific situations of gross human rights violations such as the murder of a human rights defender. In a press statement of 15 February 2002, for instance, the Commission condemned the torture and assassination in Colombia of human rights defender Ms. María del Carmen Florez on the previous day.[93] The Commission referred to a General Assembly resolution of June 2001 deploring acts directly or indirectly preventing or hampering the tasks of human rights defenders. The Assembly urged the member States to intensify their efforts to adopt the necessary measures guaranteeing the lives, personal integrity and freedom of expression of these human rights defenders. It also instructed the Permanent Council to follow up its resolution and to present to the General Assembly information about State compliance with it. In light of this resolution[94] the Commission informed the OAS Permanent Council of the extra-judicial execution of Ms. Florez.[95]

The Inter-American Commission has institutionalised its capacity to deal with the situation of human rights defenders, thereby facilitating the monitoring the implementation of its precautionary measures and the provisional measures of the Court. In December 2001 the Executive Secretariat of the Commission established the 'Human Rights Defenders Functional Unit'. As the President of the Commission noted in his presentation of the Commissions Annual Report of 2001, '(t)his Unit will be in charge of collecting information on the plight of human rights defenders in the America's, maintaining contact with governmental and non-governmental organizations, and coordinating the Secretariat's work in this area. This initiative should contribute to more comprehensive knowledge of the situation and to mechanisms to help the OAS work more effectively and with greater coordination'.[96]

---

[91] CIDH Press release 33/01 'Inter-American Commission on Human Rights concludes its visit to the Republic of Colombia', 13 December 2001, §18 and Annual Report 2001, Chapter IV, §16.

[92] See CIDH *Guantanamo Bay* case, precautionary measures of 23 July 2002, 18 March 2003, 29 July 2004 and 28 October 2005. CIDH Resolution 1/06 in Press Release 27/06, 'Inter-American Commission urges to close Guantanamo without delay', 28 July 2006, available at <http://www.cidh.org/Comunicados/English/2006/27.06eng.htm> (consulted 6 October 2006). See further Chapter VIII (Ensuring procedural rights).

[93] She was working on the alleged forced disappearance of Alcides Torres Arias whose case was pending before the Commission. Ms. Florez was preparing the next hearing before the Commission.

[94] General Assembly resolution AG/RES.1818, (XXXI-O/01), June 2001.

[95] CIDH 'IACHR deplores the assassination of Maria del Carmen Florez in Colombia', press release 6/02, 15 February 2002. In English the Inter-American Commission uses the same acronym as the Court: IACHR.

[96] Address by Dr. Juan E. Méndez, President of the Inter-American Commission on Human Rights, upon presenting the CIDH Annual Report for 2001 to the Committee on Juridical and Political Affairs of the Permanent Council of the OAS, 30 April 2002 (<www.cidh.org/discoursos/04.30.02.eng.htm>).

The Commission considers that if it publishes a final report or if the Court publishes a decision and for a long time the government does not do anything about implementation, the only option it has under the Convention is to report this to the OAS General Assembly. In order to prepare a report for the General Assembly the Commission introduced a 'reopening of the issue' for the purposes of follow-up and implementation. It may, for instance, call a hearing and ask the government what it is doing about the recommendations that had been sent to them more than a year before. Many governments have protested that the Commission does not have jurisdiction to do this but the Commission believes it is actually part of its jurisdiction, being an implied power as the Commission has to protect the integrity of the system.[97] While this relates to its follow-up on decisions on the merits and not its precautionary measures, it does show the Commission's resolve indeed to protect the integrity of the system.

The Inter-American Court has also engaged in follow-up. It has done so both in the context of its judgments on the merits and reparations and in the context of its provisional measures. It needs to know the extent to which States have complied with its rulings in order to monitor compliance with the undertaking made by the States 'to comply with the judgment of the Court in any case to which they are parties' (under Article 68) and, in particular, to inform the General Assembly of 'the cases in which a State has not complied with its judgments' (Article 65 ACHR).[98] During 2007 the Inter-American Court started a new procedure of holding private hearings on monitoring compliance with its judgments.[99]

The hearings that are held in order to decide on the use, maintenance, expansion or termination of provisional measures are important in themselves: 'besides calling public attention to the case', a hearing 'gives the provisional measures procedure a solemnity that enhanced the chances of compliance and enables the Court to better assess the need for such measures'.[100]

In its Orders for provisional measures the Court requires the State and the Commission to report to it on the implementation of its provisional measures.[101] Preparing the periodic reports on

---

[97]   Interview by author with Juan Mendez, Washington D.C., 17 October 2001.

[98]   "Accordingly, the Court must monitor that the States concerned comply with the reparations it has ordered, before informing the OAS General Assembly about any failure to comply with its decisions. The Court's monitoring of compliance with its decisions implies, first, that it must request information from the State on the actions carried out to implement compliance, and then obtain the comments of the Commission and of the victims or their representatives. When the Court has received this information, it can assess whether the State has complied with its judgment, guide the State's actions to that effect, and comply with its obligation to inform the General Assembly, in the terms of Article 65 of the Convention". IACHR Annual Report 2006, pp. 41-42.

[99]   IACHR Annual Report 2007, p. 40. As pointed out by Buergenthal (1994), pp. 91-92, already before an initial Order for provisional measures is made, 'the mere threat of a hearing' would tend 'to make the State concerned more willing to adopt on its own certain protective measures it was previously unwilling to consider'. The developments since 1994 have confirmed this. The possibility of hearings has become an important tool at different stages of the proceedings before the Court and the private hearings that have in fact taken place since 2007 monitoring compliance with the Court's judgments have reportedly already had an important positive effect in the attitude of States.

[100]   Buergenthal (1994), p. 94.

[101]   Buergenthal (1994), p. 92 notes that the Court cannot really act on the follow-up information provided by the Commission unless it is sitting. "To deal with this problem the Court in one case assigned to its own Permanent Commission the task of monitoring compliance. The Commission then began to transmit to the Court, without comment or analysis, all communications it received from the attorneys in the case relating to the provisional measures, forcing the Court to conclude

State compliance required by the Court is an enormous task for the Commission to tackle. It has to depend largely on the petitioners, usually NGOs, and it complements this, to some extent, with information gathered during on-site visits. The main problem in countries like Colombia, is losing contact with the beneficiaries. Local NGOs may be under death threats themselves and/or, because of an ongoing conflict, the Commission cannot send people to a particular area to gather information. Sometimes the Commission simply has to inform the Court that it is not in a position to give information on the current situation.[102] Information on the situation of the beneficiaries of precautionary and provisional measures is essential for any follow-up. Without such information these measures cannot be effective. Especially in cases of threats and internal displacement effectiveness is fundamentally related to access. The intended beneficiaries are often located in remote places to which the Inter-American Commission, the petitioners or even the UNHCR have no access.[103] Without access to the beneficiaries it proves very problematic to monitor a State's compliance with provisional measures. Obviously, when the Commission and the petitioners cannot find the victims, the Commission is unable to monitor compliance and without follow-up the effectiveness decreases both of its own precautionary measures and of the provisional measures ordered by the Court.

The Court also holds hearings for a follow-up on its provisional measures. It has specifically followed up on promises made by States. In the *Peace Community* case Colombia had pointed out both in 2000 and in 2002 that it was seeking to design an early warning system to be coordinated between the Community and the public security forces in order to be effective.[104] While it had already announced this in 2000, in 2002 it was still at the intentional stage. In 2002 the Court ordered that, in agreement with the beneficiaries or their representatives, the State must also establish a mechanism for continuous surveillance and permanent security in the Community, in conformity with the terms of the Court's Order.[105]

In its Order for provisional measures in the mass expulsion case the Court expressed its appreciation about the State's willingness – shown at the public hearing – to improve its procedures and practices.[106] This remark is important for the Court's follow-up of its provisional measures because at that stage it may refer to the State's promise and enquire about the results. The State assured the Court that with regard to the other people protected by the provisional measures, no deportations had occurred.

In Orders to halt an execution the Inter-American Court provides the rationale for its use of provisional measures: 'if the State were to execute the alleged victims, this would lead to an irreparable situation, as well as constitute conduct incompatible with the object and purpose of the Convention'.[107] This type of motivation may enhance compliance. The same applies to clarity: it

---

that it was being asked to perform functions it was not really competent to perform under the Convention. As a result the Court returned the matter to the Commission for further monitoring. The matter was never resubmitted to the Court". The matter was that of *Bustíos-Rojas* (Peru). See Order of 8 August 1990 for the Court's decision to monitor itself and Order of 17 January 1991 returning the matter to the Commission.

[102] See also Chapter XV (Immediacy and risk).

[103] See also Chapter XIII (Protection), section 3 on beneficiaries.

[104] IACHR *Peace Community of San José de Apartadó* case (Colombia), Order of 24 November 2000.

[105] IACHR *Peace Community of San José de Apartadó* case (Colombia), Order of 18 June 2002.

[106] IACHR *Haitians and Dominicans of Haitian Origin in the Dominican Republic*, Order of 18 August 2000.

[107] See e.g. IACHR *James et al.*, Order of 26 November 2001 (12th 'Considering' clause); *Raxcacó et al.*, 30 August 2004 (9th 'Considering' clause) and *Boyce and Joseph* v. *Barbados*, 25 November 2004 (9th 'Considering' clause).

must be very clear to the State what is expected from it. If the responses of States on previous occasions leave much to be desired, the Court's follow-up will be more specific.[108]

As noted, the references in its Orders to the State's reporting obligations show that the Court has incorporated some form of follow-up in its Orders themselves.[109] Yet in some instances the Court has also followed up the implementation of its Orders outside of the Orders themselves. In conformity with Article 65 ACHR, it informed the General Assembly of the State's failure to comply with its decisions on provisional measures. It requested the General Assembly to urge the State to comply with them. It also wished to put on record its concern about Trinidad's denunciation of the Convention, on 26 May 1998. It pointed out that this decision, which was without precedent in the history of the Inter-American human rights system, did not apply to the Court's provisional measures in this case. Finally, the Court considered that while States Parties have a right to denounce international instruments, when it concerns international human rights treaties, due to their special nature, such denunciation affects the international or regional human rights system as a whole. This particular situation justified, therefore, involvement on the part of the OAS General Assembly to request Trinidad to reconsider its decision.[110]

It appears, however, from the Court's note to the OAS Secretary General of May 1999, that the General Assembly did not properly receive the Court's request to urge Trinidad to comply with its obligations under the Convention. In this note the Court asked the Secretary General to bring its letter to the attention of the General Assembly. It quoted Article 65 and pointed out that 'it falls to the General Assembly to take formal note of the recommendations which the Court makes in its Annual Report concerning non-compliance with its decisions, and to issue such comments as it may consider pertinent'. It wrote that until then all States Parties to the ACHR had complied with its Orders. Trinidad and Tobago was the 'sole exception'.[111]

---

[108] This was the case already early on the Court's practice. Buergenthal (1994), p. 82 refers to the matter of *Bustios Rojas* regarding the protection of witnesses to the killing of a journalist in Peru, in which the IACHR, in its second Order, 17 January 1991 responded to Peru's reported manner of compliance with the Court's Order. Peru had informed the Court that it had 'established a system of military liaisons whom the protected persons could contact'. In its follow-up the Court ordered Peru to supplement this system 'in three Peruvian localities with a comparable civilian liaison system'. "This part of the order can be traced to the concern expressed by the Commission that the persons to be protected, some of whom were in hiding, accused various military officers of having been the killers. The witnesses might therefore have had a justified fear of military liaison officers affiliated with the very units that could have been involved in the murder and attempted cover-up". IACHR *Bustios Rojas* (Peru), Order of 17 January 1991. On specificity see further Chapter XIII (Protection), section 3.

[109] In its Order of August 1998, for example, the Court required the State to report every two weeks on the status of the appeals and scheduled executions. It also required the Commission to send its observations on these reports within two days of their receipt. It ordered both the State and the Commission to inform it immediately of any significant developments. *James et al.* cases, Order of 29 August 1998.

[110] CIDH Informe Anual 1998, II (Actividades Jurisdiccionales y consultivas de la Corte), K. (Estado de Cumplimiento de las Sentencias de la Corte), §7.

[111] The Court reminded the Secretary General that, in the new structure of the General Assembly, the Presidents of the Inter-American Commission and Court (and the Inter-American Juridical Committee) could no longer orally present their Annual Reports. Instead, the Assembly only received for consideration a Resolution on the observations and recommendations to the Annual Reports approved by the Permanent Council. Both the Commission on Juridical and Political Matters and the Permanent Council, however, had omitted the Court's recommendation. Thus,

"It is a matter of profound concern to the Court that, in the operative part of the recommendations concerning its 1998 Annual Report, which the Commission on Juridical and Political Matters and the Permanent Council of the Organisation are forwarding to the General Assembly, no mention is made of the Court's recommendation…".[112]

The Court decided to send copies of this letter to all Ministers of Foreign Relations of the OAS member States and also to their Permanent Representatives to the OAS in Washington D.C.[113] This proactive approach was considered necessary to ensure that all OAS Member States are aware of the situation. Still, the General Assembly adopted no resolution on this issue during its 1999 session.

---

the General Assembly would be 'precluded from considering and commenting on' the Court's recommendation to urge Trinidad to comply with the Court's Orders.

[112] IACHR *James et al.* case, Note of the Court to His Excellency Ambassador Julio César Aráoz, President of the Permanent Council, 24 May 1999. The Court emphasised that the protection of human rights is the most important function of the OAS, 'as has been acknowledged by Your Excellency'. The omission of the Court's recommendation 'affects the very essence of the Inter-American System of human rights protection, which finds its most telling expression in the binding nature of the judgements issued by the jurisdictional organ, the Inter-American Court of Human Rights'. The Court also noted that previously it had already taken steps to convince the Permanent Council, by sending two notes to its President. These notes, which the Court enclosed, remained without effect. In May 1999 the Court sent the first note to the President of the Permanent Council. This letter referred to the draft Resolution on the Court's Annual Report that the Commission on Juridical and Political Affairs had presented to the Permanent Council. "When studying the draft Resolution that will be submitted to the General Assembly, the Court noted with some surprise that, whilst its second "considering" makes mention to [sic] Article 65 and to the duty of the Court to report the cases in which a State fails to comply with its judgements, the operative exhortation to the Republic of Trinidad and Tobago to comply with the Orders of the Court has been omitted". IACHR *James et al.* case, Note of the Court to His Excellency Ambassador Julio César Aráoz, President of the Permanent Council, 24 May 1999. The Court emphasised the importance of the support of the highest organ of the OAS to help safeguard the effectiveness of the Inter-American system. It requested the inclusion in the draft Resolution of an operative paragraph in which 'the General Assembly urges the Republic of Trinidad and Tobago to comply' with the Court's Orders for provisional measures. Such inclusion would be 'in compliance with' Article 65 ACHR. The Court also requested the President to submit its note to the next session of the full Permanent Council, *James et al.* case, Note of the Court to His Excellency Ambassador Julio César Aráoz, President of the Permanent Council, 24 May 1999. The Court received a reply by the President of the Permanent Council. It did not specify its contents but acknowledged its receipt and reiterated that 'the Court esteems that it is convenient that the Permanent Council consider and decide upon the inclusion of an operative paragraph relating to Trinidad and Tobago's failure to comply with its Orders for this Tribunal', *James et al.* case, Note of the Court to His Excellency Ambassador Julio César Aráoz, President of the Permanent Council, 25 May 1999. As mentioned before, the Court included these letters in its note to the OAS Secretary General. It concluded that: "The Court is of the view that this issue which is of fundamental importance for the Organisation and the Inter-American System, should receive the benefit of a pronouncement by the General Assembly, the highest organ of the Organisation". *James et al.* case, Note of the Court to His Excellency César Gaviria T., Secretary General of the OAS, 27 May 1999.

[113] IACHR *James et al.* case, Note of the Court to His Excellency César Gaviria T., Secretary General of the OAS, 27 May 1999.

During its Thirtieth Regular Session in Windsor, Canada, which was held from 4 to 6 June 2000, the President of the Court presented the Court's Annual Report 1999 to the General Assembly. The General Assembly had once more changed its structure, at least to the extent that the Court's President was able again to personally present the Court's Report. In June 2000 the General Assembly adopted its amended Rules of Procedure. These state that the 'chairs or representatives' of, among others, the Commission and the Court 'may attend the General Assembly with the right to speak'.[114]

Upon his presentation, the General Assembly adopted a resolution in which it reiterated 'that the judgments of the Court are final and may not be appealed and that the states parties to the Convention undertake to comply with the rulings of the Court in all cases to which they are party'. The Assembly also urged States that had denounced the ACHR or withdrawn their recognition of the Court's obligatory jurisdiction to reconsider their decisions.[115] In other words, in its Session of June 2000 the General Assembly issued the Resolution the Court had requested it to take the year before. Now the Assembly itself referred to Article 65 ACHR establishing that the Court 'shall submit' to the General Assembly a Report on its work during the previous year. It pointed out that the Court 'shall specify, in particular, the cases in which a state has not complied with the Court's judgments and make any pertinent recommendations'. The Assembly also reiterated the Court's statement about the particular nature of the regional human rights system: 'bearing in mind that the denunciation of inter-American legal instruments on human rights and the withdrawal of recognition of the Court's binding jurisdiction affect the regional system as a whole, due to its particular nature'.[116]

The Court had followed up specifically the cases of Mr. Ramiah and Mr. Briggs. In these cases it only approached the State itself, but did not resort to the General Assembly. In June 1999 Trinidad had executed Joey Ramiah in violation of the Court's provisional measures. As a first response to the execution the Court pointed out that Mr. Ramiah 'was protected by the Provisional Measures ordered by the Court'.[117] The State may have thought that, in light of the attitude of the OAS Permanent Council with regard to the Court's Annual Report 1998 and the consequent lack of discussion of the Court's Report of non-compliance under Article 65 ACHR during the 1999 Session of the General Assembly, there was not much risk of General Assembly involvement if it would execute some of its prisoners in violation of the Court's provisional measures.

On 27 July 1999 the Deputy Secretary of the Court wrote to Trinidad that the President of the Court had directed him to urgently request the State to present information on the Commission's communication informing the Court that Trinidad had read Mr. Briggs a warrant of execution.[118] He reminded the State of the Court's provisional measures on behalf of Mr. Briggs, in

---

[114]   OAS General Assembly, Amendments to the Rules of Procedure, OEA/Ser.P, AG/RES. 1737 (XXX-O/00), 5 June 2000 (original: Spanish).

[115]   OAS General Assembly, Resolution AG/RES. 1716 (XXX-O/00), 5 June 2000, reproduced in: Annual Report 2000, III (Other activities of the Court), 8. (Thirtieth Regular Session of the General Assembly of the OAS) and Commission Annual Report 2000, Chapter IIa.

[116]   OAS General Assembly, Observations and Recommendations of the Member States on the Annual Report of the Inter-American Court of Human Rights, AG/RES. 1716 (XXX-O/00), 5 June 2000, reproduced in: Commission Annual Report 2000, Chapter Iia.

[117]   IACHR *James et al.* cases, Order for provisional measures, 16 August 2000.

[118]   In the Briggs case the Commission informed the Court, in June 1999, that the High Court of Trinidad and Tobago had dismissed an application to stay his execution and that the State's Court of Appeal had dismissed his appeal. The latter court indicated that 'notwithstanding the Order of the Court of 25 May 1999, it was not satisfied that any substantive issue respecting Anthony Briggs was pending before the Inter-American Court'. It also refused to grant a stay of execution

particular its Order of May 1999. In this Order 'the Court considered the circumstances of Mr. Briggs' case before the Inter-American system and after deliberation' decided to maintain the measures until such time as the Court would have issued a decision.[119] Trinidad executed Anthony Briggs that same day.

In its Order of 16 August 2000 the Court censured the State for having executed Anthony Briggs and Joey Ramiah. It pointed out that 'pursuant to the Orders of the Inter-American Court' Trinidad and Tobago 'had a duty to preserve the life and physical integrity of Anthony Briggs and Joey Ramiah'.[120] It reprimanded Trinidad for failure to submit the required fortnightly reports on the circumstances of the beneficiaries of the Court's provisional measures. The Order considered that the State 'did present its observations on the execution of Anthony Briggs and, in like manner, this Court deems important to obtain information on the circumstances that led to the execution of Joey Ramiah'. It then referred to the Court's obligation to comply in good faith with the provisions and to its duty not to take actions that may frustrate restitution in kind of the rights of the alleged victims. The Court referred to Article 65 ACHR on the recommendations the Court shall submit to the General Assembly in cases of non-compliance. Although this reference can be found in its considerations and not in its decisions, it gives an indication of the action the Court might undertake as follow-up to the State's non-compliance.

As part of its follow-up it required Trinidad to submit information, within two weeks, 'on the circumstances that led to the execution of Joey Ramiah so that the Inter-American Court of Human Rights may consider it and include it in its report to the next General Assembly of the Organisation of American States'.[121] In September 2000, 'pursuant to the Order of the Court', the State 'presented information regarding the circumstances that led to the execution of Joey Ramiah'.[122]

In February 2000 the Commission submitted to the Court the case of *Constantine et al.* v. *Trinidad and Tobago*, which encompassed the case of Joey Ramiah. In its Judgment in this case, *Hilaire, Constantine and Benjamin and others*, the Court found that the State had arbitrarily deprived Mr. Ramiah of his right to life in violation of Article 4 ACHR. "This situation is aggravated because the victim was protected by Provisional Measures ordered by this Tribunal, which expressly indicated that his execution should be stayed pending the resolution of the case by the inter-American human rights system".[123] The State had 'caused irreparable harm to the detriment of Joey Ramiah, by reason of its disregard of a direct order of the Court and its deliberate decision

---

pending an appeal to the Privy Council. Mr. Briggs' solicitors instead brought an expedited petition for special leave to appeal to the Privy Council. They sought a stay of his execution pending the determination of this petition. On 21 June the Judicial Committee of the Privy Council indeed granted him leave to appeal as well as a stay of execution. It requested 'further clarification from his solicitors as to the nature of the matter relating to him that was pending before the Inter-American Court'. On the same day the Commission informed the Court of this situation. The next month, however, the Privy Council dismissed his appeal. See further Chapter XIV (Jurisdiction).

[119] Letter of Deputy Secretary Renzo Pomi to the honourable Ralph Maharaji, M.P., Minister of Foreign Affairs of Trinidad and Tobago, 27 July 1999, REF: CDH-S/877. The Court also reproduced the relevant parts of this letter in: *James et al.* cases, Order for provisional measures, 16 August 2000.

[120] IACHR *James et al.* cases, Order of 16 August 2000. See also the Order of 24 November 2000.

[121] IACHR *James et al.* cases, Order of 16 August 2000.

[122] IACHR *James et al.* cases, Order of 24 November 2000.

[123] IACHR *Hilaire, Constantine and Benjamin et al.* v. *Trinidad & Tobago*, Judgment of 21 June 2002, §198.

to order the execution of this victim'.[124] It stressed 'the seriousness of the State's non-compliance in virtue of the execution of the victim despite the existence of Provisional Measures in his favour, and as such' found the State responsible for violating Article 4 ACHR.[125]

While the Court ordered different forms of reparation in the cases of the other victims, with regard to Mr. Ramiah this was no longer possible. Instead it ordered payment of damages for immaterial harm to his wife (to be used on behalf of their son) and mother. In light of the Court's remark about its provisional measures, its finding of an additional violation in the case of Mr. Ramiah can be seen as a form of follow-up of the Court's provisional measures in his case. Nevertheless the Court should also have found a violation of Article 63(2) ACHR on provisional measures.[126] Moreover, as has the European Court with regard to Article 34 ECHR, it could have found a violation of the right of individual petition (Article 44 ACHR).[127]

The Court did not refer to the execution of Briggs because his case was not included in the Commission's submission to the Court that resulted in the *Hilaire, Constantine and Benjamin and others* Judgment. In order to follow up the Briggs case the Commission could have instituted new proceedings on the State's non-compliance with its recommendations in the Article 51 Report and with the Court's provisional measures. It could have moved such a case quickly through and submitted it to the Court. Yet it did not do so.[128]

The Court had summoned the State and the Commission to a public hearing in August 1998 to discuss the provisional measures to halt the executions. Yet, Trinidad informed the Court that it 'must decline' its summons to appear at this public hearing. The President of the Court sent a note to the Prime Minister of Trinidad reiterating the importance of this State's appearance before the Court to fulfil its obligation as a State Party to the ACHR.

When in 1998 Trinidad announced its refusal to appear before the Inter-American Court the Court's President pointed out that the Court had always relied on the good faith and cooperation of States so that it could carry out its mandate. He expressed the following strongly worded criticism:

> "the failure of a State Party to appear at a public hearing, to which it has been duly summoned, is without precedent in the history of the Court. The Tribunal is seriously concerned by the implications of Trinidad and Tobago's decision in the present matter and its ramifications".[129]

The Court's President explained the importance of such hearing in which the Court sought to permit the Commission and the State to present their arguments in a public forum 'without compromising their positions in the proceedings which are currently pending before the Commission'. Apart from allowing both parties the opportunity to publicly present their arguments, such a hearing was also important, 'due to the urgency and complexity of these matters', to enable the Court to fully consider these arguments.[130] The Court later stressed that Trinidad's failure to appear at the public hearing 'represents a violation of its international obligations under the American Convention'.[131]

---

[124] Id., §199.

[125] Id., §200.

[126] On non-compliance with the Court's provisional measures as a violation of Article 63(2) ACHR itself, see already Buergenthal (1994), p. 88.

[127] See Chapter XVI (Legal status). See also Haeck/Burbano Herrera/Zwaak (2008), p. 46 and p. 63.

[128] See also Chapter XIV (Jurisdiction).

[129] IACHR *James et al.* case, note from the President to the Prime Minister of Trinidad and Tobago, 19 August 1998, Series E, Compendium 2.

[130] Ibid.

[131] IACHR *James et al.* cases, Order of 9 August 1998.

In its Order for provisional measures in *Boyce and Joseph* v. *Barbados* the Inter-American Court has pointed out that the State is 'under the obligation to keep this Tribunal informed regarding the actions it has taken to comply with the Order of the President. The provision of such information is essential in order to permit the Court to evaluate the State's degree of compliance with the said Order'.[132] In this case the Court decided that despite the temporary stay of execution by the High Court of Barbados, it would maintain its provisional measures. It considered the stay 'a crucial step on the part of the State' to protect the fundamental rights of the beneficiaries 'as well as to facilitate the processing of their cases in accordance with the requirements of the American Convention'. It noted, however, that the State had failed to submit the report required in the President's Order two months previously and the Court consequently decided to maintain its Order.[133]

Often the Inter-American Court follows up earlier provisional measures by confirming, specifying and/or expanding them. The Court has also *maintained* its provisional measures, in some of its cases, even after its decision on the merits of the case, because some of the witnesses involved in that case were still being threatened. In some of these cases the Court's Judgment on Reparations was still pending, but it seems that even if that were not the case, the Court does not consider a case 'closed' until a State has implemented the Court's Judgment on Reparations. Yet it now started the practice of continuing monitoring specifically as part of its procedure for supervision of Compliance of Judgments, often thereby concluding its provisional measures and instead issuing Orders on (non-)compliance.[134] At other times it decides to lift them with regard to those beneficiaries that are no longer at risk of irreparable harm to their life or personal integrity. It has also decided to lift provisional measures when it considered its monitoring was more appropriately related to compliance with a judgment on the merits or reparation.[135]

Following up on its Judgments in the cases *Fermín Ramírez* and *Raxcacó Reyes* the Inter-American Court pointed out that it is a power inherent in its jurisdictional function to supervise compliance with its decisions.[136] States must apply their obligations in good faith (*pacta sunt servanda*) and the State may not forward internal reasons for non-compliance. The obligations apply to all organs of the State. Implementation by State agents of a domestic law that violates the ACHR triggers international state responsibility. When a State has ratified an international treaty such as the ACHR its domestic courts, as part of the State apparatus, are obliged to ensure that the

---

[132]   IACHR *Boyce and Joseph* v. *Barbados*. Order of 25 November 2004, §6.

[133]   Ibid.

[134]   See also Chapter XIV (Jurisdiction and admissibility). It may also combine the two types of Orders, see e.g. IACHR *Bámaca Velásquez* v. *Guatemala*, Order of 27 January 2009, declaring Guatemala's partial compliance with the Judgment on Reparations, declaring to keep open its monitoring process until full compliance is achieved and maintaining its provisional measures of 11 March 2005 (Provisional Measures and Monitoring Compliance with Judgment).

[135]   See e.g. IACHR *Case of the Mayagna (Sumo) Awas Tingni Community* (Nicaragua), Order of 26 November 2007. In December 2008 the Commission issued a press release praising the demarcation and titling of ancestral lands belonging to the Awas Tingni. The government of Nicaragua gave them the property title to 73,000 hectares of its territory, which 'marked a critical step forwards' in the resolution of the case. See CIDH press release 62/08, 'IACHR hails titling of Awas Tingni Community lands in Nicaragua', 18 December 2008.

[136]   See e.g. IACHR Order on supervision of compliance of the cases *Fermín Ramírez* v. *Guatemala* and *Raxcacó Reyes* v. *Guatemala* and on the request to expand the provisional measures in *Raxcacó Reyes y otros*, 9 May 2008, 1st 'Considering' clause.

effects of the decisions made under the ACHR are not diminished because of the application of domestic laws that revolts against its object and purpose.[137]

In its (consecutive) Orders the Inter-American Court also follows up on the implementation of the provisional measures ordered by it and, while doing so, it refers to the particularly important role of the Commission in adequately and effectively following up on the implementation of the measures ordered by the Court. It stresses that the State's reports reflect the adoption of the priority measures established by the Court by describing the specific results achieved.[138]

The Court has pointed out that provisional measures have an exceptional character. They are ordered in function of the necessities of protection and, once ordered, they must be maintained as long as the Court considers that the basic requirements of extreme gravity and urgency and the prevention of irreparable harm to the persons protected by them, are still fulfilled.[139]

In the context of three cases against Venezuela the Court noted that the State had questioned the Court's power to supervise its provisional measures, rather than responded to the requirement to provide information. Venezuela considered that the Court exceeded its power of supervision of compliance if it demanded information from the State, on an obligatory basis, with regard to the implementation of its measures or called into question the manner in which the State was implementing them.[140] Yet, as the Court has noted, the power to supervise the compliance with its provisional measures and give instructions as requested by the parties or *proprio motu* is a power inherent to the Court's functions.[141] In other words it is simply part of the normal exercise of its jurisdictional functions.[142]

The State's duty to inform the Court has a dual character. It requires for its effective implementation the formal presentation of a document as well as specific, recent and detailed information with regard to the implementation of the specific obligations.[143] In this respect the Court has stressed that it follows a written procedure that permits it to supervise compliance with the provisional measures adopted by it and to guarantee respect for the contradictory nature of the proceedings so that all parties (the State, the Commission and the beneficiaries) must have the opportunity to provide the Court with the information they consider relevant with regard to the compliance with the Order. Often public hearings take place that allow for oral testimonies by the parties.[144]

In 2008, when faced with a request to expand the provisional measures in *Raxcacó Reyes y otros*, the Court pointed out that because Article 62(2) ACHR refers to cases of *prima facie* urgency, while the risk of irreparable harm in these cases related to violations that have already been established by judgments of the Court that have *res iudicata* status, it would not order the provisional measures requested. Instead it ordered the State simply to comply with its judgment, adding specifications and noting that it would continue to monitor the situation.[145]

---

[137]   IACHR Order on supervision of compliance of the cases *Fermín Ramírez* v. *Guatemala* and *Raxcacó Reyes* v. *Guatemala* and on the request to expand the provisional measures in *Raxcacó Reyes y otros*, 9 May 2008, 4th 'Considering' clause. The Court also referred to Article 27 VCLT.

[138]   IACHR *Matter of Mendoza prisons*, Order of 27 November 2007, 3rd 'Decisional' clause.

[139]   IACHR *Matter of Liliana Ortega et al.* (Venezuela), Order of 14 June 2005, 5th 'Considering' clause.

[140]   IACHR *Liliana Ortega et al.; Luisiana Ríos et al.; Luis Uzcátegui; Marta Colomina and Liliana Velásquez* (*Venezuela*), Order of 4 May 2004, 16th 'Considering' clause.

[141]   Id., 9th 'Considering' clause.

[142]   Id., 11th 'Considering' clause.

[143]   Id., 15th 'Considering' clause.

[144]   Id., 10th 'Considering' clause.

[145]   IACHR Order on supervision of compliance of the cases *Fermín Ramírez* v. *Guatemala* and *Raxcacó Reyes* v. *Guatemala*. See also e.g. IACHR *Matter of the persons imprisoned in the "Dr.*

In any case, as noted, the Inter-American Court has now decided, in cases in which it has already found violations on the merits, often simply to order compliance with the obligations based already on its previous Judgments rather than ordering provisional measures to halt irreparable harm. In other words it now more clearly distinguishes between supervision of its judgments on the merits and reparation and supervision, expansion or termination of its provisional measures.

2.2.8 Supervision and monitoring in the European system

The former European Commission on Human Rights has sometimes followed up specifically on its provisional measures, in the face of possible or actual non-compliance. It did so, for instance, by renewing them in response to certain developments.[146] It has also used follow-up provisional

---

Sebastião Martins Silveira" Penitentiary in Araraquara, São Paulo (Brazil), Order of 30 September 2006, *Matter of the persons imprisoned in the "Dr. Sebastião Martins Silveira" Penitentiary in Araraquara, São Paulo* (Brazil), Order of 30 September 2006 and Case of *Comunidad Indígena Sawhoyamaxa* v. *Paraguay*, Order of 2 February 2007 on supervision of compliance, 9th and 12th 'Considering' clauses. As part of the request to expand the provisional measures in *Raxcacó Reyes y otros*, 9 May 2008, the petitioners had also requested provisional measures on behalf of one person whose case was still pending in the Inter-American system, but this was a new matter that could not be dealt with as an expansion of existing provisional measures. Thus it involved a new request for provisional measures in a matter not yet pending before the Court. Therefore it was the Commission that had to request these measures and not the petitioners. See Chapter II (Systems). After the Commission indeed did so, the Court decided to order provisional measures on his behalf. IACHR Order on supervision of compliance of the cases *Fermín Ramírez* v. *Guatemala* and *Raxcacó Reyes* v. *Guatemala* and on the request to expand the provisional measures in *Raxcacó Reyes y otros*, 9 May 2008, 51st-63rd 'Considering' clauses.

[146] In EComHR *B.* v *France* (1987) the petitioner gave himself up to the French police. He explained that he himself wished to be extradited in order to be able to defend himself. Once detained, he allegedly found out he had already been sentenced to death *in absentia* in Morocco. EComHR *B.* v. *France*, 22 January 1987 (inadm.), p. 173. He feared that, upon return, he would 'not be entitled to adversarial proceedings together with the guarantees accompanying a fair trial'. "If that proved to be the case, he would not be in a position to defend himself and enforcement of the death penalty would therefore constitute treatment contrary to Article 3 of the Convention", p. 174. In August 1985 the President of the European Commission used provisional measures to halt his extradition. The next month the French Government informed the Commission that it had asked the Moroccan authorities to specify whether, in the event of Mr. B. being handed over to them, he could be retried in the Government's presence in Morocco. It had also asked for a formal undertaking that, if the death penalty were to be pronounced a second time, it would not be enforced. The Commission decided to adjourn its examination of the case in light of the information provided by France. Many months later, in July 1986, the French Government informed the Commission that, according to the Moroccan authorities, a retrial was possible. From this, it concluded that it could 'carry out the extradition in the next few weeks'. p. 175. As the Commission put it, the Government referred 'only to the first of the two conditions with which the Moroccan authorities had been asked to comply', p. 175. Accordingly, in August, October and December 1986 the President of the Commission renewed the application of Rule 36, p. 175. It specifically requested the views of the parties with regard to the question 'whether a person detained with a view to extradition who receives a communication of this kind is not justified in placing legitimate confidence in the Government's consenting to his extradition only if the Moroccan authorities give a formal undertaking that, in the event of the death penalty being pronounced a second time, it will not be enforced'. It added the question whether 'a change in the

measures to the effect that the State that ignored its provisional measures to halt an expulsion or extradition should enable the return of the petitioner. In *Cruz Varas* v. *Sweden* (1990) the European Commission specifically pointed out, under Rule 36 on provisional measures, that the State should take measures to enable the petitioner's return to Sweden as soon as possible 'given the failure of the Government to comply' with its earlier provisional measures.[147] The State responded that the National Immigration Board was responsible for granting permission to enter and remain in Sweden. A week after receipt of the Commission's provisional measures the Government had informed the Board of these measures. Two weeks later the Board rejected the request from Mr. Cruz Varas to be allowed to return to Sweden.[148] The Commission only followed up this decision when it maintained its provisional measures a few days later, but when the Board subsequently confirmed this rejection the Commission did not respond. Instead it decided, a few months later, not to prolong its provisional measures.[149]

In *Mansi* v. *Sweden* (1989) the State again ignored the Commission's provisional measures. In this case as well the Commission subsequently invoked Rule 36 so that the Government would take measures to enable the petitioner to return to Sweden as soon as possible. Sweden informed the Commission that it had transmitted these provisional measures to the National Immigration Board. This is interesting because the Government had expelled Mansi despite this Board's proposal not to do so.[150] Both Amnesty International and a representative of the Swedish Embassy in Jordan confirmed that he had been tortured upon return. Later the petitioner was allowed to return to Sweden and the case never came before the ECtHR because a friendly settlement was agreed upon.[151]

As noted, the Inter-American Court itself monitors compliance. In the European system it is the Committee of Ministers (the Permanent Representatives of the member States) of the Council of Europe that supervises the execution of the Court's judgments under Article 46(2) ECHR. It generally does so through constructive dialogue. Normally a case remains on the agenda until the State concerned has informed the Committee of the measures it has taken to implement the judgment. Following this the Committee adopts a resolution containing the information given by the State.[152]

Government's attitude' was 'liable to constitute a violation of Article 3 of the Convention, in view of the confidence awakened in the prisoner and the extreme seriousness of the issue concerning him', pp. 175-176. The case was subsequently declared inadmissible for non-exhaustion.

[147] EComHR *Cruz Varas et al.* v. *Sweden*, 7 June 1990 (Article 31 report), §§61 and 73.

[148] Id., §§62 and 38.

[149] Id., §§63 and 38. See also §§105-127 and dissenting opinion Sperduti.

[150] EComHR *Mansi* v. *Sweden*, 7 December 1989 (adm.), p. 244.

[151] EComHR *Mansi* v. *Sweden*, 9 March 1990 (Friendly settlement).

[152] See e.g. Klerk (2000), p. 154; Van der Velde (1997); VandeLanotte/Haeck (2005), pp. 733-752; Zwaak (2008) and Lodeweges (2008), pp. 949-953. Among others, within the Council of Europe a Department for the Execution of Judgments of the ECtHR has been established. Moreover, the Committee of Ministers has suggested to the Court, in its Resolution (2004) 3, 12 May 2004 to specifically identify systemic problems underlying the violations found, especially 'when it is likely to give rise to numerous applications', so as to assist states in finding the appropriate solution and the Committee of Ministers in supervising the execution of judgments'. See also Chapter XIII (Protection). This 2004 resolution also invited the Court to 'specifically notify any judgment containing indications of the existence of a systemic problem not only to the state concerned and to the Committee of Ministers, but also to the Parliamentary Assembly, to the Secretary General of the Council of Europe and to the Council of Europe Commissioner for Human Rights, and to highlight such judgments in an appropriate manner in the database of the

The Court's Rule 39 on provisional measures also specifically refers to the Committee of Minister's monitoring role. The Committee of Ministers has the role to follow up on compliance with the Court's provisional measures. Apparently one reason for including in Rule 39 a paragraph on follow-up was to compensate for the fact that legally binding provisional measures were not included as such in Protocol 11.[153] Garry notes the significance of the fact that this follow-up procedure is the same as that used after a binding final judgment has been issued under Article 46(2) ECHR.[154] The Parliamentary Assembly of the Council of Europe, by way of its Committee on Legal Affairs and Human Rights, has actively followed up on provisional measures as well.[155]

Nevertheless the fact that the Committee of Ministers does perform a task monitoring compliance of judgments as well as provisional measures and that the Parliamentary Assembly also plays a role, does not exclude the Court's own role in monitoring compliance. Lawson suggests this would apply in particular to monitoring measures directly related to the rights of the individuals involved: cessation of the violation, *restitutio in integrum* and payment of compensation, rather than changes in legislation. He also suggests that the Court should be able to keep the case on its docket to allow the national authorities, for instance, to reopen a criminal case. If this takes too long the European Court could still intervene.[156] The text of Article 41 ECHR certainly allows the ECtHR to monitor compliance with its judgments, including reparation in the form of *restitutio in integrum*. Like the Inter-American Court it could later issue a judgment on reparations taking into account the measures already taken by the State.[157] Lawson gives some additional

---

Court'. Formally the Secretary General has the power, under Article 52 ECHR, to request from the State an explanation of its implementation of the Convention. The fact that the resolution refers to the Secretary General may open up the possibilities of this provision somewhat. The reason why the Committee also refers to the Parliamentary Assembly is obviously related to the fact that the latter has already involved itself in the supervision of judgments and may employ possibilities for publicity. The Committee of Ministers itself publishes interim decisions on implementation, which may include increasingly urgent language. The fact that it makes public such decisions is a way to pressure the State through public opinion. An interesting option suggested by Zwaak (2008), p. 362 is the use of Article 17 Statute of the Council of Europe, under which the Committee of Ministers may set up advisory or technical committees or commissions, for instance 'for the purpose of taking evidence and other tasks within the context of its function under the Convention'. Indeed such committees could also assist in the follow-up on provisional measures, especially of those revealing an underlying systemic problem affecting large groups of people.

[153] See interview by Garry (2001) with Judge Pellonpää, Section IV, 16 June 2000, p. 409.

[154] Garry (2001), p. 409.

[155] See e.g. its response to Russia ignoring the Court's provisional measures to suspend the deportation of a person to Uzbekistan. The President of the Parliamentary Assembly René van der Linden wrote to the Chairman of the Russian delegation to PACE to ask for explanations, see Council of Europe Parliamentary Assembly Committee on Legal Affairs and Human Rights, 'Member states' duty to co-operate with the European Court of Human Rights', Doc. 11183, 9, February 2007, Explanatory memorandum by Rapporteur Christos Pourgourides, §52 (in footnote). In this case the ECtHR found Russia in violation of Article 3 ECHR (among others). Yet given the conflicting information with regard to the timeline of the expulsion and the moment Russia received the provisional measures, the Court felt unable to find a violation of Article 34 ECHR for disrespecting its provisional measures, *Muminov* v. *Russia*, 11 December 2008.

[156] See Lawson (Preadvies 1999), pp. 82-83, p. 85.

[157] See also Lawson (Preadvies 1999), p. 82. In the proposed 14th Protocol, awaiting ratification by Russia, it is the Committee of Ministers that can ask the Court to interpret its previous judgments in order to assist the Committee in its supervisory role. In addition the Committee of Ministers

arguments. The *effet utile* of the procedure requires implementation of the Court's judgments by the States and access to an effective procedure for the victim in case of State failure. Non-compliance, moreover, is an aggravated breach of the ECHR. The Court could reopen the case (or open a *new* case) and in its judgment on compensation it could take into account the fact that the State knowingly violates the Convention. The Committee of Ministers does not have this possibility. In this respect he emphasises that the Court should make clear in its judgment the measures it expects of the State.[158] It is suggested that these arguments for the Court's role in monitoring compliance with its judgments apply equally to its role in following up its provisional measures.

2.2.9 Follow-up on provisional measures under the Dayton Accord

Strangely, Article XI, 1(b) of Annex 6 of the Dayton Accord grants the Bosnia Chamber the power 'to include an order for provisional measures in its final decision on the merits of a case'. The Chamber seems to have found a way to interpret this provision: "This power might be used to regulate the position of the parties before the decision becomes final and binding, or pending the full implementation of the decision".[159] Indeed, pending implementation it may often be useful to follow up on the situation of the victims in order to make sure that nothing happens that could prevent further implementation.[160]

In de case of *Boudellaa et al.* (2002) the Bosnia Chamber examined on the merits the obligations of the respondent Parties in handing over the petitioners to US forces. This led to their detention at Camp X-Ray in Guantanamo Bay, Cuba. It had been done contrary to the Chamber's provisional measures.[161] In response to Bosnia and Herzegovina ignoring its provisional measures to halt the removal of the petitioners the Bosnia Chamber found 'that the expulsion was unlawful because it was carried out in violation of the Chamber's binding order for provisional measures of 17 January 2002, which ordered both respondent Parties to take all necessary steps to prevent the applicants from being taken out of the territory of Bosnia and Herzegovina. The Chamber recalls that in its previous case law, the Chamber has held that an order for provisional measures is binding and has the status of national law'.[162]

The Bosnia Chamber specifically responded to allegations by Bosnia that the order had not been delivered to it in a timely and proper manner and that it had no authority to give effect to the Orders by the Chamber.[163] It noted: "It is not necessary for the Chamber to examine these submissions. It is undisputed that the applicants were held in detention by officials of the Federation when its order was issued, that they were handed over to US forces by officials of the Federal

---

[158] may specifically refer a case to the Court asking it to determine whether a State has failed to comply with a judgment. See further Zwaak (2008), pp. 357-360.

[158] Lawson (Preadvies 1999), p. 91.

[159] See Bosnia Chamber Annual Report 2000 (under the heading 'provisional measures').

[160] Similarly, the Inter-American Court only considers a case closed once the State has fully implemented it. Before such time it may maintain provisional measures, for instance to protect witnesses. See also further Chapter XIV discussing jurisdiction.

[161] Bosnia Chamber *Boudellaa, Lakhdar, Nechle and Lahmar* v. *BiH and Fed. BiH*, 11 October 2002, §§4-5.

[162] Id., §185 (adding: 'The Chamber recalls that, for example, in the *D.K.* case, it held that the eviction of the applicant was not in accordance with the law, for the purposes of Article 8(2) of the Convention, even though the competent authorities had established that the applicant was an illegal occupant, because there was an order for provisional measures of the Chamber prohibiting the eviction (case no. CH/98/710, *D.K.* v. *Republika Srpska*, decision on admissibility and merits of 2 November 1999, paragraphs 33-37, Decisions August-December 1999)').

[163] See also Chapter XVII (Official responses).

Ministry of Interior, and that the order for provisional measures had been brought to the attention of the Federal Ministry of Interior before the hand-over of the applicants. This is sufficient to establish the unlawfulness of the expulsion in this respect as well".[164]

The Chamber found that 'the respondent Parties have not followed the requirements of a legal expulsion procedure arising from the domestic law. They thereby violated the condition set out in Article 1 paragraph 1 of Protocol No. 7 to the Convention of a decision reached in accordance with law'.[165]

The violations fell 'within the responsibility of both respondent Parties'. "The law and also the factual actions taken by both respondent Parties in regard to (...) the hand-over of the applicants to US forces, after ensuring through diplomatic contacts that those forces would take them into custody and take them out of the country, involved actions by both respondent Parties which constitute a violation of the applicants' rights".[166]

Given the possibility that US authorities might seek and impose the death penalty against the petitioners, the Chamber found that the respondent Parties should have sought assurances from the US before handing them over. The fact that they had not done so constituted a violation of Article 1 Protocol 6 to the ECHR.

Among others, Bosnia and Herzegovina was ordered to take all possible steps to prevent the death penalty from being pronounced against and executed on the petitioners. This also meant that they should seek assurances from the US, through diplomatic contacts, that they will not be subjected to the death penalty.[167] The Chamber ordered both respondent Parties to 'retain lawyers authorised and admitted to practice in the relevant jurisdictions and before the relevant courts, tribunals or other authoritative bodies in order to take all necessary action to protect the applicants' rights while in U.S. custody and in case of possible military, criminal or other proceedings involving the applicants, each of the respondent Parties bearing half the cost of the attorney fees and expenses'.[168]

In addition, if the petitioners did not return within a year, the respondent Parties were to pay the compensation in the amount of 10,000 KM to the petitioners' families in Bosnia and Herzegovina.[169] Both respondent Parties were also ordered to report to the Chamber every two months until full implementation of the Chamber's decision was achieved.[170]

2.2.10 Follow-up as part of the different reporting procedures

In the Inter-American system there are two forms of *seguimiento*. Apart from a follow-up specifically on the case law, the Commission also uses its country visits and the reports it prepares to comment on failure to comply with its precautionary measures and the Court's provisional measures.[171]

Under the Convention against Torture and the ICCPR the reporting procedure has played a role both in providing country specific information that could help make provisional measures more focused *and* in providing the adjudicators with another forum for the follow-up on compli-

---

[164] Bosnia Chamber *Boudellaa, Lakhdar, Nechle and Lahmar* v. *BiH and Fed. BiH*, 11 October 2002, §187.
[165] Id., §188.
[166] Id., §189.
[167] Id., §330.
[168] Id., §331.
[169] Id., §332.
[170] Id., §333, 20th 'Decisional' clause.
[171] This happened the first time in a report on Ecuador, providing a precedent for the later country reports on Mexico, Brazil and Colombia.

ance with their provisional measures. After all they can simply enter into dialogue directly with State representatives during the public hearings on the State reports and they can subsequently refer to non-compliance in their Concluding Observations with regard to these reports.[172] In its Concluding observations CAT has referred to the 'absolute nature' of Article 3 ICAT and expressed concern with regard to the failure by some States to comply with all provisional measures.[173] In the European system the country reporting procedure is not used, although it would be possible under Article 52 ECHR.[174]

2.3 Possible consequences attached to non-compliance with provisional measures with regard to the admissibility and merits stage

2.3.1 Introduction

Obviously there are many kinds of consequences of non-compliance with provisional measures. First and foremost it is the intended beneficiary of the provisional measures who suffers the consequences of an exposure to irreparable harm. Then obviously there the legal and political consequences for the State concerned.

One question in the context of the follow-up by the adjudicators, is whether this is still aimed at preventing (further) irreparable harm in the case at hand, or if no longer possible, whether it is aimed at preventing recurrence of non-compliance in future cases. What are the legal consequences for State of ignoring provisional measures?[175]

Is the only legal consequence of non-compliance an aggravated breach in case a violation of the substantive right is indeed found? As discussed, another possibility is finding a *procedural* violation of the substantive right, such as the non-refoulement rule. In any case most adjudicators assume that the right of petition is no longer effective when acts occur that are of an irreparable nature, which is generally seen in the light of the right to life and the prohibition of cruel treatment and torture.

---

[172] Yet the fact that most of the time and resources of the Committees is reserved to the reporting procedure also limits their capacity to deal with individual petitions.

[173] CAT Press release HR/4844 'Committee against Torture Concludes 34th session: Issues Concluding Observations on Reports of Canada, Switzerland, Finland, Albania, Uganda and Bahrain', 20 May 2005 (referring to the report of Canada), <http://www.un.org/News/Press/docs/2005/hr4844.doc.htm> (consulted 17 April 2006).

[174] See e.g. Verhey (1996), pp. 103-116, suggesting the usefulness of the country reporting procedure to complement the individual complaint procedure.

[175] Another question is what are the consequences of compliance. Often the case is then solved and may be struck out of the list of pending cases. Yet this is not always the case. See e.g. ECtHR *Sheekh* v. *the Netherlands*, 11 January 2007, where the State argued that the petitioner had an official permit to stay in the Netherlands, which 'solved' the case. The Court, on the other hand, noted that the permit was granted based on a general policy based on the Court's provisional measures. The Court considered it feasible that the petitioner would then have to reintroduce the case before the Court once the general policy is withdrawn and he can again be expelled. In fact, the use of provisional measures in this case required an final examination of the case so as to confirm or dismiss the real risk alleged. The Court declared the case admissible and held on the merits that the petitioner's expulsion would be in violation of Article 3 ECHR. See also Woltjer (2007), p. 362.

This section focuses on the impact on the admissibility decision and on the evidentiary requirements for finding a violation on the merits of the *substantive* rights invoked. While reference is made to the practice of the HRC and CAT, the focus is on the ECtHR judgment in *Mamatkulov*.

2.3.2 Deciding on admissibility

In the disappearance case of *Tshishimbi* v. *Zaire* (1996), in which it had used provisional measures, the HRC noted, using the usual expression, that 'in the circumstances, due weight had to be given to the author's allegations, to the extent that they were sufficiently substantiated'. This remark indicates a relationship between lack of co-operation. including respect for provisional measures, and the standard and burden of proof required for the final determination of the case. The HRC also referred to the impossibility to have access to Mr. Tshishimbi or to 'obtain reliable information about his whereabouts and state of health'. This explained why non-exhaustion of local remedies did not preclude it from examining the communication. In other words, the State's unresponsiveness to the request for information on his whereabouts and state of health was an additional factor establishing a lack of effective local remedies.[176]

In *Guerra and Wallen* v. *Trinidad and Tobago* (1995) the HRC deeply regretted that the State was 'not prepared to give the undertaking requested by the Committee' in its provisional measure, 'apparently because it considers itself bound by the conservatory order issued by the Court of Appeal on 29 April 1994'.[177] The HRC considered that, in fact, 'this situation should have made it easier for the State party to confirm that there would be no obstacles to acceding to the Committee's request; to do so would, in any event, have been compatible with the State party's international obligations'.[178] In view of the fact that the State was not prepared to respect the provisional measures taken pending the case, the HRC could also have decided to maintain these measures, as it did in several other cases it had declared inadmissible for non-exhaustion.[179] This case was decided after the public discussion condemning the execution of *Ashby* but before the decision on the merits in *Piandiong*.

2.3.3 Evidentiary requirements: deciding on the merits

The HRC and CAT have occasionally said something on the obligations of States on the merits in a case in which the State had ignored their provisional measures. In two cases involving Belarus the executions had already taken place when the HRC took provisional measures.[180] On the merits

---

[176] HRC *Tshishimbi* v. *Zaire,* 25 March 1996.
[177] HRC *Lincoln Guerra and Brian Wallen* v. *Trinidad and Tobago*, 4 April 1995, §2.3.
[178] Id., §6.5.
[179] See Chapter XIV (Jurisdiction and admissibility).
[180] HRC *Igor Lyashkovich and Mariya Staselovich* v. *Belarus*, 3 April 2003. In one of these cases the petitioner declared that death sentences are executed in secret in Belarus and neither the condemned prisoner nor his family are informed of the date of execution. In July 2002 the HRC addressed specific questions to the petitioner and the State party in this case to find out the exact execution date. It also requested the State to inform it 'at what time did the State party learn about the existence of the communication'. It asked the petitioner whether she had informed the State party of the submission of the case to the HRC before the registration of the case. The State party replied to the Committee's request in September 2002, but only to the question about the precise date of the execution and not about 'the exact moment from which the State party was aware of the existence of the communication'. HRC *Igor Lyashkovich and Mariya Staselovich* v. *Belarus*, 3 April 2003, §6.1; see also *Anton Bondarenko and Natalia Schedko (submitted by the latter on behalf of her deceased son and herself)* v. *Belarus*, 3 April 2003, §7.1. Counsel asserted, 'without

the HRC noted its earlier case law that a State party violated its obligations under the OP by executing a person who has submitted a communication to the HRC. This was so not only in cases where it had explicitly requested provisional measures of protection 'but also on the basis of the irreversible nature of capital punishment'.[181] Yet the relevant earlier case law, *Piandiong et al.* v. *the Philippines* (2000),[182] was decided and published *subsequent* to the execution of Lyashkevich and Bondarenko. For this reason the HRC decided it could not hold the State party responsible for a breach of the OP for the execution of the death sentence after the submission of the communication but prior to its registration. This means, however, that in new death penalty cases formal use of provisional measures by the HRC is not strictly necessary.

In *Weiss* v. *Austria* (2003) the State had extradited the petitioner to the US in contravention of the the HRC's provisional measures. Consequently, the State was 'under an obligation to make such representations to the United States' authorities as may be required to ensure that the author does not suffer any consequential breaches of his rights under the Covenant, which would flow from the State party's extradition of the author in violation of its obligations under the Covenant and the Optional Protocol'. It was also 'under an obligation to avoid similar violations in the future, including by taking appropriate steps to ensure that the Committee's request for interim measures of protection will be respected'.[183]

In *Dar* v. *Norway* (2007) the petitioner had been deported to Pakistan in spite of CAT's provisional measures. This was in violation of Article 22 ICAT, but this breach was remedied because Norway granted him a residence permit for three years upon return. CAT considered that the issue whether deportation constituted a violation of Article 3 has become moot because the petitioner had returned to Norway.[184]

After finding a violation of Articles 3 and 22 in *Brada* v. *France* (2005) CAT noted that it wished 'to be informed, within 90 days, of the steps the State party has taken in response to the views expressed above, including measures of compensation for the breach of article 3 of the Convention and determination, in consultation with the country (also a State party to the Convention) to which the complainant was returned, of his current whereabouts and state of well-being'.[185]

Part of following up non-compliance with provisional measures in non-refoulement cases should also be in the assessment on the merits whether the forced removal indeed constituted a violation of non-refoulement. The question then arises as well what should be the role of subse-

---

giving any further detail', that Mrs Staselovich 'had informed her son's lawyer, the Supreme Court and the prison authorities that she had submitted a communication to the Human Rights Committee before her son's actual execution'. HRC *Igor Lyashkovich and Mariya Staselovich* v. *Belarus*, 3 April 2003, §5.5; see also *Anton Bondarenko and Natalia Schedko* (*submitted by the latter on behalf of her deceased son and herself*) v. *Belarus*, 3 April 2003, §6.5. According to the petitioner the State had breached its obligations under the OP by ignoring the fact that she had sent a petition to the HRC and that she had informed her son's lawyer, the prison authorities and the Supreme Court about this. The State party did not specifically refute this claim. It only referred to the date it received the HRC's note verbale with the provisional measure, seven months after the execution.

[181] HRC *Igor Lyashkovich and Mariya Staselovich* v. *Belarus*, 3 April 2003, §5.5; see also *Anton Bondarenko and Natalia Schedko* (*submitted by the latter on behalf of her deceased son and herself*) v. *Belarus*, 3 April 2003, §6.5.

[182] HRC *Dante Piandiong, Jesus Morallos and Archie Bulan* (*deceased*) (*submitted by Alexander Padilla and Ricardo III Sunga*) v. *the Philippines*, 19 October 2000.

[183] See HRC *Weiss* v. *Austria*, 3 April 2003, §11.1.

[184] CAT *Nadeem Ahmad Dar* v. *Norway*, 11 May 2007, §16.5.

[185] CAT *Mafhoud Brada* v. *France*, 17 May 2005, §15.

quent information. It should be clear that when subsequent information provided by the State is taken into account, the information provided by the petitioner (if possible) or his counsel should be as well.

In *Elif Pelit* v. *Azerbaijan* (2007) CAT found a violation not just of Article 22 ICAT, but also of Article 3. It referred to the fact that Azerbaijan had ignored its provisional measures, together with the fact that the assurances provided by Turkey (the receiving State) were insufficient and the fact that Azerbaijan had not respected Conclusion No. 12 of the UNHCR Executive Committee to the effect that it should have recognized the determination of refugee status by Germany, another State party to the Refugee Convention.[186]

In *Cruz Varas* (1991) the European Court pointed out that the European Commission or its President only took provisional measures in exceptional circumstances.[187] In expulsion or extradition cases they serve the purpose of 'putting the Contracting States on notice that, in the Commission's view, irreversible harm may be done to the applicant if he is expelled and, further, that there is good reason to believe that his expulsion may give rise to a breach of Article 3 of the convention'.[188] Apparently the Court distinguished the irreparable harm which may be done to the petitioner from the breach of Article 3 of the Convention that this expulsion may give rise to. It then merely concluded that a State, when it decides not to comply with a provisional measure, knowingly assumes the risk of being found in breach of Article 3 following adjudication of the dispute. Any such finding would then have to be seen as aggravated by the failure to comply with the indication, since by way of this provisional measure the State had had its attention drawn to 'the dangers of prejudicing the outcome of the issue then pending before the Commission'.[189]

The Commission, however, had previously stated that Contracting Parties do not have a choice between either complying with their obligations, or instead trying to provide a remedy for the violation once it has been established.[190] It had referred to the text of Article 1 of the Convention, stipulating that the High Contracting Parties "shall secure" the rights and freedoms in the Convention, and to the Court's statements on the interpretation of the Convention's provisions so as to make its safeguards practical and effective. It had concluded that the primary obligation of the Contracting Parties must always be not to violate the Convention in the first place.

Yet there was something else at stake than the risk for States of being found in breach of an international rule. An interpretation of such human rights treaties necessarily must take as a point of reference the position of the (potential) victim. Sweden specifically based its refusal to take provisional measures on its view that these were not legally binding. The likelihood of being found in aggravated breach after completion of the dispute's adjudication may induce States to take provisional measures seriously, but apparently such inducements are not equal to a situation where provisional measures *are* legally binding.

The ECtHR (Grand Chamber) case *Mamatkulov* (2005) has particular relevance for the discussion of assessment of risk at the stage of provisional measures, because it illustrates the extent to which on the merits the ECtHR gave weight to its assessment of real risk at the stage of provi-

---

[186] CAT *Elif Pelit* v. *Azerbaijan*, 1 May 2007, §11. It also noted that '(b)y establishing Tunisia as the destination for the complainant, in spite of the latter's explicit request not to be returned to his country of origin, the State party failed to take account of the universally accepted practice in such cases, whereby an alternative solution is sought with the agreement of the individual concerned and the assistance of the Office of the United Nations High Commissioner for Refugees and a third country willing to receive the individual who fears for his safety', §8.5.

[187] ECtHR *Cruz Varas et al.* v. *Sweden*, Judgment of 20 March 1991, §103.

[188] Ibid.

[189] Ibid.

[190] ECtHR *Cruz Varas et al.* v. *Sweden*, Judgment of 20 March 1991, §126.

sional measures when the State subsequently ignored these.[191] In reference to this case, where the petitioners rather than the State bore the consequences, it is argued that that the minority opinion of Bratza, Bonello and Hedigan in fact took the better approach.[192]

Because the State had ignored the Court's provisional measures in *Mamatkulov* the Court had been prevented from effectively examining the complaint under Article 3 ECHR. Nevertheless, despite many indications of risk of a violation of Article 3, the Court rewarded the State for this behaviour by not finding a violation of this article.[193] Instead it only found a violation of Article 34 ECHR. In the circumstances of the case it found that the petitioners 'undeniably suffered non-pecuniary damage' that 'cannot be repaired solely by a finding that the respondent State has failed to comply with its obligations under Article 34'. In that light the Court awarded each applicant € 5,000 for non-pecuniary damage.[194]

It is doubtful, in my view, whether an award for non-pecuniary damage alone helps repair the harm done or prevent future violations. This situation is particularly grave given the serious indications of risk available at the time of extradition, indications that indeed triggered the use of provisional measures and that were borne out by subsequent facts.

At the merits stage the petitioners' counsel had pointed out the significant difference between the situation of the petitioners in Turkey, *before* extradition, when they had denied the charges against them, and their full admission of the same charges once in Uzbekistan. They referred to the lack of legal assistance and suggested they had been forced to 'confess' the crimes.[195]

According to Turkey Article 3 should only apply in extradition cases when it was *certain* that the requesting State would inflict the prohibited treatment. The petitioner should produce strong evidence that there were substantial grounds for believing he or she was facing torture or ill treatment. The State also argued that Article 3 should not be 'construed in a way that would engage the extraditing State's responsibility indefinitely'. Its responsibility 'should end once the extradited person had been found guilty and had started to serve his or her sentence'.

The Court acknowledged that the findings by international human rights organisations denouncing an administrative practice of torture and other forms of ill treatment of political dissidents described the general situation in Uzbekistan. These findings, however, did not support the *specific* allegations made by the petitioners in this particular case. Corroboration by other evidence was necessary.

The ECtHR assesses issues 'in light of all the material placed before it or, if necessary, material obtained *proprio motu*'.[196]

> "Since the nature of the Contracting States' responsibility under Article 3 in cases of this kind lies in the act of exposing an individual to the risk of ill-treatment, the existence of the risk must be assessed primarily with reference to those facts which were known or ought to have been known to the Contracting State at the time of the extradition; the Court is not precluded,

---

[191] See also Chapter XVII (Official State responses).

[192] See also Rieter (2007), p. 975.

[193] See Chapter XV on assessment of immediacy and risk.

[194] ECtHR Grand Chamber, *Mamatkulov and Askarov* v. *Turkey*, 15 December 2004, §134.

[195] During the extradition proceedings in Turkey the petitioners had denied the charges against them 'and adduced relevant evidence in their defence'. By contrast, counsel pointed out, the fact that the petitioners, once in Uzbekistan, and without legal assistance by a lawyer of their choosing, 'had fully admitted the same charges to the Uzbek authorities', 'showed that they had been forced through torture and ill-treatment to "confess" to crimes they had not committed'. ECtHR Grand Chamber *Mamatkulov and Askarov* v. *Turkey*, 4 February 2005, §60.

[196] ECtHR Grand Chamber *Mamatkulov and Askarov* v. *Turkey*, 4 February 2005, §69.

however, from having regard to information which comes to light subsequent to the extradition. This may be of value in confirming or refuting the appreciation that has been made by the Contracting Party of the well-foundedness or otherwise of an applicant's fears".[197]

When the petitioner has not been extradited or deported during the Court's examination of the case 'the relevant time will be that of the proceedings before the Court' (i.e. the relevant time for the assessment of the risk).[198] In other words, if the State had respected the provisional measures the Court would have determined whether there was a real risk on the basis of the situation at the time of its decision on the merits rather than at the time the expulsion or extradition was initially intended. The Court noted that this situation 'typically arises when deportation or extradition is delayed' as a result of a provisional measure by the Court. Such measure 'means more often than not that the Court does not yet have before it all the relevant evidence it requires to determine whether there is a real risk of treatment proscribed by Article 3 in the country of destination'.[199]

On the other hand, in this case the date that should be taken into consideration when assessing whether there was a real risk of a violation of Article 3 was 27 March 1999, when the petitioners were extradited despite the Court's provisional measure.

> "By applying Rule 39, the Court indicated that it was not able on the basis of the information then available to make a final decision on the existence of a real risk. Had Turkey complied (…) the relevant date would have been the date of the Court's consideration of the case in the light of the evidence that had been adduced".[200]

It then pointed out that 'Turkey's failure to comply with the indication given by the Court has prevented the Court from following its normal procedure. Nevertheless, the Court cannot speculate as to what the outcome of the case would have been had the extradition been deferred as it had requested. For this reason, it will have to assess Turkey's responsibility under Article 3 by reference to the situation that obtained on 27 March 1999'.[201]

When the Grand Chamber adopted its Judgment in *Mamatkulov*, on 15 December 2004, the representatives of the petitioners had still been unable to contact the petitioners.[202] The Court concluded as follows:

> "In the light of the materials before it, the Court is not able to conclude that substantial grounds existed at the aforementioned date for believing that the applicants faced a real risk of treatment proscribed by Article 3. Turkey's failure to comply with the indication given under Rule 39, which prevented the Court from assessing whether a real risk existed in the manner it considered appropriate in the circumstances of the case, must be examined below under Article 34".[203]

---

[197] Ibid., §69, referring to *Cruz Varas and others* v. *Sweden*, 20 March 1991, §§75-76 and *Vilvarajah and others* v. *the United Kingdom*, 30 October 1991, §107.

[198] See e.g. ECtHR *Chahal* v. *the United Kingdom*, Judgment of 15 November 1996, §§85-86 and ECtHR Grand Chamber, *Mamatkulov and Askarov* v. *Turkey*, 15 December 2004, §69.

[199] ECtHR Grand Chamber, *Mamatkulov and Askarov* v. *Turkey*, 15 December 2004, §69.

[200] Id., §75.

[201] Id., §75.

[202] Id., §36.

[203] Id., §77. The Court noted that Turkey had asserted that it extradited the petitioners after it had obtained an assurance from the Uzbek Government. In fact it was the Public Prosecutor of Uzbekistan who gave the assurance that the 'applicants' property will not be liable to general

With regard to Mamatkulov and Askarov the Court concluded that the facts clearly showed that their extradition prevented it 'from conducting a proper examination of their complaints in accordance with its settled practice in similar cases and ultimately from protecting them, if need be, against potential violations of the Convention as alleged'.[204] It found a violation of Article 34.[205]

In short, in *Mamatkulov and Askarov v. Turkey* the Grand Chamber confirmed (more or less) the earlier decision by the First Section[206] finding no violation of Art. 3 despite its recognition of the adverse situation with regard to respect for the prohibition of torture and cruel treatment in Uzbekistan, and notwithstanding the fact that Turkey had ignored the Court's provisional measures in violation of Article 34.

Different from the judgment of the First Section, in which there were no dissents, in the Grand Chamber three judges dissented on this issue. Judges Bratza, Bonello and Hedigan would indeed have found violations of Article 3.[207] They pointed out that the prohibition of ill-treatment 'is an absolute prohibition even in the case of expulsion and extradition and that the activities of the individual in question, however undesirable or dangerous and whether or not terrorist-related, cannot be a material consideration where a real risk of treatment contrary to Article 3 has been shown'.[208] They emphasised that when there is a real risk of a violation of Article 3 it is not allowed to extradite someone by arguing that 'a refusal to extradite would interfere with rights under international treaties or conflict with the norms of international judicial process or would inevitably involve an assessment of conditions in the requesting country which is not a Party to the Convention against the standards of Article 3 of the Convention'.[209]

---

confiscation, and the applicants will not be subjected to acts of torture or sentenced to capital punishment'. The prosecutor added that Uzbekistan 'is a party to the United Nations Convention against Torture and accepts and re-affirms its obligation to comply with the requirements of the provisions of that Convention as regards both Turkey and the international community as a whole'. ECtHR Grand Chamber *Mamatkulov and Askarov v. Turkey*, 15 December 2004, §76. Uzbekistan also produced medical reports from the doctors of the Uzbek prisons in which the applicants were subsequently held.

[204] ECtHR Grand Chamber, *Mamatkulov and Askarov v. Turkey*, 15 December 2004, §127.

[205] See Chapter XVI on legal status.

[206] ECtHR (First Section) *Mamatkulov and Abdurasulovic v. Turkey*, 6 February 2003. See also Rieter (2004).

[207] They would also have found a violation of Article 6 and Judge Rozakis (Greece) joined them in this.

[208] Joint partly Dissenting Opinion of Judges Bratza, Bonello and Hedigan, ECtHR Grand Chamber, *Mamatkulov and Askarov v. Turkey*, 15 December 2004, §2, referring to *Chahal v. UK*, 15 November 1996, §§79-80.

[209] Joint partly Dissenting Opinion of Judges Bratza, Bonello and Hedigan, ECtHR Grand Chamber, *Mamatkulov and Askarov v. Turkey*, 15 December 2004, §2, referring to *Soering v. UK*, 7 July 1989, §§83 and 88-91. The dissenters confirmed that the existence of a risk must be assessed 'primarily with reference to those facts which were known or ought to have been known to the Contracting State responsible for returning the person at the time of the extradition or expulsion at question'. "The Court is not precluded from having regard for information which comes to light subsequent to the return of the person, such information being of potential value in confirming or refuting the appreciation made by the Contracting State or the well-foundedness or otherwise of an applicant's fears". Joint partly Dissenting Opinion of Judges Bratza, Bonello and Hedigan, ECtHR Grand Chamber, *Mamatkulov and Askarov v. Turkey*, 15 December 2004, §3. At the same time they acknowledged, in reference to *Vilvarajah*, that 'evidence as to the actual treatment received by the applicant on his return to the receiving country is not conclusive, the essential question being whether it was foreseeable at the time of the expulsion that the person would be subjected to ill-treatment reaching the threshold of Article 3'. Joint partly Dissenting

They pointed out that the question to be determined was whether there were substantial grounds for believing that the applicants faced a real risk of ill-treatment on 27 March 1999, the date on which they were handed over to the Uzbek authorities.

> "By applying Rule 39 the Chamber of the Court was necessarily satisfied that there existed at least a prima facie case for the existence of such a risk. There appears to us to have been a strong basis for such a view".[210]

They added the following:

> "It is unclear to us what further corroborative evidence could reasonably be expected of the applicants, particularly in a case such as the present, where it was Turkey's failure to comply with the interim measures indicated by the Court which has prevented the Court from carrying out a full and effective examination of the application in accordance with its normal procedures. In such a situation, we consider that the Court should be slow to reject the complaint under Article 3 in the absence of compelling evidence to dispel the fears which formed the basis of the application of Rule 39".[211]

Judges Bratza, Bonello and Hedigan considered that substantial grounds had indeed been shown 'for believing that the applicants faced a real risk of ill-treatment and that, in returning the applicants despite this risk, Article 3 of the Convention has been violated'.[212]

---

[210] Opinion of Judges Bratza, Bonello and Hedigan, ECtHR Grand Chamber, *Mamatkulov and Askarov* v. *Turkey*, 15 December 2004, §3, referring to *Vilvarajah and others* v. *UK*, 30 October 1991, §112.

[211] They referred in particular to Amnesty International's briefing for CAT, made public in October 1999, noting a growing number of reports of ill-treatment and torture by law enforcement officials since 1997 of persons perceived to be members of Islamic congregations, especially suspected supporters of banned movements such as *Erk*. Moreover, the briefing noted the response in the wake of bomb explosions in the capital in February 1999 and statements of officials, including the President, that 'if not directly sanctioning the use of violence by State agents, could be perceived at the very least as condoning the use torture and ill-treatment'. The dissenters considered that the 'undisputed findings' about the general situation in Uzbekistan 'provide strong grounds for believing that the applicants were at particular risk'. "Not only were both applicants members of *Erk* but both were arrested in March 1999 (shortly after the reported terrorist bomb attacks in Tashkent) on suspicion of homicide, causing injuries by explosions and an attempted terrorist attack on the President of Uzbekistan himself". Joint partly Dissenting Opinion of Judges Bratza, Bonello and Hedigan. ECtHR Grand Chamber, *Mamatkulov and Askarov* v. *Turkey*, 15 December 2004, §7.

[211] Joint partly dissenting opinion of Judges Bratza, Bonello and Hedigan. ECtHR Grand Chamber, *Mamatkulov and Askarov* v. *Turkey*, 15 December 2004, §8.

[212] Joint partly dissenting opinion of Judges Bratza, Bonello and Hedigan. ECtHR Grand Chamber, *Mamatkulov and Askarov* v. *Turkey*, 15 December 2004, §13. They disputed the reliance by the Court on the assurances given by the Uzbek Government, the statement by the Public Prosecutor that Uzbekistan was party to the Convention against Torture and the medical reports from the doctors of the Uzbek prison in which the petitioners were being held upon extradition. They found it 'striking that the only assurance which was received prior to the applicants' surrender (namely, that of 9 March 1999) was not even communicated to the Court until 19 April 1999, well after the application of Rule 39 and after the extradition had been effected in disregard of the Court's interim measures'. See also Chapter XVII (Official State responses). "Moreover, an assurance, even one given in good faith, that an individual will not be subjected to ill-treatment is

With regard to the assurances in *Mamatkulov* the Court did not address the fact that Turkey used the Uzbek assurances as an excuse for having ignored the Court's provisional measures.[213] Moreover, it entered new information by forwarding reports by medical doctors made subsequent to the extradition. In this context the Court could have taken the opportunity to examine the value of such assurances on the basis of generally available information without adhering to its approach of taking into account only the information available at the time of extradition. After all the State did not invoke the assurances to convince the Court to withdraw its provisional measures, but instead invoked them *after* having ignored these measures. The fact that the State deprived the Court of the opportunity to assess these assurances in advance of the extradition should not provide the State the additional advantage that critical reports published subsequently could not be taken into account, if these discredit the value of such assurances, especially not when the reports by medical staff provided subsequently by the State were indeed taken into account.

Other information that became available subsequently equally confirms the European Court's assessment of real risk at the provisional measures stage. In April 2001 the HRC expressed grave concern about 'consistent allegations of widespread torture, inhuman treatment and abuse of power by law enforcement officials'.[214] In June 2002 CAT equally was concerned about the 'particularly numerous, ongoing and consistent allegations of particularly brutal acts of torture and other cruel, inhuman or degrading treatment or punishment committed by law enforcement personnel'.[215] It was also concerned about the 'lack of access for persons deprived of liberty, immediately after they are apprehended, to independent counsel, a doctor or medical examiner and family members, an important safeguard against torture'.[216] Moreover, it noted 'a lack of practical training for doctors in the detection of signs of torture or ill-treatment of persons who have been or are in custody'.[217] The Committee further expressed alarm over the 'de facto refusal of judges to take account of evidence of torture and ill-treatment provided by the accused, so that there are neither investigations nor prosecutions' and concerning 'the numerous cases of convictions based on confessions, and the continued use of the criterion of "solved crimes" as the basis

---

not of itself a sufficient safeguard where doubts exist as to its effective implementation". Joint partly dissenting opinion of Judges Bratza, Bonello and Hedigan. ECtHR Grand Chamber, *Mamatkulov and Askarov* v. *Turkey*, 15 December 2004, §§9 and 10, referring to *Chahal* v. *UK*, judgment of 15 November 1996, §105. They considered that the situation for political dissidents in Uzbekistan at the time of their surrender was such as to 'give rise to serious doubts' about the effectiveness of the assurances. The same applied to the reliance on the fact that Uzbekistan was party to the Convention against Torture. In this respect they referred in particular to the findings of Amnesty International. Joint partly dissenting opinion of Judges Bratza, Bonello and Hedigan. ECtHR Grand Chamber, *Mamatkulov and Askarov* v. *Turkey*, 15 December 2004, §§10 and 11. Finally, they noted that the medical reports were 'very brief and unspecific', following medical examinations apparently carried out 'at least 21 months after the extradition of the applicants and some 18 months after their trial and conviction'. "Insofar as any regard may be had to events occurring after the extradition had taken place we can attach very little weight to these reports which cast no light on the treatment received by the applicants in the intervening period and, more particularly, in the period leading up to their trial".

213 Generally on the controversial issue of assurances, see e.g. Chapter XV (Immediacy and risk), section 3.2.4 on non-refoulement cases.

214 HRC Concluding Observations, 4 April 2001, CCPR/CO/71/UZB, 26 April 2001, §7.

215 CAT Concluding Observations CAT/C/CR/28/7, 6 June 2002, §5a.

216 Id., §5b.

217 Id., §5d.

for promotion of law enforcement personnel, which, taken together, create conditions that promote the use of torture and ill-treatment to force detainees to "confess".[218]

A few days before publication of the judgment by the First Section the UN Special Rapporteur on the question of torture, Theo van Boven, concluded that systemic torture takes place in Uzbekistan.[219] The Concluding Observations by CAT and the HRC and the report by the Special Rapporteur all seem to indicate that the assurances such as those provided to Turkey by Uzbekistan are of little value.[220]

The rationale for taking into account only the information available at the time of the extradition relates to the fact that the human rights situation may significantly change between that time and the decision on the merits.

Indeed, if the situation is improved and the petitioners have not yet been extradited the Court may find that the extradition would now be allowed under the Convention despite the fact that it considered there was a real risk a few years previously at the provisional measures stage. If the situation has deteriorated this will also be taken into account, except when the petitioner has already been extradited, even if the petitioner was indeed subjected to ill-treatment.

Yet when the State extradited petitioners despite provisional measures, this approach gives an unfair advantage to the State. This is exacerbated in a situation such as this where the State invokes assurances to justify ignoring the Court's provisional measures.[221] In fact the State received one of the letters by Uzbekistan on 9 March, nine days before the Court used provisional measures. It could have informed the Court of these assurances and requested the Court not to maintain its provisional measures. The Court would then have been able to examine the contents of the assurances.[222] It would have noted, for instance, that Uzbekistan did not reaffirm its obligations under the ICCPR and the OP, but only referred to its obligations under the Convention against Torture. In this respect it is significant that Uzbekistan executed several petitioners to the OP in blatant disregard of the HRC's provisional measures.[223] These cases concerned complaints about confessions extracted under torture. In the context of anti-terrorism measures it is also

---

[218]   Id., §5h. In May 2002 the delegation of Uzbekistan before CAT indicated that the authorities were considering to train medical personnel in recognizing and preventing torture. It is unlikely that the physicians who provided the medical certificates on the health of the petitioners would have already received such training and would have been aware that the authorities should not pressure them. Press release, 'Committee Against Torture concludes consideration of report of Uzbekistan', CAT 28th session, 2 May 2002.

[219]   Special Rapporteur on the question of torture (Theo van Boven), E/CN.4/2003/68/Add.2, 3 February 2003.

[220]   See also Human Rights Watch (2004).

[221]   Tams (2003), p. 678 takes a different approach, considering that 'the Court sensibly opted for a relatively restrictive reading' of Article 3 and that it 'had good reason to rely on Uzbekistan's formal assurances to respect the international guarantees against torture and inhuman treatment'. Nevertheless, he finds it 'slightly surprising' that the Court 'seemed to downplay the relevance of independent assessments by bodies such as Amnesty International'. He noted that independent country reports 'seem a rather helpful (although not sufficient) source of information' to assess whether there is a real risk.

[222]   The other letter of assurances invoked by Uzbekistan was of 10 April 1999, after which the petitioners had been extradited. It was only on 19 April 1999 that Turkey informed the Court of these assurances.

[223]   Press release, 'Human Rights Committee deplores the execution of six individuals in Uzbekistan', 24 July 2003. See also Chapter III (Halting executions) and Chapter XVII (Official State responses).

noteworthy that Uzbekistan only refers to the prohibition of torture and not to that of cruel, inhuman or degrading treatment or punishment laid down in Article 7 ICCPR.

Obviously, while Uzbekistan refers to its obligations under the Convention against Torture alone, ignoring its obligations under the ICCPR that are similar to Article 3 ECHR, Turkey nevertheless has the obligation to secure the right not to be subjected to inhuman or degrading treatment or punishment in Article 3 ECHR for everyone under its jurisdiction.

Thus the ECtHR generally holds responsible the extraditing State for those violations that this State could have foreseen at the time of extradition, not taking into account subsequent events. Nevertheless, in circumstances such as these it would have been more in line with the aim of using provisional measures to protect against irreparable harm to persons if the Court would have found that the evidence available at the time of removal indeed indicated a real risk of access to counsel being blocked and of incommunicado detention and torture.

The fact that it has to assess Turkey's responsibility by reference to the situation on the day they were extradited does not mean that the Court should ignore the fact that at the time it used provisional measures it considered there was a real risk of a violation of Article 3 in the requesting State, a risk that Turkey, through its extradition in defiance of the Court's provisional measures, made impossible to assess properly. In this respect the fact that the petitioners' counsel were unable to contact them in Uzbekistan is indeed significant for the assessment whether Turkey violated Article 3 when it extradited the petitioners. The Court itself concluded that in this case the extradition 'irreversibly reduced' the level of protection it could offer to the rights asserted under Articles 2 and 3.[224]

Much weight is to be given to the initial finding of prima facie risk at the stage of provisional measures, because by ignoring these measures the State has made it impossible for the Court to examine all the evidence it needs. As to subsequent information, the Court should not pay heed just to what the State is saying, but also to publicly available information.

If, upon renewed assessment of the information available at the time of the extradition, there is credible evidence of systematic torture and ill-treatment, combined with the *individual* factors that extradition was requested specifically for these petitioners, on charge of terrorism, the balance should generally tilt in favour of the person at risk. After all, the Court used provisional measures so as to be able to examine the case properly and it was the extraditing State that ignored them. In such cases the burden should shift to the State to show that these rights have not been violated.

In a slightly different context the Court has considered that a failure to investigate allegations of ill-treatment in itself constituted a violation of Article 3.[225] Similarly, in my view a failure to fully cooperate with the ECtHR and adequately consider whether there is a real risk of a violation of Article 3, together with a failure to respect the right of individual petition by ignoring the Court's provisional measures in the context of Article 3, may in itself constitute a violation of that article.

Given the serious nature of the harm risked and the vulnerability of one party (the petitioner) vis-à-vis the other (the State), it should be the State that should bear the consequences of its non-compliance with the adjudicator's provisional measures.[226]

---

[224] ECtHR (Grand Chamber), *Mamatkulov and Askarov* v. *Turkey*, 4 February 2005, §108.
[225] ECtHR *Assenov et al.* v. *Bulgaria*, 28 October 1998.
[226] See also Rieter (2005b) and Vermeulen/De Vries (2005), §5.

3 FOLLOW-UP BY OTHER AUTHORITIES IN VARIOUS INTER-STATE SYSTEMS OF COOPERATION

As noted when discussing the legal status of provisional measures, authorities other than the HRC have also stressed that States should comply with the Committee's provisional measures.[227] The UN Rapporteur against Torture, for instance, did so in 2003 and 2004[228] and the Deputy UN High Commissioner for Human Rights equally urged respect for the Committee's provisional measures (2003). He emphasised the importance of respecting 'interim measures of protection ordered by Human Rights Treaty Bodies'.[229] With regard to executions of death sentences in violation of the provisional measures by the HRC he spoke of a 'grave breach' of the obligations under both the ICCPR and the OP.[230]

During his visit of March 2003 the Deputy High Commissioner for Human Rights, Bertrand Ramcharan, discussed with senior officials, the compliance with provisional measures 'ordered by' the HRC. He was visiting countries in Central Asia to enhance dialogue and technical cooperation.[231]

---

[227] Indeed 'there may be good reasons to utilize both avenues [urgent action under both treaty and non treaty protection system] concurrently so as to enhance the chances of relief', Van Boven (2005), p. 106.

[228] See e.g. Special Rapporteur on Torture, mission to Uzbekistan of November-December 2002, E/CN.4/2003/68/Add.2. See also official statement by the Special Rapporteur on Torture, 13 September 2004, referring to the 'interim measures ordered by the Committee and urgent appeals dispatched by United Nations monitoring mechanisms regarding persons whose life and physical integrity may be at risk of imminent and irreparable harm'.

[229] Press release Deputy United Nations High Commissioner for Human Rights Bertrand Ramcharan, 'Deputy Human Rights Chief ends visit to Uzbekistan with call for implementation of official commitments', 14 March 2003.

[230] See e.g. press release Acting High Commissioner for Human Rights Bertrand Ramcharan, 'Acting High Commissioner for Human Rights asks Uzbek government not to carry out death sentences in cases under international appeal', 4 July 2003 and 'Acting High Commissioner for Human Rights deeply concerned at executions in Uzbekistan', 25 July 2003.

[231] 'Official visit of the Deputy High Commissioner in Tajikistan', <www.unhchr.ch/news/tajikistan.htm> (consulted 6 March 2003). In April 2001 Tajikistan executed Mr. Gaibullodzhon Ilyasovich Saidov. In January of that year the Committee had used provisional measures on his behalf. The State party had not responded. While the HRC devoted a separate section of its decision on the merits to the State's failure to respect its provisional measures, reiterating the remarks made in earlier decisions, it did not issue a press release.The initial provisional measures were addressed to the State on 12 January 2001. The execution took place on 4 April 2001. The Committee was informed of this on 10 May 2001. With this knowledge, a Note Verbale was sent to the State on 18 May 2001 requesting information on the situation of Mr. Saidov and reiterating the provisional measures. On 19 June 2001 the Chairperson of the Committee addressed the State with a request for clarification on the non-compliance with the provisional measures. Finally, on 3 August 2001, a Note Verbale was addressed to the State requesting it to provide information on 'what steps were taken by the State to comply with the Committee's rule 86 request, on what grounds Mr. Saidov was executed, and what measures are being taken by the state to guarantee compliance with such requests in future'. On 5 December 2002 the State was invited, once more, to provide this information. *Barno Saidova* v. *Tajikistan*, 8 July 2004.

In July 2003 the HRC issued a press release deploring the execution of six beneficiaries of its provisional measures in Uzbekistan.[232] The UN Special Rapporteur on the question of torture had already addressed the issue of compliance with the provisional measures of the HRC during his mission to Uzbekistan (November-December 2003). In his report he noted with concern that it became clear from his discussion with the Acting Chairperson of the Supreme Court that this Court, which reviews all death penalty cases, was not aware of the Committee's provisional measures. He pointed out that a large number of the provisional measures related to death sentences based on confessions allegedly extracted under torture.[233] He recommended:

> "All competent government authorities should give immediate attention and respond to interim measures ordered by the Human Rights Committee and urgent appeals dispatched by United Nations monitoring mechanisms regarding persons whose life and physical integrity may be at risk of imminent and irreparable harm".[234]

From the press release of the HRC deploring the executions of six individuals it appears that at least one of the individual cases addressed by the UN Rapporteur was also pending before the HRC. This was the case of Ulugbek Eshov. The Rapporteur noted, among others, that it was reported that Eshov was forced to sign a confession and that he could not stand or walk during the trial. His mother saw him last in August 2001. The Rapporteur pointed out that fears had been expressed that he 'may have been' executed.[235] Subsequent to his visit the Rapporteur addressed the Chairperson of the HRC and expressed an interest in coordinating his activities with those of the HRC and exchange information on urgent cases including those in which the Committee had used provisional measures.[236]

As noted, in March 2003 the Deputy United Nations High Commissioner for Human Rights visited Uzbekistan as part of an official trip to countries of Central Asia to enhance dialogue and technical cooperation. During his visit he noted that 'in several instances, interim measures of protection ordered by Human Rights Treaty Bodies had not been respected and that persons had even been executed notwithstanding such orders'. He urged respect for such provisional meas-

---

[232]   It pointed out that their cases were pending before it. Moreover, it had issued provisional measures on their behalf. The petitioners had alleged that their death sentences were preceded by an unfair trial. The HRC noted that it had discussed the information of their execution during its plenary session. It reminded the State party of 'its position that it amounts to a grave breach of the Optional Protocol to execute an individual whose case is pending before the Committee, in particular where a request for interim protection under rule 86 of the Committee's Rules of Procedure has been issued'. It reiterated the provisional measures 'in all other cases currently pending under the Optional Protocol in respect of Uzbekistan'. The State was not to execute the persons involved before the HRC had concluded its consideration of those cases. More generally, it requested the State party's full cooperation with all cases currently pending before it. Finally, it took the opportunity to request the State to submit its second periodic report by April 2004, as requested in its Concluding Observations three years previously. Press release, 'Human Rights Committee deplores the execution of six individuals in Uzbekistan', 24 July 2003. The petitioners who were executed were Muzaffar Mirzaev (case 1170/2003), Shukrat Andasbaev (case 1166/2003), Ulugbek Ashov (case 1165/2003), Ilkhon Babadzhanov and Maksud Ismailov (case 1162/2003), and Azamat Uteev (case 1150/2003).

[233]   Special Rapporteur against Torture (Theo van Boven), Report of mission to Uzbekistan, E/CN.4/2003/68/Add.2, 3 February 2003, §§36 and 64.

[234]   Id., §70 (u).

[235]   Id., §40.

[236]   Information on file with the author.

ures.[237] In July 2003 he asked the government of Uzbekistan once more not to carry out the execution of detainees whose cases were pending before the HRC. He re-iterated the importance of respecting interim measures of protection issued by human rights treaty bodies. Indicating that Special Procedures of the Commission on Human Rights had also brought some of these cases to the attention of the government, he urged the State 'to make all necessary efforts in order to ensure strict observance of its international human rights obligations' under the ICCPR and its OP 'and to cooperate fully with the Special Procedures.[238]

Following the press release by the HRC deploring the execution of six petitioners in contravention of its provisional measures, the Acting High Commissioner equally expressed his concern and deep regret about these executions. He stressed that they 'render futile review by the Human Rights Committee of these cases, which amounts to a grave breach of Uzbekistan's obligations' under the ICCPR and the OP.[239] During its summer session (14 July-8 August 2003) the HRC discussed the situation once more, deplored the executions and 'reminded the State party of its position that it amounts to a grave breach of the Optional Protocol to execute an individual whose case is pending before the Committee, in particular where a request for interim protection under rule 86 of the Committee's Rules of Procedure has been issued'.[240]

Since the execution of these six persons, Uzbekistan has executed at least three other petitioners as well. Apparently the HRC sent several letters for clarification, but it did not issue a press release. The Special Rapporteur on Torture did. He referred to his mission to Uzbekistan at the end of 2002. He deeply regretted that he continued 'to receive information on the execution of persons whose death sentences were allegedly based on confessions extracted under torture in Uzbekistan'. He strongly deplored that 'in a number of cases the Government disregarded requests of the United Nations Human Rights Committee to stay executions pending its considerations of the cases'. He pointed out that since the publication of the report of his visit at least nine persons had been executed despite the Committee's provisional measures. On the first six executions he had already commented previously. In this press statement he referred to the last two executions, of Azizbek Karimov and Yusuf Zhumayev, on 10 August 2004. He appealed to the government to 'ensure strict observance' of its obligations under the ICCPR, the OP and the Convention against Torture as well as to co-operate fully with the Special Procedures of the Commission on Human Rights. Once more he drew attention to the recommendations on the report of his visits.

"In particular, that all competent Government authorities give immediate attention and respond to interim measures ordered by the Committee and urgent appeals dispatched by United Nations monitoring mechanisms regarding persons whose life and physical integrity may be at risk of imminent and irreparable harm".[241]

---

237 Press release Deputy United Nations High Commissioner for Human Rights Bertrand Ramcharan, 'Deputy Human Rights Chief ends visit to Uzbekistan with call for implementation of official commitments', 14 March 2003.

238 Press release Acting High Commissioner for Human Rights Bertrand Ramcharan, 'Acting High Commissioner for Human Rights asks Uzbek government not to carry out death sentences in cases under international appeal', 4 July 2003.

239 Press release Acting High Commissioner for Human Rights Bertrand Ramcharan, 'Acting High Commissioner for Human Rights deeply concerned at executions in Uzbekistan', 25 July 2003.

240 Press release 'Human Rights Committee rules on complaints of violations from individuals', 4 September 2003.

241 Press Release Special Rapporteur on Torture 'UN expert deplores Uzbekistan's lack of co-operation with UN human rights mechanisms', 13 September 2004. See also Radio Free

Reuters reports that his statements 'followed several similar critiques of the former Soviet Central Asian state's human rights record from U.N. bodies and independent international organisations'. It also notes that 'President Karimov rejects criticism of his harsh treatment of opponents and jailing of thousands of dissident Muslims'. "He says secular rule in the country is endangered by militants seeking to set up a hardline Islamic state".[242]

Tajikistan has a moratorium on the death penalty since March 2004. In 2005 the President of Uzbekistan decided to put executions on hold and the death penalty was officially abolished as of 1 January 2008.[243]

Moving to the Americas, in the case of juvenile offender Alexander Williams the Inter-American Commission had issued press releases about its precautionary measures. The EU had also sent an urgent humanitarian appeal, as had the Secretary General of the Council of Europe. The state of Georgia (US) later decided to commute Williams' death sentence, although this may have been predominantly for domestic reasons.[244]

At other times there appears to be concerted action by various international authorities that implicitly reinforces provisional measures used by human rights adjudicators. On 3 May 2002 the HRC used provisional measures requesting Australia to inform it of what measures it had taken to prevent any further acts of self-harm by at least two of the children of Mrs. Bakhtiyari detained in immigration detention.[245] In May/June 2002 the regional advisor to the UN High Commissioner

---

Europe/Radio Liberty, based on AP/Reuters, 'Uzbekistan accused of ignoring UN over death penalty', 13 September 2004, <www.rferl.org> (consulted on 14 September 2004); also referring to a statement of 13 September by the Independent Human Rights organisation of Uzbekistan that a man convicted of terrorism the previous week might have been tortured to death in prison. Authorities had said that he died of natural causes; Scoop media, 'UN human rights official deplores executions in Uzbekistan', 14 September 2004, <www.scoop.co.nz> (consulted 14 September 2004).

[242] Reuters Foundation AlertNet, 'UN sleuth hits US ally Uzbekistan on executions', 13 September 2004, <www.alertnet.org> (consulted on 14 September 2004).

[243] Associated press 'EU welcomes Uzbekistans abolition of the death penalty', 4 January 2008. In some previous HRC cases Uzbekistan had respected the provisional measures. In *Arutyunyan* v. *Uzbekistan* (2004), the HRC used provisional measures in March 2000 and in May of that year the State party informed the Committee that his sentence had been commuted to twenty years imprisonment at the end of March 2000: *Arsen Arutyunyan (submitted by his sister Karina)* v. *Uzbekistan*, 29 March 2004. In the case of Ikram Mukhtarov the State also respected the Committee's provisional measures. This was around the same time as it ignored them in two other cases. The petitioner had been sentenced to death in May 2004. 'The court reportedly ignored the claim that his "confession" to the murders was extracted in the torture'. The HRC used provisional measures on his behalf in July 2004. In August 2004 the judicial board of the Supreme Court of Uzbekistan overturned his death sentence and referred his case for further investigation. The Uzbek NGO Mothers Against the Death Penalty and Torture had been campaigning on his behalf. This Organisation believes that international pressure has 'played a crucial role in getting his case re-examined'. Amnesty International, further information on Urgent Action 234/04, 23 September 2004, AI Index: EUR 62/023/2004.

[244] See urgent humanitarian appeal of 21 August 2000, under the French Presidency and of 14 February 2002 by Spain as the current EU president, together with Denmark, the subsequent president and the European Commission to the Governor of Georgia and the Chairman of the Georgia Board of Pardons and Paroles. See also appeal of 15 February 2002 for clemency by Walter Schwimmer, Secretary General of the Council of Europe, press release 085a (2002) and press release of the Secretary General welcoming the commutation of the death sentence of Mr. Williams to a prison sentence, press release 107a (2002), 26 February 2002.

[245] HRC *Bakhtiari family* v. *Australia*, 29 October 2003. See also Chapter VII (Detention).

of Human Rights and the UN Working Group on Arbitrary Detention visited and criticized immigration detention centres and the immigration of children.[246] Some months later a Rapporteur of the UN Committee of the Rights of the Child, the UN High Commissioner for Refugees and the Executive Director of UNICEF Australia spoke out against the mandatory immigration detention of children as well.[247]

The case of minors detained in adult prisons in Honduras,[248] in which the CIDH had used precautionary measures, had also generated an international outcry. One Honduran newspaper even reported that the Italian authorities had warned the Honduran Government that the European Union would introduce, within 40 days, trade sanctions against Honduras for violation of international treaties on the rights of children.[249]

---

[246] See e.g. Cynthia Banham, 'UN deplores "tragedy" of asylum system', 1 August 2002, <www.smh.com.au> (consulted 9 April 2003), referring to regional advisor Justice Bhagwati's statement, after his visit of Woomera in May and June 2002: "These children were growing up in an environment which affected their physical and mental growth and many of them were traumatised and led to harm themselves in utter despair". He also said that the children were being 'deprived of adequate educational services appropriate to their age'. The Government responded by criticising him for including 'a number of emotive descriptions and assertions that have no foundation in the human rights instruments to which Australia is a party'; see also Grant Holloway 'UN links Australian camps to self-harm and suicide', 6 June 2002, <www.cnn.com> (consulted 9 April 2003). The Working Group expressed concern that the conditions in the detention camps could lead to a 'collective depression syndrome'. Some of the concerns already expressed by the Working Group on Arbitrary Detention in advance of the publication of its report related to the detention of vulnerable people 'especially children, pregnant women, the disabled and the elderly' and to the legality of using private security firms to run the detention camps. Chairman Joinet said that 'the use of private security reduced the care of the detained to a "bottom-line business" equation'. He also considered that the contractual relationship 'reinforced the disciplinary nature of detention'. See Michael Millett and Michael Bradley, 'criminals better off than asylum seekers', Sydney Morning Herald, 7 June 2002, <www.smh.com.au> (consulted 9 April 2003). The Immigration Minister, Philip Ruddock noted: "I would simply say that the issue of how the detention centres themselves are managed is not a matter (in which) treaties or any involvement of the UN is appropriate". He pointed out: "We make a decision in terms of certain standards that we expect will be applied. The operators have to meet those standards and we seem to get the best value for tax payers here in Australia and we do that through a competitive tendering system". Grant Holloway 'UN links Australian camps to self-harm and suicide', 6 June 2002, <www.cnn.com> (consulted 9 April 2003).

[247] See e.g. Judith Carp as quoted by Caroline Overington, 'Australia attacked for harming child asylum seekers', 2 May 2002, <www.theage.com.au> (consulted 9 April 2003); Tony Stevens, 'UN call for release of child detainees', the Age, 15 July 2002, <www.theage.com.au> (consulted on 9 April 2003) and the UN High Commissioner for Refugees pointed out, in September 2002, that 'Australia's policy of mandatory, indefinite detention of asylum seekers, particularly children, is an outrageous violation of international conventions and human rights'. See The World Today, 'Govt. grilled by UN over treatment of asylum seekers', Australian Broadcasting Cooperation 26 September 2002, <www.acc.net.au> (consulted on 9 April 2003).

[248] CIDH *Minors in detention* v. *Honduras*, 10 March 1999 (merits), §21.

[249] 'Honduras violates its Constitution by incarcerating minors with adult prisoners' in: *La Nación*, July 1995; In its footnote 57 the Commission also refers to several other articles: see 'Canada asks why children are being jailed in Honduras' in: *El Heraldo*, 2 June 1995; Letter from London's Central American Human Rights Committee to President Reina, 26 April 1996; 'They exploit international pressure exerted over the unlawful incarceration of juveniles' in: *El Heraldo*, 8 April 1995.

On the failure to comply with the Bosnia Chamber's Order for provisional measures not to hand over the petitioners to the US authorities the UN Office of the High Commissioner for Human Rights, which had been asked to submit an amicus curiae brief in this case, argued 'that the respondent Parties have no defence to their failure to comply with the Chamber's order for provisional measures. In accordance with Annex 6 to the General Framework Agreement, the Chamber's decisions are final and binding on all parties. The UN OHCHR notes that superseding the authority of the Chamber, an independent judicial body, with that of the Executive undermines the rule of law'.[250] Even more than in the context of international treaties, follow-up by various officials has occurred in the hybrid 'constitutional' system that existed under the Dayton Peace Agreement. For instance OSCE officers have played a role in monitoring compliance with Bosnia Chamber decisions, including Orders for provisional measures.[251] Both the Office of the High Representative[252] and the Organization for Security and Co-operation in Europe (OSCE) were involved in monitoring compliance with Judgments and decisions by the Bosnia Chamber.

In the context of follow-up by authorities from various inter-State systems of cooperation, general policy documents can be relevant as well. In 2001 the EU adopted *Guidelines to EU policy towards third countries on torture and other cruel, inhuman or degrading treatment or punishment.*[253] In its actions against torture the EU would 'urge third countries' to take measures, among others to "comply with the requests for interim measures of protection, rulings, decisions and recommendations of international human rights bodies" and 'ensure that no one is forcibly returned to a country where he or she risks being subjected to torture or ill-treatment' and "co-operate with the relevant Council of Europe mechanisms, in particular the decisions of the European Court of Human Rights and recommendations of the Committee for the Prevention of Torture". The EU noted it will 'support the relevant international and regional mechanisms (e.g. the Committee Against Torture, the European Committee for the Prevention of Torture, the relevant Special Rapporteurs) and stress the need for states to co-operate with the mechanisms'.[254] These Guidelines are interesting also because in order to convincingly invoke them vis-à-vis third countries, the EU members may be expected themselves to respect provisional measures.

4   FOLLOW-UP BY NGOS

The follow-up by the adjudicators can be reinforced not just by officials of international organisations, but also by NGOs.[255] Often these NGOs were actively supporting the petition in the first

---

[250] Bosnia Chamber *Boudellaa, Lakhdar, Nechle and Lahmar* v. *BiH and Fed. BiH*, 11 October 2002, §140.

[251] See e.g. Annual Reports 1999 and 2000 of the Bosnia Chamber, in its overview of cooperation with international institutions in BiH and Periodic Report of the Human Rights Field Operation in the former Yugoslavia of the Office of the High Commissioner for Human Rights, April 1998, §§27-29. See also Berg Handbook (1999), p. 10.

[252] The High Representative is at the same time the EU's Special Representative. See the website of the High Representative: <http://www.ohr.int/>.

[253] "The purpose of these guidelines is to provide the EU with an operational tool to be used in contacts with third countries at all levels as well as in multilateral human rights fora in order to support and strengthen on-going efforts to prevent and eradicate torture and ill-treatment in all parts of the world".

[254] Guidelines to EU policy towards third countries on torture and other cruel, inhuman or degrading treatment or punishment, adopted by General Affairs Council – Luxembourg, 09/04/01, <http://ec.europa.eu/external_relations/human_rights/torture/guideline_en.htm>.

[255] On the role of NGOs see e.g. Keck/Sikkink (1998).

place. In *Mamatkulov* (2003) the International Commission of Jurists had submitted an *amicus curiae* arguing for the binding nature of provisional measures.

Moreover, in the African and Inter-American systems, NGOs may themselves be the petitioners. Especially in the context of the Inter-American system NGOs (often themselves the petitioners, but not the beneficiaries of the provisional measures) regularly issue press releases condemning non-compliance with decisions by the Inter-American Commission and Court, including their precautionary and provisional measures. To give just one example, in a press release CEJIL and Amazon Watch expressed their concern regarding Ecuador's failure to comply with the Commission's precautionary measures, initially ordered in December 2005 and expanded in August 2006 in order to protect several legal counsel in domestic litigation against Chevron-Texaco who were being threatened by members of the military. As Ecuador had not done anything to protect them and the attacks were persisting the NGOs proposed the State to take the following specific measures: to install alarms and means to identify the origin of telephone calls, secure telephone lines and police surveillance. The government should study these proposals and meet with the beneficiaries that same week to discuss them.[256]

Obviously it is easier for the beneficiaries and NGOs to use provisional measures as a tool to approach governments and the media in order to prevent irreparable harm when these measures include argumentation and sufficient precision.[257]

A good illustration of the interplay between a human rights adjudicator, officials of inter-governmental organisations and NGOs as part of international rather than regional litigation is the case of Habré, the former dictator of Chad. In April 2001 CAT had decided on provisional measures to the effect that Senegal should not expel Habré and should take all necessary measures to prevent him from leaving the territory of Senegal in violation of the principle that a person suspected of torture should be either prosecuted or extradited. Subsequently President Wade of Senegal told journalists that he was still seeking Habré's departure. He claimed that the UN had not asked Senegal to hold Habré. In response Human Rights Watch (HRW) urged him to comply with the provisional measure and to hold Habré until he could be extradited to face torture charges.[258] In September 2001, following an appeal by UN Secretary-General Kofi Annan, President Wade stated that he had agreed to hold Habré in Senegal 'pending an extradition request from a country such as Belgium capable of organising a fair trial. He 'reaffirmed this pledge in a meeting with Human Rights Watch in May 2002'.[259]

This shows how different actors can reinforce each other's actions.[260] Kofi Annan had the backup of CAT determining individual complaints under the Convention against Torture with its provision on *aut dedere aut iudicare*. CAT had requested the State, as an urgent measure, to prevent Habré from leaving Senegal in any other way than through extradition. Its provisional measure, in turn, was strengthened by UN Secretary General Kofi Annan, using his authority and position. All of this was triggered by Chadian organisations, supported by international NGOs who made sure to report on these actions both domestically and internationally.

As noted, this is a case about which much information has been made available, especially by NGOs. This makes it possible to discuss what happened subsequently, between the date of the

---

[256] CEJIL, 'Ecuador no cumple con las medidas cautelares de la CIDH', press release of 6 March 2007.

[257] See also Chapter II (Systems), section 8.2.

[258] Human Rights Watch, Senegalese President urged to aid rights prosecution, 27 June 2001, <www.hrw.org> (consulted 10 April 2003).

[259] Human Rights Watch, The case against Hissène Habré, an 'African Pinochet', 2003/2006, <http://www.hrw.org/justice/habre/habre_0402.pdf> (consulted 14 June 2007).

[260] See also, more generally, Chapter XVII (Official responses).

Committee's provisional measures and of its decision on the merits. This information, as discussed below, illustrates how the provisional measures have helped prevent irreversible harm to the claim under the Convention against Torture.

In early 2002 the Belgian investigating judge and a police team visited Chad.

> "The visit was front-page news in Chad and transformed the abstract case against Habré in far-off courts into a concrete reality, touching off a minor revolution in a country where Habré's most brutal henchmen still occupy most of the key security posts".[261]

While President Déby had ousted Habré, many high ranking officials in the new government of Chad had been implicated in Habré's crimes. Thus, the new government had not sought his extradition from Senegal. Yet the fact itself that Habré was indicted in Senegal 'had an immediate impact back in Chad'. After his arrest in Senegal, President Déby of Chad met with representatives of the Chadian association of victims of political repression AVCRP and told them that 'the time for justice has come'.[262] In October 2000 seventeen victims had lodged criminal complaints in courts in Chad for torture, murder and disappearance against identified members of Habré's police. Human Rights Watch reports that 'in May 2001 a Chadian investigating judge began to hear witnesses, and in September 2002, he started calling in the defendants to testify'.[263] Public attention in Senegal to Chad's ex-dictator may also have played a role in the decision of the government of Chad to allow the victims and human rights NGOs access to the files of the Documentation and Security Directorate (DDS), Habré's political police. Subsequently, one of the aforementioned NGOs[264] examined these files and submitted them to the investigating judge in Belgium. Meanwhile, the American Association for the Advancement of Science, together with Human Rights Watch was making a statistical analysis of the document.[265]

All of this indicates that the authorities in Chad had allowed victims and organisations some measure of access to files both in order to find the truth and in order to facilitate prosecution, albeit not in Chad itself. A similar approach is evident from Chad's decision to inform the Belgian judge of its withdrawal of Habré's immunity. In a letter to the judge investigating the charges against Habré in Belgium, in October 2002, the Minister of Justice of Chad wrote that 'Habré can not claim to enjoy any form of immunity from the Chadian authorities'.[266]

At the same time, the actions before courts in Chad, Senegal and Belgium apparently have not been without risks for the victims and their representatives. HRW refers to 'security forces

---

[261] Human Rights Watch, The case against Hissène Habré, an 'African Pinochet', 2003/2006, <http://www.hrw.org/justice/habre/habre_0402.pdf> (consulted 14 June 2007).

[262] Id.

[263] Id.

[264] The association of victims of political repression (AVCRP).

[265] Human Rights Watch, The case against Hissène Habré, an 'African Pinochet', 2003/2006, <http://www.hrw.org/justice/habre/habre_0402.pdf> (consulted 14 June 2007).

[266] On 5 December 2002 HRW and FIDH received a copy of this letter and made it public. Letter of Minister of Justice, Djimain Koudj-Gaou, to the 'Juge d'Instruction' of Brussels, Tribunal First Instance, 7 October 2002: "*La Conference Nationale Souveraine tenue à N'Djaména du 15 Janvier au 7 Avril 1993 avait officiellement levé toute immunité de juridiction à Monsieur HISSEIN HABRE. Cette position a été confortée par la Loi No 010/PR/95 du 9 Juin 1995 accordant l'amnistie aux détenus et exiles politiques et aux personnes en opposition armée, à l'exclusion de 'l'ex Président de la République, HISSEIN HABRE, ses co-auteurs et/ou complices'. Dés lors, il est clair que Monsieur HISSEIN HABRE ne peut prétendre à une quelconque immunité de la part des autorités Tchadiennes et ce depuis la fin de la Conférence Nationale Souveraine*". See <www.hrw.org> (consulted on 18 April 2003).

commanded by one of the ex-DDS defendants' that threw a grenade at counsel for the International Committee for the Trial of Habré, Jacqueline Moudeina. She was severely injured and her office was later ransacked.[267] Amnesty International notes that members of the security forces reportedly enquired who was Ms. Moudeina and then threw a teargas grenade in her direction. Following this, a senior member of the security forces who had been searching for her was said to have visited twice the medical centre to which she had been brought.[268] The Vice-President of one of the NGOs, Mr. Souleymane Guengueng,[269] apparently had been tailed by uniformed men and was suspended from his civil service job just after the visit of the Belgian judge.[270] As noted, Mr. Guengueng was one of the victims on whose behalf HRW had submitted the case before CAT and requested provisional measures to prevent impunity for Habré.[271]

In September 2005 an international arrest warrant was issued and Belgium asked for Habré's extradition from Senegal. The Chairperson of the Commission of the African Union supported the request, as did the UN Special Rapporteur on Torture and the UN Secretary-General. Almost two months later he was arrested and taken into custody in Senegal. Its Court of Appeal, however, ruled that it had no jurisdiction to decide on an extradition request involving a former head of state. It was subsequently decided that he could remain in Senegal, which would request the January 2006 summit of the African Union to 'indicate the competent jurisdiction' for his trial. The African Union set up a Committee of Eminent African Jurists to consider this question. This Committee should take into account, among others, 'adherence to the principles of total rejection of impunity', to fair trial standards, efficiency, accessibility to the trial by alleged victims and by witnesses as well as priority for an African mechanism.[272] Following this Commit-

---

[267] Human Rights Watch, The case against Hissène Habré, an 'African Pinochet', 2003/2006, http://www.hrw.org/justice/habre/habre_0402.pdf (consulted 14 June 2007).

[268] Amnesty International Annual Report 2002, AI index POL 10/001/2002.

[269] Vice-President of the AVCRP.

[270] Human Rights Watch, The case against Hissène Habré, an 'African Pinochet', 2003/2006, <http://www.hrw.org/justice/habre/habre_0402.pdf> (consulted 14 June 2007).

[271] In February 2003 Human Rights Watch stated it was confident that President Wade would keep his promise to extradite Habré if a third State would guarantee him a fair trial. The President had made a commitment to the UN and Kofi Annan to keep Habré in Senegal until he could be brought to justice elsewhere. Reed Brody de Human Rights Watch sur l'affaire Habré: 'nous faisons confiance au Président Wade', Le Soleil (Senegal), 25 February 2003. In February 2003, when he was in Paris, President Wade formally excluded any possibility for trial of Habré in Senegal. A trial where the civil parties and the defence would produce two to three thousand witnesses would 'ridicule the Senegalese justice system'. He pointed out that any State that so wished could bring an extradition request before the Senegalese judiciary that, if it were up to him, would receive a favourable response. He noted, however, that, as of yet, no country had requested such extradition. Hissène Habré ne sera pas jugé au Sénégal, selon Wade, Le Soleil, 24 February 2003.

[272] Human Rights Watch, The case against Hissène Habré, an 'African Pinochet', 2003/2006, <http://www.hrw.org/justice/habre/habre_0402.pdf> (consulted 14 June 2007). See also the African Union resolution itself: Assembly/AU/Dec.103 (VI). Meanwhile Amnesty International requested the Chairperson of African Commission on Human and Peoples' Rights 'to establish contacts with the Senegalese authorities and to request information on the steps taken by Senegal to comply with its obligations under international law and to report back to the Commission at its next session'. Amnesty International, 'African Commission on Human and Peoples' Rights: Oral statement on options for trial of Hissene Habre', AI Index: AFR 01/004/2006 (Public), News Service No: 115, 11 May 2006.

tee's advice,[273] the AU mandated 'Senegal to prosecute and ensure that Hissène Habré is tried, on behalf of Africa, by a competent Senegalese court with guarantees for fair trial'.[274]

Concerted action by various international and domestic actors, intergovernmental and non governmental, is particularly warranted in situations involving death threats. As discussed in chapter IX, thus far, there is only one case in which information is available on the use of provisional measures by the HRC to protect against death threats. The Special Rapporteur of the HRC had used them in January 2004 and had requested the State to inform the Committee on the measures it had taken in compliance within thirty days.[275] On 2 February 2004 the non-governmental organisation Asian Human Rights Commission spread an urgent appeal relating to an attempt on

---

[273] Report of the Committee of Eminent African Jurists on the case of Hissene Habré, May 2006 "27. The Committee recommends that an African option should be adopted. 28. Habré should be tried by an African member State – Senegal or Chad in the first instance, or by any other African country. 29. Senegal is the country best suited to try Habré as it is bound by International law to perform its obligations. 30. Chad has the primary responsibility to try and punish Hissène Habré. It should therefore cooperate with Senegal". See <http://www.hrw.org/justice/habre/> (consulted 16 May 2008).

[274] AU Decision On The Hissene Habré Case And The African Union Doc. Assembly/Au/3 (Vii), 2 July 2006. See <http://www.hrw.org/justice/habre/> (consulted 16 May 2008). On subsequent developments, see e.g. HRW press release 'Senegal: New Law Will Permit Habré's Trial', 2 February 2007; HRW press release 'Senegal Failing to Act on Trial of Hissène Habré; One Year After Dakar Agreed to Try Chad Ex-Dictator, Victims are Still Waiting; Chadians March for Justice', 30 June 2007; HRW press release 'EU to Aid Senegal in Preparing Hissène Habré's Trial', 19 January 2008 (in response to a request by the Senegalese President for international assistance) and Open letter to the international and African communities of the Steering Committee of the International Committee for the Fair Trial of Hissène Habré, 15 April 2008 See <http://www.hrw.org/justice/habre/> (consulted 16 May 2008). See also Thijs Bouwknecht of Radio Netherlands Worldwide, 'rights Council should press Senegal over Habré; 5 February 2008, quoting petitioner Guengueng; The Human Rights Council needs to tell Senegal to comply with the UN ruling and bring Habré to justice". The article notes that the European Commission, Chad itself, France, Switzerland, Belgium and the Netherlands 'have already agreed to help fund the trial, but are still waiting for Senegal to present a detailed budget'. The State has now amended its law, including its constitution, 'to allow its courts to prosecute genocide, crimes against humanity, torture and war crimes committed in the past'. "Meanwhile, however, it has appointed the former coordinator of Habré's legal defence team, Madické Niang, as minister of justice, responsible for the organisation of the trial'. <http://www.rnw.nl/internationaljustice/specials/Universal/090905-habre> (consulted 13 February 2009). In May 2009 Belgium submitted a case against Senegal before the ICJ, requesting provisional measures. The ICJ, by a majority, decided not to grant these, *Questions relating to the Obligation to Prosecute or Extradite* (*Belgium* v. *Senegal*), Order of 28 May 2009. While Belgium's action, inspired by NGOs, can as such be interpreted as a form of follow-up, neither Belgium's submission, nor the ICJ's Order referred to the previous provisional measure by CAT. The dissenting opinion by Judge Cançado Trindade, on the other hand, did, §84. See also his reference to discussion of the matter by the United Nations Human Rights Council, §45.

[275] This meant that the Committee expected a response no later than on 9 February 2004. HRC *Michael Anthony Fernando* v. *Sri Lanka*, 1189/2003, provisional measures of 9 January 2004 as reproduced by the Human Rights Correspondence School, a project of the Asian Human Rights Commission, lesson series 33, p. 3, 14 April 2004, <www.hrschool.org> (consulted on 5 August 2004).

the petitioner's life earlier that day.[276] It called for 'a thorough inquiry into the conduct of the Sri Lankan Government in terms of Rule 86'. It also called 'for the international community to cooperate in making the Sri Lankan government accountable under the international obligations of the ICCPR'. It also called upon the government itself 'to investigate this matter thoroughly and to arrest and prosecute the offenders, provide due medical care and compensation for Mr. Fernando and to provide the utmost protection to Mr. Fernando and his family'.[277] The next day it issued an official statement. It pointed out that, while chloroform was sprayed on his face, a van pulled nearby, presumably to take him away. "This violent incident raises very serious issues as to whose responsibility it is to ensure that the Sri Lankan government implements the UNHRC's interim measures that were issued to it". It noted that the representative of Sri Lanka in Geneva would have been informed of the provisional measures on the day they were decided. It was his duty to transmit this information to the Minister of Foreign Affairs as soon as possible. The minister would then be duty-bound to 'inform the government of such an important decision by the UNHRC'.

> "Given the importance of the decision, it would have been the right of the president, the prime minister and the cabinet to know about the communication from the UNHRC. Once the government is informed about the UNHRC's decision, the relevant authorities would be informed to take immediate action on the basis of the communication. In this particular instance, the two most relevant authorities are the attorney general and the inspector general of police (IGP). If the attorney general and the IGP had been informed by the government of the interim measures, it can be presumed that under normal circumstances they would take immediate action to see that they are implemented and would report back to the government of the actions that had been taken. The fact that no action has been taken suggests that either the attorney general and the IGP were not informed about the relevant interim measures or they neglected to attend to the matter after receiving this information. Whatever the case, Mr. Fernando did not receive any form of protection despite the interim measures; and as a result of this failure, he was subjected to a brutal attack which could have ended with even more drastic consequences than those that he is presently suffering".[278]

The Asian Human Rights Commission pointed out that the State's failure to adequately implement the provisional measures raises important questions that would likely feature in the public debate, 'both locally and internationally'.

> "At what point, for instance, did the government fail to ensure its compliance with these interim measures? At whose desk did the communication from the UNHRC stop? (...) (H)as Sri Lanka developed a procedure to deal with its treaty obligations, particularly in terms of treaties to which it has become a state party in relation to the United Nations? What stipulated procedure exists for dealing with communication from the relevant international authorities? Above all, in terms of the great importance of the UNHRC, is there any existing mechanism to implement and respond to their communication specifically?"[279]

---

[276] It reported that he went to see a friend 'when a bearded person appeared and held a handkerchief to his face'. He reportedly felt dizzy, but managed to escape to a tailor shop that he knew. He collapsed there and his father was informed and took him to the hospital.

[277] Asian Human Rights Commission, Urgent Appeal of 2 February 2004, <www.derechos.org> (consulted on 5 August 2004).

[278] A statement by the Asian Human Rights Commission, 'Attack on Tony Fernando, Sri Lanka seriously embarrassed internationally', <www.ahrchk.net> (consulted on 5 August 2004).

[279] Id.

First of all, the government should immediately comply with the provisional measures 'even at this late stage'. The petitioner was now in the hospital undergoing treatment. He 'should be given the protection available to him as a citizen of Sri Lanka and in response to Sri Lanka's international obligations'.

> "The duty to provide direct protection lies with the IGP. The duty to see to the overall implementation of the interim measures lies with the attorney general. It is up to them to act promptly and boldly now to demonstrate the government's willingness and capacity to protect its citizens".[280]

The NGO noted that the perpetrators were still at large and that the government has a duty to answer these questions and to bring the perpetrators to justice.[281]

Seven days after the attack the Asian Human Rights Commission received a letter by the petitioner explaining that he had been provided with security at the hospital on 2 February (noon) until his discharge on 7 February. Two armed police officers protected him under the instruction of the ministry of defence. Upon his discharge they brought him back home, but informed him 'that they had instruction to give protection only at the hospital' and until he was brought home. They said that there was nothing more they could do and if he needed further protection he should talk to 'higher ups'. He was now in hiding, moving from place to place. He also referred to the non-compliance with the Committee's provisional measures and noted that there had been three persons in the van that had been waiting to take him following the attack the previous week.[282]

It may be expected that the HRC sent a remainder if it did not receive a response to its provisional measures by 10 February 2004. However, the Committee probably merely would take specific action with regard to the attack of 2 February 2004 following specific submissions by the petitioner or the State with regard to the incidents. The Special Rapporteur on Torture, on the other hand, did intervene on his behalf.[283] Sri Lanka is one of the few States in the Asian region that accepted the right of individual complaint to the HRC.[284]

In 2002 the Inter-American Commission took precautionary measures on behalf of several forensic anthropologists and their families in Guatemala who were receiving threats to intimidate them into stopping the exhumations of victims of the armed conflict buried in clandestine cemeteries. Guatemala had informed the Commission that it had in fact offered police protection to those beneficiaries who had 'expressly accepted it'.[285] NGOs regularly take Urgent Action through their own networks. In September 2005 Amnesty International issued an Urgent Action on behalf of one of the persons mentioned in the Commission's precautionary measures (2002) and his family. It referred to these precautionary measures and noted that concerns remained that the level of protection they were receiving was inadequate. Following a death threat received by the anthropologist's sister and her husband two policemen were initially stationed outside their

---

[280] Id.

[281] Id.

[282] Letter of Tony Fernando, 9 February 2004, urgent appeal update of 10 February 2004, <www.ahrchk.net> (consulted on 5 August 2004).

[283] UN Special Rapporteur on Torture Urgent appeal of 16 February 2004, also referring to the Committee's provisional measures. The Special Rapporteur had previously contacted the State on Fernando's behalf on 25 September 2003. Moreover, the Special Rapporteur on the Freedom of Opinion and Expression had done on 23 December 2003 (on file with the author).

[284] For other Asian States that have recognised the right of individual complaint see the e.g. Philippines, South Korea, Uzbekistan and Tajikistan.

[285] CIDH Annual Report 2002, §56.

house and she received 24 hour police protection.[286] NGOs have equally used press releases to condemn non-compliance with provisional measures.[287]

5 CONCLUSION

The practice of the adjudicators as well as that of officials from intergovernmental organisations and that of NGOs shows that follow-up is considered to be essential. Without it provisional measures can be expected to decrease in effectiveness.

Follow-up can take place by the political bodies formally assigned that task within the relevant human rights system, but in practice this is insufficient or sometimes even non-existent. The Geneva bodies and the Inter-American Commission and Court have taken it upon themselves to monitor not just compliance with their decisions on the merits, but also with their provisional measures. Apart from repeated messages to the State concerned to the effect that the provisional measures remain in force, the adjudicators have also made use of press releases, Court hearings (Inter-American Court), country visits (Inter-American Commission), hearings in the context of State reports and referring to compliance with provisional measures in Concluding Observations on these reports (the Geneva bodies HRC, CAT and CEDAW).

In addition it is argued that ignoring provisional measures has consequences for how the complaint on the merits can be examined. Not only the right of individual petition is violated, but often the right to life and the prohibition of torture and cruel treatment is too. In fact the burden should shift to the State to show that these rights have not been violated.

Finally, apart from the adjudicators themselves, officials from intergovernmental organisations and NGOs have also 'followed up' on the provisional measures taken by the adjudicators. This may indeed help increase the pressure on the State to comply after all (if still possible) or otherwise at least to comply in future. Moreover it underscores the awareness of NGOs and officials appointed by intergovernmental organisations of the serious nature of the harm risked and appears to confirm their recognition of a general principle to prevent irreparable harm to persons.

---

[286] "However, from late December 2005 onwards, the police officers stationed outside the house failed to report on duty on some days. On 7 January, three days three days before the written death threat was received, they stopped coming altogether. Since these most recent threats, the homes of Gianni Peccerelli and Bianka Peccerelli Monterroso are being guarded by police. However, as they have been threatened directly, the FAFG [the Forensic Anthropology Foundation, ER] is calling for the authorities to provide them with personal protection 24 hours a day, and to guarantee that this level of protection will be maintained". Amnesty International, Urgent Action, 13 January 2006 (referring to previous Urgent Action of 14 September); this Action was circulated by the Guatemala Human Rights Commission (Washington, D.C.) as well.

[287] See e.g. Human Rights Watch, 'Italy: halt expulsion of Tunisian at risk of torture, Respect European Court of Human Rights Ruling', 3 June 2008 and Update of 5 June 2008, <http://hrw.org/English/docs/2008/06/03/italy19016_txt.htm> (consulted 23 September 2008).

CONCLUSION

This Part dealt with the official responses by States to provisional measures and with the follow up by the adjudicators (and others). As to the first, Chapter XVII noted that States generally respect provisional measures, sometimes explicitly confirming their compliance. It then focused on those situations in which States have failed to comply. It discussed official responses by States justifying why they failed to comply with a provisional measure in which the State protested against the (temporary) outcome of the normative process, on the one hand, and official responses protesting against the development of the process as such, on the other hand. Explanations for the first category of responses may be derived from the system of implementation in domestic law, specific politics, the role of media and other actors. Explanations of non-compliance based on the second type, disagreement with the decision-making process of the adjudicator, may relate to the procedures of the adjudicator in general or to specific issues arising in the case, e.g. relating to the principle of *audiatur et altera pars* or the lack of transparency in the decision-making process.

These official responses simply present legal arguments for a decision of non-compliance that in fact is likely to be based on domestic reasons of a political rather than legal nature. Moreover, the paucity of consistent information on State responses does not allow for a clear answer to the question whether States respond more favourably to provisional measures that aim to protect those rights that are commonly considered the most fundamental.

It may be expected that governments wishing to maintain an image of democracy would generally be more receptive to provisional measures indicated by human rights adjudicators than would more authoritarian and repressive governments. Yet there is an exception to this receptiveness in relation to the execution of death sentences and decisions to expel or extradite convicted criminals or suspected terrorists. If international adjudicators consider that these persons run a real risk of irreparable harm not only to their human rights claim, but to their survival or personal integrity, domestic authorities are often less open to this assessment exactly because of a segment of public opinion that revolves around fear.

In such circumstances even the fact that the provisional measures relate to life and personal integrity may not be decisive for compliance in and of itself. For instance the decision not to halt an execution despite a provisional measure ordered by an international adjudicator may be explained by a public opinion strongly in favour of the death penalty. In fact a provisional measure protecting against irreparable harm to the claim (not involving a core right) rather than to persons may then be less controversial.

The practice of the adjudicators as well as that of officials from intergovernmental organisations and that of NGOs shows that follow-up is considered to be essential (Chapter XVIII). The follow up by the political bodies formally assigned with that task within the human rights systems is often insufficient or sometimes even non-existent. The Geneva adjudicators and the Inter-American Commission and Court have taken it upon themselves to monitor non-compliance with their provisional measures. They repeatedly send messages to the State concerned to the effect that the provisional measures remain in force. Such follow up may often require increased specificity of these provisional measures as well.[1] In addition the Inter-American Court has held Court hearings discussing implementation of its provisional measures and has assigned the Commission

---

[1]   See also Chapter XIII (Protection).

an important monitoring role in this respect. The Inter-American Commission has paid attention to implementation of its own precautionary measures and those of the Court during country visits. The Geneva bodies have asked questions on the implementation of provisional measures during hearings in the context of State reports, etc.

Chapter XVIII argued that ignoring provisional measures has consequences for how the complaint on the merits can be examined. Not only the right of individual petition is violated, but often the right to life and the prohibition of torture and cruel treatment are too. In such cases of non-compliance the burden should shift to the State to show that these rights have not been violated.

UN independent experts as well as NGOs may also play an important role in the follow-up on provisional measures. Publicity in the context of other activities (for those adjudicators that have other (non-adjudicatory) tasks in the human rights system as well) could be a useful tool to counteract non-compliance, as long as each situation is assessed individually as to the anticipated impact of such publicity on the beneficiaries, especially if domestic (or local) public opinion strongly disfavours the protection of the beneficiaries of the provisional measures.[2]

In contrast to the partly negative domestic factor of public opinion in such cases, in the long run it may also be the strength of the external disapproval for non-compliance that will help determine compliance with future cases. This external disapproval, through the follow up by the adjudicators, as well as statements by international organisations, NGOs and other States, does seem to be determined, at least partially, by the irreparable nature of the harm the provisional measures aim to prevent, thereby reaffirming the common core of the concept as it currently stands.

---

[2]　The involvement of the media is very important in this respect. Yet the impact of the media may tip the balance both ways. Especially national media may make or break compliance. In addition, in the face of negative domestic media interest in provisional measures powerful States may be less inclined to comply with them than States in transition that are counting on joining international organizations or receiving financial support and therefore more interested in avoiding external disapproval.

GENERAL CONCLUSION

1   INTRODUCTION

This book examined the legal concept of provisional measures in human rights adjudication. The General Conclusion brings together aspects of the conclusions to the various chapters, with an emphasis on the conclusion to Part II on the purpose of provisional measures. That preliminary conclusion examined the extent of the convergence or divergences in the approaches of the adjudicators. A conceptual framework was presented discussing the core common to provisional measures in the human rights systems as well as the outer limits of such measures. The framework is based, on the one hand, on the factual question whether two or more adjudicators have used provisional measures in a given context (e.g. halting executions) and on the other hand on the underlying rationale of preventing irreparable harm that the provisional measures of the various adjudicators have in common. In other words, the 'common core' refers to the types of situations in which a provisional measure is based on a common underlying rationale *and* in which more than one human rights adjudicator has in fact used provisional measures. The 'outer limits' of the concept refers to the boundaries beyond which one can no longer speak of provisional measures, as the harm risked is not irreversible. It is argued that the use of provisional measures in such situations is therefore inappropriate. In addition there is a continuum between the outer limits of the concept and its common core. Along this continuum various provisional measures can be situated as ordered by the human rights adjudicators. In this respect the contexts in which the various adjudicators operate are significant. It should be noted, moreover, that the common core of the concept is not fixed, but may change over time, when a new underlying rationale becomes apparent in the case law of the various adjudicators, backed by actual provisional measures ordered in more than one system.

By singling out some of the best practices developed in the human rights systems discussed in this book this General Conclusion also suggests steps that could be taken to improve the functioning of provisional measures. It takes into account, where relevant, the following criteria to determine how provisional measures could best assist a beneficiary: accessibility, motivation and consistency, responsiveness to the specific situation, consultation and follow-up. The criteria of accessibility, motivation and consistency were selected for use in this study as they were thought to make provisional measures more convincing vis-à-vis addressee States. Responsiveness to the specific situation and consultation were considered necessary for the effectiveness of these measures in protecting the individual and follow-up by the adjudicators was used as a criterion because it has generally been regarded as essential in treaty monitoring.

Cançado Trindade already referred to the transformation of the concept of provisional measures through international human rights law, from precautionary to protective, as an example of the humanisation of public international law.[1] Indeed, as argued in this study, the concept of provisional measures has been adapted to some extent in order to fit the context of international

---

[1]   See e.g. IACHR *Matter of the persons imprisoned in the "Dr. Sebastião Martins Silveira" Penitentiary in Araraquara, São Paulo* (Brazil), Order of 30 September 2006, individual opinion Judge Cançado Trindade, §27.

human rights law, yet this may be relevant not just in the practice of the human rights adjudicators, but also in that of other international adjudicators faced with issues involving the fate of human beings.

Interestingly, there are also situations in which human rights adjudicators take a more limited approach to provisional measures than the ICJ and ITLOS. One explanation may be the fact that several constitutive documents of the human rights adjudicators do not contain a specific reference to provisional measures, which makes the adjudicators more cautious in using them. At the same time the principles of effective protection of human rights and of prevention of irreparable harm to persons would argue for a lenient approach to, for example, evidentiary requirements at the stage of provisional measures. The fact that the approach of human rights adjudicators is not always lenient appears due more to pragmatic than to principled reasons, for fear that a 'too lenient' approach might eventually render provisional measures less effective.

Yet with regard to other aspects of provisional measures the human rights adjudicators have developed a firm practice stressing the importance of preventing irreparable harm to persons and specifying the manner in which this prevention is to take form. This could, in turn, be relevant as well to adjudicators with a general competence, not limited to human rights issues, when they are dealing with issues involving irreparable harm to persons. The value still attached to the traditional concept of State consent in the contentious procedure before the ICJ might not yet allow the ICJ to join in all aspects of the practice on provisional measures developed by the human rights adjudicators. This applies in particular to the case law on jurisdiction and admissibility. Yet on other issues the ICJ, when dealing with situations involving risk of irreparable harm to persons, may indeed draw inspiration from the practice developed by the human rights adjudicators. An example is taking into account the question whether the interests of the individuals caught up in the conflicts between States are properly represented by their States. After all, while the States are the formal beneficiaries and addressees of the provisional measures by the ICJ, when provisional measures aim at preventing irreparable harm to persons *de facto* these persons are the beneficiaries. Another, related, example would be increasing the specificity of the Orders for provisional measures, allowing for additional scrutiny and follow-up precisely to prevent irreparable harm to persons.

2 THE SETTING OF PROVISIONAL MEASURES IN HUMAN RIGHTS ADJUDICATION

2.1 Introduction

The development of the concept of provisional measures in international human rights adjudication must be seen in the context of the traditional concept as developed by the ICJ, which is also subject to the 'humanisation' of international law (Chapter I). At the same time it must be seen in the specific context of each system of human rights adjudication (Chapter II).

2.2 The humanisation of the traditional concept

The rationale behind the use of provisional measures is to ensure a meaningful outcome of a case brought before a court or other adjudicator. More specifically, the traditional purposes of provisional measures as used by the ICJ are twofold. The first is the preservation of rights, the breach of which is both imminent (or already taking place) and likely to cause irreparable harm to the rights claimed. The second, applied only incidentally, is the preservation of proper legal proceedings. In other words, in the first case there should be a link between the right and remedy claimed and the provisional measure and in the second case there should be a link between the provisional measure and the purpose of having a fair and accurate procedure.

The ICJ is not a human rights court. It does not even deal with individual complaints. Yet in spite of the limitations it is faced with as an adjudicator dealing only with inter-State complaints, it does seem to realise the importance of the protection of groups and individuals. It has used provisional measures for reasons not necessarily closely related to the rights claimed or to the proceedings. It has taken provisional measures in border conflict cases, for instance, not only to maintain the status quo in relation to the claim, but also to prevent irreparable harm to civilians living in the border area. Their rights were not the (main) subject of a State's request for provisional measures against another State. In the practice of the ICJ the traditional twofold distinction may have been extended to a threefold distinction: to prevent irreparable harm to the claim, to the procedure or to individuals not central to the dispute.

The ICJ's finding in *LaGrand* that its provisional measures are legally binding was not made dependent on the fact that basic rights of the human person were involved, but was simply part of its traditional function. The power to indicate provisional measures is required by the object and purpose of Article 41 ICJ Statute and 'based on the necessity, when the circumstances call for it, to safeguard, and to avoid prejudice to, the rights of the parties as determined by the final judgment of the Court'.[2]

At the same time some conflicts between States in which the ICJ orders provisional measures may indeed concern the rights of individuals and the (human rights) obligations of States towards them. In such cases its provisional measures may either aim to halt measures that could result in irreparable harm to a large group of people (armed activities; nuclear tests, etc), or aim at the (diplomatic) protection of specific individuals (halt execution of a death sentence; release persons held hostage).

Various aspects of the Court's orders for provisional measures specifically show its responsiveness to the fate of human beings. In the *Chorzów factory* (1927) case, concerning a request to grant a pecuniary claim at the provisional measures stage, rather than to secure rights basic to the human being, the PCIJ was strict and refused to order provisional measures because it considered that the request coincided with the claim on the merits and was in fact a request for an interim judgment. On the other hand, without breaking with *Chorzów factory*, the ICJ did take provisional measures in the *Nuclear Test* cases (1973).[3] While it did not explain the difference, it is likely, especially in light of subsequent cases, that it took into account the enormity of the possible consequences to the environment and population of the applicant States. In the *Hostages* case (1979) it again ordered provisional measures overlapping to a great extent with the main claim. What distinguishes these cases from the *Chorzów factory* case is that they involved the fate of human beings.

In some cases, at the stage of provisional measures, the ICJ was yet to determine on the merits whether a certain act or omission by a State would indeed constitute a violation of the rights invoked by the other State (e.g. the *Nuclear Test* cases). In other cases it was clear that certain acts or omissions constituted a violation of the rights invoked, but the dispute related to evidence and/or imputability (e.g. the *Hostages* case and *DRC* v. *Uganda*).

The ICJ has also taken into account the basic rights of the individual in its attitude towards *procedural* requirements. In a particularly urgent case it used provisional measures in advance of a hearing on the use of provisional measures: in an Order to halt the imminent execution of an individual it was prepared to 'reward' the requesting State for submitting the claim and request

---

[2] ICJ *LaGrand* (*Germany* v. *US*), Judgment of 27 June 2001, §102.

[3] Only two of the judges considered this approach incorrect, as rewarding an attempt to obtain an 'interim judgement'.

for provisional measures strategically late, as the individual facing execution could hardly be punished for his State being procedurally remiss. Had the claim only involved pecuniary interests, rather than the life of an individual, such decision would have been unlikely. A similar conclusion may be drawn with regard to the recent majority decision by the ICJ to order provisional measures to halt the execution of death sentences pending a case involving a request for the interpretation of its previous judgment *Avena*. This despite the fact that the respondent State had argued that there was no dispute between the parties regarding this interpretation and the Court therefore had no jurisdiction to order provisional measures.[4]

In some cases States may invoke human rights treaties. Even if they act on the basis of diplomatic protection rather than *erga omnes* obligations, they in fact ask the ICJ to interpret State obligations under human rights treaties and, therefore, to take into account the rights of the individuals concerned. In such cases the assessment of the risk involved and the role of the beneficiaries may differ from the approach normally taken by the ICJ in its use of provisional measures and approximate more closely the provisional measures taken by human rights adjudicators. At the same time, as noted, States may sometimes be involved in legal disputes that have developed into military conflicts, with their citizens caught in the middle. If the States involved bring the case before the Court and request provisional measures, not particularly invoking the rights of the individuals, the ICJ nevertheless takes into account the basic rights of the individual. As a result the provisional measures ordered may differ from those requested by the State(s). In general the Court seems to be more resourceful in drafting Orders for provisional measures different from those requested when the case involves the fate of human beings. In such cases it refers to the obligations of both Parties, it adds the obligation not to aggravate the dispute and it reminds States of their task in the maintenance of peace and security.

The more recent decisions to take provisional measures in the consular protection/death penalty cases, on the one hand, and in the cases on mass human rights violations, on the other, constitute examples of the humanisation of international law. The practice of the ICJ indicates, albeit tentatively, that adjudicators not exclusively dealing with human rights may develop sensitivity for the plight of human beings caught up in conflicts between States, with its consequent effects on the concept of provisional measures.

2.3 The principle of effective protection and the inherent authority to take provisional measures

While in most inter-State proceedings not involving human rights the principle of State sovereignty (and in particular State consent) is still important, in human rights adjudication (mostly between an individual and a State, but also inter-State) the principle of effective protection of human rights is predominant. Moreover, even in inter-State proceedings not automatically involving human rights, State sovereignty it is not the only relevant principle. Other relevant principles may be effective protection of the environment or the preservation of peace as well as preventing irreparable harm to persons.

Human rights adjudicators have the inherent authority to use provisional measures.[5] If the treaty also includes inter-State proceedings it should be possible to use provisional measures in these proceedings as well. The authority to use provisional measures includes the authority to use

---

[4] ICJ *Request for interpretation of the judgment of 31 March 2004 in the case concerning Avena and other Mexican nationals* (*Mexico* v. *US*), Order of 16 July 2008.

[5] Chapter II (Systems) discussed the authority to use provisional measures in the context of each human rights system.

them *proprio motu*. Especially in cases in which potential beneficiaries are unable to contact the adjudicator directly, the adjudicator should be able to intervene on his own motion on the basis of other credible information. The main concern in this respect should not be whether the adjudicators have the authority to do so – which is derived from their function and the purpose of provisional measures – but whether it is expected that the beneficiary will agree. In some situations involving death threats and harassment an intended beneficiary may not wish to be identified in the text of provisional measures.[6]

The inherent authority to order provisional measures, based on the principle of effective protection, also implies the possibility of delegation. Without the possibility to delegate the power to use provisional measures to one member of the court or adjudicatory body these measures will be deprived of their protective function. After all, various adjudicators only convene periodically. The member to whom the authority has been delegated should indeed report to the main body about the use of all provisional measures. An obligation to consult other members of the Court or Committee could be useful as well, but this should not be required at the cost of expedience.

2.4   Transparency or the lack thereof

This book emphasises the importance of motivation and accessibility of an adjudicator's provisional measures. In most systems the transparency of decision-making on provisional measures is insufficient. The availability of information is not very balanced over the different bodies. The Inter-American Court of Human Rights publishes its decisions on provisional measures separately and these decisions are motivated. The other systems, however, offer virtually no explanations on the use of provisional measures. The use of provisional measures is simply mentioned in the decision on the merits or inadmissibility. The unpublished letters to the parties informing them of decisions about provisional measures normally do not clarify the criteria for their use either.

Most adjudicators do not formally reject requests by petitioners to take provisional measures. Thus it is not possible to systematically trace failed attempts to convince them to take such measures. Systematic references to refusals to use provisional measures are only found in the decisions by the Inter-American Court, the Bosnia Chamber and, to some extent, the Committee against Torture. The lack of references by the other adjudicators is unfortunate because cases in which the petitioners failed to convince the adjudicators to take provisional measures could give particular insight into their approach to the concept.

It might be said that providing a motivation for the use of provisional measures would already anticipate the final determination of the case. Yet in that case it would be the use itself of the measures rather than the motivation that would anticipate the decision on the merits. Motivation only serves to clarify the basis for using provisional measures and to make visible the most important criteria applied by the adjudicator. If this already indicates a certain direction the adjudicator may take, this is very likely to happen as well if he omits making explicit such a motivation. Adjudicators like the ICJ, with a more general mandate, not only involving human rights, have also motivated their orders for provisional measures. The motivation and publication of the Orders of the Inter-American Court of Human Rights is commendable and States have not complained that this anticipated the eventual decision. In human rights cases involving the risk of irreparable harm to persons the rule of non-anticipation by the adjudicator of the decision on the merits simply means that provisional measures should not *dictate* the direction of the ultimate determination of the main conflict. This approach is based on the threat of irreparable harm to persons on the one hand and the difference in availability of evidence and time for evaluation of

---

[6]   See further Chapter XIII (Protection), section 4 (beneficiaries).

this evidence at different stages of the proceedings. The assessment of the evidence for the purpose of provisional measures should not prejudice the eventual decision. It should be clear, for instance, that the final decision is based on an evaluation of all the available evidence and arguments on the basis of the principle *audi alteram partem*. After all adjudicators should make available the information to both parties and allow them the opportunity to respond. In fact this principle should apply already *pending* the proceedings to any follow-up decision with regard to the provisional measures initially taken.

In the text of the initial decision informing the State of the provisional measure there is no need for the adjudicator to already invite the State party to suggest that the measures be lifted. As part of the written proceedings the State party would have to respond to the provisional measures by a certain deadline. In its response it has to indicate how it is complying with the provisional measures. At the same time it has the opportunity to indicate why it does not (fully) agree with them and it may suggest that the adjudicator lift them. The petitioner would have an opportunity to comment on the State party's compliance and, if need be, on the arguments of the State that the provisional measures should be lifted. Following this exchange of information and comments the adjudicator could decide to maintain, lift or adapt its provisional measures.

Hearings on requests by petitioners for provisional measures may clearly help enhance the persuasive force of provisional measures as well, and play a role in follow-up. They would offer a formalized forum for dialogue between the parties on this issue. Nevertheless, they are not always practicable in the context of international adjudication, unless there would be a fund specifically for the purpose of paying the expenses of indigent petitioners in cases considered of particular importance by the adjudicator. Moreover, the absence of such hearings does not significantly diminish the authority of provisional measures that are substantiated and publicly accessible. The initial decisions sent to the State party should already contain a brief (standard) motivation referring to the purpose of provisional measures. The decision confirming these initial decisions should contain a clear motivation similar in structure to the Orders for provisional measures by the Inter-American Court of Human Rights.

With a brief explanation for the use of provisional measures both the State and the petitioner may be able to provide a more focused response. The provisional measure would be substantiated by referring to the *authority* to use it, to the purpose of preventing irreparable harm to persons and to the applicable rights, as well as by noting that the decision is made in light of the urgency of the situation and based on *prima facie* evidence of an imminent risk of irreparable harm. The adjudicator could also refer to previous decisions on the legal status of provisional measures, indicate the follow-up information required as well as the relevant time limits. For adjudicators that do not yet motivate their use of provisional measures, substantiation in this form would not imply an inordinate increase of the workload. It would only require one extra page in a Note Verbale or Order to the government (sent for information to the petitioners) that could partially be standardised.[7]

While a certain measure of flexibility for the adjudicator is warranted, better accessibility to the public of information about the use of these measures and some explanation of their use would help increase predictability of decision-making. The practice of using them should have consistency within each system. All of this would enhance legal certainty as well as the credibility of the adjudicator and the concept of provisional measures as such. It would make these measures more persuasive and it would enhance coherence within and even among systems. Transparency on the use of provisional measures would also enhance access of potential beneficiaries to the tool

---

[7]   The Inter-American Court uses such a standardised model, adding the relevant information for the case at issue.

of provisional measures and it would provide conditions for a more informed media, which in turn could help improve State compliance.

Accessibility, transparency, coherence and consistency in the use of provisional measures should be increased, among others by making public the decisions and by including reasoning. One of the aims of the research was to assist in this process by collecting, systematizing and analysing the relevant information. This book makes reference mainly to those cases that are easily verifiable. An exception is made for the practice of the HRC because for several years it failed to mention its use of provisional measures in its final decisions altogether. Without reference to information derived from the case files the practice discussed would not be representative. Because eventually an opportunity was offered to examine case files in Geneva on the Committee's practice with regard to provisional measures it was decided to make the information retrieved more widely available in this book.

The current lack of transparency in the practice of most adjudicators made an impact on the methodology used in this book. Given the breadth of systems and subject matters discussed, and as most provisional measures are not published, exhaustive discussion of the practice with regard to all subject matters dealt with by all the adjudicators when using provisional measures was not possible. It was not necessary either since this book takes an illustrative rather than an exhaustive approach. The cases discussed were selected because they were informative about a particular aspect of provisional measures. Typical cases were discussed providing insight into the features of provisional measures that the various systems have in common. Similar cases were also mentioned in which other adjudicators confirmed the approach taken in these typical cases or in which they chose to take a different approach. The book also examined atypical cases (Chapter XI) in order to explore the outer limits of the concept.

At a more abstract level some underlying principles and ideas can be found in the human rights systems. These have been used to clarify and develop a legal concept of provisional measures in human rights cases. These principles and ideas are linked to the existing doctrine on provisional measures in general international law. Thus, based on more abstract principles that the approaches of the adjudicators have in common, this book aimed to fill gaps in the doctrine. While it did not claim to be exhaustive in discussing the practices of the different systems, the breadth and depth of the source material used made possible a comprehensive overview, allowing conclusions to be drawn about the common core and outer limits of provisional measures in human rights adjudication.

2.5   Cross-fertilization

The overview presented in Chapter II served to highlight commonalities as well as differences between the human rights systems. As to the commonalities, the systems are facing common problems and issues, which may sometimes result in converging interpretations, occasionally consciously (often referred to as 'dialogue' or 'cross-fertilization'), at other times more indirectly. As to the differences between the systems, they may help explain possible divergences in the approaches of the adjudicators with regard to provisional measures. These divergences were explored to clarify the use of provisional measures that are situated on a continuum beyond the common core, but still within the outer limits of the concept (Chapter XII).

The differences and commonalities in the systems may help to explain why the respective practices of the adjudicators converge or diverge with regard to the use of provisional measures. Awareness of convergence and divergence may in turn enhance the understanding of the common core and outer limits of the current concept of provisional measures in human rights adjudication.

As an example of an international law concept on which the approaches of the various adjudicators may differ, this research on provisional measures also contributes to the ongoing discussion on the proliferation of international adjudicators and the 'fragmentation' of international law, or in any case the importance of coherence in the application of international law. Article 31(3)(c) Vienna Convention on the Law of Treaties (VCLT) is particularly relevant as an expression of the aim of increasing coherence in the law applied to different subject matters. It reflects the principle of systemic integration, referring to 'any relevant rules of international law applicable in the relations between the parties' as an element that must be taken into account with the context when interpreting a treaty provision. A presumption exists of consistency of the text to be interpreted with general international law, unless this would undermine the object and purpose of the system.

International human rights law may to some extent be seen as a 'regime' or 'a set of implicit or explicit principles, norms, rules, and decision-making procedures around which actors' expectations converge in a given area of international relations'.[8] Indeed, human rights adjudicators, alleged victims, NGOs and States appear to have assumed, even if implicitly, the principle of effective protection to prevent irreparable harm to persons as a fundamental norm around which the human rights system is built. At the same time, in light of the principle of systemic integration, this special 'regime' does not, and should not weaken general international law.

The African Commission is explicitly authorized to 'draw inspiration from' rules of international law other than those found as such in the ACHPR or to take those 'into consideration' (see Articles 60 and 61 ACHPR). The African Court even 'shall apply' the provisions of the ACHPR as well as 'other instruments ratified by the States concerned' (Article 7 Protocol).[9] The older instruments, in particular the ECHR, are not explicit in this respect, but nevertheless cross-fertilization does appear to take place. In some cases even the ECtHR has explicitly referred to the case law of other adjudicators.

Obviously it is more difficult to find a common understanding of legal concepts and achieve convergence in interpretation with regard to a large number of States from different regions of the world. Yet if all adjudicators have a similar interpretative approach to certain phenomena and legal texts, this would validate that interpretation for the time being. Cross-fertilization can make an interpretation more convincing and more coherent from the perspective of the development of a body of international case law.

Consultation by adjudicators of the case law developed by other adjudicators and familiarity with their interpretative approaches is warranted. The practice that has been developed by human rights adjudicators in the application of the human rights treaties subsequent to their entry into force is relevant when a given treaty is applied domestically, as well as when other international adjudicators invoke the provisions of that treaty. International adjudicators may do so either directly, as the ICJ has done, or in order to inform the meaning of the particular treaty they supervise. In both cases they consider the subsequent practice of the relevant treaty bodies as well. This is so either as law applicable in the relations between the parties or as the authoritative interpretation of a treaty provision that is conceptually similar, which interpretation could therefore serve as a source of inspiration or even indicate underlying general principles of law or interpretation.

The text of Article 31(3)(b) VCLT, 'any subsequent practice in the application of the treaty which establishes the agreement of the parties regarding its interpretation', arguably could mandate a dynamic interpretation involving subsequent developments. After all, it may be assumed that States parties ratified human rights treaties, including the supervisory mechanisms, in good faith, meaning that the human rights adjudicators established by these treaties have genuinely been assigned the task of monitoring compliance therewith and therefore the task of interpreting the provisions of the treaty. Thus in a way the practice developed by the human rights adjudica-

---

[8]   Krasner (1983), p. 2.

[9]   This concerns the Protocol to the African Charter establishing an African Court on Human and Peoples' Rights, not the Protocol on the Statute of the African Court of Justice and Human Rights, see Chapter II, section 5.2.

tors could be seen as establishing the agreement of the parties regarding their interpretation as such, exactly because they created these adjudicators under the treaty in order to interpret it. Had States preferred to reserve each interpretation for themselves, their recognition of the individual complaint system would have been in bad faith. This is not to be assumed. In light of the object and purpose of the human rights treaty, which is not traditionally inter-State, as well as of the individual complaint mechanism included in the treaty, one may conclude that there is no need for the consent of each State party to each and every finding by these adjudicators. They have agreed to, and signed up for, a 'process' of treaty interpretation by an expert body functioning as an adjudicator in the context of the individual complaint procedure.[10]

Apart from the relevance of the subsequent practice developed by the adjudicators to the interpretation of treaty provisions, 'judicial decisions' also constitute 'subsidiary means for the determination of international law' (Article 38(1)(d) ICJ Statute). These may be domestic or international judicial decisions. The term 'judicial decisions' is used, rather than 'court decisions', which potentially includes the decisions made in individual cases by treaty monitoring bodies or WTO Panels. The argument is often made that such decisions are 'quasi-judicial', but even if that is the case, what could be argued to be most relevant is the range of States whose obligations are covered by the interpretation, rather than the exact legal status of the findings. In other words, a decision of a domestic court, which may be binding on one particular State, certainly has less legal authority vis-à-vis other States, than the interpretation by a treaty monitoring body. Nevertheless, the findings by domestic courts and other domestic adjudicators may be used as subsidiary means for the determination of international law. In this vein the decisions of treaty bodies on individual complaints against States could equally, and more suitably, serve as subsidiary means for the determination of this law.

Further dialogue about the concept within, as well as between the various systems, will undoubtedly enhance the quality and persuasiveness of provisional measures by human rights adjudicators. Meanwhile, for this research 'information-rich' cases were selected in order to gain insight into the concept of provisional measures in human rights adjudication. Some of them related to situations in which (almost) all human rights adjudicators have used provisional measures, others concerned unusual situations.

Most of the best practices with regard to provisional measures can be found in the Inter-American system. As noted, in this system the information is also the most accessible. The Orders for provisional measures by the Inter-American Court have been published separately. Yet it must be kept in mind that some of what this book identifies as 'best practices' might be explained by the particularities of a regional system and could not always easily be transferred to other systems.

As noted in the Introduction, when the underlying approaches of all adjudicators, as well as the specific practice of at least two of them converge, this study speaks of a common core.

It is assumed that if the adjudicators indeed move towards a more uniform approach this will make the provisional measures more persuasive to domestic courts, the executive and the legislator. In addition it presumably is more 'costly' for a State's image to ignore such provisional measures because of their enhanced legitimacy.

---

[10]   See Chapter II (Systems), §8.3.

3 THE PURPOSE OF PROVISIONAL MEASURES IN HUMAN RIGHTS ADJUDICATION

3.1 Introduction

In general international law the purposes of provisional measures relate to preserving the rights of the parties, preserving the procedure and preventing irreparable harm. In human rights adjudication preventing irreparable harm is the main purpose. This has taken on a specific meaning, relating primarily to harm to persons and only secondarily to harm to the claim or the procedure. Risk of irreparable harm to persons should normally be established by a two-prong test of (1) irreparable harm to persons and (2) irreparable harm to the rights claimed, including the possibility of reparation. The third type of irreparable harm, harm to the procedure, may play a role as well if persons other than the alleged victim(s) are risking irreparable harm.[11] This is the case when witnesses, counsel or family members of the alleged victim are harassed and receive death threats. In such cases there is no need to establish a relationship with the main claim. Here the test is (1) irreparable harm to persons and (2) irreparable harm to the integrity of the complaint procedure.

The ECtHR, the HRC and CAT adjudicate in systems that do not have an article on provisional measures included in their constitutive documents. They nevertheless use provisional measures because they consider that the power to do so is inherent in the protective function of the adjudicator, which is why they have included a reference to this power in their Rules of Procedure. Yet, maybe because of the absence of a reference in the constitutive documents themselves, they are more cautious in the use of provisional measures than the Inter-American Commission and Court.

In addition worldwide systems generally take a more limited approach than regional systems because they are further removed from the situations and have fewer possibilities for supervision. In order to determine the common core it is important to examine a system with less extensive possibilities. Thus, this book has taken the HRC as a point of departure. It is the most internationally applicable system, comparable in content to the regional systems.

The adjudicators appear to agree that in order to make provisional measures effective it is necessary, with respect to the kinds of situations in which they are taken, to draw the line somewhere. Part II of this book provided a conceptual motivation on where to draw the line. Acts or omissions by the State that are reversible cannot be irreparable, making irreversibility a threshold criterion for the use of provisional measures. Yet it is submitted in this book that acts or omissions that are irreversible are not necessarily irreparable. They are if they would result in harm for which forms of reparation other than *restitutio in integrum* would be unacceptable, while such restitution would no longer be possible.

In other words, violations of rights causing irreparable harm must be prevented since a return to the *status quo ante* is impossible after the irreversible has taken place (irreversibility),

---

[11] In addition, as noted, preventing irreparable harm to the procedure could be seen as a collateral purpose in death penalty and non-refoulement cases. The execution of a petitioner, for instance, pending the proceedings causes irreparable harm to the fairness of the proceedings before the adjudicator and, thereby, the integrity of the individual complaint procedure under the treaty in question. Clearly, when one party in a conflict kills the other party during the course of legal proceedings instituted in order to settle their conflict, that party, rather than the adjudicator, settles the conflict. Such a course of action, moreover, is not conducive to the principle of equality of arms. This form of irreparable harm to the proceedings is so serious that the use of provisional measures to prevent it could be justified even if there is no clear link with an eventual remedy preserving the life of the victim.

while the nature of the harm implies that such violations can never be repaired by financial compensation (irreparability). In human rights cases the relevance of this traditional reason for using provisional measures is particularly striking.

Based on the practices in the various systems and the principles underlying the use of provisional measures the following findings were presented about the common core and outer limits of the concept.

3.2 Within the common core: preventing irreparable harm to persons

The practice of the human rights adjudicators with regard to provisional measures is rich but often incoherent and lacking explanation. There are four situations in which international human rights adjudicators most often make use of the tool of provisional measures. The first is to halt the execution of petitioners who are sentenced to death until the adjudicator has been able to examine their complaints (Chapter III). The second is to halt the expulsion, extradition or deportation of petitioners until the adjudicator has been able to examine their complaints involving non-refoulement (Chapter V). The third is to intervene in a timely manner in detention situations involving risks to health and dignity (Chapter VII). The fourth is to order a State to provide protection to witnesses, human rights defenders and others against threats to their lives and physical integrity (Chapter IX).

The first situation, where provisional measures are used in order to halt an execution while a case is pending before an adjudicator, is a more traditional use of provisional measures by human rights adjudicators. Almost all adjudicators in international human rights cases have used provisional measures this way. For the HRC supervising the ICCPR this is the predominant situation in which it used provisional measures, at least until both Jamaica and Trinidad and Tobago withdrew their recognition of the right of individual complaint.[12]

The second situation involving their use to halt deportations, is predominant in the practice by CAT as well as in the European human rights system. The European Court of Human Rights (ECtHR), or – in the past – the Convention organs (Court and Commission), indicates provisional measures when a State should halt an extradition or expulsion until the Court has examined whether this would result in a violation of Articles 2 (right to life) and 3 (prohibition of torture and cruel treatment) ECHR. When there is a real risk that the petitioner will be subjected to torture or inhuman treatment in the requesting or receiving State, extradition or expulsion would be contrary to the international obligations of the extraditing or expelling State. If there is a chance that such situation will occur, the Court may indicate to the State that, as a provisional measure, it should not expel or extradite this person until it has been able to determine whether such a real risk does or does not exist. In that case the measure taken may be temporary, in the sense that the extradition or expulsion may nevertheless take place later if the supervisory body, once it has determined the case, concludes that this would not result in a violation of the State's international obligations. Alternatively, the final decision may cause the provisional measure to lose its temporary nature (as a provisional measure) and become permanent.[13] The same applies to the practice of CAT to order provisional measures to halt expulsion or extradition in cases involving claims under Article 3 ICAT (non-refoulement).

The third situation deals with ongoing detention situations in which detainees face risks to their lives and personal integrity. It was initially mainly the HRC that intervened in such situa-

---

tions pending the proceedings, albeit often without formally invoking its Rule on provisional measures. Currently it is mainly in the Inter-American system that provisional measures often aim at protecting the lives and personal integrity of all persons detained in, working at or visiting the premises of a certain detention facility. Nevertheless, the other adjudicators have also used provisional measures in this context.

The fourth situation, involving protection against threats, is most prominently used in the Inter-American system. This is an innovative approach to provisional measures that is still evolving, but that appears to already have saved lives. The example of the Inter-American Commission and Court to protect alleged victims, witnesses and other persons against death threats has been followed by the other adjudicators. While these have not yet built an extensive practice in this regard, their decision to intervene in these circumstances may be explained by the importance attached in all human rights systems to preventing irreparable harm to life and physical integrity (Chapter IX). Even the ECtHR may be expected to start taking a firm approach in taking provisional measures in situations of death threats and harassment as well.

Other situations in which provisional measures have been used with a similar underlying rationale of preventing irreparable harm to life and personal integrity are measures in order to halt corporal punishment or ensure the safety of persons recently disappeared. Indeed, adjudicators in human rights cases have taken most provisional measures in relation to the right to life and the prohibition of cruel treatment and torture. These fundamental rights have an exceptional position within all human rights treaties. For instance they are considered non-derogable in all treaties under examination exactly because their violation, even during a state of emergency, would defeat the whole purpose of the treaty. The exceptional nature of these non-derogable rights is also confirmed by the fact that their violation may constitute a crime against humanity. All adjudicators agree that even if the treaty in question does not explicitly provide for the use of provisional measures, the duty to protect against threats to life and personal integrity requires the State to abstain from action or take positive measures, also *pending* international proceedings.[14]

Chapter VIII argued that the few provisional measures that have been taken to ensure access to court and counsel may equally belong to the common core when these rights are accessory to the protection against ill treatment and torture and against threats to life.

As noted, the position taken in this book is that the common core of provisional measures is flexible rather than frozen in time. The right to life and the prohibition of torture and cruel treatment clearly necessitate the use of provisional measures because violations result in irreparable harm to persons threatening their very existence. Yet there are situations not involving the right to life and the prohibition of cruel treatment and torture in which human rights adjudicators have used provisional measures that have by now become part of the common core, namely to ensure cultural survival and prevent mass expulsion and forced eviction in a context of pervasive discrimination. This may be explained by the special position of indigenous peoples and of minorities in a particularly vulnerable position. For instance, an appropriate form of reparation for violations of the right to culture and religion should take into account cultural integrity and survival. Financial compensation alone would not constitute meaningful redress because the very existence as a cultural group may be at stake. Pending the proceedings provisional measures could prevent such irreparable harm (Chapter X).

Irreparable harm results from the violation of rights crucial to a person's or a group's basic existence or crucial to a person's dignity. In some contexts provisional measures may assist in alleviating the situation even of potentially large groups of people. At present the use of provisional measures to protect collective rights has been limited to protecting indigenous culture and protecting religious rights in the context of persecution of ethnic groups Combined with pervasive

---

[14]   See also Chapter XVI (Legal status).

discrimination, mass expulsion or internal displacement may indeed be so serious as to constitute not just undue hardship, but irreparable harm to the very existence of people. Such harm must be prevented rather than only redressed following the mass expulsion or displacement. Mass expulsion (and internal displacement) must be prevented exactly because the causes may be endemic (e.g. based on religious or ethnic grounds) and the consequences may have extremely long-term effects for a large group of people. The protection against forced displacement 'by expulsion or other coercive means from the area in which the persons concerned are lawfully present' is another norm recognised by the HRC for its fundamental nature.[15] The use of provisional measures to prevent or halt such violations could be warranted. At the same time international adjudicators may not be able to collect enough information to assist the potential beneficiaries with provisional measures that are sufficiently focused. Thus while the use of provisional measures in cases of mass expulsion and internal displacement may be justified normatively, in practice it does not seem to be immediately possible. If at all, in an international system such provisional measures should only be used incrementally on the basis of clearly established case law on the merits as well as an ongoing exchange of thoughts with the particular State in question and the alleged victims (Chapter XI). Nevertheless, in light of the underlying rationale and the practice of more than one adjudicator of actually using provisional measures in this context these situations now belong to the common core.

In sum, under universal treaties provisional measures are normally reserved for the prevention of irreparable harm to persons. Such provisional measures are taken in a limited set of circumstances, mainly involving claims about the right to life and the prohibition of torture and cruel treatment. Sometimes it concerns the cultural survival of indigenous peoples. In certain extreme situations the prohibition of discrimination may also trigger provisional measures, often in the context of mass expulsion, forced eviction and the right to family and private life or freedom of religion. Thus, presently the purpose of provisional measures in human rights adjudication is to prevent irreparable harm to persons and this relates to ensuring survival of persons and groups and ensuring personal integrity. This constitutes the core common to provisional measures used by international adjudicators in human rights cases.

The adjudicators have also used provisional measures in other situations, which are currently situated beyond the common core. Yet it is suggested that particularly in systems not providing for them in the text of the constitutive document, provisional measures should remain exceptional. If the authority of human rights adjudicators to use provisional measures is not based on the constituent document but derived from their function (and based on the rules of procedure),[16] the importance of preventing irreparable harm requires that they are limited to situations threatening the very existence and personal integrity.

Provisional measures should not be used to prevent human rights violations that 'simply' cause undue hardship rather than irreparable harm. This is not because this would not be possible conceptually, but because it risks devaluating the system, especially if used abruptly and without sufficient explanation and discussion.

Still the rule that provisional measures are only to be used to prevent irreparable harm to persons should be applied with a certain measure of flexibility, taking into account, for instance, the developmental rights of children and their ensuing special right to protection. If the beneficiary is a young child one might indeed speak of prevention of irreparable harm to persons in some cases that would otherwise cause undue hardship short of irreparable harm.

---

[15] See HRC General Comment 29 on states of emergency, 31 August 2001, §13, referring to Article 7(1)(d) and 7(2)(d) of the Statute of the International Criminal Court.

[16] See further Chapter XVI (Legal status).

Indeed, the risk of irreparable harm may vary depending on the vulnerability of the persons involved. Irreparable harm to persons refers not only to harm to physical integrity, but also to psychological and moral integrity, as long as the adjudicator would be likely to find a violation of the prohibition of cruel treatment and torture when dealing with such a case on the merits.

In any case in order for provisional measures to remain exceptional any expansion of their use by these adjudicators should only involve other rights essential for the very existence of persons and indigenous peoples. In fact, as noted, these rights coincide with rights recognised for their particular fundamental nature within the treaty.

When provisional measures presently belong to the common core the adjudicator may be expected to use them, whether the system is regional or international, and whether its authority to use them is based on an explicit treaty provision on provisional measures or not. On the other hand, when provisional measures do *not* belong to the common core adjudicators could still decide to take them, so long as their aim and the protection required are not beyond the outer limits of the concept by dealing with situations that are easily reversible. Whether such use of provisional measures is advisable would depend on the context. One relevant factor is the international, regional or 'constitutional' nature of the complaint system. Regional systems with a monitoring presence or at least the capacity of making country visits and organising hearings are likely to have a better chance to collect sufficient information and focus the provisional measures on the specific needs of the beneficiaries. This applies even more to the provisional measures of more 'constitutional' or hybrid adjudicators, such as the Bosnia Chamber. Another relevant factor is whether the adjudicator was established in order to deal with a broad range of rights (HRC, CIDH, IACHR, EComHR, ECtHR, Bosnia Chamber) or with one issue in particular (CAT, CEDAW, CERD).[17]

International adjudicators are generally seen as having the authority to use provisional measures, but not the obligation. In other words, it is a discretionary power. It could be argued, however, that given their function, human rights adjudicators do have the obligation to use provisional measures if they consider there is a risk of irreparable harm to persons meeting the criteria for the common core of provisional measures involving situations in which they have been used in other human rights systems as well. This indeed is the approach taken by the Inter-American Court, which is of course able to base this explicitly on the wording of Article 63(2) ('shall').[18]

This applies in particular if the case law on the merits is abundantly clear on the risk of irreparable harm to life or personal integrity. Yet provisional measures may fall within the common core even without pre-existing case law on the merits on the obligation to abstain from certain measures or instead to take certain action. Like the ICJ (e.g. in the *Nuclear Test* cases),[19] on occasion human rights adjudicators have also used provisional measures in situations where there was no case law on the merits yet. Examples are a provisional measure to protect witnesses in the first case pending before the Inter-American Court, to halt refoulement in early cases pending before the European Commission, to halt corporal punishment and halt measures destroying the natural habitat (in a case involving indigenous culture) in cases pending before the HRC, or to halt destruction of embryos in a case pending before the ECtHR. If adjudicators are too cautious in this respect and do not use provisional measures for lack of specific precedent on the merits (or even

---

[17] See also Chapter II (Systems).

[18] See e.g. IACHR *Matter of Capital El Rodeo I and El Rodeo II Judicial Confinement Center*, Order of 8 February 2008, 19th 'Considering' clause ("As is evident in the instant case, the irreparable nature of the extremely serious and urgent threat has to do with the right to life and physical integrity that the Court has the obligation to protect whenever there are circumstances such as the ones described in Article 63 (2)").

[19] See Chapter I.

for lack of a previous provisional measure in a similar case) they take the chance that irreparable harm will be caused to persons. The risk of such irreparable harm is greater in cases where previous developments, such as Concluding Observations by the UN adjudicators, already indicate the possibility that the adjudicator will find a violation on the merits.

3.3 Within or beyond the outer limits: preventing irreversible harm to the claim

This book identified the directions the various human rights adjudicators are taking to advance the scope of provisional measures in their own system. In this light it explained the outer limits of the concept in the various systems. It identified a few situations in which provisional measures were taken that are beyond the outer limits of the concept (Chapter XII). It is argued that the criteria of immediacy (Chapter XV) and irreversibility are relevant in all systems. In some situations the use of provisional measures is inappropriate, as they aim to prevent harm that would mostly be reversible. An example would be a single action hindering the freedom of expression or the independence of the judiciary. Yet in a climate of harassment against journalists or the judiciary, when single infringements add up, this could indeed result in irreversible harm to the *claim*. In such a context it could be appropriate for regional adjudicators with an explicit mandate to use provisional measures to order them to prevent irreversible harm to the claim. Moreover, such a climate of harassment would probably involve death threats and harassment against the personal integrity of the intended beneficiaries as well, bringing the provisional measures within the common core of the concept to the extent that they aim to protect the life and personal dignity of the person involved, while also specifying that this person should be able to continue his or her activities (as a journalist, judge, witness, human rights defender, etc.).

All human rights adjudicators may take steps to expand the use of provisional measures. Even an international adjudicator like the HRC, with no reference to provisional measures in its constituent document, may do so, but this requires particularly careful reasoning. Generally speaking it may be useful for all adjudicators to expand their use of provisional measures progressively rather than in a sudden and unexpected manner not based on a pre-existing rationale (Chapter II).

Some provisional measures are typical to a certain region. The most particular adjudicator dealt with in this book, the Bosnia Human Rights Chamber, may serve as an example. The Bosnia Chamber was a hybrid and non-permanent body that has been rather specific in its approaches to provisional measures, closely adapting its practice to the exigencies of the post-war situation in Bosnia and Herzegovina. The Chamber had to deal with the aftermath of a four year war with ethnic cleansing and discriminatory practices that were still pervasive after the war. It had to deal with only three addressees (the State of BiH and its constituent parts: the Federation of BiH and the Republika Srpska), all from the same geographical region. The Secretariat of the Chamber was based in the area concerned and the Chamber held its sessions there. Although it was a *sui generis* body rather than a constitutional court, its case law clearly is – and should be – more context-specific than that of an international adjudicator like the HRC. This was reflected in its use of provisional measures to halt forced eviction and in certain provisional measures involving personal integrity and religion (Chapter XII).

Adjudicatory caution may explain why human rights adjudicators only use provisional measures to prevent irreparable harm to persons and generally not for other purposes. In that sense they take a more restrictive approach than the ICJ. Yet once a situation does involve irreparable harm to persons, the approach of the adjudicators is innovative and dynamic.

3.4   The protection required

Chapter XIII discussed several issues involving protection. The first three were the type and specificity of the protective measures and the group of beneficiaries and addressees. The last issue involved the link between the protection required as part of provisional measures and the protection required on the merits (cessation, assurances of non-repetition) and as part of a judgment on reparation.

The protection required in provisional measures takes various forms. They range from formal to informal and from abstention to action, representing various types of positive measures. Not only the right to personal security but also the right to life and the prohibition of cruel treatment and torture themselves imply positive obligations in order to prevent irreparable harm. In that light, rather than abstention alone, an element of positive action is present in most provisional measures as well. This should be made explicit in cases involving ongoing situations such as adverse detention conditions, recent disappearances and death threats (Chapters IX and XIII).

Often provisional measures indicate the required result, such as to refrain from executing a death sentence or to protect persons against threats. Sometimes they are also more precise as to how the State should achieve this result, or at least they rule out certain activities that do not qualify as compliance. Thus, in the Inter-American system the provisional measures have become increasingly specific, partly in light of the experiences of the Commission and Court with certain States. In fact these measures provide insight into the ways States could or must protect persons under their jurisdiction against threats by paramilitary groups or other groups operating with the acquiescence of (certain factions of) the army, the police, or other authorities. They show, for instance, that protection against threats means that the State must protect the beneficiaries in the area in which they live and work, rather than banishing them to 'safe areas', claiming that this would absolve it from taking protective measures. Providing effective protection against death threats is not divorced from other human rights obligations, which means that States must assist internally displaced persons to return safely and allow human rights defenders or journalists to continue the activities that had triggered the threats in the first place. Generally speaking the States involved do not appear to find fault with this approach, possibly also because the provisional measures concern the most basic of rights: the right to life and the prohibition of torture and cruel treatment.

This specificity applies especially to regional systems. Nevertheless, similar to the practice in regional systems it is argued that international adjudicators should also specify their provisional measures, so as to provide clarity to States on what is expected of them, but they should do so even more gradually than the regional systems. This gradual approach is warranted exactly because of the less cohesive nature of an international as opposed to a (presumably more coherent) regional monitoring system and the diminished possibility in an international system of collecting and interpreting information. Another aspect that might play a role is the sensitivity of some States and the way these States would base their disagreement with certain provisional measures on regional doctrine, or insist on sovereignty over protection of human rights.

In a way decisions by international human rights adjudicators combine a top-down and a bottom-up approach. After all, they are initiated with the individual's (or group's) complaint to the adjudicator, following exhaustion of domestic remedies. Subsequently the international adjudicator orders provisional measures and the individuals, groups and supporting NGOs in turn invoke these measures at the domestic level.

The discussion on subsidiarity (and on the related margin of appreciation in the interpretation of treaty obligations) is more prominent in some systems than in others and plays out differently in each system. Yet especially with regard to ensuring respect for core rights specificity could become important in all systems and the provisional measures taken by the other human rights adjudicators could at least give some direction to an adjudicator regarding what the State is expected to do or to abstain from doing in order to prevent irreparable harm to persons.

In order to uphold the legitimacy of provisional measures it is vital to adhere to principles of procedural fairness. In this regard it is important to make sure that the positions and arguments of both parties are duly taken into account. Yet in the face of irreparable harm to persons adjudicators should not balance the rights of the intended beneficiaries with the general interest.

In the European system the tables have sometimes been turned by addressing the alleged victim under the Rule on provisional measures. This book argued that, given the more vulnerable procedural position of the alleged victim, it is not appropriate to address an order for provisional measures to him or her instead of to the State, suggesting a detainee that stopping a hunger strike is a prerequisite for examining the case. Of course an adjudicator may call on a petitioner to stop his hunger strike as part of his or her duty to cooperate and may draw inferences from the failure to do so even after the State has complied with the adjudicator's provisional measures to improve a detention situation, but this is not the same as using the tool of provisional measures vis-à-vis the petitioner.

Both as to purpose and as to substance the provisional measures should be consistent with similar measures already taken by the same adjudicator in order to increase their credibility and avoid discriminatory application vis-à-vis various beneficiaries and addressees. Comparable situations should be treated similarly and different situations should be treated differently.

Apart from the type (action or abstention) and specificity of provisional measures, in order to give full effect to the protective nature of provisional measures it must be clear who is included as a beneficiary and whether and how the beneficiaries have been consulted about the measures intended to protect them. Especially with regard to large groups of persons, such as those cases involving indigenous culture and in cases involving protection against death threats, the issue of consultation is important. Do the intended beneficiaries really want the provisional measures? In addition consultation is important to ensure effective implementation of the provisional measures in a manner that truly protects the beneficiaries.

The Inter-American system has developed a special approach with regard to the beneficiaries of provisional measures. It does not aim to protect the alleged victim exclusively. Sometimes it aims to protect witnesses, counsel, or others. It regularly extends the group of beneficiaries and often seeks to protect a large group. This book argued that the practice developed in the Inter-American system of using provisional measures to protect the members of a defined community, or people working at human rights organisations, as well as all other persons visiting the premises, is appropriate. While they are not identified by name, the beneficiaries of the required protective measures are clear to the State.

Sometimes beneficiaries may live in remote areas or be otherwise difficult to reach. In such cases it should not be required to have the names and addresses of each beneficiary, as long as there are indications that they are likely to agree with the provisional measures ordered on their behalf and as long as there are no (subsequent) indications of disagreement.

The wider impact of provisional measures also deserves attention. A good faith implementation of the obligations under the human rights treaty warrants a pro-active stance of the State to ensure the underlying rationale to a provisional measure is achieved as well.

States interested in supporting early warning systems could invest in this type of monitoring by international and regional adjudicators, especially if, like is often the case in the Inter-American system, the provisional measures aim to protect an extended group of beneficiaries and concrete and effective follow-up is possible.

The final issue discussed in Chapter XIII (Protection) was the link between the protection required as part of provisional measures and the protection required on the merits (cessation, assurances of non-repetition) and as part of a judgment on reparation. There should be such a link in the sense that the protection required as part of the provisional measure should never go further than that required as part of the decision on the merits or reparation.

The general purpose of the provisional measure is to safeguard a final determination that makes sense in the light of the human rights treaty. Therefore there should be a correlation between the measures required pending and upon conclusion of the procedure, in case a violation is indeed found. Without such correlation the question arises whether the object of the provisional measure was simply to postpone the suffering until after the expected finding. This would be an unsatisfactory approach to the concept of provisional measures. An obligation on the merits aimed at restoring the situation as much as possible or at least at preventing further degradation in the context of a finding of a violation of the right to life, prohibition of torture and cruel treatment, the prohibition of mass expulsion and of violations of cultural and religious rights endangering cultural survival would justify the type of provisional measure taken pending the proceedings to prevent irreparable harm to *persons*.

Thus the authority to order provisional measures and the authority to order action or abstention on the merits, as well as reparations, are closely related. In some cases it would be particularly unacceptable to await the harm and then award pecuniary damages. Prevention (or putting a halt to ongoing violations) would be the only appropriate measure exactly because the harm is irreparable. In these cases, any form of financial compensation would be insufficient in relation to the harm done. The reason for using provisional measures would then be so pressing that States would normally feel especially embarrassed to ignore them.

With regard to ordering a State to protect a person against threats, the aim seems to be identical in provisional measures and on the merits. The link between halting an execution pending the proceedings and ordering commutation or a new trial as a form of reparation as part of the decision on the merits is evident. If in the final determination of the case the adjudicator does not recommend at least the preservation of the life of the victim it seems that its provisional measures to prevent harm to persons serve little purpose.

In other words, preventing harm to the *claim* and ensuring that adequate measures can be taken upon the finding of a violation are prerequisites to preventing harm to the *person*. This book argued that this would apply as well to situations in which the alleged victim and the beneficiary do not coincide. As noted, persons who are not the alleged victims may still receive protection as beneficiaries of provisional measures, for instance because they are receiving threats as witnesses in the case at hand. What the petitioner needs to show, for purposes of such provisional measures, is the threat of irreparable harm to persons and the relationship of these persons to the alleged victim. In order to make sure that the action or abstention required of the State remains credible, the petitioner also needs to show that the provisional measures would go no further than the eventual remedy would have, if the persons involved had been the alleged victims. Yet in order to obtain an eventual form of reparation as part of a judgment on the merits, persons other than the alleged victims obviously must institute their own proceedings.

Both in provisional measures and on the merits the ultimate aim is to prevent irreparable harm to persons. The substance of the protection required is often similar as well at both stages. What is different is the function of the protection required: at the provisional measures stage reference is made to this protection in order to ensure a final outcome that makes sense *in case* a violation would be found on the merits in which it would also be determined that certain protective measures are necessary in order to prevent irreparable harm to persons.

Thus there is a continuum between the substance of provisional measures, on the one hand, and cessation, assurances and reparation, on the other hand. Whether pending the proceedings or upon a finding of a violation on the merits, States have the obligation to prevent irreparable harm to persons by taking measures of protection that may substantively coincide, even though the function of these measures differs depending on whether they are required pending the proceedings or upon the finding of a violation.

In sum, alleged victims have the right to a remedy in the sense that they should be able to initiate a meaningful procedure. The adjudicators may then use provisional measures pending this procedure in order to ensure its effectiveness. Ensuring this effectiveness means in particular that a meaningful outcome such as cessation and specific forms of reparation must not be made impossible already pending the case. At the same time provisional measures may protect beneficiaries beyond the alleged victims. In all those cases a permanent injunction would be pointless without the interim injunction.

4 THE IMPACT OF THE IRREPARABLE NATURE OF THE HARM

4.1 Introduction

The case law developed by the human rights adjudicators shows a convergence, rather than divergence of jurisprudence on provisional measures, with regard to the purpose of preventing irreparable harm to persons and the impact of this purpose on questions involving jurisdiction and legal status. This could be explained by an awareness of each other's jurisprudence, sometimes evident from conscious cross-referencing of jurisprudence, as was seen in the ECtHR judgment in *Mamatkulov*. Moreover, to the extent that they are not aware of each other's jurisprudence, it could be explained simply by the fact that all the human rights adjudicators examined in this book are dealing with similar treaty provisions, for instance on the right to life and the prohibition of torture and cruel treatment and on the right of individual petition.

The principle of preventing irreparable harm to persons involves protection of the very existence of persons and groups. The common core with regard to the purpose of provisional measures has various consequences. Part III showed that the serious nature of the harm risked has an impact on the approach of the human rights adjudicators to the requirements of *prima facie* admissibility and jurisdiction on the merits (Chapter XIV); on the requirements of immediacy and real risk (Chapter XV) and on the legal status of provisional measures (Chapter XVI).

4.2 Jurisdiction, admissibility and provisional measures

What is the standard for assuming the competence to use provisional measures in light of the likelihood of jurisdiction on the merits? The rules discussed in Chapter I on traditional international law seem to apply in human rights cases as well, but in the latter cases the adjudicator appears to take a more flexible approach, not requiring *prima facie* admissibility. Rather, only if the case were *prima facie in*admissible an adjudicator would have no competence to use provisional measures. In other words there is no need to determine admissibility and jurisdiction on the merits other than at very first glance.

More than the ICJ, human rights adjudicators have confirmed the principle that there is no need to finally establish their jurisdiction before using provisional measures. If the State has not ratified the individual complaint procedure, the adjudicator clearly has no jurisdiction on the merits and therefore no competence to use provisional measures. Yet in other situations, for purposes of provisional measures, the adjudicator is normally assumed to be competent to deal with the case. Generally speaking the human rights adjudicators are not reticent on this issue. The HRC and the Inter-American Court have used provisional measures in cases involving disputed recognition of their authority. They reserved determination of a dispute on jurisdiction, e.g. on the significance of certain reservations, to the phase of preliminary objections or admissibility and meanwhile used provisional measures.

This principle also applies, or should apply, in the context of the extraterritorial application of human rights treaties. Most adjudicators, including the ICJ, have recognized that States may have obligations under human rights treaties with regard to acts (and sometimes omissions) by their agents outside of the national borders. Some human rights adjudicators have also been faced with requests for provisional measures in this context and this may increasingly be the case in the future. While the case law on the merits is yet to fully crystallize, the adjudicators should not shrink from using provisional measures, if otherwise warranted, simply because they *might* later declare themselves incompetent to deal with such an 'extraterritorial' petition.

As to the duration of provisional measures, human rights adjudicators sometimes indicate that they apply until a given date, until 'further notice' or until a decision on admissibility has been made. In those cases, if there would still be urgency, they would extend the provisional measures just before expiry of the previous date, or upon declaring the case admissible. At other times they note that the provisional measures apply 'pending the case', meaning throughout the proceedings. One remarkable practice of the HRC has been to *maintain* its provisional measures upon declaring a case inadmissible. It did so in death penalty cases where the inadmissibility declaration related to non-exhaustion of domestic remedies and was open to review. In its decision it reminded the State, under its Rule on provisional measures, not to execute the petitioner in the period between exhaustion and a renewed petition to the HRC. Thus if it declares a death penalty case inadmissible for non-exhaustion of domestic remedies, it may maintain provisional measures to cover the period between inadmissibility and the resubmission of the case following exhaustion. If the State would execute the petitioner before he would have a chance to renew his submission, this would in fact pre-empt the use provisional measures.[20] In such cases it operates from the perspective that the case is still pending. This shows the importance the HRC attaches to the function of its provisional measures to protect against irreparable harm. It seems to have developed a *sui generis* approach to jurisdiction and admissibility for purposes of provisional measures, based on this protective function. If there is prima facie evidence of irreparable harm it would indeed be appropriate for adjudicators dealing with human rights cases to maintain their provisional measures in cases susceptible to review.

The Inter-American Court has even determined that, if necessary, its provisional measures remain applicable beyond its judgment on reparations because it considers cases closed only once they are fully implemented. Therefore it regards its jurisdiction as extending until that moment.[21] Nevertheless more recently it has begun emphasizing its system on follow-up on compliance. This possibility has now become well-established. Thus, in cases where the risk of irreparable harm related to violations that had already been established by judgments of the Court (with *res iudicata* status), it does appear even more appropriate to resort to this follow- up procedure rather than maintaining or adopting provisional measures.[22]

In general, human rights adjudicators, like other international adjudicators, consider provisional measures terminated upon inadmissibility declaration or final judgment. Yet they often deal with extreme situations of threats to life and physical integrity. In some cases this warrants an approach to jurisdiction and admissibility that is slightly different from that taken by other adjudicators, dealing with non-human rights cases. Even without formally maintaining or taking provisional measures, if there is still a threat following final determination, the follow-up proceeding could specifically indicate that the case would only be closed once it has been resolved.[23] At minimum, the adjudicator should commit actively to follow up the final decision not only through

---

[20] See also the discussion in Chapter XVI (Legal status) on the case law of the HRC to the effect that a good faith application of the ICCPR and its Optional Protocol means that States are to halt executions once they are informed that a petition has been brought before the HRC, in other words, already before the HRC has taken provisional measures.

[21] In a similar vain, the HRC has sometimes followed up its decision on the merits, urgently communicating to the State, in the face of an execution date, that at the very least its findings of a violation meant that the death sentence should not be executed. In fact this is a follow-up to its final View, finding a violation of Article 14 and, therefore, Article 6 ICCPR. On the official responses of States and the follow-up on provisional measures see Chapters XVII and XVIII.

[22] See Chapter XIV (Jurisdiction), section 2.5 and Chapter XVIII (Follow-up), section 2.2.

[23] See also Chapter XVIII (Follow-up).

regular follow-up proceedings but also through emergency proceedings and press releases. Nevertheless the latter would mainly be appropriate for the Inter-American Commission or the treaty bodies because of their range of functions going beyond the adjudicatory function alone. In exceptional cases an adjudicator could also decide *proprio motu* to ask the petitioner whether she wishes to re-institute a case and take new provisional measures. A final option would be to 'maintain' the provisional measures formally. This last option would be feasible after an adjudicator has built up a considerable practice of using provisional measures aiming to protect witnesses, human rights defenders and others against death threats and harassment, as is the case in the Inter-American system. Provisional measures could then become a tool to some extent operating independently from the main proceedings. Nevertheless, if a specific tool for follow-up has been established, this could sometimes be more appropriate, especially, as the Inter-American Court has indicated, in the context of the obligation to investigate, prosecute and punish previous violations.

Moreover it is argued that for those adjudicators that have no additional monitoring functions (i.e. the various regional courts) there should always be a real claim on the merits with which the provisional measures are connected. Turning the concept of provisional measures into a summary procedure standing on its own, disconnected from any intent by the petitioner to even continue proceedings on the merits, would move it too far from its origins as developed by the ICJ and its predecessor. While for the protection of human rights a dynamic approach is warranted, maintaining some continuity with the traditional concept is also important. Continuity has a persuasive force of its own. Thus in order to prevent irreparable harm to persons the use of strongly worded provisional measures, operating somewhat independently from the main case (jurisdiction, merits, reparation), would be warranted as long as the petitioners have brought a genuine claim on the merits as well.

As noted, thus far the Inter-American system is the only system that has on occasion maintained provisional measures even beyond the judgments on the merits or reparations. It is also a system that includes a provision on provisional measures in the treaty itself. Different from systems where the authority to use provisional measures is implied, this explicit presence may justify such 'free-standing' provisional measures. A case is treated as pending so long as it has not yet been implemented. On the other hand, if the authority is implicit the irreparable harm to persons must be linked much more clearly to the case to be dealt with on the merits, either because of irreparable harm to the claim or because of irreparable harm to the procedure.

With regard to general international law the argument has been made that because provisional measures primarily serve the legal interests of those requesting them, 'the principle of equality of parties before justice requires that the balance be restored by restraint in the practice of granting interim protection and by allowing the benefit of doubt to serve the respondent'.[24] Obviously this argument does not apply in cases involving risk of irreparable harm to persons. In such cases it is clearly not necessary nor warranted, in light of the urgency concerned, to wait until jurisdiction and admissibility are fully determined before using provisional measures.[25] Within the conceptual framework proposed in this book, and consonant with the practice of the HRC and Inter-American Court, it is suggested that if the State has withdrawn from the individual complaint proceeding and different interpretations are possible about the competence (e.g. *ratione temporis*) of the adjudicator to still deal with the case, this should be examined as part of the decision on preliminary objections or admissibility and not already at the stage of provisional measures.

---

[24] Sztucki (1983), pp. 258-259.
[25] As noted, in this respect Rule 94(3) of the CERD Rules of Procedure is an anomaly.

The ICJ itself noted in its Order in the *Nuclear Test* cases (1973) that it should be sufficient that there is no *a priori* lack of jurisdiction.[26] Clearly in light of the principle of effective protection against irreparable harm to persons[27] in human rights adjudication there should be no need to determine *prima facie* admissibility.

As discussed, only if the case were *prima facie in*admissible an adjudicator would have no competence to use provisional measures. In such cases it would be worthwhile if UN treaty body adjudicators would put in place a procedure by which their secretariats could forward to other appropriate UN bodies or special mechanisms urgent cases for which they have such *prima facie* lack of jurisdiction. In the alternative they could inform the petitioners about other possibilities.

From the analysis of the wider issue of admissibility (not just involving jurisdiction on the merits) in cases in which provisional measures were used, it is clear that at the stage of provisional measures there is no need for full evidence about admissibility either. While the case law does not explicitly say whether some measure of *prima facie* evidence for admissibility is required for the use of provisional measures, the human rights adjudicators do use provisional measures before they declare cases (in-)admissible.

If the applicable remedies have no suspensive effect, exhaustion of domestic remedies is not necessary before granting provisional measures. In decisions on admissibility human rights adjudicators have made clear that domestic remedies must only be exhausted to the extent that they have suspensive effect. If they do not have such effect, resort is warranted to an international adjudicator who can also use provisional measures *before* determining that indeed the domestic remedies lack suspensive effect. After all, it is exactly in situations in which the domestic remedies do not prevent irreparable harm that provisional measures are warranted. In this approach the international adjudicator would equally have competence to use provisional measures if the domestic proceedings are theoretically capable of halting certain measures, in other words, have suspensive effect, but not in practice. This is not contrary to the text of the respective provisions on exhaustion, while it corresponds with the principle of effective protection of persons against irreparable harm.[28]

In addition, if a complaint is submitted to more than one international adjudicator, provisional measures could initially be used. In urgent cases petitioners may resort to various international and domestic adjudicators at the same time. This does not necessarily conflict with rules on exhaustion of local remedies on the one hand and non-submission of the 'same matter' to different international adjudicators on the other hand, as long as this is done only at the early stages of the proceedings, in order to prevent irreparable harm to the persons involved. Subsequently the petitioner should indicate which claim he maintains. Any provisional measures used by the other adjudicator should then be withdrawn.

In any case, whether the authority to order provisional measures is implicit or explicit, the case law of the human rights adjudicators with regard to jurisdiction and admissibility clearly shows their awareness of the irreparable nature of the harm.

4.3   Immediacy, risk and provisional measures

In the practice of the human rights adjudicators there is a link as well between the importance attached to preventing irreparable harm to persons and the issue of imminence, immediacy or

---

[26]   ICJ *Nuclear Tests* case (*New Zealand* v. *France*), Order of 22 June 1973.
[27]   See Conclusion Part II and Chapter XVI (Legal status).
[28]   See Conclusion Part II on the purpose of preventing irreparable harm to persons and Chapter XVI on legal status.

temporal urgency. While conceptually a similar link would be expected between the importance attached to preventing irreparable harm on the one hand and assessment of risk on the other, in practice this does not always appear to be the case.

For provisional measures in human rights cases the risk to be prevented generally relates to irreparable harm to the life or physical integrity of persons and the cultural survival of indigenous groups. When the alleged risk is imminent quick action is to be preferred over lengthy deliberation about the existence of such risk. In cases where there is friction between lack of information and the risk involved, the standard of proof may have to be lowered. Given the overriding importance of protecting the very existence of people(s)[29] this applies to the assessment of risk in human rights cases even more than it does to such assessment in other cases.[30] Yet in practice it seems that the human rights adjudicators sometimes take a rather restrictive approach in their use of provisional measures.

Looking at the specific situations in which provisional measures have been used in human rights cases it is evident that they related to future or ongoing facts. Nevertheless the level of evidence available may differ considerably. In some cases of ongoing harm very concrete evidence is available already at the stage of provisional measures to show the risk of irreparable harm. In other cases, involving future harm, the adjudicators have to determine at this stage whether there is a 'real risk'.

In all these cases the factors to be taken into account in the decision on the merits coincide with those relevant for an assessment at the stage of provisional measures. The difference lies in the difficulty of proving future facts. In non-refoulement cases involving claims of a risk to life or physical integrity in the receiving or requesting State if someone would be removed to that State, the facts necessary for a risk assessment are often difficult to obtain. A combination of those facts is usually required for a risk assessment.

Some examples illustrate the various situations in which petitioners have requested the use of provisional measures. With regard to requests for provisional measures to protect persons whose life is threatened, concrete evidence of recent threats and harassment could be provided. In the eventual decision on the merits of claims involving death threats and harassment the evidence that must be provided is similar, but more definitive and establishing attribution.

A situation in which the adjudicators have to attach great importance to circumstantial evidence is that of enforced disappearances.[31] In this case as well the factors taken into account on the merits are equally important in the assessment for the use of provisional measures, again without having to establish at that stage attribution of the disappearance to the State. With regard to provisional measures, however, the adjudicator will additionally take into account the question whether the alleged disappearance is sufficiently recent to make the use of provisional measures worthwhile.

For provisional measures to put a stop to *ongoing* ill-treatment or ensure access to medical treatment in detention concrete evidence concerning ill-treatment may be provided as well. Again similar criteria of what has to be proved at the merits stage must be met. In relation to requests for provisional measures to halt corporal punishment or the execution of a death sentence it is even possible to provide very concrete evidence of material risk.[32]

In contrast, in expulsion or extradition cases the claims of irreparable harm are more uncertain because they deal with future facts. The criterion to be met on the merits is that there is a real

---

29   See Conclusion Part II.

30   See Chapter I (ICJ and ITLOS).

31   See Chapter VI (Disappearances) and Chapter XV (Immediacy and risk), section 3.2.

32   Obviously a conviction and especially an execution date may equally provide evidence of temporal urgency or, in other words, the imminence of the risk.

risk of such harm. Here the risk assessment for decision-making on provisional measures equally coincides with the assessment of 'real risk' at the merits stage. Specific factors that may be relevant in this respect are the general human rights situation in the receiving State and, if available at the stage of provisional measures, evidence that petitioners have been ill treated in the receiving State, that they belong to a specific (ethnic) group that is being targeted, that they have been politically active (in the opposition) in the receiving State or have subsequently been vocal about their State of origin while in the sending State. It is argued in this respect that in these urgent cases, all adjudicators should be able to consult and take into account information derived from publicly available reports by authorities such as UN Special Rapporteurs or by reputable NGOs, even when the parties did not provide it.

The foregoing means that the type of evidence necessary to show a real risk is similar at the merits and provisional measures stages. Thus the *type* of evidence required on the merits coincides with that required for provisional measures.

It is only the standard of proof that may be lower at the stage of provisional measures. The question arises to what extent evidence of real risk and *prima facie* evidence of such risk differ or, more generally speaking, whether and how the standard of proof on the merits could be relevant already in the assessment of risk of irreparable harm *pending* the proceedings.

The contours of the assessment of risk for the use of provisional measures may be sketched in relation to the various stages of decision-making. The strictest requirements can be found exactly in relation to the merits. At the admissibility stage the standard of evidence to be shown by the petitioner is lower than at the merits stage. Among others, there must be *prima facie* evidence of admissibility *ratione materiae*. On the premise that provisional measures may be used in advance of the admissibility declaration the level of evidence required is again lower than that required at the admissibility stage. In other words, the petitioner must be able to show evidence of risk of irreparable harm at very first sight (*prima prima facie*).

Of course in all situations referred to (disappearances, threats, treatment in detention, expulsion) the State is in a position to cover up or withhold information. In general this warrants a lowering of the standard of proof required for the petitioner before the burden shifts to the State. Yet the question arises whether the issue of burden of proof is relevant already at the provisional measures stage. In this respect there is a difference between the provisional measures that are taken for the first time in a given case and those that are taken subsequently. Initially, when an adjudicator has to decide urgently on the use of provisional measures, this is often on the basis of an urgent evaluation of the credibility and sufficiency of the information provided by the petitioner alone. Yet when the adjudicator takes a provisional measure and subsequently is called upon to confirm, adapt or withdraw this measure, the burden of proof does play a role similar to that at the merits stage. If the State provides information to the effect that the petitioner is not (or no longer) facing irreparable harm, the petitioner wishing a continuation of the provisional measures, must bring evidence to convince the adjudicator that such continuation is necessary despite the information provided by the State.

Provisional measures show that adjudicators believe the matter to be so urgent that measures should be taken, although they have not yet been able to evaluate all the evidence and arguments in relation to the main claim. The adjudicator simply tried to assess, on an urgent basis and when the case was pending, all the information available at that point of the risk of irreparable harm to the person involved.

In my view the requirement that provisional measures must not prejudice the eventual legal determination is related to the assessment of risk.[33] If provisional measures are taken this does not

---

[33] Chapter I discussed the issue of prejudgment in the context of the provisional measures by the ICJ.

mean that a violation will eventually be found. This is so exactly because pending the case the adjudicator takes decisions on the basis of urgency, without being able to examine fully the evidence in relation to the main claim.

If the adjudicator did not use provisional measures, eventually it can still find a violation of, for instance, the right to life. If it did use provisional measures it can still declare the case inadmissible or find no violations. With regard to the evidence, in other words, the decision on provisional measures is unrelated to and does not predetermine the decision on the merits.[34] What is important is that upon final determination the adjudicator is not led by the fact that provisional measures were taken pending the proceedings. After all, a full assessment of the evidence at the merits stage must be stricter than an assessment of risk at the provisional measures stage. The latter concerns a *prima facie* assessment only. Moreover, this assessment concerns those claims alone that relate to irreparable harm.[35]

4.4   The legal status of provisional measures

Chapter XVI argued that the authority of human rights adjudicators to take binding provisional measures is derived from the core rights singled out in the treaties, in light of the practice developed of attaching particular importance to the protection of personal integrity and (cultural) survival, read together with the right of individual petition.[36] After all, the principles of effectiveness and of the prevention of irreparable harm have been used by the adjudicators, either explicitly or implicitly, when interpreting these provisions. In addition it is submitted that the prevention of irreparable harm is not just a principle of treaty interpretation, but has also developed into a general principle of law, which is, as such, binding on States (Article 38 (1)(c) ICJ Statute).

The human rights adjudicators do have in common an underlying interpretative approach, both with regard to their implied power to use provisional measures and as to the binding nature of provisional measures. In fact one can speak of an 'acquis humanitaire' based on the standards of protection that all human rights adjudicators have in common,[37] which also applies to the legal status of provisional measures.

The text of the human rights treaties must be interpreted in light of their context and object and purpose, in a dynamic manner, taking into account the need to ensure that they have effect. The principle of effectiveness flowing from the object and purpose indicates that the adjudicators instituted under these treaties must have the power to use provisional measures. As discussed, the ICJ's finding in *LaGrand* that its provisional measures were legally binding was not made dependent on the fact that basic rights of the human person were involved, but was simply part of the Court's traditional function. Nevertheless the principle of effectiveness came into play. The power to indicate provisional measures was required by the object and purpose of Article 41 ICJ Statute and 'based on the necessity, when the circumstances call for it, to safeguard, and to avoid prejudice to, the rights of the parties as determined by the final judgment of the Court'.[38]

---

[34]   See Chapter XIV (Jurisdiction and admissibility).

[35]   This should also be reflected in the motivation of provisional measures that this book argues for, see e.g. Chapter II, section 8.2.

[36]   See also Conclusion Part II.

[37]   On the issue of convergence and divergence in general, see Chapter II, section 8.3. On the common core of the concept of provisional measures, see Conclusion Part II. The term 'acquis humanitaire' was also used by Simma (1995), p. 173, although not in the specific context of the concept of provisional measures.

[38]   ICJ *LaGrand* (*Germany* v. *US*), Judgment of 27 June 2001, §102.

The ECtHR has considered that 'in the light of the general principles of international law, the law of treaties and international case-law, the interpretation of the scope of interim measures cannot be dissociated from the proceedings to which they relate or the decision on the merits they seek to protect'.[39] This statement about the scope of provisional measures shows that now the ECtHR too recognises that in the context of such measures procedural and substantive law meet. The emphasis on the decision on the merits that provisional measures seek to protect underscores the binding nature of these measures. After all, otherwise States would be allowed to cause irreparable harm to the claim on the merits, and, to the extent the provisional measures relate to claims involving survival and personal integrity, which is generally the case, irreparable harm to persons.[40]

By accepting the jurisdiction of an international (including regional) adjudicator a State has committed itself to an international system of adjudication. Just like a domestic system of adjudication, an international system can, in my view, only be effective if the adjudicator has the power to order provisional measures that are legally binding. In this respect the main difference between domestic and international systems of adjudication is the all-inclusive nature of the former on the one hand and the fact that in most international systems States initially are free to accept or reject compulsory jurisdiction on the other. This difference, however, loses much of its significance once a State has accepted the jurisdiction of an adjudicator. Even if a rule on the binding character of provisional measures is not included as such in a treaty text, by accepting the competence of an adjudicator to deal with conflicts between States or between individuals and States, the State has accepted the adjudicator's judicial independence and its power to deal with these conflicts effectively. The authority to use binding provisional measures is inherent to effective adjudication.

Even if the treaty in question does not explicitly provide for the use of provisional measures, the duty to protect against threats to survival and personal integrity requires the State to take positive measures also pending international proceedings. If it is the international adjudicator who recommends such positive measures, in the form of provisional measures, respecting them is also required as part of the obligations entered into by the State's recognition of the complaint procedure.

It is argued that the human rights adjudicators have been correct to stress that the *effet utile* of their decisions on the merits necessitates respect for the provisional measures indicated by them pending the proceedings. If decisions on the merits are not considered legally binding in all respects (such as certain recommendations for reparation), at least the State's recognition of the substantive rights in the treaty and its recognition of the individual complaint system require a basic level of action and abstention on its part. The most fundamental rights in the treaty at issue require at least the protection of the petitioner from irreparable harm, as well as the good faith cooperation by the State with the relevant adjudicator.

An action or omission causing irreparable harm to persons (involving personal integrity and survival) is an aggravated breach of the human rights treaty. If a State has recognized the right of individual complaint (or of inter-State complaint for that matter) and the adjudicator decided to use provisional measures to prevent such harm, ignoring these measures is an aggravated breach of the right of petition as well.

While not an aggravated breach, ignoring other provisional measures, which may not (yet) fall within the common core, is also contrary to the obligation to cooperate with the adjudicator in good faith. If a State considers that the adjudicator was in error in using provisional measures it should still respect the measures. In most such cases the State has a different assessment of the risk (urgency), but it is ultimately for the human rights adjudicator to decide on this. In addition,

---

[39] ECtHR Grand Chamber, *Mamatkulov and Askarov* v. *Turkey*, 15 December 2004, §123.
[40] See also Conclusion Part II on the relation between irreparable harm to the claim and to persons.

the State's belief that the adjudicator was in error may be based on a genuine conviction that the risk is not irreversible, meaning that the provisional measures are situated beyond the outer limits. Even then the State must respect the provisional measures based on its obligations under the system of individual complaint. At the same time the adjudicators must take care not to go beyond the outer limits, also for the sake of the individual petition system. After all their provisional measures must be seen as worthy of compliance in the long run.

4.5   The principle of preventing irreparable harm and taking into account the inequality between the parties

The foregoing indicates that the *effet utile* of human rights treaties and the principle of preventing irreparable harm to persons not only necessitate the use of provisional measures that are legally binding, but these principles, as well as the due process principle of taking into account the *de facto* inequality between the parties, also influence the assessment of jurisdiction, admissibility and urgency at the provisional measures stage.

The further discussion deals with the principle of preventing irreparable harm and the principle of taking into account de facto inequality between the parties. The more adverse the impact of certain measures is likely to be on the well-being of people, facing a situation that would be intolerable, the more reason adjudicators have for the use of provisional measures pending the proceedings, particularly if the task of the adjudicator specifically relates to this issue or if the problem in question is endemic in the region involved.

As noted in Chapter II, international human rights law may to some extent be seen as a 'regime' or 'a set of implicit or explicit principles, norms, rules, and decision-making procedures around which actors' expectations converge in a given area of international relations'.[41] Indeed, human rights adjudicators, alleged victims, NGOs and States appear to have assumed, even if implicitly, the principle of effective protection to prevent irreparable harm to persons.

In addition, when deciding on the use of provisional measures the human rights adjudicators have also taken into account the factual inequality between the parties. Together with their awareness of the serious nature of the harm risked, this inequality has also played a role in the more lenient attitude of the human rights adjudicators towards the requirements of *prima facie* admissibility and jurisdiction on the merits and of immediacy and real risk. It does not play a similar role in the discussion on the legal status of provisional measures because, as discussed, the authority to use binding provisional measures is inherent in effective adjudication in any case.

To the extent that cases before the ICJ also involve the rights of individuals, the case law of the human rights adjudicators could also be relevant to it. The inequality between the parties is a criterion applying particularly in the context of individual complaints about human rights violations. Yet taking into account the serious nature of the harm risked to persons clearly applies in the inter-State context of the ICJ as well.

Insofar as general international law is truly in the process of humanization,[42] resort to international law rules that harm the effective protection of human rights is becoming increasingly less likely. While it is important for the human rights adjudicators, as it is for other adjudicators, to pursue consistency and coherence in the application of general concepts and principles of international law, two factors must be taken into account. The first is that in any case often the most human rights protective interpretation applies, simply based on the text of the relevant human rights treaty. The second is that the interpretation of rules of general international law by human

---

[41]   Krasner (1983), p. 2.

[42]   See also Chapter I, section 3.4.

rights adjudicators may be more correct, in the circumstances, than that of the ICJ or that expressed in certain general doctrine. Moreover, while human rights law as such may not (yet) be
seen as hierarchically higher than international law regarding other values, this is different with
regard to the law developed to prevent irreparable harm to persons. As Sands has suggested, in
some cases the object and purpose of the human rights system would be undermined by applying
the interpretation advanced by general international adjudicators.[43] Thus, in order to safeguard the
object and purpose of the human rights system, which is at minimum to protect persons against
irreparable harm, in case of differences with regard to the approach of the ICJ, e.g. on the issue of
reservations, the human rights adjudicators may have to continue to 'diverge' until the ICJ follows their lead.

5 OFFICIAL STATE RESPONSES AND FOLLOW-UP BY THE ADJUDICATORS

While the question of effectiveness is one of causality and is an empirical question that falls
outside the scope of this conceptual research, it was considered useful to give a brief overview of
the types of official responses by addressee States (Chapter XVII) and of the follow-up provided
by the adjudicators and others (Chapter XVIII).

Chapter XVII noted that States generally respect provisional measures, sometimes explicitly
confirming their compliance. It then focused on those situations in which States have failed to
comply. It discussed official responses by States justifying why they failed to comply with a
provisional measure. It distinguished two categories, one where the State protested against the
(temporary) outcome of the normative process, and another where the State protested against the
development of the process as such. Explanations for the first category of responses may be derived from the system of implementation in domestic law, specific politics, the role of media,
domestic and international NGOs and other international actors. Explanations of non-compliance
based on the second type, disagreement with the decision-making process of the adjudicator, may
relate to the procedures of the adjudicator in general or to specific issues arising in the case, e.g.
involving the principle of *audiatur et altera pars* or the lack of transparency in the decision-
making process.

These official responses simply present legal arguments for a decision of non-compliance
that in fact is likely to be based on domestic reasons of a political rather than legal nature. Moreover, the paucity of consistent information on State responses does not allow for a clear answer to
the question whether States respond more favourably to provisional measures that aim to protect
those rights that are commonly considered the most fundamental.

The adjudicators are the final interpreters of what would be irreparable harm, both during
the proceedings and in their decisions on the merits. The general authority of the supervisory
body is obviously linked with the persuasiveness of its case law. A distinction may be made,
however, between the authority of the body in general, and its authority in the specific target-
State. Apart from these types of authority and apart from residual doubts regarding the legal status
of provisional measures, there are several other aspects that play a role in the attitude of States
towards the provisional measures of the respective supervisory bodies.

Not even national courts can work miracles and protect everyone from harm. Regional and
international adjudicators are even less in position to be an Action Hero. If tested against Super-
man standards the provisional measures by the international adjudicators would fail miserably.
Their intervention against irreparable harm always takes place by proxy. They order the State to
do what it should have done already or to refrain from acting in other cases. Their powers are

---

[43]   Sands (1999), p. 104.

simply those of authority and persuasion, making use of the wish of most States to perform well internationally and of their fear of international embarrassment. This is all the more reason for adjudicators to always strive to improve the persuasiveness of their decisions on provisional measures, among others by providing reasoning and promoting dialogue.

As was the practice especially before the former European Commission, given the rationale of protecting persons against irreparable harm, where appropriate the adjudicator should also allow a State to anticipate a formal provisional measure and make such measure unnecessary by solving an urgent situation. At the same time, the follow-up of such situations as well as the follow-up on actual provisional measures should ensure also that the adjudicator is aware of the particular circumstances of the case and immediately addresses stalling techniques and evasive replies.

It may be expected that governments wishing to maintain an image of democracy would generally be more receptive to provisional measures indicated by human rights adjudicators than would more authoritarian and repressive governments, among others for fear of public opinion. Yet there is an exception to this receptiveness in relation to the execution of death sentences and decisions to expel or extradite convicted criminals or suspected terrorists. If international adjudicators consider that these persons run a real risk of a irreparable harm not only to their human rights claim, but to their survival or personal integrity, domestic authorities are often less open to this assessment exactly because of public opinion.

In such cases the fact that the provisional measures relate to life and personal integrity may not be decisive in and of itself (e.g. the decision not to halt an execution despite a provisional measure ordered by an international adjudicator may be explained by a public opinion strongly in favour of the death penalty). In fact in such a context a provisional measure protecting against irreparable harm to the claim (not involving a core right) rather than to persons may be less controversial, making it easier for the State to comply.

Chapter XVIII noted that the practice of the adjudicators, as well as that of officials from intergovernmental organisations and that of NGOs, shows that follow-up on provisional measures is considered to be essential. In practice the follow-up by the political bodies formally assigned with that task within the human rights systems is insufficient or sometimes even non-existent. The Geneva adjudicators and the Inter-American Commission and Court have taken it upon themselves to monitor non-compliance with their provisional measures. They repeatedly send messages to the State concerned to the effect that the provisional measures remain in force. Such follow-up may often require increased specificity of these provisional measures as well.[44] In addition the Inter-American Court has held Court hearings discussing implementation of its provisional measures and has assigned the Inter-American Commission an important monitoring role in this respect. This Commission has paid attention to implementation of its own precautionary measures and of those of the Court also during country visits. The Geneva bodies have asked questions on the implementation of provisional measures during hearings in the context of State reports as well.

In addition Chapter XVIII argued that ignoring provisional measures has consequences for how the complaint on the merits can be examined. Not only the right of individual petition is implicated when a State has ignored provisional measures, but often the right to life and the prohibition of torture and cruel treatment are too. In such cases of non-compliance with provisional measures, on the merits the burden should shift to the State to show that these rights have not been violated.

Follow-up could be one of the best tools to ensure compliance. In particular the Inter-American Court shows a proactive approach in this respect. Any mechanisms for resort to the

---

[44]   See also Chapter XIII (Protection).

political bodies of the organisation within which the adjudicatory system has been created should also be employed to the full. Adjudicators that have other monitoring functions as well, such as the Geneva bodies and the African and Inter-American Commissions, may refer to compliance with their provisional measures in that context, e.g. when discussing State reports. When States nevertheless do not comply, the resort to publicity by NGOs or independent UN experts could be a useful method to help counteract this. Nevertheless it is important in this respect as well that each situation is assessed individually as to the anticipated impact of such publicity on the beneficiaries, especially if domestic (or local) public opinion strongly disfavours the protection of the beneficiaries of the provisional measures.

In the long run it may also be the strength of the external disapproval for non-compliance that will help determine compliance in future cases. This external disapproval, through the follow-up by the adjudicators, as well as statements by international organisations, NGOs and other States, does seem to be determined, at least partially, by the irreparable nature of the harm the provisional measures aim to prevent, thereby reaffirming the common core of the concept as it currently stands. An 'acquis humanitaire' has now been achieved based on standards of protection that all human rights adjudicators have in common.

6   AN 'IDEAL' PROVISIONAL MEASURE

The use of provisional measures has helped protect persons against irreparable harm and their respect or disrespect has a significant impact on the integrity of the regional and international human rights systems. While the reasons for States to ignore provisional measures often are unrelated to their persuasiveness, the respect specific provisional measures command more generally does depend on their contents, the transparency of the decision-making procedure with regard to them, their purpose, the manner in which they are adapted to the situation at hand, their motivation and legal status.

The 'common core' discussed in this book refers to the types of situations in which a provisional measure appears to be based on a common underlying rationale *and* more than one human rights adjudicator has in fact used provisional measures in such situation. Currently the situations falling within the common core are those where provisional measures aim to prevent irreparable harm to persons. Such irreparable harm results from the violation of rights crucial to a person's or a group's basic existence or crucial to a person's dignity. This entails ensuring survival of persons and groups and ensuring respect for personal integrity.

Given their function, human rights adjudicators do have the obligation to use provisional measures if they consider there is a risk of irreparable harm to persons meeting the criteria for the common core of provisional measures. This applies in particular if the case law on the merits is abundantly clear on the risk of irreparable harm to life or personal integrity.

On the other hand, in some situations the use of provisional measures is inappropriate, as they aim to prevent harm that would mostly be reversible. In this book such provisional measures are considered to be situated beyond the outer limits of the concept.

There are also many measures that can be placed along the continuum between the common core and the outer limits of the concept. In order to prevent a devaluation of the human rights system in question, particularly in systems not referring to provisional measures in the text of their constitutive documents, an 'ideal' provisional measure is a measure that is taken in exceptional circumstances, preferably situated within the common core or closely gravitating towards that core.[45] At the same time an 'ideal' provisional measure is sufficiently adapted to the exigen-

---

[45]   See Chapter XII (Other situations).

cies of the situation at hand. Thus human rights adjudicators should have sufficient flexibility to be able to take steps to expand their use of provisional measures. Yet generally speaking they should do so progressively rather than in a sudden and unexpected manner not based on a pre-existing rationale.

The Inter-American system is the system this book has often referred to for best practices with regard to the protection of witnesses, displaced persons, indigenous culture, human rights defenders and peace communities. The system is innovative and, compared to the other systems, shows a closer awareness of the circumstances of the individual cases. Provisional measures by the Inter-American Court are also more persuasive than those by the other human rights systems because they are published and they provide reasoning.

The practice in the Inter-American system exemplifies the continuum between preventing and compensating for human rights violations, as well as the importance of monitoring and follow-up.

Yet provisional measures are also context specific and what works in one system does not necessarily work in another. Of course the adage applies that the smaller the group, the greater the cohesion and the tighter the *ordre public*. Nevertheless, the international mechanisms of individual complaint (the Geneva supervisory bodies) and of individual accountability as well as international rules and supervision on trade and the law of the sea demonstrate the creation of various types of larger public orders, often warranting increased cross-referencing and cooperation. This applies even more to the rules and supervisory mechanisms (including the right of individual complaint) established by regional organisations. Organisations such as the Council of Europe and the OAS have created an *ordre public* with regard to human rights. The participating States have voluntarily submitted to international supervisory mechanisms and set in motion a process that would be difficult to reverse. They cannot, at convenient times, ignore or withdraw from this supervision by insisting on their complete sovereignty without severely damaging their own reputation.

For provisional measures by the UN adjudicators to serve their purpose it is also important – and this is specific to the Geneva context – that staff members of the High Commissioner's Secretariat in Geneva maintain open and efficient lines of communication so that provisional measures by the treaty bodies and urgent appeals by special proceedings, such as the Special Rapporteurs on torture or executions, reinforce each other.

The persuasiveness of the provisional measures depends on their legitimacy, motivation, publication, consistency and follow-up. They must be credible and convincing. Another relevant factor is their precision, showing the awareness by the adjudicator of the situation in the target State suggesting the necessary measures in that particular context. This awareness of the situation in the target State also means that the adjudicator must have sufficient flexibility.

The *effet utile* of human rights treaties necessitates the use of binding provisional measures. These measures are authoritative if their use is coherent, credible and transparent and if they are at the same time closely adapted to the exigencies of the situation. All of this is warranted to ensure they effectively protect persons against irreparable harm.

Samenvatting

Voorlopige maatregelen in internationale rechtspraak over mensenrechten ter voorkoming van onherstelbare schade

Deze studie onderzoekt de ontwikkeling van het juridische concept van de voorlopige maatregel in internationale klachtprocedures ingesteld bij mensenrechtenverdragen. Is er sprake van een convergentie in de benadering van de verschillende regionale en internationale rechterlijke colleges op het gebied van de rechten van de mens? De praktijk van deze verschillende rechterlijke colleges bij het gebruik van voorlopige maatregelen is systematisch geanalyseerd met betrekking tot overtuigingskracht, waarbij de verschillende aspecten zijn belicht die een rol spelen in de discussie over het traditionele interstatelijke concept van de voorlopige maatregel. Het betreft de volgende aspecten van voorlopige maatregelen: de bevoegdheid tot het nemen ervan, de inhoud, de te beschermen personen, de rechten van de aangesproken Staten, de vraag in hoeverre de bevoegdheid van het Hof om de zaak ten gronde te behandelen een rol speelt; de beoordeling van het bewijs van risico als zodanig en van de vraag hoe onmiddellijk de dreiging is, de juridische status en de follow-up op de reacties van Staten.

De studie presenteert een conceptueel kader dat laat zien dat er inderdaad sprake is van een convergerende trend die de overtuigingskracht van voorlopige maatregelen kan vergroten. Hierbij is zowel de gemeenschappelijkheid van de onderliggende reden voor het gebruik ervan van belang, als het feit dat twee of meer juridische colleges *daadwerkelijk* in die situatie een voorlopige maatregel hebben gebruikt. Daarnaast spelen criteria als transparantie in de besluitvorming ook een rol bij de overtuigingskracht ten aanzien van Staten. Omdat voorlopige maatregelen inderdaad effectieve bescherming moeten kunnen bieden is het ook van belang dat zij qua inhoud zijn afgestemd op de concrete situatie en dat de te beschermen personen hierover worden geconsulteerd.

DEEL I
DE CONTEXT WAARBINNEN HET CONCEPT 'VOORLOPIGE MAATREGEL' ZICH ONTWIKKELT

Hoofdstuk I gaat in op het traditionele concept 'voorlopige maatregelen' zoals ontwikkeld door het Internationaal Gerechtshof. Daarnaast refereert het aan de praktijk van zijn voorganger, het Permanente Hof van International Justitie en aan de praktijk van het Zeerechttribunaal.

De focus van het hoofdstuk ligt op de humanisering van het concept, die ook al bij het Internationaal Gerechtshof kan worden waargenomen. Dit Hof, dat uitsluitend klachten behandelt van de ene Staat tegen de andere, houdt namelijk rekening met het lot van mensen die verstrikt zijn geraakt in conflicten tussen Staten. Dit blijkt niet alleen uit zijn voorlopige maatregelen in de context van klachten van de ene Staat over schending van mensenrechtenverplichtingen door de andere, maar ook uit voorlopige maatregelen die het Hof nam in de context van het Weense Verdrag inzake Consulaire Bescherming en in de context van bepaalde grensconflicten. In dit kader heeft het soms een voorlopige maatregel genomen die overeenkwam met de klacht ten gronde, of formuleerde het juist andere maatregelen dan gevraagd door de Partij(en).

Van oudsher is het doel van voorlopige maatregelen om rechten te beschermen die op het punt staan om te worden geschonden, terwijl dit onherstelbare schade aan de geclaimde rechten zou kunnen opleveren. Eventueel kunnen voorlopige maatregelen ook als doel hebben om te verzekeren dat de procedure als zodanig goed verloopt. In ieder geval moeten zij dus een zinnige einduitspraak kunnen waarborgen. Een zeker verband tussen een verzoek van een Staat om voorlopige maatregelen en de rechten die ten gronde worden ingeroepen ligt dan voor de hand. Als het gaat om serieuze situaties waar het lot van personen (en niet alleen andere belangen van Staten) in het geding is, stelt het Hof zich niet rigide op. Dit is zelfs zo als de klacht en het verzoek om voorlopige maatregelen elkaar grotendeels overlappen. Dit blijkt bijvoorbeeld uit de voorlopige maatregelen in de *Hostages* case en in de *Nuclear Test* cases. Bij een dergelijke overlap in klacht en verzoek tot voorlopige maatregelen *zonder* dat het lot van personen in het geding is, zou het Hof waarschijnlijk het verzoek afwijzen als een verkapt verzoek om een tussenvonnis.

Aan de andere kant houdt het Hof om dezelfde reden, namelijk bescherming van personen, ook niet strikt vast aan de eis dat er een duidelijk verband moet zijn met de hoofdklacht, hoewel het dus ook geen verhuld verzoek om een tussenvonnis mag zijn. In grensconflicten heeft het Hof eveneens voorlopige maatregelen genomen die vooral gericht waren op bescherming van de grensbewoners tegen geweld van beide partijen en daarnaast op het waarborgen van bewijsmateriaal. Juist ter bescherming van personen is het Hof inventief in het herformuleren van door een Partij verzochte voorlopige maatregelen. Het Hof zou zelfs ambtshalve (*proprio motu*) dergelijke voorlopige maatregelen kunnen nemen wanneer de argumenten van de partijen daar maar enigszins aanleiding toe geven.

Hoewel het Internationaal Gerechtshof eventuele procedurele strategieën van Staten (bijvoorbeeld om stukken erg laat in te dienen) niet wenst te belonen, heeft het hierop een uitzondering gemaakt toen de indiener (Duitsland) zo'n strategie had gevolgd terwijl het leven van de *de facto* te beschermen persoon (LaGrand) op het spel stond. Het Hof nam een voorlopige maatregel om zijn executie op te schorten zonder eerst een hoorzitting te houden en de argumenten van beide partijen te horen, zoals bij het Hof anders wel gebruikelijk is. Ook dit illustreert een zekere humanisering in de benadering van het Hof.

Het Hof kan zelf bij zijn gebruik van voorlopige maatregelen eveneens kijken naar de praktijk van de toezichthoudende instanties bij mensenrechtenverdragen. Het heeft in een andere context ook naar de interpretaties verwezen van die instanties. De notie 'judicial decisions' in artikel 38(1) (d) van het Statuut van het Internationaal Gerechtshof verwijst ten slotte niet alleen naar uitspraken van het Internationaal Gerechtshof als hulpmiddel voor het bepalen van rechtsregels maar naar 'judicial decisons' in het algemeen.

Hoofdstuk II belicht voorlopige maatregelen in de context van de verschillende onderzochte mensenrechtensystemen waarbinnen personen klachten kunnen indienen: drie toezichthoudende comités bij VN-verdragen (het Mensenrechtencomité, het Comité tegen foltering en het Comité tegen discriminatie van vrouwen), drie regionale Commissies en Hoven (in het Inter-Amerikaanse, het Europese en het Afrikaanse systeem) en een *sui generis* instantie (de Bosnia Chamber). Bij sommige van deze instanties staat de bevoegdheid voorlopige maatregelen te nemen letterlijk vermeld in het betreffende verdrag zelf, bij andere is dit niet het geval. Het gaat echter om een impliciete bevoegdheid die voortvloeit uit het feit dat deze instanties de functie hebben individuele klachten juridisch te beoordelen. Zij moeten de verplichtingen van een Staat bepalen, op basis van een juridische procedure, bij een juridisch conflict met een of meerdere personen. Het beginsel van effectieve mensenrechtenbescherming veronderstelt dat deze instanties ten minste onherstelbare schade moeten kunnen voorkomen, ook *proprio motu*. Bovendien is het bij instanties die slechts enkele malen per jaar bijeenkomen van belang dat de bevoegdheid tot het nemen van voorlopige maatregelen wordt gedelegeerd naar een van de leden.

Het hoofdstuk bespreekt het gebrek aan publicatie en motivatie van voorlopige maatregelen in de meeste systemen en betoogt dat het vergroten van de toegankelijkheid van informatie over voorlopige maatregelen en hun motivatie noodzakelijk is om de overtuigingskracht van deze maatregelen te vergroten. Dit maakt het ook mogelijk effectief naar deze maatregelen te verwijzen in vergelijkbare zaken voor de nationale rechter.

De mensenrechtensystemen zijn zeer divers. Dit leidt tot een verscheidenheid aan situaties waarin slechts één rechterlijk college voorlopige maatregelen heeft genomen (bijvoorbeeld de Bosnia Chamber om gedwongen uithuiszettingen op te schorten). Maar ook dit blijkt niet te zijn gebaseerd op een divergentie in de onderliggende benadering van het concept. Uit deel II blijkt dat er duidelijk meer sprake is van convergentie dan van divergentie. Dit heeft te maken met het doel van voorlopige maatregelen.

DEEL II
HET DOEL VAN DE INGESTELDE VOORLOPIGE MAATREGELEN

Dit deel presenteert een conceptueel kader met een gemeenschappelijke kern, een uiterste grens en de bandbreedte daartussen. Het gaat hierbij om een zich ontwikkelend concept, waardoor de gemeenschappelijke kern en de bandbreedte in de loop van de tijd kunnen veranderen. In de kern betreft het die situaties ter bescherming van rechten die in de verschillende systemen in eind-uitspraken zijn geselecteerd als van uitzonderlijk belang en waarbij in twee of meer systemen ook daadwerkelijk voorlopige maatregelen zijn genomen. Hierbij wordt dus zowel normatief-inhoudelijk als feitelijk getoetst. Het onderzoek stelt dat de uiterste grens van het concept 'voorlopige maatregel' wordt overschreden als deze maatregel wordt genomen in situaties die niet onomkeerbaar zijn. Een voorbeeld is een maatregel in de vorm van een opdracht aan de Staat om tijdens de procedure de klager geen boetes op te leggen. In dergelijke situaties die buiten de grenzen van het concept vallen is het gebruik van voorlopige maatregelen ongepast omdat dit de algemene overtuigingskracht van het middel kan aantasten bij de effectieve bescherming tegen ernstige schendingen.

Er zijn ook mensenrechtensituaties die niet binnen de gemeenschappelijke kern vallen maar wel binnen de uiterste grenzen blijven omdat de voorlopige maatregelen wel degelijk beogen iets onomkeerbaars te voorkomen. Deze voorlopige maatregelen liggen op verschillende punten op de bandbreedte tussen de uiterste grens en de gemeenschappelijke kern. Hoe meer het, in de situatie waarin in één van de systemen een voorlopige maatregel is genomen, rechten betreft die in de verschillende systemen zijn geselecteerd om hun uitzonderlijk belang, hoe dichter bij de gemeenschappelijke kern zo'n maatregel kan worden gesitueerd.

Momenteel wordt in alle systemen *de facto* het criterium gehanteerd dat de voorlopige maatregel 'onherstelbare schade' moet voorkomen. Het kan hierbij gaan om schade aan de eis of de procedure. In het conceptueel kader gaat het dan simpelweg om het voorkomen van onomkeerbare situaties. Daarnaast worden voorlopige maatregelen genomen met als doel werkelijk *onherstelbare* schade aan *personen* te voorkomen. Onherstelbaar wordt in dit kader gezien als een overtreffende trap van onomkeerbaar. Het gaat namelijk om de onmogelijkheid van rechtsherstel. Het gaat om onomkeerbare situaties die hoe dan ook moeten worden voorkomen omdat zij ondraaglijk zijn. Het door de Staat in het vooruitzicht stellen van herstel achteraf (met een geld-bedrag) is simpelweg onbehoorlijk.

In de praktijk gaat het bij het voorkomen van onherstelbare schade om bescherming van de rechten die in alle systemen zijn geselecteerd om hun grote belang. Wanneer een voorlopige maatregel de bescherming van eén van deze rechten betreft en wanneer in twee of meer systemen in een dergelijke situatie zo'n maatregel is genomen, spreekt dit boek dus over een gemeenschappelijke kern. Hiervan is op dit moment sprake bij het opschorten van uitvoering van de doodstraf en lijfstraffen en van uitlevering en uitzetting in de context van non-refoulement; bij het ingrijpen in detentieomstandigheden en ter bescherming van verdwenen of bedreigde personen. Daarnaast is de gemeenschappelijke kern uitgebreid met het recht op toegang tot rechtsbijstand en rechter wanneer het recht op leven en het respect voor de persoonlijke integriteit in het geding zijn; met het waarborgen van het voortbestaan van inheemse culturen en bescherming van religieuze rechten van minderheden (in Bosnië als post-conflict gebied); en in specifieke situaties van diepge-wortelde discriminatie ook met de bescherming tegen willekeurige (massale) uitzettingen en gedwongen uithuiszettingen.

Hoofdstukken III tot en met XI bespreken deze situaties, waarbij wordt gekeken of er inder-daad een verband is tussen de inhoud van de voorlopige maatregel genomen tijdens de procedure en de inhoud van de einduitspraak. Oordeelt het rechterlijke college in dergelijke gevallen meestal dat er inderdaad sprake is van een schending en is de Staat volgens de einduitspraak ook verplicht om iets te doen of na te laten om een dergelijke schending te voorkomen of stop te zetten? Er is bijvoorbeeld geen overtuigend verband tussen de voorlopige maatregel die tijdens de procedure wordt genomen ter opschorting van een executie en de klacht dat het verblijf in een dodencel in strijd is met het verbod op wrede behandeling indien het rechterlijk college in zijn einduitspraak nooit concludeert dat een dergelijk verblijf in strijd is met dit verbod. Er is ook geen overtuigend verband tussen een voorlopige maatregel en de claim ten gronde als het rechterlijk college welis-waar concludeert dat er een schending heeft plaatsgevonden (bijvoorbeeld van het verbod op wrede behandeling), maar daaraan niet de conclusie verbindt dat omzetting van de doodstraf naar een gevangenisstraf onderdeel moet zijn van het rechtsherstel waarop het slachtoffer recht heeft. Zonder een dergelijk verband kan er geen sprake zijn van het voorkomen van onomkeerbare schade aan de eis. Dan is het gebruik van voorlopige maatregelen ongepast omdat ten gronde de Staat dan nooit verplicht kan worden iets te doen of na te laten wat de voorlopige maatregelen eerder wel vorderden. De klager wordt dan bijvoorbeeld alsnog geëxecuteerd.

Hoofdstuk XII bespreekt atypische situaties waarin maar in één systeem voorlopige maatre-gelen zijn genomen en bespreekt waar op de bandbreedte deze kunnen worden geplaatst en of het gebruik van voorlopige maatregelen in sommige situaties niet buiten de uiterste grens van het concept valt. Hoofdstuk XIII gaat in op de inhoud van de voorlopige maatregelen. De Staat moet vaak niet alleen iets nalaten, maar heeft ook de positieve verplichting om iets te doen. Het Inter-Amerikaanse Hof en, meer nog, de Inter-Amerikaanse Commissie zijn hierbij het meest specifiek in de aanwijzingen aan de Staat over de vereiste bescherming. Het hoofdstuk stelt onder meer dat het subsidiariteitsbeginsel niet in de weg hoeft te staan aan het besluit van een internationaal rechterlijk college om verplichtingen van Staten in het kader van voorlopige maatregelen nader te concretiseren. Dit geldt ook voor het Europese Hof. In sommige gevallen is nader concretiseren noodzakelijk om de gewenste bescherming te bereiken. Bij voorlopige maatregelen om het voort-bestaan van inheemse culturen te waarborgen is het van belang dat de woordvoerder de groep in kwestie inderdaad vertegenwoordigt. Bij doodsbedreigingen kan het nodig zijn de lijst van te beschermen personen in vervolg-maatregelen uit te breiden naar familieleden, collega's en derge-lijke. Terecht heeft het Inter-Amerikaanse Hof bepaald dat het niet altijd nodig is alle te bescher-men personen met naam en toenaam te noemen. Soms is het niet mogelijk de namen van iedereen te achterhalen. De te beschermen personen willen bijvoorbeeld inderdaad wel beschermd worden, maar zijn bang om hun naam vrij te geven. Het is dan toch mogelijk voorlopige maatregelen te nemen om hen te beschermen. Het moet voor de Staat alleen duidelijk zijn dat iemand tot de bedreigde groep behoort, zoals een specifieke 'Peace Community', of iedereen die het gebouw van een plaatselijke mensenrechtenorganisatie bezoekt. Van groot belang is wel dat als de te beschermen personen bij naam worden genoemd, zij hiermee instemmen, dat alle te beschermen personen inderdaad beschermd willen worden en dat zij vervolgens ook worden geraadpleegd bij de implementatie van de genomen voorlopige maatregel.

DEEL III

IMPACT VAN DE ONHERSTELBARE AARD VAN DE TE VOORKOMEN SCHADE

Dit deel betreft de impact van de onherstelbare aard van de te voorkomen schade op de benadering door de rechterlijke colleges van onderwerpen zoals de ontvankelijkheid en bevoegdheid om de zaak ten gronde te beoordelen; het vereiste bewijs van risico, de onmiddellijkheid van dit risico en de juridische status van voorlopige maatregelen.

Het blijkt dat zij bij de besluitvorming over het al dan niet nemen van voorlopige maatregelen een minder strikte benadering hebben van zowel onmiddellijkheid van het risico als ontvankelijkheid en bevoegdheid ten gronde. Dit komt door het beginsel van effectieve bescherming tegen onherstelbare schade aan personen, en het beginsel dat rekening moet worden gehouden met de feitelijke ongelijkheid tussen de beoogde te beschermen persoon aan de ene kant en de Staat aan de andere. Voor het nemen van voorlopige maatregelen is het alleen nodig dat de niet-ontvankelijkheid van een zaak niet *prima facie* (op het eerste gezicht) duidelijk is en dat bevoegdheid ten gronde niet *a priori* ontbreekt. Een Staat heeft bijvoorbeeld een voorbehoud gemaakt, waardoor deze Staat de bevoegdheid van het rechterlijk college betwist om een zaak ten gronde te beoordelen. Maar er bestaat discussie over de rechtmatigheid van dit voorbehoud. In dergelijke gevallen is het wel degelijk gepast een voorlopige maatregel eerder in de procedure te nemen, voordat de besluitvorming over rechtsmacht plaatsvindt.

Voor ontvankelijkheid *ratione materiae* kijken de meeste rechterlijke colleges naar de vraag of er *prima facie* bewijs is van een reëel risico. Omdat de vraag naar het al dan niet instellen van voorlopige maatregelen nog vóór de besluitvorming over ontvankelijkheid aan de orde komt, zou daar het criterium van *prima prima facie* (op het allereerste gezicht) bewijs moeten gelden. Het beginsel van effectieve bescherming tegen onherstelbare schade aan personen, en het beginsel dat rekening moet worden gehouden met de feitelijke ongelijkheid tussen de partijen, hebben er echter in de context van uitlevering- en uitzettingszaken voor het EHRM niet toe geleid dat het vereiste bewijs van 'reëel risico' echt minder streng wordt beoordeeld. Het beginsel van effectieve bescherming tegen onherstelbare schade aan personen geeft wel voor alle internationale rechterlijke colleges de genomen voorlopige maatregelen noodzakelijkerwijs een verplichtend karakter, ook wanneer de bevoegdheid om voorlopige maatregelen te nemen niet expliciet in het verdrag is opgenomen.

DEEL IV

DE REACTIES VAN STATEN OP VOORLOPIGE MAATREGELEN EN DE REACTIES VAN ORGANISATIES EN DE RECHTERLIJKE COLLEGES ZELF OP GEVALLEN VAN NIET-NALEVING

De effectiviteitvraag is een empirische vraag die buiten de reikwijdte valt van dit conceptuele onderzoek. Wel is er in deel IV voor gekozen een kort overzicht te geven van de verschillende soorten officiële reacties van Staten op de voorlopige maatregelen van de verschillende rechterlijke colleges (hoofdstuk XVII). Normaal gesproken respecteren Staten de aan hen opgelegde voorlopige maatregelen. Er zijn echter ook notoire gevallen van niet-naleving. In hun officiële reactie proberen Staten dit te rechtvaardigen met inhoudelijke argumenten of door middel van protest tegen de manier waarop de besluitvorming heeft plaatsgevonden. De echte redenen voor niet-naleving hoeven echter niet overeen te komen met de officiële rechtvaardiging zoals gericht aan het internationale rechterlijk college.

Hoofdstuk XVIII betreft het toezicht op de naleving, waarbij verschillende rechterlijke colleges zichzelf een taak hebben toebedeeld, vaak bij gebrek aan toezicht door de politieke instanties die daarin officieel een taak hebben. Dit eigen toezicht kan verschillende vormen aannemen,

1115

van het sturen van herinneringen aan de betreffende Staat tot het nemen van steeds specifiekere vervolgmaatregelen gericht aan die Staat. Niet-naleving, bijvoorbeeld door iemand uit te zetten in strijd met een voorlopige maatregel, heeft ook consequenties voor de beoordeling van de klacht ten gronde. Naast een specifieke inbreuk op het effectief klachtrecht kunnen hierdoor ook het recht op leven en het verbod van foltering en wrede behandeling geschonden worden. Dit boek betoogt dat wanneer een Staat voorlopige maatregelen heeft genegeerd de bewijslast moet overgaan naar die Staat die dan overtuigend moet aantonen dat deze rechten toch niet zijn geschonden. Dit is dan ook een vorm van 'follow-up'. Het hoofdstuk constateert verder dat ook andere officiële instanties (bijvoorbeeld binnen de VN) en mensenrechtenorganisaties op hun manier 'toezien' op de naleving van voorlopige maatregelen. Ook dit toezicht, door de rechterlijke colleges zelf, door andere officiële instanties en door mensenrechtenorganisaties is gebaseerd op het beginsel van effectieve bescherming tegen onherstelbare schade aan personen.

CONCLUSIE

De meest overtuigende voorlopige maatregelen van internationale rechterlijke colleges zijn die welke ingrijpen in mensenrechten situaties die anders niet alleen onomkeerbaar maar ook onherstelbaar zouden zijn en die een onderliggende redenering en praktijk gemeen hebben met voorlopige maatregelen genomen door andere internationale rechterlijke colleges. Momenteel is die gemeenschappelijke onderliggende redenering de bescherming van het leven en de persoonlijke integriteit. Wanneer in de praktijk twee of meer internationaal rechterlijke colleges ook daadwerkelijk voorlopige maatregelen hebben genomen in situaties op basis van een dergelijke onderliggende redenering is er sprake van een gemeenschappelijke kern van het concept.

In de specifieke context van het rechterlijk college in kwestie kan het gebruik van voorlopige maatregelen ook gepast zijn wanneer de situatie niet binnen de gemeenschappelijke kern valt, zolang het gebruik van de voorlopige maatregel wel binnen de grenzen van het concept blijft. Voorlopige maatregelen die ingrijpen in mensenrechtensituaties die niet onomkeerbaar zijn vallen buiten de grenzen van het concept. Het gebruik van zulke voorlopige maatregelen speelt Staten die voorlopige maatregelen in andere gevallen naast zich neerleggen in de kaart omdat het aanzien van het middel hiermee wordt geschaad. Maar het zijn niet alleen de ernst van de situatie waarin wordt ingegrepen en een gemeenschappelijke redenering en praktijk van meerdere instanties die voorlopige maatregelen overtuigend maken. De voorlopige maatregelen van het Inter-Amerikaanse Hof zijn overtuigender dan die van het EHRM, Afrikaanse Commissie, de Comités in Geneve en de Bosnia Chamber simpelweg omdat zij apart worden gepubliceerd en gemotiveerd en bovendien meer zijn toegespitst op de specifieke situatie dan de voorlopige maatregelen ingesteld door de andere rechterlijke colleges.

Het feit dat de meeste voorlopige maatregelen genomen in de verschillende systemen binnen de gemeenschappelijke kern vallen, vergroot de overtuigingskracht van het concept 'voorlopige maatregel' als zodanig. Zij worden genomen om onherstelbare schade aan personen te voorkomen.

BIBLIOGRAPHY[1]

A

Abi-Saab, G., 'Fragmentation or Unification: Some Concluding Remarks', in *Symposium Issue*: 'The Proliferation of International Tribunals: Piecing Together the Puzzle', 31(4) *NYU J. Int'l L. Pol.* 679 (1999), pp. 919-933

Aceves, W.J., 'Annotation of ICJ Order and US Supreme Court *Breard v. Green*', 92 *American Journal of International Law* 517 (1998), pp. 517-523

Aceves, W.J., 'Avena and other Mexican Nationals', 97 *American Journal of International Law* 923 (2003), pp. 923-929

Aceves, W.J., 'Consular Notification and the Death Penalty: the ICJ's Judgment in Avena', *ASIL Insight*, April 2004

Ascencsio, H., 'La responsabilité selon la Cour Internationale de Justice dans l'affaire du génocide Bosniaque', 2 *RGDIP* 285 (2007), pp. 285-302

Addo, M., 'Interim Measures of Protection for Rights under the Vienna Convention on Consular Relations', 10(4) *European Journal of International Law* 713 (1999), pp. 713-732

'Agora: *Breard*' with contributions by J. Charney, W. Reisman, C. Bradley, J. Goldsmith, L. Henkin, C. Vázquez, J. Paust, L. Fisler Damrosch, F. Kirgis, A-M Slaughter, 92 *American Journal of International Law* 666 (1998), pp. 666-712

Aguiar, A., 'Apuntes sobre las medidas cautelares en la Convención Americana sobre Derechos Humanos', in: R. Nieto (ed.), *La Corte y el Sistema Interamericano de Derechos Humanos* Corte IDH, San José 1994

Ajibola B.A., 'Compliance with Judgments of the International Court of Justice', in: M.K. Bulterman, M. Kuijer (eds.), *Compliance with Judgments of International Courts*, Proceedings of the symposium organized in honour of Professor Henry G. Schermers by Mordenate College and the Department of International Public Law of Leiden University, The Hague, Boston, London 1996, pp. 7-38

Alefsen, H., 'The Council of Europe and Enforcement of Human Rights in Bosnia and Herzegovina', in: W. Benedek (ed.), *Human Rights in Bosnia and Herzegovina after Dayton: from Theory to Practice*, Human Rights Centre of the University of Sarajevo, Martinus Nijhoff Publishers, The Hague [etc.] 1999, pp. 149-154

Alfredsson, G., J. Grimheden, B.G. Ramcharan, A. de Zayas (eds.), *International Human Rights Monitoring Mechanisms: Essays in Honour of Jakob Th. Möller*, Martinus Nijhoff Publishers The Hague [etc.] 2001

Alleweldt, R., 'Protection against Expulsion under Article 3 of the European Convention on Human Rights', 4 *European Journal of International Law* 360 (1993), pp. 360-376

---

[1]   Different from the manner customary in Dutch literature, names such as 'Van Boven' can be found under 'V' rather than 'B'. This applies similarly to surnames starting with 'De' or 'Van der'.

Alleweldt, R., *Schutz vor Abschiebung bei drohender Folter oder unmenschlicher oder erniedrigender Behandlung oder Strafe: Refoulement-Verbote im Völkerrecht und im deutschen Recht unter besonderer Berücksichtigung von Artikel 3 der Europäischen Menschenrechtskonvention und Artikel 1 des Grundgesetzes*, Springer-Verlag, Berlin 1996

Alston, P. (ed.), *Peoples' Rights*, Oxford University Press, Academy of European Law, European University Institute 2001

Alston, P., Crawford, J., *The Future of UN Human Rights Treaty Monitoring*, Cambridge University Press, Cambridge 2000

Amann, D.M., 'Guantánamo Bay', 42 *Columbia Journal of Transnational Law* 263 (2004) pp. 263-348

Amerasinghe, C.F., 'The Bosnia Genocide case', 21 *Leiden Journal of International Law* 411 (2008), pp. 411-428

Amnesty International, Angel Francisco Breard: Facing Death in a Foreign Land, March 1998, AI-Index: AMR 51/14/98

Amnesty International, The Execution of Angel Breard: Apologies are not enough, 1 May 1998

Amnesty International, Using the International Human Rights System to Combat Racial Discrimination, A Handbook, 2001, AI-Index: IOR 80/001/2001

Amnesty International, 'A time for Action, Protecting Consular Rights of Foreign Nationals Facing the Death Penalty', August 2001, AI-Index: AMR 51/106/2001

Amnesty International, 'Rights at Risk, Amnesty International's Concerns Regarding Security Legislation and Law Enforcement Measures', January 2002, AI-Index: ACT 30/001/2002

Amnesty International, 'Time is Wasting: Respect for the Land Rights of the Lubicon Cree long Overdue', April 2003, AI-Index: AMR 20/001/2003

Amnesty International, Niemandsland, Opvang van Vluchtelingen in de Regio, Amnesty International, Amsterdam, 2003

Amnesty International, 'Bosnia-Herzegovina. Unlawful Detention of Six Men from Bosnia-Herzegovina in Guantánamo Bay', 30 May 2003, AI-Index Eur 63/013/2003

Amnesty International, 'USA, Human Dignity Denied, Torture and Accountability in the "War on Terror"', 27 October 2004, AI-Index: AMR 51/145/2004

Amnesty International, 'USA, Guantánamo: Trusting the Executive, Prolonging the Injustice', 26 January 2005, AI-Index: AMR 51/030/2005

Amnesty International, 'USA, Guantánamo and beyond: The Continuing Pursuit of Unchecked Executive Power', 13 May 2005, AI-Index: AMR 51/063/2005

Amnesty International, *Secret detention in CIA 'Black Sites'*, 8 November 2005, AI-Index: AMR 51/177/2005

Amnesty International, *USA: Torture and secret detention testimony of the 'disappeared' in the 'war on terror'*, 4 August 2005, AI-Index: AMR 51/108/2005

Amnesty International, *Below the radar: secret flights to torture and disappearance*, 5 April 2006, AI-Index: AMR 51/051/2006

Amnesty International, *Partners in crime: Europe's role in US renditions*, 14 June 2006, AI-Index: EUR 01/008/2006

Amnesty International, 'USA, Justice at last or more of the same? Detentions and Trials after *Hamdan* v. *Rumsfeld*', 18 September 2006, AI-Index: AMR 51/146/2006

Anaya, J.A., S. Wiessner, 'The UN Declaration on the Rights of Indigenous peoples: towards Re-empowerment', in: JURIST-Forum, *Legal News and Research*, University of Pittsburgh School of Law, 3 October 2007, at: <http://jurist.law.pitt.edu/forumy/2007/10/un-declaration-on-rights-of-indigenous.php>

Anaya, S.J., *Indigenous Peoples in International Law*, Oxford University Press, New York 1996

Anaya, S.J., C. Grossman, 'The Case of Awas Tingni v. Nicaragua, a New Step in the International Law of Indigenous Peoples', 19(1) *Arizona Journal of international and Comparative Law* 1 (2002), pp. 1-15

Anaya, S.J., R.A. Williams, 'The Protection of Indigenous Peoples' Rights over Lands and Natural Resources Under the Inter-American Human Rights System', 14 *Harvard Human Rights Journal* 33 (2001), pp. 33-86

Anaya Valencia, R., C. Jackson, L. van de Putte, R. Ellis, 'Avena and the World Court's Death Penalty Jurisdiction in Texas: Addressing the Odd Notion of Texas's Independence from the World', 23 *Yale Law & Policy Review* 455 (2005), pp. 455-507

Andreu-Guzman, F., 'The Draft International Convention on the Protection of All Persons from Forced Disappearance', 62-63 *ICJ Review* 73 (2001), pp. 73-106

Ankumah, E.A., *The African Commission on Human and People's Rights: Practices and Procedures*, Martinus Nijhoff Publishers, The Hague [etc.] 1996

Antoine, R.M.B, 'The Judicial Committee of the Privy Council – an Inadequate Remedy for Death Row Prisoners', 41 *International and Comparative Law Quarterly* 179 (1992), pp. 179-190

Aolain, F. Ni, 'The Emergence of Diversity: Differences in Human Rights Jurisprudence', 19 *Fordham International Law Journal* 57 (1995), pp. 101-142

Aolain, F. Ni, 'The Evolving Jurisprudence of the European Convention on Human Rights Concerning the Right to Life', 19(1) *NQHR* 21 (2001), pp. 21-42

d'Argent, P., 'Le droit à un recours et à réparation des victimes de violations flagrantes du droit international des droits de l'homme et de violations graves du droit international humanitaire', *Annuaire Français de Droit International* 2005, pp. 27-56

Ashworth, A., *Human Rights, Serious Crime and Criminal Procedure*, Sweet & Maxwell, London 2002

d'Aspremont, J., 'The Recommendations made by the International Court of Justice', 56 *ICLQ* 185 (2007), pp. 185-198

Association of the Bar of the City of New York & Center for Human Rights and Global Justice, *Torture by Proxy: International and Domestic Law Applicable to 'Extraordinary Renditions'*, New York 2004

Ayala Corao, C., 'La jerarquía de los Tratados de Derechos Humanos', in: J.E. Mendez, F. Cox (ed.), *El Futuro del Sistema Interamericano de Protección de Los Derechos Humanos*, Instituto Interamericano de Derechos Humanos, San José (Costa Rica) 1998, pp. 137-154

Aybay, R., 'A New Institution in the Field: The Human Rights Chamber of Bosnia and Herzegovina', 15(4) *Netherlands Quarterly of Human Rights* 529 (1997), pp. 529-558

B

Babcock, S., 'The Role of International Law in United States Death Penalty Cases', 15 *Leiden Journal of International Law* 367 (2002), pp. 367-387

Bal, P., E.R. Rieter, 'Habeas corpus in de Verenigde Staten: een ultiem maar uiterst beperkt rechtsmiddel', 31(1) *Delikt en delinkwent* 1 (2001), pp. 1-57

Barkhuysen, T., *Artikel 13 EVRM: effectieve nationale rechtsbescherming bij schending van mensenrechten*, diss. Leiden, Vermande, Lelystad 1998

Barkhuysen, T, Annotation of ECtHR (Grand Chamber) *Mamatkulov and Askarov* v. *Turkey*, 4 February 2005, in: *AB* 2005, 274 (annotation of Grand Chamber judgment on the legal status of provisional measures)

Barkhuysen, T., M.L. van Emmerik, E.R. Rieter, *Procederen over mensenrechten onder het EVRM, het IVBPR en andere VN-verdragen*, Ars Aequi Libri, Nijmegen 2002 (1st); 2008 (2nd)

Barkhuysen, T., M.L. van Emmerik, P.H.P.H.M.C. van Kempen (eds.), *The Execution of Strasbourg and Geneva Human Rights Decisions in the National legal Order*, Martinus Nijhoff Publishers, The Hague/Boston/London 1999

Barnhoorn, L., K. Wellens (eds.), *Diversity in Secondary Rules and the Unity of International Law*, Martinus Nijhoff Publishers, The Hague [etc.] 1995

Bassiouni, Ch., 'International crimes: jus cogens and obligatio erga omnes', 59(4) *Law and Contemporary Problems* 63 (1996), pp. 63-74

Bassiouni report: independent expert to prepare a revised version of the Principles and Guidelines, Bassiouni, reports E/CN.4/1999/65 and E/CN.4/2000/62

Battjes, H., *European Asylum Law and International Law*, Brill Martinus Nijhoff Publishers, Leiden 2006

Battjes, H. (HBA), Annotation of *N. v. UK*, 27 May 2008, in: *Jurisprudentie Vreemdelingenrecht JV* 2008/266

Bayefsky, A. (ed.), *The UN Human Rights Treaty System in the 21st Century*, Kluwer Law International, the Hague/London/Boston 2000

Bayefsky, A., *The UN Human Rights Treaty System: Universality at the Crossroads*, Transnational Publishers, Ardsley, N.Y. 2001

Bayefsky, A., *How to Complain to the UN Human Rights Treaty System*, Transnational Publishers, New York 2002

Bedi, S., *The Development of Human Rights Law by the Judges of the International Court of Justice*, Hart Publishing, Oxford/Portland Oregon 2007

Bedjaoui, M., 'À propos de la place des droits de la personne humaine dans la jurisprudence de la Cour internationale de Justice', in: P. Mahony et al., *Protection of Human Rights: The European Perspective, Studies in Memory of Rolv Ryssdal*, Heymans, Köln 2000, pp. 87-93

Beirlaen, A., 'De ordonnantie van 11 september 1976 gewezen in de zaak Plateau continental de la Mer Egée en de bevoegdheidsproblematiek in de fase der voorlopige maatregelen van het Internationale Hof van Justitie', 14 *Revue belge de droit international* 425 (1978-1979), pp. 425-459

Beirlaen, A., *De conservatoire maatregelen van het Internationale Gerechtshof*, diss. Free University Brussels, 1979-1980

Beirlaen, A., 'De bindende kracht en afdwingbaarheid van de door het internationale Hof van Justitie aangeduide conservatoire maatregelen', 18 *Revue belge de droit international* 739 (1984-1985), pp. 739-775

Bekker, G., 'Human Rights News: III Africa', 22(2) *Netherlands Quarterly of Human Rights* 293 (2004), pp. 293-299

Benedek, W. (ed.), *Human Rights in Bosnia and Herzegovina after Dayton: from Theory to Practice*, Human Rights Centre of the University of Sarajevo, Martinus Nijhoff Publishers, The Hague [etc.] 1999

Ben-Naftali, O., M. Sharon, 'What the ICJ Did Not Say About the Duty to Punish Genocide: The Missing Pieces in a Puzzle', 5(4) *Journal of International Criminal Justice* 859 (2007), pp. 859-874

Benvenisti, E., 'Margin of Appreciation, Consensus, and Universal Standards', 31(4) *New York University Journal of International Law and Politics* 843 (1999), pp. 843-854

Berman M.R., R.S. Clark, 'State Terrorism: Disappearances', 13 *Rutgers Law Journal* 531 (1982), pp. 531-577

Bernhardt, J.P.A., 'The Provisional Measures Procedure of the International Court of Justice through U.S. Staff in Tehran: *Fiat Iustitia, Pereat Curia?*', 20(3) *Virginia J. Int.'l L.* 557 (1980), pp. 557-613

Bernhardt, R. (1994a), 'Interim Measures of Protection under the European Convention on Human Rights', in: R. Bernhardt (ed.), *Interim Measures Indicated by International Courts*, Springer-Verlag, Berlin [etc.] 1994, pp. 95-114

Bernhardt, R. (ed.) (1994b), *Interim Measures Indicated by International Courts*, Springer-Verlag, Berlin/Heidelberg/New York 1994

Birdsong, L.E., 'Is there a Rush to the Death Penalty in the Caribbean: the Bahamas says no', 13 *Temple International and Comparative Law Journal* 285 (1999), pp. 285-308

Blaauw, M., "'Denial and Silence'' or "Acknowledgement and Disclosure'", 84 *International Review of the Red Cross* 767 (2002), pp. 767-783

Boerefijn, I. (1999a), *The Reporting Procedure under the Covenant on Civil and Political Rights*, Intersentia, Antwerp [etc.] 1999

Boerefijn, I. (1999b), 'Follow up of the Views of the United Nations Treaty Bodies', in: T. Barkhuysen et al. (eds.), *The Execution of Strasbourg and Geneva Human Rights Decisions in the National Legal Order*, Kluwer Law International, The Hague [etc.] 1999, pp. 101-112

Boerefijn, I. (2005a), Annotation of CEDAW *A.T.* v. *Hungary*, 26 January 2005, 2/2003, 30(4) *NJCM- bulletin* 470 (2005), pp. 470-480

Boerefijn, I. (2005b), 'Foltering is het probleem, niet de oplossing: het verbod van foltering en andere wrede, onmenselijke of vernederende behandeling of bestraffing in het kader van VN-verdragen', 30(3) *NJCM-bulletin* 240 (2005), pp. 240-258

Boerefijn, I. (2005c), 'Domestic Violence against Women in International Human Rights Law', in: I. Westendorp, R. Wolleswinkel (eds.), *Violence in the Domestic Sphere*, Intersentia, Antwerp [etc.] 2005, pp. 35-57

Bomhoff, J., L. Zucca, 'The Tragedy of Ms. Evans: Conflicts and Incommensurability of Rights', 2 *European Constitutional Law Review* 434 (2006), pp. 434-442

Bonifaz Tweddle, G., 'Las medidas cautelares, urgentes y provisionales en el Sistema Interamericano de Protección de los Derechos Humanos' in: Política Internacional/Academia Diplomática del Perú, n. 85, julio-setiembre 2006, pp. 55-97

Borgen, C.J., 'Transnational Tribunals and the Transmission of Norms: Hegemony of Process', St. John's University School of Law Legal studies Research Paper series, August 2005

Boulesbaa, A., *The U.N. Convention against Torture and the Prospects for Enforcement*, Martinus Nijhoff Publishers, The Hague [etc.] 1999

Böcker, R., 'Feeling the Heat in Geneva and New York, The Netherlands before the UN Treaty Bodies in Individual Complaints Procedures', in: N. Blokker, R. Lefeber, L. Lijnzaad, I. van Bladel (eds.), *The Netherlands in Court, Essays in honour of Johan G. Lammers*, Brill, Leiden 2006, pp. 125-140

Böhler, B., *De zwerftocht van een leider, Achter de schermen van de zaak Öcalan*, Arbeiderspers Amsterdam 2000

Bradley, C.A., 'Breard, our Dualist Constitution, and the Internationalist Conception', 51 *Stanford Law Review* 529 (1998-1999), pp. 529-566

Brems, E., Case note on *Evans* v. *UK* (7 March 2006), *European Human Rights Cases* 2006, pp. 428-442

Brody, R., F. Gonzáles, 'Nunca Más: an analysis of international instruments on "Disappearances"', 19 *Human Rights Quarterly* 365 (1997), pp. 365-405

Bronkhorst, D., 'Naming Names', 16(4) *Netherlands Quarterly of Human Rights* 457 (1998), pp. 457-474

Brook, J., 'Federalism and Foreign Affairs: how to Remedy Violations of the Vienna Convention and obey the U.S. Constitution, too', 37 *University of Michigan Journal of Law Reform* 573 (2004) pp. 573-597

Brown, Ch., *A Common Law of International Adjudication*, Oxford University Press, New York 2007

Bruin, R., "'More than a Mere Possibility", Risicogroepen, het Committee tegen Foltering en de bewijslast', *NAV* 145 (1998), pp. 145-150

Bruin, R., Case note of ECtHR (Grand Chamber) *Mamatkulov and Askarov* v. *Turkey*, 4 February 2005, *NAV* 2005/79

Bruin, R., Case note of ECtHR *N.* v. *UK*, 27 May 2007, *NAV* 2008/28

Bruin, R., K. Wouters, 'Terrorism and the Non-derogability of Non-refoulement', 15(1) *International Journal of Refugee Law* 5 (2003), pp. 5-29

Buergenthal, Th, 'The Revised OAS Charter and the Protection of Human Rights', 29 *American Journal of International Law* 828 (1975), pp. 828-836

Buergenthal, Th, 'The Inter-American Court of Human Rights', 76 *American Journal of International Law* 231 (1982), pp. 231-245

Buergenthal, Th, 'The Advisory Practice of the Inter-American Human Rights Court', 79 *American Journal of International Law* 1 (1985), pp. 1-27

Buergenthal, Th., 'Interim Measures in the Inter-American Court of Human Rights', in: R. Bernhardt (ed.), *Interim Measures indicated by International Courts*, Springer-Verlag, Berlin 1994, pp. 69-94

Buergenthal, Th., 'International Tribunals and National Courts: The Internationalization of Domestic Adjudication', in: U. Beyerlin et al. (eds.), *Recht Zwischen Umbruch und Bewahrung: Völkerrecht, Europarecht, Staatsrecht: Festschrift für Rudolf Bernhardt*, Springer, Berlin 1995, pp. 687-703

Buergenthal, Th., 'The Normative and Institutional Evolution of International Human Rights', 19(4) *Human Rights Quarterly* 703 (1997), pp. 703-723

Buergenthal, Th., 'Proliferation of International Courts and Tribunals: is it good or is it bad?', 14 *Leiden Journal of International Law* 267 (2001), pp. 267-275

Buergenthal, Th., *Remembering the Early Years of the Inter-American Court of Human Rights*, NYU Center for Human Rights and Global Justice No. 1, 2005

Buergenthal, Th., D. Cassell, 'The Future of the Inter-American Human Rights System', in: J.E. Mendez, F. Cox (eds.), *El Futuro del Sistema Interamericano de Protección de los derechos Humanos*, Instituto Interamericano de Drechos Humanos, San José 1998, pp. 539-571

Buergenthal, Th., D. Shelton, *Protecting Human Rights in the Americas: Cases and Materials* (4th rev. ed.) International Institute of Human Rights, Strasbourg, Engel Verlag, Kehl 1995

Bulterman, M., Case note Behrami and Behrami, 2 May 2007, *EHRC* 2007/111

Bulterman, M.K., M. Kuijer (eds.), *Compliance with judgments of international courts*, Kluwer Law Intenational, The Hague 1996

Buquicchio-de Boer, M., 'Interim Measures by the European Commission of Human Rights', in: M. de Salvia, M.E. Villiger (eds.), *The Birth of European Human Rights Law. Liber Amicorum Carl Aage Nørgaard*, Nomos, Baden-Baden 1998, pp. 229-236

Burgers, J.H., H. Danelius, *The United Nations Convention against Torture: A Handbook against Torture and other Cruel, Inhuman or Degrading Treatment or Punishment*, Nijhoff, Dordrecht 1988

C

Caflisch, L., A. Cançado Trindade, 'Les Conventions Américaines et Européennes des Droits de l'Homme et le Droit International Général', 108(1) *RGDIP* 5 (2004), pp. 5-62

Cançado Trindade, A., *Co-existence and Co-ordination of Mechanisms of International Protection of Human Rights (at Global and Regional Levels)*, 202 *Collected Courses Hague Academy* (1987-II)

Cançado Trindade, A., 'Derecho internacional de los Refugiados y derechos internacional de los derechos Humanos: aproximaciones y convergencias', 119-120 *Estudios Internacionales del instituto de estudios Internacionales* 321 (1997), pp. 321-350

Cançado Trindade, A. (1998a), 'The Operation of the Inter-American Court of Human Rights', in: D.J. Harris, S. Livingstone (eds.), *The Inter-American System of Human Rights*, Oxford Clarendon Press, Oxford 1998, pp. 133-149

Cançado Trindade, A. (1998b), 'The Consolidation of the Procedural Capacity of Individuals on the Evolution of the International Protection of Human Rights: Present State and Perspective at the Turn of the Century', 30(1) *Colombia Human Rights Law Review* 1 (1998), pp. 1-27

Cançado Trindade, A. (1998c), 'Reflexiones sobre el Futuro del sistema interamericano de Protección de los derechos Humanos', in: J.E. Mendez, F. Cox (eds.), *El Futura del Sistema In-*

teramericano de Protección de Los Derechos Humanos, Instituto Interamericano de Derechos Humanos (IIDH), San José, Costa Rica 1998, pp. 573-604

Cançado Trindade, A., 'The Inter-American System of Protection of Human Rights (1948-2000): Evolution, Present State and Perspectives at the Dawn of the XXIst Century', International Institute of Human Rights, XXXI Study session, Strasbourg, 10-13 July 2000, AACT/1-AACT/60, pp. 113-172

Cançado Trindade, A., Preface by the President of the Inter-American Court of Human Rights to Series E: Provisional Measures, No. 2, Compendium: July 1996-June 2000, Secretariat of the Court, San José, Costa Rica 2000

Cançado Trindade, A., 'The Evolution of Provisional Measures of Protection under the Case-law of the Inter-American Court of Human Rights (1987-2002)', 24(5-8) *Human Rights Law Journal* 162 (2003), pp. 162-168

Cançado Trindade, A., 'The Development of International Human Rights Law by the Operation and the Case-law of the European and the Inter-American Courts of Human Rights', speech on the occasion of the opening of the judicial year, 22 January 2004, <www.echr.coe.int/Eng/Speeches> (consulted on 14 July 2004)

Cançado Trindade, A., 'Les mesures provisoires de protection dans la jurisprudence de la cour interaméricaine des droits de l'homme', in: G. Cohen-Jonathan, J.-F. Flauss (eds.), *Mesures conservatoires et droits fondamentaux*, Bruyant, Bruxelles 2005, pp. 145-163

Carlson, S.N., G. Gisvold, *Practical Guide to the International Covenant on Civil and Political Rights*, Transnational Publishers, Ardsley, NY 2003

Caron, D.D., 'Interim Measures of Protection: Theory and Practice in Light of the Iran-United States Claims Tribunal', 46 *ZaöRV* 465 (1986), pp. 465-518

Carozza, P.G., 'Uses and Misuses of Comparative Law in International Human Rights: Some Reflections on the Jurisprudence of the European Court of Human Rights', 73(5) *Notre Dame Law Review* 1217 (1998), pp. 1217-1237

Carozza, P.G, 'Subsidiarity as a Structural Principle of International Human Rights Law', 97 *American Journal of International Law* 38 (2003), pp. 38-79

Carter, L.E., 'Compliance with ICJ Provisional Measures and the Meaning of Review and Reconsideration under the Vienna Convention on Consular Relations: Avena and other Mexican Nationals (*Mex. v. U.S.*)', 25(1) *Michigan Journal of International Law* 117 (2003), pp. 117-134

Cassel, D., 'A United States View of the Inter-American Court of Human Rights', in: P. Nikken (ed.), *The Modern World of Human Rights: Essays in Honour of Thomas Buergenthal*, IIDH/IIHR, San José, Costa Rica 1996, pp. 209-230

Cassel, D. (1999a), 'Peru Withdraws from the Court: will the Inter-American Human Rights System meet the Challenge?', 20(4-6) *Human Rights Law Journal* 167 (1999), pp. 167-175

Cassel, D. (1999b), 'Judicial Remedies for Treaty Violations in Criminal Cases: Consular Rights of Foreign Nationals in United states Death Penalty Cases', 12 *Leiden Journal of International Law* 851 (1999), pp. 851-888

Cassel, D., 'International Remedies in National Criminal Cases: ICJ Judgment in Germany v. United States', 15 *Leiden Journal of International Law* 69 (2002), pp. 69-86

Cassel, D., 'Extraterritorial Application on Inter-American Human Rights Instruments', in: F. Coomans, M. Kamminga (eds.), *Extraterritorial Application of Human Rights Treaties*, Intersentia, Antwerp/Oxford 2004, pp. 175-181

Castan, M., S. Joseph, J. Schultz, *The International Covenant on Civil and Political Rights: Cases, Materials and Commentary*, Oxford University Press, Oxford 2004

Cerna, C.M., 'International Law and the Protection of Human Rights in the Inter-American System, 19 *Houston Journal of International Law* 731 (1997), pp. 731-759

Cerna, C.M., 'Extraterritorial Application of the Human Right Instruments of the Inter-American System', in: F. Coomans, M. Kamminga (eds.), *Extraterritorial Application of Human Rights Treaties*, Intersentia, Antwerp/Oxford 2004, pp. 141-174

Cerna, C., Out of bounds? The approach of the Inter-American system for the promotion and protection of human rights to the extraterritorial application of human rights law, Working Paper 6 of the NYU Center for Human Rights and Global Justice, 2006

Cerone, J., 'The Application of Regional Human Rights Law beyond Regional Frontiers: The Inter-American Commission on Human Rights and US Activities in Iraq', *ASIL Insight* October 25, 2005

Cerone, J., Out of bounds? Considering the reach of international human rights law, Working Paper 5 of the NYU Center for Human Rights and Global Justice, 2006

Charney, J.I. (1999a), *Is International Law threatened by Multiple International Tribunals?*, 271 *Recueil des Cours, Collected courses of the Hague Academy of International Law 1998*, Martinus Nijhoff Publishers, The Hague [etc.] 1999

Charney, J.I. (1999b), 'The Impact on the International Legal System of the Growth of International Courts and Tribunals', 31(4) *New York University Journal of International Law and Politics* 697 (1999), pp. 697-708

Charney, J.I., 'The "Horizontal" Growth of International Courts and Tribunals: Challenges or Opportunities?', 96 *American Society of International Law* 369 (2002), pp. 369-380

Cheng, B., *General Principles of Law as applied by International Courts and Tribunals*, Grotius Publications Limited, Cambridge 1987 (reprint from 1953)

Chenwi, L., *Towards the Abolition of the Death Penalty in Africa, A Human Rights Perspective*, Pretoria University Law Press 2007, <http://www.pulp.up.ac.za/pdf/2007_02/2007_02.pdf>

Clark, T., 'Mainstreaming Refugees Rights. The 1951 Refugee Convention and International Human Rights Law', 17(4) *Netherlands Quarterly of Human Rights* 389 (1999), pp. 389-410

Clements, L.J., N. Mole, A. Simmons, *European Human Rights Taking a Case under the Convention*, Sweet & Maxwell, London 1999

Cohen-Jonathan, G., 'De l'effet juridique des "mesures provisoires" dans certaines circonstances et de l'efficacité du droit de recours individuel: à propos de l'arrêt de la cour de Strasbourg Cruz Varas du 20 Mars 1991', *Revue Universelle des Droits de l'homme* 205 (1991), pp. 205-209

Cohen-Jonathan, G., 'Les rapports entre la Convention européenne des Droits de l'Homme et les autres traités conclus par les Etats Parties', in: R. Lawson, M. de Blois (eds.), *The Dynamics of the Protection of Human Rights in Europe; Essays in Honour of Henry G. Schermers (Vol. 3)*, Martinus Nijhoff Publishers, Dordrecht [etc.] 1994, pp. 79-111

Cohen-Jonathan, G., 'Cour Européenne des Droits de L'Homme et Droit International Général (1998-1999)', XLV *Annuaire Français de Droit International* 767 (1999), pp. 767-789

Cohen-Jonathan, G. (2005a), 'Sur la force obligatoire des mesures provisoires, l'arrêt de la Grande Chambre du 4 février 2005, Mamatkulov et Askarov contre Turquie', 2 *RGDIP* 421 (2005), pp. 421-434

Cohen-Jonathan, G. (2005b), 'Conclusions générales', in: G. Cohen-Jonathan, J.-F. Flauss (eds.), *Mesures conservatoires et droits fondamentaux*, Bruyant, Bruxelles 2005, pp. 283-307

Cohen-Jonathan, G. (2005c), 'À propos des arrêts Assanidzé (8 avril 2004), Ilascu (8 juillet 2004) et Issa (16 novembre 2004). Quelques observations sur les notions de 'juridiction' et 'd'injonction'', 63 *Revue Trim. Dr. H.* 767 (2005), pp. 767-785

Cohen-Jonathan, G., J.-F. Flauss (eds.) (2005d), *Mesures conservatoires et droits fondamentaux*, Bruyant, Bruxelles 2005

Collins, L., *Provisional and Protective Measures in International Litigation*, 234(III) *Recueil des Cours, Academy of International Law 9 (1992)*, Martinus Nijhoff Publishers, Dordrecht [etc.] 1993

Conforti, B., 'Unité et fragmentation du droit international: Glissez mortels, n'appuyez pas', 1 *RGDIP* 6 (2007), pp. 6-18

Conte, A., S. Davidson, R. Burchill, *Defining Civil and Political Rights: the Jurisprudence of the United Nations Human Rights Committee*, Ashgate, Aldershot 2004

Coomans, F., 'The *Ogoni* Case before the African Commission on Human and Peoples' Rights', 52 *ICLQ* 749 (2003), pp. 749-760

Coomans, F., M. Kamminga (eds.), *Extraterritorial Application of Human Rights Treaties*, Intersentia, Antwerp/Oxford 2004

Crawford, J., 'The Right of Self-Determination in International Law: Its Develoment and Future', in: Ph. Alston (ed.), *Peoples' Rights*, Academy of European Law, European University Institute, Oxford University Press, Oxford [etc.] 2001, pp. 7-67

Crockett, C.H., 'The Effects of Interim Measures of Protection in the International Court of Justice', 7 *Calif. West Int.'l L.J.* 348 (1977), pp. 348-384

D

Davidson, J.S., *The Inter-American Human Rights System*, Darthmouth Publishing Company, Aldershot 1997

De Feyter, K., *World Development Law, Sharing Responsibility for Development*, Intersentia Antwerp/Groningen/Oxford 2001

De Feyter, K., S. Parmentier, M. Bossuyt, P. Lemmens (eds.), *Out of the Ashes, Reparation for Victims of Gross and Systematic Human Rights Violations*, Intersentia, Antwerpen/Oxford 2005

De Salvia, M., 'La pratique de la cour européenne des droits de l'homme relative aux mesures provisoires', in: G. Cohen-Jonathan, J.-F. Flauss (eds.), *Mesures conservatoires et droits fondamentaux*, Bruyant, Bruxelles 2005, pp. 177-194

De Salvia, M., E. Villiger (eds.), *The Birth of European Human Rights Law, Liber amicorum, Studies in Honour of Carl Aage Nørgaard*, Nomos, Baden-Baden 1998

De Schutter, O., 'Les mesures provisoires devant la Cour de justice des communautés européennes dans le domaine des droits fondamentaux', in: G. Cohen-Jonathan, J.-F. Flauss (eds.), *Mesures conservatoires et droits fondamentaux*, Bruyant, Bruxelles 2005, pp. 93-130

De Wet, E., 'The Protection Mechanism under the African Charter and the Protocol on the African Court of Human and Peoples' Rights' in: G. Alfredsson, J. Grimheden, B.G. Ramcharan, A. de Zayas (eds.), *International Human Rights Monitoring Mechanisms: Essays in Honour of Jakob Th. Möller*, Martinus Nijhoff Publishers The Hague [etc.] 2001, pp. 713-729

Decaux, E., 'Les mesures d'urgence devant la Commision des droits de l'homme des nations unies et ses organses subsidiaires', in: G. Cohen-Jonathan, J.-F. Flauss (eds.), *Mesures conservatoires et droits fondamentaux*, Bruyant, Bruxelles 2005, pp. 241-275

Denbeaux, M., J. Denbeaux, 'The Guantanamo Detainees: the Government's Story', Report on Guantanamo detainees, a profile of 517 detainees through analysis of department of defence data, 2 August 2006, <http://law.shu.edu/news/guantanamo_report_final_2_08_06.pdf#search =%22Denbeaux%20Guantanamo%22>

Devine, D.J., 'Provisional Measures ordered by the International Tribunal for the Law of the Sea in the Area of Pollution, the Mox Plant Case (Ireland v. United Kingdom) ITLOS Case No. 10, 3 December 2001', 28 *SAYIL* 263 (2003), pp. 263-275

De Zayas, A., 'The Examination of Individual Complaints by the United Nations Human Rights Committee under the Optional Protocol to the International Covenant on Civil and Political Rights,' in: G. Alfredsson et al. (eds.), *International Human Rights Monitoring Mechanisms*, Martinus Nijhoff Publishers, The Hague [etc.] 2001, pp. 67-121

Doerfel, J., 'The Convention against Torture and the Protection of Refugees', 24(2) *Refugee Survey Quarterly* 83 (2005), pp. 83-97

Dommen, C., 'Claiming environmental rights: some possibilities offered by the United Nation's human rights mechanisms', 11(1) *Georgetown International Environmental Law Review* 1 (1998), pp. 1-48

Donders, Y.M., *Towards a Right to Cultural Identity?*, Intersentia, Antwerp/Oxford/New York 2002

Douma, W., *The Precautionary Principle, its Application in International, European and Dutch Law*, Diss. Groningen 2003, T.M.C. Asser Press, The Hague 2004

Dugard, J., 'The Future of International Law; a Human Rights Perspective – with some Comments on the Leiden School of International Law', 20 *LJIL* 729 (2007), pp. 729-739

Dulitzky, A., 'La aplicación de los tratados sobre los derechos humanos por los tribunals locales: un estudio comparado', in: M. Abregú, C. Courtis (eds.), *La aplicación de los tratados sobre los derechos humanos por los tribunals locales*, CELS Centro de Estudios Legales y Sociales, Buenos Aires 1997, pp. 33-74

Dulitzky, A., 'La Duración del procedimiento: responsabilidades compartidas', in: J.E. Mendez, F. Cox (eds.), *El Futura del Sistema Interamericano de Protección de Los Derechos Humanos*, Instituto Interamericano de Derechos Humanos (IIDH), San José, Costa Rica 1998, pp. 363-390

Dumbauld, E., *Interim Measures of Protection in International Controversies*, Nijhoff, The Hague 1932

Dumbauld, E., 'Relief *pendente lite* in the Permanent Court of International Justice', 39 *AJIL* 391 (1945), pp. 391-405

Dupuy, P.M., *L'unité de l'ordre juridique international*, 297 *RCADI Recueil des Cours*, Collected courses of the Hague Academy of International Law 2002

Dupuy, P.M., 'Crime sans châtiment ou mission accomplie?', 111(2) *RGDIP* 243 (2007), pp. 243-258

Duxbury, A., 'Saving Lives in the International Court of Justice: the Use of Provisional Measures to Protect Human Rights', 31 *California Western International Law Journal* 141 (2000), pp. 141-176

E

Eissen, M.A., 'Les mesures provisoires dans la Convention européenne des droits de l'homme', 2 *Human Rights Journal* 252 (1969), pp. 252-256

Elkind, J.B., *Interim Protection, a Functional Approach*, Nijhoff, The Hague [etc.] 1981

Ergec, R., J. Velu, *La Convention Européenne des Droits de L'Homme; extrait du Répertoire pratique du droit belge Complément, tome VII*, Bruylant, Bruxelles 1990

Escher, A., 'Release of vessels and crews before the International Tribunal for the Law of the Sea', 3 *The Law and Practice of International Courts and Tribunals* 411 (2004), pp. 411-507

Evans, M., R. Murray (eds.), *The African Charter on Human and Peoples' Rights, the System in Practice: 1986-2000*, Cambridge University Press, Cambridge 2002

Evatt, E., 'Individual Communications under the Optional Protocol to the International Covenant on Civil and Political Rights', in: S. Pritchard (ed.), *Indigenous Peoples, the United Nations and Human Rights*, Zed Books Ltd. (London), the Federation Press (Annandale/Leichardt, Australia) 1998, pp. 86-115

F

Farer, T., 'The Future of the Inter-American Commission on Human Rights: Promotion versus exposure', in: J.E. Mendez, F. Cox (eds.), *El Futuro del Sistema Interamericano de Protección de los Derechos Humanos*, Instituto Interamericano de Derechos Humanos, San José 1998, pp. 515-536

Faúndez Ledesma, H., 'La Independencia e Imparcialidad de los Miembros de la Comisión y de la Corte: Paradojas y desafíos', in: J.E. Mendez, F. Cox (eds.), *El Futura del Sistema Interamericano de Protección de Los Derechos Humanos*, Instituto Interamericano de Derechos Humanos (IIDH), San José, Costa Rica 1998, pp. 185-210

Faúndez Ledesma, H., *El sistema interamericano de protección de los derechos humanos: aspectos institucionales y procesales*, Instituto Interamericano de Derechos Humanos (IIDH), San José, Costa Rica 1999 (2nd ed.)

Faure, M.G., E.I.L. Vos, *Juridische afbakening van het voorzorgsbeginsel: mogelijkheden en grenzen,* Zoetermeer, Gezondheidsraad 2003

Feria Tinta, M., 'Individual Human Rights v. State Sovereignty: the Case of Peru's Withdrawal from the Contentious Jurisdiction of the Inter-American Court of Human Rights, Current Legal Developments', 13 *Leiden Journal of International Law* 985 (2000), pp. 985-996

Feria Tinta, M., 'Due Process and the Right to Life in the Context of the Vienna Convention on Consular Relations: Arguing the LaGrand Case', 12(2) *European Journal of International Law* 363 (2001), pp. 363-366

Fitzpatrick, J., 'The Unreality of International Law in the United States and the LaGrand Case', 27 *Yale Journal of International Law* 427 (2002), pp. 427-433

Fix-Zamudio, H., 'La Protección Judicial de los Derechos Humanos en Latinoamérica y en el Sistema Interamericano', 8 *Revista IIDH* 8 (1989), pp. 8-64

Fix-Zamudio, H., 'El derecho Internacional de los derechos Humanos en law Constituciones Latinoamericanas y en la Corte Interamericana de Derechos Humanos', in: P. Nikken (ed.), *The Modern World of Human Rights: Essays in Honour of Thomas Buergenthal*, IIDH/IIHR, San José, Costa Rica 1996, pp. 19-32

Fix-Zamudio, H., 'The European and the Inter-American Courts of Human Rights: a Brief Comparison', in: P. Mahony, F. Matscher, H. Petzold, L. Wildhaber (eds.), *Protecting Human Rights: The European Perspective, Studies in memory of Rolv Ryssdal*, Carl Heymanns Verlag KG, Köln 2000, pp. 507-533

Flauss, J.-F. (2005a), 'Notule sur les mesures provisoires devant la Commission africaine des droits de l'homme et des peuples,' in: G. Cohen-Jonathan, J.-F. Flauss (eds.), *Mesures conservatoires et droits fondamentaux*, Bruyant, Bruxelles 2005, pp. 231-239

Flauss, J.-F. (2005b), 'Discussion', in: G. Cohen-Jonathan, J.-F. Flauss (eds.), *Mesures conservatoires et droits fondamentaux*, Bruyant, Bruxelles 2005, pp. 195-214

Flinterman, C., *Soevereiniteit en de rechten van de mens*, Inaugurale rede Universiteit Utrecht, 19 januari 2000 Utrecht: Studie- en Informatiecentrum Mensenrechten (SIM) 2000

Flinterman, C., 'United Nations Human Rights Reform: Some Reflections of a CEDAW-member' (Column), 21(4) *Netherlands Quarterly of Human Rights* 621 (2003), pp. 621-624

Flinterman, C., E. Ankumah, 'The African Charter on Human and Peoples' Rights', in: H. Hannum (ed.), *Guide to International Human Rights Practice*, Transnational Publishers, Ardsley, New York 2004 (4th), pp. 171-188

Fitzmaurice, G., *The Law and Procedure of the International Court of Justice, Vol 2*, Grotius, Cambridge 1986

Forder, C., 'Positieve verplichtingen in het kader van het Europees Verdrag tot Bescherming van de Rechten van de Mens en Fundamentele Vrijheden', 17(6) *NJCM-Bulletin* 611 (1992), pp. 611-637

Forder, C., J. Wittingham, Case note on Evans v. UK, 7 March 2006, *NJCM* 863 (2006), pp. 863-880

Forster, M.J.C., 'The *Mox Plant* Cases – Provisional Measures in the International Tribunal for the Law of the Sea', 16 *Leiden Journal of International Law* 611 (2003). pp. 611-619

Freestone, D., E. Hey (eds.), *The Precautionary Principle in International Law. The Challenge of Interpretation* (International Environmental Law and Policy Series, Vol. 31), Kluwer Law International, The Hague/London/Boston 1996

Froidevaux, S., 'L'humanitaire, le religieux et la mort', 848 *International Review of the Red Cross* (special issue on the missing) 785 (2002), pp. 785-801

G

Gaeta, P. (2007a), 'Genocide d'état et responsabilité pénale individuelle', 2 *RGDIP* 273 (2007), pp. 273-283

Gaeta, P. (2007b), 'On what Conditions can a State be held Responsible for Genocide?', 18(4) *EJIL* 631 (2007), pp. 631-684

Gaffikin, B., 'The International Court of Justice and the Crisis in the Balkans Case Concerning Application of the Convention on the Prevention and Punishment of the Crime of Genocide (Bosnia and Herzegovina v. Yugoslavia)', 17 *Sydney Law Review* 458 (1995), pp. 458-472

Garry, H.R., 'When Procedure involves Matters of Life and Death: Interim Measures and the European Convention on Human Rights', 7(3) *European Public Law* 399 (2001), pp. 399-432

Gathii, J. Thuo, 'Case Concerning Armed Activities on the Territory of the Congo (Democratic Republic of the Congo v. Uganda)' 101 *American Journal of International Law* 142 (2007), pp. 142-149

Gattini, A., 'Breach of the Obligation to Prevent and Reparation thereof in the ICJ's Genocide Judgment', 18(4) *EJIL* 695 (2007), pp. 695-713

Gelmamez, M.S., 'Constitution, Ombudsperson and Human Rights Chamber in 'Bosnia and Herzegovina'', 17(3) *Netherlands Quarterly of Human Rights* 277 (1999), pp. 277-329

Ghandhi, P.R., *The Human Rights Committee and the Right of Individual Communication: Law and Practice*, Ashgate, Aldershot/Brookfield (USA)/Singapore/Sydney 1998

Ghandhi, S., 'Avena and other Mexican Nationals', 53 *International & Comparative Law Quarterly* 738 (2004), pp. 738-746

Giardina, A., 'Provisional Measures in Europe: Some Comparative Observations', 4 *Diritto del commercio internazionale: pratica internazionale e diritto interno* 791 (1993), pp. 791-802

Gill, T., E. van Sliedregt, 'Guantánamo Bay: a Reflection on the Legal Status and Rights of "Unlawful Enemy Combatants"', 1 *Utrecht Law Review* 28 (2005), pp. 28-54

Gilman, D., 'Confidentiality in the Proceedings as a Topic in the Discussion of Reform', in: J.E. Mendez, F. Cox (eds.), *El Futuro del Sistema Interamericano de Protección de Los Derechos Humanos*, IIDH, San José, Costa Rica 1998, pp. 261-290

Goldie, L.F.E., 'The Nuclear Test Cases: Restraints on Environmental Harm', 5 *Journal of Maritime Law & Commerce* 491 (1973-74), pp. 491-505

Goldman R.K., 'International Human Rights and Humanitarian Law and the Internally Displaced', in: P. Nikken (ed.), *The Modern World of Human Rights: Essays in Honour of Thomas Buergenthal*, IIDH/IIHR, San José, Costa Rica 1996, pp. 517-548

Goldman, R.K., B.D. Tittemore, *Unprivileged Combatants and the Hostilities in Afghanistan: Their Status and Rights under International Humanitarian and Human Rights Law*, American Society of International Law Task Force Paper, Washington 2002

Goldstone, R.J., R.J. Hamilton, "*Bosnia v. Serbia*: Lessons from the Encounter of the International Court of Justice with the International Criminal Tribunal for the Former Yugoslavia', 21 *Leiden Journal of International Law* 95 (2008), pp. 95-112

Gómez, V. (1998a), 'Seguridad Jurídica e Igualdad Procesal ante los Órganos', in: J.E. Mendez, F. Cox (eds.), *El Futura del Sistema Interamericano de Protección de Los Derechos Humanos*, Instituto Interamericano de Derechos Humanos, San José 1998, pp. 213-240

Gómez, V. (1998b), 'The Interaction between the Political Actors of the OAS, the Commission and the Court', in: D.J. Harris, S. Livingstone (eds.), *The Inter-American System of Human Rights*, Clarendon Press, Oxford 1998, pp. 173-197

Gómez, V., 'Inter-American Commission on Human Rights and the Inter-American Court of Human Rights: New Rules and Recent Cases', 1(1) *Human Rights Law Review* 111 (2001), pp. 111-126

Gomien, D., 'Human Rights in Bosnia and Herzegovina: European Practice, Fraught Federalism and the Future', in: W. Benedek (ed.), *Human Rights in Bosnia and Herzegovina after Day-*

ton: from Theory to Practice, Human Rights Centre of the University of Sarajevo, Martinus Nijhoff Publishers, The Hague [etc.] 1999, pp. 107-120

Gomien, D., 'The Human Rights Ombudsperson for Bosnia and Herzegovina', in: G. Alfredsson, J. Grimheden, B.G. Ramcharan, A. de Zayas (eds.), *International Human Rights Monitoring Mechanisms: Essays in Honour of Jakob Th. Möller*, Martinus Nijhoff Publishers The Hague [etc.] 2001, pp. 763-770

Gomien, D., D. Harris, L. Zwaak, *Law and Practice of the European Convention on Human Rights and the European Social Charter*, Council of Europe Publishing, Strasbourg 1996

Gondek, M., 'Extraterritorial Application of the European Convention on Human Rights. Territorial Focus in the Age of Globalization?', 52 *Netherlands International Law Review* 349 (2005), pp. 349-387

González Espinoza, O.I., *La protección internacional del ser humano y las medidas provisionales dictadas en el marco de la Convención Americana sobre Derechos Humanos, con énfasis en la práctica de la Corte Interamericana de Derechos Humanos*, Tesis Universidad de Costa Rica, Facultad de Derecho, May 2002

Goodman, R, 'Human Rights Treaties, Invalid Reservations and State Consent', 96(3) *American Journal of International Law* 531 (2002), pp. 531-560

Goodwin-Gill, G.S., J. MacAdam, *The Refugee in International Law*, Oxford University Press, Oxford 2007 (3rd)

Gorlick, B., 'The Convention and the Committee against Torture; a Complementary Protection Regime for Refugees', 11(3) *International Journal of Refugee Law* 479 (1999), pp. 479-495

Gorlick, B., 'Human Rights and Refugees: Enhancing Protection through International Human Rights Law', 69(2) *Nordic Journal of International Law* 117 (2000), pp. 117-177

Goy, R., 'La Cour Permanente de Justice Internationale et les Droits de l'Homme', in: V. Berger et al. (eds.), *Liber Amicorum Marc-André Eissen*, Bruylant, Brussels 1995, pp. 199-232

Gray, C., *Judicial Remedies in International Law*, Clarendon Press, Oxford 1987

Gray, C., 'Application of the Convention on the Prevention and Punishment of the Crime of Genocide (*Bosnia and Herzegovina* v. *Yugoslavia* (*Serbia and Montenegro*)), Orders of Provisional Measures of 8 April 1993 and 13 September 1993', 43 *International and Comparative Law Quarterly* 704 (1994), pp. 704-714

Gray, C., 'The Use and Abuse of the International Court of Justice: Cases concerning the Use of Force after Nicaragua', 14(5) *EJIL* 867 (2003), pp. 867-905

Gross, L., 'Some Observations on Provisional Measures', in: Y. Dinstein, M. Tabory (eds.), *International Law at a Time of Perplexity, Essays in Honour of Shabtai Rosenne*, Nijhoff, Dordrecht 1989, pp. 308-324

Gros Espiell, H., 'Opiniones Disidentes y separadas en la Corte Interamericana de derechos Humanos', 4 *Revista Uruguaya de derecho procesal* 456 (1988), pp. 456-466

Grossman, C., 'Disappearances in Honduras: The Need for Direct Victim Representation in Human Rights Litigation', 15 *Hastings Int'l & Comp. L. Rev* 363 (1992), pp. 363-389

Grünfeld, F., *Vroegtijdig optreden van omstanders ter voorkoming van oorlogen en schendingen van de rechten van de mens*, Inaugural speech Utrecht University, 2003, available online at <http://arno.unimaas.nl/show.cgi?fid=3830>

Grünfeld, F., 'The Role of Bystanders in Human Rights Violations', in: F. Coomans et al. (eds.), *Rendering Justice to the Vulnerable: Liber Amicorum in Honour of Theo van Boven*, Kluwer Law International, The Hague/London/Boston 2000, pp. 131-143

Grünfeld, F., A. Huijboom, *The Failure to Prevent Genocide in Rwanda: the Role of Bystanders*, Martinus Nijhoff Publishers, Leiden 2007

Gubbay, A.R., 'The Protection and Enforcement of Fundamental Human Rights: The Zimbabwean Experience', 19 *Human Rights Quarterly* 227 (1997), pp. 227-254

Guggenheim, P., *Les Mesures Provisoires de Procédure Internationale et leur Influence sur le Développement du Droit des Gens*, Recueil Sirey, Paris 1931

Guggenheim, P., *Les Mesures Conservatoires Dans la Procédure Arbitrale et Judiciaire*, 40 *Recueil des Cours,* Recueil Sirey, Paris 1933

Gumedze, S., 'Bringing Communications before the African Commission on Human and Peoples' Rights', 3(1) *African Human Rights Law Journal* 118 (2003), pp. 118-148

H

Haeck, Y., C. Burbano Herrera, 'Provisional Measures in the Case Law of the European Court of Human Rights', 4 *NQHR* 625 (2003), pp. 625-676

Haeck, Y., C. Burbano Herrera, L. Zwaak, 'Strasbourg Takes Away any Remaining Doubts and Broadens its Pan-European Protection: Non-Compliance with a Provisional Measure Automatically Leads to a Violation of the Right of Individual Application... or Doesn't it?', 1 *European Constitutional Law Review* 41 (2008), pp. 41-63

Hafner, G., 'Risks Ensuing from Fragmentation of International Law', UN Doc. ILC (LII)/WG/LT/L.1/Add.1, at 24 (2000) (included as annex to UN Doc. A/55/10 (2000)

Haller, G., 'The Human Rights Regime in Bosnia and Herzegovina in the European Context', in: W. Benedek (ed.), *Human Rights in Bosnia and Herzegovina after Dayton: from Theory to Practice*, Human Rights Centre of the University of Sarajevo, Martinus Nijhoff Publishers, The Hague [etc.] 1999, pp. 25-32

Hallo de Wolf, A., 'Defending the Defenders: hoe beschermt het internationaal recht mensenrechten NGO's', 27(5) *NJCM-Bulletin* 531 (2002), pp. 531-546

Hamalengwa, M., C. Flinterman, E.V.O. Dankwa (eds.), *The International Law of Human Rights in Africa: Basic Documents and Annotated Bibliography*, Nijhoff, Dordrecht/Boston 1988

Hannum, H., 'The Protection of Indigenous Rights in the Inter-American System', in: D.J. Harris, S. Livingstone (eds.), *The Inter-American System of Human Rights*, Clarendon Press, Oxford 1998, pp. 323-344

Hannum, H. (ed.), *Guide to International Human Rights Practice*, Transnational Publishers, Ardsley, New York 2004 (4th)

Hannum, H., R.B. Lillich, *International Human Rights: Problems of Law, Policy, and Practice*, Aspen Publishers, Boulder (Co) 1995 (3rd)

Harrington, J. (Joanna), 'Punting Terrorists, Assassins and other Undesirables: Canada, the Human Rights Committee and Requests for Interim Measures of Protection', 48 *McGill L.J.* 55 (2003), pp. 55-87

Harrington, J. (Joanna), 'The Absent Dialogue: Extradition and the International Covenant on Civil and Political Rights', 32 *Queen's Law Journal* 82 (2006), pp. 82-134

Harrington, J. (Julia), 'Protecting Human Rights in Africa: Strategies and Roles of Non-Governmental Organizations by Claude Welch (book review)', 9 *Harvard Human Rights Journal* 333 (1996), pp. 333-338.

Harrington, J. (Julia), 'Special Rapporteurs of the African Commission on Human and Peoples' Rights', 1(2) *African Human Rights Law Journal* 247 (2001), pp. 247-267

Harrington, J. (Julia), 'The African Court on Human and Peoples' Rights', in: M. Evans, R. Murray (eds.), *The African Charter on Human and Peoples' Rights, the System in Practice: 1986-2000*, Cambridge University Press, Cambridge 2002, pp. 305-334

Harris, D., M. O'Boyle, C. Warbrick, *Law of the European Convention on Human Rights*, Butterworths, London 1995

Harris, D., S. Livingstone (eds.), *The Inter-American System of Human Rights*, Clarendon Press, Oxford 1998

Hathcock, J.N., 'The Precautionary Principle – An Impossible Burden of Proof', 3(4) *AgBioForum* 255 (2000), pp. 255-258, <www.agbioforum.org>

Helfer, L.R., A.-M. Slaughter, 'Why States Create International Tribunals: A Response to Professors Posner and Yoo', 93 *California Law Review* 1 (2005), pp. 1-58

Helfer, L.R., A.-M. Slaughter, 'Towards a Theory of Effective Supranational Adjudication', 107 *Yale Law Journal* 273 (1997), pp. 273-391

Helfer, L.R., 'Forum Shopping for Human Rights', 148(2) *University of Pennsylvania Law Review* 285 (1999), pp. 285-379

Henckaerts, J.M., *Mass Expulsion in Modern International Law and Practice*, Martinus Nijhoff Publishers, The Hague 1995

Henrard, K., *Devising an Adequate System of Minority Protection: Individual Human Rights, Minority Rights and the Right to Self-determination*, Nijhoff, The Hague 2000

Herdegen, M., *Völkerrecht*, Beck, München 2004 (3rd)

Hey, E., *Teaching International Law: State-Consent as Consent to a Process of Normative Development and Ensuing Problems*, Kluwer Law International, The Hague 2003

Heyns, C. (ed.), *Human Rights Law in Africa (Vol. 2)*, Martinus Nijhoff, Leyden 2004

Heyns, C. (ed.), *Compendium of Key Human Rights Documents of the African Union*, Pretoria University Law Press, Pretoria 2005

Heyns, C., M. Killander, 'The African Regional Human Rights System', in: F. Gómez Isa, K. De Feyter (eds.), *International Protection of Human Rights: Achievements and Challenges*, University of Deusto, Bilboa 2006, pp. 509-543

Heyns, C., F. Viljoen, 'Current Developments: An overview of International Human Rights Protection in Africa', 15 *SAJHR* 421 (1999), pp. 421-445

Heyns, C., F. Viljoen, 'The Regional Protection of Human Rights in Africa: An Overview and Evaluation', in: P.T. Zeleza, P.J. McConnaughay (eds.), *Human Rights, the Rule of Law, and Development in Africa*, University of Pennsylvania Press, Philadelphia 2004, pp. 129-143

Hicks, P., 'The Human Rights Role of the Office of the High Representative and Other Implementing Organizations', in: W. Benedek (ed.), *Human Rights in Bosnia and Herzegovina after Dayton: from Theory to Practice*, Human Rights Centre of the University of Sarajevo, Martinus Nijhoff Publishers, The Hague [etc.] 1999, pp. 127-148

Higgins, R., *Problems and Process, International Law and how to use it*, Clarendon Press, Oxford 1994

Higgins, R., 'Interim Measures for the Protection of Human Rights', 36 *Columbia Journal of Transnational Law* 91 (1997), pp. 91-108

Higgins, R., 'The International Court of Justice and Human Rights', in: K. Wellens (ed.), *International Law: Theory and Practice, Essays in Honour of Eric Suy*, Kluwer Law International/Martinus Nijhoff Publishers, The Hague/Boston/London 1998, pp. 691-705

Higgins, R., 'The ICJ, the ECJ, and the Integrity of International Law', 52 *International and Comparative Law Quarterly* 1 (2003) pp. 1-20

Higgins, R., 'Human Rights in the International Court of Justice', 20 *LJIL* 745 (2007), pp. 745-751

Highet, K., 'U.S. Withdrawal from Proceedings Initiated by Nicaragua', 79 *The American Journal of International Law* 438 (1985), pp. 438-441

Highet, K., 'Evidence and Proof of Fact', in: L. Fisler Damrosch (ed.), *The International Court of Justice at a Crossroads*, Transnational Publishers/Dobbs Ferry, New York 1987, pp. 355-375

Highet, K., 'Evidence, the Chamber and the ELSI Case', in: R.B. Lillich (ed.), *Fact-finding before International Tribunals*, Transnational Publishers, Inc., Ardsley-on-Hudson, New York 1992, pp. 65-68

Hirsch Ballin, E.M.H., 'De VS en het internationale recht: onthouden van consulaire bijstand aan ter dood veroordeelde Duitsers', 50(10) *Ars Aequi* 807 (2001), pp. 807-819

Hood, R., *The Death Penalty, a Worldwide Perspective*, Oxford University Press, Oxford 2002

Horn, F., *Reservations and Interpretative Declarations to Multilateral Treaties*, North-Holland, Amsterdam 1988

Huff, A., 'Resource Development and Human Rights: A Look at the Case of the Lubicon Cree Indian Nation of Canada', 10 *Colo. J. Int' l Environmental Law & Policy* 161 (1999), pp. 161-194

Human Rights First, 'Getting to Ground Truth, Investigating US Abuses in the "War on Terrror"', September 2004, <www.HumanRightsFirst.org>

Human Rights Watch, 'Empty Promises: Diplomatic Assurances no Safeguard against Torture', Vol. 16, No. 4 (D), April 2004

Human Rights Watch, *The United States' Disappeared; the CIA's long-term ghost detainees,* a Human Rights Watch briefing paper, October 2004

Human Rights Watch, 'Still at Risk: Diplomatic Assurances no Safeguard against Torture', Vol. 17, No. 4 (D), April 2005

I

ILA, 'Interim Report of the Committee on International Human Rights Law and Practice of the International Law Association (ILA), on the Impact of Findings of the United Nations Human Rights Treaty Bodies on National Courts and Tribunals, at the New Delhi Conference (2002)', 70 *International Law Association' Rep. Conf.* 508, April 2-6 (2002), pp. 507-555

ILA, 'Final Report of the Committee on International Human Rights Law and Practice of the International Law Association (ILA) on the Impact of Findings of the United Nations Human Rights Treaty Bodies, at the Berlin Conference (2004)', 71 *International Law Association' Rep. Conf.* 621 August 16-21 2004, pp. 621-702

Ingelse, C., *The UN Committee against Torture: An Assessment*, Kluwer Law International, The Hague 2001

Iwamoto, Y., 'The Protection of Human Life through Provisional Measures indicated by the International Court of Justice', 15 *Leiden Journal of International Law* 345 (2002), pp. 345-366

J

Jacobs, F.G., 'Interim Measures in the Law and Practice of the Court of Justice of the European Communities', in: R. Bernhardt (ed.), *Interim Measures Indicated by International Courts*, Springer Verlag, Berlin/Heidelberg/New York 1994, pp. 37-68

Jayawickrama, N., *The Judicial Application of Human Rights Law, National, Regional and International Jurisprudence*, Cambridge University Press, Cambridge 2002

Jennings, R., 'The LaGrand Case', 1 *The Law and Practice of International Courts and Tribunals*, 13 (2002) pp. 13-54

Joseph, S., 'Rendering Terrorists and the Convention against Torture', 5 *Hum.Rts.L. Rev.* 339 (2005), pp. 339-446

Joseph, S., J. Schultz, M. Castan, *The International Covenant on Civil and Political Rights, Cases, Materials and Commentary*, Oxford University Press, Oxford 2004 (2nd)

K

Kammerhofer, J., 'The Binding Nature of Provisional Measures of the International Court of Justice: the 'Settlement' of the Issue in the *LaGrand* Case', 16(1) *Leiden Journal of International Law* 67 (2003), pp. 67-83

Kamminga, M.T., *Inter-State Accountability for Violations of Human Rights*, University of Pennsylvania Press, Philadelphia 1992

Kamminga, M.T., 'The Precautionary Approach in International Human Rights Law: How It can Benefit the Environment', in: E. Hey, D.A.C. Freestone (eds.), *The Precautionary Principle and International Law,* Kluwer Law International, The Hague 1996, pp. 171-186

Kamminga, M.T., *De humanisering van het volkenrecht*, Inaugurele rede, Universiteit Maastricht, 2001

Kamminga, M.T., 'The Evolving Status of NGOs under International Law: a Threat to the Inter-State System?', in: G.P.H.. Kreijen et al. (eds.), *State, Sovereignty, and International Governance*, Oxford University Press, Oxford 2002, pp. 387-406

Kamminga, M.T., 'Humanisation of International Law', in: I. Boerfijn, J. Goldschmidt (eds.), *Changing Perceptions of Sovereignty and Human rights: Essays in Honour of Cees Flinterman*, Intersentia, Antwerp 2008, pp. 29-40

Kamminga, M.T., *Final Report on the Impact of International Human Rights Law on General International Law, presented on behalf of the Committee of Human Rights Law and Practice of the International Law Association (ILA)*, July 2008, made available on SSRN: <http://ssrn.com/abstract=1150664> (consulted 5 August 2008)

Kälin, W., 'Human Rights and Statehood', in: W. Benedek (ed.), *Human Rights in Bosnia and Herzegovina after Dayton: from Theory to Practice*, Human Rights Centre of the University of Sarajevo, Martinus Nijhoff Publishers, The Hague [etc.] 1999, pp. 59-66

Kazazi, M., *Burden of Proof and Related Issues, A Study on Evidence before International Tribunals*, Kluwer Law International, The Hague/London/Boston 1996

Kempees, P., N. Mol, A. van Steijn, 'Voorlopige maatregelen bij het Europees Hof voor de Rechten van de Mens', in 5 *NAV* 299 (2004), pp. 299-300

Kingsbury, B., 'Reconciling Five Competing Conceptual Structures of Indigenous Peoples' Claims in International and Comparative Law', 34 *N.Y.U. J. Int'l L. & Pol.* 189 (2001), pp. 189-250

Kirgis, F.L., 'The Supreme Court decides a Consular Convention case', 10(16) *ASIL Insight* 7 July 2006

Klabbers, J., 'Executing Mr Breard', 67(3) *Nordic Journal of International Law* 357 (1998), pp. 357-364

Klabbers, J., 'Accepting the Unacceptable? A New Approach to Reservations to Multilateral Treaties', 69 *Nordic Journal of International Law* 179 (2000), pp. 179-193

Klein, E., 'Individual Reparation Claims under the International Covenant on Civil and Political Rights: The Practice of the Human Rights Committee', in: A. Randelzhofer, C. Tomuschat (eds.), *State Responsibility and the Individual: Reparation in Instances of Grave Violations of Human Rights*, Kluwer Law International 1999, pp. 27-41

Klerk, Y., 'The Character of the Views of the Human Rights Committee', in: F. Coomans et al. (eds.), *Rendering Justice to the Vulnerable*, Kluwer Law International, The Hague/London/Boston 2000, pp. 149-159

Klerk, Y.S., *Het ECRM-Toezichtmechanisme; verleden, heden, toekomst*, dissertation, Ars Aequi Libri, Nijmegen 1995

Knoops, G.G.J., 'Het House of Lords "Torture" arrest en de gevolgen voor counter-terrorism door overheden: van "geheime vluchten", CIA tot Guantanamo Bay', 55 *Ars Aequi* 116 (2006) pp, 116-122

Koh, H. Hongju, 'Refugees, The Courts, and the New World Order', *Utah Law Review* 999 (1994a), pp. 999-1025

Koh, H. Hongju, 'America's Offshore Refugee Camps', 29 *University of Richmond Law Review* 139 (1994b), pp. 139-173

Koh, H. Hongju, 'Why do Nations Obey International Law?', 106 *The Yale Law Journal* 2599 (1997), pp. 2599-2659

Kokott, J., *The Burden of Proof in Comparative and International Human Rights Law, Civil and Common Law Approaches with Special Reference to the American and German Legal Systems*, Kluwer Law International, The Hague/London/Boston 1998

Koskenniemi, M., P. Leino, 'Fragmentation of International Law? Postmodern Anxieties', 15(3) *Leiden Journal of International Law* 553 (2002), pp. 553-580

Krisch, N., 'The Establishment of an African Court on Human and Peoples' Rights', 58(3) *ZaöRV* 713 (1998), pp. 713-726

Kritsiotis, D., 'Armed Activities on the Territory of the Congo (Democratic Republic of the Congo v. Uganda): Provisional Measures', 50(3) *International and Comparative Law Quarterly* 662 (2001), pp. 662-670

Krsticevic, V., 'Líneas de Trabajo para Mejorar la Eficacia del Sistema', in: J.E. Mendez, F. Cox (eds.), *El Futura del Sistema Interamericano de Protección de Los Derechos Humanos*, Instituto Interamericano de Drechos Humanos, San José 1998, pp. 413-448

Krüger, H.C., 'Probleme der Beweiserhebung durch die Europäische Kommission für Menschenrechte', 6 *Bulletin Des Droits De L'Homme* 43 (1996), pp. 43-56

Künzli, A., 'Case Concerning Mexican Nationals', 18(1) *Leiden Journal of International Law* 49 (2005), pp. 49-64

Küttler, E., *Die Menschenrechtskammer für Bosnien-Herzegowina*, Berliner Wirtschafts-Verlag GmbH, Berlin 2003

Kwiatkowska, B., 'The International Court of Justice and the Law of the Sea', in: J. Makarczyk (ed.), *Theory of International Law at the Threshold of the 21st Century: Essays in Honour of Krzysztof Skubiszewski*, Kluwer Law International, The Hague 1996, pp. 439-485

L

LaGrand Symposium: 'Reflections on the ICJ's *LaGrand* Decision', 27 *YaleJIL* 423 (2002), pp. 423-452

Lagrange, P., 'La protection des témoins: entre le possible et le souhaitable', in: L. Burgorgue-Larsen (ed.), *La répression internationale du génocide rwandais*, Collection du CREDHO-Université de Paris-Sud et Rouen, Bruyant, Bruxelles 2003, pp. 41-83

Lakha Sriram, C., 'Trying Habre in Senegal: An African Solution to an African Problem?, *Jurist, Legal News and Research*, University of Pittsburgh School of Law, 6 July 2006, <http://jurist.law.pitt.edu/forumy/2006/07/trying-habre-in-senegal-african.php>

Lavranos, N., 'The *Mox Plant* and *IJzeren Rijn* Disputes: which Court is the Supreme Arbiter?', 19 *Leiden Journal of International Law* 223 (2006) pp. 223-246

Lawson, R., M. de Blois (eds.), *The Dynamics of the Protection of Human Rights in Europe. Essays in Honour of Henry G. Schermers (Vol. 3)*, Martinus Nijhoff Publishers, Dordrecht 1994

Lawson, R.A., 'Positieve verplichtingen onder het EVRM – Opkomst en ondergang van de Fair Balance-test,' in 20(5) *NJCM-Bulletin* 558 (1995), pp. 558-573 and 20(6) *NJCM-Bulletin* 727 (1995), pp. 727-750

Lawson, R., E. Myjer, 'De zaak loopt volstrekt uit de hand...' Een interview met de nieuwe Nederlandse leden van het Europese Hof en de Europese Commissie voor de Rechten van de Mens, 22(2) *NJCM-Bulletin* 104 (1997), pp. 104-123

Lawson, R., *De internationale rechter en de Nederlandse rechtsorde,* Preadvies; Handelingen Nederlandse Juristen-Vereniging jrg. 129, Tjeenk Willink, Deventer 1999

Lawson, R., 'Life after Bankovic: on the Extraterretorial Application of the European Convention on Human Rights', in: F.Coomans, M. Kamminga (eds.), *Extraterritorial Application of Human Rights Treaties*, Intersentia, Antwerp [etc.] 2004, pp. 83-123

Lawson, R., 'Behrami en Behrami t. Frankrijk en Saramati t. Frankrijk, Duitsland en Noorwegen, Mission impossible, het EVRM is niet van toepassing op vn-vredesmissies, (annotation), 32 *NJCM* 39 (2007), pp. 39-63

Leach. Ph., 'The British military in Iraq – the Applicability of the espace juridique doctrine under the European Convention on Human Rights', *Public Law* (2005), pp. 448-458

Leach, Ph., *Taking a Case to the European Court of Human Rights*, Oxford University Press, Oxford 2007 (2nd)

Letsas, G., 'International Human Rights and the Binding Force of Interim Measures', 5 *European Human Rights Law Review* 527 (2003), pp. 527-538

Leuprecht, P., 'Human Rights – The Foundation of Justice and Peace', in: W. Benedek (ed.), *Human Rights in Bosnia and Herzegovina after Dayton: from Theory to Practice*, Human Rights Centre of the University of Sarajevo, Martinus Nijhoff Publishers, The Hague [etc.] 1999, pp. 15-18

Lewis-Anthony, S., M. Scheinin, 'Treaty-Based Procedures for Making Human Rights Complaints Within the UN System', in: H. Hannum (ed.), *Guide to International Human Rights Practice*, Transnational Publishers, Ardsley/New York 2004 (4th), pp. 43-64

Lijnzaad, L., *Reservations to UN-human Rights Treaties: Ratify and Ruin?*, Martinus Nijhoff Publishers, Dordrecht 1995

Lillich, R.B., 'Notes and Comments, The Soering Case', 85 *AJIL* 128 (1991), pp. 128-149

Lillich, R.B. (ed.), *Fact-finding before International Tribunals*, Transnational Publishers, Inc., Ardsley-on-Hudson/New York 1992

Lloyd, A., R. Murray, 'Institutions with Responsibility for Human Rights Protection under the African Union', 48(2) *Journal of African Law* 165 (2004), pp. 165-187

Lodeweges, A., 'Executie-impressies, ontwikkelingen in de praktijk van de tenuitvoerlegging van Hof-uitspraken', 33(7) *NJCM* 949 (2008), pp. 949-953

Lombardi, G., R. Sluder, D. Wallace, 'Mainstreaming Death-Sentenced Inmates: The Missouri Experience and Its Legal Significance', 61(2) *Federal Probation* 3 (1997), pp. 3-11

M

MacDonald, R.St.J., 'Interim Measures in International Law, with Special Reference to the European System for the Protection of Human Rights', 52(3-4) *ZaöRV* 703 (1992), pp. 703-740

Macklin, A., 'Refugee Women and the Imperative of Categories', 17(2) *Human Rights Quarterly* 213 (1995), pp. 213-277

Macklin, A., 'Mr. Suresh and the Evil Twin', 20(4) *Refuge* 15 (2002), pp. 15-22 (see <www.law.utoronto.ca> (consulted 18 July 2004)

McLachlan, C., 'The Principle of Systemic Integration and Article 31(3)(c) of the Vienna Convention', 54 *International and Comparative Law Quarterly* 279 (2005), pp. 279-320

Mahoney, P., 'Judicial Activism and Judicial Self-Restraint in the European Court of Human Rights: Two Sides of the Same Coin', 11(1-2) *Human Rights Law Journal* 57 (1990), pp. 57-88

Maison, R., 'Les ordonnances de la CIJ dans l'affaire relative à l'application de la Convention sur la prévention et la répression du crime de génocide', 5 *EJIL* 381 (1994), pp. 381-400

Malinverni, G., 'La pratique des Comités conventionnels des nations unies en matière de mesures conservatoires', in: G. Cohen-Jonathan, J.-F. Flauss (eds.), *Mesures conservatoires et droits fondamentaux*, Bruyant, Bruxelles 2005, pp. 63-75

Mampuya, A., 'Responsabilité et réparations dans le conflit des Grands-Lacs au Congo-Zaire', 108(3) *Revue générale de droit international public* 679 (2004), pp. 679-707

Mani, V.S., 'On Interim Measures of Protection: I.C.J. Practice', 13 *Indian Journal of International Law* 262 (1973), pp. 262-272

Mani, V.S., 'The Right to Consular Assistance as a Basic Human Right of Aliens – A Review of the ICJ Order dated 3 March 1999', 39(3) *Indian Journal of International Law* (1999), pp. 431-446

Maraj, R. (Minister of Foreign Affairs), 'Notice to Denounce the Optional Protocol to the International Covenant on Civil and Political Rights', 20 (4-6) *Human Rights Law Journal* 280 (1998), pp. 280-281

Marr, S., *The Precautionary Principle in the Law of the Sea: Modern Decision Making in International Law*, Nijhoff, Leiden 2003

Martin, C., "The Moiwana Village Case: A New Trend in Approaching the Rights of Ethnic Groups in the Inter-American System", 19(2) *Leiden Journal of International Law* 491 (2006), pp. 491-504

Martin, I., 'International Experiences for Human Rights Monitoring', in: W. Benedek (ed.), *Human Rights in Bosnia and Herzegovina after Dayton: from Theory to Practice*, Human Rights Centre of the University of Sarajevo, Martinus Nijhoff Publishers, The Hague [etc.] 1999, pp. 67-72

Martin, S., 'The Missing', 84 *International Review of the Red Cross* 723 (2002), pp. 723-726

Mayer, J., 'Outsourcing Torture, The Secret History of America's Extraordinary Rendition Program', *The New Yorker*, 7 February 2005

McCorquodale, R., 'An Inclusive International Legal System', 17(3) *Leiden Journal of International Law* 477 (2004), pp. 477-504

McGoldrick, D., *The Human Rights Committee: Its Role in the Development of the International Covenant on Civil and Political Rights*, Clarendon Press, Oxford 1994

McGoldrick, D., 'Extraterritorial Application of the International Covenant on Civil and Political Rights', in: F. Coomans, M. Kamminga (eds.), *Extraterritorial Application of Human Rights Treaties*, Intersentia, Antwerp/Oxford 2004, pp. 41-72

McKie, K.L., 'Executions and Apologies: The U.S., International Law and Right to Consular Notification', 11 *Critical Criminology* 199 (2002), pp. 199-215

Medina Quiroga, C., *The Battle of Human Rights: Gross, Systematic Violations and the Inter-American System*, Martinus Nijhoff Publishers, Dordrecht 1988

Medina Quiroga, C., *La Convención Americana: Teoría y jurisprudencia; vida, integridad personal, libertad personal, debido proceso y recurso judicial*, Universidad de Chile 2005

Medina Quiroga, C., C. Nash Rojas, *Sistema Interamericano de Derechos Humanos: Introducción a sus Mecanismos de Protección Universidad de Chile*, Centro de Derechos Humanos 2007

Meijknecht, A.K., *Towards International Personality: the Position of Minorities and Indigenous Peoples in International Law*, Intersentia/Hart, Antwerp/Groningen/Oxford 2001

Mendelson, M., 'Interim Measures of Protection in Cases of Contested Jurisdiction', 46 *B.Y.I.L* 259 (1972-1973), pp. 259-322

Mendelson, M., 'The international Court of Justice and the Sources of International Law', in: V. Lowe, M. Fitzmaurice (eds.), *Fifty Years of the International Court of Justice: Essays in Honour of Sir Robert Jennings*, Cambridge University Press, Cambridge 1996, pp. 63-89

Méndez, J.E., F. Cox (eds.), *El Futuro del Sistema Interamericano de Protección de los Derechos Humanos*, Instituto Interamericano de Derechos Humanos, San José 1998

Méndez, J.E., J.M. Vivanco, 'Disappearances and the Inter-American Court: Reflections on a Litigation Experience', 13 *Hamline Law Review* 507 (1990), pp. 507-577

Méndez, J.E., J.M. Vivanco, V. Krsticevic, 'Amicus Curiae', 18 *Revista IIDH* 29 (1993), pp. 29-44

Mennecke, M., C.J. Tams, 'LaGrand Case (Germany v. United States of America)', 51(2) *ICLQ* 449 (2002), pp. 449-454

Meron, Th., *The Humanization of International Law*, Hague Academy of International Law, Vol. 3 (General Course 2003), Martinus Nijhoff Publishers, Leiden 2006

Merrills, J.G., *The Development of International Law by the European Court of Human Rights*, Manchester University Press, Manchester 1993

Merrills, J.G., 'Interim Measures of Protection in the Recent Jurisprudence of the International Court of Justice', 44(1) *ICLQ* 90 (1995), pp. 90-146

Milano, E., 'Diplomatic Protection and Human Rights before the International Court of Justice: Re-fashioning Tradition?', XXXV *Netherlands Yearbook of International Law* 85 (2004), pp. 85-142

Milanović, M., 'State Responsibility for Genocide', 17(3) *EJIL* 553 (2006), pp. 553-604

Milanović, M., 'State Responsibility for Genocide: a Follow-up', 18(4) *EJIL* 669 (2007), pp. 669-694

Mol, N., 'Implications of the Special Status Accorded in the General Framework Agreement for Peace to the European Convention on Human Rights', in: M. O'Flaherty, G. Gisvold (eds.), *Post-war Protection of Human Rights in Bosnia and Herzegovina*, Martinus Nijhoff Publishers, The Hague/Boston 1998, pp. 27-69

Mole, N., '*Issa* v. *Turkey*: Delineating the Extra Territorial Effect of the European Convention on Human Rights', 1 *European Human Rights Law Journal* 86 (2005), pp. 86-91

Morel, C., 'Defending Human Rights in Africa: The Case for Minority and Indigenous Rights', 1(1) *Essex Human Rights Review* 54 (2004), pp. 54-65

Mowbray, A.R., *The Development of Positive Obligations Under the European Convention on Human Rights by the European Court of Human Rights*, Hart Publishing, Oxford 2004

Mowbray, A.R., 'A New Strasbourg Approach to the Legal Consequences of Interim Measures', 5(2) *Human Rights Law Review* 377 (2005), pp. 377-386

Mowbray, A.R., *Cases and Materials on the European Convention on Human Rights*, Oxford University Press, Oxford 2007 (2nd)

Mugwanya, G.W., *Human Rights in Africa, Enhancing Human Rights through the African Regional Human Rights System*, Transnational Publishers, New York 2003

Müller, D., 'Procedural Developments at the International Court of Justice', 3 *The Law and Practice of International courts and tribunals* 553 (2004), pp. 553-579

Murphy, S.D., 'Contemporary Practice of the United States relating to International Law', 98 *American Journal of International Law* 579 (2004), pp. 579-609

Murray, R., 'Serious or Massive Violations under the African Charter on Human and Peoples' Rights: A Comparison with the Inter-American and European Mechanisms', 17(2) *Netherlands Quarterly of Human Rights* 109 (1999), pp. 109-133

Murray, R. *The African Commission on Human and People's Rights & International Law*, Hart Publishing, Oxford/Portland Oregon 2000

Murray, R., *Human Rights in Africa, From the OAU to the African Union*, Cambridge University Press, Cambridge 2004

Murray, R., M. Evans (eds.), *Documents of the African Commission on Human and Peoples' Rights*, Hart Publishing, Oxford/Portland Oregon 2001

Murray, R., S. Wheatley, 'Groups and the African Charter on Human and Peoples' Rights', 25 *Human Rights Quarterly* 213 (2003), pp. 213-236

Mutua, M., 'African Human Rights Organizations: Questions of Context and Legitimacy', in: P.T. Zeleza, P.J. McConnaughay, *Human Rights, the Rule of Law, and Development in Africa*, University of Pennsylvania Press, Philadelphia 2004, pp. 191-215

Myjer, E., 'Straatsburgse Myj/meringen: wie het eerst komt is niet altijd urgent', 32(7) *NJCM* 1073 (2007), pp. 1073-1075

N

Naldi, G.J., *The Oganization of African Unity, an Analysis of its Role*, Mansell Publishing, New York 1999 (2nd)

Naldi, G.J., 'Notes and Comments: Limitation of Rights under the African Charter on Human and Peoples' Rights: The Contribution of the African Commission on Human and Peoples' Rights', 17 *South African Journal of Human Rights* 109 (2001), pp. 109-118

Naldi, G., 'Interim Measures of Protection in the African system for the Protection of Human and Peoples' Rights', 2(1) *African Human Rights Law Journal* 1 (2002), pp. 1-9

Naldi, G.J., 'Interim Measures in the UN Human Rights Committee', 53 *ICLQ* 445 (2004), pp. 445-454

Neussl, P., 'Bosnia and Herzegovina still far from the Rule of Law/Basic Facts and Landmark Decisions of the Human Rights Chamber', 20(7-11) *HRLJ* 290 (1999), pp. 290-302

Nicholson, F., P. Twomey, *Refugee Rights and Realities, Evolving International Concepts and Regimes*, Cambridge University Press, Cambridge 1999

Nieto Navia, R., 'Las medidas provisionales en la Corte Interamericana de Derechos Humanos: Teoría y Praxis', in: R. Nieto Navia (ed.), *La Corte y el Sistema Interamericano de Derechos Humanos*, Corte IDH, San José Costa Rica 1994, pp. 369-398

Nieto Navia, R., 'Aplicación por la Corte Interamericana de derechos Humanos de las Normas de la Convención de Viena sobre el derecho de los Tratados sobre Interpretación en Diversos Idiomas', in: P. Nikken (ed.), *The Modern World of Human Rights: Essays in Honour of Thomas Buergenthal*, IIDH/IIHR, San José, Costa Rica 1996, pp. 397-418

Nikken, P., 'Perfeccionar el Sistema Interamericano de Derechos Humanos sin Reformar al pacto de San José', in: J.E. Mendez, F. Cox (eds.), *El Futura del Sistema Interamericano de Protección de Los Derechos Humanos, The Modern World of Human Rights: Essays in Honour of Thomas Buergenthal*, IIDH/IIHR, San José, Costa Rica 1996, pp. 25-44

Nmehielle, V.O., *The African Human Rights System: Its Law, Practice, and Institutions*, Martinus Nijhoff Publishers, The Hague [etc.] 2001

Nørgaard, C.A., 'Interim Measures Under the European System for Protection of Human Rights', in: K. Thorup, J. Rosenbløm (eds.), *Festskrift til Ole Due (Liber Amicorum)*, Forlaget Tomson, Stockholm 1994, pp. 278-297

Nørgaard, C.A, H.C. Krüger, 'Interim and Conservatory Measures under the European System of Protection of Human Rights', in: M. Nowak, D. Steurer, H. Tresser (eds.), *Fortschritt im Bewusstsein der Grund- und Menschenrechte, Progress in the Spirit of Human Rights, Festschrift für Felix Ermacora*, Engel Verlag, Kehl/Strasbourg/Arlington 1988, pp. 109-117

Nowak, M., *U.N. Covenant on Civil and Political Rights: CCPR Commentary*, N.P. Engel, Kehl/Strasbourg/Arlington 1993

Nowak, M., 'The Human Rights Chamber for Bosnia and Herzegovina adopts its First Judgment', 18 *HRLJ* 174 (1997), pp. 174-178

Nowak, M. (1999a), 'Is Bosnia and Herzegovina Ready for Membership in the Council of Europe? The Responsibility of the Committee of Ministers and of the Parliamentary Assembly', 20 *HRLJ* 285 (1999), pp. 285-289

Nowak, M. (1999b), 'Shortcomings of Effective Enforcement of Human Rights in Bosnia and Herzegovina', in: W. Benedek (ed.), *Human Rights in Bosnia and Herzegovina after Dayton: from Theory to Practice*, Human Rights Centre of the University of Sarajevo, Martinus Nijhoff Publishers, The Hague [etc.] 1999, pp. 95-106

Nowak, M. (2000a), 'Lessons for the International Human Rights Regime from the Yugoslav Experience', Academy of European Law (ed.), *Collected Courses of the Academy of European Law*, Volume VIII, Book 2, Kluwer Law International, The Hague 2000, pp. 141-208

Nowak, M. (2000b), 'Is the Death Penalty an Inhuman Punishment?', in: T.S. Orlin, A. Rosas, M. Scheinin (eds.), *The Jurisprudence of Human Rights Law: A Comparative Interpretive Approach*, Turku, Finland: Institute for Human Rights, Åbo Akademi University 2000, pp. 27-45

Nowak, M., 'Individual Complaints Before the Human Rights Commission for Bosnia and Herzegovina', in: G. Alfredsson, J. Grimheden, B.G. Ramcharan, A. de Zayas (eds.), *International Human Rights Monitoring Mechanisms: Essays in Honour of Jakob Th. Möller*, Martinus Nijhoff Publishers, The Hague [etc.] 2001, pp. 771-793

O

O'Boyle, M., 'Torture and Emergency Powers under the European Convention on Human Rights: Ireland v. United Kingdom', 71 *AJIL* 674 (1977), pp. 674-691

O'Boyle, M., 'The European Convention on Human Rights and Extraterritorial Jurisdiction: a Comment on 'Life after Bankovic'', in: F. Coomans, M. Kamminga (eds.), *Extraterritorial Application of Human Rights Treaties*, Intersentia, Antwerp/Oxford 2004, pp. 125-139

O'Riordan, T., J. Cameron, A. Jordan (eds.), *Reinterpreting the Precautionary Principle*, Cameron May, London 2001

Oda, S., 'Provisional Measures, The Practice of the International Court of Justice', in: V. Lowe, M. Fitzmaurice (eds.), *Fifty Years of the International Court of Justice: Essays in Honour of Sir Robert Jennings*, Cambridge University Press, Cambridge 1996, pp. 541-556

Odinkalu, C.A., 'The Role of Case and Complaints Procedures in the Reform of the African Regional Human Rights System', 1(2) *African Human Rights Law Journal* 225 (2001), pp. 225-246

Oellers-Frahm, K., *Die einstweilige Anordnung in der internationalen Gerichtbarkeit*, Springer-Verlag, Berlin 1975

Oellers-Frahm, K., 'United States Diplomatic and Consular Staff in Tehran Case', in: R. Bernhardt (ed.), *Encyclopedia of Public International Law 2*, Max Planck Institute, North-Holland Publishing Company, Amsterdam/New York/Oxford 1981, pp. 282-286

Oellers-Frahm, K., 'Remarks Concerning the Indication of Provisional Measures by the ICJ in the Case of Bosnia and Herzegovina v. Yugoslavia (Serbia and Montenegro) of 8 April 1993 (Summary)', 53(3) *Zeitschrift für ausländisches und öffentliches Recht und Völkerrecht* 654 (1993), pp. 654-656

Oellers-Frahm, K. (2001a), 'Entscheidungen – IGH – 27.6.01 – Verbindlichkeit einstweiliger Anordnungen des IGH. Nichtbeachtung durch die USA. Individualrechte. Fall LaGrand (Deutschland gegen USA)', 28(11-13) *EuGRZ* 287 (2001), pp. 287-298

Oellers-Frahm, K. (2001b), 'Multiplication of International Courts and Tribunals and Conflicting Jurisdiction- Problems and Possible Solutions', in: J.A. Frowein, R. Wolfrum (eds.), *Max Planck Yearbook of United Nations Law 5*, Kluwer Law International, The Hague 2001, pp. 67-104

Oellers-Frahm, K, 'Verbindlichkeit einstweiliger Massnahmen: Der EGMR vollzieht – endlich – die erforderliche Wende in seiner Rechtsprechung, Anmerkung zum Fall Mamatkulov und Abdurasulovic gegen Türkei', 30 (22-23) *EuGRZ* 689 (2003), pp. 689-693

O'Flaherty, M., *Human Rights and the UN, Practice before the Treaty Bodies*, Sweet & Maxwell, London 1996

O'Flaherty, M., 'Report on the Conference on Human Rights in Bosnia and Herzegovina: From Theory to Practice', in: W. Benedek (ed.), *Human Rights in Bosnia and Herzegovina after Dayton: from Theory to Practice*, Human Rights Centre of the University of Sarajevo, Martinus Nijhoff Publishers, The Hague [etc.] 1999, pp. 6-13

O'Flaherty, M., 'Human Rights and the General Framework Agreement for Peace in Bosnia and Herzegovina', in: G. Alfredsson, J. Grimheden, B.G. Ramcharan, A. de Zayas (eds.), *International Human Rights Monitoring Mechanisms: Essays in Honour of Jakob Th. Möller*, Martinus Nijhoff Publishers, The Hague [etc.] 2001, pp. 749-762

Oguz, N., S. Miles, 'The Physician and Prison Hunger Strikes: Reflecting on the Experience in Turkey', 31 *J Med Ethics* 169 (2005), pp. 169-172

Onoria, H., 'The African Commission on Human and Peoples' Rights and the Exhaustion of Local Remedies Under the African Charter', 31(1) *African Human Rights Law Journal* 1 (2003), pp. 1-24

Orakhelashvili, A., 'Questions of International Judicial Jurisdiction in the *LaGrand* Case', 15 *Leiden Journal of International Law* 105 (2002), pp. 105-130

Orakhelashvili, A., 'Judicial Competence and Judicial Remedies in the Avena Case', 18(1) *Leiden Journal of International Law* 31 (2005), pp. 31-48

Orakhelashvili, A., *Peremptory Norms in International Law*, Oxford University Press, Oxford 2006

Ouguergouz, F., *The African Charter on Human and Peoples' Rights: A Comprehensive Agenda for Human Dignity and Sustainable Democracy in Africa*, Martinus Nijhoff Publishers, The Hague 2003

Ovey, C., R. White, *The European Convention on Human Rights*, Oxford University Press, Oxford 2006

P

Padilla, D.J., 'The Future of the Inter-American Human Rights System', 3(1) *Human Rights Brief* (American University Washington College of Law), 1995, <http://www.wcl.american.edu/hrbrief/v3i1/iahr31.htm>

Padilla, D.J., 'Provisional Measures under the American Convention on Human Rights', in: C. Gaviria (ed.), *Liber Amicorum Héctor Fix-Zamudio*, San José, Costa Rica 1998, pp. 1189-1196

Padilla, D., 'An African Human Rights Court: Reflections From the Perspective of the Inter-American System', 2(2) *African Human Rights Law Journal* 185 (2002), pp. 185-194

Pajic, Z., 'An Overview of the substantive Human Rights Regime after Dayton: A Critical Appraisal of the Constitution of Bosnia and Herzegovina', in: M. O'Flaherty, G. Gisvold (eds.), *Post-war Protection of Human Rights in Bosnia and Herzegovina*, Martinus Nijhoff Publishers, The Hague 1998, pp. 1-12

Pajic, Z., 'A Critical Appraisal of the Dayton Constitution of Bosnia and Herzegovina', in: W. Benedek (ed.), *Human Rights in Bosnia and Herzegovina after Dayton: from Theory to Practice*, Human Rights Centre of the University of Sarajevo, Martinus Nijhoff Publishers, The Hague [etc.] 1999, pp. 33-44

Palmisano, G., 'Les garanties de non-repetion entre codification et realization juridictionnelle du droit: à propos de l'affaire LaGrand', 4 *Revue Générale de Droit International Public* 753 (2002), pp. 753-789

Partsch, K.J., 'Vor- und Nachteile einer Regionalisierung des internationalen Menschenrechtschutzes', 16 (1-2) *EuGRZ* 1 (1989), pp. 1-9

Pasqualucci, J.M., 'Provisional Measures in the Inter-American Human Rights System: An Innovative Development in International Law', 26(4) *Vanderbilt Journal of Transnational Law* 803 (1993), pp. 803-864

Pasqualucci, J.M., 'Sonia Picado, First Woman Judge on the Inter-American Court of Human Rights', 17 *HRQ* 794 (1995), pp. 794-806

Pasqualucci, J.M. (1996), 'Thomas Buergenthal: Holocaust Survivor to Human Rights Advocate', 18 *Human Rights Quarterly* 877 (1996), pp. 877-899

Pasqualucci, J.M., *The Practice and Procedure of the Inter-American Court of Human Rights*, Cambridge University Press, Cambridge 2003

Pasqualucci, J.M., 'Interim Measures in International Human Rights: Evolution and Harmonization', 38(1) *Vanderbilt Journal of Transnational Law* 1 (2005), pp. 1-49

Patton, M.Q., *Qualitative Research and Evaluation Methods*, Sage, Thousand Oaks 2002 (3rd)

Paulson, C., 'Compliance with Final Judgments of the International Court of Justice since 1987', 98(3) *American Journal of International Law* 434 (2004), pp. 434-461

Paust, J. (2003), 'Judicial Power to Determine the Status and Rights of Persons Detained without Trial', 44 *Harvard International Law Journal* 505 (2003), pp. 505-532

Paust, J. (2004a), 'Post-9/11 Overreaction and Fallacies Regarding War and Defense, Guantanamo, the Status of Persons, Treatment, Judicial Review of Detention, and Due Process in Military Commissions', 79 *Notre Dame Law Review* 1335 (2004), pp. 1335-1364

Paust, J. (2004b), 'After 9/11, "No Neutral Ground" with Respect to Human Rights: Executive Claims and Actions of Special Concern and International Law Regarding the Disappearance of Detainees', 50 *The Wayne Law Review* 79 (2004), pp. 79-96

Paust, J., 'Unsafe Harbour, the G.O.P. 'compromise' on Detainee Treatment', JURIST- Forum *Legal News and Research*, University of Pittsburgh School of Law, 22 September 2006, at: <http://jurist.law.pitt.edu/forumy/2006/09/unsafe-harbor-gop-compromise-on.php> (consulted 15 October 2007)

Paust, J., 'Medellín, Avena, the Supremacy of Treaties, and Relevant Executive Authority', 31(2) *Suffolk Transnational Law Review* 301 (2008), pp. 301-333

Pauwelyn, J., *Conflict of Norms in Public International law: How WTO law relates to Other Rules of International Law*, Cambridge University Press, Cambridge 2003

Penal Reform International, *Making Standards Work, An international handbook on good prison practice*, The Hague 2001 (2nd), <www.penalreform.org>

Petzold, H., 'The Convention and the principle of subsidiarity', in: R.St.J. Macdonald, F. Matscher, H. Petzold (eds.), *The European System for the Protection of Human Rights*, Nijhoff, Dordrecht 1993, pp. 41-62

Picado Sotela, S., 'Thomas Buergenthal', in: P. Nikken (ed.), *The Modern World of Human Rights: Essays in Honour of Thomas Buergenthal*, IIDH/IIHR, San José, Costa Rica 1996, pp. 19-32

Pinto, M., 'Las relaciones entre los Órganos del Sistema', in: J.E. Mendez, F. Cox (eds.), *El Futura del Sistema Interamericano de Protección de Los Derechos Humanos*, Instituto Interamericano de Derechos Humanos (IIDH), San José, Costa Rica 1998, pp. 169-184

Pinto, M., 'De la protection diplomatique à la protection des droits de l'homme', 3 *Revue Générale de Droit International Publique* 513 (2002), pp. 513-548

Pityana, N.B., 'The Challenge of Culture for Human Rights in Africa: the African Charter in a Comparative Context', in: M. Evans, R. Murray (eds.), *The African Charter on Human and Peoples' Rights, the System in Practice: 1986-2000*, Cambridge University Press, Cambridge 2002, pp. 219-245

Pityana, N.B., 'Hurdles and Pitfalls in International Human Rights Law: The Ratification Process of the Protocol to the African Charter on the Establishment of the African Court on Human and Peoples' Rights', 28 *South African Yearbook of Internatinal Law* 110 (2003), pp. 110-129

Prakken, T., *Het laatste woord, zes opstellen over verdediging in strafzaken*, Kluwer, Deventer 2005

Pritchard, S. (ed.), *Indigenous Peoples, the United Nations and Human Rights*, Zed Books Ltd., London, the Federation Press, Annandale/Leichardt, Australia 1998

Pronto, A., 'Human-Rightism' and the Development of General International Law', 20 *LJIL* 753 (2007), pp. 753-765

Q

Quigley, J., A.S. Shank, 'Death Row as a Violation of Human Rights: Is It Illegal to Extradite to Virginia?', 30 *VJIL* 214 (1989), pp. 241-272

R

Raguz, B., 'The Ombudsman Institution of the Federation of Bosnia and Herzegovina', in: W. Benedek (ed.), *Human Rights in Bosnia and Herzegovina after Dayton: from Theory to Practice*, Human Rights Centre of the University of Sarajevo, Martinus Nijhoff Publishers, The Hague [etc.] 1999, pp. 121-124

Ramcharan, B.G., 'Complementarity between Universal and Regional Organizations/Perspectives from the UN High Commissioner for Human Rights', 21(8) *Human Rights Law Journal* 324 (2000), pp. 324-326

Ramcharan, B.G., *The United Nations High Commisioner for Human Rights, the Challenges of International Protection*, Martinus Nijhoff Publishers/Kluwer Law International, The Hague [etc.] 2002

Ratner, M., 'How We Closed the Guantanamo HIV Camp: The Intersection of Politics and Litigation', 11 *Harvard Human Rights Journal* 187 (1998), pp. 187-220

Ray, S., 'Domesticating International Obligations: How to ensure U.S. Compliance with the Vienna Convention of Consular Relations', 91 *Californian Law Revue* 1729 (2003), pp. 1729-1771

Redgwell, C.J., 'Reservations to Treaties and Human Rights Committee General Comment No. 24(52)', 46 *International and Comparative Law Quarterly* 390 (1997), pp. 390-412

Reed, L., 'Great Expectations: Where does the Proliferation of International Dispute Resolution Tribunals Leave International Law?', 96 *American Society of International Law* 219 (2002), pp. 219-237

Reichler, P.S., 'Tribute to Professor Abram Chayes: Holding America to its Own Best Standards: Abe Chayes and Nicaragua in the World Court', 42 *Harvard International Law Journal* 15 (2001), pp. 15-46

Reisman, M., *Systems of Control in International Adjudication and Arbitration: Breakdown and Repair*, Duke University Press, Durham, NC 1992

Rieter, E., 'Interim Measures by the World Court to suspend the Execution of an Individual: the Breard Case', 16(4) *Netherlands Quarterly of Human Rights* 475 (1998), pp. 475-494

Rieter, E., 'Het VN-Comité tegen foltering, interim maatregelen en de Nederlandse verplichtingen', 24(8) *NJCM-Bulletin* 1136 (1999), pp. 1136-1145

Rieter, E. (2002a), 'Het Internationaal Gerechtshof over rechtsherstel en de bindende kracht van voorlopige maatregelen: Duitsland t. VS (LaGrand)', 27(4) *NJCM-Bulletin* 481 (2002), pp. 481-491

Rieter, E. (2002b), 'ICCPR Case Law on Detention, the Prohibition of Cruel Treatment and some Issues Pertaining to the Death Row Phenomenon', 1 *Journal of the Institute of Justice and International Studies* 83 (2002), pp. 83-103 (<www.cmsu.edu/cj/journal.htm>)

Rieter, E. (2003a), 'Het recht op leven, het verbod van wrede behandeling en de voorlopige maatregelen van het EHRM: eindelijk effectief klachtrecht', 21 *Nederlands Juristenblad* 1074 (2003), pp. 1074-1076

Rieter, E. (2003b), Annotation of *Shamayev and 12 Others* t. *Georgië en Rusland*, 1 *European Human Rights Cases* 23 (2003), pp. 23-27

Rieter, E., 'Effectief klachtrecht, onherstelbaar letsel en voorlopige maatregelen door het EHRM', 29(1) *NJCM-Bulletin* 73 (2004), pp. 73-87

Rieter, E. (2005a), 'Motiveringsvereisten voor de Straatsburgse voorlopige maatregelen, het voorbeeld van de Somalische zaken', 30(1) *NJCM* 25 (2005), pp. 25-44

Rieter, E. (2005b), Annotation of *Mamatkulov en Askarov* t. *Turkije*, 4 februari 2005, 4(6) *European Human Rights Cases* (2005), pp. 320-324

Rieter, E., Annotation of Afd. Bestuursrechtspraak Raad van State, 6 januari 2006, rol nr. 200508638/1, JV 2006/189, pp. 736-739

Rieter, E., Annotation of *Paladi* v. *Moldavia*, 10 July 2007, 39806/05, *European Human Rights Cases* (EHRC) 2007/101, pp. 969-975

Rivera-Salgado, G., *Equal in Dignity and Rights: the Struggle of Indigenous Peoples of the Americas in an Age of Migration*, inaugural address Utrecht University, Utrecht 2005

Robertson, E., 'Psychological Injury and the Prison Litigation Reform Act: A 'Not exactly' Equal Protection Analysis', 37 *Harvard Journal on Legislation* 105 (2000), pp. 105-158

Rodley, Sir N.S., *The Treatment of Prisoners in International Law*, Oxford University Press, Oxford 1999 (2nd)

Rodley, Sir N.S., 'Urgent Action', in: G. Alfredsson et al. (eds.), *International Human Rights Monitoring Mechanisms*, Martinus Nijhoff Publishers, The Hague [etc.] 2001, pp. 279-283

Rodley, N.S., 'United Nations Human Rights Treaty Bodies and Special Procedures of the Commission on Human Rights – Complementarity or Competition?', 25(4) *Human Rights Quarterly* 882 (2003), pp. 882-908

Rodríguez Pinzón, D., 'Presumption of Veracity, Nonappearance and Default in the Individual Complaint Procedure of the Inter-American System on Human Rights', 25 *Revista IIDH* 125 (1998), pp. 125-148

Rodríguez Rescia, V., 'La ejecución de sentencias de la Corte', in: J.E. Mendez, F. Cox (eds.), *El Futura del Sistema Interamericano de Protección de Los Derechos Humanos*, Instituto Interamericano de Derechos Humanos, San José 1998, pp. 51-72

Rogge, K., 'Einstweilige Massnahmen in Verfahren von der Europäische Komission für Menschenrechte', 35 *Neue Jurist. Wochenschr.* 1569 (1977), pp. 1569-1570

Rosenne, S., *Provisional Measures in International Law, the International Court of Justice and the International Tribunal for the Law of the Sea*, Oxford University Press, Oxford 2005

S

Salvioli, F.O., 'Derechos, Acceso y Rol de las Víctimas', in: J.E. Mendez, F. Cox (eds.), *El Futura del Sistema Interamericano de Protección de Los Derechos Humanos*, Instituto Interamericano de Derechos Humanos (IIDH), San José, Costa Rica 1998, pp. 293-342

Sands, Ph., 'Treaty, Custom and the Cross-Fertilization of International Law', 1 *Yale Journal of Human Rights and Development Law* 85 (1999), pp. 85-105

Sands, Ph., 'Turtles and Torturers: the Transformation of International Law', 33 *NYU J. Int'l L. Pol.* 527 (2001), pp. 527-558

Sands, Ph., *Principles of International Environmental Law*, Cambridge University Press, Cambridge 2003 (2nd)

Savadogo, L., 'Case concerning Armed Activities on the Territory of the Congo (Democratic Republic of the Congo v. Uganda): the Court's Provisional Measures Order of 1 July 2000', 72 *BYIL* 357 (2002), pp. 357-380

Schabas, W., 'Soering's Legacy: the Human Rights Committee and the Judicial Committee of the Privy Council take a Walk down Death Row', 43 *International and Comparative Law Quarterly* 913 (1994), pp. 913-921

Schabas, W.A., *The Death Penalty as Cruel Treatment and Torture, Capital Punishment Challenged in the World Courts*, Northeastern University Press, Boston 1996

Schabas, W.A. (2002a), *The Abolition of the Death Penaly in International Law*, Cambridge University Press, Cambridge 2002

Schabas, W.A. (2002b), 'The ICJ ruling against the United States: Is it really about the death penalty?', 27 *Yale Journal of International Law* 445 (2002), pp. 445-452

Schabas, W., 'Discussion', in: G. Cohen-Jonathan, J.-F. Flauss (eds.), *Mesures conservatoires et droits fondamentaux*, Bruyant, Bruxelles 2005, pp. 77-90

Schachter, O., 'Creativity and Objectivity in International Tribunals', in: R. Bernhardt, W.K. Geck, G. Jaenicke, H. Steinberger, *Volkerrecht als Rechtsordnung internationale Gerichtsbarkeit Menschenrechte, Festschrift für Hermann Mosler*, Springer-Verlag, Berlin/Heidelberg/New York 1983, pp. 813-821

Scheinin, M., 'The Right to enjoy a Distinct Culture: Indigenous and Competing Uses of Land', in: Th.S. Orlin et al. (eds.), *The Jurisprudence of Human Rights: a Comparative Interpretive Approach*, Åbo Akademi University Institute for Human Rights, Turku 2000, pp. 159-222

Scheinin, M., 'How to Untie a Tie in the Human Rights Committee', in: G. Alfredsson et al. (eds.), *International Human Rights Monitoring Mechanisms, Essays in Honour of Jakob Th. Möller*, Martinus Nijhoff Publishers/Kluwer Law International, The Hague [etc.] 2001, pp. 129-145

Scheinin, M. (2004a), 'Reservations by States under the International Covenant on Civil and Political Rights and its Optional Protocols, and the Practice of the Human Rights Committee', in: I. Ziemele (ed.), *Reservations to Human Rights Treaties and the Vienna Convention Regime: Conflict, Harmony or Reconciliation*, Martinus Nijhoff Publishers, Leiden 2004, pp. 41-58

Scheinin, M. (2004b), 'Extraterritorial effect of the International Covenant on Civil and Political Rights', in: F. Coomans, M. Kamminga (eds.), *Extraterritorial Application of Human Rights Treaties*, Intersentia, Antwerp/Oxford 2004, pp. 73-81

Schermers, H.S., 'Acceptance of International Supervision of Human Rights', 12 *Leiden Journal of International Law* 821 (1999), pp. 821-831

Schiffman, H.W., 'The LaGrand Decision: The Involving Legal Landscape of the Vienna Convention on Consular Relations in U.S. Death Penalty Cases', 42 *Santa Clara Law Review* 1099 (2002), pp. 1099-1135

Schiffrin, N., 'Jamaica Withdraws the Rights of Individual Petition under the International Covenant of Civil and Political Rights', 92 *American Journal of International Law* 564 (1998), pp. 564-568

Schmidt, M., 'Individual Human Rights Complaints Based on United Nations Treaties and the Need for Reform', 41 *International and Comparative Law Quarterly* 645 (1992), pp. 645-659

Schmidt, M., 'Treaty-based Human Rights Complaints Procedures in the UN – Remedy or Mirage for Victims of Human Rights Violations?', 2 *Human Rights – Droits de l'Homme* 13 (1998), pp. 13-18

Schmidt, M., 'The Death Row Phenomenon: a Comparative Analysis', in: T.S. Orlin, A. Rosas, M. Scheinin (eds.), *The Jurisprudence of Human Rights Law: A Comparative Interpretive Approach*, Turku, Finland: Institute for Human Rights, Åbo Akademi University 2000, pp. 47-72

Schulte, C., *Compliance with Decisions of the International Court of Justice*, Oxford University Press, Oxford 2004

Schwebel, S. (1996a), 'Commentary', in: M.K. Bulterman, M. Kuijer (eds.), *Compliance with Judgments of International Courts, Proceedings of the symposium organized in honour of Professor Henry G. Schermers,* Mordenate College and the Department of International Public Law of Leiden University, Martinus Nijhoff Publishers, The Hague [etc.] 1996, pp. 39-62

Schwebel, S. (1996b), 'The Treatment of Human Rights and of Aliens in the International Court of Justice', in: V. Lowe, M. Fitzmaurice (eds.), *Fifty Years of the International Court of Justice, Essays in Honour of Sir Robert Jennings*, Cambridge University Press, Cambridge 1996, pp. 327-350

Seiderman, I., *Hierarchy in International Law: the Human Rights Dimension*, Intersentia/Hart, Antwerpen/Groningen/Oxford 2001

Sepúlveda, M., *The Nature of the Obligations under the International Covenant on Economic, Social and Cultural Rights*, Intersentia/Hart, Antwerpen/Groningen/Oxford 2003

Sevinç, M., 'Hunger strikes in Turkey', 30 *Human Rights Quarterly* 655 (2008), pp. 655-679

Shahabuddeen, M., *Precedent in de World Court, Hersch Lauterpacht Memorial Lectures*, Cambridge University Press, Cambridge 1997

Shany, Y., *The Competing Jurisdictions of International Courts and Tribunals*, Oxford University Press, Oxford 2003

Shea, M.P., 'Expanding Judicial Scrutiny of Human Rights in Extradition Cases After Soering', 17(1) *Yale Journal of International Law* 85 (1992), pp. 85-138

Shelton, D., 'The Independence of International Tribunals', in: P. Nikken (ed.), *The Modern World of Human Rights: Essays in Honour of Thomas Buergenthal*, IIDH/IIHR, San José, Costa Rica 1996, pp. 299-334

Shelton, D., 'The Legal Status of the Detainees at Guantanamo Bay: Innovative Elements in the Decision of the Inter-American Commission on Human Rights of 12 March 2002', 23 *Human Rights Law Journal* 13 (2002), pp. 13-14

Shelton, D. (2004a), 'Case concerning Avena and other Mexican Nationals', 98 *American Journal of International Law* 559 (2004), pp. 559-566

Shelton, D. (2004b), 'The Inter-American Human Rights System', in: H. Hannum (ed.), *Guide to International Human Rights Practice*, Transnational Press, Ardsley, NY 2004 (4th), pp. 127-141

Shelton, D. (2005a), *Remedies in International Human Rights Law*, Oxford University Press, Oxford 2005 (2nd)

Shelton, D. (2005b), 'Discussion', in: G. Cohen-Jonathan, J.-F. Flauss (eds.), *Mesures conservatoires et droits fondamentaux*, Bruyant, Bruxelles 2005, pp. 165-176

Shelton, D. (2006a), 'Normative Hierarchy in International Law', 100 *American Journal of International Law* 291 (2006), pp. 291-323

Shelton, D. (2006b), 'Subsidiarity and Human Rights', 27 *Human Rights Law Journal* 4 (2006), pp. 4-11

Simma, B., *The Charter of the United Nations*, Oxford University Press, Oxford 1994

Simma, B., 'International Human Rights and General International Law: a Comparative Analysis', IV(2) *Collected Courses of the Academy of European Law 1993*, Kluwer Law International, Dordrecht 1995, pp. 153-236

Simma, B., 'Introduction: Fragmentation in a Positive Light', Symposium: Diversity or Cacophony?: New Sources of Norms in International Law', 25(4) *Mich. J. Int'l L.* 845 (2004), pp. 845-847

Sivakumaran, S, 'Case Comment: Application of the Convention on the Prevention and Punishment of the Crime of Genocide (Bosnia and Herzegovina v. Serbia and Montenegro)', 56(3) *ICLQ* 695 (2007), pp. 695-708

Slaughter, A.-M., 'A Typology of Transjudicial Communication', 29 *University of Richmond Law Review* 99 (1994), pp. 99-135

Slaughter, A.-M., 'Judicial Globalization', 40 *Virginia Journal of International Law* 1103 (2000), pp. 1103-1124

Slaughter, A.-M., 'A Global Community of Courts', 44 *Harvard International Law Journal* 191 (2003), pp. 191-219

Smeulers, A., *In Staat van Uitlevering*, Intersentia, Antwerpen 2002

Smeulers, A., J. de Vries, 'Het Europees aanhoudingsbevel, gerechtvaardigd vertrouwen?', 28(4) *NJCM* 428 (2003), pp. 428-460

Sohn, L.B., 'The New International Law: Protection of the Rights of Individuals rather than States', 32 *American University Law Review* 1 (1982), pp. 1-64

Sohn, L.B., 'The Contribution of Latin American Lawyers to the Development of the United Nations Concept of Human Rights and Economic and Social Justice', in: P. Nikken (ed.), *The Modern World of Human Rights: Essays in Honour of Thomas Buergenthal*, IIDH/IIHR, San José, Costa Rica 1996, pp. 33-56

Sorel, J.-M., 'Article 31', in: O. Corten, P. Klein (eds.), *Convention de Vienne sur le droit des traités – commentaire article par article*, Bruylant, Bruxelles 2006, pp. 1289-1338

Sorel, J.-M., 'Les multiples lectures d'un arrêt: entre sentiment d'impunité et sentiment de cohérence, une décision à relativiser', 111 *RGDIP* 259 (2007), pp. 259-272

Spielmann, A., D. Spielmann, 'La cour unique et permanente et les mesures provisoires', in: P. Mahoney et al. (eds.), *Protecting Human Rights: the European Perspective, Studies in Memory of Rolv Ryssdal*, Heymanns, Köln 2000, pp. 1346-1358

Spijkerboer, Th., Case note CAT *Gamal El Rgeig* v. *Switzerland*, 22 January 2007, *JV* 160 (2007), pp. 660-661

Spijkerboer, Th., Case note ECtHR *Saadi* v. *Italy*, 23 February 2008 (Grand Chamber), 33(7) *NJCM* 1005 (2008), pp. 1005-1017

Spronken, T., *Verdediging, een onderzoek naar de normering van het optreden van advocaten in strafzaken*, diss. Maastricht, Gouda Quint, Deventer 2001

Steenbergen, H., T. Zwart, Annotation of ECtHR Cruz Varas et al. v. Sweden, *NJCM* (1991), pp. 335 ff.

Stephens, T., 'The LaGrand Case (Federal Republic of Germany v United States of America), The Right to Information on Consular Assistance under the Vienna Convention on Consular Relations: a Right for what Purpose?', 3 *Melbourne Journal of International Law* 143 (2002), pp. 143-164

Steyn, J., 'Guantanamo Bay: the Legal Black Hole', 53 *International and Comparative Law Quarterly* 1 (2004) pp. 1-15

Szabó, E., 'Provisional Measures in the World Court: Binding or Bound to be Ineffective?', 10 *Leiden Journal of International Law* 475 (1997), pp. 475-489

Sztucki, J., *Interim Measures in the Hague Court: an Attempt at a Scrutiny*, Kluwer Law International, The Hague 1983

T

Taillant, J.D., R. Picolotti, 'In the Wake of the Discussions on Reforming the Inter-Aemrican Human Rights System. Behind the Scenes at the OAS', in: J.E. Mendez, F. Cox (eds.), *El Futura del Sistema Interamericano de Protección de Los Derechos Humanos*, Instituto Interamericano de Derechos Humanos (IIDH), San José, Costa Rica 1998, pp. 117-134

Tams, C., 'Recognizing Guarantees and Assurances of Non-repetition: *LaGrand* and the Law of State Responsibility', 27 *Yale Journal of International Law* 441 (2002), pp. 441-444

Tanaka, Y., 'Prompt Release in the United Nations Convention on the Law of the Sea: Some Reflections on the ITLOS Jurisprudence', *Netherlands International Law Review* 237 (2004), pp. 237-271

Tanaka, A., Y. Nagamine, *The International Convention on the Elimination of All Forms of Racial Discrimination: A guide for NGOs*, Minority Rights Group, London 2000

Taqi, I., 'Adjudicating Disappearance Cases in Turkey: an Argument for Adopting the Inter-American Court of Human Rights' Approach', 24 *Fordham International Law Journal* 940 (2001), pp. 940-987

Tatulli, J.R., 'UN report: Resolving Africa's Longest Civil War: Updates on the Case Concerning Armed Activities in the Democratic Republic of Congo', 19 *New York Law School Journal of Human Rights* 903 (2003), pp. 903-912

Terlouw, A., 'Gepasseerd', Case note of *Salah Sheekh* v. *the Netherlands*, 32(2) *NJCM* 179 (2007), pp. 179-194

Terlouw, A., 'De zaag in de stoelpoten van het absolute karakter van artikel 3 EVRM', Case note of ECtHR *N.* v. *UK*, 27 May 2007, 33(7) *NJCM* 1034, (2008), pp. 1034-1051

Thirlway, H., 'The Indication of Provisional Measures by the International Court of Justice', in: R. Bernhardt (ed.), *Interim Measures indicated by International Courts*, Springer-Verlag, Berlin 1994, pp. 1-36

Thomassen, W., 'Het kleine verschil en de grote gevolgen', 33(7) *NJCM* 930 (2008), pp. 930-935

Thompson, J.J., 'La libertad de Prensa en el Sistema Interamericano', in: P. Nikken (ed.), *The Modern World of Human Rights: Essays in Honour of Thomas Buergenthal*, IIDH/IIHR, San José, Costa Rica 1996, pp. 231-254

Thornberry, P., *Indigenous Peoples and Human Rights*, Manchester University Press, Manchester 2002

Tittemore, B.D., 'Guantanamo Bay and the Precautionary Measures of the Inter-American Commission on Human Rights: a Case for International Oversight in the Struggle against Terrorism', 6(2) *Human Rights Law Review* 378 (2006), pp. 378-402

Tomuschat, C., 'Making Individual Communications an Effective to for the Protection of Human Rights', in: U. Beyerlin (ed.), *Recht zwischen Umbruch und Bewahrung: Völkerrecht, Europarecht, Staatsrecht; Festschrift für Rudolf Bernhardt*, Springer-Verlag, Heidelberg 1995, pp. 615-634

Tomuschat, C., 'Individual Reparation Claims in Instances of Grave Human Rights Violations: The Position under General International Law', in: A. Randelzhofer, C. Tomuschat (eds.),

State Responsibility and the Individual: Reparation in Instances of Grave Violations of Human Rights, Kluwer Law International, London 1999, pp. 1-25

Tomuschat, C., *Human Rights: Between Idealism and Realism*, Oxford University Press, Oxford 2003

Toufayan, M., 'Human Rights Treaty Interpretation: a Postmodern Account of its Claim to 'Speciality'', 2 NYU Center for Human Rights and Global Justice Working Paper 2005

Toufayan, M., 'The World Court's Distress when Facing Genocide: a Critical Commentary on the Application of the Genocide Convention Case (Bosnia and Herzegovina v. Yugoslavia (Serbia and Montenegro))', 40 *Tex. Int'l L. J.* 233 (2005), pp. 233-261

Treves, T., 'Conflicts between the International Tribunal for the Law of the Sea and the International Court of Justice', 31 *International Law and Politics* 809 (1999), pp. 809-831

Tridimas, T., *The General Principles of EC Law*, Oxford University Press, Oxford 1999

Trouwborst, A., *Evolution and Status of the Precautionary Principle in International Law*, Kluwer Law International, the Hague/London/New York 2002

Tushnet, M., L. Yackle, 'Symbolic Statutes and Real Laws: the Pathologies of the Antiterrorism and Effective Death Penalty Act and the Prison Litigation Reform Act', 47 *Duke Law Journal* 1 (1997), pp. 1-86

U

Udombana, N.J., 'Toward the African Court on Human Rights and Peoples' Rights: Better Late Than Never', 3 *Yale Human Rights and Development L.J.* 45 (2000), pp. 45-50

Udombana, N.J., 'Can the Leopard Change its Spots? The African Union Treaty and Human Rights', 17(6) *American University International Law Review* 1177 (2002), pp. 1177-1261

Udombana, N.J. (2003a), 'So far, so far: The local Remedies Rule in the Jurisprudence of the African Commission on Human and Peoples' Rights', 91(1) *The American Journal of International Law* 1 (2003), pp. 1-37

Udombana, N.J. (2003b), 'Interim Measures: a Comparative Study of Selected International Institutions', 43 *Indian Journal of International Law* 479 (2003), pp. 479-532

Umozurike, U.O., *The African Charter on Human and Peoples' Rights*, Martinus Nijhoff Publishers, The Hague 1997

Umozurike, U.O., 'The Complaint Procedure of the African Commission on Human and Peoples' Rights', in: G. Alfredsson, J. Grimheden, B.G. Ramcharan, A. de Zayas (eds.), *International Human Rights Monitoring Mechanisms: Essays in Honour of Jakob Th. Möller*, Martinus Nijhoff Publishers, The Hague [etc.] 2001, pp. 707-712

V

Van Alebeek, R. *The Immunity of States and their Officials in the Light of International Criminal Law and International Human Rights Law*, E.M. Meijers Institute of Legal Studies, Leiden University 2006

Van Boven, Th.C., *People Matter, Views on International Human Rights Policy, collected and introduced by Hans Thoolen*, Meulenhoff, Amsterdam 1982

Van Boven, Th.C., 'Facing Urgent Human Rights Cases; Legal and Diplomatic Action', in: R. Lawson, M. de Blois (eds.), *The Dynamics of the Protection of Human Rights in Europe. Essays in Honour of Henry G. Schermers*, (Vol. 3), Nijhoff, Dordrecht 1994, pp. 61-78

Van Boven, Th.C., *The Protection of Human Rights in Europe, Collected Courses of the Academy of European Law, Vol. IV(2) 1993*, Nijhoff, The Hague 1995

Van Boven, Th.C., Rapporteur, Study concerning the Right to Restitution, Compensation, and Rehabilitation for Victims of Gross Violations of Human Rights and Fundamental Freedoms, Final Report, E/CN.4/sub.2/1993/8, 2 July 1993; revised version E/CN.4/Sub.2/1996/17, 24 May 1996 and E/CN.4/1997/104, 16 January 1997

Van Boven, Th.C., 'Prevention, Early-Warning and Urgent Procedures: A New approach by the Committee on the Elimination of Racial Discrimination', in: E. Denter, N. Schrijver (eds.), *Reflections on International Law from the Low Countries, in Honour of Paul de Waart*, Kluwer Law International, The Hague 1998, pp. 165-182

Van Boven, Th.C., 'Rendering Justice to Victims: A Case for Reparations', in: W.J M. van Genugten et al. (eds.), *Realism and Moralism in International Relations*, Kluwer Law International, The Hague 1999, pp. 197-211

Van Boven, Th.C. (2000a), 'The Petition System under the International Convention on the Elimination of All Forms of Racial Discrimination, A Sobering Balance-Sheet', in: J.A. Frowein, R. Wolfrum (eds.), *Max Planck Yearbook of United Nations Law*, Kluwer Law International, The Hague 2000, pp. 271-287

Van Boven, Th.C. (2000b), ''Political' and 'Legal' Control Mechanisms: Their Competition and Coexistence', in: F. Coomans et al. (eds.), *Human Rights from Exclusion to Inclusion; Principles and Practice, An Anthology from the Work of Theo van Boven*, Kluwer Law International, The Hague 2000, pp. 49-72

Van Boven, Th.C. (2001a), 'CERD and Article 14; The Unfulfilled Promise', in: G. Alfredsson et al. (eds.), *International Human Rights Monitoring Mechanisms*, Kluwer Law International, The Hague 2001, pp. 153-166

Van Boven, Th.C. (2001b), 'Reparations; a Requirement of Justice', in: Corte Interamericana de Derechos Humanos, *El Sistema Interamericano de Protección de los Derechos Humanos en el Umbral de los Siglo xxi*, Corte Interamericana des Derechos Humanos, San José, Costa Rica 2001, pp. 653-670

Van Boven, Th.C., 'La preambule dans la Convention de la Saufegarde de Droits de l'Homme Europeenne', in: J.E. Pettiti, E. Decaux, P.-H. Imbert (eds.), *La Convention Europeenne des Droits de l'Homme, Commentaire article par article*, Economic, Paris 1995 (2nd ed. 2002), pp. 125-134, also published in: F. Coomans et al. (eds.), *Human Rights from Exclusion to Inclusion; Principles and Practice, An Anthology from the Work of Theo van Boven*, Kluwer Law International, The Hague 2000, pp. 401-411

Van Boven, Th.C., 'Agiza t. Zweden, Het Anti-Foltercomité scherpt het non-refoulement beginsel aan', 31(5) *NJCM* 746 (2006), pp. 746-758

Van Boven, Th.C., 'Reparative justice – Focus on victims', SIM lecture 2007, 25(4) *Netherlands Quarterly of Human Rights* 723 (2007), pp. 723-735

Van Boven, Th.C., C. Flinterman, F. Grünfeld, I. Westendorp (eds.), Seminar on the Right to Restitution, Compensation and Rehabilitation for Victims of gross Violations of Human Rights and Fundamental Freedoms, Maastricht, 11-15 March 1992, SIM Special No. 12

Van Boven, Th.C., C. Flinterman, E. Rieter (1999), 'Nederland wil asielzoeker uitzetten in strijd met een interim maatregel van het VN-Comité tegen Folteringen', 20 *Nederlands Juristenblad* 908 (1999), pp. 908-909

Van Boven, Th.C., E. Rieter (2000), 'Nederland, het Internationale Gerechtshof en de doodstraf', 39 *Nederlands Juristenblad* 1921 (2000), pp. 1921-1922

Vande Lanotte, J., Y. Haeck, *Handboek Europees Verdrag voor de Rechten van de Mens, deel 1, algemene beginselen*, Intersentia, Oxford 2005

Vandenhole, W., *The Procedures before the UN Human Rights Treaty Bodies: Divergence or Convergence?*, Intersentia, Antwerp 2004

Van den Wyngaert, Ch., 'Applying the European Convention on Human Rights to Extradition: Ppening Pandora's Box?', 39 *ICLQ* 757 (1990), pp. 757-779

Van der Mei, A.-P. (2005a), 'The New African Court on Human and Peoples' Rights: Towards an Effective Human Rights Protection Mechanism for Africa?', 18 *Leiden Journal of International Law* 113 (2005), pp. 113-129

Van der Mei, A.-P. (2005b), 'The Advisory Jurisdiction of the African Court on Human and Peoples' Rights', 5(1) *African Human Rights Law Journal* 27 (2005), pp. 27-46

Van der Velde, J., *Grenzen aan het toezicht op de naleving van het EVRM*, Stichting NJCM-Boekerij, Leiden 1997

Van der Velde, J., 'Positieve verplichtingen', in: A.W. Heringa, J.G.C. Schokkenbroek, J. van der Velde (eds.), *EVRM Rechtspraak en Commentaar*, Koninklijke Vermande, The Hague 2002, pp. 1-22

Van der Wilt, H., 'Après Soering: the Relationship between Extradition and Human Rights in the Legal Practices of the Netherlands, Germany and the United States', XLII (1) *NILR* 53 (1995), pp. 53-80

Van Dijk, P., F. van Hoof, A. van Rijn, L. Zwaak (eds.), *Theory and Practice of the European Convention on Human Rights*, Intersentia, Antwerpen/Oxford 2006 (4th)

Van Emmerik, M., *Schadevergoeding bij schending van mensenrechten, De rechtspraktijk onder het EVRM vergeleken met die in Nederland*, diss. Leiden, Leiden 1997

Van Kempen, P.H.P.H.M.C., *Heropening van procedures na veroordelingen door het EHRM. Over redres van schendingen van het EVRM in afgesloten strafzaken alsook afgesloten civiele en bestuurszaken*, Wolf Legal Publishers, Nijmegen 2003

Ventura Robles, M.E., La Corte Interamericana de Derechos Humanos, *San José,* Charla dictada el 20 de junio de 2001, en el XIX Curso Interdisciplinario en Derechos Humanos del Instituto Interamericano de Derechos Humanos

Verdross, A., B. Simma, *Universelles Völkerrecht, Tehorie under Praxis*, Duncker & Humblot, Berlin 1984 (3rd)

Verhey, L.F.M., 'Implementatie van het EVRM door de wetgever', in: A.W. Heringa, E. Myjer (eds.), *45 jaar EVRM 1950-1995*, Speciaal nummer NJCM-Bulletin 21(1), Leiden 1996, pp. 103-116

Vermeer-Künzli, A., 'As If: the Legal Fiction in Diplomatic Protection', 18(1) *European Journal of International Law* 37 (2007), pp. 37-68

Vermeulen, B.P., Case note ECtHR Sheekh v. the Netherlands, 11 January 2007, *JV* 30 (2007), pp. 319-323

Vermeulen, B.P., K.M. de Vries, Case note ECtHR (Grand Chamber) *Mamatkulov and Askarov* v. *Turkey*, 4 February 2005, *JV* (2005), p. 89

Viljoen, F., E. Baimu, 'Courts for Africa: Considering the Coexistence of the African Court on Human and Peoples' Rights and the African Court of Justice', 22(2) *Netherlands Quarterly of Human Rights* 241 (2004), pp. 241-267

Viljoen, F., L. Louw, 'The Status of the Findings of the African Commission: From Moral Persuasion to Legal Obligation', 48 *Journal of African Law* 1 (2004), pp. 1-22

Vivanco, J.M., 'Fortalecer o reformar el Sistema Interamericano', in: J.E. Mendez, F. Cox (eds.), *El Futura del Sistema Interamericano de Protección de Los Derechos Humanos*, IIDH San José, Costa Rica 1998, pp. 51-72

Vlemminx, F.M.C. (2002a), *Een nieuw profiel van de grondrechten: een analyse van de prestatieplichten ingevolge klassieke en sociale grondrechten*, Boom Juridische uitgevers, Den Haag 2002 (3rd Rev.)

Vlemminx, F.M.C. (2002b), 'De autonome rechtstreekse werking van het EVRM; De Belgische en Nederlandse rechtspraak over verzekeringsplichten ingevolge het EVRM – Preadvies uitgebracht voor de Nederlandse Vereniging Voor Rechtsvergelijking op 19 december 2002 te Maastricht', 62 *Geschriften van de Nederlandse Vereniging voor Rechtsvergelijking* 1 (2002), pp. 1-120

Volio Jiménez, F., 'La Protección de los Derechos Humanos', in: P. Nikken (ed.), *The Modern World of Human Rights: Essays in Honour of Thomas Buergenthal*, IIDH/IIHR, San José, Costa Rica 1996, pp. 287-298

Vos, E., G. van Calster (eds.), *Risico en voorzorg in de rechtsmaatschappij*, Intersentia, Antwerpen 2004

W

Warbrick, C., 'Interim Protection from Genocide', 52 *Cambridge Law Journal* 367 (1993), pp. 367-371

Weckel, Ph., 'Les measures conservatoires devant les jurisdictions internationals de caractère universel', in: G. Cohen-Jonathan, J.-F. Flauss (eds.), *Mesures conservatoires et droits fondamentaux*, Bruyant, Bruxelles 2005, pp. 33-53

Weckel, Ph., 'L'arrêt sur le Génocide: le souffle de l'avis de 1951 n'a pas transporté la Cour', 111 *RGDIP* 305 (2007), pp. 305-331

Weiser, I., 'Undressing the window: Treating International Human Rights Law meaningfully in the Canadian Commonwealth System', 37 *U.B.C. Law Review* 113 (2004), pp. 1-34

Welch, C.E., *Protecting Human Rights in Africa: Roles and Strategies of Non-Governmental Organizations*, University of Pennsylvania Press, Philadelphia 1995

Wellens, K., 'Diversity in Secondary Rules and the Unity of International Law: Some Reflections on Current Trends', 25 *Netherlands Yearbook of International Law* 3 (1994), pp. 3-37

Wellens, K. (1998a) (ed.), *International Law: Theory and Practice; Essays in Honour of Eric Suy*, Martinus Nijhoff Publishers, The Hague 1998

Wellens, K. (1998b), 'Reflections on some Recent Incidental Proceedings before the International Court of Justice', in: E. Denters, N. Schrijver (eds.), *Reflections on International Law from the Low Countries in Honour of Paul de Waart*, Martinus Nijhoff Publishers, The Hague 1998, pp. 417-441

Wellens, K., *Remedies against International Organisations*, Cambridge University Press, Cambridge 2002

Wellens, K., R. Huesa-Vinaixa, *L'influence des sources sur l'unité et la fragmentation du droit international,* Bruylant, Brussels 2006

Westendorp, I., *Women and Housing: Gender makes a Difference*, diss., Intersentia, Antwerp 2007

Wibisana, M.R.A.G., *Law and Economic Analysis of the Precautionary Principle*, diss., Maastricht 2008

Wiebalck, A., 'Genocide in Bosnia and Herzegovina? Exploring the Parameters of Interim Measures of Protection at the ICJ', 28(1) *Comparative and International Law Journal of Southern Africa* 83 (1995), pp. 83-106

Wijnakker, C., 'NJCM-Commentaar op de regelgeving over het toedienen van dwangvoeding, Duidelijke regelgeving met betrekking tot het toedienen van dwangvoeding aan gedetineerden broodnodig', 31(3) *NJCM* 434 (2006), pp. 434-449

Willems, J., *Wie zal de opvoeders opvoeden? Kindermishandeling en het recht van het kind op persoonswording*, diss. Maastricht, T.M.C. Asser Press, Den Haag 1998

Wilson, R.J., 'Researching the Jurisprudence of the Inter-American Commission on Human Rights: a legislator's perspective', 10 *American University International Journal of Law and Policy* 1 (1994-1995), pp. 1-18 (in 1997 this Journal was renamed *American University International Law Review*), for the text see also <http://www1.umn.edu/humanrts/cases/commissn.htm> (accessed 26 July 2005)

Wilson, R.J., 'Defying Worl Law in the Angel Breard Case, State Department Dishonored Our Treaty Obligations', *Legal Times of Washington* (27 April 1998)

Wilson, R.J., 'The Index of Individual Case Reports of the Inter-American Commission on Human Rights: 1994-1999', 16 *American University International Law Review* 353 (2001), pp. 353-647

Wiseberg, L., 'Protecting Human Rights Activists and NGOs: what more can be done?', 13(4) *Human Rights Quarterly* 525 (1991), pp. 525-544

Woltjer, A., Case note ECtHR *Sheekh* v. *the Netherlands*, 11 January 2007, *EHRC* 36 (2007), pp. 362-363

Woltjer, A, Case note ECtHR *Olaechea Cahuas* v. *Spain*, 10 August 2006, *EHRC* (2006), p. 128

Y

Yang, Q., 'Thou shalt not violate provisional measures', 60 *Cambridge Law Journal* 441 (2001) pp. 441-446

Yoo, J.C., J.C. Ho, 'The Status of Terrorists', 44 *Virginia Journal of International Law* 207 (2003), pp. 207-228

Young, K., 'UNHCR and ICRC in the Former Yugoslavia: Bosnia-Herzegovina', 83(843) *IRRC* 781 (2001), pp. 781-805

Young, K., *The Law and Process of the U.N. Human Rights Committee*, Transnational Publishers Arsdley NY 2002

Young, L., 'Setting Sail with the Charming Betsy: Enforcing the International Court of Justice's Avena Judgment in Federal habeas corpus Proceedings', 89 *Minnesota Law Review* 890, (2005) pp. 890-915

Z

Zeleza, P.T., P.J. McConnaughay, *Human Rights, the Rule of Law, and Development in Africa*, University of Pennsylvania Press, Philadelphia 2004

Ziemele, I. (ed.), *Reservations to Human Rights Treaties and the Vienna Convention Regime: Conflict, Harmony or Reconciliation*, Martinus Nijhoff Publishers, Boston/Leiden 2004

Zwaak, L., *International Human Rights Procedures: Petitioning the ECHR, CCPR and CERD*, Ars Aequi Libri, Nijmegen 1991

Zwaak, L., 'The Role of the Council of Europe and its Committee of Ministers, Analysing the Efficiency of Measures taken under Article 46(2) of the ECHR', in: I. Boerefijn, J. Gold-schmidt (eds.), *Changing Perceptions of Sovereignty and Human Rights, Essays in Honour of Cees Flinterman*, Intersentia, Antwerp 2008, pp. 355-380

Zwart, T. (1985a), 'Aan de Amerikanen overgeleverd; uitlevering, ECRM en voorlopige maatre-gelen', 10(7) *NJCM* 562 (1985), pp. 562-571

Zwart, T (1985b), 'Onrechtmatige eigenwijsheid', 10(1) *NJCM* 65 (1985), pp. 65-71

Zwart, T., *The Admissibility of Human Rights Petitions*, dissertation Leiden, Nijhoff, Dordrecht 1994

Zyberi, G., *The Humanitarian Face of the International Court of Justice, Its Contribution to Interpreting and Developing International Human Rights and Humanitarian Law Rules and Principles*, Intersentia, Antwerp/Oxford/Portland 2008

TABLE OF CASES

Judgments

Advisory Opinions

Order in the context of a request for an Advisory Opinion

3   INTERNATIONAL TRIBUNAL ON THE LAW OF THE SEA (ITLOS)

Orders granting or denying provisional measures

CAT discontinued case

CAT General Comments

8   HUMAN RIGHTS COMMITTEE (HRC)

Those situations, uncovered during the research for this book, in which the HRC used provisional measures but did not mention this in its View or inadmissibility decision, are indicated by an asterisk: *, followed by the date(s) of the provisional measure.

---

[1]   See Chapter II (Systems), section 2.4.6 on the categories of HRC decisions.

HRC documents other than inadmissibility decisions and Views

9   INTER-AMERICAN COMMISSION ON HUMAN RIGHTS (CIDH)

10 INTER-AMERICAN COURT OF HUMAN RIGHTS (IACHR)

Provisional measures[2]

---

[2]   This refers to Orders granting or denying requests for provisional measures. The provisional measures by the Inter-American Court are presented in alphabetical, rather than chronological, order, because often they are maintained for a considerable period and regularly expanded. Consecutive Orders are listed by date of first Order; the last Order mentioned may not be the last Order in the matter, as many situations are ongoing.

Orders for compliance with judgments

IACHR Judgments

11   AFRICAN COMMISSION ON HUMAN AND PEOPLE'S RIGHTS (ACHPR)[3]

---

[3]   The decisions by the African Commission are often undated.

13   EUROPEAN COURT OF HUMAN RIGHTS (ECtHR)

International Criminal Tribunal for the former Yugoslavia (ICTY)

Bosnia Human Rights Chamber

Judicial Committee of the Privy Council (JCPC)

Supreme Court of Canada

INDEX

CURRICULUM VITAE

Eva Rieter (1970) studied law at Maastricht University (Master of Dutch law, specialization international law, 1995). She went on to obtain an LL.M degree at the University of Virginia School of Law (LL.M. 1996, specializations human rights law and US law), where she also worked as a research assistant for Prof. R.B. Lillich and received the McClure Fellowship in human rights. She joined the Maastricht Centre for Human Rights in 1997. In 1999 she received a Max van der Stoel Human Rights award for her article 'Interim Measures by the World Court to Suspend the Execution of an Individual: the Breard Case', published in the *Netherlands Quarterly of Human Rights*. She has published a range of articles and is the co-author of a book on the proceedings before the European Court of Human Rights, the UN Human Rights Committee and the other three Geneva bodies (2002; revised edition 2008). She has taught public international law and human rights at Maastricht University School of Law and University College Maastricht. Currently she is assistant professor at Radboud University Nijmegen lecturing public international law and international human rights law.

SCHOOL OF HUMAN RIGHTS
RESEARCH SERIES

The School of Human Rights Research is a joint effort by human rights researchers in the Netherlands. Its central research theme is the nature and meaning of international standards in the field of human rights, their application and promotion in the national legal order, their interplay with national standards, and the international supervision of such application. The School of Human Rights Research Series only includes English titles that contribute to a better understanding of the different aspects of human rights.

Published titles within the Series:
1   Brigit C.A. Toebes, *The Right to Health as a Human Right in International Law*
     ISBN 90-5095-057-4

2   Ineke Boerefijn, *The Reporting Procedure under the Covenant on Civil and Political Rights. Practice and Procedures of the Human Rights Committee*
     ISBN 90-5095-074-4

3   Kitty Arambulo, *Strengthening the Supervision of the International Covenant on Economic, Social and Cultural Rights. Theoretical and Procedural Aspects*
     ISBN 90-5095-058-2

4   Marlies Glasius, *Foreign Policy on Human Rights. Its Influence on Indonesia under Soeharto*
     ISBN 90-5095-089-2

5   Cornelis D. de Jong, *The Freedom of Thought, Conscience and Religion or Belief in the United Nations (1946-1992)*
     ISBN 90-5095-137-6

6   Heleen Bosma, *Freedom of Expression in England and under the ECHR: in Search of a Common Ground. A Foundation for the Application of the Human Rights Act 1998 in English Law*
     ISBN 90-5095-136-8

7   Mielle Bulterman, *Human Rights in the External Relations of the European Union*
     ISBN 90-5095-164-3

School of Human Rights Research Series

8   Esther M. van den Berg, *The Influence of Domestic NGOs on Dutch Human Rights Policy.*
    Case Studies on South Africa,Namibia, Indonesia and East Timor
    ISBN 90-5095-159-7

9   Ian Seiderman, *Hierarchy in International Law: the Human Rights Dimension*
    ISBN 90-5095-165-1

10 Anna Meijknecht, *Towards International Personality: the Position of Minorities and*
    Indigenous Peoples in International Law
    ISBN 90-5095-166-X

11 Mohamed Eltayeb, *A Human Rights Approach to Combating Religious Persecution. Cases*
    from Pakistan, Saudi Arabia and Sudan
    ISBN 90-5095-170-8

12 Machteld Boot, *Genocide, Crimes Against Humanity, War Crimes: Nullum Crimen Sine Lege*
    and the Subject Matter Jurisdiction of the International Criminal Court
    ISBN 90-5095-216-X

13 Corinne Packer, *Using Human Rights to Change Tradition. Traditional Practices Harmful to*
    Women's Reproductive Health in sub-Saharan Africa
    ISBN 90-5095-226-7

14 Theo R.G. van Banning, *The Human Right to Property*
    ISBN 90-5095-203-8

15 Yvonne M. Donders, *Towards a Right to Cultural Identity?*
    ISBN 90-5095-238-0

16 Göran K. Sluiter, *International Criminal Adjudication and the Collection of Evidence:*
    Obligations of States
    ISBN 90-5095-227-5

17 Nicola Jägers, *Corporate Human Rights Obligations: in Search of Accountability*
    ISBN 90-5095-240-2

18 Magdalena Sepúlveda, *The Nature of the Obligations under the International Covenant on*
    Economic, Social and Cultural Rights
    ISBN 90-5095-260-7

19 Mitsue Inazumi, *Universal Jurisdiction in Modern International Law: Expansion of National*
    Jurisdiction for Prosecuting Serious Crimes under International Law
    ISBN 90-5095-366-2

20 Anne-Marie L.M. de Brouwer, *Supranational Criminal Prosecution of Sexual Violence: The*
    ICC and the Practice of the ICTY and the ICTR
    ISBN 90-5095-533-9

21 Jeroen Gutter, *Thematic Procedures of the United Nations Commission on Human Rights and International Law: in Search of a Sense of Community*
ISBN 90-5095-557-6

22 Hilde Reiding, *The Netherlands and the Development of International Human Rights Instruments*
ISBN 978-90-5095-654-3

23 Ingrid Westendorp, *Women and Housing: Gender Makes a Difference*
ISBN 978-90-5095-669-7

24 Quirine A.M. Eijkman, *We Are Here to Serve You! Public Security, Police Reform and Human Rights Implementation in Costa Rica*
ISBN 978-90-5095-704-5

25 Antoine Ch. Buyse, *Post-conflict Housing Restitution. The European Human Rights Perspective with a case study on Bosnia and Herzegovina*
ISBN 978-90-5095-770-0

26 Gentian Zyberi, *The Humanitarian Face of the International Court of Justice. Its Contribution to Interpreting and Developing International Human Rights and Humanitarian Law Rules and Principles*
ISBN 978-90-5095-792-2

27 Dragoş Cucereanu, *Aspects of Regulating Freedom of Expression on the Internet*
ISBN 978-90-5095-842-4

28 Ton Liefaard, *Deprivation of Liberty of Children in Light of International Human Rights Law and Standards*
ISBN 978-90-5095-838-7

29 Laura van Waas, *Nationality Matters. Statelessness under International Law*
ISBN 978-90-5095-854-7

30 Jeroen Denkers, *The World Trade Organization and Import Bans in Response to Violations of Fundamental Labour Rights*
ISBN 978-90-5095-855-4

31 Irene Hadiprayitno, *The Dialectics of Development Practice and the Internationally Declared Right to Development, with Special Reference to Indonesia*
ISBN 978-90-5095-932-2

32 Michał Gondek, *The Reach of Human Rights in a Globalising World: Extraterritorial Application of Human Rights Treaties*
ISBN 978-90-5095-817-2

33 Jeff Handmaker, *Advocating for Accountability: Civic-State Interactions to Protect Refugees in South Africa*
ISBN 978-905095-910-0

School of Human Rights Research Series

34 Anna Oehmichen, *Hazard or Right? Terrorism and Anti-Terror Legislation: The Terrorised Legislator? A Comparison of Counter-Terror Legislation and Its Implications on Human Rights in the Legal Systems of the United Kingdom, Spain, Germany and France*
ISBN 978-90-5095-956-8

35 Simon Walker, *The Future of Human Rights Impact Assessments of Trade Agreements*
ISBN 978-90-5095-986-5

36 Fleur van Leeuwen, *Women's Rights Are Human Rights: The Practice of the United Nations Human Rights Committee and the Committee on Economic, Social and Cultural Rights*
ISBN 978-90-5095-980-3